Central America & Mexico Handbook

Peter Hutchison

66 99

"Or like stout Cortez when with eagle eyes
He stared at the Pacific – and all his men
Looked at each other with a wild surmise –
Silent, upon a peak in Darien."

John Keats.

Footprint story

It was 1921

Ireland had just been partitioned, the British miners were striking for more pay and the federation of British industry had an idea. Exports were booming in South America – how about a handbook for businessmen trading in that far away continent? The Anglo-South American Handbook was born that year, written by W Koebel, the most prolific writer on Latin America of his day.

1924

Two editions later the book was 'privatized' and in 1924, in the hands of Royal Mail, the steamship company for South America, it became The South American Handbook, subtitled 'South America in a nutshell'. This annual publication became the 'bible' for generations of travellers to South America and remains so to this day. In the early days travel was by sea and the Handbook gave all the details needed for the long voyage from Europe. What to wear for dinner; how to arrange a cricket match with the Cable & Wireless staff on the Cape Verde Islands and a full account of the journey from Liverpool up the Amazon to Manaus: 5898 miles without changing cabin!

1939

As the continent opened up, The South American Handbook reported the new Pan Am flying boat services, and the fortnightly airship service from Rio to Europe on the Graf Zeppelin. For reasons still unclear but with extraordinary determination, the annual editions continued through the Second World War.

1970s

Many more people discovered South America and the backpacking trail started to develop. All the while the Handbook was gathering fans, including literary vagabonds such as Paul Theroux and Graham Greene (who once sent some updates addressed to "The publishers of the best travel guide in the world, Bath, England").

1990s

During the 1990s the company set about developing a new travel guide series using this legendary title as the flagship. By 1997 there were over a dozen guides in the series and the Footprint imprint was launched.

2000s

The series grew quickly and there were soon Footprint travel guides covering more than 150 countries. In 2004, Footprint launched its first thematic guide: *Surfing Europe*, packed with colour photographs, maps and charts. This was followed by further thematic guides such as *Diving the World*, *Snowboarding the World*, *Body and Soul escapes*, *Travel with Kids* and *European City Breaks*.

2009

Today we continue the traditions of the last 88 years that has served legions of travellers so well. We believe that these help to make Footprint guides different. Our policy is to use authors who are genuine experts who write for independent travellers; people possessing a spirit of adventure, looking to get off the beaten track.

Above: Chichicastenango, Guatemala, on market day – a spectacularly colourful event.

Images of Central America and Mexico flow as freely as tequila in a Mexican cantina: indigenous markets, chaotic cities, serene countryside, stunning beaches, pristine national parks and marine reserves filled with wildlife. Volcanoes and earthquakes have shaped and moulded these mountainous lands for millennia. Impressive tropical storms illuminate the night sky, while the wreckage left by hurricanes is a reminder of the power of nature and the fragility of life. Human impact on this land is no less impressive. Ruined remnants of ancient civilizations litter the region: from the Maya to modern times, each ruling power has commemorated its success either by building on the past or by trying to destroy its legacy. Today, modern life develops at great speed in the region's cities but, hidden in rural pockets, culture remains resolutely unchanged. People live as their forebears have for centuries.

Contents

Belizean market.

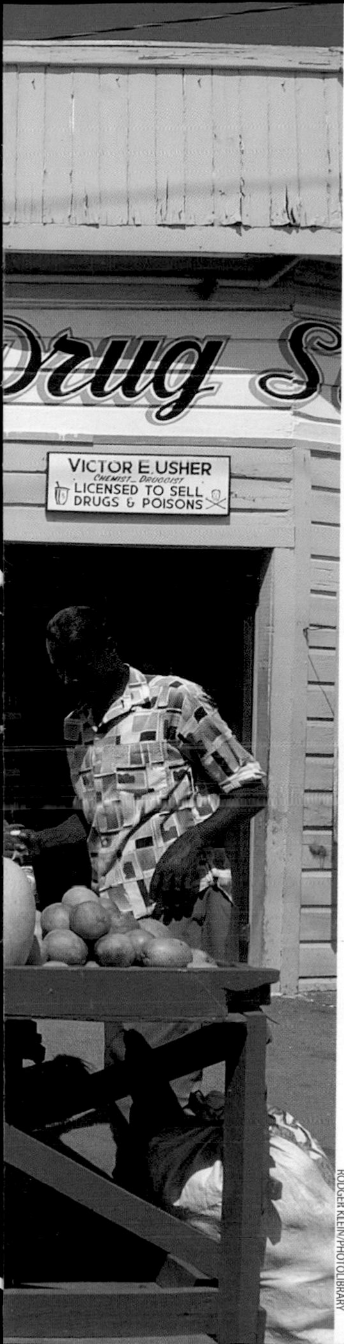

RODGER KLEIN/PHOTOLIBRARY

Where to go

The sheer variety of options in Central America and Mexico means that for once the cliché is true – there is something for everyone. The diversity of landscapes, cultures and opportunities excites, entices and, to start with, just bewilders. The scope for adventurous holidays is vast, whether it be climbing a volcano, scuba-diving and snorkelling, whitewater rafting or seeking out the elusive quetzal bird from the forests of Guatemala right down to Panama. Equally enticing is the cultural variety; the pyramids and sculptures of the Aztecs, Maya and other cultures; the Spanish colonial heritage, from the grandest cathedral to the smallest village church; the flora and fauna; Indian markets; the modern and dynamic museums and art of the region; learning the language or local cooking techniques; or the mere prospect of lazing at some palm-shaded hideaway fringed with golden sands. One especially rewarding aspect of travel in Central America is the relatively compact size of many of the countries making it easy to move from one place to the next.

Mexico

Encapsulating Mexico is difficult, but imagine countries within countries. Gloriously manic Mexico City is a world away from the serenity of the country's quieter spots. Little remains of the pre-conquest island city of Tenochtitlán but the vast ruins of Teotihuacán stand as monument to the value of this prized land. Today's capital is equally impressive. Struggling to move for congestion and gasping for air in the pollution, the Federal District remains one of the world's great cities: a living, working, just-breathing metropolis.

To the north, colonial cities founded on the wealth of silver mines, rest assuredly on their architectural laurels, while beyond

Planning your trip

Belizean market.

RODGER KLEIN/PHOTOLIBRARY

Where to go

The sheer variety of options in Central America and Mexico means that for once the cliché is true – there is something for everyone. The diversity of landscapes, cultures and opportunities excites, entices and, to start with, just bewilders. The scope for adventurous holidays is vast, whether it be climbing a volcano, scuba-diving and snorkelling, whitewater rafting or seeking out the elusive quetzal bird from the forests of Guatemala right down to Panama. Equally enticing is the cultural variety; the pyramids and sculptures of the Aztecs, Maya and other cultures; the Spanish colonial heritage, from the grandest cathedral to the smallest village church; the flora and fauna; Indian markets; the modern and dynamic museums and art of the region; learning the language or local cooking techniques; or the mere prospect of lazing at some palm-shaded hideaway fringed with golden sands. One especially rewarding aspect of travel in Central America is the relatively compact size of many of the countries making it easy to move from one place to the next.

Mexico

Encapsulating Mexico is difficult, but imagine countries within countries. Gloriously manic Mexico City is a world away from the serenity of the country's quieter spots. Little remains of the pre-conquest island city of Tenochtitlán but the vast ruins of Teotihuacán stand as monument to the value of this prized land. Today's capital is equally impressive. Struggling to move for congestion and gasping for air in the pollution, the Federal District remains one of the world's great cities: a living, working, just-breathing metropolis.

To the north, colonial cities founded on the wealth of silver mines, rest assuredly on their architectural laurels, while beyond

Opposite page: Train ride up to the Copper Canyon, Mexico: one of the world's great journeys, it climbs 2000 m in a little over 240 km. **Above:** Lake Atitlán, Guatemala; the most beautiful laundrette in the world.

are miles of endless deserts, punctuated by hot spots such as the Baja California Peninsula and the spectacular train journey to the Copper Canyon. The Pacific coast, stretching southeast from Mazatlán, entices the traveller with glorious, surf-pummelled beaches, and the Yucatán Peninsula, jutting out into the Caribbean, is home to both mega-resorts and quiet palm-backed strands, spiced up with unmissable Maya ruins.

In the southern state of Chiapas, campaigners champion the rights of Mexico's 24 million indigenous people, contributing to the continuous evolution of the country's cultural heritage.

In the wake of the global financial tremors, the merits of NAFTA membership are continuously being questioned. Mexico is continuing on a course of revolution, this time a quiet and steadily building one. People are beginning to expect change. Viva variety, viva confusion, viva Mexico!

Guatemala

Surely nobody could fail to be impressed by Guatemala. The expansive ruins of Tikal symbolize this rich and complex country, with majestic temples looking out across the endless rainforest canopy. To the south, the Maya, who once ruled these massive cities of stone, live on in hundreds of towns and villages, nestled among the intensely farmed foothills of scenic mountains and volcanoes. Each Guatemalan community has its own unique textile and its own fiesta; colourful markets welcome visitors, while packed buses ignore your pleas for a ride. But serenity and calm await. Not in the chaos of Guatemala City but amid the colonial charm of Antigua, the former capital, and in the hypnotic beauty of Lake Atitlán, which draws in even the most seasoned traveller. To the east, the lowland sierras offer trekking and hiking, while the Caribbean coast promises laid-back beach life and Garífuna culture. And, to the west, a fledgling ecotourism interest supports nesting turtles on the shores of the Pacific.

Belize

Compact and accessible, but more expensive than its immediate neighbours, tiny Belize is frequently overlooked. Yet this Caribbean

TANGWEN SANDERSON

Above: Colourful buses in Antigua. **Opposite page:** Lobster traps on Big Corn Island, off Nicaragua's Caribbean coast.

country is home to the Mesoamerican Barrier Reef – the longest in the Western Hemisphere – and offers some of the best diving in the world, not to mention a boatload of other watersports worth getting wet for. What's more, over 35% of the country is protected in national parks and reserves, including the world's only jaguar sanctuary at Cockscomb Basin. To the east, an intricate system of caves drains the rivers of Mountain Pine Ridge, many of which can be explored on foot, by boat or even inflated tube. And in the pine-clad hills to the south, Caracol, the largest of many ruins in Belize, remains mostly unexplored, revelling in the little-known fact that it once ruled over nearby Tikal.

El Salvador

Like Belize, El Salvador gets short shrift due to the popularity of its neighbours. The volcanic highlands and contrasting coastal plains are stunningly beautiful but a massive double earthquake in early 2001 ruined architectural

treasures and human lives. El Salvador is challenging for independent travellers but ultimately enjoyable thanks to its genuinely friendly people. San Salvador, the country's capital, is close to unmissable volcanoes, lakes and national parks. Northern towns are moving out from the shadows of civil war and enjoying a cultural revival, while, to the south, long sandy beaches, prized by surfers for decades, stretch along the Costa del Sol to the Gulf of Fonseca. To the west are coffee plantations and the beautiful Ruta de las Flores. And who could resist a national park called 'El Imposible'.

Honduras

One of Central America's dark horses, Honduras has been pushing for a place in the limelight for years. The Bay Islands, off the Caribbean coast, are still the cheapest place to learn to scuba dive and, onshore, the adventure continues with whitewater rafting, hiking and birdwatching. Along the Atlantic, you can relax in the coastal

communities of Omoa, Tela, La Ceiba and Trujillo and visit the isolated rainforest of La Mosquitia – Central America's 'Little Amazon'. In the west of the country, the villages are quieter and the hillside paths less travelled but there are colonial treasures and indigenous communities to discover. Close to the border with Guatemala, the stunning Copán ruins mark the southernmost reach of the Maya Empire.

Nicaragua

Although memories of the 1979 Sandinista Revolution still evoke images of work crews, comandantes and communist sympathies, 30 years on the Nicaragua of today is a very different and rapidly changing place. The country is embracing a deluge of tourist dollars that is set to increase as word gets around: Nicaragua is cool. There is a freshness about a country where the smiles are still warm, the questions still honest and the eyes undimmed by the attitudes of thoughtless travellers. Beautiful sites like the Island of Ometepe, Volcán Masaya, the Corn Islands, the Río San Juan and Pacific beaches are matched by some of Central America's oldest towns, including conservative Granada and liberal León. It's the contrasts that make Nicaragua so appealing.

Costa Rica

Peaceful, calm and 100% democratic . . . ah, that'll be Costa Rica. The wealth of national parks and biospheres, private reserves and national monuments in this country could make you believe that Ticos have a monopoly on nature. What makes the difference in Costa Rica is the sheer variety of wildlife on offer – something you only truly appreciate after pawing over large maps for ages: quetzales here, nesting turtles there, big cats at all points of the compass. World-class whitewater rafting from Turrialba, surfing on both coasts, experiencing the eruption of Arenal volcano and the steaming mudpools nearby, walking and hiking in the cloudforests of Monteverde or the rainforest of the Osa Peninsula; other

countries may offer these things, but they don't pack them into such a compact, attractive bundle as Costa Rica. And they don't do it in quite the same laid-back way as the Ticos, who espouse *la pura vida*.

Panama

Panama is the crossroads of the world. The Panama Canal may not be natural but it is spectacular and pure Panamanian since the country successfully took control of the world's greatest shortcut at the end of 1999. Beyond modern Panama City, national and international visitors are opening their eyes to new discoveries on the Azuero Peninsula and in the Chiriquí Highlands, while Bocas del Toro on the Atlantic is developing into a hip coastal destination, with glassy waters and islands full of tiny multicoloured frogs. The autonomous San Blas Islands provide a precious haven of calm and tranquillity and, for the true adventurer, the wilderness of the Darién still offers one of the great challenges this side of space travel.

Itineraries

Three to four weeks

Not long enough to cover the region, but in three or four weeks you could explore a chunk of the Ruta Maya. In Guatemala, take a week or 10 days to take in the essentials of Antigua, Tikal and Lake Atitlán then head for Belize's Cayo district, and Caye Caulker for a bit of diving, before heading north to Mexico's Yucatán and west to the indigenous homelands of Chiapas, completing the loop. Any version of the Ruta Maya, taking in the main Maya sites of Guatemala, Belize and southern Mexico is possible in four weeks but doesn't really allow time for deviation. Another three- to four-week trip could focus on Costa Rica, with a great variety of national parks on offer: the most popular include Manuel Antonio National Park, Monteverde Cloud Forest Reserve, Tortuguero National Park to the east and Corcovado National Park to the south. The explosive Volcán Arenal never disappoints (unless it is shrouded in cloud). For the active there is whitewater rafting, surfing, horse riding and trekking. You could easily pop in to Nicaragua to the north, or Panama to the south. You could just about manage an overland trip from Guatemala through to Costa Rica in three to four weeks. If you're feeling particularly manic, you could even manage a mad dash down the Pan-American Highway from Mexico City all the way to Panama City.

Six to eight weeks

Six to eight weeks is long enough to travel across a few countries without feeling you've rushed too much. Arrive in Mexico City and, after a few days spent exploring the sights and sounds, the architecture ancient and modern, and dodging the traffic, you can head south to the beaches of Oaxaca, before making your way east to Chiapas and the Maya ruins of Palenque. From here continue south to Guatemala or west out to the Yucatán Peninsula for the beautiful beaches and more Maya ruins. Dropping south, Belize is worth some time. Diving, though more expensive than Honduras, is some of the best in the world and includes the famed Blue Hole. Head west for Guatemala and the eerie cave and river trips of the Cayo District or, to the south, the serenity around Placencia, the jaguar sanctuary at Cockscomb Basin and Maya villages close to Punta Gorda.

With six weeks you could squeeze in a short Spanish language course in Antigua, Quetzaltenango or even Todos Santos – world famous for its annual festival in November. After Guatemala, Honduras draws many to the affordable diving of the

PRISMA/SUPERSTOCK

Bay Islands, which need at least a week. Other attractions include whitewater rafting on the Río Cangrejo close to La Ceiba. Inland, treks and hikes in the quiet hills around Gracias go through beautiful scenery and small indigenous communities, the very heart of Honduras. An alternative six-week trip might arrive in Guatemala City and head south overland flying out of San José, Costa Rica. While experiencing Guatemala and Costa Rica, you can travel at leisure through Honduras, dip into the lakes and volcanic beauty of El Salvador and visit Nicaragua where revolutionary history merges with colonial legacy to create one of Central America's most endearing nations. Honduras and Nicaragua are, for many travellers, the most challenging destinations, but for many the most memorable.

Three months

Three months is plenty to enter into the classic trip – to follow the Pan-American Highway from the Río Grande to the Darién Gap. Equally you could start at Panama and head north. You can cross the US-Mexico border at several points. From Laredo, the route heads south through Monterrey and the port of Tampico before veering inland through the silver-mining centre of Pachuca and on to Mexico City. From Ciudad Juárez on the border, it's a short trip to Chihuahua, the vast Copper Canyon and the glorious railroad down to the Pacific Ocean. The famous train journey is one of several options for leaving Chihuahua on a route heading south that takes in the old silver towns of Colonial Heartland of Zacatecas and San Luis Potosí. On the west coast, Tijuana offers the simplest route to the rugged desert beauty of the Baja California Peninsula, popular for beaches and whale-watching. This is also an alternative (and longer) route to the Copper Canyon via Los Mochis. After the Pacific Costa Alegre, head inland for Guadalajara and then Mexico City. Continue

Opposite page: Panama City, where old and new worlds collide. **Above:** An ornate colonial church in San Cristóbal de las Casas, Mexico.

southeast from the Mexican Central Highlands to Guatemala and follow the route south, or take in Belize after travelling through the Yucatán Peninsula.

A gentle meander through Honduras, El Salvador and Nicaragua can involve a switch of coastlines in Costa Rica, to the Caribbean coast and take in the idyllic alternative of the southern beaches and the dive sites of Bocas del Toro. Or continue south to Costa Rica's Osa Peninsula before taking the Pan-American Highway across the final border to David and on to Panama City. From David, you can blend adventure and beauty with a visit to the Chiriquí Highlands. A voyage through the Panama Canal would be the ideal way to end a trip of trans-continental travel before returning home, or heading further south through and beyond the Darién Gap – one of the great adventure challenges of the region.

Central America & Mexico highlights & itineraries

See colour maps in centre of book

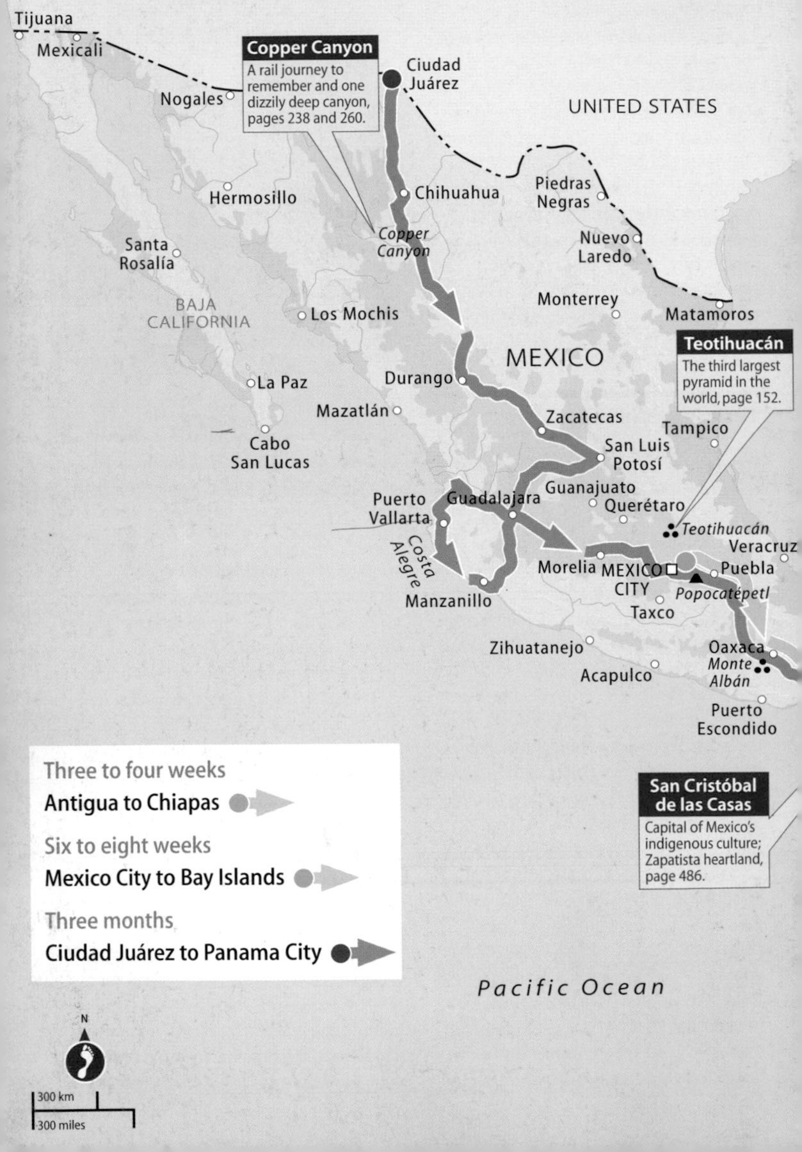

Copper Canyon
A rail journey to remember and one dizzily deep canyon, pages 238 and 260.

Teotihuacán
The third largest pyramid in the world, page 152.

San Cristóbal de las Casas
Capital of Mexico's indigenous culture; Zapatista heartland, page 486.

Tijuana
Mexicali
Nogales
Ciudad Juárez

UNITED STATES

Hermosillo
Chihuahua
Piedras Negras
Nuevo Laredo

Santa Rosalía

Copper Canyon

BAJA CALIFORNIA

Los Mochis
Monterrey
Matamoros

La Paz
Durango
MEXICO

Mazatlán
Zacatecas
Tampico

Cabo San Lucas
San Luis Potosí

Puerto Vallarta
Guadalajara
Guanajuato
Querétaro

Costa Alegre
Teotihuacán
Veracruz

Morelia
MEXICO CITY
Puebla
Popocatépetl

Manzanillo
Taxco

Zihuatanejo
Oaxaca
Monte Albán

Acapulco

Puerto Escondido

Three to four weeks
Antigua to Chiapas

Six to eight weeks
Mexico City to Bay Islands

Three months
Ciudad Juárez to Panama City

Pacific Ocean

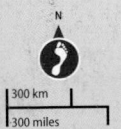

N

300 km
300 miles

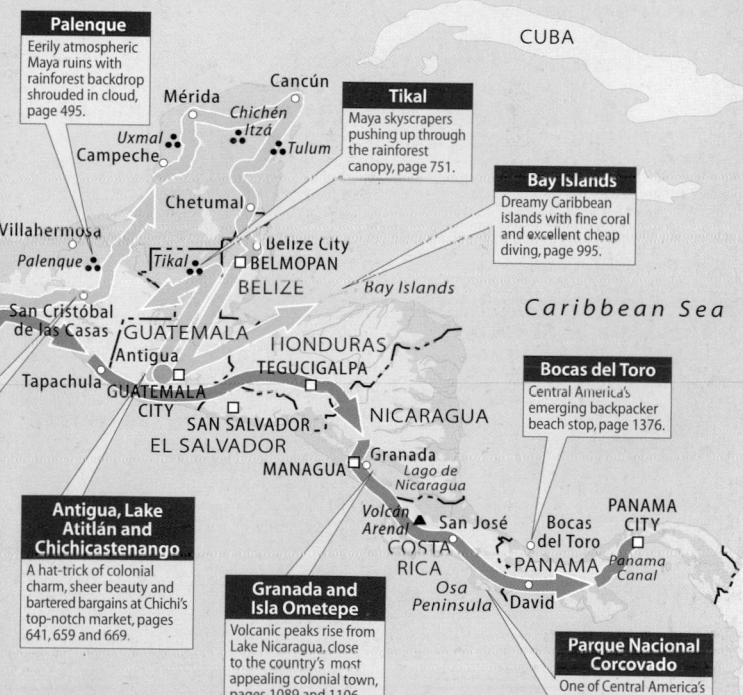

Gulf of Mexico

CUBA

Palenque
Eerily atmospheric Maya ruins with rainforest backdrop shrouded in cloud, page 495.

Mérida
Cancún
Chichén Itzá
Uxmal
Campeche
Tulum

Tikal
Maya skyscrapers pushing up through the rainforest canopy, page 751.

Chetumal

Bay Islands
Dreamy Caribbean islands with fine coral and excellent cheap diving, page 995.

Villahermosa

Palenque

Belize City
BELMOPAN
BELIZE

Tikal

Bay Islands

Caribbean Sea

San Cristóbal de las Casas
GUATEMALA
Antigua
Tapachula
GUATEMALA CITY
SAN SALVADOR
EL SALVADOR

HONDURAS
TEGUCIGALPA

NICARAGUA

Bocas del Toro
Central America's emerging backpacker beach stop, page 1376.

MANAGUA
Granada
Lago de Nicaragua
Volcán Arenal
San José
COSTA RICA
Osa Peninsula

Bocas del Toro
PANAMA
PANAMA CITY
Panama Canal
David

Antigua, Lake Atitlán and Chichicastenango
A hat-trick of colonial charm, sheer beauty and bartered bargains at Chichi's top-notch market, pages 641, 659 and 669.

Granada and Isla Ometepe
Volcanic peaks rise from Lake Nicaragua, close to the country's most appealing colonial town, pages 1089 and 1106.

Parque Nacional Corcovado
One of Central America's best-protected rainforest reserves, page 1255.

Maya sites

Palenque, Mexico

Built at the height of the Classic period on a series of artificial terraces, Palenque is one of the most beautiful of all the Maya ruins in Mexico, with a hillside setting backing onto the rainforest with whisps of cloud drifting across the site after rainfall. From about the fourth century AD, Palenque grew from a small agricultural village to one of the most important cities in the pre-Hispanic world, although it really achieved greatness between AD 600 and 800. The pyramids once held ornate tombs of Maya rulers deep within.

Chichén Itzá, Mexico

Recently voted one of the Seven New Wonders of the World, Chichén Itzá is one of the most spectacular of Maya sites. The Castillo, a giant stepped pyramid, dominates the site, watched over by Chacmool, a Maya fertility god who reclines on a nearby structure. The city was built by the Maya in late Classic times (AD 600-900). By the end of the 10th century, the city was more or less abandoned. It was re-established in the 11th-12th centuries, though much debate surrounds by whom.

Tulum, Mexico

The Maya-Toltec ruins of Tulum are perched on coastal cliffs in a beautiful setting above the azure Caribbean waters. The ruins are 12th century, with city walls of white stone. The temples were dedicated to the worship of the Falling God, or the Setting Sun, represented as a falling character over nearly all the west-facing doors (Cozumel was the home of the Rising Sun). The same idea is reflected in the buildings, which are wider at the top than at the bottom. The main structure is the Castillo, which commands a view of both the sea and the forested Quintana Roo lowlands stretching westwards.

Caracol, Belize

Caracol is a rediscovered Maya city and now part of a National Monument Reservation. The site was established about 300 BC and continued well into the Late Classic period (glyphs record a victorious war against Tikal). Why Caracol was built in such a poorly watered region is not known, but Maya engineers showed great ingenuity in constructing reservoirs and terracing the fields. The Sky

LUCARELLI TEMISTOCLE/SHUTTERSTOCK

Above: The massive stepped pyramid of Chichén Itzá in Mexico's Yucatán Peninsula.
Opposite page top: The Maya ruins of Tulum, Mexico, look out across the Caribbean Sea.
Opposite page bottom: Large mask stone carving at Tikal, Guatemala.

Palace (Caana) pyramid, climbing 42 m above the site, is being excavated and satellite mapped by members of the University of Central Florida. Excavations take place February-May but there are year-round caretakers who will show you around.

Copán, Honduras

The magnificent ruins of Copán are one of Central America's major Maya sites, certainly the most significant in Honduras, and they mark the southeastern limit of Maya dominance. When John Lloyd Stephens and Frederick Catherwood examined the ruins in 1839, they were engulfed in jungle. In the 1930s, the Carnegie Institute cleared the ground and rebuilt the Hieroglyphic Stairway, and since then the ruins have been maintained by the government with a museum exhibit in Tegucigalpa. Some of the most complex carvings are found on the 21 stelae, or 3-m columns of stones on which the passage of time was originally believed to have been recorded. The stelae are deeply incised and carved with faces, figures and animals. There are royal portraits with inscriptions recording deeds and the lineage of those portrayed as well as dates of birth, marriage and death. Ball courts were revealed during excavation, and one of them has been fully restored.

Tikal, Guatemala

With its Maya skyscrapers pushing up through the jungle canopy, the massive site of Tikal will have you transfixed. Steep-sided temples for the mighty dead, stelae commemorating the powerful rulers, inscriptions recording the noble deeds and passing of time, and burials that were stuffed with jade and bone funerary offerings, make up the greatest Maya city in this pocket of Guatemala. And when you need a break from the expansive site, the area is packed with bird and other wildlife. Overall, it's a must-see of Guatemala, and a must-see for this part of the world.

six of the best

Volcano adventures

Volcán Arenal, Costa Rica

A silent plume of smoke puffs from the peak of Arenal's perfectly symmetrical cone. The powerful landscape seems underplayed by the absence of drama, noise and fire. Treks in the national park are filled with natural surprises. But as night falls and the light and noise of the day fade, brilliant orange lines of crashing lava drizzle down the mountainside, and the eerie, crashing noise is mildly chilling. This is nature for real. Of course, nature is no TV show; it may be cloudy or Arenal may be resting for few days, but since the 1960s, she's been pushing out lava, adding layer upon layer around the summit. If you like the idea of a volcano, you have to see Arenal.

Volcán Irazú, Costa Rica

In 1963 Volcán Irazú welcomed President John F Kennedy's visit to San José with a shower of volcanic ash across the capital. The appeal of Irazú (meaning 'mountain of quakes and thunder') is in its dormant, latent mischievous power. While earthquake swarms show magma is still active, it's a peaceful meander to the 3432 m summit along a seemingly endless road. At the top, the steep sides of the lagoon-filled craters are an impressive sight. And with an early-morning trip, the summit is often above the clouds, creating a distinctly heavenly feel.

Isla Ometepe, Nicaragua

Home to a twin volcano complex, Ometepe is the largest and most enchanting of Lake Nicarauga's rustic islands. The cones of Maderas and Concepción rise from the waters in perfect symmetry, and are steeped in legend. Their forest-swathed slopes conceal mysterious stone carvings that hint at the island's pre-Columbian past. Maderas is extinct and believed to have last erupted 800 years ago; today it's wrapped in thick cloudforest, great for hiking and wildlife observation. Concepción is dryer, harsher and very much active, periodically spewing ash over the island and its inhabitants.

CELSO DINIZ/SHUTTERSTOCK

Volcán Barú, Panama

On a clear day, it's possible to see both the Caribbean Sea and the Pacific Ocean from the top of Volcán Barú, Panama's highest peak at 3474 m. Imbued with rich volcanic soil and visited by endless swathes of rolling mist, the cool lush slopes of this sleeping giant are covered by a patchwork of sleepy coffee *fincas*, strawberry plantations and diminutive farming communities. Luxuriant cloudforests flourish at this elevation, accommodating dazzling birds, delicate orchids and a host of ethereal plant life. Protected as a national park, hikers and wildlife-lovers are drawn into extended explorations. But the mountains promise adrenalin-charged thrills too, with some of Central America's best whitewater rapids waiting to be tamed.

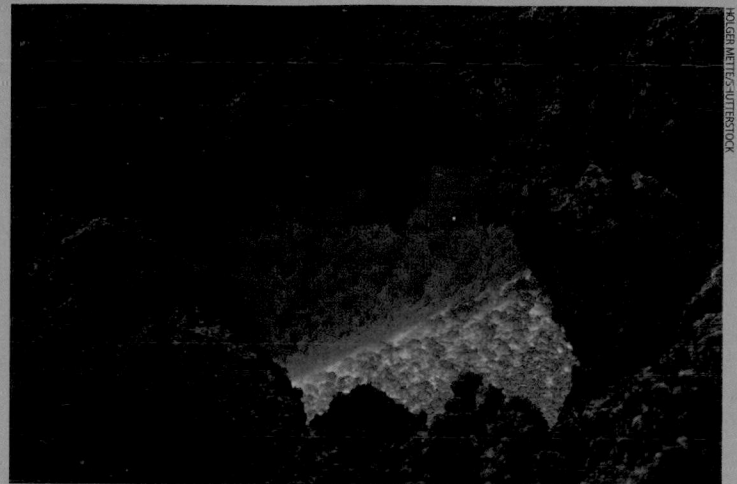

Volcán Pacaya, Guatemala

A short distance from La Antigua or Guatemala City, Pacaya Volcano is a rare and memorable opportunity to get up close and sweaty with a volcano. As gnarly, bumpy lumps of lava are squeezed out, molten boulders bump and spin down the mountain side. Take a bag of marshmallows and melt them on a stick. As the sun sets, the views across the mountainous peaks of the Guatemalan highlands are unforgettable, and as you head down, the glowing lava takes over the slope. Pacaya is very much alive.

Popocatépetl, Mexico

On a clear day, Popocatépetl can be seen from the Mexican capital and from the town of Puebla. As one of the country's most active volcanoes (Colima is probably the most active at present), Popo has been steadily puffing since the early 1990s. Linked to the Iztaccíhuatl volcano to the north by the high saddle known as the Paso de Cortés, legends about the two mountains hold an important place in Mexican culture. While the 5426-m peak is volcanically active, there are glaciers on the higher levels of the mountain. Climbing is not allowed, but you can walk on the lower slopes of this legendary volcano.

Opposite page: Volcán Arenal in northern Costa Rica; a perfect symmetrical cone.
Top: Volcán Pacaya, Guatemala; the best geology lesson on the planet. **Above**: Sleeping Volcán Irazú, near Cártago, Costa Rica, calm and beautiful, bides her time until the next eruption.

Festivals and traditions

Mardi Gras in Veracruz

The Shrovetide carnival is said to be Mexico's liveliest. The carnival starts a week before Shrove Tuesday and ends on Ash Wednesday; Saturday to Tuesday are the main days with parades. At this time of year it can be very difficult to find accommodation or transport.

Day of the Dead

Commemorated on 1 and 2 November, the Día de los Muertos is an occasion when families and friends get together to remember friends and relatives who have died. A national holiday in Mexico and throughout Central America, you can respectfully join the occasion at any cemetery. Traditions and activities vary greatly between towns and countries. Two places that have a particularly strong reputation are Mixquic, a small town on the outskirts of Mexico City, and Janitzio, a small island in the state of Michoacán.

Fiesta de Corpus Christi

The Fiesta de Corpus Christi (40 days after Easter) is a four-day feast and one of Panama's most famous and popular festivals. It's a glorious distillation of the Azuero Peninsula's strong Spanish roots and well worth attending. Troops of 'dirty devil' dancers dominate the proceedings, clad in wildly colourful (if deeply grotesque) masks and charging through the streets like imps unleashed from hell. Several other intriguing ceremonies form part of these must-see festivities, including a host of musical processions, dances and a bull hunt led by crowds of enthusiastic children (the 'bull' is actually a man inside a costume).

Semana Santa

The week-long event in Antigua, Guatemala, is a spectacular display of religious ritual and floral design. Through billowing clouds of incense, processions of floats carried by men

TRAVIS HOUSTON/SHUTTERSTOCK

ROBERT HARDING PICTURE LIBRARY/SUPERSTOCK

robed in purple make their way through town, accompanied by music. The largest processions with some of the finest floral carpets are on Palm Sunday and Good Friday. The whole occasion is one of the biggest Easter events in Latin America, so plan your trip well in advance.

Todos Santos

The horse festival of Todos Santos, Guatemala, is one of the most celebrated and spectacular in Central America. Riders race between two points, having a drink at each turn until they fall off. It's a frenzied day that usually degenerates into a drunken mass. The origin dates back to the arrival of the *conquistadores* who arrived on horseback, draped in flowing scarves.

Virgen de Suyapa

Patron Saint of Honduras, the diminutive 6-cm-high statue of the Virgin of Suyapa is one of the most worshipped idols in the country. Residing in the basilica of Suyapa, a suburb of Tegucigalpa, the town is deluged with pilgrims in the first week of February, peaking on the 3rd of the month. The Virgin travels around the country, so check locally to find out about her movements.

Opposite page left: Mexico's wonderfully gaudy Día de los Muertos celebrations.
Opposite page right: Coloured sawdust carpet on Antigua street during Semana Santa.
Top: Easter week in Antigua is rightly world famous. **Above:** Todos Santos in Guatemala has one of the most memorable festivals in the whole of Latin America.

When to go

The best time to go is between October and April, although there are slight regional variations. The rainy season works its way up from the south beginning in May and running through until August, September and even October. This is also hurricane season along the Caribbean. Despite the high-profile storm of Hurricane Wilma and a few lesser known local hurricanes and tropical storms, landfall is relatively rare. If a hurricane does arrive while you're in the area you can get details at www.nhc.noaa.gov. But don't be put off by the term 'rainy season' – in most places and in most years, heavy rain falls for an hour or two a day.

If the time and mood is right, there is little to beat a Latin American festival. Fine costumes, loud music, the sounds of firecrackers tipped off with the gentle wafting of specially prepared foods all (normally) with a drink or two. Whether you're seeking the carnival or happen to stumble across a celebration, the events – big or small – are memorable.

If you want to hit the carnivals there are a few broad dates generally significant throughout the region. Carnival is normally the week before the start of Lent. It's more important in Mexico but you'll probably find regional celebrations in most places. Semana

Above: El Salvador's volcanic landscape creates some incredible vistas.
Opposite page: Colonial window, Mexico.

Santa (Easter Week) is an understandably more spiritual affair. On 2 November is Día de los Muertos (Day of the Dead), again most popular in Mexico but significant throughout the region when families visit cemeteries to honour the dead. Christmas and New Year result in celebrations of some kind, but not always public.

Public holidays throughout the region lead to a complete shut-down in services. No banks, government offices, usually no shops and often far fewer restaurants and bars. It is worth keeping an eye on the calendar to avoid changing money or trying to make travel arrangements on public holidays.

Central America and Mexico

Activity	J	F	M	A	M	J	J	A	S	O	N	D
Whale watching in Baja California, Mexico	★	★	★									★
Monarch butterfly migration, Michoacán, Mexico	★	★										★
Green turtle nesting in Tortuguero, Costa Rica				★	★	★	★					
Leatherback turtle nesting in Tortuguero, Costa Rica						★	★	★	★	★		
Birdwatching throughout the region	★	★	★	★	★	★	★	★	★	★	★	★
Whitewater rafting and surfing throughout the region	★	★	★	★	★	★	★	★	★	★	★	★
Major festivals, especially in Guatemala and Mexico			★	★	★						★	★

Rainfall and climate charts

Mexico City

Month	Average temperature in °C max-min	Average rainfall in mm
Jan	19 - 06	13
Feb	21 - 06	05
Mar	24 - 08	10
Apr	25 - 11	20
May	26 - 12	53
Jun	24 - 13	119
Jul	23 - 12	170
Aug	23 - 12	152
Sep	23 - 12	130
Oct	21 - 10	51
Nov	20 - 08	18
Dec	19 - 06	08

Cancún

Month	Average temperature in °C max-min	Average rainfall in mm
Jan	27 - 19	04
Feb	28 - 20	02
Mar	29 - 22	02
Apr	29 - 23	02
May	31 - 25	05
Jun	32 - 26	07
Jul	32 - 26	04
Aug	32 - 25	06
Sep	32 - 24	09
Oct	31 - 23	09
Nov	29 - 22	04
Dec	28 - 21	04

Guatemala City

Month	Average temperature in °C max-min	Average rainfall in mm
Jan	23 - 12	08
Feb	25 - 12	03
Mar	27 - 14	13
Apr	28 - 14	31
May	29 - 16	152
Jun	27 - 16	274
Jul	26 - 16	203
Aug	26 - 16	198
Sep	26 - 16	231
Oct	24 - 16	173
Nov	23 - 14	23
Dec	22 - 13	08

Belmopan

Month	Average temperature in °C max-min	Average rainfall in mm
Jan	28 - 18	128
Feb	29 - 18	64
Mar	31 - 19	44
Apr	33 - 20	44
May	34 - 22	85
Jun	32 - 23	306
Jul	32 - 22	276
Aug	32 - 22	225
Sep	31 - 22	255
Oct	30 - 21	215
Nov	29 - 20	200
Dec	28 - 19	178

San Salvador

Month	Average temperature in °C max-min	Average rainfall in mm
Jan	32 - 16	08
Feb	33 - 16	05
Mar	24 - 17	10
Apr	34 - 18	43
May	33 - 19	196
Jun	31 - 19	328
Jul	32 - 18	292
Aug	32 - 19	297
Sep	31 - 19	307
Oct	31 - 18	241
Nov	31 - 17	41
Dec	32 - 16	10

Tegucigalpa

Month	Average temperature in °C max-min	Average rainfall in mm
Jan	25 - 14	12
Feb	27 - 14	02
Mar	29 - 15	01
Apr	30 - 17	26
May	30 - 18	180
Jun	28 - 18	177
Jul	27 - 18	70
Aug	28 - 17	74
Sep	28 - 17	151
Oct	27 - 17	87
Nov	26 - 16	38
Dec	25 - 15	14

Managua

Month	Average temperature in °C max-min	Average rainfall in mm
Jan	30 - 20	05
Feb	32 - 21	01
Mar	34 - 22	05
Apr	34 - 23	05
May	34 - 23	76
Jun	31 - 23	296
Jul	31 - 22	134
Aug	31 - 22	130
Sep	31 - 22	182
Oct	31 - 22	243
Nov	31 - 21	59
Dec	31 - 20	05

San José

Month	Average temperature in °C max-min	Average rainfall in mm
Jan	24 - 14	15
Feb	24 - 14	05
Mar	26 - 15	20
Apr	26 - 17	46
May	27 - 17	229
Jun	26 - 17	241
Jul	25 - 17	211
Aug	26 - 16	241
Sep	26 - 16	305
Oct	25 - 16	300
Nov	25 - 16	145
Dec	24 - 14	41

Panama City

Month	Average temperature in °C max-min	Average rainfall in mm
Jan	17 - 04	146
Feb	18 - 05	120
Mar	22 - 08	158
Apr	25 - 12	95
May	28 - 16	98
Jun	31 - 20	153
Jul	32 - 22	222
Aug	32 - 22	191
Sep	31 - 19	156
Oct	26 - 13	89
Nov	22 - 08	115
Dec	18 - 04	103

Sport and activities

Canyoning and caving

ⓘ **Mexico**: see under **Expediciones Umarike**, page 278. **Belize**: see under **Caves Branch Jungle Lodge**, page 831.

Options for caving and canyoning are developing in Mexico and Guatemala but the best caving in the region and the western hemisphere is found in Belize with some of the longest cave systems in the world.

Cenote diving

ⓘ **Mexico**: Mike Madden's CEDAM Dive Centres, PO Box 1, Puerto Aventuras, T/F873-5129; **Aquatech**, Villas de Rosa, PO Box 25, Aventuras Akumal No 35, Tulum, T875-9020, www.cenotes.com; **Cenote Dive Center**, Tulum, T871-2232, www.cenotedive.com, Norwegian-owned.

There are more than 50 cenotes in this area – accessible from Ruta 307 and often well signposted – and cave diving has become very popular. However, it is a specialized sport and, unless you have a cave diving qualification, you must be accompanied by a qualified dive master. A cave diving course involves over 12 hours of lectures and a minimum of 14 cave dives using double tanks, costing around US$600. Accompanied dives start at around US$60. Some of the best cenotes are 'Carwash', on the Cobá road, good even for beginners, with excellent visibility; 'Dos Ojos', just off Ruta 307 south of Aventuras, the second largest underground cave system in the world; it has a possible link to the Nohoch Nah Chich, the most famous cenote and part of a subterranean system recorded as the world's largest, with over 50 km of surveyed passageways connected to the sea. A word of warning: cenote diving has a higher level of risk than open-water diving – do not take risks and only dive with recognized operators.

Climbing

ⓘ See Mexico chapter, page 70, for more information. Other details are listed in the relevant chapters.

If you have a serious interest in rock climbing the place to head for is the massive limestone cliffs and big-wall appeal of Potrero Chico, just outside Monterrey in northern Mexico. There are also opportunities in Humira outside Creel. This sport requires specialist knowledge and thorough safety systems.

The main climbing in the region is found in the highlands of Mexico where there are several peaks which are over 5000 m.

In all countries further south there are several volcanic peaks, active and dormant, that give excellent views and a challenging climb all the way through the isthmus down to Panama. In Guatemala the active volcanic peak of Pacaya is a popular and safe excursion, while the Cuchumatanes Mountains in the mid-west of the country have the country's highest non-volcanic peaks. In Belize the highest climb is at Victoria Peak, best reached from the Cockscomb Basin Jaguar Sanctuary. Moving further south, climbing tends towards trekking. The peaks in Honduras include the hills around Gracias such as Celaque (the highest at 2849 m), Puca and Opulaca. Close to La Ceiba is the rarely climbed Pico de Bonito. In Nicaragua, Volcán Concepción and Madera on Isla de Omotepe are one of the highlights of any trip through the region. In Costa Rica the highest peak is Cerro Chirripó and in Panama Volcán Barú is a 'drive' from the nearby town of Boquete.

Protect the reef

Belize, Mexico, Honduras and Panama offer some of the finest marine environments in the Caribbean Basin, but the major challenge is to keep it that way. It's important that if you dive or snorkel you take responsibility for your own actions, and that your trip contributes to the preservation, rather than the destruction, of the reef. Here are a few ways to help:

1 Don't touch the reef. Even a gentle brush can remove the protective covering of mucus from a coral colony and cause the death of an animal community that has taken hundreds of years to develop.

2 Don't remove anything from the reef.

3 Be aware of your fins and where they go. It's easy to lose track of that deadly (for the coral) 50 cm on the end of your foot.

4 If you want to snorkel but haven't tried it before, practise your technique before you get close to a coral reef. A shallow bottom of a sandy beach or a swimming pool is perfect.

5 When diving, stop your initial descent before you whack straight into the reef below.

6 Lend a hand! Collect any plastic or rubbish you find on the reef or the cayes and make sure it's correctly disposed of. Lost fishing nets can be a huge problem for marine life, killing fish, turtles, even dolphins for years afterwards.

7 Support an organization working to protect coral reefs, locally or worldwide. There are many excellent small-scale grassroots organizations that deserve your support.

Previous page: Divers and sponge, Belize. **Above:** Looking out across Santa Rosa National Park, rare dry tropical forest in northwest Costa Rica. **Opposite page:** Salsipuedes, Baja California, Mexico – an excellent right-point break that works on big swells; not for the beginner.

Diving

ⓘ See full-colour diving section in the middle of this book.

Opportunities for diving and snorkelling can be found throughout the region. Overall the best diving for safety and opportunity is probably in Belize, especially in the offshore Cayes, but prices tend to be higher than elsewhere. The cheapest place to learn to dive is off the Bay Island of Utila, Honduras: just US$200, even less in low season. If arriving in Cancún, learning to dive in the area is surprisingly affordable and you can dive off Isla Mujeres on your way south. Good diving in Costa Rica is limited to the area around Puerto Viejo and Manzanillo on the Caribbean south coast, with the same good conditions continuing south to Bocas del Toro in Panama. Two diving hotspots in the region are the Blue Hole in Belize and the Cocos Islands off Costa Rica. The Blue Hole costs around US$180 for a day trip but you'll need around US$3600 for the 10-day trip to the Cocos Islands.

Fishing

ⓘ Details of the operators are listed in the relevant chapters.

Sea and freshwater fishing are world class, with marlin and sailfish in the deep waters off Costa Rica and Mexico, bonefish a little closer to shore on the flats in Belize, and the freshwater dreams of snook and tarpon lurking in tropical streams along the Caribbean. Costs, however, are generally prohibitive, running to several hundred dollars for the day.

Hiking

ⓘ Details of the trails are listed in the relevant chapters. Most Central American countries have an **Instituto Geográfico**, which sells topographical maps, scale 1:100,000 or 1:50,000. The physical features shown on these are usually accurate; the trails and place names less so. National Parks offices also sell maps.

A network of paths and tracks covers much of Central America. In Guatemala, which has a large indigenous population, you can walk just about anywhere, but in other countries, particularly Costa Rica, you can be limited to the many excellent national parks with hiking trails.

Trekking should not be approached casually. Even if you only plan to be out a couple of hours you should have comfortable, safe footwear (which can cope with the wet) and a daypack to carry your sweater and waterproof. At high altitudes the difference in temperature between sun and shade is remarkable. The longer trips mentioned in this book require basic backpacking equipment. Essential items are: a good backpack, sleeping bag, foam mat, stove, tent or tarpaulin, dried food (not tins), water bottle, compass, trowel for burying human waste.

Hikers have little to fear from the animal kingdom apart from insects; robbery and assault are rare. You are much more of a

threat to the environment than vice versa. Leave no evidence of your passing; don't litter and don't give gratuitous presents of sweets or money to rural villagers. Respect their system of reciprocity; if they give you hospitality or food, then is the time to reciprocate with presents.

Surfing

ⓘ Details of the best surf spots are listed in the relevant chapters.

It's an endless summer of surfing all the way down the Pacific coast. From the north to the south there are popular breaks. From Baja California and Cabo San Lucas down to the Mexican Pipeline at Puerto Escondido there are popular breaks along the Mexican Pacific coast. In El Salvador there are good breaks close to La Libertad, with several all down the Pacific coast of Nicaragua. Costa Rica has well-documented breaks with the main centres at Tamarindo, Malpaís, Jaco and

KATOIMOVE/SHUTTERSTOCK

ANTHONY MERCIECA/SUPERSTOCK

Above: A truly Resplendent Quetzal.
Opposite page: Whitewater rafting on Río Cangrejal, Honduras.

Dominical. Particular breaks are mentioned in the text. If looking to learn, your best chance is probably in Mexico or Costa Rica.

Two main areas provide opportunities for unskilled volunteers: childcare – often at orphanages or schools; and nature projects. Be warned, spontaneous volunteering is becoming more difficult. Organizations that use volunteers have progressed and plan their personnel needs so you may be required to make contact before you visit. Many organizations now charge volunteers for board and lodging, and projects are often for a minimum of four weeks. Guatemala and Costa Rica have fairly well-developed and organized volunteer programmes. The US Peace Corps is the most prominent in the region, working with countries on development projects with two-year assignments for US citizens in countries throughout the region. Variations on the volunteering programme are to enrol on increasingly popular gap-year programmes. These normally incorporate a period of volunteer work with a few months of free time at the end of the programme for travel. **Experiment in International Living** is the UK element of a US international homestay programme that arranges stays with families in Mexico and Central America, with social projects based on the ethos that if you want to live together you need to work together. It's an excellent way to meet people and learn the language.

Volunteering

ⓘ **US Peace Corps**, Paul D Coverdell Peace Corps Headquarters, 1111 20th St NW, Washington, DC 20526, T1-800-424-8580, www.peacecorps.gov; **Experiment in International Living**, T+44-1684-562577, www.eiluk.org. There are many more: details are given in the Essentials sections of the individual countries.

Wildlife and birdwatching

ⓘ See Background, page 1405, for an introduction to the region's wildlife.

Central America and Mexico is home to spectacular wildlife-watching opportunities. Whale watching off the coast of Baja California is popular between mid-December and mid-March, and you have the chance to dive with whale sharks between March and May in southern Belize and the Bay Islands, off Honduras. Another popular animal to see is the manatee, most likely to be in the coastal lagoons of Belize and Honduras.

On land it is the mammals, particularly monkeys and the elusive cat family, that quicken the heartbeat, while in the air, or at least close to the ground the sheer number of bird species mean ornithologists get positively over excited by the opportunities found throughout the region. From Mexico to Panama there are countless sites. Wetland lagoons in Mexico and rainforest sites provide some of the most colourful birdlife. The resplendent quetzal, with its beautifully flamboyant tail feather, is an essential sighting to start any twitcher's career.

Whitewater rafting

ⓘ Details of the operators are listed in the relevant chapters.

Being a potentially dangerous sport, whitewater rafting is not as widespread as it could be, but there are many world-class opportunities in the region. In Mexico try the Antigua/Pescados and Filo-Bobos rivers near Veracruz. In Guatemala there are operators using the Cahabón, Motagua and Esclavos. In Honduras try the Cangrejal near La Ceiba in North Honduras. In Costa Rica the Reventazón and Pacuare are popular rivers, as is the River Chiriquí in Boquete, Panama.

TANIGWEN SANDERSON

How big is your footprint?

The travel industry is growing rapidly, and the impact is becoming increasingly apparent. These impacts can seem remote and unrelated to an individual trip or holiday, but air travel is clearly implicated in global warming and damage to the ozone layer, and resort location and construction can destroy natural habitats and restrict traditional rights and activities. With this in mind, individual choice and awareness can make a difference in many instances (see box opposite); collectively, travellers can have a significant effect in shaping a more responsible and sustainable industry. In an attempt to promote awareness of and credibility for responsible tourism, organizations such as **EC3**, Suite 8, Southern Cross House, 9 McKay Street, Turner, ACT, 2612, Australia, T+61-2-6257-9102, www.greenglobe.com, offer advice on selecting destinations and sites that aim to achieve certain commitments to conservation and sustainable development. Generally, these are large mainstream destinations and resorts but they are

TANGWEN SANDERSON

Restaurants and bars on the shores of Lake Atitlán, Guatemala.

Travelling light

The point of a holiday is, of course, to have a good time, but if it's relatively guilt-free as well, that's even better. Perfect ecotourism would ensure a good living for local inhabitants, while not detracting from their traditional lifestyles, encroaching on their customs or spoiling their environment. Perfect ecotourism probably doesn't exist, but everyone can play their part. Here are a few points worth bearing in mind:

- Where possible choose a destination, tour operator or hotel with a proven ethical and environmental commitment.
- Spend money on locally produced (rather than imported) goods and services and use common sense when bargaining: your few dollars saved may be a week's salary to others.
- Use water and electricity carefully: travellers may receive preferential supply while the needs of local communities are overlooked.
- Consider staying in local accommodation rather than foreign-owned hotels: the economic benefits for host communities are far greater, and there are greater opportunities to learn about local culture.
- Protect wildlife and other natural resources; don't buy souvenirs or goods unless they are made from materials that are clearly sustainably produced and are not protected under CITES legislation (CITES controls trade in endangered species).
- Learn about local etiquette and culture; consider local norms and behaviour and dress appropriately for local cultures and situations.
- Always ask before taking photographs or videos of people.
- Make a voluntary contribution to counter the pollution caused by international air travel. Climate Concern calculates the amount of carbon dioxide you generate, and then offsets it by funding projects that reduce it; visit www.co2.org. Alternatively, you can offset CO_2 emissions from air travel through Climate Care's CO_2 reduction projects, www.climatecare.org.

destinations and resorts but they are still a useful guide and increasingly aim to provide information on smaller operations. Of course travel can have beneficial impacts and this is something to which every traveller can contribute – many national parks are part funded by receipts from visitors. Similarly, travellers can support small-scale enterprises by staying in locally run hotels and hostels, eating in local restaurants and by buying local goods, supplies and crafts. There has been a phenomenal growth in tourism that promotes and supports the conservation of natural environments

and is also fair and equitable to local communities. This 'eco-tourism' segment provides a vast and growing range of destinations and activities in Central America. For example, in Mexico, cultural heritage and ecotourism is being promoted by **Bioplanet@**, T+52-55-5661-6156, www.bioplaneta.com, and in Belize through the **Belize Ecotourism Association**, T+501-722-2119, www.bzecotourism.org, and PACT (the Protected Areas Conservation Trust), T+501-822-3637, www.pactbelize.org.

Screen and page

Books to read

Best known of the home-grown authors is **Carlos Fuentes**, whose *The Death of Artemio Cruz* is a symbolic journey from revolutionary idealism through to corrupt excesses. Another literary giant is **Miguel Angel Asturias**; his Nobel prize-winning *Hombres de Maiz* is an epic tale of the life of Guatemala's indigenous people in the early 20th century. **Juan Rulfo** has also gained an international audience with *Pedro Páramo* and the much-acclaimed *The Burning Plain and Other Stories*.

Fiction by outsiders is more accessible: among the most recommended are **DH Lawrence**'s *The Plumed Serpent* and **Graham Greene**'s *The Lawless Road* and *The Power and the Glory*, which offer great insight into Mexico. He also covers Panama in *Getting to Know the General*, looking at his friendship with dictator Torrijos from the 1960s to the early 1980s. **Paul Theroux** based *The Mosquito Coast* in Honduras, providing one take on an impossible and improbable life on the country's north shore. **Salmon Rushdie** penned *The Jaguar's Smile* on a trip to Sandanista-ruled Nicaragua in the mid-1980s, while **John Le Carré**'s *The Tailor of Panama* is a great read if you like thrillers with geographical context.

Films to watch

Until recently it was the bloody history of Central America and Mexico that represented the region in the movies. *Romero*, starring Raúl Julia, covered the story of the Salvadorian archbishop's assassination. Oliver Stone's *Salvador* takes a journalist's view of the country's civil war. British Director Ken Loach provided a harrowing view of the conflict during the Nicaraguan Revolution in *Carla's Song*. More light-hearted treatments have included *The Tailor of Panama* starring Pierce Brosnan, and *The Mosquito Coast* with Harrison Ford.

Mexico's growing cultural confidence in recent years has seen the country move beyond being just a movie set (Durango in the north of the country was one of the most commonly used settings for US Westerns). The country's film industry has produced international successes including *Como agua para chocolate*, *Danzón*, *Amores Perros* and *Y tu Mamá También*, a road movie set in southern Mexico directed by Alfonso Cuarón. Mexico's currency on the international market was ably demonstrated when Cuarón was named director for *Harry Potter and the Prisoner of Azkaban*, the third film in the series. *Frida* was another international hit, celebrating the life of Mexico's most famous artist.

Contents

Essentials

Getting there

All countries in Latin America (in fact across the world) officially require travellers entering their territory to have an onward or return ticket and may at times ask to see that ticket. Although rarely enforced, this regulation can create problems. In lieu of an onward ticket out of the country you are entering, any ticket out of another Latin American country may suffice, or proof that you have sufficient funds to buy a ticket (a credit card will do). International air tickets are expensive if purchased in Latin America.

Air

Certain Central American countries impose local tax on flights originating there. Among these are Guatemala, Costa Rica, Panama and Mexico. Details of all the main airlines flying to each country are given in the relevant country Essentials sections.

Fares from Europe and North America to Latin American destinations vary. Peak periods and higher prices correspond to holiday season in the northern hemisphere. The very busy seasons are as follows: 7 December to 15 January and July to mid-September. If you intend travelling during those times, book as far ahead as possible. Check with an agency for the best deal for when you wish to travel. There is a wide range of offers to choose from in a highly competitive environment. Check the lists of discount flight agents for UK and Ireland, North America, and Australia and New Zealand. Also check the list of airline websites here and the list of tour operators in the UK and North America, on page 61. Many airlines share passengers across different routes to increase the areas that they can claim to cover. So you many fly the transatlantic leg with one airline before changing to a different airline for the final leg.

Most airlines offer discounted (cheaper than official) fares of one sort or another on scheduled flights. These are not offered by the airlines direct to the public, but through agencies that specialize in this type of fare. An indication of cost is difficult to give due to the large number of variables, not least the current fluctuations in currency and the wide variations in oil prices in recent years. The main factors are frequency of flights and popularity of destination at a particular time of year and there is a great price fluctuation. As a rough guide a three-month London–Mexico return in August is between US$1050. In November the same flight falls to US$810. A three-month London–Costa Rica return is US$1100 in August, falling to US$1000 in November. Flying into one place and out of another can be very useful, but usually costs extra. Flying into Mexico City and out of Costa Rica in August is around US$1050, while in November look to pay around US$920. While these are prices from London, the European prices are usually similar or cheaper as flights often involve European airlines such as **Martinair** or **Iberia**.

Travellers from Australia and New Zealand are getting an increasingly better deal compared with recent years, with special offers occasionally down to AUS$1900 flying direct to Mexico City. The more regular price is close to AUS$3200.

Other fares fall into three groups, and are all on scheduled services: **Excursion** (return) fares: these have restricted validity either seven to 90 days, or seven to 180 days, depending on the airline. They are fixed-date tickets where the dates of travel cannot be changed after issue without incurring a penalty. **Yearly fares:** these may be bought on a one-way or return basis, and usually the returns can be issued with the return date left open. You must, however, fix the route. **Student** (or Under-26) fares: one way and returns

Packing for Central America and Mexico

Take as little as possible. Clothes that are quick and easy to wash and dry are a good idea. Loose-fitting clothes are more comfortable in hot climates and can be layered if it gets cooler. Sarongs are versatile: they can be used as a towel, beach mat, skirt, sheet, or scarf, to name but a few. But don't pack too many clothes; you can easily, and cheaply, buy things en route. Four musts are good walking shoes, a sun hat, sunglasses and flip-flops or sandals.

Don't load yourself down with toiletries either. They're heavy and can usually be found cheaply and easily everywhere. Items like contact lens solutions and tampons may be harder to find, but stock up in major cities as you go along and there shouldn't be a problem. Dental floss can be useful for backpack repairs as well.

Probably the most useful single item is a Swiss Army knife (with corkscrew), followed by a money belt, a headtorch/flashlight (not everywhere has 24-hour electricity), the smallest alarm clock you can find and a basic medical kit,

Pack photocopies of essential documents like passport, visas and traveller's cheque receipts, in case you lose the originals. For security, a small padlock is useful for locking up your bag, and on the doors of some of the more basic hotels. Finally, a climbing karabiner can be handy for clipping your bag on to something and foiling the grab thief.

Photographers using film will want to take all that they will require for the trip, ideally in a bag that is both water and dust proof – if not available, triple wrap them in plastic bags. As the march to digital continues, availability of film is becoming unpredictable. Digital photographers will want to find a way of clearing the camera memory either by burning to CD, downloading to a website or some other method. You'll also need to take recharging gear and related adaptors.

available, or 'open jaws' (see below). There is also a wider range of cheap one-way student fares originating in Latin America than can be bought outside the continent. There is less availability in the busy seasons. The range of student fares is wider to Mexico than elsewhere. Some airlines are flexible on the age limit, others are strict.

Open-jaw fares For people intending to travel a linear route and return from a different point from that which they entered, there are 'open-jaw' or multi-stop flights, which are available on student, yearly, or excursion fares.

Flights from Europe

Airfares from Europe to Mexico City between February and June can be very low (see above), although the same does not apply to holiday destinations like Cancún or Acapulco. Most European airlines have a regular weekly service to the capital throughout the year so it is worth considering Mexico City as an entry/exit point for a Mexican trip for the widest range of options and prices. If you do not stop over in Mexico City, low-cost add-ons are available to Mexican domestic destinations through links with the main airlines.

With the promotion of Cancún as a gateway from Europe, there has been an increase in the number of scheduled flights to Mexico (for example **Iberia** flies daily from Madrid and Barcelona to Cancún via Miami; **Air France/American Airlines** daily from Paris to Cancún;

Condor Flugdienst from Frankfurt once a week to Cancún, **British Airways** operates a daily flight from London Gatwick to Cancún via Dallas Fort Worth). If starting in the US and crossing Mexico's northern border, flights can be surprisingly cheap if you get a special offer linking with one of the US international carriers.

Moving beyond Mexico there are few direct flights and asking a local discount supplier for the cheap options is the best way of finding out about flights. Seasonal charter flights can work out to be very affordable. **Martinair**, a subsidiary of **KLM**, flies Costa Rica–Netherlands, for around US$500 return. There are several cheap French charters to Mexico and Guatemala and a number of 'packages' that include flights from Mexico to Cuba can be bought locally in Mexico, Guatemala, Costa Rica or in advance. Travellers starting their journey in continental Europe should make local enquiries about charters and agencies offering the best deals.

Flights from the US and Canada

Flying to Mexico from the US and Canada offers a very wide range of options. The main US carriers – **American Airlines**, **Continental** and **United** – offer flights to many cities in Mexico in addition to daily flights to Mexico City, Guadalajara, Cancún, Monterrey and Puerto Vallarta. Direct international flights also serve many other cities in the country; the main through points are Miami, Dallas/Fort Worth, Los Angeles and San Francisco. From Canada the options are less varied, but regular flights serve the main cities with direct flights from Montreal and Toronto. Keep an eye out for special offers, which can produce extremely cheap flights (often at very short notice). Fewer flights operate to Central America from the US and Canada.

Flights from Central and Latin America

Links throughout the isthmus are provided by **Taca**, a regional association linking five Central American national carriers. Main connections within the region and to other countries in Latin America and the Caribbean are provided through Mexico, San Salvador and Panama City. Prices for regional services are beginning to fall and are worth considering.

Flights from Australia and New Zealand

Flights to Central America and Mexico from Australia and New Zealand are with **United Airlines** and generally connect through Los Angeles.

General hints

Given complete free choice many people do not know where they will end up after several months travelling and would like to leave arranging the return leg of a ticket open in terms of date and departing airport or better still purchase a return leg when the time is right. In reality this is not a good idea. Two one-way tickets are always more expensive than a return and purchasing a ticket to the US or Europe from Central America is almost always more expensive than it would be from your home country. If you have a return ticket you can normally change the return leg date of travel and often the airport (normally at a charge) at local travel agents.

If you buy discounted air tickets always check the reservation with the airline concerned to make sure the flight still exists. Also remember that airlines' schedules change in March and October each year, so if you're going to be away a long time it's best to leave return flight coupons open. If you know that you will be returning at the very busy seasons you should make a reservation. In addition, it is vital to check in advance whether you are entitled to any refund or re-issued ticket if you lose, or have stolen, a discounted air ticket.

E-tickets are increasingly common. If you are unsure about the use of an e-ticket, telephone the company concerned. If you can't locate a telephone number to call, it's probably best not to book with the company. At the booking stage, you should be reassured that you are buying a real ticket. If you find yourself stuck somewhere, you'll want to talk to a person – not a machine.

Weight allowances if going direct from Europe are generally 22 kg for economy and business class or 30 kg for first class. If you have special baggage requirements, check with an agency about anomalies that exist on different weight allowances one way, for example. Certain carriers (for example **Iberia** and **Air France**) offer a two-piece allowance out of the UK only, each piece up to 32 kg. Many people travel to Mexico and Central America via the US, and all carriers via the USA offer this allowance in both directions. Weight limits for internal flights are often lower, so it's best to enquire beforehand. For all the discussion of allowances, you're likely to have to carry your bag at times. So perhaps your personal carrying capacity is a more useful weight consideration.

Airport information
As a general rule, try to avoid arriving at night. If that's not possible, book a hotel for the first night at least and take a taxi or shuttle bus direct to your hotel. It may not be the cheapest way out of the airport, but it is the simplest and safest. Each country in the region charges an airport departure tax – information is given in each chapter for the relevant country.

Ticket agents and airlines

Most international and several domestic airlines have websites that are useful for gaining information about flights. As yet you are unlikely to get the best price online, so use the websites in an advisory capacity only.

Airlines
AeroMéxico www.aeromexico.com
Air France www.airfrance.com
Alaska Airlines www.alaskaairlines.com
Alitalia www.alitalia.com
American Airlines www.aa.com
Avianca www.avianca.com
British Airways www.britishairways.com
Condor www.condor.de
Continental www.continental.com
Copa www.copaair.com
Cubana www.cubana.cu
Delta www.delta.com
Iberia www.iberia.com
Japan Airlines www.jal.com
KLM www.klm.com

LanChile www.lanchile.com
Lufthansa www.lufthansa.com
Martinair www.martinair.com
Mexicana www.mexicana.com
Northwest www.nwa.com
Qantas www.qantas.com.au
Taca www.taca.com
United www.united.com
Varig www.varig.com
For a full list of airline websites visit www.evasions.com/airlines1.htm.

Mexican low-cost airlines
Interjet www.interjet.com.mx
MexicanaClick www.clickmexicana.com
Mexicanalink www.mexicana.com
VivaAerobus www.vivaaerobus.com
Volaris www.volaris.com.mx

Web resources
www.expedia.com
www.lastminute.com
www.opodo.com
www.orbitz.com

www.priceline.com
www.travelocity.com

Discount flight agents
In the UK
Journey Latin America, 12-13 Heathfield Terrace, London, W4 4JE, T020-8747 8315; www.journeylatinamerica.co.uk.

South American Experience, Welby House, 96 Wilton Rd, London, SW1V 1DW, T0845-277 3366, www.southamerican experience.co.uk.

STA Travel, 45 branches in the UK (450 worldwide). Find your closest at T0871-230 0040, www.statravel.co.uk. Specialists in low-cost student/youth flights and tours, also good for student ID cards.

Trailfinders, 194 Kensington High St, London, W8 7RG, T020-7938 3939, www.trailfinders.com.

Rest of Europe
Die Reisegalerie, Grüneburgweg 84, 60323 Frankfurt, Germany, T069-9720-6000, www.reisegalerie.com.

Images du Monde, 14 rue Lahire, 75013 Paris, France, T1-4424-8788, www.imagenes-tropicales.com. Also with an office in Costa Rica.

Thika Travel, Kerkplein 6, 3628 AE, Kockengen (gem. Breukelen), Holland, T0346-242526, www.thika.nl.

North America
Air Brokers International, 685 Market St, Suite 400, San Francisco, CA94102, T01-800-883-3273, www.airbrokers.com.

Discount Airfares Databases Online, www.etn.nl/discount.htm. Discount agent links.

Exito Latin American Travel Specialists, 108 Rutgers Av, Fort Collins, CO 80525, T1-800-655-4053, www.exito-travel.com.

STA Travel, T1-800-781-4040, www.statravel.com Branches throughout the US and Canada.

Travel CUTS, 187 College St, Toronto, ON, M5T 1P7, T1-888-359-2887, www.travel cuts.com. Student discount fares.

Australia and New Zealand
Flight Centres, 82 Elizabeth St, Sydney 2000, T133-133, www.flightcentre.com.au; Unit 3, 239 Queen St, Auckland, T0800-243544, www.flightcentre.co.nz. With branches in other towns and cities.

STA Travel, 841 George St, Sydney, T02-9212-1255, www.statravel.com.au. In NZ: 267 Queen St, Auckland, www.statravel.co.nz, T0800-474-400. Also in major towns and university campuses.

Travel.com.au, 76-80 Clarence St, Sydney, T1300-130483, www.travel.com.au.

Trailfinders, 8 Spring St, Sydney, NSW 2000, www.trailfinders.com.au, T1300-780-212.

Boat

Sailing your own vessel
Following the coastal route doesn't have to be done from the land side, as thousands of sailors who follow the good-weather sailing around the coast of Mexico and Central America can confirm. Indeed there seem to be increasing numbers of people travelling this way. Between California, the Panama Canal and Florida dozens of marinas await the sailor looking to explore the region from the sea. A guide to the marinas and sailing ports of the region is *Cruising Ports: the Central American Route*, and Mexico Boating Guide by Capt Pat Rains, published by Point Loma Publishing in San Diego. Captain Rain is an experienced navigator of Mexican and Central American waters with over 30 Panama transits under her cap (www.centralamericanboating.com).

Travelling by boat to the region is really only worth considering if you are shipping a vehicle from Europe or the US. Enquiries regarding passages should be made through agencies in your own country. In the UK, **Strand Voyages** have information on occasional one-way services to the Gulf of Mexico from Europe. Details on shipping cars are given in the relevant country sections.

In Europe
The Cruise People, 88 York St, London, W1H 1QT, T020-7723-2450, www.cruise people.co.uk; 1252 Lawrence Av East, Suite 210, Toronto, Canada, M3A 1C3, T416-444-2410.

SGV Reisenzentrum Weggis, Globoship, Rütligasse 3, CH-6000 Luzern 7, Switzerland, T141-248-0048, www.frachtschiffreisen.ch.

Strand Voyages, 357 Strand, London, WC2R OHS, T020-7010-7990, www.strandtravel.co.uk.

In the USA
Freighter World Cruises, 180 South Lake Av, Suite 340, Pasadena, CA 91101-2655, T1-800-531-7774, www.freighterworld.com.

Travltips Cruise and Freighter Travel Association, PO Box 580188, Flushing, New York 11358, T1-800-872-8584, www.travltips.com.

Road

Travel from the USA
There are a multitude of entry points from the US, the main ones being Tijuana, Nogales, Ciudad Juárez, Piedras Negras, Nuevo Laredo and Matamoros. Details of these and others are provided in the Mexico chapter. Crossing the border is simple and hassle-free for foot passengers and reasonably straightforward for people travelling with their own vehicle. All border towns have bus terminals that provide long-distance bus services. Alternatively, consider catching a long-distance bus from inside the US. **Greyhound** and others offer the service from border towns and towns further north such as Los Angeles or even Chicago.

If you are thinking of travelling from your own country via the USA, or of visiting the USA after Latin America, you are strongly advised to get your visa and find out about any other requirements from a US Consulate in your own country before travelling. Although visa requirements for air travellers with round-trip tickets to the USA have been relaxed, it is advisable to have a visa to allow entry by land, or on airlines from South and Central America which are not 'participating carriers' on the Visa Waiver scheme.

Travellers are not permitted to bring any meats, fruits, vegetables, plants, animals, and plant and animal products into Mexico. Travellers who fail to declare items can be fined up to US$100 on the spot, and their exit from the airport will be delayed. Call T301-436-5908 for a copy of the helpful pamphlet, *Travelers' Tips*.

Getting around

Bus travel is the most popular style of transport for 'independent' travellers. An excellent network criss-crosses the region varying in quality from luxurious intercity cruisers with air conditioning, videos and fully reclining seats, to beaten-up US-style school buses or 'chicken buses'.

Travelling under your own steam is also very popular. Driving your own vehicle – car, camper van, motorbike and bicycle – offers wonderful freedom and may not be as expensive or as bureaucratic as you think. From the letters we receive, the ever-greater cooperation between the nations of Central America is producing dramatic benefits at border crossings for those who decide to go it alone. Indeed, since 2006, when Guatemala, El Salvador, Honduras and Nicaragua signed the **Central America-4**, it's been even easier (see box, page 41). With the comprehensive road network it's easy to miss out on other sensible choices. Don't shun the opportunity to take a short flight. While you'll need to enquire about precise costs, the view from above provides a different perspective and the difference in cost may not be as great as you think. Getting around in Central America is rarely a problem whether travelling by bus, car, bike, in fact almost any mode of transport.

There is just one caveat that stands good across all situations: be patient when asking directions. Often Latin Americans will give you the wrong answer rather than admit they do not know. Distances are notoriously inaccurate so ask a few people.

Air

With the exception of El Salvador, all countries have a domestic flight service. Prices vary but it is definitely worth considering an aerial 'hop' if it covers a lot of difficult terrain and you get the bonus of a good view. If you know the outline of your itinerary, it may be worth booking internal flights before you arrive in the country. They are often cheaper.

Air passes

An option worth exploring is the airpass, usually offered by an airline or group of airlines. The standard scheme works on system of vouchers. A voucher covers a set distance between any two destinations. You simply buy as many vouchers as you want. **Mexicana** operates one such scheme and there is **All-America Airpass**, with 27 participating airlines from the US, Mexico, the Caribbean, Central and South America. These passes must be purchased in conjunction with an international air ticket.

Low-frills airlines have arrived in the region, with five operating in Mexico. Keep an eye on websites for special offers; see page 37.

Boat

Keeping all options open, water transport has to be a consideration – although not a very realistic one in terms of reaching a set destination. Beyond the value of sightseeing particularly in small, quiet tropical rivers, genuine water transportation is on the decline. You'll find a few regular ferry schedules that avoid circuitous land routes. The main journeys are from the tip of Baja California to the Mexican mainland; between the Cayes of Belize and skipping down the coastline; from the Bay Islands of Honduras to the mainland; across Lake Nicaragua; and in Costa Rica, where there are connections between the mainland and the Osa and Nicoya peninsulas on the Pacific Coast. If heading from Panama to South America you can work your way along the Caribbean coastline to Colombia using a number of small sporadically available vessels.

Beyond this functional travel one journey stands out: travelling the Panama Canal (as opposed to just seeing it!) and crewing a private yacht. Both of these require flexible schedules and good timing, but you might get lucky. Conditions of 'employment' vary greatly – you may get paid, you may get board and lodgings, you may even have to pay. See the Panama chapter for further information.

Border cooperation

In June 2006, Guatemala, El Salvador, Honduras, and Nicaragua entered into a 'Central America-4 (CA-4) Border Control Agreement'. Under the terms of the agreement, citizens of the four countries may travel freely across land borders from one of the countries to any of the others without completing entry and exit formalities at Immigration checkpoints. US citizens and other eligible foreign nationals, who legally enter any of the four countries, may similarly travel among the four without obtaining additional visas or tourist entry permits for the other three countries. Immigration officials at the first port of entry determine the length of stay, up to a maximum period of 90 days.

Road

The dramatic change in oil prices in 2007-8 has had an impact on the cost of road travel. International currency fluctuations has complicated the impact. Whether travelling by bus or car, the price has changed. Fortunately, the price will always be cheap relative to your home country, where transport is likely to be affected in the same way.

Bus

There is an extensive road system with frequent bus services throughout Mexico and Central America. Some of these services are excellent. In mountainous country, however, and after long journeys, do not expect buses to get to their destination anywhere near on time. Avoid turning up for a bus at the last minute; if it is full it may depart early. In general travellers tend to sit near the front – going round bends and over bumps has less impact on your body near the front axle, making the journey more comfortable and reducing the likelihood of motion sickness (on some long journeys it also means you are further from the progressively smelly toilets at the back of the bus). Tall travellers are advised to take aisle seats on long journeys as this allows more leg room. When the journey takes more than three or four hours, meal stops at country inns or bars, good and bad, are the rule. Often no announcement is made on the duration of the stop; ask the driver and follow him, if he eats, eat. See what the locals are eating – and buy likewise, or make sure you're stocked up on food and drink at the start. For drinks, stick to bottled water, soft drinks or coffee (black). The food sold by vendors at bus stops may be all right; watch if locals are buying. See page 58 for security in buses. Make sure you have a sweater or blanket to hand for long bus journeys, especially at night; even if it's warm outside, the air conditioning is often fierce.

International buses link the capital cities providing an effective way of quickly covering a lot of ground. There are several companies but the main operator is **Ticabus** with headquarters in Costa Rica, www.ticabus.com. However, bear in mind that Panama–Guatemala with **Ticabus** takes almost three days and costs around US$100, plus accommodation in Managua and San Salvador. You may want to consider flying if you need to get through more than one country quickly.

Car

If driving, an international driving licence is useful, although not always essential. Membership of motoring organizations can also be useful for discounts such as hotel charges, car rentals, maps and towing charges.

The kind of motoring you do will depend on your car. A 4WD is not necessary, although it does give you greater flexibility in mountain and jungle territory. Wherever you travel you should expect from time to time to find roads that are badly maintained, damaged or closed during the wet season, and delays because of floods, landslides and huge potholes.

Be prepared for all manner of mechanical challenges. The electronic ignition and fuel metering systems on modern emission-controlled cars are allergic to humidity, heat and dust, and cannot be repaired by mechanics outside the main centres. Standard European and Japanese cars run on fuel with a higher octane rating than is commonly available in North, Central or South America. Note that in some areas gas stations are few and far between. Fill up when you see one: the next one may be out of fuel.

Documents Land entry procedures for all countries are simple though time-consuming, as the car has to be checked by customs, police and agriculture officials (see Mexico, Getting around by car). All you need is the registration document in the name of the driver, or, in the case of a car registered in someone else's name, a notarized letter of authorization. Note that Costa Rica does not recognize the International Driving Licence, which is otherwise useful. In Guatemala, Honduras and Costa Rica, the car's entry is stamped into the passport so you may not leave the country even temporarily without it. A written undertaking that the vehicle will be re-exported after temporary importation is useful and may be requested in Nicaragua, Costa Rica and Panama.

Most countries give a limited period of stay, but allow an extension if requested in advance. Of course, do be very careful to keep **all** the papers you are given when you enter, to produce when you leave. An army of 'helpers' loiters at each border crossing, waiting to guide motorists to each official in the correct order, for a tip. They can be very useful, but don't give them your papers. Bringing a car in by sea or air is much more complicated and expensive; generally you will have to hire an agent to clear it through.

Insurance for the vehicle against accident, damage or theft is best arranged in the country of origin. In Latin American countries it is very expensive to insure against accident and theft, especially as you should take into account the value of the car increased by duties calculated in real (that is non-devaluing) terms. If the car is stolen or written off, you will be required to pay very high duty on its value. A few countries (for example Costa Rica) insist on compulsory third-party insurance, to be bought at the border; in other countries it's technically required, but not checked up on (again, see Mexico, Getting around by car, for details on **Sanborn's** and other insurers, who will insure vehicles for driving in Mexico and Central America). Get the legally required minimum cover – not expensive – as soon as you can, because if you should be involved in an accident and are uninsured, your car could be confiscated. If anyone is hurt, do not pick them up (you become liable). Seek assistance from the nearest police station or hospital if you are able to do so. You may find yourself facing a hostile crowd, even if you are not to blame. Expect frequent road checks by police, military (especially Honduras, where there is a check point on entering and leaving every town), agricultural and forestry produce inspectors, and any other curious official who wants to know what a foreigner is doing driving around in his domain. Smiling simple-minded patience is the best tactic to avoid harassment.

For a good, first-hand overview of the challenges of travelling overland in your own vehicle, get hold of a copy of *Panama or Bust*, by Jim Jaillet, www.panamaorbust.com, which covers the challenges of preparing for and completing a year-long trip from the US to Panama and back.

Security Spare no ingenuity in making your car secure. Avoid leaving the car unattended except in a locked garage or guarded parking space. Remove all belongings and leave the empty glove compartment open when the car is unattended. Also lock the clutch or accelerator to the steering wheel with a heavy, obvious chain or lock. Street children will generally protect your car in exchange for a tip. Note down key numbers and carry spares of the most important ones, but don't keep all spares inside the vehicle.

Shipping a vehicle to Central America Two recommended shipping lines are **Wallenius Wilhelmsen** ① *head office in Norway at Box 33, N-1324 Lysaker, T+47-6758-4100, for other offices visit www.2wglobal.com*, and, in the US, **American Cargo Service Inc** ① *2305 Northwest 107 Av, Box 122, Miami, FL 331720, T305-592-8065*. Motorcyclists will find good online recommendations at www.horizonsunlimited.com.

Shipping from Panama to mainland South America is expensive; shop around to find the cheapest way. The shipping lines and agents, and the prices for the services from Panama and elsewhere change frequently. Current details and recommendations can be found in the Panama chapter under Shipping a vehicle, page 1295.

Car hire

While not everyone has the time or inclination to travel with their own car, the freedom that goes with renting for a few days is well worth considering, especially if you can get a group of three or four together to share the cost. The main international car-hire companies operate in all countries, but tend to be expensive. Hotels and tourist agencies will tell you where to find cheaper rates, but you will need to check that you have such basics as a spare wheel, toolkit, functioning lights, etc. If you plan to do a lot of driving and will have time at the end to dispose of it, investigate the possibility of buying a second-hand car locally; since hiring is so expensive it may work out cheaper and will probably do you just as well. For visiting Mexico and beyond, investigate the cost of buying a car in the USA and selling it there at the end of a trip (do not try to sell a car illegally in Mexico or Central America).

Car hire insurance Check exactly what the hirer's insurance policy covers. In many cases it will only protect you against minor bumps and scrapes, not major accidents, or 'natural' damage (for example flooding). Ask if extra cover is available. Also find out, if using a credit card, whether the card automatically includes insurance. Beware of being billed for scratches that were on the vehicle before you hired it. When you return the vehicle make

sure you check it with someone at the office and get signed evidence that it is returned in good condition and that you will not be charged.

Cycles and motorbikes

Cycling Unless you are planning a journey almost exclusively on paved roads – when a high-quality touring bike would probably suffice – a mountain bike is recommended. The good-quality ones are incredibly tough and rugged. Although touring bike and to a lesser extent mountain bike spares are available in the larger Latin American cities, you'll find that locally manufactured goods are often shoddy and rarely last. In some countries, such as Mexico, imported components can be found but they tend to be very expensive. Buy everything you can before you leave home. **Note** From Guatemala to Panama, border officials are likely to ask for a document of ownership and a frame number for your bicycle.

Recommended reading: *Richard's New Bicycle Book* (Pan) makes useful reading for even the most mechanically minded. Also recommended is *Latin America by Bike – A Complete Touring Guide*, Walter Sienko (The Mountaineers, 1993). For a first-hand account of travelling through the entire region by bike, look at *The Road That Has No End*, by Tim Travis (www.downtheroad.org). Tim and Cindie set out on a round the world trip in 2002 and are still going. This book covers the stretch from Mexico to Panama.

The **Expedition Advisory Centre** ① *at the Royal Geographical Society, 1 Kensington Gore, London, SW7 2AR, T+44-(0)20-7591-3030, www.rgs.org*, has published a booklet on planning a long-distance bike trip titled *Bicycle Expeditions*, by Paul Vickers. Published in March 1990, it is available as a PDF from the website or £5 for a photocopy. In the UK the **Cyclists' Touring Club** ① *CTC, Parklands, Railton Rd, Guildford, Surrey, GU2 9JX, T0844-736-8450, www.ctc.org.uk*, has information on touring, technical information and discusses the relative merits of different types of bikes.

Motorbikes People are generally very friendly to motorcyclists and you can make many friends by returning friendship to those who show an interest in you. Buying a bike in the States and driving down works out cheaper than buying one in Europe. In making your choice go for a comfortable bike. The motorcycle should be off-road capable, without necessarily being an off-road bike. A passport, International Driving Licence and bike registration document are required.

Security This is not a problem in most countries. Try not to leave a fully laden bike on its own. A D-lock or chain will keep the bike secure. An alarm gives you peace of mind if you leave the bike outside a hotel at night. Look for hotels that have a courtyard or more secure parking and never leave luggage on the bike overnight or whilst unattended. Also take a cover for the bike.

Shipping Bikes may be sent from Panama to Colombia by cargo flight. You must drain the fuel and oil and remove the battery, but it is easier to disconnect and seal the overflow tube. Tape cardboard over fragile bits and load the bike yourself. The Darién Gap is impossible unless you carry the bike. For details on Panama, see page 1295.

Border crossings All borders in Central America seem to work out at about US$20 per vehicle. The exceptions to this are Mexico (see Getting around by car in Mexico) and Panama (approximately US$4.50). All borders are free on exit, or should be on most occasions. Crossing borders on a Sunday or a holiday normally incurs double the standard charges in Central American countries. It is sometimes very difficult to find out exactly what is being paid for. If in doubt, ask to see the boss and/or the rule book.

Hitchhiking

Hitchhiking in Latin America is reasonably safe and straightforward for males and couples, provided you speak some Spanish. It is a most enjoyable mode of transport – a good way to meet the local people, to improve one's languages and to learn about the country. If trying to hitchhike away from main roads and in sparsely populated areas, however, allow plenty of time, and ask first about the volume of traffic on the road. On long journeys, set out at the crack of dawn, which is when trucks usually leave. They tend to go longer distances than cars. However, it should be said that hitchhiking involves inherent risks and should be approached sensibly and with caution.

Train

Trains are like nature – they are treasured when threatened with extinction. Now that the privatization and subsequent closure of train lines in Mexico and Central America is almost complete there is a renaissance of interest in the classic journeys including the **Copper Canyon** in northern Mexico, the **Tequila Express** running from Guadalajara to Tequila (www.tequilaexpress.com.mx), a fledgling tourist service in **Costa Rica** offering a couple of short runs and the **Trans-Isthmus** railroad in Panama. With the exception of the Copper Canyon, none of these are genuine train journeys. Trains do run in a few countries – Mexico and El Salvador– but they are slower than buses and there is no such thing as a scheduled service. Train travel is no longer a viable means of transport for the region.

Maps

Maps from the **Institutos Geográficos Militares** in capital cities are often the only good maps available in Latin America. It is therefore wise to get as many as possible in your home country before leaving, especially if travelling overland. An excellent series of maps covering the whole region and each country is published by **International Travel Maps (ITM)** ① *12300 Bridgeport Rd, Richmond, BC, Canada, T604-273-1400, www.itmb.com*, most with historical notes by the late Kevin Healey.

An excellent source of maps is **Stanfords** ① *12-14 Long Acre, Covent Garden, London, WC2E 9LP, T+44-020-7836-1321, www.stanfords.co.uk, also in Bristol and Manchester.* Internet ordering and international delivery service available.

Sleeping

Hotels

At the top end of the market, mid- and upper-range hotel chains can be found throughout the region. A cheap but not bad hotel might be US$15 a night upwards in Mexico, less in some but not all of the Central American countries. In many of the popular destinations there is often an established preferred choice budget option. The quality of these fluctuates. The good ones stay on top of the game, the mediocre ones fade and bloom with the fashions. For those on a really tight budget, it is a good idea to ask for a boarding house – *casa de huéspedes, hospedaje, pensión, casa familial* or *residencial*, according to the country; they are normally to be found in abundance near bus and railway stations and markets. The very cheapest hotels may not have 24-hour water supplies so ask when the water is available. There are often great seasonal variations in

Hotel prices and facilities

LL (over US$150) to **A** (US$46-65) Hotels in these categories can be found in most of the large cities but especially where there is a strong concentration of tourists or business travellers. They should offer pool, sauna, gym, jacuzzi, business facilities including email, restaurants and bars. A safe box is usually provided in each room. Credit cards are usually accepted and dollars cash changed occasionally at below market rates.

B (US$31-45) Hotels in this category should provide more than the standard facilities and a fair degree of comfort. Many include a good breakfast and offer extras such as a colour TV, minibar and air conditioning. They may also provide tourist information and their own transport for airport pickups. Service is generally good and most accept credit cards although a lower rate is often offered for cash.

C (US$21-30) and **D** (US$12-20) Hotels in these categories range from very comfortable to bare and functional. There are some real bargains to be had. You should expect your own bathroom, constant hot water, a towel, soap and toilet paper. Some-times there'll be a restaurant and a communal sitting area. Wi-Fi is increasingly common in the better **C**-class hotels. In tropical regions, rooms are usually equipped with air conditioning although this may be rather old. Hotels used to catering for foreign tourists and backpackers often have luggage storage, money exchange and kitchen facilities.

E (US$7-11) and **F** (under US$7) Hotels in these categories can be extremely simple with bedside or ceiling fans, shared bathrooms and little in the way of furniture. Standards of cleanliness may not be high, but it's not all gloomy; there are some spectacular places in this price range. In towns, a room with a window can often make the difference between OK and intolerable. Balance that with possible noise and security issues.

hotel prices in resorts. In Mexico, couples should ask for a room with *cama matrimonial* (double bed), which is normally cheaper than a room with two beds. Note that in the text the term 'with bath' usually means 'with shower and toilet', not 'with bath tub'.

Motels, particularly in northern Mexico, are extremely popular and tend to provide accessible, economic accommodation close to the main roads. Further south, the term 'motel' picks up an altogether seedier interpretation.

Making reservations is a good idea, particularly at times you know are going to be busy or if you are travelling a long distance and won't have the energy to look around for a room. At the lower end of the market, having reservations honoured can be difficult. Ask the hotel if there is anything you can do to secure the room. If arriving late, make sure the hotel knows what time you plan to arrive.

Youth hostels

The **International Youth Hostel Association** ⓘ *www.hihostels.com*, has a growing presence in the region with several places in Mexico and Costa Rica. With other affiliated hostels joining it is worth considering getting membership if you are staying in Mexico for a while. While there is no shortage of cheap accommodation, youth hostels do still offer a fairly reliable standard of cleanliness. Members with an ID card normally get a discount.

The web has spawned some great communities and independent travellers should take a look at www.couchsurfing.com. It's a way of making friends by kipping on their couch. It's grown rapidly in the last couple of years– and appears to be a great concept that works.

Camping
Organized campsites are referred to in the text immediately below hotel lists, under each town. If there is no organized site in town, a football pitch or gravel pit might serve. Obey the following rules for 'wild' camping: (1) arrive in daylight and pitch your tent as it gets dark; (2) ask permission to camp from a person in authority; (3) never ask a group of people – especially young people; (4) avoid camping on a beach (because of sandflies and thieves). If you can't get information, camp in a spot where you can't be seen from the nearest inhabited place and make sure no one saw you go there.

If taking a cooker, the most frequent recommendation is a multifuel stove (for example MSR International Coleman Peak 1), which will burn unleaded petrol or, if that is not available, kerosene, *benzina blanca*, etc. Alcohol-burning stoves are simple, reliable, but slow and you have to carry a lot of fuel: for a methylated spirit-burning stove buy *alcohol desnaturalizado, alcohol metílico, alcohol puro (de caña)* or *alcohol para quemar* (avoid this in Honduras as it does not burn). Ask for 95%. In Mexico fuel is sold in supermarkets; in all countries it can be found in pharmacies. Gas cylinders and bottles are usually exchangeable, but if not can be recharged; specify whether you use butane or propane. Gas canisters are not always available. Camping supplies are usually only available in the larger cities, so stock up on them when possible.

Hammocks
A hammock can be an invaluable piece of equipment, especially if travelling on the cheap. It will be of more use than a tent because many places have hammock-hooks, or you can sling a hammock between trees or posts. A good tip is to carry a length of rope and some plastic sheeting. The rope gives a good choice of tree distances and the excess provides a hanging frame for the plastic sheeting to keep the rain off. Metal S-hooks or a couple of climbing karabiners can also be very useful, as can strong cord for tying out the sheeting. Don't forget a mosquito net if travelling in insect-infected areas.

Toilets
Almost without exception, used toilet paper should be placed in the receptacle provided and not flushed down the pan. This applies even in quite expensive hotels. Failing to observe this custom blocks the pan or drain.

Eating

There is a section on each nation's food at the start of each chapter and the listings give a cross section of the type of places available, and hopefully include the best of what is on offer. Naturally the dining experience varies greatly. An excellent general rule when looking for somewhere to eat is to ask locally.

Most restaurants serve a daily special meal, usually at lunchtime called a *comida corrida* or *comida corriente*, which works out much cheaper and is usually filling and nutritious. Vegetarians should be able to list all the foods they cannot eat; saying '*Soy*

Eating price codes

🍴🍴🍴 over US$15   🍴🍴 US$8-15   🍴 under US$8

Prices refer to the cost of a meal with a drink for one person.

vegetariano/a' (I'm a vegetarian) or *'No como carne'* (I don't eat meat) is often not enough. Universally the cheapest place to eat is the local market. **Note** The golden rule is boil it, cook it, peel it or forget it, but if you did that every day, every meal, you'd never eat anywhere ... A more practicable rule is that if large numbers of people are eating in a regularly popular place, it's more than likely going to be OK.

Shopping

The range of gifts available is daunting, from the fine silver of Mexico's Colonial Heartlands to the tacky T-shirts of the more popular spots, and from the textiles and clothing of Guatemala to the leather goods from Nicaragua and the finely crafted *molas* of Panama. If buying more expensive items, research before you leave home so you know if you're getting a good deal. Best buys and regional items are highlighted in each chapter. Generally, choice is better in the capital, but the price is often steeper. Always make sure you know the price before purchasing an item. Bargaining seems to be the general rule in most countries' street markets.

Festivals and events

If the time and mood is right, there is little to beat a Latin festival. Fine costumes, loud music, the sounds of firecrackers tipped off with the gentle wafting of specially prepared foods all (normally) with a drink or two. Whether you seek out the carnival or happen to stumble across a celebration, the events – big or small – are likely to be memorable.

If you want to hit the carnivals there are a few broad dates generally significant throughout the region. Carnival is normally the week before the start of Lent. It's more important in Mexico but you'll probably find regional celebrations in most places. *Semana Santa* (Easter Week) is an understandably more spiritual affair. On 2 November is *Día de los Muertos* (Day of the Dead), again most popular in Mexico but significant throughout the region when families visit cemeteries to honour the dead. Christmas and New Year result in celebrations of some kind, but not always public.

Public holidays throughout the region lead to a complete shut-down in services. No banks, government offices, usually no shops and often far fewer restaurants and bars. It is worth keeping an eye on the calendar to avoid changing money or trying to make travel arrangements on public holidays.

Mexico

Feb/Mar Carnival/Mardi Gras Traditionally throughout Latin America, this week is a time for celebration before the hardships of Lent;

in Mexico it is particularly popular in La Paz (Baja California Sur) and the port of Veracruz.

15 Sep Cry for Independence, celebrations that are particularly impressive in Mexico City.

16 Sep Independence Day, with regional festivities and parades.

2 Nov Day of the Dead, in which the souls of the deceased return to earth and family and friends turn out in costume and festival to meet them – particularly colourful around Lake Pátzuaro.

12 Dec Pilgrimage of thousands to the Basílica de Guadalupe, in northeast Mexico City, the most venerated shrine in Mexico. Well worth a visit.

Guatemala

Mar/Apr Semana Santa, particularly colourful in Antigua with floats carrying Christ over wonderfully coloured and carefully placed carpets of flowers; also spectacular is **Santigo Atitlán**.

Nov Todos Santos Cuchumatán, All Saints' Day in the small town of Todos Santos, a colourful and drunken horse race with lots of dancing and antics.

Belize

10 Sep St George's Cay Day, with celebrations in Belize City that start with river races in San Ignacio.

19 Nov Settlement Day, celebrating the liberation (or arrival) of the Garífuna from distant shores. Also celebrated in Guatemala and Honduras.

El Salvador

29 Nov Nuestra Señora de la Paz. Big celebrations in San Miguel.

Honduras

15 May San Isidro, La Ceiba's patron saint, followed by a fortnight of celebrations. The highlight is a huge carnival on the third Sat in May.

1-4 Feb Supaya, southeast of Tegucigalpa, the most important shrine in Honduras with a tiny wooden image of the Virgen de Supaya.

Nicaragua

Keep an eye out for patron saints of villages and towns.

Dec La Purísima in honour of the patron saint of the Immaculate Virgin, celebrated with fireworks with 7 Dec being the national high point.

Costa Rica

Late Jan/early Feb Fiesta de los Diablitos in the small towns of Boruca and Rey Curre, south Costa Rica, symbolic of the fight between cultures, religion and colonization.

2 Aug Virgin of Los Angeles, celebrated with pilgrimages to the basilica in Cártago.

15 Sep Independence Day with celebrations and parades in the capital San José and throughout the country.

12 Oct Día de la Raza (Columbus Day) celebrated with particular gusto in the Caribbean city of Puerto Limón.

Panama

3 Nov Independence Day.

Essentials A-Z

Children

Travel with children can bring you into closer contact with Latin American families and generally presents no special problems – in fact, the path is often smoother for family groups. Officials tend to be more amenable where children are concerned. Always carry a copy of your child's birth certificate and passport photos. For an overview of travelling with children, visit www.babygoes2.com.

Public transport

Overland travel in Latin America can involve a lot of time spent waiting for public transport. It is easier to take biscuits, drinks, bread, etc with you on longer trips than to rely on meal stops where the food may not be to taste. All airlines charge a reduced price for children under 12 and less for children under 2. Double check the child's baggage allowance – some are as low as 7 kg. On long-distance buses children generally pay half or reduced fares. For shorter trips it is cheaper, if less comfortable, to seat small children on your knee. Often there are spare seats that children can occupy after tickets have been collected. In city and local excursion buses, small children do not generally pay a fare, but are not entitled to a seat when paying customers are standing. On sightseeing tours you should always bargain for a family rate; often children can go free. Note that a child travelling free on a long excursion is not always covered by the operator's travel insurance.

Hotels

Try to negotiate family rates. If charges are per person, always insist that 2 children will occupy 1 bed only, therefore counting as 1 tariff. If rates are per bed, the same applies. It is quite common for children under 10 or 12 to be allowed to stay for no extra charge as long as they are sharing your room.

Customs and duty free

Duty free allowances and export restrictions for each country are listed in the beginning sections of each chapter. It goes without saying that drugs, firearms and banned products should not be traded or taken across international boundaries.

Disabled travellers

In most Latin American countries, facilities for disabled travellers are severely lacking. Most airports and hotels and restaurants in major resorts have wheelchair ramps and adapted toilets. While some cities such as San José in Costa Rica are all ramped, in general pavements are often in such a poor state of repair that walking is precarious.

Some travel companies specialize in exciting holidays, tailor-made for individuals depending on their level of disability. The Global Access-Disabled Travel Network Site, www.globalaccessnews.com, provides travel information for disabled adventurers and includes a number of reviews and tips from members of the public. You might also want to read *Nothing Ventured*, edited by Alison Walsh (Harper Collins), which gives personal accounts of worldwide journeys by disabled travellers, plus advice and listings.

Drugs

Users of drugs without medical prescription should be particularly careful, as some countries impose heavy penalties – up to 10 years' imprisonment – for even the simple possession of such substances. The planting of drugs on travellers, by traffickers or the police, is not unknown. If offered drugs on the street, make no response at all and keep walking. Note that people who roll their own cigarettes are often suspected of carrying drugs and are subjected to close searches.

If you are taking illegal drugs – even ones that are widely and publically used – be aware that authorities do set traps from time to time. Should you get into trouble, your embassy is unlikely to be very sympathetic.

Gay and lesbian travellers

Most of Latin America is not particularly liberal in its attitudes to gays and lesbians. Even in the cities people are fairly conservative, and more so in provincial towns and rural areas. Having said that, things are changing and you'll find there is a gay scene with bars and clubs at least in most of the bigger cities and resorts. Helpful websites include www.gay scape.com, www.gaypedia.com and www.iglta.org (International Gay and Lesbian Travel Association).

Health

Before you go
See your doctor or travel clinic at least 6 weeks before your departure for general advice on travel risks, malaria and vaccinations. Make sure you have travel insurance, get a dental check (especially if you are going to be away for more than a month), know your own blood group and, if you suffer a long-term condition such as diabetes or epilepsy, make sure someone knows or that you have a Medic Alert bracelet/necklace with this information on it (www.medicalert.org.uk).

Recommended vaccinations
Vaccinations for tetanus, hepatitis A and typhoid are commonly recommended for all countries covered in this book. In addition, yellow fever vaccination is recommended for some areas of Panama; in most of the countries a yellow fever certificate is required if entering from an infected area. In all 8 countries vaccinations may also be advised advised against tuberculosis, hepatitis B, rabies and diptheria and, in the case of Guatemala, cholera. The final decision, however, should be based on a consultation with your GP or travel clinic. In all cases you should confirm your primary courses and boosters are up to date.

Malaria
Malaria precautions (see below) are essential for some parts of Mexico and Central America, particularly some rural areas. Once again, check with your GP or travel clinic well in advance of departure.

A-Z of health risks

Altitude sickness
The best way of preventing acute mountain sickness is a relatively slow ascent. When trekking to high altitude, some time spent walking at medium altitude, getting fit and acclimatizing is beneficial. When flying to places over 3000 m a few hours' rest and the avoidance of alcohol, cigarettes and heavy food will go a long way towards preventing acute mountain sickness.

Bites and stings
This is a very rare event for travellers, but if you are unlucky (or careless) enough to be bitten by a venomous snake, spider, scorpion or sea creature, try to identify the culprit, without putting yourself in further danger (do not try to catch a live snake).

Snake bites in particular are very frightening, but in fact rarely poisonous. Victims should be taken to a hospital or a doctor without delay. It is not advised for travellers to carry snake bite antivenom as it can do more harm than good in inexperienced hands. Reassure and comfort the victim frequently. Immobilize the limb with a bandage or a splint and get the patient to lie still. Do not slash the bite area and try to suck out the poison. This also does more harm than good. You should apply a tourniquet in these circumstances, but only if you know how to. Do not attempt this if you are not experienced.

Certain tropical fish inject venom into bathers' feet when trodden on, which can be exceptionally painful. Wear plastic shoes if such creatures are reported. The pain can be relieved by immersing the foot in hot water (as hot as you can bear) for as long as the pain persists.

Dengue fever

This is a viral disease spread by mosquitoes that tend to bite during the day. Reported cases in parts of Central America have slightly increased, but public health programmes have prevented significant outbreaks of the disease. The symptoms are fever and often intense joint pains, also some people develop a rash. Symptoms last about a week but it can take a few weeks to recover fully. Dengue can be difficult to distinguish from malaria as both diseases tend to occur in the same countries. There are no effective vaccines or antiviral drugs though, fortunately, travellers rarely develop the more severe forms of the disease (these can prove fatal). Rest, plenty of fluids and paracetamol (not aspirin) is the recommended treatment.

Diarrhoea

The standard advice to prevent diarrhoea is to be careful with water and ice for drinking. Ask yourself where the water came from. If you have any doubts then boil it or filter and treat it. Food can also transmit disease. Be wary of salads (what were they washed in, who handled them), re-heated foods or food that has been left out in the sun having been cooked earlier in the day. The golden rule is wash it, peel it, boil it or forget it. Be wary of unpasteurized dairy products as these can transmit a range of diseases.

Adults can use an anti-diarrhoeal medication such as loperamide to control the symptoms but only for up to 24 hrs.

In addition keep well hydrated by drinking plenty of fluids and eat bland foods. Oral rehydration sachets taken after each loose stool are a useful way to keep well hydrated. These should always be used when treating children and the elderly.

Bacterial traveller's diarrhoea is the most common form. Ciproxin (Ciprofloxacin) is a useful antibiotic and can be obtained by private prescription in the UK. You need to take one 500 mg tablet when the diarrhoea starts. If there are so signs of improvement after 24 hrs the diarrhoea is likely to be viral and not bacterial. If it is due to other organisms such as those causing giardia or amoebic dysentery, different antibiotics will be required.

If symptoms persist beyond 2 weeks or if there is blood in the stools and/or fever seek specialist medical attention.

Hepatitis

Hepatitis means inflammation of the liver. The most obvious symptom is a yellowing of your skin or the whites of your eyes. However, prior to this all that you may notice is itching and tiredness. There are vaccines for hepatitis A and B (the latter is spread through blood and unprotected sexual intercourse, both of which can be avoided).

Malaria

Malaria can cause death within 24 hrs and can start as something just resembling an attack of flu. You may feel tired, lethargic, headachy, feverish; or more seriously, develop fits, followed by coma and then death. Have a low index of suspicion because it is very easy to write off vague symptoms, which may actually be malaria. If you have a temperature, visit a doctor as soon as you can and ask for a malaria test. On your return home, if you suffer any of these symptoms, have a test as soon as possible. Even if a previous test proved negative, this could save your life.

Remember ABCD: Awareness (of whether the disease is present in the area you are travelling in), **Bite avoidance, Chemoprophylaxis, Diagnosis.**

To prevent mosquito bites wear clothes that cover arms and legs, use effective insect repellents in areas with known risks of insect-spread disease and use a mosquito net treated with an insecticide. Repellents containing 30-50% DEET (Di-ethyltoluamide) are recommended when visiting malaria endemic areas; lemon eucalyptus (Mosiguard) is a reasonable alternative. The key advice is to guard against contracting malaria by taking the correct anti-malarials and finishing the recommended course. If you are popular target for insect bites or develop lumps quite soon after being bitten use antihistamine tablets and apply a cream such as hydrocortisone.

Remember that it is risky to buy medicine, and in particular anti-malarials, in some countries. These may be sub-standard or part of a trade in counterfeit drugs.

Rabies

Rabies is endemic throughout certain parts of the world so be aware of the dangers of the bite from any animal. Rabies vaccination before travel can be considered but if bitten always seek urgent medical attention – whether or not you have been previously vaccinated after first cleaning the wound and treating with an iodine-base disinfectant or alcohol.

Sun

Protect yourself against the sun; over-exposure can lead to sunburn and, in the longer term, skin cancers and premature skin aging. The best advice is simply to avoid exposure to the sun by covering exposed skin, wearing a hat and staying out of the sun if possible, particularly between late morning and early afternoon. Apply a high-factor sunscreen (greater than SPF15) and also make sure it screens against UVB. A further danger in tropical climates is heat exhaustion or more seriously heatstroke. This can be

avoided by good hydration, which means drinking water past the point of simply quenching thirst. Also when first exposed to tropical heat take time to acclimatize by avoiding strenuous activity in the middle of the day. If you cannot avoid heavy exercise it is also a good idea to increase salt intake.

Underwater health

If you plan to dive make sure that you are fit do so with your national diving organisation. In the UK, the **British Sub-Aqua Club (BSAC),** Telford's Quay, South Pier Rd, Ellesmere Port, Cheshire CH65 4FL, UK, T0151-350-6200, www.bsac.com, can put you in touch with doctors who will carry out medical examinations. Check that any dive company you use is reputable and has appropriate certification from **BSAC** or **Professional Association of Diving Instructors (PADI),** Unit 7, St Philips Central, Albert Rd, St Philips, Bristol, BS2 0PD, T0117-300-7234, www.padi.com.

Water

There are a number of ways of purifying water. Dirty water should first be strained through a filter bag and then boiled or treated. Bring water to a rolling boil for several minutes. There are sterilizing methods that can be used and products generally contain chlorine (eg *Puritabs*) or iodine (eg *Pota Aqua*) compounds. There are a number of water sterilizers now on the market available in personal and expedition size. Make sure you take the spare parts or spare chemicals with you and do not believe everything the manufacturers say.

Other diseases and risks

There are a range of other insect-borne diseases that are quite rare in travellers, but worth finding out about if going to particular destinations. Examples are sleeping sickness, river blindness and leishmaniasis. Fresh water can also be a source of diseases such as bilharzia and leptospirosis and it is worth investigating if these are a danger before bathing in lakes and streams.

Take heed of advice regarding protecting yourself against the sun (see above) and remember that unprotected sex always carries a risk and extra care is required when visiting some parts of the world.

Websites and books

Websites

Fit for Travel (UK), www.fitfortravel.scot. nhs.uk This site from Scotland provides a quick A-Z of vaccine and travel health advice requirements for each country. **Foreign and Commonwealth Office** (FCO) (UK), www.fco.gov.uk. **The National Travel Health Network and Centre** (NaTHNaC) www.nathnac.org. **World Health Organisation**, www.who.int.

Books

Travellers' health. Dawood R, Ed. 3rd Ed. Oxford: Oxford University Press, 2002. *Expedition Medicine*. David Warrell and Sarah Anderson, Eds. The Royal Geographic Society.

Insurance

Insurance is strongly recommended and policies are very reasonable. If you have financial restraints, the most important aspect of any insurance policy is medical care and repatriation. Ideally you want to make sure you are covered for personal items too. Read the small print **before** heading off so you are aware of what is covered and what is not, what is required to submit a claim and what to do in the event of an emergency.

Internet

Email is very common and public access to the internet is becoming endemic with cybercafés opening in both large and small towns. Hotels and even cafes in popular places are installing Wi-Fi that you can log on to if you have your own laptop or notebook. We list cybercafés in the text, but obviously these change. One website giving information on cybercafés is **www.world66.com** but it is very difficult keep pace with the changing situation.

Language

→ *See Footnotes, page 1412, for a list of useful words and phrases.*
Spanish is spoken throughout most of Mexico and Central America and, while you will be able to get by without knowledge of Spanish, you will probably become frustrated and feel helpless in many situations. English, or any other language, is useless off the beaten track (except in Belize). A pocket dictionary and phrase book together with some initial study or a beginner's Spanish course before you leave are strongly recommended. If you have the time, book 1-2 weeks of classes at the beginning of your travels.

Some areas have developed a reputation for language classes, for instance Cuernavaca in Mexico, Antigua and Quetzaltenango in Guatemala and San José and Heredia in Costa Rica. Many other locations also provide tuition. The better-known centres normally include a wide range of cultural activities and supporting options for homestay. A less well-known centre is likely to have fewer English speakers around. For details, see Language schools in the Directory sections of individual towns and cities.

Not all the locals speak Spanish, of course; you will find that some indigenous people in the more remote areas – the highlands of Guatemala for example – speak only their indigenous languages, although there will usually be at least one person in a village who can speak Spanish.

Language tuition

Arranging language tuition internationally is increasingly popular.

AmeriSpan, 1334 Walnut St (PO Box 58129), 6th floor, Philadelphia, PA 19107, T1-215-751-1100, T1-800-879-6640, www.amerispan.com (also with offices in Antigua, Guatemala). One of the most comprehensive options, offering Spanish immersion programmes, educational tours, volunteer and internship positions throughout Latin America.

Cactus Language, 4 Clarence House, 30-31 North St, Brighton, East Sussex, BN1 1EB, T0845-130-4775, www.cactuslanguage training.com. Spanish language courses from 1 week in duration in Mexico and Central America, with pre-trip classes in the UK. Also has additional options for volunteer work, diving and staying with host families.

Institute for Spanish Language Studies, in the US on T1-800-765-0025, www.isls.com. Has schools in Mexico, Costa Rica and Panama, offering innovative and flexible programmes.

Spanish Abroad, 5112 N 40th St, Suite 101, Phoenix, AZ 85018, USA, T1-888-722-7623 (USA and Canada), T1-602-778-6791 (worldwide), www.spanishabroad.com. Intensive Spanish immersion programmes throughout Latin America for those wishing to study abroad.

Media

World Band Radio Latin America has more local and community radio stations than practically anywhere else in the world; a shortwave (world band) radio offers a practical means to brush up on the language, sample popular culture and absorb some of the richly varied regional music. International broadcasters also transmit across Central America in both English and Spanish, these include the **BBC World Service**, www.bbc.co.uk/worldservice/index.shtml for schedules and frequencies, the **Voice of America**, www.voa.gov, and Boston (Mass)-based **Monitor Radio International**, operated by Christian Science Monitor, www.csmonitor.com. **Putumayo World Music**, www.putumayo.com specialize in the exotic sounds of Mexican music.

Details of the national newspapers, television and radio are given in the Essentials section at the beginning of each chapter.

Money

While most – but not all – countries in Mexico and Central America have their own currencies, the most useful foreign currency in the region is the US dollar. Consequently, that proportion of your money you take in cash and traveller's cheques (TCs) should be in US dollars. Banks and *casas de cambio* are increasingly able to change euros but the dollar is still the most readily accepted and changed.

The 3 main ways of keeping in funds while travelling are with US dollars cash, US dollar TCs, or plastic (credit cards). It is recommended that you take all 3.

Cost of travelling

As a rough calculation budget travellers can get by on US$25-35 a day, but that means that you won't be able to afford to take many excursions. A more realistic and sustainable budget is US$35-50. Plenty of travellers manage on smaller budgets but it's probably better to spend a little longer at home saving up, and then have a good time while you're away, rather than find yourself adding up the small change on a Sat night to see if you can afford a weekly beer.

Cash

The chief benefit of taking US dollars is that they are accepted almost everywhere. They are used as national currency in El Salvador and Panama, and rates and commissions are more competitive than for other currencies.

Exchange rates (June 2009)

	Unit of currency	US$1=	€1=	£1=
Belize	Belize dollar	2.00	2.74	3.25
Costa Rica	Colón	557	804	949
El Salvador*	Colón	8.75	12.19	14.38
Guatemala	Quetzal	8.13	11.34	13.38
Honduras	Lempira	18.88	26.34	31
Mexico	Peso	13.34	18.60	21.94
Nicaragua	Córdoba	19.11	26.65	31.43
Panama*	Balboa	1.00	1.39	1.64

* US notes and coins are legal tender.

In many countries, US dollar notes are only accepted if they are in excellent condition – no small tears, rips, nicks, holes or scribbles. When ordering money at home bear this in mind. Take a selection of bills including several low-value US dollar bills (US$5 or US$10) which can be carried for changing into local currency if arriving in a country when banks or *casas de cambio* are closed, and for use in out of the way places when you may run out of local currency. They are also very useful for shopping: shopkeepers and *casas de cambio* tend to give better exchange rates than hotels or banks (but see below).

If your budget is tight it is essential to avoid situations where you are forced to change money regardless of the rate; watch weekends and public holidays carefully and never run out of local currency. Take plenty of local currency, in small denominations, when making trips away from the major towns and resorts.

Traveller's cheques

Traveller's cheques (TCs) provide reasonably accessible cash with peace of mind against theft. Denominations of US$50 and US$100 are preferable, with a few of US$20 to increase your options. Some banks will change the cheques for US dollars cash if you need to top up your supply. American Express or Visa US dollar TCs are recommended, but less commission is often charged on Citibank or Bank of America TCs if they are cashed at Latin American branches of those banks. American Express now has a plastic Traveller's Cheque Card, used in a similar way to paper TCs. While this should work in theory, experience shows that new financial ideas are not quickly adopted in Central America and you may have trouble using it.

Several banks charge a high fixed commission for changing TCs because they don't really want the bother. *Casas de cambio* are usually a much better choice for this service. Some establishments may ask to see a passport and the customer's record of purchase before accepting. Keep the original purchase slip in a separate place to the TCs and make a photocopy for security. The better hotels will normally change TCs for their guests (often at a poor rate).

Credit cards

Credit cards are ideal for travelling, providing ready access to funds without carrying large amounts of cash on your person. In an ideal world taking a couple of cards (one Visa and one MasterCard) will make sure you are covered in most options. It is straightforward to obtain a cash advance against a credit card and even easier to withdraw cash from ATMs. (Remove your credit card from the machine immediately after the transaction to avoid it being retained – getting it back can be difficult.) There are 2 acceptance systems, **Plus** and **Cirrus**. You may have to experiment to see what combination of options your require. Fortunately, most ATMs give you a 'language' option after you enter your card. The rates of exchange on ATM withdrawals are the best available for currency exchange but your bank or credit card company imposes a handling charge. If you lose a card, immediately contact the 24-hr helpline of the issuer in your home country (find out the numbers to call before travelling and keep them in a safe place). Most card issuers provide a telephone number where you can call collect from anywhere in the world in case of card loss or theft; be sure to request it before travelling.

For purchases, credit cards of the Visa and MasterCard groups, American Express (Amex), Carte Blanche and Diners Club can be used. Make sure you know the correct procedure if they are lost or stolen. Credit card transactions are normally at an officially recognized rate of exchange; they are often subject to sales tax. In addition, many establishments in Latin America charge a fee of about 5% on credit card transactions; although forbidden by credit card company rules there is not a lot you can do about this, except get the charge itemized on the receipt and complain to the card company. For credit card security, insist that imprints are made in your presence. Any imprints incorrectly completed should be torn into tiny pieces. Also destroy the carbon papers after the form is completed (signatures can be copied from them).

Changing money

Whenever possible change your money at a bank or a *casa de cambio*. Black markets and street changers have largely disappeared; avoid them if you can as you are unlikely to get a significantly better rate and you place yourself a greater risk of being ripped off. If you need to change money on the street, do not do so alone. If you are unsure about rates of exchange when you enter a country, check at the border with more than one changer, or ask locals or any traveller who may be leaving that country. Whenever you leave a country, sell any local currency before leaving – the further you get away from a country, the less the value of a country's money; in some cases you may not be able to change it at all.

Police

Probably the best advice with regards the police in Mexico and Central America is to have as little to do with them as possible. An exception to this rule are the Tourist Police, who operate in some of the big cities and resorts, and provide assistance. In general, law enforcement in Latin America is achieved by periodic campaigns, not systematically.

You may be asked for identification at any time and should therefore always have ID on you. If you cannot produce it, you may be jailed. If a visitor is jailed his or her friends should provide food every day. This is especially important for people on a special diet, such as diabetics. If you are jailed, you should contact your embassy or consulate and take advice. In the event of a vehicle accident in which anyone is injured, all drivers involved are automatically detained until blame has been established, and this does not usually take less than 2 weeks.

The giving and receiving of bribes is not recommended. However, the following advice may prove useful. Never offer a bribe unless you are fully conversant with the customs of the country. Wait until the official makes the suggestion, or offer money in some form that is apparently not bribery, for example 'In our country we have a system of on-the-spot fines (*multas de inmediato*). Is there a similar system here?' Do not assume that officials who accept a bribe are prepared to do anything else that is illegal. You bribe them to do their job, or not do it, or to do it more quickly, or more slowly. You do not bribe them to do something which is against the law. The mere suggestion would make them very upset. If an official suggests that a bribe must be paid before you can proceed on your way, be patient (assuming you have the time) and he may relent. Bear in mind that by bribing you are participating in a system that may cause you immense frustration.

Post

Postal services vary in efficiency from country to country and prices are quite high; pilfering is frequent. All mail, especially packages, should be registered. Check before leaving home if your embassy will hold mail and if so for how long, in preference to the Poste Restante/General Delivery (*Lista de Correos*) department of a country's Post Office. Cardholders can use Amex agencies. If you're expecting mail and there seems to be no mail at the *Lista* under the initial letter of your surname, ask them to look under the initial of your forename or your middle name. If your name begins with 'W', look for letters under 'V' as well, or ask. For the smallest risk of misunderstanding, use title, initial and surname only.

Punctuality

Punctuality is more of a concept than a reality in Latin countries. The *mañana* culture reigns supreme and any arrangement to meet at, say 1900, will normally rendezvous somewhere between 2000 and 2100. However, the one time you are late to catch a bus, boat or plane, it will leave on time – the rule is hurry up and wait.

Safety

Generally speaking, most places in Latin America are no more dangerous than any major city in Europe or North America and the people, if anything, are friendlier and more open. In provincial towns, main places of interest, on daytime buses and in ordinary restaurants the visitor should be quite safe. Nevertheless, in large cities (particularly in crowded places such as markets and bus stations) crime exists, mostly of the opportunistic kind. If you are aware of the dangers, act confidently and use your common sense, you will lessen many of the risks. The following tips, endorsed by travellers, are meant to forewarn, not alarm.

Keep all documents secure; hide your main cash supply in different places or under your clothes. Extra pockets sewn inside shirts and trousers, pockets closed with a zip or safety pin, moneybelts, neck or leg pouches, and elasticated support bandages for keeping money and cheques above the elbow or below the knee have been repeatedly recommended. Pouches worn outside the clothes are not safe. Keep cameras in bags (preferably with a chain or wire in the strap to defeat the slasher) and don't wear fancy wrist-watches or jewellery. Carry your small day pack in front of you.

Safety on public transport

When you have all your luggage with you at a bus or railway station, be especially careful: don't get into arguments with any locals if you can help it and clip, tie or lock all the items together with a chain or cable if you are waiting for some time, or simply sit on top of your backpack. Take a taxi between airport/bus station/railway station and hotel, if you can afford it. Keep your bags with you in the taxi and pay only when you and your luggage are safely out of the vehicle (but keep an eye on it your luggage!). Avoid night buses unless essential or until you are comfortable travelling in the area; avoid arriving at night whenever possible; and watch your belongings whether they are stowed inside or outside the cabin (rooftop luggage racks create extra problems, which are sometimes unavoidable – many bus drivers cover rooftop luggage with plastic sheeting, but a waterproof bag or outer sack can be invaluable for protecting your luggage and for stopping someone rummaging through the top of your bag). Major bus lines often issue a luggage ticket when bags are stored in the hold; this is generally a safe system. When getting on a bus, keep your ticket handy as you will probably have to show it at some point. Finally, be wary of accepting food, drink, sweets or cigarettes from unknown fellow travellers on buses or trains; although extremely rare, they may be drugged, and you could wake up hours later without your belongings. In this connection, never accept a bar drink from an opened bottle (unless you can see that the bottle is in general use); always have it uncapped in front of you.

Scams

A number of distraction techniques such as mustard smearers and paint or shampoo sprayers and strangers' remarks like 'what's that on your shoulder?' or 'have you seen that dirt on your shoe?' are designed to distract you for a few critical moments in which time your bag may be grabbed. Furthermore, supposedly friendly assistance asking if you have dropped money or other items in the street work on the same premise. If someone follows you when you're in the street, let him catch up with you and give him the 'eye'. While you should take local advice about being out at night, do not assume that daytime is any safer. If walking after dark on quiet streets, walk in the road, not on the pavement.

Be wary of 'plain-clothes policemen'; insist on seeing identification and on going to the police station by main roads. Do not hand over your identification (or money – which he should not need to see anyway)

until you are at the station. On no account take them directly back to your lodgings. Be even more suspicious if he seeks confirmation of his status from a passer-by. If someone implies they are asking for a bribe, insist on a receipt. If attacked, remember your assailants may well be armed, and try not to resist.

It is best, if you can trust your hotel, to leave any valuables you don't need in a safe-deposit. Always keep an inventory of what you have deposited. If you don't trust the hotel, lock everything in your pack and secure that in your room. If you do lose valuables, you will need to report the incident to the police for insurance purposes.

Sexual assault

This is extremely rare, but if you are the victim of a sexual assault, you are advised in the first instance to contact a doctor (this can be your home doctor if you prefer). You will need tests to determine whether you have contracted any sexually transmitted diseases; you may also need advice on post-coital contraception. You should also contact your embassy, where consular staff are very willing to help in cases of assault.

Student and teacher travellers

If you are in full-time education you will be entitled to an **International Student Identity Card** (ISIC), which is distributed by student travel offices and travel agencies in over 100 countries. ISIC gives you special prices on all forms of transport (air, sea, rail, etc), and a variety of other concessions and services. Contact **International Student Travel Confederation (ISTC)**, Herengracht 479, 1017 BS Amsterdam, The Netherlands, T+31-20-421 2800, www.isic.org. Student cards must carry a photograph if they are to be of any use for discounts in Latin America. The ISIC website provides a list of card-issuing offices around the world.

Telephone codes

	Country code	IDD code
Mexico	52	00
Guatemala	502	00 (130+00 Telefónica; 147-00 Telgua)
Belize	501	00
El Salvador	503	00 (144+00 Telefónica)
Honduras	504	00
Nicaragua	505	00
Costa Rica	506	00
Panama	507	00 Cable & Wireless (088+00 Telecarrier; 055+00 Clarocom)

Teachers may want to take an **International Teacher Identity Card** (ITIC) distributed by ISTC (above), as discounts are often extended to teachers.

Tax

When departing, don't forget you'll have to pay departure tax if it isn't already included in your ticket. Check individual chapters for further details.

Telephone

Many of the telecommunications networks have been privatized and prices have fallen considerably. In some areas, services have even improved. Consequently keeping in touch by phone is no longer prohibitive. International telecom charge cards are useful and available from most countries; obtain details before leaving home. For the US **AT&T**'s 'USA Direct', **Sprint** and **MCI** are all available for calls to the USA. It is much cheaper than operator-assisted calls. Internet calls (eg via Skype) may be possible.

Using a mobile in most of Mexico and Central America is very expensive. In addition to the hassle of having to charge your phone, research whether it is worth your while. Mobile phone calls will be cheaper if you buy a SIM card for the local network; in-country calls are likely to be considerably cheaper than using your home-based account. The initial cost of the SIM is getting more affordable (as little as US$3 in Honduras), but check the cost of calls. Also bear in mind, the number you use at home will not work.

Tour operators

In the UK

Condor Journeys and Adventures, 2 Ferry Bank, Colintraive, Argyll, PA22 3AR, T01700-841-318, www.condorjourneys-adventures.com, also offices in France.

Explore Worldwide, 55 Victoria Rd, Farnborough, Hants, GU14 7PA, T0870-333-4001, www.explore.co.uk.

Galapagos Classic Cruises, 6 Keyes Rd, London, NW2 3XA, T020-8933-0613, www.galapagoscruises.co.uk.

Journey Latin America, 12-13 Heathfield Terrace, London, W4 4JE, T020-8747-8315, www.journeylatinamerica.co.uk.

Last Frontiers, Fleet Marston Farm, Aylesbury, Buckinghamshire, HP18 0QT, T01296-653-000, www.lastfrontiers.com.

Select Latin America, 3.51 Canterbury Court, 1-3 Brixton Rd, Kennington Park, London, SW9 6DE, T020-7407-1478, www.selectlatinamerica.com.

South American Experience, Welby House, 96 Wilton Rd, London, SW1V 1DW, T0845-277-3366, www.southamericanexperience.co.uk.

Trips Worldwide, 14 Frederick Place, Clifton, Bristol, BS8 1AS, T0800-840-0850, www.tripsworldwide.co.uk.

Tucan Travel, 316 Uxbridge Rd, London, W3 9QP, T020-8896-1600, www.tucantravel.com.

Veloso Tours, 34 Warple Way, London, W3 0RG, T020-8762-0616, www.veloso.com.

In North America

Exito Travel, 108 Rutgers St, Fort Collins, CO 80525, T970-482-3019, www.exito-travel.com.

GAP Adventures, 19 Charlotte St, Toronto, Ontario, M5V 2H5, T1-800-708-7761, www.gapadventures.com.

Mila Tours, 100 S Greenleaf Av, Gurnee, Il 60031, T1-800-367-7378, www.milatours.com.

S and S Tours, 4250 S Hohokam Dr, Sierra Vista, AZ 85650, T866-780-2813, www.ss-tours.com.

International

The following have operations in the US, Canada, Europe, Australia and New Zealand.

Dragoman, T01728-861-133, www.dragoman.co.uk.

Exodus Travels, T020-8675-5550, www.exodus.co.uk.

LADATCO tours, 2200 S Dixie Highway, Suite 704, Coconut Grove, FL 33133, T1-800-327-6162, www.ladatco.com.

Tourist information

All countries in the region have a tourist board but not all have an international presence. Fortunately the internet makes

it possible to get the latest information on developments in a country.

South American Explorers, Head Office in the USA at 126 Indian Creek Rd, Ithaca, NY 14850, USA T607-277-0488, www.saexplorers.org, is a very useful resource. Despite the name, the whole of Latin America is covered and members receive help with travel planning as well as informed access on books and maps covering the region.

Useful websites

www.centralamerica.com Covers mainly Costa Rica but also touches on Guatemala, Belize, Honduras, Nicaragua and Panama.
www.latinnews.com Up-to-date site with political comment.
www.planeta.com A phenomenal resource, which is staggering for its detail on everything from ecotourism and language schools to cybercafés.
www.revuemag.com Growing regional guide in print and online, focusing on Guatemala with coverage of El Salvador, Honduras and Belize.
Google has country search engines for **Mexico** (.com.mx), **El Salvador** (.com.sv), **Honduras** (.com.hn), **Nicaragua** (.com.ni), **Costa Rica** (.com.cr) and **Panama** (.com.pa).

A couple of general travel websites that are worth a look are **www.bootsnall.com** and **www.tripadvisor.com**.

Visas and immigration

For information on visas and immigration, see the individual country chapters.

For US nationals, the implications of the **Western Hemisphere Travel Initiative**, which came into force on 1 Jan 2008 should be considered if entering Mexico. You will need a passport to reenter the US once you have left and visited Mexico.

All international travel requires that you have at least 6 months remaining on a valid passport. Beyond a passport, very little is required of international travellers to Mexico and Central America. However, there are a few little tricks that can make your life a lot easier. Latin Americans, especially officials, are very document-minded. If staying in a country for several weeks, it is worthwhile registering at your embassy or consulate. Then, if your passport is stolen, the process of replacing it is faster and easier. It can also be handy to keep some additional passport-sized photographs together with photocopies of essential documents – including your flight ticket – separately from the originals.

It is your responsibility to ensure that your passport is stamped in and out when you cross borders. The absence of entry and exit stamps can cause serious difficulties; seek out the proper immigration offices if the stamping process is not carried out as you cross. Also, do not lose your entry card; replacing it can cause you a lot of trouble and possibly expense. If planning to study in Latin America for a long period, make every effort to get a student visa in advance.

Women travellers

Some women experience problems, whether accompanied or not; others encounter no difficulties at all. Unaccompanied Western women will at times be subject to close scrutiny and exceptional curiosity. Don't be unduly scared. Simply be prepared and try not to over-react. When you set out, err on the side of caution until your instincts have adjusted to the new culture. Women travelling alone could consider taking a wedding ring to prevent being hassled. To help minimize unwanted attention, consider your clothing choices. Do not feel bad about showing offence. When accepting an invitation, make sure that someone else knows the address you are going to and the time you left. Ask if you can bring a friend (even if you do not intend to do so). A good rule is always to act with confidence, as though you know where you are going, even if you do not. Someone who looks lost is more likely to attract unwanted attention. Do not disclose to strangers where you are staying.

Working

Two main areas provide opportunities for unskilled volunteers: childcare – often at orphanages or schools – and nature projects. Be warned, spontaneous volunteering is becoming more difficult. Organizations that use volunteers have progressed and plan their personnel needs so you may be required to make contact before you visit. Many organizations now charge volunteers for board and lodging and projects are often for a minimum of 4 weeks. Guatemala and Costa Rica in particular have fairly well-developed and organized volunteer programmes.

Many developed countries have nationally organized volunteer programmes.

The **US Peace Corps**, Paul D Coverdell Peace Corps Headquarters, 1111 20th St NW, Washington, DC 20526, T1-800-424-8580, www.peacecorps.gov, is the most prominent in the region, working with countries on development projects with 2-year assignments for US citizens in countries throughout Mexico and Central America.

Variations on the volunteering programme are to enrol on increasingly popular gap-year programmes. These normally incorporate a period of volunteer work with a few months of free time at the end of the programme for travel.

Experiment in International Living, T+44-1684-562577, www.eiluk.org, is the UK element of a US international homestay programme that arranges stays with families in Mexico and Central America with social projects based on the ethos that if you want to live together, you need to work together. It's an excellent way to meet people and learn the language.

Contents

Footprint features

Border crossings

Mexico–USA
  see pages 75, 198, 234, 255 and 285
Mexico–Guatemala
  see page 504
Mexico–Belize
  see page 586

At a glance

⊙ **Getting around** Vast distances by bus, internal flights very useful.

⊙ **Time required** 3 weeks if heading south from Mexico City, 4 months for the country highlights.

⊙ **Weather** Dry and warm Dec-Apr. Rainy Jun-Oct with intensity reducing from south to north.

⊗ **When not to go** Resorts get busy in summer. Extremely crowded everywhere at Easter and Christmas; rooms very hard to find.

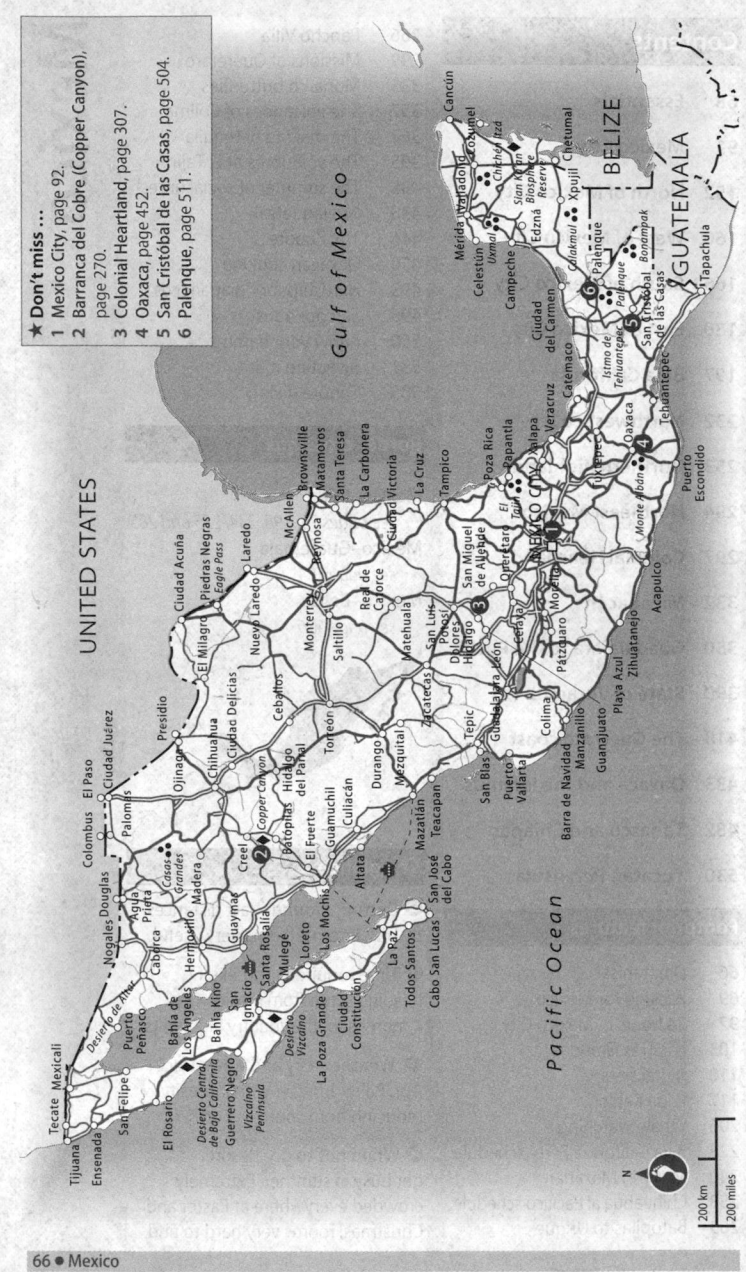

★ Don't miss ...
1 Mexico City, page 92.
2 Barranca del Cobre (Copper Canyon), page 270.
3 Colonial Heartland, page 307.
4 Oaxaca, page 452.
5 San Cristóbal de las Casas, page 504.
6 Palenque, page 511.

Embracing scorched desert in the north through to body-hugging humidity in the south, Mexico combines an invigorating cocktail of influences as diverse as the landscape. As an emerging global market, Mexico's economy ebbs and flows to the tide of world trade, the whims of its northern neighbour and as a world-class tourist destination. Yet in rural communities, market stallholders barter produce as they have for millennia. City wealth contrasts with rural poverty, and globalization creeps in through fast-food outlets, television programmes, toys and shopping malls as centuries-old cultures cling to ancient traditions.

Underlying everything in Mexico is the improvisation of history. The growth of regional powers – the Olmecs, Teotihuacán, Toltecs and Mixtecs – were precursors for the Maya in the south and the terrifying Aztecs in the Central Highlands. Later, the Spanish conquest exploited regional rivalries before eventually replacing the Aztec capital, Tenochtitlán, with the first foundations of today's Mexico City.

For the visitor it's the chaotic confusion and juxtapositions that are so invigorating: the stark barren beauty of the Vizcaíno Desert in Baja California contrasts with the natural wonder of breeding grey whales lolling in the waters of Scammon's Lagoon; along the south Pacific coastline, isolated international resorts sit unnervingly close to deserted beaches; in the colonial cities winding cobbled lanes echoing the memories of Mexico's silver-mining history are lit with the electronic flash of neon light; in Chiapas, Zapatista rebels use laptops and mobile phones to galvanize support for Mexico's indigenous population. And all over the country hundreds of vibrant festivals celebrate Mexico's rich cultural heritage.

Essentials

Mexico's size makes it impossible to see it properly all in one go. Fortunately, with so many attractions and relatively good transport links, it is not difficult to incorporate a good variety of cultures, activities and landscapes into one trip. The Pacific Coast, Gulf of Mexico and Caribbean sea provide thousands of miles of beaches on either side of the country. The bulk of the interior is made up of mountains and plateaux; in the north predominantly arid, but, in the south, more densely forested and wet. For those flying in, there are two main ports of entry, Mexico City and Cancún, several major international airports such as Puerto Vallarta and Cabo San Lucas, and several smaller airports take international flights. To the north there is one long and wonderfully permeable border across which driving traffic arrives.

Where to go

Northern Mexico If you're heading down from the US, the busiest land border is Tijuana. Most travellers take time to explore the **Baja California Peninsula**, crossing spectacular desert scenery to lay up at idyllic beaches and, if the timing is right, to watch the migrating whales. Once you hit La Paz or the Cape you are effectively on an island with a ferry service to the mainland, ideal for **Los Mochis** and the **Copper Canyon**. The shortest route from the US border to the heart of Mexico is down the east coast, staying close to the Gulf. More interesting by far is the central route from **Ciudad Juárez** through the rugged barren lands of the high Sierra Madre, with access to Chihuahua and the classic rail journey through the Copper Canyon to the Pacific. An alternative is down the west coast through the desert lowlands of the State of Sonora and then taking the train from Los Mochis, up the railway, seeing the best stretch as far as Creel and then visiting the Copper Canyon at Batópilas en route to **Hidalgo del Parral** via Guachochi. **Durango**, once the centre of the Mexican movie industry with countless Westerns and Hollywood hits filmed nearby, is seven hours away by road and then you're just a few hours from **Zacatecas**, **Guanajuato** and the towns of the Colonial Heartland.

Central Mexico One of the world's great capitals, **Mexico City's** splendour of architecture and vast public plazas survive side by side with the chaos of traffic and 20 million people. It deserves several days' stay just to visit the highlights – the Centro Histórico, Museum of Anthropology, Chapultepec Park, the cultural highlights of Coyoacán, San Angel and Xochimilco among them. Get a feel for its stirring revolutionary past through the murals of Orozco, Rivera and Siqueiros, and for its ancient history with the awesome ruins of **Teotihuacán**, an easy day-trip from the capital. A relatively short circuit north of Mexico City, possible in a week, is to the Colonial Heartland, taking in the former silver-mining towns of **Querétaro**, **Guanajuato**, **San Miguel de Allende** and **Dolores Hidalgo**. Heading west leads to colonial **Guadalajara** and nearby **Tequila** before hitting the Pacific at Puerto Vallarta. The coastline sweeps south through built-up resorts and isolated beaches.

The south A hub for travellers, **Oaxaca City** is worth several days in itself for the colonial architecture and nearby ruins of **Monte Albán**. Continuing east leads to **San Cristóbal de las Casas** with indigenous villages in the surrounding hills. From here you can sweep down to Guatemala, head north to Tikal, travel through Belize, and on to the Mexican Caribbean coast at Quintana Roo. Alternatively, you can follow the isthmus through **Palenque** and **Campeche** to the Yucatán.

Packing for Mexico

In the highlands it can be cold at night especially in winter, and most hotels do not have heating. Cheaper hotels often provide only one blanket and, while they will certainly provide a second if available, a light sleeping bag that packs up small can be useful. This applies in popular tourist centres such as San Cristóbal de las Casas and Pátzcuaro. If travelling on air-conditioned buses keep warm clothes and a blanket with you, especially if travelling overnight.

It's also worth having a keeping a small torch handy, as many Mexican streets and stairways are poorly lit.

Yucatán Peninsula If you like to party, you'll love **Cancún**, a major holiday destination, and a good alternative entry point to Mexico City. If you're looking for something a little quieter, a short journey will take you to beaches nearby where you can snorkel and dive, relaxing in the warm, soothing waters. Cancún is the perfect starting point for the Ruta Maya – an elliptical route that takes in the major Maya ruins in Mexico, Belize, Guatemala and Honduras. South of Cancún, towards Belize is **Tulum**, while heading inland to **Mérida** it's a short trip to **Uxmal** and **Chichén Itzá**, voted one of the Seven New Wonders of the World. Heading southwest towards Guatemala is the fortress city of Campeche and the fine ruins of **Palenque** are close to the waterfalls of Misol-Há and Agua Azul and the ruins of **Yachilán** and **Bonampak**.

Suggested itinerary The ultimate trip has to be from top to bottom. Start by crossing from San Diego to **Tijuana**, down the **Baja California Peninsula** and over to **Los Mochis** for the **Copper Canyon**. From there, drop into a couple of the colonial towns – **Zacatecas** and **Guanajuato** stand out – and then to **Mexico City**. After a few days in the capital, head down to **Oaxaca City** and then the **Oaxaca coast**, on to **San Cristóbal de las Casas** and nearby **Palenque**. That will take about four to six weeks, once you've added on the inevitable side trips. From Palenque you have three options. Head up to the **Yucatán Peninsula**, its beaches and the Maya ruins of **Chichén Itzá**, **Uxmal**, **Tulum** and the many lesser known sites, and then down to Belize through **Chetumal** – about three weeks. Alternatively, cross from Palenque through the **La Palma–El Naranjo** crossing, or **Frontera–Echeverría**, for good, direct access to Santa Elena and Tikal. If heading for the Guatemalan highlands, cross at Ciudad Tecún Umán or Talismán from southern Mexico, the quickest option.

When to go

The best time to visit Mexico is from October to April when there is virtually no rain. The rainy season works its way up from the south beginning in May and running until August, September and even October. This is also hurricane season in the Caribbean and on rare occasions the Yucatán and Gulf states get hit. But don't be put off by the term 'rainy season' – most years, the rains only affect travellers for an hour or two a day. In the northern states of Baja California, Sonora, Chihuahua and Coahuila, it can stay very hot and dry.

August is holiday time for Mexicans and this can make accommodation scarce in the smaller resorts and in popular places close to Mexico City. Semana Santa (Easter week) and the Christmas holidays can also affect room availability. Day of the Dead celebrations (at the beginning of November and particularly around Pátzcuaro) and other important local fiestas also make it advisable to pre-book. ▶▶ *For festival dates, see page 85.*

Sport and activities

Mexico's coastline of reefs and swells, expanse of mountain ranges cut by long rivers and protected areas make it extremely well suited to many types of outdoor adventure. The ability to do the activity is very often linked to the ability to support the discipline as much as the quality or level of the activity. If you have enough experience to support yourself, Mexico has incredible options in almost any activity imaginable. The **Asociación Mexicana de Turismo de Aventura y Ecoturismo (AMTAVE)** ① *Félix Cuevas 224-b, Col del Valle, CP 03100, México DF, T/F55-5575 7887, www.amtave.org*, is making steady progress in promoting and protecting ecotourism alongside adventure-related pursuits. The need for standards is important in some activities and **AMTAVE** is doing plenty to develop awareness in this field.

Aerial sports
See under Adventure and ecotourism specialists, page 140. **Guanajuato**, **Valle de Bravo** (for hang-gliding) and the State of **Hidalgo** are most often the backdrop.

Canyoning
Rappel, or abseiling, is often the only way to reach some sites so canyoning is frequently a part of any trip. Two of the best locations for this new sport are the **Cañadas de Cotlamani**, near Jalcomulco in Veracruz and, in the **Cumbres de Monterrey National Park**, the Recorrido de Matacanes circuit (based on the Cascada Lagunillas) and a circuit spilling out from the Cascada El Chipitín, known locally as Recorrido Hidrofobia.

Caving
Caving, or speleology, in Mexico is more than just going down into deep dark holes. Sometimes it is a sport more closely related to canyoning as there are some excellent underground river scrambles. The best of these is probably the 8-km-long **Chontalcuatlán**, a part of the Cacahuamilpa cave system near Taxco. There is an underground lagoon here in **Zacatecolotla** cave. There are also well-publicized options for caving in **Cuetzalan**, near Puebla. Beside the **Matacanes** river circuit in Nuevo León, near Monterrey (see Canyoning) there are some large caves: the **Grutas de La Tierrosa**, **La Cebolla** and **Pterodáctilo**.

For purist potholers there are many vertical caves or *sótanos* (cellars) such as **El Jabalí**, **El Nogal** and **Tilaco** in the Sierra Gorda de Querétaro and La **Purificación** near Ciudad Victoria. The biggest cave systems are in Chiapas especially around Tuxtla Gutiérrez. One of the best elsewhere is the **Sótano de las Golondrinas** on the Santa María river, San Luis Potosí (see Rafting), although perhaps the most challenging is **Pozo Verde**, 1070 m deep, near Ocotempa, Puebla.

And finally you have the option of diving in water-filled caves known as *cenotes*, a common and popular sport in the Yucatán, particularly around **Tulum**.

Climbing
The big glaciated volcanoes are within relatively easy reach of Mexico City. Although there are few technical routes, crampons, ice-axe and occasionally rope are required for safe ascents. The season is October to May. Now that **Popocatépetl** (5452 m) and **Colima Volcano** (3842 m) are sporadically erupting (although it may still be possible to climb **El Nevado** 4339 m, behind Colima Volcano), the two remaining high-altitude challenges are **Pico de Orizaba** (Citlatépetl, 5760 m, Mexico's highest volcano) and **Iztaccíhuatl** (5286 m,

the best technical climbing with great views over Popo). Two good acclimatization climbs are **Cofre de Perote** (Nouhcampatépetl, 4282 m) and **Nevado de Toluca** (Xinantécatl, 4583 m). Further afield, near Tapachula in Chiapas, **Volcán Tacaná** (4150 m) is a worthwhile but little-climbed mountain.

Rock climbing is an increasingly popular sport for Mexicans and there is good to great climbing in most parts of the country. Specialist opportunities can be found near **Pueblo Viejo** and also in the area surrounding **Creel**, in Chihuahua. Also in the north, near Hidalgo (40 km from Monterrey), is the the massive limestone cliff of **Potrero Chico**, a magnet for big-wall climbers.

Diving

This is practised off most of Mexico's coastline but two regions, **Quintana Roo** and **Baja California** at opposite ends of the country, are particularly noteworthy. Southern Baja has adventurous diving in deep waters. Quintana Roo offers warm-water reefs close to the shore and visibility of over 30 m. **Cozumel**, in Quintana Roo, has some of the best diving in the world. There are marine parks at Chankanaab and at Palancar Reef with numerous caves and gullies and a horseshoe-shaped diving arena. Also excellent on the west side of the island are Santa Rosa and sites off San Francisco beach. To the southwest are good sites off Laguna Colombia, while off Punta Sur there is excellent deep diving. There is concern, however, over the damage to the reef inflicted by the new cruise ship pier, and more of these piers are planned. At **Isla Mujeres**, also in Quintana Roo, the most dived sites include Los Manchones, La Bandera, a shallow dive south of the island, and El Frío, a deep wreck 1½ hours to the north.

Diving in the *cenotes* of the Yucatán, particularly around **Tulum**, is also popular.

Rafting

The variety of Mexico's rivers opens the activity up to all levels of experience. The attraction is not just the run but the trek or rappel to the start and the moments between rapids, drifting in deep canyons beneath hanging tropical forests, some of which contain lesser-known and inaccessible ruins. For thrills, many of the best are in the centre of the country.

The season for whitewater rafting is generally July to September, when rivers are fuller, in Central Mexico, but in Chiapas, January and February are preferred because the climate is cooler.

The most popular river is the **Río Antigua/Pescados** in Veracruz. The upper stretch, the Antigua, has some good learning rapids (Grade II) running into Grade III, but, if you have more than one day, the Pescados (the lower Antigua), nearer to Jalcomulco, can give a bigger adrenalin rush with some Grade IV whitewater. The biggest rush in the country, however, is on the **Barranca Grande** and at **Cañón Azul** where there is excellent quality Grade V water. To complete the pre-eminence of **Veracruz** as a rafting destination is the **Filo-Bobos**. The Alto Filo (Grades IV and V) and the 25-km-long Tlapacoyan to Palmilla stretch, halfway along which the Bobos enters the Filo, are the areas of most interest to rafter-archaeologists.

Rafting in **Chiapas** covers the spectrum from sedate floats on rivers such as the Lacan-Há through the Lacandón jungle to Grade IV/V rapids on the Río Jataté, which gathers force where the Lacan Tum enters it and gradually diminishes in strength as it nears the Río Usumacinta.

Sea kayaking

Sea kayaking is growing in popularity. The simplest kayaks are more like rafts and have no open compartments that you need to worry about flooding. Agencies will assess your experience when renting out more advanced equipment and for longer periods. The warm waters of the **Sea of Cortés**, off Baja California Sur, are kayak heaven. **Isla Espíritu Santo** and **Isla Partida** are easily accessible from La Paz and whether in or out of your kayak you can experience a wild party of stingrays, sea-lions, dolphins, porpoises and occasionally grey whales and hammerheads. Another good spot for kayaking is in the **Bahía de Sayulita** just north of Puerto Vallarta and around the nearby **Islas Marieta**s.

Sport fishing

There are resort-based sports fishing fleets along much of Mexico's Pacific Coast, from **Acapulco** to **Bahía Kino**, where there is a major tournament at the end of June/early July. There is also a big tournament in **Manzanillo** in February.

Surfing

Some of the world's most exhilarating surfing can be experienced along Mexico's Pacific Coast. The highlights are the huge and powerful Hawaiian-size surf that pounds the **Baja California** shoreline and the renowned *Mexican Pipeline* at **Puerto Escondido**. There are numerous possibilities, ranging from developed beaches to remote bays accessible only by 4WD. Many are to be found at the estuaries of rivers where sandbars are deposited and points are formed. It is impossible to name all the good beaches; the following is a selection starting in the north.

Isla de Todos Santos in front of Ensenada has big swells. It is much frequented by US surfers and is best in winter. A wetsuit is usually necessary when surfing in Baja. **Mazatlán** is the point on the mainland where currents escape the shielding effects of the Baja peninsula and surfing is possible. As the geographical centre point on Mexico's surfing coast it has been chosen as home to the **Surfing Association** ① *PO Box 310*. In front of the town Isla de la Piedra is good along with Playa Cerritos just north of the town and also **El Caimanero** and near **Teacapan**, 100 km to the south. **San Blas** is an excellent learning centre. The waves are normally not too big and there are few rocks or dangerous currents. Surfing is best in the spring and summer, particularly July to October.

Trekking

The **Copper Canyon** is a vast wilderness for trekking. Creel is the obvious base but an excellent trek is from Batópilas to Urique – three days in the heat of the *barranca*, through Tarahumara lands – there's no better way to experience the abyss after you have spent a day or two wondering, from a mirador on its rim, what it is like down there. Be careful about where you camp. Ask landowners' permission and don't slow down too much should you stumble across a marijuana plantation.

The best trekking within easy reach of a major city is from Monterrey, particularly in the **Cumbres de Monterrey National Park**. There are several organizations in Mexico City that arrange weekend mountain hiking excursions.

One of the attractions of more remote trekking – in the states of **Oaxaca** and **Nayarit**, for example – is to visit indigenous communities such as Cora and Huichol villages. However, one should be sensitive to local reaction to tourist intrusion. Baja California's petroglyph cave sites can often only be visited on foot, which adds to the mystical experience, but here too remember that most sites are sacred and you should be accomanied by a guide. Seek advice before trekking in **Chiapas** and **Guerrero**, both hideouts for rebel groups, with the hefty military presence that goes with them.

National parks

Mexico has an immense range of habitats and wildlife; the far south is in the Neotropical kingdom, with a wealth of tropical forest species, while the far north is very much part of the Neoarctic kingdom, with typically North American species, and huge expanses of desert with unique ecosystems. The greater part of the country is a transition zone between the two, with many strange juxtapositions of species that provide invaluable information to scientists, as well as many endemic species. Mexico's national parks were set up a long time ago primarily to provide green recreation areas for city dwellers; they are generally small and have often been planted with imported species such as eucalyptus, and are thus of no biological value. However, the country does also have a good number of biosphere reserves, which are both of great biological value and suitable for tourism.

There are 93 protected areas in Mexico covering 11.7 million hectares, roughly 6% of the country. Starting in the far south, in Chiapas, **El Triunfo Biosphere Reserve** protects Mexico's only cloud forest, on the mountains (up to 2750 m) above the Pacific Coast; the main hiking route runs from Jaltenango (reached by bus from Tuxtla) to Mapastepec on the coastal highway. Groups need to book in advance through the **Instituto de Historia Natural** ① *Calzada de Hombres de la Revolución, by the botanical garden and Regional Museum (Apdo 391, Tuxtla 29000; T961-612-3663)*.

Also in Chiapas is the immense **Selva Lacandona**, supposedly protected by the Azules Biosphere Reserve but in reality still being eaten away by colonization and logging. New plant species are still being discovered in this rainforest, best visited either from the Bonampak and Yaxchilán ruins, or by the road/boat route via Pico de Oro and Flor de Café to Montebello.

In the Yucatán the **Sian Ka'an Biosphere Reserve**, south of Cancún, is a mixture of forest, savanna and mangrove swamp, best visited on a day-trip run by **Amigos de Sian Ka'an** ① *Calle Fuego 2 SM, Cancún, T998-892 2958, www.amigosdesiankaan.org*. Also useful is the **Sian Ka'an Information Centre** ① *Av Tulum between Satelite and Geminis, Tulum, T/F984-871 2363, siankaan_tours@hotmail.com*. It is also well worth visiting the **Río Lagartos** and **Río Celestún** reserves on the north and west coasts of Yucatán, well known for their flamingos. The **Calakmul Biosphere Reserve** is important mainly for its Mayan ruins, seeming to the layman more like scrub than forest.

Across the country's centre is the **Transversal Volcanic Belt**, one of the main barriers to Nearctic and Neotropic species; it's easiest to head for the **Parque Nacional Izta-Popo** (from Amecameca), the **Parque Nacional Zoquiapan** (on the main road to Puebla) or the **Parque Nacional El Tepozteco** (on the main road to Cuernavaca), and naturally the volcanoes themselves are well worth climbing.

Only small areas of the northern deserts and sierras are formally protected. The most accessible areas are in Durango state, including **La Michilía Biosphere Reserve**, with pine, oak and red-trunked *Arbutus* and *Arctostaphylus* trees typical of the Sierra Madre Occidental. A daily bus runs to San Juan de Michis, and you should get off at a T-junction 2 km before the village and walk west, first getting permission from the Jefe de Unidad Administrativo, **Instituto de Ecología** ① *Apdo 632, 34000 Durango, T618-812 1483*; their offices are at Km 5 on the Mazatlán highway. The **Mapimí Biosphere Reserve** covers an area of desert *matorral* (scrub) that receives just 200 mm of rain a year; it lies to the east of

Ceballos, on the Gómez Palacio–Ciudad Jiménez highway. In addition to the species of bush and cactus, this is home to giant turtles, now in enclosures at the Laboratory of the Desert.

There is a great variety of protected areas in Baja California, all of considerable biological value: the highest point (3000 m) is the **Sierra de San Pedro Mártir**, in the north, which receives plenty of precipitation and has largely Californian fauna and flora. A dirt road starts at the Puente San Telmo, on the main road down the west coast, and leads almost 100 km to an astronomical observatory. Desert environments are, of course, unavoidable here, with 80 endemic cacti: the **Gran Desierto del Altar** is a dry lunar landscape, best seen from the main road along the US border, while the **El Vizcaíno Biosphere Reserve** protects a huge area of central Baja, characterized by agaves and drought-resistant scrub. However, the main reason for stopping here is to see the migration of the grey whale to its breeding grounds. In the far south, the **Sierra de la Laguna** boasts a unique type of cloud forest, with several endemic species; to get here you have to cross about 20 km of desert from just south of Todos Santos to La Burrera, and then follow a trail for 11 km to a rangers' *campamento* at about 1750 m.

Information on national parks and biosphere reserves can be obtained from the **Instituto Nacional de Ecología** ① *Periférico 5000, Col Insurgentes Cuicuilco, CP 04530, Delegación Coyoacán, México DF, T55-5424 6400, www.ine.gob.mx*, a decentralized body of the Secretaría de Medio Ambiente y Recursos Naturales.

Non-governmental conservation organizations include **Naturalia** ① *Horquillas 43, Col Santa Fe, Hermosillo, 83249, Sonora, T55-5559 5696, www.naturalia.org.mx*, and **Pronatura, Asociación Mexicano por la Conservación de la Naturaleza** ① *Aspérgulas 22, Col San Clemente, CP 01740, México DF, T/F55-5635 5054, www.pronatura.org.mx*.

Getting there

Air

Airport information There are several international airports, the two busiest are **Mexico City** and **Cancún**. Puerto Vallarta and Cabo San Lucas are increasingly popular and may have space on charter flights. Services from the US and Canada arrive at almost 30 Mexican cities. Air passes are often bought in conjunction with international flights so ask when booking if planning internal flights, see page 76. For those arriving at Mexico City who are going straight on to Córdoba, Cuernavaca, Puebla, Querétaro, Toluca or Pachuca, there are bus services at frequent intervals departing from outside Sala D of the airport. If you are likely to be returning home at a busy time (eg between Christmas and New Year, or August) a booking is advisable on open-return tickets.

When arriving in Mexico by air, make sure you fill in the immigration document before joining the queue to have your passport checked.

Departure tax Currently US$40 on international flights (dollars or pesos accepted); always check when purchasing if departure tax is included in ticket price. A sales tax of 15% is payable on domestic plane tickets bought in Mexico.

Student/youth and discount fares Some airlines are flexible on the age limit, others strict. One way and returns available, or 'Open Jaws' (flying into one point and returning from another). Do not assume student tickets are the cheapest, though they are often very flexible.

Major land border crossings Mexico–USA

Baja California
Tijuana–San Diego, see page 198.
Tijuana–Otay Mesa, see page 198.
Tecate–Tecate, see page 198.
Mexicali–Calexico, see page 199.

Northwest coast
Algodones–Andrade, see page 232.
San Luis Rio Colorado–San Luis,
    see page 232.
Sonoyta–Lukeville, see page 233.
Altar–Sásabe, see page 234.
Nogales–Nogales, see page 234.

Northern highlands
Agua Prieta–Douglas, see page 255.
Palomas–Columbus, see page 255.
Ciudad Juárez–El Paso, see page 255.
Ojinaga–Presidio, see page 255.

Northeast Mexico
Ciudad Acuña–Del Rio, see page 284.
Piedras Negras–Eagle Pass, see
    page 285.
Nuevo Laredo–Laredo, see page 285.
Matamoros–Brownsville, see page 285.
Reynosa–McAllen, see page 285.

From Europe To Mexico City: there are several airlines that have regular direct flights. From Amsterdam with KLM; from Frankfurt with Lufthansa and AeroMéxico (LTU and Condor charter flights to Mexico City or Cancún); from London and Manchester with British Airways; from Barcelona with Iberia; from Madrid with Iberia and AeroMéxico; from Paris with Air France and AeroMéxico. Most connecting flights in Europe are through Madrid or Gatwick. Fares vary from airline to airline and according to time of year. Check with an agency for the best deal for when you wish to travel. **To Cancún:** From Amsterdam with Martinair, Dusseldorf with LTU, Frankfurt with LTU and Condor, Munich with LTU and Condor; Madrid with AeroMéxico and Avianca, Milan with Lauda Air and Paris with American Airlines.

From USA To Mexico City: A large number of airlines fly this route, including American Airlines, AeroMéxico, Delta, Continental, United, Northwest, Taesa and Americawest. Flights are available from most major cities, with the cheapest generally going through Miami, Dallas, Houston and sometimes Los Angeles. **To Cancún:** Flights leave from many cities across the USA.

From Canada To Mexico City: From Montreal and Sault Ste Marie with Mexicana; from Toronto with Mexicana and United; and from Vancouver with Japan Airlines. **To Cancún:** From Montreal and Vancouver with Mexicana.

From Australia and New Zealand From Sydney with United and from Auckland with Air New Zealand, all flying through Los Angeles.

From Latin America and the Caribbean Flights from Latin America have increased in recent years. Central America is covered by the TACA network, connecting the capitals of each country to Mexico City and some of the smaller regional cities. In South America, connections are to capitals and major cities. If planning a trip to Cuba there are flights from Cancún, Mérida and Mexico City with Mexicana and Cubana.

Road

From USA There are many border crossings with the US (see box, page 75); the main ones are Tijuana, Mexicali, Nogales, Ciudad Juárez, Piedras Negras, Nuevo Laredo and Matamoros.

From Guatemala The main border town is Tapachula, with a crossing over the Talismán Bridge or at Ciudad Hidalgo. A more interesting route is via Ciudad Cuauhtémoc or heading northwest from Santa Elena/Flores towards Tenosique. There are also options for road and river travel.

From Belize The border crossing at Santa Elena is near Chetumal, where public transport can be arranged. A very quiet, and more challenging, crossing is at Blue Creek.

Getting around

It may sound obvious but Mexico is larger than many people realize. Travelling Tijuana to Cancún non-stop by bus and assuming good links would take at least three days and cost in the region of US$250-300. Be realistic about the distances you hope to travel. If time is short, consider taking an internal flight – it might seem expensive but add the cost of bus travel, food en route and recovery time, and it's worth keeping an open mind.

Air

Most medium-sized towns have an airport. If you're looking to cover a great distance in a short time it is worth exploring the option of an airpass. **Mexicana** provide an airpass covering much of the country; it is eligible only to those arriving on transatlantic flights, valid three to 90 days and must be purchased before arrival in Mexico. Fares range from US$50-400 per coupon; extra coupons may be bought and reservations may be changed. Several other airlines fly internal routes (a few with international flights as well), including **Aeromar, Aeroméxico Connect, Taesa**, and **Aviacsa**.

Low-cost airlines include: **Interjet** (www.interjet. com.mx), **Volaris** (www.volaris.com. mx), **Mexicana Airline's Mexicana Click** (www.clickmexicana.com) and **VivaAerobus** (www.vivaaerobus.com), providing services to different parts of Mexico. Toluca's Adolfo López Mateos International Airport, about 64 km west of Mexico City is the central hub for the low-cost airlines. General costs are comparable with the older airlines. You get the bargain if you can book ahead, travel at inconvenient times or if there is a special offer.

Bus → *Buses are often called camiones, hence 'Central Camionero' for bus station.*

The Mexican bus system is good, but at times complicated and confusing. When buying tickets you may be confronted with a daunting range of options, sometimes leaving from different terminals. The bottom line is that there is normally a bus going from where you are to where you want to go. The problem is trying to locate where that bus leaves from. In some cities there is a central bus terminal (in Mexico City there are four – one at each point of the compass broadly serving their respective areas), in others there are a couple – one for first-class buses, one for second. A third variation is division by companies.

Bus travel can use up a lot of your budget because the distances covered are great. As a very rough calculation bus travel works out at around US$4.80 per hour spent travelling, with tickets falling between US$4 to US$5.50 an hour depending on the level of competition on the route.

Bus services are generally organized, clean and prompt. Services range from luxury to first and second class. However, travellers should not be beguiled into thinking that it is necessary to purchase an expensive ticket in order to travel comfortably. The service varies greatly between routes. A journey between two cities will almost certainly have a luxury service; a short trip between villages may be on a battered old bus.

The superior classes, called **Primera Plus** and **Ejecutiva**, offer varying degrees of comfort and some extra services. A number of bus companies offer this option providing reclining seats, toilets, drinks, videos, etc. **ETN** has exceptional buses with very comfortable, extra-wide seats but prices are about 35-40% more than regular first class. The superior classes are probably best for journeys over six hours. First-class buses are also comfortable and have reclining seats, toilets and videos. For many long-distance routes, the second-class buses have disappeared. Second-class buses usually operate from a different terminal to first-class buses and are often antiques (interesting, but frustrating when they break down). They call at towns and villages and go up side roads that the first-class pass.

In general, it is a good idea to take food and drink with you on a long bus ride, as stops may depend on the driver. When a bus stops for refreshment, remember who your driver is and follow him; in busy terminals memorize your bus number so you don't miss it when it leaves. On daytime journeys consider whether you want to see the scenery or a video. If going on an overnight bus, book seats at the front as toilets can get smelly by morning. Also make sure you have a jacket, jumper or blanket to hand as the air conditioning can be very cold at night. You're advised to book in advance for buses travelling in the Yucatán Peninsula, especially around Christmas; it is also advisable to book if going elsewhere during Christmas. Bus seats are particularly hard to get during school holidays, August and the 15 days up to New Year when many public servants take holidays; transport from Mexico City is booked up in advance and hotels are filled too. On intercity services luggage is checked into the hold of the bus with a receipt provided, offering a degree of security. If you are putting luggage in the hold, always check that your bags are on the right bus.

Inside the bus, lock or clip your luggage to the rack with a cycle lock and chain. Luggage racks on both classes of long-distance bus are spacious and will take a rucksack with a little persuasion (either of the rucksack itself, or the bus driver).

Fares First-class fares are usually 10% dearer than second-class ones and the superior classes are even more. On a long journey you can save the price of a hotel room by travelling overnight, but in many areas this is dangerous and not recommended. Look out for special offers, including discounts at some hotel chains.

Useful bus links

Some bus tickets can be purchased at www.ticketbus.com.mx, information on T01-800-702-8000. If travelling from north of the border, you might want to hook up with **Green Tortoise**, www.greentortoise.com, which has a range of trips throughout Mexico. **ADO GL**, www.adogl.com.mx, T01-800-702-8000. The Yucatán, southeast, Gulf and northeast Mexico.

Cristóbal Colón, T01-800-702-8000. South of Mexico City. Details on the Ticketbus system.

ETN, www.etn.com.mx, T01-800-8000-386.
Estrella de Oro, www.estrelladeoro.com.mx, T01-800-9000-105. Southwest of Mexico City.
Grupo Estrella, www.estrellablanca.com.mx, T01-800-507-5500. Most of Mexico through several companies
Omnibus, www.odm.com.mx, T01-800-965-6636. North of Mexico City.
Primera Plus, www.primeraplus.com.mx, T01-800-375-7587. Mid-central to southern Mexico.
UNO, www.uno.com.mx, T01-800-702-8000. North of Mexico City.

Bicycle

Mexico offers plenty of enjoyable places for cycling. The main problems facing cyclists are the heavy traffic that will be encountered on main roads, the poor condition of these roads and the lack of specialized spare parts, particularly for mountain bikes. It is possible to find most bike spares in the big cities, but outside these places it is only possible to find the basics: spokes, tyres, tubes, etc. Traffic is particularly bad around Mexico City. The easiest region for cycling is the Gulf of Mexico coast; however, many of the roads are dead flat, straight and generally boring. The mountains may appear intimidating, but gradients are not difficult as clapped-out buses and trucks have to be able to climb them. Consequently, much of the best riding is in the sierra. If cycling in Baja, avoid riding in mid-summer; even during October temperatures can reach 45°C+ and water is always very scarce. The toll roads are generally preferable to the ordinary highways for cyclists; there is less traffic, more lanes and a wide paved shoulder. Some toll roads have 'no cyclists' signs but usually the police pay no attention. If you walk your bicycle on the pavement through the toll station you don't have to pay. If using the toll roads, take lots of water as there are few facilities. Cycling on some main roads can be very dangerous; it is useful to fit a rear-view mirror.

Car

Permits Vehicles may be brought into Mexico on a **Tourist Permit** for 180 days each year. The necessary documents are: passport, birth certificate or naturalization papers; tourist card; vehicle registration (if you do not own the car, a notarized letter from the vehicle's owner or the hire company is necessary); and a valid international or national druving licence. The original and two photocopies are required for each. It takes 10 days to extend a permit, so ask for more time than you need. Don't overstay; driving without an extension gets a US$50 fine for the first five days and then rises to half the value of the car. US$16.50 is charged for the permit, payable only by credit card (Visa, MasterCard, American Express or Diners Club), not a debit card, in the name of the car owner, as recorded on the vehicle registration. The **American Automobile Association (AAA)** issues Tourist Permits for 'credit card' entry, free to members, US$18 non-members; in California this service is available only to members. If you do not have a credit card, you have to buy a bond in cash to the value of the vehicle according to its age (a set scale exists), which is repaid on leaving Mexico. The bond is divided into two parts, the bond itself and administration; the latter, accounting for about 43% of the total cost, is retained by the authorities; the bond is refunded. The bond is issued by Afianziadora Mexicana at US/Mexican border crossings, or by **Sanborn's** (see Insurance, page 79). It may be waived if you are only going to the State of Sonora.

English versions of leaflets giving the rules on temporary importation of vehicles state you must leave at the same crossing by which you entered. The Spanish versions do not say this and in practice it is not important. The temporary importation permit is multiple entry for 180 days; within that period you can enter and leave by any crossing, and as often as you like. However, you must have a new tourist card or Visa for each new entry. The Sanborn's website (www.sanbornsinsurance.com) is an excellent source of information.

On entry, go to *Migración* for your tourist card, on which you must state your means of transport. This is the only record of how you entered the country. At the **Banjército** desk sign an *Importación Temporal de Vehículos/Promesa de retornar vehículo*, which bears all vehicle and credit card details so that if you sell your car illegally your credit card account can be debited for the import duty. Next you purchase the *Solicitud de importación temporal*, which costs US$12; it bears a hologram that matches the dated sticker, which must be displayed on the windscreen or, on a motorcycle, on some safe surface. Then go to

Copias to photocopy all necessary documents and papers issued. The sticker and other entry documents must be surrendered on departure. They can only be surrendered at a Mexican border crossing, with date stickers cancelled by **Banjército** at Immigration. If you neglect to do this, and re-enter Mexico with an expired uncancelled sticker on your car, you will be fined heavily for each 15-day period that has elapsed since the date of expiry. If you intend to return to Mexico within the 180-day period, having surrendered your sticker and documents, keep safe the *Importación Temporal de Vehículos* form and stamped *Cancelado*. If entry papers are lost there can be much delay and expense (including enforcement of the bond) in order to leave the country. **Banjército (Banco del Ejército)** offices at borders are open daily, some for 24 hours. Each vehicle must have a different licensed driver (that is, you cannot tow another vehicle into Mexico unless it has a separate driver).

On arrival, you have to find the place where car permits are issued; this may not be at the border.

Insurance In Mexico, foreign insurance will not be honoured; you must ensure that the company you insure with will settle accident claims inside Mexico. According to latest official documents, insurance for foreign cars entering Mexico is not mandatory, but it is highly recommended to be insured. Arranging insurance when crossing from the USA is very easy as there are many offices at US border crossings. Policy prices vary enormously between companies, according to age and type of vehicle. **Sanborn's Mexican Insurance Service** ⓘ *head office: 2009 S 10th St, McAllen, TX 78505-0310, T956-686-0711, toll free 1-800-222-0158, www.sanbornsinsurance.com*, provides comprehensive insurance, including full-year cover, within Mexico and other parts of Latin America, and provides free 'Travelogs' for Mexico and Central America with useful tips. It has offices in every US border town, and many more throughout the country. **Tepeyac** has offices in most Mexican cities, as well as at border towns and in the US (eg San Diego). Information in Spanish at www.mapfretepeyac.com or through English-speaking agents www.mexadventure.com, T800-485 4075.

Entering Mexico from Guatemala presents few local insurance problems now, **Tepeyac** (see above), has an office in Tapachula; and **Seguros La Provincial** ⓘ *Av General Utrillo 10A, upstairs, San Cristóbal de las Casas*, also has an office in Cuauhtémoc ⓘ *Av Cuauhtémoc 1217 ground floor, Sr García Figueroa, T5-604-0500*. Otherwise, try **Segumex** in Tuxtla Gutiérrez. In Mexico City, try **Grupo Nacional Provincial** ⓘ *Río de la Plata 48, T528-67732, www.gnp.com.mx*, which has offices in many towns.

Petrol/diesel All *gasolina* is now unleaded. All petrol stations in Mexico are franchised by Petróleos Mexicanos (PEMEX) and fuel costs the same throughout the country (approximately US$0.65 a litre) except near the US border, where it may be a bit cheaper. Unleaded petrol is classified either as *Magna*, from the green pumps, or the more expensive *Premium*, from the red ones. Diesel is also available. Petrol stations are not self-service. Make sure the pump is set at zero before your tank is filled and that your filler cap is put back on before you drive off. Specify how much you want either in litres or in money; it is normal to give the attendant a small tip.

Assistance The free assistance service of the Mexican Tourist Department's green jeeps (**Angeles Verdes**) patrol many of Mexico's main roads. Call them toll-free on T01-800-903-9200; every state also has an Angeles Verdes hotline. The drivers speak English, are trained to give first aid, make minor auto repairs and deal with flat tyres. They carry gasoline and have radio connection. All help is completely free, and you pay cost price for the gasoline. Although the idea is great, few Mexicans rely on the service in outlying areas and your best bet is to keep your vehicle in good condition and carry out the usual regular checks. More information through angelesverdes@sectur.gob.mx.

Road tolls A toll is called a *cuota*, as opposed to a non-toll road, which is a *vía libre*. There are many toll charges and the cost works out at around one peso per kilometre. Check out your route, and toll prices, on the **Traza Tu Ruta** section of www.sct.gob.mx. Some new freeways bypassing city centres charge US$4-12, or more. Because of the high cost of toll roads, they are often quite empty, which means that good progress can be made. Some tolls can be avoided if you seek local or motoring club advice on detours around toll gates (follow trucks). This may involve unpaved roads, which should not be attempted in the wet. However, the *carreteras libres* are normally perfectly acceptable and more interesting as they often travel through small towns and sometimes beautiful countryside.

In case of accident Do not abandon your vehicle. Call your insurance company immediately to inform it of the accident. Do not leave Mexico without first filing a claim in Mexico. Do not sign any contract or agreement without a representative of the insurance company being present. Always carry with you, in the insured vehicle, your policy identification card and the names of the company's adjusters (these are the recommendations of **Asemex**). If, in an accident, bodily injury has occurred or the drivers involved cannot agree who is at fault, the vehicles may be impounded. Drivers will be required to stay in the vicinity in cases of serious accidents, the insured being confined to a hotel (or hospital) until the claim is settled (according to **Sanborn's**). A helpline for road accidents is available by phoning T02 and asking the operator to connect you to T55-5684 9715 or T55-5684 9761.

Warnings On all roads, when two vehicles converge from opposite directions, or when a vehicle is behind a slow cart, bicycle, etc, the driver who first flashes his lights has the right of way. This also applies when a bus or truck wishes to turn left across the opposing traffic: if the driver flashes his lights he is claiming right of way and the oncoming traffic must give way. At *Alto* (Halt) signs, all traffic must come to a complete stop. Avoid driving at night. Night-time robberies on vehicles are on the increase especially in Guerrero and Oaxaca states. 'Sleeping policemen' or road bumps can be hazardous in towns and villages as there are often no warning signs; they are sometimes marked *zona de topes*, or incorrectly marked as *vibradores*. In most instances, their distinguishing paint has worn away.

Roadworks are usually well marked. If your vehicle breaks down on the highway and you do not have a warning triangle or a piece of red cloth to act as a warning, cut branches from the roadside and lay them in the road some distance in front of and behind your vehicle (remember to remove them when you move on).

If you are stopped by police in town for an offence you have not committed and you know you are in the right, do not pay the 'fine' on the spot. Take the policeman's identity number, show him that you have his number and tell him that you will see his chief (*jefe*) at the tourist police headquarters instead. It is also advisable to go to the precinct station anyway whenever a fine is involved, to make sure it is genuine. If stopped in a remote area, it is not advisable to get into a dispute with a policeman; drugs may be planted in your vehicle or problems may occur.

Further information A useful source of advice (whose help we acknowledge here) is the **Recreation Vehicle Owner's Association of British Columbia (RVOABC)** ① *PO Box 73046, Evergreen RPO Surrey, BC, V3R 0J2, T604-596 9788, www.rvoabc.org*. Membership costs US$35 a year and members receive a copy of the *RV Times*; Mexican insurance can be arranged. There's a vast amount of information on the web, try www.rvbasics.com for starters. *RVing in Mexico, Central America and Panamá*, by John and Liz Plaxton (ITMB Publishing, Canada, 1996), has been recommended as full of useful information, although it can be difficult to get hold of.

Car hire Car rental is very expensive in Mexico, from US$35-45 a day for a basic model with 15% sales tax added to rental costs. Rates will vary from city to city. Make sure you have unlimited mileage. Age limit is normally at least 25 and you'll need to place a deposit, normally against a credit card, for damage. It can be cheaper to arrange hire in the US or Europe. Proceed with caution. At some tourist resorts, however, such as Cancún, you can pick up a VW Beetle convertible for US$25 per day. Renting a vehicle is nearly impossible without a credit card. It is twice as expensive to leave a car at a different point from the starting point than it is to make a round trip.

Hitchhiking

Hitchhiking is usually possible for single hikers, but apparently less easy for couples. It is generally quick, but not universally safe (seek local advice). Do not, for example, try to hitch in parts of Guerrero and Oaxaca states where even driving alone is not recommended. Yet in Baja California in some ways it is the best way to travel. In more out-of-the-way parts, short rides from village to village are usually the rule, so progress can be slow. Getting out of big cities is best done by taking a local bus out of town in the direction of the road you intend to take. Ask for the bus to take the *salida* (exit) to the next city on that road. It is very easy to hitch short distances, such as the last few kilometres to an archaeological site off the main road; offer to pay something, like US$0.50.

Motorcycle

Motorcycling is good in Mexico as most main roads are in fairly good condition and hotels are usually willing to allow the bike to be parked in a courtyard or patio. In the major tourist centres, such as Acapulco, Puerto Vallarta or Cancún, motorbike parts can be found as there are Honda dealers for bike and jet ski rentals.

Taxi

To avoid overcharging, the government has taken control of taxi services from airports to cities. Only those with government licences are allowed to carry passengers from the airport and you can usually buy a ticket with a set price to your destination from a booth at the terminal. No tipping is required for airport taxis, except when the driver handles heavy luggage or provides some extra service for you. The same system has been applied at bus stations but it is possible to pay the driver direct. Avoid flagging down taxis in the street at night in Mexico City. It is safer to phone for a *sitio* taxi from your hotel.

Train

Apart from the **Chihuahua al-Pacífico**, between Los Mochis, Creel and Chihuahua, considered one of the world's greatest rail routes (see page 258), and the **Tequila Express**, a rather cutesy way of moving people from Guadalajara to Tequila so they can drink and not drive, there are no official passenger services running. However, some freight trains do have passenger wagons – they just don't publish the schedules (they were close to useless when they did). If you have a great deal of time and patience and are train mad then you probably can travel through Mexico on trains. Services are said to be ridiculously cheap and stupidly slow – walking may be quicker. Reaching your destination is also likely to be more through luck and persistence than planning.

Maps

Internationally, **ITM** (see page 45), www.itmb.com, provide several maps including one covering all Mexico, Mexico City, Baja California, Mexico North West, Mexico South East, Yucatán Peninsula and a growing selection of regional road maps. The *Mexican Government Tourist Highway* map is free at tourist offices (when in stock). If driving from the US you get a free map if you buy your insurance at **Sanborn's** in the border cities.

Guía Roji publish a wide range of regional maps, city plans and gazettes, available at most bookshops and news stands. Guia roja is online at http://guiaroji.com.mx with full street, town, city and state search facilities for the country.

The **Dirección General de Oceanografía** ① *Calle Medellín 10, near Insurgentes metro station, Mexico City*, sells excellent maps of the entire coastline of Mexico. Buy good detailed maps of states of Mexico and the country itself from **Dirección General de Geografía y Meteorología** ① *Av Observatorio 192, México 18 DF, T55-5515 1527; Observatorio metro station, go up Calle Sur 114, turn right a short distance down Av Observatorio*. Maps are also available from **Instituto Nacional de Estadística, Geografía e Informática**, which has branches in Mexico City (see page 93) and in state capitals (US$3 per sheet). **Pemex** road atlas, *Atlas de Carreteras y Ciudades Turísticas*, US$5 in bookshops, has 20 pages of city maps, almost every road one may need, contour lines, points of interest and service stations. It is rarely on sale in Pemex stations but recommended.

Sleeping

Hotels and hospedajes

Hotel prices in the lower and middle categories are still very reasonable by US and European standards. Prices of top and luxury hotels have risen more steeply as tourism has increased. English is spoken at the best hotels and is increasingly common throughout Mexico. There is a hotel tax, ranging between 1% and 4%, according to the state, although it is generally levied only when a formal bill is issued.

Always check the room before paying in advance. Also ask if there is 24-hour running water. Check-out time from hotels is commonly 1100 but bag storage is commonplace. Rooms are normally charged at a flat rate, or if there are single rooms they are around 80% the price of a double, so sharing works out cheaper. A room with a double bed is usually cheaper than one with two singles and a room with three or more sharing is often very economical even in the mid-price range.

During peak season (November to April) it may be hard to find a room. The week after Easter is normally a holiday, so prices remain high, but resorts are not as crowded as the previous week. Discounts on hotel prices can often be arranged in the low season (May to October), but this is more difficult in the Yucatán and Baja California.

Casas de huéspedes are usually the cheapest places to stay, although they are often dirty with poor plumbing. Motels and auto-hotels, especially in central and south Mexico, are not usually places where guests stay the whole night (you can recognize them by curtains over the garage and red and green lights above the door to show if the room is free). If driving, and wishing to avoid a night on the road, they can be quite acceptable (clean, some have hot water, and in the Yucatán they have a/c), and they tend to be cheaper than other, 'more respectable' establishments. Beware of 'helpers' who try to find you a hotel, as prices quoted at the hotel desk rise to give them commission.

Youth hostels

Hostels in Mexico are very much on the increase covering private hostels and International Youth Hostel endorsed accommodation. *Albergues* exist in Mexico, mostly in small towns; they are usually good value and clean. While the hostels take YHA members and non-members, members pay a slightly reduced rate and, after about four nights, it normally works out to be cost effective to become a member. Services vary from place to place. Hostels often have lockers for valuables. For information contact **Hostelling International Mexico** ① *Guatemala 4, Col Centro, Mexico City, T55-5518 1726, www.hostellingmexico.com*.

Many towns have a **Villa Deportiva Juvenil**. While these are essentially the Mexican equivalent of a youth hostel their main market is for groups of student Mexicans who may, for example, be taking part in a regional event. It's worth looking out for the option as they are normally very cheap. But while some cater very well for the international traveller, others are barely interested.

Camping

Most sites are called 'trailer parks', but tents are usually allowed. However, due to their primary role as trailer parks they're often in locations more suited for people with their own transport than people on public transport. **Playas Públicas**, with a blue and white sign of a palm tree, are beaches where camping is allowed. They are usually cheap, sometimes free and some have shelters and basic amenities. You can often camp in or near national parks, although you must speak first with the guards, and usually pay a small fee. Paraffin oil (kerosene) for stoves is called *petróleo para lámparas* in Mexico. It is available from an *expendio*, or *despacho de petróleo*, or from a *tlapalería*, but not from gas/petrol stations. Methylated spirits is called *alcohol desnaturalizado* or *alcohol del 96* and is available from chemists. Calor gas is widely available, as it is throughout Central America. *Gasolina blanca* (white gas) may be bought in *ferreterías* (ironmongers) or paint shops; prices vary widely, also ask for Coleman fuel. Alcohol for heating the burner can be obtained from supermarkets.

Eating and drinking

Food

Food for most Mexicans represents an integral part of their national identity, a fact immediately seen in their desire to offer visitors an excess of the most typical dishes and specialities. Much has been written since the 1960s about the evolution of Mexican food and experts suggest that there are three important stages: first, the combination of the indigenous and the Spanish; later, the influence of other European cuisines, notably the French in the 19th century; and finally the adoption of exotic oriental dishes and fast-food from the US in the 20th century.

Because of the use of chilli in Mexican cooking, it is usually perceived as spicy or hot. However, there is another element that is even more characteristic and which visitors become aware of as they get to know the wide range of Mexican dishes. Maize, or corn, has been a staple crop from oldest times not only in Mexico but in the continent as a whole. Maize is consumed in *antojitos* (snacks), some of the most common of which are *quesadillas, sopes, tostadas, tlacoyos* and *gorditas*, which consist of various shapes and sizes of *tortillas*, with a variety of fillings and usually garnished with a hot sauce.

Certain dishes such as *mole* (chicken or turkey prepared in an elaborate chilli-based sauce, see box, page 450) or *pozole* (a pot-au-feu with a base of maize kernels and stock) are close to their indigenous traditions. Others, however, are of more recent creation, for example the following breakfast dishes, all with eggs: *huevos rancheros* (fried, with spicy sauce on a bed of tortillas), *machaca norteña* (scrambled with dried minced beef), *huevos motuleños* (fried with sauce of tomatoes, peas, cheese and fried banana) and *huevos a la mexicana* (scrambled with chilli and tomatoes).

Usual meals are breakfast, a heavy lunch between 1400 and 1500 and a light supper between 1800 and 2000. Meals in modest establishments cost US$2-3 for breakfast, US$2.50-3.50 for set lunch (US$4-6 for a special *comida corrida*) and US$5-10 for dinner (generally no set menu). A la carte meals at modest establishments cost about US$8-12; a very good meal can be had for US$15 at a middle-level establishment. Much higher prices are charged by the classiest restaurants in Mexico City and some resorts. Some restaurants give foreigners the menu without the *comida corrida* (set meals), so forcing them to order à la carte which is often double the price.

Street stalls are by far the cheapest – although not always the safest – option and often the best chance of trying truly local food. The best value is undoubtedly in small, family-run places. If self-catering, markets are cheaper than supermarkets. In resort areas hotels often include breakfast and dinner.

Drink

The **beer** is good: brands include **Dos Equis-XX, Montejo, Bohemia, Sol, Superior** and **Tecate. Negra Modelo** is a dark beer; it has the same alcohol content as the other beers. Some beer is drunk with lime juice and a salt-rimmed glass, or *michelada* with chilli sauce (both available in Oaxaca). Local **wine** is cheap and improving in quality; try **Domecq, Casa Madero** or **Santo Tomás**; the white sold in *ostionerías*, oyster restaurants, is usually good. **Cetto Reisling Fumé** has been recommended. Some of the best wines produced in Mexico are those from Monte Xanic, produced near Ensenda, Baja California, but they are very expensive. The native drinks are *pulque*, the fermented juice of the agave plant (those unaccustomed to it should not over-indulge), **tequila**, made in Jalisco, and **mezcal** from Oaxaca; also distilled from agave plants. Mezcal usually has a *gusano de maguey* (worm) in the bottle, considered to be a particular delicacy. Tequila and mezcal rarely have an alcoholic content above 40-43%; tequila **Herradura** is particularly recommended. Also available is the Spanish aniseed spirit, *anís*, which is made locally. Imported whiskies and brandies are expensive. **Rum** is cheap and good. *Puro de caña* (called *chingre* in Chinanteca and *posh* in Chamula) is distilled from sugar cane; it is stronger than *mezcal* but with less taste; it is found in Oaxaca and Chiapas.

There are always plenty of non-alcoholic *refrescos* (soft drinks) and mineral water. *Agua fresca* – fresh fruit juices mixed with water or mineral water – and *licuados* (milk shakes) are good and usually safe. If you don't like to drink out of a glass ask for a *popote* (straw). Herbal teas, for example chamomile and mint (*manzanilla* and *hierba buena*), are readily available. There are few outdoor drinking places in Mexico except in tourist spots.

Festivals and events

If any of these holidays falls on a Thursday or a Tuesday, they are usually an excuse for a *puente*, a long weekend (which can have implications for travel, hotel accommodation and services).

National holidays
I Jan New Year
5 Feb Constitution Day
21 Mar Birthday of Benito Juárez
Mar/Apr Maundy Thu, Good Fri, Easter Sat
1 May Labour Day
5 May Battle of Puebla
1 Sep El Informe (Presidential Message)
16 Sep Independence Day
12 Oct Día de la Raza (Discovery of America)

20 Nov Día de la Revolución (Revolution Day)
25 Dec Christmas Day

Religious fiestas
There are more than 5000 religious festivals each year. The most widely celebrated are:
6 Jan Santos Reyes (Three Kings)
10 May Día de las Madres (Mothers' Day)
1-2 Nov Día de los Muertos (All Souls' Day)
12 Dec La Virgen de Guadalupe

Shopping

A useful website promoting fair trade and sustainable production is www.bioplaneta.com.

Ceramics Ceramics are generally crafted out of baked clay or plaster and are polished, glazed or polychrome. In some parts, such as Michoacán, men paint the pieces but in the main pot-making is done by women. Some of the best pots have a brilliant glaze such as the Patambán pottery found in Michoacán. The green finish comes from the oxidization of copper while its fragility comes from 'eggshell'-thin clay working.

Crafts The colourful markets and craft shops are a highlight of any visit to Mexico. *Artesanía* is an amalgam of ancient and modern design. The strongest influence are the traditional popular art forms of indigenous communities the length and breadth of the country, which pour into colonial towns such as Oaxaca, San Cristóbal, Pátzcuaro and Uruapan. These are convenient market centres for seeing the superb range of products from functional pots to scary masks hanging over delicately embroidered robes and gleaming lacquered chests.

Jewellery For silver and gold work, known as *orfebrería*, try Taxco and the markets in Mexico City. Jade jewellery is made in Michoacán while semi-precious stones such as onyx, obsidian, amethyst and turquoise are found in Oaxaca, Puebla, Guerrero, Zacatecas and Querétaro.

Masks Textile art is heavily influenced by religious ritual, particularly dances to master natural forces, but as well as being impressively robed, priests, witches and shamans are often masked in the guise of animals such as eagles, jaguars, goats, monkeys and coyotes, particularly in the states of Guerrero (for example in Chilapa), Sinaloa, Sonora and Nayarit.

Textiles Weaving and textile design go back a long way in Mexico and the variety on offer is huge. Textiles can be spun in cotton or wool on the traditional *telar de cintura*, a 'waist loom', or *telar de pie*, a pedal-operated loom introduced by the Spanish. Many woven items are on sale in the markets, from *sarapes* and *morrales* (shoulder bags) to wall-hangings, rugs and bedspreads. Synthetic fibres are often used, so make sure you know what you're getting.

Complaints If you have any complaints about faulty goods or services contact **Profeco** or **Procuraduría Federal del Consumidor** ① *T01-800-468-8722, www.profeco.gob.mx*, or visit the nearest city branch.

Essentials A-Z

Customs and duty free

The list of permitted items is extensive and generally allows for anything that could reasonably be considered for personal use. Adults entering Mexico are allowed to bring in up to 6 litres of wine, beer or spirits; 20 packs of cigarettes, or 25 cigars, or 200 g of tobacco and medicines for personal use. Goods imported into Mexico with a value of more than US$1000 (with the exception of computer equipment, where the limit is US$4000) have to be handled by an officially appointed agent. If you are carrying more than US$10,000 in cash you should declare it. There is no penalty but registration is required. Full details and latest updates are available at www.aduanas.sat.gob.mx.

Dress

Casual clothing is adequate for most occasions although men may need a jacket and tie in some restaurants. Topless bathing is increasingly acceptable in parts of Baja California, but take guidance from others.

Electricity

127 volts/60 Hz, US-style 2-pin plug.

Embassies and consulates

You'll find contact details for other embassies at www.sre.gob.mx, which has an English-language section.

Australia, 14 Perth Av, Yarralumia, 2600 ACT, Canberra, T6273-3963, www.mexico.org.au.

Belize, 3 North Ring Rd, Belmopan, T822-0406.

Canada, 45 O'Connor St, Suite 1000, Ottawa, Ont, K1P 1A4, T613-233-8988, www.sre.gob.mx/canada.

Denmark, Bredgade 65, 1st floor 1260, Copenhagen, T3961-0500, www.sre.gob.mx/dinamarca.

France, 9 rue de Longchamp, 75116 Paris, T5370-2770, www.sre.gob.mx/francia.

Germany, Klingelhöferstrasse 3, 10785 Berlin, T30-269-3230, www.sre.gob.mx/alemania.

Holland, Nassauplein 28, 2585 EC, The Hague, T360-2900, www.embamex-nl.com.

Israel, 25 Hamared St, Trade Tower 5th floor, Tel Aviv 68125, T516-3938, www.sre.gob.mx/israel.

New Zealand, 185-187 Featherston St, level 2 (AMP Chambers), Wellington, T472-5555, www.sre.gob.mx/nuevazelandia.

Switzerland, Welpoststrasse 20, 5th floor, CH-3015, Berne, T357-4747, www.sre.gob.mx/suiza.

UK, 16 St George St, London, W1S 1FD, T020-7499-8586, www.sre.gob.mx/reinounido.

USA, 1911 Pennsylvania Av, NW, 20006 Washington DC, T202-728-1600, www.sre.gob.mx/eua.

Health

Social security hospitals are restricted to members, but will take visitors in emergencies; they are more up to date than the *Centros de Salud* and *Hospitales Civiles* found in most town centres, which are very cheap and open to everyone. It's advisable to vaccinate against hepatitis, typhoid, paratyphoid and poliomyelitis if visiting the low-lying tropical zones, where there is also some risk of malaria. Dengue fever is spreading so seek advice and protect yourself against being bitten. Note also that cholera is on the rise. Hepatitis is also a problem and, if you have not been vaccinated in advance, gamma globulin is available at better pharmacies/chemists.

A vaccination certificate is generally required for travellers arriving from countries where yellow fever is present.

Identification

ID is increasingly required when visiting offices or tourist sites within government buildings. It's handy to have some form of identification (*identificación* or *credencial*), a photocopied passport will usually do.

Internet

A list of useful websites is given on page 90. Every major town and these days most small villages now has at least one internet café, with more springing up daily. The better ones can often cater for a wide range of internet services, including Skype. Prices vary from place to place but are normally around US$1.

Language

The official language of Mexico is Spanish. Outside of the main tourist centres, travelling without some knowledge of Spanish is a major hindrance. Adding to the challenges of communication, there are also some 50 indigenous languages spoken in Mexico, the most common of which are Nahuatl, Maya, Zapotec and Mixtec.

Media

The influential daily newspapers are: *Excelsior, Novedades, El Día, Uno Más Uno, El Universal, El Heraldo, La Jornada* (www.jornada.unam.mx, more to the left, *Tiempo Libre*, listing cultural activities in Mexico City), *La Prensa* (a popular tabloid, with the largest circulation), *El Nacional* (mouthpiece of the government). In Guadalajara, *El Occidental, El Informador* (www.informador.com.mx) and *Siglo 21*. There are influential weekly magazines *Proceso, Siempre, Época* and *Quehacer Político*. The political satirical weekly is *Los Agachados*.

The New York edition of the *Financial Times* and other British and European papers are available at Mexico City Airport and from the **Casa del Libro** in Calle Florencia 37 (Zona Rosa); Hamburgo 141 (Zona Rosa); and Calle Homero (Polanco), all in Mexico City. *The Miami Herald* is stocked by most newspaper stalls.

Money → *US$1=$13.34 pesos (June 2009)*

The monetary unit is the Mexican peso, represented by '$' – the dollar sign – providing great potential for confusion, especially in popular tourist places where prices are higher and often quoted in US dollars (US$).

Exchange

US dollars cash can be easily changed in all cities and towns at banks and *casas de cambio*, and in the more popular places can sometimes be used if you're running short of pesos. When changing money, ask for a mixture of large and small denominations or go to a bank and ask them to change large notes for you. You don't want to get stuck trying to change a US$100 bill in a dusty village in the middle of nowhere, or trying to pay for a local bus. While it is possible to change the euro, sterling and other currencies, not all banks or *casas de cambio* will take them.

Traveller's cheques (TCs) from any well-known bank can be cashed in most towns if drawn in US dollars; TCs from other currencies are harder to cash, and certainly not worth trying to change outside the largest of cities. If you are stuck, branches of HSBC have been known to change other currencies. *Casas de cambio* are generally quicker than banks for exchange transactions and stay open later; fees are not charged but their rates may not be as good. You may be asked to show your passport, another form of ID or even proof of purchase (but keep it separate from your TCs). Denominations of US$50 and US$100 are preferable, though you will need a few of US$20. Amex and Visa US dollar TCs are recommended as the easiest to change.

Transfer

If you need to make a transfer ask your bank if they can transfer direct to a Mexican bank without using an intermediary, which usually results in greater delays. Beware of short-changing at all times. **Western Union,** www.westernunion.com, have outlets throughout Mexico but the service is more expensive than a traditional bank wire.

Credit cards
ATMs are now found even in small towns, allowing you to travel without carrying large amounts of cash or TCs. **MasterCard, Visa** and **American Express** are widely accepted in Mexico either when paying for goods, withdrawing cash from ATMs (*cajero automático*) or obtaining cash over the counter from banks. Many banks are affiliated to MasterCard and/or Visa so travel with both if possible. Credit cards are useful in hotels, restaurants, shops and when hiring equipment to put down a deposit. There is often a 6% tax on the use of credit cards. For lost or stolen cards call: **MasterCard** T001-800-307-7309; **Visa** T001-800-847-2911.

Cost of living and travelling
A basic room is likely to set you back about US$15 on average, with occasionally cheaper prices available. Comfortable rooms will start at around US$20. Some hotels offer no single rooms, or they may charge 80% of the price of a double. If you are travelling alone this should be built into your budget. Meals start from US$10 a day for those on tight budgets. Activities will tend to be in the region of US$30 and upwards a day.

Travel eats up more of your budget. Travel in Mexico is considerably more expensive (and more comfortable) than in the rest of Central America, partly because of the vast distances covered. As an average, travel by bus costs around US$4.80 per hr travelled. See Getting around, page 76.

Budget travellers should note that there is a definite tourist economy in resort areas, with high prices and, on occasion, unhelpful service. This can be avoided by seeking out those places used by locals; an understanding of Spanish is useful.

Student cards
Although an international student (ISIC) card offers student discounts, only national Mexican student cards permit free entry to museums, archaeological sites etc (see SETEJ, page 93).

Opening hours
Banks Mon-Fri 0900-1330 (some stay open later), Sat 0900-1230.
Business 0900/1000-1300/1400, then 1400/1500-1900 or later. Business hours vary considerably according to the climate and local custom.

Photography
There is a charge of US$3-5 for the use of video cameras at historical sites. For professional camera equipment, including a tripod, the fee is much higher.

Post
Rates are raised in line with the peso's devaluation against the dollar. International service has improved and bright red mailboxes, found in many parts of the city, are reliable for letters. Parcel counters often close earlier than other sections of the post office in Mexico. Not all these services are obtainable outside Mexico City; delivery times in/from the interior may well be longer than those from Mexico City. Poste Restante (*lista de correos* in Mexico) functions quite reliably, but you may have to ask under each of your names; mail is sent back after 10 days (for an extension write to the Jefe de la Administración of the post office holding your mail, any other post office will help you do this). Address the envelope: '*Favor de retener hasta llegada*'. In Mexico, tourists can call T01-800-446-3942 to clarify problems.

Costs
To **North America**, **Central America** and the **Caribbean**: under 20 g = 10.50 pesos; 20-50 g = 17.50 pesos; 500 g-1 kg = 108.50 pesos. To **South America** and **Europe**: under 20 g = 13 pesos; 20-50 g = 20.50 pesos; 500 g-1 kg = 275 pesos. To **Asia**, **Africa** and

Oceania: under 20 g = 14.50 pesos; 20-50 g = 24.50 pesos; 500 g-1 kg = 357.50 pesos.

Safety

Mexico is generally a safe country to visit, although precautions over personal safety should be taken, especially in Mexico City. Never carry valuables visibly or in easily picked pockets. Leave passports, tickets and important documents in a hotel safety deposit, not in your room. Cars are a prime target for theft; never leave possessions visible inside the car and park in hotel car parks after dark. Avoid travelling at night; if at all possible make journeys in daylight. Avoid lonely beaches, especially if you are a single woman; some on the west coast are gaining a reputation as drug-landing points.

The police service has an equivalent to the Green Angels (see page 79), which assists stranded motorists, the **Silver Angels**, who help victims of crime to file a report. US citizens should present this report to the nearest embassy or consulate. Otherwise, it is best to avoid the police if at all possible; they are rarely helpful and tend to make complicated situations even worse. Should you come into contact with them, try to stay as calm and polite as possible. Never offer a bribe unless you are fully conversant with the customs of the country (see Warnings, page 80).

Speaking Spanish is a great asset for avoiding rip-offs targeting gringos, especially short changing and overcharging (both rife), and for making the most of cheap *comedores* and market shopping.

Telephone → *Country code T+52.*
IDD T00; operator T020; **international operator** T090; **directory enquiries** T040.

Calls made to Mexican numbers are local, regional or international. Most destinations have a 7-digit number (except Mexico DF, Guadalajara and Monterrey which have 8 digit numbers). Most regions have a 3-digit code (except Mexico DF, Guadalajara and Monterrey which have 2-digit codes).

The format of a number, depending on the type of call, should be as follows:
local 7- or 8-digit phone number;
regional long-distance access code (01) + regional code (2- or 3-digit code) + 7- or 8-digit number;
international international direct-dialling code + country code + regional code + 7- or 8-digit number.

Most public phones take phone cards only (**Ladatel**) costing 30 or 50 pesos from shops and news kiosks everywhere. AT&T has a US Direct service available; for information in Mexico dial T412-553-7458, ext 359. From LADA phones (see below), dial **01, similar for AT&T credit cards. To use calling cards to Canada T95-800-010-1990. Commercially run *casetas*, or booths (for example **Computel**), where you pay after phoning, are up to twice as expensive as private phones, and charges vary from place to place. **Computel** has offices countrywide with long opening hours. It is better to call collect from private phones, but better still to use the LADA system. Reverse-charge (collect) calls on **LADA** can be made from any blue public phone, say you want to *llamar por cobrar*; silver phones are for local and direct long-distance calls, some take coins. Others take foreign credit cards (Visa, MasterCard, not Amex; not all phones that say they take cards accept them, others that say they don't do).

Pre-paid phone cards (eg **Ladatel**) are available, but expensive for international calls. Of other pre-paid cards, the best value are those issued by **Ekofon**, available at various airport and other outlets, and through a pre-chargeable account service, which may be opened by internet; go to www.ekofon.com.

Time

Mexico City is 6 hrs behind GMT. Daylight Saving Time runs from the first Sun in Apr to the last Sun in Oct (when it is 5 hrs behind GMT).

Sonora, Sinaloa, Nayarit and Baja California Sur are 7 hrs behind GMT; Baja California Norte (above 28th Parallel) is 8 hrs behind GMT (but 7 hrs behind GMT during Daylight Saving Time).

Tipping
Normally 10-15%; the equivalent of US$0.25 per bag for porters, the equivalent of US$0.20 for bell boys, and nothing for a taxi driver unless some kind of exceptional service.

Tourist information
Tourist offices are listed throughout the text. In Europe, information is available in several different languages by calling T00-800-1111-2266. In North America call T1-800-446-3942.

Useful websites
Mexico's web presence is phenomenal, some of the reliable, informative and useful websites that have been round for a while include:
www.mexconnect.com General information.
www.mexperience.com Well-constructed site updated daily, with current affairs, feature articles and advice on travel in Mexico. Look out for the forum where comments from fellow travellers are exchanged.
www.sectur.gob.mx Tourism Secretariat's site, with less glossy links but equally comprehensive information.
www.visitmexico.com Mexico Tourist Board site, a comprehensive multilingual site with information on the entire country.

Visas and immigration
US citizens need a passport when they travel as you will need to show it to re-enter the USA. A passport is required for citizens of Western European countries, Canada, Australia, New Zealand, Hungary, Iceland, Japan, Singapore, South Korea, Argentina, Bermuda, Chile, Costa Rica, Uruguay, Venezuela and Israel.

Once proof of nationality has been verified you receive a Mexican Tourist Card (FM-T) at the point of entry or in advance at a consulate or embassy. The tourist card is issued for up to 180 days and should be returned to immigration officials when departing the country. Citizens of other countries need to obtain a visa before travelling – check in advance.

Although technically you are only supposed to stay 180 days a year on a tourist card, one correspondent lived in Mexico for 5 years on a tourist card, making short visits to the US 3-4 times a year, with no problems. Tourist cards are not required for cities close to the US border.

Renewal of entry cards or visas can be done at any **National Institute of Migration** office. In Mexico City the office is at 862 Ejército Nacional, Col Polanco, Mexico City DF, (Mon-Fri 0900-1300). You can find details of offices throughout the country at www.inm.gob.mx, which has an English-language page. Only 60 days are given, and you can expect to wait up to 10 days for a replacement tourist card. To renew a tourist card by leaving the country, you must stay outside Mexico for at least 72 hrs. Take TCs or a credit card as proof of finance.

At the border crossings with Belize and Guatemala, you may be refused entry into Mexico if you have less than US$200 (or US$350 for each month of intended stay, up to a maximum of 180 days). Likewise, if you are carrying more than US$10,000 in cash or TCs, you must declare it.

If a person **under 18** is travelling alone or with one parent, both parents' consent is required, certified by a notary or authorized by a consulate. A divorced parent must be able to show custody of a child. (These requirements are not always checked by immigration authorities and do not apply to all nationalities.) Exact details are available from any Mexican consulate (see page 86).

Weights and measures
The metric system is used.

Mexico City

→ *Colour map 3, B4. Phone code: 55. Altitude: 2240 m.*

Although very little remains of the ancient Aztec capital, the island city of Tenochtitlán that ruled the Central Highlands for a couple of hundred years, the city that has replaced it is equally impressive. Founded by the Spaniards in 1521, Mexico City is colourful, bawdy, vibrant, gaudy, cultured, noisy, sometimes dangerous, always fascinating and these days downright fashionable – a celebration of chaotic humanity, good and bad.

One of the largest cities in the world, Ciudad de México, Distrito Federal or DF as it is often called, needs some time to do it justice, especially the Centro Histórico. Monumental architecture, magnificent church interiors, museums and vibrant pulsating murals full of the optimism of the post-Revolution period, invite you to drift around savouring the delights (and pollution) of this vast metropolis. There is music, dance and theatre in parks and plazas round every corner, while beyond the city centre you can explore San Angel, Coyoacán, Xochimilco and the Villa de Guadalupe. ▶▶ *For listings, see pages 121-151.*

Ins and outs

Getting there
The airport is 13 km east of the city centre. Fixed-price taxis (US$9-11) to the centre, tickets in the departure area of the airport and at the taxi ranks. For details of international scheduled flights, see Planning your trip, page 74, and for airport information, see page 141. Domestic flights go to all major towns in Mexico. There are four long-distance bus terminals: North, South, East and West, divided, more or less, according to the regions they serve. ▶▶ *See Transport, page 141.*

Getting around
If visiting for the first time, get yourself a hotel close to the Centro Histórico or Zócalo. In the heart of everything, you can walk to many of the major sights or just sit and watch the world go by. The metro is straightforward, cheap and the most convenient form of public transport, see page 145. It is also less polluted than the alternatives, such as buses and taxis, which are frequently stuck in the congested traffic. The Centro Histórico is best managed on foot and most other sights are within easy walking distance of a metro station.

Best time to visit
Spring is the hottest time of year but because of the high altitude, the climate is usually mild save for a few days in mid-winter, when it can get quite cold. Even in summer the temperature at night is rarely above 13°C and in winter there can be frosts. The normal annual rainfall is 660 mm and most of it falls between May and October, usually in the late afternoon.

Orientation
You will find, as you explore the city, that you use two thoroughfares more than any others. The most famous is **Paseo de la Reforma**, with a tree-shaded, wide centre section and two side lanes. From the west it skirts the north edge of the Bosque de Chapultepec and then runs diagonally northeast past the Centro Histórico and on towards the Basílica de Guadalupe, still fairly wide but without side lanes. The other

24 hours in Mexico City

If you only have one day to explore Mexico City you'll struggle to do the place justice, you'll be exhausted by the altitude and dazed by the number of people. Your best bet is to jump on the **Turibus City Tour**, US$13, T55-5598 6309, www.turibus. com.mx, which provides a hop-on, hop-off service travelling a set route taking in the city's major museum and highlights.

However you travel, spend some time around the **Zócalo**, visiting the cathedral on the north side and the Palacio Nacional on the east. A short walk to the north leads to the ruins of the **Aztec Templo Mayor**; within a very short space you have an insight into the driving forces of Mexico; religion, cultural heritage and government.

Heading west from the Zócalo stop by at the **Café Tacuba** (Calle Tacuba) or **La Opera** (5 de Mayo) for a bite to eat, before continuing west to the leafy plaza of **Alameda Central**. If you've a head for heights take the lift to the 44th floor of the **Torre Latinoamericana** for a great view of the city, smog permitting.

Jump on the metro and head down to Chapultepec and the **Museo Nacional de Antropología**. This cavernous museum is a one-stop shop of Mexican culture and a useful foundation for trips you might do while exploring the country. Take your time before heading into **Chapultepec Park**, a mind-blowing experience at weekends when the entire population of the city seems to be seeking relaxation in the green lungs of the city.

In the evening head down to the **Zona Rosa** and grab a bite to eat in **La Bodeguita del Medio**, or wander back to the Zócalo and hang out at **Salón Corona**.

thoroughfare is **Avenida Insurgentes**, a diagonal north-south artery about 35 km long. Reforma and Insurgentes bisect at a *glorieta* (roundabout) with a statue of Cuauhtémoc, the last of the Aztec emperors.

Other important thoroughfares are the **Eje Central (Lázaro Cárdenas)**, which runs south to north from the Circuito Interior via Bellas Artes and the Torre Latinoamericana, through Tlatelolco, past the Terminal del Norte (North Bus Terminal); the **Calzada de Tlalpan**, which runs north-south from near the centre, past the Terminal del Sur (South Bus Terminal) and out of the city towards Cuernavaca; the **Circuito Interior**, which encircles the city about 5 km from the centre; the **Periférico** which does the same thing further out; and the **Viaducto Miguel Alemán** crossing from the east, near the airport, and joining the Periférico in the west.

Tourist information

Dotted around town are sporadically manned **tourist information booths**, operated by the Mexico City Government, which have handy maps and can provide information. **Tourist assistance** ① *T55-5250 0123*, provides information by phone. They have a **main office** ① *Nuevo León 56, 9th floor, T55-5553 1260, www.mexicocity.gob.mx*, very comprehensive website. The **Secretaría de Turismo** ① *Masaryk 172, 5th floor, between Hegel and Emerson*, is in the Colonia Polanco (bus No 32). Most museums and galleries are closed on Mondays.

Refer complaints to the tourist information centres or Tourist Police, in blue uniforms. For problems such as theft, fraud, abuse of power by officials, call **Protectur** ① *T55-5516 0490*.

Maps

The best maps of the city are from *Guía Roji* (an excellent A to Z, US$14). A very good pocket map is available free from tourist information booths – there's one on the northwest corner of the Zócalo. Metro stations have useful large-scale wall maps of the immediate area.

Specialized maps for the whole of Mexico can be bought from the **Instituto Nacional de Estadística Geografía e Informática (INEGI)** ① *Balderas 71, T55-5512 1873, www.inegi.gob.mx, Metro Juárez; and from other branches at the airport and Patriotismo 711, Metro Mixcoac.*

Students

The Mexican Students' Union, **SETEJ** ① *Hamburgo 305, Col Juárez, Metro Sevilla, T55-5211 0743, www.setej.org, Mon-Fri 0900-1800, Sat 0900-1400*, issues student cards and deals with ISIS insurance. Most museums are free to students and teachers with ID.

Safety and pollution

As with any large city there are grounds for caution at times. Take care in the centre at quiet times and in Chapultepec. At night you are advised to phone for a taxi.

The city lies in the Valley of Mexico, a huge basin roughly 110 km long by 30 km wide. Rimming this valley is a chain of peaks of the Sierra Nevada mountains that trap the air within the basin. About one in five of Mexico's population share this enclosed area with half the country's manufacturing employment breathing in much of the nation's industrial smog (worst from December to February). Common ailments that creep up over hours or days are a burning sensation in the eyes (contact lens wearers take note) and nose, and a sore throat. Local authorities advise citizens not to smoke or take outdoor exercise. Newspapers provide information on air quality, with warnings and advice.

Background

The vast metropolis of Mexico City has a history stretching back some 15,000 years when the first indigenous groups arrived in the fertile valley, eventually settling around 4000 BC with the domestication of corn. However, it was maize cultivation by the Olmec civilization on the Pacific Coast that supported the settlement of Teotihuacán, 49 km north of Mexico City. The city grew to house some 250,000 before rapidly declining in the seventh century.

Dominant cultures failed to appear until the 14th century when the warring Aztecs founded a city where an eagle was seen devouring a snake. The city of Tenochtitlán began its growth on an island located at the modern-day Plaza Santo Domingo. The city grew, fed by produce grown on irrigated islands, *chinampas*, and fuelled by an unquenchable bloodthirst that demanded ritual sacrifice to the gods.

The city state was suffering with 200,000 inhabitants – and a population of some 1.5 million in the wider Valley of Mexico – when Moctezuma's messengers informed him of the arrival of vessels off the Yucatán. Cortés' arrival in 1519 coincided with the predicted return of Quetzalcoatl, the legendary Plumed Serpent, from the east. The 33-year-old conqueror exploited friction between Mexico's regional groups and within seven months had walked into Tenochtitlán. Moctezuma was taken hostage and murdered and within two years the Aztec empire had been effectively destroyed.

Development of Mexico and the capital in the 16th and 17th century was fuelled by silver mining in what is today the Colonial Heartland to the north and the development of agriculture. New Spain flourished through trade with Europe and the Orient,

1 Mexico City orientation

To Route 57/45 & Querétaro

To Tenayuca & Tlalnepantla

To Route 45/85, Teotihuacán, Pachuca & Tampico

Los Indios Verdes

Basílica de Guadalupe

Terminal del Norte

Av Insurgentes Norte

Carranza

GUSTAVO A MADERO

Av Cuitláhuac

Paseo Jacarandas

Calz México Tacuba

Plaza de las Tres Culturas

Av Río Consulado

Calz Legaria

CENTRO HISTÓRICO

Av Argentina

Terminal del Oriente (TAPO)

Via Tapo

Blvd Puerto Aéreo

To Route 150/190, Puebla & Veracruz

Hipódromo de las Américas

Pres Masaryk

POLANCO

Paseo de la Reforma

Zócalo Alameda

Calz I Zaragoza

To Route 134, Toluca & Miguel Hidalgo

Paseo de la Reforma

ZONA ROSA

Chapultepec

Av Río de la Loza

Bosque de Chapultepec

Av Constituyentes

Poliforum Cultural Siqueiros

Av Cuauhtémoc

Eje Central Lázaro Cárdenas

Calz de Tlalpan

Viaducto

Eje 2 Sur

CARRANZA

Terminal del Poniente

Anillo Periférico

Av Revolución

Plaza México Bullring

Av Insurgentes Sur

Eje 2 Pte

Av Patriotismo

Eje 4 Sur

IZTACALCO

Calz de la Viga

Circuito Interior

Eje 5 Sur

To Route 15, Toluca & Guadalajara

Teatro de los Insurgentes

BENITO JUÁREZ

Av Plutarco Elías Calles

Eje 1 Ote

IZTAPALAPA

Calz Ermita Iztapalapa

San Angel

Frida Kahlo Museum

Av Río Churubusco

Museo de las Intervenciones

CHURUBUSCO

Av MA de Quevedo

Terminal del Sur

COYOACAN

Av San Jerónimo

Ciudad Universitaria

Anahuacalli/ Diego Rivera Museum

To Desierto de los Leones

Olympic Stadium

Calz de Tlalpan

Anillo Periférico Sur

Estadio Azteca

To Route 95 & Cuernavaca

To Xochimilco

N

1 km
1 mile

while Spain suffered a steady decline. By Independence in 1821 the city's population was around 160,000.

Mexico City boomed under the industrialization of the 20th century, and the promise of employment through the 1930s depression pushed the population to over 1.5 million by the 1940s. Sheer numbers created pressure on services and shanty towns sprung up around the city. The momentum was set and the die cast of a city infrastructure that struggles to cope with a population that now numbers some 20 million – and counting.

Sights

Starting at the Zócalo (main square) and the streets around it the following route takes you through the main highlights of Mexico City, moving westwards, to the Palacio de Bellas Artes, through the Alameda Central, down Reforma and skirting the Zona Rosa, eventually leading to Chapultepec Park, and the fashionable area of Polanco, to the north of the park.

Centro Histórico

Much of the historic centre has been refurbished in recent years and **Calle Tacuba** is especially fine. This central area forms a rough rectangle bordered by Alhóndiga/Santísma to the east of the Zócalo, Guerrero to the west of the Alameda, República de Honduras (by Plaza Garibaldi) to the north, and Arcos de Belén/Izazaga to the south. A good way of familiarizing yourself quickly with the Centro Histórico is to take a ride on a *bicitaxi* (form of rickshaw) (see page 148) from the Zócalo, US$2 for 30 minutes. The tourist information booth on the northwest corner of the Zócalo provides free city maps.

Zócalo
This great main square, or Plaza Mayor, is centre of the oldest part of the city and always alive with people and often vivid with official ceremonies and celebrations, or with political demonstrations and marches. The huge flag in the centre of the square is raised at 0600 (0500 in winter), and taken down, with great pomp and ceremony, at 1800 (1700 in winter) on most days. On the north side, on the site of the Great Teocalli (temple of the Aztecs), is the cathedral.

Cathedral
① *Open daily 0800-2000, free.*
This is the largest and oldest cathedral in Latin America. First built in 1525, rebuilding began in 1573; it was consecrated in 1667 but wasn't finished until 1813. It is singularly harmonious considering the many architects employed and time taken to build it. There is an underground crypt reached by stairs in the west wing of the main part of the building (closed for restoration since 1993). You might not be able to go down, but it's possible to go up to the bell-towers which provide spectacular views of the Zócalo. Ask inside – trips leave when there are enough people. Next to the cathedral is the **Sagrario Metropolitano**, 1769, with a fine churrigueresque façade. Unlike the cathedral, it was built on the remains of an Aztec pyramid and is more stable than the former.

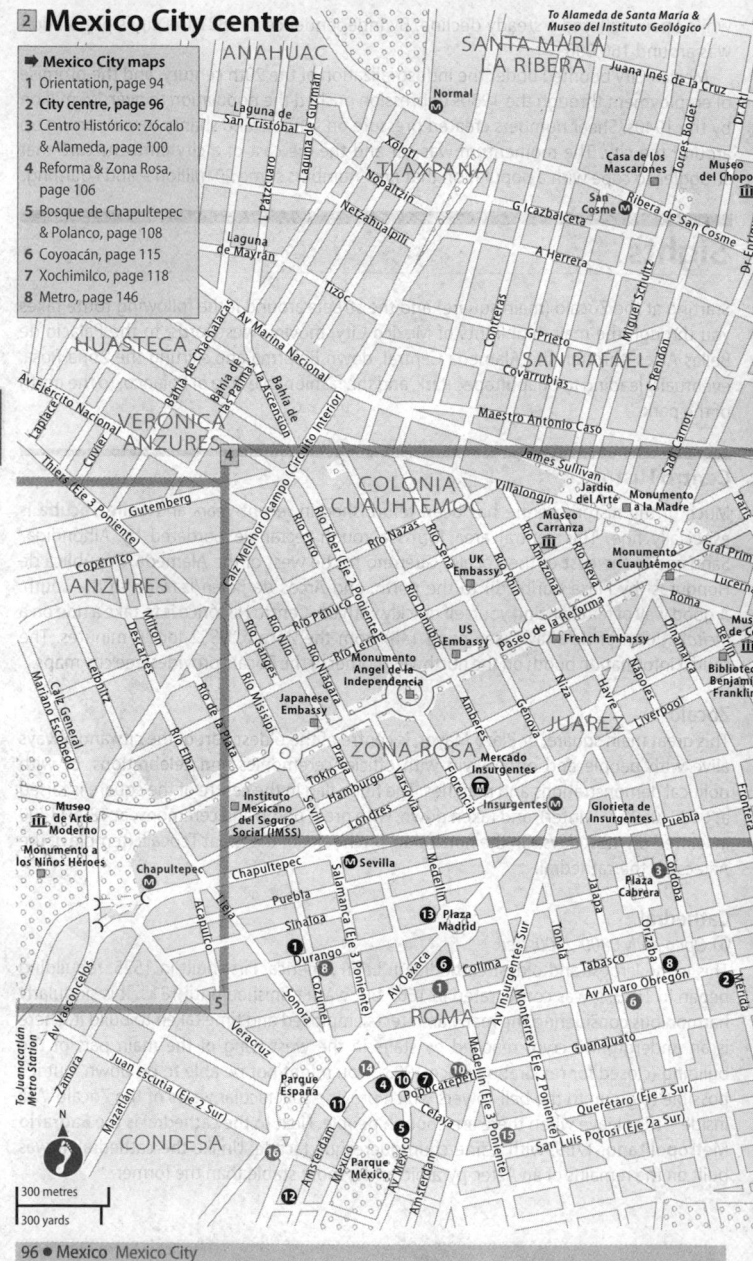

2 Mexico City centre

ANAHUAC

SANTA MARIA LA RIBERA

To Alameda de Santa María & Museo del Instituto Geológico

Juana Inés de la Cruz

Laguna de San Cristóbal

Normal

TLAXPANA

Xólotl

Nopaltzin

Netzahualpilli

Casa de los Mascarones

Museo del Chopo

San Cosme

Ribera de San Cosme

G Icazbalceta

A Herrera

Laguna de Mayrán

Tizoc

Conteras

G Prieto

SAN RAFAEL

Covarrubias

Maestro Antonio Caso

HUASTECA

Av Marina Nacional

Miguel Schultz

S. Rendón

VERÓNICA ANZURES

Av Ejército Nacional

Bahía de Chachalaca

Bahía de la Palma

Bahía de la Ascensión

James Sullivan

Villalongin

Jardín del Arte

Monumento a la Madre

Laplace (Eje 3 Poniente)

Thiers (Eje 3 Poniente)

Gutemberg

COLONIA CUAUHTÉMOC

Museo Carranza

Monumento a Cuauhtémoc

Gral Prim

Lucerna

Copérnico

ANZURES

Calz Melchor Ocampo (Circuito Interior)

Río Ebro

Río Tíber (Eje 2 Poniente)

Río Nazas

Río Sena

Río Amazonas

Roma

Milton

Descartes

Río Pánuco

UK Embassy

Río Rhin

Paseo de la Reforma

French Embassy

Museo de Ce...

Leibnitz

Río Nilo

Río Ganges

Río Lerma

US Embassy

Nza

Havre

Dinamarca

Biblioteca Benjamin Franklin

Calz General Mariano Escobedo

Río de la Plata

Río Misisipi

Río Elba

Monumento Angel de la Independencia

Amberes

Génova

Nápoles

Liverpool

JUÁREZ

Japanese Embassy

ZONA ROSA

Tokio

Praga

Varsovia

Florencia

Mercado Insurgentes

Insurgentes

Glorieta de Insurgentes

Puebla

Museo de Arte Moderno

Instituto Mexicano del Seguro Social (IMSS)

Sevilla

Hamburgo

Londres

Frontera

Monumento a los Niños Héroes

Chapultepec

Chapultepec

Puebla

Sinaloa

Sevilla

Medellín

Sevilla

Plaza Cabrera

Av Vasconcelos

Acapulco

Llaa

Durango

Salamanca (Eje 3 Poniente)

Plaza Madrid

Colima

Tabasco

Av Álvaro Obregón

Mérida

To Juanacatlán Metro Station

Zamora

Veracruz

Juan Escutia (Eje 2 Sur)

Mazatlán

Sonora

Cozumel

Av Oaxaca

ROMA

Av Insurgentes Sur

Monterrey (Eje 2 Poniente)

Guanajuato

Querétaro (Eje 2 Sur)

Orizaba

Jalapa

Córdoba

CONDESA

Parque España

Amsterdam

Parque México

Popocatépetl

Celaya

Medellín (Eje 3 Poniente)

San Luis Potosí (Eje 2a Sur)

300 metres

300 yards

Sleeping

Benidorm 2
Casa de la Condesa 3
Casa de los Amigos 4
Carlton 5
Colonia Roma 6
El Paraíso 7
Hostel Home 1
La Casona 8
Palace 9
Roosevelt 10
Stanza 11
Texas 12

Eating

Bisquet Obregón 2
El Tigre 3
Flor de Lis 4
Hip Kitchen 5
Ixchel 6
La Bodega 7
La Bodeguita del Medio 1
Lamm 8
La Parilla Argentina 9
Orígenes Orgánicos 10
Rojo Bistrot 11
Tacos Hola 12
Tierra de Vinos 13

Bars & clubs

El Mitote 14
Mamá Rumba 15
Pata Negra 16

Templo Mayor

① Seminario 4 y Guatemala, entrance in the northeast corner of the Zócalo, T55-5542 4784, www.templomayor.inah.gob.mx, Tue-Sun 0900-1700, last tickets 1630, museum and temple US$4; guided tours in Spanish, audio guides in English and other languages; there is a café, bookshop and left-luggage office.

Directly east of the cathedral are the Aztec ruins of the Templo Mayor, which were discovered in 1978 when public works were being carried out. The Aztecs built a new temple every 52 years, and seven have been identified here, one on top of the other. Behind the temple, the **Museo Arqueológico del Sitio** houses sculptures found in the main pyramid of Tenochtitlán and others, including a huge, circular monolith representing the dismembered body of Coyolxauhqui, who was killed by her brother Huitzilopochtli, the Aztec tutelary god.

Palacio Nacional

① Tue-Sun 1000-1700, free, photo ID requested.

The national palace takes up all the eastern side of the Zócalo. Built on the site of the Palace of Moctezuma and rebuilt in 1692 in colonial baroque, it has a façade of the red volcanic stone called *tezontle*; the top floor was added by President Calles in the 1920s. Today it houses various government departments. Over the central door hangs the Liberty Bell, rung every year at 2300 on 15 September by the president, who commemorates independence from Spain and gives **El Grito**: *'¡Viva México!'*

The staircase leading to the first floor of the inner courtyard and two of the walls of the first floor are decorated with superb frescoes by Diego Rivera. The right-hand panel on the staircase (1929) depicts pre-Hispanic Mexico; the large central panel (275 sq m, started 1929, finished 1935) shows the history of Mexico from 1521 to 1930 and the panel on the left is known as *El mundo de hoy y de mañana* (The World Today and Tomorrow, 1934). The first fresco (4.92 m x 9.71 m) on the first floor is known variously as *La gran Tenochtitlán* and *El mercado de tlatelolco* (1945), and shows the market of Tlatelolco against a background of the ancient city of Tenochtitlán. There follow representations of various indigenous cultures – Purépecha, Mixteca-Zapoteca, Totonaca and Huasteca (the last showing the cultivation and worship of maize) – culminating in the final fresco, which shows in narrative form the arrival of Hernán Cortés in Veracruz. These murals were done between 1942 and 1951. There are knowledgeable guides who speak English. They also sell postcards of the murals, but much better reproductions of the same works are available in most museums in the city.

On the first and second floors of the Palacio Nacional, on the left as one enters the great courtyard, an area formerly occupied by government offices has been transformed into elegant galleries open to the public and housing temporary exhibitions. The **Museo Nacional de Culturas** *① Moneda 13, Tue-Sun 0930-1745, free, on the same block as the Palacio Nacional to the north*, holds exhibitions from countries worldwide.

Around the Zócalo

The **Suprema Corte de Justicia de la Nación** *① directly south of the Palacio Nacional on the southeast corner of the Zócalo, Mon-Fri 0900-1700, free, ID required*, has frescoes by Orozco (*National Riches* and *Proletarian Struggle*). The ornate building in the southwest corner of the Zócalo, the **Antiguo Ayuntamiento** (old city hall), is now used for ceremonial purposes and is where visiting dignitaries are granted the Keys to the City.

On the west side of the Zócalo are the **Portales de los Mercaderes** (arcades of the merchants), which have been very busy since they were built in 1524. North of them, opposite the cathedral, is the **Monte de Piedad** (national pawnshop), established in the 18th century and housed in a 16th-century building. Prices are government controlled and bargains can often be found. Auctions are held each Friday at 1000 (first, second and third Friday for jewellery and watches, fourth for everything else). US dollars are accepted.

North of the Zócalo

On Calle Justo Sierra, north of cathedral between Guatemala and San Ildefonso, is the **Mexican Geographical Society**, in whose courtyard is a bust of Humboldt and a statue of Benito Juárez, plus a display of documents and maps (ask at the door to be shown in); opposite are the **Anfiteatro Simón Bolívar**, with murals of his life in the lobby and an attractive theatre, entered through the former **Colegio de San Ildefonso** ① *Justo Sierra 16, 2 blocks north and ½ block east of the Zócalo's northeast corner, www.sanildefonso.org.mx, Tue-Sun 1000-1700, US$4, free Tue*, which was built in splendid baroque style in 1749 as a Jesuit school and later became the Escuela Nacional Preparatoria. There are important frescoes by Orozco (including *Revolutionary Trinity* and *The Trench*) and, in the Anfiteatro Bolívar, by Diego Rivera (*Creation*) and Fernando Leal, all in excellent condition. There is another Leal mural, *Lord of Chalma*, in the stairwell separating the two floors of Orozco works, as well as Jean Charlot's *Massacre in the Templo Mayor*. In a stairwell of the Colegio Chico there are experimental murals by Siqueiros. The whole interior has been magnificently restored. There are occasional important temporary exhibitions. More Orozco frescoes can be seen at the **Biblioteca Iberoamericana** ① *Cuba, between República de Brasil and Argentina*. For more information on the muralists, see pages 103 and 110.

Just along the road is the **Museo de la Caricatura** ① *Donceles 99, Tue-Sun 1000-1800, US$2*. Housed in the former Convento de Cristo, this collection includes works by contemporary cartoonists as well as the influential artist José Guadalupe Posada, famous for his skeletal images that moved well beyond Day of the Dead references.

The **Secretaría de Educación Pública** ① *Argentina 28, 3 blocks from the Zócalo, daily 0900-1800, free*, was built in 1922. For lovers of Mexican murals there are over 200 to view by a number of different painters, including some of Diego Rivera's masterpieces. Painted between 1923 and 1928, they illustrate the lives and sufferings of the common people, as well as satirizing the rich. Look out for *Día de Muertos* (Day of the Dead) on the ground floor (far left in second courtyard) and, on the first floor, *El pan nuestro* (Our Daily Bread) showing the poor at supper, *El banquete de Wall Street* (The Wall Street Banquet) and the splendidly restored *La cena del capitalista* (The Capitalist's Supper). A long passageway connecting the Secretaría with the older Antigua Aduana de Santo Domingo (see below) displays the dynamic Siqueiros mural, *Patriots and Parricides*.

Plaza Santo Domingo, two blocks north of the cathedral, is an intimate little plaza surrounded by fine colonial buildings. There is the former customs house **Antigua Aduana** ① *daily 1000-1730, US$2, Sun US$1.30*, on the east side; the **Portales de Santo Domingo**, on the west side, where public scribes and owners of small hand-operated printing presses are still just about carrying out their business; the church of **Santo Domingo**, in Mexican baroque (1737) on the north side (note the carving on the doors and façade); and the old **Edificio de la Inquisición**, where the tribunals of the Inquisition were held, at the northeast corner. By standing on tiptoe in the men's room one can see – if tall enough – through the window into the prison cells of the Inquisition, which are not yet open to the public. It became the Escuela Nacional de la Medicina and is now the **Museo de la Medicina Mexicana** ① *Brasil 33, daily 0900-1800, free*. There is a remarkable staircase in the patio.

③ Centro Histórico: Zócalo & Alameda

Sleeping

Canadá **4** B4
Catedral **7** B5
Congreso **10** B4
Cortés **11** B2
Cuba **12** B4
Detroit **1** A1
El Roble **14** C5
Fleming **16** C2
Fornos **17** D2
Frimont **18** B1
Gillow **20** B4
Gran Hotel de México **3** C4
Habana **19** B4
Hostal Amigo **15** C4

Hostal Moneda **31** B5
Hostel Catedral **8** B4
Isabel la Católica **21** C4
Juárez **23** B4
Lafayette **24** C4
La Marina **25** A4
Majestic **26** C4
Marlowe **27** C3
Meave **28** C3
Mexico City Hostel **2** B4
Mina **29** A1
Monaco **30** A1
Oxford **34** B1
Ramada **22** B1
República **37** B4

Río de Janeiro **38** A4
Rioja **39** B4
Royalty **40** B1
San Antonio **41** B4
San Francisco **42** C2
Sheraton Centro
   Histórico **43** B2
Texas **9** B1
Tuxpan **44** A4
Washington **46** B4
Zamora **46** B4

Eating

Al Andalus **14** D6
Bar la Opera **2** B3

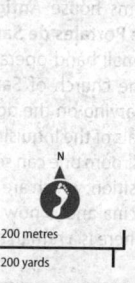

200 metres
200 yards

Café del Centro **22** *C4*
Café El Popular **3** *B4*
Café La Blanca **4** *B4*
Café La Pagodo **29** *B3*
Café Tacuba **5** *B4*
Comida Económica
  Verónica **34** *B4*
Costillitas el Sitio **20** *C4*
Danubio **25** *C3*
Dulcería de Celaya **6** *B4*
El Cardenal **18** *B4*
Fonda Santa Rita **26** *C3*
Gili's Pollo **30** *B4*
Gran Café del Centro **28** *B3*
Hong Kong **27** *C3*

Hostería Santo
  Domingo **31** *A4*
La Casa de las Sirenas **7** *B5*
La Habana **9** *C1*
Los Girasoles **8** *B3*
Los Vegetarianos **23** *B3*
Maple **35** *C5*
Mariscos **24** *C3*
Mercaderes **10** *B4*
Panadería La
  Vasconia **32** *B4*
Pastelería Ideal **21** *C1*
Pastelería Madrid **33** *C4*
Rex **19** *C4*
Salon Sol **1** *B2*

Sanborn's Casa de los
  Azulejos **11** *B3*
Super Soya **12** *C4*
Sushi Roll **13** *B3*
Trevi **15** *B2*

Bars & clubs 🎵
La Perla **16** *A4*
Pervert Lounge **37** *C4*
Salón Corona **17** *C4*
Zinco Jazz Club **36** *B4*

➡ **Mexico City maps**
1 Orientation, page 94
2 City centre, page 96
3 **Centro Histórico: Zócalo & Alameda, page 100**
4 Reforma & Zona Rosa, page 106
5 Bosque de Chapultepec & Polanco, page 108
6 Coyoacán, page 115
7 Xochimilco, page 118
8 Metro, page 146

Two blocks east of Santo Domingo are the church and convent of **San Pedro y San Pablo** (1603), both massive structures now turned over to secular use. A block north is the Mercado Rodríguez, a public market with striking mural decorations.

The **Church of Loreto**, built 1816 and now tilting badly but being restored, is on a square of the same name, surrounded by colonial buildings. Its façade is a remarkable example of 'primitive' or 'radical' neoclassicism. A little further south, on Moneda, **La Santísima Trinidad** (1677, remodelled 1755) should be seen for its fine towers and the rich carvings on its façade. **Museo José Luis Cuevas** ① *Academia 13, Tue-Sun 1000-1700, US$1.50*, is a large colonial building, housing a permanent collection of paintings, drawings and sculptures (one is two storeys high) by the controversial, contemporary Cuevas.

La Merced

The **Mercado Merced** (Metro Merced), said to be the largest market in all the Americas, dates back over 400 years. Its activities spread over several blocks and it is well worth a visit. In the northern quarter of this market are the ruins of La Merced monastery. The fine 18th-century patio is almost all that survives; the courtyard, on Avenida Uruguay, between Calle Talavera and Calle Jesús María, opposite No 171, is nearly restored.

Heading back towards the centre, three blocks south of the Zócalo the oldest hospital in continental America, **Jesús Nazareno**, is at 20 de Noviembre 82. It was founded in 1526 by Cortés and was remodelled in 1928, save for the patio and staircase. Since 1974 Cortés' bones have been kept in the adjoining church, on the corner of Pino Suárez and República de El Salvador, diagonally opposite the Museo de la Ciudad.

Museo de la Ciudad ① *Pino Suárez 30 and República de El Salvador, Tue-Wed 1000-1800, US$1.50, bring photo ID*, shows the geology of the city with life-size figures in period costumes depicting the history of different peoples before Cortés. The permanent exhibition is sometimes inaccessible during temporary shows. In the attic above the museum is the studio of Joaquín Clausell, with walls covered with Impressionist miniatures. Two blocks south of this museum at Mesones 139 is the **Anglican (Episcopal) Cathedral**, called the Catedral de San José de Gracia. Built in 1642 as a Roman Catholic church, it was given by the Benito Juárez government to the Episcopal Mission in Mexico. Juárez himself often attended services here.

Zócalo to La Alameda

Head back up to the Zócalo. On Avenida Madero, which leads from the Zócalo west to the Alameda, is the late 16th-century **La Profesa** church with a fine high altar and a leaning tower. The 18th-century **Palacio de Iturbide** ① *Av Madero 17, Tue-Sun 1000-1700, free*, once the home of Emperor Agustín (1821-1823), has been restored and has a clear plastic roof. Wander around; it is now the head office of a bank.

Also on Avenida Madero, near the Alameda, is the 16th-century **Casa de los Azulejos** (House of Tiles). It is brilliantly faced with blue and white 18th-century Puebla tiles. Occupied by the Zapatista army during the Revolution, it is now home to **Sanborn's** restaurant. The staircase walls are covered with an Orozco fresco *Omniscience* (1925). Opposite is the **Church of San Francisco**, founded in 1525 by the 'Apostles of Mexico', the first 12 Franciscans to reach the country. It was by far the most important church in colonial days, attended by the Viceroys themselves. Cortés' body rested here for some time, as did the body of 'Emperor' Iturbide.

The **Museo Nacional de Arte** ① *Tacuba 8, Tue-Sun 1030-1730, US$2.50, www.munal.com.mx*, is one block north opposite the Palacio de Minería, near the main

Los Tres Grandes

The story of muralism in Mexico has largely been that of 'Los Tres Grandes', Diego Rivera, José Clemente Orozco and David Alfaro Siqueiros, although there were many other artists involved from the start. In 1914 Orozco and Siqueiros were to be found in the Carranza stronghold of Orizaba fomenting social and artistic revolution through the mouthpiece of the pamphlet *La Vanguardia*. Seven years later, out of the turmoil and divisiveness of the Revolution emerged a need for a visual expression of *mexicanidad* (Mexican identity) and unity, and in 1921 Orozco and Siqueiros answered the call of the Minister of Education, José Vasconcelos, to provide a visual analogue to a rapidly changing Mexico. Rivera was brought onto the team that in buildings like the National Preparatory School and the Ministry of Education, attempted to produce a distinctly Mexican form of modernism, on a monumental scale, accessible to the people. These were ideas forged in Orizaba and later clarified in Europe (where Rivera and Siqueiros saw Italian frescoes) but which derived their popular form from paintings on the walls of *pulquerías* and in the satirical broadsheet engravings of José Guadalupe Posada. Themes were to include pre-Columbian society, modern agriculture and medicine and a didactic Mexican history pointing to a mechanized future for the benefit of all. Siqueiros in particular was keen to transform the working practice of artists who would henceforth work as members of cooperatives.

The 'movement' fell apart almost from its inception. There were riots objecting to the communist content of murals and the beginnings of a long ideological and artistic disagreement between Siqueiros and Rivera, which would culminate on 28 August 1935 at the Palacio de Bellas Artes with Rivera, brandishing a pistol, storming into a Siqueiros lecture and demanding a debate on what the Mexican Mural Renaissance had all been about! The debate ensued over several days before they agreed to disagree.

Despite the failings of the 'movement' many outstanding murals were painted over a long period. With Siqueiros frequently off the scene, in jail or in exile, Los Tres Grandes became the big two; Rivera carving up much of Mexico City as his territory and Orozco taking on Guadalajara. However, Siqueiros outlasted both of them and carried the torch of Muralism and Revolution into the early 1970s. See also Mural sites, page 110.

post office. It was built in 1904 and designed by the Italian architect Silvio Contri as the Palacio de Comunicaciones. The building has magnificent staircases made by the Florentine firm Pignone. It houses a large collection of Mexican paintings, drawings, sculptures and ceramics dating from the 16th century to 1950. It has the largest number of paintings (more than 100) by José María Velasco in Mexico City, as well as works by Miguel Cabrera, Gerardo Murillo, Rivera, Orozco, Siqueiros, Tamayo and Anguiano. The museum building has been completely restored and modernized.

On the corner of Tacuba and the Eje Central (Lázaro Cárdenas) is the magnificent **Correo Central** (central post office) ① *Mon-Fri 0900-1800, Sat 1000-1400, free*, commissioned in 1902 and completed in 1907.

Palacio de Bellas Artes

① *Tue-Sun 1000-1800, US$3, performances by the Ballet Folklórico de México, Sun 0930 and 2030, Wed 2030; tickets US$37-65, T55-5529 9320, www.balletamalia.com, for details.*

A large, showy building, interesting for art deco lovers (see the fabulous stained-glass skylight in the roof), it houses a museum, theatre, a *cafetería* at mezzanine level (serving average continental food at moderate prices) and an excellent bookshop on the arts. The museum has old and contemporary paintings, prints, sculptures and handicrafts. There are spirited Riveras in the room of oils and watercolours. The fresco by Rivera is a copy of the one rubbed out in disapproval at Radio City, New York. Other frescoes are by Orozco, Tamayo and Siqueiros. There are also prestigious temporary fine art exhibitions (no extra charge). On the top floor is a museum of architecture, which holds temporary exhibitions and shows the building's history. The most remarkable thing about the theatre is its glass curtain designed by Tiffany. It is solemnly raised and lowered before each performance of the Ballet Folklórico de México. Operas are also performed here and there are frequent orchestral concerts. The Palacio was refurbished, inside and out, in 1994 to celebrate its diamond jubilee; the garden in front of the marble apron has been laid out as originally designed. But the Palacio is listing badly and has sunk 4 m since it was built.

La Alameda

Across the road is the **Torre Latinoamericana** ① *daily 0930-2230, US$4.50 to go up,* which has a viewing platform with telescopes on the 44th floor, remodelled in 2006 to celebrate the tower's 50th anniversary. This great glass tower dominates the gardens of the **Alameda Central**, once the Aztec market and later the place of execution for the Spanish Inquisition. Beneath the broken shade of eucalyptus, cypress and ragged palms, wide paths link fountains and heroic statues. The Alameda became a popular area for all social classes to stroll casually in the 19th century. It is now much more a common thoroughfare, with many temporary stalls at certain festive times of year. The park is illuminated at night.

Along the south side of the Alameda runs Avenida Juárez, a broad street with a mixture of old and new buildings. Opposite the Palacio de Bellas Artes is a building known as **La Nacional**, which was Mexico City's first skyscraper in the 1930s. Look carefully at its perpendicularity, a result of the 1985 earthquake.

Also on the south side of the Alameda is the **Hemiciclo a Juárez** statue (now on the 20 peso note), designed by Guillermo de Heredia in white marble and inaugurated in 1910 to mark the centenary of Independence. Opposite, the colonial church of Corpus Christi is used to display and sell folk arts and crafts. Further west is the **Plaza de las Esculturas** (1998), with 19th-century sculptures. A stroll down Calle Dolores, a busy and fascinating street, leads to the market of San Juan. Three blocks west, on Plaza Ciudadela, is the lively **Mercado de la Ciudadela**, which sells crafts from all over Mexico. The new **Museo de Arte Popular** ① *Revillagigedo 11, 1 block south of the Alameda, Tue-Sun 1000-1700, free,* exhibits *artesanías* from all the country and is great introduction to Mexican craft traditions.

Diego Rivera's huge (15 m by 4.8 m) and fascinating mural, the *Sueño de una Tarde Dominical en la Alameda Central*, was removed from the earthquake-damaged **Hotel del Prado** on Avenida Juárez in 1985 and now occupies its own purpose-built museum, the **Museo Mural Diego Rivera** ① *north side of the Jardín de la Solidaridad at the west end of the Alameda Central, Tue-Sun 1000-1800, US$1.50.* One of Rivera's finest works, it presents a pageant of Mexican history from the Conquest up to the 1940s with vivid portraits of national and foreign figures, heroes and villains as well as his wife, Frida Kahlo (see box, page 117) and characters from everyday life. It is highly recommended.

On the northern side of the Alameda, on Avenida Hidalgo, is the Jardín Morelos, flanked by two old churches: **Santa Veracruz** (1730) to the right and **San Juan de Dios** to the left. The latter has a richly carved baroque exterior; its image of San Antonio de Padua is visited by those who are broken-hearted from love. Next door, the **Museo Franz Mayer** ① *T55-5518 2265, Tue-Sun 1000-1700, US$2*, in the former Hospital de San Juan de Dios, was built in the 17th century. Recently rebuilt and exquisitely restored, it houses a library and an important decorative arts collection of ceramics, glass, silver, timepieces, furniture and textiles, as well as Mexican and European paintings from the 16th to the 20th centuries. Its cloister is an oasis of peace in the heart of the city.

North of La Alameda

Plaza Garibaldi
About four blocks north of the post office off Eje Central Lázaro Cárdenas is Plaza Garibaldi, an absolute must one evening, ideally on a Friday or Saturday (it tends to be quiet on Mondays) when up to 200 *mariachis* in their traditional costume of huge sombrero, tight silver-embroidered trousers, pistol and *sarape*, will play your favourite Mexican serenade for between US$5 (for a bad one) and US$10 (for a good one). If you arrive by taxi you will be besieged. The whole square throbs with life and the packed bars are cheerful. On one side of the plaza is a gigantic and very entertaining eating hall where different stalls sell different courses. The **Lagunilla** market is held about four blocks northeast of the plaza, a hive of activity particularly on Sundays.

Plaza de las Tres Culturas
Further north still, Lázaro Cárdenas leads to Santa María la Redonda, at the end of which is **Plaza Santiago de Tlatelolco** (metro line 3 to Tlatelolco), the city's oldest plaza, after the Zócalo. The main market of the Aztecs was here, and on it, in 1524, the Franciscans built a huge church and convent. It is now known as the Plaza de las Tres Culturas since it shows elements of Aztec, colonial and modern architecture. The Aztec ruins have been restored and the magnificent Franciscan church of Santiago Tlatelolco, completed in 1609, is now the focus of the massive, multi-storey Nonoalco-Tlatelolco housing scheme (heavily damaged in the 1985 earthquake), a garden city within a city, with pedestrian and wheeled traffic entirely separate. In October 1968, the Plaza de las Tres Culturas was the scene of serious disturbances between the authorities and students, in which a large number of students were killed.

West of La Alameda

West of the Paseo de la Reforma is the **Monumento a la Revolución**, a great copper dome, soaring above supporting columns set on the largest triumphal arches in the world. Beneath the monument, the **Museo Nacional de la Revolución** ① *Tue-Sun 1000-1700, US$1.50*, which deals with the period 1867-1917, is very interesting and has lots of exhibits, original photographs and videos.

The **Museo de San Carlos** ① *Puente de Alvarado 50 (Metro Revolución), Wed-Mon 1000-1800, US$2, www.mnsancarlos.com*, reached by crossing Reforma near Metro Hidalgo, is in a 19th-century palace, with fine Mexican colonial painting and a first-class collection of European paintings. It was the home of Señora Calderón de la Barca who wrote *Life in Mexico* while living there.

Santa María la Ribera and San Cosme

These are two wards north of Metro San Cosme that became fashionable residential areas in the late 19th century. Many elegant, if neglected, façades can still be seen. On the corner of Ribera de San Cosme and Naranjo next to San Cosme metro note the **Casa de los Mascarones**. Built in 1766, this was the country house of the Conde del Valle de Orizaba, later the Escuela Nacional de Música. Recently restored, it now houses a university computer centre. The **Museo Universitario del Chopo** ① *Enrique González Martínez 10, between Metro San Cosme and Av Insurgentes Norte, Wed-Sun 1000-1400, 1600-1900*, holds contemporary international photography and art exhibitions in a church-like building designed by Eiffel. In the pleasant **Alameda de Santa María**, between Pino and Torres Bodet, stands an extraordinary Moorish pavilion designed by Mexicans for the Paris Exhibition in 1889. On its return to Mexico, the *kiosko* was placed in the Alameda Central before being transferred to its present site in 1910. On the west side of this square, on Torres Bodet, is the **Museo del Instituto Geológico**

4 Reforma & Zona Rosa

Sleeping 🛏
Casa González 1
María Cristina 4
NH México 5
Prim 7
Royal Zona Rosa 2
Suites Amberes 8
Suites Havre 9
Uxmal 10
Viena 11

Eating 🍴
Arles 1
Beatricita 2
Bella Luna 3
Chalet Suizo 4
Fonda del Refugio 5
La Puerta del Angel 6
Les Moustaches 7
Quebracho 8
Sushi Itto 9
Yug 10

Bars & clubs 🍸
Milán 11

① *Tue-Sun 1000-1700, free.* In addition to its collection of fossils and minerals (and magnificent early 20th-century showcases), the building itself (1904) is worth a visit for its wrought-iron staircases and unusual stained-glass windows of mining scenes by Zettler (Munich and Mexico).

Paseo de la Reforma and Zona Rosa

The wide and handsome Paseo de la Reforma continues southwest from the Alameda to the Bosque de Chapultepec. It is lined with shops, offices, hotels and some striking modern buildings: the Hotel Crowne Plaza, the Mexican Stock Exchange (*Bolsa de Valores*) and the Hotel María Cristina, as well as a red-and-black cuboid office structure on the left. Along it are monuments to Columbus, Cuauhtémoc and, at the intersection with Tiber/Florencia, a 45-m marble column supporting the golden form of a female angel representing Independence. Known as 'El Angel', the statue, which used to be on an even higher column, fell to the ground in the 1957 earthquake. This is a favourite spot for political demonstrations, as well as sporting and national celebrations. One block north of Reforma, the **Museo Carranza** ① *Lerma y Amazonas*, is a museum with items linked to the life of Venustiano Carranza, the famous revolutionary and constitutionalist, and to the Revolution itself. It is worth a visit and could be combined with a trip the Basílica de Guadalupe, see page 120, further north.

Zona Rosa

The famous Zona Rosa (pink zone) lies to the south of Reforma, contained approximately by Reforma, Sevilla, Avenida Chapultepec and Insurgentes Sur. This was formerly the setting for Mexico City's most fashionable stores, restaurants and nightclubs. It suffered considerable damage in the 1985 earthquake and subsequently lost ground to Polanco (see below). In recent times it has seen a revival and is once again a very pleasant area in which to stroll, shop (or window-shop) and dine, in the many open-air or half-covered restaurants.

Bosque de Chapultepec and Polanco

The park, with its thousands of *ahuehuete* trees (so sacred to the Aztecs), is beautiful and kept litter free. It is well policed (park closes at 1700). The best day to visit is Sunday when it is at its most colourful (and crowded). The park is divided into three sections. The first, the easternmost, was a wood inhabited by the Toltecs and Aztecs. Most of the interesting sites are in this section (see below).

The second section, west of Bulevar Manuel Avila Camacho, was added in 1964. It has a large **amusement park** ① *Wed and Fri-Sun, 1030-2000, US$1*, with a wonderful

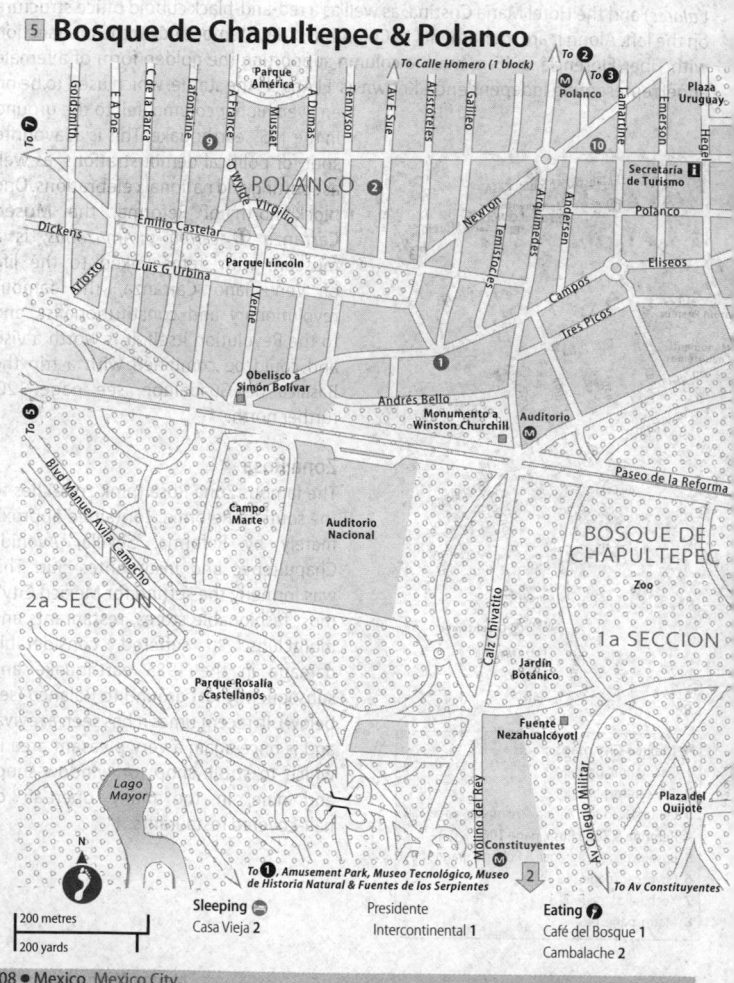

⑤ **Bosque de Chapultepec & Polanco**

Sleeping 🛏	Presidente	Eating 🍴
Casa Vieja 2	Intercontinental 1	Café del Bosque 1
		Cambalache 2

200 metres
200 yards

section for children and another for adults. The **Montaña Rusa** ⓘ *Sat and Sun only, US$1*, is one of the world's largest roller coasters. There are bridle paths and polo grounds. Diego Rivera's famous fountain, the **Fuente de Tlaloc**, is near the children's amusement park. Close by are the **Fuentes de las Serpientes** (snake fountains). Both the Lago Menor and Lago Mayor are popular for boating; on the shore of each is a restaurant.

The third section, which was added in 1974, stretches a long way beyond the **Panteón Civil de Dolores** (cemetery) and has little to interest the tourist.

The first section contains a maze of pathways, the **Plaza del Quijote** and **Monumento a los Niños Héroes**, a large lake and a smaller one (with an outdoor

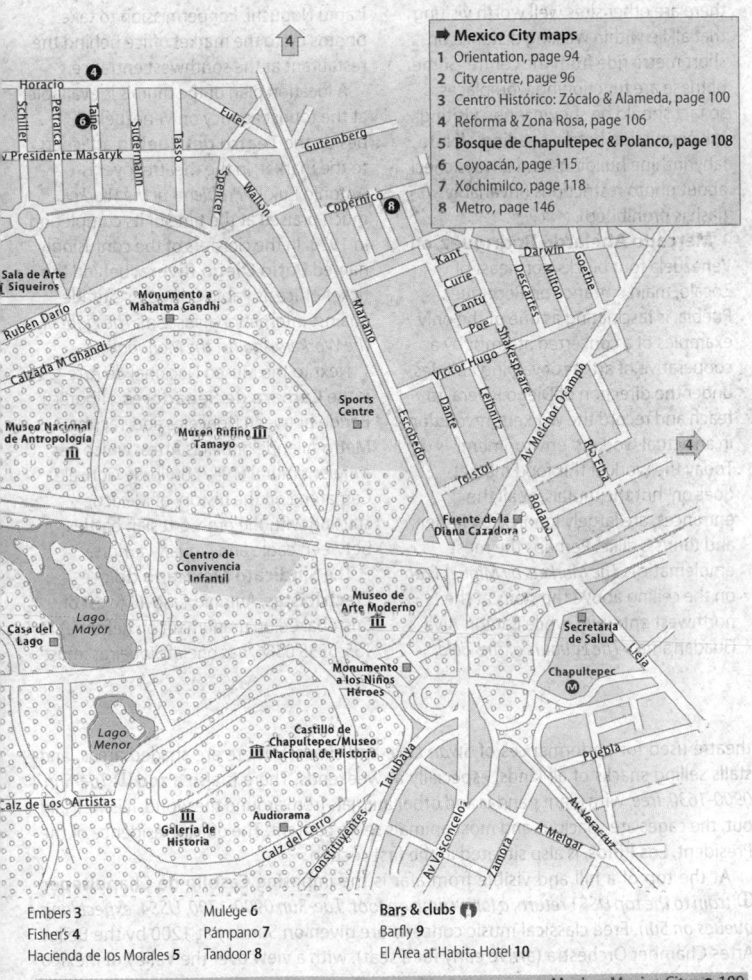

➡ **Mexico City maps**
1 Orientation, page 94
2 City centre, page 96
3 Centro Histórico: Zócalo & Alameda, page 100
4 Reforma & Zona Rosa, page 106
5 Bosque de Chapultepec & Polanco, page 108
6 Coyoacán, page 115
7 Xochimilco, page 118
8 Metro, page 146

Embers **3**
Fisher's **4**
Hacienda de los Morales **5**

Mulége **6**
Pámpano **7**
Tandoor **8**

Bars & clubs 🍸
Barfly **9**
El Area at Habita Hotel **10**

Mural sites

Apart from the main centres of mural painting already listed geographically in the text (Palacio Nacional, Suprema Corte de Justicia, Palacio de Bellas Artes, Museo Mural Diego Rivera, Escuela Nacional Preparatoria-San Ildefonso, Secretaría de Educación, Castillo de Chapultepec and below Polyforum Cultural Siqueiros), there are other sites well worth visiting that all lie within walking distance or short metro ride from the centre. Some of these are functioning workplaces, so tact should be shown when visiting: ask permission before heading off into labyrinthine buildings and always check about photo restrictions (invariably flash is prohibited).

Mercado Abelardo Rodríguez, on Venezuela four blocks northeast of Zócalo, main entrance on Rodríguez Puebla, is fascinating as one of the only examples of a concerted attempt by a cooperative of artists of varying abilities, under the direction of Diego Rivera, to teach and record the workers' revolution in an actual workers' environment. Today the work of this food market goes on, but the murals, at all the entrances, are largely ignored by traders and tourists alike. Perhaps the most emblematic is *The Markets by Miguel Tzab* on the ceiling above the stairs at the northwest entrance, while Ramón Alva Guadarrama's *The Labours of the Field*, at the southeast corner, reflects the market's agricultural base. Most elaborate are the murals of the American Greenwood sisters, Marion and Grace, showing *Industrialization of the Countryside and The Mine*, on the stairs either side of the main entrance. Opposite, upstairs, is a relief mural by Isamu Noguchi. For permission to take photos go to the market office behind the restaurant at the southwest entrance.

A location plan of the murals is available at the tourist agency on Venezuela 72, beside the **Teatro del Pueblo** attached to the market. In the theatre foyer is Antonio Pujol's *Problems of the Worker*, much praised at the time of its completion in 1936. In the cloisters of the confusingly named **Patio Diego Rivera**, behind the ticket office, is Pablo O'Higgins's tirade against international fascism, *The Fight of the Workers Against the Monopolies*.

Next to the Museo Nacional de Arte is the **Cámara de Senadores**, Hipoteca Beride between Donceles and Tacuba, Metro Allende or Bellas Artes, which has a violent mural (1957) by Jorge González Camarena on the history of Mexico, starting with the pre-Cortesian battles between eagle and jaguar warriors.

The **Sindicato Mexicano de Electricistas**, Antonio Caso 45 (west of Cristóbal Colón monument on Reforma), T55-5535 0386, has one of Siqueiros' most

theatre used for performances of *Swan Lake* and similar). There are shaded areas, and stalls selling snacks of all kinds, especially at weekends. There is also a **zoo** ① *Tue-Sun, 0900-1630, free,* with giant pandas and other animals from around the world; it is well laid out, the cages are spacious and most animals seem content. The official residence of the President, **Los Pinos**, is also situated in the first section.

At the top of a hill and visible from afar is the imposing **Castillo de Chapultepec** ① *train to the top US$1 return, a long climb on foot, Tue-Sun 0900-1700, US$4, expect long queues on Sun.* Free classical music concerts are given on Sunday at 1200 by the Bellas Artes Chamber Orchestra (arrive early for a seat), with a view over the Valley of Mexico

important murals, *Portrait of the Bourgeoisie* (1939-1940), located up the second floor stairwell to the left of the entrance. It depicts the revolutionary struggle against international fascism and is considered a seminal work for its use of cinematic montage techniques and viewing points. Before taking photos ask permission in the secretaría office on the right at the end of the corridor on the second floor.

A 15-minute walk away at Altamirano 118, Colonia San Rafael, T55-5535 2246, is the **Teatro Jorge Negrete**, in the foyer of which is a later Siqueiros mural, *Theatrical Art in the Social Life of Mexico* (1957), precursor in its expression of movement to his mural in Chapultepec Castle. Ask permission to see it in the office at No 128. No photos (nearest Metro San Cosme).

At the **Hospital de La Raza** in what was once an outer entrance hall (but is now at the centre of the building) is Rivera's *History of Medicine* (1953), and to the left of the main entrance, in a naturally lit theatre foyer (usually locked but you can see it through the large frontal windows if there is nobody about with keys), is Siqueiros' *For the Complete Safety of All Mexicans at Work* (1952-1954). Ask a security guard or at main reception for directions to the murals. Take Metro La Raza and from the station head south along the right side of Insurgentes Norte,

cross the railway, go straight ahead and then cross the freeway by the footbridge to the hospital. For permission to take photos here and at other medical centres you must ask at the **Sede IMSS**, Hidalgo 230, Metro Bellas Artes.

Another hospital with a relevant themed mural is the **Centro Médico Nacional**, Avenida Cuauhtémoc, where Siqueiros' *Apology for the Future Victory of Medicine over Cancer* (1958) has been restored following damage in the 1985 earthquake. Since 1996 it has been on display in the waiting area of the oncology building beyond the main entrance building on the right. At the entrance, as you come up the stairs from the metro station Centro Médico, is a mural by Chávez Morado commemorating the rebuilding of the hospital in which many died during the earthquake.

Before or after visiting the mural sites we recommend reading one or more of the following: *The Murals of Diego Rivera*, by Desmond Rochfort, London, 1987; *Mexican Muralists*, same author, New York, 1984. *Dreaming with his Eyes Open*, by Patrick Marnham, New York and London, 1998, is an immensely readable though not entirely scholastic biography of Diego Rivera, which deals with Orozco, Siqueiros and the other muralists as well as Rivera. See also box, page 103.

from its beautiful balconies. The castle now houses the **Museo Nacional de Historia** ① *Tue-Sun 0900-1700, US$4.* Its rooms were once used by the Emperor Maximilian and the Empress Carlota during their brief reign. There is an impressive mural by Siqueiros, *From the Dictatorship of Porfirio Díaz to the Revolution* (in Sala XIII, near the entrance), and a mural by O'Gorman on the theme of Independence, as well as several by Camarena.

Halfway down the hill is the **Galería de Historia**, which has dioramas, with audio explanations of Mexican history, and photographs of the 1910 Revolution. Below the castle are the remains of the **Arbol de Moctezuma**, known as *El Sargento*. This immense tree, which has a circumference of 14 m, was about 60 m high before it was cut down to 10 m.

Also in the first section of the Bosque de Chapultepec, and on the same side of Reforma as Chapultepec Castle, is the **Museo de Arte Moderno** ① *Tue-Sun 1000-1800, US$1.50, free with ISIC card.* There is a good bookshop, gift shop and an open-air cafeteria behind the first building. The museum has a permanent collection of modern Mexican art and regularly stages temporary national and international exhibitions. It consists of two circular buildings pleasantly set among trees with sculptures in the grounds. The temporary exhibitions are usually held in the smaller of the two buildings; entrance is through the larger one. The delightfully light architecture of the larger building is balanced by a heavy, marble staircase, with a curious acoustic effect on the central landing under a translucent dome, which must have been unplanned.

The **Museo Rufino Tamayo** ① *on the other side of Reforma, cross near the Museo de Arte Moderno, on the way to the Anthropological Museum, Tue-Sun 1000-1800, US$1.70, free to students with ISIC card, www.museotamayo.org,* has a fine collection of works by Rufino Tamayo and shows contemporary Mexican and other painters. The interior space of the museum is unusual in that it is difficult to know which floor you are on. There is a very pleasant restaurant.

Museo Nacional de Antropología

① *Tue-Sun 0900-1900, US$4.50, free on Sundays, www.mna.inah.gob.mx. The nearest metro is Auditorio or Chapultepec, or take a colectivo down Reforma marked 'Auditorio'. Written explanations in Spanish and English, audio guide in English, US$4, describes 130 of the exhibits. Guided tours in English or Spanish free with a minimum of 5 people. If you want to see everything, you need at least 2 days. Permission to photograph (no tripod or flash allowed) US$1, US$5 for video camera. On sale are English and Spanish guide books plus a few in French and German, and guides to Mexican ruins including maps. The cafeteria on site is good, recommended, but pricey. Added attractions outside include voladores spiralling downwards off high poles and musicians.*

The crowning glory of Chapultepec Park was built by architect Pedro Ramírez Vásquez to house a vast collection illustrating pre-Conquest Mexican culture. It has a 350-m façade and an immense patio shaded by a gigantic concrete mushroom measuring 4200 sq m, the world's largest concrete and steel expanse supported by a single pillar. The largest exhibit (8.5 m high, weighing 167 tonnes) is the image of Tlaloc, the rain god, removed (accompanied by protesting cloudbursts) from near the town of Texcoco to the museum. Upstairs is a display of folk costumes, which may be closed on Sundays.

Inside, the museum is very well organized; each major culture that contributed to the evolution of Mesoamerican civilization is well represented in its own room or *sala*: pre-Classic, Teotihuacán, Toltec, Aztec, Oaxaca, Gulf Coast, Maya, Northwestern and Western Mexico. Two areas are often missed by visitors: the Torres Bodet Auditorium, where visiting archaeologists, art historians, anthropologists etc give seminars, often in English and usually free; and the Temporary Exhibitions Hall, which is also worth checking out.

Polanco

① *To get to Polanco, take a colectivo marked 'Horacio' from Metro Chapultepec or Metro Polanco. To get to Lomas de Chapultepec, take a bus marked 'Km 15' or 'Cuajimalpa' from Antropología or the bus station by Metro Chapultepec. To get to Las Palmas, take a colectivo or bus marked 'Las Palmas' from Antropología or from the bus station by Metro Chapultepec.*

To get to Santa Fe, take a colectivo marked 'Centro Comercial Santa Fe' from Antropología or a bus from Metro Chapultepec.

Directly northwest of the Museo de Antropología, lies the luxury residential area known as Polanco, with many interesting art galleries and shops. It does not suffer from the tourists that crowd the Zona Rosa and other so-called chic areas. Many of the old houses have carved stone façades, tiled roofs and gardens, especially on **Calle Horacio**, a pretty street lined with trees and parks. Polanco also contains some of the most modern (and conspicuous) hotels in the city, such as the **Nikko, Presidente, Camino Real**, and **W**, which are at least worth a walk-in visit. Also here are exclusive private residences, commercial art galleries, fashion stores, expensive restaurants and various other establishments that are collectively a monument to the consumer society; one glaring example of this is the huge **Palacio de Hierro** department store and offices along **Mazaryk**. There are also a couple of fairly unremarkable modern churches and, in fact, little of cultural value, with the exception of the **Sala de Arte Siqueiros** ① *Tres Picos 29*. Traffic is frequently very congested; avoid taking a taxi if possible; Metro Polanco on Horacio is centrally situated.

Beyond the Auditorio Nacional, Reforma continues west towards the area known as **Lomas de Chapultepec** (or simply 'Las Lomas'), which gradually rises through broad tree-lined avenues to an altitude that leaves most of the pollution behind. It is mostly residential, including many embassies and ambassadorial residences.

To the north, taking a right at the Fuente de Petróleos (Petróleos bridge) up Bulevar Manuel Avila Camacho, you come to the modern office and commercial area of **Las Palmas**, while straight ahead, some 8 km further, beyond Lomas de Chapultepec and on the way out towards Toluca, lies the district of **Santa Fe**, perched on some of the highest ground and therefore in one of the least polluted areas in the city, with some extraordinary, futuristic architecture.

South of the city centre

When you have exhausted the centre of Mexico City, or perhaps when it has exhausted you, the surrounding areas have much to offer in the way of museums, colonial architecture, markets, shops, restaurants and parks. At Xochimilco you can float in a colourful *trajinera* and enjoy a picnic on the banks of the *chinampas*, or floating gardens. The enormous Ciudad Universitaria should not be missed, nor should the botanical gardens. Visit the Saturday bazaar in San Angel, try a glass of *pulque* or take in a performance at Coyoacán.

Insurgentes Sur

Heading out of the city centre along Insurgentes towards the delightful suburbs, or *colonias*, of San Angel and Coyoacán, there are several sites that should not be missed. A little to the west of where Insurgentes crosses Chapultepec, and on Avenida Chapultepec itself between Calle Praga and Calle Varsovia, are the remains of the old **aqueduct** built in 1779. South of the Viaducto and next door to the towering World Trade Center, the **Polyforum Cultural Siqueiros** ① *Insurgentes Sur 701, US$0.40, daily 1000-1900, closed for lunch*, includes a 500-seat theatre, art gallery and art museum, with huge frescoes by Siqueiros, one of the largest in the world, inside the ovoid dome.

A little further south is the **Plaza México**, the largest bullring in the world, with capacity for some 55,000 spectators. It is situated in the **Ciudad de los Deportes** ① *just off*

Insurgentes Sur, T55-5563 1659, US$1-18 in the cheaper sol (sun) half of the Plaza; seats in the sombra (shade) are more expensive, up to US$35 in the barreras. It's best to buy tickets, especially for important fights, early on Saturday morning from the *taquillas* at the plaza. The 'México' is one of the world's three most important bullfighting venues and, as virtually every great matador comes to fight in Mexico in the winter months, the chances of seeing an important event are high. The closest metro station is San Antonio or take a *colectivo* to junction of Insurgentes Sur with Eje 5.

Further south still on Avenida Insurgentes Sur 1587 at the corner of Mercaderes is a remarkable building by Alejandro Prieto: the **Teatro de Los Insurgentes**, a theatre and opera house seating 1300 people. The main frontage consists of a high curved wall covered with mosaic decoration, the work of Diego Rivera.

San Angel

① *Go by bus from Chapultepec Park or by metro Line 3 to Miguel Angel de Quevedo.*
Villa Obregón, popularly known as San Angel, is 13 km southwest of the centre, has narrow, cobblestone streets, many old homes, huge trees and the charm of an era now largely past. Most of the distinguished architecture is from the 19th century. See the triple domes of its **Iglesia del Carmen**, covered with coloured tiles, and the former Convento del Carmen, now the **Museo Colonial del Carmen** ① *daily 1000-1700, US$3, free Sun,* which houses 17th- and 18th-century furniture and paintings. In the crypt, several mummified bodies are displayed in glass-topped cases. The **Centro Cultural San Angel** ① *Revolución opposite Museo del Carmen,* stages exhibitions, concerts, lectures and cultural events. See also the beautifully furnished and preserved 18th-century **Casa del Risco** ① *Callejón de la Amargura, near the Bazar del Sábado, Tue-Sun 1000-1700, free; library Mon-Fri 0900-2000, Sat 1000-1400, photographic ID required for entry.* The house contains a collection of Mexican and European paintings from the 15th to the 20th centuries as well as a library devoted to international law and the Mexican Revolution. Also worth a visit is the **Church of San Jacinto**, once belonging to a Dominican convent (1566). The **Museo de Arte Carrillo Gil** ① *Av Revolución 1608, US$3.35,* has good changing exhibits and a permanent collection including paintings by Orozco and Siqueiros as well as several of Diego Rivera's Cubist works. There is a good bookshop and *cafetería.*

The **Museo Casa Estudio Diego Rivera** ① *Av Altavista and Calle Diego Rivera, Tue-Sun 1000-1800, US$1, free Sun,* is where Diego and his wife, Frida Kahlo lived and worked. It contains several works by Rivera, as well as belongings and memorabilia. The building was designed by Juan O'Gorman. Opposite is the **Antigua Hacienda de Goicoechea** – now the **San Angel Inn**. Many residents and tourists alike come to San Angel on a Saturday to visit the **Bazar del Sábado** ① *0900-1400,* a splendid folk art and curiosity market. Between San Angel and Coyoacán is the monument to Alvaro Obregón on the spot where the former president was assassinated in 1928 (by the junction of Avenida Insurgentes Sur and Arenal).

Coyoacán

① *From the city centre, it is easiest to take the metro to Viveros, Miguel Angel de Quevedo or General Anaya. The colectivo from Metro General Anaya to the centre of Coyoacán is marked 'Santo Domingo', get off at Abasolo or at the Jardín Centenario.*
The oldest part of Mexico City, Coyoacán is the place from which Cortés launched his attack on the Aztec city of Tenochtitlán. It is also one of the most beautiful and best-preserved parts of the city, with hundreds of fine buildings from the 16th to 19th

centuries, elegant tree-lined avenues and carefully tended parks and, in the Jardín Centenario and the Plaza Hidalgo, two very attractive squares. It's best explored on foot, which will take most of a day, although it's often combined with a visit to San Angel.

Coyoacán is culturally one of the liveliest parts of Mexico City and with its attractive cafés and good shops it is much frequented by the inhabitants of the capital, particularly at weekends. From San Angel, you can get to Coyoacán via a delightful walk through Chimalistac, across Avenida Universidad and down Avenida Francisco Sosa; or you can take a bus or *pesero* marked 'Taxqueña' as far as Calle Caballocalco.

If coming from Metro Viveros (a large park in which trees are grown for other city parks) or Miguel Angel de Quevedo it is worth making a slight detour in order to walk the length of **Francisco Sosa**, said to be the first urban street laid in Spanish America. At the beginning of this elegant avenue is the 18th-century church of **San Antonio Panzacola** by the side of Río Churubusco. Nearby, on Universidad, is the remarkable, beautiful (and modern) chapel of **Nuestra Señora de la Soledad**, built in the grounds of the 19th-century ex-hacienda El Altillo. A little way down is the **Museo Nacional de la Acuarela** ① *Salvador Novo, Tue-Sun 1000-1800, free*, the National Watercolour Museum, founded in 1967 and something of a pioneer. The terracotta-fronted residence at **Francisco Sosa 383** ① *Tue-Sun, free; courtyard and garden Mon-Fri 0900-1600*, is said to

6 Coyoacán

➡ **Mexico City maps**
1 Orientation, page 94
2 City centre, page 96
3 Centro Histórico: Zócalo & Alameda, page 100
4 Reforma & Zona Rosa, page 106
5 Bosque de Chapultepec & Polanco, page 108
6 Coyoacán, page 115
7 Xochimilco, page 118
8 Metro, page 146

Sleeping
Suites Coyoacán 1

Eating
Churros Rellenos Jordan 1
El Jarocho 5
El Jardín del Pulpo 2

El Caracol de Oro 3
Fabio's 7
El Globo 8
El Morral 9
Hacienda de Cortés 10
La Guadalupana 4
Los Danzantes 11

Mastropiero Café 12
Mesón Antiguo Santa Catarina 6
Moheli 13

Bars & clubs
El Hijo del Cuervo 14

have been built by Alvarado. Many fine houses follow, mostly built in the 19th century. **Santa Catarina**, in the square of the same name, is a fine 18th-century church; on Sunday, at about one o'clock, people assemble under the trees to tell stories (all are welcome to attend or participate). In the same square, the **Casa de la Cultura Jesús Reyes Heroles** should not be missed, with its delightful leafy gardens. Just before arriving at the **Jardín Centenario**, with its 16th-century arches, is the 18th-century **Casa de Diego Ordaz**.

The centre of Coyoacán, with its two adjacent plazas, is dominated by the 16th-century church of **San Juan Bautista**, with later additions and a magnificent interior. Jardín Centenario was once the atrium of this 16th-century Franciscan monastery. On the north side of Plaza Hidalgo, the **Casa de Cortés** was in fact built 244 years after the Conquest, on the site of Cortés' house.

The **Museo Nacional de Culturas Populares** ⓘ *Av Hidalgo, Tue-Sun 1000-1600, free*, just off Plaza Hidalgo, houses exhibitions on popular Mexican culture.

At weekends there are many open-air events especially on Plaza Hidalgo and in the *artesanía* market, off Plaza Hidalgo, which is well worth a visit.

The beautiful 18th-century church of **La Conchita** ⓘ *Fri evenings and Sun mornings*, in a pretty square of the same name is reached by walking down Higuera from Plaza Hidalgo; the interior, especially the altarpiece, is magnificent. On the corner of Higuera and Vallarta is what is reputed to be the **Casa de La Malinche**, Cortés' mistress and interpreter.

Admirers of Frida Kahlo will want to visit the **Museo Frida Kahlo**, or **Casa Azul** ⓘ *Allende and Londres 247, Tue-Sun 1000-1800, US$4, no photographs*. Two rooms are preserved as lived in by Frida Kahlo and her husband Diego Rivera, and the rest contain drawings and paintings by both. Frida was very interested in folk art, an interest that is illustrated by the small collection of regional costumes on display. In the **Jardín Cultural Frida Kahlo**, near Plaza de La Conchita, there is a striking bronze statue of Frida by the contemporary Mexican sculptor Gabriel Ponzanelli.

La Casa de Trotsky ⓘ *Río Churubusco 410, between Gómez Farías and Morelos, Tue-Sun 1000-1700, US$2, half-price with ISIC card*, is where the Russian revolutionary lived before he was murdered in the study in 1940. The house is dark and sombre, and there is a tomb in the garden where his ashes were laid.

To reach the centre of Coyoacán from Metro General Anaya, there is a pleasant walk along Héroes del 47 (one block along on the left is the 16th-century **church of San Lucas**), across División del Norte and down Hidalgo (one block along on the left, and two blocks down San Lucas is the 18th-century **church of San Mateo**).

☾ *If time in Coyoacán is limited, take in La Casa de Trotsky, Museo Frida Kahlo, Museo de las Culturas Populares and the church of San Juan Bautista.*

Ciudad Universitaria
ⓘ *Take a bus marked 'CU', along Eje Lázaro Cárdenas; also bus 17, marked 'Tlalpan', which runs the length of Insurgentes (about 1 hr); alternatively, take metro Line 3 to Copilco station (20 mins' walk to University) or to Universidad station (30 mins' walk). At University City free buses ferry passengers to the different areas of the campus.*

The world-famous University City, 18 km from the centre via Insurgentes Sur on the road towards the Cuernavaca highway, was founded in 1551. The modern era construction was built from 1949 to 1952 and in 2007 the ensemble was declared a World Heritage Site. Perhaps the most notable building is the 10-storey **Biblioteca** (library), by Juan O'Gorman, its outside walls iridescent with mosaics telling the story of scientific knowledge, from Aztec astronomy to molecular theory.

Frida Kahlo

Frida Kahlo was one of the most significant Mexican painters of the 20th century. She painted using vibrant colours in a style that was influenced by the indigenous cultures of Mexico as well as by European movements such as Symbolism, Realism and Surrealism. Her life was not a happy one; she questioned her European and Mexican roots, very much like the artists of an earlier era who were took ideas and subjects originating in the Old World, which they attempted to express in New World terms.

Frida suffered greatly because her treatment after an accident when she was young went terribly wrong, added to which she and her spouse, Diego Rivera, were not a compatible couple. Her anguish is expressed in her paintings on display at the Museo Frida Kahlo, in Coyoacán. Many of her works are self-portraits.

Frida's life was the subject of the film *Frida*, filmed on location in San Luis Potosí with Salma Hayek in the title role and Alfredo Molina as Diego Rivera.

Across the highway is the **Estadio Olímpico**, with seats for 80,000 and a sculpture-painting by Diego Rivera telling the story of Mexican sport. In shape, colour and situation a world's wonder, but now closed and run down. Beyond the Olympic stadium is the **Jardín Botánico Exterior** ① *daily 0700-1630, 30-min walk, ask directions*, which displays all the cactus species in Mexico. Beyond the Ciudad Universitaria, but still a part of the university, is a complex which includes the **Museo Universitario Contemporáneo de Arte** and the extraordinary **Espacio Escultórico**, a large circular area of volcanic rock within a circle of cement monoliths; on the opposite side of the road is another large area with many huge sculptures; stick to the path as it is possible to get lost in the vegetation.

Anahuacalli

① *Off División del Norte, Museo 150, T55-5617 4310, Tue-Sun 1000-1800, closed Holy Week, US$4, www.anahuacallimuseo.org. The museum is reached by Combi 29 from the Tuxquena metro station to Estadio Azteca, or take the bus marked División del Norte from outside Metro Salto del Agua.*

Further east is the Museo Diego Rivera Anahuacalli, usually shortened to just Anahuacalli. There is a fine collection of pre-Columbian sculpture and pottery, effectively displayed in a pseudo-Mayan tomb purpose built by Diego Rivera. There is a big display here for the Day of the Dead at the beginning of November.

Churubusco

① *Reached from the Zócalo by Coyoacán or Tlalpan buses; or from Metro General Anaya.*

Situated 10 km southeast in the area of Churubusco is the picturesque and partly ruined convent (1762) that is now the **Museo de las Intervenciones** ① *General Anaya y 20 de Agosto, Tue-Sun 0900-1800, US$3*. The museum's 17 rooms are filled with mementoes, documents, proclamations and pictures recounting foreign invasions, incursions and occupations since Independence. It also holds temporary exhibitions. The site of the museum was chosen because it was the scene of a battle when the US Army marched into Mexico City in 1847. This was where the San Patricios, the famous Saint Patrick's Brigade who fought as volunteers on the Mexican side, were captured by the US Army. Next door is the 16th-century church of **San Diego**, with 17th- and 18th-century additions. Near the church, on the other side of Calzada General Anaya, is the delightful **Parque de Churubusco**. One block from Tlalpan along Héroes del 47, to the left, is the 18th-century church of **San Mateo**.

Tlalpan

A further 6.5 km, or direct from San Angel (see page 114), is this suburb with colonial houses, gardens and, near the Plaza de la Constitución, the early 16th-century **church of San Agustín** with a fine altar and paintings by Cabrera. It can be reached by bus or trolley bus from the Taxqueña metro station. The suburb of **Peña Pobre** is 2.5 km west, near which, to the northeast, is the **Pyramid of Cuicuilco** ① *Insurgentes Sur Km 16 y Periférico,*

7 Xochimilco

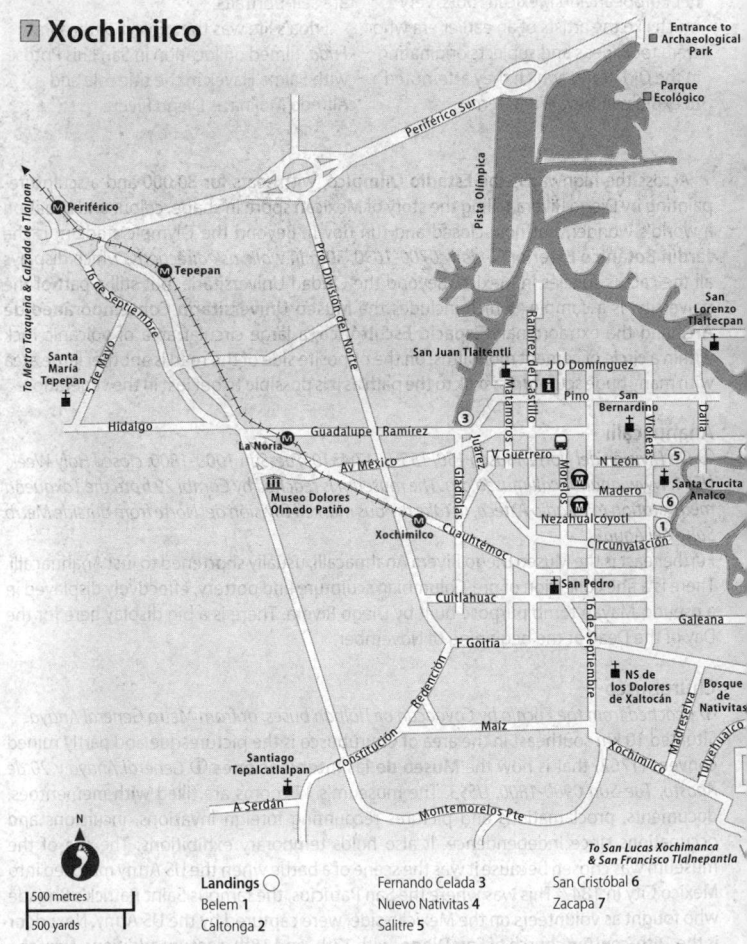

Landings ○	Fernando Celada **3**	San Cristóbal **6**
Belem **1**	Nuevo Nativitas **4**	Zacapa **7**
Caltonga **2**	Salitre **5**	

To San Lucas Xochimanca & San Francisco Tlalnepantla

Tue-Sun 0800-1800, believed to be the oldest pyramid in Mexico. It dates from the fifth or sixth century BC and is over 100 m in diameter but only 25 m high. There is an archaeological museum on site.

Xochimilco → *Colour map 3, B5.*
① *Easiest access is by bus, colectivo or metro to Metro Taxqueña, then tren ligero (about 20 mins). Get off at the last stop.*

Around 20 km to the southeast of the city centre, Xochimilco has many attractions, not least the fact that it lies in an unpolluted area. Meaning 'the place where flowers grow', Xochimilco was an advanced settlement long before the arrival of the Spaniards. Built on a lake, it developed a form of agriculture using *chinampas* (floating gardens); the area is still a major supplier of fruit and vegetables to Mexico City. The Spaniards recognized the importance of the region and the need to convert the indigenous population; evidence of this is the considerable number of 16th- and 17th-century religious buildings in Xochimilco and in the other 13 *pueblos* that make up the present-day *delegación* (municipality).

Xochimilco is famous for its canals and colourful punt-like boats, *trajineras*, which bear girls' names. There are seven landing-stages, or *embarcaderos*, the largest of which are **Fernando Celada** and **Nuevo Nativitas** (the latter is a large craft market where most coachloads of tourists are set down). All are busy at weekends, especially Sunday afternoon. Official tariffs operate, although prices are sometimes negotiable. In addition to the trajineras Xochimilco: It should be mentioned that besides the expensive *trajineras* there are *colectivo*-boats operating for US$1-2 for a trip around the canals starting from *embarcadero* San Cristóbal. For the private boats six passengers costs US$10 per hour (a trip of at least 1½ hours is desirable); floating *mariachi* bands will charge US$3.50 per song, *marimba* groups US$1.50. There are reasonably priced tourist menus (lunch US$2) from passing boats or, even better, stock up with a picnic and beers before setting off.

The indisputable architectural jewel of Xochimilco is the church of **San Bernardino de Siena** (begun in 1535, completed 1595;

> ### ➡ Mexico City maps
> 1 Orientation, page 94
> 2 City centre, page 96
> 3 Centro Histórico: Zócalo & Alameda, page 100
> 4 Reforma & Zona Rosa, page 106
> 5 Bosque de Chapultepec & Polanco, page 108
> 6 Coyoacán, page 115
> 7 **Xochimilco, page 118**
> 8 Metro, page 146

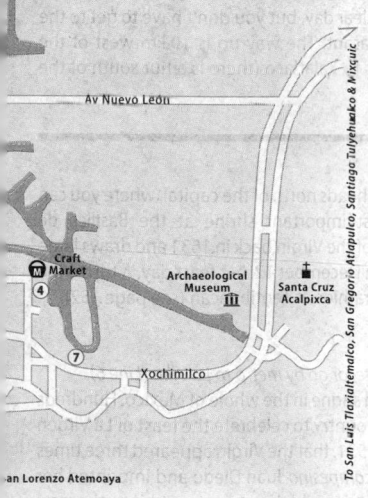

magnificent Renaissance-style altarpiece, 1580-1590) and its convent (circa 1585). The oldest Spanish-built religious edifice is the tiny **Capilla de San Pedro** (1530). Also worthy of mention are **Nuestra Señora de los Dolores de Xaltocán** (17th-century façade, 18th-century retable), **Santa Crucita Analco** and **San Juan Tlaltentli**. All are within walking distance of the centre of Xochimilco. For those interested in church architecture, the villages to the west, south and east of Xochimilco are worth visiting, all reachable by *colectivo* or bus from the centre of Xochimilco. In nearby **Míxquic**, famous for its **Día de los Muertos** (Day of the Dead) celebrations, the church of **San Andrés** (second quarter of 16th century; façade 1620; many alterations) was built on the site of an earlier temple using some of the original blocks, with traces of pre-Hispanic designs.

Museo Dolores Olmedo Patiño ① *Av México 5843 and Antiguo Camino a Xochimilco, 1 block southwest from La Noria tren ligero station, Tue-Sun 1000-1800, US$3.50, students US$1.50, T55-5555 1016, www.md op.org.mx*, is highly recommended. It is set in 3 ha of beautiful garden and grassland on the site of an old estate, probably dating from the 16th century. Rare Mexican hairless dogs and peacocks parade through the grounds. The museum houses 137 works by Diego Rivera, 25 by Frida Kahlo, and an important collection of drawings by Angelina Beloff. There are also pre-Hispanic artefacts, 19th-century antiques and Mexican folk art. There is also a very pleasant open and covered café and a **tourist office** ① *Pino 36, daily 0800-2100*.

Ajusco
Another excursion can be made to Ajusco, a mountain on the southern edge of the Mexico City basin about 20 km southwest of the city. To get there: catch a bus from Estadio Azteca on Calzada Tlalpan direct to Ajusco. From the summit of the extinct **Volcán Ajusco** (3929 m) there are excellent views on a clear day, but you don't have to get to the top as a stroll through the foothills is also pleasant. The way up is 10 km west of the village, 400 m west of where the road branches to Xalatlaco (there is a hut south of the road where the path goes to the mountain).

North of the city centre

Another worthwhile escape from the city centre heads north of the capital, where you can make your own pilgrimage to Mexico's most important shrine at the Basílica de Guadalupe. The site celebrates two apparitions of the Virgin back in 1531 and draws large numbers throughout the year, and especially on December 12, her feast day. A trip to the Basílica is easily combined with a visit to the pyramids at Teotihuacán (see page 152).

Basílica de Guadalupe
① *US$3, buses marked 'La Villa' go close to the site, or go by metro to La Villa (Line 6).*
The Basílica de Guadalupe is the most venerated shrine in the whole of Mexico. Hundreds of thousands of people come from all over the country to celebrate the feast of La Virgen de Guadalupe, on 12 December. It was here, in 1531, that the Virgin appeared three times in the guise of an indigenous princess to local *campesino* Juan Diego and imprinted her portrait on his cloak. The cloak is preserved, set in gold, but was moved into the new basilica next door as a massive crack had appeared down the side of the old building. The huge, modern basilica, completed in 1976, was designed by architect Pedro Ramírez Vázquez (who was also responsible for the Museo Nacional de Antropología). It's an impressive building and holds over 20,000 people (very crowded on Sunday) and an

estimated 20 million pilgrims visit the shrine every year. The original basilica has been converted into a **museum**. It still houses the original magnificent altar, but otherwise it mostly has representations of the image on the cloak, plus interesting painted tin plates offering votive thanks for cures, etc from about 1860. A chapel stands over the well that gushed at the spot where the Virgin appeared. Indigenous dance groups provide entertainment in front of the basilica. There are, in fact, about seven churches in the immediate neighbourhood, including one on the hill above, the **Iglesia del Cerrito** (which has excellent views over the city); most of them are at crazy angles to each other and to the ground, because of subsidence. The **Templo de los Capuchinos** has been the subject of a remarkable feat of engineering in which one end has been raised 3.4 m so that the building is now horizontal.

Northern suburbs

The **pyramid of Tenayuca** ① *10 km to the northwest of the city centre, daily 1000-1645, US$1.50*, is about 15 m high and the best preserved in Mexico. The Aztecs rebuilt this temple every 52 years; the one that stands today was reconstructed around 1507 and is well worth seeing, for it is surrounded with serpents in masonry. To get there, take the metro to the Terminal de Autobuses del Norte, La Raza, and catch the bus from there. By bus from Tlatelolco, ask the driver and passengers to advise you on arrival as the site is not easily visible. Not far from Tenayuca is the old town of **Tlalnepantla** where you can see the ancient convent (ask for the Catedral) on the Plaza Gustavo Paz, and the church (1583), which contains the first image, a Christ of Mercy, brought to the New World. The smaller pyramid of **Santa Cecilia Acatitlán** ① *US$2*, which is interesting for its restored sanctuary, is 2.5 km to the north. It is difficult to find; head for the church tower visible from the footbridge over the highway.

In **Naucalpan**, northwest of the city just outside the city boundary on Bulevar Toluca, pre-Classic Olmec-influenced figurines can be seen in the **Museo de la Cultura de Tlatilco** ① *opposite the Hotel Naucalpan on Vía Gustavo Paz, Tue-Sun*. This is said to be the oldest settlement in the Cuenca de México; now a rather grim suburb. These sites are only worth visiting if you are seriously interested; it's a bit of a trek to reach them.

ⓜ Mexico City listings

Hotel and guesthouse prices
LL over US$150 **L** US$100-150 **AL** US$66-99
A US$46-65 **B** US$31-45 **C** US$21-30
D US$12-20 **E** US$7-11 **F** under US$7
Restaurant prices
ⓣⓣⓣ over US$15 **ⓣⓣ** US$8-15 **ⓣ** under US$8
See pages 45-48 for further information.

available, especially in low season or at weekends. Breakfast is rarely included in the room price unless otherwise stated. There are hotel reservation services at the airport and bus stations. Tourist information offices can also help you with reservations.

⊜ Sleeping

Prices of the more expensive hotels do not normally include 15% tax; service is sometimes included but it's always safest to check in advance. Discounts are often

Centro Histórico *p95, map p100*
LL-L Gran Hotel de México, 16 de Septiembre 82, Metro Zócalo, T55-1083 7700, www.granhotelciudaddemexico.com. One of the city's most elegant hotels with an incredible 1930s-style foyer, superb wrought-iron furnishings and an antique

elevator. The 4th-floor restaurant and balcony are superb for Zócalo-watching, especially on Sun morning (breakfast buffet US$10).

LL-L Sheraton Centro Histórico, Juárez 70, Metro Hidalgo, T55-5130 5300, www.sheratonmexico.com. A very well-appointed hotel with a great location overlooking the Alameda Central. Built on the site of the former Hotel del Prado, which collapsed in the 1985 earthquake. It boasts a wealth of amenities and an interesting collage of Diego Rivera murals.

L-AL Hotel de Cortés, Av Hidalgo 85, T55-5518 2181, Metro Hidalgo, www.hoteldecortes.com.mx. This is the only baroque-style hotel in Mexico City and a former pilgrims' guesthouse. The rooms are tasteful and attractive with lots of extras including safes, computer ports and satellite TV. There's a restaurant and a pleasant patio, but no pool.

L-AL Majestic (Best Western), Madero 73, Metro Zócalo, T55-5521 8600, www.majestic.com.mx. Another beautiful historic building on the Zócalo with a stunning interior of Puebla tiles, antique furnishings and carved wooden beams. The rooms are quiet, interesting and comfortable, with large beds and views of a courtyard. Some of them overlook the Zócalo, as does the magnificent restaurant on the 7th floor.

A Catedral, Donceles 95, Metro Zócalo, T55-5518 5232, www.hotelcatedral.com. A good, professional hotel with a high standard of service and amenities including restaurant, bar, taxi, laundry and internet. Rooms are clean, carpeted and spacious with telephone, cable TV and room service. Suites have jacuzzis. Recommended.

A Gillow, Isabel la Católica 17 and 5 de Mayo, Metro Allende, T55-5510 8585, www.hotel gillow.com. A large, elegant hotel that's centrally located. The rooms are not quite as plush as the lobby, but comfortable and attractive all the same. The best are on 6th floor. Lots of services, hospitable and good value, but the restaurant is only mediocre.

A San Francisco, Luis Moya 11, T55-5521 8960, Metro Juárez, www.delangel.com.mx. Friendly, good-value hotel with excellent views. Rooms are comfortable and have the usual amenities. Takes credit cards and serves good set meals.

B Canadá, Av 5 de Mayo 47, Metro Allende, T55-5518 02106, www.hotelcanada.com.mx. Smart, modern place with lots of slightly overpriced rooms equipped with bath, hot water, telephone, TV and safe. Services include laundry, money exchange and Wi-Fi. There's a good buffet breakfast. Friendly and helpful.

B Fleming, Revillagigedo 35, T55-5510 4530, Metro Juárez, www.hotelfleming.com.mx. Comfortable mid-range lodgings with a host of pleasant if unremarkable rooms. Bar, restaurant, Wi-Fi in reception and internet terminals. Suites have jacuzzis. Reliable.

B Marlowe, Independencia 17, T55-5521 9540, Metro San Juan de Letrán, www.hotelmarlowe.com.mx. A clean, modern hotel, finished to a high standard. It has safe parking and a good restaurant, but the service is slow (tourist office at airport refers many travellers here). If this one is too expensive, the cheaper Concordia is around the corner.

B-D Hostal Amigo, Isabel la Católica 61, Metro Isabel la Católica, T55-5512 3496, www.hostelamigo.com. Same ownership as Hostal Moneda, with identical rates and services, although they have a crazier barman, reportedly. The private rooms also lack private bathrooms and there's less of them. Otherwise a fun, funky and youthful place. Part of the Ciaro/Amigo Hostel Group, T01800-746 7835, www.amigohostelgroup.com, with hostels in Oaxaca, Campeche, Cancún and Tulum. Book online for up to 15% off.

B-D Hostel Catedral, Guatemala 4, Metro Zócalo, T55-5518 1726, www.hostel catedral.com. A thriving hostel with an attractive location just behind the cathedral. It has 204 beds including a mixture of private rooms (**C**) and dorms (**E**). A wealth of amenities including restaurant, kitchen, bar, laundry, internet centre, secure storage, travel agency and roof terrace. The bar livens up Tue-Fri with live music or dance classes. The front desk is open 24 hrs and there's lots of tourist info and tours on offer. Cheaper for YHI members or when booked online.

B-D Hostal Moneda, Moneda 8, 1 block east of the cathedral, Metro Zócalo, T55-5522 5803 (or 01800-221 7265, free in DF), www.hostalmoneda.com.mx. Clean, friendly and safe hostel in a great location. Dorms have 3-6 beds (**E**) and private rooms have bath (**C**). There's a great rooftop terrace restaurant used for serving inclusive breakfasts and dinners with a beautiful view of the cathedral and surroundings. There's free internet, a wide range of tours and complimentary city centre walking tour. Friendly and recommended.

C El Roble, Uruguay 109, Metro Zócalo, T55-5522 7830, www.hotelroble.com. Popular hotel with clean, modern rooms, all equipped with bath, TV, telephone, safe

and Wi-Fi. Good restaurant attached, although it closes early. Recommended.
C Washington, Av 5 de Mayo 54, Metro Allende, T55-5512 3502. Clean, small rooms with cable TV. A regular cheap hotel in the centre of town. Credit cards accepted. Euro changed.

C-D Isabel la Católica, Isabel la Católica 63, Metro Isabel la Católica, T55-5518 1213, www.hotel-isabel.com.mx. This big old colonial building has large shabby rooms with bath and hot water. Pleasant, popular, clean, helpful and safe (taxi drivers must register at desk before taking passengers). There's a roof terrace and quite good restaurant too. Rooms on top floor with shared bathroom are cheaper (**E**). Central and a bit noisy but still recommended.

C-D Mexico City Hostel, República de Brasil 8, Metro Zócalo, T55-5512 3666, www.mexicocityhostel.com. Neat, tidy and one of the newer hostels in town. Housed in a beautiful colonial building and

generally quieter than **Catedral** or **Moneda**. Interesting tours include a visit to a *Lucha Libre* wrestling match and a crawl around the local nightclubs. Private rooms (**D**) have no bath but are large; dorms have 8, 10 or 12 beds (**E**). Breakfast and Wi-Fi included.

C-D San Antonio, 2o Callejón, 5 de Mayo 29, Metro Allende, T55-5512 1625. Clean, pleasant, popular, friendly, TV in room. Recommended, but get a receipt if staying for several days and paying in advance.

D Congreso, Allende 18, Metro Allende, T55-5510 4446. 80 comfortable rooms with bath, TV and telephone. Good value and clean. Parking available.

D Cuba, Cuba 69, Metro Allende, T55-5518 1380, www.hotelcuba.com.mx. Good-value rooms with wooden floors, big beds, writing desks, telephones and cable TVs. There's a suite with a jacuzzi too.

D Fornos, Revillagigedo 92, Metro Balderas, 5 mins' walk to Alameda, T55-5521 9594. This hotel is extremely clean, but the rooms are slightly small. Each is equipped with carpets, TV, radio and writing desk. There's also parking space and a double with a jacuzzi (**B**). The staff are friendly and the Spanish owner speaks Dutch. Recommended.

D Habana, República de Cuba 77, Metro Allende, T55-5518 1589. Spacious, clean carpeted rooms with huge beds, writing desks, cable TV and telephone. The staff are friendly and helpful. Can be noisy, but a good location if you're looking to avoid the crowds. Excellent value and highly recommended.

D Juárez, up a quiet alley off 5 de Mayo 17, Metro Allende, T55-5512 6929, hoteljuarez@prodigy.net.mx. Great location near the Zócalo. Rooms are clean and comfortable with marble bathrooms, phone, radio and TV. Try to book in advance as often full. A very good budget choice – friendly, helpful and highly recommended. Ask for room with window.

D Lafayette, Motolinia 40 and 16 de Septiembre, Metro Allende, T55-5521 9640. Simple rooms with bath, TV, hot water and telephone. Clean and quiet (pedestrian

precinct), but check rooms; there is a variety of sizes.

D La Marina, Allende 30 y Blv Domínguez, Metro Allende, T55-5518 2445. Rooms here are clean and functional. They have large beds, TVs and simple writing desks. Soft drinks available in the lobby. Not bad, good value and friendly.

D Rioja, Av 5 de Mayo 45, next door to **Canadá**, Metro Allende, T55-5521 8333. Rooms are located around a high-ceiling central courtyard. They have shared or private baths, reliable hot water, telephone. Clean, popular and well placed. Normally recommended, but we have received a report of theft from rooms in the hotel – watch your gear just to be safe.

D-E Zamora, 5 de Mayo 50, Metro Allende, T55-5512 1832. Slightly gloomy but generally OK and friendly. Some big rooms work out very economical with more than 2 people. Cheaper rooms without bath also available (**F**).

E República, Cuba 57, Metro Allende, T55-5512 9517. Wonderful old colonial building with very cheap, if tired, rooms. Charming in a run-down sort of way and in the process of remodelling at the time of research. Rooms have bath and hot water and are even cheaper without TV. Upstairs is quieter. Recommended for budget travellers.

E Río de Janeiro, Brasil 451, near Colombia close to Plaza Santa Domingo, Metro Allende, T55-5526 2905. Grubby and extremely basic lodgings, head up the stairs and through the metal door. OK if money is really tight. Ultra-cheap without bath.

E Tuxpan, Colombia 11, near Brasil, close to Plaza Santo Domingo, Metro Allende, T55-5526 1118. This hotel is in the heart of a street market, so it's a lively spot. The interior is darkened with rooms set around a central courtyard. Rooms are clean with double beds, TV, hot showers and mirrors on the ceiling. Classy, and economical too.

West of La Alameda p105, map p96

A fairly run-down part of town, but close to the working heart of the city.

AL Ramada, Jesús Terán 12, Metro Hidalgo, T55-5566 0277, www.ramada international.com. Formerly **Hotel Jena**, the Ramada is clean, professional and well appointed, boasting all the amenities you'd expect from a modern, upmarket hotel. The rooms are large and comfortable; the lobby is airy and attractive.

B Mayaland, Maestro Antonio Caso 23, Metro Juárez, T55-5566 6066, www.hotelmayaland.com.mx. A large, modern and professional hotel with 100 clean, comfortable, if slightly generic, rooms. There's a convention centre, restaurant, computing hall and travel agency too. Recommended.

B Monaco, Guerrero 12, Metro Hidalgo, T55-5566 8333, www.hotel-monaco.com.mx. Professional, modern hotel with a marble interior. Rooms are large, clean and carpeted with amenities including cable TV, a/c and safe. There's a buffet breakfast for US$5.

C Palace, Ignacio Ramírez 7, Metro Revolución, T55-5566 2400. Clean, comfortable, carpeted rooms with striking blue walls, cable TV, Wi-Fi and phone. Helpful reception has a taxi service and there's a travel agency in the building.

C-E Casa de los Amigos, Ignacio Mariscal 132, Metro Revolución, T55 5705 0521, near Metro Revolución, www.casadelos amigos.org. Dormitory accommodation, slightly more in a double room, pay 2 nights in advance, use of kitchen, maximum 15-day stay, separation of sexes, run by Quakers for Quakers, or development-work-related travellers; other travellers taken only if space is available, good information on volunteer work, travel and language schools, breakfast and laundry facilities on roof, safe-keeping for luggage, English library; advance booking advisable. Recommended.

D Carlton, Ignacio Mariscal 32-bis, Metro Revolución, T55-5566 2911. A bit dusty and run-down, verging on shabby, but generally OK. Basic furniture and worn-out carpets. Small rooms, but some have fine views (those at the front are noisy). Good restaurant.

D Detroit, Zaragoza 55, Metro Revolución, T55-5566-0755. Hourly rental place with marble floors, perfumed ambience, plastic flowers and contraceptives on reception. Still, it's very clean, central and economical.

D El Paraíso, Ignacio Mariscal 99, Metro Revolución, T55-5566 8077. A bit rough around the edges and fading. Rooms are clean and simple with hot water, private bath, TV and phone. Popular with working class Mexicans.

D Frimont, Jesús Terán 35, Metro Revolución, T55-5705 4169. The corridors are slightly musty, but the rooms aren't bad. They're smallish but comfortable, clean and equipped with desk, phone and TV. Good views from up on the 5th floor. There's also a good, cheap restaurant.

D Mina, José T Salgado 18, esq Mina, Metro Hidalgo, T55-5703 1682. Clean, modern rooms come fitted with marble sinks, carpets, dressers and phones. For the lonely, there are mirrors on the ceiling too. Good value.

D Oxford, Ignacio Mariscal 67, Metro Revolución, T55-5566 0500. Dark and slightly seamy with adult movies broadcast in the evenings. Some rooms are huge and have interesting views of the plaza. Friendly, helpful and really excellent value. Recommended for budget travellers, but no advance reservations.

E Royalty, Jesús Terán 21, Metro Hidalgo, T55-5566 9255. Gloomy and rundown and hardly fit for a king, as their name might suggest. Rooms are basic with TV and bath, shabby and unwelcoming, but OK if you're desperate, poor or jaded.

D Texas, Ignacio Mariscal 129, Metro Revolución, T55-5705 6496, www.gran hoteltexas.com. Reasonably comfortable, carpeted rooms have bath, cable TV, hot water, dresser and Wi-Fi. Sofas and snacks in reception. Parking.

Paseo de la Reforma and Zona Rosa
p107, map p106

LL-L NH México, Liverpool 155, Metro Insurgentes, T55-5228 9928, www.nh-hotels.com. A reputable chain of hotels with professional service, lots of amenities and predictably high standards. This one is particularly aimed at the North American business traveller. Recommended.

LL-L Royal Zona Rosa, Amberes 78, Metro Insurgentes, T55-9149 3000, www.hotel royalzr.com. A tower of glass and steel, this modern hotel has fine rooms and suites ideal for both businesspeople and holiday-makers. The usual Best Western quality.

A María Cristina, Lerma 31, Metro Insurgentes, T55-5566 9688, www.hotel mariacristina.com.mx. This handsome colonial-style hotel has 150 comfortable rooms, helpful staff, safe parking, bookstore and restaurant. Recommended.

A Prim, Versalles 46, Metro Cuauhtémoc, T55-5592 4600, www.hotelprim.com.mx. Clean, comfortable hotel with lots of rooms and staff, including a doorman on the lobby. Bar, restaurant, laundry, parking and Wi-Fi. Recommended.

A Viena, Marsella 28, Metro Cuauhtémoc, T55-5566 0700, www.posadavienahotel.com. An attractive, colourful hotel with lots of Mexican art, stained-glass windows and impressive craft pieces adorning the corridors and enclaves. Rooms are pleasantly comfortable and are equipped with telephone, hot water, shaving mirrors and Wi-Fi. There's a good café and restaurant on-site. Friendly, helpful and recommended.

A-B Casa González, Lerma y Sena 69, Metro Insurgentes, T55-5514 3302, casa.gonzalez@prodigy.net.mx. A very quiet and secluded hotel with peaceful, flower-filled inner courtyards. Breakfast and other food is available in the 24-hr café, with laundry, Wi-Fi and TV options too. The interior rooms are more attractive and expensive (**A**). Very helpful, friendly and highly recommended.

C Uxmal, Madrid 13, quite close to Zona Rosa, Metrobus Reforma. Clean rooms, same owner as more expensive **Madrid** next door (**AL**), with access to their better facilities. Recommended.

Apartments
Suites Amberes, Amberes 64, Metro Insurgentes, T55-5533 1306, www.suites amberes.com.mx. Attractive and comfortable suites with a wealth of amenities including gym, room service and cable TV.

Suites Havre, Havre 74, Metro Insurgentes, T55-5533 5670, near Zona Rosa. 56 suites with kitchen, phone and service for around US$150 per week or US$515 per month. Recommended for longer stays.

Bosque de Chapultepec and Polanco
p108, map p108

LL Casa Vieja, Eugenio Sue 45, Metro Polanco, T55-5282 0067, www.casavieja.com. Beautiful boutique hotel in a converted mansion. Lodgings include 6 junior suites, 3 master suites and 1 presidential suite. Each is equipped with bar, kitchen, jacuzzi and steam sauna.

LL-L Presidente Intercontinental, Campos Elíseos 218, overlooking Chapultepec Park, Metro Auditorio, T55-5327 7700, www.interconti.com. Typical Intercontinental quality with great service, comfort and amenities. The ideal hotel for business and pleasure.

South of the city centre

Insurgentes Sur *p113, map p94*
LL-L La Casona, Durango 280, Col Roma, Metro Sevilla, T55-5286 3001, www.hotel lacasona.com.mx. This elegant, converted early-20th-century mansion has spacious, attractive rooms and plenty of amenities, including gym, Wi-Fi, spa and valet parking.

AL Benidorm, Frontera 217, Col Roma, Metro Hospital General, T55-5265 0800, www.benidorm.com.mx. A very large 5-star hotel on a busy road with predictably comfortable rooms and lots of amenities including events room, parking, gym, gift shop, lobby bar and laundry. More modern than the **Marbella** next door.

A Stanza, Obregón 13, corner of Morelia, Col Roma, Metro Cuauhtémoc, T01800-9089-600, www.stanzahotel.com. Professionally run and appointed, the Stanza has an elegant marble lobby and a wealth of amenities including restaurant, gym, bar and Wi-Fi. The rooms are clean and modern with coffee-makers, mini-bars, telephones, safes and spotless bathrooms. Recommended.

B Hotel Roosevelt, Insurgentes Sur 287, Col Hipódromo Condesa, Metrobus Alvaro Obregón, T55-5208 6813, www.roosevelt.com.mx. Rooms at the Roosevelt are clean and modern and equipped with cable TV, phone, safe, writing desk, carpets and Wi-Fi. Some are bigger than others, so ask to see a few. The restaurant downstairs serves tasty Mexican food. Very friendly and helpful. Good.

D Colonia Roma, Jalapa 110, Col Roma, Metrobus Alvaro Obregón, T55-5584 1396, F55-5264-7975. This big pink building on the corner has 60 clean rooms, all with private bath, cable TV and telephone. Not bad.

D Hostel Home, Tabasco 303, Col Roma, Metrobus Alvaro Obregón, T55-5511 1683, www.hostelhome.com.mx. Great little hostel with the cleanliness and services you expect (such as a kitchen, friendly staff, dormitory accommodation) in a quiet part of town, so not as crowded as the hostels in the Centro Histórico, and with a more relaxed atmosphere.

Apartments
Casa de la Condesa, Plaza Luis Cabrera 16, Col Roma Sur, Metro Insurgentes, T55-5574 3186, www.extendedstaymexico.com. Very comfortable and attractive suites owned by the Mousalli family. Some have great views overlooking the plaza. They also own and rent slightly cheaper apartments on Calle Madrid and Calle París, very close to Insurgentes and the Zona Rosa.
Hotel Suites del Parque, Dakota 155, Col Nápoles, T55-5536 1450, hotelsuites

delparque@prodigy.net.mx. Extremely spacious suites with the usual amenities, the price is good if sharing with up to 4 people, very convenient for the World Trade Center (across the street), good restaurant. Any length of stay.

Coyoacán *p114, map p115*
L-AL Suites Coyoacán, Av Coyoacán 1909, Col del Valle T55-5534 8353, www.suites coyoacan.com. One of the few hotels in the area with a restaurant, catering facilities and gym.

Apartments
Suites Quinta Palo Verde, Cerro del Otate 20, Col Romero de Terreros, México 21 DF, T55-5554 3575. Pleasant, diplomatic residence turned guesthouse, near the university; run by a veterinary surgeon, Miguel Angel who is very friendly and speaks English and German, but the dogs are sometimes noisy.

North of the city centre *p120, map p94*
A Brasilia, near Terminal del Norte bus station, on Av Cien Metros 48-25, T55-5587 8577. Excellent modern hotel with king-size beds and TV. There's a 24-hr traffic jam out the front.
B La Villa de los Quijotes, Moctezuma 20, near Basílica de Guadalupe (Metro La Villa), T55-5577 1088, www.hotelvillaquijotes.com. Modern and quiet, with clean rooms, expensive restaurant.

Elsewhere *map p94*
L-AL JR Plaza, Blv Puerto Aéreo 390, T55-5785 5200. Free airport transport, expensive restaurant, quiet, good rooms with solid furniture, close to metro.

Youth hostels and campsites
Asociación Mexicana de Albergues de la Juventud, Madero 6, Oficina 314, México 1, DF. Contact by post for information.
Comisión Nacional del Deporte (Condep), runs the **Villas Deportivas Juveniles**;

information office at Glorieta del Metro Insurgentes, Local C-11, T55-5525 2916. Condep will make reservations for groups of 10 or more; to qualify you must be aged between 8 and 65 and have a *Tarjeta Plan Verde* membership card, US$6, valid for 2 years, obtainable within 24 hrs from office at Tlalpan 583, esq Soria, Metro Xola, or a IYHF card.

See also **SETEJ**, page 93, for information on hotels and other establishments offering lodging for students.

For the nearest camping, see Tepozotlán, page 157, and the road to Toluca, page 164.

❼ Eating

All the best hotels have good restaurants. The number and variety of eating places is vast; this is only a small selection.

Centro Histórico

Zócalo and around *p95, map p100*
₮₮₮ Bar La Opera, 5 de Mayo, Metro Allende, T55-5512 8959. Mon-Sat 1300-2400, Sun 1300-1800. One of the city's most elegant watering holes, open since 1870. Relaxing atmosphere, Mexican appetizers and entrées, and an expensive drinks list. The bullet hole in the ceiling was left by Mexican revolutionary hero Pancho Villa, allegedly.
₮₮₮ Café Tacuba, Tacuba 28, Metro Allende. A very old restaurant with stunning tile decor, not touristy and specializing in Mexican food. Very good *enchiladas*, excellent meat dishes, *tamales* and fruit desserts although portions are a little small and service a bit slow. Live music and mariachis, very popular with local business people. It's also where renowned Mexican politician Danilo Fabio Altamirano was assassinated in 1936. Expensive but recommended.
₮₮₮ El Cardenal, Palma 23, Metro Allende. Excellent Mexican food impeccably served in an elegant mansion. Interesting seasonal specialities include *gusanos de maguey*

(maguey worms) *flores de maguey* (maguey flowers) and *chiles en nogada*. Breakfasts are tasty too, including a traditional feast of hot chocolate and sweet rolls.
₮₮₮ Hostería Santo Domingo, 70 and 72 Belisario Domínguez, 2 blocks west of Plaza Santo Domingo, Metro Allende, T55-5510 1612. The oldest restaurant in town with former diners creating a who's who of Mexican history. Good food and service and excellent live music.
₮₮₮ La Casa de las Sirenas, Tacuba y Seminario, Metro Zócalo, behind the cathedral. This lovely old colonial building houses a classic Mexican restaurant with a fantastic selection of tequilas. Excellent food and service with great views from the rooftop terrace. Recommended.
₮₮₮ Mercaderes, 5 de Mayo 57, Metro Allende. Supposedly located where the Aztec emperor's former palace once stood, this elegant old restaurant serves a range of international dishes and a handful of obscure Mexican specialities too.
₮₮₮ Sanborn's Casa de los Azulejos, Av Madero 17, Metro Bellas Artes. Known as the foreigners' home-from-home, **Sanborn's** has 36 locations in Mexico, with soda fountain, drugstore, restaurant, English, German and Spanish-language magazines, handicrafts, chocolates, etc. This, the most famous branch, is in the 16th-century 'house of tiles'. Service can be poor, but there are many delicious local dishes in beautiful high-ceilinged room, with an Orozco mural on staircase. About US$10-15 per person without wine (also has handicraft shops).
₮₮-₮₮ Danubio, Uruguay 3, Metro San Juan de Letrán. Founded over 60 years ago by 2 chefs from Spain's Basque region, this well-regarded restaurant is most famous for its seafood – perhaps the best in the city. Some 110 dishes grace the menu, many prepared on the traditional coal and wood stove that's been burning since 1936.
₮₮ Al Andalus, Mesones 171, Metro Pino Suárez. The best Lebanese food in the city served in a secluded old colonial building

that's mercifully free of tourists. Fare includes kebabs, hummus, *shwarma*, falafel and sweet baklava pastries.

♥♥ Los Girasoles, corner of Tacuba and Gante, Metro Allende. Long-standing and popular restaurant serving Mexican cuisine in a big, airy old colonial building that's painted bright yellow to match the flowers. Reasonable food and a few interesting dishes, *chapulines* (roasted crickets) and *escamoles* (ant larvae) among them. There's also some pleasant outdoor seating on the plaza.

♥♥ Sushi Roll, 5 de Mayo and Filomeno Mata, about 5 blocks west of the Zócalo, Metro Allende. This Japanese eatery has a clean and pleasant interior. It serves a large selection of sushi rolls, unsurprisingly. Very good.

♥♥-♥ Café El Popular, 5 de Mayo 52, on corner of alley to **Hotel Juárez**, Metro Allende. Cheap, busy and popular with Mexicans. Fare includes a plethora of breakfasts and Mexican staples, Oaxacan omelettes, tacos and enchiladas. There's a selection of fresh baked pastries too. Open 24-hours.

♥♥-♥ Café La Blanca, 5 de Mayo 40, Metro Allende. Popular and busy atmosphere at this unpretentious eatery with a large menu of breakfasts, Mexcian staples, and the usual meat, chicken and fish fare. Recommended.

♥♥-♥ Café La Pagoda, 5 de Mayo and Filomeno Mata, behind Bar La Opera, Metro Bellas Artes. Unassuming diner with cosy booth seating and friendly waitresses in 1950s American-style uniforms. Breakfasts, Mexican staples and economical *menú del día*. Clean.

♥♥-♥ Gran Café del Centro, 5 de Mayo 10, Metro Bellas Artes. Smart little café with a chequered floor, reminiscent of a European coffee house. Sweet pastries, set breakfasts, *comida corrida*, fresh coffee, the usual Mexican staples and bar service.

♥ Comida Económica Verónica, República de Cuba, 2 doors from **Hotel Habana** (No 77), close to Plaza Santo Domingo , Metro Allende. For tasty breakfasts, set *comida corrida* and very hot *chilaquiles*. Good value and delightful staff. Recommended.

♥ Costillitas el Sitio, Uruguay 84, Metro Isabel la Católica. Popular lunch-time taco joint, feeding the locals since 1970.

♥ Glll's Pollo, 5 de Mayo, opposite **Hotel Rioja**, Metro Allende. Excellent chicken, eat in or takeaway, cheap, filling and friendly.

♥ Maple, Uruguay 109, next to **Hotel Roble**, Metro San Juan de Letrán. Clean, pleasant restaurant that's recommended for its economical *comida*.

♥ Mariscos, República de Uruguay 29a, Metro San Juan de Letrán. Bustling lunch stop and hole in the wall serving good seafood including ceviche, conch, prawn cocktails, fillets and fish soup.

♥ Restaurante Los Vegetarianos, Filomeno Mata 13, Metro Allende. Open 0800-2000. Relaxed outdoor seating and good, cheap vegetarian fare including salads, soups, juices, breakfasts and *menú del día*.

♥ Rex, 5 de Febrero 40, Metro Isabel la Católica. Unpretentious grub including rotisserie chickens, *tortas*, ultra-economical *comida corrida* and other wholesome fare for working class Mexicans and budget-conscious travellers.

Cafés, bakeries and sweet shops

Café del Centro, Bolívar 26, Metro Allende. Interesting little café. Dark, intimate and open front, with great views of the street and the passing people.

Dulcería de Celaya, 5 de Mayo 39, Metro Allende. Famous traditional (and expensive), handmade candy store in lovely old premises.

Panadería La Vasconia, Tacuba 73, Metro Allende. Good bread, also sells cheap chicken and fries.

Pastelería Ideal, Uruguay 74, Metro San Juan de Letrán. Large, popular bakery with a huge array of cakes, breads, sweet rolls and pastries.

Pastelería Madrid, 5 de Febrero 25, 1 block from **Hotel Isabel la Católica**, Metro Pino Suárez. Good pastries and breakfasts.

Super Soya, Bolívar 29, Metro Allende. Health-food shop with good juices and fruit salads.

La Alameda and around *p104, map p100*

Hong Kong, Dolores 25a, Metro San Juan de Letrán. One of several Chinese joints in the area, if you've had your fill of Mexican food and need new flavours.

Trevi, Dr Mora y Colón, Metro Hidalgo. Mediocre diner-style place serving Italian, US and Mexican grub at reasonable prices. An Alameda institution.

Salon Sol, Juárez 52, Metro Bellas Artes. Economical breakfasts and Mexican staples with plastic chairs and booth seating. Overlooks the Alameda.

Fonda Santa Rita, Independencia 10, Metro San Juan de Letrán. Bustling locals' haunt serving mole *poblano*, quesadillas, soups, *tortas* and tacos.

West of La Alameda *p105, map p96*

You'll find lots of good street stalls in the residential roads west of La Alameda. They're often busy with hungry lunch crowds.

La Parilla Argentina, Lafragua 4, corner of Revolution Monument, Metro Revolución. Tasty Argentine steaks and other carnivorous fare.

La Habana, Bucareli y Morelos, Metro Juárez. Not cheap but good, and famed for its excellent coffee and *banderilla* pastries. Popular with journalists and a great place for breakfast.

El Tigre, Iglesias and Mariscal, Metro Revolución. Great *torta* stand that's popular with locals. They also do refreshing fruit *licuados*.

Paseo de la Reforma and Zona Rosa *p107, map p106*

Chalet Suizo, Niza 37, Metro Insugentes. Swiss fondues, shredded veal fillet and German-style beef pot roast are some of the wholesome offerings at this popular Swiss restaurant, established by a celebrity chef. Several European languages spoken.

Les Moustaches, Río Sena 88, Metro Insurgentes. Mon-Sat 1300-2330. This award-winning French restaurant is one of Mexico City's finest. Classic French dishes like foie gras, onion soup and Gruyère prawns compliment more exotic fare like crocodile with kiwi and walnuts. The epitome of elegance and therefore suitably pricey.

Quebracho, Río Lerma 175, Metro Insurgentes. Succulent Argentine steaks for all your carnivorous needs. Popular with middle-class Mexicans.

Fonda del Refugio, Liverpool 166, Metro Insurgentes. Founded by writer Judit Van Beuren in the 1950s, this popular Mexican restaurant serves classic national dishes in a colonial setting. Loved by tourists.

Sushi Itto, Hamburgo 141, Metro Insurgentes. Fresh, reliable Japanese fare from this famous chain. Clean and tasty, if somewhat generic.

Bella Luna, Río Lerma and Río Sena, Metro Insurgentes. Tasty, affordable and authentic Oaxacan specialities at this modest little restaurant, including dishes featuring the famous *moles* particular to the region.

Yug, Varsovia 3, Metro Insurgentes. This large vegetarian restaurant has an extensive menu of juices, fruits, yogurts, salads and soups. The breakfast options are especially impressive and there's Mexican fare too, *sin carne*, of course.

Arles, Río Sena 30, Metro Insurgentes. Clean, busy eatery that serves buffet breakfasts, *comida del día* and other unpretentious fare. Popular with the locals.

Beatricita, Londres 188, Metro Insurgentes. Busy locals' haunt that's been serving up economical Mexican food since 1910. Tacos, breakfasts, national dishes and good-value *comida corrida* are on the menu.

La Puerta del Angel, Varsovia y Londres, Metro Insurgentes. Large and slightly faded locals' eatery where economical food and spirited Latin music come in equally hearty measures.

Bosque de Chapultepec and Polanco
p108, map p108

Mexico City's very finest restaurants are concentrated in Polanco and Chapultepec. Prices are steep, reflecting the high quality on offer.

¶¶¶ Cambalache, Arquimedes north of Presidente Masaryk, Metro Polanco. This Argentine steakhouse serves some excellent cuts and stocks a wide selection of wines. Cosy atmosphere.

¶¶¶ Fisher's, Taine 311, Metro Polanco. They serve superb seafood here, and not expensive considering the quality and presentation. No reservations accepted.

¶¶¶ Hacienda de los Morales, Vásquez de Mella 525, Metro Polanco (but many blocks west of the station, consider a taxi), T55-5281 4703. Housed in an old 16th-century hacienda, this famous restaurant has lots of style and atmosphere. They serve Mexican specialities like chiles *en nogada* and roasted goat. Wear a tie and jacket in the evening.

¶¶¶-¶¶ Café del Bosque, Lago Menor 2da, Metro Constituyentes, T55-5515 4652, www.cafedelbosque.com.mx. Located inside Chapultepec park, this smart little restaurant overlooks a lake. It's a popular spot for breakfast and serves international fare the rest of the time.

¶¶¶-¶¶ Mulegé, Taine 324, Metro Polanco, T55-5203 4988. Trendy, ambient oyster bar. The place to sip martinis and be seen.

¶¶¶-¶¶ Pámpano, Moliere 42, Metro Polanco, T55-5281 2010. Fine cuisine from Mexican chef Richard Sandoval. Contemporary and interesting.

¶¶ Embers, Séneca y Ejército Nacional, Metro Polanco. Get past the gaudy 'Disney World' exterior and this young, popular restaurant serves 43 types of excellent hamburger. Good French fries too. Recommended.

¶¶ Tandoor, Copérnico 156, Metro Polanco, 155-5203 0045, www.tandoor.com.mx. Reportedly the best Indian and Pakistani food in the city – and possibly the country. A good range of vindaloos and other delicious, spicy fare.

South of the city centre

Insurgentes Sur *p113, map p94*

Roma and Condesa are DF's trendiest eating-out districts and a great place to sample the city's culinary talents.

¶¶¶ Bistrot Mosaico, Michoacán 10, Condesa, Metrobus Campeche, T5584-2932. Closed Mon. Elegant French restaurant serving pricey, but authentic cuisine. Lots of ambience and dusty wine bottles on display.

¶¶¶ Hip Kitchen, México 188, Condesa, Metrobus Alvaro Obregón, T55-5212-2110. Closed Sun. A very fine and popular restaurant serving top-notch Asian-Mexican cuisine. Located in the **Hippodrome Hotel**.

¶¶¶ Restaurante Lamm, Alvaro Obregón 99, Roma, Metrobus Alvaro Obregón, T55-5514 8501. Closed Mon. Located within the **Casa Lamm Cultural Centre**, this widely revered fine-dining establishment serves excellent Mexican and international cuisine.

¶¶¶-¶¶ El Chisme, México 111, Condesa, Metrobus Campeche, T55-5584 0032, www.elchisme.com.mx. Occasional live events at this popular restaurant, including dance and comedy. They serve well-presented international fare including pasta, pizzas, crêpes and fondue. Open for breakfast, but closed all day Fri.

¶¶¶-¶¶ Ixchel, Medellín 65, Roma, Metrobus Durango, T55-3096 5010, www.ixchel.com.mx. Clean, crisp interior at this nightclub turned trendy restaurant. Specialities include squash flowers stuffed with Oaxacan cheese and ravioli filled with spinach and goats' cheese. There are also steaks and fish, all well prepared.

¶¶¶-¶¶ La Bodega, Popocatépetl 25, Condesa, Metrobus Alvaro Obregón, 55-5511 7390, www.labodega.com.mx. Closed Sun. Founded in 1973, this famous, bohemian restaurant is housed in an atmospheric colonial building. They serve Mexican specialities like *mole poblano* and *nopal* soup. The wine list is reasonably extensive. Occasional live music.

ⵟⵟ-ⵟ Lion Wok, Tamaulipas 136, Condesa, Metro Patriotismo, T55-5256 1579. A trendy, young restaurant with a modern interior. They serve sushi and wok-fried treats.

ⵟⵟ-ⵟ Litoral, Tamaulipas 55, Condesa, Metrobus Sonora, 55-5286 2015, www.restaurantelitoral.com. Smart, popular restaurant serving well-presented contemporary dishes, including a range of seafood, red meats, soups, pastas and chicken. Crisp white table cloths, wooden floors and well-attired waiting staff.

ⵟⵟ-ⵟ Mama Rosa's, Atlixco 105, Condesa, Metro Patriotismo, T55-5211 1640, www.mamarosas.com.mx. Italian-Mexican fusion and international fare at this highly popular and often buzzing eatery on the corner. Dishes include 'Rock Burgers', Filete Sauvignon, stone-baked pizzas and pastas.

ⵟⵟ-ⵟ Rojo Bistrot, corner of Parras and Amsterdam, Condesa, Metrobus Sonora, T55-5211 3705. Closed Sun. European-style café with dimmed lighting, tasteful decor and French cuisine.

ⵟⵟ-ⵟ Tierra de Vinos, Durango 197, Roma, Metrobus Durango, T55-5208 5133, www.tierradevinos.com. Closed Sun. Spanish and Mediterranean cuisine. As the name suggests, they keep a sensational wine cellar with bottles from around the world.

ⵟ Agapi Mu, Alfonso Reyes 96, Condesa, Metro Patriotismo, T55-5286 1384. Closed Mon. Intimate and hospitable Greek restaurant serving classic dishes like tsatsiki, moussaka and sweet baklava. It can get spirited in the evenings when the ouzo flows liberally.

ⵟ El Japonez, Suárez 42a, Condesa, Metro Patriotismo, T55-5286 0712. Open daily 1300-2300. This Japanese restaurant has a crisp, attractive interior and pavement tables outside. Great sushi and spicy rolls.

ⵟ El Ocho, Ozuluama 14, Condesa, Metro Patriotismo. This fun, bright 'creative café' serves burgers, baguettes, bagels, other light meals and international fare. There's lots of board games to keep you entertained too.

ⵟ Flor de Lis, Huichapan 21, Condesa, Metrobus Sonora, T55-5211 3040, www.flordelis.com.mx. Open for breakfast. Well-established haunt serving lovingly prepared and presented Mexican cuisine, including delicious *chiles en nogada* and *tamales de chicharrón*.

ⵟ Orígenes Orgánicos, Plaza Popocatépetl, 41a, Col Condesa, Metrobus Sonora. This small, busy café-restaurant and health food store serves wholesome organic meals including soups, salads and snacks. Some tables outside and free Wi-Fi for clients.

ⵟ-ⵊ Bisquet Obregón, Alvaro Obregón and Mérida, Roma, Metrobus Alvaro Obregón. A hugely popular spot for breakfast and lunch with queues of Mexican families at the weekend. This well-established city-wide chain serves economical national staples.

ⵊ Amore Pizza, Michoacán 78, Condesa, Metro Patriotismo. Hole in the wall selling pizza by the slice. Quick food on the go.

ⵊ El Tizoncito, Tamaulipas and Campeche, Condesa, Metro Patriotismo. This well-established and popular eatery serves tacos and other wholesome fast food, all cooked on the grills in front of you and filling the air with delicious smells. There's a 2nd branch at Campeche and Cholula.

ⵊ Tacos Hola, Amsterdam 135, corner of Michoacán, Condesa, Metrobus Campeche. There's often a small crowd gathered around this little taco joint. Popular and tasty.

Cafés

Café Malafama, Michoacán 78, Condesa, Metrobus Campeche. Large, slick pool hall with a plethora of trendy black and white photos. They serve coffee by day and beer by night.

Café María, México and Iztaccíhuatl, Condesa, Metrobus Campeche. This popular café has tables on the pavement so you can sip your frappuccino and watch the world go by. Close to the park and relaxing.

El Péndulo, Nuevo León 115, Condesa, Metrobus Campeche. Great little coffee shop inside a bookstore, for those who are (or wish to appear) intellectual. They also serve light snacks.

San Angel *p114, map p94*

San Angel Inn, Diego Rivera 50, T55-5616 2222, www.sanangelinn.com. Mon-Sat 1230-0030, Sun 1300-2130. Top-quality dining in the former Carmelite monastery. If you can't afford a meal, it's worth going for a drink.

Coyoacán *p114, map p115*

There are several pleasant *cafeterías* in the Jardín Centenario, some of which serve light snacks and *antojitos*.

Los Danzantes, south side of Jardín del Centenario, Metro Viveros. Highly regarded as a bastion of culinary creativity. They serve Mezcal from their own distillery and Mexican fusion from the European-trained chef.

Hacienda de Cortés, Fernández Leal 74, behind Plaza de la Conchita, Metro Viveros, T55-5659 3741, www.haciendade cortes.com.mx. Exceptionally pleasant surroundings with a large shaded, outdoor dining area. They serve excellent breakfast and good value *comida corrida* US$5; try the *sábana de res con chilaquiles verdes*. Come at the weekend (book in advance) and see the heart of Mexican family life.

El Caracol de Oro, Higuera 22, Metro Viveros. Photos, artwork and beautifully painted furniture create a relaxed and bohemian atmosphere at this youthful café-restaurant, imaginatively named 'The Golden Snail' Juices, energy drinks, pastas and Mexican dishes on the menu.

Mesón Antiguo Santa Catarina, Plaza Santa Catarina, Metro Viveros. This delightfully situated restaurant in the square of the same name serves good Mexican cuisine at reasonable prices. There's a splendid atmosphere, especially for breakfast or supper, and the interior is adorned with Mexican art and wooden beams. Upstairs there's a terrace overlooking the plaza.

Moheli, Sosa and Tres Cruces, west side of the Jardín Centenario, Metro Viveros. This popular café-delicatessen serves bagels, baguettes and pastas and has pleasant outdoor seating along the pavement. A great breakfast spot.

El Morral, Allende 2, Metro Viveros. A good Mexican restaurant with an attractive tiled interior, an array of interesting old photos and other memorabilia. The toilets are palatial. Prices double at weekends, no credit cards. Highly recommended.

Fabio's, overlooking Plaza Hidalgo and the Delegación, Metro Viveros. Chequered table clothes and hanging baskets adorn this Mediterranean restaurant with views. Good *comida corrida*, credit cards accepted.

La Guadalupana, Higuera and Caballocalco, a few steps behind the church of San Juan Bautista in the centre of Coyoacán, Metro Viveros, T55-5554 6253. Mon-Sat 0900-2300. One of the best-known *cantinas* in Mexico, dating from 1932, fantastic food and a great atmosphere and no apologies for the passionate interest in bull fighting.

Churros Rellenos 'Jordan', Aguayo and Cuauhtémoc, Metro Viveros. Wholesome home-cooked *comida corrida*, tacos and other fast food. Just 1 of several economical places in this area.

Mercado, between Malintzin and Xicoténcatl, opposite Jardín del Carmen, Metro Viveros. Exquisite *quesadillas* at Local 31, outside try the seafood at El Jardín del Pulpo if you can get a seat. Fruit and vegetable sellers are ready to explain the names and uses of their goods; frequent musical entertainment particularly lunchtime and weekends.

Cafés and bakeries

El Globo, Caballocalco and Hidalgo, east side of Plaza Hidalgo, Metro Viveros. A stunning bakery with a wide selection of cakes, pastries and breads. Check out the wedding cakes in the windows.

El Jarocho, Allende and Cuauhtémoc, Metro Viveros. Buzzing little coffee shop with locals queuing up in the street and filling the surrounding benches. The interior is filled with coffee sacks and processing paraphernalia. Snacks and pastries on offer too.

Mastropiero Café, Higuera 31, next to the post office, Metro Viveros. A new café that serves as a cultural space with books, dance classes and music. Specialities include *tamales*, chocolate truffles and pizza with white chocolate! Young, friendly owners.

Xochimilco *p119, map p118*
† **Beto's**, opposite Fernando Celada, Metro Xochimilco. Good, clean and cheap restaurant, US$2 for lunch.
† **Restaurante del Botas**, Pino, to the left of the cathedral, Metro Xochimilco. 1st-rate cheap lunch (US$2).

Bars and clubs

Nightlife in Mexico City is as lively and varied as everything else the city has to offer. From gentle supper clubs with floorshows to loud, brash nightclubs, and from piano bars to *antros* (disco-bars) and bars that offer traditional Mexican music – all tastes are catered for. The most popular districts are Condesa, Roma, Zona Rosa, Polanco, San Angel and Coyoacán. You can go for a drink at any time, clubbing starts late with most just getting going by 2400. Prices of drinks and admission vary enormously depending on the area. Remember that, because of the high altitude, 1 alcoholic drink in Mexico City can have the effect of 2 at lower altitudes. Many bars and nightclubs are closed on Sun.

Centro Histórico *p95, map p100*
Plaza Garibaldi, Eje Central Lázaro Cárdenas, 5 blocks north of Bellas Artes, Metro Bellas Artes, is the place to experience live and spirited mariachi performances, most vociferous on Fri and Sat nights. Take a taxi and watch out for thieves.
Bar la opera, 5 de Mayo 10, Metro Allende. Fantastic old bar-restaurant with a range of national drinks and a bullet hole in the ceiling left by Pancho Villa. Dark, cosy and possessing great ambience.
Bar Mata, Filomeno Mata 11, Alameda Central, Metro Bellas Artes, T55-5518 0237,

Thu-Sat. On the 4th and 5th floors of a colonial building near Palacio de Bellas Artes. Atmosphere conducive to dancing and mingling, especially in the rooftop (5th-floor) bar, with great views of the city at nights.
Casa de las Sirenas, Guatemala 32, Metro Zócalo, www.lacasadelassirenas.com. Home to an astonishing stock of over 250 tequilas, this is the place to develop your knowledge and appreciation of the Mexico's proud alcoholic heritage. Great views too.
El Nivel, Moneda 2, Metro Zócalo. Colourful and boozy little cantina that's been around for centuries. 100% local, with the odd tourist popping in. Try it.
La Perla, República de Cuba 44, Metro Allende. Thu-Sat 2000-0400, cover US$4. Seedy but popular little club in the centre. Everything from dance to freaky cabaret has been reported.
Pervert Lounge, Uruguay 70, Metro Isabel la Católica. Thu-Sat 2230-0500. Famous dance venue attracting world-class DJs and crowds of revellers. Techno, house and trance plays. Cover US$10.
Salón Corona, Bolívar 24, betwen Madero and 16 de Septiembre, Metro Allende. Closes around 2400. Big, basic bar full of locals (and watching visitors). Good atmosphere.
Zinco Jazz Club, Motolinia 20, Metro Allende, www.zincojazz.com. Wed-Sat 2100-0330. Atmospheric jazz hall located in the basement of an art deco building. Great ambience and captivating live performances. Popular, so book ahead.

Paseo de la Reforma and Zona Rosa *p107, map p106*
Bar Milán, Milán 18, Metro Cuauhtémoc. Tue-Sat from 2100. Intimate little drinking hole that attracts a bright, young international crowd. They use a ticket system to dispense drinks at the bar. Eclectic music.
Casa Rasta, Insurgentes 149, Metro Insurgentes, T55-5705 0086. Thu-Sat from 2200. US$20 for men, US$5 for women, but with free bar. For reggae lovers, as the name suggests.

El Colmillo, Versailles 52, Metro Cuauhtémoc, T55-5553 0262. Thu-Sat from 2200-0400. Attracting a young, chic crowd with techno music downstairs and an exclusive jazz bar upstairs.

El Taller, Florencia and Reforma. Tue-Sun, 2200. Underground gay bar, one of the 1st in Mexico City.

Yuppie's Sports Café, Génova 34, Metro Insurgentes, T55-5208 2267. Daily 1300-0100. Good Tex-Mex and American-style fare in a pub with every corner adorned with sports memorabilia, TVs broadcast games from Mexico and around the world.

Bosque de Chapultepec and Polanco
p108, map p108

Barfly, Plaza Mazarik Mall, Metro Polanco, T55-5282 2906. Tue-Sat from 2000. Cosy bar with small dance floor and Cuban dance bands from 2300.

El Area, Habita Hotel, Masaryk 201, Metro Polanco, www.hotelhabita.com. Mon-Sat, from 1900. Swanky roof-top bar where hipsters and jet-set chosen ones congregate for evening cocktails.

Mezzanote, Masaryk 407, Metro Polanco, T55 5282 0130. Daily from 1400. Art nouveau decor, ideal for drinking, dining or dancing, especially later in the night. Franchise from the original in Miami, frequented by 30-somethings.

Insurgentes Sur *p113, map p94*

El Mitote, Amsterdam 33, Condesa, Metrobus Sonora, www.elmitote.com. Tue-Sat, from 2000. Popular with locals, a pleasant watering hole set in a charming old building.

Hookah Lounge, Campeche 284, Condesa, Metro Chilpancingo, Mon-Sat, from 1300. Styled on an Arabic smoking den with water-pipes and molasses tobacco for your consumption. DJs spin electronic tunes in the evenings.

La Bodeguita del Medio, Cozumel 37, Roma, Metro Sevilla, T55-5553 0246. Extremely popular Cuban bar-cum-restaurant where drinks like *mojitos*

became famous, and graffiti an art form.

Malafama, Michoacán 78, Condesa, Metro Patriotismo. Busy billiards hall with bottled Coronas and an array of stylish black and white photography.

Mamá Rumba, Querétaro 230 and Medellín, Roma, Metrobus Sonora, T55-5564 6920. One of the first places in Mexico City with Cuban rhythms, famous for its *rumba*, now with a couple of floors. Live music Thu-Sat from 2300. Also a new branch opened in San Angel (T55-5550 8099) with live music Wed-Sat from 2100. Get there early, it gets packed. US$6.

Pata Negra, Tamaulipas 30, Condesa, Metro Patriotismo. Daily 1330-0200. 2 floors of popular bar space that attracts moneyed Mexicans and crowds of international hipsters. Tapas is available too.

Rexo, Saltillo 1 and Nuevo León, Condesa, Metro Patriotismo, T55-5553 5337. Daily from 1330. Restaurant-bar with Mediterranean food, one of the most popular places in the area.

Coyoacán *p114, map p115*

El Hijo del Cuervo, Jardín Centenario 17, Metro Viveros, T55-5658 5306. Daily 1300-2400. Small cover (up to US$7) depending on show. Attracting students and hip intellectuals of all ages for an interesting mix of rock and *nueva canción*, and the occasional theatre show.

La Guadalupana, Higuera and Caballocalco, Metro Viveros. Atmospheric Coyoacán institution. See Eating, page 133.

Entertainment

For all cultural events, consult *Tiempo Libre*, every Thu from news-stands, US$1, or monthly programmes from **Bellas Artes** bookshop.

Cinema
A number show non-Hollywood films in original language (Spanish subtitles); check *Tiempo Libre* magazine for details.

Most cinemas, except **Cineteca Nacional**, offer reduced prices on Wed.

Cine Diana, Av Reforma, at the end where Parque Chapultepec starts, Metro Sevilla, T55-5511 3236.

Cinemax Plaza Insurgentes, San Luis Potosi 214, Metro Insurgentes, T55-5257-6969, www.cinemex.com.

Cinemex Palacio Chino, Iturbide 21, in the Chinese *barrio* south of Av Juárez (also an interesting area for restaurants), Metro Juárez, T55-5512 0348, www.cinemex.com.

Cinemex Real, Colón 17, Metro Hidalgo, T55-5257 6969, www.cinemex.com.

Lumiere Reforma, Río Guadalquivir 104, Metro Sevilla, T55-5514 0000.

For art-house films, courses in film appreciation or an otherwise more involved look at the cinematic form, try:

Cinematógrafo del Chopo, Dr Atl 37, Metro San Cosme, T55-5702 3494. Non-commercial films daily.

Cinemex Casa de Arte, France 120, Metro Polanco, T55-5280 9156, www.cinemex.com. Alternative, independent and art-house films.

Cineteca Nacional, Av México-Coyoacán 389, Metro Coyoacán, T55-1253 9390, www.cine tecanacional.net. Excellent bookshop on the cinema and related topics. They usually screen films by theme and also host the city's international film festival every Nov.

Ciudad Universitaria, Insurgentes Sur 3000, T55-5665 0709, www.filmoteca.unam.mx. The university's cultural centre has 2 good cinemas that regularly screen art-house films.

Theatre

Centro Histórico *p95, map p100*

Tickets for many shows can be acquired online from Ticket Master, www.ticketmaster.com.mx, whilst Mejor Teatro, www.mejorteatro. com.mx, has some information on current Spanish-language performances.

Centro Cultural Helénico, Revolución 1500, Metrobus Altavista, T55-4155 0919,

www.helenico.gob.mx. 450 seats with occasional Spanish-language productions.

Palacio de Bellas Artes, Hidalgo 1, Metro Bellas Artes, T55-5512 2593, www.bellasartes.gob.mx. For Ballet Folklórico, opera and classical concerts. For more information see page 104).

Teatro la Blanquita, Av Lázaro Cárdenas Sur near Plaza Garibaldi, Metro Bellas Artes, T55-5512 8264. Variety show nightly with singers, dancers, comedians, magicians and ventriloquists, very popular with locals.

Teatro de la Ciudad, Donceles 36, Metro Allende, T55-5510 2197. Has the Ballet Folklórico Nacional Aztlán, US$3-US$15, very good shows Sun morning and Wed.

Bosque de Chapultepec and Polanco *p108, map p108*

Auditorio Nacional, Paseo de la Reforma 50, Metro Auditorio, www.auditorio.com.mx. Major concerts and spectaculars (eg presidential inauguration) are often staged here. There are a couple of theatres behind the Auditorio (check at tourist office for details of programmes).

Insurgentes Sur *p113, map p94*

Teatro de los Insurgentes, Av Insurgentes Sur 1587, T55-5611 5047, south of the centre. Mostly Spanish-languange.

Teatro Universitario, Insurgentes Sur 3000, T55-5665 0709, www.difusion.cultural. unam.mx, at the UNAM's Centro Cultural has 5 theatres for music, dance and drama (see page 116).

Coyoacán *p114, map p115*

On the edge of the Delegación Coyoacán, at the southeast corner of Churubusco and Tlalpan (Metro General Anaya) is the **Central Nacional de las Artes**, T55-4155 0000, www.cenart.gob.mx, a huge complex of futuristic buildings dedicated to the training and display of the performing and visual arts. It has a good bookshop, library and *cafeterías*.

Coyoacán also has several small and medium-sized theatres, for example:

Teatro Coyoacán and Teatro Usigli, Eleuterio Méndez, 5 blocks from Metro General Anaya; Foro Cultural de Coyoacán, Allende (most events free of charge); Museo Nacional de Culturas Populares, Hidalgo; Foro Cultural Ana María Hernández, Pacífico 181; Teatro Santa Catarina, Plaza Santa Catarina; the Teatro Rafael Solana, Miguel Angel de Quevedo (nearly opposite Caballocalco; Casa del Teatro, Vallarta 31; and Foro de la Conchita, Vallarta 33.

Also note El Hábito, Madrid, and El Hijo del Cuervo, Jardín Centenario, for live music, avant-garde drama and cabaret; Los Talleres de Coyoacán, Francisco Sosa, for dance and ballet; CADAC, Centenario, for traditional and experimental drama.

❂ Festivals and events

17 Mar Día de San José. Several districts commemorate this date with music and processions.
Mar/Apr Festival del Centro Histórico, www.fchmexico.com. The Centro Histórico becomes a stage for vibrant international performances, concerts and gastronomic gatherings during this annual festival.
Mar/Apr Semana Santa. A joyous occasion across the country, but the Passion Play in Ixtapalapa district is particularly memorable, where the crucifixion is vividly re-enacted.
Mar/Apr Feria de la Flor Más Bella del Ejido. Xochimilco's annual festival of flowers sees a wealth of events including a beauty contest.
5 May Cinco de Mayo. National celebration commemorating the failed French invasion. Ixtapala is reported to be the most festive.
25 Jul Día de Santiago. In commemoration of St James, with a slew of folkloric performances at the Plaza de las Tres Culturas.
13 Aug The Fall of Tenochtitlán. In honour of Emperor Cuauhtémoc and the fallen Aztec Empire, troupes of *conchero* dancers convene on the Plaza de las Tres Culturas.
15 Sep Independence celebration; largest in the capital when the president gives the *Grito*: 'Viva México' from the Palacio Nacional on the Zócalo at 2300, and rings the Liberty Bell (now, sadly, electronic). This is followed by fireworks. Just as much fun, and probably safer, is the *Grito* that takes place at the same time in the plaza in Coyoacán.
16 Sep Military and traditional regional Independence parades in the Zócalo and surrounding streets, 0900-1400, great atmosphere.
1-2 Nov Día de los Muertos. Mexico's national celebration of the dead is a memorable and spirited affair in the capital. Locals compete for the most beautiful and artistic *ofrendas* (altars) with impressive public displays in the Zócalo and across the city. Night-time vigils take place in various locations including the Panteón Civil, Bosque de Chapultepec 2a Sección, San Andrés Mixquic, San Lucas Xochimanca, Santa Cecilia Tepetlapa and San Antonio Tecómitl.
22 Nov Fiesta de Santa Cecilia. In honour of the patron saint of musicians, with lots of crooning at plaza Garibaldi and around.
12 Dec Guadalupana at the Basílica de Guadalupe, is definitely worth a visit if you're in town (see page 120). The festival honours the patron saint of Mexico with millions of pilgrims descending upon the sacred site.

❍ Shopping

Art and handicrafts

Fonart, Fondo Nacional para el Fomento de las Artesanías, a state organization founded in 1974 in order to rescue, promote and diffuse the traditional crafts of Mexico. Main showroom at Av Patriotismo 691, Metro Mixcoac, T55-5598 1666, and branches at Av Juárez 89, Metro Hidalgo, and Paseo de la Reforma 116, Metro Cuauhtémoc. Competitive prices and superb quality.
Mercado de Artesanías Finas Indios Verdes, Galería Reforma Norte SA, González Bocanegra 44 (corner of Reforma Norte, near statue of Cuitláhuac, Tlatelolco). Good prices and quality but no bargaining.

Uriarte, Emilio Castelar 95-E, Polanco, T55-5282 2699, and Pabellón Altavista, Calzada Desierto de los Leones 52 D-6, San Angel, T55-5616 3119, www.uriarte talavera.com.mx. For Talavera pottery from Puebla.

There are many gift shops in **Coyoacán**: **Mayolih**, Aldama with Berlín, 2 blocks from Museo Frida Kahlo; and **La Casita** on Higuera.

Bicycle shops
Benolto, near Metro Polanco, stocks almost all cycle spares.

Escuela Médico Militar, near Metro Pino Suárez, has a very good shop, stocking all the best-known makes for spare parts.

Hambling González Muller, Ezequiel Ordóñez 46-1, Col Copilco el Alto, Coyoacán, Metro Viveros, T/F55-5658 5591. The best cycle repair in Mexico City. Builds wheels and frames for Mexican racers, reasonable prices. Highly recommended.

Tecno-Bici, Av Manuel Acuña 27 (Metro Camarones, line 7), stocks almost all cycle spares, parts. Highly recommended.

Books, posters and music
American Bookstore, Bolívar 23Metro San Juan de Letrán, has large stocks of Penguins and Pelicans, low mark-up.

Casa Libros, Monte Athos 355, Lomas, large stock of second-hand English books, staffed by volunteers, gifts of books welcome, all proceeds to the American Benevolent Society.

El Parnaso, Jardín Centenario, Coyoacán, Metro Viveros. One of the most famous bookshops in Mexico City (its coffee is equally well known).

Fondo de Cultura Económico, Miguel Angel de Quevedo. Inexpensive editions in Spanish.

Gandhi has several shops with a big selection and keen prices. Large branches on Miguel Angel de Quevedo, another opposite Palacio de Bellas Artes. Good range of music, excellent prices.

John Gibbs Publications, T/F55-5658 5376, www.johngibbs.com. Supplies fine art posters, including images by Diego Rivera and Frida Kahlo, to the city's principal museums and bookshops.

La Torre de Papel, Filomeno Mata 6-A, in Club de Periodistas, sells newspapers from all over Mexico and US.

Librería del Sótano, several branches: Av Juárez, Antonio Caso, Miguel Angel de Quevedo). Inexpensive editions in Spanish.

Librería Madero, Madero 12, Centro. Good, stocks antiquarian books.

Libros y Arte is a good chain of literary and art bookshops with branches in the Palacio de Bellas Artes, the airport (area D), the Centro Nacional de Las Artes, the Cineteca Nacional, Coyoacán (Av Hidalgo), Museo del Carmen (San Angel) and the Museo Nacional de las Culturas (Moneda 13, Centro).

Sanborn's chain has the largest selection of English-language magazines in the country and stocks some best-selling paperbacks in English.

Second-hand book market, Independencia just past junction with Eje Lázaro Cárdenas. Has some English books; also Puente de Alvarado, 100 m from Metro Hidalgo, and Dr Bernard 42, Metro Niños Héroes. Second-hand Spanish and antiquarian booksellers on Donceles between Palma and República de Brasil, about 1½ blocks from Zócalo.

UNAM bookshop, Ciudad Universitaria. Has a comprehensive range of books in Spanish.

Clothing and accessories
Mexican jewellery and handmade silver can be bought everywhere. Among the good silver shops are **Sanborn's**, **Calpini**, **Prieto**, and **Vendome**.

Joyería Sobre Diseño, Local 159, at the Ciudadela market. Helpful and will produce personalized jewellery cheaply. There are also good buys in perfumes, quality leather and suede articles.

Many small tailors are found in and around República de Brasil; suits made to measure in a week or less at a fraction of European prices. Also many off-the-peg tailors, eg **Beleshini**, Juárez 12, opposite the Palacio de Bellas Artes.

At Metro Pino Suárez are several shops selling *charro* clothing and equipment (leggings, boots, spurs, bags, saddles, etc), eg **Casa Iturriaga**. Recommended.

Markets

Bazar del Sábado, San Angel (page 114), Metrobus La Bombilla, Sat only from about 1100. Although expensive, many items are exclusive to it; good leather belts, crafts and silver.

Buena Vista craft market, Aldama 187 y Degollado, Metro Guerrero. Mon-Sat 0900-1800, Sun 0900-1400. Excellent quality.

La Ciudadela, Mercado Central de Artesanías, beside Balderas 95 between Ayuntamiento y Plaza Morelos, Metro Balderas. Mon-Sat 1100-1800, Sun 1100-1400. Government-sponsored with fixed prices and good selection. Reasonable and uncrowded, and generally cheaper than San Juan, but not for leather. Craftworkers from all Mexico have set up workshops here (best for papier mâché, lacquer, pottery and Guatemalan goods), but prices are still cheaper in places of origin.

Mercado Insurgentes, Londres, Metro Insurgentes. Good for silver, but other items are expensive. The stallholders pester visitors – the only place where they do so.

Mercado Jamaica, Metro Jamaica, line 4 Has a huge variety of fruits and vegetables, also flowers, pottery, canaries, parrots, geese, and ducks, indoor and outdoor halls.

Mercado La Lagunilla, near Glorieta Cuitláhuac, take a *colectivo* from Metro Hidalgo. Open daily, but Sun is the best day. A flea market covering several blocks where antique and collectable bargains are sometimes to be found, also a lot of rubbish. Good atmosphere, but watch your bag.

Mercado Merced (page 102), Metro Merced. Vast general market that covers several city blocks and sells everything. Beware of thieves.

Mercado San Juan, Ayuntamiento and Arandas, Metro Salto del Agua. Mon-Sat 0900-1900, Sun 0900-1600 (don't go before 1000). Good prices for handicrafts, especially leather goods and silver (also cheap fruit and health food).

Mercado Sonora, Metro Merced. Sells secret potions, spells and remedies, animals and birds as well as *artesanías*. Resist the wizened old ladies beseeching you in the darkness.

Tianguis del Chopo, Aldama, No 211, between Sol and Luna, Metro Buenavista. Sat 1000-1600. Clothes, records, etc, frequented by hippies, punks, rockers and police.

Photography

Foto Regis, Balderas 32, 4th floor, T55-5521 5010, www.fotoregis.com. Mon-Fri 0900-1800, Sat 0900-1400. Good service on a range of makes including Canon, Minolta, Pentax, Hasselblad, Konica and Leica. Reasonably priced as well. Also provides good-quality, reliable development at shop on Juárez 80, T55-5521 0346.

▲ Activities and tours

Hiking

At weekend with Alpino and Everest clubs.

Club Alpino Mexicano, Coahuila 40 esq Córdoba, Roma, T55-5574 9683, www.clubalpinomexicano.com.mx. Small shop (if club door is closed ask here for access). Helpful, also arranges (free) mountain hiking at weekends, runs ice-climbing courses.

Club de Exploraciones de México, Juan A Mateos 146, Col Obrero, Metro Chabacano, T55-5740 8032, www.cemac.org.mx. Meetings Wed and Fri 1930-2200, organizes several walks in and around the city on Sat and Sun, cheap equipment hire.

Supplies and repairs

Coleman Camping Gear, Vicente Guerrero No 3, local 3, casi esq Gustavo Baz, Col El Mirador, T55-2628 0622. Coleman camping supplies.

Deportes Rubens, Venustiano Carranza 17, T55-5518 5636, www.dscorp.com.mx/rubens. Supplies good selection of outdoor gear including climbing kit.

Vertimania, Federico T de la Chica 12, Plaza Versailles, Local 11-B, Col Satélite, T/F55-5393 5287. Supplies equipment.

Spectator sports
Bullfights
Monumental Plaza México, Rodin 241, Nápoles, T55-5563 3961. One of the world's largest bull-rings with a near 50,000 capacity. Professional fights run every Sun, Nov-Mar. Aspiring professionals practise Jun-Oct. As usual the cheapest seats are in the sunny section, around US$20.

Football
Estadio Azteca, south of the city. Sun 1200. To get to the Aztec Stadium take metro to Taxqueña terminus, then tram en route to Xochimilco to Estadio station; about 75 mins from Zócalo. To find out what's on visit www.esmas.com/estadioazteca (Spanish only).

Horse races
Hipódromo de las Américas, west of Blv Avila Camacho, off Av Conscriptos, www.hipodromo.com.mx. Beautiful track with infield lagoons and flamingos, and plenty of atmosphere. Incorporates exhibition and convention centre.

Lucha Libre
There are 2 principle arenas where you can catch a theatrical Lucha Libre wrestling performance, something of a national 'sport': **Arena Coliseo**, Perú 77, Metro Lagunilla, T55-5526 1687. Tue and Sun from 1700. **Arena de México**, Dr Lavista 197, Col Doctores, Metro Cuauhtémoc, T55-5588 0508, www.arenamexico.com.mx. Every Fri from 2030.

Tour operators
Shop around as prices vary considerably, although deals regularly available in Europe or the USA are rare or impossible to find. If possible, use a travel agent that has been recommended to you, as not all are efficient or reliable. Hotels and hostels are often able to book excursions and in some cases flights. This is often more convenient. **American Express**, Reforma 350, T55-5207 7282. Mon-Fri 0900-1800, Sat 0900-1300. Helpful.

Corresponsales de Hoteles, Pilares 231 Local 6, del Valle, T55-5575 5500, www.corresponsales.com.mx. For upmarket hotel reservations.

Grey Line Tours, Londres 166, T55-5208 1163, www.mexitours.com.mx. Reasonably priced tours, car hire, produces This is Mexico book (free).

Hivisa Viajes, Av Paseo de la Reforma 505 PB Loc 7, Col Cuauhtémoc, T55-5212 0812, www.hivisaviajes.com.mx. One of the most reliable. Good for flights to Europe, Central and South America, and for changing flight dates, English spoken, ask for Icarus Monk.

Mundo Joven Travel Shop, Guatemala 4, Col Centro, T55-5518 1755, www.mundo joven.com. Issues ISIC card, agents for International Youth Hostel Federation.

Protures Viajes, Av Baja California 46, Col Roma Sur, T55-5482 8282. Recommended agency for flights to Central and South America and Cuba.

Turibus, www.turibus.com.mx, 0900-2100. This open-top double-decker tour bus departs every 30 mins from near the Zócalo and trawls the major sights, including Paseo de la Reforma. Tickets are sold as 1-, 2- or 3-day passes and allow users to get on and off at will. A complete circuit takes around 3 hrs.

Viajes Tirol, José Ma Rico 212, Depto 503, T55-5534 5582. English and German spoken, recommended.

Adventure and ecotourism specialists
Al Aire Libre, Centro Comercial Interlomas, Local 2122, Lomas Anáhuac Huixquilucan, T55-5291 9217. Rafting (Ríos Pescados-Antigua, Santa María, Amacuzac), climbing, caving (Chontalcuatlán, Zacatecoltla, La Joya), ballooning, parapenting.

Asociación Mexicana de Turismo de Aventura y Ecoturismo (AMTAVE), Río y Montaña, Prado Norte 450-T, Lomas de Chapultepec, T/F55-5520 2041, www.am tave.org. Regulates and promotes many of the agencies listed. Not all areas of adventure sport come under their umbrella, for instance specialist diving agencies remain unattached to any Mexico-based organization, as diving is a mainly regional activity. But a very good wide-ranging list of members.

⊖ Transport

Air
Airport information
The well-equipped and expanding **Benito Juárez International Airport**, 155-5571-3214, www.aicm.com.mx, with 2 terminals is divided into sections, each designated by a letter. A row of shops and offices outside each section provides exchange, ATMs and shopping services. Information available at:

Sala A Domestic Arrivals; AeroMéxico, post office, city of Mexico tourist office, exit to taxis and metro, INAH shop, telecommunications office.
Sala A-B AeroMéxico; Bancomer ATM.
Sala B Click Mexicana, Aeromar, Mexicana.
Salas B-C Entrance to Continental Plaza hotel, *casa de cambio*.
Sala C Aviacsa; map shop.
Salas C and D Ladatel phones just after C. **Exposición Diego Rivera** exhibition hall. Other national airline offices; bookshop.
Sala D National and International Departures; *cambio* opposite; more national airline desks; long-distance phones; a bar and restaurant.
From Sala D you must leave the building to get to:
Salas F1-3 International check-in; banks.
Sala G International Departures.

Money exchange
Pesos may be bought at any of the bank branches liberally spread throughout the airport. Most foreign currencies or TCs are accepted, also most credit cards.

Telephones
Many phones at the airport, you'll have to keep looking until you find one that works. Look for the Lada *multi-tarjeta* phones. There is a phone office at the far end of Sala F, which accepts Amex and, in theory, Visa, MasterCard and other cards.

Hotel bookings
There are airport information kiosks at Salas A and E1 (interational arrivals). There is a hotel desk before passing through customs. The tourist office at A has phones for calling hotels, no charge, helpful, but Spanish only. The travel agency at east exit will book hotels or reconfirm flights.

Transport from the airport
Taxi Fixed-price 'Transporte Terrestre' taxis by zone, buy tickets from booths at exits by Salas A, E and F; you can buy tickets before passing customs but they are cheaper outside the duty-free area; rates vary, around US$15 to the **Centre/Zócalo**, according to distance (per vehicle, not per person), drivers may not know or may be unwilling to go to cheaper hotels. For losses or complaints about airport taxis, T55-5571 3600 ext 2299; for reservations T55-5571 9344, daily 0800-0200. The fixed-price taxi system is efficient and safe. A cheaper alternative (about 50%) if you don't have too much luggage is to cross the Blv Puerto Aéreo by the Metro Terminal Aérea and flag down an ordinary taxi outside the **Ramada** hotel.

Bus There are regular buses from the city centre to the airport (eg No 20, along north side of the Alameda), but the drawback is that you have to take one to Calzada Ignacio Zaragoza and transfer to a trolley bus at the Blv Puerto Aéreo (ie at Metro Terminal Aérea). Buses to the airport may be caught every 45 mins until 0100 from outside **Hotel de Carlo**, Plaza de la República 35. It takes 1 hr from downtown (and, in the rush hour, most of the day, it is jam-packed), but you can take baggage if you can squeeze it in.

Long-distance buses Frequent long-distance buses to **Cuernavaca**, **Puebla**, **Querétaro**, **Toluca**, **Pachuca** and **Córdoba** direct from the airport. See map, page 94, for location of terminals. For details of bus services, see destinations in text.

Metro To get to the airport cheaply, take the metro to Terminal Aérea and walk, or take metro to Blv Puerto Aéreo and then a *pesero* marked 'Oceanía', which will leave you at the Terminal metro station.

Airline offices

See page 37 for web addresses. Many airline offices are on Paseo de la Reforma or Hamburgo.
Aero California, Reforma 332, T55-5207 1392. **Air Canada**, Reforma 398-14, T55-5207 6611. **AeroMéxico**, Reforma 445, T55-5133 4010. **Air France**, Edgar Allan Poe 90, T55-5627 6011. **Alitalia**, Río Tiber 103, 6th floor, T55-5533 1240. **American Airlines**, Reforma 300, T55-5209 1400. **Avensa**, Reforma 325, T55-5208 4998. **Avianca**, Reforma 195, T55-5566 8580. **British Airways**, Jaime Balmes 8, Los Morales, T55-5387 0321. **Canadian Airlines**, Reforma 390, T55-5207 6611. **Continental**, Andrés Bello 45, T55-5280 1567. **Delta**, Horacio 1855 1st floor, Polanco, T55-5279 0820. **El Al**, Paseo de las Palmas, T55-5735 1105. **Iberia**, Av Ejército Nacional 436, 9th floor, T55-1101 1515. **Japan Airlines**, Reforma 295, T55-5533 6580. **KLM**, Paseo de las Palmas 735, T55-5202 4444. **Lufthansa**, Paseo de las Palmas 239, T55-5230 0000. **Mexicana**, Xola 535, Col del Valle, T55-5448 3000. **Northwest Airlines**, Reforma y Amberes 312, T55-5511 3579, Reforma 300, T55-5525 7090. **SAS**, Hamburgo 61, T55-5533 0098. **Swissair**, Hamburgo 66, T55-5533 6363. **Taca**, Morelos 108, Col Juárez, T55-5546 8807. **United Airlines**, Hamburgo 213, loc 23-24, T55-5250 1657.

Bus
Local

An efficient new bus service, Metrobus, runs the length of Insurgentes from Metro Indios Verdes to San Angel. Plans are underway to extend it further south. The Metrobus runs 0430-2400 and is particularly useful for getting to and from the restaurants in Roma and Condesa, as well as the Ciudad Universitaria. You'll need to buy a rechargeable smartcard at one of the stops, US$1, and 'touch in' at the barriers. Fares are US$0.50 per journey – 'top up' using the automated machines.

The city's other buses have been coordinated into a single system: odd numbers run north–south, evens east–west. Fares on large buses, which display routes on the windscreen, are US$0.20, exact fare only. There are 60 direct routes and 48 feeder (SARO) routes. Thieves and pickpockets haunt the buses along Reforma and Juárez. A useful route for tourists (and well known to thieves) is No 76, which runs from Uruguay (about the level of the Juárez Monument at Parque Alameda) along Paseo de la Reforma, beside Chapultepec Park. A *Peribus* service goes round the entire Anillo Periférico. Most buses run 0500-2000; some routes on Reforma run 24 hrs.

Long distance

This is how Mexico travels. At all bus stations there are many counters for the bus companies, not all are manned and it is essential to ask which is selling tickets for the destination you want (don't take noticeboards at face value). On the whole, the bus stations are clean and well organized. Book ahead where possible.
Terminal del Norte, Av Cien Metros 4907, T55-5587 1552, www.centraldel norte.com.mx, for destinations in north Mexico, including US borders. There is a *casa de cambio*, 24-hr cafés, left luggage, pharmacy, bakery and phone offices for long-distance calls (often closed and poorly informed, very high charges). The bus station is at Metro Autobuses del Norte, Line 5.

City buses marked 'Cien Metros' or 'Central del Norte' go directly there.

Terminal del Sur, at corner of Tlalpan 2205, across from Metro Taxqueña, Line 2, serves **Cuernavaca**, **Acapulco**, **Oaxaca** and **Zihuatanejo** areas. Direct buses to centre (Donceles) from Terminal del Sur, and an express bus connects the Sur and Norte terminals. It can be difficult to get tickets to the south, book as far in advance as possible; the terminal can be chaotic.

Terminal Poniente is situated opposite the Metro Observatorio, Line 1 of the metro, to serve the west of Mexico. You can go to the centre by bus from the *urbano* outside the bus station, Terminal Poniente (US$0.10).

Terminal Oriente, known as TAPO, Calzada Ignacio Zaragoza, Metro San Lázaro, Line 1 for buses to **Veracruz**, **Yucatán** and southeast, including **Oaxaca** and **Puebla** (2 hrs). It has a tourist information office open from 0900; luggage lockers, US$2.65 per day; key is left with guard; post office, *farmacia* changes TCs. To **Guatemala**, from TAPO, take a bus to Tapachula, Comitán or Cd Cuauhtémoc, pesos only accepted.

Mexico City Airport There are also buses departing from the airport (outside Sala D) to **Cordoba**, **Cuernavaca**, **Pachuca**, **Puebla**, **Querétaro** and **Toluca**, very convenient if you don't want to head into town.

Schedules and fares

Bus frequencies, prices, terminals of departure and journey times are given below. Note that schedules are subject to seasonal changes, as are prices, which also vary with the vagaries of exchange rates and oil prices. They are given here only approximately. As a general rule, you should expect to pay US$3.50-US$4.50 per hr of 1st-class travel (50-60 pesos). Luxury services are generally around 30% more expensive than 1st class; 2nd-class buses are around a 3rd cheaper than 1st class. Services from the airport to **Cuernavaca**, **Puebla**, **Querétero**, **Pachuca** and **Toluca** are around US$5 more expensive than standard services from the city.

To **Acapulco**, Sur/Norte, every 30 mins-1 hr, 5 hrs, US$22.50. To **Aguascalientes**, Norte, every 1-2 hrs, 6 hrs, US$27. To **Bahías de Huatulco**, Sur/Norte/TAPO, 1-2 daily from each terminal, 15 hrs, US$52.50. To **Campeche**, TAPO, 5 daily, 17 hrs, US$76.50. To **Cancún**, TAPO, 5 daily, 24 hrs, US$108. To **Chetumal**, TAPO, 4 daily, 19 hrs, US$95. To **Chihuahua**, Norte, 10 daily, 20 hrs, US$90. To **Ciudad Juárez**, Norte, 10 daily, 24 hrs, US$108. To **Cuernavaca**, Sur/Airport, every ½ hr, 1½ hrs, US$7. To **Durango**, Norte, 10 daily, 12 hrs, US$54. To **Guadalajara**, Norte/Poniente, hourly, 7 hrs, US$31.50. To **Guanajuato**, Norte, 11 daily, 5 hrs, US$25. To **Guaymas**, Norte, 12 daily, 30 hrs, US$135. To **León**, Norte, hourly, 5 hrs, US$22.50. To **Malinalco**, Norte, 3 daily, 2 hrs, US$9. To **Manzanillo**, Norte, 3 daily, 12 hrs, US$54. To **Matamoros**, Norte, 10 daily, 14 hrs, US$63. To **Matehuala**, Norte, 10 daily, 8 hrs, US$36. To **Mazatlán**, Norte, hourly, 16 hrs, US$72. To **Mérida**, TAPO, 5 daily, 20 hrs, US$90. To **Mexicalli**, Norte, hourly, 48 hrs, US$216. To **Monterrey**, Norte, every hour, 12 hrs, US$54. To **Morelia**, Poniente/Norte, every ½ hr, 5 hrs, US$22.50. To **Nuevo Laredo**, Norte, every hour, 16 hrs, US$72. To **Oaxaca**, TAPO, every hour, 6 hrs, US$27. To **Orizaba**, TAPO, every hour, 5 hrs, US$22.50. To **Pachuca**, Norte, every 15 mins, 1½ hrs, US$6.75. To **Palenque**, TAPO, 2 daily, 14 hrs, US$63. To **Papantla**, Norte, 4 daily, 5 hrs, US$22.50. To **Pátzcuaro**, Poniente, every 1-2 hrs with some from Norte also, 5 hrs, US$22.50. To **Puebla**, TAPO/Norte/Airport, every 15 mins, 2 hrs, US$9. To **Puerto Escondido**, Sur/TAPO, 3-4 daily, 14 hrs, US$63. To **Puerto Vallarta**, Norte, 4 daily, 13 hrs, US$58.50. To **Querétaro**, Norte/ Airport, every 30 mins, 3 hrs, US$13.50. To **Saltillo**, Norte, 12 daily, 10 hrs, US$45. To **San Cristóbal de las Casas**, TAPO, 4 daily, 13 hrs, US$58.50. To **San Luis Potosí**, Norte, every hr, 5 hrs, US$22.50. To **San Miguel de**

Allende, Norte, every hr, 4 hrs, US$18. To Tapachula, TAPO, 6 daily, 18 hrs, US$81. To Taxco, Sur, every hr, 2½ hrs, US$11.25. To Tehuantepec, TAPO, 2 daily, 11 hrs, US$49.50. To Teotihuacán, Norte, every 15 mins, 1 hr, US$4.50. To Tepic, Norte, every hr, 10 hrs, US$45. To Tepoztlán, Sur, every ½ hr, 1½ hrs, US$6.75 To Tijuana, Norte, every hr, 41 hrs, US$184.50. To Tlaxcala, TAPO, every ½ hr, 2 hrs, US$9. To Toluca, Poniente/Airport, every 15 mins, 1 hr, US$4.50. To Tula, Norte, every ½ hr, 1½ hrs, US$6.75. To Tuxpan, Norte, every hr, 5 hrs, US$22.50. To Tuxtla Gutiérrez, TAPO, 10 daily, 12 hrs, US$54. To Uruapan, Poniente/Norte, every 1-2 hrs, 6 hrs, US$27. To Valle de Bravo, Poniente, every ½ hr, 3 hrs, US$13.50. To Veracruz, TAPO, every hr, 5-6 hrs, US$22.50. To Villahermosa, TAPO, 12 daily, 11 hrs, US$49.50. To Xalapa, TAPO, every hr, 5 hrs, US$22.50. To Zacatecas, Norte, every hr, 8 hrs, US$36. To Zihuatanejo, Sur, 6 daily, 9 hrs, US$40.50.

Booking
Advance booking is recommended for all trips over 6 hrs. You can book tickets for some destinations through Ticket Bus, www.ticketbus.com.mx, either on-line or through one of their many offices. Otherwise you must go and queue at the bus stations. This is usually painless, but can occasionally involve a long wait during peak periods. It is essential to book very early if travelling to fiestas during Easter Week or other important celebrations, including all regional festivals. Expect crowds and chaos during such times. At Christmas, many Central American students return home via Tapachula, and buses to and from Mexico City are booked solid for 2 weeks beforehand (except for those lines that do not make reservations). Note that many bus companies require luggage to be checked in 30 mins in advance of departure.

Transport from terminals
All bus terminals operate taxis with voucher system and there are long queues (check change carefully at the taxi office). It is much easier to pay the driver, although beware of extra charges. The terminals are connected by metro, but this is not a good option at rush hour, or if carrying too much luggage.

Bus companies
Mexico's long-distance bus network is privately owned by a plethora of competing companies, including a staggering array of 2nd- and 1st-class subsidiaries. As such, the system is complex and initially baffling. In practice though, shopping around for 1st-class fares – where possible – does not yield significant differences in cost or service. The most expensive luxury lines are comfortably kitted out with reclining seats and icy a/c (not so comfortable).
Estrella de Oro, T55-5649 8520, www.auto bus.com.mx, runs to Guerrero state and coast, Cuernavaca, Puebla and Veracruz.
Estrella Roja, T55-5130 1800, www.estrella roja.com.mx, operates services between Puebla State and the capital.
ETN, T55-5089 9200, www.etn.com.mx, is a reputable operator and runs to major destinations in Western, Central and Northeast Mexico.
Grupo ADO, T55-5133 2424, www.ado.com.mx, is a major player with several 1st-class and luxury lines: ADO, ADO GL, UNO, OCC and AU. They serve Eastern and Southern Mexico, including the states of Puebla, Veracruz, Oaxaca, Chiapas, Tabasco and the Yucatán Peninsula.
Grupo Estrella Blanca, T55-5729 0807, www.estrellablanca.com.mx, is also a formidable empire: Estrella Blanca, Futura Primera, Futura Plus, Transportes Chihuahuenses, Elite, Oriente, Autobuses Americanos, Transportes Frontera, Pacifico and Norte de Sonora are among their lines. They travel widely throughout Central, Western and Northern Mexico, with some limited services to Oaxaca and Guerrero too.

Omnibus de México, T800-765 6636, www.odm.com.mx, is also a big name and runs extensive services throughout Western, Central and Northern Mexico.

Primera Plus and **Flecha Amarilla**, T55-5567 7887, www.flecha-amarilla.com.mx, operate throughout central and western Mexico.

Pullman de Morelos, www.pullman.com.mx, is a minor company that serves Cuernavaca and other Morelos destinations.

Car

If you have a car in the city, find a cheap hotel to park and explore the city by bus, metro or on foot. If you are planning to hire a car, it is generally cheaper to organize it from the USA or Europe. To reduce pollution, cars are required to stay off the road for 1 working day a week. When driving in the capital you must check which *hoy no circula* applies to your vehicle's number plate; if your car is being driven when its number is prohibited, you could be fined US$80. This should not apply to foreign-licensed cars. The regulation covers the State of México as well as the Distrito Federal. The ban applies to the last digit of your number plate: **Mon** 5 & 6; **Tue** 7 & 8; **Wed** 3 & 4; **Thu** 1 & 2; **Fri** 9 & 0. Occasionally, when contamination levels are even worse than usual, the programme runs at weekends too: **Sat**, all even numbers and 0; **Sun**, all odd numbers. Normally, you can drive freely in 'greater' Mexico City on Sat, Sun and between 2200 and 0500 all week.

Car hire

Most car hire firms are concentrated in the Zona Rosa, particularly along Reforma. Local companies tend to be cheaper. **Avis**, Reforma 308 (across from US Embassy), T55-5511 2228. **Budget**, Atenas 40, T55-5566 8815. **Hertz**, Versalles 6, T55-5128 1699. **National**, Reforma 107, T55-5703 2222.

Metro

An efficient, modern system and the best method of getting around the city,

especially when the pollution is bad. Trains are fast, frequent, clean and quiet although over-crowded during rush hours, 0730-1000 and 1500 2000. Look out for the colourful *vendedores* with loud speakers strapped to their backs. Between 1800 and 2100 men are separated from women and children at Pino Suárez and certain other central stations. 2 pieces of medium-sized luggage are permitted.

Beware of pickpocketing on the metro. It's not especially dangerous, more a natural aspect of large numbers of people. Pino Suárez, Hidalgo and Autobuses del Norte are particularly infamous for thieves.

Tickets and times

Tickets cost 2 pesos, and it's best to buy several to avoid queuing every time you take a trip. Check train direction before entering turnstile or you may have to pay again.

The service operates Mon-Fri 0500-2400, Sat 0600-2400 and Sun and holidays 0700-2400.

Metro information

Maps of the metro are included in the city maps distributed by the City Tourist Information Booths. There is also a metro information service at Insurgentes station on the Pink Line 1, which dispenses maps, and most interchange stations have information kiosks. All the stations have a symbol, eg the grasshopper signifying Chapultepec, and there is a detailed local street map of the immediate vicinity – *planos de barrio* – at every station. There are 9 lines in service.

Line 1 (pink) from **Observatorio** (by Chapultepec Park) to **Pantitlán** in the eastern suburbs. It goes under Av Chapultepec and not far from the lower half of Paseo de la Reforma, the Mercado Merced, and 3 km from the airport.

Line 2 (blue) from **Cuatro Caminos** in the northwest to the Zócalo and then south above ground to **Taxqueña**.

Line 3 (olive) from Indios Verdes south

8 Mexico City metro

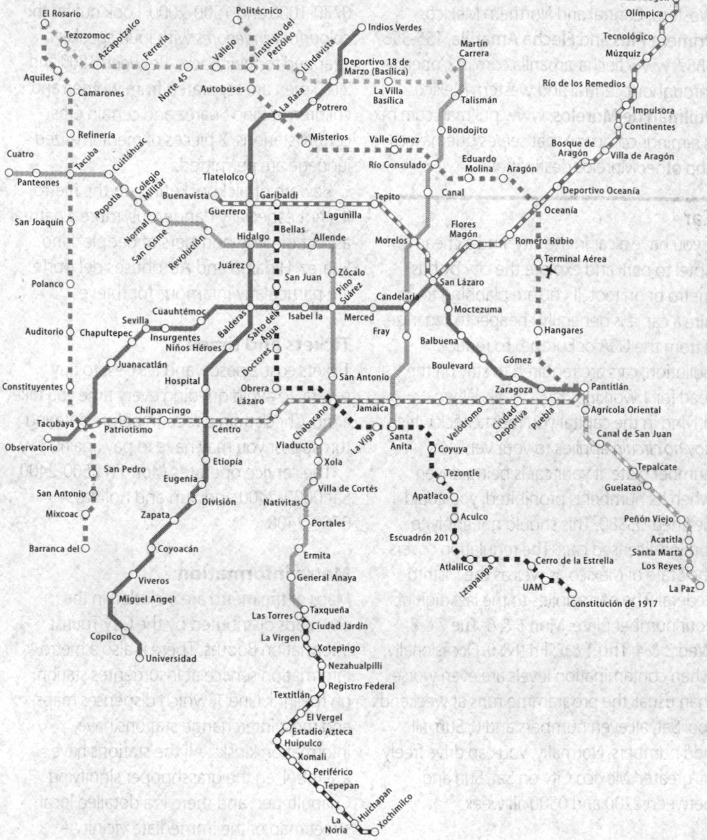

Ciudad Azteca
Plaza Aragón
Olímpica
Tecnológico
Múzquiz

El Rosario
Tezozomoc
Azcapotzalco
Ferrería
Vallejo
Instituto del Petróleo
Lindavista
Indios Verdes
Martín Carrera

Aquiles
Camarones
Norte 45
Autobuses
La Raza
Deportivo 18 de Marzo (Basílica)
La Villa Basílica
Talismán
Río de los Remedios

Refinería
Potrero
Impulsora
Continentes

Cuatro
Tacuba
Cuitláhuac
Misterios
Valle Gómez
Bondojito
Bosque de Aragón
Villa de Aragón

Panteones
Popotla
Colegio Militar
Tlatelolco
Río Consulado
Eduardo Molina
Aragón
Deportivo Oceanía

San Joaquín
Buenavista
Garibaldi
Tepito
Canal
Oceanía

Normal
Guerrero
Lagunilla
Flores Magón
Romero Rubio

San Cosme
Hidalgo
Bellas Artes
Allende
Morelos
Terminal Aérea

Revolución
Juárez
San Juan
Zócalo
Pino Suárez
Candelaria
San Lázaro
Hangares

Polanco
Cuauhtémoc
Balderas
Isabel la Católica
Merced
Moctezuma

Auditorio
Sevilla
Insurgentes
Salto del Agua
Fray
Balbuena
Gómez

Chapultepec
Niños Héroes
Doctores
Pantitlán

Juanacatlán
Hospital
San Antonio
Boulevard
Agrícola Oriental

Constituyentes
Obrera
Lázaro
Jamaica
Velódromo
Ciudad Deportiva
Puebla
Canal de San Juan

Chilpancingo
Zaragoza

Tacubaya
Patriotismo
Centro
Chabacano
La Viga
Santa Anita
Coyuya
Tepalcate

Observatorio
Viaducto
Xola
Guelatao

San Pedro
Etiopía
Tezontle

Eugenia
Villa de Cortés
Apatlaco
Aculco
Peñón Viejo

San Antonio
Zapata
División
Nativitas
Portales
Escuadrón 201
Atlalilco
Cerro de la Estrella
Acatitla
Santa Marta
Los Reyes

Mixcoac
Coyoacán
Ermita
Iztapalapa
UAM
La Paz

Barranca del
Viveros
General Anaya
Constitución de 1917

Miguel Angel
Taxqueña

Copilco
Las Torres
Ciudad Jardín

Universidad
La Virgen
Xotepingo
Nezahualpilli
Registro Federal

Textitlán
El Vergel
Estadio Azteca
Huipulco
Xomali
Periférico
Tepepan
La Noria
Huichapan
Xochimilco

➡ Mexico City maps

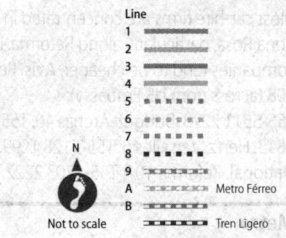

Line
1
2
3
4
5
6
7
8
9
A — Metro Férreo
B — Tren Ligero

N
Not to scale

to the **University City** (free bus service to Insurgentes).

Line 4 (turquoise) from **Santa Anita** on the southeast side to **Martín Carrera** in the northeast.

Line 5 (yellow) from **Pantitlán**, via Terminal Aérea (which is within walking distance of gate A of the airport, but some distance from the international gates – opens 0600), up to **Politécnico** (if using La Raza to connect with Line 3, note that there is a long walk between Lines 5 and 3, through the Tunnel of Knowledge).

Line 6 (red) from **El Rosario** in the northwest to **Martín Carrera** in the northeast.

Line 7 (orange) from **El Rosario** (northwest) to **Barranca del Muerto** in the southwest.

Line 8 (green) from **Garibaldi** (north of Bellas Artes, Line 2), through Chabacano (Line 9) and Santa Anita (Line 4), to **Constitución de 1917** in the southeast.

Line 9 (brown) parallel to Line 1 to the south, running from **Tacubaya** in the west (where there are interesting paintings in the station) to **Pantitlán** in the east.

In addition to the numbered lines:

Line A (*metro férreo*) southeast from Pantitlán as far as **La Paz** (10 stations in all).

Line B, from Buenavista to Cd Azteca in **Ecatepec**, north of the city.

Tren ligero From Taxqueña to **Xochimilco**, a very convenient route.

Art in the metro

At the **Zócalo** metro station there is an interesting permanent exhibit about the city. At **Pino Suárez**, the station has been built around a small, restored Aztec temple. Other places of interest in the network include Line 1, Pino Suárez and Tacubaya; Line 2, Bellas Artes and Panteones; Line 3, La Raza, scientific display In the Tunnel of Knowledge, and south of Coyoacán; Line 4, Santa Anita; Line 5, Terminal Aérea; Line 6, all stations, Line 7, Barranca del Muerto; Line 9, Mixuca.

Taxi

Turismo taxis Operate from 1st-class hotels, the Museo Nacional de Antropología, etc and are the most expensive.

Sitio taxis (fixed ranks) Operate from bus terminals, railway station and other locations; no meters. About double the normal price but safer. You pay in advance at a booth (check your change); they charge on a zone basis, US$4.60 for up to 4 km, rising to US$22 for up to 22 km (the same system applies at the airport – see above). You can also phone for a sitio taxi: **Radiotaxi**, T55-5566 077, **Servitaxis** T55-5271 2560, **Taximex** T55-5519 7690, **Transportación Terrestre al Aeropuerto**, for trips to and from the airport, T55-5571 3600.

Taxis on unfixed routes (Green or white with a broad red horizontal band; yellow ones should be avoided as they are supposed to have been phased out). These can be flagged down anywhere; tariffs US$0.35 plus 5 cents for each 250 m or 45 seconds; between 2200 and 0600 they charge 20% extra. They have meters (check they are working properly and set at zero); if you do not bargain before getting in, or if the driver does not know the route well, the meter will be switched on, which usually works out cheaper than negotiating a price. Some drivers refuse to use their meter after 1800.

Drivers often do not know where the street you want is because the city's numbering is erratic. Try to give the name of the intersection between 2 streets rather than a number.

Warning Lone travellers, especially female, are advised to take only official *sitio* taxis (not VW ones) from hotels or ordered by phone, particularly at night. Tourist police advise that you make a note of registration and taxi numbers before getting in.

Tips and complaints

A tip is not normally expected, except when special help has been given.

For information, or complaints, T55-5605 5520; if complaining, make sure you take the taxi's ID number.

Bicitaxi
Another type of taxi travel, the tricycle, is now being encouraged to counter exhaust pollution, and is a good way to see the architecture of the city centre. There are many outside the Palacio Nacional.

Colectivos
Colectivos (often called *peseros* – they used to cost 1 peso) run on fixed routes, often between metro stations and other known landmarks; destination and route displayed on the windscreen. Fares are US$0.20 up to 5 km, US$0.25 up to 10 km and US$0.35 beyond. If a bus runs on the same route, it may be preferable as it has fixed stops.

⊖ Directory

Banks and currency exchange
Banks
Opening hours are generally Mon-Fri 0930-1700, Sat 0900-1300. Bancomer, head office at Av Universidad 1200, also Venustiano Carranza y Bolívar, good quick *cambio*, same rate for cash and TCs. Banamex's offices at Av Isabel la Católica 44, are in a converted baroque palace, ask the porter for a quick look into the magnificent patio. Another worthwhile building is the bank's branch in the Casa Iturbide, Madero 17 and Gante, where Agustín de Iturbide lived as emperor. HSBC recommended, they deal with MasterCard (Carnet) and Visa (usually quicker than Bancomer or Banamex for cash advances against credit card). Banca Serfín, corner of 16 de Septiembre y Bolívar, or Madero 32, near Bolívar. Citibank, Paseo de la Reforma 390, for Citicorp TCs, they also give cash advances against credit cards with no commission. American Express emergency number, T55-5326 2626; office at Reforma 350 esq Lancaster, T55-5207 7049, will

change cheques on Sat 0930-1330, also Mon-Fri until 1800 (there are 10 other Amex offices in Mexico City, including at the Hotel Nikko at Campos Elíseos 204, Local 5, T55-5283 1900, and Centro Comercial Perisur, Periférico Surrey 4690, T55-5606 9621). For more details on Visa and MasterCard, see Credit cards, page 88.

Casas de cambio
There are many *casas de cambio*, especially on Reforma, Madero and throughout the city centre. Their hours may be more convenient, but their rates can be poor. Central de Cambios (Suiza), Madero 58, west of Zócalo, and Casa de Cambio Plus, Av Juárez, have been recommended for rates. The Perisur shopping centre, Insurgentes and Periférico Sur, has a *casa de cambio*, T55-5606 3698, which is usually open until 1900, with a better exchange rate in the morning. Exchange services also available at the airport.

Currency exchange
Always see if there is a special counter where currency transactions can be effected to avoid standing in long queues. Branches of all major Mexican banks proliferate in most parts of the city. Cash advances on credit cards are easy with good rates. TCs in most major currencies can be cashed at any branch of Bancomer or Banca Serfín without undue delay. Banks do not charge commission for changing TCs. The exchange of foreign currency notes, other than dollars, can be difficult apart from at the airport and main bank branches in the city centre. Before buying or selling currency, check the day's exchange rate from a newspaper and then shop around. There is often a great disparity between different banks and *casas de cambio*, particularly in times of volatile currency markets. Hotels usually offer very poor rates.

Cultural centres and international libraries
Amistad Británico-Mexicana, Montes Escandinavos 405, Lomas de Chapultepec,

155-2623 0603, www.amistadbm.org.mx.
Anglo-Mexican Cultural Institute, Maestro Antonio Caso 127, T55-5566 6144. **Biblioteca Benjamin Franklin**, Liverpool 31, T55-5080 2733, Mon-Fri 1000-1900, has books and English-language papers. ID required.
British Council, Lope de Vega 316, Polanco, T55-5263 1900, www.britishcouncil.org.mx.
Goethe-Institut, Liverpool 89, T55-5207 0487, www.goethe.de/mexiko. German books and papers. **Instituto Francés de América Latina**, Campos Elíseos 339, free films Thu at 2030, T55-9171 9703, www.paginas culturales.org.mx. **Instituto Italiano**, Francisco Sosa 77, Coyoacán, T55-5554 0044, www.iicmessico.esteri.it, has 3-week intensive yet painless courses in Spanish, 3 hrs a day.

Embassies and consulates

For up-to-date information, check: www.sre.gob.mx/acreditadas.
Australia, Rubén Darío 55, Polanco, T55-1101 2200, www.mexico.embassy.gov.au.
Belize, Bernardo de Gálvez 215, Lomas Chapultepec, T55-5520 1346, Mon-Fri 0900-1330. **Canada**, Schiller 529, near Anthropology Museum, T55-5724 7900, www.canada.org.mx. **Costa Rica**, Río Po 113, Col Cuauhtémoc, T55-5525 7765. **Denmark**, Tres Picos 43, T55-5255 3405, Mon-Thu 0830-1600, Fri 0830-1300. **El Salvador**, Temístocles 88, T55-5281 5725. **France**, Campos Elíseos 339, 155-9171 9700, www.ambafrance-mx.org. **Germany**, Horacio 1506, T55-5283 2200, www.mexiko.diplo.de, Mon-Thu, 0730-1530, Fri 0730-1500.
Guatemala, Explanada 1025, Lomas de Chapultepec, T55-5540 7520, Mon-Fri 0900-1300. **Honduras**, Alfonso Reyes 220, T55-5211 5250. **Ireland**, Cda Blv Manuel Avila Camacho 76, 3rd floor, T55-5520 5803, Mon-Fri 0900-1700. **Israel**, Sierra Madre 215, T55-5201 1500, www.mfa.gov.il, Mon-Thu 0900-1600, Fri 0900-1400. **Italy**, Paseo de las Palmas 1994, T55-5596 3655. **Japan**, Paseo de la Reforma 395, T55-5211 0028. **Netherlands**, Vasco de Quiroga No 3000, piso 7, Edificio Calakmul, T55-5258 9921, www.paises bajos.com.mx. **New Zealand**, Jaime Balmer 8, 4th floor, Edificio Corporativo, T55-5283 9460. **Nicaragua**, Prado Norte 470, T55-5540 5625, **Panama**, Sócrates 339, T55-5280 7857, www.embpanamamexico.com. **Poland**, Cravovia 40, T55-5481 2050, www.meksyk. polemb.net. **Russia**, Vasconcelos 204, T55-5273 1305, www.embrumex.com.mx.
Sweden, Paseo de las Palmas 1375, T55-9178 5010, www.suecia.com.mx.
Switzerland, Paseo de las Palmas 405, 11th floor, Edificio Torre Optima, T55-9178 4385, Mon-Thu 0830-1300 and 1400-1630, Fri 0800-1145. **UK**, Río Lerma 71, T55-5242 8500, www.embajada britanica.com.mx, Mon-Thu 0800-1600, Fri 0800-1330. **USA**, Paseo de la Reforma 305, T55-5080 2000, www.usembassy-mexico.gov, Mon-Fri 0830-1730. If requiring a visa for the USA, it is best to get it in your home country.

Immigration

The **Instituto Nacional de Migración**, of the Secretaría de Gobernación, is at Ejército Nacional 862, Polanco, T55-2581 0100. Nearest metro is Polanco, then taxi. Mon-Fri 0900-1330. Get there early, usually long queues, little English spoken. Here you can extend tourist cards for stays over 90 days or replace lost cards; new cards can take just a couple of hours, but charges are as high as US$40; you may be given 10 days to leave the country.

This is also where you have to come to exchange a tourist card for a student visa and for any other immigration matter concerning foreigners. It is essential to be armed with a lot of patience, and to attend with a Spanish speaker if you don't speak the language. The normal procedure is to fill out a form indicating which service you need; you are then given a receipt with a number. See page 90 for more information on visas.

Internet

Rates are US$1-3 per hr, with many to choose from throughout the city – ask your hotel for the nearest.

Language schools

The UNAM (see page 116) has excellent classes of Spanish language and Mexican culture: Centro de Enseñanza para Extranjeros, Av Universidad 3002, T55-5622 2470, www.cepe.unam.mx, US$340 for 6 weeks, 5 different programmes, free additional courses in culture, free use of medical service, swimming pool, library, a student card from here allows free entry to all national monuments and museums and half price on many bus lines (eg ADO during summer vacations). See also Language tuition, page 55, and Cultural centres, page 148.

Laundry

Laundrette, Río Danubio, between Lerma and Pánuco and at Chapultepec and Toledo, near Metro Sevilla, expensive. Lavandería at Chapultepec y Toledo. Lavandería Automática Edison, Edison 91 (Metro Revolución), between José María Iglesias y Ponciano Arriaga, Col Tabacalera (centre). Mon-Fri 0900-1900, Sat 0900-1800. Has automatic machines, US$1.50 per 3 kg, US$1.50 drying. Lavandería at Parque España 14 and Antonio Caso 82, near the British Council, US$4 for 3 kg, quick service.

Medical services
Doctors

Dr Goldberg, Av de Las Palmas 745, ground floor, pb, Col Lomas de Chapultepec, T55-5540 7300, emergencies T55-5727 7979. Dr César Calva Pellicer (who speaks English, French and German), Copenhague 24, 3rd floor, T55-5514 2529. Dr Smythe, Campos Elíseos 81, T55-5545 7861, recommended by US and Canadian embassies.

Hospitals and clinics

Most embassies have a list of recommended doctors and dentists who speak languages other than Spanish. Try the US embassy website for a complete list of hospitals, www.usembassy-mexico.gov/medical_lists.html. American British Cowdray Hospital (also known as El Hospital Inglés, or ABC), on Observatorio past Calle Sur 136, T55-5230 8161, also at Santa Fe; very helpful. Hospital de Jesús Nazareno, 20 de Noviembre 82, Spanish-speaking, friendly, drugs prescribed cheaply. It is a historical monument (see page 102).

Vaccination centres

Vaccination centre Benjamín Hill 14, near Metro Juanacatlán (Line 1), Mon-Fri 0830-1430, 1530-2030, avoid last 30 mins, Sat 0830-1430. Typhoid (free throughout Mexico), cholera and yellow fever (US$2), Tue and Fri only; will give a prescription for gamma globulin. For hepatitis shots you have to buy gamma globulin in a pharmacy (make sure it's been refrigerated) and then an injection there, at a doctor's surgery or the ABC Hospital (see above).

Pharmacies

Farmacia Homeopática, Mesones 111-B. Farmacia Nosarco, corner of 5 de Febrero and República de El Salvador, stocks a wide range of drugs for stomach bugs and tropical diseases, may give 21% discount. Sanborn's chain and El Fénix discount pharmacies are the largest chains with the most complete selection. Many supermarkets have good pharmacies.

Post office

Correo Central Tacuba y Lázaro Cárdenas, opposite Palacio de Bellas Artes, open for letters Mon-Fri 0800-2400, Sat 0800-2000, Sun 0900-1600. For parcels Mon-Fri 0800-1800, Sat 0800-1600. Parcels up to 2 kg (5 kg for books) may be sent. It is an interesting historic building with a stunning interior, worth a visit.

EMS Mexpost, accelerated national and international postage, is available at the Central Post Office, the airport, Zona Rosa, Coyoacán and 13 other post offices in the city; payable by weight.

Other post offices (Mon-Fri 0800-1900, Sat 0800-1300), which travellers may find useful: **Centre**, Nezahualcóyotl 184 and Academia 4; **P Arriaga** and Ignacio Mariscal, 2 blocks north of Monumento a la Revolución; **Zona Rosa**, Londres 208; **Tlatelolco**, Flores Magón 90; **San Rafael**, Schultz 102; **Lomas de Chapultepec**, Prado Norte 525; **Buenavista**, Aldama 216; **San Angel**, Dr Gálvez 16; **Coyoacán**, Higuera 23; **Iztapalapa**, Calzada Ermita Iztapalapa 1033; **Xochimilco**, Prolongación Pino 10; also at the **airport** and bus terminals. In all there are 155 branches in the federal capital, so there is no need to go to the Correo Central.

Telephone

Finding a public phone that works can be a problem. Most now take phone cards (**Ladatel**, provided by **Telmex**), costing 30, 50 and 100 pesos, from shops and news kiosks everywhere. Calls abroad can be made from phone booths with credit cards (via **LADA** system), but this is very expensive. See page 89 for details of the **LADA** phone system. International calls can be made easily from the phone offices in bus terminals. There are several places, including some shops, all officially listed, with long-distance phones. One of the best options for international calls is an **Ekofon** card or account (see page 89). Also look out for Internet cafés that are set up to handle internet calls (ie Skype).

North of Mexico City

Right in the centre of the country, Mexico City is well suited for exploring the colonial towns, villages, national parks, pre-Hispanic sites, volcanoes, caves and hot springs that are within easy reach for a day or weekend trip. Everyone heads north to see Mexico's most visited pyramids at the vast and awe-inspiring site of Teotihuacán, 'the place of the gods'. Less crowded are the towering Atlantes at Tula, the Toltec capital, and the pretty villages in the hills near Pachuca where you can eat the Cornish pasties that are a legacy of the English who once mined gold in the region. ⏩ *For listings, see pages 157-159.*

Acolman

Acolman, 35 km northeast of Mexico City, is easily visited after the Basílica de Guadalupe (see page 120) and on the way to Teotihuacán. It has the formidable fortress-like convent and church of **San Agustín**. This dates from 1539-1560, with much delicate detail on the façade and some interesting murals inside. Note the fine portal and the carved stone cross at the entrance to the atrium. An interesting architectural feature is the open chapel just above and to the right of the main entrance. While Mass was being celebrated inside the monastery for the benefit of the Spaniards, the spiritual needs of the indigenous worshippers were catered for by the friar who celebrated the Mass in this tiny balcony chapel. Acolman can be reached by bus from Metro Indios Verdes, or from the zócalo.

Teotihuacán ⊜⊘▲⊜ ⏩ *pp157-159. Colour map 3, B4.*

ⓘ *Daily 0800-1700, US$3.50 (extra charge for videos, tripods not permitted). Son et lumière display, US$4 per person, 45 mins, 1900 in Spanish, 2015 in English (Oct-Jun only); take a blanket or rent one. Arrive early before the vast numbers of ambulantes (wandering vendors) and the tour groups at 1100. Allow 2-3 hrs, longer if you're really keen. There is a perimeter road with a number of car parking places. The simplest way to visit Teotihuacán is on an organized tour although you can catch an ordinary buses from Terminal del Norte and Indios Verdes.* ⏩ *For Transport, see page 158.*

This site, 49 km north of Mexico City, has some of the most remarkable relics of an ancient civilization in the world. Thought to date from around 300 BC-AD 600, the builders of Teotihuacán, or 'place of the gods', remain a mystery. Where they came from and why the civilization disappeared is pure conjecture. It seems that the city may have housed 250,000 people who were peace-loving but whose influence spread as far as Guatemala. However, the 'peace-loving' theory is constantly being challenged. There are definite indications that human sacrifice was being practised at Teotihuacán long before the arrival of the Aztecs to the Valley of Mexico. Recent research indicates that an individual from Teotihuacán arrived at Copán in Honduras and usurped the power of the rightful ruler, thus continuing to spread the influence of Teotihuacán throughout the Maya region. Teotihuacán was not just a ceremonial centre; vast areas of enclaves have been excavated showing that, apart from those zones designated as sacred, there were also areas occupied by artisans, labourers, merchants and representatives of those crafts and professions that contribute to a functioning city. One zone housed merchants from the Maya area, another was occupied by representatives from Monte Albán in Oaxaca. Some time in the seventh century, Teotihuacán was ravaged by fire and may also have been looted, causing an exodus of its inhabitants. So completely was it abandoned that it was left to the Aztecs to give names to its most important features. There are many questions still to be answered about Teotihuacán culture and new discoveries are being made all the time.

Teotihuacán

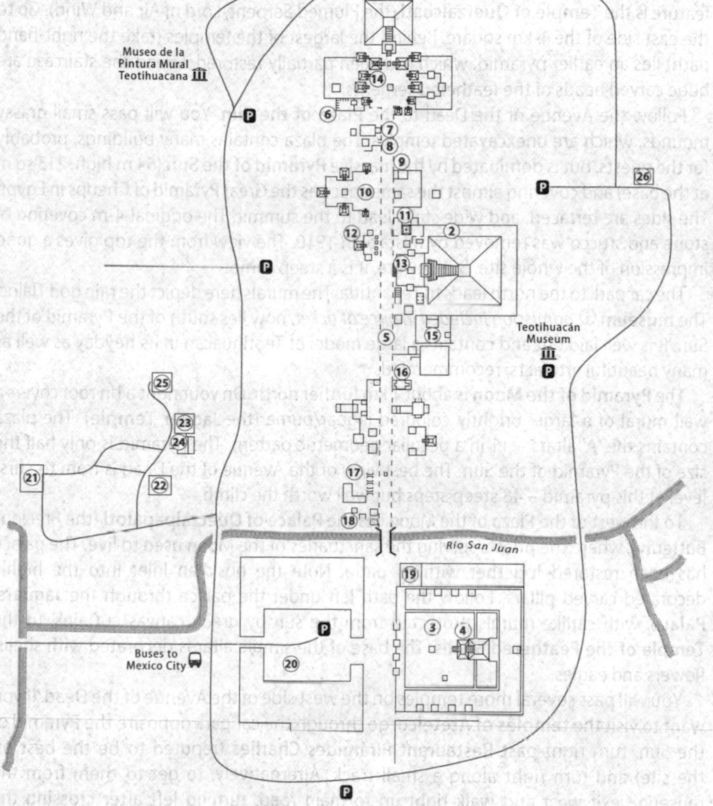

Museo de la
Pintura Mural
Teotihuacana 🏛

Teotihuacán
Museum 🏛

Río San Juan

Buses to
Mexico City 🚌

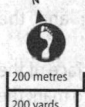

N

200 metres
200 yards

Pyramid of the Moon 1
Pyramid of the Sun 2
Ciudadela 3

Temple of Quetzalcoatl 4
Avenue of the Dead 5
Palaces of Quetzalpapalotl,
  Jaguars & Feathered
  Shells 6
Temple of Agriculture 7
Mural of the Mythological
  Animals 8
Jaguar Temple & Mural 9
Plaza of the Columns 10
Palace of the Sun 11

Patio of the Four Little
  Temples 12
Plaza of the Sun 13
Plaza of the Moon 14
House of the Priest 15
Viking Group 16
Avenue of the Dead
  complex with
  'Superimposed Buildings'
  group 17
Northwest Cluster 18

Plaza Two 19
Great Compound 20
Palace of Atetelco 21
Palace of Tetitla 22
Palace of Zacuala 23
Patio of Zacuala 24
Palace of Yayahuala 25
Palace of Tepantitla 26

Sights

There are three main areas: the **Ciudadela**, the **Pyramid of the Sun** and the **Pyramid of the Moon**. The whole is connected by the Avenue of the Dead, which runs almost due north for nearly 4 km. To the west lie the sites of Tetitla, Atetelco, Zacuala and Yayahuala (see below). To the northeast lies Tepantitla, with fine frescoes. The old city is traceable over an area of 3.5 km by 6.5 km. Capable of holding 60,000 people, the citadel's main feature is the **Temple of Quetzalcoatl** (the Plumed Serpent, Lord of Air and Wind). Go to the east side of the 1-km square. Behind the largest of the temples (take the right-hand path) lies an earlier pyramid, which has been partially restored. Lining the staircase are huge carved heads of the feathered serpents.

Follow the Avenue of the Dead to the **Plaza of the Sun**. You will pass small grassy mounds, which are unexcavated temples. The plaza contains many buildings, probably for the priests, but is dominated by the massive **Pyramid of the Sun** (64 m high, 213 sq m at the base) and covering almost the same space as the Great Pyramid of Cheops in Egypt. The sides are terraced, and wide stairs lead to the summit. The original 4-m covering of stone and stucco was removed by mistake in 1910. The view from the top gives a good impression of the whole site. But beware, it is a steep climb.

The car park to the north leads to Tepantitla. The murals here depict the rain god Tlaloc. The **museum** ① *admission included in price of ticket*, now lies south of the Pyramid of the Sun. It is well laid out and contains a large model of Teotihuacán in its heyday as well as many beautiful artefacts; recommended.

The **Pyramid of the Moon** is about 1 km further north. On your right a tin roof covers a wall mural of a large, brightly coloured jaguar/puma (the **Jaguar Temple**). The plaza contains the 'A' altars – 11 in a peculiar geometric pattern. The pyramid is only half the size of the Pyramid of the Sun. The best view of the Avenue of the Dead is from the first level of this pyramid – 48 steep steps but well worth the climb.

To the west of the Plaza of the Moon lies the **Palace of Quetzalpapalotl** (the Precious Butterfly), where the priests serving the sanctuaries of the Moon used to live. The palace has been restored together with its patio. Note the obsidian inlet into the highly decorated carved pillars. Follow the path left under the palace through the **Jaguars' Palace**, with catlike murals protected from the sun by green canvas curtains, to the **Temple of the Feathered Shells**. The base of the simple altar is decorated with shells, flowers and eagles.

You will pass several more temples on the west side of the Avenue of the Dead. If you want to visit the **temples of Atetelco**, go through the car park opposite the Pyramid of the Sun, turn right past **Restaurant Pirámides Charlies** (reputed to be the best on the site) and turn right along a small track. Alternatively, to get to them from the museum, exit west and walk right up to main road, turning left after crossing the stream. They are well worth a visit: **Tetitla**, a walled complex with beautiful frescoes and paintings; **Atetelco** with its three tiny temples and excellent murals; and the abandoned sites of **Zacuala** and **Yayahuala**.

At the spring equinox, 21 March, the sun is perfectly aligned with the west face of the Pyramid of the Sun; many ad hoc sun worshippers hold unofficial ceremonies to mark the occasion. This is also Benito Juárez's birthday so entry is free.

At the exit to the rear of the Jaguars' Palace (which is the usual way out), and across the road, is the delightful **Museo de Pintura Mural Teotihuacana** ① *daily 1000-1700, free*, which contains collections and explanations of ancient wall painting.

Pachuca ●●●● ➤➤ pp157-159. Colour map 3, B4.

➜ *Phone code: 771. Altitude: 2445 m.*

Capital of Hidalgo state (www.turismo.hidalgo.gob.mx), Pachuca, 94 km northeast of Mexico City, is also one of the oldest silver mining centres in Mexico. The Aztecs, the Spaniards and more recently the English all mined here leaving the hills honeycombed with old workings and terraced with tailings. The English left a small culinary legacy with a Mexicanized version of a Cornish pasty, available in some of the town's cafés.

The town centre is partly pedestrianized and, although the centre is largely modern, there are a number of colonial buildings among its narrow, steep and crooked streets. These include the treasury for the royal tribute, **Las Cajas Reales** (1670), Venustiano Carranza 106, now used as offices, and **Las Casas Coloradas** (1785), on Plaza Pedro María Anaya, now the Tribunal Superior de Justicia. The 400-year-old former **Convento de San Francisco** (1596) on Arista and Hidalgo next to Parque Hidalgo is an attraction in itself, and now houses the **Centro Cultural de Hidalgo** ① *Tue-Sun 0900-1800, may close early on Sun afternoon.* The outstanding **photographic museum** ① *T771-714 3653, Tue-Sun 1000-1800, free,* is in the cloister on the far side of the convent; it has international and historical images from renowned photojournalists. Nearby is the **Fototeca**, with an archive of over a million images that you can search and print for a small fee. The **Museo Regional de Hidalgo** displays chronological exhibits of the state's history. In the complex there is a souvenir shop with reproductions of anthropological items and recordings of indigenous music.

Casa de las Artesanías for Hidalgo state is at the junction of Avenida Revolución and Avenida Juárez. In the Plaza Independencia is a huge clock with four Carrara marble figures.

If Pachuca's mining history interests you, the **Museo de la Minería** ① *Mina 110, Tue-Sun 1000-1400, 1500-1800, US$1,* has an excellent display of the history of mining in Pachuca. An industrial heritage programme is under way to restore some of the old mining settlements; up-to-date information is available in the museum.

The modern buildings include a **theatre**, the **Palacio de Goblerno** (which has a mural depicting ex-President Echeverría's dream of becoming Secretary-General of the UN), and the **Banco de Hidalgo**. For information contact the **tourist office** ① *Av Revolución 1300, T771-718 3937.*

Getting there A four-lane highway runs from Mexico City to Pachuca via Venta de Carpio, Km 27, from which a road runs east to Acolman, 12 km, and Teotihuacán, another 10 km. ➤➤ *See Transport, page 159.*

Around Pachuca

North of Pachuca via Atotonilco el Grande there is a chapel and convent halfway down a beautiful canyon, the impressive **Barranca de Metztitlán**, which has a wealth of different varieties of cacti, including the 'hairy old man' cactus, and a huge 17th-century monastery. The death of Ome Tochtli (Two Rabbit) at the hands of Tezcatlipoca (Smoking Mirror) occurred at Metztitlán. Further north on a difficult road is **Molango**, where there is a restored convent, Nuestra Señora de Loreto. **San Miguel Regla**, 34 km northeast of Pachuca, is a mid-18th-century hacienda built by the Conde de Regla, and now run as a resort. A road continues towards **Tulancingo** on the Pachuca–Poza Rica road, Route 130, with a handful of hotels. **Epazoyucan**, 17 km east of Pachuca, and a further 4 km off Route 130 to the right, is a village with the interesting convent of San Andrés. After Tulancingo, Route 119 branches off to the right to **Zacatlán**, famous for its apple orchards, plums, pears and cider. Its alpine surroundings include an impressive national park, the **Valle de las Piedras Encimadas** (stacked rocks), where camping is possible. Some 16 km south of Zacatlán and about 1½ hours from Puebla (see page 182) is **Chignahuapan**, a leading producer of *sarapes*, surrounded by several curative spas.

Real del Monte, a very interesting and attractive small town, is one of a number of mining centres in the area, most of which are no longer in operation. Cornish miners came here from England in large numbers in the second quarter of the 19th century. Traces of their presence can still be seen in blue-eyed inhabitants, surnames and, of course, the pasties or *pastes*. Most of the buildings have sloping roofs or *techos de dos aguas* and are carefully preserved. The **Panteón Inglés** (English cemetery) is on a wooded hill opposite the town; the caretaker will recite stories about families buried there. No lodging is available at present; take a *colectivo* from Pachuca, 10 minutes' drive.

Tepotzotlán ●❶❷❸ ▶▶ *pp157-159. Colour map 3, B4.*

→ *Phone code: 55.*

The town of Tepotzotlán is about 43 km northwest of Mexico City – not to be confused with Tepoztlán, to the south of Mexico City near Cuernavaca. Just off the road to Querétaro is the splendid Jesuit church of **San Francisco Javier** in churrigueresque style and with fine colonial paintings in the convent corridors. The old Jesuit monastery has been converted into the **Museo Nacional del Virreinato** ① *Plaza Hidalgo, www.munavi.inah.gob.mx, Tue-Sun 0900-1800, US$4,* a comprehensive and well-displayed collection covering all aspects of life under Spanish rule. It is also a tourist centre with restaurants. There is a big market on Wednesday and Sunday when the town gets very congested; there is a good selection of handicrafts and jewellery, as well as meat, cheese and other foods. In the third week of December, *pastorelas* (plays based on the temptation and salvation of Mexican pilgrims voyaging to Bethlehem), are held. Tickets (US$10) are very much in demand and can be bought at www.ticketmaster.com.mx.

Tula ●❶❷❸ ▶▶ *pp157-159. Colour map 3, B4.*

→ *Phone code: 773.*

① *Tue-Sun 0900-1700. Site and museum, US$3. The small restaurant is not always open. Guidebooks in many languages are available at the entrance, fizzy drinks on sale.*

A half-day excursion from Mexico City can be made to Tula, 65 km north of Mexico City, thought to be the most important Toltec site in Mexico. In all, two ball courts, pyramids, a frieze in colour, and remarkable sculptures over 6 m high have been uncovered. There are four huge warriors in black basalt on a pyramid, these are the great Atlantes anthropomorphic pillars. One is a reproduction; the original is on display at the Museo Nacional de Antropología in Mexico City (see page 112). The platform on which the four warriors stand is encircled by a low relief frieze depicting jaguars and coyotes, and Tlaloc masks adorn the walls. Note the butterfly emblem on the chests of the warriors and the *atlatl* (spear-thrower) held by their sides. The butterfly, so important an element in Toltec iconography, was once more to become associated with the warrior class during the Aztec period, when dead warriors became butterflies who escorted the sun to midday. The museum is well worth visiting and there is a massive fortress-style church, dating from 1553, near the market.

The town of Tula itself is pleasant, clean and friendly. If driving from Mexico City, take the turn for Actopan before entering Tula, then look for the Parque Nacional sign (and the great statues) on your left.

⊙ North of Mexico City listings

For Sleeping and Eating price codes and other relevant information, see Essentials pages 45-48.

● Sleeping

Teotihuacán *p152, map p153*
AL Villas Arqueológicas, San Juan Teotihuacán, T594-956 0909, www.teotihuacaninfo.com. 40 attractive rooms with arched enclaves, whitewashed walls and wooden furniture. Services include restaurant, bar, pool and sky TV. A good location close to the pyramids.
B Posada Sol y Luna, Cantu 13, San Juan Teotihuacán, T594-956 2368, www.posadasolyluna.com. 16 straightforward rooms with colour TV, private bath and hot water. Services include restaurant and parking. Comfortable enough, but unexciting.

Pachuca *p155*
A Emily, Plaza Independencia, T771-715 0828, www.hotelemily.com.mx. A smart and tidy hotel with comfortable rooms, marbled floors and a plethora of services including Wi-Fi, cable TV, restaurant, gym, parking and conference room. Weekend deals sometimes available.
B Gran Hotel Independencia, Plaza Independencia 116, T771-715 0515, www.granhotelindependencia.com. This historic building, formerly **Hotel Grenfell**, has clean, pleasant, carpeted rooms with large colonial-style windows, cable TV and tasteful furnishings. Parking and Wi-Fi available.
C Hotel Noriega, Matamoros 305, T771-715 0150. Fantastic building with curved staircases, arched corridors and exuberant foliage spilling over the railings. The rooms are tired though, with basic furniture and ancient TV sets. Restaurant attached.

C Juárez, Barreda 107, just before Real del Monte. Set in superb wooded surroundings. Rooms have bath, some are without windows.
C San Antonio, 6 km from Pachuca on road to Mexico City (ask for directions), T771-711 0599. Spacious rooms at this hotel on the highway, good value, clean and quiet. They have a restaurant.
D Hotel America, 3ra de Victoria 203, T771 715 0055. A bright orange building with economical rooms around a courtyard. All have bath, hot water and cable TV.

Around Pachuca *p155*
A Hacienda San Miguel Regla, San Miguel Regla, T01800-201-1287, www.sanmiguel regla.com. A fine atmosphere, excellent service, pool, lush gardens, tennis, horse riding and log fires. Highly recommended.
A Mi Ranchito, Xicotepec de Juárez, T771-764 0212, www.hotelmiranchito.com.mx. A very pleasant, hospitable little hotel with a family atmosphere. A range of services include pool, tennis court, playground, and games room.
A Posada Don Ramón, T797-975 0315, Zacatlán. Best hotel in town, with pleasant furnished rooms in a colonial-style building.

Tepotzotlán *p156*
AL Tepotzotlán, Inés de la Cruz, T55-5876 0340. Good views at this hotel. Services include restaurant, swimming pool and secure parking. Recommended.
C Posada San José, Plaza Virreinal No 13, T55 5876 0520. An old colonial building with pleasant rooms and a good atmosphere, if sometimes lacking authenticity.

Camping
Pepe's, Eva Sámano de López, Mateos 62, T55-5876 0515/0616. The nearest trailer park

to the capital, it costs about US$12 per night, 55 pads with full hook-ups, very friendly, clean, hot showers, Canadian run. Recommended. Owner has a hotel in Mexico City so you can leave your trailer here and stay in the capital.

Tula *p156*
AL-A Real Catedral, Zaragoza No 106, T773-732 0813, www.hotelrealcatedral.com. Attractive colonial building with a renovated modern interior, lots of ambient lighting and a wide range of rooms and suites. Gym, valet parking, Wi-Fi, tour guides and transport available.

🍴 Eating

Teotihuacán *p152, map p153*
♥ Los Pinos, Guadalupe Victoria, in the village of San Juan Teotihuacán, is one of a few decent eating options, and the village makes an interesting detour.

Pachuca *p155*
♥♥ Reforma, Matamoros 111. This old restaurant has a wood-panelled interior and serves breakfasts and Mexican fare.
♥♥-♥ La Blanca, Plaza de la Independencia. Atmospheric restaurant with lots of old photos and an interesting interior. They serve breakfasts, Mexican specialities and the ubiquitous pasty.
♥ Pastes Grenfell, Plaza Independencia. One of the city's better pasty shops, with great value, tasty Cornish-style pasties filled with meat or vegetables – good for a quick bite or food on the go. Recommended.

Tepotzotlán *p156*
♥♥ Hostería del Monasterio, Plaza Virreinal 1. This atmospheric old restaurant serves very good Mexican food and stages a band on Sun; try their *café de olla* (sweet coffee with cinnamon).

♥ Restaurant Artesanías, opposite church. Cheap, economical grub. Recommended.

Tula *p156*
♥♥ Casa Blanca, Hidalgo 114. Always busy and popular, this large dining hall has lots of character and serves tasty Mexican fare.
♥♥ Los Negritos, Heroes de Chapultepec and Moctezuma. Good, clean, popular and often recommended for its Mexican food. Pleasant outdoor seating with a courtyard and arches.
♥♥-♥ Cocina Las Cazuelas, Pasaje Hidalgo 3. Wholesome home-cooked fare prepared on grills in front of you. Very affordable *comida corrida*.
♥ Azcatimolli Tortas, Rojo del Río 24. *Tortas*, fast food and Aztec grub. Tasty!

▲ Activities and tours

Teotihuacán *p152, map p153*
Tour operators
Mexbus, T594-5514 2233 or T01800-523 9412, provides day trips, including a stop at the Basílica de Guadalupe, pick-up and return from central hotels, English-speaking guide and lunch for US$30.
Mundo Joven Adventures, Guatemala 4 at Hostal Catedral behind the Catedral, T594-5518 1726, www.mundojoven adventures.com, also provide daily trips to Teotihuacán with a Guadalupe stop-off.

⊖ Transport

Teotihuacán *p152, map p153*
When using public transport, the site is more generally known as 'Pirámides'. 'Teotihuacán' usually refers to the nearby village of the same name.

Bus
Buses leave from **Terminal del Norte, Mexico City** for Las Pyramides every

15-30 mins, 0700-1800, US$3, 1 way. You can also take the metro to Indios Verdes (last stop on line 3), then a public bus (US$3) to the pyramids. Bus returns from Door 1 (some others from 2 and 3) at the site, supposedly every 30 mins. Some return buses to the capital terminate in the outskirts in rush hour without warning. You can also ride back to town with one of the tourist buses for about US$5.

Taxi
To reach the ruins from the village of San Juan Teotihuacán, *combis*, US$0.60, and taxis, US$1.50, depart regularly from the plaza.

Pachuca *p155*
Bus
There are frequent departures from **Terminal del Norte**, US$5, 1½ hrs. In Pachuca the bus terminal is out of town; take any *colectivo* marked 'Centro', 20 mins, US$0.40, and exit at the main plaza. To **Tula**, hourly from the main bus station, 2 hrs, US$5, and an interesting backdoor route.

Tepotzotlán *p156*
Bus
From near Metro El Rosario, *colectivo*, US$1.50, 1-hr ride. Many Querétaro or Guanajuato buses from **Terminal del Norte** pass the turn-off at 'Caseta Tepotzotlán' from where you can take a local bus, US$0.40, or walk (30 mins) to the town.

Tula *p156*
Bus
Regular 1st-class bus from **Terminal del Norte**, Av de los Cien Metros, which goes to Tula bus terminal in 1½ hrs; US$5, every 40 mins, 0600-2100.

Tula bus terminal is 3 km from the site, take a 'Chapantago' bus (every 20 mins) to the entrance, 5 mins (ask where to get off), or a taxi, US$3. It's also possible to walk, turning right out of the bus station. At the main road, cut diagonally left across road and take first right, which will take you to a bridge over an evil-smelling river. Carry on to the main highway, then turn left.

To **Pachuca** US$5, 2 hrs; safe to leave belongings at bus station. There are also services to **Queretaro** (2¼ hrs), **Guanajuato** and **León**.

West of Mexico City

Heading west takes you through the mountains that form the western fringe of the Central Valley and which, on clear days (quite rare), provide spectacular views of the city. Time it right and go on a Friday, travelling through cool pine forests, for Toluca's massive street market. You can hike on the slopes of Nevado de Toluca, explore the forests of Ixtapan de la Sal or visit the lesser-known ruins of Malinalco. ➤➤ *For listings, see pages 164-165.*

Toluca ⊜🍴🚌 ➤➤ *pp164-165. Colour map 3, B3.*

➔ *Phone code: 722. Altitude: 2639 m.*

From Mexico City head towards **Parque Nacional Miguel Hidalgo**, or **La Marquesa**, with lakes suitable for watersports and other activities such as hiking and camping in nearby hills. Turning south off Route 15 leads to Chalma and Santiago Tianguistenco with incredible panoramic views of the city and the Valley of Mexico, smog permitting. Entering the Basin of Toluca, the ice-capped Toluca volcano (see page 161) dominates the landscape.

At 2680 m, Toluca – 64 km west of Mexico City by dual carriageway – is the highest city in Mexico and capital of the state of the same name. It's a friendly, busy place that's not much visited by tourists. Well known for confectionery and the local *chorizo* sausage, Toluca's real fame is down to the huge Friday market, close to the bus station on Paseo Tollocán and Idisro Fabela. Spreading out across several blocks, modern manufactured goods are sold alongside traditional woven baskets, *sarapes*, *rebozos*, pottery and embroidered goods. Also look out for an orange liqueur known as *moscos*, a local speciality. Toluca is easily visited as a day trip starting early from Mexico City (very regular

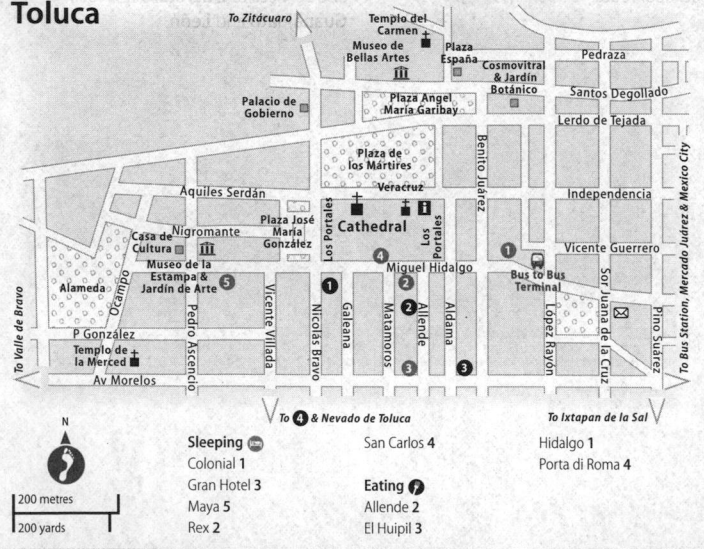

Toluca

Sleeping ⊜
Colonial 1
Gran Hotel 3
Maya 5
Rex 2
San Carlos 4

Eating 🍴
Allende 2
El Huipil 3

Hidalgo 1
Porta di Roma 4

buses from Terminal Poniente, one hour). The municipal **tourist office** ① *Palacio Municipal, Plaza de los Mártires, www.edomexico.gob.mx*, has a free *Atlas Turístico* of the State of México, including street maps of towns of interest. Outside the city centre is the **state tourist office** ① *Urawa and Tollocan, T722-212 5998*, also with good information.

Sights

At the heart of the city is the **Plaza de los Mártires**, a large, open public square that's named after the insurgents who were executed there during the War of Independence. On its south side is the **cathedral**, one of the largest in the country, begun in 1870 but not completed until 1978. Incorporated into its interior is the baroque façade of the 18th-century church of the **Tercera Orden**. Also on the south side is the **Palacio Municipal**, site of the tourist office, and next door, the **Church of Veracruz**, housing a Black Christ and very attractive interior. Flanking these three structure to the south, west and east are **Los Portales** – a parade of arcaded shops, restaurants and three art galleries. On the east side of the plaza stands the **Palacio de Poder Ejecutivo**. On the north side lies the stately **Palacio de Gobierno**, with a small park to the east, Plaza Angel María Garibay, complete with trees and fountains.

Just north of Plaza Garibay is the **Museo de Bellas Artes** ① *Tue-Sat 1000-1800, Sun 1000-1500, US$0.70, concessions half price, booklet US$1.35*, formerly the Convento del Carmen, with seven halls of paintings from 18th-century colonial baroque to the 20th century. Next door to the ex-Convento is the **Templo del Carmen**, a neoclassical church with a gold and white interior, and next to that is Plaza España.

Four blocks west of Los Portales is the **Alameda**, a large park with a statue of Cuauhtémoc and many tall trees. On Sunday morning it is popular with families strolling among the many stalls. The entrance is at the junction of Hidalgo and Ocampo.

The **Centro Cultural Mexiquense** ① *Bulevar Jesús Reyes Heroles 302, San Buenaventura, T722-274 1200, Tue-Sat 1000-1800, Sun 1000-1500, US$0.70, located 4.5 km west of the centre, to get there, take a 'Centro Cultural' bus from Mercado Juárez and exit at the large roundabout by the University, 20 mins*, is one of the most interesting attractions in Toluca. This large, modern cultural centre, built on the site of the Hacienda de la Pila, houses a historical archive, the public library and three cultural museums; the **Museo de Culturas Populares** explores local crafts, folklore and lifestyles; the **Museo de Arte Moderno** has a small collection of Mexican art and, the best of the three, the **Museo de Antropología y História**, home to some 7000 archaeological artefacts from the state of Mexico.

Around Toluca ●❶❷❸ ⇝ *pp164-165*.

A road branches off the Toluca to Valle de Bravo road at Km 75 to the Toluca volcano, **Nevado de Toluca**, or Xinantécatl. At 4583 m, this is the fourth highest mountain in Mexico. The road climbs to the deep blue lakes of the Sun and the Moon in its two craters, at about 4270 m, from which there is a wide and awe-inspiring view. It is 27 km from the turning off the main road to the heart of the craters. During winter it is possible to ski on the slopes; 2 km from the entrance is an *albergue* with food and cooking facilities. From here it is 10 km to the entrance, where there is a smaller *albergue* (cooking facilities, food sold at weekends only, no bathroom or water, dirty), and then a further 6 km to the lakes. A shortcut from the small *albergue* takes 20 minutes to the crater; it is not possible to drive. At the third refuge, 21 km from the turn-off is an attendant. Trips to the volcano are very popular at weekends. You can stay overnight at any of the refuges (**F**), although they are sometimes closed during the week; there is a restaurant, but the trip can be done in one day from Toluca. If walking remember the entrance to the crater, as you face it, is on the far left side of the volcano.

To reach the Toluca volcano take the first bus to Sultepec from Toluca at about 0700 (every two hours thereafter). Leave the bus where the road to the radio station branches off, just after Raíces village (US$1); from there it is about 20 km to the crater. Aim to get to the crater by midday before the clouds set in. Visitors must leave by 1700.

North of Toluca

From Toluca take a bus north to the pyramids and Aztec seminary of **Calixtlahuaca** ① *US$4.35*, 2 km off the road to Ixtlahuacan. The most notable building is Structure 3, a circular temple dedicated to the Aztec wind god Ehecatl. They are just behind the village, 10 minutes' walk from the final bus stop. Forty-five minutes north of Toluca by car, near the town of **Temoaya**, is the **Centro Ceremonial Otomí**, a modern site for cultural events in a beautiful setting.

South of Toluca

Route 55 south of Toluca provides access to a number of interesting art and craft villages, all with fine old churches. The first is **Metepec**, a pottery-making centre of the valley, 1.5 km off the road to Tenango. Clay figurines are painted bright fuchsia, purple, green and gold, are unique. This is the source of the *árboles de la vida*, the gaudily painted pottery 'trees of life and death' sold all over Mexico. Craft workshops are very spread out; market day is Monday.

A detour east off Route 55 or south from Route 15, the Toluca–Mexico City highway, goes to the town of **Santiago Tianguistenco**, where there are good pottery bowls, baskets and *sarapes*. Try blue corn *gordas* or *tlacoyos* which are stuffed with a bean paste. If you're feeling brave, try *atepocates*: embryo frogs with tomato and chillies, boiled in maize leaves. Market day is Wednesday and the town is crowded at weekends.

San Mateo Atenco (altitude 2570 m) is situated south of the Toluca–Lerma 'corridor'. Settled in ancient times, it has featured in several important historical moments by virtue of occupying a bridge-head between lagoons: Axayácatl, Cortés and Hidalgo all passed this way. There is a Franciscan church and monastery, dating from 1550. The town is famous for its shoes, and leather goods of all descriptions and you can pick up some excellent bargains. On 25 October St Crispin, the patron saint of shoemakers, is honoured in the open chapel of the church in the presence of the local bishop. Market is on Friday and Saturday.

Route 55 descends to **Tenango de Arista**, where there are hotels and a car park by the main road, where one can walk (20 minutes) to the ruins of Teotenango. **Teotenango** ① *US$1 museum and ruins*, shows the Matlazinca culture and is reminiscent of La Ciudadela at Teotihuacán, with five plazas, 10 structures and one ball court.

Tenancingo → *Phone code: 714. Altitude: 1830 m.*

West of Mexico City, just 48 km south of Toluca, the road descends abruptly through gorges to Tenancingo, which has a warm climate year round. Thirty minutes by bus to the south along an unpaved road is the magnificent 18th-century Carmelite convent of **El Santo Desierto**, where they make beautiful *rebozos* (shawls). The townspeople also weave fine *rebozos* and make delicious fruit wine. Overlooking the busy town is a statue of Christ on a hill. The daily market is two blocks from the bus terminal (continue one block, turn left for two further blocks to the main square); market day is Sunday, with excellent local cheese.

Malinalco → *Phone code: 714.*

About 11 km east of Tenancingo is Malinalco, a friendly, colourful little town that's an increasingly popular weekend trip from the capital. A path winds up 1 km, 20 minutes, to the partly excavated **Malinalco ruins** ① *Tue-Sun 1000-1800, US$2.60*, dating from 1188, and one of the most remarkable pre-Hispanic ruins in Mexico. A fantastic rock-cut temple in the side of a mountain, 430 steps up, conceals in its interior eagle and jaguar effigies. Apparently, you can feel movement in the rock if you lie on it. The site, which shows Matlatzinca culture with Aztec additions, is very small, but in a commanding position overlooking the valley.

The site is visible from the town as a ledge on the hillside; the walk up passes a tiny, blue colonial chapel. For a better view of the ruins carry straight on where the path leading to the ruins branches off right. This old road is cobbled in places and rises up the mountainside pretty steeply, arriving at a small shrine with two crosses (1½ hours' walk). It is possible to camp here but there is no water. Breathtaking views can be seen off both sides of the ridge. The trail carries on down the other side, past avocado trees, for 20 minutes, to the paved road to Tenancingo, almost opposite a brick house with arches. It is possible to catch a bus back over the mountains to Malinalco. It would also be much easier, a downhill walk mostly, to do this whole hike in reverse; catch the bus out, ask for the old road, and walk back.

You should also visit the Augustinian **Templo y Ex-convento del Divino Salvador** (1552), in the centre of town, the nave of which has a patterned ceiling, while the two-storey cloisters are painted with elaborate, early frescoes. Just below the convent, in the main square, a market is held on Wednesdays. There is a fiesta in Malinalco on 6 August.

By public transport, most people arrive at Malinalco via Tenancingo, but you can also get to there through **Chalma**. This is a popular pilgrimage spot and one of Mexico's most famous shrines. From the bus stop, walk uphill past the market to the crossroads where blue *colectivos* run until 2000 (10 km, 20 minutes, US$1).

Ixtapan de la Sal → *Colour map 3, B3. Phone code: 721.*

On Route 55, 23 km from Tenancingo, is Ixtapan de la Sal, a pleasant leisure resort with medicinal hot springs surrounded by forest. In the centre of this quiet whitewashed town is the **municipal spa** ① *daily 0700-1800, US$3*. At the edge of town is the privately run **Spa y Parque Acuático** ① *0900-1800, US$11*, which has a train running around it and numerous picnic spots. For the hedonist there are 'Roman' baths; for the stiff-limbed, a hot-water pool; for the vain, mud baths. There's also an Olympic pool and rowing boats. Market day is Sunday; a fiesta is held on the second Friday in Lent. Several other luxury spa facilities are dotted around town.

Tonatico, 5 km past Ixtapan de la Sal, is more pleasant and has a municipal *balneario* with medicinal hot water supposed to help blood circulation, rheumatism and other illnesses. There is also a waterslide (weekends only). Close to town flows the impressive Tzompantitlán waterfall, at a height of 50 m, and La Estrella caves, with rock formations, creepy stalactites and stalagmites.

Valle de Bravo → *Colour map 3, B3. Phone code: 726.*

The mountain resort of Valle de Bravo, located on a branch road of Route 134, is a charming old town on the edge of an attractive artificial lake and close to an important Monarch butterfly wintering area. Valle de Bravo's fiesta is 26 February to 14 March. From Valle del Bravo it's an easy excursion to **Colorines** with rock paintings dating from AD 800.

For Sleeping and Eating price codes and other relevant information, see Essentials pages 45-48.

⦿ Sleeping

Toluca *p160, map p160*

A El Gran Hotel, Allende 124, T722-213 9888. A decent, professionally run hotel with clean, carpeted rooms, wooden furniture, cable TV, heating and a/c. The lobby is glass-fronted and strewn with antiques. Bar-restaurant on site.

B Colonial, Hidalgo Ote 103, T722-215 9700, bus 'Terminal de Autobuses–Centro' passes in front. This big, airy colonial building has an attractive exterior with carved stone details. The interior is dominated by a courtyard and balconies, whilst rooms are comfortable and tidy, all equipped with clean bathrooms, TV, telephone, hot water. Coffee is available in the morning.

B San Carlos, Portal Madero 210, T722-214 9419, www.hotelsancarlos.com. Nice big rooms with carpets, drinking water, cable TV and hot water. Friendly and recommended. Check out the giant fish in the lobby!

C Rex, Matamoros Sur 101, T722-215 9300, hotelrex@prodigy.net.mx. Basic rooms have TV, hot water and bath. Ask to see a few, as some are reported to be shabby. Refreshments sold in the lobby.

D Maya, Hidalgo Pte 413, T722-214 4800. Cosy budget lodgings at this little blue house. Rooms are small, but comfortable enough, some cheaper ones have shared bath. Some doors don't have locks. Simple and family-run.

Camping

Campo Escuela Nacional de Tantoco, Km 29.5 on Mexico City–Toluca road, T722-5512 2279. Cabins and campsite.

Tenancingo *p162*

C Lazo, Guadalupe Victoria 100 (1½ blocks from market), T714-402 0083. Clean rooms with shower, leafy courtyard, restaurant.

D Don Ale, corner of Insurgentes y Netzahualcóyotl, T714-402 0516. Good value, with clean rooms, nice balcony and garden and no bugs. Loud TV may annoy.

Malinalco *p163*

B Santa Mónica, Hidalgo 109, T714-147 0031. A lovely little hotel with a peaceful courtyard. Close to the steps for the ruins. Rooms have bath, TV, hot water. Parking facility.

Ixtapan de la Sal *p163*

L-AL Ixtapan Spa, Blv Arturo San Román, T721-143 2440, www.spamexico.com. Gargantuan hotel and golf resort with 220 rooms, 3 restaurants, pools, gym, tennis courts and spa facilities. Discounts available for longer stays, check the website for more. Rooms are comfortable, predictably.

A Vista Hermosa, T721-143 0092, www.hotel-vistahermosa.com.mx. Next door to Ixtapan, this small, pleasant hotel has 16 comfortable rooms, a restaurant, green spaces and pool. Rates include 3 meals. Good and friendly.

C Casa de Huéspedes Margarita, Juárez. Clean and simple. Recommended.

C Casa Guille, José María Morelos 12, T721-143 0220. Clean, simple rooms with bath.

Valle de Bravo *p163*

Cheap *posadas familiares* by the plaza.

L-AL Los Arcos, Bocanegra 310, T726-262 0042. Some rooms with excellent view, swimming pool, restaurant at weekends, but unhelpful staff.

C Blanquita's, opposite church off main plaza. Basic, fairly clean, OK.

Camping

Trailer park, Av del Carmen 26, T726-262 1972. Recommended.

ⓔ Eating

Toluca p160, map p160

ᵮ El Huipil, Morelos 102. Good, traditional Mexican cuisine prepared before you at this atmospheric restaurant. Very affordable. Good breakfasts too.

ᵮ Porta di Roma, Nicolás Bravo Sur 540A. Pastas, pizzas, antipastos and other Italian fare.

ᵮ-ᵮ Hidalgo, Hidalgo 229. A good spot for breakfast. They also serve steaks, meats, Mexican food and hamburgers.

ᵮ Café de Allende, Allende 102. A bright little locals' café serving coffee, sweet rolls and Mexican staples.

South of Toluca p162

ᵮ Mesón del Cid, Santiago Tianguistenco. Serves local food, try *sopa de hongos* (mushroom soup).

Malinalco p163

ᵮ Los Placeres, Plaza Principal. A Bohemian space with interesting artwork and a pleasant garden with potted cacti, shade and stunning mountain views. *Chiles en nogada*, meat and the ubiquitous trout are on the menu.

Cafés

Mazinqui Café, Hidalgo, between Progreso and Comercio. Chilled out coffee shop serving caffeinated beverages, baguettes and snacks.

Valle de Bravo p163

Restaurants on the pier are expensive.
ᵮ Los Pericos, Embarcadero Municipal, T726-262 0558. Daily 0900-2000. International menu, specializes in fish dishes.
ᵮ Alma Edith, zócalo. Breakfast from 0900. Very good, but slow service, *comida corrida*.
ᵮ El Monarca, Juárez 203. Tasty *comida corrida*.
ᵮ Mercado. Good, cheap food. The *cecina* (salted beef) in this region is magnificent.

ⓔ Transport

Toluca p160, map p160

Bus

Local The bus station is away from the centre and confusing. Buses marked 'Centro' run to the centre, US$0.50; to the bus station buses marked 'Terminal' leave from Ignacio Rayón Norte and Hidalgo Ote (yellow or orange bus).

Long distance To **Mexico City** (Terminal Poniente, near Metro Observatorio), every 10 mins, 1 hr, US$4. To **Pátzcuaro**, 6 hrs, US$28, several daily. To **Taxco**, hourly, 3 hrs, US$8, a spectacular journey. To **Morelia**, several buses daily, 4 hrs, US$13. Many 2nd-class buses to **Tenango de Arista**, 30 mins, US$1.50; also regular buses to **Calixtlahuaca** 1 hr, US$3.50.

Malinalco p163

To reach Malinalco, travel to Tenango or Tenancingo, 2nd-class buses depart from **Toluca** every 30 mins, 1½-2 hrs, US$1.50. From there, catch a local *colectivo* to Malinalco, US$1.50, 1-1½ hrs. Alternatively, there a handful of daily departures to Tenancingo from Mexico City's **Terminal Poniente**, as well as a few direct services to Malinalco from Toluca, Sat and Sun only.

Ixtapan de la Sal p163

Bus To **Mexico City** (Terminal Poniente) every 30 mins, 3 hrs, US$11. To **Toluca** every 30 mins, 2 hrs, US$7. Also to **Taxco**, **Coatepec**, and **Cuernavaca**.

Car 2 hrs from Mexico City: turn off Route 15 (Toluca Hwy) at La Marquesa, go through Santiago Tianguis Tenco and join Route 55 at Tenango. The road goes on to the **Grutas de Cacahuamilpa** (see page 173), from where you can continue to Cuernavaca or Taxco.

Valle de Bravo p163

Bus To Mexico City's **Terminal Poniente**, hourly, US$10, 3 hrs. To **Toluca**, hourly, 2 hrs, US$5. 2 direct buses a day from **Zitácuaro**, 1½ hrs, US$5.

South of Mexico City

Heading south has been a popular route for centuries. Visit Cuernavaca and follow in the footsteps of Aztec nobility, Cortés and modern Mexicans who have used the gentle climate of the 'city of eternal spring' as a bolt-hole to relax and get away from the metropolis. As a centre of learning it is one of the most popular spots for Spanish-language schools in Mexico. Further south lies the colonial mining centre of Taxco with red-tiled roofs and pretty up-and-down cobbled streets; the magnificent Santa Prisca church is one of the most elaborate in all Mexico. The shops and market stalls are an attraction too, and you can seek out bargains in beautifully crafted silver. ▸▸ For listings, see pages 173-179.

Cuernavaca ●❷❷●▲●❸ ▸▸ pp173-179. Colour map 3, B4.

→ *Phone code: 777. Altitude: 1542 m.*

Cuernavaca lies just outside the Valley of Mexico. It is more than 700 m lower than Mexico City and the mild climate has made the town a popular escape from the heat of the city, and gets busy at weekends. With the Náhuatl name of Cuauhnáhuac, meaning 'adjacent to the tree', the area was popular with the Aztec nobility, and Hernán Cortés built a palace here, a tradition that continues today with the modern walled homes of rich *capitalinos*. The town is a buzzing centre of arts and intellectuals, with visitors from foreign lands joining the quest for knowledge at the town's many language schools.

Ins and outs

Getting there Buses leave the capital from the Terminal del Sur to one of Cuernavaca's four bus stations, each serving a different bus company. To drive the 89 km from Mexico City to Cuernavaca, follow Insurgentes Sur all the way south beyond Ciudad Universitaria and then take either the fast *cuota* (toll road), or the picturesque *libre*. Beyond Cuernavaca, Routes 95 and 95D continue south towards Taxco and Acapulco, or you can head east to Tepoztlán, Cuautla and on to the State of Puebla. There is a small airport at Cuernavaca with some domestic flights. ▸▸ *See Transport, page 177.*

Getting around Most of the sights in Cuernavaca are near the centre of town, within easy walking distance of each other. Local buses can be confusing as they take long, roundabout routes through the *colonias*. Buses marked 'Centro' or 'Buena Vista' all go to the cathedral. Taxis are plentiful and easy to flag down; agree the price before travelling.

Tourist information There is a state **tourist office** ① *Av Morelos Sur 187, T777-314 3872*, and a **tourist kiosk** ① *Vicente Guerrero outside Posada San Angelo*. For cultural activities, the best place for information is the university building behind the cathedral on Morelos Sur.

Sights

West of the centre, Calle Hidalgo leads to one of the main areas of historical interest in the city. The **cathedral**, finished in 1552 by Spanish architect Fransisco Becerra, who also designed Cortés' palace, has a stern and imposing exterior. Inside, the interior is bathed in different colours from the modern stained-glass windows. At the west end is a stone font full of water; at the east end, painted gold, stands the modern altar. In the entrance to the chapel of the Reserva de la Eucarista is a black and white fresco of the crucifixion. There are also two-storey cloisters with painted friezes and a fragment of massed ranks of monks and nuns. Some 17th-century murals were discovered in the interior during restoration. They depict the martyrdom of the Mexican saint San Felipe de Jesús on his journey to Japan, with renditions of monks in open boats and mass crucifixions. By the cathedral entrance stands the charming small church of the **Tercera Orden** (1529), whose quaint façade, carved by local indigenous craftsmen, contains a small figure suspected to

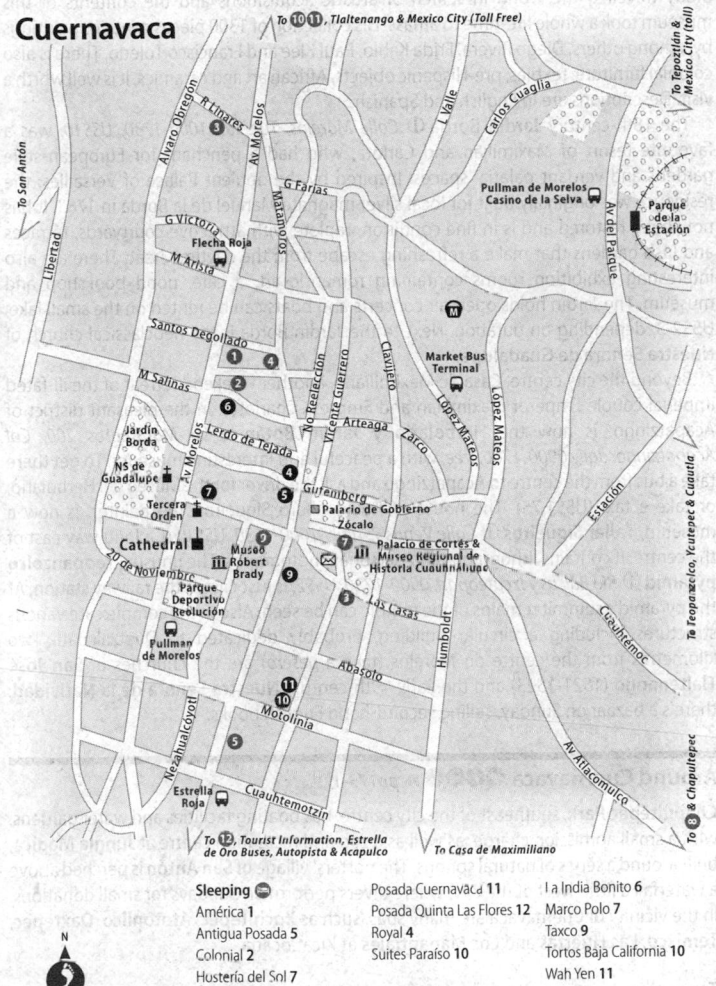

Cuernavaca

Sleeping

América **1**
Antigua Posada **5**
Colonial **2**
Hostería del Sol **7**
Hostería Las Quintas **8**
Las Hortensas **9**
Las Mañanitas **3**

Posada Cuernavaca **11**
Posada Quinta Las Flores **12**
Royal **4**
Suites Paraíso **10**

Eating

La Cavocha **4**
La Cueva **5**

La India Bonito **6**
Marco Polo **7**
Taxco **9**
Tortos Baja California **10**
Wah Yen **11**

be one of only two known statues of Cortés in Mexico. (The other is a mounted statue near the entrance of the **Casino de la Selva** hotel.) The gates to the cathedral and the Tercera Orden are closed each day at 1400.

Next to the cathedral, in the Casa de la Torre is the **Museo Robert Brady** ① *Calle Nezahualcoyotl 4, www.bradymuseum.org, Tue-Sun 1000-1800, US$2, café and shop*, housing the extensive collection of works and artefacts belonging to the American artist. Brady travelled the world in search of artistic acquisitions and the contents of this museum took a whole life-time to amass. His collection of 1300 pieces contains paintings by, among others, Diego Rivera, Frida Kahlo, Paul Klee and Francisco Toledo. There is also colonial furniture, textiles, pre-Hispanic objects, African art and ceramics. It is well worth a visit. Descriptions are in English and Spanish.

The 18th-century **Jardín Borda** ① *Calle Morelos, Tue-Sun 1000-1730, US$10*, was a favourite resort of Maximilian and Carlota, who had a penchant for European-style gardens and verdant palatial spaces. Inspired by the opulent Palace of Versailles, the residence was originally built for local silver magnate Manuel de la Borda in 1783. It has now been restored and is in fine condition, replete with attractive courtyards, terraces and lush gardens that make a refreshing escape from the daytime heat. There are also interesting exhibition rooms containing romantic art, a café, good bookshop and museum. The Jardín holds open-air concerts and boats can be rented on the small lake, US$2-3, depending on duration. Next to the Jardín Borda is the neoclassical church of **Nuestra Señora de Guadalupe**.

Beyond the city centre, Casa de Maximiliano, another weekend retreat of the ill-fated imperial couple Emperor Maximilian and Empress Charlotte, in the pleasant district of Acapatzingo, is now the **Herbolario y Jardín Botánico** ① *Matamoros 200, Col Acapatzingo, daily 0900-1700, free*, with a peaceful and interesting museum. To get there take a bus from the centre to Acapatzingo and ask the driver for the Museo del Herbolario, or take a taxi (US$1.75). The house of David Alfaro Siqueiros, the painter, is now a museum, **Taller Siqueiros** ① *Calle Venus 7, daily 1000-1630, US$1.50*, a long way east of the centre. It contains lithographs and personal photographs. The unusual **Teopanzolco pyramid** ① *Río Balsas y Ixcateopan, 0900-1730, US$2*, is just east of the railway station. At the pyramid's summit remains of the temple can be seen. Also in the complex are various structures including a circular building, probably dedicated to Quetzalcoatl. Two kilometres from the centre on Morelos (take a *pesero*) are the churches of **San José Tlaltenango** (1521-1523) and the early 19th-century **Nuestra Señora de la Natividad**; there's a bazaar on Sunday, selling second-hand English books.

Around Cuernavaca 😀🚗🍴🛏️ ›› *pp173-179*.

Chapultepec Park, southeast of the city centre, has boating facilities and water gardens, with a small admission charge, as well as a zoo and recreation centre at **Jungla Mágica**, built around a series of natural springs. The potters' village of **San Antón** is perched above a waterfall a little west of the city, where divers perform on Sundays for small donations. In the vicinity of Cuernavaca are many spas, such as **Xochitepec**, **Atotonilco**, **Oaxtepec**, **Temixco**, **Las Huertas** and **Los Manantiales** at Xicatlocatla.

Tepoztlán → *Colour map 3, B4. Phone code: 739.*
Tepoztlán, meaning 'where copper abounds', is 24 km northeast of Cuernavaca, with steep cobbled streets, bustling markets and interesting historical architecture. As a

bastion of Náhua traditions, this was the village studied by anthropologist Robert Redfield and later by Oscar Lewis, who wrote the classic *Life in a Mexican Village*. Increasingly, it caters to wealthy weekenders, tourists and a growing hippie contingent, perhaps drawn by the mystical energies of the surrounding hills and the fact that Tepoztlán was the mythical birthplace of Quetzalcoatl, the feathered serpent. If you're in the area on 7 September there's a raucous festival in honour of Náhua Pulque gods, whilst in the first week of November there is an arts festival with films and concerts held outdoors and in the main church's cloister.

The town is home to a remarkable 16th-century church and convent, **María de la Natividad**. Here, the Virgin and Child stand upon a crescent moon above an elaborate plateresque portal. A mural by Juan Ortega (1887) covers the eastern end of the church. Behind the church there is a small **archaeological museum** ① *Tue-Sun 1000-1800, US$0.75*, with objects from all over Mexico that were collected and donated by Tabascan poet Carlos Pellicer Cámara. There is an arts and crafts market on the plaza at the weekend with a good but expensive selection of handicrafts from Mexico, Guatemala and East Asia.

Tepoztlán lies at the foot of the spectacular **Parque Nacional El Tepozteco**, with the small **Tepozteco pyramid** ① *0900-1730, US$2.70, free on Sun*, high up in the mountains. The only way into the park is on foot. It takes 40 to 60 minutes to climb from the car park at the end of Avenida de Tepozteco. Be warned, the 2 km ascent is quite strenuous, so go before the sun is too high. Signs remind you on the way that you must pay at the top, and five minutes before the entrance a steel ladder has to be scaled. The altitude at the top is 2100 m and the view of the valley expansive. The pyramid here was dedicated to the Pulque deity, Tepoztecatl.

Cuautla → *Colour map 3, B4. Phone code: 735.*

Take Route 160 from Cuernavaca via Yautepec to the semi-tropical town of Cuautla, meaning 'where trees abound'. This crowded weekend resort for the capital is a popular sulphur spring, known as *aguas hediondas* or stinking waters. The tourists' Cuautla is divided from the locals' Cuautla by a wide river and the locals have the best deal; it is worth crossing the stream. The plaza is pleasant, traffic free and well maintained. There is a market in the streets around 5 de Mayo. The **tourist office** ① *Av Obregón*, is opposite Hotel Cuautla. The **Casa de la Cultura** ① *3 blocks north of the zócalo*, has information and maps. There is a **museum** and ex-convent next door.

Xochicalco → *Colour map 3, B4.*

① *Daily 0900-1800, US$4, tickets must be bought at the museum.*

The ruined ceremonial centre of Xochicalco lies 36 km southwest of Cuernavaca and is a UNSECO World Heritage Site. It is one of the oldest known fortresses in Mesoamerica and was an important trading point as well as religious centre. The name means 'Place of the flower house' although now the hilltops are barren. The site is topped by a pyramid on the peak of a rocky hill, dedicated to the Plumed Serpent, whose coils enfold the whole building and enclose fine carvings that represent priests. Xochicalco was at its height between AD 650 and 900. It was the meeting place of northern and southern cultures and, it is believed, both calendar systems were correlated here. The sides of the Pyramid of the Plumed Serpent are faced with andesite slabs, fitted invisibly without mortar. After the building was finished, reliefs up to 10 cm deep were carved into the stone as a frieze. There are some interesting **underground tunnels** ① *daily 1100-1400*. One of them served as a solar observatory where, as the sun nears the tropic of cancer on 14/15 May and 28/29 July, a hexagonal-shaped chimney casts a shaft of light directly over an image of the sun. There are also ball courts, the remains of 20 large circular altars and of a palace and dwellings. Xochicalco is well worth the 4-km walk from the bus stop; take a torch for the underground part. There is a **museum** about 500 m from the ruins, incorporating many ecological principles and housing magnificent items from the ruins; descriptions in Spanish only.

South to Guerrero state
If heading south on super-highway 95D towards Acapulco or Guerrero state, there are a number of sights and back-road diversions to break your journey. South of Cuernavaca, **Alpuyeca**, Km 100, has a church with indigenous murals. From here, a road runs south towards **Lago Tequesquitengo** and the lagoon and sulphur baths of **Tehuixtla**. East of the lake is **Jojutla** and the nearby old Franciscan convent of **Tlaquiltenango** (1540) (frequent bus service from Cuernavaca, US$1.75, **Pullman de Morelos**). West of the lake, the highway branches towards the silver town of Taxco, which is well worth a visit (see below), but back on super-highway 95D, it's 278 km to Acapulco from the Morelos–Guerrero state border. You'll pass through Chilpancingo en-route.

Taxco ⬤🅟🅕🅔🅑🅒 ⟫⟫ pp173-179. Colour map 3, C4.
Surrounded by steep slopes and awesome mountain views, Taxco is a popular colonial town with twisting, cobbled streets and many handsome buildings. It's now almost wholly dedicated to tourism. The first silver shipped to Spain came from the mines of Taxco. José de la Borda made and spent three fortunes here in the 18th century; he founded the present town and built the magnificent twin-towered, rose-coloured parish church of Santa Prisca, which soars above everything but the mountains. The picturesque town is now a national monument and all modern building is forbidden.

Ins and outs
Getting there Buses to Taxco leave from Mexico City's **Terminal del Sur** and arrive at terminals on the edge of town. You should book onward or return bus tickets to Mexico City on arrival. Some buses en route to Mexico City drop passengers on the main highway, some way from the centre. Taxco is connected to Mexico City and Acapulco via Route 95 and the fast *supercarretera* Route 95D. For international flights, Mexico City or Acapulco airports are the closest. Some domestic routes are served by Cuernavaca airport. ⟫⟫ See Transport, page 177.

Getting around Taxco is a fairly small town and, although hilly and cobbled, is best experienced on foot. *Combis* or taxis will take you up the hill from the bus terminals.

Tourist information You can take a city tour from the **tourist office** ⓘ Av de los Plateros 1, T762-622 2274, daily 0900-1400, 1600-2000, inconveniently located on the north side of town.

Sights
The central area of Taxco is quite hectic. Roaring taxis, vociferous silver merchants, crowds of shoppers and gawping tourists all contribute to the sense of chaos. The district between the four-storey Mercado and the Carretera Nacional is much quieter, as are those parts up from the main streets where taxis can't go. There are silver markets all over

Taxco

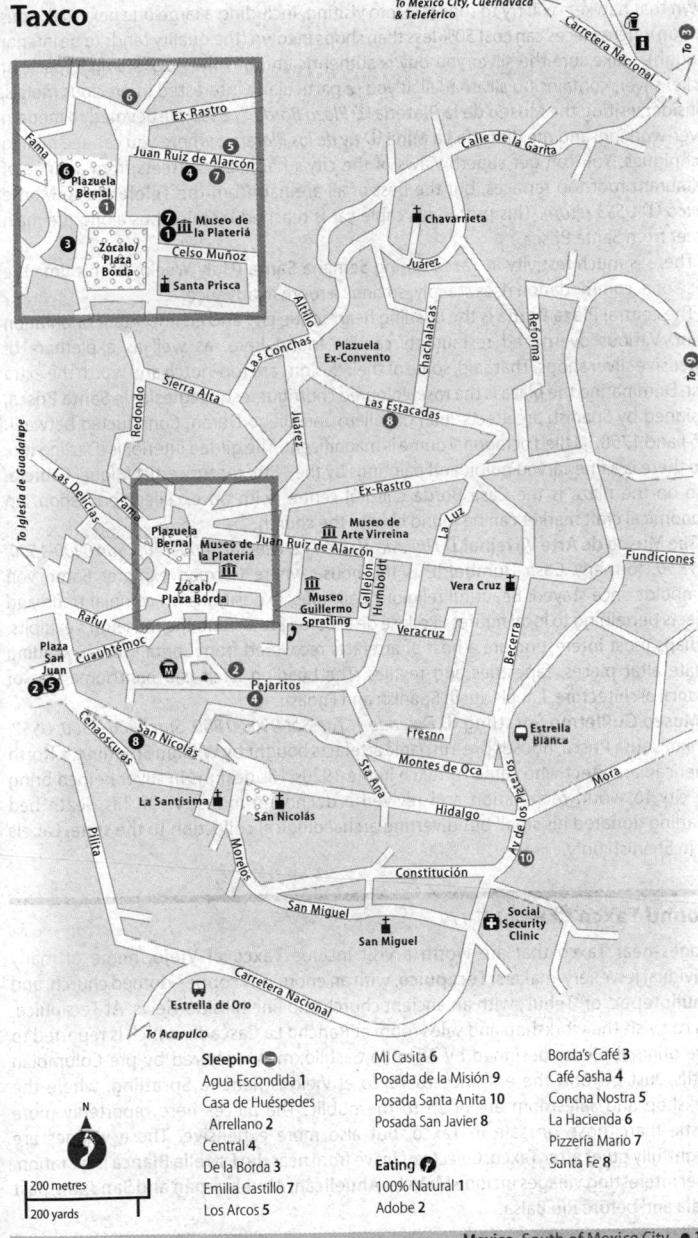

To Mexico City, Cuernavaca & Teleférico

Carretera Nacional

Inset (top):
Ex Rastro
Fama
Juan Ruiz de Alarcón
Plazuela Bernal 6
Zócalo/Plaza Borda 3
Celso Muñoz
Museo de la Platería 1
Santa Prisca

Calle de la Garita
Chavarrieta
Juárez
Chachalacas
Reforma

Plazuela Ex-Convento
Las Conchas
Altitio
Sierra Alta
Las Estacadas 8
Redondo
Ex-Rastro
La Luz
Las Delicias
Fama
Plazuela Bernal
Museo de la Platería
Juan Ruiz de Alarcón
Museo de Arte Virreina
Fundiciones
Zócalo/Plaza Borda
Museo Guillermo Spratling
Callejón Humboldt
Vera Cruz
Raful
Veracruz
Becerra
Plaza San Juan
Cuauhtémoc
Pajaritos
Fresno
Estrella Blanca
Cenaoscuras
San Nicolás
Montes de Oca
Mora
La Santísima
San Nicolás
Hidalgo
Av de los Plateros
Pilita
Sta Ana
Morelos
Constitución
San Miguel
Social Security Clinic
San Miguel
Carretera Nacional
Estrella de Oro
To Acapulco

To Iglesia de Guadalupe

200 metres
200 yards

Sleeping 🛏
Agua Escondida 1
Casa de Huéspedes Arrellano 2
Central 4
De la Borda 3
Emilia Castillo 7
Los Arcos 5
Mi Casita 6
Posada de la Misión 9
Posada Santa Anita 10
Posada San Javier 8

Eating 🍴
100% Natural 1
Adobe 2
Borda's Café 3
Café Sasha 4
Concha Nostra 5
La Hacienda 6
Pizzería Mario 7
Santa Fe 8

town that hawkers will try to rope you into visiting, including a large one next to the bus station where pieces can cost 50% less than shops in town (the quality tends to be inferior though). Make sure the silver you buy is authentic and has the '925' stamp. Alpaca, or nickel silver, contains no silver at all. If you're particularly interested in precious metals, consider visiting the **Museo de la Platería** ① *Plaza Borda 1, US$1.50*, devoted to modern silver-working; and the **Platería La Mina** ① *Av de los Plateros*, where you can see mining techniques. You can get superb views of the city's haphazard streets from a range of restaurant roof-top terraces, but the best of all are had from the **Teleférico to Monte Taxco** ① *US$3 return*. This precarious cable car is reached by microbus along the main street from Santa Prisca.

There is much festivity in Taxco during **Semana Santa** (Holy Week). At this time the price of accommodation rises steeply, so book a room in advance.

The central **Plaza Borda** is the bustling heart of the city and an important orientation point. Various overpriced restaurants can be found here, as well as a plethora of expensive silver shops. That said, some of their designs are top-notch and worth the extra cost. Dominating the plaza is the rose-coloured churrigueresque **Iglesia de Santa Prisca**, designed by Spanish architects Juan Caballero and Diego Durán. Constructed between 1751 and 1758, its tiled octagonal dome is magnificent. The gilded interior is dazzling too, and there is a fine carved pulpit and paintings by the 18th-century artist Miguel Cabrera. Also on the plaza is the **Casa Borda** cultural centre, with an excellent bookshop. An economical craft market can be found behind the church.

The **Museo de Arte Virreinal** ① *J Ruiz de Alarcón 12, Tue-Sat 1000-1700, Sun 0900-1500, US$1.50*, formerly **Casa Humboldt**, is the house where German explorer Baron von Humboldt once stayed. Beautiful religious paintings, expositions on colonial trade and objects pertaining to local figures like José de la Borda are among the museum's exhibits. Perhaps most interesting are a host of artefacts recovered from Santa Prisca, including ornate altar pieces, tapestries and textiles. The building itself is a handsome feat of colonial architecture. Labels are in Spanish and English.

Museo Guillermo Spratling ① *Delgado 1, Tue-Sat 0900-1800, Sun 0900-1500, US$2*, behind Santa Prisca, houses pre-Hispanic artefacts bought by William Spratling, a North American architect who came to Taxco in the 1920s. His designs in silver helped bring the city to world recognition and revived a dwindling industry. On his death bed Spratling donated his small but diverting archaeological collection to the state. Labels are in Spanish only.

Around Taxco ❸ ↠ *pp173-179*.

Villages near Taxco that are worth a visit include **Taxco el Viejo**, home of many individual jewellery-makers; **Tecapulco**, with an enormous copper-domed church; and **Tehuilotepec**, or 'Tehui', with an ancient church and fine hillside views. At Tecapulco, you can visit the workshop and sales room at **Rancho La Cascada**, which is reported to have original pieces designed by Antonio Castillo, many inspired by pre-Columbian motifs. Just beyond the entrance to Taxco el Viejo is **Rancho Spratling**, where the workshop and salesroom are open to the public. The pieces here reportedly more artistic than those on sale in Taxco, but also more expensive. These villages are delightfully quiet after Taxco. *Colectivos* leave from near the **Estrella Blanca** bus station. Other interesting villages include **Maxela**, **Ahuelicán**, **Ahuehuepán** and **San Juan**, past Iguala and before Río Balsa.

Ixcateopan de Cuauhtémoc, Cuauhtémoc's birthplace, is a beautiful and peaceful village where most of the buildings, and even the cobblestones, are made of marble. A statue honouring Cuauhtémoc, the last Aztec emperor, stands at the entrance to town. The old church has been converted into a museum where Cuauhtémoc's skeleton is said to rest in the glass-covered altar-like tomb. 22-23 February is the anniversary of Cuauhtémoc's death, called *Día de la Mexicanidad*, the date when he was executed by Cortés. In rememberance, runners come from Mexico City to Ixcateopan via Taxco, carrying a torch representing the identity of the Mexican people. Meanwhile, Aztec dancers, in traditional dress and colourful plumed headdresses, arrive from all over to dance all night and most of the following day. To get here, take a *pesero* from the road out of Taxco towards Acapulco, a one-hour drive west through beautiful mountain scenery.

Cacahuamilpa

ⓘ *www.cacahuamilpa.conanp.gob.mx, daily 1000-1700, US$2.50, children US$4, including 2¼-hr tour, Spanish only, every hr on the hr up to 1600 (crowded after 1100 and at weekends), take a torch.*

The Cacahuamilpa caverns, known locally as 'Las Grutas', are some of the largest caves in North America and are well worth a visit. They have enormous chambers, as well as some strange and rather stunning stalactites and stalagmites. Steps lead down from the near the entrance to the caverns and onto the double opening in the mountainside far below, from which an underground river emerges. Guided tours take you 2 km inside; some excursions have gone 6 km. Note that some visitors have reported underwhelming experiences with these guides, who generally do not speak English. Don't miss the descent to the river exits at the base of the cliff, called Dos Bocas, which is tranquil and less frequently visited.

◉ South of Mexico City listings

For Sleeping and Eating price codes and other relevant information, see Essentials pages 45-48.

◉ Sleeping

Cuernavaca *p166, map p167*
LL Hacienda de Cortés, Plaza Kennedy 90, T777-315 8844, www.hotelhaciendade cortes.com. A historic 16th-century sugar hacienda with magnificent colonial architecture, atmospheric gardens, suites, pool and an excellent restaurant. Access by car.
LL Las Mañanitas, Ricardo Linares 107, T777-362 0000, www.lasmananitas.com.mx. This is 1 of the best hotels in Mexico, sumptuously decorated and built in colonial style, with many birds in the lovely gardens, elegant suites, excellent food and spa facilities. Reservations necessary.

L-AL Hostería Las Quintas, Av Díaz Ordaz 9, Col Cantarranas, T777-362 3949, www.hosterialasquintas.com.mx. Built in traditional Mexican style with a magnificent setting and beautiful bougainvillea embracing the exterior. Facilities include restaurant, 2 pools, spa and outdoor jacuzzi. The owner also has a splendid collection of bonsai trees. Fine reputation.
L-AL Posada Quinta Las Flores, Tlaquepaque 210, Col Las Palmas, 30 mins' walk from centre, T777-314 1244, www.quintalasflores.com. You'll find comfortable, tasteful rooms and a splendid, flower-filled garden at this pleasant hotel. Services include pool, restaurant and parking. Rates include breakfast. Helpful and highly recommended.
AL Antigua Posada, Galeana 69, T777-310 2179, www.hotelantiguaposada.com. This mid-range hotel looks much better on the

inside than the outside. Each room has its own terrace where breakfast is served in the morning. Services include pool, Wi-Fi, phone, taxi service and tourist information. Clean, comfortable and helpful. There's a 10% discount during the week.

AL Posada Cuernavaca, Paseo del Conquistador, T777-313 0800, www.hotel posadacuernavaca.com. Motel-style place with restaurant, pool and pleasant grounds.

AL Suites Paraíso, Av Domingo Díaz 1100, T777-313 2444, www.suitesparaiso.com.mx. Modern hotel with pool, restaurant and pleasant patio. Rooms are comfortable and carpeted, if fairly unremarkable. Some have reported poor service.

B Hostería del Sol, Fray Bartolomé de las Casas 5, close to the Palacio de Cortés, T777-312 6892. Loaded with charm and authentically Mexican, this friendly and secluded hotel has lots of tiles, courtyards, patios and flowers. They have just 6 rooms, including a suite (**A**). An events room is also available. Friendly and recommended.

C América, Aragón y León 14, T777-318 6127, www.tourbymexico.com/hotelamerica. In the words of the owners, 'bueno, bonito, barato.' Simple, clean rooms surround a central courtyard, equipped with basic furniture, fan, hot water and bath, and some cheaper beds have shared bath. Friendly and comfortable enough. OK. Not bad.

C Colonial, Aragón y León 19, T777-318 6414, hotelcolonialcortes@hotmail.com. Clean, simple rooms overlooking a quiet courtyard filled with plants. Rooms have TV, fan and bath. OK.

C Las Hortensias, Hidalgo 13, T777-318 5265, www.hotelhortensias.com. A simple and very slightly grubby hotel with carpeted rooms and cable TV. Still, the courtyard is pretty and it's central. They take Visa.

C Royal, Matamoros 11, T777-318 6480, www.hoteles-royal.com. Motel-style joint with parking, fan, cable TV and hot water. Rooms are a bit tired and grubby.

Tepoztlán p168

LL Posada del Tepozteco, T739-395 0010, www.posadadeltepozteco.com. A very good historic inn, quiet and old fashioned, with an excellent atmosphere and superlative views. Rooms are very comfortable and tasteful, services include pool and terraced restaurant. Patronized by celebrities and highly recommended.

LL Posada del Valle, Camino a Meztitla 5, T739-395 0521, www.posadadelvalle.com.mx. A very pleasant, romantic retreat with attractive stonework, great views, colourful gardens and tastefully presented rooms. Services include restaurant, pool and spa facilities for those needing a pamper.

A Posada Ali, Nezahualcóyotl 2 C, off Av del Tepozteco, T739-395 1971. A comfortable choice with good value and attractive rooms, pool, suites, views and courtyard.

Cuautla p169

B Jardín de Cuautla, 2 de Mayo 94, opposite Colón bus station, T735-352 0088. Modern and clean, but subject to bad traffic noise. There's a pool.

D Casa de Huéspedes Aragón, Guerrero 72. A basic, friendly hotel, good value, where clean rooms have hot water. Recommended.

D España, 2 de Mayo 22, 3 blocks from bus station, T735-352 2186. Very good and clean with 30 comfortable rooms. Recommended.

D Hotel Colón, main square. Good, clean and basic budget lodging.

South to Guerrero state p170

Several lakeside hotels at Tequesquitengo.
LL-L Hacienda Vista Hermosa, Tequesquitengo, T734-345 5362, www.hac iendavistahermosa.com.mx. Hernán Cortés' original *ingenio* (sugar mill) is a popular resort, with swimming, boating, waterskiing and fishing on the lake. Rooms are very attractive and filled with unfussy, tasteful furnishings.

Taxco p170, map p171

L Posada de la Misión, Cerro de la Misión 32, T762-622 0063, www.posadamision.com.

A very attractive, secluded hotel with elegant finishes, good atmosphere and astounding hill-top views. Services include restaurant, Wi-Fi, pool, jacuzzi and parking.

A Hotel de la Borda, on left as you enter Taxco, T762-622 0225, www.hotelborda.com. An elegant, attractive hotel with atmospheric colonial architecture, great views and over 100 comfortable rooms. Services include restaurant, pool and 4 events rooms.

A Posada Don Carlos, Consuelo 8, T762-622 0075. A converted old mansion with a restaurant and good views.

A-C Agua Escondida, Plaza Borda 4, T762-622 1166, www.aguaescondida.com. Great terraces, arches and corridors at this centrally located lodging. There's Wi-Fi, a good pool, restaurant, café, and a bar with great views of the plaza. Rooms are plain and comfortable, cheaper downstairs without TV (**B-C**). Prices rise at weekends. Professional and helpful.

B Hotel Emilia Castillo, Alarcón 7, T762-622 1396, www.hotelemiliacastillo.com. A charming, colonial-style hotel, just off the main square. Services include bar, massage and silver shop. Very friendly and good value. Book ahead if possible.

B Hotel Mi Casita, Altos de Redondo 1, T762-627 1777, www.hotelmicasita.com. This hospitable and historic colonial townhouse has very 12 pleasant rooms, all complimented by tiled bathrooms, attractive wooden furniture and other tasteful details. Comfortable and charming.

B Los Arcos, Juan Ruiz de Alarcón 4, T762-622 1836, www.hotellosarcos.net. A beautifully reconstructed 17th-century ex-convent with a tree growing out of the central courtyard. Very tastefully decorated with fountains, wooden furniture and Mexican *artesanías*. The best rooms for views are 18 and 19, the rooms overlooking street are noisy. Lots of character and highly recommended.

B Posada San Javier, Estacadas 32, T762-622 3177, posadasanjavier@ hotmail.com. Lots of cooling, plant-filled patios, secluded little bungalows and a pool. Centrally located, with Wi-Fi.

B-C Posada Santa Anita, Av de los Plateros 320, T762-622 0752, hpsta54@hotmail.com. Located on a busy main road, rooms here are smallish and straight-forward, slightly overpriced, but comfortable enough. They're cheaper without TV (**D**), parking and sun terrace available. Friendly.

C Casa de Huéspedes Arrellano, Pajaritos 23, below Santa Prisca and Plaza Borda, inside the *artesanía* market, T762-622 0215. Basic, friendly hotel with patios and nice little budget rooms, with or without bath and hot water.

D Central, Pajaritos 27, around the left-hand corner of **Casa de Huéspedes Arrellano**, T762-622 0365. Reasonable budget lodgings, but most suitable for thrifty backpackers. Rooms come with or without bath, those upstairs are better, and some have little balconies. A room for 7 people works out very economically (**F**). Hot water 24 hrs. Friendly.

❼ Eating

Cuernavaca *p166, map p167*
Fruit juices are sold from stalls beneath the bandstand on the *zócalo*.

🍴🍴🍴 Las Mañanitas, see Sleeping, above. This beautiful and highly reputable restaurant serves imaginatively prepared, delicious Mexican food. Smart, romantic and excellent, but expensive, and only Amex accepted. A pleasant garden setting replete with exotic birds.

🍴🍴-🍴 Marco Polo, opposite cathedral. A good Italian restaurant serving fine pizzas. Also a popular meeting place with great views from the upper floor balconies. Recommended.

🍴 La India Bonita, Morrow 20. Fine Mexican food served in a lush colonial garden complete with trees, plants and bubbling fountain. Breakfasts are excellent, with a Sunday buffet 0900-1300. Recommended.

🍴 Wah Yen, Juárez 306. Tasty Cantonese food, including set menus, fish, vegetable and chicken dishes.

¶¶-¶ Taxco, Galeana 12. Bustling little locals' restaurant with colourful chairs and tablecloths. They serve enchiladas, *mole poblano*, *chiles en nogada*, *quesadillas* and other classic Mexican fare.

¶ La Cavocha, Rayon 2. Unpretentious and ultra-cheap. *Comida corrida*, plastic chairs and Telenovelas blasting from the TV.

¶ La Cueva, Galeana. Locals' haunt under the arches. The usual cheap, high-carb fare.

¶ Tortas Baja California, corner of Motolinía and Juárez. Small and bustling fast food joint with lots of locals. *Tortas*, burritos and fish-filled tacos are on the menu.

Tepoztlán *p168*

¶¶¶-¶¶ El Ciruelo, Zaragoza 17. A quiet restaurant with nice decor and good mountain views. Popular with wealthy Mexicans.

¶¶ La Costa de San Juan, by plaza on opposite side of street. Mostly meat and seafood.

¶¶ Los Colorines, Av del Tepozteco 13-B. Good Mexican and vegetarian food in brightly painted, cheery surroundings.

¶¶-¶ Axitla, at beginning of path up to Tepozteco. Open Fri, Sat, Sun and holidays. Mexican and international food in atmospheric, natural surroundings.

Taxco *p170, map p171*

¶¶¶-¶¶ 100% Natural, Plaza Borda. This famous franchise, found throughout Mexico, specializes in wholesome, healthy food, all prepared with love. Recommended.

¶¶¶-¶¶ La Ventana, in La Hacienda del Solar, T762-622 0587. Wonderful views of the city and an Italian-Mexican menu.

¶¶ Adobe, Plazuela de San Juan. A Mexican restaurant with good decor and atmosphere, if a bit touristy. Dishes include Oaxacan *enchiladas*, garlic soup and shrimp specials, and Guerrero-style chicken cooked with paprika, onions and miniature potatoes. Excellent *chilaquiles* and other breakfasts.

¶¶ La Hacienda, Plaza Borda 4 (entrance is off the square). A fabulous interior with chic decor and a good atmosphere. Excellent

Mexican food and wine at reasonable prices. Also accessible from **Hotel Agua Escondido**.

¶¶ Pizzería Mario, Plaza Borda. Opened 30 years ago, Mario's was the 1st pizzeria in town, with beautiful view over city, excellent pizzas and pleasant service. Highly recommended, and not to be confused with either **Café** or **Restaurant Mario**.

¶¶-¶ Café Sasha, Alcarón 1. A bohemian café adorned with swirling fractals and other trippy artwork. They serve baguettes, burgers, breakfasts, coffee and beer. Speciality of the house is vegetable crêpes in coconut curry sauce.

¶¶-¶ Concha Nostra, Plazuela San Juan (above **Hotel Casa Grande**). Pizza, lasagne, burgers and live rock on Sat. Good views of the plaza below, but some have reported that the food is mediocre and the service poor. Cheap for breakfasts, other meals are pricey.

¶¶-¶ Santa Fe, Hidalgo 2, opposite **Hotel Santa Prisca**, T762-622 1170. Excellent *comida corrida* (US$6) but disappointing enchiladas. Frequented by the locals.

¶ Borda's Café, Plaza Borda 6a. A friendly little café adorned with black and white film memorabilia. They serve snacks and light meals, including pork chops, tacos, enchiladas and salads. Lots of good coffee too, including drowsy alcoholic brews laced with Kahlua. English-speaking.

¶ Mercado, cheap *comida corrida* in the market and good cheap restaurants on San Nicolás.

O Shopping

Cuernavaca *p166, map p167*

Bookshops Particularly good on art and history in the **Palacio de Cortés**, to the left of the main entrance; also at **Jardín Borda** in Morelos. Another good bookshop, **Gandhi Colorines**, Av Teopanzoclo 401, not far from the archaeological site of the same name. Second-hand English books at **Guild House**, Tuxtla Gutiérrez, Col Chipitlán, T777-312 5197.

Handicrafts Market behind Palacio de Cortés, moderately priced and interesting silver, textiles and souvenirs.

Taxco p170, map p171

You'll find no shortage of silver shops in Taxco with from the exclusive all the way down to basic, poor quality and even fake items. Some of the most reputable shops are on the **Plaza Borda**, particularly in the **Patio de Artesanías**. You'll find cheaper bustling markets on the main road close to the Estrella Blanca bus station, as well as on side streets around town. Wherever you buy, always look for the '.925' mark, which confirms that the silver is of sterling quality, that is, 92.5% pure. Silver that's 100% pure is only half as strong as sterling silver and is unsuitable for most jewellery pieces.

▲ Activities and tours

Cuernavaca p166, map p167
Travel agents
Marín, Centro Las Plazas, Local 13, Amex agent, changes Amex TCs but poorer rate than *casas de cambio*, charges US$1 to reconfirm flights.
Pegaso, also in Centro Las Plazas, French, Italian, German, English spoken (the sign says), charges US$2 to reconfirm.
Viajes Adelina, Pasaje Bella Vista, on zócalo.

● Transport

Cuernavaca p166, map p167
Bus
Each bus company has its own terminal: **Estrella de Oro**, Morelos Sur 900, Col Las Palmas, T777-312 3055; **Pullman de Morelos**, Abasolo 106 y Netzahualcóyotl in the centre, T777-318 0907, with a 2nd terminal at **Casino de la Selva**, Plan de Ayala 102, opposite Parque de la Estación, T777-318 9205; **Estrella Blanca** on Morelos Norte 503 y Arista, T777-312 5797, also with

Futura and **Flecha Roja** departures; and **Estrella Roja**, Galeana y Cuauhtemotzín, south of the centre. Many minibuses and 2nd-class buses leave from a terminal by the market.

To **Acapulco**, every 2 hrs, **Futura**, US$25, 4 hrs, or **Estrella de Oro**, every 2 hrs, book well in advance. To **Cuautla**, every 15 mins, **Estrella Roja**, 0600-2200, 1½ hrs, US$4, or take a minibus from the market terminal, 1 hr via Yautepec, intresting trip. To **Guadalajara**, 5 daily, **Estrella Blanca**, US$38. To **Mexico City**, every 10 mins, **Pullman** (Casino de la Selva), 1½ hrs, US$7. To **Mexico City airport**, 10 daily, **Pullman** (Casino de la Selva), 2 hrs, US$12. To **Puebla**, hourly, **Estrella Roja**, 0510-1910, US$12, 3 hrs, or **Estrella de Oro**, hourly. To **Queretero**, 5 daily, **Estrella Blanca**, US$15. To **San Luis Potosí**, 4 daily, **Estrella Blanca**, US$32. To **Taxco**, hourly, **Estrella de Oro**, 1st class, US$6, 1½ hrs, or **Estrella Blanca**, hourly, 2nd class (not recommended). To **Tepoztlán**, every 30 mins, **Estrella Roja**, 30 min, US$2.

Tepoztlán p168
Pullman de Morelos operate services between Mexico City's Terminal Sur and Tepoztlán every 30 mins, US$5, 1½ hrs. More frequent buses pass the toll booth just outside downtown Tepoztlán, including rapid services to **Mexico City** and **Cuautla**. Regular 2nd-class services to **Cuernavaca** depart from downtown.

Cuautla p169
Cuautla has 4 bus terminals serving various companies: OCC, Sur and Volcanes, 2 de Mayo and Bravo; **Pullman de Morelos**, also on 2 de Mayo and Bravo; **Estrella de Oro**, 2 de Mayo and Mongoy; **Estrella Roja**, Costena and 2 de Mayo.

To **Cuernavaca**, every 20 mins, **Estrella Roja**, 1½ hrs, US$4. To **Mexico City**, every 20 mins, **Estrella Roja**, 2½ hrs, US$7, or OCC. To **Puebla**, hourly, **Estrella de Oro**, 2½ hrs, US$10, or **Estrella Roja**. To **Tepoztlán**, every 15 mins, **Pullman**, 15 mins, US$2.

Xochicalco *p169*

Bus 2nd-class 'Cuautepec' buses depart from Cuernavaca market and go directly to the site entrance. Alternatively, take a **Pullman de Morelos** bus from Cuernavaca en route to El Rodeo (every 30 mins), Coatlán or Las Grutas; get off at the turn-off 4 km from the site, then take a *colectivo*, US$0.35-US$1.20 per person, or walk up the hill. From Taxco, take bus to Alpuyeca (US$1.60, 1 hr 40 mins) and pick up the bus from Cuernavaca to the turn-off, or taxi from the junction at Alpuyeca directly to ruins (12 km, US$2.50).

Taxco *p170, map p171*
Bus
Local *Combis* take you up the hill from the bus terminal, US$0.35, same fare across town.

There are 2 bus stations: **Estrella Blanca**, Av de los Plateros, serving **Estrella Blanca**, **Futura** and **Costa** lines; and **Estrella de Oro**, Carretera Nacional, further south on the edge of town.

To **Acapulco**, 4 daily, **Estrella Blanca**, 5 hrs, US$16, or with **Costa**, 4 daily, or **Estrella de Oro**, 7 daily. To **Chilpancingo**, 7 daily, **Estrella de Oro**, 3 hrs, US$11. To **Cuernavaca**, 5 daily, **Estrella de Oro**, 1½ hrs, US$5. To **Mexico City**, 4 daily, **Estrella Blanca**, 2½ hrs, US$10, or with **Costa**, 6 daily, or **Estrella de Oro**, 5 luxury services daily, US$12. Spectacular journey to **Toluca**, avoiding Mexico City, 2nd-class buses only, 3 hrs, US$8, change at Toluca for **Morelia**.

Cacahuamilpa *p173*
Estrella Blanca buses from Taxco to the caves run 6 times daily. Alternatively, catch a Toluca or Ixtapan-bound service (**Estrella Blanca** terminal), US$2, 45 mins; ask the driver for 'las grutas' and walk 400 m downhill from the crossroads. Alternatively, catch an hourly *colectivo* from outside the terminal, US$1.50.

There are direct **Pullman de Morelos** buses from **Cuernavaca**, 1 hr, US$2; or **Flecha Roja**, usually overcrowded at weekends.

❶ Directory

Cuernavaca *p166, map p167*
Banks Cambio Gesta, Morrow 9, T777-318 3750, daily 0900-1800. Divisas de Cuernavaca, Morrow 12; many banks in the vicinity of the zócalo. **Internet** Axon Cyber Café, Av Cuauhtémoc 129-B. California Cybercafé, Lerdo de Tejada 10b, Mon-Sat 0800-2000, Sun 0900-1400. **Language schools** Spanish courses start from about US$180-300 per week for 5-6 hrs a day. Some schools also have a registration fee of as much as US$100. Staying with a local family will be arranged by a school and costs US$25-40 a day including meals; check with individual schools, as this difference in price may apply even if you stay with the same family. Many schools include excursions within the programme, adding to the cost. The peak time for tuition is summer: at other times (Mar, Apr and Sep-Nov) it may be possible to arrive and negotiate a reduction of up to 25%. Choosing a school is best done on personal recommendation. If that's not an option, make sure your objective (college credits for example) are the same as the course and language school. Financially, total up the full cost. Some schools may have a cheaper weekly rate, but higher registration and coursework fees. **Cemanahuac**, San Juan 4, Col Las Palmas, CP 62051, T777-318 6407, www.cemanahuac.com. Claims high academic standards, field study, also weaving classes. **Centro de Artes y Lenguas**, Nueva Tabachín 22-A, T777-317 3126, scale@infosel.net.mx. 5 hrs a day, registration US$100, 1 week minimum, classes US$160, US$300 a week accommodation with families including meals. **Centro de Lengua, Arte e Historia para Extranjeros**, Universidad Autónoma del Estado de Morelos, Río Pánuco 20, Col Lomas del Mirador, T777-316 1626 (accommodation with families can be arranged). **Cetlalic**, Madero 721, Col Miraval, CP 62270, T777-313 5450, www.cetlalic.org.mx. Themed courses, plus Mexican and Central American history and culture. Non-profit

making. Various levels. Small groups (maximum 5 people). Stay with families. Recommended. **Cuauhnáhuac**, Morelos Sur 123, Col Chipitlán, CP 62070, T777-312 3673, www.cuauhnahuac.edu.mx. A cooperative language centre offering standard and intensive Spanish options, and private classes, registration US$100, US$350 per week or US$880 per month high season, US$280/US$750 low season, family stays US$25 per day shared room with meals or US$35 single room with meals, efficient, helpful. **Cuernavaca Language School**, Azalea 3, Jardines de Reforma, CP 62269, T777-311 8956, www.cls.com.mx, or PO Box 4133, Windham, New Hampshire, USA. **Encuentros**, Morelos 36, Col Acapantzingo, CP 62440, T777-312 5088, www.learnspanishin mexico.com. A fun, functional approach to acquiring Spanish including twice-weekly visits to places in Cuernavaca. Registration US$100, tuition US$210. **Experiencia**, Leyva 200, Col Miguel Hidalgo, CP 62050, T777-312 6579, www.experiencia spanish.com. 1-to-1, class and hourly sessions. From US$200 per week. Free *intercambios* (Spanish-English practice) Tue and Wed afternoon, open 5 days a week. **Fenix Language Institute**, Nueva Francia 8, Col Recursos, T/F777-313 3285, www.fenix mex.com. **Ideal Latinoamerica**, Privada Narciso Mendoza 107, Col La Pradera, CP62170, T777-311 7551, www.ideal-school.com. A variety of courses, including a professional vocabulary program; family homestay is an option. **Idel**, Apdo 1271-1, Calz de los Actores 112, Col Atzingo, T777-313 0157, www.del-site.Tripod.com/idel.html, 5 levels of course. **IMEC**, Copalhuacán 107, Col Amatitlan, CP62410, T777-312 1448, www.imeccuerna vaca.com.mx. A variety of packages are offered and homestay can be arranged. Are planning to move – make sure the street

address is correct. **Instituto Chac-Mool**, Privada de la Pradera 108, Col Pradera, T777-317 1163, www.chac-mool.com. Family homestay arranged. **KUKULCAN**, Manuel Mazarí 208, Col Miraval, CP62270, T777-312 5279, www.kukulcan.com.mx. **Universidad Internacional**, San Jerónimo 304, Cuernavaca, Apdo Postal 1520, T777-317 1087, www.spanishschool.uninter.edu.mx. A variety of Spanish courses, including one for healthcare professionals, and free cultural activities such as salsa, folk dancing and cooking. **Spanish Language Institute** (SLI), La Pradera 208, Col La Pradera, CP 62170, T777-311 0063, www.asli.com.mx. Minimum 6 hrs per day, classes start every Mon. **Universal**, JH Preciado 171, Col San Antón, CP 62020, T777-312 4902, www.universal-spanish.com, 3 levels of language course, tutorials and mini courses on culture. **Laundry** On Galeana, 1½ blocks from the zócalo. **Post office** On Hidalgo, just off the Alameda. **Telephone** Telmex on Hidalgo, just off the Alameda, LADA phones are outside, almost opposite junction of Nezahualcóyotl.

Tepoztlán *p168*
Language schools Tepoztlán is a definite alternative to Cuernavaca. Try **Spanish Communications Institute**, Cuauhtemotzín, T739-315 1709, USA T956-994-9977.

Taxco *p170, map p171*
Banks Good rates at Cambio de Divisar Argentu on Plazuela San Juan 5. **Bancomer**, between Plazuela San Juan and Plaza Principal, is OK. **Internet** Azul Cybercafé, Hidalgo, near Plaza San Juan, Mon-Sat 0900-2200. **Laundry** Lavandería La Cascada, Delicias 4. **Post office** On Carretera Nacional about 100 m east of Estrella de Oro bus terminal.

East of Mexico City

Snow-capped Popocatépetl, the smoking-mountain warrior, and his princess Iztaccíhuatl rise majestically to the east of the capital en route to Puebla, City of the Angels, or tucked-away Tlaxcala, delightful capital of Mexico's smallest state. Nearby are the dramatic murals of Cacaxtla and Cholula's artificial 'mountain', in fact the largest pyramid in all Mesoamerica. ▶▶ *For listings, see pages 189-196.*

Amecameca → *Colour map 3, B4. Phone code: 597. Altitude: 2315 m.*

At Km 29 on Route 190 is **Ixtapaluca**, where a road heading south leads to the small town of Amecameca, the starting point for exploring Iztaccíhuatl, the white woman. On the way to Amecameca, see the restored 16th-century convent and church at **Chalco**, and the fine church, convent and open-air chapel of the same period at **Tlalmanalco**.

From the zócalo at Amecameca, 60 km from Mexico City, a road heads to the sanctuary of El Sacromonte, 90 m above the town. This small but very beautiful church, built round a cave, was once inhabited by Fray Martín de Valencia, a conquistador who came to Mexico in 1524. It is, after the shrine of Guadalupe, the most sacred place in Mexico and has a much-venerated full-sized image of Santo Entierro weighing only 1.5 kg. To get there, take the exit under the arch and head for the first white station of the cross; the stations lead to the top where a magnificent view awaits. Market day in Amecameca is Saturday, and there is an excellent non-touristy market on Sunday. The **tourist office** ① *near the plaza, daily 0900-1500*, can provide information and guides for Iztaccíhuatl. To get to Amecameca from Mexico City, take a second-class Volcanes or Sur bus from the TAPO terminal, every 20 minutes, 1½ hours, US$2.

Popocatépetl

In December 2000, Popocatépetl (5452 m), known familiarly as Don Goyo, had its largest eruption for 500 years. The crater lid, which was in part blown sky-high, had increased, according to experts, to 14 million cubic metres; not only did smoke and ash rise to a height of more than 10 km, but the volcano also threw out incandescent rocks for a radius of up to 2 km. There was another similar eruption less than a month later, and since then, it has suffered a string of mostly moderate eruptions. Its last strong explosion was in January 2008, when an 8-km-long ash plume was thrown into the sky. For the foreseeable future it will not be possible to climb, or get close to, Popocatépetl. The volcano has been closed to climbers since 1994; access is restricted in a radius of 12 km from the crater. Furthermore, outsiders should exercise discretion about visiting villages in the danger area out of respect for the inhabitants. Ask locally for up-to-date information and advice. Fortunately, nearby Iztaccíhuatl (5286 m) has remained reassuringly dormant and still makes for a reasonably challenging climb.

Iztaccíhuatl

Climbing Iztaccíhuatl has been described as 'an exhilarating roller coaster of successive summits', but before venturing out to the volcano, check into the offices of the **Parque Nacional Itzaccihuatl-Popocatépetl** ① *Plaza de la Constitución 9B, in Amecameca, T597-978 3829, Mon-Fri 0900-1800, Sat 0900-1500*. They will be able to advise you on accomplishing your climb, as well as supply you with any necessary permits. For the purposes of search and rescue, you should also notify them of your intended route. Due to the changeable, rugged and glacial nature of the terrain, it is highly recommended that you use a guide, and these can be hired from various agencies in Amecameca. Note also that some rock climbing is required, so crampons and ice-picks are necessary, and these too will need to be acquired in town. If you hope to summit the volcano, you will need to spend at least one night in the park.

From Amecameca, drive (or catch a taxi or *colectivo*) to the Paso de Cortés, a refreshing space between the two volcanoes through which Cortés once passed on his way to Aztec Tenochititlán. From here, a road goes north along a dirt road, past a TV station, for 8 km to **La Joya**, the nearest parking to the summit of Iztaccíhuatl. Near the antennae is a *refugio* called **Atzomani**, which is the safest place to park, and there is a *buzón* (box) for notifying potential rescue groups of your intended route. From there you find various routes to the summit (12 to 15 hours return) and three to four refuges in which to stay overnight (no furniture, bare floors, dirty). The first two huts are at 4750 m (space for 30 people), the third at 4850 m (10-15 people), and the last hut is at 5010 m (in poor condition, 10-12 people); the Luis Menéndez hut is the most salubrious. From the last hut it is 2½ to three hours to the top; set off at 0400, over two glaciers.

A more technical route starts at the *buzón* and at first descends left into the valley. Walk three to four hours from La Joya to the Ayoloco glacier before which is a refugio for eight to 10 people at 4800 m. From here it is three to four hours to the summit. You'll definitely need a guide here, as walking on glaciers without knowing the conditions is hazardous.

It's also possible to climb Iztaccíhuatl from Puebla. Take a second-class bus to Cholula from Puebla, then a *combi* from the centre to San Nicolás de los Ranchos. From here bargain with one of the few local taxis for a ride to La Joya (US$20).

Mexico City to Puebla

Heading east from Mexico City you could make a small detour to **Chapingo**, where there are some fine Rivera frescoes in the **college chapel** ① *Mon-Fri 0900-1800*. You can get there by *colectivo* from General Anaya y San Ciprián or by bus from TAPO (Auto transportes Mexico-Texcoco, US$0.70).

Near Chapingo a road runs to **Huexotla**, which has an Aztec wall, ruined fortifications and pyramid, and the 16th-century Franciscan convent of San Luis Obispo. Another road from the town of Texcoco runs through the public park of **Molino de las Flores**. From the old hacienda buildings, now in ruins, a road (right) runs up the hill of Tetzcotzingo, near the top of which are the **Baños de Nezahualcóyotl**, the poet-prince. **San Miguel de Chiconcuac**, on the road to San Andrés and left at its church, 4 km away, is famous for its rugs, sweaters and *sarapes*. Tuesday is market day and there is a rousing fiesta in honour of their patron saint on 29 September.

Beyond Ixtapaluca, southeast of Los Reyes on Route 190, the road climbs through pine forests to reach 3196 m, about 63 km from Mexico City, and then descends in a series of sharp bends to the town of **San Martín Texmelucan**, Km 91. The old Franciscan convent here has a beautifully decorated interior, and a former hacienda displays weaving and old machinery. The zócalo too is beautiful, with benches covered in ceramic tiles and a central gazebo. Market day is Tuesday.

Puebla ⬤⬤⬤⬤⬤⬤⬤ ➤➤ pp189-196. Colour map 3, B4.

➔ *Phone code: 222. Population: 1,346,176. Altitude: 2060 m.*

'City of the Angels', Puebla de los Angeles is one of Mexico's oldest and most famous cities and the capital of Puebla state. It was founded in 1531 by Fray Julián Garcés who saw angels in a dream indicating where the city should be built, hence its name. It is also one explanation of why Puebla wasn't built over pre-Hispanic ruins like many other colonial cities. Talavera tiles are an outstanding feature of Puebla's architecture and their extensive use on colonial buildings distinguishes Puebla from other colonial cities. Puebla is a charming, pleasant and friendly city, always popular with travellers.

Ins and outs

Getting there Aeropuerto Hermanos Serdán (**PBC**) ⓘ *Km 91.5 Carretera Federal México–Puebla, T222-774 2804, www.aeropuertopuebla.com*, has mostly domestic flights and is located 22 km northwest of the city. The **CAPU** bus station, Blv Norte 4222, is 4 km to the north. Taxis from the terminal to the city centre leave from outside the departure terminal, US$3.60 with a pre-paid voucher. 'Centro' buses pass on the other side of Blv Norte. From the centre to the terminal, take any form of public transport marked 'CAPU'. Puebla is on the main Highway 150 from Mexico City to the Gulf Coast, the same *supercarretera* that branches south, beyond Puebla, to Oaxaca. An important commercial centre, Puebla is also the hub of other lesser routes to towns and villages in the surrounding area. Buses to Cholula depart from the corner of 6 Poniente and 13 Norte; transport to Cacaxtla leaves from 10 Poniente, between 13 Norte and 11 Norte.

Getting around Although Puebla is a big city, most of the major sites are around the centre, within easy walking distance of each other. City buses, *colectivos* or taxis will take you to any of the more distant sites.

Tourist information The **state tourist office** ⓘ *Calle 5 Ote 3, Av Juárez, T222-777 1519, www.puebla.gob.mx, Mon-Fri 0900-2000, Sat-Sun 0900-1500*, is behind the cathedral, next to the post office. They are helpful and friendly. The **municipal tourist office** ⓘ *Portal Hidalgo 14, Mon-Fri 0900-2000, Sat-Sun 0900-1500*, is in the Palacio Municipal on the zócalo. The best time to visit the volcano is late October to early March when skies are clear; from May to October the weather is good before noon only.

Orientation

Puebla was laid down according to a grid plan and is very logical to navigate with a few simple rules. The northwest corner of the zócalo, Plaza de Armas, marks the intersection of four major arteries: Reforma to the west; Palafox y Mendoza to the east; 5 de Mayo to the north; and 16 de Septiembre to the south. Around this central axes, roads are assigned their appropriate suffix. For example, those running north of the Reforma/Palafox y Mendoza axis terminate Norte; those running south of it terminate Sur. Conversely, the 5 de Mayo/16 de Septiembre axis marks the change from Poniente to Oriente. Note also that roads running east-west are Avenidas, while roads running north-south are Calles. Simple!

Sights

Puebla's centre, although beautifully colonial, is cursed with traffic jams and pollution, except in those shopping streets reserved for pedestrians. Still, it's a great city for strolling, and home to an abundance of beautiful churches. Previously, the din from their bells was so loud that the residents requested that it be toned down since they were driven to distraction on Sundays and feast days.

Puebla's zócalo, Plaza de Armas, marks the historical centre of the city. A thronging marketplace until the 19th century, this large, shady plaza still attracts crowds of tourists and Poblanos with its leafy trees, exuberant street performers, arcaded shops, terraced restaurants, and architecturally worthy buildings, some dating from the early colonial period. The **Palacio Municipal** is on the north side, to the right of which is the entrance to the **Biblioteca del Palacio**, opened 1996, with some tourist information and books on the city. To the left is the **Teatro de la Ciudad**, opened 1995, where music and drama are performed. There is also an art gallery in the building. The tiled façade of the **Casa de los Muñecos**, on the northeast corner of the square, is famous for its caricatures in tiles of the enemies of the 18th-century builder. Inside, in the **Museo Universitario** ① *2 Norte 1, Tue-Sun 1000-1700, US$1*, some rooms contain old physics instruments, seismographs, cameras and telescopes, another has stuffed animals, but most contain religious paintings from the 17th and 18th centuries. Puebla's fine cathedral is on the south side of the zócalo (see below), while 1½ blocks west, the **Museo Bello** ① *Av 3 Pte 302, Tue-Sun, US$2, free Tue, guided tours available*, is the house of the collector and connoisseur Bello who died in 1938. It has good displays of Chinese porcelain and Talavera pottery and is beautifully furnished.

Puebla's majestic **cathedral** ① *Av 3 Ote y 16 de Septiembre, 0700-12.30 and 1615-1930*, is one of Mexico's most beautiful religious structures. Construction began in 1575 under the direction of architect Fransisco Becerra, but most work was accomplished some 65 years later, by Bishop Juan de Palafox. The finished building exhibits a range of architectural styles including early Baroque and renaissance. The interior is particularly notable for its marble floors, onyx and marble statuary and gold-leaf decoration. There are statues flanking the altar, designed by Tolsá, which are said to be of an English king and a Scottish queen. The bell tower, the tallest in Mexico, gives a grand view of the city and snow-capped volcanoes, although recently visitors have not been allowed access.

Opposite the cathedral and also worth visiting is the **Biblioteca Palafoxiana** ① *Av 5 Ote 5, inside the Casa de la Cultura, www.bpm.gob.mx, 1000-1600, US$0.70*, or the library of Bishop Palafox; it has 46,000 antique volumes and is one of the oldest libraries in the Americas. It is housed by a colonial building with a large courtyard, also home to paintings and art exhibitions. Next door at 5 Oriente 9 is another

1 Puebla

➡ Puebla maps
1 Puebla, page 183
2 Puebla centre, page 184

attractive structure, the **Tribunal Superior de Justicia**, built in 1762; you may go into the courtyard. The **Congreso del Estado** ① *Av 5 Pte 128*, formerly the Consejo de Justicia, near the post office, is a converted 19th-century Moorish-style town house. The tiled entrance and courtyard are very attractive and it had a theatre inside, shown to visitors on request. It is now the seat of the state government.

The modest but interesting **Casa del Dean** ① *16 de Septiembre y 7 Pte, US$2.20 plus tip for the guide if wanted*, was built in 1580. The walls of the two remaining rooms are covered with 400-year-old murals in vegetable and mineral dyes, which were discovered in 1953 under layers of wallpaper and paint. In 1984, the house, previously used as a cinema, was taken over by the government and opened to the public. The murals were inspired by the poems of the Italian poet and humanist Petrarch, and are believed to have been painted by indigenous craftsmen under the direction of the Dean, Don Tomás de la Plaza, whose house it was. The murals contain a mixture of classical Greek, pagan (indigenous) and Christian themes. About 40% have been restored.

The **Patio de los Azulejos** ① *3 Sur between 9 and 11 Pte 110*, should also be visited; it has fabulous tiled façades on the former almshouses for old retired priests of the order of San Felipe Neri. The colours and designs are beautiful. The tiny entrance on 16 de Septiembre is hard to find; ring the bell on the top right and you may get a guided tour.

② Puebla centre

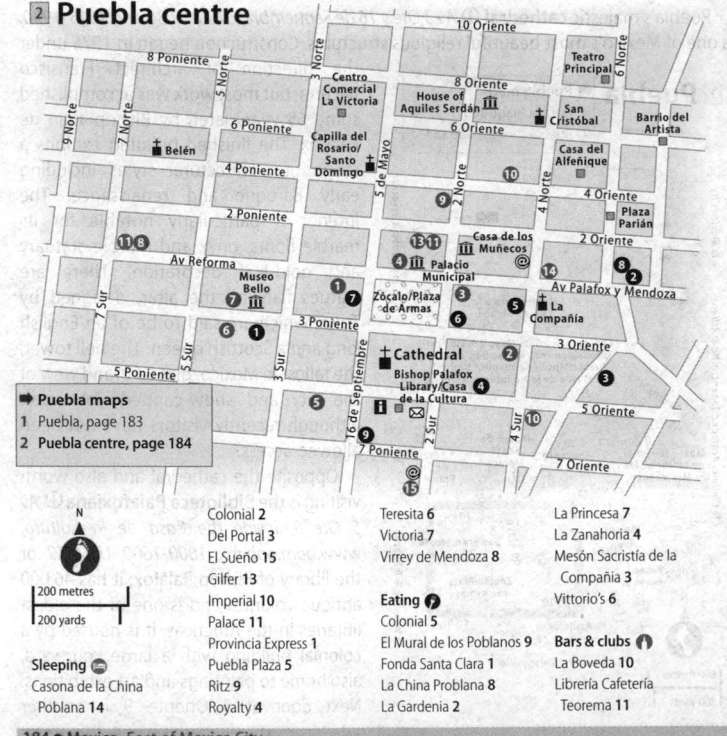

➡ **Puebla maps**
1 Puebla, page 183
2 Puebla centre, page 184

	Colonial **2**	Teresita **6**	La Princesa **7**
	Del Portal **3**	Victoria **7**	La Zanahoria **4**
	El Sueño **15**	Virrey de Mendoza **8**	Mesón Sacristía de la
	Gilfer **13**		Compañía **3**
200 metres	Imperial **10**	**Eating** 🍴	Vittorio's **6**
200 yards	Palace **11**	Colonial **5**	
	Provincia Express **1**	El Mural de los Poblanos **9**	**Bars & clubs** 🍸
Sleeping 🛏	Puebla Plaza **5**	Fonda Santa Clara **1**	La Boveda **10**
Casona de la China	Ritz **9**	La China Problana **8**	Librería Cafetería
Poblana **14**	Royalty **4**	La Gardenia **2**	Teorema **11**

The **Museo Amparo** ① *2 Sur 708, esq 9 Ote, www.museoamparo.com, Wed-Mon 1000-1730, US\$3, students half price, free Mon, audioguides available, US\$0.70, English language tours on request, US\$13,* housed by handsome 16th- and 17th-century buildings, has an excellent anthropological exhibition spanning eight rooms. Punctuated by relaxing colonial courtyards, this is one of the best pre-Hispanic collections in Mexico and particularly aesthetic. There is a strong Olmec contingent, but artefacts from all the country are displayed too. Audiovisual explanations are available in Spanish, English, French and Japanese. Sombre colonial art and furniture are on show upstairs, also worth a look. The Museo Amparo is privately owned and run, the legacy of local philanthropist Manuel Espinosa Iglesias. Recommended.

At the heart of Puebla's most bohemian neighbourhood is the **Plaza y Mercado El Parián**, between Avenida 2 y 4 Oriente and Avenida 6 y 8 Norte, where there are many small shops selling paintings, *artesanías* and onyx souvenirs. Note that Onyx figures and chess sets are more attractive and cheaper than elsewhere in Mexico, but the *poblanos* are hard bargainers. In the adjoining Barrio del Artistas are artists' studios. Live music and refreshments can be enjoyed at various bars and cafés nearby.

Just north of the Barrio del Artistas, the **Teatro Principal** (1550) ① *Av 8 Ote y Calle 6 Norte,* is possibly the oldest in the Americas, although it was badly damaged by fire in 1902 and had to be rebuilt. West of the barrio, the fragile-looking and extravagantly ornamented **Casa del Alfeñique** (Sugar Candy House) ① *Av 4 Ote 418, Tue-Sun 1000-1700, US\$1.50,* now the Museo Regional del Estado, is worth seeing.

A couple of blocks of west of the Teatro Principal is the house of Aquiles Serdán, a liberal activist who opposed the dictatorship of Porfirio Díaz. A conflict that took place in this house – in which he and about 17 others were killed – is said to have sparked the 1910 Revolution. It is now full of memorabilia and houses the **Museo de la Revolución Mexicana** ① *6 Ote 206, Tue-Sun 1000-1630, US\$1.* Two blocks west of El Parián is the **Museo Poblano de Arte Virreinal** ① *Calle 4 Norte 203, Tue-Sun 1000-1700, US\$1, free Tue,* with a fine collection of vice-regal art. It housed in the Hospital de San Pedro, dating from the 16th century.

The **Museo de Artesanías del Estado** ① *5 Norte 1203, Tue-Sun 1000-1630, US\$1.50* in the **ex-Convento de Santa Rosa**, several blocks north of the zócalo, is well worth a visit for its good display of the many crafts produced in the State of Puebla. However, the real highlight is a priceless collection of 16th-century Talavera tiles on the walls and ceilings of its extraordinary vaulted kitchen. It was here that the nuns are said to have invented the famous *mole poblano.*

The **Museo de Santa Mónica** ① *Av 18 Pte 103, on the corner of 5 de Mayo, Tue-Sun 1000-1800, US\$2.50,* is housed in a former convent where generations of nuns hid after the reform laws of 1857 made the convent illegal. An underground network of secret tunnels and hidden corridors concealed them for over 60 years while they continued to practise their faith, and furthering the fine accomplishments of Poblano cuisine, invented the local speciality and national dish, *chiles en nogada.* The nuns were 'discovered' in 1935 (it's likely they were already known of) and the building was subsequently converted into a religious museum.

One of the most stunning sights in Puebla is the **Capilla del Rosario** of the church of **Santo Domingo** (1596-1659) ① *5 de Mayo 407, 0700-1230 and 1615-1930, free.* The baroque here displays a beauty of style and prodigality of form that served as example and inspiration for all later baroque in Mexico. Inside, the chapel is a riot of detailed gold leaf. The altar of the main church is also decorated with gold leaf, with four levels from floor to ceiling of life-size statues of religious figures. There is a strong indigenous flavour to Puebla's baroque; this can be seen in the churches of Tonantzintla and Acatepec (see page 186). It is not so evident but still present in the opulent decorative work in the cathedral. Beyond the church, up towards the Fuerte Loreto (see below), there is a spectacular view of the volcanoes.

The Jesuit church of **La Compañía** ① *Av Don Juan de Palafox y Mendoza y 4 Sur*, has a plaque in the sacristy showing where China Poblana is said to be buried. Other places well worth visiting are the churches of **San Cristóbal** (1687) ① *4 Norte y 6 Ote*, with modern churrigueresque towers and Tonantzintla-like plasterwork inside, as well as the 18th-century **San José** ① *2 Norte y 18 Ote*, with attractive tiled façade and decorated walls around the main doors and beautiful altarpieces inside. One of the most famous and oldest local churches is **San Francisco** ① *14 Ote 1009*, with a glorious tiled façade and a mummified saint in its side chapel; see also the pearl divers' chapel, given by the divers of Veracruz. The **Capilla de Dolores** ① *the other side of Blv 5 de Mayo from San Francisco*, is small but elaborately decorated. **Santa Catalina** ① *3 Norte with 2 Pte* has beautiful altarpieces. **Nuestra Señora de la Luz** ① *14 Norte and 2 Ote*, has a good tiled façade and so has **San Marcos** ① *Av Reforma and 9 Norte*. The Maronite church of **Belén** ① *7 Norte and 4 Pte*, has a lovely old tiled façade and a beautifully tiled interior. The church **La Puerta del Cielo** ① *at the top of the Cerro de San Juan in Col La Paz*, has over 80 figures of angels inside.

In the suburbs of Puebla the **Cinco de Mayo Civic Centre**, with a stark statue of Benito Juárez, is, among other things, a regional centre of arts, crafts and folklore. It is near the **Museo Regional de Puebla** ① *daily 1000-1700, US$3*, which has magnificent collections but little information. Also nearby is the **Museo de Historia Natural**, auditorium, planetarium, fairgrounds and an open-air theatre. In the same area, the forts of Guadalupe and Loreto were the scene of the Battle of Puebla, in which 2000 Mexican troops defeated Maximilian's 6000 European troops on 5 May 1862 (although the French returned victorious 10 days later). This is why 5 May is a holiday in Mexico. Inside the **Fuerte Loreto**, which has views of the city (and of its pollution), is a small museum, **Museo de la No Intervención** ① *Tue-Sun 1000-1700, US$3*, depicting the battle of 1862.

Around Puebla ⊖🕜🕜🕜 ➤ *pp189-196*.

The small, somnolent town of **Cholula**, home to the Universidad de las Américas, was once as influential as Teotihuacán. When Cortés arrived, it was a holy centre with 100,000 inhabitants and 400 shrines, or *teocallis*, grouped round the great pyramid of Quetzalcoatl. After the Cholulans tried (and failed) to ambush Cortés, he slaughtered the population and razed their shrines, vowing to build a chapel for each one destroyed. In fact, there are 'only' about 70 churches in Cholula. At the centre of town lies the zócalo, with the Franciscan fortress church of **San Gabriel** (1552) ① *Mon-Sat 0600-1200, 1600-1900, Sun 0600-1900*, built over the pyramid of Quetzalcoatl and housing an interesting library of antique books. Next to it is the **Capilla Real** ① *Mon-Sat 1000-1200, 1530-1800, Sun 0900-1800*, a Moorish-style construction with 49 domes. The **Museo de la Ciudad de Cholula** *5 de Mayo y Calle 4 Pte, Thu-Tue 0900-1500*, has archaeological artefacts recovered from the pre-Hispanic settlement, as well colonial art dating from its evangelisation. Cholula, now a virtual suburb of Puebla, has quite a lively nightlife thanks to the local student population.

Cholula's archaeological zone is home to the gargantuan **Pirámide Tepanapa** ① *0900-1800, US$2.70, guides US$6.50, to get there from the zócalo, follow Av Morelos and* *cross the railway*, resembling a small naturally formed mountain, in spite of its excavation. Its base measures 350 m by 350 m, making it the world's largest pyramid, but at 66 m high, it is not the tallest. Some 8 km of tunnels have been dug into the structure to explore its architecture. Some of them are open to the public, giving a clearer idea of the layers that were superimposed through its various phases of construction. Near the tunnel entrance is a the **Patio de los Altares**, with sacrificial altars and large stone carvings reminiscent of Gulf Coast cultures. There is also a **museum**, with scale models of the site and reproduction frescoes. The 16th-century chapel of **Los Remedios**, on top of the pyramid, gives a fine view of the town, valleys and mountains.

In the neighbouring village of **Tonantzintla** the 16th-century church of **Santa María de Tonantzintla** ① *daily 1000-1800*, or 'the place of our venerable mother', is one of the most beautiful churches in Mexico. It can be reached by paved road from **San Francisco Acatepec**, another village with an equally beautiful but less ornate 16th-century **church** ① *daily 0900-1800 (supposedly, but not always so), the key is held by José Ascac, ask for his shop*. Its interior has been restored following a fire, but the wonderful tiled façade is still intact. These two tiny churches are exquisite and should not be missed; they are resplendent with Poblano tiles and their interiors, especially that of Tonantzintla, are a riot of indigenous stucco work and carving. Best light for photography is after 1500; photography *inside* the churches is frowned upon.

Tlaxcala ●●●● ►► *pp189-196. Colour map 3, B4.*

→ *Phone code: 246. Altitude: 2240 m.*

North of Puebla the quaint old town of Tlaxcala, 'red city' and capital of Mexico's smallest state, has a very pleasant centre of simple buildings washed in ochre, pink and yellow, and vast not-so-quaint suburbs. It is a place where wealthy ranchers breed fighting bulls, but the landless peasants are still poor. Tlaxcala is most famous for the treacherous alliance it struck with Cortés. Supplying him with valuable warriors and tactical information, the Tlaxcalans had hoped to undermine their eternal enemies, the Aztecs. Tlaxcala's **tourist office** ① *Av Juárez y Landizábal, T246-465 0960, www.tlaxcala.gob.mx/ turismo*, has many maps, leaflets and is very helpful. The annual fair is held 29 October-15 November each year.

Tlaxcala's sights are modest but diverting. In the Palacio de Gobierno on the main square are some extremely colourful murals depicting the indigenous story of Tlaxcala, the history of Mexico and of humankind. The **Church of San Francisco**, dating from 1521, is the oldest in Mexico, from whose pulpit the first Christian sermon was preached in New Spain (Mexico). Of course, the sermon would have been for the benefit of the Spanish residents; the local indigenous people would have congregated outside at the open chapel. Almost next door is the **Museo del Estado de Tlaxcala** ① *Tue-Sun 0900-1700, US$3*, with two floors of interesting historical and artistic exhibits. The **Museo de Memoria** ① *Independencia 3, Tue-Sun 1000-1700, US$0.70*, has exhibits on indigenous culture, while the **Museo de Artes y Tradiciones Populares** ① *Sánchez 1, 1000-1800, Tue-Sun, US$1*, is a 'living museum' where local Otomí people demonstrate traditional arts and customs including the sweat bath, cooking, embroidery, weaving and pulque-making. Highly recommended.

Around Tlaxcala

The churrigueresque **Santuario de Ocotlán** (1541), on a hill in the outskirts of Tlaxcala (a stiff 20-minute climb from Juárez via Guribi and Alcocer), commands a view of valley and volcano. It was described by Sacheverell Sitwell as "the most delicious building in the world". Its façade of lozenge-shaped vermilion bricks, framing the white stucco portal and surmounted by two white towers with fretted cornices and salomonic pillars, is beautiful. The sumptuous golden interior, comparable with those of Taxco and Tepotzotlán, was worked on for 25 years by the indigenous artist Francisco Miguel.

The ruined pyramid of **Xicoténcatl** at **San Esteban de Tizatlán**, 5 km from Tlaxcala, has two sacrificial altars with original colour frescoes preserved under glass. The pictures tell the story of the wars with Aztecs and Chichimecs. Amid the archaeological digs at Tizatlán are a splendid 19th-century church and the 16th-century chapel of San Esteban. To get there, take a *colectivo* to Tizatlán from 1 de Mayo y 20 de Noviembre, Tlaxcala; at the main square, alight when you see a yellow church dome on the left.

Cacaxtla → *Colour map 3, B4.*
① *Tue-Sun 1000-1630, US$3.50, which also includes access to the nearby ruins of Xochitécatl. From Puebla take a Flecha Azul bus marked 'Nativitas' from Calle 10 Pte y Calle 11 Norte to just beyond Nativitas where a sign on the right points to San Miguel del Milagro and Cacaxtla. Walk up the hill or take a colectivo to a large sign with its back to you, turn left here for the ruins.*

A remarkable series of pre-Columbian frescoes are to be seen at the ruins of Cacaxtla near San Miguel del Milagro, between Texmelucan and Tlaxcala. The colours are still sharp and some of the figures are larger than life size. To protect the paintings from the sun and rain, a huge roof has been constructed. An easily accessible visitor centre has been opened but there is disappointingly little published information on the site. In theory there is a 'per picture' charge for photography, but this is not assiduously collected although flash and tripod are strictly prohibited. It can be very foggy at Curetzalan, even when it is fine in Puebla.

Cuetzalan and around → *Colour map 3, B5. Phone code: 233.*
An interesting day trip from Puebla is to Cuetzalan market (via Tetela–Huahuaxtla), which is held on Sunday in the zócalo (three hours' walk up). In the first week of October each year dancers from local villages gather and *voladores* 'fly' from the top of their pole. The Nahua sell *huacales* (cradles) for children, machetes and embroidered garments. Women decorate their hair with skeins of wool. The **Día de los Muertos** (2 November) is interesting here. Big clay dogs are made locally: unusual stoves that hold large flat clay plates on which *tortillas* are baked and stews are cooked in pots; these are also available in nearby Huitzilán. You can also go via Zaragoza, Zacapoaxtla and Apulco, where you can walk along a path, left of the road, to the fine 35-m waterfall of **La Gloria**. The **tourist office** ① *Calle Hidalgo y Bravo*, is helpful and can provide a good map.

From Cuetzalan it is a 1½-hour walk to the well-preserved pyramids of **Yohualichan** ① *Wed-Sun, US$3*, from the Totonac culture. There are five excavated pyramids, two of them equivalent to that at El Tajín (see page 393), and three still uncovered. There has been earthquake damage, though. Take a bus from Calle Miguel Alvarado Avila y Calle Abosolo, more frequent in morning and market days, to San Antonio and get off at the sign Pirámides Yohualichan (30 minutes, bad road), then walk 2 km to the site. In the Cuetzalan area are 32 km of caverns with lakes, rivers and wonderful waterfalls. These include Tzicuilan (follow Calle Emiliano Zapata, east of town) and Atepolihuit (follow Carretera Antigua up to the Campo Deportivo, west of town). Children offer to guide visitors to the ruins and caves.

South to Oaxaca ⊜🅿🅕🅢🅒 ⇥ *pp189-196.*

From Puebla, Route 150 continues to **Amozoc**, where tooled leather goods and silver decorations on steel are made, both mostly as outfits for the *charros*, or Mexican cattlemen. Beyond Amozoc lies **Tepeaca** with its late 16th-century monastery, well worth a visit; its weekly market is very extensive. On the main square is **Casa de Cortés** ① *daily 1000-1700*, where Hernán Cortés signed the second of five *Cartas de Relación* in 1520. An old Spanish tower (1580) stands between Tepeaca's main square and the parish church. Beyond Tepeaca, 57 km from Puebla, lies **Tecamachalco**, where the vast 16th-century Franciscan monastery church has beautiful murals on the choir vault, in late medieval Flemish style, by a local indigenous artist.

Tehuacán → *Colour map 3, C5. Phone code: 238. Altitude: 1676 m.*

This charming town, southeast of Puebla, has a pleasant, sometimes cool, climate. Water from the mineral springs is bottled and sent all over the country by **Garci Crespo**, **San Lorenzo** and **Peñafiel**. From the small dam at Malpaso on the Río Grande, an annual race is held for craft without motors as far as the village of Quiotepec. The central plaza is pleasant and shaded. The **Museo de Minerología Romero** ① *Av Reforma, 7 Norte 356, daily 0900-1200, 1600-1800, morning only on Sat, free*, is in the ex-Convento del Carmen. It has one room with a good collection of minerals from all over the world. The *ayuntamiento* (town hall) on the zócalo is decorated inside and out with murals and tiles. A short bus ride beyond Peñafiel Spa is the spa of **San Lorenzo** ① *US$2*, with spring-fed pools surrounded by trees.

Huautla de Jiménez

From Teotitlán it is possible to drive into the hills to the indigenous town of Huautla de Jiménez, where the local Mazatec population consume the hallucinogenic 'magic' mushrooms made famous by Dr Timothy Leary. Huautla has all four seasons of the year in each day: spring-like mornings, wet, foggy afternoons, fresh, autumn evenings and freezing nights. Hiking in the mountains here is worthwhile. There are many police and military. Drivers may be waved down by people in the road up to Huautla; do not stop for them, they may be robbers.

⦿ East of Mexico City listings

For Sleeping and Eating price codes and other relevant information, see Essentials pages 45-48.

⊜ Sleeping

Amecameca *p180*

D San Carlos, Constitución 10, T597-978 0746. The only hotel, simple basic rooms.

Camping

Permitted at the railway station, ask the man in the office (leaving town, it's after the road to Tlamacas, on the right, 1-2 km away).

Puebla *p182, maps p183 and p184*
Puebla has a plethora of hotels with everything from dusty old cheapies to luxury boutiques.
LL Casona de la China Poblana, Palafox and Mendoza, T222-242 5336, www.casona delachinapoblana.com. This sumptuous and exclusive boutique hotel sports a range of stylish rooms, all decorated differently. They have a fine restaurant and bar. Comfortable, luxurious and very expensive.
LL-L El Sueño, 9 Ote 12, T222-232 6423, www.elsueno-hotel.com. This bastion of

minimalist beauty offers romantic and luxurious rooms, delectable suites, restaurant and spa facilities. Great services, comfort and impeccable taste.

LL-L Puebla Marriott Real, Hermanos Serdán 807, near 1st Puebla interchange on Mexico City–Puebla motorway, T222-141 2000, www.marriott.com. Standards and services at the Marriott are high, with a wealth of amenities including gym, pool, restaurant, bar, events room and attractive gardens. Rooms and suites are attractive, comfortable and tasteful. One of the best hotels in town, but far from the centre.

LL-AL Camino Real, 7 Pte 105, T222-229 0909, www.caminoreal.com/ puebla. A very elegant and atmospheric hotel housed by the historic and beautifully restored 16th-century ex-Convento de la Concepción. There are 84 rooms and suites, all adorned with antiques and sumptuous details, all different. Services include bar, restaurant, room service, boutiques and business centres. Quiet and luxurious.

A Colonial, 4 Sur 105, across pedestrian street from La Compañía church, T222-246 4612, www.colonial.com.mx. A superb colonial building, old-fashioned and charming, replete with big paving stones, colonial art, antique fixtures, history and character. All rooms have bath, Wi-Fi, safe, electronic locks and good double-glazing. Some have high-ceilings and original paintwork. Most have bath tubs and antique sinks. Helpful and recommended.

A Del Portal, Portal Morelos 205, T222-404 6200, www.hoteldelportal.com. An attractive old building with a pleasant colonial courtyard and atmospheric corridors. The rooms are plain, some have noisy views of the zócalo. Services include colour TV, Wi-Fi, hot water, safes, laptop storage, parking, night porter, restaurant and bar. A bit overpriced and slightly disappointing.

A Puebla Plaza, 5 Pte 111, near cathedral, T222-246 3175, www.hotelpuebla plaza.com.mx. Formerly **Hotel Santander**, the Puebla Plaza has an attractive, royal blue colonial façade. They have 48 plain but comfortable rooms with phone, TV, Wi-Fi and hot showers. Some big, bright rooms face the street. Enclosed parking.

B Gilfer, 2 Ote 11, T222-309 9800, www.gilferhotel.com.mx. An attractive, modern building with large rooms and a reasonable restaurant. Abrupt, unhelpful reception.

B Imperial, 4 Ote 212, T222-242 4980, www.hotelimperialpuebla.com. Good-sized plain rooms around a central courtyard. The executive suites are a little roomier and have more character. All are clean, with TV, phones and hot shower. Services include restaurant, gym, parking and Wi-Fi. 30% discount for Footprint owners. Continental breakfast included, good value, recommended.

B Palace, 2 Ote 13, T222-242 4030, www.hotelpalace.com.mx. A modern hotel with marble floors and a restaurant, **El Ranchito**, serving Mexican food. Rooms are clean and comfortable, if fairly unremarkable.

B Provincia Express, Reforma 141, close to the zócalo, T222-246 3557, provincia express_puebla@hotmail.com. Formerly **Hotel Alamada**, the interior of this building is beautifully painted in Moorish style. The rooms are plain, most are windowless, all are clean, with TV, phone and bath. Services include parking, Wi-Fi, and café.

B Royalty, Portal Hidalgo 8, T222-242 4740, www.hotelr.com. Pleasant and central with straightforward rooms and a comfortable suite. Rooms on the zócalo have fine views, but the windows are thin. The restaurant is good, but expensive and slow, with table under the *portales* where a marimba band often plays. OK overall, but pricey for what it is.

C Granada, Blv de la Pedrera 2303, T222-232 0966. A quiet, comfortable hotel with restaurant, room service and TV in the rooms. Very close to bus terminal; the bus to the centre leaves from front door.

C Virrey de Mendoza, Reforma 538, T222-242 3903. This old colonial house has a beautiful wooden staircase and lots of plants. Rooms are plain and fairly basic, with high ceilings, TV and bath.

C-D Ritz, 2 Norte 207 y 4 Ote, 2 blocks from zócalo, T222-232 4457, www.hotelritz puebla.com. Reasonable, but drab exterior at this centrally located budget hotel. Some good rooms have balconies.
D Teresita, 3 Pte 309, T222-232 7072. Small, clean, simple rooms with hot water and bath (although the 'comedy showers' manage to get everything soaked). Friendly.
D Victoria, near zócalo, 3 Pte 306, T222-232 8992, www.hotelesenpuebla.com/victoria.htm. Small, basic and windowless, but clean. Reasonable budget lodgings. Friendly and recommended for thrifty travellers.

Around Puebla *p186*
Cholula
LL-L Estrella de Belem, 2 Ote 410, T222-261 1925, www.estrelladebelem.com.mx. This luxurious B&B with spa facilities has an impressive roof-top terrace with views, hydro-massage pool, solarium and heated swimming pool. Lots of atmosphere, with courtyards, fountains and decorative antiques.
LL-L La Quinta Luna, 3 Sur 702, T222-247 8915, www.laquintaluna.com. Formerly a 17th-century mansion, La Quinta Luna is a sumptuous and immaculately presented high-end option with lots of style and character. A library containing 3000 books takes pride of place in this establishment, and rooms and services are impeccable.
AL-A Villas Arqueológicas, 2 Pte 501, Cholula, T222-247 1966. Close to the pyramid and affiliated with Club Med, this hotel has 44 comfortable rooms, lush gardens, tennis court and a French Restaurant. Rooms have heating, TV and phone. English and French Spoken. Prices rise at the weekends (**AL**).
B Casa Calli, on zócalo, Portal Guerrero 11, Cholula, T222-261 5607, www.hotel casacalli.com. Attractive, colonial-style lodgings with 37 rooms, Wi-Fi, cable TV, pool, restaurant and spa facilities. Chic and affordable.
D Hostal Cholollan, 2 Calle Norte 2003, Barrio de Jesús, Cholula, T222-247 7038. Dormitory accommodation in a lively place

with great views of Popo and Izta from the terrace. Free use of kitchen, and a great meeting spot.
D Las Américas, 14 Ote 6, San Andrés, Cholula, T222-247 0991. Near the pyramid, actually a motel, with modern rooms off galleries around a paved courtyard (car park). They have a small restaurant. Clean and good value.
D Trailer Park Las Américas, 30 Ote 602, Cholula. Hot showers and secure, as are the furnished apartments.

Tlaxcala *p187*
AL Posada San Francisco (Club Med), Plaza de la Constitución 17, T246-462 6022, www.posadasanfrancisco.com. Lavishly decorated in colonial style, this hotel has a plethora of good services including 2 restaurants, Wi-Fi, dance hall, secure parking, swimming pool and tennis courts. Rooms are comfortable, but not astounding. Promotional deals sometimes available, check the website. Highly recommended.
B Alifer, Morelos 11, uphill from plaza, T246-462 5678, www.hotelalifer.com.mx. Central, comfortable and affordable, but slightly characterless. Rooms are spacious, carpeted and equipped with Wi-Fi. Restaurant and safe parking.

Cuetzalan and around *p188*
A Hotel La Casa de la Piedra, García 11, T233-331 0030, www.lacasadepiedra.com. A very beautiful and atmospheric property, formerly a coffee-processing plant. The rooms are rustic yet comfortable, with attractive wooden floor boards and beams. The stonework is gorgeous. Recommended.
B Posada Cuetzalan, Zaragoza 12, T233-331 0154, www.posadacuetzalan.com. A colourful, charming hotel with lush courtyards and lots of exuberant plant life. Rooms are comfortable and equipped with cable TV and phone. There's also a pool, laundry service, internet and bilingual guides.
C-E Hotel Taselotzin, by La Gloria waterfall, near Cuetzalan, T/F233-331 0480. Owned

and operated by an association of Nahua craftswomen, this hotel has both rooms (**D**) and a set of dormitory-style *cabañas*, very clean with great views (**F** per person per night). Recommended.

D-E Hotel Rivello, G Victoria 3, T233-331 0139, 1 block from zócalo. Basic, friendly and clean. Rooms have bath (cheaper without).

Tehuacán *p189*

B México, Reforma Norte and Independencia Pte, 1 block from zócalo, T238-382 0019. This renovated colonial building is one of the town's better options, with attractive rooms, parking, TV, restaurant. Quiet, charming and comfortable.

C-D Iberia, Independencia Ote 217, T238-383 1500. Clean and airy, with a pleasant restaurant and nearby public parking at reduced fee with a voucher from the hotel. Recommended, but can be noisy at weekends.

D Inter, above restaurant of same name, close to the bus station (ask there), T238-383 3620. Modern and clean with hot showers.

D Madrid, 3 Sur 105, T238-382 0272, opposite Municipal Library. Cheap and comfortable with a pleasant courtyard. Rooms are cheaper without bath. Recommended.

⊘ Eating

Amecameca *p180*
There are several eating places and a good food market. A good-quality *pulque* is available at the *pulquería* on the main plaza.

Puebla *p182, maps p183 and p184*
Local specialities include *chiles en nogada* (poblano chillies stuffed with minced meat and almonds and topped with a sweet cream sauce made with ground nuts, then topped with pomegranate seeds; the green, white and red colours are supposed to represent the Mexican flag); and *mole poblano* (chicken or turkey with sauce of chillies, spices, nuts and chocolate).

††† El Mural de los Poblanos, 16 de Septiembre 506, T222-242 0503, www.elmuraldelospoblanos.com. Fabulous food in the fabulous setting of a 17th-century courtyard. Fantastic paintings feature scenes and characters from Mexican history whilst freshly prepared regional specialities are served with impeccable grace. Not cheap.

††† Mesón Sacristía de la Compañía, 6 Sur 304, T222-242 3554. Located in the old sacristy, this elegant restaurant has a marvellous patio and lots of plants. They serve regional specialities like *quesadillas de flor de calabaza* and a fiery hot *cazuelita poblana* – spicy fajitas, basically. *Consomé de enfermo* is a kind of chicken soup with 'restorative' properties.

†††-†† Restaurant Colonial, 4 Sur 105, across pedestrian street from La Compañía church. Hotel Colonial's restaurant is the locals' favourite and best at Sun lunch time, when it really fills up with diners. They serve international food and regional specialities. The menu changes daily and there's also a reasonable *comida corrida*. The kitchen is good and clean, and the interior is elegant.

†† Fonda Santa Clara, 3 Pte 307, with parking a couple of blocks west on 3 Pte. A good, popular place to sample local specialities and classic Puebla dishes. Excellent *mole*, *mixiote* (lamb with chilli, wrapped in paper with spicy sauce) and *chiles en nogada* (best Jul-Sep). They also serve more exotic fare like *escamoles* (ant eggs) and *gusanos de maguey* (maguey grubs). A pleasant, atmospheric interior.

†† Hotel Royalty, Portal Hidalgo 8. Pleasant restaurant, busy restaurant on the plaza, under the *portales*. Sometimes serenaded by a marimba band. They serve traditional dishes including *platillos poblanos*. Packed at weekends.

†† Vittorio's, Morelos 106. Italian restaurant on the zócalo with live music on Friday and Saturday night. Good atmosphere and pizzas.

††-† La China Poblana, 6 Norte 1. An open-front restaurant decorated in attractive puebla tiles and serving tasty, home-cooked, regional food.

♦-♦ La Gardenia, Palafox 416. A busy little locals' haunt serving good regional cuisine. Affordable and unpretentious, if a little cramped.

♦-♦ La Zanahoria, 5 Ote 206. A big, popular vegetarian place that serves juices, salads, shakes and other wholesome fare. Economical set meals are also available.

♦ La Princesa, Portal Juárez 101. Good variety and good prices, several other similar places nearby to choose from on the zócalo.

♦ Mercado El Alto, in the San Francisco quarter. Beautiful market covered with *azulejos*, with good local cuisine. Breakfast and lunch, 8 different menus.

Cafés, sweet shops and ice cream parlours

Nieves – drinks made of alcohol, fruit and milk – are worth trying. **Calle 6 Ote** specializes in shops selling traditional handmade *dulces* (sweets), *camotes* (candied sweet potatoes) and *rompope* (egg nog).

Café Britannia, Reforma 528. Cheap and good coffee. Recommended.

Cafetería Tres Gallos, 4 Pte 110. Good coffee and pastries.

Super-Soya, 5 de Mayo. Good for fruit salads and juices. Several other good places for *comidas corridas* on 5 de Mayo.

Tepoznieves, 3 Pte 150, esq 3 Sur. Rustic Mexican decor, serves all varieties of tropical fruit ice cream and sherbet.

Around Puebla *p186*
Cholula

There are many good restaurants and food stops in Cholula. Try the *licuados* at market stalls (fruit and milk and 1 or 2 raw eggs if you wish); *mixiote* is a delicious local dish of spicy lamb or goat barbecued in a bag.

♦♦ Café Enamorada, southwest corner of the zócalo. Popular place with outdoor seating, live music most nights and a Sun breakfast buffet.

♦♦ La Lunita, 6 Norte and Calzada San Andrés. An Interesting joint that serves Mexican food and cold cerveza. A busy bar atmosphere takes over in the evenings.

♦ Restaurant Choloyán, Av Morelos. Good, clean and friendly. They also sell handicrafts.

♦-♦ Los Jarrones, Portal Guerrero 7. Outdoor seating, breakfast buffet and loud music in the evenings. Popular with locals.

Tlaxcala *p187*

♦♦ Fonda del Convento, San Francisco 1. Intimate restaurant serving excellent 4-course traditional meals.

♦♦ Los Portales, main square. Popular, with regional dishes.

♦ Oscar's, Av Juárez, by corner of Zitlalpopocatl. Excellent sandwiches and juices.

Cuetzalan and around *p188*

♦ Yoloxochitl, 2 de Abril, Cuetzalan. Old jukeboxes and views of the cathedral. Good for breakfasts, huge juices.

Cafés

Café-Bazar Galería, in centro, Cuetzalan. Good sandwiches and tea, nice garden, English magazines. Recommended.

Tehuacán *p189*

There are many reasonably priced eating places on the zócalo.

♦♦ Restaurant Santander. Good but pricey.

♦ Pizzería Richards, Reforma Norte 250. Good pizzas, good fresh salads.

Cafés, bars and juice stalls

Cafetería California, Independencia Ote 108. Excellent juices and *licuados*.

La Pasita, 5 Ote between 2 y 4 Sur, in front of Plaza de los Sapos. The oldest bar in Puebla, sells a drink by the same name, a local speciality. Recommended.

✪ Entertainment

Puebla *p182, map p183 and p184*
For the latest cultural happenings,
see www.andonepuebla.com.

Bars and clubs

La Bóveda, 6 Sur 503. Beery student
haunt with live rock.
La Cantina de los Remedios, Juárez 2504.
Crowded and popular. One of several
drinking holes on this stretch of Juárez.
Librería Cafetería Teorema, Reforma
540, esq 7 Norte. Café, books and art
and live music at night. They also serve
good coffee and snacks, pastries,
and *platillos mexicanos*. Recommended.

✪ Festivals and events

Puebla *p182, map p183 and p184*
Mid-Apr Feria for 2 weeks.
Sep-Nov The Fiesta Palafoxiana runs
from the last Fri in Sep until mid-Nov for
9 weekends of dancing, music, theatre,
exhibitions, etc; some free performances.

✪ Shopping

Puebla *p182, map p183 and p184*
5 de Mayo is a pedestrian street closed to
traffic from the zócalo to Av 10. The entire
block containing the Capilla del Rosario/
Templo de Santo Domingo in the southeast
corner has been made into a shopping mall
(opened 1994), called the **Centro Comercial
La Victoria** after the old La Victoria market.
The old market building still exists.

   Bookshops Librería Británica,
Calle 25 Pte 1705-B, T222-240 8549.

   Crafts The famous Puebla Talavera
tiles may be purchased from factories
outside Puebla, or from the famous
Taller Uriarte, Av 4 Pte 911 (spectacular
building, tours at 1100, 1200 and
1300). Recommended.

Other government-sponsored shops
include **Tienda Convento Santa Rosa**,
3 Norte 1203, T222-240 8904; **Talavera de la
Reyna**, Camino a la Carcaña 2413, Recta a
Cholula. Recommended (also in **Hotel Mesón
del Angel**); **Centro de Talavera**, Calle 6 Ote
11; **D Aguilar**, 40 Pte 106, opposite Convento
de Santa Mónica; and **Casa Rugerio**, 18 Pte
111. **Margarita Guevara**, 20 Pte 30.

✪ Transport

Amecameca *p180*
Bus
From Mexico City with **Cristóbal Colón**.
Los Volcanes 2nd-class bus 1-1½ hrs,
US$2.80, from the Terminal del Oriente.

Puebla *p182, map p183 and p184*
Air
Aeropuerto Hermanos Serdán (PBC) has
flights to **Guadalajara**, **León**, **Mexico City**,
Monterrey and **Tijuana**. For airline website
addresses, see page 37.
   Airline offices Aero California,
Blv Atlixco 2703, Locales B y C, Col Nueva
Antequera, T222-230 4855. AeroMéxico,
Av Juárez 1514, Col La Paz, T222-232 0013.
Aeromar, T222-232 9633. **Lufthansa** and
LanChile, Av Juárez 2916, Col La Paz,
T222-248 4400. **Mexicana**, Av Juárez
2312, between Calle 23 Sur y 25 Sur,
T222-248 5600.

Bicycle
There are several bike shops in 7 Norte, north
of 4 Pte, with a good selection of parts.

Bus
The huge **CAPU** bus terminal is north of city.
From the centre take any form of transport
marked 'CAPU', many *colectivos* and buses
(route 12) on Av 9 Norte, US$3.50 per person
flat rate; or bus 37 or 21 at Av Camacho.
To the centre from the terminal take *combi*
No 14, US$0.30, which stops at 11 Norte and
Reforma at Paseo de Bravo (make sure it's a

No 14 'directo', as there is a No 14 that goes to the suburbs). The departure terminal has banking services (with ATM), and a good practical mix of shops including gift shops, phone booths, food shops and luggage storage. The arrivals terminal has some shops including small grocery, free toilets, long-distance pay phones and taxi ticket booth (but you have to take ramp to the departure terminal to get the taxi).

Bus services from Puebla run to most parts of Mexico. To **Mexico City**, ADO GL to TAPO (eastern) terminal every 20 mins from 0430 to 2010, 2 hrs, US$9. To **Terminal del Sur** every hour from 0635 to 2135, US$6.50; to **Terminal del Norte** every 20-40 mins from 0520-2150, US$6.50. 2nd-class service to Mexico City every 10 mins, US$5, plus service US$5.50; AU, every 12 mins from 0510 to 2300. **Estrella Roja** to **Mexico City airport** every hour from 0300 to 2000, 2 hrs, US$9. To **Acapulco**, Estrella Blanca, 10 daily, US$37. To **Chetumal**, ADO, 1145, US$66, 17 hrs. To **Cuernavaca**, ADO, hourly, 3 hrs, US$12. To **Mérida**, ADO, 1305, 1955, 2005, US$69-83, 17½ hrs. To **Oaxaca**, ADO, 12 daily, US$24, 4½ hrs. To **Reynosa**, ADO, 1100, US$64. To **San Cristóbal de las Casas**, Cristóbal Colón plus service, 6 daily, US$66-79. To **Tapachula**, UNO, 2015, 16 hrs, US$102; Cristóbal Colón plus service, 4 a day, US$68. To **Tehuacán** direct ADO every 30-45 mins 0600-2100, US$6. To **Tuxtla Gutiérrez**, ADO, 1930, 2205, 10 hrs, US$59. To **Villahermosa**, ADO GL plus service via autopista, 1835 and 2200, 8½ hrs, US$57; 1st-class; 1145, 2045, 2145, 8¼ hrs, US$50; UNO at 2130, 2350, 8 hrs, US$82. To **Xalapa**, ADO GL plus service at 0745, 1645 and 2015, US$14, 1st class, 8 a day, 3 hrs, US$12; AU, 2nd class, 13 daily, 3½ hrs, US$11

Bus companies Autobuses de Oriente (ADO), T01800-7028000. Mercedes Benz buses, 1st class and ADO GL plus service. Autobuses Unidos (AU), T222-249 7366, all 2nd class without toilets. Cristóbal Colón, T222-249 7144 ext 2860, plus service. Estrella Blanca, T222-249 7561, 1st class,

plus and elite services. Estrella Roja, T222-249 7099, 2nd class, 1st class and plus service. Oro, T222-249 7775, gran turismo or 1st-class service. UNO, T222-230 4011, luxury service.

Taxi
Radio Omega, T222-240 6299, radio taxi service, with new Chevrolet cars, 24-hr service, will deliver packages or pick up food or medicine and deliver it to your hotel.

Train
The train station is a long way from the centre, so before going there check at the tourist office to see if any passenger services are running.

Around Puebla p186
Cholula
Bus Frequent 2nd-class **Estrella Roja** buses from **Puebla** to Cholula from 6 Pte y 13 Norte, 9 km on a new road, 20 mins, also 1st- and 2nd-class **Estrella Roja** buses from CAPU bus terminal hourly (be ready to get out, only a quick stop in Cholula); from Cholula take a 'Pueblo Centro' bus to the city centre, or a 'Puebla-CAPU' bus for the terminal; colectivos to Cholula. From **Mexico City**, Estrella Roja buses leave for Cholula from Terminal del Oriente every 30 mins, 2½-3 hrs, US$4.20, 2nd class every 20 mins, a very scenic route through steep wooded hills. Good views of volcanoes.

Tlaxcala p187
Bus
Tlaxcala's bus station is about a 10-min walk from the centre. Frequent **Flecha Azul** buses from **Puebla**, central bus station (platform 81/82) between 0600 and 2130, 45 mins, US$1.50. To **Cacaxtla** US$0.55.

Cuetzalan p188
Bus
Direct buses from **Puebla** (Tezuitecos line only), 5 a day from 0500 to 1530, US$8.50; quite a few return buses, but if none direct,

go to Zaragoza and change buses there. There are many buses to **Zacapoaxtla** with frequent connections for Cuetzalan.

Tehuacán p189
Bus
ADO bus station on Av Independencia (Pte). Direct to **Mexico City**, hourly service, 5 hrs, US$15-17. To **Puebla**, every 30 mins, 2-2½ hrs, US$7-8. To **Oaxaca**, 1220, 3 hrs, US$19, Autobuses Unidos at 1430, coming from Mexico City, may be full, **Veracruz**, 0150, 1345 and 1645, 4½ hrs, US$14; **Autobuses Unidos**, 2nd class on Calle 2 Ote with several buses daily to Mexico City and Oaxaca. Local bus to **Huajuapan**, 3 hrs, US$7; from there, frequent buses to Oaxaca.

Huautla de Jiménez p189
Bus
Several daily buses to/from **Mexico City** and **Oaxaca** (US$6.50); children meet buses offering lodging in their homes.

● Directory

Puebla p182, map p183 and p184
Banks Bancomer, 3 Pte 116, changes TCs 0930-1300, good rates. On the zócalo are Banco Santander Mexicano; Banco Inverlat at Portal Benito Juárez 109, changes money 0900-1400; and a *casa de cambio* at Portal Hidalgo 6 next to Hotel Royalty. On Av Reforma are: Banamex, No 135; Bancomer, No 113; HSBC, across the street. Most banks have ATMs. **Internet** Escuela Sandoval, 5 Ote. Soluciones Alternativas, Calle 4 Norte 7, No 101, 1st floor, no sign. At the BUAP University, Av San Claudio esq 22 Sur, T222-244 4404, Mon-Fri 0700-2100, Sat

and Sun 0800-1800, 48 PCs, but slow. **Laundry** Commercial centre on Av 21 Pte and Calle 5 Sur, US$4 wash and dry, 3 hrs. Another on 9 Norte, between 2 and 4 Pte, US$2.80, good service wash. **Medical services** Dentist: Dr A Bustos, 2 Pte 105-8, T222-232 4412, excellent, recommended. Doctors: Dr Miguel Benítez Cortázar, 11 Pte 1314, T222-242 0556, US$15 per consultation; Dr Cuauhtémoc Romero López, same address and phone. Hospitals: Beneficiencia Española, 19 Norte 1001, T222-232 0500. Betania, 11 Ote 1826, T222-235 8655. UPAEP, 5 Pte 715, T222-246 6099. The cheapest is **Universitario de Puebla**, 25 Pte y 13 Sur, T243-1377, where an outpatient consultation is US$5. **Post office** 5 Ote between 16 de Septiembre and 2 Sur, Mon-Fri 0800-2000.

Around Puebla p186
Cholula
Banks There is a *casa de cambio* on the corner of the main plaza in Cholula.

Tlaxcala p187
Internet Café Internet, Independencia 21, south of Av Guerrero. **Laundry** Servi-Klim, Av Juárez, 1½ blocks from plaza, dry cleaners, will launder but at dry-cleaning prices. Lavandería Acuario, Alonsa Escalona 17, between Juárez and Lira y Ortega, 3 kg US$3, self-service 4 kg US$1, daily 0830-2000.

South to Oaxaca p189
Language school Escuela de Español en Tecamachalco, Calle 29 Sur 303, Barrio de San Sebastián, Tecamachalco, CP 75480, Apdo Postal 13, T249-422 1121, run by Patricia Martínez, very good; homestays available.

Baja California

Baja California (Lower California) is the long, narrow appendage that dangles southwards from the US border between the Pacific Ocean and the Gulf of California for 1300 km. Rugged and almost uninhabited mountains split its tapering length, which has an average width of only 80 km. The tourist hotspots are found at the far north and south. Bordering the US is the brassy and gaudy Tijuana and nearby northern beaches, and in the far south the upmarket resorts of Cabo San Lucas and San José del Cabo of the southern Cape zone and La Paz with its colourful carnival. In between is the wilderness that attracts visitors to watch the whales and dolphins at Guerrero Negro or nearby San Ignacio, comb the beaches, explore the national parks, discover the ancient cave paintings and enjoy the awe-inspiring and ever-changing desert landscapes. For them the peninsula, with its hundreds of kilometres of virgin coastline, is a magical place of blue skies, fresh air, solitude and refuge from the rat race north of the border. ▸▸ *For listings, see pages 214-231.*

Background

Cortés attempted to settle at La Paz in 1534 after one of his expeditions had brought the first Europeans to set foot in Baja, but the land's sterile beauty disguised a chronic lack of food and water; this, and sporadic hostility from local tribes, forced the abandonment of most early attempts at settlement. Jesuit missionary fathers arrived at Loreto in 1697 and founded the first of their 20 missions. The Franciscans and then Dominicans took over when the Jesuits were expelled in 1767. The fathers were devoted and untiring in their efforts to convert the peninsula's ethnic groups, but diseases introduced unknowingly by them and by ships calling along the coasts soon decimated the local population. Some indigenous people remain today, but without tribal organization. Scattered about the sierras are the remains of these missions, some beautifully restored, others no more than eroded adobe foundations.

Ins and outs

Food and accommodation tend to be more expensive than the rest of Mexico, but cheaper than the US. Tijuana, Ensenada and La Paz have a good range of duty-free shopping. Make a note of departure times of buses in Tijuana or Ensenada when travelling south: between Ensenada and Santa Rosalía it can be difficult to obtain bus information. Don't ask for menus in English if you can help it; prices are often cheaper in the Spanish version. Check change as overcharging is not uncommon. Note that hotels have widely divergent winter and summer rates; between June and November tariffs are normally lower than those given in the text (especially in expensive places). The US dollar is preferred in most places north of La Paz.

If you're planning the 'big trip' from Mexico to Panama you have to start or end at the Mexican border with the US. It's long, stretching from Tijuana on the Pacific Coast east to the outlet of the Río Grande near Matamoros in the Gulf of Mexico.

Stretching 1704 km from Tijuana to Cabo San Lucas, Highway 1 is generally in good repair, although slightly narrow and lacking hard shoulders. Roads in Baja California Norte are more potholed than those in Baja California Sur. Service stations are placed at adequate intervals along the route, but motorists should fill their tanks at every opportunity and carry spare fuel, particularly if venturing off the main roads. Stations in small towns may not have fuel, or may sell from barrels at inflated prices. The same conditions apply for Highway 5

Border essentials: Baja California–USA

At all borders Mexican authorities will issue and stamp **tourist cards** and process **car permits**. There is a buffer zone for about 120 km south of the border allows US citizens to travel without a tourist card. If you are travelling beyond Baja California, do not forget to go through immigration and customs checks or you will have serious problems at police checks later on. The same applies if you are travelling with a vehicle. In addition to those detailed below, immigration authorities are also encountered at Ensenada, Quitovac (28 km south of Sonoyta, Sonora on Highway 2), and when boarding the ferries to cross the Gulf of California, see box, page 228.

Tijuana–San Diego (California)

US freeways funnelling 12 lanes of traffic into three on the Mexican side means great congestion, particularly at weekends. It is worth considering staying in San Diego for a couple of nights, and popping over the border to orientate yourself, check out bus times and so forth without weighty baggage. A tourist office at the border gives out maps of the area explaining money-changing, buses, etc. The border is open 24 hours.

Leaving Mexico Be prepared for tough immigration procedures.

Leaving USA Due to the sheer volume of people crossing the border, it is very easy to enter Mexico without completing exit and entry formalities. Be sure to get an entry stamp on your tourist card as well as your passport. Pedestrians can get a tourist card from the immigration office just over the bridge (difficult to find; you will have to look around). After completing immigration procedures walk over another pedestrian bridge before you get to Tijuana proper where you're greeted by money changers. From there, it's a short walk to the downtown bus terminal. The main terminal is 5 km southeast of town.

Crossing with a vehicle Follow the right-hand lane marked 'Customs'. You should also be able to obtain your tourist card/vehicle permit at this office, then get a stamp from the vehicle registry office about 100 m south. Officials will ask for copies of your documents, including the vehicle permit. For insurance try **Baja Bound Insurance Services**, 750 11th Av 101, San Diego, T619-702 4292, www.bajabound.com, which also has good information on travelling requirements in Mexico.

Crossing by bicycle Note that cyclists are not allowed on Highway 1-D (the toll road), so head for Highway 1 (*libre*) to Ensenada.

Tijuana–Otay Mesa (California)

A quieter recommended alternative to Tijuana is the Otay Mesa crossing 8 km east of Tijuana, reached from the US side by SR-117. The border is open 0600-2200. Car insurance and vehicle permit facilities are no longer available here. From the Mexican side it is harder to find; continue on the bypass from Highway 1-D to near the airport and the 'Garita de Otay' sign.

Tecate–Tecate (California)

The border is open 0600-2400, but immigration and customs officers will only process vehicle papers 0800-1600; at other hours, continue to Mexicali or Sonoyta. All documents are obtainable at the border. Tourist cards may also be obtained at the bus terminal.

Leaving Mexico Immigration facilities are three blocks north, uphill, from the west side of the parque. Mexican immigration offices, Lázaro Cárdenas and Callejón Madero, T665-654 0280, are on the left.
Leaving USA US immigration facilities are opposite the Mexican offices, above.

Mexicali–Calexico (California)
The border is open 24 hours a day. Southbound flow is generally better than northbound. There is no immigration check on the Mexican side of the border.
Leaving Mexico Pedestrians travelling to Calexico should take the underpass beneath Calzada López Mateos, which passes through the Mexican immigration office before continuing to the US side.
Leaving USA Follow the diagonal Calzada López Mateos, which leads to the tourist office and train and bus stations. Highway 2 runs east from Mexicali through San Luis Río Colorado, Sonoyta and Caborca to join the Pacific Highway at Santa Ana; see page 234.

(Mexicali–San Felipe), Highway 3 (Tecate–Ensenada–San Felipe) and Highway 2 (Tijuana 196, Mexicali–San Luis-Sonoyta). Hitchhiking is not difficult although you may have long waits, and there is very little public transport off the main highway.

Border towns ●❼❸❸❶ ▶▶ pp214-231. Colour map 1, A1.

Mexicali → Phone code: 686.
Capital of Baja California, Mexicali is not as geared to tourism as Tijuana and thus retains its busy, business-like border-town flavour. There is a **tourist office** ① Obregón 1257, local 12 altos Col. Nueva, www.mexicaliturismo.com, Mon-Fri 0800-1900, with the usual flyers and brochures. The University of Baja California's **Museo Regional** ① Av Reforma y Calle L, Tue-Fri 0900-1800, weekend 1000-1500, free, has interesting exhibits illustrating Baja's archaeology, ethnography and missions.

Calexico (California)
Opposite Mexicali, Calexico, the much smaller city on the California side of the border, is so thoroughly Mexicanized that it can be difficult to find a newspaper from San Diego or Los Angeles. Mexican shoppers flock here for clothing bargains. Day visitors may prefer to park on the California side, since the extremely congested Avenida Cristóbal Colón in Mexicali, which parallels the frontier fence, is the access route to the US port of entry.

Tecate
The road west from Mexicali to Tijuana is fast and well surfaced, running across barren desert flats, below sea level and with organ-pipe cacti in abundance, until reaching the eastern escarpment of the peninsula's spine; it winds its way up the Cantú Grade to **La Rumorosa**, giving expansive, dramatic vistas of desert and mountain.

The border town of Tecate is more like a Mexican city of the interior than a gaudy border town, perhaps because there is no town centre on the US side. Bus services to the interior resemble those from Tijuana. The **Baja California Secretary of Tourism** ① opposite the park at Libertad 1305, T665- 654 5892, provides a useful map of the town and other information. English spoken. Tecate is the birthplace of Tecate beer and the only real reason for stopping in town is to make a pilgrimage to the world-famous brewery, **Cerverceria Cuautémoc Moctezuma** ① *Arturo Guerra 70, T665-654 9478, www.ccm.com.mx*. Call ahead for a tour of the facilities, where fresh locally sourced spring water is transformed into golden nectar.

San Diego (California)
Arriving in **San Diego International Airport**, bus No 992 stops outside all terminals and gets you from the airport to the downtown Gaslamp district and the **Greyhound station** ① *120 W Broadway, T619-239 6737, www.greyhound.com*, with many services to Los Angeles. The trolley bus service that covers most of the city goes to the border at San Ysidro.

Tijuana ☺⊙⊙⊙▲⊙⊙ ⇒ pp214-231. Colour map 1, A1.

→ *Phone code: 664.*

Sitting on the south side of the River Tijuana, 35 million people annually cross the border to Tijuana, fuelling the city's claim to be 'the world's most-visited city'; this is the frontline at which the US and Mexico face up to each other in pleasure and politics. Often criticized as 'not being the real Mexico', it is nevertheless an historic and impassioned place. It came to prominence with Prohibition in the US in the 1920s when Hollywood stars and thirsty Americans flocked to the sleazy bars and enterprising nightlife of Tijuana and Mexicali, both at this time little more than large villages.

Although countless bars still vie for the visitor's dollar, it is the duty-free bargains, horse racing, cheap medicines and inexpensive English-speaking dentists that attract many visitors. Modern Tijuana is Mexico's fourth largest city and one of the most prosperous. However, a walk along the *barrio* beside the border (don't go alone) to see the breached fence will demonstrate the difference between the developed and developing worlds.

Ins and outs
Getting there It is cheaper to fly south from Tijuana's airport, **Aeropuerto Rodríguez (TIJ)** ① *east of downtown, 17 km (20 mins) from San Diego, CA*, than it is from any US airport. The **bus station** is 5 km southeast of the centre at the end of Vía Oriente (at La Mesa); take any local bus marked 'Central Camionera' or 'Buena Vista'. Local buses marked 'La Línea/Centro' go from the bus station to the border. ⇒ *See Transport, page 226.*

Getting around In the centre a selection of long distance buses leave from Calle 2 near Revolución. When taking a taxi in Mexico (unless it is a fixed-price airport service), it is often a good idea to agree on a price before travelling (some bargaining may be acceptable).

Tourist information The main **tourist office** ① *Revolución, between calles 3a and 4a, T664-685 2210, www.seetijuana.com, Mon-Thu 1000-1600, Fri-Sun 1000-1900*, is in the heart of downtown. There are two other offices at the border, and one at the airport. Some of the staff speak English.

Sights
The main drag, **Avenida Revolución**, runs directly south from the tourist kiosk on the edge of the red-light district, with many bars and restaurants and souvenir shops (generally open 1000-2100). The **Centro Cultural** ① *Paseo de los Héroes y Av Independencia, T664-687 9600,*

www.cecut.gob.mx, 1000-1900, US$2, contains the excellent **Museo de las Identidades Mexicanas**, which lets visitors know in no uncertain terms that they are in Mexico. There are also handicraft shops, restaurant, concert hall, and the ultra-modern spherical **Omnimax Cinema** ① *1664-684 1111, English performance 1400 daily, Spanish version 1900*, where three films are shown on a 180° screen; it is best to sit at the back/top so you don't have to lean too far back. There is a small **Wax Museum** ① *Calle 1 y Madero, daily 1000-1800, US$1.80*, with historical figures and movie stars. The **Catedral of Nuestra Señora de Guadalupe** is at Calle 2. Perhaps unsurprisingly, devotees of alcoholic beverages are well catered to in Tijuana. The **Cerveceria Tijuana** ① *Fundadores 2951, T664-638 8662, www.tjbeer.com, Mon-Fri 0800-1730*, offers tours of their micro-brewery; call in advance. **LA Cetto** ① *Cañón Johnson 2180, T664-685 3031, Mon-Fri 1000-1200, 1500-1700*, is a local winery that also offers tastings and tours. Tijuana has two bullrings: the **Plaza de Toros Monumental** ① *Playas de Tijuana, www.plazamonumental.com*, is the only one in the world built on the sea shore; and **El Toreo** ① *3 km east of downtown, Blv Agua Caliente, T664-680 1808, May-Sep Sun 1600, tickets from US$11 in the sol (sun) to US$14 in the sombra (shade)*. Corridas alternate between the two. Charreadas (rodeos) take place at one of four grounds (every Sunday from May to September, free).

Tijuana

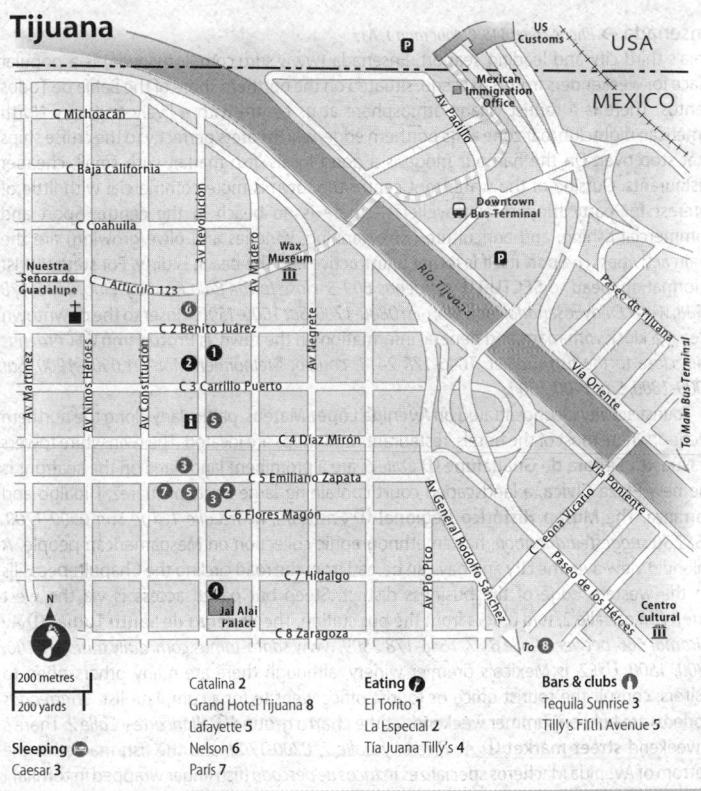

200 metres	Catalina **2**
200 yards	Grand Hotel Tijuana **8**
	Lafayette **5**
Sleeping	Nelson **6**
Caesar **3**	Paris **7**

Eating 🍴
El Torito **1**
La Especial **2**
Tía Juana Tilly's **4**

Bars & clubs 🍸
Tequila Sunrise **3**
Tilly's Fifth Avenue **5**

South of Tijuana ●●●●● ‣ *pp214-231. Colour map 1, A1.*

A dramatic 106-km toll road (Highway 1-D) leads along cliffs overhanging the Pacific to Ensenada; the toll is in three sections of US$2 each. There are emergency phones approximately every 2 km on the toll road. This is the safest route between the two cities and 16 exit points allow access to a number of seaside developments and villages along the coast.

Rosarito ‣ *Phone code: 661. Colour map 1, A1.*

Rosarito is variously described as a drab resort strung out along the old highway, or 'a breath of fresh air after Tijuana', with numerous seafood restaurants and curio shops. There is a fine swimming beach and horse riding. In March and April accommodation is hard to find as college students in great numbers take their holiday here. Essential for lovers of the big screen is **Foxploration** ① *2 km beyond the La Paloma toll, T661-614 9444, www.foxploration.com, daily, US$12, Wed-Sun 1000-1630*. This is where *Titanic* was filmed. There is also a **tourist office** ① *Quinta Plaza Mall, Benito Juárez 96, T661-612 0396, daily 0900-1600*.

Ensenada ‣ *Phone code: 646. Colour map 1, A1.*

Baja's third city and leading seaport, Ensenada (www.sdro.com/cotucoeda) is a popular place for weekenders from San Diego, situated on the northern shore of the Bahía de Todos Santos. There is a tourist village atmosphere at its centre with a lively and very North American nightclub/bar zone at its northern edge, which caters perfectly to the cruise ships that stop over. On the harbour fringe is a good locals' fish market with small, cheaper restaurants. Outside of the waterfront centre the town is more commercial with little of interest for party trippers or travellers – there is no beach in the centre. Sport and commercial fishing, and agriculture (with canning, wineries and olive growing) are the main activities. The port itself is rather unattractive and the beach is dirty. For state tourist information, head to **SECTUR** ① *Cárdenas 609-5, close to the Baja Country Club, T646-178 8588, www.EnjoyEnsenada.com, Mon-Fri 0800-1700, Sat 1000-1500*. Closer to the downtown area is a kiosk with maps and general information on the town, is **Proturismo** ① *Cárdenas 540, close to the fish market, T646-178 2411, cotucoe@telnor.net, Mon-Fri 0900-1900, Sat 1000-1800, Sun 1100-1500*.

Tourist activity is concentrated on **Avenida López Mateos**, particularly along the northern section, where most of the hotels, restaurants and shops are located. The twin white towers of **Nuestra Señora de Guadalupe** ① *Calle 6*, are a prominent landmark; on the seafront is the new **Plaza Cívica**, a landscaped court containing large busts of Juárez, Hidalgo and Carranza. The **Museo Histórico Regional** ① *Gastelum, near Calle 1, Tue-Sun 0900-1700, US$2.50 suggested donation*, has an ethnographic collection on Mesoamerican people. A splendid view over the city and bay can be had from the road circling the Chapultepec Hills on the western edge of the business district. Steep but paved access is via the west extension of Calle 2, two blocks from the bus station. The **Bodegas de Santo Tomás** ① *Av Miramar 666, between Calle 6 y 7, T646-178 2509, www.santo-tomas.com, daily tours at 1100, 1300, 1500, US$2*, is Mexico's premier winery, although there are many others open to visitors; consult the tourist office or tourist office website for a complete list. *Charreadas* (rodeos) are held on summer weekends at the **charro ground** ① *Blancarte y Calle 2*. There's a weekend **street market** ① *Av Riverol y Calle 7, 0700-1700*, and the fish market at the bottom of Avenida Macheros specializes in *tacos de pescado* (fish finger wrapped in tortilla).

Highway 1 south from Ensenada passes turn-offs to several beach resorts. Just before the agricultural town of **Maneadero**, a paved highway runs 23 km west on to the Punta Banda pensinsula, where you can see **La Bufadora** blowhole, one of the most powerful on the Pacific, apparently best seen on a rising tide. Air sucked from a sea-level cave is expelled as high as 16 m through a cleft in the cliffs.

Southeast to San Felipe ⊖⊙⊙ ⧉ *pp214-231. Colour map 1, A1.*

Highway 3 heading east to San Felipe leaves Ensenada at the Benito Juárez *glorieta* monument on the Calzada Cortés. At Km 39, a paved road leads off 3 km to **Ojos Negros**, continuing east (graded, dry weather) into scrub-covered foothills. It soon climbs into the *ponderosa* pine forests of the Sierra de Juárez. The road enters the **Parque Nacional Constitución de 1857**, 37 km from Ojos Negros. The jewel of the park is the small Laguna Hanson, a sparkling shallow lake surrounded by Jeffery pines; camping here is delightful, but note that the lake is reduced to a boggy marsh in dry seasons and that the area receives snow in midwinter.

Highway 3 descends along the edge of a green valley to the rapidly developing town of Valle de Trinidad. A reasonable dirt road runs south into the **Parque Nacional Sierra San Pedro Mártir** (see below).

After leaving the valley, Highway 3 follows a canyon covered in dense stands of barrel cacti to the **San Matías Pass** between the Sierras Juárez and San Pedro Mártir, which leads on to the desolate **Valle de San Felipe**. The highway turns east and emerges on to open desert hemmed in by arid mountains; 201 km from Ensenada it joins Highway 5 at the La Trinidad T-junction, 142 km south of Mexicali and 51 km north of San Felipe.

Mexicali to San Felipe
Highway 5 heads south from Mexicali for 193 km to San Felipe, passing at about Km 34 the Cerro Prieto geothermal field. After passing the Río Hardy and the **Laguna Salada** (Km 72), a vast, dry alkali flat sometimes turned into a muddy morass by rare falls of rain, the road runs straight across sandy desert until entering San Felipe around a tall, white, double-arched monument. Floods can cut the road across the Laguna Salada; when it is closed, motorists have to use Highway 3 from Ensenada (see above) to get to San Felipe.

San Felipe → *Phone code: 686. Colour map 1, A2.*
San Felipe is a pleasant, tranquil fishing and shrimping port on the Gulf of California although at weekends it can become overcrowded and noisy. Long a destination for devoted sportfishermen and a weekend retreat for North Americans, San Felipe is now experiencing a second discovery, with new trailer parks and the paving of many of the town's sandy streets. The **tourist office** ⓘ *Mar de Cortés y Manzanillo, opposite Motel El Capitán, T686-577 1600, Tue-Sun 0900-1400 and 1600-1800, www.sanfelipe.com.mx,* is helpful. **Navy Day** is celebrated on 1 June with a carnival, street dancing and boat races.

South from Ensenada ⊖ ⧉ *pp214-231. Colour map 1, A1.*

Santo Tomás
Chaparal-clad slopes begin to close in on the highway as it winds its way south, passing through the small town of Santo Tomás. Nearby are the ruins of the Dominican Mission of 1791 (local Santo Tomás wine is cheaper out of town). A little north of San Vicente a road

heads west to **Eréndira**, a beach resort made popular and accessible by **Coyote Cal's** (see Sleeping, page 216). **San Vicente** comes next, with two Pemex stations, cafés, tyre repairs and several stores. **Colonet**, further south, is a supply centre for surrounding ranches with several services. A dry-weather dirt road runs 12 km west to **San Antonio del Mar** where there are many camping spots amid high dunes fronting a beautiful beach renowned for surf fishing and clam-digging.

A reasonable, graded road branches east, 7 km south of Colonet, to San Telmo and climbs into the mountains. At 50 km it reaches the **Meling Ranch** (also called San José), which offers resort accommodation for about 12 guests. About 15 km beyond, the road enters the **Parque Nacional Sierra San Pedro Mártir** and climbs through forests (4WD recommended) to three astronomical observatories perched on the dramatic eastern escarpment of the central range. The view is one of the most extensive in North America: east to the Gulf, west to the Pacific, and southeast to the granite mass of the **Picacho del Diablo** (3096 m), Baja's highest peak. Turning west off the main road goes to **Campo 4 Casas** ⓘ *small entrance fee*, a good beach resort with services and good surfing.

El Rosario → *Colour map 1, B1.*
After leaving the San Quintín valley the scenery starts to get spectacular, bypassing Santa María (fuel available), the Transpeninsular Highway (officially the Carretera Transpeninsular Benito Juárez) runs along the Pacific before darting inland at Rancho El Consuelo. It climbs over a barren spur from which there are fine views, then drops in a succession of tight curves into El Rosario, 58 km from San Quintín. This small, agricultural community has a Pemex station, small supermarket, a basic museum, and meals, including Espinosa's famous lobster *burritos* (expensive and not particularly good) and omelettes.

Central desert of Baja California ⬤𝕗 ⟫ *pp214-231.*
Highway 1 makes a sharp 90° turn at El Rosario and begins to climb continuously into the central plateau; gusty winds increase and astonishingly beautiful desertscapes gradually become populated with many varieties of cacti. Prominent are the stately cardones; most intriguing are the strange, twisted cirios growing to heights of 6-10 m. They are unique to this portion of Baja California and extend as far south as the Vizcaíno Desert, and to a small area of Sonora state on the mainland. At Km 62, a 5-km track branches south to the adobe remains of **Misión San Fernando Velicatá**, the only Franciscan mission in Baja, founded by Padre Serra in 1769. About 26 km north of Cataviña is the start of a strange region of huge boulders, some as big as houses, interspersed by cacti and crouching elephant trees. This area is one of the most picturesque on the peninsula.

Cataviña → *Colour map 1, A2.*
Cataviña only has a small grocery store/**Café La Enramada** and the only Pemex station on the 227-km stretch from El Rosario to the Bahía de Los Angeles junction (there are in fact two fuel stations, but do not rely on either having supplies). Approximately 2 km north of Cataviña there are some easily accessible cave paintings near Km 170 on the Transpeninsular Highway.

Highway 1 continues southeast through an arid world of boulder-strewn mountains and dry salt lakes. A new graded road branches off east to Bahía San Luis Gonzaga.

Bahía de los Angeles → *Colour map 1, B2.*

The side road runs 68 km through cirios and datilillo cactus-landscapes and crosses the Sierra de la Asamblea to Bahía de los Angeles (no public transport but hitchhiking possible), a popular fishing town, which, despite a lack of vegetation, is one of Baja's best-known beauty spots. The bay, sheltered by the forbidding slopes of **Isla Angel de la Guarda** (Baja's largest island), is a haven for boating, although winds can be tricky for kayaks and small craft. There is good clamming and oysters. There are facilities in town and also a modest but interesting **museum**, which provides good background information on the many mines and on mining techniques used in the region around the turn of the 20th century.

There are thousands of dolphins in the bay between June and December. Some stay all year round. There are large colonies of seals and many exotic seabirds. Fishing is excellent. **La Gringa**, a beautiful beach 13 km north of town, charges a small fee for its many camping sites, pit toilets and rubbish bins. The series of tiny beaches at the foot of **Cabañas Díaz** are good for swimming, but watch out for stingrays when wading.

Baja California Sur ●●●● ⟫ *pp214-231. Colour map 1, B2.*

Back on the main route, Highway 1 now runs due south. Before you enter Baja California Sur you pass Rosarito (shop and restaurant) and go through **Villa Jesús María** (fuel station, shop, cafés) to the 28th parallel, which marks the state border (with a soaring stylized eagle monument) between Baja California and Baja California Sur. Note that minor Bajan roads require high-clearance, preferably 4WD, vehicles carrying adequate equipment, water and fuel. Clocks go forward one hour to Mountain time when entering Baja California Sur, but Northern Baja observes Pacific Daylight Saving Time from the first Sunday in April to the last Sunday in October; time in both states and California is thus identical during the summer.

Guerrero Negro → *Phone code: 615. Colour map 1, B2.*

Three kilometres beyond the state line and 4 km west of the highway, Guerrero Negro is the halfway point between the US border and La Paz. It's a rather unattractive little strip town with little to recommend it. There are gas stations, bank (**Banamex**, does not change traveller's cheques), hospital, cafés, stores, an airport, and the headquarters of **Exportadora de Sal**, the world's largest salt-producing firm and a cause for much concern among environmentalists.

At the far western end of town is the skeleton of a grey whale, a fitting memorial to a town that is recognized for whale watching. At times, you can hear the whales breathe as you stand on shore. Many hotels and agencies in town thrive or die on the backs of the tourists who migrate to the region from mid-December to mid-March. The alternative base for whale-watching tours is San Ignacio 142 km to the east. See box, page 206.

Desierto Vizcaíno → *Colour map 1, B2.*

After Guerrero Negro the highway enters the grim Vizcaíno Desert. A gravel road branches off due east for 42 km to El Arco and other abandoned mining areas. The road then crosses the peninsula to **San Francisquito** on its beautiful bay overlooking the Gulf of California (77 km). A new gravel road from Bahía de Los Angeles (135 km) gives easier road access than from El Arco and opens up untouched stretches of the Gulf Coast.

Whale watching

Whale watching is the main attraction on **Laguna Ojo de Liebre**, usually known as **Scammon's Lagoon** after the whaling captain who entered in 1857. California grey whales mate and give birth between the end of December and January, in several warm-water lagoons on central Baja's Pacific Coast. The whales stay a couple of months until their calves have built up enough strength. Most leave by the beginning of April, but some stay as late as May or June. They can be seen cavorting and sounding from the old salt wharf 10 km northwest of Guerrero Negro on the Estero San José, or from a designated 'whale-watching area' with observation tower on the shore of Scammon's Lagoon, 37 km south of town. The access road branches off Highway 1, 8 km east of the junction (if going by public transport, leave bus at the turn-off and hitch). There is a small fee for camping at the watching area, which pays to keep it clean.

The shores of Scammon's Lagoon are part of the **Parque Natural de la Ballena Gris**. *Pangas* are available for hire (US$10 per person), but a more straightforward way of seeing the whales is on one of the daily tours from Guerrero Negro including a 1½-hour boat trip, sandwiches and transport to the lagoon, US$40-45 per person, with departures at 0800 and 1100, between mid-December and mid-March, when as many as 50 whales are in the lagoon. One reader saw a dozen on a trip in mid-January. There are also some trips from San Ignacio.

Whale conservation

Mexico was the first country in the world to set aside habitat for whales. In 1971, Scammon's Lagoon was designated a grey whale refuge. A few years later, two more grey whale lagoons were protected – Guerrero Negro and San Ignacio. Whale watching and some fishing is still permitted in the lagoons under special regulations but other industrial activities are prohibited.

In 1988, a new biosphere reserve and world heritage site was created, which included all of Laguna Ojo de Liebre, Laguna Guerrero Negro and Laguna San Ignacio as well as the desert areas all around – a total area of more than 2.5 million hectares. Called the **Vizcaíno Desert Biosphere Reserve**, it is the largest nature reserve in Latin America. It is definitely worth visiting. Besides whales and dolphins, it is possible to see California sea lions, black and green turtles, osprey, brown pelicans, Caspian terns, great blue herons, great egrets and peregrine falcons.

With such habitat protection, the return of grey whale numbers, and the sightings of more and more hump-back, blue, fin and Bryde's whales in the Gulf of California, Mexico's whales seemed to be in good shape.

In 1995, however, the Mexican government in partnership with Mitsubishi, the Japanese conglomerate, announced plans to build the largest salt mine in the world inside the reserve, greatly expanding existing salt factories. The US$120 million development, which would create 208 permanent jobs in a relatively underdeveloped area. Direct impact from the construction and operation of the facility on the shore of Laguna San Ignacio would impact the temperature and salinity of the critical grey whale habitat. Intervention and pressure from Mexican and international conservation bodies has led to expansion plans being shelved.

Vizcaíno Peninsula → *Colour map 1, B2.*

Vizcaíno Peninsula, which thrusts into the Pacific south of Guerrero Negro, is one of the most remote parts of Baja. Although part of the Vizcaíno Desert, the scenery of the peninsula is varied and interesting; isolated fishing camps dot the silent coast of beautiful coves and untrodden beaches. A dry-weather road cuts west through the peninsula to Bahía Tortugas and the rugged headland of Punta Eugenia. It leaves Highway 1, 70 km beyond Guerrero Negro at the Vizcaíno Junction (also called Fundolegal). The new road is paved for 8 km to Ejido Díaz Ordaz. It passes **Rancho San José** (116 km) and the easily missed turn-off to Malarrimo Beach (where beachcombing is unparalleled). After another bumpy 50 km is **Bahía Tortugas**, a surprisingly large place considering its remoteness. Two roads leave the Vizcaíno–Bahía Tortuga road for Bahía Asunción. From here there is a coast road south to **Punta Prieta**, **La Bocana** and **Punta Abreojos** (93 km). A lonely road runs for 85 km back to Highway 1, skirting the Sierra Santa Clara before crossing the salt marshes north of Laguna San Ignacio and reaching the main road 26 km before San Ignacio.

San Ignacio → *Phone code: 615. Colour map 1, B2.*

The highway continues southeast and, 20 km from the Vizcaíno Junction, reaches the first of 23 microwave relay towers that follow Highway 1 almost to the cape. They are closed to the public but make excellent landmarks and, in some cases, offer excellent views. The turn-off right for the oasis town of San Ignacio, marked by a grey whale skeleton, is at **San Lino**, 143 km from Guerrero Negro. A road of about 3 km (US$2 in a taxi) leads to a small, attractive town with pastel-coloured commercial buildings and a good old mission church; there is a service station with mechanical assistance. Whale-watching tours can be arranged from here and it's a far more enjoyable place to spend time than Guerrero Negro. The best season for whale-watching is January to March.

Several tours can be arranged around town, including whale watching and seeing nearby cave paintings. Whale-watching trips are US$40 per person for 2½ hours, with transport costs of US$130 shared between the number of people travelling. Try **Ecoturismo Kuyima** ① *on the main plaza, T/F615-154 0070, Morelos 23, www.kuyima.com*, who can organize this trip and other excursions.

Around San Ignacio → *Colour map 1, B2.*

A 70-km road from San Ignacio leads to Laguna San Ignacio, one of the best whale-viewing sites; mothers and calves often swim up to nuzzle boats and allow their noses to be stroked. The **Cooperativa Laguna de San Ignacio** ① *Juárez 23, off the zócalo in San Ignacio*, takes fishermen to the lagoon every day and can sometimes accommodate visitors.

There are many **cave painting** sites around San Ignacio; colourful human and animal designs left by Baja's original inhabitants still defy reliable dating or full understanding. To reach them, most require a mule trek over tortuous trails. Oscar Fischer at **Motel La Posada** arranges excursions into the sierras (about US$10 per person to Santa Teresa cave). The cave at the **Cuesta del Palmarito**, 5 km east of **Rancho Santa Marta** (50 km northwest of San Ignacio), is filled with designs of humans with uplifted arms, in brown and black; a jeep and guide (if one can be found) are required. A better road leads east from the first microwave station past Vizcaíno Junction up to **San Francisco de la Sierra**, where there are other paintings and petroglyphs.

Santa Rosalía ⊜❶❷❸❹ ›› pp214-231. Colour map 1, B3.

→ *Phone code: 615.*

Some 72 km from San Ignacio is Santa Rosalía, squeezed into a narrow bottleneck valley running off the harbour. It was built by the French **El Boleo Copper Company** in the 1880s, laid out in neat rows of wood-frame houses, many with broad veranda. There is something intangible about Santa Rosalía that doesn't quite make it French but neither is it Mexican in appearance. In many ways, it is actually reminiscent of the Caribbean.

Up the hill near the **Hotel Francés**, the dusty street of shaded verandas is split down the middle by six rusting old engines. Subject to the fierce elements, their display is both nostalgic and pointless, but still good to see. There is a small museum, **Museo Histórico Minero de Santa Rosalía** ① *Mon-Fri 0800-1400, US$1.50*, off Calle Francisco next to the **Impecsa** warehouse, with historic exhibits of mining. The church of **Santa Bárbara** ① *Obregón y Calle 3*, a block north of the main plaza, was built of galvanized iron for the 1889 Paris World Fair from a design by Eiffel, then shipped around the Horn to Baja. Also visit the *panadería* **El Boleo**, which has been baking and selling bread for over 100 years.

The Pemex station is conveniently located on the highway, unlike the one at Mulegé, so larger RVs and rigs should fill up here. There is a 24-hour store a couple of hundred metres south. Santa Rosalía's streets are narrow and congested; larger vehicles should park along the highway or in the ferry dock parking lot. The Santa Rosalía– Guaymas ferry has recommenced, running four times a week in each direction. ›› *See Transport, page 228.*

Mulegé and around ⊜❶▲❸❹ ›› pp214-231. Colour map 1, B3.

→ *Phone code: 615.*

Some 61 km south of Santa Rosalía is another oasis community, a tranquil retreat outside of spring break, which is an increasingly popular hideaway for US and Canadian retirees. There are lovely beaches, good diving, snorkelling and boating in Bahía Concepción. The old Federal prison (**La Cananea**) has been converted into a museum. It became known as the 'prison without doors' because the inmates were allowed out during the day to work in the town. A pleasant walk leads for 3 km out of town to the stony beach complete with lighthouse with good views. The tidal lagoons are popular for collecting clams.

Just upstream from the highway bridge on the south side of the river is the **Misión de Santa Rosalía de Mulegé**, founded by the Jesuits in 1705. Above the mission there is a good lookout point over the town and its sea of palm trees. Looking the other way there is a fine view at sunset over the inland mesas. Locals swim at an excellent spot about 500 m inland from the bridge and to the right of the track to the mission. There are tours to cave-painting sites, US$40 per person including drinks; a guide is necessary; recommended is **Salvador Castro**, ask for him at the taxi rank in the plaza. The Pemex station is in Calle General Martínez, one block before plaza in the centre; not convenient for large vehicles, which also have a one-way system to contend with. But there is another Pemex station 4.5 km south of the bridge, on the road out of town towards Loreto, with restaurant and mini-market. There is good free **tourist information** in the town centre. There are no banks, but you can change dollars so make sure you bring enough cash.

South of Mulegé

Beyond Mulegé the highway runs along the shores of Bahía Concepción for 50 km. This stretch is the most heavily used camping and boating area on the peninsula; the water is beautiful, swimming safe, camping excellent and there is varied marine life. **Playa Santispac**, in **Bahía Coyote** cove, 23 km south of Mulegé (about a 30-minute ride) is recommended. There are many small restaurants (for example **Ana's**, which sells water and bakes bread, good value; and **Ray's**, good food, a bit pricey) and *palapas* (shelters) for hire (day or overnight, US$2.50). You can get to Santispac from Mulegé on the La Paz bus (taxi, US$12); it is also quite easy to hitch. Just south of here, in the next cove, at **Playa Concepción**, tents, *palapas* and kayaks can be hired at **Ecomundo**, see page 217.

Further south from El Coyote is **Playa Buenaventura**, which has rooms at **A George's Olé**, *palapas* and three *cabañas* for rent (US$20), and an expensive restaurant. From the entrance to the beach at Requesón, veer to the left for **Playa La Perla**, which is secluded.

A new graded dirt road branches off Highway 1 to climb over the towering **Sierra Giganta**, whose desert vistas of flat-topped mesas and cardón cacti are straight out of the Wild West. The road begins to deteriorate after the junction (20 km) to San José de Comondú and limps another 37 km into San Isidro, after a spectacular drop into the **La Purísima** valley. The paved road leads on southwards to **La Poza Grande** (52 km) and **Ciudad Insurgentes** (85 km).

Loreto and around 😊🏧🏕️😊😊 ➤ *pp214-231. Colour map 1, C3.*

➤ *Phone code: 613.*

Some 1125 km from Tijuana, Loreto is one of the most historic places in Baja. Here, the Spanish settlement of the peninsula began with Father Juan María Salvatierra's founding of the **Misión de Nuestra Señora de Loreto** ① *zócalo, Tue-Sun 0900-1300, 1345-1800, US$1.80*, on 25 October 1697. It was the first capital of the Californias. Nestled between the slopes of the Sierra Giganta and the offshore Isla del Carmen, Loreto has recently experienced a tourist revival that's particularly focused on outdoor activities. The nearby marine park, Parque Nacional Bahía de Loreto, offers great diving possibilities, while the sports fishing is some of the best in Baja California. The mission is the largest structure in town and perhaps the best restored of all the Baja California mission buildings. It has a gilded altar. The **museum** next door is also worth a visit. Inside the Palacio de Gobierno you'll find the **tourist office** ① *Plaza Cívica, T613-135 0411, www.gotoloreto.com, Mon-Fri 0800-1500*, with useful flyers and info on Loreto and surroundings.

South of Loreto

Just south of Loreto a rough road runs 37 km through impressive canyon scenery to the village of **San Javier**, tucked in the bottom of a steep-walled valley. This settlement of just 120 people has only one store, but the **Misión de San Javier** is one of the best preserved in North America; it was founded by the Jesuits in 1699 and took 59 years to complete. The thick volcanic walls, Moorish ornamentation and bell tower are most impressive in so rugged and remote a location. Taxis from Loreto can be arranged at roughly US$65 for the day, but hitching is quite possible. The trip is worth the effort.

The highway south of Loreto passes a picturesque stretch of coast. There are three lovely public beaches between Loreto and Puerto Escondido (none has drinking water): **Notrí**, **Juncalito** and **Ligüí** are palm-lined coves, which are a far cry from the bustle of the new resort developments nearby. Beyond Ligüí (36 km south of Loreto), Highway 1 ascends the eastern escarpment of the Sierra Giganta (one of the most fascinating legs of Highway 1) before leaving the Gulf to strike out southwest across the peninsula again to Ciudad Constitución.

Ciudad Constitución and around → *Colour map 1,C3. Phone code: 613.*

The highway passes by **Ciudad Insurgentes**, a busy agricultural town with two service stations, banks, auto repairs, shops, cafés and a few accommodation options, then runs dead straight for 26 km to Ciudad Constitución, which is the marketing centre for the Magdalena Plain agricultural development and has the largest population between Ensenada and La Paz (50,000). It has department stores, restaurants, banks, service stations, car repairs, hospital and airport.

Whales can be seen at **Puerto López Mateos** further north (access from Ciudad Insurgentes or Ciudad Constitución); there's no hotel, but ask for house of María del Rosario González who rents rooms, or take a tent and camp at the small harbour near the fish plant. 'Mag Bay' is considered the finest natural harbour between San Francisco and Acapulco.

La Paz ●❼❸❀❍▲❸❸ → *pp214-231. Colour map 1, C3.*

→ *Phone code: 612.*

Capital of Baja California Sur, La Paz is a relaxed modern city nestled at the southern end of **Bahía La Paz** (where Europeans first set foot in Baja in 1533). Sunsets can be spectacular. Prices have risen as more tourists arrive to enjoy its winter climate, but free port status ensures that there are plenty of bargains (although some goods, like certain makes of

La Paz

Lorimar **3**	Café El Callejón **3**	Los Magueys **12**
Los Arcos **4**	Café Gourmet **6**	Señor Sushi **7**
Mediterráneo **5**	Carlos 'n' Charlies **2**	
Pensión California **6**	Delís **8**	**Bars & clubs** ❶
Plaza Real **8**	El Dragón **6**	Bowk **13**
Posada del Cortez **7**	El Quinto **4**	Jungle Bar **13**
	Giulietta y Romeo **10**	La Casa de Villa **14**
Sleeping ●	Kiwi **5**	Osha **15**
Hostería del Convento **1**	**Eating** ❼	La Boheme **10**
La Perla **2**	Adriana **1**	

camera, are cheaper to buy in the US). Oyster beds attracted many settlers in the 17th century, but few survived long. The **Jesuit mission**, founded in 1720, was abandoned 29 years later. La Paz became the territorial capital in 1830 after Loreto was wiped out by a hurricane. Although bursting with new construction, there are still many touches of colonial grace, arched doorways and flower-filled patios. The early afternoon siesta is still observed by many businesses, especially during summer.

If you're looking for a challenging way to move on, hang around a while and visit one of the marinas at the northern end of town to see if you can get a crewing job with a boat heading down the coast.

Head to the Palacio Municipal for **tourist information** ① *16 de Septiembre and Domínguez, T612 125-6844, www.vivalapaz.com, Mon-Fri 0900-1700*, who have helpful staff and a profusion of flyers. In high season there is also a **tourist office** ① *Tourist Wharf, at the bottom of 16 de Septiembre, Mon-Fri 0800-1500, Sat 0900-1300, 1400-1500*, which will make hotel reservations. Staff speak English and can provide tourist literature and town maps. There's a noticeboard for rides offered, crew wanted, etc.

Sights

The street grid is rectangular. Westerly streets run into the Paseo Alvaro Obregón, the waterfront **Malecón**, where the commercial and tourist wharves back on to a tangle of streets; here are the banks, **Palacio Municipal**, **Chinatown** and many of the cheaper *pensiones*. The local landmark is **Carlos 'n' Charlies** restaurant from where you can find most things within a couple of blocks. The more expensive hotels are further southwest. The heart of La Paz is the **Plaza Constitución**, a little east of the main tourist area, facing which are the government buildings and the graceful **Catedral de Nuestra Señora de la Paz**, built in 1861-1865 on or near the site of the original mission. The **Museo Antropológico de Baja California Sur** ① *Ignacio Altamirano y 5 de Mayo, Mon-Fri 0800-1800, Sat 0900-1400, free*, is well worth a visit for the small but admirable display of Peninsular anthropology, history and pre-history, folklore and geology. The bookshop has a wide selection on Mexico and Baja. The **Museum of the Whale** ① *Navarro and Ignacio Altamirano, Tue-Sat 0900-1300, free*, and a carved mural depicting the history of Mexico, can be seen at the **Palacio de Gobierno** ① *Isabel La Católica, corner of Bravo*.

Beaches

There are many beaches around La Paz, the most popular are on the **Pichilingüe Peninsula**. Most have restaurants (good seafood restaurant under a *palapa* at Pichilingüe). Going north from La Paz to the ferry terminal on Highway 11 you will pass **Palmira**, **Coromuel**, popular with *paceños* (residents of La Paz), **El Caimancito**, and **Tesoro**. Windsurfing and catamaran trips can be arranged. Buses to Pichilingüe run from 1000-1400 and 1600-1730, US$1.30 from station at Paseo Alvaro Obregón and Independencia. About 100 m north of ferry terminal is a public beach. **Balandra** ① *palapas US$2*, and **Tecolote** ① *camping free under palapas*, are reached by the road beyond the ferry terminal (paved for some distance beyond this point; some buses on this route run beyond the ferry terminal at weekends). The road ends at a gravel pit at **Playa Cachimba** (good surf fishing), 13 km northeast of Pichilingüe; the north facing beaches are attractive but can be windy, and there are some sandflies. **El Coyote** (no water or facilities), on the east coast, is reached by a road/track from La Paz running inland along the middle of the peninsula. Southwest of La Paz on the bay are the tranquil, no-surf beaches of **Comitán** and **El Mogote**. In October (at least) and after rain, beware of stinging jellyfish in the water.

Around La Paz

There are boat tours from the Tourist Wharf on the Malecón around the bay and to nearby islands like **Espírtiu Santo**. Travel agencies offer a daily boat tour to **Los Lobos Islands** ranging from US$40-80; the tour should include lunch and snorkelling, and last about six hours. You can see pelicans, sea-lions and dolphins, with luck whales, too. About 17 km west of La Paz a paved road branches northwest off Highway 1 around the bay leading to the mining village of **San Juan de la Costa**, allowing a closer look at the rugged coastal section of the Sierra de la Giganta. After San Juan (45 km), the road is passable for medium-size vehicles to **Punta Coyote** (90 km), closely following the narrow space between mountains and coast with wonderful untouched camping spots. From Coyote to **San Evaristo** (27 km) the track is poor and a rugged vehicle is recommended. San Evaristo is a sleepy fishing village on a delightful cove sheltered on the east by Isla San José. This is a rewarding excursion for those with smaller, high-clearance vehicles (vans and pickups) for the steep final 32-km stretch.

State Highway 286 leads southeast out of La Paz 45 km to **San Juan de Los Planes**. A fair road continues another 15 km to the beautiful **Ensenada de los Muertos**, where there is good fishing, swimming and 'wild' camping. A further 11 km is the headland of **Punta Arena de la Ventana**, with a magnificent view of the sterile slopes of Isla Cerralvo. Six kilometres before Los Planes, a graded road leads to the **Bahía de la Ventana** and the small fishing villages of La Ventana and El Sargento, which have lovely beaches facing **Isla Cerralvo**.

South of La Paz ⊜❼❶⦿▲⊜❶ ▸▸ pp214-231. Colour map 2, C1.

South of La Paz, the central mountain spine rises again into the wooded heights of the **Sierra de la Laguna** and bulges out into the 'Cape Region', Baja's most touristically developed area.

Eight kilometres beyond **El Triunfo** is the lovely mountain town and farming centre of **San Antonio** (gasoline, groceries, meals), which was founded in 1756 and served briefly as Baja's capital (1828-1830) when Loreto was destroyed. Eight kilometres south of San Antonio was the site of **Santa Ana**, where silver was first discovered in 1748. It was from this vanished village that the Viceroy and Padre Junípero Serra planned the expedition to establish the chain of Franciscan missions in Alta California.

Highway 1 climbs sharply from the canyon and winds past a number of ancient mines, through the peaceful orchard-farming town of **San Bartolo** (groceries and meals) and down to the coastal flats around **Los Barriles**. A number of resort hotels are situated near here along the beautiful **Bahía de Palmas** and at nearby **Buena Vista**; none are in the budget class, but all are popular.

The highway turns inland after Los Barriles (106 km from La Paz). An 'East Cape Loop' turns east off the highway through **La Rivera**. A new spur leads towards **Cabo Pulmo**, running parallel to the coast until San José del Cabo. Off Cabo Pulmo, a beautiful headland, is the Northern Pacific's only living coral reef. This is an excellent area for fishing, diving and snorkelling; enquire locally about renting equipment.

Santiago is a pleasant, historic little town 3 km off Highway 1 (bus stop at junction, two hours from La Paz, US$3.50 in a taxi from the highway). A Pemex station, café and stores grouped around the town plaza. The Jesuits built their tenth mission in Santiago in 1723 after transferring it from Los Barriles. The town was one of the sites of the uprising of the Pericué people in 1734. There are warm springs, behind a mini dam, in a pleasant setting,

12 km away along a dirt road at the foot of the mountains. Head towards the village of **Aguascalientes** (8 km) and the springs are 4 km beyond this. You can walk on from the spring to a waterfall.

Some 3.5 km south of the Santiago turn-off, Highway 1 crosses the Tropic of Cancer, marked by a large concrete sphere, and runs south down the fertile valley between the lofty **Sierra de la Laguna** (west) and the **Sierra Santa Clara** (east), to Los Cabos International Airport. San José del Cabo is 14 km further south.

San José del Cabo → Colour map 2, C1. Phone code: 624.

The largest town south of La Paz and founded in 1730, San José del Cabo is now a modern town divided into two districts: the very Americanized resort sectors and new **Fonatur** development on the beach, and the downtown zone to the north, with the government offices and many businesses grouped near the tranquil **Parque Mijares**. The attractive church on the **Plaza Mijares** was built in 1940 on the final site of the mission of 1730; a tile mosaic over the entrance depicts the murder of Padre Tamaral by rebellious locals in 1734.

Cabo San Lucas → Colour map 2, C1. Phone code: 624.

The resort town of Cabo San Lucas has grown rapidly in recent years from the sleepy fishing village of 1500 inhabitants it was in 1970. It is now an expensive international resort with a permanent population of 8500. The place is full of North Americans who come for the world-famous fishing or to find a retirement paradise.

Ringed by pounding surf, columns of fluted rock enclose **Lover's Beach** (be careful if walking along the beach, as huge waves sweep away several visitors each year), a romantic sandy cove with views out to the seal colonies on offshore islets. At the very tip of the Cabo is the distinctive natural arch, **El Arco**; boats can be hired to see it close up, but care is required because of the strong currents. At the harbour entrance is a pinnacle of rock, **Pelican Rock**, which is home to vast shoals of tropical fish; it is an ideal place for snorkelling and scuba-diving, and glass-bottomed boats can be rented at the harbour.

Todos Santos → Phone code: 612. Colour map 2, C1.

Highway 9 was not paved until 1985 and the superb beaches of the west coast have yet to suffer the development of the east. The road runs due south through a cactus-covered plain from just after **San Pedro** to Todos Santos. This quiet farming town just north of the Tropic of Cancer is slowly becoming a tourist and expat centre.

West coast beaches

Two kilometres from Todos Santos is a stretch of the Pacific Coast with some of the most beautiful beaches of the entire Baja California Peninsula. Nearest to the town is **Playa Punta Lobos** where the local fishermen shore up (the *pangas* come in early afternoon); it is a popular picnic spot, but with too much rubbish and too many unfriendly dogs for wild camping. Next comes **Playa Las Palmas**, which is good for swimming. Cleaner for camping is the sandy cove at **Playa San Pedrito** (4 km southeast). Backed by groves of Washingtonia fan palms and coconut palms, this is one of the loveliest wild camping spots anywhere; it is also good for surfing. Opposite the access road junction is the **Campo Experimental Forestal**, a botanical garden with a well-labelled array of desert plants from all regions of Baja. Here too is the **Trailer Park San Pedrito** (see Sleeping, page 220), an open area on the beach and one of the most beautifully sited RV parks in Baja California.

Parque Nacional Sierra de la Laguna

In the rugged interior east of Todos Santos is the Parque Nacional Sierra de la Laguna. Its crowning peak is the **Picacho La Laguna** (2163 m), which is beginning to attract a trickle of hikers to its 'lost world' of pine and oak trees, doves and woodpeckers, grassy meadows and luxuriant flowers; there is nothing else like it in Baja. The trail is steep but straightforward; the panoramic view takes in La Paz and both the Gulf and Pacific coasts. It gets cold at night. The park can be reached from Todos Santos; three-day guided pack trips are also offered by the **Todos Santos Inn**. Alternatively, take a taxi from Todos Santos to **La Burrera**, from where it is eight hours' walk along the littered path to La Laguna.

◉ Baja California listings

For Sleeping and Eating price codes and other relevant information, see Essentials pages 45-48.

● Sleeping

Mexicali p199

B Azteca de Oro, Industria 600, T686-557 1433, www.hotelaztecadeoro.com. Motel opposite train station and only a few blocks from bus terminal. Rooms have a/c, TV and phone. Services include a restaurant and bar. A bit scruffy, but convenient.
B Del Norte, Melgar y Av Madero, T686-552 8102, www.hoteldelnorte.com.mx. Big hotel across from the border. Rooms are generic, some have a/c and TV. Pleasant but a little noisy, with free parking for guests and discount coupons for breakfast and dinner. There are 2 sections, rates are reduced when booked online.
B Hotel De Anza, motel on the Calexico side. Excellent value for money.
C Rivera, near the railway station. Best of the cheaper hotels, with a/c.

Tecate p199

D Frontera, Callejón Madero 131, T665-654 1342. Basic, but clean and friendly (Antonio Moller Ponce, who resides here, knows a lot about the area's history).
D Juárez, Juárez 230. Rooms with or without bath, hot water.

Tijuana p200, map p201

L-A Grand Hotel Tijuana, Blv Agua Caliente 4500, T01-800-026-6007 (toll free in Mexico), www.grandhoteltij.com.mx. A 1st-rate high-rise hotel with 28 floors and a plethora of very comfortable rooms and suites. Amenities include business centre, golf course, pool and tennis court. Check online for discounts and packages.
A-C San Diego Downtown Hostel, 521 Market St, T619-525 1531, www.sandiego hostels.org. A very clean, well-organized hostel in the heart of the San Diego's historic Gaslamp Quarter. They have tidy dorms (**D**) and private rooms (**B**), breakfast included. It's a good spot and close to the Greyhound station. Discounts for HI members.
B Nelson, Av Revolución 721, T664-685 4302. Clean, spacious rooms, some with views of the action below. Very noisy Fri-Sat with crooning Mariachis and discos downstairs. Coffee shop.
C Caesar, Calle 5 y Av Revolución, T664-685 1606. A unique character, decorated with bullfight posters and at the heart of the action. Rooms have a/c and there's a restaurant. Good.
C Catalina, Calle 5 and Madero, T664-685 9748. Clean, and a good standard for Tijuana.
C Lafayette, Av Revolución 325, between Calle 3 and 4, T664-685 3940. Clean, safe straight-forward rooms, and right in the centre of things. Wi-Fi and drinking water in the lobby.
D París, Calle 5, No 8181, T664-685 3023. A large, adequate, good-value budget hotel.

Ensenada p202

Some of the larger hotels have different rates for summer and winter; check in advance. All hotels are filled at weekends, so get in early.

LL-AL Las Rosas Hotel and Spa, 7 km west of town, Highway 1 at Km 105.5, T/F646-174 4310, www.lasrosas.com. Comfortable *casitas* (**LL**) with spectacular ocean views, rooms (**AL**) and suites (**L**). Amenities include pool, sauna, gym, spa and restaurant. Good rates mid-week in the low season (**A**).

L-AL El Rey Sol, Av Blancarte 130, T646-178 1601, www.ensenadaexperience.com. Formerly the Ensenada Travelodge, this boutique hotel has pleasant, comfortable rooms and suites, all equipped with a plethora of gadgets and eco-technology. Amenities include spa, jacuzzi, gym, restaurant, pool and parking. Continental breakfast and a free Welcome Margarita Hour included, all you can drink.

L-A Quintas Papagayo, 1.5 km north on Hwy 1, T646-174 4575, www.hussongs. com.mx. Landscaped beach resort complex with all facilities and **Hussong's Pelícano** restaurant. Comfortable cottages (**L**), suites (**AL**), and rooms (**A**) are among the lodgings.

AL Bahía, Blv Costero and Av Alvarado, T646-178 2101, www.hotelbahia.com.mx/ing. Suites (**AL**) and rooms (**A**) with balconies, a/c and fridges. Quiet, clean, good value and popular, with parking. Free Margarita upon registration and good promotional rates, check the website for more.

C América, López Mateos, T646-176 1333. Good, cosy beds, powerful showers and cable TV. Comfortable and functional.

C Ritz, Av Ruiz y Calle 4, No 379, T646-174 0501. Central location with cable TV, carpet and phone. Straightforward and economical.

D Hostal Sauzal, El Sauzal de Rodríguez, 9.5 km before Ensenada, 2½ blocks from the highway up Av L (get off the bus at the traffic light in El Sauzal and walk) T646-174 6381, http://hostelsauzal.tripod.com. Price per person. Has 4-bed dorms, hot water, storage lockers, use of kitchen and a library of books and maps on Baja – a good place to stop, chill, and pick up info before rushing south. María is very friendly and welcoming and will give you the complete lowdown on the latest developments throughout Baja.

D-F Río, Av Miramar 231 and Calle 2. Basic, but the cheapest place to stay in town. Some ultra-cheap rooms have no TV (**F**).

Southeast to San Felipe *p203*

B-C Mike's Sky Rancho, Parque Nacional Sierra San Pedro Mártir, T664-681 5514 (Tijuana), www.totalescape.com/lodge/ADS/mikes.html. A working ranch that offers motel-style accommodation, pool, camping and guided trips into the surrounding mountains. Good meals.

San Felipe *p203*

AL Castel, Av Misión de Loreto 148, T686-577 1282. A/c, 2 pools, tennis. Best in town.

A Cortez, on Av Mar de Cortés, T686-577 1055. Beachside esplanade. Motel with a/c, pool, *palapas* on beach, launching ramp, disco, restaurant. Comfortable, if uninspiring rooms, with cable TV, a/c and ocean views.

A La Trucha Vagabunda, Mar Báltico, near Motel Cortez, T686-577 1333. Also a few RV spaces and **Restaurant Alfredo** (Italian), seafood, international cuisine.

C El Pescador, T686-577 1044, Mar de Cortés and Calzada Chetumal. A modest but comfortable motel with a/c.

Camping

Many trailer parks and campgrounds in town and on coast to north and south.

El Faro Beach and RV Park, on the bay 18 km south at Km 14.

La Jolla, Playa de Laura. US$12.

Mar del Sol, Av Misión de Loreto, T686-577 1088. US$18 per site.

Playa Bonita, Golfo de California 784, T686-577 1215, playabonita@aol.com. US$15-25.

Ruben's, Golfo de California 703, T686-577 1442. Nice beach. US$12.

South from Ensenada *p203*

AL-A Meling Ranch (also called San José), www.melingguestranch.com. Pleasant ranch accommodation for about 12 guests. They have a pool and can help arrange outdoor activities like birdwatching.

A-D Coyote Cal's, Eréndira, T646-154 4080, www.coyotecals.com. Fun international hostel with rooms (**B**), dorms (**E**), RV and tent sites. Good range of activities available including beaches, surfing, whale watching and hiking.

C El Palomar Motel, Santo Tomás, T/F646-178 8002. Adequate but overpriced rooms, restaurant, bar, general store and gas station, RV park with full hook-ups, campsite with swimming pool, clean and refurbished.

D Campo 4 Casas, Punta San Telmo, T646-165 0010. International hostel. Good beach resort with services and good surfing.

D Motel El Cammo, Hwy 1, south of San Vicente. Rooms without bath, friendly, OK restaurant.

El Rosario *p204*

C Sinai. Comfortable, very clean, small RV park, friendly owner makes good meals, but beware of overcharging.

Bahía de los Angeles *p205*

B-E Camp Gecko, T664-151 9454, www.campgecko.com. Good, quiet spot, *cabañas* and camping under *palapas*.

Camping

Guillermo's Trailer Park, T664-650 3209. Flush toilets, showers, restaurant, gift shop, boat ramp and rentals. It has a restaurant on main street, above the gift shop, well-prepared Mexican food, attractive, reservations advised at weekends. US$8-12.

Sal y Mauro, campsite. First gravel road on left before entering town, friendly.

Guerrero Negro *p205*

AL-A Desert Inn, T615-157 1304, www.desertinns.com/GuerreroNegro. A comfortable hotel with pool, dining room, bar and trailer park attached, 60 spaces, full hook-ups, laundry and gasoline at hotel.

B-C Malarrimo, east end of town, T615-157 0100, www.malarrimo.com. A mix of comfortable family rooms, *cabañas*, standard rooms, an RV park and a good surf 'n' turf

restaurant. Very clean and quiet, with TV, fan and Wi-Fi. A good deal overall. Also the site of a good tour operator that arranges whale-watching tours.

C El Morro, Zapata 5 y División del Norte, on road into town from highway, T615-157 0414. Modest, clean lodgings with private bath, hot water, cable TV, private parking and restaurant.

D Las Dunas, few doors from **El Morro**, T615-157 0650. Friendly, modest, clean. Rooms have TV and private bath.

D San José, opposite bus terminal, T615-157 1420. This hotel has 13 clean, straightforward rooms, including singles, doubles and triples. Will help organize whale-watching tours.

San Ignacio *p207*

AL-A Desert Inn, on road leading into town, T615-154 0300, www.desertinns.com/SanIgnacio. Built in the mission colonial style, this comfortable hotel has a pool and all facilities. Attractive but overpriced.

C Motel La Posada, on rise 2 blocks from the zócalo, just ask in town, T615-154 0313. Well maintained, with fans and shower. Best value in town, worth bargaining.

D Chalita, south side of the plaza, T615-154 0082. Cheap and cheerful.

Santa Rosalía *p208*

A Francés, Jean Michel Cousteau 15, up the hill, T615-152 2052. This charming 2-storey French colonial building is a living piece of history – you can visit, but there is a charge. A/c, restaurant, bar, pool and excellent views overlooking the Gulf.

C Real, Av Manuel Montoya near Calle 1, T615-152 0068. Rooms at the front are grubby with ancient TV sets, bath and cable. The ones at the back are nicer, and more expensive. Friendly and talkative management.

C-D Blanco y Negro, Calle 3 and Serabia, T615-152 0080. Very basic and ramshackle, but friendly, with or without bath. A few pricier rooms have a/c and TV.

D Olvera, on plaza at entrance to town, 2nd floor, T615-152 0057. Basic and shabby, with a/c, hot water and TV.

Camping

It's possible to camp on the beach under *pulpus*, access via an unmarked road 500 m south of El Morro, free, no facilities, a beautiful spot.

Las Palmas, 3 km south of town. Trailer park, 30 spaces, showers, laundry, good value.
San Lucas RV Park, on beach, San Lucas. No hook-ups, flush toilets, boat ramp, ice available, restaurant, US$6 per vehicle, 75 spaces. Recommended.

Mulegé *p208*

Prices change dramatically between high and low season.

L-A Serenidad, 4 km south of town near the river mouth on beachside road, T615-153 0530, www.hotelserenidad.com. Good views over the Gulf and a relaxing away-from-it-all ambience. Cottages (**AL**), rooms (**A**), and RV hook-ups.
B Las Casitas, Callejón de los Estudiantes y Av Madero 50, T615-152 3023, www.historicolascasitas.com.mx. A pleasant, older hotel, well run, with shady garden patio, restaurant and bar. Fishing trips arranged.
C Vieja Hacienda, Madero 3, T615-153 0021, hotelhacienda_mulege@hotmail.com. Refurbished rooms around a lovely courtyard, with pool and bar. Trips to cave paintings offered. Recommended.
C Suites Rosita, Av Madero near main plaza, T615-153 0270. A bit run-down but good value, clean and pleasant, with a/c, kitchenettes and hot water.
D Manuelita's, Moctezuma, T615-153 0175. Simple rooms around a beautiful patio.
D-E Nachita, **Canett** and **Sorpresa**. *Casas de huéspedes* on the road into town. All basic but reasonably clean.

Camping

The Orchard (Huerta Saucedo) RV Park, on river south of town, partly shaded, off Hwy 1, T615-153 0300. Pool, free coffee, book exchange, boat ramp, fishing, discount with AAA/AA membership. Recommended.

Villa María Isabel RV Park, on river and highway east of Orchard, T615-153 0246. Pool, recreation area, disposal station, American-style bakery.

South of Mulegé *p208*

C Ecomundo, T615-153 0409, Apdo Area 60, ecomundo@aol.com (office in Mulegé at Las Casitas hotel). Tents, *palapas* and kayaks can be hired, and there is also a bookshop, gallery, bar and restaurant. Idyllic place to hang out, run by an American couple.

Loreto *p209*

LL-L Posada de Flores, Salvatierra y Madero s/n, T613-135 1162, www.posadadelas flores.com. Very tasteful and attractive colonial-style lodgings with comfortable rooms and suites. All are equipped with a/c, satellite TV, mini-bar and a host of other amenities. Welcome cocktails and continental breakfast included.
L-AL El Oasis, Baja California y López Mateos s/n, T613-135 0211, www.hoteloasis.com. Comfortable rooms and suites overlooking the sea of Cortés. Amenities include private beach, parking, Wi-Fi, pool, restaurant, spa and car rental. Pleasant tropical gardens and sports fishing offered.
AL-A Coco Cabañas, Davis 71, T613-135 1729, www.coco-cabanas.com. Comfortable self-contained cottages with a/c and cooking facilities. Pool.
AL-A Desert Inn, on Sea of Cortés, 2 km north of the zócalo, T613-135 0025, www.desertinns.com/loreto. A comfortable ocean-front hotel with pool, tennis, golf and fishing boat hire. Considered by many the best of the original 'Presidente' *paradores*. Recommended.
A Plaza Loreto, Paseo Hidalgo 2, T613-135 0280, www.loreto.com/hotelplaza. An attractive, centrally located hotel with comfortable, well-equipped rooms. They also have a travel agency and offer activities including sports fishing and whale watching.
B Motel El Dorado, Paseo Miguel Hidalgo y Pipila, T613-135 1500, www.motelel

dorado.com. Large comfortable rooms with Wi-Fi, cable TV, a/c and comfortable beds. Services include restaurant and sports fishing charters. Friendly, helpful, and not at all bad. Recommended.

C Salvatierra, Salvatierra, on south approach to town, T613-135 0021. Economical motel-style place near the bus station. Clean rooms have a/c, hot showers but poor water pressure, limited cable TV. Good value.

D Posada San Martín, Juárez and Calle Davis 4, 2 blocks from the beach, T613-135 0792. Clean motel with small patio and very friendly owner. The most economical rooms have fan, bath, hot water, cable TV and Wi-Fi. Laundry and parking service (extra), coffee in the morning and breakfast on request. Simple and recommended.

Camping
Ejido Loreto RV Park, on beach 1 km south of town. Full hook-ups, toilets, showers, free coffee, laundry, fishing and boat trips. Butter clams are plentiful in the sand.

South of Loreto p209
Camping
Tripui Trailer Park, 25 km south of Loreto, PO Box 100, Loreto, T613-133 0818, www.tripui.com. Claimed to be the best in Mexico. Landscaped grounds, paved roads, coin laundry, groceries, restaurant and pool, lit tennis court, playground; 31 spaces, US$15.

Ciudad Constitución and around p210
C Casino, Guadalupe Victoria, a block east of the Maribel, Cd Constitución, T613-132 0455. Quiet, with 36 clean rooms, restaurant and bar.
C Maribel, Guadalupe Victoria and Hwy 1, T613-132 0155, 2 blocks south of San Carlos road junction, Cd Constitución. Services include a/c, TV, restaurant, bar, suites available, clean, fine for overnight stop.
C-D El Arbolito, Hidalgo, Cd Constitución, T613-132 0431. Basic, clean and central.
D Motel Las Brisas, Bahía Magdalena, 1 block behind the bus station, T613-136 0152. Clean, friendly, quiet.

D Reforma, Obregón, 2 blocks from the plaza, Cd Constitución, T613-132 0988. Basic, with bath. Friendly.

Camping and RV parks
Campestre La Pila, 2.5 km south of Cd Constitución on unpaved road off Hwy 1, T613-132 0562. Farmland setting, full hookups, toilets, showers, pool, laundry, groceries, tennis courts, ice, restaurant, bar, no hot water, US$12.
RV Park Manfred, on left of main road going north into Cd Constitución, T613-132 1103. Very clean, friendly and helpful, Austrian owner (serves Austrian food). US$13-18.

La Paz p210, map p210
AL-A Los Arcos, Alvaro Obregón 498 at Allende, T612-122 2744, www.losarcos.com. Pleasant rooms and *cabañas* with a/c. Amenities include pool, jacuzzi, bar, sauna, massage, laundry and business centre. In the throes of industrial action during the time of research, hopefully now resolved. Good value.
A-B Mediterráneo, Allende 36, T/F612-125 1195, www.hotelmed.com. Beautiful Greek-style hotel with classic standards as you would expect. Great service, outstanding La Pazta restaurant with Greek and Italian dishes. Internet access, café and kayaks.
A-B La Perla, Obregón 1570, on the waterfront, T612-122 0777, www.hotelperla baja.com The first hotel in La Paz, founded in 1940. They have a wealth of amenities including restaurant, pool, jacuzzi and car rent. Also the site of a popular night club, La Cabaña. Rooms are comfortable and cute.
B Plaza Real, Esquerro y Callejon La Paz, T612-122 9333. Rooms are straightforward and clean, with private bath, hot water, phone and a/c. The restaurant is open until 1500, with other eateries nearby. OK, but rather underwhelming.
C Posada del Cortez, Av 16 de Septiembre, T612-122 8240. Clean, basic and slightly tired rooms with TV, hot fan and electric showers. Some have a/c, others are quite spacious, so ask to see a few. Free coffee in the morning. Not bad value for La Paz.

C-D Lorimar, Bravo 110, T612-125 3822, Lorimar@prodigy.net.mx. Run by a Mexican-American couple, very clean and helpful, and a good place to meet fellow travellers. Standard rooms (**D**) have good furniture, the cheaper rooms (**E**) are grubby and lightly crumbling. Wi-Fi in the courtyard.

D Hostería del Convento, Madero 85, T612-122 3508. Friendly enough but pretty basic, with fans, shower and tepid water between 0700 and 0900. Cheapest in town and not terribly clean.

D Pensión California, Degollado 209, near Madero, T612-122 2896, pensioncalifornia@prodigy.net.mx. Described by the owner as a 'Backpacker Paradise', rooms at this family-run hotel are certainly economical. There's a communal kitchen with a fridge, garden patio, Wi-Fi and hot water. Friendly, noisy and not too clean. Good budget choice.

Camping

El Cardón Trailer Park, 4 km southwest on Hwy 1, T613-122 0078. Partly shaded area away from beach, full facilities.

La Paz Trailer Park, 1.5 km south of town off Hwy 1, access via Calle Colima, T613-122 8787. Deluxe, nearest RV park to La Paz.

South of La Paz *p212*

B Palomar, by the hot springs, 12 km from Santiago. A/c, hot showers, restaurant, bar, on main street, modest, good meals. Camping in hotel grounds, with cold shower and toilets.

D La Rivera RV Park, La Rivera, in palm grove next to beach. Excellent swimming in the sea, hot showers, laundry facilities, friendly. Recommended.

San José del Cabo *p213*

Several top-quality hotels along the beach front, about 1 km south of town, of varying excellence and seclusion. All are booked as part of resort holidays; some won't even allow passing trade to enter.

LL One & Only Palmilla, 8 km west at Punta Palmilla T624-146 7000, www.oneandonlyresorts.com. One of the top resorts in Baja with outstanding surf nearby. Services include a/c, showers, pool, beach, tennis, restaurant, bar, skin diving, fishing cruisers and skiffs for hire (daily happy hour allows mere mortals to partake of margarita and appetizers and see how royalty and film stars live).

LL-AL El Encanto Inn, Calle Morales and Alvaro Obregón, T624-142 0388, www.elencanto inn.com. Easy Mediterranean feel with stylish 'upscale rustic' decor. Amenities include spa facilities, pool and leafy gardens. A good choice.

AL-A Posada Terranova, Degollado between Doblado and Zaragoza, T624-142 0534, www.hterranova.com.mx. Pleasant rooms in a quietly professional atmosphere. There's a fine mid-price restaurant with patio dining.

A Collí, close to the centre, T624-142 0725, hotelcolli@hotmail.com. Some 30 adequate rooms at this family-run hotel, with a/c and cable TV. Other amenities include parking and Wi-Fi.

B Yuca Inn, Alvaro Obregón 1, just off the main square, T/F624-142 0462, www.yuca inn.com.mx. This ramshackle hotel is home to a sweet and playful Pitbull called Lulu. Several room options, ranging from basic to quite comfortable. None are fantastic, but the small pool, use of kitchen and hammock area make it a good choice for the cheaper rooms.

C Brisa del Mar, Hwy 1, 3 km southwest of town. Motel with 10 rooms, restaurant, bar, pool, modest but comfortable, behind trailer park on outstanding beach.

C Ceci, Zaragoza 22, 1 block west of plaza, T624-142 0051. A basic budget place with fans, hot showers (occasionally), cable TV and parking. Clean and good value.

C Hotel Diana, Zaragoza 30, T624-142 0490. Spacious, straightforward, windowless rooms with TV, bath and hot water.

C-D Nuevo San José, Alvaro Obregón. A range of economical options. The cheapest rooms have just a bed, hot water and fan (**D**). The most expensive have cable TV, bath and a/c (**C**).

Camping

Unofficial camping is possible on those few beaches not fronted by resort hotels.
Brisa del Mar Trailer Park, 100 RV sites in fenced area by great beach. Full hook-ups, flush toilets, showers, pool, laundry, restaurant, bar, fishing trips arranged, popular, good location. Recommended. US$18-25.

Cabo San Lucas *p213*

Cheap accommodation doesn't exist in Cabo.
LL-L Finisterra, perched on promontory near Land's End, T624-143 3333, www.finisterra.com. A very upmarket hotel with comfortable rooms. The poolside bar has an unsurpassed view of the ocean. Amenities include restaurant and sport-fishing cruisers.
L-A Marina, Blv Marina y Guerrero, T624-143 0030, www.loscabosguide.com/hotels/marina1.htm. Pricey, central hotel with comfortable if slightly generic rooms. Services include a/c, restaurant and bar. Can be noisy.
A-B Dos Mares, Calle Emiliano Zapata, T624-143 0330, www.loscabosguide.com/hotels/dosmares.htm. Various comfortable units with a/c, telephone and TV. Clean, with a small pool and parking space. Don't get drunk and fall down the stairs – survival is unlikely. Recommended.
A-B Mar de Cortés, Cárdenas and Guerrero, town centre, T1-800-347 8821 (US), www.mardecortez.com. Good-value suites and rooms with wooden beams, attractive furniture, a/c and showers. There's also a pool and an outdoor bar/restaurant.
B San Antonio, Av Morelos between Obregón and Carranza, 3 blocks back from the main street, T624-143 7353. Cheapest option in town really, and much better than the rest.
C El Dorado, Morelos, 4 blocks from bus terminal. Clean, with fan, hot water, private bath.

Camping

El Faro Viejo Trailer Park, 1.5 km northwest at Matamoros y Morales, T624-143 4211. Shade, laundry, ice, restaurant, bar, clean, out of town but good. US$15.

Todos Santos *p213*

LL-AL Hotel California, formerly the Misión de Todos Santos Inn, Juárez and Morelos, T612-145 0525, www.hotelcaliforniabaja.com. An historic building near the town centre, a block north of Hwy 9. The interior is very elegant, adorned with artwork and antiques. Very comfortable and popular, with a good restaurant and expensive craft shop.
LL-AL Todos Santos Inn, Calle Legaspi 33, 2 blocks north of Plaza T/F612-145 0040, www.todossantosinn.com. This elegant brick building is a refurbished 19th-century house with lots of character and stylish touches. Very tranquil and worth splashing out on.
C Miramar, south end of village, T612-145 0341. New, with bath, hot water, fan, pool, clean, safe, parking. Recommended.
D Motel Guluarte. Calle Morelos, T612-145 0006. Spacious, if rather plain, white rooms with blinkered TV sets, hot water and fan. There's a laundrette conveniently located downstairs. Comfortable, but nothing special.

Camping

El Molino Trailer Park, off highway at south end of town, 30 mins from beach, T612-124 0140. Full hook-ups, flush toilets, showers, laundry, American owner, very helpful, US$8 for 4. No camping here but apparently OK to use the beach (clean, but look out for dogs).

West Coast beaches *p213*
Camping

Trailer Park San Pedrito, several kilometres south of Todos Santos, T612-125 0170. This is a great location on the beach. Full hook-ups, flush toilets, showers, pool, laundry, restaurant, bar, US$13 for RVs.

● Eating

Tijuana *p200, map p201*
†††-†† Tía Juana Tilly's, Av Revolucion at Calle 7, T664-685 6024. Excellent food, popular local open-air spot, reasonably priced.

El Torito, Av Revolución between Calle 2 and 3. Mexican-diner style, with rock music in the evenings.

La Especial, Av Revolución 718, T664-685 6654. Surprisingly authentic Mexican food by Tijuana standards.

Ensenada *p202*

Plenty of places to choose from down the Blv Costero promenade, or the upper section of Av López Mateos.

El Rey Sol, López Mateos 1000 y Blancarte. Award-winning cuisine including Mexican and seafood specialities.

Mandarín, López Mateos 2127, between Soto and Balboa (Chinese). Elegant surroundings, good food, expensive, considered to be the best *chifa* in Ensenada.

Casamar, Lázaro Cárdenas 987. Popular place serving fine seafood and steaks, including lobster. A lively atmosphere.

Cantina Hussong's, Av Ruiz 113, open 1000-0100. An institution in both the Californias, more of a bar than a restaurant.

El Charro, López Mateos 475. Spit-roast chicken, fish tacos, beef *fajitas* and other fine Mexican fare.

El Pollo Feliz, Macheros y Calle 2. Daily 1000-2200. Grilled chicken 'Sinaloa style', fast food.

Mi Kaza, Riveroll 87. Low-key, friendly restaurant serving breakfasts, Mexican and international food.

Lonchería La Terminal, opposite bus station. Cheap and filling *comida corrida*, good but basic.

San Felipe *p203*

George's, 336 Av Mar de Cortés. Steaks, seafood and live music. Pleasant, friendly and popular with US residents. Recommended.

Green House, Av Mar de Cortés 132 y Calzada Chetumal. Daily 0730-0300. Good food, beef or chicken *fajitas* a speciality, friendly service, cheap breakfasts, 'fish fillet for a fiver'.

Las Misiones in Mar del Sol RV park. Small menu, moderately priced, seafood crêpes a speciality, popular with families, good service.

Clam Man's Restaurant, Calzada Chetumal, 2 blocks west of Pemex station. Used to belong to the late, famous Pascual 'The Clam Man'. Oddly decorated, but excellent clams, steamed, fried, barbecued, at budget prices.

Bahía de los Angeles *p205*

Restaurant Las Hamacas, on north edge of town. Budget café with bay view, slow service, popular for breakfast.

Guerrero Negro *p205*

Malarrimo Restaurant-Bar, east end of town, T615-157 0100, www.malarrimo.com. In hotel of the same name. Good fish and steak menu, moderate prices, music, open for breakfast.

Mario's Restaurant-Bar, next to El Morro. Modest surroundings and fare, disco.

Taco stall, a few blocks towards town from El Morro. Excellent.

San Ignacio *p207*

Lonchería Chalita, zócalo. Excellent value.

Rice'n'Beans, zócalo. Good, cheap.

Santa Rosalía *p208*

El Muelle, Constitución and Plaza. Nautically themed seafood restaurant, for a pleasant sit-down meal.

Terco's Pollito, Obregón y Playa, opposite Parque Morelos. BBQ chicken, Mexican staples and breakfasts. Moderately priced. OK.

Panadería El Boleo, Av Constitución. A Santa Rosalía institution. This bakery was selling bread when the West was Wild.

Mulegé *p208*

A few bars in town will offer you the full range of tequilas.

Patio El Candil, Zaragoza. Simple outdoor dining with good breakfasts.

El Mezquite, Zaragoza. Good burgers and live music.

Equipales, Zaragoza, upstairs. Recommended for good local cooking and for breakfasts.

Jungle Jim, signed turn-off from highway, 2 km south. Rustic, Mexican, friendly.

♥♥-♥ Donna Moe's Pizza, Zaragoza, on corner of Plaza Corona. Pleasant rooftop breakfast patio and bar.

Loreto p209
♥♥♥ 1697, Davis 13, on the plaza. Good Italian food, including pizzas and pastas, but not cheap. Pleasant outdoor seating.
♥♥♥ Pachamama, Zapata 3, 1700-2200. Very good Argentine cuisine. Cosy and rustic.
♥♥♥-♥♥ La Palapa, Av Hidalgo, ½ block from seafront. Great ambience, food and service. Delicious fresh seafood served under a giant *palapa*. Recommended.
♥♥♥-♥♥ Mediterraneo, Malecón, near the corner of Hidalgo. Gourmet Mexican food, a large selection of wine and great views of the Sea of Cortez. Downstairs you'll find the Backyard Texas BBQ restaurant.
♥♥♥-♥♥ Mita Gourmet, Davis 11, on the plaza. A pleasant setting by a rock fountain where you can sometimes see hummingbirds taking a drink. A good breakfast spot, with Mexican food at other times.
♥♥ César's, Zapata y Juárez. Good food and service, candlelit, moderate prices.
♥♥-♥ Café Olé, Madero 14. Mexican and fast food, *palapa*-style, open-air breakfasts and budget rates. Order and collect from counter.

Juice bars
El Cañaveral, just off the plaza and close to the mission. A great juice bar with baskets of fruit outside.

Ciudad Constitución p210
♥♥ Nuevo Dragón de Oro, Av Olachea with Esgrima, 5 blocks north of plaza. Chinese.
♥ Panadería Superpan, north of market hall. Bakery selling excellent pastries.

La Paz p210, map p210
♥♥♥ La Bohéme, Esquerro y 16 de Septiembre. French-style place with great ambience, wine list and romantic garden setting. Pastas, pizzas, fish, chicken and salads.
♥♥♥ Los Magueys, Allende y Prieto. Excellent Mexican food and beverages, including good

tequila and margaritas. Popular, atmospheric.
♥♥♥-♥♥ Carlos 'n' Charlies, right on the seafront. A popular Mexican staple, good to know where it is, but probably not the best food.
♥♥♥-♥♥ Kiwi, Obregón y 5 de Mayo, on the sea front. 0800-2400. A mix of Mexican and international dishes, including meat and seafood. Good prices through the day.
♥♥ Adriana, Obregón y Constitución, on beachfront. Candle-lit ambience that's sort of romantic in spite of the plastic chairs. They serve mostly seafood and shrimp, but some meat and chicken too. Live music Tue-Sun, happy hour at 1800.
♥♥ Café El Callejon, Callejón de la Paz. They do a good burger, Mexican snacks and seafood. Outdoor seating, internet access and revolutionary photos. Evening music.
♥♥ El Dragón, Esquerro 1520 y 16 de Septiembre, 2nd floor. Good, reliable Chinese.
♥♥ Señor Sushi, Madero and Degollado. Good sushi, eat in or takeaway.
♥♥-♥ El Quinto, Independencia y Belisario Domínguez. Very good vegetarian with lots of wholesome foodstuffs.
♥ Taquerías. Superb seafood tacos at stands outside **Pensión California** and **Posada San Miguel**.

Cafés and ice cream parlours
Café Gourmet, Esquerro 1520 y 16 de Septiembre, under El Dragón. Sophisticated little coffee house.
Delís, La Paz y Esquerro. Snacks, baguettes, breakfasts, coffee and cakes.
Giulietta y Romeo, Callejón de la Paz. Italian ice cream and outdoor seating on the pedestrian street.

San José del Cabo p213
The town is full of tasty options, many of them courting the dollars of holidaymakers over travellers on a budget. For budget options, you have to head west of the centre.
♥♥♥ Baan Thai, Morelos and Comonfort, opposite **Encanto Inn**, T624-142 3344. Pricey Thai restaurant with a wonderful atmosphere and quiet patio at the back.

Casa Natalia, Blv Mijares, in the hotel of the same name. A stylish setting with a chic approach to romance.

El Vaquero, Juárez 31 and Doblado. This restaurant is almost stately with its high-backed chairs. The menu is certainly aimed at royal wallets, with expensive meat dishes that include 20 oz steaks and slow-roasted prime-rib.

Damiana, Mijares 8. Gourmet Mexican food served in a converted 18th-century colonial mansion. The candle-lit patio makes for a romantic setting.

La Dolce, Hidalgo and Zaragoza. Italian restaurant with a pleasant ambience, nice artwork and high wood beam ceilings. Pastas include Fettucine alla Romana and Spaghetti Diavola. Good list of antipastos and pizzas.

Salsitas, Obregón y Hidalgo. Closed Tue. Good Mexican food and a well-decorated interior filled with Mexican art. Open for breakfast, lunch and dinner. The *chilaquiles con pollo* are sensational.

Café La Sirena, Doblado, behind **Hotel Ceci**. Pleasant arty little place serving economical breakfasts, lunches and dinners, including Mexican staples.

La Choza, Delgallado s/n, between Zaragoza and Obregón. Open-air joint serving BBQ burgers, grilled fare and, strangely, sushi.

Cafés

Café El Armario, Imperial y Obregón. Open-air café on the corner, with plants, parasols and baguettes.

Cabo San Lucas *p213*

Many expensive but good eateries, particular on the promenade in front of the marina.

The Giggling Marlin, Marina Blvd. A landmark used for directions, and a fine place to experience what makes Cabo San Lucas tick. The food is good, the prices reasonable and the self-deprecating humour on the walls refreshing.

Flor de Guadalajara, Lázaro Cárdenas, on the way out of town a few blocks

beyond 'Skid Row'. Good local dishes.

Rays Tequila – The Corner Café, Los Cabos. Does what is says on the tin a fine chap called Ray serves fine tequila.

Paty's Garden, Niños Héroes between Zaragoza and Ocampo, T624-143 0689. Authentic atmosphere, with pool table, and tasty as well. A good budget choice.

Todos Santos *p213*

Café Santa Fe, on main plaza. Gourmet Italian food, pricey but very highly rated restaurant.

La Buena Vida, Centenario 40. A beautiful colonial building with wooden beams and exotic lanterns. Great ambience and great pizzas, but expensive for what it is.

Tequila Sunrise, opposite the Hotel California. A colourful spot with graffiti on the walls. They serve dishes like peppers stuffed with lobster, as well as drinks and snacks to those venturing up from Cabo San Lucas.

Miguel's, Degollado and Rangel. Friendly little joint that's famous for its stuffed chilles. Good, but not fine dining.

Shut up Frank's, Degollado, opposite Miguel's. US expat hang-out serving burgers and snacks. A good place to glug down some cold beers.

Cafés

Cafélix, Juárez 4. Good smoothies, cappuccinos, breakfasts and Wi-Fi, but not cheap, like everything else in Todos Santos.

⊙ Entertainment

Tijuana *p200, map p201*
Bars and clubs

Recommended nightclubs include **Flamingos**, south on old road to Ensenada, and **Chantecler**.

Tequila Sunrise, Av Revolución, between Calle 5 and 6. Balcony bar with great opportunity to get your

bearings without being hassled on the street.
Tilly's Fifth Avenue, Revolución and Calle 5, T664-685 9015. Good lively bar.

La Paz p210, map p210
Bars and clubs
Bowk, Alvaro Obregón y 16 de Septiembre, next to Jungle Bar. White-leather lounge space with ultra-violet lighting.
Jungle Bar, Alvaro Obregón y 16 de Septiembre, on the seafront. An open-air bar with big TVs and wildlife themes, including animal murals, abundant plants and zebra stripes. Popular.
La Casa de Villa, Alvaro Obregón y 16 de Septiembre. A rowdy open-air terrace with drinks specials, big-screen TVs and green lighting.
Osho, 16 de Septiembre, ½ block from the Malecón. Cosy, dimly lit and atmospheric. Doubles up as a sushi bar.

San José del Cabo p213
Bars and clubs
Plenty of drinking options, mostly geared towards moneyed foreign travellers. Beer fans should try:
Baja Brewing Company, Morelos 1227, between Comonfort y Obregón, next to Baan Thai. Unique beers brewed on site, including *Raspberry Lager*, *Cactus Wheat Brew* and *Oatmeal Stout*, to name a few. There's also a good internationally flavoured restaurant.

✹ Festivals and events

La Paz p210, map p210
Feb/Mar Pre-Lenten **Mardi Gras** (carnival), inaugurated in 1989, is one of Mexico's finest. The Malecón is converted into a swirling mass of dancing, games, restaurants and stalls, and the street parade is happy and colourful.

○ Shopping

Tijuana p200, map p201
Plaza Río Tijuana Shopping Centre, Paseo de Los Héroes; opposite are the **Plaza Fiesta** and **Plaza del Zapato** malls, the latter specializing in footwear. Nearby is the colourful public **market**. Downtown shopping area is **Av Revolución** and **Av Constitución**. Bargaining is expected at smaller shops; and everyone is happy to accept US currency.

La Paz p210, map p210
A duty-free port. Tourist shops are concentrated along the Malecón between the tourist and commercial wharves.

Crafts
Bazar del Sol, Obregón 1665. Quality ceramics and good Aztec art reproductions.
Casa de las Artesanías de BCS, Paseo Alvaro Obregón at Mijares, just north of **Hotel Los Arcos**. Souvenirs from all over Mexico.
Centro de Arte Regional, Chiapas y Encinas, 5 blocks east of Isabel la Católica. Pottery workshop, reasonable prices.
Fortunato Silva, Hwy 1 (Abasolo) y Jalisco at south end of town. Good-quality woollen and hand-woven cotton garments and articles.
Solco's, Obregón y 16 de Septiembre. Large selection of Taxco silver, leather, onyx chess sets.

General supplies
CCC Supermarket, opposite Palacio de Gobierno, is good for supplies.
Ferretería, across from the main city bus terminal. Hardware store, sells white gas stove fuel (*gasolina blanca*).
La Perla de la Paz department store, Arreola y 21 de Agosto. General camping supplies.
Mercado Central, Revolución y Degollado, and another at Bravo y Prieto. Wide range of goods (clothes, sandals, guitars, etc), plus fruit and vegetables.

Todos Santos *p213*
El Tecolote Libros is an excellent bookshop selling good maps, books, book swap and very useful general information on the area.

▲▲ Activities and tours

Tijuana *p200, map p201*
Honold's Travel, Av Revolución 828, T664-688 1111. Provides all standard services and plane ticketing services.

Mulegé *p208*
Diving
Diving is off Punta Concepción or Isla Santa Inés. The best snorkelling from the shore is just past the point, opposite way up from beach by lighthouse.
Cortez Explorers, Calle Moctezuma 75A, T/F615-153 0500, www.cortez-explorer.com. Mon-Sat 1000-1300, 1600-1900. Friendly, English spoken, US$90 for 2-tank boat dive excluding equipment. US$45 snorkelling from boat with minimum of 3 people. A PADI Gold Palm centre with training up to Dive Master.

Tour operators
There is a small sports fishing fleet operating out of the harbour here. Also hires out quadbikes (must be 16 or over), mountain bikes, horse riding and fishing tours.
Day trips to nearby cave paintings at La Trinidad can be arranged from Mulegé. US$40 per person, slightly less with groups. T/F615-153 0232 or book through **Hotel Las Casitas**.

Loreto *p209*
Diving
Scuba and snorkelling information and equipment booth on municipal beach near the fishing pier; the beach itself stretches for 8 km, but is dusty and rocky. Beware of stingrays on the beach.
Cormorant Dive Center, Paseo Miguel Hidalgo s/n, T613-135 1146. A typical 2-tank

dive costs US$95, including entrance fees, cooler, lunch, dive master and all equipment (5-6 hrs). Most trips go to Cormorant island, where you might see I lammerhead sharks (poor visibility in winter). There's also SSI certification, including open-water and dive specialist. Whale-watching tours cost US$110, including box lunch, cooler, drinks and English-speaking naturalist. A range of other land-based tours are available.

Fishing
You can catch dorado, marlin, sailfish, yellowtail, snapper and seabass.
Late Mar-early Sep are the best times.
Arturo's Sport Fishing Fleet, T613-135 0766, www.arturosport.com. Sports fishing and tours to the islands with a fleet of pangas and cruisers. They also offer a range of eco-tours, including whale watching, kayaking and trips to the rock-paintings.
Baja Big Fish Company, Calle Juárez, T613-135 1603, www.bajabigfish.com. Specializes in fly fishing, light tackle and lure, as well as conventional bait fishing. A standard panga for 2 people is US$268 per day, including water, marine tickets, tax and fish handling. A panga for 4 costs US$354 per day. Additional costs include license and bait. Fly-fishing equipment available for rent and they make their own flies, which they sell. The Baja Big Fish Company is an International Game Fishing Association weigh station, where various fly-fishing records have been recorded.

Tour operators
Desert & Sea Expeditions, Paseo Miguel Hidalgo s/n, between Colegio and Pino Suárez. A range of 'eco-friendly' packages, including whale watching and naturalist tours of Cormorant island. Cultural trips to the rock art and San Javier mission are also available.

La Paz *p210, map p210*
Biking
You can hire a bike and head out on your own, or take a tour – all-day tour around

mountains visiting local ranches (US$55) – it's worth the effort.

Katun Tours, El Malecón, in Baja Outdoor Adventure office, next to Hotel El Moro, T612-125 5636, www.katuntours.com. Professional mountain-bike tours through Baja's arid semi-desert regions.

Diving
Aug-Nov are the best months for diving. During winter, the wind ruins visibility. You might see moray eels, hammerhead sharks, whale sharks and sea lions on a good dive. **Baja Diving and Service**, Obregón 1680, T612-122 1826, www.clubcantamar.com. Dive operator that also runs a resort and marina, where they offer accommodation as part of some packages. A standard 3-tank dive is US$105. A week-long expedition costs US$1600. They also offer whale watching, kayaking and sports fishing.

Kayaking
Baja Outdoor Activities, on the seafront, T612-125 5636, www.kayactivities.com. Run by Ben and Alejandra Gillam. Simple half-day tours or full trips out to Espíritu Santo Island in the Gulf, also whale watching. Prices start at US$45. Excellent.

Cabo San Lucas p213
There's absolutely no shortage of sporting activities, including scuba-diving (US$80 for a 2-tank dive), snorkelling (US$45), horse riding (US$65 for 2 hrs), parasailing (US$45) and so on. The latest craze is personal submarines (US$85 for 30 mins). Plenty of operators.

Todos Santos p213
Surfing
Todos Santos surf shop, Rangel and Zaragoza. Board hire at US$10.50 per day, US$5.25 for body board. They have kiosk at Playa Los Cerritos beyond El Pescadero. They also hire out tents (US$5.50 per day) and mountain bikes (US$10) at the main shop.

⊖ Transport

Mexicali *p199*
Air
Airport (MXL) 25 km east, Blv Aviación. Flights to **Chihuahua**, **Cd Obregón**, **Guadalajara**, **Hermosillo**, **Mexico City**, **Monterrey** and **Torreón**.

Airline offices AeroMéxico, Pasaje Alamos 1008D, T686-557-2551. **Click** and Mexicana, Obregón 1170, T686-553-5920.

Bus
All buses leave from the central bus station (**Camionera Central**) on Av Independencia. 'Central Camionera' bus to Civic Centre and bus station. Local buses are cheap, about US$0.55. To **Ensenada**, 4 a day, 4 hrs, US$27. To **Guadalajara**, 1 service, 34 hrs, US$100. To **Hermosillo**, regular service, 10 hrs, US$29. To **La Paz**, daily 1630, 24 hrs, US$150. To **Mazatlán**, every 30 mins, 24 hrs, US$75. To **Mexico City**, 1 a day, 40 hrs, US$120. To **San Felipe**, 4 a day, 3 hrs, US$17. To **Tijuana** every 30 mins, 3 hrs, US$20.

To USA Golden State buses to **Los Angeles** (US$44) tickets available at trailer/ kiosk across from Hotel del Norte, also with services within Mexico. **Greyhound** from **Los Angeles** to **Calexico** (901 Imperial Av), US$37, 6 hrs. **San Diego** to **Calexico** via **El Centro**, US$27, 3 hrs.

Tijuana *p200, map p201*
Air
Aeropuerto Rodríguez (TIJ), T664-607 8210. Flights to **Mexico City**, with connections to regional airports. Also international flights to **Las Vegas**, **Los Angeles** in the US and **Panama City**. Taxi between airport and centre US$15.

Airline offices Aero California, Plaza Río Tijuana, T664-684 2100. AeroMéxico, Plaza Río Tijuana, T664-683 8444. **Click** and Mexicana, Diego Rivera 1511, T664-634 6566.

Bus

Local General information at bus station, T664 621 2606. It is possible to get buses to most destinations from Tijuana's **Downtown** station, Calle 2 near Av Revolución, with the office close to the pedestrian bridge. Local buses go to the border from the bus station, every 30 mins up to 2300, marked 'La Línea/Centro', US$0.50.

Long distance There are local buses to the Central Camionera, the main bus station 5 km southeast of the centre at the end of Vía Oriente, from Constitución and Calle 3, about US$0.50, taxis ask US$10. Good facilities including *casa de cambio*, ATM, pharmacy and a couple of fast-food outlets. Services provided by **Estrella Blanca**, T664-683 5681, **TAP**, T664-621 3903, and **Transportes del Pacífico**, T664-621 2606, for services throughout Mexico. For **Baja California**, the main option is ABC, T664-621 2424. All services hourly unless stated. To **Culiacán**, 22 hrs, US$65. To **Guadalajara**, 34 hrs, US$92. To **Hermosillo**, 11 hrs, US$40. To **Los Mochis**, 19 hrs, US$55. To **Mazatlán**, 26 hrs, US$72. To **Mexicali**, 2 hrs, US$20. To **Mexico City**, 38 hrs, US$131. To **Sonoyta**, 2½ hrs, US$30.

Heading down the peninsula from north to south, with ABC departures every 30 mins, the options are: **Ensenada**, 1½ hrs, US$10; **El Rosario**, 6½ hrs, US$28; **Guerrero Negro**, 12 hrs, US$59; **Santa Rosalía**, 17 hrs, US$76; **Mulegé** 18 hrs, US$81; **La Paz**, 24 hrs, US$121.

To USA From Tijuana bus terminal **Greyhound** has buses every hour, US$15, 1 hr 10 mins, to **San Diego** via the Otay Mesa crossing, except after 2200, when it uses the Tijuana crossing; coming from **San Diego** stay on the bus to the main Tijuana terminal, entry stamp given at border (ask driver to get it for you), or at bus station. Long queues for immigration at lunchtime. Walk across La Línea (border) and catch a **Golden State** bus to downtown **Los Angeles**, US$13 (buy ticket inside McDonald's restaurant), 12 a day, or take trolley to downtown **San Diego** and get a **Greyhound**, US$20, or

Amtrak train, US$25, to **Los Angeles**. **Golden State** is the cheapest and fastest; its terminal is about 1 km from **Greyhound** terminal in downtown LA, but stops first at **Santa Ana** and elsewhere if requested.

Ensenada *p202*
Bus

The bus terminal is located at Av Riveroll 1075, several blocks north of López Mateos. **Estrella Blanca** operate services to mainland destinations including Guadalajara, 1000, around 35 hrs, US$100; and Mexico City, 1000, around 40 hrs, US$140. ABC head south through the peninsula with 1st-class services departing at 1420, 1815 and 2015, subject to change, including **Guerrero Negro**, 9 hrs, US$49; and **Laz Paz**, 20 hrs, US$112. There are cheaper and more frequent 2nd-class fares also, particularly for journeys under 5 hrs. **Transportes ABC** and TNS buses run to **San Felipe**, direct, over the mountains, at 0800 and 1800, 3½ hrs, US$17.

Hitchhiking

Hitching is a great way to get around the Baja and used by many budget travellers. There seems to be a slightly different approach on the peninsula to the 'mainland'. Hitching out of Tijuana would range between pointless and dangerous; Ensenada would be a good starting point if heading south.

San Felipe *p203*
Bus

Bus station is on Mar Báltico near corner of Calzada Chetumal, in town centre.

Transportes ABC and TNS buses to **Ensenada**, direct, over the mountains, at 0800 and 1800, 3½ hrs, US$17. To **Mexicali**, 4 a day from 0730, 2 hrs, US$12.

Guerrero Negro *p205*
Air

Airport (GUB), 3 km from town, very handy if you want to go to **Hermosillo**. There are regular flights to **Isla Cedros** and **Bahía Tortugas**; info from airfield downtown.

Ferry schedule from Baja California

	La Paz–Topolobampo	Topolobampo–La Paz
Duration	6 hours	6 hours
Frequency	Mon-Fri 1500, Sat 2300	Sun-Fri 2300
Adult (one-way)	US$81	US$81
Child (3-11 years)	US$40	US$40
Cabin (1-4 passengers)	US$58	US$58
Car	US$79	US$79

	La Paz–Mazatlán	Mazatlán–La Paz
Duration	12 hours	12 hours
Frequency	Mon, Wed, Fri 1700	Tue, Thu 2000, Sun 1700
Adult one way	US$91	US$91
Children (3-11 years)	US$45	US$45
Cabin (1-4 passengers)	US$58	US$58
Car	US$186	US$186

Baja Ferries, www.bajaferries.com.mx (English section not always updated – check the Spanish area of the website if you're unsure, La Paz: T612-125 6324; Mazatlán: T669-985 0470; Los Mochis: T668-818 6893. If travelling with a vehicle, allow plenty of time to sort out the documentation. See also box, Border essentials, page 198.

Bus

Northbound **ABC/Aguila** buses depart at 0800, 1100, 1940, 2200 and 0100. Southbound buses pass at 0600, 0900, 1200, 1630, 2100 and 0100. All schedules are subject to change, so it pays to visit the bus station in advance. To **La Paz**, 11 hrs, US$63. To **Mulegé**, 4½ hrs, US$22. To **Santa Rosalía**, 3 hrs, US$17. To **Tijuana**, 11 hrs, US$58.

Santa Rosalía *p208*
Bus

ABC/Autobus Aguila station, T615-152 0150, next to the ferry terminal, is the stop for most Tijuana-La Paz buses, around 5 daily each way. To **La Paz**, 1100, US$45. To **Tijuana**, US$76.

Ferry

Ferries to Guaymas on Tue and Wed at 0900, and Fri and Sat at 2000, returning on Mon, Tue, Thu and Sat at 2000, US$65 per person, US$248 for cars and pickups. Full details at www.ferrysantarosalia.com. Fares and

schedules are subject to change at all times, but particularly during winter, when the Tue sailing is sometimes cancelled. Plan ahead, and remember to check your watch when arriving in Guaymas. Get a vehicle permit from Banjercito bank, if you need one.

Mulegé *p208*
Bicycle Bike repairs near **Doney's Tacos**, 1 block before Casa de la Cultura, on left.

Bus Around 5 buses per day travel in each direction, although rarely to scheduled times. Ask in town as everyone knows when they come through. Allow plenty of time for your journey. Bus stop is on highway, north of bridge, at entrance to town. There is an airstrip for private planes beside the currently closed **Hotel Vista Hermosa**.

Loreto *p209*
Air Airport 7 km south of town. Flights to **Cd Obregón**, **Guadalajara**, **Hermosillo**,

La Paz and internationally to **Los Angeles**. Other destinations in high season.

Bus Station at Salvatierra opposite intersection of Zapata. Several north and southbound buses throughout the day, although often to irregular schedules. To **La Paz**, 6 a day, from 0700, 5 hrs, US$24. To **Tijuana** throughout the day, US$75, 19 hrs. To **Mulegé** with Aguila, 2½ hrs, US$12.

La Paz *p210, map p210*
Air
General Manuel Márquez de León International Airport (LAP), 11 km southwest on paved road off Hwy 1, T612-122 2959. Taxi fare US$20, *colectivo* US$14. Flights within Mexico to **Chihuahua, Cd Obregón, Culiacán, Guadalajara, Hermosillo, Loreto, Los Mochis, Mazatlán, Mexico City, Monterrey, Tijuana**. US destinations include **Los Angeles** and **Phoenix**. More charter flights in high season.

    Airline offices Aero California, Alvaro Obregón 55, T612-125 4353. AeroMéxico, T612-124 6366.

Bicycle
Viajes Palmira, Av Obregón, opposite Hotel los Arcos, T612-122 4030. Rents bikes/mopeds.

Bus
Local Buses about US$0.50, depot at Revolución de 1910 y Degollado by the Mercado Central. The Central Camionera (main bus station) is at Jalisco y Héroes de la Independencia, about 16 blocks from centre (taxi US$2). However, you can get most buses you need from the promenade Aguila terminal on Obregón between Independencia and 5 de Mayo, 1 block up from Carlos 'n' Charlies. **Long distance** Buses heading for the Cape go clockwise or counter clockwise. Head counter clockwise if going for **Todo Santos** or **Cabo San Lucas**. Services at 0730, 1030, 1130, 1530 and 1930, 2½ hrs, US$10. Head clockwise if going to **San José del Cabo**. Services at 0800, 1000, 1200, 1430, 1630 and

1830, 3 hrs, US$10. Information T122-7094 ext 111.

    For most long-distance journeys you will have to go to the main terminal. To **Guerrero Negro**, 6 per day, US$63. To **Loreto**, 3 per day, US$25. To **Tijuana**, 1300 and 2000, 22 hrs, US$121. Try to book at least 2 weeks ahead (6 weeks at Christmas, Easter and in Jul and Aug).

Car
Budget, Avis, Hertz, Auto Renta Sol and Auto Servitur booths at airport.

Ferry
For schedule to **Mazatlán** and **Topolobampo**, see above. Modern ferry terminal at Pichilingüe, 21 km north on paved highway.

    Tickets for the same day are sold at the terminal. Advance tickets may be bought at **Baja Ferries** at Isabel la Católica y Navarro, toll free on T01-800-337-74337, www.baja ferries.com.mx, and some local travel agents. They also have offices in Los Mochis and several other towns in the area.

    In general book in advance whenever possible, especially if travelling by vehicle and your journey time is critical. **Tourist cards** must be valid, allow 2 hrs as there are long queues when buying tickets and boarding. In the past, many motorists have had difficulty getting reservations or having them honoured. Vehicles must have **car permits**, obtainable at ferry terminal or at **Registro Federal de Vehículos** in Tijuana; automobile clubs will provide information. Service and conditions on the ferry are improving. Bus to **Pichilingüe** from seafront terminal in La Paz. Reasonable facilities at terminal but crowded; large parking lots, officials may permit RVs to stay overnight while awaiting ferry departures. On all ferry crossings, delays can occur from Sep if there is bad weather. Keep a flexible schedule if travelling to the mainland.

San José del Cabo *p213*
Air To Los Cabos International Airport (SJD), 14 km, take a local bus, US$3, which drops at the entrance road to the airport, leaving a 2-km walk, otherwise take a taxi. Airport to San José del Cabo in *colectivo*, US$7. Good regional connections and international to the US.
Airline offices Aero California, T624-146 5252. Click and Mexicana, T624-143 5353. Aeromexico, T624-146 5097. American Airlines, T624-146 5300.
Bus Bus station on Valerio González Canseco, about 600 m south of the main road into town. To **Cabo San Lucas** with Tres Estrellas, daily from 0700, US$1.25, 30 mins. To **La Paz** daily from 0630, US$10, 3 hrs.

Cabo San Lucas *p213*
Bus Bus station at 16 de Septiembre y Zaragoza, central, few facilities. Regular service to **San José del Cabo**, 30-45 mins, US$2. To **La Paz**, 6 a day from 0630, US$10.

Todos Santos *p213*
Buses
The bus stop is located at Heróico Colegio Militar, Between Zaragoza and Morelos, a few mins from the centre of town. Several buses pass on the La Paz–Cabo San Lucas loop. To La Paz, hourly, 2 hrs, US$5.50. To Cabo San Lucas, 1 hr, US$4.50.

🌐 Directory

Mexicali *p199*
Banks All major banks; currency exchange 0900-1330 only. *Casas de cambio* in Calexico give a slightly better rate. There are several on López Mateos.
Immigration Mexican Consulate in Calexico, T686-357 3863.

Tijuana *p200, map p201*
Banks Many banks, all dealing in foreign exchange. For Visa TCs, go to **Bancomer**. Better rate than *casas de cambio* but less

convenient. Countless *casas de cambio* throughout Tijuana open day and night. Most *cambios* charge a commission (up to 5%), even for cash dollars; ask before changing. **Embassies and consulates** Canada, Germán Gedovius 10411-101, T664-684 0461, tijuana@ canada.org.mx. **France**, Av del Bosque y Calle Fresno, T664-681 3133. **Spain**, Av de los Olivos 3401, T664-686 5780. **UK**, Blv Salinas 1500, Fraccionamiento Aviación, T664-686 5320, www.britishconsulate tijuana.com. **US**, Tapachula 96, between Agua Caliente racetrack and the Country Club, Mon-Fri 0800-1630, T664-622 7400.
Emergencies Fire: T135. Police: T134.
Immigration Mexican Consulate-General, San Diego, CA, 1549 India St, T619-231 8414, portal.sre.gob.mx/sandiego, Mon-Fri 0900-1400, for visas and tourist information. **Internet** Revolución just beyond Calle 3. **Medical services** Red Cross: T132 and T066; valid for Tijuana, Rosarito, Ensenada, Tecate, Mexicali and San Luis Río Colorado. **Telephone** Computel, Calle 7 y Av Negrete, metered phones, fax, computer facilities.

Ensenada *p202*
Immigration Beside the shipyard, for tourist entry permits. **Internet** Equinoxio, Blv Lázaro Cárdenas 267 in front of Plaza Marina, T646-179 4646, US$1 per hr, with a mighty fine cappuccino served on the side. **Language schools** Baja California Language College, east of the town towards San Quintín, PO Box 7556, San Diego, CA 92167, USA T1-877-444-2252, www.bajacal.com. Spanish immersion for business executives, teachers, travellers and students.

Santa Rosalía *p208*
Banks Banamex and Bancomer, both with ATMs. **Internet** Centcom, Obregón and Calle 9, with another place just behind the main junction entrance to the town, and at Obregón and Playa. **Laundry** Opposite

Hotel Central, wash and dry US$2.50 per load.
Post office Only from here and La Paz can parcels be sent abroad; customs check necessary first, at boat dock.

Mulegé *p208*
Banks There are none in town and very few places take TCs. You can change dollars at most stores. **Laundry** Claudia, Zaragoza and Moctezuma, next to Hotel Terrazas, self-service and with good information boards. **Post office** and **police** in old city hall, 1 block up from Pemex. **Telephone** Mini-supermarket Padilla, Zaragoza, 1 block from Pemex station (also fax); also from video store, nearby.

Loreto *p209*
Bank Bancomer on southwest corner of plaza. **Internet** Gigante, estate agent above shoe shop, on Salvatierra. **Laundry** Lavandería Casa de Lucy, Calle Zenith y Alborada 68.

La Paz *p210, map p210*
Banks Plenty of banks and ATMs on 16 de Septiembre: Banamex, Arreola y Esquerro. 2 *casas de cambio* on 5 de Mayo off Obregón, 0800-2000, better rates than banks.
Immigration 2nd floor of large building on Paseo Alvaro Obregón, opposite the pier, very helpful, able to extend visa here. **Internet** Espacio Don Tomás, Obregón between 5 de Mayo and Constitución. In an art gallery with fine snacks and coffee; and Café el

Callejón, Callejón La Paz 51, with restaurant.
Laundry Laundromat Yoli, 5 de Mayo y Rubio. Also at Marina de La Paz; and La Paz Lava, Ocampo y Mutualismo.

San José del Cabo *p213*
Banks Several *casas de cambio* around town. There is a branch of **Bancomer** on Zaragoza and a branch of **BanCrecer** with an ATM, just off the junction of the Transpeninsular Highway and Doblado.
Internet Several places in town, many asking ridiculous prices. Try inside Plaza Catedral, Zaragoza, just off main plaza near Hidalgo; or **Espacio Café Internet** (discounts for students) on the 2nd floor opposite the hospital on Doblado. **Laundry** Lavamática San José, on Valerio González. **Post office** A few blocks from the town centre down Blv Mijares.

Cabo San Lucas *p213*
Banks Plenty of branches with ATMs in town. **Internet and laundry** Kill 2 birds with one stone, log on while doing your washing at the laundromat on Leona Vicario and 20 de Noviembre, 30 mins US$2.40, 1 load wash and dry US$2.40. Cafés on the main drag are pricey. **Post office** Morelos y Niños Héroes.

Todos Santos *p213*
Banks BanCrecer, with ATM but doesn't change TCs, *casa de cambio* on Colegio Militar with Hidalgo does. **Laundry** Lavandería Misión. US$3.50 wash and dry.

Northwest coast

The Northwest coast of Mexico includes the scenic Sierra de Pintos, the copper-mining centre at Cananea, the longest sand dunes in North America at Algodones, the desert conditions of the Desierto de Altar, and the beaches and watersports of Puerto Peñasco. At the Pinacate Natural Park the moonscape of volcanic craters and lava fields is very impressive and so is the wildlife. With a little more time, you can explore the Kino Missions and enjoy sportfishing at Kino Nuevo, participate in fishing tournaments at La Choya and San Carlos or take a boat excursion from Rocky Point. There are many opportunities to take boat trips to the islands just off the coast and you can take an overnight ferry to Baja California.

Heading south, detour to the beautiful colonial town of Alamos, declared a national historic monument in 1952 and home of the original Mexican jumping bean. Relax in the streets of Los Mochis and enjoy the music of the roaming mariachis before boarding the famous Copper Canyon train for the journey of a lifetime. The popularity of Mazatlán as a holiday resort is well established; from here, you can travel northeast to Durango and the Colonial Heartland, or southeast to Tepic and Guadalajara, pleasant resting places on the way to Mexico City.

Like the west coast of all continents between latitudes 20° and 30°, the whole area is desert, but fruitful wherever irrigated by water flowing from the mountains. Summers are very hot, sometimes rainy, winters are mild and very dry. ▶▶ For listings, see pages 242-252.

Northwest border ●❼❺❻ ▶▶ pp242-252. Colour map 1, A2.

Route 2 from Tijuana runs close to the border, going through Mexicali (see page 199), San Luis Río Colorado, Sonoyta and Caborca to Santa Ana, where it joins the West Coast Highway (Route 15) to Mexico City.

San Luis Río Colorado–San Luis (Arizona) → Phone code: 653.

East of Mexicali the fast four-lane highway crosses the fertile Mexicali Valley to a toll bridge over the diminished Colorado River, and continues to San Luis Río Colorado, a cheerfully tourist-oriented border town in the 'free zone' and serving cotton country. There are summer bullfights and small nightlife districts like those of the Old West, including a so-called Zona de Tolerancia.

Algodones–Andrade (California) → Colour map 1, A2.

North of San Luis (35 km) is Baja California's last international border-crossing point, the farming town of Algodones. The border is open 0600-2000, but motor vehicle documents are only processed Monday to Friday 0800-1500. The road north from San Luis skirts the Algodones dunes, the longest in North America. Algodones has one hotel, Mexican car insurance is readily available, and there are several casas de cambio. At **Andrade**, on the California side, the Quechan people from the nearby Fort Yuma Reservation operate an RV park and campground (see Sleeping, page 242).

Desierto de Altar

After leaving San Luis Río Colorado, Route 2 crosses the sandy wastes of the Desierto de Altar – Mexico's own mini-Sahara. The desert, home to the largest dunes in the Western Hemisphere, was used to train US astronauts during the lunar missions. One look at the landscape and it's easy to see why. The road is very narrow in places; watch out for overloaded Mexican trucks. For 144 km there are no facilities (petrol at Los Vidrios), only three houses and an enveloping landscape of sand dunes, cinder cones and a dark lava flow from the Cerro del Pinacate. All the area around the central range is protected by the **El Pinacate Biosphere Reserve**. A gravel road 10 km east of **Los Vidrios** gives access to the northern sector of the park, which contains much wildlife, including puma, deer, antelope, wild boar, Gila monster, wild sheep, quail and red-tailed eagle. The reserve's most impressive crater is 'El Elegante', 1 km wide and 120 m deep. Cerro el Pinacate at 1190 m offers amazing views but is several hours' hike from the park's closest road.

Sonoyta–Lukeville (Arizona) → Colour map 1, A2.

After a hot and monotonous 205 km from San Luis de Colorado, Route 2 reaches the sun-bleached bordertown of **Sonoyta**, a short distance from **Lukeville** (Arizona). Sonoyta has little of interest itself, but there are several American-style hotels. Arizona's picturesque Organ Pipe Cactus National Monument, is just across the border from Sonoyta. The border is open 0800-2400. Camping is possible at the Twin Peaks campground near the visitor centre at **Organ Pipe National Monument** ① T520-387 6849, www.nps.gov/orpi, US$12 (US$8 visitor permit valid for 7 days).

Highway 8 goes southwest from Sonoyta through 100 km of sand dunes; a sign, 'Dunas – 10 km', at Km 80, points along a sandy road that leads to dramatic, desolate inland dunes through mountain-rimmed black lava fields; a 4WD is recommended.

Puerto Peñasco → Phone code: 638. Colour map 1, A2.

Once upon a time, Puerto Peñasco was no more than a middle-of-nowhere fishing village. It has blossomed in recent years to become an overpriced resort replete with high-rise condos and luxury hotels. As with much of the Pacific coast, the pace of development has been astonishing. The town's main visitors are two widely divergent groups: beach-starved Arizonans and young gringos out to exploit lax liquor laws on the one hand, (so expect a healthy array of beer drenched, North American style bars)), and retirees and 'snow birds' from further north seeking to escape the US and Canadian winters. There are also plenty of RV parks and campgrounds, many overlooking the beautiful, desert-backed beaches. Fishing, diving and sailing are possible and best arranged at the old port. The **Centro Intercultural de Estudios de Desiertos y Océanos (CEDO)** ① in the Las Conchas residential zone, T638-382 0113, www.cedointercultural.org, Mon-Sat 0900-1700, has a wealth of information on the interesting local wildlife (rapidly diminishing thanks to unsympathetic construction projects). It runs excellent, informative tours of the region's natural highlights, including El Pinacate Biosphere Reserve.

Caborca → Phone code: 637. Colour map 1, A3. Altitude: 286 m.

Route 2 runs from Sonoyta to Caborca (150 km), passing through a number of small towns (San Emeterio, San Luisito) and a more mountainous but still arid land. There is a customs and immigration station near the gold mine centre of Quitovac (28 km south of Sonoyta). The paved State Highway 37 continues southeast, roughly following the rail line to Caborca (180 km) – an alternative to the inland Highway 2 route.

Caborca lies on the Mexicali–Benjamín Hill railway in the midst of a gently sloping plain. Caborca's restored church of **Nuestra Señora de la Concepción** (1693) was one of the 25 Jesuit missions founded by the legendary missionary and explorer Padre Kino in Sonora and Arizona between 1687 and 1711. Caborca is the best base for exploring the **Kino Missions**.

Border essentials: northwest coast–USA

Nogales–Nogales (Arizona)

This is the most popular crossing along this stretch and the border is open 24 hours. There's no checkpoint on the Mexican side although there is a customs area that is staffed occasionally. After you cross into Mexico, walk straight ahead for about 50 m until you get to the immigration office (on your right) where you can pick up a tourist card (FM-T) and get it stamped. For transport to/from the border, see page 248.

Crossing with a vehicle Motorists are advised to use the truck crossing (0600-2000, currency exchange available) to avoid congestion. It is reached by the Mariposa Avenida exit from Interstate 19, 4 km north of downtown Nogales, Arizona. From Mexico to the US, follow the sign to the 'Periférico', which avoids the downtown area.

Motor vehicle documents can be obtained at the Mexican customs post 21 km south of Nogales, on Highway 15 to Santa Ana, along with US insurance (which may also be obtained at the border). There is a **tourist office** and a *casa de cambio* here. You need to have title to the car with you (ie you can't drive someone else's car into Mexico). You also need two photocopies of vehicle registration, driver's licence, insurance papers, credit card and visitor permit (approved); a photocopy machine is available. In the same building as the immigration office on the border is a **Seguros Tepeyac**, www.mapfretepeyac.com.mx, outlet where you can buy car insurance. There are also a few other insurance agencies around town.

Altar–Sásabe (Arizona) → Colour map 1, A3.

Highway 2 continues east through Altar (café, gas station) to join Highway 15 at **Santa Ana**, a small town of little note. The **Fiesta de Santa Ana** is held 17-26 July, with horse racing and fireworks.

The border is open 0800-2000, but there is no public transport on either side, nor is there any Mexican automobile insurance agency. For information as to road conditions, phone US Customs, T602-823 4231; although they appear not to encourage traffic over this route.

Nogales → Colour map 1, A3.

Much like its border town cousins to the east and west, Nogales is a scruffy, unattractive place with little to offer the casual visitor. Still, as border towns go it's not deeply unpleasant, and makes a good place to rest before venturing further into Mexico's interior. The town lies astride a mountain pass at 1120 m across from Nogales, Arizona, and is the largest settlement in the Pimería Alta, the area of southern Arizona and northern Sonora occupied by the Pima people at the arrival of the Spaniards. The **tourist office** is just past the immigration office at the border (see box page 234). The staff are friendly, helpful and have brochures. The **Pimería Alta Historical Society** ① *Mon-Fri 0900-1700, Sat 1000-1600, Sun 1300-1600, free*, a block from the border in Nogales, Arizona, has excellent exhibits on the history of the region, a valuable library and archives, and also organizes tours to the Sonoran missions.

The Nogales border crossing is open 24 hours at the Deconcini Gate for non-commercial vehicle traffic. Day trippers can take advantage of the shopping arcades, which are within walking distance from the parking lots on the US side of the border.

South of the border ● ▶ pp242-252.

Nogales to Mazatlán: the Pacific Highway

Route 15 along the Pacific coast gives access to several resorts (Guaymas, Mazatlán and via Route 200, Puerto Vallarta, Manzanillo, Ixtapa–Zihuatanejo, and Acapulco), to ferry terminals for Baja California, and to the Los Mochis end of the Chihuahua al Pacífico railway passing beside the Copper Canyon. From Nogales to Guaymas on the Gulf of California, the road runs along the western slopes of the Sierra Madre, with summits rising to 3000 m. From Guaymas on to Mazatlán it threads along the lowland, with the Sierra Madre Occidental's bold and commanding escarpment to the east.

The Pacific Highway down the coast to Acapulco and Salina Cruz is completely paved but has military searches in the State of Guerrero (for narcotics and arms). There are many motels along the whole route; every town of any importance has one or more nearby.

Magdalena Valley

South of the border at Nogales, Route 15 passes through the Magdalena Valley. The Cocóspera mines are near **Imuris** and there are famous gold and silver mines near Magdalena, which has a great indigenous fiesta in the first week of October.

From Imuris, Route 2 heads east (to Naco and Agua Prieta) through the scenic Sierra de Pintos to the historic and still important copper mining centre of **Cananea**. This was the site of a 1906 miners' strike against the American-owned **Cananea Consolidated Copper Company**, one of the critical events in the last years of the Porfirio Díaz dictatorship. Hundreds of Arizona Rangers crossed the border to join the Sonora militia in putting down the strike, which is commemorated at the **Museo de La Lucha Obrera** ① *Av Juárez*, the former city jail. Back on Route 15, 120 km from Nogales, is Santa Ana, where the road enters from Tijuana and Mexicali.

Hermosillo ●❶❷❸● ▶ pp242-252. Colour map 1, B3.

→ *Phone code: 662. Altitude: 237 m.*

Capital of Sonora state, Hermosillo is a thriving, modern city with only sparse mementos of its illustrious colonial past. These can be found around the central Plaza Zaragoza (invaded by noisy birds at sunset). The imposing neoclassical **Catedral de La Asunción** (1779), has a baroque dome and three naves, and the **Palacio de Gobierno** has intricately carved pillars and pediment, historical murals and grandiose statues amid landscaped gardens. The **Sonora Museum**, Jesús García Final, inside the old town prison, Tue-Sun, 0900-1800, US$3, charts the historical development of the state and is worth a look. You'll find it at the base of the **Cerro de la Campana**, a distinctive, surreally illuminated hill that rises from the centre of the city; locals call it El Caracol, The Snail. Not far north of downtown (Rosales y Transversal) is **University City**, with its modern buildings of Mexican architecture blended tastefully with Moorish and Mission influences. There is an active fine arts and cultural life in Hermosillo, with many events throughout the year open to visitors (check at the tourist office for details). Two kilometres south of Plaza Zaragoza, near the Periférico Sur, is the wonderful **Centro Ecológico de Sonora** ① *www.centroecologico.gob.mx, 0800-1700, US$3*, a botanical garden and zoo displaying Sonoran and other desert flora and fauna in well-cared-for surroundings. Hermosillo has a helpful **tourist office** ① *Paseo del Canal y Comonfort Edificio Sonora, 3rd floor, T662-217 0060, www.visitasonora.com.*

Bahía Kino → *Phone code: 662. Colour map 1, B3.*

A paved 118-km road runs west past the airport to Bahía Kino, divided into the old, somnolent and somewhat down-at-heel fishing village, and the new **Kino Nuevo**, a 'winter gringoland' of condos, trailer parks and a couple of expensive hotels. Although the public beaches are good, most North American visitors come for the sportfishing. The Seri people, who used to live across El Canal del Infiernillo (Little Hell Strait) on the mountainous **Isla Tiburón** (Shark Island), have been displaced by the Navy to the mainland. They come into Kino on Saturday and Sunday to sell their ironwood animal sculptures and traditional basketware. They can usually be found at the **Posada del Mar Hotel**. For the visitor interested in exploring nature reserves, Isla Tiburón is of especial interest. Protected in the nearly 400 sq m preserve, the population of both the big horn sheep and mule deer has grown enormously. On the south end of the island, water depths of 50 m or more are common. It is an excellent area not only for scuba-diving but also for fishing, and **Dog Bay** provides shelter and ideal anchorage for spending the night. **Isla Patos** (Duck Island), 30 minutes north of Isla Tiburón, offers the opportunity to explore the submerged Spanish vessels that once sailed the Sea of Cortés. Other islands worth visiting are **Alcatraz** (also known as **Pelican Island**), **Turner**, and **San Esteban**. In Kino Nuevo, there is the fine **Museo Regional de Arte Seri** on Mar de Cortés, the main boulevard.

Guaymas ⬤⬤⬤⬤ ⯈⯈ *pp242-252. Colour map 1, B3.*

→ *Phone code: 622.*

Guaymas was once a grotty port town, but set on a lovely bay backed by desert mountains the area is being tipped, by some, as Mexico's next big resort. There's little to keep you here, but it does have excellent deep-sea fishing and seafood for the gourmet. **Miramar beach**, on **Bocachibampo Bay** with its blue sea sprinkled with green islets, is the resort section. The climate is ideal in winter but unpleasant in summer. The 18th-century church of **San Fernando** is worth a visit; so, too, outside the town, is the 17th-century church of **San José de Guaymas**. The port area also boasts some worthy buildings, among which are the **Templo del Sagrado Corazón de Jesús**, the **Banco de Sonora**, the **Palacio Municipal** (constructed in 1899), the **Ortiz Barracks** and the **Antigua Carcel Municipal** (old Municipal Prison) constructed in 1900. Guaymas acquired the title 'heroic' in 1935, in memory of the valiant defence by its inhabitants during the French Invasion of 1854.

Bahía San Carlos

Some 15 km north of Guaymas (12 km from Highway 15), Bahía San Carlos is very touristy and Americanized. *Catch 22* was filmed here and the sunsets are stunning. Above the bay a twin-peaked hill, the **Tetas de Cabra**, is a significant landmark. There is good fishing with an international tournament in July. There's a **tourist office** ⓘ *Av Serdán.*

South to Sinaloa

Head south on the highway from Guaymas and you'll reach **Ciudad Obregón**, a rather dull agricultural centre, unless you're in the market for leather goods. Further south is **Navojoa**, another farming town. West of Navojoa, on **Huatabampo Bay**, are the survivors of the Mayo people; their festivals are in May. You'll find a small museum dedicated to their culture in Navojoa; the **Museo Regional del Mayo** ⓘ *Leona Vicario between Morales and No Reelección.* However, most travellers continue south along four-lane highway into Sinaloa, or east to Alamos, which is served by hourly buses from Navajoa.

Alamos → *Phone code: 647. Colour map 2, B1.*

Fifty-two kilometres into the hills is the delightfully crumbling old colonial town of Alamos, now declared a national monument and home to increasing numbers of North American artists. It is set in a once famous mining area, fascinating for rock enthusiasts. Although the area was explored by the Spanish in the 1530s, development did not begin for another 100 years when the Jesuits built a mission nearby. With a rich history in silver mining, trips to old mine sites can easily be arranged. Fabulous old mansions also recall the town's glory days, with house tours departing every Saturday from outside the bank on the Alameda, 1000, US$12. You can also hire an English-speaking guide from outside the tourist office on the main plaza. A short, sharp hike up to the mirador is worth the effort, with wonderful views of the town and surrounding mountains.

Another, altogether more lighthearted reason for visiting Alamos, in June in particular, is to see the famous jumping beans: a symbiotic relationship between a plant and a moth larvae. The two develop simultaneously giving the impression that the seed pod or bean is actually jumping. The **Alamos Music Festival** is an annual event held for seven days at the end of January, www.alamosmexico.com.

Los Mochis and around ⬤🅱🅰⬤🅲 ↠ *pp242-252. Colour map 2, B1.*

→ *Phone code: 668.*

In spite of being 25 km from the sea, Los Mochis in Sinaloa is a fishing resort with a sizeable US colony. The name is derived either from a local word meaning 'hill like a

Los Mochis

Sleeping 🛏
Beltrán **2**
Fénix **3**
Las Fuentes **4**
Los Arcos **5**
Santa Anita **8**

Eating 🍴
El Farallón **3**
El Taquito **4**

España **5**
Mi Cabaña Tacos **2**

turtle', or possibly, from *mocho*, meaning one-armed, perhaps after a cowboy thus mutilated. The city, in a sugar-cane area, was founded in 1904 around a sugar mill built by the American, Benjamin Johnson, and his wife was responsible for building the Sagrado Corazón church. The family lost everything in the Revolution. This is the starting point for the uphill railway journey passing the Copper Canyon.

There isn't a great deal to see in Los Mochis, but if you're bored, the **Museo Regional del Valle Fuerte** ① *Obregón and Rosales, Mon-Sat 0900-1300, Sun 1000-1300, US$1.20*, has mildly diverting displays on local history (in Spanish), whilst the **Parque Sinaloa** has a mediocre botanical collection and large trees that offer some respite from the heat. There are also plenty of nightspots and bars visited by mariachis, who play excellent music.

Tourist information is available for Los Mochis and the State of Sinaloa in the **Unidad Administrativa building** ① *Allende and Cuauhtémoc, T668-816 2015, www.vivesinaloa.com, Mon-Fri 0900-1600*.

Topolobampo → *Phone code: 668. Colour map 2, B1.*

A side road, running southwest from Los Mochis, crosses the salt flats to Topolobampo (20 km, 30 minutes). The town is built on several hills facing the beautiful bay- and lagoon-indented coast. In the bay, which has many outlets, there are a number of islands; sunsets here are lovely. Note that there are few lodgings in Topolobampo itself; it's best to stay the night in Los Mochis.

You can get a ferry from here to La Paz. Show up early, purchase tickets as soon as possible (as space is limited). The ferry starts boarding three hours early, and departs 2300, Sunday to Friday, arriving in La Paz 0600 the next day.

Towards Chihuahua by train → *For information on Creel and the Copper Canyon, see page 261.*

The famous *Chihuahua al Pacífico* train journey shows the spectacular scenery of the Sierra Madre and the Barranca del Urique/Cobre (Urique/Copper Canyon). The **Servicio Estrella** train should leave daily at 0600 (but often at 0700), US$67 to Creel (about 10 hours), US$122 to Chihuahua (about 16½ hours, but expect delays). For train information and prices, check www.chepe.com.mx. Bring your own food, drinking water and toilet paper for the journey.

For this very popular trip, tickets **must** be bought in advance either on the morning of departure or, in high season (July/August, Christmas/New Year, Holy Week), a day or more before. **Estrella**-class tickets can be bought from tour operators in Los Mochis, with an 8% surcharge, but they will try to persuade you to book into expensive hotels. It may be worth buying tickets from them to avoid long queues at the station. If you are only going as far as Creel, buy return tickets as it is impossible to reserve seats from Creel back to Los Mochis. Local buses leave from Los Mochis on Obregón and Zaragoza (US$0.30) for the train station, departing 0515.

On the **Primera Especial** the windows do not open, so, to take photos, stand between the carriages. Motorists taking the train to Creel are advised to park in front of the station as there are lights and people at all times. There is more expensive parking downtown.

The ordinary economy-class train, **Tarahumara**, aims to leave at 0700, with prices roughly half that of the first class, but it is not possible to reserve seats. Second-class trains make many stops but are reasonably comfortable and it is possible to open the windows. On either train, sit on the right for the best views, except when approaching Temoris when it's all jump to the left, then return to the right until the first tunnel after Temoris when the views are good on both sides.

South to Mazatlán

Roughly halfway between Los Mochis and Mazatlán you'll encounter Sinaloa state's capital, **Culiacán**, founded in 1531 by Beltrán de Guzmán. It can no longer be called a colonial city, but it is attractive and prosperous, and has a university. That said, there's little reason for stopping here apart from breaking the journey; the city is geared much more towards business visitors than tourists. Continue south beyond Culiacán and you'll soon pass the Tropic of Cancer. The change from temperate to tropical is marked by a shift in vegetation and atmosphere, both becoming denser and wetter. Just 20 km south of the tropical divide lies Mazatlán itself.

Mazatlán ⊜🏠🏖🏔⊜🌡 » pp242-252. Colour map 2, C2.

→ *Phone code: 669.*

Mazatlán, spread along a peninsula at the foot of the Sierra Madre, is the largest Mexican port on the Pacific Ocean. The beauty of its setting and its warm winters have made it a popular resort, but unfortunately with expansion it has lost some of its attraction. But while the big developments attract international tourists, in the heart of the old town you can join Mexicans taking their vacations and enjoying the city, without the hard sell. The

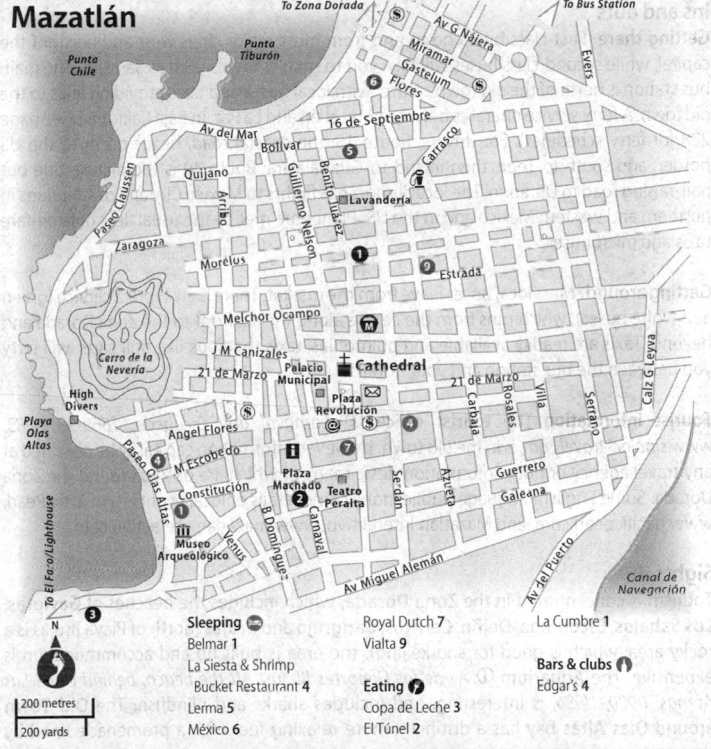

Mazatlán

Sleeping
Belmar 1
La Siesta & Shrimp
Bucket Restaurant 4
Lerma 5
México 6
Royal Dutch 7
Vialta 9

Eating
Copa de Leche 3
El Túnel 2
La Cumbre 1

Bars & clubs
Edgar's 4

Music in Mazatlán

Mazatlán is the epicentre of what is now one of Mexico's major music forms: La Banda – tuba-dominated and exuberantly-spirited music bands that include saxophones, trumpets, clarinets, several types of percussion as well as very direct voices. The polka is a preferred rhythm of "La Banda". The expert can tell the difference between the regional variations. Mariachi, from Jalisco, is the "national" form. Musica Norteña is dominated by harmonica and La Banda formerly from the State of Sinoloa but now popular throughout north and central west Mexico. Whichever form you hear, this music permits you an insight into the spirit and character of Mexicans in this region.

old town overlooks **Olas Altas (High Waves) Bay**, which has a very strong current. The area of extensive development, called the **Zona Dorada**, stretches for several kilometres to the north of the **Old Town**. Entering Mazatlán by sea from Baja shows the city at its most impressive – two pyramid-shaped hills, one topped by a lighthouse (150 m above sea level), the other the 'rock' of **Isla Piedra**, guards the harbour entrance.

Ins and outs

Getting there First-class buses go to and from most major cities west and north of the capital, while second-class buses will take you to smaller towns such as San Blas. The main bus station is north of the old town centre, with local buses and taxis providing links to the old town. A ferry service operates between Mazatlán and La Paz, in Baja California (see page 228 for ferry schedules). For drivers, Route 15, the coastal road, heads north to the US border, and south to Tepic then inland to Guadalajara; Route 40 is the picturesque but hair-raising road to Durango. The local airport has flights to Mexico City and destinations in northern and western Mexico and in the US. Planes are met by the usual fleet of fixed-fare taxis and microbuses.

Getting around Most local buses leave from the market. There is an express service (green and white buses), which runs from the centre along the seafront to the Zona Dorada and beyond. Taxis are readily available and pulmonias, taxis that look like golf carts, will ferry you between the bus station and your hotel.

Tourist information The **tourist office** ① *Carnaval and Escobedo, T669-981 8883, www.sinaloa-travel.com*, is in the old town. However, information can easily be obtained at any travel agency or hotel information desk, many of which are dotted around the Zona Dorada. Some English-language publications carry details of local events. Try Pacfic Pearl, www.pacificpearl.com, and Mazatlán Interactivo, www.mazatlaninteractivo.com.

Sights

Tourism is concentrated in the **Zona Dorada**, which includes the beaches of **Gaviotas, Los Sábalos, Escondida, Delfín, Cerritos, Cangrejo** and **Brujas** (north of Playa Brujas is a rocky area, which is good for snorkelling); the area is built up and accommodation is expensive. The **Aquarium** ① *Av de los Deportes III, just off the beach, behind Hotel Las Arenas, 0900, US$6*, is interesting, and includes sharks and blindfish. The **Old Town** around **Olas Altas** bay has a distinctly more relaxing feel with a promenade lined by hotels; a long beach at its foot, curves northwards around the bay, first as Paseo Claussen, then Avenida del Mar, which leads to Avenida Camarón Sábalo in the Zona Dorada (take bus from Juárez – best from in front of market – marked Sábalo Centro US$0.50). The sunsets are superb seen from this side of the peninsula; at this time of day high divers can be watched and the fishermen return to the north beach. There are many good beach bars from which to view the setting sun. Buses from Calle Arriba go to the Zona Dorada for US$0.40. See www.mazatlan.com.mx for more online information on options in and around town.

The old part of Mazatlán is around Plaza Machado, on Calle Carnaval. This is by far the most interesting part of Mazatlán. While it does not give the same emphasis to its architecture and history as to its recreational side, the baroque (although constructed in the late 19th century) **Basilica de la Purísima Concepción** at the heart of the old town on the plaza is well worth a visit, with its elegant interior and two slender spires.

Half a block from the plaza is the **Teatro Peralta**, the 19th-century opera house, which was restored in 1987 and since 1992 has been open to the public. The **Museo Arqueológico de Mazatlán** ① *Sixto Osuna 115, ½ block from Hotel Freeman, US$1*, is small, covering the State of Sinaloa. Recommended.

Around Mazatlán

To reach **Isla de la Piedra** (which is in fact a peninsula), take a small boat from the south side of town from Armada (naval station near Pacífico brewery, reached by 'Zaragoza' bus from Juárez outside market), regular service, US$1.50 return ticket. The 30-km beach on the Mazatlán side is now littered but you can walk across the peninsula either side of the hill (10 minutes) to a clean beach where there is good surfing. There is also a ferry that goes from near the lighthouse to the Isla de la Piedra (until 1700). Local *comedores* on the beach provide primitive accommodation, or ask for permission to camp on the beach. Try smoked fish sold on a stick; **Victor's comedor** has been recommended. Beware of sandflies.

Mazatlán to Durango

About 20 km beyond Mazatlán, the coast-to-coast highway heads east to Durango (a spectacular stretch in good condition – a must-see road section) turning left at Villa Unión. Heading east, after another 21 km, the road reaches **Concordia**, a delightful colonial town with a well-kept plaza and a splendid church, then after 24 km climbs the foothills of the Sierra Madre Occidental past **Copala**, another former mining town. On this road, 40 km from Concordia, 3 km before **Santa Lucía**, at La Capilla del Taxte, 1240 m, there is a good German hotel and restaurant (see Listings, page 242). Before reaching La Ciudad (one very basic hotel) and the plains, the road goes through a spectacular section, winding through many vertical-sided canyons with partly forested slopes. The road is a phenomenal feat of engineering, as it is cut into the cliff side with steep drops below.

At one point, called **El Espinazo del Diablo** (Devil's Spine), the road crosses a narrow bridge (approximately 50 m long) with vertical drops either side and superb views to the south and north. No signs, just ask on the bus and the locals will tell you when it's coming up. If you're lucky you may be able to get the bus driver to stop. After reaching the high plateau, the road passes through heavily logged pine forests to Durango (see page 267). Cyclists will find this road hard work in this direction, as there are many bends and steep hills. Trucks are frequent but they travel at very reduced speeds.

South of Mazatlán

Route 15 continues south from Villa Unión. At **Rosario**, 68 km south of Mazatlán, an old mining town riddled with underground workings. There is an attractive and generally clean beach at **Playas El Caimanero**, about 45 km southwest of Rosario. Try the fish. Be careful of hiking around the Baluarte River valley as there are *caimanes* (alligators), hence the name of the beach. There is a good seafood restaurant on the left at the entrance to **Escuinapa** coming from Mazatlán.

Teacapan → *Phone code: 695.*

In **Escuinapa** a good road turns off 30 km to the coast at Teacapan. There is a bus that connects the two towns. The fishing is excellent and you can buy fresh fish directly from the fishermen on Teacapan beach. There are fine beaches such as **Las Cabras**, **La Tambora** and **Los Angeles**, with occasional visits from dolphins. Buses run from Escuinapa; tours from Mazatlán cost US$45.

South of Escuinapa the road passes several quaint little towns: **Acaponeta** (turn-off for El Novillero beach, large waves and many sandflies), **Rosamorada**, **Tuxpan** and **Santiago Ixcuintla** (several hotels), all with colonial religious buildings and archaeological museums. Nearby is the tiny island of **Mexcaltitán** and, further south, the beaches at San Blas (see page 365). After Tepic, Route 15 heads inland to Guadalajara (see page 350).

⊚ Northwest coast listings

For Sleeping and Eating price codes and other relevant information, see Essentials pages 45-48.

⊜ Sleeping

Algodones *p232*
E Motel Olímpico. Algodones' only hotel, rather misnamed.

Camping
RV park and campground, run by the Quechan people from the nearby Fort Yuma Reservation, US$12 per site with electricity, US$8 without; including hot showers and access to laundry room.

Puerto Peñasco *p233*
Accommodation is no longer cheap in Puerto Peñasco and you'll be hard pressed to find a room for under US$30. Prices can double or triple on weekends, during high season, spring break, Christmas and Semana Santa.
LL-AL Viña del Mar, Calle 1 de Junio y Blv Malecón Kino, T638-383 3600, www.vinadel marhotel.com. Swanky, modern resort with

attractive rooms, cliffside jacuzzi, disco and a plethora of little luxury details.
A Motel Peñasco, Encinas, between C14 and C15, T638-383 3101. The best 'budget' motel in town. Rooms are large with bath, a/c and cable TV. Friendly.
B Posada La Roca, 1 de Junio 2, old port, T638-383 3199. The oldest building in the port, where Al Capone used to hang out. Rooms are slightly pokey, but it's a friendly, interesting place.

Camping
You'll find many more RV parks fronting the beach on Matamoros.
Playa Bonita Resort and RV Park, on lovely Playa Bonita, T638-383 2596. With 300 spaces. There's a restaurant, shop and laundry. US$20-25.
Playa de Oro Trailer Resort, Matamoros 36, T638-383 2668, 2 km east. 200 sites with laundry and boat ramp. US$20-25.

Caborca *p233*
C Casa Blanca Hotel, Blv Aviación 280 y Carretera Internacional México (Route 2),

T637-372 4119, www.casablanca caborca.com. Friendly staff, a/c, cable TV, Wi Fi in all 28 rooms, RV hook-ups.
C-D Hotel Plaza, Av Quiroz y Mora Sur 33, T637-372 5095. On the main square.

Altar *p234*
B Motel San Francisco, T641-324 1380. With a/c, shower and baths. Also has a restaurant.

Camping
Canadian-Mexican trailer park, south of town, on the right going south. A rustic sport with space for 9-10 trailers. Also makes a useful overnight stop.

Nogales *p234*
There is a wide selection of cheap hotels on Juárez, a 1-block extension of Av López Mateos between Campillo and the border, 2 blocks from the Mexican port of entry.
B Miami, Campillo and Ingenieros, T631-312 5450. Friendly hotel with a good restaurant attached. Recommended.
C Fray Marco de Niza, Campillo 91, T631-312 1651, www.hotelfraymarcos deniza.com. Excellent restaurant, central location, otherwise a nondescript building.

Magdalena Valley *p235*
B-C El Cuervo, Av 5 de Mayo 316. Various rooms, cheaper without TV.
B-C El Toro, Av Niños Héroes y Misión de Dolores, T632-322 0375. Centrally located, largest in town, probably the best of the lot.

Hermosillo *p235*
A-B San Sebastian, Pereférico Sur 96 esq, Blv Vildósola, T662-259 9550, www.hotelsan sebastian.com.mx. On its way to becoming best hotel in town in this range; with all amenities/services.
C Monte Carlo, Juárez y Sonora, T662-212 3354. Popular old hotel with a/c, clean rooms and adjoining restaurant.
C San Alberto, Serdán y Rosales, T662-213 1840. Good-value hotel with a/c, cable TV and pool. Breakfast served.

C Santiago Plaza, Blv Luis Encinas 545, T662-289 8990, www.hotelsantiago plaza.com. Downtown location, pool, restaurant, gym, all rooms a/c, TV.
D Washington, Dr Noriega Pte 68, T662-213 1183. The best budget hotel in town. Clean, basic rooms lie off narrow courts, some have a/c. Parking for motorbikes.
E Casa de los Amigos, contact the Asociación Sonorense de los Amigos, Felipe Salido 32, T/F662-217 0142. Various dorms, living room, library, garden, laundry and kitchen.

Cheap hotels and *casas de huéspedes* can be found around Plaza Zaragoza and along Sonora near Matamoros.

Bahía Kino *p236*
A Hotel Saro, Av Mar de Cortés, north of Posada del Mar, Kino Nuevo, T662-242 0216. Sicilian-run establishment with large, cool, self-contained, apartment-style lodgings. Just over the road from the beach.
C Geko Apartments, Av Mar de Cortés 1120, Kino Nuevo, T662-360 1387. 6 apartments and 4 suites for an alternative to hotel living. Wi-Fi in main building, comfortable, great location on water and quiet.

Camping
It's possible to camp on the beaches with or without a tent.
Kino Bay RV Park, Av Mar de Cortés, northernmost end of Kino Nuevo, T662-242 0216, www.kinobayrv.com, US$20.

Guaymas *p236*
B Santa Rita, Serdán and Calle 9, T622-222 8100. This comfortable hotel has clean rooms with bath and a/c. There's another more expensive motel with the same name.
C Playa de Cortés, Bahía de Bacochibampo 66, T622-221 1048. Great views of ocean from this old hacienda-style hotel. Highly recommended.
D Motel Cominse, Calle 14. Clean and simple motel, but a good choice.

F Casa de Huéspedes Martha, Calle 13, T622-222 8332. Run-down but reliable old cheapie. Rooms have bath, fan and hot water.

Camping

At Km 13 the road forks: left 1 km to 2 secluded bays with limited trailer camping, and right to the **Marina Real** on Sonora Bay, and beyond a beach with open camping.

Bahía San Carlos *p236*
A Fiesta San Carlos, T622-226 1318, hotelfiesta10@hotmail.com. Clean hotel with a pool. Good food.
B-C Best Western Hacienda Tetakawi, Paseo Escénico Km 8.8, T622-226 0220. Directly across from ocean, clean, and quiet.
C Dorada Rental Units, T622-226 0307, PO Box 48. After 10 km from the highway a road branches here. On the beach and pleasant.

South to Sinaloa *p236*
AL Best Western Hotel San Jorge, M Alemán 929 Norte, Cd Obregón, T644-410 4000, www.bestwestern.com. Colonial Spanish decor at this clean, friendly, reliable hotel. There's a restaurant, bar, pool, safe and safe parking. Rooms have a/c and TV.
C Valle Grande Obregón, Miguel Alemán y Tebatiate, T644-410 6500, www.vallegrande obregon.com. Bilingual, friendly staff, gym, pool, restaurant. Charges for internet use.

Camping

Navojoa RV and Camping, in the north of Navojoa on Route 15 Km 159, T642-421 5203. Run-down, shaded, US$13 for full hook-up (50 available), US$5 for car or small jeep, dollars preferred to pesos.

Alamos *p237*
LL-L Hotel Colonial, Obregón 4, T647-428 1371, www.alamoshotelcolonial.com. Beautifully decorated colonial house with 10 very different rooms and hospitable, North American management.
A Los Portales Hotel, Juárez 6, T647-428 0211. Beautiful 300-year-old hacienda on the plaza with atmospheric courtyard and wonderful murals. The 9 big rooms have bath but fan only.
C Enrique, Juárez, on the plaza, T647-428 1199. Big, crumbling rooms at this dilapidated hotel, favoured by backpackers. Some rooms have a bath.

Camping

El Caracol Trailer Park, Navojoa–Alamos Hwy Km. 37. Rustic, good swimming pool, not always open (US$15).

Los Mochis *p237, map p237*
AL Santa Anita, Leyva and Hidalgo, T668-818 7046, www.santaanitahotel.com. Big, comfortable hotel with pleasant, modern rooms. Lots of services, including restaurant, bar, Wi-Fi and travel agency, where you can book your rail tickets and lodgings.
B Beltrán, Hidalgo 281 Pte, T668-812 0688, www.losnmochishotel.com. Clean, tidy, efficient hotel with comfortable, if somewhat generic rooms.
B Fénix, A Flores 365 Sur, T668-815 8948, hotelfenix@email.com. Clean, if sometimes pokey quarters. Some rooms have impressive big screen TVs, so ask to see a few.
C Las Fuentes, Blv Adolfo López Mateos 1251-A Norte, T668-818 8871, lasfuenteshotel@lmm.megared.net.mx. Very friendly, a/c, TV, private parking, close to downtown. Recommended.
C Nuevo Hotel Montecarlo, Gen Angel Flores 322 Sur, T668-812 1818. One of the cheapest in its range. Recently remodelled and centrally located. Recommended.
D-E Los Arcos, Allende 524, between Castro and Obregón, T668-817 1424. Rock-bottom rates, with an atmosphere to match. Rooms are dingy and without bath. Not very friendly and slightly dubious area, so take care.

Camping

RV Park Copper Canyon, Ruta 15, on the right side of the road when entering town. Good place to leave vehicles when visiting the Copper Canyon.

Topolobampo *p238*

For other accommodation, go to Los Mochis.
B Yacht Hotel, 3-4 km south of town. Modern, clean, quiet hotel with a/c, good food and views, but seems to close for the winter.
E Estilo Europeo Poama, at the ferry terminal, 10 mins' walk from Los Mochis bus.

South to Mazatlán *p239*

AL Los 3 Ríos, 1 km north of town on Hwy 15, at Km 1423, Culiacán, T667-750 5280. Trailer park, US$10, pool, resort-style, good restaurant.
A Los Caminos, Blv Colegio Militar y Blv Leyva Solano, T667-715 3300. With a/c, phone, satellite TV, restaurant, pool, nightclub, safe parking, clean rooms.
B San Francisco, Hidalgo 227, T66/-713 5863. Good, functional hotel. Rooms have a/c, bath and cable TV. Clean, friendly, free parking.

Mazatlán *p239, map p239*
Zona Dorada

LL-L Océano Palace, Av Camarón Sábalo, T669-913 0666, www.oceanopalace.com, north end of Zona Dorada. Big all-inclusive resort with 200 rooms, pool, restaurant and abundant service.
AL Aguamarina, Av del Mar 110, across the road from the beach. T669-981 7080, www.aguamarina.com. Big, comfortable, 4-star hotel with pool and all amenities. Front rooms are likely to be noisy.
A Las Arenas, Av del Mar, across the road from the beach, T669-982 0000, www.sands arenas.com. Front rooms are likely to be noisy. With swimming pool, a/c, TV, fridge, garden, good restaurant, on beach.
A-D Apartmentos Fiesta, Ibis 502, T669-913 5355, www.mazatlanapartments.com. A range of pleasant, good-value apartments surrounding a pleasant patio, some are budget (**D**). Diving and fishing tours available.
C Suites Linda Mar, Av Rodolfo Loaiza 226, T669-913 5533. Very clean, much in demand (book well ahead) and straight on the ocean. The only option in this range, and a good one.

Old Town

AL Royal Dutch, Constitución 627, T669-981 4396, www.royaldutchcasadesanta maria.com. Pleasant and traditional Dutch-owned B&B. Rooms are very comfortable and the management is helpful, friendly and informative. Book in advance.
A La Siesta, No 11 Sur, T669-981 2640, www.lasiesta.com.mx. Good, reliable hotel with comfortable a/c rooms. Some have sea views and are more expensive. There's a decent, if noisy, restaurant downstairs.
C Belmar, Paseo Olas Altas 166 Sur, T669-985 1113, http://hotelbelmar.googlepages.com. In the Old Town but also on beach, 1 block from La Siesta, with spectacular views, with pool, Wi-Fi in lobby, baby-sitting services. Accepts US, Canadian and Mexican currency. Special rates for backpackers. English spoken. Reputedly haunted. Highly recommended.
D Lerma, Simón Bolívar 622 and Aquiles Serdán, near beach, T669-981 2436. Best deal in the Old Town. Rooms are simple and quiet, with fan and hot showers. Secure parking.
D México, México 201 and Aquiles Serdán, T669-981 3806. Tidy, sometimes small rooms, basic, but a popular budget option. Ask for a quieter room facing away from the street.
D Vialta, Azueta 2006, 3 blocks from market, T669-981 6027. Plain, simple rooms with bath and fan, all set around a pleasant central patio. Friendly and helpful.

Camping

North of the city there are undeveloped beaches with free overnight camping; it is safer to camp in a group (take bus to Sábalos and get out where it turns round). There are at least 10 trailer parks on Playa del Norte/Zona Dorada and on towards the north.
Las Palmas Trailer Park Camarón Sábalo, T669-983 6424. Next to Las Palmas Suites, with full hook-ups, hot showers and coin laundry.
RV Park Villas al Mar, quiet place directly on the beach at the Camarón Sábalo. Good shade amongst the palms and bamboo.

Mazatlán to Durango *p241*
D Villa Blanca, La Capilla del Taxte, 3 km from Santa Lucía, T244-442 1628. A good hotel and restaurant.

South of Mazatlán *p242*
B Motel Virginia, Carretera Internacional Km 1107, south of Rosario and several kilometres north of Escuinapa, T694-953 2755. Good clean, *palapa* restaurant next door, possible trailer parking.

Teacapan *p242*
A Rancho Los Angeles, Km 25 Carretera Escuinapa–Teacapán, T695-953 1344). Former home of a drug baron (deceased), 16 km north from Teacapan towards Escuinapa, on beach. Good value, luxurious swimming pool. Recommended.
D Hotel Denisse, on square, T/F695-954 5266, José Morales and Carol Snobel. Clean, next to phone office, noisy, local trips arranged.

Camping
Oregon. US$8, no signs, on beach in town, run-down but one of better places to stay, new Mexican hotel next door.

● Eating

Puerto Peñasco *p233*
♦♦ **Costa Brava Restaurant**, Kino y 1 de Junio. Exotic menu, modest prices. Best in town.
♦♦ **La Casa del Capitán**, on top of the mountain overlooking town, follow the path for 15 mins. Great views, tasty international food and seafood. One of the best.
♦♦ **Lily's**, Malecón 31, T638-383 2510. Popular outdoor terraced restaurant, frequented by gringos.
♦ **Gamma's**, C Armada Nacional 28, right on the water. Popular locals' joint that serves very good seafood. Often noisy and colourful.

Nogales *p234*
♦♦♦ **La Roca**, Elias 91. A very fine, romantic restaurant serving decent Sonoran cuisine. Probably the best place in town.
♦♦ **Café Olga**, Juárez 37 next to bus station. A Nogales institution, open all hours.
♦ **Leo's Café**, Obregón and Capillo. Cheap and cheerful eaterie serving Mexican staples.
♦ **San San**, Av López y Ateos 171. Chinese (nice alternative to fast foods and taco joints), usually crowded. Recommended.

Hermosillo *p235*
♦♦♦ **Jardín Xochimilco**, Obregón 51, T662-250 4052. A Hermosillo favourite. Good beef and top range Mexican fare.
♦♦♦ **San César**, Plutarco Elías Calles 71 Pte. Excellent chop sueys, seafood and expensive gringo food.
♦♦♦-♦♦ **Mariscos Los Arcos de Hermosillo**, Michel y Ocampo (4 blocks south of Plaza), T662-213 2220. Fresh seafood, attractive and expensive.
♦ **El Marcos**, Av Rodríguez, T662-215 4710. International, children's menus, very popular and crowded.

Bahía Kino *p236*
♦♦ **El Pargo Rojo**. Recommended for seafood.
♦♦ **La Palapa**, Old Kino. Reasonably priced meals are available.

Guaymas *p236*
Food in Guaymas tends to be down-to-earth.
♦♦ **Los Barcos**, Av 11 and Calle 20. Excellent seafood is served here, under a giant *palapa* overlooking the bay.
♦ **Froggy's**, Nuevo Guaymas. Sports bar open daily 1100-0200. Cheap eats. Live music at weekends.

Bahía San Carlos *p236*
Restaurants here tend to be overpriced.
♦♦ **Piccolo**, Creston 305, T622-226 0503. Good pasta, salads, original dishes, good value.
♦♦-♦ **Jax Snax**, San Carlos. Open early. Good, tasty breakfasts and filling staples.

Los Mochis *p237, map p237*
Many *birrierías* serving *birria*, a local beef dish.
▥▥ España, Av Alvaro Obregón 525 Pte,
T668-812 2221. Oldest eatery in town,
upscale, very good steak and seafood,
especially paella, served with style and grace.
▥▥ El Farallón, Flores and Obregón. Good
seafood and service, the best place in
town, reasonably priced.
▥▥-▥ El Taquito, Leyva, 1 block from
Santa Anita. Open 24 hrs.
▥ Leñador, Rendón y Guillermo Prieto 301
Norte, T668-812 6600. Grilled meat,
popular with locals.
▥ Mi Cabaña Tacos, corner of Obregón
y Allende. Popular with locals, friendly
atmosphere. Recommended.

Mazatlán *p239, map p239*
There are many cheap street places selling
fruit shakes and simple Mexican dishes at the
beach end of Av Manuel G Nájera.
▥▥ Shrimp Bucket, Olas Altas 11 and Av del
Mar. Rightly famous for seafood, good
environment, popular, good.
▥▥-▥ Copa de Leche, Av Olas Altas 1220 A Sur,
T669-982 5753. Mexican food. Quaint, rustic
ambience. Sidewalk tables are perfect for
enjoying your meal amid the sights and
sounds of the crashing waves.
▥▥-▥ El Túnel, opposite Teatro Angela Peralta.
Open 1200-000. Good Mexican food in this
legendary old restaurant, popular with locals
and tourists. Great specialities.
▥▥-▥ La Cumbre, Benito Juárez and Hidalgo.
Few seats, very busy, not many tourists,
1100-1500. Recommended.
▥ Pura Vida, Laguna 777, T669-916 5815.
Another breakfast/brunch eatery, this one
emphasising vegetarian food. Simple and
cozy, omelets and wholewheat pancakes as
well as a variety of yogurt and muffins, soy
burgers and fruit plates for brunch.
▥ Mercado. The best deal is at the market,
where you can get an excellent fish lunch
for US$1.50.

☻ Entertainment

Mazatlán *p239, map p239*
Bars and clubs
Edgar's Bar, Aquiles Serdán. 1 of Mazatlán's
oldest drinking joints.
Joe's Oyster Bar, Av Rodolfo T Loaiza 100,
T669-983 5333. Probably Mazatlán's best
known bar. Open-air, US$5 cover charge
on weekends (includes 3 drinks). Good
music and busy in the tourist season.

▲ Activities and tours

Los Mochis *p237, map p237*
Aracely, Obregón 471 Pte, T668-812 5090.
Amex agents, and full services with
reservations for 1st-class train.
Viajes Flamingo, www.mexicoscopper
canyon.comin the lobby of **Hotel Santa Anita**,
Leyva and Hidalgo, T668-812 1613. Bookings
for the trains attract a commission of 8%.

Mazatlán *p239, map p239*
Always check with the locals whether
swimming is safe, since there are strong rip
currents in the Pacific, which run out to sea
and are extremely dangerous. **Fishing** is
the main sport (sailfish, tarpon, marlin, etc).
Mazatlán's famous fishing tournament
follows Acapulco's and precedes the one at
Guaymas. **Birdwatching** is popular too: in
the mangrove swamps are egrets, flamingos,
pelicans, cranes, herons and duck. Nearby at
Camarones there is **parasailing**, drawn by
motorboats. The northern beach tourist strip
offers boat trips to nearby deserted islands,
snorkel hire and paragliding. **Bungee
jumping** is done at junction Camarón Sábalo
y Rafael Buelna opposite McDonald's. There is
a 3-hr **harbour cruise** run by Yate Fiesta,
Calzado Joel Montes Camarena 7, T668-982
3130, www.yatefiesta.com, it departs Tue-Sun
from the ferry dock, 1100, US$14.
There are **bullfights** at Mazatlán,
Sun at 1600, very touristy.

Tour operators
Explora Tours, Centro Comercial Lomas, Av Camarón Sábalo 204-L-10, T669-913 9020. Very helpful. Recommended.
Hudson Tours, T669-913 1764, good for mountain biking.
Ole Tours, Camarón Sábalo 7000, T669-916 6288, www.oletours.com, runs regular city tours, baseball tours and sport-fishing trips.
Zafari Tours, Paseo Claussen 25. Ferry bookings, helpful.

● Transport

Nogales *p234*
Bus
Nogales' main bus terminal is 8 km south of the city centre, along the highway to Magdalena and Hermosillo; parking US$1 per hr. There are several other small terminals nearby, including the TBC terminal, where Albatros buses go to Puerto Peñasco.

Taxis at the border ask US$5 to take you to the bus station, but on the return journey the booth selling taxi vouchers charges less than US$4. A local bus, 1 peso, leaves 1 block from the border. Bus 46 from Juárez goes to the terminal (US$0.25). The bus station has a booth to change money.

There are 3 bus lines that go into Mexico using the main terminal: **Norte de Sonora, Transportes y Autobuses del Pacífico (TAP)** and **Elite**. They all seem to have high-quality buses and prices are almost always identical between carriers; **Transportes y Autobuses del Pacífico (TAP)** also runs 2nd-class buses to most of their destinations. To **Chihuahua**, Elite, US$50. To **Cd Obregón**, TAP, 9 daily, US$23. To **Culiacán**, TAP, 7 daily, US$44. To **Durango**, 1530, US$75. To **Guadalajara** (**Tonalá**, outside of city), every couple of hrs, US$96. To **Guaymas**, hourly, US$18. To **Hermosillo**, hourly, US$11. To **Los Mochis**, hourly, US$35. To **Mazatlán**, hourly, US$63. To **Mexicali**, TAP, 1930, US$28. To **Tepic**, hourly, 23 hrs, US$76. To **Zacatecas**, direct, US$87.

To USA To Los Angeles, **Autobuses Crucero**, 3 daily, US$84. **Phoenix**, 5 daily, US$27. **Tucson**, 4 daily, US$23. There are also links to the **Greyhound** network in the USA.

To get to the USA border, turn left as you leave the bus station and walk to the 1st traffic light, then cross the street. You can pick up the buses to the border, referred to by the locals as *La Línea*. The buses run along the same street you'd be walking on.

On the Arizona side, 1 block from the port of entry, **Citizen Auto Stage Company**, T287-5628, runs 10 buses daily between **Tucson** and Nogales; stops at Tucson airport en route. Stopovers (no additional charge) are possible to visit **Tumacacori Mission**.

If you're entering the US from Mexico, you'll see a ramp and stairs on your left on the street after you've crossed the border. The **Greyhound** station is at the top of the stairs, where you can catch buses to Tucson and points beyond. Buses leave for **Tucson** almost hourly 0630-2000. There are smaller vans that leave at 0800, 1200, and 1600. Buses leave for **Phoenix**, AZ (Arizona's largest city, about 2 hrs north of Tucson) at 0745, 1015, 1415 and 2045, US$32. They also have buses for **Hermosillo** and **Cd Obregón** that don't require a transfer in Nogales, which stop across the border on the Mexican side to pick up passengers. The **Greyhound** bus station is a small; a 1-room building with toilets, lockers, pay phones and a few fast-food outlets.

Car
Road tolls If driving from Nogales to **Mazatlán** by the 4-lane, divided toll road (Route 15), there are 12 toll gates. The first is 88 km south of Nogales. No motorcycles, bikes (but see page 78), pedestrians or animals are allowed on the highway, which is fenced and patrolled. The toll stations are well lit, have good public conveniences, fuel and food. The total distance from Nogales to Mazatlán is 1118 km. Most deviations are dirt roads and should not be taken in the rainy season. On toll routes and their avoidance, seek advice from

US motoring associations and clubs (see page 76) as costs and conditions change rapidly.

Hermosillo *p235*
Air The Gen Pesquira/García airport (HMO) is 12 km from town. Daily flights to **Mexico City** AeroMéxico T662-216 8415, and Aviacsa T662-216 5278. Good domestic connections. International flights to **Los Angeles**, **Tucson** and **Phoenix**.

Bus Bus station on Blv Encinas 400, between Los Pinos and Jaffa. To **Agua Prieta**, 6 a day, 7 hrs, US$16. To **Guaymas**, hourly round the clock, 2½ hrs, US$8. To **Kino**, 4 a day, 1½ hrs, US$6. To **Los Mochis**, TAP, hourly, 7½ hrs through scrubland and wheat fields, US$21. To **Mazatlán**, every 1-2 hrs, 10-12 hrs, US$44. To **Nogales**, 9 daily, 4 hrs, US$12. To **Tijuana**, every 1-2 hrs, 11 hrs, US$43.

Guaymas and Bahía San Carlos *p236*
Air The Gen José M Yáñez airport (GYM) is 5 km from Guaymas on the way to San Carlos. AeroMéxico (T622-226 0123) has flights to **La Paz**, **Mexico City** and **Phoenix**.

Bus 1st class bus to **Hermosillo**, 2½ hrs, US$6. To **Mazatlán**, frequent, 12 hrs, US$42. To **Tijuana**: 18 hrs, US$51. To **Culiacán**, hourly, 9 hrs, US$25. To **Los Mochis**, TAP, every 1-2 hrs, 5½ hrs, US$15.

Alamos *p237*
Bus Navojoa-Alamos every hour on the ½ hr from 0630-1830, 1 hr, US$2, good road. Bus station for Alamos is about 8 blocks from main bus station in Navojoa, but you must ask directions because it is a confusing route.

Los Mochis *p237, map p237*
Air
Aeropuerto Federal (LMM) is 6.5 km from town. Flights to **Mexico City** and major towns in Northern Mexico. International flights to **Los Angeles**, **Phoenix** and **Tucson** with AeroMéxico.

Airline offices Aero California, T668-818 1616.

Bus
Local Buses to the train station leave from the corner of Obregón and Zaragoza, first leaves at 0515 in time to get tickets for the train, US$0.40. Local buses to destinations around Sinaloa, eg Topolobampo, Guasave, San Blas (Sufragio) and Culiacán leave from Cuauhtémoc, near the post office.

Long distance The main bus station is on the corner of Castro and Constitución, to the south of town, about 10 mins' walk. **Estrella Blanca** companies (**Futura** and **Elite**) with long-distance services leave from here as well as international services coming down from the US. The terminals of **Norte de Sonora**, T668-812 1757, 2nd-class **Estrella Blanca** and 1st-class **Tufesa**, T668-818 2222, for services along the western coast leave from several terminals clustered together near Degollado and Juárez, to the east of town. Buses to El Fuerte depart regularly from inside the market on the corner of Independencia and Degollado, US$1.40. Check locally for the best option for your destination if it is slightly unusual. Many other destinations are served by a combination of regional and local buses, but tickets must be purchased separately.

To **Cd Obregón**, hourly or better, 3 hrs, US$10. To **Guadalajara**, hourly, 13 hrs, US$47. To **Guaymas**, 6 hrs, US$15. To **Mazatlán**, hourly or better, 6 hrs, US$24. To **Mexico City**, every couple of hrs, 24 hrs, US$87. To **Monterrey**, 0900 and 2000, 24 hrs, US$72. To **Nogales**, TAP, 8 daily, 12 hrs, US$36. To **Tepic**, hourly, 10 hrs, US$40. To **Tijuana**, hourly, 20 hrs, US$60.

Train
For **Creel** and **Chihuahua**, see page 281. If coming from Chihuahua and you don't want to stay in Los Mochis (assuming the train is not over-delayed), you can take a night bus to Mazatlán at 2200, arriving 0630. Los Mochis station has toilets and local phones; ticket office is open 1 hr before train leaves.

The station is 8 km from town; do not walk there or back in the dark. There is a bus service from 0500, US$0.10 from corner of hotels **Hidalgo** and **Beltrán**, otherwise take the 0500 bus from **Hotel Santa Anita**, US$2.25 (for house guests only), or taxi. Taxis in the centre go from Hidalgo y Leyva; fare to station US$5 per car, bargaining not possible, make sure price quoted is not per person, rip-offs are common. Bus to town from corner of 1st junction from station from 0530.

Topolobampo *p238*
Ferry To **La Paz**, Baja California Sur. For schedule, fares and information, see page 228. Enquiries in Los Mochis on T668-817 3752 or on day of travel at Muelle Topolobampo office, opens 3 hrs prior to departure (be there at least 2 hrs before sailing), T668-862 0141.

South to Mazatlán *p239*
Air The Aeropuerto Federal de Bachi-gualato (CUL) is 10 km from Culiacán. AeroMéxico, T667-715 3772; have flights to **Mexico City**, **Acapulco** and major cities in northern Mexico. International flights to **Los Angeles** and **Tucson**.

Bus Buses from Culiacán to all places along the west coast, including **Guaymas**, 9 hrs, US$25. **Tepic**, 8½ hrs, US$29.

Car North of the city, the north and southbound carriageways are on different levels with no divide (very dangerous). A toll section of freeway heads nearer to the coast, past Navolata, bypasses Culiacán and rejoins Hwy 15 a few kilometres south of that city.

Mazatlán *p239, map p239*
Air
Aeropuerto General Rafael Buelna (MZT), 3 km from centre. Domestic flights to **Guadalajara**, **Mexico City**, and major cities in Northern Mexico. International connections to **San José** (Costa Rica), **Calgary** (Canada), **Denver**, **Houston**, **Los Angeles**, **Phoenix**,

Portland, **Salt Lake City**, **San Francisco**, **Seattle** and **Spokane** (Washington).
Airline offices AeroMéxico, T669-984 1111. Mexicana, T669-913 0770.

Bicycle
Beware, the Mazatlán–Tepic–Guadalajara road has been described as 'the most dangerous in the world for cyclists'.

Bus
Local Green and white express buses on the 'Sábalo Centro' route run from Playa Cerritos to the city centre along the seafront road, US$0.20.
Long distance A big central terminal, making travel a bit easier, is just off the Carretera Internacional and Ferrusquilla s/n, about 3 km north of the Old Town, 4 km south of the Zona Dorado. Take 'Insurgentes' bus from terminal to Av Ejército Mexicano for the centre, via market at Aquiles Serdán.

To **Chihuahua**, 1400 and 1800, 16 hrs, US$44. To **Durango**, hourly 0600-1900, 7 hrs, US$27. To **Guadalajara**, hourly, 8 hrs, US$30. To **Guaymas**, hourly, 11 hrs, US$42. To **Los Mochis**, hourly or better, 6 hrs, US$24. To **Mexicali**, TAP, 13 daily, 24 hrs, US$70. To **Mexico City**, 17 hrs, US$71. To **Navojoa**, every 1½ hrs, 8 hrs, US$30. To **Nogales**, every 1½ hrs, 18 hrs, US$63. To **Puerto Vallarta**, TAP, 2300, 2430, 8 hrs, US$25. To **Tepic**, hourly, 5 hrs, US$15. To **Tijuana**, hourly, 26 hrs, US$78. To **Rosario**, US$1.25, you can then (with difficulty) catch bus to **Caimanero** beach. Terminal Alamos, Av Guerrero Ote 402, 2 blocks from market, buses to **Alamos** every hour on the ½ hr.

Bus companies Transporte Norte de Sonora, T669-981 2335, Transportes del Pacífico, T669-981 5156, Estrella Blanca, T669-982 1949.

Car
AGA, Camarón Sábalo 316, T669-914 4405. Budget, Camarón Sábalo 402, T669-913 2000. National, Camarón Sábalo 7000, T669-913 6000, US$277 per week.

Ferry

La Paz (Baja California Sur), see schedule, page 228. Allow plenty of time for booking and customs procedure. Tickets from **Hotel Aguamarina**, Av del Mar 110, with 10% commission, also from travel agents. Ferry terminal is at the southern end of Av del Puerto, quite a way from the centre (take bus marked 'Playa Sur', which also goes from the street corner opposite ferry terminal to Av Ejército Mexicano near bus station).

Ticket office for La Paz ferry 0830-1300 only, on day of departure, arrive before 0800, unclaimed reservations on sale at 1100. Don't expect vehicle space for same-day departure.

Taxi

Taxis charge an average US$3.50-5 between Zona Dorada and city centre. From Bahía del Puerto Viejo to centre, taxi US$1, bus US$0.15.

❶ Directory

Puerto Peñasco p233
Banks There are 4 banks in town, most with ATMs. **Laundry** Laundromat Liz, Altamirano y Simón Morua. Also Lavamatic Plus, Fco León de la Barra and San Luis.

Nogales p234
Banks Casas de cambio: Money Exchange, Campillo y López Mateos. 'El Amigo', Campillo y López Mateos, local 14. **Compra-venta de Dólares Serfín**, Av López Mateos y Calle Pierson 81, 1st floor. **Medical services** According to the tourist office, the best private hospital in Nogales is the **Hospital del Socorro**, Dirección Granja, T631-314 6060. Any taxi driver will know how to get there. **Pharmacy: Farmacia Benavides**, behind the immigration office. They give injections. There are other pharmacies nearby.

Bahía Kino p236
Banks There is no bank in the area, ATMs at most petrol stations and some supermarkets in Old Kino. The nearest bank is **Bancomer** in Miguel Alemán, between Kino and Hermosillo, 48 km away.

Guaymas and Bahía San Carlos p236
Bank (Banamex, Mon-Fri 0830-1630), phone and fax after 10 km, near the Pemex station in San Carlos. **Post office and police station** 7 km from the highway, behind the shops.

Los Mochis p237, map p237
Banks Many banks on Leyva, with ATMs, and a casa de cambio open a little later.
Internet Hugo's Internet Café, Leyva 537, with printers/ scanners. Also **Cyber Más**, Independencia 421. **Laundry** Lavamatic, Allende 218; **Lavarama** at Juárez 225.
Medical services Hospital Fátima, Loaizo 606 Pte, T668-815-5703, private, English spoken. **Post office** Ordóñez Pte, between Prieto y Zaragoza Sur, south of centre, Mon-Fri 0900-1400, 1600-1800.

Mazatlán p239, map p239
Banks Many in the centre, near the plaza. Banamex, Juárez and Angel Flores, also Av Camarón Sábalo 434. Open 0900-1330, 1530 1730. Casas de cambio on Camarón Sábalo 109, 1009 and at junction with RT Loaiza; also at R I Loaiza 309. **American Express**, Camarón Sábalo, T669-913 0600, Mon-Fri 0900-1700, Sat 0900-1400.
Embassies and consulates Canada, Hotel Playa Mazatlán, Av Playa Gaviotas 202, Local 9, Zona Dorado, T669-913 7320. France, B Domínguez 1008, T669-985 1228. Netherlands, Av Sábalo Cerritos, T669-913 5155. Germany, Jacarandas 10, T669-981 2077. Italy, Av Olas Altas 66-105, T669-981 4855. Norway, F Alcalde 4, T981-3237. USA, RT Loaiza, opposite Hotel Playa Mazatlán, T/F669-916 5889, Mon-Fri 0930-1300, T669-913 4455 ext 285. **Internet and telephone** Mail Boxes Etc, Camarón Sábalo 310, T669-916 4009, mail boxes, courier service; across the street at Centro Comercial Lomas. In the Old Town, a couple of internet

cafés on the south side of the main plaza, US$1.50 per hr. Also cheap international calls (US$1.80 per hr) and international calls and faxes, Mon-Fri 0600-2200, Sat-Sun 0900-1700. **Laundry** Lavandería, on Zúñiga and Juárez, near Hotel Lerma. **Medical services** General emergency T06; Red Cross T669-981 3690; **Ambulance** T669-985 1451; **Police** T669-982 1867. Hospitals: Hospital General, Av Ferrocarril, T669-984 0262. **Cruz Roja Mexicana**, Alvaro Obregón 73, T669-981 3690. There is a free Red Cross treatment station on Camarón Sábalo, opposite the Beach Man. **Post**

office Juárez y 21 de Marzo, opposite Palacio Municipal, T669-981 2121. **DHL** is a couple of doors from Mail Boxes Etc (see above), Mon-Fri 0900-1330, Sat 1500-1800, 0830-1330. **Telephone** Camarón Sábalo, 1 block from American Express; also 21 de Marzo y Juárez. **Computel** phone and fax service, Aquiles Serdán 1512, T669-985 0109. Phone rental, **Accetel**, Camarón Sábalo 310-4, T669-916 5056. There are public phones taking international credit cards all along Camarón Sábalo and RT Loaiza in the Zona Dorada for long-distance calls.

Northern highlands

The imposing Sierra Madre highlands of northern Mexico are rarely a destination in their own right. But these vast landscapes, at times barren and monotonous, hold some of Mexico's most spectacular surprises. The most important archaeological site in Northern Mexico is just a couple of hours' drive south of the border at Casas Grandes or Paquimé, a maze of multi-storeyed adobe buildings, once a thriving community with over 3000 inhabitants. Don't expect to see too many dainty little dogs in Chihuahua; this, Mexico's biggest state, is the rugged land of Pancho Villa and there are museums and memorabilia dedicated to the Bandido-turned-Hero of the Revolution – even the bullet-ridden Dodge car he was finally gunned down in. It's dramatic stuff; and so is the Chihuahua al Pacífico, billed as 'the world's most scenic railroad', which wends its way across bridges, through tunnels and over the Sierra Madre down to the Pacific coast at Los Mochis. It's a journey of a lifetime. Hikers will want to stop off at Creel or Divisadero to absorb the views, discover the awe-inspiring landscapes, strange rock formations and wildlife, visit Mexico's tallest waterfall and penetrate the vertiginous depths of the Barranca del Cobre, the Copper Canyon, bigger than Colorado's Grand Canyon. This is the craggy land of the Tarahumara people, and some 60,000 live in the Sierra where you can buy their hand-carved and woven crafts in any of the towns or villages. And if you're still looking for action, why not try some of the Wild-West kind and walk the streets of real Western film sets in the State of Durango. ** For listings, see pages 268-283.

Border towns ●❶❷❸❹ ** pp268-283. Colour map 2, A2.

Ciudad Juárez → *Phone code: 656. Altitude: 1150 m.*

Crossing the border from El Paso, Texas you'll reach Ciudad Juárez. Ciudad Juárez and El Paso have over 1.2 million people each; the cross-border industry has made Ciudad Juárez the largest *maquiladora* or workshop city in the world. Twin plant assembly and manufacturing operations now supersede tourism and agriculture in the city.

The Spanish conquistador Cabeza de Vaca discovered the Paso del Norte (Northern Pass) on the Camino Real. The name was retained until 1888 when Porfirio Díaz renamed the city after Benito Juárez. Today four bridges link the two cities.

Note that Juárez is notorious for its violent crime. Over 400 women have been murdered here since 1993, whilst the brutal antics of the infamous Juárez cartel, who manage the multi-million dollar business of trafficking cocaine to the US, only further affirms this city's nasty reputation. You're unlikely to encounter any trouble as long as you stick to the main roads and don't wander off, especially at night. It can be intimidating by the Santa Fe bridge at any hour, and female travellers should take care when choosing a hotel. The Pronaf (Programa Nacional Fronterizo) zone is the safest place for visitors.

The **tourist office** ⓘ *Av de las Américas 2551, T656-611 3174, www.visitajuarez.com, Mon-Fri 0900-1700, Sat-Sun 1000-1400*, is a good source of information, but located away from the centre in the Pronaf zone.

In Ciudad Juárez, the **Nuestra Señora de Guadalupe de El Paso del Norte** mission was the first established in the region; the building was completed in 1668. The mission, and the nearby **cathedral**, are two blocks west of Avenida Juárez on 16 de Septiembre. At the junction of Avenida Juárez and 16 de Septiembre is the Aduana, the former customs building, now the **Museo Histórico** ⓘ *Tue-Sun 1000-1700*. In Parque Chamizal, just across the Córdova bridge, are the **Museo de Arte Prehispánico** ⓘ *Tue-Sun 1000-1700*, with exhibits from each Mexican state, the **Botanic Gardens** and a **memorial to Benito Juárez**. Continuing south down Avenida Lincoln, you come to the Pronaf zone with the **Museo de Arte e Historia** ① *Tue-Sun 1000-1700*. The **University Cultural Centre** and the **Fonart artisan centre**, which acts as a Mexican 'shop window', are well worth a look for the uninitiated tourist. The **Plaza Monumental de Toros** ① *López Mateos y Triunfo de la República*, holds bullfights between April and August, and *charreadas* (rodeos) are held at the **Lienzo Charro** ① *Av del Charro*. The main street is **Avenida Juárez**, on or near which are most of the souvenir shops, hotels, cheap and expensive restaurants, clubs and bars.

To the east of **El Paso**, over the border, the **Ysleta Mission** is the oldest in Texas (1680), built by Franciscan monks and local Tigua tribesmen, who have a 'reservation' (more like a suburb) nearby; the **Socorro Mission** (1681) and **San Elizario Presidio** (1789, rebuilt 1877-1887) are in the same direction. There are a number of museums, including the **Americana Museum** in the **Civic Centre** (which also houses a performing arts centre, convention centre and tourist office), the **Museum of Art** ① *1211 Montana, T915-544 0062, www.elpaso artmuseum.org, Tue-Sat 0900-1700, Thu 0900-2100, Sun 1200-1700*, and the **Fort Bliss Air Defence Museum** of the nearby Air Base. The **Border-jumper trolley** ① *T915-544-0062*, conducts tours of El Paso and Ciudad Juárez, US$12.50, departing from the Convention Centre, Santa Fe street, El Paso. **El Paso Tourist** Office ① *Civic Centre Plaza, T915-534-0601; also at the airport.*

There is a new border crossing at Santa Teresa (New Mexico), west of El Paso. It is good for trucks and southbound travellers avoiding the congestion of Ciudad Juárez.

Ojinaga → *Phone code: 626.*

The State of Chihuahua may also be reached from the border at Ojinaga, east of El Paso/Ciudad Juárez. This route is recommended not only for the ease of crossing, but also for the spectacular scenery either side of the border.

Ciudad Juárez/El Paso

N

500 metres
500 yards

Sleeping
El Paso International
Hostel **2**
Impala **3**
Imperial **4**
Moran **5**
Plaza Continental **1**
Santa Fé **6**

Eating ⓐ
Kentucky Club **1**
La Cueva de Chucho **2**
La Fiesta del Pueblo **3**
Martino **4**
Tacos Lucas **5**
Villa del Mar **6**

Border essentials: northern highlands–USA

If you cross into the US and will be leaving by plane, you must ask for an immigration card. Make sure you have a US visa if you need one.

Agua Prieta–Douglas (Arizona)

Winter Arizona time is the same as Agua Prieta time but during summer Agua Prieta is one hour ahead. Immigration and customs are on the right just as you cross the border. You can pick up your FM-T (tourist card) here, as well as car documentation and insurance. If you keep walking straight ahead you'll cross a street, which has buses running to the Agua Prieta bus station. Take buses running east, which have '13-20', 'Ejidal' or 'P Nuevo' on their front windows. Taxis cost US$3 from the border to the bus station (10 minutes).

Palomas–Columbus (New Mexico)

This modern border, 5 km south of Columbus on Highway 11, is open 24 hours. Palomas is just across the border. The Mexican immigration office is on the right as you cross the border. If driving, park just before the border and walk across to get your documents stamped. Customs is 60 m south of immigration.

Ciudad Juárez–El Paso (Texas)

El Paso is on Mountain Standard Time, which is one hour behind Central Standard Time and General Mexican Time. Border formalities are minimal. From El Paso you can get on a bus outside Gate 9 of the Greyhound terminal, they depart at least every hour, 0600-2200, US$9.50; as you cross the border the driver should stop and wait for your documents to be processed. You are given 30 days entry, unless you ask for longer. Trolley buses cross the border for short trips. Alternatively, you can walk across (US$0.35 toll per person). Walking from Mexico to the US costs US$0.55 (toll for cars leaving Mexico US$2.05).

Ojinaga–Presidio (Texas)

The border is open 24 hours.
Leaving USA Follow signs to Ojinaga; pass US immigration on left (if you need to, surrender US visa waiver form here). On the Mexican side, a guard will check your passport. Those with vehicles then park before doing paperwork. There are separate desks for personal and vehicle papers. Photocopying can be done for US$1. Get insurance before Presidio, no one sells it there, but you could ask **Stella McKeel Agency**, T915-229 3221/5.
Leaving Mexico The bus station is 2 km from the border. Make sure all your papers are stamped correctly.

Some 42 km from Ojinaga on Route 16 towards Chihuahua is **El Peguis**, overlooking an extraordinary canyon. There is also a *garita*, where vehicle papers are checked.

Palomas

Route 2 runs west from Ciudad Juárez, roughly parallel with the Mexico–US border. Between Juárez and Janos, at the northern end of lateral Mexico 24, is the dusty border town of **Palomas** (Chihuahua), opposite **Columbus** (New Mexico, USA).

Palomas itself has few attractions apart from limited duty-free shopping for liquor and pharmaceuticals, but Columbus was the site of Pancho Villa's 1916 incursion into New Mexico, which led to reprisals by the forces of American General John J Pershing. The **Columbus Historical Museum** ① *daily 1000-1600*, on the southeast corner of the highway intersection, contains many old photos of Pancho Villa, a copy of his death mask, and one of his *sombreros*; it also has exhibits on Villa's sacking and burning of Columbus. There is a small shelf of books on the history of the town that you can browse through. The father of the museum's curator played a part in the battle.

Janos and around → *Phone code: 636. Colour map 2, A2.*

At the intersection of border Route 2 and Chihuahua Route 10 to Nuevo Casas Grandes is Janos. Nearby are the northernmost Mennonite colonies in Mexico; numerous vendors sell Mennonite cheese, which also has a market in upscale restaurants across the border in New Mexico. The German-speaking Mennonites are very conspicuous, the men in starched overalls and the women in long dresses and leggings, their heads covered with scarves.

Agua Prieta → *Phone code: 633. Colour map 2, A1.*

Northwest of Janos, via border Route 2, are the border crossings of Agua Prieta (opposite Douglas, Arizona) and **Naco** (adjacent to its Arizona namesake and a short distance south of the historic, picturesque copper mining town of Bisbee). Agua Prieta is growing rapidly with the proliferation of *maquiladoras* on both sides of the border.

On the Douglas side, the **Chamber of Commerce** ① *T633-364 2477, at 1125 Pan American*, has good information on Mexico as well as Arizona, with a wealth of maps (including Agua Prieta) and brochures.

Agua Prieta is 162 km from Janos via Route 2, which crosses the scenic Sierra San Luis, covered by dense woodland, to the continental divide (elevation 1820 m) at **Puerto San Luis**, the border between the states of Sonora and Chihuahua. There are outstanding views of the rangelands to the west. Southbound motorists from the US must present their papers to Mexican customs at **La Joya**, a lonely outpost 70 km northwest of Janos.

South of Ciudad Juárez ●❶❷❸❹ ▸▸ *pp268-283*.

The road between Ciudad Juárez and Chihuahua is wide, mostly flat, easy to drive, and not as interesting as the Gulf and Pacific routes. From Ciudad Juárez for some 50 km along the Río Bravo there is an oasis that grows cotton of an exceptionally high grade. The next 160 km of the road to Chihuahua are through desert.

Casas Grandes (Paquimé) → *Colour map 2, A2. Phone code: 636.*

① *Tue-Sun, 1000-1700, US$3.50, inc. museum, free Sun.*

The archaeological site of Casas Grandes (Paquimé) can be reached from Chihuahua, Ciudad Juárez or Agua Prieta, roughly 60 km south of Janos on Route 2. **Nuevo Casas Grandes** is a town built around the railway; it is very dusty when dry, the wind blowing clouds of dust down the streets, and when wet the main street becomes a river. There is not much to do, but there are cinemas that show US and Mexican films.

Casas Grandes/Paquimé was probably a trading centre, reaching its peak between 1210 and 1261. The city was destroyed by fire in 1340. Its commercial influence is said to have reached as far as Colorado in the north and into southern Mexico. At its height, it had multi-storeyed buildings; the niches that held the beams for the upper floors are still visible in some structures. A water system, also visible, carried hot water from thermal springs to the north, and acted as drainage. Most of the buildings are of a type of adobe, but some are faced with stone. You can see a ball court and various plazas among the buildings. The site is well tended. To get there take a yellow bus from outside the furniture shop at 16 de Septiembre y Constitución Poniente, US$0.20, 15 minutes. From the square in Casas Grandes village either take Calle Constitución south out of the square past the school, walk to the end of the road, cross a gully, then straight on for a bit, turn right and you will see the site, or take Avenida Juárez west out of the square and turn left at the sign to Paquimé, 1 km.

Paquimé ceramics, copying the original patterns, either black on black, or beige with intricate red and grey designs, are made in the village of **Mata Ortiz**, 21 km southwest of Nuevo Casas Grandes.

Madera and around → *Phone code: 157. Colour map 2, A2. Altitude: 2100 m.*
Madera is in the Sierra Madre, northwest of Chihuahua, surrounded by rugged mountain scenery. It is high enough to receive snow in winter (rainy season September-March, best time to visit May-August). The region around Madera has ample scope for tourism: archaeological sites, birdwatching, fine landscapes and good infrastructure.

Madera is on an important waterfowl migratory route, with white-fronted, blue and snow geese, mallard, pintail, teal, widgeon and redhead duck, and sandhill crane passing through. This does mean that it has become a popular centre for shooting (season mid-November to February), but birdwatching expeditions can be arranged at **Motel Real del Bosque**.

Taking Calle 3 in a northerly direction out of town you come to a signed turning right to Las Varas, which leads to Casas Grandes (there is another, unsigned turning to Las Varas further on). Straight on is **El Salto**, a 35-m waterfall, best seen after the spring thaw (March-April). The fall is along a track to the left; to see it you have to walk around the rim of a little canyon. It is possible to hike down to the river below (about one hour). Ask at the house on the track to the fall if you want to camp (no facilities).

Four kilometres from the turn-off to El Salto is the entrance to **Cuarenta Casas (40 houses)** ① *1½ hrs from Madera, daily 0900-1500 (except 16 Sep), free.* Cuarenta Casas is a series of cave dwellings, inhabited originally by indigenous people of the Paquimé culture. Some of the houses have the palet-shaped windows/doorways also seen at Casas Grandes (called here La Cueva de las Ventanas); some are two storeys high. There is a good view of the cave houses from the visitors' hut at the entrance. A trail descends to the river before climbing steeply to the cave, a hike that takes 45 minutes to one hour one way. Camping is possible only when personnel are staying the night; there are no facilities other than water. (Tour from **Motel Real del Bosque**, Carretera Chihuahua-Madera, T157-572 0066, takes six hours, US$65, minimum four people; alternatively, hitchhiking is possible.)

South of Madera is the **Misión Tres Ojitos**, where the Spanish priest, Padre Espronceda, makes ham. Take the road to La Junta from Madera and at the signpost, turn off right. On the dirt road, take the left fork through the village. Go past the church and on the right the Mission is signed (10 km from Madera).

In Madera there is a sign indicating **Zona Arqueológica Huapoca** ① *0900-1500, free,* going west on Independencia. At Km 13 on this good dirt road is Lago Campo 3, shallow

Chihuahua al Pacífico Primera Express timetable

From Chihuahua to Los Mochis

Chihuahua	0600		2045	US$130
Cuauhtémoc	0815	US$27	1823	US$104
Creel	1115	US$59	1524	US$71
Divisadero	1234	US$72	1345	US$60
Posada	1300	US$72	1340	US$60
San Rafael	1318	US$74	1320	US$57
Bahuichivo	1417	US$80	1227	US$51
Temoris	1515	US$88	1126	US$43
El Fuerte	1810	US$130	0830	US$24
Los Mochis	2050	US$130	0600	

From Los Mochis to Chihuahua

and marshy, with wildlife. Eighteen kilometres from town you reach an altitude of 2500 m, with stunning views of the Sierra Madre. Plenty of birdlife can be seen from the road. At Km 41 is the entrance to the **Zona Arqueológica Anasazi** ① *0900-1500, free,* which contains the Nido del Aguila (Eagle's Nest) cave dwellings and the Cueva del Serpiente (Serpent's Cave). The 2-km road to the site is terrible and about 300 m are impassable (you have to find somewhere to leave your car before the so-called 'car park'). There is no path to the Nido del Aguila, and a guide is recommended.

Chihuahua ⊖❼❶⊙▲⊖❶ » *pp268-283. Colour map 2, B2.*

→ *Phone code: 614. Altitude: 1420 m.*

The capital of Chihuahua state and centre of a mining and cattle area, Chihuahua City, 375 km from the border, is mostly a modern and rather run-down industrial city, but has strong historical connections, especially with the Mexican Revolution. Pancho Villa operated in the surrounding country, and once captured the city by disguising his men as peasants going to market. There are also associations with the last days of Independence hero Padre Hidalgo. Unfortunately there's none of the handsome colonial architecture that characterizes the cities further south, but Chihuahua does have an abundance of attractive 19th-century edifices. Summer temperatures often reach 40°C but be prepared for ice at night in winter. Rain falls from July to September.

The **tourist office** ① *Palacio de Gobierno, Aldama y Guerrero, T614-429 3596, www.ah-chihuahua.com, Mon-Fri 0900-1700, Sat-Sun 1000-1500,* is small, helpful and English speaking.

Sights

The old tower of the Capilla Real where Hidalgo awaited his execution is in the former **Palacio Federal**, now the **Museo Casa Chihuahua** ① *Libertad y Guerrero, 1000-1700, US$2.80,* with an array of cultural exhibits, gallery and convention halls. The dungeon itself (*calabozo*) is fairly unremarkable. Nearby, the **Palacio de Gobierno** is in fine condition, with a dramatic set of murals by Aaron Piña Morales depicting Chihuahua's history. There are a number of old mansions and the **Paseo Bolívar** area is pleasant. **Calle**

Libertad is for pedestrians only from Plaza Constitución to the Palacio de Gobierno and Palacio Federal. Calle 4 and streets that cross it northwest of Juárez are bustling with market stalls and restaurants. The **cathedral**, on Plaza Constitución, was built 1717-1789 and has a baroque façade dating from 1738. The interior is mostly unadorned, with square columns, glass chandeliers and a carved altarpiece. The crypt beneath it is home to the **Museo de Arte Sacro** ① *Mon-Fri 0900-1300 and 1500-1700, US$0.70*. In the southeast of town near Calle Zarco are ancient **aqueducts**. Walk north along Ocampo and over the river for fine views of the city at sunset.

Chihuahua

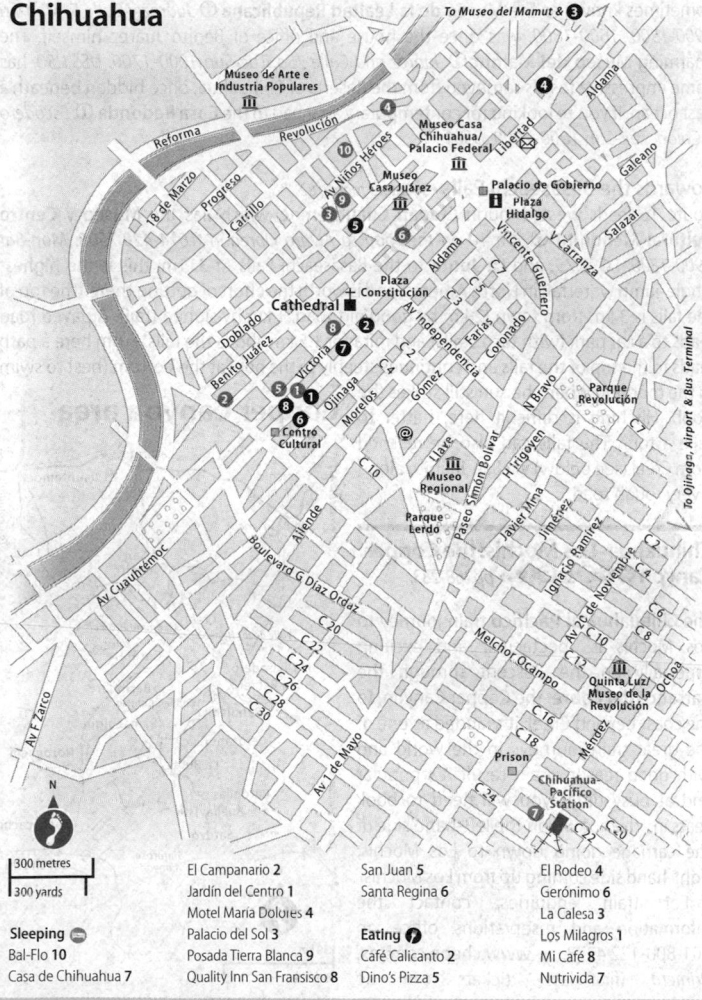

El Campanario **2**	San Juan **5**	El Rodeo **4**
Jardín del Centro **1**	Santa Regina **6**	Gerónimo **6**
Motel María Dolores **4**		La Calesa **3**
Palacio del Sol **3**	**Eating ⑦**	Los Milagros **1**
Sleeping ⚇	Posada Tierra Blanca **9**	Café Calicanto **2**	Mi Café **8**
Bal-Flo **10**	Quality Inn San Fransisco **8**	Dino's Pizza **5**	Nutrivida **7**
Casa de Chihuahua **7**			

The **Quinta Luz** (1914), where Pancho Villa lived, now the **Museo de la Revolución** ① *Calle 10 No 3014, Tue-Sat 0900-1900, Sun 0900-1600, US$0.70*, is well worth a visit, with many old photographs, the car in which Villa was assassinated (looking like a Swiss cheese from all the bullet holes), his death mask and postcards of the assassinated leader. The **Museo Regional** ① *Bolívar 401, Tue-Sun 1100-1400, 1600-1900, US$1.50*, in the former mansion Quinta Gameros, has interesting exhibits and extremely fine art nouveau rooms, an exhibition of Paquimé ceramics, and temporary exhibitions. The **Museo de Arte e Industria Populares** ① *Av Reforma 5, Tue-Sat 0900-1300, 1600-1900, free*, has displays Tarahumara art and lifestyle as well as shops. The **Museo Casa Juárez**, sometimes known as the **Museo de la Lealtad Republicana** ① *Juárez y Calle 5, Mon-Fri 0900-1500, 1600-1800*, was once the house and office of Benito Juárez himself. The charming **Museo del Mamut** ① *Juárez and Calle 25a, Tue-Sun 1000-1700, US$1.50*, has some impressive fossils retrieved from the deserts of Chihuahua, once hidden beneath a vast ocean. If you're looking for contemporary art, head to the **Casa Redonda** ① *Escodero y Colón, Tue-Sun 1000-2000, US$1*.

Towards the Basaseachi Falls → *Colour map 2, B2.*
Route 16 leads west through **Ciudad Cuauhtémoc**, which has the **Museo y Centro Cultural Menonita** ① *Km 10 on the road to Alvaro Obregón, T614-428 7508, Mon-Sat 0900-1800, US$1.75*, and **La Junta** to the Basaseachi Falls At 311m, this is the highest single-jump waterfall in North America and is worth the effort of getting there. The top of the falls is 3 km from town (2 km by good dirt road, 1 km by signed trail). A paved road leads to a car park (with taco stalls) and mirador 1.5 km above the falls. From here a path leads to the top of the falls and continues steeply to the pool at the bottom (best to swim in the morning when the sun still strikes the pool). Hitching is difficult here; better to take a tour. The falls can also be reached from Creel (see below) via San Juanito along a very rough road.

Chihuahua–Los Mochis: the Copper Canyon ⊖❶❷❸▲❶❶ » *pp268-283.*

The **Chihuahua al Pacífico** train journey to Los Mochis is spectacular and exciting especially on the descent through the **Barranca del Cobre**, the Copper Canyon, to the coast beyond Creel: it's lauded as one of the great train journeys in the world and with good reason. As a result it's popular and at busy times you will need to book seats in advance. Sit on the left-hand side of the carriage going down to Los Mochis; right-hand side coming up from Los Mochis.

For train enquiries, contact the information and reservations office on T01-800-122 4373, www.chepe.com.mx. *Primera* (first-class) tickets can be

Copper Canyon area

30 km
30 miles

pre-booked at travel agents in Chihuahua, Los Mochis (see page 237) and some stations along the way. The schedule is an approximation of intent, but check details as they are subject to change. On average trains are about one hour late by the time they arrive in Los Mochis and are rarely (if ever) on schedule to meet the La Paz ferry. Bring your own drinking water and toilet paper. Do not take large amounts of cash or jewellery, there can be security problems on the railway.

A second-class train (*mixto* or *clase económica*) also runs but travelling on it is much more difficult. You can only buy tickets in person; they are sold once the first train has left or passed through; the train leaves in theory about one hour after the first-class train and the timetable is quintessentially latino – the train may be along today. Or it may be along tomorrow. It's really only worth taking the second-class heading west to east; if you travel east to west, it's likely to be dark by the time you reach the best sections. Prices are roughly half that of the first-class train.

The most interesting part of the journey is between Creel and Los Mochis. If wishing to see the best scenery, there is little point in taking the train Chihuahua-Creel-Chihuahua (on this stretch, the cheaper train is just as good as the *Primera Especial*). If planning to spend a few days in Creel, there are frequent buses Chihuahua-Creel. Delays are possible in the rainy season.

West of Chihuahua are high, windy and sparsely populated plains. From Chihuahua, the railway and road (Route 16, *cuota* and *libre* after Km 45; the latter is good) cross the Sierra of the **Tarahumara** people, who call themselves the **Rarámuri** ('those who run fast'). They were originally cave-dwellers and nomads, but now work as labourers in the logging stations and have settled around the mission churches built by the Spanish in the 17th century.

Creel

To Chihuahua

Av Tarahumara

Noreste — Misión Tarahumara

Estrella Blanca

E Zapata

Francisco Villa

To San Juanito, Cristo Rey, San Rafael, Divisadero, Cusárare & Lag.nc Arareco

Town Map

Parroquia

Main Plaza

E Creel

Presidencia Municipal

Av López Mateos

Oscar Flores

Elfido Batista Caro

Amigos Canyon Expeditions

To Cerro Chepultepec

To Divisadero & Los Mochis

Av Cuesta

Comercial de Creel Supermarket

To ⑨⑩⑪ & Cusárare

N

50 metres
50 yards

Sleeping
Bertis 12
Casa de Huéspedes
 Margarita 1
Cascada Inn 7
Korachi 5
Lodge at Creel 3

Los Valles 6
Margarita's Plaza
 Mexicana 2
Parador La Montaña 4
Posada de Creel 8
Quinto Misión 9
Sierra Bonita 10
Villa Mexicana 11

Eating
Mi Café 1
Pizza del Rey 3
Tío Molcas 4
Verónica 2

Creel and around → Phone code: 635.

Colour map 2, B2. Altitude: 2356 m.

Creel is the commercial centre of the Tarahumara region and is named after Enrique Creel (1854-1931), economist and entrepreneur, and governor of Chihuahua state in 1907. He initiated the building of the railway and planned to improve the Tarahumara's lives by establishing a colony here. Increasingly, tourism is growing dominate this sleepy, pine-scented mountain town, the starting point for most planned forays into the wilderness, including the Barranca del Urique and the Barranca del Cobre. This is also the place to take an unforgettable bus ride to the even sleepier village of Batopilas.

In lieu of an official tourist office, good maps and information are available from **Three Amigos Canyon expeditions** ① *López Mateos 46, T635-456 0179, www.amigos3.com, 0900-1900*. This is the most helpful and professional outfit in Creel, and can help arrange everything from bike tours to truck rentals.

There's not much to actually do in town, but it's worth checking out the **Museo de la Casa Artesanías** ① *opposite the plaza, Mon-Sat 0900-1800, Sun 0900-1300, US$1*, which has interesting exhibitions on Rarámuri culture. Several good hikes can be had in the **San Ignacio ejido**, a land-owning cooperative just outside town. The **San Ignacio mission**, a series of eerie rock formations and serene **Lake Arareco** are among the attractions, all easily reached independently. **Recohuata hot springs** is 22 km south of town, for which you'll need a bike or a horse, and some degree of physical fitness.

Cusárare → *Colour map 2, B2.*
Twenty kilometres south of Laguna Arareco, is Cusárare (place of the eagles), with a **Jesuit church** ① *US$1*, dating back to 1767 and painted by indigenous craftsmen. To get to the 30-m waterfall, continue 100 m after the junction to Cusárare where there is a hotel sign on the right; turn right, pass the hotel and then the bridge, at the junction turn right; it's about 45 minutes' walk and is not well-signposted. The falls are at their best from July to September. There is very good hiking around Cusárare, but a guide may be necessary (Sr Reyes Ramírez and his son have been recommended for tours to the canyon). Allow four days to see the canyon properly, as hiking is tough. The canyon is hot by day and cold by night. The American guide Cristóbal, at **Margarita's**, has also been recommended.

Guachochi → *Phone code: 649. Colour map 2, B2.*
Guachochi, 156 km south of Creel, has a Wild West appearance. Fresh trout is the local speciality, which you should endeavour to try. There is a bank. From Guachochi you can walk four hours to the impressive **Barranca de Sinforosa**, widely regarded as the most beautiful of all the region's canyons. It's not actually visible until you reach the edge. From a point several hundred metres above the Río Verde you can see an unforgettable extended system of immense canyons, grander (according to some) than the view you can see from El Divisadero or on crossing the Barranca del Cobre. There's a path down to the river.

Barranca del Urique/Copper Canyon → *Colour map 2, B2.*
The road south out of Cusárare leads eventually to Batópilas, passing a turn-off to El Tejabán above the Barranca del Urique/Cobre (this is claimed to be the 'real' Copper Canyon); **Basíhuare** ('Sash') village, surrounded by pink and white rock formations (40 km from Creel); and the **Puente del Río Urique**, spanning the Urique Canyon. The climate is ideal for camping. At the junction Creel-Guachochi-Bufa, near Samachique, is a small restaurant/ hotel, **La Casita (F)**, which is very primitive and romantic. The road is paved as far as the junction but is bumpy from then on. Just after the junction, 3 km down into the valley is **Samachique**, where the *rari-pame* race, kicking a wooden ball for 241 km without rest, often takes two or three days and nights in September. Stranded travellers can find a room and food at the bus stop (no more than a shack) in Samachique, which is

Batópilas to Urique

A three-day hike goes from the Batópilas Canyon to Urique (once known as the Camino Real), from where you can get a ride to Bahuichivo for a train to Creel or Los Mochis (colour map2, B2).

Routes Batópilas–Cerro Colorado–Piedra Redonda–Cerro El Manzano–La Estación–Los Alisos–Urique. You climb from 500 m, reaching 2200 m before descending to Urique at 600 m. It can be very hot in the canyons; drink at least four litres of water a day (you can fill up at settlements along the way) and take plenty of sunblock. There are many junctions of paths and so if you are without a guide it is vital to check that you are on the correct route as often as possible (try not to wander into marijuana plantations). One recommendation if you are using the 'Batópilas' survey map (1:50,000 sheet G13A41, covering the entire route, available from the Misión Tarahumara in Creel US$5) is that you take the ridge path (not marked on the 1979 edition) after Cerro El Manzano to La Estación, both for the views and directness.

Horse riding A recommended guide (not cheap) is Librado Balderrama Contreras who will guide you to Urique or to surrounding attractions such as Mesa Quimoba, Mesa de San José and Monerachi. There are several places in town where you can hire mules (with a handler) for carrying gear.

1 km off the main route to Batópilas (1330 bus from Guachochi arrives at 1500 after the Creel bus has gone through). If wishing to hitch to Batópilas (2½-hour drive) take the right fork as you walk back out of Samachique; it rejoins the route at a junction where you can wait for traffic both coming through and by-passing the village. **Quírare**, 65 km from Creel, offers views of the beautiful Batópilas Canyon. After Quírare there is an awesome 14-km descent to **La Bufa**, in the Batópilas canyon, and on to Batópilas, possibly the most scenic road in northern Mexico.

Batópilas and around

Batópilas, 120 km from Creel, is a delightful little palm-fringed town of 1100 inhabitants hemmed in by the swirling river and the cactus-studded canyon walls. It is an excellent centre for walking and within easy reach of the Urique Canyon (see box, above). The **Mina de Guadalupe** was discovered in 1780 by Pedro de la Cruz. Batópilas became a thriving silver-mining centre, with mines owned by the Shepard family. Their mansion (near the bridge), abandoned during Pancho Villa's campaign, must be one of the most elaborate adobe houses anywhere, but it is now overgrown and dilapidated.

The **Porfirio Díaz Mine** above the bridge into town can be explored to about 3 km into the mountain (take torch); as you get into the mine there is the sickly, sweet smell of bat droppings, after about 1 km the air is thick with disturbed bats. There is a Jesuit mission at **Satevo**, a 7-km walk from Batópilas along the river.

Towards Divisadero → Colour map 2, B2.

Beyond Creel, the Chihuahua al Pacífico train passes its highest point, **Los Ojitos** and, soon after, the **Lazo loop**, in which the track does a 360° turn. At Divisadero there is a too brief 20-minute stop to view the canyon and buy souvenirs from the Tarahumara women. Five minutes further on, the train comes to **Hotel Posada Barrancas**. See page 258 for schedule.

For those who aren't travelling on the train the Barranca de Urique/Cobre (Urique/Copper Canyon) is quite a long way from Creel. Apart from the access from Batópilas (see box, page 263), or from Bahuichivo (see below), the simplest way to see the canyon is to take a bus or hitch to Divisadero or **Posada Barrancas** on the rough road, paved halfway from Creel, or else take the train.

The **Balancing Rock** is at the edge of the canyon; it wobbles in a stomach-churning way as you stand on it. Reached by *camioneta* from **Hotel Divisadero Barrancas**, or walk 1-2 km from Divisadero (away from Creel) and on the left you will see the wooden entrance gate. From there it is 45 minutes to the rock with stops at the canyon viewing points. The canyon can also be reached on foot from Divisadero or **Posada Barrancas**; from the former it is 6 km (walk or hitch) along the dirt road that runs beside the railway to the house of Florencio Manzinas (at the first group of houses you come to). From there it's a day's hike along narrow, slippery, often steep and sometimes overgrown trails into the canyon, descending from cool pine forest into gradually more subtropical vegetation as you approach the river and the canyon floor. Take plenty of water for the hike as, after descending the first section following a stream, you have to go over another hill before getting down to the river, which means several hours without access to water.

Divisadero to Bahuichivo → *Colour map 2, B2.*
Twenty-five minutes beyond the **Hotel Posada Barrancas** the **Chihuahua al Pacífico** reaches **San Rafael**, where there is a 10-minute stop, and then passes the **La Laja** bridge and tunnel. It is a further 20 minutes to **Cuiteco**. Next on the line comes Bahuichivo; if you don't want to go all the way to Los Mochis you can return from here. From Bahuichivo to Los Mochis is five hours on the train.

Urique → *Phone code: 635. Colour map 2, B2.*
From Bahuichivo, bus and pickups make the five-hour journey to Urique, in the heart of the Barranca de Urique. At the lip of the canyon is a mirador offering fine views. The road into the canyon is spectacular, only rivalled by the road to Batópilas.

Témoris → *Phone code: 635.*
Near Témoris, the train track enters a tunnel in which the railway turns through 180°. Témoris, an attractive town 11 km above the train station, in the mining and cattle country of the lower western Sierra Madre, is a good base for visiting working ranches, Tarahumara villages, waterfalls and swimming holes, on foot, horse or mountain bike. *Colectivos* make the trip or you may be able to hitch with local merchants. There are three hotels in the area and several cheap restaurants.

El Fuerte → *Phone code: 698. Colour map 2, B1.*
El Fuerte is the more atmospheric gateway to the Copper Canyon – wonderfully tranquil and rich in colonial architecture, and far more enticing than Los Mochis. Founded on the verdant banks of the Río Fuerte in 1564, it's located 1½ hours by train from Los Mochis (also accessible by bus, two hours) and is a destination in its own right. The station is 10 km from town, taxis cost around US$6.

Aside from strolling the attractive streets, it's particularly worth visiting the **El Fuerte Mirador Museum** ① *Tue-Sun 0900-1700, US$0.50*, housed in the town's old fort that was designed to withstand attacks from local tribes. The views are commanding. Birdwatching is possible here, with over 150 species, best encountered by river boat in the early morning. You can also visit local petroglyphs and the **Mayo Indigenous Mission**. For information, contact **El Fuerte Eco-Adventures** ① *Posada del Hidalgo, www.hotelposadadelhIdalgo.com*.

For those travelling on the train, the high, long bridge over the Río Fuerte heralds the beginning of more interesting scenery (this is the first of 37 major bridges); three hours from Los Mochis the first, and longest, of the 86 tunnels is passed, then, 10 minutes later, the **Chinapas bridge** (this is approximately the Sinaloa/Chihuahua state border, where clocks go forward an hour).

South from Chihuahua ⬤⬤ » pp268-283.

Ciudad Delicias to Zacatecas → *Phone code: 639. Colour map 2, B3-C4.*
At Ciudad Delicias, the first major town southeast of Chihuahua on Route 45, Ciudad Delicias, there is a **Museo de Paleontología** ① *Av Río Chuvíscar Norte y Círculo de la Plaza de la República, T639-472 8513, Mon-Sat 0900-2000*, with fossils from the Zona de Silencio (see below) and from the inland sea that covered the area 80 million years ago.

Further south is **Ciudad Camargo** (phone code: 648), famous for its eight days of **Fiesta de Santa Rosalía** beginning on 4 September, when there are cockfights, horse racing and dancing.

From **Ciudad Jiménez** (1263 km from Mexico City) there are two routes south to Fresnillo and Zacatecas: the Central Highway through Durango, or a more direct route via Torreón (237 km from Ciudad Jiménez), passing Escalón, **Ceballos**, **Yermo** and **Bermejillo**, on Route 49.

Between Escalón and Ceballos is the **Zona del Silencio** (the Silent Zone), a highly magnetic area where, it is claimed, electrical appliances fall silent, aircraft radar goes haywire, and so on. It inspires much interest and research.

Between Gómez Palacio and Zacatecas are **Cuéncame**, **Río Grande** and **Fresnillo**. This last town is the birthplace of the artist Francisco Goitia and musician Manuel M Ponce.

Hidalgo del Parral ⬤⬤⬤⬤ » pp268-283. Colour map 2, B3.

→ *Phone code: 627.*
Connecting to the north through Ciudad Jiménez (77 km), Hidalgo del Parral (often known just as Parral), is an old mining town with narrow streets. In 1629, Juan Rangel de Viezma discovered La Negrita, the first mine in the area. Now known as La Prieta, it overlooks the city from the top of Cerro la Prieta. Rangel founded the town in 1631 under the name of San Juan del Parral. The mine owners were generous benefactors to the city, leaving many beautiful buildings that still stand. On 8 September 1944, severe damage was caused by a flood. The decrease in population, either through drowning or flight, led to a recession. Hidalgo del Parral is a pleasant, safe, affluent city with a compact centre with a string of shaded plazas, many bridges over the sinuous, and often dry, Río del Parral, and several churches. The city's history is split between its mining heritage and the fact that Pancha Villas was assasinated here. You'll find a modest tourist information module on the main plaza, www.hdelparral.gob.mx.

Sights
On the Plaza Principal is the **Parroquia de San José**, with a beautiful interior. Plaza Baca has a statue to *El Buscador de Ilusiones* (the Dream Seeker), a naked man panning for gold.

The assassination of Pancho Villa

The infamous assassination of Pancho Villa took place in the centre of Hidalgo del Parral on 20 July 1923. Villa owned a house on Calle Zaragoza (now a shop called Almacenes Real de Villa, painted bright pink) and was making his way from there to the Hotel Hidalgo, which he also owned, when he was ambushed on Avenida Juárez. The house chosen by the assassins is now the **Museo Pancho Villa** (Monday-Friday 0900-2000, Saturday 0900-1300.) Twelve of the 100 bullets fired hit Villa, who was taken immediately to the Hotel Hidalgo. The death mask taken there can be seen in the museum and also in the museum in Chihuahua. His funeral took place the next day and he was buried in the Panteón Municipal; his tomb is still there even though the body has been transferred to Mexico City.

The **cathedral** is on this square and, on the opposite side, is the **Templo San Juan de Dios** with an exuberant altarpiece, painted gold. Across the road from the cathedral is the former **Hotel Hidalgo** (not in use), built in 1905 by mine owner Pedro Alvarado and given to Pancho Villa in the 1920s. Next door is **Casa Stallforth** (1908), the shop and house of a German family who supplied everything imaginable to the city. It is still a shop, with the original interior. Continuing on Mercaderes, before the bridge, is **Casa Griensen**, now the **Colegio Angloamericano Isaac Newton**. Griensen, another German, married Alvarado's sister. Behind this house is **Palacio Pedro Alvarado** ① *1000-1800, US$1.45*, Alvarado's colonial mansion, recently restored and containing his personal effects. The building hides some tragic stories and sensitive souls might sense a melancholy presence in the bedroom. Crossing the bridge at the end of Mercaderes, you come to the site of Villa's death, on the corner of Plaza Juárez, where you'll find a museum commemorating the great 'Centaur of the North', **Museo Fransisco Villa** ① *Juárez and Barreda, Tue-Sun 1000-1700, US$0.70*. Overlooking the town is the old mine, **La Prieta** ① *Tue-Sun 1000-1700, US$1.80*, which is part ruin, part mining museum.

Around Hidalgo del Parral

Twenty-six kilometres east of Parral on the Jiménez road, a well-signed road leads 5 km south to **Valle de Allende**. Originally called Valle de San Bartolomé, it was the site of the first **Franciscan mission** in Chihuahua, founded in the late 16th century by Fray Agustín Rodríguez. The original monastery building still stands on the main square, but it is unused (it has been used as a *refrigeradora* to store apples).

Hidalgo del Parral to Durango

Route 45 is in good condition all the way to Durango. At **Villa de Nieve**, 3 km down a winding road, well signed, is Pancho Villa's hacienda, with an excellent **museum** ① *give a donation to the man who opens the door*. Villa was given the hacienda in exchange for promising to lay down his arms and retire to private life (28 July 1920).

Cinema enthusiasts can visit the Western sets of **Villa del Oeste** ① *9 km from Durango, T618-112 2882, www.villadeloeste.com, Tue-Fri 1200-1900, Sat-Sun 1100-1900*, and **Chupaderos** (14 km). The former is a small theme park that lays on cheesy cowboy shows; the latter is abandoned and dilapidated but at least smells authentically of horse manure. San Juan del Río buses go there or take a taxi, US$14; 4 km east off the road, at San Juan del Río, is a Pemex station. Halfway down the side road to San Juan is a signed road to **Coyotada**, off which is a 4-km road to **Pancho Villa's birthplace and museum** ① *free, donation welcome*, which is modest, with a few artefacts and photos.

Santiago Papasquiaro is three hours north of Durango on Route 23. On the way, In Canatlán, are Mennonite colonies. There are a number of hot springs in the area; **Hervideros** is the most popular, take the bus to Herreras, then it's a 30-minute walk. **Tepehuanes**, one hour further on, is a small pleasant town with a couple of hotels. Walk to Purísima and then to a small, spectacular canyon. A dirt road continues to **Guanacevi**, a mining town in the Sierra.

Seven kilometres north of the Durango road, 12 km before Sombrerete, is the **Sierra de los Organos** (Valley of the Giants), now a national park, where John Wayne made several of his westerns. It is named after the basalt columns, which are supposed to resemble organ pipes.

Durango ⊖🟡🛆🖐️🟢🟢 ►► pp268-283. Colour map 2, C3.

→ *Phone code 618. Altitude: 1924 m.*

Victoria de Durango, capital of Durango state was founded in 1563. It is a modernizing city but with many beautiful old buildings, including the 18th-century **Casa de los Condes de Suchill**, now Bancomer, on 5 de Febrero, and the French-style Teatro Ricardo Castro, with wonderfully calming murals in the auditorium, a cathedral (1695) and a famous iron-water spring.

The town is all pretty much within a couple of blocks of the main plaza. The main street is Avenida 20 de Noviembre, a wide dominating thoroughfare that reflects the 'Wild West' image of the State of Durango, so often a backdrop to not only Hollywood movies but also the Mexican film industry at its height. Lest you think the city rests on the laurels that

Durango

100 metres / 100 yards

Sleeping ⊖
California 2
Casablanca 1
Florida Plaza 3
Gallo 7
Hostel de la Monja 8
Plaza Catedral 4
Posada San Jorge 5
Reforma 6
Rincón Real 9
Roma 10

Eating 🟡
Corleone's Pizza 1
El Paraíso Michoacano 4
El Zocabón 5
Gorditas Gabino 5
Fonda de la Tía Chonda 3
La Esquina de Café 8
La Fogata 9
La Tostada 10

Los Esquipules 11
Los Farolitos 7
Los Quatros Vientos 12
Pizzaly 13
Quattros Grados 14
Samadhi 2

Bars & clubs 🟢
La Malquerida 15

made such classics as *The Wild Bunch* by Sam Peckinpah (1968), more recent films include The *Mask of Zorro I* (1998) and *Bandidas* (2006). The **tourist office** ① *Florida 1106, T618-811 2139, www.vistadurango.com.mx*, is helpful and friendly and has a supply of good new promotional materials.

Sights

Durango is home to several museums that you'll need a couple of days to fully appreciate. The **Museo Regional de Durango** ① *Victoria 100, T618-812 5605, Tue-Sun 0900-1600, Sun 1000-1500, US$0.70*, is devoted to the historical development of Durango with fourteen galleries, temporary exhibits and a library. The building dates from the 19th century when the vogue was for all things European. The **Museo de Arqueología de Durango Garnot-Peschard** ① *Zaragoza 315 Sur, Tue-Fri 1000-1830, Sat-Sun 1100-1800, US$0.35*, contains interesting archaeological finds belonging to Durango's northern cultures. The **Museo de Las Culturas Populares** ① *5 de Febrero 1107, Tue-Fri 0900-1800, Sat-Sun 1200-1800, US$0.35*, is a small but compelling museum dedicated to local indigenous groups. The **Instituto de Cultura del Estado de Durango (ICED)** ① *16 de Septiembre 130, T618-128 6008, www.iced.gob.mx, Tue-Fri 0900-1800, Sat-Sun 1000-1800*, is a newly opened complex of several modest cultural museums. They include the **Museo de Cine Rafael Trujillo**, with memorabilia and old film equipment commemorating Durango's golden age as a centre for cinematic productions; the rather obscure **Museo de la Revolucion 'General Domino Arrieta'**, with personal effects, old weapons and historical displays relating to the General; the **Museo de Arqueología**, with an array of archaeological finds; and the **Pinacoteca del Estado**, containing historic art works. There is a nominal charge to enter each one.

◉ Northern Highlands listings

For Sleeping and Eating price codes and other relevant information, see Essentials pages 45-48.

● Sleeping

Ciudad Juárez *p253, map p254*
AL-B Holiday Inn Express, Paseo Triunfo de la República 3745, T656-629 6000, www.ichotelsgroup.com/h/d/ex/1/en/ hotel/juaex. Reliable Holiday Inn quality. Comfortable, generic rooms are equipped with satellite TV, internet, coffee-makers and other gadgets. Pool and restaurant are among the amenities. Best rates online.
B Hotel Santa Fé, Lerdo 675, T656-615 1558, www.hotel-santafe-juarez.com. A large, modern hotel with 76 good comfortable rooms, all with a/c and satellite TV. Private parking, restaurant and bar are among the amenities. Recommended.

C Hotel D'Manely, Blv Oscar Flores 4431, T656-610 7330, close to bus station. Go out of the west (taxi) entrance, walk straight across the parking lot to the street, cross the street, and walk left 2 blocks. Rooms have heating and private bath. Clean, but the atmosphere is slightly sketchy and depressing. Good if you need an early morning bus though.
C Hotel Impala, Lerdo 670 Norte, T656-615 0431, www.hotel-impala.com. This hotel, close to the bridge, has 56 straightforward rooms with a/c, heating, carpet, TV, phone and hot water. Enclosed parking available. Helpful.
C Hotel Imperial, Guerrero 206, T615-0323. At the bustling heart of downtown, a big hotel with straightforward rooms, all with phone, TV and a/c. Not as attractive as some other lodgings in this price bracket.
C Plaza Continental, Lerdo Sur 112, T656-615 0259. Clean and comfortable hotel

with 65 rooms, all equipped with cable TV and a/c. Other services include late night restaurant, Wi-Fi parking and bar.
D Hotel Moran, Juárez 264 Norte, T656-0862. On the main drag, close to the bars and restaurants, with basic, clean rooms for those on a budget.

El Paso (Texas)
A-D El Paso International Hostel, 311 East Franklin Av, T656-532 3661, www.elpasohostel.com. Also known as the Gardner hotel, this El Paso institution has been serving travellers since the 1920s. They have dorm accommodation (**D**), common room, coffee, internet, hot water and TV. They have some private rooms also, with (**A**) or without bath (**B**).
B International Hotel, Oregon. Clean rooms with a/c and TV. Recommended.

Ojinaga p254
C Armendariz, Zaragoza 713, near the zócalo, T626-453 1198. Clean rooms and safe parking.

Palomas p256
C Hotel Restaurant San Francisco. Reasonable accommodation.
D Motel Santa Cruz, behind seafood restaurant, opposite gas station. Fairly basic with prices to match.

Columbus (New Mexico)
B Martha's Place, Main Stand Lima St, T505-531 2467, marthas@vtc.net. It has a very attractive lobby and a pleasant breakfast area.
B Suncrest Inn, Hwy 11, just north of Hwy 9. TV and phones in rooms.
Camping Pancho Villa State Park, opposite the Columbus Historical Museum, Excellent, well-maintained sites, additional charge for electrical hook-up.

Agua Prieta p256
B Motel Arizona, Av 6 between Calle 17 and 18, T633-338 2522. Pleasant place. Rooms have heating.

B Motel La Hacienda, Calle Primera and Av 6, T633-338 0621, a few blocks from the border. The best in town.

Douglas (Arizona)
AL-B Gadsden Hotel, 1046 G Av, T520-364 4481, www.hotelgadsden.com. A registered historical landmark used as a location for Western films. Fabulous lobby, completely unexpected to find such a place in a border town. Recommended.
Camping RV parks on the Arizona side charge about US$10 per night for vehicle, US$5 for tent camping: **Double Adobe Trailer Park** off Hwy 80; **Copper Horse Shoe RV Park** on Hwy 666.

Naco
C Motel Colonial The only formal accommodation, often full, but the manager may tolerate a night's auto camping within the motel compound.

Casas Grandes (Paquimé) p256
A Las Guacamayas, 20 de Nov y Zona Arqueologica 1101, T636-692 4144, www.mataortizollas.com. An adobe-style B&B, located right next to the archaeological site. Interesting and comfortable, with traditional rooms, hammocks, wood beams, flowers and tiled floors. Peaceful and hospitable. Breakfast included.
B Paquimé, Av Benito Juárez 401, T636-694 4720, paquime_hotel@hotmail.com. Large, clean rooms with cable TV, fan or a/c.
B Piñon, Av Juárez 605, T636-694 0655, hotelpinon@prodigy.net.mx. Pleasant, friendly hotel with comfortable rooms, pool, and a selection of Paquimé pottery. Tours of the ruins occasionally offered. Recommended.
D Juárez, Obregón 110, T636-694 0233. The only budget lodgings in town. Rooms cheap and relatively nasty. At least the management is friendly and English-speaking.

Madera p257
B María, Calle 5 y 5 de Mayo. Clean rooms have heating, some cheap ones available.

Limited parking. Restaurant open 24 hrs. Good.
E Motel Maras, Calle 5, 1 block south of Mirmay. Noisy, dusty, but otherwise clean rooms with hot water.

Chihuahua *p258, map p259*
Lodgings in Chihuahua are comfortable, but not great value. The cheaper hotels are on Juárez and its cross-streets; the cheapest (and nastiest) are behind the cathedral.
AL Palacio del Sol, Independencia 116, T614-412 3456, www.hotelpalaciodelsol.com. High-rise hotel with views over the city. Rooms and suites are predictably comfortable, cable TV, telephone and gadgetry. Facilities include Wi-Fi, 2 restaurants, gym, bar and 7 events rooms. Group discounts sometimes available.
A-B Posada Tierra Blanca, Niños Héroes 102, T614-415 0000, www.posadatierra blanca.com.mx. Large motel-style lodgings with lots of balconies and 94 clean, carpeted rooms, all equipped with cable TV, heating and a/c. There's also a gym, pool, restaurant, Wi-Fi, bar and events room. Check out the interesting mural with esoteric themes.
A-B Quality Inn San Francisco, Victoria 409, T614-415 3538, www.qualityinn chihuahua.com. A very comfortable hotel with pleasant rooms and suites. A plethora of amenities including gym, café and executive centre. Good service, and centrally located close to the cathedral.
B Bal-Flo, Niños Héroes y 5a, T614-201 4571, www.hotelbalflo.com. Clean, comfortable rooms with a/c, telephone, heating and satellite TV. The carpets could use a bit of a scrub, but otherwise not bad. Internet available.
B El Campanario, Blv Díaz Ordaz 1405, southwest of cathedral, T614-415 4979. Good clean mid-range option. Rooms have cable TV, heating and a/c. Wi-Fi and restaurant among the amenities. Recommended.
B-D Santa Regina, C3 No 102, www.hotel elsantaregina.com This hotel has 2 sections: economical (**D**) and standard (**B**). Rooms are

comfortable enough, if uninspiring, with cable TV, a/c and phone. There's also private parking and a daily buffet breakfast.
C Motel Maria Dolores, 9a No 30, T614-410 4770, motelmadol@hotmail.com. Motel-style place with small but immaculately clean rooms, quite new and tiled. Services include cable TV, hot water, coffee, Wi-Fi, drinking water and parking. Good value and recommended.
C-D Jardín del Centro, Victoria 818, T614-415 1832. Clean, comfortable, modern rooms with heating and a/c, all overlooking a pleasant, plant-filled courtyard where lots of little birds are jumping around (some of them are in cages though). For those on a budget, there's also slightly cheaper, less attractive quarters (**D**), many with colonial-style high ceilings. Economical restaurant attached. Recommended.
C-E Casa de Chihuahua, www.casade chihuahua.com. A clean, pleasant hostel conveniently located opposite the train station. They have a mixture of dormitory accommodation (**D**) and private rooms (**C**), all with shared bath. Facilities include giant DVD screen and tourist information. Discount for students.
D-E San Juan, Victoria 823, T614-410 0035. An old, dark, gloomy colonial house. Some rooms are nicer and newer than others. Some are in a state of neglect (**F**). Services include Wi-Fi, cable TV, phone, bath and hot water. A backpacker haunt, but not terribly friendly and truthfully, a bit of a dump.

Creel *p261, map p261*
You'll need to make reservations in advance during high season. As Creel's popularity is increasing, hotel prices are inflating.
LL-A Sierra Bonita, Gran Visión s/n, T635-456 0615, www.sierrabonita.com. A way out of town with a great hill-top location, this hotel has a mixture of comfortable cabins (**LL-L**) and cosy rooms (**A**). There's a restaurant, bar and disco on-site, as well as a pair of caged Bengal tigers, reportedly.

AL Quinta Mision, López Mateos, T635-456 0021, www.quintamision.com. Newly opened luxury lodgings with 10 tastefully attired suites. All are equipped with flat screen TVs, heating, soft duvets, terraces, fridges, microwaves, elegant furniture and wooden beams. Some have a separate childrens' room with bunk beds. Recommended.

AL Villa Mexicana, López Mateos s/n, T635-456 0665, www.vmcoppercanyon.com. Luxury log cabins and suites with flat screen TVs, satellite and heating. They have a good international restaurant, bar, Wi-Fi and laundry facilities. RV hook-up for trailers. A 20-min walk out of town, although transport is provided.

AL-A The Lodge at Creel, Av López Mateos 61, about 1 km from the plaza and railway station, T635-456 0071, www.thelodgeat creel.com. Owned by Best Western and one of the most luxurious places in town. Wooden, cabin-style rooms, spa facilities and an excellent restaurant.

A Parador La Montaña, Av López Mateos 44, T635-456 0023, www.hotelparadorcreel.com. A very comfortable, tasteful hotel with big rooms and fireplaces. There's also a good restaurant, bar, Wi-Fi and childrens' play area.

A-B Cascada Inn, López Mateos 49, T635-456 0253, www.motelcascadainn.com. This hotel has 30 clean, comfortable rooms with 2 beds each, TV, heating and 24-hr hot water. There's a restaurant serving international and Mexican food, an indoor pool, 2 events rooms and parking. Friendly and English speaking, but a little overpriced.

B Margarita's Plaza Mexicana, Elfida Batista Caro, off López Mateos, T635-456 0245, www.hoteles-margaritas.com. Part of Margarita's hotel empire, which extends to Batopilas and Cerocahui. Plaza Mexicana is a comfortable hotel with pleasant, colourful rooms and lots of murals. Some rooms have been recently remodelled with big bath tubs, great for a soak after a long day hiking. There are also 2 suites with cooking facilities, large enough for 6 persons. Services include Wi-Fi, tours and information, and a simple breakfast and dinner is included in the price.

C Korachi, Francisco Villa 116, T635-456 0064. Right beside the station, with small, spartan, but comfortable rooms. The rustic cabins outside are much better.

C Los Valles, Elfido Batista Caro s/n, next to Margarita's Plaza Mexicana, T635-456 0092. A motel-style place with parking, restaurant, and pokey, clean, unremarkable rooms; all have heating, private bath and TV. Reasonable value, although rates might vary. The office is in their restaurant at the corner of Elfido Batista and López Mateos.

C-D Hotel Bertis, López Mateos 31, T635-456 0287. A bit shabby on the outside, but rooms are clean and comfortable, some with chimney, all with TV, writing desk, heating and bath. Simple and reasonable. Parking.

C-F Casa de Huéspedes Margarita, López Mateos 11, T635-456 0045. Popular backpacker joint that's packed in high season. A mix of dorms (**E**), mattresses (**F**) and more expensive double rooms (**C**). Lots of services, including bike rental, tours, laundry, Wi-Fi, hiking orientation, free maps and water refills. Breakfast and dinner included. Margarita's reps meet arriving train passengers and can be quite pushy. Book in advance in high season.

D-E Posada de Creel, Ferrocarril s/n. A low-key hostel with dorms (**E**) and economical private rooms (**D**), tours and vouchers for food. An alternative to the long-reigning Margarita.

Camping

Villa Mexicana, López Mateos s/n, T635-456 0665, www.vmcoppercanyon.com. Full RV hook-up for US$20. They also have luxury cabins (see above) and a restaurant on site.

Sierra Bonita, Gran Visión s/n, T635-456 0615, www.sierrabonita.com. Full RV hook-up May-Oct, as well as rooms and cabins (see Sleeping, above).

Guachochi *p262*

B Melina, Belisario Domínguez 14, 1649-543 0255. Clean and comfortable rooms with hot water. Adjoining restaurant.

C Chaparro, Francisco Villa 1, T649-543 0004. Cosy, but overpriced rooms, with cable TV and hot water. Good restaurant attached.
D Hotel Mansion, 20 de Noviembre 14, T649-543 0089. A good budget choice, with clean, straightforward rooms.

Copper Canyon *p262*
E La Casita, at the junction Creel-Guachochi-Bufa, near Samachique. A small restaurant/hotel, very primitive and romantic.

Batópilas *p263*
AL-A Copper Canyon Riverside, T800-648 8488, www.coppercanyonlodges.com. The Copper Canyon Riverside is open irregularly. It is also so exclusive that it won't open its doors to passersby, let alone travel writers. Rooms are beautifully adorned with antique furniture. Definitely book in advance.
A La Hacienda, on the road into town, T635-456 0245 (Creel), www.hoteles-margarita.com. Very comfortable lodgings that are the jewel of Margarita's empire. This 19th-century house retains much of its Victorian character, the rooms are simple but elegant, with antique furniture and beautiful tiled bathrooms. Located outside of town, half an hour away.
B Casa Real de Minas Aranasaina, just off the plaza, T649-456 9045. Beautifully decorated and colourful rooms set around a central courtyard. The best mid-range option in town.
C Juanita, on the plaza principal, T649-456 9043. Large clean rooms and lots of relaxing little enclaves. Peaceful and recommended.
D-E Batopilas, 2 blocks north of the plaza. The cheapest place in town. Simple lodgings with fan and private bath. Prices per person.
E Casa Monse, on the plaza principal, T649-456 9027. Basic rooms around a plant-filled courtyard. Lots of character, albeit it slightly off-beat.

Towards Divisadero *p263*
LL-AL Cabañas Divisadero Barrancas, close to the train station, Divisadero, T614-415 1199, www.hoteldivisadero.com. Stunning views of the canyon at this luxury hotel where the rooms are beautiful and tasteful. Prices include 3 daily meals and 2 walking tours.
LL-AL Posada Barrancas Mirador, www.hotelmirador.hotelesbalderrama.com. Another exceptional lodging, 3 km down the road from Divisadero Barrancas. Awesome views, beautiful rooms with fireplaces and excellent service.
C Casa de Huéspedes Díaz, Posada Barrancas, T614-578 3008. Rooms with 2 double beds, hot water on request. Prepares meals.
C-E Trail Head Inn, T614-578 3007. Run by Rogelio Domínguez who often meets the train saving the 2 km walk from town. Basic, dormitory accommodation. Great location for canyon hikes to the river and great views.

Divisadero to Bahuichivo *p264*
A Hotel Cuiteco, Cuiteco. This quiet, delightful hotel has a patio with an unimpeded view of the mountains. Oil lamps and gas stove in courtyard.

Témoris *p264*
C-E Campamento Adame, a good choice for backpackers, has *cabañas*, dormitories and tent sites with shower and cooking facilities.

El Fuerte *p264*
AL Posada del Hidalgo, Hidalgo 101, T698-893 0242, www.hotelposadadelhidalgo.com. Housed by a historic mansion, Posada del Hidalgo is a very big, professional hotel with spa facilities and a legion of staff. Rooms can be booked through Hotel Santa Anita in Los Mochis. Often visited by large tour groups, who may take priority over other guests.
A El Fuerte, Monteclaros 37, T698-893 0226, www.hotelelfuerte.com.mx. A very beautiful hotel with exquisite rooms and a jacuzzi fed by illuminated waterfalls. Tours, Wi-Fi, bar and restaurant are among the services. The best in town and recommended, even if the decor is slightly overpowering.
A La Choza, 5 de Mayo 101, T698-893 1274, www.hotellachoza.com.mx. Rooms are

comfortable and spacious with attractive domed ceilings. Restaurant, pool, parking, hot water, cable TV and a/c are among the amenities. Can help arrange tours.

B Real de Carapoa, Paseo de la Juventude 102, T698-893 1796. A new place with a handful of comfortable, good value rooms.

B Río Vista, Cerro de las Pilas, T698-893 0413, www.hotelriovista.com.mx. Housed in the old fort stables with excellent views over the river. Lots of rusty old antiques and a good restaurant. Other services include transport to the train station, Wi-Fi, birdwatching on the river and visits to indigenous communities. Recommended.

C La Herradura, Montesclaros s/n, T698-893 0512. Reasonable rooms with a/c, cable TV and Wi-Fi. Not stunning, but quite adequate, and friendly.

D-F San José, Juárez 108, T698-893 0845. For the budget explorer, small, basic rooms with fan. The most expensive have bath, TV and a/c. Friendly and scruffy.

Ciudad Delicias to Zacatecas *p265*

A Hotel Santa Fe, south edge of Ciudad Camargo on highway, T648-462 4022. Very quiet hotel with secure parking and good breakfasts. Some English spoken. Recommended.

A Motel La Fortuna, Panamericana Km 724, Fresnillo, T493-932 5664, www.motella fortuna.com. Clean, comfortable, hotel with pleasant rooms and hot water.

B Hacienda del Norte, Av Agricultura Norte 5, Cd Delicias, T639-472 0200. Good all-round comforts.

B Motel La Siesta, Av Madero 320 Norte, Gómez Palacio, Torreón, T871-714 0291. Clean hotel with hot water and safe parking. Good.

B-C Posada de Sol, Blv Revolución 3501, Torreón, T871-720 2991. Modern motel with secure parking, small restaurant, bar and hot showers. Rooms range from basic, windowless, clean *cabañas* to large, US-style rooms with TV. Good value.

C Baeza, Calle 2 Norte 309, Cd Delicias, T639-472 1000. Also a good choice.

C La Posta, Gral Ceniceros 68 Norte, Cuéncame, T671-763 0029. Has hot water and parking.

C Maya, Ensaye 9, Fresnillo, T493-932 0351. A good travelling option.

D Victoria, Comonfort y Jiménez, Cd Camargo, T648-462 0801. Clean and cheap motel.

Hidalgo del Parral *p265*

B Adriana, Colegio 2, between Plaza Principal and Plaza Baca, T627-522 2570, www.hoteladriana.com.mx. This modern hotel has good carpeted, comfortable rooms with a/c, heating and TV. Services include Wi-Fi, restaurant, bar, parking.

C Acosta, Agustín Barbachano 3, T627-522 0221, off Plaza Principal. Quiet, clean, centrally located hotel with an excellent rooftop terrace overlooking a plaza. Friendly, helpful and good value. Internet and heating among the amenities. Recommended.

C San José, Santiago Méndez 5, near Plaza Principal, T627-522 2453. Big, clean, carpeted rooms with a/c, heating, cable TV, writing desk, hot water and phone. Central, with safe parking.

C Margarita, Independencia 367, near bus station, T627 523 0063. The good, clean, carpeted rooms are a good size, with cable TV, hot water, a/c and heating. If arriving at night, a large green neon sign lights the way. 24-hr parking available in supermarket next door. Friendly, helpful and recommended.

D Chihuahua, Jesús García and Colón 1, T627-522 1513. Clean and simple with parking and restaurant. Tiled rooms have TV, hot water, heating and phone. Not bad. There's another cheapie, **San Miguel**, just across the street.

D Hotel Fuentes, Mercaderes 79, T627-522 0016, hotelfuentes79@hotmail.com. Clean, simple rooms with a/c, telephone cable TV and hot water. Parking and restaurant available. Cheaper without TV.

Hidalgo del Parral to Durango *p266*
C Hotel División del Norte, Madero 35, Santiago Papasquiaro, T674-862 0013. In a former convent; the owner's husband was in Pancho Villa's División del Norte.

Durango *p267, map p267*
There are a handful of cheaper places near the market.
AL-A Hostel de la Monja, Constitución 214 Sur, T618-837 1719, www.hostaldela monja.com.mx. Attractive, luxurious lodgings in the typical colonial style of Durango. There are 20 rooms with high ceilings, DVD players, cable TV, a/c, crisp white sheets and wooden furniture. Very polite and courteous. Restaurant and valet parking are among the services.
A Posada San Jorge, Constitución 102 Sur, T618-811 3257, www.hotel posadasanjorge.com.mx. One of the best places in town. Housed in a big old colonial building, this hotel has lots of character and style, attractive courtyards and rooms. There's Wi-Fi, parking and an excellent Brazilian restaurant. Continental breakfast included. Recommended.
A-B Florida Plaza, 20 de Noviembre y Independencia, T618-825 0421, www.hotel floridaplaza.com. A large 4-star hotel with good comfortable rooms, carpets and pleasant furnishings. Services include restaurant, parking and gym.
B-C Casablanca, 20 de Noviembre 811 Pte, at Zaragoza, T618-811 3599, www.hotelcasa blancadurango.com.mx. A big old hotel with rather iffy decor. The rooms are spacious and comfortable, with cable TV, safe, carpet, a/c, Wi-Fi and hot water. Clean and friendly.
B-C Rincón Real, Zarco 309 Sur, T618-837 0723, www.rinconreal.com. Very spacious and comfortable apartment-style suites with kitchen, sofas, a/c, TV and alarm clock. Laundry service, restaurant and parking are among the amenities. Safe and secure, with reduced rates at the end of the week (**C**).
C Roma, 20 de Noviembre 705 Pte, T618-812 0122, www.hotelroma.com.mx. An old hotel, since 1918, with an interesting antiquated lift.

Rooms are on the small side, but comfortable enough, with cable TV, clean bath, carpets and writing desks. Some rooms are windowless. Wi-Fi in the lobby.
C-D Plaza Catedral, Constitución 216 Sur, T618-813 2480. A big old atmospheric building that's great value for its central location. Some rooms are pokey, others are spacious, so ask to see before accepting. Services include Wi-Fi in the lobby and parking. Some TV sets are blinkered. Rooms with cathedral views are more expensive (**C**). Friendly and helpful.
D Reforma, 5 de Febrero y Madero, T618-813 1622. This hotel has an authentic 1960s lobby and clean, comfortable, straight-forward rooms with cable TV and hot water. Free indoor parking.
E Hotel California, Zarco 317, T618-811 4561. Ultra-cheap, basic and clean. Rooms are pokey and windowless, but equipped with TVs. For the impoverished traveller, and not bad. Also known as Hotel Oasis. Friendly.
E Hotel Gallo, 5 de Febrero 117 Pte, T618-811 5920. Another cheapie with very basic quarters and limited hot water.

● Eating

Ciudad Juárez *p253, map p254*
A plethora of places do deep fried chicken, rotisserie and other spit-roasted meats, particularly along 16 de Septiembre. That said, the smell isn't very appetising.
♥♥ Kentucky Club, Juárez 629. The Kentucky club harks back to the prohibition era when Kentucky whisky was produced in Juárez and smuggled over the border. An atmospheric bar and grill with sports TV.
♥♥ La Fiesta del Pueblo, Juárez y González. Fun, touristy Mexican-themed restaurant serving t-bone steaks, tacos and shrimp cocktails, among other international offerings. A very well-stocked bar.
♥♥ Villa del Mar, Villa Sur 130. Clean and popular seafood joint with booth seating. They serve some meat dishes too.

La Cueva de Chucho, Villa Sur 136. Economical breakfasts and Mexican food, including *pollo con mole* and *milanesa de res*.
Tacos Lucas, Mejía and Juárez. Popular fast-food joint serving tacos, as the name suggests. Also *tortas*, burritos and other cheap grub.

Janos *p256*
Restaurant Durango, de facto bus station at the intersection. Good inexpensive food.

Agua Prieta *p256*
El Pollo Loco, Agua Prieta, near the plaza, for roasted chicken.
Mariscos y Carnes 'La Palapa', Calle 6 between Av 11 and 12. Seafood and meat.

Casas Grandes (Paquimé) *p256*
Constantino, Juárez y Minerva. Since 1954, serving wholesome Mexican fare.
Dinno's Pizza, Constitución and Minerva. Tasty pizzas and an excellent breakfast buffet.

Chihuahua *p258, map p259*
The smartest and best are in the 'zona dorada', northeast of the centre on Juárez, near Colón.
La Calesa, Juárez 3300. Elegant, upmarket restaurant serving Northern-style steaks. Smart and fancy.
Café Calicanto, Aldama 411. Friendly, popular establishment serving meaty Chihuahuan specialities. Live Mexican music Tue-Sun. Recommended.
El Rodeo, Libertad 1705. Regional cuisine with a carnivorous emphasis. Wooden booths, tables and wild west photos.
Gerónimo, Aldama y C10a. Good clean diner with a pricey but good buffet breakfast of fresh fruit, chilled juices, *huevos al gusto* and hot meat dishes, US$7. There's Wi-Fi too, so you can check your emails over a coffee. Skip the lunchtime buffet, which is mediocre at best.

Los Milagros, Victoria 812. Young people's meeting place serving light snacks and cocktails around a pleasant colonial courtyard. Good atmosphere.
Dino's Pizzas, Doblado 301. Pizzas, as the name suggests, adequate but not excellent and slightly over-sweet. They also do spaghetti and light snacks.
Mi Café, Victoria 1000. Economical diner-style place with reasonable breakfasts, Mexican staples and working-class Mexicans.
Nutrivida, Victoria 420. Health food and economical meals, for those seeking respite from the heavy Norteño cuisine.

Creel and around *p261, map p261*
Not much fine dining Creel, but there are plenty of economical cafés. Try the Best Western hotel for a better sit-down meal.
Tío Molcas, López Mateos 35. Mexican staples and wholesome Norteño fare. One of the better ones, but still, nothing outstanding.
Pizza del Rey, López Mateos. Reasonable enough pizza.
Verónica, López Mateos 33. Good *comida corrida* and northern specialities. **Lupita**, a few doors down, is of a similar standard.
Mi Café, López Mateos 21. Locals' haunt serving good, cheap food. Try the apple *empanadas*, friendly.

Batópilas and around *p263*
Carolina, Plaza de la Constitución. Tasty, affordable Mexican staples. Friendly and pleasant. Recommended.
Doña Mica, Plaza de la Constitución. Opposite Carolina's, with a similar selection of appetizing home-cooked fare. Friendly.
El Puente Colgante, off the main plaza. Cold beer, wine, steaks and seafood. Try the Plato Norteño, with excellent, full-flavoured local beef that's best washed down with a cool Tecate, salt and lime. A raucous local atmosphere in the evening. Recommended.
Quinto Patio, inside Hotel Mary's, near the church. Economical fare, Mexican staples and breakfast.

El Fuerte *p264*

♦♦♦-♦♦ La Canastilla, Juárez 510. A reputable riverside restaurant serving tasty seafood and locally caught black bass. Recommended.
♦♦-♦ Mi Casita, Robles y Zaragoza. Try the baked potato and taco stuffing, served with a tray of guacamole and other tasty dips.

Hidalgo del Parral *p265*

Little gourmet dining in Parral, but there are plenty of reasonable places and plenty others serving wholesome, high-carb economical grub. There are lots of bars and big restaurants on Independencia, over the bridge and close to the centre of town.
♦♦ La Parroquia in Hotel San José. Good-value meals, including breakfast.
♦♦ Morelos, Plazuela Morelos 22, off Plaza Principal, 0700-2300, Fri and Sat open 24 hrs. Reasonably good, if slightly overpriced all-you-can-eat buffet, with fruit, eggs, lots of hot meat, stews, soups, desserts and coffee, US$6.
♦♦-♦ Café Corales, Flores Magón opposite Buses Ballezano. Good beef sandwiches.
♦♦-♦ La Fuente, Colegio and 20 de Noviembre. Bright chequered tablecloths help brighten the slightly tired interior, whilst smartly attired waiters disguise a run-of-the-mill menu of Mexican staples and breakfasts.
♦ Mercado Hidalgo, Méndez, opposite Hotel San José. Lots of cheap restaurants and breakfast places inside the market.

Cafés and bakeries

El Parralense, off Independencia on Calle Los Ojitos. Wide choice of bread and cakes.

Durango *p267, map p267*

You'll find economical restaurants along 5 de Febrero and around the market.
♦♦♦-♦♦ Fonda de la Tía Chonda, Nogal 110. An elegant Durango establishment, usually packed. Serves expensive, but tasty, traditional Mexican food. Recommended.
♦♦♦-♦♦ La Fogata, Cuauhtémoc 200 y Negrete. Long-standing Durango favourite, the place to get great cuts of meat, steaks and sizzling carnivorous fare.

♦♦♦-♦♦ Pampas, Constitución 102 Sur, inside Hotel Posada San Jorge. Brazilian buffet with 18 salads and 21 types of meat cuts.
♦♦ Corleone's Pizza, Constitución 110 Norte, at Serdán. Sweet pizzas and cocktails. Busy, popular, family place.
♦♦ El Zocabón, 5 de Febrero 513 Pte. Warm and cosy diner that has a good atmosphere at breakfast time when locals and cowboys fill the tables. Very spicy *huevos rancheros* and good fluffy hotcakes.
♦♦ La Tostada, Florida Norte 1125. Pleasant place with lots of light and brightly painted furniture. Home-cooked Mexican fare is rustled up before you, breakfast and lunch only. Good meat tacos.
♦♦ Los Esquipules, Florida y Negrete. A popular Mexican restaurant serving traditional dishes. Well presented.
♦♦ Los Quatros Vientos, Constitución 154 Norte. This seafood restaurant has a high-ceiling colonial interior with square wooden tables and historic photos.
♦♦-♦ Gorditas Gabino, Constitución 112 Norte. Mexican food in a US-diner style. Cheap, good and central.
♦♦-♦ Pizzaly, 20 de Noviembre 1004. A fairly charmless place, but the pizza isn't bad. Quick, cheap, greasy and filling food for those in need of an unpretentious dining experience.
♦♦-♦ Samadhi, a couple of blocks from the cathedral on Negrete 403 Pte. Good-value vegetarian food, delicious soups and popular with locals. Small, quiet and friendly, but not outstanding.
♦ Los Farolitos, Martínez and 20 de Noviembre. An unpretentious locals' haunt serving exquisite tacos and *burritos*.

Cafés and ice cream parlours

El Paraíso Michoacano, 20 de Noviembre, between Juárez and Victoria. For those craving a fix, ice cream and other sugary fare.
La Esquina del Café, Nogal y Florida. A cosy little coffee-shop on the corner.
Quattros Grados, Negrete y Florida. Clean and modern design, serving smoothies and coffees.

☻ Entertainment

Creel and around *p261, map p261*
Bars and clubs
Creel is lacking in decent watering holes. Most tend to be orientated to locals, who may or may not be welcoming, especially to unaccompanied women. Be discreet and you should be OK.
Tío Molcas, López Mateos 35. The one and only place geared towards foreign travellers and a great place to unwind after a long day in the canyons. It's cosy and intimate, with a roaring log fire. Recommended.

Durango *p267, map p267*
Durango has a varied night-life, although much of it is catered towards students and young folk. Sun afternoons and early evenings often feature itinerant musicians on the main plaza, who will walk you around town and entertain you. This is a traditional form of entertainment known as a *callejoneada*.

Bars and clubs
Club Cien, Paseo del Peñón Blanco 101, Thu-Sat from 2100. Disco lounge that's very popular with Durango's in-crowd. Good dance music.
La Jarra, Nogal 112. Live music on Thu, Fri, Sat, usually of the hard rock variety, including Doors covers.
La Malquerida, Florida, opposite the Tourist Office. Named after a film made in Durango and adorned with pictures of actress Dolores del Río. A fun, popular bar.

☻ Festivals and events

Ciudad Juárez *p253, map p254*
2-5 May Festival de la Raza; with music, dance and various cultural events.
5 May Celebrations take place on Av Juárez (Battle of Puebla).
1-4 Jun Festival Ojinaga.
Jun-Jul Feria Juárez, Parque Chamizal.
15 Sep Independence Day.

Creel and around *p261, map p261*
12 Dec Tarahumara festival.

○ Shopping

Chihuahua *p258, map p259*
Chihuahua is a good place to pick up cowboy boots (head for Calle Libertad, between Independcia and Díaz Ordaz).
Artesanías Tarahumaras, Calle 5 y Doblado 312, T614-413 0627. Crafts, baskets, wood carvings, jewellery.
Mexican Vanilla Gallery, Victoria 424. Sells vanilla in all shapes and forms.

Creel and around *p261, map p261*
There's no shortage of *artesanía* shops in Creel. The **Artesanías Misón** on the plaza has an array of rustic crafts, as well as topographical maps of the canyons. Proceeds go to the Mission Hospital. Alternatively, buy directly from the Rarámuri. Children often make the rounds with simple belts and embroidered pieces.

▲ Activities and tours

Chihuahua *p258, map p259*
Tour operators
Conexion a la Aventura, Melgar y Miguel Schultz 3701, T614-413 7929, www.conexionalaaventura.com. A wide range of tours and outdoor activities throughout the state of Chihuahua, including canyon excursions, kayaking, sand-boarding, hiking and visits to Paquimé. Some trips further afield too.
Guillermo Bechman, T614-413 0253. Arranges stays at cabins above Bahuichivo, near Copper Canyon.
Turismo Al Mar, T614-416 5950. Rail packages and accommodation to Copper Canyon, 5 nights and some meals, US$500 for 2 people.

Creel and around *p261, map p261*
Horse riding
Eco Paseos El Adventurero, next to hotel
Pueblo Viejo, T635-294 4585 (mob),
www.ridemexico.com. A very professional
outfit managed by Norberto, who speaks
English and cares for his horses. Over 15
riding packages are available, with day tours
to local rock formations, Arareco lake and San
Ignacio Mission. A 2-hr ride starts at around
US$15. Longer, more exciting excursions can
also be arranged in advance, with 2- to 9-day
adventures to Ekarine hot springs, various
canyons, waterfalls and villages. Norberto also
has a *cabaña*, which is part of his Ranchito,
where you can stay overnight and partake in
cowboy activities. Finally, his new language
school lets you learn Spanish whilst getting a
horsemanship experience. See website for
more. Recommended.

Rock climbing
Expediciones Umarike, T635-456 0632,
www.umarike.com.mx. Owned by Chito
Arturo, who has over 10 years' experience
navigating the canyons. In addition to rock
climbing, Chito can organize extensive
hiking and canyoning trips. For the hardcore
adventure enthusiast. Reservations and queries
in advance, and through the website only.

Tour operators and guides
Many people hang around the square
offering tours in a variety of vehicles,
or other means of transport. Most hotels
also offer packages that are very similar to
each other. If you don't speak Spanish, always
check your guide is English-speaking before
agreeing to anything. It's worth shopping
around, particularly if you have a longer
excursion in mind.
3 Amigos Canyon Expeditions, López Mateos
46, T635-456 0179, www.amigos3.com. The
best tour operator in town and something of a
Creel institution. As well as offering guided
hikes, customised tours, bike rides and
romantic picnic lunches with canyon views,
they will inform and advise on how best to

explore the region independently. They rent
out good vehicles, bikes and scooters, with
free maps, tools and picnic lunch, if desired.
They also have extensive professional
contacts, including experts in wildlife
and geology. Anything is possible.
Helpful and highly recommended.
César González Quintero, T635-456 0108, or
enquire at Margarita's Plaza Mexicana Hotel,
Elfida Batista Caro. Margarita's son, César, is a
qualified English-speaking guide who offers
tours of all the major canyon attractions,
including Batopilas. He once guided a
Discovery Channel expedition to Urique.
Roberto Venegas, T635-456 0049, who
has a van, is recommended.

Batópilas and around *p263*
Tour operators
Several people in Creel offer trips to Batópilas.
An overnight trip for 4 (minimum) starts at
around US$60 per person, plus lodging and
meals, and includes a trip to Jesuit Mission
at Satevo. A recommended guide is **Pedro
Estrada Pérez** (limited English but patient),
T649-456 0079. Also recommended is
3 Amigos Canyon Expeditions (see above),
who will drive you to the rim of Batopilas
canyon and let you ride a bicycle downhill
through all the turns and switch-backs.
Julio, one of their guides, is particularly
recommended.

El Fuerte *p264*
Tour operators
3 Amigos Canyon Expeditions, Reforma
100, on the waterfront, follow signs from the
plaza, T698-893 5028, www.amigos3.com. This
branch of the legendary canyon specialists is
professionally managed by Ivan and Yolanda.
They specialize in guided kayak tours, with river
rides ranging from 'short and sweet' to 'rough
and tumble'. Recommended.
Amigo Trails, Reforma 100, same office as
3 Amigos above, T698-893 5029,
www.amigotrails.com. Same reputable
management as 3 Amigos, they organize
specialized, all-inclusive packages to Canyon

country, including chartered flights over the mountains.

Chal, Hotel Rio Vista, T698-893 0413, www.hotelriovista.com.mx. Chal is a gregarious English-speaking guide who also owns the Hotel Rio Vista. He offers bird-watching, sports fishing, village tours and trips to the petroglyphs.

Durango p267, map p267
Tour operators
Durango is just awakening to its potential as a centre for adventure activities. The tourist office has a complete list of guides and operators.

Durango Xtremo, Zaragoza 203, local 9, T618-185 0460, www.durangoxtremo.com. Specializes in guided excursions, wilderness training and activities like hiking and rapelling. They rent out camping equipment. **Excursiones Pantera**, Pino Suárez 436 Ote, 2nd floor, T618-813 9875, www.aventurapantera.com.mx. Good selection of outdoor and adventure tours in the area, including expeditions to the Zona del Silencio, birdwatching, biking, camping and canyoning.

⊖ Transport

Ciudad Juárez p253, map p254
Air
Abraham González (CJS) airport is 19 km south of the city (T656-619 0734). Flights to **Mexico City**, **Chihuahua**, **Cd Obregón**, **Culiacán**, **Durango**, **Guadalajara**, **Hermosillo**, **Ixtapa**, **León**, **Los Cabos**, **Mazatlán**, **Monterrey**, **Torreón**, **Tijuana** and **Zacatecas**.

El Paso Airport (ELP) is near Fort Bliss and Biggs Field military airbase with flights by American, Delta, America West Airlines and Southwest Airlines to all parts of the US. There are also flights to El Paso from **Chihuahua** and **Guadalajara**. *Colectivo* from Cd Juárez airport to El Paso or El Paso airport, US$15.50.

Airline offices Aero California, T618-3399. AeroMéxico, T656-613 8719.

Bus
The **long-distance terminal** is at Blv Oscar Flores 4010, T656-613 2083, south of the centre. There is a taxi information booth, which can sell you a ticket before you approach a driver. From the terminal to centre or Santa Fe bridge, taxi fare is about US$7. If you walk from the terminal to the highway, take any bus going to the right marked 'Centro' for US$0.30. Shuttle bus to **El Paso** Greyhound Terminal, US$11, hourly.

From the **Greyhound Terminal** in El Paso, corner of San Antonio and Santa Fe streets, you can get buses to **Laredo** and **Tucson**, etc, and other connections in the US. They have buses every hr on the ½ hr to **Cd Juárez**, 0630-2130, US$11. You can buy your ticket on the bus. It stops at the Mexican side of the border for immigration, where you can pick up your FM-T (tourist card).

The **Cd Juárez bus station** has good services including long-distance telephones, money-changing facilities and left-luggage. Exit the west side (the same door you use to get taxis) and cross the parking lot to take any northbound bus to the city centre. Ticket counters are on the north side of the terminal. The main bus lines are Estrella Blanca and its subsidiaries, Grupo Senda, Greyhound, Autobuses Americanos, ETN and Omnibus.

To **Chihuahua**, every ½ hr, 4½ hrs, US$22. To **Durango**, every 2 hrs, US$50. To **Guadalajara**, 8 daily, US$80. To **León**, 8 daily, US$73. To **Mexico City**, every 1-2 hrs, 25 hrs, US$93. To **Monterrey**, 1130, 1330, 1630 and 2145, US$57. To **San Luis Potosí**, every 2 hrs, US$71. To **Zacatecas**, every 1-2 hrs, US$60.

To USA Check Autobuses Americanos and Greyhound website, www.greyhound.com.mx, for the best fares. To **Alburquerque**, **NM**, 4 daily, 7½ hrs, US$45-63. To **Denver, Colorado**, 4 daily, 15 hrs, US$73-133. To **Los Angeles, CA**, 6 daily, 17 hrs, US$80-144.

Car

Sanborn's, for insurance and information, 440 Raynolds, El Paso, T1-800-222-0158, www.sanbornsinsurance.com, Mon-Fri 0830-1700.

Taxi

Charged by zone, from US$2 to US$8. You can also negotiate with the driver for hourly rates. The going rate about US$20 per hour. Some are allowed to cross the border and take you to downtown El Paso; US$40; or to El Paso Airport, US$50.

Agua Prieta p256
Bus

The bus station in Agua Prieta is one small room with an adequate restaurant called Don Camione, and a phone service. To Chihuahua, every couple of hrs from 0600, US$33. To Cd Juárez, 0900, 0930 and 2230, US$26. To Durango, 2010, US$59. To Hermosillo, every couple of hours from 0600-1400, US$25. To Mexico City, Omnibus, 1630, US$103. To Nogales, every couple of hours from 0830-1600, US$13. To Phoenix: every 3 hrs from 0515-1630, US$42. To Zacatecas, Cabellero Azteca (all 2nd class), 2130, US$56.

Douglas has a small bus terminal, 538 14th St, between Av F and Av G, operated by Greyhound and Autobuses Crucero. Tucson, US$19. Phoenix, US$30. Los Angeles: US$65. The schedules for all the buses are the same: 0545, 1145, 1515, and 1715. The terminal closes at 1600 so you'd have to wait outside for the 1715 bus.

Taxi

Armando Chávez, T633-335 2162. Recommended. If you are crossing the border, when you come to the first cross street, take a left and the office is just around the corner on the north side of the street.

Casas Grandes (Paquimé) p256

To Cd Juárez, several daily, 4 hrs, US$12.50. To Chihuahua, every 1-2 hrs, 5 hrs, US$18.

To Mexico City, 1 a day via El Sueco, 1 via Cuauhtémoc, US$98. 3 a day to Agua Prieta. Also 1 a day to Cuauhtémoc, Hermosillo, Madera, Monterrey, Nogales and Tijuana.

Madera and around p257

Bus Estrella Blanca, T157-572 0431, to/from Chihuahua every hour, 5 hrs, bus stop on Calle 5. Also infrequent services to Ciudad Juárez and Casas Grandes, 1-2 daily.

Chihuahua p258, map p259
Air

Airport Gen Fierro Villalobos (CUU) on Blv Juan Pablo II, 18 km from centre on road to Ojinaga. Airport buses collect passengers from hotels, fare US$1.10. Also minibuses. Taxi US$16 (no other transport at night). Flights to Cd Juárez, Cd Obregón, Culiacán, Guadalajara, Hermosillo, La Paz, Loreto, Los Cabos, Los Mochis, Manzanillo, Mazatlán, Mexico City, Monterrey, Tijuana and Torreón. AeroMéxico to Los Angeles daily, and Aerolitoral to Dallas and El Paso in the US.

Airline offices AeroMéxico, T614-423 4715, American Eagle, T614-446 8211, Interjet, T614-446 8233.

Bicycle

Bicycle spares Independencia 807, 0900-2000.

Bus

Local Town buses cost US$0.20.
Long distance Bus terminal on Blv Juan Pablo II, 8 km from centre on way to airport, southeast of town, T614-420 2286, 20 mins by bus to centre (US$0.40), or taxi US$6 (fixed price). Buses from centre at Niños Héroes between Ocampo and Calle 10. There is an exchange office (beware short-changing), cafetería and left luggage. The main bus lines include Grupo Senda, Omnibus, Estrella Blanca and its subsidiaries.

To Aguascalientes, hourly, 13 hrs, US$50. To Ciudad Juárez, every 30 mins from 0530, 5 hrs, US$21. To Creel, 5 daily, 5 hrs, US$15. To Durango, hourly, US$30. To

Guadalajara, several, US$61, including Estrella Blanca, which also goes to Acapulco and Puerto Vallarta. To Hidalgo del Parral, 9 daily, 2½ hrs, US$9. To Nuevo Casas Grandes, 13 daily, 4 hrs, US$16. To Nuevo Laredo, 2030, US$35. To Monterrey, every 1-2 hrs, US$38. To Mazatlán, 2 companies, US$38, 19 hrs, heart-stopping view. To Mexico City (and intermediate destinations), frequent services with several companies, 20 hrs, US$75. To Querétaro, every 1-2 hrs, US$65. To San Luis Potosí, 7 daily, US$52. To Saltillo, 5 daily, US$37 (or go to Monterrey and backtrack). To Torreón, every ½ hr, US$25. To Zacatecas, every ½ hr, 12 hrs, US$43.

Taxi
Taxis operate on a zone system.

Train
For schedules, see box, page 258. The station for the 631-km Chihuahua al Pacífico railway is 1 block behind the prison (take bus marked Rosario, or walk); in the early morning you may have to take a taxi.

Creel and around p261, map p261
Bicycle
Bikes from several places roughly US$13 for the day; look around if you need better bikes. 3 Amigos (see tour operators) has the best.

Bus
There are 2 bus stations in Creel, Noreste and Estrella Blanca, both located close to each other outside, across the railway track and opposite the square, near hotel Korachi. To Chihuahua, 13 daily, 5 hrs, US$15. To Cd Juárez, 0800. To Guachochi, 1200, 1730, US$4. To Hidalgo del Parral, 1210, 5 hrs. To San Rafael and Divisadero, 5 daily, US$3. Buses to Batopilas depart from López Mateos, Mon-Sat, see below.

Train
For schedule, see page 258. Station office Mon 0800-1000, 1100-1600, Tue-Fri

1000-1600, Sat 1000-1300. From Creel to Los Mochis takes about 8 hrs.

Guachochi p262
Bus
To Creel 2 daily from Estrella Blanca terminal, 0730 and 1330, US$4 (1210 and 1730 from Creel); also reached from Hidalgo del Parral, bus leaves for Parral several times a day with Transportes Ballezanos..

Batópilas and around p263
Bus/lorry
From Creel, Tue, Thu and Sat at 0730, and Mon, Wed, Fri at 0930, 5-6 hrs (paved as far as Samachique turn-off) depending on weather, US$15. Buy ticket the day before from the El Two Artesanía shop, López Mateos, as it can be very crowded. Returns to Creel at 0500, Mon-Sat (have a torch handy as it is very dark). Supply lorry leaves for Chihuahua Tue, Thu, Sat at 0600, takes passengers. A stunning trip.

Towards Divisadero p263
Bus
Regular daily buses run from Divisadero to Creel (US$2.30) connecting with buses to Chihuahua.

Train
The train pauses at Divisadero for 15 mins, allowing you to snap some stunning pictures and grab a burrito.

Ciudad Delicias p265
Air
Torreón airport (14.5 km from the centre) has domestic flights to Chihuahua, Ciudad Juárez, Culiacán, Durango, Guadalajara, Hermosillo, Ixtapa, Mazatlán, Mexico City, Monterrey, Piedras Negras and Tijuana. International flights to Houston and Los Angeles in the US, Panama City and São Paulo, Brazil.

Bus
To/from Chihuahua hourly, US$4; Omnibus de México, Av 6 y Calle 2 Norte,

T639-472 1020; **Estrella Blanca**, Av 6 Norte 300, T639-472 1509; **Rápidos Delicias**, Av 5 Norte 301, T639-472 1030.

From Torreón to **Chihuahua**, 6 hrs, US$34. To **Ciudad Juárez**, hourly, US$46. To **Durango**, hourly, 4½ hrs, US$17. To **Tepic**, US$42.

Gómez Palacio has its own bus station, without a shuttle to the centre. City buses outside have frequent services to all 3 city centres, US$0.33.

Hidalgo del Parral *p265*
Bus
The bus station is 20 mins' walk out of town on Av Independencia, east of centre, taxi about US$2. Few bus lines start here so it is difficult to reserve seats. The main players are **Estrella Blanca**, **Omnibus** and **Grupo Senda**. To **Ciudad Juárez**, several daily, 8 hrs, US$27. To **Durango**, 6 hrs, US$20. To **Zacatecas**, 9 hrs, US$37. To **Chihuahua**, frequent departures, 2½ hrs, US$9. Also to **Guachochi**. Buses Ballezano to Guachochi leave from office on Carlos Fuero y Flores Magón at 0800, 1230, 1545, US$4.

Durango *p267, map p267*
Air
Guadalupe Victoria Airport (DGO), 12 km from centre (taxi US$8.50). To **Chihuahua**, **Guadalajara**, **Mazatlán**, **Mexico City**, **Monterrey**, **Tijuana** and **Torreón**. There are international flights to **Chicago**, **El Paso** and **Los Angeles**.

Airline offices Aero California, T618-817 7177. AeroMéxico, next to cathedral, T618-817 8828. Mexicana, T618-813 3030.

Bus
The bus station is out of town: minibuses marked 'centro' go downtown, every 5 mins from 0600 to 2130, US$0.25. Take 'camionera' buses from 20 de Noviembre to get back to the terminal.

Services with **Omnibus de México** and **Estrella Blanca**. Across the Sierra Madre Occidental to **Mazatlán** there are several

buses daily, 7 hrs, US$19. The views are fantastic and recommended if you cannot do the Chihuahua–Los Mochis train journey; sit on left side.

To **Chihuahua**, 5-6 daily, 8 hrs, US$30. To **Hidalgo del Parral**, 7 hrs, US$20. To **Guadalajara**, 2000 and 2200, 8 hrs, US$40. To **Mexico City**, every couple of hrs, 12 hrs, US$58. To **Zacatecas**, hourly, 4½ hrs, US$15.

❶ Directory

Ciudad Juárez *p253, map p254*
Banks Most *cambios* are on Av Juárez and Av de las Américas; there is also a *cambio* at the bus terminal. Rates vary little. The best and most convenient exchange houses are in El Paso: **Valuta Corp**, 301 Paisano Drive, buys and sells all foreign currencies but at poor rates, wires money transfers, open 24 hrs including holidays. **Melek Corp**, 306 Paisano Drive, offers most of the same services as Valuta but only dollars and pesos, not open 24 hrs. If coming from US Immigration, when you reach Paisano Drive/Hwy 62, turn east for these places. (In El Paso, banks are closed on Sat.)
Embassies and consulates Mexico, 910, E San Antonio, El Paso, T656-533 4082. **US**, Victoria 3650, Cd Juárez, T656-227 3000. **UK**, Fresno 185, Campestre Juárez, T656-617 5791. **Internet** Compurent, 16 de Septiembre and Villa, US$1 per hr; also at Juárez 243. **Post office** Corner of Lerdo Sur and Ignacio de la Peña.

Presidio (Texas)
Banks Bancomer on zócalo, changes TCs, no commission; opposite is **Casa de Cambio Allende**, cash only, poorer rates.

Agua Prieta *p256*
Medical services Cruz Roja, corner of Calle 17 and Av 6. From there they can take you to other hospitals. Pharmacies: open 24 hrs, 1 on the corner of Calle 3 and Av 8, and another on the corner of Av 5 and 7.

Casas Grandes (Paquimé) *p256*
Banks Several on 5 de Mayo and Constitución Ote; Casa de Cambio California next to hotel of that name.
Telephone Long-distance calls from Rivera bus office, on Alvaro Obregón.

Madera and around *p257*
Banks Banamex, Bancomer and Banrural with ATMs and will change dollars (and TCs).

Chihuahua *p258, map p259*
Banks Bancomer on Plaza Constitución offers better rates than Multibanco Comermex on same square. Casa de Cambio Rachasa, Independencia y Guadalupe Victoria, on Plaza, poorer rates, no commission on cash, 2 on TCs, Mon-Sat 0900-2100 (also at Aldama 711). Exchange is available in the bus terminal, but rates are slightly better downtown. **Internet** Not terribly numerous. Try the computer shop at Ocampo 1433. Or Mi Café (see Eating, page 275), which has a few terminals with bad keyboards. Most places charge around US$1 per hr. **Laundry** Ocampo 1412. Julián Carrillo 402. **Telephone** Libertad, in the Palacio Federal. Also in Central Camionera. Credit card phone outside AeroMéxico office on Guadalupe Victoria, ½ block from Plaza Constitución (towards Carranza). Main phone office on Av Universidad.

Creel and around *p261, map p261*
Banks Banca Serfín, on the square, very friendly, 0900-1300, changes dollars cash with no commission, but commission

charged on TCs (US$1 per cheque), TCs must be authorized by manager, Visa and MasterCard advances, no commission.
Internet Try Cascada.net, López Mateos 49 or Compucenter, López Mateos 33. Connections tend to be poor. **Laundry** Pink house opposite side of tracks from square, US$3 per load, 2 hrs, good, Mon-Sat 0900-2000, restricted hours on Sun. **Post office** On main square in Presidencia Municipal, no sign. **Telephone** Long-distance phone office in Hotel Nuevo.

Batópilas and around *p263*
Banks Tienda Grande (Casa Morales), the store on the plaza, can change TCs at a poor rate. No ATMS, carry all the cash you need.

Hidalgo del Parral *p265*
Banks Banco Unión, in Hotel Adriana complex, exchange until 1200, poor rates, similarly at Banamex opposite. Good rates at Bancomer, Plaza Principal until 1200. Opposite is Cambios de Oro, no commission, good rates, Mon-Fri 0900-1900, Sat until 1400. Also at Gasolinera Palmilla on road to Santa Bárbara, 3 km out of town.
Internet Ciber, Jiménez 1, US$1 per hr.
Post office Calle del Rayo, just over bridge from centre, 0800-1500.

Durango *p267, map p267*
Banks Bancomer, and many others with ATMs neatly on the west side of the plaza by cathedral. **Internet** El Cactus, Constitución, 1 block past the cathedral heading north, open 1000-2200. Many others in town. **Post office** Av 20 de Noviembre 500 B Ote.

Northeast Mexico

Some of the most crucial battles of the 1846-1848 War between Mexico and the United States were fought in the northeast of Mexico. Brownsville and Matamoros experienced the first outbreak of hostilities and it was here that many US troops deserted and joined the Mexican forces, giving rise to the St Patrick's Battalion. Museums in the towns and cities along the way tell this and other stories of the region. On a more contemporary note, the galleries of Monterrey are at the cutting edge of modern Mexican art. Outside the city you can explore Mexico's largest national park, venture into vast caves with stalactites and stalagmites, try rock climbing on mountains that tower above chasms, or set out on a two-day adventure circuit involving river canyoning, abseiling or swimming through tunnels. Further south you can enjoy tropical bird sanctuaries, jungle and even cloudforest and visit archaeological sites of the enigmatic Huastec civilization. You could even take in some deep-sea fishing before finally reaching Tampico and the Gulf coast or heading inland to the Colonial Highlands.

The Gulf Route from Laredo, along the Pan-American Highway, takes in the major industrial centre of Monterrey and the port of Tampico. The route passes through the coastal state of Tamaulipas before entering the regions of the Huastec and Otomí people. Then there is a choice of either continuing south or heading west to the Central Highlands via the old silver-mining centre of Pachuca. ❯❯ *For listings, see pages 291-296.*

Border towns ⊖⊜❶ ❯❯ *pp291-296.*

The first route to be opened to Mexico was the Gulf Route. It's not the most inspiring introduction to Mexico, but it is the fastest way to the south. Traffic can enter northeast Mexico through six gateways along the Río Bravo. They run from west to east: Ciudad Acuña, opposite Del Río; Piedras Negras, opposite Eagle Pass, Nuevo Laredo, opposite Laredo; Ciudad Miguel Alemán, opposite Roma; Reynosa opposite McAllen; Matamoros, opposite Brownsville. The roads from these places all converge upon Monterrey (a toll road from Nuevo Laredo is the quickest route, US$12).

By car, the best way is over the Colombia Bridge, north of Laredo: on Interstate 35, take the exit to Milo (the first exit north of the tourist bureau, then take Farm Road 1472 west). This crossing has little traffic and friendly staff, but it does involve a 40-km detour (it is well signposted on the Mexican side). There is a toll on the international bridge. Once in Mexico, you can continue to Monterrey either on Route 85 via Nuevo Laredo, or by following the railway line via Ciudad Anáhuac and Lampazos.

Ciudad Acuña–Del Rio (Texas)
Most of the time, Ciudad Acuña is an unassuming, if slightly ugly, middle-of-nowhere sort of town. It comes to life at weekends when rowdy Texans pop over the border to quench their thirsts. Sadly, there's little to do but join them under the neon signs, soaking up the seamy undertones. Nearby, the **Parque Internacional del Río Bravo** is a vast protected area accessible only by 4WD, and just over the border there's the **Big Bend National Park**, www.nps.gov/bibe, which is worth a visit. Otherwise there's little reason to hang around.

Nuevo Laredo → *Colour map 2, B6. Phone code: 867.*
Nuevo Laredo is a rather sleazy, charmless town – part tourist trap, part den of iniquity. If you enjoy illicit activities you can call it home, otherwise it's best to move on quickly.

Border essentials: northeast Mexico–USA

Piedras Negras–Eagle Pass, Texas
Piedras Negras is a small, friendly border town, often eerily quiet. Crossing the border is a quick, painless process. Many of the hotels are in decline or outright dilapidation, and there is the sense that few strangers ever stay long.

Nuevo Laredo, Tamaulipas–Laredo, Texas
This is the most important town of the eastern border crossings and sees a lot of traffic, legal and illegal. The World Trade Bridge crosses the Rio Grande. It currently operates Mon-Fri 24 hours Sat 0800-1600, Sun 1000-1400. Formalities are straightforward if your paperwork is in order.

Matamoros, Tamaulipas–Brownsville, Texas
Crossing the border by car here is quick and easy. Permission is usually granted for six months (multiple entry) for passengers and vehicle, paperwork takes only about 10 minutes if everything is in order. Visas can be obtained in Brownsville on the US side of the border from the Mexican Consulate at 940 East Washington.

After 120 km of grey-green desert, the road from Nuevo Laredo climbs the Mamulique Pass, which it crosses at 700 m, before descending to Monterrey. From Laredo to Monterrey there is a toll road (*cuota*) and a non-toll road (*vía libre*). The latter goes through **Sabinas Hidalgo**. There is a toll bypass around Monterrey.

Reynosa–McAllen (Texas) → *Phone code: 899.*
Opposite McAllen on the border, Reynosa has a population of just over 400,000 but there's not much to see. This is a small, but busy, industrial city; friendly enough but rather dull and unappealing.

Matamoros → *Colour map 2, B6. Phone code: 868.*
Matamoros is the most attractive of the eastern border towns, although that's not saying much. Once you get past the industrial outskirts, the centre has a certain energy and friendliness, and if you want to acclimatize, this is the best place to do it. Founded in 1774 by families from nearby Reynosa, Matamoros nowadays is best known for its annual autumn international festival (www.fiomat.org), held at various cultural venues throughout the city for two weeks in October.

Saltillo ⬤🅿🅗🅘🅞 » *pp291-296. Colour map 2, B5.*

→ *Phone code: 884. Altitude: 1600 m.*
The capital of Coahuila state is a cool, dry, popular resort noted for the excellence of its *sarapes*. Its 18th-century **cathedral**, a mixture of romanesque, churrigueresque, baroque and plateresque styles, is the best in northern Mexico. College students from the US attend the popular **Summer School** ① *T884 416 3049, www.summerschool.com.mx*. There's a **tourist office** ① *Blv Venustiano Carranza 8520, T884-432 3690*, located outside the centre.

The **Museo de las Aves (Bird Museum)** ① *Hidalgo y Bolívar 151 (a few blocks north of sarape factory), www.museodelasaves.org, Tue-Sat 1000-1800, Sun 1100-1900, US$1, guides available*, contains hundreds of stuffed birds. Also check out the **Museo del Desierto** ① *Prolongación Pérez Treviño 3745, www.museodeldesierto.org, Tue-Sun 1000-1700, US$6.50*, to learn all you need to know about the Mexican desert. The house of the artist **Juan Antonio Villarreal Ríos** ① *Blv Nazario Ortiz Garza, Casa 1, Manzana 1, Col Saltillo 400, T884-415 2707, free*, has an exhibition in every room of Dali-esque work; visitors are welcome, phone first. There are good views from **El Cerro del Pueblo** overlooking the city. An 87-km road runs east to Monterrey (both toll and non-toll).

Matehuala → *Phone code: 488.*

From Saltillo, two roads run south: one heads southwest to Zacatecas (see page 309) and the other south to Matehuala and San Luis Potosí (see page 312). Along the Saltillo–

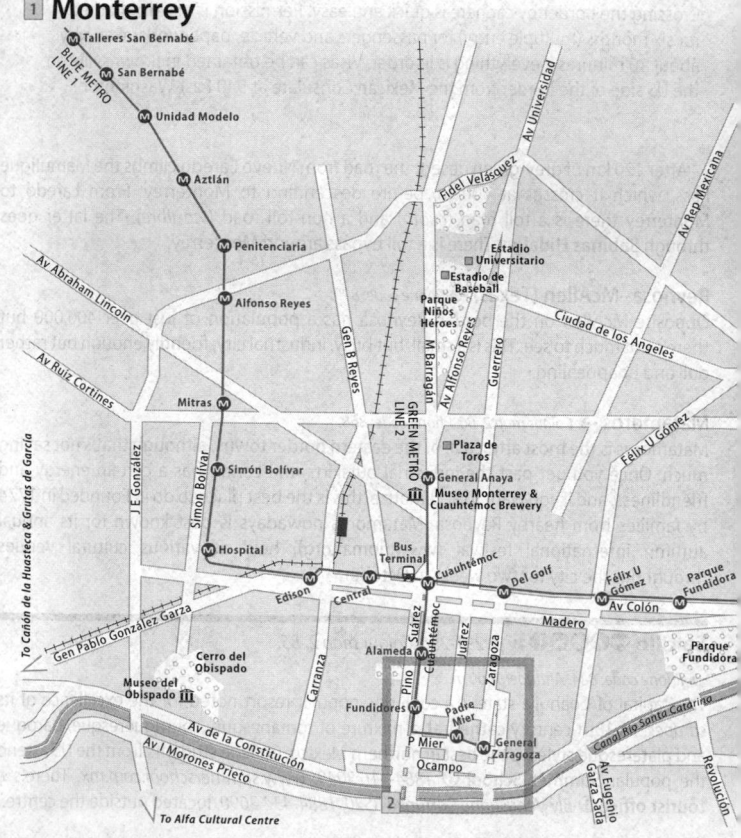

1 Monterrey

Matehuala section the scenery is worthwhile, as the road winds its way through wooded valleys. The final section passes through undulating scrub country to Matehuala, an important road junction with a fiesta from 6-20 January. It's also a good jumping-off point to visit the important mining town of Real de Catorce (see page 315). From Matehuala you go via the Colonial Heartland route to Mexico City.

Monterrey and around ⊜❼▲❺❻ ⟫ pp291-296. Colour map 2, B5.

→ *Phone code: 81. Altitude: 538 m.*

Capital of Nuevo León state and third largest city in Mexico, Monterrey, 253 km south of the border, is dominated by the **Cerro de la Silla** (saddle) from the east and the **Cerro de las Mitras** in the west. It is an important cultural centre in Mexico and there are many fine museums to visit. Its streets are congested, its layout seems unplanned and its architecture uninspiring, except in the centre, which has undergone remodelling in recent years. This is a bold, forward-looking city, home to thriving industries and challenging modern styles.

> ➡ **Monterrey maps**
> 1 Monterrey, page 286
> 2 Monterrey centre, page 288

Ins and outs

Getting there Aeropuerto Internacional General Mariano Escobedo (MTY), T81-8345 4434, 24 km from city centre, has flights to most cities in Mexico and to many in the US, Canada, Caribbean and Latin America. A taxi from the airport to the city centre costs around US$20. The vast, long-distance bus terminal is north of the city centre on Avenida Colón (Metro Cuauhtémoc). Several major routes converge at Monterrey, connecting the industrial city to the rest of Mexico and to Nuevo Laredo, Reynosa and Matamoros on the US border (see box, page 285).

Getting around The Monterrey metro system has two intersecting lines, which run north–south and east–west of the city. Buses run to all areas within the city; ask at the tourist office for a map.

Tourist information Best obtained from the **State Tourist Office**① *Washington 648 Ote, inside the old Palacio Federal, Mon-Fri 0900-1800, T81-8152 3333*. Look out for a quarterly English-language publication, *Explore Monterrey*, which has details on local attractions.

Map labels: López Mateos; Bernardo Reyes; Av Félix Galván; Av Las Américas; Av Ruiz Cortines; To Airport; Villareal; Av Miguel Alemán; Griega; Av Benito Juárez; Palacio Federal; Lerdo de Tejada; Exposición; Av Chapultepec; N; 1 km; 1 mile

Best time to visit Monterrey climate is fairly unattractive: it's too cold in winter, too hot in summer (though evenings are cool), dusty at most times and a there's shortage of water.

Sights

The centre lies just north of the Río Santa Catarina. Plaza Zaragoza, Plaza 5 de Mayo, the Explanada de los Héroes and Parque Hundido link with the Gran Plaza to the south to form the **Macro Plaza**, claimed to be the biggest civic square in the world. Its centrepiece is the **Faro de Comercio** (Commerce Beacon). To the east of the Faro is the 18th-century **cathedral**, badly damaged in the war against the US in 1846-1847, when it was used by Mexican troops as a powder magazine. Running along the west side of the northern part of the Plaza are the **Torre Latina**, **High Court** and **State Congress**; opposite, on the east side are the **Biblioteca** and the **Teatro de La Ciudad**, all modern buildings. The Macro Plaza is bordered at its southern end by the **Palacio Municipal**, and at its northern limit is the **Palacio de Gobierno**. East of the macroplaza lies the bohemian **Barrio Antiguo**, the best surviving evidence of Monterrey's colonial past. The district comes alive on Friday and Saturday evenings when the city's student population takes to its bars and clubs. **Parque Fundidora**, www.parquefundidora.org, east of the centre, is a surreal parkland of rolling greenery, old warehouses converted to cultural spaces, and crumbling, industrial chimneys.

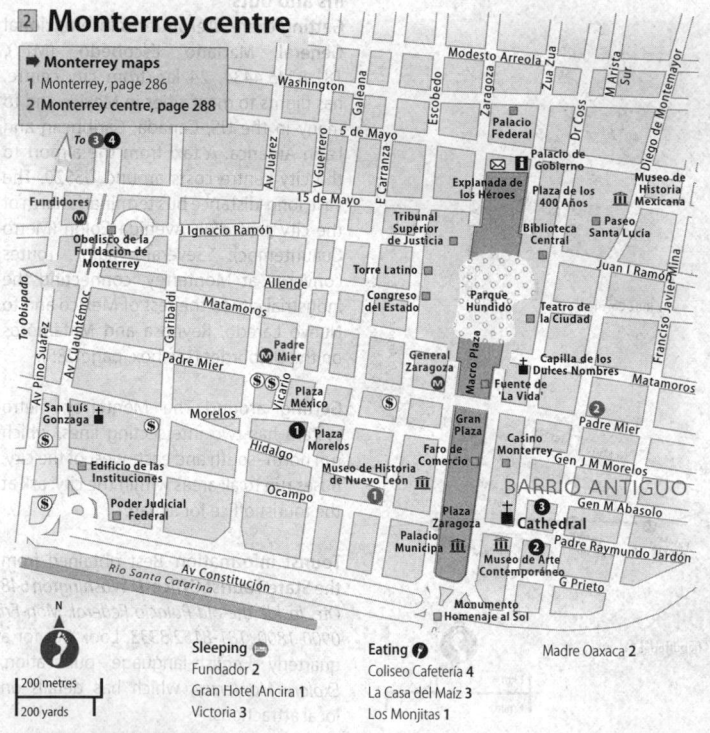

2 Monterrey centre

➡ **Monterrey maps**
1 Monterrey, page 286
2 Monterrey centre, page 288

Sleeping 🛌
Fundador 2
Gran Hotel Ancira 1
Victoria 3

Eating 🍴
Coliseo Cafetería 4
La Casa del Maíz 3
Los Monjitas 1

Madre Oaxaca 2

The **Museo de Arte Contemporáneo (MARCO)** ① *Zua Zua y PR Jardon, T818-262 4500, www.marco.org.mx, Wed and Sun 1000-2000, Tue-Sun 1000-1800, US$1.50, free Wed*, is one of the best modern art galleries in Mexico; it holds temporary shows and has a good bookshop. Other art galleries with temporary shows are the **Pinacoteca de Nuevo León** ① *Parque Niños Héroes, T81-8331 5462, Tue-Sun 1000-1800*; the **Museo Metropolitano** ① *Zaragoza and Corregidora, T81-8344 1971, Mon-Sun 1000-2000, free*; the **Centro Cultural de Arte** ① *Belisario Domínguez 2140 Pte, Col Obispado, T81-8347 1128, Mon-Fri 0900-1300, 1500-1800*; and the **Cineteca-Foteca** ① *Parque Fundidora, 1000-1700, free*, a photo gallery and art house cinema. There are several other galleries dotted around **Parque Fundidora**.

The famous **Instituto Tecnológico** ① *Av Garza Sada 2501*, has valuable collections of books on 16th-century Mexican history. The **Museo de la Historia Mexicana** ① *Dr Coss 445 Sur, off the north end of the plaza, T81-8342 4820, 1000-1900, Tue-Sun, US$1.50, free on Tue*, is an excellent interactive museum, good for children. Regional history is the focus of the museum inside the elegant **Obispado** ① *Tue-Sun 1000-1700, US$3*, the wonderful old Bishop's palace that overlooks the city from atop Chepe Vera hill.

The **Salón de Fama de Beisbol** ① *Av Alfonso Reyes 2202 Norte (500 m north of Metro Central), T81-8328 5746, www.salondelafama.com.mx, Tue-Sun 1100-2000, Wed 1000-2000*, commemorates Mexico's heroes of baseball and is in the grounds of the **Cuauhtémoc Brewery** ① *visits to the brewery Mon-Fri 0930-1530, Sat 0930-1300*. The **Casa de los Tieres** ① *Jardón 968, T81-8343 0604, www.baulteatro.com, Mon-Fri 0900-1300, 1400-1600, US$1.20*, contains an interesting, if slightly weird, collection of marionettes. If glassware is your passion, there's a comprehensive **Museo del Vidrio** ① *Zaragoza and Magallanes, Tue-Sun 0900-1800, US$1.50, free Tue*.

The **Centro Cultural Alfa** ① *Roberto Gaza Sada 1000, T81-8356 5696, Tue-Fri 1500-2100, Sat 1400-2100, Sun 1200-2100, closed Mon*, has a fine **planetarium** ① *T81-8303 0001, www.planetarioalfa.org.mx*. In a separate building is a Rufino Tamayo stained-glass window. The centre is reached by special bus from the west end of the Alameda, which runs hourly on the hour 1500-2000, free.

Around Monterrey

In the hills around Monterry is the bathing resort of **Topo Chico**, 6.5 km to the northwest; water from its hot springs is bottled and sold throughout Mexico. Reached by a road heading south (extension of Avenida Gómez Morín), is **Chipinque** ① *T81-8303 2190, www.chipinque.org.mx, 0600-2000, US$2, cars US$3*, an ecological park in the Sierra Madre, with magnificent views of the Monterrey area. It is popular for hiking, mountain biking and climbing, with peaks reaching 2200 m.

West of Monterrey, off the Saltillo road, are the **Grutas de García** ① *about 10 km from Villa García, which is 40 km from Monterrey*. The entrance to the caves is 800 m up, by cable car, and inside are beautiful stalagmites and stalactites. A tour of the caves takes 1½ hours, and it is compulsory to go in a group with a guide. You can take a bus to Villa García, but it is a dusty walk to the caves. On Sunday, **Transportes Saltillo-Monterrey** run a bus to the caves at 0900, 1000 and 1100. Otherwise, take an agency tour, for example **Osetur**; book at **Hotel Ancira**.

Hidalgo is a small town 38 km northwest of Monterrey on the Monclova road (Route 53). Dominating the area are the massive limestone cliffs of **Potrero Chico** (4 km west of town, take road leading on from Calle Francisco Villa). The cliffs are a magnet for big-wall climbers, particularly during the US winter, and have some of the hardest pitches in the world (up to 5.12d), including the 650-m-long **Sendero Luminoso** route on the central pillar of **El Toro**. The climbing school here is the best in Mexico. A sheet guide by Jeff Jackson describing 80 of the best climbs and places to camp is available at the store on the left before you reach the *balneario*. There is accommodation, see Sleeping, page 292. **Autobuses Mina** leave at hourly intervals from Monterrey bus station to Hidalgo (bus station on plaza).

Monterrey to the Colonial Heartland ⊖❻▲❻❻ ➤ *pp291-296.*

Heading south from Monterrey, the road threads through the narrow and lovely **Huajuco Canyon**; from the village of Santiago, a road runs to within 2 km of the **Cola de Caballo**, or Horsetail Falls, in the **Parque Nacional Cumbres de Monterrey** ① *US$2.40; cost of guide US$5*, the largest in Mexico. There is a first-class hotel on the way, and you can take a *colectivo*, US$1.65, from the bus stop to the falls, and hire a horse to take you to the top. Deeper into the park are other waterfalls: the 75-m **Cascada El Chipitín** and **Cascada Lagunillas**. There is a two-day circuit, *Recorrido de Matacanes*, starting at Las Adjuntas, taking in both these falls and involving river canyoning, abseiling and swimming through tunnels. Ask at **Asociación de Excursionismo y Montañismo** in Monterrey (see page 294).

Ciudad Victoria ➤ *Colour map 2, C6. Phone code: 834. Altitude: 336 m.*
Capital of Tamaulipas state, Ciudad Victoria is a quiet, clean, unhurried city with a shaded plaza. The Parque Siglo 21 is the same end of town as the bus station. The centrepiece is a planetarium, which looks like a huge red ball that landed on the banks of the Río San Marcos. The **Museo de Antropología e Historia** ① *on the plaza*, has a good section on the Huastec culture. There's a **tourist office** ① Calle *8 Anaya y Olivia Ramírez 1287, T/F934-316 1074*. The north–south streets (parellel to the Sierra) have names and numbers, the east–west streets have only names.

Ciudad Mante and around ➤ *Colour map 2, C6. Phone code: 831.*
After crossing the Tropic of Cancer the road enters the solid green jungle of the tropical lowlands. Ciudad Mante (Route 85), 137 km south of Ciudad Victoria, is almost exactly the mid-way point between Matamoros and Mexico City and makes a convenient stopover place despite being a grubby city. It has a **Museo de Antropología e Historia**, with objects from the Huastec culture.

Forty-five kilometres north of Ciudad Mante is the village of **Gómez Farías**, an important centre for ornithological research: the highlands above the village represent the northernmost extent of several tropical vegetation formations. Many tropical bird species reach the northern limit of their range. Gómez Farías is reached by turning west off the main highway, 14 km over a paved road to the town plaza. From there, an easy 2-km walk provides excellent views of bird habitats.

South of Ciudad Mante, at Km 548 from Mexico City, is **Antiguo Morelos** where a road turns off west to San Luis Potosí (see page 312) and Guadalajara (see page 350).

Tampico ➤ *Colour map 2, C6. Phone code: 833.*
The port of Tampico, on the Gulf of Mexico, is definitely not a tourist attraction, although fishing (both sea and river) is excellent. It is reached by a fine road from Ciudad Mante, in a rich sugar-growing area. Tampico was founded in 1522 by Gonzalo de Sandoval but was sacked by pirates in the 17th century and refounded in 1823.

Ciudad Valles → *Colour map 2, C6. Phone code: 481.*

Ciudad Valles, on a winding river, is a popular stopover with many hotels. **Museo Regional Huasteco** ① *Rotarios y Artes (or Peñaloza), Mon-Fri 1000-1200, 1400-1800*, is the centre of archaeological and ethnographic research for the so-called Huasteca region.

Ixmiquilpan and around → *Colour map 3, B4. Phone code: 759.*

An area of 23,300 sq km north and south of Ixmiquilpan (Km 169 from Mexico City), just off the highway, is inhabited by 65,000 Otomí people. The beautifully worked Otomí belts and bags may sometimes be bought at the Monday market, and also in the *artesanía* shop in the main street. See early indigenous frescoes in the main church, one of several 16th-century battlemented Augustinian monastery-churches; the monastery is open to the public. At sunset each day white egrets come to roost in the trees outside the church; it's worth going up on to the battlements to see them swoop down. The church of **El Carmen** has a lovely west façade and gilded altars inside. There is a 16th-century **bridge** over the river and a great walk along the *ahuehuete* tree-lined banks.

The **Barranca de Tolantongo** ① *37 km northeast of Ixmiquilpan, US$2, car parking US$2 at entrance to recreational area*, is about 1500 m deep with a waterfall and thermal spring; camping is permitted and at weekends there is a small eating place. To get there take the road towards **El Cardonal**, then an unpaved turn-off about 3 km before El Cardonal (there is a bus from Pachuca).

Actopan to Tula → *Colour map 3, B4. Phone code: 772.*

Actopan (Km 119 from the capital) has another fine 16th-century Augustinian church, convent, and an impressive open chapel and the **Hotel Rira** (**B**). From Actopan a 56-km branch road runs to one of Mexico's great archaeological sites: Tula, capital of the Toltecs (see page 156).On the way to Tula there is an interesting cooperative village, **Cruz Azul**, where there are free Sunday-morning concerts at 1000 in front of main market. At **Colonia** (Km 85), a road runs left for 8 km to Pachuca (see page 155).

⓪ Northeast Mexico listings

For Sleeping and Eating price codes and other relevant information, see Essentials pages 45-48.

⊜ Sleeping

Ciudad Acuña *p284*
Few hotels are good value here.
B Best Western Hotel Villa Real, Bravo 643 Sur, T877 772 7100. Formerly the Hotel Ciudad Acuña, modern-looking, downtown location (5 blocks from bridge). Very clean, good food, and best by far in this range.

Nuevo Laredo *p281*
Many hotels including international chains with reduced rates at weekends.

B-C Motel Romanos, Doctor Mier 2420, T867-712 2391. Filled with rather cheesy mock-Romanesque decor, but the rooms are comfortable and have excellent beds.
C-D Diamante, Av Reforma 3760, T867-711 1596. Small, quiet, and excellent restaurant. Best in range.
E Calderón García Ana, Hermenegildo Galeana 508, T867-712 0948. In centre, run-down but friendly. Rooms have bath, hot water and fan.

Piedras Negras *p285*
Hotels are rather neglected and overpriced.
A Best Western Autel Río, Padre de las Casas 121 Norte, T878-782 7064, autelrio@

prodigy.net.mx. The best place in town, with comfortable rooms, beautiful gardens, a pool, parking space and internet.

Camping
The better of the 2 trailer parks is on the east side of Interstate 35, Main St, exit, 10 mins from border.

Reynosa *p285*
Like elsewhere on the border, hotels are generally poor value in Reynosa.
C Virrey, Blv Miguel Hidalgo y Práxedis Balboa, T899-923 1049, www.hvirrey.com.mx. Reynosa's largest and best in this range by far. Bland, but on main strip and with all amenities. Highly recommended.

Matamoros *p285*
A Colonial, Calle 6 and Matamoros, T868-816 5975, www.hcolonial.com. A very attractive hotel with a beautiful colonial interior and comfortable rooms. Very traditional and recommended.
C Majestic, Abasolo 131, T868-813 3680. This is budget range for Matamoros. Large, clean rooms with hot water and friendly staff.

Saltillo *p285*
There are several hotels a short distance from the plaza at the intersection of Allende and Aldama, the main streets. Saltillo is a conference centre with many hotels in the luxury range.
A Rancho El Morillo, Prolongación Obregón Sur y Echeverría, T884-417 4376, www.elmorillo.com. An attractive old converted hacienda with a beautiful, sunny garden. Meals available.
C Garden Express, Blv Los Fundadores 2001, T844-430 1300. Economical and best in range.
D Brico, Ramos Arizpe Pte 552, T884-412 5146. Cheap, noisy and clean. Tepid water.

Camping
Trailer park, turn right on road into town from Monterrey between **Hotel del Norte**

and **Kentucky Fried Chicken**. Basic, with hook-ups and toilets.

Matehuala *p286*
C Del Parque, Bocanegra 232, T488-882 5200. Best in range, large rooms, breakfast, secure parking, Wi-Fi. Recommended.
C El Dorado, nearby, T88-882 0174. Cheaper, and recommended.
E Alamo, Guerrero 116, T88-882 0017. Very pleasant rooms, clean, with hot showers. Safe motorcycle parking. Friendly, recommended.

Monterrey *p287, maps p286 and p288*
Accommodation in Monterrey is notoriously expensive. There are many hotels between Colón and Reforma, but nothing below US$15. Most of the cheap hotels are in the area around the bus station (metros Central and Cuauhtémoc).
LL Gran Hotel Ancira, Ocampo 443 Oeste, T81-8150 7000, www.hotel-ancira.com. A very sumptuous, regal hotel with a beautiful marble staircase that's perfect for a James Bond-style entrance. Now a national historic monument. Not cheap, but a picture of elegance.
B Fundador, Montemayor 802, T81-8342 1694. A good location in the Barrio Antiguo. Rooms are comfortable, clean and unremarkable. Lots of wood panelling.
C Motel/Trailerpark Nueva Castilla, on Hwy 85 before Saltillo bypass. Motel with spaces for RVs, pool, hot showers, clean but drab.
C Victoria, Bernado Reyes 1205 Norte, T81-8375 6919. Fading bus station 'cheapie' that's relatively economical for Monterrey. Noisy, so get a room away from the street.

Around Monterrey *P289*
D Posada El Potrero Chico, Camino al Potrero Chico 825, Hidalgo, T81-8362 6672, www.elpotrerochico.com.mx.

Ciudad Victoria *p290*
There are several cheaper hotels by the bus station and in the centre.

AL Best Western Santorín, Cristóbal Colón Norte 349, T834-318 1515. Typical Best Western comfort. Rooms have a/c and TV. There's parking and a restaurant.
C Las Fuentes Misión, Cra Nacional Km 227, T834-312 5655. On Route 85, centrally located, pool, restaurant, room service, internet. Best in this range.

Camping
Victoria RV Trailer Park, Libramiento 101-85 (follow signs), T/F834-312 4824. Good service, electricity and hot showers. US$15.

Ciudad Mante and around *p290*
A Mante, Guerrero 500 Norte, T831-232 0990. Probably the best hotel, in shaded grounds at north edge of business sector.
C Monterrey, Av Juárez 503 Ote, T831-232 2712, in old sector. Manager speaks English here. Rooms have bath, hot water, a/c and cable TV. The restaurant isn't so good. Recommended.

Tampico *p290*
A-B Brisas del Mar, Blv Costero 504 Pte, T833 269-0100, www.brisasdelmar.com.mx. Nice waterfront location. Restaurant, all mod cons, clean and bright. Highly recommended.
E Hawaii, Héroes del Cañonero 609, 2 blocks east of Plaza Libertad, T833-234 1887. Dark rooms, but clean. There are other cheapies on this street.

Camping
RVs can stay in the parking lot of the airport, US$15 per vehicle, noisy from traffic.

Ciudad Valles *p291*
B San Fernando, Blv México–Laredo 17 Norte, T481-382 0184. Clean, large rooms with a/c and TV. Parking.
D Condesa, Av Juárez 109, T481-382 0015. Clean, friendly and basic. Rooms have fan. OK.

Camping
El Bañito, 11 km south of town. With warm sulphur pools.

Ixmiquilpan *p291*
C Hotel Diana, Av Insurgentes Pte 5, T759-723 0758. Rooms at the rear of the building are slightly more expensive. Safe parking. Recommended.
E Hotel/Restaurant Los Portales, 1 block from main square. Clean, with safe parking.

❶ Eating

Saltillo *p285*
🍴 **El Campanario Saloon and Grill**, Ocampo, 1200-2400. Recommended.
🍴 **El Tapanco**, Allende Sur 225, T844-414 0043. Saltillo's most popular restaurant, local dishes served with flair in beautiful surroundings. Downtown location.
🍴 **Arcasa**, Victoria. Good local food.
🍴 **Victoria**, Padre Flores 221, by **Hotel Hidalgo**. Has reasonable *comida* and good breakfasts.

Monterrey *p287, maps p286 and p288*
🍴 **El Regio**, Gonzalitos y Vancouver, T81-8346 8650. Traditional upscale local cuisine. One of Monterrey's best restaurants.
🍴 **Madre Oaxaca**, Jardón 814 Ote. A beautiful, upmarket restaurant serving fine Oaxacan cuisine.
🍴-🍴 **La Casa del Maiz**, Abasolo 870B Ote, at Dr Coss. Great, arty decor at this restaurant specializing in creative Mexican fare. Very pleasant.
🍴-🍴 **Los Monjitas**, Morelos 240 Ote. The waitresses serve your food dressed as nuns. Good Mexican dishes with a religious twist. Recommended.
🍴 **Coliseo Cafetería**, Colón 235. Cheap and cheerful 24-hour joint near the bus station. Tasty, reliable staples.

Ciudad Victoria *p290*
🍴 **Daddy's** on the plaza. A sort of **Denny's**, with a Mexican touch for the homesick North American.

Tampico *p290*
¶ **Centro Gastronómico Mercado de Comida** east of the market, for many cheap restaurants.
¶ **Emir**, Olmos, between Díaz Mirón and Madero. Good for breakfast.

☻ Festivals and events

Saltillo *p285*
30 May and **30 Aug** Indigenous dances and picturesque ceremonies.
Aug Local feria during the 1st half of the month; cheap accommodation impossible to find at this time.
Oct Bullfights during fiestas.
Dec Pastorelas, telling the story of the Nativity, are performed in the neighbourhood in Christmas week.

▲ Activities and tours

Monterrey *p287, maps p286 and p288*
Adventure sports
Asociación de Excursionismo y Montañismo, Washington Pte 2222-B, Col María Luisa, T81-8327 1929 (ask for Sr Angel Medina).

Spectator sports
Baseball Estadio de Baseball Monterrey, Parque Niños Héroes, T81-8351 8022.
Bullfighting Plaza de Toros, M Barragán y Alfonso Reyes, north of bus station, T81-8374 0505.
Football Estadio Tecnológico, off Av Garza Sada, southeast of centre, T81-8375 8200; **Estadio Universitario**, Parque Niños Héroes, north of centre, T81-8376 2238.

Tampico *p290*
Fishing
Apr-Aug is the **Deep-Sea Fishing** competition season, with several major competitions.

☻ Transport

Nuevo Laredo *p284*
Bus
The Nuevo Laredo bus station is not near the border; take a bus to the border, then walk across. You cannot get a bus from the Laredo **Greyhound** terminal to the Nuevo Laredo terminal unless you have an onward ticket. Connecting tickets from Houston via Laredo to Monterrey are available, 14 hrs. Some buses to Laredo connect with **Greyhound** buses in the US.

Grupo Senda and **Estrella Blanca** manage all regional buses in and out of Nuevo Laredo.

To **Guadalajara**, 13 daily, 18 hrs, US$28, executive class US$61. To **Mexico City**, 18 daily, 16 hrs, US$65. To **Monterrey**, every ½ hr or better, 4 hrs, US$12. To **San Luis Potosí**, Estrella Blanca, 13 daily, US$23. To **Tampico**, Estrella Blanca, 1445, 1745, 1915, 2045, 17 hrs, US$52.

Car
Car insurance Johnson's Mexico Insurance, Tepeyac Agent, Lafayette and Santa Ursula (59 and Interstate 35), US$2 per day, open 24 hrs, recommended. **Sanborn's**, 2212 Santa Ursula (Exit 16 on Interstate 35), T867-723 3657, www.sanbornsinsurance.com. Expensive, open 24 hrs.

Matamoros *p285*
Bus
Several lines run 1st-class buses to **Mexico City**, 14 hrs, US$35-69. Estrella Blanca to **Cd Victoria** regular departures, 4 hrs, US$20.

Saltillo *p285*
Air
The airport (SLW) is 16 km from town. Flights to **Mexico City** daily with Mexicana. Aerolitoral flies regularly to **Guadalajara** and **Monterrey**.

Bus

The terminal is on Blv Echeverría, 3 km south of centre (yellow bus marked 'Periférico' from Allende y Lerdo de Tejada in centre); minibuses to Pérez Treviño y Allende (for centre) will take luggage. Bus to **Cd Acuña**, Grupo Senda, 12 daily, 8 hrs, US$25-30. To **Mexico City**, Estrella Blanca and Grupo Senda, 7 daily, 11 hrs, US$30. To **San Luis Potosí**, Estrella Blanca, 1745, US$21. To **Monterrey**, almost constantly, US$5-8. For **Torreón** 3 hrs, US$12-16, all buses originate in Monterrey and tickets are only sold when bus arrives; be prepared to stand.

Matehuala *p286*
Bus

Mexico City, 8 hrs, US$32. **Monterrey**, 4 hrs, US$12. **Real de Catorce**, US$4. **San Luis Potosí**, with Estrella Blanca, 2½ hrs, US$6.

Monterrey *p287, maps p286 and p288*
Air

Gen Mariano Escobedo airport (MTY), 24 km from centre. Daily flights from **Mexico City** take 1 hr 20 mins. Good links to many other Mexican cities and numerous flights to the **US** and **Canada** and to **Havana**, Cuba.

Airline offices AeroMéxico, T81 8343 5560. American Airlines, T81-8342 9717. Aviacsa, T81-8153 4304. Mexicana, T800-715 0220.

Bus

Terminal on Av Colón, between Calzada B Reyes and Av Pino Suárez (Metro Cuauhtémoc), T318-3737. Grupo Senda and Estrella Blanca are the main companies. To **Santiago**, for Cola de Caballo falls, US$2. To **Mexico City**, hourly, 12 hrs, US$32-61. A more scenic trip is from Mexico City (northern bus terminal) to **Cd Valles**, 10 hrs, from where there are many connecting buses to Monterrey. To **Chihuahua**, 11 daily, 12 hrs, US$44. To **Guadalajara**, 15 daily, US$74; executive 2100, US$51. To **Matamoros**, hourly, 4 hrs, US$18. To **Nuevo Laredo**, hourly, 4 hrs, US$8-11. Constant buses to

Saltillo, US$355-0480. To **San Luis Potosí**, hourly, US$18-34. To **Tampico**, hourly, 7-8 hrs, US$27-38. To **Torreón**, hourly, US$17-25.

Car

If driving to **Saltillo**, there is nothing to indicate you are on the toll-road until it is too late. The toll is US$7. Look for the old road.

Car rental Monterrey, Serafín Peña 740-A Sur, T81-344 6510. **Payless**, Escobedo Sur 1011 Local 8, T81-344 6363.

Metro

There are 2 metro lines. The **blue line**, the longer one, runs south from the suburb of San Bernabé and then makes a right-angle turn traversing the city eastwards passing by the bus and train stations. It connects with the **green line** (at Cuauhtémoc near the bus station), which runs south into the centre. Tickets bought from machines (2 pesos a ticket, discount for more than one).

Ciudad Victoria *p290*
Bus

The terminal is on the outskirts near the ring road northeast of the town centre. Omnibuses Blancos to **Cd Valles**, US$12. To **Mexico City**, 10 hrs, US$41-44.

Tampico *p290*
Air

The Francisco Javier Mina Airport (TAM), T833-238 0571, is 8 km from the centre. Mexicana has daily flights to **Mexico City** and Aerolitoral flies to **San Antonio** (Texas). There are good links with towns in Northern Mexico and on the Gulf coast flies to **Los Angeles** via **Mexico City**, **Tepic** and **Tijuana**. Continental Express flies to **Dallas** and **Houston**.

Airline offices Aero California, T833-213 8400. AeroMéxico, T833-217 0939. Mexicana, T833-213 9600.

Bus

The bus station is several kilometres from the centre on Av Ejército Mexicano on the far side of Laguna del Carpintero. *Colectivos* to bus station leave from Olmos between market and plaza. To **Cd Valles**, US$9.50. To **Mexico City**, 8 hrs, US$34. To **Monterrey**, 7-8 hrs, US$27-28. To **San Luis Potosí**, 7 hrs, US$25.

Ciudad Valles *p291*
Bus Omnibus Oeste to **San Luis Potosí**, US$18, 4 hrs; **Mexico City**, US$24.30, 10 hrs.

① Directory

Nuevo Laredo *p284*
Banks UNB Convent and Matamoros charges 1% commission on TCs, Mon-Fri 0830-1600. IBC, no commission under US$500. **Embassies and consulates** Mexican Consulate, Farragut and Maine, 4th light on the right after leaving Interstate 35, Mon-Fri 0800-1400, helpful.

Saltillo *p285*
Banks Bancomer, Allende y Victoria. Banamex, Allende y Ocampo. **Post office** Victoria 223. **Telephone** Long-distance calls from **Café Victoria**, Padre Flores 221, near market.

Monterrey *p287, maps p286 and p288*
Banks Plenty of ATMs in town.
Embassies and consulates Canada, T81-8344 3200. Mon-Fri 0900-1330 and 1430-1730. French, T81-8336 4498. Germany, T81-8338 5223. Guatemala, T81-8372 8648. Holland, T81-8342 5055. Israel, T81-8336 1325. Sweden, T81-8346 3090. Switzerland, T81-8338 3675. US, T81-8345 2120. UK (Honorary), T81-8333 7598. **Medical services** Hospital General de IMSS, Pino Suárez y J I Ramón, T81-8345 5355. Angeles Verdes, T81-8340 2113. Red Cross, T81-8375 1212.
Post office Palacio Federal, Av 5 de Mayo y Zaragoza (behind Government Palace), T81-342 4003.

Tampico *p290*
Embassies and consulates Germany, 2 de Enero, 102 Sur-A, T833-212 9784. Also deals with British affairs.
Medical services Red Cross, T833-212 1313. **Post office** Madero 309 Ote, T833-212 1927.

Colonial Heartland

For centuries, the mines of Central Mexico churned out much of the world's silver and a fair amount of gold and precious stones. Spanish-style architecture, built with the amassed fortunes, is at its most opulent and impressive in the magnificent towns and cities of the colonial highlands. While the mines of Zacatecas, San Luis Potosí and Guanajuato supplied the precious metal to the Spanish crown, the states of Aguascalientes and Querétaro were important supply centres and stopovers on the silver route to the capital and the port of Veracruz. The years of heavy-handed Spanish rule and obvious inequalities led to discontent and in the early 19th century this region was the Cradle of Independence; nearly every town or village played a part in the break with Spain and many museums and monuments tell the story. Mining is still important in this area and many of these old cities are today important modern industrial centres, mostly with sprawling suburbs; but they mostly manage to retain at their core the magnificence of their colonial past. The 'ghost towns' of Pozas and Real de Catorce, once thriving mining centres, have not fared so well, but it is fascinating to wander through their semi-deserted streets. Colonial rule relied heavily on the work of the missionaries and a tour of the 18th-century Missions of Querétaro, well off the beaten track, with a stop-off at the thermal baths and opal mines of Tequisquiapan, is well worth the hair-raising journey of '700 curves'. ❯❯ *For listings, see pages 315-331.*

Querétaro ●❷❼❹❽❺❻❼ ❯❯ *pp315-331.*

→ *Colour map 3, B3. Phone code: 442. Altitude: 1865 m.*

As gateway to the Colonial Heartland, Querétaro hides a treasured city centre of pedestrian walkways and colonial architecture. Meaning 'Place of Rocks' in Tarascan, the city was found in 1531 and has grown to be an important albeit sprawling industrial centre and state capital. Sights are somewhat limited, but the ambience makes a visit worthwhile and provides time to contemplate the historical significance of the city. Hidalgo's rising in 1810 was plotted here, and it was here that Emperor Maximilian surrendered after defeat. He was tried and shot on 19 June 1867, on the **Cerro de las Campanas** (the Hill of Bells), outside the city. It's also a good base to plan trips to the **Peñón de Bernal** and the rarely visited **Missions of Querétaro** in the Sierra Gorda to the east.

Ins and outs

Getting there The Central Camionera (bus station) is 5 km southeast of the centre on the Mexico City-León highway. There are regular services to Mexico City's Terminal del Norte and the airport (Sala D). Querétaro is at the crossroads of Route 57 (San Luis Potosí–Mexico City) and Route 45 to Celaya, León and Aguascalientes.

Getting around Querétaro centre is reasonably compact; walking tours are very popular. City buses 8 and 19 link the town centre and bus station; make sure they say 'Central Camionera' or 'Terminal de Autobuses'. There is a **tourist office** ① *Pasteur Norte 4, on Plaza Independencia at the junction with Libertad, T442-212 1412.*

Sights

In 1810, Doña Josefa Ortiz de Domínguez, wife of the mayor and prominent member of a group plotting for Independence, got word to Father Hidalgo that their plans for revolt had been discovered. Hidalgo immediately gave the cry (*El Grito*) for Independence. Today, every 15 September at 2300, *El Grito* is given from the balcony of the **Palacio Municipal** ① *T442-238 5000, Mon-Fri 0800-2000, Sun 0800-1800*, which was once home of Doña Josefa La Corregidora. (*El Grito* is echoed on every civic balcony throughout Mexico). The **Santa Rosa de Viterbo** church and monastery was remodelled by Francisco Tresguerras. He also reconstructed the **Templo de Santa Clara**, one of the loveliest churches in Mexico, with fine gilded carvings. The 16th-century church and monastery of **Santa Cruz** served as the headquarters of Maximilian and his forces and later as the emperor's prison before he faced the firing squad in 1867. There is a good view from the bell tower. The church of **San Felipe**, recently restored, is now the cathedral. The splendid **Palacio Federal**, once an Augustinian convent with exceptionally fine cloisters, has been restored and houses an art gallery containing some beautiful works. The **Teatro de la República**, by Jardín Zenea, is where Maximilian and his generals were tried, and where the Constitution of 1917 (still in force) was drafted.

A little out of town to the west on Avenida Zaragoza **Los Arcos** form an impressive **aqueduct**, built in 1726, and the enduring symbol of Querétaro.

The important and elegant **Museo Regional** ① *main plaza, Tue-Sun 1000-1900, US$3*, is known as Plaza de Armas or Jardín Obregón. It contains material on the

Querétaro

Sleeping 🛏
Hidalgo 1
Hostal Jirafa Roja 2
La Casa de la Marquesa 3
Mesón de Santa Rosa 4
Plaza 5
San Agustín 8

Eating 🍴
Alda Café 1
Bisquetes 2
Café 1810 4
El Arcangel 5
Italian Coffee Company 8

Mesón de Chucho el Roto 6
Ostionería Tampico 7
Vegetariano Natura 9

Missions of Querétaro

A little-known feature of Querétaro is the existence of five 18th-century missions in the far northeast of the state justly made a Unesco World Heritage Site in 2003. The missions were founded by Fray Junípero de la Serra, who later went on to establish missions in California. He is also said to have planted a miraculous tree in the convent of Santa Cruz in the city of Querétaro by thrusting his staff into the ground. The tree is apparently the only one of its kind in the world to have cruciform thorns.

The Missions of Querétaro are distinguished by the profusion of baroque carving, their superb location and the care with which they have been conserved. All five missions – Jalpan, Concá, Landa de Matamoros, Tilaco and Tancoyol – have been restored, and two of them have hotels nearby.

The journey itself requires something of a head for heights – while it is a dramatic and scenic journey climbing the massif of the Sierra Gorda, there are said to be 700 curves en route. There is a slightly shorter route, but that has more than 1000 curves! If travelling by bus, allow at least three days to enjoy the tour of the missions. Alternatively they can be visited as day trips from Jalpan.

Independence movement and the 1864-1867 period leading to the imprisonment and death of Maximilian.

Around Querétaro ●❶❷❸❹ ⟫ pp315-331.

There are two routes up to the Missions of Querétaro, both of which pass through the small market town of **Ezequiel Montes**. The first road is reached by turning northeast from the main highway, 21 km east of Querétaro, and has two towns of interest along the way: **Colón**, 14 km off the road, has a 17th century Templo de Nuestra Señora de los Dolores de Soriana; and **Bernal**, 75 km from Querétaro, which is a centre for clothing, blankets, wall hangings and carpets.

Near Bernal is the remarkable **Peñón de Bernal**, a massive rocky outcrop 350 m high. On the night before and the day of the spring equinox (21 March) there is a festival held here. Local indigenous people believe the mountain is an energy point, because of its distinctive shape, and come to get strength from the first sun of the year. It is considered the third largest of its kind, after the Rock of Gibraltar and the Sugarloaf Mountain in Rio de Janeiro. The second route to the Missions is reached by Route 120 from San Juan del Río (see below).

San Juan del Río → Colour map 3, B3. Phone code: 427.

Forty-eight kilometres from Querétaro is San Juan del Río, where some of the best fighting bulls are raised; the town is a centre for handicrafts, and also for polishing gemstones: opals and amethysts.

Tequisquiapan → Colour map 3, B3. Phone code: 414.

A branch road runs northeast from San Juan to the picturesque town of Tequisquiapan, with thermal baths, a fine climate, watersports, weekend residences and expensive, good hotels. The town is deserted from Monday to Thursday so look for reductions in hotel prices. There is a geyser, at **Tecozautla**, 1¼ hours from Tequisquiapan.

Cadereyta → *Colour map 3, B3. Phone code: 441.*

North of Tequisquiapan is Cadereyta (Km 75), colonial in style, with two noteworthy churches in the main square, one dedicated to St Peter, the other to St Paul. The latter houses an important collection of colonial religious art.

San Joaquín → *Colour map 3, B3. Phone code: 441.*

East of Route 120, the ruins at San Joaquín (Km 138), Ranas and Toluquilla, have been only partially excavated. You must register upon arriving and a donation is requested. The sites have been attributed to the Toltecs and the Chichimecs. **Ranas** ① *US$1*, is a 30-minute walk from the village and has stupendous views from a series of terraced platforms and pyramids; **Toluquilla** is 10 km from the village along a poorly marked road. Although there were only, at most, 200 inhabitants, there are six ball courts. Tarantulas abound! **San Joaquín** is famous for the annual **Huapango** dance festival on 15 April. Fifteen minutes' walk from San Joaquín is a beautiful cave (**Las Grutas**).

The road to the ruins is steep and the ruins are often swathed in mist. The bends really start after Vizarrón. Much of the journey from here on is through rather arid and dramatic terrain with gorges and panoramic views. The high point is called **La Puerta del Cielo** (Door to the Sky), which is apt as you can actually look down on the clouds. As the road begins to descend, so the vegetation becomes more tropical and the weather gets much warmer. If driving there are plenty of petrol stations, but keep topping up just to be safe.

Jalpan → *Colour map 3, B4. Phone code: 441. Altitude: 700 m.*

Jalpan, the first and the largest of the missions in the high valleys spreading out from the town, becomes visible way below in a broad, lush valley. It was founded in 1744 and has cloisters in addition to the main church. The town itself is picturesque without being spoilt. There are also pleasant walks along tree-lined riverbanks. The town **museum** ① *daily 1000-1500, US$0.50*, is worth a visit.

Jalpan makes a good base for day-trips to the other missions. **Landa de Matamoros**, 18 km east of Jalpan; **Tilaco**, 25 km beyond Landa to the east; and **Tancoyol**, 37 km to the north of Landa. The roads are good apart from the last 15 km into Tilaco.

Concá → *Altitude: 500 m.*

Thirty-eight kilometres northwest of Jalpan is Concá. At the bridge of Concá a hot-water river flows into one with cold water. The mission is built on a ridge, creating a dramatic skyline when viewed from below. The village is very small with two restaurants. *Acamaya* (freshwater crayfish) are a local speciality. There's an hourly bus to Concá from Jalpan, US$1.30.

Xilitla → *Colour map 3, B4. Phone code: 489.*

About 87 km west of Jalpan is the charming village of Xilitla which would normally be overlooked but for the lush tropical valley and comfortable climate. The late Edward James, born 1907, millionaire heir to the Phelps Dodge copper fortune and with connections to the British royal family, fell in love with the place and built Las Pozas, a house and gardens of architectural eccentricity that are matched only by their setting. Las Pozas is 30 minutes' walk from Xilitla and is fascinating with extravagant concrete structures intertwined with exuberant vegetation, waterfalls, birds and butterflies.

Celaya ⬤❶❷❸❹ → pp315-331. Colour map 3, B3.

→ *Phone code: 461. Altitude: 1800 m.*

Celaya is famous for its confectionery, especially a caramel spread called *cajeta* or *dulce de leche*, and its churches, built by Mexico's great architect Francisco Eduardo Tresguerras (1759-1833), a native of the town. His best is considered to be **El Carmen**, with an elegant tower and dome. He also built a fine bridge over the Río de la Laja. Founded on 1 January 1571, the city's prosperity came from the fertile soils of the region, which helped the growing town to develop as an important trade and supply centre for mining communities in the region. The **tourist office** ⓘ *Casa del Diezmo, Juárez 204, T/F461-613 4313*, is helpful.

Not surprisingly the appeal of the town lies in the architecture of Tresguerras. **Templo del Carmen** was built by Tresguerras in 1802-1807; the interior and exterior are neoclassical with a simple elegance, and you can see Tresguerras' own paintings inside. **Convento de San Francisco** is one of the largest in the country, with a 17th-century baroque interior; the façade of the cloisters was rebuilt by Tresguerras. **Templo de San Francisco** was rebuilt in 1683 after the original chapel was demolished. The façade is neoclassical and was rebuilt, together with the altars, by Tresguerras in 1810-1820. **Claustro Agustino** dates from the beginning of the 17th century and was the municipal prison until 1961, but now doubles as the Casa de la Cultura. **Templo de San Agustín** was built in 1609 in the plateresque style. **Templo de la Tercera Orden** is another of Tresguerras' neoclassical works, built in 1820 with marvellous altars. The **Columna de la Independencia** was designed by Tresguerras and was the first monument in the country to celebrate Mexico's freedom in 1828. **Torre Hidráulica**, also known as the *bola de agua* (ball of water), has been adopted as the symbol of the city; it was inaugurated on the centenary of Mexico's Independence from Spain and holds one million litres of water. **Casa del Diezmo**, built at the end of the 17th century, now houses the **tourist office**. The **Presidencia Municipal** has impressive murals up the stairways in the entrance off the main square, a metamorphosis of people and events in Mexico's history, created in 1980 by local artist Octavio Ocampo González. The **Mausoleo de Tresguerras** is a baroque chapel where the famous architect is buried

Irapuato ⬤ → pp315-331. Colour map 3, B3.

→ *Phone code: 462.*

Irapuato is 'World Strawberry Capital' and is justly noted for the delicious fruit. In the town centre, around **Plaza de los Fundadores** and the **Jardín Hidalgo**, there is a cluster of historic buildings. The **Templo del Hospital**, built around 1550, rebuilt 1617, façade completed 1733, is said to have the country's largest chandelier. Outside, the **Cruz Monolítica** commemorates the visit of San Sebastián of Aparicio. The façade of the **Templo de San Francisco**, also known as El Convento (1799), is a mixture of baroque and neoclassical. The huge **Parroquia** (parish church) was rebuilt in the mid-18th century. The 19th-century **Presidencia Municipal** incorporates a former 18th-century school, the **Colegio de Enseñanza para Niños**. The fountain, **Fuente de los Delfines**, was given to the town by Emperor Maximilian. There's a **tourist office** ⓘ *Escuela Médico Militar 60, Col Jardines, T462-624 7174, www.irapuato.gob.mx.*

Unfortunately, the centre of town has been invaded by unsightly and incongruous modern buildings, but just to the edge is the 16th-century church of **San José**, with fine examples of American indigenous art, and the **Templo of Nuestra Señora de Guadalupe** (1890), with a striking late neoclassical gold-leaf-decorated interior.

San Miguel de Allende and around 😊🚗🏨🌐🅿️🔺🚌🏛️ ➤➤ *pp315-331.*
Colour map 3, B3.

➔ *Phone code: 415. Altitude: 1850 m.*

This charming old town on a steep hillside facing the broad sweep of the Río Laja and the distant blue of the Guanajuato mountains is 50 km north of Querétaro by paved road and has pretty much been taken over by North Americans seeking the combination of language schools and relaxed living with an arty edge that this pleasant colonial town has. It was founded as San Miguel in 1542, with 'Allende' added in honour of the Independence patriot who was born there. Its twisting cobbled streets rise in terraces to the mineral spring of **El Chorro**, from where the blue and yellow tiled cupolas of some 20 churches can be seen. It has been declared a national monument.

Ins and outs
Getting there The long-distance bus station is west of the town centre along Calle Canal. The town centre can be reached by taxi or bus. The nearest airport is at Silao, close to León, also called **Aeropuerto del Bajío**.

Getting around Most places of interest can be reached on foot. Walking tours of old houses and gardens leave from the **Jardín** ① *Insurgentes 25, between Reloj and Hidalgo, T415-152 0293, Sun 1200, 4 hrs, US$10.* The **tourist office** ① *Plaza Prinicpal, next to the church, T415-152 6565,* is good for finding hotels, English spoken, city map.

Sights
Social life revolves around the market and the Jardín, or Plaza Principal, an open-air living room for San Migueleans. Around it are the colonial **Palacio Municipal**, several hotels and **La Parroquia** (parish church), adorned in the late 19th century by Zeferino Gutiérrez, an indigenous stonemason who provided the austere Franciscan front with a beautiful façade and a Gothic tower. There is an interesting mural in the chapel. The church of **San Felipe Neri**, with its fine baroque façade, is at the southwest end of the market. Notable among the baroque façades and doors rich in churrigueresque details are the **Casa del Mayorazgo de Canal** and the

San Miguel de Allende

N
100 metres
100 yards

Sleeping 🛏️
Casa de Huéspedes 1
Casa de Sierra Nevada 11
Casa Luna B&B 2
Hostal Alcatraz 4
La Mansión del Bosque 5
Parador San Sebastián 7
Posada Carmina 8
Posada de las Monjas 9
Posada 'El Mayorazgo' 3
Rincón del Cielo 12

Sautto 13
Vista Hermosa Taboada 14

Eating 🍴
Café etc 1
Casa Mexas 2
El Buen Café 3
El Infierno 4
El Jardín 5
El Tomate 6
La Fonda 11
La Piñata 7
Mama Mía 8
Mesón de San José 9
Rincón Español 12
San Agustín 13
Tío Lucas 10

San Francisco church, which was designed by Tresguerras. The convent of **La Concepción**, built in 1734, now houses an art school, the **Centro Cultural Ignacio Ramírez Nigromonte**, locally known as Escuela de Bellas Artes (good *cafetería* in its courtyard). The summer residence of the Condes de Canal, on San Antonio, contains the art school and a language school, the **Instituto Allende**, started by Stirling Dickinson (which has an English-language library and runs Spanish courses). A magnificent view of the city can be gained from the mirador on the Querétaro road.

Around San Miguel de Allende

A good all-day hike can be made to the **Palo Huérfano** mountain on the south side of town. Take the road to just before the radio pylon then take the trails to the summit, where there are oaks and pines. **El Charco del Ingenio** ① *T415-154 4715, daily, US$2.75*, are botanical gardens that cover an area of 64 ha, with lovely views, a deep canyon, an artificial lake and cacti garden of many species. There are great views and hikes around the canyon and lakes, and it's a good spot for watching the sunset – but don't wander too far, it closes at dusk. To get there, take a bus to El Gigante shopping centre, turn left and continue for 15 minutes, or go up Calle Homobono, a more interesting and attractive route.

Dolores Hidalgo and around ●●●●● ➤➤ *pp315-331. Colour map 3, B3.*

➔ *Phone code: 418.*

This attractive, tranquil small town, 54 km from Guanajuato, was the home of Father Hidalgo, the Mexican Roman Catholic priest and revolutionary rebel leader. His statue stands in the lovely main square, known as the Jardín. The square is lined with restaurants, cafés and banks. On one side is the church of **Nuestra Señora de los Dolores** (1712-1778) ① *not always open*, in which Hidalgo gave *El Grito de la Independencia* (the Cry for Independence from Spain); the façade is impressive, and the churrigueresque side altar pieces, one of gold leaf, one of wood, are more ornate than the main altar. The **tourist office** ① *main square, T/F418-182 1164*, can direct you to places making traditional Talavera tiles and ceramics, available at very good prices. Dolores Hidalgo can be a good, quiet base for visiting livelier Guanajuato and more expensive San Miguel de Allende (above).

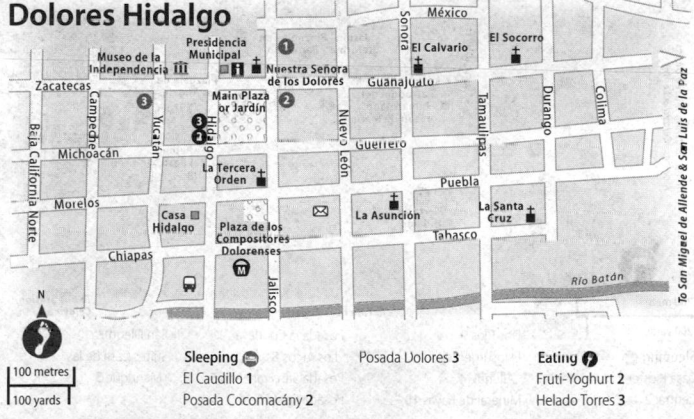

Dolores Hidalgo

Sleeping 🛏
El Caudillo **1**
Posada Cocomacány **2**
Posada Dolores **3**

Eating 🍴
Fruti-Yoghurt **2**
Helado Torres **3**

The **Iglesia de La Asunción** ① *Puebla y Sonora*, has a large tower at one end, a dome at the other, extensive murals and a tiled floor inside. Two blocks away, at Puebla and Jalisco, is **Plaza de los Compositores Dolorenses** with a bandstand. Between these two sites on Puebla is the post and telegraph office. Visit Hidalgo's house, the **Museo Casa Hidalgo** ① *Morelos and Hidalgo, Tue-Sat 1000-1800, Sun 1000-1700, US$4.35*, a beautiful building with a courtyard and wells, memorabilia and one room almost a shrine to the 'Father of Independence'. The **Museo de la Independencia** ① *Zacatecas, US$0.70*, was formerly a jail, but now has displays of striking paintings of the path to Independence.

Around Dolores Hidalgo

About 5 km southeast of town on a dirt track are the ruins of the **Hacienda de la Erre** ① *free entrance to the untended ruins and grounds*, Padre Hidalgo's first stop on the Independence route after leaving Dolores. The standing walls are only 3-4 m high; there are about four rooms with ceilings, the patio is overgrown, but the chapel has been rebuilt. Outside is the huge mezquite tree under which Hidalgo is supposed to have said Mass for his insurgent troops. The walk to the ruins (1½-2 hours) starts from the plaza. Take Calle Guerrero to the east, then Tamaulipas to the main road. Turn left for 1 km to a gravel road on the left on a long curve. Follow this to the hacienda in a fertile area with plenty of trees.

Guanajuato

Sleeping 🛏
Casa Kloster 1
Central 2
Dos Ríos 9
El Insurgente
Allende 4
Mineral de Rayas 10
Posada la Condesa/
Los Arcos 8
Posada San Francisco 5
Posada Santa Fe 6
San Diego 7
Suites Casa de las
Manrique 3

→ *Phone code: 461. Altitude: 2010 m*

The beautiful university city in the central state of Guanajuato, declared a UNESCO World Heritage Site, has been important for its silver since 1548. Its name derives from the Tarascan Quanax-Huato, 'place of frogs'. It stands in a narrow gorge amid wild and striking scenery. The Guanajuato River, which cuts through the city, has been covered over and several underground streets wind their way underneath the city like a human rabbit warren – an unusual and confusing system, especially if you're driving.

Ins and outs

Getting there The international **Aeropuerto del Bajío** (BJX), 40 km west of Guanajuato near the town of Silao, receives internal flights and from the USA. The long-distance bus terminal is on the outskirts, southwest of town; taxis or buses ('Centro') will ferry you into town. ▸▸ *See Transport, page 326.*

Getting around Many of the interesting places are along and around Juárez and can be visited on foot in a day or two. Some streets, like Padre Belaunzarán, are not entirely enclosed; others, such as Hidalgo, are, so they fill with traffic fumes. The Túnel Los Angeles leads from the old subterranean streets to the modern roadway that connects with the Carretera Panorámica and the monument to Pípila (see below). Taking traffic underground has not relieved the congestion of the surface streets, which are steep, twisted and narrow. Parking for hotels is often a fair distance away.

Tourist information The **tourist office** ⓘ *Plaza de la Paz 14, beside the Basílica, T01 800-714-1086, www.guanajuato.gob.mx,* sells maps and has information about the area. The **Festival Cervantino**, said to be Latin America's biggest arts festival, takes place in October each year.

Sights

The best of many colonial churches are the Jesuit **La Compañía** (1765), by the university, note the brick ceiling; **San Diego** (1663) on the Jardín de la Unión; the **Parroquia del Inmaculado Corazón de María**, on Juárez, opposite Mercado Hidalgo, which has interesting statues on the altar; and the cathedral, or **Basílica de Nuestra Señora de Guanajuato** (1693), on Plaza de la Paz, which has a beautiful yellow interior and an ornately painted vaulted

[Map of Guanajuato city centre showing streets including Compañía, Plaza Baratillo, Baratillo, Nueva, Teatro Principal, Plaza Mexiamora, Mexiamora, Cantarranas, Alonso, Calle del Truco, Alderete, Constancia, Basílica, Jardín de la Unión, Sopeña, San Antonio, Teatro Juárez, San Diego, San Francisco, Museo Iconográfico del Quijote, To Presa de la Olla, Monumento a Pípila, Panorámica, To Presa de la Olla]

Eating 🍴
Café Las Musas **6**
Café Truco 7 **5**
El Mexicano **2**
El Retiro **3**
La Lonja **1**
La Mancha **4**

ceiling. **San Roque** (1726), on Plazuela de San Roque, a park between Juárez and Pocitos, has a vaulted ceiling, reached by a walkway that goes from the northeast side of the Jardín Reforma. The **Templo de San Francisco** (1671), on Sopeña, is also worth visiting.

Probably the most famous of Guanajuato's alleys and lanes is the **Callejón del Beso** (Alley of the Kiss), which is so narrow that, according to legend, two lovers kept apart by their families were able to exchange kisses from opposite balconies.

Guanajuato has a series of fine museums too. One most interesting building is the massive **Alhóndiga de Granaditas** ① *US$2.80*, built as a granary, turned into a fortress, and now a museum with artefacts from the pre-Columbian and colonial periods. When Father Hidalgo took the city in 1810, the Alhóndiga was the last place to surrender, and there was a wanton slaughter of Spanish soldiers and royalist prisoners. Later when Hidalgo was himself caught and executed, along with three other leaders, in Chihuahua, their severed heads were fixed, in revenge, at the four corners of the Alhóndiga.

An unusual sight shown to visitors is of mummified bodies in the small **Museo de las Momias** ① *daily 0900-1800, US$2.60, long queues on Sun,* in the Panteón Municipal, above the city off Tepetapa; buses go there ('Momias', signposted Panteón Municipal, 10 minutes, along Avenida Juárez), but you can walk. The **Museo Iconográfico del Quijote** ① *Manuel Doblado 1, Tue-Sat 1000-1830, Sun 1000-1430, US$2, free Sun,* is highly recommended for its paintings, drawings and sculptures of the Don. The painter **Diego Rivera** was born at Pocitos 47, now a **museum** ① *Tue-Sat 1000-1900, Sun 1000-1500, US$1.40,* with a permanent collection of his work on various floors, showing his changing styles; on the ground floor are his bed and other household objects. Also on Pocitos, just across from the university, is the **Museo del Pueblo** ① *Tue-Sat 1000-1900, Sun 1000-1500, US$1.40,* in a beautiful 17th-century mansion; it has one room of work by the muralist **José Chávez Morado**, a room of selected items of all Mexican art forms and temporary exhibitions. The **university** was founded in 1732; its façade of coloured stone, above a broad staircase, glows richly at sunset.

Around Guanajuato

Crowning the high hill of Hormiguera is the **Monumento a Pípila**, the man who fired the door of the Alhóndiga so that the patriots could take it. There is a fine view from the top. Look for the 'Al Pípila' sign. A number of cobbled stairways through picturesque terraces, such as Callejón del Calvario, leading off Sopeña, go up to the monument. It's a steep but short climb (about 15 minutes) rewarded with fine panoramic views of the city. Otherwise take a local bus from **Hotel Central**, on Juárez. The Carretera Panorámica, which encircles the city, passes the Pípila monument. At its eastern end the Panorámica goes by the **Presa de la Olla**, a favourite picnic spot with good cheap food available from roadside stalls. From the dam, Paseo de la Olla runs to the city centre, passing mansions of the wealthy silver barons and the **Palacio de Gobierno** (note the use of local stone).

Over the city looms the shoulder of **La Bufa** mountain. You can hike to the summit up a trail, which takes one hour: from the Pípila monument, follow the main road for about 1 km to the hospital. Walk past the hospital to a power station where the main trail starts; if you pass the quarry, note the quality of the stonemasonry on the mason's shelter.

The splendid church of **La Valenciana**, one of the most impressive in Mexico, is 5 km out of town on the Dolores Hidalgo road; it was built for the workers of the Valenciana silver mine, once the richest in the world. The church, dedicated to San Cayetano, has three huge gilt altars and a wooden pulpit of sinuous design. The style is churrigueresque, done in grey-green and pink stone; the façade is also impressive.

The **Valenciana mine** ① *daily 0900-1700, US\$1*, which has functioned since 1548, is surrounded by a wall with triangular projections on top, said to symbolize the crown of the King of Spain. The huge stone walls on the hillside, supported by enormous buttresses, created an artificial level surface from earth excavated higher up the slope. The mine is still working with both gold and silver being extracted. With care you can walk freely in the whole area. Guides are available to take you round on an interesting 30-minute tour. It is a 10-minute walk between the church and the mine pit-head.

At the old site of **La Cata** silver mine (local bus near market) is a church with a magnificent baroque façade and the shrine of **El Señor de Villa Seca** (the patron saint of adulterers) with *retablos* and crude drawings of miraculous escapes from harm, mostly due to poor shooting by husbands.

León ⊖🕐🕹⊛🅾⚠🅶🅲 ⮞⮞ *pp315-331. Colour map 3, B3.*

→ *Phone code: 477. Altitude: 1885 m.*

In the fertile plain of the Río Gómez, León is now said to be Mexico's fifth city. Nuño de Guzmán reached the area on 2 December 1530 and subsequently local farms and estates were granted to the Spaniards. Eventually Don Martín Enríquez de Almanza decreed on 12 December 1575 that a city, called León, would be founded if 100 volunteers could be persuaded to live there for 10 years, or a town if only 50 could be found. On 20 January

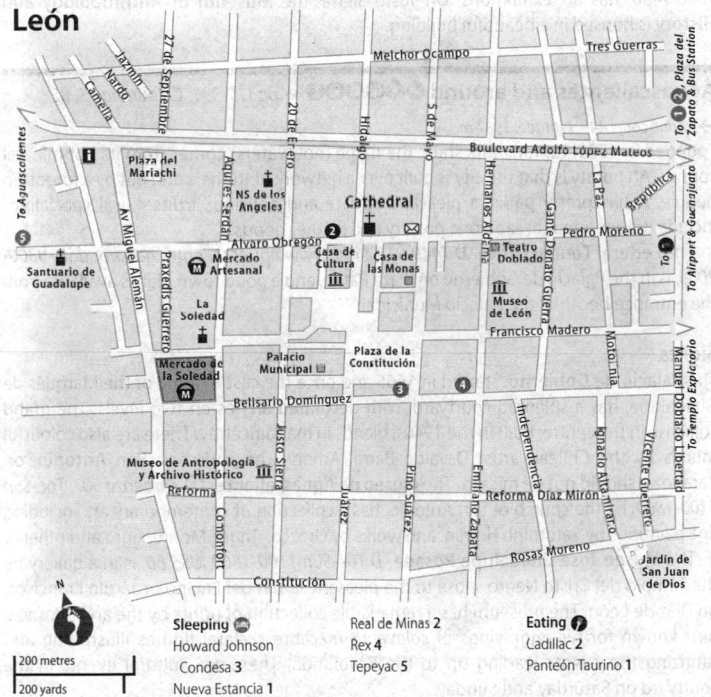

León

Sleeping 🛏
Howard Johnson
Condesa 3
Nueva Estancia 1

Real de Minas 2
Rex 4
Tepeyac 5

Eating 🍴
Cadillac 2
Panteón Taurino 1

200 metres
200 yards

1576 a town was founded by Dr Juan Bautista de Orozco, and it wasn't until 1830 that León became a city. The business centre is the delightful **Plaza de la Constitución**. León is the main shoe centre of the country and is noted for its leather work, fine silver-trimmed saddles and *rebozos* (shawls).

The **tourist office** ① *Edificio Cielo 501, López Mateos Poniente and M Alemán, www.leon-mexico.com*, provides helpful but limited information; a good city map is available free at the Palacio Municipal.

Sights

There are many shaded plazas and gardens in León. The **Palacio Municipal**, by the Plaza de la Constitución, is said to have been built as a result of a winning lottery ticket bought by a local doctor. The small **cathedral** was started by Jesuits in 1744, but they were expelled from Mexico in 1767 by Carlos III. It was eventually finished in 1837 and consecrated in 1866. The catacombs are well worth seeing at the **Templo Expiatorio** ① *Thu-Sun 1000-1200*, which has been under construction for most of the last century. The **Teatro Doblado** ① *Av Hermanos Aldama*, stages events. There is also a **Casa de Cultura**, which houses exhibitions and is buzzing at night. Also worth seeing is the **Casa de Las Monas** ① *5 de Mayo 127-29*, where Pancho Villa issued the Agrarian Reform Law on 24 May 1915, and the beautiful **Santuario de Guadalupe**.

The **Museo de León** ① *Hermanos Aldama, Tue-Sat 1000-1400 and 1630-1930, Sun 1000-1400*, has art exhibitions. On Justo Sierra, the **Museum of Anthropology and History** is housed in a beautiful building.

Aguascalientes and around ⬤⬤⬤⬤⬤⬤ ➤➤ *pp315-331. Colour map 3, B2.*

➔ *Phone code: 449. Altitude: 1987 m.*

Founded in 1575, capital of its state, the name (hot waters) comes from its hot mineral springs. An oddity is that the city is built over a network of tunnels dug out by a forgotten people. It has pretty parks, a pleasant climate and delicious fruits. Local specialities include drawn-linen threadwork, pottery and leather goods.

The **Federal Tourist Office** ① *T449-915 1155, www.aguascalientes.gob.mx, daily 0800-2000*, is in the Palacio de Gobierno on Plaza Patria, and a good town plan is available from the entrance booth of the Palacio Municipal.

Sights

The **Palacio de Gobierno**, started in 1665 and once the castle home of the Marqués de Guadalupe, has a splendid courtyard, with decorated arches on two levels. The grand staircase in the centre, built in the 1940s, blends in magnificently. There are also colourful murals by the Chilean artist Osvaldo Barra. Among the churches, **San Antonio**, on Zaragoza, should not be missed. The **Museo de Aguascalientes** ① *Zaragoza 507, Tue-Sun 1100-1800*, by the church of San Antonio, has a collection of contemporary art, including fine paintings by Saturnino Herrán, and works by Orozco, Angel, Montenegro and others.

The **Museo José Guadalupe Posada** ① *Tue-Sun 1100-1800, US$.60*, is in a gallery by the Templo del Cristo Negro, close to the pleasant Jardín del Encino or Jardín Francisco, on Díaz de León. The museum has a remarkable collection of prints by the artist Posada, best known for his engravings of *calaveras*, macabre skeletal figures illustrating and satirizing the events leading up to the Revolution. There are cultural events in the courtyard on Saturday and Sunday.

Next to the cathedral **Teatro Morelos** ① *T449-915 0097*, is where the revolutionary factions led by Pancho Villa, Emiliano Zapata and Venustiano Carranza attempted to find some common ground on which they could all work together. The attempt ended in failure.

Also worth visiting is the Carmelite **Templo de San Marcos**, with a baroque façade, built 1655-1765 on the site of a chapel that had existed since the mid-16th century, in the *barrio* of San Marcos west of the centre.

The **Casa de la Cultura**, on Venustiano Carranza and Galeana Norte, is a fine colonial building. It holds a display of *artesanía* during the April **feria**. The **university** is 30 minutes from the city centre. Its administrative offices are in the ex-Convento de San Diego, by the attractive Jardín del Estudiante, and the Parián shopping centre.

Around Aguascalientes

Hacienda de San Blas, 34 km away, contains the **Museo de la Insurgencia**, with murals by Alfredo Zermeño. Forty-two kilometres southwest en route to Guadalajara is the colonial town of **San Juan de los Lagos**, a major pilgrimage centre and crowded during Mexican holidays. There is also a fine view on entering this town: as the road descends you see the twin-towered church with its red, blue and yellow tiled dome. San Juan is famous for glazed fruits. There are many hotels in the town.

Zacatecas and around ●●●●○▲●● ⯈ *pp315-331. Colour map 3, B2.*

→ *Phone code: 492. Altitude: 2495 m.*

Founded in 1546, and capital of Zacatecas state, this picturesque up-and-down former mining city is built in a ravine with pink stone houses scattered over the hills. The largest silver mine in the world, processing 10,000 tonnes of ore a day or 220 tonnes of silver, is at nearby Real de Angeles. Silver has bestowed an architectural grandeur on Zacatecas to match that of Guanajuato. Many travellers believe it to be the most pleasant town in this part of Mexico, if not of all of Mexico. Less oriented toward (and much less overrun by) North American retirees and backpackers than San Miguel de Allende or Guanajuato, Zacatecas' laid-back atmosphere, multitude of cultural attractions, and ideal climate make it the rival of several better-known cities. You could easily spend days soaking up the atmosphere. There's also a lively nightlife with bars and discos.

Ins and outs

Getting there The international **Aeropuerto La Calera** (ZCL) is 27 km north of the city, with flights to domestic locations and several cities in the USA. Alternatively, the city can also be reached via the larger airport of San Luis Potosí, with daily bus and car rental service to Zacatecas. The bus terminal is 4 km south of town. Bus No 8 from outside the terminal leaves for the town centre every 10-15 minutes.

Getting around Blvd Adolfo López Mateos, a busy highway, runs close to the centre of town from the bus station (4 km south of town) and down the ravine. Driving in the historic centre can be a nightmare with many one-way systems. The **tourist office** ① *Av Hidalgo 403, 2nd floor, T492-925 1277, www.turismozacatecas.gob.mx*, is friendly and helpful with free maps and good information on hotels and language classes. Throughout the centre are yellow-, green-, and blue-shirted tourism office representatives ('Amigos de Turismo') who can provide free information, and a kiosk at the intersection of Hidalgo and Allende.

Sights

For a city of fewer than 150,000 inhabitants, Zacatecas has a disproportionately large number of sights, especially for those interested in colonial architecture and history. The **cathedral** (1730-1752) is the centrepiece of town with a fine churrigueresque façade. To the west is the former **San Agustín** church, constructed in 1617 (now an art gallery maintained by the Autonomous University of Zacatecas), with interior carvings. East of San Agustín is the **Museo Zacatecano** ① *Ignacio Hierro 301, Wed-Mon 1000-1700, US$1.50*, containing religious paintings, Huichol handicrafts and some colonial items.

Zacatecas

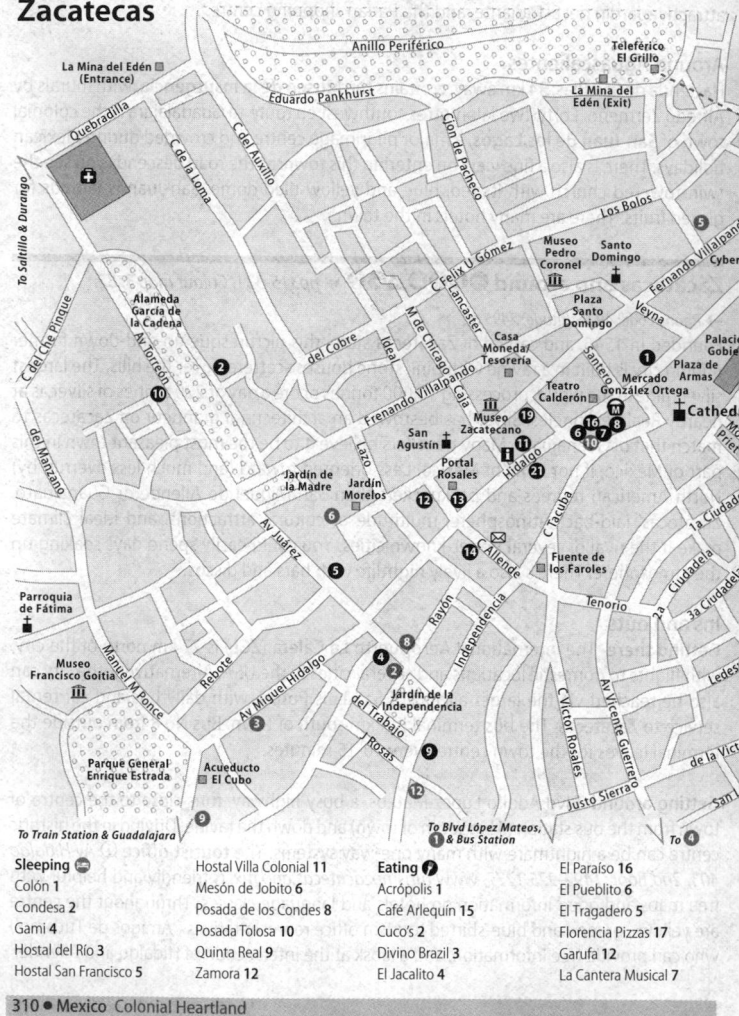

Sleeping	Hostal Villa Colonial **11**	Eating	El Paraíso **16**
Colón **1**	Mesón de Jobito **6**	Acrópolis **1**	El Pueblito **6**
Condesa **2**	Posada de los Condes **8**	Café Arlequín **15**	El Tragadero **5**
Gami **4**	Posada Tolosa **10**	Cuco's **2**	Florencia Pizzas **17**
Hostal del Río **3**	Quinta Real **9**	Divino Brazil **3**	Garufa **12**
Hostal San Francisco **5**	Zamora **12**	El Jacalito **4**	La Cantera Musical **7**

North of the cathedral is the imposing Jesuit church of **Santo Domingo** built between 1746-1749 and featuring eight gorgeous baroque retablos (see also frescoes in the sacristy by Francisco Martínez; ask the sacristan to turn the lights on). Nearby is the **Museo Pedro Coronel** ① *Plaza Santo Domingo, Fri-Wed 1000-1700, US$2.50*, which houses an excellent collection of European and modern art (including the largest collection of Goya and Miró outside of the Prado, and several by Hogarth and Tàpies), as well as folk art from Mexico and around the world (take a guide to make the most of the collections). Also worth seeing are the **Casa Moneda** (better known as the **Tesorería**), founded 1810, and the **Teatro Calderón**, opposite the cathedral.

To the north of the centre the **Museo Rafael Coronel** ① *Wed-Mon 1000-1700, US$2.50*, housed in the ex-Convento de San Francisco, has a vast collection of masks and puppets, primarily Mexican, some Rivera sketches, and an attractive garden perfect for a small picnic.

The **Mina del Edén** ① *Av Torreón y Quebradilla, daily 1000-1800, US$2.50*, at the western side of town, is an old mine with a short section of mine railway in operation; the tour is in Spanish and lasts one hour. In the mine there is also a **disco** ① *Thu, Fri and Sat, 2200-0230, varied music.* You can leave the mine the way you went in or work your way through to the end and the Swiss-built **El Teleférico**, cable car which carries you over the city, with spectacular views, to Cerro de la Bufa and the **Capilla de Los Remedios** (1728).

Up on the hill, best visited after going through Mina El Edén and El Teleférico, is **Museo de la Toma de Zacatecas** ① *daily 1000-1700, US$1.50*, on the Cerro de la Bufa, commemorates Pancho Villa's victory over Huerta's forces in 1914. The hill, northeast of the centre, is recommended for views over the city. It is a pleasant walk, although crowded on Sundays. There are equestrian bronze statues of Villa and his generals Angeles and Natera, an observatory and the **Mausoleo de Los Hombres Ilustres**. It's a 10- or 15-minute walk back down, with a small café on the first road you meet.

Heading south, near the fine old **Acueducto El Cubo**, is the **Museo Francisco Goitia** ① *Tue-Sun 1000-1700, US$2.50*, housed in what was once the governor's mansion, by the Parque General Enrique

Map labels: Juan Tolosa, Lavandería Laubasólo, To Museo Rafael Coronel, Paseo La Bufa, Lavandería El Indio Triste, Cerro de La Bufa, C de la Mantequilla, Capilla de Los Remedios, Museo de la Toma de Zacatecas, Rebote de Barbosa, Camino Ancho de la Bufa, C Altamira, Donato Guerra, 100 metres, 100 yards

Estrada, Colonia Sierra de Alicia. The museum has modern paintings by Zacatecans, but its main attractions are the paintings of small-town poverty in Mexico by Francisco Goitia. Behind the museum is the spectacular and modern **Parroquia de Fátima**; built in 1975, which pays tribute to the heritage of the city.

Around Zacatecas

Beyond Zacatecas to the east lies the **Convento de Guadalupe**, a national monument, with a fine church and convent, which now houses a world-class **Museum of Colonial Religious Art** ① *daily 1000-1700, US$1.50*. The galleries of the convent are full of paintings covering the life of St Francis and huge frescoes. The labyrinthine convent is well worth a visit and the church contains the Virgin as a child set in gold. To get there, take bus No 13 from López Mateos y Salazar, near the terminal, US$0.15, 20 minutes.

Also worth a visit are the **Chicomostoc** ruins, also known as **La Quemada** ① *56 km south, US$3.50*. To get there, take the 0800 or 1100 **Línea Verde** bus from the main terminal to Adjuntas (about 45 minutes, US$0.60), on the Villanueva road. Walk 30 minutes through beautiful, silent, nopal-cactus scenery to the ruins, which offer an impressive view. There is the Palace of the Eleven Columns, a Pyramid of the Sun and other remains on a rocky outcrop, in various stages of restoration. In themselves the ruins are not spectacular, but together with the setting they are worth the trip. For the return from the junction at Adjuntas, wait for a bus or hitch back to Zacatecas.

Jerez is an old colonial town about 54 km from Zacatecas, where the wide-brimmed *sombrero charro* and *serape* are still worn, and travel is as often on horseback as by car. There are two interesting churches in the town. **La Soledad**, begun in 1805 and completed later that century, has a baroque façade and three elaborate gateways – composites of all manner of over-the-top classical styles. **La Inmaculada** (1727), also has a baroque façade but with a neo-Romanesque interior. Also in the historic centre are the beautiful **De La Torre House** (now the town's cultural activities centre), the grand Victorian **Hinojosa Theatre**, and the exquisite **Rafael Páez Garden**, with its architectural homage to Ramón López Velarde, one of Mexico's most beloved poets.

San Luis Potosí and around ●❶❷❸❹❺ » *pp315-331. Colour map 3, B3.*

→ *Phone code: 444. Altitude: 1880 m.*
San Luis Potosí, 423 km from Mexico City, is famous for its colourful glazed tiles. The main plaza is covered with them, as are the domes of many of the city's churches, and one of its shopping streets. It became an important centre after the discovery of the famous San Pedro silver mine in the 16th century. There is a festival in the second half of August.

The helpful **tourist office** ① *Obregón 520, ½ a block west of Plaza de los Fundadores, T444-812 9906, www.visitasanluispotosi.com*, in a beautiful colonial house with lovely gardens, has good brochures and maps. Parking in San Luis Potosí is very difficult. There is a car park near the police station on Eje Vial, US$1 for the first hour, US$0.65 for each subsequent hour.

The **cathedral** is on the east side of **Plaza Hidalgo**. It has a beautiful exterior of pink cantera (local stone), with ornately carved bell towers. The interior is beautiful with rows of stone columns, approximately 2 m in diameter, running down the length of each side. Just north of the cathedral, is the **Palacio Municipal**. Inside, above the double branching staircase, you can admire glasswork of the city's coat of arms. On the upper floor, the Cabildo Hall has a ceiling painted by Italian artist Erulo Eroli, featuring mythological Christian themes.

Don't miss the church of **San Francisco**, which fronts the very pleasant plaza of the same name. This church is one of the baroque jewels of the city. The construction dates back to 1686. In that year, the work of the beautiful pink limestone façade was begun but it wasn't until the next century that some of its most important features were added, such as the baroque tower and the main altar. The interior is embellished with wonderful paintings, among which the works by Miguel Cabrera and Antonio Torres are the most outstanding. Worthy of admiration is the sacristy, the most magnificent in San Luis Potosí.

The **Museo Regional de Arte Popular** ① *Mon 1000-1500, Tue-Sat 1000-1345, 1600-1745, Sun 1000-1400,* next to the church of San Francisco, is housed in what used to be a private residence. Handicrafts from various parts of the state can be seen and bought, including ceramics, woodwork, *rebozos* and textiles. Nearby is the **Museo Regional Potosino** ① *Tue-Fri 1000-1300, 1500-1800, Sat 1000-1200, Sun 1000-1300,* located in a building that was originally a Franciscan convent. The ground floor has an exhibition of pre-Hispanic artefacts, mainly from the Huastec culture. The baroque

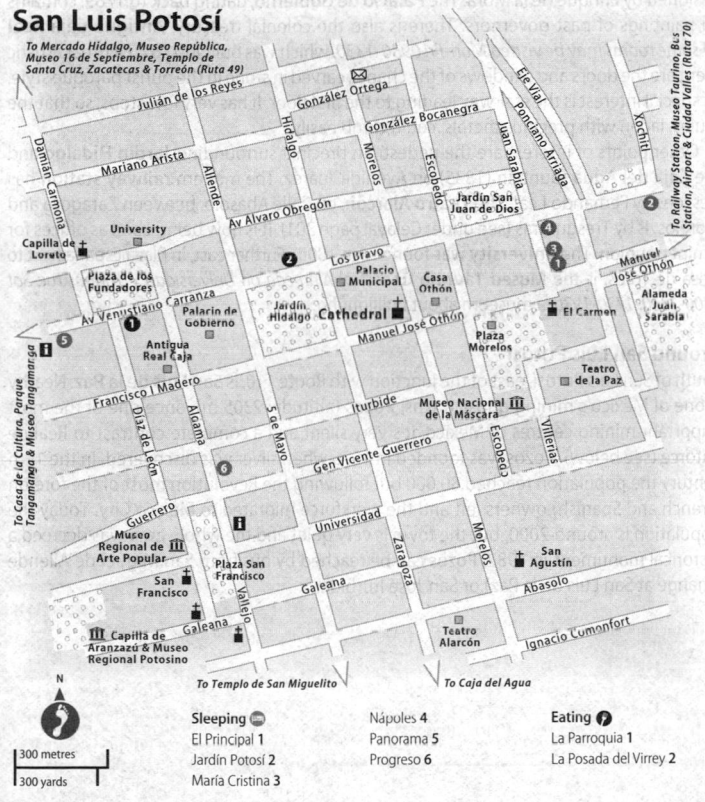

San Luis Potosí

To Mercado Hidalgo, Museo República, Museo 16 de Septiembre, Templo de Santa Cruz, Zacatecas & Torreón (Ruta 49)

Sleeping	Nápoles 4	Eating
El Principal 1	Panorama 5	La Parroquia 1
Jardín Potosí 2	Progreso 6	La Posada del Virrey 2
María Cristina 3		

Capilla de Aranzazú, inside the regional museum, should not be missed; the carved stone framework of the chapel window is one of the most beautiful pieces of baroque art in the city.

Further west, in Parque Tangamanga is the **Museo Tangamanga** ① *daily 0600-1800*, in an old hacienda, and also a planetarium, observatory and open-air theatre.

East of the cathedral, the **Templo del Carmen**, in **Plaza del Carmen**, has a grand tiled dome, an intricate façade, and a fine pulpit and altar inside. The room to the left of the main altar has another exquisite, and very striking, altar covered in gold leaf. The **Teatro de la Paz** is next door.

The **Museo Nacional de la Máscara** ① *daily 1000-1400, 1600-1800, US$0.50 plus US$0.50 for use of camera*, in what used to be the Palacio Federal, has an excellent collection of masks. The most impressive are the masks used in colonial and pre-Hispanic times in pagan religious ceremonies.

Also well worth seeing are the **Capilla de Loreto** with a baroque façade; the **Templo de San Miguelito**, in the oldest part of the city; **San Agustín**, with its ornate baroque tower; and the modern **Iglesia de la Santa Cruz**, in the Industria Aviación district, designed by Enrique de la Mora. The **Palacio de Gobierno**, dating back to 1789, contains oil paintings of past governors. There is also the colonial treasury, **Antigua Caja Real** ① *some rooms may be visited Mon-Fri 0930-1330*, which was built in 1767. Of great artistic merit are the doors and windows of the chapel, carved in stone in the purist baroque style. Of special interest is the stairway leading to the first floor. It has very low steps, so that the mules, laden with precious metals, could climb easily.

Other points of interest are the pedestrian precinct surrounding **Jardín Hidalgo** and the **Caja del Agua** fountain (1835) on Avenida Juárez. The modern **railway station** has frescoes by Fernando Leal. The **Teatro Alarcón**, on Calle Abasolo, between Zaragoza and Morelos, is by Tresguerras (see under Celaya, page 301). It is now being used as offices for a miners' union. The **university** was founded in 1804. Further east, in Plaza España next to Plaza de Toros, is the **Museo Taurino** ① *east of Alameda on Universidad y Triana, Tue-Sat 1100-1330, 1730-1930*, a museum about bullfighting.

Around San Luis Potosí

South of San Luis Potosí, east of the junction with Route 110, is **San Luis de la Paz**. Nearby is one of Mexico's mining ghost-towns, **Pozos** (altitude: 2305 m), once one of the most important mining centres of Mexico. It's very silent and a complete contrast to Real de Catorce (see below). Pozos was founded in 1576 when silver was discovered. In the 19th century the population reached 80,000 but following the Revolution most of the foreign (French and Spanish) owners left and the workforce migrated to Mexico City. Today the population is around 2000, but the town is very quiet and the whole area was decreed a historical monument in 1982. Pozos can be reached by bus from San Miguel de Allende (change at San Luis de la Paz) or San José Iturbide.

Real de Catorce ⭕🔵🔶🔴 ▸▸ *pp315-331. Colour map 3, A3.*

➔ *Phone code 488. Altitude: 2765 m.*

Real de Catorce, 56 km west of Matehuala, is one of Mexico's most interesting old mining towns. This remarkable city, founded in 1772, clustering around the sides of a valley, used to be so quiet that you could hear the river in the canyon, 1000 m below. It is becoming increasingly popular as a tourist destination and new hotels are being built.

The first church was the **Virgen del Guadalupe** (1779), a little way out of town. Beautiful ceiling paintings remain, as well as the black coffin used for the Mass of the Cuerpo Presente. Many of the images were moved to the church of **San Francisco** (1817), where miracles are believed to have occurred. The floor of the church is made of wooden panels, which can be lifted to see the catacombs below. In a room to one side of the main altar are *retablos*, touchingly simple paintings on tin, as votive offerings to the saint for his help. Next to the church is a small but worthwhile **museum** displaying mining equipment.

⭕ Colonial Heartland listings

For Sleeping and Eating price codes and other relevant information, see Essentials pages 45-48.

⬤ Sleeping

Querétaro *p297, map p298*
LL-L La Casa de la Marquesa, Madero 41, T442-212 0092, www.lacasadela marquesa.com. Opulence and comfort as it should be with 3 categories of room, the cheapest is a steal at US$135. Mid-priced rooms are equally luxurious.
L-AL Mesón de Santa Rosa, Pasteur Sur 17, Centro, T442-224 2623, www.mesonsanta rosa.com. Small, 300-year-old inn, crammed with colonial detail but tastefully modernized, good restaurant with international and Mexican cuisine.
B Hidalgo, Madero 11 Pte, near zócalo, T442-212 0081, www.hotelhidalgo.com.mx. With bath, quiet, friendly, excellent value for 2 or more, restaurant.
C Plaza, Juárez Norte 23, T442-212 1138. With bath, TV and phone, good location, airy, lovely inner patio, modernized, safe, clean, comfortable. Recommended.
C San Agustín, Pino Suárez 12, T442-212 3919. Small, dark rooms, handy restaurant next door.

D El Cid, Prolongación Corregidora Sur 10, T442-214 1165. More of a motel, clean, good value.
E Hostel Jirafa Roja, Calle 20 de Noviembre 72, T442-212 4825. Promising hostel, reasonably close to the centre of town. Kitchen facilities available. Reception desk not always staffed, call in advance to say what time you're going to arrive. Good local information.
E Posada Familiar, Independencia 22, T442-212 0584. Basic but OK, courtyard.

San Juan del Río *p299*
AL Hotel Mansión Galindo, just outside town, T427-272 0050. Beautiful restored hacienda; apparently given by Cortés to his mistress, La Malinche.
C Layseca, Av Juárez 9 Ote, T427-272 0110. Colonial building, large rooms, nice furniture, excellent, car parking, no restaurant.

Tequisquiapan *p299*
L-AL El Relox, Morelos 8, T414-273 0006, www.relox.com.mx. Attractive with spa pool, open to non-residents.
A Posada Los Arcos, Moctezuma 12, T414-273 0566. Pleasant spot, well maintained. Private bath, fan and TV.
B Posada Tequisquiapan, Moctezuma 6, T414-273 0010. Large rooms with bath

and TV, some with balconies looking out
onto gardens.

San Joaquín p300
D Mesón de Joaquín, T441-272 5315, next
to bus park. Good-value rooms for 4 and a
campground with shelters and barbecue
stands on the outskirts above the town.

Jalpan p300
A Hotel Inn Misión Jalpan, main square
next to the mission, T441-296 0255,
www.hotelesmision.com. Best place in
town, good-sized rooms, tastefully decorated,
good restaurant and swimming pool.
C Posada Fray Junípero, Ezequiel Montes
124, opposite church, T441-412 1241. With
bath and TV, clean, friendly, credit cards,
colonial style, pool, restaurant, good value
but noisy because of bus station.
D El Aguaje del Morro, down walkway on
north side of the main plaza, just before the
bridge, T441-296 0245. Very friendly staff,
can be noisy. Excellent, cheap local food.
D El Económico, on main road just
downhill of first Pemex in town, T441-441
2960. Clean, basic with laundry. Helpful staff.
E Posada Aurora, Calle Hidalgo. With bath,
hot water, fan, clean, friendly. Recommended.

Concá p300
AL Hotel Misión Hacienda Conca, Carretera
Jalpan-Río Verde, Km 57, T01-800-029-4240,
www.hotelesmision.com. A refuge of all-
inclusive luxury in the middle of nowhere.

Xilitla p300
AL-B El Castillo, T489-365 0038.
Breakfast, pool, fine views.
C El Lobo, in El Lobo, between the northern
missions and Xilitla, T441-234-9103. Simple
but OK hotel if you need to stop.

Celaya p301
Many of the better hotels are out of the centre.
B Plaza Bajío Inn, Libertad 133, T461-613
8600. With 80 rooms, central, restaurant,
parking, medical service, laundry.

C Isabel, Hidalgo 207, T461-612 2096.
Restaurant, bar, laundry, parking.
E Guadalupe, Portal Guadalupe 108, T461-
612 1839. Very old historic hotel, central,
cheaper rooms without bath.

Irapuato p301
B-C Hotel Real de Minas, Portal Carrillo
Puerto 1, T462-627 7330. Overpriced rooms
and restaurant, quiet rooms on church side.
C Kennedy, Kennedy 830, T462-627 4110.
Simple rooms with TV.

San Miguel de Allende p302, map p302
Many weekend visitors, so book ahead.
A good source of information about
cheap rooms is the English-language
paper published weekly by the
Anglo-Mexican Library on Insurgentes.
LL Casa de Sierra Nevada, Hospicio 42,
T01-800-701-1561, www.casadesierra
nevada.com. Best hotel in town combining
colonial grace and top service.
LL-L Casa Luna B&B, Pila Seca 11,
T/F415-152 1117, www.casaluna.com.
American run, excellent breakfast included,
beautiful themed rooms, no smoking inside.
Also operates Casa Luna Quebrada.
LL-L Rincón del Cielo, Correo 10, next
to main plaza, T415-152 1647. Rooms are
large and have 2 storeys, the bedroom is
upstairs with fireplace and huge bathroom
with tub, living room has a bar, attractive
and good value.
LL-AL Posada Carmina, Cuna de Allende 7,
T415-152 8888, www.posadacarmina.com.
Colonial building, courtyard for meals.
Recommended.
L-B La Mansión del Bosque, Aldama 65,
T415-152 0277, www.infosma.com/mansion.
Possibly the most relaxing and friendly guest-
house in San Miguel. The rooms are normally
fully booked. Service is very welcoming.
A La Siesta, Salida a Celaya 82, near Jardín,
T415-152 0207, www.hotellasiesta.com. Pool,
fireplaces in rooms (US$34 with breakfast).
A Posada de las Monjas, Canal 37, T415-
152 0171, www.posadalasmonjas.com.

With shower, excellent set meals in restaurant, bar, clean and attractive, very good value, a converted convent.
B Sautto, Dr Macías 59, T415-152 0052. Rooms with fridge, fireplace and bath, new rooms best, rustic, garden, hot water, parking. Recommended.
B Vista Hermosa Taboada, Allende 11, T415-152 0078. Popular, pleasant old colonial building.
C Hotel Posada 'El Mayorazgo', Hidalgo 8, T415-152 1309. If you stay 6 days, the 7th is free. Monthly rental available, also has 1-bed apartments.
C Parador San Sebastián, Mesones 7, near market, T415-152 7084. With bath, charming, large rooms with fireplace, clean, car park, noisy at front (most rooms are at the back), and beautiful courtyard. Recommended.
D Casa de Huéspedes, Mesones 27, T415-152 1378. Looks grubby on the outside but it's clean and has hot water, popular, roof garden, nice location, good value.
E Hostal Alcatraz, Relox 54, T415-152 8543, alcatrazhostel@yahoo.com. Clean and tidy dormitory accommodation, hot water and kitchen available. Very friendly and helpful. Recommended.
F La Villa de Pancho, Quebrada 12 (1 block west of Hotel Sautto), T415-152 1247. Tidy little rooms up a cranky set of stairs, but good value and very friendly.

Camping
KAO campgrounds further out than Siesta on road to Guanajuato. Quiet, grassy site, all facilities, pleasant, Dutch owner.
Siesta, on road to Guanajuato, with trailer park, gardens.

Dolores Hidalgo *p303, map p303*
B El Caudillo, Querétaro 8, just off plaza, opposite the church of Nuestra Señora de los Dolores, T418-182 0198. Clean, good value.
B Posada Cocomacán, T418-182 6087, on the Jardín. Pleasant colonial house where Juárez once stayed, rooms are

comfortable, good value, good food, parking. Recommended.
D Posada Dolores, Yucatán 8, T418-182 0642. With bath, clean, OK, small rooms.

Guanajuato *p305, map p304*
Hotel rooms can be hard to find after 1400. For holidays and weekends it is advisable to book ahead.
L-AL Parador San Javier, Plaza Aldama 92, http://hotelmex.com/paradorsanjavier, T461-732 0696. Very extensive grounds, some rooms have fireplaces.
L-AL Posada Santa Fe, Jardín de la Unión 12, T461-732 0084, www.posada-santafe.com. Plain regular rooms but very attractive suites with colonial-style furniture. Good restaurant on open terrace with excellent service. Dining tables on the plaza. Recommended.
AL San Diego, Jardín de la Unión 1, T461-732 1321. Good bar and restaurant but slow, colonial style, very pleasant.
AL Suites Casa de las Manrique, Juárez 116 (between the Mercado and the Callejón del Beso), T461-732 7678. Large, attractive suites, colonial decor, very good value for price.
A El Insurgente Allende, Juárez 226, T461-732 3192. Pleasant, clean, avoid rooms on 4th floor where there is a disco, good breakfasts.
B Alhóndiga, Insurgentes 49, T461-732 0525. Good, clean, quiet, TV in rooms, parking, restaurant La Estancia.
B La Fragua, Juárez, T461-732 2715, at the western end. Very clean, good staff, 5 mins' walk from the centre of town.
B Socavón, Alhóndiga 41A, T461-732 6666. Pretty restaurant/bar. Colonial decor, attractive interior courtyard, nice rooms for price, with TV and phones.
C Central, Juárez 111, T461-732 0080, near Cine Reforma. Friendly, good restaurant but noisy for rooms beside it.
C Dos Ríos, Alhóndiga 29, T461-732 0749. TV in rooms, good value, rooms on street noisy.
C Posada San Francisco, Juárez 178, corner of Gavira, on zócalo, T461 732 2084. Good value but outside rooms noisy, lovely inner patio.

D Mineral de Rayas, Alhóndiga 7, T461-732 1967. With bath, linen, pool, garage, restaurant, bar and **Danny's Bar**. Recommended.

D Posada La Condesa/Los Arcos, Plaza de La Paz 60 (west end of plaza), T461-732 1462. Small, basic rooms, clean, hot water, drinking water available.

D-E Casa Kloster, Alonso 32, T461-732 0088. Book ahead, good location, very friendly, dormitory rooms for 4, a few with private bath, some without windows, clean, very good value. Often recommended, but not right for all. Have a look and see.

F Marilú Ordaz, Barranca 34, T461-732 4705. Accommodation in private home. Price per person. Friendly, 5 mins' walk from market.

Around Guanajuato *p306*
D Hotel El Crag, Santa Rosa. Wonderful setting in the forest.

León *p307, map p307*
AL Real de Minas, López Mateos 2211, T477-710 4090, www.realdeminaspoli forum.com.mx. Comfortable hotel with reliable services, including pool and business centre. Recommended.

A Howard Johnson Condesa, on Plaza, Portal Bravo 14, T477-713 1120, www.hjleon.com. In the centre of town overlooking the main square, 3 star, good, recommended.

A Nueva Estancia, López Mateos 1317 Pte, T477-637 0000, www.nehotel.com.mx. Chic boutique hotel, with a couple of stylish restaurants.

B-C Rex, 5 de Febrero 104, near Plaza, T477-714 2415, www.hotelrealrex.com. Great value for the quality, aimed more at the business travellers. Recommended.

C Fundadores, Ortiz de Domínguez 218, T477-716 1727. Better than similarly priced hotels in centre.

C Monte Carlo, Justo Sierra 432, T477-713 1597. Clean, friendly, central.

D Posada de Fátima, Belisario Domínguez 205. Clean, central.

D Tepeyac, Obregón 727, T477-716 8365. 1 star, OK, rooms a bit dark.

Aguascalientes *p308*
LL Gran Hotel Hacienda de la Noria, Av Héroe de Nacozari Sur 1315, Col La Salud, T449-918 4343, www.granhotella noria.com.mx. Very comfortable, jacuzzi in all rooms. Mexican, Japanese and international cuisine, gardens, swimming pool.

AL Hotel de Andrea Alameda, Alameda esq Av Tecnológico, T449-970 3800. Old hacienda, large rooms, good restaurant.

B Imperial, Moctezuma y 5 de Mayo 106, on plaza, T449-915 1650. Large, sparse rooms.

D Señorial, Colón 104, T449-915 1630. Rooms with phone, helpful lady speaks English.

D-E Don Jesús, Juárez 429, T449-915 5598. Hot water 3 hrs morning and evening, good value.

E Brasil, Guadalupe 110, T449-915 1106. With bath, quiet. One of several cheap hotels around Juárez market.

E Reforma, Nieta y Galeana, 1 block west of main plaza. Colonial style, large courtyard, rooms a bit dark, friendly, clean.

F Casa Belén, López Mateos y Galeana, T449-915 8593. Central, hot water, clean, friendly.

Around Aguascalientes *p309*
B Posada Santa Cecilia, Constitución/San Francisco 4, Jerez, T494-945 2412. Old style, pleasant atmosphere.

C Hotel Casa Blanca, Anguiano 107 on the plaza, Encarnación de Díaz, T475-953 2007. Hot water, secure parking nearby, reasonable restaurant) is halfway to Lagos de Moreno.

Zacatecas *p309, map p310*
L Hostal del Rio, Hidalgo 116, at epicentre of Centro Histórico. T493-922 7833. Very small (10 rooms), smart rooms and great service.

L Mesón de Jobito, Jardín Juárez 143, in the heart of Centro Histórico, T493-924 1722, www.mesondejobito.com. Small, select and very stylish hotel, attractive restaurant with international and Mexican cuisine.

L Quinta Real, Av Rayón 434, T493-922 9104. Beautiful, built around old bullring (said to be the 2nd oldest in Latin America), aqueduct goes past the front door. Excellent.

B Condesa, opposite Posada de los Condes (below), Av Juárez 102, T493-922 1160. OK, quiet with good views of Cerro de la Bufa, cheap restaurant.

B Hotel Posada Tolosa, Juan de Tolosa 811, also in Centro Histórico, T493-922 5105, www.hotelposadatolosa.com. Quiet, large rooms, group rates,

C Colón, Av López Velarde 508, Barrio La Paz, near old bus station, T493-922 8925. Clean, with showers.

C Hostal San Francisco, Calle del Angel 415, also in Centro Histórico, T493-925 3974, www.hostalsanfrancisco.com.mx. Eco-friendly suites, extended-stay discounts.

C Hostal Villa Colonial, 1 de Mayo y Callejón Mono Prieto, just south of the cathedral, right in the historic centre, T/F493-922 1980. Shared bath in a mix of dorms and private rooms. Great views from the rooftop patio. Information on sites and transport. Kitchen, internet access. Good deal, recommended. Also runs **Hostal Plata** to meet demand.

C Posada de los Condes, Juárez 18, T493-922 1093. A bit noisy, rooms darkish except those at front with balconies.

C-D Gami, Av López Mateos 309, southeast of town, near old bus station, T493-922 8005. Rooms with TV, OK.

D Zamora, Plaza de Zamora 303, T493-922 1200. With bath, central, very basic.

E Youth hostel, Parque del Encantado 103, CP 98000, on bus route to centre from bus station, T493-922 1151. No single rooms.

Camping

Trailer park, at Morelos junction, about 20 mins northwest of the city, where Route 54 Saltillo–Guadalajara crosses Route 49. Hook-ups, basic, behind Pemex.

San Luis Potosí p312, map p313

There are many hotels between the railway station and the cathedral.

AL Panorama, Av Venustiano Carranza 315, T444-812 1777, www.hotelpano rama.com.mx. Price includes breakfast and a 20% discount on other meals.

Large, attractive rooms. Great views of the city from the upper floors.

A Mansión Los Arcos, Hwy 57, Km 191, a few kilometres south of San Luis Potosí, signposted, T444-824 0530. Motel with restaurant and safe parking.

A María Cristina, Juan Sarabia 110, Altos, T444-128 8550. Modern, clean, small rooms with phone and TV, restaurant, good value.

A Nápoles, Juan Sarabia 120, T444-812 8418. Good restaurant, TV, phones, ceiling fans. Recommended.

B Hotel Guadalajara, Jiménez 253, near train station, T444-812 4404. Small rooms with TV and phone, off-street parking.

C El Principal, Juan Sarabia 145 opposite María Cristina, T444-812 0784. With bath. OK, loud TV in hall.

C Progreso, Aldama 415, less than a block from Plaza San Francisco, T444-812 0366. Attractive colonial façade. Rooms are large but rather dark and a little run-down. Not bad for the price.

D Universidad, Universidad 1435, between train and bus station, T444-816 0707. Clean, friendly, hot showers.

D-E Jardín Potosí, Los Bravo 530, T444-812 3152. Good, hot water, restaurant. Recommended.

Around San Luis Potosí p314

L Casa Montana, Pozos, T478-293 0032, www.casa montanahotel.com. Extreme comfort blended with great style. A wonderful place to stay in the heart of the colonial centre, but away from the crowds.

Real de Catorce p315

Accommodation is easy to find: boys greet new arrivals and will guide motorists through the peculiar 1-way system (otherwise possible police fine).

A El Corral del Conde, Morelos, close to Mesón de la Abundancia, T488-887 5048. 6 rooms, fine furniture, clean, big bathrooms.

A Hotel El Real, Morelos 20. Clean, nice atmosphere, friendly owner, good restaurant. Recommended.

B Quinta Puesta del Sol, Calle del Cementerio 16, T488-887 5050. With bath, TV, beautiful views, poor restaurant.
E Providencia, on main street. Hot water, clean, restaurant. Several other hotels nearby and various restaurants.

🍴 Eating

Querétaro *p297, map p298*
¶¶¶ **Mesón de Chucho el Roto**, Plaza Independencia. Very popular at night with drinks, music, good food and service. Surprisingly affordable and good value.
¶¶¶ **Mesón de Santa Rosa**, Pasteur 17, in the courtyard of the hotel of same name (see Sleeping). Good but expensive, restored colonial building.
¶¶ **Alda Café**, Río de la Loza 4, T442-224 4077. Modern, breezy and stylish Italian café/restaurant. Chic and popular.
¶¶ **Bisquetes**, in arcade of old **Gran Hotel** on zócalo. Good value. Try local Hidalgo Pinot Noir wine.
¶¶ **Café 1810**, Plaza Independencia. Enjoyable plaza-side restaurant perfect for watching the world go by.
¶¶ **El Arcangel**, Plaza Jardín Guerrero. Stylish spot with a good *menú del día*.
¶¶ **Lonergan's**, Plaza de Armas. Pleasant café with small art gallery; magazines in English, French and German.
¶¶ **Ostionería Tampico**, Corregidora Norte 3. Specialists in fish, and with good reason.
¶ **The Italian Coffee Company**, on the plaza. Pure Italian heaven in a cup.
¶ **La Mariposa**, A Peralta 7. Excellent coffee, *tortas* and fruit shakes.
¶ **Leo's**, at La Cruz market. Excellent tacos and *quesadillas*, popular.
¶ **Vegetariano Natura**, Av Juárez 47. Good, cheap vegetarian food, with health-food supplements available for sale.

Tequisquiapan *p299*
¶¶¶ **K'puchinos**, north side of main square. Excellent Mexican dishes in a stylish

restaurant. The place to sit and watch the world go by.
¶¶ **Maridelphi**, on south side of main square. Popular local choice.

Jalpan *p300*
¶ **Las Cazuelas**, to right of church. Delicious tacos, very clean.
¶ **Las Jacarandas**, next to bus station. Good *comida corrida*, reasonably priced, clean. Shrimp cocktails at stalls on plaza.

Xilitla *p300*
¶ **Restaurant Los Cayos**. Good view. Try *enchiladas huastecas* and local coffee.

Celaya *p301*
¶¶¶ **El Mezquital**, Blv López Mateos 1113 Ote. Meat and traditional barbeque.
¶¶ **La Mansión del Marisco**, Blv López Mateos 1000, esq Juárez. Fish and seafood, live music at weekends.

San Miguel de Allende *p302, map p302*
¶¶¶-¶¶ **Mesón de San José**, Mesones 38, T415-152 3848. Open 0800-2200. Live music on Sun. Mexican and international cuisine including vegetarian dishes, excellent breakfast, in a pleasant patio. Gift shop. Well hidden so quiet at times.
¶¶ **Café etc**, Calle Reloj 37. Mon-Sat 0800-2100, Sun 1000-1800. Great café atmosphere in a gallery, with internet and excellent music – some 2000 CDs from classical to the very latest sounds – most of which is available to buy.
¶¶ **Casa Mexas**, Canal 15. Good American food, clean, popular with gringos.
¶¶ **El Buen Café**, Jesús 23, T415-152 5807. Good quiche, pies, cakes and juices.
¶¶ **El Infierno**, Mesones, just below Plaza Allende. Excellent *sopa azteca*, good value.
¶¶ **El Jardín**, San Francisco, close to plaza. Friendly service, good food including vegetarian options. Violinist plays upstairs at weekends.
¶¶ **El Tomate**, Mesones. Vegetarian restaurant, attractive, spotless, excellent food, generous helpings, not cheap.

Mama Mía, Umarán, west of main square. Main meals good but not cheap, free live folk music or films in the afternoon, excellent cheap breakfasts.

Restaurant La Fonda, Hidalgo 28 between Insurgentes and Mesones. Excellent Mexican food and very friendly staff. Impromptu music and readings.

Rincón Español, opposite post office. Good *comida corrida*, flamenco at weekends. Recommended.

San Agustín, on San Francisco. Good food with *fajitas*, excellent *churros* and Mexican hot chocolate, lively music and quirky decor.

Tío Lucas, Mesones 103, opposite Teatro Angela Peralta, T415-152 4996. Very good. Recommended.

Chicken restaurant, corner of Juárez and Mesones. Good for a snack.

La Piñata, Umarán. One of the few cheap, family-run Mexican restaurants left in town. No airs and graces, but great food.

Dolores Hidalgo *p303, map p303*
Cafés and ice cream parlours
Fruti-Yoghurt, Hidalgo y Guerrero, just off Jardín. Delicious yoghurt, wholefood cakes and biscuits.

Helado Torres, southwest corner of Jardín. Excellent ice cream.

Guanajuato *p305, map p304*
Tourists are often given the à la carte menu; ask for the *menú del día* or *comida corrida*. You can eat well and cheaply in the market (eg sandwiches and fresh fruit juices) and in the *locales* behind Mercado Hidalgo.

La Lonja, on the corner of the Jardín de la Unión, opposite **Hotel San Diego**. Pleasant and lively bar, beers come with complimentary dish of tacos with salsa.

El Mexicano, Juárez 214. Good *comida corrida* with dessert and drink, a little overpriced.

Café Truco 7, Callejón Truco, off Plaza de la Paz. *Menú del día* US$3, relaxed family atmosphere. Theatre in back room Fri and Sat afternoon. Recommended.

El Retiro, Sopeña 12, near Jardín de la Unión. Reasonable food, *comida corrida* very good value.

La Mancha, Galarza 7. Reasonable price. Recommended for *comida corrida*.

Pizza Piazza, Plaza San Fernando and several other locations. Cheap and good.

Café Las Musas, Plaza Baratillo. Good-value breakfast.

El Unicornio Azul, Plaza Baratillo. Good healthfood shop, *pan integral*, also sells cosmetic products.

Vegetariano, Callejón Calixto 20. Inexpensive, sells wholewheat bread.

Around Guanajuato *p306*
Rancho de Enmiedo, Santa Rosa. Good dried meat specialities and beautiful scenery.

León *p307, map p307*
Panteón Taurino, Calzado de Los Héroes 408, T477-713 4969. Expensive but worth visiting for the incredible decor.

Cadillac, Hidalgo, ½ a block from the cathedral. Good *comida corrida*.

La Pagoda de Ling Choy, López Mateos 1501 Ote, T477 714 9026. Chinese.

Lupillos, López Mateos 2003 Ote, opposite the stadium, T477-771 1868. Pasta and pizza.

GFU, López Mateos, near IMSS building. Vegetarian snacks.

Aguascalientes *p308*
Try the area around 5 de Mayo for *pollo rostizado*.

Freeday, near Benito Juárez statue. Video bar and restaurant, lively at weekends.

Mitla, Madero 220. Good breakfast, moderate prices.

Café Parroquia, Hidalgo, 1 block west of Madero. Good, cheap.

Jacalito, López Mateos, also near Plaza Crystal. Cheap *tortas*, clean.

Jugos Acapulcos, Allende 106. Good *comida corrida*.

Lonchería Gorditas Victoria. Popular with locals especially for tacos.

Zacatecas *p309, map p310*

Ħ Divino Brazil, Hidalgo 802, T493-922 9710. Open until 0230. Good Brazilian food with live music in the evenings.

Ħ El Jacalito, Juárez 109. Daily 0800-2230. Excellent *comida corrida* and breakfast.

Ħ El Paraíso, Av Hidalgo y P Goitia, corner of market. Closed Sun. Bar/restaurant, good atmosphere.

Ħ La Cuija, Av Tacuba, in old Centro Comercial. Good food, music and atmosphere.

Ħ La Gaviota, Callejón de Rosales 101 upstairs, T493-925 4040. Brilliant decor, exemplary service. Best seafood restaurant in the region.

Ħ La Leyenda, 2da, De Matamoros 216, T493-922 3853. Fantastic local cuisine with avant-garde ambience; gaining reputation as city's best restaurant.

Ħ-Ħ Garufa, Callejón de Cuevas, T493-921 2357. Argentine food, al fresco, charming atmosphere, popular with tourists.

Ħ-Ħ La Cantera Musical, Av Tacuba. Good atmosphere, poor a/c, good Mexican food but drinks limited after 2000.

Ħ-Ħ La Traviata, Callejón de Cuevas 109, T493-924 2030. Wonderful Italian dishes. Outside seating, smart interior and bar.

Ħ-Ħ Nueva Galicia, Plazuela Goitia 102. Wide range of Mexican food, also offers delicious sushi. Recommended.

Ħ El Pueblito, Hidalgo 403-D, T493-924 3818. Open daily. Typical Mexican food and bar. Clean and cheap.

Ħ El Tragadero, Juárez 232. Open 0900-2100, 365 days of the year, with special dishes on Christmas Day. Pretty basic café set-up but good local Zacatecan dishes, veggie dishes, very friendly, cheap and excellent value.

Ħ Florencia Pizzas, off of Gerano Codina, T493-925 1241. Daily 0900-2300. Best pizza in town, in a charming little family-run place.

Ħ La Unica Cabaña, Jardín de la Independencia. Cheap, excellent set meals.

Ħ Las Costillas de Sancho, Blv José López Portillo 218 (Tres Cruces neighbourhood), T493-899 1144. Good pan-Mexican cuisine and music. Crowded on weekends.

Ħ Locanda la Tana, Genaro Codina 714, T493-925 4621. Sun-Fri 1330-1700, 1930-2200, Sat 1930-2200 only. Excellent Italian dishes made from scratch and good wine list.

Ħ Recovedi, facing Plaza Alameda. All-you-can eat buffets, good veggie options, good wholesome food. Cheap.

Cafés

Acrópolis, opposite cathedral. 50-year-old café and diner, good breakfast, slow service but great art inside.

Café Arlequín, Hidalgo 814. Much-loved café/lending library/mini art gallery and all-purpose gathering place for city's intellectuals (of which there are many).

Cuco's, Alameda 404, T493-924 4333. Open late. Popular with the student crowd.

Healthfood store, Rayón 413. Excellent food at reasonable prices.

San Patricio Caffe, Av Hidalgo. Wonderful but expensive coffees, where the smart, young and rich Zacatecanos hang out.

Sanborn's, Av Hidalgo 212 and Allende, 2nd floor. Coffees, deserts and free internet access for patrons, with restaurant attached. 1950s-era shopping store on 1st floor.

San Luis Potosí *p312, map p313*
Many reasonably priced eating places at western end of Alameda Juan Sarabia.

Ħ Los Molinos, in Hostal del Quijote. Excellent, well-served food.

Ħ-Ħ Café Pacífico, corner of Los Bravo and Constitución, a couple of blocks from the train station. Open 24 hrs. Good hot chocolate. Nice atmosphere.

Ħ-Ħ La Parroquia, Plaza de los Fundadores, corner of Díaz de León and Carranza. Old building but modern inside. Good food and *comida corrida*.

Ħ-Ħ La Posada del Virrey, north side of Jardín Hidalgo. Set in the beautiful covered courtyard of an old colonial building. Also has a dining room facing the plaza.

Real de Catorce *p315*
††† El Eucalyptus, on way to zócalo. Italian/Swiss-run. Excellent home-made pasta, vegetarian food, cakes. Pricey but recommended.

⊕ Entertainment

Querétaro *p297, map p298*
Music
Mariachis play in the Jardín Corregidora, 16 de Septiembre y Corregidora, in the evenings. The town band plays in the Jardín Obregón on Sun evening, lovely atmosphere.

Theatre
Corral de Comedias, Carranza 39, T442-212 0765. An original theatre company, colonial surroundings and suppers.

San Miguel de Allende *p302, map p302*
Cinema
Villa Jacaranda, hotel video bar. English-language films, US$5 including alcoholic drink and popcorn.

Theatre
Teatro Angela Peralta, Mesones 82. Theatre, musical events and dance. There's a coffee house in the front entrance hall.

Guanajuato *p305, map p304*
Bars and clubs
Recommended nightclubs include **Disco El Grill**, Calle Alonso (100 m from Casa Kloster) and **Disco Los Comerciales**, Juan Valle.

Music
A live band plays in Jardín de la Unión 3 times a week.

Theatre
Theatre sketches from classical authors out of doors in lovely old plazas from Apr-Aug.
Teatro Juárez, on Sopeña. A magnificent French-type Second Empire building (US$0.50 to view, US$0.35 to take

photos), shows art films and has symphony concerts.
Teatro Principal, Cantarranas, by Plaza Mexiamora.

León *p307, map p307*
Bars and clubs
Good bars include **Fut-bol Bar**, Hidalgo 923-B, T477-717 8020; **JJ Sport**, Rocío 115-A, Jardines del Moral; **Pepe's Pub**, Madero 120, Zona Centro.

Nightclubs include **Domus**, López Mateos 2611 Ote, T477-711 6614; **La Iguana**, Centro Comercial Insurgentes, Local 4 y 5B, T477-718 1416; **Ossy's**, Av Paseo de los Insurgentes, on exit road to Lagos de Moreno, T477-717 6880; **Piano Bar Maya**, Prolongación Calzada 112, T477-716 9734.

⊛ Festivals and events

Querétaro *p297, map p298*
Dec Feria Agrícola (agricultural fair) from 2nd week of Dec until Christmas with bullfights and cockfights.
31 Dec New Year's Eve there is a special market and performances in the main street.

Celaya *p301*
10-20 Jan Fiesta of the appearance of the Virgen de Guadalupe in the Tierrasnegras barrio, one of the oldest districts of Celaya. There is theatre, dancing, fireworks and eating a typical local *antojito*: *gorditas de Tierrasnegras*.
Mar/Apr Easter is marked by visiting several *balnearios* in the area and there are processions through the streets, much eating of local delicacies, and on Easter Sun, a **Judas** image is burned in many places in the city.
16 Jul The Virgen del Carmen.

San Miguel de Allende *p302, map p302*
Feb Pre-Lenten carnival.
Jun Corpus Christi.
End-Jul to mid-Aug Classical Chamber Music Festival; information from Bellas Artes.

15-16 Sep Independence Day.
28 Sep-1 Oct Fiesta de San Miguel, with *conchero* dancers from many places.
2 Nov Day of the Dead.
16-24 Dec Christmas Posadas, celebrated in the traditional colonial manner. There is a Christmas season musical celebration, which attracts musicians of an international level.

Dolores Hidalgo *p303, map p303*
15-16 Sep Independence celebrations.

Guanajuato *p305, map p304*
Mar/Apr Viernes de las Flores (Fri of Flowers) is held on the Fri before Good Fri, starting with the Dance of the Flowers on Thu night at about 2200 right through the night, adjourning to Jardín de la Unión to exchange flowers. Very colourful and busy.
End Oct Festival Cervantino de Guanajuato, T461-731 1161, www.festivalcervantino. gob.mx, is an important cultural event in the Spanish-speaking world, encompassing theatre, song and dance over the last 2 weeks of Oct. There is a mixture of free, open-air events and paying events. Well-known artists from around the world perform. The festival, in honour of Cervantes, is highly recommended and crowded; book accommodation in advance.
Dec During the Christmas period, students dress up in traditional *estudiantina* costumes and wander the streets singing carols and playing music. Groups leave from in front of the theatre at 2030.

León *p307, map p307*
19-24 Jan Fiesta de San Sebastián, very crowded and good fun.

Aguascalientes *p308*
Mid-Apr Start of a 3-week wine festival, Feria de San Marcos (the area is famous for viticulture and the local wine is named after San Marcos). There are processions, cockfights (in Mexico's largest *palenque*, seating 4000), bullfights, agricultural shows, etc. Plaza de Armas is lavishly decorated for

the occasion. The *feria*, covered by national TV networks, is said to be the biggest in Mexico. Book accommodation in advance.

Zacatecas *p309, map p310*
Mid-Mar Semana Santa (Holy Week) processions and events are innumerable. Festival Cultural is now Mexico's most popular festival, transforming the city into a 24-hr extravaganza with a large number of free events, performers from many countries, light shows, fireworks, poetry readings, classical music, traditional arts, and internationally known musicians.
Jun Folklore Festival, very popular.
Sep The fiestas spread over most of the month. There are bullfights on Sun, but given the growth in popularity of the town you could stumble across an impromptu celebration at any time of year. Also in Sep is an agricultural fair.

Real de Catorce *p315*
Mar/Apr On Good Fri, thousands of visitors gather to watch a lively Passion play, with realistic Roman soldiers and very colourful Jews and apostles.
3-4 Oct Pilgrimage for San Francisco, on foot from Matehuala. Take the local bus from Matehuala to La Paz and join the groups of pilgrims who set out from early evening onwards.

O Shopping

Querétaro *p297, map p298*
Gems and jewels There are local opals, amethysts and topazes for sale; mineral specimens are shaped into spheres and then polished until they look like jewels. Prices are cheaper than San Juan del Río, but more expensive than Taxco. Recommended is Joyería Villalón, Andador Libertad 24a, for fine opals at good prices. La Cruz market, 10 mins' walk from the centre, is very well stocked, busy and clean. Open daily, with a street market on Sun.

San Juan del Río *p299*
Gems and jewels La Guadalupana,
16 de Septiembre 5. A friendly shop.
Recommended.

San Miguel de Allende *p302, map p302*
Bookshop El Tecolote, Calle Jesús. Good
selection of French and English books.

Handicrafts Pottery, cotton cloth and
brasswork are the main local crafts. **Mercado
de Artesanías**, tends to sell tacky souvenirs
rather than real handicrafts; prices are high
and the selection poor. **La Casa del Vidrio**,
Correo 11, offers an excellent selection of
brown-glass items at fair prices (sale prices
in the summer, 40% off).

Dolores Hidalgo *p303, map p303*
Crafts Artesanías Castillo, Ribera del Río,
between Hidalgo and Jalisco. Beautiful
ceramics at low prices. Visits to the factory
can be arranged.

Markets Tabasco, south side, between
Jalisco and Hidalgo. There's another market,
near Posada Dolores, on Yucatán.

Guanajuato *p305, map p304*
Crafts Fonart, opposite La Valenciana
church (see above) has an excellent selection
of handicrafts; high prices but superb quality.
Local pottery is for sale in the **Mercado
Hidalgo** (1910), in the centre of town, and
there is a **Casa de Artesanías** behind the
Teatro Juárez (see Entertainment, above).

León *p307, map p307*
Leatherwork Shops along **Belisario
Domínguez** and **Plaza Piel**, Hilario Medina
y López Mateos.

Shopping centres La Gran Plaza, Blv
López Mateos 1902 Pte; **Plaza Mayor**, Av de
las Torres, corner of Prolongación Morelos;
Plaza León, Blv López Mateos 1102 Ote.

Aguascalientes *p308*
Bootmakers Zapatería Cervantes,
Guerrero 101 Sur y Nieto, T449-915 1943. One
of many shops selling boots made to order.

Market The main market is at 5 de Mayo y
Unión, large and clean, toilet on upper floor.

Zacatecas *p309, map p310*
Market Between Hidalgo and Tacuba the
elegant 19th-century market building has
been converted into a pleasant shopping
centre (popular café on balcony). The market
is now dispersed in various locations a few
blocks to the southwest. Zacatecas is famous
for its *sarapes* (now hard to find outside of
Jerez, Sombrerete) and has 2 delicacies: the
local cheese, and *queso de tuna*, a candy
made from the fruit of the nopal cactus
(don't eat too much, as it has powerful
laxative properties). There are many shops
along Av Hidalgo that sell excellent silver,
which is still mined locally.

San Luis Potosí *p312, map p313*
Markets Head north on Hidalgo and you
come to **Mercado Hidalgo**, then **Mercado
República** and **Mercado 16 de Septiembre**.
Locally made *rebozos* (the best are from Santa
María del Río) are sold in the markets.
Chalita, a 3-storey hypermarket, is on
Jardín San Juan de Dios between Av
Alvaro Obregón and Los Bravo.

Food Casa de Nutrición, 5 de Mayo 325,
is a healthfood store.

▲▲ Activities and tours

San Miguel de Allende *p302, map p302*
Tour operators PMC, Hidalgo 18,
T415-152 0121, www.pme xc.com.
A wide range of tours and trips from
walking tours of the town, workshops
and language classes, through to adventure
and nature tours and visits to nearby
archaelogical sites. **Viajes Vertiz**,

Hidalgo 1A, T415-152 1856, vvertiz@
unisono.net.mx. Good travel agent,
Amex agent.

Guanajuato *p305, map p304*
Tour operators
Tours of the city and outskirts and south
of the state are possible; if you want an
English-speaking guide, prices multiply.
Transportes Turísticos de Guanajuato,
underneath the Basílica on Plaza de la
Paz, T461-732 2838, offers tours to sites
outside the city.

León *p307, map p307*
Tour operators
Jovi de León, Madero 319 Centro,
T477-714 5094.
Viajes Sindy de León, 20 de Enero 319,
T477-713 1224.

Zacatecas *p309, map p310*
Tour operators
Cantera Tours, Centro Comercial El Mercado,
Av López Velarde 602-6, Local A-21,
T493-922 9065.
Delao Tours, Av Hidalgo 613-3, T493-922
3464. Excellent daily tours of city and
surrounding historic towns.
Operadora Zacatecas, T924-0050, offers
several interesting tours.
Viajes Masoco, Enlace 115, Col Sierra de Alca,
T493-922 5559, tours to Chicomostoc and
Jerez, US$15.50.

● Transport

Querétaro *p297, map p298*
Air
Flights to **Guadalajara**, **Mexico City**,
Monterrey and **San Luis Potosí**.
   Airline offices Aeromar, T442-220 6936.

Bus
The bus station is 5 km southeast of the
centre, near Estadio Corregidora. Terminal A,
modules 1 and 2, 1st class and *plus*; Terminal

B, modules 3, 4 and 5, 2nd class. No buses
run directly to the centre; the closest you'll
get is the south end of Corregidora. There are
fixed-price taxis and buses. The bus station
has luggage storage, restaurants (with a
bar upstairs), travel agency, newsagents,
telephones and toilets.
   There are good connections with
most towns on the US border if you are
heading north. Likewise, if heading south,
Querétero is transport hub, with good
connections. To **Acapulco**, 1100 and 2200,
US$46. To **Aguascalientes**, 6 a day, 4½ hrs,
US$23. To **Chihuahua**, 1930 and 2030,
US$70. To **Cd Juárez**, 16 a day, 20-22 hrs,
US$110. To **Durango**, 1130, 1145 and 2100,
10 hrs, US$40-50. To **Guadalajara**, frequent
services, 5-6 hrs, US$29. To **Guanajuato**,
6 a day between 0800 and 1700, 3 hrs,
US$11. To **León**, every couple of hours,
2½ hrs US$13. To **Mazatlán**, 1000, 1210
and 1830, US$64. To **Mexico City**, an
endless stream of buses of all classes,
3 hrs, US$13-17. To **Monterrey**, 15 per day,
8 hrs, US$36. To **Morelia**, 16 per day, 4 hrs
US$12. To **Nogales**, 0015 and 1815, 25 hrs,
US$125. To **Piedras Negras**, 1540, 1900
and 1955, US$84. To **San Juan del Río**,
every 15 mins, 1 hr. To **San Luis Potosí**,
regular throughout the day, 3 hrs, US$15.
To **San Miguel de Allende**, hourly, 1 hr,
US$6. To **Tula**, 2¼ hrs, US$10. To **Zacatecas**,
almost hourly, 5 hrs US$32.

Car
There is a 4-lane motorway from Irapuato past
Querétaro to Mexico City. The Mexico City
motorway passes close to Tula and Tepozotlán.

Tequisquiapan *p299*
Bus
San Juan del Río–Tequisquiapan, regular
services, 40 mins, US$1.50.

San Joaquín *p300*
Bus
San Joaquín can be reached in 3 hrs by car
or bus on a windy road going through desert

and then misty pine forests. **Flecha Amarilla** runs 6 buses a day, earliest from **Querétaro** 0620, last 1620, US$5; **Flecha Azul** also runs buses San Joaquín–**San Juan del Río**.

Jalpan *p300*
Bus
To **Mexico City**, 3 direct, 6 hrs, US$21, beautiful trip. To **Landa de Matamoros**, hourly, US$1, 20 mins. To **Tilaco** and **Tancoyol**, 40-min bus journey to **La Lagunita**, hourly, then *combis* (on market day, Sat) or hitchhike. To **Querétaro**, every hour, 5 hrs, US$6. To **Cd Valles**, frequent, via Landa de Matamoros and Xilitla.

Xilitla *p300*
Bus
From **Jalpan** every hour, US$3, 2½ hrs.

Celaya *p301*
Bus
Hourly buses to **Mexico City** with Primera Plus. US$21.

San Miguel de Allende *p302, map p302*
Bus
The bus station is on the outskirts, regular bus to the centre US$0.25, returns from the market or outside Posada San Francisco on the Jardín. A taxi costs about US$1 to the centre. Buses to the centre leave from in front of the terminal.

To **Aguascalientes**, 1235 and 1435, 2 hrs, US$13. To **Celaya**, every 15 mins, 1 hr, US$3. If there are no buses leaving for Guadalajara from San Miguel at the time you want to go, it's best to go to Celaya and catch a bus from there. To **Guadalajara**, 0730, 0930 and 1730, 5 hrs, US$30. To **Guanajuato**, 0745, 0945, 1245 and 1700, US$9. To **León**, 0730, 0930 and 1730, US$11. To **Mexico City** (northern terminal), 0940 and 1600, US$21, cheaper services every 40 mins from 0520 to 2000, US$15. To **Querétaro**, every 40 mins 0520-2000, US$6. To **San Luis Potosí**, 7 a day, US$12.

International Daily buses to **Laredo**, Texas, US$49, **San Antonio** and on to **Dallas**, US$74, at 1800. Also daily buses to **Houston** at 1800. And every Wed at 1800 to **Chicago**, US$125.

Dolores Hidalgo *p303, map p303*
Bus
Station is at Hidalgo y Chiapas, 5 mins from main square; with restaurant, toilets, left-luggage and telephones. Frequent buses to **Guanajuato**, US$4; **Querétaro**, US$4.50; **León**, US$4.50; **Mexico City**, US$14; **San Luis Potosí**, US$6; **San Luis de la Paz**, US$2.50; and **San Miguel de Allende**, US$4. To **Aguascalientes**, US$8, 2nd class, via San Felipe.

Guanajuato *p305, map p304*
Bus
Local Set fare for city buses US$0.25.

Long distance A bus terminal has opened on the road to Silao, near toll gate, 20 mins from centre by bus, US$0.30. Taxi to centre, US$2. Buses leave for the centre from right outside the front of the terminal. Look for 'Centro' on the front window of the bus, or the sign above the front window. To get to the bus station from the centre, you pick up buses on Av Juárez in front of the **Hotel Central**, about a block west of the Mercado Hidalgo. The bus stop has a sign saying 'C Camionera'. The bus terminal has a place for storing luggage.

To **Cuidad Juárez**, transferring in León 1015, US$115. To **Guadalajara**, 19 buses a day between 0900 and 2330, US$24. To **Irapuato**, 5 daily between 0530 and 1830, US$5. To **León**, 0830, 1230 and 1730, 45 mins, US$4.50. To **Mexico City**, regular service, 4½ hrs, US$29. To **Monterrey**, 7 a day, all in the afternoon, US$47. To **Morelia**, 0700, 0820, 1210 and 1620, US$13. To **Nuevo Laredo**, 1930, US$74. To **Querétaro**, 6 daily between 0710 and 1820, US$11. To **San Luis Potosí**, 5 throughout the day, US$15. To **San**

Miguel de Allende, regular service from 0700 until 1915, 1½ hrs, US$6. To **Tijuana**, 1800, US$135.

For many destinations it is better to go to León and pick up the more frequent services from there (buses every 10 mins Guanajuato–León, US$1.30).

Around Guanajuato p306
Bus
For **La Valenciana** mine, a local 'Valenciana' bus starts in front of **Hotel Mineral de Rayas**, Alhóndiga 7, leaving every 30 mins during the day, US$0.10, 10 mins' ride.

For **Cerro del Cubilete**, take local buses from Guanajuato, 1½ hrs, US$1.15, 0700, 0900, 1100, 1400, 1600 (also from **Silao**, US$0.75). Last bus up leaves at 1600 from Silao and Guanajuato.

León p307, map p307
Air
International airport, **Del Bajío (BJX)**, 18 km from León, 6 km from Silao. Good domestic connections, international flights to several US cities, also to Guatemala and South American cities.

Airline offices AeroMéxico, Madero 410, T477-716 6226. **Continental**, Blv López Mateos 2307 Pte, T477-713 5199. **Mexicana**, Blv López Mateos 401 Ote, T477-714 9500.

Bus
The terminal has a post office, long-distance phones, restaurant and shops. To **Chihuahua**, US$57. Many buses run to **Cd Juárez**, US$56. To **Durango**, US$16.50. To **Guadalajara**, every 30 mins, first at 0600, 4 hrs, US$29. To **Guanajuato**, all the time, 40 mins, US$4. To **Mexico City**, more buses than you can count, 5 hrs, US$28. To **Monterrey**, US$28. To **Poza Rica**, US$24. To **Querétaro**, hourly, 2 hrs, US$9. To **Zacatecas**, 3½ hrs, US$16.

Taxi
Taxis are expensive from the airport to León; take one to Silao, US$10, and then take a bus to León or Guanajuato, or walk 1½ km to the main road and take a bus from there.

Aguascalientes p308
Air
The airport (AGU) is 21 km from the town centre. Good domestic flights and flights to **Los Angeles** with AeroMéxico.

Airline offices Aero California, Juan de Montoro 203, T449-915 2400. AeroMéxico, Madero 474, T449-916 1362.

Bus
Bus station about 1 km south of centre on Av Circunvalación Sur with post office and pharmacy, take city bus from Galeana near López Mateos. To **Cd Juárez**, US$75. To **Chihuahua**, US$88. To **Guadalajara**, several through the day, 6 hrs, US$21. To **Guanajuato**, 5 daily, 3½ hrs, US$11. To **León**, 21 a day, 2 hrs, US$10. To **Mexico City**, 9 a day, 7 hrs, US$37. To **Monterrey**, US$53. To **Morelia**, Primera Plus, 4 a day, US$20. To **Nuevo Laredo**, US$81. To **Puerto Vallarta**, at 2230, US$51. To **Querétaro**, 8 a day, 6 hrs, US$23. To **San Luis Potosí**, Futura, 16 a day 0600-2300, US$11. To **Tijuana**, 1530 and 2100, US$145. To **Zacatecas**, every 30 mins, 2½ hrs, US$6.

Zacatecas p309, map p310
Air
Aeropuerto La Calera (ZCL), 27 km north of city, flights daily to **Mexico City**, **Tijuana**, **Guadalajara**, **Cd Juárez**, **Morelia**, **Aguascalientes** and direct flights to several US cities.

Airline offices Mexicana, T493-922 3248.

Bus
New terminal 4 km south of town; taxi US$1.20; red No 8 buses from Plaza Independencia (US$0.15) or white *camionetas* from Av González Ortega (old bus station on Blv López Mateos

only serves local destinations). Apart from buses to Mexico City, Chihuahua and a few other major towns, most routes do not have bookable seats. Frequent buses passing through Jerez back to Zacatecas with Rojo de Los Altos, US$2.80.

To **Aguascalientes**, every 30 mins, 2½ hrs, US$6. To **Chihuahua**, via Torreón, 12 hrs, US$50. To **Durango**, 5 hrs, many throughout the day, US$10 (if continuing to Mazatlán, stay the night in Durango in order not to miss the views on the way to the coast). To **Guadalajara**, hourly, 4 hrs, US$22. To **Hidalgo del Parral**, 10 hrs, US$44. To **León**, 3½ hrs, US$16. To **Mexico City**, almost hourly, 8 hrs, US$45. To **San Luis Potosí**, 7 daily, 2½ hrs, US$11.

Train
Zacatecas is on the **Mexico City–Querétaro–Chihuahua** line. No scheduled trains are running, but if a cargo train is passing through, there may be a passenger wagon.

San Luis Potosí p312, map p313
Air
The airport (SLP) is 6 km from the centre. Many daily to **Mexico City**, also flights to **Aguascalientes**, **Guadalajara**, **Monterrey**, **Tampico** Flights to **Chicago**, **San Antonio** (Texas).

Airline offices Aeromar, Av Carranza 1160-2, T444-911 4671. Aero California, T444-911 8050. Mexicana, T444-917 8836. Mexicana de Aviación, T444-917 8920.

Bus
Bus station on outskirts of town 1.5 km from centre. Left-luggage, telephone office and a few shops at the terminal. Also taxi ticket booth, US$2 to centre. For local buses to the centre, walk out the front door of the terminal and turn right. Walk down the street to the first traffic light. Then take buses heading south on the cross street (ie to your right as you're facing it) marked 'de Mayo' or 'Los Gómez'.

To **Aguascalientes**, hourly, 2½ hrs, US$18. To **Chihuahua**, 9 buses per day, US$73. To **Cd Juárez**, 9 buses per day, US$98. To **Durango**, 1405, 2045 and 2330, US$32. To **Guadalajara**, hourly service, 5 hrs, US$27. To **Guanajuato**, regular service, 4 hrs, US$13. To **Nuevo Laredo**, 10 hrs, US$51. To **Mexico City**, very regular service, 5 hrs, US$31. To **Monterrey**, 14 daily, 6 hrs, US$32. To **Morelia**, regular service, US$21. To **Querétaro**, hourly from 0900, 2½ hrs, US$16. To **San Miguel de Allende**, 6 a day, 3 hrs. To **Tijuana**, 1530 and 1830, US$140. To **Zacatecas**, 7 buses daily, 2½ hrs, US$11.

International Autobuses Americanos run 2 buses daily, stopping at **Laredo**, **San Antonio**, Dallas, and **Houston**, in Texas, and **Chicago**.

Real de Catorce p315
Bus
Many buses a day to **Matehuala**, from the corner of Guerrero and Mendiz, US$2 1 way. Local buses from office 1 block north of the zócalo.

❶ Directory

Querétaro p297, map p298
Banks There is a Banamex ATM on the Jardín Obregón at Juárez and 16 de Septiembre that accepts Visa and MasterCard. Banco Inverlat ATM (that should accept Amex cards) at Corregidora Norte 60. *Casa de cambio* at Corregidora Norte 134. **Internet** Café Internet Asodi, Francisco Márquez 219, Col Las Campanas. **Café Internet Cibers Pace**, Av Universidad 297, Col Las Brujas. **Café Internet Welo**, Ezequiel Montes 67 Sur (close to corner of Constituyentes), T442-212 7272. **Wave Internet**, Carraza, open daily 0900-2200 or thereabouts, US$1 per hr. Simple set-up but good machines. **Language school** Centro Intercultural de Querétaro, Reforma 41, Centro, T/F442-212 2831. **Post office** Arteaga Pte 5.

San Miguel de Allende *p302, map p302*
Banks Casa de Cambio Deal, on Correo, opposite post office, and on Juárez.
Cookery classes Mexican Cooking Classes, ask at El Buen Café, Jesús 23, different menu every week.**Embassies and consulates** US Consular Agent, Plaza Golondrinas arcade, Hernández Macías, interior 111, T415-152 2357, Mon-Fri 0900-1300. **Immigration** 2nd floor Plaza Real del Conde, T415-152 2542, daily 0900-1300. For tourist card extensions, etc, take 2 copies of passport, tourist card and credit card or TCs. **Internet** Border Crossings, Correo 19, phone, fax, and email service. Café etc, Calle Reloj 37, Mon-Sat 0800-2100, Sun 1000-1800. Good machines and so much more than an internet café with excellent music and coffee. Estación Internet, Recreo 11. La Conexión, Aldama 1, T/F415-152 1599. **Language schools** Many of the schools demand payment in US dollars (technically illegal) and you may prefer to arrange private tuition for US$3-4 per hr. Academia Hispanoamericana, Mesones 4, T415-152 0349, www.ahaspeak spanish.com, recommended for language lessons and sessions on Mexican history, folklore, literature, singing and dancing; very helpful; accommodation with families. Habla Hispana Spanish School, Calzada de la Luz 25, T415-152 1535, www.mexico spanish.com, has also received good reports. Warren Hardy Spanish, San Rafael 6, T415-152 4728, www.warrenhardy.com, intensive courses for beginners or intermediate level, run by Warren Hardy, the inventor of the Card Game method. **Laundry** On Pasaje de Allende, same-day service; unnamed laundry at Correo 42, good. **Libraries** English-language library Biblioteca Pública on Insurgentes has an excellent selection on Mexico; very extensive bilingual library, with computer centre and English-speaking staff. They distribute the weekly *Atención San Miguel*, which has listings of Spanish classes, tutors and local events.
Telephone There is a long-distance phone service at Diez de Sollano 4, just off the plaza.

Guanajuato *p305, map p304*
Banks Bancomer, Banca Serfín, Banamex, daily 0900-1100. **Internet** Alonso 70B, Mon-Sat 0900-1800. **Language schools** Academia Falcón, Paseo de la Presa 80, Guanajuato, 36000, T461-731 0745, www.academiafalcon.com. Good-quality instruction, regular recommendations. Universidad de Guanajuato, T461-732 0006, montesa@quijote.ugto.mx. The university has many US exchange students. **Laundry** Lavandería Internacional, Alhóndiga 35A, self or service wash. La Burbuja Express, Plazuela Baratillo. Lavandería Automática Internacional, Manuel Doblado 28. **Post office** Corner of Subida San José, by La Compañía church. **Telephone** International phone calls from phone booths with coins, or collect. Long-distance offices in Miscelánea Unión shop, by Teatro Principal and on Pocitos, opposite Alhóndiga de Granaditas.

León *p307, map p307*
Banks Bancomer, Belisario Domínguez 322, and HSBC on the plaza. **Post office** Obregón y 5 de Mayo, Mon-Fri 0800-1900.

Aguascalientes *p308*
Banks On Plaza Inverlat, ATM takes Amex. Banamex, ATM. **Cultural centres** El Centro Cultural Los Arquitos, Narcozari y Alameda, T449-917 0023, formerly a 19th-century bathhouse, restored 1993, museum, bookshop, café. **Internet** Acnet, Edificio Torreplaza Bosques 2nd floor, Av Aguascalientes near university, bus from Rivero Gutiérrez. Sistemas Alt 64, Vásquez del Mercado 206, T449-915 7613, Mon-Sat 1000-1400, 1600-2100. **Medical services** Red Cross, T449-915 2055. **Post office** Hospitalidad, near El Porián shopping centre.

Zacatecas *p309, map p310*
Banks Banamex, Av Hidalgo. **Bancomer,**
Av Hidalgo, has a Visa cash dispenser and
gives cash (pesos) on Visa cards. Several
other banks with ATMs on Av Hidalgo.
Cultural centres Alianza Francesa,
Callejón del Santero 111, T493-924 0348,
French film every Tue at 1900 (free).
Internet Café@rroba, Félix U Gómez
520 B, daily 0900-2200. @Internet,
Hidalgo 737, daily. Cybertech, Hidalgo 771,
T493-922 0870, Mon-Sat 0930-2130.
Language school Fénix Language
Institute, T493-922 1643, www.fenixlanguage
institute.com. **Laundry** At the north end
of town are Lavandería El Indio Triste, Juan
de Tolosa 828 and **Lavasolo**, similar prices.
Medical services Santa Elena Clinic,
Av Guerrero, many specialists, consultation,

US$15. **Post office** Allende between
Independencia and Hidalgo, across from
Sanborn's. **Telephone** Telégrafos,
Av Hidalgo y Juárez.

San Luis Potosí *p312, map p313*
Internet Café Cibernético, Av Carranza
416. **Medical services** Clínica Díaz
Infante (private), Arista 730, T444-912 3737.
Hospital Central (public), Av Carranza 2395,
T444-913 0343. Hospital de Nuestra Señora
de la Salud (private), Madre Perla 435, Frac
Industrias (4 blocks behind Holiday Inn Hostal
del Quixote), T444-924 5424. Red Cross,
Av Juárez and Diez Gutiérrez, T444-915 3332.
Sociedad de Beneficios Española (private),
Av V Carranza 1090, T444-913 4048.
Post office Morelos y González Ortega.

Michoacán

West of Mexico City the State of Michoacán, home to the Purépecha (or Tarascan) people, is a country of deep woods, fine rivers and great lakes, with abundant fruit, fish and game. Visitors are drawn by the Tarascan customs, folklore, way of life, craft skills (pottery, wood work and lacquer), music and especially dance. Try to catch one of the festivals. The Day of the Dead, an important date in the Mexican calendar of festivals, is prominent in Michoacán, particularly around Pátzcuaro, where on 1 November every village around the lake honours its dead; it is a festive occasion, but also profoundly spiritual. People flock to El Campanario Ecological Reserve each year to see millions of Monarch butterflies take to the wing, one of the most impressive sights in all of Mexico.

There are many small pre-Hispanic sites to be explored en route, and the open chapel at Cuitzeo is well worth a stop. As elsewhere in Mexico, the colonial architecture will impress and the natural beauty of Volcán Paricutín will bemuse. A few days relaxing on the almost deserted beaches of Playa Azul will prepare you for the next stage of your journey.
▶▶ For listings, see pages 340-349.

Morelia ⊕❼❽▲⊕❻ ▶▶ pp340-349. Colour map 3, B3.

→ *Phone code: 443. Altitude: 1950 m.*
Founded in 1541, Morelia, capital of Michoacán state, is a rose-tinted city with grand, attractive colonial buildings, delightful courtyards and shady plazas.

Ins and outs

Getting there The airport is about 27 km north of Morelia. Blue and white 'Aeropuerto' buses run to the centre. The new bus terminal is a long way from town. It is best to get a taxi for the 15- to 20-minute drive, US$2; or take a local bus. Morelia is connected by Route 43 to Salamanca, Route 14 to Uruapan and Route 15 to Zamora and Mexico City.

Tourist information You'll find limited tourist information at the booths outside the Cathedral. There is also an inconveniently located **main tourist office** ① *Tata Vasco 80, T443-317 8032, www.turismomichoacan.gob.mx, Mon-Fri 0800-2000, Sat and Sun 0900-1900*. There are some good language schools in Morelia (see Directory, page 349).

Sights

The **cathedral** (1640) sits between the two main plazas, with graceful towers and a fine façade, in what is called 'sober baroque' style. The **Santuario de la Virgen de Guadalupe**, east of the aqueduct, has an ornate interior of terracotta garlands and buds, painted in pastels. There are four huge oil paintings of the missionaries 'Christianizing the Indians'. Other important churches are the modernized **Templo de la Cruz** and the 18th-century **Templo de las Rosas** in the delightful plaza of the same name (its ex-Convento now houses the Conservatorio de Música). The oldest of Morelia's churches is the **Templo de San Francisco** of the Spanish Renaissance period, although it lacks many of the decorative features of that style. The **Templo de las Monjas** has an extravagant baroque façade, constructed in 1727. The **Templo de San Agustín** (16th century) has a more Gothic influence but is also imposing.

Even more interesting than the colonial churches are the many fine colonial secular buildings still standing. The Independence hero José María Morelos, the reformer Melchor Ocampo and the two unfortunate emperors of Mexico (Agustín de Iturbide and the Archduke Maximilian of Austria) are commemorated by plaques on their houses. **Morelos' birthplace** ① *Corregidora 113, 0900-1900, free,* can be visited. The **Colegio de San Nicolás** (1540) is the oldest surviving institution of higher education in Latin America. (It has a summer school for foreign students.) Opposite is the **Centro Cultural Universitario**, with many free events. The fine former Jesuit college, now called the **Palacio Clavijero** ① *corner of Madero and Nigromante,* contains government offices and an extensive market selling *artesanía* and sweets in the arcades. At the east edge of the downtown area, on the road to Mexico City, are the 224 arches of a ruined **aqueduct**, built in 1788 (walk 11 blocks east from cathedral along Avenida Madero). Both **Banamex** and **Bancomer** have their offices in magnificent old houses on Madero Poniente, near the plaza; the patio of the former is especially fine. Also notable are the **Law School**, in the former monastery of **San Diego**, next to the **Santuario de la Virgen de Guadalupe**, past the aqueduct; the **Palacio de Gobierno** (1732-1770), facing the cathedral; the **Palacio Municipal**; and the **Palacio Federal**, built in the 18th century, and formerly a convent. Visit also the churches of **La Merced**, with its lovely tower and strange, bulging *estípites* (inverted pyramidal supports), **Las Capuchinas** ① *Ortega y*

Morelia

Sleeping 🛏
Catedral 1
Colonial 5
Concordia 6
Don Vasco 7
Fenix 8
Hostel Allende 9
Los Juaninos 3
Mintzicuri 10

Posada del Cortijo 11
Posada de la Soledad 4
Qualitel 2
Señorial 12

Eating 🍴
Boca del Río 1
Café Colón 2
Café de Conservatorio 3

El Rincón de los Sentidos 4
La Flor de las Mercedes 5
Lilian's Coffee 6
Los Milagritos 7
Los Mirasoles 8
Los Pioneros 9
Mercado de Dulces 10
Michoacana 11
Viandas de San José 12

100 metres
100 yards

Montaño, southeast of the centre, which has some churrigueresque *retablos*, and **Santa María**, on a hilltop south of the city.

Next to the Plaza de Morelos is the **Calzada Fray Antonio de San Miguel**, a shady pedestrianized walkway with restored mansions leading three blocks to the **Fuente Tarasca**, a fountain with three bare-breasted women holding up a giant basket of fruit.

Thursday and Sunday are market days: specialities are pottery, lacquer work, wood-carving, jewellery, blankets and leather sandals. The **Casa de Artesanías de Michoacán**, in the ex-Convento de San Francisco, next to the church of the same name, sells fine regional products (but not cheap). The small shops upstairs, some of which have local artisans at work, have better quality crafts than the shops downstairs. The masks are particularly fine.

Museums

The **Museo de Michoacán** ① *Calle Allende 305, Mon-Sat 0900-1900, Sun 0900-1400, US$3*, has a collection of objects relating to the history of Michoacán from pre-Hispanic times to the present day. The **Casa de la Cultura** ① *Av Morelos Norte, daily, free*, housed in the ex-Convento del Carmen, has a good collection of masks from various regions, and also of crucifixes. The centre hosts arts workshops (nominal fee), daily music, dance performances and exhibitions. The **Museo del Estado** ① *southeast corner of Jardín de las Rosas, Mon-Sat 0900-1400, 1600-2000, Sun 0900-1400, 1600-1900, free*, in the house of Empreror Iturbide's wife (Casa de la Emperatriz), is well worth a visit. Most of the ground floor is dedicated to Tarascan history and culture, with lots of information about Michoacán and, at the front, an old pharmacy with all its bottles, cabinets and scales intact. The **Museo Casa de Morelos** ① *Morelos Sur, daily 0900-1900, US$1.80*, about three blocks south of the cathedral, has exhibits on the Independence movement and its hero, José María Morelos. **Museo de Arte Contemporáneo Alfredo Zalce** ① *Av Acueducto 18, Mon-Fri 1000-2000, Sat-Sun 1000-1800*, in a 19th-century French-style building, has temporary exhibitions. For a guided tour of the city, contact David at the front desk of the **Villa Montaña Hotel**, where there are many other tours on offer, including one to the Monarch Butterfly Reserve (see box, page 335).

Around Morelia ●❶❷❸ ⇢ *pp340-349.*

The road east of Morelia soon climbs through 50 km of splendid mountain scenery of forests, waterfalls and gorges, to the highest point (Km 253), Puerto Gartan, and **Mil Cumbres** (2886 m), with a magnificent view over mountain and valley, and then descends into a tropical valley. A four-lane highway avoids the Mil Cumbres pass.

Zitácuaro is a small town with a pleasant plaza and a good covered market. The **tourist office** ① *T715-153 0675, www.zitacuaro.com.mx*, is at Km 4 on the Zitácuaro-Toluca road. North of here, a turning off the main road at **Angangueo** brings you to a unique site, the wintering grounds of the Monarch butterfly in **Reserva Ecológica El Rosario** ① *Mid-Nov to March, daily 0900-1700, US$2, plus a tip for your guide, Spanish only, see box, page 335*, above the village of **El Rosario**. Try to form a small group to go round the reserve. There is a visitor centre and food kiosks near the entrance. Be warned, the air is thin and it's a fairly tough climb to reach the butterfly colonies.

Just north of Morelia there is a good road to two lakeside villages in the neighbouring state of Guanajuato. At **Cuitzeo**, the first one, there is a fine Augustinian church and convent (begun in 1550), with a cloister, a huge open chapel, and good choir stalls in the sacristy. The church houses a collection of Mexican graphic art, spanning four centuries, in a gallery in the basement. **Laguna de Cuitzeo**, beside which it stands, is the second

Monarch butterflies

The wintering ground of the Monarch butterfly In Reserva Ecológica El Campanario is one of the natural wonders of the world. Every year millions of bright orange butterflies gather to enjoy the warm climate having migrated from southeast Canada and northeast USA. Huge clusters of butterflies hang from branches, which bow under their weight, eventually rising in a swirling mass of red clouds when warm air blows through the reserve. Most impressive is the sound of their wings, like a strong breeze blowing through the trees. The butterflies arrive between December and March, with the best time of year to visit being January and February. They leave in March, after which there is nothing to see until the following November/ December. The reserve is at a high altitude and you need to walk a few kilometres (30 minutes) to see the butterflies. Bring warm clothes as it is very cold at night. It gets very busy at weekends, when all the accommodation will be full; your best bet is to arrive at the sanctuary when it opens at 0900 to avoid the rush of tourists, US$2.

The reserve can be visited most easily from the village of Angangueo or from Zitácuaro, both of which cater for the influx of butterfly-watchers (see Sleeping, page 341). Alternatively, you can arrange transport from Mexico City. Half-hourly local bus (marked 'Angangueo') from Zitácuaro (Avenida Santos Degollado Oriente, or from bus station on outskirts of town) to Ocampo, one hour, and from Ocampo take a *camionetas* from Hidalgo and Ocampo, 45 minute journey, US$2, 12 km on a mountainous dirt road) to the parking lot below the reserve from where it is a 15-minute walk to the reserve. A truck from Ocampo to the butterfly refuge costs US$19; this can be shared, especially at weekends. All hotels will arrange transport to the reserve, about US$22 per vehicle, one hour. Four direct buses a day to Mexico City (west).

largest lake in Mexico; the road crosses it on a causeway. From here one can go through the attractive mountain scenery around **Valle de Santiago**. The second village, 33 km to the north, **Yuriria**, has a large-scale indigenous version of the splendid church and convent at Actopan. It is on Laguna de Yuriria, which looks like a grassy swamp.

Quiroga heart of Tarascan (Purépecha) country, is named after Bishop Vasco de Quiroga, who was responsible for most of the Spanish building in the area and for teaching the Purépecha people the various crafts they still practise: work in wool, leather, copper, ceramics and cane. There are many indigenous people here and few tourists. There is a fair and craft exhibitions in December.

Tzintzuntzan (pronounced rapidly *sin-sun-san*) was the pre-Conquest Tarascan capital; the **ruins** ① *daily 0900-1700, US$3*, are just behind the village; a Purépecha ceremonial centre, with five pyramids, is across the road and up the hill (10 minutes' walk) from the monastery. The **monastery**, on Magdalena, was built in 1533 but closed over 250 years ago. It has been restored, but its frescoes have deteriorated badly. The church bells date from the 16th century; a guard will show you around. In the grounds are some very old olive trees, still bearing fruit, said to have been planted by Vasco de Quiroga. Fortuitously they were missed in a Spanish edict to destroy all Mexican olive trees when it was thought that Mexican olive oil would compete with Spain's. A most interesting **Passion play** depicting the trial, suffering and death of Jesus Christ is given at Tzintzuntzan and fiestas, such as **El Señor del Rescate** on 1 February, are very colourful. Beautiful, hand-painted pottery, displayed everywhere, is very cheap but also brittle. (It is also available in other markets in Mexico.) Other handicrafts on sale include woodcarving, leather and basket-woven Christmas tree ornaments; good bargaining opportunities.

Pátzcuaro and around ⊜❶❷❸❀▲⊖⊙ ▶▶ pp340-349. Colour map 3, B2.

→ *Phone code: 434. Altitude: 2110 m.*

Twenty-three kilometres south of Quiroga, Pátzcuaro is one of the most picturesque towns in Mexico, with narrow cobbled streets and deep overhanging eaves. The houses are painted white and brown. It is built near Lago de Pátzcuaro, about 50 km in circumference, with Tarascan villages on its shores and many islands. At these villages, the Day of the Dead commemorations are worth visiting.

Ins and outs

Getting there The nearest airports are at Morelia to the east and Uruapan to the west. The bus station is on the outskirts of town. A local bus, *colectivo* or taxi will take you to the centre. Pátzcuaro is connected by Route 14 to Morelia and Uruapan.

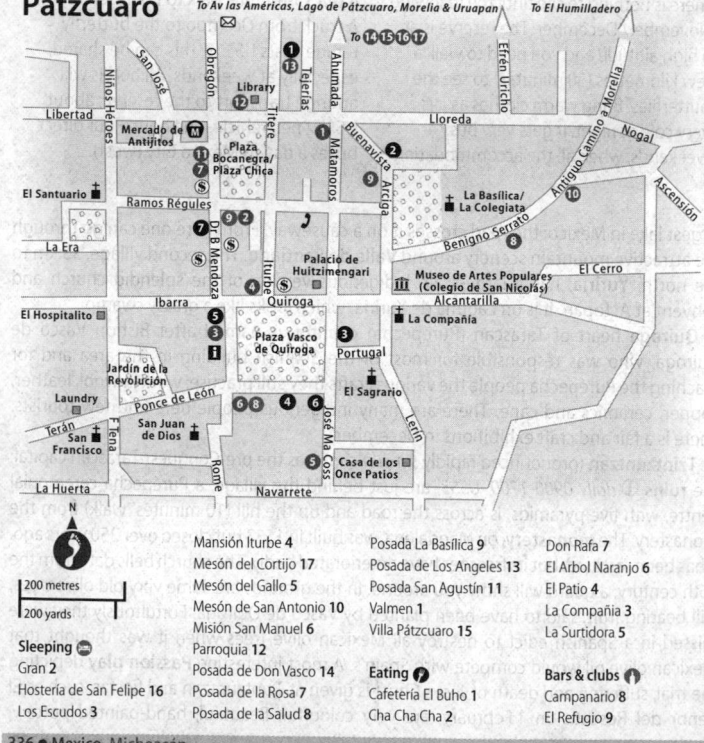

Pátzcuaro

To Av las Américas, Lago de Pátzcuaro, Morelia & Uruapan · To El Humilladero

To ❶❹❺❻❼

Sleeping ⊜
Gran 2
Hostería de San Felipe 16
Los Escudos 3
Mansión Iturbe 4
Mesón del Cortijo 17
Mesón del Gallo 5
Mesón de San Antonio 10
Misión San Manuel 6
Parroquia 12
Posada de Don Vasco 14
Posada de la Rosa 7
Posada de la Salud 8
Posada La Basílica 9
Posada de Los Angeles 13
Posada San Agustín 11
Valmen 1
Villa Pátzcuaro 15

Eating ❷
Cafetería El Buho 1
Cha Cha Cha 2
Don Rafa 7
El Arbol Naranjo 6
El Patio 4
La Compañía 3
La Surtidora 5

Bars & clubs ❶
Campanario 8
El Refugio 9

Getting around It is a steep 3-km walk uphill from the lake shore to the plaza; *colectivos* run every few minutes to Plaza Chica.

Tourist information The **tourist office** ① *north side of Plaza Grande, next to Banco Serfín, Mon-Fri 0900-1500, variable opening hours in afternoon, usually 1700-1900, Sat and Sun 0900-1500*, is friendly and provides good information. For information on the Day of the Dead, see Festivals and events, page 347.

Sights

There are several interesting buildings: the unfinished **La Colegiata** (1603), known locally as La Basílica, with its much-venerated Virgin fashioned by an indigenous craftsman from a paste made with cornstalk pith and said to have been found floating in a canoe. Behind the Basílica there are remains of the pre-Columbian town and of a pyramid in the precincts of the Museo de Artes Populares; the restored Jesuit church of **La Compañía** (and, almost opposite, the early 17th-century church of the **Sagrario**) at the top of Calle Portugal. Behind this street are two more ecclesiastical buildings: the **Colegio Teresiano** and the restored **Templo del Santuario**; on Calle Lerín is the old monastery, with a series of small patios. There are murals by Juan O'Gorman in the **library**, formerly San Agustín. On Calle Allende is the residence of the first governor. On Calle Lerán is the church of **San Francisco**; nearby is **San Juan de Dios**, on the corner of Calle Romero. Visit also the **Plaza Vasco de Quiroga**. The chapel of **El Calvario** is 15 minutes' walk outside the town, on the summit of Cerro del Calvario, a hill giving wide views. The views are also good from the old chapel of the **Humilladero**, above the cemetery on the old road to Morelia. This chapel is said to have been built on the spot where the last Tarascan emperor knelt in submission to the Spanish conquistador, Cristóbal de Olid.

The very well arranged **Museo de Artes Populares** ① *Tue-Sat 0900-1900, Sun 0900-1430, English speaking, friendly guide, US$2.50*, is in the former Colegio de San Nicolás (1540) and is excellent for seeing regional ceramics, weaving, woodcarving and basketware. Ask there for the **Casa de los Once Patios**, which contains boutiques selling handicrafts; you can see weavers and painters of lacquerware in action.

Around Pátzcuaro

The best-known lake island is **Janitzio**, which has been spoilt by the souvenir shops and the tourists (visit during the week if possible). It is 45 minutes by motorboat; boats leave when full from 0800 onwards, US$3 return from Muelle General; cheaper from Muelle San Pedrito, 500 m further on, tickets from office at dock, last boat back (return by any boat) at 2000. It is a 45-minute walk from the centre of Pátzcuaro or take a bus marked 'Lago' from Plaza Bocanegra. There is an unfortunate **Monumento a Morelos** ① *US$0.50*, crowning a hill on the island, with a mural glorifying Independence inside. It nevertheless affords magnificent views although there are often queues to climb the spiralling stairs inside to the top. A circular path goes around the island where there are lots of good restaurants; those on the waterfront charge more than those on the hill, same quality.

Another lake island to visit, less touristy than Janitzio, is **Yunuen**, boat from Muelle General, US$3. The island is clean and quiet. There are few *lanchas* during the week, so be sure to arrange a return trip unless you want to spend the night. Bring provisions. On a lakeside estate (formerly the country house of General Lázaro Cárdenas) is the **Educational Centre for Community Development in Latin America** ① *Av Cárdenas 525, Pátzcuaro, T434-342 8200, www.crefal.edu.mx*, better known as CREFAL (free films every Wednesday).

For a truly spectacular view of the lake, the islands and the surrounding countryside, walk to **Cerro del Estribo**; an ideal site for a quiet picnic. It is a 1½-hour walk to the top from the centre of Pátzcuaro. The areas round Pátzcuaro are also recommended for birdwatching.

From Pátzcuaro, you can also visit Tzintzuntzan and Quiroga by regular bus service. Thirty minutes by local bus from Plaza Chica are the ruins of **Ihuatzio** ① *US$1.80, leaflets in Spanish or English, US$0.40*, on a peninsula 12 km north of Pátzcuaro town, 8 km from Tzintzuntzan. This was the second most important Tarascan city; two pyramids are well preserved and afford good views of the lake. The pyramids are signposted, 1 km from the village, but the road is very bad. To get to Tzintzuntzan from Ihuatzio, take bus or hitch back to main road and wait for Pátzcuaro–Quiroga bus.

Uruapan and around ⬤🏨🎒🍴🛏️ ⟫ pp340-349. Colour map 3, B2.

→ *Phone code: 452. Altitude: 1610 m.*

From Pátzcuaro, the road continues southwest to Uruapan, the 'place where flowers are plentiful'. The most attractive of its three plazas is the **zócalo**, which has the **Jardín de los Mártires** at its west end. Opposite the Jardín is part of the former Collegiate church of **San Francisco** (17th century with later additions such as an interesting 1960s modern art interior), which houses the attractive **Casa de la Cultura** (small museum upstairs, free, with excellent display of the history of Uruapan). Local crafts can be bought in the *portales* or at the market. At the east end of the zócalo is the restored hospital, built by Fray Juan de San Miguel in the 16th century; now a ceramics museum, the **Museo La Huatápera**. Adjoining it is a 16th-century chapel now converted into a craft shop. Behind the chapel and museum is the **Mercado de Antojitos** and, beyond it, the clothes and goods market permanently occupying several streets. The **food market** has now moved out of the centre to two sites, one at Obregón and Francisco Villa with cheap eateries upstairs, and the other on Calzada Benito Juárez at the end of the goods market that extends up Constitución from the centre. On M Treviño, between A Isaac and Amado Nervo, there is a house just 1.5 m wide and several storeys high – possibly Mexico's narrowest building. The **tourist office** ① *Ayala 16, T452-524 7199, Mon-Sat 0900-1400 and 1600-2000, Sun 1000-1400*, is between Independencia and Pino Suárez.

The town suffers badly from traffic fumes although it is set beside streams, orchards and waterfalls in the **Parque Nacional Eduardo Ruiz** ① *US$0.85*, which is cool at night, and well worth a visit. To get there, walk or catch a bus one block south of the zócalo marked 'El Parque'. At the entrance to the Parque, on the corner of Independencia and Culver City, 1 km from the town centre, is a **Mercado de Artesanías** selling wooden boxes and bracelets. Local foods are sold in the park.

It is 10 km through coffee groves and orchards along Río Cupatitzio (meaning Singing River) to the **Tzararacua Falls** ① *www.tzararcua.com.mx, US$0.70*. There are restaurants at the bus stop where you can hire a horse to the falls; it is not advisable to walk to the falls alone. A bus (marked 'Tzararacua', or 'Zupomita'; but ask if it goes all the way) will take you from the zócalo at Uruapan to Tzararacua, US$1 (15-25 minutes), weekends and public holidays only.

Volcán Paricutín → Colour map 3, B2.

The volcano of Paricutín can be visited from Uruapan. It started erupting on 20 February 1943, became fiery and violent and rose to a height of 1300 m above the 2200-m-high region, and then died down after several years into a quiet grey mountain (460 m) surrounded by a sea of cold lava. The church tower of **San Juan**, a buried village, thrusting up through cold lava is a fantastic sight (the lava flow stopped at the foot of the altar). If you are not taking an organized tour (with horses and guides included), Paricutín is best reached by taking a 'Los Reyes' bus on a paved road to **Angahuan**, 34 km from Uruapan, US$0.85, one hour, nine a day each way (from 0500 to 2000) with **Galeana**, then hire a horse or mule or walk (one hour).

A full day's excursion with mules to the area costs about US$40, with US$3-4 tip for the guide (six to seven hours); shorter journeys cost less. To go on foot with a guide costs US$25. It is 3 km from Angahuan to the San Juan ruins, an easy walk: as you enter the village square from Uruapan (the church is south of that street) follow the road and after the square take the second street to you left (it is the only road that goes at an angle of 45°) and follow this cobbled street with telegraph poles on the left-hand side for 750 m to a stone pillared gateway. At the gate turn right down a dirt path that leads to a parking area and a viewpoint of the site (overnight parking possible). Just before you enter the parking lot a wide, dirt path with many horse tracks and footprints leads to your right and down through the forest and directly to the lava field and the church. Alternatively, start at the new hostel from where you can also see the church. Guide on foot to church US$5 per group.

To the crater of the volcano is 10 km, a long, tough walk (also a long day on horseback for the unaccustomed, especially if you get a wooden saddle). Walk westwards round the lava field, through an avocado plantation. Wear good walking shoes with thick soles as the lava is very rough and as sharp as glass in places (some people find they cannot make the last stretch over the tennis-ball size rocks); bear in mind the altitude too, as the return is uphill. It takes seven to nine hours to the volcano and back. The cone itself is rather small and to reach it there is a stiff 30-minute climb from the base. A path goes around the tip of the crater, where activity has ceased. If going in one day, leave Uruapan by 0800 so that you don't have to rush. Go even earlier in the rainy season as clouds usually build up by midday. Take a sweater for the evening and for the summit where it can be windy and cold after a hot climb. The last bus back to Uruapan leaves at 1900; but it's best not to rely on it. Much better is to stay the night in Angahuan, where there is an *albergue*. It is possible to drive to the *albergue* where they try to charge US$1.60 for the free car park. Camping is possible near the hostel. In the village are shops selling food and drink and there is a good local restaurant in the street behind the church. Two reasonable restaurants are on the road to the *albergue*. There is a water tap near the church; follow the signs. Just outside the village, on the dirt track to the main road, is the cemetery.

Zamora and Paracho → *Colour map 3, B2. Phone codes: Zamora 351, Paracho 423.*

Zamora (58 km east of Jiquilpan) is an agricultural centre founded in 1540. In the centre is the **Catedral Inconclusa**, a large, interesting Gothic-style church, started in 1898, but work was suspended during the Revolution. There are several other fine churches, and a market on Corregidora. Much of the area around the plaza is pedestrianized. Nearby is tiny Laguna de Camécuaro, with boats for hire, restaurants and wandering musicians; popular at holiday times. There is a **tourist office** ① *Morelo Sur 76, T351-512 4015.*

South east of Zamora is **Charapán** where a branch road runs 32 km south through pine woods to **Paracho**, a quaint, very traditional village of small wooden houses; in every other one craftworkers make guitars, violins and mandolins, worth from US$15 to US$1500. A recommended workshop is that of **Ramiro Castillo** ① *Av Independencia 259, Galeana 38*, good value, friendly. Bargaining is possible in all workshops.

Pacific coast ⬤⬤ ⟶ pp340-349. Colour map 3, B2.

The Pacific Coast of Michoacán is only just coming under development. From Uruapan, Route 37 goes to Playa Azul, 350 km northwest of Acapulco (bus US$12, 10½ hours minimum) and 122 km from Zihuatanejo. **Playa Azul** is a coconut-and-hammock resort (reported dirty and dilapidated) frequented much more by Mexicans than foreigners, with a few large hotels. The town of **La Mira**, on the main road, is larger than Playa Azul. Forty kilometres of excellent deserted beaches stretch to the north of Playa Azul. At night there is beautiful phosphorescence at the water's edge.

Northwest up the coast, 76 km from Playa Azul, is **Caleta de Campos**. Buses run along the coast road to La Mira, then a short distance to Caleta de Campos. In this poor village perched above a beautiful bay, there is little to eat other than seafood. At the beach here, five minutes from the village, there are bars and restaurants, popular with surfers. Be careful as there are strong currents. The main fiesta runs from 10-13 December; at 0200 on 13 December **El Torito**, a bull mask and sculpture loaded with fireworks, makes its spectacular appearance (watch out for elaborate, if dangerous, fireworks at fiesta time).

Eighty-six kilometres further up the coast, to the northwest, is **Maruata**, unspoilt and beautiful. This is a turtle conservation area. There are floods in the rainy season and the river has washed away some of the beach. There are *cabañas* for rent and *palapas* under which you can camp. For southbound traffic seeking Maruata, road signs are inadequate.

Lázaro Cárdenas is the connecting point for buses from Uruapan, Manzanillo and Zihuatanejo. There is a **tourist office** ① *120-E Rector Hidalgo, T753-532 1547*.

⦿ Michoacán listings

For Sleeping and Eating price codes and other relevant information, see Essentials pages 45-48.

⬤ Sleeping

Morelia *p332, map p333*
Some of the cheaper hotels may have water only in the morning; check. Prices drop by 15-20% in low season.

LL-L Los Juaninos, Morelos Sur 39, T443-312 0036, www.hoteljuaninos.com.mx. A very luxurious and elegant hotel that was once the Episcopal Palace (1685), beautifully restored. They offer golf and spas services and have a wonderful rooftop restaurant overlooking the zócalo.

LL Villa Montaña, Patzimba 201, T443-314 0231, www.villamontana.com.mx. On Santa María hill, south of the city, with glorious views. This gorgeous colonial-style hotel, run by French aristocrats, has 36 *casitas*. Each is unique and assuredly comfortable. Very expensive but worth it. Superb restaurant.

L Posada de la Soledad, Zaragoza 90 and Ocampo, T443-312 1888, www.hsoledad.com. Off Plaza de Armas and quiet. Luxurious rooms, most fitted with antique furniture and fireplaces, surrounding beautiful, lightly crumbling courtyards filled with pots, palms, red flowers and colonial art. The chapel has been converted into a dining room and a plethora of services include Wi-Fi and parking. Rooms on the 2nd patio are cheaper. Recommended.

AL-A Catedral, Zaragoza 37, T443-313 0406, www.hotelcatedralmorelia.com. A very well appointed, attractive colonial building with spacious rooms, bar and restaurant, although they close quite early. Some (more expensive) rooms have good cathedral views. Recommended.

B Colonial, Morelos Norte, corner with 20 de Noviembre 15, T443-312 1897. Pleasant, clean and friendly, with lots of hot water, cable TV and parking.

B Concordia, Gómez Farías 328, around the corner from the old bus station, T443-312 3052, www.hotelconcordiamorelia.com.mx. A good, clean, modern hotel with pastel shades of yellow. Rooms are clean and comfortable, if unexciting, with desk, complimentary water and clean bath. Services include, restaurant, parking, tours and internet.
B Villa Centurión, Carretera Morelia Km 4.5, T443-313 2272. Hotel on the highway with good antiques, pool and comfortable rooms.
C Don Vasco, Vasco de Quiroga 232, T/F443-312 1484, www.galeon.com/hotel posadadonvasco. Simple, comfortable rooms with TV and writing desk, a bit pokey, but clean and OK. Nothing great. Local and national calls are free, there's Wi-Fi and free coffee in the morning.
C Mintzicuri, Vasco de Quiroga 227 (opposite **Don Vasco**), T443-312 0664. Small, clean, carpeted rooms overlooking a courtyard, with hot water and cable TV. Parking and restaurant.
C Posada del Cortijo, E Ruiz 673, T443-312 9642, reservaciones@posadadelcortijo.com. Smallish, but well cared for, and comfortable enough. Rooms have hot water, cable TV and phone. Parking.
C-D Fenix, Madero Pte 537, T443-312 0512. Nice little cheapie with lots of plants, parking and clean, basic rooms. Popular with European backpackers, friendly and helpful. Cheapest rooms are without bath or TV.
C-D Hostel Allende, Allende 843, T443-312 2246, hostelallende@msn.com. Friendly hostel with 33 rooms and 2 dorms, kitchen, lockers, luggage store, tourist information and a pleasant, leafy courtyard too.
D Qualitel, E Ruiz 531, opposite the old bus station, T/F443-312 464, www.qualitel.com.mx. Formerly hotel Matador, this clean, modern hotel has reasonable, characterless rooms with hot water and cable TV. There's a restaurant, parking, business centre and Wi-Fi. Breakfast included.
E-F Señorial, Santiago Tapiá 543, 1 block south from the old bus terminal. Shabby and

ultra-basic rooms around a crumbling central courtyard, but OK if you're poor. Cheapest rooms (**E**) are without bath or TV.

Around Morelia p334
Zitácuaro
AL-A Rancho San Cayetano, Carretera a Huetamo Km 2.3, T715-153 1926, www.ranchosancayetano.com. Attractive chalets in pleasant, green grounds with views. Friendly, clean and knowledgeable about the butterflies and the sanctuary. English spoken. Highly recommended.
AL-A Villa Monarca Inn, Carretera Toluca–Morelia Km 103.5, T715-153 5346, www.villamonarca.com. Pleasant hotel on the highway with a pool, restaurant, playground and straightforward, comfortable rooms.
C América, Revolución Sur 8, Zitácuaro, 1st block, T715-153 1116. Clean, straightforward rooms with TV and hot water. Parking.
C Lorenz, Av Hidalgo Ote 14, 9 blocks from bus station, T715-153 8458. Very friendly, gregarious and helpful, with clean, newly furnished doubles, hot water, cable TV, parking, luggage store, restaurant and cooking facilities on request. Good. Recommended.
C Mary, Revolución Norte 4, Zitácuaro, T715-153 0847. Clean, simple rooms with TV and hot water.
C México, Revolución Sur 22, T715-153 2811. Large, slightly grubby rooms, some overlooking the street. Services include hot water, TV, restaurant and parking.
C Posada Michoacán, 5 de Mayo Sur 26a, main square, Zitácuaro, T715-153 1246. Small, clean, carpeted rooms with hot water and drinking water. Coffee and tours available.
E Carolina, Zitácuaro, 1 block north of the plaza between Revolución. Basic, grubby and friendly, with big rooms and hot water until 2100, cheap option.

Angangueo
A-B Albergue Don Bruno, Morelia 92, T715-156 0026. Good, comfortable

rooms, but a little overpriced. Nice setting and restaurant.

B La Margarita, Morelia. Very clean and highly recommended. Owner runs tours to butterfly sanctuary.

C-D Real Monarca, Nacional 20, Angangueo, T715-158 0187. Large comfortable rooms, hot water, friendly, meals. Highly recommended.

Quiroga
C Quiroga, Vasco de Quiroga Pte 340, Quiroga, T454-354 0035. Modern with parking.

C Tarasco, Vasco de Quiroga Ote 9, Quiroga, T454-354 0100, eduardo_carreon_valadez@ yahoo.com.mx. Colonial style, with a courtyard, clean, hot water, pleasant but front rooms noisy. Parking.

Camping Trailer park 3 km north of Quiroga. Old summer residence of a former Mexican president, good view over Lake Pátzcuaro.

Pátzcuaro and around *p336, map p336*
Rooms in some hotels are reserved 4 weeks prior to Día de los Muertos; other hotels do not take reservations, so it's pot luck at this time.

L-AL Mansión Iturbe, Portal Morelos 59, T434-342 0368, www.mansioniturbe.com. This beautifully restored 1790s mansion on the main plaza has lots of character and 12 individually decorated rooms. They have an excellent Argentine restaurant, living room, solarium, parking, Wi-Fi and bike rental. Recommended.

L-AL Posada La Basílica, Arciga 4, T434-342 1108, www.posadalabasilica.com. This charming, colonial-style hotel has pleasant patios and 12 very tasteful rooms with wooden floor boards and beams. They also have a nice restaurant with views.

AL-A Hotel Parroquia, Plaza Bocanegra 24, T434-342 5280, reserva_laparroquia@ hotmail.com. Rooms overlook an attractive central courtyard at this pleasant colonial hotel, formerly the Fiesta Plaza. Services include cable TV, phone, hot water, events room, business centre and Wi-Fi.

AL-A Posada de don Vasco, Av Lázaro Cárdenas 450, towards the lake, T434-342 0227. Attractive, colonial-style Best Western hotel (halfway between lake and town). Breakfast is good, other meals are poor, presents the *Baile de los Viejitos* (Dance of the Old Men) on Wed and Sat at 2100 at no charge, non-residents welcome but drinks very expensive. Plenty of other services, including conference hall, pool, games room and Wi-Fi.

AL-A Villa Pátzcuaro, Av Lázaro Cárdenas 506, 1 km from centre, T434-342 0767, www.villapatzcuaro.com. Very quiet and pleasant with 12 traditional rooms with fireplaces and cable TV, peaceful gardens, lots of birds and flowers. Also a camping and caravan site. Good low season reductions.

A Mesón de San Antonio, Serrato 33, T434-342 2501, www.mesondesan antonio.com. An elegant, 300-yr-old building with a pleasant sunny garden, cacti and lemon trees. The high-ceilinged rooms are comfortable, equipped with great fire places and adorned with Mexican art and crafts. Wi-Fi and meeting room available. Continental breakfast included. Friendly, helpful and recommended.

A-B Gran Hotel, Portal Regules 6, on Plaza Bocanegra, T434-342 0443, www.granhotel patzcuaro.com.mx. Rooms are small, clean and comfortable, but hardly a great value. The suites are nice and spacious and well equipped. Prices include continental breakfast, parking, Wi-Fi and restaurant.

A-B Hostería de San Felipe, Av Lázaro Cárdenas 321, T/F434-342 1298, www.mexon line.com/hosteria-sanfelipe.htm. Friendly, clean, lodgings with attractive stone-work and other interesting features. Rooms have fireplaces. A good restaurant, but closes early (2030). Highly recommended.

A-B Mesón del Cortijo, Obregón, just off Américas, towards the lake, T434-342 1295. Often fully booked at weekends. Recommended.

A-B Misión San Manuel, Portal Aldama 12 on main plaza, T434-342 1050, www.misionsanmanuel.com. A beautiful colonial building with spacious rooms, all decorated with rustic wooden beams, attractive tiled showers and sinks. Services include hot water, internet, cable TV, restaurant, café and bar.

A-C Los Escudos, Portal Hidalgo 73, T434-342 1290. A 17th-century building with comfortable, attractive rooms, valet parking, restaurant and Wi-Fi. The suites (**A**) are very spacious with interesting furniture and wooden beams. There are cheaper rooms in the other section, very good value and comfortable, ask for one with a fireplace. *Baile de los Viejitos* (Dance of the Old Men) every Sat at 2000. Recommended, and often full at the weekends.

B Mesón del Gallo, Dr Coss 20, T434-342 1474, hmeson@yahoo.com. 25 comfortable, pleasant rooms with tasteful furnishings. Services include bar and restaurant. Good value.

B Posada de los Angeles, Títere 16, T434-342 2440. A pleasant sunny garden and very clean, carpeted, comfortable rooms, equipped with all the usual amenities. Friendly and recommended.

C Posada de la Salud, Benigno Serrato 9, T434-342 0058, www.posadadelasalud. A clean, quiet hotel with tidy little rooms, attractive wooden furniture and a pleasant garden. 2 rooms have fireplaces. Sometimes the hot water is off in the middle of the day. Recommended.

D Posada San Agustín, Portal Juárez 27 (Plaza Chica), T434-342 1108, www.mexo line.com/sanagustin.htm. Simple, basic, economical rooms, with bath, hot water and cable TV. Some rooms with windows and views, some without. Not bad.

D Valmen, Padre Lloreda 34-A, T434-342 1161. Clean, reasonable budget lodgings with nice tiles and plants in the courtyard. Rooms have cable TV, bath and hot water.

D-E Posada de la Rosa, Portal Juárez 29 (Plaza Chica), T434-342 0811. Simple, windowless rooms, colonial-style, cheaper with bath and TV (**F**), although the doors are not very secure. Parking.

Camping

See also Villa Pátzcuaro, above.

Trailer Park El Pozo, on lakeside, opposite Chalamu, Km 20, Carretara 15, T434-342 0937. Hot showers am, large, delightful, well equipped, owner speaks English, also camping.

Uruapan and around *p338*

LL-L Mansión del Cupatitzio, motel on the road to Guadalajara, T452-523 2100, www.mansiondel cupatitzio.com. A beautiful colonial-style hacienda with sumptuous rooms and grounds. Services include pool, gym, Wi-Fi, restaurant and spa. Outstanding quality.

L-AL El Tarasco, Independencia 2, T452-524 1500, contacto_hoteleltarasco@hotmail.com. Comfortable lodgings with pool, mountain views and a good restaurant.

AL Mi Solar, Juan Delgado 10, 1452-522 0912, www.hotelmisolar.com. The oldest hotel in Uruapan with 14 individually decorated rooms and 3 junior suites. There are pleasant shaded patios, a fine restaurant and a plethora of services including sauna, Wi-Fi and gym. Rooms are tasteful and well-appointed.

A Pie de la Sierra, Km 4 Carretera a Charapán, on north outskirts, T452-524 2510, www.piedelasierra.com. Good motel with a moderately priced restaurant, comfortable rooms, pool and pleasant, well-tended grounds. There's also a trailer park.

B Concordia, Portal Carrillo 8, on the main plaza, T/F452-523 0400, www.hotelcon cordia.com.mx. Comfortable, if unremarkable rooms with TV, phone and bath. There's a nice restaurant and a buffet breakfast each day for US$5. Parking and laundry service.

B Nuevo Hotel Alameda, Av 5 de Febrero, T452-523 4100, nhalameda@yahoo.com.mx. A clean, modern hotel with comfortable rooms. All have bath, a/c, TV, phone and heating. Other services include laundry and parking.

B Villa de Flores, Emilio Carranza 15, west of centre, T452-524 2800. You'll find lots of lovely flowers in the courtyard of this pleasantly furnished, quiet hotel. 28 rooms have cable TV and hot water. Parking. Recommended.

C Del Parque, Av Independencia 124, T452-524 3845. Quiet, simple rooms with hot water and cable TV, some cheaper ones without TV. A bit faded but perfectly adequate. Located by the entrance to national park with enclosed parking. Friendly and recommended.

C Posada Morelos, Morelos 30, T452-523 2302. A clean, adequate cheapie with a big courtyard. Rooms have cable TV and hot water. Those upstairs are slightly larger.

D Betty's, near bus station. Basic lodgings with prices per person. Rooms have bath. Good if you need an early bus, but otherwise better to head into the centre. A few other budget lodgings in the area.

D Moderno, main plaza. A very basic place on the east side of the plaza, a lovely old building with great murals. Water is spasmodic. Just one of a few cheapies here.

Volcán Paricutín p338

B-E Cabañas, Angahuan. Sleep 6, with a log fire, or cheaper per person in dormitory with bunk beds (dormitories closed in low season). Both have hot showers; meals available, restaurant closes 1900 in low season, basic facilities, but clean and peaceful, warm and recommended but service poorer when few people are staying.

C Alberque Centro Turístico de Angahuan, T452-523 3934 (Uruapan). The *albergue* is signposted from the bus stop, and is about 30-min walk from there.

Zamora and Paracho p339

L-B Fénix, Madero Sur 401, Zamora, T351-512 0266, www.hotelfenix.com. A big, clean hotel with a pool, poor ventilation and pleasant balconies. Lots of tariffs and varying qualities of room.

B-C Posada Fénix, Morelos y Corregidora Ote 54, T351-515 1265, 1 block from zócalo, Zamora. Rooms of varying quality, nice owner (also owns Fénix, see above), good laundry service.

D San Sebastián, Piedad de Cabadas. Central, hot water, old but nice, parking across the street.

Pacific Coast p340

AL-A De la Curva, Nicolás Bravo 235, Lázaro Cárdenas, T753-537 3658, www.hoteldela curva.com. Good services across the board, including pool, laundry, parking, restaurant, internet and beauty salon. 76 spacious rooms, including 6 suites.

A Playa Azul, Venustiano Carranza s/n, Playa Azul, T753-536 0089. Comfortable rooms and a trailer park with 20 spaces, full hook-up, bathrooms, cold shower, 2 pools, bar and restaurant, US$13 for car and 2 people.

B Delfín, Venustiano Carranza s/n, Playa Azul, T753-536 0007. No a/c, but clean, pleasant and there's a swimming pool.

B Hotel Yuritzi, Caleta de Campos, T753-531 5010, www.hotelyuritzi.com. Comfortable rooms with bath, a/c and TV, but cheaper without. Clean, with pool and good views from out front. Changes TCs at reasonable rates.

B Los Arcos, Caleta de Campos, T753-531 5038. Acceptable rooms with bath, most also have good views. Parking.

C Del Pacífico, Blv Francisco Villa, Playa Azul, opposite beach, T753-536 0106. Simple rooms with bath and fan. A bit run-down, but clean, friendly and recommended. Hammocks on the roof.

D Cabañas, Caleta de Campos. With hammock space at US$1 per person, northwest of village, where Río Nexpa reaches the coast.

D Costa Azul, 5 de Mayo 276, Lázaro Cárdenas, T753-532 0780. With bath.

E Cabañas, Maruata. There are *cabañas* for rent and *palapas* under which you can camp.

● Eating

Morelia p332, map p333

♥♥♥-♥♥ La Flor de las Mercedes, León Guzmán 47. A smart, colonial-style house with beautiful decor, well-attired waiters and a romantic ambience. They have an international menu with steaks, crêpes and trout.

♥♥♥-♥♥ Los Mirasoles, Madero Pte 549. A good restaurant that specializes in regional good and interesting Mexican dishes like *sopa Tarasca* and *chiles capones* – black chillies stuffed with salsa and served on a bed of fried green tomatoes and cheese. They also have a selection of international fare.

♦♦ Boca del Río, Gómez Farías185. Good, clean restaurant serving fish fillets, shrimps in garlic butter, and octopus cocktails, among other seafood fare. They have cold Coronas too, to wash it down.

♦♦ Café Catedral, Zaragoza 37, opposite the cathedral. One of several places on the plaza, good for a breakfast and people-watching, although you'll be approached by beggars if you sit outside. Neighbouring restaurants are similar in style and cost, but this one has Wi-Fi, so you can check your email over a morning coffee.

♦♦ El Rincón de los Sentidos, Madero Pte 485. A young, hip space in a colonial building. They serve burgers, enchiladas, other snacks and bar food. Drinks promotions usually on, and a good spot for an evening beer.

♦♦ La Bodega de la Iguana, Av Camelinsa 3636, T443-314 4204. Very good traditional cuisine. Highly recommended.

♦♦ Viandas de San José, Alvaro Obregón 263 and Zapata. Pleasant dining around a pleasant, sunny colonial courtyard. There serve good cheap *comida corrida* and specialize in regional offerings. Excellent service, recommended.

♦ Los Milagritos, Galeana 103. Cheap and cheerful *torta* joint dishing out fast food and other economical fare. Check out the murals and *lucha libre* artwork. OK.

♦ Los Pioneros, Aquiles Serdán y Morelos Norte 110. Clean, pleasant and economical taco house that's popular with the locals.

Cafés, bakeries and ice cream parlours
Café Colón, Aquiles Serdán 265. An obscure locals' haunt with breakfast, sandwiches and a good selection of coffee.
Café de Conservatorio, on Plaza de las Rosas (opposite music academy). Not cheap but great atmosphere and tasty cakes.
Casa de la Cultura. Has a good café with delicious home-made cakes.

Lilian's Coffee, Madero Pte 388. Clean-cut coffee house with a corporate style, cakes and gourmet roasts.
Mercado de Dulces, Gómez Farías at the western end of the Palacio Clavijero. Famous for *ates* (fruit jellies), candies and *rompope* (an alcoholic drink similar to advocaat).
Michoacana, Madero Pte 327. For sweet, cold ice creams.

Around Morelia *p334*
Zitácuaro
♦♦ La Trucha Alegre, Revolución Norte 2. Specializes in trout, as the name suggests.

Angangueo
♦♦ Los Arcos. One of several cafés and restaurants near the plaza, serving wholesome food, but not gourmet.

Pátzcuaro and around *p336, map p336*
Local speciality is *pescado blanco* (white fish), and several lakeside restaurants serve fish dishes. Economical breakfast available from small stands in the market, usually 0600-0700 (milk shakes, rice pudding, etc). *Comida corrida* at restaurants around Plaza Grande and Plaza Chica is usually the same each day. Many places close before 2000. Most good hotels have their own restaurants.

♦♦♦-♦♦ El Gaucho Viejo, Mansión Iturbide (see Sleeping, above). Argentine *churrasco* and other carnivorous fare. Wed-Sun 1800-2400, folk music.

♦♦♦-♦♦ La Compañia, Portal Matamoros 355. One of the better plaza options. They serve grilled meats, steaks, fish and fajitas. The wine and tequila selection is healthy. Good service, and a clean, pleasant colonial interior. The steak is tasty, recommended.

♦♦ Cha Cha Cha, Buenavista 7. A cheery little patio laden with plants and *artesanías*. Dishes include salmon poached in white wine sauce, lasagne, and trout in pistachio sauce. Very pleasant and highly recommended.

♦♦ El Arbol Naranjo, Plaza Vasco de Quiroga, Head upstairs for views of the plaza. A laid-back little restaurant where they serve fresh fish and regional specialities, all home-cooked. Pretty good.

¶¶ La Surtidora, Portal Hidalgo 71. Very good coffee, well-presented breakfasts and tables on the plaza. The shop inside sells little delicacies. Good service and a Patzcuaro institution, but not fine dining.

¶¶-¶ Don Rafa, Mendoza 30. Small, intimate and economical dining space with *sopa Tarasca* and *pescado blanco* among the regional offerings.

¶¶-¶ El Patio, Plaza Vasco de Quiroga 19, T434-342 0484. Daily 0800-2200. Fruit and yoghurt for breakfast, also serves good meals, good service too. Recommended.

¶ Cafetería El Buho, Tejerías 8, tucked away down an alley. Service is slow but the food is very tasty and good value. Stylish and friendly. Recommended.

¶ Mercado de Antijitos, Plaza Chica. Good chicken with vegetables and *enchiladas* over the market (budget restaurants here are usually open in the evening).

Cafés and ice cream parlours
Paletería, Codallos 24. Excellent ice cream parlour that also sells frozen yoghurt.

Uruapan and around *p338*
The local speciality is *cecina*, dried meat. Not much in the way of fine dining downtown, but plenty of acceptable places.

¶¶ La Terraza de la Trucha, Rodilla del Diablo 13, next to the national park. As the name suggests, this is the place for rainbow trout. Try it stuffed with squash flowers.

¶¶-¶ Boca del Río, Delgado 2. Since 1974, a rough-and-ready, locally flavoured seafood joint. Soups and prawn cocktail on offer.

¶¶-¶ Café Tradicional, Carranza 5B. Filled with delicious coffee aromas, the interior of this restaurant is adorned with beautifully crafted wooden pillars, beams and doors. The staircase is particularly nice. Coffee by the cup or sack, breakfasts and *comida típica*.

¶¶-¶ Concordia, Portal Carrillo 8, on the main plaza, inside Hotel Concordia. Good for a buffet breakfast.

¶¶-¶ Cox-Hanal, Carranza, close to the corner Miguel Treviño. The name means 'let's go eat' in Yucatec. A clean, unpretentious restaurant serving Yucatec specialities. Photo art features the region's premier ruins and *cenotes*.

¶ Bambino's, Carranza 8. Brightly lit, busy, unpretentious eatery serving fast food like burgers, burritos, quesadillas and pizzas.

¶ Cocina Mary, Independencia 63. Very popular spot serving great value and diverse *comida corrida*, breakfasts, Mexican staples and economical fare. Nice mural.

¶ La Pérgola, on plaza. An interesting old place, vaguely reminiscent of a mafia den, with lots of weary characters smoking cigarettes and imbibing black coffee. Food includes mediocre Mexican staples, but the people-watching makes up for it.

¶ Mercado de Antojitos, behind the church. Cheap meals from *comedores*. Locals eat at open-air food stalls, very picturesque.

Cafés and ice cream parlours
Several ice cream parlours can be found on the zócalo.

Café La Lucha, Ortiz 22. Atmospheric little coffee house with 8 decades of tradition and lots interesting old photos on the wall.

Zamora and Paracho *p339*
¶¶ Carnes Toluca, Madero Sur and Leonardo, Zamora, and **Antigua Carnes Toluca** over the road. Not much more than meat, but plenty of it.

¶ Café D'Gribet, on main street, cheap and good snacks. Try local pancakes.

¶ El Patio, La Piedad de Cabadas, near church. Very good, dish of the day good value.

🎭 Entertainment

Morelia *p332, map p333*
Peña Bola Suriana, Allende 355. Live traditional guitar music, open courtyard, small cover charge.

Teatro Municipal. Free weekly concerts are performed.

Patzcuaro and around *p336, map p336*

A handful of bars can be found on the main plaza, which fills up with people in the evening. Try:

Campanario, Plaza Grande 14. Atmospheric and cavernous drinking hole with occasional live music.

El Refugio, Portal Régules 9. Sports TV, beer and cosy corners to escape the chilly highland evening.

⊛ Festivals and events

Pátzcuaro and around *p336, map p336*
1 Jan Los Viejitos (Old Men), in Janitzio.
2 Feb Los Sembradores (The Sowers).
4 Feb Los Apaches (at the churches).
Feb Carnaval in the Lake Pátzcuaro region; the Danza de los Moros (The Moors) is performed.
12 Oct Día de la Raza, when Columbus reached America, there is also a procession with the Virgin and lots of fireworks.
1-2 Nov Día de los Muertos (All Souls' Day), ceremony at midnight, at almost every village around the lake; it is well worth experiencing. The ceremony is most touristy on Janitzio island and at Tzintzuntzan, but at villages such as Ihuatzio, Jarácuaro and Urandén it is more intimate. The tourist office has leaflets listing all the festivities.
6-9 Dec Virgen de la Salud, when Tarascan dances performed in front of the Basílica.
12 Dec There is an interesting fiesta for the Virgen de Guadalupe.

Uruapan and around *p338*
1st week of Apr The zócalo is filled with pottery, brought from all the surrounding indigenous villages.
Jun Las Canacuas (Crown Dance), on Corpus Christi.
16 Sep In nearby village of San Juan, to celebrate the saving of an image of Christ from the San Juan church at the time of the Paricutín eruption.
15 Sep Feria in Uruapan (2 weeks either side).

▲ Activities and tours

Morelia *p332, map p333*
Tour operators
Tour de Leyendas de Morelia, T443-337 0350, viajescasamayavip@hotmail.com. Tours recalling Morelia's legendary past depart 2100 daily from Portal Galeana, opposite the cathedral. The same company runs trips throughout the state too. Spanish only.
Tours en Michoacán, Pino Suárez 524, T443-262 3782. Tours throughout the state, including Pátzcuaro, the Monarch butterfly sanctuary and lakeside villages. Trips further afield run to Guanajuato, Queretaro and San Miguel de Allende.

Pátzcuaro and around *p336, map p336*
Fishing
Winter is the best time for fishing in the somewhat fish-depleted lake, where locals traditionally threw nets shaped like dragonflies, now a rather rare event.

Tour operators and guides
Jorge Guzmán Orozco, T434-342 2579, Jorge_guzman_orozco@hotmail.com. Guided tours to Janitzio, Tzinzuntzan, Santa Clara del Cobre and Volcán Paricutín , among others. Spanish tours depart daily from Plaza Vasco de Quiroga; enquire about English tours. Fully licensed.
Jorge Méndez, T434-100 5783. Trips to lake-side communities, kayaking, boat trips, archaeological sites and culinary tours are among the offerings. French, English and Spanish spoken.
Miguel Angel Núñez, T434-344 0108, casadetierra@hotmail.com. Miguel, a writer and anthropologist by trade, offers truly excellent personalized tours to local communities, the butterfly sanctuary and archaeological sites. He is very knowledgeable about local cultures having spent many years immersed in them. Rates are US$12 per hr, excluding transportation costs. English-speaking and highly recommended.

☐ Transport

Morelia p332, map p333

Air

Mexican destinations include **Cuernavaca**, **León**, **Mexico City**, **Tijuana**, **Uruapan**, **Veracruz** and **Zacatecas**. There are international flights to **Chicago**, **LA**, **San Francisco** and **San José** (CA).

Airline offices Aeromar, Pirindas 435, T443-324 6777; AeroMéxico, Plaza Morelia Local C-18, T443-324 3604; Aviacsa, Av Camelinas 2630 Local 4, T443-324 5775; Continental, T443-317 9218; Mexicana, Enrique Ramiríz 200, T443-324 5400.

Bus

The new terminal is out of town, a 15- or 20-min taxi ride, US$3. The terminal is divided into 3 sections: **A**, for 1st class; **B**, for 2nd class; and **C**, for 3rd class. Parkhuni, ETN, Estrella Blanca and Omnibus are among the 1st-class lines. To **Aguascalientes**, 5 daily, 7 hrs, US$26. To **Celaya**, 18 per day, US$11. To **Colima**, 0740, 1200, US$23. To **Guadalajara**, at least hourly, 3-5 hrs, quicker on the *autopista*, US$23. To **Guanajuato**, 8 daily from 0650 to 1525, 3½ hrs, US$11. To **León**, regular throughout the day, 4 hrs, US$14. To **Mexico City**, very regular services, some to the North terminal, some to the West terminal, 4 hrs, US$27. To **Monterrey**, 1745, 2000, 2045, US$72. To **Pátzcuaro**, hourly, 1 hr, US$4; or every 15 mins with 2nd class autobuses **Purhépaca**. To **Querétaro**, very regular, 4 hrs, US$11. To **San Luis Potosí**, hourly, US$22. To **Toluca airport**, hourly, 0500-1800. To **Uruapan**, very regular departures, 2 hrs, US$10. To **Zitácuaro**, hourly, US$10, 3 hrs.

Around Morelia p334

Zitácuaro

Bus The bus station is about 1 km from downtown. Fixed price taxi to and from town, US$1.50; minibuses US$0.40. Buses to Angangueo, every ½ hr, 1½ hrs, US$1. To **Mexico City**, 1½ hrs, US$11. To **Morelia**,

hourly, 3½ hrs, US$10. For the **El Rosario butterfly sanctuary**, take the Angangueo bus and exit at Ocampo. From there, *camionetas* to the reserve depart from Hidalgo and Ocampo, 45 mins, US$2.

Angangueo

Bus To reach Angangueo, go to Zitácuaro and catch a bus, every ½ hr, 1½ hrs, US$1. Comfortable *colectivo* taxis also travel between the 2 towns; ask around. To reach the **El Rosario butterfly sanctuary**, catch a bus towards Zitácuaro and exit at Ocampo (see above).

Pátzcuaro and around p336, map p336

Bus The bus station (called Central) is 1.5 km out of town, with a left-luggage office. Buses run between Plaza Chica and the terminal, US$0.50. Taxis are US$2.

To **Guadalajara**, late morning service, 6 hrs, US$17. To **Lázaro Cárdenas**, hourly from 0600, 8 hrs, long but spectacular ride through mountains and lakes (police checks likely), US$19. To **Quiroga**, every ½ hr, 40 mins, US$1.50. To **Mexico City**, regular constant service, 6 hrs, US$25. To **Morelia**, every 15 mins with 2nd-class Purépecha, 1 hr, US$4. To **Santa Clara del Cobre**, every 30 mins, 30 mins, US$1. To **Toluca**, from 0915, 5 hrs, 1st class US$20. To **Tzintzuntzan**, every 15 mins, 30 mins, US$1. To **Uruapan**, every 30 mins, 1 hr, US$3. To the **lake**, local buses depart from the corner of the market on Plaza Chica. *Combis* run between the lakeside villages.

Uruapan and around p338

Air

Daily flights to **Mexico City**. Also flights to **Culiacán**, **Guadalajara** and **Tijuana**.
Airline offices Aeromar, T452-523 5050.

Bus

Bus station on the northeast edge of town, necessary to get a city bus into town (US$0.25), finishing at about 2100, or a taxi to the plaza, US$3. Left-luggage.

To **Colima**, 4 daily, 6 hrs, US$22. To **Guadalajara**, roughly hourly, 4½ hrs, US$20. To **Lázaro Cárdenas**, every 30 mins, 6 hrs, US$22. To **Mexico City**, more than 1 per hr, 6 hrs, US$32. Tto **Morelia**, every 20 mins, 2½ hrs, US$9. To **Pátzcuaro**, frequent, 1 hr, US$4.

Zamora and Paracho *p339*
Bus Bus station at north edge of Zamora, local bus to centre US$0.25, taxi US$3.50, from centre to bus station from 5 de Mayo in front of Catedral Inconclusa. Bus to **Mexico City** and to **Guadalajara**, US$19. To **Morelia**, US$18. To **Pátzcuaro**, 2½ hrs. To **Tamazula**, for Cd Guzmán, 3½-4 hrs, US$11.

From Paracho there are buses to **Uruapan**, 45 mins, US$1. Also to **Morelia** via Pátzcuaro.

Pacific Coast *p340*
Bus Buses ply up and down the coast road, stopping at the road junction 4 km from Plaza Azul. *Colectivos* take you between town and junction. If driving north it is 5 hrs to **Tecomán** (where the road from Colima comes down to the coast).

From Lázaro Cárdenas **Galeana** to **Manzanillo** 7¾ hrs, US$18. To **Uruapan**, 6½ hrs, US$19. To **Guadalajara**, US$35 with **La Línea**. To **Mexico City** US$48, luxury.

❶ Directory

Morelia *p332, map p333*
Banks Bancomer, Av Madero Oriente, Visa ATM. There is an ATM just east of the Hotel Casino that accepts Visa and MasterCard. There is a Banco Inverlat ATM next to the bus station that accepts Amex cards. **Internet** La Central, Matamoros 72A, Mon-Sat 0900-2200. Chatroom Cybercafé, Nigromante 132A, Mon-Sat 0900-2200, Sun 1200-2100, spacious, tranquil. Shareweb Cybercafé, Av Madero Ote 573-C, Mon-Sat 0900-2200, Sun 1400-2200. **Language schools** Centro Mexicano de Idiomas, Calzada Fray Antonio de San Miguel 173, T443-312 4596. Intensive weekly classes; other courses available include handicrafts.

Accommodation with families. Baden-Powell Institute, Antonio Alzate 565, T443-312 4070, www.baden-powell.com. Courses for all levels, plus cultural, social science and extracurricular courses. Highly recommended.
Laundry Lavandería Chapultepec, Ceballos 881. Lavandería on Santiago Tapiá towards the old bus station. **Medical services** Dentist: Dr Leopoldo Arroyo Contreras, Abraham González 35, T443-312 0751, near the cathedral. Recommended. **Post office** Madero Ote 369. Long- distance phone and fax, Gómez Farías 113, near sweet market.

Pátzcuaro and around *p336, map p336*
Banks Several ATMs in the centre. Banamex, Portal Juárez 32. **Promex**, Portal Regules 9. Serfín, Portal Allende 54. Bancomer, Zaragoza 23; *casa de cambio* at Benito Mendoza 7.
Internet Several places on or around the Plaza Grande, most charge US$0.50-US$1.
Laundry Lavandería San Francisco, Terán 16, Mon-Sat 0900-2000. **Medical services** Dentist: Dr Antonio Molina, T434-342 3032. Doctors: Dr Jorge Asencio Medina, T434-342 4038. Dr Guadalupe Murillo, T434-342 1209. Pharmacy: Gems, Benito Mendoza 21, T434-342 0332, daily 0900-2100. **Post office** Obregón 13, 1 block from Plaza Chica, Mon-Fri 0800-1600, Sat 0900-1300.

Uruapan and around *p338*
Banks Banamex, Cupatitzio y Morelos, Visa agent. Bancomer, Carranza y 20 de Noviembre. Serfín, Cupatitzio. **Internet** Logicentro Cyber Café, Av Juárez 57, T452-524 9494, Mon-Sat 0900-1400, 1600-2100. Computer shop, basement of Hotel Plaza. **Laundry** Carranza 47, Mon-Sat 0900-1400, 1600-2000. Mujer Santayo Lavandería, Michoacán 14, T452-523 0876. **Medical services** Red Cross, 1452-524 0300. **Post office** Jalisco 81. **Telephone** Computel, Ocampo, on plaza, daily 0700-2200.

Zamora *p339*
Internet In small mall on Morelos, between Colón and Ocampo.

Guadalajara to the Pacific coast

If it's the Mexican stereotype you're after, make your way to the State of Jalisco. This is where you'll find the town of Tequila, the lasso-swinging charros, the swirling Jarabe Tapatío (Mexican hat dance) and the romantic mariachis, those roving musicians dressed in fine, tight-trousered gala suits and massive sombreros of the early 19th-century rural gentry. All these originated in Jalisco, but there are other attractions worth making a song and dance about.

Guadalajara, the state capital, is today a huge, modern metropolis. But the 'pearl of the west' has a magnificent and elegant Spanish core with shady plazas, impressive colonial architecture, some fine museums and the vast Mercado Libertad. A short visit to the famous craft centre suburbs of Tlaquepaque or Tonalá is relaxing and rewarding. Take a boat ride on Mexico's largest lake, Lago de Chapala, go and see the volcanically active Nevado de Colima, cool off in the pine forests around the delightful old town of Tapalpa, or visit a distillery in Mexico's most famous small town, Tequila.

Jalisco is also gateway to the Pacific coast and the mega resorts of Puerto Vallarta and its recent northern spin-off, Nuevo Vallarta, both on the vast Bahía de Banderas. But there are other beautiful and secluded beaches to the north and south of Vallarta. Up the coast, in the neighbouring state of Nayarit, sleepy San Blas is popular with surfers and birdwatchers. Away from the resorts, remote in the Sierra Madre Occidental, live the Cora and Huichol people, renowned for their stunningly beautiful chaquira beadwork and colourful nierika yarn paintings, as well as for the ancestral ritual that takes them hundreds of miles every year on a pilgrimage to the sacred peyote grounds near Real de Catorce to collect the hallucinogenic cactus. **▸▸** *For listings, see page 368-389.*

Guadalajara ⬤🅿🅕🅖🅧🅞▲🅔🅒 ▸▸ *pp368-389. Colour map 3, B2.*

→ *Phone code: 33. Population: 5,000,000. Altitude: 1650 m.*

Guadalajara, Mexico's second city, was founded on 14 February 1542. In the Centro Histórico, graceful colonial arcades, or portales, flank scores of old plazas and shaded parks. Efforts are being made to preserve the colonial atmosphere and restore noteworthy buildings. At weekends and on public holidays, the town fills with people from all over the state meandering through the streets.

Ins and outs

Getting there Aeropuerto Internacional Miguel Hidalgo (**GDL**), 20 km south of the city, receives frequent flights from Mexico City and many other domestic and international airports. Fixed-rate taxis will take you into the city; tickets are available in the airport. Two local bus routes also service the airport. ▸▸ *See Transport, page 381.*

An important commercial centre, Guadalajara is the hub of several major land routes. The appropriately vast **bus terminal** is 10 km southeast of the centre; allow at least 30 minutes to get there on one of the luxury bus services (**Línea Azul** and **Línea Cardenal**). The terminal is a nightmare if you try to understand it; fortunately that's not too important. Simply put, there are seven modules at the terminal, each serving different bus companies within four towns or regions within Mexico.

The **old bus station**, a few blocks south of the city centre, serves towns within 100 km of Guadalajara, mainly with second-class buses and *colectivos* that run to the towns on

Lake Chapala. There is a train station at the south end of Calzada de la Independencia operating the **Tequila Express**.

Getting around The most pleasant way of seeing the city is by horse-drawn carriage; these are to be found outside the Museo Regional at the corner of Liceo and Hidalgo and a few other places. More conventional buses and *colectivos* run to most areas of the city, although regular services can be frustratingly bad. Trolley buses and the new luxury buses with guaranteed seats on a few fixed routes are a much better option. The city also has two 'metro', or rather *tren ligero* lines, one running north-south and the other west-east. Taxis tend not to use meters so agree on a price before setting off.

Best time to visit The climate is mild, and clear all through the year, although in summer it can be thundery at night. Pollution from vehicles can be bad downtown and the winter is the worst time for smog. However, afternoons are usually clear and sunny and during the rainy summer season, smog is less of a problem.

Guadalajara

	Azteca 3 *B3*	**Eating** 🍴	La Rinconada 6 *B3*
	Francés 5 *B2*	Café D'Oslo 1 *C1*	
	Hostal Guadalajara 7 *B3*	Café Madoka 2 *B1*	**Bars & clubs** 🍸
	Janeiro 10 *B3*	Carnes Asadas	Femina La Latina 8 *B2*
	León 11 *C2*	El Tapatío 7 *B3*	La Jaula 9 *B2*
	Plaza Génova 15 *B2*	Carnes Asadas	La Maestranza 12 *B2*
	Posada San Pablo 16 *C1*	Rigo's 3 *C3*	La Mansión 10 *B2*
	Posada Tapatía 17 *B1*	El Mexicano 4 *B3*	La Maskara 11 *B2*
Sleeping 🛏	Rotonda 18 *A2*	La Playita 5 *B2*	
Aranzazú 2 *C2*			

N

200 metres / 200 yards

To Old Bus Station, Parque Agua Azul, Museo de Arqueología del Occidente de México, Train Station, Airport & Chapala

To Bus Terminal, Tlaquepaque, Tonalá & Mexico City

Tourist information State and federal tourist office (Sectur) ① *Morelos 102, Plaza Tapatía, T33-3668 1602, Mon-Fri 0800-2000, Sat and Sun 1000-1600,* has information in German and English, including a good walking tour map of the historic centre, helpful. There are also tourist booths in front of the cathedral and at the eastern end of Plaza Tapatía. The newspaper *Siglo 21* has daily music, film and arts listings, as well as a good entertainments section *Tentaciones* on Friday. Guadalajara is generally a safe city. Normal precautions are required against pickpockets, but little more.

Cathedral and Plaza de Armas
The heart of the city is the Plaza de Armas. On its north side is the **cathedral** (1561-1618), which incorporates a medley of styles. Its two spires are covered in blue and yellow tiles. There is a reputed Murillo Virgin inside (painted 1650), and the famous *Virgen del Carmen*, painted by Miguel Cabrera, a Zapotec artist from Oaxaca. In the dome are frescoes of the four gospel writers and in the Capilla del Santísimo are more frescoes and paintings of the Last Supper. From inside you can see the evening sun's rays streaming through the dome's stained glass. The cathedral's west façade is on Plaza de los Laureles, on the north side of which is the **Palacio Municipal** (1952), which contains murals by Gabriel Flores depicting the city's founding.

Also on Plaza de Armas is the **Palacio de Gobierno** (1643) where, in 1810, Hidalgo issued his first proclamation abolishing slavery. **José Clemente Orozco**'s great murals can be seen on the central staircase; they depict social struggle, dominated by Hidalgo, with the church on the left, fascism on the right and the suffering peasants in the middle. More of Orozco's work can be seen in the **Congreso** (free), an integral part of the Palacio de Gobierno; and also at the university Rectoría, the Instituto Cultural Cabañas, and the Casa Taller José Clemente Orozco (see below) as well as at the university's main library, Glorieta Normal, north of the centre.

East of the cathedral
East of the cathedral is the **Plaza de la Liberación**, with a statue of Hidalgo, where the national flag is raised and lowered daily (with much ceremony). On the north side, the **Museo Regional de Guadalajara** ① *Liceo 60, between Hidalgo and Independencia, Tue-Sat 0900-1730, Sun 0900-1700 US$2, free on Sun, Tue and holidays, free for children and senior citizens,* is in an old seminary (1710), with a good prehistoric section (including the complete skeleton of a mammoth found in Jalisco). This museum has an interesting display of shaft tombs, an excellent display of Colima, Nayarit and Jalisco terracotta figures (but less extensive than the Museo de Arqueología, see below), and one of the finest displays of 17th- to 18th-century colonial art in Mexico. There are also musical instruments, indigenous art and one room devoted to the history of Jalisco from the conquistadors to Iturbide; highly recommended.

The **Palacio Legislativo** ① *Plaza de la Liberacón, open to the public 0900-1800,* a neo-classical building, remodelled in 1982, has a list of the names of all the Constituyentes, from Hidalgo to Otero (1824-1857 and 1917). At the eastern end of this plaza is the enormous and fantastically decorated **Teatro Degollado** ① *daily 1000-1400,* dating back to 1866. It's well worth seeing even if you don't go to a performance. ►► *See Entertainment, page 377.*

A pedestrian mall, **Plaza Tapatía**, has been installed between the Teatro Degollado and the Hospicio Cabañas, crossing the Calzada de la Independencia, covering 16 blocks. It has plants, fountains, statuary and a tourist office. The massive **Hospicio Cabañas** near the Mercado Libertad, to the east is now known as **Instituto Cultural Cabañas** ① *Tue-Sat*

1000-1600, Sun 1000-1500. The ex-orphanage is a beautiful building with 22 patios, which is floodlit at night. The contents of the former Museo Orozco in Mexico City have been transferred here. See also Orozco's famous *Man of Fire* painted in the dome. The Cabañas also has exhibitions of Mexican and international art and other events.

Facing the Cabañas, on Morelos, is a sculpture in bronze by Rafael Zamarripa of Jalisco's symbol: two lions supporting a tree. Immediately in front of the Instituto Cultural Cabañas are four bronze seats/sculptures by local artist Alejandro Colunga, which could be regarded as amusing or macabre, depending on your sense of humour. They include skeletons, an empty man's suit topped by a skull and a large pair of ears. Just south of the Cabañas is the vast **Mercado Libertad** (see Shopping, page 379), known locally as San Juan de Dios. Opposite, on Obregón and Leonardo Vicario, is the **Plaza de los Mariachis**.

Museo de la Ciudad ① *Calle Independencia 684, Tue-Sun 1000-1730, Sat 1000-1400, US$0.50*, in a pretty colonial building with two columned patios, has information on the city from its founding to the present day, including maps and population statistics.

West of the cathedral

West of the cathedral, along Avenida Juárez, is the *Rectoría* of the **University of Guadalajara** ① *Av Juárez y Tolsá (Enrique Díaz de León)*. Inside, in the *paraninfo* (main hall), is another Orozco mural portraying 'man asleep, man meditating, and man creating'; lie on your back or look in a mirror. The building also houses the **Museo de Arte** ① *Tue-Fri 1000-1800, Sat-Sun 1000-1600*, with a good café.

Not far from the university is the strange-looking **Templo Expiatorio** ① *Av Enrique Díaz de León y Madero*, with fine stained glass and intricate ceiling, Gothic style but still unfinished after a century.

Further west along Avenida Vallarta, the **Casa Taller José Clemente Orozco** ① *Aurelio Aceves 29, Tue-Sat 1000-1600, Sun 1000-1500*, on a pedestrian street half a block from Los Arcos, was built in the 1940s and donated to the State of Jalisco by the family after the artist's death in 1951.

South of the cathedral

Not far from the centre a couple of churches are worth visiting. **San Francisco Neri** (1550), off Avenida 16 de Septiembre, has a three-tiered altar with columns, a feature repeated on the façade. To the north is the **Jardín San Francisco**, a pleasantly shaded plaza, and the starting point for horse-drawn carriages. To the west is the old church of **Nuestra Señora de Aranzazú**, with three fantastic churrigueresque altarpieces; equally impressive are the coloured ceilings and the finely carved dado, the only light coming from high-up windows and from the open east door.

The **Museo de Arqueología de Occidente de México** ① *Av 16 de Septiembre 889, Zona Agua Azul, Tue-Sun 1000-1330, 1700-1900, Sat 1200-1400, 1600-1900, US$0.50*, has a comprehensive collection of objects from Jalisco, Colima and Nayarit, including pottery, ornaments, weapons, figures and illustrations of tombs. A small booklet in English is available. Nearby, is **Parque Agua Azul** ① *Calzada Independencia Sur, Tue-Sun 0800-1900, US$0.20*, a park with a good aviary, trees, flowers and fountains. It also contains an outdoor concert bowl, the **Teatro Experimental** and the **Casa de las Artesanías de Jalisco** (see Crafts, page 379). It's about 15 blocks south of the centre at the intersection of Constituyentes and González Gallo; to get there take bus No 52 or 54 up Avenida 16 de Septiembre or No 60 or 62 up Calzada Independencia back to centre.

North of the cathedral

North of the cathedral, is the **Museo de Periodismo y Artes Gráficas** ① *Av Alcalde 225, Tue-Sat 1000-1800, Sun 1100-1500, US$1, students with ID half price, over 60s free*. The building is known as the Casa de los Perros because of two large dog statues on the roof. The first printing shop in Guadalajara was here and the first *periódico insurgente* (insurgent newspaper) in the Americas, *El Despertador Americano*, was published here in 1810. The museum contains old printing presses and newspapers. When Avenida Alcalde was widened in 1950, the building's façade was moved back 9 m. **Casa Museo López Portillo** ① *Calle Liceo 177, Tue-Sat 1000-1700, Sun 1000-1500*, formerly the family home of the ex-president, was restored in 1982 when he was in office. It is a colonial house with a large tiled courtyard, and surrounding rooms furnished with 18th- and 19th-century Italian and French furniture. It is also used as a cultural centre with classes in music, dance, literature, chess, indigenous culture and languages.

Churches worth seeing north of the cathedral include **Santa Mónica** ① *Santa Mónica y Reforma* (1718), which is small, but very elaborate with impressive arches full of gold under a clear atrium and a richly carved façade. Nearby, is the church of **San José** ① *Alcalde y Reforma*, a 19th-century church with a fine gilded rococo pulpit, has eight pillars in a semi-circle around the altar, painted deep red and ochre behind, giving an unusual effect, the overall light blue gives an airy feel; in the plaza outside is a statue of Núñez, defender of the Reforma who was killed in 1858. The **Santuario de Guadalupe** ① *Av Alcalde and Juan Alvarez*, is lovely inside; outside, in the Jardín del Santuario, are massive celebrations on 12 December, the day of the Virgin of Guadalupe, with fireworks, musicians, vendors and games. Five minutes' walk away, **San Miguel de Belén** ① *Hospital 290*, is enclosed in the Hospital Civil Viejo and contains three fine late 18th-century *retablos*; behind the hospital is the **Panteón de Belén** ① *entrance at Calle Belén 684 at the corner of Eulogio Parra, open until 1500*, a beautiful old cemetery closed to new burials for many years.

Parque Alcalde ① *Jesús García y Av de los Maestros, small entry fee*, is a pleasant enough park with a lake, rowing boats and a children's playground.

On the way out of the city going north along Calzada Independencia, near the Barranca de Oblatos, a huge canyon, there is a large and well-kept **Jardín Zoológico** ① *US$0.50, take bus Nos 600, 60 and 62 heading north on Independencia*, with plenty of Central American animals and aviaries in a delightful atmosphere. **Selva Mágica** amusement park is inside the zoo; it has a dolphin and seal show three or four times a day. There is also a **Planetarium** nearby.

Zapopan

In a northwest suburb of Guadalajara is the **Basílica de Zapopan**, completed 1690, with a miraculous image of Nuestra Señora, known as *La Generala* on the main altar, given to the local people in 1542. There is a huge **Fiesta de la Virgen de Zapopan** on 12 October. Next door is the **Museo de Arte Huichol Wixárica** ① *Mon-Sat 0930-1330, 1500-1800, Sun 1000-1500*. At one end of the pedestrian street, **Paseo Teopitzintli**, leading to the plaza and basilica, is the colonial-style **Arco de Ingreso**. The **tourist office** ① *Guerrero, T33-3110 0754, Mon-Fri 0900-2100, Sat 0900-1300*, is in the Casa de la Cultura, two blocks behind the Basílica. To get to Zapopan, take bus No 275 on Avenida Alcalde, or take line 1 of the *tren ligero* to the Avila Camacho stop and pick up bus No 175 to Zapopan (there are several different 175s, so check with driver that the bus goes all the way to Zapopan).

Tlaquepaque

About 7 km southeast of the city centre is the attractive suburb of Tlaquepaque, which is well worth a visit. Calle Independencia runs from Bulevar Tlaquepaque (the main avenue into Guadalajara) to the main plaza where you can see the restored **Parroquia de San Pedro Tlaquepaque** and the **Basílica La Teranensis**. Further on is the **Parián**, a very large, square building occupying most of another plaza, with bars (pretty woodwork and tiling) and kitchens around the perimeter. The rest is an open courtyard. By day Tlaquepaque is a fusion of craft ideas ranging from red-hot and pricey minimalist style through to stack-it-high and sell-it-cheap tack (see Shopping, page 379); at night the boulevards and main square fill with diners and *mariachis*, who play Friday, Saturday, Sunday, 1530 and 2130; also roving *mariachis* play for a fee. If you're looking to stay in the area for a couple of days there is good accommodation, see Sleeping, page 369. The **Museo Regional de la Cerámica** ① *Independencia 237, T33-3635 5404, Tue-Sat 1000-1800, Sun 1000-1500*, in a beautiful colonial building displays examples of Jalisco's ceramics and other handicrafts. There are also items for sale. Tlaquepaque can be combined with a visit to Tonalá (see below) for an easy day-trip from Central Guadalajar.

Around Guadalajara ●❷❸❹❺❻❼ ▶ *pp368-389. Colour map 3, B2.*

Tonalá → *Phone code: 33.*

Fifteen kilometres southwest of Guadalajara on the road to Mexico City is Tonalá, noted for its Sunday and Thursday markets, where you can pick up bargains in pottery, glass and ceramics. The market is held on the central avenue, where all the buses from Guadalajara stop. Calle Benito Juárez intersects this avenue and is a main shopping street. It runs to the main plaza (where it intersects with Calle Madero, the other main shopping street in the centre) and on another block to the **Parroquia de Santiago de Tonalá**, a very beautiful church built in the mid-17th century. On the plaza is the cream-coloured **Iglesia del Sagrado Corazón**. The walls are lined with crucifixion paintings. Also on the plaza are the **Presidencia Municipal**, a pastel blue-green colonial-style building, and the municipal market (food and crafts).

Chapala → *Colour map 3, B2. Phone code: 376.*

Chapala town, 64 km to the southeast of Guadalajara on the northern shore of **Laguna de Chapala** (113 km long, 24-32 km wide), has thermal springs, several good and pricey hotels, three golf courses, and is a popular resort particularly with retired North Americans and Mexican day-trippers.

Laguna de Chapala is set in beautiful scenery. There are boats of all kinds for hire, some go to the **Isla de los Alacranes** (restaurant), and there is water-fowl shooting in autumn and winter. Most fish in the lake have been killed by pollution, but the 5-cm 'XYZ' fish, called *charales*, are a delicacy similar to whitebait. There is a market on the east side of the zócalo with stalls selling handicrafts, some places to eat, and dirty public conveniences (1 peso); entrance on street behind the market. There is a regional **tourist office** ① *Aquiles Serdán 26, T376-765 3141.* A free English-language newspaper, *El Ojo del Lago*, is available at hotels and online at www.chapala.com.

Ajijic to Jocotepec → *Colour map 3, B2. Phone code: 376.*

Seven kilometres to the west of Chapala, Ajicjic a smaller, once indigenous village, has an arty-crafty American colony with many retired North Americans. The village is pleasant, with cobbled streets, a pretty little plaza and many single-storey villas. One block east of the plaza at the end of Calle Parroquia is the very pretty church of San Andrés, started in 1749. On Colón, in the two blocks north of the plaza, are several restaurants, boutiques and galleries. Going south from the plaza, Colón becomes Morelos, crossing Calle Constitución and continuing some five blocks to the lake with lots of restaurants, galleries and shops. The lake shore has receded about 200 m from the original shoreline and is a bit smelly. The Way of the Cross and a Passion Play are performed at Easter in a chapel high above the town. **House and garden tours** ① *T376-766 1881, Thu 1030, 2½ hrs, US$10*, in aid of Lakeside School for the Deaf.

Beyond Ajijic to the west lies the small town of **San Juan Cosalá**, less prosperous than Ajijic but pleasant, with cobblestone streets and fewer gringos. There are thermal springs (varied temperatures, crowded and noisy at weekends, five pools of different sizes). Fish restaurants are squeezed between the carretera and the lake at **Barrenada**, 1 km east of town.

Forty kilometres due south of Lake Chapala is the colonial town of **Mazamitla** (2200 m), a pleasant place on the side of a range of mountains, but cold at night. It has a charming zócalo.

Tapalpa → *Colour map 3, B2. Phone code: 343.*

About 130 km south of Guadalajara off Route 54 to Sayula and Ciudad Guzmán is Tapalpa, a very pretty village indeed and a popular place for weekend homes for rich Tapatíos. It is a 3½-hour drive from Guadalajara. The bus makes several detours into the hills to stop at small places such as **Zacoalco** (Sunday market) and **Amacueca**. The road up to Tapalpa is winding and climbs sharply and the air becomes noticeably cooler. The town itself, with only 11,000 inhabitants, shows ample signs of the influx of prosperity. There are two churches (one with a curious atrium) and an imposing flight of stone steps between them, laid out with fountains and ornamental lamps. Tapalpa is in cattle country; the rodeo is a popular sport at weekends. The main street is lined with stalls, selling *sarapes* and other tourist goods on Sunday and fresh food the other days of the week. The local speciality is *ponche*, an improbable blend of tamarind and mezcal, which is sold in gallon jars and recommended only for the curious or foolhardy.

Colima and around ●❼❷❸❺❶ ⟩⟩ *pp368-389. Colour map 3, B2.*

→ *Phone code: 312. Altitude: 494 m.*

The capital of the State of Colima is a most charming and hospitable town, but it lives in the shadow of the active volcano, which can be seen smoking 30 km to the north. The town also suffers from earthquakes, the latest of which was in January of 2003. It damaged many buildings and killed at least 25 people, but the town is recovering quickly and is rebuilding and repairing its churches and historical buildings. The main square is the focal point of the town, with a 19th-century Moorish-style arcade and a strange rebuilt Gothic ruin on the road beyond the **cathedral** (late 19th century). Also on the east side of the main square is the **Palacio de Gobierno**, which contains interesting murals of the history of Mexico. Behind them is the **Jardín Torres Quintero**, another pretty plaza but smaller.

The **Museo Regional de Historia** ① *on the zócalo, Tue-Sat 0900-1800, Sun 1700-2000*, has a comprehensive collection of pre-Hispanic ceramics; look out for the figurines of dogs, which were clearly being fattened for the supper table. The ceramicists attained a high level of perfection in portraying the facial expressions of people engaged in their daily tasks.

The volcanoes of Colima

Protected by Parque Nacional Volcán Nevado de Colima, the Volcano of Colima (3860 m) and El Nevado de Colima (4330 m) are to the north of the city of Colima. The former, which erupted with great loss of life in 1941, used to be one of the most exciting climbs in Mexico. However, in recent years, activity increased dramatically, peaking in 1999 with explosions that sent columns of dust 8 km into the sky. In 2003, a huge earthquake measuring 7.8 on the Richter scale hit the State of Colima and 10,000 homes were damaged.

Colima volcano has been erupting periodically for 500 years with over 30 major eruptions dating as far back as 1585. This latest period of activity puts the volcano off limits for the time being – you can check on the current situation at www.ucol.mx/volcan.

Andador Constitución is a pedestrian street, with people selling paintings, several small, attractive restaurants and a state-run artisan's shop at the north end on the corner of Zaragoza. Crossing Zaragoza, Constitución is open to traffic and one block north on the corner with Vicente Guerrero is the church of **San Felipe de Jesús** (early 18th-century plateresque façade) where Miguel Hidalgo was at one time parish priest. There is a public swimming pool in the **Parque Regional Metropolitano** on Calle Degollado about five to six blocks from the southwest corner of the main plaza. **Teatro Hidalgo** on the corner of Degollado and Morelos, has a pink colonial façade and large carved wooden doors (only open during functions). Parque Núñez, five blocks east of the plaza is also attractive and twice the size of the plaza. There's also a **tourist office** ① *Hidalgo 96, corner of 27 de Septiembre, T312-312 4360, www.visitacolima.com.mx, Mon-Fri.*

The **Museo de las Culturas de Occidente María Ahumada** ① *Calzada Pedro Galván, Tue-Sun 0900-1900,* in the Casa de Cultura complex, deserves a visit if only for its ample collection of pre-Hispanic figurines. The region specialized in the production of pottery figures concerned with earthly problems and not cosmological events, as in other areas. The **Museo Universitario de Artes Populares 'Ma Teresa Pomar'** ① *Calle 27 de Septiembre y Manuel Gallardo, Tue-Sun 1000-1300, 1700-2000,* exhibits folklore and handicrafts and has items for sale.

Around Colima

El Chanal ① *Tue-Sun 0100-1700,* is an archaeological site 15 km north of Colima, which has a small pyramid with 36 sculptured figures, discovered in 1944. Another site, closer by, is **La Campana** ① *just off Av Tecnológico, Tue-Sun 1000-1700, US$1.30.* These largely unexcavated remains include a ball court and a few temples and platforms aligned with Colima Volcano. **El Hervidero**, 22 km southeast of Colima, is a spa in a natural lake of hot springs (25°C).

Comala, a pretty colonial town near Colina with whitewashed adobe buildings, has a cooler and more comfortable climate. There are excellent views of the volcanoes, especially the active Volcán de Fuego. The surrounding vegetation is lush with coffee plantations. There are regular buses, US$0.25, 20 minutes, from Colima's Suburbana bus station.

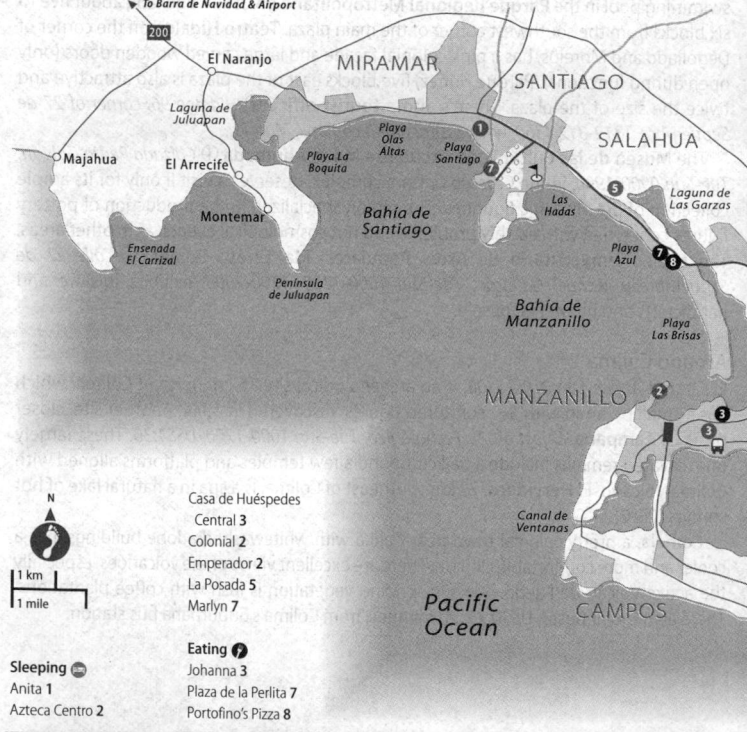
→ *Phone code: 314.*

A beautiful, three-hour hilly route runs from Colima to Manzanillo, which has become an important port on the Pacific. A fast toll road has been opened between Guadalajara and Manzanillo. It is not a touristy town and activities include deep-sea fishing (US$250 to hire a boat for a day, with beer, *refrescos* and *ceviche*), bathing, and walking in the hills. There is a good snorkelling trip starting at the beach of **Club Las Hadas**, US$40 includes soft drinks and equipment. The water is clear and warm, with lots to see. The best beach is the lovely crescent of **Santiago**, 8 km north, but there are three others, all of which are clean, with good swimming, frequent buses serve these from the centre. There's a **tourist office** ⓘ *Blv Miguel de la Madrid 4960, T314-333 2277, Mon-Fri 0900-1500.*

Southeast of Manzanillo

Southeast of Manzanillo is **Tecomán**, which has a delightful atmosphere although some of the buildings still show evidence of the 2003 earthquake. To the west of Tecomán, the small coastal resort of **Cuyutlán**, on the fast highway between Colima and Manzanillo,

Manzanillo

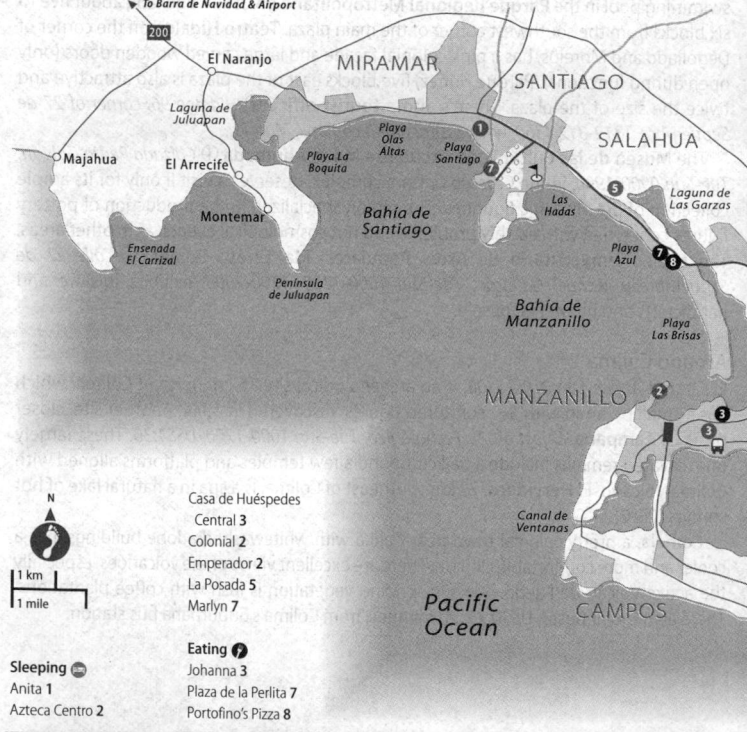

N
1 km
1 mile

Casa de Huéspedes
  Central **3**
Colonial **2**
Emperador **2**
La Posada **5**
Marlyn **7**

Sleeping 🛏
Anita **1**
Azteca Centro **2**

Eating 🍴
Johanna **3**
Plaza de la Perlita **7**
Portofino's Pizza **8**

has a pleasant, black-sand beach. The coast road continues southeast to the unspoilt fishing village of **Boca de Apiza** (no hotels but some seafood restaurants). There is abundant birdlife at the mouth of the river. Further south still the road reaches Playa Azul, Lázaro Cárdenas, Zihuatanejo and, eventually, Acapulco. For 80 km beyond Manzanillo it is good, then the condition of Route 200 deteriorates and for long stretches you cannot see the ocean. About one hour south of Tecomán is the village of **San Juan de Lima**, on a small beach. Halfway between Tecomán and Playa Azul is another uncrowded beach, **Maruata**, where you can ask the restaurant owner if you can camp or sling a hammock.

North of Manzanillo

San Patricio Melaque is in a bay which is one of the most beautiful on the Pacific Coast, but it is very commercialized, crowded at holiday times and targets long-stay residents. The beach is long, shelving and sandy with a rocky coast at each end and pelicans diving for fish. The waves are not so big at **Playa San Patricio**. The week leading up to St Patrick's Day is fiesta time, when there are fireworks, dances and rodeos. There's a **tourist office** ① *Sonora 15, T314-357 0100*, but it is better to visit Mari Blanca Pérez at **Paraíso Pacífico Tours** ① *Hotel Barra de Navidad, T314-355 5122, May-Dec 0900-1400, Jan-Apr 0900-1800*, who is very helpful.

Barra de Navidad, just along the beach from Melaque, is commercial but pleasant and has a monument to the Spanish ships that set out in 1548 to conquer the Philippines. Barra is about 1½ hours from Manzanillo; the beach is beautiful and good for swimming, but crowded during holiday times. The **Colorín** liquor store, opposite **Hotel Barra de Navidad**, changes money and sells stamps. A friendly and useful resource is at **Ciber@net** internet café, one block from the bus terminal at Veracruz 212, where Pedro Flores can change money and offer friendly advice. There is a book exchange on Mazatlán between Sinaloa and Guanajuato. The **tourist office** ① *Jalisco 67, T314-355 5100, www.barradenavidad.com, Mon-Fri 0900-1700, Sat and Sun 1000-1400*, is helpful, English is spoken.

La Manzanilla is quite a pretty seaside village 14 km north of the Routes 200/80 junction. Three kilometres north of the beach is Boca de Iguanas with two trailer parks: **Boca de Iguanas** and **Tenacatita**. For both places take the unpaved road from Highway 200 as far as the abandoned **Hotel Bahía de Tenacatita**; at the T-junction, turn right, pass the hotel, and the campsites are about 500 m further on the left. This place is nothing to do with the village of **Tenacatita**, which is further up the coast, and has a perfect beach complete with palm huts and tropical fish among the rocks; good for snorkelling. Route 200, a little rough in places, links Barra de Navidad with Puerto Vallarta, the second largest resort in Mexico. There are beaches and hotels on this route and places to stay in Perula village at the north end of **Chamela** beach (see Sleeping, page 371). The Pemex station at Chamela is closed and there's no other for miles.

Puerto Vallarta and around 😊🚹🚺😊🅾️⛰️😊🚊 ➤➤ pp368-389. Colour map 3, B1.

➔ *Phone code: 322.*

Now a highly commercialized sun-and-sand holiday resort increasingly marred by congestion and widespread condominium developments, Puerto Vallarta still has its advantages. With a wonderful location on the Bahía de Banderas (Bay of Flags), one of the most striking bays in Mexico, it has wonderful beaches and dolphins frolicking in the clear waters. The resort caters to low-end mass tourism as well as high-end member-only visitors. In the spring, Vallarta is also a top destination for college students. While the weather is pleasant year-round, the high season runs from November to April. Prices drop considerably during the low season, although they remain high compared to less developed areas of the country.

The stepped and cobbled streets of the old centre, particularly around the well-preserved Zona Romántica, are picturesque, and accommodation and restaurants are varied enough to suit most budgets. There is plenty of good hiking in the surrounding hills and watersports and diving are easily accessible. Increasingly it has become a base for excursions and for special-interest trips including ornithology and whale watching. And of course there are the beaches – more than 50 of them ranging from pristine, deserted shores (mostly to the north) to ultra-luxurious strands that flank the private marinas closer to the city. Development is heading north towards the still relatively untouched fishing villages that dot the bay. Travellers wishing to see what Puerto Vallarta was like 30 years ago, before the arrival of international tourism, should take a trip north to any of these villages.

Ins and outs

Getting there The **Aeropuerto Internacional Ordaz** (**PVR**), 6 km north of the town centre, is served by national and international airlines with flights to destinations in Mexico, the US and Europe (mostly package). Buses from the airport can be caught by taking the walkway to the other side of the street and walking to the main road and getting buses for the centre, US$0.40. Steer clear of the low-price timeshare touts.

The long-distance **bus station**, almost directly opposite the airport, is a 30-minute ride from town, buses from the bus terminal may take the long way into the centre, it is worth changing buses on the main road to get a direct bus into the centre. Puerto Vallarta is on the Carretera Costera, Route 200, which runs south along the Pacific Coast, all the way to the Guatemalan border. If you want to get a taxi into town they're half the price if you get them from across the main road outside the airport.

Getting around Taxis are expensive in Puerto Vallarta. Local buses operate on most routes north to Nuevo Vallarta, and south to Mismaloya and Boca de Tomatlán. Buses marked 'Centro' go through town, while those marked 'Túnel' take the bypass. Taxis and buses have come under fire from local authorities for their poor driving habits. Only take official taxis.

Tourist information The **tourist office** ① *Independencia 123, T322-223 2500 ext 230, www.visitpuertovallarta.com*, is in the government building on the main square.

Sights

Greater Puerto Vallarta is drawn out along 25 km of the west-facing curve of the deeply incised Banderas Bay. It can be split into six sections: **North Central** is the oldest, with the main plaza, cathedral and seafront Malecón boulevard as well as an uninviting strip of pebble/sand beach; **South Central**, across the Río Cuale, is newer but similarly

Puerto Vallarta

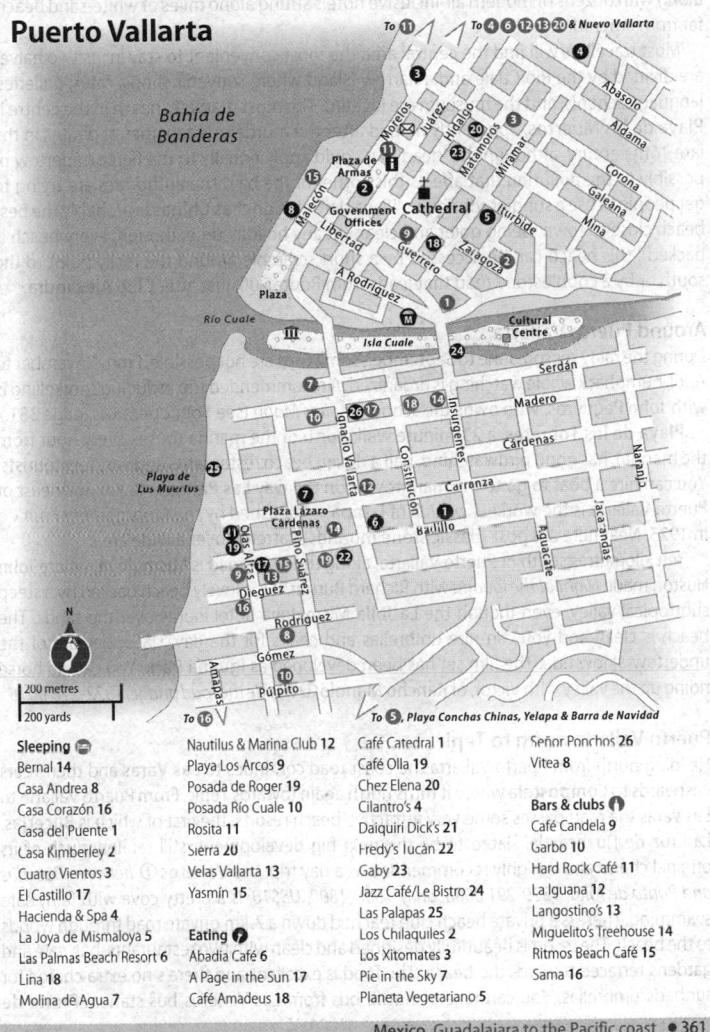

Sleeping	Nautilus & Marina Club **12**	Café Catedral **1**	Señor Ponchos **26**
Bernal **14**	Playa Los Arcos **9**	Café Olla **19**	Vitea **8**
Casa Andrea **8**	Posada de Roger **19**	Chez Elena **20**	
Casa Corazón **16**	Posada Río Cuale **10**	Cilantro's **4**	**Bars & clubs**
Casa del Puente **1**	Rosita **11**	Daiquiri Dick's **21**	Café Candela **9**
Casa Kimberley **2**	Sierra **20**	Fredy's Tucán **22**	Garbo **10**
Cuatro Vientos **3**	Velas Vallarta **13**	Gaby **23**	Hard Rock Café **11**
El Castillo **17**	Yasmín **15**	Jazz Café/Le Bistro **24**	La Iguana **12**
Hacienda & Spa **4**		Las Palapas **25**	Langostino's **13**
La Joya de Mismaloya **5**	**Eating**	Los Chilaquiles **2**	Miguelito's Treehouse **14**
Las Palmas Beach Resort **6**	Abadía Café **6**	Los Xitomates **3**	Ritmos Beach Café **15**
Lina **18**	A Page in the Sun **17**	Pie in the Sky **7**	Sama **16**
Molina de Agua **7**	Café Amadeus **18**	Planeta Vegetariano **5**	

packed with shops and restaurants and bordered by the fine, deep sand of Playa de los Muertos; **South Shore** is where the mountains come to the sea, there are several cove beaches and a scattering of big hotels; **North Hotel Zone** is a long stretch from town towards the cruise ship terminal and the airport, with mediocre beaches, many big hotels and several commercial centres; **Marina Vallarta**, further north, has a dazzling array of craft, a golf course, smart hotels and poor quality beach (you can't walk far because of condominiums built around the marina); and **Nuevo Vallarta**, 15 km north of centre, in the neighbouring state of Nayarit (time difference), which has a golf course and marina, along with dozens of modern all-inclusive hotels strung along miles of white-sand beach, far from amenities.

Most travellers will find the central area the most convenient to stay in; its two halves are divided by the Río Cuale and a narrow island where souvenir shops, cafés, galleries, language schools, and the museum are located. The most dramatic beach in the centre is **Playa de los Muertos**, apparently named after the murderous activities of pirates in the late 16th century, although the 'dead' tag could apply equally to the fierce undertow or possibly to the pollution that affects this corner of the bay. The authorities are trying to get people to use a sunnier sobriquet: 'Playa del Sol'. **Conchas Chinas** is probably the best beach close to town, being quiet and clean (at any holiday time, though, every beach is packed); this beach can be accessed by a short scramble around the rocky point to the south or by a cobblestone road that leads from Route 200, just after **Club Alexandra**.

Around Puerto Vallarta

During the rainy season, June to September, some trips are not possible. From November to April, humpback whale watching is organized. A recommended trip including snorkelling is with John Pegueros, who owns the schooner *Elías Mann* (see Tour operators, page 381.)

Playa de los Tomates, a 25-minute walk north of the marina (buses every hour from the marina), has good birdwatching, half a dozen beach restaurants and very few tourists. You can hire a boat to go to the mangroves. On the way **Las Palmas**, 40 km northeast of Puerto Vallarta is the workers' *pueblo* of **Ixtapa**, established by the Montgomery Fruit Co in 1925. Near here are post-Classic stone mounds scattered over a wide area.

Ten kilometres south of Puerto Vallarta, along the coast road is **Mismaloya**, where John Huston made *Night of the Iguana* with Richard Burton. It is a lovely beach backed by a steep subtropical valley, even though the **La Jolla Mismaloya** hotel looms over the sands. The beach is clean and you can hire umbrellas and chairs for the day, US$1; beware of the undertow at low tide. The film set has been developed as **Iguana Park**. You can go horse riding up the valley with Victor, of **Rancho Manolo** ① *beside the road bridge, T322-228 0018*.

Puerto Vallarta north to Tepic

Heading north from Puerto Vallarta the coast road continues to **Las Varas** and then veers eastwards to **Compostela** where it turns north again towards Tepic. From Puerto Vallarta to Las Varas the road passes some very attractive beach resorts, the first of which is **Bucerías**. La Cruz de Huancaxtle, slated to be the next big development, still retains much of its original charm and is highly recommended as a day trip. **Los Veneros** ① *between Bucerías and Punta de Mita, T329-291 0088, daily 1000-1800, US$10,* is a pretty cove with fairly safe swimming. There is a private beach club reached down a 7-km private road through woods to the beach. The resort is beautifully designed and clean with two restaurants, bar, café and gardens terraced towards the beach. The food is excellent and there's no extra charge for sunbeds/umbrellas. You can take a shuttle bus from Los Veneros bus station. **Punta de**

Mita, a fishing village and beach resort at the tip of a peninsula, has fish restaurants, miles of beach and abundant birdlife. At **Playa Destiladeros** (daily 0700-1900, ample parking US$3.50) there is an excellent restaurant. **Medina** or **Pacífico** buses from Puerto Vallarta pass every 15 minutes. There are boat trips to the nearby **Islas Marietas**, where there are caves and birds. Camping is possible on the beach. Simple accommodation is also available. North of Punta de Mita are beaches on the coast road include **Chacala**, a nice free beach lined with coconut palms, good swimming, cold showers and a restaurant; it is reached by an unsurfaced road through jungle.

Tepic to Guadalajara ⊜🌳🏠🔺⊜🊐 ›› pp368-389. Colour map 3, B1.

Tepic → Phone code: 311. Altitude: 900 m.

Capital of Nayarit state, Tepic was founded in 1531 at the foot of the extinct Sangagüey. It is a clean but slightly scruffy town with many little squares, filled with trees and flowers.

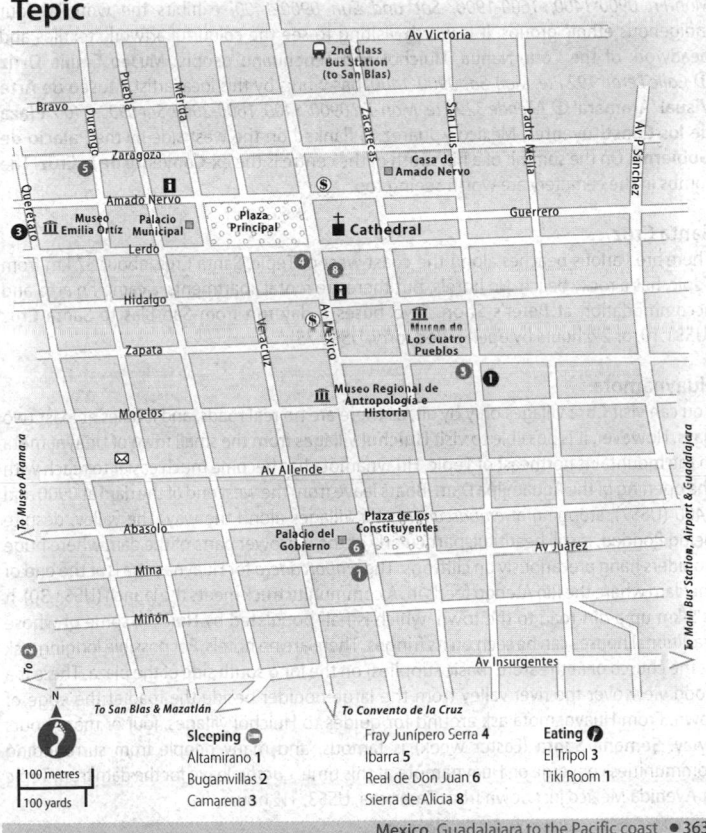

Tepic

Sleeping
Altamirano 1
Bugamvillas 2
Camarena 3

Fray Junípero Serra 4
Ibarra 5
Real de Don Juan 6
Sierra de Alicia 8

Eating
El Tripol 3
Tiki Room 1

The landscape around Tepic is wild and mountainous; access is very difficult. The Huichol and Cora people live in this region. Their dress is very picturesque; their craftwork – bags (carried only by men), scarves woven in colourful designs, necklaces of tiny beads (*chaquira*) and wall-hangings of brightly coloured wool – is available from souvenir shops. You may see them in Tepic but it is best to let them approach you when they come to town if you want to purchase any items.

The **tourist office** ① *Av México and Calzada del Ejército, 1 block from the cathedral, T311-213 9203, daily 0900-2000*, is helpful and English is spoken. The **Municipal Tourist Office** ① *Puebla and Amado Nervo, T311-216 5661*, is also very helpful.

The **cathedral** (1891), with two fine Gothic towers, on the Plaza Principal, has been restored; it is painted primrose yellow, adorned with gold. Worth seeing are the **Palacio Municipal**, painted pink and the **Casa de Amado Nervo** ① *Zacatecas Norte 281, Mon-Fri 1000-1400, Sat 1000-1300*, the house of the great Mexican poet and diplomat. The **Museo Regional de Antropología e Historia** ① *Av México 91 Norte, Mon-Fri 0900-1900, Sat 0900-1500*, has a fine collection of Aztec and Toltec artefacts and some beautiful religious paintings from the colonial period. **Museo de Los Cuatro Pueblos** ① *Hidalgo y Zacatecas, Mon-Fri 0900-1400, 1600-1900, Sat and Sun 0900-1400*, exhibits the work of four indigenous ethnic groups. It is worth visiting to see the colourful artwork, textiles and beadwork of the Cora, Nahua, Huichol and Tepehuano people. **Museo Emilia Ortiz** ① *Calle Lerdo 192 Pte, Mon-Sat 0900-1400*, has works by this local artist. **Museo de Arte Visual 'Aramara'** ① *Allende 329 Pte, Mon-Fri 0900-1400, 1600-2000, Sat 0900-1400*. **Plaza de los Constituyentes**, México y Juárez, is flanked on the west side by the **Palacio de Gobierno**. On the summit of a hill south of the centre is the **ex-Convento de la Cruz**. The tombs in the cemetery are worth seeing too.

Santa Cruz
There are various beaches along the coast west of Tepic. Santa Cruz, about 37 km from Tepic, has a rocky beach. No hotels, but there are rental apartments, a camping area and accommodation at **Peter's Shop**. Two buses a day run from San Blas to Santa Cruz (US$1.10, or 2½ hours by open-sided lorry, US$0.75).

Huaynamota
You can visit **Cora** villages only by air, as there are no real roads, and it takes at least two days. However, it is possible to visit **Huichol** villages from the small town of Huaynamota in the mountains northeast of Tepic. Huaynamota has become much easier to reach with the opening of the Aguamilpa Dam. Boats leave from the west end of the dam at 0900 and 1400 (US$7), stopping at *embarcaderos* for villages along the way. The valley, despite being flooded, is still beautiful, particularly at the narrower parts of the dam where huge boulders hang precariously on clifftops. The *embarcadero* for Huaynamota is at the end of the dam where the Río Atengo feeds in. A community truck meets the launch (US$1.30). It is 8 km up a dirt road to the town, which is half populated by Huichol, some of whose traditional houses can be seen on its fringes. There are no hotels. For possible lodging, ask at the church or at the store (basic supplies) on the long south side of the plaza. There is a good view over the river valley from the large boulder beside the road at the edge of town. From Huaynamota ask around for guides to Huichol villages, four or more hours away. **Semana Santa** (Easter week) is famous, and many people from surrounding communities converge on Huaynamota at this time. *Combis* leave for the dam from Tepic at Avenida México just down from Zaragoza, US$3, 1½ hours.

San Blas and around → *Phone code: 328. Colour map 3, B1.*

This old colonial town, built as a fortress against piracy, is 69 km from Tepic and overcrowded during US and Mexican summer holidays. Founded in 1768, little is left of the old Spanish fortress, **Basilio**. It is from here that the Spanish set off to colonize Baja California and North America. Above the town are **La Contaduría** ① *US$0.60*, the Spanish counting house (1773), and **La Marinera**, a ruined church. The views over the town, estuaries and mangrove swamps from beside an incredibly ugly statue on the battlements, are superb.

In town, near the harbour, is the old **Customs House** (1781-1785) and a stone and adobe church (1808-1878) on the plaza. Up to the mid-19th century, San Blas was a thriving port and it still has a naval base and a (smelly) harbour.

There are few tourists early in the year or in August when it becomes very hot and is famous for its many mosquitoes. The beach, 2 km from the village, doesn't suffer from mosquitoes but there are other biting insects, so take repellent anyway. The two worst bugs are *jejenes* or *no sees* during the dry season, and *sancudos*, the big black monsters, during the wet season. But don't be too put off, as they are diminishing year by year, and if you don't linger around vegetation and still water they are not so bad.

Quieter than the dirty town beach is the extensive and often-deserted **Playa El Rey** on the north side of the estuary of the same name, beyond the lighthouse. Take a boat across the river from just west of the harbour, US$0.60 each way; the boatman works until 1730, but stops at lunchtime. Tell him when you want to return so that he knows to look out for your frantic waving from the other bank. The best beach is **Playa de las Islitas** reached by bus marked 'Las Veras' from the bus station, or 'El Llano' from Paredes y Sinaloa, just off the plaza. There is some threat of resort development here. At the beach of **Matanchén**, 7 km from San Blas (taxi US$3), there is good swimming but, again, many mosquitoes. Good home-made fruitcakes and bread are sold here. Surfing can be done at these beaches, but rarely at any one time is the surf up at all of them. Check at **Juan Bananas** (see Activities and tours, page 380). San Blas also claims to be home to the world's longest wave. About three times a year it is possible to surf non-stop for over a mile, from town towards Las Islitas, relaying on a series of point breaks.

Four-hour boat trips to see whales and dolphins are available in the San Blas area. Ask at the tourist office. Armando is a good guide; he charges US$52 for three people. It is also possible to take a three-hour jungle trip in a boat (bus to *embarcadero* on Matenchén road) to **La Tovara**, a small resort with a freshwater swimming hole brimming with turtles and catfish, a restaurant and not much else. The mangrove swamps can be visited on the way to La Tovara. Tour buses leave from the bridge 1 km out of town and cost US$30 for a canoe with six passengers, but it is cheaper to arrange the trip at **Embarcadero El Aguada**. Official prices are posted but it still seems possible to shop around. Away from the swimming hole there are coatis, raccoons, iguanas, turtles, boat-billed herons, egrets and parrots. Avoid fast motorized boats as the motor noise will scare any animals. Tours on foot are even better. Crocodiles are kept in caves along the route. Twilight tours enable naturalists to see potoos and, if very lucky, an ocelot. La Tovara is crowded at midday during the summer. A cheaper 1½- to two-hour cruise is also possible from the **Embarcadero El Aguada** (reached by Las Islitas bus – see above), US$17 per boat, but US$4.25 each if more than four people; it goes through a tunnel of mangroves, to the swimming hole 20 minutes away. You can take a bus from San Blas towards Santa Cruz and get off at Matanchén beach (see above). From here, a boat for half-day hire includes the best part of the jungle cruise from San Blas.

Sixteen kilometres south from San Blas is the beautiful **Playa Los Cocos**, which is empty except at weekends. The **tourist office** ① *Mercado, 1 block from plaza, T328-255 0021, Mon-Sat 0900-1300, 1800-2000, Sun 0900-1300. www.visitsanblas.com*, has information in English on the history of San Blas as well as a town map.

Inland towards Guadalajara

The old Route 15 leaves Tepic for Guadalajara. About 50 km from Tepic, off the Guadalajara road, is an attractive area of volcanic lagoons. Take the bus to **Santa María del Oro** for the lagoon of the same name. On the south side of the toll road is the Laguna Tepetiltic and near Chapalilla is another lake at San Pedro Lagunillas. There is a turn-off at Chapalilla to Compostela and Puerto Vallarta. At **Ahuacatlán**, 75 km from Tepic, the 17th-century ex-Convento de San Juan Evangelista stands on the Plaza Principal; handicrafts are on sale here. Nearby, the village of **Jala** has a festival mid-August. From here the **Ceboruco volcano** can be reached in a day. On the main road a lava flow from Ceboruco is visible at El Ceboruco, Parador Turístico, with restaurant, information, toilets and a shop.

Ixtlán del Río, 84 km from Tepic (one hour 15 minutes by bus), has a few souvenir shops, a Museo Arqueológico in the Palacio Municipal, and a *casa de cambio*. Harvest (maize) festival is mid-September. Two kilometres out of town are the ruins of **Los Toriles** ① *US$2.35*, a Toltec ceremonial centre on a warm, wind-swept plain. The main structure is the Temple of Quetzalcoatl, noted for its cruciform windows and circular shape. The ruins have been largely restored and some explanatory notes are posted around the site. There is a caretaker but no real facilities. Two kilometres beyond the Los Toriles site is **Motel Hacienda**, with pool. The road climbs out of the valley through uncultivated land, where trees intermix with prickly pear and chaparral cactus.

The journey from Tepic to Guadalajara cannot easily be broken at Ixtlán for sightseeing since buses passing through in either direction tend to be full; the bus on to Guadalajara takes three hours.

Tequila → *Colour map 3, B2. Phone code: 374. Altitude: 1300 m.*

Tequila can be visited as a day-trip from Guadalajara, by car, bus or Tequila Express (see page 386). As the bus approaches the town, the aroma of the blue agave, from which the famous Mexican drink is distilled, fills the air and then the plants in neat rows can be seen growing in the pleasant, hilly countryside. Tours of the tequila distilleries are available (see box, opposite) and stores will let you sample different tequilas before you buy. Often around 20 bottles are open for tasting.

The town is attractive, a mix of colonial and more modern architecture. It is a pleasant place to stay but there is not much to do other than tour the distilleries and there is little in the way of nightlife other than imbibe the local produce and recover the following morning. Along Calle Sixto Gorjón, where the arriving buses drop you, there are several liquor stores selling tequila, restaurants where you can eat for under US$5, pharmacies, doctors, dentists and the **Rojo de los Altos** bus ticket office at No 126A.

In the town centre there are two plazas next to each other. On one is the **Templo de Santiago Apóstol**, a large, pretty, old stone building, with a 1930s municipal market next to it. Also on this plaza is the post office and Banamex. About a block behind Banamex, where Sixto Gorjón ends, is the entrance to the **José Cuervo distillery**. Along Calle Ramón Corona is the **Sauza distillery**. Both provide tours. The **Museo Nacional del Tequila** ① *Calle Ramón Corona 34, Tue-Sun 1000-1700, US$1, 50% discount for students*, is full of the history of tequila, along with details of the origins, processes, cultivation and distilling

"A field of upright swords" – the making of tequila

The quote from Paul Theroux's *The Old Patagonian Express* describes the swathes of blue agave grown in the dry highlands of the State of Jalisco and a few neighbouring areas. Agave is the raw material for tequila and, although there are some 400 varieties of agave, only the blue agave is suitable. After eight years growing in the fields, the spiky leaves are hacked off and the central core, weighing around 45 kg, is crushed and roasted. The syrup extracted is then mixed with liquid sugar, fermented for 30-32 hours and then distilled twice. **White** tequila is the product of a further four months in vats. It can be drunk neat, with a pinch of salt on the back of your hand, followed by a suck on a wedge of lime, or mixed into cocktails such as the margarita. **Gold** tequila is a blend of white tequila and tequila aged in wooden casks. **Añejo**, aged tequila, is a golden brown from spending at least two years in oak casks. Special premium tequila has no sugar added.

In pre-Conquest times, the local people used the agave sap to brew a mildly alcoholic drink, *pulque*, still drunk today. The Spaniards, however, wanted something more refined and stronger. They developed mezcal and set up distilleries to produce what later became tequila. The first of these was established in 1795 by royal decree of King Charles IV of Spain. It is still in existence today: **La Rojena**, the distillery of José Cuervo, known by its black crow logo, is the biggest in the country.

In recent years tequila exports have increased but not without problems. Demand has outstripped supply – not enough blue agave was planted eight years ago.

Tequila, like many other spirits, is blended. While the best tequila is 100% *puro de agave*, a couple of distilleries appear to have been blending more than they would like to admit. Some years ago the *Consejo Regulador del Tequila*, whose job it is to check and monitor standards on the industry, made a couple of surprise calls on well-established distilleries and were denied entry – suggesting strongly they had something to hide.

Around the town of Tequila there are 12 distilleries, of which 10 produce 75% of the country's tequila. Tours of the distilleries can be arranged with a free sample at the end, and of course shopping opportunities. Tours are hourly 1000-1400, US$4, lasting about one hour. Tours in English are available – check locally for precise times. For tours of **Tequila Cuervo**, T33-3634 4170 (Guadalajara), or T374-742 0076 (Tequila), contact Srta Clara Martínez. Tours of **Tequila Sauza**, T374-742 0244, or in Guadalajara on T33-3679 0600. Dating from 1873, you can see the famous fresco illustrating the joys of drinking tequila. **Herradura**, T374-3614 9657, 8 km from Tequila, is in an old hacienda outside Amatitlán village, which has adobe walls and cobblestone streets and is worth a visit.

If buying tequila most of the liquor available in town should be drunk quickly and kept off the palate as much as possible. If you're looking for quality there are a few things to look out for. Look for the stamp of CRT (the *Consejo Regulador del Tequila* mark), look for 100% agave and finally, for the very best, look for *reposada* (matured). If it has all three, it's a fine tequila – and you should sip it gently.

processes. Apparently 100% agave tequila blends in well with the human metabolism to the extent that if it's good stuff you don't get a hangover. Years of personal experience suggests otherwise, but buy the best you can. The **Palacio Municipal** on the main square puts out a stall by the map, which supposedly offers tourist information. In reality, it just sells tours of the distilleries, which include trips to the fields.

Guadalajara to the Pacific Coast

For Sleeping and Eating price codes and other relevant information, see Essentials pages 45-48.

Sleeping

Guadalajara *p350, map p351*
The smart business hotels are in the modern western part of the city, around the Plaza del Sol, roughly 2 km west of the Centro Histórico.
LL Presidente Intercontinental, López Mateos Sur and Av Moctezuma, T33-3678 1234, www.ichotelsgroup.com/h/d/icon/hd/gdlha. Some deluxe suites with private patio, high-rise tower with built-in shopping centre, cavernous lobby.
LL Quinta Real, Av México 2727 y López Mateos, T33-3615 0000. Designed as colonial manor, convenient location, good, 78 large, well-furnished rooms, original artwork, good restaurant.
AL Aranzazú, Av Revolución 110 Pte, T33-3942 4040, www.aranzazu.com.mx. Central, very good but a bit overpriced, full business services. See the bats departing from the roof eaves at dusk.
AL Plaza Génova (Best Western), Juárez 123, T33-3613 7500, www.hplazagenova.com. In the Centro Histórico, includes continental breakfast and welcome cocktail. Clean, good service, good restaurant. Recommended.
AL Villa Ganz, López Cotilla 1739, T800-508 7923, www.mexicoboutiquehotels.com/villaganz/index.html. Converted century-old mansion with 10 rooms, each beautifully appointed. Close to Av Chapultepec, but an oasis of tranquillity.
A Francés, Maestranza 35, T33-3613 1190, www.hotelfrances.com. Colonial building with central patio, oldest hotel in the city, built in 1610, have a drink there at 'happy

hour' 1800-1900, to enjoy the bygone atmosphere, disco and bar music noisy at night, some rooms small but very good-value penthouse suite, free parking underneath adjoining Plaza de la Liberación; 3 blocks away.
A Rotonda, Liceo 130, T/F33-3614 1017, central, near cathedral. Remodelled 19th-century building, attractive, dining area in courtyard, cheap set lunches, nice public areas, rooms OK, with TV, phones, covered parking.
B Azteca, Javier Mina 311, 1½ blocks east of Mercado Libertad, T33-3617 7465. Clean, very friendly, some rooms with good views, parking around the corner.
C Canadá, Estadio 77, ½ block west of old bus station, T33-3619 4014. All rooms with bath, hot water, some with TV, clean, good value.
D Janeiro, Av Obregón 95, 1 block south of Mercado Libertad, T33-3617 5063. Best value in the market area. A few rooms have balconies overlooking the busy market street, close to Plaza de los Mariachis. Ideal for people-watching or insomnia.
D La Hacienda, Circunvalación Pte 66, a long way from the centre of town, in Col Cd Granja, off Av Vallarta on left before the *periférico* and head to Tepic, T33-3627 1724, ext 117. Motel with shaded, pool, clubhouse, hook-ups.
D Posada San Pablo, Madero 429 (no sign), T33-3614 2811. A family home that's been welcoming backpackers for years. No sign, just ring the bell and Lilia will let you in if she thinks you look OK. Quiet, informal and friendly. A small charge for laundry and use of kitchen.
D Posada Tapatía, López Cotilla 619, T33-3614 9146. Colonial-style house, 2-3 blocks

from Federalismo, one of the better budget places, although traffic can be a problem.
E Estación, Independencia Sur 1297, across the main boulevard beside train station, T33-3619 0051. Quiet, clean, safe, luggage store, hot water, small, limited restaurant. Recommended.
E Hostel Guadalajara, Maestranza 147, close to the centre, T33-3562 7520, www.hostelguadalajara.com. Youth Hostel-affiliated, with good facilities including kitchen, laundry, internet and lounge area.
E León, Independencia Sur 557. Bath, towels, hot water, clean, staff friendly and helpful.

Tlaquepaque *p355*
Consider staying in Tlaquepaque if stocking up on gifts before heading home.
L El Tapatío, Blv Aeropuerto 4275, en route to airport, T33-3837 2929. Fine view of city, extensive grounds, very attractive and comfortable rooms.
L-AL La Villa del Ensueño, Florida 305, T33-3635 8792, www.villadel ensueno.com. 8 rooms, 2 suites, pool, breakfast, no smoking, English spoken.
B La Posada de la Media Luna, off Juárez 1 block east of the Parián, T33- 3635 6054. Delightful rooms, with private bath, TV and telephone, includes breakfast on colourful patio. Excellent value.

Tonalá *p355*
D Hotel Tonalá, Madero 22. Plain but in good shape, some rooms with TV.

Chapala *p355*
A Villa Montecarlo, west edge of town on Av Hidalgo at Calle Lourdes, T376-765 2120. Family rooms or suites, very comfortable, in beautiful grounds with palms and mangoes.
B Chapala Haciendas, Km 40, Chapala-Guadalajara highway, T376-765 2720. Live music Wed and Sat. Unheated pool.
B Nido, Av Madero 202, close to lake, T376-765 2116. Brick building, old photos in reception hall, clean, cheaper without TV, accepts Visa and MasterCard, good

restaurant, swimming pool, parking for motorcycles beside pool.

Camping
PAL, 1 km from the lake between Chapala and Ajijic, Apdo Postal 1-1470, Guadalajara, T376-766 0040. Trailer park, 1st class, pool, good.

Ajijic to Jocotepec *p355*
L-A Posada del Pescador, Miguel Arana 611, Jocotepec outskirts, T387-763 0028. *Cabañas* with bedroom, living room, kitchen and bathroom, set in a lovely garden.
AL La Nueva Posada, Donato Guerra 9, Ajijic, T376-766 1444. Breakfast included, vast rooms, Canadian management, horse riding, golf, tennis, theatre, gardens, swimming pool, restaurant, attractive outdoor seating in garden overlooking lake, colonial decor, delightful.

Tapalpa *p356*
B Posada Hacienda, Raúl Quintero 120, T343-432 0193. Nice bungalows with fireplace and small kitchen.
D Hotel Tapalpa. With huge holes in the floor, but clean and fairly cheap.

Colima *p356*
AL-A Hotel América, Morelos 162, T312-312 9596. A/c, cable TV, phone, pretty interior gardens, travel agency, steam baths, good restaurant, central, friendly.
A Ceballos, Torres Quintero 12, T312-312 4449, main square, www.hotelceballos.com. A fine building with attractive *portales*, some huge rooms with a/c, clean, good food in its 2 restaurants (pricey), secure indoor parking, very good value. Highly recommended.
C Gran Hotel Flamingos, Av Rey Colimán 18, near Jardín Núñez, T312-312 2525. Pleasant small rooms with fan, bath, simple, clean, breakfast expensive, disco below goes on till 0300 on Sat and Sun.
C-D La Merced, Hidalgo 188 (entrance at Juárez 82), T312-312 6969. Pretty colonial house with rooms around patio filled with

plants, all rooms same price, TV, bath. Highly recommended for budget travellers.
E Núñez, Juárez 88 at Jardín Núñez, T312-312 7030. Basic, dark, with bath.

Manzanillo p358, map p358

AL La Posada, Calzada Lázaro Cárdenas 201, near the end of Las Brisas peninsula, T314-333 1899. American owned, beautifully designed rooms, some back into the very rock of an outcrop.
A Marlyn, Santiago Beach, T314-333 0107. 3rd-floor rooms with balcony overlooking the beach. Recommended.
B Anita, Santiago Beach, T314-333 0161. Built in 1940, has a certain funky charm, clean and on the beach.
B Colonial, González Boncanegra 28 and México, at the port, T314-332 1080. Colonial building with good restaurant, good central location and friendly.
C Azteca Centro, Madero 265, at the port, T314-332 7343. Fairly new, fan, TV, clean, opposite the market, good value.
D Emperador, Dávalos 69, at the port, T314-332 2374. Good value, friendly, fan, TV, cheap restaurant.
E Casa de Huéspedes Central, behind bus station, in town. With bath, fan, OK.

Camping

La Marmota trailer park, at junction of Hwys 200 and 98, Manzanillo. Cold showers, bathrooms, pool, laundry facilities.
Trailer Park El Palmar, Miramar and Santiago beaches, 4.5 km north of Manzanillo, T314-333 5533. With a large swimming pool, run-down, very friendly, coconut palms.

Southeast of Manzanillo p358

B Hotel Bucanero, Cuyutlán, near the north end of the seafront, T313-326 4005. Clean rooms, good restaurant, games room and souvenir shop. Swimming here is excellent and umbrellas and wooden walkways protect feet against the hot sun and sand.
C Gran Fénix, Javier Mina 460, Tecomán, T313-324 0791. Larger rooms have a/c,

smaller rooms are noisier but hotel is recommended.
D-E Yeza, Lázaro Cárdenas 59, Tecomán. Very clean, spacious rooms in a quiet spot on the corner from the bus station, the owner's son speaks English.

North of Manzanillo p359

L-AL Villas Camino del Mar, San Patricio Melaque, T315-355 5207. Rooms or villas on beach, 2 pools, discounts for long stays.
AL Hotel Barra de Navidad, López de Legazpi 250, Barra de Navidad, T315-824 4043, www.hotelbarradenavidad.com. With balcony on beach, or bungalows where you can cook, with pool.
AL-A Los Artistas Bed and Breakfast, Isla Navidad, reached by ferry, T315-355 6441, www.islanavidad.com/meson. Spectacular private mansion converted into an exclusive hotel, 27 golf holes, private beaches, pools, individualized service, good value.
A Delfín, Morelos 23, Barra de Navidad, T315-355 5068, http://hoteldelfinmx.com. Very clean, pool, gym, hot water, friendly. Recommended.
A Hacienda Melaque, Morelos 49, San Patricio Melaque, T315-355 5334. Tennis court, kitchen, pool.
B Monterrey, Gómez Farías 27, San Patricio Melaque, T315-355 5004, on beach. Clean, fan, bath, parking, superb view.
B Posada Pablo de Tarso, Gómez Farías 408, San Patricio Melaque, T315-355 5117, facing beach. Pretty, galleried building, tiled stairs, antique-style furniture.
B Santa María, Vallarta, San Patricio Melaque, T315-357 0338. Friendly. Recommended.
C San Lorenzo, Av Sinaloa 7, T315-355 5139, Barra de Navidad. Very clean, hot water, friendly staff, good restaurant opposite.
C San Nicolás, Gómez Farías 54, San Patricio Melaque, T315-357 0066, beside **Estrella Blanca** bus station. Noisy but clean. Off season, very pleasant.
D Caribe, Sonora 15, Barra de Navidad. Fan, friendly, kitchen facilities, family-run.

D Posada Pacífico, Mazatlán 136, Barra de Navidad, T315-355 5359, 1 street behind bus terminal. Clean, fan, friendly, good restaurant opposite, good value.
E Posada Carmelita, Tomatlán, Km 103 south of Puerto Vallarta and 12 km inland, has a few modest hotels with bath, clean.

Camping

Melaque Follow the 'Melaque' signs and at the end of the main road is a free camping place on the beach at the bay, very good, easily accessible for RVs, popular for vehicles and tents. **Trailer Park La Playa**, San Patricio Melaque, T315-357 0065, in the village, on beach. US$13 for car and 2 people, full hook-up, toilets, cold showers.

Tenacatita Take the unpaved road from Hwy 200 north of Barra de Navidad as far as the abandoned **Hotel Bahía de Tenacatita**; at the T-junction, turn right, pass the hotel, and the following 2 campsites are about 500 m further on the left: **Boca de Iguanas**, trailer park, vehicle free, hook-ups, cold showers, toilets, laundry facilities, clean, pleasant location. **Tenacatita**, trailer park, hook-ups, cold showers, toilet, laundry facilities, restaurant.

Chamela Villa Polonesia Trailer Park, near Chamela, full hook-ups, hot showers, on lovely beach (follow signs from Route 200 on unmade road). Recommended. Restaurant on road to trailer park, clean, good food.

Puerto Vallarta *p360, map p361*
LL Sierra, Nuevo Vallarta, T322-297 1300. Colourful building-block hotel, smart, modern, all inclusive.
LL Velas Vallarta, Marina Vallarta, North Hotel Zone, T322-221 0091, www.velas vallarta.com. Rustic with Moorish touches, part timeshare hotel with verdant gardens, golf course opposite, all-inclusive options.
L Casa Kimberley, Zaragoza 445, North Central, T322-222 1336. Former home of

Richard Burton and Elizabeth Taylor, 10 rooms full of memorabilia of the actors, breakfast included, bar, great views, pool, much cheaper in low season.
L Hacienda and Spa, Blv Francisco Medina Ascencio, North Hotel Zone, T322-224 6667. Modern, with colonial influence, gym, Temazcal treatments, pleasant pool, is nicest in zone but 100 m to beach and on main road, discounts out of season.
L Las Palmas Beach Resort, Blv Medina Ascencio, North Hotel Zone, Km 2.5, T322-226 1220. Castaway-on-a-desert-island theme, all rooms with sea view.
L Molina de Agua, Ignacio L Vallarta 130, South Central, T322-222 1957. Cabins in pleasant wooded glade on bank of river, a/c, good service, 2 pools. Recommended.
L Nautilus and Marina Club, Marina Vallarta, T322-221 1015. Olympic pool and dive tank in this resort. Most rooms have private balcony or patio.
L Playa Los Arcos, Olas Altas 380, South Central, T322-222 0583. Good location for restaurants, undersized pool terrace overflows to Playa Los Muertos.
AL Casa Andrea, Rodríguez 174, South Central, 1322-222 1213, www.casa-andrea.com. Small hotel suites, close to cafés and restaurants, pleasant garden with bar, pool, owner operated, good friendly service with attention to detail. Reduced rates in low season.
AL Rosita, Paseo Díaz Ordaz 901, north end of Malecón, North Central, T322-223 2000, hrosita@zonavirtual.com.mx. Puerto Vallarta's original holiday hotel (1948) with pool, on town beach.
AL-B Casa del Puente, North Central, by bridge opposite market, enter through the restaurant, T322-222 0749, www.casadel puente.com. Suites with kitchen in a private villa suspended above river, delightful, book months ahead, cheaper in low season, good value.
A Casa Corazón, Amapas 326, South Central, T/F322-222 6364, corazon@zianet.com. US-owned hideaway on steep slope above

southern end of Playa Los Muertos, overpriced but 3 big rooms on top terrace with spectacular views worth the premium, including big breakfast, beach access with bar and restaurant.

A Cuatro Vientos, Matamoros 520, North Central, T322-222 0161, www.cuatro vientos.com. Up steep cobbled street from church, spectacular views, good restaurant perched high above city, plunge pool, breakfast included, friendly and relaxed atmosphere. Recommended.

A Hotel Los Tulipanes, Panamá 272, Col 5 de Diciembre, Zona Este, T322-223 4128. hoteltulipanes@pvnet.com.mx. Quiet and with parking, swimming pool. Good value and a wise choice for those wishing to stay in Vallarta but away from the crowds.

A Posada Río Cuale, Aquiles Serdán 242, South Central, near new bridge, T/F322-222 0450. Small pool in front garden, not very private, pleasant, colonial-style rooms.

B Bernal, Francisco I Madero 423, South Central, T322-222 3605. Friendly, large rooms, fan, good showers. Recommended.

B Posada de Roger, Basilio Badillo 237, South Central, T322-222 0836. Communal kitchen, pool, cable TV, a/c, great breakfast restaurant (**Freddy's Tucan**).

C-D Yasmín, Basilio Badillo 168, South Central, T322-222 0087. Plant-filled courtyard arrangement behind **Café Olla**, a/c, clean, restaurant, 1 block from the beach, noisy till at least 2300.

D-E El Castillo, Francisco I Madero 273, South Central. Fan, hot water, cable TV, cheaper without bath. Convenient for restaurants, a few blocks from the beach.

D-E Lina, Francisco I Madero 376, South Central, T322-222 1661. With bath, hot water, fan, run-down, rooms on street noisy.

Camping
Puerto Vallarta, north of centre, just north of bypass then east 2 blocks. Popular. **Tacho**, 2 trailer parks, on road to Pitillal, opposite Marina. 60 spaces but spacious.

Around Puerto Vallarta *p362*
LL La Joya de Mismaloya, Mismaloya, Km 11.5, T322-228 0660. Romantic but over-developed setting on filmset beach.

LL Majahuitas Resort, between Quimixto and Yelapa beaches, only accessible by boat, transfers included, T322-221 2277, www.mexicoboutiquehotels.com/majahuita, run by Margot and Lirio González. All-inclusive resort, 8 guesthouses, on cove, sandy beach, rustic furniture, solar energy, horse riding and snorkelling available portion of profits go to indigenous community of Chacala, good value.

B Lagunita, Yelapa, T322-209 5055, www.hotel-lagunita.com. Cabin hotel with pool.

C Mateo and Elenita, Yelapa, breakfast included in price. Visit their waterfall.

Camping
Beto and Felicidad, camping available 30 mins' walk up valley from **Yelapa**, US$4 per person, in beautiful setting (Felicidad's home-made *tortillas* are 'the best in Mexico').

Camping is also possible in the fishing village of Yelapa, best reached by boat from **Hotel Rosita** at 1130: camp under *palapas*, about US$4 per person.

Puerto Vallarta north to Tepic *p362*
A Hotel and Trailer Park Piedras Blancas, Punta de Mita. Good, also camping, hook-ups US$12-14, restaurants.

C Coca, Rincón de Guayabitos, among several hotels and restaurants on a rocky peninsula to the south of the beach.

C Tía Adriana's bed and breakfast, Sayulita, T/F329-291 3029, www.tiaadrianas.com Nov-Jun, good, central, good value.

E Hotel Contreras, Las Varas. With fan and bath, clean, small rooms.

Camping
Trailer Park, Sayulita, 2.5 km off Route 200, contact T55-5572 1335 (Mexico City). On beautiful beach, German owner, very friendly, also has bungalows. Highly recommended.

Tepic to Guadalajara *p363*
C-D Bungalows and Trailer Park Koala,
La Laguna, Santa María del Oro. Bungalows
accommodating up to 4 people, several
trailer sites and a large campground.
Good cheap meals available. Fishing
and waterskiing on nearby lagoon.
D Hotel Colonial, Hidalgo 45 Pte, Ixtlán
del Río. Very friendly. Recommended.

Tepic *p363, map p363*
AL Fray Junípero Serra, Lerdo Pte 23,
T311-212 2525, main square. Comfortable,
big rooms, clean, a/c, good restaurant,
friendly, good service. A little noisy with
the new road, but still recommended.
AL Real de Don Juan, Av México 105 Sur,
on Plaza de Los Constituyentes, T/F311-
216 1888. Charming, traditional style.
With parking.
A Bugamvillas, Av Insurgentes y Libramiento
Pte, T311-218 0225. Very comfortable rooms
with a/c, TV, pool, restaurant with great food
and good wine list.
A Sierra de Alicia, Av México 180 Norte, T311-
212 0322. With fan, tiled stairways, friendly.
B Santa Fe, Calzada de la Cruz 85, near
Parque La Loma, a few mins from centre,
T311-213 1966. With TV, clean, comfortable,
good restaurant.
C Ibarra, Durango Norte 297A, T311-212
3870. Luxurious rooms, with bath and fan
(some rooms noisy) and slightly spartan,
cheaper rooms without bath, very clean.
C-D Tepic, Dr Martínez 438, T311-213 1377,
near bus station outside town. With bath,
clean, friendly but noisy.
D Altamirano, Mina 19 Ote, T311-212
7131, near Palacio de Gobierno. Noisy,
good value. Parking.
E-F Camarena, San Luis Norte 63,
4 blocks southeast of zócalo. Without
bath, clean, friendly.
E-F Pensión Morales, Insurgentes y Sánchez,
4 blocks from bus station. Clean and friendly,
hotel is now closed but family still put up
backpackers in what is now a private house.

San Blas *p365*
Accommodation becomes scarce and
more expensive around Semana Santa
and other holidays.
L Garza Canela, Paredes 106 Sur, T328-285
0112, www.garzacanela.com. Very clean,
excellent restaurant, small pool, nice garden.
Highly recommended.
B Casa Mañana, Los Cocos beach. Austrian-
run, hotel and restaurant, good food. Many
apartments for rent.
B Posada del Rey, Campeche, T328-285 0123.
Very clean, swimming pool, excellent value.
C Marino Inn, Batallón, T328-285 0340.
With a/c, friendly, pool, fair food.
C-D El Tesoro de San Blas, 50 m south of
dock, 5 mins from centre. Rooms and villas,
hot water, satellite TV, US owners.
D Posada Irene, Batallón 122, 4 blocks
southwest of zócalo. Basic with a fan,
few rooms with a shower and hot water.
Kitchen, friendly.
D-E Posada Azul, Batallón 126, 4 blocks
from plaza towards beach, T328-285 0129.
3-bedded rooms with fan and hot water,
cheaper for simple 2-bedded rooms without
bath, cooking facilities.
E Hotel Delfín, Los Cocos beach. With
bath, balcony, good view, good value
but some beds a bit lumpy.

Camping
No camping or sleeping permitted on
beaches but several pay campsites available.
All trailer parks in the town centre are
plagued by mosquitoes.
Playa Amor, Los Cocos beach. The best trailer
park, good beach, on a narrow strip of land
between road to Santa Cruz and cliff, good,
popular, 16 km south of town.

Tequila *p366*
C Abasolo, Abasolo 80, T374-742 0195.
Well (over) decorated, rooms have TV.
C Posada del Agave, Sixto Gorjón 83,
T374-742 0774. Excellent value with
private bath, TV, very comfortable.

D Motel Delicias, Carretera Internacional 595, on the highway to Guadalajara about 1 km outside Tequila, T374-742 1094. Best available, TV, off-street parking.

E Colonial, Morelos 52, corner of Sixto Gorjón, T374-742 0355. Characterless, but central, clean and not run-down, some rooms with private bath. A good deal.

❼ Eating

Guadalajara *p350, map p351*
As can be expected in a city of this size there is a wide variety of restaurants on offer, look in local tourist literature for the flavour of the month. There are also fast-food outlets, *pizzerías* and Mexican *cafeterías* and bars. The cheapest restaurants are in the streets near the old bus station, especially in Calle de Los Angeles, and upstairs in the large Mercado Libertad (San Juan de Dios) in the centre. There are also plenty of cheap *loncherías*.

♈♈♈ Piaf, Marsella 126. Closed Sun. French cuisine, live music, friendly. Excellent.

♈♈♈-♈♈ El Ganadero, on Av Américas. Excellent beef, reasonable prices.

♈♈♈-♈♈ El Mexicano, Plaza Tapatía, Morelos 81. Rustic Mexican decor. Recommended.

♈♈♈-♈♈ La Rinconada, Morelos 86 on Plaza Tapatía, Open until 2130. A beautiful colonial building, columned courtyard, carved wood doors, separate bar.

♈♈♈-♈ La Trattoria, Niños Héroes 3051. Very good, reasonably priced Italian, very popular (queues form for lunch from 1400).

♈♈ Carnes Asadas El Tapatío, Mercado Libertad (there are 3). Strictly for carnivores, try delicious *carne en su jugo* (beef stew with potatoes, beans, bacon, sausage, onion and avocado, garnished with salsa, onion and coriander).

♈♈ Carnes Asadas Rigo's, Independencia 584A. Popular. Goat is a speciality, roasted each day and served with radish, onion and chilli.

♈♈ Cortijo La Venta, Federación 725, T33-3617 1675. Daily 1300-0100. Invites customers to fight young bulls (calves) after their meal (the animals are not harmed; guests might be), restaurant serves meat, soups, salads.

♈♈ La Pianola, Av México 3220 and several other locations. Good, reasonable prices, serves *chiles en nogada*. Excellent.

♈♈-♈ Café Madoka, Enrique González Martínez 78, T33-3613 3134, just south of Hidalgo. Excellent very early breakfasts, well known for the men who play dominoes there. Friendly, a Guadalajara institution.

♈ Búfalo, Calderón de la Barca and Av Vallarta. Tacos and cheap *comida corrida*, very friendly.

♈ Café D'Osio, around the corner from **Hotel Hamilton**, on corner of Prisciliano Sánchez and Ocampo. Daily 0900-1800. Excellent breakfast and delicious *tortas*, especially the roast pork, not expensive.

♈ La Bombilla, López Cotilla y Penitenciaría. Very good for *churros* and hot chocolate.

♈ La Catedral del Antojito, Pedro Moreno 130, a pedestrian street. Colonial-style house, restaurant upstairs above bridal gown shop, serves tacos, *tortas*, etc, good meal for under US$2.

♈ La Playita, Av Juárez between Corona and Maestranza, also one at Morelos 99, by the tourist office. Very good; try *tortas de lomo doble carne con aguacate* (pork and avocado special).

Zapopan *p354*
♈♈ El Asadero, opposite the Basílica in Zapopan. Very good.

Tonalá *p355*
♈♈ El Rincón del Sol, 16 de Septiembre 61. An attractive restaurant serving steaks and Mexican food.

♈♈ Restaurant Jalapeños, Madero 23. Serves pizza, beer and regular meals.

Chapala *p355*
♈♈♈-♈♈ La Langosta Loca, Ramón Corona. Good seafood.

♈♈ La Leña, Madero 236. Open air, serves *antojitos* and steaks, bamboo roof.

¶ Café Paris, Madero 421. Sidewalk tables, popular, *corrida corrida* US$3, also breakfast and sandwiches.

Cafés and ice creams
Bing's, Madero, by the lake. Ice cream parlour. Try the *mamey* flavour!

Ajijic to Jocotepec *p355*
Jocotepec is famous for its ice cream.
₮₮₮-₮₮ Posada Ajijic, Morelos, Ajijic, T376-766 0744. Bar and restaurant, accept credit cards, indoor and outdoor seating and bar, used to be over water but stilts are now over dry land.
₮₮ Ajijic, pavement café on corner of plaza. Cheap drinks, Mexican snacks, hearty *parrillada* Sat, Sun.
₮₮ Los Girasoles, 16 de Septiembre 18, Ajijic. Mexican food in walled courtyard.
¶ Lonchería, on plaza, Ajijic. Clean, good simple meals, cheap, grilled chicken, used by locals and Americans.

Tapalpa *p356*
The more expensive restaurants have tables on balconies overlooking the square and all are visited by *mariachis*.
₮₮₮-₮₮ Posada Hacienda, overlooking the square (which has a US$1 cover charge) is well placed.

Colima *p356*
₮₮ El Vivero, Constitución 61, Colima. Nice open-air plant-filled courtyard, moderately priced specialities including seafood, Mexican and Italian, live music Thu-Sun.
₮₮ La Troje, on southeast of Colima heading to Manzanillo, T312-2680. Good, *mariachis*, very Mexican.
₮₮ Los Naranjos, Gabino Barreda 34, ½ block north of Jardín Torres Quintero, Colima. Going since 1955, nice, well known.
¶ El Trébol, southwest corner of zócalo. Probably the best of several restaurants on the zócalo serving inexpensive meals.

Cafés, bakeries and ice cream parlours
Centro de Nutrición Lakshmi, Av Madero 265, Colima. Good yoghurt and wholemeal bread run by Hari Krishnas.

Around Colima *p357*
₮₮-₮ Los Portales and **Comala**, both in the town of Comala. Popular restaurants, with *mariachis* and local specialities; open until 1800. If you sit and drink you will usually be brought complementary food until you wilt from *mariachi* overload.

Manzanillo *p358, map p358*
₮₮₮-₮₮ Carlos 'n' Charlie's, Blv M de la Madrid Km 6.9, on the beach. Seafood and ribs, great atmosphere.
₮₮₮-₮₮ Chantilly, Juárez, closed Sat. Popular café serving big traditional meals and good coffee.
₮₮ Plaza de la Perlita, next door to Portofino's Pizza. Good food, live music.
₮₮ Portofino's Pizza, Blv M de la Madrid, Km 13. Italian, very good pizza.
¶ Johanna, opposite bus station entrance. Good food, cheap.
¶ Mercados, There are central markets with *fondas* for good cheap seafood, clean.

Southeast of Manzanillo *p358*
₮₮₮ Willy's Seafood Restaurant, Playa Azul, on the beach. French owner, primarily seafood, some meat, very good.

North of Manzanillo *p359*
There are many restaurants on the beach at San Patricio Melaque but most close at 1900.
₮₮₮ Antonio's, on grand bay, Barra de Navidad. Serves gourmet food, award-winning restaurant.
₮₮₮-₮₮ Ambar, Veracruz 101, Barra de Navidad. Half menu vegetarian, real coffee, good breakfast and crêpes, closed lunchtime. Recommended.
₮₮₮-₮₮ Seamaster, on the beach, Barra de Navidad. Best ribs.
₮₮ Koala's at the Beach, Alvaro Obregón 52, San Patricio Melaque, 2 blocks from **Camino**

del Mar. Small, good, great food in walled garden compound off dusty street. Canadian/Australian run.

Ŵ Maya Melaque, on the beach, San Patricio Melaque, T315-355 6881. Fine inexpensive cuisine, Mediterranean style, open during high season, reservations recommended for beachside tables.

Ŵ Velero's, Barra de Navidad. Delicious snapper and good views.

Ŵ-Ŵ Banana's, on the beach, Barra de Navidad. Good breakfast and coffee.

Puerto Vallarta *p360, map p361*
Most restaurants in Nuevo Vallarta are not freestanding but instead are located in the many hotels that line the shore. Most are open to the public, but during high season may be reserved for hotel guests only.

ŴŴŴ Café des Artistes, Guadalupe Sánchez 740, T322-222 3228, www.cafedes artistes.com. Daily 1800-2330. Considered by many as Puerto Vallarta's best restaurant. French gourmet bistro owned by chef Thierry Blouet. Amazing (and expensive). Must reserve.

ŴŴŴ Chez Elena, Matamoros 520, T322-222 0161, up lots of steps but worth it. Beautiful view over town from large balcony, popular well-established restaurant, award-winning food. Recommended.

ŴŴŴ Daiquiri Dick's, Olas Altas 314, T322-222 0566, www.ddpv.com. Restaurant and bar open for breakfast, lunch and dinner, opposite Playa Los Muertos, excellent cooking, classical harp and guitar music Sun 1300-1500.

ŴŴŴ-ŴŴ Jazz Café/Le Bistro, by the bridge on Insurgentes. Garden, bamboo, beside river, pleasant for coffee and classical music (piano or harp) in morning, crowded and expensive in evening, many vegetarian dishes, clean.

ŴŴŴ-ŴŴ Señor Ponchos, Madero 260 and Vallarta. Authentic Mexican, typical breakfast, seafood and lobster, moderate prices.

Ŵ A Page in the Sun, Olas Altas opposite Los Arcos hotel on corner. Coffee is excellent, cakes home-made, second-hand bookshop.

Ŵ Abadia Café, Basilio Badillo and I L Vallarta, T322-222 6720. Open for breakfast lunch and dinner 0800-2400. Mexican-Continental Cuisine. Rave reviews for years, now in new location.

Ŵ Black Forest German Restaurant, further north in La Cruz de Huancaxtle, Marlín 16, Nuevo Vallarta T329-295 5203. Daily 1800-2400. Just what the name implies.

Ŵ Café Amadeus, Miramar 271, up steps from Guerrero. Classical music, books, board games in delightful whitewashed rooms or balcony perched above old town, coffee, delectable cakes. Recommended.

Ŵ Café Catedral, Basilio Badillo and Insurgentes. Very good breakfasts, fine coffee, good value.

Ŵ Cilantro's, Abasolo 169, T322-222 7147. Canadian-owned, unusual Mexico-meets-Pacific Northwest cuisine, paired with good wines.

Ŵ Frascati, further north in La Cruz de Huancaxtle, Av Langosta 10 and Coral, Nuevo Vallarta T329-295 618. Daily 1700-2400. Great Italian food in delightful setting near beach.

Ŵ Las Palapas, on the beach near Playa de los Muertos. Good food, service, value, decor and atmosphere.

Ŵ Los Arbolitos, east end of Lázaro Cárdenas. 3 balconied floors above river. Mexican, good atmosphere.

Ŵ Los Xitomates, Morelos 570, T322-222 1695. Daily 1900-2330. Mexican cuisine with eclectic (pre-Columbian and colonial) items as well.

Ŵ Mark's, further north in Bucerías, Lázaro Cárdenas 56, Nuevo Vallarta T329-298 0303. American-owned, highly regarded seafood and California-based cuisine.

Ŵ Planeta Vegetariano, Iturbide 270, T322-222 3073. Cash-only vegetarian restaurant recently named one of world's best by *Bon Appétiti* magazine. Remarkably low-priced. Second location at Marina Del Rey L-4.

Ŵ Rico Mac Taco, Av México, corner with Uruguay. Busy, cheap and widely popular.

ⵟⵟ Roberto's and **Chante Clair**, Nuevo Vallarta. Closed Sun. Both good food and near Parque La Loma.

ⵟⵟ Vitea, Libertad 2 and Malecón, T322-222 8703, www.viteapv.com. Open from early morning until 2400. Smart oceanfront bistro.

ⵟⵟ-ⵟ Café Olla, lower end Basilio Badillo. Good-value Mexican and barbecue in cramped open-fronted dining room, very popular.

ⵟⵟ-ⵟ El Arrayán, Allende 344, T322-222 7195, www.elarrayan.com.mx. Wed-Mon 1800-2300. Consistently voted best Mexican restaurant in Vallarta for many years running. Excellent folk music.

ⵟⵟ-ⵟ Fredy's Tucán, Basilio Badillo 237. Good courtyard dining, mainly Mexican menu, good breakfast with bottomless coffee.

ⵟⵟ-ⵟ Hacienda Xóchitl, off the beaten path on Río Nazas 388, T322-222 3344, www. Haciendaxochitl.com. Daily 1300-2400. Huge portions of Mexican dishes, great margaritas; bilingual staff. Highly recommended.

ⵟⵟ-ⵟ Juanita's, Av México 1067. Attracts locals as well as value-seeking gringos, good.

ⵟⵟ-ⵟ Las Milagros, Juárez and Pipila. Forget the queues at the popular gringo restaurants, this one is excellent, moderately priced, cosmopolitan, live music, colonial-style courtyard. Recommended.

ⵟⵟ-ⵟ Los Chilaquiles, Zaragosa 160, 4th floor, in Vallarta Plaza, T322-223 9482. Mon-Fri 0800-2400 only. Excellent new Jalisciense restaurant with upstairs water views. Reasonably priced.

ⵟ Gaby, Mina. Small, family-run, eat in the garden, excellent food, cheap and clean.

ⵟ Pepe's Tacos, Calle Honduras, opposite Pemex at northern end of downtown. Cheap, ethnic and delicious in spartan pink/white dining room, open all night.

ⵟ Pie in the Sky, Lázaro Cárdenas 247, Zona Romántica, T322-223 8083. Daily 0830-2200. Also has 2nd location further north in Bucerlas. Very highly recommended, especially for desserts. Bakery as well.

Tepic *p363, map p363*
The restaurant in the bus terminal is overpriced. There are lots of fish stalls by market on Puebla Norte.

ⵟⵟ El Tripol, in mall, near plaza. Excellent for vegetarian food.

ⵟⵟ Tiki Room, San Luis Norte opposite Hotel Camarena. Restaurant, art gallery, video bar, fun.

San Blas *p365*
On Sun women prepare delicious pots of stew *al fresco* on the plaza.

ⵟⵟ Las Islitas. With a distinctly nautical feel, good value seafood, also sells banana bread. Recommended.

ⵟⵟ Tumba de Yako, on way to beach. Yoghurt and health foods, and the original version of *pan de plátano* (banana bread), advertised all over town.

ⵟⵟ-ⵟ Las Olas. One of many seafood restaurants on the beach. Good and cheap with good local dishes.

Tequila *p366*
ⵟⵟ El Marinero, Albino Rojas 16B. Nice seafood restaurant with strolling musicians.

ⵟⵟ El Sauza, Juárez 45, beside Banamex. Restaurant/bar, Mexican atmosphere.

ⵟⵟ-ⵟ El Callejón, Sixto Gorjón 105. Rustic Mexican decor, à la carte, *antojitos* and hamburgers.

⊕ Entertainment

Guadalajara *p350, map p351*
Bars and clubs
Just stroll down Maestranza south of Juárez from about 0830 and listen for the noise. La Maestranza is very popular, and brings out the *machismo* with distinctive themes of the matador. La Maskara and La Jaula are on the same block, and gay friendly. La Mansión is round the corner, and Femina La Latina offers an altogether more cultured approach to the whole drinking/socializing malarkey.

Cinema
Good-quality films, some in English, are shown at the *cine-teatro* in the Instituto Cultural Cabañas (see page 352), which also has a good *cafetería*.

Music
Concerts and theatre in the ex-Convento del Carmen. A band plays every Thu at 1800 in the Plaza de Armas, in front of the Palacio de Gobierno, free. There are organ recitals in the cathedral.
Peña Cuicacalli, Av Niños Héroes almost at corner of Av Chapultepec, T33-3825 4690, opens 2000, US$5, food and drink available, fills up fast; local groups perform variety of music including Latin American folk music Fri and Sat.

Theatre
Instituto Cultural Cabañas, see page 352. The Ballet Folklórico del Instituto Cultural Cabañas performs Wed 2030, US$5. The Instituto is also an art school, with classes in photography, sculpture, ceramics, literature, music, theatre and dance.
Teatro Degollado, Plaza de la Liberación, T33-3658 3812. Ballet Folklórico de la Universidad de Guadalajara, performs every Sun at 1000, superb, highly recommended, pre-Hispanic and Mexican-wide dances, and other cultural shows, US$2-10 (check before you go). The theatre is open to the public Mon-Fri 1000-1300, just to look inside.
Grupo Folklórico Ciudad de Guadalajara performs here every Thu at 2000.

Chapala *p355*
Bars and clubs
Beer Garden, where Madero reaches the lake. Restaurant/bar with live amplified Mexican music, dancing, tables on the beach.

Around Colima *p357*
Bars and clubs
Botanero Bucaramanga, outside the town of Comala, on the Colima road. Bar with *botanas* (snacks) and more *mariachis*.

Puerto Vallarta *p360, map p361*
Bars and clubs
There are many clubs and late bars throughout the central area.
Cafe Candela, Guerrero 311 and Matamoros, Centro, T322-222 0743. Eclectic pizzeria and bar with unique (for Puerto Vallarta) ambience.
Carlos O'Brian's, Malecón and Andale, Olas Altas. Attracts a motley crowd of revellers and starts hopping after 2200.
Club Nitro, Av de las Garzas, Zona Hotelería, T322-226 6800. One of Vallarta's more popular spots, with frequently change musical themes. Everything from Banda to Blues.
Encuentros, Lázaro Cardénas 312, Zona Romántica, T322-222 0643. Sophisticated pizza bar and lounge, cash only.
Garbo, Púlpito 142, Zona Romántica, T322-223 5753. Quiet piano jazz bar, good drinks.
Hard Rock Café, Paseo Díaz Ordaz 652, along Malecón, T322-222 2230. Hughly popular with tourists. Avoid during spring beak but otherwise good music late at night.
La Iguana, Lázaro Cárdenas 311, Zona Romántica, T322-222 2733. Popular with locals, many traditional Mexican mariachi and regional bands.
Langostino's, Manuel M. Diéguez 109, Zona Romántica, T322-222 0894. Popular rock club somewhat apart from the din of the Malecón.
Miguelito's Treehouse, Basilio Badillo 287, Zona Romántica. T322-223 1263. Country and blues bar, cheap beer.
Ritmos Beach Cafe, Malecón 177, Zona Romántica, www.ritmoscafe.com. Afternoon-only (1400-1700) bar on beach with excellent music.

Sama, Olas Altas 510, Zona Romántica, T322-223 3182. Martini bar with sidewalk seating; arrive early for best seats.

✹ Festivals and events

Guadalajara *p350, map p351*
21 Mar Benito Juárez's birthday; everything closes.
Jun-Oct In Jun, the **Virgen de Zapopan** (see page 354), leaves her home to spend each night in a different church where fireworks are let off. The virgin has a new car each year but the engine is not started; men pull it through the beautifully decorated streets with ropes. The climax is 12 Oct when the virgin leaves the cathedral for home, there are great crowds along the route.
Oct Fiestas de Octubre; throughout the month there is a great fiesta with concerts, bullfights, sports and exhibitions of handicrafts from all over Mexico.
Late Nov/early Dec Feria Internacional del Libro, the 3rd largest book fair in the world, is held in Guadalajara's Gran Salón de Exposiciones. As well as the usual gathering of publishers, there are around-the-clock readings of poetry and fiction, music, dance, theatre, games, food and drink. For information, write (in English or Spanish) to FIL Guadalajara, Francia 1747, Col Moderna, Guadalajara, Jal 44190, México, T523-810 0331, www.fil.com.mx.

Chapala *p355*
2-3 Oct Fiesta de Francisco de Asís, with fireworks and excellent food served in the streets.

Ajijic to Jocotepec *p355*
11-18 Jan There is a local fiesta in Jocotepec.

Colima *p356*
Oct-Nov The annual feria of the region (agriculture, cattle and industry, with much additional festivity) runs from the last Sat of Oct until the 1st Sun of Nov. Traditional local potions (all the year round) include *jacalote* (from black maize and pumpkin seeds), *bate* (*chía* and honey), *tuba* (palm tree sap) and *tecuino* (ground, germinated maize).

○ Shopping

Guadalajara *p350, map p351*
The best shops are no longer in the centre, although a couple of department stores have branches there. The best stores are in the shopping malls, of which there are many, small and large, mainly on the west side.

Bookshops
Librería La Fuente, Medellín 140, near Juan Manuel in the centre, T33-3613 5238. Sells used books and magazines in English and Spanish, interesting to browse in, some items quite old, from 1940s and 1950s.
Librería México, Plaza del Sol, local 14, area D, on Av López Mateos side, T33-3121 0114. Has US magazines and newspapers.
Sanborn's, several branches: Av Vallarta 1600 and Gen San Martín; Juárez and 16 de Septiembre; Plaza Bonita and López Mateos Sur 2718 (near Plaza del Sol). English books and magazines are available at a reasonable mark-up.

Crafts, furniture and textiles
Casa de Artesanías de Jalisco, González Gallo 20, Parque Agua Azul, T33-3619 4664. Mon-Sat 1000-1900, Sun 1000-1400. High-quality display (and sale) of handicrafts, ceramics, paintings, hand-blown glass, dresses, etc (state-subsidized, reasonably priced but not cheap).
Casa de los Telares, Hidalgo 1378, some way from the main shopping area. Traditional textiles are woven on hand looms.
La Casa Canela, Independencia 258, near Cruz Verde, T33-3635 3717. Sells furniture and crafts, don't miss the colonial kitchen at the back of the house.

Markets

Mercado Libertad (also known as **San Juan de Dios**), Javier Mina, has colourful items for souvenirs with lots of Michoacán crafts including Paracho guitars and Sahuayo hats, leather jackets and *huaraches* (sandals). Delicious food is served upstairs on the 1st level (particularly goat meat, *birria*, also very sweet coconut called *cocada*), fruit juices and other soft drinks.

Tlaquepaque *p355*
Crafts

The blue, green, amber and amethyst blown-glass articles are made at 2 glass factories. Many other crafts are available in Tlaquepaque, and you can watch the potters at work. Although you may sometimes find better bargains in Tonalá (see below), overall Tlaquepaque is the cheapest and most varied source of local crafts, with attractive shops set in old colonial villas; best buys are glass, papier-mâché goods, leather (cheapest in Mexico), and ceramics.

Antigua de México, Independencia 255. Beautiful, expensive furniture in a lovely building, used to be a convent, the family has branches in Nogales and Tucson so furniture can be shipped to their shops there.

Museo Regional de la Cerámica, Independencia 237. See page 355.

Jewellery

Sergio Bustamante, Independencia 238. Zona Centro, Tlaquepaque. Good modern jewellery; expensive but well worth a look, a stream runs through this house with a colonial façade.

Tonalá *p355*

In Tonalá, market days are Sun and Thu. For shopping in the centre of town, **Aldana Luna**, Juárez 194, T33-3683 0302, sells wrought-iron furniture. **Artesanías Nuño**, Juárez 59, T33-3683 0011, sells brightly painted wooden animals. **Plaza Juárez**, Juárez 141, is a large building with several craft shops in it.

Puerto Vallarta *p360, map p361*
Shopping opportunities are endless, including armies of non-aggressive beach vendors. The flea market is grossly overpriced; the many shops often offer better value, but not much. Guadalajara is cheaper for practically everything. The market, by the bridge at the end of Insurgentes, sells silver, clothes and souvenirs as well as meat and fish. There's a large, well-stocked supermarket nearby.

Bookshops Rosas Expresso, Olas Altas 399. Second-hand books, English and some in German.

Jewellery Olas de Plata, Francisco Rodríguez 132. Plaza Malecón has 28 curio shops, restaurant, music, etc.

Supermarket GR, Constitución 136, is reasonable for basics.

San Blas *p365*
Crafts Huichol Cultural Community store, Juárez 64. For Huichol art; it claims to be non-profit making. Great freehand beadwork with glass beads, yarn paintings, decorated masks and scented candles.

▲▲ Activities and tours

Guadalajara *p350, map p351*
Golf

Rancho Contento, 10 km out on Nogales road; **San Isidro**, 10 km out on Saltillo road, noted for water hazards; **Santa Anita**, 16 km out on Morelia road, championship course.

Hiking

Club Colli, bulletin board Av Juárez 460, details from **Café Madrid**, Juárez 264 or T33-3623 3318.

Rafting

Expediciones México Verde, José Ma Vigil 2406, Col Italia Providencia, T/F33-3641 5598.

Rafting specialists (Actopan, Jatate, Santa María, Antigua-Pescados, Filobobos and Usumacinta rivers).

Spectator sports
Baseball Apr-Sep.
Bullfights Oct-Mar. Plaza de Toros is on Calzada de la Independencia.
Charreadas (rodeos) are held in mid-Sep at Unión de San Antonio; *lienzo charro* near Parque Agua Azul at Aceves Calindo Lienzo, Sun at 1200.
Football is played all year round. The Estadio Jalisco is on Calzada de la Independencia.

North of Manzanillo *p359*
Tour operators
Donatours, Veracruz, next to bus terminal, Barra de Navidad. Travel agent.
Nautimar, Hamberto, Barra de Navidad, T315-355 5790. Snorkel, scuba-diving and waterskiing.

Puerto Vallarta *p360, map p361*
Tour operators
Many agents and hotel tour desks offer boat trips, car hire and tours at big discounts if you accept a timeshare presentation. Worthwhile savings are to be made for those prepared to brazen out the sales pitch, and many do.
American Express, Morelos 660, esq Abasolo, T322-223 2955. Town guide available.
John Pegueros, Lázaro Cárdenas 27, Apdo Postal 73, Bucerías, Nayarit, CP63732, T329-298 0060. Whale watching and snorkelling trips on the schooner *Elías Mann*. Tickets from Marina Vallarta, US$60, includes some meals, starts 0800.
Open Air Expeditions, Guerrero 339, T322-222 3310, openair@vivamexico.com, Oscar and Isabel run hiking trips (mountain or waterfall), whale watching (winter), kayaking, birdwatching and other trips from US$40, knowledgeable guides.
Vallarta Adventure, Av las Palmas 39, Nueva Vallarta, T/F322-297 1212, www.vallarta-adventures.com. Boat trips,

whale-watching (US$65-80), Sierra Madre expedition (US$75), jeep safari (US$75), dolphin encounter (US$128), Las Caletas by night or by day (US$78), also scuba-diving, PADI certificate.

Cycling
Bikemex Adventures, Guerrero 361, T322-223 1834. Offers trips for cyclists of varying grades of competence, from local environs up to 3-4 days in old silver towns of Sierra Madre, all equipment provided including good, front-suspension bikes, from US$45, also offers hiking adventures.

Horse riding
Rancho El Charro, T322-224 0114, www.ranchoelcharro.com. Horse-riding expeditions to jungle villages and Sierra Madre silver towns. Independent guides and horses congregate at lower end of Basilio Badillo; also occasionally at fishermen's wharf, by **Hotel Rosita** for short beach and mountain trips, agree price beforehand.

Tepic *p363, map p363*
Tour operators
Tovara, Ignacio Allende 30.
Viajes Regina, tours to San Blas, Playas de Ensueño, and Tepic city tour.

San Blas *p365*
Tumba de Yako (see Eating, page 377) rents out surf boards. Owner, Juan Bananas, was coach to the Mexican surfing team, gives lessons, speaks English. Mountain bike and kayak hire (for estuaries) also available.

⊝ Transport

Guadalajara *p350, map p351*
Air
Miguel Hidalgo (GDL), 20 km from town; 3 classes of taxi (*especial, semi-especial* and *colectivo*) charge fixed rates for 3 city zones; no tip necessary. To reach the airport, bus

No 176 'San José del 15' (grey) leaves from intersection of Corona and Calzada de la Independencia every 20 mins, US$0.25. **Autotransportes Guadalajara-Chapala** runs 2nd-class buses from old bus terminal every 15 mins, 0655-2125, US$0.35, stop at airport on way to/from Chapala.

Airline offices Mexicana, reservations T33-3678 7676, arrival and departure information T33-3688 5775, ticket office: Av Mariano Otero 2353, by Plaza del Sol, T33-3112 0011. AeroMéxico, reservations T33-3669 0202, airport information T33-3688 5098, ticket offices: Av Corona 196 and Plaza del Sol, Local 30, Zona A. **Air France**, Vallarta 1540-103, T33-3630 3707. **American**, Vallarta 2440, T33-3616 4090 for reservations, T33-3688 5518 at airport. **Continental**, ticket office Astral Plaza, Galerías del Hotel Presidente Intercontinental, Locales 8-9, T33-3647 4251 reservations, T33-3688 5141 airport. **Delta**, López Cotilla 1701, T33-3630 3530. **KLM**, Vallarta 1390-1005, T33-3825 3261. **United**, Plaza Los Arcos, Av Vallarta 2440, local A13, T33-3616 9489.

Bus

Local Tourist office in Plaza Tapatía has a full list of local and long-distance buses. If in doubt ask the bus driver. Regular buses cost US$0.20, *Línea Azul* 'luxury' bus US$0.45.

Some useful lines: **Route 275**, on 16 de Septiembre and Revolución, from Zapopán–Plaza Patria–Glorieta Normal–Av Alcalde–Av 16 de Septiembre–Av Revolución–Tlaquepaque–new bus station–Tonalá (there are different 275s, from A to F; most follow this route, check with the driver). **Route 707** also goes to Tonalá (silver-blue bus with Tur on the side). **Route 60** goes along Calzada de la Independencia from zoo, passing Estadio Jalisco, Plaza de Toros, Mercado Libertad and Parque Agua Azul to the old bus terminal and the railway station (if you are going to Parque Mirador, take bus 62 northbound. There is also a trolley bus that

runs along the Calzada de la Independencia to the entrance to the Mirador, better than 60 or 62. For the old bus station, take minibus 174 south along Calzada de la Independencia from Mercado Libertad, or bus 110 south along Av Alcalde. **Route 102** runs from the new bus terminal along Av Revolución, 16 de Septiembre and Prisciliano Sánchez to Mercado Libertad. **Route 258 or 258A** from San Felipe (north of cathedral) or **258D** along Madero go to **Plaza del Sol. Route 371** runs from Tonalá to Plaza del Sol. A shuttle bus runs between the 2 bus stations.

There is a luxury bus service **Línea Azul** running from Zapopán, along Avila Camacho, past Plaza Patria shopping centre to the Glorieta La Normal, south down Av Alcalde, through Tlaquepaque, to the new bus station and ending in Tonalá. Another luxury bus service to the centre is **Línea Cardenal**. No buses after 2230.

Long distance The **old bus station**, Los Angeles and 28 de Enero, city centre, serves towns roughly within 100 km of Guadalajara. You have to pay 20 centavos to enter the terminal (open 0545-2215). It has 2 *salas* (wings): A and B, and is shaped like a U. The flat bottom of the U fronts Dr R Michel, where the main entrances are. There is a side entrance to Sala A from Los Angeles and to both A and B from 15 de Febrero via a tunnel. Taxi stands are on both sides of the terminal. By the entrances to the *salas* is a **Computel** outlet with long-distance and fax service. Shuttle buses to the new bus station leave from here, US$0.20. In Sala A there are 2nd-class buses to **Tepatitlán** and **Zapotlanejo** and *'La Penal'* (the prison), with Oriente. 1st-class buses to the same destinations leave from the new bus terminal. Buses to **Chapala** (every 30 mins, 0600-2140, US$1.60) and Ajijic (every 30 mins, 0700-2100, US$1.80) leave from here with **Autotransportes Guadalajara-Chapala**. Round-trip package to the *balneario* at **San Juan Cosalá**, US$5.25 including admission to the baths.

In Sala B, **Omnibus de Rivera** sells tickets to the same *balneario* for US$1.50 and at **La Alteña** booth for the *balnearios* **Agua Caliente** and **Chimulco**. A Primera Plus/Servicios Coordinados booth sells tickets to places served by the new bus terminal. Buses to **Tequila** every 30 mins, US$3. Both *salas* have several food stands serving *tortas*, etc, and there are toilets, luggage store and magazine stand.

The **new bus station** is 10 km from the centre, near the El Alamo junction; buses 102 and 275 go to the centre, US$0.25, frequent service (see Local transport, above), journey takes at least 30 mins.

In the centre of town information and tickets are available at 2 offices on Calzada de la Independencia underneath Plaza Tapatía (access from Independencia), daily 0900-1400, 1600-1900. Very handy because of the distance from the centre of town although it is worth getting your departure information at the bus station before you go into town. Most services sold are for the higher-class travel.

The terminal is in the shape of a big U, with modules 1 to 7 evenly spaced around the outside. Buses enter the U at Module 1, following through to 7 at the other end of the U. Different companies have a presence in several modules and while they will sell you a ticket to any destination, you have to get to the correct module. So, shop around, preferably without your bag. Most terminals now have baggage storage, along with telephones, toilets, restaurants, shops and occasionally staffed tourist information booths.

There are probably direct buses to every conceivable destination in Mexico. The schedules for the most commonly used are below, with modules. To **Acapulco**, 1730 and 1900, 17 hrs, US$63, Mod 7. To **Aguascalientes**, hourly 0500-2000, 4 hrs, US$18, Mods 1, 2, 6 and 7. To **Barra de Navidad**, every 2 hrs 0700-1500, and 2200 and 0100, 5 hrs, US$21, Mods 1 and 2. To **Chihuahua**, 8 between 0600 and 2000,

16 hrs, US$72, Mod 7. To **Colima**, hourly, 3 hrs, US$14, Mods 1, 2 and 6. To **Guanajuato**, hourly, 4 hrs, US$21, Mods 1, 2 and 7. To **Hermosillo**, every couple of hrs, 23 hrs, US$85, Mods 3 and 4. To **Lagos de Moreno**, very regular, 3 hrs, US$13, best service from Mod 5. To **León**, hourly, 4 hrs, US$18, Mods 1 and 2. To **Los Mochis**, almost hourly through the day, 15 hrs, US$67, Mods 3 and 4. To **Manzanillo**, hourly, more regular in the afternoon, 6 hrs, US$18, Mods 1, 2 and 3. To **Mazatlán**, every hour day and night, 8 hrs, US$36, Mods 3 and 4. To **Mexicali**, every hr day and night, 34 hrs, US$119, Mods 3 and 4. To **Mexico City** (North Terminal), every 15 mins, 8-9 hrs, US$37, most often at Mod 1. To **Morelia**, every 2 hrs, 4 hrs, US$19, Mods 1 and 2. To **Puerto Vallarta**, every 2 hrs in the morning, 6 hrs, US$32, Mods 1, 2, 3 and 4. To **Querétaro**, every 30 mins, 5 hrs, US$24, most often at Mod 1. To **San Luis Potosí**, every 2 hrs, 5 hrs, US$21, Mod 5. To **San Miguel de Allende**, 1300 and 1500, 6 hrs, US$33, Mod 1. To **Tepic**, every 30 mins, day and night, 3½ hrs, US$18, Mods 3, 4, 6 and 7. To **Tijuana**, hourly, day and night, 33 hrs, US$125, Mods 3 and 4. To **Uruapan**, every 2 hrs, 4½ hrs, US$15, Mods 1 and 2. To **Zacatecas**, roughly every 3 hrs, 5 hrs, US$23, Mods 6 and 7.

Car

Car hire Avis, at airport, T33-3688 5656. Budget, Av Niños Héroes, esq 16 de Septiembre, T33-3613 0027. Hertz, office at Hotel Quinta Real, other at airport, others scattered throughout city, T33-3614 6162. National, Niños Héroes 961, by Hotel Carlton, and other offices at the hotels Fiesta Americana, Holiday Inn Select, and the airport, T33-3614 7175. Quick, Av Niños Héroes, esq Manzano, T33-3614 2247.

Metro

The metro, or *tren ligero*, has **Línea 1** running under Federalismo from Periférico Sur to Periférico Norte. **Línea 2** runs from Juárez station westbound and passes Mercado Libertad. Fare US$0.40, 1-peso coins needed to buy tokens.

Taxi
No meters are used. A typical ride in town costs US$2-4. From the centre to the new bus station is about US$6; if the taxi ticket booths are open at the bus station it costs around US$4. A taxi to the airport costs US$10.

Horse-drawn carriages
US$22 per hour from the Museo Regional de Guadalajara at the corner of Liceo and Hidalgo, or on Independencia just below Plaza Tapatía.

Train
For the **Tequila Express**, see page 386.

Tonalá *p355*
Bus
Bus No 275 from the centre goes through **Tlaquepaque** en route to the bus station and then, to Tonalá; it's a bumpy 45-min journey.

Chapala *p355*
Bus
The station is on Av Madero at the corner of Miguel Martínez. Buses from **Guadalajara** every 30 mins, 0515-2030, 1 hr. 2 blocks south of bus station, minibuses leave every 20 mins for **Ajijic**, 2 pesos, and **San Juan Cosalá**, 3 pesos.

Taxi
Stand on zócalo and at the bus station.

Ajijic to Jocotepec *p355*
Bus
Buses run between **Chapala** and Ajijic (or taxi US$3.20). Jocotepec can be reached from Ajijic or from the Mexico City–Guadalajara highway. Bus **Chapala-Jocotepec** US$2, every hour in each direction.

Colima *p356*
Air
Airport (CLQ) 19 km from centre, T312-314 4160. Flights to **Mexico City** and **Tijuana**.
   Airline offices Aeromar, T312-313 1340. AeroMéxico, T312-313 1340.

Bus
2 bus stations on the outskirts: 'Suburbana' for buses within Colima state – urban buses and *combis* run to centre, US$0.50; take Routes 1 or 19, or taxi, about US$1.40; and, 'Foránea' for buses out of state, take Route 4 or 5 from Jardín Nuñez. If going to **Uruapan** it is best to go to **Zamora** (7-8 hrs, although officially 4 hrs) and change there. To **Guadalajara**, hourly service, 2½-3 hrs, US$15. To **Manzanillo**, 3 hrs, US$9. To **Mexico City**: US$54.

Manzanillo *p358, map p358*
Air
Frequent flights from airport (ZLO), 19 km from town, to **Mexico City** and **Guadalajara**. Other domestic destinations include **Chihuahua**, **Monterrey**, **Puerto Vallarta** and **Saltillo**. US destinations: **Los Angeles**.
   Airline offices Aerolíneas Aeromar, T314-333 0151. Mexicana, T314-332 1972.

Bus
To **Miramar**, US$0.45, leave from J J Alcaraz, 'El Tajo' and can be picked up anywhere along the Av Niños Héroes. Several to **Guadalajara**, 6 hrs, US$19. To **Mexico City**, 11 hrs, US$57. To **Barra de Navidad**, 1½ hrs, US$5. To **Colima**, 3 hrs, US$11. Down the coast to **Lázaro Cárdenas** and crossroads for Playa Azul with **Autobus de Occidente** or **Galeana**, 7 hrs. To **Acapulco**, US$24. To **Zihuatanejo**, 2130, US$21. To **Puerto Vallarta**, 1st class with Trans Cihuatlán at 0800 and 1200, 4½ hrs. Bus terminal in Av Hidalgo outside centre, local buses go there. Taxi to centre US$1.50.

Car

Car hire Budget, Blv Miguel de la Madrid Km 10, 1314-333 1445. **National**, Km 7, Carretera Manzanillo–Santiago, T314-333 0611.

North of Manzanillo *p359*
Barra de Navidad

Bus Buses from terminal on Calle Veracruz, to **Manzanillo**, 1st class, 1215, 1615, 1815 and 2000, US$6, 2nd class; hourly from 0745, US$4.50. To **Puerto Vallarta**, 1st class, 0915 and 1315, 4 hrs, US$18; 2nd class 0900, 1000, 1200, 1400, 1600 and 1800, 5½ hrs, US$15.

Puerto Vallarta *p360, map p361*
Air

International Ordaz airport (PVR), 6 km from centre, T322-221 1325. If you walk 100 m to the highway and catch a local bus to town, it will cost far less than the US$10 taxi fare. Excellent international connections to the USA, Europe, Central and South America.

Airline offices AeroMéxico, T322-224 2777. Aero California, T322-209 0645. Alaska Airlines, T95-800-426-033. America West, T800-235-9292, T800-533-6862. American Airlines, T91-800-90460. Continental, 191-800-90050. Delta, T91-800-90221. Mexicana, T322-224 8900. United, T911-800-00307, T800-426-5561.

Bus

Local Mismaloya to Marina, US$0.40, but complicated routing. The main southbound artery through town is México–Morelos–Vallarta; the main northbound is Juárez–Insurgentes. Plaza Lázaro Cárdenas is the main terminal in south of town and starting point for Mismaloya–Boca buses going south. Buses marked 'Olas Altas' go to South Central, those marked 'Hoteles' or 'Aeropuerto' go to North Hotel Zone and beyond. Buses are also marked for 'Marina' and 'Mismaloya/Boca' (Boca de Tomatlán). The ones marked 'Centro' go through town, those with 'Túnel' take the bypass. Buses

to outlying villages with **Medina** bus line, terminal at Brasil, between Brasilia and Guatemala, regular (15-20 mins) service to **Nuevo Vallarta, San José, San Juan, Bucerías, Manzanilla, Punta de Mita** and others. Fares US$0.75-$1.50.

Long distance All buses leave from bus station almost opposite the airport (turn left when you exit from arrivals, then it's a short walk), 30 mins from centre depending on the route. Taxis from the airport to the main bus station charge inflated prices.

There are frequent services to **Guadalajara**, 6 hrs, US$26. To **Tepic**, every 20 mins, 3 hrs, US$12. To **Barra de Navidad**, 4 hrs, US$18, and **Manzanillo**, 4½ hrs, US$23, every couple of hrs. Other regular services to **Acapulco, Aguascalientes, Cd Guzmán, Cd Juárez, Colima, León, Mazatlán, San Patricio Melaque, Mexico City, Monterrey, Querétaro, Tecomán, Tijuana** and **Zihuatanejo**.

Around Puerto Vallarta *p362*
Water taxi

To reach **Yelapa**, take the tourist water taxi from pier – Los Muertos – US$18 return, leaves 1030, 1100. From fisherman's quay on Malecón, by **Hotel Rosita**, opposite McDonald's, US$10 1 way, leaves 1130. From **Boca de Tomatlán** (bus, US$0.40) water taxi from beach is US$4 1 way, leaves 1030.

Tepic *p363, map p363*
Air

Airport Amado Nervo airport (TPQ) with flights to **Los Angeles, Mexico City, Tampico** and **Tijuana** daily with Aero California, T311-216 1636 or AeroMéxico, T311-213 9047.

Bus

Bus station is a fairly short walk from town centre, T311 213 6747; bus from centre to terminal from Puebla Norte by market. At bus station there are phones, post office, left-luggage and tourist information (not always open). Bus to **San Blas** from main bus terminal and from local bus station on park at Av Victoria y México, from 0615 every hour US$4.50. To **Guadalajara**, frequent departures, 3½ hrs, US$18. To **Mazatlán**, 4½ hrs, US$16. To **Los Mochis**, US$64. To **Puerto Vallarta**, every 20 mins, 3 hrs, US$11. To **Mexico City**, 13 hrs, US$48.

San Blas *p365*
Bus
Bus station on corner of Plaza. To **Tepic**, frequent from 0600, 1½ hrs, US$3.60. To **Guadalajara**, 8½ hrs, US$16.

Tequila *p366*
Bus
2nd class from the old terminal, Sala B, in **Guadalajara**, Rojo de los Altos, every 45 mins, up to 2 hrs, US$2.80. Return from outside Rojo de los Altos ticket office, Sixto Gorjón, 126A, every 20 mins, 0500-1400, then every 30 mins until 2030.

Taxi
To **Guadalajara** US$19, plus US$9 in tolls if you take the expressway.

Train
The **Tequila Express**, T33-3880 9099 (Guadalajara), www.tequilaexpress.com.mx, is a rather comfortable way of visiting the town from Guadalajara. It's all jazzed up and smart-looking – not how the Mexican rail industry used to be that's for sure – but you spend the day drifting towards the town, exploring one of the plantations and then returning with no fear of driving. Sat and/or Sun only, leaving about 1000, returning around 2000, US$60 for adults, US$32 for kids. Book from tour operators in Guadalajara (or see website for options).

❶ Directory

Guadalajara *p350, map p351*
Banks
There are many *casas de cambio* on López Cotilla between Independencia and 16 de Septiembre and 1 in Plaza del Sol. **American Express**, Plaza Los Arcos, Local 1-A, Av Vallarta 2440, esq Francisco García de Quevedo, about 5 blocks east of Minerva roundabout, T33-3630 0200, daily 0900-1800 for the travel agency and 0900-1430, 1600-1800 to change money. Across Prisciliano Sánchez from the Jardín San Francisco is a **Banco Inverlat** with ATM. There are many others arouind town.

Cultural centres
Alliance Française, López Cotilla 1199, Sector Juárez, T33-3825 2140. **Instituto Cultural Mexicano-Norteamericano de Jalisco**, Enrique Díaz de León 300 (see Language schools, below). **Instituto Goethe**, Morelos 2080 y Calderón de la Barca, T33- 3615 6147, library, nice garden, newspapers.

Embassies and consulates
Australia, López Cotilla 2030, T33-3615 7418, 0800-1330, 1500-1800. **Austria**, Montevideo 2695, Col Providencia, T33-3641 1834, 0900-1330. **Belgium**, Metalúrgica 2818, Parque Industrial El Alamo, T33-3670 4825, Mon-Fri 0900-1400. **Canada**, trade officer and consul, Hotel Fiesta Americana, local 31, T33-3616 5642, 0830-1400 and 1500-1700. **Denmark**, Lázaro Cárdenas 601, 6th floor, T33-3669 5515, 0900-1300, 1600-1800. **El Salvador**, Fermín Riestra 1628, between Bélgica and Argentina, Col Moderna, T33-3810 1061, hours for visas 1230-1400, normally visas will be received the same day. **France**, López Mateos Norte 484 entre Herrera y Cairo y Manuel Acuña, T33-3616 5516, 0930-1400. **Germany**, Corona 202, T33-3613 9623, 1130-1400. **Guatemala**, Mango 1440, Col del Fresno, T33-3811 1503, 1000-1400. **Honduras**, Ottawa 1139, Col Providencia, T33-3817 4998, 1000-1400,

1700-1900. **Israel**, Av Vallarta 2482 Altos, Sector Juárez, T33-3616 4554, 0930-1500. **Italy**, López Mateos Norte 790-1, T33-3616 1700, Tue-Fri 1100-1400. **Netherlands**, Lázaro Cárdenas 601, 6th floor, Zona Industrial, T33-3811 2641, 0900-1400, 1630-1900. **Nicaragua**, Eje Central 1024, esq Toreros, Col Guadalupe Jardín, behind Club Atlas Chapalita, T33-3628 2919, 1600-1800. **Spain**, Av Vallarta 2185, T33-3630 0450, 0830-1330. **Sweden**, J Guadalupe Montenegro 1691, T33-3825 6767, 0900-1400, 1600-1900. **Switzerland**, Av Revolución 707, Sector Reforma, T33-3617 5900, 0800-1400, 1600-1900. **UK**, Eulogio Parra 2539, T33-3616 0629, 0900-1500, 1700-2000. **US**, Progreso 175, T33-3825 2700.

Immigration

Mexican tourist cards can be renewed at the immigration office (1st floor) in the Palacio Federal on Av Alcalde between Juan Alvarez and Hospital, across the avenue from the Santuario de Guadalupe. The Palacio Federal also contains a post office and fax service.

Internet

Arrobba, Av Lázaro Cárdenas 3286, just west of intersection with López Mateos, Mon-Sat 1000-2200, drinks, snacks, salads. **Cyber café**, López Cotilla, southwest corner of Parque Revolución, 1st floor, T33-3826 3771, also with pizza, snacks, beer and soft drinks. **Futurama**, Pedro Moreno 570, Local 1, T33-3613 7318. **Imprenta Rápida**, Local J in the mall on Juárez 323, T33-3613 5258. **Mr Ch@t**, Madero between Ocampo and Guerra, printers and scanners too.

Language schools

Centro de Estudios para Extranjeros de la Universidad de Guadalajara, Tomás V Gómez 125, between Justo Sierra and Av México, T33-3616 4399, www.cepe.udg.mx, with or without homestay. The **Instituto Cultural Mexicano-Norteamericano de Jalisco**, at Enrique Díaz de León 300, T33-3825 5838, 5 levels of instruction, cultural lectures on Fri,

homestays possible. The **Universidad Autónoma de Guadalajara (UAG)**, a private university, offers Spanish classes through their Centro Internacional de Idiomas, T33-3641 7051, ext 32251, 0800-1800, at Edificio Humanidades 1st floor, on the main campus at Av Patria 1201, Col Lomas del Valle, 3a sección, 7 levels of instruction, each lasting 4 weeks, homestays possible. **Vancouver Language Centre**, Av Vallarta 1151, Col América, T33-3826 0944 (T1-604-687-1600-Vancouver), www.study-mexico.com, 1-week intensive programmes. See also **National Registration Center for Study Abroad** under Learning Spanish in Essentials, page 54.

Laundry

Aldama 125 (walk along Independencia towards train station, turn left into Aldama).

Medical services

Dentists: **Dr Abraham Waxtein**, Av México 2309, T33-3615 1041, speaks English. Doctors: **Dr Daniel Gil Sánchez**, Pablo Neruda 3265, 2nd floor, T33-3642 0213, speaks English (1st consultation, 2½ hrs, including thorough physical, US$50). Hospitals: **Hospital del Carmen**, Tarascos 3435, Fraccionamiento Monraz (behind Plaza México), T33-3813 0042, a good private hospital (take credit cards). **Hospital Angel Leaño**, off the road to Tesistán, T33-3834 3434, affiliated with the University (UAG). For those who cannot afford anything else there are the **Hospital Civil**, T33-3614 5501, and the **Nuevo Hospital Civil**, T33-3618 9362. Pharmacies: There are 3 big chains: **Farmacias Guadalajara**, **Benavides** and **ABC**. **Farmacia Guadalajara**, Av Américas and Morelos, has vaccines and harder-to-find drugs, T33-3615 5094. Vaccinations: For *antirrábico* (rabies), T33-3643 1917; to receive the vaccine you have to go to **Clinic 3 of the Sector Salud**, T33-3823 3262, at the corner of Circunvalación División del Norte and Federalismo, across the street from a Telmex office, near the División del Norte Station,

Line 1, *tren ligero*; you can also get an HIV test here. Sidatel (AIDS), T33-3613 7546.

Post office

Main post office, V Carranza, just behind Palacio de Justicia, Mon-Fri 0800-1900, Sat 0900-1300. There are also branches at the Mercado Libertad (San Juan de Dios) and at the old bus station. To send parcels abroad go to Aduana Postal in same building as main post office, Mon-Fri 0800-1300, T33-3614 9002. FedEx has 3 outlets: Av Américas 1395; Plaza del Sol Locales 51-55; Av Washington 1129, next to Bolerama 2000, T33-3817 2502. UPS, Av Américas 981, Local 19, T01-800-902-9200.

Telephone

International collect calls can be made from any coin-box phone kiosk and direct dial calls can be made from LADA pay phones. You can also make long-distance calls and send faxes from Computel outlets: one in front of old bus station, one on Corona y Madero, opposite Hotel Fénix. Mayahuel, Paseo Degollado 55, has long-distance service, fax, sells Ladatel cards, postcards and maps. There is a credit card phone at Ramón Corona y Av Juárez, by the cathedral. 2 USA Direct phones, 1 within and 1 beyond the customs barrier at the airport.

Chapala *p355*

Banks *Casa de cambio*, Av Madero near Beer Garden, Mon-Sat 0830-1700. HSBC, Madero 208, ATM taking Visa, MasterCard, and cards of Cirrus and Plus networks. Nearby is a Banamex with ATM. Bancomer, Hidalgo 212 near Madero, ATM taking Visa; across the street is a Banca Serfín, ATM. Lloyds, Madero 232, is a real estate office, *casa de cambio*, travel agency and *sociedad de inversión*; many Americans keep their money here. **Laundry** Zaragoza y Morelos. Dry cleaners at Hidalgo 235A, also repairs shoes and other leather items. **Medical services** IMSS clinic on Niños Héroes between Zaragoza and 5 de Mayo. Centro de Salud, Flavio Romero de

V and Guerrero. Red Cross, Parque de la Cristina. **Post office** The post office is at Hidalgo 223. Nearby is a UPS office. Mail Box Etc, Carretera Chapala-Jocotepec 155, opposite PAL Trailer Park, T376-766 0747. Shipping office at Hidalgo 236 uses FedEx and DHL. **Telephone** Computel on the plaza, long distance and fax, accepts Amex, MasterCard, AT&T. Also pay phones for long-distance calls on zócalo and outside bus station.

Ajijic to Jocotepec *p355*

Banks Opposite taxi stand at Colón 29, Ajijic is a *casa de cambio*. On southwest corner of plaza is Banco Promex with 2 ATMs. **Immigration** Castellanos 4, Ajijic, T376-766 2042. **Laundry** About ½ block north at Colón 24A is a *lavandería*. **Medical services** Dentists: 2 dentists' offices on Colón, just south of plaza, Ajijic. Doctors: Dr Alfredo Rodríguez Quintana, T376-766 1499 (home). Hospitals and clinics: Clínica Ajijic, Carretera Ote 33, T376-766 0662, with 24-hr ambulance service. **Post office** 1 block south of plaza, corner of Colón and Constitución. Ajijic Real Estate, Morelos 4, T376-766 2077, is an authorized UPS outlet. **Telephone** On the northwest corner of the plaza is a Computel booth for long-distance phone and fax, daily 0800-2100.

Colima *p356*

Banks Banco Inverlat, Juárez 32, on west side of Jardín Núñez, ATM takes Amex, Visa, Diner's Club. Casa de cambio at Morelos and Juárez on southwest corner of same park. Bacomer at Madero and Ocampo 3 blocks east of plaza, ATM takes Visa and Plus. Casa de cambio across the street. Banamex, one block south on Ocampo at Hidalgo, has an ATM. **Internet** Cyber café, Plaza Country, Av Tecnológico, 15 blocks north of centre, Mon-Fri 0900-2200, Sat and Sun 1000-2200. **Laundry** Lavandería Shell, 27 de Septiembre 134, daily 0900-2000, inexpensive, quick. **Medical services** Hospitals and clinics: Hospital Civil,

T312-312 0227. **Red Cross**, T312-312 1451.
Pharmacy: Farmacia Guadalupana on
northeast corner of Jardín Torres Quintero
behind cathedral. Another pharmacy on
northeast corner of zócalo. **Post office**
Av Francisco I Madero and General Núñez,
northeast corner of Jardín Núñez.
Telephone Computel, Morelos 234 on
south side for long-distance phone and fax,
and at bus station, daily 0700-2200, accepts
Visa, MasterCard, Amex and AT&T cards.
Fax not always in use.

Manzanillo *p358, map p358*
Medical services Hospital Civil,
T314-332 4161. Red Cross, T314-336 5770.

North of Manzanillo *p359*
Internet Cybernet between beachfront
and Gómez Farías, near Hotel Monterrey,
San Patricio Melaque. **Medical services**
Dra Herlinda Rubio, English speaking, Barra
de Navidad. **Internet** Ciber@net, Veracruz
212, Barra de Navidad.

Puerto Vallarta *p360, map p361*
Banks *Casas de cambio* on nearly every
street in tourist areas. Rates inferior to
Guadalajara. Check Bancomer's *cambio* at
Juárez 450, for good rates, open late. Banks
offer slightly better rates (but slower service)
and ATMs for Visa, MasterCard. **Embassies
and consulates** Canada, Edif Vallarta
Plaza, Zaragoza 160, 1st floor, T322-222 5398,
daily 1000-1400. USA, T322-222 0069.

Immigration In front of the Marina
terminal, T224-7970. **Internet** Numerous
internet cafés normally charging around
US$2 per hr. **Laundry** Practically one on
every block in South Central; numerous
throughout resort. **Medical services** Dra
Irma Gittelson, Juárez 479, speaks French and
English, very helpful. **Emergency**: T915-724
7900. **Post office** Mina between Juárez and
Morelos. **Telephone** Long-distance phone
(*casetas*) and fax at Lázaro Cárdenas 267, daily
to 2300, also in lobby of Hotel Eloisa. Many
shops bear *Larga distancia* sign, check tariffs.

Tepic *p363, map p363*
Banks *Casas de cambio* at México 91 and
140 Norte, Mon-Sat 0900-1400, 1600-2000.
Telephone Credit card phone at Veracruz
Norte y Zapata Pte.

San Blas *p365*
Banks Banamex just off zócalo, exchange
daily 0830-1000. **Comercial de San Blas**
on the main square will change money.
Laundry 2 blocks down toward the beach
from La Familia. Will take your clothes and
return them, very clean, later or the next day.

Tequila *p366*
Banks Banamex, corner of Sixto Gorjón
and Juárez, 24-hr ATM accepts Visa and
MasterCard. Many ATMs in town. *Casa de
cambio*, Sixto Gorjón 73, daily 0900-1400,
1600-2000, change cash and TCs.

State of Veracruz

Often overlooked by tourists, the State of Veracruz is off the usual beaten track. Maybe it hasn't got the best beaches in Mexico but for almost everything else it's hard to beat. Inland, there's adventure tourism with Mexico's highest mountain, deepest caves and fastest rapids. Temperatures rise as the land drops to the green, fertile coastal plain and the endless plantations. To the south, beyond the plains of the vast Río Papaloapan, the Tuxtla mountains, tropical and lush, are a birdwatcher's paradise and contrast dramatically with the wilderness of the massive oil refineries at Minatitlán and Coatzacoalcos. In the north are the Huastec people, best known for their traditional huapango music and falsetto singing. In the vanilla-growing Papantla area, the spectacular volador ritual, an example of surviving Totonac traditions, is performed regularly in Papantla and outside the ruins of El Tajín, one of the most magnificent archaeological sites in all America. Xalapa, the lively state capital and an important university city, has one of the best museums in the whole country. But it's the rich cultural mix that makes Veracruz so special. For 300 years, the port was Spain's gateway to the riches of the New World. The arrival of black slaves profoundly influenced the people and culture – most notably the music – of this region. Veracruz is a popular destination for Mexican tourists who enjoy the famous hospitality of the Veracruzanos, known as jarochos, and the eternally festive, tropical-port atmosphere that crescendoes each spring during the liveliest carnival in all Mexico. ▸▸ For listings, see pages 405-417.

Mexico City to Veracruz ●●●●● ▸▸ pp405-417.

Much of the area east of Mexico City constituted the eastern tribute quarter conquered by the Mexica, formerly the Aztecs, who derived great wealth from those subject nations that stretched from the Basin of Mexico to the Guatemalan border.

By road, the principal route to the coast from Mexico City is paved all the way, a distance of about 150 km. A fast toll road runs all the way from Mexico City to Veracruz.

Orizaba → *Colour map 3, B5. Phone code: 272. Altitude: 1283 m.*

The favourite resort of the Emperor Maximilian, on the eastern edge of the mountains, lost much of its charm in the 1973 earthquake, when the bullring, many houses and other buildings were lost; the city is now heavily industrialized. The setting, however, is lovely. In the distance is the majestic volcanic cone of Orizaba.

The town developed because of the natural springs in the valley, some of which are used by the textile and paper industries and others are dammed to form small pools for bathing beside picnic areas. The **Cerro del Borrego**, the hill above the Alameda park, is a favourite early-morning climb. On the north side of the zócalo is the market, with a wide variety of local produce and local women in traditional dress, and the many-domed **San Miguel** church (1690-1729). There are several other interesting churches. The **ex-Palacio Municipal**, now the Palacio de Hierro, is a cast-iron pavilion designed by Gustave Eiffel, brought piece by piece from France after the famous 19th-century Paris Exhibition and an odd sight. The **Museo de Arte del Estado** ① *4 Ote y 23 Sur, Tue-Sun 10001700, US$1*, in the Oratorio de San Felipe Neri, has a delightful collection of colonial to contemporary paintings. The **tourist office** ① *Palacio de Hierro, T272-728 9136, www.orizaba.gob.mx, Mon-Fri 0800-1500 and 1600-2000*, has maps and general information.

Around Orizaba

A road leaves Orizaba southwards, up into the mountains of **Zongolica**, a dry, poor and isolated region, cold and inhospitable, inhabited by various indigenous groups who speak Náhuatl, the language of the Aztecs. Zongolica village is a good place to buy *sarapes* (shawls); take the early bus from Orizaba (ask for direct one) to get clear views of the mountains.

Beyond Orizaba, en route to the coast, the scenery is magnificent. The road descends to coffee and sugar-cane country and a tropical riot of flowers. It is pleasant except when a northerly blows, or in the heat and mugginess of the wet season.

Córdoba → *Colour map 3, B5. Phone code: 271. Altitude: 923 m.*

Eight kilometres beyond Fortín in the rich valley of the Río Seco is the old colonial city of Córdoba, which is crazy with flowers. Its zócalo is spacious, leafy and elegant; three sides are arcaded; two of them are lined with tables. On the fourth is an imposing church with a chiming clock. There are several hotels in the zócalo, which is lively but relaxed at night. In **Portal de Zavallos**, General Iturbide signed the Treaty of Córdoba in 1821, which was instrumental in freeing Mexico from Spanish colonial rule. There's a local **museum** ① *Calle 3, No 303, daily 0900-1400, 1600-2000, free* with a small collection of archaeological and anthropological artefacts. Cordoba has the highest rainfall in Mexico, falling between April and November. Rainfall is usually fierce and brief in the afternoon. The **tourist office** ① *Palacio Municipal, zócalo, T271-717 1700, 0800-1900,* has maps and info.

Xalapa ⬤🄿🄵🄾🄼🄾🄲 ↠ *pp405-417. Colour map 3, B5.*

→ *Phone code: 228. Altitude: 1425 m.*

The capital of Veracruz state since 1885 and 132 km from the port, Xalapa (also spelt **Jalapa**) is in the *tierra templada* and is a lively town in keeping with its climate. It is yet another 'City of Flowers', with walled gardens, stone-built houses, wide avenues in the newer town and steep, cobbled, crooked streets in the old. The world-famous *xalapeño* (*jalapeño*) chilli originally comes from the this region.

A settlement called Xallac ('the place of the sandy waters') is known to have existed here in the 12th century. It has always been a good place to break the journey from the coast to the highlands and, in the 18th century, development was helped by the creation of a huge annual trading fair. There was a passion for building and renovation in the flamboyant Gothic style during the first part of the 19th century.

The excellent, modern **Anthropology Museum** ① *Tue-Sun 0900-1700, US$3.50, Tue free, half price for students with ID, guided tours included in fee,* second only to the one in Mexico City, is in the northern suburbs of Xalapa, on the road out towards Mexico City. The museum concentrates on exhibits from the region's three major pre-Hispanic civilizations, showing treasures of the Olmec, Totonac and Huastec coastal cultures. It has the best collection of Olmec monumental stone sculptures in all Mexico, including several of the magnificent colossal heads from the south of Veracruz and Tabasco, and the exquisite *Señor de las Limas*.

The **Pinacoteca Diego Rivera** ① *Herrera 5, on the zócalo, Tue-Sun 1000-1800, free,* has a small permanent collection of Rivera's paintings. Pico de Orizaba is visible from hotel roofs or Parque Juárez very early in the morning, before the haze develops. There is a **tourist office kiosk** ① *in the Palacio Municipal, T228 842 1200, www.xalapa.gob.mx* with local maps and information. The Palacio de Gobierno, south of Enríquez on Dr Lucio, is the place for information on attractions in Veracruz state.

Around Xalapa

Coatepec is a sleepy coffee town just 12 km south of Xalapa and well worth a visit. The zócalo is lined with good restaurants and open-front cafés where the aroma of fresh ground coffee permeates the air. Stock up on beans, wander the colonial streets or otherwise sample the gentle atmosphere. Northwest of the zócalo, the Cerro de Culebra offers commanding views, whilst the tourist office, also on the zócalo, has good information and maps. To get to Coatepec, catch a bus from Xalapa's Los Sauces terminal (30 minutes, $0.40), or take a taxi, 20 minutes, US$10-15.

The **Texolo** waterfalls are some 15 km southwest of Xalapa and 5 km from the pretty village of **Xico**. There is a deep ravine and a good, cheap restaurant at the falls. The old bridge is still visible but a new bridge across the ravine has been built. It is a pleasant place for a cold swim, birdwatching and walking. To get there, take a bus from Xalapa (US$0.60, every 30 minutes).

Naolinco is 30 minutes' ride, 40 km northeast of Xalapa up a winding hilly road. Two waterfalls, with various pools, tumble several thousand feet over steep wooded slopes. **Restaurant La Fuente** serves local food and has a nice garden. **Las Cascadas** has a mirador to admire the falls from. Both restaurants are on the way into town.

Two hours northwest from Xalapa is the archaeological site of **Filobobos** ① US$2. It includes El Cuajilote, a 400-m-wide ceremonial centre, and Vega de la Peña, an area of basalt rocks decorated with bas reliefs, a ball court and several pyramids by the river banks. Abundant wildlife here includes toucans, parrots and otters.

Route 140 towards the capital, renowned for being foggy, continues to climb to **Perote**, 53 km from Xalapa. The **San Carlos fort** here, now a military prison, was built in 1770-1777; there is a good view of Cofre de Perote volcano (known, in Aztec times, as *Nauhtecuhtli*, 'Four Times Lord'). A road branches north to **Teziutlán**, with a Friday market, where good *sarapes* are sold. A local fair, **La Entrega de Inanacatl**, is held in the third week in June. The old convent at **Acatzingo**, 93 km beyond Perote on Route 140, is worth seeing. Another 10 km and you join the road to Puebla and Mexico City.

Papantla ●❶❷❸❹ ▶▶ pp405-417. Colour map 3, B5.

→ *Phone code: 784.*

Some 40 km inland from Tecolutla is Papantla ('Where banners abound'), built on the top of a hill overlooking the lush plains of northern Veracruz. It was the stronghold of a Totonac rebellion in 1836. Traditional Totonac dress is still worn: the men in baggy white trousers and sailor shirts and the women in lacy white skirts and shawls over embroidered blouses. Papantla is also the centre of one of the world's largest vanilla-producing zones, although production has decreased in recent years due to the proliferation of mass-produced synthetic vanilla. The vanilla is processed in **Gutiérrez Zamora**, a small town about 30 km east (close to Tecolutla), and a 'cream of vanilla' liqueur is also produced. The **Fiesta de la Vainilla** is held throughout the area in early June. The **tourist office** ① *Azueta 101, northwest of the zócalo, T784-842 3837, Mon-Fri 0900-1400, 1800-2100*, is helpful, with good information, maps and bus schedules; English is spoken.

Sights

The zócalo, formally known as **Plaza Téllez**, is bordered by Enríquez on its downhill north edge; on the south uphill side the **Catedral de Nuestra Señora de la Asunción** (1700) has a remarkable 50-m-long mural on its northern wall called *Homenaje a la Cultura Totonaca*, by Teodoro Cano García (1979), with the plumed serpent Quetzalcoatl along its entire length. *Voladores* perform in the church courtyard each Sunday at 1100, and as many as three times daily during the colourful 10 days of **Corpus Christi** (late May or early June), along with games, fireworks, artistic exhibitions, dances and cockfights. For a sweeping view of the area, walk up Reforma to the top of the hill where the giant **Monumento al Volador** was erected in 1988. Murals and mosaic benches in the zócalo also commemorate Totonac history and their conception of creation. Northeast of the plaza is the **Mercado Hidalgo** ① *20 de Noviembre, daily 0600-2000*, off the northwest corner of the zócalo, where traditional handmade clothing is sold alongside fresh produce and livestock.

El Tajín → *Colour map 3, B5.*

① *2 km from Papantla. Daily 0900-1700, except mid-Aug 0800-1900. US$3.50. There is a small modern museum, a cafetería and souvenir shops. In the wet season beware of a large, poisonous creature like a centipede. El Tajín can be visited either from Papantla (see page 392) or from Poza Rica (see page 396).*

The great city of El Tajín once covered approximately 1050 ha at the heart of which are four major groupings of structures: **Tajín proper** covers the valley floor; most of the major temples are located here. This is also the location of most of the carved and plain ball courts as well as ceremonial and market plazas. This area was the religious and commercial centre of the city. **Tajín Chico** is a huge terraced acropolis dominated by an elaborate multi-storeyed palace and administrative structures for the city's elite. The largest buildings erected at El Tajín are on the upper levels of Tajín Chico. Along with its Annex, the 'Building of the Columns' is the greatest architectural complex in the city. It was the special domain of the ruler 13 Rabbit, who governed at the city's zenith. The **West Ridge** is mostly an artificially tiered natural hill. The structures here are thought to be elite residences, modest temples and, perhaps, small ball courts. The **East Ridge** is very similar to the West Ridge but with fewer structures.

The suggested timescale for El Tajín's construction is AD 300-900, with a great surge of energy around AD 600, the time when Teotihuacán and Monte Albán were experiencing collapse and abandonment. Although impressive, the architecture of El Tajín is less informative than the rich corpus of iconography that decorated the Pyramid of the Niches, the North Ball Court, the South Ball Court and the Building of the Columns. Most of the imagery associated with these structures tells of conquest, ball games, the interplay between human existence and that of the gods, the dignified sacrifice of warriors and ball players and the undignified sacrifice of captive enemy lords.

The ball game was the single most important activity expressed in the imagery of El Tajín, as emphasized by the presence of at least 11 ball courts at the site. The obsession with the ball game and its related iconography suggests that the city was an immense academy where young men were trained in the skills and rules associated with the game. As yet, no evidence supports this suggestion, but it is tempting to speculate that the residences on the East and West Ridges were intended to house young trainees.

Associated almost exclusively with the ball game and players, the cult of the maguey plant (from which the intoxicant pulque is made) and pulque deities at El Tajín presents a puzzle, perplexing because the maguey will not grow in the general area. The probability is that the city was the creation of a small enclave of Huastecs rather than the Totonacs who then inhabited and still inhabit the region. The maguey proliferates throughout the Highlands, and in the mythology of the Central Highlands it was a Huastec who drank more than the stipulated four cups, became drunk, stripped naked and had to return in disgrace to his homeland.

Pyramid of the Niches
The form of the pyramid, one of the earliest structures at El Tajín, is very distinctive, and said to have 365 niches, one for each day of the year. Dated approximately AD 600, it is

El Tajín

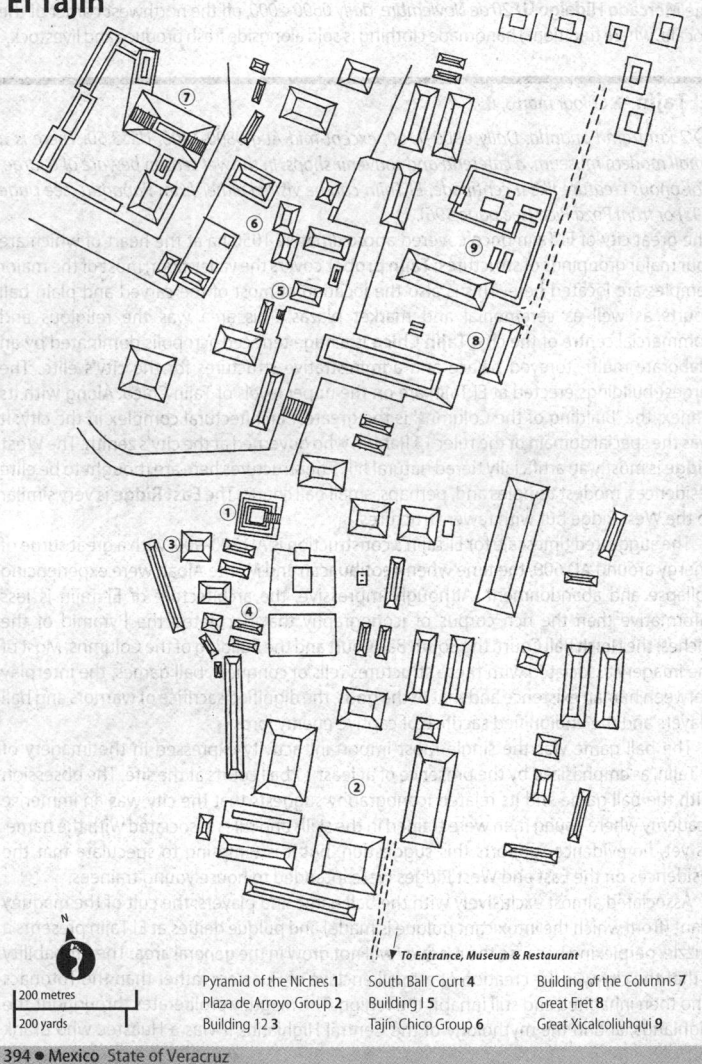

200 metres	Pyramid of the Niches **1**	South Ball Court **4**	Building of the Columns **7**
200 yards	Plaza de Arroyo Group **2**	Building I **5**	Great Fret **8**
	Building 12 **3**	Tajín Chico Group **6**	Great Xicalcoliuhqui **9**

▼ To Entrance, Museum & Restaurant

394 • Mexico State of Veracruz

The voladores of El Tajín

Traditionally, on Corpus Christi, Totonac rain dancers erect a 30-m mast with a rotating structure at El Tajín. Four *voladores* (flyers) and a musician climb to the top of the surmounting platform. There, the musician dances to his own pipe and drum music, while the roped *voladores* throw themselves into space to make a dizzy spiral descent, head first, to the ground. Each *voladore* makes 13 revolutions, symbolizing the 52-year cycle of the Aztec calendar.

Voladores are now in attendance at El Tajín every day during high season (other times just weekends), and fly if and when they think there are enough tourists (donations expected).

crowned with a sanctuary that was lined with engraved panels, one of which shows a cacao plant bearing fruit. Cacao was precious and of great commercial value to the people of the area. There is some evidence that the rulers of El Tajín controlled its cultivation in the zones surrounding the site. Another trapezoidal panel depicts a priest or ruler adorned with ball game accoutrements and holding a knife ready to perform a ritual sacrifice, the scene being set within the confines of a ball court. The depiction of a skull at the foot of the executioner indicates sacrifice by decapitation.

North Ball Court

The imagery of the North Ball Court is only partially understood. Most of the problems associated with this zone derive from erosion and mutilation of the engravings. Men in bat costumes are a major theme in these panels and suggest influence from the Maya region where men dressed in this way were common images on ceramics of the Classic period. Also present in the North Ball Court is the imagery of the ball game and human sacrifice.

South Ball Court

The South Ball Court offers a fascinating glimpse into the philosophy that underpinned the whole ritual life of El Tajín. Central to the narrative is the role of the ball player who acts as an intermediary between this world and that of the gods. In the engravings, the ball player is presented to the executioner and decapitated while the gods look on. Two of the panels are bordered with the image of a laughing pulque deity with two bodies, and there are many Venus symbols. The death god, Mitlantecuhtli, emerges from an urn of pulque, and many of the known gods of the Mesoamerican pantheon are represented. In some of the painted books of the Central Highlands, the powerful gods Quetzalcoatl and Tezcatlipoca oppose each other in a ball game; at El Tajín, it is possible that the human players represented the earthly aspects of these gods. The imagery of the engravings of the South Ball Court is extremely complex, but it does imply that, through the ball game, humans can approach the realm of the gods by means of the decapitation of the principal players.

Tajín Chico

The Building of the Columns is another area with a very complex iconographical narrative. However, while the iconography of the South Ball Court expresses a communion between gods and men, the iconography of the Building of the Columns refers to themes that are much more mundane. The focus of attention is the ruler 13 Rabbit, whose glyph is repeated many times on the surface of the column drums, always with the image of a rabbit and the number 13 expressed by two bars, each counting as five, and three dots. 13 Rabbit had clearly been on a conquest campaign because a number of prisoners are lined up in preparation for the decapitation ritual. They have been divested of almost all their clothes and thus divested of their dignity. They are named by glyphs above or near their persons, which indicates that they were chiefs of opposing polities; the common warrior was rarely identified by name. Whereas the warrior/ball player of the South Ball Court approached his death with calm dignity, the prisoners of the Building of the Columns are forced toward the sacrificial block, some held by the hair. Two sacrificial sequences but two very different approaches to death. The narrative of 13 Rabbit is now in the site museum. Although seen and depicted as all-powerful, 13 Rabbit was not omnipotent enough to prevent the destruction of the city and probably the State of El Tajín, which occurred shortly after the engraving of the Building of the Columns was completed. The great centre of the ball game, like so many others, perished, but at whose hands has yet to be discovered.

Poza Rica and south to Veracruz ◉❶❷❸❶ ➤ pp405-417. Colour map 3, B5.

→ Phone code: 782.

Twenty-one kilometres northwest of Papantla is **Poza Rica**, a fairly ugly oil city formed out of four old *rancherías*, which happened to lie on top of the then second largest oil strike in the world. It has an old cramped wooden market and a simple mural by O'Higgins (*From Primitive Prehispanic Agricultural Works to the Present Day Oil Industry Development*, 1959) on the outside of the **Palacio Municipal**. The **tourist office** ① *T782-822 1390 ext 129*, is at the back of the Palacio Municipal on the ground floor.

From Poza Rica you can head north to visit the **Castillo de Teayo**, a pyramid with the original sanctuary and interesting carvings on top (buses run every 30 minutes, change halfway).

Coast road to Veracruz

East of Papantla, a side road branches off the main Route 180 to the coast at **Tecolutla**, a very popular resort on the river of that name, toll bridge US$2.50. The fiesta that takes place two days before the carnival (February to March) in Veracruz is recommended.

Forty-two kilometres further south, Route 180 passes through **Nautla**, a pleasant town. Three kilometres before Nautla, Route 131 branches inland to Teziutlán. **El Pital** (15 km in from the Gulf along the Nautla River, 80 km southeast of Papantla), was identified early in 1994 as the site of an important, sprawling pre-Columbian seaport (approximately AD 100-600), which lay hidden for centuries under thick rainforest. Now planted over with bananas and oranges, the 100 or more pyramid mounds (some reaching 40 m in height) were assumed by plantation workers to be natural hills. Little excavation or clearing has yet been done, but both Teotihuacán-style and local-style ceramics and figurines have been found.

The ruins of **Cempoala** ① *US$2.50*, are 40 km north of Veracruz. Cortés was welcomed by the inhabitants of the coastal city who became his allies against the Aztecs. The ruins are interesting because of the round stones uniquely used in construction. Sundays can be very crowded. It is a pleasant site and setting and *voladores* are often in attendance. To get there take a second-class bus to Cardel, and then a micro to Cempoala.

Chachalacas is a fine uncrowded beach. There's a swimming pool and changing facilities (US$1 adults) in an expensive but spotless hotel of the same name. Local delicacies, including *robalito* fish, are sold from *palapas* on the beach. It is worth asking the restaurants on the beach to let you hang up your hammock, most have showers and toilets. They charge US$2 if you agree to eat at their restaurant.

La Antigua, the site of what was thought to be Cortés' house, is 1.5 km off the road to Cardel, some 30 km north of Veracruz. Take a Cardel bus from the second class part of the bus station (US$0.40) and get off at La Antigua Caseta, the first toll booth the bus comes to. It is an easy 10- or 15-minute walk from there. The house is worth visiting just to see the large ceiba roots growing all over the walls.

Veracruz ●❼❷❸❸● » *pp405-417. Colour map 3, B5.*

→ *Phone code: 229.*

Veracruz is a mixture of the very old and the new; there are still many picturesque white-walled buildings and winding side streets. The centre is at the back of the harbour and has something of a 1950s feel about it. It is very much a port town, noisy and congested, but lively, full of music and dance, and with a definite Caribbean air.

Ins and outs

Getting there and around **Aeropuerto Las Bajadas (VER)** is 12 km from the city centre with a shuttle service into town. The bus terminals (first and second class) are about 3 km from the town centre, on Avenida Díaz Mirón. Highways 150 and 150D (*supercarretera*) link Mexico City to the Gulf coast at the port of Veracruz. Route 180 runs north-south along the coast. All places of interest are within easy walking distance of Plaza de Armas. Frequent buses run along the seafront to Mocambo or Boca del Río during the day, but at night you may have to take a taxi. » *See Transport, page 415.*

Best time to visit It is generally hot, however, if visiting between July and September, check the weather forecast because tropical storms, known as *nortes*, blow themselves out in this region, bringing heavy rain. From October to January the weather is changeable, with cold, damp winds. At this time the beaches and Malecón are empty and many resorts close, except over Christmas and New Year when all road transport is booked up five days in advance.

Tourist information The helpful **tourist office** ① *Palacio Municipal, T229-989 8817 or freephone on T01-800-VERATUR, or www.veracruzturismo.com, 1000-1800*, is on the zócalo.

Background

The principal port of entry for Mexico lies on a low alluvial plain bordering the Gulf Coast. Cortés landed near here at Isla de los Sacrificios on 17 April 1519. The first settlement was called Villa Rica de la Vera Cruz; its location was changed several times, including to La Antigua (see above). The present site was established in 1599.

Culturally, Veracruz is a Caribbean city, home to the *jarocho* costume, dance and music, which features harps and guitars. The most famous dances, accompanied by the *conjunto jarocho* dressed in white, are the *bamba* and *zapateado*, with much stamping and lashing of feet related to the flamenco of Andalucía in Spain. Mexico's version of the Cuban *danzón* music and the *música tropical* add to the cultural richness. Many cultural events can be seen at the **Instituto Veracruzano de Cultura**, a few blocks from the zócalo, which is a great place to relax with a good café and library.

Sights

The heart of the city is **Plaza de Armas** (zócalo). The square is white-paved, with attractive cast-iron lampstands and benches, and surrounded by the cathedral (with an unusual cross, depicted with hands), the **Palacio Municipal** and colonial-style hotels. The plaza comes alive in the evenings with an impressive combination of the crush of people, colour and marimba music, *danzón* or *son veracruzano* in the floodlit setting. From 15 July to the end of August there is jazz in the zócalo from 1900. At night, too, the Malecón (seafront) is very lively, with performers entertaining the public.

The city's two most interesting buildings are the very fine 17th-century **Palacio Municipal** (1627), on Plaza de Armas, with a splendid façade and courtyard, and the **Fortress of San Juan de Ulúa** (1565) ① *Tue-Sun 0900-1700, US$2.50*, built on Isla Gallega to deter the buccaneers but now joined by a causeway to the mainland. It later became a political prison and Mexico's 'Robin Hood', Chucho el Roto, famously managed to escape three times. Benito Juárez was also incarcerated here between 1858 and 1861. In 1915, Venustiano Carranza converted it into a presidential palace. Take the bus marked Ulúa from Malecón/Avenida República, or catch a *lancha* from the malecón, US$2.50. The **Baluarte de Santíago** ① *Francisco Canal y Gómez Farías, Tue-Sun 1000-1630, US$2.20*, a bastion that once formed part of the city walls, contains a small pre-Hispanic gold collection recovered from a wreck. The market on the Salvador Díaz Mirón triangle (Ignacio Allende/Miguel Alemán/Hernán Cortés) is a fascinating experience.

1 Veracruz

➡ **Veracruz maps**
1 Veracruz, page 398
2 Veracruz centre, page 400

| 500 metres | **Sleeping** | Mar y Tierra 3 | **Eating** |
| 500 yards | Lois 2 | Mocambo 1 | Doña Carmen Pardiños 3 |

The **Museo de la Ciudad** ① *Zaragoza 397, Mon-Sat 1000-1800, free,* has a good, well-displayed collection of photographs; it traces the history of Veracruz from the Conquest to 1910. Plazuela de la Campana, by Serdán and Zaragoza, is an attractive small square where locals like to dance in the evenings. The **Museo Carranza** ① *Malecón, Tue-Sun 0900-1700, free,* has photos of the Revolution, the life of Carranza and his battles against the Huerta regime. The **Museo Histórico Naval** ① *Gómez Farías and Morales, Tue-Sun 0900-1700, free,* has an excellent and extensive collection of naval memorabilia, especially from the 1914 resistance to US invasion. Back on the zócalo, the **Fototeca** ① *www.fototecadeveracruz.org, Tue-Sun 1000-1900,* has interesting temporary photographic exhibits and is worth a look.

On the way to Mocambo beach, where Bulevar Avila Camacho meets Bulevar Ruiz Cortines, is the **Museo Agustín Lara (La Casita Blanca)** ① *US$2, free on Sun,* a must for anyone interested in Mexican popular music. It was the home of the greatest 20th-century Mexican songwriter, Agustín Lara, who wrote more than 700 songs (*Solamente una vez, Veracruz, Granada* and *María Bonita* among the most famous), many of which still reverberate around the streets and squares of Veracruz. A pianist plays Tuesday to Saturday 1100-1400, 1600-1900; at other times visitors are welcome to play Lara's piano.

Zona Hotelera and Boca del Río
The high-rise and heavily sanitised Zona Hotelera skirts the shores south of the downtown area. The beaches along this stretch of waterfront, and the sea, are polluted

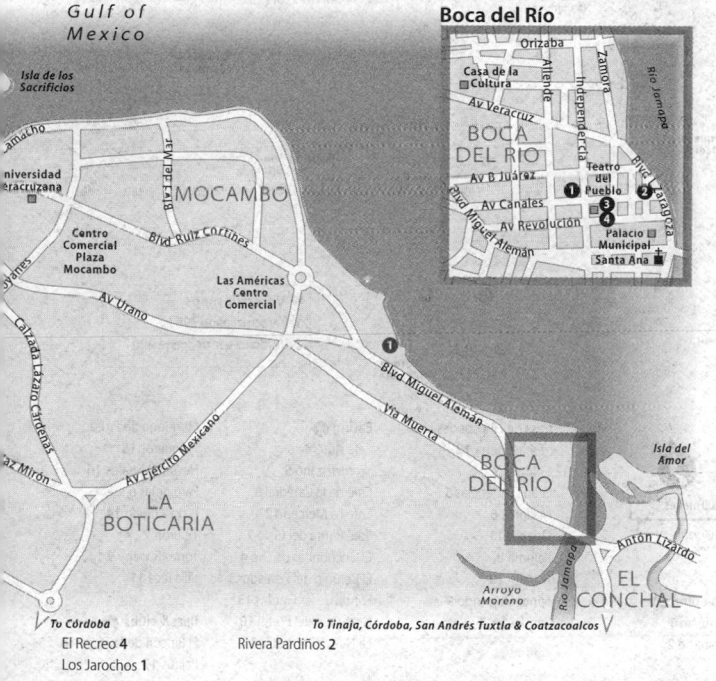

El Recreo **4**　　　　Rivera Pardiños **2**
Los Jarochos **1**

from the heavy shipping. A short bus ride from the fish market takes you to **Mocambo** beach, which has a superb, 50-m swimming pool (with restaurant and bar), restaurants, Caribbean-style beach huts and dirty sand; the water is quite a bit cleaner but still rather uninviting. There are crabs and mosquitoes and much pestering by sellers. The beach is

2 Veracruz centre

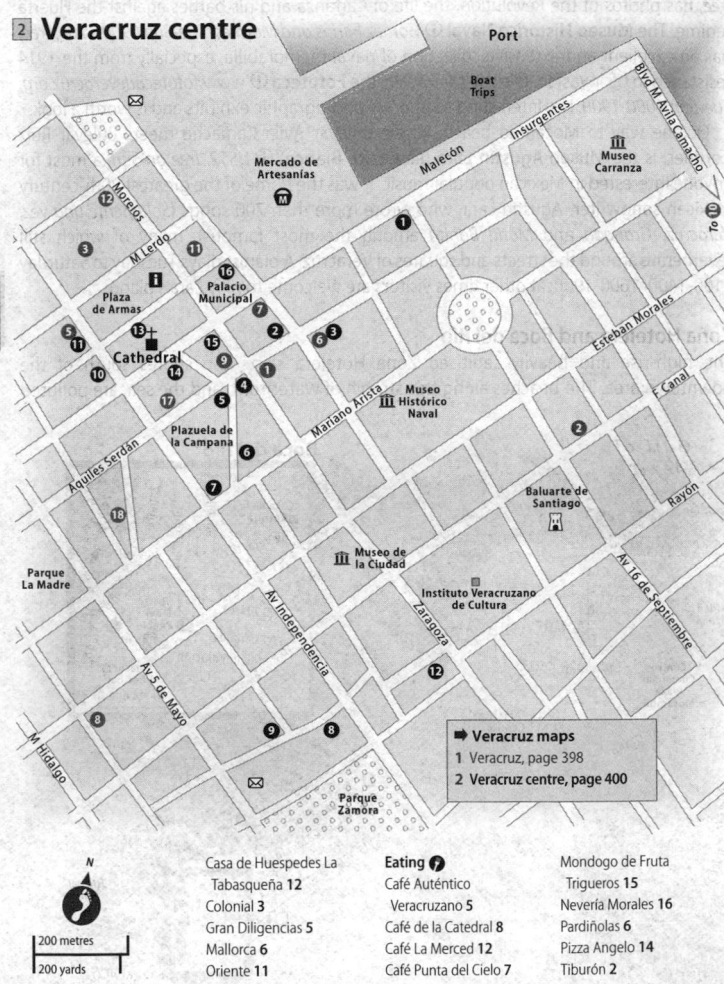

Sleeping	
Amparo 1	
Baluarte 2	
Casa de Huespedes La Tabasqueña 12	
Colonial 3	
Gran Diligencias 5	
Mallorca 6	
Oriente 11	
Paloma 8	
Royalty 10	
Santo Domingo 9	
Santander 7	

Eating	
Café Auténtico Veracruzano 5	
Café de la Catedral 8	
Café La Merced 12	
Café Punta del Cielo 7	
Chanchonitas de Oro 4	
El Refugio del Pescador 3	
Fonda de las Gordas 13	
Gran Café del Portal 10	
La Nueva Parroquia 1	
Mondogo de Fruta Trigueros 15	
Nevería Morales 16	
Pardiñolas 6	
Pizza Angelo 14	
Tiburón 2	
Tortas Royalty 9	
Villa Rica 1	

Bars & clubs	
El Rincón de la Trova 18	
Palitos 17	

200 metres
200 yards

➡ Veracruz maps
1 Veracruz, page 398
2 Veracruz centre, page 400

crowded, and at holiday time cars race up and down with music blaring. Take a bus marked 'Boca del Río' on Avenida Zaragoza.

Harbour trips are available from the Malecón. On Sunday, there are trips to **Mandinga** for cheap fresh seafood (big prawns) and local entertainment.

Some 6 km to the south of Veracruz (*colectivo* from Avenida Zaragoza) is **Boca del Río**, beyond Mocambo, on the left bank of the mouth of Río Jamapa. In 1518, the Spaniard Grijalva gave the already existing settlement the name of Río de Banderas as the inhabitants carried small flags in order to transmit messages. Worthy of a visit is the church of Santa Ana (1716). Modern buildings of interest include the Palacio Municipal, Teatro del Pueblo and the Casa de la Cultura, but most people come to Boca del Río to eat at one of its many fish restaurants.

A 10-minute bus ride from Boca del Río to the other side of the river is **El Conchal**, a small residential development overlooking picturesque lagoons with a number of attractive restaurants. The bus continues along a low sandy spit to Punta Antón Lizardo, where there is a small village with a few beach restaurants and good sand and bathing.

Papaloapan region ●❶❷❸❹ ▶▶ *pp405-417. Colour map 3, C5/C6.*

Route 180 heads southeast from the port of Veracruz along the flat, wet coastal plain through Alvarado and on the Tuxtla mountains and the Isthmus of Tehuantepec. An alternative route is to turn inland through the fertile Papaloapan region and on south into the State of Oaxaca. **Puerto Alvarado** is a modern fishing port 1½ hours south from Veracruz by bus, none too pleasant for women on their own as there are many bars and drunks. Crossing the **Río Papaloapan** (Butterfly River) by a toll bridge along Route 180 leads to the sugar-cane area around Lerdo de Tejada and Angel R Cavada. At **El Trópico** shop a dirt road turns left to some quiet beaches such as Salinas and Roca Partida.

Tlacotalpan → *Colour map 3, C6. Phone code: 288.*

About 15 km from Alvarado, Route 175 crosses the over the Río Papaloapan at Buenavista, and heads southwards to the town of Tlacotalpan where the Papaloapan and San Juan rivers meet. This small town, once the main town in southern Veracruz, and an important international port in the steamship era, is regarded as the centre of Jarocho culture. It has many picturesque streets with one-storey houses all fronted by stuccoed columns and arches painted in bright colours. The fusion of Spanish and Caribbean traditions are preserved as a UNESCO World Heritage Site. There are two churches in the zócalo, the Parroquia de San Cristóbal and the Capilla de la Candelaria, and a Casa de las Artesanías on Chazaro, 1½ blocks from the zócalo. The **Museo Salvador Ferrando** ① *US$1.50*, contains interesting local 19th-century paintings, furniture, artefacts and Jarocho costume. The **tourist office** ① *T884-2050, Mon-Fri 0800-1400, 1500-1900, Sat and Sun 1000-1400,* is on the main plaza.

Otatitlán

Another 40 km, beyond Cosamaloapan, is a ferry to Otatitlán, also on the east bank of the river (US$0.25, leaves when enough people). The town, also known as **El Santuario**, dates back to early colonial times. Its houses have tiled roofs supported by columns, but most interesting is the church. The priest maintains that the gold-patterned dome is the largest unsupported structure of its kind in Mexico, measuring 20 m wide and 40 m high.

Tuxtepec is the natural place for a stay in the Papaloapan area. It is an important supply centre in the State of Oaxaca, a large commercial city, untouristed and tranquil. Prices here are lower than in other parts of Oaxaca. The region has significant agricultural activity with local industries including a sugar mill, brewery and paper mill. The city is built on the left bank of the Río Santo Domingo. Avenida Independencia runs along the riverfront and has the market, shops and several miradors with good views. A small ferry crosses the river from below the viewpoint next to **Hotel Mirador**. The people of Tuxtepec consider themselves more *jarochos* (ie from the State of Veracruz) than *oaxaqueños*; the mixture of the music and exuberance of Veracruz with the food and handicrafts of Oaxaca is fascinating. The **tourist office** ① *Cámara Nacional de Comercio Serytour, Libertad esq Allende, opposite Parque Benito Juárez, T287-875 0886, Mon-Fri 0900-1400, 1700-2000, Sat 0900-1300,* has limited information.

Parque Benito Juárez, the main plaza, has a monument to the mother and child, an ample Palacio Municipal to the south, and a modern cathedral to the east. Further west is Parque Hidalgo, with a statue of the father of Mexico's Independence. The modern **Casa de la Cultura** is on Daniel Soto by Bulevar Benito Juárez.

Around Tuxtepec

The **Presa Miguel Alemán**, a lake formed by the Miguel Alemán and Cerro de Oro dams, is very scenic. There are several points of access, the most widely used being that of **Temascal**, a small town near the Alemán dam, with shops and a few places to eat.

The road west of Tuxtepec towards the State of Puebla is quite scenic; along it are a number of towns and villages that maintain an indigenous flavour, *huípiles* and crafts can be found here, especially on market day. The road is paved as far as **Jalapa de Díaz** and then continues to **San Bartolomé Ayautla** and **Huautla de Jiménez**. **San Lucas Ojitlán** is a Chinantec town, 42 km from Tuxtepec, with a hilltop church dominating the surroundings.

Jalapa de Díaz is 70 km from Tuxtepec, near the base of Cerro Rabón, a mountain with a spectacular 500-m sheer cliff face. The town is built on several small hills, with the church on the highest.

Tuxtepec to Oaxaca

The road from Tuxtepec to Oaxaca, Route 175, is a spectacular steep and winding route, cars need good brakes and it is reported to be difficult for caravans and cyclists; the latter are recommended to take a bus. It is mostly a paved road, but sections near the high passes can at times be badly potholed and rutted. The ride up from Tuxtepec to Oaxaca takes six to seven hours, a bit less in the opposite direction. From Tuxtepec, at 30 m above sea level, the road climbs 30 m gradually to Valle Nacional (see below). Just after crossing the Río Valle Nacional it climbs steeply into the Sierra Juárez, reaching the El Mirador pass (2900 m) in 2½ hours. The transition from lush lowland forest to pines is splendid, there are lovely views of the ridges and valley far below (sit on the right if travelling south to Oaxaca). From here the road drops in two hours to Ixtlán de Juárez and San Pablo Guelatao, the birthplace of Benito Juárez (gas station, restaurants). The route continues to drop to the dry valley of the Río Manzanillo, at 1500 m, before climbing again to La Cumbre pass (2700 m), from which there are fine views of Oaxaca below, one hour further.

Valle Nacional Set in the beautiful valley of the Río Valle Nacional, 48 km south of Tuxtepec, the small town of Valle Nacional (Colour map 3, C5, altitude: 60 m) sees few visitors, but offers basic services and excellent opportunities for birding and walking in the surrounding hills. The town is laid out along the main road; there is a gas station at the Tuxtepec end. Nearby are several rubber plantations (for example just across the bridge on the road to Oaxaca) and tappers may be seen at work early in the morning, especially in the dry season. This area had a horrific reputation as the 'Valle de los Miserables' in the era of Porfirio Díaz, for political imprisonment and virtual slavery.

Los Tuxtlas ⊜🖉🖴🖸 ➻ *pp405-417. Colour map 3, C6.*

Back on the coastal Route 180, southeast of Alvarado and the Papaloapan, is Tula where there is a spectacular waterfall, **El Salto de Tula**; a restaurant is set beside the falls. The road then climbs up into the mountainous volcanic area of Los Tuxtlas, known as the Switzerland of Mexico for its mountains and perennial greenness.

Santiago Tuxtla → *Colour map 3, C6. Phone code: 294.*

This pleasant town of colonial origin is set on a river. In the main square is the largest known Olmec head, carved in solid stone, and also a museum, **Museo Tuxtleco** ① *Mon-Sat 0900-1800, Sun 0900-1500, US$2.50, tourist info available,* containing examples of local tools, photos, items used in witchcraft (*brujería*), the first sugar-cane press used in Mexico and another Olmec head. There is dancing to *jarana* bands in the Christmas fortnight. In June and July, dancers wear jaguar masks to perform the *danza de los liseres*.

Travellers with plenty of time, could also consider a trip to the archaeological site of **Tres Zapotes**, to the west of Santiago Tuxtla. It is reached by leaving the paved road south towards Villa Isla and taking either the dirt road at Tres Caminos (signposted) in the dry season (a quagmire May to December), or in the wet season access can be slowly achieved by turning right at about Km 40, called Tibenal, and following the dirt road north to the **museum** ① *daily 0900-1700, US$2 (if it is closed, the lady in the nearby shop has a key).* The site, once the centre of the Olmec culture, is a 1-km walk (the bus cannot reach Tres Zapotes if rain has swollen the river that the road has to cross). At the museum there is an Olmec head, also the largest carved stela ever found and stela fragments bearing the New World's oldest Long Count Date, equal to 31 BC. In this region of Mexico there are other Olmec sites at Cerro de las Mesas, Laguna de los Cerros and San Lorenzo Tenochtitlán.

San Andrés Tuxtla → *Colour map 3, C6. Phone code: 294.*

A further 15 km beyond Santiago lies San Andrés Tuxtla, the largest town of the area, with narrow winding streets, bypassed by a ring road. It has a well-stocked market with Oaxacan foods such as *carne enchilada* (spicy meat) and *tamales de elote* (cakes of maize-flour steamed in leaves). It is the centre of the cigar trade. One factory beside the main road permits visitors to watch the process and will produce special orders of cigars (*puros*) marked with an individual's name. The **tourist office** is at the Palacio Municipal.

Catemaco ●○●●● ➤➤ pp405-417. Colour map 3, C6.

➔ *Phone code: 294.*

Catemaco town is famed for its traditional *brujos* (sorcerers) who have become a great tourist attraction. The first Friday of March sees a grand convention of sorcerers from around the region. Catemaco is a pleasant town with a large colonial church and picturesque setting on the lake, 13 km from San Andrés Tuxtla (irregular bus service). There are stalls selling handicrafts from Oaxaca, and boat trips out on the lake to see the shrine where the Virgin appeared, the spa at Coyamé and the Isla de los Monos (boat owners charge US$30-35 per boat). The **Isla de los Monos** is home to a colony of macaque monkeys introduced from Thailand for the University of Veracruz. Launches to the island charge US$12.50, or you can pay US$3.20 to be rowed there by local fishermen – cheaper and more peaceful. At Easter time many people camp on the beach, however for most of the year it is not recommended because of the potential for assaults and robberies.

Around Catemaco

The **Reserva Ecológica Nanciyaga** ① *T294-943 0808*, 7 km round the northern shore of the lake, has rainforest with rich birdlife, including toucans. The film *Medicine Man*, with Sean Connery, was filmed using the ecological park as a 'jungle' backdrop.

Catemaco to Playa Hermosa

The Gulf Coast may be reached from Catemaco along an 18 km road to **Sontecomapan**, crossing over the pass at Buena Vista and looking down to the *laguna* where, it is said, Francis Drake sought refuge. The village of Sontecomapan lies on an entry to the *laguna* and boats may be hired for the 20-minute ride out to the bar where the *laguna* meets the sea. A large part of the lagoon is surrounded by mangrove swamp, and the sandy beaches, edged by cliffs, are almost deserted except for local fishermen and groups of pelicans. Beaches such as **Jicacal** and **Playa Hermosa** are accessible to those who enjoy isolation.

Coatzacoalcos, Minatitlán and around ●○ ➤➤ pp405-417. Colour map 3, C6.

➔ *Phone codes: Coatzacoalcos 921; Minatitlán 922.*

The road from Catemaco heads south to Acayucan then east to Minatitlán and Coatzacoalcos. The latter is the Gulf coast gateway for the Yucatán Peninsula, 1.5 km from the mouth of its wide river. It is hot, humid and lacking in culture. The beach is dangerous at nights, do not sleep there or loiter. Minatitlán, the oil and petrochemical centre, is 39 km upriver. The road between the two towns carries very heavy industrial traffic and both cities are often under a pall of smog. There is a high incidence of lung disease. Not many foreigners visit either town, but there are hotels and restaurants in both places should you choose to stay.

Acayucan, at the junction of Highway 180 and 185, makes a great place to stop if you're driving from Mexico City to points south. There's not a great deal to do, apart from wander the streets, watch the municipal game of basketball, log on in an internet café, or watch a movie, but it's a decent town.

About 40 km east of Coatzacoalcos, on a side road off Route 180 is **Agua Dulce**, where there is a campground (see Sleeping, below). Further east along the Gulf coast is **Sánchez Magallanes** (turn off Route 180 at Las Piedras, 70 km from Coatzacoalcos, signposted), a pleasant, friendly town where you can camp safely on the beach.

State of Veracruz listings

For Sleeping and Eating price codes and other relevant information, see Essentials pages 45-48.

Sleeping

Orizaba p390

B-C Trueba, Ote 6 No 485 and Sur 11, T272-724 2730, www.hoteltrueba.com. A large, modernist building with 1960s decor. They have 5 floors, with services including business centre, bar, coffee shop and car rental. Rooms are well equipped with cable TV, internet access and room service. Breakfast included in the price.

C De France, Ote 6, No 186, T272-725 2311. This charming 19th-century building has clean, comfortable rooms and a reasonable restaurant. Friendly.

D América, Ote 6, No 269. Very friendly and good value. Simple and economical.

Córdoba p391

A Hotel Layfer, Av 5 No 908, between Calle 9 y 11, T271-714 0099. A 4-star hotel with swimming pool, gymnasium, video games, restaurant, bar and secure parking. Rooms are comfortable and have a/c and cable TV. Highly recommended.

B Mansur, Av 1, No 301, y Calle 3, on square, T271-712 6000, www.hotelmansur.com.mx. Rooms have cable TV, hot water, a/c, cable TV, room service. The restaurant serves breakfast only. Wi-Fi in the lobby and terrace.

B Virreynal, Av 1 No 309 and Calle 1, T271-712 2377. A good central spot on the main plaza. There are 2 good restaurants and rooms have Wi-Fi, hot water, phone and a/c.

C Iberia, Av 2 No 919, T271-712 1301. The best of the budget options with good-value clean rooms around a central courtyard, with Wi-Fi and cable TV. Recommended.

E Hotel los Reyes, Calle 3 No 10, T271-712 2538, losreyes@prodigy.net.mx. Good, clean comfortable budget lodgings with fan, cable TV, hot water. Some bathrooms are bigger than others. Some have comedy

showers that soak everything. Get a quieter interior room, if possible.

Xalapa p391

Cheaper hotels are up the hill from the market. Town centre hotels are generally noisy, but there's plenty to choose from and they're generally good value.

L-AL Misión Xalapa, Victoria y Bustamante, T228-818 2222. A large, modern and comfortable hotel, some 5-10 minutes from downtown Xalapa. They have attractive grounds and a good restaurant. A mixture of rooms and suites.

AL-A Mesón del Alférez, Zaragoza y Sebastián Camacho 2, T/F228-818 6351, www.pradodelrio.com. Charming colonial rooms with wooden beams and tasteful, hand-crafted furniture. They have 18 rooms (**A**) and 5 excellent suites (**AL**). Services include cable TV, phone, safe, restaurant, parking, Wi-Fi and laundry. Recommended.

B María Victoria, Zaragoza 6, T228-818 6011, www.hotelmariavictoriaxalapa.com. A large, reasonably modern business hotel with a marbled lobby, comfortable rooms, good restaurant, bar and meeting room.

B Salmones, Zaragoza 24, T228-817 5431. The carpet on the stairs is a bit tired and shabby, but the rooms are very comfortable and spacious with lots of light, good sinks, bathrooms and kitsch details. Some have balconies and mountain views. They have a good little restaurant serving comida del día, sandwiches, breakfasts and snacks.

C Limón, Av Revolución 8, behind the cathedral, T228-817 2204, hotellimon@prodigy.net.mx. Lots of echo and noise from the hallways, but otherwise not bad for budget lodgings. Rooms are smallish, attractively tiled, with good hot showers and TV. Some have nice views.

C México, Lucio 4, T228-817 3365. Clean and simple motel-style place with parking. Rooms are straightforward and comfortable enough; some have views.

C Principal, Zaragoza 28, T228-817 6400. Although it could use a lick of paint, a lot of the rooms at this hotel aren't bad. Check to see a few, because they're all different. Wi-Fi in the lobby.

D Plaza, Enríquez 4, T228-817 3310. Rooms are clean and bright, all have private bath and TV, although some mattresses look a bit tired. Clean, safe and friendly, with a good view of Pico de Orizaba from the roof. Not bad. Recommended.

D-E Hostal de la Niebla, C Gutiérrez Zamora No 24, T228-817 2174, www.delaniebla.com. A good budget choice with 6 bed single-sex dorms (**E**) and private rooms (**D**). They have hot water, internet, kitchen, fridge and lockers. Discounts for HI members. Tourist information available.

Around Xalapa *p392*
Coatepec
LL-AL Posada Coatepec, Hidalgo 9, T228-816 0544, www.posadacoatepec. com.mx. A very old, beautiful colonial house with antique furnishings and a sumptuous central courtyard complete with bubbling stone fountain and an old carriage. The lovely big rooms have double glazing and elegant details. The restaurant serves seafood. There's bikes for rent, jacuzzi, sauna, massage and a beautiful pool. Good, but a little overpriced.

AL-A El Retoño Ecolodge, Calle Tlanalapa s/n, T228-816 1428. A very decent, environmentally conscious project with bird-watching platforms, spa facilities and workshops in paper-making, ceramics and yoga. Wooden cabins are clean and cosy and surrounded by nature. A plethora of tours available including coffee and birding trips.

C-D Angelina Carolina, Nicolas Bravo 108, T228-816 3863. Quiet, friendly and brightly painted. Rooms are simple and good, equipped with TV and hot water. King-size rooms (**D**).

Perote
B Hotel Central, near plaza, T228-825 1462. Quiet and friendly, with bath and TV.

D Gran Hotel, on plaza. Basic, with only limited water.

Papantla *p392*
B El Tajín, Nuñez and Domínguez 104, T784-842 0121, hoteltajin@hotmail.com. Clean, straightforward rooms with hot water, cable TV, a/c and writing desks. The rooms with 2 beds are better. Services include parking, 2 restaurants and a recreation centre with pool. Drinking water and room service available.

B Totonocapan, 20 de Noviembre y Olivo, T784-842 1220, www.hotelsenpapantla.com. Clean and fine, with hot water, TV, a/c and bar-restaurant. Some rooms have interesting views. Good value.

C-D Hotel Pulido, Enríquez 205, T784-842 0036. Basic, spartan lodgings with hot water and parking. Cheaper rooms have fan (**D**), others have cable TV and a/c (**C**). Long-term stay available, if for some strange reason you should require it.

D México, Obispo de Las Casas y Núñez (opposite *Cine Tajín*), T784-842 0086. Basic. One of the cheapest in town.

Poza Rica *p396*
AL Poza Rica, 2 Norte, between 10 and 12 Ote, T782-822 0112. A friendly Best Western with reliable service and fairly comfortable rooms. Good restaurant.

B-C Salinas, Blv Ruiz Cortines 1905 y Cazones, T782-822 0706. Good rooms with a/c and TV. Services include restaurant, pool and secure parking.

C Nuevo León, Av Colegio Militar, T782-822 0528, opposite market. Spacious rooms, fairly clean and quiet. Recommended.

D Fénix, 6 Norte (near Av Central Ote), T782-822 3572. Basic, but one of the better cheap places.

Camping
Trailer Park Quinta Alicia, Km 84, T232-321 0042. Very clean, plenty of shade in the palms. Helpful and friendly.

Coast road to Veracruz *p396*
C Casa de Huéspedes Malena, Av Carlos Prieto, Tecolutla. Pleasant, clean rooms.
C Hotel Malinche, La Antigua. Quiet, laid-back and peaceful.
D Los Buhos, Tecolutla, close to the beach. Very good rooms with hot shower and TV.

Camping
Torre Molino trailer park, 16 km from Nautla on coastal Route 180 (towards Veracruz). Electricity, sewage disposal, hot showers, pool, on beach. Recommended.

Veracruz *p397, maps p398 and p400*
High season runs Jul-Oct. Prices can drop by 10-40% at other times of the year. The zócalo is very lively at night, so rooms overlooking the square can be noisy.

Downtown
LL-L Gran Hotel Diligencias, Independencia 115, on the zócalo, T229-933 0280, www.granhoteldiligencias.com. A very historic and comfortable hotel that's easily the best of the plaza lodgings. Rooms are tasteful and comfortable, and there's a wide range of services including business centre, pool, gym, jacuzzi, Wi-Fi and bar. Superb restaurant.
AL Colonial, on zócalo, T229-932 0193, www.hcolonial.com.mx. A long-standing zócalo option with terrace, solarium, parking, pool, restaurant, Wi-Fi and tourist services like car rental. Good and helpful, if slightly past its prime. Significant low season discount.
A Baluarte, opposite the small fort of Baluarte, Canal 265, T229-932 5222, www.hotelbaluarte.com.mx. Good, clean, efficient rooms, all located around a central courtyard and equipped with TV, phone and a/c. Services include pool and restaurant. Recommended.
B Mar y Tierra, Figueroa y Malecón, T/F229-931 3866, www.hotelmarytierra.com. Close to downtown with the best bay views in Veracruz. Friendly and helpful, with a restaurant serving good breakfasts. Good low-season discount.

B Santander, Landero y Coss 123, T229-932 4529. Recently remodelled, with good, clean rooms and pleasant bed spreads. Top-floor rooms are slightly nicer. 46 rooms in total, all with a/c, bath and TV. Very clean.
B-C Royalty, Abasolo 34, T229-932 3988, www.hotel-royalty.com.mx. A Large, average quality hotel near the beach and 20 mins walk from the zócalo. Rooms are comfortable, but the hotel can be noisy as it caters mainly to student groups. Good value in the low season. Cheaper with fan (**D**).
C Amparo, Aquiles Serdán 482, T229-932 2738, www.hotelamparo.com.mx. Clean, economical rooms with fan, cable TV, insect screens and hot water. Friendly and good value. Parking available. Recommended.
C Casa de Huéspedes La Tabasqueña, Av Morelos 325, T229-931 9437. All rooms have a fan, 2 have a/c. The upper rooms are less good, front rooms are noisy, and some have no windows. Cheap, clean, safe and helpful, if simple and slightly shabby.
C Mallorca, Aquiles Serdán 424, T229-932 7549. Basic rooms with bath, fan and radio. Very clean and highly recommended.
C Oriente, M Lerdo 20, T/F229-931 2490. Simple rooms, clean and spacious, with a/c, cable TV, phone and bath. Some have noisy street balconies, others have fan. Wi-Fi and drinking water in the lobby. OK.
C-D Impala, Orizaba 658, T229-937 1257. Straightforward rooms with bath, cold water and mosquitoes, but clean. Near bus station.
D Paloma, Av Morales y Reforma, T229-932 4260. Clean, basic and friendly. Good value, the choice of itinerant hippies.
D Hotel Santo Domingo, Serdán 481, T229-931 6326. Good, if small, budget rooms with reliable hot water, Wi-Fi and fan. Friendly, but very noisy at night.

Zona Hotelera
Upmarket lodgings are concentrated in the Zona Hotelera, most are quiet and sterile, but usually with access to a beach.
L-AL Hotel Lois, Ruiz Cortines 10, T229-937 8290, www.hotellois.com.mx. A slick, modern

high-rise hotel perched on the coast.
107 rooms and 17 suites, all comfortable
and well equipped. A plethora of facilities
include gym, sauna, squash court,
car rental, parking and pool.
LL-AL Mocambo, Calzada Ruiz Cortines 4000,
south of the port on Playa Mocambo, T229-
922 0200, www.hotelmocambo.com.mx. A
1930s palace on the beach with good service
and a reputable restaurant. Rooms are large
and comfortable, well equipped, many with
good ocean views. Highly recommended.

Tlacotalpan *p401*
B Posada Doña Lala, Carranza 11, T288-884
2580, www.hoteldonalala.com. Centrally
located on the zócalo, this hotel has
comfortable rooms with a/c and TV,
cheaper with fan. A good restaurant too.
B Tlacotalpan, R Beltrán 35, T/F288-884
2063, hoteltlacoptalpan@tlaco.com.mx.
Clean, good-value rooms around a central
courtyard, with bath and a/c. There's also
a restaurant. Good value.
D Reforma, Carranza 2 (sometimes known
as **Viajero**), T288-884 2022. Good budget
lodgings, if a little grubby. Some rooms
have good views.
D-E Jarocho, Carranza 22. Seedy, but large
rooms in an old house. A good view of town
from the roof.

Tuxtepec *p402*
B El Rancho, Avila Camacho 435, T287-875
0722, elrancho@prodigy.net.mx. Rooms
with a/c. Services include pool, restaurant,
parking. Recommended.
B Hacienda, Blv Benito Juárez 409, T287-875
1500. A/c, restaurant, pool, gardens, parking.
B-C Playa Bruja, Independencia 1531, T287-
875 0325. With a/c, pool, cafeteria, parking.
C María de Lourdes, 5 de Mayo 1380, T287-
875 0410. A/c, cheaper with fan, hot water,
good parking. Recommended.
C-D Tuxtepec, Matamoros 2 corner of
Independencia, T287-875 0934. A/c or fan,
hot water, restaurant, good value.
Recommended.

D-E Casa de Huéspedes Ocampo, Ocampo
285 y Libertad. With bath, fan, friendly.
E Catedral, Guerrero, near zócalo, T287-875
0764. Very friendly, fan and shower.

Santiago Tuxtla *p403*
B Castellanos, on Plaza, T294-947 0300.
Clean, comfortable rooms with hot shower.
There's a pool too. Recommended.
C Estancia Olmeca, No 78 on main highway
just north of **ADO** office, T294-947 0737.
Clean and friendly, with parking.
D Morelos, Obregón 13 and Morelos,
T294-947 0474. Family-run, quiet and
nicely furnished.

San Andrés Tuxtla *p403*
Expect good reductions in low season.
A Del Parque, Madero 5, T294-942 0198,
www.hoteldelparque.com. The best place
in town. Del Parque has comfortable rooms
with a/c, cable TV, phone, bath and Wi-Fi.
Very clean, with a good restaurant too.
B Hotel de los Pérez, Rascón 2, T294-942
0777. A newish hotel with clean, comfortable
rooms, Wi-Fi, parking and a/c.
C Posada San José, Belisario Domínguez 10,
T294-942 1010, close to plaza. Run by a lovely
family and staff, this hotel has comfortable
rooms with cable TV, hot water and a/c,
restaurant and pickup truck for excursions,
as well as a 2nd hotel at Monte Pío. Rooms
with fans are slightly cheaper.
C San Andrés, Madero 6, just off plaza,
T294-942 0604. The economical rooms here
aren't bad. They're clean and equipped with
a/c and cable TV, slightly cheaper with fan.
The restaurant is OK, with Wi-Fi to check
your emails. Parking.
D Figueroa, Pino Suárez 10, T294-942 0257.
In better shape than its neighbour, Figueroa
has straightforward rooms with hot water,
fan and cable TV, just 1, a triple, has a/c (**A**).
Parking and tourist information.
E Colonial, Pino Suárez opposite **Figueroa**,
T294-942 0552. Faded and run-down, but not
without character. Rooms have bath and hot
water. The lobby is filled with dozens of plants.

Catemaco *p404*

There are a number of hotels at the lakeside. High season runs Jul-Aug and Dec.

A-AL La Finca, just outside town, T294-947 9700, www.lafinca.com.mx. A luxury resort hotel and spa with treatments like temazcal steam baths, massages and mineral mud baths. It has a beautiful setting on the lake, with comfortable rooms that are often full at the weekend. There's also a pool, restaurant and café, although the food and service are poor, reportedly.

A Catemaco, on main square, T294-943 0203, hcatemaco@yahoo.com.mx. This hotel has old and new sections, Wi-Fi, a pool, cigar shop and restaurant. Rooms are comfortable and equipped with TV, bath and phone. Low-season reductions are available, just ask.

A Los Arcos, Madero 7, T294-943 0003, www.arcoshotel.com.mx. A good little hotel with pleasant, clean, comfortable rooms, Wi-Fi, cafeteria, pool and parking. Significant reductions in low season.

B Del Brujo, Ocampo y Malecón, T294-943 0071. This hotel has definitely seen better days and could use a bit of remodelling. However, rooms are spacious and equipped with noiseless a/c. Some have good balconies overlooking the lake. Friendly.

B-C Juros, Playa 14, T294-943 0084. A fine, clean, motel-style place with a pool. Will allow trailers and use of parking. A good deal when staying in rooms with fan (**D**). Hot water, TV and a/c as standard.

C Acuario, corner of plaza, T294-943 0418. Family atmosphere at this friendly hotel. Rooms have a/c, hot water and fan. Parking.

E San Francisco, Matamoros 26, T294-943 0398. Friendly little cheapie with rooms in 2 separate buildings, all with TV and hot water. Basic, but good and clean. Some have a/c (**D**).

Camping **Solotepec trailer park** by the lake on the road to Playa Azul. US$6.50 per vehicle, very clean. Recommended.

Coatzacoalcos, Minatitlán and around *p404*

B Kinaku, corner of Ocampo and Victoria, Acayucan, T924-245 0016. Clean, modern rooms, with a/c and TV. Restaurant and pool.

C Ritz, Acayucan, a better deal, has many new rooms, with good showers, a/c, TV, very clean, spacious and comfortable.

Camping **Rancho Hermanos Graham**, Agua Dulce. Nice location, full hook-up, cold showers, US$6.50 for car and 2 people.

🍴 Eating

Orizaba *p390*

In the market, try the local morning snack, *memelita picadita*.

♥ Radha's, on Sur 5 between Ote 1 and 3. Indian vegetarian restaurant serving excellent *comida corrida*.

♥ Romanchú, main street. Excellent international cuisine.

♥ Crazy Foods, opposite **Hotel de France**. Good and cheap, nice sandwiches.

Córdoba *p391*

♥♥♥-♥♥ Cantábrico, Calle 3, No 9, 1 block from zócalo, T271-712 7646. Excellent meat and fish dishes, fine wines and good service, 'worth a trip from Mexico City'. Highly recommended.

♥♥♥-♥♥ Portal de la Jaiba, on the zócalo. Mostly seafood with some meats, snacks and pastas. Specialities include paella and octopus. Breakfasts are cheapish. The bar upstairs, **La Divina Comedia**, is good for an evening tipple.

♥♥♥-♥♥ Zevallos, on the zócalo. The smartest place on the plaza with crisp table cloths, superb views and attentive staff.

♥♥-♥ Las Delicias, Av 2 No 307, between C3 and C5. Economical breakfast packages and Mexican staples. Clean, with bright table cloths and slack, even unhelpful service. Several city-wide branches.

Cafés and bakeries
La Colonial, Calle 5 y Av 2. A good selection of cakes, sweet rolls and breads. There are many other bakeries on the surrounding streets, most serve hot coffee too.

Xalapa *p391*
There are several good cafés on Carrillo Puerto for good-value *comida corrida*.
†††† Le Bistrot, Miguel Palacio 1. Closed Mon. Expensive French and international cuisine including fondues, peppered steak, quiche Lorraine, snails and crème brulée.
††††-†† La Casona del Beaterio, Zaragoza 20. A tastefully restored colonial-style house with patios, fountain and historic photos of Xalapa. They serve various seafood and meat dishes, economical comida del dia and breakfasts. The food is OK, but nothing great.
†††-†† Tango, Pánuco 7. Mon-Sat 1330-0030, Sun 1330-1800. Tasty Argentine food including meat cuts to delight any carnivore. There's live music most nights and tango on Fri.
†† La Fonda, Callejón Diamante 1. Atmospheric Mexican restaurant serving traditional food in vibrant surroundings. Popular.
††-† La Parroquia, Zaragoza 18, and another on Av Camacho. A big dining hall where *café lechero* is served with typical flamboyance. Similar menu and prices as the famous restaurant of same name in Veracruz.
† La Sopa, Callejón Diamante 3a. Economical locals' haunt serving Mexican staples.
† Mi Tierra, Enríquez 24. Greasy taco joint with giant spit-roasted meats, *tortas* and other quick, cheap, filling fare that probably tastes better after several beers.

Cafés, ice-cream parlours and juice bars
Calí Cafe, Callejón Diamante. Coffee house that's always buzzing with arty types.
Angelo Casa de Té, Primo Verdad 21A. Interesting herbal teas, cakes and snacks.
Tepoz Nieves, Enríquez, between Revolución and Clavijero. Ice creams and fruit juices.

Around Xalapa *p392*
Coatepec
In Coatepec there are several good cafés and restaurants around the main plaza.
†††-†† Casa Bonilla, Juárez 20 esq Cuauhtémoc. Award-winning restaurant renowned for its delicious and varied langostine dishes. It's worth coming to Coatepec just to eat here.
†† Arcos de Belem, Lerdo 9. A pleasant place on the plaza with faded murals and open windows. They serve breakfasts, seafood and regional dishes, including trout.
†† El Tío Yeyo, Degollado 4. *Trucha* (trout) is the speciality of the house here, with over 2 dozen preparations. Good wine list, and an interesting interior filled with plants and *artesanías*.

Papantla *p392*
Lots of little locals' places. Dive in.
†††-†† Mesón del Quijote, Serdán 700. Smartish place with good wines and spirits, steaks, cuts, paella and salmon. Well-staffed, tidy and clean.
††-† El Totonaco, Núñez y Domínguez 104, inside Hotel Tajín. Buffet breakfasts every day for US$5 and an à la carte menu that includes spaghetti, *milanesa* and *mariscos*. A nice, clean restaurant. The hotel's other restaurant, **La Parroquia**, is also good, serving cuts of meat, fajitas and Mexican fare.
††-† Sorrento, zócalo. Covered in decorative tiles and serving good, cheap seafood and *comida corrida*. Recommended.
† Taquería del Parque, Artes y Azuela. Open-front joint serving tacos and Mexican fast food.

Poza Rica and south to Veracruz *p396*
† Café Manolo, 10 Ote 60 y 6 Norte, Poza Rica. Good breakfast.
† Lonchería El Petrolero, Plaza Cívica 18 de Marzo y Av Central Ote, Poza Rica. Excellent bread baked on premises, popular with locals.

Veracruz *p397, maps p398 and 400*

Downtown
In the main market, Cortés y Madero, there are cheap restaurants in the mezzanine. *Toritos* are a local drink made of egg, milk, fruit and alcohol, delicious and potent. If you eat outside, expect an array of hawkers to approach you.

₮₮₮ Villa Rica, on the zócalo. The most upmarket seafood restaurant in Veracruz, with a branch in the Zona Hotelera too, where Bill Clinton once dined. The one in the plaza is very smart, with great views and atmosphere. Recommended.

₮₮₮-₮₮ Gran Café del Portal, Independencia and Zamora, open 0700. An historic, grand old dining hall just off the zócalo and under the arches. They serve breakfasts, cordon bleu chicken, filete mignon and an array of seafood including *filete a la Veracruzana*, prawns and whole fish.

₮₮ Café de la Catedral, Ocampo 202. An interesting and unpretentious eatery with lots of fascinating local colour and pavement seating. Try the fish stuffed with shrimps.

₮₮ Café La Merced, Rayón 609. Another big Veracruz dining hall with lots of character. The menu has lots of meat dishes as well as Mexican snacks, seafood and *tortas*. Popular.

₮₮ Chanchonitas de Oro, Serdán and Morelos. An unpretentious seafood joint. They breakfasts too.

₮₮ La Nueva Parroquia, on Malecón, is famous throughout Mexico (it used to be called Café La Parroquia, on Plaza de Armas). 2 coffee houses in same block, very popular, with excellent coffee, good food and lots of atmosphere. You haven't been to Veracruz until you've been here, or so they say.

₮₮ Pardiñolas, Plazuela de la Campana. Locals' joint that serves oysters among other fresh seafood offerings. Outdoor seating offers great views of the evening's entertainment (see Entertainment, below).

₮₮ Pizza Angelo, Molina, behind the cathedral. When you've had enough of seafood. Take-away available.

₮₮ Tiburón, Landero y Coss 167, corner of Aquiles Serdán, 2 blocks from zócalo. An interesting place, run by 'Tiburón' González, the 'Rey de la Alegría', or 'Rey Feo' of carnival; the walls are covered in pictures of him and his *comparsas*, dating back to at least 1945. The food is good and inexpensive too. The restaurant was being remodelling during our last visit, but should be reopen soon.

₮₮-₮ El Refugio del Pescador, Serdán and Landero y Cos. The gastronomic plaza occupies the old fish market and is a great place to sample good, fresh seafood with the locals. Recommended.

₮ Fonda de las Gordas, on the zócalo. A good, clean, economical eatery that's popular with locals. They serve *gorditas*, enchiladas and other snacks.

₮ Tortas Royalty, Ocampo 215. Cheap *tortas* and fast food from this hole in the wall.

Cafés, bakeries and ice cream parlours
Café Auténtico Veracruzano, off Plazuala de la Campana. A low-key coffee shop that often has chess players at its tables outside.
Café Punta del Cielo, Independencia and Arista. Modern and slightly pretentious coffee shop with a vast array of hot and cold caffeinated drinks, tasty snacks and cookies. In the vein of corporate franchises.
Mondogo de Fruta Trigueros, Morelos and Molina. Fresh fruit smoothies and snacks.
Nevería Morales, Zamora, between Zaragoza and Landero y Cos. Just one of a few ice cream parlours on this stretch of road.

Boca del Río *p399*
Boca del Río is famous for its relatively cheap and decent seafood.

₮₮₮-₮₮ Doña Carmen Pardiños, Canales and Zamora. A large dining establishment with crisp white tablecloths and well-dressed musicians.

₮₮ El Recreo, Revolución and Zamora. Under the arches, this seafood restaurant is good for watching the lazy activity on the plaza.

₮₮ Rivera Pardiños, Zaragoza 127. Good-value seafood including fillets stuffed with prawns and served a la Veracruzano. Generally quiet, with few hawkers approaching the outside seating.

₹₹-₹ Los Jarochos, Independencia, between Juárez and Canales. Seafood, *tortas*, breakfasts and *comida del día*.

Tlacotalpan *p401*

₹₹-₹ Brisas de Tlacotalpan, one of several good fish restaurants with terraces on the riverfront.

₹₹-₹ La Flecha. Excellent *sopa de mariscos* and *jaiba a la tlacotalpina* (crab).

Tuxtepec *p402*

₹₹ El Estero, Benito Juárez by Independencia. Fish dishes and local cuisine. Excellent.

₹₹ La Tablita, Matamoros 2. Good *comida corrida* and à la carte. Long hours.

₹₹ Taquería Gambrinos, 5 de Mayo 438, 1½ blocks from Parque Juárez. Excellent tacos, very popular, busy every evening.

₹₹ Villa de Carvajal, Muro Blv esq Nicolás Bravo, on the riverfront. Seafood and grill.

₹₹-₹ Los Caporales, Independencia 560. Good-value *comida corrida* and à la carte.

₹ La Mascota de Oro, 20 de Noviembre 891. Cheap and very friendly.

San Andrés Tuxtla *p403*

₹₹ La Carreta, near the town centre, otherwise known as **Guadalajara de Noche**. It appears small from the outside but is large and pleasant inside. Well recommended. Sells *tepache*, a drink made from fermented pineapple, similar in flavour to cider, and *agua de jamaica* (hibiscus juice).

₹₹-₹ Caperucita, Juárez 108. Delicious home-cooked food prepared with love. They serve breakfasts, lunches and seafood, but specialize in snacks like enchiladas, tacos and gringas. Try the *misantleca*, a salsa-topped fried tortilla filled with ham and cheese. Drinks include coffee, hot chocolate and amazing *licuados*. Good value and highly recommended.

₹₹-₹ Refugio La Casona, Madero 18. Tasty Mexican food and lush garden.

₹₹-₹ Winni's, Madero 10, on the plaza. A very popular spot for breakfast, with a range of good-value *menú del día*. Some outdoor seating, good for people-watching.

Catemaco *p404*

Despite what some locals may tell you, *carne de chango* is not monkey meat. It's smoked pork.

On the promenade are a number of good restaurants. The best value are those not directly on the lake. At the rear of the market are some inexpensive, good restaurants serving *comida corrida* for US$2-2.50.

₹₹₹ El Fiorentino, Malecón s/n, near the ADO terminal. Tue-Fri from 1830. The pasta at this slightly pricey Italian restaurant is good. Skip the pizzas and tiramisu.

₹₹ Café Catemaco, Carranza 8, on the plaza. A great spot for morning coffee and breakfast. They've got Wi-Fi, so you can check your emails too.

₹₹ Jorge's, Malecón s/n, next to La Ola. One of the better malecón restaurants, serving breakfasts, chicken and *pescado* as you like.

₹₹ La Ola, Malecón s/n. Fish fillets, shrimp cocktails, barbeque chicken and carne de chango. OK, but not amazing. Nice owners and a big deck overlooking the water.

₹₹ Pizzeteria, Malecón s/n, under **Hotel de Brujo**. Open Wed-Sat, evenings only. A humble little pizza joint.

₹₹-₹ La Casita, Matamoros 64. This good, clean, open-air eatery serves decent economical food.

₹₹-₹ La Casona, Aldama 4. Home-cooked Mexican fare including breakfasts, meat, chicken and fish dishes. Nice interior with Mexican art and plants. You can hear the birds first thing in the morning.

Coatzacoalcos, Minatitlán and around *p404*

Soyamar, Guerrero 23, Acayucan. Good vegetarian snack option.

🎭 Entertainment

Xalapa *p391*
Bars and clubs
Xalapa's large student population ensures there's plenty of vibrant night-life.
Catedral, Leandro Valle 3. This popular place fills up with students and beer-guzzlers each evening. They sell coffee during the day.
Café Lindo, Primo Verdad 21. A café by day and a bustling watering hole by night, popular with students and often featuring live music.
Cubanías, Callejón González Aparicio, an alley off Primo Verdad. A busy little joint that's good for a mojito, Cuban snacks and meeting local students. Lots of other bustling places nearby.
Kbar, Camacho 54. Fancy a sing along? Then check out this popular karaoke bar.

Veracruz *p397, maps p398 and 400*
Bars and clubs
Most discos and night-clubs are located in and around the Zona Hotelera. Several places have been recommended, including **Coralinos**, **City Bamba** and **La Comedia**. Drinking in the town centre can be an interesting experience, often coloured by raucous local characters. Head for the zócalo and the portales and see where the evening takes you.
El Rincón de la Trova, Callejón de la Lagunilla, an alley off Serdán. Great live trova music, dancing and Cuban food.
Palitos, Tlapacoyan and Serdán. Busy, young, downtown bar with screens and jukebox, occasional drunken crooning and live music of the pop-rock variety. Ladies free Tue-Wed. Slightly sketchy.
Plazuela de Campana. Each night the plaza fills with locals who dance to live music. Pure 1950s ambience. Fantastic.

✹ Festivals and events

Veracruz *p397, maps p398 and 400*
Feb/Mar The Shrovetide carnival is said to be Mexico's liveliest. The carnival starts a week before **Shrove Tue** and ends on Ash Wed; Sat-Tue are the main days with parades. At this time of year it can be very difficult to find accommodation or transport.

Tlacotalpan *p401*
31 Jan There is a well-known **Candelmas** fiesta here, when accommodation is impossible to find.

Tuxtepec *p402*
Jun The **fiestas patronales** in honour of St John the Baptist are held 24 and 25 Jun. There are fairs, fireworks and dances, including the *flor de piña* folk dance for which the Papaloapan region is well known.

▲ Activities and tours

Xalapa *p391*
Rafting is available with a number of operators, including:
Amigos del Río, Chilpancingo 205, T228-815 8817, www.amigosdelrio.com.mx. Established rafting operation with offices in Xalapa and Jalcomulco.
Expediciones Mexico Verde, Carretera Jalcomulco-Coatepec Km 4, T279-832 3734, www.mexicoverde.com. A rafting and adventure resort around 40 mins from Xalapa, just outside the town of Jalcomulco.
Viajes de Aventura, Jalcomulco, T279-832 3655, www.viajesdeaventura.com.mx. All-inclusive rafting trips including stays at their comfortable resort facilities. Based outside Xalapa in Jalcomulco.

Veracruz *p397, maps p398 and 400*
Diving
Mundo Submarino, Camacho 3549, T229-980 6374, www.mundosubmarino.org. Day and night dives, snorkelling trips and various diving courses available, including PADI and NAUI certification.

Tour operators
Harbour tours and trips to the islands depart from the malecón every hour or so.

Amphibian, Lerdo 117, inside **Hotel Colonial**, T229-931 0997, www.amphibian veracruz.com. Adventure and eco-tours throughout the state of Veracruz, including birdwatching, hiking, rafting, diving, climbing and cycling, among others. English spoken. **Tranvías**, T229-817 3425. Musical trolley bus tours of the city, departing from the zócalo every hour and usually quite rowdy in the evenings.

Tuxtepec p402
Boating and fishing
The Papaloapan River and its tributaries, as well as the Presa Miguel Alemán, offer plenty of opportunities for watersports. Motor-boating and rowing are popular on the rivers and artificial lake; races are held in May.

The most common fish species are *robalwo* (sea bass), *mojarra* (carp), and on the Río Tonto (Puente de Caracol) *sábalo* (tarpon).

Rodeo
Tuxtepec has a *lienzo charro* with capacity for 5000 spectators, where rodeos are held; this is an important regional tradition.

⊖ Transport

Orizaba p390
Bus To **Córdoba**, every ½ hr, 40 mins, US$2. To **Mexico City (TAPO)**, 15 daily, 4 hrs, US$19. To **Oaxaca**, 3 daily, 0105, 1010, 1740, 4½ hrs, US$21. To **Puebla**, 13 daily, 2 hrs, US$11. To **Veracruz**, between every 30 mins and hourly, 2½ hrs, US$9. To **Xalapa**, 10 daily, 4 hrs, US$12.

Córdoba p391
Bus Bus station is at the end of Av 6. To **Mexico City (TAPO)**, huly, 5 hrs, US$20. To **Oaxaca**, 4 daily, 5½ hrs, US$22. To **Orizaba**, every ½ hr, 40 mins, US$2. To **Puebla**, every ½ hr, 3 hrs, US$12. To **Veracruz**, every ½ hr, 1½ hrs, US$8. To **Xalapa**, 10 daily, 3 hrs, US$11.

Xalapa p391
Air
There is a small airport serving a few national destinations, 15 km southeast of the city.

Bus
Local Buses marked 'Xalapa' or 'Museo' run north to the **Anthropology Museum**. To reach nearby towns of **Coatepec** and **Xico** take a bus from Mercado Los Sauces, 2 km south of the city centre on Circuito Presidentes. From the bus station, buses marked 'Centro' will take you into town from nearby Av 20 de Noviembre, just downhill from the terminal. To return, take a 'Camacho-CAXA-SEC' bus from Camacho or Hidalgo.

Long distance Bus station, CAXA, is on the outskirts. To **Coatzacoalcos**, 11 daily, 6-8 hrs, US$25. To **Mexico City (TAPO)**, hourly, 5-6 hrs, US$22. To **Poza Rica**, 18 daily, 5 hrs, US$16. To **Papantla**, 11 daily, 4½ hrs, US$14. To **Puebla**, 11 daily, 2½ hrs, US$12. To **Veracruz**, frequent, 0500-2300, 2 hrs, US$7. To **Villahermosa**, 5 daily, 8-10 hrs, US$33.

Papantla p392
Bus ADO terminal, Juárez 207, 5 blocks from centre, T228-842 0218. To **Mexico City (Norte)**, 6 daily, US$19, 6 hrs. To **Poza Rica**, hourly, 45 mins, US$1.70. To **Tuxpan**, 7 daily, 2 hrs, US$5. To **Veracruz**, 6 daily, 4 hrs, US$13. To **Xalapa**, 11 daily, 4½ hrs, US$15.

Many services to local destinations, including **El Tajín**, buses leave when full. Occasional minibus to El Tajín from southwest corner of zócalo, unreliable schedule about every 1-1½ hrs. Transportes Urbano-TUSPA buses for **El Tajín** leave from office on 16 de Septiembre near Obispo de las Casas (US$0.50).

Taxi Taxi rank on Enríquez between 5 de Mayo and zócalo, and on Juárez.

Poza Rica and south to Veracruz *p396*

Air

Airport **El Tajín**, 3 km south of Poza Rica, T782-822 2119; several flights daily to **Mexico City**.

Airline offices Aeromar, T782-824 3001. **AeroMéxico**, Av 6 Norte No 8, 1st floor, Local 102, Edif Anabel, T01-800-021-4010.

Bus

Local El Tajín, buses leave every 20-30 mins, 0700-2000, from behind Monumento de la Madre statue, marked 'Chote' or 'Chote Tajín'. Ask driver for Las Ruinas, US$0.50, 20-25 mins, most go to the entrance. **Barra de Cazones**, Transportes Papantla or Autotransportes Cazones, 1 hr, US$1.20 (often waits 30 mins in Cazones on way back until bus fills). It is not always necessary to go to bus station to catch your bus: buses to Barra de Cazones pass through the centre along Blv Cortines.

Long distance All buses leave from new terminal referred to as **ADO**, about 1.5 km from centre. Take white bus from centre, or taxi. Terminal is divided into ADO (T782-822 0085, also office in centre, 6 Norte opposite **Hotel Fénix**, open daily) and all others, good facilities, tourist office.

To **Mexico City**, almost hourly, 5 hrs, US$17. To **Tampico**, every ½ hr, 4-5 hrs, US$20. To **Pachuca**, 0250 and 1340, 4½ hrs, US$11. To **Papantla**, almost hourly, 1 hr, US$1.70, bus may be caught on Av Central Ote by Plaza Cívico 18 de Marzo. To **Tecolutla**, 7 daily, 1¾ hrs, US$4. To **Tuxpan**, hourly, 1 hr, US$1.70. To **Veracruz**, hourly, 4-5 hrs, US$15. To **Xalapa**, 15 daily, 4-5 hrs, US$16.

Veracruz *p397, maps p398 and 400*

Air

Airport **Las Bajadas (VER)**, 12 km from the centre, several flights daily to the capital and flights to coastal cities. Flights also to **Houston**, **San Antonio** and **Havana**.

Airline offices AeroMéxico, Bolívar No 952, T229-937 1765. **Mexicana**, Av 5 de Mayo y Aquiles Serdán, T229-932 2242.

Bus

The majority of buses are booked solid for 3 days in advance throughout summer and holiday periods; at other times queues of up to 2 hrs possible at Mexico City booking offices of bus companies (best company: **ADO**). Book outward journeys on arrival in Veracruz, as the bus station is some way out of town and there are often long queues. Referred to as **ADO** the bus station is divided into 1st and 2nd class; the 1st-class part, mostly **ADO** company, is on the main street, Díaz Mirón y Xalapa, T229-938 2968; **Autobuses Unidos**, mostly 2nd class, is on Lafragua y Xalapa (2 blocks from ADO), T229-937 2376.

For local buses, get accurate information from the tourist office. Buses to the main bus station along Av 5 de Mayo, marked **ADO**, and from the station to the centre, blue and white or red and white buses marked Díaz Mirón, pass 1 block from the zócalo, US$0.50, or *colectivos*, also US$0.50. Taxi to **ADO** terminal from centre, US$3.

To **Catemaco**, 9 daily, 3½ hrs, US$9. To **Córdoba**, every ½ hr, 1½ hrs, US$8. To **Mexico City**, hourly, 0600-0200, 5-6 hrs, US$30. To **Mérida**, 4 daily, 14-18 hrs, US$59-71. To **Oaxaca**, 3 daily, 0800, 1515, 2230, 7 hrs, US$30. To **Orizaba**, every ½-1 hr, 2½ hrs, US$9. To **Papantla**, 6 daily, 4 hrs, US$13. To **Puebla**, 12 daily, 3½ hrs, US$18. To **San Andrés**, 14 daily, 3 hrs, US$8.50. To **Santiago Tuxtla**, 9 daily, 2½ hrs, US$8. To **Tampico**, every 1-2 hrs, 9½ hrs, US$30. To **Tapachula**, 2 daily, 1345 and 1830, 13-15 hrs, US$56. To **Tuxpan**, 13 daily, 6 hrs, US$17. To **Villahermosa**, 18 daily, 6-8½ hrs, US$30. To **Xalapa**, frequent, 24 hrs, 2 hrs, US$7.

Connections with Guatemala

For Guatemala take bus to Tapachula and then from the border into Guatemala City; quicker than the much more mountainous route further north. Alternatively, take ADO bus to **Oaxaca**, then carry on to Tapachula.

Tlacotalpan *p401*
Bus

To/from **Santiago Tuxtla**, 7 daily, 1 hr 20 mins, US$4, **San Andrés Tuxtla**, 7 daily, 1½ hrs, US$5.

Tuxtepec *p402*
Air

The airport is in Loma Bonita, 36 km east on the road to Sayula. Veracruz, 165 km to the north, has the main airport in the area.

Car

The Tuxtepec–Palomares road, Route 147, provides a shortcut to the Transístmica. The road via Sayula is 20 km longer, but much safer. AU buses covering the route from Tuxtepec to **Tehuantepec**, **Juchitán** and **Salina Cruz**, take only the Sayula road.

Bus

There is a joint bus station for ADO, AU and Cuenca at Matamoros by Blv Avila Camacho. Other 2nd-class companies have their own stations.

To **Juchitán**, 3 daily with AU, 0200, 2205, 2335, 6 hrs, US$13. To **Tehuantepec**, 2 daily, 0200 and 2335, AU, 6½ hrs, US$14. To **Salina Cruz** 2 daily, 0200 and 2335, AU, 7 hrs, US$15. To **Oaxaca**, 2 daily, 2225 and 2315, 7½ hrs, US$22. To **Mexico City**, 4 daily, 7½ hrs, US$28 . To **Puebla**, 2 daily, 0630 and 2315, 6 hrs, US$20. To **San Andrés Tuxtla**, 4 daily, 4 hrs, US$9. To **Valle Nacional**, every 15 mins 0500-2100, 1 hr, US$2.50. To **Veracruz**, 5 daily, 3 hrs, US$10.

Santiago Tuxtla *p403*
Bus

Plenty of 2nd-class buses run between Santiago, San Andrés and Catemaco. Departures below are all 1st class. To **Catemaco**, 12 daily, 1 hr, US$1.70. To **Córdoba**, 1 daily, 2335, 3½ hrs, US$14. To **Mexico City** (TAPO), 2 daily, 0005 and 2235, 8h rs, US$32. To **Puebla**, 2 daily, 0005 and 2335, 5½ hrs, US$25. To **San Andrés**, 12 daily, ½ hr, US$1.20. To **Veracruz**, 8 daily,

2½ hrs, US$8. To **Xalapa**, 3 daily, 0710, 1410, 1925, 4½ hrs, US$14.

San Andrés Tuxtla *p403*
Bus

Plenty of 2nd-class buses run between Santiago, San Andrés and Catemaco. Departures below are all 1st class. To **Catemaco**, 12 daily, ½ hr, US$1. To **Córdoba**, 1 daily, 2305, 4 hrs, US$15. To **Mexico City** (TAPO), 2 daily, 2205 and 2235, 8½ hrs, US$33. To **Minatitlán**, 1845, 3 hrs, US$7.50. To **Puebla**, 2 daily, 2205 and 2335, 6 hrs, US$26. To **Santiago**, 12 daily, ½ hr, US$1.20. To **Veracruz**, 15 daily, 3 hrs, US$9. To **Xalapa**, 3 daily, 0710, 1410, 1925, 4-5 hrs, US$15.

Catemaco *p404*
Bus

Plenty of 2nd-class buses run between Santiago, San Andrés and Catemaco. Departures below are all 1st class. To **Coatzacoalcos**, 1 daily, 1915, 3 hrs, US$8. To **Córdoba**, 1 daily, 2330, 4½ hrs, US$16. To **Mexico City** (TAPO), 2 daily, 2130 and 2300, 9 hrs, US$34. To **Minatitlán**, 1 daily, 1915, 2½ hrs, US$6.50. To **Puebla**, 2 daily, 2130 and 2300, 6½ hrs, US$27. To **San Andrés**, 12 daily, ½ hr, US$1. To **Santiago**, 12 daily, 1 hr, US$1.70. To **Veracruz**, 8 daily, 3½ hrs, US$10 . To **Xalapa**, 4 daily, 0710, 1410, 1925, 4-5½ hrs, US$16

❶ Directory

Córdoba *p391*
Banks *Casa de cambio*, Av 3, facing Bancomer.

Xalapa *p391*
Banks Banca Serfín on Enríquez will change TCs in major currencies. **Santander** on Carrillo Puerto changes dollar TCs. **American Express** at Viajes Xalapa, Carrillo Puerto 24, T228-817 6535, in centre, sells cheques against Amex card. *Casa de cambio*, on right side of Zamora going down hill. Rates vary enormously, so shop around. Quick service and good rates at

Dollar Exchange, Gutiérrez Zamora 36.
Cultural centres Centro de Recreación
Xalapeño has exhibitions. El Ágora, under-
neath Parque Juárez, cultural centre with live
music, films and exhibitions. **Internet**
Serviexpress, Zaragoza 14B. Café Chat, on
Camacho opposite Parque Bicentenal,
another in shopping arcade off Enríquez.
Most charge US$2.50 per hr. **Laundry**
Several on Allende and Ursulo Galván, all
charge by weight, usually US$3 per 3 kg.
Medical services There are 2 dentists
on Ursulo Galván. The hospital is on **Nicolás
Bravo. Post office** On Diego Leño.
Telephone Long-distance phone
in shop on Zaragoza with sign outside,
others behind the government palace.

Papantla p392
Banks Bancomer and Banamex, on zócalo,
0900-1300, change cash and TCs till 1200.
Medical services Hospital Civil, Madero
518, T784-842 0094. Red Cross, T842-0126.
Farmacia Aparicio, Enríquez 103, daily 0700-
2200. **Post office** Azueta 198, 2nd floor,
Mon-Fri 0900-1300, 1500-1800, Sat 0900-1200.

Poza Rica and south to Veracruz p396
Banks Bancomer, opposite Hotel Poza Rica.
Serfín, 4 Norte y 2 Ote. **Cultural centres**
Casa de la Cultura, Guatemala 502, T782-
822 3185. **Medical services** Cruz Roja,
Blv Lázaro Cárdenas 106, T782-823 6871.
Laundry Yee del Centro, Prolongación
20 de Noviembre.

Veracruz p397, maps p398 and 400
Banks Bancomer, Independencia y Juárez,
has *casa de cambio* for dollars and TCs, good
rates, Mon-Fri 0930-1730, Sat-Sun 1100-1400.
Banca Serfín, Díaz Mirón, 2 blocks from bus
station, changes US$ cash and TCs. Banamex

is at Independencia esq Juárez. Amex agency
is Viajes Olymar, Blv Avila Camacho 2221,
T229-931 3406. La Amistad, Juárez 112
(behind the hotels on the zócalo), *casas de
cambio* rates not as good as the banks but
quicker; Hotel Veracruz changes money at
similar rates. **Embassies and consulates**
US Consular Agency, Francisco Javier Mina
No 506, T229-932 0227. **Internet** Plenty to
choose from in the downtown and tourist
areas, US$0.50-1. Networld Café, Callejón
Clavijero 173, near Francisco. Stationet, 5 de
Mayo, between Lerdo and Zamora, Mon-Sat
0900-2100. Micro Café, Ruiz Cortines, 100 m
on from Museo Agustín Lara, Mon-Sat 1000-
2300. **Laundry** Madero 616, US$4 per 3 kg,
open 0730-2300. **Post office** Main post
office by bridge to San Juan de Ulúa fortress,
a fine building inaugurated in 1902 by Porfirio
Díaz, Mon-Fri 0900-1200; also Palacio Federal,
5 de Mayo y Rayón, Mon-Fri 0800-1900.

Tuxtepec p402
Banks Bancomer, Independencia 437, cash
and TCs, 0900-1400. HSBC, Independencia
895, cash and TCs. Agencia de Divisas Greco,
Independencia 269, cash and TCs, poor rates.
Internet Tuxcom, Guerrero esq Blv Muro,
by riverfront. Tux Net, Morelos 200. **Laundry**
Lava Sec, Guerrero esq Independencia 1683
and Blv Muro, wash and dry US$5 per 4 kg.

Santiago Tuxtla p403
Banks Exchange at Banco Comermex
on Plaza, TCs 0900-1330.

San Andrés Tuxtla p403
Internet 'Ri' Chat, Constitución Norte 106.

Catemaco p404
Banks Bancomer, opposite cathedral,
open Mon, Wed, Fri 0900-1400.

The Guerrero coast

Punctuated by miles and miles of entrancing beaches, Guerrero's coastline is as alluring as it is legendary. Its intense natural beauty had made it the focus of several resort developments, Acapulco the first and foremost among them once the paragon of sun-kissed hedonism is now wanton and decayed, but its love of a great party has not abated. Further west, Zihuatanejo offers a calmer, low-key alternative to Acapulco's excesses, whilst the resort of Ixtapa is a bleak example of planned touristic development. At all these places you can partake in ocean-bound activities like sailing, sports fishing, jet-skiing and diving. And the seafood, freshly caught and prepared with all the flare and exuberance you'd expect, is delicious.

Fortunately, Guerrero's rugged topography means that it has remained, in part, relatively secluded from the world. Between the high-rise hotels and gaudy souvenir shops, there are pockets of lavish natural activity. Teeming estuaries and emerald lagoons are populated by brightly coloured birdlife, weird amphibians and carnivorous reptiles. A sublime underwater world plays host to psychedelic coral reefs, whales, dolphins and schools of tropical fish. Turtles, too, lay their eggs on Guerrero's shores.

A plethora of sleepy rural villages are home to obscure local cultures, gregarious fishermen and a way of life that hasn't changed for centuries. What better places to sling a hammock and soak up the sunset. ▸▸ *For listings, see page 425-432.*

Mexico City to Acapulco
The 406-km four-lane toll freeway from Mexico City runs west of the old highway, bypassing Chilpancingo, continuing as far as **Tierra Colorada** (where there is an exit), and on to Acapulco. It takes about 3½ hours to drive from the capital to Acapulco on the freeway, although the toll is very high.

Warning You are advised not travel by car at night in Guerrero, even on the Mexico City–Acapulco highway and coastal highway.

Chilpancingo → *Colour map 3, C4. Phone code: 747. Altitude: 1250 m.*
The journey from Mexico City to Acapulco and the Pacific coast often includes a stop-off at Cuernavaca, the 'city of eternal spring' (see page 166) and a detour to the silver town of Taxco (see page 170). Further south, beyond the Mexcala River, the road passes for some 30 km through the dramatic canyon of **Zopilote** to reach the university city of Chilpancingo, capital of Guerrero state at Km 302. There is a small but grandly conceived plaza with solid neoclassical buildings and monumental public sculptures commemorating the workers' struggle: *El hombre hacia el futuro* and *El canto al trabajo* by Victor Manuel Contreras. In the **Palacio de Gobierno** there is a museum and murals. The colourful reed bags from the village of Chilapa (see below) are sold in the market. The **Casa de las Artesanías** for Guerrero is on the right-hand side of the old main Mexico City-Acapulco highway. It has a particularly wide selection of Olinalá lacquerware. The local fiesta starts on 16 December and lasts a fortnight.

Around Chilpancingo
Olmec cave paintings can be seen at the **Grutas de Juxtlahuaca** ① *3-hr tour US$25*, east of Chilpancingo. The limestone cavern is in pristine condition; it has an intricate network of large halls and tunnels, stalagmites and stalactites, a huge underground lake, cave drawings from about AD 500, a skeleton and artefacts. Take a torch, food and drink and a

sweater if going a long way in. To reach the caves, drive to Petaquillas on the non-toll road then take a side road (paved, but poor in parts) through several villages to Colotlipa (*colectivo* from Chilpancingo, US$1.50, 1½ hours). Ask at the restaurant on the corner of the zócalo for a guide to the caves.

Acapulco ⊖❶❷▲⊖❶ ⊁ pp425-432. Colour map 3, C3.

→ *Phone code: 744.*

Acapulco, the jewel of Guerrero's coast, is slung over a wide undulating bay. Once upon a time, this was the place to be seen – a place to flaunt wealth and partake in starry cocktail parties – a place of glamour, elegance and style. But since then, this once-great international playground has been devoured by insatiable corporate interests, grotesquely overweight fast-food franchises and flocks of drunken tourists adorned in shorts, white socks, sandles and straw sombreros.

If you like to drink and dance, you can't do worse. And beyond the high-rise hotels and time-share complexes, there are glimpses of a more interesting, dignified age. Old Acapulco is home to a lively central plaza and a handful of diverting museums. And don't miss the iconic cliff-divers, who plunge from rocks as high as 45 m. The bay itself, host to a plethora of fine sandy beaches, is an assuredly seductive spectacle at night-fall. In spite of its commercialism and stench, there is still great fun to be had in Acapulco.

Ins and outs

Getting there Aeropuerto Alvarez Internacional (ACA) is 23 km east of Acapulco. Airport shuttle is US$6 one way. It is possible to find a microbus for Puerto Marquez, where you can connect with buses for Costera Miguel Alemán. A private taxi from the airport to the centre should cost US$20-25. It's worth negotiating.

There are several bus stations around town. To get to the zócalo from the main **Estrella Blanca** terminal, Central Ejido, Ejido 97, 3 km north of downtown, catch a 'Centro' or 'Caleta' bus. Estrella Blanca's other first-class terminal is located next to Parque Papagayo, Central Papagayo, Cuauhtémoc 1605; it's connected to the downtown area by 'Caleta' buses or to the Zona Hotelera by 'Río-Base' buses. **Estrella de Oro**, Cuauhtémoc 1490, has its own terminal and is located two blocks east of Parque Papagayo. Taxis can be found outside all terminals.

Getting around The most useful bus route runs the length of Costera Miguel Alemán, linking the older part of town to the different beaches and hotels. Bus stops are numbered, so find out which number you need to get off at.

Tourist information You'll find a handy municipal tourist information kiosk on the Malecón, just opposite the zócalo, with leaflets and simple maps. The **Acapulco Convention and Visitors Bureau** ① *Av Costera M Alemán 38-A, opposite Oceanic 2000, T744-484 8555, www.vistacapulco.com*, is larger and better equipped.

Sights and beaches

Acapulco has all the paraphernalia of a booming resort: swanky shops, nightclubs, red-light district, golf clubs, tennis courts, touts and street vendors. The city is divided into two broad areas. Old Acapulco, sometimes known as Acapulco Náutico, is located on the western side of the bay. This is the working heart of the city, filled with busy streets, crowded shops, people, hotels and traffic. Activity focuses on the zócalo, Acapulco's lively central plaza, populated by shady trees, tourists and occasional musicians. It is also the site of the city cathedral, built in the 1930s and dedicated to Nuestra Señora de la Soledad. It sports a mosque-style dome and Byzantine towers. East of Old Acpuclo stretches the Zona Hotelera, or Hotel Zone, also known as the Zona Dorada, replete with beaches, international restaurants and expensive hotels. This is a world away from the dirt and bustle of Old Acapulco, but the overall effect can be somewhat tacky and sterile. The two areas are joined by a single coast road that flanks the shore; Avenida Costera Miguel Alemán, also known as La Costera.

One sight that should not be missed is that of the iconic cliff divers at **La Quebrada** ① *daily at 1300, 1930, 2030, 2130 and 2230, US$2.70*, who plunge up to 45 m into the water below, timing their dives to coincide with the incoming waves. Nearby, **Hotel El Mirador Acapulco** offers a package including great views of the show, drinks and food (expensive). Don't forget to tip the divers at the end.

Close to La Quebrada is a **Diego Rivera mural** ① *Inalámbrica 6, Cerro de la Pinzona*, adorning the former home of Mexican businesswoman and philanthropist, Dolores Olmedo Patiño, who once owned the world's largest collection of Rivera paintings, now mostly housed by a museum in Mexico City.

The **Fuerte de San Diego** ① *Calle Hornitos s/n, esq. Morelos, 744-482 3828, Tue-Sun 1000-1800, museum entrance US$3*, was built in 1616 to defend the terminal for the Manila convoy from marauding Dutch and British pirates in Colonial times. It was destroyed in 1776 and rebuilt in 1783, and the last battle for Mexican Independence was also fought here. Today, the pentagonal structure has been transformed into an attractive museum of the history of Acapulco and Mexico. It has 12 exhibition rooms with objects pertaining to

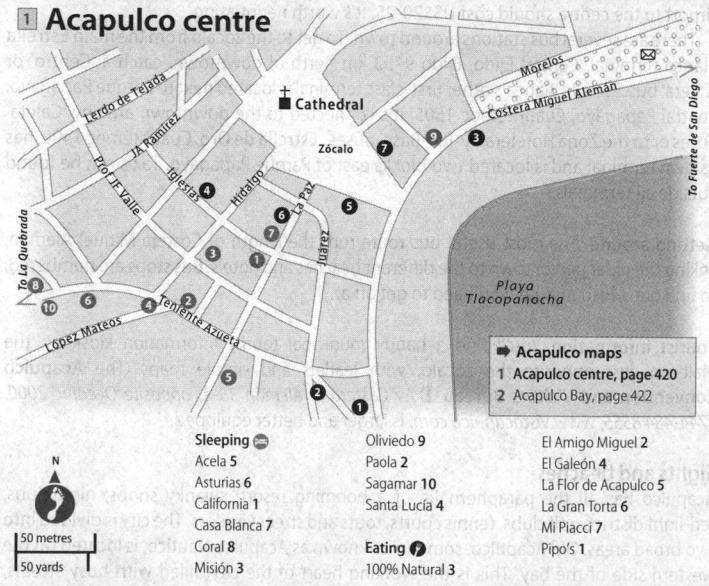

1 Acapulco centre

Cathedral

Zócalo

Playa Tlacopanocha

➡ **Acapulco maps**
1 Acapulco centre, page 420
2 Acapulco Bay, page 422

N
50 metres
50 yards

Sleeping	Oliviedo 9	El Amigo Miguel 2
Acela 5	Paola 2	El Galeón 4
Asturias 6	Sagamar 10	La Flor de Acapulco 5
California 1	Santa Lucía 4	La Gran Torta 6
Casa Blanca 7		Mi Piacci 7
Coral 8	**Eating**	Pipo's 1
Misión 3	100% Natural 3	

Spanish maritime affairs, old maps and drawings, textiles and religious artefacts. There is a sound and light show during summer evenings, and the museum is well worth a visit.

La Casa de la Máscara ① *Corredor Cultrual s/n, next to the Fuerte de San Diego, Tue-Sun 1000-1400, entrance by donation*, houses a colourful collection of masks in seven rooms – a good introduction into the exuberant world of Mexican folklore. Sadly, signs are in Spanish only. The **Jardín Botánico** ① *Av Heróico Colegio Militar 52-52, www.acapulcobotanico.org, US$2.20*, was inaugurated in March 2002, and occupies 6 ha of land in the grounds of the University. Well-marked paths snake through the boulder-strewn terrain where you will encounter several different microclimates. A range of plant life is supported, including palms, orchids, cacti, fruit trees and bromeliads. Six kilometres beyond Acapulco the Palma Sola Petroglyphs are in the 4-ha **El Veladero** ecological zone. Some 400 m above sea level, you'll get commanding views of the bay. Little is known of these stone carvings, dating 200 BC to AD 600, except that they occupy a sacred space where rituals took place. These were most likely connected with fertility and agriculture. There are 18 rocks in total, depicting everything from historical events to myths to aspect of daily life. Of course, these depictions are highly stylized and subject to interpretation. Bring water for the hike.

There are at least 20 beaches in and around Acapulco, all with fine sand. West of the zócalo, the Península de Las Playas arcs across the bay and is home to several good locations. The shielded, sickle-curved Playa Caleta and neighbouring Playa Caletilla are very popular with families. The waters are smooth, sheltered and dirty, but the sand is clean. Just off shore is the **Mágico Mundo Marina** ① *US$4.50*, on Isla Yerbabuena, with an aquarium, a swimming pool with waterchute, and a breezy bar. Also off shore is **Isla la Roqueta**, where you can practise snorkelling or kayaking, or just languish on the busy sands. Boats to Roqueta, some of them glass-bottomed, depart from Caleta every 20 minutes, US$3 return. The hidden, sheltered beach of **Playa Angosta** offers a smaller, more secluded option a short walk from Caleta. To get to the Peninsula and its beaches, walk 20 minutes from the zócalo or catch a Caleta bus from the coast road.

The majority of Acapulco's beaches, however, are slung along the shores east of the zócalo. The straight, gentle shores of Playa Tamarindo soon give way to the more popular, surf-pounded beaches of **Los Hornos** and Los Hornitos. Note the surf is sometimes dangerous and the beaches are unsafe at night. Swimmers should also look out for motorboats close to the shore. As the bay arcs around, Playa Condesa is located roughly in the centre, at the heart of the hotel zone. Beyond **Playa Icacos** (complete with marine-land amusement park) are Playa Guitarrón, flanked by wealthy vacation homes and palm trees, and the sheltered waters of Bahía Puerto Marqués. Fishing, sailing and other water-sports are popular here. Beyond, at **Playa Revolcadero**, up-scale development has blossomed, with scores of new luxury hotels, roads and carefully sculpted landscapes. This is Acapulco Diamante, now the city's most exclusive – and most soulless – neighbourhood. It is possible to reach Puerto Marqués by boat, US$3 return, or by bus from La Costera.

Coast northwest of Acapulco ●❶❷▲❸ ▶ *pp425-432.*

Pie de la Cuesta

Some 12 km northwest of the city, Pie de la Cuesta is preferred by many travellers to Acapulco, but it is also commercialized. There are several bungalow-hotels and trailer parks, a lagoon, and long, clean, sandy beaches. Here, you can swim and fish year-round, drink delicious *coco loco* (fortified coconut milk) and watch the sunsets from your hammock. If Acapulco's hedonistic sprawl isn't to your taste, here is a recommended alternative.

Just beyond town, **Laguna Coyuca** (also known as La Barra or Laguna Pie de la Cuesta), over 10 km long, has interesting birdlife, water hyacinths and tropical flowers. These can be explored by motorboat, or by tour. **Coyuca de Benítez**, near the Laguna Coyuca, is a market town selling exotic fruit, cheap hats and shoes. Pelicans fly by the lagoons, there are passing dolphins and plentiful sardines. Locals are now trying to protect the turtle eggs that young boys (and dogs) like to hunt.

The lesser travelled stretches of Guerrero's Costa Chica reach southeast from Acapulco as far as the state border with Oaxaca. The shores here are almost completely undeveloped and you will need your own vehicle – or at the very least a tent, a good map and some degree of patience – to fully explore them. If you're looking for beaches, **Playa Ventura**, close to the village of **Copala**, is possibly one of the best, home to a handful of cheap, basic lodgings. **Ometepec** is a peaceful colonial town that also has basic hotels, good for breaking a journey. If you're interested in the region's Afro-Mestizo inhabitants, their population is concentrated in one of the region's largest settlements, **Coajinicuilapa**, where you will find a local museum dedicated to their culture and history.

Acapulco to Zihuatanejo: La Costa Grande

Guerrero's Costa Grande, or 'Big Coast', is a sublime stretch of Pacific shoreline punctuated by placid lagoons and drowsy villages. It reaches west of Acapulco for over 300 km and is

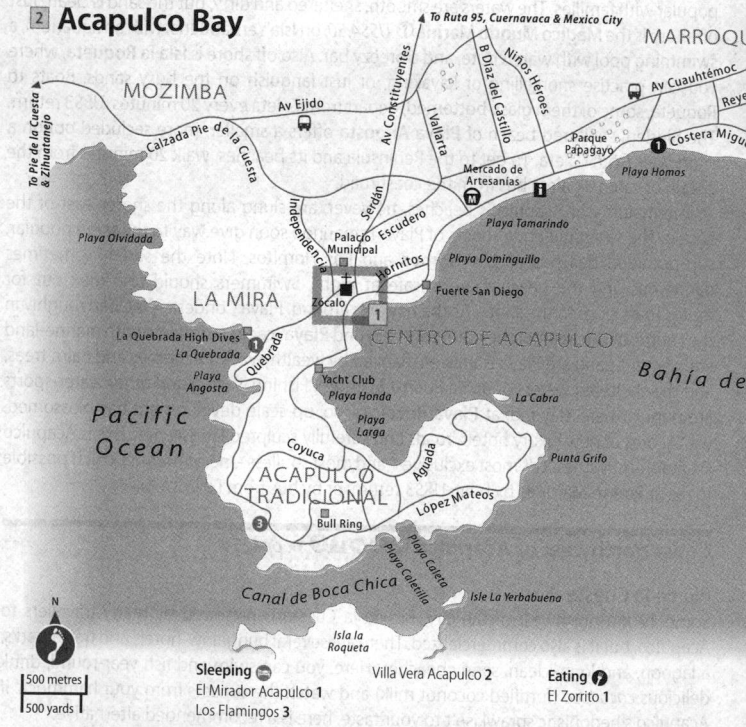

2 Acapulco Bay

Sleeping
El Mirador Acapulco 1
Los Flamingos 3
Villa Vera Acapulco 2

Eating
El Zorrito 1

home to the twin resorts of Ixtpa and Zihuatanejo, now almost a single contiguous settlement. Flanked by rolling mountains and verdant palm plantations, it is traversed by Highway 200, giving drivers access to a wealth of obscure and lesser visited attractions, including deserted beaches and luxuriant estuaries resplendent with chattering birds.

West of Acapulco, transit along coastal Highway 200 is simple, smooth and generally quite rapid. Increasingly, however, there are military checkpoints. Beyond Coyuca, the road heads inland and the first place of any real size is **San Jerónimo**, roughly 100 km west of Acapulco. Here, a detour leads to a verdant lagoon and wind-swept beaches of **Paraíso Escondido**; turn south before crossing the bridge into town and continue through the villages of **Arenal de Alvarez** and **Hacienda de Cabañas**.

Back on Highway 200, west of San Jerónimo, the next sizeable settlement is **Técpan**, capital of the municipality with the same name. Nearby there is a beach at Michigan; take a southbound detour to get there. As Highway 200 continues west, it skirts the shores of Laguna El Veinte before passing the small towns of **San Luis Pedro** and **San Luis de la Loma,** almost a single settlement. Further on, it dips briefly towards the shore, offering access to the rugged beaches of **Piedra Tlalcoyunque**, **Ojo de Agua**, and the small community of **Puerto Vincente Guerrero**.

Inland, **Papanoa** is the next sizeable settlement, followed by **Coyuquila Norte**, after which the Highway dips back to the ocean. Some of the coast here is quite rugged, and there are good surf beaches around the village of **Loma Bonita**; basic accommodation is available, ask around.

Next, the highway passes through the small town of **Juluchuca** before arriving at the more sizeable settlement of **Petatlán**. Just beyond town, a turning heads to the village of **Soledad de Maciel**, also known as La Chole, site of an important pre-Hispanic settlement. Archaeologists have uncovered some pyramids, plazas and a ball court here. Back on Highway 200, you will pass a string of small settlements before arriving at Zihuatanejo. At Los Achotes is the turning for the popular fishing settlement of **Barra de Potosí**, an easy day trip from Zihuatanejo. It's a great contrast to the some of the more densely populated stretches of the Guerrero coast. Wonderfully rustic and utterly devoid of high-rise settlements, this beautiful sandy beach arcs around a vast curved bay.

Zihuatanejo

Once little more than an obscure fishing village, the low-key beach resort of Zihuatanejo is an increasingly popular alternative to overdeveloped Acapulco. It owes much of its fame and prosperity to its

To Ruta 95, Cuernavaca & Mexico City
Paseo del Farallón
LAS CUMBRES
tólicos
La Diana
Alemán
ACAPULCO MODERNO
COSTA AZUL
Zona Hotelera
Playa Condesa
Farallón del Obispo
La Redonda
Convention Centre
Playa Icacos
CV/Ci Recreation Centre
Acapulco
COLONIA ICACOS
Punta del Guitarrón
Naval Base
Carretera Escénica
PLAYA GUITARRÓN
To Puerto Márques, Playa Revolcadero & Airport
Playa La Paloma

➡ **Acapulco maps**
1 Acapulco centre, page 420
2 **Acapulco Bay, page 422**

Bars & clubs 🎧
Baby O **2**
Disco Beach **3**

less attractive neighbour, Ixtapa, a planned resort that brought unprecedented wealth and attention to the area. But despite being spruced up, 'Zihua', as it is called locally, retains much of its Mexican village charm. For now, it remains reassuringly quiet, low-rise, laid-back and friendly. Perched inside a sheltered bay, the town centre is compact and

Zihuatanejo

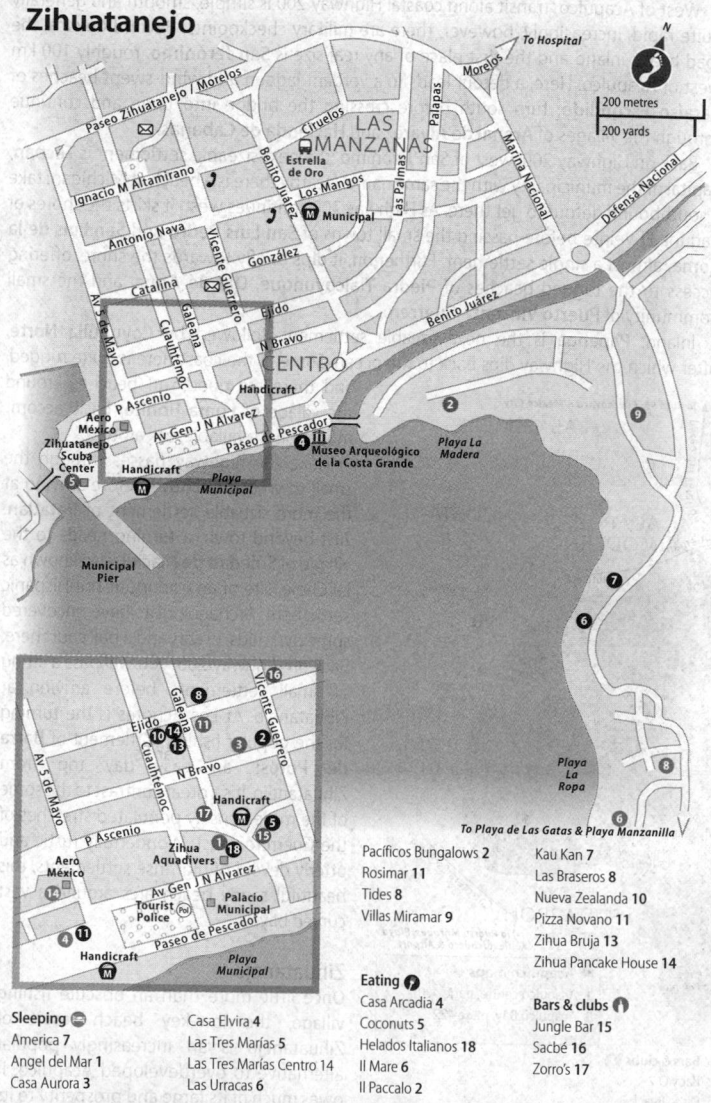

Sleeping
America **7**
Angel del Mar **1**
Casa Aurora **3**
Casa Elvira **4**
Las Tres Marías **5**
Las Tres Marías Centro **14**
Las Urracas **6**
Pacíficos Bungalows **2**
Rosimar **11**
Tides **8**
Villas Miramar **9**

Eating
Casa Arcadia **4**
Coconuts **5**
Helados Italianos **18**
Il Mare **6**
Il Paccalo **2**
Kau Kan **7**
Las Braseros **8**
Nueva Zealanda **10**
Pizza Novano **11**
Zihua Bruja **13**
Zihua Pancake House **14**

Bars & clubs
Jungle Bar **15**
Sacbé **16**
Zorro's **17**

easily explored on foot. There are an abundance of gaudy souvenir shops, little art galleries, and, thanks to its burgeoning popularity, some very decent restaurants. The small **Museo Arqueológico** ① *Av 5 de Mayo, US$0.60*, in the old Customs and Immigration building, has exhibits on state history and anthropology, and at the town entrance, the **Plaza de Toros** has seasonal *corridas*. Various watersports can be pursued in Zihuatanejo, especially sports fishing, diving and snorkelling. **Tourist information** ① *T755-554 2001, Zihuatanejo Pte s/n, Colonia La Deportiva, www.ixtapa-zihuatanejo.com, Mon-Fri 0800-1600, with bilingual assistance*, can be obtained from the Palacio Municipal, 2 km northeast of the centre. There is a smaller office on Paseo de la Bahia, near Playa La Ropa, and a kiosk during high season, Alvarez s/n.

There are four beaches in the bay, starting with **Playa Principal** in the centre of town. The waters here are a bit dirty and hawkers often traipse the sands, but there are bars and restaurants too, and it can be a sociable place to enjoy a few cocktails at sunset. From here, follow the walkway to reach nearby **Playa La Madera**, also a bit unclean but relatively sheltered. Much better is **Playa La Ropa**, 20 minutes' walk away climbing the steps into hills and follow the road past the cliffs. Otherwise you can catch a bus from the centre of town. La Ropa (the clothes) derives its name from the silks that washed up here when a Chinese trading ship sunk off-shore. It is a long sandy stretch flanked by various hotels and restaurants, and is possibly the bay's best beach. But also good is **Playa Las Gatas**, secluded, sheltered, and a haven for aquatic sports.

Ixtapa → *Colour map 3, C2. Phone code: 755.*

Ixtapa, 244 km northwest of Acapulco and meaning 'where there are salt lakes', is one of Mexico's most odious resort developments. Built in the 1980s and intended as an alternative to Cancún, its modern hotels, manicured lawns and overpriced international restaurants are as unglamorous as they are devoid of soul. Unless you've got money to burn or a perverse sense of aesthetics, there's little point spending time here.

◉ The Guerrero Coast listings

For Sleeping and Eating price codes and other relevant information, see Essentials pages 45-48.

● Sleeping

Acapulco *p419, maps p420 and p422*
Downtown
Most cheaper hotels are grouped around the zócalo, especially on La Paz and Juárez. In the high season you should make reservations, at least for 1 night, before arriving. For the better hotels you can make reservations at the bus terminal in Mexico City. Take care with the numbering along the Costera Miguel Alemán; basically it means nothing, a better reference is to the beach names and major hotels.

B Misión, Felipe Valle 12, close to zócalo, T744-482 3643, hotelmision@hotmail.com. Very cool and quiet with a pleasing plant-filled patio. Rooms are comfortable, clean and tasteful, with good sinks, hot water and fan, but no TV or phone. The best ones are on the ground floor. Breakfast is served, but not included in the price.
B-C Asturias, Quebrada 45, T744-483 6548, gerardomancera@aol.com. Clean, comfortable, friendly and decent. Rooms have a/c, cheaper without (**C**), hot water and TV. Good pool and free coffee, parking available. Recommended.
B-C Paola, Teniente Azueta 16, 2 blocks from zócalo, T744-482 6243. Perfectly adequate budget lodgings with a small pool and roof terrace. Rooms have hot water, the cheapest is without TV or a/c (**D**). Very pink.

B-F Oliviedo, Costera Miguel Alemán 207, 1 block from zócalo, T744-482 1511, www.paginasprodigy.com/hotel.oviedo. acapulco. A big old 1950s building with great views from the top rooms. They have a mixture of economical (**D**) and standard (**C**) rooms, as well as dormitory beds (**F**) for backpackers. The better rooms have a/c.

C Acela, La Paz 29, T744-482 0661. Clean, blue rooms with fan, bath, cold water and TV. Family-run and friendly, and the owner speaks English. A good little budget place.

C Coral, Quebrada 56, T744-482 0756. Fading and a bit shabby, but OK. Rooms have a/c, TV, bath and fan, get one with a balcony. Beds are slightly thin and hard. There's a pool and parking outside is not entirely secure. Reasonably quiet.

C Sagamar, Quebrada 51, T744-482 9992. Basic and a bit shabby, but helpful and friendly, with some English spoken. Rooms have fan, hot water and TV. There's a small pool.

C Santa Lucía, López Mateos 33, T744-482 0441. Family owned and operated, slightly run-down, but helpful and clean. Rooms have fan, hot water, TV, bath. OK.

C-D California, La Paz 12, T744-482 2893, 1½ blocks west of zócalo. A mix of singles, double, triples, and 1 family room for 5-6 persons. The rooms are good value, simple and comfortable, equipped with fan and hot water, and surrounding a patio. The owner is a good source of information for sport fishing. English and French spoken. TV available for longer stays.

La Costa and the Zona Hotelera

The coastline north and south of downtown has a concentration of upmarket high-rise hotels.

LL Villa Vera Acapulco, Lomas del Mar 35, T744-109 0570, www.clubregina.com. Formerly a private vacation home, this 'spa and racquet club' resort has been a celebrity spot since the 1950s, where Elvis once stayed. They have some 17 swimming pools, 2 tennis courts, gym, beauty parlour and jacuzzi among their extensive facilities.

AL El Mirador Acapulco, Plazoleta La Quebrada 74, at the top next to the cliff divers, T744-483 1155, www.hotelelmirador acapulco.com.mx. Hotel with a long tradition and a great place to view the divers at La Quebrada. They have a private seawater pool (no beach), a/c, some rooms with jacuzzi, restaurant and bar.

AL Los Flamingos, Av López Mateos s/n, T744-482 0690, www.hotellosflamingos.com. One of the finest locations in Acapulco with glorious cliff-top views. In the 1950s it was a retreat for John Wayne. Facilities include gardens, pool, restaurant and Wi-Fi. Breakfast included.

A El Tropicano, Costera Miguel Alemán 20, on Playa Icacos, T744-484 1332, www.eltropicano. com.mx. A large hotel with 137 clean, comfortable rooms, all with a/c, cable TV and phone. Facilities include well-tended gardens, 2 pools, bars and restaurant. Very friendly and helpful. Recommended.

Camping

Acapulco West KDA, Barra de Coyuca. Beachfront, security patrol, pool, restaurant, hot showers, laundry, store, volleyball, basketball, Spanish classes, telephones.

Quinta Dora Pie de la Cuesta,13 km up the coast on Highway 200. *Palapas*, bathrooms, cold showers, hook-ups, US$12 for 2 plus car, US$4 just to sling hammock.

Trailer Park El Coloso, La Sabana. Small swimming pool, secure.

Trailer Park La Roca, on road from Puerto Marqués to La Sabana. Secure.

Pie de la Cuesta *p421*

Most hotels are strung along a single road and conveniently marked by big orange signs.

AL-A Casa Blanca, Playa Pie de la Cuesta 370, T744-460 0324, www.acapulco casablanca.net. Friendly place with good management. They have a range of rooms and rates, from older, smaller rooms to good new rooms with sea views. All have a/c. There's also a restaurant, pool, beach access, sun loungers and hammocks.

A-B Villa Nirvana, Playa Pie de la Cuesta, T744-460 1631, www.lavillanirvana.com. A very friendly, hospitable hotel that works with local clinics to supply children with medicine. They have a wide range of rooms, all pleasant and comfortable, including family apartments equipped with kitchens (**B**). Quiet and peaceful and good for couples, families and young people. Direct beach access, pool and restaurant. Highly recommended.

C Brisa de Oro, Playa Pie de la Cuesta, L7 Mz 56, T744-460 0829, mariocg20@ hotmail.com. Terraces with hammocks, a pool, good sea views and a restaurant under a *palapa* can be found at this small, friendly hotel. A handful of rooms have sofas and bed. OK.

C La Cabañita, Playa Pie de la Cuesta, L17, Mz 56, T744-460 0946, aca_master@ hotmail.com. A handful of basic, straightforward rooms with fan and TV, but no hot water. There's parking, pool, restaurant and a talkative parrot. OK.

Zihuatanejo *p423, map p424*
It's difficult to find accommodation during Semana Santa and around Christmas and New Year, when prices can double and the town is booked out.

A Las Tres Marías Centro, Juan Alvarez 52, T755-554 6706. An annexed and slightly pricier version of the **Las Tres Marías** on the riverside. Rooms are simple, but comfortable, and the best are on the 2nd floor. Note that prices double during Christmas holidays.

B-C Rosimar, Ejido 35, T755-554 2139. Starting to fade, but not bad. Standard rooms (**C**) have fan, hot water and TV, some have a/c (**B**), others have kitchen facilities (**B**). Clean and reasonable. Plants in the courtyard.

C Casa Aurora, Nicolás Bravo 42, T755 554 3046, www.zihuatanejo.com.mx/aurora. Clean, comfortable, straightforward rooms with fan, shared fridge and access to a microwave. Only some have hot water. Some also have a/c.

C Casa Elvira, Alvarez 29, in older part of town on waterfront, T755-554 2061. A very basic hotel with lots of lovely plants draped around the inner courtyard. Rooms are simple, but clean, with fan, bath and cold water only. The restaurant on the beach is a good place to watch the world go by. Good and reasonable, particularly for backpackers.

C-D Las Tres Marías, La Noria 4, cross the wooden footbridge, T755-554 2191. A very pleasant place with large communal balconies overlooking town and harbour. Rooms are clean but sparsely decorated, with tiny baths and cold water. You may get woken by the roosters and early morning activity on the river. Some rooms have a/c (**C**).

D-E Angel del Mar, Pedro Ascenio 10, T755-554 5084. Formerly **Angela's**, this backpacker hostel has 3 dorms with 6 beds each (**E**), and 6 private rooms with bath, hot and cold water (**D**). Facilities include kitchen, hammocks, fridge, lockers and communal room. The restaurant opposite, **Fonda Tertulia**, serves cheap *comida corrida* for a few dollars. The most economical place in town. Clean.

Playa La Madera
L Villas Miramar, T755 554 3350, www.hotelvillasmiramar.com. A comfortable 4-star hotel with rooms spread across 4 buildings. Good amenities, including a golf course, 2 pools, massage, car rentals, tours and lovely gardens.

AL-A Bungalows Pacíficos, T755-554 2112, www.bungalows pacificos.com. Advance reservation necessary. This hotel has a huge terrace with expansive ocean views, hammocks and colourful flowers, steps from the beach. The owner, Anita, is very friendly, helpful and speaks English and German. Highly recommended.

Playa La Ropa
LL The Tides, T755-555 5500, www.tides zihuatanejo.com. A highly regarded and award-winning hotel with 2 world-class restaurants, daily events, tennis courts, fitness centre and 4 pools. The rooms and beach front suites are luxurious. If you can't afford to

stay here but want a taste of the high life, you can buy a day pass for US$25 entitling you to use the bar, restaurant, sun loungers and pool. Recommended, if you can afford it.
A Las Urracas, T755-554 2049. 17 cosy bungalows with fridge, kitchen, fan, comfortable little lounges, fully equipped ovens, utensils, hot water, cold water and pleasant verandas. Friendly and good value. No a/c.

Ixtapa *p425*
Accommodation in Ixtapa is exclusively high-end.
LL Barcelo, Blv Ixtapa, T755-553 1858. www.barceloixtapa.com. A 5-star hotel with predictably high standards and a plethora of amenities including a panoramic lift and everything else you could possibly want or need. Reductions for AAA members. Recommended.
LL Las Brisas, 5-min drive from downtown Ixtapa, T755-553 2121. A vast luxury complex with contemporary architectural design and a spectacular setting in a small jungle. Services and amenities are 1st class.

Camping
Playa Linda Trailer Park, on Carretera Playa Linda at Playa Linda Hotel, just north of Ixtapa. 50 spaces, full hook-ups, restaurant, recreation hall, babysitters, on beach, US$14 for 2, comfortable.

● Eating

Acapulco *p419, maps p420 and p422*
Fish dishes are a speciality of Acapulco. There are a number of variously priced restaurants along and opposite Playa Condesa, another group of restaurants along Playa Caleta walkway, and yet another group with mixed prices on the Costera opposite the **Costa Club Acapulco** – 250 or so to choose from. Many cheap restaurants in the blocks surrounding the zócalo, especially along Juárez. As the coast road climbs south towards Las Brisas,

there are a number of restaurants with truly spectacular views (particularly after dark) over the bay.

Downtown
ⲧⲧⲧ Pipo's, Almirante Bretón 3 (off Costera near zócalo). One of the 1st-established and best restaurants in Acapulco. Fine seafood. There are 2 other branches: Costera and Plaza Canadá; and Calle Mahahual, Puerto Marqués.
ⲧⲧⲧ-ⲧⲧ 100% Natural, Costera Miguel Alemán s/n, on the bay. Excellent *licuados* and energy drinks, as well as very good pasta and Mexican dishes. All healthy and well prepared, with several branches around town. Wi-Fi. Recommended.
ⲧⲧ El Amigo Miguel, Juárez 16. Popular and often buzzing seafood haunt with a 2nd branch on the opposite side of the road. Good and clean.
ⲧⲧ El Galeón, Iglesias 8. Bar and seafood restaurant that's heavy on the nautical theme. Popular with tourists.
ⲧⲧ Mi Piaci, on the zócalo. Busy terrace on the plaza where they do average pizzas and pretty reasonable breakfasts, including a fairly tasty fruit salad with honey, yoghurt and granola. Lots of other economical packets available. Always busy with Mexican tourists. OK, but not fantastic.
ⲧ La Gran Torta, La Paz 6. Sandwiches, tacos, *tortas* and economical Mexican fare. An unpretentious locals' haunt that's often buzzing with interesting characters.

La Costa and the Zona Hotelera
The coast, and Zona Hotelera particularly, are home to an abundance of international restaurants, some good, some bland.
ⲧⲧⲧ Fairmont Acapulco Princess, Costera de la Palmas, T744-469 1000, A famous luxury hotel that lays on a Sun lunch buffet, including champagne and seafood. An event worth saving space for! Casual dress, but no shorts or jeans. Reservations on the day.
ⲧⲧⲧ Madeira, Las Brisas. Recommended for its cuisine, its atmosphere and the inspirational view.

El Zorrito, opposite the Costa Club Acapulco. Excellent local food with live music, a 2nd branch 1 block west (opposite the Howard Johnson Hotel) is open 24 hrs and very popular late after the clubs close.

Zihuatanejo p423, map p424

There are plenty of decent restaurants in Zihuatanejo, although some of them are perched on cliffs out of town, requiring a taxi or own transport to reach them. Look out for cheaper dining near and in the market.

Coconuts, Pasaje Ramírez 1, www.restaurantcoconuts.com. Established in 1979 and housed by Zihuatanejo's oldest building, this fine restaurant serves creative offerings by Australian chef David Dawson. Seafood and meat dishes include *filet in hoja* sauce, filet mignon and chargrilled pork in mango chutney. One of the best.

Il Mare, Playa Escénica Playa La Ropa. Great Mediterranean food and impeccable views of the bay.

Kau-Kan, Carretera Escéncia 7. Highly regarded gourmet restaurant serving creative international dishes and seafood. Up on the cliffs with views.

Pizza Novana, Bahía de Zihuatanejo Alvarez. Great pizzeria with red and white chequered table cloths and an attractive interior adorned with fairy lights.

Casa Arcadia, Paseo del Pescador. Cheapish seafood place. The food isn't out of this world, but it's fresh and tasty, and it's served right on the beach. One of a few similar places on this stretch. Wear mosquito repellent.

Il Paccolo, Bravo 38. Various steak cuts, pastas, pizza and fish dishes.

Nueva Zealanda, Cuaultémoc 30. Pleasant little diner with clean counter space and tables, some outside. Good coffees, breakfasts and enchiladas.

Stall 27 at marketplace. Very popular, cheap and good, try local lobster for about US$10; most meals cost around US$3.

Zihua Pancake House, Galeana and Ejido. A great breakfast spot that's popular with foreign tourists and expats.

Las Braseros, Ejido 26. Busy little joint serving Mexican food, including a wide range of tacos.

Cafés and ice cream parlours

Helados Italianos, Alvarez 28. Tasty, flavoursome Italian ice-cream.

Zihua Bruja, Galeana, between Ejido and Bravo. Owned and operated by a music and art teacher, Miguel Angel Quimiro, who gives free classes to the town's underprivileged kids. The space functions as an art and music school by day and a café by night, when there's often live acoustic music. They serve coffee, *refrescos*, cervezas and snacks.

Ixtapa p425

Villa de la Selva, T755-553 0362. Recommended for food and views, book in advance.

Two Fat & Tropical Boys, Centro Comercial Los Arcos, T755-553 0160. A popular bar/restaurant with live music and a varied menu.

Super Tacos, west of the commercial centre by the roundabout. Great hot sandwiches.

⊙ Entertainment

Acapulco *p419, maps p420 and p422*
Bars and clubs

Acapulco has a superb, varied nightlife at the weekends, and every major hotel has at least 1 disco. Others worth trying include:

Baby O, towards the naval base on Costera Miguel Alemán.

Disco Beach, Costera Miguel Alemán, between the Diana and Hotel Fiesta Americana Condesa. By the beach, informal dress – open till 0500, good.

Karaoke, close to the zocaló, famous for its Les Girls-style show on Thu-Sat at 2300.

La Casa Blanca, La Paz 8. Bar popular with locals.

Las Puertas, behind the cathedral by stairs on Ramírez, disco and live music.

Mangos, Costera Miguel Alemán, American sports-style bar, popular, food.

Zihuatanejo p423, map p424

Jungle Bar, Ramírez 6. Funky, popular bar with a young crowd, crazy decor, colourful murals and ice cold beers. Recommended.
Sacbé, Guerrero and Ejido. Youthful disco-lounge that's popular with Mexican students.
Zorro's, Ascenio and Galeana. Interesting bar with a slightly dingy ambience and incipient alcoholics. Their slogan: Hey my beer's a buck, so get in here you lazy …

Ixtapa p425

Bars and clubs
Every hotel without exception has at least 1 nightclub/disco and a bar.

▲▲ Activities and tours

Acapulco p419, maps p420 and p422

As you'd expect of a well developed beach resort, a host of watersports are available. These include jet-skiing, waterskiing, banana-boating and parasailing, with operators in the upmarket hotel zone. You can also rent masks and snorkels on the beach for a simple splash around.

Bay Cruises depart from the malecón close to the zócalo. Most cruises tend to be fun, boozy affairs, usually with a bilingual guide (but check). Try:
Acarey, malecón, opposite the zócalo, T744-482 3763. Low-season jaunts include the Sunset Cruise, departing at 1630, with live disco music, games.
Fiesta & Bonanza, Costera Alemán, Gloreita Tlacopanocha, T744-482 2055, yatesfb@ yahoo.com.mx. Romantic after-dinner cruises depart at 1630 with live music, dance party, open bar and views of the sunset.

Diving and snorkelling isn't huge in Acapulco, but there some interesting sites, including sunken ships, caves and rock formations. You might see coral, sea stars,

mackerel, sea horses, turtles, rays and whale sharks. Visibility is best Nov-Feb.
Acapulco Scuba, Paseo del Pescador 13 y 14, T744-482 9474, www.acapulcoscuba.com. 2-tank dives cost US$70 and depart 0900 daily.

Sports fishing is quite popular in Acapulco with sailfish, tuna and dorado in the waters. Smaller game includes bonito, roosterfish and mahi-mahi.
Fish R Us, Costera 100, T744-482 8282, www.fish-r-us.com. A well-established sports-fishing outfit managed by Captain Parker, who has 20 years' experience fishing the waters off Acapulco.

Zihuatanejo p423, map p424

There are some great dive sites around Zihuatanejo. Off Playa Las Gatas is an underwater wall built, according to one legend, by the Tarascan King Calzonzin, to keep the sharks away while he bathed; the wall is fairly massive and can be seen clearly. Try **Carlo Scuba**, Playa Las Gatas, T755-554 6003, www.carloscuba.com. **Zihua Aquadivers**, Alvarez 30-4, opposite the basketball court, T755-544 6666, www.divezihuatanejo.com, or **Zihuatanejo Dive Center**, La Noria 1, over the bridge, T755-554 8554, www.zihuatanejodive center.com. Dive trips include full equipment, a 2-tank trip costs around US$85; single tank costs US$65.

Fishing Boats can be commissioned from the pier, roughly US$180 for up to 4 people. Otherwise, try **Temo Sport Fishing**, Cuauhtémoc y Alvarez, T755-112 1779, temosportfishing@yahoo.com.mx.

Small-scale **kayak tours** of mangrove reserve at Laguna de Potosí with **Zoe Kayak Tours**, T755-553 0496, www.zoe kayaktours.com.

Ixtapa p425

Activities are numerous and much the same as for Zihuatanejo, above.
Adventours, Hotel Villas Paraíso, T755-556 3322. Arranges walks, cycling, sea-kayaking, birdwatching and rappelling.

Ixtapa Aqua Paradise, Hotel Barceló, Local 2, T755-553 1510, www.ixtapa aquaparadise.com. Scuba-diving; PADI diving courses, excursions and night dives.

⊖ Transport

Acapulco p419, maps p420 and p422
Air
Acapulco's **Juan Alvarez International** airport, T744-435 2060, www.oma.aero, lies 23 km southeast of the city, with direct connections to many US cities and charter flights from Europe in the summer. Good domestic connections with **Mexico City, Cd Juárez, Cuernavaca, Culiacán, Guadalajara, León, Monterrey, Puerto Vallarta, Toluca** and **Tijuana**.

Airline offices Aeromar, Blv de Las Naciones s/n, Plan de Los Amates, T744-446 9394. AeroMéxico, Av Costera Miguel Alemán, No 286, T744-485 2280. American Airlines, airport, T744-446 9232. Aviacsa, Av Costera Miguel Alemán 178, T744-481 3240. Avolar, Blv de las Naciones s/n, Poblado de los Amates, T744-466 9373. Click Mexicana, La Gran Plaza, Locales 8, 9 and 10, T744-486 7569. Continental, airport, T744-446 9063. Delta, airport, T800-123 4710. Interjet, Prolongación Farrallón y Av Costera Miguel Alemán, Centro Comercial Plaza Marbella 26, T744-484 5124. US Airways, airport, T800-428 4322.

Bus
Local Several bus routes, with 1 running the full length of Costera Miguel Alemán and linking the older part of town to the latest hotels, marked 'Caleta-zócalo-Base', US$0.50. Bus to **Pie de la Cuesta**, 12 km, US$0,60. From Ejido bus terminal to the zócalo for the 'zócalo-Caleta' bus.

Long distance There are several bus stations. Estrella Blanca has 2 1st-class terminals: **Terminal Ejido**, Ejido 97, for **Mexico City, Taxco, Puerto Escondido**,

Zihuatanejo and other coastal destinations; and **Terminal Papagayo**, Cuauhtémoc 1605, with buses for **Mexico City, Cuernavaca, Puebla, Guadalajara** and **Tijuana**, among others. Nearby, the 1st-class **Estrella de Oro** terminal, Cuauhtémoc 1490, esq Massieu, has services to **Chilpancingo, Mexico City, Taxco** and **Zihuatanejo**. The 2nd-class **Estrella Blanca** Terminal, Cuauhtémoc 97, serves mostly local destinations in Guerrero state. To **Chilpancingo**, hourly or better, 2-3 hrs, US$7. To **Cuernavaca**, 7 daily, 5 hrs, US$22. To **Mexico City**, 6 hrs, US$30-45. To **Oaxaca**, no direct bus, so take a bus to **Puerto Escondido**, 7 a day, US$24, or **Pochutla**, 5 a day, US$28; also via Pinotepa Nacional at 2100, but worse road. To **Puerto Escondido**, 7 a day, 9½ hrs, US$24. To **Tapachula**, take Impala 1st-class bus to **Huatulco**, arriving 1930; from there **Cristóbal Colón** at 2030 to **Salina Cruz**, arriving about 2400, then take 1st- or 2nd-class bus. To **Taxco**, 10 daily, 4 hrs, US$16. To **Zihuatanejo**, 4-5 hrs, hourly, US$12.

Car
Car hire many car hire outlets, especially in the Zona Hotelera. Avis, Av Costera M Alemán 139-C, T744-484 5720; Budget, Av Costera M Alemán 93, Local 2, T744 481 2433; Hertz, Av Costera M Alemán 137-A, corner of Sandoval, T744-485 8947.

Taxi
Most fares around town cost US$2-5, airport shuttle to Zona Hotelera costs around US$6 (private taxi US$20-25). Taxis are more expensive from outside bus terminals; walk ½ a block around the corner and catch one on the street, around US$3 to zócalo. Acapulco's taxis are ruthless, so take care and beware scams, rip-offs and overcharging, especially if travelling from the bus station or airport.

Zihuatanejo p423, map p424
Air
Ixtapa-Zihuatanejo international airport (ZIH), 20 km from town, T755-554 2070.

Many direct domestic flights from **Mexico City** and **Guadalajara**, with other destinations by connection. International from **Houston**, **Los Angeles**, **Phoenix**, **San Francisco** and **Seattle**.

Airline offices AeroMéxico, Centro Comercial Los Patios, T755-553 0555; **Delta** (airport), T755-554 3386; **Click-Mexicana**, Nicolás Bravo 64, T755-554 2208.

Bus

Estrella de Oro operates its own terminal on Paseo Palmar, serving **Mexico City**, with services at 0640, 2000, 2210, 2300, 9 hrs, US$45. Services to **Acapulco** (4-5 hrs) calling at Petatlán and Tecpan de Galeana, at 0600, and on the hr until 1800, US$14. To **Lázaro Cárdenas**, 0630, 0830, 0930, 1200 then hourly until 2000, 2 hrs, US$5.50.

The **Central de Autobuses** is on the Zihuatanejo–Acapulco highway opposite Pemex station (bus from centre US$0.40); **Estrella Blanca** and a range of smaller lines – **TAP Parhikuna, Turistar** and **Costa** included – operate from here. The terminal is clean, with several snackbars and services. Next door is the **Estrella de Oro** terminal.

To **Acapulco**, hourly, US$13. To **Manzanillo**, 1000, 1050, 2000, 8 hrs, US$28. To **Puerto Vallarta**, 1020 and 2235. To **Mexico City**, 12 daily with various lines, US$38. To **Laredo**, at 1730, 30 hrs, US$78. To **Lárazo Cárdenas**, hourly after 1230, 2 hrs, US$5. To **Puerto Escondido** and **Huatulco**, at 1920, 12 hrs US$25.

Car

Car hire Hertz, Nicolás Bravo and airport, T755-554 3050; several others with offices at the airport and in Ixtapa hotels including Avis, Budget, Dollar and Economy.

① Directory

Acapulco *p419, maps p420 and p422*

Embassies and consulates Canada, T744-484 1306, Local 23, Centro Comercial Marbella, corner of Prolongación Farallón and Miguel Alemán, Mon-Fri 0900-1400. **France**, Av Costera M Alemán 91, T744-484 4580. **Norway**, Maralisa Hotel, T744-484 3525. **Spain**, Av Costera Miguel Alemán, T744-435 1500. **Sweden**, Av Insurgentes 2, T744-485 2935. **UK** Edificio Hemisphere, Migel Aleman 49, T744-484 3331. **USA**, Hotel Continental, Av Costera M Alemán, T744-469 0556, 0900-1400.

Immigration Juan Sebastián el Cuno 1, Costa Azul el Lado, T744-484 9021, 0800-1400, take a 'Hornos Base' bus from Miguel Alemán, US$0.35, 30 mins, visa extensions possible. **Internet** Cafés normally charge US$1 per hr, good speeds. **Laundry** Tintorería Bik, 5 de Mayo. Lavadín, José María Iglesias 11a, T744-482 2890, next to Hotel Colimense, recommended. Various other places on the streets around the zócalo. **Post office** Costera 125, 2 blocks south of zócalo. **Telephone** Public offices will not take collect calls; try from a big hotel (ask around, there will be a surcharge).

Zihuatanejo *p423, map p424*

Banks Several around town, including Banamex, Ejido y Guerrero, Bancomer, Juárez y Bravo, Banorte, and Juárez y Ejido. **Internet** Most places charge around US$1 per hr. Try Zihuatanejo Bar Net, ground floor, Hotel Zihuatanejo, Ramírez 2, and **Infinitum Internet**, Bravo 12. **Laundry** Lavandería del Centro, Guerrero 17, US$2 for 1.5kg.

Oaxaca and the Isthmus

Oaxaca is a place of brilliant colours, rich indigineous heritage and scintillating culinary traditions. At its heart lies the capital, Oaxaca City, a UNESCO World Heritage Site replete with bold colonial architecture. Some of Mexico's finest historic churches can be found here – testaments to baroque at its most grandiose. But beyond historical appeal, Oaxaca City has an irresistable bohemian charm. A plethora of galleries and craft stores pay testament to a thriving arts scene, often overlooked by the casual visitor.

Travel beyond the terraced cafés and plazas of the capital and an intriguing and entirely different world unfolds. The dusty Central Valleys are a land of crumbling, pre-Columbian ruins, teeming indigenous villages and otherworldly natural wonders. A visit to the hilltop ruins of Monte Albán is obligatory, but Mitla also, with its fascinating stonework, pays homage to the splendour of Oaxaca's ancient civilizations. The villages scattered throughout the valleys also conceal several interesting attractions including El Tule, one of the world's oldest trees, and countless dizzying markets. The state's finest crafts are produced in the valleys, including sleek black pottery, dazzling tapestries and psychedelic animal sculptures called alebrijes.

South of the Capital, the Pacific Ocean pounds an exceptionally vivid shoreline with violent, crashing waters. A plethora of beach communities have blossomed here, all very different in character. Puerto Escondido is a well-established surfers' haven, where the Mexican Pipeline provides some of the world's most spectacular waves. The party town of Zipolite has long drawn an alternative crowd, while the secluded hideaway of Mazunte is only just developing its tourist potential. Puerto Angel is an old Oaxaca favourite, formerly a fishing village and popular with an older crowd. The beauty of this region has not been overlooked by big business either; the resort of Huatulco offers a convenient, if sanitised, experience of Oaxaca's Pacific coast.

East, towards the Yucatán Peninsula and Central America, Oaxaca state narrows into the Isthmus of Tehuantepec – a region characterized by strong local culture and an absence of foreign tourists. Stop here to encounter everyday life in a variety of forms: Salina Cruz is a busy industrial port, Tehuantepec a bustling Zapotec village, and Juchitán a thriving commercial centre. ►► *For listings, see page 456-481.*

Mexico City to Oaxaca

The express toll road from Mexico City to Oaxaca first runs generally eastwards to Puebla (see page 182), where it turns south to wind through wooded mountains at altitudes of between 1500 m and 1800 m, emerging at last into the warm, red-earth Oaxaca valley. It has been described as a stunning bus ride along a new motorway through cactus-filled valleys and plains. The route described here, however, avoids the new motorway in favour of the less sophisticated but equally attractive Route 190, which continues from Oaxaca to Tehuantepec. The road, although paved throughout and in good condition, serpentines unendingly over the sierras and is quite beautiful. The alternative coastal route is also very attractive and of special interest to visitors who wish to engage in the many watersports available. Buses on the new express toll road now take six hours from Mexico City to Oaxaca.

Atlixco → *Phone code: 244.*

Route 190 heads south from Puebla to Izúcar de Matamoros. A side road leads to **Huaquechula** where there's a 16th-century Renaissance and plateresque chapel. The road passes through Atlixco ('the place lying on the water'), which has interesting baroque examples in the **Capilla de la Tercera Orden de San Agustín** and **San Juan de Dios**. The annual **Atlixcayotl festival** is on San Miguel hill. Nearby are the curative springs of **Axocopán**.

Izúcar de Matamoros and around → *Colour map 3, C4. Phone code: 243.*

After Atlixco, Route 190 continues to the town of Izúcar de Matamoros (from *itzocan*, meaning 'his dirty face'), famous for its clay handicrafts, the 16th-century convent of **Santo Domingo**, and two nearby spas, **Los Amatitlanes** (about 6 km away) and **Ojo de Carbón**.

A road leads southwest from Izúcar to **Axochiapan**, Morelos state and to a paved road to the village of **Jolalpan** with the baroque church of Santa María (1553). There are very few restaurants in Jolalpan; ask where you can get a meal. The bus from Axochiapan stops in front of the church in Jolalpan. The road (and bus) continues to **Atenango del Río** in Guerrero state; the last 20-30 km are unpaved.

Acatlán to Oaxaca

From Izúcar de Matamoros, Route 190 switchbacks to **Tehuitzingo**. Then the landscape is fairly flat to Acatlán, a friendly village where black and red clay figures, and palm and flower hats are made.

Carry on to Petlalcingo, then ascend to **Huajuapan de León**, an important centre for palm products. To the southeast (12 km) is the Yosocuta Dam with fish farms and recreational facilities. Second-class bus from Oaxaca to Huajuapan, four a day, US$3.50.

After Huajuapan de León, Route 125 leads to **Pinotepa Nacional**. The next town on Route 190 is **Tamazulapan** with a 16th-century church and a pink stone arch in front of the city hall.

Yanhuitlán, 72 km northwest of Oaxaca on Route 190, has a beautiful 400-year-old church, part of the Santo Domingo monastery, built on a pre-Hispanic platform – it is considered one of the best examples of 16th-century New World Hispanic architecture. Yanhuitlán is in the Sierra Mixteca, where Dominican friars began evangelizing in 1526. Two other important centres in the region were San Juan Bautista at **Coixtlahuaca** and the open chapel at Teposcolula. The scenery and the altars, the huge convents in such a remote area are a worthwhile day trip from Oaxaca. The new highway from **Nochixtlán** to Oaxaca (103 km) has been recommended for cyclists: it has wide hard shoulders and easy gradients.

Oaxaca city ⊖❼❻❀⊙▲⊙❶ ❱❱ *pp456-481. Colour map 3, C5.*

→ *Phone code: 951. Altitude: 1546 m.*

Founded by the Spanish as Antequera in 1521 on the site of a Zapotec and Mixtec settlement, Oaxaca gracefully combines its colonial and native roots. Fine stone buildings, churches, arcades and airy patios speak for its importance during the colonial period, while its markets, crafts, dances and feast days point to a more indigenous past. Relaxing with a coffee or beer on one of the many street cafés of Oaxaca, it's easy to while away the hours. Once you've explored the museums, cathedrals, markets and surrounding streets, you can sit down with another beer to plan your days exploring the surrounding hills and valleys.

Ins and outs

Getting there Aeropuerto Xoxocotlán (OAX) is 9 km south of the city. **Transportación Terrestre Aeropuerto**, T951-514 4350, run *colectivos* to the centre for US$3; a private

The summer of social unrest

In the summer of 2006, Oaxaca City became the setting for a violent battle that left the region stunned. Several thousand armed police clashed with over 40,000 protestors in an unprecedented collision of wills. The worst social unrest in Oaxaca's recent history began as an innocuous protest over teachers' pay. Every summer for 25 years running, teachers had congregated on Oaxaca City's zócalo to rally over poor conditions and wages. Usually, the protests ended after a few weeks. What made 2006 so different? In short, Oaxaca's governor, Ulises Ruiz Ortiz.

Ortiz's reputation as a repressor of political enemies was confirmed on 14 June 2006, when he issued an order to break up the encampment on the zócalo. 3000 police stormed the square, attacking tens of thousands of teachers and their supporters. Rumours of police brutality fuelled public sympathy for the teachers who were quickly supported by other non-governmental groups, organizations and co-ops.

The first move of the newly created **Popular Assembly for the Peoples of Oaxaca (APPO)** was to reoccupy the zócalo, barricade the streets and declare their political aims. Primarily, they demanded the removal from office of Governor Ortiz. They boycotted the annual Guelaguetza festival, seized local radio stations and blockaded the bus terminals against a backdrop of frequent clashes with the police.

Events reached a climax in October when US journalist Bradley Roland Will was shot and killed in an alleged shoot-out. President Vincente Fox intervened sending federal police to quell the chaos. Six thousand five hundred police dispersed the crowds at the zócalo, resulting in yet more deaths, violence and injuries.

Today, Oaxaca is recovering from its brief foray into mayhem. Ironically, the hardest hit were the poorest members of the community, whose fledgling businesses could not withstand several months without trade.

taxi will cost around US$15. The first-class bus terminal is northeast of the zócalo on Calzada Niños Héroes (some second-class buses also leave from here). The second-class terminal is west of the zócalo on Calzada Valerio Trujano, near the Central de Abastos market. **Autobuses Unidos** (AU) has its own terminal northwest of the zócalo at Prolongación Madero.

Getting around Local town minibuses mostly charge US$0.20. For the first-class bus terminal, buses marked 'VW' leave from Avenida Juárez; for the second-class terminal, buses are marked 'Central'. Most of the important sites are in or near the city centre and can be reached on foot.

Tourist information Sedetur Tourist Office ① *Murguía 206, T951-516 0123, daily 0800-2000, www.aoaxaca.com*, with maps, posters, postcards and information about the city and state; ask here about the **Tourist Yú'ù** hostel programme in local communities (see Sleeping, page 443). There's a **second tourist office** ① *inside the Palacio Municipal, Independencia 607, T951-516 0123*. Visit the **Instituto Nacional de Estadística, Geografía e Informática** (INEGI) ① *Emiliano Zapata No 316, corner of Escuela Naval Militar, T951-512 4823*, for topographic maps and information about the state. Useful publications include *Oaxaca Times*, English monthly, www.oaxacatimes.com; *Oaxaca*, monthly in

Oaxaca

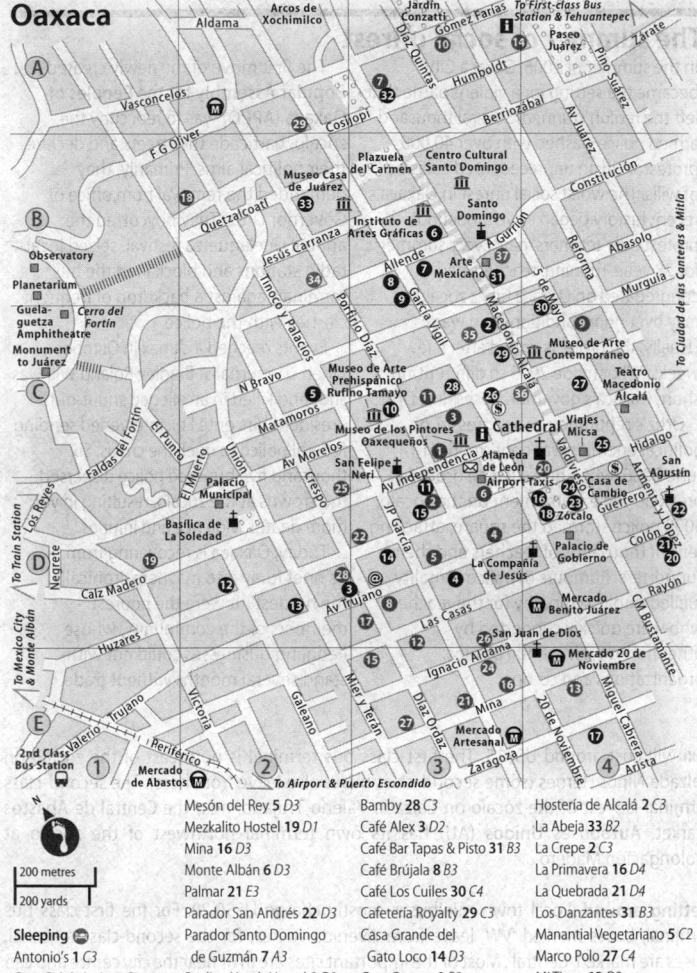

Mesón del Rey 5 *D3*
Mezkalito Hostel 19 *D1*
Mina 16 *D3*
Monte Albán 6 *D3*
Palmar 21 *E3*
Parador San Andrés 22 *D3*
Parador Santo Domingo
  de Guzmán 7 *A3*
Paulina Youth Hostel 8 *D3*
Posada Catarina 24 *E3*
Posada del Centro 25 *D2*
Posada Don Matías 26 *D3*
Posada Las Casas 15 *E3*
Principal 9 *C4*
Rivera del Angel 27 *E3*
Valle de Oaxaca 28 *D2*

Eating 🍴
Amarantos 24 *D4*
Asador Vasco 18 *D4*

Sleeping 🛏
Antonio's 1 *C3*
Casa Cid de León 3 *C3*
Casa Conzatti 10 *A3*
Casantica 11 *C3*
Central 2 *D3*
Ferri 12 *D3*
Hostal Pochon 18 *B2*
La Cabaña 13 *E4*
La Casona del Llano 14 *A3*
La Casona de Tita 29 *A2*
Las Rosas 4 *D3*
Lupita 17 *D3*
Marqués del Valle 20 *C4*

Bamby 28 *C3*
Café Alex 3 *D2*
Café Bar Tapas & Pisto 31 *B3*
Café Brújula 8 *B3*
Café Los Cuiles 30 *C4*
Cafetería Royalty 29 *C3*
Casa Grande del
  Gato Loco 14 *D3*
Casa Oaxaca 9 *B3*
Comala 7 *B3*
D'Florencia 17 *E4*
El Chef 20 *D4*
El Mesón 25 *C4*
El Naranjo 4 *D3*
El Shaddai 12 *D2*
Flor de Loto 10 *C3*
Flor de Oaxaca 22 *D4*
Gaia Organic Food 30 *C4*
Girasoles 11 *D3*
Hipocampo's 15 *D3*

Hostería de Alcalá 2 *C3*
La Abeja 33 *B2*
La Crepe 2 *C3*
La Primavera 16 *D4*
La Quebrada 21 *D4*
Los Danzantes 31 *B3*
Manantial Vegetariano 5 *C2*
Marco Polo 27 *C4*
Mi Tierra 13 *D2*
Pizza Nostrana 6 *B3*
Pizza Rústica 32 *A3*
Terranova, Taco Inn, Sushi Itto
  & Altos de Terranova 23 *D4*
Tito's 26 *C3*

Bars & clubs 🍸
Fandango 34 *B2*
La Cantinita 36 *C4*
La Divina 37 *B3*
La Tentación 35 *C3*

Spanish, English and French; *Comunicación*, in Spanish, with a few articles translated into English and French; *Guía Cultural*, published monthly by the Instituto Oaxaqueño de las Culturas, has a complete listing of musical events, exhibitions, conferences, libraries, etc.

Safety Oaxaca is a generally safe city; however, sensible precautions are advised. The **Tourist police** ① *zócalo, near the cathedral*, are friendly and helpful; or you can contact the **Centro de Protección al Turista** ① *T951-516 7280*.

Sights

The zócalo with its arcades is the heart of town, a pleasant park with new paving around the central bandstand. It's a pleasant place to sit and watch the world from one of the street cafés, or take a stroll. It is always active, and the surrounding cafés and restaurants are always busy. Free music and dance events are often held in the evenings. In the daytime vendors sell food; in the evening they offer tourist wares. It is especially colourful on Saturday and Sunday nights when indigenous women weave and sell their goods. The colourful markets and varied crafts of Oaxaca are among the main attractions of the region. ►► *See Shopping, page 468.*

Avenida Independencia is the main street running east-west, the nicer part of the old city is to the north of it; a simpler area, housing the cheaper hotels, lies to the south. Independencia is also a dividing line for the north-south streets, which change names here. Calle Macedonia Alcalá is a cobbled pedestrian walkway, which joins the zócalo with the church of Santo Domingo, many colonial buildings can be seen along this mall; this street and Calle Bustamante, its continuation to the south, are the dividing line for east-west streets, which change names here.

Worth visiting is the **Palacio de Gobierno**, on the south side of the zócalo; it has beautiful murals and entry is free. There are often political meetings or protests outside. The **Teatro Macedonio Alcalá** ① *5 de Mayo with Independencia*, is an elegant theatre from Porfirio Díaz's times. It has a Louis XV-style entrance and white marble staircase; regular performances are held here. Visit also the **Arcos de Xochimilco** on García Vigil, starting at Cosijopi, some eight blocks north of the zócalo. In this picturesque area are the remains of an aqueduct, cobbled passageways under the arches, flowers and shops. The house of the Maza family, for whom Benito Juárez worked and whose daughter he married, still stands at Independencia 1306 and is marked by a plaque. Porfirio Díaz birthplace is similarly remembered at the other end of Independencia, in a building that is now a kindergarten, near La Soledad. DH Lawrence wrote parts of *Mornings in Mexico* in Oaxaca, and revised *The Plumed Serpent*; the house he rented is on Pino Suárez. The bar **El Favorito**, on 20 de Noviembre, a couple of blocks south of the zócalo, is supposedly the original that inspired Malcolm Lowry in his novel *Under the Volcano*.

There is a grand view from **Cerro de Fortín**, the hill to the northwest of the centre; here is the Guelaguetza amphitheatre; a monument to Juárez stands on a hillside below. Atop the hill are an observatory and **planetarium**, damaged during the social unrest of 2006 and currently closed to the public. Check with the tourist office about its imminent reopening. It is a pleasant walk from town to the hill as far as the planetarium and antennas, but muggings have been reported in the trails that go through the woods and the dirt road that goes beyond. Best to take a taxi.

Ciudad de las Canteras, the quarries from where the stone for the city's monumental churches and public buildings was extracted, has been converted into a beautifully landscaped park. It is located on Calzada Niños Héroes de Chapultepec, at the east end of

Guelaguetza or Lunes del Cerro

This impressive annual celebration in July is where all the colour and variety of Oaxaca's many different cultural groups come together in one place. For those with an interest in native costumes, music and dance, it must not be missed.

The word Guelaguetza originally means something like 'reciprocity' in Zapotec, the interchange of gifts or favours. Some elements of the celebration may well date from pre-Hispanic times, however the contemporary event is a well-organized large-scale folklore festival.

The main event is a grand folk dance show held at the Guelaguetza stadium on the slopes of Cerro del Fortín, on Monday morning. The performance is lively and very colourful, with the city below serving as a spectacular backdrop.

Among the favourite presentations are always *Flor de Piña*, danced by women from the Tuxtepec area with a pineapple on their shoulder, and *Danza de la Pluma*, performed by men from the Central Valleys using enormous feather headdresses. The most elaborate costumes are those of the women from the Isthmus of Tehuantepec, including stiffly starched lace *resplandores* (halos) on their heads. At the end of each performance, gifts are thrown from the stage to the audience – watch out for the pineapples!

Los Lunes del Cerro are usually the last two Mondays in July. The performance begins 0900 and ends around 1300. Tickets for seats in the lower galleries (A and B) are sold in advance through Sedetur and cost US$35. Details from the Oaxaca State Tourism Department, Murguía 206, Centro Histórico, Oaxaca, T951-514 8501.

Advance tickets go on sale from early May. The upper galleries (C and D) are free, line up before 0600, gates open around 0700, the performance begins at 1000 and finishes around 1400. Take a sweater as it is chilly in the morning, but the sun is very strong later on. A sun hat and sunscreen are essential, a pair of binoculars is also helpful in the upper galleries. Drinks and snacks are sold.

In addition to the main event, there are scores of other happenings in Oaxaca at this time of year, ranging from professional cycling races to classical music concerts, a Feria del Mezcal, and several smaller celebrations in nearby villages. Many events are free and a complete programme is available from Sedetur.

On the Saturday before Lunes del Cerro, at around 1800, participating groups parade down the pedestrian mall on Macedonio Alcalá, from Santo Domingo to the zócalo. This is a good opportunity to see their splendid costumes close up and to meet the participants. On Sunday is the election of the Diosa Centeotl (goddess of the new corn), who presides over the following week's festivities. Candidates are chosen based on their knowledge of native traditions.

On Monday night, following the Guelaguetza, the Donají legend is presented in an elaborate torchlight performance at the same stadium starting around 2000. Donají was a Zapotec princess who fell in love with a Mixtec prince, Nucano, and eventually gave her life for her people. Some claim that the two lovers are buried in the same grave in Cuilapan de Guerrero.

Calzada Eduardo Vasconcelos; several city bus lines go there. There is a small stadium here and the site of the **Expo Feria Oaxaca**, a fair with rides, craft exhibits, food and various live performances, held throughout the year (check in the tourist information office for details).

Churches

On the zócalo is the 17th-century **cathedral** with a fine baroque façade (watch the raising and lowering of the Mexican flag daily at 0800 and 1800 beside the cathedral), but the best sight by far, about four blocks from the square up the pedestrianized Calle Macedonio Alcalá, is the church of **Santo Domingo** ① *daily 0700-1300, 1700-2000, no flash photographs allowed*, with its adjoining monastery, now the Centro Cultural Santo Domingo (see below). The church is considered one of the best examples of baroque style in Mexico. It first opened to worship in 1608 and was refurbished in the 1950s. Its gold leaf has to be seen to be believed. The ceilings and walls, sculptured and painted white and gold, are stunningly beautiful.

The massive 17th-century **Basílica de La Soledad** (between Morelos and Independencia, west of Unión) has fine colonial ironwork and sculpture (including an exquisite Virgen de la Soledad). Its interior is predominantly fawn and gold; the plaques on the walls are painted like cross-sections of polished stone. The fine façade is made up of stone of different colours, pinks and greens; it is considered the best example of carved stonework in the city. The church was built on the site of the hermitage to San Sebastián; begun in 1582, it was recommenced in 1682 because of earthquakes. It was consecrated in 1690 and the convent was finished in 1697. The **Museo Religioso de la Soledad** ① *Independencia 107, daily 1000-1745, US$0.35 donation requested*, at the back of the church, has a display of religious artefacts. In the small plaza outside the encircling wall, refreshments and offerings are sold. There are elaborate altars at the church of **San Felipe Neri** ① *Av Independencia y García*. At **San Juan de Dios** ① *20 de Noviembre y Aldama*, there is an indigenous version In paint of the conquistadors' arrival in Oaxaca and of an anti-Catholic uprising in 1700. This was the first church in Oaxaca, originally dedicated to Santa Catalina Mártir. The church of **San Agustín** ① *Armenta y López at Guerrero*, has a fine façade, with bas relief of St Augustine holding the City of God above adoring monks (apparently modelled on that of San Agustín in Mexico City, now the National Library). The church of **La Compañía de Jesús** ① *Trujano, diagonal to the zócalo*, first built in 1579, has a wooden altarpiece; in the central niche is an image of the Virgin of the Immaculate Conception, hence it is also known as the **Iglesia de la Inmaculada**.

Museums

The **Centro Cultural Santo Domingo** is a cultural complex that includes a museum, exhibit halls, botanical garden, library, newspaper archives and bookstore; concerts are also performed here. It is housed in the former convent of Santo Domingo (Macedonio Alcalá y Gurrión), next to the Santo Domingo church. Construction of the convent started in 1575. It was occupied by the Dominican friars from 1608 to 1812. After the expulsion of the church it was occupied by the Mexican army between 1812 and 1972; later it housed the regional museum. Between 1994 and 1998, the convent was very beautifully restored, using only original materials and techniques. The **Museo de las Culturas de Oaxaca** ① *Tue-Sun, 1000-1900, US$4.50, use of video US$3*, housed in the Centro Cultural Santo Domingo, and sometimes referred to as 'the Louvre of Oaxaca', is a superb museum that requires at least four hours to visit; exhibits are beautifully displayed and explained in

Spanish (with plans to implement a system of recorded explanations in other languages); highly recommended. Fourteen galleries cover the history of Oaxaca from pre-Hispanic times to the contemporary period; the archaeology collection includes spectacular riches found in Tomb 7 of Monte Albán. There are also exhibits of different aspects of Oaxacan culture, such as crafts, cooking, traditional medicine etc, as well as temporary exhibits.

Also in the Centro Cultural is the interesting **Jardín Etnobotánico** ① *free guided tours in Spanish daily at 1300 and 1800, in English Tue, Thu and Sat at 1100 and 1600, 1 hr, sign up in advance*. This garden aims to preserve different species of plants that are native to southern Mexico and have played and continue to play a role in the lives of different ethnic groups in Oaxaca. You can learn about the different species of *agaves* used to make mezcal, pulque and tequila; the trees used to make crafts; the *grana cochinilla*, an insect that lives in certain cacti and is used to dye cloth; the plants used in folk medicine; and many more species.

The **Museo de Arte Prehispánico Rufino Tamayo** ① *Morelos 503, Mon, Wed-Sat 1000-1400, 1600-1900, Sun 1000-1500, US$3*, has an outstanding display of pre-Columbian artefacts dating from 1250 BC to AD 1100, donated by the Oaxacan painter Rufino Tamayo in 1974. Information is in Spanish only and is not comprehensive. The **Museo Casa de Juárez** ① *García Vigil 609, Tue-Sat 1000-1730, Sun 1000-1700, US$3.50*, is where Benito Juárez lived. It contains some of his possessions, historical documents and some bookbinding tools. The **Museo de Filatelia** ① *Reforma 504, Tue-Sun 1000-1930, free*, has temporary exhibits, a philatelic library and tours by appointment.

Oaxaca City is home to a thriving arts scene, and there are dozens of galleries and workshops about town. The Museo de Arte Contemporáneo ① *Alcalá 202, 1030-2000, closed Tue, US$2*, hosts regional exhibits in range of media, with a library and café, housed in a late 17th-century house. The **Instituto de Arte Gráficas de Oaxaca** ① *Alcalá 507, 0900-2000, closed Tue, donation requested*, is housed in a grand old 18th-century building. It has interesting exhibitions of national artists, a good reference library and beautiful courtyards. **Museo de los Pintores Oaxaqueños**, ① *Independencia 607 and Vigil*, is a state-run gallery that features local artists, past and present. **Colectivo Plan B** ① *2nd Privada Av Universitaria*, is a new gallery for avant-garde works and cutting edge media, while **Arte Mexicano** ① *Alcalá 407*, is a renowned workshop that specializes in high quality prints and popular crafts. **Arte de Oaxaca** ① *Murguía 105*, was partly founded by Rudolfo Morales, a famous artist from Ocotlán. It has good exhibits of local talents. **Galería Quetzalli** ① *Alcalá 203*, also features gifted locals, including Fransisco Toledo.

Monte Albán ⊖ ⇥ *pp456-481. Colour map 3, C5.*

① *Daily 0800-1800, US$4.50. A charge of US$3 is made to use video cameras; fees for the guides who hang around the site are variable, ask several of them and beware of overcharging. Monte Albán receives many visitors during high season. Most people go in the morning, so it may be easier to catch the afternoon bus.* ⇥ *To get there, see Transport, page 476.*

Monte Albán is situated about 10 km (20 minutes) west of Oaxaca, on a hilltop dominating the surrounding valley. Monte Albán features pyramids, walls, terraces, tombs, staircases and sculptures of the ancient capital of the Zapotec culture, and the ruins were declared a UNESCO World Heritage Site in 1987.

Although the city of Monte Albán extended far beyond the confines of the **Main Plaza**, it is this that archaeologists, art historians, historians and tourists have looked to, when assessing and interpreting the raison d'être of this fascinating site. Constructed 400 m up a steep mountain, without immediate access to water or cultivable land, the Main Plaza has at times been considered the site of a regional marketplace or ceremonial centre. The marketplace theory becomes less convincing when access to the site is considered: not only would the visitor have had to haul merchandise up the back-breaking hill, but entrance to the plaza was severely restricted. In ancient times the only way into the site was through three narrow passageways, which could easily have been guarded to restrict entry. The modern ramp cuts across what was the ball court to the southeast of the **North Platform**. The space at the centre of the Main Plaza would seem ideal for religious ceremonies and rituals: the absence of religious iconography contradicts this interpretation. The imagery at Monte Albán is almost exclusively militaristic, with allusions to tortured captives and captured settlements.

To the right, before getting to the ruins, is **Tomb 7**, where a fabulous treasure trove was found in 1932; most items are in the Centro Cultural Santo Domingo in Oaxaca and the entrance is closed off by a locked gate. **Tomb 172** has been left exactly as it was found, with skeleton and urns still in place, but these are not visible. Tombs 7 and 172 are permanently closed.

There are tri-lingual (Spanish, English and Zapotec) signs throughout the site, as well as a good **museum** (explanations in Spanish only), exhibiting stone glyphs and sculptures as well as smaller artefacts; flash photography is prohibited. Informative literature and videos in several languages are sold in the bookstore in the visitor centre, which also houses a small restaurant. From the ruins at Monte Albán there are paths leading to the valleys below. If you're in reasonable shape consider hiring a bike for the day, and enjoy the ride down at least.

Main Plaza

The Main Plaza at Monte Albán is delineated north and south by the two largest structures in the city, which have been interpreted as palace and/or public building (North Platform) and temple (South Platform). Apart from these two impressive structures, the ball court and the arrow-shaped building in front of the South Platform, the Main Plaza has 14 other structures, six along the west side of the Plaza, three in the middle and five along the east side. One structure, known as Edificio de los Danzantes (Dancers), has bas reliefs, glyphs and calendar signs (probably 5th century BC). During the period AD 450-600, Monte Albán had 14 districts beyond the confines of the Main Plaza: it has been proposed that each of the 14 structures located within the Main Plaza corresponded with one of the districts outside. Each pertained to a distinct ethnic group or polity, brought together to create a pan-regional confederacy or league. The arrow-shaped structure functioned as a military showcase; it also has astronomical connotations.

Confederacy

The presence of a number of structures in or bordering the Main Plaza that housed representatives of distinct ethnic groups supports the theory that Monte Albán came into being as the site of a confederacy or league. Its neutral position, unrelated to any single polity, lends credence to this suggestion. The absence of religious iconography, which might have favoured one group over the others, emphasizes the secular role of the area, while the presence of the Danzantes sculptures suggests a trophy-gathering group. However, although Monte Albán may have served defensive purposes, the presence of the Danzantes and the captured town glyphs argues for an offensive and expansionist role. In all, about 310 stone slabs depicting captives, some of whom are sexually

Monte Albán

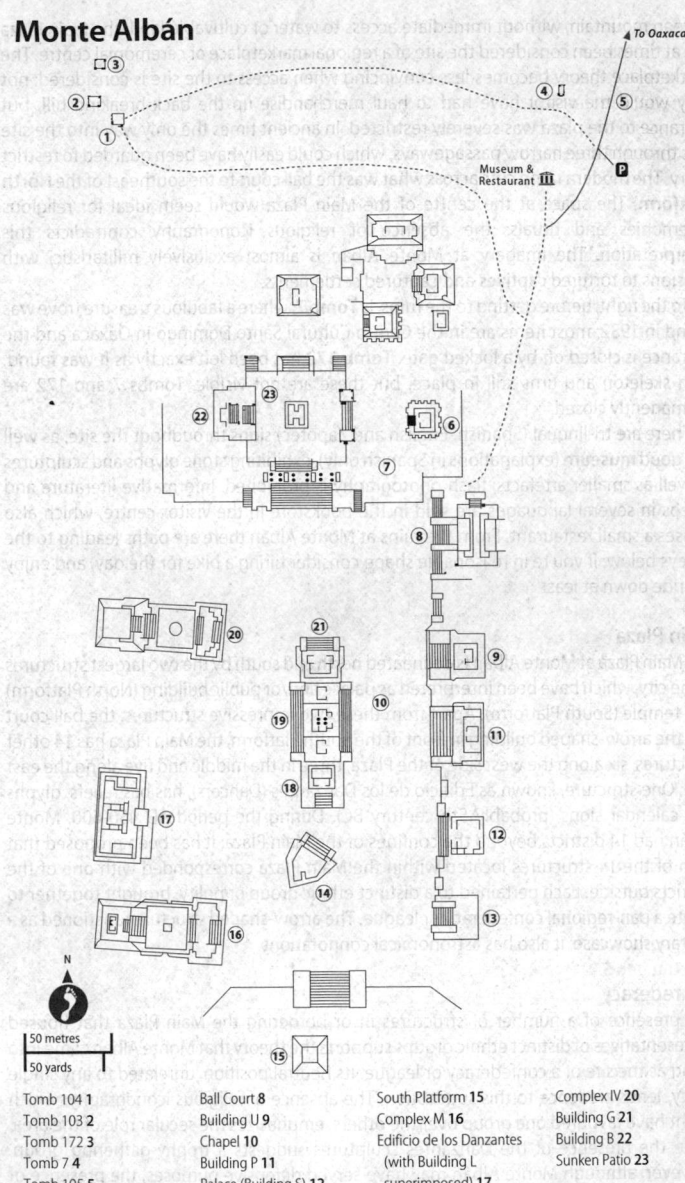

To Oaxaca

Museum & Restaurant

Tomb 104 **1**	Ball Court **8**	South Platform **15**	Complex IV **20**
Tomb 103 **2**	Building U **9**	Complex M **16**	Building G **21**
Tomb 172 **3**	Chapel **10**	Edificio de los Danzantes	Building B **22**
Tomb 7 **4**	Building P **11**	(with Building L	Sunken Patio **23**
Tomb 105 **5**	Palace (Building S) **12**	superimposed) **17**	
Mound A **6**	Building Q **13**	Building I **18**	
North Platform **7**	Observatory (Building J) **14**	Building H **19**	

mutilated with streams of blood (flowers) flowing from the mutilated parts, have been found. Some of these woeful captives are identified by name glyphs, which imply hostilities against a settlement and the capture of its warriors. The fact that most of them are nude denotes the disdain and contempt with which they were treated by their captors: nudity was considered shameful and undignified by the peoples of Mesoamerica. It is very likely that the rulers of Monte Albán were determined to bring into the confederacy as many polities as possible in order to extract tribute, which would permit the expansion of the capital. The growth of Monte Albán was a direct response to events in the Valley of Mexico, where Teotihuacán was exercising dominion over most of the area. Although Monte Albán had been developing a policy of offence and capture as early as 200 BC, the growth of the city really gained impetus with the growth of Teotihuacán, whose administrators must have cast an avaricious eye on the rich soil of the Valley of Oaxaca. From the ceramics and architecture analysed at Monte Albán, it is clear that Teotihuacán never realized its ambitions in that area; the confederacy functioned well.

Collapse

Monte Albán reached its maximum size around AD 600, with a population estimated at between 15,000 and 30,000. Shortly after that date, the city changed dramatically in form and function. There was a decrease in population of nearly 82%, the Main Plaza was abandoned and the majority of the people moved nearer to the valley floor, but behind protective walls. They were much closer to major roads, implying that Monte Albán was now becoming more commercially minded and aspired to be self-sufficient, which it had never been in its long history.

The abandonment of the Main Plaza was a direct result of the collapse of the political institution centred there. This collapse has been seen as a consequence of the fact that, beginning early in the seventh century AD, Teotihuacán was already showing signs of decadence. Gaining momentum, the decadence led to the massive abandonment of that great centre. It is unlikely to have been coincidental that the Main Plaza at Monte Albán was abandoned around this time. The removal of the Teotihuacán threat made redundant the Confederacy that was so costly to maintain: the collapse was complete.

Route to Mitla 🍴🚗❄️🛏️🚌 » pp456-481.

It is 42 km from Oaxaca to Mitla, on a poor paved road (Route 190) with many potholes and occasional flooding. On the way you pass **El Tule** ① *US$3, 12 km east of Oaxaca*, which in the churchyard has what is reputed to be the **world's largest tree**, a savino (*Taxodium mucronatum*), estimated at 2000 years old. It is 40 m high, 42 m round at its base, weighs an estimated 550 tonnes, and is fed water by an elaborate pipe system. **Casa Breno**, has unusual textiles and spindles for sale, the owners are happy to show visitors around the looms. Bus from Oaxaca, second-class bus station, every 30 minutes, US$1.

Continuing east along Route 190, 5 km from El Tule is **Tlacochahuaya**, with a 16th-century **church** ① *US$0.45*, and vivid indigenous murals; visit the cloisters at the back and see the decorated organ upstairs. Bus from Oaxaca second-class terminal, US$0.35.

Teotitlán del Valle

Five km further, a paved road leads off Route 190 to Teotitlán del Valle, where wall hangings and *tapetes* (rugs) are woven, and which is now becoming touristy. There is an artesans' market near the church, and a **Museo Comunitario** ① *Mon-Sat 1000-1800*,

US$0.50. The best prices for weavings are to be had at the stores along the road as you come into town, but they may be even cheaper in Oaxaca where competition is stronger. Make sure you know whether you are getting all wool or a mixture and check the quality. A well-made rug will not ripple when unfolded on the floor. Buses leave every hour from 0700-2100, from second-class bus terminal (US$0.45); the second-class bus may provide the contacts you need to buy all the weavings you want! From the town of Teotitlán del Valle you can walk up to the nearby hills across the river or hike north to the town of Benito Juárez.

Tlacolula → *Colour map 3, C5.*

Tlacolula has a most interesting Sunday market and the renowned Capilla del Santo Cristo in the church. The chapel is similar in style to Santo Domingo in Oaxaca, with intricate white and gold stucco, lots of mirrors, silver altar rails and sculptures of martyrs in gruesome detail. Two beheaded saints guard the door to the main nave (Fiesta: 9 October). There is a pleasant walled garden in front of the church. A band plays from 1930 every evening in the plaza (take a sweater, cold wind most evenings). On the main street by Parque Juárez is **Casa de Cambio Guelaguetza**, cash only, fair rates. The townspeople are renowned for their mezcal preparation. The indoor market next to the church is very interesting. Between the church and the market you might see a local lady selling dried grasshoppers. Tlacolula can be reached by bus from Oaxaca, from the second-class bus station every 10 minutes, daily 0600-1900, US$1.10. Taxis stop by the church, except on Sunday when they gather on a

Around Oaxaca

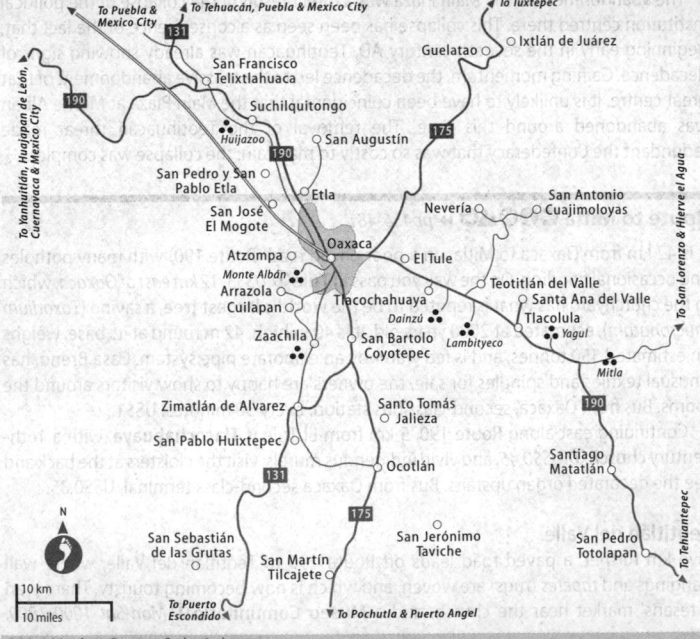

To Puebla & Mexico City
To Tehuacán, Puebla & Mexico City
To Tuxtepec
131
Guelatao
Ixtlán de Juárez
San Francisco
Telixtlahuaca
To Yanhuitlán, Huajapan de León, Cuernavaca & Mexico City
190
Suchilquitongo
175
Huijazoo
190
San Augustín
San Pedro y San Pablo Etla
Etla
Nevería
San Antonio Cuajimoloyas
San José El Mogote
Oaxaca
El Tule
Atzompa
Monte Albán
Teotitlán del Valle
Arrazola
Tlacochahuaya
Santa Ana del Valle
Cuilapan
Dainzú
Tlacolula
To San Lorenzo & Hierve el Agua
Zaachila
San Bartolo Coyotepec
Lambityeco
Yagul
Mitla
190
Zimatlán de Alvarez
Santo Tomás Jalieza
Santiago Matatlán
San Pablo Huixtepec
Ocotlán
131
175
To Tehuantepec
N
10 km
10 miles
San Sebastián de las Grutas
San Jerónimo Taviche
San Pedro Totolapan
San Martín Tilcajete
To Puerto Escondido
To Pochutla & Puerto Angel
To Tehuantepec

street behind the church; ask directions. Tlacolula's bus station is just off the main highway, several blocks from the centre; pickpockets are common here, be especially careful at the Sunday market and in the scrum to board the bus.

Santa Ana del Valle

Quality weavings can be found at Santa Ana del Valle, 3 km from Tlacolula. The village is peaceful and friendly with a small museum showing ancient textile techniques; ask any villager for the keyholder. There are two fiestas, each lasting three days. One during the second week of August, the other at the end of January. Buses leave from Tlacolula every 30 minutes.

Yagul

ⓘ *Daily 0800-1700, US$3. Tours in English on Tue, US$15, from Oaxaca agencies.*
Further east along Route 190 is the turn-off north for Yagul, an outstandingly picturesque archaeological site where the ball courts and priests' quarters are set in a landscape punctuated by candelabra cactus and agave. Yagul was a large Zapotec and later Mixtec religious centre. The ball court is said to be the second largest discovered in Mesoamerica; it also one of the most perfect discovered to date. There are fine tombs (take the path from behind the ruins, the last part is steep) and temples, and a superb view from the hill behind the ruins. Recommended. Take a bus to Mitla from the Oaxaca second-class terminal and ask to be put down at the paved turn-off to Yagul (five minutes after Tlacolula terminal). You will have to walk 1 km uphill from the bus stop to the site and you can return the same way or walk 3 km west to Tlacolula along Route 190 to catch a bus to Oaxaca.

Mitla → *Colour map 3, C5. Phone code: 951.*
ⓘ *42 km southeast of Oaxaca, Turn left off Ruta 190, 5 km after Yagul and and continue for 4 km, daily 0800-1700, US$3, use of video US$3.50, literature sold at entrance.*
At Mitla (meaning 'place of the dead') there are ruins of four great palaces among minor ones. Some of the archaeology, outside the fenced-in site, can be seen within the present-day town.

Magnificent bas-reliefs, the sculptured designs in the Hall of Mosaics, the Hall of the Columns and, in the depths of a palace, *La Columna de la Muerte* (Column of Death), which people embrace and then measure what they can't reach with their fingers to know how many years they have left to live (rather hard on long-armed people). We have been informed that the column can no longer be embraced but do not know if this is a temporary or permanent arrangement.

Hierve el Agua

From Mitla take a bus to San Lorenzo Albarradas (one hour, US$1). Three kilometres from there (57 km from Oaxaca) is the village of Hierve el Agua. Due to the concentration of minerals and a prehispanic irrigation system, various waterfalls are now petrified over a cliff, forming an enormous stalactite. You can swim in the mineral pools in the dry season.

South of Oaxaca

Along Route 175 to Pochutla are several towns that specialize in the production of different crafts. **San Bartolo Coyotepec**, 12 km southeast of Oaxaca, is known for its black pottery. Doña Rosa de Nieto accidentally discovered the technique for the black-glazed

The Zapotecs

The Zapotec language is used by over 300,000 people in the state as a first or second language (about 20% of Oaxaca State population speaks only an indigenous language). The Zapotec people, who weave fantastic toys of grass, have a dance, the *Jarabe Tlacolula Zandunga*, performed by barefoot girls splendid in becoming coifs, short, brightly coloured skirts, ribbons and long lace petticoats, while the men, all in white with colourful handkerchiefs, dance opposite them with their hands behind their backs. Only women, from Tehuantepec or Juchitán, dance the slow and stately *Zandunga*, costumes gorgeously embroidered on velvet blouse, full skirts with white pleated and starched lace ruffles and *huipil*.

ceramics in the 1930s, and her family continues the tradition, as do many other potters in town. **San Martín Tilcajete**, 21 km from Oaxaca, 1 km west of the main road, is the centre for the *alebrije* production, animals carved from copal wood, painted in bright colours and often having a supernatural look to them. **Santo Tomás Jalieza** is the centre for cotton and wool textiles, produced with backstrap looms and natural dyes in the surrounding villages. Market day is Friday.

Cuilapan de Guerrero

In Cuilapan, 12 km southwest of Oaxaca, there is a vast unfinished 16th-century **convent** ① *daily 0900-1700, US$2.20*, now in ruins, with a famous nave and columns, and an 'open chapel', whose roof collapsed in an earthquake. The last Zapotec princess, Donaji, daughter of the last ruler Cosijoeza, married a Mixtec prince at Tilantengo and was buried at Cuilapan. On the grave is an inscription with their Christian names, Mariana Cortez and Diego Aguilar. Reached by bus from Oaxaca from second-class bus station, on Calle Bustamante, near Arista (US$0.50).

North of Cuilapan and 6 km west of the main road is **San Antonio Arrazola**, another town where *alebrijes*, mythical animals made of copal wood are sold. **Zaachila** ① *daily 0800-1700, US$2.20*, 5 km beyond Cuilapan, was the last capital of the Zapotec empire. Today this town still maintains some of its ancestral traditions in the local cooking (several restaurants). There is black pottery production, and market day is Thursday. Here are the partially excavated ruins of Zaachila, with two Mixtec tombs; the outer chamber has owls in stucco work and there are carved human figures with skulls for heads inside. Take bus to Zaachila (US$0.60), which leaves every 30 minutes, then walk to unexcavated ruins in the valley.

Eighty kilometres south on Route 131 is **San Sebastián de las Grutas** ① *guide obligatory, US$2*, about 10 km northwest of El Vado, off the main road, where there is a system of caves. One 400-m-long cave, with five chambers up to 70 m high, has been explored and is open to visitors. Ask for a guide at the Agencia Municipal next to the church. Take a **Solteca** bus bound for Sola de Vega or San Pedro del Alto, from the second-class terminal, leaves 0500, 0600, 1100, 1400 and returns 0600, 0700, 0800, 1200 – you may find that this will more than likely leave you high and dry! Also note there are no hotels but camping is possible.

San Felipe del Agua

Oaxaca is a growing hotbed of ecotourism, with many options for tours. For good hikes, take local bus to San Felipe del Agua, north of the city. To the left of where the buses stop at the end of the line is a car parking area, just below it starts a dirt road; follow this road and in five minutes you will reach the San Felipe Park entrance and a booth where you register with the guard. Several trails fan out from here; one follows the river valley, it goes by some picnic areas and a swimming pool, continues upstream crossing the river several times before reaching a waterfall in about one hour. There are longer walks to the mountain to the north, crossing through several vegetation zones, from low dry shrub to pleasant pine forest: allow five or six hours to reach the summit.

Santa María Atzompa

At Santa María Atzompa, 8 km northwest of Oaxaca, at the foot of Monte Albán, green glazed and terracotta ceramics are produced. You can see the artisans at work; their wares are sold at **La Casa del Artesano**. Buses leave from the second-class terminal.

Etla Valley

The Etla Valley, along which Route 190 runs, had a number of important settlements in pre-Hispanic times. Seventeen kilometres along this road and 2 km to the west is **San José el Mogote**, an important centre before the rise of Monte Albán; there is a small museum housing the artefacts found at this site. **San Pedro y San Pablo Etla**, 19 km from Oaxaca, has an important Wednesday market specializing in Oaxacan foods such as *quesillo* (string cheese), *tasajo* (dried meat) and different types of bread; the town has a 17th-century church and convent. At **Santiago Suchilquitongo**, 27 km from Oaxaca and atop a hill, are the ruins of **Huijazoo**, once an important centre that controlled the trade between the Central Valleys and the Cañada region; the local museum has a reproduction of a Huijazoo polychromatic mural, which has been compared to those at Bonampak. The town of **San Agustín Etla** (turn off east from Route 190 at Guadalupe Etla) was once an important industrial centre and in the 19th century it had two large cotton mills; with the introduction of synthetic fibres came a decline to this area. Since 1998, the town has found a new use for the cotton and other natural fibres available in the region, with the production of handmade paper for artists. Cotton, agave fibres, pineapple, nettle, ash, limestone and other raw materials are used in the workshop, which welcomes visitors. Further information from the **Instituto de Artes Gráficas** on Alcalá 507 in Oaxaca city.

Sierra Juárez

The Sierra Norte or Sierra Juárez is a region of beautiful landscapes and great biological diversity; seven of the nine types of vegetation that exist in Mexico can be found in this area. The region is starting to develop ecotourism with community participation; permits are required to camp on community land. The mountains gradually drop to the Papaloapan valley to the north. There are two access roads, Route 175 from Oaxaca to Tuxtepec, and the small roads that go north from Route 190, past Teotitlán and Santa Ana del Valle (see page 445). The Oaxaca–Tuxtepec road has been recommended as exhilarating for cyclists.

Puerto Escondido → *Colour map 3, B5. Phone code: 954.*

The town and its surroundings offer some stunningly beautiful beaches with world-class surfing, good facilities for visitors, and the town is a good base for various interesting excursions. Sadly, however, Puerto Escondido is at risk of becoming a case study in unsustainable tourism development. It was a small and sleepy fishing village as recently as the 1980s, until the population rapidly increased, perhaps in response to grandiose plans for Acapulco-style development. These never panned out and tourism instead developed low-rise and haphazardly, creating considerable environmental and social impact. The state tourist police now patrol both the main beach and tourist areas. They are English speaking and helpful.

Puerto Escondido

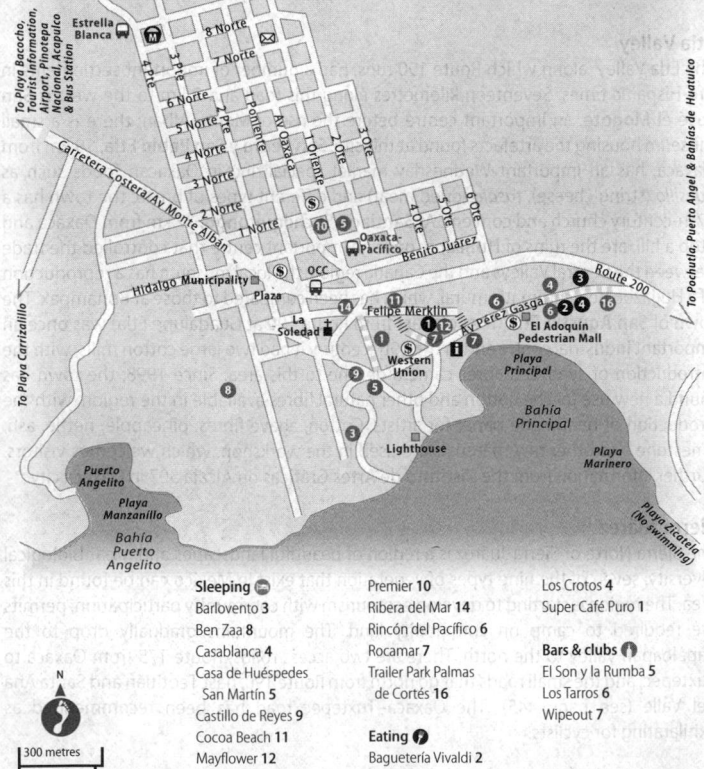

Sleeping 🛏️
Barlovento **3**
Ben Zaa **8**
Casablanca **4**
Casa de Huéspedes
 San Martín **5**
Castillo de Reyes **9**
Cocoa Beach **11**
Mayflower **12**
Paraíso Escondido **1**

Premier **10**
Ribera del Mar **14**
Rincón del Pacífico **6**
Rocamar **7**
Trailer Park Palmas
 de Cortés **16**

Eating 🍴
Bagueteria Vivaldi **2**
Benditos **3**

Los Crotos **4**
Super Café Puro **1**

Bars & clubs 🍸
El Son y la Rumba **5**
Los Tarros **6**
Wipeout **7**

At present, Puerto Escondido is a bustling and very commercial seaside resort. El Adoquín, the city's pedestrian tourist mall along Avenida Pérez Gasga near the beach teems with Mexican families in season, sunburnt foreigners and hard-core surfies throughout the year; December to January are the most crowded, May to June are the quietest (and hottest) months. A handful of luxury hotels and resorts are clustered above Playa Bacocho. Playa Zicatela, home to the Mexican Pipeline, is where surfers and their crowd hang out.

The real town, where prices are lower and there is less of a hard-sell atmosphere, is located up the hill on the other side of the highway. There is an ample selection of hotels and restaurants in all areas. Many fast-talking '*amigos*' are found at all the nearby beaches and other sites frequented by tourists offering an impressive array of goods and services for sale or hire; be polite and friendly (as are most of the vendors) but also wary, since there is no shortage of overpricing and trickery. **Sedetur information kiosk** ① *at the west end of El Adoquín, T954-582 1186, delpuerto@aoaxaca.com*, is run by Gina Machorro, a very helpful, friendly person who possesses in-depth knowledge about the town and the region. She speaks English, Spanish and French, giving a two-hour walking tour of Puerto Escondido on Wednesday and Saturday, US$20, including food, refreshments and souvenirs. They leave at 0800 from outside the kiosk.

Safety Even with the vast improvements in security, safety is an especially important issue in and around Puerto Escondido. A safe and pleasant stay here is possible with the appropriate precautions, but carelessness can have severe consequences. Never walk on any beach at night, alone or in groups. The ocean currents at Zicatela can be treacherous and although there are life-guards now paid by the government, there are easier ways to meet them than by getting drowned.

The **Playa Principal**, abutting El Adoquín pedestrian mall, has the calmest water but it is very close to the city and not clean. A few fishermen still bring in the catch of the day here. The local government began building a small pier for them and the tourist craft, but it remains unfinished, and a monument to poor planning. Immediately to the south is **Playa Marinero**, with slightly stronger surf (reportedly a good place for beginners), also built up with hotels, bars and restaurants. Further south, past a rocky point called Rocas del Morro, lies the long expanse of **Playa Zicatela**, which claims to be the best surfing beach in Mexico, with the Mexican Pipeline producing the fastest-breaking waves, at times over 3.5 m high, anywhere in the world. It makes for breathtaking viewing. It is suitable only for experienced surfers and very dangerous for swimming. To the west of the main bay, past a lovely headland (being built up with condominiums) and a lighthouse, are a series of picturesque bays and beaches, all accessible by road or boat from town. **Playa Manzanillo** and **Puerto Angelito** share the Bahía Puerto Angelito and are the closest, an easy 15-minute walk; they are pretty with reasonably safe swimming but very commercial; every square millimetre of shade is proprietary here. Further west is **Playa Carrizalillo**, with swimming and more gentle surfing than Zicatela, accessible along a steep path of 170 steps, or by boat or taxi. **Playa Bacocho** is next, a long beautiful stretch of less developed beach, where the ocean, alas, is too dangerous for swimming but makes for a great sunset.

Around Puerto Escondido

Seventy-four kilometres west of Puerto Escondido is the 140,000-ha **Parque Nacional Lagunas de Chacahua**, a wildlife refuge of sand dunes, interconnected lagoons, mangroves and forest. La Pastoría is the largest lagoon, connected to the sea by an

Oaxacan cooking

The food of the state of Oaxaca is a fine representation of the complexity and variety of its cultures. The region's cuisine ranges from sublime to highly unusual.

A stroll through any of Oaxaca's markets will quickly bring you into contact with vendors selling *chapulines*. These small grasshopper-like creatures are fried, turning them bright red, and then served with lime. Another interesting ingredient in the diet is *gusanito*, a small red worm that is used to make a special sauce or ground with salt to accompany mezcal.

There are local curiosities for vegetarians as well. *Flor de calabaza*, squash flowers, are used in soup, *empanadas*, or as a garnish. Soup is also prepared from *nopales*, the young leaves of the prickly-pear cactus.

The most typical regional snacks are *tlayudas*, huge crispy tortillas, covered with a variety of toppings (beef, sausage, beans or cheese) and grilled over the coals. Oaxacan string cheese, known as *quesillo*, is also famous, as is the area's excellent chocolate, best enjoyed as a hot beverage. A slightly fermented drink made from corn flour is known as *atole*.

Barbacoa is a pork, lamb or beef dish combining several different types of chillies and special condiments such as avocado leaves. The colour of the resulting sauce is a very deep red, reminiscent of another platter appropriately called *mancha manteles* (tablecloth stain).

The essence of Oaxacan cooking, however, and the recipes for which the state is most famous, are its many *moles*, which come in all colours of the rainbow. They are served as sauces accompanying beef, chicken, turkey or pork. The most complex by far is *mole negro* (black), combining at least 17 different ingredients including cocoa beans and sesame seeds. *Mole colorado* (red), or just *coloradito*, is also very typical and quite spicy. *Almendrado* (also red) is milder and slightly sweet. *Mole verde* (green) is a bit tangy, while *mole amarillo* (yellow) rounds out Oaxaca's culinary chromatic spectrum.

---

estuary; it has nine islets that harbour thousands of birds, both resident and migratory. On the shores of the lagoon is the village of Chacahua, home to some of the area's small Afro-Mexican population. There is a crocodile hatchery nearby, aimed at preserving this native species. A tour is the easiest way to see the park and learn about its wildlife (see Activities and tours). To go independently you need two days; take a minibus to Río Grande (from 2a Norte and 3a Poniente, every 20 minutes), then another one to Zapotalito from where there are boats (US$12 per person if there are enough passengers) to the village of Chacahua. It's best to leave early to avoid the tour groups and if you plan to stay the night, take a mosquito net.

Closer and easier to access than Chacahua are the **Lagunas de Manialtepec**, 16 km west of Puerto Escondido, also a good place for birdwatching and watersports. Tours are available or take the same minibus towards Río Grande. Get off at the village of Manialtepec; at restaurants **Isla de Gallo** and **Puesta del Sol** you can hire a boat for four people (US$33 for two hours).

Pochutla → *Colour map 3, C5. Phone code: 958.*

Sixty-six kilometres east of Puerto Escondido and 240 km south of Oaxaca is San Pedro Pochutla, a hot and busy supply town with an imposing church set on a small hill. Its pleasant **Plaza de las Golondrinas**, where people stroll in the cool of the evening, is filled with many singing birds; countless swallows line up on the electric wires here every night. There is a prison in Pochutla, and the inmates carve crafts out of coconut husks for sale by their families and local shops. The **Fiesta de San Pedro** takes place on 29-30 June.

From Oaxaca, Highway 175 to Pochutla is a very scenic but extremely winding paved road. In the Central Valleys it goes through the craft towns of **Ocotlán de Morelos** (**Posada San Salvador**) and **Ejutla de Crespo** (**Hotel 6** and several other places to stay), before climbing the Sierra Madre del Sur to its pine-clad ridges and the pass. Just south of the pass is **San José del Pacífico**, a hamlet with nice views and a restaurant where buses make a rest stop.

Puerto Angel → *Colour map 3, C5. Phone code: 958.*

Twenty minutes south of Pochutla along a pretty road that winds through hilly forest country before dropping to the sea is Puerto Angel. Until the 1960s it was a busy port from which coffee and timber were shipped to Asia; with the fall in coffee prices, the local population turned to selling turtle skins until 1990, when this activity was banned in Mexico. Tourism and fishing are currently the main economic activities here. The town lies above a beautiful flask-shaped bay; unfortunately the turquoise water is polluted, but there are hopes for improvement if a planned sewage system is installed. Because of its lovely setting it has been described as 'the ideal place to rest and do nothing'. The beach, right in town, is an ideal spot to watch the activity of the small charming dock. A short walk away, either along the road or on a concrete path built on the rocks (not safe at night), is **Playa del Panteón**, a small beach in a lovely setting, but crowded with restaurants (touts await visitors on arrival) and many bathers in season. There are cleaner and more tranquil nearby beaches east of town. **Estacahuite**, with simple *cabañas*, 1 km from town, about a 20-minute walk, has good snorkelling (gear rental from hut selling drinks and snacks) but beware of strong waves, currents and sharp coral that can cut you; La Boquilla, with comfortable Canadian-run bungalows, is 3 km away, off a signed track on the road to Pochutla. There is a fiesta on 1 June to celebrate the Día de la Marina and another on 1 October, the Fiesta de San Angel.

Zipolite and San Agustinillo → *Phone code: 958.*

The fabled haunt of Zipolite has long-drawn an alternative crowd. Located 4 km west of Puerto Angel, it overlooks a stretch of ocean so ferocious, the waves seem to be possessed by some violent, raging spirit. If you don't break your neck trying to swim here, you'll be carried off to sea by wildly shifting rip-tides. Indeed, the name 'Zipolite' is believed to be derived from a Zapotec word meaning 'beach of the dead'.

But most people don't come here to swim, they come to be entertained. And Zipolite's reputation as a party town is deserved. Hordes of young gringos, backpackers, bongo-toting crusties and burnt-out old hippies descend en masse during high season. Young Mexicans too, are making their presence felt, and a string of beach bars provide the nightly entertainment, sousing the crowds with beer, tequila and other intoxicating liquors. Illicit drugs are readily available too, and the usual penalties for possession apply, including a long and not very comfortable stay in a Mexican prison.

The west end of the beach is reserved for nudists, so you may see naked men (they are almost always men) congregating around the rocks. Generally, the west side of the beach is the more lively and hedonistic side, with the greatest development and the most popular places. You'll find internet cafés and paved roads here. There's a quieter, family atmosphere at the less developed eastern side. Note that low season can be eerily quiet everywhere.

Another 3 km west lies **San Agustinillo**, a long, pretty beach, with an extraordinary cave in the cliffs. The western end is quite built up with private homes. Swimming is safest at the west end of the beach, surfing best near the centre. Nude bathing is prohibited.

Mazunte → *Phone code: 958.*

One kilometre further west is Mazunte, perhaps the least developed major beach in the area but rapidly changing, so responsible tourism is especially important. The beach is on federal land and drug laws are strictly enforced; nude bathing is prohibited, the safest swimming is at either end of the bay. At the east end of Mazunte is the **Centro Mexicano de la Tortuga** ① *guided tours in Spanish and English, Tue-Sat 1000-1630, Sun 1000-430, US$15, crowded with tour buses from Huatulco 1100-1300 during high season; interested researchers may contact the director at http://centromexicano delatortuga.org*, a government institute that studies sea turtles and works to conserve these frequently endangered species, as well as to educate visitors and the local population. There are interesting viewing tanks to observe many species of turtles underwater. A trail leads from the west end of the beach to **Punta Cometa**, a spit of land with lovely views of the thundering breakers below, a popular spot to view the sunset and well worth the 30-minute walk.

La Ventanilla

Two kilometres west of Mazunte is a signed turn-off for Ventanilla. It is 1.5 km from here to the village and visitor centre on the shores of a lagoon. Tours are run by local residents who are working on a mangrove reforestation project (in 1997 Hurricane Pauline wiped out part of the mangroves here) and have a crocodile farm to repopulate the area. The tour combines a rowing boat ride through the mangroves for up to 10 people, a visit to the crocodile farm and a walk on the beach, US$5 per person, many birds, crocodiles and iguanas may be seen; the guides speak Spanish only. Recommended. Horse-riding tours along the beach are also available for US$25 per hour. Those wishing to spend the night can camp or stay with a family. Simple meals are available in the village.

Huatulco → *Colour map 3, C5. Phone code: 958.*

East of Pochutla (50 km, one hour), and 112 km west of Salina Cruz on the coast road is Huatulco, a meticulously engineered and environmentally aware resort complex surrounded by 34,000 ha of forest reserve and nine splendid bays (where pirate ships used to shelter). It offers golf, swimming pools, international and Mexican cuisine, nightlife, beaches, watersports, excursions into the forest and exploration of archaeological sites. The final product is safe, clean, efficient, an international vacation resort in a lovely setting with a mild Mexican flavour. Huatulco's high seasons include Holy Week, July to August and November to March, with regular charter flights from the USA and Canada during the latter months; prices can as much as double during these periods.

The Sedetur tourist office ① *Blv Benito Juárez, Tangolunda, T958-581 0176, sedetur6@oaxaca.gob.mx*, is near the golf course, helpful and informative. An auxiliary **information booth** ① *Parque Central*, a *Crucecita*, run by Señor Cipriano, is a handy alternative source of information. A useful **website** is *www.bahiasdehuatulco.com.mx*. ▶ *See Activities and tours, page 472.*

The Huatulco complex encompasses several interconnected towns and development areas; and there are many taxis, some of which operate as *colectivos*. Prices for journeys can be found on signs at the main plaza in Crucecita. **Tangolunda** (meaning 'beautiful woman' in Zapotec), on the bay of the same name and also known as the Zona Hotelera, is set aside for large luxury hotels and resorts; it also has the golf course and the most expensive restaurants, souvenir shops and nightlife. **Chahué**, on the next bay west, where development only began in 1999, has a town park with spa and beach club, a marina and a few hotels. Further west (6 km from Tangolunda) is **Santa Cruz Huatulco**, once an ancient Zapotec settlement and Mexico's most important Pacific port during the 16th century (later abandoned). It has the marina where tour boats leave for excursions, as well as facilities for visiting yachts, several upscale hotels, restaurants, shops and a few luxury homes. An open-air chapel by the beach here, the Capilla de la Santa Cruz, is attractive; nearby is a well-groomed park.

La Crucecita, located 2 km inland, is the functional hub of the Huatulco complex, with housing for the area's employees, bus stations, banks, a small market, ordinary shops, bars, plus the more economical hotels and restaurants. It also doubles as a Mexican town, which the tourists can visit, more cosmetic by the manicured Plaza Principal, less so towards the highway. The old-looking but brand-new Templo de Guadalupe church stands on a small hill next to the plaza.

Huatulco's coastline extends for almost 30 km between the Río Copalita to the east and the Río Coyula to the west. Hills covered in deciduous forest – very green during the rainy season (June to September), yellow and parched in the dry – sweep down to the sea. Nine turquoise bays with 36 golden beaches line the shore, some bays have road access while others can only be reached by sea.

Around Huatulco

In the Huatulco area the **Sierra Madre del Sur** mountains drop from the highest point in the state of Oaxaca (3750 m) right down to the sea. There are ample opportunities for day-hiking, see Activities and tours. In the hills north of Huatulco are a number of coffee plantations that can be visited. Huatulco travel agencies arrange for full-day plantation tours, which include a meal with traditional dishes at the farm and bathing in fresh water springs or waterfalls; US$44 per person.

Bays of Huatulco

Day trips to the different coastal attractions to the west, including Puerto Angel and Mazunte, are offered by travel agencies for US$20. Much ground is covered; it's a long day.

Isthmus of Tehuantepec ●🛈⊗●🛈 ⇒ pp456-481. Colour map 3, C6.

From the city of Oaxaca, Route 190 heads southeast, through the towns of **San José de Gracia** and **El Camarón**, towards the Golfo de Tehuantepec and the Pacific.

Only about 210 km separate the Atlantic and the Pacific at the hot, once heavily jungled Isthmus of Tehuantepec, where the land does not rise more than 250 m. This narrowest point of Mexico is also the geographic boundary between North and Central America. There is the Trans-Isthmian Highway between Salina Cruz and Coatzacoalcos, the terminal cities on the two oceans.

The Isthmus has a strong cultural character all of its own. The people are *mestizo* and descendants of several different indigenous groups, but Zapotecs predominate. Once a matriarchal society, Zapotec women continue to play a very important role in local affairs. Their typical dress is intricate and beautiful, and they are high-pressure saleswomen. The men generally work in the fields, or as potters or weavers, or at the Salina Cruz oil refinery.

The Isthmian region of Oaxaca is dominated by three neighbouring cities: Salina Cruz is a modern industrial city and port; Tehuantepec is the smallest and most authentic; while Juchitán has the largest and most interesting market. The climate throughout the area can be oppressive, very hot and quite humid, hence the region's cultural events usually take place late in the evening. Winds are very strong on and near the Isthmus, due to the intermingling of Pacific and Caribbean weather systems. Take extra care in the sea as the currents are very dangerous. Also watch your belongings.

Salina Cruz → Colour map 3, C6. Phone code: 971.

A modern and industrial city and port, with broad avenues and a large central plaza. Salina Cruz is surrounded by hills and many poor neighbourhoods. Some of the nearby beaches are quite scenic but oil pollution, high winds, dangerous surf and sharks all conspire against would-be bathers. Do not park close to the beach, as your vehicle may be sandblasted.

Ten kilometres to the southeast is a picturesque fishing village with **La Ventosa** beach, which, as the name says, is windy. In 1528 the Spanish conquerors established a shipyard here; the old lighthouse, **El Faro de Cortés**, can still be seen. Buses go to the beach every 30 minutes from a corner of the main square.

The coast west of Salina Cruz is quite scenic, with several high sand dunes and lagoons; shrimp farms have been set up in this area. Just west of the city is the village of Salinas del Marquez; the beach of **Las Escolleras** in Salinas is popular with locals. Urban bus service from the park in Salina Cruz every 30 minutes.

Tehuantepec → Colour map 3, C6. Phone code: 971. Altitude: 150 m.

Santo Domingo Tehuantepec, 257 km from Oaxaca, is a colourful town that conserves the region's indigenous flavour. Robust Zapotec matrons in bright dresses ride standing in the back of motorized tricycles known as *moto-carros*. Life moves slowly here, centered on the plaza, which has arcades on one side, and an adjacent market, the best place to admire the Zapotec dress. In the plaza is a statue of Máximo Ramón Ortiz

(1816-1855) composer of the *zandunga*, the legendary music of the Isthmus, which is still very popular. The meandering Río Tehuantepec is two blocks from the plaza, by the highway. Due to the importance of Tehuantepec during the early colonial period, many churches were built here; attractive white churches with coloured trim dot the landscape. Houses are low, in white or pastel shades.

The **Casa de la Cultura** is housed in the 16th-century Dominican ex-convent Rey Cosijopi. The building is quite run down, but original frescoes can still be seen on some walls. There is a library and some simple exhibits of regional archaeology, history and costumes. Ask the caretaker to open the exhibits for you. The **Museo Casa de la Señora Juana C Romero** is a chalet built entirely with materials brought from France; Señora Romero's great-granddaughter lives there today, ask for permission to visit the house.

There are two tourist offices, **SEDETUR** ① *Carretera Transístmica, next to the bridge into town*, the regional office for the Isthmus and the **Regiduría de Turismo** ① *Palacio de Gobierno*.

Around Tehuantepec

To the northwest of town, off the road to Oaxaca, are the unrestored ruins of **Guiengola**, 'the Mexican Machu Picchu', so called because of its lonely location on a mountain. It has walls up to 3 m high, running, it is said, for 40 km; there are the remains of two pyramids and a ball court. This last fortress of the Zapotecs was never conquered (*guiengola* is the Zapotec word for fortress); Alvarado and his forces marched past it in 1522. Take the 0500 bus from Tehuantepec towards Oaxaca and get off at the Puente las Tejas bridge (8 km from Tehuantepec); this is the last place to buy water on the way to the ruins. Take the turning at the signpost 'Ruinas Guiengola 7 km'. Walk 5 km then turn left, uphill, to the car park. From here it is 1½ hours' walk to the ruins, there are no facilities or entry fees. Try to return before 0900 because it gets very hot; take plenty of water. Alternatively, take a taxi to the car park and ask the driver to return for you three hours later (US$5.50 each trip).

Juchitán and around → *Colour map 3, C6. Phone code: 971.*

Twenty-seven kilometres from Tehuantepec is the larger and more modern city of Juchitán de Zaragoza, an important commercial and cultural centre on the Isthmus. It has a nice plaza next to impressive colonial municipal buildings and many churches including that of **San Vicente Ferrer**, the city's patron saint. Many Zapotec women here still wear traditional costumes as everyday dress. The **tourist office** is at the Palacio de Gobierno. The **Mercado Central 5 de Septiembre** is the largest market on the Isthmus; traditional barter still takes place here. The meat and produce section is dirty, but the crafts section on the second floor is well worth a visit; this is the best place to see the elaborate embroidered Zapotec dresses, which sell for up to US$600.

South of Juchitán and stretching for some 100 km to the east are three very large, shallow lagoons. On the shores of Laguna Superior, the closest one, 10 km south of the city, is the fishing village of **Playa Vicente**; across from here are several scenic islands. In Laguna Mar Muerto, the furthest one to the east, there are salt pans.

For Sleeping and Eating price codes and other relevant information, see Essentials pages 45-48.

☺ Sleeping

Oaxaca *p434, map p436*
There are over 160 hotels in Oaxaca in all price categories. If you wish to stay at a particular hotel reservations are recommended during peak holiday periods (Easter, Jul-Aug, Christmas and New Year).

There are many cheap hotels in the block formed by the streets Mina, Zaragoza, Díaz Ordaz and JP García; also on Trujano (4 blocks from the zócalo).
LL Casa Cid de León, Av Morelos 602, 2 blocks from the zócalo, T951-514 1893, www.casaciddeleon.com. This intimate and interesting boutique hotel offers 4 different suites, all luxurious and lavishly decorated. The service is 1st rate and personal, overseen by the gracious and hospitable Leticia Ricardez. The hotel organizes tours and offers massage. Low-season and longer-stay discounts. Highly recommended.
LL-L La Casona de Tita, García Vigil 805, T951 516 1400, www.lacasonadetita.com. 6 individually decorated, spacious rooms, set around a beautiful terracotta courtyard, right next to a craft centre. 1 room is wheelchair accessible. Stylish and eco-friendly with all the mod cons. Recommended.
L Marqués del Valle, Portal de Clavería, right on the zócalo by cathedral, T951-514 0688, www.hotelmarquesdelvalle.com.mx. An elegant lobby precedes far less interesting and somewhat overpriced rooms. However, some of them have exceptional views over the zócalo, which makes up for it some way. The staff are friendly and courteous. Also has a good restaurant, **Portal del Marqués**.
AL Casa Conzatti, Gómez Farías 218, T951-513 8500, www.casaconzatti.com.mx. 45 rooms in refurbished colonial house, a/c, safety deposit box, exchange, restaurant.

AL Parador Santo Domingo de Guzmán, Alcalá 804, T951-514 2171, www.paradorstodomingo.com.mx. An all-suite hotel with secure car parking, pool, cable TV and internet access. Suites have bedroom, sitting room and kitchen, daily maid included. Good mid-week rates. Recommended.
AL-A La Casona del Llano, Juárez 701, T951-514 7719. Clean, modern rooms in this secluded hotel, all with cable TV. There's an elegant restaurant attached that overlooks Paseo Juárez. Secure parking. Good low season discounts.
A Ferri, Las Casas 405, T951-514 5290. Pretty motel-style option with clean, modern rooms, internet and parking.
A Hotel Casantica, Av Morelos 601, T951-516 2673, www.hotelcasantica.com. Handsome hotel set in a beautifully restored 200-year-old colonial convent with quiet courtyards replete with palms and greenery, bubbling fountains and an inviting – if modest – pool. There's a restaurant attached, open 0730-2200, but service is reportedly slow.
A Posada Catarina, Aldama 325, T951-516 4270, www.travelbymexico.com/oaxaca/catarina. Modern colonial mid-range option, comfortable, with parking.
B Antonio's, Independencia 601, 1 block from zócalo, T951-516 7227, antonios_hotel@hotmail.com. Colonial patio, hot water, very clean.
B Hotel Monte Albán, Alameda de León 1, T951-516 2777, www.travelbymexico.com/oaxa/montealban. Friendly, colonial-style hotel with some elegant rooms overlooking the cathedral. Folk dance performances every night at 2030. (see Entertainment, page 467).
B Las Rosas, Trujano 112, T951-514 2217, hlrosasoax@hotmail.com. Plenty of charm at this friendly hotel. There's a nice patio, a good view from the roof, free internet, free tea and coffee for guests. Good family rooms.
B Mesón del Rey, Trujano 212, 1 block from zócalo, T951-516 0033, mesonrey@

prodigy.net.mx. This colonial-style hotel offers clean, modern and often cosy rooms, all quiet except for street-facing ones. Restaurant attached.

B Parador San Andrés, Hidalgo 405, 2 blocks from the zócalo, T951-514 1011, www.hotelesdeoaxaca.com. Comfortable, colonial-style hotel with just 6 quiet rooms, all with lovely wood beam ceilings. There's a tranquil and secluded terrace. Discounts for longer stays.

B Posada del Centro, Independencia 403, T951-516 1874, www.mexonline.com/posada.htm. Pretty, colourful posada set around courtyard, with spacious rooms. Friendly and able to organize tours. Over US$10 cheaper with shared bath. Highly recommended.

B Posada Don Matías, Aldama 316, T951-501 0084, www.donmatias.net. Very pleasant, tastefully decorated hotel with a beautiful, plant-filled patio and clean, attractive rooms, free internet.

B Posada Las Casas, Las Casas 507 y Díaz Ordaz, T951-516 2325. Clean and tidy hotel with rooms set around a central courtyard. Cheaper without bath (**C**), friendly and good value.

B Principal, 5 de Mayo 208, 2 blocks from the zócalo, T951-516 2535, hotelprincipal@gmail.com. Colonial house, slightly run-down, private shower, morning coffee and cookies included. English spoken, friendly, rooms overlooking street are a bit noisy but still heavily booked.

B Rivera del Angel, Francisco Javier Mina 518, T951-516 6666, www.hotelrivera delangel.com. Large and friendly, if a bit impersonal, hotel takes over a whole block so you can't miss it. Lush garden, swimming pool and volleyball court. Parking and tours available. Popular with Mexicans.

B Valle de Oaxaca, Díaz Ordaz 208, T951-516 3707, www.travelbymexico.com/oaxaca/hotelvalledeoaxaca. Clean, comfortable hotel with some tranquil patio space, sofas and table soccer. Friendly. Good restaurant attached.

B-C Lupita, Díaz Ordaz 314, T951-516 5733. Lovely, large, clean and brightly coloured rooms. Upstairs rooms have brilliant views across the city and mountains from the flat rooftop. Rooms cheaper without bath.

C Central, 20 de Noviembre 104, 1 block from the zócalo, T951-514 9425. This well-located cheapie has simple rooms with bath and hot water, although it isn't especially good value. Rooms cheaper without bath. Slightly scruffy and run down.

C Mina, Mina 304, T951-516 4966. This clean and basic hotel has rooms with shared bath only. There is hot water.

C-D La Cabaña, Mina 203, T951-516 5918, F514-0739. This good value, economical hotel has rooms with and without bath. Clean, but can be noisy.

C-E Hostal Pochon, Callejón del Carmen 102, T951-516 1322, www.hostalpochon.com. 5 dormitories and several private rooms, including a new junior suite in quiet part of town near Santo Domingo. Cheap long-distance calls, breakfast with home-made bread, free drinking water, Wi-Fi, internet, cooking lessons, excursions arranged, bike hire and bike tours. Good friendly atmosphere and multilingual staff. Highly recommended.

C-E Mezkalito Hostel, Independencia 101, T951-514 3001, www.mezkalitohostel.com. Clean, professionally managed hostel with various sized dorms or private rooms, laundry services, internet, kitchen and. Good low season and long-stay discounts.

D-F Paulina Youth Hostal, Trujano 321, T951-516 2005, www.paulinahostel.com. This immaculate and professionally run youth hostel has large, clean, attractive dorms and a few private rooms. There's a pleasant garden and the interior is tastefully decorated. A simple breakfast is included.

E Palmar, JP García 504 y Mina, T951-514 9889. Family-run and slightly run-down cheapie offers comfortable enough rooms, even cheaper without bath. Hot water in morning, safe motorcycle parking. Long-stay discounts.

Camping

Oaxaca Trailer Park, Violeta 900, Col Reforma, north of town off the road to Mitla at a sign marked 'Infonavit' (corner of Pinos and Violetas). US$4.50 for a tent, US$12 for a camper van, secure; bus 'Carmen-Infonavit' from downtown. Slightly run-down these days.

Route to Mitla *p443*

In 13 towns, throughout the Central Valleys around Oaxaca, including Tlacolula, there is tourist accommodation known as **Tourist Yú'ù** run by local communities (**D** per person, US$5 to camp). Each house has a room with 6 beds, equipped kitchen, bathroom with hot water. For details contact the **Sedetur** office, see page 435.

B Hotel y Restaurante Mitla, Mitla town square, T951-968 0112. Private bath, simple, clean, friendly, local food.

C Hotel y Restaurante La Zapoteca, Mitla, before bridge on road to ruins, T951-958 0026. Private bath, hot water, parking, friendly, good food.

Puerto Escondido *p448, map p448*

Puerto Escondido and Playa Zicatela have some180 hotels in all categories.

Downtown

L Aldea del Bazar, Benito Juárez 7, T954-582 0508, www.aldeadelbazar.mexico-hoteles.com. A veritable Sultan's palace, complete with Middle Eastern dress for the staff. There's a huge garden with palms, pool, large rooms and a good restaurant.

A Barlovento, Camino al Faro, Calle 6a Sur, No 3, T954-582 0220, www.oaxaca-mio.com/hotelbarlovento.htm. Large, comfortable and secluded hotel on the way to the lighthouse offers a/c rooms with telephone and TV. There's a pool, and cheaper rooms with fans. Great views over the bay.

A Paraíso Escondido, Unión 10, Centro, T954-582 0444, www.hotelpe.com. Away from the beach, this colonial-style hotel has suites and rooms, a/c, pool, and a great garden filled with statues in the style of pre-Columbian artefacts; the restaurant open in high season serves international cuisine.

A-B Casablanca, Av Pérez Gasga 905 (Adoquín), T954-582 0168, www.ptohcasablanca.com. A/c in some rooms, fan, hot water, clean, well furnished with balconies and a pool.

A-B Rincón del Pacífico, Av Pérez Gasga 900 (Adoquín), T954-582 0193, www.rincondelpacifico.com.mx. Clean and simple rooms with fan, TV and bathroom. **Danny's Beach Bar** is attached.

B Rocamar, Av Pérez Gasga 601, T954-582 0339. Decent, nicely decorated and economical rooms, most of them with a/c and cable TV.

C Ben Zaa, 3a Sur 303, T954-582 0523, www.hotelben-zaa.com, on hill climbing to the lighthouse. 30 rooms with cable TV and economical *cabañas*, complete with cooking facilities, fridges and bathrooms – daily, weekly and monthly rates available. The hospitable manager, Steve Posing, can organize sport fishing, horse riding and bikes. There's international cuisine and daily specials. The view from the roof is sublime.

C Casa de Huéspedes San Martín, 1a Oriente 106, T954-582 0883. Bit grotty and very basic, but close to bus stations. Private bath and fan not especially good value.

C Castillo de Reyes, Av Pérez Gasga 210, T/F954-582 0442 Clean, nice rooms, hot water, quiet, good beds, friendly, good value. Recommended.

C Cocoa Beach, de los Fundadores s/n, also access from Felipe Merklin, T954-582 0428, behind the church. Small, clean and simple rooms with fan or a/c and mosquito nets. Also has 2 self-catering flats. Friendly and family-run.

C Hotel Premier, Hidalgo and 1er ote, T954-582 0116. Another clean and basic cheapie near the bus station. Some rooms are large and offer good ocean views.

C Mayflower, Andador Libertad, on pedestrian walkway perpendicular to El Adoquín, T954-582 0367. Minnemay7@

hotmail.com. This excellent hostel has dorms and rooms and offers its guests Wi-Fi, free internet, lockers, safety deposit box, kitchen facilities and pool table. There's a great terrace and upstairs sitting area with a grand piano and views over the bay. The owner, Minne Dahlberg, is a very attentive hostess. Recommended.

C Ribera del Mar, Felipe Merklin 205, T954-582 0436, behind Iglesia de la Soledad (beware early morning church bells). Fan, hot water, pool, clean, quiet, laundry facilities, some rooms with great views of the sea. Good value. Recommended.

C Villa Mozart y Macondo, Av Tortugas 77, Carrizalillo, T954-104 2295, www.villa mozart.de. Hotel with rooms, apartments and bungalows close to Playa Carrizalillo. Beautiful location, German-run.

Camping Trailer Park Palmas de Cortés, Av Pérez Gasga and Andador Azucena, near Playa Principal, T954-582 0774. Clean bathrooms, shade, US$5 per car, US$6 per person. Recommended.

Playa Zicatela

LL Santa Fe, Calle del Moro, T954-582 0170, www.hotelsantafe.com.mx. 4-star Mediterranean-style hotel concealing pleasant patios, courtyards and pool. Good seafood restaurant attached.

A Bungalows Acuario, Calle del Moro, T954-582 0357, www.hotelbungalows acuariozicatela.com.mx. Rooms and bungalows. Prices drop considerably off-season, and are generally cheaper with shared bath. There's a pool, gym, good travel agent, *casa de cambio* and internet facilities.

A Bungalows Zicatela, Calle del Moro, T954-582 0798, www.bungalows zicatela.com.mx. Ocean-front rooms with terraces, kitchenettes and fridge. Rooms have a/c, but are cheaper with fan. There are 2 larger and 2 smaller pools and a small restaurant. Low season prices much lower.

B Casa de las Iguanas, Av Bajada las Brisas s/n, T954-582 1995, www.casadelas iguanas.com.

Friendly new surfers' hotel. Has comfortable rooms with a/c, jacuzzis, pool and funky bar. Clean and professionally managed. Organizes surf lessons and excursions.

B Inés, Calle del Moro, T954-582 0792, www.hotelines.com. Colourful, pleasant rooms and a chilled-out garden slung with hammocks. Also has *cabañas*, apartments and suites. There's a bar, pool and travel agency.

B Rockaway, Calle del Moro, T954-582 0668, www.hotelrockaway.com. Popular hangout with hippie twist where *cabañas* and rooms overlook a pool. *Cabañas* are completely self-contained with bathroom, showers and mosquito nets. Rooms have a/c and hot water.

Pochutla *p450*

There are several hotels in Pochutla if you need to stay. But with all those miles of beautiful coast just a short ride away, why would you want to?

C Costa del Sol, Lázaro Cárdenas 47, T958-584 0318. Parking and pool at this hotel. Rooms have a/c (cheaper with fan) and cable TV.

C Izala, Lázaro Cárdenas 59, T958-584 0115. Slightly tired rooms have a/c, cheaper with fan (**C**), TV, hot water, nice patio, clean, comfortable.

D Santa Cruz, Lázaro Cárdenas 88, across from Oaxaca terminal (shuttle to Oaxaca leaves from here), T958-584 6214. Very basic and run down, cheaper with fan.

Puerto Angel *p451*

A La Cabaña, Pedro Saenz de Baranda s/n, Playa del Panteón, T958-584 3105, www.lacabanapuertoangel.com. Clean and comfortable rooms with a/c. There's a pleasant terrace and pool.

B Soraya de Puerto Angel, José Vasconcelos s/n, Playa Principal, T958-584 3009. Beautiful views, clean, spacious terraces, a/c, parking.

B Villa Florencia, Calle Virgilio Uribe s/n across from town beach, T/F958-584 3044. A/c, cheaper with fan, clean, comfortable, friendly, Italian/Mexican-run, restaurant, bar, library with terrace.

B-C Casa de Huéspedes Gundi y Tomás, central and up the hill opposite old military base, T958-584 3068, www.puerto angel-hotel.com. Pleasant hotel with colourful rooms and tranquil terraces. There's a book exchange, hammocks for chilling out in, communal fridge and bar. Good rates for weekly and monthly stays. Changes TCs.

C Capy's, Pedro Saenz de Baranda, on road to Playa del Panteón, T958-584 3240. Basic rooms with fan. Nice restaurant attached. Cheap for a single person.

C Posada Rincón Sabroso, Uribe s/n, near Villa Florencia, T958-584 3095. Clean rooms with hot water. Beautiful views and a terrace with hammocks. Quiet. Friendly management.

C Puesta del Sol, on road to Playa del Panteón, T958-584 3315, www.puerto angel.net. Friendly German management has a wealth of information on the area. Comfortable rooms, movies and internet available. Rooftop terrace with hammocks, light breakfast and snacks. Recommended.

D Casa de Huéspedes Leal, central, T958-584 3081. Very economical and basic. Shared bath, washing facilities, friendly.

Zipolite *p451*

The shore is lined with *palapas* offering cheap meals, accommodation and informal discos. The western end of the beach is more lively and popular than the quieter eastern end.

B El Neptuno, T958-584 3219, www.hotelneptunozipolite.com, eastern end of beach. If sleeping in a hut isn't your thing, then come here. You'll find nice, bright rooms surrounded by solid walls, balconies, sea-views and a restaurant serving good Mexican food.

AL Nude Bungalows and Sky Lounge, on the western end of beach opposite the nude beach, hence the name. This is the latest addition to Zipolite with upmarket *cabañas* boasting excellent views, an international restaurant and über-cool bar, perfect for sundowners. Most *cabañas* have TV, private bathrooms and kitchen, beach chairs and there's a nice pool.

C Lo Cósmico, www.locosmico.com, western end of beach. Lovely, rustic *cabañas* with excellent views. There are hammocks (**F**) if you're very impoverished (or just enjoy sleeping outdoors). Friendly owner.

C Lola's Linos, along the quieter eastern end of the beach, T958-584 320131. Colourful rooms on several floors. There's a bar and restaurant, with reasonably priced meals (**¶¶-¶**). Quiet setting and brightly painted pinky-purple building, can't be missed. Spacious rooms, friendly.

C Posada Brisa Marina, T958-584 3193, brisamarinaca@yahoo.com, western end of beach. Large, simple rooms and hammock space **G**. Friendly owner will help with bus tickets. Free Wi-Fi. Recommended.

C Posada México, T958-584 3194, www.posadamexico.com, western end of beach. Nice, spacious, comfortable *cabañas* in gorgeous colours, all kitted out with nets and hammocks. There's an attractive cactus garden and an Italian restaurant that serves authentic stone-baked pizzas in high season.

C Shambhala, T958-584 3152, shambhala_vision@excite.com, western end of beach near the rocks. "Where the 60s never end" – and they mean it. There's a strong hippie ethos at this long-standing Zipolite favourite. It has dorms (**E**) and rooms, social spaces and inspiring views over the Pacific. Café Bohemia, attached, serves good fish and Mexican dishes.

San Agustinillo *p451*

A Punta Placer, on main beach, www.puntaplacer.com. Well-kept, clean and popular. Owner also runs Coco Loco surf club (www.cocolocosurfclub.com) – surf board rental, surfing lessons in English, Spanish and French, surfing tours (also in 3 languages); mountain hikes, restaurant attached. Recommended.

C Posada San Agustín, San Agustinillo. This place has been slowly left to crumble into a ruin, but it still has the best views in San Agustinillo.

C-D Palapa Olas Altas, western end of the beach. 3 rooms with bath and several cheaper *cabañas*. Economical, but a bit basic. Restaurant attached does reasonable meals including good seafood.

Mazunte *p452*

Several *palapas* offer simple accommodation along the middle of the beach.
A Posada Alta Mira, on a wooded hillside overlooking the western end of the beach, T958-101 8332, www.labuenavista.com/alta_mira. Beautiful, tidy bungalows overlooking the ocean – the views are spectacular.
B Balamjuyuc, next to Posada Alta Mira, T958-101 1808, balamjuyuc@hotmail.com. Friendly owners Emiliano and Gaby run this tranquil eco-tourism venture with gorgeous views. Different types of massage and temazcal are available and their restaurant Pacha Mama does home-made veggie food with everything from the bread to the pasta made on location. There's tent space or hammocks (**G**). English, German and Italian spoken. Highly recommended.
C Ziga, www.posadaziga.com, at the eastern end near the Centro Mexicano de la Tortuga. Rooms are cheaper without bath, but not that good value (**C**). There's a great terrace with hammocks and views of the Pacific.
D Restaurant and Cabañas Yuri. Beach *palapa* with basic rooms, some have separate bath. There's also hammock space. Friendly and family-run.

Huatulco *p452*

Discounts of up to 50% can be expected in low season.
L Marina Resort, Tehuantepec 112, Santa Cruz, T958-587 0963, www.hotelmarina resort.com. Various high quality suites and a plethora of facilities including pools, restaurants, pre-Hispanic-style spa, and disco.
L Quinta Real, Blv Benito Juárez 2, Tangolunda, T958-581 0428, www.quintareal.com. Exclusive and very secluded resort with inspirational views over the bay. There's a golf club, beach club, pool, bar and restaurant. The suites are 1st rate.
AL Gran Hotel Huatulco, Carrizal 1406, La Crucecita, at the entrance to town, T01-800-712 7355, www.granhotel huatulco.com. 32 comfortable, if unremarkable rooms, all with double beds, a/c and cable TV. Also pool, restaurant bar and parking. Good reductions in low season.
AL Meigas Binniguenda, Blv Sta Cruz 201, Santa Cruz, T958-587 0077, binniguenda@ prodigy.net.mx. Colonial-style hotel with gardens, pool, restaurant and beach club.
AL Plaza Huatulco, Blv Benito Juárez 23, Tangolunda, T958-581 0035, www.hotelplaza huatulco.com.mx. Small luxurious hotel with comfortable suites and personalized service.
AL Posada Chahué Best Western, Mixie and Mixteco, Chahué, T958-710 7889, www.bwhuatulco.com. Good, if predictable rooms with a/c and all the usual extras. There's a pool and terrace restaurant.
A Busanvi I, Carrizal 601, La Crucecita, T958-587 0739. A/c, fan and hot water.
A Misión de los Arcos, Gardenia 902 and Tamarindo, La Crucecita, T958-587 0165, www.misiondelosarcos.com. Elegant suites with Wi-Fi and a/c. Guests have use of Chahué beach club. Restaurant attached.
A Posada de Rambo, Guarumbo 307, La Crucecita, near main plaza, T958-587 0958. Clean and quiet with pleasant rooms. A/c, cable TV and hot water.
C Benimar, Bugambilia and Pochote, La Crucecita, T958-587 0447. Simple rooms with bath, fan and hot water.
C Casa de Huéspedes Koly, Bugambilia 301, La Crucecita, near Plaza, T958-583 1985. Very central, cheap, basic and clean rooms with fan, bath and cable TV. Fair for the price.
C Posada del Carmen, Palo Verde 307, La Crucecita, 1958-587 0593. Clean, simple, straightforward rooms in this small hotel. Acceptable.
C San Agustín, Carrizal No 1102 and Macuil, La Crucecita, T958-587 0368. Clean, basic rooms with bath and fan.

Salina Cruz *p454*
You'll find cheap lodgings on La Ventosa beach, where you can sling a hammock for a few dollars.
B Avistmo, Trabajo 699C, T971-714 5236, near the bus station. Motel-style place with large rooms, cable TV and secure parking. The owner speaks English and is helpful.
B Costa Real, Progreso 22, near Avila Camacho, T971-714 0293. Clean, spacious rooms with a/c. There's a restaurant attached, but it's pricey. Parking.
B María del Carmen, Manzanillo 17 and Tampico, T971-714 5625. Modern rooms with a/c. Cheaper with fan.
C Pacífico, Avila Camacho 709, T/F971-714 5552. Simple rooms with a/c, cheaper with fan. Restaurant attached.
C Posada del Jardín, Avila Camacho 108, T971-714 0162. As the name might suggest, there's a good, lush garden. Rooms have a/c and bath, cheaper with fan.

Tehuantepec *p454*
B Donají del Istmo, Juárez 10, T971-715 0064, in centre. Clean and friendly hotel with hot water in the mornings. Rooms with a/c more expensive (**B**).
B Guiexhoba, on road to Oaxaca, T971-715 0416, guiexhoba@prodigy.net.mx. A/c, mini-fridge, pool, restaurant, parking.
C Oasis, Melchor Ocampo 8, 1 block from plaza, T971-715 0008, h.oasis@hotmail.com. Clean, simple rooms with bath and fan, more expensive with a/c (**B**). The owner is helpful and has good information on local history. There's safe parking, an internet café and restaurant attached. Look out for the toucan.
D Casa de Huéspedes Istmo, Hidalgo 31, 1½ blocks from the main plaza, T971-715 0019. Very basic and quiet. There's a patio and hammocks.

Juchitán and around *p455*
The Casa de Cultura can help if you want to stay with local people and learn about their culture.

A-B Santo Domingo, Carretera Juchitán – Tehuantepec s/n 1era sección,, Juchitán, T971-711 1959. Good rooms with a/c. There's a restaurant and pool.
B Hotel López Lena Palace, 16 de Septiembre 70, Juchitán, T971-711 1388. Clean, modern, comfortable rooms with a/c. Cheaper in older wing and with fan, restaurant.
C Alfa, Carretera Panamericana Km 821, T971-711 0327. Basic, economical room with a/c and bath. Cheaper with fan.
D Modelo, 2 de Abril 64, T971-711 1241, Juchitán, near market. With bath, fan, basic.

❶ Eating

Oaxaca *p434, map p436*
Around the zócalo
Most restaurants on the main square cater for tourists, and can be pricey. Generally standards are good.
†††-†† Asador Vasco, above Bar Jardín. www.asadorvasco.com. Live Mexican music in the evening, good regional, international and Basque food and good service.
††† Portal del Marqués, part of Hotel del Marqués, on the north side of the zócalo. Fine dining on the plaza with exciting adaptations of regional food.
††-† La Primavera. Good-value meals, international and traditional dishes, good snacks and espresso coffee, slow.
††-† Restaurante Amarantos and **Terranova Restaurant**, **Taco Inn**, **Sushi Itto** and **Altos de Terranova**, the last 4 under 1 roof, Hidalgo, at east side of zócalo. Good food and snacks, friendly but **Terranova** can be pricey.
† El Mesón. Buffets 0800-1830, good at US$2.50, breakfast, *comida corrida* poor value, good tacos, clean, quick service.

North of Independencia
††† Café Bar Tapas & Pisto, Macedonio Alcalá 403, upstairs. Opens 1800. Artfully renovated colonial house, excellent view

from top terrace, more pricey but worth visiting just for the bathroom.

Casa Oaxaca, García Vigil 407. Where food is art, fine courtyard, excellent service and food, reservations very necessary, popular with artists and writers such as Gabriel García Márquez, excellent value. Also does accommodation.

Hostería de Alcalá, Macedonio Alcalá 307. Excellent food and quiet atmosphere in a beautiful colonial courtyard. Mostly meat and fish dishes. Good service and expensive.

Los Danzantes, next door to Café Bar Tapas & Pisto, Macedonio Alcalá 403. Open 1430-2330, Mexican fusion cooking in a stylish courtyard, well-stocked bar, particularly good for mezcal.

Marco Polo, 5 de Mayo 103. 0800-2100. Reputable seafood restaurant. Specialities include crab in chilli sauce, seafood shish kebab and red snapper fillet.

La Abeja, Porfirio Díaz 610 and Carranza. Traditional breakfasts and lunches, also good set vegetarian meals, bakery, garden setting.

La Crepe, Macedonio Alcalá 307. This clean, modern restaurant has a great 1st-floor location, with some tables overlooking the street. Good fresh salads, crêpes and cheap breakfast combos.

Pizza Rústica, Alcalá 804A and Humboldt. This decent and popular Italian restaurant dishes out fine pasta and pizza, as well as antipastos, meat and fish dishes. Friendly and authentic.

Comala, Plaza Allende 109. Trendy café inspired by Juan Rulfo's novel *Pedro Páramo*. Themed cocktails and excellent Mexican dishes. Try the cucumber margarita. Good nightspot.

Flor de Loto, Morelos 509, next to Museo Rufino Tamayo. Good value, clean, vegetarian and Mexican. *Supesteka* is delicious, also breakfast.

Manantial Vegetariano, Matamoros with Tinoco and Palacios. Tables occupy a pleasant, fountain-filled courtyard at this renowned restaurant. There's a buffet Sat lunchtime and *comida corrida* during the week. Also serves meat dishes. Good value, recommended.

Pizza Nostrana, corner of Allende close to Santo Domingo church. 1300-2300. Delicious Italian cuisine.

Tito's, García Vigil No 116. Good, reasonably priced food including Mexican and Oaxacan staples, sandwiches and a set menu at lunch time.

Cafetería Royalty, Matamoros 100B. Cheap, simple dishes including a lunch menu for just US$3.

Cafés and bakeries

Bamby, García Vigil 205. Big, cheap bakery where you can pick up bread and sweet rolls for a couple of pesos a piece. The place for breakfast on a budget.

Café Brújula, García Vigil 409D. The place for really excellent, carefully sourced Oaxacan coffee, as well as breakfasts, smoothies, sandwiches, salads, pizzas and other freshly prepared, home-made snacks. American-owned, friendly and popular with local artists.

Café Los Cuiles, Labastida 115. Breezy little café with Oaxacan artwork on the wall. A good place to tap away on your laptop. Very friendly and popular with gringos.

Gaia Organic, Food next door, is also worth a visit for a dose of healthy food. Asking for fries will horrify the owner.

South of Independencia

The most popular place to eat *tlayudas* (oversized tortillas) and other local snacks in the evening is from stalls and restaurants along Aldama, between Cabrera and 20 de Noviembre.

Flor de Oaxaca, Armenta y López 311. Pricey but good Oaxacan cuisine, including tasty platters, *moles*, meat cuts and *tlayudas*. They serve chocolate and several interesting mezcals too. Friendly and attentive staff. Recommended.

El Naranjo, Trujano 203. A pleasant restaurant set in the plant-filled courtyard of a 17th-century house. They serve tasty Oaxacan fare, and their specialities include an interesting dessert of dark chocolate torte filled with mezcal crème. Also does cooking lessons.

¶¶ La Quebrada, Armenta y López 410. Open 1000-1900. A reputable and well-established seafood restaurant, open since 1964. Their menu includes various fish fillets, shrimp cocktails and a seafood curry.

¶¶-¶ Café Alex, Díaz Ordaz 218 and Trujano. Over 20 different breakfasts are offered at this pleasant restaurant, including pancakes with fruit and various Oaxacan specialities. There's also a good *comida corrida* with 4 different menus to choose from. Recommended.

¶¶-¶ Casa Grande del Gato Loco , Hidalgo 410, 2 blocks from zócalo. Restaurant-bar with big screen TVs and mostly economical meals. Live music and karaoke in the evenings.

¶¶-¶ Coronita, Díaz Ordaz 208 below **Hotel Valle de Oaxaca**. Affordable Oaxacan specialities including various *mole*-based recipes, meat and fish dishes.

¶¶-¶ Hipocampo's, Hidalgo 505. This rough-and-ready locals' haunt offers basic, economical set meals at lunchtime. Mon-Sat 0800-2200, Sun 1000-1900.

Comedores Some of the most authentic Oaxacan food is found in the *comedores familiares,* such as **Clemente, Los Almendros, La Juchita,** but they are way out of town and could be difficult to get to, or in *comedores populares* in the market.

¶ D'Florencia, Zaragoza 205L. Very friendly restaurant with excellent Oaxacan specialities, run by Angel and Antonia. Good breakfasts, economical meals. Highly recommended.

¶ El Chef, Armenta and López 422. Economical *comida corrida*, Mexican staples and simple, unpretentious meals.

¶ El Shaddai, Av Hidalgo 121 and Galeano. Busy family-run restaurant serving tacos, other Mexican fare and set menus. Popular with locals, friendly, busy, good and cheap.

¶ Girasoles, 20 de Noviembre 102. Popular, slightly scruffy vegetarian restaurant that offers a decent set menu at lunchtime and karaoke in the evening.

¶ Hermanas Jiménez, Mercado de Abastos. Recommended for a local bread called *pan de yema*, made with egg yolk.

¶ Mi Tierra, Mier and Terán 222B. Another good spot for economical home-cooking. Breakfast and lunch only, closes 1830.

Route to Mitla *p443*

Teotitlán del Valle has 1 simple restaurant. **Tlacolula** has several simple restaurants. The market at El Tule, has good food.

¶ La Sonora, on eastern edge of El Tule. Quite tasty food.

¶ María Teresa, Mitla, 100 m from site towards village. Good *comida corrida*.

Puerto Escondido *p448, map p448*
Downtown

There are over 400 restaurants of wide-ranging standards in the area, so there's plenty of choice. Many line Av Pérez Gasga, but for really cheap fare you should head to the market on 8 Norte and 3 Pte, for *comida corrida* and varied local food.

¶¶ Super Café Puro, off top flight of stairs of walkway that starts at the tourist information kiosk. Good for breakfast, pleasant terrace, Mexican, family-run, free Wi-Fi and an excellent spot to while away some time over a cup of fresh Oaxacan coffee.

¶¶-¶ Baguetería Vivaldi, Av Pérez Gasga. Good breakfast, coffee, crêpes and sandwiches.

¶¶-¶ Benditos, Av Pérez Gasga. *The* place for pizza, pasta and other authentic Italian dishes. Good value.

¶¶ Los Crotos, Av Pérez Gasga (Adoquín), fresh seafood and fish dishes, Mexican traditional. Access to the beach from restaurant. Friendly.

Playa Zicatela

Restaurants front the beach all the way along. Stroll down and see what appeals.

¶¶¶ Hotel Santa Fé. Excellent, expensive vegetarian. Worth it for the views at sunset.

¶¶¶-¶¶ La Galería, in Hotel Arcoris. Specialities include lobster, jumbo prawns and stuffed peppers.

₦ Cabo Blanco, Calle del Moro. Crazy happening place with accommodation, restaurant and bar. Big party on Mon nights, cover charge US$2 after 2200, always packed. Cajun prawns to die for and a good range of mezcals from sister company Sivayaa, www.mezcalsivayaa.com.

₦ El Greko, beach restaurant and bar opposite Cabo Blanco. Nice seafood and friendly staff, lovely for lunch by the sea. Popular with families at weekends. Recommended.

₦ El Tabachín, Playa Marinero, behind Hotel Santa Fe. Vegetarian, café, breakfast and lunch.

₦ Sabor a Mar, Calle del Moro. Delicious seafood served under a beachfront *palapa* that overlooks the crashing waves of the Mexican pipeline. Great fillets, good service.

₦-₸ El Cafecito, Calle del Moro. This popular restaurant does excellent breakfasts and wholesome, home-cooked Mexican fare. Recommended.

Carmen's Bakery, Calle del Moro. Great pastries baked on the premises, next door to El Cafecito.

Puerto Angel *p451*

₦ Beto's by turn-off for Playa del Panteón. Good fish (fresh tuna), lobster and chicken, cheap beer and nice views.

₦ Villa Florencia. Calle Virgilio Uribe s/n across from town beach. Hotel with an excellent restaurant serving good Italian and Mexican dishes, charming place.

₸ Cangrejo, by Naval Base gate. Popular bar, also good breakfasts and excellent tacos.

₸ Mar y Sol. Cheap, good seafood.

₸ Sirenita. Popular for breakfast and bar, friendly.

Zipolite *p451*

The majority of hotels strung along the beach have a restaurant or bar attached. They mostly serve breakfasts, pizzas, seafood and good, cold beer.

₦₦-₦₦ El Alquimista, western end of beach near rocks, overlooking the nudist beach and violently crashing waves. Quality of food has

gone downhill a bit, but still good for pizzas and breakfast. Also has *cabañas* for rent.

₦-₸ Pacha Mama, western end of beach at Balamjuyuc hostel (see Sleeping, above). Vegetarian, home cooked, organic food.

₸ Café Maya, eastern end of beach. Good sushi and cocktails. Chilled out spot.

₸ El Pelicano, western end of town, away from the beach One set menu for US$2 serving the best barbecued chicken with rice, pasta, salad, tortillas, avocado and salsa. Very popular with locals and visitors alike.

San Agustinillo *p452*

₦-₸ El Sueño de Frida, on main road, San Agustinillo. Closed Mon and 1300-1600 daily. Frida Kahlo-themed café and ice cream parlour with outside terrace. Breakfast and dinner.

₦ Un Secreto, eastern end of main road, off the beach. Salad and seafood in pleasant setting.

Mazunte *p452*

Some of the best food and the best views can be had at the **Posada Alta Mira**, see Sleeping, above.

₦-₸ La Dolce Vita, on main road at western end. Open Wed-Sun 1600-2300. Good Italian pizza and home-made pasta, pricey.

₦-₸ La Tortuguita, opposite the turtle centre. Breakfasts, *comida corrida*, *tortas*, snacks and Oaxacan specialities.

₦ Brisa, good seafood, including excellent steamed squid. **Arbolito** next door does good pizzas.

Huatulco *p452*

Restaurants on the beach, out of town, tend to be the cheapest. There are luxury restaurants at the Tangolunda hotels. In La Crucecita, prices get cheaper as you get away from the plaza; there are several restaurants along Gardenia.

₦₦ Don Porfirio, Blv Benito Juárez s/n, Tangolunda. Lobster, shrimps, octopus, fish fillets and other fine sea fare. Specialities including shrimp fajitas with brandy.

¶¶¶ Il Giardio del Papa, Flamboyán 204, La Crucecita. Italian chef was once the Pope's cook, expensive.

¶¶¶ Jardín del Arte, Paseo Mitla 107 at **Hotel Marlín**, Santa Cruz. Menu a bit basic, popular with Mexican families.

¶¶¶ Las Cúpulas, Blv Benito Juárez 2 in **Hotel Quinta Real**, Tangolunda. Fine dining with panoramic view of the harbour, also popular breakfast venue. Entertainment Fri and Sat evenings. Recommended.

¶¶-¶ Oasis Café, Flamboyán 211 and Bugambilia, by main plaza, La Crucecita. Varied menu including snacks, grilled meats, sushi, soups, seafood and regional cuisine. Japanese lunchtime specials. Recommended.

¶ La Crema, Gardenia and Guanacastle, La Crucecita. Popular bar restaurant, pizzas, bar food, games. Recommended.

¶¶-¶ Agave, Bugambilia 701 A, on main plaza, La Crucecita. Restaurant and bar serving tasty Mexican fare and Italian frittatas, good breakfasts, lunches and dinners.

¶¶-¶ El Sabor de Oaxaca, Guamúchil 206, La Crucecita. Tasty *tlayundas*, *moles* and other Oaxacan specialities. Burgers and regular Mexican fare too.

¶¶-¶ La Crucecita, Bugambilia and Chacah, La Crucecita. Seafood and regional cuisine, breakfast, snacks and set meals. Economical.

¶¶-¶ Los Portales, Bugambilia 603, Plaza Principal, La Crucecita. Attached to the Iguana bar, this restaurant does beef, fish, chicken, burgers and steaks. Specialities include *nopal* cactus with melted cheese and salad.

¶ Café Huatulco, near the marina, Santa Cruz. Regional coffee and snacks.

¶ Mercado 3 Mayo, Guamúchil, La Crucecita. Market *stalls* serving typical dishes at very cheap prices, great value.

¶ Toñita, Gardenia and Chacah, La Crucecita. *Comida corrida* and à la carte menus. All home-cooked, economical fare. Very friendly.

Salina Cruz *p454*

¶ Aloha, Wilfrido Cruz 13-A. Seafood and regional dishes.

¶¶ Casa Flor, Miramar 3. Reportedly the best food in town. Breakfast specials include crêpes and eggs.

¶¶-¶ La Pasadita, Avila Camacho 603. Large, breezy restaurant serving shrimp, lobster and other seafood.

Tehuantepec *p454*

The local *quesadillas* made of maize and cheese are delicious; sold at bus stops.

¶¶¶-¶ Restaurant Scaru, Leona Vicario 4. Good food, fish and seafood specialities, upscale, nice courtyard and mural.

¶¶ Mariscos Angel, 5 de Mayo No 1, by entrance from Salina Cruz. Cheap food on top floor of market, here you can get the local speciality, pork or chicken stuffed with potatoes.

¶¶-¶ Cafetería Almendro, Melchor Ocampo 8, near the plaza. Economical breakfasts, sandwiches, tacos, pizzas and burgers.

Juchitán and around *p455*

¶¶¶-¶ Casa Grande, Juárez 125, on the main square, Juchitán. In a beautifully restored colonial house, good food, live music.

¶¶¶-¶ Deyaurihe, 5 de Septiembre corner of Aldama, Juchitán. Mexican food, *comida corrida* and à la carte.

¶¶ Los Chapulines, 5 de Septiembre and Morelos, Juchitán. Regional and international food, *comida corrida* and à la carte, a/c.

¶¶ Pizzería La Vianda, 5 de Septiembre 54-B, Juchitán. Pizza and seafood, tasty, if slightly overpriced.

● Entertainment

Oaxaca *p434, map p436*
Bars and clubs

Fandango, Díaz and Allende. Grungy vibes at this friendly, cavernous bar. Popular with students and rockers. Open very late.

La Candela, Murguía 413 and Pino Suárez. Salsa, merengue, live music from 2200, restaurant, popular with visitors and locals, cover US$5.

La Cantinita, Alcalá 303. Large and often buzzing bar with live music and mixed clientele. Popular and loud.

La Casa de Mezcal, Flores Magón 209, in front of the market. Popular drinking hole.

La Divina, Gurrión 104. Dark, grungy bar with a gothic interior, sticky carpets and young, bohemian clientele. They play salsa, chillout, house, trance and reggae.

La Farola, 20 de Noviembre 3C, old-fashioned mezcal joint, with snacks and live music.

La Tentación, Matamoros 101, between Macedonio Alcalá and García Vigil. Salsa and merengue. Live music starting 2230, open late, friendly atmosphere. Cover US$5.

Cinemas
Multimax, Plaza del Valle. Shopping mall with a massive multi-screen complex.

Folk dancing
Guelaguetza-style shows, when there are enough people, at:
Casa de Cantera, Murguía 102, T951-514 9522, www.casadecantera.com. Shows cost US13, with dinner US$26.
Hotel Monte Albán, Alameda de León 1, T951-516 2777, nightly at 2030, US$7, photography permitted. Book if you can. Special group prices.

Puerto Escondido *p448, map p448*
Bars and clubs
It is not advisable to stay at bars and discos in Playa Zicatela past 0300.
Art and Harry's Surf Inn, Calle del Morro. Popular surfers' bar that does 2-for-1 specials. There's a pool table and views of the ocean.
Barfly, Calle del Morro. Above the popular Banana's restaurant plays good, lively music and regularly screens films.
Casa Babylon, Calle del Morro. Funky little bar with shelves of books and an assortment of strange, other-worldly masks.
El Son y la Rumba, Av Marina Nacional. Rooftop bar with live salsa and rumba at night. Restaurant serves *comida corrida* during the day.

Los Tarros, Av Pérez Gasga 604. Lively bar with pool table, staff are nice and friendly.
Wipeout, Av Pérez Gasga. Rowdy, popular bar playing rock and techno music.

Huatulco *p452*
Several luxury hotels have shows such as the **Barcelo's Fiesta Mexicana with Mariachis**, folk dancing and Mexican buffet. Live music in the lobby bar every night.
La Guelaguetza folklore show at **Noches Oaxaqueñas**, Blv Benito Juárez, Tangolunda, US$12, reservations T958-581 0001.
Latin dancing at **Magic Tropic**, Santa Cruz. Also **La Papaya**, Benito Juárez, Manzana 3, Lote 1, Bahía de Chahué, T958-587 2589. Popular, US$7 cover, European-style disco, big screen.

⊛ Festivals and events

Oaxaca *p434, map p436*
Jul Guelaguetza, also called Los Lunes del Cerro, is the city's most important festival. A festive atmosphere permeates the city for over 2 weeks, particularly the last 2 Mon in Jul (see page 438).
Oct El Señor del Rayo, a 9-day event in the 3rd week of Oct, including excellent fireworks.
2 Nov Day of the Dead, a mixture of festivity and solemn commemoration, best appreciated at the Panteón General (main cemetery). Always ask before photographing. In recent years Oaxaca has hosted a rugby 'tournament of death' in conjunction with the festival, for information, www.planeta.com.
8-18 Dec Fiesta de la Soledad, patroness of Oaxaca, with fine processions centred around the Basílica and throughout the city.
Dec During the 9 days before Christmas, the Novenas are held. Groups of people go asking for shelter, *posada*, as Joseph and Mary did, and are invited into different homes. This is done in the centre as well as other neighbourhoods like San Felipe (5 km north) and at Xoxo, to the south. The *posadas* culminate on the night of 24 Dec with what

is known as **Calendas**, a parade of floats representing allegories from the birth of Christ; every church in town prepares a float honouring its patron saint, the groups from all the parishes converge at the cathedral at 2300 (best seen from balcony of the restaurants around the zócalo; go for supper and get a window table).

23 Dec Noche de Rábanos, outside the Palacio de Gobierno, is a unique contest of figures carved out of radishes. Stands made of flowers and corn stalks have been added in recent years to this old tradition.

Teotitlán del Valle *p443*
3 May Fiesta de las Cruces, when people climb to a cross on a beautiful summit above town (across the river); good hiking at any time of the year.
Jul Since 1999 a Fiesta Antigua Zapoteca is celebrated here to coincide with the Guelaguetza in Oaxaca.
8 Sep Feast of Virgen de la Natividad.

Puerto Escondido *p448, map p448*
Jan-Feb blues festival at various venues.
Feb Marlin fishing tournament.
Mar Long board tournament.
Aug Master World Surf Championship.
Nov The city's festivities are held throughout the month, along with a **surfing tournament** and a fishing tournament. The Festival Costeño de la Danza, with colourful, lively folk dances is held in the middle of the month.
Dec Large-scale *posada* takes place, visitors welcome to participate.

Huatulco *p452*
1st week Apr Fiesta del Mar
3 May Fiesta de la Santa Cruz.
1st week May International sail-fishing tournament.
8-12 Dec Fiesta de la Virgen de Guadalupe.

Tehuantepec *p454*
Festivals and traditions are very important in Tehuantepec. There are many colourful and

ceremonious celebrations throughout the year, when the women don their elaborate embroidered dresses and lace halos, known as *resplandores*. The town is divided into 15 wards; each one has a patron saint. **Fiestas patronales** are held in each neighbourhood for several days in honour of the local saint, culminating on the saint's day. Another type of celebration are *velas*, which are very formal dances in a decorated setting resembling a European palace, where the attendees wear traditional dress.
19 May Vela Zandunga.
1st week Aug Fiestas of Santo Domingo are held in the centre of Tehuantepec.
Mid-Aug Velas de Agosto are held throughout the Isthmus.
24 Jun Fiestas in honour of St John the Baptist in the San José neighbourhood.
26 Dec Vela Tehuantepec.

Juchitán and around *p455*
Although every birth and wedding provides a reason for a colourful celebration, best known are the *velas*. There are *velas* throughout the year, the most important ones are held during **May** in honour of **San Vicente Ferrer**.

O Shopping

Oaxaca *p434, map p436*
Bookshops
Amate, Alcalá 307, best selection of English-language books and magazines and a nice selection of books about Oaxaca and Mexico.
Proveedora Escolar, Independencia 1001 and Reforma, large, excellent selection on all subjects, cheaper.

Crafts
Many crafts are produced throughout the state of Oaxaca. Crafts are sold in nearby villages or they may be purchased in the city of Oaxaca, at the markets listed below. There are endless shopping temptations, such as green and black pottery, baskets and bags made from

cane and rushes, embroidered shirts, skirts, painted wooden animals called *alebrijes*, hammocks, tooled leather goods, woven wall hangings and rugs.

Blackbox, 5 de Mayo 412, www.la-black box.com. An interesting new store with unique and experimental creations fusing traditional techniques with modern designs. The owner, Gustavo Friedke, works closely with indigenous communities.

Casa de las Artesanías, Matamoros 105, www.casadelasartesanias.com.mx. This large, successful co-op displays the craftwork of over 60 artists. Goods include fine *alebrijes*, weavings and pottery.

Fábrica de Papel de San Agustín Etla, downhill from the University. This factory produces handmade paper. There's a small exhibit in the powerhouse nearby, as well as an attractive range of items for sale including journals, notebooks and sketch pads. Has a small museum and school.

Hecmafer, 5 de Mayo y Murguía. Good selection of jewellery, rugs and pottery, somewhat overpriced.

Instituto Oaxaqueño de las Artesanías, García Vigil 809, T516-9211. Government-run, cheaper and better than most, service good, with very good small **market** nearby on junction of García Vigil and Jesús Carranza, for beautiful coloured belts and clothes.

La Mano Mágica, Alcalá 203. The highest-quality rug collection in Oaxaca. Some of these dazzling creations fetch thousands of dollars.

Mineralia, Alcalá 207. Shimmering mountains of gems, crystals and stones are on sale at this popular jewellery store. Also has branches in other parts of the country.

Mujeres Artesanas de las Regiones de Oaxaca (MARO), 5 de Mayo 204, T951-516 0670, daily 0900-2000, a regional association of Oaxacan craftswomen with a sales and exhibition store.

Markets

The city has 4 main markets, all of which are worth a visit, and several smaller ones; polite bargaining is the rule everywhere.

Mercado de Abastos, also known as the **Central de Abastos**, near the 2nd-class bus station, is the largest; a cacophony of sights, sounds and aromas, busiest on Sat and not to be missed. Prices here tend to be lower than in the smaller markets, and it's a good place to find cheap crafts. If all that shopping makes you hungry, why not sample the grasshopper-like creatures called *chapulines*? They're fried in huge vats of oil around the market with garlic, chilli and lime juice added.

Mercado 20 de Noviembre (Aldama on the corner of 20 de Noviembre), in the centre of town, has clean stalls selling prepared foods, cheese and baked goods. Try the *quesadillas de flor de calabaza* (pumpkin flower quesadillas).

Mercado Artesanal, Zaragoza and JP García, has a good selection of crafts intended for the tourist trade.

Mercado Benito Juárez, next door to Mercado 20 de Noviembre, has a selection of household goods, fruits, vegetables, crafts and regional products, such as *quesillo* (string cheese), bread and chocolate.

Mercado Orgánico, also known as El Pochote, García Vigil 817. Fri-Sat, 0900-1800. This new, organic market sells tasty local produce including honey, chocolate, mezcal and coffee.

Photography

Centro Fotográfico Alvarez Bravo, Bravo and García Vigil, for photo exhibits and sales. You'll also find the newly opened 'Fonoteca' inside. This cultural project comprises a vast music collection from around the world. A true audio feast.

Foto Rivas, Juárez 605, opposite Parque Juárez and 20 de Noviembre 502C, has an excellent collection of photographs of Oaxacan themes, new and old, also sells postcards and film.

Regional food and drink

On Mina and 20 de Noviembre, opposite the 20 de Noviembre market, are several mills where they grind cacao beans, almond, sugar and cinnamon into a paste for making delicious hot chocolate, the cacao smell permeates the air in this area. Some of the brands sold are **Mayordomo** (very good), **Guelaguetza** and **La Soledad**. These same outlets sell Oaxacan *mole*, a thick paste used for preparing sauces. *Mole* and *quesillo*, the regional, white string cheese, are sold at the Benito Juárez market, where **La Oaxaqueña** stalls are recommended. Also at Mina and 20 de Noviembre is **La Casa del Dulce** sweet shop. Mezcal is readily available throughout town.

Puerto Escondido *p448, map p448*
Crafts and souvenirs are available from shops all along **El Adoquín**, stalls on the main street, east of El Adoquín and on **Andador Libertad**, a walkway going uphill from about the middle of El Adoquín. Vendors on the beach are likely to ask for higher prices and you may find better value in shops north of the highway.
Ahorrara, 3a Pte y 5a Norte, large well-stocked supermarket.
Oasis, Adoquín, opposite the tourist kiosk, fine accessories and gifts.
Papi's souvenir shop has a small selection of foreign books for sale or trade.
Super Che, Hidalgo and 1a Ote, a new supermarket, long anticipated by the locals.
Surfing gear and clothing are best bought from shops in Zicatela.

San Agustinillo *p452*
Arte Sano Craftshop, main road away from the beach, opposite Hotel Malex, has a good selection of handicraft products.

Mazunte *p452*
Cosméticos Naturales de Mazunte.
Women's Cosmetics Collective, affiliated to the Body Shop, main road out of Mazunte. Good-value cosmetics and toiletries.

Huatulco *p452*
Mercado de Artesanías de Santa Cruz,
Blv Santa Cruz, corner Mitla, has a variety of regional crafts.

Museo de Artesanías Oaxaqueñas,
Flamboyán 216, Plaza Principal, La Crucecita, also exhibits and sells Mexican crafts. Has a good display of regional dresses from the Guelaguetza.

▲▲ Activities and tours

Oaxaca *p434, map p436*
Art classes
Centro de los Artes de San Agustín,
Independencia s/n, T951-521 3043 www.centrodelasartesdesanagustin.com, downhill from the University, part of the Fábrica de Papel de San Agustín Etla. Open 0900-1800.Courses in various art forms from painting to photography to ceramics to video. Different levels are available, including beginner and professional. Always check what language the classes are taught in.

Birdwatching
Almost 700 species of bird can be found in the state of Oaxaca. Its strategic location at the junction between North and Central America and its geographic diversity, spanning the Pacific and Atlantic watersheds, result in great diversity. There are birding opportunities in the Central Valleys, in the mountain range separating the Central Valleys from the Pacific coast, in the coastal lagoons, the thorn forests along Route 190, and in the cloud forests and lowlands of the Atlantic coast.

Cooking classes
Susan Trilling, T951-508 0469, www.seasonsofmyheart.com. Instruction in the sublime art of Oaxacan cooking, culinary tours and week-long courses. Half-day classes start at US$50. Recommended.

Cycling
Zona Bici, García Vigil 406, T951-516 0953, www.oaxacawebs.org/zonabici. Mon-Sat 1000-1430 and 1630-2030. New aluminium-

frame bikes, front suspension, US$12 for 24-hr rental. They also sell them, along with general cycling supplies. Tours cost US$33, make reservations. Recommended.

Public baths
Baños Reforma, Reforma 407, daily 0700-1800, steam bath US$4, sauna US$4.
Baños San Rafael, Tinoco y Palacios 514, Mon-Sat 0600-1800, Sun 0600-1530, hot water.

Tour operators
There are many in town, most running the same tours, eg daily to Monte Albán; El Tule, Mitla and, sometimes, another village on this route; city tour; Fri to Coyotepec, Jalietza and Ocotlán; Thu to Cuilapan and Zaachila; Sun to Tlacolula, Mitla and El Tule. Basically, the tours tie in with local markets. Regular day tours cost US$15 per person. If visiting archaeological sites, check if entry is included in the price.
Eugenio Cruz Castaneda, T951-513 4790, offers excellent guided trips to Monte Albán, other archaeological sites and can arrange custom itineraries throughout Oaxaca state.
Expediciones Sierra Norte, Manuel Bravo 210. T951-514 8271, www.sierranorte.org.mx. Hikers and bikers should check out this reputable eco-tourism agency. They organize expeditions to the mountains and Los Pueblos Mancomunados, 1-5 days in length. Tours depart daily; call in advance for information and reservations
Tierraventura, Abasolo 217 and Av Juárez, T951-501 1363, www.tierraventura.com. A long-standing eco-tourism agency that runs a range of tours all over the state, from the sierras to the coast. Wildlife, indigenous medicine, birds, botany and ecology are some of their environmentally aware themes. This is a small-scale company, so best to book at least 1 week in advance.
Viajes Xochitlán, Manuel Bravo 210 Int A, T951-514 3628, www.xochitlan-tours.com.mx. This reputable, well-established agency runs tours to the Central Valleys, visiting

all the sights including Mitla and Hierve el Agua.

Puerto Escondido p448, map p448
Diving
The region's coastline offers good opportunities for snorkelling and scuba-diving; snorkelling from the beach is easiest at Puerto Angelito. There are some 70 boats available for trips, dolphin and whale watching in the area.
Aventura Submarina, Av Pérez Gasga, at western end of El Adoquín, T954-582 2353, asubmarina@hotmail.com. Tours and diving lessons with Jorge Pérez Bravo. Diving lessons, US$75 for 1 tank; if qualified, US$43 for 1 tank.
Puerto Dive Center, T01954-102 7767, www.puertodivecenter.com. NAUI and PADI certification, equipment rental and tours. 1 tank US$45, 2 tanks US$65, 2-hr snorkel tour with gear US$25, Open Water diving lessons, US$320 for a 4-day course.

Fishing
Boats can be hired for fishing at Playa Principal or through travel agencies for approximately US$40 per hr for up to 4 passengers.
Omar Sportfishing, T954-559 4406, www.tomzap.com/omar.html. Fishing charters with Captain Omar Ramírez. He also runs dolphin-watching tours.
Janine II, T954-101 1264, josmarlin1@hotmail.com. Boat trips and fishing.

Horse riding
El Caballerango, T954-582 3460. Tours and rental.

Pelota Mixteca
A modern version of an ancient Mixtec ball game is played on Sat or Sun, check dates with tourist information kiosk, in Bajos de Chila, 15 mins from Puerto Escondido, on the road to Acapulco. In a 9-m by 35-m court, teams of 5-7 players propel a rubber ball weighing almost 1 kg, using elaborately decorated leather mitts that weigh between 3.5 kg and 6 kg. A game can take up to

4 hrs. Bajos de Chila also has an annual festival every Feb, with many games and firework displays. Best to go with a local if possible, as it can get quite drunken and rowdy.

Surfing
Playa Zicatela is a surfer's haven, but dangerous for the novice. Board rental from US$13 a day from **360 Surf Shop** and **Carri Surf and Oasis**. Lessons from the lifeguards on the towers, US$28.

Tour operators
Gina Machorro (speaks English and French), offers a 2-hr gastro walking tour of Puerto Escondido on Sat, US$18 per person, taking in the history of coffee in the region, visiting the house of tamales and the house of chocolate. On Sun she does an archaeology tour, both tours held in winter only. The fee goes directly to the local community. Contact through the tourist information kiosk, El Adoquín. **Hidden Voyages Ecotours**, Pérez Gasga 905B, T954-582 2305, www.peleewings.ca/ecco.php, inside **Turismo Dimar Travel Agency**. This agency offers recommended tours to the lagoons with Canadian ornithologist Michael Malone, in winter only. **Lalo Ecotours**, T954-588 9164, www.lalo-ecotours.com. This truly eco-touristic tour operator is managed by knowledgeable locals who know the region's lagoon s, such as nearby Laguna de Manialtepec, intimately. Birdwatching expeditions, kayak trips and tours to bio-luminiscent waters are among their services. Highly recommended.

Puerto Angel *p451*
Azul Profundo, next door to **Cordelia's** on Playa del Panteón, T958-584 3109, www.tomzap.com/azulprofundo.html. Scuba-diving with experienced instructors, up-to-date equipment, PADI service available. Introduction to diving US$33. Also runs snorkelling trips that visit beaches along the coast. English spoken.

Huatulco *p452*
Cycling
A mountain bike is a good way to get around this area and to reach the high points with many views of the bays. You'll find rental stores in and around the hotel zones. In La Crucecita, try **Erick Tours**, Flamboyán 207, T958-587 1936, just off Plaza Principal, renting bicycles and motorcycles by the day or hour.

Diving and snorkelling
There are good snorkelling areas on reefs by the beach at **La Entrega** (Bahía Santa Cruz), **Riscalillo** (Bahía Cachacual) and **San Agustín** (Bahía San Agustín). The islands of **Cacaluta** (Bahía Cacaluta) and **La Montosa** (Bahía Tangolunda) are also surrounded by reefs with several species of coral, many different organisms can be seen here in relatively shallow water. Snorkel and fins at **Santa Cruz marina**, US$5 or through agencies who organize tours. There are good scuba-diving opportunities and the cliffs that separate the different bays continue underwater an average of 30 m.
Diving lessons and tours
Buceo Sotavento, Flamboyán No 310 , La 18, Crucecita, T958-587 2166, www.tomzap.com/sotavento.html. Well-established dive shop with a branch at Tangolunda (T958-581 0051).
Hurricane Divers, Playa Santa Cruz, Manzana 19, Lote 8, T958-587 1107, www.hurricanedivers.com. Package diving tours, if you have your certificate.

Fishing
Launches and yachts for deep-sea fishing charge US$100 per hr, minimum rental 3 hrs.
Coorporativo Tangolunda, T958-587 0081, Bahía Santa Cruz, near the beach, cheaper option.

Golf

The Tangolunda golf course offers 18-hole, par-72 golf with good views. Reservations T958-581 0037.

Health spa

Xquenda Huatulco Spa, Vialidad Lambda s/n, Bahía Chahué, T958-583 4448, www.huatulcospa.com. Massage, beauty salon, gym, 25-m pool, temazcal treatments. **Baño de Temazcal de Santa Cruz**, near the cruise port. Ritual herbal bath from US$8, additional treatments US$16 (aromatherapy, hydrotherapy, etc), full package US$24, bring sandals, towel and bathing suit.

Hiking

There are opportunities for hiking in the forested hills to the north of Huatulco. Because part of the forest is deciduous, the experience is very different in the rainy season, when it is green, and in the dry season when the area is brown and some cacti even change from green to violet. The Río Copalita to the north and east of Huatulco is quite scenic. It has waterfalls and rapids, walking here can be combined with a visit to the Punta Celeste Zapotec archaeological site. See Tour operators, below.

Rafting

Several companies run tours down the Copalita and Zimatán rivers. These can be as basic as a float down the river or as challenging as Grade IV-V rapids; ask enough questions to find the tour that best suits you. Half-day tours cost around US$44, full-day tours US$85-65 per person. Note that from Feb-May there may not be enough water. See Tour operators, below.

Rock climbing

There are rock-climbing opportunities at **Piedra de los Moros**, a few km north of Route 200, on the road to Pueblo Viejo, the turn-off is west of the Bahías de Huatulco entrance road; by the **Copalitilla waterfall**, on the Copalita river canyon, 65 km from

Huatulco; and in **Punta Celeste**, at the Botazoo Park, 8 km from Huatulco. See Tour operators, below.

Sailing

Luna Azul, day and evening sailing trips and private charter. Contact Jack Hennessey on T958-587 0945, or drop in at the **Hotel Posada Chahué**, Calle Mixie L 75, Sector R Bahía de Chahué, T958-587 0945, www.lunaazul.netfirms.com.

Tour operators

Full-day boat tours to see the different bays are offered by travel agencies for US$15 per person, with stops for swimming, snorkelling and a meal; there are catamarans, sail boats, yachts and small launches. Trips can also be arranged at the Santa Cruz marina directly with the boatmen, who will probably speak Spanish only. Some of the bays can also be reached by land, and there are tours on all-terrain quad bikes (*cuatrimotos*).
Aquaterra, Plaza las Conchas 6, Tangolunda, T958-581 0012. For adventure sports including hiking, rock-climbing, birdwatching, canyoneering and biking.
Bahías Plus, Carrizal 704, La Crucecita, T/F958-587 0932, and at **Hotel Binniguenda**, Santa Cruz, T/F958-587 0216, www.bahias plus.com, does everything from horse riding to conference organising and airline reservations. Numerous specialist tours and excursions. Helpful.
Explora Mexico, Sierra Juárez Edif. 13 A, Dept 202, Chahué, T958-587 2058, exploramex@ prodigy.net.mx. Various river tours/rafting trips, including 4- to 5-day excursions.
Jungle Tour, at Blv Chahué, Lote 22, Manzana 1, T958-581 0491. Quad-bike tours through the jungle.
Rancho Tangolunda, Blv Benito Juárez Local No 5, Tangolunda, T958-587 2126, www.ranchotangolunda.com, 10 mins from the hotel zone. This well-established adventure sports agency can organize rafting, hiking and climbing trips. Also rents kayaks, horses and quad bikes.

Watersports

Wind surfing, sailing, wave running and waterskiing equipment can be rented at the major hotels and beach clubs.
Zax Aventura Extrema, Av Bahía San Augustín, Lote17, Mz 24, Coyul, T958-587 1264, tubing.

◉ Transport

Oaxaca *p434, map p436*

Air

Xoxocotlán (OAX) airport is about 9 km south, direction Ocotepec. Airport taxis cost US$3.50 per person. Book at **Transportación Terrestre Aeropuerto** on Alameda de León No 1-G, opposite the cathedral in the zócalo (T951-514 4350) for collection at your hotel to be taken to airport, office open Mon-Sat 0900-1400, 1700-2000. All prices and timetables are subject to change. The flights listed below are 1 way, and the cheapest fares are web fares. To **Huatulco** with **Aerotucán**, Mon-Sat 0900, Sun 1000, 1 hr, US$156. To **Mexico City** with AeroMexico, Mon-Sat 3 flights daily, Sun 4 flights, US$84; with **Click Mexicana** , 5 daily, US$47. To **Puerto Escondido** with Aerotucán, Mon-Sat 0700, Sun 1200, 1 hr, US$56; and with **Aerovega**, 0900 daily, US$79. To **Tuxtla** with Click Mexicana, 1435, 1 hr, US$89. To most other destinations it is necessary to make a connection in Mexico City.

Airline offices For airline websites, see page 37. **Click Mexicana**, Fiallo 102 y Av Independencia, T951-516 5797, Mon-Sat 0800-2000. **AeroMéxico**, Av Hidalgo 513 Centro, T951-516 3765. **Aviacsa**, Pino Suárez 604, T951-518 4555. **AeroTucán**, Emiliano Carranza 303, T951-502 0840. **AeroVega**, Hotel Monte Albán, Alameda de León 1, T951-516 4982.

Bus

Local Buses mostly charge US$0.50. To the 1st-class bus station, buses marked 'VW' go from Av Juárez. Many lines marked 'Central' go by the 2nd-class bus station.

Long distance For 1st-class buses, buy tickets in advanced at the Ticket Bus Office, 20 de Noviembre 103, T951-514 6655, 0800-2000 daily. There is a new 1st-class terminal, also referred to as **ADO** terminal, northeast of zócalo on Calzada Niños Héroes de Chapultepec with left-luggage facilities. Taxi from centre US$3. **ADO, OCC, Sur** and **Cuenca** operate from here. Note that many 2nd-class buses leave from here too. 2nd-class terminal is west of zócalo on Calzada Valerio Trujano, just west of the Periférico, across from the Central de Abastos; it is referred to as the 'Central Camionera' (has left-luggage office, open until 2100). Some 2nd-class companies also offer superior service on some runs. The **Autobuses Unidos (AU)** terminal (2nd class, 2 levels of service, 1 is very good, modern buses but without a/c) is at Santa Rosa, near the Teatro Alvaro Carillo. 1st-class terminal is the only one for **Villahermosa** and the **Yucatán**. Tickets for ADO, OCC, AU, Sur and Cuenca can also be purchased at Periférico 152, T516-3222, by the pedestrian crosswalk across from the Mercado de Abastos. To **Mexico City**, most go to **TAPO** (Mexico City east bus terminal) but there are also services to the North (**Terminal Norte**) and South (**Tasqueña**) terminals. Many buses throughout the day and night, prices from US$28. To **Puebla**, 1st-class buses take the *autopista*, 4½ hrs, 2nd-class buses go on the old road, 5-6 hrs, good scenery in both cases, many buses throughout the day, US$20-25. To **Veracruz**, ADO services at 0830, 2215, 2400, it is 7½ hrs via the *autopista* US$28. AU service 2230 and ADO GL 2245 on Fri and Sun, 6 hrs, US$31-22. To **Villahermosa**, ADO services 1700, 1900, 2130, 12 hrs, US$35, book well ahead. To **Mérida**, ADO, Sun at 0900 and ADO GL 1130, 21 hrs, US$63.

The route to Chiapas from Oaxaca is via **Tehuantepec** and the 1st 2 hrs are on very windy roads. To **Tuxtla Gutiérrez**, OCC services at 1900, 2100 and 2230, 10 hrs, US$26; and luxury services at 2000, US$31, also luxury service with **Línea 1**; 2nd-class services with **Oaxaca-Istmo** and **Fletes y Pasajes**, US$18. To **San Cristóbal de las Casas**, OCC services at 1900 and 2100; 11 hrs, US$29 and a luxury service at 2000, US$33. To **Tapachula**, an OCC service at 1910, US$26, 13 hrs; and a luxury ADO service at 2100, 11½ hrs, US$33.To **Tehuantepec**, frequent OCC and ADO services, US$12, 4½ hrs; 2nd class: with **Oaxaca-Istmo** and **Fletes y Pasajes**, every 30 mins 0600-2400, US$9, 5½ hrs To **Arriaga**, an OCC service at 1910, 9 hrs, US$15.

1st-class services to the Pacific coast go via the Isthmus of Tehuantepec, taking a long detour that's best accomplished overnight. 2nd-class services are direct but unpleasant, twisting and turning on their descent to sea level; pack Dramamine and a sick bag, and avoid alcohol the night before. All in all, it's worth considering a shuttle van. To **Pochutla**, 1st-class OCC services at 0930, 2130, 2300, 2350, 10 hrs, US$1; a direct 2nd class **Oaxaca Pacífico** and **Estrella del Valle** at 2300, 6 hrs, US$9; indirect services at 0900, 1330 and 1630 To **Puerto Escondido**, 1st-class OCC services at 0930, 2130, 2300, 0010, 12 hrs, US$22. Direct 2nd-class **Oaxaca Pacífico** and **Estrella del Valle** services (via **Pochutla**) at 0930, 2130 and 2300, 8 hrs, US$19; **Transol** services at 0600 and 1330, US$9 and 7 daily with **Estrella Roja**, US$11. To **Huatulco**, 6 OCC 1st-class services, 0930, 2130 and 2300, 7 hrs, US$18; 1 2nd-class service with **Oaxaca Pacífico** and **Estrella del Valle**, US$10.

To Monte Albán, **Autobuses Turísticos** depart from **Hotel Rivera del Angel**, Mina 518 near Díaz Ordaz (bus tickets available from hotel lobby), every 30 mins between 0830 and 1530, US$3 return, 3 hrs at the

site, allowing only just enough time to visit ruins before returning (you are permitted to come back on another tour on 1 ticket for an extra US$1 but you will not, of course, have a reserved seat). Last bus back at 1800, but double-check as this is subject to change. It's possible to walk to the site by catching a local bus marked 'Colonia Monte Albán' from in front of the **Panadería México**, next to the Mercado de Abastos, which will drop you at the foot of the mountain. From there, it's tough uphill climb that should not be attempted alone or without water. It's much more feasible to walk the 4 km downhill on the return journey. The views over Oaxaca are superb.

To **Mitla**, buses depart from the 2nd-class stations every 10 mins, 0600-1900, 1½ hrs, US$1.50, The ruins are 10 mins' walk across the village from the bus stop on the highway. Other destinations in the Central Valleys, including **Teotitlán de Valle**, **Tlacolula** and **Santa Ana del Valle**, are also served by frequent 2nd-class buses. To **Hierve el Agua**, there is 1 2nd-class bus, 0800, returning at 1430, subject to change.

Shuttles To **Pochutla** with Minibuses Atlántida, hourly. Reservations and tickets at Oficina Matriz, La Noria 101, T951-514 7077, 9 departures daily, 5½ hrs, US$12; and with **Eclipse 70**, Armenta y López 504, T951-516 1068, 12 departures daily, 5½ hrs, US$12. To **Puerto Escondido**, minibuses leave from Arista 116 several times a day, 6 hrs, US$13.

Car
Car hire Phone ahead to book, a week before if possible.
Alamo Rent a Car, 5 de Mayo 203, T951-514 8534, airport, T951-511 6220
Hertz, La Bastida 115, T951-514 2434.
TTN, 5 de Mayo 217-7 y Murguía, T951-516 2577.

Monte Albán *p440*
Bus
Autobuses Turísticos operate services between Monte Albán and **Oaxaca** (see above).

Route to Mitla *p443*
Bus
To **Oaxaca**, 2nd-class buses depart from the highway every 10 mins, 0600-1900, 1½ hrs, US$1.50,

Hierve el Agua *p445*
Bus
2nd-class buses to **Oaxaca** depart daily at 1430, subject to change.

Puerto Escondido *p448, map p448*
Air
Airport (PXM) 10 mins' drive west of town. All fares and timetables are subject to change. Consult the web for the best deals. To **Mexico City** with **Click Mexicana**, T954-582 2023, daily at 1525, 1 hr, US$142; To **Oaxaca City** with **Aerovega**, T954-582 0151, daily at 0730, US$79. Most other flights via Mexico City. *Colectivo* from airport, US$3 per person.

Bus
Local To Pochutla, from corner Carretera Costera and Av Oaxaca, every 15 mins, 0530-2000, 1 hr, US$2.20. For **Puerto Angel**, **Zipolite** and other beaches: transfer in Pochutla to pickup or *colectivo* taxi, or alternatively get off at the crossroads at San Antonio and take a *colectivo* (US$0.50, every 30 mins) or taxi (US$3-4, usually waiting at the bus stop) from there, avoiding Pochutla altogether.

Long distance To **Acapulco**, with Estrella Blanca, a/c, semi-direct service every couple of hrs from 0400, 7½ hrs, US$18.50; or regular service, hourly 0500-1730, 9 hrs, US$14. To **Mexico City**, 1st class services at 1535, to the Southern Terminal (Tasqueña) and 1800 to TAPO and Northern terminal, US$46, 18 hrs; Oaxaca-Pacífico/Estrella del

Valle, 1st class, at 1800, US$33, 12 hrs via Oaxaca, arrives at **Fletes y Pasajes** terminal near TAPO (east terminal). To **Oaxaca**, with Estrella del Valle, Av Hidalgo 400 near Av Oaxaca, direct service at 0815, 1245, 2215 US$8.50, 1st class at 2230, US$10.50. OCC, 3 daily, ,0700, 1430 and 2045, US$19, 10 hrs. To **Huatulco**, via Pochutla, afternoon departures only, 2¼ hrs, US$6, 2nd class with SUR, frequent, 2½ hrs, US$3.50. To **Puebla**, with Oaxaca-Pacífico/Estrella del Valle, 1st class, at 1800, US$28, 10 hrs via Oaxaca, leaves you by the highway, not CAPU. 1st-class service 1535 and 1800, 16 hrs, US$49.To **Salina Cruz**, frequent 1st-class departures, 5½ hrs, US$12; Estrella Blanca, Av Oaxaca, 5 a day, 5 hrs, US$6.50. To **Tapachula**, with ADO, 1730, 15 hrs, US$33. To **Tuxtla Gutiérrez** and **San Cristóbal de las Casas**, with OCC, 1830 and 2130. To **Tuxtla** US$27, 12 hrs. To **San Cristóbal**, US$30, 13 hrs. To **Zihuatanejo**, with Estrella Blanca, 1 direct bus daily.

Shuttles To **Oaxaca** depart from Hotel Luz del Angel on Av Oaxaca, T582-0122, 6 hrs, US$13.

Car hire
Dimar Travel Agency, Av Pérez Gasga 905B, T954-582 1551.

Pochutla *p450*
Bus
Pochutla is a transport hub for the region, with **OCC** and **Estrella Blanca** as the main 1st-class operators. There are also several 2nd-class lines including Estrella del Valle and **Transportes Rápidos de Pochutla**.

Local To **Huatulco** (La Crucecita), with OCC, frequent, 1 hr, US$3. To **Puerto Escondido**, with small buses from side street near church, every 15 mins 0530-2000, 1½ hrs, US$2.20; also with through buses coming from Oaxaca or Salina Cruz.

Long distance To **Acapulco**, with Estrella Blanca, 0630, 0930, 1530, 1830, 2100, 9 hrs, US$28. To **Mexico City**, with 1930, 16 hrs, US$46. To **Oaxaca**, with OCC, direct service 0820, 1550, 2200, 9 hrs, US$18. 2nd-class service, 11 daily, 9 hrs, US$7. To **San Cristóbal de las Casas**, with OCC at 2000 and 2245, 12 hrs, US$27. To **Salina Cruz**, with OCC, 9 daily, US$9; with **Estrella Blanca**, 5 daily, 4 hrs, US$10. To **Tapachula**, with OCC, 1850, 13 hrs, US$30. To **Tuxtla Gutiérrez**, with OCC, 2000 and 2245, 10 hrs, US$23.

Shuttles To **Oaxaca** include Minibuses Atlántida, departing from Hotel Santa Cruz, Lázaro Cárdenas 88, T958-584 0116, 9 daily, 6 hrs, US$12; and **Eclipse 70** departing from Lázaro Cárdenas 85, T958-516 0840, 12 daily, 6 hrs, US$12.

Taxi and colectivo
For **Puerto Angel**, **Zipolite** and other beaches, pickup trucks with benches in the back and shared taxis (*colectivos*) do round trips on the coastal road in both directions; these taxis also offer private service (*carreras*); in Pochutla, wait at marked bus stops along the main road. To **Puerto Angel**, truck US$0.50, *colectivo* US$1 per person, taxi US$4. To **Zipolite**, truck US$0.50, *colectivo* US$1, taxi US$6. To **Mazunte**, truck US$1, *colectivo* US$1, taxi US$8. Beware of overcharging, which is especially common in this area.

Huatulco *p452*
Air
Aeropuerto Bahías de Huatulco (HUX), is located 17 km northwest of Huatulco along Route 200, T958-581 9099; airport van service 1958-581 9014, US$27. Taxi US$12, 20 mins. All fares and timetables are subject to change. To **Mexico City** with Click Mexicana, T958-587 0223, 3 daily at 1115, 1510, 1905, 1½ hrs, US$74.

Bus
Local 2nd-class buses to **Pochutla** from Blv Chahué and Riscalillo, La Crucecita, every 15 mins 0500-2000, US$1.20, 1 hr. 2nd-class buses to **Salina Cruz** from Blv Chahué and Bugambilia, frequent departures, 3 hrs. *Colectivo* taxis run from Tangolunda and Crucecita (main plaza), US$0.40. Autotransportes Istmeños, Carrizal and Blv. Chahué, have frequent 2nd-class departures to **Salina Cruz**, **Juchitán** and **Tehuantepec**.

Long distance To **Acapulco**, with Estrella Blanca, 1st class, 4 daily, 9 hrs, US$28; 2nd class, 3 daily, 11 hrs, US18. To **Mexico City**, with OCC at 1520, 1620 and 2020, 14 hrs, US$56. To **TAPO** with ADO GL, 1520, 14 hrs, US$55. With OCC to **TAPO** and **Northern terminal**, 1610 and 2020, 14 hrs, US$46. To **Tasqueña** with OCC, 1755, 14 hrs, US$46. To **Oaxaca**, 1st class with OCC, La Crucecita OCC/ADO terminal, 0920, 1650, 2305, 8 hrs, US$18. To **Puerto Escondido**, with OCC, 1st class, frequent departures mornings and evenings, US$67, 2 hrs; with **Estrella Blanca**, Gardenia corner Palma Real, La Crucecita, 1st class, 5 daily, 2½ hrs, US$6, 2nd class, 3 daily, US$4. To **Juchitán** with OCC, frequent departures afternoon and evening, US$9, 3½ hrs. ADO GL, 1520, US$11. To **Salina Cruz**, with OCC, 1st class, 0920, 1610 and frequent evening departures, 2½ hrs, US$7. To **Tapachula**, with OCC, 1st class, 1950, 13 hrs, US$27. To **Tuxtla Gutiérrez**, with OCC, 1st class, 2050 and 2350, 8 hrs, US$21. To **Pochutla** from Blv Chahué and Riscalillo, La Crucecita, *microbuses* every 15 mins, 0500-2000, US$2. Make connections at the crossroads at Pochutla for *colectivos*, minibuses and taxis for **Puerto Angel**, **Mazunte**, **Puerto Escondido** and **Zipolite**.

Salina Cruz *p454*
Bus
Regional service to **Tehuantepec** (US$1) and **Juchitán** (US$2.50) every 10 mins with Autotransportes Istmeños, 0500-2400,

from Progreso west of Tampico, by train tracks. Frequent 2nd-class service to **Huatulco**, 3 hrs. There is a joint bus station for OCC, ADO, AU and Sur at the north end of town, by the Carretera Transístmica. The **Estrella Blanca** station is at Frontera 25.

To **Coatzacoalcos**, 8 daily, 6 hrs, US$15. To **Oaxaca**, 1st class: OCC, 7 daily including 1 luxury service, 5-6 hrs, US$13; 2nd class: Oaxaca-Istmo, 3 daily, 6 hrs, US$10. To **Pochutla**, 1st class with OCC and ADO, 7 daily, 4 hrs, US$19; 2nd class; with Estrella Blanca, 5 daily, 3-4 hrs, US$10. To **Puerto Escondido**, 1st class, with OCC and ADO, 8 daily, 5 hrs, US$12. To **Tapachula**, with OCC at 2245, 9 hrs, US$20. To **Tuxtla Gutiérrez**, with OCC and ADO , 0255, 0750, 1415, 2245, 2345, 5½ hrs, US$15, better to book in advance. To **San Cristóbal de las Casas**, with OCC at 0255 and 2345, 9 hrs, US$18, better to book in advance.

Tehuantepec *p454*
Bus
Regional **Istmeños** buses leave from the highway (Carretera Cristóbal Colón), at the end of 5 de Mayo. To **Salina Cruz**, every 10 mins, 0500-2400, US$1, 45 mins. To **Juchitán**, every 10 mins, 0500-2400, US$1.50, 1 hr. There is a joint bus station for OCC, ADO, AU and Sur on the outskirts of town; taxi to zócalo US$1, *moto-carro* US$0.50 or 15 mins' walk (walking not recommended at night).

For **Chiapas** destinations, it is not always possible to get a 1st-class reservation; you have a better chance from Salina Cruz or Juchitán, where more buses stop. To **Arriaga**, with OCC, 2355, 4 hrs, US$8. To **Cancún**, with ADO at 1330, 22 hrs, US$65. To **Coatzacoalcos**, with ADO and Sur, 10 daily, 5½-6 hrs, US$14. To **Oaxaca**, frequent OCC services, 4½ hrs, US$12. To **Pochutla**, with OCC, 2355, 0225, 0700, 4½ hrs, US$10. To **Puerto Escondido**, with OCC, 2355, 0225, 0530, 0700, 4½-6 hrs, US$13. To **Huatulco**, with OCC, 2355, 0225,

0530, 0700, 3½ hrs, US$8. To **Mexico City**, with ADO GL, luxury service, 1850, 2040, US$52; 6 1st class daily, US$44-39. To **Tonalá** and **Tapachula**, with OCC, 2355, 4½ hrs, US$9 (Tonalá), 8½ hrs, US$19 (Tapachula). To **Tuxtepec**, with AU, 1035 and 2135, 6½ hrs, US$13. To **Veracruz**, 1st class, 1035, 2130, 2135, 7-10 hrs, US$25; ADO GL luxury service, 2110, 6¾ hrs, US$27. To **Tuxtla Gutiérrez**, with OCC, 0315, 0825, 1445, 2315, 4½ hrs, US$14. To **Villahermosa**, with OCC, 0225, 1330, 1515, 1830, 2230, US$17, 8-9 hrs, US$22.

Car
Tehuantepec is at the junction of the Carretera Transístmica (185) and Route 190, which connects it with Oaxaca, 257 km away.

Taxis
3-wheeled motorized rickshaws (*moto-carros*) take locals around town; you have to stand and hold on to the railing.

Juchitán and around *p455*
Bus
Regional bus service to **Tehuantepec** (US$1) and **Salina Cruz** (US$1.50). Every 15 mins with Istmeños, 0500-2400, from Prolongación 16 de Septiembre, by the highway to Tehuantepec. Joint bus station for OCC, ADO, Sur and AU at Prolongación 16 de Septiembre, just south of the highway to Tehuantepec. To **Huatulco**, 1st-class, 7 daily, 4 hrs, US$9-11. To **Coatzacoalcos**, frequent 1st-class services, 5 hrs, US$12. To **Mexico City (TAPO)**, 13 1st-class services, 12 hrs, US$43; and a luxury service, US$75. To **Oaxaca**, frequent 1st-class services, 5 hrs, US$13; and a luxury service, US$16. To **Pochutla**, 1st class, 6 daily, 4½ hrs, US$12. To **Puerto Escondido**, 1st class, 6 daily, 6 hrs, US$15. To **San Cristóbal de las Casas**, with OCC, 0015, 0345, 7 hrs, US$17. To **Tapachula**, 1st class, 2400, 0025, 0150, 0235, 1540, 7 hrs, US$20. To **Tuxtepec**, with AU , 1110, 2210, 6 hrs, US$12. To **Tuxtla Gutiérrez**, 1st class,

6 daily, 5 hrs, US$13. To **Veracruz**, with AU, 1110, 2210, 9 hrs, US$22; and an ADO luxury at 2125, 2200, 7-6 hrs, US$29-24.

Car
Juchitán is 26 km northeast of Tehuantepec. At La Ventosa, 14 km northeast of Juchitán, the road splits: the Carretera Transístmica (Route 185) continues north towards Coatzacoalcos on the Gulf of Mexico, and the Carretera Costera (Route 200) goes east to San Pedro Tapanatepec, where it splits again, one road going to Tuxtla Gutiérrez and the other to Tapachula.

● Directory

Oaxaca *p434, map p436*
Banks Bancomer, on García Vigil, 1 block from zócalo, exchanges TCs in own *casa de cambio*, 0900-1700, and Visa ATM. **Banco Santander Mexicano**, Independencia 605, cash and TCs, good rates, TCs changed Mon-Fri 0900-1330. **Amex** office **Viajes Micsa**, Valdivieso 2, T951-516 2700, just off zócalo. **Escotiabank**, Periférico near Mercado de Abastos, best rates, main branch in Independencia 801. *Casa de cambio* at Armenta y López 203, near corner with Hidalgo, Mon-Sat 0900-1700, shorter hrs on Sun. No problem to change TCs at weekends as there are many *casas de cambio* around the zócalo. **Embassies and consulates** Canada, Pino Suárez 700-Loc 11B, T951-513 3777; France, 3ers Privada José López Alvarez 5, T951-514 2184; Italy, Alacalá 400, T951-515 3176; Spain, Porfirio Díaz 340, T951-515 5058; USA, Alacalá 207, T951-514 3054.
Immigration Independencia 709, Mon-Fri 0900-2000, on the 2nd floor.
Internet Many cyber cafés around town, most charge US$1 per hr. **Language schools** There are many schools in the city, many of which can offer homestays, which can enhance your learning. The following have all been recommended: Académia

Vinigúlaza, Abasolo 503, T951-513 2763, www.vinigulaza.com, small groups, US$11 per 20-hr week, good place to talk to Mexican students, also cooking and salsa classes. **Amigos del Sol**, Calzada San Felipe del Agua 322, T951-133 6052, www.oaxacanews.com/amigos delsol.htm, small groups, US$105 per week; cooking classes US$20, accommodation can also be arranged, recommended. **Becari**, M Bravo 210, Plaza San Cristóbal, CP 68000, T951-514 6076, www.becari.com.mx, 4 blocks north of zócalo, US$120 for a 15-hr week with fully qualified teachers, courses including culture, history, literature and politics, with workshops on dancing, cooking or art, flexible programmes, recommended. **Centro de Idiomas**, Universidad Autónoma Benito Juárez, Burgoa, 5 blocks south of zócalo, weekly or monthly classes (US$200 per month), or private tuition, very professional and good value for money, recommended. **Español Interactivo**, Armenta and López 311B, T951-514 6062, www.studyspanish inoaxaca.com, small groups, US$105 per week, 3 hrs per day, cooking, dancing. **Instituto Cultural Oaxaca**, Av Juárez 909, T951-515 3404, www.icomexico.com, in addition to Spanish classes, local crafts and culture (including dance, cooking, weaving and pottery) are taught. 4 hrs of formal Spanish teaching are complemented with 2 hrs spent in cultural workshops and 1 hr of informal conversation with a native speaker; US$115 per week, 3 hrs per day. **Instituto de Comunicación y Cultura**, M Alcalá 307, 2nd floor, T951-516 3443, www.iccoax.com, cultural workshops and field trips included in the programme, US$150 per week, 3 hrs per day. **Soléxico Language and Cultural Center**, Abasolo 217 and Juárez, T951-516 5680, www.solexico.com, variable programme with options for homestay, excursions and volunteering. Has branches in Playa del Carmen and Puerto Vallarta. See also Language tuition in Essentials, page 55.
Laundry Lavandería Azteca, Hidalgo 404

between Díaz Ordaz y J P García, Mon-Sat 0830-2000, quick service, delivers to nearby hotels, 3.5 kg US$6.50. **Lavandería Hidalgo**, Hidalgo and J P García, Mon-Sat 0800-2000, 3.5 kg US$6.50. **ELA, Super Lavandería Automática**, Antonio Roldán 114, Col Olímpica, washes and irons. **Libraries** Biblioteca Circulante Benedict Crowel Memorial, also known as The American Lending Library, Pino Suárez 519, lending library with very good English books, a few French and Spanish, used books and magazines for sale (Mon-Fri 1000-1300, 1600-1900, Sat 1000-1300), US$13 per year plus US$13 returnable deposit. Biblioteca Pública Central, Alcalá 200 (no sign), has a lovely courtyard and a reading room with Mexican newspapers and magazines. Next door is the library of the Museo de Arte Contemporáneo. There are also libraries at the Centro Cultural Santo Domingo and the Instituto de Artes Gráficas. **Luggage storage** Servicio Turístico de Guarda Equipaje y Paquetería, Av Tinoco y Palacios 312, Centro, T951-516 0432, open 24 hrs, US$15 for 30 days. **Medical services** English-speaking doctors can be found at Clínica del Carmen, Abasolo 215, T951-516 2512, close to centre; and at Hospital Molina, García Vigil 317, T951-516 3836. **Pharmacies**: beneath Hospital Molina and all over town. **Post office** Alameda de León, Independencia y 20 de Noviembre. **Telephone** Public card phones are the easiest way to make long-distance calls, otherwise shop around for rates at long-distance phone establishments.

Puerto Escondido p448, map p448
Banks ATMs are all over town. Bancomer, 1a Norte y 2a Pte, cash and TCs 0800-1400. HSBC, 1a Norte y 3a Pte, cash and TCs, cash advance on Visa and MasterCard, Mon-Sat 0800-1900. Banamex, Av Pérez Gasga east of El Adoquín, 0900-1300. Bannorte, Oaxaca and Hildago, cash and TCs, reliable service. 2 *casas de cambio* on El Adoquín, open

until 2000, poor rates. **Internet** Some 35 internet cafés about town all charge US$1.50 per hr. **Laundry** Lavandería at east end of El Adoquín, US$1 per kg or US$3.25 per load, self-service, Mon-Sat 0900-2100. Also Mangos at Av Pérez Gasga by Hotel Nayar, US$2 per kg. **Medical services** Doctors: Dr Max, Av Oaxaca and 5a Norte, no emergency service, Spanish only, but recommended. Dr Mario Fransisco de Alba, Av Pérez Gasga 609, T954-582 3581. Hospitals and clinics: Clínica de Especialidades del Puerto, Av Oaxaca, has been recommended. Clínica de Loredes, 1a Pte y 1a Norte, surgery and emergency. Clínica Santa Fe, Av 5a Pte, Red Cross T954-582 0550. Opticians: Optica Nuestra Señora de la Luz, 3a Pte, T954-582 1844. Emergency prescription glasses, contacts. Pharmacies: Farmacia San Antonio, Av Pérez Gasga 203, T954-582 0214, has a physician in-house, open 24 hrs. **Post office** 7a Norte by Av Oaxaca, good telegraph service to wire money (need transfer number from sender), Western Union office next door.

Pochutla p450
Banks All on main street: Bancomer, 0830-1400, cash and TCs. Banorte, 0830-1400, cash and TCs. HSBC, 0830-1700, cash and TCs. Banamex, opposite plaza, ATM and Western Union office. **Internet** Email in a couple of places on Lázaro Cárdenas. **Medical services** Public hospital just south of town.

Puerto Angel p451
Banks Cash and TCs changed at Hotel Soraya. Banks in Pochutla. **Internet** Caseta Puerto Angel, Calle José Vasconcelos 3 (next to Hotel Soraya), T958-584 3038.

Huatulco p452
Banks HSBC, Bugambilia corner Sabalí, La Crucecita, cash and TCs, cash advances through ATM only. Bancomer, Blv Santa Cruz y Otitlán del Valle, Santa Cruz, cash

and TCs. **Scotiabank Inverlat**, Blv Santa Cruz, Santa Cruz, cash and TCs. **American Express**, Bahías Plus, Carrizal 704, La Crucecita, cash and TCs at good rates, Mon-Sat 0900-1400. *Casa de cambio*, Guamúchil near the Plaza, La Crucecita, poor rates. **Internet** Informática Mare, Guanacastle 203, 2nd floor, near market, US$3 per hr. **Laundry** Laundrettes are all over La Crucecita, and the upmarket hotels will wash your clothes if you're a guest.
Medical services Especialidades Médicas Santa Cruz, Flamboyán at Plaza, La Crucecita, private, English spoken. **Central Médica Huatulco**, Flamboyán 205, La Crucecita, T958-587 0104, private. **IMSS**, social security hospital, Blv Chahué, just south of La Crucecita. **Post office** Blv Chahué, at south end of La Crucecita.

Salina Cruz *p454*
Banks Bancomer, Avila Camacho. HSBC, Avila Camacho and Coatzacoalcos. Both change cash and TCs. **Internet** Cafés all over town, they charge around US$1 per hr. **Laundry** Laundry Carvel, Avila Camacho 503, US$1.80 per kg. **Medical services** Hospital Civil, Avila Camacho, Centre, T971-714 0110.

Tehuantepec *p454*
Banks HSBC, Juana C Romero, 0800-1700. Bancomer, 5 de Mayo. Banorte, 5 de Mayo. All change cash and TCs. **Internet** Ciber Kalipso, Melchor Ocampo s/n, near the plaza, US$1 per hr.

Juchitán and around *p455*
Banks Bancomer, 16 de Septiembre by the main plaza, Mon-Fri 0830-1400, cash and TCs. HSBC, 16 de Septiembre y Alvaro Obregón, Mon-Fri 0800-1900, Sat 0900-1400, cash and TCs. **Internet** Many places along 16 de Septiembre, most charge around US$1 per hr.

Tabasco and Chiapas

The states of Tabasco and Chiapas merge to form a geographical block that separates Mexico from Guatemala and the Yucatán Peninsula. Until recently, low-lying, jungly Tabasco was considered an oil state with little appeal for tourists, but oil wealth has brought Villahermosa, the state capital, a certain self-assurance and vibrancy, and the parks, nature reserves and huge meandering rivers in the eastern and southern regions of the state are beginning to attract visitors. Its lands once gave rise to the first great civilization of Mesoamerica, the Olmec, whose influence was felt through vast zones of Mexico and further afield.

In Chiapas, the land of the Classic Maya (whose descendants still inhabit the highland villages today), the attractions are better known: San Cristóbal de las Casas is the end of the line for many travellers who base themselves in this delightful colonial and indigenous town while they soak up the atmosphere and explore the jungle waterfalls; the dramatic Sumidero Canyon; the multi-coloured lakes, and – highlight of any trip to Mexico – the ruins at Palenque, with a jungle setting that is arguably the most atmospheric and beautiful of all the Maya sites. Chiapas is also a good entry point for Guatemala. You can head straight for northern Guatemala and the ruins of Tikal or take a more genteel entry through the western highlands and idyllic Lake Atitlán.

Although in some ways Chiapas has fallen victim to the progress bug, it nevertheless seems impervious to the intrusion of outsiders. The Lost World feeling is created by indigenous inhabitants and their villages which make everything seem timeless. The appalling treatment the inhabitants have suffered over centuries was the fundamental cause of the rebellion on 1 January 1994, which led to the occupation of San Cristóbal by the revolutionaries of the EZLN (Zapatista Army of National Liberation) and their continuing struggle in and beyond the boundaries of Chiapas. ►► For routes to Guatemala, see page 502; for listings, see pages 506-529.

Villahermosa ⚫🅟🅕🅧🅞▲🅖🅒 ►► pp506-529. Colour map 4, B1.

→ Phone code: 993. Population: 275,000.

Capital of Tabasco state, hot and humid Villahermosa is a busy, prosperous and attractive city on the Río Grijalva, which is navigable to the sea. Prices here tend to be high, although it is possible to find cheaper alternatives.

The **cathedral**, ruined in 1973, has been rebuilt, its twin steeples beautifully lit at night; it is not in the centre. There is a warren of modern colonial-style pedestrian malls throughout the central area. The **Centro de Investigaciones de las Culturas Olmecas** (CICOM) is set in a new modern complex with a large public library, expensive restaurant, airline offices and souvenir shops, a few minutes' walk south, out of town along the river bank. The **Museo Regional de Antropología Carlos Pellicer** ① Tue-Sun 0900-1700, US$2.50, on three floors, has well-laid-out displays of Maya and Olmec artefacts. Two other museums worth visiting are the **Museo de Cultura Popular** ① Zaragoza 810, Tue-Sun 0900-2000, free, and the **Museo de Historia de Tabasco** ① Av 27 de Febrero corner of Juárez, Tue-Sun 0900-1900, US$1.50. **Mercado Pino Suárez** ① Pino Suárez corner of Bastar Zozaya, offers a sensory overload as every nook and cranny is taken up with a variety of goods; everything from barbecued *pejelagarto* to cowboy hats, colourful handmade fabrics, spices and dangling naked chickens en route to the kettle. The local drink, *pozol*, is believed to cure a hangover. You can watch it being made here as the *pozoleros* grind the hominy into a thick dough to then mix it with cacao and water; its grainy starchiness is somewhat of an acquired taste. Nonetheless it is popular, and the *pozoleros* will serve you the drink *al gusto*, that is, with as much or as little sugar as you want. The **Institute of Tourism** ① *Av de los Ríos y Calle 13, T993-316 3633, www.vistetabasco.com, daily 0800-1800, English spoken*, is good for maps and advice on Tabasco state. Be sure to take insect repellent.

Parque Nacional La Venta

① *Blv Adolfo Ruiz Cortines, T993-314 1652, Tue-Sun 0800-1600, US$4; it takes up to 2 hrs to do the park justice; excellent guides speak Spanish and English, recommended.*

In 1925 an expedition of archaeologists discovered huge sculptured human and animal figures, urns and altars in almost impenetrable forest at **La Venta**, 120 km west of Villahermosa, and once the centre of the ancient Olmec culture. In the 1950s the monuments were threatened with destruction by the discovery of oil nearby. The poet Carlos Pellicer got them hauled all the way to a woodland area near Villahermosa, now the Parque Nacional de La Venta, also called the Museo Nacional de la Venta. The park, with scattered lakes, next to a children's playground, is almost opposite the old airport entrance (west of downtown). There, the 33 exhibits are dispersed in various small clearings. The huge heads, one of them weighing 20 tonne, are Olmec, a culture that flourished about 1150-150 BC. The figures have suffered a certain amount of damage through being exposed to the elements (those in the Xalapa Anthropological Museum are in far better condition) but to see them here, in natural surroundings, is an experience not to be missed. There is also a zoo with creatures from the Tabasco jungle, including monkeys, alligators, deer, wild pigs and birds. There is nothing to see at the original site of La Venta. Outside the park, on the lakeside, is an observation tower, **Mirador de las Aguilas** ① *free*, with excellent views, but only for the fit as there are lots of stairs. Taxis charge US$2 to the Parque. Bus Circuito No 1 from outside second-class bus terminal goes past Parque La Venta. From Parque Juárez in the city, take a 'Fraccionamiento Carrizal' bus and ask to be let off at Parque Tomás Garrido, of which La Venta is a part.

Parque Yumká

① *T993-356 0107, daily 0900-1600, US$5, most tour agencies offer round trips for about US$14,* a safari park containing 108 ha of Tabasco's three major habitats – jungle, savannah and lagoon, is a 'zoo without cages' offering walking, trolley and boat tours of each habitat. While the ecological park partly promotes the diversity of the region's flora and fauna, there are also animals from Asia and Africa. It's an easy day trip; take the *colectivo* to the airport and the park is next door.

South of Villahermosa ①① ▶ pp506-529. Colour map 4, B1.

→ *Phone codes: Teapa 932; Bochil 932.*

South of Villahermosa on Route 195 the nice, clean little town of **Teapa** has several hotels and beautiful surroundings. Also in Teapa are the **Grutas de Cocona** ① *Tue-Sun 0900-1700, US$2.50,* which house a stunning array of stalagmites and beautiful displays of colour. The caves are approximately 500 m deep and a fresh and inviting river runs through them. There is a restaurant and campsite in the area.

Southwest of Teapa on Route 195 is **Pichucalco**, an affluent town with a lively and safe atmosphere. The zócalo throngs in the evening with people on after-dinner *paseos*. Buses run hourly to Villahermosa, US$4. There are hotels, restaurants and bars here. South of Pichucalco on Highway 195 on the way to Tuxtla Gutiérrez, is **Bochil**, an idyllic stopover.

Tuxtla Gutiérrez ⊕⊘▲⊖☰ ⤞ pp506-529. Colour map 4, B1.

→ *Phone code: 961. Altitude: 522 m.*

The street system here is as follows: Avenidas run from east to west, Calles from north to south. The Avenidas are named according to whether they are north (Norte) or south (Sur) of the Avenida Central and change their names if they are east (Oriente) or west (Poniente) of the Calle Central. The number before Avenida or Calle means the distance from the Centre measured in blocks. You know whether it's an Avenida or a Calle by the order of the address: Avenidas have their number, then Sur or Norte followed by east or west; Calles have the east or west position first. For example, 1 Norte Oriente is the eastern part of the first avenue north of Avenida Central; 2 Oriente Norte is the north part of the second street west of Calle Central. It sounds complicated, but as long as you check map and road signs very carefully, it is not difficult to navigate your way around. ⤞ *See Transport, page 521.*

The capital of Chiapas, Tuxtla Gutiérrez is a busy, shabby city with a couple of points of interest to the tourist. The main sights are a long way from the centre and too far to walk; the gem is the zoo. The feast of the Virgen de Guadalupe is celebrated on 12 December. To get to the state **tourist office** ① *Belisario Domínguez 950, Plaza Instituciones, T961-602 5127, www.turismo chiapas.gob.mx, daily 0800-1900*, take a *colectivo* from the junction of Avenida Central and Calle 2 Oriente. There is also a more convenient **municipal tourist office** ① *4th floor of the Edificio Balencio, Av Central, between Calle 4a and 5a Pte Norte, Mon-Fri 0800-2000, Sat 0800-1400.*

Sights

In the Parque Madero at the east end of town (Calzada de los Hombres Ilustres) is the **Museo Regional de Chiapas** ① *Tue-Sun 0900-1700, US$3.30*, with a fine collection of Maya artefacts, an auditorium and a library. Nearby is the **Jardín Botánico** (**botanical garden**) ① *Mon-Fri 0900-1500, Sat 0900-1300, free.*

Tuxtla is best known for its superb **zoo** ① *Tue-Sun 0900-1700, US$2; in Spanish only*, some 3 km south of town up a long hill. It was founded by Dr Miguel Alvarez del Toro, who died in 1996. His philosophy was to provide a free zoo for the children and

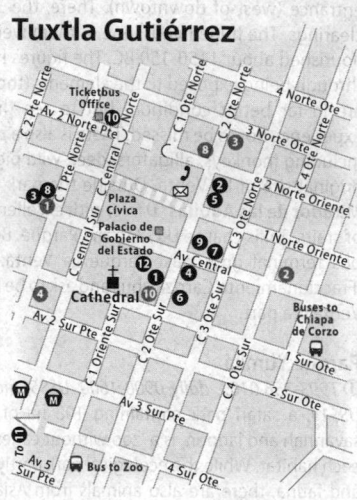

Tuxtla Gutiérrez

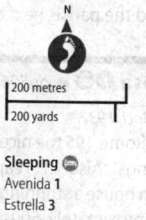

200 metres
200 yards

Sleeping ⊝
Avenida **1**
Estrella **3**
Maria Eugenia **2**
Plaza Chiapas **8**
Posada de Chiapas **4**
Regional San Marcos **10**

Eating ⊘
Antigua Fonda **1**
Bonampak **11**
Café Avenida **3**
Cherry's Liquados y Tortas **4**
El Borrego Lider **2**
El Huipil **5**
El Mesón de Quijote **7**
La Chata **6**
Los Molcajetes **12**
Mi Café **8**
Taquería Chano y Chon **9**
Tuxtla **10**

indigenous people of the area. The zoo is very large and many of the animals are in open areas, with plenty of room to run about. Monkeys are not in cages, but in areas of trees pruned back so they cannot jump out of the enclosure. Some birds wander along the paths among the visitors. The zoo makes for a very pleasant and educational afternoon. Recommended. Take mosquito repellent. *Colectivos* to 'Zoológico' and 'Cerro Hueco' from Mercado (Calle 1a Oriente Sur y 7 Sur Oriente), pass the entrance every 20 minutes; taxis charge around US$3 from centre or town buses charge US$0.20. When returning, catch the bus from the same side you were dropped off as it continues up the hill to the end of the line where it fills up for the return journey.

Sumidero Canyon ⚫⚫⚫ ▶ *pp506-529. Colour map 4, B1.*

① *Daily 0600-1800, www.sumidero.com.*

The Sumidero Canyon, 1000-m deep, is a truly impressive spectacle. Native warriors, unable to endure the Spanish conquest, hurled themselves into this hungry chasm rather than submit to foreign domination. Fortunately, you don't have to do the same to experience the awesome energy of this place. There are two ways do it: from below, as a passenger on a high-speed boat; or from above, by visiting a series of miradors. The former method is highly recommended.

Boats depart from the river in **Chiapa de Corzo** (see below) when full, but you shouldn't have too wait long for other passengers. Tickets are available at the **Turística de Grijalva office** ① *west side of the plaza, 0800-1700, US$10.* There is a second departure point beneath Cahuaré bridge, but it is hard to get to without your own vehicle. It takes two to three hours to traverse the canyon, where you'll see prolific wildlife including crocodiles, monkeys and vultures. The trip concludes near a hydroelectric dam – the engineering structure responsible for majority of the water in the canyon. Pack a sweater for the ride, as it gets chilly when you're speeding along.

Alternatively, you can view the canyon from a sublime series of miradors. **Autobús Panorámico** visits the main ones, Tuesday to Sunday 0900-1300, check with Tuxtla tourist office for more details. Otherwise you'll need your own vehicle or an expensive taxi. The best views are at La Coyota, especially at sunset, and there is a restaurant at the final Mirador. A trip to the Sumidero Canyon is a highlight of any visit to Chiapas. Organized tours including all transport costs are widely available in San Cristóbal and Tuxtla.

Chiapa de Corzo → *Colour map 4, B1. Phone code: 961. Altitude: 456 m.*

Fifteen kilometres beyond the canyon, Chiapa de Corzo, a colonial town on a bluff overlooking the Grijalva River, is more interesting than Tuxtla. In the centre is a fine 16th-century crown-shaped **fountain**; the 16th-century church of **Santo Domingo** with an engraved altar of solid silver; and craftsmen who work with gold, jewellery and lacquerwork. Chiapa de Corzo was a pre-Classic and proto-Classic Maya site and shares features with early Maya sites in Guatemala, the ruins are behind the Nestlé plant, and some unrestored mounds are on private property in a field near modern houses.

The waterfall at the **Cueva de El Chorreadero** is well worth a detour of 1 km. The road to the cave is 10 km past Chiapa de Corzo, a few kilometres after you start the climb up into the mountains to get to San Cristóbal. Camping is possible but there are no facilities; take a torch.

➔ *Phone code: 967. Altitude: 2110 m.*

One of Mexico's most beautiful towns, San Cristóbal de las Casas is stunningly located in the fertile Jovel valley, with the mountains of Huitepec to the west and Tzontehuitz to the east. The city is a charming blend of colonial architecture and indigenous culture, laid out in the colonial period with 21 indigenous *barrios* on the city's perimeter, which were later integrated into the totally *mestizo* city that existed by the 18th century. The indigenous population is today an important part of San Cristóbal's atmosphere, many of them earning a living by selling handicrafts in the town's two markets. The centre is rich in architectural variety, with excellent examples of baroque, neoclassical and plateresque, a Mexican style characterized by the intricate moulding of façades, resembling the work of silversmiths, hence the name, which means 'like a silversmith's'.

Ins and outs

Getting there The first class **OCC** and **ADO** bus terminal is at the junction of Insurgentes and Blv Sabines Gutiérrez, several blocks south of the centre. Other second-class lines and shuttle operators, including **AEXA** and **Rodolfo Figueroa**, also have nearby terminals on Gutiérrez, which soon becomes the Pan-American highway. The airport serving San Cristóbal is now closed to commercial traffic; Tuxtla is the nearest point of entry. Those travelling to Palenque by car will have fine views but should avoid night-time journeys because of armed robberies. ➤➤ *See Transport, page 522.*

Getting around Most places are within walking distance of each other although taxis are available in town and to the nearby villages; the cheaper *colectivos* run on fixed routes only.

Best time to visit Due to its altitude, San Cristóbal has a pleasantly mild climate compared to the hotter Chiapas towns such as Palenque and Tuxtla. During June, July and August, it is warm and sunny in the morning, while in the afternoon it tends to rain, with a sharp drop in temperature. Warm, waterproof clothes are needed, although the heavy rains conveniently stop in the evening, when you can enjoy San Cristóbal's many cheap restaurants and friendly bars and cafés.

Tourist information The **tourist office** ⓘ *Hidalgo 1, at the government offices, T967-678 6570, Mon-Sat 0800-2000, Sun 0900-1400*, is very helpful with all types of information and provides good maps; usually someone there speaks English. The **Municipal Office** ⓘ *on the main plaza, in the Palacio Municipal, T967-678 0665*, has a good free map of the area.

Sights

The main square, **Plaza 31 de Marzo**, has a gazebo built during the era of Porfirio Díaz. In front of the plaza is the neoclassical **Palacio Municipal**, built in 1885. A few steps away is the **Catedral de San Cristóbal**, built in the 16th century, painted in ochre, brown and white, with a baroque pulpit added in the 17th century. Adjacent to the cathedral is the church of **San Nicolás**, which houses the historical archives of the diocese. The building dates from 1613, and is believed to be the only church in Mexico to preserve its original design in the architectural style of indigenous people's churches. Just off the plaza, at the beginning of Insurgentes, is the former **Casa de la Sirena**, now the **Hotel Santa Clara**. Built at the end of the 16th century, this is a rare example of colonial residential architecture in the plateresque

San Cristóbal de las Casas

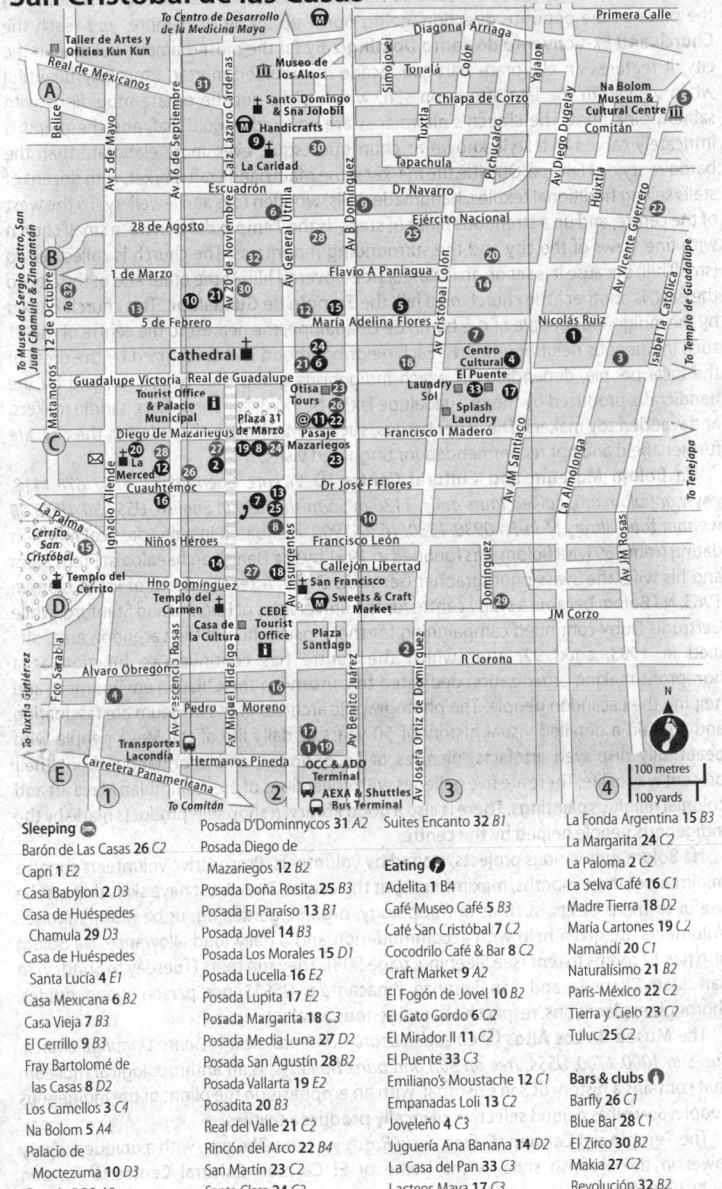

Sleeping

Barón de Las Casas **26** C2
Capri **1** E2
Casa Babylon **2** D3
Casa de Huéspedes
  Chamula **29** D3
Casa de Huéspedes
  Santa Lucía **4** E1
Casa Mexicana **6** B2
Casa Vieja **7** B3
El Cerrillo **9** B3
Fray Bartolomé de
  las Casas **8** D2
Los Camellos **3** C4
Na Bolom **5** A4
Palacio de
  Moctezuma **10** D3
Posada 5 **30** A2

Posada D'Dominnycos **31** A2
Posada Diego de
  Mazariegos **12** B2
Posada Doña Rosita **25** B3
Posada El Paraíso **13** B1
Posada Jovel **14** B3
Posada Los Morales **15** D1
Posada Lucelia **16** E2
Posada Lupita **17** E2
Posada Margarita **18** C3
Posada Media Luna **27** D2
Posada San Agustín **28** B2
Posada Vallarta **19** E2
Posadita **20** B3
Real del Valle **21** C2
Rincón del Arco **22** B4
San Martín **23** C2
Santa Clara **24** C2

Suites Encanto **32** B1

Eating 🍴

Adelita **1** B4
Café Museo Café **5** B3
Café San Cristóbal **7** C2
Cocodrilo Café & Bar **8** C2
Craft Market **9** A2
El Fogón de Jovel **10** B2
El Gato Gordo **6** C2
El Mirador II **11** C2
El Puente **33** C3
Emiliano's Moustache **12** C1
Empanadas Loli **13** C2
Joveleño **4** C3
Juguería Ana Banana **14** D2
La Casa del Pan **33** C3
Lacteos Maya **17** C3

La Fonda Argentina **15** B3
La Margarita **24** C2
La Paloma **2** C2
La Selva Café **16** C1
Madre Tierra **18** D2
María Cartones **19** C2
Namandí **20** C1
Naturalísimo **21** B2
París-México **22** C2
Tierra y Cielo **23** C2
Tuluc **25** C2

Bars & clubs 🍸

Barfly **26** C1
Blue Bar **28** C1
El Zirco **30** B2
Makia **27** C2
Revolución **32** B2

style. The interior has the four classic corridors of renaissance constructions. Heading off the plaza in the opposite direction, going north up 20 de Noviembre, you reach the **Church and Ex-Convento de Santo Domingo**. By far the most dramatic building in the city, it features an elaborate baroque façade in moulded mortar, especially beautiful when viewed in the late afternoon sun, which picks out the ornate mouldings with salmon pink hues. The church's altarpieces are covered in gold leaf, and the pulpit is intricately carved in a style known as churrigueresque, even more elaborate than the baroque style of Europe. Outside the market is the main handicraft market, with dozens of stalls selling traditional textiles, handmade dolls, wooden toys and jewellery. To the west of the centre, and up a strenuous flight of steps, is the **Templo del Cerrito**, a small church with fine views of the city and the surrounding mountains. The church is called *cerrito* (small hill) because it is set on an isolated, tree-covered hill. At the other end of the city, to the east, is another little church on a hill, the **Templo de Guadalupe**. This church is used by the indigenous people of the barrio de Guadalupe, the nearest to the centre of the 21 such indigenous neighbourhoods. Each neighbourhood is characterized by the dress of the local people, depending on which indigenous group they belong to, and by the handicrafts produced by them. Guadalupe is the barrio of candle makers, saddle makers, and wooden toy makers. The other barrios, such as Mexicanos, the oldest in the city, are further afield and not recommended for unguided visits.

Na Bolom Museum and Cultural Centre ① *Vicente Guerrero 33, T967-678 1418, www.nabolom.org, guided tours daily, 1130 in Spanish, 1630 in English, US$4.50, US$3.50 without tour; library Mon-Fri 0930-1330, 1630-1900*, is situated in a neoclassical mansion dating from 1891. Na Bolom was founded in 1951 by the Danish archaeologist Frans Blom and his wife, the Swiss photographer Gertrudis Duby. After the death of Frans Blom in 1963, Na Bolom became a study centre for the universities of Harvard and Stanford, while Gertrudis Duby continued campaigning for the conservation of the Lacandón area. She died in 1993, aged 92, after which the centre has continued to function as a non-profit-making organization dedicated to conserving the Chiapan environment and helping the Lacandón people. The photographic archives in the museum are fascinating and contain a detailed visual history of 50 years of daily life of the Maya people with beautifully displayed artefacts, pictures of Lacondones, and information about their present way of life. There are five galleries with collections of pre-Columbian Maya art and colonial religious paintings. There is also a good library. A shop sells products made by the indigenous people helped by the centre.

Na Bolom runs various projects, staffed by volunteers. Prospective volunteers spend a minimum of three months, maximum six, at the centre. They must have skills that can be useful to the projects, such as anthropology, organic gardening, or be multi-linguists. Volunteers are given help with accommodation and a daily food allowance. Na Bolom also has 12 rooms to rent (see Sleeping, page 508). They run tours (Tuesday to Sunday) to San Juan Chamula and San Lorenzo Zinacantán; US$15 per person, good guides, thorough explanations, respectful to indigenous locals.

The **Museo de Los Altos** ① *Calzada Lázaro Cárdenas, next to Santo Domingo church, Tue-Sun 1000-1700, US$4, free on Sun and bank holidays*, is an anthropological museum that contains a history of San Cristóbal, with an emphasis on the plight of the indigenous people, as well as a good selection of locally produced textiles.

The **Templo del Carmen** ① *Crescencio Rosas y Alvaro Obregón*, with a unique archery tower in the Moorish style, is the home of **El Carmen Cultural Centre** ① *Tue-Sun 0900-1700, free*.

The **Centro de Desarrollo de la Medicina Maya** ① *Salomón González Blanco, Mon-Fri 0900-1800, Sat and Sun 1000-1600, US$2*, has a herb garden with detailed displays on the use of medicinal plants by the Maya for various purposes, including child delivery.

Villages near San Cristóbal

Travellers are strongly warned not to wander around in the hills surrounding San Cristóbal, as they could risk assault. Warnings can be seen in some places frequented by tourists. Remember that locals are particularly sensitive to proper dress (that is neither men nor women should wear shorts or revealing clothes) and manners; persistent begging should be countered with courteous, firm replies.

You are recommended to call at Na Bolom (see above) before visiting the villages, to get information on their cultures and seek advice on the reception you are likely to get. **Photography** is resisted by some of the indigenous people because they believe the camera steals their souls, and photographing their church is stealing the soul of God; it is also seen as invasive and sometimes profiteering. Either leave your camera behind or ask your guide to let you know when you can and cannot take pictures. Cameras have been taken by villagers when photography has been inappropriate. Much of the population does not speak Spanish. You can visit the villages of San Juan Chamula, Zinacantán and Tenejapa. While this is a popular excursion, especially when led by a guide, several visitors have felt ashamed at going to look at the villagers as if they were in a zoo; there were many children begging and offering to look after private vehicles.

Zinacantán

Zinacantán is reached by VW bus from the market, US$0.75, 30 minutes' journey, sometimes with frequent stops while the conductor lights rockets at roadside shrines; taxi US$4. The Zinacantán men wear pink/red jackets with embroidery and tassels, the women vivid pale blue shawls and navy skirts. Annual festival days here are 6 January, 19-22 January, 8-10 August; visitors are welcome. At midday every day the women prepare a communal meal, which the men eat in shifts. The main gathering place is around the **church** ① *US$1.50 for entering, official ticket from tourist office next door; photography inside is strictly prohibited*; the roof was destroyed by fire. There are two museums, but both have closed. Check before planning a visit. **Ik'al Ojov** ① *off Calle 5 de Febrero, 5 blocks down Av Cristóbal Colón from San Lorenzo church, and 1 block to the left; donation requested*, includes two traditional *palapas* (huts) that people used to live in and there is a small collection of regional costumes. It occasionally holds shows and there is an annual festival on 17 February. There is also a tiny gift shop. The second museum is the **Museo Comunitario Autzetik ta jteklum** ① *1 block from San Lorenzo church*, which is run by women from Zinacantán and also has exhibits on local culture.

Above the municipal building on the right, creative, resourceful Antonia has opened **Antonia's House** ① *Isabel la Católica 7*. There is a small crafts shop and she and her family will demonstrate back-strap weaving, the making of tortillas and many other aspects of life in the village. She usually has some *posh* on the go – it's strong stuff, and the red variant will set your throat on fire... Be ready with a couple of litres of water! Antonia is very easy going and she may not charge for a sample of *posh*, however bear in mind that she makes her living from the shop, so buy something or leave a contribution. Tours from San Cristóbal cost US$15.

San Juan Chamula → *Colour map 4, B1.*

Signs in Chamula warn that it is dangerous to walk in the area on your own; robberies have occurred between Chamula and both San Cristóbal and Zinacantán. It's generally best to seek full advice on any travel outside San Cristóbal de las Casas.

In this Tzotzil village 10 km northwest of San Cristóbal the men wear grey, black or light pink tunics, while the women wear bright blouses with colourful braid and navy or bright blue shawls. One popular excursion is to visit the brightly painted **church** ① *a permit (US$1) is needed from the village tourist office and photographing inside the church is absolutely forbidden*. There are no pews but family groups sit or kneel on the floor, chanting, with rows of candles lit in front of them, each representing a member of the family and certain significance attached to the colours of the candles. The religion is centred on the 'talking stones' and three idols as well as certain Christian saints. Pagan rituals are held in small huts at the end of August. The pre-Lent festival ends with celebrants running through blazing harvest chaff. This happens just after Easter prayers are held, before the sowing season starts. Festivals in Chamula should *not* be photographed; if you wish to take other shots ask permission, people are not unpleasant, even if they refuse (although children may pester you to take their picture for a small fee). For reasons of cultural understanding and safety it is recommended that you visit Chamula on a tour.

There are many handicraft stalls on the way up the small hill southwest of the village. This has a good viewpoint of the village and valley. Take the road from the southwest corner of the square, turn left towards the ruined church then up a flight of steps on the left.

To get to Chamula, you can catch a VW bus from the market in San Cristóbal every 20 minutes, last at 1700, last one back at 1900, US$1 per person (or taxi, US$4). It is an interesting walk from San Cristóbal to Chamula along the main road to a point 1 km past the crossroads with the Periférico ring road (about 2.5 km from town centre); turn right on to an old dirt road, not signposted but it is the first fork you come to between some farmhouses. Then head back via the road through the village of Milpoleta, some 8 km downhill; allow five hours for the round trip (one hour for Chamula). Best not done in hot weather. Also, you can hike from Chamula to Zinacantán in 1½ hours: when leaving Chamula, take the track

Around San Cristóbal de las Casas

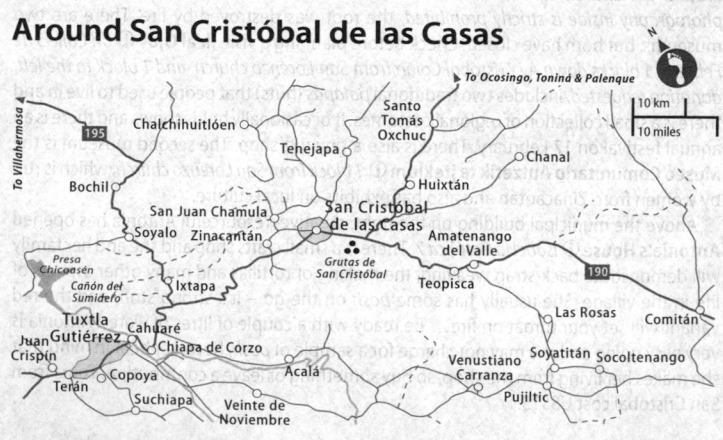

straight ahead instead of turning left onto the San Cristóbal road; turn left on a small hill where the school is (after 30 minutes) and follow a smaller trail through light forest. After about an hour you reach the main road 200 m before Zinacantán (but see warning, above).

Tenejapa → *Phone code: 967.*
Few tourists visit Tenejapa. The village is very friendly and many men wear local costume. Ask permission to take pictures and expect to pay. The Thursday market is traditionally for fruit and vegetables, but there are a growing number of other stalls. The market thins out by noon. Excellent woven items can be purchased from the weavers' cooperative near the church. They also have a fine collection of old textiles in their regional ethnographic **museum** adjoining the handicraft shop. The cooperative can also arrange weaving classes.

Other excursions from San Cristóbal
Two other excursions can be made, by car or local bus, from San Cristóbal. The first goes south on the Pan-American Highway (30 minutes by car) to **Amatenango del Valle**, a Tzeltal village where the women make and fire pottery in their yards, and then southeast (15 minutes by car) to **Aguacatenango**, a picturesque village at the foot of a mountain. Continue one hour along this road past **Villa Las Rosas** (hotel) to **Venustiano Carranza**, where the women wear fine costumes, and there is an extremely good view of the entire valley. There is a good road from Las Rosas to Comitán as an alternative to the Pan-American highway. There are frequent buses.

   Las Grutas de San Cristóbal ① *daily 0900-1700, US$1*, are caves 10 km southeast of the town, which contain huge stalagmites and are 2445 m deep but only lit for 750 m. Refreshments are available. Horses can be hired at Las Grutas for US$15 for a five-hour ride (guide extra) on lovely trails in the surrounding forest. Some of these are best followed on foot. Yellow diamonds on trees and stones mark the way to beautiful meadows. Stay on the trail to minimize erosion. The land next to the caves is taken up by an army football pitch, but once past this, it is possible to walk most of the way back to San Cristóbal through woods and fields. Las Grutas are reached by **Autotransportes de Pasaje '31 de Marzo'** *colectivos* every 15 minutes (0600-1900, US$1) from Avenida Benito Juárez 37B, across the Pan-American Highway just south of the **Cristóbal Colón** bus terminal (or take a *camioneta* from Pan-American opposite San Diego church 500 m east of Cristóbal Colón). *Colectivos* are marked 'San Cristóbal, Teopisca, Ciudad Militar, Villa Las Rosas', or ask for minibus to 'Rancho Nuevo'. To the bus stop take 'San Diego' *colectivo* 1 block east of zócalo to the end of Benito Juárez. When you get to Las Grutas, ask the driver to drop you at Km 94; the caves are poorly signed.

   Tours from San Cristóbal to the Sumidero Canyon (see page 485) including boat trip cost around US$20 with numerous travel agencies, 0900-1600. San Cristóbal can also serve as a base for exploring the Maya ruins at Palenque (210 km away, see page 495), Bonampak and Yaxchilán, near the Guatemalan border (see page 499).

Route to Palenque ⊙▲⊙ ➤➤ *pp506-529.*

Ocosingo → *Colour map 4, B1. Phone code: 919.*
Palenque can be reached by paved road from San Cristóbal de las Casas, a beautiful ride via Ocosingo, which has a local airport, a colourful market and several hotels. It was one of the centres of fighting in the Ejército Zapatista de Liberación Nacional (EZLN) uprising in January 1994.

Toniná → Colour map 4, B1.

① Daily 0900-1700, US$3.30, drinks are available at the site; also toilets and parking.

The Maya ruins at Toniná are 12 km from Ocosingo, with bus links to San Cristóbal de las Casas. A tour from San Cristóbal to Toniná costs US$15; it is possible to drive in an ordinary car, or take a taxi (US$6). There are also *colectivos* (15 minutes, US$1) running from the market, or you can walk from Ocosingo

Toniná is one of the last Classic Maya sites, with the palace high on a hill to your left. It is well worth visiting the ruins, which were excavated by a French government team. The temples are in the Palenque style with internal sanctuaries in the back room, but influences from many different Maya styles of various periods have been found. The huge pyramid complex, seven stone platforms making a man-made hill, is 10 m higher than the Temple of the Sun at Teotihuacán and is the tallest pyramidal structure in the Maya world. Stelae are in very diverse forms, as are wall panels, and some are in styles and of subjects unknown at any other Maya site. Ask the guardian to show you the second unrestored ball court and the sculpture kept at his house. He will show you round the whole site; there is also a small **museum**.

Agua Azul

① Entry US$1.50, US$4 for cars. Entry price is not always included in day trips from Palenque, which allow you to spend up to 3 hrs at Agua Azul. Violent robberies have been reported so don't go alone; groups of at least 4 are best.

The series of jungle waterfalls and rapids at Agua Azul run for 7 km and are breathtakingly beautiful. They are easily visited on a day trip from Palenque. All the travel agencies, and many hotels, offer a tour there for about US$10, including a visit to the waterfall at Misol-Há and Agua Clara (see below). Agua Azul's main swimming area has many restaurants and indigenous children selling fruit. Swimming is good, in clear blue water during good weather, in muddy brown water during bad (but still refreshing if very hot, which it usually is). Swimmers should stick to the roped areas where everyone else can see them; the various graves on the steep path up the hill alongside the rapids are testament to the dangers of swimming in those areas. One of the falls is called 'The Liquidizer', an area of white water in which bathing is extremely dangerous. On no account should you enter this stretch of water; many drownings have occurred. Even in the designated areas, the currents can be ferocious. Beware of hidden tree trunks in the water if it is murky. The path on the left of the rapids can be followed for 7 km, with superb views and secluded areas for picnics. There are also several *palapas* for hammocks, plenty of space for free camping and some rooms to rent.

Agua Clara and Misol-Há

Eight kilometres from Agua Azul along the river is **Agua Clara** ① entry US$1, a nature reserve. At Misol-Há there is a stunning waterfall usually visited first on day trips from Palenque. A narrow path winds around behind the falls, allowing you to stand behind the immense curtain of water. Swimming is possible in the large pool at the bottom of the tumbling cascade of water, but it is usually better to wait until you get to Agua Azul for a good swim. However, during the rainy season swimming is reported to be better at **Misol-Há** ① entry US$1, so go by bus or check with your tour operator, as some only allow a brief stop at Misol-Há.

Hardship for the Chiapanecos

For the visitor to Chiapas, the state's wonders are many: lush tropical jungle, quaint colonial villages, or the modern, prosperous capital, Tuxtla Gutiérrez. However, the peacefulness masks the troubles of the state's indigenous peoples. Their plight was splashed across the world's press with the Zapatista uprising of January 1994 and has remained a photogenic story ever since.

Chiapas, the southernmost state and one of Mexico's poorest, appears much like its neighbour, Guatemala, and shares many of the same problems. Subsistence has been a way of life for centuries, illiteracy and infant mortality are high, particularly among those who have retained their languages and traditions, shunning the Spanish culture. The Chiapas government estimates that nearly one million indigenous people live in the state, descendants of the great Maya civilization of AD 250-900. The indigenous Chiapanecos of today are spread out across the state, they do not speak the same language, nor dress alike, have the same customs nor the same types of tribal government.

The Tzotziles and Tzeltales total about 626,000 and live mainly on the plateau and the slopes of the high altitude zones. The Choles number 110,000 and live in the towns of Tila, Tumbalá, Salto de Agua, Sabanilla and Yajalón. The 87,000 Zoques live near the volatile Chichonal volcano.

The 66,000 Tojolabales live in Margaritas, Comitán, La Independencia, La Trinitaria and part of Altamirano. On the high mountains and slopes of the Sierra Madre are the 23,000 Mames and the 12,000 Mochós and Kakchikeles. The Lacandones, named after the rainforest they occupy, number only 500 today. Along the border with Guatemala are 21,500 Chujes, Kanjobales and Jacaltecos, although that number includes some refugees still there from the Guatemalan conflict, which ended in late 1996.

A minority of the indigenous population speaks Spanish, particularly in the Sierra Madre region and among the Zoques. Many have dropped their traditional clothing. Customary positions of authority along with stewardships and standard bearers have been dropped from tribal governance, but medicine men continue to practise. They still celebrate their festivals and they think about their ancestors as they have for centuries. Many now live in the large cities, but those who remain in *el campo* are, for the most part, poor. They get by, eating tortillas, some vegetables and occasionally beans. Many who leave for the city end up as domestic servants, labourers or street pedlars. The scarcity of land for indigenous people has been a political issue for many decades and limited land reform merely postponed the crisis that eventually erupted in the 1990s, and continues to cause the government difficulties.

Palenque town → *Colour map 4, B2. Phone code: 916.*
A friendly and, at times, hot, humid and airless little town whose sole reason to exist is to accommodate the tourists heading for the famous archaeological site nearby. There is plenty of accommodation for every budget, with dozens of cheap *posadas* around the centre, and a new tourist barrio, **La Cañada**, with more expensive hotels, restaurants and bars. Souvenirs are available at lower prices than elsewhere on the Ruta Maya, making Palenque a convenient place to stop off en route to the southerly Chiapan towns of San

Cristóbal and Tuxtla Gutiérrez. Travellers coming to Palenque from Mérida, Campeche and other cities in the Yucatán Peninsula will find it much hotter here, particularly in June, July and August. The **Fiesta de Santo Domingo** is held on the first week of August.

The **tourist office** ① *daily 0900-2100*, is on Juárez, a block below the plaza and next to the craft market. They are fairly useless but provide a good free map of Palenque and the ruins.

Five kilometres from Palenque town, but 3 km before the ruins, **El Panchán** ① www.palenquemx.com/elpanchan, is host to a fascinating mix of philosophies, foods and intellectual interests. Don Moisés, founder of El Panchán, first came to Palenque as an archaeologist and was one of the first guides to the ruins. He bought a plot of land, named it El Panchán – Maya for 'heaven on earth' – and started to raise a family. Now he has divided lots among his children who run various businesses. It is about 10°C cooler at El Panchán than Palenque town due to the dense foliage cover. Although vastly different, all businesses at Panchan have intertwined themselves into the natural jungle that surrounds them, creating an almost Robinson Crusoe setting – if you don't want to stay in town and like the idea of being based in the forest, get a bus or taxi here soon after arriving in Palenque town. **»** *See listings, pages 506-529.*

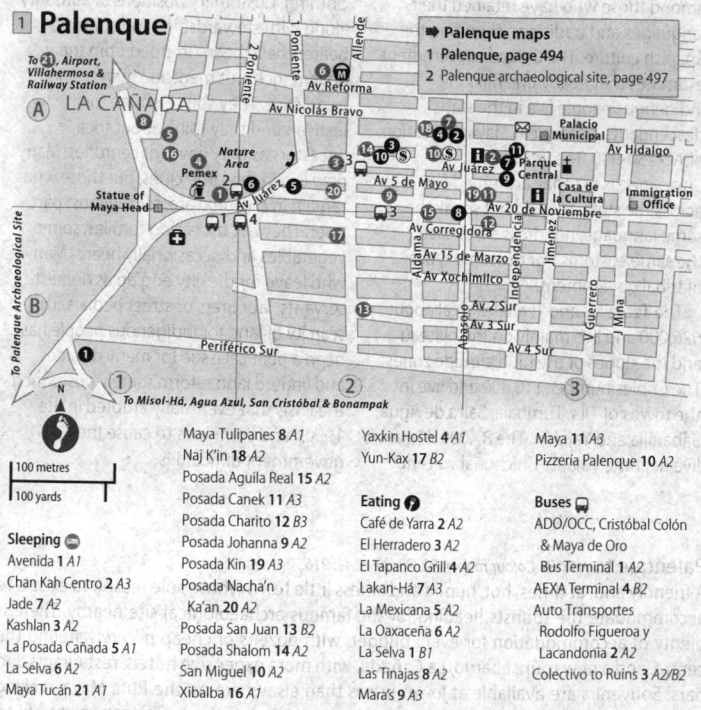

① Palenque

➡ **Palenque maps**
1 Palenque, page 494
2 Palenque archaeological site, page 497

To ② Airport, Villahermosa & Railway Station

LA CAÑADA

Nature Area

Statue of Maya Head

Pemex

To Palenque Archaeological Site

Periférico Sur

To Misol-Há, Agua Azul, San Cristóbal & Bonampak

100 metres
100 yards

Av Reforma
Av Nicolás Bravo
Av Juárez
Av 5 de Mayo
Av Corregidora
Av 15 de Mayo
Av Xochimilco
Av 2 Sur
Av 3 Sur
Av 4 Sur
Av 20 de Noviembre
Av Hidalgo

Palacio Municipal
Parque Central
Casa de la Cultura
Immigration Office

Sleeping 🛏
Avenida 1 *A1*
Chan Kah Centro 2 *A3*
Jade 7 *A2*
Kashlan 3 *A2*
La Posada Cañada 5 *A1*
La Selva 6 *A2*
Maya Tucán 21 *A1*
Maya Tulipanes 8 *A1*
Naj K'in 18 *A2*
Posada Aguila Real 15 *A2*
Posada Canek 11 *A3*
Posada Charito 12 *B3*
Posada Johanna 9 *A2*
Posada Kin 19 *A3*
Posada Nacha'n
  Ka'an 20 *A2*
Posada San Juan 13 *B2*
Posada Shalom 14 *A2*
San Miguel 10 *A2*
Xibalba 16 *A1*

Yaxkin Hostel 4 *A1*
Yun-Kax 17 *B2*

Eating 🍴
Café de Yarra 2 *A2*
El Herradero 3 *A2*
El Tapanco Grill 4 *A2*
Lakan-Há 7 *A3*
La Mexicana 5 *A2*
La Oaxaceña 6 *A2*
La Selva 1 *B1*
Las Tinajas 8 *A2*
Mara's 9 *A3*

Maya 11 *A3*
Pizzería Palenque 10 *A2*

Buses 🚌
ADO/OCC, Cristóbal Colón
  & Maya de Oro
  Bus Terminal 1 *A2*
AEXA Terminal 4 *B2*
Auto Transportes
  Rodolfo Figueroa y
  Lacandonia 2 *A2*
Colectivo to Ruins 3 *A2/B2*

Palenque ▶ Colour map 4, B1.

① *Daily 0800-1700, US$4.50, entrance to national park US$1; guided tours possible. There are lots of souvenir stalls at the main entrance. Water at the site is expensive, so bring your own. The cheapest food is the tacos from the stalls. Colectivos back to the town leave from outside the main entrance, US$1, every 6-18 mins. From Palenque town, take a colectivo from the main road near the 1st-class bus station.*

Built at the height of the Classic period on a series of artificial terraces surrounded by jungle, Palenque is one of the most beautiful of all the Maya ruins in Mexico. It was built for strategic purposes, with evidence of defensive apertures in some of the retaining walls. In the centre of the site is the Palace, a massive warren of buildings with an asymmetrical tower rising above them, and fine views to the north. The tower was probably used as an astronomical observatory and a watchtower. The outer buildings of the palace have an unusual series of galleries, offering shade from the jungle heat of the site.

From about the fourth century AD, Palenque grew from a small agricultural village to one of the most important cities in the prehispanic world, although it really achieved greatness between AD 600 and 800. During the long and illustrious reign of Lord Pacal, the city rapidly rose to the first rank of Maya states. The duration of Pacal's reign is still a bone of contention among Mayanists because the remains found in his sarcophagus do not appear to be those of an 81-year-old man, the age implied by the texts in the Temple of the Inscriptions.

Since its discovery, choked by the encroaching jungle that pushed against its walls and scaled the stairs of its temples once climbed by rulers, priests and acolytes, the architecture of Palenque has elicited praise and admiration and begged to be reconstructed. The corbelled vaults, the arrangement of its groupings of buildings, the impression of lightness created by walls broken by pillars and open spaces make Palenque-style architecture unique. It was only later that archaeologists and art historians realized that the architecture of Palenque was created mainly to accommodate the extraordinary sculptures and texts that referred not only to historical individuals and the important events in their lives, but also to mythological beings who endorsed the claims of dynastic continuity or 'divine right' of the rulers of this great city. The structures most illustrative of this function are the Palace, a group of buildings arranged around four patios to which a tower was later added, the Temple of the Inscriptions that rises above the tomb of Lord Pacal, and the temples of the Group of the Cross, used by Chan Bahlum, Pacal's successor, who made claims in the inscriptions carved on the tablets, pillars and balustrades of these exceptional buildings, claims which, in their audacity, are awe inspiring.

Warning The ruins are surrounded by thick, mosquito-infested jungle so wear insect repellent and make sure you're up to date with your tablets (May to November is the worst time for mosquitoes). It is extremely hot and humid at the ruins, especially in the afternoon, so it is best to visit early. Unfortunately, as well as mosquitoes, there have also been reports of criminals hiding in the jungle. As ever, try and leave valuables at home to minimize any loss.

The Palace

The Palace and Temple XI are located in the centre of the site. The Palace stands on an artificial platform over 100 m long and 9 m high. Chan Bahlum's younger brother, Kan Xul, was 57 when he became king. He devoted himself to enlarging the palace, and apparently built the four-storey tower in honour of his dead father. The top of the tower is

Sarcophagus

Pacal's sarcophagus, or coffin, is carved out of a solid piece of rock, with a carved slab covering it. Every element in the imagery of the sarcophagus lid is consistent with Maya iconography. It is exquisitely beautiful. The central image is that of Lord Pacal falling back into the fleshless jaws of the earth monster who will transport him to Xibalba, the realm of the dead. A cruciform world-tree rises above the underworld maw. The same world-tree appears on the tablets in the sanctuaries at the backs of the buildings known as the Group of the Cross. A long inscription runs around the edge of the lid, which includes a number of dates and personal names that records a dynastic sequence covering almost the whole of the seventh and eight centuries.

Four plugs in the corners of the lid filled the holes used with ropes to lower the lid into place; the plug in the southeast corner had a notch cut in it so that the channel, built into the stairway leading to the upper world, would allow spiritual communion between the dead king and his descendants above. Although the imagery of the sarcophagus lid refers to Pacal's fall into Xibalba, the location of the tower of the palace ensures that he will not remain there. The sun, setting over the crypt on the winter solstice, will have to do battle with the Nine Lords of the Night before re-emerging triumphantly in the east; the nine tiers of the pyramid represent the nine battles to be fought during his downward journey. Pacal, who awaits the sun at the point where the final battle had been fought, will accompany the sun as he re-emerges from Xibalba in the east. Palenque, the westernmost city of the Classic Maya, was in the 'dead zone', which placed it in the perfect position to accommodate the descent of the sun and Lord Pacal into the underworld.

almost at the level of Pacal's mortuary temple, and on the winter solstice the sun, viewed from here, sets directly above his crypt. Large windows where Maya astronomers could observe and chart the movement of the planets, ancestors of the royal lineage of Palenque, pierce the walls of the tower. Kan-Xul reigned for 18 years before being captured and probably sacrificed by the rulers of Toniná. During his reign Palenque reached its greatest degree of expansion, although recent excavations at the site may prove differently.

Temple of the Inscriptions

The Temple of the Inscriptions, along with Temple XII and Temple XIII, lies to the south of the Palace group of buildings and is one of the rare Maya pyramids to have a burial chamber incorporated at the time of its construction. This building was erected to cover the crypt in which Lord Pacal, the founder of the first ruling dynasty of Palenque, was buried. Discovered in 1952 by Alberto Ruz-Lhuillier, the burial chamber measured 7 m long, 7 m high and 3.75 m across, an incredible achievement considering the weight of the huge pyramid pressing down upon it. According to the inscriptions, Lord Pacal was born in AD 603 and died in AD 684. Inside, Ruz-Lhuillier discovered his bones adorned with jade jewellery. Around the burial chamber were various figures carved in stucco, depicting the Bolontikú, the Nine Lords of the Night of Maya mythology. There was a narrow tube alongside the stairs, presumably to give Pacal spiritual access to the outside world. Pacal also left a record of his forebears in the inscriptions. These three great tablets contain one of the longest texts of any Maya monument. There are 620 glyph blocks; they tell of Pacal's ancestors, astronomical events and an astonishing projection into the distant future (AD 4772). One of the last inscriptions reveals that, 132 days after Pacal's death, his son, Chan Bahlum, ascended to power as the new ruler of Palenque.

While finishing his father's funerary monument, Chan Bahlum had himself depicted as a child being presented as heir by his father. The portraits of Chan Bahlum, on the outer pillars of the Temple of the Inscriptions, display features that are both human and divine. He took and assumed attributes that rightly belong to the gods, thus ensuring that the heir to the throne was perceived as a divine human.

2 Palenque archaeological site

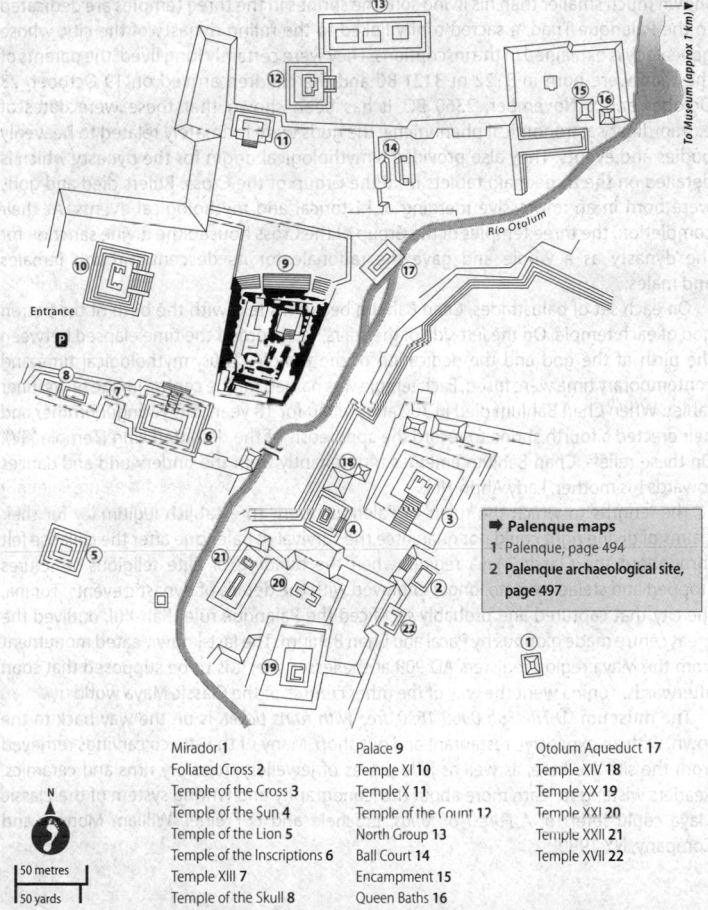

➡ **Palenque maps**
1 Palenque, page 494
2 Palenque archaeological site, page 497

Mirador 1	Palace 9	Otolum Aqueduct 17
Foliated Cross 2	Temple XI 10	Temple XIV 18
Temple of the Cross 3	Temple X 11	Temple XX 19
Temple of the Sun 4	Temple of the Count 12	Temple XXI 20
Temple of the Lion 5	North Group 13	Temple XXII 21
Temple of the Inscriptions 6	Ball Court 14	Temple XVII 22
Temple XIII 7	Encampment 15	
Temple of the Skull 8	Queen Baths 16	

50 metres
50 yards

Group of the Cross

To the extreme southeast of the centre of the site lie Temple XIV and the buildings known as the *Grupo de la Cruz*. These include the Temple of the Sun, with beautiful relief carvings, which would probably have been painted in their day. The three temples in this group all have dramatic roof-combs, originally believed to have a religious significance, although traces of roof-combs have been found on buildings now known to have been purely residential. In all of the temples there was discovered a huge stone tablet with bas-relief, now removed to the museum, from whose images the name of each temple was taken.

Human and mythological time come together in the inscriptions of these temples. In each tableau carved on the tablets at the back of the temples, Chan Bahlum, the new ruler, receives the regalia of office from his father, Pacal, now in the underworld and shown much smaller than his living son. The shrines in the three temples are dedicated to the Palenque Triad, a sacred trinity linked to the ruling dynasty of the city, whose genealogy is explained in the inscriptions. They were certainly long lived: the parents of the triad were born in 3122 or 3121 BC and the children arrived on 19 October, 23 October and 6 November, 2360 BC. It has been shown that these were dates of extraordinary astronomical phenomena: the gods were intimately related to heavenly bodies and events. They also provided a mythological origin for the dynasty which is detailed on the three main tablets from the Group of the Cross. Rulers died and gods were born in an impressive merging of historical and mythological events. At their completion, the three temples of the Group of the Cross housed the divine sanction for the dynasty as a whole and gave the rationale for its descent through females and males.

On each set of balustrades, Chan Bahlum began his text with the birth of the patron god of each temple. On the left side of the stairs, he recorded the time elapsed between the birth of the god and the dedication of the temple. Thus, mythological time and contemporary time were fused. Each temple was named for the central image on its inner tablet. When Chan Bahlum died in 702 after ruling for 18 years, his younger brother and heir erected a fourth shrine to record the apotheosis of the departed king (Temple XIV). On these reliefs, Chan Bahlum emerges triumphantly from the underworld and dances towards his mother, Lady Ahpo-Hel.

The lengths to which the rulers of Palenque went to establish legitimacy for their claims of divine right could not guarantee the survival of Palenque after the collapse felt throughout the Classic Maya region, when the building of elite religious structures stopped and stelae were no longer engraved with the details of dynastic events. Toniná, the city that captured and probably sacrificed the Palenque ruler Kan-Xul, outlived the great centre made glorious by Pacal and Chan Bahlum. The last-known dated monument from the Maya region registers AD 909 at the lesser site; it is to be supposed that soon afterwards, Toniná went the way of the other centres of the Classic Maya world.

The **museum** ① *Tue-Sun 0900-1630, free with ruins ticket*, is on the way back to the town, with an expensive restaurant and gift shop. Many of the stucco carvings retrieved from the site are here, as well as jade pieces of jewellery, funerary urns and ceramics. Readers wishing to learn more about the iconography and writing system of the Classic Maya could refer to: *A Forest of Kings*, L Schele and D Freidel, William Morrow and Company, NY 1990.

Yaxchilán, Bonampak, Lacanjá and around ⊜⊘⊿⊖⊕ » pp506-529.
Colour map 4, B2.

ⓘ Yaxchilán 0800-1600, US$4.50; Bonampak 0800-1645, US$3.70 (free for under 13s, students and over 60s) plus US$11.50 for optional transport with the Jach Winik coop to the site; this includes toilet and locker and entry to the small museum. It's a 1-hr journey from Frontera Corozal to Bonampak.

Yaxchilán

Yaxchilán is a major Classic Maya centre built along a terrace and hills above the Río Usumacinta, where there are more howler monkeys than people. The temples are ornately decorated with stucco and stone and the stone lintels are carved with scenes of ceremonies and conquests. Bonampak, originally under the political domination of Yaxchilán, was built in the late-Classic period on the Río Lacanjá, a tributary of the Usumacinta. It is famous for its murals, dated at AD 800, which relate the story of a battle and the bloody aftermath with the sacrificial torture and execution of prisoners.

From around AD 200 to the early 10th century, the era known as the Classic Maya witnessed the growth of many small settlements into great centres noted for wonderful architecture, sculpture, painted ceramics, impressive advances in mathematics and hieroglyphic writings, and the growth of an elite who often created alliances with other polities through marriage. Wide causeways, sacbés, were built between centres enabling the inhabitants to maintain contact with those of other towns. All these great advances came to an end around AD 909, when the Classic Maya civilization collapsed. For many years Mayanists have postulated about the cause of the collapse: some have suggested land exhaustion, others have suggested invasion from the Central Highlands, while still others believe in a peasant revolt against the conspicuous consumption of an expanding elite. The painted walls of Structure 1 at Bonampak illustrate well the extravagance indulged in by the elite of this centre on the margins of the Lacandón rainforest.

Bonampak

The murals at Bonampak are very realistic with an excellent use of colour and available space. Painted on the walls, vault rises and benches of three adjoining but not interconnecting rooms, they describe the rituals surrounding the presentation at court of the future ruler. Some of the rituals were separated by considerable intervals, which adds to the solemnity of the ceremony. It is very possible that the rituals illustrated were only a small selection of a far greater series of events. The people participating were mainly elite, including the royal family, and a strict hierarchy was observed in which eminent lords were attended by minor nobility.

In Room 1, the celebration opens with the presentation of the young prince, a simple act in which a porter introduces the child to an assembly of lords, dressed for the occasion in white robes. The king, dressed simply, watches from his throne. Also present are two representatives from Yaxchilán, one male and one female. It is probable that the female is the wife or consort of Chaan-Muan, the ruler of Bonampak. After this simple opening, the spectacle begins. Lords are represented dressing in sumptuous clothing and jewellery, musicians appear playing drums, turtle carapaces, rattles and trumpets and they all line up for a procession, which will bemuse the peasantry, labourers and artisans waiting outside. We never see the lower orders, but, open-mouthed, we can stand with them to observe the spectacle. The headdresses alone are enough to bedazzle us and the great diversity in the attire of the participants illustrates the wide spectrum of social functions fulfilled by those attending the ceremony.

The imagery and text of the sculptured lintels and stelae at nearby Yaxchilán proclaim the right of the heir to accede to the throne while emphasizing the need to take captives to be sacrificed in honour of the king-to-be. This need is echoed in the paintings of Room 2, Structure 1, at Bonampak. A ferocious battle is in progress in which the ruler, Chaan-Muan, proves his right to the throne. In the midst of battle, he shines out heroically. The local warriors pull the hair of those of the opposite side, whose identity is not known. Many captives were taken. In the ensuing scene, the full horror of the fate of those captured by the Maya is illustrated.

On a stepped structure, the ruler Chaan-Muan oversees the torture and mutilation of the captives taken in the recent battle. This event is clearly in the open air and surely witnessed by the inhabitants of Bonampak, whose loyalty is rewarded by admission to the bloody circus. The torture of the captives consisted of mutilation of the hands; some disconsolate individuals hold up their hands dripping blood, while one has clearly been decapitated, his head resting on a bed of leaves. It is to be supposed that the torture of the captives would be followed by death, probably by decapitation. The gods demanded sacrifice, which was provided by the rulers in an extravaganza of bloodletting. It must be understood that what appears to be outright bloodthirstiness was a necessary part of Maya ritual and probably accepted by all the polities throughout the Classic Maya region. It is very probable that the heir would not have been acceptable without this gory ritual.

The murals of the third room at Bonampak express the events that were meant to close the series of rituals designed to consolidate the claim to the throne by the son of the ruler. At first sight, the paintings that cover the walls of room three of Structure 1 appear to celebrate the sacrifices of the previous depictions in an exuberant public display of music, dance and perhaps song. The background is a pyramid, and ten elegantly dressed lords dance on different levels, colourful 'dance-wings' sprouting from their hips. The dominant dancer on the uppermost level is believed to be the ruler, Chaan-Muan. However, it has been noted that a very strong element of sacrifice accompanies the extrovert display. In a more private corner, the royal family is portrayed preparing to engage in blood sacrifice; a servant proffers them a container that the sacred bloodletting instruments. There are also indications that the male dancers had already drawn blood by means of penis perforation. As at Yaxchilán, blood endorsed the dynastic claims of the royal family.

The rituals portrayed on the walls of Structure 1 at Bonampak are thought to have been performed between 790 and 792, a time when the collapse of the Classic Maya was beginning to be felt. The extravagant use of enormous amounts of fine cloth, expensive jaguar pelts, jade beads and pectorals, elegant costumes, headdresses made from rare feathers, and spondylus shells was not enough to reverse the decadence of the civilization that had produced magnificent works in art, architecture, jewellery, mathematics, astronomy and glyphic writing: within a hundred years, the jungle was to claim it for its own.

Lacanjá

At Lacanjá (9 km from Bonampak) there is a community of Lacandones. For more details ask at **Na-Bolom** in San Cristóbal de las Casas. Local guides can be hired for hikes in the jungle and to the ruins of Bonampak. Lucas Chambor at the **Casa de Cultura** is a good source of advice. Lacanjá to Bonampak with locals costs US$6.50-9. The walk through the jungle is beautiful and crosses several streams. Another walk in the area is to the **Cascadas de Moctuniha** (one hour each way, US$6.50 with guide).

Comitán and around → *Phone code : 963.*

Comitán de Domínguez is a small but handsome colonial city located close to the border. It's a tranquil and elevated place, offering cool respite from the stifling lowlands and a good place to relax before or after visiting Guatemala. A large, shady zócalo marks the centre of town, where you'll find a **tourist office** ① *Juárez 6, just inside Pasaje Morales on the east side, Mon-Fri 0800-1800, Sat 0800-1600.* Visit the **Guatemalan Consulate** ① *1a Calle Sur Pte 26, T963-632 2979, Mon-Fri 0900-1700,* if you need a visa. There's a handful of small museums in town including the **Museo de Arte Hermila Domínguez de Castellanos** ① *Av Central Sur and 3a Sur Pte, Tue-Sat, 1000-1800, Sun 0900-1245, US$0.50,* with a collection of modern art; and **Casa Museo Belisario Domínguez** ① *Av Central Sur and 2a Sur Pte, Mon-Sat 1000-1800, Sun 0900-1245, US$0.50,* filled with memorabilia and dedicated to a local doctor who was assassinated after speaking out against President Huerta.

Lagunas de Montebello and Chinkultic

Six kilometres south of Comitán take a right turn for the Maya ruins of **Tenán Puente** (5 km), situated in a forest, 0900-1600, US$2.50; there is a shortcut on foot. In 1996 the tomb of a Maya nobleman (AD 1000) was discovered here. The buildings at Tenán are more restored than those at Chinkultic (see below). A road branches off the Pan-American Highway, 16 km further on, to a very beautiful region of vari-coloured lakes and caves, the **Lagunas de Montebello** (a national park). Off the road to Montebello, 30 km from the Pan-American Highway, lie the ruins of **Chinkultic** ① *0900-1700, US$3,* with temples, ball court, carved stone stelae and a *cenote* (deep round lake, good swimming) in beautiful surroundings; from the signpost the ruins are about 3 km along a dirt road. Watch and ask for the very small sign and gate where the road to the ruins starts (about 1 km back along the main road, towards Comitán from **Doña María's**, don't attempt any short cuts); worth visiting when passing. *Colectivo* from Comitán US$2.50.

Combi vans or buses marked 'Tziscao' or 'Lagos' to the Lagunas de Montebello National Park (60 km from Comitán, US$1.30 about one hour), via the **Lagunas de Siete Colores** (so called because the oxides in the water give varieties of colours), leave frequently from Avenida 2 Ponientete Sur y Calle 3 Sur Poniente, four blocks from the plaza in Comitán; buses go as far as Laguna Bosque Azul, a one-hour journey. For those with their own transport there are several dirt roads from Comitán to the Lagunas; a recommended route is the one via La Independencia, Buena Vista, La Patria and El Triunfo (beautiful views), eventually joining the road west of the Chinkultic ruins.

Tziscao

Tziscao is 9 km along the road leading right from the park entrance, which is 3 km before Bosque Azul; hourly buses Comitán-Tziscao; the last bus and *colectivo* back connecting with the 1900 bus to San Cristóbal is at 1600. The last *combi* to Comitán is at 1700. A trip to the Lagunas de Siete Colores from Comitán can be done in a day (note that the less-accessible lakes are hard to get to even if staying in the vicinity). It is also possible to hire a *combi*, which takes 12 people, to go to the Lakes and Chinkultic for US$15 per hour. A day trip to Chinkultic and the lakes from San Cristóbal de las Casas is also possible, if exhausting (take passport and tourist card). The **Bosque Azul** area is now a reserve. The area is noted for its orchids and birdlife, including the famous *quetzal*, but it gets very busy at weekends and holidays. There are small caves nearby.

Routes to Guatemala ●❼▲●● ➾ *pp506-529*.

There are two main border crossings into Guatemala: one at Ciudad Cuauhtémoc (La Mesilla in Guatemala), reached via Route 190 from San Cristóbal de las Casas, and the other at Tapachula along the coastal Route 200 from the neighbouring state of Oaxaca. A third option is to cross the border by boat, east of Palenque, along the rivers Usumacinta or San Pedro. Note: if planning on returning to Mexico after an excursion to Guatemala, ensure you get an exit stamp, at the immigration office. Pick up your tourist card and a slip of paper, take this to any bank, pay US$23 and the slip is stamped. Not doing this can lead to problems when you try to leave Mexico again.

Ciudad Cuauhtémoc

South of San Cristóbal and heading for Guatemala, follow the 170-km paved road via **Teopisca** to **Comitán de Domínguez**. From Comitán the road winds down to the Guatemalan border at Ciudad Cuauhtémoc via La Trinitaria (near the turn-off to Lagunas de Montebello, restaurant but no hotel).

Ciudad Cuauhtémoc, despite its name, is not a city, but just a few buildings; the **Cristóbal Colón** bus station is opposite Immigration, with an overpriced restaurant and an excellent hotel. Be sure to surrender your tourist card and get your exit stamp at Mexican Immigration in Ciudad Cuauhtémoc before boarding a pickup for Guatemalan immigration; you will only have to go back if you don't. A pickup to the Guatemalan border, 4 km, costs US$0.65 per person. Walk 100 m to Immigration and Customs (open until 2100). Beyond the Guatemalan post at La Mesilla, see box, page 694, a beautiful stretch of road leads 85 km to Huehuetenango. This route is far more interesting than the one through Tapachula; the border crossing at Ciudad Cuauhtémoc is also reported as easier than that at Talismán.

Tapachula crossings: Talismán and Ciudad Hidalgo

The Talismán bridge lies 8 km from Tapachula and provides good onward connections to the western highlands and Quetzaltenango. It's a fairly grubby crossing with plenty of aggressive moneychangers who you should avoid doing business with. Further south, 37 km from Tapachula, Ciudad Hidalgo is a busy border town that connects with Guatemala's Pacific Highway.

Río Usumacinta route

The Río Usumacinta route takes you by road to Benemérito (southeast of Yaxchilán and Bonampak), boat to Sayaxché, Guatemala and then road to Flores. **Autotransportes Comitán Lagos de Montebello** buses (Avenida Manuel Velasco Suárez, Palenque, three blocks from food market) run eight a day starting at 0400 until 1530 to **Benemérito**, on the Mexican side of the Usumacinta, seven to 12 hours but will be quicker when the new paved road is completed; basic buses, dreadful road, crowded (it's about half the time in a *camioneta* if you can hitch a ride). You must visit immigration, about 3 km from Benemérito, to sign out of Mexico (the bus will wait).

Once in Benemérito where there is a 2100 curfew (two basic *pensiones*), hope for a boat to Guatemala; this may take a couple of days. The boat goes to Sayaxché and should stop at Pipiles for immigration. A trading boat takes two days, US$4-5; a motorized canoe eight hours, US$5-10. You can also charter a fast boat for about US$200. From Sayaxché, buses run to Flores.

For an alternative (and much easier) route, take the bus from Palenque to Frontera Corozal with Transportes Chamoan, Hidalgo 141, roughly hourly from 0500-1700, US$6. About an hour down this route at Km 61 is an excellent breakfast stop, Valle Escondido. Keep an eye out for hummingbirds. In Corozal there is an immigration post, two hotels and restaurants. It's a 30-minute *lancha* ride to Bethel, US$30 for one to two people, US$40 for three to four people; or a cheap five-minute ride to La Técnica, see box, page 758.

Tenosique and Río San Pedro route

The Río San Pedro route starts at Tenosique, a friendly place east of Palenque (money exchange at clothing shop, Ortiz y Alvarez at Calle 28 No 404, good rates for dollars to quetzales, poor for dollars to pesos). From here, the classic route takes you by road to La Palma, boat to El Naranjo, in Guatemala, and then road to Flores. A newer, more convenient route begins at El Ceibo, 60km southeast of Tenosique.

From Tenosique to **La Palma** on the Río San Pedro, *colectivos* starting at 0600 from in front of the market, one hour, US$1, two hours by bus (from Tenosique bus station, which is outside town, take taxi, US$1.70 or *colectivo* to 'Centro', or walk 20 minutes). Taxi to La Palma US$7, shared by all passengers. From La Palma boats leave to El Naranjo when they have enough passengers, but timings are very irregular (they wait for a minimum of five passengers), at least 4½ hours, US$22. Be at the boat one hour early, it sometimes leaves ahead of schedule; if this happens ask around for someone to chase it, US$3-4 per person for three people. If there are fewer than five passengers, the boat may be cancelled, in which case you must either wait for the next one, or hire a *rápido* (US$125, maximum four people). You may be able to arrange a slower boat for up to six people for US$100. In La Palma, one restaurant will change money at weekends at a reasonable rate.

It is a beautiful boat trip, through mangroves with flocks of white herons and the occasional alligator, dropping people off at homesteads. There is a stop at the border post two hours into the journey to sign out of Mexico, a lovely spot with a lake and lilies. In the rain, your backpack will get wet; take waterproofs and a torch/flashlight. There are no officials on arrival at the jetty in El Naranjo; Immigration is a short way uphill on the right (entry will cost US$5 in quetzales or dollars, beware extra unofficial charges at customs); bus tickets to Flores are sold here.

For the newer, more reliable route, take an hourly bus from Tenosique to El Ceibo. They depart from calle 45 and 16, behind the market, 0600-1700, one hour. Once at the border, catch a pickup to Río San Pedro. There are frequent *lanchas* to El Naranjo until 1700, US$3.50, 30 minutes.

Route to Tapachula ● ⊮ *pp506-529.*

Travelling from the neighbouring state of Oaxaca, Routes 190 and 200 merge to cross the Isthmus of Tehuantepec. Accommodation is available at **Zanatepec**, and **Tapanatepec**, which is where Highway 190 heads northeast to Tuxtla Gutiérrez and Highway 200 continues southeast along the coast of Chiapas to the Guatemalan border.

Border essentials: Mexico–Guatemala

Ciudad Cuauhtémoc
Tourist cards and visas are available at the border; some reports say only 15 days are being given, but extensions are possible in Oaxaca or Mexico City. It is forbidden to bring in fruit and vegetables.

Drivers entering Mexico At the border crossing your vehicle is fumigated, US$7.25, get a receipt (if re-entering Mexico, with documents from a previous entry, papers are checked here). Proceed 4 km to Migración to obtain tourist card or visa, or have existing visa checked. Then go to **Banjército** to obtain the necessary papers and windscreen sticker or, if re-entering Mexico, to have existing papers checked. Monday to Friday 0800-1600, Saturday to Sunday 0900-1400. Mexico is one hour ahead of Guatemala.

Talismán
It is 8 km from Tapachula to the 24-hour border at Talismán.

Immigration The Mexican Customs post is 200 m from the Guatemalan one.

Guatemalan consulate See Tapachula.

Crossing into Guatemala By car can take several hours. If you don't want your car sprayed inside it may cost you a couple of dollars. Do not park in the car park at the control post, as it is very expensive.

Driving into Mexico See Essentials, page 42, for information about the temporary import of vehicles. Car papers are issued at the Garita de Aduana on Route 200 out of Tapachula. There is no other road; you can't miss it. Photocopies of documents must be made in town; there are no facilities at the Garita. Reported to be a frustrating procedure – be prepared and patient.

Exchange Change money in town rather than with men standing around Customs on the Guatemalan side (check rates before dealing with them, and haggle; there is no bank on the Guatemalan side).

Ciudad Hidalgo
There is a border crossing south of Tapachula, at Ciudad Hidalgo, opposite Tecún Umán with connections to Coatepeque, Mazatenango and Retalhuleu. A few blocks from the town plaza is Mexican Immigration, at the foot of the 1-km-long bridge across the Río Suchiate; cycle taxis cross the bridge for about US$1, pedestrians pay US$0.15. You cannot change TCs here.

Arriaga → *Colour map 3, C6. Phone code: 966.*
Arriaga is a good stopping place just across the state border that separates Oaxaca from Chiapas; many banks around zócalo for exchange. The road from Arriaga to Tapachula is a four-lane divided freeway.

From Arriaga, Route 200 continues to Tonalá, formerly a very quiet town but now noisy and dirty. Bus Tonalá–Tapachula, three hours, US$6.75; also buses to Tuxtla. This is by far the most direct road for travellers seeking the quickest way from Mexico City to Guatemala.

Puerto Arista → *Colour map 3, C6. Phone code: 961.*

Along the coast from Tonalá to Tapachula there are several fine-looking and undeveloped beaches, although waves and currents are dangerous. Puerto Arista (17 km south of Tonalá) is now being built up, but it is still a relatively peaceful area with 32 km of clean beach to relax on with no salespeople; bus/*colectivo* from Tonalá every hour, 45 minutes, US$0.60, taxi US$2; plenty of buses to Arriaga, US$0.75. Many hotels, motels and restaurants on the beach, which is hot and, in the wet season, has sandflies.

Buses also from Tonalá to **Boca del Cielo** further down the coast, which is good for bathing and has *cabañas* with hammocks, and similarly **Cabeza del Toro**. **Paredón**, on the huge Laguna del Mar Muerto, 14 km west of Tonalá, has excellent seafood and one very basic guesthouse. You can take a local fishing boat out into the lagoon to swim; the shore stinks because fishermen clean fish on the beach among dogs and pigs. There are frequent buses.

On the way to Tapachula you pass through **Pijijiapan** where there is the **Hotel Pijijilton** next to the **Cristóbal Colón** bus station. From **Huixtla**, a good, scenic road winds off into the mountains parallel to the border, towards Ciudad Cuauhtémoc and Comitán.

Tapachula and around ⬤🅿🅰⬤🅖 ➤➤ *pp506-529. Colour map 4, C1.*

→ *Phone code: 962.*

Once little more than an obscure border town in a lesser visited corner of Chiapas, more than US$70 million has recently been invested in Tapachula, with a view to exploiting its strategic location on the Pacific coast. The result? Puerto Chiapas: a major new port large enough to receive the latest generation cruise, container and cargo ships. It's hoped that this ambitious new development will bring unprecedented visitors to Tapchula and Chiapas, and the tourist board's slick new brochures are an exercise in shameless self-promotion. Yet beyond the manicured lawns of the port, Tapachula is still the same shambling old border town it's always been, more characteristic of Central America than Mexico. For now, at least, this city has yet to blossom.

For orientation, **avenidas** run north-south, calles east-west (Oriente-Poniente). Odd-numbered **calles** are north of Calle Central, odd **avenidas** are east of Avenida Central. For information, contact the **municipal tourist office** ⓘ *8a Av Norte and 3a Pte, T962-625 0441, www.turismotapachula.gob.mx*; or the **state tourist office** ⓘ *Plaza Kamico, Central Ote, T962-625 5409*, away from the centre. Tapachula has an airport and is a major crossing junction for Guatemala.

There's little to see in town itself, save a small but captivating archaeological museum, **Museo Regional del Soconusco**, west side of the plaza. But beyond the city, a flurry of new attractions have opened in anticipation of the big tourist influx.

Around Tapachula

La Ruta Café is a new agro-tourism development that includes 13 coffee *fincas*, many of German origin. Some of them are stunningly positioned, with luxury, mountain-top accommodation and spas; others have facilities for adventure sports like biking and zip-lining. Speak to the tourist office for more details.

Caicrochis ⓘ *F962-642 6692, Tue-Sun, 1000-1700, US$3*, is the oldest crocodile reserve in Mexico and home to around a thousand of the beasts. Don't dangle the kids too close! A couple of 'eco-parks' have opened that are really just touristy playgrounds with opportunities for activities like swimming, rock climbing and quad-biking. They include

Club Catay Maya ① *Carretera a Carillopuerto San Agustín Jitotol, www.cataymaya.com*; and **Parque Ecoturístico La Changa** ① *Carretera a la Presa José Cecilio del Valle s/n, T626-5592, www.lachanga.com.mx*.

There are several beaches near Tapachula, including Playa Linda, San Benito, Las Escolleras and Barra Cahoacán. 5 km from Playa Linda you'll find **Laguna de Pozuelos**, a lagoon with rich mangroves and wildlife including snakes, lizards and aquatic birds. Similarly, **La Encrucijada Biosphere Reserve** is home to various species of local fauna.

The ruins of **Izapa** (proto-Classic stelae, small museum) lie just off the road to Talismán; the part of the site on the north is easily visible but a larger portion is on the south side of the highway, about 1 km away, ask caretaker for guidance. To reach Izapa take a *combi* from Unión Progreso bus station.

Forty-five kilometres northeast of Tapachula, beyond the turning to Talismán, is **Unión Juárez**, where you can have your papers stamped and proceed on foot via Talquián to the Guatemalan border at Sibinal.

A worthwhile hike can be made up the **Tacaná volcano** (4150 m), which takes two to three days from Unión Juárez. Ask for the road to Chiquihuete; no cars. The Tapachula tourist office can help; in Unión Juárez ask for Sr Umberto Ríos at **Restaurante Montaña**, he will put you in touch with guide Moisés Hernández, who charges US$15 a day. It is possible to stay overnight in Don Emilio Velásquez's barn halfway up, US$2; he offers coffee and *tortillas*. At the top are some *cabañas* in which you sleep for free; sleeping bag essential.

⊕ Tabasco and Chiapas listings

For Sleeping and Eating price codes and other relevant information, see Essentials pages 45-48.

⊜ Sleeping

Villahermosa *p482*
The price difference between a reasonable and a basic hotel can be negligible, so you might as well go for the former. Try to book hotel rooms in advance, especially during the holiday season (May onwards). Hotels tend to be full Mon-Thu; arrive before nightfall if you can. For cheaper options there are a number of hotels and guesthouses of varying standards and cleanliness along Av Constitución, in the centre, 1 block from the river.
AL Olmeca Plaza, Madero 418, T993-358 0102, www.hotelolmecaplaza. Large, central, professionally managed hotel with good services including restaurant, gym and pool. Some rooms have good views.
AL Quality Inn Villahermosa Cencali, Juárez 105, T993-313 6611, www.qualityinn villahermosa.com. Secluded and wonderfully

a/c business hotel. It's located away from the centre, but close to commercial developments. Excellent breakfast. Highly recommended.
B Madero, Madero 301, T993-312 0516. Clean, if slightly damp and smelly rooms with hot water, fan and cable TV.
B Provincia Express, Lerdo 303, T993-314 5376, provincial_express@hotmail.com. Good, comfortable rooms with a/c and cable TV. Restaurant and bar, good value
C Chocos, Lino Merino 100 and Constitución, T993-312 9444. Signposted from far away, not too hard to find. Clean, good-value rooms with a/c and telephone. Restaurant attached.
C Hotel San Francisco, Av Madero 604, T993-312 3198. Reasonable central hotel, with adequate rooms, hot water, and fan.
C Oriente, Madero 425, T993-312 0121, hotel-oriente@hotmail.com. The rooms smell clean and fresh at this tidy hotel. They have hot showers and fan, pricier with a/c.
D San Miguel, Lerdo 315, T993-312 1426. Friendly, but rather smelly and run-down place on a noisy street.

D-E Hotel Lino, Lino Merino 823, very close to **ADO** terminal. T993-148 1924. Basic rooms with good showers, quiet despite its location, more expensive with a/c.

E Del Río, Av Constitución 206 and Reforma, on plaza off Madero, T993-312 8262. Simple, slightly odd hotel with cheap rooms. You're greeted by an enormous sign telling you the management is not responsible for your belongings, so take care. The price matches the rooms.

Tuxtla Gutiérrez *p484, map p484*
There is plenty of budget accommodation near the former 1st-class ADO terminal, Av 2 Norte Ote Pte 323, beyond the plaza. (Some of them also have left-luggage for a small fee even if you're not a hotel guest. Look for signs outside.)

A Hotel María Eugenia, Av Central Oriente 507, T961-613 3767, www.maria eugenia.com.mx. Pleasant rooms in the heart of town. Internet, a/c, cable TV, parking, pool and restaurant.

A Palace Inn, Blv Belisario Domínguez 1081, 4 km from centre, T961 615 0574, palaceinn@hotmail.com. Generally recommended, lovely garden, pool, noisy video bar.

C Regional San Marcos, 1 Sur y 2 Ote Sur 176, T961-613 1940, hotelsanmarcos@ prodigy. net.mx. Simple, but comfortable rooms with bath, fan or a/c, cheaper without TV.

C-D Posada de Chiapas, 2 Pte Sur 243. Small, basic rooms with bath, fan or a/c, TV, friendly.

D Estrella, 2 Ote Norte 322, T961-612 3827. Friendly, clean hotel, slightly run-down, but good value. Rooms with bath and free drinking water, recommended.

D Hostal San Miguel, 3a Av Sur Poniente No 510, T961-611 4459, www.hostalsan miguel.com.mx. Nice, modern hostel with internet access, TV room, kitchen and lockers.

D Hotel Avenida, Av Central Poniente 224, T961-612 0807, mauriciog994@hotmail.com.

Private bath, hot water, tv and fan. Nice and central, if a bit basic.

D Plaza Chiapas, Av 2 Norte Ote y 2 Ote Norte, T961-613 8365. Small, clean rooms with hot showers, cable TV and a/c. Cheaper with fan. Enclosed car park. Recommended.

E Posada del Sol, 3a Pte Norte and 2a Pte Norte, T961-614 6220, 1 block from former bus terminal. Rooms with hot shower and fan. Good service, good value, but quite basic. Under refurbishment, so a bit noisy daytime.

Camping

E La Hacienda, Belisario Domínguez 1197 (west end of town on Route 190), T961-602 6946, www.lahaciendahotel.com. 4 spaces with hook-up, hot showers, restaurant, mini-pool, a bit noisy and not easily accessible for RVs over 6 m; owner speaks English.

San Cristóbal de las Casas *p486, map p487*
Look on the bulletin board outside the tourist office for guesthouses advertising cheap bed and breakfast.

AL Casa Mexicana, 28 de Agosto 1, T967-678 0698, www.hotelcasamexicana.com. This hotel is filled with art work and Mexican crafts. Services include sauna, Wi-Fi, parking and babysitters. The master suite has a jacuzzi, and the attractive courtyard is lush and filled with plants. There is a newer wing on the opposite side of the road with a good craft shop attached. Restaurant Los Magueys and Bar Cucaracha attached to old wing, open 0700-2200. Highly recommended.

AL Casa Vieja, María A Flores 27, T967-678 6868, www.casavieja.com.mx. Elegant and relaxing converted colonial house, with TV, good restaurant, hot water, radiators in rooms if weather cold, Wi-Fi, parking and laundry service.

L Posada Diego de Mazariegos, 5 de Febrero 1, 1 block north of plaza, T967-678 0833, www.diegodemazariegos.com.mx. Comfortable and quiet, almost convent-like atmosphere. Comfy common room. There's a travel agency and restaurant inside, as well as a bar, **Tequila Zoo**. Sun buffet at 1400. Recommended.

A Na Bolom, Vicente Guerrero 33, T967-678 1418, www.nabolom.org. Beautiful, 17-room guesthouse in a cultural centre (see page 488). Rooms have bath and fireplace. Insightful tours available. Traditional Mexican meal every night at 1900 in the courtyard restaurant. Recommended.

A Posada El Paraíso, Av 5 de Febrero 19, T967-678 0085, www.hotelposada paraiso.com Mexican-Swiss owned. Impeccable, light and airy rooms, many open onto pretty patio. Excellent, atmospheric restaurant, parking nearby beneath cathedral. Very friendly and highly recommended.

A Rincón del Arco, Ejército Nacional 66, 8 blocks from centre, T967-678 1313. Simply gorgeous tasteful, friendly hotel with 58 rooms and 2 junior suites, some with fireplaces. There's a pleasant garden, bar and nice restaurant. Recommended.

A Santa Clara, Insurgentes 1, on plaza, T967-678 1140, www.travelbymexico.com/chis/santaclara. Colonial-style hotel with clean rooms; some are noisy. Breakfast included. Good restaurant, Wi-Fi, travel agency, swimming pool and pool bar. Recommended.

B El Cerrillo, Belisario Domínguez 27, T967-678 1283, www.hotelesjardines.com. Nice carpeted rooms and a lovely rooftop patio. Wi-Fi and cable TV. Recommended.

B Palacio de Moctezuma, Juárez 16, T967-678 0352, www.travelbymexico.com/chis/moctezuma. Colonial-style hotel founded in 1727. Rooms have hot water and cable TV, good Mexican food is served in the restaurant. Rooms downstairs sometimes damp – 1st floor much better. Long-stay discounts and parking. Highly recommended.

B Posada Jovel, Flavio Paniagua 28, T967-678 1734, www.mundochiapas.com/hotelposadajovel. Villa-style hotel with clean, comfortable rooms. Beautiful garden with fruit trees, and the roof terrace has fine views. There's a restaurant, and rooms over

the road get a discount. Hotel is being expanded. Recommended.

B Posada Los Morales, Ignacio Allende 17, T967-678 1472, www.hotelhaciendalos morales.com. This brightly painted, elegant hotel can be spotted from afar, scaling Cerrito San Cristóbal and has beautiful views over the city. The cottages have open fires, kitchen and hot showers. The owner is a collector and exporter of rustic-style Mexican furniture and the interior richly reflects this. Substantial low-season discounts. Recommended.

B Posada Margarita, Real de Guadalupe 34, T967-678 0957, www.laposada margarita.com. This popular professionally managed hotel is spotless. Comfortable rooms have safes, cable TV and 24-hr hot water. There's a terrace, travel agency, free internet and an expensive restaurant serving wholefood.

B Real del Valle, Av Real de Guadalupe 14, next to plaza, T967-678 0680, hrvalle@mundo maya.com.mx. Very clean and friendly. Avoid noisy room next to the kitchen. Rooms have hot water and Wi-Fi. Well maintained and good value.

C Barón de Las Casas, Belisario Domínguez 2, T967-678 0881, www.chiapas.turista. com.mx. Clean, comfortable, good value. Recommended.

C Fray Bartolomé de las Casas, Insurgentes and Niños Héroes, T967-678 0932. Clean, comfortable quarters, set around an attractive courtyard. The better rooms have cable TV and 24-hr hot water (**B**), otherwise it runs only at set times.

C Posada Media Luna, Hermano Domínguez 5, T967-631 5590, www.hotel-lamedia luna.com. Italian-run, cheery, brightly coloured hotel with hot water, free Wi-Fi, free water, cable TV and an Italian fish restaurant, **Creuza de Ma'**. Also organizes tours to nearby sights and villages. Recommended.

C San Martín, Real de Guadalupe 16, in the centre of the city near the plaza, T967-678 0533, www.travelbymexico.com/chis/sanmartin. Clean hotel with 24-hr hot water, internet for guests, cable TV and left luggage. Once excellent, standards falling.

C Suites Encanto, 10 de Marzo 42, T967-672 2679, suitesencanto5@gmail.com. This new hotel has comfortable suites with fireplaces, cookers, fridges and sofas. There are cheap dorm beds too (**F**), and the manager can organize other accommodation if full. Excellent value. Highly recommended.

D Hotel Posada D'Dominnycos, corner of Lázaro Cárdenas and Real de Mexicanos, 1-D, T967-674 0534, www.travelbymexico.com/ chis/dominnycos. Comfy rooms right next to Santo Domingo church and craft market.

D Posada Lucella, Av Insurgentes 55, T967-678 0956, opposite Iglesia Santa Lucía (the bells can be noisy). Clean, economical rooms set around a patio, with bath, fan and hot water. Cheaper with shared bath.

D Posada San Agustín, Ejército Nacional 7, T967-678 1816. Large, clean, comfortable rooms, some with shared bath. Family-run and friendly. Recommended.

D Posada Vallarta, Hermanos Pineda, near 1st-class bus terminal, T967-678 0465. Quiet, clean, tidy, nice plants. Hot water and parking.

D-F Casa Babylon, on Josefa Ortiz de Domínguez and Ramón Corona, T967-678 0590, www.casababylon.wordpress.com. Funky youth hostel with bargain dorm beds and private rooms (cheaper without bath). Breakfast included. Communal kitchen, patio space, lockers, book exchange, free Wi-Fi and laundry. Hot showers and free drinking water.

D-F Los Camellos, Real de Guadalupe 110, T967-116 0097, loscamellos@hotmail.com. Popular backpackers' hostel with dorms and private rooms. There's 24-hr hot showers, free coffee and drinking water, book exchange, shisha café and hammocks. French-Mexican run, friendly and hospitable staff.

E Capri, Insurgentes 54, T967-678 3018, hotelcapri81@hotelmail.com, near first-class bus terminal. Large, reliable hotel with plenty of rooms and differing tariffs. Quieter rooms at the back. Clean and helpful. Chinese restaurant next door, if you're fed up with Mexican grub. Recommended.

E Casa de Huéspedes Chamula, Julio M Corzo 18, 1967-678 0321. Clean, hot showers, washing facilities, friendly, parking, noisy, with shared bath, some rooms without windows.

E Casa de Huéspedes Santa Lucía, Clemente Robles 21, 1 block from the Transportes Lacondia bus terminal, T967-678 0315. Basic rooms, some with bath, some without. There's hot water 24 hrs.

E Posadita, Flavio Paniagua 30. With bath, clean, laundry facilities. Recommended.

E-F Posada 5, Comitán No 13, T967-674 7660, www.posada5.com. Dorms and private rooms, with or without shared bath, nice garden, tours organized, book exchange, free internet, free coffee and tea, communal kitchen, friendly and laid-back.

E-F Posada Doña Rosita, Ejército Nacional 13, T967-678 8676, posadadn_rosita@ hotmail.com. 3 blocks from main plaza. This economical *posada* is more like a friendly and caring family home, presided over by Doña Rosita – an experienced healer who knows about herbs and local affairs. She heals sick guests, offers healthy organic breakfasts, and runs courses in cooking and natural medicine. Her dorms and rooms are basic, but there's hot water 24 hrs, just ask Rosita to switch it on as she has a good water-saving scheme. Highly recommended.

F Posada Lupita, near bus terminal on Insurgentes 46. Nice plant-filled courtyard, popular, often full, despite being a bit scruffy.

Camping

Rancho San Nicolás, T967-678 0057, at end of Francisco León, 1.5 km east of centre. Trailer park in a beautiful, quiet location, take warm blankets or clothing as the temperature really drops at night, hot showers, US$7 for room in *cabaña*, US$5 to camp, US$12 for camper van with 2 people (electricity hook-up), children free, laundry facilities. Recommended.

Trailer park Bonampak, Route 190 at west end of town, T967-678 1621. Full hook-up, hot shower, heated pool in season, restaurant, US$10 per vehicle, US$5 per person.

Agua Azul p492

There are 2 places with *cabañas* for hammocks (hammock rental US$1.50 and up, US$3.50 per person in beds in dormitory); if staying, be very careful of your belongings; thefts have been reported.

Camping

Camping Casa Blanca is popular and reliable, opposite the parking lot; camping costs US$3.50, for a tent or hammock, and US$0.15 for use of toilets (all Agua Azul toilets charge up to US$0.50). You can also camp at the **Estación Climatológica at Paso del Cayuco (F)**; it's about 15-20 mins' walk up the falls to the wire fence station.

RVs can stay overnight at Agua Azul, using the facilities, without paying extra (as long as you do not leave the park). Follow the path up the falls to a 2nd campsite, cheaper, less crowded. There are more *cabañas* and pleasant places to sling a hammock further upstream, all cheaper and less touristy than lower down.

Palenque town p493, map p494

Palenque town has a plethora of cheap lodgings, but it's generally a hot, dirty and unappealing place to stay. The only exception is La Cañada district in the northwest; a burgeoning (and more expensive) tourist zone buffeted by lush jungle foliage and trees. With a number of new places opening up though, the jungle setting is getting a bit thinner. Remember that humidity and bugs can be a real scourge in Palenque – always check the room for dampness, odours and creepy-crawlies.

B Chan Kah Centro, corner of Juárez and Independencia, T916-345 0318. Restaurant and terrace bar overlooking the main plaza, www.chan-kah.com.mx. Sister hotel and convention centre (**AL**) with a pleasant pool and verdant setting, on the road to the ruins.

C Avenida, Juárez 173, T916-345 0116. Large rooms with fan, cable TV and hot water. Some have a/c (**A**) and balcony.

Not very friendly, but convenient for bus station.

C Jade, Hidalgo 61, T916-345 0463. Family-run hotel with clean, comfortable rooms. Hot water, a/c and cable TV. Recommended. Peaceful. Will store luggage.

C Naj K'in, Hidalgo 72, T916-345 1126. Clean, comfortable, well-decorated rooms with bath, fan and 24-hr hot water. Safe parking. Some rooms with a/c.

C Posada Aguila Real, 20 de Noviembre s/n, T916-345 0004, www.posadaaguilareal.com. Very comfortable, attractive lodgings. Rooms are clean with hot water, cable TV and a/c. Helpful staff.

C Posada Kin, Abasolo s/n, 20 de Noviembre y 5 de Mayo, very near zócalo, T916-345 1714, posada_kin@hotmail.com. Clean and large doubles with bathroom, fan, safe and luggage store. Recommended. Organizes tours in the area.

C Posada Shalom, Av Juárez 156, T916-345 0944. Economic rooms with hot water, bath and cable TV. Friendly and clean. Stores luggage. If full, there is also a **Posada Shalom II** a couple of blocks away with further accommodation.

C-D San Miguel, Hidalgo and Aldama, above **Union Pharmacy**, T916-345 0152. Big clean rooms with balcony, hot water and fan. Pricier with TV and a/c. There are cheap dorms too. Good value.

D Kashlan, 5 de Mayo 116, T916-345 0297, www.palenque.com.mx/kashlan. Long-standing Palenque favourite. Clean, mostly quiet rooms (except those facing the street) have bath, fan or a/c (**A**). The owners are helpful and friendly and offer a 25% discount to holders of this book. Recommended.

D Posada Nacha'n Ka'an, 20 de Noviembre 25 and Allende, T916-345 4737. Rooms with hot water and fan, more expensive with a/c (**C**), but there are also cheaper dorms (**G**).

D Posada San Juan, T916-345 0616, Emilio Robasa, corner of Allende, (from **ADO** go up the hill and 1st right, it's on the 4th block on the left). With bath, cheaper without, cold water, fan, clean, quiet, firm beds, secure locks, pleasant courtyard, very good for budget accommodation, safe parking available. Dorms also available (**F**).

D Yun-Kax, Av Corregidora 87 (behind Santo Domingo). Quiet, clean, large rooms with, hot water and fan (**C** with a/c). Recommended.

D-E Posada Canek, 20 de Noviembre 43. Nice rooms and dorm beds (**F**). More expensive rooms have bath. English spoken, recently refurbished rooms have TV and a/c. Friendly, chatty and helpful owner. Restaurant set to open end of 2009.

E La Selva, Av Reforma 69, T916-345 3707. Economical rooms with fan, bath and hot water. Some have TV. Good prices for groups. The owner also has a tour company working in the area.

E Posada Charito, 20 de Noviembre 15B, T916-345 0121. Clean, friendly, family-run. The rooms are basic and good value, although sometimes airless. The ground floor is best.

E Posada Johanna, 20 de Noviembre and Allende, T916-345 0687. Tidy, family-run joint with basic, good value rooms.

La Cañada

AL Maya Tulipanes, Cañada 6, T916-345 0201, www.mayatulipanes.com.mx. The slightly impersonal rooms have a/c and cable TV, and vary in price, size and quality. There's a garage, pool, bar and restaurant. The restaurant does karaoke in the evenings, but luckily also has sound-proof walls.

B La Posada Cañada, Nicolás Bravo, La Cañada, T916-345 0437, nochepat@ hotmail.com. Cheapish, basic rooms, with hot water and fan. Brand new kitchen facilities available to guests.

B Xibalba, Merle Green 9, T916-345 0411, www.hotelxibalba.com. A pleasant, hospitable hotel with 2 separate wings, 1 older, 1 newer. Clean, comfortable, bug-free rooms, with safes and a/c. There's an impressive reproduction lid of Pacal's tomb, somewhat larger than the original. The owner is friendly and knowledgeable. Recommended.

D Yaxkin Hostel, Av Hidalgo corner with 5 a Pte, T916-345 0102, www.hostalyaxkin.com. This is a new, economical alternative to the more upmarket hotels in La Cañada. Dorms and bungalows include a nice breakfast, popular with backpackers, free internet, movie lounge, *palapa*-style bar and restaurant area, kitchen, parking, laundry and luggage storage. Recommended.

Road to the ruins

Exuberant rainforest flanks the road to the ruins, making the accommodations interesting and attractive; **El Panchán**, a collection of budget *cabañas* is the most famous and popular. This area is plagued with bugs, ants and creepy-crawlies, in addition to raging humidity. Ensure your room or *cabaña* has secure screens and a net. Bring repellent, especially in the wet season.

AL Maya Tucán, Carretera Palenque, km 0.5, T916-345 0290, www.tucan sihoplaya.com/palenque. Clean, pleasant hotel with swimming pool, bar and restaurant. Rooms have a/c and lovely views.

C-D Margarita and Ed's, El Panchán, edcabanas@yahoo.com (although the internet connection here is erratic). The plushest *cabañas* at El Panchán, all with private bath. If you don't fancy getting too close to nature, there are also modern rooms (**A**). A friendly, restful place oozing good vibes. The mattresses are amazing.

D Chato's, El Panchán, panchan@yahoo. com.mx, inside **Don Mucho's** restaurant. Cabins with private or shared bath.

D-E Jungle Palace, part of Chato's Cabañas. Economical rooms with private or share bath.

D-F La Palapa, 1.5 km from the ruins inside the national park. *Cabañas*, camping with or without roof cover, space for hammocks. A bit basic, but the new owners are restoring this pretty site right by a lake. They grow organic fruit and veg and run a Mexican restaurant where the food is prepared right in front of you on a grill. There is also an all-night bar with dancing, which can make it a bit noisy. All toilets are separate from the *cabañas* in order to keep the nearby lake clean. Group discounts.

E Betos, El Panchán. Cheap cabins and space to sling a hammock (**F**). Prepare for loud dance music at night.

E Jaguar, on the quieter side, across over the road from El Panchán, but the philosophy is still the same. Shared bath only.

E-F Rakshita, El Panchán. Delightful Rakshita has seen better days – the meditation area has been dismantled, the hippies have fled and the vegetarian restaurant has closed. Still, the cabins are intact and it remains a friendly, economical place to stay. Dorm beds (**G**) and very cheap hammock spaces (**F**) are also available.

F Elementos Naturales, past El Panchán, www.elementosnaturales.org. Youth hostel, can sling hammock or camp. Includes breakfast. Pleasant outdoor feel.

Camping Trailer Park Mayabell, 2 km before entrance to ruins, T916-341 6977, www.mayabell.com.mx. Space for tents, hammocks and caravans. There are also comfortable *cabañas* with a/c and private bath. Pool and live music in the evenings. Recommended.

Yaxchilán, Bonampak, Lacanjá and around *p499*

There is basic accommodation at Bonampak; take hammock and mosquito net. Thieving has been reported. Camping is restricted to the INAH site on the Usumacinta.

At Lacanjá there are 4 campsites where you can sling a hammock: **Kin Bor**, **Vicente K'in**, **Carlos Chan Bor** and **Manuel Chan Bor**.

Comitán and around *p501*

Accommodation is inferior in quality and almost twice the price of San Cristóbal.

B Internacional, Av Central Sur Belisario Domínguez 22, near plaza, T963-632 0110. Comfortable, attractive rooms with cable TV. There's a decent restaurant attached. Rooms cheaper in older part of hotel.

B Los Lagos de Montebello, Belisario Domínguez 144, corner of 3 Av, T963-632 0657, www.hotellagosdemontebello.com. Noisy but good.

C Pensión Delfín, Av Domínguez 21, T963-632 0013, www.hotel-delfin-comitan.com, on plaza. Pleasant colonial-style building with comfortable rooms, garden and courtyard. There's parking and cable TV. Recommended, but don't leave valuables near windows even if they appear closed.

D Hospedaje Montebello, 1a Calle Norte Pte 10, T963-632 3572, 1 block from Delfín. Clean, sunny courtyard, laundry, TV, internet and parking, friendly. Recommended.

D San Fransisco, 1a Av Ote Norte 13A, T963-110 6244. The rooms are clean and economical, but still slightly pokey. There's cable TV and hot water 24 hrs.

Río Usumacinta route *p502*

D Centro Turístico and Grutas Tsolk'in, Benemérito, www.ecoturlacandona.com. Clean, well-kept rooms with communal bathrooms. Much more friendly and helpful than the nearby Escudo Jaguar (which is overpriced and unfriendly). Less than 5 mins' walk from the dock. Take a right turning opposite immigration office.

Tenosique and Río San Pedro route *p503*

D Rome, Calle 28, 400, T934-342 2151. Clean, will change dollars for residents, bath, not bad.

E Azulejos, Calle 26, 416. With bath, fan, clean, hot water, friendly, helpful owner speaks some English, opposite church.

E Casa de Huéspedes La Valle, Calle 19. With bath, good, but a little grubby.

Route to Tapachula *p503*

C Galilea, Av Hidalgo 111 and Callejón Ote, Tonalá, T966-663 0239. With bath, a/c, good, basic cheap rooms on 1st floor, balconies, on main square, with good restaurants.

C Hotel El Estraneo, Av Central, Pijijiapan, T918-645 0264. Very nice, parking in courtyard.
C Ik Lumaal, 1era Av Norte 6, near zócalo, Arriaga, T966-662 1164. A/c, clean, quiet, good restaurant.
C Posada San Rafael, Zanatepec. Motel. Very comfortable, safe parking.
D Motel La Misión, Tapanatepec, on Hwy 190 on northern outskirts, T971-717 0140. Fan, hot water, clean, TV, hammock outside each room, affiliated restaurant, very good.
D-E Colonial, Callejón Ferrocarril 2, Arriaga, next to bus station, T966-662 0856. Clean, friendly, quiet, limited free parking.
E Sabrina, Pijijiapan. Nice, clean and quiet, safe parking.
F Hotel Iris, Callejón Ferrocarril, Arriaga, near bus station. Bath, fan, basic.

Camping

José's Camping Cabañas (ask *colectivo* from Tonalá to take you there, US$0.60 extra), at east edge of Puerto Arista, follow signs. Canadian-run, well organized, clean, laundry, restaurant (including vegetarian), library.

Tapachula and around *p505*
AL Loma Real, Carretera Costera 200, Km 244, T962-626 1440, www.hotel lomareal.com.mx, 1 km north of city. Large, upmarket hotel with comfortable rooms, suites and bungalows. With pool, gym and parking.
A-B San Francisco, Av Central Sur 94, T962-620 1000, www.sucasaentapachula.com, 15 mins from centre. This large, professional hotel has clean, modern rooms with a/c and hot water. With pool, gym, bar and restaurant.
B Galieras Hotel & Arts, 4a Av Norte 21, T962-642 7596, www.galeriasartshotel.com. Modern hotel with an arty focus, 5% discount if paying by cash, a/c, cable TV, hot and cold water, Wi-Fi and parking in the centre of town.
C Santa Julia, next to OCC terminal, T962-626 2486. Bath, phone, TV, a/c, clean, good. Unusually does discounts in high

season. Its location next to main road and bus station can make it very noisy, particularly early mornings.
C Hotel Plaza Guizar, 4a Av Norte 27, T962-626 1400. Clean, tidy and basic, with fan. Plenty of rooms and sitting space. Good views over the city from balcony.
E San Román, Calle 9 Pte between Av 10 y 12 Norte. Very cheap motel-style place. Parking for cars and bikes. Friendly.
E Cinco de Mayo, Calle 5 Pte y Av 12 Norte. Dirt cheap rooms in need of a good clean. Convenient for Talismán *colectivos*, which leave half a block away.

● Eating

Villahermosa *p482*
In high season a number of eateries, bars and discos open up along the riverfront. Good for sunset drinks and dining, but take mosquito repellent.
₸₸₸-₸₸ Los Manglares, Madero 418, inside **Hotel Olmeca Plaza**. Attractive restaurant serving seafood, meat, chicken and breakfast. Excellent 4-course lunch buffet.
₸₸₸-₸₸ Los Tulipanes, Malecón, south of Paseo Tabasco, 2 blocks from the bridge Puente Grijalva 2. Thu-Sun 0800-1800, Mon-Wed 1300-1800, not open for dinner. Nice location, friendly staff, good fish and seafood. Recommended.
₸₸₸-₸₸ Villa Rica, Corredor Turístico Malecón. Open 1200-2000, sometimes closed in low season. A pleasant, modern restaurant with an enticing waterfront location. Tasty seafood including fish fillets and shellfish.
₸₸ Capitán Beuló II, Malecón Carlos A. Madrazo, kiosko I, 1993-314 4644, Ventas3@hotelolmecaplaza.com. A novel dining experience, with gastronomic cruises along Villahermosa's waterways, accompanied by the sounds of live Marimba. Gastro tour Sun, 1430, sightseeing tour Wed-Fri 1700 and Sat-Sun 1200, 1430, 1730 and 1930. Children under 10 pay half price.

El Matador, Av César Sandino No 101a, www.elmatador.com.mx. Open daily 24 hrs. Local meat dishes, *tacos al pastor*, good value.

Hotel Madan, Madero 408, has a restaurant serving good breakfast, inexpensive fish dishes, a/c, newspapers, a pleasant and quiet place to escape from the heat. Also has free Wi-Fi.

Vips, next door to **Hotel Madan**. This is a well-known Mexican chain with many branches across the country. Good-value breakfasts, set lunches and Mexican staples. Always popular, open early until late and has free Wi-Fi in many of its restaurants.

Rodizio do Brasil, Parque la Choca, Stand Grandero, T993-316 2895, informacion@ restauranterodizio.com. Speciality *espadas*, good Brazilian food.

For good tacos head to Calle Aldama, Nos 611, 613 and 615, where there are 3 decent places. These are cheap and cheerful, but very good value, with great selections.

Cafés

Café La Cabaña, Juárez 303-A, across the way from the Museo de Historia de Tabasco. Has outdoor tables where town elders congregate to debate the day's issues over piping cups of cappuccino. Very entertaining to watch. No meals.

El Café de la Calle Juárez, Juárez 513, indoor/outdoor café. Great for breakfast, good coffee, a new menu every month. Outdoor tables are great for people-watching.

South of Villahermosa *p483*

Restaurante Familiar El Timón, Carretera Villahermosa–Teapa Km 52.5 s/n, Teapa.

Tuxtla Gutiérrez *p484, map p484*

Bonampak, Blv Belisario Domínguez 180, T961-602 5916. Formerly an upmarket hotel, now only the restaurant remains. Decent Mexican and North American dishes, quite pricey.

El Borrego Lider, 2 Ote Norte 262. Breakfasts and meat dishes, popular with locals.

El Mesón de Quijote, Central Ote 337. Clean, cheap place on the central avenue, serves Mexican fare, tacos for less than US$1.

Las Pichanchas. Av Central Ote 857, T961-612 5351, www.laspichanchas.com.mx. Open daily 1200-2400. Pretty courtyard, typical food, live marimba music 1430-1730 and 2030-2330 and folkloric ballet 2100-2200, daily. Sister restaurant at **Mirador Copoya**, overlooking the Sumidero Canyon.

Antigua Fonda, 2 Ote Sur 182, opposite La Chata. *Tortas*, *licuados*, breakfasts and general Mexican fare.

El Huipil, 2 Ote Norte 250a. Clean locals' place serving *comida corrida* and *menú del día*. Also has a good breakfast selection.

La Chata, opposite **Hotel San Marcos**. One of the few touristy places, grilled meat and *menú del día*, OK.

Los Molcajetes, in the arches behind the cathedral. Cheap all-day meal deals incl tacos, *suizas*, *chilaquiles* and other staples. Several other restaurants lining the arches offer similar good value.

Taquería Chano y Chon, 2 Ote Norte 120. Locals' joint serving cheap tacos.

Tuxtla, Av 2 Norte Pte y Central, near plaza. Good *comida corrida* and fruit salad.

Cafés and ice cream parlours

Café Avenida, Central Pte 230. Good coffee shop, does cappuccino and espresso.

Mi Café, 1a Pte Norte 121. Interesting locals' place serving organic coffee by the bag or cup.

Cherry's Licuados and Tortas, Central Ote 214 L1. Fresh fruit ice creams and *licuados*.

Chiapa de Corzo *p485*

There are good seafood restaurants by the river.

Parachic's near the main plaza, opposite the church Does excellent breakfasts and good lunches.

San Cristóbal de las Casas *p486, map p487*

There are several cheap, local places on Madero east of Plaza 31 de Marzo.

Agapandos, Calzada Roberta 16, inside Parador San Juan de Dios. This elegant restaurant is very secluded and quiet, overlooking a fragrant garden at the foot of the mountains. They serve sumptuous crêpes, eggs, chicken and meat dishes with a local flavour and Mediterranean twist.

La Fonda Argentina, Adelina Flores 12, Good selection of steaks, fillets and other carnivorous, Argentine cuisine.

El Fogón de Jovel, Av 16 Septiembre 11, opposite the Jade Museum. One of the best restaurants in town and a great place to experiment and try out a variety of local dishes. Try the local liquor, *posh*. Colourful vibe with 2 themed rooms – **Revolution** and **Mask**. Live music at night.

La Casa del Pan, part of El Puente, Real de Guadalupe 55, has a restaurant with good food and a great atmosphere. There's a lunchtime buffet.

La Paloma, Hidalgo 3, a few doors from zócalo. Inventive regional dishes at reasonable prices; international cuisine. Classy place, popular with tourists, best coffee, good breakfast, good pasta, art gallery next door, live music at weekends.

Madre Tierra, Insurgentes 19 (opposite Franciscan church), T967-678 4297. Anglo-Mexican owned, European dishes, vegetarian specialities, good breakfasts, wholemeal breads from bakery (also takeaway), pies, brownies, chocolate cheesecake, Cuban and reggae music in the evenings, popular with travellers.

Tierra y Cielo, Juárez 1, www.tierray cielo.com.mx. International food, with a menu that changes every Sun. Modern and clean. Good breakfast buffets Thu, Sat and Sun.

Tuluc, Insurgentes 5. Good value especially breakfasts, fresh *tamales* every morning, near plaza, popular, classical music, art for sale and toys on display.

Cocodrilo Café & Bar, Plaza 31 de Marzo. Smart café/bar on the south side of the plaza serving snacks, cocktails and cappuccinos. They host live music, salsa and merengue.

Emiliano's Moustache, Av Crescencio Rosas 7. *Taquería*, popular with Mexicans, tacos from US$0.40. Excellent-value lunch menu. Recommended.

Joveleño, Real de Guadalupe 66, T674-6278. Pretty setting, fountain inside restaurant. Breakfast, lunch and dinner. Excellent selection of Thai, Arab and Indian dishes. Great service. A nice change from the usual beans, good value. Great atmosphere. Highly recommended.

La Margarita, inside Posada Margarita (see Sleeping) at Real de Guadalupe 34. Open from at 0700. Live music in the evenings, flamenco, rumba and salsa, good tacos.

María Cartones, Plaza 31 de Marzo, T967-631 6002. Old-time favourite, with tables overlooking the plaza. Breakfasts, *comida típica*, coffee and sandwiches.

París-México, Madero 20. Smart, French cuisine vegetarian dishes, excellent breakfasts, reasonably priced *comida corrida*, classical music. Tequilas for US$1 in the evenings. Highly recommended.

Craft market, Insurgentes. The stalls here are the cheapest places for lunch in San Cristóbal. They do set meals for US$1.20, usually beef or chicken. Numerous stalls nearby sell punch, often made with *posh*.

El Gato Gordo, Real de Guadalupe 20, T962-678 8313. Funky place, popular with backpackers. Cheap set breakfast, crêpes, *tortas*, vegetarian options.

El Mirador II, Madero. Good local and international food, excellent *comida corrida* US$3 and pizzas US$2.50. Recommended.

Juguería Ana Banana, Av Miguel Hidalgo 9B, good typical Mexican food and fresh juices.

Restaurante Adelita, María Adelina Flores No 49. Great selection of tacos in a traditional, *charro*-themed restaurant. 2 for 1 tacos on Tue and tacos from US$0.30 any day.

Tierradentro, Real de Guadalupe 24 Small cultural centre serving economical breakfasts, lunch menus, baguettes, snacks and coffee.

Cafés, juice stalls and bakeries

Café Centro, Real de Guadalupe. Popular for breakfast, good *comida corrida*.

Café Museo Café, Flores 10. Big, breezy café selling fine coffee by the bag or cup. There's an interesting museum inside charting the history of coffee in Chiapas – both café and museum are open daily.

Café San Cristóbal, Cuauhtémoc 2. Good coffee sold in bulk too, chess hangout.

Empanadas Loli, Cuauhtémoc. Sweet, home-made *empanadas*.

La Casa del Pan, Dr Navarro 10 with B Domínguez. Excellent wholemeal bread, breakfasts, live music, closed Mon. Has another branch at El Puente and in Real de Guadalupe 55. Highly recommended but not cheap.

La Selva Café, Crescencio Rosas and Cuauhtémoc. 30 types of really delicious organic coffees, owned by growers' collective, art gallery, lively in evenings. Good healthy breakfast and cakes. Recommended.

Lacteos Maya, Av J M Santiago, has excellent locally made yogurt.

Namandí, Diego de Mazariegos 16. Crêpes, baguettes, juices, coffee and cake. They have Mexican staples too, if you fancy something more substantial. Has several branches in town including one in Insurgentes opposite El Templo del Carmen.

Naturalísimo, 20 de Noviembre 4. Healthy, low-fat vegetarian food, fresh (delicious) yoghurt, fruit sherbet and juices, wholewheat bread and home-baked goodies, pleasant courtyard inside. Recommended.

Palenque town *p493, map p494*

The classier restaurants are in the barrio La Cañada, behind the Maya head as you enter town.

♦♦♦ El Tapanco Grill, Av Hidalgo 65, 2 blocks below plaza above **Bing** ice cream shop. Good steak, balcony dining.

♦♦ Pizzería Palenque, Juárez 168 and Allende, T916-345 0332. Good pizzas and prices.

♦♦-♦ Lakan-Há, Juárez 20. Good tacos, fast and efficient. Also serves breakfast, Mexican staples and *menú del día*.

♦♦-♦ Mara's, Juárez 1, by the zócalo, cheap set menus.

♦♦-♦ Restaurante Maya, Hidalgo and Independencia. Popular, set-menu lunches and à-la-carte dinner. Good meat dishes, efficient service and free Wi-Fi.

♦ Café de Yarra, Hidalgo 68. Clean, stylish café serving good value, tasty breakfasts. Occasional live music.

♦ El Herradero, Av Juárez 120. Breakfast and reasonably priced meals, fast service, open 24 hrs. Recommended.

♦ La Oaxaceña, Juárez 122, opposite the **ADO** bus station. Economical Mexcian staples and *menú del día*.

♦ La Mexicana, RR Juárez and 5 de Mayo. Typical Mexican fare and breakfasts.

♦ Las Tinajas, 20 de Noviembre 41 and Abasolo. Good, family-run, excellent food, huge portions, recommended.

♦ Mundo Maya, Juárez 10, friendly, good and cheap Mexican fare.

Road to the ruins

♦♦♦♦ La Selva, Km 0.5 on Hidalgo. Open 1300-2300. Excellent, smart dress preferred, live music at weekends, recommended.

♦♦-♦ Don Mucho, El Panchán. Outdoor restaurant serving excellent Italian-Mexican food and fantastic breakfast. There's good evening entertainment, including fire dancing; quite exotic given the forest backdrop. They also host 'passing through' travelling musicians.

♦ El Mono Blanco, El Panchán. Cheaper than Don Mucho's and much lower key. They serve Mexican food, breakfasts and à la carte menus.

Comitán *p501*

♦♦ Café Gloria II, 1a Calle Sur Pte 47. The place for a wholesome evening meal.

♦ Restaurant Acuario, Belisario Domínguez 9, on the plaza opposite the church. In league with Vick's/Vicky restaurant (the sign has 2 different names) next door. Good Mexican standard grub, *tortas* and *comida corrida*, but do double check your bill before paying.

♥-♥ Doña Chelo, Calle Central Pte 67. Traditional Mexican fare and seafood.

Café
Café Quiptic, part of **Centro Cultural Rosario Castellanos**, on the plaza. Good Chiapanecan coffee and snacks.

Tapachula and around *p505*
There are a couple of decent and reasonably priced eateries along the south side of the main plaza, for breakfasts lunch and dinner.
♥♥♥-♥♥ Vainilla Cous Cous, 4a Av Sur No 6, T962-118 0083. Open Tue-Sat 0930 -2330 and Sun 0930-1700, with live music Fri and Sat 2100-2200. Run by a chef and a photographer this is a new stylish place with some of the nicest dining in town. International cuisine with a North African twist, fine wines and a gallery next door. Also does yoga classes Mon and Thu.
♥♥ El 7 Mares, Díaz Ordáz 11. Decent seafood, sometimes pricey.
♥ Restaurant Prontos, 1a Calle Poniente 11, T962-626 5680. Open 0600-2200. Meat and more meat dishes.

⊕ Entertainment

San Cristóbal de las Casas *p486, map p487*
Bars and clubs
Barfly, Crecencio Rosas 4. Open 2000-2400. DJs play reggae, house and funk. Free drink on entry.
Bar Makia, Hidalgo, just off plaza, above a shop. Fri and Sat from 2200 until very late.
Blue Bar, Av Crescencio Rosas 2, live music after 2300, salsa, rock, reggae, pool table, good atmosphere.
Cocodrilo, Insurgentes 1, T967-678 0871. Cappuccinos, cocktails, beer and live music every night: reggae, *trova*, flamenco and rumba.
El Zirko, 20 de Noviembre 7; couple of blocks north of the zócalo. Live music.
Emiliano's Moustache (see page 515) has a bar open until 0100.

Revolución, 20 de Noviembre and 1 de Marzo. Café, bar with internet upstairs, happy hour 1200-1900, live soul, blues and rock music at 2000, good atmosphere.

Cinema and theatre
Centro Bilingüe at the Centro Cultural El Puente (see Cultural centres, page 528), Real de Guadalupe 55. Films Mon-Sat 1800, US$2, with later showings Fri and Sat, 2000. Film schedules are posted around town.
La Ventana, Real de Guadalupe 46. Cinema club showing a good range of films.
Teatro Municipal Daniel Zebadúa, 20 de Noviembre and 1 de Marzo, film festivals each month, films at 1800 and 2100 US$2 (US$1.50 students).

Palenque town *p493, map p494*
Road to the ruins
La Palapa (see Sleeping), has an all-night bar with dancing. Also numerous new bars and restaurants are springing up in the La Cañada district.

⊕ Festivals and events

Villahermosa *p482*
Feb Ash Wednesday is celebrated from 1500 to dusk by the throwing of water bombs and buckets of water at anyone who happens to be on the street!

Chiapa de Corzo *p485*
The fiestas here are outstanding.
Jan Daylight fiestas, **Los Parachicos**, on 15, 17 and 20 Jan to commemorate the miraculous healing of a young boy some 300 years ago, and the **Chunta Fiestas**, at night, 8-23 Jan. There are parades with men dressed up as women in the evenings of the 8, 12, 17 and 19 Jan. All lead to the climax, 20-23 Jan, in honour of **San Sebastián**, with a pageant on the river.
25 Feb El Santo Niño de Atocha.
25 Apr Festival de San Marcos, with various *espectáculos*.

San Cristóbal de las Casas *p486, map p487*
Jan/Feb Carnival is held during the 4 days before Lent, dates vary.
Mar/Apr There is a popular spring festival on Easter Sun and the week after.
Early Nov Festival Maya-Zoque, which lasts 4 days, promoting the 12 different Maya and Zoque cultures in the Chiapas region, with dancing and celebrations in the main plaza.
12 Dec La Fiesta de Guadalupe.

O Shopping

Villahermosa *p482*
A small number of shops along Madero sell Tabasqueña handicrafts and souvenirs of varying quality and there are also some stalls set up daily along the same street. Bargain.

San Cristóbal de las Casas *p486, map p487*
Bookshops
La Pared, Av Miguel Hidalgo 2, T967-678 6367, lapared9@yahoo.com, opposite the government tourist office. Open daily, 1000-1400 and 1600-2000. Books in English and a few in other European languages, many travel books including **Footprint** handbooks, book exchange, American owner Dana Gay very helpful.
Soluna, Real de Guadalupe 13B, has a few English guidebooks, a wide range of Spanish titles and postcards.

Crafts
Amber Museum Diego de Mazariegos, next la Merced. There are many shops on Av Real de Guadalupe for amber and jade plus other *artesanías*. The market north of Santo Domingo is worth seeing as well.
Casa de Artesanías, Niños Héroes and Hidalgo. Top-quality handicrafts. Shop is also a museum.
Ex-Convento de Santo Domingo has been partly converted into a cooperative, Sna Jolobil, selling handicrafts from many local villages especially textiles (best quality

and expensive); also concerts by local groups. Well worth a visit.
La Casa del Jade, Av 16 de Septiembre 16. The shop, which sells top-quality jade, also has a museum with replicas of jade relics and the Tomb of Pakal (Maya King of Palenque), which is now more difficult to visit at Palenque.
Taller Leñateros, Flavio A Paniagua 54, T967-678 5174, www.tallerlenateros.com. A paper-making workshop run primarily by a Maya group. Their paper and prints are made from natural materials and their profits help support around 30 Maya families. Souvenir markets on Utrilla between Real de Guadalupe and Comitán.

The **craft market** at Parque Fray Bartolomé de las Casas has stands offering an assortment of local sweets such as *cocada*, balls of sweet and caramelized shredded coconut, as well as small, perfectly shaped animal figurines made, strangely enough, of sweetened hard-boiled egg yolks. Different, yet tasty.

Palenque town *p493, map p494*
Av Juárez is lined with souvenir shops selling hammocks, blankets, Maya figurines and hats. Sales staff are less pushy than in towns in the Yucatán Peninsula; bargain for the best prices.

▲ Activities and tours

Villahermosa *p482*
Tour operators
Creatur Transportadora Turística, Paseo Tabasco 715, T993-317 7717, www.creaturviajes.com. Tour operator organizing tours along the 7 new touristic routes of the state, including a gastronomic tour, the cacao route, whitewater rafting. Tours only run at weekends in low season. Recommended.

Tuxtla Gutiérrez *p484, map p484*
Tour operators
Carolina Tours, Sr José Narváez Valencia (manager), Av Central Pte 1138, T961-612

4281; reliable, recommended; also coffee shop at Av Central Pte 230.

Lacandona Tours, 6a Sur Pte 1276, T961-612 9872, www.lacantours.com. Tours to all the attractions in Chiapas including the Lacandon rainforest, Bonampak and the Sumidero canyon.

Viajes Miramar, Av Central Pte 1468, T961-613 3983, www.viajesmiramar.com.mx. Good, efficient service for national flight bookings.

San Cristóbal de las Casas *p486, map p487*
Horse riding

Horse-riding tours are widely available in San Cristóbal, most going to Chamula and costing US$8-12 for 4-5 hrs. Hotels, tourist offices and travel agencies can easily organize them, or look for advertising flyers in touristy cafés and restaurants. Also Señor Ismael rents out horses and organizes treks. T961-678 1511.

Rafting

There are several rivers in the San Cristóbal area that offer great rafting opportunities. **Explora-Ecoturismo y Aventura**, 1 de Marzo 30, T967-674 6660, www.ecochiapas.com. Eco-sensitive company with good recommendations offer rafting, caving, sea kayaking, river trips and multi-day camping expeditions on a variety of rivers.

Tour operators and guides

There are many agencies to choose from. As a rough guide to prices: to San Juan Chamula and Zinacantán, US$12. Horse riding to San Juan Chamula, US$12. Sumidero Canyon, US$15. Montebello Lakes and Amatenango del Valle, US$18. Palenque ruins, Agua Azul and Misol-Há, US$22. Toniná ruins, US$26. There's also a 3-day jungle trip option taking in Agua Azul, Misol-Há, the ruins at Bonampak, Cedro River Falls, Yaxchilán and Palenque ruins. Camping in the jungle, US$250. Day trips to Bonampak and Yaxchilán are also possible, but they are much cheaper if booked in Palenque; take care to check what is included in packages.

Na Bolom Museum and Cultural Centre, Vicente Guerrero 33, T967-678 1418, www.nabolom.org. This internationally renowned and widely respected cultural centre has close, long-standing ties with Mayan communities. They run superlative tours to the villages and expeditions to the Lacandon rainforest (see page 488).

Otisa Travel, Real de Guadalupe 3, T967-678 1933, otisa@otisatravel.com. Daily tours to Sumidero Canyon, San Juan Chamula and Zinacantán, Lagunas de Montebello, Yaxchilán and Bonampak, among other places.

Pronatura , Pedro Moreno 1, organizes guided bird walks with Javier Gomez, 2½ hrs starting at 0700, from US$7 and plant walks, leaving at any time of day depending on demand. These last 1½ hrs, from US$5.

Raúl and Alejandro, T967-678 3741, alexyraultours@yahoo.com.mx. Tours to San Juan Chamula, Zinacantán and other villages. They depart from in front of the cathedral at 0930 and return at 1400, in blue VW minibus, US$15, in English, Spanish and Italian. Friendly, very good, highly recommended.

Roberto Molina, T967-672 2679. Roberto has good knowledge of medicinal plants and the ancient art of pulse-reading. He offers a spiritual interpretation of the land around San Cristóbal and can organize tours to the outlying villages, horse riding or hiking trips in the surrounding mountain areas. Find him at **Posada Doña Rosita** (see page 509).

Travesía Maya, 20 de Noviembre 3, T967-674 0824, www.travesiamaya.com.mx. This friendly agency offers informative, economical tours to attractions in Chiapas, as well as private planes and direct buses to Guatemala.

Viajes Pakal, Cuauhtémoc 6-A, T967-678 2818, www.pakal.com.mx. A reliable agency with culturally friendly tours, several branches in other cities. Good for flight bookings, though some require 4 days' notice. Recommended.

Misol-Há *p492*
Tour operators
All the travel agencies in Palenque do a cheap tour to both Misol-Há and Agua Azul, about US$10 per person. Most tours allow about 30 mins at Misol-Há and 3-4 hrs at Agua Azul. Bring a swimsuit and plenty of drinking water. *Colectivos* from Hidalgo y Allende, Palenque, for Agua Azul and Misol-Há, 2 a day, US$8; *colectivos* can also be organized between Misol-Há and Agua Azul, in either direction. Taxi US$45 with 2 hrs at Agua Azul, or to both falls US$55.

Palenque town *p493, map p494*
Horse riding
Tours can be booked at the **Clínica Dental Zepeda**, Juárez s/n – the dentist owns the horses. Also through **Cabañas de Safari** in Palanque archaeological zone Km 1, T916-345 0026. **Gaspar Alvaro** also hires horses. He can be located at his house on the road to the ruins, directly in front of Mayabel. Gaspar will take you on a 3-hr ride through rainforested trails in the surrounding area of the ruins. Good chance of seeing monkeys and toucans. US$15 for 3 hrs. Tell him specifically that you want to go through the rainforest and not on the road.

Tour operators and guides
Alonso Méndez is a well-versed guide with extensive knowledge of flora, fauna, medicinal uses of plants and an intimate knowledge of the Palenque ruins. A respected authority on Chiapanecan ethnobotany, Alonso has a gift of academic and spiritual understanding of the rainforest. He speaks English, Spanish and Tzeltzal and can be found at his home in **El Panchán** camping site. Full-day hiking trips US$50 for a group of 6-8 people. Highly recommended. **Fernando Mérida**, T044 916-103 3649 (mobile). Fernando is a Lacandón guide with some interesting and unconventional views of the Maya and Mayan prophecies. He runs a range of unusual tours not offered by other companies, across Chiapas, including

birdwatching expeditions on Sun lagoon. He speaks English and Italian. Look for his desk set up near Chan Kan Centro, Av Juárez. **José Luis Zúñiga Mendoza**, T916-341 4736, tentzun@hotmail.com. Very easy going, José has excellent knowledge of the Palenque area and in addition to guided trips around the ruins offers jungle walks and stays with local communities. **Na Chan Kan**, corner of Hidalgo and Jiménez, across from Santo Domingo church, T916-345 0263, www. nachankan.com /viajesnachan. Offers a wide selection of packages ranging from tours to Agua Azul to excursions to the Yaxchilán and Bonampak ruins as well as transport to Guatemala. **Shivalva** (Marco A Morales), Merle Green 9, La Cañada, T916-345 0411, www.hotelxibalba.com. Tours of Palenque, Yaxchilán, Bonampak and waterfalls. Friendly and well established. **Turistica Maya Chiapas**, Av Juárez 123, T916-345 0798, www.mayachiapas.com.mx. Tours to the waterfalls, Lacandon jungle. Tikal and other parts of Guatemala, as well as Belize. English spoken. Recommended.

Yaxchilán, Bonampak, Lacanjá and around *p499*
Tour operators
Operators from Palenque offer 1- and 2-day trips to Bonampak and Yaxchilán, all transport and food included. To see both sites independently, it's recommended you take at least 2 days and stay overnight in Lacanjá. Otherwise, be prepared for a long, tough day of at least 14 hours.

Local Spanish-speaking guides can be found by asking around in Lacanjá or enquiring at the entrance to Bonampak. The entire area is beautiful and worth exploring.

Tenosique and Río San Pedro route *p503*
Several agencies in Palenque offer tours to Flores by minibus and/or taxi, boat and public bus, via Tenosique, La Palma and

El Naranjo. You probably won't meet any other travellers, so be prepared to fund the whole trip yourself, especially in low season.

Tapachula and around p505
Tour operators
Agencia de Viajes Chávez Tours, a few doors down from the OCC terminal, past Hotel Santa Julia, does tours of the area.

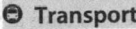 Transport

Villahermosa p482
Air
Airport Carlos R Pérez (VSA), 18 km from town, receives international flights from **Havana** and **Houston**, and has good national connections. VW bus to town US$5 each, taxi US$11.

   Airline offices AeroMéxico, Blv Ruiz Cortines 102 local 8, T993-352 4129. Aviacsa, Vía 3 No 120, T993-316 5731. Mexicana, Av Vía 3 No 120 locales 5 y 6 Tabasco 2000, T993-316 3132.

Bus
Reserve your seat as soon as you can; buses to Mexico City can sometimes be booked up well in advance. 1st-class **ADO** bus terminal is on Javier Mina and Lino Merino, 12 blocks north of centre, computerized booking system. Beware of long queues at the 1st-class ticket counters. The Central Camionera 2nd-class bus station is on Av Ruiz Cortines, near roundabout with fisherman statue, 1 block east of Javier Mina, opposite Castillo, 4 blocks north of ADO.

   To **Mexico City** (TAPO, Norte or Tasqueña), regular departures, 10-12 hrs, US$52-US$84. To **Cancún**, many daily, 12 hrs, US$52.50. To **Chetumal**, 7 daily, 8½ hrs, US$27. To **Campeche**, many daily, 6 hrs, US$18. To **Mérida**, many daily, 8 hrs, US$25-US$36. To **Palenque**, OCC 2 daily, ADO 6 daily, 2½ hrs, US$8. To **Puebla**, 4 ADO services daily, US$40; and 4 luxury services, US$49. To **San Andrés Tuxtla**, ADO services, 0255, 0930, 1100, 1925, 6 hrs, US$16. To **San Cristóbal de las Casas**, 2 OCC services at 0930 and 1230, 7 hrs, US$16. Tto **Tapachula**, 1 OCC at 1915, 10 hrs, US$41; and 1 ADO luxury at 0335, US$50. To **Veracruz**, many daily including luxury services, 8 hrs, US$26. To **Xalapa**, with **ADO** at 1055, 1800, 1925, 2230, 8 hrs, US$31; and 2 luxury services at 2100 and 2120, US$37 and US$48. To **Emiliano Zapata**, many daily, 2½ hrs, US$8. To **Tenosique** (for Río San Pedro crossing into Guatemala, see page 526), many daily 3½ hrs, US$10.

Car
Car hire Hertz car rental is available from the airport. **Agrisa**, Paseo Tabasco corner of El Malecón, T993-312 9184, good prices, eg US$40 per day including taxes and insurance, but it is expensive to return the car to another city.

Taxi
City taxis charge US$1 for journeys in the centre.

South of Villahermosa p483
Bus There are buses between Teapa and **Villahermosa**, 50 km, 1 hr, US$2.20. Also to **Chiapa de Corzo** at 0730, through lovely, mountainous landscape.

Tuxtla Gutiérrez p484, map p484
Air
Aeropuerto Angel Albino Corzo is Tuxtla's new international airport, 27 km south of the city. A taxi into town costs around US$15 and from town to airport US$8 ADO buses to the airport from the OCC terminal, US$3.50.

   Airline offices Aviacsa, Av Central Pte 1144, T961-612 8081; Mexicana, Belisario Domínguez 1748, T961-602 5771. All lines also have ticket offices at the airport.

Bus
There is a brand new 1st-class **ADO** and **OCC** bus terminal at 5a Norte Poniente, corner of Angel Albino Corzo, next to the new, large Plaza del Sol mall Plaza del Sol. There's a 2nd-class terminal at 3a Av Sur Ote and 7a Oriente Sur, about 1 km southeast of the centre.

To **Cancún**, OCC, 1055 and 1310, US$53; and **ADO GL**, 1430 and 1800, US$66. To **Córdoba**, 1st class (OCC and ADO), 1720, 1950, 7½ hrs, US$38. To **Chetumal**, OCC, 1310, 13 hrs, US$37; and **ADO GL**, 1430, US$44. To **Cd Cuauhtémoc**, Guatemalan border, OCC, 0630, 1015, 1615, 4½ hrs, US$13. To **Comitán**, OCC, many daily, 3 hrs, US$6. To **Mexico City**, 1st class, many daily, 12 hrs, US$57. To **Villahermosa**, 1st class, many daily, 4-7 hrs, US$17. To **Mérida**, OCC, 1500, 14 hrs, US$40; and **ADO GL**, 1800, US$48; otherwise change at Villahermosa. The scenery between Tuxtla and Mérida is very fine, and the road provides the best route between Chiapas and the Yucatán. To **Oaxaca**, OCC, 1130, 1920, 2355, 10 hrs, US$25; and **ADO GL**, 2130, US$30. To **Palenque**, 7 with OCC, 6 hrs, US$12; and **ADO GL**, 1430, US$15. To **Pochutla**, OCC, 2025 and 2310, 10 hrs, US$23. To **Puebla**, 1st class, many daily, same times as Mexico City, 10 hrs, US$50. To **Salina Cruz**, 1st class and luxury services, 1410, 1645, 2025, 2245, US$14.50. Take travel sickness tablets for Tuxtla–Oaxaca road if you suffer from queasiness. To **San Cristóbal de las Casas**, OCC, frequent services, 1 hr, US$3. To **Tapachula**, 1st class, many daily, 7½ hrs, US$183. To **Tonalá**, 1st and 2nd class, many daily, US$7-9. To **Tulum**, OCC, 1055, 1310, 17 hrs, US$48; and an **ADO GL**, 1430, US$57. To **Veracruz**, OCC, 2255, 2335, US$47; and an **ADO GL**, 2245, US$46.

Shuttles To **Chiapa de Corzo**, from 1 Sur Ote and 5a Ote Norte; and from the Transportes Chiapa–Tuxtla station, 2a Oriente Sur and 1a Av Sur Ote, 20 mins,

US$0.70. To **San Cristóbal de las Casas**, from 2a Sur Ote 1203, between 11 and 12 Oriente Sur, 1 hr, US$2.50.

Taxis
Easy to flag down anywhere. US$3 within the centre, US$4 to the zoo, US$6 to Chiapa de Corzo (for Sumidero Canyon).

Chiapa de Corzo *p485*
Bus
Frequent buses to Tuxtla depart from Avenida 21 de Octubre on the plaza. Buses to San Cristóbal now bypass Chiapa de Corzo, meaning you'll have to pick one up on the highway or go via Tuxtla.

San Cristóbal de las Casas *p486, map p487*
Air
San Cristóbal has a small airport about 15 km from town, but at present does not serve passenger planes. Tuxtla Gutiérrez is now the principal airport.

Bicycle
Bike hire Los Pingüinos, Av Ecuador 4B, T967-678 0202, www.bikemexico.com/pinguinos, 0915-1430, 1600-1900, rents mountain bikes for US$10 for 4 hrs or US$14 per day. Guided biking tours half or full days, as well as longer guided tours. English, German spoken, beautiful countryside and knowledgeable guides, highly recommended.

Bus
For reasons of cultural sensitivity, it is recommended that you visit Mayan villages as part of a tour. A good guide will explain the workings of a Mayan community and introduce you to villagers personally, making your visit welcome and enlightening. If you go independently, be prepared for culture shock and some suspicious treatment. Crowded microbuses to Chamula, Zinacantán, San Andrés Larráinzar, Tenejapa and other villages depart from around the market, north of the centre on Utrilla. Don't get stranded, as there isn't any tourist infrastructure.

There is a **Ticketbus** office in the pedestrianised part of Real de Guadalupe in the centre of San Cristóbal that stays open until 2200, daily. Very convenient for booking tickets without venturing as far as the OCC terminal.

Long distance The 1st-class OCC and ADO bus terminal is at the junction of Insurgentes and Blvd Sabines Gutiérrez, several blocks south of the centre. Other 2nd-class lines and shuttle operators, including **AEXA** and **Rodolfo Figueroa**, also have nearby terminals on Gutierrez, which soon becomes the Pan-American highway. There's also a variety of smaller bus companies and shuttles services that leave from the main road near the OCC bus station, with departures as far afield as Tijuana and other parts of northern Mexico, as well as Ocosingo, Palenque and nearby villages.

From the 1st-class terminal to **Campeche**, OCC, 1820, 10 hrs, US$25. To **Cancún**, OCC, 1215, 1430, 17 hrs, US$46; and ADO GL, 1545, US$58. To **Chetumal**, 1st class (OCC and ADO), 1215, 1430, 1605, 12 hrs, US$33, ADO GL, 1545, US$40. To **Cd Cuauhtémoc**, OCC, 0745, 1130, 1730, 3 hrs, US$6. To **Comitán**, OCC, frequent services, 1½ hrs, US$3. To **Mérida**, OCC, 1820, 13 hrs, US$36. To **Mexico City**, OCC, 1610, 1740, 1810, 2230, 14 hrs, US$60 and ADO GL 1700, 13 hrs, US$72. To **Oaxaca**, OCC, 1805, 2000, 10 hrs, US$34; and ADO GL, 2000, US$33. To **Palenque**, 8 daily with OCC and ADO GL, 5 hrs, US$9-11. To **Playa del Carmen**, OCC, 1215, 1430, US$56; and ADO GL, 1545, US$68. To **Pochutla**, OCC, 1915, 2200, 12 hrs, US$27. To **Puebla**, 4 daily with OCC and 2 with ADO GL daily, 11 hrs, US$64-53. To **Puerto Escondido**, OCC, 1915, 2200, 13 hrs, US$30. To **Tapachula**, 7 OCC daily, 8 hrs, US$16. To **Tuxtla Gutiérrez**, OCC, many daily, 1 hr, US$2. To **Tulum**, OCC, 1215, 1430, 1605, 14½ hrs, US$44; and ADO GL, 1545, 16 hrs, US$52. To **Veracruz**, OCC, 2045, 8½ hrs, US$40; and ADO GL, 2115, 9 hrs, US$47. To

Villahermosa, OCC, 1120, 2300, 7 hrs, US$16. AEXA buses to **Palenque**, 0630, 1150, US$6. To **Agua Azul**, 0630, 1150, US$4. To **Tuxtla Gutiérrez**, *combis* every 10 mins from outside AEXA terminal from 0500, US$2. 50. 1st-class OCC buses depart for **Ciudad Cuautémoc** and the border daily. Alternatively, there are frequent departures to **Comitán**, from where you can catch a pickup or *colectivo*, hourly from 0700, around US$1. For details on crossing the border at **La Mesilla**, see page 694.

Shuttles Shuttles to **Tuxtla** regularly depart from the terminals on Gutiérrez, near the 1st-class bus terminal, 1 hr, US$3. You'll find shuttles to **Ocosingo** in the same area. Several operators run direct shuttles to the Guatemalan border and beyond, including **Travesia Maya**. Destinations include **La Mesilla**, **Quetzaltenango**, **Antigua**, **Flores** and **Panajachel**, US$30-60. It's a convenient and comfortable option if you can afford it. There are also regular departures to **Guatemala** from the OCC terminal itself, all departing at 0745 daily. To **Huehuetenango**, US$14. To **Los Encuentros**, US$19. To **Cuatro Caminos**, US$17 and to **Guatemala City**, US$24.

Car
Car hire Optima, Diego de Mazariegos 39, T967-674 5409; and **Hertz**, Villas Mercedes, Panagua 32, T967-678 1886.

Scooters
Croozy Scooters, Belisario Domínguez 7, www.prodigyweb.net.mx/croozyscooters. Swiss-British run, Open Tue-Sun 0900, closing times vary. Rents out bikes and small scooters, a good way of moving around. Minimum payment US$14, 2 hrs, US$25 per day. They provide maps and suggested routes. Deposit and ID required. Bikes US$2 per day. Friendly. Recommended.

Taxi
US$1.40 anywhere in town, *colectivo* US$0.70.

Ocosingo *p491*
Many buses and *colectivos* to **Palenque**, 2½ hrs, US$3.30 and **San Cristóbal de Las Casas**.

Misol-Há *p492*
Several buses from Palenque daily (direction San Cristóbal de las Casas or Ocosingo), to crossroads leading to the waterfall, such as **Transportes Chambalu** to both Misol-Há and **Agua Azul**, leaving at 0900, 1000 and 1200, US$8.50, 2nd class, 1½ hrs. You can also purchase bus tickets from **Transportes Figueroa**, about 100 m from the ADO bus station (in direction of the town centre) in Palenque. Bus time is approximately 1½ hrs from Palenque to the turn-off to the Agua Azul road. From the crossroads walk the 4 km downhill to the falls on a beautiful jungle-lined road (or hitch a ride on a minibus for US$1). If, after a long day at the falls, you have no desire to walk the 4 km back to the main road (steep) you can always catch a ride back to Palenque on tour buses that have extra space, US$4. They leave from the Agua Azul parking lot 1500-1800. Back from the junction 1400-1600 with **Transportes Maya** buses. There are buses between San Cristóbal de las Casas and Palenque (to 2nd-class bus station, **Transportes Maya**), which will stop there, but on a number of others you must change at Temo, over 20 km away, north of Ocosingo. Tour companies can also arrange bus tickets with **AEXA** from the crossroads to San Cristóbal and other places if you don't wish to return all the way to Palenque to catch an onward bus.

Palenque town *p493, map p494*
Air
Commercial traffic through Palenque's small airport has dwindled, and it's now mainly used for specially chartered planes. Speak to a tour agent if you would like to organize flights within Chiapas (including Yaxchilán and Bonampak), Yucatán or Guatemala.

Bus
Local Micro buses run back and forth along the main street, passing the bus station area, to and from the ruins, every 10 mins, US$0.70 (taxi US$6). Catch one of these for **El Panchán** and other nearby accommodations.

Long distance There are 3 bus terminals. The 1st class **ADO/OCC** terminal is at the western end of Juárez. The Rodolfo Figueroa y Lacandonia terminal is on the opposite side of the road, with a few 2nd-class departures to San Cristóbal. An **AEXA** terminal is almost next door to the 1st-class terminal, serving a handful of destinations in Chiapas. Also on Juárez is **Autotransportes Tuxtla**, with 2nd-class departures to **Quintana Roo**.

To **Cancún**, 1st class (ADO and OCC), 1720, 1935, 2100, 13 hrs, US$40; and ADO GL, 2100, US$48. To **Campeche**, 1st class, 0800, 2100, 2200, 2325, 5 hrs, US$17.50. To **Escárcega**, 1st class, 6 daily, 3 hrs, US$10. To **Mérida**, 1st class, 0800, 2100, 2200, 2325, 8 hrs, US$26. To **Mexico City**, ADO, 1830 (TAPO), 2100 (Norte), 14 hrs, US$55. To **Oaxaca**, ADO, 1730, 15 hrs, US$39. To **San Cristóbal**, 1st class, 8 daily, 5 hrs, US$9.50; and an ADO GL. Also some 2nd-class departures. To **Tulum**, 1st class, 1720, 1935, 2000, 2110, 11 hrs, US$34; and ADO GL, 2100, US$40. To **Tuxtla Gutiérrez**, OCC, 8 daily, 6 hrs, US$12; and an ADO GL, US$14.50. To **Villahermosa**, 1st class, 11 daily, 2 hrs, US$7.50.

Shuttles To **Agua Azul** and **Misol-ha**, Transportes Chambalú, Allende and Juárez, 0900, 1000, 1200, US$8.50. They stop for 30 mins at Misol-Há and 3 hrs at Agua Azul. To **Frontera Corozal** (for **San Javier**, **Bonampak**, **Lacanjá** and **Yaxchilán**), Transportes Chamoan, Hidalgo 141, roughly hourly from 0500-1700, US$5. To **Tenosique**, Transportes Palenque, Allende and 20 de Noviembre, hourly, US$5. **Playas de Catazajá** (for Escárcega and Campeche) Transportes Pakal, Allende between 20 de Noviembre and Corregidora, every 15 mins, US$1.50.

Taxi
Taxis charge a flat rate of US$1.50 within the town, US$4 to **El Panchán** and nearby **Maya Bell** camping areas.

Yaxchilán, Bonampak, Lacanjá and around *p499*
Air
Flights from **Palenque** to Bonampak and Yaxchilán, in light plane for 5, about US$600 per plane, to both places, whole trip 6 hrs. Prices set, list available. **Viajes Misol-Há**, Juárez 48 at Aldama, T916-345 1614, run charter flights to Bonampak and Yaxchilán for US$150 per person return, minimum 4 passengers.

Boat
From **Bethel**, Guatemala, *lanchas* charge US$93 per boat return to visit Yaxchilán. From Palenque to Bethel US$20 and there are also connection direct to Flores US$25. From **La Técnica**, Guatemala, US$53 return. From **Frontera Corozal** to Yaxchilán it costs between US$50-60 per boat, although you may find other tourists to share the cost. Bargain the boatmen down (be warned, they're stubborn), or hitch a ride with a tour group. If you are travelling from Frontera Corozal to **Guatemala**, register with the immigration office before crossing the border and have your documents stamped. River crossings at Río Usumacinta US$3.50.

Bus
A few different companies run hourly *colectivo* services between **Palenque** and **Frontera Corozal**, including Transportes Chamoan (see Palenque shuttles, above). For Lacanjá or Bonampak, catch one of these and exit at the junction and military checkpoint at San Javier. From there, you will need to hike or take a taxi, if you can find one. Bear in mind this is a remote destination, so pack water, travel light and plan your time accordingly. For Yaxchilán, take a boat from **Frontera Corozal**.

Car
Bonampak is over 30 km from Frontera Corozal and can be reached from the San Javier crossroads on the road to Corozal.

Comitán *p501*
Bus
Buses to **San Cristóbal de las Casas**, OCC, many daily, 2 hrs, US$3, also 2 luxury services US$4. To **Mexico City** (TAPO and Norte), OCC, 1410, 1550, 1640, 2040, 15½ hrs, US$64. To **Puebla**, same timings as for Mexico City, 13 hrs, US$57.To **Palenque**, OCC, 1345, 2115, 6½ hrs, US$14.50. **Tapachula**, OCC, 6 daily, 5½ hrs, US$12. To **Tuxtla Gutiérrez**, OCC, many daily, 3 hrs, US$5. To Cancún, OCC, 1345, 20½ hrs, US$56.

Frequent *combis*, shuttles and taxis for nearby **Ciudad Cuauhtémoc**, US$2, every 15 mins. To **San Cristóbal**, US$2.50 *combi*, US$3 taxi, 1 hr 10 mins, **Tuxtla** and other nearby places, transport leaves from the main boulevard, Belisario Domínguez, a few block north from the OCC terminal. Since these are only marginally cheaper than the much more comfortable buses, this is only worth it if you're strapped for cash or time.

Ciudad Cuauhtémoc *p502*
Bus
Long distance OCC 1st-class buses to **Comitán**, 1215, 1240, 1855, 200, 1½ hrs, US$3. There are also frequent **de paso** 2nd-class buses and *combis*. To **Mexico City**, OCC, 1240, 17 hrs, US$68. To **San Cristóbal de las Casas**, OCC, 1215, 1240, 1855, 2200, 3 hrs, US$6. To **Tuxtla Gutiérrez**, OCC, 1240, 1855, 2200, 4½ hrs, US$12. To **Tapachula** (via Arriaga), OCC, 1100, 1445, 1755, 2045, 4½ hrs, US$8. If crossing the border, there are hourly buses to **Huehuetenango** or **Quetzaltenango** departing from the Guatemalan side.

Shuttles To **Comitán**, various operators, frequently from the border, 1½ hrs, US$3. More national connections in Comitán, including services to **San Cristóbal** and **Tuxtla**.

Río Usumacinta route p502

Shuttles From Frontera Corozal to **Palenque**, hourly, 0400-1600, 2½ hrs US$5. Operators include **Transportes Chamoan**. Crossing the Río Usumacinta at Frontera Corozal by *lancha*, US$3.50.

Boat

Lanchas to **Yaxchilán**, 30 mins, US$50-60. To **Bethel**, 30 mins, US$30 for 2 people, US$40 for 4. To **Técnica**, US$5 per person. To **Piedras Negras**, 2-3 days, prices negotiable (around US$100-US$150 per person), and best organized as a group. Ensure your papers are in order before crossing the border. Visit immigration offices on both sides for exit and entry stamps, and keep a photocopy of your passport handy for possible military inspection.

Tenosique and Río San Pedro route p503

To **Emiliano Zapata**, ADO, many daily, 1 hr, US$3. To **Mexico City**, ADO, 1700, 15 hrs, US$57. To **Villahermosa**, ADO, frequent services, 3½ hrs, US$10.
Shuttles To **Palenque**, hourly with Transportes Palenque, US$3.50. Or, catch a Villahermosa bus to **El Crucero de la Playa** and pick up a frequent *colectivo* from there.

Border with Guatemala: Talismán p504

Bus There are few buses between the Talismán bridge and **Oaxaca** or **Mexico City**; it is advisable therefore to travel to **Tapachula** for connection; delays can occur at peak times.

 Taxi *Combi* vans run from near the Unión y Progreso bus station, about US$1; *colectivo* from outside **Posada de Calú** to Talismán, US$0.60, also from Calle 5 Pte between Av 12 y Av 14 Norte. Taxi **Tapachula–Talismán**, negotiate fare to about US$2. A taxi from Guatemala to Mexican Immigration will cost US$2,

but it may be worth it if you are in a hurry to catch an onward bus.
 Hitchhikers should note that there is little through international traffic at the Talismán bridge.

Border with Guatemala: Ciudad Hidalgo p504

Bus
From Calle 7 Pte between Av 2 Norte and Av Central Norte, Tapachula, buses go to 'Hidalgo', US$1.

Arriaga p504

Bus To many destinations, mostly 1st class. To **Mexico City**, 1600, 1705, 1930, 2150, 12-13 hrs, US$50. To **Tuxtla**, with Fletes y Pasajes at 1400 and 1600, 4 hrs, US$7. To **Oaxaca**, 6 hrs, US$7.

Tapachula p505
Air

Tapachula airport is 25 mins from town centre and has flights to **Mérida** and **Mexico City**, daily, for other destinations connect via Mexico City. *Combis* to airport from Calle 2 Sur No 40, T962-625 1287, US$1, taxis US$7. From airport to border, minibuses charge US$26 for whole vehicle, so share with others, otherwise take *colectivo* to 2nd-class bus terminal and then a bus to Cd Hidalgo.

 Airline offices Aviacsa, Central Norte and 1a Pte, T962-625 4030. AeroMéxico, Central Ote, T962-626 7757.

Bus

OCC bus **Mexico City–Guatemala City** takes 23 hrs, with a change at the border to **Rutas Lima**. There is a variety of direct buses to many parts of Central America from Tapachula all leaving from the OCC Terminal. TICA Bus has some of the best connections. To **Guatemala City**, US$12. To **San Salvador**, US$24. To **Managua**, US$43. To **San José**, US$59. To **Panama City**, US$79. Also Línea Dorada, www.tikalmayanworld.com, operates buses between Tapachula and **Flores**, **Guatemala City** and **Río Dulce**.

Guatemala and Galgos go to **Guatemala City** and **San Salvador**. To **Mexico City**, OCC, 9 daily, 17 hrs, including 3 luxury services from US$64. To **Oaxaca**, OCC, 1915, 12 hrs, US$25. To **Puebla**, OCC, 5 daily, 14½ hrs, US$55; and 3 luxury services, US$65-82. To **San Cristóbal de las Casas**, OCC, 0730, 0915, 1430, 1730, 2120, 7½ hrs, US$16. To **Tuxtla Gutiérrez**, OCC, 12 daily, 7 hrs, US$18; many 2nd-class and 2 luxury services, 1545 and 2359, US$33. To **Salina Cruz**, OCC, 2245, 7 hrs, US$20. To **Tehuantepec**, OCC, 1915, 7½ hrs, US$19.

● Directory

Villahermosa *p482*
Banks American Express, Turismo Nieves, Sarlat 202, T01800-504 0400. **Banamex**, Madero and Reforma, Mon-Fri 0900-1700. HSBC, Juárez and Lerdo, changes TCs at good rates. There is also a good branch on Constitución and Merino, 0900-1700, Mon-Fri. **Cultural centres** Centro Cultural, Corner of Madero and Zaragoza, T993-312 5473. Presentations of local artists and photographers. Live music, workshops in literature, local handicrafts and musical interpretation, among others. El Jaguar Despertado, Sáenz 117, T993-314 1244, forum for artists and local Villahermosino intellectuals. Hosts concerts, art exhibitions and book presentations. Friendly. **Internet** Many along the pedestrianised section of Benito Juárez, all charging about US$1.50 per hr. Others scattered around town. **Post office** On Sáenz and Lerdo in the centre. DHL, parcel courier service, Paseo Tabasco and Malecón Carlos A Madrazo.

Tuxtla Gutiérrez *p484, map p484*
Banks Most banks open 0900-1600, HSBC has longer opening hours. Bancomer, Av Central Pte y 2 Pte Norte, for Visa and TCs, 0900-1500. HSBC, Mon-Fri 0900-1900, Sat 0900-1500, good rates and service. For cheques and cash: 1 Sur Pte 350, near zócalo.

There are ATMs in various branches of Farmacia del Ahorro, all over the city. **Immigration**, 1 Ote Norte. **Internet** Free at library of Universidad Autónoma de Chiapas, Route 190, 6 km from centre. Various other internet cafés all over town, especially on Av Central, costing about US$1 per hr. **Post office** On main square. **Telephone** International phone calls can be made from 1 Norte, 2 Ote, directly behind post office, 0800-1500, 1700-2100 (Sun 1700-2000).

San Cristóbal de las Casas *p486, map p487*
Banks Banamex, Insurgentes 5, changes cheques without commission, 0900-1300. Banca Serfín on the zócalo, changes euro, Amex, MasterCard, TCs. **Bancomer**, Plaza 31 de Marzo 10, charges commission, cash advance on Visa, Amex or Citicorp TCs, good rates and service. **Casa Margarita** will change dollars and TCs. Banks usually open for exchange 0900-1600. HSBC, Diego de Mazariegos 6, good rates for cash and TCs (US$ only), fast, efficient, cash advance on MasterCard, open Sat afternoons. **Casa de Cambio Lacantún**, Real de Guadalupe 12, Mon-Fri 0900-1400, 1600-1900, Sat and Sun 0900-1300 (may close early), no commission, at least US$50 must be changed and much lower exchange than at the banks. 24-hr ATM at **Banorte**, 5 de Febrero, adjacent to cathedral. Quetzales can be obtained for pesos or dollars in the *cambio* but better rates are paid at the border. **Cultural centres** The Casa de Cultura, opposite El Carmen church on junction of Hermanos Domínguez and Hidalgo, has a range of activities on offer: concerts, films, lectures, art exhibitions and conferences. They also do marimba music and danzón on the plaza outside the centre some evenings. **Casa/Museo de Sergio Castro**, Guadalupe Victoria 47 (6 blocks from plaza), T967-678 4289, 1800-2000 (but best to make appointment), entry free but donations welcome. Excellent collection of indigenous garments, talks (in English, French or Spanish)

and slide shows about customs and problems of the indigenous population. **El Puente**, Real de Guadalupe 55, 1 block from the plaza, T967-678 3723, www.elpuenteweb.com, Spanish lessons with a restaurant, internet centre and a small cinema. Check their notice board for forthcoming events. A good place to meet other travellers. **Na Bolom Museum and Cultural Centre**, see page 488 and Sleeping, above. **Immigration** On Carretera Panamericana and Diagonal Centenario, opposite Hotel Bonampak. From zócalo take Diego de Mazariegos west, after crossing bridge take Diagonal on the left towards Hwy, 30-min walk. **Internet** There are many internet cafés all over town with rates around US$0.80 per hr. Service is generally good. **Language schools** Centro Cultural El Puente, Real de Guadalupe 55, T967-678 3723, www.elpuente web.com (Spanish programme), rates around US$10 per hr, US$145/week, 1-to-1 lessons, homestay programmes available from US$230 per week, registration fee US$35. Mixed reports. **Instituto Jovel**, Francisco Madero 27, T967-678 4069, www.institutojovel.com. Group or 1-to-1 classes, homestays arranged, said to be the best school in San Cristóbal as their teachers undergo an obligatory 6-week training course; very good reports from students, all teachers bilingual to some extent. **Universidad Autónoma de Chiapas**, Av Hidalgo 1, Dpto de Lenguas, offers classes in English, French and Tzotzil. **Laundry** Superklin, Crescencio Rosas 48, T967-678 3275, US$1.30 per kg, for collection after 5 hrs. La Rapidita, Insurgentes 9, coin-operated machines for self-service or they will launder clothes for you 1-3 kg US$3.50. **Medical services** Doctors: Servicio Médico Bilingüe, Av Juárez 60, T967-678 0793, Dr Renato Zarate Castañeda speaks English, is highly recommended and if necessary can be reached at home, T967-678 2998. Hospitals and clinics: Red Cross, Prolongación Ignacio Allende,

T967-678 0772. Recommended. **Pharmacies:** Widely available around town. **Post office** Allende and Mazariegos, Mon-Fri 0800-1600, Sat 0900-1200. **Telephone** Casetas Telefónicas can be found all over the city. There are also **Ladatel** phones on the plaza, but these are generally more expensive than *casetas*.

Palenque town *p493, map p494*
Banks Exchange rate only comes through at 1000. **Bancomer**, changes TCs, good rates, Mon-Fri 0830-1600, Sat 0900-1500. Banamex, Juárez 28, Mon-Fri 0830-1600, Sat 0900-1500, slow. ATMs at **Bancomer** and **Banamex**, but often with long queues. Many travel agencies also have *casas de cambio*, but don't usually change TCs. **Internet** Several internet cafés along Juárez with good service and prices ranging from US$1-1.50 per hr. **Laundry** Opposite Hotel Kashlan, US$2 per 3 kg, 0800-1930. At the end of Juárez is a laundry, US$3 per 3 kg. **Post office** Independencia, next to Palacio Municipal, helpful, Mon-Fri 0900-1300. **Telephone** Long-distance telephones at *casetas* along Juárez and at the bus terminals.

Comitán *p501*
Banks Bancomer, on plaza will exchange Amex TCs, bring ID; 2 others on plaza, none change dollars after 1200; also a *casa de cambio*. **Embassies and consulates** Guatemala, 1era Calle Sur Pte 35, 3rd floor (hard to spot, look for Guatemalan flag on top of building), T963-672 0491. Mon-Fri 0800-1300, 1400-1700, visas US$25 (not needed by most nationalities); tourist card US$10 (even for those for whom it should be free), valid 1 year, multiple entry. **Internet** Several internet cafés in the streets near the main plaza, US$0.50 per hr. **Post Office** In Av Central Sur Belisario Domínguez, 2 blocks south of main plaza.

Ciudad Cuauhtémoc *p502*
Banks Don't change money with the Guatemalan customs officials: the rates they

offer are worse than those given by bus drivers or in banks (and these are below the rates inside the country). There is nowhere to change TCs at the border and bus companies will not accept cheques in payment for fares. However, 300 m after the border you can get good rates for TCs at the **Banco de Café**. The briefcase-and-dark-glasses brigade changes cash on the Guatemalan side only, but you must know in advance what the rates are.

Tapachula *p505*

Banks Avoid the crowds of streetwise little boys at the border; exchange is better in the town, bus station gives a good rate (cash only). **Banamex**, Blv Díaz Ordaz, 0830-1230, 1400-1600, disagreement over whether TCs are changed. **HSBC** is the only bank open Sat, changes TCs. **Casa de Cambio Tapachula**, Av 4 Norte y Calle 3 Pte, changes dollars, TCs, pesos, quetzales and lempiras

(open late Mon-Sat), but not recommended, poor rates. Very difficult to change money or find anywhere open at weekends. Try the supermarket. **Embassies and consulates** El Salvador, Calle 2 Ote 31 and Av 7 Sur, T962-626 1252, Mon-Fri 0900-1700. **Guatemala**, Av 5a Norte, No 5, 3rd floor, Mon-Fri 1000-1500 and 1600-1800; tourist card US$10, friendly and quick, take photocopy of passport, photocopier 2 blocks away. **Immigration** Av 14 Norte 57, T962-626 1263. **Laundry** There is a laundry, at Av Central Norte 99 between Calle 13 y 15 Ote, US$3 wash and dry, 1 hr service, about 2 blocks from OCC bus station, open Sun. Also on Av Central Norte between Central Ote y Calle 1, opens 0800, closed Sun. **Telephone** Several long-distance phone offices, eg Esther, Av 5 Norte 46; La Central, Av Central Sur 95; **Monaco**, Calle 1 Pte 18.

Yucatán Peninsula

The Yucatán Peninsula, which includes the states of Campeche, Yucatán and Quintana Roo, is sold to tourists as the land of Maya archaeology and Caribbean beach resorts. And there's no denying it, the warm turquoise sea, fringed with fine white-sand beaches and palm groves of the 'Mayan Riviera' are second to none. And it would be a crime not to tread the beaten path to the sensational ruins at Chichén Itzá, Uxmal and Tulum. But it more than pays to explore beyond the main itineraries to visit some of the lesser-known Maya sites such as Cobá, Edzná or Dzibilchaltún, or the imposing Franciscan monastery and huge pyramid at Izamal. There are flamingo feeding grounds at Celestún and Río Lagartos and over 500 other species of bird, many of which are protected in Sian Ka'an Biosphere Reserve, which covers 4500 sq km of tropical forest, savanna, and coastline. Ever since Jacques Cousteau filmed the Palancar Reef in the 1960s, divers have swarmed to the clear waters of Cozumel, the 'Island of the Swallows', to wonder at the many species of coral and other underwater plants and creatures, at what has become one of the most popular diving centres in the world. Also popular and specialized is diving in the many cenotes (sink holes), including the famous Nohooch Nah Chich, part of the world's largest underground cave system.

Background

After the Maya arrived in Yucatán about 1200 BC, they built monumental stone structures during the centuries leading up to the end of the pre-Classic period (AD 250). Later they rebuilt their cities, but along different lines, probably because of the arrival of Toltecs in the ninth and 10th centuries. Each city was autonomous, and in rivalry with other cities. Before the Spaniards arrived the Maya had developed a writing system in which the hieroglyphic was somewhere between the pictograph and the letter. Fray Diego de Landa collected their books, wrote a very poor summary, the *Relación de las Cosas de Yucatán*, and with Christian but unscholarly zeal burnt most of the codices, which he never really understood.

The Spaniards found little to please them when they first arrived in the Yucatán: no gold, no concentration of natives; nevertheless Mérida was founded in 1542 and the few natives were handed over to the conquerors in *encomiendas*. The Spaniards found them difficult to exploit: even as late as 1847 there was a major revolt, fuelled by the inhumane conditions in the *henequén* (sisal) plantations, and the discrimination against the Maya in the towns, but it was the expropriation of Maya communal lands that was the main source of discontent. In July 1847 a conspiracy against the *Blancos*, or ruling classes from Mexico, was uncovered in Valladolid and one of its leaders, Manuel Antonio Ay, was shot. This precipitated a bloody war, known as the *Guerra de Castas* (Caste War) between the Maya and the *Blancos*. The first act was the massacre of all the non-Maya inhabitants of Tepich, south of Valladolid. The Maya took control of much of the Yucatán, laying siege to Mérida, only to abandon it to sow their crops in 1849. This allowed the governor of Yucatán to counter-attack, driving the Maya by ruthless means into southern Quintana Roo. In Chan Santa Cruz, now called Felipe Carrillo Puerto, one of the Maya leaders, José María Barrera, accompanied by Manuel Nahuat, a ventriloquist, invented the 'talking cross', a cult that attracted thousands of followers. The sect, called Cruzob, established itself and renewed the resistance against the government from Mexico City. It was not until 1901 that the Mexican army retook the Cruzob's domain.

People

The people are divided into two groups: the Maya, the minority, and the *mestizos*. The Maya women wear *huípiles*, or white cotton tunics (silk for fiestas), which may reach the ankles and are embroidered round the square neck and bottom hem. Their ornaments are mostly gold. A few of the men still wear straight white cotton (occasionally silk) jackets and pants, often with gold or silver buttons, and when working protect this dress with aprons. Carnival is the year's most joyous occasion, with concerts, dances and processions. Yucatán's folk dance is the *jarana*, the man dancing with his hands behind his back, the woman raising her skirts a little, and with interludes when they pretend to be bullfighting. During pauses in the music the man, in a high falsetto voice, sings *bambas* (compliments) to the woman. The Maya are a courteous gentle people. They drink little, except on feast days, speak Mayan languages, and profess Christianity laced with a more ancient nature worship.

Access to sites and resorts

Many tourists come to the Yucatán, mostly to see the ancient **Maya sites** and to stay at the new coastal resorts. A good paved road runs from Coatzacoalcos through Villahermosa, Campeche and Mérida (Route 180). An inland road from Villahermosa to Campeche gives easy access to Palenque (see page 495). If time is limited, take a bus from Villahermosa to Chetumal via Escárcega, which can be done overnight as the journey is not very interesting (unless you want to see the Maya ruins off this road). From Chetumal travel up the coast to Cancún, then across to Mérida. Route 307, from Chetumal to Cancún and Puerto Juárez is all paved and in very good condition. Air services from the US and Mexico City are given under Mérida, Cancún and Cozumel.

The state of Quintana Roo is on the eastern side of the Yucatán Peninsula and has recently become the largest tourist area in Mexico with the development of the resort of Cancún, and the parallel growth of Isla Mujeres, Cozumel and the 100-km corridor south of Cancún to Tulum. Growth has been such, In both Yucatán and Quintana Roo, that there are insufficient buses at peak times; old second-class buses may be provided for first-class tickets and second-class buses take far too many standing passengers. There is also a lack of information services. Where beaches are unspoilt they often lack all amenities. Many cheaper hotels are spartan.

Warning So many of the tourists coming to the coastal resorts speak no Spanish so price hikes and short-changing have become very common, making those places very expensive if you are not careful. In the peak, winter season, prices are increased anyway, by about 50%.

Quintana Roo (and especially Cozumel) is the main area for **diving** and **watersports** in the Yucatán Peninsula, and the options are mentioned in the text. However, watersports in Quintana Roo are expensive and touristy, although operators are generally helpful; snorkelling is often in large groups. On the more accessible reefs the coral is dying and there are no small coral fish, as a necessary part of the coral life cycle. Further from the shore, though, there is still much reef life to enjoy.

A useful website on places and activities in the Yucatán is www.yucatantoday.com, the web version of the monthly *Yucatán Today* magazine.

State of Campeche

Take time out to explore the State of Campeche. Colonial architecture is plentiful, there are several fortified convents and Campeche city itself was fortified to protect its citizens from pirate attacks. There are many archaeological sites, most demonstrating influences of Chenes-style architecture. Relax at the resorts of Sihoplaya and Seybaplaya while watching pelicans dive and iguanas scurry. You can try the beaches at Ciudad del Carmen, eat delicious red snapper and buy a cheap, but sturdy, Panama hat. The exhibits at several museums reflect the seafaring nature of the area and the pre-Conquest civilization that occupied these lands. The official government website is at www.campeche.gob.mx. ▸▸ *For listings, see pages 540-544.*

Tabasco to Campeche ⊖❶❷❸ ▸▸ *pp 540-544.*

There are two routes to Campeche from the neighbouring state of Tabasco: the inland Highway 186, via Escárcega, with two toll bridges (cost US$5), and the slightly longer coastal route through Ciudad del Carmen, Highway 180; both converge at Champotón, 66 km south of Campeche. Highway 186 passes Villahermosa's modern international airport and runs fast and smooth in a sweeping curve 115 km east to the Palenque turn-off at Playas del Catazajá; beyond, off the highway, is **Emiliano Zapata** (fiesta 26 October), a busy cattle centre, with a Pemex station.

Francisco Escárcega → *Colour map 4, B2. Phone code: 982.*
Escárcega is a major hub for travellers on their way south to the states of Tabasco and Chiapas, north to Mérida in the state of Yucatán, east to Maya sites in Campeche and Quintana Roo states, and further east to the city of Chetumal. The town itself is not particularly enticing, set on a busy highway with a dusty wild west atmosphere. If stuck here overnight, there are a couple of hotels, a bank and several cheap restaurants.

Coast road to Campeche ⊖❶❷❸❹ ▸▸ *pp540-544.*

Although Highway 180 via Ciudad del Carmen is narrow, crumbling into the sea in places and usually ignored by tourists intent on visiting Palenque, this journey is beautiful and more interesting than the fast toll road inland to Campeche. The road threads its way from Villahermosa 78 km north through marshland and rich cacao, banana and coconut plantations, passing turnings to tiny coastal villages with palm-lined but otherwise mediocre beaches. It finally leads to the river port of **Frontera**, where Graham Greene began the research journey in 1938 that led to the publication of *The Lawless Roads* and later to *The Power and the Glory*. The **Feria Guadalupana** is held from 3-13 December, with an agricultural show, bullfights, *charreadas* and regional dances.

The road touches the coast at the Tabasco/Campeche state border. It then runs east beside a series of lakes (superb birdwatching) to the fishing village of **Zacatal** (93 km), at the entrance to the **Laguna de Términos** (named for the first Spanish expedition, which thought it had reached the end of the 'island' of Yucatán). Just before Zacatal is the lighthouse of **Xicalango**, an important pre-Columbian trading centre. Cortés landed near here in 1519 on his way to Veracruz and was given 20 female slaves, including 'La Malinche', the indigenous princess baptized as Doña Marina who, as the Spaniards' interpreter, played an important role in the Conquest. A bridge crosses the lake's mouth to Ciudad del Carmen.

Ciudad del Carmen → *Colour map 4, B1. Phone code: 938.*

This is the hot, bursting-at-the-seams principal oil port of the region. The site was established in 1588 by a pirate named McGregor as a lair from which to raid Spanish shipping; it was infamous until the pirates were wiped out by Alfonso Felipe de Andrade in 1717, who named the town after its patroness, the Virgen del Carmen.

Most streets in the centre are numbered; even numbers generally run west-east, and odd south-north. Calle 20 is the seafront *malecón* and the road to the airport and university is Calle 31. There's a tourist office at the main plaza, near the seafront malecón, 0800-1500.

The attractive, cream-coloured **cathedral** (Parroquia de la Virgen del Carmen), begun 1856, is notable for its stained glass. **La Iglesia de Jesús** (1820) opposite Parque Juárez is surrounded by elegant older houses. Nearby is the Barrio del Guanal, the oldest residential quarter, with the church of the **Virgen de la Asunción** (1815) and houses with spacious balconies and tiles brought from Marseilles.

There are several good beaches with restaurants and watersports, the most scenic being Playa Caracol (southeast of the centre) and Playa Norte, which has extensive white sand and safe bathing. Fishing excursions can be arranged through the **Club de Pesca** ① *Nelo Manjárrez, T938-382 0073, at Calle 40 and Calle 61.* Coastal lagoons are rich in tarpon (*sábalo*) and bonefish. The town's patroness is honoured with a cheerful fiesta each year between 15 and 30 June.

Maya ruins in south Campeche ● ▶▶ *pp 540-544.*

Calakmul → *Colour map 4, B2.*

① *Daily 0800-1700, US$3.70, cars US$4, entrance to biosphere reserve US$4.*

Three hundred kilometres southeast from Campeche town, and a further 60 km off the main Escárcega-Chetumal road, the ruins of Calakmul are only accessible by car. The site has been the subject of much attention in recent years, due to the previously concealed scale of the place. It is now believed to be one of the largest archaeological sites in Mesoamerica, and certainly the biggest of all the Maya cities, with somewhere in the region of 10,000 buildings in total, many of them as yet unexplored. There is evidence that Calakmul was begun in 300 BC, and continually added to until AD 800. At the centre of the site is the Gran Plaza, overlooked by a pyramid whose base covers 2 ha of ground. One of the buildings grouped around the **Gran Plaza** is believed, due to its curious shape and location, to have been designed for astronomical observation. The **Gran Acrópolis**, the largest of all the structures, is divided into two sections: **Plaza Norte**, with the ball court, was used for ceremonies; **Plaza Sur** was used for public activities. The scale of the site is vast, and many of the buildings are still under excavation, which means that information on Calakmul's history is continually being updated. To reach Calakmul, take Route 186 until Km 95, then turn off at Conhuás, where a paved road leads to the site, 60 km.

Xpujil → *Colour map 4, B2. Phone code: 983.*

① *Tue-Sun 0800-1700, US$3.40, US$3 to use a video camera.*

The name means a type of plant similar to a cattail. The architectural style is known as Río Bec, characterized by heavy masonry towers simulating pyramids and temples, usually found rising in pairs at the ends of elongated buildings. The main building at Xpujil features an unusual set of three towers, with rounded corners and steps that are so steep they are unscalable, suggesting they may have been purely decorative. The façade features the open jaws of an enormous reptile in profile on either side of the main entrance, possibly representing Itzamná, the Maya god of creation. Xpujil's main period of activity was AD 500-750; it began to go into decline around 1100. Major excavation on the third structure was done as recently as 1993, and there are still many unexcavated buildings dotted about the site. It can be very peaceful and quiet in the early mornings, compared with the throng of tourist activity at the more accessible sites such as Chichén Itzá and Uxmal. To get there, see Transport, page 543.

The tiny village of Xpujil, on the Chetumal–Escárcega highway, is conveniently located for the three sets of ruins in this area, Xpujil, Becán and Chicanná. There are two hotels and a couple of shops. Guided tours to the more remote sites, such as Calakmul and Río Bec, can be organized through either of the two hotels, costing about US$20-30 per person for the whole day.

Becán → *Phone code: 996. Colour map 4, B2.*
ⓘ *Daily 0800-1700, US$3.70.*
Seven kilometres west of Xpujil, Becán is another important site in the Río Bec style. Its most outstanding feature is a moat, now dry, which surrounds the entire city and is believed to be one of the oldest defence systems in Mesoamerica. Seven entrance gates cross the moat to the city. The large variety of buildings on the site are a strange combination of decorative towers and fake temples, as well as structures used as shrines and palaces. The twin towers, typical of the Río Bec style, feature on the main structure, set on a pyramid-shaped base supporting a cluster of buildings that seem to have been used for many different functions.

Chicanná → *Colour map 4, B2. Phone code: 981.*
ⓘ *Daily 0800-1700. US$3.40.*
Located 12 km from Xpujil, Chicanná was named upon its discovery in 1966 in reference to Structure II: chi – mouth, *can* – serpent, and *ná* – house, 'House of the Serpent's Mouth'. Due to its dimensions and location, Chicanná is considered to have been a small residential centre for the rulers of the ancient regional capital of Becán. It was occupied during the late pre-Classic period (300 BC-AD 250); the final stages of activity at the site have been dated to the post-Classic era (AD 1100). Typical of the Río Bec style are numerous representations of the Maya god Itzamná, or Earth Mother. One of the temples has a dramatic entrance in the shape of a monster's mouth, with fangs jutting out over the lintel and more fangs lining the access stairway. A taxi will take you from Xpujil bus stop to Becán and Chicanná for US$10, including waiting time.

Hormiguero → *Colour map 4, B2.*
ⓘ *Daily 0800-1700, US$2.50.*
Twenty kilometres southwest of Xpujil, Hormiguero is the site of one of the most important buildings in the Río Bec region, whose elaborate carvings on the façade show a fine example of the serpent's-mouth entrance, with huge fangs and a gigantic eye.

Río Bec
Río Bec is south off the main highway, some 10 km further along the road to Chetumal. Although the site gave its name to the architectural style seen in this area, there are better examples of it at the ruins listed above. Río Bec is a cluster of several smaller sites, all of which are very difficult to reach without a guide.

Champotón → *Colour map 4, A2.*

Back near the west coast of Campeche state, Route 261 runs 86 km due north from Escárcega through dense forest to the Gulf of Mexico, where it joins the coastal route at Champotón, a relaxed but run-down fishing and shrimping port spread along the banks of Río Champotón. In pre-Hispanic times it was an important trading link between Guatemala and Central Mexico; Toltec and Maya mingled here, followed by the Spaniards; in fact blood was shed here when Francisco Hernández de Córboba was fatally wounded in a skirmish with the inhabitants in 1517. On the south side of town can be seen the remnants of a 1719 fort built as a defence against the pirates who frequently raided this coast. The Feast of the Immaculate Conception (8 December) is celebrated with a joyous **festival** lasting several days.

Sihoplaya and Seybaplaya → *Colour map 4, A2. Phone code: 982.*

Continuing north, Highways 180 and 261 are combined for 17 km until the latter darts off east on its way to Edzná and Hopelchen (bypassing Campeche, should this be desired). A 66-km toll *autopista*, paralleling Highway 180, just inland from the southern outskirts of Champotón to Campeche, is much quicker than the old highway. Champotón and Seybaplaya are bypassed. But from the old Highway 180, narrow and slow with speed bumps, you can reach the resort of **Sihoplaya** (regular buses from Campeche US$1). A short distance further north is the larger resort of **Seybaplaya**. This is an attractive place where fishermen mend nets and pelicans dry their wings along the beach. On the highway is the open-air **Restaurant Veracruz**, serving delicious red snapper (fresh fish at the seafront public market is also good value), but in general there is little to explore. Only the **Balneario Payucán** at the north end of the bay makes a special trip worthwhile; this is probably the closest decent beach to Campeche (33 km), although a little isolated, as the water and sand get filthier as one nears the state capital. Nevertheless, there is still much reef life to enjoy.

Campeche ●❷✿✪●▲✦● ›› *pp540-544. Colour map 4, A2.*

→ *Phone code: 981.*

Campeche's charm is neatly hidden behind traffic-blocked streets, but once inside the city walls it reveals itself as a good place to break your journey out to the Yucatán. At the end of the 20th century, the town of Campeche was declared a World Heritage Site by UNESCO. The clean streets of brightly painted houses give the town a relaxed Caribbean feel. The Malecón is a beautiful promenade where people stroll, cycle, walk and relax in the evening in the light of the setting sun.

Ins and outs

Like many Yucatán towns, Campeche's streets in the Old Town are numbered rather than named. Even numbers run north/south beginning at Calle 8 (no one knows why) near the Malecón, east to Calle 18 inside the walls; odd numbers run east (inland) from Calle 51 in the north to Calle 65 in the south. Most of the points of interest are within this compact area. A full circuit of the walls is a long walk; buses marked 'Circuito Baluartes' provide a regular service around the perimeter.

The **state tourist office** ① *T981-811 9229, www.campechetravel.com, 0800-2100 daily,* is on the Malecón in front of the Palacio de Gobierno (walk down Calle 61 towards the sea). There is another smaller **tourist office** ① *on the northeastern corner of the zócalo,* *next to the cathedral, daily 0900-2100.* For a good orientation take the Centro Histórico tour, a regular **tourist tram** ① *daily on the hour from 0900-1200 and 1700-2000, 45 mins, US$7.50, English and Spanish spoken,* running from the main plaza.

Background

Highway 180 enters the city as the Avenida Resurgimiento, passing either side of the huge **Monumento al Resurgimiento**, a stone torso holding aloft the Torch of Democracy. Originally the trading village of Ah Kim Pech, it was here that the Spaniards, under Francisco Hernández de Córdoba, first disembarked on Mexican soil (22 March 1517) to replenish their water supply. For fear of being attacked by the native population, they quickly left, only to be attacked later by the locals further south in Champotón, where they were forced to land by appalling weather conditions at sea. It was not until 1540 that Francisco de Montejo managed to conquer Ah Kim Pech, founding the city of

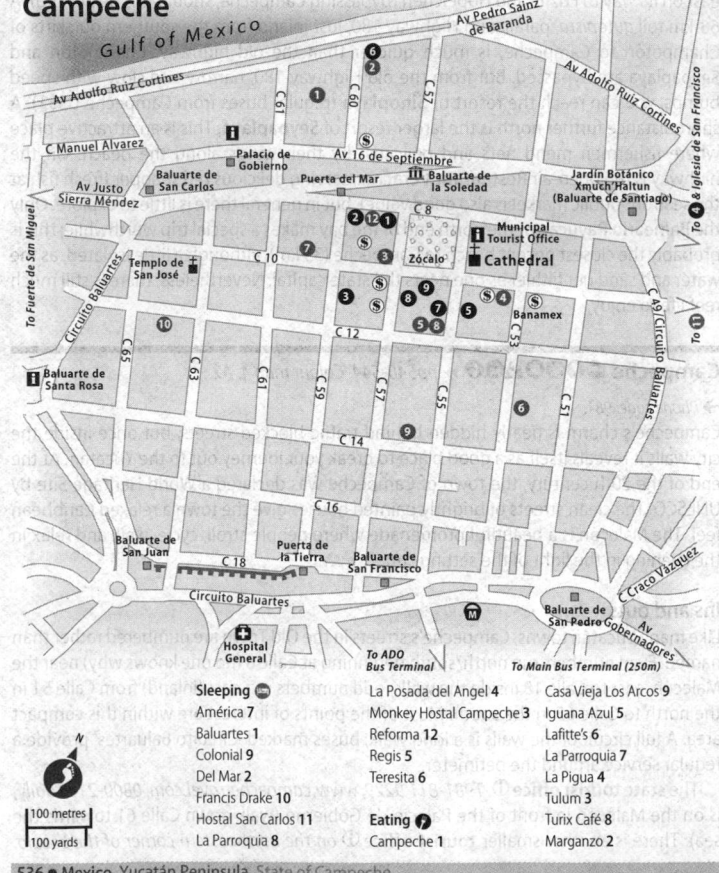

Campeche

Sleeping		La Posada del Angel 4	Casa Vieja Los Arcos 9
América 7		Monkey Hostal Campeche 3	Iguana Azul 5
Baluartes 1		Reforma 12	Lafitte's 6
Colonial 9		Regis 5	La Parroquia 7
Del Mar 2		Teresita 6	La Pigua 4
Francis Drake 10			Tulum 3
Hostal San Carlos 11		Eating	Turix Café 8
La Parroquia 8		Campeche 1	Marganzo 2

Campeche on 4 October 1541, after failed attempts in 1537 and earlier in 1527. The export of local dyewoods, *chicle*, timber and other valuable cargoes soon attracted the attention of most of the famous buccaneers, who constantly raided the port from their bases on Isla del Carmen, then known as the Isla de Tris. Combining their fleets for one momentous swoop, they fell upon Campeche on 9 February 1663, wiped out the city and slaughtered its inhabitants. Five years later the Crown began fortifying the site, the first Spanish colonial settlement to be completely walled. Formidable bulwarks, 3 m thick and 'a ship's height', and eight bastions (*baluartes*) were built in the next 36 years. All these fortifications soon put a stop to pirate attacks and Campeche prospered as one of only two Mexican ports (the other was Veracruz) to have had the privilege of conducting international trade. After Mexican Independence from Spain, the city declined into an obscure fishing and logging town. Only with the arrival of a road from the 'mainland' in the 1950s and the oil boom of the 1970s has Campeche begun to see visitors in any numbers, attracted by its historical monuments and relaxed atmosphere (*campechano* has come to mean an easy-going, pleasant person).

Sights

Of the original walls, seven of the *baluartes* and an ancient fort (now rather dwarfed by two big white hotels on the seafront) remain. Some house museums (see below).

The heart of the city is the zócalo, where the austere Franciscan **cathedral** (1540-1705) has an elaborately carved façade; inside is the Santo Entierro (Holy Burial), a sculpture of Christ on a mahogany sarcophagus with a silver trim. There is plenty of shade under the trees in the zócalo, and a small pagoda with a snack bar.

Right in front of the zócalo is the **Baluarte de Nuestra Señora de la Soledad**, the central bulwark of the city walls, from where you can do a walking tour of the **Circuito Baluartes**, the remains of the city walls. Heading east, you will come to the **Puerta del Mar**, formerly the entrance for those permitted to enter the city from the sea, which used to come up to this point. Next along the *Circuito* is a pair of modern buildings, the **Palacio de Gobierno** and the **Congreso**. The latter looks like a flying saucer, and makes for a bizarre sight when viewed with the 17th-century **Baluarte de San Carlos** in the background. Baluarte de San Carlos now houses a museum. Heading west on the continuation of the *Circuito*, you will come to **Templo de San José**, on Calle 10, an impressive baroque church with a beautifully tiled façade. It has been de-consecrated, and is now an educational centre. Back on to the *Circuito*, you will next reach the **Baluarte de Santa Rosa**, now the home of the tourist information office. Next is **Baluarte de San Juan**, from which a large chunk of the old city wall still extends, protecting you from the noisy traffic on the busy road beyond it. The wall connects with **Puerta de la Tierra** ① *Tue, Fri and Sat 2000 (for information, contact the tourist office)*, where a *Luz y Sonido* (Light and Sound) show takes place, US$4. The continuation of the *Circuito* will take you past the **Baluarte de San Francisco**, and then past the market, just outside the line of the city walls. **Baluarte de San Pedro** flanks the northeast corner of the city centre, and now houses a museum. The *circuito* runs down to the northwest tip of the old city, where the **Baluarte de Santiago** houses the Botanical Gardens.

Further from the city walls is the **Batería de San Luis**, 4 km south from the centre along the coast road. This was once a lookout post to catch pirates as they approached the city from a distance. The **Fuerte de San Miguel**, 600 m inland, is now a museum. A 20-minute walk along Avenida Miguel Alemán from Baluarte de Santiago is the **San Francisco** church, 16th century with wooden altars painted in vermilion and white. Nearby are the

Portales de San Francisco, a beautifully restored old entrance to the city, with several good restaurants in its shadow.

The **Museo de la Escultura Maya** ① *Baluarte de Nuestra Señora de la Soledad, Tue-Sun, 0800-1930, US$2.50*, has three well-laid-out rooms of Maya stelae and sculpture. **Jardín Botánico Xmuch'Haltun** ① *Baluarte de Santiago, Tue-Sun 0900-1600*, is a small, but perfectly formed collection of tropical plants and flowers in a peaceful setting. The **Fuerte de San Miguel** ① *Tue-Sun 0900-1930, US$2.50*, on the Malecón 4 km southwest, is the most atmospheric of the forts (complete with drawbridge and a moat said to have once contained either crocodiles or skin-burning lime, take your pick!); it houses the **Museo Arqueológico**, with a well-documented display of pre-Columbian exhibits including jade masks and black funeral pottery from Calakmul and recent finds from Jaina.

🌙 *The word 'cocktail' is said to have originated in Campeche, where 17th-century English pirates enjoyed drinks adorned with palm fronds resembling cocks' tails.*

Around Campeche

Lerma is virtually a small industrial suburb of Campeche, with large shipyards and fish-processing plants; the afternoon return of the shrimping fleet is a colourful sight. The **Fiesta de Polk Kekén** is held on 6 January, with traditional dances. The nearest decent beaches are at Seybaplaya (see page 535), 20 km south of Campeche. There, the beaches are clean and deserted; take your own food and drink as there are no facilities. Crowded, rickety buses marked 'Lerma' or 'Playa Bonita' run from Campeche, US$1, 8 km.

Maya sites east of Campeche ⊛ ➤➤ *pp540-544.*

A number of city remains (mostly in the Chenes architectural style) are scattered throughout the rainforest and scrub to the east of Campeche; little excavation work has been done and most receive few visitors. Getting to them by the occasional bus service is possible in many cases, but return trips can be tricky. The alternatives are one of the tours run by some luxury hotels and travel agencies in Campeche (see Tour operators) or renting a vehicle (preferably with high clearance) in Campeche or Mérida. Whichever way you travel, carrying plenty of drinking water is strongly advised.

Edzná → *Colour map 4, A2.*
① *Tue-Sun 0800-1700, US$3; local guides available.*

The closest site to the state capital is Edzná ('House of Grimaces'), reached by the highway east to Cayal, then a right turn onto Highway 261, a distance of 61 km. A paved shortcut southeast through China and Poxyaxum (good road) cuts off 11 km; follow Avenida Nacozari out along the railway track. Gracefully situated in a lovely, tranquil valley with thick vegetation on either side, Edzná was a huge ceremonial centre, occupied from about 600 BC to AD 200, built in the simple Chenes style mixed with Puuc, Classic and other influences. The centrepiece is the magnificent, 30-m-tall, 60-sq-m **Temple of the Five Storeys**, a stepped pyramid with four levels of living quarters for the priests and a shrine and altar at the top; 65 steep steps lead up from the Central Plaza. Opposite is the **Paal U'na**, Temple of the Moon. Excavations are being carried out on the scores of lesser temples by Guatemalan refugees under the direction of Mexican archaeologists, but most of Edzná's original sprawl remains hidden away under thick vegetation. Imagination is still needed to picture the network of irrigation canals and holding basins built by the Maya along the valley below sea level. Some of the stelae remain in position (two large stone faces with grotesquely squinting eyes are covered by a thatched shelter); others can be seen in various Campeche museums. There is also a good example of a *sacbé* (sacred road). There is a small *comedor* at the entrance. Edzná is well worth a visit especially in July (exact date varies), when a Maya ceremony to honour Chac is held, to encourage or to celebrate the arrival of the rains. To get there see Transport, page 543.

Hochob
① *Daily 0800-1700, US$2.70.*

Of the more remote and even less-visited sites beyond Edzná, Hochob and Dzibilnocac are the best choices for the non-specialist. Hochob is reached by turning right at Hopelchén on Highway 261, 85 km east of Campeche. This quiet town has an impressive fortified 16th-century church but only one hotel. From here a narrow paved road leads 41 km south to the village of **Dzibalchén**. Don Willem Chan will guide tourists to Hochob (he also rents bikes for US$3.50 per day), helpful, speaks English. Directions can be obtained from the church here (run by Americans); you need to travel 18 km southwest on a good dirt road (no public transport, hopeless quagmire in the rainy season) to the village of Chenko, where locals will show the way (4 km through the jungle). Bear left when the road forks; it ends at a small *palapa* and, from here, the ruins are 1 km uphill with a magnificent view over the surrounding forest. Hochob once covered a large area but, as at Edzná, only the hilltop ceremonial centre (the usual Plaza surrounded by elaborately decorated temple buildings) has been properly excavated; although many of these are mounds of rubble, the site is perfect for contemplating deserted, yet accessible Maya ruins in solitude and silence. The one-room temple to the right (north) of the plaza is the most famous structure: deep-relief patterns of stylized snakes moulded in stucco across its façade are designed to resemble a mask of the ferocious rain god Chac. A door serves as the mouth. A fine reconstruction of the building is on display at the Museo de Antropología in Mexico City. Early morning second-class buses serve Dzibalchén, but, returning to Campeche later in the day is often a matter of luck.

Dzibilnocac
① *Daily 0800-1700, free.*

Twenty kilometres northeast of Dzibalchén at Iturbide, this site is one of the largest in Chenes territory. Only three temples have been excavated here (many pyramidal mounds in the forest and roadside *milpas*); the first two are in a bad state of preservation, but the third is worth the visit: a unique narrow edifice with rounded corners and remains of a stucco façade, primitive reliefs and another grim mask of Chac on the top level. Much of the stonework from the extensive site is used by local farmers for huts and fences. A bus leaves Campeche at 0800, three hours, return 1245, 1345 and 1600, US$3.35. If driving your own vehicle, well-marked 'km' signs parallel the rocky road to Iturbide (no accommodation); bear right around the tiny zócalo and its attendant yellow church and continue (better to walk in the wet season) for 50 m, where the right branch of a fork leads to the ruins. Other sites in the region require 4WD transport and appeal mostly to archaeologists.

Becal
Becal is the centre for weaving Panama hats, here called *jipis* (pronounced 'hippies') and ubiquitous throughout the Yucatán. Many of the town's families have workshops in cool, moist backyard underground caves, which are necessary for keeping moist and pliable the shredded leaves of the *jipijapa* palm from which the hats are made. Most vendors give

the visitor a tour of their workshop, but are quite zealous in their sales pitches. Prices are better for *jipis* and other locally woven items (cigarette cases, shoes, belts, etc) in the **Centro Artesanal**, **Artesanías de Becaleña** ① *Calle 30 No 210*, than in the shops near the plaza, where the hat is honoured by a hefty sculpture of three concrete *sombreros*! More celebrations take place on 20 May during the **Feria del Jipi**.

◉ State of Campeche listings

For Sleeping and Eating price codes and other relevant information, see Essentials pages 45-48.

● Sleeping

Francisco Escárcega *p532*
C Escárcega, Justo Sierra 86, T982-824 0187, around the corner from the bus terminal (turn left twice). Clean, bath, parking, hot water, good restaurant, small garden.
C María Isabel, Justo Sierra 127, T982-824 0045. A/c, restaurant, comfortable, back rooms noisy from highway.
C Motel Akim Pech, T982-824 0240, on Villahermosa highway. A/c or fans and bath, reasonable rooms, restaurant in motel, another across the street, also a Pemex station opposite.

Coast road to Campeche *p532*
D Chichén Itzá, Aldama 671, Frontera, T913-332 0097. Not very clean, fan, shower, hot water.
C San Agustín, Pino Suárez, Frontera, T913-332 0037. Very basic, fan, no mosquito net.

Ciudad del Carmen *p533*
Hotel accommodation is generally poor value and can be difficult to come by Mon-Thu; book in advance and arrive early. For convenience sake, you'll find a handful of 'economical' hotels opposite the ADO bus station.
A EuroHotel, Calle 22 No 208, T938-382 3044, reganem@prodigy.net.mx. Large and modern, 2 restaurants, pool, a/c, disco, built to accommodate the flow of Pemex traffic.
B Lino's, Calle 31 No 132, T938-382 0788 A/c, pool, restaurant, also has 10 RV spaces with electricity hook-ups.

D Hotel Playa Dorna, on Playa Norte. Clean, friendly, pool, TV, hot water, 2 strip bars loud and late at weekends.
D Zacarías, Calle 24 No 58B, T938-382 3506. Modern, some cheaper rooms with fans, brighter a/c rooms are better value. Recommended.

Campeche *p535, map p536*
In general, prices are high. Beware of over-charging and, if driving, find a secure car park.
AL Baluartes, Av 16 de Septiembre 128, T981-816 3911, www.baluartes.com.mx. The rooms in this large and professionally managed hotel are well maintained and comfortable, if lacking personality. There's a host of services including pool, restaurant and a weekend disco.
AL Hotel Del Mar, Av Ruiz Cortines No 51 near El Malecón, T981-811 9191, www.del marhotel.com.mx. 5-star hotel on the waterfront, has pleasant rooms with seaview and balconies, all mod cons and free Wi-Fi in the rooms. Pool, gym, good bar and restaurant.
A Hotel Francis Drake, Calle 12 No 207, between Calle 63 and Calle 65, T981-811 5626, www.hotelfrancisdrake.com. Classy colonial hotel with well-equipped rooms, restaurant, bar and a good business centre.
B América, Calle 10 252, T981-816 4588, www.hotelamericacampeche.com. This centrally located hotel is clean, tidy and well-staffed. The rooms here have Wi-Fi and breakfast is included in the price. An attractive mid-range option.
C Hotel Reforma, Calle 8, No257, between Calle 57 and Calle 59, T981-816 4464. Has a/c, hot water, TV and internet. Bit grotty, but right in the centre just a minute from the main plaza.

C La Posada Del Angel, Calle 10 No 307, T981-816 7718 (on the side entrance of the cathedral). Clean, carpeted, comfortable rooms, some without windows, some with a/c (**B**). Friendly and recommended.
C Regis, Calle 12 148, between 55 and 57, T981-816 3175. Housed in a lovely old colonial building, the reception is a bit dark and dingy, but the hotel sports clean, spacious rooms and a stylish chequered floor.
D Hotel Colonial, Calle 14, No 122, between Calle 55 and Calle 57, T981-816 2630. Rooms have fans or a/c (more expensive) and hot water. A nice old colonial building, this quaint old hotel open since 1946, is living up to its name. Slightly scruffy, but very friendly.
D-E Hostal San Carlos, Calle 10, No 255, Barrio Guadalupe, a few blocks out of town, T981-816 5158, info@hostelcampeche. com.mx. Private rooms and dorms, continental breakfast included. Well-kept hostel with hot water, internet, currency exchange, laundry service and bike rental.
D-E La Parroquia, Calle 55, between 10 y 12, T981-816 2530, www.hostalparroquia.com. 3 dorms and rooms in one of Campeche's historic buildings. Services include free breakfast, kitchen, internet, bike rental book exchange, TV room with DVDs, and a tranquil terrace complete with sun loungers.
D-E Monkey Hostel Campeche, Calle 57 No 10 overlooking the zócalo, T981-811 6605, www.hostalcampeche.com. Dorms and private rooms. There are lockers, laundry, internet, bike hire, kitchen and book exchange. Price includes breakfast and can arrange local tours. Luggage storage US$2.
E Teresita, Calle 53 No 31, 2 blocks east of plaza, T981-816 4534. Very basic rooms with fans, no hot water. Cheapest in town, but good if you're on a tight budget – ask for a room with shared bath for extra savings.

Camping
Club Náutica, 15 km south of town, on the highway out of Campeche, km 180, T981-816 7545. Big campsite with good facilities. Good spot for a few days.

⊕ Eating

Francisco Escárcega *p532*
There are few places used to serving tourists, but there is a good and cheap *lonchería* opposite the bus terminal.
¶¶ Titanic, corner of the main highway and the road to the train station (first turning on the right after turning right out of the bus terminal), for a more expensive meal with a/c.

Ciudad del Carmen *p533*
¶¶ El Kiosco Calle 33 s/n, between Calle 20 and Calle 22, in **Hotel del Parque** with view of zócalo. Modest prices, eggs, chicken, seafood and Mexican dishes.
¶¶ Vía Veneto, in the **EuroHotel** (see Sleeping). Good, if quite pricey, breakfasts.
¶¶-¶ El Pavo, tucked away down Calle 36A, in Col Guadalupe. This superb, family-run restaurant serves excellent seafood dishes at cheap prices. Very popular with the locals.
¶¶-¶ La Fuente, Calle 20. 24-hr snack bar with view of the Laguna.
¶ La Mesita, outdoor stand across from the old ferry landing. Well-prepared shrimp, seafood cocktails, extremely popular all day.

Cafés
There are several tiny cafés along the pedestrian walkway (Calle 33) near the zócalo.
Café Vadillo, Calle 33. The 'best coffee in town'.
Casa Blanca, Calle 20, between Calle 29 and 27. This popular and modern café-bar overlooks the seafront malecón. It serves filter coffee, cappuccinos and espressos.
Mercado Central, Calle 20 and 37, not far northwest of zócalo. Inexpensive snacks are available in the thriving market.

Campeche *p535, map p536*
Campeche is known for its seafood, especially *camarones* (large shrimps), *esmedregal* (black snapper) and *pan de cazón* (baby hammerhead shark sandwiched between corn tortillas with black beans). Food stands in the market serve *tortas*,

tortillas, *panuchos* and *tamales* but hygiene standards vary widely; barbecued venison is also a marketplace speciality.

₮₮₮-₮₮ Casa Vieja Los Arcos, Calle 10, No 319A, on the zócalo, T981-100 5522. Beautiful balcony dining on top of the portales overlooking the main plaza. Specializes in local dishes, including *camarones*. Romantic setting.

₮₮₮-₮₮ Lafitte's Restaurant, inside Hotel del Mar. Pirate-themed restaurant with excellent Mexican dishes and good bar. There's a terrace overlooking the sea for outdoor dining. Recommended.

₮₮ La Pigua, Av Miguel Alemán 179A, www.lapigua.com.mx. A locally renowned, clean, modern restaurant that specializes in seafood. It's open for lunch and dinner, and there's a pleasant garden setting.

₮₮ Restaurante Tulum, Calle 59 No 9, between Calle 10 and Calle 12. This friendly, modern restaurant employs emerging talent from Campeche's gastronomic college. The menu is varied and international, offering white and red meats, baguettes, crêpes and salads. Open from lunchtime.

₮₮-₮ Iguana Azul, Calle 55, between C10 and C12. Bar with live music and dancing, snacks and good selection of drinks.

₮₮-₮ La Parroquia, Calle 55 No 8, part of the hotel with the same name. This busy locals' joint – staffed by smartly attired and friendly waiters – is open 24 hrs. It serves meat, fish and Mexican staples. Good breakfasts and a decent and economical *menú del día*. Free Wi-Fi. Recommended.

₮₮-₮ Marganzo, Calle 8. An elegant and widely respected fine-dining establishment. It boasts a very interesting menu of seafood and *comida típica*, and regularly lays on music with a trio of musicians and regional dancing.

₮₮-₮ Restaurant Campeche, right on the zócalo, opposite the cathedral, has an extensive menu, big portions and is very good value.

₮ Turix, Calle 57 between Calle 10 and Calle 12. Arts and crafts centre combined with gourmet. This little cute café and art space a short hop from the zócalo does a variety of salads, sandwiches and good desserts. Art and crafts for sale.

⊛ Festivals and events

Campeche *p535, map p536*
Feb/Mar Good Carnival.
7 Aug State holiday.
Sep Feria de San Román, 2nd fortnight.
4-13 Oct Fiesta de San Francisco.

Maya sites east of Campeche *p538*
13-17 Apr A traditional Honey and Corn Festival is held in Holpechén.
3 May Día de la Santa Cruz.

O Shopping

Campeche *p535, map p536*
Excellent cheap **Panama hats** *(jipis)*, finely and tightly woven so that they retain their shape even when crushed into your luggage (within reason); cheaper at the source in Becal. Handicrafts are generally cheaper than in Mérida. There are souvenir shops along Calle 8, such as **Artesanía Típica Naval**, Calle 8 No 259, with exotic bottled fruit like *nance* and *marañón*. Many high-quality craft items are available from the **Exposición** in the Baluarte San Pedro, **and Casa de Artesanías Tukulná**, Calle 10 No 333, between C59 and C31, open daily 0900-2000.

The **market**, from which most local buses depart, is beside Alameda Park at the south end of Calle 57. Plenty of bargains here. Try the ice cream, although preferably from a shop rather than a barrow. **Super 10** supermarket behind the post office has an excellent cheap bakery inside.

▲ Activities and tours

Campeche *p535, map p536*
Tour operators
Intermar Campeche, Av 16 de
Septiembre 128, T981-816 9006,
www.travel2mexico.com. Tours, ground
transport, flights and car rental.
Viajes Chicanná, Av Augustín Melgar,
Centro Comercial Triángulo del Sol, Local 12,
T981-811 3503. Flight bookings to Cuba,
Miami and Central America.
Viajes del Golfo, Calle 10 No 250 D,
T981-816 1745, viajesdelgolfo@hotmail.com.
Domestic and international flights; tours to
archaeological sites.
Viajes Xtampak Tours, Calle 57 No 14,
T981-816 6473, www.xtampak.com. Daily
transport to ruins including Edzná, Calakmul,
Uxmal and Palenque – they'll collect you
from your hotel with 24 hrs' notice. There's
a discount for groups and guide services
at an extra cost. Recommended.

● Transport

Tabasco to Campeche *p532*
Bus Buses from Emiliano Zapata, all ADO.
To **Tenosique**, almost hourly, 1½ hrs US$3. To
Villahermosa, frequent services, 2½ hrs, US$7.
To **Mérida**, 0900, 1120, 1500, 2215, 7 hrs,
US$23.50. To **Escárcega**, 0900, 1500, 2 hrs,
US$7.50. To **Chetumal**, 2100, 6 hrs, US$20.

Francisco Escárcega *p532*
Bus Most buses from Chetumal or Campeche
drop you off at the 2nd-class terminal on the
main highway. To buy tickets, you have to wait
until the outgoing bus has arrived; sit near the
ticket office and wait for them to call out your
destination, then join the scrum at the ticket
office. There is an ADO terminal west of the
2nd-class terminal, a 20-min walk. From there,
1st-class buses go to **Palenque**, 0410, 0630,
1250, 2335, 3 hrs, US$10. To **Chetumal**,
frequent services, 4 hrs, US$13. To **Campeche**,
frequent services, 2 hrs, US$7.50. From the

2nd-class terminal, there are buses to
Campeche, 16 a day, 2½ hrs, US$5.60. To
Chetumal, 3 a day, 4 hrs, US$11. To **Playas
de Catazajá**, connecting with *colectivos* to
Palenque, frequent, US$5. To **Villahermosa**,
12 a day, 4 hrs, US$12.50. *Colectivos* to
Palenque leave from outside the 2nd-class
terminal, US$5.50. From 1st class terminal
to **Mérida**, frequent, 4½ hrs, US$16.50.

Ciudad del Carmen *p533*
Air
Carmen's airport (CME, 5 km east of the
plaza) currently only has direct flights to
Mexico City, from where there are
connections to the rest of the country.
    Airline offices Mexicana, Calle 22
y 37, T938-382 1171.

Bus
The ADO bus terminal is some distance from
the centre. Take bus or *colectivo* marked
'Renovación' or 'ADO'; they leave from around
the zócalo. There are frequent ADO and ATS
services to **Campeche**, 2½-3 hrs, US$11. To
Mérida, 6 hrs, US$21. To **Villahermosa** via the
coast, 3 hrs, US$9, where connections can be
made to **Palenque**. Buses also travel via
Escárcega, where you can connect to
Chetumal and **Belize**.

Car
Car hire Budget, Calle 31 No 117, T938-382
0908. Auto-Rentas del Carmen, Calle 33
No 121, T938-382 2376.

Xpujil *p533*
Bus 2nd-class buses from **Chetumal** and
Escárcega stop on the highway in the
centre of Xpujil, some 800 m east of the
2 hotels. There are 4 buses a day to
Escárcega, between 1030 and 1500, 3 hrs,
US$6. 8 buses a day to **Chetumal**, 2 hrs,
US$5. Change at Escárcega for buses to
Palenque or **Campeche**. 1st-class buses
will not stop at Xpujil.

Campeche *p535, map p536*
Air
Modern, efficient airport (CPE) on Porfirio, 10 km northeast. **AeroMéxico** direct daily to **Mexico City**, T981-816 3109. If on a budget, walk 100 m down service road (Av Aviación) to Av Nacozari, turn right (west) and wait for 'China–Campeche' bus to zócalo.

Bus
The easiest way to reach **Edzna** is on a tourist minibus. They depart hourly and operators include Xtampak, Calle 57 No 14, between Calle 10 and Calle 12, T981-812 8655, xtampac_7@hotmail.com, US$21.50 (prices drop depending on no of passengers); and **Transportadora Turística Jade**, Av Díaz Ordaz No 67, T981-827 4885, Jade_tour@hotmail.com, US$14. To get there on public transport, catch a morning bus to Pich and ask to be let out at Edzna – it's a 15-min walk from the highway. Ask the driver about return schedules, as services are quite infrequent and subject to change. There's no accommodation at Ednzá and hitchhiking isn't recommended. Buses to **Seybaplaya** leave from the tiny Cristo Rey terminal opposite the market, 9 a day from 0615, 45 mins, US$1.

Long distance The bus station is about 3 km south of the centre. Buses from outside the terminal travel the *circuito* road. A taxi costs US$2.20. The 2nd-class bus terminal is about 1 km east of the centre along Av Gobernadores, but services are steadily moving to the main terminal. To **Cancún**, 7 daily with **ADO** and ADO GL, 7 hrs, US$32-24.50. To **Chetumal**, 1200, 6 hrs, US$42. To **Ciudad del Carmen**, frequent ADO services, 3 hrs, US$11. To **Escárcega**, frequent, 2 hrs, US$7.50. To **Mérida**, frequent ADO services, 2½ hrs, US$9.50. To **Mexico City**, ADO at 1230, 2225, 2345, 18 hrs, US$68, and 2 ADO GL services at 1430 and 1635, 16 hrs, US$82. To **San Cristóbal de las Casas**, OCC at 2145, 11 hrs, US$25. To **Veracruz**, luxury only, ADO GL at 2215, 11½ hrs, US$52.50. To **Villahermosa**, frequent ADO services, 6-7 hrs, US$21.

Car
Car hire Maya nature, Av Ruiz Cortines 51, inside Hotel del Mar, T981-811 9191. Hertz and **Autorent** car rentals at airport.

❶ Directory

Ciudad del Carmen *p533*
Banks Banamex, Calle 24 No 63 or Banorte, Calle 30 and 33. **Post office** Calle 22 No 136.

Campeche *p535, map p536*
Banks Banorte, Calle 8 No 237, between C57 and C59; Mon-Fri 0900-1700; HSBC, Calle 10 No 311, Mon-Fri 0900-1700, Sat 0900-1500; Santander Serfín, Calle 57 No 8; **American Express**, T981-811 1010, Calle 59, Edificio Belmar, oficina 5, helpful for lost cheques, etc. Plenty of ATMs and places to get cash on credit cards. **Cultural centres** Casa del Teniente de Rey, Calle 59 No 38 between 14 and 16, houses the **Instituto Nacional de Antropología e Historia (INAH)**, dedicated to the restoration of Maya ruins in the state of Campeche, as well as supporting local museums. INAH can be visited for information regarding any of the sites in the state, T981-811 1314, www.inah.gob.mx. The Centro Cultural Casa 6, Calle 57, between Calle 8 and Calle 10, 0900-2100 daily, US$0.35, is housed in a handsome building on the main plaza. It conjures the opulence and splendour of Campeche's golden days. **Immigration** The Oficina de Migración is inside the Palacio Federal. **Internet** Many internet places around town, including Cybercafé Campeche, Calle 61 between Calle 10 and 12, 0900-1300, US$1.50 per hr. **Laundry Antigua** Calle 57 between Calle 12 and 14, US$1 per kg. **Medical services** Red Cross, T981-815 2411. **Post office** Av 16 de Septiembre (Malecón) and Calle 53 in Edificio Federal); Mon-Fri 0800-2000, Sat 0900-1300 for *Lista de Correos*, registered mail, money orders and stamps. **Telephone** Telmex, Calle 8 between Calle 51 y 53, free; Calle 51 No 45, between Calle 12 and 14.

Diving Central America & Mexico

Introduction

To the uninitiated diver, the waters off Central America's eastern coastline may seem to be just another part of the Caribbean, yet these coastal nations have a secret that sets them apart. They sit along the edge of the planet's second largest barrier reef, the Mesoamerican Barrier Reef, which runs down Mexico's Yucatán Peninsula, south past Belize, Guatemala and Honduras, before finally petering out just off Nicaragua. Along this coast there are three well known dive destinations: Mexico's Yucatán, Belize, and Honduras' Bay Islands. The reefs in this region consist of a basic structure of hard corals decorated with pastel-toned soft coral seaplumes, rods and whips. Marine animals range from typical angels and butterflyfish all the way up to reef sharks, turtles and eagle rays. Dive styles vary, with calm, shallow reefs, exciting drift dives and some amazing and unique caves. Right across the region there is a good selection of diver-orientated facilities, with many professional operators and schools and recompression chambers in each. No matter where you go, you will find good visibility, usually running from 20-30 m + while the water temperature is a balmy 25-28°C.

Beth and Shaun Tierney, authors of Footprint's Diving the World.

Above: An 8-ft long tarpon in Mexico.

ii **Previous page:** Diver and barrel sponge in Belize.

Along the Yucatán coast lies a highly westernized vacation area nicknamed the Mayan Riviera. While mainstream tourism centres around purpose-built, high-octane Cancún, more discerning divers tend to head south to the once sleepy fishing village of Playa del Carmen. There's some good diving both north and south of the town. Offshore reef top plateaux are swept by strong currents and these attract a fair number of pelagic species, while the shallower inshore reefs are a little more protected and colourful reef fish congregate over small walls. The ancient *cenotes* are also a feature for the more adventurous. The land beneath the peninsula is riddled with extensive natural caves filled with freshwater. Over the centuries, the bedrock has literally dissolved leaving a vast network of subterranean rivers, underground caverns and sinkholes (*cenotes*) that extend miles inland. After the last ice age ocean levels rose and flooded the caverns that lay closest to the coast with seawater, while those further inland filled with rainwater. The Maya tapped this resource by digging sacred *cenotes* – or wells – down into them. These have since become some of the most unusual and fascinating dive sites on the planet, let alone the region!

🌊 Dos Ojos

Dos Ojos, meaning two eyes, refers to two circular *cenotes* that sit beside each other. The dives here are popular and suitable for most divers and snorkellers with well organized facilities. Entry is via a wooden platform built under the overhang of a small cave and between the two eyes. The water feels icy as you jump in, especially as the surrounding jungle is so humid. And it is mosquito heaven! The cave system has guidelines to follow but divers are obliged to go with a qualified guide. The first descent into an enormous yawning cave is breathtaking but soon changes to a dark and gloomy passage. Divers are led past fragile rock formations and through ancient tunnels that sometimes have shafts of daylight shining through. The experience becomes far more surreal once you enter tunnels that are completely black, lit only by your torch beam. You round corners to discover weird and wonderful formations, swim past rocky towers that glitter with minerals then into cathedral-like chambers. Although there are masses more tunnels leading away from the route you will take, exploration of these is restricted to professional divers. There is so much to see that hardly matters: limestone formations with arches and doorways lead to huge, cavernous rooms. Stalactites hang from every available space on the ceiling, sometimes converging to form thick columns.

Exploring Dos Ojos.

■ The Inner Reefs

Less than an hour from Belize City and only a mile or so offshore are a series of ever-popular holiday islands. The most popular and busiest for divers are Caye Caulker and Ambergris Caye but just to the south of these are many more small cayes and reefs, often with evocative names like Drowned Caye, Hen and Chicken Caye and Spanish Lookout Caye, all a reflection of their illustrious pasts. There is good diving around these islands, and some excellent snorkelling,

although it's perhaps not so challenging as being on the reefs that are further from the coast. This is because a deep-water trench parallels the coast creating a lagoon-like feel: these waters are shallow and mostly calm. The reef geography is less sculpted than further afield, but all the same these dive sites have pretty coral formations, swim-throughs, small tunnels and caverns and there are occasional encounters with larger animals like turtles, sharks and rays. Hol Chan Marine Reserve protects the southern tip of Ambergris Caye and both novice divers and snorkellers can be surprised by a face-to-face encounter with an adult nurse shark or spotted eagle ray. These animals take advantage of the seagreass beds for an easy meal.

Top right: Spotted eagle ray in Belize's Inner reefs.
Below left: Foureye butterflyfish.
Below right: School of snappers in Honduras.

🐚 The Blue Hole

Made famous by Jacques Cousteau, this is almost a pilgrimage, one of those tick-off-the-list dive sites. The Blue Hole gained celebrity status after the 1970s *Calypso* expedition. Sitting at the midpoint of Lighthouse Reef, it was believed to be a cave whose roof collapsed at the end of the ice age. Now the deep blue, perfectly circular opening is over 300 metres across and drops to around 150 metres deep. This is a completely unique dive experience – an adrenaline rush – especially for beginners who have rarely, if ever, been to such depths. Entering the water and looking down you see absolutely nothing. The dive is all about a quick descent through pure blue water to over 40 m. It's dark and cold, with almost no fish life, but you can glimpse the stalactites that hang from a hidden ledge. As limestone can't form under water, and stalactites are created by fresh water dripping through limestone rock, these are evidence that the cave was once above sea level. After a few short minutes, you are signalled to ascend for a safety stop. It is all a bit spooky and it's certainly not a traditional dive, until you get back to the shallows to find the waiting grey reef sharks. Operators have picked up on the fact that the area is visited by these beautiful animals and now use bait to attract them. They circle divers during their safety stop hoping for further handouts.

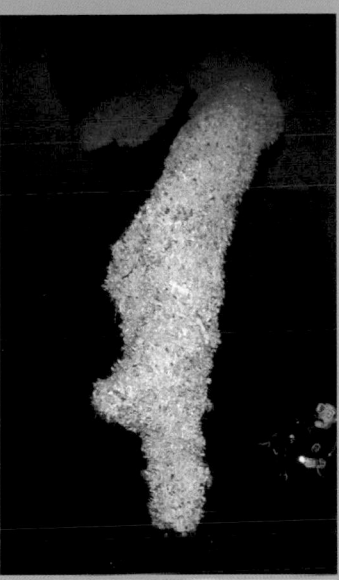

Stalactite in the Blue Hole.

■ Turneffe Atoll and Lighthouse Reef

Sailing east from Belize City and past the barrier to the Inner reef, are another series of atolls which are divided by even deeper marine trenches. The diving is more exciting than on the coastal reefs as the topography is more varied and the marine life more prolific. Turneffe Atoll sits on the first, and shallower, of two submarine ridges. There are hundreds of tiny islands and mangrove-covered islets here. It's an idyllic environment with several lovely resorts.

A little further east lies Lighthouse Reef. Although this reef system is smaller than Turneffe, the diving is the country's best. The area consists of just two cayes, Half Moon and Long, each with its own marine ecosystem. Ringed by sharp walls and cut by deep grooves and channels, caves and caverns, the dives here can be very exciting: sites all have a similar profile but some are backed by shelves with seagreass beds attracting ever more species. The biggest bonus is, of course, the famous Blue Hole (see below).

Arrow blenny on hard coral.

■ **Roatán** The largest and most popular of the Bay Islands is jungle bound and lush, with a central ridge of hills falling steeply to the sea. The coast is ringed by palm-clad sandy beaches, riddled with tiny cayes and mangroves and studded by deep-water inlets called blights. It was these that gave birth to the island's notorious history. A safe haven for boats, they were once used by huge numbers of pirate ships but, nowadays mostly by dive resorts. Just offshore, a barrier reef sits just below the surface and rings the entire island, meandering it's way around the entire coast. Inside this reef, a protected lagoon has calm and comfortable diving, while outside, especially in the south, there are steep walls, fissures, overhangs and ledges. Northern coastal sites tend to be gentler with sloping walls and reefs. Steep walls are painted in a coulourful array of sponges and fans. Lagoon dives are plentiful and right around the island conditions are similar and never very difficult.

■ **Utila** The next of the Bay Islands, Utila, is a completely different proposition to its near neighbour – flat as a pancake, dry and sandy on land, but surprisingly prolific beneath the surface. Utila sits on the edge of the continental shelf so the marine real is different to Roatán, especially on the south side, where the town is situated. Here, the dives are shallow – rarely over 25 m – but there are lots of interesting cracks and crevices along the reef walls which have created overhangs, swim-throughs and sand channels to investigate. The marine species are naturally similar, there seems to be far more critter life. There is also a wreck in the bay, the *Halliburton*, which was sunk specifically to create an artificial reef.

On the north side of the island, the reefs are more dramatic, with steep walls and drop-offs. However, this side is affected by weather conditions, so you may not get up there as much as you would like. It is also recognized as a whaleshark highway and there are regular sightings in the dry season. Utila is well loved by backpackers and has become known for training divers: course rates are cheap and there are many schools to choose from, just ensure you pick a well-respected operation. Prices that are too low may mean your operator is cutting corners.

vi Red hind grouper on a reef.

Top left: Grey reef shark at the Blue Hole. Top right: Swim-throughs in Honduras.
Middle left: The flamingo tongue mollusc. Middle right: Diamond blenny.
Below: Giant barracuda resting on a reef.
Next page: Turtle munching on sponges.

State of Yucatán

The archaeological sites of Chichén Itzá, Oxkintoc, Uxmal, Kabah and Labná are just a few of the many strewn throughout the State of Yucatán. Try not to miss Dzibilchaltún; the intrusion of European architecture is nowhere more startling than here. The region's many cenotes (deep pools created by the disintegration of the dry land above an underground river) were sacred to the Maya, who threw precious jewels, silverware and even humans into their depths; many are perfect for swimming. On the coast, boat trips are organized to observe pelicans, egrets and flamingoes in their natural habitat. It is possible to visit some of the impressive henequén (sisal) haciendas in the more rural areas and admire the showy mansions that line the Paseo de Montejo in Mérida. ➤ *For listings, see pages 558-570.*

North to Mérida

At **Maxcanú**, the road to Muná and Ticul branches east; a short way down it is the recently restored Maya site of **Oxkintoc** ① *US$3*. The Pyramid of the Labyrinth can be entered (take a torch) and there are other ruins, some with figures. Ask for a guide at the village of Calcehtoc, which is 4 km from the ruins and from the Grutas de Oxkintoc (no bus service). These, however, cannot compare with the caves at Loltún or Balankanché (see pages 551 and 556). Highway 180 continues north towards Mérida through a region of numerous *cenotes*, soon passing a turn-off to the turn-of-the-century Moorish-style *henequén* (sisal) hacienda at **San Bernardo**, one of a number in the state that can be visited; an interesting colonial museum chronicling the old Yucatán Peninsula tramway system is located in its lush and spacious grounds. Running beside the railway, the highway continues 47 km to its junction with the inland route at **Umán**, a *henequén* processing town with another large 17th-century **church** and convent dedicated to St Francis of Assisi; there are many *cenotes* in the flat surrounding limestone plain. If driving Highway 180/261 is a divided four-lane motorway for the final 18-km stretch into Mérida. There is a ring road around the city.

Mérida ⊖⊘⊗⊛⊗▲⊖⊙ ➤➤ *pp558-570. Colour map 4, A2.*

→ *Phone code: 999.*

The capital of Yucatán state and its colonial heart, Mérida is a bustling, tightly packed city full of colonial buildings in varying states of repair. There is continual activity in the centre, with a huge influx of tourists during the high season mingling with busy Meridanos going about their daily business. Although the city has been developed over many years for tourism, there is plenty of local flavour for the traveller to seek out off the beaten track. Attempts to create a sophisticated Champs Elysées-style boulevard in the north of the city at Paseo Montejo have not been quite successful; the plan almost seems to go against the grain of Mérida's status as an ancient city, which has gradually evolved into a place with its own distinct identity.

Ins and outs

Getting there All buses from outside Yucatán State arrive at the CAME terminal on Calle 70 between Calle 69 y 71, a few blocks from the centre. There is another bus terminal around the corner on Calle 69, where buses from local destinations such as Uxmal arrive.

Mérida

To Progreso

C 35
C 37
Felipe Carrillo
Puerta Monument
C 39
C 60
Paseo de la Reforma
C 39
Museo de
Antropología
e Historia
C 41
C 43
Paseo de Montejo
Parque
Santa Ana
C 45
A
C 47
C 49
C 51
Plaza
Santa Lucía
C 53
C 55
Museo de
la Canción
Yucateca
C 55
C 50
B
C 55
C 57
Mercado
Municipal 2
Teatro Peón
Contreras
La Mejorada
C 57
Museo
de Arte
Popular
Museum of
Peninsular
Culture
C 59
Jesús
C 59
Casa
Catherwood
C 76
Parque
Hidalgo
C 61
C 61
Palacio
Municipal
Palacio de
Gobierno
Cathedral
C 72
C 52
C 63
Zócalo
Museo Macay
Las
Monjas
C 58
C
Casa de
Montejo
To Campeche & Mexico City
Colectivos to
Plaza de Los
Americas
Combis to
Izamal
LOCK buses to
Celestún,
Izamal etc.
C 65
C 70
C 68
Municipal
C 67
San
Cristóbal
To Chichén-Itzá & Cancún
CAME
Parque
San Juan
C 69
D
C 71
Terminal de
Autobuses
C 73
C 64
C 66
C 60
C 75
E
C 74
Parque
San
Sebastián
C 77
La Ermita
N
300 metres
300 yards

Sleeping
Casa Becil **1** *D2*
Casa Bowen **2** *D2*
Casa MExilio **10** *B1*
Casa San Angel **18** *A3*
Casa San Juan **16** *D2*
Colonial **3** *B2*
Dolores Alba **4** *C4*
El Caminante **8** *D2*
Gobernador **5** *B2*
Gran **6** *C3*
Hostal Zócalo **17** *C2*
La Misión de
Fray Diego **7** *C2*
Las Monjas **9** *C2*
Margarita **11** *C2*
Medio Mundo **19** *B2*
Mucuy **12** *B3*
Nómadas Youth
Hostal **13** *B2*
Posada Toledo **14** *B3*
San José **15** *C2*
Trinidad **22** *B2*

Eating
Alberto's Continental **5** *B2*
Amaro **1** *B2*
Café Alameda **16** *B3*
Café Chocolate **23** *B3*
Café El Hoyo **15** *B2*
Café La Habana **8** *B2*
Café Petropolis **2** *D2*
El Colón Sorbetes y
Dulces Finos **10** *C3*
El Nuevo Tucho **4** *B3*
El Trapiche **3** *C2*
Flor de Santiago **14** *B1*
Italian Coffee
Company **9** *C2*
Jugos California **6** *C2*
La Casa de Frida **24** *C2*
La Vía Olympo **11** *C2*

Los Almendros **7** *B4*
Marlín Azul **18** *B2*
Marys **21** *C3*
Mérida **20** *C2*
Pórtico del Peregrino **17** *B2*
Villa Maria **13** *B1*
Vito Corleone's Pizza **19** *B2*

Bars & clubs
La Parranda **22** *C3*
Panchos **12** *B2*

The airport is 8 km from the city, bus 79 takes you to the centre. Taxis to the centre from the airport charge US$9.

Getting around You can see most of Mérida on foot. Although the city is big, there is not much to concern the tourist outside a few blocks radiating from the main plaza. The VW Beetle taxis are expensive, due to their scarcity; fares start at US$3 for a short journey. *Colectivo* buses are difficult to locate; they appear suddenly on the bigger roads in the city, you can flag them down anywhere. They terminate at the market; flat fare US$0.25.

Tourist information The main **tourist office** ① *Calle 60 y Calle 57 (just off Parque Hidalgo), daily 0800-2000*, is very helpful. There are other tourist offices on the main plaza by the Palacio Municipio and at the airport. You'll find good information online at www.mayayucatan.com.mx and www.yucatantoday.com.

Safety Mérida is a safe city, with its own **tourist police** ① *T999-930 3200*, recognizable by their brown and white uniforms.

Best time to visit During July and August, although very hot, Mérida is subject to heavy rains during the afternoon.

Background

Mérida was originally a large Maya city called Tihoo. It was conquered on 6 January 1542, by Francisco de Montejo. He dismantled the pyramids of the Maya and used the stone as the foundations for the cathedral of San Ildefonso, built 1556-1559. For the next 300 years, Mérida remained under Spanish control, unlike the rest of Mexico, which was governed from the capital. During the Caste Wars of 1847-1855, Mérida held out against the marauding forces of indigenous armies, who had defeated the Mexican army in every other city in the Yucatán Peninsula except Campeche. Reinforcements from the centre allowed the Mexicans to regain control of their city, but the price was to relinquish control of the region to Mexico City.

Sights

The city revolves around the large, shady zócalo, site of the **cathedral**, completed in 1559, the oldest cathedral in Latin America, which has an impressive baroque façade. It contains the Cristo de las Ampollas (Christ of the Blisters), a statue carved from a tree that burned for a whole night after being hit by lightning, without showing any damage at all. Placed in the church at Ichmul, it then suffered only a slight charring (hence the name) when the church was burned to the ground. To the left of the cathedral on the adjacent side of the plaza is the **Palacio de Gobierno**, built 1892. It houses a collection of enormous murals by Fernando Castro Pacheco, depicting the struggle of the Maya to integrate with the Spanish. The murals can be viewed until 2000 every day. **Casa de Montejo** is on the south side of the plaza, a 16th-century palace built by the city's founder, now a branch of Banamex. Away from the main Plaza along Calle 60 is Parque Hidalgo, a charming tree-filled square, which borders the 17th-century **Iglesia de Jesús**. A little further along Calle 60 is the **Teatro Peón Contreras**, built at the beginning of the 20th century by an Italian architect, with a neoclassical façade, marble staircase and Italian frescoes.

There are several 16th- and 17th-century churches dotted about the city: **La Mejorada**, behind the Museum of Peninsular Culture (Calle 59 between 48 and 50),

Tercera Orden, San Francisco and San Cristóbal (beautiful, in the centre). The Ermita, an 18th-century chapel with beautiful grounds, is a lonely, deserted place 10 to 15 minutes from the centre.

Museo de Antropología e Historia ① *Paseo de Montejo 485, Tue-Sat 0800-2000, Sun 0800-1400, US$3.70*, housed in the beautiful neoclassical Palacio Cantón, has an excellent collection of original Maya artefacts from various sites in the Yucatán state. The displays are very well laid out, and the explanations are all in Spanish. There are many examples of jade jewellery dredged from *cenotes*, and some examples of cosmetically deformed skulls with sharpened teeth. This is a good overview of the history of the Maya.

Museo Macay ① *Calle 60, on the main plaza, www.macay.org, daily 1000-1730, free*, has a permanent exhibition of Yucatecan artists, with temporary exhibits by contemporary local artists. Museo de Arte Popular ① *Calle 59 esq 50, Barrio de la Mejorada, Tue-Sat 0900-2000, Sun 0800-1400, free*, has a permanent exhibition of Maya art, handicrafts and clothing, with a good souvenir shop attached. Museo de la Canción Yucateca ① *Calle 57 between 50 and 48, Tue-Sun 0900-1700, US$1.50*, in the Casa de la Cultura, has an exhibition of objects and instruments relating to the history of music in the region. Pinacoteca Juan Gamboa Guzmán ① *Calle 59 between Calle 58 and 60, Tue-Sat 0800-2000, Sun 0800-1400, free*, is a gallery showing old and contemporary painting and sculpture. Fans of John Lloyd Steven's seminal travelogue *Incidents of Travel in Central America, Chiapas and Yucatán* should check out Casa Catherwood, Calle 59 between 72 and 74, daily 0900-1400 and 1700-2100, US$5. Dedicated to Steven's companion and illustrator, Mr Catherwood, this museum contains stunning colour lithographs of Mayan ruins, as they were found in the 19th century.

Around Mérida ●●❷●● ➤➤ *pp558-570. Colour map 4, A2.*

Celestún → *Phone code: 988.*

A small, dusty fishing resort west of Mérida much frequented in summer by Mexicans, Celestún stands on the spit of land separating the Río Esperanza estuary from the ocean. The long beach is relatively clean except near the town proper, with clear water ideal for swimming, although rising afternoon winds usually churn up silt and there is little shade; along the beach are many fishing boats bristling with *jimbas* (cane poles), used for catching local octopus. There are beach restaurants with showers. A plain zócalo watched over by a simple stucco church is the centre for what little happens in town. Cafés (some with hammock space for rent) spill onto the sand, from which parents watch offspring splash in the surf. Even the unmarked post office ① *Mon-Fri 0900-1300*, is a private residence the rest of the week.

The immediate region is a biosphere reserve, created to protect the thousands of migratory waterfowl who inhabit the lagoons; fish, crabs and shrimp also spawn here, and kingfishers, black hawks, wood storks and crocodiles may sometimes be glimpsed in the quieter waterways. In the winter months Celestún plays host to the largest flamingo colony in North America, perhaps more than 20,000 birds – in the summer most of the flamingoes leave Celestún for their nesting grounds in the Río Lagartos area. Boat trips to view the wildlife can be arranged at the visitor centre ① *below the river bridge 1 km back along the Mérida road* (US$60 for one six people, plus US$4 per person for the reserve entrance fees, 1½ hours). Make sure your boatman takes you through the mangrove channel and to the Baldiosera freshwater spring in addition to visiting the flamingoes. It is often possible to see flamingoes from the bridge early in the morning and the road to it may be alive with egrets, herons and pelicans. January to March is the best time to see them. It's important to wear a hat and use sunscreen. Hourly buses to Mérida's terminal at Calle 50 and 67, 0530-2000, two hours, US$4.

Progreso and around → *Phone code: 969.*
Thirty-six kilometres north of Mérida, Progreso has the nearest beach to the city. It is a slow-growing resort town, with the facilities improving to service the increasing number of US cruise ships that arrive every Wednesday. Progreso is famous for its industrial pier, which at 6 km is the longest in the world. It has been closed to the public since someone fell off the end on a moped. The beach is long and clean and the water is shallow and good for swimming.

A short bus journey (4 km) west from Progreso are **Puerto Yucalpetén** and **Chelem**. Balneario Yucalpetén has a beach with lovely shells, but also a large naval base with further construction in progress.

Five kilometres east of Progreso is another resort, **Chicxulub**; it has a narrow beach, quiet and peaceful, on which are many boats and much seaweed. Small restaurants sell fried fish by the *ración*, or kg, served with tortillas, mild chilli and *cebolla curtida* (pickled onion). Chicxulub is reputed to be the site of the crater made by a meteorite crash 65 million years ago, which caused the extinction of the dinosaurs. (The site is actually offshore on the ocean floor.) The beaches on this coast are often deserted and, between December and February, 'El Norte' wind blows in every 10 days or so, making the water turbid and bringing in cold, rainy weather.

Dzibilchaltún
① *0800-1700, US$5.80*
Halfway between Mérida and Progreso turn right for the Maya ruins of Dzibilchaltún. This unique city, according to carbon dating, was founded as early as 1000 BC. The site is in two halves, connected by a *sacbé* (sacred road). The most important building is the **Templo de Las Siete Muñecas** (Temple of the Seven Dolls), at the east end, which is partly restored. At the west end is the ceremonial centre with temples, houses and a large plaza in which the open chapel, simple and austere, sticks out like a sore thumb. The evangelizing friars had clearly hijacked a pre-Conquest sacred area in which to erect a symbol of the invading religion. At its edge is the **Cenote Xlaca** containing very clear water that is 44 m deep (you can swim in it, take mask and snorkel as it is full of fascinating fish); there's a very interesting nature trail starting halfway between the temple and the *cenote*; the trail rejoins the *sacbé* halfway along. The **museum** is at the entrance by the ticket office (site map available). *Combis* stop here en route to **Chablekal**, a village along the same road.

The Convent Route ⊜⦿⦿⦿ ↠ *pp558-570.*
The route takes in Maya villages and ruins, colonial churches, cathedrals, convents and *cenotes*. It is best to be on the road by 0800 with a full gas tank. Get on the Periférico to Ruta 18 (signs say Kanasín, not Ruta 18). At **Kanasín**, **La Susana** is known especially for local delicacies like *sopa de lima*, *salbutes* and *panuchos*. Clean, excellent service and abundant helpings at reasonable prices. Follow the signs to **Acanceh**. Here you will see the unusual combination of the Grand Pyramid, a colonial church and a modern church, all on the same small plaza (see Tlatelolco in Mexico City, page 105). About four blocks

Know your hammock

Different materials are available for hammocks. Some you might find include **sisal**, which is very strong, light, hard-wearing but rather scratchy and uncomfortable, and is identified by its distinctive smell; **cotton**, which is soft, flexible, comfortable, not as hard-wearing but, with care, is good for four or five years of everyday use. It is not possible to weave cotton and sisal together, although you may be told otherwise, so mixtures are unavailable. **Cotton/silk** mixtures are offered, but will probably be an artificial silk. **Nylon** is very strong and light but it's hot in hot weather and cold in cold weather.

Never buy your first hammock from a street vendor and never accept a packaged hammock without checking the size and quality. The surest way to judge a good hammock is by weight: 1500 g (3.3 lb) is a fine item, under 1 kg (2.2 lb) is junk (advises Alan Handleman, a US expert). Also, the finer and thinner the strands of material, the more strands there will be, and the more comfortable the hammock. The best hammocks are the so-called 3-ply, but they are difficult to find. There are three sizes: single (sometimes called *doble*), *matrimonial* and family (buy a *matrimonial* at least for comfort). If judging by end-strings, 50 would be sufficient for a child, 150 would suit a medium-sized adult, 250 a couple. Prices vary considerably so shop around and bargain hard.

---

away is the Temple of the Stuccoes, with hieroglyphs. Eight kilometres further south is **Tecoh**, with an ornate church and convent dedicated to the Virgin of the Assumption. There are some impressive carved stones around the altar. The church and convent both stand at the base of a large Maya pyramid. Nearby are the caverns of **Dzab-Náh**; you must take a guide as there are treacherous drops into *cenotes*. Next on the route is **Telchaquillo**, a small village with an austere chapel and a beautiful *cenote* in the plaza, with carved steps for easy access.

Mayapán and around
① *US$2.40.*

A few kilometres off the main road to the right you will find the Maya ruins of Mayapán, a walled city with 4000 mounds, six of which are in varying stages of restoration. Mayapán, along with Uxmal and Chichén Itzá, once formed a triple alliance, and the site is as big as Chichén Itzá, with some buildings being replicas of those at the latter site. The restoration process is ongoing; the archaeologists can be watched as they unearth more and more buildings of this large, peaceful, late-Maya site. Mayapán is easily visited by bus from Mérida (every 30 minutes from terminal at Calle 50 y 67 behind the municipal market, one hour, US$1 to Telchaquillo). It can also be reached from Oxcutzcab.

Thirty kilometres along the main road is **Tekit**, a large village containing the church of San Antonio de Padua, with many ornate statues of saints. The next village, 7 km further on, is called **Mama**, with the oldest church on the route, famous for its ornate altar and bell-domed roof. Another 9 km is **Chumayel**, where the legendary Maya document *Chilam Balam* was found. Four kilometres ahead is **Teabo**, with an impressive 17th-century church. Next comes **Tipikal**, a small village with an austere church.

Maní

Twelve kilometres further on is Maní, the most important stop on this route. Here you will find a large church, convent and museum with explanations in English, Spanish and one of the Maya languages. It was here that Fray Diego de Landa ordered important Maya documents and artefacts to be burned, during an intense period of Franciscan conversion of the Maya people to Christianity. When Diego realized his great error, he set about trying to write down all he could remember of the 27 scrolls and hieroglyphs he had destroyed, along with 5000 idols, 13 altars and 127 vases. The text, entitled *Relation of Things in Yucatán*, is still available today, unlike the artefacts. To return to Mérida, head for Ticul, to the west, then follow the main road via Muná.

Ticul and Oxkutzcab → *Colour map 4, A2. Phone code: 997.*

Eighty kilometres south of Mérida, Ticul is a small, pleasant little village known for its *huípiles*, the embroidered white dresses worn by the older Maya women. You can buy them in the tourist shops in Mérida, but the prices and quality of the ones in Ticul will be much better. It is also a good base for visiting smaller sites in the south of Yucatán state, such as Sayil, Kabah, Xlapak and Labná (see below).

Sixteen kilometres southeast of Ticul is Oxkutzcab, a good centre for catching buses to Chetumal, Muná, Mayapán and Mérida (US$2.20). It's a friendly place with a market by the plaza and a church with a 'two-dimensional' façade on the other side of the square.

Grutas de Loltún and around

① *Tue-Sun 0930, 1100, 1230 and 1400. US$3 with obligatory guide, 1 hr 20 mins. Recommended. Caretaker may admit tours on Mon, but there is no lighting.*

Nearby, to the south, are the caverns and pre-Columbian vestiges at Loltún (supposedly extending for 8 km). Take pickup (US$0.30) or truck from the market going to Cooperativa (an agricultural town). For return, flag down a passing truck. Alternatively, take a taxi, US$10 (can be visited from Labná on a tour from Mérida). The area around Ticul and Oxkutzcab is intensively farmed with citrus fruits, papayas and mangoes. After Oxkutzcab on Route 184 is **Tekax** with restaurant **La Ermita** serving excellent Yucatecan dishes at reasonable prices. From Tekax a paved road leads to the ruins of **Chacmultún**. From the top you have a beautiful view. There is a caretaker. All the towns between Muná and Peto, 14 km northeast of Oxkutzcab off Route 184, have large old churches. Beyond the Peto turn-off the scenery is scrub and swamp as far as the Belizean border.

The Puuc Route

Taking in the four sites of Kabah, Sayil, Xlapak and Labná, as well as Uxmal, this journey explores the hilly (or *puuc* in Maya) region to the south of Mérida. All five sites can be visited in a day on the 'Ruta Puuc' bus, which departs from the first-class bus station in Mérida every day at 0800, US$11, entry to sites not included. This is a good whistle-stop tour, but does not give you much time at each of the ruins, but five sites in one day is normally enough for most enthusiasts; if you want to spend longer seeing these sites, stay overnight in Ticul.

Kabah

① *0800-1700, US$3.*

On either side of the main road, 37 km south of Uxmal and often included in tours of the latter, are the ruins of Kabah. On one side there is a fascinating **Palace of Masks**

(*Codz-Poop*), whose façade bears the image of Chac, mesmerically repeated 260 times, the number of days in the Almanac Year. Each mask is made up of 30 units of mosaic stone. Even the central chamber is entered via a huge Chac mask whose curling snout forms the doorstep. On the other side of this wall, beneath the figure of the ruler, Kabal, are impressive carvings on the door arches, which depict a man about to be killed, pleading for mercy, and two men duelling. This side of the road is mostly reconstructed; across the road the outstanding feature is a reconstructed arch marking the start of the *sacbé* (sacred road), which leads all the way to Uxmal, and several stabilized, but unclimbable mounds of collapsed buildings being renovated. The style is Classic Puuc.

Sayil, Xlapak and Labná
① *Entrance US$3 at each site.*
Sayil means 'The Place of the Ants'. Dating from AD 800-1000, this site has an interesting palace, which in its day included 90 bathrooms for some 350 people. The simple, elegant colonnade is reminiscent of the architecture of ancient Greece. The central motif on the upper part of the façade is a broad mask with huge fangs, flanked by two serpents surrounding the grotesque figure of a descending deity. From the upper level of the palace you can see a tiny ruin on the side of a mountain called the Nine Masks.

Thirteen kilometres from Sayil, the ruins of Xlapak have not been as extensively restored as the others in this region. There are 14 mounds and three partially restored pyramids.

Labná has a feature that ranks it among the most outstanding sites of the Puuc region: a monumental arch connecting two groups of buildings (now in ruins), which displays an architectural concept unique to this region. Most Maya arches are purely structural, but the one at Labná has been constructed for aesthetic purposes, running right through the façade and clearly meant to be seen from afar. The two façades on either side of the arch differ greatly in their decoration; the one at the entrance is beautifully decorated with delicate latticework and stone carving imitating the wood or palm-frond roofs of Maya huts.

Uxmal ●❷❸❸ ➤ *pp558-570. Colour map 4, A2.*

→ *Phone code: 997.*
① *Daily 0800-1700, US$9.50 including light and sound show; rental of translation equipment US$2.50. Shows are at 2000 in summer and 1900 in winter. Mixed reports. Guides available with 1½ hour tours. Tours in Spanish US$40, in English, French, German and Italian US$45.* ➤ *For transport to Uxmal, see page 569.*
Built during the Classic period, Uxmal is the most famous of the ruins in the Puuc region. The characteristic features of Maya cities in this region are the quadrangular layout of the buildings, set on raised platforms, and an artificially created underground water-storage system. The **Pyramid of the Sorcerer** is an unusual oval-shaped pyramid set on a large rectangular base; there is evidence that five stages of building were used in its construction. The pyramid is 30 m tall, with two temples at the top. The **Nunnery** is set around a large courtyard, with some fine masks of Chac, the rain god, on the corners of the buildings. The east building of the Nunnery is decorated with double-headed serpents on its cornices. There are some plumed serpents in relief, in excellent condition, on the façade of the west building. The **House of the Governor** is 100 m long, and is considered one of the most outstanding buildings in all of Mesoamerica. Two arched passages divide the building into three distinct sections that would probably have been

covered over. Above the central entrance is an elaborate trapezoidal motif, with a string of Chaac masks interwoven into a flowing, undulating serpent-like shape extending to the façade's two corners. The stately two-headed jaguar throne in front of the structure suggests a royal or administrative function. The **House of the Turtles** is sober by comparison, its simple walls adorned with carved turtles on the upper cornice, above a short row of tightly packed columns, which resemble the Maya *palapas*, made of sticks with a thatched roof, still used today. The **House of the Doves** is the oldest and most damaged of the buildings at Uxmal. It is still impressive: a long, low platform of wide columns topped by clusters of roof combs, whose similarity to dovecotes gave the building its name.

Izamal and around ⊖🕖⊖◐⊜ ➤ *pp558-570. Colour map 4, A3.*

➔ *Phone code: 988.*
Sixty-eight kilometres east of Mérida is the friendly little town of Izamal. Once a major Classic Maya religious site founded by the priest Itzamná, Izamal became one of the centres of the Spanish attempt to Christianize the Maya.

Fray Diego de Landa, the historian of the Spanish conquest of Mérida (of whom there is a statue in the town), founded the huge **convent** and **church**, which now face the main **Plaza de la Constitución**. This building, constructed on top of a Maya pyramid, was begun in 1549 and has the second largest atrium in the world. If you carefully examine the walls that surround the magnificent atrium, you will notice that some of the faced stones are embellished with carvings of Maya origin, confirming that, when they had toppled the pre-Columbian structures, the Spaniards re-used the material to create the imported architecture. There is also a throne built for the Pope's visit in 1993. The image of the Inmaculada Virgen de la Concepción in the magnificent church was made the Reina de Yucatán in 1949, and the patron saint of the state in 1970. Just 2½ blocks away, visible from the convent across a second square and signposted, are the ruins of a great mausoleum known as the **Kinich-Kakmo pyramid** ① *0800-1700, free, entrance next to the tortilla factory.* You climb the first set of stairs to a broad, tree-covered platform, at the end of which is a further pyramid (still under reconstruction). From the top there is an excellent view of the town and surrounding *henequén* and citrus plantations. Kinich-Kakmo is 195 m long, 173 m wide and 36 m high, the fifth highest in Mexico. In all, 20 Maya structures have been identified in Izamal, several on Calle 27. Another startling feature about the town is that the entire colonial centre, including the convent, the arcaded government offices on Plaza de la Constitución and the arcaded second square, is painted a rich yellow ochre, giving it the nickname of the 'golden city'.

From Izamal you can go by bus to **Cenotillo**, where there are several fine *cenotes* within easy walking distance from the town (avoid the one *in* town), especially **Ucil**, excellent for swimming, and **La Unión**. Take the same bus as for Izamal from Mérida. Past Cenotillo is Espita and then a road forks left to Tizimín (see page 557).

The cemetery of **Hoctún**, on the Mérida-Chichén road, is also worth visiting; indeed it is impossible to miss, there is an 'Empire State Building' on the site. Take a bus from Mérida (last bus back 1700) to see extensive ruins at **Aké**, an unusual structure. Public transport in Mérida is difficult: from an unsigned stop on the corner of Calle 53 y 50, some buses to Tixkokob and Ekmul continue to Aké; ask the driver.

ⓘ *Daily 0800-1730, US$9.50 including light and sound show, free bag storage, free for Mexicans on Sun and holidays, when it is incredibly crowded; you may leave and re-enter as often as you like on day of issue. Guided tours US$40 per group of any size; it is best to try and join one, many languages available. Best to arrive before 1030 when the mass of tourists arrives. There's a tourist centre at the entrance to the ruins with a restaurant and small museum, bookshop and souvenir shop with exchange facilities. Drinks, snacks and toilets are available at the entrance and at the cenote. The site is hot, take a hat, suncream, sunglasses, shoes with good grip and drinking water.*

Chichén Itzá means 'mouth of the well of the water-sorcerer' and is one of the most spectacular of Maya sites. The Castillo, a giant stepped pyramid dominates the site, watched over by Chacmool, a Maya fertility god who reclines on a nearby structure. The city was built by the Maya in late Classic times (AD 600-900). By the end of the 10th century, the city was more or less abandoned. It was re-established in the 11th to 12th centuries, but much debate surrounds by whom. Whoever the people were, a comparison of some of the architecture with that of Tula, north of Mexico City (see page 156), indicates they were heavily influenced by the Toltecs of Central Mexico.

The major buildings in the north half display a Toltec influence. Dominating them is **El Castillo** ⓘ *1100-1500, 1600-1700, closed if raining*, its top decorated by the symbol of Quetzalcoatl/Kukulcán, the plumed serpent god. The balustrade of the 91 stairs up each of the four sides is also decorated at its base by the head of a plumed, open-mouthed serpent. The interior ascent of 61 steep and narrow steps leading to a chamber is currently closed; the red-painted jaguar that probably served as the throne of the high priest once burned bright, its eyes of jade, its fangs of flint.

There is a **ball court** with grandstand and towering walls, each set with a projecting ring of stone high up; at eye-level is a relief showing the decapitation of the winning captain (sacrifice was an honour; some theories, however, maintain that it was the losing captain who was killed). El Castillo stands at the centre of the northern half of the site, and almost at a right angle to its northern face runs the *sacbé* (sacred road), to the **Cenote Sagrado** (Well of Sacrifice). Into the Cenote Sagrado were thrown valuable propitiatory objects of all kinds, animals and human sacrifices. The well was first dredged by Edward H Thompson, the US Consul in Mérida, between 1904 and 1907; he accumulated a vast quantity of objects in pottery, jade, copper and gold. In 1962 the well was explored again by an expedition sponsored by the National Geographic Society and some 4000 further artefacts were recovered, including beads, polished jade, lumps of *copal* resin, small bells, a statuette of rubber latex, another of wood, and a quantity of animal and human bones. Another *cenote*, the Cenote Xtoloc, was probably used as a water supply. To the east of El Castillo is the **Templo de los Guerreros** (Temple of the Warriors) with its famous reclining **Chacmool** statue. This pyramidal platform is closed off to avoid erosion.

Chichén Viejo (Old Chichén), where the Maya buildings of the earlier city are found, lies about 500 m by path from the main clearing. The famous **El Caracol**, or Observatory, is included in this group, as is the **Casa de las Monjas** (Nunnery). A footpath to the right of the Casa de las Monjas leads to the **Templo de los Tres Dinteles** (Temple of the Three Lintels) after 30 minutes' walking. It requires at least one day to see the many pyramids, temples, ball courts and palaces, all of them adorned with astonishing sculptures. Excavation and renovation is still going on. Interesting birdlife and iguanas can also be seen around the ruins.

Chichén Itzá

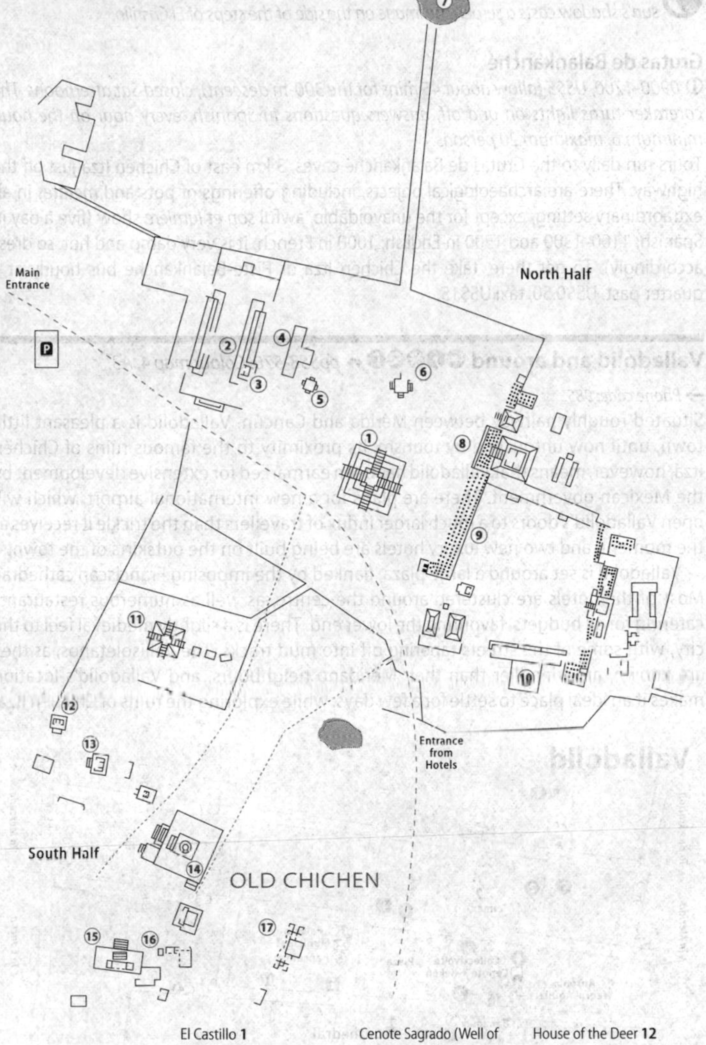

Main Entrance

North Half

P

Entrance from Hotels

South Half

OLD CHICHEN

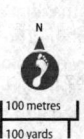

N

100 metres

100 yards

El Castillo **1**
Ball Court **2**
Temple of the Jaguar **3**
Platform of the Skulls
  (Tzompantli) **4**
Platform of Eagles **5**
Platform of Venus **6**

Cenote Sagrado (Well of
  Sacrifice) **7**
Temple of the Warriors
  & Chacmool Statue **8**
Group of a Thousand
  Columns **9**
Market **10**
Tomb of the High Priest **11**

House of the Deer **12**
Red House **13**
El Caracol (Observatory) **14**
Casa de las Monjas
  (Nunnery) **15**
'Church' **16**
Akabdzilo **17**

> *On the morning and afternoon of the spring and autumn equinoxes, the alignment of the sun's shadow casts a serpentine image on the side of the steps of El Castillo.*

Grutas de Balankanché

ⓘ *0900-1700, US$5 (allow about 45 mins for the 300-m descent), closed Sat afternoons. The caretaker turns lights on and off, answers questions in Spanish, every hour on the hour, minimum 6, maximum 20 persons.*

Tours run daily to the Grutas de Balankanché caves, 3 km east of Chichén Itzá just off the highway. There are archaeological objects, including offerings of pots and *metates* in an extraordinary setting, except for the unavoidable, awful *son et lumière* show (five a day in Spanish; 1100, 1300 and 1500 in English; 1000 in French; it is very damp and hot, so dress accordingly). To get there, take the Chichén Itzá or Pisté-Balankanché bus hourly at a quarter past, US$0.50, taxi US$15.

Valladolid and around ⊜❼✳❷❶❶ ▸ *pp558-570. Colour map 4, A3.*

▸ *Phone code: 985.*

Situated roughly halfway between Mérida and Cancún, Valladolid is a pleasant little town, until now untouched by tourism. Its proximity to the famous ruins of Chichén Itzá, however, means that Valladolid has been earmarked for extensive development by the Mexican government. There are plans for a new international airport, which will open Valladolid's doors to a much larger influx of travellers than the trickle it receives at the moment, and two new luxury hotels are being built on the outskirts of the town.

Valladolid is set around a large plaza, flanked by the imposing Franciscan cathedral. Most of the hotels are clustered around the centre, as well as numerous restaurants catering for all budgets, favouring the lower end. There is a slightly medieval feel to the city, with some of the streets tapering off into mud tracks. The Vallisoletanos, as they are known, are friendlier than their Meridano neighbours, and Valladolid's location makes it an ideal place to settle for a few days, while exploring the ruins of Chichén Itzá,

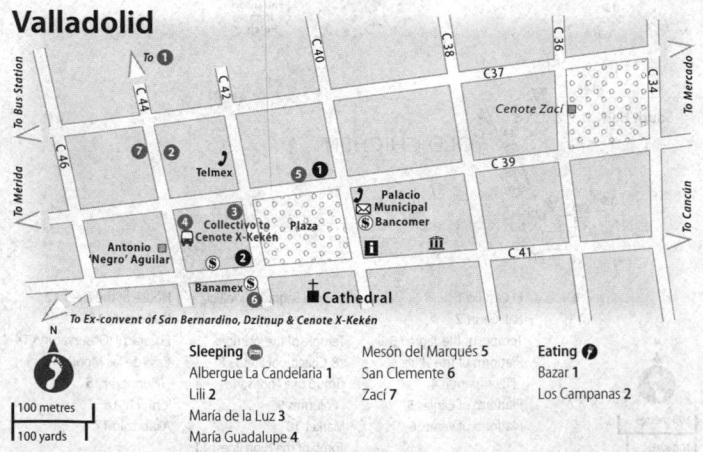

Valladolid

Sleeping		Mesón del Marqués **5**	Eating
Albergue La Candelaria **1**		San Clemente **6**	Bazar **1**
Lili **2**		Zací **7**	Los Campanas **2**
María de la Luz **3**			
María Guadalupe **4**			

To Ex-convent of San Bernardino, Dzitnup & Cenote X-Kekén

100 metres / 100 yards

the fishing village of Río Lagartos on the north coast, and the three beautiful *cenotes* in the area, one of which is right in the town itself, on Calle 36 y 39.

The **tourist office** ① *southeast corner of the plaza*, is not very helpful but they give a useful map. Much more helpful information can be obtained from **Antonio 'Negro' Aguilar** ① *Calle 44 No 195*. Something of a local celebrity, he was a baseball champion in the 1950s and 60s, playing for the Leones de Yucatán and the Washington Senators. Now he runs a shop selling sports equipment, rents bicycles and rents very cheap accommodation (see Sleeping, page 562). He is glad to offer information on any of the tourist attractions in the area; if cycling around, he will personally draw you a map of the best route you should take. Antonio can also help organize tours in a minivan to the ruins at Ek-Balam, minimum four people, US$3 per person.

Cenote Zací ① *Calle 36 between Calle 37 and 39, daily 0800-1800, US$2, half price for children*, right in town, is an artificially lit *cenote* where you can swim, except when it is occasionally prohibited due to algae in the water. There is a thatched-roof restaurant and lighted promenades. A small town **museum** ① *Calle 41, free*, housed in Santa Ana church, shows the history of rural Yucatán and has some exhibits from recent excavations at the ruins of Ek-Balam.

Seven kilometres from Valladolid is the beautiful **Cenote X-Kekén** ① *daily 0800-1800, US$2.50*, at **Dzitnup**, the name by which it is more commonly known. It is stunningly lit with electric lights, the only natural light source being a tiny hole in the cavernous ceiling dripping with stalactites. Swimming is excellent, the water is cool and refreshing, although reported to be a little dirty, and harmless bats zip around overhead. Exploratory walks can also be made through the many tunnels leading off the *cenote*, for which you will need a torch. *Colectivos* leave when full from in front of **Hotel María Guadalupe**, US$1, they return until 1800, after which you will have to get a taxi back to Valladolid, US$4. Alternatively, hire a bicycle from Antonio Aguilar (see above) and cycle there, 25 minutes. Antonio will explain the best route before you set off. There is also the newly discovered, easily reached *cenote* close by, called **Samulá** ① *US$2.25*.

Ek-Balam
① *Daily 0800-1700, US$2.50.*
Twenty-five kilometres north of Valladolid are the recently opened Maya ruins of Ek-Balam, meaning 'Black Jaguar'. The ruins contain an impressive series of temples, sacrificial altars and residential buildings grouped around a large central plaza. The main temple, known as 'The Tower', is an immaculate seven-tiered staircase leading up to a flattened area with the remains of a temple. The views are stunning, and because they are not on the tourist trail, these ruins can be viewed at leisure, without the presence of hordes of tour groups from Cancún. To get there by car, take Route 295 north out of Valladolid. Just after the village of Temozón, take the turning on the right for Santa Rita. The ruins are some 5 km further on. A recommended way for those without a car is to hire a bike, take it on the roof of a *colectivo* leaving for Temozón from outside the Hotel María Guadalupe, and ask to be dropped off at the turning for Ek-Balam. From there, cycle the remaining 12 km to the ruins. There are also minivans to Ek-Balam run by Antonio Aguilar (see above).

Río Lagartos and around → *Colour map 4, A3.*
Tizimín is a dirty, scruffy little town en route to Río Lagartos, where you will have to change buses. If stuck, there are several cheap *posadas* and restaurants, but with frequent buses to Río Lagartos, there should be no need to stay the night here.

Río Lagartos is an attractive little fishing village on the north coast of Yucatán state, whose main attraction is the massive biosphere reserve containing thousands of pink flamingos, as well as 250 other species of bird. The people of Río Lagartos are extremely friendly and very welcoming to tourists. The only route is on the paved road from Valladolid; access from Cancún is by boat only, a journey mainly made by tradesmen ferrying fish to the resort. Development in Río Lagartos, however, is on the horizon.

Boat trips to see the flamingo reserve can be easily arranged by walking down to the harbour and taking your pick from the many offers you'll receive from boatmen. You will get a longer trip with fewer people, due to the decreased weight in the boat. As well as flamingoes, there are 250 other species of bird, some very rare, in the 47-sq-km reserve. Make sure your boatman takes you to the larger colony of flamingos near **Las Coloradas** (15 km), recognizable by a large salt mound on the horizon, rather than the smaller groups of birds along the river. Early morning boat trips can be arranged in Río Lagartos to see the flamingos (US$35, in eight to nine seater, 2½ to four hours, cheaper in a five-seater, fix the price before embarking; in mid-week few people go so there is no chance of negotiating, but boat owners are more flexible on where they go; at weekends it is very busy, so it may be easier to get a party together and reduce costs). Check before going whether the flamingos are there; they usually nest here during May and June and stay through July and August (although salt mining is disturbing their habitat).

◉ State of Yucatán listings

For Sleeping and Eating price codes and other relevant information, see Essentials pages 45-48.

◉ Sleeping

Mérida *p545, map p546*

The prices of hotels are not determined by their location with budget hotels close to the plaza and the better hotels often further away. If booking into a central hotel, always try to get a room away from the street side, as noise on the narrow streets begins as early as 0500.

LL Hacienda Xcanatún, Km 12, Carretera Mérida–Progreso, T999-941 0273, www.xcanatun.com. Carefully restored hacienda, 10 mins out of town, relaxed atmosphere, full breakfast included, restaurant, **Casa de Piedra**, possibly the best in Mérida without an expensive price tag, located in a converted machine room with ceilings high enough to give you vertigo, live music Thu, Fri and Sat. Highly recommended.

L Hotel Casa San Angel, Paseo de Montejo No 1 with Calle 49, T999-928 1800, www.hotelcasasanangel.com. An old colonial building with gorgeous, high-ceilinged rooms on the ground floor and more rooms upstairs. Quiet, tranquil relaxation pool, restaurant and craft shop. Pleasant.

AL Colonial, Calle 62 No 476, on the corner of Calle 57, T999-923 6444, www.hotelcolonial.com.mx. Great location 2 blocks from the plaza. Small but comfortable rooms with TV and a/c, with small pool. Busy and popular with friendly and efficient staff. Restaurant serves good buffet meals, including a highly recommended breakfast. Sometimes gives good discounts in low season.

AL Gobernador, Calle 59 No 535, corner of 66, T999-930 4141, www.gobernador merida.com.mx. Good clean hotel with 2 small pools. All rooms with a/c, cable TV and phone. 'Executive' rooms are better. Restaurant offers buffet breakfast. Promotional rates and free Wi-Fi. Recommended.

AL La Misión de Fray Diego, Calle 61 No 524 between 64 and 66, T01-800-221-0599, www.lamisiondefraydiego.com. Very pleasant colonial-style hotel situated around

2 shady courtyards. Section nearest the road is original 17th century, formerly connected to the convent behind. Mini-bar and TV in all rooms, small pool and restaurant.

A Casa MExilio, Calle 68, between C 59 and 57, T999-928 2505, casamexilio@earthlink.net. This fabulous, old-fashioned colonial building has 3 floors complete with antique sitting room, lush courtyard and a pleasant pool. Part of a bygone world and a soothing place to stay. Breakfast included. Friendly hosts. Recommended.

A Medio Mundo, Calle 55, No 533 between 64 and 66, T999-924 5472, www.hotelmediomundo.com. Renovated old home now a charming hotel with 12 tasteful, high-ceiling rooms, lush garden patio and swimming pool. Friendly, pleasant and quaint. Nice handicraft shop forms part of the hotel. Recommended.

B Casa San Juan, Calle 62 No 545A between 69 and 71, T999-986 2937, www.casasanjuan.com. This restored 19th-century house, close to the bus station, has a pleasant, tranquil atmosphere. The multilingual owner is helpful and friendly, the rooms are large, and prices include American breakfast. Book ahead in high season.

B Dolores Alba, Calle 63 No 464 between 52 and 54, T999-858 1555, www.doloresalba.com. This large, modern hotel has 2 sections and price bands. The more comfortable and expensive rooms are recently remodelled and overlook the pool and courtyard. The cheaper rooms are slightly smaller and have no views. Cool, airy atmosphere and a nice pool. All rooms have are a/c, and there's a sister establishment in Chichén Itzá.

B Posada Toledo, Calle 58 No 487 esq 57, T999-923 1690, hptoledo@prodigy.net.mx. This charming old hotel has a strong, if slightly tired, character. Elegant, high-ceiled rooms surround a plant-filled courtyard, all adorned with interesting woodwork and occasionally weathered, antique furniture. Cheap breakfast, parking (US$4) and colour TV.

B-C Gran Hotel, Parque Hidalgo, Calle 60 No 496, with Calle 59, T999-923 6963, www.granhoteldemerida.com.mx. A great place to stay with a good atmosphere. Popular with the stars of film and stage, and politicians including Fidel Castro. All rooms are clean and have a/c, TV, hot water and phone, but not all have windows. Free parking.

B-D Trinidad, Calle 62 No 464 esq 55, T999-923 2033, www.hotelestrinidad.com. This old house, popular with budget travellers and backpackers, has a relaxed, friendly vibe. Pool table, DVDs, courtyard and rooftop jacuzzi – the perfect way to unwind after a hard day pounding the streets. Continental breakfast included in the price. Simply lovely and highly recommended.

C-E Nómadas Youth Hostal, Calle 62 No 433, end of Calle 51, 5 blocks north of the plaza, T999-924 5223, www.nomadastravel.com. A clean and friendly hostel with private rooms and dorms. General services include hot water, full kitchen, drinking water, hammocks and internet. Owner Raúl speaks English and is very helpful. Good value and a great place to meet other travellers. Free salsa classes every night. Pool opening in 2009. Live 'trova' music Mon, Wed and Fri. Recommended.

D Casa Becil, Calle 67 No 550 C, between 66 and 68, T999-924 6764, hotelcasabecil@yahoo.com.mx. The rooms are bright and clean, if simple. They all have fan, bath, hot water and cable TV. The owner is English-speaking and hospitable. There's also a communal kitchen. Conveniently located for the bus station. Recommended.

D Casa Bowen, restored colonial house, corner of Calle 66, No 521-B, esq 65, T999-928 6109. Open 24 hrs, if locked ring bell. The staff are friendly and English-speaking, and rooms have bath and hot water, cheaper with fan. Often full at weekends. Avoid rooms overlooking the main street – they're noisy. Nicely located between the **CAME** 1st-class bus terminal and the centre.

D Hotel El Caminante, Calle 64 No 539, between 65 and 67, T999-923 6730.

Motel-style joint with parking, close to the bus station. Large rooms with 1 or 2 double beds, bath, colour TV, hot water 24 hrs. Clean and good value, if unexciting.
D Las Monjas, Calle 66A No 509 between 61 and 63, T999-928 6632. Simple, family-run lodgings. Clean, quiet, friendly and good value. Can organize tours. Recommended.
D Margarita, Calle 66 No 506 and 63, T999-923 7236. With shower, clean, good, rooms a bit dark and noisy downstairs, cheaper rooms for 5 (3 beds), parking, friendly, excellent value. Some rooms have TV and a/c (pricier).
D Mucuy, Calle 57 No 481, between 56 and 58, T999-928 5193, www.mucuy.com. Good, but 1st-floor rooms are very hot. There's a pool and garden, hot water and optional TV. Run by a lovely English-speaking, elderly woman and her daughter. Highly recommended.
D San José, west of plaza on Calle 63 No 503 with 64 and 66, T999-928 6657, san_jose92@latinmail.com. Bath, hot water, basic, clean, friendly, rooms on top floor are baked by the sun, one of the cheapest, popular with locals, will store luggage, good cheap meals available, local speciality *poc chuc*.
D-E Hostal Zócalo, on the south of the plaza, T999-930 9562, hostel_zocalo@yahoo.com. Popular hostel with economical rooms and big, clean dormitories. There's TV, DVD, kitchen, laundry and internet. Full breakfast included with the private rooms. Friendly management and good location.

Camping
Trailer Park Rainbow, Km 8, on the road to Progreso, T999-926 1026 US$18 for 1 or 2, hot showers, all facilities and good bus connection into town. Reports of excessive charging for use of amenities.

Celestún *p548*
LL Hotel Eco Paraíso Xixim, Km 10 off the old Sisal Hwy, T988-916 2100, www.ecoparaiso.com. In coconut grove on

edge of reserve, pool, tours to surrounding area including flamingos, turtle nesting, etc.
C Gutiérrez, Calle 12 (the Malecón) No 127, T988-916 2609. Large beds, fans, views, clean.
C San Julio, Calle 12 No 92, T988-916 2062. Large bright rooms and clean bathrooms, owner knowledgeable about the area.

Progreso and around *p549*
B Progreso, Calle 29 No 142, T969-935 0039. Simple rooms in the centre.
B Tropical Suites, Calle 19 No 143, T969-935 1263. Suites and rooms with cable TV, a/c, sea views.

Ticul and Oxkutzcab *p551*
B Motel Bugambilias, Calle 23 No 291, Ticul, T997-972 1368. Clean, basic rooms.
B Sierra Sosa, Calle 26, near zócalo, Ticul, T997-972 0008. Cheap rooms that are dungeon-like, but friendly, clean and helpful.
C Trujeque, Calle 48 No 102-A, Oxkutzcab, T997-975 0568. A/c, TV, clean, good value, discount for stays over a week.
D Casa de Huéspedes, near bus terminal, Oxkutzcab. Large rooms with bath, TV, fan, friendly. Recommended.
D Hotel Rosalía, Calle 54 No 101 Oxkutzcab, T997-975 0167, turn right out of bus station, right again. Double room, shower, cable TV.

Uxmal *p552*
There is no village at Uxmal, just the hotels. For cheap accommodation, go to Ticul, 28 km away (see above).
L Hacienda Uxmal, T997-976 2012, www.mayaland.com/HaciendaUxmal, 300-400 m from ruins. Good, efficient and relaxing, good Yucatecan restaurant, a/c, gardens, pool.
L The Lodge at Uxmal, at entrance to ruins, T997-976 2102, www.mayaland.com/LodgeUxmal. Same owners as **Hacienda Uxmal**. Comfortable, a/c, bath, TV, fair restaurant.
A Misión Uxmal, 1-2 km from ruins on Mérida road, Km 78, T997-976 2022, www.hoteles mision.com.mx. Rooms a bit dark, with a pool.

B Rancho Uxmal, Carretera Mérida – Uxmal, Km 70, about 4 km north of ruins, T997-977 0254. Comfortable rooms, hot and cold water, camping for US$5, pool, reasonable food but not cheap (no taxis to get there).

C-E Sacbé Hostel, at Km 127 on Hwy 261, T997-858 1281. A mix of private rooms (private bath), dorms and campsite, with space for hammocks, and solar-powered showers, with breakfast and dinner for a little more.

Camping

No camping allowed at the site, but there is a campsite at **Sacbé Hostel**, see above. 2nd-class buses from Mérida to Campeche pass by, ask to be let out at the **Campo de Baseball**. French and Mexican owners, beautiful park, fastidiously clean and impeccably managed. 9 electric hook-ups (US$7-10 for motor home according to size), big area for tents (US$2.75 per person with tent), *palapas* for hammocks (US$2.65 per person), for cars pay US$1, showers, toilets, clothes-washing facilities, also 3 bungalows with ceiling fan (**E**), breakfast, vegetarian lunch and dinner available (US$2.65 each). Highly recommended.

Izamal and around *p553*

C Macan-Che, Calle 22 No 305 between 33 and 35, T988-954 0287, www.macanche.com. 4 blocks north of plaza, pleasant bungalows, breakfast. Recommended.

Chichén Itzá *p554*

LL Hacienda Chichén, T999-924 8407, www.haciendachichen.com. Luxury resort and spa, close to the ruins, with tasteful rooms, suites and bungalows. There's a garden, library and restaurant, all contained by historic colonial grounds.

L-AL Villas Arqueológicas, T997-974 6020, Apdo Postal 495, Mérida. Close to the ruins. Pool, tennis, restaurant (expensive and poor). Both are on the other side of the fenced-off ruins from the bus stop; you cannot walk

through ruins, either walk all the way round, or take taxi (US$1-1.50).

AL Hotel Chichén Itzá, Pisté, T999-851 0022, www.mayaland.com. 3 types of rooms and tariffs. The best are clean, tasteful, overlook the garden and have a/c, internet, phone and fridge. Cheaper rooms (**A**) overlook the street.

B Dolores Alba, Km 122, T985-858 1555, www.doloresalba.com. Small, Spanish-owned hotel, 2.5 km on the road to Puerto Juárez (bus passes it), 40 clean bungalows with shower, a/c and cable TV. Pool, restaurant, English is spoken. Sister hotel in Mérida.

B Pirámide Inn, 1.5 km from ruins, at the Chichén end of Pisté, Km 117, T999-851 0115, www.chichen.com. This long-standing Pisté favourite has been remodelled. It has many clean, comfortable rooms, a pool, hammocks and *palapas*. Temazcal available, book 24 hrs in advance. Camping costs US$5, or US$15 with a car. Friendly owner, speaks English.

B Posada Olalde, 100 m from the main road at the end of Calle 6, between Calle 15 and 17. This lovely, family-run hotel has a handful of economical rooms and basic Yucatecan *cabanas* built the old-fashioned way. There's a lush, tranquil garden and the Mayan owners are kind and friendly.

B Stardust Posada Annex, Pisté, about 2 km before the ruins if coming from Mérida (taxi to ruins US$2.50). Simple, basic rooms and a range of tariffs to suit your budget. Slightly run-down, but acceptable. There's also a pool and an average restaurant.

C Posada Maya, Calle 8 No 70, just off the main road. Small, simple rooms, desperately in need of a deep clean. However, there's space to sling a hammock if you're terribly impoverished (**F**).

Valladolid *p556, map p556*

A María de la Luz, Calle 42 No 193-C, Plaza Principal, T985-856 1181, www.mariadeluz hotel.com. Good clean rooms, tours to Chichén Itzá and Río Lagartos, excellent restaurant.

A Mesón del Marqués, Calle 39 with Calle 40 and 42, north side of Plaza Principal, T985-856

2073, www.mesondelmarques.com. Housed in a handsome old colonial edifice, this hotel has 90 tasteful rooms, all with a/c and cable TV. There's a swimming pool, Wi-Fi, garden and laundry service. Recommended.

A Zací, Calle 44 No 191, T985-856 2167. A clean, comfortable mid-range option. Rooms have a/c (cheaper with fan) and TV. There's a pool.

B María Guadalupe, Calle 44 No 198, T985-856 2068. Simple, clean rooms with fan. Good value, hot water, washing facilities. Recommended.

B San Clemente, Calle 42 No 206, T985-856 2208, www.hotelsanclemente.com.mx. Many clean, comfortable rooms with a/c (cheaper with fan) and cable TV. There's a pool, restaurant, garden and free parking. Recommended.

C Antonio 'Negro' Aguilar rents rooms for 2, 3 or 4 people. The best budget deal in the town for 2 or more, clean, spacious rooms on a quiet street, garden, volleyball/basketball court. The rooms are on Calle 41 No 225, before the Maya Hotel, but you need to book them at Aguilar's shop on Calle 44 No 195, T985-856 2125. If the shop is closed, knock on the door of the house on the right of the shop.

C Lili, Calle 44 No 192, T985-856 2163. Large, basic rooms with cable TV and fan. There's hot water and the management is friendly.

D Albergue La Candelaria, Calle 35 No 201-F, T985-856 2267, candelaria_hostel@hot mail.com. Good cheap option, especially for solo travellers. Single-sex dorms with fan, clean, hot water, kitchen, washing facilities, hammocks out the back in the garden, TV room. Recommended.

Río Lagartos and around *p557*
D Tere and Miguel, near the harbour (ask at the bus terminal). 3 rooms for rent, very nicely furnished, double and triple rooms, 1 with an extra hammock, sea views.

⊕ Eating

Mérida *p545, map p546*
There are a number of taco stands, pizzerías and sandwich places in Pasaje Picheta, a small plaza off the Palacio de Gobierno.

₥₥₥ Alberto's Continental, Calle 64 No 482 corner Calle 57. Yucatecan, Lebanese and international food, mouth-watering steaks and seafood, all inside a colonial mansion. Highly recommended.

₥₥₥ Casa de Piedra 'Xcanatún', in Hacienda Xcanatún (see Sleeping). Km 12 Carretera Mérida–Progreso, T999-941 0213. Fine dining, best restaurant in the area (although a bit out of town). Popular with locals. Reserve if possible. Highly recommended.

₥₥₥ Villa María, Calle 59 No 553 and Calle 68, T999-923 3357, www.villamariamerida.com. Classical music spills over the white tablecloths at this sophisticated, fine-dining establishment. The interior is beautiful and they serve French, Mediterranean and Mexican cuisine.

₥₥-₥ Café La Habana, Calle 59 y Calle 62. Neither the coffee nor the food is fantastic, but it's OK for a snack. A fine spot for people-watching, open 24 hrs. Free Wi-Fi.

₥ El Nuevo Tucho, Calle 60 near University. Good local dishes, mostly meat and fish, and occasional live music. Healthy and extensive drinks menu. Evening entertainment also.

₥ La Casa de Frida, Calle 61, between 66 and 66A, www.lacasadefrida.com.mx. Open Mon-Sat 1800-2200. Frida Kahlo-themed restaurant in a colourful courtyard setting, traditional Mexican cuisine, including mole and *chiles en nogada*.

₥ Los Almendros, Calle 50A No 493 esq 59. Housed in a high-vaulted, white-washed thatched barn, this award-winning restaurant specializes in 1st-rate traditional Yucatecan cuisine, serving tasty dishes like *pollo pibil* and *poc chuc*. Confusingly, the entrance is through the car park.

₥ Pórtico del Peregrino, Calle 57 between 60 and 62. Dining indoors or in an attractive leafy courtyard, excellent food.

¶-¶ Amaro, Calle 59 No 507 between 60 and 62, near the plaza. Open late daily. With open courtyard and covered patio, good food, especially vegetarian, try *chaya* drink from the leaf of the *chaya* tree; their curry, avocado pizza and home-made bread are also very good.

¶-¶ Café Chocolate, Calle 60 No 442 y Calle 49, T999-928 5113, www.cafe-chocolate.com.mx. This new café and art space does good *mole*, as well as an excellent breakfast buffet, a lunchtime menu and evening meals. They also have home-made fresh bread and pasta, and an excellent selection of fruit drinks and teas. Cosy and classy at the same time, with antique furniture, free Wi-Fi and art and photography exhibitions in beautiful surroundings, with sofas indoors or outdoor courtyard seating. Highly recommended.

¶-¶ Flor de Santiago, Calle 70 No 478, between 57 and 59. Reputedly the oldest restaurant in Mérida. There's a cafeteria and bakery in one section, serving cheap snacks and à la carte meals. The patio out back is sophisticated and serves Yucatecan specialities. Breakfast buffet is good value.

¶-¶ La Vía Olympo, (formerly **La Valentina**) on main plaza opposite cathedral. Good-value Mexican and Yucatecan dishes, brisk service and outdoor seating. Good for breakfasts, free Wi-Fi.

¶-¶ Restaurant Colonial, Calle 62 and 57. Average coffee, but this place lays on an 'all you can eat' breakfast buffet for US$6, with fruit, coffee, good juice, eggs, cereal and other offerings. Fill up on several courses and then come back for the lunch buffet – this time there are steaks, but drinks aren't included.

¶ Café Alameda, Calle 58 No 474 between Calle 57 and 55. Arabic and Mexican cuisine, breakfast and lunch only, 0730-1700.

¶ El Trapiche, near on Calle 62 half a block north of the plaza. Good local dishes, excellent pizzas, sandwiches, omelettes, *tortas*, tacos, burgers and freshly made juices.

¶ Marlín Azul, Calle 62, between 57 and 59. The place for cheap seafood fare, mostly

frequented by locals. Get a shrimp cocktail breakfast for a couple of dollars.

¶ Marys, Calle 63 No 486, between 63 and 58. Mainly Mexican customers. Possibly the cheapest joint in town. *Comida corrida* for US$2.50. Recommended.

¶ Restaurant Mérida, Calle 62 between 59 and 61. Full 3 course for US$2.50 – a bargain, and it's tasty Yucatecan fare as well.

¶ Vito Corleone's Pizza, Calle 59 No 508, between 62 and 60. Open from 1800. Serves pop and pizza, by the slice or whole, eat in or take away. Popular with students and young Mexicans.

Cafés, juices and ice cream parlours
Café El Hoyo, Calle 62, between 57 and 59. A chilled out spot with a patio, popular with students, serving coffee, beer and snacks.

Café Petropolis, Calle 70 opposite CAME terminal. Existed long before the terminal was built, family-run, turkey a speciality, excellent quality, good *horchata* and herb teas.

El Colón Sorbetes y Dulces Finos, Calle 61 and 60. Serving ice cream since 1907, great sorbets, *meringue*, good menu with explanation of fruits in English. Highly recommended. About 30 different flavours of good ice cream.

Italian Coffee Company, Calle 62 between 59 and 61. A bit like a Mexican Starbucks, but nevertheless serves excellent coffee, decent toasted baguettes, and tasty cakes for those feeling a trifle decadent.

Jugos California, Calle 62 and 63 good fruit salads and juices. Next door **Jugos Janitzio** also good.

There's a good *panadería* at Calle 62 y 61. Parque Santa Ana, is good for cheap street fare. Closed middle of the day.

Celestún *p548*
Many beachside restaurants along Calle 12, but be careful of food in the cheaper ones; recommended is **La Playita**, for fried fish, seafood cocktails. Food stalls along Calle 11 beside the bus station should be approached with caution.

† Chivirico, across the road from **Playita**, offers descent fish, shrimp and other seafood.
† El Lobo, Calle 10 and 13, on the corner of the main square. Best spot for breakfast, with fruit salads, yoghurt, pancakes, etc. Celestún's best pizza in the evenings.

Progreso and around *p549*
The Malecón at Progreso is lined with seafood restaurants, some with tables on the beach. For cheaper restaurants, head for the centre of town, near the bus terminal.
††-† Las Palmas and **El Cocalito** are 2 of several reasonable fish restaurants in Chelem.
† Casablanca, **Capitan Marisco** and **Le Saint Bonnet**, Malecón, Progreso, all recommended.

Ticul and Oxkutzcab *p551*
†† Los Almendros, Calle 23 207, Ticul. Nice colonial building with patio, good Yucatecan cuisine, reasonable prices.
†† Pizzería La Góndola, Calle 23, Ticul. Good, moderately priced pizzas.
† El Colorín, near **Hotel Sierra Sosa** on Calle 26, Ticul. Cheap local food.

Uxmal *p552*
†††-†† Restaurant at ruins, good but expensive.

Izamal and around *p553*
There are several restaurants on Plaza de la Constitución.
†† Kinich-Kakmó, Calle 27 No 299 between 28 and 30. Near ruins of same name, local food.
†† Tumben-Lol, Calle 22 No 302 between 31 and 33. Yucatecan cuisine.
† El Norteño at bus station. Good and cheap.
† Wayane, near statue of Diego de Landa. Friendly, clean.

Chichén Itzá *p554*
Mostly poor and overpriced in Chichén itself (cafés inside the ruins are cheaper than the restaurant at the entrance, but are still expensive). Restaurants in Pisté close 2100-2200.
†† Fiesta Maya, Calle 15 No 59, Pisté. Reportedly the best restaurant in town. Serves

Yucatecan food, tacos, meat and sandwiches. Lunch buffet every day at 1200, US$10.
† Pollo Mexicano on the main road in Pisté. One of several simple places that serves mouth-watering, barbequed chicken.
† Sayil in Pisté. Serves Yucatecan dishes like *pollo pibil*, as well as breakfast *huevos al gusto*.

Valladolid *p556, map p556*
There is a well-stocked supermarket on the road between the centre and bus station.
†† El Mesón del Marqués, Calle 39, between 40 and 42, This award-winning restaurant serves seafood and Yucatecan cuisine in a tranquil setting. Intimate and romantic.
†† La Sirenita, Calle 34N, between 29 and 31, T985-856 1655, few blocks east of main square. Closes 1800, closed Sun. Highly recommended for seafood, popular and friendly.
†† Plaza Maya, Calle 41 No 235, a few blocks east of main square. Great regional food and good *comida corrida*, step up from the rest.
† Bazar, northeast corner of Plaza Principal, next to **Mesón del Marqués**. Wholesome grub.

Cafés
Los Campanas, Calle 41 and 42, opposite the plaza, serves various types of coffee.

Río Lagartos and around *p557*
For a fishing village, the seafood is not spectacular, as most of the good fish is sold to restaurants in Mérida and Cancún.
†† Isla Contoy, Calle 19 No 134, average seafood, not cheap for the quality.
†† Los Negritos, off the plaza, moderately priced seafood.

❸ Entertainment

Mérida *p545, map p546*
See the free listings magazine *Yucatán Today* for evening activities.

Bars and clubs
There are several good bars on the north side of the plaza, beer is moderately priced

at US$1, although food can be expensive. There are a number of live-music venues around Parque Santa Lucía, a couple of blocks from the main plaza.

El Cielo, Paseo de Montejo and Calle 25, www.elcielobar.com. Sexy, white leather lounge-bar that plays house, techno and pop. Don your dancing shoes and say 'buenas noches' to the young, beautiful people.

El Tucho, also known as El Nuevo Tucho, Calle 55 between Calle 60 and 58. A restaurant open till 2100 only, with live music, often guest performers from Cuba play. Good food as well.

La Parranda, Calle 60, between 59 and 61. This touristy cantina is always buzzing with atmosphere in the evenings. Live music Thu-Sat and always a steady flow of beer.

Mambo Café, Plaza Las Americanas Shopping Mall, T999-987 7533, www.mambocafe. com.mx. Big club in Mérida, mainly salsa but all kinds of music. Wed-Sat from 2100.

Panchos, Calle 59 between 60 and 62. Very touristy, staff in traditional gear, but lively and busy, live music, patio.

Cinema

There is a cinema showing subtitled films in English on Parque Hidalgo.

Teatro Mérida, Calle 62 between 59 and 61, shows European, Mexican and independent movies as well as live theatre productions. The 14-screen multiplex **Cinepolis** is in the huge Plaza de las Américas, north of the city; *colectivo* and buses take 20 mins and leave from Calle 65 between 58 and 60. Hollywood Cinema, near Parque Santiago has 4 screens.

Theatre

Teatro Peón Contreras, Calle 60 with 57. Shows start at 2100, US$4, ballet, etc. The university puts on many shows.

⊛ Festivals and events

Mérida *p545, map p546*
Every **Thu** there is a cultural music and dance show in Plaza Santa Lucía. **Sat** brings En El Corazón de Mérida, with music and dance in bars, restaurants and in the street. Every **Sun** the central streets are closed off to traffic, live music and parades abound.
6 Jan Mérida celebrates its birthday.
Feb/Mar Carnival takes place the week before Ash Wed (best on Sat). Floats, dancers in regional costume, music and dancing around the plaza and children dressed in animal suits.

Chichén Itzá *p554*
21 Mar and 21 Sep On the morning and afternoon of the spring and autumn equinoxes, the alignment of the sun's shadow casts a serpentine image on the side of the steps of El Castillo. This occasion is popular and you'll be lucky to get close enough to see the action. Note that this phenomenon can also be seen on the days before and after the equinox, 19th-23rd of the month.

Río Lagartos *p557*
17 Jul A big local fiesta, with music, food and dancing in the plaza.
12 Dec Virgen de Guadalupe. The whole village converges on the chapel built in 1976 on the site of a vision of the Virgin Mary by a local non-believer, who suddenly died, along with his dog, shortly after receiving the vision.

○ Shopping

Mérida *p545, map p546*
Bookshops
Amate, Calle 60 453A, between 49 and 51, T999-924 2222, www.amatebooks.com. You'll find a superb stock of literature here, covering everything from architecture to Yucatecan

cuisine, but anthropology, archaeology, history and art are the mainstay. Another branch in Oaxaca.
Librerías Dante, Calle 59, No 498 between 58 and 60. Calle 61 between 62 and 64 (near **Lavandería La Fe**), used books.

Cameras and film
You can get films processed at Omega, Calle 59 and 60; camera repairs at **Fotolandia**, Calle 62 No 479G y 57, T999-924 8223; and also at a little shop on Calle 53 and 62.

Crafts and souvenirs
You'll find an abundance of craft shops in the streets around the plaza. They sell hammocks (see box, page 550), silver jewellery, Panama hats, *guayabera* shirts, *huaraches*, baskets and Maya figurines. The salesmen are ruthless, but they expect to receive about half their original asking price. Bargain hard, but maintain good humour, patience and face. And watch out for the many touts around the plaza, using all sorts of ingenious ploys to get you to their shops.

There are 2 main craft markets in the city: the **Mercado Municipal**, Calle 56a and 67 and the **Garcia Rejón Bazaar**, also known as Casa de la Artesanía, Calle 65 and 60. As for the former, it sprawls, it smells and it takes over several blocks, but it's undeniably alive and undeniably Mexican. It sells everything under the sun and it's also good for a cheap, tasty meal, but check the stalls for cleanliness. The latter is excellent for handicrafts and renowned for clothing, particularly leather *huaraches* and good-value cowboy boots. Good, cheap Yucatecan fare to be had.

If you're looking for a hammock, several places are recommended, but shop around for the best deal. **El Mayab**, Calle 58 No 553 and 71, are friendly, have a limited choice but good deals available; and **La Poblana**, Calle 65 between 58 and 60, will bargain, especially for sales of more than 1 – they also have a huge stock. **El Aguacate**, Calle 58 No 604, corner of Calle 73, good hammocks and no hard sell. Recommended.

Casa de Artesanías Ki-Huic, Calle 63, between Calle 62 and 64, is a nice, friendly store with all sorts of handicrafts from silver and wooden masks, to hammocks and batik. Shop owner Julio Chay is very knowledgeable and friendly, sometimes organizes trips for visitors to his village, Tixkokob, which specializes in hammocks. Open daily, 0900-2100. Julio can also organize trips to other nearby villages and the shop has tequilas for sampling.

For silver, there are a handful of stores on Calle 60, just north of the plaza.

Mexican folk art, including Day of the Dead skeletons, is available from **Minaturas**, Calle 59 No 507A; and **Yalat**, Calle 39 and 40.

If you're in the market for a *guayabera* shirt, you'll find stores all over the city, particularly on Calle 62, between 57 and 61.

Supermarkets
Supermaz, Calle 56, between 65 and 63.

Progreso and around *p549*
Mundo Marino, Calle 80 s/n, 1 block from the beach, T969-915 1380. Shark-related souvenirs.

Izamal and around *p553*
Market, Calle 31, on Plaza de la Constitución, opposite convent, closes soon after lunch.
Hecho a mano, Calle 31 No 332 between 36 and 38. Folk art, postcards, textiles, jewellery, papier-mâché masks.

▲ Activities and tours

Mérida *p545, map p546*
Tour operators
Most tour operators can arrange trips to popular local destinations including Chichén Itzá, Uxmal, Celestún and nearby *cenotes*.
Amigo Yucatán, Av Colón No 508-C and offices in 3 hotels, T999-920 0104, www.amigoyucatan.com. Interesting gastronomy and tasting tours of Yucatán,

as well as excursions to Maya ruins, Izamal, Puuc Route and Celestún. It's possible to book all tours online, 24 hrs in advance recommended, but also possible before 0830 on the same day (best to do this in person or on the phone). Friendly. Recommended.

Carmen Travel Services, Calle 27, No 151, between 32 and 34, T999-927 2027, www.carmentravel.com, 3 other branches. This well-established agency can organize flights, hotels and all the usual trips to the sights. Recommended.

Ecoturismo Yucatán, Calle 3 No 235, between 32A and 34, T999-920 2772, www.ecoyuc.com.mx. Specializes in educational and ecotourism tours to the natural world, including jungle trips, birding expeditions and turtle-hatching tours. Also offers adventure and archaeological packages.

Yucatan Connection, Calle 33 No 506, T999-163 8224, www.yucatan-connection.com. Tours to lesser visited Mayan sites like Mayapán, Tecoh and Ochil. Staff are fluent in English, Czech and Slovak.

Yucatán Trails, Calle 62, No 482, Av 57-59, T999-928 2582, www.yucatantrails.com. Canadian owner Denis Lafoy is friendly, English-speaking and helpful. He runs tours to all the popular local destinations, stores luggage cheaply, has a book exchange and throws famous parties on the first Fri of every month.

● Transport

Mérida p545, map p546
Air
Aeropuerto Rejón (MID), 8 km from town. From Calle 67, 69 and 60, bus 79 goes to the airport, marked 'Aviación', US$0.35, roughly every 20 mins. Taxi set price voucher system US$8; *colectivo* US$2.50. Good domestic flight connections. International flight connections with **Belize City**, **Houston**, **Miami** and **Havana**. Package tours Mérida–Havana–Mérida available (be sure to have a confirmed return flight). For return to Mexico ask for

details at Secretaría de Migración Av Colón and Calle 8.

Airline offices Aerolíneas Aztecas, T01-800-229-8322. AeroMéxico, Av Colón 451 and Montejo, T999-920 1260, www.aeromexico.com. Aviacsa, T999-925 6890, www.aviasca.com.mx. Aviateca, T999-926 9087. Continental, T999-926 3100, www.continental.com. Delta, T01-800-123-410, www.delta.com. Mexicana and Click, T01-800-502-200, www.mexicana.com.

Bus
There are several bus terminals in Mérida.

The **CAME terminal** Buses to destinations outside Yucatán State, Chichén Itzá and Valladolid operating ADO and UNO buses leave from the 1st-class CAME terminal at Calle 70, No 555, between Calle 69 and 71. The station has lockers and is open 24 hrs, left luggage charges from US$0.30 per bag, depending on size. About 20 mins' walk to centre, taxi US$2.50. Schedules change frequently.

The **ADO terminal** Around the corner, has left luggage open 24 hrs, and is for Yucatán destinations except Chichén Itzá with fleets run by Mayab, ATS, Sur and Oriente.

There are also 1st class departures from the Hotel Fiesta Americana, Calle 60 and Colón, which are mostly luxury services to Cancún.

Buses to **Progreso** depart every 15 mins, US$1.50, from their own terminal at Calle 62 No 524, between 65 and 67.

There is another 2nd-class terminal near the market at Calle 50 and 65. It deals with obscure local destinations, including **Timzimín**, **Cenotillo**, **Izamal** and many Maya villages specialising in different crafts, including **Tixkokob**.

To **Cancún**, hourly 1st-class ADO services, 4 hrs, US$18, and frequent 2nd-class services, US$15. To **Campeche**, frequent ADO and 2nd-class services, 2 hrs, US$7-10. To **Chichén Itzá** (ruins and Pisté), ADO services at 0630, 0915, 1240, 2 hrs, US$7, and cheaper, frequent 2nd-class buses stop on their way to

Cancún. To **Celestún**, frequent 2nd-class Oriente services, 2 hrs, US$3.50. To **Coatzacoalcos**, ADO services at 1210, 1830, 1930 and 2130; 12 hrs, US$38. To **Palenque**, ADO services at 0830, 1915, 2200, 8 hrs, US$26. To **Ruta Puuc**, 2nd-class ATS service, 0800, US$10. To **Tulum**, ADO services at 0630, 1040, 1240, 1745, 1945 6 hrs, US$9-14. To **Uxmal**, 2nd-class SUR services at 0600, 0905, 1040, 1205, 1705, 1½ hrs, US$3. To **Valladolid**, hourly ADO services, 1½ hrs, US$9, and 5 2nd-class buses, all in the afternoon and evening, US$5.50. To **Villahermosa**, frequent ADO services, 9 hrs, US$30.50 and several ADO GL services, US$36. To **Tuxtla Guitérrez**, an OCC service at 1915, 15 hrs, US$40, and ADO GL services at 1900 and 2315, US$55. To **San Cristóbal de las Casas**, an OCC service at 1915, 13 hrs, US$36. To **Tenosique**, an **ADO** service at 2100, US$29.

To Guatemala Take a bus from Mérida to San Cristóbal and change there for Comitán, or to Tenosique for the route to Flores. Another alternative would be to take the bus from Mérida direct to Tuxtla Gutiérrez (times given above), then connect to Cd Cuauhtémoc or to Tapachula.

To Belize Take a bus to **Chetumal**, ADO services at 0730 (except Wed and Sat), 1300, 1800, 2300, 6 hrs, US$21 and cross the border. **Premier** operate services from Chetumal to **Belize City** at 1145, 1445 and 1745, 5 hrs, US$10, schedules are subject to change.

Car
Car hire Car reservations should be booked well in advance if possible. Hire firms charge around US$45-50 a day although bargains can be found in low season. All agencies allow vehicles to be returned to Cancún for an extra charge, and most have an office at the airport where they share the same counter and negotiating usually takes place. Agencies include: Budget, at the airport, T999-946 1323; Executive, Calle 56A No 451, corner of Av Colón, at the Hotel Fiesta Americana, T999-925 8171, www.executive. com.mx; Easy Way Car Rental, Calle 60,

between 55 and 57, T999-930 9500, www.easywayrentacar-yucatan.com; Mexico Rent a Car, Calle 57A Depto 12, between 58 and 60, T999-923 3637, mexicorentacar@hotmail.com

Car service Servicios de Mérida Goodyear, Calle 59, near corner of Av 68. Very helpful, competent, owner speaks English, good coffee while you wait for your vehicle. Honest car servicing or quick oil change.

Taxi
There are 2 types: the Volkswagens, which you can flag down, prices range from US$3.50-7; cheaper are the 24-hr radio taxis, T999-928 5328, or catch 1 from their kiosk on Parque Hidalgo. In both types of taxi, establish fare before journey; there are set prices depending on the distance, the minimum is an expensive US$2.50 even for a few blocks.

Celestún *p548*
Bus Buses leave every 1-2 hrs from the local bus station on Calle 65 between 50 and 52, in Mérida, 2-hr journey, 1st class US$3.50, 2nd class US$3.

Progreso and around *p549*
Boat Boats can be hired to visit the reef of **Los Alacranes** where many ancient wrecks are visible in clear water.
Bus Buses from **Mérida** leave from the terminal on Calle 62 between 67 and 65, next to Hotel La Paz, every 10 mins. US$0.80 1-way/ US$2 return. Returns every 10 mins until 2200.

Dzibilchaltún *p549*
Bus
5 direct buses a day on weekdays, from Parque San Juan, marked 'Tour/Ruta Polígono'; returns from the site entrance on the hour, passing the junction 15 mins later, taking 45 mins from the junction to **Mérida** (US$0.60).
Shuttles Leave from Parque San Juan in Mérida, corner of Calle 62 y 67A, every 1 or 2 hrs between 0500 and 1900.

Ticul and Oxkutzcab *p551*
Colectivo There are frequent VW *colectivos* to Ticul from Parque San Juan, in **Mérida**, US$2.50.

Uxmal *p552*
Bus 5 buses a day from **Mérida**, from the terminal on Calle 69 between 68 and 70, US$4. Return buses run every 2 hrs, or go to the entrance to the site on the main road and wait for a *colectivo*, which will take you to Muná for US$0.50. From there, many buses (US$1.70) and *colectivos* (US$1.40) go to Mérida.

Car Parking at the site costs US$1 for the whole day. Uxmal is 74 km from **Mérida**, 177 km from **Campeche**, by a good paved road. If going by car from Mérida, there is a circular road round the city: follow the signs to Campeche, then 'Campeche via ruinas', then to 'Muná via Yaxcopoil' (long stretch of road with no signposting). Muná–Yaxcopoil is about 34 km. Parking US$1.

Izamal and around *p553*
Bus Bus station is on Calle 32 behind government offices, can leave bags. 2nd class to **Mérida**, every 45 mins, 1½ hrs, US$1.50, lovely countryside. Bus station in Mérida, Calle 67 between Calle 50 and 52. 6 a day to/from **Valladolid** (96 km), about 2 hrs, US$2.30-3.

Chichén Itzá *p554*
ADO bus office in Pisté is between **Stardust** and **Pirámide Inn**. Budget travellers going on from Mérida to Isla Mujeres or Cozumel should visit Chichén from Valladolid (see below), although if you plan to go through in a day you can store luggage at the visitor centre.

Bus Frequent 2nd-class buses depart from Mérida to Cancún, passing Chichen Itzá and Pisté. Likewise, there are frequent departures to/from Valladolid. The bus station in Pisté is between Stardust and Pirámide Inn. To **Mérida**, 2nd class, hourly, US$5; and 1st class, 1420 and 1720, US$7. To **Cancún**, 2nd class, hourly, US$9. To **Valladolid**, 2nd class, hourly, US$2.50.

To **Tulum**, 2nd class, 0810, 1420, 1615, US$11. The ruins are a 5-min ride from Pisté – the buses drop off and pick up passengers until 1700 at the top of the coach station opposite the entrance.

Valladolid *p556, map p556*
Bus The main bus terminal is on Calle 37 and Calle 54. To **Cancún**, ADO, frequent, 2½ hrs, US$9; and many 2nd class, 3-4 hrs, US$5.50. To **Chichén Itzá**, ADO, many daily, 30 mins; US$3; and many 2nd class, US$1.50. To **Mérida**, ADO, 16 daily, 2½ hrs, US$9. To **Playa del Carmen**, 1st and 2nd class, 11 daily, 3½ hrs, US$8.50. To **Tizimín** (for Río Lagartos), frequent 1 hr, US$1.30. To **Tulum**, frequent ADO and ATS services, 3 hrs, US$5.

Río Lagartos and around *p557*
Bus There are 2 terminals side by side in Tizimín. If coming from Valladolid en route to Río Lagartos, you will need to walk to the other terminal. Tizimín–Río Lagartos, 7 per day, 1½ hrs, US$2. To **Valladolid**, frequent, 1 hr, US$1.30. To **Mérida**, several daily, 4 hrs, US$4. There are also buses to **Cancún**, **Felipe Carrillo Puerto** and **Chetumal**.

It is possible to get to Río Lagartos and back in a day from **Valladolid**, if you leave on the 0630 or 0730 bus (taxi Tizimín–Río Lagartos US$25, driver may negotiate). Last bus back from Río Lagartos at 1730.

● Directory

Mérida *p545, map p546*
Banks Banamex, at Calle 56 and 59 (Mon-Fri 0900-1300, 1600-1700), ATM cash machine. Many banks on Calle 65, off the plaza. Most have ATM cash machines, open 24 hrs. The beautiful **Casa de Montejo**, on the main plaza is also a Banamex branch. Open 0900-1600, Mon-Fri. **HSBC** usually changes TCs and stays open later than other banks, 0900-1900, Mon-Fri and 0900-1500 Sat.
Cultural centres Alliance Française, Calle 56 No 476 between 55 and 57, T999-927

2403. Has a busy programme of events, films (Thu 1900), a library and a *cafetería* open all day. **Embassies and consulates** Austria, Av Colón No 59, T999-925 6386. Belize, Calle 53 No 498, corner of 58, T999-928 6152. Cuba, Calle 42 No 200, T999-944 4216. France, Calle 60 No 385, between 41 and 43, T999-930 1542. Germany, Calle 49 No 212, between 30 and 32, T999-944 3252. Honduras, Instituto Monte Líbano, Calle 54 No 486, between 57 and 59, T999-926 1922. Netherlands, Calle 64 No 418 between 47 and 49, T999-924 3122. USA, Calle 60 No 338, T999-942 5700. **Internet** Multitude of internet cafés, most charging US$1-1.50. **Language schools** Centro de Idiomas del Sureste, Calle 52 No 455, between 49 and 51, T999-923 0083, www.cisyucatan.com.mx, is a well-established Spanish school offering tried and tested language and cultural programmes. Modern Spanish Institute, Calle 15 No 500B, between 16A and 18, T999-911 0790, www.modernspanish.com, courses in Spanish, Maya culture, homestays. **Laundry** Lavandería, Calle 69 No 541, 2 blocks from bus station, about US$4.50 a load, 3-hr service. La Fe, Calle 61, No 518, between Calle 62 and 64. US$4.50 for 3 kg. Highly recommended (shoe repair next door). Self-service hard to find. **Libraries** Mérida English Library, Calle 53 No 524 between 66 and 68, T999-924 8401, www.meridaenglish library.com. Many books on Mexico, used book for sale, bulletin board, magazines, reading patio. Mon-Fri 0900-1300; Mon 1830-2100; Thu 1600-1900; Sat 1300-1300. **Medical services** Hospitals: Centro Médico de las Américas (CEMA), Calle 54 No 365 between 33A and Av Pérez Ponce, T999-926 2111, emergencies T999-927 3199, www.cmasureste.com, affiliated with Mercy Hospital, Miami, Florida, US. Red Cross, T999-924 9813. Dentists: Dr Javier Cámara Patrón, Calle 17 No 170, between 8 and 10,

T999-925 3399, www.dentistyucatan.com. **Post office** Calle 53, between 52 and 54. Will accept parcels for surface mail to US only, but don't seal parcels destined overseas; they have to be inspected. For surface mail to Europe try Belize, or mail package to US, Poste Restante, for collection later if you are heading that way. **Telephone** International calls are possible from caseta telefónicas. You'll find them all over town, but especially on Calle 62 and 60, north of the plaza. Calls to Europe cost around 4 pesos a minute, 2-3 pesos to the USA.

Izamal and around *p553*
Banks Bank on square with statue to Fray Diego de Landa, south side of convent.
Post office On opposite side of square to convent.

Chichén Itzá *p554*
Banks ATMs on the main street.
Internet Available in Pisté.
Telephone International calls may be placed from Teléfonos de México, opposite Hotel Xaybe.

Valladolid *p556, map p556*
Banks Santander Serfin, Calle 39 No 229; Bancomer, Calle 40 No 196; HSBC, Calle 41 No 201; Banamex, Calle 42, No 206.
Internet Phonet, west side of the plaza, daily 1000-2100, internet costs US$1 per hr and there are long-distance call facilities. There are many other internet cafés.
Laundry Teresita, Calle 33 between 40 and 42, US$6 for 5.5 kg. **Post office** On east side of plaza, 0800-1500 (does not accept parcels for abroad). **Telephone** Telmex phone office on Calle 42, just north of square; expensive Computel offices at bus station and next to Hotel San Clemente; Ladatel phonecards can be bought from *farmacias* for use in phone booths.

State of Quintana Roo

The burgeoning international destinations of Cancún, Playa del Carmen, Isla Mujeres and Cozumel overshadow the eastern coast of the Yucatán and the State of Quintana Roo. Resorts: you either love them, hate them or simply enjoy the beautiful beaches, package tours and reliable restaurants. If Cancún is your port of entry for a trip through Mexico and Central America, it will certainly make for a good contrast to other regions. Diving in the area is popular, either off the coast of Isla Mujeres or Cozumel, or in the underwater caves or cenotes found in the region. The Maya ruins of Tulum are gloriously located, and the quieter spot of Cobá is worth a trip, as is the wilderness reserve of Sian Ka'an. To the far south, Chetumal seems a world away from the tourist hot spots, but it is the stepping-off point for travel to Belize and Guatemala. ›› *For listings, see pages 589-609.*

Isla Holbox → *Colour map 4, A3. Phone code: 984.*

Also north of Valladolid, but in the neighbouring state of Quintana Roo, turn off the road to Puerto Juárez after Nuevo Xcan to Isla Holbox. Buses to **Chiquilá** for boats, three times a day; also direct from Tizimín at 1130, connecting with the ferry, US$2.20. The ferry leaves for Holbox 0600 and 1430, one hour, US$1, returning to Chiquilá at 0500 and 1300. A bus to Mérida connects with the 0500 return ferry. If you miss the ferry a fisherman will probably take you (for about US$14). You can leave your car in the care of the harbour master for a small charge; his house is east of the dock. Take water with you if possible. During 'El Norte' season, the water is turbid and the beach is littered with seaweed.

There are five more uninhabited islands beyond Holbox. Beware of sharks and barracuda, although very few nasty occurrences have been reported. Off the rough and mostly unpopulated bulge of the Yucatán coastline are several islands, once notorious for contraband. Beware of mosquitoes in the area.

Cancún ⬤⬤⬤⬤▲⬤⬤ ›› *pp589-609. Colour map 4, A3.*

→ *Phone code: 998.*

In 1970, when Cancún was 'discovered' by the Mexican tourist board, it was an inaccessible strip of barren land with beautiful beaches; the only road went straight past Cancún to Puerto Juárez for the ferry to Isla Mujeres, which had been a national tourist destination since the 1950s. Massive international investment and government sponsorship saw the luxury resort of Cancún completed within 25 years. The 25-km hotel zone, set on a narrow strip of land in the shape of a number seven alongside the coast, is an ultra-modern American-style boulevard, with five-star hotels, high-tech nightclubs, high-class shopping malls and branches of McDonald's, Burger King and Planet Hollywood.

Love or hate Cancún, its presence on the international tourism market is indisputable. From all-in-one package tours to international government conferences, Cancún has an enviable record. It's worth a trip just to see what it's like. Jump on a Ruta 1 or Ruta 2 bus and you'll quickly see the international hotel chains with hundreds of rooms, packed along the sinuous sand bar. Spotted along the way Hotel Zone international shopping brands, restaurants and entertainment centres provide the complete holiday experience.

Ins and outs

Getting there Cancún airport, www.cancun-airport.com, is 16 km south of the city. A fixed price *colectivo* taxi to the **Hotel Zone** or the centre costs US$9; pay at the kiosk outside airport. Drivers go via the Hotel Zone, but must take you to whichever part of the city centre you want. If going to the centre, make sure you know the name and address of your hotel before you get in the taxi, or the driver will offer to take you to a budget hotel of his own choice. **ADO** shuttle buses go to the centre via Avenida Tulum every 30 minutes from the airport. There is a tourist information kiosk in the airport, and a *casa de cambio*.

Getting around Ruta 1 and Ruta 2 buses go from the centre to the Hotel Zone, US$0.60; Ruta 1 runs 24 hours and goes via Avenida Tulum; Ruta 2 runs 0500-0330 and goes via

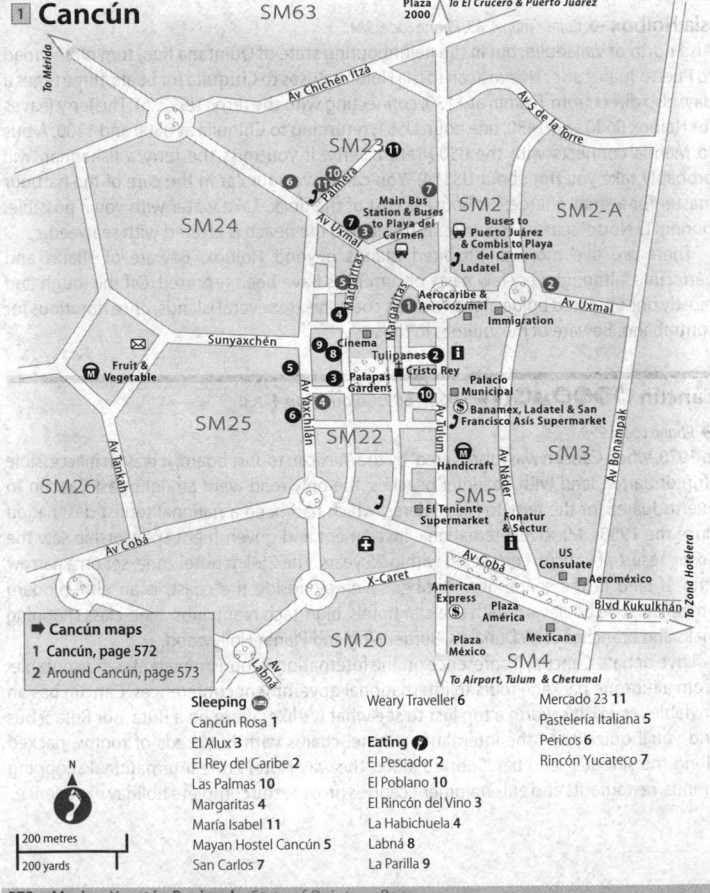

1 Cancún

➡ Cancún maps
1 Cancún, page 572
2 Around Cancún, page 573

Sleeping
Cancún Rosa 1
El Alux 3
El Rey del Caribe 2
Las Palmas 10
Margaritas 4
María Isabel 11
Mayan Hostel Cancún 5
San Carlos 7

Weary Traveller 6

Eating
El Pescador 2
El Poblano 10
El Rincón del Vino 3
La Habichuela 4
Labná 8
La Parilla 9

Mercado 23 11
Pastelería Italiana 5
Pericos 6
Rincón Yucateco 7

Avenida Cobá to the bus terminal. Buses to the Hotel Zone can be caught from many stops along Avenida Tulum. Buses to **Puerto Juárez** for the boat to Isla Mujeres leave from outside **Cinema Royal**, across Avenida Tulum from the bus terminal, US$0.55. To get around in the centre, board a bus at Plaza 2000 and ask the driver if he's going to Mercado 28; those buses go along Avenida Yaxchilán; all others go to the Hotel Zone. Taxis are cheap and abundant in Cancún. Flat rate for anywhere within the centre is US$1.50; Hotel Zone from centre US$10-20. Many taxis stop at **El Crucero**, the junction of Avenida Tulum and Avenida López Portillo outside Plaza 2000, but there are often queues.

Downtown Cancún is a world apart from the Hotel Zone. It evolved from temporary shacks housing the thousands of builders working on the Hotel Zone, and is now a massive city with very little character. The main avenue is Tulum, formerly the highway running through the city when it was first conceived. It is now the location of the handicraft market, the main shops, banks and the municipal tourist office. There are also restaurants, but the better ones are along Avenida Yaxchilán, which is also the main centre for nightlife.

2 Around Cancún

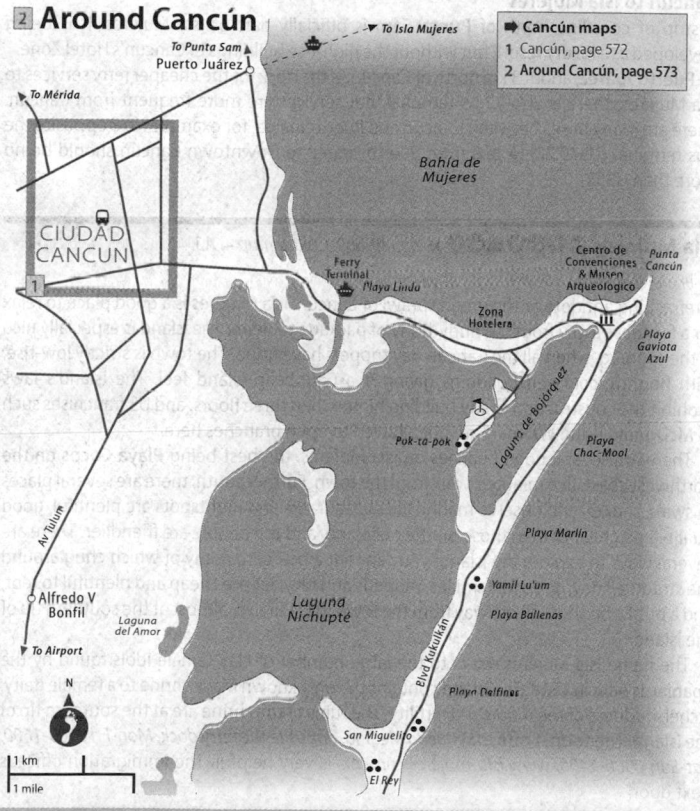

➡ Cancún maps
1 Cancún, page 572
2 Around Cancún, page 573

The cheaper end of the city, and a good area for budget travellers to base themselves, is around **El Crucero** (see above). The rest of the city is fairly expensive, but not as much as the Hotel Zone. The city is laid out in *supermanzanas* (SM), the blocks of streets between avenues, with smaller *manzanas* (M), or blocks, within them. Often the address you are given is, for example, SM24, M6, L3. L stands for *lote*, and is the precise number of the building within its *manzana*. This can lead to confusion when walking about, as the streets also have names, often not mentioned in the addresses. Look closely at street signs and you will see the SM and the M numbers. Taxi drivers generally respond better to addresses based on the *manzana* system.

Tourist information The **tourist office** ① *Av Tulum 26, www.qroo.gob.mx, in a building that also houses local government offices*, is not very helpful; you'll get a glossy pocket guide to Cancún full of adverts for expensive restaurants. There is a new and well-equipped office at the **Conventions and Visitor Bureau** ① *corner of Av Cobá and Av Bonampak, T884-6531.* Here the staff are helpful and friendly with information on new attractions, hotels and excursions.

Cancún to Isla Mujeres
A strip of coastline north of **Punta Sam** is officially part of Isla Mujeres. It is being developed as a luxury resort, but without the high-rise buildings of Cancún's Hotel Zone.

Puerto Juárez, about 3 km north of Cancún, is the dock for the cheaper ferry services to Isla Mujeres; there is also a bus terminal, but services are more frequent from Cancún. There are many buses between Cancún and Puerto Juárez, for example No 8 opposite the bus terminal (US$0.70). A taxi from Puerto Juárez to Downtown Cancún should be no more than US$2.

Isla Mujeres ⬤⬤⬤⬤⬤⬤⬤ » *pp589-609. Colour map 4, A3.*

→ *Phone code: 998.*
A refreshing antidote to the urban sprawl of Cancún, Isla Mujeres is a good place to relax for a few days away from the hurly-burly of package tourism. The island is especially nice in the evening, when all the Cancún day trippers have gone. The town is strictly low-rise, with brightly coloured buildings giving it a Caribbean island feel. The island's laws prohibit the construction of any building higher than three floors, and US franchises such as **McDonald's** and **Walmart** are not allowed to open branches here.

There are several good beaches on Isla Mujeres, the best being **Playa Cocos** on the northwest coast, five minutes' walk from the town. Further south, there are several places to swim, snorkel and observe marine life. Restaurants and nightspots are plentiful, good quality and cheaper than those on the mainland, and the people are friendlier. There are several ways to explore the island: you can rent a golf cart, many of which chug around the streets all day, good for families; mopeds and bicycles are cheap and plentiful to rent, and a public bus runs all the way from the town to El Paraíso, almost at the southern tip of the island.

The name Isla Mujeres refers to the large number of clay female idols found by the Spaniards here in 1518. The island contains the only known Maya shrine to a female deity: Ixchel, goddess of the moon and fertility. The ruins of the shrine are at the southern tip of the island. The **tourist office** ① *Rueda Medina, opposite the ferry dock, Mon-Fri 0900-1600, Sat-Sun 0900-1400, www.isla-mujeres.com.mx*, is very helpful. The immigration office is next door.

In October there is a festival of music, with groups from Mexico and the US performing in the main square, and from 1-12 December, during the fiesta for the Virgin of Guadalupe, there are fireworks and dances until 0400 in the plaza.

Sights

Most of the sights south of the town can be seen in a day. The first of these, 5 km from the town, is the **Turtle Farm** ① *daily 0900-1700, US$2*, with hundreds of sea turtles weighing from 170 g to 270 kg in a humane setting. To get there, take the bus to the final stop, Playa Paraíso, double back and walk five minutes along the main road.

At the centre of the island are the curious remains of a pirate's domain, called **Hacienda Mundaca** ① *daily 0900-1700, US$2*. A big, new arch gate marks its entrance. Paths have been laid out among the large trees, but all that remains of the estate (called Vista Alegre) are one small building and a circular garden with raised beds, a well and a gateway. Fermín Mundaca, more of a slave-trader than a buccaneer, built Vista Alegre for the teenage girl he loved. She rejected him and he died, broken-hearted, in Mérida. His epitaph there reads *Como eres, yo fui; como soy, tu serás* ('What you are I was; what I am you shall be'). See the poignant little carving on the garden side of the gate, *La entrada de La Triguena* (the girl's nickname). To get there, get off the bus at the final stop, and turn the opposite way to the beach; the house is a short walk away.

El Garrafón ① *T998-877 1100, www.garrafon.com*, is a snorkelling centre 7 km from the town, being developed into a luxury resort in the style of Xcaret on the mainland. Snorkelling is still possible, with a 12-m bronze cross submerged offshore for your exploration; by tour only. There is an expensive restaurant and bar at El Garrafón, and a small beach. The snorkelling is good past the pier, along a reef with some dead coral. Large numbers of different coloured fish can be seen at very close range. If you want to walk to El Garrafón from the bus stop at Playa Paraíso, take the second path on the right to the beach from the main road. The first path leads through **Restaurant Playa Paraíso**, which charges US$1 for the privilege of walking through their premises to the beach. Once on the beach, you can walk all the way to El Garrafón along the coast, although it gets very rocky for the final part. It is easier to go as far as the cluster of beach villas, then cut through one of them (ask for permission) to the main road. The whole walk takes about half an hour. When you arrive at El Garrafón, turn right at the building site, go down the hill to **Hotel Garrafón** del Castillo, which is the entrance to the snorkelling centre.

A further 15 minutes' walk from El Garrafón, at the tip of the island, are the ruins of the Maya shrine **Santuario Maya a la Diosa Ixchel**, US$2, dedicated to Ixchel the goddess of fertility. These were once free to visit, but unfortunately they have been bought and developed as part of the **El Garrafón 'National Park'** ① *US$5.50*. A cultural centre has also been built here with large sculptures by several international artists.

South of Cancún ⊖⊕⊘⊖⊙▲⊕⊙ ➤➤ pp589-609. Colour map 4, A3.

Puerto Morelos → *Phone code: 998.*

A quiet little village 34 km south of Cancún, Puerto Morelos is one of the few places that still retains some of the charm of an unspoilt fishing village (but not for much longer), making it a good place to stop over en route to larger towns further south, such as Playa del Carmen. The village is really just a large plaza right on the seafront with a couple of streets going off it. If on arrival at Cancún airport you don't wish to spend the night in the city, you could get a taxi directly to Puerto Morelos. This is also the place to catch the car ferry to the island of Cozumel (see below). The **Sinaltur** office on the plaza offers a range of good snorkelling, kayak and fishing trips. **Goyos**, just north of the plaza, offers jungle adventures and rooms for rent, although erratic hours are maintained.

Playa del Carmen → *Phone code: 984.*

What used to be a pleasant little town on the beach has lost the charms of its former existence as a fishing village. Recent development for tourism has been rapid, but Playa, as it is known locally, has not had the high-rise treatment of Cancún. The beach is dazzling white, with crystal-clear shallow water, ideal for swimming, and further out there is good

Playa del Carmen

Sleeping 🛏		Eating 🍴	
Alhambra 1 *B4*	Las Molcas 6 *D3*	Glass Bar 12 *A4*	**Bars & clubs** 🍷
Blue Parrot 2 *A4*	Maya Bric 10 *A4*	Habita Bookshop &	Beer Bucket 13 *A3*
Casa Tucán 5 *B3*	Mom's 11 *B2*	Café 18 *A4*	Carlos 'n' Charlies 19 *D3*
Cielo & El Carboncito	Playacar Palace 3 *D3*	Java Joe's 2 *A4*	Coco Maya 16 *A4*
Restaurant 7 *B3*	Posada Marinelly 13 *C2*	Karen's 9 *C3*	El Cielo 17 *A4*
Happy Gecko 4 *A3*	Urban Hostel 14 *B3*	La Parrilla 11 *A4*	OM 15 *A4*
Hostel Playa 8 *A2*		Los Comales 10 *B3*	Señor Frog's 20 *D3*
	Eating 🍴	Tortas del Carmen 3 *B2*	Tequila Barrel 14 *A4*
	Billy the Kid 1 *B2*	Pez Vela 5 *C3*	
	Buenos Aires 6 *B3*	Rolandi 4 *D3*	
	El Fogon 8 *A2*	Yaxche 7 *A3*	

scuba-diving. There is lodging for every budget, and plenty of good restaurants and bars of every type. Many travellers choose Playa as their base for trips to the ruins of Tulum in the south, and archaeological sites such as Cobá in the interior.

The town is laid out in a grid system, with the main centre of tourist activity based on Avenida 5 (pedestrianized in the central section at night between 1800 and 0200), one block from and parallel with the beach. This is where the more expensive hotels and restaurants are, as well as being the centre for nightlife. Cheaper accommodation can be found up Avenida Juárez and further north of the beach.

Tourist information is scant, although there is a **tourism office** ① *corner of Av Juárez and Av 15, T984-873 2804,* which has useful information and maps, and the kiosk on the main plaza will provide a copy of *Destination Playa del Carmen,* a useful guide with maps produced by US residents.

Cozumel ⊖②⊕▲⊖❶ ›› *pp589-609. Colour map 4, A3.*

→ *Phone code: 987.*

The town, San Miguel de Cozumel, is a seedy, overpriced version of Playa del Carmen. Daily tour groups arrive on cruises from Miami and Cancún, and the town's services seem geared towards this type of tourist. But Cozumel is a mecca for scuba divers, with many beautiful offshore reefs to explore, as well as much interesting wildlife and birdlife. Travellers looking for a beach holiday with some nightlife will find the island disappointing compared to Playa del Carmen. There is only one nice beach on the west side, and the eastern, Atlantic coast is far too rugged and choppy for swimming.

Ins and outs

The airport is just north of San Miguel with a minibus shuttle service to the hotels. There are 10-minute flights to and from the airstrip near Playa del Carmen, as well as flights linking to Mexico City, Cancún, Chichén Itzá and Houston (Texas). The passenger ferry from Playa del Carmen runs every two hours (see above), and the car ferry leaves twice daily from Puerto Morelos (see page 575). There are no local buses, but Cozumel town is small enough to visit on foot. To get around the island, there are organized tours or taxis; otherwise, hire a jeep, moped or bicycle.

San Miguel de Cozumel

The island's only town has very little character, mainly due to the construction of a US air base during the Second World War, whose airfield has now been converted for civilian use. There is a variety of accommodation, with a few budget hotels, but mainly focusing on the luxury end of the market.

On the waterfront between Calle 4 and 6, the **Museo de la Isla** ① *US$3.30,* provides a well-laid-out history of the island. There is a bookshop, art gallery and rooftop restaurant, which has excellent food and views of sunset, good for breakfast, from 0700 (**The Quick** is excellent value). Recommended.

Beaches

In the north of the island the beaches are sandy and wide, although those at the Zona Hotelera Norte were damaged in 1989 and are smaller than they used to be. At the end of the paved road, walk up the unmade road until it becomes 'dual carriageway'; turn left for the narrow beach, which is a bit dirty. Cleaner beaches are accessible only through the hotels. South of San Miguel, **San Francisco** is good if narrow (clean, very popular, lockers at **Pancho's**, expensive restaurants), but others are generally narrower still and rockier.

All the main hotels are on the sheltered west coast. The east, Caribbean coast is rockier, but very picturesque; swimming and diving on the unprotected side is very dangerous owing to ocean underflows. The only safe place is at a sheltered bay at **Chen Río**. Another bay with possibilities is **Punta Morena**, which is a good surf beach, there is good accommodation (contact Matt at **Deep Blue**, on Salas 200, for more information and transport) and seafood (try the *ceviche*). Three good (and free) places for snorkelling are: the beach in front of **Hotel Las Glorias**, 15 minutes' walk south from ferry (you can walk through the hotel's reception); **Playa Corona**, further south, is too far to walk, so hitch or take a taxi

1 Cozumel

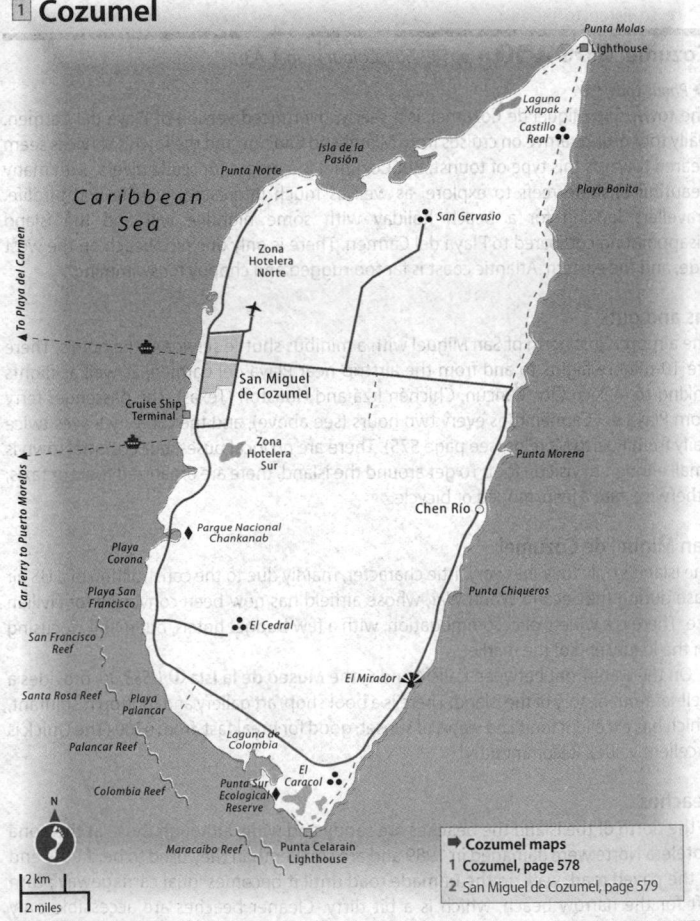

Caribbean Sea

To Playa del Carmen

Car Ferry to Puerto Morelos

Punta Molas
Lighthouse

Laguna Xlapak
Castillo Real

Isla de la Pasión

Punta Norte

Playa Banita

San Gervasio

Zona Hotelera Norte

San Miguel de Cozumel

Cruise Ship Terminal

Zona Hotelera Sur

Punta Morena

Chen Río

Parque Nacional Chankanab

Playa Corona

Playa San Francisco

San Francisco Reef

Punta Chiqueros

El Cedral

El Mirador

Santa Rosa Reef

Playa Palancar

Laguna de Colombia

Palancar Reef

Colombia Reef

El Caracol

Punta Sur Ecological Reserve

Maracaibo Reef

Punta Celarain Lighthouse

N

2 km
2 miles

➡ **Cozumel maps**
1 Cozumel, page 578
2 San Miguel de Cozumel, page 579

(there is a small restaurant and pier); and **Xul-Ha**, further south still, which has a bar and comfortable beach chairs.

Archaeological sites

There are some 32 archaeological sites on Cozumel; those on the east coast are mostly single buildings (thought to have been lookouts, navigational aids). The easiest to see are the restored ruins of the Maya-Toltec period at **San Gervasio** ① *0900-1800, US$6, guides are on hand, or you can buy a self-guiding booklet at the bookshop on the square in San Miguel, or at the flea market, for US$1.* It is in the north of the island (7 km from Cozumel town, then 6 km to the left up a paved road, toll US$1), an interesting site, quite spread out, with *sacbés* (sacred roads) between the groups of buildings. There are no large structures, but a nice plaza, an arch, and pigment can be seen in places. It is also a pleasant place to listen to birdsong, see butterflies, animals (if lucky), lizards, land crabs and insects. **Castillo Real** is one of many sites on the northeastern coast, but the road to this part of the island is in very bad condition and the ruins themselves are very small. **El Cedral** in the southwest (3 km from the main island road) is a two-room temple, overgrown with trees, in the centre of the village of the same name. Behind the temple is a ruin, and next to it a modern church with a green and white façade (an incongruous

2 San Miguel de Cozumel

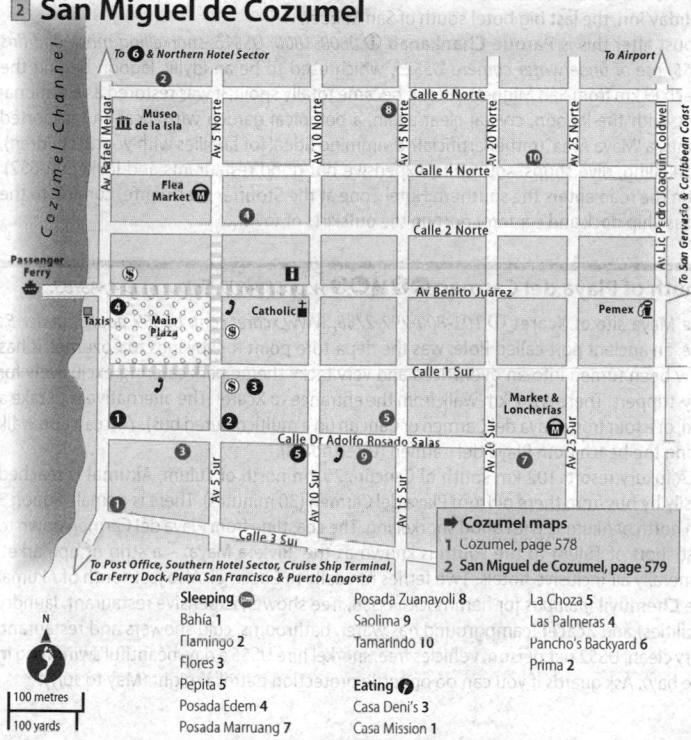

To Post Office, Southern Hotel Sector, Cruise Ship Terminal, Car Ferry Dock, Playa San Francisco & Puerto Langosta

➡ **Cozumel maps**
1 Cozumel, page 578
2 San Miguel de Cozumel, page 579

100 metres
100 yards

Sleeping
Bahía 1
Flamingo 2
Flores 3
Pepita 5
Posada Edem 4
Posada Marruang 7

Posada Zuanayoli 8
Saolima 9
Tamarindo 10

Eating
Casa Deni's 3
Casa Mission 1

La Choza 5
Las Palmeras 4
Pancho's Backyard 6
Prima 2

pairing). In the village are large, permanent shelters for agricultural shows, rug sellers and locals who pose with *iguanas doradas* (golden iguanas). **El Caracol**, where the sun, in the form of a shell, was worshipped, is 1 km from the southernmost Punta Celarain. At Punta Celarain is an old lighthouse.

Around the island

A circuit of the island on paved roads can easily be done in a day. Head due east out of San Miguel (take the continuation of Avenida Juárez). Make the detour to San Gervasio before continuing to the Caribbean coast at **Mescalito's** restaurant. Here, turn left for the northern tip (road unsuitable for ordinary vehicles), or right for the south, passing Punta Morena, Chen Río, Punta Chiqueros (restaurant, bathing), El Mirador (a low viewpoint with sea-worn rocks, look out for holes) and Paradise Cove. At this point, the paved road heads west while an unpaved road continues south to Punta Celarain. Here there is the **Punta Sur Ecological Reserve** ① *T987-872 0914, www.cozumelparks.com.mx, 1000-1700, US$10,,* an ecotourism development, with a variety of natural landscapes with lagoons and mangrove jungles. A snorkelling centre has opened here as well as a viewing platform. On the road west, opposite the turn-off to El Cedral, is a sign to **Restaurante Mac y Cía**, an excellent fish restaurant on a lovely beach, popular with dive groups for lunch. Next is Playa San Francisco (see above). A few more kilometres leads to the former **Holiday Inn**, the last big hotel south of San Miguel.

Just after this is **Parque Chankanab** ① *0800-1800, US$16, snorkelling mask and fins US$5, use of underwater camera US$25,* which used to be an idyllic lagoon behind the beach (9 km from San Miguel). After it became totally spoilt, it was restored as a National Park, with the lagoon, crystal clear again, a botanical garden with local and imported plants, a 'Maya Area' (rather artificial), swimming (ideal for families with young children), snorkelling, dive shops, souvenirs, expensive but good restaurants and lockers (US$2). Soon the road enters the southern Hotel Zone at the **Stouffer Presidente**, coming to the cruise ship dock and car ferry port on the outskirts of town.

South of Playa del Carmen ●❼▲●● ➤➤ *pp589-609. Colour map 4, A3/B3.*

The Maya site of **Xcaret** ① *T01-800-292-2738, www.xcaret.com, US$59 adults, under 5s free*, an ancient port called Polé, was the departure point for voyages to Cozumel. It has now been turned into an overpriced and very tacky theme park catering exclusively for day-trippers. There is a 1-km walk from the entrance to Xcaret. The alternative is to take a taxi, or a tour from Playa del Carmen or Cancún (in a multicoloured bus). You can also walk along the beach from Playa del Carmen (three hours).

A luxury resort, 102 km south of Cancún, 20 km north of Tulum, **Akumal** is reached easily by bus from there or from Playa del Carmen (30 minutes). There is a small lagoon 3 km north of Akumal, with good snorkelling. The coastline from Playa del Carmen down to just short of Tulum to the south is known as the 'Riviera Maya' – a strip of upmarket, generally all-inclusive hotels. Two ferries run daily to Cozumel. Also just south of Akumal are **Chemuyil** (*palapas* for hammocks, US$4, free shower, expensive restaurant, laundry facilities) and **Xcacel** (campground has water, bathrooms, cold showers and restaurant, very clean, US$2 per person, vehicles free, snorkel hire US$5 a day, beautiful swimming in the bay). Ask guards if you can go on turtle protection patrol at night (May to July).

Sweating it out

The *temazcal* is a ritual ceremony that has been practised by the indigenous peoples of Mexico for hundreds of years. The Mexican version of the sweat lodge, it is a thanksgiving to the four elements, and a healing for the spirit as well as the body. You enter the womb of mother earth when you enter the *temazcal*, and when you exit you are born a new being. Traditionally, it was done in a square- or dome-shaped building constructed from branches and then covered with blankets, and was preceded by a day of fasting. There are *temazcal* sessions open to newcomers all over Mexico. Done properly, the experience can be very intense.

Red-hot rocks are placed in the centre of the construction, and a group sits around them. The door is closed, and a medicine man leads the group in prayer and songs, all designed to connect the insiders to each of the four elements. During the ceremony, the door is opened four times, to allow people who want to leave (there is no returning), and to bring in more hot rocks. Different emotions and thoughts come up for different people, and everyone is encouraged to contribute something from their own traditions if they feel the need. After each contribution, herbal water is poured over the rocks to create more healing steam. This continues till everyone is in agreement to open the fourth and final door. Everyone then leaves, rinses off (hopefully in the sea or lagoon if you're near the coast), then shares soup and tea to break their fast.

Thirteen kilometres north of Tulum, 122 km from Cancún (bus from Playa del Carmen, 45 minutes), the beautiful clear lagoon of **Laguna Xel-Há** ① *daily 0800-1630, US$10*, is full of fish, but fishing is not allowed as it is a national park. Snorkelling gear can be rented at US$7 for a day, but it is often in poor repair; better to rent from your hotel. Lockers cost US$1. Arrive as early as possible to see fish as the lagoon is full of tourists throughout most of the day. Snorkelling areas are limited by fencing. Bungalows, first-class hotels and fast-food restaurants are being built. The food and drink is very expensive. There is a marvellous jungle path to one of the lagoon bays. Xel-Há ruins, known also as **Los Basadres** ① *US$3.35*, are located across the road from the beach of the same name. Few tourists but not much to see. You may have to jump the fence to visit; there is a beautiful *cenote* at the end of the ruins where you can have a lovely swim.

Tulum → *Colour map 4, A3. Phone code: 984.*
① *Daily 0800-1800, entry US$4.50, parking US$1.50, students with Mexican ID free.*
The Maya-Toltec ruins of Tulum are perched on coastal cliffs in a beautiful setting above the azure sea. The ruins are 12th century, with city walls of white stone. The temples were dedicated to the worship of the Falling God, or the Setting Sun, represented as a falling character over nearly all the west-facing doors (Cozumel was the home of the Rising Sun). The same idea is reflected in the buildings, which are wider at the top than at the bottom.

The main structure is the **Castillo**, which commands a view of both the sea and the forested Quintana Roo lowlands stretching westwards. All the Castillo's openings face west, as do most, but not all, of the doorways at Tulum. Look for the alignment of the **Falling God** on the temple of that name (to the left of the Castillo) with the pillar and the back door in the **House of the Chultún** (the nearest building in the centre group to the entrance). The majority of the main structures are roped off so that you cannot climb the Castillo, nor get close to the surviving frescoes, especially on the **Temple of the Frescoes**.

Tulum is crowded with tourists (best time to visit is between 0800 and 0900). Take towel and swimsuit if you wish to scramble down from the ruins to one of the two beaches for a swim (the larger of the two is less easy to get to). The reef is from 600 m to 1000 m from the shore, so if you wish to snorkel you must either be a strong swimmer, or take a boat trip.

There is a tourist complex at the entrance to the ruins. Guide books can be bought in the shops, local guides can also be hired. About two hours are needed to view at leisure. The parking area is near Highway 307, and there's a handicraft market. A small train takes you from the parking area to the ruins for US$2, or it is an easy 500 m walk. The paved road continues down the coast to **Boca Paila** and beyond, access by car to this road from the car park is now forbidden. To reach the road south of the ruins, access is possible 1 km from Tulum village. Public buses drop passengers at El Crucero, a crossroads 500 m north of the car park for Tulum Ruinas (an easy walk) where there is an ADO bus terminal that is open for a few hours from 0800; at the crossroads are some hotels, a shop (will exchange traveller's cheques), on the opposite side of the road a naval base and airstrip, and a little way down Highway 307 a Pemex station.

If staying in the area, the beach running south of the ruins is dotted with quiet, isolated *palapas*, *cabañas* and hotels to fit most budgets. Alternatively the village of **Tulum** (as opposed to the ruins) is 4 km south of El Crucero. A taxi from the village to the ruins costs US$3. It is not very large but is growing rapidly and has a bus station, post office, bank (HSBC), several grocery shops, two bakeries, hotels and restaurants. There is a **tourist information office** in the village, next to the police station, two blocks north of the bus terminal. The information centre set up by the *Weary Traveller* backpacker centre has taken over as the primary source of information for this area. Located at the southern end of town a block away from the ADO bus terminal. Friendly and knowledgeable staff give fairly impartial information on hotels, excursions and restaurants. Another source of information is the **Sian Ka'an Information Centre** ① *Av Tulum between Satélite and Géminis, Tulum, T984-871 2363, siankaan_tours@hotmail.com*, which has information about visiting the reserve (see below) and several other areas of interest.

Cobá → *Colour map 4, A3. Phone code: 985.*
① *Daily 0800-1700, US$4.50.*

An important Maya city in the eighth and ninth centuries AD, whose population is estimated to have been between 40,000 and 50,000, Cobá was abandoned for unknown reasons. The present-day village of Cobá lies on either side of Lago Cobá, surrounded by dense jungle, 47 km inland from Tulum. It is a quiet, friendly village, with few tourists staying overnight.

The entrance to the ruins of this large but little-excavated city is at the end of the lake between the two parts of the village. A second lake, **Lago Macanxoc**, is within the site. There are turtles and many fish in the lakes. It is a good birdwatching area. Both lakes and their surrounding forest can be seen from the summit of the **Iglesia**, the tallest structure in the **Cobá Group**. There are three other groups of buildings to visit: the **Macanxoc Group**, mainly stelae, about 1.5 km from the Cobá Group; **Las Pinturas**, 1 km northeast of Macanxoc, with a temple and the remains of other buildings that had columns in their construction; the **Nohoch Mul Group**, at least another kilometre from Las Pinturas. Nohoch Mul has the tallest pyramid in the northern Yucatán, a magnificent structure,

Tulum to Chetumal

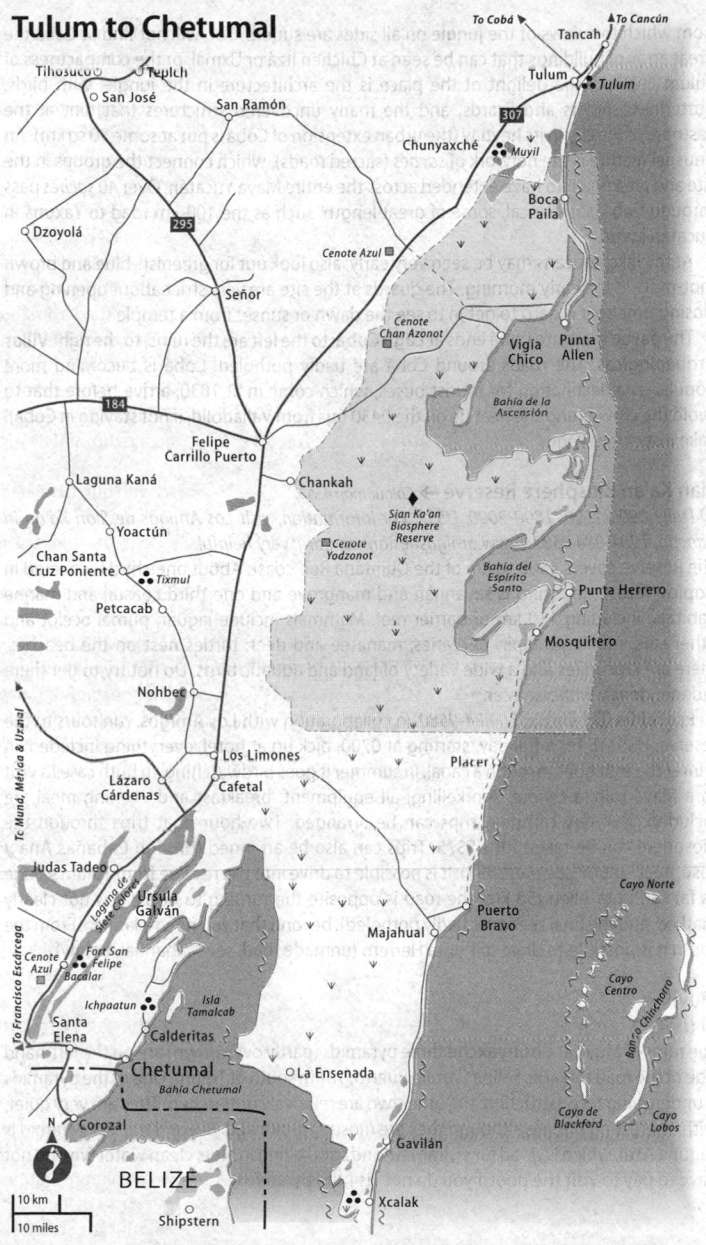

To Cobá
To Cancún
Tancah
Tihosuco
Tepich
San José
San Ramón
Tulum
San Ramón
307
Chunyaxché
Muyil
Dzoyolá
295
Boca Paila
Cenote Azul
Señor
Cenote Chan Azonot
Vigía Chico
Punta Allen
184
Bahía de la Ascensión
Felipe Carrillo Puerto
Chankah
Laguna Kaná
Sian Ka'an Biosphere Reserve
Yoactún
Cenote Yodzonot
Chan Santa Cruz Poniente
Tixmul
Bahía del Espíritu Santo
Petcacab
Punta Herrero
Mosquitero
Nohbec
Los Limones
Placer
Lázaro Cárdenas
Cafetal
Judas Tadeo
Ursula Galván
Cayo Norte
Laguna de Siete Colores
Fort San Felipe
Cenote Azul
Bacalar
To Francisco Escárcega
Ichpaatun
Isla Tamalcab
Puerto Bravo
Majahual
Cayo Centro
Santa Elena
Calderitas
Chetumal
Bahía Chetumal
La Ensenada
Cayo de Blackford
Cayo Lobos
N
Corozal
Gavilán
BELIZE
10 km
10 miles
Shipstern
Xcalak

To Mérida, Mérida & Uxmal

from which the views of the jungle on all sides are superb. You will not find at Cobá the great array of buildings that can be seen at Chichén Itzá or Uxmal, or the compactness of Tulum. Instead, the delight of the place is the architecture in the jungle, with birds, butterflies, spiders and lizards, and the many uncovered structures that hint at the vastness of the city in its heyday (the urban extension of Cobá is put at some 70 sq km). An unusual feature is the network of *sacbés* (sacred roads), which connect the groups in the site and are known to have extended across the entire Maya Yucatán. Over 40 *sacbés* pass through Cobá, some local, some of great length, such as the 100-km road to Yaxuná in Yucatán state.

At the lake, toucans may be seen very early; also look out for greenish-blue and brown mot-mots in the early morning. The guards at the site are very strict about opening and closing time so it is hard to get in to see the dawn or sunset from a temple.

The paved road into Cobá ends at **Lago Cobá**; to the left are the ruins, to the right **Villas Arqueológicas**. The roads around Cobá are badly potholed. Cobá is becoming more popular as a destination for tourist buses, which come in at 1030; arrive before that to avoid the crowds and the heat (ie on the 0430 bus from Valladolid, if not staying in Cobá). Take insect repellent.

Sian Ka'an Biosphere Reserve → *Colour map 4, A3.*
① *Daily 0900-1500, 1800-2000, US$2. For information, visit Los Amigos de Sian Ka'an in Cancún, T984-884 9583, www.amigosdesiankaan.org; very helpful.*
The Reserve covers 4500 sq km of the Quintana Roo coast. About one-third is covered in tropical forest, one-third is savannah and mangrove and one-third coastal and marine habitats, including 110 km of barrier reef. Mammals include jaguar, puma, ocelot and other cats, monkeys, tapir, peccaries, manatee and deer; turtles nest on the beaches; there are crocodiles and a wide variety of land and aquatic birds. Do not try to get there independently without a car.

Ecocolors ① *Cancún, T/F884-9580*, in collaboration with **Los Amigos**, run tours to the reserve, US$115 for a full day, starting at 0700, pick up at hotel, everything included; in winter the tour goes through a canal, in summer it goes birdwatching, in both cases a visit to a Maya ruin, a *cenote*, snorkelling, all equipment, breakfast and evening meal are included. Two-day camping trips can be arranged. Two-hour boat trips through the biosphere can be taken for US$75. Trips can also be arranged through **Cabañas Ana y José**, near Tulum (see page 593). It is possible to drive into the reserve from Tulum village as far as Punta Allen (58 km; the road is opposite the turning to Cobá; it is not clearly marked, and the final section is badly potholed); beyond that you need a launch. From the south it is possible to drive to Punta Herrero (unmade road, see Mahahual, below).

Muyil
① *US$4.*
The ruins of Muyil at **Chunyaxché** three pyramids (partly overgrown) are on the left-hand side of the road towards Felipe Carrillo Puerto, 18 km south of Tulum. One of the pyramids is undergoing reconstruction; the other two are relatively untouched. They are very quiet, with interesting birdlife although they are mosquito-infested. Beyond the last pyramid is Laguna Azul, which is good for swimming and snorkelling in blue, clean water (you do not have to pay to visit the pool if you do not visit the pyramids).

Cenote diving

There are more than 50 *cenotes* in this area – accessible from Ruta 307 and often well signposted – and cave diving has become very popular. However, it is a specialized sport and, unless you have a cave diving qualification, you must be accompanied by a qualified dive master. A cave diving course involves over 12 hours of lectures and a minimum of 14 cave dives using double tanks, costing around US$600. Accompanied dives start at around US$60. Specialist dive centres offering courses are: Mike Madden's **CEDAM Dive Centres**, PO Box 1, Puerto Aventuras, T/F984-873 5129; **Aquatech**, Villas de Rosa, PO Box 25, T984-875 9020, www.cenotes.com. **Aventuras Akumal No 35**, Tulum, T984-875 9030; **Aktun Dive Centre**, PO Box 119, Tulum, T984-871 2311,

and **Cenote Dive Center**, Tulum, T984-871 2232, www.cenotedive.com, Norwegian owned.

Two of the best *cenotes* are 'Carwash', on the Cobá road, good even for beginners, with excellent visibility; and 'Dos Ojos', just off Ruta 307 south of Aventuras, the second largest underground cave system in the world. It has a possible link to the Nohoch Nah Chich, the most famous cenote and part of a subterranean system recorded as the world's largest, with over 50 km of surveyed passageways connected to the sea.

A word of warning: *cenote* diving has a higher level of risk than open-water diving – do not take risks and only dive with recognized operators.

Felipe Carrillo Puerto → *Colour map 4, A3.*

The cult of the 'talking cross' was founded here. The **Santuario de la Cruz Parlante** is five blocks west of the Pemex station on Highway 307. The beautiful main square, which has playground equipment for children, is dominated by the Catholic church, built by the Cruzob in the 19th century (see page 530). Legend has it that the unfinished bell tower will only be completed when the descendants of those who heard the talking cross reassert control of the region.

Mahahual and around → *Colour map 4, A3.*

Further south on Route 307, at Cafetal, a good road heads east to Mahahual (Majahual) on the coast (56 km from Cafetal), a peaceful, unspoilt place with clear water and beautiful beaches. The cruise ship dock gives a clue to the occasional interruption to the peace and calm with Mahahual welcoming cruise ships travelling up and down the Mexican and Central American coast. A *combi* leaves from downtown at 0600, and from the bus terminal in Chetumal at 0600 and 1515, returning at 0630, 0845 and 1600. An offshore excursion is possible to **Banco Chinchorro**, where there is a coral bank and a white-sand beach.

About 2 km before Mahahual a paved road to the left goes to **Puerto Bravo** and on to Placer and **Punta Herrero** (In the Sian Ka'an Biosphere Reserve, see above).

Just over 3 km along this road a right turn goes to the **Sol y Mar** restaurant, with rooms to rent, coconut palms and beach. Another 10.5 km along the Punta Herrero road, again on the right, is **Camidas Trailer Park**, see Sleeping, page 595.

Xcalak → *Colour map 4, B3.*

Across the bay from Chetumal, at the very tip of Quintana Roo, is Xcalak, which may be reached from Chetumal by private launch (two hours), or by the unpaved road from

Border essentials: Mexico–Belize

Chetumal

Customs and immigration Procedure can be slow, particularly at peak holiday times when Belizeans come on charter buses for cheap shopping; over the bridge is Belizean passport control. For people entering Mexico, tourist cards are available at the border. It has been reported that only 15 days are given but you can get an additional 30 days at the Servicios Migratorios in Chetumal. Note that fresh fruit cannot be imported into Belize.

Driving Leaving Mexico by car, go to the Mexican immigration office to register your exit and surrender your vehicle permit and tourist card; very straightforward, no charges. Go to the office to obtain compulsory Belizean insurance (also money changing facilities here). Entering Belize, your car will be registered in your passport.

Exchange Money is checked on entering Belize. Excess Mexican pesos are easily changed into Belizean dollars with men waiting just beyond customs on the Belize side, but they are not there to meet the early bus. You can change US for Belizean dollar bills in the shops at the border, but this is not necessary as US$ are accepted in Belize. If you can get a good rate (dollars to pesos) in the bank, it is sometimes better to buy Belizean dollars with pesos in *casas de cambio* than to wait until you enter Belize where the US dollar/Belize dollar rate is fixed at 1:2.

Cafetal to Mahahual, then turning south for 55 km (186 km by road from Chetumal, suitable for passenger cars but needs skilled driver). *Colectivos* from Chetumal, daily 0700-1900, 16 de Septiembre 183 and Mahatma Ghandi, check return times. Bus runs Friday 1600 and Sunday 0600, returning Saturday morning and Sunday afternoon (details from Chetumal tourist office). Xcalak is a fishing village with a few shops selling beer and basic supplies and one small restaurant serving Mexican food. A few kilometres north of Xcalak are two hotels, **Costa de Cocos** and **Villa Caracol**, both American-run; the latter is good, with comfortable *cabañas*, although expensive. From here trips can be arranged to the unspoiled islands of Banco Chinchorro or to San Pedro, Belize. **Villa Caracol** has sport fishing and diving facilities. In the village you may be able to rent a boat to explore Chetumal Bay and Banco Chinchorro. Do *not* try to walk from Xcalak along the coast to San Pedro, Belize; the route is virtually impassable.

Chetumal ⊖🄿🄾🅰🄼🄱🄶 ➤ *pp589-609. Colour map 4, B3.*

→ *Phone code: 983.*

The state capital of Quintana Roo, Chetumal, is a necessary stopover for travellers en route to Maya sites in the south of the peninsula, and across the frontier to Belize and Guatemala. Although attractions are thin on the ground, Chetumal does have the advantage of being a small Mexican city not devoted to tourism, and thus has a more authentic feel than other towns on the Riviera Maya. It is 240 km south of Tulum. The Chetumal bay has been designated a natural protected area for manatees, and includes a manatee sanctuary.

The avenues are broad, busy and in the centre lined with huge shops selling cheap imported goods. The main local activity is window-shopping, and the atmosphere is more like a North American city, with an impression of affluence that can be a culture shock to the visitor arriving from the much poorer country of Guatemala. The **tourist office** ① *on the main plaza, opposite the Museo de Cultura Maya, Mon-Fri 0900-1900, Sat 0900-1300*, is mainly for trade enquiries. There is very little tourist information in Chetumal; it is usually best to go to a travel agent such as **Tu-Maya** (see page 603).

The *paseo* near the waterfront on Sunday night is worth seeing. The State Congress building has a mural showing the history of Quintana Roo. The **Museo de la Cultura Maya** ① *Av Héroes de Chapultepec by the market, Tue-Sun 0900-1900, US$5*, is highly recommended. It has good models of sites and touch screen computers explaining the Maya calendar and glyphs. Although there are few original Maya pieces, it gives an excellent overview; some explanations are in English, guided tours are available, and there's a good bookshop with English magazines.

Chetumal

Sleeping 🏨
Caribe Princess 2
Cristal 3
El Dorado 4
Los Cocos 6
María Dolores 7
Palma Real 1
Real Azteca 8
Ucum 10

Eating 🍴
El Emporio 2
El Fenicio 3
Los Milagros 4
Pantoja 5
Sergio Pizza 1

Around Chetumal 🚌🚗🏔
▶▶ *pp589-609.*

Towards Bacalar

Six kilometres north of Chetumal are the stony beaches of **Calderitas**, bus every 30 minutes from Colón, between Belice and Héroes, US$1.80, or taxi US$5, many fish restaurants. There is camping at Calderitas, signposted, OK, US$2.75. Beyond are the unexcavated archaeological sites of **Ichpaatun** (13 km), **Oxtancah** (14 km) and **Nohochmul** (20 km). Sixteen kilometres north on Route 307 to Tulum is the **Laguna de los Milagros**, a beautiful lagoon for swimming. Further on, 34 km north of Chetumal, is **Cenote Azul**, over 70 m deep, with a waterside restaurant serving inexpensive and good seafood and regional food (but awful coffee) until 1800. Both the *laguna* and the *cenote* are deserted in the week.

About 3 km north of Cenote Azul is the village of **Bacalar** (nice, but not special) on the **Laguna de Siete Colores**, which has swimming and skin-diving; *colectivos* from terminal (Suchaa) in Chetumal, corner of Miguel Hidalgo and Primo de Verdad, 0700-1900 every 30 minutes, US$1.60, return from plaza when full; also buses from Chetumal bus station every two hours or so, US$1.60. There is a Spanish fort there overlooking a beautiful shallow, clear, freshwater lagoon, and abundant birdlife on the lake shore. This is the fort of **San Felipe**, said to have been built around 1729 by the Spanish to defend the area from the English pirates and smugglers of logwood. There is a plaque praying for protection from the British and a small **museum** ① *US$0.70*. The British ships roamed the islands and reefs, looting Spanish galleons laden with gold, on their way from Peru to Cuba. There are many old shipwrecks on the reef and around the Banco Chinchorro, 50 km out in the Caribbean (information kindly provided by Coral Pitkin of the **Rancho Encantado**, see page 595). There is a dock for swimming from north of the plaza, with a restaurant and disco next to it. North of Bacalar a direct road (Route 293) runs to Muná, on the road between Mérida and Uxmal. Gasoline is sold in a side-street.

Towards Francisco Villa

From Chetumal you can visit the fascinating Maya ruins that lie west on the way (Route 186) to Francisco Villa and Escárcega, if you have a car. There are few tourists in this area and few facilities. Take plenty of drinking water. About 25 km from Chetumal at **Ucum** (where fuel is available), you can turn off 5 km south to visit **Palmara**, located along the Río Hondo, which borders Belize; there are swimming holes and restaurant.

Just before Francisco Villa (61 km from Chetumal), the ruins of **Kohunlich** ① *0800-1700, US$3*, lie 8.5 km south of the main road, 1½ hours' walk along a sweltering, unshaded road; take plenty of water. Descriptions in Spanish and English. Every hour or so the van passes for staff working at **Explorer Kohunlich**, a luxury resort hotel halfway to the ruins, which may give you a lift, but you'll still have 4 km to walk. There are fabulous masks (early Classic, AD 250-500) set on the side of the main pyramid, still bearing red colouring; they are unique of their kind (allow an hour for the site). About 200 m west of the turning for Kohunlich is an immigration office and a stall selling beer; wait here for buses to Chetumal or Xpujil, which have to stop, but first-class buses will not pick up passengers. *Colectivos* 'Nicolás Bravo' from Chetumal, or bus marked 'Zoh Laguna' from bus station pass the turning.

Other ruins in this area are **Dzibanché** and **Knichná** ① *0900-1700, US$3*. Both are recent excavations and both are accessible down a dirt road off the Chetumal–Morocoy road. In the 1990s the remains of a Maya king were disinterred at Dzibanché, which is thought to have been the largest Maya city in southern Quintana Roo, peaking between AD 300 and 1200. Its discoverer, Thomas Gann, named it in 1927 after the Maya glyphs he found engraved on the sapodilla wood lintels in Temple VI – *Dzibanché* means 'writing on the wood' in Maya. Later excavations revealed a tomb in Temple I, believed to have belonged to a king because of the number of offerings it contained. This temple is also known as the **Temple of the Owl** because one of the artefacts unearthed was a vase and lid carved with an owl figure. Other important structures are the **Temple of the Cormorants** and **Structure XIII**, known as 'The Captives', due to its friezes depicting prisoners. Knichná means 'House of the Sun' in Maya, christened by Thomas Gann in reference to a glyph he found there. The **Acropolis** is the largest structure. To reach these sights follow the Chetumal-Escárcega road, turn off at Km 58 towards Morocoy, 9 km further on. The road to Dzibanché is 2 km down this road, crossing the turning for Knichná.

State of Quintana Roo listings

For Sleeping and Eating price codes and other relevant information, see Essentials pages 45-48.

Sleeping

Isla Holbox *p571*

AL Faro Viejo, Av Juárez, on the beach, T984-875 2217, www.faroviejo holbox.com.mx. Large, breezy rooms looking over the beach. Some rooms with kitchens.

AL Villa Delfines, on the beach, T984-875 2196, www.villasdelfines.com. 20 romantic palm-roofed bungalows, leading onto the beach, pool, garden and bar, expensive but nice.

A La Palapa, Av Morelos 231, T984-875 2121, www.hotellapalapa.com. Very clean cabins, leading onto the beach.

A-B Mawimbi, T984-875 2003, www.mawimbi.com.mx. Stylishly decorated *cabañas* with kitchenette, stepping out onto the beach.

Camping

Best camping on beach east of village (north side of island).

Cancún *p571, maps p572 and p573*

Accommodation in the Hotel Zone starts at around US$75, rises quickly and is best arranged as part of a package holiday. The beaches are supposedly public so you don't have to stay in a hotel to hang out on the beach. The centre or Downtown area has many cheaper options, but prices are still higher than other parts of the Yucatán Peninsula.

Hotel Zone

Some of these hotels have special offers during Jul and Aug, listed in *Riviera Maya Hotels Guide*, available free at the airport. Discounts can be considerable. 2 good options are:

LL Le Meridien, Retorno del Rey Km 14, T998-881 2200.

L Presidente Inter-Continental, Av Kukulcán Km 7.5, T998-848 8700.

Town centre

Many hotels, especially the budget ones, tend to be full during Jul. It is best to get to them as early as possible in the morning, or try to make a reservation if planning to return to Cancún after a trip to the interior or Isla Mujeres. Prices drop considerably in the low season. El Crucero, location of some of the budget hotels, is said by locals to be safe during the day, but unsafe at night.

AL-A El Rey del Caribe, Av Uxmal 24 and Náder, T998-884 2028, www.reycaribe.com. This hotel has clean, comfortable a/c rooms, some with cooker and fridge. There's a lush garden slung with hammocks and the spa has interesting treatments, such as chocolate or honey and milk massage.

AL-A Margaritas, Yaxchilán 41 and Jasmines, T998-884 7870, www.margaritas cancun.com. A clean and modern hotel with a range of efficient services including restaurant, bar, car rental, laundry and pool. There are over 100 rooms, all with a/c, balcony and cable TV.

B Cancún Rosa, Margaritas 2, local 10, T998-884 0623. Located close to the bus terminal, this hotel has tidy rooms of various sizes (including family size), all with cable TV and a/c. Management is friendly.

B-D Mayan Hostel Cancún, Margaritas 17 SM22, T998-892 0103, www.mayan hostel.com. Price per person. *Palapa*-style dorms, private rooms, fan or a/c. Breakfast, dinner and internet included in the price. Laundry and kitchen. Good service.

C El Alux, Av Uxmal 21, T998-884 0556, www.hotelalux.com. Turn left and first right from bus station. Clean rooms with a/c and bath. Some are cheaper and good value. Beware of the persistent tout outside, trying to take you to a cheap hovel. Recommended.

C María Isabel, Palmera 59, T998-884 9015, hotelmariaisabelcancun@yahoo.com.mx, near bus station and Av Tulum. A small hotel with clean and relatively economical rooms, all with a/c and TV. Friendly and recommended, but can be noisy.

C San Carlos, Cedro 40 (5th turning onto Cedro from bus terminal), opposite Mercado 23, T998-884 0602, www.hotelsancarlo scancun.com, near and handy for the bus terminal. Mixed bag of rooms, with mixed tariffs. Some rooms are a bit noisy and smelly, the upper floor is OK and a bit cheaper, but beware of very rickety stairs.

C-D Hotel Mary Tere, Calle 7 norte and Calle 10 oriente, T998-884 0496, www.hotel marytere.com. Lots of cheap, basic rooms. Get one upstairs, as the ones downstairs can be cramped and gloomy. There are few other budget places in this street.

C-E Las Palmas, Palmeras 43, T998-884 2513, www.hotel-laspalmascancun.com. This friendly family-run hotel has very clean, good-value rooms with cable TV and a/c, and they'll store luggage. Breakfast is included and there's a cheap dormitory too. Recommended.

E The Weary Traveller, Palmera 30, entrance in Av Uxmal, T998-887 0191, reservations@ wearytravelerhostel.com. Funky budget hostel with dormitories and private rooms (**C**). There's free internet, breakfast included in the price, TV, lockers and chillout space.

Camping

A big trailer park has been built opposite Punta Sam, 150 spaces, camping (**E** per person), shop selling basic commodities. Irregular bus service there, or hitchhike from Puerto Juárez. Check to see if restaurant is open evenings. Take mosquito repellent.

Isla Mujeres p574

LL Condominio Nautibeach, Playa Los Cocos, T998-877 0606, www.nautibeach.com. This hotel feels a bit like a giant warren, but has comfortable, a/c apartments and condos, right on the beach, facing the sunset. **Sunset**

Grill, attached, is perfect for sundowners and there's a nice pool too.

L María del Mar, Av Carlos Larzo 1, on the road down to the north beach, T998-877 0179, www.cabanasdelmar.com. Good clean rooms and *cabañas*, close to the best beach. There's a restaurant, pool, beach bar, hammocks and a cool, tranquil garden for chilling out. Organizes fishing excursions and cultural tours.

AL Rocamar, Nicolás Bravo and Zona Marítima, T998-877 0101, www.rocamar-hotel.com. A large, well-established hotel, located on the quieter, eastern side of the island, where the sea is wilder and swimming not recommended. There's a range of rooms; the more expensive overlook the sea and the Caribbean sunrise and also have jacuzzi.

A Hotel Bucaneros, Hidalgo 11, T998-877 1222, www.bucaneros.com. A pleasant, professionally managed hotel, right in the heart of town. It has 18 modern rooms, all with calm, neutral interiors. There's a good restaurant attached.

B Hotel El Caracol, Matamoros 5, T998-877 0150, www.isla-mujeres.net/hotelelcaracol. Slightly tired, but acceptable rooms with fridge, fan and cable TV. Get one upstairs where there's more light. Low season prices almost 50% cheaper.

C Hotel Carmelina, Guerrero 4, T998-877 0006. Motel-style place with parking. The rooms are good and clean, with fridge, bath and fan. Good value.

C María José, Madero 25, T877-0130, close to the dock. Clean, fans, friendly, reasonably quiet, scooter hire next door.

C Posada Edelmar, Hidalgo, next to Bucanero hotel and restaurant. Economical alternative slap-bang in the middle of the pedestrianized section of town, seconds from the main restaurants and bars. Spacious rooms with good showers. Ask for a room at the back if you want some peace and quiet.

C Vistalmar, Av Rueda Medina on promenade close to the ferry dock and Pemex station, T998-877 0209 (**D** for longer stays). Clean, comfortable rooms with fan, bath, balcony and TV. Some have a/c (**C**). Ask for a room on the top floor.

C-E Pocna Hostel (price per person), top end of Matamoros on the northeast coast, T998-877 0090, www.pocna.com. This is an island institution. Large, busy and warren-like Pocna has a plethora of dorms and rooms. There's internet access, lounge and beach bar, space to sling a hammock (**F**), yoga lessons and live music in the evenings. Book in advance – this is one of few hostels on the island, and as such is popular.

D Osorio, Madero, 1 block from waterfront. Clean, simple rooms with fan, bath and hot water.

D-E Hostel Posada del Mar, Av Juárez s/n, T998-100 0759. This brand new hostel, features dorms and a couple of private rooms, all with fan, hot water and safety boxes. Continental breakfast included.

Puerto Morelos *p575*
AL Rancho Sak-Ol Libertad, next door to **Caribbean Reef Club**, T009-871 0181, www.rancholibertad.com. Thatched *cabañas*; the price includes breakfast, scuba-diving and snorkelling gear for rent.

B Posada Amor, Av Javier Rojo Gómez, opposite the beach, T998-871 0033. Very pleasant, well-built *cabañas* with good mosquito nets, the cheaper ones have outdoor communal showers, there is also a good restaurant and prices are reduced considerably out of season.

Playa del Carmen *p576, map p576*
Accommodation in Playa del Carmen is generally expensive and poor value, particularly around the beach and Av 5. The prices given below are for the high season, and can drop by as much as 50% at other times of the year.

LL Playacar Palace, T984-873 4960, www.palaceresorts.com. A huge luxury development just south of the ferry terminal, excellent in every respect, non-residents can use swimming pool

if they buy a day pass for US$84 – perhaps best to head for the beach.

LL Tides Riviera Maya, Rivera Maya Playa, Xcalacoco, Fracc 7, T984-877 3000, www.tidesrivieramaya.com. This boutique hotel boasts 30 well-designed villas in a jungle garden, and unpretentious service. The beach here is rocky, but they have built decking out to the sea so you can swim away from the rocks. See Activities and tours, page 602.

LL-L Alhambra, Calle 8 Norte, on corner with the beach, T984-873 0735, www.alhambra-hotel.net. Nice, airy palatial feel at this hotel with spiritual inclinations. All rooms have balcony or sea view, and general services include yoga instruction, jacuzzi, massage and there is a spa. Quiet and peaceful, despite its setting near beach bars. Family-run, French and English spoken. Recommended.

LL-AL Blue Parrot, at the north end of town, on a popular stretch of beach between Calle 12 and Calle 14, T01-800-022-3206. A large complex of luxury studios and suites, all stylishly rendered. There's excellent services and facilities, including a popular nightclub. This is the place for sexy, young, successful people. Slightly snooty.

AL Tropical Casablanca Hotel, Av Primera, between Calle 12 and 10, T984-873 0057, www.tropicalcasablanca.com. Clean, white, minimalist rooms. There's a garden, pool, *cenote* and impressive 6 room house for groups.

A Casa Tucán, Calle 4 Norte, between Av 10 and 15, T984-873 0283, www.casatucan.de. German-owned hotel with simple, rustic *cabañas* and rooms. Rambling and labyrinthine, but there's a lovely lush garden, beautifully painted murals, and a deep pool where diving instruction takes place. There's also a restaurant, internet café and other handy outlets attached.

A Hotel Cielo, Calle 4, between Calle 5 and 10, T984-873 1227, www.hotelcielo.com. Right in the centre of town, rooms have a/c, cable TV, safe and also throw in beach towels and breakfast. The corridors are a bit dark and narrow, but the views from the roof terrace superb. Restaurant **Carboncito** attached does great tacos.

A Hotel Las Molcas, T984-873 0070, www.molcas.com.mx, near ferry pier. Strange but interesting architecture at this hotel, where some of the Moorish-style corridors seem to recede into infinity. There's a pool and staff are friendly.

A Maya Bric, Av 5, between Calle 8 and 10, T984-873 0011, www.mayabric.com. A friendly hotel with comfortable (if unremarkable) rooms, all with Wi-Fi and safes. There's a good garden and pool.

A Mom's Hotel, Calle 4 and Av 30, T984-873 0315, www.momshotel.com, about 5 blocks from bus station or beach. Excellent value, friendly, family-run hotel with a pool. There are studios and apartments and good rates for long-term stays. Recommended.

B Happy Gecko, Av 10 between Calle 6 and 8, T984-147 0692, happygeckohotel @yahoo.com. Canadian-owned, this hotel has good rooms with kitchen, fan and bath, some with a/c. Laundry service and movies available.

C Posada Marinelly, Av Juárez between Calle 10 and 15, T984-873 0140. Centrally located with light, bright, comfortable rooms. More expensive with a/c (**A**). Handy for the **ADO** terminal. Friendly, bit basic.

C-E Urban Hostel, Av 10 between 4 and 6, T984-803 3378, urbanhostel@gmail.com Funky backpackers' place with private rooms and dorms. Price includes breakfast. There's DVD, X-Box, internet and Wi-Fi, 2 terraces and kitchen.

D-E Hostel Playa, Av 25 with Calle 8, T984-803 3277, www.hostelplaya.com. A clean, professionally run hostel with various dorms, private rooms, kitchen and lounge space. There's a comfortable, friendly atmosphere. Prices per person, not per room.

Camping
Punta Bete, 10 km north, the right-hand one of 3 campsites at the end of a 5-km road, on beach. US$3 for tent, also 2 restaurants and *cabañas*.

Cozumel *p577, map p578 and p579*
Hotels are generally expensive and poor value. Expect prices to drop up to 50% during low season.

AL Bahía, Av Rafael Melgar and Calle 3 Sur, T987-872 9090, www.suitesbahia.com. Comfortable, a/c rooms with cable TV, kitchenette and fridge. Some have ocean views.

AL Flamingo, Calle 6 Norte 81, T954-315 9236, www.hotelflamingo.com. Tasteful, comfortable rooms with a/c, Wi-Fi, balcony and fridge. There's a penthouse on the roof, good for families. Friendly staff.

A Amaranto, Calle 5 Sur, Av 15-20, T987-564 4262,www.cozumel.net/bb/amaranto. Lovely thatched-roof Mayan-style bungalows and suites, complete with hammocks. Spanish, English and French are spoken by the owners, Elaine and Jorge. There's a pool, and childcare is available on request.

A Tamarindo, Calle 4 Norte 421, between Av 20 and 25, T987-872 3614, www.cozumel.net/bb/tamarind. Intimate bed and breakfast, also owned by Elaine and Jorge. There's a shared kitchen, hammocks, dive gear storage and rinse tank, purified drinking water, laundry, and safe-deposit box.

B Pepita, Av 15 Sur 120 y Calle 1 Sur, T987-872 0098, www.hotelpepitacozumel.com. Very pleasant rooms around a plant-filled courtyard. Modern fittings, a/c, cable TV, fridge in all rooms. Free coffee in the morning. Recommended.

B Posada Marruang, A R Salas 440, between Av 20 Sur and 25 Sur, T987-872 1678. Very spick and span, large spartan rooms set back from road; barking dog ensures occasional noise and total security.

B Posada Zuanayoli, Calle 6 Norte 272 between Av 10 and Av 15 Norte, T987-872 0690. Tall, old and slightly knackered

building in a quiet street. Clean rooms have TV, fridge, fan, some with a/c (**B**). Free coffee and drinking water for guests.
B Saolima, A R Salas 260, T987-872 0886. Clean, basic rooms with fan, showers, hot water.
C Flores, A R Salas 72, off plaza, T987-872 1429. A range of basic, acceptable rooms with cable TV, fan or a/c (**B**). Only 50 m from the sea and very cheap for the location.
C Posada Edén, Calle 2 Norte 124, T987-872 1166, gustarimo@hotmail.com. Clean, economical rooms with the usual bare necessities, including fan or a/c (**B**). There are apartments for long-term rental, 1 month min.

Tulum *p581*
Tulum village
Tulum village is a blossoming, but still relatively uninspiring destination. Scores of new budget hotels and restaurants are opening apace, making it a good base for backpackers and cost-conscious travellers. However, expect to offset those lower hotel rates with additional transport costs. There are no buses to the beach, only taxis and infrequent *colectivos*. For places to stay in Sian Ka'an Biosphere Reserve, see page 594.
C Hotel Maya, T984-871 1234, Av Tulum near the bus station. Large hotel with plenty of economical rooms, all with fan and bath. There's a restaurant next door serving home-cooked Mexican fare.
C-E Rancho Tranquilo, 1984-871 2784, www.ranchotranquilo.com.mx, far south end of town. Friendly backpackers' place with dorms, *cabañas* and large rooms with private bath. There's also a lounge, library, shared kitchen and verdant garden. Friendly and highly recommended.
D-E Mayan Hostel Tulum, Carretera Coba – Boca Paila SN, 400 m from El Crucero, T998-112 1282, www.mayanhostel.com. Private rooms in *palapas*, dorms with a/c, breakfast and internet included in price. Bike rentals, book exchange, free short-term luggage storage.

D-E Weary Traveller Hostel, T984-871 2390, www.wearytravelerhostel.com, 1 block south of ADO bus terminal. Tulum's premier backpackers' hostel has bunk dorms, a book exchange and internet. They run transport to the beach, regular salsa classes and you can even cook your own food on the bbq. A good place to meet fellow travellers. Breakfast included.

Tulum beach
A plethora of lodgings run the length of the coast from Tulum ruins to the Sian Ka'an Biosphere reserve. Development has been mercifully low-key, with ramshackle *cabañas* existing alongside luxury eco-lodges. There is little infrastructure beyond these hotels, and it's best to reach them by taxi; official rates are posted on a sign at the rank in the village. Expect room costs to vary with views and proximity to the sea. Bear in mind this is a long stretch of beach and it's not always plausible to walk from hotel to hotel.
LL Ana y José, T984-880 5629, www.anayjose.com, 7 km south of ruins. Once only a collection of humble *cabañas*, Ana y José now offer elegant suites and luxurious spa accommodation. First-rate service and attention.
L Dos Ceibas, T984-877 6024, www.dosceibas.com, 9 km from the ruins. This verdant eco-lodge on the edge of the Sian Ka'an Biosphere reserve has a handful of comfortable *cabañas*. Massage and yoga instruction available. Friendly and tranquil ambience.
L Posada Lamar, T984 116-6386, www.posadalamar.com, 4.5 km from ruins. Beautiful, tranquil *cabañas*, simple yet elegant. Best to reserve in advance. Friendly management.
L Posada Margherita, T984-801 8493, www.posadamargherita.com. A decent, hospitable hotel with complete wheelchair access. There's 24-hr electricity and an excellent Italian restaurant attached. Recommended.

L-AL Eco Tulum, T01-800-514 3066, www.ecotulum.com. 3 beachside resorts: Cabañas Copal, Azulik and Zahra. Each resort shares the rustic Maya Spa (www.maya-spa.com), based at Cabañas Copal, which specializes in affordable local Maya treatments. See Activities and tours, page 603.

AL Cabañas Diamante K, T984-876 2115, www.diamantek.com, on the beach quite near the ruins. Rustic and friendly, with an array of interesting statues and hints of The Crystal Maze. Cabaña prices vary according to location and amenities, much cheaper with shared bath. There's a good bar and restaurant.

AL-B Los Arrecifes, T984-155 2957, www.losarrecifestulum.com, 7 km from ruins. Cabañas, trampoline, live music and shows, restaurant.

A Hotel Zazil-Kin, T984-124-0082, www.zazilkintulum.com, near the ruins. Zazil-Kin is a popular, well-established Tulum favourite. A bit basic for the price, it offers a wide range of lodgings from rooms to cabañas, as well as restaurant, bar and gift shop.

B Playa Condesa, next door to Diamante K. Simple, airy wooden cabañas, not particularly good value for the price. Electricity a few hrs each evening. There's a basic, but pricey grocery shop attached.

B-F Mar Caribe, near the ruins. Smaller complex than its neighbour, Zazil-Kin, but a friendly atmosphere, and much more peaceful. Very cheap if you bring your own hammock or tent. Organizes tours.

Cobá p582

A-B Villas Arqueológicas (Club Méditerranée), about 2 km from site on lake shore, T985-858 1527. Open to non-members, excellent, clean and quiet, a/c, swimming pool, good restaurant with moderate prices, but expensive beer. Don't arrive without a reservation, especially at weekends; and yet making a reservation by phone seems to be practically impossible.

E-F Hotel Restaurant El Bocadito, in the village, on the street leading to the main road, T984-876 3738, www.cancunsouth.com/bocadito/. Run-down, spartan rooms with fan, intermittent water supply, poor security, good but expensive restaurant (which is popular with tour groups), books and handicrafts for sale. Recommended.

Sian Ka'an Biosphere Reserve p584

AL Rancho Sol Caribe, Punta Allen. 4 comfortable cabañas, with bath, restaurant. Recommended.

A Centro Ecológico Sian Ka'an, T984-871 2499, www.cesiak.org. Environmentally considerate and sensitive accommodation in the heart of the Reserve. Tours, kayaking and fly fishing arranged.

Felipe Carrillo Puerto p585

B Chan Santa Cruz, Calle 68, 782, just off the plaza, T983-834 0021, www.hotelchansantacruz.com. Good, clean and friendly. A/c, cable TV, handicap accessible, fridge (Restaurante 24 Horas is open, as you'd imagine, 24 hrs).

B El Faisán y El Venado, Av Benito Juárez, Lote 781, 2 blocks northeast of main square. Mixed reports on cleanliness, but hot water and good-value restaurant, popular with locals.

B San Ignacio, Av Benito Juárez 761, near Pemex. Good value, a/c, bath, towels, TV, secure car park.

C María Isabel, near the plaza. Clean, friendly, laundry service, quiet, safe parking.

Mahahual and around p585

There are plenty of options for sleeping with hammocks, camping and cabañas.

B-E Kabah-na, T983-838 8861, kabahna@yahoo.com. Cabañas or space to hang a hammock, right on the beach.

C Sol y Mar restaurant, en route to Puerto Bravo, near Mahahual, with rooms to rent, bathrooms and spaces for RVs, also coconut palms and beach.

D-E Kok Hal, Mahahual, on the beach close to the old wharf. Shared bath and hot showers.

Camping
Camidas Trailer Park, Punta Herrero road, with palm trees, *palapas*, restaurant and space for 4 RVs, US$5 per person, car free.

Chetumal *p586, map p587*
AL Los Cocos, Av Héroes de Chapultepec 134, T983-835 0430, www.hotellos cocos.com.mx. Large, professionally managed hotel with clean, comfortable rooms and suites. There's a pool, bar and restaurant. Recommended.
A Caribe Princess, Av Obregón 168, T983-832 0520, www.caribeprincess chetumal.com. Good, clean rooms with a/c and TV. Recommended.
B Hotel Palma Real, Obregón 103, T983-833 0963. Friendly and helpful place with big, clean rooms. Bath, cable TV and a/c.
B Ucúm, Gandhi 167 cnr of 16 de Septiembre, T983-832 6186, www.hotel ucumchetumal.com. Rooms with a/c, fan and bath. Pool and enclosed car park. Good-value restaurant next door.
C El Dorado, Av 5 de Mayo 42, T983-832 0315. Comfortable rooms with hot water and a/c. Friendly and quiet. Recommended.
C Hotel Cristal, Cristóbal Colón 207, T983-832 3878. Simple rooms with fan and bath. Parking available.
C-D Real Azteca, Av Belice 186, T983-832 0720. Cheerful, friendly, but no hot shower. 2nd-floor rooms best, but still not too good.
D María Dolores, Av Alvaro Obregón 206, T983-832 0508. Bath, hot water, fan, clean, windows don't open, noisy, restaurant **Solsimar** downstairs good and popular. Recommended.

Towards Bacalar *p587*
LL Akal Ki, Carretera Federal 307, km 12.5, Bacalar Lagoon, T983-106 1751, www.akalki.com. A marvellously peaceful retreat with *palapas* built right over the water. Though surrounded by jungle, this strip of the lagoon has few rocks and little vegetation, making it crystal clear and ideal for swimming. Minimum stay 3 days. See Activities and tours, page 603.
LL-L Rancho Encantado, 3 km north of Bacalar, on the west shore of the lagoon. Resort hotel, half-board available, Apdo 233, Chetumal, T983-101 3358, www.encantado.com. With private dock, tour boat, canoes and windsurf boards for rent, private cabins with fridge and hammock, very good. See Activities and tours, page 603.
A-B Hotel Las Lagunas, Bvl Costero 479, about 2 km south of Bacalar (on left-hand side of the road going towards the village), T983-834 2206. It is very good, wonderful views, helpful, clean, comfortable, hot water, swimming pool and opposite a freshwater lake; restaurant is poor and overpriced.
C Hotel América, Av 5 258, Bacalar, 700 m north of the bus stop on the plaza (walk in the opposite direction to Chetumal). Recommended.

Camping
Camping possible at the end of the road 100 m from the lagoon, toilets and shower, US$0.10, but lagoon perfect for washing and swimming.

Eating

Cancún *p571, maps p572 and p573*
The **Hotel Zone** is lined with expensive restaurants, with every type of international cuisine imaginable, but with a predominance of Tex-Mex and Italian. Restaurants in the centre are cheaper, and the emphasis is on local food.

The cheapest area for dinner is SM64, opposite **Plaza 2000**. Popular with locals, especially on Sun when it is hard to get a table; there are 4 or 5 small, family-run restaurants serving local specialities. *Comida corrida* for as little as US$2. **Mercado 28** is the best budget option for breakfast or lunch, with many cheap outdoor and

indoor *loncherías* serving *comida corrida*,
very popular with locals, quick service.
Another good option os Mercado 23,
5 blocks north of the ADO terminal,
along Calle Cedro.

ΨΨΨ El Pescador, Tulipanes 28. Good
seafood, well established with excellent
reputation. Expensive.

ΨΨΨ La Habichuela, Margaritas 25.
Award-winning restaurant serving delicious
Caribbean seafood in a tropical garden
setting. Great ambience and jazz music.

ΨΨΨ La Parilla, Yaxchilán 51. Mouth-watering
grill platters, ribs and steaks. A buzzing, lively
joint, always busy and popular. Try the
enormous margaritas in exotic flavours –
hibiscus flower and tamarind.

ΨΨΨ Pericos, Av Yaxchilán 71, T998-884 3152,
www.pericos.com.mx. Chicken, meat, fish
fillets and seafood platters at this themed
Mexican restaurant where the staff wear
fancy dress. It's touristy, it's cheesy,
but the atmosphere is great.

ΨΨΨ-ΨΨ El Rincón del Vino, Alcatraces 29.
Tapas with a seafood emphasis. As the
name suggests, there's a healthy stock of
wine. A tranquil and pleasant place, with
a range of international food.

ΨΨΨ-ΨΨ Labná, Margaritas 29. The best in
Yucatecan cooking, serving dishes like *poc
chuc* and *pollo pibil*. Try the platter and
sample a wide range of this fascinating
regional cuisine. Good lunchtime buffet.

ΨΨ El Poblano, Tulum and Tulipanes. Tacos,
kebabs, grilled meats and steaks – carnivores
call it dinner. A friendly, unpretentious
restaurant, popular with Mexicans.

ΨΨ Rincón Yucateco, Av Uxmal 24. Good grills
and traditional Mexican grub from lunchtime.

Cafés

Pastelería Italiana, Yaxchilán, just before
turning of Sunyaxchén. Excellent coffee and
pastries, friendly. A few other cheap eateries
along Yaxchilán, tucked away between the
pricey themed restaurants, some open
during the day only.

Isla Mujeres *p574*

The most popular street for restaurants
is Hidalgo.

ΨΨΨ Mesón del Bucanero, Hidalgo, opposite
Rolandis. Steaks, seafood, pasta and crêpes
at this classy restaurant. There's a rich offering
of cocktails too. Nice al fresco seating.

ΨΨ Bamboo, Hidalgo. A sleek and trendy
restaurant-bar serving sushi, Thai curries,
seafood and fresh fruit juices. Live music
at the weekends.

ΨΨ Comono, Hidalgo. Open 1400-2230,
Mon-Fri. Israeli-run kitchen and bar that
serves Mediterranean food, beer and shakes.
There are nightly movies, live music on Fri,
and hookah pipes if you fancy smoking some
molasses. Popular with backpackers.

ΨΨ Los Amigos Restaurant, Hidalgo.
Small, with 2 tables outside, excellent
pizzas and pasta.

ΨΨ Mamma Rosa, Hidalgo and Matamoros.
Formerly La Malquerida. Italian-run restaurant
serving pasta and seafood with a good
selection of Italian wines.

ΨΨ Miguel's Moon Lite, Hidalgo 9. Good
hospitality at this lively restaurant-bar.
When the booze isn't flowing, there's
tacos, steaks and seafood. Ask for a
free shot of pomegranate tequila.

ΨΨ Rolandis, Hidalgo, T998-877 0700.
Terrace overlooking the street. Excellent
Italian food, including a good range of
tasty pizzas and pastas, seafood and meat
dishes. Has many branches across Mexico.

Ψ La Susanita, Juárez 5. Excellent home
cooking, at this cute little locals' place;
when closed it is the family's living room.

Ψ Lonchería La Lomita, Juárez 25B. Nice
and clean and at US$3, quite possibly the
best value, tasty food in town.

Ψ Loncherías, northwest end of Guerrero,
surrounding the municipal market, open till
1800. Busy and bustling, good for breakfast,
snacks and lunch. All serve the same local fare
at similar prices.

Ψ Poc-Chuc, Juárez y Madero. Somewhat
rough and ready locals' joint, serving up
big portions and good *tortas*.

Cafés

Aluxes Café, Av Matamoros, next to Aquí Estoy Pizza. A cheery little place serving cappuccinos, filter coffee and home-made snacks.

Cafecito, Matamoros 42. Cool and tranquil. A nice breakfast place, serving waffles, juice, sandwiches.

Puerto Morelos *p575*

Johnny Cairo, with good typical food.

Pelícano. Serves very good seafood.

Playa del Carmen *p576, map p576*

The majority of the town's restaurants line Av 5, where most tourists limit themselves and a meal costs no less (and usually a bit more) than US$10. Popular, big name restaurants dominate the southern end of the street. Quieter, subtler settings lie north, beyond Calle 20. For budget eating, head west, away from the main drag.

Buenos Aires, Calle 6 Norte between Av 5 and Av 10, on Plaza Playa. Speciality Argentine meats, run by Argentines, nice for a change from Mexican food.

The Glass Bar, Calle 10, between Av1-5, www.theglassbar.com.mx. A sophisticated Italian restaurant serving fine wine, Mediterranean cuisine and seafood. The place for an intimate, romantic dinner.

Karen's, Av 5, between Calle 2 and 4. Always a lively, family atmosphere here. The menu includes Mexican staples, good pizzas, grilled meats and tacos. There's live music most nights. Popular.

La Parrilla, Av 5 y Calle 8. Large portions, good service, live mariachi band every night, popular.

Yaxche, Calle 8 between Av 5 and Av 10. Traditional Maya cuisine. Cheaper lunchtime menu (₩).

Los Comales, Av 5 and Calle 4. Popular seafood restaurant. Dishes include Veracruz fish fillet, seafood platters, surf n turf, fajitas and other Mexican fare. There's a good-value breakfast buffet for US$5.50.

Maktub, Av 5, between Calle 28 and 30. Arab and Lebanese cuisine, clean and pleasant, with outdoor seating.

Sushi-Tlan, Av 5, between Calle 28 and 30. Something different; a clean, fresh, brightly-lit sushi bar.

El Famolito, Busy taco joint, popular with Mexicans. Bright, clean and modern.

Pez Vela, Av 5 y Calle 2. Good atmosphere, food, drinks and music.

Rolandi, Av 5, close to the ferry dock. Superb pasta and pizza at this popular Italian place. Branches across Mexico.

Billy the Kid, Av 15 and Calle 4. This very cheap, rough-and-ready locals' haunt does tacos and *tortas*.

El Fogon, Av 30 and Calle 6. Locals' taco joint that serves grilled meat, wholesome *tortas* and *quesadillas*.

Tortas del Carmen, Av 15, between Calle 4 and 2. Tasty *tortas* and *licuados*, open from 0830.

Cafés and bakeries

Java Joe's, Calle 10, between Av 5 and 10. Italian and gourmet coffees, sandwiches, pastries. Next door's café/bookshop **Habita** is worth a peak for its art, books and alternative cultural space.

Cozumel *p577, map p578 and p579*

There are few eating options for budget travellers. The cheapest places for breakfast, lunch or an early dinner are the *loncherías* next to the market on A R Salas, between Av 20 and 25. They serve fairly good local *comida corrida*, 0800-1930.

Lobster's Cove, Av Rafael Melgar 790. Quality seafood, live music, happy hour 1200-1400.

Pancho's Backyard, Rafael Melgar 27, in Los Cinco Soles shopping complex in big courtyard out the back. Mexican food and wine elegantly served, good food.

Prima, Salas 109. Open 1600-2400. Northern Italian seafood, handmade pasta, brick oven pizzas, non-smoking area.

ĦĦ-ĦĦ Casa Mission, Av 55, between Juárez and Calle 1 Sur, www.missioncoz.com. Open daily 1700-2300. Established in 1973, this restaurant survived hurricanes Wilma and Gilbert and is now a Cozumel institution. Fine Mexican, international and seafood in an elegant hacienda setting.

ĦĦ-ĦĦ La Choza, Salas 198 and Av 10, www.lachozarestaurant.com. Decent Mexican and regional cuisine. Popular.

ĦĦ Las Palmeras, at the pier (good people-watching spot), Av Melgar. Open 0700-1400. Very popular for breakfast, always busy. Recommended.

ĦĦ-Ħ Casa Deni's, Calle 1 Sur 164, close to plaza. Open-air restaurant, very good, cheapish prices.

Tulum *p581*
Tulum village
Testament to Tulum's growing popularity, a plethora of new restaurants have opened in town, mostly along Av Tulum. Wander along in the evening and take your pick of everything from Argentine *parrillas* to seafood and pizzas.

ĦĦ-ĦĦ El Pequeño Buenos Aires, Av Tulum, Argentine steak and grill house, one great meat feast, open air setting on the main drag.

ĦĦ Don Cafeto, Av Tulum 64. Popular place serving Mexican fare. Usually buzzing in the evenings. Beach branch currently shut, but set to re-open in late 2009.

ĦĦ La Nave, Av Tulum. Italian restaurant and pizzeria, set on 2 floors, nice rustic wooden decor. Cosy in the evenings.

Ħ Doña Tinas, good basic and cheap, in a grass hut at southern end of town. El Mariachito next door also does good, cheap and cheerful grub.

Ħ El Mariachi, cheap taco bar with good *fajitas*.

Tulum beach
Restaurants on the beach tend to be owned by hotels. For dinner, book in advance where possible. Strolling between establishments after dark isn't really feasible.

ĦĦ-ĦĦ La Zebra, Carretera Tulum–Boca Paila Km 7.5, www.lazebratulum.com. Fresh, tasty barbequed fish, shrimps, *ceviche* and Mexican fare. Lashings of Margarita at the **Tequila Bar**.

ĦĦ-ĦĦ Mezzanine, Carretera Tulum–Boca Paila Km 1.5. Excellent authentic Thai cuisine and Martini bar attached.

ĦĦ-ĦĦ Restaurant Margherita, Carretera Tulum–Boca Paila Km 4.5, in **Posada Margeherita**. Closed Sun. Excellent, freshly prepared Italian food in an intimate setting. Hospitable, attentive service. Book in advance. Recommended.

Cobá *p582*
There are plenty of restaurants in the village, on the road to **Villas Arqueológicas** and on the road to the ruins, all quite pricey. There's also a grocery store by El Bocadito and souvenir shops.

ĦĦ Pirámides, on corner of track leading to Villas Arqueológicas. Highly recommended.

Ħ Nicte-Ha, good and friendly.

Sian Ka'an Biosphere Reserve *p584*
ĦĦ-Ħ La Cantina, Punta Allen, a good, non-touristy restaurant (US$3-4 for fish).

Felipe Carrillo Puerto *p585*
ĦĦ Danburger Maya, next door to hotel San Ignacio. Good food, reasonable prices, helpful.

Ħ Restaurant Addy, on main road, south of town. Good, simple.

Chetumal *p586, map p587*
ĦĦ-ĦĦ El Emporio, Merino 106. Delicious Uruguayan steaks served in a historic old house near the bay.

ĦĦ Barracuda, about 4 blocks north of market, then 3 blocks west (another area with many restaurants). Good seafood.

ĦĦ Sergio Pizza, Av Obregón 182. Pizzas, fish, and expensive steak meals, a/c, good drinks, excellent service.

ĦĦ-Ħ El Fenicio, Héroes and Zaragoza, open 24 hrs, with mini-market at the back. Chicken, steaks, burgers and Mexican grub.

¶ Los Milagros, Zaragoza and 5 de Mayo. This locals' café serves economical Mexican fare, *comida corrida* and breakfasts.
¶ Mercado. Cheap meals in the market at the top of Av Héroes, but the service is not too good and tourists are likely to be stared at.
¶ Pantoja, Ghandi 87. Busy locals' joint serving the usual economical fare.

Towards Bacalar *p587*
¶¶ La Esperanza, 1 block north from plaza. Thatched barn, good seafood.
¶¶ Punta y Coma, Orizaba, 3 blocks from zócalo. Inexpensive, large menu including vegetarian. Recommended.

● Entertainment

Cancún *p571, maps p572 and p573*
Bars and clubs
The action happens in the Zona Hotelera, around 9 km from downtown on Kukulcan Blv, where big clubs play to big crowds. Girls will often drink for free, and there's a distinctly North American flavour. Downtown has a thriving scene too, mostly focused on Yaxchilán and the surrounding streets. If you get the chance to see local dance band **Balancé** (balancelabanda.com), don't miss it.
Bulldog, Blv Kukulcán Km 9, www.bulldog cafe.com/cancun.html. Plays rock, hip-hop, pop and salsa. A popular, well-organized mega club with sophisticated light and sound rigs.
Coco Bongo, Forum by the sea mall, www.cocobongo.com.mx. Open Wed-Sat. Cancún's most famous nightclub. Expect wild theatrical displays, including dance, acrobatics, laser shows and gallons of dry ice. Loud, pumping dance music is played.
Dady Rock, Blv Kukulcán Km 9.5, www.dady rock.com.mx. 2 floors, 4 bars, DJs, MCs and live bands. Dady Rock lays on the entertainment with boundless paternal generosity. There's frequent bikini, 'sexy legs' and 'wet body' contests too, if that's your sort of thing.
Señor Frog's, Blv Kukulcán km 9.5, www.senorfrogs.com. You'll get a yard

glass on entry, fill it with the booze of your choice, open wide and drink. Señor Frogs is a long-standing Cancún favourite; it's spawned branches in most Mexican resorts and across the Caribbean with an array of dubious, themed merchandise to match. Cover US$5.

Cinemas
Cinepolis, Tulum 260, SM7. Large complex showing English-language, subtitled films.

Isla Mujeres *p574*
Bar and clubs
Most of the bars have a permanent happy hour, with 2 drinks for the price of 1. Happy Hour here also tends to favour women, who sometimes get to drink for free. There are many bars along Hidalgo and the beach – take your pick.
Chile Locos, along the beach, with live marimba music.
La Adelita, Hidalgo 12. Adelita stocks really over 200 types of tequila, the bar staff really know their stuff and are happy to make recommendations. Pull up a stool, roll up your sleeves – it's going to be a long night.
La Palapa, on Playa Los Cocos. Serves cocktails and snacks and is busy during the day until everyone leaves the beach, then fills up again after midnight for drinking and dancing.
Om Bar, Matamoros 15. Open Wed-Sat, from 1900. Chilled-out hippy lounge. Drink beer and cocktails under the *palapa*, relax to reggae or Latin Jazz. Free shots.

Playa del Carmen *p576, map p576*
Bars and clubs
Nightlife in Playa del Carmen is famously hedonistic. The best clubs are situated on Calle 12 and 14. There are also some bars in the 'gringo zone' by the ferry dock – **Señor Frog's** and **Carlos 'n' Charlies**, most notably.
Beer Bucket, Calle 10, between Av 5 and 10. Want a simple, unpretentious beer? Try this place, popular with expats, where the grog and conversation flow cheaply.

The Blue Parrot Inn, Calle 12 y Av 1, next to beach. Dance, trance and house at this famous, sexy nightclub on the beach. Ladies night on Mon and Thu, with free drinks.
Coco Maya, Calle 12 and the beach. Beach club playing R and B, hip-hop, house and dance. Lots of TV screens, all under a *palapa*.
El Cielo, Calle 12, between Av 5 and the beach. Swanky disco playing dance and pumping tunes. Popular and well-known. Cover for men US$5, women free.
Habibi and Los Aguachiles, next door to OM (below) are new, upmarket and trendy watering holes for the hip and happening. Worth a peak, if a bit pricey.
OM, Calle 12, between Av 5 and the beach. Suave lounge-bar with sofas, sheeshas and ethereal white drapes. Electronic music.
Tequila Barrel, Av 5 between Calles 10-12. Tex-Mex Bar and grill, friendly owner (Greco) and staff. Girls who dance on the bar get a free shot of tequila.

Cozumel *p577, map p578 and p579*
Bars and clubs
1.5 Tequila Lounge, Melgar and Calle 11 Sur. Boozy, sociable lunch bar, popular with visitors straight off the cruise-ships.
Carlos 'n Charlies, Plaza Punta Langosta. Big-name chain bar, always busy with tourists.
Neptuno, Melgar and Calle 11 Sur. Long-standing Cozumel disco, playing salsa, dance and reggae.
Señor Frog's, Plaza Punta Langosta, www.senorfrogs.com. Chain bar popular with North Americans and other tourists.

O Shopping

Cancún *p571, maps p572 and p573*
There are several US-style shopping malls in the Hotel Zone. The main one, **Plaza Kukulcán**, known as Luxury Avenue, www.luxuryavenue.com, has over 200 shops, restaurants, a bowling alley and video games. It is open from 1000-2200 daily, and the prices are high for most things, including souvenirs. The main **craft market** is on Av Tulum near Plaza Las Américas; it is a huge network of stalls, all selling exactly the same merchandise: silver jewellery from Taxco, ceramic Maya figurines, hammocks, jade chess sets. Prices are hiked up to the limit, so bargain hard: most vendors expect to get half what they originally ask for. The market called **Mercado 23** (at the end of Calle Cedro, off Av Tulum) has cheaper souvenirs and less aggressive salesmen it's a bit tatty and tacky, although good for cheap food; *guayabera* shirts are available on one of the stalls. Several smoking shops have appeared, cashing in on the craze for Cuban cigars; these are all located on or just off Av Tulum. Cheaper clothes shops than the Hotel Zone can be found at the north end of Av Tulum, near Plaza 2000. Pricey leather goods, clothes and jewellery can be bought in the **Plaza 2000** shopping mall.

Isla Mujeres *p574*
Cigars
Tobacco & Co, Hidalgo 14. Cuban cigars and smoking paraphernalia. There are several other shops in the centre selling Cuban cigars.

Souvenirs
Av Hidalgo is lined with souvenir shops, most of them selling the same things: ceramic Maya figurines and masks; hammocks; blankets; and silver jewellery from Taxco. Bargaining is obligatory – try and get the desired item for half the original asking price, which is what the vendors expect to receive. There are more souvenir shops along the harbour front, where the salesmen are more pushy, and more shops along **Av Morelos**.

Playa del Carmen *p576, map p576*
Lots of expensive souvenir shops clustered around the plaza; cheaper shops, for day-to-day items, are on Av Juárez. There's a cheap *panadería* at the beginning of Av Juárez. For developing photos and buying film, there are several places along Av 5.

Chetumal *p586, map p587*

Shops are open 0800-1300, 1800-2000. Av Heroes is the main shopping street. Good for foreign foodstuffs – cheaper at the covered market in the outskirts than in the centre.

▲ Activities and tours

Cancún *p571, maps p572 and p573*
Boat trips and cruises
Aquaworld, Blv Kukulcán 15.2, T998-848 8327, www.aquaworld.com.mx. A range of boat trips and cruises including day-trips to Isla Mujeres and Cozumel; dinner cruises on the 'Cancun Queen'; and underwater explorations on their 'Sub See Explorer' submarine. They also organize parasailing, jungle tours and swimming with dolphins.

Bullfighting
Plaza de Toros, Av Bonompak south, has a folkloric show and bullfight every Wed at 1530, 2½ hrs. Admission US$38, tickets available at travel agents and the ring.

Dolphin encounters
Dolphin Discovery, Kukulcán Km 5, T998-849 4748, www.dolphindiscovery.com. Splash around with dolphins, manatees and seals, and get in touch with your inner sea mammal. A real winner for families.

Golf
Club de Golf Cancun, Kukulcán Km 7.5, T998-883 1230, www.cancungolfclub.com, 18-hole championship course, driving range and putting greens.
Hilton Cancun Beach and Golf Resort, Kukulcán Blvd Km 17, T998-881 8000, www.hlltoncancun.com/golf.htm. An attractive 18-hole course on the banks of a lagoon.

Scuba-diving and snorkelling
See also Aquaworld, above.
Scuba Cancun, Kukulcán Km 5, T998-849 5226, www.scubacancun.com.mx. A

medium-sized dive centre run by Captain Luis Hurtado who has 54 years diving experience. It offers a range of dives, snorkelling tours and accelerated PADI courses.

Tour operators
American Express, Av Tulum 208, esq Agua, SM 4, T998-884 5441.
Mayan Destinations, Cobá 31, Edificio Monaco, SM22, T998-884 4308, www.mayan destinations.com. All the usual destinations, such as Chichén Itzá, Xcaret, Tulum, as well as flights to Cuba. Many others in the centre and at larger hotels. Most hotels on the hotel zone have their own travel agency.

Watersports
A variety of watersports can be organized on the beaches along the hotel zone, including parasailing, waterskiing, windsurfing and jet-skiing.

Isla Mujeres *p574*
Birdwatching
Amigos de Isla Contoy, T998-884 7483, www.amigosdeislacontoy.org and www.islacontoy.org. This environmental organization keeps lists of authorized tour boats to Isla Contoy – a protected bird sanctuary, 30 km north of Isla Mujeres. More than 10,000 birds spend the winter on this island, including cormorants, frigates, herons, boobies and pelicans.

Scuba-diving and snorkelling
Carey, Av Matamoros 13-A, T998-877 0763. Small groups, bilingual staff and good range of dives, including reef dives, night dives, cenote dives and whale shark swimming.
El Garrafón, T998-193 3360, www.garrafon.com, southern tip of the island. This watersports centre offers a range of diving and snorkelling programmes, with a sunken cross off-shore for divers to explore. They also do dolphin encounters, kayaking and cycling.
Sea Hawk, Zazil-Ha (behind Hotel Na-Balam) T998-877 1233, seahawkdivers@

hotmail.com. Certified PADI instructors, 2-tank dive US$50, introductory course including shallow dive US$85. Also snorkelling trips and fishing trips.

Tour operators
Mundaca Travel, Av Rueda Medina, T998-877 0845, inside the ferry terminal. Tours to Chichén Itzá, Tulum, Xel-Ha and Xcaret. Bus tickets and flights to Cuba. Friendly and helpful.

Playa del Carmen *p576, map p576*
Massage
Tides Riviera Maya, see Sleeping, page 591. Offers yoga, *temazcal*, massage, a range of other therapies, jacuzzis and steam rooms.

Scuba-diving and snorkelling
Abyss, Av 1a, between Calle 10 and 12, T984-873 2164, www.abyssdiveshop.com, inside Hotel Tropical Casablanca. Said to be the best. Run by fully certified Canadian Instructor David Tomlinson. Services include PADI courses; reef, night and cenote dives. Good value dive packages.
Tank-Ha, Calle 10, between Av 5 and 10, T984-873 0302, www.tankha.com. Experienced and well-established dive centre offering a range of packages.
Yucatek Divers, Av 15 Norte, between Calle 2 and 4, T984-803 2836, www.yucatek-divers.com. Open 0730-1730. General diving and snorkelling, including programmes for disabled people. Also a snorkelling with whale sharks option.

Tour operators
Alltournative, Avenida 5, between Calle 12 and 14 and another office between calle 2 and 4 (opposite the **ADO** terminal), T984-803 9999, www.alltournative.com. Open daily 0900-1900. Culturally and ecologically sensitive tours have won this company several awards. Services include tours to archaeological sites, Mayan villages, forests, lagoons and *cenotes*.

Viajes Felgueres, Calle 6 between Av 5 and Av 10, T984-873 0142. Long-standing and reliable agency with a branch in Cancún, tours to Chichén Itzá, including transport from hotel, guide, entry, food, also bookings for national and international flights, helpful staff.

Cozumel *p577, map p578 and p579*
Scuba-diving
See box, Cenote diving, page 585. The island is famous for the beauty of its underwater environment. The best reef for scuba-diving is **Palancar**, reached only by boat. Also highly recommended are **Santa Rosa** and **Colombia**. For more experienced divers the reefs at **Punta Sur**, **Maracaibo** and **Baracuda** should not to be missed. There are at least 20 major dive sites. Almost all Cozumel diving is drift diving, so if you are not used to a current, choose an operator you feel comfortable with.

Dive centres There are 2 different types of dive centre: the larger ones, where the divers are taken out to sea in big boats with many passengers; the smaller, more personalized dive shops, with a maximum of 8 people per small boat.

The best of the smaller centres is said to be **Deep Blue**, A R Salas 200, corner of Av 10 Sur, T987-872 5653, www.deepblue cozumel.com. Matt and Deborah, an English/Colombian couple, run the centre. All PADI and NAUI certifications, eg 3-5-day dive packages US$207-325; cavern and *cenote* diving, including 2 dives, transport and lunch.

Other small dive centres are: **Black Shark**, Av 5 between A R Salas and Calle 3 Sur, T987-872 5657, www.blackshark.com.mx; **Blue Bubble Divers**, Carretera Costera Sur Km 3.5, T987-872 4240, www.blue bubble.com; **Diving Adventures**, Calle 15 Sur, between Av 19 and 21, T987-872 3009, www.divingadventures.net.

Decompression centres Buceo Médico Mexicano, Calle 5 Sur No 21B, T987-872 1430, immediate localization (24-hr) VHF 16 and 21. It is supported by

US$1 per day donations from divers with affiliated operators. **Cozumel Hyperbarics** in Clínica San Miguel, Calle 6 Norte No 135 between Av 5 and Av 10, T987-872 3070, VHF channel 65.

Tulum *p581*
Diving
Several dive shops all along the Tulum corridor. See box page 585 for cavern diving operators and specialist courses – highly recommended if you like diving. There are many untrained snorkelling and diving outfits, so take care.

Massage
Eco Tulum, see Sleeping, page 594, www.ecotulum.com. Offers affordable local Maya treatments including clay massage. Yoga, *temazcal* and holistic massage also available.

Chetumal *p586, map p587*
Tour operators
Bacalar Tours, Alvaro Obregón 167A, T987 832 3875, Tours to Mayan ruins and car rental.
Tu-Maya, Alvaro Obregón 312, T983-832 0555, www.casablancachetumal.com/tumaya. 1 day tours to Guatemala, Belize and Calakmul.

Towards Bacalar *p587*
Massage
Akal Ki (see Sleeping, page 595), www.akalki.com. A retreat offering yoga, meditation, *temazcal* and *jenzu*, a seawater massage.
Rancho Encantado (see Sleeping, page 595), www.encantado.com. A holistic resort offering *lomi lomi*, a form of massage, *temazcal*, *qigong* and meditation.

⊖ Transport

Cancún *p571, maps p572 and p573*
Air
Cancún airport (CUN) has expensive shops and restaurant, exchange facilities, double check your money, especially at busy times, poor rates too, 2 hotel reservation agencies (no rooms under US$45). 2 terminals: **Main** and **South** (or 'FBO' building), white shuttle minibuses between them. From Cancún there are domestic flights and connections throughout the country. For international connections, see Getting there on page 34 and 74. For airline websites, see page 37.

    Airline offices Aviacsa, Aerocosta, Tulum 29, T998-884 0383; Aeromar, airport, T998-886 1100; AeroMéxico, Cobá 80, T998-287 1868; Aviasca, Cobá 39, T01-800-284-2272; **Click Mexicana**, Tulum 269, T998-886 0042; **Continental Airlines**, airport, T998-886 0006; **Delta airlines**, airport, T998-886 0668, Mexicana de Aviación, Tulum 269, T998-991 9090.

Bus
For ferries to Isla Mujeres, several buses to the terminals at Gran Puerto and Puerto Juárez run from Av Tulum – try R-13, or R-1 marked Pto Juárez, US$0.80. Taxi to Puerto Juárez, US$2.50.

    Long distance Cancún bus terminal, at the junction of Av Tulum and Uxmal, is small, well organized and handy for the cheaper hostels. The bus station is the hub for routes west to Mérida and south to Tulum and Chetumal, open 24 hrs, left luggage from US$0.30 per small bag, per hr, prices rising depending on size of bag, open 0600-2200. To **Cancún Airport**, every 30 mins, 30 mins, US$3.50. To **Chetumal**, ADO, frequent departures, 6 hrs, US$17.50. To **Chichén Itzá**; all 2nd-class buses to Mérida stop here, fewer 1st-class buses, 4 hrs, US$7.50-11.50. To **Mérida**, ADO, frequent departures, 4½ hrs, US$15. To **Palenque**, 1st class (ADO and OCC), 1415, 1545, 1930, 2030, 12½ hrs,

US$40; and an **ADO GL**, 1745, 13 hrs, US$48. To **Playa del Carmen** ADO shuttle, every 10 mins, 1 hr, US$3. To **Puerto Morelos**, ADO, frequent departures, 30 mins, US$1. To **San Cristóbal**, OCC, 1415, 1545, 2030 18 hrs, US$49, **ADO GL**, 1745, US$58. To **Tulum**, ADO, frequent departures, 2½ hrs, US$5, and many cheaper 2nd-class buses. To **Valladolid**, frequent departures, 2½ hrs, US$9. To **Villahermosa**, 1st class, many departures, 13 hrs, US$52.50-73.50. To **Xcaret**, frequent departures, 1 ¾ hrs, US$3. To **Xel-Há**, frequent departures, 2 hrs, US$4. **Expreso de Oriente** also has services to the more obscure destinations of **Tizimín** (3 hrs, US$8), **Izamal**, **Cenotillo** and **Chiquilá**.

Car

Car hire There are many car hire agencies, with offices on Av Tulum, in the Hotel Zone and at the airport; look out for special deals, but check vehicles carefully. They include: Budget, Av Tulum 231, T998-884 6955; **Alamo**, Cancún Airport, T998-886 0179; **Payless**, Blvd Luid Colosio Km 12, T998-886 2812; **Master Car**, Av Uxmal 20, T01-800-711-3344; **Top Rent a Car**, Blv Kukulcán Km 14.5.

Car parking Do not leave cars parked in side streets; there is a high risk of theft. Use the parking lot on Av Uxmal.

Ferry

Ferries to Isla Mujeres depart from terminals at Gran Puerto and nearby Puerto Juárez, north of Av Tulum, every 30 mins between 0600-2300, 20 mins by fast ferry, US$2.50, US$5 return (doesn't need to be on the same day). The car ferry departs from Punta Sam, US$18.50 for a driver and vehicle, US$1.50 for each additional passenger.

Isla Mujeres *p574*
Air

The small airstrip in the middle of the island is mainly used for private planes, best arranged with a tourist office in Cancún

Bicycle and moped

Many touts along Hidalgo offer moped rentals at similar rates: US$7 per hr, US$25 full day. **Sport Bike**, Av Juárez y Morelos, has good bikes. **Cárdenas**, Av Guerrero 105, T/F998-877-0079, for mopeds and golf carts. Bicycles are usually offered by the same places as mopeds for about US$11 per day.

Bus

A public bus runs from the ferry dock to Playa Paraíso every 30 mins, US$0. 30. Timings can be erratic, especially on Sun.

Ferry

For information on ferries to and from the island, see Cancún above.

Taxi

A taxi from town to **El Garrafón** and vice versa is US$4.30. For the return journey, sharing a taxi will work out marginally more expensive than the bus for 4 people. A taxi from El Garrafón to the bus stop at Playa Paraíso is US$1. Taxis charge an additional US$1 at night. Beware that the prices are fixed, but inflated on this stretch and a taxi ride to the southernmost tip of the island, a short walk from El Garrafón, is cheaper at US$2.80. There are several places renting **golf carts**, eg Ciros, on Matamoros near Playa Cocos. Rates are generally US$32-39 per day. A credit card is usually required as a deposit.

Puerto Morelos *p575*
Bus

There are buses to **Cancún** and **Playa del Carmen** every 30 mins. Buses depart from the main road, taxi to bus stop US$3.

Ferry

Car ferries to **Cozumel** depart at 0500, 1030, 1600, the dock is 500 m south of the plaza. They return at 0800, 1330, 1900, but always check schedules in advance. Taxi from Cancún airport to Puerto Morelos costs US$25-35.

Playa del Carmen p576, map p576

Air

There are flights to **Cozumel** from the nearby airstrip, speak to a tourist office in Playa del Carmen about chartering a plane.

Bus

The **ADO** bus terminal is on Av Juárez between Av 5 and 10. All buses depart from here. The following prices and times are for ADO buses (1st class, a/c, usually showing a video on longer journeys); **Premier**, also 1st class; **Maya de Oro**, supposed to be 1st class but quality of buses can be poor; **OCC**, good 1st-class service. To **Cancún**, frequent departures, 1½ hrs, US$3; 2nd-class services with **Mayab**, less frequent, US$2. To **Cancún airport**, Riviera, frequent between 0700 and 1915, 1 hr, US$6.50. To **Chetumal**, ADO, frequent departures, 4½ hrs, US$14.50; and many 2nd-class buses. To **Chichén Itzá**, 4 departures, 0610, 0730, 0800, 1150, 4 hrs, US$8.50-15.50. To **Mérida**, frequent departures, 5 hrs, US$20.50. To **Mexico City**, ADO, 1230, 1930, 2130, 24½ hrs, US$87. To **San Cristóbal de las Casas**, OCC, 1545, 1715, 2200, 16 hrs, US$46.50; an ADO GL, 1900, US$55.50; and 3 TRF departures, US$30. To **Tulum**, frequent departures, 1 hr, US$3.50. To **Valladolid**, frequent, 3 hrs, US$8.50 (most buses going to Mérida stop at Valladolid. 2nd-class buses to Valladolid go via Tulum). To **Xcaret**, frequent departures, 15 mins, US$0.80. To **Xel Há**, frequent departures, 1 hr, US$3.50.

Car

Car hire Avis, T984-873 1964; **Budget**, 3s and 5a, T984-873 2772; **Executive**, 5a and 12N, T984-873 2354, **Happy Rent a Car**, 10a and Constituyentes, 1984-873 1739; **Hertz Rent-a-Car**, Plaza Marina, T984-873 0703; **Rodar**, 5a between 2 and 4, T984-873 0088.

Ferry

Ferries to **Cozumel** depart from the main dock, just off the plaza. There are 2 competing companies, right next to

each other, journeys take 30 mins with both, hourly departures on the hour from 0500 until 2200, US$20 return, more to bring a car across. Buy ticket 1 hr before journey.

Taxi

Cancún airport US$35. Beware of those who charge only US$5 as they are likely to charge an extra US$20 for luggage. Tours to **Tulum** and **Xel-Há** from kiosk by boat dock US$30; tours to Tulum, Xel-Há and **Xcaret**, 5-6 hrs, US$60; taxi to Xcaret US$6.65. Taxis congregate on the Av Juárez side of the square (**Sindicato Lázaro Cárdenas del Río**, T998-873 0032).

Cozumel p577, map p578 and p579

Air

To **Mexico City** direct with **Mexicana**, or via Cancún; **Continental** to **Houston**.

Airline offices Most are based at the airport, 2 km north of the town. Continental, T987-872 0847. Mexicana, P Joaquín between Salas and Calle 3 Sur, next to Pemex, T987-872 0157.

Bicycle and moped

There is no bus service, but taxis are plentiful. The best way to get around the island is by hired moped or bicycle. Mopeds cost US$25-35 per day, credit card needed as deposit; bicycles are around US$15 per day, US$20 cash or TC deposit. **El Aguila**, Av Melgar, between 3 and 5 Sur, T987-872 0729; and **El Dorado**, Av Juárez, between 5 and 10, T987-872 2383.

Car

Car rental There are many agencies, including **Avis**, airport, T987-872 0219; **Budget**, Av 5 between 2 and 4 Norte, T987-872 0219; **Hertz**, Av Melgar, T987-872 3955; **Ejecutivo**, 1 Sur No 19, T987-872 1308.

Tulum p581

Bicycle

Bikes can be hired in the village from **Iguana Bike Shop**, Calle Satélite Sur and **Andrómeda**,

T984-119-0836 (mobile) or T984-871 2357; a good way to visit local centres (Cristal and Escondido which are recommended as much cheaper, US$2, and less commercialized than Xcaret).

Bus

Regular buses go up and down the coastal road travelling from Cancún to Tulum en route to Chetumal, stopping at most places in between. Some buses may be full when they reach Tulum; very few buses begin their journeys here. To **Chetumal**, frequent departures, 4 hrs, 2nd class, US$10, 1st class US$12. To **Cobá**, 8 departures daily, 45 mins, US$3. To **Escárcega**, ADO, 1645, 1715, 7 hrs, US$24.50. To **Felipe Carrillo Puerto**, frequent departures, 1½ hrs, US$5. To **Mérida**, ADO, 2400, 0140, 0500, 1240, 1430, 4 hrs, US$14; and several 2nd-class departures. To **Mexico City**, ADO, 1340, 23½ hrs, US$85. To **Palenque**, OCC, 1655, 1825, 10-11 hrs, US$34; and ADO GL, 2015, US$40.50. To **San Cristóbal**, OCC, 1655, 1825, 15 hrs, US$43.50; and an ADO GL, 2015, US$52. To **Villahermosa**, ADO, 1340, 2324, 11 hrs, US$38.

Taxi

Tulum town to Tulum ruins US$3.50. To the *cabañas* US$3.50. To **Cobá** about US$25 1 way – bargain hard. Tucan Kin run shuttles to Cancún airport, T01-800-702-4111 for reservations, about US$20-25 for 2 people, 1 hr 45 mins.

Cobá *p582*
Bus

Buses into the village turn round at the road end. To **Cancún**, ADO, 1330, 1530, 3 hrs, US$8. To **Playa del Carmen**, ADO, 1330, 1530, 2 hrs, US$5. To **Tulum**, ADO, 1330, 1530, 1 hr, US$2.50.

Taxi

A taxi to **Tulum** should cost you around US$25. If you miss the bus there is a taxi to be found at El Bocadito.

Felipe Carrillo Puerto *p585*
Bus

Bus station opposite Pemex. To **Cancun**, frequent 1st and 2nd-class departures, 4 hrs, US$13. To **Chetumal**, frequent departures, 2½ hrs, US$8. To **Playa del Carmen**, frequent departures, 2½ hrs, US$9. To **Tulum**, frequent departures, 1½ hrs, US$5.

Chetumal *p586, map p587*
Air

Airport (CTM) 2.5 km from town. Flights to **Cancún**, **Mérida**, **Belize City** (Click Mexicana), **Mexico City**, **Monterrey** and **Tijuana**.

   Airline offices Click Mexicana, Plaza Varudi, Av Héroes 125. Aviacsa, T983-832 7765.

Bus

Bus information T983-832 5110. The main bus terminal is 3 km out of town at the intersection of Insurgentes y Belice. Taxi into town US$1.50. There is a bus into the centre from Av Belice. **Left-luggage** lockers cost US$0.20 per hr. If buying tickets in advance, go to the ADO office on Av Belice esq Ghandi, 0800-1600. There are often more buses than those marked on the display in the bus station. Always ask at the information desk. Many buses going to the border, US$0.30; taxi from Chetumal to border, 20 mins, US$6 for 2. Long-distance buses are often all booked a day ahead, so avoid unbooked connections. Expect passport checks on buses leaving for Mexican destinations.

   To **Bacalar**, very frequent 1st- and 2nd-class departures, 1 hr, US$2. To **Campeche**, ADO, 1200, 6 hrs, US$20. To **Cancún**, many 1st-class departures, 6 hrs, US$17.50. To **Córdoba**, ADO, 1130, 16 hrs, US$57. To **Emiliano Zapata**, 1st class (OCC and ADO), 2150, 2345, 6½ hrs, US$20.50. To **Escárcega**, ADO, 11 daily, 4 hrs, US$13. To **Felipe Carrillo Puerto**, many 1st- and 2nd-class departures, 2½ hrs, US$8. To **Mérida**, ADO, 0730, 1330, 1700,

2330, 5½ hrs, US$21. To **Mexico City**, ADO, 1130, 1630, 20½ hrs, US$73.50. To **Minatitlán**, ADO, 2000, 12 hrs, US$36. To **Palenque**, OCC, 0220, 2020, 2150, 7 hrs, US$23; and ADO GL, 2350, US$27. To **Playa del Carmen**, frequent 1st- and 2nd-class departures, 5 hrs, US$14.50. To **Puebla**, ADO, 2300, 17 hrs, US$66.50. To **San Cristóbal**, OCC, 0220, 2020, 2150, 12 hrs, US$33; and ADO GL 2350, US$39.50. To **Tulum**, frequent 1st- and 2nd-class departures, 4 hrs, US$12. To **Tuxtla Gutiérrez** OCC, 2030, 2150, 13 hrs, US$36.50; and ADO GL 2350, US$43.50. To **Veracruz**, 1830, 17 hrs, US$50. To **Villahermosa**, ADO, 6 daily, 8½ hrs, US$27. To **Xpujil**, 13 ADO , Sur and OCC, 2 hrs, US$6.

To Belize Premier run buses between Chetumal and **Belize City**, 1145, 1445, 1745, 5 hrs, US$10. En-route, they stop at **Orange Walk**, 2½ hrs, US$5. Money-changers in the bus terminal offer marginally poorer rates than those at the border. If intending to stay in Belize City, do not take a bus that arrives at night as you are advised not to look for a hotel in the dark.

To Guatemala Línea Dorada operate daily buses to **Flores** in Guatemala at 0600, US$29. Schedules are very subject to change, so always check times in advance, and be prepared to spend a night in Chetumal if necessary.

Car
There's a petrol/gas station just outside Chetumal on the road north at the beginning of the road to Escárcega, and another at Xpujil.

Garage Talleres Barrera, helpful, on Primo de Verdad; turn east off I Iéroes, then past the electrical plant.

Taxi
There are no city buses; taxis run on fixed-price routes, US$1.50 on average. Cars with light-green licence plates are a form of taxi.

Colectivos To **Bacalar** and **Francisco Villa** (for Kohunlich and Xpujil) depart from the junction of Av Miguel Hidalgo and Francisco Primo de Verdad.

❻ Directory

Cancún *p571, maps p572 and p573*
Banks There are 11 Mexican banks along Av Tulum, all in SM4 and SM5. **American Express**, for changing their own TCs at better rates than anywhere else, is on Av Tulum, just south of Av Cobá. Many *casas de cambio* in the centre, mainly around the bus terminal and along Av Tulum. *Casas de cambio* in the Hotel Zone give slightly lower rates for TCs than those in the centre. **Cultural centres** Casa Tabasco, Av Tulum 230, displays and handicrafts for sale from the state of Tabasco, a good place to go if bored of the same old souvenirs in Cancún. **Embassies and consulates** Austria, Cantera 4, SM15, Centro, T998-884 7505. Canada, Plaza Caracol, 3rd floor, Hotel Zone, T998-883 3360. France,Fonatur St, T998-267 9722. Germany, Punta Conoco 36, SM24, Centro, T998-884 1508. Italy, Alcatraces 39, SM22, Centro, T998-884 1261. Netherlands, Hotel Presidente, Hotel Zone, T998-883 0200. Spain, Oasis Corporativo, Hotel Zone, T998-848 9900. Sweden, Switzerland, Av Cobá 12, T998-884 8446. UK, Hotel Royal Sands, Hotel Zone, T998-881 0100. US, Plaza Caracol, 3rd floor, Hotel Zone, T998-883 0272. **Immigration office** On the corner of Av Náder and Av Uxmal. There is also an office in the airport, T998-886 0492, where the staff are better trained and speak English. **Internet** Numerous cafés charging US$1-1.50 per hr. Generally good servers, open until around 2300. **Language schools** El Bosque del Caribe, Av Náder 52 and Uxmal, T998-884 1065, www.cancun-language.com.mx. **Laundry** Alborada, Nader 5, behind tourist information building on Av Tulum. Cox-boh, Av Tankah 26, SM24. **Medical services** American Hospital

(24-hr), Viento 15, Centro, T998-884 6133. **Total Assist** (24-hr) Claveles 5, Centro, T998-884 1058. **American Medical Centre**, Plaza Quetzal, Hotel Zone Km 8, T998-883 0113. **Post office** At the end of Av Sunyaxchén, near Mercado 28, Mon-Fri 0800-1900, Sat 0900-1300. **Telephone** Many public phones and call shops everywhere, phone cards available from general stores and pharmacies. Collect calls can be made without a card. Also many public phones designed for international calls, which take coins and credit cards. Fax at post office, Mon-Sat, and at **San Francisco de Asís** shopping mall, Mon-Sat until 2200.

Isla Mujeres *p574*
Banks HSBC, Av Reuda Medina, opposite the ferry dock. Good rates, varying daily, are offered by several *casas de cambio* on Av Hidalgo. The one opposite **Rolandis** is open daily 0900-2100. **Internet** Several internet cafés operate on the island US$1.50 per hr, but speeds can be a little slow. Many cafés and restaurants have free Wi-Fi. **Laundry** Tim Pho, Juárez y Abasolo. **Medical services** Doctors: Dr Antonio Salas, Hidalgo, next to **Farmacia**, T998-877 0477. 24 hrs, house calls, English spoken, air ambulance. **Post office** At the end of Guerrero towards the beach. **Telephone** Phone cards can be bought at some of the souvenir shops along Hidalgo.

Puerto Morelos *p575*
Internet There is an internet café on the corner of the plaza opposite **Posada Amor**, US$2.50 per hr, Mon-Sat 1000-1400, 1600-2100.

Playa del Carmen *p576, map p576*
Banks Bancomer, Av Juárez between Calle 25 and 30. **Banamex**, Av Juárez between Calle 20 and 25. A few doors down is **Santander. Banorte**, Av 5 between Av Juárez and the beach. **Inverlat**, Av 5 between Av Juárez and Calle 2. HSBC, Av Juárez between Calle 10 and 15, also at Av 30 between Calle

4 and 6. There are several *casas de cambio* along Av 5, which change TCs with no commission. Count your money carefully as short changing is not uncommon and rates can be hit and miss. **Immigration office** Centro Comercial, Plaza Antigua, Av 10 Sur, T984-873 1884. **Internet** All the cybercafés in town charge between US$1.50-2 per hr. **Language schools** Playalingua,Calle 20 between Av 5 and 10, T984-873 3876, www.playa lingua.com, weekend excursions, a/c, library, family stays, US$85 enrolment fee, US$220 per wk (20 hrs). **Solexico Language and Cultural Center**, Av 35 between 6 and 6 bis, T984-873 0755, www.solexico.com. Variable programme with workshops, also have schools in Oaxaca and Puerto Vallarta. **Laundry** Av Juárez, 2 blocks from bus station; another on Av 5. **Maya Laundry**, Av 5 between Calle 2 and Calle 4, Mon-Sat 0800-2100. Laundry in by 1000, ready in the afternoon, many others around town. **Medical services** Dentist: Perla de Rocha Torres, Av 20 Norte between 4 and 6, T984-873 0021, speaks English. Recommended. International Medical Services: Dr Victor Macías Orosco, Av 35 between Calle 2 and 4, T984-873 0493. 24-hr emergency service, land and air ambulance, ultrasound, most major insurance accepted. **Tourist Divers Medical Centre**, Dr Mario Abarca, Av 10 between Av Juárez and Calle 2, T984-873 0512. Air and land ambulance service, hyperbaric and diving medicine, affiliated with South Miami Hospital, all insurance accepted. **Police** Av Juárez, T984-873 0291. **Post office** Calle 2 and Av 20, Mon-Fri 0800-1700, Sat 0900-1300.

Cozumel *p577, map p578 and p579*
Banks 4 banks on the main square (all with ATMs), all exchange money in morning only, but not at same hours: HSBC, on Juárez, Bancomer, Banamex, Banorte. *Casas de cambio* on Av 5 Norte and around square. **Internet** Several internet cafés charging

around US$1.50 per hr. **Laundry** Express, Salas between Av 5 and Av 10, T987-872 3655. Coin-op, service washes, US$9 medium load, collection service and dry cleaning. **Medical services** Dentist: Dr Hernández, T987-872 0656. Hospitals and clinics: Red Cross, A R Salas between Calle 20 and Calle 25 Sur, T987-872 1058. Centro Médico de Cozumel, Calle 1 Sur No 101, esq Av 50, T987-872 3545. English spoken, international air ambulance, 24-hr emergency service. Pharmacy: Salas between Av 12 and Av 20, 0700-2400. **Post office** Av Rafael Melgar y Calle 7 Sur, Mon-Fri 0900-1800, Sat 0900-1200. **Telephone** Ladatel phones (if working) on main square at corner of Av Juárez and Av 5, or on Salas, just up from Av 5 Sur, opposite **Roberto's Black Coral Studio**. For calls to the US, go to **The Stadium**. Telmex phone offices on the main square next to Restaurant Plaza Leza, 0800-2300, and on Salas between Av 10 and 15. There are also expensive **Computel** offices in town, eg at the cruise ship dock. **Telephone centre** for long distance on corner of Rafael Melgar and Calle 3 Sur. Also public telephone *caseta* at Av 5 esq Calle 2, 0800-1300, 1600-2100.

Tulum *p581*
Banks HSBC, Av Tulum open 0900-1900, has an ATM, but doesn't change TCs. Scotiabank further along the same road is open Mon-Fri, 0900-1600, changes TCs and cash. Several *casas de cambio* in Av Tulum closer to the ADO terminal. **Telephone and internet** Long-distance phones n oAv Tulum near and opposite the ADO terminal in town. Internet cafés on the same road.

Chetumal *p586, map p587*
Banks The banks all close at 1430. There are several ATMs. For exchange, **Banamex**, Obregón y Juárez, changes TCs. **Banco Mexicano**, Juárez and Cárdenas, TCs or US$ cash, quick and courteous service. Several on, or near, Av Héroes with ATMs. Banks do not change quetzales into pesos. **Embassies and consulates** Guatemala, Av Héroes de Chapultepec 354, T983-832 6565. Open for visas, Mon-Fri 0900-1700. It is best to organize your visa, if required, in your home country before travel. Belize, Hon Consul, Lic Francisco Lechón Rosas, Rotondo Carranza 562 (behind Super San Francisco), T983-878 7728; visas can take up to 3 weeks to get, and many are only issued in Mexico City. **Internet** Eclipse, 5 de Mayo 83 between PE Calles and Zaragoza. 0930-1500, 1800-2100, not very friendly but cheap at US$3 per hr. Los Cebollones, Calzada Veracruz 452, T983-832 9145, also restaurant and cocktail bar. **Laundry** Lavandería Automática 'Lava facil', corner of Héroes and Confederación Nacional Campesina. **Medical services** Malaria prophylaxis available from Centro de Salud, opposite hospital (request tablets for paludismo). **Post office** 16 de Septiembre y PE Calles. Mon-Fri 0800-1730, Sat 0900-1300. Packets to be sent abroad must be taken unwrapped to the bus terminal to have them checked by customs before taking them to the post office. Better to wait until another town. Parcel service not available Sat. **Western Union** office attached to post office, same hours.

Contents

Footprint features

Border crossings

At a glance

◒ **Getting around** Bus and the odd flight for long distances, minibus shuttles for shorter distances. Boats to Belize on the Caribbean coast.

◓ **Time required** 3-4 weeks; any less and you'll have to rush around.

☼ **Weather** Mid-20°Cs, but chilly at higher altitudes. Wet season is May-Oct.

✗ **When not to go** Lowlands in the wet season, if you don't like rain.

Guatemala

★ **Don't miss ...**

1 **Antigua**, page 641.
2 **Lake Atitlán**, page 659.
3 **Todos Santos Cuchumatán**, page 692.
4 **Around Quetzaltenango**, page 699.
5 **Lívingston and Río Dulce**, pages 723 and 726.

Guatemala has a monopoly on colour – from the red lava tongues of the volcanoes in the Western Highlands to the creamy shades of the caves in the southern Petén, and from the white sand of the Caribbean coast near Lívingston to the black sand and fabulous orange sunsets over the Pacific. And that's just nature's palette. Completing this work of art are traditional Maya fiestas, arcane religious rituals where idol worship and Roman Catholicism merge, and jungle temples where ancient ruins tell of long-lost civilizations. Deep in Guatemala's northern jungle, the majestic cities of the Maya are buried. Temples, stelae and plazas have been discovered here, along with evidence of human sacrifice and astronomical genius, to reveal their dynastic history and traditions.

Antigua is the colonial centre of the New World. Gracefully ruined after an 18th-century earthquake, its cobbled streets are lined with columned courtyards, toppled church arches, preserved pastel-coloured houses, flowers and fountains galore.

Formed by an explosion that blew the lid off the top of a volcanic mountain, Lake Atitlán and its three volcanoes are truly breathtaking. Further west, the bustling city of Quetzaltenango makes an excellent base from which to explore the volcanoes, markets and villages of the Western Highlands, such as the mountain community of Todos Santos, where the colourful clothes of the Maya and the All Saints' Day horse race are major attractions. In the Verapaces, rivers run through caves stuffed with stalagmites and stalactites. On the humid lower slopes of the Pacific, Olmec-influenced ruins are buried among coffee bushes and turtles nest on the shore, while on the Caribbean coast, the Garífuna rock to the sound of the punta and dolphins frolic in the sea.

Essentials

Where to go

Guatemala City is a modern, polluted capital. It is the main entry point for travellers by air and long-distance bus. While there are some sites of interest, a couple of excellent museums in the city centre and some great nightlife, few stay long, preferring to head west to the clean air and relaxed atmosphere of **Antigua**. Once the capital, Antigua was built by the Spanish *conquistadores*. Later destroyed by several huge earthquakes, the grand ruins of colonial architecture remain, the dramatic location at the foot of three volcanoes and its prominence as a centre for Spanish studies, make Antigua a justifiably popular destination.

Heading northeast from Guatemala City, lie the highlands of the Verapaz region. **Cobán** is the main focus, with access to nearby traditional villages, the caves at Lanquín, the natural bridge of Semuc Champey and, at Purulhá, the Mario Dary Rivera Reserve which protects the habitat of the quetzal, Guatemala's national bird. Skirting the northern shores of Lago de Izabal is the Bocas del Polochic Wildlife Reserve, which is full of monkeys, avifauna and other wildlife.

South of the lake, the highway runs close to **Quiriguá**, which once competed with Tikal and nearby Copán, in Honduras, for dominance of the Maya heartlands. On Guatemala's short Caribbean shore is **Lívingston**, popular with young travellers and, near **El Golfete Biotopo Chocón-Machacas**, a manatee and wildlife reserve and the fabulous Río Dulce gorge. From Lívingston boats go inland to Rio Dulce, north to Punta Gorda in Belize, or head for Puerto Barrios for Placencia in Belize, or south overland to Honduras.

The forested northern lowlands of **El Petén** hide most of Guatemala's archaeological sites. The majestic **Tikal** is the most developed for tourism, but many others can be reached including Uaxactún, Yaxhá and El Ceibal. **Flores**, sitting on an island in Lago Petén Itzá, is the centre for exploring El Petén with routes from here to Belize and Mexico.

West of Guatemala City, beyond La Antigua, the mountainous highlands overflow with Maya communities. Market days filled with colour, fiestas crammed with celebrations, and each community characterized by unique clothes and crafts. Several villages are dotted around the shores of **Lago de Atitlán**, a spectacular and sacred lake protected on all sides by silent volcanic peaks. From **Panajachel**, ferries and trails link the small communities. **San Pedro La Laguna** is the chief chill-out and hang-loose spot on the lake's shores, with **San Marcos** the favourite for true relaxation; but there are other less touristy and more interesting options to explore.

An hour north of Lake Atitlán is the famous market of **Chichicastenango**, a town where Maya and visitors converge in a twice-weekly frenzy of buying general goods and produce, alongside textiles and tapestry. The market is alive with colour and is a must for any visitor.

Towards the Mexican border, the towns of **Quetzaltenango**, **Retalhuleu** and **Huehuetenango** provide good opportunities for discovering the charms of western Guatemala, including volcanoes and Maya towns. To the north, in the heart of the Cuchumatanes mountains, **Todos Santos Cuchumatán** stands firm as a town that has restricted western influences and is increasingly popular as a place to learn about the Mam way of life, including language and weaving classes. Along the Pacific coastline, the turtle-nesting sites of **Monterrico** are attracting visitors to this little-explored district of Guatemala.

Packing for Guatemala

Most of the areas you are likely to visit in Guatemala are above 1500 m. While temperatures may well be comfortably warm in the day, it will be cold in the evening and at night. Bad weather may bring noticeable drops in temperature.

In many tropical areas where mosquitoes and other biting insects are common, take long trousers and long-sleeved shirts for after dusk. The sun is strong everywhere at midday, so have a hat to hand.

Suggested itinerary The most natural trip in Guatemala, if you're travelling through the region, is to enter the country from the north from Mexico or Belize, visit Tikal and then head south. After some time in La Antigua and around Lake Atitlán, explore the towns of the Guatemalan highlands. Continuing south, there are many options for crossing the border. Head for El Florido, for best access to Copán, or out to the Caribbean and the crossing at Entre Ríos–Corinto near Puerto Barrios for the Bay Islands. Three to four weeks is a good stay in Guatemala; any less and you'll have to rush around.

When to go

Climate is dependent upon altitude and varies greatly. Most of the population lives at between 900 m and 2500 m, where the climate is healthy – with warm days and cool nights, so you'll need warm clothes at night. The majority of visitors spend most of their time in the highlands, where the dry season lasts from November to April. The central region around Cobán has an occasional drizzle-like rain called *chipi chipi* in February and March. Some places enjoy a respite from the rains (the *canícula*) in July and August. On the Pacific and Caribbean coasts you can expect rain all year round, heaviest on the Pacific in June and September with a dry spell in between, but with no dry season on the Caribbean. In the lowlands of El Petén, the wet season is roughly May to October, when the mosquitoes are most active. December to February are cooler months, while March and April are hot and dry. All of this is increasingly settled, according to Guatemalans, who say that the clear divisions of the seasons are blurring. In terms of festivals, the key events are **Semana Santa** at Easter in Antigua, see page 646 and **All Saints' Day**, in Todos Santos, see page 693.

Sport and activities

Archaeology

Archaeology is the big attraction. Consequently there is a huge number of organizations offering tours. Some companies operate out of Flores and Santa Elena in the Petén using local villagers to help with expeditions. Try **Maya Expeditions** ① *15 Calle "A", 14-07, Zona 10, T2363-4955, www.mayaexpeditions.com*, which offers trips to Piedras Negras (with archaeologists who worked on the 1990s excavation of the site), Río Azul, the Petexbatún area, El Mirador, led by Dr Richard Hansen (the chief archaeologist of the site) and a trip to the recently discovered Cancuén site, led by its chief archaeologist, Dr Arthur Demarest. **Explorations** ① *in the USA, T1-239-992-9660, www.explorationsinc.com*, has tours led by archaeologist and Maya specialist Travis Doering.

Mountain biking

Mountain biking is an increasingly popular activity in Guatemala. There are numerous tracks and paths that weave their way across the country, passing hamlets as you go. One recommended operator in Antigua, which also deals in the gear, is **Old Town Outfitters** ① *5 Av Sur 12 "C", T7832-4171, www.adventureguatemala.com*, who offer mountain-bike tours starting at US$25 for a half day.

Mountain and volcano climbing

Guatemala represents a wealth of opportunity for climbers, with more than 30 volcanoes on offer. There are also the heights of the Cuchumatanes Mountains in the highlands, which claims the highest non-volcanic peak in the country at 3837 m, and those of the relatively unexplored Sierra de Las Minas in eastern Guatemala close to the Río Motagua Valley. For climbing in the Sierra de las Minas, a biosphere reserve, contact **Fundación Defensores de la Naturaleza** ① *7 Av, 7-09, Zona 13, T2440-8138*, to obtain a *permiso*. **Turismo Ek Chuah** ① *3 Calle 6-24, Zona 2, www.ekchuah.com*, offer volcano-specific tours. For information on volcano climbing around Guatemala City and Antigua see pages 635 and 654.

Nature tourism

The majority of tour operators listed in this guide will offer nature-oriented tours. There are several national parks, biotopos and protected areas in Guatemala, each with their highlights. CECON (Centro de Estudios Conservacionistas) and INGUAT have set up conservation areas for the protection of Guatemalan wildlife (the quetzal, manatee, jaguar, etc) and their habitats. Several other national parks (some including Maya archaeological sites) and forest reserves have been set up or are planned. Many of these are administered by the national parks and protected areas authority **CONAP (Consejo Nacional de Areas Protegidas)** ① *Av, 6-06, Zona 1, Guatemala City, T2238-0000, http://conap.online.fr*. Another useful organization is the non-profit-making project **Proyecto Ecológico Quetzal** ① *2 Calle, 14-36, Zona 1, Cobán, T7952-1047, www.ecoquetzal.org*.

Spiritual interest

There is a spiritual centre on the shores of Lake Atitlán that offers courses in accordance with the cycle of the moon: **Las Pirámides del Ka** is in San Marcos La Laguna and offers yoga, meditation as well as spiritual instruction year round (see also page 677). At the **Takilibén Maya Misión** in Momostenango, day keeper **Rigoberto Itzep** ① *leave a message for him on T7736-5537, 3 Av "A", 6-85, Zona 3*, offers courses in Maya culture.

Textiles and weaving

It is possible to get weaving lessons in many places across the highlands. Weaving lessons can also be organized through Spanish schools.

Watersports

You can **dive** in Lake Atitlán with ATI Divers at **La Iguana Perdida** ① *Santa Cruz, T5706-4117, www.laiguanaperdida.com*. **Kayak** tours are run by **Old Town Outfitters** ① *Antigua, www.adventure guatemala.com*. **Waterskiing** is possible from **La Iguana Perdida** in Santa Cruz La Laguna, see above for contact info. **Whitewater rafting** is possible on a number of rivers in Guatemala across a range of grades. However, none of the trips are turn-up-and-go – they have to be arranged in advance. In general, the larger the group, the cheaper the cost. The country's best outfitter is **Maya Expeditions**, see address under Archaeology, above. It rafts the Río Cahabón in Alta Verapaz (Grade III-V), the Río Naranjo close to Coatepeque (Grade III), the Río Motagua close to Guatemala City (Grade III-IV), the Río

Esclavos, near Barbarena (Grade III-IV), the Río Coyolate close to Santa Lucía Cotzumalguapa (Grade II-III) and the Río Chiquibul in the Petén (Grade II-III). It also runs a rafting and caving tour in the Petén and a combined archaeology and rafting tour where you would raft through a canyon on the Río Usumacinta (Grade II). For a little extra excitement, Maya Expeditions also arrange bungee jumping in Guatemala City.

Getting there

Air
From the USA American (Atlanta; Chicago; Dallas Forth Worth; Miami), **Continental** (Houston), **Delta** (Atlanta), **United** (Los Angeles), **Grupo Taca** (Miami). From Canada, connections are made through San Salvador, Los Angeles or Miami.
From Europe Iberia flies directly from Madrid and via Miami, with connecting flights from other European cities. Long-haul operators from Europe will share between airlines, taking passengers across the Atlantic normally to Miami, and using **Taca**, for example, to link to Guatemala City.
From Central America Connections available throughout Central America, in most cases travelling through the capital city. There are exceptions with connections to Belize from Flores. See page 40 for regional airpasses. **Taca** from the Caribbean and **Cubana** from Havana.
From South America Lacsa from Bogotá via San José, **Copa** via Panama.

Road
There are good road crossings with all of Guatemala's neighbouring countries. There are several crossing points to southern **Mexico** from western Guatemala with additional routes through the jungle from Palenque. From **Belize** it is possible to cross from Benque Viejo del Carmen. Links with **Honduras** are possible on the Caribbean near Corinto, and for the ruins at Copán the best crossing is El Florido. There are four road routes into **El Salvador**.
There is sometimes an unofficial tourist tax charge (10-30 quetzales) at some borders, charged on leaving or entering overland (borders may not be open 24 hours). Bribery is now less common at border crossings. Ask for a receipt and, if you have time and the language ability, do not give in to corrupt officials. Report any problems to INGUAT.

Sea
Connections be sea with daily boats between **Punta Gorda** in Guatemala and **Lívingston**.

Getting around

Air
Grupo Taca, www.taca.com, links Guatemala City with Flores/Santa Elena. **TAG**, www.tag.com.gt, also flies this route daily, US$123 one way. See page 751 for (overland) services to Tikal. Private charters are on the increase.

Road
Bus There is an extensive network of bus routes throughout the country. The chicken buses (former US school buses) are mostly in a poor state of repair and overloaded. Faster and more reliable Pullman services operate on some routes. Correct fares should be

posted. We receive regular complaints that bus drivers charge tourists more than locals, a practice that is becoming more widespread. One way to avoid being overcharged is to watch for what the locals pay or ask a local, then tender the exact fare on the bus. Many long-distance buses leave very early in the morning. Make sure you can get out of your hotel/*pensión*. For international bus journeys make sure you have small denomination local currency or US dollar bills for border taxes. At Easter there are few buses on Good Friday or the Saturday and buses are packed with long queues for tickets for the few days before Good Friday. Many names on bus destination boards are abbreviated: (Guate – Guatemala City; Chichi – Chichicastenango; Xela/Xelajú – Quetzaltenango, and so on). On many tourist routes there are **minibus shuttles**; quick, comfortable, and convenient, they charge a little more than the regular buses, but can be useful. They can be booked through hotels and travel agencies and will pick you up from your hotel.

Car and motorcycle Think carefully before driving a vehicle in Guatemala as it can be hazardous. Of the 14,000 km of roads, the 30% that are paved have improved greatly in recent years and are now of a high standard, making road travel faster and safer. Even cycle tracks (*ciclovías*) are beginning to appear on new roads. However, a new driving hazard in the highlands is the deep gully (for rainwater or falling stones) alongside the road. High clearance is essential on many roads in remoter areas and a 4WD vehicle is useful.

Bringing a vehicle into Guatemala requires the following procedure: presentation of a valid International Driving Licence; a check by **Cuarantena Agropecuaria** (Ministry of Agriculture quarantine) to check you are not importing fruit or veg; at **Aduana** (Customs) you must pay US$4.50 for all forms and a tourist vehicle permit for your vehicle. A motorcycle entry permit costs the same as one for a car. The description of your vehicle on the registration document must match your vehicle's appearance exactly. You must own the car/motorcycle and your name must be on the title papers. When entering the country, ask the officials to add any important accessories you have to the paper. Car insurance can be bought at the borders.

On leaving the country by car or motorcycle, two stamps on a strip of paper are required: surrender of the vehicle permit at customs and the **Cuarantena Agropecuaria** (quarantine) inspection, which is not always carried out. It is better not to import and sell foreign cars in Guatemala, as import taxes are very high.

Gasoline 'Normal' costs US$2.66, 'premium' US$2.80, and diesel is US$2.40 for the US gallon. Unleaded (*sin plomo*) is available in major cities, at Melchor de Mencos and along the Pan-American Highway, but not in the countryside, although it is gradually being introduced across the country.

Security Spare no ingenuity in making your car or motorbike secure. Try never to leave the car unattended except in a locked garage or guarded parking space. Lock the clutch or accelerator to the steering wheel with a heavy, obvious chain or lock. Street children will generally protect your car fiercely in exchange for a tip. Don't wash your car: smart cars attract thieves. Be sure to note down key numbers and carry spares of the most important ones. Try not to leave your fully laden motorbike on its own. An Abus D or chain will keep a bike secure. A cheap alarm gives you peace of mind if you leave the bike outside a hotel at night. Most hotels will allow you to bring the bike inside. Look for hotels that have a courtyard or more secure parking and never leave luggage on the bike overnight or whilst unattended. Also take a cover for the bike. Just about all parts and accessories are available at decent prices in Guatemala City at FPK, 5 Calle 6-75, Zona 9.

Border crossings From Mexico to Western Guatemala: **Ciudad Tecún Umán/Ciudad Hidalgo** is the main truckers' crossing. It is very busy and should be avoided at all costs by car. **Talismán**, the next border crossing north, is more geared to private cars. **La Mesilla** is the simplest for private cars and you can do your own paperwork with ease. All necessary documents can be obtained here.

Car hire Average rates are US$35-100 per day. Credit cards or cash are accepted for rental. Local cars are usually cheaper than those at international companies; if you book ahead from abroad with the latter, take care that they do not offer you a different vehicle claiming your original request is not available. Cars may not always be taken into neighbouring countries (none are allowed into Mexico or Belize); rental companies that do allow their vehicles to cross borders charge for permits and paperwork. If you wish to drive to Copán, you must check this is permissible and you need a letter authorizing you to take the vehicle in to Honduras. **Tabarini** and **Hertz** allow their cars to cross the border.

Cycling The scenery is gorgeous, the people friendly and colourful, but the hills are steep and sometimes long. The Pan-American Highway is OK from Guatemala City west; it has a shoulder and traffic is not very heavy. Buses are frequent and it is easy to load a bicycle on the roof; many buses do so, charging about two-thirds of the passenger fare. On the road, buses are a hazard for cyclists; Guatemala City is particularly dangerous. Look out for the cycle tracks (*ciclovías*) on a few main roads.

Hitchhiking Hitching is comparatively easy, but risky, especially for single women. Also beware of theft of luggage, especially in trucks. The best place to try for a lift is at a bridge or on a road out of town; be there no later than 0600, but 0500 is better as that is when truck drivers start their journey. Trucks usually charge US$1-1.50 upwards for a lift/day. Recently, travellers suggest it can be cheaper by bus. In remote areas, lifts in the back of a pickup are usually available; very crowded, but convenient when bus services are few and far between, or stop early in the day.

Sea

You can get around Lake Atitlán and from Puerto Barrios to Livingston by public boat services. Private boat services are possible from Puerto Barrios to Belize and Honduras and around El Estor and Río Dulce and around Lake Petén Itzá.

Sleeping

The tourist institute INGUAT publishes a list of maximum prices for single, double and triple occupancy of hundreds of hotels throughout the country in all price ranges, though the list is thin at the budget end. They will deal with complaints about overcharging if you can produce bills or other proof. Room rates should be posted in all registered hotels. Ask if taxes (*impuestos*) are included when you are given the room rate. INGUAT tax is 10% and service charge is usually an additional 12%. Busiest seasons are Easter, December and July to August. Most budget hotels do not supply toilet paper, soap or towels. There are no official campsites in Guatemala.

Eating and drinking

Traditional Central American/Mexican food such as tortillas, tamales, tostadas, etc are found everywhere. Tacos are less spicy than in Mexico. *Chiles rellenos*, chillies stuffed with meat and vegetables, are a speciality in Guatemala and may be *picante* (spicy) or *no* picante. *Churrasco*, charcoal-grilled steak, is often accompanied by *chirmol*, a sauce of tomato, onion and mint. *Guacamole* is also excellent. Local dishes include *pepián* (thick meat stew with vegetables) in Antigua, *patín* (tomato-based sauce served with *pescaditos*, small fish from Lake Atitlán wrapped in leaves), *cecina* (beef marinated in lemon and bitter orange) from the same region. *Fiambre* is widely prepared for families and friends who gather on All Souls' Day (1 November). It consists of all kinds of meat, fish, chicken, vegetables, eggs or cheese served as a salad with rice, beans and other side dishes. Desserts include *mole* (plantain and chocolate), *torrejas* (sweet bread soaked in egg and *panela* or honey) and *buñuelos* (similar to profiteroles) served with hot cinnamon syrup. For breakfast try *mosh* (oats cooked with milk and cinnamon), fried plantain with cream, black beans in various forms. *Pan dulce* (sweet bread), in fact bread in general, and local cheese are recommended. Try *borracho* (cake soaked in rum).

Drink

Local beers are good (Monte Carlo, Cabra, Gallo and Moza, a dark beer); bottled, carbonated soft drinks (*gaseosas*) are safest. Milk should be pasteurized. Freshly made *refrescos* and ice creams are delicious made of many varieties of local fruits; *licuados* are fruit juices with milk or water, but hygiene varies, so take care. Water should be filtered or bottled. By law alcohol cannot be consumed after 2000 on Sundays.

Festivals and events

1 Jan New Year

Mar/Apr Holy Week (4 days). Easter celebrations are exceptional in Antigua and Santiago Atitlán. Bus fares may be doubled.

1 May Labour Day.

15 Aug (Public holiday Guatemala City only).

15 Sep Independence Day.

12 Oct Discovery of America. (Not a business holiday)

20 Oct Revolution Day.

1 Nov All Souls' Day. Celebrated with abandonment and drunkenness in Todos Santos. In Santiago Sacatepéquez, the *Día de los Muertos* is characterized by colourful kite-flying (*barriletas*).

24 Dec Christmas Eve (from noon, although not a business holiday).

25 Dec Christmas Day.

31 Dec (Public holiday from noon).

Although specific dates are given for fiestas, there is often a week of jollification beforehand.

Shopping

Visiting a **market** in Guatemala can be one of the most enjoyable and memorable experiences of any trip. Bartering in the markets is the norm and is almost expected and unbelievable discounts can be obtained. You won't do better anywhere else in Central America, but getting the discount is less important than paying a fair price. Woven goods are normally cheapest bought in the town of origin. Try to avoid middlemen and buy direct from the weaver. Guatemalan **coffee** is highly recommended, although the best is exported; coffee sold locally is not vacuum-packed.

Essentials A-Z

Customs and duty free

You are allowed to take in, free of duty, personal effects and articles for your own use, 2 bottles of spirits and 80 cigarettes or 100 g of tobacco. Temporary visitors can take in any amount in quetzales or foreign currencies. The local equivalent of US$100 per person may be reconverted into US dollars on departure at the airport, provided a ticket for immediate departure is shown.

Drugs

If caught with drugs you'll wind up in prison where the minimum penalty is 5 years. In the traditional laid-back travellers' drug haven of San Pedro on Lake Atitlán, a number of police have been installed.

Electricity

Generally 110 volts AC, 60 cycles, US-style plug. Electricity is usually reliable in the towns but can be a problem in more remote areas like Petén.

Embassies and consulates

Belgium, Av Winston Churchill 185, 1180, Brussels, T(+322) 345-9058 (also covers Luxembourg).

Belize, 8 A St, Belize City, T223-3150.

Canada, 130 Albert St, Suite 1010, Ottawa, Ontario, K1P 5G4, T613 233-7237.

Costa Rica, Del Gimnasio Fitsimons 100 m sur, 50 m oeste Sabana Sur, San José, T291-6208.

El Salvador, 15 Av Norte, No 135, between C Arce and 1 C Pte, San Salvador, T2271-2225.

France, 2 rue Villebois Mareuil, 75017, Paris, T422 77 863 (also covers Portugal and Switzerland).

Germany, Joachim-Karnatz-Allee 45-47 D-10557, Berlin, T30 206-4363.

Honduras, Col Lomas del Guijaro, Calle Alfonso XIII, casa no.3716, Tegucigalpa, T231-1543.

Israel, Medinat Hayeydim 103, Ackerstein building, entry B, floor 2, Herzliya Pituah, T957-7335.

Italy, Vía dei Colli della Farnesina 128, 1-00194, Rome, T3638-1143.

Japan, 38 Kowa Bldg, 9th floor, room 905, Nishi-Azabu, Tokyo 106-0031, T3 3800-1830.

Mexico, Av Explanada No 1025, Col Lomas de Chapultepec, 11000 México DF, T5540-7520.

Nicaragua, Km 11.5 on road to Masaya, Managua, T799-609.

Panama, Edificio Altamira, 9th floor, office 925, Vía Argentina, El Cangrejo, Corregimiento de Bella Vista, Panama City, T269-3475.

Spain, Calle Rafael Salgado No 3, 10a derecha, 28036, Madrid, T1-344-1417 (also covers Morocco).

UK, 13 Fawcett St, London SW10 9HN, T020-7351-3042, embaguategtm@btconnect.com.

USA, 2220 R St NW, Washington DC, 20008, T202 745-4952, www.guatemala-embassy.org.

Health

Guatemala is healthy enough if precautions are taken about drinking water, milk, uncooked vegetables and peeled fruits; carelessness on this point is likely to lead to amoebic dysentery, which is endemic. In Guatemala City 2 good hospitals are **Bella Aurora**, 10 Calle, 2-31, Zona 14, T2368-1951 and **Herrera Llerandi**, 6 Avenida, 8-71, Zona 10, T2334-5959, but you must have full medical insurance or sufficient funds to pay for treatment. English and other languages are spoken. Most small towns have clinics. At the public hospitals, which are seriously underfunded and where care for major problems is not good, you may have an examination for a nominal fee, but drugs are expensive.

Internet

Internet cafés are found in all tourist destinations, ask around in the cities for the best rates. Rates are US$0.50-1.50 per hr.

Language

The official language is Spanish and Guatemala is one of the biggest centres for learning Spanish in Latin America. Outside the main tourist spots few people speak English. There are over 20 Mayan languages.

Regarding pronunciation in Guatemala, 'X' is pronounced 'sh', as in Xela (shay-la).

Media

The main newspaper is *Prensa Libre* (www.prensalibre.com). The *Guatemala Post* is published in English online, www.guatemalapost.com. *Siglo Veintiuno* is a good newspaper, www.sigloxxi.com. Mega popular is *Nuestro Diario*, a tabloid with more gory pics than copy. The *Revue*, www.revuemag.com, produced monthly in Antigua, carries articles, advertisements, lodgings, tours and excursions, covering Antigua, Panajachel, Quetzaltenango, Río Dulce, Monterrico, Cobán, Flores and Guatemala City.

Money→ *US$1=8.13 quetzales (June 2009)*
The unit is the quetzal, divided into 100 centavos. There are coins of 1 quetzal, 50 centavos, 25 centavos, 10 centavos, 5 centavos and 1 centavo. Paper currency is in denominations of 5, 10, 20, 50 and 100 quetzales.

There is often a shortage of small change; ask for small notes when you first change money to pay hotel bills, transport, etc.

ATMs and exchange

There are numerous banks in Guatemala and in cities and towns most have ATMs (*cajeros automáticos*). All will change US dollars cash into quetzales, the majority will change traveller's cheques and accept Visa to obtain cash. MasterCard is less commonly accepted. Banco Industrial in Guatemala City and at the international airport will change sterling, Canadian dollars and yen. Banco Uno will change euros and Mexican pesos.

Banks usually charge up to 2% per transaction to advance quetzales on a credit

card. Citicorp and Visa traveller's cheques are easier to change outside the main cities than Amex. Your passport is required and in some cases the purchase receipt as well, especially in the capital.

Credit cards

Visa is the most widely recognized and accepted bank card. If you have a MasterCard try G&T Continental or Credomatic/Banco de América Central, which are few and far . between. It is common for establishments to make a charge for use of credit cards – usually about US$3. Check before you sign. In the main it is only higher-class hotels and restaurants that accept cards. Amex cards are not very widely accepted. Visa assistance, T1-800-999-0115/T2331-8720; MasterCard T1-800-999-1480/T2334-0578. American Express T1-800-999-0245/T2470-4848.

Cost of living and travelling

Guatemala is one of the cheapest Central America countries, and those travelling on a tight budget should be able to get by on US$25 a day or less. With shorter distances, especially compared with Mexico to the north, travel becomes much less of a demand on your budget with the exception of the trip north to Tikal.

Opening hours

Banks Mon-Fri 0900-1500, some city banks are introducing later hours, up to 2000; in the main tourist towns, some banks are open 7 days a week.
Shops 0900-1300 and 1500-1900, often mornings only on Sat.

Post

Airmail to Europe takes 10-14 days. Letters cost US$1.10 for the first 20 g, US$3.40 for up to 100 g and US$37 for up to 2 kg. Airmail letters to the US and Canada cost US$0.1.10 for the first 20 g. Airmail parcel service to US is reliable (4 to 14 days) and costs US$2.70 for up 100 g and US$30 for up to 2 kg. Parcels over 2 kg can be sent from Guatemala

City, Correos y Telégrafos, 7 Avenida y 12 Calle, Zona 1, and Antigua. See under Panajachel and Chichicastenango (pages 687 and 688) for alternative services.

Prohibition

Take care with gambling in public places and do not take photos of military installations.

Safety

In some parts of the country you may be subject to military or police checks. Local people can be reluctant to discuss politics with strangers. Do not necessarily be alarmed by 'gunfire', which is much more likely to be fireworks and bangers, a national pastime, especially early in the morning.

Robberies and serious assaults on tourists are becoming more common. While you can do nothing to counter the bad luck of being in the wrong place at the wrong time, sensible precautions can minimize risks. Single women should be especially careful. Tourist groups are not immune and some excursion companies take precautions. Do not travel at night if at all possible and take care on roads that are more prone to vehicle hijacks – the road between Flores and the Belizean border, the highway between Antigua and Panajachel and the principal highway between the capital and El Salvadorian border. Assaults and robberies on the public (former US) buses have increased. There have been a high number of attacks on private vehicles leaving the airport.

Consult www.fco.gov.uk, http://guatemala.usembassy.gov/recent_incidents.html and http://travel.state.gov.

Asistur, T1500/2421-2810 is a 24-hr, year-round tourist assistance programme for any problem or question. There is also a national tourist police force, **POLITUR**, T5561-2073. Other useful numbers include: **National police** T110; and **tourist police** in Antigua T832-7290.

Tax

There is a 17% ticket tax on all international tickets sold in Guatemala. There is also a US$30 or quetzal equivalent international departure tax.

The tourist institute **INGUAT** tax is 10%. Service charge is usually an extra 12%.

Telephone → *Country code T+502, Directory enquiries T+154.*

All phone numbers in the country are on an 8-figure basis. There are 2 main service providers – **Telgua** and **Telefónica**. Telefónica sells cards with access codes, which can be used from any private or public Telefónica phone. Telgua phone booths are ubiquitous and use cards sold in values of 20 and 50 quetzales. From a Telgua phone, dial 147 before making an international call.

Most businesses offering a phone-call service charge a minimum of US$0.13 for a local call, making a phone card a cheaper option.

International calls can be made from phone booths, however, unlike the local calls, it is cheaper to find an internet café or shop, which tend to offer better rates.

Mobile phone sim cards are affordable, with good deals costing around US$6-7 for the card, which includes free calls. Comcel and PCS offer mobile-phone services. Rates are around US$0.13 a minute for a national call, US$1.06 for international.

Operator calls are more expensive. For international calls via the operator, dial T147-110. For calling card and credit-card call options, you need a fixed line in a hotel or private house. First you dial 9999 plus the following digits: For **Sprint USA**, dial 136; **AT&T Direct**: 190; **Germany**: 049; **Canada**: 198; **UK (BT)**: 044; **Switzerland**: 041; **Spain**: 034, **Italy**: 039.

Collect calls may be made from public Telgua phones by dialling T147 120.

Time
- 6 hrs GMT.

Tipping
Tip hotel and restaurant staff 10% in the better places (often added to the bill). Tip airport porters US$0.25 per bag.

Tourist information
Instituto Guatemalteco de Turismo (INGUAT), 7 Av, 1-17, Zona 4, Centro Cívico, Guatemala City, T2421-2800, www.visit guatemala.com. INGUAT provides bus times, hotel lists and road maps. Staff are helpful. Open Mon-Fri 0800-1600. Also office at the airport, open for all arrivals. The INGUAT airport office is open daily 0600-2400.

The Guatemalan Maya Centre, 94b Wandsworth Bridge Rd, London SW6 2TF, T020-7371-5291, www.maya. org.uk, has information on Guatemala, the Maya, a library, video archive and a textile collection.

INGUAT offices outside Guatemala
See also Embassies and consulates, page 621.
Germany, Joachim Karntaz-Alle 45-47, 10557, Berline Tiergarten.
Italy, Viale Prassilla 152, 00124, Rome, T390-6-5091-6626.
Mexico, T00-52-5202-1457, turismo embagua@prodigy.net.mx.
Spain, Calle Rafael Salgado 9, 4th Izquierda, 28036 Madrid, T/F34-91-457-3424.
USA, T001-202-518-5514.

Useful websites
Regional websites covering some of the more popular areas include **www.atitlan.com**, **www.mayaparadise.com** (Río Dulce/Lívingston), **www.cobanav.net** (Cobán) and **www.xelapages.com** (Quetzaltenango). **Posada Belén** in Guatemala City run a very informative site packed with information, www.guatemalaweb.com.

Of the several publications with websites, the *Revue*, **www.revuemag.com**, is probably the most useful to the visitor.

Visas and immigration
Only a valid passport is required for citizens of all Western European countries; USA, Canada, Mexico, all Central American countries, Australia, Israel, Japan and New Zealand. The majority of visitors get 90 days on arrival.

Visa renewal must be done in Guatemala City after 90 days, or on expiry. Passport stamp renewal on expiry for those citizens only requiring a valid passport to enter Guatemala must also be done at the immigration office at **Dirección General de Migración**, 6 Avenida, 3-11, Zona 4, Guatemala City, T2411-2411, Mon-Fri 0800-1600 (0800-1230 for payments). This office extends visas and passport stamps only once for a further period of time, depending on the original time awarded (maximum 90 days). Since 2006, when Guatemala signed a Central America-4 (CA-4) Border Control Agreement with El Salvador, Honduras, and Nicaragua you will have to visit a country outside of these 3 to re-enter and gain 90 days. These rules have been introduced to stop people leaving the country for 72 hrs (which is the legal requirement) every 6 months and returning, effectively making them permanent residents.

Working and volunteering
If you would like to volunteer, it is best to try and make contact before arriving, if only by a few days. Such is the demand for positions that unskilled volunteers very often have to pay for board and lodgings. Work needs to be planned and, although there is always work to do, your time will be used most efficiently if your arrival is expected and planned for. **Asociación de Rescate y Conservación de Vida Silvestre (ARCAS)**, T2478-4096, www.arcasguatemala.com. Runs projects involving working with nature and wildlife, returning wild animals to their natural habitat.

Casa Alianza, 13 Av, 0-37, Zona 2 de Mixco, Col la Escuadrilla Mixco, Guatemala City, T2250-4964, www.casa-alianza.org. A project that helps street kids.

Casa Guatemala, 14 Calle, 10-63, Zona 1, Guatemala City, T2331-9408, www.casa-guatemala.org. Runs a project for abandoned and malnourished children at Río Dulce.

Comité Campesino del Altiplano, on Lake Atitlán, 10 mins from San Lucas, T5804-9451, www.ccda.galeon.com. This Campesino Cooperative now produces Fair Trade organic coffee buying from small farmers in the region; long-term volunteers are welcome but Spanish is required.

Fundación Mario Dary, Diagonal 6, 17-19, Zona 10, Guatemala City, T2333-4957, fundary@intelnet.net.gt. Operates conservation, health and education projects on the Punta de Manabique and welcomes volunteers.

Proyecto Ak' Tenamit, 11 Av 'A', 9-39, Zona 2, Guatemala City, T2254-1560, ww.aktenamit.org, based at Clínica Lámpara, 15 mins upriver from Lívingston. This project was set up to help 7000 civil-war-displaced Q'eqchi' Maya who now live in the region in 30 communities.

Proyecto Mosaico Guatemala, 3 Av Norte 3, Antigua. T7832-0955, www.promosaico.org. An information centre and clearing house for volunteers, with access to opportunities all over the country.

Quetzaltrekkers, T7765-5895, www.quetzal trekkers.com. Volunteer hiking guides might be required.

UPAVIM, Calle Principal, Sector D-1, Col La Esperanza, Zona 12, Guatemala City, T2479-9061, www.upavim.org. This project helps poor families, providing social services and education for the workers using fair-trade principles.

There are also opportunites to work in children's homes in Quetzaltenango (Xela). 2 organizations are **Casa Hogar de Niños** and the **Asociación Hogar Nuevos Horizontes**. See page 711. Also check out Xela-based volunteering information organization www.entremundos.org. Several language schools in Xela fund community development projects and seek volunteers. Make enquiries in town or via www.xelapages.com.

The London-based **Guatemala Solidarity Network**, www.guatemalasolidarity.org.uk, can assist with finding projects that look at human rights issues.

Guatemala City

→ *Colour map 5, C2. Altitude: 1500 m.*

Smog-bound and crowded, Guatemala City is the commercial and administrative centre of the country. It is a sprawl of industrial activity lightly sprinkled with architectural treasures and out-of-place tributes to urban sculpture. Rarely rated by visitors, this is the beating heart of Guatemala and is worth a couple of days if you have time and can bear the noise and pollution in Zona 1. Guatemala City is surrounded by active and dormant volcanoes easily visited on day trips. ➤ See listings, pages 631-640.

Ins and outs

Getting there

The airport is in the south part of the city at La Aurora, 4 km from the Plaza Central, T2331-8392. It has banks, ATMs, internet, bars and restaurants. A taxi to Zona 10 is US$8, Zona 1, US$10 and from Antigua, US$25-30. Shuttles from outside airport to Antigua meet all arriving flights, US$10. The Zona 4 chicken bus terminal between 1-4 Avenida and 7-9 Calle serves the Occidente (west), the Costa Sur (Pacific coastal plain) and El Salvador. The area of southern Zona 1 contains many bus offices and is the departure point for the Oriente (east), the Caribbean zone, Pacific coast area towards the Mexican border and the north, to Flores and Tikal. First-class buses often depart from company offices in Zona 1 (see map). Note that some companies have been moved from Zona 1 and Zona 4 out to Zona 7 and 12. ➤ *See Transport, page 636.*

Getting around

Any address not in Zona 1 – and it is absolutely essential to quote zone numbers in addresses – is probably some way from the centre. Addresses themselves, being purely numerical, are usually easy to find. For example, 19 Calle, 4-83 is on 19 Calle between 4 Avenida and 5 Avenida at No 83.

Tourist information

INGUAT ① *7 Av, 1-17, Zona 4 (Centro Cívico), 24 hrs T1801-464-8281, T2421-2800, www.visitguatemala.com, Mon-Fri 0800-1600. English is sometimes spoken.* They are very friendly and provide a hotel list, a map of the city, and general information on buses, market days, museums, etc. They also have an office in the **airport arrivals hall** ① *T2331-4256, 0600-2100,* where staff are exceptionally helpful and on the ball.

Background

Guatemala City was founded by decree of Carlos III of Spain in 1776 to serve as capital after earthquake damage to the earlier capital, Antigua, in 1773. Almost completely destroyed by earthquakes in 1917-1918, it was rebuilt in modern fashion, or in copied colonial, only to be further damaged by earthquake in 1976. Most of the affected buildings have been restored.

Sights

The old centre of the city is Zona 1. It is still a busy shopping and commercial area, with some good hotels and restaurants, and many of the cheaper places to stay. However, the main activity of the city has been moving south, first to Zona 4, now to Zonas 9, 10 and 14. With the move have gone commerce, banks, embassies, museums and the best hotels and restaurants. The best residential areas are in the hills to the east, southeast and west.

Around Zona 1

At the city's heart lies the **Parque Central**. It is intersected by the north-to-south-running 6 Avenida, the main shopping street. The eastern half has a floodlit fountain; on the west side is **Parque Centenario**, with an acoustic shell in cement used for open-air concerts and public meetings. The Parque Central is popular on Sunday with many *indígenas* selling textiles.

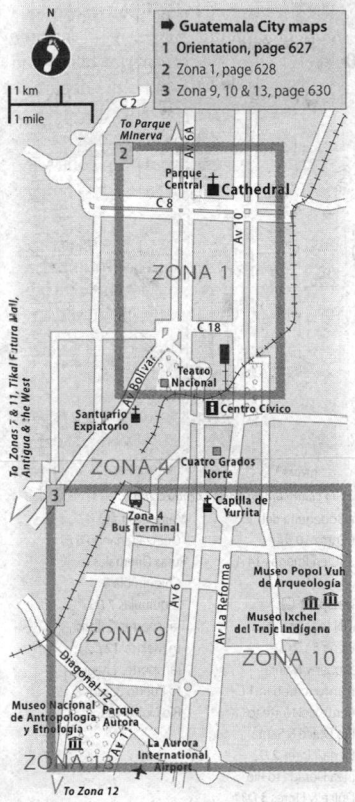

1 Guatemala City orientation

➡ **Guatemala City maps**
1 Orientation, page 627
2 Zona 1, page 628
3 Zona 9, 10 & 13, page 630

To the east of the plaza is the **cathedral** (www.catedral.org.gt). It was begun in 1782 and finished in 1815 in classical style with notable blue cupolas and dome. Inside are paintings and statues from ruined Antigua. Solid silver and sacramental reliquary are in the east side chapel of the Sagrario. Next to the cathedral is the colonial mansion of the Archbishop. Aside from the cathedral, the most notable public buildings constructed between 1920 and 1944, after the 1917 earthquake, are the **Palacio Nacional** ⓘ *visits every 15 mins Mon-Fri 0900-1645; every 30 mins Sat and Sun, 0900-1630*, built of light green stone, the Police Headquarters, the Chamber of Deputies and the Post Office. To the west of the cathedral are the Biblioteca Nacional and the Banco del Ejército. Behind the Palacio Nacional is the Presidential Mansion.

Museums in Zona 1 include the **Museo Nacional de Historia** ⓘ *9 Calle, 9-70, T2253-6149, Mon-Fri 0900-1600, Sat-Sun 0900-1200 and 1300-1600, US$6*, which has historical documents and objects from Independence onward. **Museo de la Universidad de San Carlos de Guatemala (MUSAC)** ⓘ *9 Av, 9-79, T2232-0721, www.musacenlinea.org, Mon, Wed-Fri 0930-1730, Sat 0930-1700, closed Tue and Sun, US$1; guided tours at 1000 and 1400*, charts the history of the university. The

② Zona 1

➡ **Guatemala City maps**
1 Orientation, page 627
2 **Zona 1, page 628**
3 Zona 9, 10 & 13, page 630

Eating ⊘
Altuna **1** *C2*
Arrin Cuan **2** *A2*
Café de Imeri **3** *A1*
Helados Marylena **5** *A1*
Los Canalones **6** *B2*
Vegetariano
 Rey Sol **7** *A2*

Bars & clubs ⊙
El Portal **12** *A2*
Europa **4** *B2*

Spring **9** *C2*

La Bodeguita del
 Centro **10** *B1*
Las Cien Puertas **14** *A2*

Transport ⊟
ADN to Santa
 Elena **5** *C2*
Escobar y Monja
 Blanca to Cobán **1** *C2*
Fuente del Norte to
 Río Dulce & Santa
 Elena/Flores **2** *D2*
Línea Dorada to Río
 Dulce & Flores **3** *D3*

Marquensita to
 Quetzaltenango **6** *E1*
Rutas Orientales to
 Chiquimula &
 Esquipulas **7** *D3*
Transportes Galgos
 to Mexico **12** *D2*
Transportes Litegua
 to Puerto Barrios &
 Río Dulce **13** *C3*

Sleeping ⊜
Chalet Suizo **4** *C2*
Colonial **5** *C2*
Continental **6** *B2*
Pan American **7** *A2*
Pensión Meza **8** *B3*
Posada Belén **1** *C3*

Salón Mayor is where Guatemala signed its independence from Mexico in 1823, and in 1826, the Central American Federation, with Guatemala as the seat of power, abolished slavery in the union. Also, Doctor Mariano Gálvez, the country's president from 1831-1838, is buried behind part of the salon wall and a marble bust of him sits outside the door. The Universidad de San Carlos was the first university in Guatemala City. **Casa MIMA** ① *8 Av, 14-12, T2253-6657, casamima@hotmail.com, Mon-Sat 0900-1230, 1400-1500, US$1, no photography,* is the only authentic turn-of-the-19th-century family home open to the public, once owned by the family Ricardo Escobar Vega and Mercedes Fernández Padilla y Abella. It is furnished in European-influenced style with 15th- to mid-20th-century furniture and ornaments.

Most of the churches worth visiting are in Zona 1. **Cerro del Carmen** ① *11 Av y 1 Calle A,* was built as a copy of a hermitage destroyed in 1917-1918, containing a famous image of the Virgen del Carmen. Situated on a hill with good views of the city, it was severely damaged in the earthquake of 1976 and remains in poor shape. **La Merced** ① *11 Av y 5 Calle,* dedicated in 1813, has beautiful altars, organ and pulpit from Antigua as well as jewellery, art treasures and fine statues. **Santo Domingo** ① *12 Av y 10 Calle,* built between 1782 and 1807, is a striking yellow colour, reconstructed after 1917, with an image of Nuestra Señora del Rosario and sculptures. **Sagrado Corazón de Jesús,** or **Santuario Expiatorio** ① *26 Calle y 2 Av,* holds 3000 people; the colourful, exciting modern architecture was by a young Salvadorian architect who had not qualified when he built it. Part of the complex, built in 1963 (church, school and auditorium) is in the shape of a fish. The entrance is a giant arch of multicoloured stained glass, wonderfully illuminated at night. The walls are lined with glass confessionals. **Las Capuchinas** ① *10 Av y 10 Calle,* has a very fine St Anthony altarpiece, and other pieces from Antigua. **Santa Rosa** ① *10 Av y 8 Calle,* was used for 26 years as the cathedral until the present building was ready. The altarpieces are from Antigua (except above the main altar). **San Francisco** ① *6 Av y 13 Calle,* a large yellow and white church that shows earthquake damage outside (1976), has a sculpture of the Sacred Head, originally from Extremadura, in Spain. **Carmen El Bajo** ① *8 Av y 10 Calle,* was built in the late 18th century; again the façade was severely damaged in 1976.

North of the centre

Parque Minerva ① *Av Simeón Cañas, Zona 2, 0900-1700, US$1.50,* has a huge relief map of the country made in 1905 to a horizontal scale of 1:10,000 and a vertical scale of 1:2,000. The park has basketball and baseball courts, bar and restaurant and a children's playground (unsafe at night). To get there, take bus V21 from 7 Avenida, Zona 4. Just beyond is a popular park, the **Hipódromo** which is packed on Sundays with bumper cars and mechanical games, and a great little train for kids.

South of the centre: Avenida La Reforma

The modern **Centro Cívico**, which links Zona 1 with Zona 4, includes the Municipalidad, the Palacio de Justicia, the Ministerio de Finanzas Públicas, the Banco de Guatemala, the mortgage bank, the social-security commission and the tourist board. The curious **Teatro Nacional** ① *Mon-Fri 0800-1630 for tours, US$4,* with its blue and white mosaic, dominates the hilltop of the west side of the Centro Cívico. There is an excellent view of the city and surrounding mountains from the roof. An old Spanish fortress provides a backdrop to the open-air theatre adjoining the Teatro Nacional.

Cuatro Grados Norte, located on Vía 5 between Ruta 1 and Ruta 2, is a pedestrianized area that has grown up around the IGA theatre and bookshop (a cultural centre, which sometimes has interesting concerts and exhibitions). Cafés and bars have tables on the street and it's safe and fun to wander around at night. The **Centro Cultural de España** is located here with live music, films, exhibitions and conferences, there is also a branch of **Sophos**, an excellent bookshop. On Saturdays there is a street market with craft and jewellery stalls, often cultural events in the street. On Sundays there are clowns and events for children. It's a strange mix of wealthy Guatemalans strolling with their poodles and alternative street-market types; sit back and enjoy watching the people.

To see the finest residential district go south down 7 Avenida to Ruta 6, which runs diagonally in front of Edificio El Triángulo, past the orange **Capilla de Yurrita** (Ruta 6 y Vía 8). Built as a private chapel in 1928 on the lines of a Russian Orthodox church, it has been described as an example of "opulent 19th-century bizarreness and over-ripe

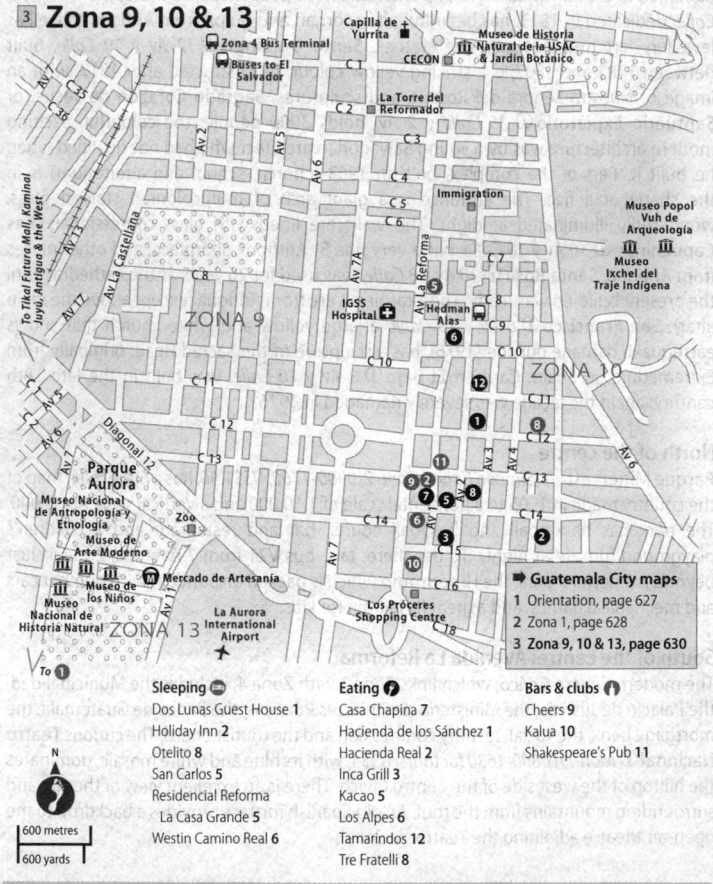

3 Zona 9, 10 & 13

Sleeping
Dos Lunas Guest House 1
Holiday Inn 2
Otelito 8
San Carlos 5
Residencial Reforma
La Casa Grande 5
Westin Camino Real 6

Eating
Casa Chapina 7
Hacienda de los Sánchez 1
Hacienda Real 2
Inca Grill 3
Kacao 5
Los Alpes 6
Tamarindos 12
Tre Fratelli 8

Bars & clubs
Cheers 9
Kalua 10
Shakespeare's Pub 11

➡ **Guatemala City maps**
1 Orientation, page 627
2 Zona 1, page 628
3 Zona 9, 10 & 13, page 630

extravagance". There are many woodcarvings, slender white pillars, brown/gold ornamentation and an unusual blue sky window over the altar. Ruta 6 runs into the wide tree-lined Avenida La Reforma.

To the east, in Zona 10, are some excellent museums. **Museo Ixchel del Traje Indígena** ① *Campus of Universidad Francisco Marroquín, 6 Calle Final, T2331-3638, www.museo ixchel.org, Mon-Fri 0900-1700, Sat 0900-1300, US$5*, has a collection of indigenous dress. In addition to the clothes there are photos from the early 20th century, paintings and very interesting videos. A shop sells beautiful textiles that aren't available on the tourist market, prices are fixed, and quality costs. **Museo Popol Vuh de Arqueología** ① *6 Calle Final, T2361-2301, www.populvuh.ufm.edu.gt, Mon-Fri 0900-1700, Sat 0900-1300, US$5, US$3 charge to take photographs*, has an extensive collection of pre-Columbian and colonial artefacts, as well as a replica of the Dresden Codex, one of the only Maya parchment manuscripts in existence. **Museo de Historia Natural de la USAC y Jardín Botánico** ① *Calle Mcal Cruz 1-56, T2334-6065, Mon-Fri 0800-1600, Sat 0830-1230, US$1.30*, has gardens, stuffed animals and live snakes.

In **Parque Aurora**, Zona 13, in the southern part of the city, are La Aurora International Airport, the Observatory, racetrack and **Parque Zoológico La Aurora** ① *T2472-0507, Tue-Sun 0900-1700, US$1.10*. The newer areas show greater concern for the animals' well-being. There are also several museums: **Museo Nacional de Antropolgía y Etnología** ① *Salón 5, Parque Aurora, Zona 13, T2472-0478, Tue-Fri 0900-1600, Sat-Sun 0900-1200, 1330-1600, US$4, no photos*. Outstanding Maya pieces including stelae from Piedras Negras and typical Guatemalan dress, as well as good models of Tikal, Quiriguá and Zaculeu. There are sculptures, murals, ceramics, textiles, a collection of masks and an excellent jade collection. Around the corner is the **Museo Nacional de Historia Natural** ① *6 Calle, 7-30, Zona 13, T2472-0468, Mon-Fri 0900-1600, Sat-Sun 0900-1200, 1400-1600, US$1.30*, which houses a collection of national fauna, including stuffed birds, animals, butterflies, geological specimens, etc. Opposite the archaeology museum, the **Museo de Arte Moderno** ① *Salón 6, Parque Aurora, Zona 13, T2472-0467, US$1.30, Tue-Fri 0900-1600*, has a modest but enjoyable collection. Next door is the **Museo de los Niños** ① *T2475-5076, Tue-Fri 0800-1200, 1300-1700, Sat-Sun 1000-1330, 1430-1800, US$4.50*, an interactive museum with a gallery of Maya history and the Gallery of Peace which houses the world's largest single standing artificial tree – a ceiba.

⦿ Guatemala City listings

Hotel and guesthouse prices
LL over US$150 **L** US$100-150 **AL** US$66-99
A US$46-65 **B** US$31-45 **C** US$21-30
D US$12-20 **E** US$7-11 **F** under US$7
Restaurant prices
♥♥♥ over US$15 **♥♥** US$8-15 **♥** under US$8
See pages 45-48 for further information.

⦿ Sleeping

You can get better prices in the more expensive hotels by booking corporate rates through a travel agent or simply asking at the desk if any lower prices are available. Hotels are often full at holiday times, eg Easter and Christmas. At the cheaper hotels, single rooms are not always available. There are many cheap *pensiones* near bus and railway stations and markets; those between Calle 14 and Calle 18 are not very salubrious.

Hoteles Villas de Guatemala, reservations 8 Calle 1-75 Zona 10, T2223-5000, www.villasdeguatemala.com, rents luxury villas throughout Guatemala.

Zona 1 *p627, map p628*

AL-A Pan American, 9 Calle, 5-63, T2232-6807, www.hotelpanamerican.com.gt. Quiet and comfortable rooms with TV, but try to avoid rooms on the main-road side. Parking, and breakfast included. Restaurant with good food in the mid-range price bracket.

B Posada Belén, 13 Calle "A", 10-30, T2232-9226, www.posadabelen.com. A colonial-style house run by the friendly Francesca and René Sanchinelli, who speak English. Laundry, email service, luggage store and good dining room. Parking. Tours available. A lovely place to stay.

B-C Colonial, 7 Av, 14-19, T2232-6722, www.hotelcolonial.net. Rooms are quiet with TV and nice dark cedar wood furniture. It's pleasant, friendly and with parking too.

B-D Spring, 8 Av, 12-65, T2230-2858. Bright rooms with TV in this quiet haven of tranquillity and flowers amid the pollution of Zona 1. Rooms without private shower are cheaper. Patio garden, good breakfasts, and parking near by. Free coffee, email service, phone calls, luggage store. Probably the best choice in Zona 1 at this price.

C Continental, 12 Calle, 6-10, T2230-5814. 2 floors up with a very secure street entrance. It has vast, comfortable rooms, but they're spartan; some quadruples available. All are very clean with private bath. Credit cards accepted.

C-D Chalet Suizo, 7a Calle, 14-34, T2251-3786, chaletsuizo@gmail.com. In a good central position with constant hot-water showers (cheaper with shared bathroom). It is popular, so often crowded. There is a locked luggage store, safety box, and the rooms are secure. Those rooms facing the main street are noisy. Avoid rooms 9-12 as a noisy pump will disturb sleep and 19-21 have very thin walls. Free parking.

D-E Pensión Meza, 10 Calle, 10-17, T2232-3177. A large ramshackle place with beds in dorms. It's popular with helpful staff and English is spoken. It's

sometimes noisy and some rooms are damp. Other rooms are darker than a prison cell, but cheered by graffiti, poetry and paintings. There is a ping-pong table, book exchange, internet at US$80 per hr, or free Wi-Fi.

South of the centre: Avenida La Reforma *p629*

LL-L Holiday Inn, 1 Av, 13-22, Zona 10, T2421-0000, www.ichotelsgroup.com. Good value with a pool, gym, bar, email centre, and free airport shuttle available.

LL-L Westin Camino Real, Av La Reforma y 14 Calle, Zona 10, T2333-3000, www.starwoodhotels.com. Excellent value, good restaurants open 0600-2330, gym, pool, spa, airport shuttle, piano bar and live Cuban music Fri and Sat at 2100.

L Otelito, 12 Calle, 4-51, T2339-1811, Zona 10, www.otelito.com. 12 lovely rooms in this small boutique hotel. Includes breakfast, shuttle to hotel and internet. Restaurant open Mon-Wed 0630-2100, Thu-Sat 0630-2230, Sun 0630-2030.

AL Residencial Reforma La Casa Grande, Av La Reforma, 7-67, Zona 10, T2332-0914, www.casagrande-gua.com. Near US Embassy, with nicer rooms than the next door **San Carlos**. Colonial style, all rooms come with TV. Good, small restaurant, open 0630-2100, a bar and internet service. Good value.

AL San Carlos, Av La Reforma, 7-89, Zona 10, T2332-6055, www.hsancarlos.com. A small, charming hotel, with pool and plant-filled patio. Includes breakfast and free airport transfer.

B Hincapié Guest House, Av Hincapié, 18-77, Zona 13, T2332-7771, ruedapinillos@ yahoo.com. On the far side of the airport runway. Continental breakfast included and free airport transport. Cable TV in the rooms.

B Hotel Aeropuerto Guest House, 5 mins' walk from the airport at 15 Calle "A", 7-32, Col Aurora 1, Zona 13, T2332-3086, www.aeropuertoguesthouse.com. Free transport to and from the airport.

With or without bath, and is clean and safe, breakfast included. Free internet.
B-D Dos Lunas Guest House, 21 Calle, 10-92, Zona 13, T2261-4248, www.hoteldoslunas.com. Private rooms and dorms in a comfy B&B. Very close to the airport with free transport to or from the airport. Storage service, free breakfast and water and tourist information. Lorena, the landlady, also organizes shuttles and taxis and tours. English spoken. Reservations advisable as often full.

● Eating

Zona 1 *p627, map p628*
There are all kinds of food available in the capital, from the simple national cuisine to French, Chinese and Italian food. There is a plethora of fast-food restaurants and traditional *comedores* where you will get good value for money; a reasonable set meal will cost no more than US$3. The cheapest places to eat are at street stalls and the various markets – take the normal precautions.
TTT Altuna, 5 Av, 12-31. Serves tasty Spanish food in huge portions. Lobster available but expensive. Delicious coffee. This hotel has a beautiful traditional Spanish bar interior. There is a branch in Zona 10 at 10 Calle, 0-45.
TTT Hotel Pan American, 9 Calle, 5-63 (see Sleeping). Best lunchtime menu.
TT Arrin Cuan, 5 Av, 3-27. A famous local institution specializing in traditional food from Cobán (*subanik*, *gallo en chicha*, and *kak ik*). The restaurant is centred around a small courtyard with a little fountain and live lunchtime marimba music. Breakfast available. Also on 16 Calle, 4-32, Zona 10.
TT-T Café de Imeri, 6 Calle, 3-34. Closed Sun. Sandwiches, salads, soups and pastries in a patio garden. Set lunch and excellent cakes. It's popular with young professional Guatemalans. Try the *pay de queso de elote* (maize cheesecake). Its bakery next door has a rare selection of granary breads, birthday cakes, etc.

TT Los Canalones – Parrillada Argentina, 6 Av A, 10-39. Open Mon-Sat 1200-1630. Barbecue on the street outside, for serious meat eaters. Alejandro *El Argentino* does tasty chunks of meat and chorizo served with excellent salad, get there early. Meals include soup, endless tortillas and *refresco*.
T Restaurante Vegetariano Rey Sol, 8 Calle, 5-36. Closed Sun. A prize vegetarian find – wholesome food and ambience oasis amid the fumes of Zona 1, and popular with the locals. Delicious veggie concoctions at excellent prices served canteen-style by friendly staff. Breakfasts and *licuados* also available. Newer, larger and brighter branch at 11 Calle, 5-51.

Ice cream parlours
T Helados Marylena, 6 Calle, 2-49. Open daily 1000-2200. Not quite a meal but almost. This establishment has been serving up the weirdest concoctions for 90 years. From the probably vile – fish, chile, yucca and cauliflower ice cream – to the heavenly – beer and sputnik (coconut, raisins and pineapple). The *elote* (maize) is good too. This city institution is credited with making children eat their vegetables! Anyone travelling with fussy eaters should stop by here.

South of the centre: Avenida La Reforma *p629*
Most of the best restaurants are in the 'Zona Viva', within 10 blocks of the Av La Reforma on the east side, between 6 Calle and 16 Calle in Zona 10. **Zona 9** is just across the other side of Av La Reforma.

There are several options in the area around **Cuatro Grados Norte** providing tapas, sushi, *churros* and chocolate. Lively, especially on Fri and Sat nights.
TTT Hacienda de los Sánchez, 12 Calle, 2-25, Zona 10. Good steaks and local dishes, but seriously crowded at weekends, and so not the most pleasant of settings compared with other steakhouses in the vicinity.
TTT Hacienda Real, 15 Calle, 15, Zona 10, recently moved. An excellent steak selection.

Candles and palms create a garden-like atmosphere. Nice little bar with Mexican leather chairs on one side.

††† Inca Grill, 2 Av 14-32, Zona 10. Tasty Peruvian food, live Andean music.

††† Kacao, 2 Av, 13-44, Zona 10. A large variety of delicious local and national dishes, which are attractively prepared and served in ample portions. The setting is fantastic – a giant thatched room, *huípiles* for tablecloths, beautiful candle decorations; some options are expensive.

††† Tamarindos, 11 Calle, 2-19A, Zona 10, T2360-2815. Mixed Asian, sushi, Vietnamese rolls, mushrooms stuffed with almonds and crab are some of the tantalizing options at this very smart Asian restaurant with spiral shades and soothing bamboo greens.

††† Tre Fratelli, 2 Av 13-25, Zona 10. Good Italian food; tasty bread and parmesan cheese; very lively and popular, some outside tables.

†† Café Vienés, in the **Camino Real**, Zona 10. One of the best places for German-style coffee and cakes, your chance to try a chocolate fondu.

†† Casa Chapina, 1a Av, 13-42, Zona 10, T4212-2746. Near the quality hotels, friendly service, reasonable prices and a wide range of traditional and international dishes to choose from.

†† Los Alpes, 10 Calle, 1-09, Zona 10. Closed Mon. A Swiss/Austrian place with light meals, which also offers a smorgasbord of excellent cakes and chocolates. Popular with Guatemalan families.

††-† Cafesa, 6 Av, 11-64, Zona 9. 24-hr diner serving Western and Guatemalan food with some seriously cheap options.

Cuatro Grados Norte

††† Café Rouge, Cuatro Grados Norte, Vía 5 between Ruta 1 and Ruta 2. Good cappuccinos, chocolate things and apple pie.

††† L'Ostería, Vía 5 between Ruta 1 and Ruta 2. Italian on the corner with leafy terrace; popular; brick pizza oven.

†† Arguileh, Vía 5 between Ruta 1 and Ruta 2. Eastern-style kebabs and *pan árabe*, wooden decor, looks good.

†† Tarboosh, Vía 5 between Ruta 1 and Ruta 2, not far from **L'Ostería**. Mediterranean cuisine in a funky upstairs setting with loud live music acts.

● Entertainment

Bars and clubs

Cheers, 13 Calle, 0-40, Zona 10. A basement sports bar with pool tables, darts, and large cable TV. Mon-Sat 0900-0100, Sun 1300-2400ish. Happy hour until 1800.

El Portal, Portal del Comercio, 8 Calle, 6-30, Zona 1. Mon-Sat 1000-2200. This was a favourite spot of Che Guevara and you can imagine him sitting here holding court at the long wooden bar. A stuffed bull's head now keeps watch over drinkers. To get there, enter the labyrinths of passageways facing the main plaza at No 6-30 where there is a Coke stand. At the first junction bear round to the left and up on the left you will see its sign. *Comida típica* and marimba music, beer from the barrel.

Europa, 11 Calle, 5-16, Zona 1. Mon-Sat 0800-0100. Popular peace-corps/travellers' hang-out, sports bar, shows videos, books for sale.

Kalua, 1 Av, 15-06. Huge club, 3 floors with different tunes, stylish.

La Bodeguita del Centro, 12 Calle, 3-55, Zona 1, T2239-2976. The walls of this hip place in an old stockhouse are adorned with posters of Che Guevara, Bob Marley and murdered Salvadorian Archbishop Romero. There's live music Thu-Sat at 2100, talks, plays, films, exhibitions upstairs. Wooden tables are spread over 2 floors; seriously cheap nachos and soup on the menu. It's an atmospheric place to spend an evening. Call in to get their **Calendario Cultural** leaflet.

Las Cien Puertas, Pasaje Aycinea, 7 Av, 8-44, just south of Plaza Mayor, Zona 1. Daily 1600-2400. Has a wonderful atmosphere with political, satirical and love missives covering its walls. There's excellent food and outdoor seating and it's friendly.

Sabor Latino, 1 Av, 13 Calle, Zona 10. A club that's under **Rock and Salambo** on the same block as **Mi Guajira**. The night begins with salsa and graduates to a more hip-hop beat.

Shakespeare's Pub, 13 Calle, 1-51, Zona 10. Mon-Fri 1100-0100, Sat and Sun 1400-0100. English-style basement bar with a good atmosphere, American owner, a favourite with ex-pats and locals, safe for women to go and drink.

Cinema and theatre
There are numerous cinemas and they often show films in English with Spanish subtitles. **Teatro Nacional**, Centro Cívico. Most programmes are Thu-Sun.

O Shopping

Bookshops
Museo Popol Vuh bookshop has a good selection of books on pre-Columbian art, crafts and natural history. The Museo Ixchel also has a bookshop.

Maps
Maps can be bought from the **Instituto Geográfico Nacional** (IGN), Av Las Américas, 5-76, Zona 13, T2332-2611. Mon-Fri 0900-1730. The whole country is covered by about 200 1:50,000 maps available in colour or photocopies of out of print sections. None is more recent than 1991. There is, however, an excellent 1996, 1:15,000 map of Guatemala City in 4 sheets. A general *Mapa Turístico* of the country is available here, also at INGUAT.

Markets and supermarkets
The **Central Market** operates underground behind the cathedral, from 7 to 9 Av, 8 Calle, Zona 1. One floor is dedicated to native textiles and crafts, and there is a large, cheap basketware section on the lower floor. Silverware is cheaper at the market than elsewhere in Guatemala City. Other markets include the **Mercado Terminal** in Zona 4, and the **Mercado de Artesanía** in the Parque Aurora, near the airport, which is for tourists. Large shopping centres have been opened in the last few years, which are good for a wide selection of local crafts, artworks, funky shoes, clothes and the local scene. Don't miss the *dulces*, candied fruits and confectionery.

The best shopping centres are **Centro Comercial Los Próceres**, 18 Calle and 3 Av, Zona 10, the **Centro Comercial La Pradera**, Carretera Roosevelt and Av 26, Zona 10. There is a large **Paiz** supermarket on 18 Calle and 8 Av and a vast shopping mall **Tikal Futura** at Calzada Roosevelt and 22 Av, Zona 11. *Artesanías* for those who shop with a conscience at the fair-trade outlet **UPAVIM**, Calle Principal, Col La Esperanza, Mesquital Zona 12, T2479-9061, www.upavim.org, Mon-Fri 0800-1800, Sat 0800-1200.

▲ Activities and tours

Aire, Mar y Tierra, Plaza Maritima, 6 Av, 20-25, Zona 10, T2337-0149. Recommended.
Clark Tours, Plaza Clark, 7 Av 14-76, Zona 9, T2412-4700, www.clarktours.com.gt, and several other locations. Long-established, very helpful, tours to Copán, Quiriguá, etc.
Four Directions, 1 Calle, 30-65, Zona 7, T2439-7715, www.fourdirections.com.gt. Recommended for Maya archaeology tours. English spoken.
Maya Expeditions, 15 Calle "A", 14-07, Zona 10, 12363-4955, www.mayaexpeditions.com. Very experienced and helpful, with varied selection of short and longer river/hiking tours, whitewater rafting, bungee jumping, cultural tours, tours to Piedras Negras.
Setsa Travel, 8 Av, 14-11, Zona 1, T2230-4726, karlasetsa@intelnet.net.gt, very helpful, tours arranged to Tikal, Copán, car hire.

Tourama, Av La Reforma, 15-25, Zona 10, T2368-1820. English spoken. Recommended.
Trolley Tour, T5907-0913, Tue-Sat 1000-1300, Sun 1000. Pick-ups from Zona 10 hotels for 3-hr city tours, US$20, children, US$10.
Turismo Ek Chuah, 3 Calle 6-24, Zona 2, T2220-1491, www.ekchuah.com. Nationwide tours as well as some specialist and tailor-made tours.

⊖ Transport

Air
Flights to **Flores** with Grupo Taca 0820, 1605 and 1850, and **TAG** at 1630 daily.

Airline offices
Charter airlines Aero Ruta Maya, Av Hincapié and 18 Calle, Zona 13, T2339-0502.

Domestic airlines Aerocharter, 18 Calle and Av Hincapié, Zona 13, T5401-5893, to **Puerto Barrios**. Phone for schedule. **Aeródromo**, Av Hincapié and 18 Calle, Zona 13, T5539-9364, to **Huehuetenango**. Phone for schedule. **Aerolucía**, 18 Calle and Av Hincapié, T5959-7008 to **Quetzaltenango**. Phone for schedule. **Grupo Taca** at the airport and Av Hincapié, 12-22, Zona 13, T2470-8222, www.taca.com. **Tag**, Av Hincapié y 18 Calle, Zona 13, T2361-1180, www.tag.com.gt.

International airlines American Airlines, Hotel Marriot, 7 Av, 15-45, Zona 9, T2422-0000. Continental Airlines, 18 Calle, 5-56, Zona 10, Edif Unicentro, T2385-9610. Copa, 1 Av, 10-17, Zona 10, T2385-5555. Cubana de Aviación, Edificio Atlántis, 13 Calle, 3-40, Zona 10, T2361-0857. Delta Airlines, 15 Calle, 3-20, Zona 10, Edif Centro Ejecutivo, T2263-0600. Iberia, Av La Reforma, 8-60, Zona 9, Edif Galerías Reforma, T2332-7471/ 2332-0911, www.iberia.com. Inter Jet, T1-800-835-0271, www.inter jet.com.mx. Mexicana,13 Calle, 8-44, Zona 10, Edif Plaza Edyma, T2333-6001.

Spirit Air, www.spiritair.com. **Taca** (includes Aviateca, Lacsa, Nica and Inter), see above.
United, Av La Reforma, 1-50, Zona 9, Edif La Reformador, 2nd floor, T1-800-835-0100.

Bus
Local
Buses operate between 0600-2000, after which you will have to rely on taxis.

In town, US$0.13 per journey on regular buses and on the larger red buses known as *gusanos* (worms) except on Sun and public holidays when they charge US$0.16.) One of the most useful bus services is the **101**, which travels down 10 Av, Zona 1, and then cuts across to the 6 Av, Zona 4, and then across Vía 8 and all the way down the Av La Reforma, Zona 10. The **82** also travels from Zona 1 to 10 and can be picked up on the 10 Av, Zona 1 and the 6 Av, Zona 4. Bus **85**, with the same pickup points, goes to the cluster of museums in Zona 13. Buses **37**, **35**, **32** all head for the INGUAT building, which is the large blue and white building in the Centro Cívico complex. **R40** goes from the 6 Av, Zona 4, to the Tikal Futura shopping complex – a good spot to catch the Antigua bus, which pulls up by the bridge to the complex. Buses leaving the 7 Av, Zona 4, just 4 blocks from the Zona 4 bus terminal, for the Plaza Mayor, Zona 1, are *gusano* **V21, 35, 36, 82**, and **101**.

Long distance
Watch your bags everywhere, but like a hawk in the Zona 4 terminal.

There are numerous bus terminals in Guatemala City. The majority of 1st-class buses have their own offices and departure points around Zona 1. Hundreds of chicken buses for the south and west of Guatemala leave from the Zona 4 terminal, as well as local city buses. However, there was a plan, at the time of writing, to redirect all buses for the southern region to leave from Central sur, Col Villalobos. International buses have their offices scattered about the city. (The cheaper Salvador buses leave from near the Zona 4 terminal.) The Zona 4 bus terminal has to be the dirtiest and grimmest public area in the whole of the city.

The main destinations with companies operating from Guatemala City are:

Antigua, every 15 mins, 1 hr, US$1, until 2000 from Av 23 and 3 Calle, Zona 3. To **Chimaltenango** and **Los Encuentros**, from 1 Av between 3 y 4. Calle, Zona 7. **Chichicastenango** hourly from 0500-1800, 3 hrs, US$2.20 with **Veloz Quichelense**. **Huehuetenango**, with Los Halcones, Calzada Roosevelt, 37-47, Zona 11, T2439-2780, 0700, 1400, 1700, US$7, 5 hrs, and Transportes Velásquez, Calzada Roosevelt 9-56, Zona 7, T2440-3316, 0800-1630, every 30 mins, 5 hrs, US$7. For La Mesilla, see below.

Panajachel, with Transportes Rebulí, 41 Calle, between 6 y 7 Av, Zona 8, T2230-2748, hourly from 0530-1530, 3 hrs, US$2.20; also to **San Lucas Tolimán** 0530-1530, 3 hrs US$2.10 **San Pedro La Laguna** with Transportes Méndez, 41 C, between 6 y and Av, Zona 8, 1300, 4 hrs. **Santiago Atitlán**, with various companies, from 4 C, between 3 y 4 Av, Zona 12, 0400-1700, every 30 mins, 4 hrs, US$4.

Quetzaltenango (Xela) and **San Marcos**. 1st-class bus to Xela with Transportes Alamo, 12 Av "A", 0-65, Zona 7, T2471-8626, from 0800-1730, 6 daily 4 hrs, US$7. Líneas Américas, 2 Av, 18-47, Zona 1, T2232-1432, 0500-1930, 7 daily, US$7. Galgos, 7 Av, 19-44, Zona 1, T2232-3661, between 0530-1700, 5 daily, 4 hrs, US$7 to **Tapachula** in Mexico through the El Carmen border. Marquensita, 1 Av, 21-31, Zona 1, T2230-0067. From 0600-1700, 8 a day, US$6.10, to Xela and on to San Marcos. To **Tecpán**, with Transportes Poaquileña, 1 Av corner of 3 and 4 Calle, Zona 7, 0530-1900, every 15 mins, 2 hrs, US$1.20.

To **Santa Cruz del Quiché**, Sololá and Totonicapán, buses depart from 41 Calle between 6 and 7 Av, Zona 8.

To **Biotopo del Quetzal** and **Cobán**, 3½ hrs and 4½ hrs respectively, hourly from 0400-1700, US$6 and US$7.50, with **Escobar y Monja Blanca**, 8 Av, 15-16, Zona 1, T2238-1409. **Zacapa**, **Chiquimula** (for **El Florido**, Honduras border) and **Esquipulas** with Rutas Orientales, 19 Calle, 8-18, Zona 1, T2253-7282, every 30 mins 0430-1800. To **Zacapa**, 3¼ hrs, to **Chiquimula**, 3½ hrs, to **Esquipulas**, 4½ hrs, US$6.

Puerto Barrios, with Transportes Litegua, 15 Calle, 10-40, Zona 1, T2220-8840, www.litegua.com, 0430-1900, 31 a day, 5 hrs, US$6.80, 1st class US$12 and **Río Dulce**, 0600, 0900, 1130, 5 hrs, US$6.20.

El Petén with Fuente del Norte (same company as Líneas Máxima de Petén), 17 Calle, 8-46, Zona 1, T2251-3817, going to **Río Dulce** and **Santa Elena/Flores**. There are numerous departures 24 hrs; 5 hrs to Río Dulce, US$6.50; to Santa Elena, 9-10 hrs, US$12; buses vary in quality and price, breakdowns not unknown. The 1000 and 2130 departures are a luxury bus **Maya del Oro** with snacks, US$18, the advantage being it doesn't stop at every tree to pick up passengers. Linea Dorada, 16 Calle, 10-03, Zona 1, T2220-7990, www.tikalmayanworld.com, at 1000, US$16 to **Flores**, 8 hrs and on to **Melchor de Mencos**, 10 hrs. To **Santa Elena** ADN, 8 Av, 16-41, Zona 1, T2251-0050, www.adnautobuses delnorte.com, luxury service, 2100 and 2200, returns at 2100 and 2300, US$19, toilets, TV and snacks.

To **Jalapa** with Unidos Jalapanecos, 22 Calle 1-20, Zona 1, T2251-4760, 0430-1830, every 30 mins, 3 hrs, US$2.50 and with Transportes Melva Nacional, T2332-6081, 0415-1715, every 30 mins, 3 hrs 30 mins, US$2.50. Buses also from the Zona 4 terminal. To **San Pedro Pinula** between 0500-1800.

To **Chatia Gomerana**, 4 Calle y 8 Av, Zona 12, to **La Democracia**, every 30 mins from 0600-1630 via Escuintla and Siquinala, 2 hrs. Transportes Cubanita to **Reserva Natural de Monterrico** (La Avellana), 4 Calle y 8 Av,

Zona 12, at 1030, 1230, 1420, 3 hrs, US$2.50. To **Puerto San José** and **Iztapa**, from the same address, 0430-1645 every 15 mins, 1 hr. To **Retalhuleu** (Reu on bus signs) with **Transportes Fortaleza del Sur**, Calzada Aguilar Batres, 4-15, Zona 12, T22230-3390, between 0010-1910 every 30 mins via Escuintla, Cocales and Mazatenango, 3 hrs, US$6.80. Numerous buses to **Santa Lucía Cotzumalguapa** go from the Zona 4 bus terminal.

International buses

Reserve the day before if you can. Taking a bus from Guatemala City as far as, say, San José, is tiring and tiresome (the bus company's bureaucracy and the hassle from border officials all take their toll).

To **Honduras** avoiding El Salvador, take a bus to **Esquipulas**, then a minibus to the border. Hedman Alas, 2 Av, 8-73, Zona 10, T2362-5072, www.hedmanalas.com, to **Copán** via El Florido, at 0500 and 0900, 5 hrs, US$30. Also goes on to **San Pedro Sulas**, US$45, and **La Ceiba**, US$52. Pullmantur to **Tegucigalpa** daily at 0700 via San Salvador, US$66 and US$94. Ticabus to **San Pedro Sula**, US$34 and **Tegucigalpa**, US$34 via San Salvador. Rutas Orientales, 19 C, 8-18, T2253-7282 goes to **Honduras** at 0530 via Agua Caliente, 8 hrs, US$28.

To **Mexico** with Trans Galgos Inter, 7 Av, 19-44, Zona 1, T2223-3661, www.transgalgos inter.com.gt to **Tapachula** via **El Carmen**, 0730, 1330, and 1500, 7 hrs. Línea Dorada, address above, to **Tapachula** at 0800, US$24. Transportes Velásquez, 20 Calle, 1-37, Zona 1, T2221-1084, 0800-1100, hourly to **La Mesilla**, 7 hrs, US$5. Transportes Fortaleza del Sur, Calzada Aguilar Batres, 4-15, Zona 12, T2230-3390 to **Ciudad Tecún Umán**, 0130, 0300, 0330, 0530 via **Retalhuleu**, 5 hrs.

To **Chetumal** via **Belize City**, with Línea Dorada change to a minibus in Flores. Leaves 1000, 2100, 2200 and 2230, 2 days, US$42. Journey often takes longer than advertised due to Guatemala–Belize and Belize–Mexico border crossings.

Shuttles

Shuttles are possible between Guatemala City and all other destinations, but it's a case of reserving them first. Contact shuttle operators in Antigua (see Antigua Transport). Guatemala City to **Antigua**, US$10, **Panajachel** US$25, Chichicastenango US$25, **Copán Ruinas**, US$35, **Cobán**, US$26 and **Quetzaltenango**, US$21.

Car

Avenidas have priority over *calles* (except in Zona 10, where this rule varies).

Car hire companies Hertz, at the airport, T2470-3800, www.hertz.com. Budget, at the airport; also at 6 Av, 11-24, Zona 9, www.budget.co.uk. Tabarini, 2 Calle "A", 7-30, Zona 10, T2331-2643, airport T2331-4755, www.tabarini.com. Tally, 7 Av, 14-60, Zona 1, T2232-0421, very competitive, have pickups. Recommended.

Car and motorcyle repairs Mike and Andy Young, 27 Calle, 13-73, Zona 5, T2331-9263, Mon-Fri 0700-1600. Excellent mechanics for all vehicles, extremely helpful. Honda motorcycle parts from FA Honda, Av Bolívar, 31-00, Zona 3, T2471-5232. Some staff speak English. Car and motorcycle parts from FPK, 5 Calle, 6-75, Zona 9, T2331-9777. David González, 32 Calle, 6-31, Zona 11, T5797-2486, for car, bike and bicycle repairs. Recommended.

Taxi

If possible call a taxi from your hotel or get someone to recommend a reliable driver; there are hundreds of illegal taxis in the city that should be avoided.

There are 3 types of taxis – **Rotativos**, **Estacionarios** and the ones that are metered, called **Taxis Amarillos**. *Rotativos* are everywhere in the city cruising the length and breadth of all zones. You will not wait more than a few mins for one to come along. They are numbered on their sides and on their back windscreen will be written TR (*Taxi Rotativo*) followed by 4 numbers. Most of them have a company logo stamped on the side as well. *Estacionarios* also have numbers on the sides but are without logo. On their back windscreen they have the letters TE (*Taxi Estacionario*) followed by 4 numbers. They are to be found at bus terminals and outside hotels or in other important places. They will always return to these same waiting points (good to know if you leave something in a taxi). Do not get in a taxi that does not have either of these labels on its back windscreen. *Rotativos* and *Estacionarios* are unmetered, but *Estacionarios* will always charge less than *Rotativos*. The fact that both are unmetered will nearly always work to your advantage because of traffic delays. You will be quoted an inflated price by *Rotativos* by virtue of being a foreigner. *Estacionarios* are fairer. It is about US$8 from the airport to Zona 1. From Zona 1 to 4 is about US$4. The metered *Taxi Amarillo* also moves around but less so than the *Rotativos*, as they are more on call by phone. They only take a couple of minutes to come. **Amarillo Express**, T2332-1515, are 24 hr.

⊙ Directory

Banks

The legal street exchange for cash may be found on 7 Av, between 12 and 14 Calle, near the post office (Zona 1), but be careful; don't go alone. Banks change US dollars into quetzales at the free rate, but actual rates and commission charges vary; if you have time, shop around. **Banco Industrial**, Av 7, opposite the central post office, Visa cards only, Mon-Fri 0900-1530. **Bancared**, near Parque Centanario on 6 Calle and 4 Av has 24-hr ATM for Visa/Cirrus. **Lloyds Bank plc**, 6 Av, 9-51, Zona 9, Edif Gran Vía, also at 14 Calle and 4 Av, Zona 10, with ATM. Mon-Fri 0900-1500. **Banco Uno**, 10 Calle, 5-40, Visa and ATM. Mon-Fri 0930-1730, Sat 1000-1300. Quetzales may be bought with MasterCard

at **Credomatic**, beneath the Bar Europa, at 11 Calle, 5-6 Av, Zona 1. Mon-Sat 0800-1900. MasterCard ATM also at **Banco Internacional**, Av La Reforma and 16 Calle, Zona 10. **Western Union**, T2360-1737, collect T1-800-360-1737.

Embassies and consulates

Australia, Australians should report loss or theft of passports at the Canadian Embassy. Nearest Australian embassy is in Mexico. **Austria**, in Mexico (T+52) 55 52 510806, www.embajadadeaustria.com.mx. **Belgium**, in Costa Rica, T(+506) 225 6433. **Belize**, 5 Av 5-55, Zona 14, Europlaza Torre II, office 1502, T2367-3883. Mon-Fri 0900-1200, 1400-1600. **Canada**, 13 Calle, 8-44, Zona 10, T2363-4348. Mon-Thu, 0800-1700, Fri 0800-1330. **Costa Rica**, 15 C 7-59, Zona 10, T2366-9918. Mon-Fri 0900-1400. **El Salvador**, Av de las Américas 16-46, Zona 13, T2360-7670. Mon-Fri 0800-1500. **France**, 5 Av, 8-59, Zona 14, Edif Cogefar, T2421-7370. Mon-Fri 0900-1200. **Germany**, 20 Calle, 6-20, Zona 10, T2364-6700. Mon-Fri 0900-1200. **Honduras**, 19 Av "A", 20-19, Zona 10, T2363-5495. Mon-Fri 0900-1700. **Israel**, 13 Av, 14-07, Zona 10, T2333-6951. Mon-Fri 0800-1600. **Japan**, Av La Reforma, 16-85, Zona 10, Edif Torre Internacional, T2367-2244. Mon-Fri 0930-1230, 1400-1630. **Mexico**, 2 Av, 7-57, Zona 10, T2420-3430. Mon-Fri 0900-1300, 1400-1700. **Netherlands** 16 Calle, 0-55, Zona 10, T2381-4300. Mon-Fri 0800-1700. **Nicaragua**, 10 Av, 14-72, Zona 10, T2368-0785. Mon-Fri 0900-1300. **Panama**, 12 Av, 2-65, Zona 14, T2366-3331. Mon-Fri 0900-1400. **Spain**, 6 Calle, 6-48, Zona 9, T2379-3530. Mon-Fri 0800-1400. **Switzerland**, 16 Calle, 0-55, Zona 10, Edif Torre Internacional, 14th floor, T2367-5520. Mon-Fri 0900-1130. **UK**, 16 Calle, 0-55, Zona 10, T2367-5425-29. Embassy open Mon-Thu 0800-1230, 1330-1700, Fri 0800-1200. Consulate Mon-Thu 0830-1200, Fri 0830-1100. **USA**, Av La Reforma, 7-01, Zona 10, T2326-4000, http://guatemala. usembassy.gov, Mon-Fri 0800-1700.

Emergency
T128 for ambulance, T122 for the *bomberos*, the fire brigade who also get called to accidents.

Immigration
Immigration office Dirección General de Migración, 6 Av, 3-11, Zona 4, T2411-2411. For extensions of visas. If you need new entry stamps in a replacement passport (ie if one was stolen), a police report is required, plus a photocopy and a photocopy of your passport. They also need to know your date and point of entry to check their records.

Internet
There's an internet café in Edificio Geminis in Zona 10.

Medical services
Doctors Dr Boris Castillo Camino, 6 Av, 7-55, Zona 10, Of 17, T2334-5932. 0900-1230, 1430-1800. Recommended.
Dentists Centro Médico, 6 Av, 3-47, Zona 10, T2332-3555, English spoken by some staff.
Hospitals Hospital de las Américas, 10a. Calle 2-31, Zona 14, T2384-3535, info@hospitalesdeguatemala.com. Private hospital, must be able to demonstrate you have funds for treatment. Roosevelt Hospital, Calzada Roosevelt, Zona 11, T2471-1441. Public hospital affiliated with University San Carlos School of Medicine.
Opticians Optico Popular, 11 Av, 13-75, Zona 1, T2238-3143, excellent for repairs.

Post office
The main post office is at 7 Av and 12 Calle, Zona 1. Mon-Fri 0830-1700.

Antigua and around

→ *Colour map 5, C2.*

Antigua is rightly one of Guatemala's most popular destinations. It overflows with colonial architecture and fine churches on streets that are linked by squat houses, painted in ochre shades and topped with terracotta tiles, basking in the fractured light of the setting sun. Antigua is a very attractive city and is the cultural centre of Guatemala; arts flourish here. Maya women sit in their colourful clothes amid the ruins and in the Parque Central. In the late-afternoon light, buildings such as Las Capuchinas are beautiful, and in the evening the cathedral is wonderfully illuminated as if by candlelight. Around Antigua are a cluster of archaeological sites, highland villages and volcanoes to explore. ▶▶ *See listings, pages 648-658.*

Ins and outs

Getting around *Avenidas* run north to south and *calles* run from east to west. House numbers do not give any clue about how far from the Parque Central a particular place is. ▶▶ *See Transport, page 655.*

Tourist information INGUAT office ① *inside Casa Antigua El Jaulón, 4 Calle Oriente No10 Sur, 0800-1300, 1400-1700, Sat and Sun 0900-1300, 1400-1700, T7832-5681, info-antigua@ inguat.gob.gt, www.visitguatemala.com,* is very helpful, with lots of maps and information. Volunteer work information available. English, Italian and a little German spoken. The monthly magazine *The Revue* is a useful source of information with articles and advertisements in English, and is free.

Safety Unfortunately, despite its air of tranquillity, Antigua is not without unpleasant incidents. Take care and advice from the tourist office on where to go or not to go. There are numerous tourist police (green uniforms) who are helpful and conspicuous; their office is at 4 Avenida Norte at the side of the Municipal Palace. If you wish to go to Cerro de la Cruz (see page 645), or the cemetery, they will escort you, leaving 1000 and 1500 daily. Antigua is generally safe at night, but it's best to keep to the well-lit area near the centre. Report incidents to police and the tourist office. Tourist assistance 24 hours, T2421-2810. ▶▶ *See also page 623.*

Background

Until it was heavily damaged by an earthquake in 1773, Antigua was the capital city. Founded in 1543, after the destruction of an even earlier capital, Ciudad Vieja, it grew to be the finest city in Central America, with numerous great churches, a university (1676), a printing press (founded 1660), and a population of around 50,000, including many famous sculptors, painters, writers and craftsmen.

Antigua has consistently been damaged by earthquakes. Even when it was the capital, buildings were frequently destroyed and rebuilt, usually in a grander style, until the final cataclysm in 1773. For many years it was abandoned, and most of the accumulated treasures were moved to Guatemala City. Although it slowly repopulated in the 19th century, little was done to prevent further collapse of the main buildings until late in the

Antigua

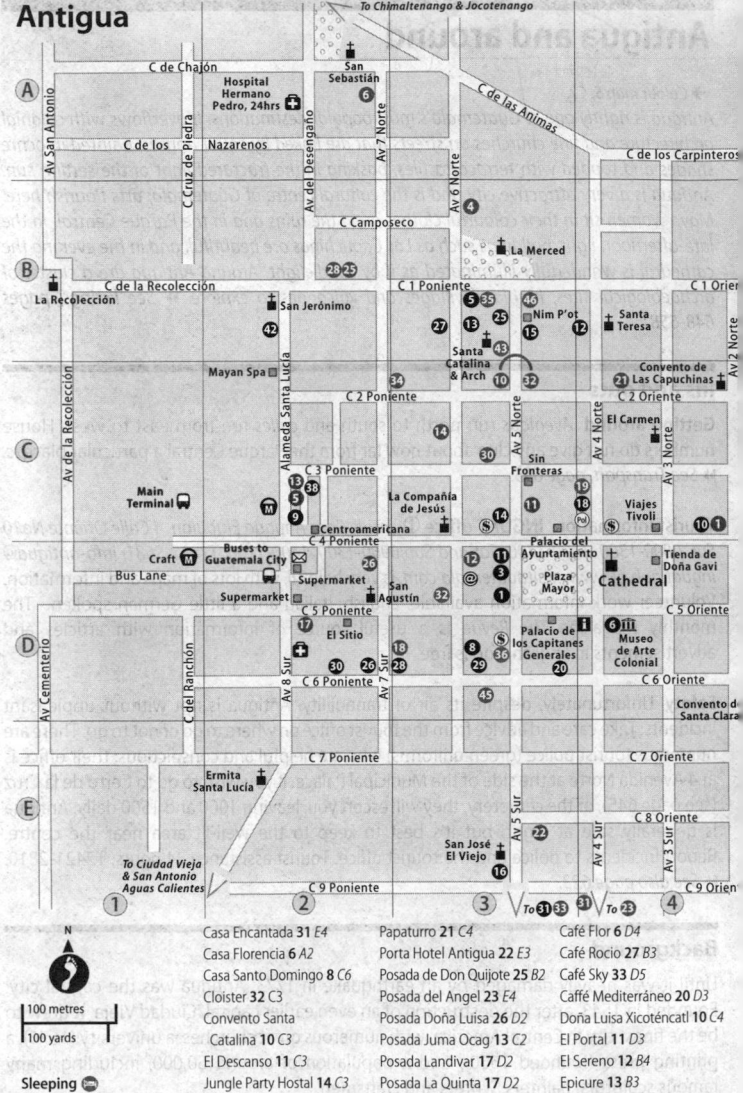

Sleeping	
Aurora 1 *C4*	
Base Camp 7 *D5*	
Black Cat Hostel 12 *D3*	
Casa Capuchinas 3 *B4*	
Casa de Santa Lucía 3 4 *B3*	
Casa de Santa Lucía 4 5 *C2*	

Casa Encantada 31 *E4*
Casa Florencia 6 *A2*
Casa Santo Domingo 8 *C6*
Cloister 32 *C3*
Convento Santa
  Catalina 10 *C3*
El Descanso 11 *C3*
Jungle Party Hostal 14 *C3*
La Casa de los Sueños &
  Azafrán Restaurant 16 *D5*
Las Camelias Inn 2 *C5*
La Tatuana 18 *D3*
Mesón de María 30 *C3*
Mesón Panza Verde 33 *E3*

Papaturro 21 *C4*
Porta Hotel Antigua 22 *E3*
Posada de Don Quijote 25 *B2*
Posada del Angel 23 *E4*
Posada Doña Luisa 26 *C2*
Posada Juma Ocag 13 *C2*
Posada Landivar 17 *D2*
Posada La Quinta 17 *D2*
Yellow House 28 *B2*

Eating 🍴
Bagel Barn 1 *D3*
Café Barroco 2 *C5*
Café Condesa 3 *D3*

Café Flor 6 *D4*
Café Rocio 27 *B3*
Café Sky 33 *D5*
Caffé Mediterráneo 20 *D3*
Doña Luisa Xicoténcatl 10 *C4*
El Portal 11 *D3*
El Sereno 12 *B4*
Epicure 13 *B3*
Fonda de la Calle Real 14 *C3*
Frida's 15 *B3*
Hector's 5 *B3*
Helas Taberna Griega 18 *C4*
La Antigua Vinería 16 *E3*

To Cerro de la Cruz   To Guatemala City

C de la Candelaria

■ La Candelaria

✝ Santa Rosa

Plazuela
Santa Rosa

C de la Beatas Indias

C de los Duelos

■ Santo Domingo

Av 1 Norte

❽

C 3 Oriente

❷ ㉒   ❷   ㊶

C 4 Oriente

■ La Concepción

⓰

C del Hermano Pedro

❼

⓭

C 1 Sur

San
Francisco

C del Hermano Pedro

C de los Pasos

To Escuela
de Cristo &
El Calvario

✝ Santa Cruz

To Santa Isabel, San Juan
del Obispo & Santa María
de Jesús ❻

❺

La Casa de los
Mixtas 38 C2
La Casserole 41 C5
La Fuente 10 C4
Nicolás 44 C5
Ni-Fu Ni-Fa 22 C5
Peroletó 42 B2
Quesos y Vinos 25 B3
Rainbow Café &
Travel Center 26 D2
Sabe Rico 8 D3
Típico Antigüeño 9 C2
Tostaduría Antigua 28 D3
Travel Menu 29 D3

Tre Fratelli 30 D2
Vivero y Café de
la Escalonia 31 E3

Bars & clubs ❶
Café 2000 32 D3
Casbah 43 B3
La Chiminea 34 C3
La Sala 45 D3
Monoloco 36 D3
Reds 35 B3
Reilly's Irish Pub 46 B3
Rikki's 19 C4

20th century when the value of the remaining monuments was finally appreciated. Since 1972, efforts to preserve what was left have gained momentum, and it is now a UNESCO World Heritage Site. The major earthquake of 1976 was a further setback, but you will see many sites that are busy with restoration, preservation or simple clearing. If the city was not treasure enough, the setting is truly memorable. Volcán Agua (3766 m) is due south and the market is to the west, behind which hang the imposing peaks of Volcán Acatenango (3976 m) and Volcán Fuego (3763 m), which still emits the occasional column of ash as a warning of the latent power within.

Sights

In the centre of the city is the **Parque Central**, the old Plaza Real, where bullfights and markets were held in the early days. The present park was constructed in the 20th century though the fountain dates back to the 18th century. The **Cathedral** ① US$0.40, to the east, dates from 1680 (the first cathedral was demolished in 1669). Much has been destroyed since then and only two of the many original chapels are now in use. The remainder can be visited. The **Palacio de los Capitanes Generales** is to the south. The original building dates from 1558, was virtually destroyed in 1773, was partly restored in the 20th century, and now houses police and government offices. The **Cabildo**, or **Municipal Palace**, is to the north and an arcade of shops to the west. You can climb to the second floor for a great view of the volcanoes (Monday to Friday 0800-1600). The **Museo de Santiago** ① Tue-Fri 0900-1600, Sat-Sun 0900-1200, 1400-1600, US$4, is in the municipal offices to the north of the plaza, as is the **Museo del Libro Antiguo** ① same hours and price, which contains a replica of a 1660 printing press (the original is in Guatemala City), old documents and a collection of 16th- to 18th-century books (1500 volumes in the library). The **Museo de Arte Colonial** ① *Tue-Fri 0900-1600, Sat-Sun 0900-1200, 1400-1600, US$4*, is half a block from Parque Central at Calle 5 Oriente, in the building where the San Carlos University was first housed. It now has mostly 17th- to 18th-century religious art, well laid out in large airy rooms around a colonial patio.

Hotel Casa Santo Domingo is one of Antigua's most beautiful sights – a converted old Dominican church and also monastery property. Archaeological excavations have turned up some unexpected finds at the site. During the cleaning out of a burial vault in September 1996, one of the greatest finds in Antigua's history was unearthed. The vault had been filled with rubble, but care had been taken in placing stones a few feet away from the painted walls. The scene is in the pristine colours of natural red and blue, and depicts Christ, the Virgin Mary, Mary Magdalene and John the Apostle. It was painted in 1683, and only discovered by placing an ultraviolet light over it. Within the monastery grounds are the **Colonial Art Museum**, with displays of Guatemalan baroque imagery and silverware and the **Pre-Columbian Art Museum, Glass Museum, Museum of Guatemalan Apothecary** and the **Popular Art and Handicrafts of Sacatepequez Museum** ① *3 Calle Ote 28, 0900-1700, US$5 for each museum*.

There are many fine colonial religious buildings: 22 churches, 14 convents and 11 monasteries, most ruined by earthquakes and in various stages of restoration. Top of the list are the cloisters of the convent of **Las Capuchinas** ① *2 Av Norte y 2 Calle Ote, 0900-1700, US$3.90*, with immensely thick round pillars (1736) adorned with bougainvillea. The church and convent of **San Francisco** ① *1 Av Sur y 7 Calle Ote, 0800-1200, 1400-1700, US$0.40*, with the tomb of Hermano Pedro, is much revered by all the local communities. He was canonized in 2002. The church has been restored and now includes the **Museo de Hermano Pedro** ① *Tue-Sun 0900-1200, 1300-1630, US$0.40*. The convent of **Santa Clara** ① *6 Calle Ote y 2 Av Sur, 0900-1700, US$3.90*, was founded in about 1700 and became one of the biggest in Antigua, until the nuns were forced to move to Guatemala City. The adjoining garden is an oasis of peace. **El Carmen** ① *3 Calle Ote y 3 Av Norte*, has a beautiful façade with strikingly ornate columns, tastefully illuminated at night, but the rest of the complex is in ruins. Likewise **San Agustín** ① *5 Calle Pte y 7 Av Norte*, was once a fine building, but only survived intact from 1761 to 1773; earthquake destruction continued until the final portion of the vault collapsed in 1976, leaving an impressive ruin. **La Compañía de Jesús** ① *3 Calle Pte y 6 Av Norte, 0930-1700*, at one time covered the whole block. The church is closed for restoration but you can access the rest of the ruins from 6 Avenida Norte. The church and cloisters of **Escuela de Cristo** ① *Calle de los Pasos y de la Cruz*, a small independent monastery (1720-1730), have survived and were restored between 1940 and 1960. The church is simple and has some interesting original artwork. **La Recolección** ① *Calle de la Recolección, 0900-1700, US$3.90*, despite being a late starter (1700), became one of the biggest and finest of Antigua's religious institutions. It is now the most awe-inspiring ruin in the city. **San Jerónimo** ① *Calle de la Recolección, 0900-1700, US$3.90*, was a school (early 1600s) for La Merced, three blocks away, but later became the local customs house. There is an impressive fountain in the courtyard. **La Merced** ① *1 Calle Pte y 6 Av Norte, 0800-1700*, with its white and yellow façade dominates the surrounding plaza. The church (1767) and cloisters were built with earthquakes in mind and survived better than most. The church remains in use and the **cloisters** ① *US$0.80*, are being further restored. Antigua's finest fountain is in the courtyard. **Santa Teresa** ① *4 Av Norte*, was a modest convent, but the church walls and the lovely west front have survived. It is now the city's men's prison.

Other ruins including **Santa Isabel, Santa Cruz, La Candelaria, San José El Viejo** and **San Sebastián** are to be found round the edges of the city, and there is an interesting set of the Stations of the Cross, each a small chapel, from San Francisco to **El Calvario** church, which was where Pedro de Betancourt (Hermano Pedro) worked as a gardener and planted an esquisuchil tree. He was also the founder of the **Belén Hospital** in 1661, which was destroyed in 1773. However, some years later, his name was given to the **San Pedro Hospital**, which is one block south of the Parque Central.

There is a fabulous panorama from the **Cerro de la Cruz**, which is 15 minutes' walk from the northern end of town along 1 Avenida Norte.

Around Antigua ⊖⊖ ▸▸ *pp648-658*

Ciudad Vieja – the former capital – is 5.5 km southwest of Antigua at the foot of Volcán Agua. In 1527, Pedro de Alvarado moved his capital, known then as Santiago de Los Caballeros, from Iximché to San Miguel Escobar, now a suburb of Ciudad Vieja. On 11 September 1541, after days of torrential rain, an immense mudslide came down the mountain and swallowed up the city. Alvarado's widow, Doña Beatriz de la Cueva, newly elected governor after his death, was among those drowned. Today Ciudad Vieja is itself a suburb of Antigua, but with a handsome church, founded in 1534, and one of the oldest in Central America. There's a fiesta on December 8. Between Ciudad Vieja and San Miguel de las Dueñas is the **Valhalla macadamia nut farm** ① *T7831-5799, www.exvalhalla.net, free visits and nut tasting, 0800-1700.*

About 3 km northwest of Ciudad Vieja is **San Antonio Aguas Calientes**. The hot springs unfortunately disappeared with recent earthquakes, but the village has many small shops selling locally made textiles. **Carolina's Textiles** is recommended for a fine selection, while on the exit road **Alida** has a shop. You can watch the weavers in their homes by the roadside. Local fiestas are 16-21 January, Corpus Christi (a moveable feast celebrated around June) and 1 November.

Beyond San Juan del Obispo, beside Volcán Agua, is the charming village of **Santa María de Jesús**, with its beautiful view of Antigua. In the early morning there are good views of all three volcanoes from 2 km back down the road towards Antigua. Colourful *huípiles* are worn, made and sold from a couple of stalls, or ask at the shops on the plaza. The local fiesta is on 10 January.

Just north of Antigua is **Jocotenango** . The music museum, **Casa K'ojom** ① *Mon-Fri 0830-1630, Sat 0830-1600, US$4,* is in the **Central Cultural La Azotea**, with displays of traditional Maya and colonial-era instruments. The village also has public saunas at the **Fraternidad Naturista Antigua**.

Five kilometres beyond San Lucas Sacatepéquez, at Km 29.5, Carretera Roosevelt (the Pan-American Highway), is **Santiago Sacatepéquez**, whose fiesta on 1 November, *Día de los Muertos* (All Souls' Day), is characterized by colourful kite-flying (*barriletas*). They also celebrate 25 July. Market days are Wednesday and Friday.

Visiting a **coffee farm** is an interesting short excursion. **Tour Finca Los Nietos** ① *San Lorenzo El Cubo, T7831-5438, www.fincalosnietos.com, by appointment only Mon-Fri 0800-1100,* is 6 km from Antigua. A 1½-hour tour including processing, roasting and tasting (US$6.50) can be arranged.

North of Guatemala City is **Mixco Viejo**, the excavated site of a post-Classic Maya fortress, which spans 14 hilltops, including 12 groups of pyramids. Despite earthquake damage it is worth a visit and is recommended. It was the 16th-century capital of the Pokomam Maya.

Semana Santa

This week-long event is a spectacular display of religious ritual and floral design. Through billowing clouds of incense, accompanied by music, processions of floats carried by purple-robed men make their way through the town.

The cobbled stones are covered in carpets known as *alfombras*, made up of coloured sawdust and flowers.

The day before the processions leave from each church, Holy Vigils (*velaciones*) are held, and the sculpture to be carried is placed before the altar (*retablo*), with a backdrop covering the altar. Floats (*andas*) are topped by colonial sculptures of the cross-carrying Christ. He wears velvet robes of deep blue or green, embroidered with gold and silver threads, and the float is carried on the shoulders by a team of 80 men (*cucuruchos*), who heave and sway their way through the streets for as long as 12 hours. The processions, arranged by a religious brotherhood (*cofradía*), are accompanied by banner and incense carriers, centurions, and a loud brass band.

The largest processions with some of the finest carpets are on **Palm Sunday** and **Good Friday**. Not to be missed are the procession leaving from **La Merced** on **Palm Sunday** at 1200-1300; the procession leaving the church of **San Francisco** on **Maundy Thursday**; the 0200 sentencing of Jesus and 0600 processions from **La Merced** on **Good Friday**; the crucifixion of Christ in front of the **cathedral** at noon on **Good Friday**; and the beautiful, candlelit procession of the crucified Christ which passes the **central park** between 2300 and midnight on **Good Friday**.

This is the biggest Easter attraction in Latin America, so accommodation is booked far ahead. If you plan to be here and haven't reserved a room, arrive a few days before Palm Sunday. If unsuccessful, commuting from Guatemala City is an option. Don't rush: each procession lasts up to 12 hours. The whole week is a fantastic opportunity for photographs – and if you want a decent picture remember the Christ figure always faces right. Arm yourself with a map (available in kiosks in the central park) and follow the processional route before the procession to see all the carpets while they are still intact. (There are also processions into Antigua from surrounding towns every Sunday in Lent.)

Volcanoes ○ ↠ *pp648-658.*

Each of the four volcanoes that are immediately accessible from Antigua provides a unique set of challenges and rewards. Agua, Fuego and Acatenango volcanoes directly overlook Antigua whilst Volcan Pacaya is about an hour's drive away. All of these volcanoes can be experienced either as part of a day trip (a cheaper and faster option that requires only light-weight packs) or with an overnight excursion (heavier packs making climbing times longer, but with better light conditions for lava viewing and enhancing already spectacular views with beautiful sunset and sunrises). Whatever option you choose, it is important to prepare properly for the unique features of each volcano (Pacaya is a relatively quick climb in a secure national park, while the three volcanoes on Antigua's perimeter are longer climbs with much greater risk of robberies and attacks). At a minimum, ensure that you have appropriate clothing and footwear (as summits are cold and volcanic ash is sharp bring fleeces and ideally use climbing boots), enough water (very important) and snacks for the trip and make informed decisions about safety (although you can climb each of these volcanoes independently, you will significantly decrease your risks of getting lost, attacked or not finding shelter by using a professional guiding service – Outdoor Excursions (OX), which runs trips with expert guides and armed security is particularly recommended). Remember that altitude takes its toll and for the longer hikes it is important to start early in the morning to allow enough time to ascend and descend in daylight. As a general rule, descents take from a third to a half of the ascent time.

Volcán Pacaya

① *Tours are available for US$6 upwards and are sold in most tour companies in Antigua. The popular and best time for organized trips is to leave Antigua at 1300 and return at 2100. Departures also 0600 returning 1300. There is also a US$3.50 fee to be paid at the entrance to the Volcán Pacaya National Park in San Francisco de Sales (toilets available). It is strongly recommended that you do not climb all the way to the crater.*

At 2552 m, the still-active Volcán Pacaya can't be missed and is the most exciting volcano to climb. Pacaya has erupted about 20 times since 1565, but since the mid-1960s it has been continuously active, meaning it can reward climbers with some spectacular lava flows. From where the shuttle bus leaves you, it's about 1½-2 hours hiking to the base of the crater – making Pacaya by far the quickest and easiest climb of the volcanoes near Antigua. Try to avoid going on a mid-morning departure, which usually results in an arrival at the summit just as it is covered in cloud. Take torch/flashlight, refreshments and water and – it may sound obvious – wear boots or trainers, not sandals. If you bring marshmallows to toast on the lava, make sure you have a long stick – lava is (rather unsurprisingly) very hot! Security officers go with the trips and police escorts ensure everyone leaves the area after dark. Check the situation in advance for **camping** (well below the crater lip). Sunrise comes with awesome views over the desolate black lava field to the distant Pacific (airborne dust permitting) and the peaks of Fuego, Acatenango and Agua.

Volcán Agua

① *Most organized tours with Antigua tour operators are during the day – you should enure that costs include both a guide and security. Trips normally leave Antigua about 0500.*

At 3760 m, Agua Is the easiest but least scenic of the three volcanoes overlooking Antiqua. The trail, which can be quite littered, begins at **Santa María de Jesús**. Speak to Aurelio Cuy Chávez at the **Posada El Oasis**, who offers a guide service or take a tour with a reputable agency. For Agua's history, see Ciudad Vieja. The crater has a small shelter (none too clean), which was a shrine, and about 10 antennae. There are great views of Volcán Fuego. It's a three- to five-hour climb if you are fit, and at least two hours down. To get the best views before the clouds cover the summit, it is best to stay at the radio station at the top. Agua can also be climbed from **Alotenango**, a village between Agua and Fuego, south of Ciudad Vieja. It's 9 km from Antigua and its name means 'place surrounded by corn'. Alotenango has a fiesta from 18-20 January.

Volcán Acatenango

① *If you do this climb independently of a tour agency, ask for a guide in La Soledad. However, it is strongly recommended that you use a professional guiding service, ideally with security.*

Acatenango is classified as a dormant volcano and is the third tallest in the country (3975 m) with two peaks to its name. Its first recorded eruption was in 1924. Two other eruptions were reported in 1924-1927 and 1972. The best trail heads south at **La Soledad**, 2300 m (15 km west of Ciudad Vieja), which is 300 m before the road (Route 5) turns right to Acatenango (see Sleeping). A small plateau, La Meseta on maps, known locally as **El Conejón**, provides a good camping site half way up (three or four hours). From here it is a further three or four hours' harder going to the top. The views of the nearby (lower) active crater of Fuego are excellent.

Volcán Fuego

ⓘ *This is an active volcano with trails that are easy to lose – it is recommended that you use a guiding service and do not venture up to the crater.*

This volcano (3763 m) can be climbed via Volcán Acatenango, sleeping between the two volcanoes, then climbing for a further two to three hours before stopping a safe distance from the crater. This one is for experienced hikers only. Do not underestimate the amount of water needed for the climb. It is a seven-hour ascent with a significant elevation gain – it's a very hard walk, both up and down. There are steep, loose cinder slopes, which are very tedious, in many places. It is possible to camp about three-quarters of the way up in a clearing. Fuego has regular eruptions that shoot massive boulders from its crater – often without warning. Check in Antigua before attempting to climb. If driving down towards the south coast you can see the red volcanic rock it has thrown up.

ⓦ Antigua and around listings

For Sleeping and Eating price codes and other relevant information, see Essentials pages 45-48.

ⓢ Sleeping

Antigua *p641, map p642*
In the better hotels, advance reservations are advised for weekends and Dec-Apr. During Holy Week, hotel prices are significantly higher, sometimes double for the more expensive hotels. In the Jul-Aug period, find your accommodation early in the day.
LL Porta Hotel Antigua, 8 Calle Pte 1, T7832-2801, www.portahotels.com. Has all the benefits associated with a hotel in this range as well as beautiful gardens and a pool, parking. It is some 4 blocks from the plaza on a quiet street. Non-residents can use the pool for a small fee.
LL Posada del Angel, 4 Av Sur 24-A, T7832-5244, www.posadadelangel.com. Breakfast included, dining room, exercise pool, fireplaces, 5 suites individually decorated, roof terrace, romantic, exclusive and private. Bill Clinton stayed here.

LL-AL Casa Santo Domingo, 3 Calle Ote 28, T7820-1220, www.casasanto domingo.com.gt. This is a beautifully designed hotel with 126 rooms in the ruins of a 17th-century convent with pre-Hispanic archaeological finds, with good service, beautiful gardens, a magical pool, good restaurant with breakfast included. Worth seeing just to dream. See Sights, page 644.
LL-L The Cloister, 5 Av Norte 23, T7832-0712, www.thecloister.com. 7 big rooms around luscious patio garden, inviting sitting room, library, view of the clock tower, breakfast available.
LL-L Mesón Panza Verde, 5 Av Sur 19, T7832-2925, www.panzaverde.com. Colonial indulgence at its height, breakfast included for the 12 rooms – 3 doubles, 9 suites. The bathrooms are pamper palaces in their own right. All with cupolas and arresting designs. There is a slither of a swimming pool for your morning work out.
LL-AL Hotel Mesón de María, 3 Calle Pte 8, T7832-6068, www.hotelmesondemaria.com. Great little place with a wonderful roof terrace. 20 stylish rooms are decorated with local

textiles. Free internet and breakfast included at a local restaurant. Friendly and attentive service. Showers have large skylights.

LL-AL La Casa de los Sueños, 1 Av Norte 1, T7832-9897, www.lacasadelossuenos.com. A richly furnished, beautiful, colonial building, with friendly and helpful owners. Some rooms are grander than others so make sure you know what you're getting. Breakfast is included and served at a vast table, medieval-style. The gardens have a swimming pool and patio. Restaurant **Azafrán** on the premises.

LL-A Casa Encantada, 9 Calle Pte1, esq Av 4 Sur, T7832-7903, www.casaencantada-antigua.com. This sweet colonial boutique hotel with 10 rooms is a perfect retreat from the centre of Antigua. It has a small rooftop terrace where breakfast is served and a comfortable sitting room with open fire, books, lilies and textile-lined walls. 2 rooms are accessed by stepping stones in a pond. The suite, with jacuzzi, enjoys views of the 3 volcanoes.

L-AL Hotel Convento Santa Catalina, 5 Av Norte 28, T7832-3080, www.convento.com. 12 rooms with lovely bedspreads, wooden ceilings and quarry tiled floors, plus 4 apartments in this converted convent. Good deal for longer stays. Las Catalinas restaurant on premises.

L-A Las Camelias Inn, 3 Calle Ote 19, T/F7832-5780, www.cameliasinn.com. 16 rooms, some with bath. There's a small patio and balconies to hang out on. There are also 3 apartments for rent. Parking.

AL-A Casa Capuchinas, 2 Av Norte 7, T7832-0121, www.casacapuchinas.com. 5 large, colonially furnished rooms, with fireplaces and massive beds, adjoining beautiful tiled bathrooms and special touches. A continental breakfast is included.

AL Aurora, 4 Calle Ote 16, T7832-0217, www.hotelauroraantigua.com. The oldest hotel in the city with old plumbing (but it works) and 1970s features. Quieter rooms face a patio overflowing with beautiful flowers. Continental breakfast included, English spoken.

A Casa Florencia, 7 Av Norte 100, T7832-0261, www.cflorencia.net. A sweet little hotel enjoying views towards Volcán Agua. 11 rooms with all the usuals including safety box and kitchen for guests. The balcony has *cola de quetzal* plants lining it. Staff are very welcoming. Recommended.

B Papaturro, 2 Calle Ote 14, T7832-0445. Family atmosphere, rooms around attractive restaurant/bar area, run by a Salvadorian couple, 5 rooms, 1 with bath and mini kitchen, breakfast included, full board available, good deals for longer stays.

B Posada de Don Quijote 1 Calle Pte 22 A and B, T7832-0775, www.posadaquijote.com. Old colonial house, with or without bath, patio, friendly, good value.

B Posada Landivar, 5 Calle Pte 23, close to the bus station, T7832-2962. Rooms with private bathroom and a/c. It's safe and in a good position. Discounts for longer stays. Parking. Recommended.

B-D La Tatuana, 7 Av Sur 3, T7832-1223. Small hotel that's friendly, clean and safe; discounts are available off season. Some rooms are a little dark. Choose carefully. (Allegedly Tatuana was a witch condemned to death by the Spanish Inquisition and burnt in the central plaza in the capital.)

C El Descanso, 5 Av Norte 9, T7832-0142. Rents 4 clean rooms on the 2nd floor, with private bath. There's a family atmosphere here and the place is extremely friendly and welcoming.

C Posada Doña Luisa, 7 Av Norte 4, T7832-3414, posadadoluisa@hotmail.com. Near the San Agustín church; good view of romantically lit ruins at night, a clean and very friendly place with a family atmosphere. It has 8 rooms with private bath and a small cafeteria. Parking.

D Casa de Santa Lucía No 3, 6 Av Norte 43A, T7832-1386. There are 20 standard clean rooms here all with private bathrooms, towels, soap, hot water and free drinking water. Beautiful views of La Merced and Volcán de Fuego. Parking.

D Casa de Santa Lucía No 4, Alameda Sta Lucía Norte 5, T7832-3302. Way more attractive than Nos 2 and 3, with 30 rooms for the same price. Only 14 years old, it has been built in a colonial style, with dark wood columns and is decorated with large clay bowls in the patio. Parking.

D Casa Los Arcos, 7a Av Norte and Callejón Camposeco '5A. T7832-7813. Great family place, simple, basic and friendly. Use of small kitchen, internet downstairs, Wi-Fi throughout. Good for longer stays.

D Posada Juma Ocag, Calzada Santa Lucía Norte 13, T7832-3109. A small, but clean and nicely decorated hotel, using local textiles as bedspreads. It has an enclosed roof terrace, is quiet and friendly, shared bathrooms.

D Yellow House, 1 Calle Pte 24, T7832-6646. 8 clean rooms in this hostel run by the welcoming Ceci. Breakfast included. Colonial style, laundry service, free internet. 3 rooms with bath, kitchen, patio, parking. Recommended.

D-E Base Camp, 1 Avenida 4b, T7832-0074, www.basecamphostel.com. 6 dorm beds and 2 double rooms with lots of shared space. Runs adventure tours through Outdoor Excursions.

E The Black Cat Hostel, 6 Av Norte 1, T7832-1229. A hostel with dorm rooms. Services include a bar, free breakfasts and DVD screenings. There's also an upmarket option at 9 Calle Ote 5, T7832-2187 with private rooms, free breakfast and a terrace bar.

E Jungle Party Hostal and Café, 6 Av Norte 20, T7832-0463, www.junglepartyhostal.com. Price per person. 33 beds spread across 6 rooms and 3 shared showers. Friendly management. Hot water, lockers, small patio, TV, free breakfast and movies. BBQ on Sat.

E Posada La Quinta, 5 Calle Pte 19, T7832-1713, basic. Some single rooms are cell-like but they have their own shower and are a good deal for single travellers who want their own bathroom. Luggage stored. Coffee and purified water available, small patio area.

E Primavera, 3 Callejón, off 3 Calle Pte near Alameda Sta Lucía, T7832-1479. 15 rooms with shared bathrooms that are clean. Good

for the price though and in a quiet location. 2 rooms have private bathroom.

Apartments
Look on the notice boards in town. Rooms and apartments are available from about US$25 a week up to US$500 per month. One recommended family is **Estella López**, 1 Calle Pte 41A, T7832-1324, who offer board and lodging on a weekly basis. The house is clean, and the family friendly.

Around Antigua p645
E Restaurante Posada El Oasis, Santa María de Jesús. The owner hires horses and offers a volcano-guiding service. Basic rooms, welcoming.
F Pensión, Volcán Acatenango. Basic, with good cheap meals.

❷ Eating

Antigua p641, map p642
For the cheapest of the cheap go to the stalls on the corner of 4 Calle Pte and 7 Av Norte, and those at the corner of 5 Calle Pte and 4 Av Sur. During the Easter period, the plaza in front of La Merced is transformed into a food market. At all these places you can pick up *elote, tortillas, tostadas* and *enchiladas*.

♈♈♈ Azafrán, La Casa de los Sueños, 1 Av Norte 1, T7832-5215. Tue-Sun 1200-1500, 1900-2200. Serves international cuisine with tables on the patio. Recommended.

♈♈♈ El Sereno, 4 Av Norte 16, T7832-0501. 1200-1500, 1800-2300. Grand entrance with massive imposing heliconia plants in the courtyard. It has a lovely terrace bar up some stone steps and a cave for romantic dining; it's popular at weekends. International/Italian cuisine.

♈♈♈ Hotel Casa Santo Domingo, 3 Calle Ote 28, T7832-0140. Sun-Thu 0600-2200, Fri and Sat 0600-2400. A range of international and national food (mixed reports) in superb surroundings. Very good service and music.

La Casserole, Callejón de Concepción 7, T7832-0219 close to **Casa Santo Domingo**. Tue-Sat 1200-1500, 1900 2200, Sun 1200-1500, closed Mon. Sophisticated French cooking with fresh fish daily served at tables set in a beautiful courtyard, exclusive. Rigoberta Menchú dined with Jacques Chirac here!

Nicolás, 4 Calle Ote 20, T7832-0471, www.nicolas.com.gt. Thu-Mon 1230-1500, 1900-2200. Swish restaurant in lovely surrounds with occasional live music and newly opened lounge.

Tre Fratelli, 6 Calle Pte 30, T7832-7730. Good Italian food, family atmosphere, romantic candlelit roof terrace, excellent bread with cumin seeds made on the premises for sale, delicious lasagna served with a mound of spinach cooked in garlic.

Caffé Mediterráneo, 6 Calle Pte 6A, T7832-7180. Wed-Mon 1200-1500, 1830-2200. 1 block south of the plaza. Mouth-watering Italian cuisine with great candlelit ambience. Recommended.

Fonda de la Calle Real, 5 Av Norte 5 and No 12, also at 3 Calle Pte 7 (which wins over the others for the setting). Its speciality is *queso fundido*. It also serves local dishes including *pepián* (and a vegetarian version) and *Kak-ik*, a Verapaz speciality.

Ni-Fu Ni-Fa, 3 Calle Ote 21, T7832-6579. Great Argentinian-style steaks, excellent salad bar included in price, candle-lit garden, good service.

Frida's, 5 Av Norte 29, Calle del Arco, T7832-0504. Daily 1200-0100. Ochre and French navy colours decorate this restaurant's tribute to Mexico's famous female artist. It is quite dark inside but Frida memorabilia and colander-like lampshades lighten the interior. Efficient service. 2nd-floor pool table, Wed and Thu ladies' night.

Hector's, 1 Calle Poniente No.9, 783-9867. Small, busy and welcoming restaurant that serves wonderful food at good prices. Highly recommended.

La Antigua Vinería, 5 Av Sur 34A, T7832-7370. Mon-Thu 1800-0100, Fri-Sun 1300-0100. Owned by Beppe Dángella, next door to San José ruins. Amazing photographic collection of clients in various stages of inebriation, excellent selection of wines and grappa, you name it. Very romantic, feel free to write your comments on the walls, very good food, pop in for a reasonably priced *queso fundido* and glass of wine if you can't afford the whole hog.

Quesos y Vinos, 5 Av Norte 32, T7832-7785. Wed-Mon 1200-1600, 1800-2200. Authentic Italian food and owners, good selection of wines, wood-fired pizza oven, sandwiches, popular.

Sabe Rico, 6 Av Sur No 7, 7832-0648. Herb garden restaurant and fine-food deli that serves healthy, organic food in tranquil surroundings.

Café Flor, 4 Av Sur 1, T7832-5274. Full-on delicious Thai/Guatemalan style and Tandoori food, delivered up between 1100-2300. The stir-fries are delicious, but a little overpriced. Discounts sometimes available. Friendly staff.

Café Rocio, 6 Av Norte 34. This is a palace of Asian food delight. Virtually everything on the menu is mouth-wateringly delicious. Don't leave without indulging in the *mora crisp*: hot blackberry sauce sandwiched between slices of vanilla ice cream! Highly recommended.

Helas Taberna Griega, 4 Av Norte 4, inside La Escudilla, see below. Open 1800-0100, from 1300 weekends, closed Wed. Delicious food including pitta bread stuffed with goodies, Greek olives, tzatsiki, all surrounded by a Greek ruin and sea mural, fishing net and shells.

Rainbow Café, 7 Av Sur, on the corner of 6 Calle Pte. Consistently delicious vegetarian food served in a pleasant courtyard surrounded by hanging plants, good filling breakfasts, indulgent crêpes, popular, live music evenings, good book exchange. Bar at night with happy hour and ladies' nights. Recommended.

In front of La Merced, in the back of the shop opposite La Merced, open until about 1900. Where local people eat it's ridiculously cheap, large proportions. Arrive respectfully and enjoy a real Guatemalan experience.

La Casa de los Mixtas, 3 Calle Pte 3 Callejón 2A. Mon-Sat 0900-1900. Cheap Guatemalan fodder with a few tables on the pavement next to Casa de Don Ismael, good breakfasts, set lunch way above average, friendly family. Recommended.

Típico Antigüeño, Alameda Sta Lucía 4, near the PO, T7832-5995. This locally run place offers an absolute bargain of a *menú del día* (fish, chicken), which includes soup and sometimes a drink. It is extremely popular and can get ridiculously busy, so best to turn up before 1300 for lunch. Recommended.

Travel Menu, 6 Calle Pte 14. Big fat juicy sandwiches and tofu stir-fry, in candle-lit place, friendly.

Cafés and delis

Bagel Barn, 5 Calle Pte 2. Open 0600-2200. Popular, breakfast, snack deals with bagels, videos shown no charge.

Café Barroco, Callejón de la Concepción 2, T7832-0781. Peaceful garden, stylish, delicious cakes, coffees, huge selection of English teas for the deprived.

Café Condesa, 5 Av Norte 4. Open 0700-2100. West side of the main plaza in a pretty courtyard, popular, a little pricey for the portions, breakfast with free coffee fill-ups, desserts, popular Sun brunches.

Café Sky, 1 Av Sur 15. Daily 0800-2300. Rooftop café-cum-bar with panoramic views over town, happy hour Tue-Sat.

Cafetería Alemana Charlotte, Callejón de los Nazarenos 9, between 6 and 7 Av Norte. Good breakfasts, cakes, good coffee, German books, newspapers, and films.

Doña Luisa Xicoténcatl, 4 Calle Ote 12, 1½ blocks east of the plaza, 0700-2130 daily. Popular meeting place with an excellent bulletin board, serving breakfasts, tasty ice cream, good coffee, burgers, large menu, big portions. Good views of Volcán Agua upstairs. Shop sells good selection of wholemeal, banana bread, yogurts, etc; don't miss the chocolate and orange loaf if you can get it.

El Portal, 5 Av Norte 6. 0700-2100. Latest hangout for the young and beautiful, coffee from their own **Finca Filadelfia**, home-made cakes, pies, pasties, cappuccinos, espressos, *licuados*, take away.

Epicure, 6 Av Norte 35-A, T7832-1414. This deli serves lovely sandwiches and renowned scotch eggs. All bread baked on the premises.

La Fuente, 4 Calle Pte 14 next to Doña Luisa, sandwiches, light meals and cakes at tables set around fountain, colourful and popular, excellent service. Amazing selection of *huíplies* and *cortes* for sale Sat.

Peroleto, Alameda Sta Lucía 36. Run by a Nicaraguan, next to San Jerónimo church, stop by here for the wickedest *licuados* in town and you probably won't be able to bypass the cake cabinet either. It has a *ceviche* restaurant next door open until 1800.

Tostaduría Antigua, 6 Calle Pte/Av Sur Esquina. 0900-1300,1430-1800. Roasts and brews good Antiguan coffee, many say the best in town. You can smell the coffee half a block away in each direction.

Vivero y Café de La Escalonia, 5 Av Sur Final 36 Calle, T7832-7074. This is a delightful place, well worth the walk – a café amid a garden centre with luscious flowers everywhere, pergola, classical music, *postres*, herb breads, salads andcold drinks. Bird of paradise flowers and tumbergia. Daily 0900-1800.

⊕ Entertainment

Antigua *p641, map p642*

Bars and clubs

Café 2000, 6 Av Norte 8, between 4 and 5 Calle Pte. Daily 0800-0100. Happy hour Tue-Sat 1930-2300. Kicking most nights with indie music, and hard, cool lines in decor, but the free films or sports events shown on a giant screen can alter the balance in the bar between those on a bender and those glued to the screen. Good salads.

Cafe No Sé, 1 Av y 11 Calle. Small, dimly lit bar, proving popular on the travelling circuit.
Casbah, 5 Av Norte 30. Mon-Sat 1800-0100. Cover charge includes a drink. Gay night Thu. Has a medium-sized dance floor with a podium and plays a mix of good dance and Latin music, the closest place to a nightclub atmosphere in Antigua.
La Chiminea, 7 Av Norte 18. Mon-Sat 1700-2430. Happy hour every day, seriously cheap, relaxed atmosphere, mixed young crowd, dance floor, salsa, rock.
La Sala, 6 Calle Pte, T5671-3008. One of the most popular salsa dancing and watering holes in town.
Monoloco, 5 Av Sur 6. Daily 1100-0100. Rooftop veranda, heaving at weekends, happy hour 1700-2000, also good food – huge plates of nachos go down well with the booze, excellent burritos, burgers, Tue is ladies' night.
Reds, 1 Calle Pte 3. Daily 0800-2400. All decorated in red, pool table, satellite TV fireplace, 100 things on the menu from Thai to steak. Good frozen *licuados*. Happy hour every day 1900-2400. Patio out back, free films.
Reilly´s Irish Pub/ Bar, 5 Av Norte 32. Daily 1400-0100, happy hour 1600-2000. Guinness available, very popular night spot with reasonably priced food.
Rikki's Bar, 4 Av Norte 4, inside La Escudilla. Usually packed full of gringos, but attracts a young Guatemalan crowd as well, popular with students and visitors and the gay fraternity. Good place to meet people. A good mix of music, including jazz.

Cinemas

Antigua must be the home of the lounge cinema. All show films or videos in English, or with subtitles.
Café 2000, 6 Av Sur, shows free films daily and is the most popular spot in town to watch movies.
Cine Sin Ventura, 5 Av Sur 8. The only real screen in town, auditorium can get cold, and they could do with hitting the brightness button.

⊕ Festivals and events

Antigua *p641, map p642*
Feb International Culture Festival: dance, music and other top-quality performers from around the globe come to Antigua
Mar/Apr Semana Santa: see box, page 646.
21-26 Jul The feast of San Santiago.
31 Oct-2 Nov All Saints and All Souls, in and around Antigua.
7 Dec Quema del Diablo (burning of the Devil) by lighting fires in front of their houses and burning an effigy of the Devil in the Plazuela de La Concepción at night, thereby starting the Christmas festivities.
8 Dec Fiesta in Ciudad Vieja
15 Dec The start of what's known as the Posadas, where a group of people leave from each church, dressed as Mary and Joseph, and seek refuge in hotels. They are symbolically refused lodging several times, but are eventually allowed in.

O Shopping

Antigua *p641, map p642*
Antigua is a shopper's paradise, with textiles, furniture, candles, fabrics, clothes, sculpture, candies, glass, jade and ceramics on sale. The main municipal market is on Alameda Santa Lucía next to the bus station, where you can buy fruit, clothes and shoes. The *artesanía* market is opposite, next to the bus lane.

Art
Galería de Arte Antigua, 4 Calle Ote 27 y 1 Av. Tue-Sat. Large art gallery.

Bookshops
Numerous bookshops sell books in English and Spanish, postcards, posters, maps and guides including Footprint Handbooks.
Un Poco de Todo, near Casa del Conde on the plaza. **Casa del Conde**, 5 Av Norte 4; has a full range of books from beautifully

illustrated coffee-table books to guides and history books. **Rainbow Cafe**, 7 Av Sur 18, second-hand books. **Hamlin and White**, 4 Calle Ote 12A. Books on Guatemala are cheaper here than at **Casa del Conde**.

Crafts, textiles, clothes and jewellery

Many other stores sell textiles, handicrafts, antiques, silver and jade on 5 Av Norte between 1 and 4 Calle Pte and 4 Calle Ote. **Casa Chicob**, Callejón de la Concepción 2, www.casachicob.com. Beautiful textiles, candles, ceramics for sale, **Casa de Artes**, 4 Av Sur 11, www.casadeartes.com.gt, for traditional textiles and handicrafts, jewellery, etc. Very expensive. **Casa de los Gigantes**, 7 Calle Ote 18, for textiles and handicrafts. **Diva**, at 5 Av Norte 16. For western-style clothes and jewellery. **El Telar**, Loom Tree, 5 Av Sur 7, all sorts of coloured tablecloths, napkins, cushion covers and bedspreads are sold here. **Huipil market** held in the courtyard of La Fuente every Sat 0900-1400. The display is very colourful and if the sun is out this is an excellent place for photos. **Mercado de Artesanías**, next to the main market at the end of 4 Calle Pte. **Nativo's**, 5 Av Norte, 25 "B", T7832-6556. Sells some beautiful textiles from such places as Aguacatán. **Nim P'ot**, 5 Av Norte 29, T7832-2681, www.nimpot.com, a mega-warehouse of traditional textiles and crafts brought from around the country. Excellent prices. **Textura**, 5 Av Norte 33, T7832-5067 for lots of bedroom accessories.

Food

Doña María Gordillo, 4 Calle Ote 11. Famous throughout the country. It is impossible to get in the door most days but, if you can, take a peek, to see the *dulces*, as well as the row upon row of yellow wooden owls keeping their beady eyes on the customers. **La Bodegona**, 5 Calle Pte 32, opposite Posada La Quinta, on 5 Calle Pte and with another entrance on 4 Calle Pte, large supermarket. **Tienda de Doña Gavi**, 3 Av Norte 2, behind the cathedral, sells all sorts of lovely potions and herbs, candles and home-made biscuits. Doña Gaviota also sells Guatemala City's most famous ice creams in all sorts of weird and wonderful flavours (see **Helados Marylena**, page 633).

▲ Activities and tours

Antigua *p641, map p642*

Spas

Antigua Spa Resort, San Pedro El Panorama, lote 9 and 10 G, T7832-3960. Daily 0900-2100. Swimming pool, steam baths, sauna, gym, jacuzzi, beauty salon. Reservations advised. **Mayan Spa**, Alameda Sta Lucía Norte 20, T7832-3537. Mon-Sat 0900-1800. Massages and pampering packages, including sauna, steam baths and jacuzzi, are available.

Riding

Ravenscroft Riding Stables, 2 Av Sur 3, San Juan del Obispo, T7830-6669. You can also hire horses in Santa María de Jesús.

Swimming

Porta Hotel Antigua, non-residents may use the pool for a charge. **Villas de Antigua** (Ciudad Vieja exit), T7832-0011-15, for buffet lunch, swimming and marimba band.

Tour operators

Adrenalina Tours, 5 Av Norte 31, Portal Hotel Posada Asjemenou, T7832-1108, www.adrenalinatours.com. Xela's respected tour operator has opened up in **Posada Asjemenou**. As well as in-country shuttles, there are minibuses to San Cristóbal de las Casas, US$50. Also customized packages, week end trips to Xela and discounted Tikal trips. Recommended. **Adventure Travel Center Viareal**, 5 Av Norte 25B, T7832-0162, daily trips to Guatemalan destinations (including Río Dulce sailing, river and volcano trips), Monterrico, Quiriguá, El Salvador and Honduras.

Antigua Tours, Casa Santo Domingo, 3 Calle Ote 22, T7832-5821, www.antiguatours.net. Run by Elizabeth Bell, author of 4 books on Antigua. She offers walking tours of the city (US$20 per person), book in advance, Mon, Thu 1400-1700, Tue, Wed, Fri, Sat 0930-1230. During Lent and Holy Week there are extra tours, giving insight into the processions and carpet making. Highly recommended.

Aventuras Naturales, Col El Naranjo No 53, Antigua, T7832-3328, http://aventuras naturales.tripod.com. Specialized trips including guided birding tours.

Aventuras Vacacionales, end of 2 Av Sur, turn left for 20 m, on the right is Residencial San José, No 4, T7832-6056, www.sailing-diving-guatemala.com. Highly recommended sailing trips on *Las Sirenas* with Captain John Clark (see also under Río Dulce, page 733).

CA Tours, 6 Calle Oriente Casa 14, T7832-9638, www.catours.co.uk. British-run motorbike tour company. Recommended.

Eco-Tour Chejo's, 3 Calle Pte 24, T832-5464, ecotourchejos@hotmail.com. Well-guarded walks up volcanoes. Interesting tours also available to coffee fincas, flower plantations, etc, shuttle service, horse riding, very helpful.

Gran Jaguar, 4 Calle Pte 30, T7832-2712, www.guacalling.com/jaguar/. Well-organized fun volcano tours with official security. Also shuttles and trips to Tikal. Very highly recommended for the Pacaya trip.

Old Town Outfitters, 5 Av Sur 12 "C", T7832-4171, www.adventureguatemala.com. Mountain bike tours (½-day tour, US$39), kayak tours, outdoor equipment on sale, maps, very helpful.

Outdoor Excursions, 1 Av Sur 4b, T7832-0074, www.guatemalavolcano.com. Professional, knowledgeable and fun Volcano tour company with private security. Overnight tours to Fuego (US$79), Acatenango (US$79) and Pacaya (US$59).

Rainbow Travel Center, 7 Av Sur 8, T7832-4202, www.rainbowtravelcenter.com.

Full local travel service, specialists in student flights and bargain international flights, they will attempt to match any quote. It also sells ISIC, Go25 and teachers' cards. English, French, German and Japanese spoken.

Sin Fronteras, 5a Av Norte 15 "A", T7720-4400, www.sinfront.com. Local tours, shuttles, horse riding, bicycle tours, canopy tours, national and international air tickets including discounts with ISIC and Go25 cards. Also sells travel insurance. Agents for rafting experts **Maya Expeditions**. Reliable and highly recommended.

Tivoli Travel, 4 Calle Ote 10, T7832-4274, antigua@tivoli.com.gt. Closed Sun. Helpful with any travel problem, English, French, Spanish, German, Italian spoken, reconfirm tickets, shuttles, hotel bookings, good-value tours. Useful for organizing independent travel as well as tours.

ViaVenture, 2 Calle Ote 2, T7832-2509, www.viaventure.com. Professional tour operator offering special interest and tailor-made tours.

Vision Travel, 3 Av Norte 3, T7832-3293, www.guatemalainfo.com. Closed Sun. A wide range of tours. Frequently recommended. Also has guidebooks for reference or to buy, along with a water bottle-filling service to encourage recycling. Cheap phone call service. Shuttles and tours.

⊖ Transport

Antigua *p641, map p642*
Bus
To **Guatemala City**. Buses leave when full between 0530 and 1830, US$1, 1-1½ hrs, depending on the time of day, from the Alameda Santa Lucía near the market, from an exit next to **Pollo Campero** (not from behind the market). All other buses leave from behind the market. To **Chimaltenango**, on the Pan-American Hwy, from 0600-1600, every 15 mins, US$0.65, for connections to **Los Encuentros** (for **Lake Atitlán** and **Chichicastenango**), **Cuatro Caminos**

(for **Quetzaltenango**) and **Huehuetenango** (for the Mexican border). It is possible to get to Chichicastenango and back by bus in a day, especially on Thu and Sun, for the market. Get the bus to Chimaltenango and then change. It's best to leave early. See Chimaltenango for connections. The only direct bus to **Panajachel** is Rebuli, leaving at 0700, from 4 Calle Pte, in front of **La Bodegona** supermarket, US$5, 2½ hrs, returning 1100. Other buses to **Pana** via Chimaltenango with **Rebuli** and **Carrillo y Gonzalez**, 0600-1645, US$2.50. To **Escuintla** 0530-1600, 1 hr, US$1.25. **International** To **Copán**, with Hedman Alas, www.hedmanalas.com, from Posada de Don Rodrigo to its terminal in Guatemala City for a connection to Copán. The bus leaves at 0330 and 0630 from Antigua, US$41, US$77 return and then 0500 and 0900 from Guatemala City, US$35, US$65 return. Return times are 1330 and 1800 to Guatemala City; the earlier bus continues to Antigua.

Shuttles Hotels and travel agents run frequent shuttle services to and from **Guatemala City** and the **airport** (1 hr) from 0400 to about 2000 daily, US$6-10 depending on the time of day: details from any agency in town. There are also shuttles to **Chichicastenango**, US$6-18, **Panajachel**, US$5-12; **Quetzaltenango**, US$16, **Monterrico**, US$15, **Flores**, US$20-40, **Copán**, US$10-25 and other destinations, but check for prices and days of travel.

Around Antigua *p645*
Bus
To **Ciudad Vieja**, US$0.30, every 30 mins, 20 mins. **San Miguel de las Dueñas**. Take a bus marked 'Dueñas', every 30 mins, 20 mins, US$0.30. To **San Antonio Aguas Calientes**, every 30 mins, 30 mins, US$0.30. To **Santa María de Jesús** every 30 mins, 45 mins, US$0.50. There are a few buses a day between **Mixco Viejo** and the Zona 4 terminal, Guatemala City. The bus goes to Pachalum; ask to be dropped at ruins entrance.

Volcán Agua *p647*
Bus
From Antigua to **Alotenango** from 0700-1800, 40 mins.

Volcán Acatenango *p647*
Bus To reach **La Soledad**, take a bus heading for Yepocapa or Acatenango village and get off at La Soledad.

Car Tabarini, 6 Av Sur 22, T7832-8107, also at the Hotel Radisson Villa Antigua, T7832-7460, www.tabarini.com.

Motorcycle hire La Ceiba, 6 Calle Pte 15, T7832-0077.

Taxi Servicio de Taxi 'Antigua', Manuel Enrique Gómez, T5417-2180, has been recommended.

Horse-drawn carriage Available at weekends and during fiestas around the plaza.

Tuk-tuk Motobike taxis with a seat for 2 will whizz you around town for US$1.50.

⊙ Directory

Antigua *p641, map p642*
Banks
Banks are closed Wed-Sun of Holy Week and none change money between Christmas and New Year. Most banks are open Mon-Fri 0900-1800, some until 1900 and Sat 0900-1300. **Banco de América Central**, on the plaza, Visa and MasterCard ATM (Cirrus and Plus), but bank hours only. **Banco Industrial**, 5 Av Sur 4, near plaza, gives cash on Visa ATM (24 hr) and Visa credit card at normal rates, no commission. Extremely quick service. **Banco Industrial** on plaza, good rates, no commission, MasterCard (Cirrus) ATM.

Internet
Some internet cafés offer discount cards, which are worth buying if you are in town

Learning the lingo

Antigua is overrun with language students and so some say it is not the most ideal environment in which to learn Spanish. There are about 70-plus schools, open year-round. At any one time there may be 300-600 overseas students in Antigua. Not all schools are officially authorized by INGUAT and the Ministry of Education. INGUAT has a list of authorized schools in its office. Rates depend on the number of hours of tuition per week, and vary from school to school. As a rough guide, the average fee for four hours a day, five days a week is US$95-180, at a reputable school, with homestay, though many are less and some schools offer cheaper classes in the afternoon. You will benefit more if you have done a bit of study of the basics before you arrive. There are guides who take students around the schools and charge a high commission (make sure this is not added to your account). They may approach tourists arriving on the bus from the capital.

All schools offer one-to-one tuition; if you can, meet the teachers in advance, so much the better, but don't let the director's waffle distract you from asking pertinent questions. Paying more does not mean you get better teaching and the standard of teacher varies within schools as well as between schools. Beware of 'hidden' extras and be clear on arrangements for study books. Some schools have an inscription fee. Several schools use a portion of their income to fund social projects and some offer a programme of activities for students such as dance classes, Latin American film, tours, weaving and football. Before making any commitment, find somewhere to stay for a couple of nights and shop around. Schools offer accommodation with local families, but check the place out before you pay a week in advance. Average lodging rates with a family with three meals a day are US$75-100 per week. Some schools organize group accommodation; if you prefer single, ask for it.

for any length of time. The following are recommended: **Enlaces**, 6 Av Norte 1. **Funky Monkey**, Paseo de los Corregidores, 5 Av Sur 6.

Language schools

Footprint has received favourable reports from students for the following language schools: **Academia Antigüeña de Español**, 1 Pte 10, T7832-7241, www.spanishacademy antiguena.com. **Alianza Lingüística 'Cano'**, Av El Desengaño 21A, T7832-0370. Private classes are also available. **Amerispan**, 6 Av Norte 40 and 7 Calle Ote, T7832-0164, www.amerispan.com. In the US, 1334 Walnut St, 6th floor, Philadelphia PA 19107. **Centro Lingüístico Maya**, 5 Calle Pte 20, T7832-1342, www.clmmaya.com. **CSA** (Christian Spanish Academy), 6 Av Norte 15, Aptdo Postal 320,

T7832-3922, www.learncsa.com. **Don Pedro de Alvarado**, 6 Av Norte 39, T5872-2469, www.donpedro spanishschool.com. 25 years' experience. **Proyecto Bibliotecas Guatemala** (PROBIGUA), 6 Av Norte 41B, T7832-2998, www.probigua.org. Gives a percentage of profits towards founding and maintaining public libraries in rural towns; frequently recommended. **Proyecto Lingüístico Francisco Marroquín**, 6 Av Norte, www.plfm-antigua.org. **Sevilla Academia de Español**, 1 Av Sur 8, T7832-5101, www.sevillantigua.com. **Tecún Umán**, 6 Calle Pte 34A, T7832-2792, www.tecunuman.centramerica.com.

Private Lessons Check ads in Doña Luisa's and others around town and the tourist office. Recommended: Julia Solís, 5 Calle Pte 36, T7832-5497, julisar@

hotmail.com (she lives behind the tailor's shop). **Armalia Jarquín**, Av El Desengaño 11, T7832-2377. There are, unbelievably, numerous No 11s on this road. Armalia's has a sign up and is opposite No 75, which has a tiled plaque.

Laundry
All charge about US$1 per kg and most close Sun and half-day Sat. **Delilah** in La Unión on 1 Av Sur provides an excellent service. **Lavandería Gilda**, 5 Calle Pte between 6 and 7 Av, very good and can do a wash and dry in 2 hrs. **Central**, 5 Calle Pte 7B.

Medical services
Hospitals and clinics Casa de Salud Santa Lucía, Alameda Sta Lucía Sur 7, T7832-3122. Open 24 hrs, good and efficient service. Consultation prices vary. **Hospital Privado Hermano Pedro**, Av El Desengaño 12A, T7832-6419. **Opticians** Optica Santa Lucía, 5 Calle Pte 28, T7832-0384. Sells contact-lens solution and accessories.

Police
Tourism police, Rancho Nimejay, 6 Calle, between 8 Avenida and 4 Calle del Ranchon, T7832-7290. The office is open 24 hrs. Just knock on the door or ring their number. **National Police** are based in Antigua, in the Palacio de los Capitanes General, on the south side of the plaza.

Post office
At Alameda Sta Lucía and 4 Calle Pte, near the market. Mon-Fri 0800-1830, Sat 0830-1400. **Courier services** There are several in town, including DHL, 6 Calle Pte and 6 Av Sur.

Telephones
Telgua, 5 Av Sur, corner of the plaza for international and local calls. There are public phone boxes inside the **Telgua** building, which are quieter to use than the couple under the arches on the west side of the square. Mon-Fri 0800-1800, Sat 0800-1200. Try **Funky Monkey** for internet calls.

Lake Atitlán and around

→ *Colour map 4, C2.*

Beautiful scenery stretches west of the capital through the Central Highlands. Here, volcano landscapes are dotted with colourful markets and the Maya wearing traditional clothes in the towns and villages. Aldous Huxley called Lake Atitlán "the most beautiful lake in the world" and attractive villages flank its shores. Further north you can explore the streets of Chichicastenango as the town fills with hawkers and vendors at the weekly markets serving tourists and locals alike. North of Chichicastenango, the Quiché and Ixil Triangle regions have small, very traditional, hamlets set in beautiful countryside that are easily explored by bus.
▸▸ *For listings, see pages 674-688.*

Ins and outs

The easiest way to get to the Lake Atitlán area is by the numerous buses that ply the Pan-American Highway, changing at Los Encuentros or El Cuchillo junctions. Alternatively, shuttles go to Panajachel from most big tourist centres. Villages around the lake are connected to Panajachel by boat services. Some are served by buses. Some Hurricane Stan damage from October 2005 is still visible and some small roads remain unrepaired. Access is not affected, though. Panabaj, the village that was completely destroyed behind Santiago Atitlán, was declared a mass graveyard.
▸▸ *See Transport, page 684.*

Towards Lake Atitlán

The Pan-American Highway heads west out of the capital passing through Chimaltenango and on to Los Encuentros where it turns north for Chichicastenango, Santa Cruz del Quiché, Nebaj and the Ixil Triangle, and south for Sololá and the Lake Atitlán region. It continues to the western highland region of Quetzaltenango (see page 699), Totonicapán, Huehuetenango and the Cuchumatanes Mountains (see page 692).

Chimaltenango and around

Chimaltenango is busy with traffic. Here, another road runs south for 20 km to Antigua. This tree-lined road leads to Parramos where it turns sharp left. Straight on through the village, in 1.5 km, is a well-known inn and restaurant (see Sleeping, page 674). This road continues through mountains to Pastores, Jocotenango and finally to Antigua. At **San Andrés Itzapa**, which is well worth a visit, there is a very interesting **chapel to Maximón** ① *6 km south of Chimaltenango, open till 1800 daily.* Shops by the chapel sell prayer pamphlets and pre-packaged offerings. Beyond Chimaltenango is **Zaragoza**, a former Spanish penal settlement, and beyond that a road leads 13 km north to the interesting village of **Comalapa**. This is the best place to see *naïf* painting and there are plenty of galleries. There's a colourful market on Monday and Tuesday.

Routes west: Tecpán and Los Encuentros

Returning to the Pan-American Highway the road divides 6 km past Zaragoza. The southern branch, the old Pan-American Highway, goes through Patzicía and Patzún (see below) to Lake Atitlán, then north to Los Encuentros. The northern branch, the new Pan-American Highway, which is used by all public transport, goes past Tecpán (see below) and then to Los Encuentros. From Los Encuentros there is only the one road west to San Cristóbal Totonicapán, where it swings northwest to La Mesilla/Ciudad Cuauhtémoc, at the Mexican border.

From Zaragoza the Pan-American Highway runs 19 km to near **Tecpán**, which is slightly off the road at 2287 m. It has a particularly fine church with silver altars, carved wooden pillars, odd images and a wonderful ceiling that was severely damaged by the

Lake Atitlán

1976 earthquake. There is accommodation, restaurants and banks. Near Tecpán are the important Maya ruins of **Iximché** ① *5 km of paved road south of Tecpán, 0800-1700, US$3.25*, once capital and court of the Cakchiqueles. The first capital of Guatemala after its conquest was founded near Iximché; followed in turn by Ciudad Vieja, Antigua and Guatemala City. The ruins are well presented with three plazas, a palace and two ball courts on a promontory surrounded on three sides by steep slopes.

To Las Trampas, Guatemala
City & Zaragoza

Río Panajachel

San Andrés
Semetabaj

Las Canoas

Santa Catarina
Palopó

Godínez

San Antonio
Palopó

To Patzún

Tzampetey

Agua Escondida

Pachitulúl

Panaranjo

San Lucas
Tolimán   San Gabriel

To Cocales & Pacific Highway

The old and new Pan-American Highways rejoin 11 km from Sololá at the **El Cuchillo** junction. About 2 km east is **Los Encuentros**, the junction of the Pan-American Highway and the paved road 18 km northeast to Chichicastenango, see page 669.

To Lake Atitlán along the old Pan-American Highway

With amazing views of Lake Atitlán and the surrounding volcanoes, travellers of the southern road from Zaragoza to Lake Atitlán encounter a much more difficult route than the northern option, with several steep hills and many hairpin bends. Nevertheless, if you have both the time and a sturdy vehicle, it is an extremely rewarding trip. Note that there is no police presence whatsoever along the old Pan-American Highway.

The route goes through **Patzicía**, a small Maya village founded in 1545 (no accommodation). Market days are Wednesday and Saturday and the local **fiesta** is 22-27 July. The famous church, which had a fine altar and beautiful silver, was destroyed by the 1976 earthquake. Beyond is the small town of **Patzún**; its church, dating from 1570, is severely damaged and is not open to the public. There is a Sunday market, which is famous for the silk (and wool) embroidered napkins and for woven *fajas* and striped red cotton cloth; other markets are on Tuesday and Friday and the town fiesta is 17-21 May. For accommodation, ask at the *tiendas*.

The road leaves Patzún and goes south to Xepatán and on to **Godínez**, the highest community overlooking the lake. From Godínez, a good paved road turns off south to the village of San Lucas Tolimán and continues to Santiago Atitlán.

The main (steep, paved) road continues straight on for Panajachel. The high plateau, with vast wheat and maize fields, now breaks off suddenly as though pared by a knife. From a viewpoint here, there is an incomparable view of Lake Atitlán, 600 m below. The very picturesque village of **San Antonio Palopó** is right underneath you, on slopes leading to the water. It is about 12 km from the viewpoint to Panajachel. For the first 6 km you are close to the rim of the old crater and, at the point where the road plunges down to the lakeside, is **San Andrés Semetabaj** which has a beautiful ruined early-17th-century church. Market day is Tuesday. Buses go to Panajachel.

Sololá → *Colour map 5, C1. Altitude: 2113 m.*

On the road down to Panajachel is Sololá, which has superb views across Lake Atitlán. Outside the world of the tourist, this is the most important town in the area. A fine, modern, white church, with bright stained-glass windows and an attractive clocktower dominates the west side of the plaza. Sololá is even more special for the bustling market that brings the town to life every Tuesday and Friday, when the Maya gather from surrounding commuities to buy and sell local produce. Women and particularly men wear traditional dress. While it is primarily a produce market, there is also a good selection of used *huípiles*. Even if you're not in the market to buy, it is a colourful sight. Markets are mornings only; Friday market gets underway on Thursday. There's a fiesta 11-17 August.

From Sololá the old Pan-American Highway weaves and twists through a 550-m drop in 8 km to Panajachel. The views are impressive at all times of day, but particularly in the morning. Time allowing, it is quite easy to walk down direct by the road (two hours); you also miss the unnerving bus ride down (US$0.40).

Panajachel ⊜⊘⊘⊚⊙▲⊚⊙ » *pp674-688. Colour map 5, C1.*

The old town of Panajachel is charming and quiet but the newer development, strung along a main road, is a tucker and trinket emporium. It's busy and stacked cheek by jowl with hundreds of stalls and shops along the main road. Some of the best bargains are here and textiles and crafts from across the country can be found. Panajachel is a gringo magnet, and if you want to fill up on international cuisine and drink then it's a good place to stay for a few days. There are also stunning views from the lakeshore.

Ins and outs

Getting there and around Good connections from most large town in the highlands, including Antigua, Chichicastenango and Quetzaltenango. The town centre is the junction of Calle Principal and Calle (or Avenida) Santander. The main bus stop is here, stretching south back down Calle Real, and it marks the junction between the old and the modern towns. It takes about 10 minutes to walk from the junction to the lake shore. Calle Rancho Grande is sometimes called Calle del Balneario and other streets have variants. » *See Transport, page 684.*

Tourist information INGUAT ⓘ *Calle Santander 1-87, T7762-1106, daily 0900-1500 and 1600-1800.* Helpful with information about buses, boats and good local knowledge. Also see www.atitlan.com.

Safety There have been reports from travellers who have suffered **robbery** walking around the lake between San Juan and San Pablo and between San Marcos and Tzununá. Seek local advice from **INGUAT**, other travellers and local hotels/hostels before planning a trip.

Panajachel

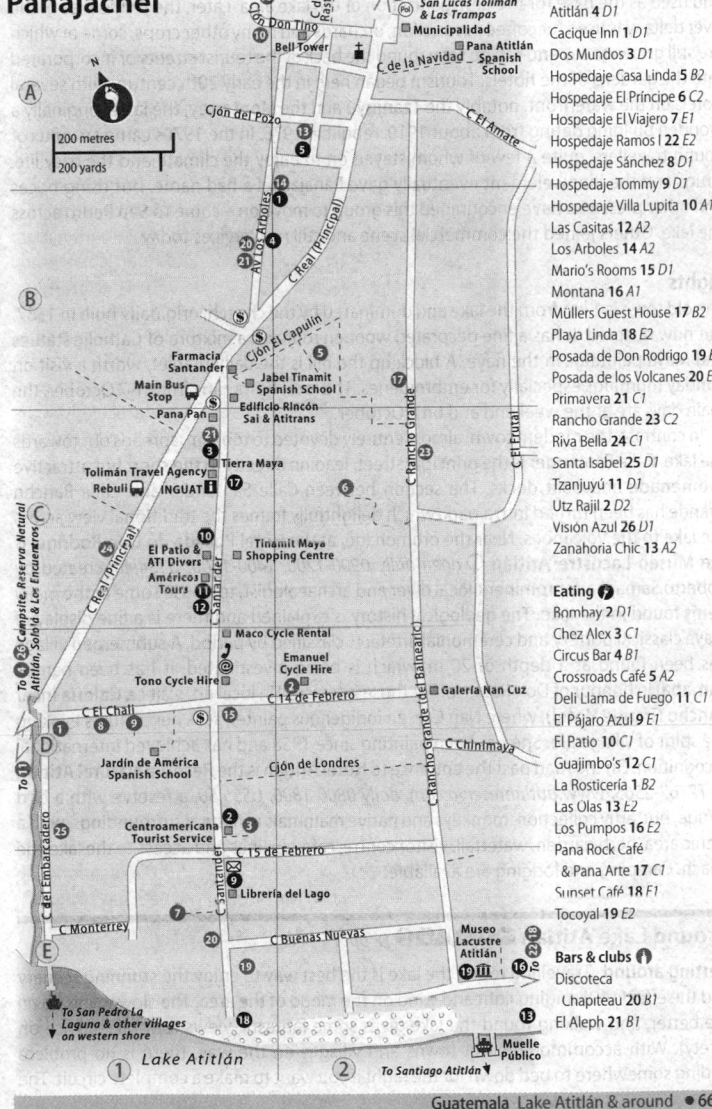

Background

The original settlement of Panajachel was tucked up against the steep cliffs to the north of the present town, about 1 km from the lake. Virtually all traces of the original Kaqchikel village have disappeared, but the early Spanish impact is evident with the narrow streets, public buildings, plaza and church. The original Franciscan church was founded in 1567 and used as the base for the Christianization of the lake area. Later, the fertile area of the river delta was used for coffee production, orchards and many other crops, some of which are still grown today and can be seen round the back of the tourist streets or incorporated into the gardens of the hotels. Tourism began here in the early 20th century with several hotels on the waterfront, notably the **Tzanjuyú** and the **Monterrey**, the latter originally a wooden building dating from about 1910, rebuilt in 1975. In the 1970s came an influx of young travellers, quite a few of whom stayed on to enjoy the climate and the easy life. Drugs and the hippy element eventually gave Panajachel a bad name, but rising prices and other pressures have encouraged this group to move on – some to San Pedro across the lake. Others joined the commercial scene and still run services today.

Sights

The old town is 1 km from the lake and dominated by the **church**, originally built in 1567, but now restored. It has a fine decorated wooden roof and a mixture of Catholic statues and Maya paintings in the nave. A block up the hill is the daily market, worth a visit on Sunday mornings especially for embroideries. The local fiesta runs from 1-7 October, the main days are at the weekend and on 4 October.

In contrast, the modern town, almost entirely devoted to tourism, spreads out towards the lake. Calle Santander is the principal street, leading directly to the short but attractive **promenade** and boat docks. The section between Calle Santander and Calle Rancho Grande has been turned into a park, which delightfully frames the traditional view across the lake to the volcanoes. Near the promenade, at the **Hotel Posada de Don Rodrigo**, is the **Museo Lacustre Atitlán** ① *open daily 0900-1200, 1400-1800, US$4.40*, created by Roberto Samayoa, a prominent local diver and archaeologist, to house some of the many items found in the lake. The geological history is explained and there is a fine display of Maya classical pottery and ceremonial artefacts classified by period. A submerged village has been found at a depth of 20 m, which is being investigated. It has been named **Samabaj** in honour of Don Roberto. For those interested in local art, visit **La Galería** (near **Rancho Grande Hotel**), where Nan Cuz, an indigenous painter, sells her pictures evoking the spirit of village life. She has been painting since 1958 and has achieved international recognition. On the road past the entrance to **Hotel Atitlán** is the **Reserva Natural Atitlán** ① *T7762-2565, www.atitlanreserva.com, daily 0800-1800, US$5.50*, a reserve with a bird refuge, butterfly collection, monkeys and native mammals in natural surroundings, with a picnic area, herb garden, waterfall, visitor centre, café, zip lines and access to the lakeside beach. Camping and lodging are available.

Around Lake Atitlán ◉🅟🅞▲🅞🅒 » *pp674-688.*

Getting around Travelling round the lake is the best way to enjoy the stunning scenery and the effect of changing light and wind on the mood of the area. The slower you travel the better, and walking round the lake gives some fantastic views (but take advice on safety). With accommodation at towns and villages on the way, there is no problem finding somewhere to bed down for the night if you want to make a complete circuit. The lake is 50 km in circumference and you can walk on or near the shore for most of it. Here and there the cliffs are too steep to allow for easy walking and private properties elsewhere force you to move up 'inland'. For boat information see Transport, Panajachel. At almost any time of year, but especially between January and March, strong winds (*El Xocomil*) occasionally blow up quickly across the lake. This can be dangerous for small boats. ▶▶ *For further details, see Transport, page 684.*

Santa Catarina Palopó
The town, within easy walking distance (4 km) of Panajachel, has an attractive adobe church. Reed mats are made here, and you can buy *huípiles* (beautiful, green, blue and yellow) and men's shirts. Watch weaving at **Artesanías Carolina** on the way out towards San Antonio. Bargaining is normal. There are hot springs close to the town and an art gallery. Houses can be rented and there is at least one superb hotel, see Sleeping. The town fiesta is 25 November.

San Antonio Palopó
Six kilometres beyond Santa Catarina, San Antonio Palopó has another fine 16th-century church. Climbing the hill from the dock, it lies in an amphitheatre created by the mountains behind. Up above there are hot springs and a cave in the rocks used for local ceremonies. The village is noted for the clothes and head dresses of the men, and *huípiles* and shirts are cheaper than in Santa Catarina. A good hike is to take the bus from Panajachel to Godínez, take the path toward the lake 500 m south along the road to Cocales, walk on down from there to San Antonio Palopó (one hour) and then along the road back to Panajachel via Santa Catarina Palopó (three hours). You can walk on round the lake from San Antonio, but you must eventually climb steeply up to the road at Agua Escondida. The local fiesta is 12-14 June.

San Lucas Tolimán
San Lucas is at the southeastern tip of the lake and is not so attractive as other towns. It is known for its fiestas and markets especially Holy Week with processions, arches and carpets on the Thursday and Friday, and 15-20 October. Market days are Tuesday, Friday and Sunday (the best). There are two banks and an internet centre. **Comité Campesino del Altiplano** is based in the small village of Quixaya, 10 minutes from San Lucas. This Campesino Cooperative now produces fair trade organic coffee buying from small farmers. You can visit its organic processing plant on a small coffee *finca* and learn about its *café justicia*, and political work ① *T5804-9451, www.ccda.galeon.com,* long-term volunteers welcome, Spanish required.

Volcán Atitlán and Volcán Tolimán
① *Ask Father Gregorio at the Parroquia church, 2 blocks from the Central Plaza, or at the Municipulidad for information and for available guides in San Lucas. Father Greg has worked in the area for more than 40 years so has a vested interest in recommending safe and good guides. One such is Carlos Huberto Alinan Chicoj, leaving at 2400 with torches to arrive at the summit by 0630 to avoid early cloud cover.*
From San Lucas the cones of **Atitlán**, 3535 m, and **Tolimán**, 3158 m, can be climbed. The route leaves from the south end of town and makes for the saddle (known as Los Planes, or Chanán) between the two volcanoes. From there it is south to Atitlán and north to the double cone (they are 1 km apart) and crater of Tolimán. Though straightforward, each

climb is complicated by many working paths and thick cover above 2600 m. If you are fit, either can be climbed in seven hours, five hours down. Cloud on the volcano is common, but least likely from November to March. There have been reports of robbery so consider taking a guide, and ask local advice before setting out.

Santiago Atitlán

Santiago is a fascinating town, as much for the stunningly beautiful embroidered clothing of the locals, as for the history and character of the place with its mix of Roman Catholic, evangelical and Maximón worship. There are 35 evangelical temples in town as well as the house of the revered idol Maximón. The Easter celebrations here rival Antigua's for interest and colour. These are some of the most curious and reverential ceremonies in the world. If you only visit Guatemala once in your lifetime and it's at Easter and you can't bear to leave Antigua, come to Santiago at least for Good Friday. Commemorative events last all week and include Maximón as well as Christ.

You will be taken to the house of Maximón for a small fee. The fine church, with a wide nave decorated with colourful statues, was founded in 1547. The original roof was lost to earthquakes. There is a plaque dedicated to priest Father Francis Aplas Rother who was assassinated by the government in the church on 28 August 1981. At certain times of the year, the square is decked with streamers gently flapping in the breeze. The Tz'utujil women wear fine clothes and the men wear striped, half-length embroidered trousers (the most beautiful in Guatemala). There is a daily market, best on Friday and all sorts of art work and crafts can be bought. **Asociación Cojol ya weaving centre** ⓘ *T5499-5717, Mon-Fri 0900-1600, Sat 0900-1300, free, weaving tours also*. As well as Holy Week, the local fiesta takes place 23-27 July.

Near town is the hill, **Cerro de Oro**, with a small village of that name on the lake. The summit (1892 m) can be reached from the village in 45 minutes.

For more information on the **Lake Atitlán Medical project** and volunteer opportunities, see www.puebloapueblo.org.

San Pedro La Laguna

San Pedro is a small town set on a tiny promontory with coffee bushes threaded around tracks lined with hostels and restaurants on the lakeside fringes. The tourists and long-term gringos have colonized the lakeside while the **Tz'utujil Maya** dominate the main part of the town up a very steep hill behind. San Pedro is now the favourite spot to hang out in for a couple of days or longer. It's a place to relax, to soak in hot baths, learn a bit of Spanish, horse ride and trek up Nariz de Maya. Some of the semi-permanent gringo inhabitants now run bars and cafés or sell home-made jewellery and the like. The cobbled road from the dock facing Panajachel (known as the *muelle)* climbs up to the centre and another goes down, more or less at right angles, to the other dock (known as the *playa* – beach) facing Santiago with the town arranged around. There's a mazy network of callejones and paths that fringe the shoreline between the two ferries. Market days are Thursday and Sunday (better) and there's a fiesta 27-30 June with traditional dances.

The town lies at the foot of the **Volcán San Pedro** (3020 m), which can be climbed in four to five hours, three hours down. It is now in the Parque Ecológico Volcán San Pedro, and the US$15 entrances includes a guide. **Politur** also work in the park and there have been no incidents of robbery since the park's inauguration. Camping is possible. Go early (0530) for the view, because after 1000 the top is usually smothered in cloud; also you will be in the shade all the way up and part of the way down.

Descubre San Pedro has set up a museum of local culture and coffee, with natural medicine and Maya cosmovision tours.

Evangelical churches are well represented in San Pedro, and you can hardly miss the yellow and white **Templo Evangelico Bautista Getsemaní** in the centre. A visit to the

San Pedro La Laguna

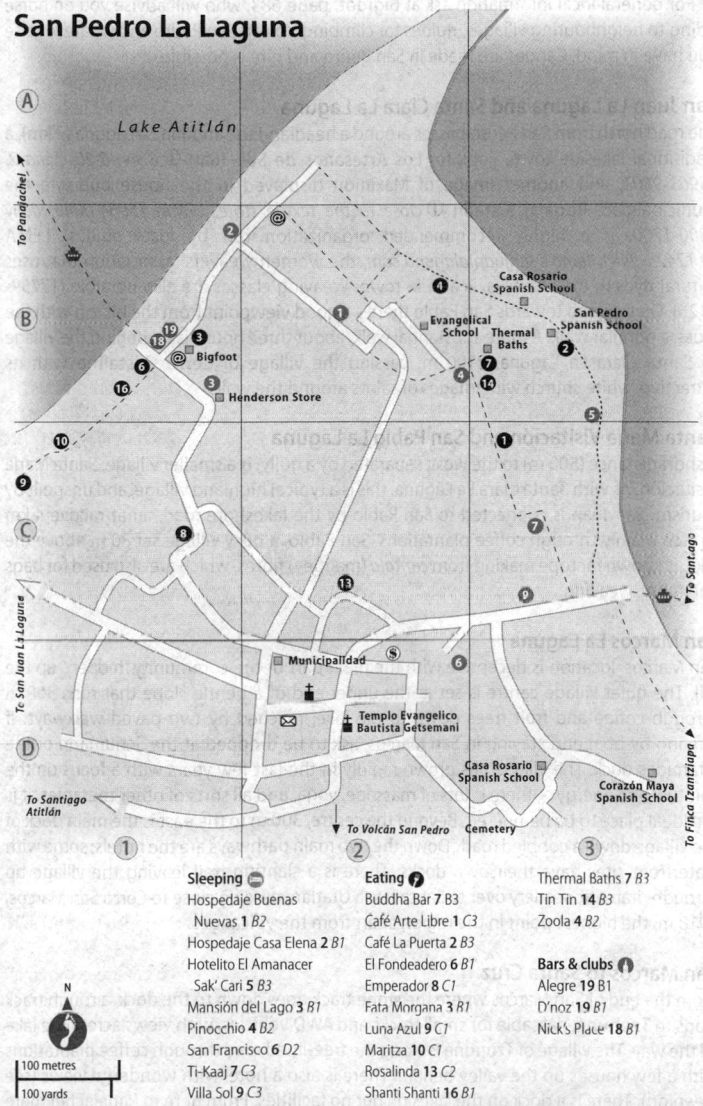

Lake Atitlán

To Panajachel

Casa Rosario
Spanish School

Evangelical
School

Thermal
Baths

San Pedro
Spanish School

Bigfoot

Henderson Store

Municipalidad

Templo Evangelico
Bautista Getsemani

Casa Rosario
Spanish School

To Santiago
Atitlán

To Volcán San Pedro

Cemetery

Corazón Maya
Spanish School

To Finca Tzantziapa

To San Juan La Laguna

To Sant.ago

N

100 metres
100 yards

Sleeping 🛏
Hospedaje Buenas
  Nuevas **1** B2
Hospedaje Casa Elena **2** B1
Hotelito El Amanacer
  Sak' Cari **5** B3
Mansión del Lago **3** B1
Pinocchio **4** B2
San Francisco **6** D2
Ti-Kaaj **7** C3
Villa Sol **9** C3

Eating 🍴
Buddha Bar **7** B3
Café Arte Libre **1** C3
Café La Puerta **2** B3
El Fondeadero **6** B1
Emperador **8** C1
Fata Morgana **3** B1
Luna Azul **9** C1
Maritza **10** C1
Rosalinda **13** C2
Shanti Shanti **16** B1

Thermal Baths **7** B3
Tin Tin **14** B3
Zoola **4** B2

Bars & clubs 🍸
Alegre **19** B1
D'noz **19** B1
Nick's Place **18** B1

rug-making cooperative on the beach is of interest and backstrap weaving is taught at some places. A visit to the **thermal baths** ① *about US$10 a session, Mon-Sat 0800-1900*, is a relaxing experience. Note that the water is solar heated, not chemical hot springs. Best to reserve in advance. Massage also available, US$10.

For general local information ask at **Bigfoot**, page 683, who will advise you on horse riding to neighbouring villages, guides for climbing Volcán San Pedro and whatever else you have in mind. Canoes are made in San Pedro and hire is possible.

San Juan La Laguna and Santa Clara La Laguna
The road north from San Pedro passes around a headland to San Juan La Laguna (2 km), a traditional lakeside town. Look for **Los Artesanos de San Juan** ① *8 Av, 6-20, Zona 2, T5963-9803*, and another image of Maximón displayed in the house opposite the Municipalidad. **Rupalaj Kistalin** ① *close to the textile store, LEMA, T5964-0040, daily 0800-1700*, is a highly recommended organization run by local guides. **LEMA** ① *T2425-9441, lema@sanjuanlalaguna.com*, the women weavers' association that uses natural dyes in their textiles, is also in town. Weaving classes are also possible (T7759-9126). On the road towards San Pablo there's a good viewpoint from the hilltop with the cross; a popular walk. A more substantial walk, about three hours, is up behind the village to Santa Clara La Laguna, 2100 m, passing the village of **Cerro Cristalino** with its attractive, white church with images of saints around the walls.

Santa María Visitación and San Pablo La Laguna
A short distance (500 m) to the west, separated by a gully, is a smaller village, Santa María Visitación. As with Santa Clara La Laguna, this is a typical highland village, and unspoilt by tourism. San Juan is connected to San Pablo by the lakeshore road, an attractive 4 km stretch mainly through coffee plantations. San Pablo, a busy village set 80 m above the lake, is known for rope making from *cantala* (maguey) fibres, which are also used for bags and fabric weaving.

San Marcos La Laguna
San Marcos' location is deceptive with the main part of the community 'hidden' up the hill. The quiet village centre is set at the upper end of a gentle slope that runs 300 m through coffee and fruit trees down to the lake, reached by two paved walkways. If arriving by boat and staying in San Marcos, ask to be dropped at the Schumann or the Pirámides dock. The village has grown rapidly in the last few years with a focus on the spiritual and energy – there is lots of massage, yoga, and all sorts of other therapies. It is the ideal place to be pampered. Beyond the centre, 300 m to the east is the main dock of the village down a cobbled road. Down the two main pathways are the hotels; some with waterfront sites have their own docks. There is a slanting trail leaving the village up through dramatic scenery over to Santa Lucía Utatlán, passing close to Cerro San Marcos, 2918 m, the highest point in the region apart from the volcanoes.

San Marcos to Santa Cruz
From the end of San Marcos where the stone track goes down to the dock, a rough track leads to **Tzununá**, passable for small trucks and 4WD vehicles, with views across the lake all the way. The village of Tzununá is along the tree-lined road through coffee plantations with a few houses up the valley behind. There is also a hotel with wonderful views (see Sleeping). There is a dock on the lakeside but no facilities. From here to Panajachel there

are no roads or vehicular tracks and the villages can only be reached by boat, on horse or on foot. Also from here are some of the most spectacular views of the lake and the southern volcanoes. **Jaibalito** is smaller still than Izununá, and hemmed in by the mountains with wonderful accommodation, see Sleeping. Arguably the best walk in the Atitlán area is from Jaibalito to Santa Cruz.

Santa Cruz La Laguna

Santa Cruz village is set in the most dramatic scenery of the lake. Three deep ravines come down to the bay separating two spurs. A stone roadway climbs up the left-hand spur, picks up the main walking route from Jaibalito and crosses over a deep ravine (unfortunately used as a garbage tip) to the plaza, on the only flat section of the right spur, about 120 m above the lake. The communal life of the village centres on the plaza. The hotels, one of them overflowing with flowers, are on the lake shore. Behind the village are steep, rocky forested peaks, many too steep even for the locals to cultivate. The fiesta takes place 7-11 May.

There is good walking here. Apart from the lake route, strenuous hikes inland eventually lead to the Santa Lucía Utatlán–Sololá road. From the left-hand (west) ravine reached from the path that runs behind the lake shore section, a trail goes through fields to an impossible looking gorge, eventually climbing up to Chaquijchoy, **Finca María Linda** and a trail to San José Chacayá (about four hours). In the reverse direction, the path southwest from San José leads to the Finca María Linda, which is close to the crater rim from where due south is a track to Jaibalito, to the left (east) round to the trail to Santa Cruz. Others follow the ridges towards San José and the road. These are for experienced hikers, and a compass (you are travelling due north) is essential if the cloud descends and there is no one to ask. From Santa Cruz to Panajachel along the coast is difficult, steep and unconsolidated, with few definitive paths. If you do get to the delta of the Río Quiscab, you may find private land is barred. The alternatives are either to go up to Sololá, about 6 km and 800 m up, or get a boat.

Chichicastenango ●◐❼❸❽▲❸❻ ›› pp674-688. Colour map 5, B1.

→ Altitude: 2071 m.

Chichicastenango is a curious blend of mysticism and commercialism. It is famous for its market where hundreds come for a bargain. On market mornings the steps of the church are blanketed in flowers as the women, in traditional dress, fluff up their skirts, amid baskets of lilies, roses and blackberries. But, with its mixture of Catholic and indigenous religion readily visible, it is more than just a shopping trolley stop. On a hilltop peppered with pine, villagers worship at a Maya shrine; in town, a time-honoured tradition of brotherhoods focuses on saint worship. Coupled with the mist that encircles the valley in the late afternoon, you can sense an air of intrigue. There is a local tourist information committee in the town.

Ins and outs

Getting there Chichicastenango is served by numerous chicken buses that head north from Los Encuentros or south from Santa Cruz del Quiché. There are direct buses from Xela and Guatemala City and shuttles from Antigua, the city and Pana. ›› See Transport, page 684.

Background

Often called 'Chichi' but also known as Santo Tomás, Chichicastenango is the hub of the Maya-K'iche' highlands. The name derives from the *chichicaste*, a prickly purple plant-like a nettle, which grows profusely, and *tenango*, meaning 'place of'. Today the locals call the town 'Siguan Tinamit' meaning 'place surrounded by ravines'. The townsfolk are also known as *Masheños*, which comes from the word *Max*, also meaning Tomás. About 1000 *ladinos* live in the town, but 20,000 Maya live in the hills nearby and flood the town for the Thursday and Sunday markets. The town itself has winding streets of white houses roofed with bright red tiles, which wander over a little knoll in the centre of a cup-shaped valley surrounded by high mountains. The men's traditional outfit is a short-waisted embroidered jacket and knee breeches of black cloth, a woven sash and an embroidered kerchief around the head. The cost of this outfit, now over US$200, means that fewer and fewer men are wearing it. Women wear *huípiles* with red embroidery against black or brown and their *cortes* have dark blue stripes.

Chichicastenango

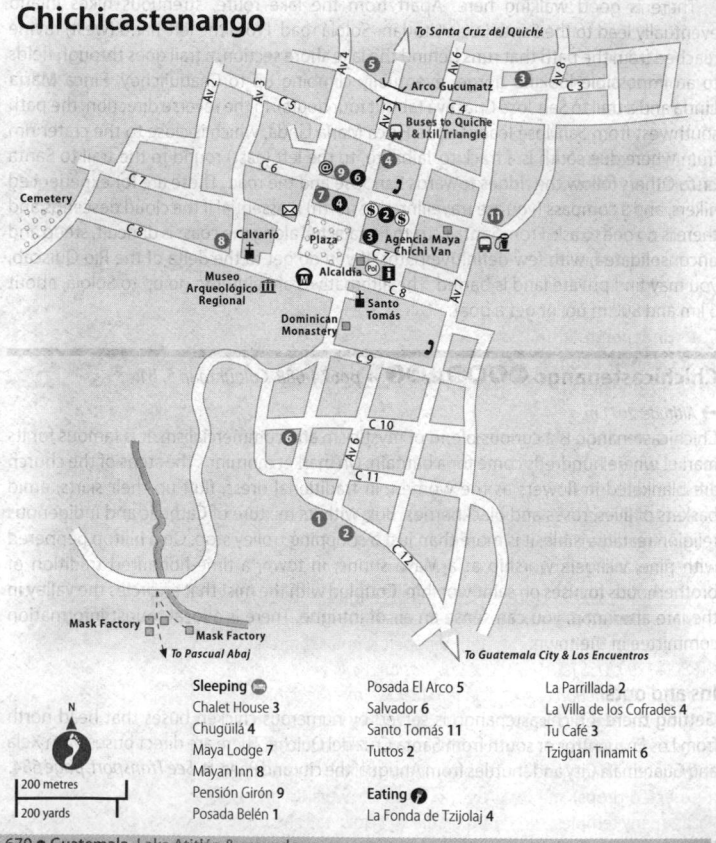

Sleeping	Posada El Arco 5	La Parrillada 2
Chalet House 3	Salvador 6	La Villa de los Cofrades 4
Chugüilá 4	Santo Tomás 11	Tu Café 3
Maya Lodge 7	Tuttos 2	Tziguan Tinamit 6
Mayan Inn 8		
Pensión Girón 9	**Eating**	
Posada Belén 1	La Fonda de Tzijolaj 4	

Sights

A large plaza is the focus of the town, with two white churches facing one another: **Santo Tomás** the parish church and **Calvario**. Santo Tomás, founded in 1540, is open to visitors, although photography is not allowed, and visitors are asked to be discreet and enter by a side door (through an arch to the right). Next to Santo Tomás are the cloisters of the Dominican monastery (1542). Here the famous *Popol Vuh* manuscript of the Maya creation story was found. A human skull wedged behind a carved stone face, found in Sacapulas, can be seen at the **Museo Arqueológico Regional** ① *main plaza, Tue, Wed, Fri, Sat 0800-1200, 1400-1600, Thu 0800-1600, Sun 0800-1400, closed Mon, US$0.70, photographs and video camera not permitted*. There's also a jade collection once owned by 1926-1944 parish priest Father Rossbach.

The Sunday and Thursday markets are both very touristy, and bargains are harder to come by once shuttle-loads of people arrive mid-morning. Articles from all over the Highlands are available: rugs, carpets and bedspreads; walk one or two streets away from the main congregation of stalls for more realistic prices, but prices are cheaper in Panajachel for the same items and you won't find anything here that you can't find in Panajachel.

The idol, **Pascual Abaj**, a god of fertility, is a large black stone with human features on a hill overlooking the town. Crosses in the ground surrounding the shrine are prayed in front of for the health of men, women and children, and for the dead. Fires burn and the wax of a thousand candles, flowers and sugar cover the shrine. One ceremony you may see is that of a girl from the town requesting a good and sober husband. If you wish to undergo a ceremony to plead for a partner, or to secure safety from robbery or misfortune, you may ask the *curandero* (US$7 including photographs). To reach the deity, walk along 5 Avenida, turn right on 9 Calle, down the hill, cross the stream and take the second track from the left going steepest uphill, which passes directly through a farmhouse and buildings. The farm now belongs to a mask-maker whom you can visit and buy masks from. Follow the path to the top of the pine-topped hill where you may well see a Maya ceremony in progress. It's about half an hour's walk. The site can be easily visited independently (in a small group), or an INGUAT-approved guide arranged through the local tourist committee can take you there and explain its history and significance (US$6.50, one or two hours, identified by a license in town).

Santa Cruz del Quiché and around → *Population: 7750. Altitude: 2000 m.*

Santa Cruz del Quiché, often simply called Quiché, is a quaint, friendly town, with a colourful daily market covering several blocks. There are few tourists here and prices are consequently reasonable. Its main attraction is **Utatlán**, the remains of the Maya K'iche' capital. The large Parque Central has a military garrison on the east side with a jail on the lower floor and a sinister military museum with reminders of recent conflicts above. The town's fiesta – about 14-20 August – varies around the Assumption.

Three kilometres away are the remains of temples and other structures of the former Quiché capital, **Gumarcaj**, sometimes spelt **K'umarkaaj**, and now generally called **Utatlán** ① *0800-1700, US$1.30, from the bus station, walk west along 10 Calle for 40 mins until you reach a small junction with a blue sign (SECP), take the right lane up through gates to the site*. The city was largely destroyed by the Spaniards, but the stonework of the original buildings can be seen in the ruins, which can be reached on foot; the setting is very attractive and well maintained. There are two subterranean burial chambers (take a torch, as there are unexpected drops) still used by the Maya for worship and chicken sacrifices. The seven plazas, many temples, ball court, gladiator's archway and other features are marked.

There is a paved road east from Quiché to (8 km) **Santo Tomás Chiché**, a picturesque village with a fine, rarely visited Saturday market (fiesta 25-28 December). There is also a road to this village from Chichicastenango. Although it is a short-cut, it is rough and virtually impassable in any vehicle. It makes a good, three- to four-hour walk, however. Further east (45 km) from Chiché is **Zacualpa**, where beautiful woollen bags are woven. The church has a remarkably fine façade and there is an unnamed *pensión* near the plaza. Market days are Sunday and Thursday.

At **Joyabaj** women weave fascinating *huípiles* and there is a colourful Sunday market, followed by a procession at about noon from the church led by the elders with drums and pipes. This was a stopping place on the old route from Mexico to Antigua. There is good walking in the wooded hills around, for example north to Chorraxaj (two hours), or across the Río Cocol south to Piedras Blancas to see blankets being woven. During fiesta week (9-15 August) Joyabaj has a *Palo Volador* and other traditional dances. There is a restaurant next to the Esso station on the Santa Cruz end of the plaza with a bank opposite (will change US dollars cash).

The road east to Cobán

The road east from **Sacapulas** is one of the most beautiful mountain roads in all Guatemala, with magnificent scenery in the narrow valleys. There is accommodation in **Uspantán** and this is the place to stay for the night enroute to Cobán. The road is not paved beyond Uspantán. ▶▶ *See Transport, page 684.*

It's a five-hour walk from Uspantán south to **Chimul**, the birthplace of **Rigoberta Menchú**, Nobel Peace Prize winner in 1992. The village was virtually wiped out during the 1980s, but the settlement is coming to life again. Only pickups go to the village.

The Ixil Triangle ⊝⊕⊿⊝⊙ ▶▶ *pp674-688.*

The Ixil Triangle is made up of the highland communities of Nebaj, Chajul and Cotzal. The forested mountainous scenery provides great walking opportunities, although sadly, out of local necessity, many of the slopes have been badly deforested and the wood burnt for fires. The traditional dress of the Nebaj women – an explosion of primary colours – is spectacular. Much of this area was decimated during the Civil War and then repopulated with the introduction of 'model villages' established by the government. Evidence of wartime activities can still be seen and more remote Maya Ixil-speaking villages are gradually opening up to visitors with the introduction of hostel and trekking facilities.

Nebaj and around → *Colour map 5, B1.*

The town of Nebaj is high in the Cuchumatanes Mountains and its green slopes are often layered with mist. It is coloured by the beautiful dress worn by the local women, in an extravaganza of predominantly green, with red, yellow, orange, white and purple. The *corte* is mainly maroon with vertical stripes of black and yellow; some are bright red, and the *huipil* is of a geometric design. The women also wear a headdress with colourful bushy pom-poms on them. The men hardly ever wear the traditional costume; their jacket is red and embroidered in black designs. The main plaza is dominated by a large, simple white church. At the edge of the plaza there are weaving cooperatives selling *cortes, huípiles* and handicrafts from the town and the surrounding area – bargaining is possible. When you arrive, boys will meet you from incoming buses and will guide you to a *hospedaje* – they expect a tip. Nebaj has Sunday and Thursday markets and a fiesta on

12-15 August with traditional dancing. There is an excellent website for Nebaj, www.nebaj.com, run by **Solidaridad Internacional**, with useful phrases in Ixil and your daily Maya horoscope.

La tumba de la Indígena Maya is a shrine just outside Nebaj (15 minutes) where some of those massacred during the war were buried. Take the same route as to Ak'Tzumbal, but at the bottom of the very steep hill, immediately after the bridge over the river, take a left, walk straight on over a paved road, then you come to a small junction – carry straight on until you see a minor crossroads on a path with an orange house gate to your left. Look up and you will see a small building. This is the shrine. Walk to your right where you will see a steep set of stairs leading to the shrine.

There is a walk to **Ak'Tzumbal**, through fields with rabbits, and through long, thin earth tunnels used by the military and guerrillas during the war. You need a guide to walk this cross-country route. Alternatively you can take the road to Ak'Tzumbal, where the new houses still display signs warning of the danger of land mines. Walk down 15 Avenida de Septiembre away from the church, and take a left just before **El Triangulo** gas station past **El Viajero Hospedaje**, then left and then right down a very steep hill and keep walking (1½ hours). When you reach a small yellow tower just before a fork – take the right (the left goes to Salquil Grande) to reach the 'model village'. Above the village of Ak'Tzumbal is **La Pista**, an airstrip used during the war. Next to it bomb craters scar the landscape. Only a few avocado trees, between the bomb holes, survive, and the *gasolinera* to refuel planes, is still there, although it is now covered in corrugated iron. Ask around for directions.

Chajul and Cotzal

Chajul, the second largest village in the Ixil Triangle, is known for its part in the Civil War, where Rigoberta Menchú's brother was killed in the plaza, as relayed in her book *I, Rigoberta Menchú*. According to the Nobel Peace Prize winner on 9 September 1979, her 16-year-old brother Petrocinio was kidnapped after being turned in for 15 quetzales. He was tortured in the plaza by the army along with numerous others. Villagers were forced to watch the torture under threat of being branded communists. People were set on fire, but the onlookers had weapons and looked ready to fight. This caused the army to withdraw. Chajul's main fiesta is the second Friday in Lent. There is also a pilgrimage to Christ of Golgotha on the second Friday in Lent, beginning the Wednesday before (the image is escorted by 'Romans' in blue police uniforms). Market day is Tuesday and Friday. It is possible to walk from Chajul to Cotzal. It is a six-hour walk from Nebaj to Chajul. A couple of very basic *hospedajes* are in town.

Cotzal is spread over a large area on a number of steep hills. The village's fiesta is 21-24 June, culminating in the day of St John the Baptist (24 June). Market days are Wednesday and Saturday. You can hire bikes from **Maya Tour** on the plaza next to the church. Nebaj to Cotzal is a pleasant four-hour walk. There's no accommodation or restaurants in other small villages and it is difficult to specify what transport is available in this area as trucks and the occasional pickup or commercial van are affected by road and weather conditions. For this reason, be prepared to have to spend the night in villages.

For Sleeping and Eating price codes and other relevant information, see Essentials pages 45-48.

● Sleeping

Chimaltenango and around *p659*

A-B La Posada de Mi Abuelo, Carretera a Yepocapa, Parramos, T7849-5930, www.laposadademiabuelo.com. A delightful inn formerly a coffee farm, good restaurant. Packages with horse riding, biking and meals are available.

E Pixcayá, 0 Av, 1-82, Comalapa, T7849-8260. Hot water, parking.

Sololá *p662*

D Del Viajero, 7 Av, 10-45, on Parque Central (also annexe around the corner on Calle 11) T7762-3683. Rooms with bath, cheaper without, spacious, clean and friendly, good food in restaurant on plaza (El Cafetín).

E El Paisaje, 9 Calle, 5-41, 2 blocks from Parque Central, T7762-3820. Pleasant colonial courtyard, shared baths and toilets, clean, hot water, restaurant, good breakfast, family-run, laundry facilities.

Panajachel *p662, map p663*

LL Atitlán, 1 km west of centre on lake, 2nd turning off the road to Sololá, T7762-1441, www.hotelatitlan.com. Full board available, colonial style, excellent rooms and service, beautiful gardens with views across lake, pool, private beach, top-class restaurant.

L Posada de Don Rodrigo, Final Calle Santander, overlooks the lake, T7762-2326, www.posadadedonrodrigo.com. Pool, sauna, terrace, gardens, good restaurant, excellent food and service, comfortable and luxurious bathrooms, fireplaces.

AL Los Arboles (Apart-Hotel), Av de los Arboles 0-42, lakeside, T7762-0544/48. Fully equipped apartments for 2-3 people, swimming pool, gardens, TV, fireplace, colonial style, parking.

AL Rancho Grande, Calle Rancho Grande, Centro, T7762-1554, www.ranchograndeinn.com. Cottages in charming setting, 4 blocks from beach, popular for long stay, good, including breakfast with pancakes. Pool with café in spacious gardens with good children's play equipment. Staff are helpful. Recommended.

A Cacique Inn, Calle del Embarcadero, Centro, T7762-1205, caciqueinn@hotmail.com. Large, comfortable rooms some with fireplace, credit cards accepted, swimming pool, magnificent house and spacious gardens, English spoken, good food.

A Posada de los Volcanes, Calle Santander, 5-51, Centro, T7762-0244, www.posadadelosvolcanes.com. 12 rooms with bath, hot water, clean, comfortable, quiet, friendly owners, Julio and Jeanette Parajón.

A Visión Azul, on road to Hotel Atitlán, T/F7762-1426. Restaurant, pool, attractive gardens, campground on lakeside US$2 per person, US$4 per tent.

A-B Dos Mundos, Calle Santander 4-72, Centro, T7762-2078, www.hoteldosmundos.com. Pool, cable TV, some rooms surround pool, good Italian restaurant (La Lanterna). Breakfast included.

B Müllers Guest House, Calle Rancho Grande 1-81, Centro, T7762-2442. Comfortable, quiet, good breakfast included. Recommended.

B Playa Linda, on main promenade, T7762-0096, www.hotelplayalinda.com. Nicely decorated large rooms, comfortable, TV, fireplaces, cheaper without lake view, pool and jacuzzi.

B Primavera, Calle Santander, Centro, T7762-2052, www.primaveratitlan.com. Clean, bright rooms, with TV, cypress wood furniture, gorgeous showers, washing machine available, friendly. Recommended. **Chez Alex** next door serves French food but lovely patio setting at the back. Don't get a room overlooking the street at weekends.

B Tzanjuyú, first left on road to Sololá, T7762-1318. Superb position on bluff overlooking lake, In need of renovation but good value, flower gardens, restaurant, pool, romantic spot, quiet, camping possible.

C Montana, Callejón Don Tino, near bell tower in the old town, T7762-2180, www.hotelmontanapanajachel.com. Comfortable, TV, hot water, parking, Wi-Fi, large patio filled with plants.

C Riva Bella, Calle Real, 2-21, Centro, T7762-1348. Bungalows with parking, with bath, good, clean, nice garden. Recommended.

D Hospedaje El Príncipe, Callejón Los Yach, off Calle Rancho Grande (follow signs, worth the walk), T7762-0228. 14 rooms, hot water shower, clean, good budget option, garden.

D Hospedaje El Viajero, final Calle Santander, Centro, T7762-0128, www.sleeprentbuy.com/elviajero. With bath, comfortable large, clean rooms, hot water, friendly, laundry facilities, nice flower garden.

D Hospedaje Ramos I, close to public beach, T7762-0413. Run by Maya family, friendly, safe, loud music from nearby cafés, with bath, hot water, clean, good value, some rooms have TV. View from 2nd floor.

D Hotel Utz Rajil, Calle 14 de Febrero, T7762-0303, gguated@yahoo.com. Neat, tidy hotel off the main street leading down to the lake. Good choice.

D Las Casitas, Calle Real 1-90, old town, T7762-1224. Neat bungalows, breakfast available, with bath, hot shower, gardens, friendly, next to police station and market, buses stop outside but it's quiet at night.

D Mario's Rooms, Calle Santander esq Calle 14 Febrero, Centro, T7762-1313. Cheaper without bath, with garden, clean, bright rooms, hot showers, good breakfast, but not included, popular and friendly.

D Santa Isabel, Calle del Embarcadero 8-86, Centro, T7762-1462. 2 rooms in large house, quiet, hot water, with bath, friendly, nice gardens, parking, also fully equipped bungalow for longer rent. Recommended.

D-E Hospedaje Casa Linda, Callejón El Capulín, Centro, T7762-0386. Hot shower in shared or private bathrooms, garden, friendly, clean and quiet. Good value. Recommended.

D-E Zanahoria Chic, 3 Av 0-46, Av de los Arboles, old town, T7762-1249, www.zanahoriachic.com. Restaurant, rooms above, clean, TV, hot water in shared or private bathrooms, colonial style, friendly, coffee, luggage store.

F Hospedaje Sánchez, Calle El Chali 3-65, Centro, T7762-2224. Clean, friendly, hot shower, family-run, quiet, comfortable. Recommended.

E Hospedaje Tommy, Calle El Chali 3-43, Centro, T7762-0799. Clean shared bathroom, small attractive garden, 6 rooms.

E Hospedaje Villa Lupita, Callejón Don Tino, old town, T5054-2447. Pretty courtyard, hot showers, clean, friendly, parking, good value. Recommended.

Apartments
Ask around for houses to rent; available from US$125 a month for a basic place, to US$200, but almost impossible to find in Nov and Dec. Break-ins and robberies of tourist houses are not uncommon. Water supply is variable.

Apartamentos Bohemia, Callejón Chinimaya, rents furnished bungalows.

Camping
Possible in the grounds of **Hotel Visión Azul** and **Tzanjuyú** – see above for details.

Santa Catarina Palopó *p665*
You can stay in private houses (ask around) or rent rooms (take sleeping bag).

LL Tzam Poc Resort, Via Rural Km 6.5, T7762-2680, www.atitlanresort.com. Resort on the slopes above Santa Catarina with an amazing infinity pool. Lovely villas and spa. There's also a bow and arrow range.

LL-L Casa Palopó, Carretera a San Antonio Palopó, Km 6.8, less than 1 km beyond Santa Catarina, on the left up a steep hill, T5773-7777, www.casapalopo.com. One of the finest hotels in the country, 9 beautiful rooms all richly furnished, flowers on arrival, excellent service, heated pool, spa, gym, top-class restaurant overlooking the lake – reservations necessary.

A Villa Santa Catarina, T7762-1291, www.villasdeguatemala.com. 36 comfortable rooms with balconies around the pool, most with view of the lake. Good restaurant.

B Hotel Terrazas del Lago, T7762-0157, www.hotelterrazasdellago.com. On the lake with view, bath, clean, restaurant, a unique hotel built up over the past 30 plus years.

San Lucas Tolimán p665

A Toliman, Av 6, 1 block from the lake, T7722-0033, www.atitlanhotel.com. 18 rooms and suites in lovely colonial-style washed in terracotta colours with some lovely dark wood furniture. Suite No 1 is very romantic with lit steps to a sunken bath, good but expensive restaurant (reservations), fine gardens, pool, partial lake views. Recommended.

D Casa Cruz Inn, Av 5 4-78, a couple of blocks from the park. Clean, comfortable beds, run by an elderly couple, garden, quiet, good value.

D Hotel y Restaurante Don Pedro, Av 6, on lakeside, T7722-0028. Unattractive building – a sort of clumsy rustic, 12 rooms, a little rough around the edges, restaurant, bar.

D La Cascada de María, Calle 6, 6-80, T7722-0136. With bath, TV, parking, garden, restaurant, good.

Santiago Atitlán p666
Book ahead for Holy Week.

AL-D Posada de Santiago, 1.5 km south of town, T7721-7366, www.posadade santiago.com. Highly recommended relaxing lakeside lodge with comfortable stone cottages (some cheaper accommodation), restaurant with home-grown produce and delicious food, tours and pool. Massage and language classes arranged. Friendly and amusing management – David, Susie and his mum, Bonnie – quite a trio. Has its own dock or walk from town.

A Bambú, on the lakeside, 500 m by road towards San Lucas, T7721-7332,

www.ecobambu.com. 10 rooms, 2 bungalows and 1 *casita* in an attractive setting with beautifully tended gardens, restaurant, a secluded pool, a few mins by *lancha* from the dock. Kayaks available.

D-E Chi-Nim-Ya, walk up from the dock, take the first left and walk 50 m and it's there on the left, T7721-7131. Good, clean, comfortable and friendly, cheaper without bath, good value, good café, cheap, large helpings.

E Tzutuhil, on left up the road from the dock to centre, above Ferretería La Esquina, T7721-7174. With bath and TV, cheaper without, restaurant, great views, good.

Camping
Camping is possible near **Bambú**.

San Pedro La Laguna p666, map p667
Accommodation is mostly cheap and laid-back; your own sleeping bag, etc, will be useful.

D Hotelito El Amanacer Sak' Cari, T7721-8096, www.hotelsakcari.com. With bath, hot water, lovely rooms with great garden – get those with fabulous lake views. Extremely good value. Recommended.

D Mansión del Lago, T7721-8041, www.hotelmansiondellago.com. Up a hill with good views, with bath, hot water, TV costs more, very good value.

E Hospedaje Casa Elena, along the path behind **Nick's Place**. With large bathrooms or shared bath (some are nicer than others), clean, excellent views of lake. Recommended.

E Hotel San Francisco. Rooms with lake view, garden, cooking facilities, cold water, helpful owner, washing facilities, cheaper without bath, good value. Tours offered.

E Pinocchio. Rooms with private bath, nice garden and use of kitchen. Hammocks available.

E Ti-Kaaj, uphill from Santiago dock, 1st right. Simple rooms, hammock space, popular with backpackers, lovely garden and small pool; basic, but worth it for pool.

E Villa Sol, T2334-0327. With bath, cheaper shared, but the rooms aren't

as nice. The newer part is a lot nicer.
There are 2 bungalows with kitchen facilities,
friendly staff, nice rooms. Recommended.
F Hospedaje Buenas Nuevas.
Small, friendly, with hot shower.

San Juan La Laguna *p668*
AL-A Hotel Uxlabil, T5990-6016/2366-9555
(in Guatemala City), www.uxlabil.com. This is
an eco-hotel set up on the hill with its own
dock, a short walk from the town centre.
It's run by very friendly people with a small
restaurant. It is a perfect, relaxing getaway,
with Maya sauna and tended gardens, in this
most unassuming and interesting of towns.
It has links with the ecotourism association
in town. Recommended.

San Marcos La Laguna *p668*
AL-B Aaculaax, Las Pirámides dock, on a
path from the **Centro Holístico**, T5287-0521,
www.aaculaax.com. A Hansel-and-Gretel
affair on the lake shore. It is a blend of cave
work with Gaudí-type influence from the
stained-glass work down to the sculptures
and lamp shades. A corner of artistic Nirvana
on Lake Atitlán – this place is highly
recommended. Each of the 7 rooms with
private bathroom is different, with quirky
decor. It is run on an eco-basis, compost
toilets and all. It is run by a German, Niels.
There is a restaurant, bar, bakery and massage
room. Also glass and papier mâché workshops.
A-D Posada Schumann, 2nd dock,
T5202-2216, www.posadaschumann.com.
With waterfront and dock, bungalows in
attractive gardens, some with kitchenettes,
sauna, restaurant, comfortable.
B-D Hotel Jinava, 2nd dock, left at the top
of first pathway, T5299-3311, www.hotel
jinava.com. This is heaven on a hill. With
fabulous views, it clings to a steep slope
with lovely rooms, restaurants, terraces
and a patio. Books and games and solitude
if you want it. Close to the lakeshore with
its own dock where launches will drop you.
Only 5 rooms, breakfast included.
German-owned. Recommended.

D La Paz, 2nd dock, first pathway, T5702-
9168. Bungalows and 1 dorm (**F** per person),
vegetarian restaurant, quiet with nice
communal area, popular.
D Las Pirámides del Ka, Las Pirámides dock,
www.laspiramidesdelka.com, a residential,
meditation centre. See also page 616.
E Unicornio, Las Pirámides dock, 2nd
pathway. With self-catering, bungalows,
shared kitchen and bathrooms. Has a
little post office.
F Quetzal, Las Pirámides dock, 2nd pathway,
T5306-5039. Price per person. 4 bunk rooms,
shared bath, restaurant.

San Marcos to Santa Cruz *p668*
AL Lomas de Tzununá, Tzununá,
T7820-4060, www.lomasdetzununa.com.
This hotel enjoys a spectacular position
high up above the lake. The views from
the restaurant terrace are magnificent. The
10 spacious rooms, decorated with local
textiles, have 2 beds each with lake views and
a balcony. The hotel, run by a friendly Belgian
family, offers walking, biking, kayaking and
cultural tours. The restaurant (¶¶-¶) uses
home-made ingredients, the hotel is run
on solar energy and the pool does not use
chlorine. Board games, internet, bar and giant
chess available. The family are reforesting
a hill. Breakfast and taxes included.
A-B La Casa del Mundo, Jaibalito,
T5218-5332, www.lacasadelmundo.com.
Enjoys one of the most spectacular positions
on the entire lake. Room No 15 has the best
view followed by room No 1. Cheaper rooms
have shared bathrooms. Many facilities,
standard family-style dinner, lakeside hot
tub, a memorable place with fantastic
views. Repeatedly recommended.

Santa Cruz La Laguna *p669*
L-A Villa Sumaya, Paxanax, beyond the
dock, about 15 mins' walk, T5810-7199,
www.villasumaya.com. Including breakfast,
with its own dock, sauna, massage and healing
therapies, yoga, comfortable, peaceful.

A-C La Casa Rosa, to the right as you face the dock from the water, along a path, T5416-1251, www.atitlanlacasarosa.com. Bungalows and rooms, with bath, cheaper without, home-made meals, attractive garden, sauna. Candlelit dinners at weekends.
B-D Arca de Noé, to the left of the dock, T5515-3712. Bungalows, cheaper rooms with shared bathrooms, good restaurant, BBQ, lake activities arranged, nice atmosphere, veranda overlooking a really beautiful flower-filled gardens and the lake. Low-voltage solar power.
B-E La Iguana Perdida, opposite dock, T5706-4117, www.laiguanaperdida.com. Rooms with and without bathroom and dorm (**F** per person) with shared bath, lively, especially weekends, delicious vegetarian food, BBQ, popular, friendly, great atmosphere. ATI Divers centre (see page 682), water-skiing; kayaks and snorkelling. Bring a torch.

Chichicastenango *p669, map p670*
You won't find accommodation easily on Sat evening, when prices are increased. As soon as you get off the bus, boys will swamp you and insist on taking you to certain hotels.
L Santo Tomás, 7 Av, 5-32, T7756-1061. A very attractive building with beautiful colonial furnishings. It is often full at weekends, pool, sauna, good restaurant and bar. Buffet lunch (US$14) on market days in stylish dining room, with attendants in traditional dress.
AL Mayan Inn, corner of 8 Calle, 1-91, T7756-1176, www.mayaninn.com.gt. A classic, colonial-style courtyard hotel, filled with plants, polished antique furniture, beautiful dining room and bar with fireplaces. Gas-heated showers and internet The staff are very friendly and wear traditional dress. Secure parking.
B-C Maya Lodge, 6 Calle, 4-08, T7756-1167. 9 rooms with bath, courtyard, right on the corner of the plaza, quaint dining room, breakfast available.
B-C Posada El Arco, 4 Calle, 4-36, T7756-1255. Clean, very pretty, small, friendly,

garden, washing facilities, negotiate lower rates for stays longer than a night, some large rooms, good view, parking, English spoken.
C Chalet House, 3 Calle, 7-44, T7756-1360, www.chalethotelguatemala.com. A clean, guesthouse with family atmosphere, hot water. Don't be put off by the dingy street.
C Chugüilá, 5 Av, 5-24, T7756-1134, hotelchuguila@yahoo.com. Some rooms with fireplaces. Avoid the front rooms, which are noisy, restaurant.
D Tuttos, 12 Calle, near *Posada Belén*, T7756-7540. Reasonable rooms.
D Pensión Girón, Edif Girón on 6 Calle, 4-52, T7756-1156. Clean rooms with bath, cheaper without, hot water, parking, 17 rooms.
E Posada Belén, 12 Calle, 5-55, T7756-1244. With bath, cheaper without, hot water, clean, will do laundry, fine views from balconies and hummingbirds in attractive garden, good value. Recommended.
E Salvador, 10 Calle, 4-47. 55 large rooms with bath, a few with fireplace (wood for sale in market), good views over town, parking. Cheaper, smaller rooms without bath available.

Santa Cruz del Quiché and around *p671*
Several very basic options around the bus arrival/departure area.
C Rey K'iché, 8 Calle, 0-9, 2 blocks from bus terminal. Clean, comfortable, hot water, parking, restaurant, TV.
D Maya Quiché, 3 Av 4-19, T7755-1667. With bath, hot water, restaurant.
D-E San Pascual, 7 Calle, 0-43, good location two blocks south of the central plaza, T5555-1107. With bath, cheaper without, quiet, locked parking.
F La Cascada, 10 Av, 10 Calle. Friendly, clean.

The road east to Cobán *p672*
There are a couple of *hospedajes* in Uspantán.
E Galindo, 4 blocks east of the Parque Central. Clean, friendly, recommended.

The Ixil Triangle *p672*

F Solidaridad Internacional supports 6 hostels in the villages of Xexocom, Chortiz, Xeo, Cocop, Cotzol and Parramos Grande where there is room for 5 people. Contact them at the PRODONT-IXIL office, Av 15 de Septiembre (www.nebaj.org).

Nebaj and around *p672*

C-E Hotel Turansa, 1 block from plaza down 5 Calle, T7775-8219. Tiny rooms, but very clean, soap, towels, 2nd-floor rooms are nicer, TV and parking, little shop in entrance, phone service.

D-E Hotel Mayan Ixil, on north side of main square, T7755-8168. Just 5 rooms with private bath and gas hot water. Small restaurant overlooking the plaza, internet service downstairs.

D-E Ilebal Tenam, bottom of Av 15 de Septiembre, road to Chajul, T7755-8039. Hot water, shared and private bath, very clean, friendly, parking inside, attractive decor.

E Hospedaje Esperanza, 6 Av, 2-36. Very friendly, clean, hot showers in shared bathroom, noisy when evangelical churches nearby have activities, hotel is cleaner than it looks from the outside.

F Hostal Ixil Don Juan, 0 Av A, 1 Calle B, Canton Simocol. Take Av 15 de Septiembre and take a left at Comedor Sarita, opposite grey office of PRODONT-IXIL, then it's 100 m to the right, on the right, T7755-4014/1529. Part of Programa Quiché, run with the support of the EU, there are 6 beds in 2 rooms, each bed with a locked strongbox, and hot showers. The colonial building has a traditional sauna, *chuj*.

F Media Luna MediaSol, T5749-7450, www.nebaj.com/hostel.htm. A backpackers' hostel close to El Descanso restaurant with dorms and private rooms. The hostel's also got a little kitchenette, DVD player and Wi-Fi.

Cotzal *p673*

F Cafetería and Hospedaje Christian, alongside the church. Basic.

F Hostal Doña Teresa. Has a sauna, patio and honey products for sale.

❶ Eating

Panajachel *p662, map p663*

♦♦♦ Chez Alex, Calle Santander, centre, T7762-0172. Open 1200-1500 and 1800-2000. French menu, good quality, mainly tourists, credit cards accepted.

♦♦♦ Tocoyal, annexe to Hotel del Lago. A/c, groups welcome, buffet on request but tourist prices.

♦♦ Circus Bar, Av Los Arboles 0-62, T7762-2056. Open 1200-2400. Italian dishes including good pizzas, good coffee, popular. Live music from 2030, excellent atmosphere. Recommended.

♦♦ Crossroads Café, Calle de Campanario 0-27. Tue-Sat 0900-1300, 1500-1900. Global choice of quality coffee, but you can´t go wrong with Guatemalan! Excellent cakes.

♦♦ El Patio, Calle Santander. Good food, very good large breakfasts, quiet atmosphere but perfect for people-watching from the garden. Try the amaretto coffee.

♦♦ Guajimbo's, Calle Santander. Good atmosphere, excellent steaks, fast service, popular, live music some evenings. Recommended.

♦♦ La Rosticería, Av Los Arboles 0-42, T7762-2063. Daily 0700-2300. Good food, try eggs 'McChisme' for breakfast, good fresh pasta, excellent banana cake, good atmosphere, popular, a bit pricey. Live piano music at weekends, friendly service.

♦♦ Los Pumpos, Calle del Lago. Varied menu, bar, good fish and seafood dishes.

♦♦ Pana Rock Café with Pana Arte upstairs, Calle Santander 3-72. Buzzing around happy hour (2 for 1), salsa music, very popular, international food, pizza.

♦♦ Sunset Café, superb location on the lake. Open 1100-2400. Excellent for drinks, light meals and main dishes, live music evenings, but you pay for the view.

¶-¶ Bombay, Calle Santander near Calle 15 Febrero, T7762-0611. Open 1100-2130. Vegetarian recipes, German beer, Mexican food, good food and wines, set lunch popular, good service. Very highly recommended.

¶-¶ El Pájaro Azul, Calle Santander 2-75, T7762-2596. Café, bar, crêperie with gorgeous stuffed sweet or savoury crêpes, cakes and pies. Vegetarian options available. Reasonable prices, good for late breakfasts, occasional slow service. 1000-2200. Recommended.

¶ Deli Llama de Fuego, Calle Santander, T7762-2586. Thu-Tue 0700-2200. Sweet little café with a giant cheese plant as its focus. Breakfasts, muffins, bagels, pizzas, pasta, Mexican food and vegetarian sandwiches.

¶ Restaurante Las Olas, overlooking the lake at the end of Calle Santander, down by the dock. Serves the absolute best nachos, great for just before catching the boat.

Bakeries

Pana Pan, Calle Santander 1-61. Excellent wholemeal breads and pastries, banana bread comes out of the oven at 0930, wonderful, cinnamon rolls and internet too. Recommended.

San Lucas Tolimán *p665*

¶ La Pizza de Sam, Av 7, 1 block down from the plaza towards the lake. Pizzas and spaghetti.

¶ Restaurant Jardín, orange building on corner of plaza. *Comida típica* and *licuados*.

Santiago Atitlán *p666*

There are many cheap *comedores* near the centre. The best restaurants are at the hotels.

¶¶¶ El Pescador, on corner 1 block before Tzutuhil. Full menu, good but expensive.

¶¶¶ Posada de Santiago, 1.5 km south of town, T/F7721-7167. Delicious, wholesome food and excellent service in lovely surroundings. Highly recommended.

¶ Restaurant Wach'alal, close to Gran Sol. Daily 0800-2000. A small yellow-painted café serving breakfasts, snacks and cakes. Airy and pleasant.

San Pedro La Laguna *p666, map p667*

Be careful of drinking water in San Pedro; both cholera and dysentery exist here.

¶-¶ Café Arte Libre, up the hill from Hotel San Pedro. All meals, vegetarian dishes, good value.

¶-¶ Luna Azul, along shore. Popular for breakfast and lunch, good omelettes.

¶-¶ Restaurant Maritza, with commanding views over lake. Chilled place to hang out with reggae music. Service is slow though. 5 rooms also to rent with shared bath. (**F**).

¶-¶ Tin Tin. Good value, Thai food, delightful garden. Recommended.

¶ Buddha Bar. Shows movies every night and has a rooftop and sports bar.

¶ Café La Puerta, on the north shore coastal path. Open daily 0800-1700. Cheap, tasty dishes, with tables in a quirky garden, or looking out over the lake. Beautiful.

¶ Comedor Sta Elena, near Nick's Italian. Seriously cheap and filling breakfasts.

¶ El Fondeadero. Good food, lovely terraced gardens, reasonable prices.

¶ Emperador, up the hill. *Comedor* serving good local dishes.

¶ Fata Morgana, near the Panajachel dock, great foccacia bread sandwiches, with pizza and fine coffee too.

¶ Rosalinda, near centre of village. Friendly, breakfasts (eg *mosh*), local fish and good for banana and chocolate cakes.

¶ Shanti Shanti. Run by Israelis, Italian dishes.

¶ Thermal Baths, along shore from *playa*. Good vegetarian food and coffee, expensive.

¶ Zoola. Open 0900-2100. Close to the north shore, a quiet, hideaway with pleasant garden. A great spot.

San Marcos La Laguna *p668*
All hotels and hostels offer food.
†††-† Il Giardino, up the 2nd pathway.
Attractive garden, Italian owners,
good breakfasts.

Chichicastenango *p669, map p670*
The best food is in the top hotels, but is
expensive. On market days there are plenty
of good food stalls and *comedores* in the
centre of the plaza that offer chicken in
different guises or a set lunch for US$1.50.
There are several good restaurants in the
Centro Comercial Santo Tomás on the
north side of the plaza (market).
††† La Fonda de Tzijolaj, on the plaza.
Great view of the market below, good meals,
pizza, prompt service, reasonable prices.
††† Las Brasas Steak House, 6 Calle 4-52,
T7756-2226. Nice atmosphere, good steak
menu, accepts credit cards.
†††-† La Villa de los Cofrades, on the plaza.
Café downstairs, breakfasts, cappuccinos,
espressos, good value. There is a 2nd
restaurant up the street and upstairs,
more expensive, great people-watching
location and an escape during market
days, popular for breakfast.
†††-† Tziguan Tinamit, on the corner of 5 Av,
esq 6 Calle. Some local dishes, steaks, tasty
pizzas, breakfasts, good pies but a little
more expensive than most places, good.
† Caffé Tuttos, 12 Calle, near Posada Belén.
Daily 0700-2200. Good breakfast deals, pizzas,
and *menú del día*, reasonable prices.
† La Parrillada, 6 C 5-37, Interior Comercial
Turkaj. Escape the market bustle, courtyard,
reasonable prices, breakfast available.
† Tu Café, 5 Av 6-44, on market place, Santo
Tomás side. Open 0730-2000. Snacks, budget
breakfast, sandwiches, set lunch, good value.

Santa Cruz del Quiché
and around *p671*
Try *sincronizadas*, hot tortillas baked with
cubed ham, spiced chicken and cheese.
† La Cabañita Café, 1 Av, 1-17. Charming,
small café with pinewood furniture,
home-made pies and cakes, excellent
breakfasts (pancakes, cereals, etc), eggs
any way you want 'em, great snacks, for
example *sincronizadas*.
† La Toscan, 1 Av just north of the church,
same road as **La Cabañita**. A little pizza and
pastelería with checked cloth covered tables.
Lasagne lunch a bargain with garlic bread
and pizza by the slice also.

Nebaj and around *p672*
Boxboles are squash leaves rolled tightly with
masa and chopped meat or chicken, boiled
and served with salsa and fresh orange juice.
† El Descanso. Popular volunteer hang-out,
good food and useful information about
their other community-based projects
(see www.nebaj.com).
† Maya Inca, on the plaza. Substantial food,
run by Peruvians hence the name.
† Pizza del César. Daily 0730-2100. Breakfasts,
mouth-wateringly good strawberry cake.

Cotzal *p673*
† Comedor and Hospedaje El Maguey.
Bland meal, but decent size, plus drink, are
served up for for US$1.70. Don't stay here
though, unless you're desperate.

🎭 Entertainment

Panajachel *p662, map p663*
Circus Bar, Av los Arboles. Open daily
1200-0200. Good live music from 2030.
Discoteca Chapiteau, Av los Arboles
0-69, nightclub Thu-Sat 1900-0100.
El Aleph, Av los Arboles. One of a number
of bars, Thu-Sat 1900-0300.

San Pedro La Laguna *p666, map p667*
Nick's Place, overlooking the main dock, is
popular, and well frequented in the evening.
Nearby are **Bar Alegre**, a sports bar
(www.thealegrepub.com) and **D'noz**.
Ti Kaaj is another popular spot.

O Shopping

Panajachel *p662, map p663*
Bartering is the norm. There are better bargains here than in Chichicastenango. The main tourist shops are on Calle Santander.
Tinamit Maya Shopping Centre, part way down Calle Santander, with many stalls for typical items, bargain for good prices. Maya sell their wares cheaply on the lakeside; varied selection, bargaining is easy/expected.
Librería del Lago, Calle Santander Local A-8, T7762-2788. Open 0900-1800 daily. Great bookshop selling a good range of quality English-language and Spanish books.

Chichicastenango *p669, map p670*
Chichicastenango's markets are on Sun and Thu. See page 671.

⊛ Festivals and events

Chichicastenango *p669, map p670*
1 Jan Padre Eterno.
20 Jan San Sebastián.
19 Mar San José.
Feb/Apr Jesús Nazareno and María de Dolores (both Fri in Lent).
Mar/Apr Semana Santa (Holy Week).
29 Apr San Pedro Mártir.
3 May Santa Cruz.
29 Jun Corpus Christi.
18 Aug Virgen de la Coronación.
14 Sep Santa Cruz.
29 Sep San Miguel.
30 Sep San Jerónimo Doctor.
1st Sun of Oct Virgen del Rosario.
2nd Sun in Oct Virgen de Concepción.
1 Nov San Miguel.
13-22 Dec Santo Tomás, with 21 Dec being the main day. There are processions, traditional dances, the *Palo Volador* (19, 20, 21 Dec) marimba music, well worth a visit – very crowded.

▲▲ Activities and tours

Panajachel *p662, map p663*
Diving
ATI Divers, round the back of El Patio, Calle Santander, T5706-4117, www.laiguana perdida.com. A range of options including PADI Open Water US$220, fun dive US$30, 2 for US$50. PADI Rescue and Dive Master also available. Altitude speciality, US$80. Dives are made off Santa Cruz La Laguna and are of special interest to those looking for altitude diving. Here there are spectacular walls that drop off, rock formations you can swim through, trees underwater, and because of its volcanic nature, hot spots, which leaves the lake bottom sediment boiling to touch. Take advice on visibility before you opt for a dive.

Fishing
Lake fishing can be arranged, black bass (*mojarra*) up to 4 kg can be caught. Boats for up to 5 people can be hired for about US$15. Check with INGUAT for latest information.

Hang-gliding
Rogelio, contactable through **Americo's Tours**, Calle Santander, and other agencies will make arrangements, at least 24 hrs' notice is required. Jumps are made from San Jorge La Laguna or from above Santa Catarina, depending on weather conditions.

Kayaking and canoing
Kayak hire is around US$2 per hr. Ask at the hotels, INGUAT and at lakeshore. **Diversiones Acuáticos Balán**, in a small red and white tower on the lakeshore, rent out kayaks. Watch out for strong winds that occasionally blow up quickly across the lake; potentially dangerous in small boats.

Tour operators
All offer shuttle services to Chichicastenango, Antigua, the Mexican borders, etc, and some to San Cristóbal de las Casas (see Transport) and can arrange most activities on and around the lake. There are a number of tour

operators on Calle Santander, including those listed below. **Americo's Tours**, T7762-2021. **Centroamericana Tourist Service**, T7832-5032. **Tierra Maya**, T7725-7320. Friendly and reliable tour operator, which runs shuttles to San Cristóbal de las Casas as well as within Guatemala. **Toliman Travel**, T7762-1275. Also **Atitrans** on Edif Rincón Sai, T7762-2336, www.atitrans.com.

Waterskiing
Arrangements can be made with **ATI Divers** at **Iguana Perdida** in Santa Cruz.

Santiago Atitlán *p666*
Aventura en Atitlán, Jim and Nancy Matison, Finca San Santiago, T7811-5516. 10 km outside Santiago. Riding and hiking tours.
Francisco Tizná from the Asociación de Guías de Turismo, T7721-7558, is extremely informative. Ask for him at the dock or at any of the hotels. Payment is by way of donation.

San Pedro La Laguna *p666, map p667*
A growing list of activities from hiking up the Nariz de Maya (5 hrs, US$13) and other local trips, through to local crafts. Yoga for all levels is available down towards the shore (US$5 for 1½ hrs).
Bigfoot, 0800-1900. Run by the super-helpful Juan Baudilio Chipirs, T7721-8203. Also close to the small streets away from the docks.

San Juan La Laguna *p668*
Rupalaj Kistalin, T5964-0040, rupalajkistalin@ yahoo.es, offers interesting cultural tours of the town visiting painters, weavers, *cofradias* and traditional healers. As well as this cultural circuit there is an adventure circuit taking in Panan forest and a canopy tour at Park Chuiraxamolo' or a nature circuit taking in a climb up the Rostro de Maya and fishing and kayaking. Highly recommended. Some of the local guides speak English.

San Marcos La Laguna *p668*
Wellbeing
Casa Azul Eco Resort, T5070-7101, www.casa-azul-ecoresort.com, is a gorgeous little place offering yoga and reiki, among other therapies and writers' workshops hosted by Joyce Maynard There's also a sauna, campfire and café/restaurant serving vegetarian food. You can reach it from the first dock, or from the centre of the village.
Las Pirámides del Ka, www.laspiramides delka.com. The month-long course costs US$420, or US$15 by the day if you stay for shorter periods, accommodation included. Courses are also available for non-residents. In the grounds are a sauna, a vegetarian restaurant with freshly baked bread and a library. This is a relaxing, peaceful place.
San Marcos Holistic Centre, up the 2nd pathway, beyond **Unicornio**, www.sanm holisticcentre.com. Mon-Sat 1000-1700. Offers iridology, acupuncture, kinesiology, Indian head massage, reflexology and massage. Classes in various techniques can also be taken.

Chichicastenango *p669, map p670*
Maya Chichi Van, 6 Av, 6-45, T7756-2187, mayachichivan@yahoo.com. Shuttles and tours ranging from US$10-650.

Nebaj and around *p672*
Guías Ixiles (El Descanso Restaurant), www.nebaj.com ½- to 3-day hikes, bike rental. There's also a 3-day hike to Todos Santos.
Solidaridad Internacional, Av 15 de Septiembre, www.nebaj.org. Inside the PRODONT-IXIL (Proyecto de Promoción de Infraestructuras y Ecoturismo) office, in a grey building on the right 1 block after the **Gasolinera El Triángulo** on the road to Chajul. For further information call in to see the director Pascual, who is very helpful. 2-, 3- and 4-day hikes, horses available. Options to stay in community *posadas*.

Chajul and Cotzal p673

Ask Teresa at Hostal Doña Teresa about trips from the Cotzal or ask for Sebastián Xel Rivera who leads 1-day camping trips.

🚌 Transport

Chimaltenango p659
Bus

Any bus heading west from Guatemala City stops at Chimaltenango. To **Antigua** leave from the corner of the main road and the road south to Antigua where there is a lime green and blue shop – Auto Repuestos y Frenos Nachma, 45 mins, US$0.34. To **Chichicastenango**, every 30 mins, 0600-1700, 2 hrs, US$2. To **Cuatro Caminos**, 2½ hrs, US$2.50. To **Quetzaltenango**, every 45 mins, 0700-1800, 2½ hrs, US$2.80. To **Tecpán** every 30 mins, 0700-1800, 1 hr.

Routes west: Tecpán and Los Encuentros p659
Bus

From Tecpán to **Guatemala City**, 2¼ hrs, buses every hr, US$2.20; easy day trip from Panajachel or Antigua.

To Lake Atitlán along the old Pan-American Highway p661
Bus

To and from **Godínez** there are several buses to Panajachel, US$0.45 and 1 bus daily Patzún-Godínez. To **San Andrés Semetabaj**, bus to Panajachel, US$0.40.

Sololá p662
Bus

To **Chichicastenango**, US$0.50, 1½ hrs; to **Panajachel**, US$0.38, every 30 mins, 20 mins, or 1½-2 hrs' walk. To **Chimaltenango**, US$1.20. To **Quetzaltenango**, US$1.8. *Colectivo* to **Los Encuentros**, US$0.20. To **Guatemala City** direct US$2.50, 3 hrs.

Panajachel p662, map p663
Boat

There are 2 types of transport – the scheduled ferry service to Santiago Atitlán and the *lanchas* to all the other villages. The tourist office has the latest information on boats. The boat service to **Santiago Atitlán** runs from the dock at the end of Calle Rancho Grande (Muelle Público) from 0600-1630, 8 daily, 20 mins in launch, US$3.10, 1 hr in the large **Naviera Santiago** ferry, T7762-0309 or 20-35 mins in the fast *lanchas*. Some *lanchas* to all the other villages leave from here, but most from the dock at the end of Calle Embarcadero run by *Tzanjuyú* from 0630-1700 every 45 mins or when full (min 10 people). If you set off from the main dock the *lancha* will pull in at the Calle Embarcadero dock as well. These *lanchas* call in at **Santa Cruz, Jaibalito, Tzununá, San Marcos, San Pablo, San Juan** and **San Pedro**, US$1.20 to US$2.50 to **San Marcos** and beyond. To **San Pedro** US$3.10. The first boat of the day is at 0700. If there is a demand, there will almost always be a boatman willing to run a service but non-official boats can charge what they like. Virtually all the dozen or so communities round the lake have docks, and you can take a regular boat to any of those round the western side. Note that, officially, locals pay less. The only reliable services back to Panajachel are from **Santiago** or **San Pedro** up to about 1600. If you wait on the smaller docks round the western side up to this time, you can get a ride back to Panajachel, flag them down in case they don't see you, but they usually pull in if it's the last service of the day. Only buy tickets on the boat – if you buy them from the numerous ticket touts on the dockside, you will be overcharged. There are no regular boats to Santa Catarina, San Antonio or San Lucas: pickups and buses serve these communities, or charter a *lancha*, US$30 return to Santa Catarina and San Antonio. Bad weather can, of course, affect the boat services. Crossings are generally rougher in the afternoons, worth bearing in mind if you suffer from sea-sickness.

Boat hire and tours *Lanchas* can be hired to go anywhere round the lake, about US$100 for 5 people for a full day. For round trips to **San Pedro** and **Santiago** and possibly **San Antonio Palopó**, with stopovers, go early to the lakefront and bargain. Trip takes a full day, eg 0830-1530, with stops of 1 hr or so at each, around US$6-7, if the boat is full. If on a tour, be careful not to miss the boat at each stage – if you do, you will have to pay again.

Bus
Rebuli buses leave from opposite Hotel Fonda del Sol on Calle Real, otherwise, the main stop is where Calle Santander meets Calle Real. Rebuli to **Guatemala City**, 3½ hrs, US$3.30, crowded, hourly between 0500 and 1500. To **Guatemala City** via **Escuintla** south coast, 8 a day plus 3 **Pullman** a day. Direct bus to **Quetzaltenango**, 7 a day between 0530 and 1415, US$2.70, 2½ hrs. There are direct buses to **Los Encuentros** on the Pan-American Hw (US$0.75). To **Chichicastenango** direct, Thu and Sun, 0645, 0700, 0730 and then hourly to 1530. Other days between 0700-1500, US$2, 1½ hrs. There are 4 daily direct buses to **Cuatro Caminos**, US$1.60 from 0530, for connections to Totonicapán, Quetzaltenango, Huehuetenango, etc. To **Antigua** take a bus up to Los Encuentros through Sololá. Change for a bus to **Chimaltenango** US$3.10, and change there for Antigua. There is also a direct bus (Rebuli) to **Antigua** leaving 1030-1100, daily, US$4.40. To **Sololá**, US$0.40, 20 mins, every 30 mins. You can wait for through buses by the market on Calle Real. The fastest way to southern **Mexico** is probably by bus south to Cocales, 2½ hrs, 5 buses between 0600 and 1400, then many buses along the Pacific Hwy to **Tapachula** on the border. For **La Mesilla**, take a bus up to Los Encuentros, change west for Cuatro Caminos. Here catch a bus north to La Mesilla. Some travel agencies go direct to

San Cristóbal de las Casas via La Mesilla, daily at 0600. See Tour operators, above.

Shuttles Services are run jointly by travel agencies, to **Guatemala City**, **Antigua, Quetzaltenango, Chichi** and more. Around 4 a day. **Antigua**, US$14, **Chichicastenango**, on market days, US$15, **Quetzaltenango** US$20 and the Mexican border US$40.

Bicycle
Several rental agencies on Calle Santander, eg **Maco Cycle Rental** and **Tono Cycle Rental**. Also **Alquiler de Bicicletas Emanuel**, on Calle 14 de Febrero. The cost is upwards of US$2 up per hr or about US$10 for a day.

Motorcycle
Motorcycle hire About US$6 per hr, plus fuel and US$100 deposit. Try **Maco Cycle** near the junction of Calle Santander and 14 de Febrero, T7762-0883.

Motorcycle parts **David's Store**, opposite Hotel Maya Kanek, has good prices and also does repairs.

Santa Catarina Palopó *p665*
There are frequent pickups from Panajachel and boat services.

San Antonio Palopó *p665*
Frequent pickups from Panajachel. Enquire about boats.

San Lucas Tolimán *p665*
Boat Enquire about boats. Private *lancha*, US$35.
Bus To **Santiago Atitlán**, hourly and to **Guatemala City** via **Panajachel**.

Santiago Atitlán *p666*
Bus To **Guatemala City**, US$2.60 (5 a day, first at 0300). 2 **Pullmans** a day, US$3.40. To **Panajachel**, 0600, 2 hrs, or take any bus and change on main road south of San Lucas.

Boat 4 sailings daily to Pana with *Naviera*, 1¼ hrs, US$1.80, or by *lancha* when full,

20-35 mins, US$1.30-2. To **San Pedro** by *lancha* several a day, enquire at the dock for times, 45 mins, US$1.80.

San Pedro La Laguna *p666, map p667*
Boat
Up to 10 *lanchas* to **Panajachel**. To **Santiago**, leave when full (45 mins, US$2.50). To **San Marcos**, every 2 hrs. Private *lanchas* (10 people at US$2 each).

Bus
There are daily buses to **Guatemala City**, several leave in the early morning and early afternoon, 4 hrs, US$4.50, to **Antigua** and to **Quetzaltenango**, in the morning, 3½ hrs, US$3.

San Marcos La Laguna *p668*
Boat Service roughly every ½ hr to **Panajachel** and to **San Pedro**. Wait on any dock. Fare US$1.80 to either.
Bus San Pedro to Pan-American Hwy can be boarded at San Pablo. **Pickup** Frequent pickups from the village centre and anywhere along the main road. To **San Pedro**, US$0.50, less to villages en route.

Chichicastenango *p669, map p670*
Bus
Buses passing through Chichi all stop at 5 Av/5 Calle by the **Hotel Chugüilá**, where there are always police and bus personnel to give information. To **Guatemala City**, every 15 mins 0200-1730, 3 hrs, US$3.70. To **Santa Cruz del Quiché**, every ½ hr 0600-2000, US$0.70, 30 mins or 20 mins, if the bus driver is aiming for honours in the graduation from the School of Kamikaze Bus Tactics. To **Panajachel**, ½ hr, US$2, several until early afternoon or take any bus heading south and change at Los Encuentros. Same goes for **Antigua**, where you need to change at Chimaltenango. To **Quetzaltenango**, 5 between 0430-0830, 2½ hrs, US$3.80. To **Mexico**, and all points west, take any bus to Los Encuentros and change. To **Escuintla** via Santa Lucía Cotzumalguapa, between

0300 and 1700, 3 hrs, US$2.80. There are additional buses to local villages especially on market days.

Shuttle Chichi **Turkaj Tours**, see Tour operators, above. Shuttles to the capital, **Xela**, **Panajachel**, **Huehuetenango** and Mexican border. **Maya Chichi Van**, see Tour operators, above.

Santa Cruz del Quiché and around *p671*
Bus
Terminal at 10 Calle y 1 Av, Zona 5. To **Guatemala City**, passing through Chichicastenango, at 0300 until 1700, 3 hrs, US$4.50. To **Nebaj** and **Cotzal**, 8 a day, US$3.20, 2 hrs. Buses leave, passing through Sacapulas (1 hr, US$2.50), roughly every hour from 0800-2100. To **Uspantán**, via **Sacapulas**, for **Cobán** and **San Pedro Carchá** every hours, 2 hrs, US$3.90. To **Joyabaj**, several daily, via Chiché and Zacualpa, US$1.80, 1½ hrs. First at 0800 with buses going on to the capital. Last bus back to Quiché at 1600. It is possible to get to **Huehuetenango** in a day via Sacapulas, then pickup from bridge to **Aguacatán** and bus from there to Huehuetenango. Last bus to Huehue from Aguacatán, 1600. Daily buses also to **Quetzaltenango**, **San Marcos**, and to **Panajachel**. To **Joyabaj**, Joyita bus from **Guatemala City**, 10 a day between 0200 and 1600, 5 hrs, US$1.80. There are buses from **Quiché** to **San Andrés Sajcabaja**.

The road east to Cobán *p672*
Bus and truck
Several trucks to Cobán, daily in the morning from **Sacapulas**; 7 hrs if you're lucky, usually much longer. Start very early if you wish to make it to Cobán the same day. **Transportes Mejía** from Aguacatán to **Cobán** stops in Sacapulas on Tue and Sat mornings. Also possible to take Quiché–Uspantán buses (0930, 1300, 1500), passing Sacapulas at about 1030, 1400, 1600. Then take the early morning buses at 0300 and 0500 from Uspantán to Cobán or the **Transportes**

Mejía buses. After that, pickups leave when full. Hitchhiking to Cobán is also possible. Buses to Quiche 0300, 2200, other early-morning departures.

Nebaj and around p672
Bus
The bus ride to Quiché is full of fabulous views and hair-raising bends but the road is now fully paved. Buses to **Quiché** (US$3.20, 2½ hrs) passing through **Sacapulas** (1¾ hr from Nebaj, US$1.30) leave hourly from 0500-1530. Bus to **Cobán** leaves Gazolinera Quetzal at 0500, 4-5 hrs, US$6.50. Cobán to Nebaj at 1300. Alternatively get to Sacapulas on the main road, and wait for a bus.

Chajul and Cotzal p673
Bus
Buses to Chajul and Cotzal do not run on a set schedule. It is best to ask the day before you want to travel, at the bus station. There are buses and numerous pickups on Sun when villagers come to Nebaj for its market, which would be a good day to visit the villages. Alternatively, bargain with a local pickup driver to take you on a trip.

● Directory

Panajachel p662, map p663
Banks Banco Industrial, Calle Santander (TCs and Visa ATM), Calle Real, US$, TCs and cash, Visa ATM opposite. There is a *cambio* on the street near **Mayan Palace** for US$ cash and TCs. **Internet** Many in centre, shop around for best prices; standard is US$1 per hr. Cheaper in the old town. **Medical services** Centro de Salud Calle Real, just downhill from the road to San Antonio Palopó. **Farmacia Santander**, top end of Calle Santander, very good and helpful. **Post office** Calle Santander. Difficult but not impossible to send parcels of up to 1 kg abroad as long as packing requirements are met. **Get Guated Out**, Centro Comercial, Av Los Arboles, T/F7762-0595, good but

more expensive service, they use the postal system but pack and deal with formalities for you. DHL, Edif Rincón Sai, Calle Santander. **Telephone** Telgua, Calle Santander and internet cafés. **Language schools** Jardín de América, Calle 14 de Febrero, T7762-2637, www.jardindeamerica.com. US$80 for 20 hrs per week tuition, lodging with family costs an additional US$60 per week. **Jabel Tinamit**, behind Edif Rincón Sai, T7762-0238, www.jabeltinamit.com. Similar tariff.

San Lucas Tolimán p665
Banks Banrural and Corpobanco.
Internet Available in the plaza.

Santiago Atitlán p666
Banks G&T Continental, opposite the church. **Internet** Next to Chim-ni-ya.

San Pedro La Laguna p666, map p667
Banks Banrural changes cash and TCs; Visa ATM. **Internet** There are several internet and phone offices. **Language schools** This is a popular place for learning Spanish. Students may make their own accommodation arrangements but homestays are possible. Casa Rosario, www.casarosario.com, offers classes from US$70 a week for 20 hrs a week. Corazón Maya, T7721-8160, www.corazonmaya.com, from US$49 a week. Tz'utujil classes also. Run by the welcoming Marta Navichoc. San Pedro, T5715-4604, www.sanpedrospanish school.org, from US$75 per week. School has a great location with gardens close to the lakeshore. **Medical services** Centro Médico opposite Educación Básica school has a good doctor who does not speak English.

San Juan La Laguna p668
Banks Banrural, diagonally opposite Nick's Place. Changes cash and TCs.
Internet There are a couple of places in town.

San Marcos La Laguna *p668*
Language schools Casa Rosario, T5613-6401. San Marcos Spanish School, T5852-0403, www.sanmarcos spanishschool.com. From US$76 per week.

Chichicastenango *p669, map p670*
Banks There are a number of banks in town taking Visa and MasterCard. **Mayan Inn** will exchange cash. **Internet** Aces, inside Hotel Girón, 6 Calle, 4-52. **Post office** 7 Av, 8-47. Cropa Panalpina, 7 Av, 8-60, opposite post office, T7756-1028, www.cropa.com.gt. Will pack and ship your purchases back home by air cargo.
Telephone Telgua, 6 Calle between 5 y 6.

Santa Cruz del Quiché and around *p671*
Banks Banco Industrial, 3 Calle y 2 Av, top corner of Parque Central, cash on Visa cards and TCs; **G&T Continental**, 6 Calle y 3 Av, Visa and MasterCard TCs. **Post office** 3 Calle between 1 Av and 0 Av, Zona 5. Telgua: 1 Av/2 Calle, Zona 5.

Nebaj and around *p672*
Banks Banrural, TCs and Visa ATM. There are now a couple of ATMS. **Internet** There are a couple of internet services in town.
Language schools The Nebaj Language School, www.nebajlanguageschool.com, US$145 a week including accommodation.
Post office Behind the bank.

Western highlands

Just before the volcanic highlands reach their highest peaks, this part of the western highlands takes the form of scores of small market towns and villages, each with its own character – the loud animal market at San Francisco El Alto, the extra-planetary landscape at Momostenango, and its Maya cosmovision centre, and the dancing extravaganzas at Totonicapán. The modern ladino town of Huehuetenango sits at the gateway to the Sierra de los Cuchumatanes, within which hides, in a cold gash in a sky-hugging valley, the indigenous town and weaving centre of Todos Santos Cuchumatán. ➤ *For listings, see pages 695-698.*

Ins and outs

This area is well connected by buses from the Cuatro Caminos junction, Quetzaltenango or Huehuetenango. The road from Cobán is another access option, although a much slower one. ➤ *See Transport, page 697.*

Nahualá and Cuatro Caminos

Before the major four-way junction of Cuatro Caminos, the Pan-American Highway runs past Nahualá, a Maya village at 2470 m. The traditional *traje* is distinctive and best seen on market days on Thursday and Sunday, when finely embroidered cuffs and collars are sold, as well as very popular *huípiles*. The **Fiesta de Santa Catalina** is on 23-26 November (25th is the main day). There is an unpaved all-weather road a little to the north and 16 km longer, from Los Encuentros (on the Pan-American Highway) through Totonicapán (40 km) to San Cristóbal Totonicapán. The route from Chichicastenango to Quiché, Xecajá and Totonicapán takes a day by car or motorcycle, but is well worth taking and recommended by cyclists. There are no buses. There is also a scenic road from Totonicapán to Santa Cruz del Quiché via San Antonio Ilotenango. It takes one hour by car or motorcycle and two hours by pickup truck. There are no buses on this route either.

Cuatro Caminos is a busy junction with roads, east to Totonicapán, west to Los Encuentros, north to Huehuetenango and south to Quetzaltenango. Buses stop here every few seconds so you will never have to wait long for a connection. There is a petrol station and lots of vendors to keep you fed and watered. Just north of Cuatro Caminos is **San Cristóbal Totonicapán**, noted for its *huípiles*.

Totonicapán → *Colour map 5, B1. Altitude: 2500 m.*

The route to San Miguel Totonicapán, the capital of its department, passes through pine-forested hillsides, pretty red-tiled roofs and *milpas* of maize on the road side. The 18th-century beige church stands on one of the main squares, unfortunately now a parking lot, at 6 y 7 Avenida between 3 and 4 Calle. The market is considered by Guatemalans to be one of the cheapest, and it is certainly very colourful. Saturday is the main market noted for ceramics and cloth, with a small gathering on Tuesdays. There is a traditional dance fiesta on 12-13 August, music concerts and a chance to see *cofradía* rituals. The annual **feria** is on 24-30 September in celebration of the Archangel San Miguel, with the main fiesta on 29 September. The **Casa de Cultura** ① *8 Av, 2-17, T7766-1575* , run by Carlos Humberto Molina, displays an excellent collection of fiesta masks, made on site at the mask factory, and for sale. It has a cultural programme with a number of tour options. You need to reserve in advance.

San Francisco El Alto

San Francisco stands high on a great big mound in the cold mountains at 2640 m above the great valley in which lie Totonicapán, San Cristóbal and Quetzaltenango. It is famous for its market, which is stuffed to capacity, and for the animal market held above town, where creatures from piglets to kittens to budgies are for sale. The town's fiesta is on 1-6 October, in honour of St Francis of Assisi.

The market is packed to bursting point on Fridays with locals buying all sorts, including woollen blankets for resale throughout the country. It's an excellent place for buying woven and embroidered textiles of good quality, but beware of pickpockets. Go early to see as much action as possible. Climb up through the town for 10 minutes to see the animal market (ask for directions all the time as it's hard to see 5 m ahead, the place is so packed).

The **church** on the main square is magnificent; notice the double-headed Hapsburg eagle. It is often full on market days with locals lighting candles, and their live purchases ignoring the 'Silencio' posters. The white west front of the church complements the bright colours of the rest of the plaza, especially the vivid green and pink of the Municipalidad.

Momostenango → *Colour map 5, B1.*

Momostenango is set in a valley with ribbons of houses climbing higgledy-piggledy out of the valley floor. Momostenango, at 2220 m, represents *Shol Mumus* in K'iche', meaning 'among the hills', and on its outlying hills are numerous altars and a hilltop image of a Maya god. Some 300 medicine men are said to practise in the town. Their insignia of office is a little bag containing beans and quartz crystals. Momostenango is the chief blanket-weaving centre in the country, and locals can be seen beating the blankets (*chamarras*) on stones, to shrink them. There are also weird stone peaks known as the *riscos* – eroded fluted columns and draperies formed of volcanic ash – on the outskirts of town.

The town is quiet except on Wednesday and Sunday market days, the latter being larger and good for weaving, especially the blankets. On non-market days try **Tienda Manuel de Jesús Agancel** ① *1 Av, 1-50, Zona 4, near bank*, for good bargains, especially blankets and carpets. There is also **Artesanía Paclom** ① *corner of 1 Calle and 3 Av, Zona 2*, just five minutes along the road to Xela. This family have the weaving looms in their back yard and will show you how it's all done if you ask.

The **Feast of Wajshakib Batz' Oj** (pronounced 'washakip'), is celebrated by hundreds of *Aj Kij* (Maya priests) who come for ceremonies. New priests are initiated on this first day of the ritual new year; the initiation lasting the year. The town's very popular fiesta is between 21 July and 4 August, with the town's patron saint of Santiago Apóstol celebrated on 25 July. The **Baile de Convites** is held in December with other dances on 8, 12 and 31 December and 1 January. At **Takilibén Maya Misión**, 3 Avenida "A", 6-85, Zona 3, T7736-5537 (just after the Texaco garage on the right on the way in from Xela) Chuch Kajaw (day keeper) Rigoberto Itzep welcomes all interested in learning more about Maya culture and cosmology. He offers courses in culture and does Maya horoscope readings. He also has a **Maya sauna** (*Tuj*).

Just outside town are three sets of *riscos* (eroded columns of sandstone with embedded quartz particles), creating a strange eerie landscape of pinnacles that look like rocket lollipop ice creams. To get there, take the 2 Calle, Zona 2, which is the one to the right of the church, for five minutes until you see a sign on a building pointing to the left. Follow the signs until you reach the earth structures (five to 10 minutes).

→ *Altitude: 1905 m.*

Huehuetenango – colloquially known as Huehue – is a pleasant, large town with little to detain the visitor. However, it is a busy transport hub serving the Cuchumatanes Mountains and the Mexican border. Its bus terminal, 2 km from town, is one of the busiest in the country. There are Maya ruins near the town, which were badly restored by the infamous **United Fruit Company**, and new adventure tourism opportunities opening up nearby. Trips, including horse rides, to more remote spots in the Huehuetenango region to see forests, haciendas and lakes are organized by **Unicornio Azul**. A useful website is www.interhuehue.com.

The neoclassical **cathedral** was built between 1867-1874; destroyed by earthquake in 1902, and took 10 years to repair. In 1956, the image of the patron saint, the Virgen de la Concepción was burnt in a fire. Then, during the 1976 earthquake, 80% of it was damaged, save the bells, façade and cupola. The skyline to the north of the city is dominated by the Sierrra de los Cuchumatanes, the largest area over 3000 m in Central America.

Huehuetenango

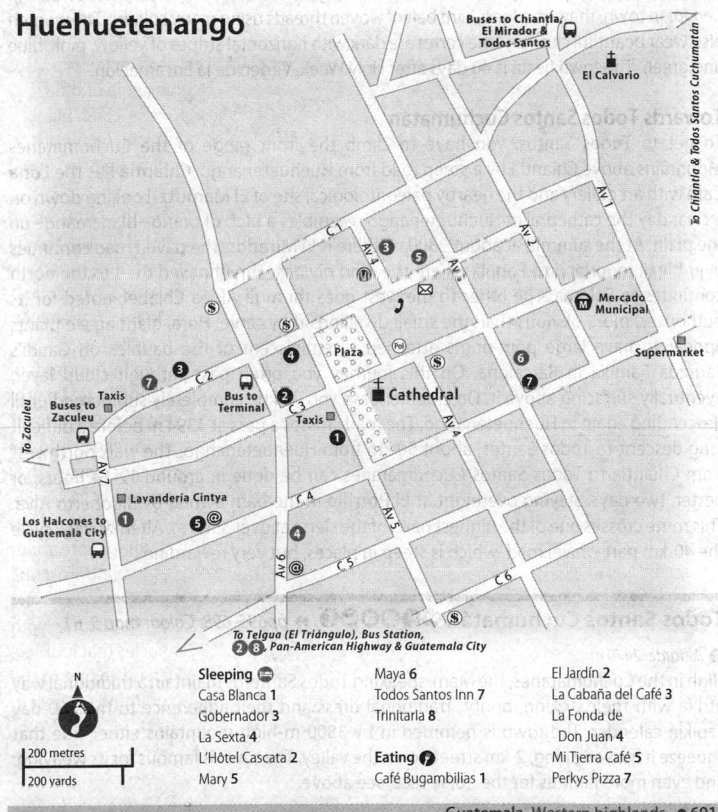

To Zaculeu

To Chiantla & Todos Santos Cuchumatán

Buses to Chiantla, El Mirador & Todos Santos

El Calvario

Mercado Municipal

Supermarket

Buses to Zaculeu

Taxis

Bus to Terminal

Plaza

Cathedral

Taxis

Lavandería Cintya

Los Halcones to Guatemala City

To Telgua (El Triángulo), Bus Station, Pan-American Highway & Guatemala City

N

200 metres
200 yards

Sleeping 😊
Casa Blanca **1**
Gobernador **3**
La Sexta **4**
L'Hôtel Cascata **2**
Mary **5**

Maya **6**
Todos Santos Inn **7**
Trinitaria **8**

Eating 🍴
Café Bugambilias **1**

El Jardín **2**
La Cabaña del Café **3**
La Fonda de
Don Juan **4**
Mi Tierra Café **5**
Perkys Pizza **7**

The ruins of **Zaculeu** ① *0800-1800, US$6.40*, the old capital of the Mam Maya, are 5 km west of Huehuetenango on top of a rise with steep drops on three sides – a site chosen because of these natural defence measures. Its original name in Mam was *Xinabajul*, meaning 'between ravines'. In K'iche' it means 'white earth'. It was first settled in the Early Classic period (AD 250-600), but it flourished during the late post-Classic (AD 1200-1530). In July 1525, Gonzalo de Alvarado, the brother of Guatemala's conqueror, Pedro de Alvarado, set out for Zaculeu with 80 Spaniards, 40 horses and 2000 indigenous fighters, passing Mazatenango and Totonicapán on the way. The battle lasted four months, during which time the soldiers and residents of Zaculeu were dying of hunger, and eating their dead neighbours. The weakened Kaibil Balam, the Zaculeu *cacique* (chief), called for a meeting with Gonzalo. Gonzalo told the Mam chief that peace was not on the cards. Negotiations followed with the outcome being that Kaibil Balam be instructed in Christianity, obey the Spanish king and leave the city, whereupon Gonzalo de Alvarado would take possession of the Mam kingdom settlement in the name of the Spanish crown.

Aguacatán → *Colour map 5, B1. Altitude: 1670 m.*
The women of Aguacatán wear the most stunning headdresses in the country. On sale in *tiendas* in town, they are a long, slim belt of woven threads using many colours. The women also wear beautiful clothes – the *cortes* are dark with horizontal stripes of yellow, pink, blue and green. The town fiesta is 40 days after Holy Week, Virgen de la Encarnación.

Towards Todos Santos Cuchumatán
To get to Todos Santos, you have to climb the front range of the Cuchumatanes Mountains above Chiantla by a steep road from Huehuetenango. **Chiantla** has the **Luna Café** with art gallery and the nearby paleontological site of **El Mamutz**. Looking down on a clear day the cathedral at Huehuetenango resembles a blob of orange blancmange on the plain. At the summit, at about 3300 m, there is **El Mirador**. The paved road continues over bleak moorland to Paquix where the road divides. The unpaved road to the north continues to Soloma. The other to the west goes through Aldea Chiabel, noted for its outhouses, more obvious than the small dwellings they serve. Here, giant agave plants appear to have large pom-poms attached – reminiscent of the baubles on Gaudí's Sagrada Familia in Barcelona. On this journey you often pass through cloud layer, eventually surfacing above it. On cloudier days you will be completely submerged until descending again to Huehuetenango. The road crosses a pass at 3394 m before a difficult long descent to Todos Santos, about 50 km from Huehuetenango. The walk northwest from Chiantla to Todos Santos Cuchumatanes can be done in around 12-14 hours, or better, two days, staying overnight at **El Potrillo** in the barn owned by Rigoberto Alva. This route crosses one of the highest parts of the sierra at over 3500 m. Alternatively, cycle the 40-km part-gravel road, which is steep in places, but very rewarding.

Todos Santos Cuchumatán ●❷❸❹❺❻ ➤➤ *pp695-698. Colour map 5, B1.*
→ *Altitude: 2470 m.*
High in the Cuchumatanes, the Mam-speaking Todos Santeros maintain a traditional way of life with their striking, bright, traditional dress and their adherence to the 260-day Tzolkin calendar. The town is hemmed in by 3800-m-high mountains either side that squeeze it into one long, 2-km street down the valley. The town is famous for its weaving, and even more famous for the horse race, see above.

Todos Santos festival

The horse racing festival of Todos Santos is one of the most celebrated and spectacular in Central America – it is also a frenzied day that usually degenerates into a drunken mess. Quite simply, riders race between two points, having a drink at each turn until they fall off.

According to Professor Margarito Calmo Cruz, the origins of the fiesta lie in the 15th or 16th century with the arrival of the *conquistadores* to Todos Santos. They arrived on horses wearing large, colourful clothes with bright scarves flowing down their backs and feathers in their hats. The locals experimented, imitating them, enjoyed it and the tradition was born.

When the day begins, the men are pretty tipsy, but sprightly and clean. The race is frantic and colourful with scarves flying out from the backs of the men. As the day wears on, they get completely smashed, riding with arms outstretched – whip in one hand and beer bottle in the other. They are mudspattered, dishevelled and are moaning and groaning from the enjoyment and the alcohol, which must easily reach near-comatose level.

At times the riders fall, and look pretty lifeless. They are dragged by the scruff of the neck, regardless of serious injury or death, to the edge of the fence as quickly as possible, to avoid trampling.

The men guzzle gallons of beer and the aim is to continue racing all day. A fall means instant dismissal from the race. There are wardens on the side lines with batons, whose primary job is the welfare of the horses, changing them when they see necessary. But they also deal with protesting fallen riders, who try and clamber back onto their horses. By the end of the day the spectacle is pretty grotesque. The horses are drenched with sweat and wild-eyed with fear. The men look hideous and are paralytic from booze. The edge of the course and the town is littered with bodies.

The race takes place on the road that winds its way out of town, not the incoming road from Huehue. It starts at 0800. There are about 15 riders on the course at any one time. It continues until noon, stops for *cerveza* guzzling and begins again at 1400, ending at 1700.

Some of Guatemala's best weaving is done in Todo Santos. Fine *huipiles* may be bought in the cooperative on the main street and direct from the makers. The men wear the famous red-and-white striped trousers. Some wear a black wool over-trouser piece. Their jackets are white, pink, purple and red-striped with beautifully coloured, and intricately embroidered, collars and cuffs. Their straw hat is wrapped with a blue band. You can buy the embroidered cuffs and collars for men's shirts, the red trousers, and gorgeous colourful crocheted bags made by the men. The women wear navy blue *cortes* with thin, light blue, vertical stripes.

There is a colourful Saturday market and a smaller one on Wednesday. The **church** near the park was built in 1580.

Around Todos Santos

The closest walk is to **Las Letras**, where the words 'Todos Santos' are spelt out in white stone on a hillside above the town. The walk takes an hour. To get there take the path down the side of **Restaurant Cuchumatlán**. The highest point of the Cuchumatanes, and the highest non-volcanic peak in the country, **La Torre** at 3837 m, is to the northeast of Todos Santos and can be reached from the village of **Tzichem** on the road to Concepción

Border essentials: Guatemala–Mexico

La Mesilla–Ciudad Cuauhtémoc
The Pan-American Highway runs west, from the junction to Huehuetenango to La Mesilla.

Guatemalan immigration Open 0600-2100. The Mexican border post is in Ciudad Cuauhtémoc (just a few buildings, not a town), about 4 km from the Guatemalan border. If you are crossing into Mexico and will be there less than seven days there is no departure fee. If you stay more than seven days, the charge is US$16 and must be paid at a bank listed on the immigration papers before departure. There are pickups during the day. Crossing by private vehicle is reported to be fairly simple.

Sleeping There are a couple of *pensiones* at the border inside Guatemala, including **Hotel Mily's (F)**, 10 rooms, hot water.

Transport Buses La Mesilla–Huehuetenango run 0330-1800, two hours, US$1.40. Express buses run by **Transportes Velásquez** go to Guatemala City (US$6.80, seven hours).

Banks Rates are not usually favourable at the border in either currency. Banrural in La Mesilla with ATM and at the border, or haggle in the street.

Entering Guatemala A tourist card for Guatemala can be obtained at the border. Guatemalan immigration are currently charging an unofficial 30-quetzal fee to enter Guatemala. Point out that this is not official and insist on a receipt.

Crossing by private vehicle Full details under Getting around by car, page 618.

Mexican consulates Mexican visas are available at the border. See also Quetzaltenango, Embassies and consulates.

Car insurance For Mexico and Guatemala, arrange at Banco G&T Continental's agent, Edif Villa Rosa opposite Mi Tierra Café Internet.

Huista. When clear, it's possible to see the top of Volcán Santa María, one of the highest volcanoes in Guatemala. The hike takes about five hours. The best way to do it is to start in the afternoon and spend the night near the top. It is convenient for camping, with wood but no water. A compass is essential in case of mist. From Todos Santos, you can also hike south to **San Juan Atitán**, four to five hours, where the locals wear an interesting *traje típico*. Market days are on Mondays and Thursdays. From there you can hike to the Pan-American Highway – it's a one day walk. The local fiesta is 22-26 June.

From Jacaltenango to the Mexican border
The road from Todos Santos continues northwest through **Concepción Huista**. Here the women wear towels as shawls and Jacalteco is spoken. The fiesta, 29 January-3 February, has fireworks and dancing. The hatmaker in Canton Pilar supplies the hats for Todos Santos, he welcomes viewers and will make a hat to your specifications (but if you want a typical Todos Santos leather *cincho*, buy it there).

Beyond Jacaltenango is **Nentón**, and **Gracias a Dios** at the Mexican border. When the road north out of Huehue splits at Paquix, the right fork goes to **San Mateo Ixtatán**, with ruins nearby. The road from Paquix crosses the roof of the Cuchumatanes, before descending to **San Juan Ixcoy, Soloma** and **Santa Eulalia**, where the people speak O'anjob'al as they do in Soloma. East along a scenic route is **Barillas**. There are several *pensiones* in these places and regular buses from Huehue.

For Sleeping and Eating price codes and other relevant information, see Essentials pages 45-48.

⦿ Sleeping

Totonicapán *p689*
D-E Hospedaje San Miguel, 3 Calle, 7-49, Zona 1, T7766-1452. Rooms with or without bath, hot water, communal TV.
E Pensión Blanquita, 13 Av and 4 Calle. 20 rooms, hot showers, good. Opposite this *pensión* is a Shell station.

San Francisco El Alto *p690*
D-E Vista Hermosa, 2 Calle, 2-23, T7738-4010. 36 rooms, cheaper without bathroom, hot water, TV.
F Hotel Vásquez, 4 Av, 11-53, T7738-4003. Rooms all with private bathroom. Parking.

Momostenango *p690*
E Hospedaje y Comedor Paclom, close to central plaza, at 1 Calle, 1-71, Zona 4. Pretty inner courtyard with caged birds and plants, hot water in shared bathrooms.
E Ixcel (Estiver), downhill away from plaza at 1 Calle, 4-15, Zona 4, T7736-5036. 12 rooms, hot water, cheaper without bath, clean.
E-F La Villa, 1 Av, 1-13, Zona 1, below bank, T7736-5108. 6 rooms, warm water only, clean and nicely presented.

Huehuetenango and around *p691*, *map p691*
B Casa Blanca, 7 Av, 3-41, T7769-0777. Comfortable, good restaurant in a pleasant garden, buffet breakfast, set lunch, very popular and good value, parking.
C L'Hôtel Cascata, Lote 4, 42, Zona 5, Colonia Alvarado, Calzada Kaibil Balam, close to the bus station, T7769-0795, www.hotelcascata.ya.st. Newish hotel with 16 rooms and private bathrooms. Rooms have Wi-Fi. It is owned by Dutch, French and English folk and the service is excellent.

C-D Maya, 3 Av, 3-55, T7764-0369. This former basic hotel has been remodelled with spa facilities, offering free coffee in reception, hot water and cable TV in rooms. It is ultra-clean, but some rooms are a little small; accepts credit cards.
D La Sexta, 6 Av, 4-29, T7764-6612. With bath, cheaper without, cable TV, restaurant, good for breakfast, clean, good value, phone call facility, stores backpacks without charge.
D Mary, 2 Calle, 3-52, T7764-1618. With bath, cheaper without, good beds, hot water, cable TV, parking, clean, quiet, safe, well-maintained, good value. Recommended.
D-E Trinitaria, Cda Kaibil Balam 9-30, Zona 5, near bus terminal, T7764-3922. 13 rooms with bath, cheaper without, hot water.
E Hotel Gobernador, 4 Av 1-45, T7764-1197. Garden, parking, with bath cheaper without, clean, good value.
E Todos Santos Inn, 2 Calle, 6-74, T7764-1241. Shared bath and private bath available, hot water, TV, helpful, clean, laundry, some rooms a bit damp, luggage stored. Recommended.

Todos Santos Cuchumatán *p692*
Reservations are necessary in the week before the Nov horse race, but even if you turn up and the town is full, locals offer their homes.
E Casa Familiar, up the hill, close to central park, T7783-0656. Run by the friendly family of Santiago Mendoza Pablo. Hot shower, sauna, breakfast, dinner, delicious banana bread, spectacular view, popular. The Mendoza family make and sell *típicas* and give weaving lessons.
E Hotel Mam, above the central park, next to **Hotelito Todos Santos**. Friendly, clean, hot water, but needs 1 hr to warm up, not too cold in the rooms as an open fire warms the building, good value.
E Hotelito Todos Santos, above the central park. Hot water, clean, small café, but beware

of boys taking you to the hotel quoting one price, and then on arrival, finding the price has mysteriously gone up.

E-F Hospedaje El Viajero, around the corner and then right from **Hotelito Todos Santos**, 5 rooms, 2 shared baths with hot water.

E-F Hotel La Paz. Friendly, great view of the main street from balconies, excellent spot for the 1 Nov fiesta, shared showers have seen better days, enclosed parking.

San Juan Atitán *p694*
F Hospedaje San Diego. Only 3 beds, basic, friendly, clean, food available.

🍴 Eating

Totonicapán *p689*
🍴 **Comedor Brenda 2**, 9 Av, 3-31. Good, serving local food.
🍴 **Comedor Letty**, 3 Calle, 8-18. Typical Guatemalan fare.

Momostenango *p690*
🍴 **Comedor Santa Isabel**, next door to Hospedaje y Comedor Paclom. Friendly, cheap and good breakfasts.
🍴 **Flipper**, 1 Calle y 2 Av A. Good *licuados* and a range of fruit juices.
🍴 **Hospedaje y Comedor Paclom**, close to the central plaza and where buses arrive from Xela, 1 Calle, 1-71, Zona 4. Cheap meals, including snacks in a pretty inner courtyard.

Huehuetenango and around *p691*, *map p691*
🍴-🍴 **Casa Blanca**, 7 Av, 3-41. Open 0600-2200. Try the breakfast pancake with strawberries and cream. The plate of the house is a meat extravaganza, fish and good salads served, set lunch good value.
🍴-🍴 **La Cabaña del Café**, 2 Calle, 6-50. Log cabin café with to-die-for cappuccino, snack food and good *chapín* breakfasts, good atmosphere. Recommended.

🍴 **Café Bugambilias**, 5 Av 3-59, on the plaza. large, unusual 4-storey building, most of which is a popular, cheap, restaurant, very good breakfasts, *almuerzos*, sandwiches. Recommended.
🍴 **El Jardín**, 6 Av 2-99, Zona 1. Meat dishes, breakfasts, good pancakes and local dishes. It's worth eating here just to check out the toilets, which are right out of the 3rd-and-a-half floor of the office in the movie *Being John Malkovich*!
🍴 **La Fonda de Don Juan**, 2 Calle, 5-35. Italian restaurant and bar (try the *cavatini*), sandwiches, big choice of desserts, *licuados*, coffees, good pizzas, also *comida típica*, with reasonable prices all served in a bright environment with red and white checked tablecloths.
🍴 **Mi Tierra Café**, 4 Calle, 6-46, T7764-1473. Good drinks and light meals, Mexican offerings – try the *fajitas*, nice setting, popular with locals and travellers. Recommended.
🍴 **Perkys Pizza**, 3 Av esq, 4 Calle. Wide variety of pizzas, eat in or takeaway, modern, clean, good value.

Todos Santos Cuchumatán *p692*
There are *comedores* on the 2nd floor of the market selling very cheap meals.
🍴 **Comedor Katy**. Will prepare vegetarian meals on request, good-value *menú del día*.
🍴 **Cuchumatlán**. Has sandwiches, pizza and pancakes, and is popular at night.

🎉 Festivals and events

Todos Santos Cuchumatán *p692*
1 Nov Horse race. The festival begins on 21 Oct. See box, page 693.
2 Nov Day of the Dead, when locals visit the cemetery and leave flowers and food.

O Shopping

Todos Santos Cuchumatán *p692*
The following shops all sell bags, trousers, shirts, *huípiles*, jackets and clothes. Prices have more or less stabilized at the expensive end, but the best bargains can be had at the **Tienda Maribel**, further up the hill from Casa Familiar and the **Cooperativa Estrella de Occidente**, on the main street. **Casa Mendoza**, just beyond Tienda Maribel, is where Telésforo Mendoza makes clothes to measure. **Domingo Calmo** also makes clothes to measure. His large, brown house with tin roof is on the main road to the Ruinas (5 mins) – follow the road up from Casa Familiar. Ask for the **Casa de Domingo**.

▲ Activities and tours

Huehuetenango and around *p691*,
map p691
Unicornio Azul, based in Chancol, T5205-9328, www.unicornioazul. com. Horse-riding trips, trekking, mountain biking and birdwatching in the Cuchumatanes.

O Transport

Totonicapán *p689*
Bus
Every 15 mins to **Quetzaltenango**, US$0.40, 45 mins. To **Los Encuentros**, US$2.20. To **Cuatro Caminos**, 30 mins, US$0.30.

San Francisco El Alto *p690*
Bus
2 km along the Pan-American Hwy heading north from Cuatro Caminos is a paved road, which runs to San Francisco El Alto (3 km) and then to Momostenango (19 km). Bus from **Quetzaltenango**, 50 mins on Fri, US$0.75. The last bus back is at 1800.

Momostenango *p690*
Bus
From **Cuatro Caminos** (US$0.50) and **Quetzaltenango**, 1-1½ hrs. Buses to Xela every 30 mins from 0430-1600.

Huehuetenango and around *p691*,
map p691
Bus
Local From the terminal to town, take 'Centro' bus (minibus), which pull up at cathedral, 5 mins. Taxis from behind the covered market building. Walking takes 20-25 mins. Bus leaves Salvador Osorio School, final Calle 2, every 30 mins, 15 mins, to **Zaculeu**, last return 1830. Taxi, US$8, including waiting time. To walk takes about 1 hr – either take 6 Av north, cross the river and follow the road round to the left, through Zaculeu modern village to the ruins, or go past the school and turn right beyond the river. The signs are barely visible.

Long distance To **Guatemala City**, 5 hrs, US$11, **Los Halcones**, 7 Av, 3-62, Zona 1 (they do not leave from the terminal) at 0430, 0700, 1400, reliable. From the bus terminal there are numerous services daily to the capital from 0215-1600 via **Chimaltenango**, 5 hrs, US$4. Via **Mazatenango** there are 5 daily.

North To **Todos Santos Cuchumatán**, 10 daily until 1630, 2-3 hrs, US$3.60. To **Barillas**, via **San Juan Ixcoy** (2½ hrs), **Soloma** (3 hrs), and **San Mateo Ixtatan** (7 hrs), 10 daily from 0200-2330, US$7. There are also buses to **San Rafael la Independencia** passing through Soloma and Sta Eulalia.

Northwest To **La Mesilla** for Mexico, frequent buses between 0530-1800, US$3.50, 2½ hrs, last bus returning to Huehue, 1800. To **Nentón**, via La Mesilla twice a day. To **Gracias a Dios**, several times a day.

South To **Quetzaltenango**, 13 a day from 0600-1600, US$3, 2-2¼ hrs. To **Cuatro Caminos**, US$2, 2 hrs. To **Los Encuentros**, for Lake Atitlán and Chichicastenango, 3 hrs.

East To **Aguacatán**, 12 daily, 0600-1900, 1 hr 10 mins, US$1.20. To **Nebaj** you have to get to Sacapulas via Aguacatán. To **Sacapulas**, 1130, 1245. To **Cobán**, take the earliest bus/pickup to Aguacatán and then Sacapulas and continue to Uspantán to change for Cobán.

Aguacatán *p692*
Bus
From **Huehue**, 1 hr 10 mins. It is 26 km east of Huehuetenango on a semi-paved route (good views). Returning between 0445 and 1600. Buses and pickups for **Sacapulas** and for onward connections to Nebaj and Cobán leave from the main street going out of town. Wait anywhere along there to catch your ride. It is 1½ hrs from Aguacatán to Sacapulas. To **Guatemala City** at 0300, 1100.

Todos Santos Cuchumatán *p692*
Bus
To **Huehuetenango**, 2-3 hrs, crowded Mon and Fri, 0400, 0500, 0600, 0615-0630, 1145, 1230, 1300. Possible changes on Sat so ask beforehand. For petrol, ask at **El Molino**.

From Jacaltenango to the Mexican border *p694*
Bus
From **Huehuetenango** at 0330, 0500, returning at 1130 and 1400; also pickups.

❶ Directory

San Francisco El Alto *p690*
Banks G&T Continental, 2 Av, 1-95, takes MasterCard and changes TCs; **Banco Industrial**, 2 Calle, 2-64, cashes TCs, takes Visa.

Momostenango *p690*
Banks Banrural, on plaza, TCs only.
Language schools Patzite, 1 Calle, 4-33, Zona 2, T7736-5159, www.patzite.20m.com.

Huehuetenango and around *p691,*
map p691
Banks Many local banks taking Visa and MasterCard, some open Sat morning. The bigger banks change TCs. Mexican pesos can be got from **Camicard**, 5 Av, 6-00.
Internet Several places around town.
Language schools Some operate in the summer months only (see box, page 657). Huehuetenango would be a good spot to learn Spanish, as there are fewer chances of meeting gringos and conversing in your own tongue. **Señora de Mendoza**, 1 Calle, 1-64, Zona 3, T7764-1987. **Rodrigo Morales** (at Sastrería La Elegancia), 9 Av, 6-55, Zona 1. Recommended. **Spanish Academy Xinabajul**, 4 Av, 14-14, Zona 5, T7764-6631, www.world wide.edu/guatemala/xinabaj/index.html. **Abesaida Guevara de López**, 10 Calle 'A', 10-20, Zona 1, T7764-2917. Recommended. Information on schools and other tourist information is posted in **Mi Tierra Café**. **Post office** 2 Calle, 3-54. **Telephone** Telgua, Edif El Triángulo, 9 Av, 6-142, on main road out of town.

Todos Santos Cuchumatán *p692*
Bank Banrural TCs and dollars cash only.
Language schools All the local coordinators are on friendly terms with each other but all are competing for your business. Take your time and visit all 3 schools. **Hispano Maya**, opposite Hotelito Todos Santos, www.hispanomaya.org. **Nuevo Amanecer**, escuela_linguistica@ yahoo.com. Working There is also a volunteer project to teach English in a nearby village where food and board is provided. Weaving can be taught.
Post office Central park.

Quetzaltenango and around

→ *Colour map 5, C1. Altitude: 2335 m.*
Quetzaltenango (commonly known as Xela – pronounced 'shayla') is the most important city in western Guatemala. The country's second city is set among a group of high mountains and volcanoes, one of which, Santa María, caused much death and destruction after an eruption in 1902. The bulk of the city is modern, but its 19th-century downtown revamp and its narrow streets give the centre more of a historic feel. There are breathtaking views and a pleasant park with its beautifully restored façade of the colonial church. It is an excellent base from which to visit nearby hot springs, religious idols, volcanoes and market towns. ➤➤ *For listings see pages 706-711.*

Ins and outs

Getting there Most visitors arrive by bus, a 30-minute (14.5 km) journey southwest of Cuatro Caminos. Buses pull into the Zona 3 Minerva Terminal. To get a bus into the city centre, take a path through the market at its far left or its far right, which brings you out in front of the Minerva Temple. Watch out for very clever pickpockets walking through this market. Buses for the town centre face away (left) from the temple. All Santa Fe services go to Parque Centro América, US$0.15. Alternatively take a taxi. ➤➤ *See Transport, page 709.*

Getting around The town centre is compact and all sites and most services are within walking distance. The Santa Fe city bus goes between the terminal, the *rotonda* and the town centre. Out of town destination buses stop at the *rotonda* and it is quicker to get here from the town centre than to the Minerva Terminal. City buses for the terminal leave from 4 Calle and 13 Avenida, Zona 1, and those straight for the *rotonda* leave from 11 Avenida and 10 Calle, Zona 1, US$0.15. A taxi within Zona 1, or from Zona 1 to a closer part of Zona 3, is between US$3.20.

Tourist information INGUAT ① *7 Calle, 11-35, on the park, T7761-4931, Mon-Fri 0900-1600, Sat 0900-1300.* Not recommended. Try the recommended tour operators for information instead. General information can be found at www.xelapages.com and www.xelawho.com, which has good listings.

Background

The most important battle of the Spanish conquest took place near Quetzaltenango when the great K'iche' warrior Tecún Umán was slain. In October 1902 the Volcán Santa María erupted, showering the city with half a metre of dust. An ash cloud soared 8.6 km into the air and some 1500 people were killed by volcanic fallout and gas. A further 3000 people died a short while later from malaria due to plagues of mosquitoes which had not been wiped out by the blast. Some 20 years on, a new volcano, born after the 1902 eruption, began to erupt. This smaller volcano, Santiaguito, spews clouds of dust and ash on a daily basis and is considered one of the most dangerous volcanoes in the world. The city's prosperity, as seen by the grand neoclassical architecture in the centre, was built on the back of the success of the coffee *fincas* on the nearby coastal plain. This led to the country's first bank being established here. The town's fiestas are 9-17 September, Holy Week and the October fiesta of La Virgen del Rosario.

Sights

The central park, **Parque Centro América**, is the focus of the city. It is surrounded by the cathedral, with its beautifully restored original colonial façade, and a number of elegant neoclassical buildings, constructed during the late 19th and early 20th century. The modern cathedral, **Catedral de la Diócesis de los Altos**, was constructed in 1899 and is set back behind the original. The surviving façade of the 1535 **Catedral del Espíritu Santo** is beautiful, intricately carved and with restored portions of murals on its right side. On the south side of the park is the **Casa de la Cultura**. Inside are the **Museo de la Marimba** with exhibits and documents relating to the 1871 Liberal Revolution. On the right-hand

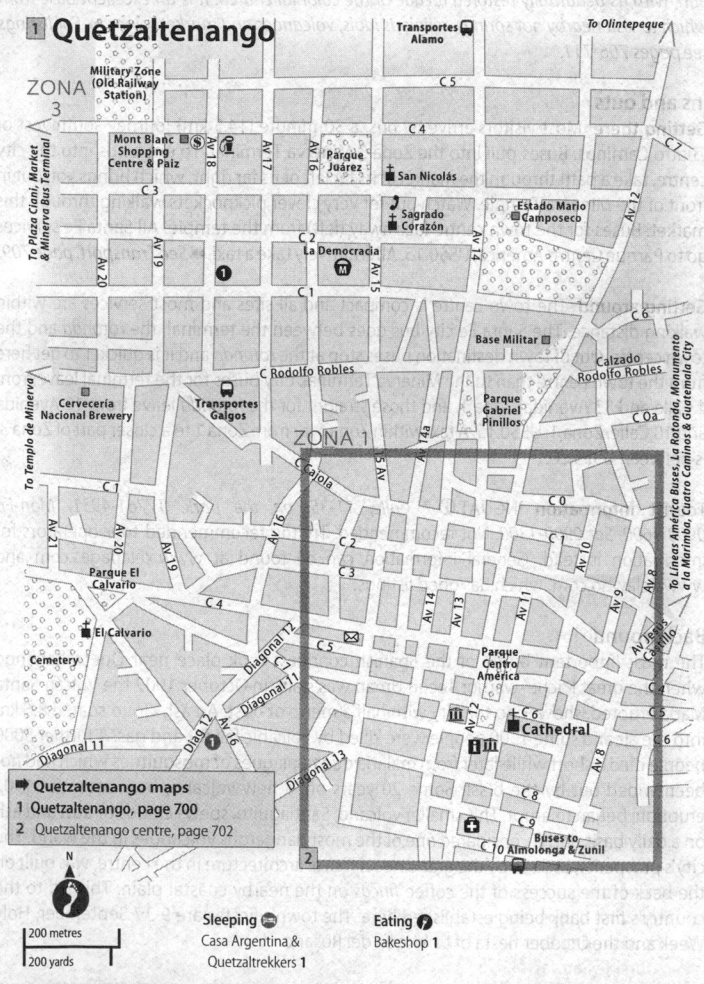

1 Quetzaltenango

Transportes Alamo

To Olintepeque

ZONA 3

Military Zone (Old Railway Station)

Mont Blanc Shopping Centre & Paiz

Parque Juárez

San Nicolás

Estado Mario Camposeco

Sagrado Corazón

La Democracia

To Plaza Cioni, Market & Minerva Bus Terminal

Base Militar

C Rodolfo Robles

Calzado Rodolfo Robles

Cervecería Nacional Brewery

Transportes Galgos

ZONA 1

Parque Gabriel Pinillos

To Templo de Minerva

To Lineas América Buses, La Rotonda, Monumento a la Marimba, Cuatro Caminos & Guatemala City

Parque El Calvario

El Calvario

Cemetery

Parque Centro América

Cathedral

Buses to Almolonga & Zunil

Diagonal 11

➡ **Quetzaltenango maps**
1 Quetzaltenango, page 700
2 Quetzaltenango centre, page 702

N

200 metres
200 yards

Sleeping 🛏
Casa Argentina & Quetzaltrekkers **1**

Eating 🍴
Bakeshop **1**

side of the building is the totally curious **Museo de Historia Natural** ① *Mon-Fri 0800-1200, 1400-1800, US$0.90*. Deformed stuffed animals are cheek by jowl with pre-Columbian pottery, sports memorabilia, fizzy drink bottles, a lightning-damaged mirror and dinosaur remains. It satisfies the most morbid of curiosities with displays of a two-headed calf, Siamese twin pigs, an eight-legged goat, and a strange sea creature that looks like an alien, known as *Diabillo del Mar* (little sea devil). On the park's southwest side is the **Museo de Arte**, with a collection of contemporary Guatemalan art, and the **Museo del Ferrocarril Nacional de los Altos** ① *7 Calle and 12 Av, Mon-Fri 0800-1200, 1400-1800, US$0.90*, recounting the story of an electric railway between Xela and the Pacific slope. The **Banco de Occidente**, founded in 1881, and the first bank to opened in Guatemala, dominates the northern edge of the park. The overly wired-up **Municipalidad** straddles the eastern edge of the park with its neoclassical columns. Its first building blocks were laid in 1881, but it wasn't completed until 1897. The stately **Teatro Municipal** (1892-1896) is on 14 Avenida y 1 Calle and can be visited outside of performance hours. Restored at a cost of four million quetzales, it has an imposing presence. To its left, on Avenida 14 "A", is the Teatro Roma. Building began in 1898, but was not completed until 1931, when it became the first cinema to open in Guatemala. It was restored in 2000 as a theatre with a capacity for 1400 and is open for performances.

There is a sickly green modern church, the **Sagrado Corazón**, on the Parque Benito Juárez near the market. Inside is a gigantic, free-standing, Chagall-influenced painting with swooping angels, and Christ in a glass box, built into the picture. The church of **La Transfiguración** ① *near the corner of 11 Calle and 5 Av, Zona 1*, houses the largest crucified Christ figure (San Salvador del Mundo) to be found in Central America – it is almost 3 m in height and now housed behind glass. At 20 Avenida and 4 Calle is the city's **Cementerio** ① *0700-1900*. Inside are the remains of the Quetzalteco President, Estrada Cabrera (1898-1920) in a small cream neoclassical temple. Behind his tomb are the unmarked graves of a large number of cholera victims wiped out in a 19th-century epidemic. Manuel Lisandra Barillas (Guatemalan President 1885-1892) is also entombed here. There is a small patio area known as Colonia Alemana lined with graves of German residents; a large area where those that died as martyrs in the civil war lie; and a memorial to those that perished in the September Revolution of 1897.

North of Quetzaltenango ○○ » *pp706-711*.

Heading south to Quetzaltenango from Cuatro Caminos you pass the small *ladino* town of **Salcajá**, where *jaspé* skirt material has been woven since 1861. If you fancy a taste or a whiff of some potent liquor before bracing yourself for an entry into Quetzaltenango, then this is the place to halt. It is worth a visit not only for the booze but its famous church – the oldest in Central America – and for its textiles, often seen being produced in the streets. In 1524 the first church in Central America was founded by the conquering Spaniards. **San Jacinto** is a small church on 6 Avenida y 2 Calle; it may not always be open. *Caldo de frutas*, a highly alcoholic drink with quite a kick, is not openly sold but is m̶ ̶ in the town and drunk on festive occasions. It is illegal to drink it in public pl̶ ̶ ̶ concoction of nances, cherries, peaches, apples and quinces and is left to̶ ̶ There is also *rompope*, a drink made with eggs. Salcajá is a town that̶ ̶ textiles, with shops on every street. Yarn is tied and dyed, u̶ ̶ stretched around telephone poles along the road or on th̶ ̶ seen outside San Jacinto church. Market day is Tues̶

San Andrés Xecul is a small village in stunning surroundings with an extraordinarily lurid coloured church, 8 km north of Xela. Painted a deep-mustard yellow in 1900, its figurines, including angels, have been given blue wings and pastel-pink skirts. Climb the hill a bit above the town and catch a glimpse of the fantastic dome – mulitcoloured like a

2 Quetzaltenango centre

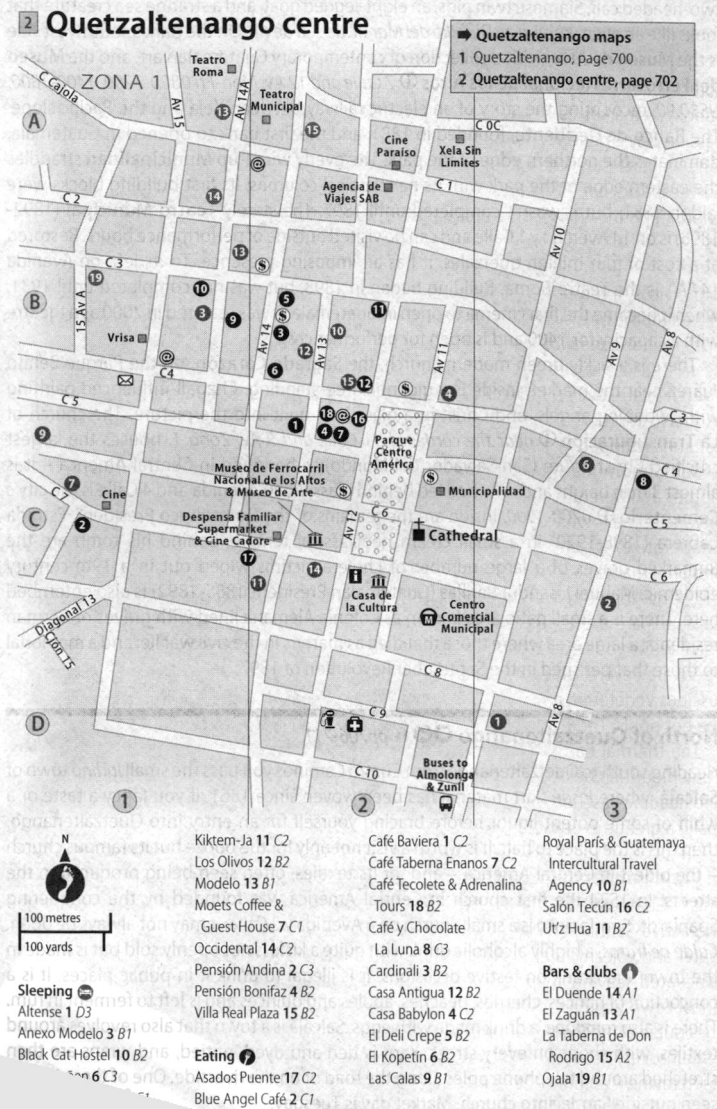

➡ **Quetzaltenango maps**
1 Quetzaltenango, page 700
2 Quetzaltenango centre, page 702

Sleeping 🛏
Altense 1 D3
Anexo Modelo 3 B1
Black Cat Hostel 10 B2
⌐ⁿⁿⁿⁿ 6 C3

Eating 🍴
Asados Puente 17 C2
Blue Angel Café 2 C1

Kiktem-Ja 11 C2
Los Olivos 12 B2
Modelo 13 B1
Moets Coffee &
  Guest House 7 C1
Occidental 14 C2
Pensión Andina 2 C3
Pensión Bonifaz 4 B2
Villa Real Plaza 15 B2

Café Baviera 1 C2
Café Taberna Enanos 7 C2
Café Tecolote & Adrenalina
  Tours 18 B2
Café y Chocolate
  La Luna 8 C3
Cardinali 3 B2
Casa Antigua 12 B2
Casa Babylon 4 C2
El Deli Crepe 5 B2
El Kopetín 6 B2
Las Calas 9 B1

Royal París & Guatemaya
  Intercultural Travel
  Agency 10 B1
Salón Tecún 16 C2
Ut'z Hua 11 B2

Bars & clubs 🍸
El Duende 14 A1
El Zaguán 13 A1
La Taberna de Don
  Rodrigo 15 A2
Ojala 19 B1

beach ball. With your back to the church climb the cobbled street leading up the right-hand side of the plaza to a yellow and maroon chapel peering out across the valley. The view from here is spectacular. Market day is Thursday, opposite the church. The town's fiestas are on 21 November, 30 November and 1 December.

South of Quetzaltenango ●▲●● » pp706-711.

Souteast of Xela is **Cantel** which has the largest and oldest textile factory in the country. Sunday is market day and the town's fiesta is 12-18 August (main day 15). At Easter a passion play is performed. A little further on, on the outskirts of town, on the right-hand side (one minute on the bus), is the white **Copavic glass factory** ① T7763-8038, www.copavic.com, Mon-Fri 0500-1300, Sat 0500-1200, where you can watch and photograph the workers blow the recycled glass.

Zunil

Pinned in by a very steep-sided valley is the town of Zunil, 9 km from Quetzaltenango. It is visited for the nearby hot thermal baths that many come to wallow in, and for its worship of its well-dressed idol San Simón (Maximón). The market is held on Mondays. The town's fiesta is 22-26 November (main day 25) and there is a very colourful Holy Week. The **church** is striking both inside and out. It has a large decorated altarpiece and a small shrine to murdered Bishop Gerardi at the altar. The façade is white with serpentine columns wrapped in carved ivy.

San Simón (Maximón) is worshipped in the town and is often dressed in different clothes at different times. A small charge is made for the upkeep and to take photos; ask anyone in the town to escort you to his house. To the left of the church is the **Santa Ana Cooperative**, which sells beautiful *huipiles*, shirt and skirt materials, as well as bags and bookmarks.

The nearby extinct **Volcán Pico Zunil**, rises to 3542 m to the southeast of the town. On its slopes are the **thermal baths of Fuentes Georginas** ① 0700-1900, US$2.70, which you'll know you're approaching by the wafts of sulphurous fumes that come your way. There are several different-sized pools set into the mountainside surrounded by thick, luscious vegetation and enveloped in the steam that continuously rises up in wafts from the hot pools. There are spectacular views on the way to the baths.

The thermal baths of **Aguas Amargas** ① 0800-1700, US$2, children, US$1.30, are on Zunil Mountain below Fuentes Georginas. They are reached by following the road south and heading east (left) by Estancia de La Cruz. This road passes fields of flowers and would make a great trip on a bike.

El Viejo Palmar

This is Guatemala's Pompeii. The river that cuts through here flows directly down from the active Santiaguito volcanic cone following a series of serious lahars (mudflows of water and volcanic material) that took place in the 1990s. The small town of 10,000 was evacuated, leaving an extraordinary legacy. In August 1998, the whole south end of the ghost town was destroyed by a massive lahar that crushed the church. This also shifted the course of the Río Nimá I, which began to flow directly through the centre of the church remains. Very heavy erosion since has left the west front and the altar separated by a 30-m deep ravine – an unbelievable sight.

Volcán Santa María and Santiaguito

Santiaguito's mother, Santa María (3772 m), is a rough 5½-hour climb (1500 m). You can see Santiaguito (2488 m) below, erupting mostly with ash blasts and sometimes lava flows from a mirador. It is possible to camp at the summit of Santa María, or on the saddle west of the summit, but it is cold and windy, but worth it because dawn provides views of the entire country's volcanic chain and an almighty shadow is cast across the area by Santa Maria's form. Santiaguito is a fairly new volcano that formed after the eruption of Santa María out of its crater. Do not attempt to climb Santiaguito: it erupts continuously on a daily basis throwing up ash and is considered one of the most dangerous volcanoes in the world. To see it erupting you need to climb Santa María, where you can look down on this smaller volcano. ▶▶ See Tour operators, page 708.

Laguna Chicabal

San Martín rangers' station ① 0700-1800, US$2, is where the two-hour climb to Laguna Chicabal starts. This is a lime-green lake, at 2712 m, in the crater of the extinct volcano (2900 m) of the same name, with wild white lilies, known as *cartucho*, growing at the edges. The Maya believe the waters are sacred and it is thought that if you swim in the lake you will become ill. The highlight of a trip here is the sight of the clouds tumbling down over the circle of trees that surround the lake, and then appearing to bounce on the surface before dispersing. Ceremonies of Maya initiation are held at the lake in early May, known as *Jueves de la Ascensión*. The walk from San Martín takes about two hours.

West of Quetzaltenango ⊖ ▶▶ pp706-711.

To Mexico from Quetzaltenango

It takes half an hour to reach **San Juan Ostuncalco**, 15 km away. It's a pleasant, prosperous town with a big white church noted for its good weekly market on Sunday and beautiful sashes worn by men. Its fiesta, Virgen de la Candelaria, is held on 29 January to 2 February. The road, which is paved, switchbacks 37 km down valleys and over pine-clad mountains to a plateau looking over the valley in which are San Pedro and San Marcos. **San Marcos** has a few places to stay and eat. It is a transport hub with little to see. **San Pedro Sacatepéquez** has a huge market on Thursday. The Maya women wear golden and purple skirts.

The extinct **Volcán Tajumulco**, at 4220 m, is the highest in Central America. Start very early in the day if you plan to return to San Marcos by nightfall. It's about a five-hour climb and a three-hour descent. Once you have reached the ridge on Tajumulco, turn right along the top of it; there are two peaks, the higher is on the right. The peak on the left (4100 m) is used for shamanistic rituals.

Dormant **Volcán Tacaná** (4093 m) on the Mexican border may be climbed from the village of Sibinal. Its last eruption was 1949, but there was activity in 2001, so check before climbing. It is the second highest volcano in Guatemala with a 400-m wide crater and fumaroles on its flanks. Take a bus to Sibinal from San Marcos. It is a six-hour difficult climb to the summit and it's recommended that you ask for a guide in the village. About 15 km west of San Marcos the road begins its descent from 2500 m to the lowlands. In 53 km to **Malacatán** it drops to 366 m. It is a winding ride with continuous bends, but the scenery is attractive. There is accommodation.

Border essentials: Guatemala–Mexico

El Carmen–Talismán

The international bridge over the Río Suchiate at Talismán into Mexico is 18 km west of Malacatán. The last staging post in Guatemala is El Carmen.

Guatemalan immigration Open 24 hours. It is a 200-m walk between the two border posts. If entering by car, especially a rented car, be prepared for red tape, miscellaneous charges, vehicle fumigation and frustration.

Sleeping Hospedaje El Paso (**B-C**), T7776-9474, 13 rooms with bath, TV, a/c, cheaper without.

Transport For long-distance travel see Transport, Guatemala City. Travelling by bus to Mexico is quicker from Quetzaltenango than from San Marcos. Most traffic seems to go via Coatepeque and not via San Marcos. However, from Quetzaltenango, there are frequent buses to Talismán via San Marcos or Coatepeque; buses from Xela marked 'Talismán' usually involve a change in Malacatán, 40 mins from the border. From San Pedro Sacatepéquez, there are frequent local buses from 0430-1630 to Malacatán, from where *colectivos*, often crowded, will get you to the border. Or, take a bus from Quetzaltenango to Retalhuleu, 1½ hours, US$1, and then another to the border, two hours, US$2.30. Línea Dorada, www.tikalmayaworld.com, goes from Guatemala City to Tapacuhula at 0800, US$20. This border is not used much by heavy transport.

The road to the coastal plain from San Juan Ostuncalco is the most attractive of all the routes down from the highlands, bypassing most of the small towns through quickly changing scenery as you lose height. After San Juan, go south for 1.5 km to **Concepción Chiquirichapa**, with a bright blue and yellow church, which is one of the wealthiest villages in the country. It has a small market early every Thursday morning and a fiesta on 5-9 December. About 6 km beyond is **San Martín Sacatepéquez**, which used to be known as San Martín Chile Verde, and is famous for its hot chillies. This village appears in Miguel Angel Asturias' *Mulata de Tal*. It stands in a windy, cold gash in the mountains. The slopes are superbly steep and farmed, giving fantastic vistas on the climb up and down from Laguna Chicabal (see above). The men wear very striking long red and white striped tunics, beautifully embroidered around the hem. Market day is Sunday. The fiesta runs from 7-12 November (main day 11 November).

For Sleeping and Eating price codes and other relevant information, see Essentials pages 45-48.

● Sleeping

Quetzaltenango *p699, maps p700 and p702*
At Easter, 12-18 Sep and Christmas, rooms need to be booked well in advance.
A Casa Mañen, 9a Av, 4-11, Zona 1, T7765-0786, www.comeseeit.com. Reports are consistently good, serves great breakfasts and friendly staff offer a very warm welcome. Room 2 is a great option with a bed on a mezzanine. Some rooms have microwave, fridge and TV. All are comfortable, and furnished with attractive wooden accessories. There is a small, pretty courtyard area and secure parking.
A Modelo, 14 Av "A", 2-31, Zona 1, T7761-2529. Friendly hotel with 20 rooms with TV, some set around a garden patio. Hot showers, restaurant and bargain breakfasts. Safe parking.
A Pensión Bonifaz, 4 Calle, 10-50, Zona 1, T7765-1111. 75 clean, comfortable rooms with TV. Pool (noisy at times) which is occasionally heated. Good restaurant and bar. Parking.
B Anexo Hotel Modelo, 14 Av "A", 3-22, Zona 1, T7761-2529. 9 rooms with private bath and TV, good value. Part of Modelo.
B Villa Real Plaza, 4 Calle, 12-22, Zona 1, T7761-4045. Dignified colonial building, 58 rooms with TV. Restaurant has good vegetarian food, and is good value. Parking.
C Kiktem-Ja, 13 Av, 7-18, Zona 1, T7761-4304. A central location with 16 colonial-style rooms, nicely furnished, locally made blankets on the beds, wooden floors, all with bath, hot water, open fires, car parking inside gates.
C Los Olivos, 13 Av, 3-22, T7761-0215, Zona 1. 26 pleasant rooms above parking area with private bathroom, TV and a restaurant with cheap breakfasts and meals.
D Occidental, 7 Calle, 12-23, Zona 1, T7765-4069. 10 rooms, 1 of the cheapest

budget rooms right in the town centre. Rooms lack natural light, but there's hot water and the town's on your doorstep.
D-E Altense, 9 Calle, 8-48, Zona 1, T7765-4648. 16 rooms with bath, hot water, parking, secure and friendly. However, if your room is on the 9 Av side, you'll be woken by rush-hour traffic. This is a good town centre deal for single travellers. Recommended.
D-F Black Cat Hostel, 13 Av, 3-33, Zona 1, T7761-2091, www.blackcathostels.net. A hostel in the old Casa Kaehler. Dorms (**F** per person) and private rooms all with shared bathrooms. Breakfast included.
E Hostal Don Diego, 6 Calle, 15-12, Zona 1, hostaldondiego@gmail.com. Sweet hostel, set about an interior courtyard with rooms with shared bathroom. Hot water and breakfast included. Bright and clean. Weekly and monthly rents available.
E Moets Coffee & Guest House, 7 Calle 15-24, T5585-4213. 4 single (**F** per person) and 1 double room. Long-stay discounts possible. Restaurant and bar.
E Pensión Andina, 8 Av, 6-07, Zona 1, T7761-4012. Private bathrooms, hot water, friendly, clean, sunny patio, restaurant, good value, parking.
F Casa Argentina, Diagonal 12, 8-37, Zona 1, T7761-2470. 25 clean rooms, hot water, 10 shared bathrooms, cheaper in 18-bed dorm, rooms with private bath, cooking facilities with purified water, friendly, laundry service. Monthly room rates, US$100.

Zunil *p703*
C-D Las Cumbres Eco-Saunas y Gastronomía, T5399-0029, www.lascumbres.com.gt. Daily 0700-1800. Just beyond Zunil on the left-hand side of the road heading to the coast (Km 210). This is just the place for some R&R with saunas emitting natural steam from the geothermal activity nearby. There are 12 rooms, with sauna, cheaper without sauna. There are separate saunas and jacuzzis for day visitors

(US$2.50 per hr) and a restaurant serving wholesome regional food and natural juices. Highly recommended. See Transport for transfers.

D Turicentro Fuentes Georginas, 6 cold bungalows with 2 double beds and 2 bungalows with 3 single beds. They have cold showers, fireplaces with wood, electricity from 1700-2200 and barbecue grills for guests' use near the baths. Guests can use the baths after public closing times. Reasonably priced restaurant with breakfasts, snacks and drinks, 0800-1800.

❶ Eating

Quetzaltenango *p699, maps p700 and p702*
¶¶¶-¶¶ Cardinali, 14 Av, 3-25, Zona 1. Owned by Benito, a NY Italian, great Italian food, including large pizzas with 31 varieties: 2 for 1 on Tue and Thu; tasty pastas of 20 varieties, extensive wine list. Recommended. Also does home delivery in 30 mins (T7761-0924).
¶¶¶-¶¶ El Kopetín, 14 Av, 3-51, Zona 1. Friendly, good, meat and seafood dishes, try the fish cooked in garlic.
¶¶¶-¶ Las Calas, 14 Av "A", 3-21, Zona 1. Mon-Sat. Breakfasts, salads, soups, paella and pastas served around a courtyard with changing art hanging from walls. The food is tasty with delicious bread to accompany, but small portions are served. The breakfast service is far too slow. Adjoining bar.
¶¶¶-¶ Restaurante Royal París, 14 Av "A", 3-06, Zona 1. Delicious food (try the fish in a creamy mushroom sauce), excellent choices, including vegetarian. Also cheap options. Run by Stéphane and Emmanuelle. Recommended. Live music from 2000 on Fri.
¶¶ Ut'z Hua, Av 12, 3-02, Zona 1. This prettily decorated restaurant with purple tablecloths does typical food, which is always very good and filling. Don't miss the *pollo con mole* or fish. Recommended.
¶¶-¶ Asados Puente, 7 Calle, 13-29. Lots of veggie dishes with tofu and tempeh. Also ceviche. Popular with expats. Run by Ken

Cielatka and Eva Melgar. Some profits go towards helping ill children.
¶¶-¶ Casa Antigua, 12 Av, 3-26. Savoury and sweet crêpes, baguettes and light meals served up in an 1814 house in a courtyard or inside. Bar available.
¶¶-¶ Salón Tecún, Pasaje Enríquez, off the park at 12 Av y 4 Calle, Zona 1. Bar, local food, breakfasts also, TV. Always popular with gringos and locals.
¶ Café Taberna Enanos, 5 Calle near Av 12 and Parque Central, Zona 1. Mon-Sat 0715-2000. Good cheap breakfast, also has *menú del día*.
¶ El Deli Crepe, 14 Av, 3-15, Zona 1. Good tacos, *almuerzo* with soup, great milkshakes, savoury and sweet crêpes, juicy *fajitas* that arrive steaming.

Cafés and bakeries
Bakeshop at 18 Av, 1-40, Zona 3. A Mennonite bakery that is Xela's answer to *dulce* heaven. They bake a whole range of cookies, muffins, breads and cakes and sells fresh yoghurt and cheeses. Tue and Fri 0900-1800 so get there early as the goodies go really fast.
Blue Angel Café, 7 Calle, 15-79, Zona 1. Great salads, light meals, service a little slow though, movies shown on a monthly rotation, useful noticeboard.
Café Baviera, 5 Calle, 13-14, Zona 1. Open 0700-2000. Good cheap meals and excellent pies, huge cake portions (try the carrot cake) and coffee in large premises, with walls lined from ceiling to floor with old photos and posters. Good for breakfasts, but a little on the expensive side. Popular, but lacks warmth.
Café Tecolote, a new place above Adrenalina Tours. While sipping coffee and eating cake, access wireless internet and pick up tourist information from the staff.
Café y Chocolate La Luna, 8 Av, 4-11, Zona 1. Delicious hot chocolate with or without added luxuries, good cheap snacks, also top chocolates and *pasteles* (the strawberry and cream pie is recommended), pleasant atmosphere in a colonial house

decorated with moon symbols, fairy lights, and old photos; a good meeting place.
Casa Babylon, 13 Av y 5 Calle, Zona 1. Daily 1230-2230. Enormous sandwiches (with veggie options) and crêpes. Recommended.

⊕ Entertainment

Quetzaltenango *p699, maps p700 and p702*
Bars and clubs
El Duende, 14 Av "A", 1-42, Zona 1. Popular café-bar, 1800-2330. A favourite among Guatemalans and gringos.
El Zaguán, 14 Av "A", A-70, Zona 1. A disco-bar Wed, Thu 1900-2430, Fri, Sat 2100-2430, US$3.25, drink included; plays salsa music.
La Taberna de Don Rodrigo, 14 Av, Calle C-47, Zona 1. Cosy bar, reasonable food served in dark wood atmosphere, draught beer.
Ojala, 15 Av "A", 3-33, an entertainment venue, popular with locals and gringos, which also shows films.
Salón Tecún, Pasaje Enríquez, 12 Av y 4 Calle, Zona 1. See Eating, above.

Cinemas
Cine Sofía, 7 Calle 15-18. Mon-Fri 1800. See Blue Angel and Ojala, above.

Dance
Tropica Latina, 5 Calle 12-24, Zona 1, T5892-8861, tropicalatina@xelawho.com. Classes Mon-Sat.

Theatre
Teatro Municipal, 14 Av and 1 Calle, main season May-Nov, theatre, opera, etc.

○ Shopping

Quetzaltenango *p699, maps p700 and p702*
Bookshops
Vrisa, 15 Av, 3-64, T7761-3237, a good range of English-language second-hand books.

Markets
The **main market** is at Templo de Minerva on the western edge of town (take the local bus, US$0.10); at the southeast corner of Parque Centro América is the **Centro Comercial Municipal**, a shopping centre with craft and textile shops on the upper levels, food, clothes, etc below. There is another **market** at 2 Calle y 16 Av, Zona 3, south of Parque Benito Juárez, known as La Democracia. Every first Sun of the month there also is an art and handicrafts market, around Parque Centro America.

Supermarkets
Centro Comercial Mont Blanc, Paiz, 4 Calle between 18-19 Av, Zona 3.
La Pradera, near the Minerva Terminal.
Despensa Familiar, 13 Av, 6-94.

North of Quetzaltenango *p701*
The smallest bottle of bright yellow *rompope* is sold in various shops around Salcajá, including the **Fábrica de Pénjamo**, 2 Av, 4-03, Zona 1, US$1.55, and it slips down the throat very nicely!

▲ Activities and tours

Quetzaltenango *p699, maps p700 and p702*
When taking a tour up any of the volcanoes make sure your guides stay with you all the time; it can get dangerous when the cloud rolls down.
Adrenalina Tours, inside Pasaje Enríquez, T7761-4509, www.adrenalinatours.com. Numerous tours are on offer including bike, fishing, rafting, horse riding, rock climbing and volcano tours as well as packages to Belize, Honduras and the Petén and trips to Huehue and Todos Santos. Highly recommended. Also offers Central American packages via Andamos Travel, www.andamostravel.com.
Agencia de Viajes SAB, 1 Calle, 12-35, T7761-6402. Good for cheap flights.

Guatemaya Intercultural Travel Agency, 14 Av "A", 3-06, T7765-0040. Very helpful. **Mayaexplor**, T7761-5057, www.maya explor.com. Run by Thierry Roquet, who arranges a variety of trips around Xela and around the country. He can also arrange excursions into Mexico, Belize and Honduras and treks, eg Nebaj–Todos Santos. French-speaking. His website offers useful information for travellers. A proportion of funds goes towards local development projects. Recommended.

Quetzaltrekkers, based inside **Casa Argentina** at Diagonal 12, 8-37, T7765-5895, www.quetzaltrekkers.com. This recommended, established, non-profit agency is known for its 3-day hike (Sat am-Mon pm) from Xela across to Lake Atitlán. Proceeds go to the **Escuela de la Calle School** for kids at risk, and a dorm for homeless children. Also offers trek from Nebaj–Todos Santos, 6 days, full-moon hike up Santa María and others. Hiking volunteers are also needed for a 3-month minimum period: hiking experience and reasonable Spanish required.

Tranvia de los Altos, www.tranviadelos altos.com, provides daytime and nighttime walking tours in Xela as well as excursions. Guided city tour is only US$4. Recommended.

Zunil p703

See **Las Cumbres EcoSaunas y Gastronomía**, T5399-0029, under Sleeping, above.

⊙ Transport

Quetzaltenango p699, maps p700 and p702
Bus
Local City buses run between 0600 and 1900. Between the town centre and Minerva Terminal, bus No 6, Santa Fe, US$0.20, 15-30 mins, depending on traffic. Catch the bus at the corner of 4 Calle and 13 Av by Pasaje Enríquez. Buses to the Rotonda leave from the corner of 11 Av and 10 Calle, US$0.20, or catch bus No 6, 10 or 13, from Av 12 y 3 Calle as they come down to the park, 15 mins. To

catch buses to **San Francisco El Alto**, **Momostenango**, the **south coast** and **Zunil**, get off the local bus at the Rotonda, then walk a couple of steps away from the road to step into a feeder road where they all line up.

Long distance To **Guatemala City**, Galgos, Calle Rodolfo Robles, 17-43, Zona 1, T7761-2248, 1st-class buses, at 0400, 1230, 1500, US$5, 4 hrs, will carry bicycles; **Marquensita** several a day (office in the capital 21 Calle, 1-56, Zona 1), leaves from the Minerva Terminal, US$4.60, comfortable, 4 hrs. **Líneas América**, from 7 Av, 3-33, Zona 2, T7761-2063, US$5, 4 hrs, between 0515-2000, 6 daily. **Línea Dorada**, 12 Av and 5 C, Zona 3, T7767-5198, 0400 and 1800, US$9. **Transportes Alamo** from 14 Av, 5-15, Zona 3, T7763-5044, between 0430 and 1430, 7 a day, US$5, 4 hrs.

The following destinations are served by buses leaving from the Minerva Terminal, Zona 3 and the Rotonda. For **Antigua**, change at Chimaltenangoby either taking a chicken bus or pullman. To **Almolonga**, via **Cantel**, every 30 mins, US$0.50, 10 mins. (Buses to Almolonga and Zunil not via Cantel, leave from the corner of 10 Av and 10 Calle, Zona 1.) To **Chichicastenango** with Transportes Veloz Quichelense de Hilda Esperanza, several from 0500 to 1530, US$3.80, 2½ hrs. To **Cuatro Caminos** US$0.50, 30 mins. To **Huehuetenango** with **Transportes Velásquez**, every 30 mins 0500-1730, US$2.50, 2½ hrs. To **La Mesilla** at 0500, 0600, 0700, 0800, 1300, 1400 with Transportes Unión Fronteriza, US$3.60, 4 hrs. To **Los Encuentros**, US$2.20. To **Malacatán**, US$3.60, 5 hrs. To **Momostenango**, US$1.20, 1½ hrs. To **Panajachel**, with Transportes Morales, at 0500, 0600, 1000, 1200, 1500, US$3.20, 2½-3 hrs. To **Retalhuleu**, US$1.20, 1½ hrs. To **Salcajá**, every 30 mins, US$0.40, 15 mins. To **San Andrés Xecul** every 2 hrs, US$0.60, 30 mins. To **San Cristóbal Totonicapán**, every 30 mins, US$0.40, 20 mins. To **San Francisco El Alto**, US$0.70. **San Marcos**, every 30 mins, US$1, 1 hr. **San Martín Sacatepéquez/San Martín Chile**

Verde, US$0.70, 1 hr. **Santiago Atitlán**, with Ninfa de Atitlán at 0800, 1100, 1230, 1630, 4½ hrs. To **Ciudad Tecún Umán** every 30 mins, 0500-1400, US$3.60, 4 hrs. To **Totonicapán**, every 20 mins, US$1.20, 1 hr. To **Zunil**, every 30 mins, US$0.70, 20-30 mins.

Shuttle Adrenalina Tours, see Tour operators, above, runs shuttles. To **Cobán**, US$33 and also to **Fuentes Georginas** and **Las Cumbres Eco-Saunas y Gastronomía**, by its own chicken bus at 0800, 1100, 1400 returning 0900, 1200, 1800, US$5 return. Returning from the Eco-Saunas at 0920, 1230 and 1820.

International: Adrenalina Tours, see Tour operators, runs a shuttle to and from San Cristóbal de las Casas, Mexico, US$30.

Car
Car hire Tabarini Renta Autos, 9 Calle, 9-21, Zona 1, T7763-0418.
Mechanic José Ramiro Muñoz R, 1 Calle, 19-11, Zona 1, T7761-8204. Also Goodyear **Taller** at the Rotonda and for motorbikes **Moto Servicio Rudy**, 2 Av, 3-48, Zona 1, T7765-5433.

Taxi
Found all over town, notably lined up along Parque Centro América.
Taxis Xelaju, T7761-4456.

North of Quetzaltenango *p701*
Bus All buses heading to Quetzaltenango from Cuatro Caminos pass through **Salcajá**, 10 mins. From Xela to **San Andrés Xecul**, US$0.60, 30 mins. Or take any bus heading to Cuatro Caminos and getting off at the Esso station on the left-hand side, and then almost doubling back on yourself to take the San Andrés road. There are pickups from here.

South of Quetzaltenango *p703*
Bus Cantel is 10-15 mins by bus (11 km), and US$0.24 from Xela on the way to Zunil, but you need to take the bus marked for Cantel Fábrica and Zunil, not Almolonga and Zunil. From **Zunil** to Xela via Almolonga leaves from the bridge. Walk down the left-hand side of the church to the bottom of the hill, take a left and you'll see the buses the other side of the bridge, US$0.60. **Fuentes Georginas** is reached either by walking the 8 km uphill just to the south of Zunil, 2 hrs (300 m ascent; take the right fork after 4 km, but be careful as robbery has occurred here), by pickup truck in 15 mins (US$10 return with a 1 hr wait), or hitch. If you come by bus to Zunil and are walking to the Fuentes, don't go down into town with the bus, but get off on the main road at the Pepsi stand and walk to the entrance road, which is visible 100 m away on the left. See also Shuttles, left, for transfer to the thermal pools.

El Viejo Palmar *p703*
Bus Just before San Felipe, and just before the Puente Samalá III, if you're heading south, is the turn to the right for El Viejo Palmar. Take any bus heading to the south coast, and asked to be dropped off at the entrance and walk. Or, take a pickup from San Felipe park. Ask for Beto or Brígido.
Taxi From Xela round trip is US$20, or take a tour from town.

Volcán Santa María and Santiaguito *p704*
Bus To reach the volcano take the bus to **Llano del Pinal**, 7 km away, from the Minerva Terminal (every 30 mins, last bus back 1800). Get off at the crossroads and follow the dirt road towards the right side of the volcano until it sweeps up the right (about 40 mins), take the footpath to the left (where it is marked for some distance); bear right at the saddle where another path comes in from the left, but look carefully as it is easily missed.

Laguna Chicabal *p704*
Bus/car The last bus to **Quetzaltenango** leaves at 1900, 1 hr. Parking at the entrance, US$2. It is a 40-min walk from the car park (and you'll need a sturdy vehicle if you attempt the steep first ascent in a car).

To Mexico from Quetzaltenango *p704*
Bus Volcán Tajumulco can be reached by getting to the village of **San Sebastián** from San Marcos, which takes about 2 hrs.

❶ Directory

Quetzaltenango *p699, maps p700 and p702*
Banks Many banks on Parque Centro América. Non-Amex TCs are difficult to change here. Maestro can't be used in ATMs. There is a **Bancard**, 24 hr Visa ATM on the park next to **Banrural** which has a MasterCard ATM **Banco Industrial**, corner of 5 Calle y 11 Av, 24 hr Visa ATM, Visa accepted. **G&T Continental**, 14 Av, 3-17. Advances on MasterCard. **Embassies and consulates** Mexican Consulate, 21 Av, 8-64, Zona 3, T7767-5542, Mon-Fri 0800-1100, take photocopies of your passport. **Emergencies** Police: T7761-5805; Fire: T7761-2002; Red Cross: T7761-2746. **Internet** Lots of places around town. **Language schools** See also the box on page 657. Many of Xela's schools can be found at www.xelapages.com/schools.htm. There are many schools that offer individual tuition, accommodation with families, extra-curricular activities and excursions. Some also offer Mayan languages. Several schools fund community-development projects, and students are invited to participate with voluntary work. Some schools are non-profit making; enquire carefully. Extra-curricular activities are generally better organized at the larger schools. Prices start from US$130 per week including accommodation, but rise in Jun-Aug to US$150 and up. The following have been recommended: **Centro de Estudios de Español Pop Wuj**, 1 Calle, 17-72, T7761-8286, www.pop-wuj.org. **Guatemalensis**, 19 Av, 2-14, Zona 1, T7765-1384, www.geocities.com/spanland/. **Instituto Central América (ICA)**, 19 Av, 1-47 Calle, Zona 1, T/F7763-1871. **INEPAS** (Instituto de Estudios Español y Participación en Ayuda Social), 15 Av, 4-59, T7765-1308, www.inepas.org. Keen on social projects and has already founded a primary school in a Maya village, extremely welcoming. **Juan Sisay Spanish School**, 15 Av, 8-38, Zona 1, T7761-1586, www.juansisay.com. **Kie-Balam**, Diagonal 12, 4-46, Zona 1, T7761-1636, kie_balam@hotmail.com. Offers conversation classes in the afternoon in addition to regular hours. **La Paz**, Diagonal 11, 7-36, T7761-2159, xela.escuelalapaz@gmail.com. **Minerva Spanish School**, 24 Av, 4-39, Zona 3, T7767-4427, www.minervaspanish school.com. **Proyecto Lingüístico Quetzalteco de Español**, 5 Calle, 2-40, Zona 1, T7765-2140, hermandad@plqe.org. Recommended. **Proyecto Lingüístico 'Santa María'**, 14 Av "A", 1-26, T/F7765-1262. Volunteer opportunities and free internet access. **Sakribal**, 6 C, 7-42, Zona 1, T7763-0717, www.sakribal.com. Community projects are available. **Ulew Tinimit**, 4 C, 15-23, Zona 1, T7761-6242, www.spanish guatemala.org. **Utatlán**, 12 Av, 14-32, Pasaje Enríquez, Zona 1, T7763-0446, utatlan_ xela@hotmail.com. Voluntary work opportunities, one of the cheaper schools. **Laundry** Minimax, 14 Av, C-47. Lavandería Pronto, 7 Calle, 13-25, good service. Lavandería El Centro, 15 Av, 3-51, Zona 1, very good service. **Medical services** San Rafael Hospital, 9 Calle, 10-41, T7761-2956. Hospital Rodolfo Robles, a private hospital on Diagonal 11, Zona 1, T7761-4229. Hospital Privado Quetzaltenango, Calle Rodolfo Robles, 23-51, Zona 1, T7761-4381. **Post office** 15 Av y 4 Calle. **Telephone** Telgua, 15 Av "A" y 4 Calle. Kall Shop, 8 Av, 4-24, Zona 1. **Voluntary work** Asociación Hogar Nuevos Horizontes, www.ahnh.org, T7761-6140. EntreMundos, El Espacio, 6 Calle, 7-31, Zona 1, T7761-2179, www.entre mundos.org, puts people in touch with opportunities. Hogar de Niños, Llanos de Urbina, Cantel, T7761-1526, hogardeninos@hotmail.com.

Southern Guatemala

The southern coastal plain of Guatemala supports many plantations of coffee, sugar and tropical fruit trees and its climate is unbearably hot and humid. Amid the fincas some of the most curious archaeological finds have been unearthed, a mixture of monument styles such as Maya and Olmec, including Abaj Takalik, the cane field stones at Santa Lucía Cotzumalguapa and the big 'Buddhas' of Monte Alto.

On the coast are the black-sand beaches and nature reserves of the popular and laid-back Monterrico and Sipacate resorts, where nesting turtles burrow in the sand and masses of birds take to the skies around. Casting a shadow over the coast, the Central Highland volcanoes of Lake Atitlán, and the Antigua trio of Fuego, Acatenango and Agua, look spectacular, looming on the horizon above the lowlands. ▶▶ *For listings, see pages 717-720.*

Ins and outs
Numerous buses travel from Guatemala City and along the CA2 Highway that runs through the transport hub of Escuintla and through towns either side to the Mexican and El Salvadorian borders. ▶▶ *See Transport, page 719.*

Guatemala City to the Pacific coast
The main road from the capital heads to Escuintla, which connects Guatemala City with all the Pacific ports. There is also a direct route to Escuintla from Antigua. South of Guatemala City is **Amatitlán** on the banks of the lake of the same name. The lake is seriously polluted. The main reason for coming here would be for the **Day of the Cross** on 3 May, when the Christ figure is removed from the church and floated out of a boat amid candles and decorations. A *teleférico* has opened on the lake. **Palín** has a Sunday market in a plaza under an enormous ceiba tree. The textiles are exceptional, but are increasingly difficult to find. There are great views of Pacaya to the east as you head down to the coast, Volcán Agua to the northwest, and the Pacific lowlands to the west. An unpaved road runs northwest from here to Antigua via **Santa María de Jesús**. The town's fiesta is on 24-30 July. **Escuintla** is a large, unattractive provincial centre in a rich tropical valley. It is essentially a transport hub for travellers in the area.

Puerto San José, Chulamar and Iztapa
South of Escuintla the fast tarmacked highway heads to Puerto San José. Puerto San José used to be the country's second largest port and first opened for business (especially the coffee trade) in 1853. The climate is hot, the streets and most of the beaches dirty, and at weekends the town fills up with people from the capital. Fishing is available (see under Iztapa, below), and there are swimming beaches near by, but beware of the strong undercurrent. Some 5 km to the west of Puerto San José is Chulamar, a popular beach at weekends with good bathing. Iztapa is world-renowned for deep-sea fishing. Sail fish, bill fish, marlin, tuna, dorado, roosterfish, yellowfin and snapper are to be found in large numbers. See Tour operators, page 718 for further details. The **Chiquimulilla Canal** runs either side of Puerto San José parallel to the coast, for close to 100 km. From here a trip can be taken through the canal by *lancha* to the old Spanish port of Iztapa, now a bathing resort, a short distance to the east.

Monterrico ⊜🅱️🅖🅐🅜🅖🅘 ➤➤ *pp717-720. Colour map 5, C2.*

Monterrico is a small, black-sand resort where the sunsets are a rich orange and the waves crash spectacularly on to the shore. If you are in the area between September and January, you can sponsor a baby turtle's waddle to freedom.

Ins and outs

The landing stage is 10 minutes' walk from the ocean front, where you'll find the main restaurants and places to stay. When you step off the dock take the first left, and keep left, which heads directly to the main cluster of beach hotels. This road is known as Calle del Proyecto or Calle del Muelle. Walking straight on from the dock takes you to the main drag in town. When you get to the main drag and want to walk to the main group of hotels, take a left along the beach or take the sandy path to the left one block back from the beach where the sand is a tiny bit easier to walk on.

Sights

Monterrico's popularity is growing fast but mainly as a weekend and holiday resort with views that are undisturbed by high-rise blocks. All the hotels, mostly rustic and laid-back, are lined up along the beach, and there are a few shops and *comedores* not linked to hotels, in this village of just 1500 people. The village is surrounded by canals carpeted in aquatic plants and mangrove swamps with bird and turtle reserves in their midst. These areas make up the **Monterrico Nature Reserve**. Anteater, armadillo, racoon and weasel live in the area. It is worth taking a boat trip at sunrise or sunset, to see migratory North and South American birds, including flamingo. However, the real stars in this patch are the olive ridleys – *Parlama blanca* and *Parlama negra* turtles, which lay eggs between July and October, and the Baule turtle, which lays between between October and February. There is a **turtle hatchery** ① *daily 0800-1200, 1400-1700, US$1*. Just behind the hatchery there are 300 breeding crocodiles, 150 turtles and iguanas. The turtle liberation event takes place every Saturday night between October and February.

Santa Lucía Cotzumalguapa ⊜🅱️🅖🅘 ➤➤ *pp717-720. Colour map 5, C2.*

Amid the sugar-cane fields and *fincas* of this Pacific town lie an extraordinary range of carved stones and images with influences from pre-Maya civilizations, believed mostly to be ancient Mexican cultures, including the Izapa civilization from the Pacific coast area of Mexico near the Guatemalan border. The town is just north of the Pacific Highway, where some of the hotels and banks are.

Ins and outs

You can visit all the sites on foot. However, you are advised not to go wandering in and out of the cane fields at the Bilbao site as there have been numerous assaults in the past. You can walk along the tarmacked road north to the El Baúl sites (6 km and 8 km respectively from town), but there is no shade, so take lots of water. Ask for directions. There is an occasional 'Río Santiago' bus, which goes as far as Colonia Maya, close to the El Baúl hilltop. Only workers' buses go to **Finca El Baúl** in the morning, returning at night. To get to the museum, walk east along the Pacific Highway and take a left turn into the *finca* site. Alternatively, take a taxi from town (next to the plaza) and negotiate a trip to all four areas. They will charge around US$20. **Note** Do not believe any taxi driver who tells

Border essentials: Guatemala–Mexico

Tecún Umán–Ciudad Hidalgo

The Pacific Highway goes west from Escuintla to the Mexican border at Ciudad Tecún Umán, some 200 km away, passing Siquinalá, where there is a brand-new bypass that emerges the other side of Santa Lucía Cotzumalguapa (buses run through the centre of these places), and on to Mazatenango (see page 715) and Retalhuleu (see page 715). The border is separated by the Río Suchiate from the Mexican town of Ciudad Hidalgo.

Guatemalan immigration The 1 km bridge over the river separates the two border posts. For a fee, boys will help you with your luggage. Normally open 24 hours.

Mexican consulates See Quetzaltenango and Retalhuleu.

Sleeping Hotel Don José (**D**), Calle Real del Comercio, T7776-8164, rooms with bath. Hotel Villazul (**D**), 3 Av, 5-28, T7776-8827. Rooms with bath and a/c.

Transport Buses run from the Mexican side of the border to Tapachula, 30 mins. To Guatemala City, US$6.50, run by **Fortaleza**, four direct buses daily, five hours. Frequent slower buses via Reu and Mazatenango. *Colectivo* from Coatepeque, US$0.70. See also Talismán, page 705, for crossing into Mexico.

Directory There are numerous banks and money changers.

---

you that Las Piedras (the stones) have been moved from the cane fields to the museum because of the increasing assaults.

Sights

There is considerable confusion about who carved the range of monuments and stelae scattered around the town. However, it's safe to say that the style of the monuments found in the last 150 years is a blend of a number of pre-Columbian styles. Some say that the prominent influence is Toltec, the ancestors of the Maya K'iche', Kaqchikel, Tz'utujil and Pipiles. It is thought the Tolteca-Pipil had been influenced in turn by the Classic culture from Teotihuacán, a massive urban state northeast of the present Mexico City, which had its zenith in the seventh century AD. However, some experts say that there is no concrete evidence to suggest that the Pipiles migrated as early as AD 400 or that they were influenced by Teotihuacán. All in all, the cultural make-up of this corner of Guatemala may never be known.

Four main points of interest entice visitors to the area. **Bilbao, El Baúl, Finca El Baúl** and the **Museo de Cultura Cotzumalguapa**. The remnants at **Bilbao**, first re-discovered in 1860, are mainly buried beneath the sugar cane but monuments found above ground show pre-Maya influences. It is thought that the city was inhabited 1200 BC-AD 800. There are four large boulders – known as *Las Piedras* – in sugar-cane fields, which can be reached on foot from the tracks leading from the end of 4 Avenida in town. **El Baúl** is a Late Classic ceremonial centre, 6 km north of Santa Lucía, with two carved stone pieces to see; most of its monuments were built between AD 600-900. **Finca El Baúl** has a collection of sculptures and stelae gathered from the large area of the *finca* grounds. The **Museo de Cultura Cotzumalguapa** ① *Finca Las Ilusiones, Mon-Fri 0800-1600, Sat 0800-1200, US$1.30, less than 1 km east of town, ask the person in charge for the key*, displays numerous artefacts collected from the *finca* and a copy of the famous Bilbao Monument 21 from the cane fields.

From Santa Lucía Cotzumalguapa to the Mexican border

Beyond Santa Lucía Cotzumalguapa is **Cocales**, where a good road north leads to Patulul and after 30 km, to Lake Atitlán at San Lucas Tolimán. The Pacific Highway continues through San Antonio Suchitepéquez to **Mazatenango** (where just beyond are the crossroads for Retalhueleu and Champerico) and on to Coatepeque and Ciudad Tecún Umán for the Mexican border. Mazatenango is the chief town of the Costa Grande zone. While not especially attractive, the Parque Central is very pleasant with many fine trees providing shade. There is a huge fiesta in the last week of February, when hotels are full and double their prices. At that time, beware of children carrying (and throwing) flour.

Retalhuleu and around → *Colour map 5, C1.*

Retalhuleu, normally referred to as 'Reu' (pronounced 'Ray-oo') is the capital of the department. The entrance to the town is grand with a string of royal palms lining the route, known as Calzada Las Palmas. It serves a large number of coffee and sugar estates and much of its population is wealthy. The original colonial church of **San Antonio de Padua** is in the central plaza. Bordering the plaza to the east is the neoclassical **Palacio del Gobierno**, with a giant quetzal sculpture on top. The **Museo de Arqueología y Etnología** ① *Tue-Sat 0830-1300, 1400-1800, Sun 0900-1230, US$1.30 next to the palacio*, is small. Downstairs are exhibits of Maya ceramics.

Fancy cooling off? Near Reu are the **Parque Acuático Xocomil** ① *Km 180.5 on the road from Xela to Champerio, T7722-9400, www.irtra.org.gt, Thur-Sun 0900-1700, US$9.60.* Nearby is the enormous theme park with giant pyramids of **Xetulul** ① *T7722-9450, www.irtra.org.gt, Thur-Sun 100-1800, US$26.*

Abaj Takalik

① *Daily 0700-1700, US$3.25, guides are volunteers so tips are welcomed.*

One of the best ancient sites to visit outside El Petén is Abaj Takalik, a ruined city that lies, sweltering, on the southern plain. Its name means 'standing stone' in K'iche'. The site was discovered in 1888 by botanist Doctor Gustav Brühl. It is believed to have flourished in the late pre-Classic period of 300 BC to AD 250 strategically placed to control commerce between the highlands and the Pacific coast. There are some 239 monuments, which include 68 stelae, 32 altars and some 71 buildings, all set in peaceful surroundings. The environment is loved by birds and butterflies, including blue morphos, and by orchids, which flower magnificently between January and March. The main temple buildings are mostly up to 12 m high, suggesting an early date before techniques were available to build Tikal-sized structures.

Towards the Mexican border

The main road runs 21 km east off the Pacific Highway to **Coatepeque**, one of the richest coffee zones in the country. There is a bright, modern church in the leafy Plaza Central. The local fiesta takes place from 11-19 March. There are several hotels, *hospedajes* and restaurants. **Colomba**, an attractive typical village east of Coatepeque in the lowlands, has a basic *hospedaje*.

Routes to El Salvador

Three routes pass through Southern Guatemala to El Salvador (see box, page 716, for border-crossing information). The main towns are busy but scruffy with little to attract the visitor. If travelling by international bus to El Salvador, see page 636.

Border essentials: Guatemala–El Salvador

Frontera–San Cristóbal
This is the principal crossing. Heavy transport and international buses favour this route.
Guatemalan immigration Open 0600-2000 but usually possible to cross outside these hours with extra charges.

Valle Nuevo–Las Chinamas
Since the construction of the Santa Ana bypass, this has become a popular route for lighter traffic.
Guatemalan immigration Officially open 0800-1800.

Ciudad Pedro de Alvarado–La Hachadura
This is becoming a busier crossing as roads on both sides have improved.
Sleeping There are several cheap *hospedajes* (all **G**, basic), but it is not recommended that you plan to stay here.
Transport The last bus for Sonsonate in El Salvador leaves at 1800.

Route 1 The Pan-American Highway: The first route heads directly south along the paved Pan-American Highway from Guatemala City (CA1) to the border at San Cristóbal Frontera. **Cuilapa**, the capital of Santa Rosa Department, is 65 km along the Highway. About 9 km beyond Los Esclavos is the El Molino junction. Beyond, just off the Pan-American Highway, is the village of **El Progreso**, dominated by the imposing Volcán Suchitán, at 2042 m, now part of the Parque Regional Volcán Suchitán run by La Fundación de la Naturaleza. There is accommodation. The town fiesta with horse racing is from 10-16 November. From El Progreso, a good paved road goes north 43 km to Jalapa through open, mostly dry country, with volcanoes always in view. There are several crater lakes including **Laguna del Hoyo** near Monjas that are worth visiting. The higher ground is forested. Beyond Jutiapa and El Progreso the Pan-American Highway heads east and then south to Asunción Mita. Here there is a turning left to Lago de Güija. Before reaching the border at **San Cristóbal Frontera** (see box, above), the Pan-American Highway dips and skirts the shores (right) of **Lago Atescatempa**, with several islands set in heavy forest.

Route 2 Via Jalpatagua: The second, quicker way of getting to San Salvador is to take a highway that cuts off right from the first route at El Molino junction, about 7 km beyond the Esclavos bridge. This cut-off goes through El Oratorio and Jalpatagua to the border at **Valle Nuevo** (see above), continuing then to Ahuachapán and San Salvador.

Route 3 El Salvador (La) via the border at Ciudad Pedro de Alvarado: This coastal route goes from Escuintla to the border bridge over the Río Paz at La Hachadura (El Salvador). It takes two hours from Escuintla to the border. You pass **Auto Safari Chapín** ① *Km 87.5, T2363-1105, Tue-Sun 0900-1700, US$5,* east of Escuintla, an improbable wildlife park, but busy at weekends and holidays. **Taxisco** is 18 km beyond and just off the road. It's a busy place, which has a white church with a curious hearts and holly design on the façade. To the east is Guazacapán, which merges into **Chiquimulilla**, 3 km to the north, the most important town of the area, with good-quality leather goods available. There is accommodation on offer. A side excursion can be made from Chiquimulilla up the winding CA 16 through coffee *fincas* and farmland. About 20 km along there is a turning to the left down a 2- to 3-km steep, narrow, dirt road that goes to **Laguna de Ixpaco**, an impressive, greenish-yellow lake that is 350 m in diameter. It is boiling in some places, emitting sulphurous fumes and set in dense forest. This trip can also be made by heading south off the Pan-American Highway after Cuilapa (just before Los Esclavos) towards Chiquimulilla on the CA 16, with old trees on either side, some with orchids in them, where you will reach the sign to Ixpaco, after 20 km. Thirty kilometres beyond on the Pacific Highway is **Ciudad Pedro de Alvarado** on the border. See box, opposite.

● Southern Guatemala listings

For Sleeping and Eating price codes and other relevant information, see Essentials pages 45-48.

● Sleeping

Puerto San José, Chulamar and Iztapa *p712*

There are a number of *comedores* in town.
LL Soleil Pacífico, Chulamar, T7879-3131, www.gruposoleil.com. Usual luxuries with day passes available.
AL Hotel y Turicentro Eden Pacific, Barrio El Laberinto, Puerto San José, T7881-1605. 11 a/c rooms with TV, private beach and pools.
C Hotel Club Sol y Playa Tropical, 1 Calle, 5-48, on the canal, Iztapa, T7881-4365. With pool, friendly staff and standard rooms with fans. Good food at restaurant.

Monterrico *p713*

Most hotels are fully booked by Sat midday and prices rise at weekends – book beforehand if arriving at the weekend.
A Hotel Pez de Oro, at the end of main strip to the east, T2368-3684, www.pezdeoro.com. 18 spacious bungalows attractively set around a swimming pool. All rooms have private bathroom, mosquito lamps, pretty bedside lights and fan. Some with a/c. Recommended.
A-B San Gregorio, Calle del Proyecto, behind El Kaimán, T2238-4690. 29 modern rooms with bath, fan and mosquito nets. There is a large part-shaded pool, a restaurant set around the pool. Non-guests can pay to use the pool.

A-C El Mangle, main strip, T5514-6517. Rooms with fans, bathrooms, and mosquito nets (some are a little dark), centred around a nice, clean pool, set a little back from the beach front. It's quieter than some of the others. Recommended.
B Eco Beach Place, 250 m west of the main drag, T5611-6637, ecobeachplace@ hotmail.com. Facing the ocean, take a right off Calle Principal down the path opposite **Las Margaritas**, on the beach. This cosy place has 10 rooms with bath, mosquito nets and fans. There is a pool, and restaurant. Breakfast included in the room price. There is a discount on stays of 3 nights or more.
B-C Café del Sol, 250 m west of the main drag next to **Eco Beach Place**, T5810-0821, www.cafe-del-sol.com. 13 rooms pleasant rooms. Rooms across the road in an annexe are much more spartan. There is a pleasant bar area and a restaurant.
B-F Johnny's Place, main strip. Equipped bungalows, rooms with bath, cheaper without, and a dorm (**F** per person). All windows have mosquito netting. Internet, table tennis, swimming pools, fishing and a restaurant with free coffee fill-ups. Recommended.
C Hotel Restaurante Dulce y Salado, some way away from the main cluster of hotels and a 500-m hard walk east through sand if you are on foot, T5817-9046. The sea view and the uninterrupted view of the highland volcanoes behind is fantastic. Run by a friendly Italian couple, Fulvio and Graziella. Clean, nice rooms, with bath,

fans and mosquito nets, set around a pool. Breakfast included, good Italian food.
D-E El Delfín, T5904-9167, eldelfin99@yahoo.com. Bungalows, with mosquito nets, fans and private bathroom and rooms. Restaurant with vegetarian food. Organizes shuttles at any hour. Recommended.
E Hotel y Restaurant Kaiman, on the beach side, T5617-9880, big bar ('1000 'til you're done' at the weekends) and restaurant. The rooms are very clean, with bath, fan, and mosquito nets. There are 2 pools for adults and children, but they're not in top shape. Discounts for longer stays.

Santa Lucía Cotzumalguapa *p713*
A Santiaguito, Pacific Hwy at Km 90.4, T7882-5435. A/c, TV and hot and cold water, pool and restaurant. Non-guests can use the pool for US$2.60.
C-D Hotel El Camino, diagonally opposite Santiaguito across the highway at Km 90.5, T7882-5316. Rooms with bath, tepid water, fan, some rooms with a/c (more expensive). All have TV. Good restaurant.
E Hospedaje La Reforma, a stone's throw from the park on 4 Av, 4-71. Lots of dark box rooms and dark shared showers. Clean.

Retalhuleu and around *p715*
A La Colonia, 1.5 km to the north at Km 180.5, T7772-2048. Rooms with a/c and TV, pool, and good food.
B Astor, 5 Calle, 4-60, T7771-2559, hotelastor@intelnett.com. A colonial-style place with with 27 rooms, a/c, hot water, TV, set around a pretty courtyard where there's a pool and jacuzzi. Parking and restaurant. Bar La Carreta is inside the hotel. Non-guests can use the pool and jacuzzi here (nicer than the one at Posada de Don José) for a fee.
B Posada de Don José, 5 Calle, 3-67, T7771-0180, posadadonjose@hotmail.com. Rooms with a/c and fan, TV. Also a very good restaurant serving such mouth-watering temptations as lobster sautéed in cognac. Restaurant and café are set

beside the pool. Non-guests can use the pool for a small fee.
B Siboney, 5 km northwest of Reu in San Sebastián, Km 179, T7772-2174, www.hotelsiboney.com. Rooms are with bath, a/c and TV, set around pool. Try the *caldo de mariscos* or *paella* in the excellent restaurant. Non-guests can pay to use the pool.

❼ Eating

Monterrico *p713*
Be careful especially with *ceviche*. There are lots of local *comedores* along Calle Principal, which leads to the beach.
☗ Restaurant Italiano, at the end of the main strip to the east, at Hotel Pez de Oro. Popular and consistently good. Recommended.

Santa Lucía Cotzumalguapa *p713*
☗ Pastelería Italiana, Calzada 15 de Septiembre, 4-58. Open early for bakery.

Retalhuleu and around *p715*
☗ Restaurante La Luna, 5 Calle, 4-97, on the corner of the plaza. Good *típico* meals served.
☗ El Patio, corner of 5 Calle, 4 Av. *Menú del día* and cheap breakfasts. Limited.

❽ Entertainment

Monterrico *p713*
El Animal Desconocido, on beach close to Johnny's Place. Open from 2000 in the week.

▲ Activities and tours

Monterrico *p713*
Tour operators
Those preferring to stay on land can rent horses for a jaunt on the beach. *Lancha* and turtle-searching tours are operated by a couple of agencies in town.

⊖ Transport

Guatemala City to the Pacific coast p712

Bus To and from Guatemala City to **Amatitlán** (every 30 mins, US$0.50) from 0700-2045 from 14 Av, between 3 y 4 Calle, Zona 1, Guatemala City. From **Escuintla** (1½ hrs), to the capital from the 8 Calle and 2 Av, Zona 1, near the corner of the plaza in Escuintla. However, buses that have come along the Pacific Hwy and are going on to the capital pull up at the main bus terminal on 4 Av. From the terminal there are buses direct to **Antigua** every 30 mins, 1-1½ hrs, US$1.20. To **Taxisco** from Escuintla, every 30 mins, 0700-1700, 40 mins, for connections onwards (hourly) to La Avellana, for boats to Monterrico. Frequent buses to **Iztapa** with the last bus departing at 2030.

If you are changing in Escuintla for **Santa Lucía Cotzumalguapa** to the west, you need to take a left out of the bus terminal along the 4 Av up a slight incline towards the police fortress and take a left here on its corner, 9 Calle, through the market. Head for 3 blocks straight, passing the **Cinammon Pastelería y Panadería** on the right at 9 Calle and 2 Av. At the end here are buses heading to Santa Lucía and further west along the Pacific Hwy. It is a 5- to 10-min walk. Buses leave here every 5 mins. To **Santa Lucía Cotzumalguapa** (the bus *ayudantes* shout 'Santa'), 35 mins, US$1.20. On the return, buses pull up at the corner of the 8 Calle and 2 Av, where Guatemala City buses also pass.

Puerto San José, Chulamar and Iztapa p712

Bus Regular buses from the capital passing through **Escuintla**, 2-3 hrs. If you are heading further east by road from Iztapa along the coast to **Monterrico** (where the road is lined with loofah plantations), you need to cross the toll bridge to **Pueblo Viejo**, US$1.60 per vehicle (buses excluded), pedestrians, US$0.85. See below for Transport information.

Monterrico p713
Bus and boat

There are 3 ways of getting to Monterrico, 2 by public transport, the 3rd by shuttle. The **first route** to Monterrico involves heading direct to the Pacific coast by taking a bus from the capital to **Puerto San José**, 1 hr, and changing for a bus to **Iztapa**. Or take a direct bus from Escuintla to Iztapa. Then cross river by the toll bridge to **Pueblo Viejo** for US$1.60 per vehicle (buses excluded), or US$0.80 per foot passengers, 5 mins. The buses now continue to Monterrico, about 25 km east, 1 hr. Buses run to and from Iztapa between 0600-1500, from the corner of main street and the road to Pueblo Viejo to the left, 3 blocks north of the beach, just past the Catholic church on the right.

The **second route** involves getting to Taxisco first and then La Avellana. There are also direct buses to La Avellana from Guatemala City. See Transport, Guatemala City. If you are coming from Antigua, take a bus to **Escuintla** 1-1½ hrs. From there, there are regular departures to **Taxisco**, 40 mins. From Taxisco to La Avellana, buses leave hourly until 1800, US$1, 20 mins. If you take an international bus from Escuintla (45 mins), it will drop you off just past the Taxisco town turnoff, just before a bridge with a slip road. Walk up the road (5 mins) and veer to the right where you'll see the bus stop for **La Avellana**. At La Avellana take the **motor boats** through mangrove swamps, 20-30 mins, US$0.60 for foot passengers, from 0630 and then hourly until 1800. The journey via this route from Antigua to Monterrico takes about 3¼ hrs if your connections are good. Return boats to La Avellana leave at 0330, 0530, 0700, 0800, 0900, 1030, 1200, 1300, 1430, 1600. Buses leave La Avellana for Taxisco hourly until 1800. Buses pull up near the **Banco Nor-Oriente** where numerous buses heading to Guatemala and Escuintla pass.

Shuttles Alternatively, numerous travel agencies in Antigua run shuttles, US$10-12 1 way. You can book a return shuttle journey in Monterrico by going to the language school on the road that leads to the dock. There are also mini buses operating from Monterrico to **Iztapa** and vice-versa.

Santa Lucía Cotzumalguapa *p713*
Bus Regular departures to the capital. Buses plying the Pacific Hwy also pass through, so if you are coming from Reu in the west or Escuintla in the east you can get off here.
Car If you are driving, there are a glut of 24-hr **Esso** and **Texaco** gas stations here. See under Guatemala City to the Pacific coast for catching transport from **Escuintla**.

From Santa Lucía Cotzumalguapa to the Mexican border *p715*
Bus 5 a day **Cocales-Panajachel**, between 0600 and 1400, 2½ hrs. Frequent buses to **Mazatenango** from Guatemala City, US$5. To the border at **Ciudad Tecún Umán**, US$2.10, an irregular service with Fortaleza del Sur.

Retalhuleu and around *p715*
Bus Services along the Pacific Hwy to Mexico leave from the main bus terminal, which is beyond the city limits at 5 Av 'A'. To **Coatepeque** (0600-1800), **Malacatán**, **Mazatenango** and **Champerico** (0500-1800). Buses also leave from here to **El Asintal**, for Abaj Takalik, 30 mins, every 30 mins from 0600-1830, last bus back to Reu 1800. Or catch them before that from the corner of 5 Av 'A' and the Esso gas station as they turn to head for the village. Leaving from a smaller terminal at 7 Av/10 Calle, there are regular buses to **Ciudad Tecún Umán**, **Talismán** and **Guatemala City** via the Pacific route, and to Xela (1¾ hrs, every hr 0500-1800).

Abaj Takalik *p715*
Bus Take a bus to El from **Retalhuleu** and walk the hot 4 km to the site entrance. Or, take any bus heading along the Pacific Hwy

and get off at the **El Asintal** crossroads. Take a pickup from here to El Asintal; then a pickup from the town square to Abaj Takalik. As there are only *fincas* along this road, you will probably be on your own, in which case it is US$5 to the site or US$10 round trip, including waiting time. Bargain hard.
Taxi and tour A taxi from central plaza in Reu to the site and back including waiting time is US$13. Alternatively, take a tour from Xela.

Towards the Mexican border *p715*
Bus From Quetzaltenango to **Coatepeque**, catch any bus heading to Ciudad Tecún Umán from Reu.

⊙ Directory

Monterrico *p713*
Language school Proyecto Lingüístico Monterrico, http://monterrico-guatemala.com/spanish-school.htm. **Medical services** There is a clinic behind El Delfín open at weekends. **Post office** Near Hotel Las Margaritas on the Calle Principal.

Santa Lucía Cotzumalguapa *p713*
Banks Banco G&T Continental, on the highway, accepts MasterCard. Banco Industrial, accepts Visa, 3 Av between 2 and 3 Calle. There's a **Bancared** Visa ATM on the plaza. **Telephone** Telgua, Cda 15 de Septiembre near the highway.

Retalhuleu and around *p715*
Banks There are plenty of banks in town taking Visa and MC. ATMs also. **Embassies and consulates** México, inside the Posada de Don José. Mon-Fri 0700-1230, 1400-1800. **Medical services** Hospital Nacional de Retalhuleu, Blvd Centenario, 3 Av, Zona 2, 10 mins along the road to El Asintal, T7771-0116. **Post office** On the plaza. **Telephone** 5 Calle, 4-18.

Guatemala City to the Caribbean

From the capital to the Caribbean, the main road passes through the Río Motagua Valley, punctuated by cacti and bordered by the Sierra de Las Minas mountains rising abruptly in the west. Dinosaur remains, the black Christ and the Maya ruins of Quiriguá can be found on or close to the highway. The banana port of Puerto Barrios is a large transport and commercial hub and jumping-off point for the Garífuna town of Lívingston. Trips down the lush gorge of the Río Dulce are a highlight; nearby are some great places to see and stay on its banks, as well as accommodation around Lago de Izabal. ▶▶ *For listings, see pages 728-736.*

Ins and outs
Getting there The Carretera al Atlántico, or Atlantic Highway, stretches from Guatemala City all the way to Puerto Barrios on the Caribbean coast in the department of Izabal. Most of the worthwhile places to visit are off this fast main road, along the Río Motagua valley, where cactus, bramble, willow and acacia grow. There are numerous buses plying the route. ▶▶ *See Transport, page 733.*

Along the Atlantic Highway
Before Teculután is **El Rancho** at Km 85, the jumping-off point for a trip north to Cobán (see page 740). There are a few places to stay here. Geologists will be interested in the **Motagua fault** near Santa Cruz, between Teculután and Río Hondo. Just before Río Hondo (Km 138), a paved road runs south towards Estanzuela. Shortly before this town you pass a monument on the right commemorating the 1976 earthquake, which activated a fault line that cut across the road. It can still be seen in the fields on either side of the road. The epicentre of this massive earthquake, which measured 7.5 on the Richter scale, and killed 23,000 people, was at **Los Amates**, 65 km further down the valley towards Puerto Barrios.

Estanzuela
Estanzuela is a small town fronting the highway. Its **Museo de Palaeontología, Arqueología y Geología** ① *daily 0800-1700, free*, displays the incredible reconstructed skeletal remains of a 4-m prehistoric giant sloth found in Zone 6, Guatemala City and a giant armadillo among others. Take a minibus heading south from Río Hondo and ask to be dropped at the first entrance to the town on the right. Then walk right, into the town, and continue for 600 m to the museum, 10 minutes. When you reach the school, walk to the right and you will see the museum.

Chiquimula, Volcán de Ipala and the Honduran border
Chiquimula is a stop-off point for travellers who stay here on their way to or from Copán Ruinas, Honduras, if they can't make the connection in one day (see page 724 for border crossing). The fiesta, which includes bullfighting, is from 11-18 August.

An alternative route to Chiquimula and Esquipulas is from the southeast corner of Guatemala City (Zona 10), where the Pan-American Highway heads towards the Salvadorian border. After a few kilometres there is a turning to **San José Pinula** (fiesta: 16-20 March). After San José, an unpaved branch road continues for 203 km through fine scenery to Mataquescuintla, Jalapa (several *hospedajes*, good bus connections; fiesta: 2-5 May), San Pedro Pinula, San Luis Jilotepeque, and Ipala to Chiquimula. Southwest of

Anguiatú
This border is 19 km from the Padre Miguel Junction on the main road and
33 km from Esquipulas.
Immigration Open 0600-1900.
Transport There are *colectivos* to/from Padre Miguel junction connecting with
buses to Chiquimula and Esquipulas. From Esquipulas, minibuses run every
30 minutes, 0600-1720, US$1.05, 40 minutes. By taxi, US$30. From Chiquimula there
are minibuses every 30 minutes from 0515-1700, 1½ hours, US$1.20.

Chiquimula, the extinct Volcán de Ipala (1650 m) can be visited. The crater lake is cool and
good for swimming.

At **Vado Hondo**, 10 km south of Chiquimula on the road to Esquipulas, a smooth dirt
road branches east to the Honduran border (48 km) and a further 11 km to the great Maya
ruins of Copán. The border is 1 km after the village.

Esquipulas → *Colour map 5, C3.*
Esquipulas is dominated by a large, white basilica, which attracts millions of pilgrims from
across Central America to view the image of a Black Christ. The town has pulled out the
stops for visitors, who, as well as a religious fill, will lack nothing in the way of food, drink
and some of the best kitsch souvenirs on the market. If it's possible, stop at the mirador,
1 km from the town, for a spectacular view on the way in of the basilica, which sits at the
end of a 1.5-km main avenue. The history of the famous *Cristo Negro* records that in 1735
Father Pedro Pardo de Figueroa, suffering from an incurable chronic illness, stood in front
of the image to pray, and was cured. A few years later, after becoming Archbishop of
Guatemala he ordered a new church to be built to house the sculpture. The **basilica**
① *open until 2000*, was completed in 1758 and the *Cristo Negro* was transferred from the
parish church shortly after that. Inside the basilica, the Black Christ is on a gold cross,
elaborately engraved with vines and grapes. It was carved by Quirio Cataño in dark
balsam wood in 1595. The image attracts over 1,000,000 visitors per year, some crawling
on their hands and knees to pay homage. The main pilgrimage periods are 1-15 January
(with 15 January being the busiest day), during Lent, Holy Week and 21-27 July.

Quiriguá
① *Daily 0730-1630, US$4. Take insect repellent. There are toilets, a restaurant, a museum
and a jade store and you can store your luggage with the guards. There is no accommodation
at the site (yet), but you can camp (see Sleeping). The site is reached by a newly paved road
from the Atlantic Highway. The village of Quiriguá is about half way between Zacapa and
Puerto Barrios on the highway, and about 3 km from the entrance road to the ruins.*
The remarkable Late Classic ruins of Quiriguá include the tallest stelae found in the Maya
world. The UNESCO World Heritage Site is small, with an excavated acropolis to see, but
the highlight of a visit is the sight of the ornately carved tall stelae and the zoomorphic
altars. The Maya here were very industrious, producing monuments every five years
between AD 751-806, coinciding with the height of their prosperity and confident rule.
The earliest recorded monument dates from AD 480.

Border essentials: Guatemala–Honduras

Agua Caliente
Guatemalan immigration Open 0600-1900.
Honduran consulate In Hotel Payaquí, Esquipulas, very helpful, 0930-1800, T7943-1143.
Transport Minibuses run from Esquipulas, US$0.65, 15 minutes. By taxi US$6.50. From Chiquimula, US$1.80, every 10 minutes.

It is believed that Quiriguá was an important trading post between Tikal and Copán, inhabited since the second century, but principally it was a ceremonial centre. The Kings of Quiriguá were involved in the rivalries, wars and changing alliances between Tikal, Copán and Calakmul. It rose to prominence in the middle of the eighth century, around the time of Cauac Sky who ascended to the throne in AD 724. Cauac Sky was appointed to the position by 18 Rabbit, powerful ruler of Copán (now in Honduras), and its surrounding settlements. It seems that he was fed up with being a subordinate under the domination of Copán, and during his reign, Quiriguá attacked Copán and captured 18 Rabbit. One of the stelae tells of the beheading of the Copán King in the plaza at Quiriguá as a sacrifice after the AD 738 battle. After this event 18 Rabbit disappears from the official chronicle and a 20-year hiatus follows in the historical record of Copán. Following this victory, Quiriguá became an independent kingdom and gained control of the Motagua Valley, enriching itself in the process. And, from AD 751, a monument was carved and erected every five years for the next 55 years. The tallest stelae at Quiriguá is **Stelae E**, which is 10.66 m high with another 2.5 m or so buried beneath. It is 1.52 m wide and weighs 65 tonnes. One of its dates corresponds with the enthronement of Cauac Sky, in AD 724, but it's thought to date from AD 771. All of the stelae, in parkland surrounded by ceiba trees and palms, have shelters, which makes photography difficult. Some monuments have been carved in the shape of animals, some mythical, all of symbolic importance to the Maya.

Thirteen kilometres from Quiriguá is the turn-off for **Mariscos** and Lago de Izabal (see page 728). A further 28 km on are the very hot twin towns of Bananera/Morales. From Bananera there are buses to Río Dulce, Puerto Barrios and the Petén.

Puerto Barrios → *Colour map 5, B3.*

Puerto Barrios, on the Caribbean coast, is a hot and dusty port town, still a central banana point, but now largely superseded as a port by Santo Tomás. The launch to the Garífuna town of Lívingston leaves from the municipal dock here. While not an unpleasant town, it is not a destination in itself, but rather a launch pad to more beautiful and happening spots in Guatemala. It's also the departure point for the Honduran Caribbean. On the way into town, note the cemetery on the right-hand side, where you will pass a small Indian mausoleum with elephant carvings. During the 19th century, *cull* (coolies) of Hindu origin migrated from Jamaica to Guatemala to work on the plantations. The fiesta is 16-22 July.

Lívingston and around ⊕⊕⊘⚠⊛⊝⊙ → *pp728-736. Colour map 5, B3.*

Lívingston, or La Buga, is populated mostly by Garífuna, who bring a colourful flavour to this corner of Guatemala. With its tropical sounds and smells, it is a good place to hang out for a few days, sitting on the dock of the bay, or larging it up with the locals,

Border essentials: Guatemala–Honduras

El Florido

Open 0700-1900. If you are going to Copán for a short visit, the Guatemalan official will give you a 72-hour pass, stapled into your passport. You must return through this border within this period, but you will not require a new visa. Exit fees of US$1.30 are being charged.

Honduran consulate If you need a visa to enter Honduras, go to the lobby of the Hotel Payaquí, Esquipulas, where there is a consulate office, manned by helpful staff. It's reportedly quicker to get your Honduran visa here than in the capital.

Honduran immigration At El Florido on the border. They charge a small entry and exit fee.

Transport See page 733. Taxi to the Chiquimula border is US$18. Chiquimula–Copán and back the same day in a taxi costs US$35. It is impossible to visit Copán from Guatemala City by bus and return the same day; travel agents do one-day or overnight minibus trips. Pickup trucks run all day every day when full until 1700 between Copán Ruinas and the border, 30 minutes, connecting with buses to Guatemalan destinations. The cost is around US$2.50. Bargain for a fair price. They leave from one block west of the park, near the police station. There are direct minibus shuttle services Copán–Antigua.

Crossing by private vehicle If crossing by car make sure you have all the right paperwork. If you are in a Guatemalan hire car you will need a letter of authorization from the hire company allowing you to take the car across the border to Honduras. You can leave your car at the border and go on to Copán by public transport, thus saving the costs of crossing with a vehicle. If leaving Honduras for Guatemala with a vehicle, you need three stamps on your strip from Migración, Tránsito (where they take your *Proviso Provisional*), and Aduana (where they take your *Pase Fronterizo* document and cancel the stamp in your passport). For a better road to Honduras from Chiquimula, see Agua Caliente, page 723.

Exchange There are many money changers but for US$ or TCs, change in Copán, as there are better rates.

---

punta-style. *Coco pan* and *cocado* (a coconut, sugar and ginger *dulce*) and locally made jewellery are sold in the streets. The town is the centre of fishing and shrimping in the Bay of Amatique and only accessible by boat. It is nearly 23 km by sea from Puerto Barrios and there are regular daily boat runs that take 35 minutes in a fast *lancha*. The bulk of the town is up a small steep slope leading straight from the dock, which is at the mouth of the Río Dulce estuary. The other part of town is a linear spread along the river estuary, just north of the dock and then first left. The town is small and everything is within walking distance. The Caribbean beach is pretty dirty nearer the river estuary end, but a little further up the coast, it is cleaner, with palm trees and accommodation. Closer to the town are a couple of bars and weekend beach discos. The town's **Centro Cultural Garífuna-Q'eqchi'** is perched on a hillock, and has the best views in the whole of Livingston. The town's fiestas are 24-31 December, in honour of the Virgen del Rosario, with dancing including the *punta*, and Garífuna Day, 26 November. For local information see www.livingston.com.gt.

Around Lívingston

Northwest along the coastline towards the Río Sarstún, on the border with Belize (where manatee can be seen), is the **Río Blanco beach** (45 minutes by *lancha* from Lívingston), followed by **Playa Quehueche** (also spelt Keueche). Beyond Quehueche, about 6 km (1½ hours) from Lívingston, are **Los Siete Altares**, a set of small waterfalls and pools hidden in the greenery. They are at their best during the rainy season when the water cascades down to the sea. In the drier seasons much of the water is channelled down small, eroded grooves on large slabs of grey rock, where you can stretch out and enjoy the sun. Early *Tarzan* movies were filmed here. Don't stroll on the beach after dark and be careful of your belongings at the Siete Altares end. Police occasionally accompany tourists to the falls; check on arrival what the security situation is. Boats can be hired in Lívingston to visit beaches along the coast towards San Juan and the Río Sarstún.

Lívingston

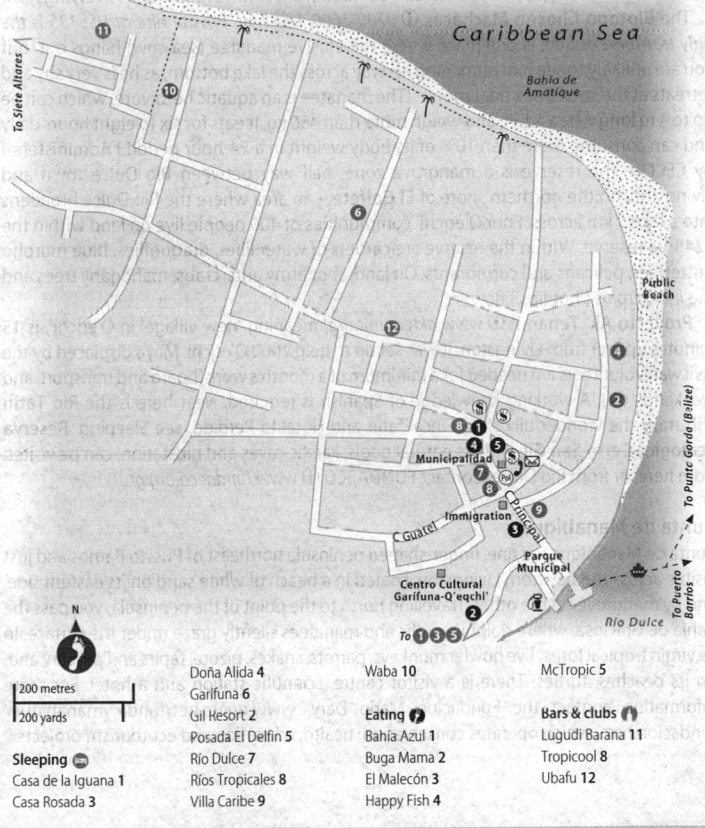

	Doña Alida **4**	Waba **10**	McTropic **5**
200 metres	Garífuna **6**		
200 yards	Gil Resort **2**	**Eating**	**Bars & clubs**
	Posada El Delfín **5**	Bahía Azul **1**	Lugudi Barana **11**
Sleeping	Río Dulce **7**	Buga Mama **2**	Tropicool **8**
Casa de la Iguana **1**	Ríos Tropicales **8**	El Malecón **3**	Ubafu **12**
Casa Rosada **3**	Villa Caribe **9**	Happy Fish **4**	

Border essentials: Guatemala–Belize

Puerto Barrios/Lívingston–Punta Gorda

Guatemalan immigration Offices are in Puerto Barrios and Lívingston, both open 24 hours. Exit fees to leave Guatemala by boat are US$10. You must have your exit stamp from immigration before you can buy a ticket. If you come to Guatemala by boat, you must go straight to the Puerto Barrios or Lívingston immigration offices.

For one of the best trips in Guatemala take a boat up the **Río Dulce** through the sheer-sided canyon towards El Golfete, where the river broadens. Trees and vegetation cling to the canyon walls, their roots plunging into the waters for a long drink below. The scenery here is gorgeous, especially in the mornings, when the waters are unshaken. Tours can be arranged from Lívingston for US$12. You can also paddle up the Río Dulce gorge on *cayucos*, which can be hired from some of the hotels in Lívingston.

The **Biotopo Chocón Machacas** ① *0700-1600, US$2.50. Private hire at US$125 is the only transport option*, is one place where the elusive manatee (sea cow) hangs out, but you are unlikely to see him munching his way across the lake bottom, as he is very shy and retreats at the sound of a boat motor. (The manatee is an aquatic herbivore, which can be up to 4 m long when adult, and weigh more than 450 kg. It eats for six to eight hours daily and can consume more than 10% of its body weight in a 24-hour period.) Administered by CECON, the reserve is a mangrove zone, half way between Río Dulce town and Lívingston, on the northern shore of **El Golfete** – an area where the Río Dulce broadens into a lake 5 km across. Four Q'eqchi' communities of 400 people live on land within the 6245-ha reserve. Within the reserve are carpets of water lilies, dragonflies, blue morpho butterflies, pelicans and cormorants. On land, spot army ants, crabs, mahogany trees and the *labios rojos* ('hot lips') flower.

Proyecto Ak' Tenamit ① *www.aktenamit.org*, meaning 'new village' in Q'eqchi', is 15 minutes upriver from Lívingston. It was set up to help 7000 Q'eqchi' Maya displaced by the civil war. Volunteers are needed for a minimum of a month's work (board and transport, and weekends off). A working knowledge of Spanish is required. Near here is the **Río Tatín tributary** the wonderfully sited Finca Tatín and Hotelito Perdido, see Sleeping. **Reserva Ecológica Cerro San Gil**, with its natural pools, karstic caves and biostation, can be visited from here, or from Río Dulce. Contact **FUNDAECO** ① *www.fundaeco.org.gt*.

Punta de Manabique

Punta de Manabique is a fine, finger-shaped peninsula northeast of Puerto Barrios and just visible across the bay from Lívingston, coated in a beach of white sand on its eastern side, and by mangrove on the other. Travelling north to the point of the peninsula, you pass the Bahía de Graciosa, where dolphins frolic and manatees silently graze under the surface. In its virgin tropical forest live howler monkeys, parrots, snakes, pizote, tapirs and peccary and, on its beaches, turtles. There is a visitor centre, scientific station and a hotel. For more information contact the Fundacíon Mario Dary, www.guate.net/fundarymanabique/fundacion.htm, which operates conservation, health, education and ecotourism projects.

Border essentials: Guatemala–Honduras

Entre Ríos–Corinto

Guatemalan immigration You can get your exit stamp at the Guatemalan immigration in Puerto Barrios or Lívingston if you are leaving by boat to Honduras. If you arrive in Guatemala by boat, go straight to either of these offices.

Honduran consulate If you need a visa, you must obtain it in Guatemala City, or at Esquipulas.

Transport Minibuses leave the market on 8 Calle in Puerto Barrios for Entre Ríos every 15 minutes from 0630-1800, US$1.90. They pull up at the immigration post beyond Entre Ríos at El Cinchado and wait for you to complete formalities. The minibus continues the journey (15 minutes) over a bridge over the Río Motagua. It's a short walk to Honduran immigration and on to Corinto and buses for your onward journey.

Honduran immigration Buses travel the coastal road to Corinto, from where it is a short walk to Honduran immigration. Complete formalities, cross the border and wait for a bus to Puerto Barrios that will stop at Guatemalan immigration on the way.

Lago de Izabal ●❷▲●❶❶ ›› *pp728-736. Colour map 5, B3.*

The vast Lago de Izabal narrows to form a neck at the town of Fronteras. Better known as Río Dulce, it is famed for its riverside setting and there are some beautiful places around the lake and river in which to stay. Just south of Río Dulce on the lake is the Castillo de San Felipe. On the northern shore of the lake is the town of El Estor, and on its southern shore the smaller town of Mariscos (see Sleeping for a complete getaway). Further east, beyond Río Dulce, the river broadens out to El Golfete, where there is the Biotopo Chacón Machacas, see above. It then narrows into one of the finest gorges in the world, and opens out at its estuary, with Lívingston at its head. This area can be wet in the rainy season, but it experiences a lull in July, known as the *canícula*.

Fronteras/Río Dulce and around

Río Dulce is a good place to stop and kick back for a couple of days. Allow yourself to be tempted to laze on a boat for the afternoon, walk in the nearby jungle, or eat and drink at one of several dockside restaurants. Río Dulce, www.mayaparadise.com, is 23 km upstream from Lívingston at the entrance to Lago de Izabal, is easily accessible from Puerto Barrios by road, and is the last major stop before the Petén. It's also a good place to collect information about the area stretching from El Estor to Lívingston.

On the shore of Lago de Izabal is **Casa Guatemala** ① *14 Calle, 10-63, Zona 1, Guatemala City, T2231-9408, www.casa-guatemala.org, or the Hotel Backpacker's,* an orphanage where you can work in exchange for basic accommodation and food. At the entrance to Lago de Izabal, 2 km upstream, is the old Spanish fort of **Castillo de San Felipe** ① *0800-1700, US$2.30.* The fortification was first built in 1643 to defend the coast against attacks from pirates. Between Río Dulce and El Estor is **Finca El Paraíso**, a hot waterfall with waters that plunge into a cool-water pool below.

El Estor and around → *Colour map 5, B3.*

El Estor enjoys one of the most beautiful vistas in Guatemala. It is strung along the northwest shore of Lago de Izabal, backed by the Santa Cruz mountain range and facing the Sierra de las Minas. The lake is the largest in Guatemala at 717 sq km. It's a great place to relax, swim (down a nearby canyon), go fishing and spot manatee. Some businesses are expecting the new road to bring a surge of tourists visitors. For the next few years, you'll still have the place mostly to yourself. The town dates back to the days when the Europeans living in the Atlantic area got their provisions from a store situated at this spot, now the **Hotel Vista al Lago**. Briton Skinner and Dutchman Klee used to supply the region from *el store* from 1815 to 1850. Nickel-mining began just outside town in 1978, but was suspended at the **Exmibal plant** after the oil crisis of 1982, because the process depended on cheap sources of energy.

You can hire a boat from Río Dulce to El Estor, passing near the hot waterfall, inland at Finca El Paraíso, which can be reached by a good trail in about 40 minutes. The Río Sauce cuts through the impressive **Cañón El Boquerón**, where you can swim with the current all the way down the canyon, which is brilliant fun. It's a deep canyon with lots of old man's beard hanging down, strange rock formations and otters and troops of howler monkeys whooping about. One of the locals will paddle you upstream for about 800 m (US$1). Exploring the Río Zarco, closer to town, also makes for a good trip, with cold swimming. The **Refugio de Vida Silvestre Bocas del Polochic** (Bocas del Polochic Wildlife Reserve) is a 23,000-ha protected area on the western shores of the lake. Howler monkeys are commonly seen. In addition to over 350 bird species, there are iguanas, turtles and the chance of sighting crocodiles and manatees. The NGO **Defensores de la Naturaleza** ① *2 Calle and 5 Av, El Estor, T2440-8138 in the capital, www.defensores.org.gt*, has a research station at Selempim with bunk beds (**F** per person), food, showers and kitchen. Its a two- or three-hour boat ride from El Estor to Ensenada Los Lagartos. Tours available from town for US$30 for two people. Contact the office in El Estor or ask at a hotel about boat services.

Mariscos is on the southern shore of Lago de Izabal. The best reason to come here is the nearby **Denny's Beach**.

⦿ Guatemala to the Caribbean listings

For Sleeping and Eating price codes and other relevant information, see Essentials pages 45-48.

⊜ Sleeping

Chiquimula *p721*
B Posada Perla del Oriente, 2 Calle between 11 and 12 Av, T7942-0014. All rooms with TV, some with a/c, parking, pool, quiet. Restaurant. Recommended.
D Hernández, 3 Calle, 7-41, T7942-0708. Cheaper without bathroom, fans. TVs in rooms and a pool add to its attractions. Family-run, quiet and friendly.

D Hotel Posada Don Adán, 8 Av, 4-30, T7942-0549. All rooms with private bathroom, a/c, TV. Run by a friendly, older couple.
D Victoria, 2 Calle, 9-99, next to the bus station (so ask for rooms away from street), T7942-2732. All rooms have bath, cold water, fan, cable TV, towels, soap, shampoo, some rooms have a/c, drinking water provided, good restaurant, good value, will store luggage. Recommended.

Esquipulas *p722*
There are plenty of hotels, *hospedajes* and *comedores* all over town, especially in and around 11 Calle, also known as Doble Vía

Quirio Cataño. Prices tend to double before the Jan feast day. They also rise at Easter and at weekends. When quiet, midweek, bargain for lower room prices.

A Hotel Chortí, on the outskirts of town at Km 222, T7943-1148. All 20 rooms have a/c, TV, phone and *frigobar*. There are 2 pools, a restaurant and bar.

A Payaquí, 2 Av, 11-26, T7943-1143, www.hotelpayaqui.com. The 40 rooms are lovely, with *frigobars*, full of beers for the pilgrims to guzzle, hot-water showers and free drinking water, swimming pool, parking, restaurant, bar; credit cards, Honduran lempiras and US dollars accepted.

A-C Hotel El Peregrino, 2 Av, 11-94, T7943-1054. Clean rooms in the newer part.

B Hotel Villa Zonia, 10 Calle, 1-84, T7943-1133. Looks a little Alpine and very nice.

B Legendario, 3 Av and 9 Calle, T7943-1824, www.portahotels.com. Built around a garden with 2 pools, restaurant, parking.

B Los Angeles, 2 Av, 11-94, T7943-1254. Spotless rooms with bath, TV and fans, parking, friendly service. Recommended.

C Hotel Calle Real, 3 Av, 10-00, T7943-2405. Rooms all with private bathroom, with TV, hot water, clean.

E Pensión Casa Norman, 3 Av, 9-20, T7943-1503. Rooms with bath and hot water.

E San Carlos 2, used to be known as París, 2 Av, 10-48, T7943-1276. 28 very clean rooms. Cheaper without bath, hot water showers.

Quiriguá *p722*

B Hotel Restaurante Santa Mónica, in Los Amates, 2 km south of Quiriguá village on the highway, T7947-3838. 17 rooms all with private bath, TV and fan, pool, restaurant. It is opposite a 24-hr Texaco gas station. Convenient if you don't want to walk the 10-15 mins into Quiriguá village for the 2 hotels there. There are a couple of shops, banks, and *comedores* here.

E Hotel y Cafetería Edén, T7947-3281. Helpful, cheaper with shared bath, basement rooms are very dark, clean. The bus comes

as far as here, which is where the back route walk to the ruins starts.

E Hotel y Restaurante Royal, T7947-3639. With bath, cheaper without, clean, mosquito netting on all windows, good place to meet other travellers, restaurant.

Camping

You can camp in the car park of the ruins for free, but facilities are limited to toilets and very little running water. There is a restaurant and a project in the pipeline to open a hotel and waterpark opposite the entrance.

Puerto Barrios *p723*

A Hotel Valle Tropical, 59 rooms on 12 Calle between 5 and 6 Av, T7948 7084, vtropical@guate.net. All rooms with a/c and private bathroom, inviting pool and restaurant, parking. Non-guests can use pool (US$7).

A-C El Reformador, 16 Calle and 7 Av 159, T7948-5489. 51 rooms with bathroom, a/c and TV, some with a/c, restaurant, laundry service, clean, quiet, accepts credit cards. Recommended. The same management run the **Oguatour** travel agency across the road.

B-D Hotel del Norte, at the end of the 7 Calle, T7948-2116. A rickety, old wooden structure with sloping landings on the seafront side. All rooms have bath, some with a/c. There's a pool and expensive restaurant, but worth it for the English colonial tearoom atmosphere, no credit cards, but will change dollars.

C-D Hotel Europa, 8 Av, between 8 and 9 Calle, T7948-1292. 23 clean rooms, with bath, fan, 2 more expensive rooms with a/c, good restaurant, parking, friendly Cuban management.

D-E Hotel Xelajú, 9 Calle, between 6 and 7 Av, T7948-0482. Rooms, with bath, cheaper without, fans, quiet, and ultra-clean shared bathrooms.

E Hotel Lee, 5 Av, between 9 and 10 Calle, T7948-0830. Convenient for the bus station and dock, 24 rooms with fan and TV, with private bath, cheaper without. Noisy restaurant opposite. Friendly service.

Lívingston *p723, map p725*
L-AL Hotel Villa Caribe, up Calle Principal
from the dock on the right, T7947-0072,
www.villasdeguatemala.com. All rooms have
sea view and baths. There is a swimming pool
(available to non-guests when the hotel is
not busy for US$6.50), and a large restaurant
overlooking the sea.
A Gil Resort, T7947-0990, www.gil
resorthotel.com. 14 clean, attractive rooms
with private bath and air conditioning,
most with TV.
A Posada El Delfin, T7947-0694,
www.posadaeldelfin.com. Good-quality
hotel, with over 20 attractive rooms with
a/c and hot water.
B Hotel Doña Alida, in a quiet location,
T7947-0027, hotelalida@yahoo.es. Direct
access to the beach, some rooms with great
sea views and balconies, with restaurant.
C Hotel Ríos Tropicales, T7947-0158,
www.mctropic.com. This place has some nice
touches to distinguish it from the majority of
other places in town, like terracotta-tiled
floors. 11 rooms, with fans, 5 with private
bath, book exchange and the **McTropic**
restaurant up the road with internet and
a tour operator.
D Casa Rosada, a pastel-pink house set
on the waterfront, 600 m from the dock,
T7947-0303, www.hotelcasarosada.com.
10 bungalows furnished with attractive
hand-painted furniture. The room upstairs
overlooks the bay. Meals are set for the day,
ranging from pasta to delicious shrimps
bathed in garlic. Reservations advisable.
D-E Casa De La Iguana, T7947-0064.
Very cool hostel with jungle hut style
accommodation and hot showers. 3 private
rooms, each with bath as well as dorms and
space for tents and hammocks.
E Garífuna (see map), T7947-0183.
8 comfortable, ultra-clean rooms with
private bath, laundry and internet.
Recommended.
E Hotel Río Dulce, main street, T7947-0764,
An early 19th-century wooden building, with
a seriously sloping landing on the 1st floor, a

good place from which to watch life pass by.
Try and get a room upstairs rather than
behind the old building. Rooms with or
without bathrooms. There is a restaurant
on the ground floor with some tables
directly on the street.
E Waba, barrio Pueblo Nuevo, T7947-0193.
Run by a friendly family offering upstairs
rooms with a balcony and sea views. All
rooms have private bath and are clean and
cool, with fan. *Comida típica* is served at a
little wooden restaurant (0700-2130) on site.
Good value and recommended.

Around Lívingston *p725*
D-E Finca Tatin, Río Tatin tributary,
with great dock space to hang out on,
T5902-0831, www.fincatatin.centro
america.com. It's B&B, whether you opt
for a room with private bath, or a dorm
bed. Tours available. Take a *lancha* from
Lívingston (US$4) to get there.
C-D Hotelito Perdido, hideaway on
the River Lampara, can be dropped off
on the Lívingston–Río Dulce boat service,
T5725-1576, www.hotelitoperdido.com.
Quiet hideaway, with rustic, basic and
clean accommodation. Food extra at around
US$15 a day (no local alternatives available).
E Hotel Ecológico Salvador Gaviota,
along the coast, towards Siete Altares,
beyond **Hotel Ecológico Siete Altares**,
T7947-0874, www.hotelecologicosalvador
gaviota.com. Rooms are with shared bath,
but the bungalows for 2 or 4 people have
private bath. Rooms available for monthly
rent. All set in lush surroundings. There is
a bar and restaurant (0730-2200), and free
lancha service – just ring beforehand.
Tours available. The beach here is lovely,
hummingbirds flit about and the owner
Lisette is friendly. Highly recommended.

Camping
Biotopo Chocón Machacas, 400 m from
the entrance, next to a pond, with grills
for cooking on, and toilets, but no food
or drink for sale.

Punta de Manabique *p726*
D Eco-Hotel El Saraguate, www.quate.net/
fundarymanabique/saraguate.htm. Rooms
and a restaurant run by Fundación Mario Dary.

Fronteras/Río Dulce and around *p727*
AL Catamaran Island Hotel, T7930-5494,
www.catamaranisland.com. Finely decorated
cabañas, 40 rooms set around the lake edge,
an inviting pool, large restaurant with good
food, lancha from Río Dulce, 10 mins downstream, or call for a pickup. Recommended.
AL Hotel La Ensenada, Km 275,
in town 500 m to the right at the Shell
station on road to Petén, T7930-5340.
Riverside location, breakfast included,
restaurant, pool, nice gardens, camping
and campervan facilities.
A-C Hacienda Tijax, T7930-5505,
www.tijax.com. 2 mins by *lancha* from the
dock, jungle lodges and cabins (a/c costs
extra). There is a beautiful jungle trail, a
rubber plantation, bird sanctuary, pool with
whirlpool and jacuzzi, natural pools to swim
in, horse riding, kayaking, sailing and rowboat
hire and a medicine trail. Excellent food in the
riverside bar and restaurant, tranquil and
beautiful. Highly recommended.
B-D Tortugal Marina, T5306-6432,
www.tortugal.com. 3 beautifully presented
bungalows with gorgeous soft rugs on the
floor and other types of accommodation.
Plentiful hot water. There is a riverside
restaurant and bar, pool table in a cool
upstairs attic room with books, satellite
TV, internet, phone and fax service.
Very highly recommended.
B-F Bruno's, in town on the lake, a stone's
throw from the where the buses stop,
T7930-5721, www.mayaparadise.com/
brunoe.htm. Best rooms overlook the lake,
also dorms, camping, campervan parking,
pool, restaurant. Non-guests can pay to use
pool. The marina has 28 berths. Restaurant
service is consistently not up to scratch.
D La Cabaña del Viajero, 500 m from the
castle, T7930-5062. Small place with pool,
traditional *cabañas* as well as larger family-

style *cabañas* with private bathroom and
some cute little attic rooms as well.
E Café Sol, in town 500 m north of the
bridge on the road to Tikal, T7930-5143.
Friendly, clean, fans, good-value rooms,
cheaper without bath, TV costs a bit extra.
Useful if you have to catch an early bus.
E-F Hotel Backpacker's, in town by the
bridge on the south bank of the river,
T7930-5169, www.hotelbackpackers.com.
Restaurant and bar, dorms (**F** per person)
with lockers, and private rooms with
bathroom, internet and telephone
service, profits go to **Casa Guatemala**
(see page 727). Recommended.

El Estor and around *p728*
B-C Marisabela, 8 Av and 1 Calle on the
waterfront, T7949-7215. Large rooms with
tiled private bathrooms, some with TV,
internet service.
C-E Denny's Beach, T5398-0908,
www.dennysbeach.com. With its gorgeous
lakeside location, accessible by *lancha* from
Río Dulce (minimum fee US$41), or free from
Mariscos if you call ahead. Tours, wake
boarding and horse riding arranged. Internet
service. A remote and complete get away.
D Hotel Vista al Lago, 6 Av, 1-13,
T7949-7205. 21 clean rooms with private
bath and fan. Ask for the lakeview rooms,
where there is a pleasant wooden balcony
on which to sit. Friendly owner Oscar Paz will
take you fishing, and runs ecological
and cultural tours.
D Villela, 6 Av, 2-06, T7949-7214. 9 big
rooms with bath, clean, some quite dark
though. Flower-filled garden with chairs
to sit out in. Recommended.

🍽 Eating

Chiquimula *p721*
🍴 **Magic**, corner of 8 Av and 3 Calle. A good
place from which to watch the world go by,
and most of what's on offer is seriously cheap.
Sandwiches, *licuados* and burgers.

Pastelería Las Violetas, 7 Av, 4-80, and another near **Hotel Victoria**. An excellent cake shop with a fine spread, good-value sandwiches too, plus great cappuccino, and a/c. Next door is its bakery.

Esquipulas *p722*

There are plenty of restaurants, but prices are high for Guatemala.

††† La Hacienda, 2 Av, 10-20. Delicious barbecued chicken and steaks. Kids' menu available, breakfasts available. One of the smartest restaurants in town.

†† Restaurante Payaquí, 2 Av, 11-26, inside the hotel of the same name. Specialities include turkey in *pipián*, also lunches and breakfasts. A poolside restaurant makes a pleasant change.

† Café Pistachos, close to **Hotel Calle Real**. Clean, cheap snack bar with burgers, hotdogs, etc.

Puerto Barrios *p723*

†††-†† Restaurante Safari, at the north end of 5 Av and 1 Calle, overlooking the bay with views all around. Basically serving up oceans of fish, including whole fish, *ceviche* and fishburgers.

†† La Fonda de Quique, an orange and white wooden building at 5 Av and corner of 12 Calle. Nicely a/c with handmade wooden furniture, serving lobster, fish and meats, plus snacks.

Lívingston *p723, map p725*

Fresh fish is available everywhere; ask for *tapado* in restaurants – a rich soup with various types of seafood, banana and coconut. Women sell *pan de coco* on the streets.

†† Bahía Azul, Calle Principal. Excellent breakfasts, but dreadful coffee. Tables on the street as well as a dining-room. Specializes in salsas, *camarones* and *langosta*. There is a tourist service and the **Exotic Travel Agency**.

†† Buga Mama, an excellent example of an innovative development project. Local Mayan young people staff this large restaurant located next to the water as part of their training with the Ak'Tenamit project

(www.aktenamit.org). The food is OK, the service excellent, and a great spot too – well worth checking out.

†† El Malecón, 50 m from the dock on the left. Serves *chapín* and Western-style breakfasts, seafood and chicken *fajitas*, all in a large, airy wooden dining area.

†† Happy Fish, just along from the **Hotel Río Dulce**. A popular restaurant with internet café. Serves a truckload of fish (not quite so happy now) with good coffee. Occasional live music at weekends.

†† Hotel Río Dulce, see Sleeping. The restaurant serves delicious Italian food prepared with panache. Recommended.

† McTropic, opposite the **Hotel Río Dulce**. Street tables, great breakfasts, and cocktails. Good service and popular.

† Rasta Mesa Restaurant, in Barrio Nevago, just past the cemetery, www.site.rasta mesa.com. Garífuna cultural centre and restaurant. Music, history, classes in cooking and drumming. Great place to hang out.

Fronteras/Río Dulce and around *p727*

There are restaurants in the hotel – **Bruno's** is a relaxing location – and a couple along the main road.

El Estor and around *p728*

††-† Restaurante Típico Chaabil, lakeside. A thatched restaurant with plenty of fish to eat. Cheap breakfasts.

† Dorita. A *comedor* serving seafood, very good meals, excellent value and popular with the locals.

† Marisabela, 8 Av and 1 Calle. Good and cheap spaghetti, as well as fish and chicken, with lake views.

† Restaurant del Lago, west side of main square. New restaurant overlooking the main square. Popular with local dishes.

† Restaurant Elsita, 2 blocks north of the market on 8 Av. This is a great people-watching place. There's a large menu and the food is good.

⦿ Entertainment

Puerto Barrios *p723*
The Container, just past the Hotel del Norte overlooking the sea, is an unusual bar constructed from the front half of an old ship equipped with portholes, and a number of banana containers from the massive banana businesses just up the road. Open 0700-2300.
Mariscos de Izabal, one of the most popular spots in Puerto Barrios. A thatched bar that is mostly a drinking den but with tacos, tortillas and burgers served amid beating Latin rhythms. You can hang out until here 0100.

Lívingston *p723, map p725*
Lugudi Barana, a disco that's also on the beach and popular with visitors and locals. Sun only, 1500-0100.
Ubafu, on the main road of the town, is unmissable. It is heaving most nights as locals and travellers dance the *punta*. A live band plays nightly from about 2100 with drums, a conch shell and turtle shells, the *punta*'s instrument ensemble. This large, wooden bar, decked out in Bob Marley posters and Rastafarian symbols, is definitely worth a visit. Try the *coco loco*, rum and coco milk served up in a coconut.

▲ Activities and tours

Lívingston *p723, map p725*
Exotic Travel Agency, in the Bahía Azul restaurant, T7947-0133, www.blue caribbeanbay.com.
Happy Fish, on the main road, T7947-0661, www.happyfishresort.com.
Captain Eric, located at the Pitchi Mango snack bar on the main street, 14265-5278. Will arrange 1- to 2-day boat tours for groups of up to 5 people to the surrounding region.
You can also contract any of the *lancheros* at the dock to take you to Río Dulce, Playa Blanca and Siete Altares.

Fronteras/Río Dulce *p727*
Sailing
Captain John Clark's sailing trips on his 46-ft Polynesian catamaran, *Las Sirenas*, are highly recommended. Food, taxes, snorkelling and fishing gear, and windsurf boards included. Contact **Aventuras Vacacionales SA**, Antigua, www.sailing-diving-guatemala.com

Tour operators
Atitrans Tours, on the little road heading to the dockside. To **Finca Paraíso** for US$20.
Otiturs, opposite Tijax Express, T5219-4520. Run by the friendly and helpful Otto Archila. Offers a minibus service as well as tours to local sites, internal flights and boat trips.
Tijax Express, opposite Atitrans, T7930-5505, info@tijax.com. Agent for Hacienda Tijax (over the river)
Lancheros offer trips on the river and on Lago de Izabal. They can be contacted at the muelle principal, under the bridge. Ask for Cesár Mendez, T5819-7436, or ask at **Atitrans** for collection.

⦿ Festivals and events

Lívingston *p723, map p725*
24-31 Dec In honour of the Virgen del Rosario, with traditional dancing.
26 Nov Garífuna Day.

⦿ Transport

Estanzuela *p721*
Bus From **Guatemala City** to Zacapa, with Rutas Orientales, 0430-1800, every 30 mins, 2¾-3 hrs. To **Esquipulas** with same service that continues from Zacapa, US$6, 1½ hrs.

Chiquimula, Volcán de Ipala and the Honduran border *p721*
Bus Take an early bus to **Ipala** from Chiquimula; stay on the bus and ask the driver to let you off at Aldea El Chaparroncito (10 mins after Ipala). From here it's a 1½-hr

ascent, following red arrows every now and then. Another ascent goes via Municipio Agua Blanca. Take a minibus to **Agua Blanca** from Ipala and get out at the small village of El Sauce, where the trail starts. The last bus from Ipala to Chiquimula is 1700.

Chiquimula *p721*
Bus
There are 3 terminals in Chiquimula, all within 50 m of each other. To **Guatemala City**, Transportes Guerra and Rutas Orientales, hourly, US$4, 3¼-3½ hrs, leave from 11 Av between 1 and 2 Calle, as do buses for **Puerto Barrios**, several companies, every 30 mins, between 0300-1500, 4 hrs, US$6.50. To **Quiriguá**, US$3.20, 1 hr 50 mins. Take any Puerto Barrios-bound bus. On to **Río Dulce** take the Barrios bus and get off at La Ruidosa junction and change, or change at Bananera/ Morales. To **Flores** with **Transportes María Elena**, 8 hrs, 0400, 0800, 1300. Buses to **Ipala** and **Jalapa** also leave from here; 4 buses daily to Jalapa between 0500-1230, 4½ hrs, US$5.80; to Ipala, US$2.20. Supplemented by minibuses 0600-1715 to Ipala. To **Zacapa**, 25 mins, from the terminal inside the market at 10 Av between 1 and 2 Calle. Same for those to **Esquipulas**, every 10 mins, US$2.70, until 1900. To and from **Cobán** via El Rancho (where a change must be made). Buses to **El Florido** (Honduras border) leave with **Transportes Vilma** from inside the market at 1 Calle, between 10 and 11 Av, T7942-2253, between 0530-1630, US$2.70, 1½ hrs. Buses return from the border at 0530, 0630 and then hourly 0700-1700. See box, page 724, for border-crossing information.

Esquipulas *p722*
Bus Rutas Orientales. Leaving Esquipulas, 1 Av "A" and 11 Calle, T7943-1366, for **Guatemala City** every 30 mins from 0200-1700, 4½ hrs, US$8.50. To **Chiquimula** by minibus, every 30 mins, 0430-1830, US$1.40.

Quiriguá *p722*
Bus
Emphasize to the bus driver if you want Quiriguá *pueblo* and not the *ruinas*. Countless travellers have found themselves left at the ruins and having to make a return journey to the village for accommodation.

To get to the **ruins** directly, take any bus heading along the highway towards Puerto Barrios and ask to be let off at the *ruinas*. At this ruins crossroads, take a pickup (very regular), 10 mins, US$0.50, or bus (much slower and less regular) to the ruins 4 km away. Last bus back to highway, 1700. You can walk, but take lots of water, as it's hot and dusty with little shade. To get to the **village** of Quiriguá, 3 km south from the ruins entrance road, it is only a 10-min walk to the **Hotel Royal**. Keep to the paved road, round a left-hand bend, and it's 100 m up on the left. Or take a local bus heading from the highway into the village. The **Hotel Edén** is a further 5 mins on down the hill. There is a frequent daily bus service that runs a circular route between Los Amates, Quiriguá village and then on to the entrance road to the ruins. You can also walk through the banana plantations from Quiriguá village to the ruins as well. From **Hotel Royal** walk past the church towards the old train station and the **Hotel Edén**, and follow the tracks branching to the right, through the plantation to the ruins.

Puerto Barrios *p723*
Boat
It's a 10-min walk to the municipal dock at the end of Calle 12, from the **Litegua** bus station. Ferries *(barca)* leave for Lívingston at 1030 and 0500 (1½ hrs, US$2.50). *Lanchas* also leave when a minimum of 12 people are ready to go, 30 mins, US$3.80. The only scheduled *lanchas* leave at 0630, 0730, 0900 and 1100, and the last will leave, if there are enough people, at 1800. **Transportes El Chato**, 1 Av, between 10 and 11 Calle, T7948-5525, pichilingo2000@yahoo.com, also does trips from here to Punta de Manabique, and other places near and far.

To Belize *Lanchas* leave for **Punta Gorda** at 1000 with **Transportes El Chato**, address above, returning at 1400, 1 hr 20 mins, US$22. Also services with Requena to Punta Gorda at 1400, returning at 0900.

Bus
To **Guatemala City**, with Litegua, 6 Av between 9 and 10 Calle, T7948-1002, www.litegua.com. 18 a day, 5 hrs, US$11-7.50. Bus to **El Rancho** (turn-off for Biotopo del Quetzal and Cobán), 4 hrs, take any bus to Guatemala City. To **Quiriguá**, 2 hrs, take any capital-bound bus. To **Chiquimula**, operated by **Carmencita**, 4 hrs. Alternatively, catch a bus to Guatemala City, getting off at Río Hondo, and catch a *colectivo* or any bus heading to Chiquimula. For **Río Dulce**, take any bus heading for Guatemala City and change at **La Ruidosa** (15 mins). For minibuses to **Entre Ríos**, for the El Cinchado border crossing to **Honduras (Corinto)**, with connections to **Omoa**, **Puerto Cortés** and **La Ceiba**, see page 727.

Lívingston *p723, map p725*
Boat
Ferry to **Puerto Barrios** to (22.5 km), 1½ hrs, US$1.60 at 0500 and 1400 Mon-Sat. Private *lanchas* taking 16-25 people also sail this route, 30 mins, US$4. They leave at 0630 and 0730 each day and at 0900 and 1100 Mon-Sat to Puerto Barrios and then when full. Lívingston to **Río Dulce**, with short stops at **Aguas Calientes** and the **Biotopo Chacón Machacas**, US$15.50 1 way. *Lanchas* definitely leave at 0900 and 1430 for **Río Dulce**, but these make no stops. To **Honduras** (Omoa, Puerto Cortés, La Ceiba), *lanchas* can be organized at the dock or through tour operators, see above. To **Belize** (Punta Gorda, Placencia, Cayos Zapotillos), check with tour operators, see above, about boats to Belize. Anyone who takes you must have a manifest with passengers' names, stamped and signed at the immigration office. On Tue and Fridaysdays fast *lanchas* make the trip to Punta Gorda (US$22).

Enquire at the dock and negotiate a fare with the *lanchero* association. Boats to Placencia and the Zapotilla cayes can also be arranged.

Fronteras/Río Dulce and around *p727*
Boat
Lanchas colectivas leave for **Lívingston** at 0930 and 1300, US$15.50. Private *lanchas* can be arranged at the dock to any of the river or lakeside hotels.

Bus
Local To get to **Castillo de San Felipe**, take a boat from Río Dulce, or *camioneta* from the corner of the main road to Tikal, and the first turning left after the bridge by **Pollandia**, 5 mins, or a 5-km walk. From Río Dulce to **Finca El Paraíso**, take the same road, 45 mins, US$1.70. Buses to Río Dulce pass the *finca* between 40 and 50 mins past the hour. To **El Estor**, from the same Pollandia turn-off, US$2.50, 1½ hrs on a newly paved road, 0500-1600, hourly, returning 0500-1600. To **Puerto Barrios**, take any bus to **La Ruidosa** and change, 35 mins to junction then a further 35 mins to Puerto Barrios.

Long-distance To **Guatemala City** and **Flores**: through buses stop at Río Dulce. To **Guatemala City** with Litegua, T7930-5251, www.litegua.com, 7 a day between 0300 and 1515, US$7.54, 6 hrs. **Fuente del Norte**, T5692-1988, 23 services daily, US$6.30. Luxury service 1300, 1700 and 2400, US$13. **Línea Dorada**, at 1300, luxury service, 5 hrs, US$13. To **Flores** from 0630-0300, 25 buses daily, 4½ hrs with **Fuente del Norte**, US$8. Luxury service, 1430, US$13. This bus also stops at **Finca Ixobel** and **Poptún**, US$3.90. Línea Dorada, to Flores, 1500, 3 hrs, luxury service with a/c, TV and snacks, US$13, and on to **Melchor de Mencos** for Belize. Fuente del Norte, also to **Melchor de Mencos**, at 1300, 2130 and 2330, 6 hrs, US$12.50. Also to, **Sayaxché** at 2200 and one to **Naranjo** at 2100.

Shuttles Atitrans, T7930-5111, www.atitrans.com, runs shuttles to **Antigua**, **Flores**, **Copán Ruinas** and **Guatemala City**.

El Estor and around *p728*
Bus
The ferry from Mariscos no longer runs, but a private *lancha* can be contracted.

To **Río Dulce**, 0500-1600, hourly, 1 hr, US$2.20. Direct bus to **Cobán**, at 1300, 7 hrs, US$5.60. Also via either Panzós and Tactic, or Cahabón and Lanquín, see page 745. For the **Cañón El Boquerón**, take the Río Dulce bus and ask to be dropped at the entrance. Or hire a bike from town (8 km) or a taxi, US$6.50, including waiting time.

To **Cobán**, with **Transportes Valencia**, 1200, 0200, 0400 and 0800, 8 long and dusty hrs, with no proper stop. To **Guatemala City**, 0100 direct, via Río Dulce, 7 hrs, US$6.30, or go to Río Dulce and catch one. At 2400 and 0300 via Río Polochic Valley. For **Santa Elena, Petén** take a bus to Río Dulce and pick on up from there.

❶ Directory

Chiquimula *p721*
Banks There are several banks accepting MasterCard and Visa, and ATMs. **Post office** Close to the bus terminal inside the market. **Telephone** Office on the plaza.

Esquipulas *p722*
Banks There are a number of banks and ATMs in town close to the park, Visa and MasterCard accepted. There are money changers in the centre if you need *lempiras*. Better rates than at the borders. **Post office** End of 6 Av, 2-43.

Puerto Barrios *p723*
Banks Banco G&T Continental, 7 Calle and 6 Av, with ATMs. TCs. Banco Industrial, 7 Av, 7-30, 24-hr Visa ATM and cash on Visa

cards. **Immigration** Corner of 12 Calle and 3 Av, open 24 hrs. **Internet** A couple of places in town. **Post office** Corner of 6 Calle and 6 Av. **Telephone** Telgua, corner of 10 Calle and 8 Av.

Lívingston *p723, map p725*
Banks Banco Reformador, cash advance on Visa and MasterCard, TCs and cash changed. Has a 24-hr Visa-only ATM. There is also a Banrural. Some hotels will change cash, including Casa Rosada. **Immigration** Calle Principal, opposite Hotel Villa Caribe, T7947-0240. Just knock if the door is shut. **Internet** There are a couple of places in town – Gaby's in Barrio Marcos Sánchez Díaz is open 0900-2100 daily and charges US$1.25 an hour. **Laundry** Lavandería Doña Chila, opposite Casa Rosada. **Language Schools** Livingston Spanish School, T5715-4604, www.livingstonspanishchool.org. 1-2-1 classes, 20 hrs a week, US$95 a week including food and lodging. **Post office** Next to Telgua, behind the Municipalidad, take the small road to the right. **Telephone** Telgua, behind the Municipalidad, 0800-1800.

Fronteras/Río Dulce and around *p727*
Banks There are 2 banks: Visa, TCs and cash only. ATMS available. **Internet** Captain Nemo's Communications behind Bruno's, and phone call service and Tijax Express. **Post office** Near the banks.

El Estor *p728*
Banks Banco Industrial and Banrural have ATMs. **Internet** Xbox 360 open 0800-2100, Mon-Sat. Good machines with a/c keeping machines and people cool. **Post office** In the park.

The Verapaces

Propped up on a massive limestone table eroded over thousands of years, the plateau of the Verapaz region is riddled with caves, underground tunnels, stalagtites and stalagmites. Cavernous labyrinths used by the Maya for worship, in their belief that caves are the entrances to the underworld, are also now visited by travellers who marvel at the natural interior design of these subterranean spaces. Nature has performed its work above ground too. At Semuc Champey, pools of tranquil, turquoise-green water span a monumental limestone bridge; beneath the bridge a river thunders violently through. The quetzal reserve also provides the opportunity to witness a feather flash of red or green of the elusive bird, and dead insects provide curious interest in Rabinal, where their body parts end up on ornamental gourds. The centre of this region – the imperial city of Cobán – provides respite for the traveller with a clutch of museums honouring the Maya, coffee and orchid, and a fantastic entertainment spectacle at the end of July with a whirlwind of traditional dances and a Maya beauty contest. ▸▸ *For listings, see pages 742-746.*

Ins and outs

The principal road entrance to the Verapaces leaves the Atlantic Highway at El Rancho heading up to Cobán. This junction is one hour from Guatemala City. ▸▸ *See Transport, page 744.*

Background

Before the Spanish conquest of the region, Las Verapaces had a notorious reputation – it was known as Tezulutlán (land of war) for its aggressive warlike residents, who fought repeated battles with their neighbours and rivals, the K'iche' Maya. These warring locals were not going to be a pushover for the Spanish conquerors and they strongly resisted when their land was invaded. The Spanish eventually retreated and the weapon replaced with the cross. Thus, Carlos V of Spain gave the area the title of Verdadera Paz (true peace) in 1548. The region's modern history saw it converted into a massive coffee- and cardamom-growing region. German coffee *fincas* were established from the 1830s until the Second World War, when the Germans were invited over to plough the earth by the Guatemalan government. Many of the *fincas* were expropriated during the war, but some were saved from this fate by naming a Guatemalan as the owner of the property. The area still produces some of Guatemala's finest coffee – served up with some of the finest cakes! The Germans also introduced cardamom to the Verapaces, when a *finquero* requested some seeds for use in biscuits. Guatemala is now the world's largest producer of cardamom.

Baja Verapaz ●● ▸▸ *pp742-746.*

The small region of Baja Verapaz is made up of a couple of Achi'-Maya speaking towns, namely Salamá, Rabinal, San Jerónimo and Cubulco. The department is known for the quetzal reserve, the large Dominican *finca* and aqueduct, and the weird decorative technique of the crafts in Rabinal.

Sierra de las Minas Biosphere Reserve → *Colour map 5, A2.*

① *To visit, get a permit in San Augustín from the office of La Fundación de Defensores de la Naturaleza, Barrio San Sebastián, 1 block before the Municipalidad, T7936-0681, ctot@ defensores.org.gt, www.defensores.org.gt. The contact is César Tot. Alternatively, contact the Fundación offices in Santa Elena, Petén, at 5 Calle, 3 Av "A", Zona 2, T7926-3095, lacandon@ defensores.org.gt, or in the capital at 7 Av, 7-09, Zona 13, T2440-8138.*

Just north of El Rancho, in the Department of El Progreso, is **San Agustín Acasaguastlán**, an entrance for the Sierra de las Minas Biosphere Reserve, one of Guatemala's largest conservation areas with peaks topping 3000 m and home to the quetzal, harpy eagle and peregrine falcon, puma, jaguar, spider monkey, howler monkey, tapir and pizote.

Biotopo del Quetzal

① *Daily 0700-1600, US$2.60, parking, disabled entrance. Run by Centro de Estudios Conservacionistas (CECON), Av Reforma, 0-63, Zona 10, Guatemala City, T2331-0904, cecon@usac.edu.gt.*

The Biotopo del Quetzal, or **Biosphere Mario Dary Rivera**, is between Cobán and Guatemala City at Km 160.5, 4 km south of Purulhá and 53 km from Cobán. There are two trails. Increasing numbers of quetzals have been reported in the Biotopo, but they are still very elusive. Ask for advice from the rangers.

Salamá, Rabinal and Cubulco

Just before Salamá is **San Jerónimo**, where there is a Dominican church and convent, from where friars tended vineyards, exported wine and cultivated sugar. There is an old sugar mill (*trapiche*) on display at the *finca* and a huge aqueduct of 124 arches to transport water to the sugar cane fields and the town. Salamá sits in a valley with a colonial cathedral, containing carved gilt altarpieces as its centrepiece. The town also has one of a few remaining *Templos de Minerva* in the country, built in 1916. Behind the Calvario church is the hill Cerro de la Santa Cruz, from where a view of the valley can be seen. Market day is Monday and is worth a visit. The village of **Rabinal** was founded in 1537 by Fray Bartolomé de las Casas. It has a 16th-century church, and a busy Sunday market, where lacquered gourds, beautiful *huípiles* and embroidered napkins are sold. The glossy lacquer of the gourd is made from the body oil of a farmed scaly insect called the *niij*. The male *niij* is boiled in water to release its oil, which is then mixed with soot powder to create the lacquer. The **Museo Rabinal Achí** ① *2 Calle y 4 Av, Zona 3, T5311-1536, museoachi@hotmail.com*, displays historical exhibits and has recently produced bilingual books about the Achí culture. West of Rabinal, set amid maize fields and peach trees, Cubulco is known for its tradition of performing the pole dance, *Palo Volador*, which takes place every 20-25 July. Men, attached by rope, have to leap from the top of the pole and spiral down, accompanied by marimba music. There are three basic *hospedajes* in town.

Alta Verapaz ◎◎ ▶▶ *pp742-746.*

The region of Alta Verapaz is based on a gigantic mountain, Sierra de Chamá. Dinosaurs roamed the area more than 65 million years ago before it was engulfed by sea. It later emerged, covered with limestone rock, which over millions of years has left the area riddled with caves, and dotted with small hills. In the far northwest of the department are the mystical, emerald-green waters of **Laguna Lachuá**.

Santa Cruz Verapaz and around

Santa Cruz Verapaz has a fine white 16th-century church with a fiesta between 1-4 May when you can see the wonderful Danza de los Guacamayos (scarlet macaws). This **Poqomchi' Maya** village is 15 km northwest of Tactic, at the junction with the road to Uspantán. To get there, take the San Cristóbal Verapaz bus, 25 minutes, or take a bus heading to the capital, get off at the junction and walk 200 m into town. The local fiestas are 15, 20 January, 21-26 July with the *Palo Volador*. 8th of December is when the devil-burning dance can be seen. Six kilometres west towards Uspantán is **San Cristóbal Verapaz**, which has a large, white, colonial church. From the church, a 1-km long, straight, road (Calle del Calvario) slopes down and then curves upwards to a hilltop **Calvario Church**. At Easter, the whole road is carpeted in flowers that rival those on display in Antigua at this time of year. There is **Museo Katinamit** ① *T7950-4039, cecep@ intelnet. net.gt, Mon-Fri 0900-1200, 1500-1700, run by the Centro Comunitario Educativo Poqomchi'*, dedicated to the preservation and learning of the Poqomchi' culture.

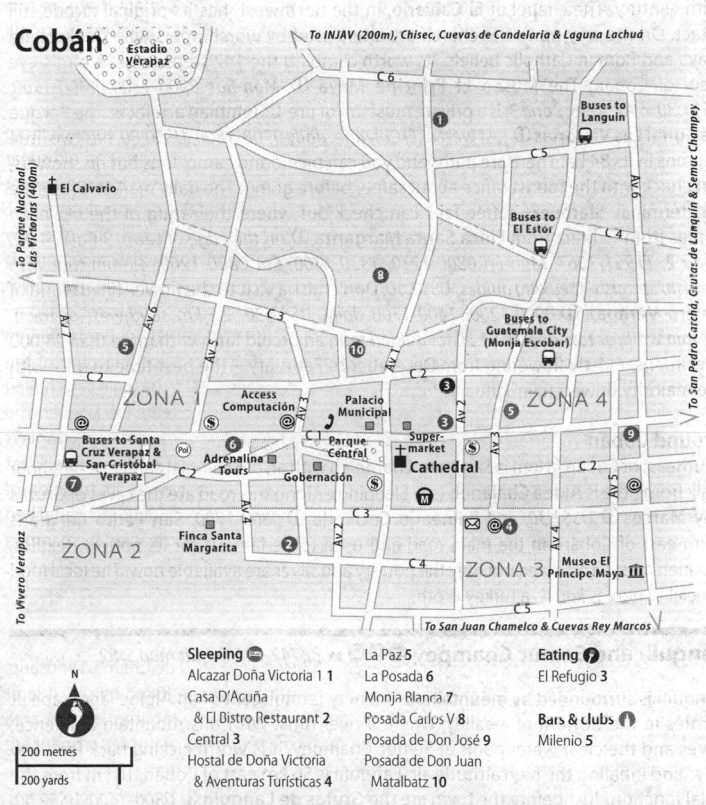

Sleeping 🛏
Alcazar Doña Victoria 1 **1**
Casa D'Acuña
& El Bistro Restaurant **2**
Central **3**
Hostal de Doña Victoria
& Aventuras Turísticas **4**

La Paz **5**
La Posada **6**
Monja Blanca **7**
Posada Carlos V **8**
Posada de Don José **9**
Posada de Don Juan
Matalbatz **10**

Eating 🍴
El Refugio **3**

Bars & clubs 🍸
Milenio **5**

Cobán and around ⊜🚻🚲❀🅰️🅾️🅲 ➤ *pp742-746. Colour map 5, B2.*

➔ *Altitude: 1320 m.*

The cathedral and centre of the Imperial City of Cobán (www.cobanav.net), is perched on a long, thin plateau with exceptionally steep roads climbing down from the plaza. To the south the roads are filled with the odd, well-preserved colonial building and a coffee *finca*. There is year-round soft rainfall, known as *chipi-chipi*, which is a godsend to the coffee and cardamom plants growing nearby. Most visitors use the city as a base for visiting sights in the surrounding area, trips to Semuc Champey, Languin and as a stepping off point for rafting trips on the Río Cahabón. There's a **tourist office** on the Parque Central. English is spoken, they have lots of information and can help organize tours. For information on northern Alta Verapaz and the southern Petén, check www.puertamundomaya.com.

Sights

The **cathedral** is on the east side of the Parque Central and dates from the middle of the 16th century. The chapel of **El Calvario**, in the northwest, has its original façade still intact. On the way up to the church are altars used by worshippers who freely blend Maya and Roman Catholic beliefs. Its worth climbing the 142 steps to get a bird's-eye view of Cobán. The **Museo El Príncipe Maya** ① *Mon-Sat 0900-1300, 1400-1800, US$1.30, 6 Av, 4-26, Zona 3*, is a private museum of pre-Columbian artefacts. The **Parque Nacional Las Victorias** ① *just west of El Calvario, daily 0700-1800, US$0.80*, has two little lagoons in its 84 ha. There are paths and you can picnic and camp, loos but no showers, but check with the tourist office about safety before going. The daily market is near the bus terminal. Starbucks coffee fans can check out where their mug of the old bean comes from – direct from **Finca Santa Margarita** ① *on the edge of town, 3 Calle, 4-12, Zona 2, T7951-3067, Mon-Fri 0800-1230, 1330-1700, Sat 0800-1200, 45-min tour with English/Spanish-speaking guides, US$2.50*. Don't miss a visit to the flower-filled world of **Vivero Verapaz** ① *0900-1200, 1400-1700 daily, US$1.30, 2.5 km southwest of town, 40-min walk, or taxi ride; US$1.30 for guided tour*, an orchid farm with more than 23,000 specimens, mostly flowering from December to February – the best time to go – with the majority flowering in January.

Around Cobán

Southeast of Cobán (8 km) is **San Juan Chamelco** with an old colonial church. A one-hour walk from here is **Aldea Chajaneb** (see Sleeping). Along this road are the caves of **Grutas Rey Marcos** ① *US$1.30*, and **Balneario Cecilinda** ① *0800-1700*. **San Pedro Carchá** is 5 km east of Cobán on the main road and used to be famous for its pottery, textiles, wooden masks and silver, but only the pottery and silver are available now. The local food speciality here is *kaq lk*, a turkey broth.

Lanquín and Semuc Champey ⊜🚻🚲 ➤ *pp742-746.Colour map 5, B2.*

Lanquín is surrounded by mountainous scenery reminiscent of an Alpine landscape. It nestles in the bottom of a valley, where a river runs. With this mountain ambience, caves and the clear water pools at Semuc Champey, it is worth kicking back for a few days and inhaling the high altitude air. Lanquín is 56 km east of Cobán, 10 km from the Pajal junction. Just before the town are the **Grutas de Lanquín** ① *0800-1600, US$2.60,*

30-min walk from town. The caves are lit for 200 m and strange stalactite shapes are given names, but it's worth taking a torch. The cave, whose ceiling hangs with thousands of stalactites, is dangerously slippery, although handrails will help you out. The sight of the bats flying out at dusk is impressive. Outside the cave you can swim in the river and camp for free.

From Lanquín you can visit the natural bridge of **Semuc Champey** ① *0600-1800, US$2.60, parking available*, a liquid paradise stretching 60 m across the Cahabón Gorge. The limestone bridge is covered in stepped, clear blue and green water pools, that span the length and breadth of it. Upstream you can see the water being channelled under the bridge. As it thunders through, it is spectacular. At its voluminous exit you can climb down from the bridge and see it cascading. You can swim in all the pools and little hot flows pour into some of them. Tours of Semuc Champey from Cobán cost around US$31.

Parque Nacional Laguna Lachuá

① *T5704 1509 to hire a guide for the day, US$4, main entrance, US$5.20, Mon-Sat 0900-1700.* Near **Playa Grande**, northwest of Cobán, is Parque Nacional Laguna Lachuá. The deep velvet-green lake, formed by a meteor impact, is 5 sq km and 220 m deep in places. It is surrounded by virtually unspoilt dense jungle, and the chances of seeing wildlife at dawn and dusk are high. There is a guided nature trail and camping and a basic guesthouse. In this area is the **Río Ikbolay**, a green river that runs underground through caves. When it emerges the other side it is blue. The river has changed its course over time leaving some of its run-through caves empty, making it possible to walk through them. The **Proyecto Ecológico Quetzal**, see page 744, runs jungle hikes in this area.

North of Cobán and the southern Petén crossroads ⊖⊖ ⊷ pp742-746.

About 100 km northeast of Cobán is **Sebol**, reached via **Chisec** (www.visitchisec.com with information on the Grutas de Candelaria and Laguna Lachuá, see above) and unappealing **Raxrujá**. From here roads go north to Sayaxché and east to Modesto Méndez via Fray Bartolomé de las Casas. West of Raxrujá are the **Grutas de Candelaria** ① *US$5.35 including a guided tour*, an extensive cavern system with stalagmites. Tubing is available. Take the road to Raxrujá and look for the Candelaria Camposanto village at Km 310 between Chisec and Raxrujá or look for a sign saying 'Escuela de Autogestión Muqbilbe' and enter here to get to the caves and eco-hotel. Camping is possible. Both points of access offer activities for visitors. North of Raxrujá is the Maya site of **Cancuén** ① *www.puertamundomaya.com, ask in Cobán about tours*, reached by *lancha* in 30 minutes (US$40 for 1-12 people), from the village of La Unión (camping and meals are available at the site). Ten kilometres east of Sebol, and 15 minutes by bus, is **Fray Bartolomé de las Casas**, a town that is just a stop-off for travellers on the long run between Poptún and Cobán or Sayaxché. A road (that is nearly all tarmacked) links Fray Bartolomé de las Casas, Sebol and Sayaxché via Raxrujá. The scenery is beautiful with luscious palms, solitary sheer-sided hills and thatched-roofed homes.

For Sleeping and Eating price codes and other relevant information, see Essentials pages 45-48.

Sleeping

Sierra de las Minas *p738*
B La Cabaña de Los Albores, Chilascó. A 130-m-high waterfall, el salto de Chilascó, is near this ecotourism project with 2 cabins and 8 beds with shared hot water showers.

Biotopo del Quetzal *p738*
A-B Posada Montaña del Quetzal, at Km 156, www.hposadaquetzal.com. Bungalows or rooms with private bathrooms, hot water, café, bar, swimming pool and gardens.
B Ram Tzul, km 185.5, S5908-4066, http://m-y-c.com.ar/ramtzul. Lovely bedrooms in wooden *cabañas*. Dozens of excursions can be arranged.
E-F Hospedaje Ranchitos del Quetzal, Km 160.8, near the Biotopo entrance, T2434-5919. Clean rooms with shared or private bathrooms, hot water, *comedor*.

Salamá, Rabinal and Cubulco *p738*
D San Ignacio, 4 Calle "A", 7-09, Salamá, T7940-1797. Behind the Telgua building, with bath and TV, clean and friendly.
E-F Posada San Pablo, 3 Av, 1-50, T7938-8025, Rabinal. Clean and friendly, will do laundry, but hard beds.

Santa Cruz Verapaz and around *p739*
A-B Hotel Park, km 196, on the main road south of the junction to the Poqomchi' Maya village, Santa Cruz, Verapaz, T7952-0807, www.parkhotelresort.com. Rooms of varying prices with TV, restaurant, bar, gym and excellent gardens.
D Eco Hotel Chi' Ixim, Km 182.5, just beyond Tactic, T7953-9198. Rooms with private bath, hot water and fireplaces, restaurant.
F Hotel El Portón Real, 4 Av, 1-44, Zona 1, Santa Cruz Verapaz, T7950-4604. Dreary from the outside, but inside this hotel is lovely

with lots of wood furnishings. It's run by a very friendly *señora*. Rooms with bath, cheaper without, hot water and free drinking water. The hotel closes its doors at 2130.

Cobán *p740, map p739*
Accommodation is extremely hard to find on the Fri and Sat of **Rabin Ajau** (last week of Jul) and in Aug. For Rabin Ajau you need to be in town a few days beforehand to secure a room, or ring and reserve.
A Alcazar Doña Victoria 1, 1 Av 5-34, Zona1 T7952-1143. More expensive than the original **Doña Victoria** (see below), modern colonial style, handy for the bus.
A La Posada, 1 Calle, 4-12, Zone 2, T7952-1495, www.laposadacoban.com. 16 attractively decorated rooms all with private tiled bathrooms and fireplaces, colonial hotel with well-kept flourishing gardens, credit cards accepted, stylish restaurant with terrace and fireplace, stop by for a drink if nothing else. Café too, see Eating.
A-B Hotel Posada de Don Juan Matalbatz, 3 Calle, 1-46, Zona 1, T7952-1599, info@discoveryguate.com. A colonial-style hotel with rooms set around a courtyard. Despite the nearby bus terminal it is very quiet and safe. All rooms have TV and there's a restaurant, pool table and parking. Tours offered.
B-C Hotel de Posada Carlos V, 1 Av 3-44, Zona 1, T7951-1133, victormoino@hotmail.com. Lantern-lined entrance, Swiss-chalet style, eclectic, Italian family, fireplace in lounge, restaurant, bar, cosy, modern annex not as nice.
C Hostal de Doña Victoria, 3 Calle, 2-38, Zona 3, T7951-4213. In a 400-year-old former Dominican convent with colonnaded gallery, attractive gardens and a good restaurant (see Eating). Excursions arranged, recommended.
D Central, 1 Calle, 1-79, T7952-1442. A stone's throw from the cathedral. 15 very clean large rooms, around a patio,

with hot shower. Rooms with TV cost
a little extra.

D Monja Blanca, 2 Calle, 6-30 Zona 2,
T7952-1712. All rooms are set around a pretty
courtyard, very peaceful, old-fashioned dining
room, breakfast good value. The place is run
by a slightly eccentric *señora* and looks shut
from the outside. Recommended.

D-E Hotel Posada de Don José, 6 Av, 1-18,
Zona 4, T7951-4760. 13 rooms with private
bathroom, TV, cheaper without, clean general
bathrooms, laundry, friendly, courtyard,
good budget option.

D-F Casa D'Acuña, 4 Calle, 3-11, Zona 2,
T7951-0482, casadeacuna@yahoo.com.
2 bunk beds to a room, ultra-clean bathrooms with hot water, laundry service,
internet, excellent meals, tempting goodies
and coffee in El Bistro restaurant in a pretty
courtyard (see Eating). The owners run a
tourist office, shop and tours. Recommended.

E La Paz, 6 Av, 2-19, T7952-1358. Hot water,
safe parking, pleasant, 35 rooms, cheaper
without bath, laundry, café, garden, popular.

Around Cobán p740

B Don Jerónimo's, Km 5.3 Carretera a
Chamil, Aldea Chajaneb, T5301-3191,
www.dearbrutus.com/donjeronimo.
Bungalows to rent, with full board including
3 vegetarian meals a day and activities such
as hiking, swimming and tubing included,
massage available, a great place for
relaxation. From Cobán in a taxi, 30 mins,
about US$8. Or, take a bus from Cobán to
Chamelco, then bus or pickup to Chamil
and ask to be let off at Don Jerónimo's.

Lanquín and Semuc Champey p740

C El Recreo, Lanquín, at the village entrance,
T7983-0056, hotel_el_recreo@hotmail.com.
Clean, good meals, friendly.

C-E El Retiro, 5 mins from Lanquín on the
road to Cahabón, T7983-0090. Campsite,
cabañas, dorms and restaurant, in a gorgeous
riverside location. There's an open fire for
cooking, hammocks to chill out in, and inner
tubes for floating on the river. To get there

don't get off in town, continue for
5 mins and ask to be dropped off.
Highly recommended.

F Hospedaje El Centro, Lanquín,
close to the church. Friendly, good simple
dinner, basic.

Camping

It is possible to camp for as long as you
want at Semuc Champey once you've
paid the entrance fee. There are toilets
and cooking areas. Take insect repellent,
a mosquito net, and all food and water.
See also El Retiro, above.

Parque Nacional Laguna Lachuá p741

E National park accommodation,
T5704-1509. Price per person. Bunk beds with
mosquito netting or camping (tents available).
Bring your own food and rubbish bags. There
are fireplaces, showers and toilets.

F Finca Chipantun, on the borders
of the national park on the bank of the
Río Chixoy, T7951-3423, www.geocities.com/
chipantun/main.html. With rooms,
hammocks or camping space. 3 meals
a day are provided at extra cost but at
excellent value – the most expensive is
dinner at US$3.50. Horse riding, boating,
kayaking and guided tours possible.

North of Cobán and the southern Petén crossroads p741

**C-D Complejo Cultural y Ecoturístico
Cuevas de Candelaria**, T7861-2203,
www.cuevasdecandelaria.com. Thatched
cabañas in a country setting with one
large room with 10 beds and private
rooms. Restaurant and café on site.
Full board available.

E Las Diamelas, Fray Bartolomé de
las Casas, just off park, T5810-1785.
Cleanest rooms in town. Restaurant
food is OK and cheap.

F Rancho Ríos Escondidos, near
Grutas de Candelaria, on the main
road. Camping possible at this farmhouse.
Ask for Doña América.

❶ Eating

Cobán *p740, map p739*

₩₩₩-₩₩ El Bistro, in Casa D'Acuña (see Sleeping), T7951-0482. Excellent menu and massive portions. Try the blueberry pancakes, great yogurt, don't walk through the restaurant without putting your nose into the cake cabinet! Recommended.

₩₩ El Refugio, 2 Av, 2-28, Zona 4, T7952-1338, 1030-2300. Excellent waiter service and substantial portions at good-value prices – steaks, fish, chicken and snacks, set lunch. Also cocktails, big screen TV and bar.

₩₩ Hostal de Doña Victoria, restaurant inside on 3 Calle, 2-38, Zona 3. Serves up breakfast, lunch and supper in a semi-open area with a pleasant, quiet ambience. Good Italian food, including vegetarian options, is the speciality of the house. Also mini cellar bar.

Cafés

Café Fantasia, 1 Calle, 3-13, western end of the main park. Handy spot open for breakfast.
Café La Posada, part of La Posada (see Sleeping). Divine brownies and ice cream, sofas with a view of the Parque Central. Open afternoons.

Lanquín and Semuc Champey *p740*
There are *tiendas* in Lanquín selling good fruit and veg, and there are a couple of bakeries, all open early, for stocking up for a trip to Semuc Champey.
₩ Comedor Shalom, Lanquín. Excellent value, if basic, including drink.

❸ Entertainment

Cobán *p740, map p739*
Bars and clubs
Milenio, 3 Av 1-11, Zona 4, 5 rooms, dance floor, live music weekends, beer by the jug, pool table, big screen TV, week ends minimum consumption US$3, popular place with a mature crowd.

Cinema
At Plaza Magdalena, a few blocks west of town. Multi-screen cinema with latest releases usually showing.

❖ Festivals and events

Cobán *p740, map p739*
Mar/Apr Holy Week.
Last week of Jul Rabin Ajau, the election of the Maya Beauty Queen. Around this time the **Paa banc** is also performed, when the chiefs of brotherhoods are elected for the year.
1-6 Aug Santo Domingo, the town's fiesta in honour of its patron.

▲ Activities and tours

Cobán *p740, map p739*
Adrenlina Tours, west of the main square. Reliable tour operator, with a national presence.
Aventuras Turísticas, 3 Calle, 2-38, Zona 3, T7952-2213, www.aventurasturisticas.com. Also offers tourist information.
Proyecto Ecológico Quetzal, 2 Calle, 14-36, Zona 1, Cobán, T7952-1047, www.ecoquetzal.org. Contact David Unger. Trips are organized to the multicoloured Río Ikbolay, northwest of Cobán, see page 741, and the mountain community of Chicacnab.

❍ Transport

Biotopo del Quetzal *p738*
Bus
From **Guatemala City**, take a Cobán bus with **Escobar-Monja Blanca** and ask to be let out at the Biotopo, hourly from 0400-1700, 3½ hrs, US$3.50. From **Cobán**, 1 hr, US$0.80, take any capital-bound bus or a minibus from Campo 2 near football stadium every 20 mins, US$0.80. From **El Rancho**–Biotopo, 1¼ hr. Cobán–Purulhá,

local buses ply this route between 0645-2000 returning until 1730, 1 hr 20 mins.

Salamá, Rabinal and Cubulco p738
Bus
Salamá-Rabinal, 1-1½ hrs. Rabinal is reached by travelling west from Salamá on a paved road. From **Guatemala City**, 5½ hrs, a beautiful, occasionally heart-stopping ride, or via El Progreso, and then Salamá by bus. Buses leave 0330-1600 to Guatemala City via Salamá from Cubulco. There is a bus between Rabinal and Cubulco, supplemented by pickup rides.

Santa Cruz Verapaz and around p739
Bus
From **Cobán** between 0600-1915 every 15 mins, US$0.700, 40 mins. All capital-bound buses from Cobán run through **Tactic**, or take a local bus between 0645-2000, returning between 0500-1730, 40 mins, US$0.80. Bus from Cobán to **Senahú**, 6 hrs, from opposite INJAV building, from 0600-1400, 4 daily, US$2.90. If you are coming from El Estor, get off at the Senahú turn-off, hitch or wait for the buses from Cobán. Trucks take this road, but there is little traffic, so you have to be at the junction very early to be in luck.

Cobán p740, map p739
Bus
A new central bus terminal has attempted to coral the multitude of bus stations into one place. While many now depart from this bus terminal, there are still a number of departure points scattered around town. Seek local advice for updates or changes.

To **Guatemala City** with Transportes Escobar-Monja Blanca, T7951-3571, every 30 mins from 0200-1600, 4-5 hrs, US$7, from its own offices near the terminal. **El Estor**, 4 daily from Av 5, Calle 4, first at 0830, and mostly morning departures, but check in the terminal beforehand, 7 hrs, US$5.60.

To **Fray Bartolomé de las Casas**, between 0600-1600 by bus, pickup and trucks, every 30 mins. Route **Raxrujá-Sayaxché-Flores** there are minibuses Micro buses del Norte that leave from the terminal del norte near INJAV 0530 and 0630, 5 hrs, US$7.20. In Sayaxché you take a passenger canoe across the river (there is also a car ferry) where minibuses will whisk you to Flores on a tarmacked road in 45 mins. To **Uspantán**, 1000 and 1200, 5 hrs, US$2 from 1 Calle and 7 Av, Zona 2. Cobán can be reached from **Santa Cruz del Quiché** via Sacapulas and Uspantán, and from **Huehuetenango** via Aguacatán, Sacapulas and Uspantán.

Around Cobán p740
Bus
Every 20 mins from Cobán to **San Juan Chamelco**, US$0.25, 20 mins from Wasen Bridge, Diagonal 15, Zona 7 To **San Pedro Carchá**, every 15 mins, US$0.25, 20 mins from 2 Calle and 4 Av, Zona 4.

Lanquín and Semuc Champey p740
Bus
From **Cobán** there are minibuses that leave from the 3 Av, 5-6 Calle, 9 a day 0730-1745, US$3.80. From Lanquín to Semuc Champey hire a pickup, see below. From Lanquín to **Flores**, take a Cobán-bound bus to **Pajal**, 1 hr, then any passing bus or vehicle to **Sebol**, 2-2½ hrs (there are Las Casas–Cobán buses passing hourly in the morning only) and then pickup, hitch or bus to Sayaxché and then Flores.

Semuc Champey is a 10-km walk from the south from Lanquín, 3 hrs' walking along the road, which is quite tough for the first hour as the road climbs very steeply out of Lanquín. If planning to return to Lanquín the same day, start very early to avoid the midday heat. To get there in a pickup start early (0630), US$0.85, or ask around for a private lift (US$13 return). Transport is very irregular so it's best to start walking and keep your fingers crossed. By 1200-1300 there are usually people returning to town to hitch a lift with. If you are on your own and out of season, it would be wise to arrange a lift back.

Car
There is a gas station in Lanquín near the church.

Parque Nacional Laguna Lachuá *p741*
Heading for **Playa Grande** from Cobán, also known as **Ixcan Grande**, ask the bus driver to let you off before Playa Grande at 'la entrada del parque', from where it's a 4.2-km (1-hr) walk to the park entrance. Minibuses leave Cobán every 30 mins via Chisec, 4 hrs, US$8 opposite INJAV.

North of Cobán and the southern Petén crossroads *p741*
Bus
Local transport in the form of minibuses and pickups connects most of these towns before nightfall.

Bus to **Poptún** from Fray Bartolomé de las Casas leaves at 0300 from the central park, 5¾ hrs, US$5.10. This road is extremely rough and the journey is a bone-bashing, coccyx-crushing one. Buses to **Cobán** at 0400 until 1100 on the hour. However, do not be surprised if one does not turn up and you have to wait for the next one. To **Flores** via Sebol, Raxrujá and Sayaxché at 0700 (3½ hrs) a further 30 mins-1 hr to Flores. The road from **Raxrujá** via Chisec to Cobán is very steep and rocky. **Chisec**

to Cobán, 1½ hrs. The Sayaxché–Cobán bus arrives at Fray Bartolomé de las Casas for breakfast and continues between 0800 and 0900. You can also go from here to Sebol to Modesto Méndez to join the highway to **Flores**, but it is a very slow, killer of a journey. Buses leave from Cobán for Chisec from Campo 2 at 0500, 0800, 0900.

❶ Directory

Cobán *p740, map p739*
Banks Most banks around the Parque Central will change money. MasterCard accepted at **G&T Continental**, corner of 1 Calle and 2 Av. **Internet** Access Computación, same building as Café Tirol. Fax and collect-call phone service only. Infocel, 3 Av, between 1-2 Calle, Zona 4. **Language schools** Active Spanish School, 3 Calle, 6-12, Zona 1, T7952-1432 (Nirma Macz). La Escuela de Español Muq'bil' B'e, 6 Av, 5-39, Zona 3, T7951-2459 (Oscar Macz), muqbilbe@ yahoo.com. Offers Spanish and Q'eqchi'. **Laundry** Lavandería Providencia, opposite Café Tirol. **Medical services** Policlínica y Hospital Galen, a private institution on 3 Av, 1-47, Zona 3, T7951-2913. **Post office** Corner of 2 Av and 3 Calle. **Telephone** You can make international calls from **Telgua** and **Access Computación** (see above).

El Petén

Deep in the lush lowland jungles of the Petén lie the lost worlds of Maya cities, pyramids and ceremonial centres, where layers of ancient dust speak ancient tales. At Tikal, where battles and burials are recorded in intricately carved stone, temples push through the tree canopy, wrapped in a mystical shroud. Although all human life has vanished from these once-powerful centres, the forest is humming with the latter-day lords of the jungle: the howler monkeys that roar day and night. There are also toucans, hummingbirds, spider monkeys, wild pig and coatimundi. Jaguar, god of the underworld in Maya religion, stalks the jungle but remains elusive, as does the puma and tapir. Further into the undergrowth away from Tikal, the adventurous traveller can visit El Mirador, the largest Maya stronghold, as well as El Zotz, El Perú, El Ceibal and Uaxactún by river, on foot and on horseback. ▸▸ *For listings, see pages 761-768.*

Ins and outs

Best time to visit The dry season and wet season offer different advantages and disadvantages. In the months of November through to early May, access to all sites is possible as tracks are bone-dry. There are also less mosquitoes and if you are a bird lover, the mating season falls in this period. In the rainy winter months, from May to November, tracks become muddy quagmires making many of them impassable, also bringing greater humidity and mosquitoes. Take plenty of repellent, and reapply frequently. It's also fiercely hot and humid at all times in these parts so lots of sun screen and drinking water are essential.

Background

Predominantly covered in jungle, the Petén is the largest department of Guatemala although it has the smallest number of inhabitants. The northern area was so impenetrable that its Maya settlers, the Itzás, were not conquered by the Spaniards until 1697. In 1990, 21,487 sq km of the north of the Petén was declared a *Reserva de la Biósfera Maya* (Maya Biosphere Reserve), by **CONAP**, the National Council for Protected Areas. It became the largest protected tropical forest area in Central America. Inside the boundaries of the biosphere are the Parque Nacional Tikal, Parque Nacional Mirador–Río Azul and Parque Nacional Laguna del Tigre.

Poptún → *Colour map 5, B3.*

Poptún is best known for its association with **Finca Ixobel**, see Sleeping. Otherwise, it is just a staging-post between Río Dulce and Flores, or a stop-off to switch buses for the ride west to Cobán.

Flores and Santa Elena ⊜❼▲⊜❻ ▸▸ *pp761-768. Colour map 5, A2.*

Flores is perched on a tiny island in Lake Petén Itzá. Red roofs and palm trees jostle for position as they spread up the small hill, which is topped by the white twin-towered cathedral. Some of the streets of the town are lined with houses and restaurants that have been given lashings of colourful paint, giving Flores a Caribbean flavour. *Lanchas*, drifting among the lilies and dragonflies, are pinned to the lake edges. Santa Elena is the dustier, less elegant and noisier twin town on the mainland where the cheapest hotels, banking services and bus terminal can be found.

Ins and outs

Getting there and around Flores is 2 km from the international airport on the outskirts of Santa Elena. The airport departures hall has an internet place. Tour operator and hotel representatives are based in the arrival halls. A causeway links Flores with Santa Elena. A taxi from the airport into Santa Elena or Flores costs US$1.30 and takes five minutes, but bargain hard. If you arrive by long-distance bus from Guatemala City, Mexico or Belize, the terminal is 10 blocks south of the causeway. There are hotels in Santa Elena and Flores across the causeway (10 to 15 minutes from Santa Elena). Chicken buses run between the two, US$0.35. Tuc-tucs charge US$0.90 for journeys between the two.

Flores

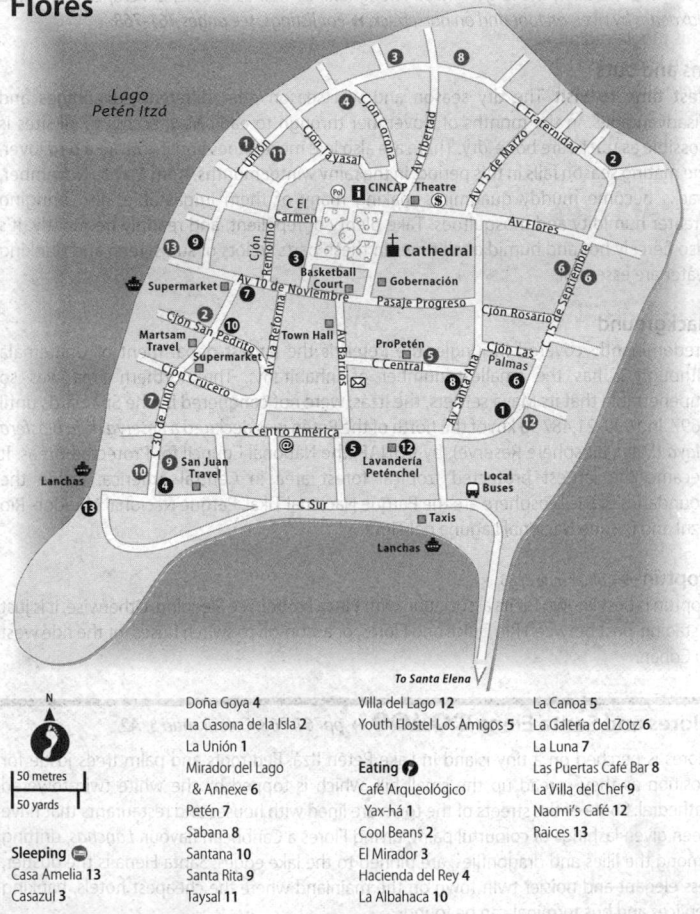

Sleeping		Villa del Lago 12	La Canoa 5
Doña Goya 4		Youth Hostel Los Amigos 5	La Galería del Zotz 6
La Casona de la Isla 2			La Luna 7
La Unión 1		**Eating**	Las Puertas Café Bar 8
Mirador del Lago & Annexe 6		Café Arqueológico Yax-há 1	La Villa del Chef 9
Petén 7		Cool Beans 2	Naomi's Café 12
Sabana 8		El Mirador 3	Raíces 13
Casa Amelia 13	Santana 10	Hacienda del Rey 4	
Casazul 3	Santa Rita 9	La Albahaca 10	
	Taysal 11		

Tourist information INGUAT ① *in the airport, T7956-0533, daily 0700-1200, 1500-1800.* ProPetén ① *Calle Central, T7867-5155, www.propeten.org,* associated with **Conservation International.** CINCAP (Centro de Información sobre la Naturaleza, Cultura y Artesanía de Petén) ① *on the plaza, T7926-0718, www.alianzaverde.org,* has free maps of Tikal, and other local information. Housed in the same building is the **Alianza Verde** ① *closed Mon,* an organization promoting sustainable eco-tourism. If you wish to make trips independently to remote Maya sites, check with **ProPetén** to see if they have vehicles making the journey.

Safety Roadside robbery used to be a problem on the road to Tikal and to Yaxhá. Get independent, up-to-date advice before visiting these places and leave all valuables at your hotel. **Asistur,** see page 623, can assist and have a base at Tikal.

Background

This jungle region was settled by the Maya Itzá Kanek in about AD 600, with their seat then known as La Isla de Tah Itzá (Tayasal in Spanish), now modern-day Flores. The Itzás were untouched by Spanish inroads into Guatemala until the Mexican conquistador Hernán Cortés and Spanish chronicler Bernal Díaz del Castillo dropped by in 1525 on their way from Mexico to Honduras. In 1697 Martín Urzua y Arismendi, the governor of the

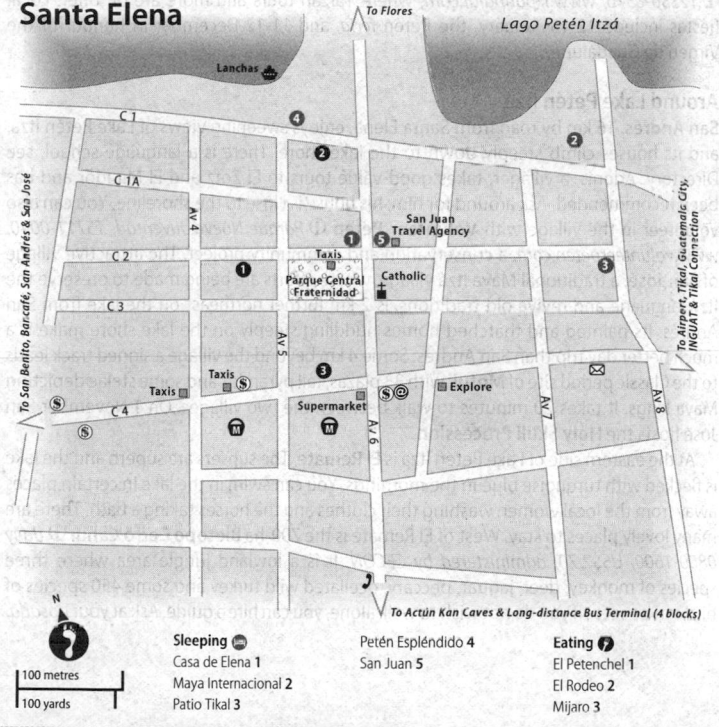

Santa Elena

To Flores

Lago Petén Itzá

Lanchas

To San Benito, Barcafé, San Andrés & San José

To Airport, Tikal, Guatemala City, INGUAT & Tikal Connection

Av 4 · Av 5 · Av 6 · Av 7 · Av 8

C 1 · C 1A · C 2 · C 3 · C 4

San Juan Travel Agency

Taxis

Parque Central Fraternidad

Catholic

Taxis · Taxis

Supermarket

Explore

To Actún Kan Caves & Long-distance Bus Terminal (4 blocks)

N

100 metres
100 yards

Sleeping
Casa de Elena 1
Maya Internacional 2
Patio Tikal 3
Petén Espléndido 4
San Juan 5

Eating
El Petenchel 1
El Rodeo 2
Mijaro 3

Yucatán, fought the first battle of the Itzás, crossing the lake in a galley killing 100 indigenous people in the ensuing battle, and capturing King Canek. He and his men destroyed the temples and palaces of Tayasal and so finished off the last independent Maya state.

Sights

The **cathedral**, Nuestra Señora de los Remedios y San Pablo del Itzá, is plain inside, and houses a Cristo Negro, part of a chain of Black Christs that stretches across Central America, with the focus of worship at Esquipulas. **Paraíso Escondido** is home to the **zoo** ① *US$2.70*. A dugout to the island costs US$16 round trip. Near the zoo is **ARCAS** (**Asociación de Rescate y Conservación de Vida Silvestre**) ① *US$2, T5208-0968, www.arcasguatemala.com*, where they care for rescued animals and release them back into the wild. Volunteers are welcome. There is a centre and interactive trails at the site. Boat tours of the whole lake cost from about US$10 per boat, calling at the zoo and **El Mirador** on the Maya ruin of **Tayasal** ① *US$2.70*. **Actún Kan caves** ① *0800-1700, US$2.70*, are a fascinating labyrinth of tunnels where, legend has it, a large serpent lived. They are 3 km south of Santa Elena and a 30 to 45 minutes' walk. To get there take the 6 Avenida out of Santa Elena to its end, turn left at a small hill, then take the first road to the right where it is well marked. South of Santa Elena is **Parque Naturual Ixpanpajul** ① *T2336-0576, www.ixpanpajul.com*, where Tarzan tours and more are on offer. Local fiestas include 12-15 January, the Petén *feria*, and 11-12 December in honour of the Virgen de Guadalupe.

Around Lake Petén Itzá

San Andrés, 16 km by road from Santa Elena, enjoys sweeping views of Lake Petén Itzá, and its houses climb steeply down to the lake shore. There is a language school, see Directory. Adonis, a villager, takes good-value tours to El Zotz and El Mirador and has been recommended. Ask around for him; his house is close to the shoreline. You can also volunteer in the village with **Volunteer Petén** ① *Parque Nueva Juventud, T5711-0040, www.volunteerpeten.com*, a conservation and community project. The attractive village of **San José**, a traditional Maya Itzá village, where efforts are being made to preserve the Itzá language and revive old traditions, is 2 km further northeast on the lake from San Andrés. Its painted and thatched homes huddling steeply on the lake shore make it a much better day trip than San Andrés. Some 4 km beyond the village a signed track leads to the Classic period site of **Motul**, with 33 plazas, tall pyramids and some stelae depicting Maya kings. It takes 20 minutes to walk between the two villages. On 1 November San José hosts the **Holy Skull Procession**.

At the eastern side of Lake Petén Itzá is **El Remate**. The sunsets are superb and the lake is flecked with turquoise blue in the mornings. You can swim in the lake in certain places away from the local women washing their clothes and the horses taking a bath. There are many lovely places to stay. West of El Remate is the 700-ha **Biotopo Cerro Cahuí** ① *daily 0800-1600, US$2.70, administered by CECON*. It is a lowland jungle area where three species of monkey, deer, jaguar, peccary, ocellated wild turkey and some 450 species of bird can be seen. If you do not wish to walk alone, you can hire a guide. Ask at your *posada*.

Parque Nacional Tikal ⊕ ↦ *pp761-768. Colour map 5, A2.*

ⓘ *Open daily 0600-1800, US$19 per day, payable at the national park entrance, 18 km from the ruins (park administration, T7920-0025). An overall impression of the ruins may be gained in 5 hours, but you need at least 2 days to see them properly. If you enter after 1600 your ticket is valid for the following day. If you stay the night in the park hotels, you can enter at 0500 once the police have scoured the grounds. This gives you at least a 2-hr head start on visitors coming in from Flores. At the visitor centre there is a post office, which stores luggage, a tourist guide service (see below), exchange facilities, toilets, a restaurant and a few shops that sell relevant guidebooks. Take a hat, mosquito repellent, water and snacks with you as it's extremely hot, drinks at the site aren't cheap and there's a lot of legwork involved.*

With its Maya skyscrapers pushing up through the jungle canopy, Tikal will have you transfixed. Steep-sided temples for the mighty dead, stelae commemorating the powerful rulers, inscriptions recording the noble deeds and the passing of time, and burials that were stuffed with jade and bone funerary offerings, make up the greatest Maya city in this tropical pocket of Guatemala.

Ins and outs

Getting there From Flores, it's possible to visit Tikal in a day. **San Juan Travel Agency** minibuses leave hourly between 0500 and 1000, one at 1400 and return at 12.30 and hourly between 1400 and 1700 (though on the way back from Tikal, buses are likely to leave 10-15 minutes before scheduled), one hour, US$7.50 return. Several other companies also run trips such as **Línea Dorada** at 0500, 0830, 1530, returning 1400 and 1700. If you have not bought a return ticket you can often get a discounted seat on a returning bus if it's not full. Minibuses also meet Guatemala City–Flores flights. A taxi to Tikal costs US$60 one way. You can also visit Tikal with a one-day or two-day package tour from Guatemala City or Antigua.

Best time to visit Try to visit the ruins after 1400, or before 0900, as there are fewer visitors. From April to December it rains every day for a while; it is busiest November to January, during the Easter and summer holidays and most weekends. The best time for bird tours is December to April, with November to February being the mating season. Mosquitoes can be a real problem even during the day if straying away from open spaces.

Tourist information A guide is highly recommended as outlying structures can otherwise be missed. The official **Tourist Guide Association** offers tours of varying natures and in different languages. A private guide can be hired for US$60 or you can join up with a group for US$15 per person. Tours are available in Spanish, English, Italian, German and French. The guidebook *Tikal*, by W R Coe, in several languages, has an excellent map.

Background

At its height, the total 'urban' area of Tikal was more than 100 sq km, with the population somewhere between 50,000 and 100,000. The low-lying hill site of Tikal was first occupied around 600 BC during the pre-Classic era, but its buildings date from 300 BC. It became an important Maya centre from AD 300 onwards, which coincided with the decline of the mega power to the north, El Mirador. It was governed by a powerful dynasty of 30-plus rulers between about the first century AD until about AD 869, with the last known named ruler being Hasaw Chan K'awill II.

Tikal's main structures, which cover 2.5 sq km, were constructed from AD 550 to AD 900 during the Late-Classic period. These include the towering mega structures of temples – shrines to the glorious dead – whose roof combs were once decorated with coloured stucco figures of Tikal lords. Doorways on the temple rooms were intricately carved – using the termite-resistant wood of the sapodilla tree – with figures and symbols, known as lintels. Tikal's stelae tell of kings and accessions and war and death. Its oldest stela dates from AD 292. Many Central Mexican influences have been found on the stelae imagery, in burial sites at Tikal and in decorative architectural technique, which led archaeologists to conclude that the city was heavily influenced from the west by forces

Tikal

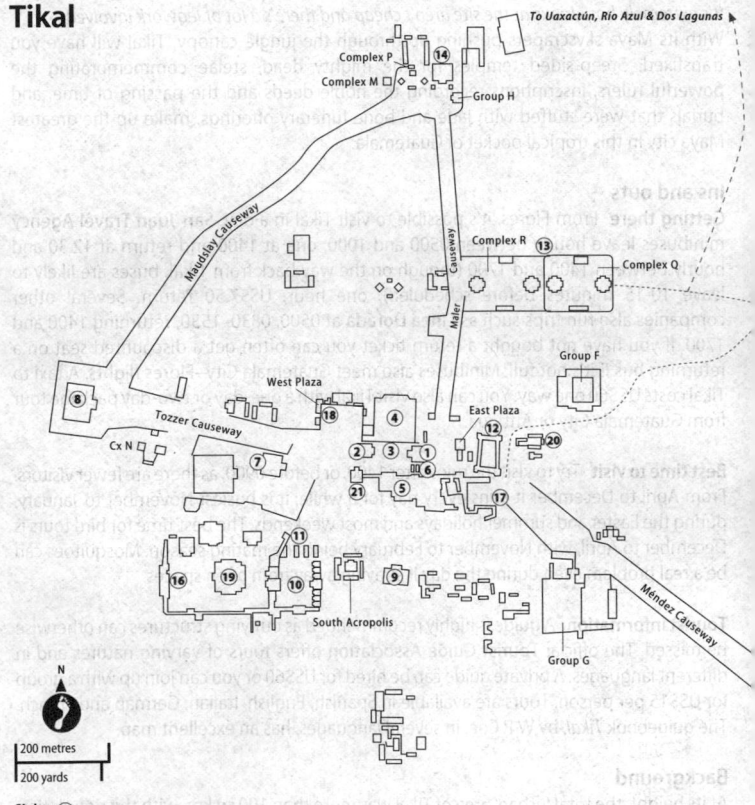

Sights ○

Temple I (Temple of the Great Jaguar) **1**

Temple II (Temple of the Masks) **2**

Great Plaza **3**

North Acropolis **4**

Central Acropolis **5**

Ball Court **6**

Temple III (Temple of the Jaguar Priest) **7**

Temple IV (Temple of the Double-Headed Serpent) **8**

Temple V **9**

Plaza of the Seven Temples **10**

Triple Ball Court **11**

Market **12**

Twin Pyramid Complexes Q & R **13**

North Group **14**

Temple VI (Temple of Inscriptions) **15**

El Mundo Perdido (Lost World) **16**

from the great enclave of Teotihuacán, now just outside Mexico City. This war-like state bred a cult of war and sacrifice and seemed intent on spreading its culture. After the collapse of Teotihuacán in AD 600, a renaissance at Tikal was achieved by the ruler Ah Cacao (Lord Cocoa, Ruler A, Moon Double Comb, Hasaw Chan K'awil I, Sky Rain) who succeeded to the throne in AD 682 and died sometime in the 720s. However, in the latter part of the eighth century the fortunes of Tikal declined. The last date recorded on a stela is AD 889. The site was finally abandoned in the 10th century. Most archaeologists now agree the collapse was due to warfare with neighbouring states, overpopulation, which resulted in environmental destruction, and drought. Tikal's existence was first reported by Spanish monk Andrés de Avendaño, but its official discovery is attributed to Modesto Méndez, Commissioner of the Petén, and Ambrosio Tut, Governor of the Petén, in 1848. They were both accompanied by the artist Eusebio Lara.

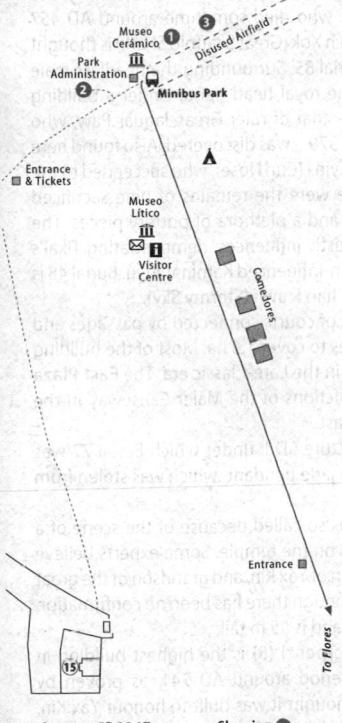

Wildlife

Tikal is a fantastic place for seeing animal and bird life of the jungle. Wildlife includes spider monkeys, howler monkeys, three species of toucan (most prominent being the keel-billed toucan), deer, foxes and many other birds and insects. Pumas have been seen on quieter paths and coatimundis (pizotes), in large family groups, are often seen rummaging through the bins. The ocellated turkeys with their sky blue heads with orange baubles attached are seen in abundance at the entrance, and at El Mundo Perdido.

The ruins

The **Great Plaza (3)** is a four-layered plaza with its earliest foundations laid around 150 BC and its latest around AD 700. It is dwarfed by its two principal temples – Temples I and II. On the north side of the plaza between these two temples are two rows of monuments. It includes Stela 29, erected in AD 292, which depicts Tikal's emblem glyph – the symbol of a Maya city – and the third century AD ruler Scroll Ahau Jaguar, who is bearing a two-headed ceremonial bar.

Temple I (Temple of the Great Jaguar) (1) on the east side of the Great Plaza rises to 44 m in height with nine stepped terraces. It was ordered to be built by the

Structure 5D 38 **17**
Structure 5D II **18**
Great Pyramid **19**
Sweat House **20**
Structure 5D 73 **21**

Sleeping 🛏
Jaguar Inn **1**
Jungle Lodge **2**
Tikal Inn **3**

Museo Cerámico **1**
Park Administration **2**
Minibus Park
Disused Airfield
Entrance & Tickets
Museo Lítico
Visitor Centre
Comedores
Entrance
To Flores
15

ruler Ah Cacao, who ruled between AD 682 to around AD 720-724, who probably planned it for use as his shrine. His tomb, the magnificent Burial 116, was discovered beneath Temple I in 1962 with a wealth of burial goods on and around his skeleton. The display is reconstructed in the Museo Cerámico/Tikal.

Temple II (Temple of the Masks) (2) faces Temple I on the Great Plaza and rises to 38 m, although with its roof comb it would have been higher. It's thought Ah Cacao ordered its construction as well. The lintel on the doorway here depicted a woman wearing a cape, and experts have suggested that this could be his wife.

The **North Acropolis (4)** contains some 100 buildings piled on top of earlier structures in a 1-ha area and is the burial ground of all of Tikal's rulers until the break with royal practice made by Ah Cacao. In 1960, the prized Stelae 31, now in the Museo Cerámico/Tikal, see below, was found under the Acropolis. It was dedicated in AD 445. Its base was deliberately burnt by the Maya and buried under Acropolis buildings in the eighth century. This burning was thought to be like a 'killing', where the burning ritual would 'kill' the power of the ruler depicted on the monument, say, after death. It's thought to depict the ruler Siyah Chan K'awil (Stormy Sky), who died sometime around AD 457 having succeeded to the throne in AD 411. Yax Moch Xok (Great Scaffold Shark) is thought to be entombed in the first century AD grave, Burial 85. Surrounding the headless male body were burial objects and a mask bearing the royal head band. Under a building directly in the centre of this acropolis Burial 22 – that of ruler Great Jaguar Paw, who reigned in the fourth century, and died around AD 379 – was discovered. Also found here was Burial 10, thought to be the tomb of Nun Yax Ayin I (Curl Nose), who succeeded to the throne in AD 379 after Great Jaguar Paw. Inside were the remains of nine sacrificed servants as well as turtles and crocodile remains and a plethora of pottery pieces. The pottery laid out in this tomb had Teotihuacán artistic influences, demonstrating Tikal's links to the powers of Teotihuacán and Teotihuacán-influenced Kaminal Juyú. Burial 48 is thought to be the tomb of Curl Nose's son, Siyah Chan K'awil (Stormy Sky).

Central Acropolis (5) is made up of a complex of courts connected by passages and stairways, which have expanded over the centuries to cover 1.6 ha. Most of the building work carried out took place between AD 550-900 in the Late-Classic era. The **East Plaza** behind Temple I is the centre of the highway junctions of the Maler Causeway in the north, and the Méndez Causeway heading southeast.

On the western side of the **West Plaza** is structure 5D II under which Burial 77 was brought to light. The skeleton was adorned with a jade pendant, which was stolen from the site museum in the 1980s.

Temple III (Temple of the Jaguar Priest) (7) is so called because of the scene of a figure in a glamorous jaguar pelt on a lintel found on the temple. Some experts believe this figure is Ah Chitam (Nun Yax Ayin II, Ruler C), son of Yax Kin, and grandson of the great Ah Cacao, and so propose that this is his shrine, although there has been no confirmation of this. Temple III was constructed around AD 810 and is 55 m tall.

Temple IV (Temple of the Double-Headed Serpent) (8) is the highest building in Tikal at 70 m. It was built in the Late-Classic period around AD 741, as proven by hieroglyphic inscriptions and carbon dating. It's thought it was built to honour Yax Kin, the son of Ah Cacao, who became ruler in AD 734. A date on the lintel is AD 741, the same year that Temple I was dedicated.

Temple V (9) constructed between AD 700-750 during the reign of Yax Kin, is 58 m high. It is the mortuary temple of an unknown ruler.

El Mundo Perdido (The Lost World) (16) The Great Pyramid is at the centre of this lost world. At 30 m high, it is the largest pyramid at Tikal. It is flat topped and its stairways are flanked by masks. From the top a great view over the canopy to the tops of other temples can be enjoyed. Together with other buildings to the west, it forms part of an astronomical complex. The Lost World pyramid is a pre-Classic structure, but was improved upon in the Early Classic. East of El Mundo Perdido is the Plaza of the **Seven Temples (10)**, constructed during the Late Classic period (AD 600-800). There is a triple ball court lying at its northern edge.

Temple VI (Temple of the Inscriptions) (15) was discovered in 1951. The 12 m-high roof comb is covered on both sides in hieroglyphic text and is the longest hieroglyphic recording to date. It was carved in AD 766, but the temple was built under the rule of Yax Kin some years before. Altar 9 is at the base of the temple as is Stela 21, said to depict the sculptured foot of the ruler Yax Kin to mark his accession as ruler in AD 734. Unfortunately because of the location of this temple away from the rest of the main structures it has become a hideout for robbers and worse. Some guides no longer take people there. Take advice before going, if at all.

The North Group There are several twin pyramid complexes at the site, including Complexes Q and R, marking the passing of the *katun* – a Maya 20-year period.

The **Museo Cerámico (Museo Tikal)** ① *near the Jungle Lodge, Mon-Fri 0900-1700, Sat and Sun, 0900-1600, US$1.30*, has a collection of Maya ceramics, but its prize exhibits are Stela 31 with its still clear carvings, and the reconstruction of the tomb of Tikal's great ruler, Ah Cacao. In the **Museo Lítico** ① *in side the visitor centre, Mon-Fri 0900-1700, Sat and Sun, 0900-1600*, there are stelae and great photographs of the temples as they were originally found, and of their reconstruction, including the 1968 rebuild of the Temple II steps. **Note** Photography is no longer permitted in either of these museums.

Other Maya ruins ●●●▲●» *pp761-768.*

There are literally hundreds of Maya sites in the Petén. Below are a handful of sites, whose ruins have been explored, and of whose histories something is known.

Uaxactún → *Colour map 5, A3.*

In the village of Uaxactún (pronounced Waash-ak-tún) are ruins, famous for the oldest complete Maya astronomical complex found, and a stuccoed temple with serpent and jaguar head decoration. The village itself is little more than a row of houses either side of a disused airstrip. Uaxactún is one of the longest-occupied Maya sites. Its origins lie in the Middle pre-Classic (1000 BC-300 BC) and its decline came by the early post-Classic (AD 925-1200) like many of its neighbouring powers. Its final stelae, dated AD 889, is one of the last to be found in the region. The site is named after a stela, which corresponds to Baktun 8 (8 x 400 Maya years), carved in AD 889 – *uaxac* means 8, *tun* means stone. South of the remains of a ball court, in **Group B**, a turtle carving can be seen, and Stela 5, which marks the takeover of the city, launched from Tikal. Next door to this stela under Temple B-VIII were found the remains of two adults, including a pregnant woman, a girl of about 15 and a baby. It is believed this may have been the governor and his family who were sacrificed in AD 378. From Group B, take the causeway to **Group A**. In Group A, Structure A-V had 90 rooms and there were many tombs to be seen. The highest structure in the complex is Palace A-XVIII, where red paint can still be seen on the walls. In **Group E** the oldest observatory (E-VII-sub) ever found faces structures in which the equinoxes and

Border essentials: Guatemala–Belize

Melchor de Mencos–Benque Viejo

Border open 0500-2100. There is a US$18.75 fee to leave Belize and a US$1.25 charge to leave Guatemala. If you need a visa for either Belize or Mexico, obtain it at their consulates in Guatemala City. As a back-up there are 72-hour transit visas available at the border, which will cover you to the Mexican border at Chetumal, but not into Mexico. If you intend to stay in Belize, you may be able to get a visa at the border but there could be extra charges when you leave the country.

Transport The road is semi-paved. There are several buses from Santa Elena to Melchor de Mencos, starting at 0500, two to three hours. Also *colectivos* from new station in Santa Elena, 1½ hours, US$2. On the return to Santa Elena there there are regular *colectivos* and **Rosita** buses at 1100, 1400, 1600, 1800, US$1.30. For Tikal, alight at Ixlu cruce. Heading to Belize: if you catch the 0500 bus from Santa Elena you can be in Belize City by 1200 having caught a bus from Benque de Viejo bus station. In addition, there is a non-stop minibus service from Santa Elena to Belize City, with **San Juan Travel Agency**, see page 766. This service terminates at the Marine Terminal in Belize, from where boats to the cayes leave. Also **Línea Dorada** at 0600, US$19, four hours, returning 0900 to Flores. Between Melchor de Mencos and Benque Viejo, the first town in Belize, there are taxis to take you the couple of kilometres, US$0.75, but rip-offs are common – so bargain hard. You can also catch taxis from the border to San Ignacio (US$15), Belmopan (US$50), Belize City (US$90) and Belize City Airport (US$100). To Mexico through Belize: there is a bus from Flores direct to Chetumal, Mexico, with San Juan Travel Agency and with **Línea Dorada**. This bus connects with an **ADO** bus to Playa del Carmen.

Exchange There are good rates for quetzales, Belizean dollars and Mexican pesos on the street; or try Banrural at the border (0700-2000).

---

solstices were observed. When the pyramid (E-VII) covering this sub-structure was removed, fairly well preserved stucco masks of jaguar and serpent heads were found flanking the stairways of the sub-structure. The ruins lie either side of the village, the main groups **(Group A and B)** are to the northwest (take a left just before **Hotel El Chiclero** and follow the road round on a continuous left to reach this group). A smaller group **(Group E)** with the observatory is to the southwest (take any track, right off the airstrip, and ask. This group is 400 m away. The site is 24 km north of Tikal on an unpaved road. It is in fairly good condition taking less than one hour in any vehicle.

El Zotz

El Zotz, meaning bat in Q'eqchi', is so called because of the nightly flight from a nearby cave of thousands of bats. There is an alternative hiking route as well (see below). Incredibly, from Temple IV, the highest in the complex at 75 m, it is possible to see in the distance, some 30 km away, Temple IV at Tikal. The wooden lintel from Temple I (dated AD 500-550) is to be found in the Museo Nacional de Arqueología y Etnología in the capital. Each evening at about 1850 the sky is darkened for 10 minutes by the fantastic spectacle of tens of thousands of bats flying out of a cave near the camp. The 200-m-high cave pock-marked with holes is a half-hour walk from the camp. If you are at the cave

Border essentials: Guatemala–Mexico

El Naranjo–La Palma

Immigration Near the landing stage, 0700-1800.

Sleeping Posada San Pedro (**C**) has simple *cabañas* with mosquito nets, restaurant, T2334-8136/39, reservations in Guatemala City.

Transport Fuente del Norte from the Santa Elena bus station to El Naranjo 0300, 1400, five hours, US$3.30. Return the same. **Transportes Pinita** buses leave from **Hotel San Juan** at 0500, 0900, five hours, US$3.25, returning 1400-1500, 1700-1800. Naranjo Frontera at 0300-1830, every 30 minutes returning 0430-1730. **Rosío** buses to El Naranjo at 0500, 0700, 0900. From El Naranjo, daily boats at 0600 and around 1300-1400, for La Palma, Mexico, US$22, cheaper to pay in quetzales, four to five hours, including Mexican border crossing, from where buses go to Tenosique and on to Palenque. The 1300 boat will often get you to La Palma just in time to miss the last bus to Tenosique; be prepared to stay the night. If there are fewer than five passengers for the boat, it may be cancelled and your alternatives are to wait for the next boat, or hire a *rápido*, US$125. Return from La Palma to El Naranjo at 0800. Bus La Palma–Tenosique at 1700, also *colectivos*; it is not possible to get to Palenque the same day unless you hire a taxi in La Palma. Mexican tourist cards can be obtained at the border.

Exchange You can change money at the grocery store opposite immigration at a better US dollar-quetzal rate than the Mexican side of the border.

you'll see the flight above you and get doused in falling excrement. If you remain at the campsite you will see them streaking the dark blue sky with black in straight columns. It's also accessible via Uaxactún. There is some basic infrastructure for the guards, and you can camp.

One of the best trips you can do in the Petén is a three-day hike to El Zotz and on through the jungle to Tikal. The journey, although long, is not arduous, and is accompanied by birds, blue morpho butterflies and spider monkeys chucking branches at you all the way.

El Perú and the Estación Biológica Guacamayo

A visit to El Perú is included in the **Scarlet Macaw Trail**, a two- to five-day trip into the **Parque Nacional Laguna del Tigre**, through the main breeding area of the scarlet macaw. There is little to see at the Maya site, but the journey to it is worthwhile. In 2004 the 1200 year old tomb and skeleton of a Maya queen were found. A more direct trip involves getting to the Q'eqchi'-speaking isolated community of **Paso Caballos** (1¾ hours). Here, the **Comité de Turismo** can organize transport by *lancha* along the Río San Pedro. From Paso Caballos it is one hour by *lancha* to the El Perú campsite and path. It's possible to stop off at the **Estación Biológica Guacamayo** ① *US$1.30, volunteers may be needed, contact Propeten, www.propeten.org*, where there is an ongoing programme to study the wild scarlet macaws (*ara macao*). The chances of seeing endangered scarlet macaws during March, April and May in this area is high because that's when they are reproducing. A couple of minutes upriver is the landing stage, where it's a 30-minute walk to the campsite of El Perú: howler monkeys, hummingbirds, oropendola birds and fireflies abound. From there, it is a two-hour walk to the El Perú ruins. Small coral snakes slither

Border essentials: Guatemala–Mexico

Bethel/La Técnica–Frontera Echeverría (Corozal)

Bethel immigration Open 24 hours. You are advised to get your visa or Mexican tourist card in advance if you need one. You can get your Mexican immigration stamp at Corozal (24 hours).

Transport Take a bus from Santa Elena via La Libertad to Bethel. **Transportes Pinita** bus, 0500, 3½-4 hours, US$4, returns 1100. With **Fuente del Norte** at 0600, five hours, US$3.30. Returns the same time. At 0500 to La Técnica with **Pinita**, returning at 0400. (Buses return to Flores at 0400, 1100, 1700, but ask at the immigration point to be sure). The bus will then continue to the *lancha* point for the boat ride, 30 minutes, US$33-40 per boat. However, if the bus does not wait you will have to walk 10-15 minutes to the river. A further 12 km from Bethel, 25 minutes, is La Técnica where the boat ride to Corozal is US$2.90 per person, three minutes. However, apparently the Bethel *lancha* co-op does not like the La Técnica *lanchas* taking its trade and robberies on the road to La Técnica have reportedly taken place. At Corozal a paved road leads up 18 km to the Frontier Highway (35 km to the San Javier junction for Lacanjá and Bonampak). From the border it is four hours by bus to Palenque. To get to Palenque in one day, take the 0500 bus from Santa Elena and catch a pickup, bus or tour bus. There is also a daily shuttle service to Palenque, Mexico, 0500, US$30. Contact **San Juan Travel Agency** (see Tour operators, page 766). Línea Dorada also plies this route for US$30, 0600, seven hours.

Sleeping In Corozal you can choose between the unfriendly **Escudo Jaguar** and the **Centro Turístico & Grutas Tsolk'in**.

Pipiles–Benemérito

Immigration and transport Get to Sayaxché, 60 km, and then take a boat down the Río de la Pasión to the military post at Pipiles (exit stamps must be given here – if you need a Mexican tourist card it's advisable to get it in advance to avoid paying bribes at the border) and on to the town of Benemérito. There are trading boats which take eight hours, US$5; motorized cargo canoe US$5-10, eight hours; private launch US$100, four hours.

Sleeping At Benemérito, there are a couple of basic *hospedajes*.

Transport From Benemérito, buses at 0600, 0700, 0800 and 1300 to immigration just past the Río Lacantún (or hitch in a truck); buses wait here before continuing to Palenque on an unpaved road; seven to 12 hours by bus Benemérito–Palenque (more in the wet). Take a hammock, mosquito net, food and insect repellent; the only accommodation between Sayaxché and Palenque are these few rooms in Benemérito, and dollars cannot be exchanged.

about, howler monkeys roar, spider monkeys chuck branches down on the path. White-lipped peccaries, nesting white turtles, eagles, fox and kingfishers have also been seen. The trip may be impossible between June and August because of rising rivers during the rainy season and because the unpaved road to Paso Caballos may not be passable. Doing it on your own is possible, though you may have to wait for connections and you will need a guide, about US$20 per day.

El Mirador, El Tintal and Nakbé → *Colour map 5, A2.*

El Mirador is the largest Maya site in the country. It dates from the late pre-Classic period (300 BC-AD 250) and is thought to have sustained a population of tens of thousands. It takes five days to get to El Mirador. From Flores it is 2½ to three hours to the village of Carmelita by bus or truck, from where it is seven hours walking, or part horse riding to El Mirador. It can be done in four days – two days to get there and two days to return. The route is difficult and the mosquitoes and ticks and the relentless heat can make it a trying trip. Organized tours are arranged by travel agents in Flores – get reassurance that your agents have enough food and water. If you opt to go to El Mirador independently, ask in Carmelita for the **Comité de Turismo**, which will arrange mules and guides. Take water, food, tents and torches. It is about 25 km to El Tintal, a camp where you can sling a hammock, or another 10 km to El Arroyo, where there is a little river for a swim near a *chiclero* camp. It takes another day to El Mirador, or longer, if you detour via Nakbé. You will pass *chiclero* camps on the way, which are very hospitable, but very poor. In May, June and July there is no mud, but there is little chance of seeing wildlife or flora. In July to December, when the rains come, the chances of glimpsing wildlife is much greater and there are lots of flowers. It is a lot fresher, but there can be tonnes of mud, sometimes making the route impassable. The mosquitos are also in a frenzy during the rainy season. Think carefully about going on the trip (one reader called it "purgatory"). The site, which is part of the Parque Nacional Mirador-Río Azul, is divided into two parts with the **El Tigre Pyramid** and complex in the western part, and the **La Danta** complex, the largest in the Maya world, in the east, 2 km away. The larger of two huge pyramids – La Danta – is 70 m high; stucco masks of jaguars and birds flank the stairways of the temple complex. The other, El Tigre, is 55 m in height and is a wonderful place to be on top of at night, with a view of endless jungle and other sites, including Calakmul, in Mexico. In **Carmelita** ask around for space to sling your hammock or camp. There is a basic *comedor*. **El Tintal**, a day's hike from El Mirador, is said to be the second largest site in Petén, connected by a causeway to El Mirador, with great views from the top of the pyramids. **Nakbé**, 10 km southeast of El Mirador, is the earliest known lowland Maya site (1000-400 BC), with the earliest examples of carved monuments.

Río Azul and Kinal

From Uaxactún a dirt road leads north to the campamento of Dos Lagunas. It's a lovely place to camp, with few mosquitoes, but swimming will certainly attract crocodiles. The guards' camp at Ixcán Río, on the far bank of the Río Azul, can be reached in one long day's walk, crossing by canoe if the water is high. If low enough to cross by vehicle you can drive to the Río Azul site, a further 6 km on a wide, shady track. It is also possible to continue into Mexico if your paperwork is ok. A barely passable side track to the east from the camp leads to the ruins of Kinal. The big attraction at Río Azul are the famous black and red painted tombs, technically off limits to visitors without special permission, but visits have been known.

Yaxhá, Topoxte, Nakum and Melchor de Mencos

About 65 km from Flores, on the Belize road ending at Melchor de Mencos, is a turning left, a dry weather road, which brings you in 8.5 km to Laguna Yaxhá. On the northern shore is the site of Yaxhá (meaning Green Water), the third largest known Classic Maya site in the country, accessible by causeway. Open 0600-1700. This untouristy site is good for birdwatching and the views from the temples of the milky green lake are outstanding.

In the lake is the unusual Late Post Classic site (AD120-1530) of Topoxte. (The island is accessible by boat from Yaxhá, 15 minutes.) About 20 km further north of Yaxhá lies Nakum, which it's thought was both a trading and ceremonial centre. You will need a guide and your own transport if you have not come on a tour. For the Belize border crossing, see box, page 756.

Northwest Petén and the Mexican border

An unpaved road runs 151 km west from Flores to **El Naranjo** on the Río San Pedro, near the Mexican border. Close by is **La Joyanca**, a site where the chance of wildlife spotting is high. You can camp at the *cruce* with the guards.

Parque Nacional Laguna del Tigre and Biotopo

The park and biotopo is a vast area of jungle and wetlands north of El Naranjo. The best place to stay is the CECON camp, across the river below the ferry. This is where the guards live and they will let you stay in the bunk house and use their kitchen. Getting into the reserve is not easy and you will need to be fully equipped, but a few people go up the Río Escondido. The lagoons abound in wildlife, including enormous crocodiles and spectacular bird life. Contact CECON.

Sayaxché → *Colour map 5, B2.*

Sayaxché, south of Flores on the road to Cobán, has a frontier town feel to it as its focus is on a bend on the Río de la Pasión. It is a good base for visiting the southern Petén including a number of archaeological sites, namely El Ceibal. You can change US dollar bills and traveller's cheques at **Banoro**.

El Ceibal

This major ceremonial site is reached by a 45-minute *lancha* ride up the Río de la Pasión from Sayaxché. It is about 1.5 km from the left bank of Río de la Pasión hidden in vegetation and extending for 1.5 sq km. The height of activity at the site was from 800 BC to the first century AD. Archaeologists agree that it appears to have been abandoned in between about AD 500 and AD 690 and then repopulated at a later stage when there was an era of stelae production between AD 771 and 889. It later declined during the early decades of the 10th century and was abandoned. You can sling a hammock at El Ceibal and use the guard's fire for making coffee if you ask politely – a mosquito net is advisable, and take repellent for walking in the jungle surroundings. Tours can be arranged in Flores for a day trip to Sayaxché and El Ceibal (around US$65) but there is limited time to see the site. From Sayaxché the ruins of the **Altar de los Sacrificios** at the confluence of the Ríos de la Pasión and Usumacinta can also be reached. It was one of the earliest sites in the Péten, with a founding date earlier than that of Tikal. Most of its monuments are not in good condition. Also within reach of Sayaxché is **Itzán**, discovered in 1968.

Piedras Negras

Still further down the Río Usumacinta in the west of Petén is Piedras Negras, a huge Classic period site. In the 1930s Tatiana Proskouriakoff first recognized the periods of time inscribed on stelae here coincided with human life spans or reigns, and so began the task of deciphering the meaning of Maya glyphs. Advance arrangements are necessary with a rafting company to reach Piedras Negras. **Maya Expeditions** (address on page 615) run expeditions, taking in Piedras Negras, Bonampak, Yaxchilán and Palenque. This trip is a real adventure. The riverbanks are covered in the best remaining tropical forest in Guatemala, inhabited by elusive wildlife and hiding more ruins. Once you've rafted down to Piedras Negras, you have to raft out. Though most of the river is fairly placid, there are the 30-m **Busilhá Falls**, where a crystal-clear tributary cascades over limestone terraces and two deep canyons, with impressive rapids to negotiate, before reaching the take-out two days later.

Petexbatún

From Sayaxché, the Río de la Pasión is a good route to visit other Maya ruins. From **Laguna Petexbatún** (16 km), a fisherman's paradise can be reached by outboard canoe from Sayaxché. Excursions can be made from here to unexcavated ruins that are generally grouped together under the title Petexbatún. These include **Arroyo de la Piedra**, Dos Pilas and Aguateca. **Dos Pilas** has many well-preserved stelae, and an important tomb of a king was found here in 1991 – that of its Ruler 2, who died in AD 726. Dos Pilas flourished in the Classic period when as many as 10,000 lived in the city. There are many carved monuments and hieroglyphic stairways at the site, which record the important events of city life. **Aguateca**, where the ruins are so far little excavated, gives a feeling of authenticity. The city was abandoned in the early ninth century for unknown reasons. Again, a tour is advisable. It's a boat trip and a short walk away. The site was found with numerous walls (it's known the city was attacked in AD 790) and a chasm actually splits the site in two. The natural limestone bridge connects a large plaza with platforms and buildings in the west with an area of a series of smaller plazas in the east. These places are off the beaten track and an adventure to get to.

⊙ El Petén listings

For Sleeping and Eating price codes and other relevant information, see Essentials pages 45-48.

● Sleeping

Poptún p747

B-F Finca Ixobel, T5410-4307, www.finca ixobel.com. A working farm owned by Carole Devine, widowed after the assassination of her husband in 1990. This highly acclaimed 'paradise' has become the victim of its own reputation and is frequently crowded especially at weekends. However, you can still camp peacefully and there are great treehouses, dorm beds, private rooms and bungalows. One of the highlights is the food. The *finca* offers a range of trips that could keep you there for days. Recommended.

Flores p747, map p748

AL Hotel Casona del Lago, overlooking the lake, T7952-8700, www.hotelesdepeten.com. 32 spacious rooms, some with balcony, in this lovely duck-egg blue and white hotel. Pool, restaurant, internet and travel agency.

A La Casona de la Isla, Callejón San Pedrito, on the lake, T7867-5163, www.hotelesde peten.com. Elegant rooms, fans, TV, clean, friendly, good restaurant, nice breakfasts, bar, garden, pool.

A Petén, 30 de Junio, T7867-5203, www.hotelesdepeten.com. Lake view, clean, pool inside the foyer area, luggage stored, ask for rooms at the front. All with a/c and TV. Internet service.

A-B Hotel Casazul, Calle Fraternindad, T7867-5451, www.hotelesdepeten.com. 9 rooms, all blue and most with lakeside view. All with cable TV, a/c and fan.

A-B Hotel Santana, Calle 30 de Junio, T7867-5123, www.santanapeten.com. Lakeside restaurant, pool, clean rooms, all with their own terrace and TV.

B Sabana, Calle La Unión, T7867-5100. Huge, spartan rooms, good service, clean, pleasant, good view, caters for European package tours, lakeside pool and restaurant.

B Villa del Lago, 15 de Septiembre, T7926-0508. Very clean, cheaper with shared bath. There's a terrace with lake view where breakfast is served, but the service is excruciatingly slow. The breakfast menu is open to non-guests, but avoid it in high season unless you don't mind a long wait.

D Doña Goya, Calle Unión, T7926-3538. 6 clean rooms, 3 with private bath, cheaper without, 3 with balcony, terrace with superb views, friendly, family-run.

D-F Tayasal, Calle Unión, T7867-5333. Rooms of various sizes, fan, showers downstairs, some with private bath as well as dorms, roof terrace, very accommodating, can arrange a Tikal trip. Travel agency in reception.

E El Tucán, on the lakeside, T7926-0536, eltucan2@elsitio.com. 4 internal rooms only, fan, shared bathroom, comfortable. It's OK here, but can be very noisy because of the restaurant, and the shared bathroom means walking by some of the punters and cooks.

E Mirador del Lago, Calle 15 de Septiembre, T7926-3276. Beautiful view of the lake and a jetty to swim from. All with private bathrooms and (irregular) hot water. One of the better budget hotels and it has lake access. New annexe opposite, quiet. All with fan.

E Santa Rita, Calle 30 de Junio, T7926-3224. Bath, clean, excellent service. 3rd-floor rooms have view of the lake, but rooms can get quite stuffy, despite the fans.

E-F Youth Hostal Los Amigos, Calle Centro América and Av Barrios, T7867-5075, www.amigoshostel.com. Dorms with 20 beds, private rooms, luxury dorms and hammocks with a funky courtyard. Good, cheap restaurant; bar and internet available. Very helpful and friendly. Highly

recommended. It also rents out hammocks and mosquito nets for tours to Tikal.

Santa Elena *p747, map p749*

L-AL Petén Espléndido, 1 Calle, T7926-0880, www.petenesplendido.com. A great lakefront restaurant setting (0600-2200), with beautiful pool on the lake. Pool open to non-guests for a small fee. Range of business services available.

AL-A Maya Internacional, lakefront, T7926-2083, www.villasdeguatemala.com. Bungalows and rooms beautifully situated and with all services. Room 52 is particularly delightful. Restaurant and pool open to non-guests, 0630-2100.

A Hotel del Patio Tikal,corner of Calle 2 and Av 8, T7926-0104, www.hoteldelpatio.com.gt. Clean, modern rooms with a/c, TV, expensive restaurant, beautiful pool and gym. It's best booked as part of a package for cheaper rates.

B Casa de Elena, Av 6, just before the causeway, T7926-2235. With a beautiful tiled staircase, rooms have cable TV, pool, restaurant 0630-2100.

D-F San Juan, Calle 2, close to the Catholic church, T7926-0562, sanjuanttravel@ hotmail.com.gt. Full of budget travellers in the older rooms, cheaper with shared bath, not always spotless. Some remodelled rooms with a/c and TV. Exchanges US dollars and Mexican pesos and buys Belizean dollars. It's not the nicest place to stay but it's safe, there's a public phone inside and parking. Note that the Tikal minibuses leave from 0500 so you will probably be woken early.

Around Lake Petén Itzá *p750*
To reach the lodgings along the north shore of the lake can be up to a 2-km walk from El Remate centre, depending on where you stay (turn left, west on the Flores–Tikal main road). There is street light up to the Biotopo entrance until 2200.

LL Bahía Taitzá Hotel and Restaurant, Barrio El Porvenir, San José, T7928-8125, www.taitza.com. 8 lovely rooms decorated with local furnishings set behind a beautiful lawn that sweeps down to the lakeshore.

Rates include breakfast and transfer. Restaurant on site.

LL-AL La Lancha, T7928-8331, www.blancaneaux.com. Francis Ford Coppola's attractive, small hotel has 10 rooms, 4 of which have lake views. There's a pool and terrace restaurant and local arts and crafts have been used to decorate the rooms. Quiet and friendly in a lovely setting.

L Camino Real, 1.8 km from the western entrance of the Biotopo Cerro Cahuí, El Remate, T7926-0204, www.caminoreal tikal.com.gt. All rooms have views, good restaurant, a/c, cable TV, lovely pool in an attractive setting.

AL Hotel Ni'tun, 2 km from San Andres on the Santa Elena road, T5201-0759, www.nitun.com. Luxury *cabañas* on a wooded hillside above the lake, run by friendly couple Bernie and Lore, who cook fantastic vegetarian meals and organize expeditions to remote sites.

B Hotel Casa Amelia, Calle La Unión, T7867-5430, www.hotelcasamelia.com. Cheerful and friendly hotel with 15 comfortable, a/c rooms – 6 of which have lake views. Guests can enjoy a terrace and pool table.

C-D La Casa de Don David, 20 m from the main road, on the El Remate side, T7928-8469, www.lacasadedondavid.com. Clean and comfortable; all rooms with private bath and some with a/c. Great view from the terrace restaurant with cheap food, bike hire free. Transport to Tikal and other tours offered. There's a wealth of information here and helpful advice is offered.

C-E Hotel y Restaurante Mon Ami, on the El Remate side, T7928-8413, www.hotelmon ami.com. Guided tours to Yaxhá and Nakum organized with the owner who is a conservationist. Lovely bungalows, dorms (**E** per person) and hammocks for sleeping. English, French and Spanish spoken. Restaurant 0700-2130, with wines and seriously cheap chicken, pastas and other dishes served.

D La Unión, Calle Unión, T7867-5634, quizam75@hotmail.com Formerly a restaurant and now a hotel with 14 rooms, all with hot water and private bathroom. Internet café in lobby and also rents kayaks.

D-E Sun Breeze Hotel, exactly on the corner, on the El Remate side, T7928-8044. Run by the very friendly Humberto Castro. Little wooden rooms with views over the lake. Fans and *mosquiteros* in each room. 2 rooms with private bathroom. He runs a daily service to Tikal and can run other trips.

E La Casa Doña Tonita, on the El Remate side, T5701-7114. One of the most chilled out places along the shore and popular, with a friendly, warm family running the place. Shared bathroom, rooms and a dorm. Enormous portions of good food. Highly recommended.

E-F La Casa Roja, on the El Remate side, T5909-6999. A red house with a tranquil, oriental feel. Rooms are under thatched roofs, with separate bathrooms in attractive stone and wood design. The rooms don't have doors but there are locked trunks. Hammock space and camping possible. Kayaks for rent and trips arranged. Recommended.

F El Mirador del Duende, on the main Flores–Tikal road in El Remate Village, T7926-0269, miradordelduende@gmail.com. Overlooks lake, camping, cabins, veggy food, jungle trips, canoes, boat trips, mountain bikes, horses and guides are available.

F La Casa de Don Juan, on the main Flores–Tikal road in El Remate Village, T5309-7172, casadonjuan@hotmail.com. Rooms out the back behind the restaurant. Owner Don Juan offers tours.

Camping
Campsite with hammock facilities at El Sotz, just before El Remate.

Parque Nacional Tikal *p751*
You are advised to book when you arrive; in high season, book in advance. Take a torch: 24-hr electricity is not normally available.

AL-A Tikal Inn, T7926-1917. Bungalows and rooms, hot water 1800-1900, electricity 0900-1600, 1800-2200, beautiful pool for guest use only. Natural history tours at 0930 for US$10, minimum 2 people, helpful.

AL-B Jungle Lodge, T5361-4098, www.quik. guate.com/jltikal/index.html. Spacious, comfortable bungalows, with bath, 24-hr hot water and fan (electricity 0700-2100), pool; cheaper without bath. It will cash TCs, full board available (although we've had consistent reports of unsatisfactory food, slow service and small portions). Jungle Lodge's Tikal tours have been recommended.

A Jaguar Inn, T7926-0002, www.jaguar tikal.com. Full board, less without food. There is also a dorm with 6 beds. Hammocks with mosquito nets and lockers. Electricity 1800-2200, hot water in the morning or on request Mar-Oct and Nov-Feb, 0600-2100. It will provide a picnic lunch and stores luggage.

Camping

F Camping Tikal, run by the **Restaurante del Parque**, reservations T2370-8140, or at the **Petén Espléndido**, T7926-0880. If you have your own tent or hammock it is US$3.25. If you need to rent the gear it is US$6.50. There are also *cabañas* with mattresses and mosquito nets for US$6.50 per person. It also does deals that include breakfast, lunch and dinner ranging from US$13-US$27 for a double. Communal showers available. Take your own water as the supply is very variable.

Uaxactún *p755*

D-F El Chiclero, T7926-1095. Neat and clean, hammocks and rooms in a garden, also good food by arrangement.

F Aldana's Lodge, T5801-2588, edeniaa@ yahoo.com. Little white *casitas*, tent and hammock space behind **El Chiclero**. Just before **El Chiclero** take a left on the road to the ruins and then first right until you see a whitewashed *casita* on the right (2 mins). Clean and run by a friendly family.

Sayaxché *p760*

C-D Guayacán, close to ferry, T7928-6111. Owner Julio Godoy is a good source of information.

C-E Hotel Posada Segura, turn right from the dock area and then first left, T7928-6162. Some rooms with bath, TV, clean; one of the best options in town.

Petexbatún *p761*

AL Chiminos Island Lodge, T2335-3506, www.chiminosisland.com. Remote, small eco-lodge close to a Maya site on a peninsula on the river. Great for exploring local sites, fishing and wildlife spotting. Includes all food.

A Posada Caribe, T7928-6117, including 3 meals, comfortable *cabañas* with bathroom and shower, excursion to **Aguateca** by launch and a guide for excursions.

Camping

Camping is possible at Escobado, on the lakeside.

❶ Eating

Flores *p747, map p748*

♥♥♥-♥♥ Raices, T5521-1843 raicesrestaurante@gmail.com. Excellent waterfront restaurant beside the lanchas near the far West end of Calle Sur. Specialities include parillas and kebabs. Great seafood.

♥♥-♥ Café Arqueológico Yax-há, Calle15 de Septiembre, T5830-2060, www.cafeyaxha.com. Cheap daily soups and home-made nachos. Offers tours to little-known Maya sites and works with local communities to protect them.

♥♥-♥ Hacienda del Rey, Calle Sur. Expensive Argentinian steaks are on the menu, but the breakfasts are seriously cheap.

♥♥-♥ La Albahaca, Calle 30 de Junio. 1st-class home-made pasta and chocolate cake.

♥♥-♥ La Luna, Av 10 de Noviembre. Closed Sun. Refreshing natural lemonade, range of fish, meat and vegetarian dishes. The restaurant has a beautiful courtyard with blue paintwork set under lush pink bougainvillea. Recommended.

† La Villa Del Chef, T4366-3822, lavilladelchef guatemala@yahoo.com. Friendly German-owned restaurant at the South end of Calle Union that specializes in *pescado blanco*. Has a happy hour and also rents canoes.

† The Mayan Princess Restaurant Café Bar and Cinema, Reforma and 10 de Noviembre. Closed Sun. Has the most adventurous menu on the island including daily specials, many with an Asian flavour, relaxed atmosphere, with bright coloured textile cloths on the tables. Internet and free films.

†-† La Galería del Zotz, 15 de Septiembre. A wide range of food, delicious pizzas, good service and presentation, popular with locals.

†-† Las Puertas Café Bar, Av Santa Ana and Calle Central, T7867-5242. Closes at 2300 for food and 2400 completely. Closed Sun. Cheap breakfasts, huge menu, good large pasta portions. It's popular at night with locals and travellers and is in an airy building, chilled atmosphere, games available.

† Cool Beans, Calle Fraternidad, T5571-9240, coolbeans@itelgua.com. Cheap food with homemade bread and pastries.

† El Mirador, overlooking the lake but view obscured by restaurant wall. Seriously cheap food and snacks but service slow.

† La Canoa, Calle Centro América. Good breakfasts (try the pancakes), dinners start at US$1.50, with good *comida típica*, very friendly owners.

† Naomi's Café, Calle Centro América. Open from 0600. Filling breakfasts and meals.

Santa Elena *p747, map p749*
† El Rodeo, 1 Calle. Excellent, reasonable prices but occasional slow service, classical music and sometimes impromptu singing performances.

† El Petenchel, Calle 2. Vegetarian food served here as well as conventional meats and meals. Excellent breakfasts. Good-value *menú del día*. Music played, prompt service.

† Restaurante Mijaro, Calle 2 and Av 8. Great filling breakfasts and a bargain *menú del día* at US$1.70, all in a thatched-roofed roadside location.

Uaxactún *p755*
† Comedor Imperial, at village entrance. Bargain *comida típica* for US$1.30.

Sayaxché *p760*
† El Botanero Café Restaurante and Bar, straight up from the dock and 2nd left. A funky wooden bar with logs and seats carved from tree trunks.

† Restaurant La Montaña, near dock. Cheap food, local information given.

† Yakín, near dock. Cheap, good food; try the *licuados*.

▲ Activities and tours

Flores and Santa Elena *p747, maps p748 and 749*
Conservation Tours Tikal, Calle 15 de Septiembre, opposite Oficina Contable Tayasal, run by Lucía Prinz, T7926-0670, http://rareconservation.org/news/article. php?id=3 (or ask at Las Puertas). This organization, funded by UNESCO, employs people from Petén communities to take visitors on tours to local sites. English and Spanish spoken. Also walking tours in the jungle, birdwatching, horse and kayak tours also. 5% of profits go to conservation.
Equinoxio, Calle Centro América, T4250-6384, sergioequinoxio@yahoo.es. Bus and airline tickets as well as Tikal tours
Explore, Calle Principal, Sta Elena, T7926-2375, www.exploreguate.com. Very helpful, reliable and professional operator offering tours to Tikal, Aguateca, Dos Pilas, Ceibal and Yaxhá.
Martsam Travel, Calle 30 de Junio, T7867-5377, www.martsam.com. Guided tours to Tikal, El Zotz, El Mirador, El Perú, Yaxhá, Nakum, Aguateca, Ceibal and Uaxactún. Guides with wildlife and

ornithological knowledge in addition to archaeological knowledge. Highly recommended.

San Juan Travel Agency, T7926-0042, www.corporacionsanjuandelnorte.com, offers transport (US$7.50 return) to Tikal and excursions to Ceibal, Uaxactún, and Yaxhá (US$80). Service to Belize, US$20, 0500 and 0700, 5 hrs. Also to Chetumal, Mexico, at 0500 and 0730, US$20, 7 hrs. To Palenque at 0500, US$35, 7 hrs.

Tikal Connection, International Airport, T7926-1537, www.tikalcnx.com, runs tours to El Perú, El Mirador, Nakbé, El Zotz, Yaxhá, Dos Aguadas, Uaxactún. It also sells bus tickets.

Viajes de Tivoli, Calle Centroamerica, T5436-6673, www.tivoli.com.gt. Trips to local sites as well as general agency services.

Uaxactún p755

For guided walks around the ruins ask for one of the trained guides, US$10. For expeditions further afield, contact Elfido Aldana at **Posada Aldana**. Neria Baldizón at **El Chiclero** has high-clearance pickups and plenty of experience in organizing both vehicle and mule trips to any site. She charges US$200 per person to go to Río Azul.

Sayaxché p760

Viajes Don Pedro, on the river front near the dock, T7928-6109, runs launches to El Ceibal (US$35 for up to 3), Petexbatún and Aguateca (US$60 for up to 5), Dos Pilas (US$50 for small group). Trip possible by jeep in the dry season, Altar de los Sacrificios (US$100 minimum 2 people) and round trips to Yaxchilán for 3 days (US$400). Mon-Sat 0700-1800, Sun 0700-1200.

⊖ Transport

Poptún p747
Bus

Take any **Fuente del Norte** bus or any bus heading to the capital from **Flores**, 2 hrs. To

Flores catch any Flores-bound bus from the capital. To **Río Dulce**, 2 hrs. Buses will drop you at the driveway to **Finca Ixobel** if that's your destination, just ask. From there it's a 15-min walk. Or, get off at the main bus stop and arrange a taxi there or through **Finca Ixobel**. To **Guatemala City** there are plenty daily, 7-8 hrs, US$10-13. The only bus that continues to **Fray Bartolomé de las Casas** (Las Casas on the bus sign) leaves at 1030, 5¾ hrs, US$8.

Flores and Santa Elena p747,
maps p748 and p749
Air

Be early for flights, as overbooking is common. The cost of a return flight is between US$180-220, shop around. **Grupo Taca**, T2470-8222, www.taca.com, leaves **Guatemala City** daily at 0645, 0955, 1725, 1 hr, returns 0820, 1605 and 1850. **Tag**, T2360-3038, www.tag.com.gt, flies at 0630 returning 1630. To **Cancún**, **Grupo Taca**. To **Belize City**, **Tropic Air**, www.tropicair.com.

Boat

Lanchas moor along Calle Sur, Flores; behind the **Hotel Santana**; from the dock behind **Hotel Casona de Isla**; and beside the arch on the causeway.

Bus

Local Local buses (chicken buses), US$0.26, Flores to Santa Elena, leave from the end of the causeway in Flores.

Long distance All long-distance buses leave from the relocated bus terminal, 6 blocks south of the Calle Principal in Santa Elena. It has a snack bar, toilets, seating and ATM. Opposite are restaurants, *comedores*, and a bakery. Banrural is down the side. To **Guatemala City**, Línea Dorada, daily office hours 0500-2200, www.tikalmayan world.com, leaves 1000, 2100, 1st class, US$30; 2200, US$16, 8 hrs. Autobuses del Norte (ADN), T7924-8131, www.adnauto busesdel norte.com, luxury service, 1000,

2100, 2300, US$23. **Fuente del Norte**, T7926-0666, office open 24 hrs, buses every 45 mins-1 hr, 0330-2230, US$12, 9 hrs. At 1000, 1400, 2100, 2200, US$20, 7-8 hrs. 2nd-class buses, **Rosita**, T7926-5178 and **Rápidos del Sur**, T7924-8072, also go to the capital, US$13. If you are going only to **Poptún**, 2 hrs, or **Río Dulce**, 3½-4 hrs, make sure you do not pay the full fare to Guatemala City. To **Sayaxché** with **Pinita**, T9926-0726, at 1100, returns next day at 0600, US$2.50. With **Fuente del Norte** at 0600, US$1.70, returning 0600. *Colectivos* also leave every 15 mins 0530-1700, US$2.40. Buses run around the lake to **San Andrés**, with one at 1200 with **Pinita** continuing to **Cruce dos Aguadas**, US$2.90 and **Carmelita**, US$3.30 for access to El Mirador. Returning from Carmelita at 0500 the next day. Minibuses also run to San Andrés. To **Chiquimula**, take Transportes María Elena, T5550-4190, at 0400, 0800, 1300, US$3. The **María Elena** bus continues onto **Esquipulas**, 9 hrs, US$12. Fuente del Norte to **Cobán**, 0530, 0630, 1230, 1330, 5 hrs, US$8. Or take a minibus to Sayaxché and change. Shuttle transfers may also be possible. To **Jutiapa**, 0500, 0530, 7 hrs, returning 0900, US$10-12.

International To **Belize City**, see page 756. To **Melchor de Mencos** at the Belize border, 0500, 0600, 1630, 2300, 1½ hrs, US$3.30. Returning 0200, 0500, 0600, 1630, 2300. Also with **Línea Dorada** and on to **Chetumal**, **Mexico**, see also box page 756. To **Copán Ruinas**, **Honduras**, take Transportes María Elena, T5550-4190, to Chiquimula at 0400, 0800, 1300, US$13 then from Chiquimula to El Florido (see page 724) and finally on to Copán Ruinas. Alternatively, take any bus to the capital and change at Río Hondo. To **Mexico**, see box, page 757. To **San Salvador**, 0600, 8 hrs, US$26.70.

Car
There are plenty of agencies at the airport, mostly Suzuki jeeps, which cost about

US$65-80 per day. **Hertz**, at the airport, T7926-0332. **Garrido** at Sac-Nicte Hotel, Calle 1, Santa Elena, T7926-1732.

Petrol is sold in Santa Elena at the 24-hr Texaco garage on the way to the airport.

Around Lake Petén Itzá *p750*
Boat
Public *lanchas* from San Benito have virtually come to a stop. Visitors can still charter a *lancha* from Flores for about US$10.

Bus
There's a bus ticket and internet office opposite the turning to El Remate. Any bus/shuttle heading for Tikal can stop at El Remate, US$2.50, last bus around 1600; taxi around US$10. Returning to **Flores**, pick up any shuttle heading south (this is a lot easier after 1300 when tourists are returning). There is a bus service heading to **Flores** from El Remate at 0600, 0700, 0830, 0930, 1300 and 1400. Shuttles leave every 30 mins for San Andrés, US$0.70, 30 mins and go on to San José.

Uaxactún *p755*
Bus
To Uaxactún from Santa Elena at 1200 arriving between 1600-1700, US$2.60, returning 0500 with Transportes Pinita. Foreigners have to pay US$2 to pass through Parque Nacional Tikal on their way to Uaxactún, payable at the main entrance to Tikal.

El Mirador, El Tintal and Nakbé *p759*
Bus
1 bus daily with **Transportes Pinita** to **Carmelita**. See Flores for information.

Northwest Petén and the Mexican border *p760*
Boat and bus
To **El Naranjo** at 0500 and 1000, returning at 0500, 1100 and 1300, US$4. Or hire a *lancha* from Paso Caballos.

Sayaxché *p760*
Bus

There are buses to **Flores**, 0600, 0700, 1-2 hrs, and microbuses every 30 mins. To **Raxrujá** and on to **Cobán** via **Chisec** at 0400, US$.80, 6½ hrs direct to Cobán. There are pickups after that hourly and some further buses direct and not via Chisec. For **Lanquín** take the bus to Raxrujá, then a pickup to Sebol, and then a pickup to Lanquín, or the Lanquín *cruce* at Pajal, and wait for onward transport. If you are heading to **Guatemala City** from here it could be quicker to head north to Flores rather than take the long road down to Cobán. However, this road has now been entirely tarmacked.

Petexbatún *p761*
Boat

It is 30-40 mins in *lancha* from Sayaxché to the stop for **Dos Pilas** to hire horses. It's 50 mins-1 hr to **Chiminos** lodge and 1 hr 20 mins to the **Aguateca** site. To Dos Pilas and Aguateca from Chiminos, US$27 return to each site.

❶ Directory

Flores and Santa Elena *p747*, *maps p748 and 749*
Banks Banrural, Flores, next to the church. TCs only. **Banco del Café**, Santa Elena, best

rates for Amex TCs. Do not use its ATM: it eats cards by the dozen. Banco de los Trabajadores, Santa Elena, MasterCard accepted. **Banco Agromercantil**, Santa Elena, open until 1800. **Banco Industrial**, MasterCard only. The major hotels and travel agents change cash and TCs. There's a bank opposite the bus terminal. **Immigration** at the airport, T7926-0984. **Internet** There are plenty of places. Hotel internet terminals tend to have fairer prices than the internet shops. **Laundry** Lavandería Petenchel, wash and dry. Open 0800-1900. **Medical services** Hospital Nacional, in San Benito, T7926-1333, open 24 hrs. **Centro Médico Maya**, 4 Av 335, Santa Elena, T7926-0810, speaks some English. Recommended. **Post office** In Flores and in Santa Elena. **Telephone** Telgua in Santa Elena and some travel agencies. **Volunteering** See ARCAS, page 624. Also www.volunteer peten.com, and Women's Association for the Revival of Traditional Medicine, T5514-8889.

Around Lake Petén Itzá *p750*
Language schools Eco-Escuela Español, San Andrés, T5940-1235, www.ecoescuelaespanol.org. 20 hrs of classes, homestay and extra curricular activities for a week, US$150. The Escuela Bio-Itzá, San José, www.ecobioitza.org offers classes, homestay and camping for the same price.

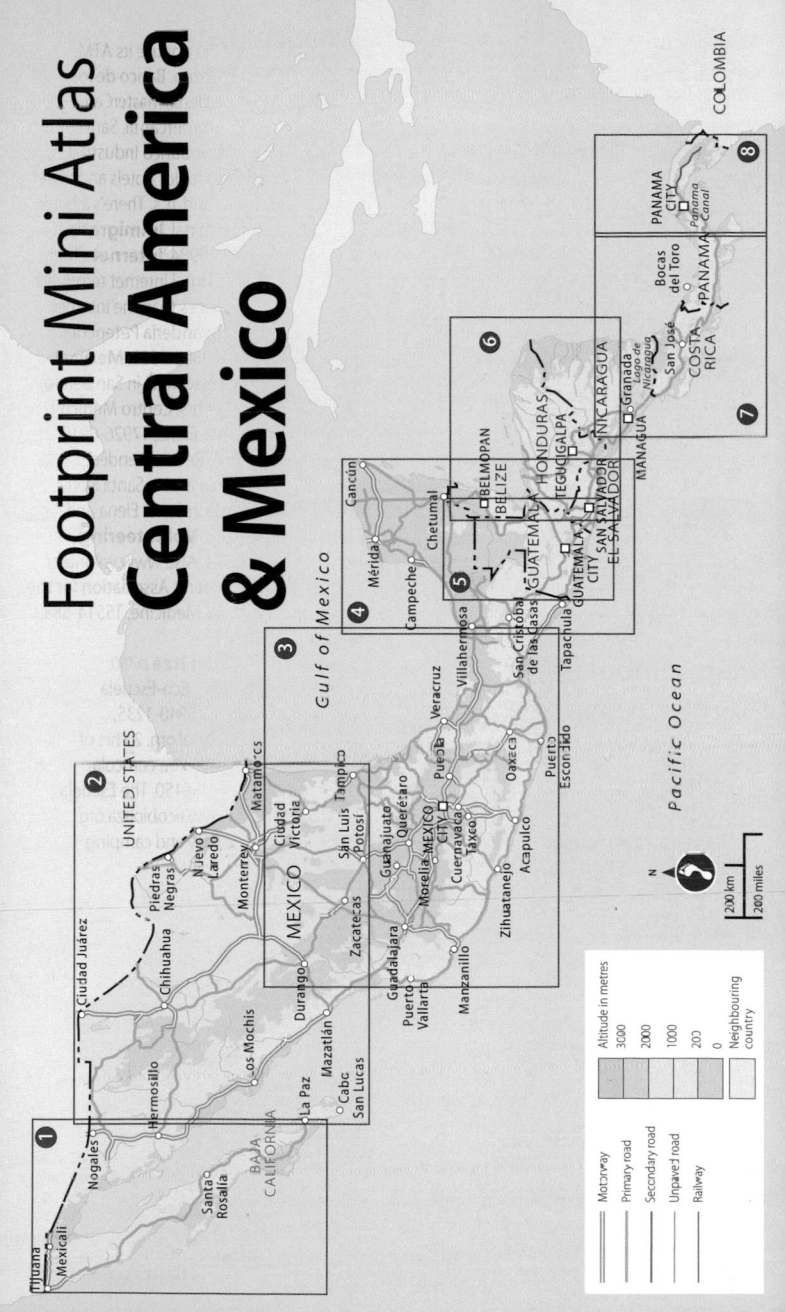

Footprint Mini Atlas
Central America & Mexico

Mexico distance chart

Acapulco

1818	**Chetumal**													
1746	2931	**Chihuahua**												
2179	3292	375	**Ciudad Juárez**											
984	2066	1160	1552	**Guadalajara**										
1459	2485	1022	1397	505	**Mazatlán**									
1828	294	2904	3279	1982	2543	**Mérida**								
411	1479	1445	1820	580	1085	1458	**Mexico City**							
1280	2468	818	1108	777	928	2061	989	**Monterrey**						
2534	3698	969	708	1697	1192	3735	2277	1707	**Nogales**					
711	1405	1933	2308	1068	1573	1408	488	1441	2685	**Oaxaca**				
828	1896	1028	1403	351	789	1918	417	537	1997	1105	**San Luis Potosí**			
1089	1257	2440	2977	1775	2280	1274	1247	1850	3212	689	1594	**Tapachula**		
3135	4299	1570	1309	2298	1758	4338	2880	2388	817	3438	2582	4145	**Tijuana**	
1136	572	2334	2605	1494	1839	545	913	1516	3223	835	1198	685	3834	**Villahermosa**

Distances in kilometres   1 kilometre = 0.62 miles

Map symbols

- □ Capital city
- ○ Other city, town
- International border
- Regional border
- ⊖ Customs
- Contours (approx)
- ▲ Mountain, volcano
- Mountain pass
- Escarpment
- Glacier
- Salt flat
- Rocks
- Seasonal marshland
- Beach, sandbank
- ⑧ Waterfall
- Reef
- Motorway
- Main road
- Minor road
- Track
- Footpath
- Railway
- Railway with station
- ✈ Airport
- Bus station
- Ⓜ Metro station

- ---- Cable car
- +++++ Funicular
- Ferry
- Pedestrianized street
- Σ C Tunnel
- One way-street
- Steps
- Bridge
- Fortified wall
- Park, garden, stadium
- Sleeping
- Eating
- Bars & clubs
- Building
- Sight
- Cathedral, church
- Chinese temple
- Hindu temple
- Meru
- Mosque
- Stupa
- ☆ Synagogue
- Tourist office
- 🏛 Museum
- ✉ Post office
- Police

- ⑤ Bank
- @ Internet
- ♪ Telephone
- Market
- Medical services
- P Parking
- Petrol
- Golf
- Archaeological site
- ◆ National park, wildlife reserve
- Viewing point
- ▲ Campsite
- Refuge, lodge
- Castle, fort
- Diving
- Deciduous, coniferous, palm trees
- Hide
- Vineyard, winery
- Distillery
- Shipwreck
- Historic battlefield
- A Detail map
- Related map

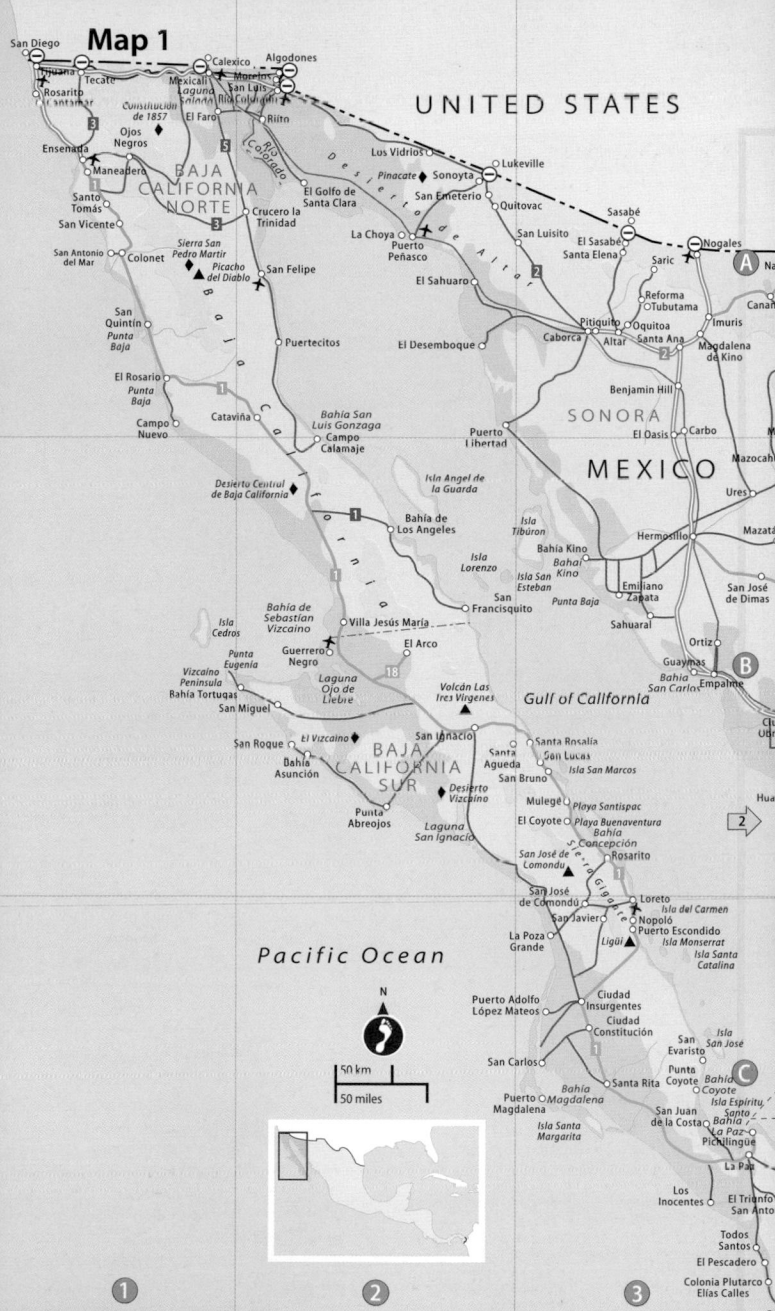

Map 2

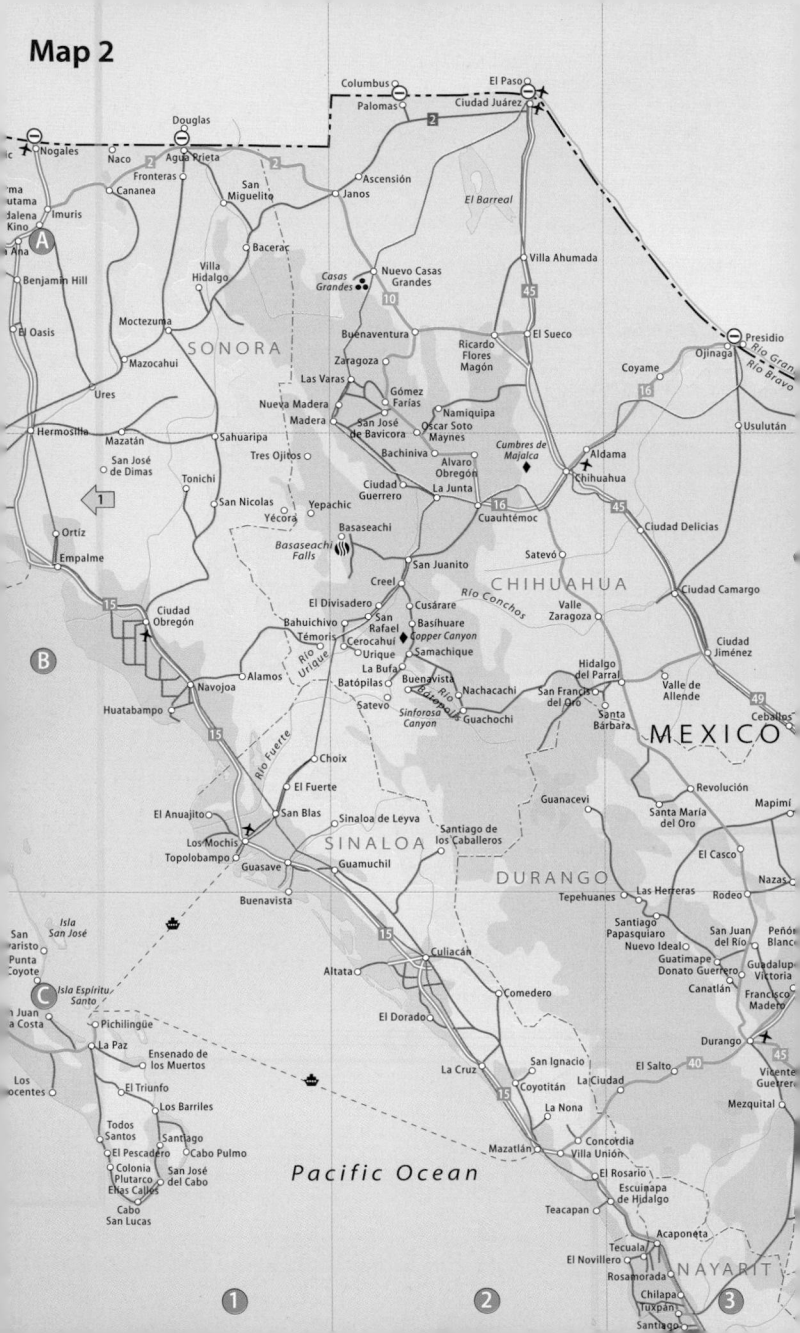

Map 4

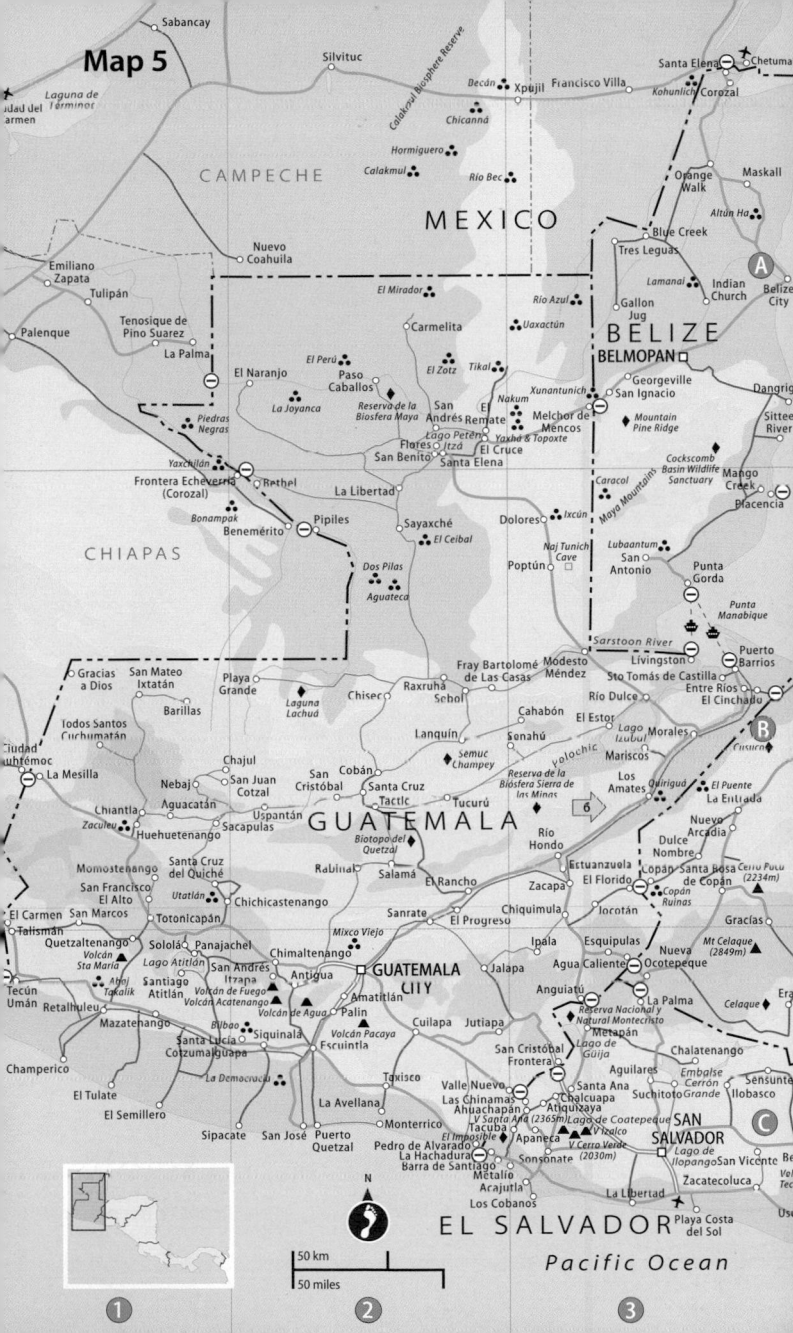

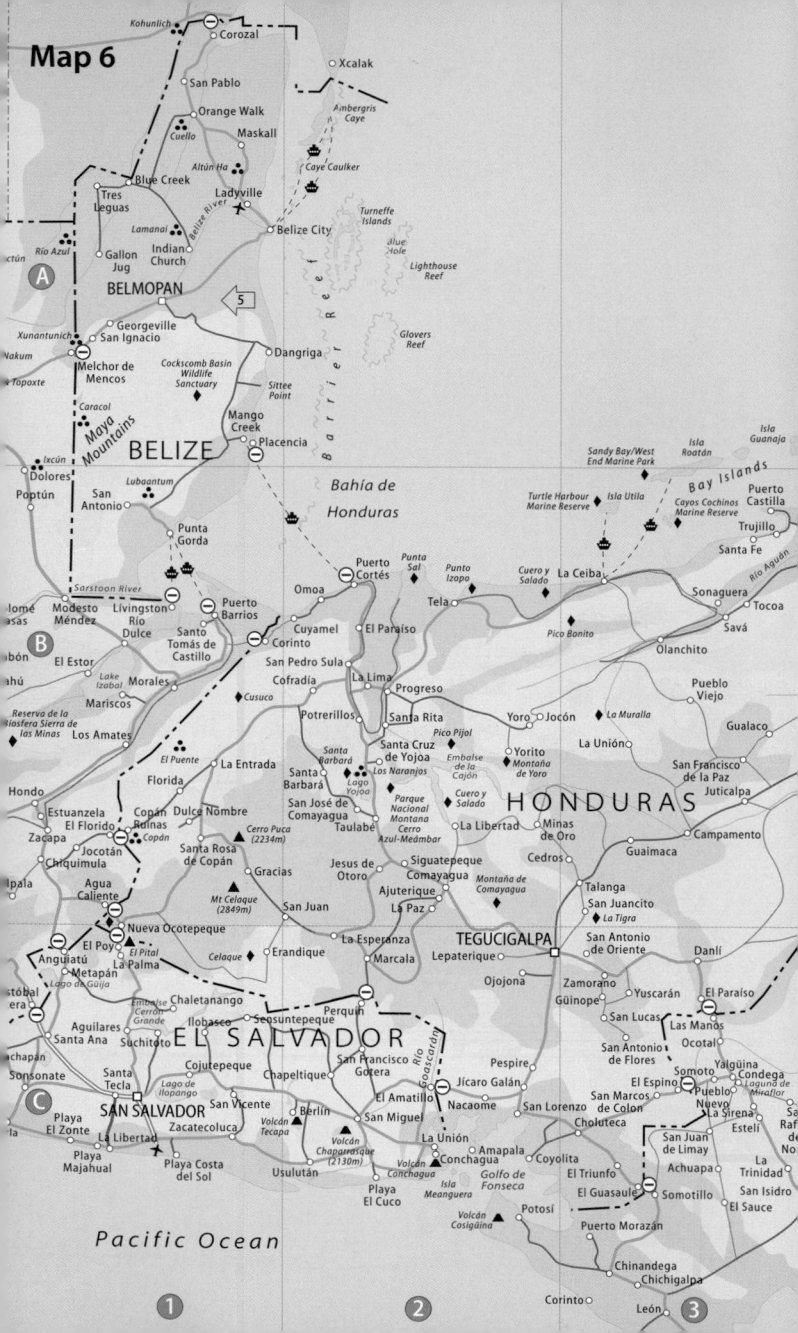

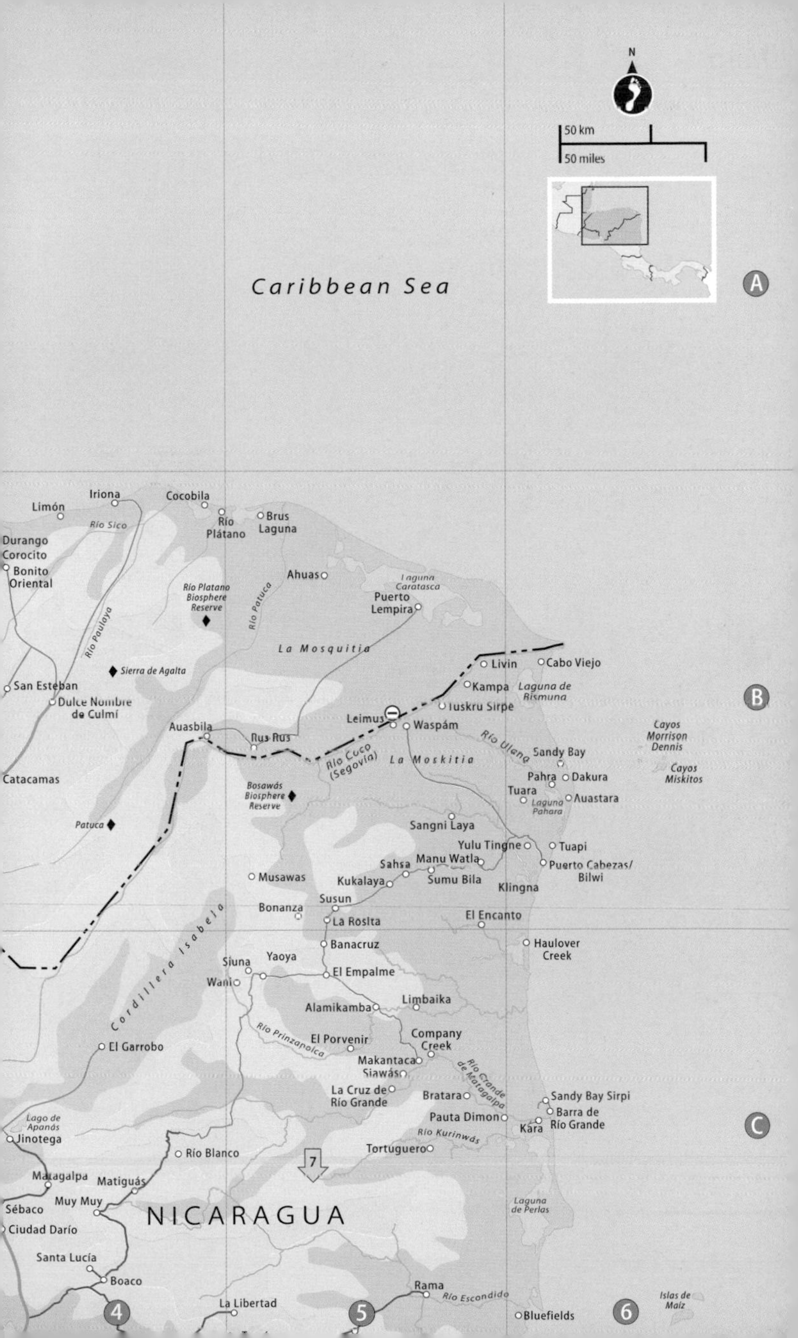

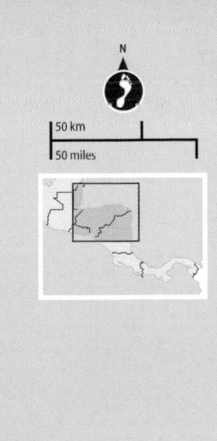

Caribbean Sea

50 km
50 miles

A

B

C

Limón
Iriona
Cocobila
Río Sico
Durango
Corocito
Bonito
Oriental
Río Plátano
Brus
Laguna
Ahuas
Laguna
Carataska
Puerto
Lempira
Río Platana
Biosphere
Reserve
Río Patuca
San Esteban
Sierra de Agalta
La Mosquitia
Livin
Cabo Viejo
Kampa
Laguna de
Rismuna
Dulce Nombre
de Culmí
Auasbila
Ñus Ñus
Leimus
Tuskru Sirpe
Waspám
Cayos
Morrison
Dennis
Río Cuco
(Segovia)
La Moskitia
Río Ulang
Sandy Bay
Catacamas
Pahra
Dakura
Cayos
Miskitos
Bosawds
Biosphere
Reserve
Tuara
Auastara
Laguna
Pahara
Patuca
Sangni Laya
Yulu Tingne
Tuapi
Musawas
Sahsa
Manu Watla
Kukalaya
Sumu Bila
Puerto Cabezas/
Bilwi
Bonanza
Susun
Klingna
La Rosita
El Encanto
Cordillera Isabela
Banacruz
Haulover
Creek
Siuna
Yaoya
El Empalme
Wani
Alamikamba
Limbaika
El Garrobo
Río Prinzapolca
El Porvenir
Company
Creek
Makantaca
Siawás
Río Grande de Matagalpa
Lago de
Apanás
La Cruz de
Río Grande
Bratara
Sandy Bay Sirpi
Barra de
Río Grande
Jinotega
Pauta Dimon
Kara
Río Kurinwás
Matagalpa
Matiguás
Río Blanco
Tortuguero
Muy Muy
Sébaco
NICARAGUA
7
Ciudad Darío
Laguna
de Perlas
Santa Lucía
Boaco
4
La Libertad
Rama
Río Escondido
5
Islas de
Maíz
6
Bluefields

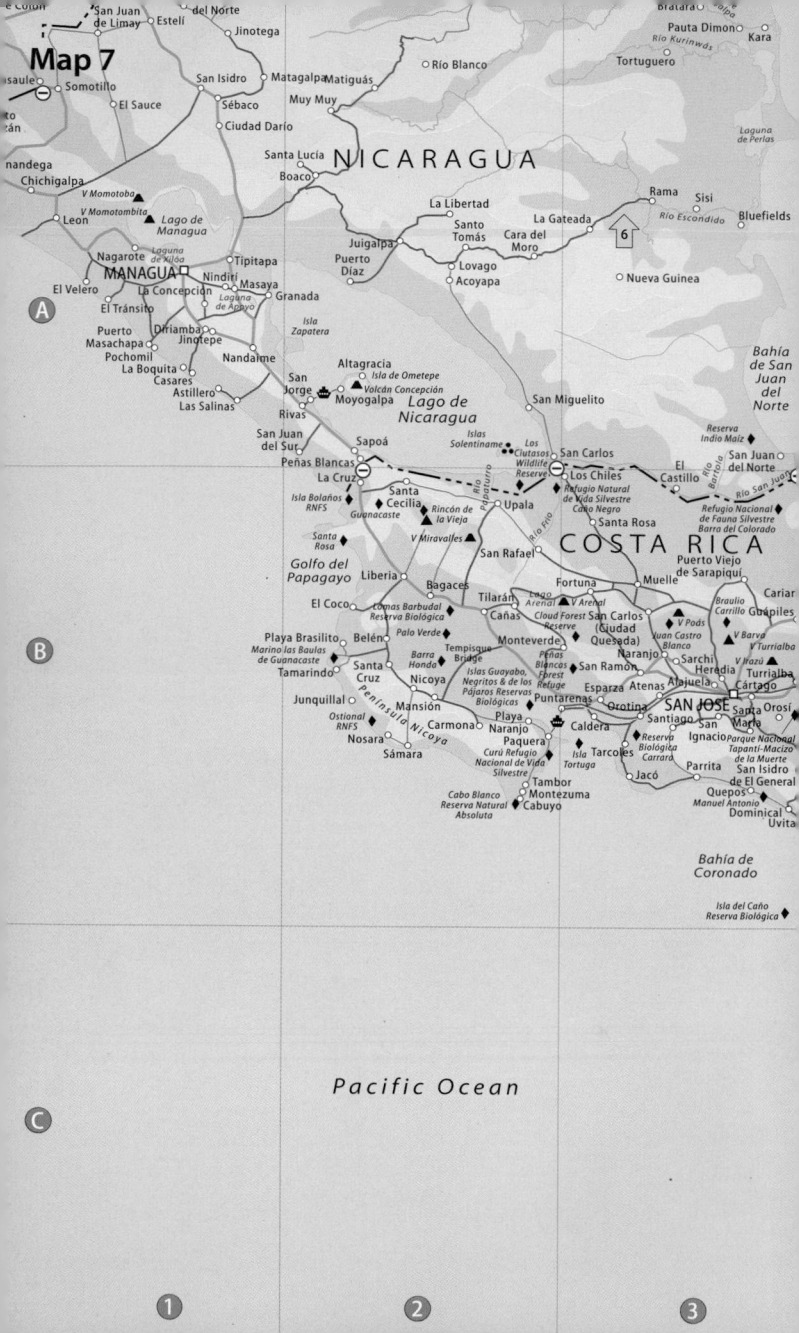

Map 8

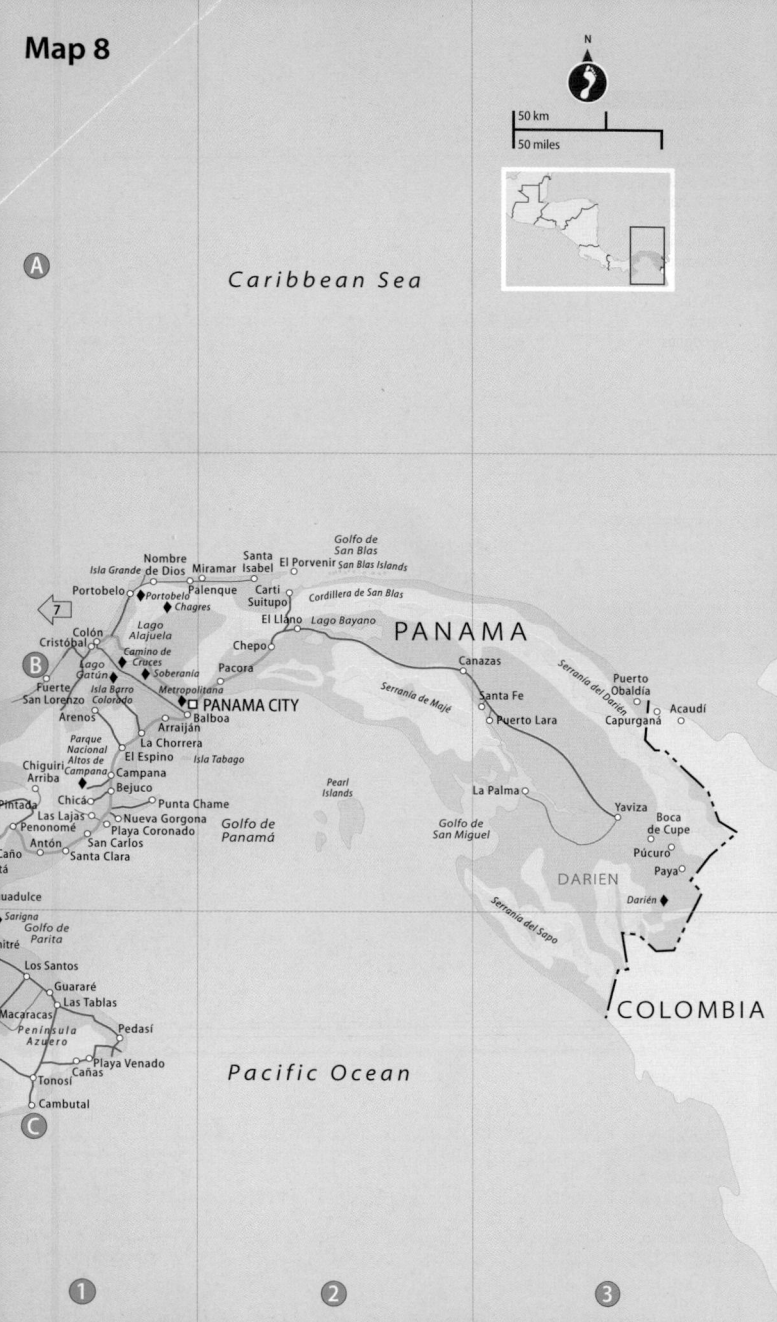

N

50 km
50 miles

A

Caribbean Sea

B

Nombre de Dios · Miramar · Santa Isabel · El Porvenir · *San Blas Islands*
Golfo de San Blas
Isla Grande
Portobelo ◆ Portobelo · Palenque · Carti Suitupo
◆ Chagres
Cordillera de San Blas
Colón
Cristóbal
Lago Alajuela
El Llano · *Lago Bayano*
Chepo
Pacora
PANAMA
Camino de Cruces
Lago Gatún
◆ Soberanía
Fuerte San Lorenzo · *Metropolitana*
Isla Barro Colorado
□ **PANAMA CITY**
Balboa
Árenos
Arraiján
La Chorrera
Parque Nacional Altos de Campana
El Espino
Chiguirí Arriba · Campana
Isla Tabago
Chicá
Bejuco
Pintada
Las Lajas · Nueva Gorgona · Punta Chame
Penonomé · Playa Coronado
Antón · San Carlos
Caño tá · Santa Clara
aguadulce
Canazas
Santa Fe
Puerto Lara
Serranía de Majé
Puerto Obaldía
Capurganá
Acaudí
Yaviza
Boca de Cupe
Púcuro
Paya
La Palma
Golfo de San Miguel
Serranía del Darién
DARIEN
◆ Darién
Serranía del Sapo
Pearl Islands
Golfo de Panamá

C

◆ Sarigna
Golfo de Parita
hitré
Los Santos
Guararé
Las Tablas
Macaracas · Pedasí
Península Azuero
Playa Venado
Tonosí · Cañas
Cambutal
Pacific Ocean
COLOMBIA

1   2   3

Index

Contents

Border crossings

Belize–Mexico
see page 805
Belize–Guatemala
see page 829

Belize

At a glance

⊖ **Getting around** Bus and plane, with the odd boat trip out to the cayes. Boats to Guatemala and Honduras.

◉ **Time required** You'll get a feel for the country in a fortnight – but longer is better.

☼ **Weather** Warm throughout the year, wettest from Jun-Oct.

✖ **When not to go** Jun and Jul are the wettest months – a real dampener if you're on the beach.

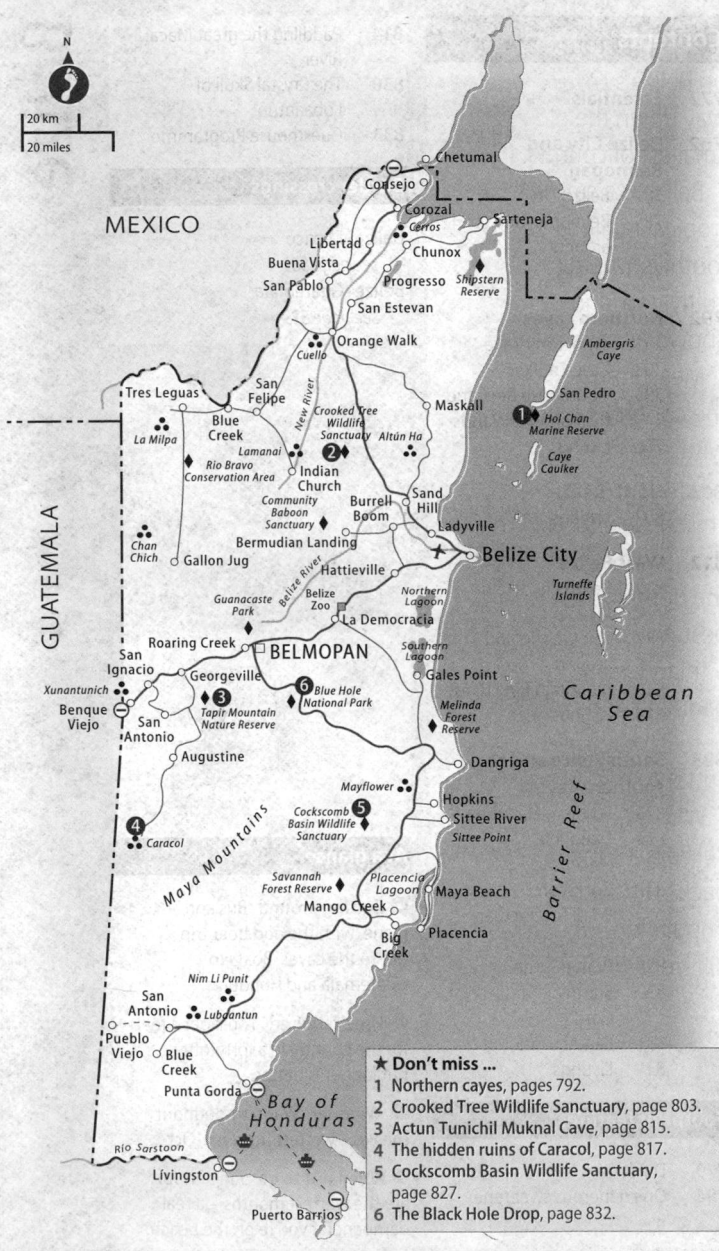

MEXICO

N

20 km
20 miles

Chetumal
Consejo
Corozal
Cerros
Sarteneja
Libertad
Chunox
Buena Vista
San Pablo
Progresso
San Estevan
Shipstern Reserve
Orange Walk
Cuello
Tres Leguas
San Felipe
Maskall
La Milpa
Blue Creek
Crooked Tree Wildlife Sanctuary
Altún Ha
Ambergris Caye
San Pedro
1 Hol Chan Marine Reserve
Rio Bravo Conservation Area
Lamanai
Indian Church
2
Caye Caulker
Chan Chich
Community Baboon Sanctuary
Burrell Boom
Sand Hill
Gallon Jug
Bermudian Landing
Ladyville
Hattieville
Belize City
Guanacaste Park
Belize Zoo
Northern Lagoon
Turneffe Islands
Roaring Creek
La Democracia
BELMOPAN
Georgeville
6 Blue Hole National Park
Southern Lagoon
Gales Point
San Ignacio
Xunantunich
3
Tapir Mountain Nature Reserve
Melinda Forest Reserve
Caribbean Sea
Benque Viejo
San Antonio
Augustine
Mayflower
Dangriga
4 Caracol
Cockscomb Basin Wildlife Sanctuary
5
Hopkins
Sittee River
Sittee Point
Barrier Reef
Savannah Forest Reserve
Placencia Lagoon
Mango Creek
Maya Beach
Big Creek
Placencia
Nim Li Punit
San Antonio
Lubaantun
Pueblo Viejo
Blue Creek
Punta Gorda
Bay of Honduras
Río Sarstoon
Livingston
Puerto Barrios

GUATEMALA

New River
Belize River
Maya Mountains

★ **Don't miss ...**
1 Northern cayes, pages 792.
2 Crooked Tree Wildlife Sanctuary, page 803.
3 Actun Tunichil Muknal Cave, page 815.
4 The hidden ruins of Caracol, page 817.
5 Cockscomb Basin Wildlife Sanctuary, page 827.
6 The Black Hole Drop, page 832.

"Be kind to tourists," says the big friendly voice in the advert on Belize's *Love FM*, as the beaten-up school bus works its way down the old Hummingbird Highway. Sometimes this smallest of countries appears innocent, naïve and relaxed.

Belize is a smorgasbord of landscapes, from mountainous, tropical rainforests with abundant wildlife to fertile subtropical foothills where cattle are rearer, sugar, rice, and fruit trees are cultivated, and bird-filled coastal wetlands and small islands – known as cayes – with beautiful beaches.

Measuring 174 miles north to south and just 80 miles across, the country nestles on the coast between Mexico and Guatemala, with a land area of about 8860 sq miles, including hundreds of cayes. The reefs and cayes form a 184-mile barrier reef with crystal-clear water and are a major attraction for world-class diving, snorkelling and sport fishing. And hidden beneath the depths is the magnificent Blue Hole, one of the world's best dives.

Inland, rivers and rainforest invite you to head out, trekking, paddling and biking, to visit the ancient ruins of the Maya, or to cave in their spiritual underworld. For the beginner and the specialist birdwatching is an endless pleasure.

With a Caribbean history and a Central American geography, Belize is a subtle blend of cultures that encourages the laid-back attitude of the small (just 311,000) but ethnically diverse population, who paint an intriguing picture in this culturally different, English-speaking Central American nation.

Essentials

Where to go

The reputation of **Belize City** is not good but the authorities are working hard to clean it up and present a better face to tourists. Special tourist police have been introduced and crime is much less widespread than it was. That said, you may still be offered drugs on the streets. It is worth spending a day or two having a look around Belize City and getting a feel for the old town – it's not possible to really know Belize if you haven't spent some time in the city. Generally, the longer people stay the better they like it and resident Belizeans are friendly and welcoming. The short journey to visit **Belize Zoo** is definitely worthwhile. A little further on is the tiny capital of **Belmopan**, an hour from Belize City.

The **northern cayes**, a series of paradise islands with crystal-clear waters, palm-fringed beaches and mangroves, are the main hub of tourism. **Ambergris Caye**, more upmarket, and **Caye Caulker**, popular with budget travellers, are the two most-developed cayes, from where you can take trips to the smaller cayes and marine parks. They attract a wide range of travellers wishing to sample the delights of a Caribbean island. The atmosphere is laid-back with plenty of watersports for the active, spectacular diving and snorkelling on the barrier reef and outlying cayes and the world-famous **Blue Hole**.

On the mainland, the Northern Highway leads from Belize City to the Mexican border through some of the most productive farmland in the country. There is still plenty of room for wildlife at the **Community Baboon Sanctuary**, for black howler monkeys; the **Crooked Tree Lagoons and Wildlife Sanctuary**, for birds. The archaeological remains of **Lamanai** with a 112-ft temple (the tallest known pre-Classic Maya structure) is easily visited from Orange Walk, and **Altún Ha**, once a major Maya ceremonial site, are essential visits for 'Maya-philes'. The largest town in the north, **Orange Walk**, is a multi-racial city of Mennonites, Creoles, Maya and other Central Americans making their living from agriculture.

The Western Highway leads from Belize City, skirting the capital Belmopan, to **San Ignacio** and the Guatemalan border. San Ignacio and its twin town Santa Elena have a pleasant climate and are in a beautiful setting of wooded hills straddling the Macal River. A side trip to the **Mountain Pine Ridge** area offers great hiking, amid spectacular broadleaf forests, rivers, rapids, waterfalls and caves, making a worthwhile excursion with much to be enjoyed along the entire route to Caracol. There are several Maya sites, notably **Cahal Pech**, on the edge of town; **El Pilar**, north through Bullet Tree Falls; **Xunantunich**, across the Mopan River by hand-cranked ferry at San José Succotz with plazas, temples, ball court and *castillo*; and **Caracol**, the country's largest site to date rivalling Tikal in size, where the Sky Palace pyramid reaches a height of 138 ft.

The Southern Highway runs along the eastern edge of the Maya Mountains, through sparsely populated countryside dotted with indigenous settlements, to Dangriga and Hopkins Village and then past the world-famous **Cockscomb Basin Wildlife (Jaguar) Sanctuary**. The coastal area around **Placencia** offers idyllic palm-fringed beaches, diving and sport fishing, with plenty of accommodation choices for all budgets. Offshore cayes are reached by boat from **Dangriga** or Mango Creek. In the far south is **Punta Gorda** with the ruins of **Lubaantun**, a late-Maya ceremonial site where the infamous Crystal Skull was discovered. You can stay at guesthouses in Maya villages nearby as part of a community tourism project.

Suggested itineraries There are two simple options: coming from Mexico's Yucatán Peninsula, head south into Belize City, pop out to the cayes then make your way south through Placencia to Punta Gorda and on to Guatemala or Honduras; or go west through San Ignacio visiting the caves of the highlands, and then to Tikal in Guatemala. If coming from Guatemala, visit San Ignacio, Belize City and the cayes before heading south. You can get a good feel for Belize in a fortnight.

When to go

The high season runs from mid-December to March and pushes into May with clear skies and warm temperatures (25-30°C). Inland, in the west, day temperatures can reach 38°C, but the nights are cooler and usually pleasant. Between November and January there are cold spells during which the temperature at Belize City may fall as low as 13°C. Humidity is normally high, making it 'sticky' most of the time in the lowlands.

There are sharp annual variations in rainfall. From 1270 mm in the north and around 1650 mm in Belize City, there is a huge increase up to 4310 mm down in the south. The driest months are April and May; in June and July there are heavy showers followed by blue skies. Around August the *mauger* occurs, a mini-dry season of about six weeks. September to November tend to be overcast and there are more insects during these months.

Hurricanes threaten the country from June to November along the coast. An efficient warning system was put in place after Hurricane Mitch and most towns and large villages have hurricane shelters. 'Hurricane Preparedness' instructions are issued annually. Do not ignore local instructions about what to do following a forecast.

Sport and activities

Archaeology

The protection of Belize's Maya heritage and its development into tourism sites is high on the agenda. Further excavation and protection of sites, better access, construction of tourist facilities like visitor centres and small souvenir shops, the availability of brochures and knowledgeable guides are all part of the plan. For information contact the **Archaeology Department** ① T822-2106, in Belmopan, where there are plans underway for a Museum of Archaeology.

Caving

Belize has some of the longest caving systems in the world. Main attractions in caves are crystal formations, but most of the caves in Belize were also used by the Maya, and in some Maya artefacts have been found. While government permission is required to enter unexplored systems, simple cave exploration is easy. From San Ignacio, tours go to Chechem Ha, Barton Creek and Actun Tunichil Muknal Cave, known for their Maya artefacts. The best one-stop shop for all levels is the Caves Branch Jungle Lodge (see page 831) on the Hummingbird Highway close to the entrance to the Blue Hole National Park.

Diving

The shores are protected by the longest barrier reef in the Western Hemisphere. The beautiful coral formations are a great attraction for scuba-diving, with canyons, coves, overhangs, ledges, walls and endless possibilities for underwater photography.

Lighthouse Reef, the outermost of the three north-south reef systems, offers pristine dive sites in addition to the incredible Blue Hole. Massive stalagmites and stalactites are found along overhangs down the sheer vertical walls of the Blue Hole. This outer reef lies beyond the access of most land-based diving resorts and even beyond most fishermen, so the marine life is undisturbed. An ideal way to visit is on a live-aboard boat. An exciting marine phenomenon takes place during the full moon each January in the waters around Belize when thousands of the Nassau groupers gather to spawn at Glory Caye on Turneffe Reef.

Note There are decreasing numbers of small fish – an essential part of the coral lifecycle – in the more easily accessible reefs, including the underwater parks. The coral reefs around the northerly, most touristy cayes are dying, probably as a result of tourism pressures, so do your bit to avoid further damage.

Fishing

Belize is a very popular destination for sport fishing, normally quite pricey but definitely worth it if you want to splash out. The rivers offer fewer and fewer opportunities for good fishing, and tilapia, escaped from regional fish farms, now compete with the catfish, tarpon and snook for the food supply. The sea still provides game fish such as sailfish, marlin, wahoo, barracuda and tuna. On the flats, the most exciting fish for light tackle – the bonefish – is found in great abundance.

In addition to the restrictions on turtle and coral extraction, the following regulations apply: no person may take, buy or sell crawfish (lobster) between 15 February and 14 June, shrimp between 15 March and 14 July, or conch between 1 July and 30 September.

Nature tourism

Conservation is a high priority in Belize. Tourism vies for the top spot as foreign currency earner in the national economy, and is the fastest-growing industry. Nature reserves are supported by a combination of private and public organizations including the Belize Audubon Society, the government and international agencies.

The **Belize Audubon Society** ① *PO Box 1001, 12 Fort St, Belize City, T223-5004, www.belizeaudubon.org*, manages seven protected areas including Half Moon Caye Natural Monument (3929 ha), Cockscomb Basin Wildlife Sanctuary (41,800 ha – the world's only jaguar reserve), Crooked Tree Wildlife Sanctuary (6480 ha – swamp forests and lagoons with wildfowl), Blue Hole National Park (233 ha), Guanacaste National Park (20.25 ha), Tapir Mountain Nature Reserve (formerly known as Society Hall Nature Reserve (2731 ha – a research area with Maya presence) and the Shipstern Nature Reserve (8910 ha – butterfly breeding, forest, lagoons, mammals and birds, contact BAS or the International Tropical Conservation Foundation, through www.shipstern.org).

The **Río Bravo Management and Conservation Area** (105,300 ha) bordering Guatemala to the northwest of the country, covers some 4% of the country and is managed by the **Programme for Belize** ① *PO Box 749, 1 Eyre St, Belize City, T227-5616, www.pfbelize.org*.

Other parks include the Community Baboon Sanctuary at Bermudian Landing, Bladen Nature Reserve (watershed and primary forest), Hol Chan Marine Reserve (reef eco-system). Recently designated national parks and reserves include: Five Blue Lakes National Park, based on an unusually deep karst lagoon, and a maze of exotic caves and sinkholes near St Margaret Village on the Hummingbird Highway; Kaax Meen Elijio Panti National Park, at San Antonio Village near the Mountain Pine Ridge Reserve; Vaca Forest Reserve (21,060 ha); and Chiquibul National Park (107,687 ha – containing the Maya ruins of Caracol). There's also Laughing Bird Caye National Park (off Placencia), Glovers Reef Marine Reserve, and Caye Caulker now has a marine reserve at its north end.

Belize Enterprise for Sustained Technology (BEST) ⓘ *Mile 54 Hummingbird Highway, PO Box 35, Belmopan, T822-3043, www.best.org.bz*, is a non-profit organization committed to the sustainable development of Belize's disadvantaged communities and community-based ecotourism, for example Gales Point and Hopkins Village.

On 1 June 1996 a **National Protected Areas Trust Fund (PACT)** ⓘ *www.pactbelize.org*, was established to provide finance for the "protection, conservation and enhancement of the natural and cultural treasures of Belize". Funds for PACT come from a US$3.75 conservation fee paid by all foreign visitors on departure by air, land and sea, and from 20% of revenues derived from protected areas entrance fees, cruise ship passenger fees, etc. Visitors pay only one PACT tax every 30 days, so if you go to Tikal for a short trip from Belize, show your receipt in order not to pay twice.

Getting there

Air
From North America and Europe With the exception of neighbouring countries, international services to Belize go through the USA, with **American Airlines**, **Continental**, **Delta** and **United**. There are no direct flights from Europe. Most flights from Europe go through the US and require an overnight stop in Miami or Houston.

From Central America There are daily connections to San Salvador with **Grupo Taca** and Flores (Guatemala) with **Maya Island Air**, www.mayaisland air.com, and **Tropic Air**, www.tropicair.com.

Road
The most commonly used routes are with the Petén Department of Guatemala at Benque Viejo del Carmen and, to the north, at the border with Chetumal on Mexico's Yucután Peninsula. Both immigration offices have been remodelled, reducing the waiting times. A less widely used crossing, for non-vehicular travellers, is at La Unión, where there are immigration facilities.

Sea
Boat services link the south of the country with Honduras and Guatemala. From Puerto Barrios, Guatemala, there is a boat service to Punta Gorda; from Puerto Cortés, Honduras, a boat goes to Placencia, via Mango Creek. Obtain all necessary exit stamps and visas before sailing – see under each town for details.

Getting around

Air
Maya Island Air and **Tropic Air** (see page 789) both provide in-country flights to the cayes, Corozal, Dangriga, Placencia and Punta Gorda; both have good safety records and regular schedules. It costs less to fly from the Municipal Airport in Belize City than from the International Airport to the same destination. There is one exception: if making a connection for an international flight, it is cheaper to arrive at the International Airport, than to take a taxi the 10 miles from the Municipal Airport to the International Airport.

Airport information The main international airport and arrival point is at Ladyville, 10 miles northwest of Belize City. For airport details, see page 782. When leaving by air you'll pay US$31.50 (payable in US dollars only) including PACT conservation tax (see page 775) plus a US$1.50 security bag fee per person. Departing overland costs US$18.75; by boat, US$3.75.

Road

Bus Public transport between most towns is by bus and, with the short distances involved, there are few long journeys to encounter. Trucks carry passengers to many isolated destinations. Most buses are ex-US school buses with small seats and limited legroom. There are a few ex-**Greyhounds**, mostly used for 'express' services and charters. It is recommended to buy tickets for seats in advance at the depot before boarding the bus. Most bus companies were acquired by **Novelos**, which went bust and is now called the **National Transportation Company** ① *T222-4250, www.nationaltransportbelize.com*. Most buses have no luggage compartments so bags that do not fit on the luggage rack are stacked at the back. Get a seat at the back to keep an eye on your gear, but rough handling is more of a threat than theft.

Car Motorists should carry their own driving licence and certificate of vehicle ownership. Third-party insurance is mandatory and can be purchased at any border: US$12.50 a week, US$25 a month, cars and motorbikes are the same, cover up to US$10,000 from the **Insurance Corporation of Belize** ① *7 Daly St, Belize City, T224-5328, www.icbinsurance.com*. Border offices are open Monday-Friday 0500-1700, Saturday 0600-1600. There are also offices in every district. Valid International Driving Licences are accepted in place of Belize driving permits. Fuel costs about US$4.95. Unleaded gasoline is now available in Belize.

Car hire Only one car rental company (**Crystal** – see page 790) will release registration papers to enable cars to enter Guatemala or Mexico. Without obtaining them at the time of hire it is impossible to take hire cars across national borders. Car hire cost is high in Belize owing to the heavy wear and tear on the vehicles. You can expect to pay between US$65 for a Suzuki Samuri and US$125 for an Isuzu Trooper per day. Drive carefully as road conditions are constantly changing and totally unpredictable, with speed bumps, cyclists and pedestrians appearing around every bend. When driving in the Mountain Pine Ridge area it is prudent to check carefully on road conditions at the entry gate; good maps are essential. Emory King's annually updated *Drivers' Guide to Belize* is helpful when driving to the more remote areas.

Hitchhiking While practised freely by locals, hitchhiking is risky and not recommended for travellers. If, however, this is your preferred mode of travel, be prepared for long waits and break the journey down into smaller legs.

Sea

Boats Several boats ferry passengers to the most popular cayes of Caye Caulker and Ambergris Caye, with regular daily services from the Marine Terminal by the swing bridge in Belize City. Further south, boat transport is available at Dangriga to nearby cayes, with a service to Puerto Cortés, Honduras, also stopping at Placencia, as well as from Punta Gorda, with service to Puerto Barrios and Lívingston, Guatemala. In the north there is a daily service between Corozal and San Pedro, Ambergris Caye.

Sleeping

Accommodation throughout the country varies greatly. For the budget traveller there are options in most towns of interest, although prices are higher than in neighbouring countries. While standard hotel options exist, the area around San Ignacio offers several secluded hideaways of varying price and to the south there are options for staying in Maya communities which helps to maintain the cultural identity of the region. The Belize Tourist Board promotes good hotels under US$60 a night through the **Toucan Trail**, www.toucantrail.com. All hotels are subject to 9% government hotel tax (on room rate only) and 10% service charge is often added. Camping sites are gaining in popularity, and there are private camping facilities to be found in most tourist areas, with a variety of amenities offered. Camping on the beaches, in forest reserves or in any other public place is not allowed. Butane gas in trailer/Coleman stove-size storage bottles is available in Belize, and white gas for camp stoves is available at **Brodies** in Belmopan.

Eating and drinking

Dishes suffer a wonderful preponderance of rice'n'beans – a cheap staple to which you add chicken, fish, beef and so on. For the cheapest meals, order rice which will come with beans and (as often as not) banana or plantain, or chicken, vegetables or even a blending of beef with coconut milk. Belize has some of the best burritos in Central America but you have to seek them out, normally in hidden-away stalls in the markets. Along the coastal region and on the cayes seafood is abundant, fresh and reasonably cheap, but avoid buying lobster between 15 February and 14 June (out of season) as stocks are worryingly low. (Conch is out of season between 1 July and 30 September; Nassau grouper, between 1 December and 31 March.) Better restaurants offer a greater variety and a break from the standards, often including a selection of Mexican dishes; there are also many Chinese restaurants, which are not always good and are sometimes overpriced.

Belikin beer is the local brew, average cost US$3 a bottle. Many brands of local rum are available too. Several local wines and liqueurs are made from available fruit. One favourite, called *nanche*, is made from *crabou* fruit and is very sweet, as is the cashew wine, made from the cashew fruit rather than the nut. All imported food and drink is expensive. A 9% sales tax is added to meals and a 10% service charge may be added as well.

Festivals and events

1 Jan New Year's Day.
Feb Weekend before or after Valentine's Day, Annual Sidewalk Arts Festival, Placencia.
9 Mar Baron Bliss Day; see also page 814.
Early Mar San José Succotz Fiesta.
Mar/Apr Good Fri and Sat and Easter Mon.
Late Apr or May National Agricultural and Trade Show (Belmopan).
1 May Labour Day.
May (variable) **Cashew Festival** (Crooked Tree), Cayo Expo (San Ignacio), Coconut Festival (Caye Caulker).

24 May Commonwealth Day.
23-25 Jun Lobster Fest, Placencia.
Early to Mid-Jul Benq ue Viejo Fiesta.
Aug International Costa Maya Festival (San Pedro, Ambergris Caye).
10 Sep St George's Caye Day.
21 Sep Belize Independence Day.
11 Oct Pan-American Day.
19 Nov Garífuna Settlement Day, festival normally over the weekend.
25 Dec Christmas Day.
26 Dec Boxing Day.

Most services throughout the country close down Good Friday to Easter Monday; banks close at 1300 on the Thursday, buses run limited services Holy Saturday to Easter Monday, though local flights and boats to the cayes are available. Christmas and Boxing Day are also limited in terms of services. Many shops will open for a few hours on holiday mornings, but still may have limited choices for food. Independence Celebrations begin on St George's Caye Day, 10 September, and there are events occurring daily through to Independence Day, 21 September. The 'September Celebrations', as they are locally called, often start two or three days in advance and require a lot of energy. The most colourful of Belizean festivals is Garífuna Settlement Day in November with celebrations concentrated around Dangriga, Seine Bight and Placencia. The tone of the festival varies greatly with a more public celebration of music and dance in Dangriga, with a more spiritual and quieter ambience in Seine Bight.

Shopping

Indigenous arts and crafts are noticeable primarily for their absence. Carved hardwood objects are widely available. Jewellery made of black coral is occasionally offered but should not be bought. There are some fine Belikin/diving T-shirts. If you want to buy music, Andy Palacio is one of the best punta rock artists.

Essentials A-Z

Customs and duty free

Clothing and articles for personal use are allowed in without payment of duty, though laptop computers, video cameras, mobile phones and CD players and radios that you bring may be stamped on your passport to ensure they leave with you. Other import allowances are: 200 cigarettes or ½ lb of tobacco; 1 litre of alcohol; 1 bottle of perfume. Visitors can take in an unspecified amount of other currencies. No fruit or vegetables may be brought into Belize; searches are infrequent, but can be thorough. Pets must have proof of rabies inoculations and a vet's certificate of good health.

Electricity

110/220 volts single phase, 60 cycles. Some hotels use 12-volt generators.

Embassies and consulates

For the latest information, visit www.governmentofbelize.gov.bz .
El Salvador, Calle El Bosque Norte and Calle Las Lomas, Candeleria No 1, Block P, Col Jardines de la Cima 1st Stage, San Salvador, T+503-248 1423.

European Communities, Blvd Brand Whitlock 136, 1200 Brussels, Belgium, T+32-2-732 6246, embelize@skynet.be.
Guatemala, 5 Av 5-55, Zona 14, Europlaza, Torre II, Oficina 1502, Guatemala City, T+502-2367 3883, F2367-3884.
Honduras, Hoteles de Honduras, R/do Hotel Honduras Maya, Tegucigalpa, Honduras CA, T+504-238 4614, F238-4617.
Mexico, 215 Calle Bernardo de Galvez, Col Lomas de Chapultepec, Mexico DF 11000, T+52-5-520 1274.
Panama, Calle 22, Villa de Las Fuentes, No 1, F-32, Panama City, R de P, T/F+507-236 4132.
UK, 3rd floor, 45 Crawford Place, London, W1H 4LP, T/F+44-20-7723 3603.
USA, 2535 Massachusetts Av, NW Washington DC 20008, T1-202-332-9636.

Health

Those taking standard precautions will find the climate pleasant and healthy. There are no mandatory inoculations required to enter the country unless coming from a country where yellow fever is a problem. Malaria prophylaxis is necessary only if staying in rural areas with poor medical care. Dengue fever is also rare but possible for travellers, and using insect repellent for mosquitoes is the best prevention for both diseases. Insect bites should be carefully scrutinized if not healing or if odd symptoms occur, as the possibilities of Chagas, leishmaniasis, or botfly larvae are all present. **Medical services** have improved in recent years with the completion of the **Karl Heusner Memorial Hospital** in Belize City, though many Belizeans still seek medical care for serious ailments in Mérida or Guatemala City. The **British High Commission** in Belmopan (T822-2146) has a list of doctors and dentists. See page 51 for further information.

Internet
The relatively high cost of telephone calls makes internet surfing and cafés prohibitive. With the exception of San Ignacio, Ambergris Caye and Caye Caulker, internet cafés are less common than in neighbouring countries. When you do find one, the cost is upwards of US$2 per hr.

Language
English is the official language, but Spanish is very widely used, especially in border areas. Creole is spoken by some throughout the country. Mennonite settlers in the north speak a Low German dialect. Several Mayan languages and Garífuna are spoken by ethnic groups to the south.

Media
There are no daily newspapers in Belize. News is available in the weeklies, which generally come out on Friday morning, with the forthcoming Sunday's date: *The Belize Times* (PUP supported), *The Guardian* (UDP supported), *The Reporter* and *Amandala*. Good coverage of Ambergris Caye is provided by *The San Pedro Sun*, likewise *Placencia Breeze* covers Placencia. Small district newspapers are published sporadically. Radio station *Love FM* (95.1FM) is the perfect summary of Belize on the airwaves. Try www.belizeweb.com for Belizean internet radio.

Money
→ *US$1=Bz$2 (stabilized)*.
The monetary unit is the **Belize dollar**. Currency notes issued by the Central Bank are in denominations of 100, 50, 20, 10, 5 and 2 dollars, and coins of 2 dollars and 1 dollar; 50, 25, 10, 5 and 1 cent coins are in use. The American expressions quarter (25c), dime (10c) and nickel (5c) are used, although 25c is sometimes referred to as a shilling. US dollars are accepted everywhere. A common cause for complaint or misunderstanding is uncertainty about which currency you are paying in. The price tends to be given in US$ when the hundred Belizean dollar mark is breached; make sure it is clear from the start whether you are being charged in US or Belizean dollars.

Exchange
See Banks, Belize City, page 790. The government has recently restricted the exchange of foreign currency to government-licensed *casas de cambio*, but these only operate in major towns. You can still find some money changers at the borders, but the exchange rate is not as high as it has been, and there is a risk of both you and the money changer being arrested and fined.

Cost of living and travelling
The cost of living is high, compared to neighbouring countries, because of the heavy reliance on imports and extra duties. Budget travellers will still be able to get by on about US$45 per person per day if travelling in pairs. Budget travellers can find exploring the interior difficult because public transport is limited to main highways and car hire is beyond the means of many. VAT has been replaced by a 9% sales tax, which is charged on all services, but should not be charged on top of the 9% hotel tax charged on your room. A 1% 'Environmental Tax' is levied on all goods brought into the country.

Opening hours

Businesses 0800-1200, 1300-1600 and Fri 1900-2100, with half day on Wed. Small shops open additionally most late afternoons and evenings, and some on Sun 0800-1000. **Government and commercial offices** Mon-Fri 0800-1200, 1300-1600.

Post

Airmail to Europe takes 8 days and costs US$0.38 for a letter, US$0.20 for a postcard. A letter to USA costs US$0.30 and a postcard costs US$0.15. A letter to Australia costs US$0.50 and a postcard costs US$0.30, and takes 2-3 weeks. **Parcels:** US$3.50 per 0.5 kg to Europe, US$0.38 per 0.5 kg to USA. The service to Europe and USA has been praised, but surface mail is not reliable. Belize postage stamps are very attractive, much in demand, and a trip to the **Philatelic Bureau** in Belize City may provide you with your most treasured souvenir.

Safety

While attacks on foreigners are extremely rare, precautions are still advised, particularly if travelling alone or at night or in deserted areas. Crimes against travellers are harshly punished. Despite the apparent availability of illegal drugs, the authorities are keen to prevent their use. The penalties for possession of marijuana are 6 months in prison or a US$3000 fine, minimum.

Telephone → *Country code T+501*

Information T113. International operator T115.

If you have many calls to make, a card phone works out much cheaper. There is a direct-dialling system between the major towns and to Mexico and USA. Local calls cost US$0.25 for 3 mins, US$0.12 for each extra min within the city, US$0.15-0.55 depending on zone. **Belize Telemedia Ltd**, 1 Church St, Belize City, Mon-Sat 0800-1800, Sun and holidays 0800-1200, has an international telephone, telex and internet service. The entire

country's telephone directory is online at www.belizetelemedia.net

The much-maligned Belizean telephone system is steadily modernizing. Formed in 2007 out of the old BTL, Belize Telemedia is promising to provide the world down the phone line.

Most people now have a mobile phone and most parts of the country have coverage. All towns have a telephone office and in most villages visitors can use the community phone. Payphones and card phones are fairly commonplace in Belize City and elsewhere.

Time

- 6 hrs GMT.

Tipping

In restaurants, 10% of the bill. Taxi drivers are tipped depending on the length of the transfer, whether 'touring' took place or for extra stops, from US$1-10.

Tourist information

The quality and quantity of tourist information in Belize varies greatly. In the popular centres of the cayes, Placencia and the developed sections of Cayo there is a steady supply of information available. Moving away from these popular areas the information is less reliable.

There is an ID card system to validate official tourist guides, which works well in the popular areas. Off the main routes there is less government checking of guides so a more ad hoc system works.

Maps of the country are limited and topographical maps have not been readily available for several years. The best internationally available maps are from ITMB.

Belize Tourism Board, 64 Regent St, Belize City, T227-2420, www.travelbelize.org, also with an office in the Tourism Village, provides information on hotels and a variety of handouts on parks and reserves.

Useful websites

www.belizenet.com, **www.belize.net** and **www.belize.com** Good search engines with general information.

www.governmentofbelize.gov.bz The government site on the country, packed with information on the official angle.

www.belizeaudubon.org and **www.pfbelize.org** Cover many protected areas and have a strong conservation focus.

www.ambergriscaye.com, **www.gocaye caulker.com**, **www.placencia.com** and **www.southernbelize.com** Useful sites.

www.belizex.com Covers the Cayo area.

www.belizereport.com The online version of the *Belize Report*.

www.belizenews.com. Local news and links to the local newspapers (*Amandala*, *The Belize Times*, *The Reporter* and *The Guardian*).

Visas and immigration

All nationalities need passports, as well as sufficient funds and, officially, an onward ticket, although this is rarely requested for stays of 30 days or less. Visas are not usually required by nationals from countries within the EU, Australia and New Zealand, most Caribbean states, the USA and Canada. Citizens of India, Israel, Austria and Switzerland do need a visa. There is a Belizean Consulate in Chetumal, Mexico, at Armada de México 91, T+52-983-8321803, US$25. If you need a visa it is best to obtain one in Mexico City or your home country before arriving at the border.

Weights and measures

Imperial and US standard weights and measures.

Belize City and Belmopan

Hardly large enough to warrant the title 'city', in any other country Belize City would be a dusty backwater, but in Belize it is the centre of the country, a blend of Latin American and Caribbean influences. Clapboard houses line dusty streets while people huddle in groups as the world drifts idly by. Born of the Belize River when the logs used to float downstream, it is still the main hub for maritime communications with boat services to the cayes. Nearby Belize Zoo is a model for zoos throughout the world. The capital, Belmopan, enjoys the cursed pleasure of being a planned city. Founded after a devastating hurricane struck Belize City, it has survived as the country's political centre, and has recently grown after several hurricanes have hit the country. ▸▸ *For listings, see pages 786-791.*

Belize City ⊖🅞🅟🅞🅞🅐🅑🅒 ▸▸ *pp786-791. Colour map 6, A1.*

→ *Population: 63,670.*

Belize City is the old capital and the largest town in Belize. Many of the houses are wooden, with galvanized-iron roofs. Most stand on seven-ft-high piles – signs of a bygone age when the city used to experience regular flooding. The city has improved greatly in recent years with the cleaning of the canals. Reclaimed land and a spate of building around the Eyre Street area, the new Museum of Belize, renovation of the Bliss Institute and the House of Culture suggest plans to improve the city are well underway. The introduction of tourist police has had a marked effect on crime levels, and the situation now requires sensible caution rather than paranoia. However, some areas of the city – particularly to the South and West – are neither particularly safe nor pleasant. Just under a quarter of the total population live here. Humidity is high, but the summer heat is offset by the northeast trades.

Hurricane Keith hit Ambergris Caye in October 2000 and Hurricane Iris in 2002, both acting as reminders of the inherent risks of Belize City's lowland location.

Ins and outs

Getting there International flights arrive at **Phillip Goldson International Airport**, 10 miles from Belize City along the northern highway. Facilities in the check-in area include toilets, a restaurant, internet, bank (daily 0830-1200 and 1230-1800), viewing deck and duty-free shop. There are no facilities on the arrivals side but you can just walk round to the check-in area. Taxi fares to town are US$20, 30 minutes; taxi drivers strongly discourage sharing so team up, if need be, before getting outside. Make sure your taxi is legitimate by checking for the green licence plates. Taxis all operate on a fixed rate, so you should get the same price quoted by every driver. Ask to see a rate sheet if you have doubts about the price. Any bus going up the Northern Highway passes the airport junction (US$1), then it's a 1½-mile walk.

The main **bus station** is on West Collette Canal Street to the west of town, an area that requires some caution. If taking an early morning bus, arrange for a taxi as walking through this part of town in darkness with luggage can be dangerous. Likewise, if arriving after dark take a taxi from outside the station; approximately US$3 to the centre. ▸▸ *See Transport, see page 789.*

Belize City

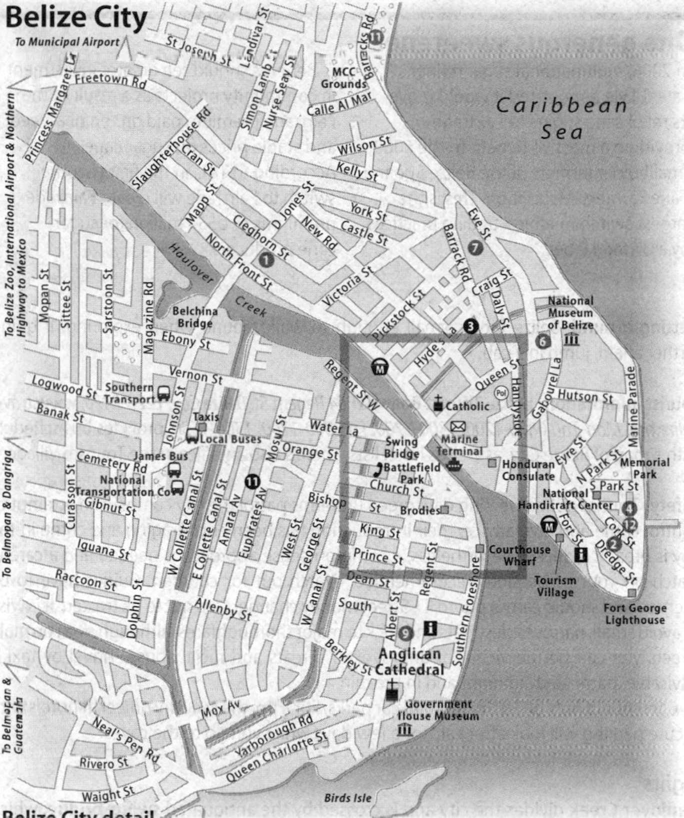

To Municipal Airport

St Joseph St — Landivar St

Freetown Rd

Princess Margaret

To International Airport & Northern Highway to Mexico

MCC Grounds

Calle Al Mar

Simon Lamb St

Nurse Seay St

Wilson St

Kelly St

Slaughterhouse Rd

Cran St

Mapp

Cleghorn St

North Front St

Haulover Creek

Mopan St

Sittee St

Sarstoon Rd

Magazine Rd

Belchina Bridge

Ebony St

Vernon St

York St

Castle St

D Jones St

New Rd

Victoria St

Pickstock St

Caribbean Sea

Eve St

Barrack Rd

Craig St

Daly St

National Museum of Belize

Regent St W

Hyde's La

Queen St

Handyside

Gabourel La

Hutson St

Marine Parade

Catholic

Marine Terminal

Honduran Consulate

Tyre St

N Park St

Memorial Park

Park St

Logwood St

Banak St

Southern Transport

Johnson St

Taxis

Local Buses

Water La

Swing Bridge

Battlefield Park

Church St

Brodies

National Handicraft Center

Cork St

Cemetery Rd

James Bus

National Transportation Co

Gibnut St

Iguana St

Raccoon St

Curasson St

Dolphin St

W Collette Canal St

E Collette Canal St

Amata Av

Euphrates Av

West St

George St

W Canal St

Bishop St

King St

Prince St

Dean St

Albert St

Regent St

South

Southern Foreshore

Courthouse Wharf

Tourism Village

Fort George Lighthouse

To Belmopan & Dangriga

To Belmopan & Guatemala

Neal's Pen Rd

Mox Av

Rivero St

Waight St

Allenby St

Berkley St

Yarborough Rd

Queen Charlotte St

Anglican Cathedral

Government House Museum

Birds Isle

Belize City detail

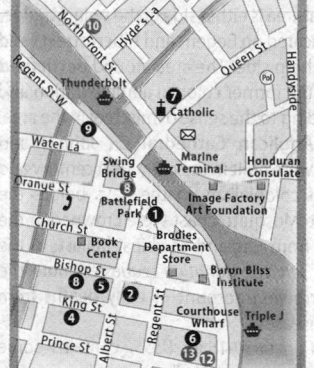

North Front St

Hyde's La

Queen St

Regent St W

Thunderbolt

Catholic

Handyside

Water La

Marine Terminal

Honduran Consulate

Swing Bridge

Orange St

Battlefield Park

Image Factory Art Foundation

Church St

Book Center

Brodies Department Store

Bishop St

Baron Bliss Institute

King St

Courthouse Wharf

Prince St

Albert St

Regent St

Triple J

N

200 metres

200 yards

Sleeping
Bakadeer Inn 1
Chateau Caribbean 4
Freddie's 7
Great House 2
Isabel Guest House 8
Ma Ma Chen 6
Mopan 9
North Front Street
  Guest House 10
Princess 11

Radisson Fort George 12
Seaside Guest House 13

Eating
Big Daddy's 1
Blue Bird Café 2
Dario's 3
DIT's 4
El Centro 5
Jambel's Jerk Pit 6
Judith's Pastries 7
Macy's 8
Marlin 9
New Chon Saan 11

Bars & clubs
Bellevue Hotel 12

One generous sweetener

In 2008, multinational sugar refiner Tate & Lyle announced it would move its retail cane sugars to Fairtrade providing a massive benefit to the 6000 smallholder farmers of the Belize Sugar Cane Farmers Association. This is the largest switch to ethical trading practices by a UK food label.

Benefits should see greater investment in community projects as a result of the Fairtrade premium paid on top of agreed and stable prices for sugar cane. According to T&L, in the first year the switch to Fairtrade will create Fairtrade premiums of US$4 million for sugar cane producers.

Getting around Belize City is small enough to walk around when exploring. If going further afield, jump in a cab.

Tourist information Belize Tourist Board ① *64 Regent St, Belize City, T227-2420, www.travel belize.org, Mon-Thu 0800-1200, 1300-1700, Fri 0800-1200, 1300-1630,* provides bus schedule with a map of Belize City, as well as hotel lists. There's also an office in the Tourism Village.

Safety Tourist police wearing dark green uniforms patrol the city centre in an attempt to control crime and give advice; their introduction has been encouraging and crime in the city is greatly reduced. Nevertheless, a common-sense approach is needed and a careful watch on your possessions recommended. Watch out for conmen. Guides have to be licensed and should carry a photo ID. Street money changers are not to be trusted. It is wise to avoid small, narrow sidestreets and stick to major thoroughfares, although even on main streets you can be the victim of unprovoked threats and racial abuse. Travel by taxi is advisable, particularly at night and in the rain.

Cars should only be left in guarded car parks. For a tip, the security officer at hotels with secure parking will look after cars for a few days while you go to the cayes.

Sights

Haulover Creek divides the city and is crossed by the antiquated **swing-bridge**, which opens to let large vessels pass, if required, usually between 1730 and 1800. Three narrow canals further divide the city. The main commercial area is either side of the swing-bridge, with most shops on the south side, many being located on Regent and Albert streets and with offices and embassies generally on the northern side. The area around **Battlefield Park** (formerly Central Park) is always busy, with the former colonial administration and court buildings bordering the overgrown park adding to the sense of mischief in the area. At the southern end of Regent Street, the **Anglican Cathedral** (St John's) and **Government House** nearby are interesting. Both were built in the early 19th century and draw on the romantic and grand memories of colonialism. In the days before the foundation of the Crown Colony, the kings of the Mosquito coast were crowned in the cathedral, which was built with bricks brought from England as ships' ballast. In the **cathedral** ① *Mon-Fri 0900-1500 and during Sun services, donation requested,* note the 19th-century memorial plaques that give a harrowing account of early deaths from 'country fever' (yellow fever) and other tropical diseases.

In Government House, the **museum** ① *Mon-Fri 0830-1630, US$5,* contains some interesting pictures of colonial times, displays of furniture and silver and glassware, as well as a one showing fishing techniques and model boats. There are pleasant gardens surrounding the museum if you are looking for somewhere quiet.

The **jail building** (1857) in front of the Central Bank on Gabourel Lane has been beautifully renovated and is now the **National Museum of Belize** ① *T223-4524, Mon-Thu 0800-1700, Fri 0800-1630, US$5*, with exhibits on the history of Belize City and a permanent exhibit on the Maya sites of Belize.

Continuing to the right on North Front Street, pop into the **Image Factory Art Foundation** ① *Mon-Fri 0900-1700*, for a peek at exhibitions by local artists – more grassroots than the other galleries. Moving towards the end of the peninsula is the **Tourism Village** consisting of souvenir and gift shops and snack bars, along with several handicraft shops. This development caters to tourists arriving from cruise ships. A little further on, at the tip of the peninsula, is **Memorial Park** ① *on Marine Parade* with a small obelisk, two cannon and concrete benches peppered with the holes of land crabs. The views across the bay can be spectacular in the early morning. The park by the **Fort George Lighthouse** has a children's play area and is a popular meeting place. Baron Bliss' tomb is also here. **Belize Zoo** (see page 812) is definitely worth a visit and not far from Belize City. The trip is very easy with buses from Belize City passing the entrance every half hour.

Belmopan and around ⊜❼❷❶ » *pp786-791. Colour map 6, A1.*

→ *Population: 16,435.*

As capital of Belize, Belmopan has been the seat of government since August 1970. It is 50 miles inland to the west of Belize City, near the junction of the Western Highway and the Hummingbird Highway to Dangriga (Stann Creek Town). Following the devastation caused in Belize City by Hurricane Hattie in 1961, plans were drawn up for a town that could be a centre for government, business and study away from the coast: Belmopan is the result.

The hurricanes of recent years have prompted a renewed interest in plans to develop the capital, and several government organizations are in the process of relocating to the city, injecting a desperately needed 'heart' to this most eerie of capitals. One possible site of interest would be the **Department of Archaeology**, in the government plaza, which has a vault containing specimens of the country's artefacts. Unfortunately, the vault is currently closed and there are no plans to open it in the near future, although there is a small display and plans to build a museum. Part of the collection is displayed in the **National Museum of Belize** (see above).

Belmopan has the National Assembly building, two blocks of government offices (with broadly Maya-style architecture), the national archives, police headquarters, a public works department, a hospital, over 700 houses for civil servants, a non-governmental residential district to encourage expansion and a market. The Western Highway from Belize City is now good (a one-hour drive), continuing to San Ignacio, and there is an airfield (for charter services only).

Guanacaste National Park

One very good reason for stopping nearby is Guanacaste National Park (US$2.50), just outside Belmopan, which is well worth a visit. As Belmopan's accommodation is so expensive it may be better to take an early bus to the park from Belize City or San Ignacio rather than go from the capital. See also page 812.

Belize City and Belmopan listings

Hotel and guesthouse prices
LL over US$150 **L** US$100-150 **AL** US$66-99
A US$46-65 **B** US$31-45 **C** US$21-30
D US$12-20 **E** US$7-11 **F** under US$7
Restaurant prices
🍴🍴🍴 over US$15 🍴🍴 US$8-15 🍴 under US$8
See pages 45-48 for further information.

Sleeping

Belize City *p782, map p783*
On the north side of the swing-bridge, turn left up North Front St for some of the cheaper hotels.
LL Radisson Fort George, 2 Marine Parade, T223-3333, www.radisson.com/belizecitybz. In 3 wings (**Club Wing**, where rooms have marble floors and panoramic views of the Caribbean; the **Colonial Section** with balconies overlooking the sea and **Villa**), rooms with partial sea view or pool view. Rooms are excellent with a/c, TV, and bathtubs. The staff are helpful and service is good. Good main restaurant (and **Stonegrill Restaurant** where food is cooked on hot, volcanic stones). 2 lovely pools, fitness room and small garden. Fri pm live music. Bar with large TV screen, open until 2400 at weekends. Le Petit Café also on the premises.
LL-L The Great House, 13 Cork St, T223-3400, www.greathousebelize.com. A beautifully maintained white colonial building with 16 rooms furnished in homey style. 2 rooms have ocean view. Ask to read about its interesting history from 1927.
LL-A Princess, King's Park, T223-2670, www.princessbelize.com. On seafront (but not central), marina facilities, casino and bowling, cinema, a/c, good food and service in restaurant and bar (a/c with sea views, expensive), good business facilities, informal calypso bar near the dock is lively at night, nice pool and children's play area.

AL Chateau Caribbean, 6 Marine Parade, by Fort George, T223-0800, www.chateaucaribbean.com. Main building is colonial. Rooms looking a little dated with a/c, good bar, restaurant (excellent Chinese and seafood), sea view, good service, parking.
A-B Mopan, 55 Regent St, T227-7351, www.hotelmopan.com. 14 rooms with bath, a/c, cheaper with fan, TV, in historic house, has restaurant and bar, management very keen to help.
A-D Bakadeer Inn, 74 Cleghorn St, T223-0659, www.bakadeerinn.com. Private bath, a/c, TV, fridge, friendly. Recommended.
B-C Isabel Guest House, 3 Albert St, above Matus Store, T207-3139. Just 3 double rooms, 1 huge triple room, fans and fridges, quiet except when nearby disco operating at weekends, private shower, clean, friendly, safe, Spanish spoken. Isabel is very friendly. Highly recommended.
B-D Seaside Guest House, 3 Prince St, T227-8339. 6 rooms with private and shared baths, very clean, pleasant veranda with view out to the bay, a great place to stay and meet other travellers. Breakfast, drinks, book swap, credit cards accepted, internet access on site. Consistently recommended.
C Freddie's, 86 Eve St, T223-3851, freddies@btl.net. 3 double rooms with shower and toilet, fan, hot water, clean, very nice, secure, very small.
C Ma Ma Chen, 5 Eve St, T223-4568, jessicachen1222@hotmail.com. 4 clean rooms with a/c or fan and private and shared bath. Run by quiet Chinese family with restaurant next door.
D North Front Street Guest House, 124 North Front St, T227-7595. 1 block north of post office, 4 rooms, no hot water, some have fans, friendly, good information, keep windows closed at night and be sure to lock your door, on street and a bit noisy. Laundry and internet across street.

Belmopan and around *p785*
Belmopan has been described as a disaster for the budget traveller.
L-AL Belmopan Hotel, Constitution Drive, opposite bus stop and market, T822-2130. A/c, hot water, swimming pool, restaurant, bars.
A Bull Frog, 25 Half Moon Av, a 15-min walk east of the market through the parliament complex or a short taxi ride from the bus station, T822-2111. A/c, good, reasonably priced, laundry, karaoke nights on Thu (popular with locals).
B-C El Rey Inn, 23 Moho St, T822-3438, www.belmopanhotels.com. Big rooms with fan, hot and cold water, basic, clean, friendly, laundry on request, central.

❶ Eating

Belize City *p782, map p783*
It can be difficult to find places to eat between 1500-1800.
₸₸₸ Harbour View Restaurant, Customs House, Fort St, T223-6420. Mon-Fri 1000-2200, Sat and Sun 1700-2200. With fine views of the bay and some tasty dishes but overpriced for the portions.
₸₸₸ Jambel's Jerk Pit, 2 King St, T227-6080. Excellent variety of Belizean and Jamaican dishes, including fresh seafood and vegetarian dishes. Outdoor patio.
₸₸₸-₸₸ Celebrity, Marine Parade, T223-7272, www.celebritybelize.com. Well-recommended restaurant that serves a wide range of food, from burgers to seafood.
₸₸₸-₸₸ Smoky Mermaid, 13 Cork Street, T223-4759. Popular with locals and specializes in snapper and pasta dishes.
₸₸ El Centro, 4 Bishop St, T227-2413. Local dishes and burgers. A/c dining room and delivery available.
₸₸ Macy's, 18 Bishop St, T227-3419. Recommended for well-prepared local game, Creole cooking, different fixed menu daily, charming host.

₸₸ Marlin, 11 Regent St West, overlooking Belize River, T227-3913. Varied menu, good seafood.
₸ Big Daddy's, 2nd floor of market building, Church St, opposite BTL office. Good food, with pleasant view over the harbour. Closes when the food runs out.
₸ Blue Bird Café, Albert St. Cheap fruit juices, specialities, basic, clean, reasonable. Inside tables are perfect for people-watching.
₸ Dario's, 33 Hyde's Lane. Classic Belizean hot meat pies, try 1 and then buy in bulk if you like them.
₸ DIT's, 50 King St. Good for pastries, rice'n'beans and desserts.
₸ Judith's Pastries, south end of Queen St. Good cakes and pastries.

Belmopan and around *p785*
Eating options are limited in Belmopan. There are several cheap *comedores* at the back of the market and a couple of bakeries near Constitution Drive. Cafés are closed on Sun.
₸₸ Caladium, next to market. Limited fare, moderately priced, small portions.
₸₸ El Rey Inn, see Sleeping.
₸ Aloha Café, next to Scotiabank. Friendly staff, good for breakfast or lunch, coffee, snacks, ice cream. Local newspapers to read.

❷ Entertainment

Belize City *p782, map p783*
Bars and clubs
Lots of bars, some with jukeboxes, poolrooms and karaoke nights. Try the local drink, anise and peppermint, known as 'A and P'; also the powerful 'Old Belizeno' rum. The local beer, Belikin, is good, as is the 'stout', strong and free of gas.

Fri night is the most popular night for going out in Belize. Clubs often have a cover charge of US$5 and drinks are expensive once inside. Happy hour on Fri starts at 1600 at **Radisson Fort George** and continues at **Biltmore, Calypso** and elsewhere. The best and safest bars are found at major hotels, **Fort George**, **Biltmore Plaza**, **Bellevue** and **Princess**. **Bellevue Hotel Bar**, south of the swing bridge, on the waterfront, has multiple entertainment options for Fri nights, including 1 or 2 live bands and karaoke. **Club Calypso**, at the **Princess Hotel**, see Sleeping, has top bands at weekends. **Eden Nightclub**, 190 Newtown Barracks, T223-6888, DJs or live music from 2200 Thu-Sat nights.

The Wet Lizard, near the Tourism Village, has good American/Creole fare, reasonable prices, great view.

Cinema
Princess Hotel, see Sleeping, has a 2-theatre modern cinema, showing recent movies for US$7.50.

O Shopping

Belize City p782, map p783
The whole city closes down on Sun except for a few shops open in the morning, eg **Brodies** in the centre of town. Banks and many shops and offices are also closed on Sat afternoons.

Books
Book Center, 4 Church St, T227-7457, books@btl.net, above **Thrift Center**. Excellent selection of books including second-hand books and back issues of some US magazines. **Brodies**, Albert St, has decent selection of books on Belize and some paperback novels.

Markets and supermarkets
The **market** is by the junction of North Front St and Fort St.
Brodie's has widest grocery selection, though prices are slightly higher. Closed Sun.
Thrift Center, 2 Church St. Good food store, especially for dry goods at competitive prices.

Souvenirs
Handicrafts, woodcarvings and straw items are all good buys.

Zericote (or Xericote) wood carvings can be bought at **Brodies**, Central Park end of Regent St (which also sells postcards), the **Fort George Hotel**, see Sleeping, above, or **Egbert Peyrefitte**, 11a Cemetery Rd. Such wood carvings are the best buy, but to find a carver rather than buy the tourist fare in shops, ask a taxi driver. The wood sculpture of **Charles Gabb**, who introduced carving into Belize, can be seen at the Art Centre, near Government House. Wood carvers sell their work in front of the main hotels.
National Handicraft Center, South Park St. The Belize Chamber of Commerce's showcase promotes craftspeople from all over Belize; come here first for an overview of Belizean art and crafts.
Belize Audubon Society, across from the Tourist Village near the lighthouse, has a small but good selection of posters, T-shirts, gifts, and jewellery, all locally made in villages, and all at very reasonable prices.

▲ Activities and tours

Belize City p782, map p783
Diving
Hugh Parkey's **Belize Dive Connection**, www.belizediving.com, is based at the Radisson's dock and is a professional outfit.

Tour operators
Discovery Expeditions, 5916 Manatee Dr, Buttonwood Bay, T223-0748, www.discovery belize.com. An efficient and professional outfit offering interesting cultural and adventure tours out of the city and across the country. Recommended.
The Green Dragon, based out near Belmopan, but covering most of the country, T822-2124, www.greendragonbelize.com, is very helpful and will arrange hotel bookings and tours all over Belize.
Island Expeditions Co, 1767 Magoon St, Southern Foreshore, T522-3328, www.island expeditions.com. Adventure and multi-sport wilderness, rainforest and reef trips.

Maya Travel Services, 42 Cleghorn St, T223-1623, www.mayatravelservices.com, gets positive reports.

S&L Guided Tours, 91 North Front St, T227-7593, www.sltravelbelize.com. Recommended group travel (groups of 4 people for most tours, 2 people for Tikal). If booking tours in Belize from abroad it is advisable to check prices and services offered with a reputable tour operator in Belize first.

● Transport

Belize City p782, map p783
Air

The International Airport is 10 miles from Belize City (see page 782). The municipal airstrip for local flights is 15 mins' drive from the centre on the northern side of town, taxi, US$5, no bus service. Domestic services with **Tropic Air** and **Maya Island Air**, flights every 30 mins, 0700-1630. Flights to and from the islands can be taken from the international airport and companies link their flights to international arrivals and departures; flights from the international airport cost about US$15 more each way. **Maya** and **Tropic** also have services to **Flores**, Guatemala.

Airline offices American Airlines, San Cas Plaza, T223-2522 (reservations), Mon-Fri 0800-1800, Sat 0800-1200. **Continental** Airlines, 32 Albert St, T227-8309. **Belize Global Travel Services**, 41 Albert St, T227-7363, www.belizeglobal.bz, provides services for **Grupo Taca** and **US Airways**. Maya Island Air, Municipal Airstrip, Belize City, T223-1140, www.mayaislandair.com. Tropic Air, Albert St, Belize City, T226-2012, www.tropicair.com.

Boat

Boats to **Caye Caulker** continuing to **San Pedro** (Ambergris Caye) leave from the Marine Terminal on North Front St with the **Caye Caulker Water Taxi Association**, T223-5752, www.cayecaulkerwatertaxi.com. Departures at 0730, 0800, 0900, 1030, 1200, 1330, 1500, 1600 (to Caye Caulker only), 1630 and 1730 (to Caye Caulker only), Caye Caulker US$7.50, return US$12.50, San Pedro US$10, return US$17.50. Check website for changes in the schedule.

Departures also with **Triple J** in covered boats from their terminal at Courthouse Wharf, T207-7777, wwwtriplejbelize.com, office hours 0700-1630, boats at 0800, 1030, 1200, 1330, 1500, 1630 to **Caye Caulker** and then **San Pedro**. To Caye Caulker, US$7.50, return US$12.50, to San Pedro US$10, US$20 return, Caye Caulker to San Pedro, US$5.

Bus

Within the city the fare is US$0.50 run by **Belize in Transit** services. They originate next to the taxi stand on Cemetery Rd.

There are bus services to all the main towns. The **National Transportation Co** operates Northern Transport from West Collette Canal St (can store luggage, US$0.50).

North to **Chetumal** (see Mexico, page 586), about 15 daily each way, roughly every 30 mins, starting at 0500 until 1800, 3 hrs, US$2.50, express buses from 0600 stopping at **Orange Walk** and **Corozal** only, US$6.50, 2½ hrs. If taking a bus from Chetumal which will arrive in Belize City after dark, decide on a hotel and go there by taxi.

West towards **Guatemala** by bus to **Belmopan** and **San Ignacio**, express bus 0900, US$3, with a/c and refreshments, ordinary bus every 30 mins, Mon-Sat frequent 0600-1900, Sun 0630-1700. The 0600, 0630 and 1015 buses connect at the border with services to **Flores**, Guatemala. To **San Ignacio**, **Benque Viejo** and the **Guatemalan border** via Belmopan, US$2.50 to Belmopan, US$4 to San Ignacio, US$4.50 to Benque, hourly Mon-Sat, 1100-1900. The last possible bus connection to **Flores** leaves the border at 1600, but it is better to get an earlier bus to arrive in daylight. Many buses leave for **Melchor de Mencos**, 0600-1030. To **Flores**, Guatemala, minibuses leave the Marine

Terminal on Front St in Belize City; make reservations the previous day.

1st-class express buses from Belize City to **Flores/Tikal** with **Mundo Maya/Línea Dorada**, www.tikalmayanworld.com, leave from Belize City daily at 1000 and 1700, with buses connecting to Guatemala City and beyond. Also with services heading north to **Chetumal**. Check the **Mundo Maya** counter in the Marine Terminal on North Front St.

South to **Dangriga**, via Belmopan and the Hummingbird Hwy. **Southern Transport** (T227-3937), from the corner of Vernon and Johnson St near the Belchina Bridge, several daily on the hour 0800-1600, plus Mon 0600, US$5. **James** (T702-2049), to **Punta Gorda** via **Dangriga**, **Cockscomb Basin Wildlife Sanctuary** and **Independence**, every hour from 0515 to 1015 and 1215 to 1515 with the last bus at 1545, 6-8 hrs, US$14.

Car
Car hire Cars start at US$75 plus insurance of around US$15 a day. Most rental firms have offices in Belize City and opposite the international airport terminal building.
Avis, T203-4619, avisbelize@btl.net. **Budget**, 2½ miles, Northern Hwy, T223-2435, www.budget-belize.com. **Crystal Auto Rental**, Mile 5 Northern Hwy, T223-1600, www.crystal-belize.com, cheapest deals in town, but not always most reliable, wide selection of vehicles, will release insurance papers for car entry to Guatemala and Mexico. **Hertz**, 11a Cork St, beside Radisson Fort George Hotel, T223-5395, www.hertz belize.com, and International Airport, T225-3300. **Pancho's**, 5747 Lizarraga Av, T224-5554, www.panchosrentalbelize.com, locally owned rental company.

Taxi
Official cabs have green licence plates (drivers have ID card); within Belize, US$4 for 1 or 2 people; slightly more for 3 or more. There is a taxi stand on Central Park, another on the corner of Collet Canal St and Cemetery Rd, and a number of taxis on Albert St, Queen St and around town. Outside Belize City, US$1.75 per mile, regardless of number of passengers. Belize City to the resorts in Cayo District approximately US$100-125, 1-4 people. No meters, so beware of overcharging and make sure fare is quoted in Bz$ not US$.

Belmopan and around *p785*
Bus
To **San Ignacio**, hourly on the hour 0500-2100, 1 hr, US$2.50. To **Belize City**, Mon-Sat, every 30 mins, 0600-1900, hourly on Sun, 1 hr, US$3.50. Heading south hourly buses Mon-Sat 0830-1630 (fewer on Sun) to **Dangriga**, 1 hr, US$3, **Mango Creek**, 3 hrs, US$8 and **Punta Gorda**, 4½ hrs, US$9. James Bus leaves for **Belize City** and **Punta Gorda** from opposite the National Transportation Co bus station. To **Orange Walk** and **Corozal** take an early bus to Belize City and change.

● Directory

Belize City *p782, map p783*
Banks
All banks have facilities to arrange cash advance on Visa. Guatemalan quetzales and Mexican pesos are best bought at the border. There are several ATMs in Belize City **Atlantic Bank**, 6 Albert St, quick efficient service, small charge for Visa/MasterCard, smaller queues than **Belize Bank Belize Bank**, 60 Market Sq, is particularly efficient and modern, US$0.50 commission on Amex cheques but a big charge for cash against Visa and MasterCard. It is easy to have money wired to Belize City.

Cultural centres
Audubon Society, see page 774. **Baron Bliss Institute**, public library, temporary exhibitions; has 1 stela and 2 large discs from Caracol on display. **The Image Factory**, 91 Front St, has exhibitions of contemporary art, Mon-Fri 0900-1800. **The Belize National**

Handicraft Center sales room on South Park St has a good supply of books about Belize culture. **Programme for Belize**, 1 Eyre St, T227-5616, www.pfbelize.org, is a conservation organization that manages land reserves including Río Bravo. **Society for the Promotion of Education and Research (SPEAR)**, 5638 Gentle Av, T223-1668, www.spear.org.bz, with a great reference library for everything Belizean.

Embassies and consulates
Many Embassies and consulates are now located in Belmopan. For more countries visit www.mfa.gov.bz (see also Belmopan Directory, below). **Canada** (consulate), represented through Guatemala. **France**, covered by San Salvador. **Guatemala**, 8A St, T223-3150, 0830-1230, will not issue visas or tourist cards here; will tell you to leave it till you reach your exit point. **Honduras**, 114 Bella Vista, T224-5889, 0900-1200, 1300-1600. **Italy** (consulate), 18 Albert St, T227-8449. **Nicaragua**, 124 Newtown Barracks, T223-3868. **Panama**, consular services at Central American Blv and Mahogany St, T222-4551.

Internet
Service at BTL and in some hotels; prices around US$4 per hr. Keep an eye out for cheaper options. **Mailbox**, on Front St.

Laundry
Northside Laundromat, North Front St, 0900-2000, US$4 for 6 kg wash and dry. **Belize Dry Cleaners and Launderomat**, 3 Dolphin St.

Post office
The main post office is at Queen St and North Front St, 0800-1700 (1630 Fri). Letters held for a month. Beautiful stamps for collectors around the corner on Queen St.

Telephone
Belize Telemedia Ltd, 1 Church St, just off Central Park, Mon-Sat, 0800-1800, Sun 0800-1200. Also public fax and booths for credit card and charge calls.

Belmopan and around p785
Banks
Scotia Bank 1915 Constitution Dr and **Belize Bank**, Constitution Dr, also provide cash advances.

Embassies and consulates
Costa Rica, Mountain View Apartments, Apartment 2, University Blv, Belmopan, T822-1582. **El Salvador**, 49 Nanche St, T822-3404. **Mexico**, Embassy Sq, Belmopan, T822-0406. **UK High Commission**, North Ring Rd, next to the Governor's residence, T822-2146, www.britishhighbze.com, Mon-Thu 0800-1200 and 1300-1600, Fri 0800-1400. Has a list of recommended doctors and dentists. **USA**, Floral Park Rd, Belmopan, T822-4011, http://belize.usembassy.gov/; consulate is round the corner on Hutson St, office hours, Mon-Fri, 0800-1200, 1300-1700.

Internet
Techno Hub at bus station, US$4.50 per hr.

Post office
The post office is next to the market (opposite the immigration office).

Northern cayes

The cayes off the coast are attractive, relaxing, slow and very 'Caribbean' – an excellent place for diving, sea fishing or just lazing about. Palm trees fringe the coastline, providing day-long shade for resting in your hammock looking out at the stunning azure seas. They are popular destinations, especially in August and between December and May.

There are some 212 sq miles of cayes. The cayes and atolls were home to fishermen and resting points to clean the catch or grow coconuts. But they have always been valued. The Maya built the site of Marco Gonzalez on the southwestern tip of Ambergris Caye, the largest and most populated of the islands. Nearby Caye Caulker is a popular destination for the more budget-minded visitor, while serious divers head for the Turneffe Islands. Other, smaller cayes are home to exclusive resorts or remain uninhabited, many being little more than mangrove swamps. St George's Caye, nine miles northeast of Belize, was once the capital and the scene of the battle in 1798 that established British possession. ▸▸ *For listings, see pages 796-802.*

Ins and outs

Most boats to Caye Caulker and Ambergris Caye leave from the Marine Terminal or the Triple J terminal. Boats leave regularly from 0630 to 1730 if you're just turning up. Otherwise check at your hotel as timetables change frequently. For the southern cayes, see page 840.

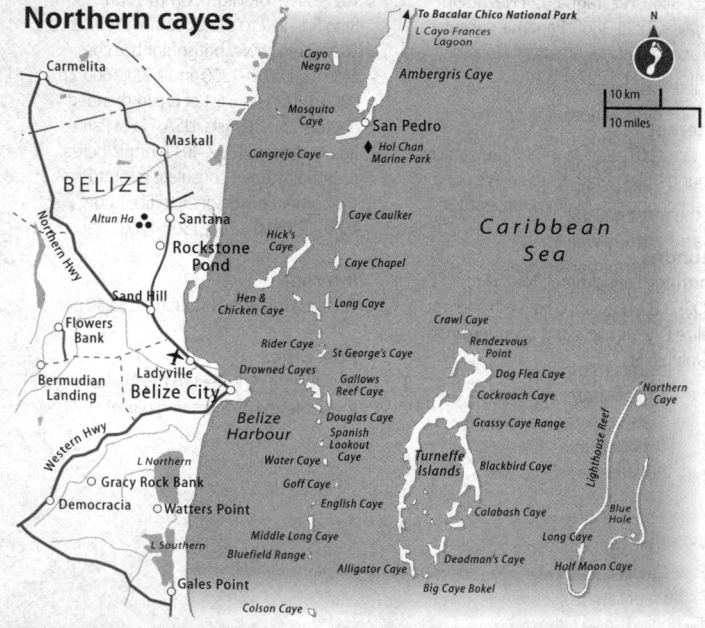

Northern cayes

Ambergris Caye ⬤❶❸⬤🅜⬤❸ ▸▸ *pp796-802. Colour map 6, A2.*

→ *Population: 10,445.*

This island (pronounced Am-*ber*-gris), along with the town of **San Pedro**, has grown rapidly over the last couple of years, with over 50 hotels and guesthouses on the island. Buildings are still restricted to no more than three storeys in height, and the many wooden structures retain an authentic village atmosphere. The very helpful **Ambergris tourist information office** ⓘ *Mon-Sat 1000-1300, 1400-1900*, is next to the the town hall.

Although sand is in abundance, there are few beach areas around San Pedro town. You cannot, in practice, walk north along the beach from San Pedro to Xcalak, Mexico. The emphasis is on snorkelling on the nearby barrier reef and **Hol Chan Marine Park**, and the fine scuba-diving, sailing, fishing and board sailing. The main boat jetties are on the east (Caribbean Sea) side of San Pedro. It can be dangerous to swim near San Pedro as there have been serious accidents with boats. Boats are restricted to about 5 mph within the line of red buoys about 25 yards offshore, but this is not always adhered to. There is a 'safe' beach in front of the park, just to the south of the government dock. A short distance to the north and south of San Pedro lie miles of deserted beachfront, where picnic barbecues are popular for day-tripping snorkellers and birders who have visited the nearby small cayes hoping to glimpse rosets, spoonbills or white ibis. If you go north you have to cross a small inlet with hand-pulled ferry, US$0.50 for foreigners. **Note** Only very experienced snorkellers should attempt to swim in the cutting between the reef and the open sea.

Around Ambergris Caye

Just south of Ambergris Caye, and not far from Caye Caulker, is the **Hol Chan Marine Park** ⓘ *US$10 entry fee; the park office (with reef displays and information on Bacalar Chico National Park to the north) is on Caribeña St, T226-2247*. This underwater natural park is divided into three zones: Zone A is the reef, where fishing is prohibited; Zone B is the seagrass beds, where fishing can only be done with a special licence (the **Boca Ciega** blue hole is here); Zone C is mangroves where fishing also requires a licence. Only certified scuba-divers may dive in the reserve. Fish feeding, although prohibited, takes place at Shark Ray Alley, where about 15 sharks and rays are fed for the entertainment of tourists. Not the most natural of experiences.

San Pedro is well known for its diving. Long canyons containing plenty of soft and hard coral formations start at around 50-60 ft going down to 120 ft. Often these have grown into hollow tubes, which make for interesting diving. **Tackle Box**, **Esmeralda**, **Cypress**, **M & Ms** and **Tres Cocos** are only some of the dive sites. The visibility in this area is usually over 100 ft. There is a recompression chamber in San Pedro and a US$1 tax on each tank fill insures treatment throughout the island.

Although offshore, Ambergris Caye airport makes arranging tours to visit places on the mainland very easy (for example Altún Ha US$60 per person; Lamanai US$125 per person) while still being able to enjoy other water experiences (catamaran sailing, deep-sea fishing, manatee and Coco Solo).

Caye Caulker ⬤❶❸⬤🅜⬤❸ ▸▸ *pp796-802. Colour map 6, A2.*

On Caye Caulker, a thin line of white sandy beach falls to a sea of turquoise blue and green, while the reef can be seen a mile and a half from the shore. By day on this laid-back island, it's diving and snorkelling, sea and sand; at dusk everyone heads up to the 'split' to watch the sunset; by night it's eating, drinking and dancing. A quiet lobster-fishing island (closed season 15 February to 14 June) until fairly recently, its extremely relaxing atmosphere, gentle climate, postcard-perfect views and the myriad small restaurants and bars have drawn increasing numbers of tourists.

The caye is actually two islands separated by a small channel (the 'split'); swimming is possible here but beware of fishing and powerboats. All services are on the southern island and, in the north, is a **marine reserve** ⓘ *free for school parties, tourists are asked for a US$2 donation to help expansion and to increase the work in ecology education*. In the south, next to **Shirley's** is the **Caye Caulker Mini Reserve**.

Tour operators and hotels on the island have worked hard to improve services for visitors. The atmosphere is friendly and easy-going, but the usual common sense rules apply with regards to personal safety. Drugs are readily available, but they are illegal and you shouldn't expect any sympathy should you get into difficulties. Some think the atmosphere is more relaxed

Caye Caulker

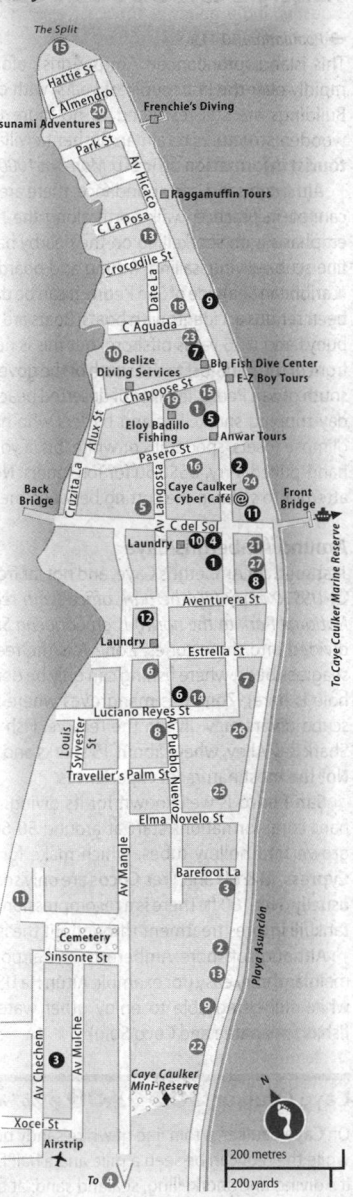

Sleeping
Albert's 1
Anchorage Resort 2
Barefoot Beach 3
Belize Odyssey 4
Caye Caulker Plaza 5
China Town 6
Daisy's 7
Edith's 8
Ignacio Beach Cabins 9
Iguana Reef Inn 10
Lazy Iguana 11
Lorraine's 13
Mira Mar 15
Pancho's Villa 16
Rainbow 18
Sandy lane 19
Sea Dreams 20
Seaside Cabañas 21
Shirley's Guest House 22
Tina's Backpackers 24
Tree Tops 25
Tropical Paradise Resort 26

Tropics 23
Vega Inn 27

Eating
Amor y Cafe 1
Cáfe Coco Loco 2
Coco Plum Gardens 3
Habanero's 4
Happy Lobster 5
Lighthouse 2
Marin's 6
Oceanside 7
Popeye's 8
Rainbow 9
Rose's Bar & Grill 10
Sandbox 11
Syd's 12

Bars & clubs
Herbal Tribes 13
I & I 14
Lazy Iguana 15

out of high season. Sandflies can be ferocious in season (December to February); take long trousers and a good repellent. Make sure you fix prices before going on trips or hiring equipment and, if you pay the night before, get a receipt.

A walk south along the shore takes you to the airstrip, the Caye Caulker Mini Reserve and to mangroves where the rare black catbird can be seen and its sweet song heard.

Around Caye Caulker

Reef trips are the same as those found on Ambergris Caye; for more details see under San Pedro (pages 793 and 800).

Generally all trips are offered at the same price by agreement between tour operators, eliminating the need to shop around for a good price. Tour operators share clients if numbers are not sufficient. This means that you can be certain there is always a trip, but make sure that the boat operator is reliable. Tour organizers must be licensed by the **Belize Tourist Board** and should have a licence to prove it. To encourage high standards, and for your own safety, insist on seeing proof that your guide is licensed.

Protect against sunburn on reef trips, even while snorkelling. Tours are slightly cheaper from Caye Caulker than Ambergris Caye. ▶▶ See Activities and tours, page 800.

Lighthouse Reef and Turneffe Islands ●▲▶▶ pp796-802. Colour map 6, A2.

ⓘ On arrival you must register near the lighthouse with the warden who will provide maps and tell you where you can camp.

Lighthouse Reef is the outermost of the three north-south reef systems off Belize and is some 45 miles to the east of Belize City. Trips out here are not cheap, but if you like diving and have the money, this is one of the most interesting and exciting dive sites in the world. There are two cayes of interest: Half Moon Caye (on which the lighthouse stands) and, 12 miles to the north, the atoll in which the diving shrine of the Blue Hole (see below) is found. **Half Moon Caye** is the site of the **Red-Footed Booby Sanctuary** ⓘ US$20, a national reserve. Besides the booby, magnificent frigate birds also nest on the island. The seabirds nest on the western side, which has denser vegetation (the eastern side is covered mainly in coconut palms). Of the 98 other bird species recorded on Half Moon Caye, 77 are migrants. The iguana, the wish willy (smaller than the iguana) and the Anolis allisoni lizard inhabit the caye, and hawksbill and loggerhead turtles lay their eggs on the beaches. The **Belize Audubon Society** in Belize City maintains the sanctuary, providing a lookout tower and a trail. The lighthouse on the caye gives fine views of the reef. It was first built in 1820: the present steel tower was added to the brick base in 1931 and nowadays the light is solar powered. Around sunset you can watch the boobies from the lookout as they return from fishing. They land beside their waiting mates at the rate of about 50 a minute, seemingly totally unperturbed by humans.

In Lighthouse Reef is the **Blue Hole** ⓘ US$20, US$40 to snorkel or dive, a National Monument that is a circular sinkhole, 1000 ft across and with depths exceeding 400 ft. The crater was probably formed by the collapsed roof of a submerged cave, and was studied by Jacques Cousteau in 1984. Stalagmites and stalactites can be found and it is rated as one of the best dives in the world. Scuba-diving is outstanding at Lighthouse Reef, and includes two walls that descend almost vertically from 30-40 ft to a depth of almost 400 ft.

Caye Chapel was once a small, quiet caye dotted with palms and devoid of sandflies, close to its busier neighbour Caye Caulker, where you could escape to a bit of quiet and solitude. That has all changed, as it is now exclusive as well as secluded.

For Sleeping and Eating price codes and other relevant information, see Essentials pages 45-48.

⚫ Sleeping

Ambergris Caye p793

San Pedro

LL Victoria House Resort, T226-2067, T1-800-247-5159 (US toll free) www.victoria-house.com. Offers a variety of stylish rooms and private villas in well-kept gardens, with good facilities and sea views.

LL-L Ramon's Village, T226-2071, www.ramons.com. 61 rooms, a diving and beach resort, highly recommended even for non-divers (fishing, swimming, boating, snorkelling), comfortable rooms, pool with beach-club atmosphere.

LL-L Sun Breeze, T226-2191, www.sun breeze.net. Near airport, Mexican-style building, a/c, comfortable, all facilities, good dive shop. Recommended.

L Mayan Princess, T226-2778, www.mayan princesshotel.com. Centre of town on seafront, clean, comfortable.

L-AL Changes in Latitude, T226-2986, toll free T1-800-631-9834, www.ambergriscaye. com/latitudes. Sweet B&B with 6 rooms decorated in retro style. Guests have free use of bikes, a golf cart and the yacht club pool. Local artists occasionally hang out in the courtyard.

L-AL San Pedro Holiday Hotel, T226-2014, www.sanpedroholiday.com. 16 rooms and a suite in good central location, fun atmosphere with good facilities. Children 2-12 US$10.

L-A Spindrift, T226-2018, www.ambergris caye.com/spindrift. 24 rooms, 4 apartments, unattractive block but central location, good bar and restaurant, popular meeting place, a/c, comfortable.

AL-A Coral Beach, T226-2013, www.coralbeachhotel.com. Central location and good local feel.

AL-A Hotel San Pedrano, T226-2054, sanpedrano@btl.net. Another small hotel with a/c and fan rooms with private bathrooms. Children 6-12 years, US$5.

AL-A Lily's Caribbean Lodge, T206-2059, www.ambergriscaye.com/lilys. 6 rooms with sea view, 2 with partial view and 3 without view, all with a/c, clean and friendly.

B Tomas, 12 Barrier Reef Dr, T226-2061. 7 airy rooms with a/c, cheaper with fan, bath, drinking water, clean, friendly and family-run. Children under 6 stay free.

B-D Pedro's Inn, T226-1825, www.back packersbelize.com. The island's only real budget place with onsite bar, BBQ and pool. Rooms have shared bathroom.

B-D Ruby's, San Pedro Town on the beach, T226-2063, www.ambergriscaye.com/rubys.

26 a/c or fan rooms, with private or shared bath, good views, central. Recommended as best value in town.

Outside San Pedro

Several resort-style complexes outside the town offer seclusion and an ambience that borders on paradise.

LL Capricorn Resort, 3 miles north of town, T226-2809, www.ambergriscaye.com/capricorn. Wooden cabins on beach with great restaurant.

LL Mata Chica Resort, 4 miles north of town, T220-5010, www.matachica.com. European owned and managed, beautiful and stylish stucco and thatched cabins on a lovely beach, fantastic **Mambo** restaurant.

LL Victoria House, San Pedro, T226-2067, www.victoria-house.com. This stunning resort, 2 miles south of town, offers 4 different types of stylishly decorated rooms. There are also fully fitted villas in the grounds. Excellent facilities, lovely pool, good dive shop and watersports. Highly recommended.

LL-L El Pescador, on Punta Arena beach 3 miles north, Belize City, T226-2398, www.elpescador.com. Specialist fishing lodge with good reputation, a/c, good food and service. Access by boat.

Caye Caulker p793, map p794

In all accommodation, take precautions against theft. The arrival pier is just about in the centre of town, with all the accommodation on or within a 15-min walk of the main street. The southern end of town is slightly quieter and has a smattering of mangrove and bird life, but it's quite a walk from the 'split' for swimming or snorkelling. Camping on the beach is forbidden.

LL-L Iguana Reef Inn, T226-0213, www.iguanareefinn.com. Probably the best place on the island, relaxing and quiet as it's on the back side. With 13 rooms, a bar and a pool.

L-AL Lazy Iguana, southwest side of the island, a block from the cemetery. T226-0350. Beautifully designed B&B with great views.

Collects and uses rainwater. Offers onsite massages for guests.

LL-B Belize Odyssey, south end of island, T671-1558. Clean, old fashioned but well-run resort hotel set on 4 acres of land. Owner Tony Vega has a wealth of knowledge about Caye Caulker, its history and local tours.

L-AL Sea Dreams, at north end of the island, T226-0602, www.seadreamsbelize.com. Cosy rooms with good facilities in well-located hotel next to a dock. 10% of profits go to a community school established by co-owner Heidi Curry.

L-AL Seaside Cabañas, first place you reach off the boat, T226-0498, www.seasidecabanas.com. 16 comfortable rooms and cabins in Mexican style with Moroccan furnishings – some with their own roof terraces set around a pool. Excellent tours and very helpful.

L-A Barefoot Beach, Playa Asuncion, T2260205. Inviting, attractive establishment with nice rooms, all with private bath and some with kitchen.

L-B Vega Inn, T226-0142, www.vegabelize.com. Suites, houses and budget rooms, camping (**E** per person) and credit cards accepted. All doubles, with ceiling fan, fresh linen and hot showers. Camping ground is guarded, hot water, clean toilets.

AL Anchorage Resort, to the south, near Ignacio's, T206-0304, www.anchorageresort.com. 3-storey building with 18 comfortable, tiled rooms with private bathrooms, pleasant atmosphere, friendly family, drinks served under shade on the beach.

AL Caye Caulker Plaza Hotel, Av Langosta, T226-0780, www.cayecaulkerplazahotel.com. New hotel with 32 rooms, all with a/c. Good views from the roof-top.

AL Pancho's Villa, Pasero St, T226-0304, www.panchosvillasbelize.com. 6 attractive rooms with good facilities and Wi-Fi. Has sundeck with views of all the island.

AL-A Shirley's Guest House, T226-0145, www.shirleysguesthouse.com, south end of the village on the beach. Very relaxing with 5 green and white raised cabins, with private and shared bath. No kids.

AL-A Tree Tops, T226-0240, www.treetops
belize.com. Spotless, spacious rooms and
suites, most with private bath, comfortable
beds with beach views, German spoken,
powerful fan or ac, cable TV, friendly, good
value. Children over 10 only. Recommended.

A-B China Town Hotel, Estrella St, T226-
0228, www.chinatownhotelbelize.com.
Efficient, matter-of-fact hotel with clean
rooms and good facilities. Decent value.

A-B Rainbow Hotel, T226-0123, www.rain
bowhotel-cayecaulker.com. Good street-front
location facing the beach and the popular
Rainbow Grill. 17 rooms and 2 apartments,
with shower, hot water, good.

A-C Tropical Paradise Resort, T226-0124,
www.tropicalparadisehotel.com. Cabins
with hot showers, clean, restaurant,
good excursions.

A-C Tropics Hotel, on the main street,
T226-0374, www.thetropicshotel.com.
Recently rennovated hotel, with private bath
and hot water. Cheaper for longer stays and
discounts available on local tours. Good value.

A-D Ignacio Beach Cabins, T226-0175.
19 small purple huts raised very high on
the beach just outside town to the south.
Cheaper rooms are smaller with cold water
bathrooms. Quiet and clean. Book exchange
and kayak and bike rental. Recommended.

C Edith's, 2 blocks from the beach and close to
the I and I Bar, T206-0069. Offering 11 rooms
with bath, hot water, fan. Recommended.

C-D Mira Mar, 2 Front St, 2 blocks up from
the dock, T206-0307. 2nd-floor rooms best,
clean showers, helpful owner Melvin Badillo.

C-D Sandy Lane, 1 block back from main
street, T226-0117. Bungalow-type cabins,
clean, private and cheaper shared bathrooms,
hot showers, run by Rico and Elma Novelo.
Also more expensive rooms with kitchen
and TV for longer stays. Recommended.

D Albert's, Front St, 1½ blocks north of dock,
T226-0277. A dependable cheapie, very clean
shared bathroom, OK for the first night. Above
a minimart in the centre of the main strip.

D Daisy's, T226-0150. Clean, friendly, safe,
cheaper rooms downstairs. All rooms with

communal bathroom. Reductions for longer
stays, will store valuables.

D Lorraine's Guest House, south end of the
village, on the beach, T206-0162. A handful of
simple yellow cabins, basic and a little tatty
with fans and tables, but friendly and quiet.

D Marin's, 1½ blocks from the beach at the
southern end, T226-0444. Good-sized rooms
with private and shared facilities in wooden
cabins on stilts in a small compound.

D-E Tina's Backpackers, T206-0019,
www.tinashostel.blogspot.com. Cheapest
on the caye, with dorms, 3 private rooms,
or sling a hammock. Very popular and noisy –
great for meeting people, but not the place
if you want peace and quiet. Dirty at times.

Lighthouse Reef and the
Turneffe Islands *p795*

Many cayes have package deals for a few
days or a week.

LL Caye Chapel Island Resort, Caye Chapel,
T226-8250, www.cayechapel.com. 22 villas
with tennis courts, private airstrip and golf.

LL Turneffe Flats, Turneffe Islands (56 Eve St,
Belize City), T220-4046, www.tflats.com. In a
lovely location, offers week-long packages
for fishing and scuba; takes 20 guests.

LL Turneffe Island Lodge, Big Caye Bokel,
Turneffe Islands, T220-4142, www.turneffe
lodge.com. Can accommodate 16 guests for
week-long fishing and scuba packages.

LL-L Blackbird Caye Resort, Turneffe Islands
(c/o Blackbird Caye Co, 8 Front St, Belize City),
T223-2767, www.blackbird.com. An ecological
resort on this 4000-acre island is used by the
Oceanic Society and is a potential site for a
biosphere reserve underwater project. Weekly
packages arranged. Diving or fishing packages
available, no bar, take your own alcohol.

🍴 Eating

Ambergris Caye *p793*
🍴 **Celi's**, behind Holiday Hotel. Good
seafood. Recommended. Closed Wed
when there is a beach BBQ.

¶¶¶ Elvi's Kitchen, popular, upmarket, live music, roof built around flamboyant tree, can be very busy, has won international awards.
¶¶¶ Jade Garden Restaurant, south of town. Chinese, sweet and sour everything, expensive drinks .
¶¶¶ Wild Mango's, south of main strip, T226-2859. Closed Mon. Run by Amy Knox, former chef at **Victoria House**. Rustic setting over looking the sea. Try the rum-soaked bacon wrapped shrimp. All the delicious meals are tastefully presented. Recommended.
¶¶¶-¶¶ Ambergris Delight, 35 Pescador Dr. Closed Tue. Pleasant place serving up Belizean cuisine and burgers.
¶¶¶-¶¶ Fido's Courtyard, towards north end of Front St. Lively bar-restaurant often with live music, good lunch and dinner. Sushi bar upstairs.
¶¶ El Patio, south of town, beyond Belize Yacht Club. Good, Mexican-style food, live music in evenings.
¶¶ Estel's Dine by the Sea on the beach close to water taxi terminal. Good food and 1940s-50s music.

Caye Caulker p793, map p794
Beer is sold by the crate at the wholesaler on the dock by the generator; ice for sale at **Tropical Paradise**.
¶¶¶ Habanero's, very close to main dock. Closed Thu. Excellent and tasty food, the best in Belize according to some. Highly recommended.
¶¶¶-¶¶ Rainbow Bar and Restaurant, with the restaurant on its own jetty. Delicious burritos good value, beautiful view.
¶¶¶-¶¶ Happy Lobster, Av Hicaco. Good food with majority fish dishes and pasta. Recommended.
¶¶¶-¶¶ Syd's Restaurant, Middle St. Closed Sun. Family-run and very popular with locals.
¶¶¶-¶¶ Tropical Paradise, on the beach. Excellent seafood, varied menu, slightly more expensive than others.
¶¶ Amor Y Cafe, Av Hicaco. Open 0600 to 1130, closed Mon. Some say it is the best place on the island for breakfast.

¶¶ Coco Plum Gardens, at the southern end of the island, with spa and art gallery. Open for breakfast and dinner, Mon-Sat and does a fabulous omelette.
¶¶ Glenda's, old time island favourite. Good breakfast and lunches. Mornings only.
¶¶ Marin's, 3 blocks south 1 west of the dock. Good seafood all day everyday, cable TV
¶¶ Oceanside, most popular bar on the island. Food OK, music and dancing until midnight.
¶¶ Popeye's, on the beach. Live music some nights, opens at 0600 for breakfast.
¶¶ Rose's Bar & Grill, Front Street, a great grill with good seafood and burgers.
¶¶ Sandbox, T226-0200. With a good atmosphere and sandy floors for that complete beach experience.
¶¶-¶ Romie's Sidewalk Restaurant and Bar. Closed Thu. Good, cheaper seafood options than some of the island restaurants and very popular, especially in the evenings. Bagels and granola for breakfast. Recommended by locals.
¶ Café Coco Loco, next door to the Lighthouse. Delicious bagels, brownies and coffee. Try the fruit sorbet cooler made with ginger ale.
¶ Lighthouse. Real ice cream in cones.

⊕ Entertainment

Ambergris Caye p793
Big Daddy's Disco, open evenings but cranks up at midnight. For entertainment, try 'Chicken Drop' in Pier Lounge at **Spindthrift Hotel** on a Wed night: you bet US$1 on which square the chicken will leave its droppings. **Jaguar's Temple** and **Barefoot Iguana** are current popular nightspots.

Caye Caulker p793, map p794
Many of the restaurants become bars in the evenings.
Herbal Tribes is a bar and restaurant near the North end of the island with a good atmosphere.

Lazy Lizard, right at the North tip of the island is an excellent place to watch the sunset.

I and I Bar, which used to be the **Swing Bar** and still has the swings, should be tried later at night.

Sunset cranks up big style after **Oceanside** closes at 2400 and is a lot of fun.

O Shopping

Ambergris Caye *p793*
Island Supermarket, across from Ramon's, has a good range of supplies. There are many gift shops in the centre of town.
Fidos has Belizean Arts (paintings and prints by local artists) and **Ambar Jewelry**.
Kasbah and **Orange** sell local crafts and jewellery.

Caye Caulker *p793, map p794*
There are at least 4 small 'markets' on the island where a variety of food can be bought; prices are 20-50% higher than the mainland. **Chan's Supermarket,** 1 street back from main street, open daily including Christmas and New Year's Day. There are a couple of gift shops and a gallery in the same building as **Coco Loco**.

▲ Activities and tours

Ambergris Caye *p793*
Diving and snorkelling
Park fees are not included in prices quoted. US$10 for Hol Chan, US$30 for Blue Hole, US$10 Half Moon Caye and US$10 for Bacalar Chico. Be clear on what's included. You will likely be charged extra for equipment. Instruction to PADI Open Water level available, from US$350. Local 2-tank dive US$60, Turneffe US$140-160, Blue Hole US$185. Many operators practice chumming to attract fish and sharks; divers should discourage operators from doing this. Accommodation and dive packages at some

hotels are very good value. All dive operators offer snorkelling trips from US$25 for **Shark Ray Alley** to US$125 for the **Blue Hole**.
Ambergris Divers, T226-2634, www.amber grisdivers.com, will collect divers from Caye Caulker for Blue Hole trip. Very good-value dive and accommodation packages with a number of hotels on the island.
Amigos del Mar, T226-2706, www.amigos dive.com, opposite **Lily's**, gets a lot of return customers and has been recommended, but practices chumming at the Blue Hole.
Protech, at the **Belize Yacht Club**, T226-3008, www.protechdive.com, is the only operator offering overnight trips to the Blue Hole, US$340.
Ramon's Village, www.ramons.com, T649-1990. A bit more expensive than other operators. Check the diving shop's recent safety record before diving.

Fishing
Freedom Tours, T603-0357, hillyboo1991@ yahoo.com, run by Gilbert 'Hilly Boo' Lara, has been recommended.

Other watersports
Board Crazy Watersports, T226-2283, wakeboarding, skiing, sumo tubing.
Karibbean Water Sports, behind **Spindrift Hotel,** T226-3205, www.karibbean watersports.com, rents out jet-skis for US$30 per 30 mins, or take a tour!
Parasail Fun Sports, T226-3513,.
Sailsports, Holiday Hotel, T226-4488, www.sailsportsbelize.com. Windsurfing, sailing, kitesurfing lessons and rentals.

Therapies
Asian Garden Day Spa, T226-4072, www.asiangardendayspa.com, **The Art of Touch,** T226-357, www.touchbelize.com, **Sol Spa,** T226-2410, www.belizesolspa.com and **Spa Shangri-La,** T226-3755.

Tour operators
Travel and Tour Belize in town, T226-2031, www.traveltourbelize.com. Helpful, all services

and can arrange flights, with a request stop at Sarteneja (for the Shipstern Nature Reserve). **Tanlshas Tour**, Daniel Nunez, does trips to the Maya sites on the north of the caye in the Bacalar Chico National Park with his company.

Caye Caulker p793, map p794
Diving and snorkelling
Mask and snorkel hire from several dive and tour operators; normally US$2.50 per day.
Belize Diving Services, T226-0143, www.belizedivingservice.com, is a dive shop on the island with similar prices to **Frenchie's**.
Big Fish Dive Center, T226-0450, bigfish dive@btl.net, go to the Blue Hole, US$175, Lighthouse Reef and Turneffe. Also does PADI refresher courses and works with **Frenchie's**.
Frenchie's Diving, T226-0234, www.frenchiesdivingbelize.com, charges US$310 for a 4-day PADI course, friendly and effective, 2-tank dive US$90, also advanced PADI instruction. Day excursion diving Blue Hole, etc, US$190, snorkellers welcome.

Fishing
Fishing can be arranged through tour operators or by ringing Eloy Badillo T226-0270.

Kayaking
Tour agencies on the main street rent kayaks.

Manatee watching
Available with most tour operators.

Sailing
Several sailing trips. **Raggamuffin Tours**, T226-0348, www.raggamuffintours.com, do a fun sunset cruise, US$25 per person, with booze and music on a sail boat as well as offering a 3-day all-inclusive sailing tour to Placencia leaving Tue and Fri, US$300 per person, minimum 8 people including all food and 2 nights' camping on Rendezvous Caye and Tobacco Caye. Beats travelling by bus and is an increasingly popular excursion. See also **Ras Creek** and **E-Z Boy Tours**, below, for their sailing trips.

Tour operators
Prices are consistent across all operators, so find someone you connect with and feel you can trust. The main excursion is snorkelling in Hol Chan Marine Park and visiting Shark Ray Alley and San Pedro US$45, equipment included. Further afield there are other snorkelling trips, river and Maya site tours. Manatees and Goff Caye (a paradise-perfect circular island with good snorkelling around), US$60; fishing trips US$175. Snorkelling excursions to the Turneffe Islands, Half Moon Caye, Bird Sanctuary and Blue Hole on request. **Sunset Tours** are popular with snorkelling until dusk, US$30.
E-Z Boy Tours, on main street, T226-0349. As well as the usual snorkelling tours, E-Z offers a seahorse, a Maya archaeology and croc-spotting tour.
Javier at Anwar, T226-0327, javi66_novelo@ hotmail.com is locally recommended for a range of snorkelling tours.
Raggamuffin, see above, run tours to the Caye Caulker Marine Reserve and Hol Chan. It can also arrange fishing tours with local fishermen, full day, US$275.

Guides Recommended guides include **Ras Creek**, 'a big man with a big heart', in his boat, based at the water taxi dock, US$27.50 including lunch and entrance fee to the Caye Caulker Marine Reserve; seahorse trips, fishing trips, US$37.50, booze cruise, US$10 per person; canoe and snorkel rental. **Neno Rosado**, of Tsunami Adventures, T226-0462, www.tsunamiadventures.com, has been approved by the guide association and is reliable and knowledgeable.

Lighthouse Reef and the Turneffe Islands p795
Tour operators
Dive operators on Ambergris and on Caye Caulker run trips to Half Moon Caye, the Blue Hole and Turneffe Islands, see Tour operators.

It's also possible to go from Belize City with **Hugh Parkey's Belize Dive Connection**, based at the Radisson's dock, www.belize

diving.com. The main dive in the Blue Hole is very deep, at least 130 ft; the hole itself is 480 ft deep. Check your own qualifications as the dive operator probably will not – you should be experienced and it is advisable to have at least the Advance Open Water PADI course, although an Open Water qualification is fine if you feel confident and don't have major problems equalizing. **Sunrise Travel**, Belize City, T227-2051 or T223-2670, helps arrange trips, advance book.

● Transport

Ambergris Caye *p793*

Air Tropic Air, T226-2012, and Maya Island Air, T226-2435, have flights to/from both **Belize City** airports, many hourly, to **Caye Caulker** and **Corozal**. Charter services are available.

Bicycle and golf cart Bicycles US$2.50 per hr, negotiate for long-term rates.

Golf carts from US$15 per hr and up to US$300 per week, battery or gas powered, driver's licence needed.

Boat More interesting than going by air are the boats. All these call at **Caye Caulker** (**Caye Chapel** and **St George's Caye** on request). Caye Caulker Water Taxi Association to Caye Caulker and **Belize City** at 0700 (express to Belize City), 0800, 0930, 1130, 1300, 1430, 1530, 1630 (Belize City on weekends and holidays only). With **Triple J** at 0800, 1030, 1200, 1330, 1500 and 1630. Many regular boats between **Ambergris Caye** and Caye Caulker.

There are boats to **Corozal** leaving from the lagoon side with *Thunderbolt*, T422-0026, thunderbolttravels@yahoo.com at 0700 and 1500, returning at 0700 and 1500, US$22.50 1 way. The *Island Ferry*, T226-3251, from Fido's dock, services the north of the island every 2 hrs from 0700-1700 then hourly 1800-2200. Also at 2400 and 0200 on Wed, Fri and Sat. Returns 0600-2200 every 2 hrs, US$10-25.

Caye Caulker *p793, map p794*

Bicycle and golf cart Island Boy Rentals, T226-0229. Golf cart rental for US$10 per hr. Bike hire for US$7.50 per day.

Air Maya Island Air flies to/from **Belize City**, **Corozal** and **San Pedro**, several daily. Also flights with **Tropic Air**, T226-2439.

Boat Boats leave from the main dock in front of **Seaside Cabañas** to **Belize City** with the Caye Caulker Water Taxi Association at 0630, 0730, 0830, 1000, 1100, 1200, 1330, 1500, 1600, 1700, 45 mins 1 way (can be 'exciting' if it's rough). To **San Pedro** 0700, 0820, 0845, 0950, 1120, 1250, 1420, 1550 and 1720. Triple J leave from the **Rainbow Hotel** dock.

● Directory

Ambergris Caye *p793*

Banks Atlantic Bank and Bank of Belize, Mon-Thu 0800-1500, Fri 0800-1630. ATMs. Small denominations of US$ in regular use. **Internet** Caribbean Connection, Barrier Reef Dr. **Medical services** San Pedro Polyclinic II, T226-2536. Emergencies, T226-2555. Hyperbaric chamber, T226-2851.

Caye Caulker *p793, map p794*

Banks Rates for cash and TCs are reasonable. Atlantic Bank Visa advances; US$5 commission and now with 24-hr ATM with Visa and MasterCard, Mon-Fri 0800-1400, Sat 0830-1200, and many other places for exchange. Gift shops will charge a commission. **Internet** Caye Caulker Cyber Café, 0700-2200, or Cayeboard Connection 0800(ish) to 2100(ish), both about US$7.50 per hr. **Laundry** There are 3 laundries with self-service options, the one next to Rose's Cafe being the most central. **Post office** ½ block west of Big Fish Dive Center. **Telephone** International service from the telephone exchange (0900-1230, 1400-1630); cardphone outside the BTL office can be used for international calls. Collect calls possible at least to North America at no charge.

North Belize

North Belize is notable for the agricultural production of sugar, fruit and vegetables and for providing much of the country's food. But among the fields of produce are some well-hidden sights and wildlife magnets. The Maya ruins of Lamanai are just about visible in the spectacular setting of the dense jungle. Wildlife can easily be seen at the Community Baboon Sanctuary, the Crooked Tree Wildlife Sanctuary – home to thousands of beautiful birds – and the wildlife reserves of Shipstern near Sartaneja. The vast Río Bravo Conservation Area nudges up to the Guatemalan border and contains the truly isolated ruins and lodge of Chan Chich.

Heading north out of Belize City, the Northern Highway leads to the Mexican border. You can do the journey in just a few hours, passing through Orange Walk and Corozal, but you won't see a thing. It's definitely worth stopping off if you have time. »» For listings, see pages 807-811.

Bermudian Landing and the Community Baboon Sanctuary

About 15 miles out of Belize City a road heading west leads to the small Creole village of Bermudian Landing (12 miles on a rough road from the turn-off), which has been thrust into the global conservation spotlight. This was once a transfer point for the timber that floated down the Belize River, but now there's a local wildlife museum sponsored by the WWF, and the **Community Baboon Sanctuary** ① *www.howlermonkeys.org*.

Crooked Tree Wildlife Sanctuary

① *US$4; you must register at the visitor centre, drinks are on sale, but take food. There is a helpful, friendly warden, Steve, who will let you sleep on the porch of the visitor centre. It is easy to get a lift to the sanctuary, and someone is usually willing to take visitors back to the main road for a small charge.*

The Northern Highway continues to **Sand Hill**, and a further 12 miles to the turn-off for the Crooked Tree Wildlife Sanctuary, which was set up in 1984 and is a rich area for birds. The network of lagoons and swamps is an internationally protected wetlands under the RAMSAR programme, and attracts many migrating birds. The dry season, October to May, is a good time to visit. You may see the huge jabiru stork, the largest flying bird in the Western Hemisphere at a height of 5 ft and a wingspan of 11-12 ft, which nests here, as well as herons, ducks, vultures, kites, ospreys, hawks, sand pipers, kingfishers, gulls, terns, egrets and swallows. In the forest you can also see and hear howler monkeys. Other animals include coatimundi, crocodiles, iguanas and turtles. Glenn Crawford is a good guide as is Sam Tillet (see Sleeping, page 808).

The turn-off to the sanctuary is signposted but keep an eye out for the intersection, which is 22 miles from Orange Walk and 33 miles from Belize City. There is another sign further south indicating the sanctuary but this just leads to the park boundary, not to the Wildlife Sanctuary. The mango and cashew trees in the village of Crooked Tree are said to be 100 years old. Birdwatching is best in the early morning but, as buses do not leave Belize City early, for a day trip take an early Corozal bus, get off at the main road (about 1¼ hours from Belize City) and hitch to the sanctuary. The village is tiny and quaint, occupied mostly by Creoles. Boats and guides can be hired for approximately US$80 per boat (maximum four people). It may be worth bargaining as competition is fierce. Trips include a visit to an unexcavated Maya site.

Altún Ha → *Colour map 6, A1.*

① *Daily 0900-1700, US$5, insect repellent necessary.*

The Maya remains of Altún Ha, 31 miles north of Belize City and 2 miles off the Old Northern Highway, are worth a visit. Altún Ha was a major ceremonial centre in the Classic period (AD 250-900) and also a trading station linking the Caribbean coast with Maya centres in the interior. There are two central plazas surrounded by 13 partially excavated pyramids and temples. What the visitor sees now is composite, not how the site would have been at any one time in the past. The largest piece of worked Maya jade ever found, a head of the Sun God Kinich Ahau weighing 9½ lb (4.3 kg), was found here in the main temple (B-4) in 1968. It is now in a bank vault in Belize City. Nearby is a large reservoir, now called **Rockstone Road**.

Orange Walk → *Colour map 6, A1. Population: 15,990.*

The Northern Highway runs to Orange Walk (66 miles), the centre of a district where Creoles, Mennonites and Maya earn their living from timber, sugar planting and general agriculture. Nearby, the impressive ruins of Lamanai make a good day trip – see below. This is also the departure point for Sartaneja and the Shipstern Peninsula and for the long overland trip to Río Bravo Conservation Area, Chan Chich and Gallon Jug.

There is little to draw the visitor for an extended stay in Orange Walk. An agricultural centre and the country's second city, it is busy with the comings and goings of a small town. Orange Walk is a truly multicultural centre with inhabitants from all over Central America, making Spanish the predominant language. Originally from Canada, Mennonites live in nearby colonies using the town as their marketing and supply centre. The only battle fought on Belizean soil took place here, during the Yucatecan Caste Wars (1840-1870s): the Maya leader, Marcus Canul, was shot in the fighting in 1872. The **House of Culture** on Main Street shows a history of the town's development.

Buses plying the route from Belize City to the Mexican border stop on Queen Victoria Avenue, the main street, close to the town hall. While a few pleasant wooden buildings remain on quiet side streets, most are worn out and badly in need of repair. Many have been pulled down and replaced by the standard concrete box affairs, which lack both inspiration and style.

A toll bridge now spans the New River a few miles south of the town at Tower Hill. There is a market overlooking New River, which is well organized with good food stalls and interesting architecture.

West and south of Orange Walk

From Orange Walk a road heads west, before turning south, running parallel to the Mexican and then Guatemalan border, where it becomes unpaved. Along this road are several archaeological sites. First is **Cuello**, 4 miles west on San Antonio road, behind Cuello Distillery (ask there for permission to visit); taxi about US$3.50. The site dates back to 1000 BC, but, although it has yielded important discoveries in the study of Maya and pre-Maya cultures, there is little for the layman to appreciate and no facilities for visitors. At **Yo Creek** the road divides, north to San Antonio, and south through miles of cane fields and tiny farming settlements as far as **San Felipe** (20 miles via San Lázaro, Trinidad and August Pine Ridge). At August Pine Ridge there is a daily bus to Orange Walk at 1000. You can camp at the house of Narciso Novelo or 'Chicho' (T323-3019), a little-known secret and a relaxing place to stay set amongst bananas, pine tres, bushes and flowers; no fixed cost, just pay what you think. Chicho will meet you off the bus if you call ahead. At San Felipe, a branch leads southeast to Indian Church/Lamanai, 35 miles from Orange Walk

Santa Elena–Chetumal

Eight miles north of Corozal is the Mexican border at Santa Elena, where a bridge across the Río Hondo connects with Chetumal, 7 miles into Mexico. The border can be very busy, and therefore slow, especially at holiday times when chartered coaches bring shoppers to Mexico.

Border crossing formalities are relatively relaxed. The border is open 24 hours a day and there is an exit tax including PACT (see page 775) of US$13.75.

Mexican tourist cards for 30 days are available at the border. To extend the tourist card beyond 30 days, go to immigration in Cancún. The Mexican Embassy is in Belize City if you need a visa. If driving to Belize, third-party insurance is obligatory. It can be purchased from the building opposite the immigration post. The Northern Highway is in good condition and driving time to the capital is roughly 3 hrs. There are frequent buses from the border and Corozal to Belize City, see under Corozal. All northbound buses from Belize City go to Chetumal.

Money changers are on the Belize side of the border. You can buy pesos at good rates with US and Belizean currency. Rates for Belizean dollars in Mexico will be lower. Coming from Mexico, get rid of pesos at the border – changing them in Belize can be difficult.

(one hour driving, 4WD needed when wet). Another road heads west to Blue Creek Village on the Mexican border (see below).

Lamanai → *Colour map 6, A1.*
① *US$5.*

Near **Indian Church**, one of Belize's largest archaeological sites, Lamanai is on the west side of New River Lagoon, 22 miles by river south of Orange Walk. Difficult to reach and hidden in the jungle, it is a perfect setting to hide the mysteries of the Maya and definitely worth a visit. While the earliest buildings were erected about 700 BC, culminating in the completion of the 112-ft major temple, N10-43, about 100 BC (the tallest known pre-Classic Maya structure), there is evidence the site was occupied as long ago as 1500 BC. As a Maya site, it is believed to have the longest history of continuous occupation and, with the Spanish and British sites mentioned below and the present-day refugee village nearby, Lamanai's history is impressive. The Maya site has been partially cleared, but covers a large area so a guide is recommended. The views from temple N10-43, dedicated to Chac, are superb; look for the Yin-Yang-like symbol below the throne on one of the other main temples, which also has a 12-ft-tall mask overlooking its plaza. Visitors can wander freely along narrow trails and climb the stairways. There is a very informative museum housing the only known stela found at the site. There is also a fine jungle lodge, see Sleeping, page 808.

At nearby Indian Church, a Spanish mission was built over one of the Maya temples in 1580, and the British established a sugar mill here. The remains of both buildings can still be seen. The archaeological reserve is jungle and howler monkeys are visible in the trees. There are many birds and the best way to see them is to reach Lamanai by boat, easily arranged in Orange Walk or by taking a day trip from Belize City, see Tour operators, page 788. The earlier you go the better, but the trips from Orange Walk all leave at pretty standard times. The mosquitoes are vicious in the wet season (wear trousers, take repellent). The community phone for information on Indian Church, including buses, is T309-3015.

Blue Creek and around → *Colour map 6, A1.*

West of San Felipe is Blue Creek (10 miles), the largest of the Mennonite settlements. Many of the inhabitants of these close-knit villages arrived in 1959, members of a Canadian colony that had migrated to Chihuahua, Mexico, to escape encroaching modernity. They preserve their Low German dialect, are exempt from military service, and their industry now supplies the country with most of its poultry, eggs, vegetables and furniture. Some settlements, such as Neustadt in the west, have been abandoned because of threats by drug smugglers in the early 1990s. Belize and Mexico have signed an agreement to build an international bridge from Blue Creek across the river to La Unión, together with a river port close to the bridge. It is not known when work will start; at present there is a canoe-service for foot passengers across the Blue Creek.

A vast area to the south along the **Río Bravo** has been set aside as a conservation area (see page 774). Within this, there is a study and accommodation centre near the Maya site of **La Milpa**. The site is at present being excavated by a team from the University of Texas and Boston University, USA.

A good road can be followed 35 miles south to **Gallon Jug**, where a jungle tourism lodge has been built in the **Chan Chich** Maya ruin, see Sleeping. The journey to Chan Chich passes through the Río Bravo Conservation Area, is rarely travelled and offers some of the best chances to see wildlife. Chan Chich is believed to have the highest number of jaguar sightings in Belize, and is also a birdwatchers' paradise. Another road has recently been cut south through Tambos to the main road between Belmopan and San Ignacio, but travel in this region is strictly a dry-weather affair.

Sarteneja and northeast of Orange Walk

From Orange Walk a complex network of roads and tracks converge on **San Estevan** and Progresso to the north. The Maya ruins near San Estevan have reportedly been 'flattened' to a large extent and are not very impressive. Ten miles from San Estevan is a road junction; straight on is **Progresso**, a village picturesquely located on the lagoon of the same name. The right turn, signposted, runs off to the Mennonite village of **Little Belize** and continues (in poor condition) to **Chunox**, a village with many Maya houses of pole construction. In the dry season it is possible to drive from Chunox to the Maya site of Cerros (see below).

Three miles before Sarteneja is the visitor centre for Shipstern Nature Reserve, which covers 22,000 acres of this northeastern tip of Belize. Hardwood forests, saline lagoon systems and wide belts of savannah shelter a wide range of mammals (coatis and foxes, and all the fauna found elsewhere in Belize, except monkeys), reptiles and 200 species of bird. There are mounds of Maya houses and fields everywhere. The most remote forest, south of the lagoon, is not accessible to short-term visitors. There is a botanical trail leading into the forest with trees labelled with Latin and local Yucatec Maya names; a booklet is available. At the visitor centre is the **Butterfly Breeding Centre** ① *daily 0800-1700, US$5 including excellent guided tour.* Visit on a sunny day if possible; on dull days the butterflies hide themselves in the foliage. There is rather poor dormitory accommodation at the visitor centre, US$10 per person. A day-trip by private car is possible from Sarteneja or Orange Walk. Mosquito repellent is essential.

Leaving the Northern Highway, a road heads east to **Sarteneja**, a small fishing and former boat-building settlement founded by Yucatán refugees in the 19th century. The main catch is lobster and conch. On Easter Sunday there is a popular regatta, with all types of boat racing, dancing and music. There are the remains of an extensive Maya city scattered throughout the village, and recent discoveries have been made and are currently being explored to the south around the area of Shipstern Lagoon.

Corozal and around → *Colour map 5, B3. Population: 9110.*

The Northern Highway continues to Corozal (96 miles from Belize City), formerly the centre of the sugar industry, now with a special zone for the clothing industry and garment exports. Much of the old town was destroyed by Hurricane Janet in 1955 and it is now a mixture of modern concrete commercial buildings and Caribbean clapboard seafront houses on stilts. Like Orange Walk it is economically depressed but Corozal is much the safer place. It is open to the sea with a pleasant waterfront where the market is held. There is no beach but you can swim in the sea and lie on the grass. You can check out the local website at www.corozal.com.

Between Orange Walk and Corozal, in San José and San Pablo, is the archaeological site of **Nohmul**, a ceremonial centre whose main acropolis dominates the surrounding cane fields (the name means 'Great Mound'). Permission to visit the site must be obtained from Sr Estevan Itzab, whose house is opposite the water tower.

From Corozal, a road leads 7 miles northeast to **Consejo**, a quiet, seaside fishing village on Chetumal Bay. No public transport, taxi about US$10.

Six miles northeast of Corozal, to the right of the road to Chetumal, is **Four Mile Lagoon**, about a quarter of a mile off the road (buses will drop you there). Clean swimming, better than Corozal bay, some food and drinks available; it is often crowded at weekends.

Across the bay to the south of Corozal stand the mounds of **Cerros**, once an active Maya trading port whose central area was reached by canal. Some of the site is flooded but one pyramid, 69 ft high with stucco masks on its walls, has been partially excavated. Take a boat from Corozal, walk around the bay (a boat is needed to cross the mouth of the New River) or do the dry-season vehicular trail from Progresso and Chunox (see above). Trips can be arranged with **Hotel Maya** and **Hok'Ol K'in Guest House**, from US$60 for a water taxi carrying up to six people.

◉ North Belize listings

For Sleeping and Eating price codes and other relevant information, see Essentials pages 45-48.

● Sleeping

Bermudian Landing and the Community Baboon Sanctuary *p803*
L-B Black Orchid Resort, T225 9158, www.blackorchidresort.com. Selection of rooms with shared bath through to luxury villas on the banks of the Belize River. Restaurant, fresh water swimming pool, and usual tours for the area. Great choice.

A-B Howler Monkey Lodge, 400 m from museum, T220-2158, www.howlermonkey lodge.com. Screened windows, fans, shared bath cheaper, student discount, TCs, Visa, MasterCard accepted, camping US$5 per person, bring tent, river tours US$25 per person, recommended. Transport from Belize City in pickup US$40, 1-4 people, on request. Breakfast, lunch and dinner, US$5-9. Many good tours including nighttime crocodile adventures US$40. Canoe rentals in Burrell Boom for trips on Belize River to see birds, howler monkeys, manatee, and other wildlife.

C Community Baboon Sanctuary, *cabañas* are available alongside the visitor centre, bath, hot water. Basic lodging is also available with families in the village and can be arranged through the Baboon Sanctuary office.

Crooked Tree Wildlife Sanctuary *p803*
AL-A Paradise Inn, T225-7044, advcam@ aol.com. Run by the Crawfords, cabins with hot showers, restaurant, well maintained, friendly, boat trips, fishing, horse riding and tours.
AL-B Bird's Eye View Lodge, T203-2040, www.birdseyeviewlodge.com (owned by the Gillett family; in USA T/F570-588-0843). Single and double rooms, shower, fan, meals available, boat trips, horse riding, canoe rental, nature tours with licensed guide, ask for information at the **Belize Audubon Society** (see page 774).
AL-B Sam Tillet's Hotel, in centre of village, T220-7026, www.crookedtreebelize.com. Wood and thatch cabin, restaurant, great trips. Cabins may be rented, up to 4 people. Also cheap rooms and camping (**F**) can also be arranged if requested.

Orange Walk *p804*
Parking for vehicles is very limited at hotels.
AL-A Mi Amor, 19 Belize-Corozal Rd, T302-2031. With shared bath, with bath and fan, or with a/c, nice, clean, restaurant.
A-B Hotel de la Fuente, 14 Main St, T322-2290. With 12 rooms and winner of Belize's 2006 Small Hotel of the Year award.
B D'Victoria, 40 Belize Rd (Main St), T322-2518, www.dvictoriabelize.com. A/c, shower, hot water, parking, quite comfortable, pool, but somewhat run-down.
B-C St Christopher's, 12 Main St, T/F302-1064. Beautiful clean rooms and bathrooms, highly recommended and the best in town.
C-D Akihito Japanese Hotel, 22 Belize Corozal Rd, T302-0185, akihitolee@ hotmail.com. An affordable place in the centre of town.
D-E Lucia's Guest House, 68 San Antonio Rd, T322-2244, osiris-rod@yahoo.com. One of the newer budget places in town

that gets recommendations, 5 mins west of town.

Lamanai *p805*
AL Lamanai Outpost Lodge, at Indian Church, T223-3578, www.lamanai.com. Run by the incredibly friendly Howells, this beautiful lodge is a short walk from Lamanai ruins, overlooking New River Lagoon, package deals available, day tours, thatched wooden cabins with bath and fan, hot water, 24-hr electricity, restaurant, excellent and well-informed guides. Juvenile crocodile study underway and guests are invited to participate.

Camping
Nazario Ku, the site caretaker, permits camping or hammocks at his house, opposite path to Lamanai ruins, good value for backpackers.

Blue Creek and around *p806*
LL Chan Chich, Chiun Chah, T223-4419, www.chanchich.com. A beautifully sited lodge in the midst of Maya ruins with an extensive trail system in the grounds, delicious food, fantastic birdwatching and wildlife-watching opportunties; very good guides; pool. Recommended. Phone before setting out for Chan Chich for information on the roads.
AL La Milpa Field Station, La Milpa, for information call T323-0011, or contact the Programme for Belize in Belize City (T227-5616, www.pfbelize.org). Makes a good base for exploring trails in the region and birdwatching. To reach La Milpa, go 6 miles west from Blue Creek to Tres Leguas, then follow the signs south towards the Río Bravo Escarpment. The reserve is privately owned and you will need proof of booking to pass the various checkpoints. 4 double *cabañas*, spacious, comfortable, with a thatched roof overhanging a large wooden deck, or a dormitory sleeping up to 30.

C Hill Bank Field Station, on the banks of the New River Lagoon. Also a good base for exploring trails in the region and birdwatching, and with a dormitory sleeping up to 30. See **La Milpa Field Station**, above, for contact details.

Sartaneja and northeast of Orange Walk p806

AL Krisami's Bay View, T423-2283, www.krisamis.com. Rooms with private bath, a/c and TV.

B-C Fernando's Guest House, on seafront near centre of Sartaneja, T423-2085, sartenejabelize@hotmail.com.

D Diani's, on the seashore. Restaurant, seems to be undergoing eternal refurbishment. Houses can be rented for longer stays.

E Backpacker's Paradise, www.cabanasbelize.com, 5 mins from the village. Newish place with cabins or camping, use of kitchen or eat in the restaurant. Range of activities. We didn't get to see it, but it seems like what Sarteneja's been waiting for.

Corozal and around p807

AL-A Las Palmas Hotel, 123, 5th Av South, T422-0196, www.laspalmashotelbelize.com. With bath and fan, OK, *refrescos* available, good food, lively bar downstairs.

AL-B Tony's, South End, T422-2055, www.tonysinn.com. With a/c, clean, comfortable units in landscaped grounds. Recommended, but restaurant overpriced.

A Copa Banana, 409 Corozal Bay Rd, T422-0284, www.copabanana.bz. Newest place in town, with 5 suites all with private bathrooms. US-owned so complimentary coffee each morning. Ask the bus driver to drop you off.

A Hok'Ol K'in Guest House, 4th Av and 4th St South, T422-3329, www.corozal.net. Immaculate rooms. Runs tours to Cerros.

C Corozal Guest House, 22 6th Av, T422-2358, www.corozal.bz. Basic, clean rooms, shared area with TV, lots of information about Belize and the area. Close to the bus terminal.

D Caribbean Village Resort, South End, T422-2045. Hot water, US$5 camping, US$12 trailer park, restaurant, recommended.

F Papa's Guest House, 5th Av South, next door to Las Palmas. Very basic but cheap.

Camping

Caribbean Motel and Trailer Park, see **Caribbean Village Resort**, above. Camping possible but not very safe (US$4 per person), shaded sites, restaurant.

Eating

Orange Walk p804

Most restaurants in town are Chinese. We've received encouraging reports about **La Hacienda Steakhouse** and **Marvias**.

King Fu, Baker's St. Chinese, excellent and filling.

Juanita's, 8 Santa Ana St (take road beside Shell station). Open 0600 for breakfast and all meals. Good, inexpensive Creole cooking. Same at **Julie's**, near police station.

Central Plaza Restaurant, behind the main bus terminal. A popular choice in a handy location.

Diner, Clarke St, behind the hospital. Good meals, very friendly, taxi US$4 or walk.

Corozal and around p807

There are many Chinese restaurants in town.

Café Kela, in a beachfront *palapa* on the shore. Best restaurant in town, intimate setting, fine food, good value, just sit back and enjoy.

Cactus Plaza, 5th Av South. A loud bar with lots of fluorescent lighting and great a/c. Worth trying if you're stuck in town for the night.

Purple Toucan, No 52, 4th Av North. Good restaurant and lively bar with pool table and good music. Opposite is **Marcelo's**, which serves good pizza.

Border, 6th Av South. Friendly Chinese, good food.

Corozal Garden, 4th Av, 1 block south. Good, quick local food.

Gongora's Pastry, southwest corner of main square. Hot pizza pieces, cakes and drinks.

Newtown Chinese, 7th Av, just north of the gas station on the other side of the main road. Large portions, good quality, slow service.

▲ Activities and tours

Orange Walk *p804*
Jungle River Tours, 20 Lovers Lane, T302-2293, lamanaimayatour@btl.net, in *Lovers' Café* on the southeastern corner of the park. Organizes and runs trips to Lamanai (US$40 plus entrance of US$5 including lunch departing 0900 returning 1600), Altún Ha and New River area, regular trips, *the* specialists on the region and consistently recommended. It also provides trips to any destination in Belize with a minimum of 4 people.

⊖ Transport

Bermudian Landing and the Community Baboon Sanctuary *p803*
Bus From **Belize City** Mcfadzean Bus from corner of Amara Av and Cemetery Rd at 1215 and 1715 Mon-Fri; 1200 and 1400 Sat. **Rancho Bus (Pook's Bus)** from Mosul St, 1700 Mon-Fri, 1300 Sat, check details, US$1.50-2, 1 hr. Alternatively, any bus travelling the Northern Hwy can drop you off at the turn-off to Bermudian Landing where you can wait for a bus, or hitch a ride. A day trip giving any meaningful time in the sanctuary is difficult by public transport, so it is best to stay the night.

Crooked Tree Wildlife Sanctuary *p803*
Bus Buses from **Belize City** with JEX (1035); return from Crooked Tree at 0600-0700.

Altún Ha *p804*
Bus With little transport on this road, hitching is not recommended – best to go in a private vehicle or a tour group. Vehicles leave **Belize City** for the village of **Maskall**, 8 miles north of Altún Ha, several days a week, but same-day return is not possible.

Orange Walk *p804*
Bus Bus station is on street beside the fire station, on the main road. All buses travelling from Belize City to Corozal and beyond to Chetumal stop in Orange Walk; from **Belize**, US$3. From **Corozal**, US$1.50, 50 mins. For **Lamanai** take bus to Indian Church (Mon, Wed, Fri 1600). Buses to **Sarteneja** (which is 40 miles away) outside Zeta's Store on Main St, 5 between 1300 and 1900, US$2.50. Also to Progresso at 1100 and 1130.

Blue Creek and around *p806*
Air Flights to Chan Chich from **Belize City** can be chartered.

Sarteneja and northeast of Orange Walk *p806*
Boat The Thunderbolt service linking San Pedro and Corozal will stop at Sarteneja on request at no extra charge. The service departs **Corozal** at 0700 and 1500, and leaves **San Pedro** at 0700 and 1500, full trip cost is US$22.50. For enquiries call T422-0026, thunderbolt travels@yahoo.com.

Bus Bus from **Belize City** at 1200, US$4.50, from the corner of Victoria and North Front St. Buses also leave from **Corozal** (1400), via Orange Walk (1530).

Corozal and around *p807*
Air Maya Island Air, daily from Belize City via Caye Caulker and San Pedro (Ambergris Caye); **Tropic Air** daily from San Pedro. Airstrip 3 miles south, taxi US$1.50. Private charters to **Sarteneja** cost about US$75 for the 30-min journey (compared with 3 hrs by road).

Boat To **Orange Walk**, leaving at 1400.

Bus Heading south, buses leave every 30 mins, starting at 0400 running until 1830. Regular service 3 hrs, US$2.50, faster express service, 2½ hrs, US$3.50, leaves at 0600, 0700, 1200, 1500 and 1800. If heading north, buses from **Belize City** continue north to **Chetumal** terminal, with stopping time to allow for immigration procedures.

For those coming from Mexico who are interested in **Tikal** in Guatemala, it is possible to make the journey border to border in a day, with a change of bus in Belize City.

Taxi Leslie's Taxi Service, T422-2377. Transfers from Corozol to the Mexican border, US$22 for a 4-person taxi. Ask for a quote for other services. Reliable and professional.

● Directory

Orange Walk *p804*
Banks Belize Bank on Main St (down Park St from Park, turn left). Scotia Bank on Park, US$0.50 commission. Shell Station will change TCs. **Internet** K&M, on Main St.

Corozal and around *p807*
Banks Atlantic Bank (charges US$2.50 for Visa cash advances), Bank of Nova Scotia, and Belize Bank. For exchange also ask at the bus station.
Internet Charlotte's Web, 5th Av between 5th and 6th St South, cyber café and book exchange.

West Belize

Impressive sights – artificial and natural – line the route from Belize City to the Guatemalan border, starting with Belize Zoo – a pleasant break from the norm. Monkey Bay Wildlife Sanctuary and Guanacaste National Park are both worth a visit. From the bustling town of San Ignacio, there are canoe trips down the Macal River and dramatic cave systems, journeys into the impressive limestone scenery of Mountain Pine Ridge, and the spectacular Maya ruins of Caracol, Xunantunich and Cahal Pech to explore. Day trippers can also cross the border for a quick visit to Tikal in Guatemala. ➤➤ *For listings, see pages 818-822.*

Belize City to San Ignacio ⊕ ➤➤ *pp818-822.*

The Western Highway leaves Belize City past the cemetery, where burial vaults stand elevated above the boggy ground, running through palmetto scrub and savannah landscapes created by 19th-century timber cutting. At Mile 16 is **Hattieville**, originally a temporary settlement for the homeless after Hurricane Hattie in 1961. The highway roughly parallels the Sibun River, once a major trading artery where mahogany logs were floated down to the coast in the rainy season; the place name 'Boom' recalls spots where chains were stretched across rivers to catch logs being floated downstream.

The small but excellent **Belize Zoo** ① *daily 0900-1700, US$7.50, www.belizezoo.org, take any bus from Belize City along the Western Highway (1 hr)*, is at Mile 28½, watch out for the sign or tell the driver where you're going. It is a wonderful collection of local species (originally gathered for a wildlife film), lovingly cared for and displayed in wire-mesh enclosures amid native trees and shady vegetation, including jaguar and smaller cats, pacas (called gibnuts in Belize), snakes, monkeys, parrots, crocodile, tapir (mountain cow), peccary (wari) and much more. Highly recommended, even for those who hate zoos. Get there early to miss the coach party arrivals. Tours by enthusiastic guides, T-shirts and postcards sold for fundraising.

At Mile 31½, the **Monkey Bay Wildlife Sanctuary** protects 1070 acres of tropical forest and savannah between the highway and the Sibun River (great swimming and canoeing). Birds are abundant and there is a good chance of seeing mammals.

Forty-seven miles from Belize City, a minor road runs 2 miles north to **Banana Bank Lodge and Jungle Equestrian Adventure** (see Sleeping, page 818).

A mile beyond the **Banana Bank Lodge and Jungle Equestrian Adventure** turning is the highway junction for Belmopan and Dangriga. At the confluence of the Belize River and Roaring Creek is the 50-acre **Guanacaste National Park** ① *US$2.50*, protecting a parcel of 'neotropical rainforest' and a huge 100-year-old *guanacaste* (tubroos) tree, which shelters a wide collection of epiphytes including orchids. Many mammals (jaguarundi, kinkajou, agouti etc) and up to 100 species of bird may be seen from the 3 miles of nature trails cut along the river. This is a particularly attractive swimming and picnicking spot at which to stop or break the journey if travelling on to Guatemala. It has a visitor centre, where luggage can be left. To get there, take an early morning bus from Belize City, see the park in a couple of hours, then pick up a bus going to San Ignacio or Dangriga.

Soon after the junction to Belmopan is **Roaring Creek**, once a thriving town but now rather overshadowed by the barely illuminated capital nearby. At Camelote, a dirt road southwards takes you to **Roaring River**. At Teakettle, turn south along a dirt road for 5 miles to **Pook's Hill Reserve** (see Sleeping, page 818).

The important but unimpressive **Floral Park** archaeological site is just beyond the bridge over **Barton Creek** (Mile 64). Just 2 miles further is **Georgeville**, from where a gravel road runs south into the Mountain Pine Ridge Forest Reserve (see page 816). The highway passes the turn-off at Norland for **Spanish Lookout**, a Mennonite settlement area 6 miles north (B & F Restaurant, Centre Road, by Farmers' Trading Centre, clean, excellent value). The **Central Farm Agricultural College**, the village of **Esperanza** and other small settlements along the way keep the road interesting until it reaches **Santa Elena**. Formerly only linked by the substantial Hawkesworth suspension bridge to its twin town of San Ignacio, it now has a small, one-lane 'temporary bridge' you must take to cross the river to San Ignacio.

San Ignacio and around ⊖🚐🛈🅿🅟🛐🛑🛈 ➤➤ pp818-822. Colour map: 6, A1.

Some 68 miles from Belize City and 10 miles from the border, San Ignacio (locally called **Cayo**) is the capital of Cayo District and Western Belize's largest town, an agricultural centre serving the citrus, cattle and peanut farms of the area, and a good base for excursions into the Mountain Pine Ridge and west Belize. It stands amid attractive wooded hills at 200-500 ft, with a good climate, and is a nice town to rest in if coming from Guatemala. The town is on the eastern branch of the Old, or Belize River, known as the Macal. The 180-mile river journey down to Belize City is internationally famous as the

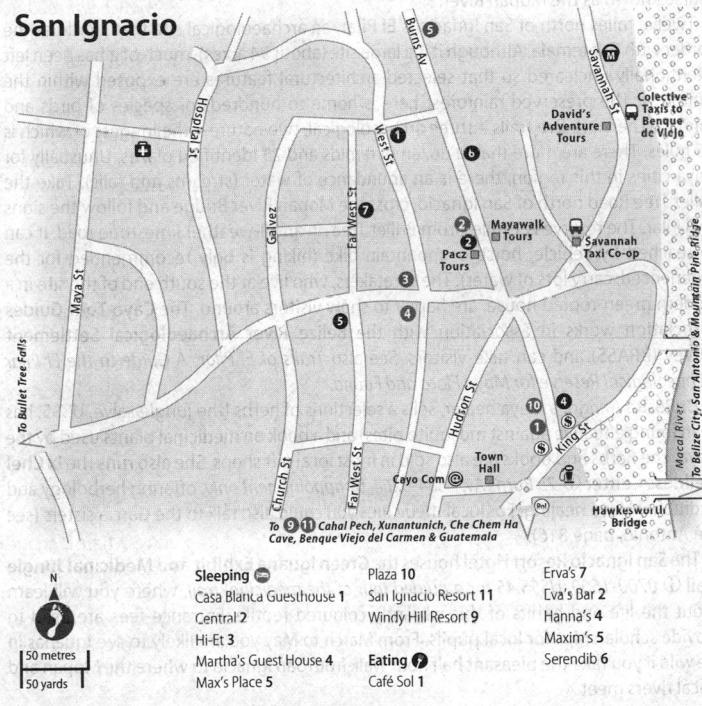

San Ignacio

Sleeping 🛏
Casa Blanca Guesthouse **1**
Central **2**
Hi-Et **3**
Martha's Guest House **4**
Max's Place **5**

Plaza **10**
San Ignacio Resort **11**
Windy Hill Resort **9**

Eating 🍴
Café Sol **1**

Erva's **7**
Eva's Bar **2**
Hanna's **4**
Maxim's **5**
Serendib **6**

To Bullet Tree Falls
To 9 11 Cahal Pech, Xunantunich, Che Chem Ha Cave, Benque Viejo del Carmen & Guatemala
To Belize City, San Antonio & Mountain Pine Ridge
Macal River
Hawkesworth Bridge

50 metres
50 yards

Paddling the great Macal River

Time it right and you can paddle down the length of the Macal River taking part in La Ruta Maya canoe race. It's a gruelling three-day open canoe race, starting in San Ignacio covering 180 miles along the river before ending in Belize City on Baron Bliss Day (early March). All food and water is provided for the trip, but you'll need to be fit and healthy.

You'll struggle to compete at the racing end of the field unless you're a top athlete and have a canoe of modern design, but plenty of people enter the race for the challenge and with a bit of luck it's possible to turn up, talk with people around town and find yourself a place on a boat. For information, visit www.larutamayabelize.com.

route for the annual 'Ruta Maya Belize River Challenge', a gruelling three-day canoe race held the weekend of Baron Bliss Day, 9 March, see box, above.

A short walk from San Ignacio (800 m from **Hotel San Ignacio**) is **Cahal Pech** ① *daily 0600-1700, US$5*, an interesting Maya site and nature reserve on a wooded hill overlooking the town, with a visitor centre and small museum.

Four miles west of San Ignacio on a good road is **Bullet Tree Falls**, a pleasant cascade amid relaxing surroundings on the western branch of the Belize River, here in its upper course known as the Mopan River.

Twelve miles north of San Ignacio is **El Pilar**, an archaeological site that straddles the border with Guatemala. Although it is a large site (about 94 acres), much of it has been left intentionally uncleared so that selected architectural features are exposed within the rainforest. The preserved rainforest here is home to hundreds of species of birds and animals. There are five trails – three archaeological, two nature – the longest of which is 1.5 miles. There are more than a dozen pyramids and 25 identified plazas. Unusually for Maya cities in this region, there is an abundance of water (streams and falls). Take the Bullet Tree Road north of San Ignacio, cross the Mopan River Bridge and follow the signs to El Pilar. The reserve is 7 miles from Bullet Tree on an all-weather limestone road. It can be reached by vehicle, horse or mountain bike (hiking is only recommended for the experienced; carry lots of water). The caretakers, who live at the south end of the site in a modern green-roofed house, are happy to show visitors around. The **Cayo Tour Guides Association** works in association with the **Belize River Archaeological Settlement Survey (BRASS)** and can take visitors. See also *Trails of El Pilar: A Guide to the El Pilar Archaeological Reserve for Maya Flora and Fauna*.

Dr Rosita Arvigo, a Maya healer, sells a selections of herbs (the jungle salve, US$5, has been found effective against mosquito bites) and a book on medicinal plants used by the Maya. The herbs and books are also sold in most local gift shops. She also runs the **Ix Chel Wellness Center** ① *25 Burns Av, T804-0264, by appointment only*, offering herbology and traditional Maya healing. For local medicines you could also talk to the García sisters (see San Antonio, page 816).

The **San Ignacio Resort Hotel** houses the **Green Iguana Exhibit and Medicinal Jungle Trail** ① *0700-1600, US$5.45 for a guided tour of the medicinal trail*, where you will learn about the life and habits of this vibrantly coloured reptile. Entrance fees are used to provide scholarships for local pupils. From March to May you are likely to see Iguanas in the wild if you take the pleasant half hour walk from San Ignacio to where the Mopan and Macal rivers meet.

Local tour operators (see below) generally offer similar tours at similar prices. Canoe trips up the **Macal River** are worthwhile. They take about three hours upstream, 1½ hrs on return. Hiring a canoe to go upstream without a guide is not recommended unless you are highly proficient as there are Grade II rapids one hour from San Ignacio. Another trip is to **Barton Creek Cave**, a 1½-hour drive followed by a 1½-hour canoe trip in the cave. The cave vault system is vast, the rock formations are beautiful, the silence is eerily comforting and all can be explored for a considerable distance by canoe (US$55 per person minimum two people). Tours can be arranged at almost every place in San Ignacio.

For a more adventurous caving tour, you shouldn't leave without going to **Actun Tunichil Muknal (ATM) Cave** (the Cave of the Stone Sepulchre), a one-hour drive from San Ignacio to the Tapir Mountain Nature reserve, a 45-minute jungle hike in the reserve and then 3½ hours of adventurous, exhilarating caving, US$75. Besides the beautiful rock formations, this cave is full of Maya artefacts and sacrificial remains. The guides from both **Emilio Awe's Pacz Tours** and **Mayawalk**, are recommended. Mayawalk also run an overnight ATM tour (US$180). Under 8s and pregnant women are discouraged from taking this tour. ▶▶ *See Activities and tours, page 821.*

Maya artefacts can be seen in **Che Chem Ha Cave** ① *T820-4063*, on the private property of the Moralez family on the Vaca Plateau, south of San Ignacio (Benque). In contrast to Barton Creek and Actun Tunichil Muknal this is a so-called dry cave. The family offers trips into the cave, a half-hour hike to the entrance, followed by a one- to 1½-hour walk in the cave. The view from the property is stunning and the family serves lunch. Tours start at 0900 and 1300. If you go by private transport be there in time for the tour and call the family in advance or, better still, book a tour with an agency in San Ignacio.

Trips to the nearby ruins of **Xunantunich** (see below) are very easy by bus, regular traffic going to the Guatemalan border. Tours of **Mountain Pine Ridge** are available (see below), but shop around carefully – if you decide to go with a taxi you probably won't get far in the wet season. Trips to **Caracol** are best arranged from San Ignacio, see page 821, and if you only want to visit Tikal in Guatemala, you can arrange a day trip that will maximize your time spent at the ruins. On a good road 9 miles west of San Ignacio is the tranquil town of **Benque Viejo del Carmen**, near the Guatemalan border. Many of the inhabitants are Maya Mopan. For information on the Benque Viejo–Melchor de Mencos border crossing, see page 756.

South of San Ignacio, halfway between Clarissa Falls turn-off and Nabitunich is Chial Road, gateway to adventure. A half-mile down the road is a sharp right turn that takes you through Negroman, the modern site of the ancient Maya city of **Tipu** which has the remains of a Spanish Mission from the 1500s. Across the river from here is **Guacamallo Camp**, rustic jungle camping and starting point for canoe trips on the Macal River. Two miles further up, also across the river, is Ek Tun (see Sleeping, page 818). **Belize Botanic Gardens** ① *T824-3101, www.belizebotanic.org, daily 0700-1700, US$2.50, guided walks 0730-1500, US$7.50*, on 50 acres of rolling hills, is next to the **Du Plooys'** lodge (see Sleeping, page 818) with hundreds of orchids, dozens of named tree species, ponds and lots of birds. Recommended.

Xunantunich → *Colour map 6, A1.*
① *Daily 0730-1600, US$5; a leaflet on the area is available from the site for US$4. Apart from a small refreshment stand, there are no facilities for visitors, but a museum has been built and a couple of stelae have been put on display in a covered area. It is an extremely hot walk up the hill, with little or no shade, so start early. Last ferry (free) back is at 1630.*

At Xunantunich ('Maiden of the Rock') there are Classic Maya remains in beautiful surroundings. The heart of the city was three plazas aligned on a north-south axis, lined with many temples, the remains of a ball court, and surmounted by the Castillo. At 130 ft, this was thought to be the highest artificial structure in Belize until the Sky Palace at Caracol was measured. The impressive view takes in the jungle, the lowlands of Petén and the blue flanks of the Maya Mountains. Maya graffiti can still be seen on the wall of Structure A-16 – friezes on the Castillo, some restored in modern plaster, represent astronomical symbols. Extensive excavations took place in 1959-1960 but only limited restoration work has been undertaken.

Just east of the ferry, **Magaña's Art Centre** and the **Xunantunich Women's Group** sell locally made crafts and clothing in a shop on a street off the highway. About 1.5 miles further north are the ruins of **Actuncan**, probably a satellite of Xunantunich. Both sites show evidence of earthquake damage.

Mountain Pine Ridge ⊖ ➤➤ *pp818-822. Colour map 6, A1.*

Mountain Pine Ridge is a Forest Reserve (146,000 acres) that covers the northwest section of the Maya Mountains, an undulating landscape of largely undisturbed pine and gallery forest, and valleys of lush hardwood forests filled with orchids, bromeliads and butterflies. The devastation to large swathes of the pine forest first caused by an infestation of the southern pine bark beetle in 2001 continues to impact on the area. Note the frequent changes of colour of the soil and look out for the fascinating insect life. If lucky, you may see deer. There's river scenery to enjoy, high waterfalls, numerous limestone caves and shady picnic sites; it's a popular excursion despite the rough roads. The easiest way of visiting is on a trip from San Ignacio. Hitching is difficult but not impossible. Try contacting the **Forestry Conservation Officer** ① *T824-3280*, who may be able to help.

Two roads lead into the reserve: from Georgeville to the north and up from Santa Elena via Cristo Rey. These meet near **San Antonio**, a Mopan Maya village with many thatched-roof houses and the nearby Pacbitun archaeological site (where stelae and musical instruments have been unearthed). At San Antonio, the García sisters have their workshop, museum and shop where they sell carvings in local slate. They also have a guesthouse (**D**). You can sample Maya food and learn about the use of medicinal plants. This is a regular stop on tours to the Mountain Pine Ridge. A donation of US$0.50 is requested; US$12.50 is charged to take photos of the sisters at work. Two buses a day from San Ignacio, 1000 and 1430, from market area; check times of return buses before leaving San Ignacio.

1000-ft falls

The main forest road meanders along rocky spurs, from which unexpected and often breathtaking views emerge of jungle far below and streams plunging hundreds of feet over red-rock canyons. A lookout point (with a small charge) has been provided to view the impressive falls, said to be 1000 ft high (often shrouded in fog October to January). On a clear day you can see Belmopan from this viewpoint. It is quite a long way from the main road and is probably not worth the detour if time is short, particularly in the dry season (February to May) when the flow is restricted. At this time of year, there is an ever-present danger of fire and open fires are strictly prohibited. Eighteen miles into the reserve the road crosses the **Río On**. Here, where the river tumbles into inviting pools over huge granite boulders; is one of Belize's most beautiful picnic and swimming spots. The rocks form little water slides and are fun for children.

Augustine

Five miles further on is the tiny village of Augustine (also called Douglas D'Silva or **Douglas Forest Station**), the main forest station where there is a shop, accommodation in two houses (bookable through the Forestry Dept in Belmopan, the area Forestry Office is in San Antonio) and a **camping ground** ① *US$1, no mattresses (see rangers for all information on the area), keep your receipt, a guard checks it on the way out of Mountain Pine Ridge*. A mile beyond Augustine is a cluster of caves in rich rainforest. The entrance to the **Río Frío Cave** (in fact a tunnel) is over 65 ft high, and there are many spectacular rock formations and sandy beaches where the river flows out. Trees in the parking area and along the Cuevas Gemelas nature trail, which starts one hour from the Río Frío cave, are labelled. It's a beautiful excursion and highly recommended.

Forestry roads continue south further into the mountains, reaching **San Luis** (6 miles), the only other inhabited camp in the area, with post office, sawmill and forest station, and continuing on over the granite uplands of the Vaca Plateau into the **Chiquibul Forest Reserve** (460,000 acres).

The four forest reserves that cover the Maya Mountains are the responsibility of the Forestry Department, who have only about 20 rangers to patrol over a million acres of heavily forested land. A hunting ban prohibits the carrying of firearms. Legislation, however, allows for controlled logging; all attempts to have some areas declared national parks or biosphere reserves have so far been unsuccessful. You can stay in the area at **Las Cuevas Research Station and Explorers Lodge** (see Sleeping).

Caracol → *Colour map 6, A1.*

About 24 miles south-southwest of Augustine, Caracol (about one hour by 4WD) is a rediscovered Maya city. The area is now a National Monument Reservation. Caracol was established about 300 BC and continued well into the Late Classic period (glyphs record a victorious war against Tikal). Why Caracol was built in such a poorly watered region is not known, but Maya engineers showed great ingenuity in constructing reservoirs and terracing the fields. The **Sky Palace** (*Caana*) pyramid, which climbs 138 ft above the site, is being excavated by members of the University of Central Florida. Excavations take place between February and May, but there are year-round caretakers who will show you around. Currently very knowledgeable guides escort groups around the site twice daily and a new information centre and exhibition hall has been built. The road has been improved and is passable for much of the year with normal vehicles and year-round with 4WD. It is an interesting journey as you pass through the Mountain Pine Ridge, then cross the Macal River and immediately enter a broadleaf tropical forest. Take your own food as there is none at the site. Otherwise **Pine Ridge Lodge, Five Sister's Lodge** or **Blancaneaux Lodge** are open for lunch (see Sleeping).

For Sleeping and Eating price codes and other relevant information, see Essentials pages 45-48.

⊖ Sleeping

Belize City to San Ignacio *p812*
L Jaguar Paw Jungle Resort, near Belize Zoo on curve of Caves Branch River on road south at Mile 31, T820-2023, www.jaguarpaw.com, with meals.
L-A Pook's Hill Lodge, Pook's Hill Reserve, T820-2017, www.pookshillbelize.com. A 300-acre nature reserve on Roaring Creek, 6 *cabañas*, horses and rafting.
AL Banana Bank Lodge and Jungle Equestrian Adventure, Guanacaste National Park, T820-2020, www.bananabank.com. Resort accommodation, with meals, horse riding on river side and jungle trails, birding and river trips.
C-E Tropical Education Centre, at Belize Zoo. Basic-style accommodation.
E Monkey Bay Wildlife Sanctuary, Mile 31 Western Hwy, Belmopan, T820-3032, www.watershedbelize.org. Dormitory accommodation or you can camp on a wooden platform with thatched roof, swim in the river, showers available, take meals with family.

San Ignacio and around *p813, map p813*
Some hotels in town and on Cahal Pech Hill may be noisy at weekends from loud music, and during the day from traffic and buses. In the area surrounding San Ignacio there are many jungle hideaways. Ranging from secluded and exclusive cottages to full activity resorts, and covering a wide range of budgets, these places are normally an adventure on their own. Before going, make sure you know what's included in the price; food is often extra.
LL Blancaneaux Lodge, Mountain Pine Ridge Rd, east of San Ignacio, Central Farm, Cayo District, T824-3878, www.blancaneaux lodge.com. Once the mountain retreat of

Francis Ford Coppola and his family, now one villa and wonderful, huge *cabañas* decorated in Guatemalan textiles, horse riding, croquet, spa, hot pool, overlooking a stream, private air strip. Access to Big Rock Falls. Italian restaurant and bar. Recommended.
LL The Lodge at Chaa Creek, on the Macal River, south of San Ignacio off the Chial Rd, after the turn to Ix Chel Farm, T824-2037, www.chaacreek.com, or hotel office at 56 Burns Av, San Ignacio. Upscale accommodation, amenities and tours, with spa, conference centre, butterfly breeding centre, natural history movement and an adventure centre. Strong supporters of environmental groups and projects. Tours and excursions offered.
LL-L San Ignacio Resort Hotel, 18 Buena Vista Rd, T824-2125, www.sanignacio belize.com. Southern end of town, on the road to Benque Viejo. Rooms with bath, a/c, hot water, some with balconies. Helpful staff, clean, swimming pool, tennis court, excellent restaurant. Live music every weekend at the **Stork Club**. **Green Iguana Exhibit** on site, see page 814, and tour agency.
L Du Plooys', south of San Ignacio, past the Chaa Creek road, then follow (including one steep hill) to its end above the Macal River, T824-3101, www.duplooys.com. Choices of accommodation and packages are available, enjoy the **Hangover Bar** with cool drinks on the deck overlooking trees and river. The **New Belize Botanic Gardens** (see page 815) is also run by the du Plooy family.
L Ek Tun, south of San Ignacio, T820-3002, in USA T303-4426150, www.ektunbelize.com. A 500-acre private jungle retreat on the Macal River, boat access only, 2 very private deluxe thatched guest cottages, excellent food, spectacular garden setting. Great spot for romantic adventurers. Advance reservations only, no drop-ins, adults only and 3-night minimum.
L-AL Five Sisters Lodge, east of San Ignacio, 2½ miles beyond **Blancaneaux Lodge** (see above), T820-4005, www.fivesisterslodge.com.

Rustic cottages lit by oil lamps, great views, good-value restaurant. Recommended.

L-A Midas Resort, Branch Mouth Rd, T824-3172, www.midasbelize.com. An attractive 7-acre family-run resort, located on the edge of town, yet with a more remote wilderness feel. *Cabaña* accommodation with Wi-Fi service and access to the river for swims.

AL Las Cuevas Research Station and Explorer's Lodge, in the Chiquibul Forest, T822-2149, www.mayaforest.com. Isolated research station open to non-researchers. Rivers, caves, archaeological sites nearby, a genuine wilderness experience.

AL Martha's Guest House, 10 West St, T804-3647, www.marthasbelize.com. 10 comfortable rooms, 2 with balcony, TV, a/c, cheaper without, lounge area, good restaurant, friendly, clean, kitchen facilities, the family also runs **August Laundromat**.

AL Mountain Equestrian Trails, Mile 8, Mountain Pine Ridge Rd (from Georgeville), Central Farm PO, Cayo District, T820-4041, www.metbelize.com. Accommodation in 4 double *cabañas* with bath, no electricity, hot water, mosquito nets, good food in *cantina*, ½-day, full-day and 4-day adventure tours on horseback in Western Belize, packages, birdwatching tours and other expeditions offered, excellent guides and staff.

AL Pine Ridge Lodge, east of San Ignacio, on the road to Augustine, just past turning to Hidden Valley Falls, T606-4557, www.pineridgelodge.com. *Cabañas* in the pinewoods, including breakfast.

AL Windy Hill Resort, 2 miles west of San Ignacio, on Graceland Ranch, T824 2017, www.windyhillresort.com. 14 cottage units, all with bath, dining room, small pool, nature trails, horseriding and river trips can be arranged, expensive.

AL-A Cohune Palms River Cabanas, Bullet Tree Falls, T824-0166, www.cohune palms.com. 4 *cabañas* separated by a fabulously beautiful garden walk.

AL-A Mopan River Resort, Benque Viejo, T823-2047, www.mopanriverresort.com. Belize's 1st all-inclusive, luxury resort on the Mopan River, opposite Benque Viejo, boat access only 12 thatched *cabañas* with verandas nestled in a lush coconut grove, pool, water garden, 7-night minimum.

AL-B Maya Mountain Lodge (Bart and Suzi Mickler), ¾ mile east of San Ignacio at 9 Cristo Rey Rd, Santa Elena, San Ignacio, T824-2164, www.mayamountain.com. Welcoming, special weekly, monthly and family rates. Restaurant, expensive excursions, self-guided nature trail, swimming, hiking, riding, canoeing, fishing can be arranged.

A-B Iguana Junction, Bullet Tree Falls, T824-2249, www.iguanajunction.com. British-run with good-quality *cabaña* accommodation in a tropical riverbank location. Hammocks available for kids.

A-C Casa Blanca Guesthouse, 10 Burns Av, T824-2080, www.casablancaguesthouse.com. 8 clean rooms with 2 beds in each, private shower, fan or a/c, TV, use of kitchenette, free coffee, friendly.

B Cahal Pech Village, south of town, near Cahal Pech, T824-3740, www.cahalpech.com. Thatched cabins or a/c rooms, restaurant, bar, meeting facilities.

B Elvira's Dinner & Guest House, 6 Far West St, T804-0243. Good clean rooms, with traditional Belizean food in the restaurant.

B Parrot Nest, near village of Bullet Tree Falls, 3 miles north of San Ignacio, T820-4058, www.parrot-nest.com. Family run with small , comfortable tree houses in beautiful grounds by the river. Breakfast and dinner are available, as well as free tubing. Can arrange local tours.

B-C Plaza, 4a Burns Av, T824-3332. Rooms in family house run by friendly couple. All 8 rooms have 2 beds, balconies, TVs, a/c, cheaper without, all with bath, parking. Free coffee.

C Aguada Hotel, Santa Elena, across the river, T804-3609, www.aguadahotel.com. Full-service hotel, 12 rooms, private baths, a/c costs more, fresh water pond and heart-shaped swimming pool, quiet part of town, excellent restaurant and bar.

C Cosmos Camping & Cabanas, ½ mile beyond **Mida's** (see below), T824-2116, cosmo scamping@btl.net. 4 very simple units, or camp on the site alongside the Macal River. Tents for rent, washing and cooking facilities, run by friendly Belizean family, good breakfasts, canoe and bikes for hire, good. Cabins available (**E**).

C Venus Hotel, Burns Av, T824-3203, www.venushotelbelize.com. Family-run hotel providing 32 rooms with private bathroom and tv.

C-D Clarissa's Falls, on Mopan River, down a signed track on the Benque road, around Mile 70, T824-3916, www.clarissafalls.com. Owned by Chena Galvez, thatched cottages on riverbank by a set of rapids, also bunkhouse with hammocks or beds, camping space and hook-ups for RVs, rafting, kayaking and tubing available, wonderful food in the restaurants.

C-D Hi-Et, 12 West St, T824-2828, thehiet@yahoo.com. Lovely, red and cream old wooden building with 10 rooms and private shower, cheaper without. Reportedly noisy, nice balcony, friendly, helpful, family-run, stunning orchids in patio. Free coffee.

D-E Max's Place, 49 Burns Av, T621-0556, maxcaballeros@yahoo.com. 5 basic rooms including a bunk room with shared bath room above family home. Communal TV. Shuttles and guided tours offered. Bike rental.

E Central, 24 Burns Av, T824-3134, easyrider@btl.net. Clean, secure, fans, shared hot showers, book exchange, friendly, veranda with hammocks, uncomfortable beds but recommended.

Camping

D-E Barton Creek Outpost, T662-4797, www.bartoncreekoutpost.com. Located in a gloriously beautiful jungle setting, this excellent campsite is worth the minor adventure of getting to it (the best bet is to contact the owners Jimmy and Jacqueline a few days prior to arrival). Camping is free if you have your own gear, and you can also rent mattresses and camp gear. Campers are offered discounts on a range of tours (most notably to Barton Creek itself). Hot meals are available for purchase.

D-E Inglewood Camping Grounds, west of San Ignacio at Mile 68¼, T824-3555, www.inglewoodcampingground.com. *Palapas*, camping, RV hook-ups, hot and cold showers, maintained grounds, some highway noise.

F Mida's, ½ mile from town on Branch Mouth Rd, near river, T824-3172, www.midasbelize.com. Down Burns Av, turn right down unpaved road after wooden church, after 200 yd turn left, campground is 300 yd on right. Hot showers, electricity, restaurant, very helpful, good value, cabins available (**B-C**), also organize trips to Tikal.

❼ Eating

San Ignacio and around *p813, map p813*

♥♥♥ **Running W**, in the San Ignacio Resort Hotel. One of the best restaurants in town. Also live music every 2nd Sat in the bar of the same hotel.

♥♥ **Café Sol**, between Burns Av and West St. Serves coffee and pastries, with vegetarian, chicken and seafood dishes for lunch and dinner. Also has bookstore and gift shop.

♥♥ **Erva's**, 6 Far West St, T824-2556. Vegetarian available, reasonable prices and proud of their pizza and seafood.

♥♥ **Eva's Bar**, 22 Burns Av, T804-2267, Mon-Sat 0800-1500, 1800-late. Good diner-style restaurant, local dishes, helpful with good local information, bike rental, internet facilities, tours.

♥♥ **Hanna's**, 5 Burns Av. Daily 0600-2100. Popular with locals and foreigners, very good Indian-Belizean food, as well as curries, vegetarian and excellent fish. Many ingredients are fresh from their own farm, good value. Friendly staff, highly recommended.

♥♥ **Sanny's Grill**, several blocks down the hill off the Western Hwy past the Texaco station. Serves the 'world's best conch ceviche', full dinner menu, charming setting.

♥♥ **Serendib**, 27 Burns Av. Mon-Sat, 1030-1500, 1830-1100. Good food and good value, Sri Lankan owners, Indian-style food.

♨-♨ Martha's Kitchen, below Martha's Guest House. Very good breakfasts and Belizean dishes, plus pizzas and burger. Garden patio.
♨ Hode's Place, Branch Mouth Rd, facing the basketball field, just outside town. Open daily. Popular with locals and good value, Belizean food arriving in huge portions, pleasant yard to sit outside.
♨ Long Luck Chinese restaurant, George Price, up the hill on the left, just after the Hydro road, Benque Viejo. Best Chinese in town.
♨ Maxim's, Bullet Tree Rd and Far West St. Chinese, good service, cheap, very good food, popular with locals, noisy TV at the bar.
♨ Old French Bakery, JNC building. Good pastries for days out exploring.
♨ Terry's, north of San Ignacio, near the village of Bullet Tree Falls. Restaurant with limited menu but good food.

⊕ Entertainment

San Ignacio and around *p813, map p813*
Cahal Pech, on a hill, with TV station, beside the road to Benque Viejo before the edge of town. Music and dancing at weekends, *the* place to be, live bands broadcast on TV and radio, good views. On a hill across the track from the club is Cahal Pech archaeological site.
Culture Club, same building as Pitpan, upstairs, live reggae Thu-Sat night, popular with foreigners and the local Rasta crowd.
Legends 200, Bullet Tree Rd. Disco, popular with locals.
Pitpan, right turn off King St to river. Open daily. The open-air bar is at the back of the building, popular spot.
Stork Club, San Ignacio Resort Hotel, see Sleeping, live music every 2nd Sat in the bar.

⊖ Shopping

San Ignacio and around *p813, map p813*
Black Rock Gift Shop, near Eva's, linked to Black Rock Lodge, luggage can be left here if canoeing from Black Rock to San Ignacio, arts and crafts, workshop. **Celina's Supermarket**, Burns Av, next to the bus station. Not the cheapest but wide selection. Open Mon-Sat 0730-1200, 1300-1600, 1900-2100. **Maxim's**, West St, small, cheap supermarket. Fruit and veg market every Fri and Sat morning. Book exchange at **Snooty Fox**, Waights Av (opposite Martha's).

▲ Activities and tours

San Ignacio and around *p813, map p813*
Many of the resorts and lodges in this area organize a variety of tours and expeditions.

Therapies
See **Dr Rosita Arvigo**, page 814. **Therapeutic Massage Studio**, 38 West St, T604-0314. Mon-Fri 0800-1200, 1300-1630. Sat 0830-1200.

Tour operators
David's Adventure Tours, near bus terminal, T804-3674. Recommended for visits to Barton's Creek Cave, US$37, Mountain Pine ridge and Barton, US$67, Caracol, US$75, or guided canoe trips along the Macal River, including the medicinal trail and overnight camping, US$127. Always gets a good report.
Easy Rider, Bullet Tree Rd, T824-3734, horse riding. Full-day tours for US$40 with lunch.
Hun Chi'ik Tours, Burns Av, T670-0746, www.hunchiiktours.com. Cave and other tours, specialising in small groups but providing discounts for groups of more than 6 people.
Pacz Tours, 30 Burns Av, T824-0536, www.pacztours.net, offers great trips to Actun Tunichil Muknal Cave, US$75 including lunch and reserve fee of US$30. Excellent guides. Bob who runs the bar, is the best starting point for information on any of the trips and is very helpful. Your hotel will also have details and suggestions. Canoe trips on the Macal River, with bird and wildlife watching, medicinal plant trail, good value, US$65; Barton Creek Cave, US$55 for ½-day tour, Mountain Pine Ridge, US$65, Caracol and trip to pools, US$75, Tikal, US$135. Highly recommended.

Mayawalk Tours, 19 Burns Av, T824-3070, www.mayawalk.com, has received good recommendations. Similar rates to **Pacz**, also offer overnight rainforest and cave packages if you're looking for some true adventure.
Maya Mystic Tours, Savannah St, T804-0055. All trips organized including El Pilar, US$45 per person and river canoeing. Shuttles arranged.

⊖ Transport

San Ignacio and around *p813, map p813*
Bus
National Transport Company Bus Station is on Burns Av. To **Belize City**, Mon-Sat 0430-1800 every hr, Sun hourly 0700-1800, 3½-4 hrs, US$2.50. To **Belmopan**, same schedule as Belize City, 1 hr, US$1.70. To **Benque Viejo**, every 2 hrs, Mon-Sat 0730-2300 (less on Sun), 30 mins, US$0.75. Change at Belmopan for Dangriga and the south. From the bus station at Benque, you need to get a taxi to the immigration post at **Melchor de Mencos**, US$1.25, 2 mins.
 Minibuses also run to **Tikal**, making a day trip possible. Organized tours cost about US$70.

Taxi
Savannah Taxi Drivers' Co-op, T824-2155, T606-7239 (Manuel, 24 hrs). To **Guatemalan border**, US$15 (*colectivo* US$2.50, on the road, but US$12.50 if you pick them up from their base opposite David's. To **Xunantunich** US$30 return, to **Belize City** US$75, to **Tikal** US$175 return, to **Mountain Pine Ridge**, US$75, **Chaa Creek**, US$30, **Caracol**, US$175 return.

Xunantunich *p815*
Bus
Bus from San Ignacio towards the border as far as **San José Succotz** (7 miles), US$0.75, where a hand-operated ferry takes visitors and cars across the Mopan River (0800-1600, free); it is then a 20-min walk uphill on an all-weather road. Return buses to San Ignacio pass throughout the afternoon.

Mountain Pine Ridge *p816*
Taxi
There's no public transport. Apart from tours, the only alternatives are to take a taxi or hire a vehicle or mountain bike. Everything is well signposted. The private pickups that go into San Ignacio from Augustine are usually packed, so hitching is impossible. Taxis charge around US$75-80 for 5 people. Roads are passable but rough Jan-May, but after Jun they are marginal and are impossible in the wet (Sep-Nov). It's essential to seek local advice at the time.

❶ Directory

San Ignacio and around *p813, map p813*
Banks Banks open Mon-Fri 0830-1500, Sat 0830-1300, all bunched together at the southern end of Burns Av, **Belize Bank** offers full service, TCs, Visa and MasterCard cash advance plus ATM. **Atlantic Bank**, also does cash advances and has an ATM. Both charge commission for cash advances. **Scotia Bank**, opposite Atlantic Bank, doesn't charge for cash advances. **Western Union**, has a branch in Celina's (supermarket), Burns Av, Mon-Thu 0800-1200 1300-1600, Fri and Sat also 1900-2100. **Eva's Bar** and **Martha's** both change TCs at good rates. Changers in the town square give better rates of exchange for US$ cash and TCs than you can get at the border with Guatemala. Change US$ into quetzales in Guatemala. **Internet** High charges from BTL mean internet services come and go. Cheapest places in town are Cayo Community Computer Centre, Hudson St, Mon-Sat 0800-2100, Sun 1000-1800 and Tradewinds Eva's Bar, US$3 for 30 mins.
Laundry August Laundromat at Martha's and Mike's, and Laundromat at Burns Av.
Post office Hudson St, reliable parcel service, Mon-Thu 0800-1200 and 1300-1700, Fri 0800-1200 and 1300-1600. **Telephone** BTL office at further end of Burns Av, opposite **Venus Hotel**, long-distance calls and fax service.

South Belize and the southern cayes

Southern Belize is the most remote part of the country and has poor roads, but it is worth exploring. Dangriga is the largest of several Garífuna settlements that burst into life every year on Settlement Day. The paradise beaches of Hopkins and Placencia are perfect for watersports and relaxing. Cockscomb Basin Wildlife (Jaguar) Sanctuary offers one of the best chances of seeing a big cat in the wild, while the sparsely populated far south around Punta Gorda has many Maya settlements to visit in a region dotted with impressive Maya ruins.
➤➤ *For listings, see pages 831-842.*

South to Dangriga ⊜▲⊜ ➤➤ *pp831-842. Colour map 6, A1.*

About 2 miles beyond the Belize Zoo on the Western Highway, the Coastal Highway (a good dirt road) runs southeast to **Gales Point**, a charming fishing village on a peninsula at the south end of Manatee Lagoon, 15 miles north of Dangriga. The villagers are keen to preserve natural resources and there are still significant numbers of the endangered manatee and hawksbill turtles. Boat tours of the lagoon are recommended.

Along the Hummingbird Highway

The narrow Hummingbird Highway branches off the Western Highway 48 miles west of Belize City, passes Belmopan and heads south. Skirting the eastern edge of Mountain Pine Ridge, the newly surfaced highway meanders through lush scenery of cohune palms, across

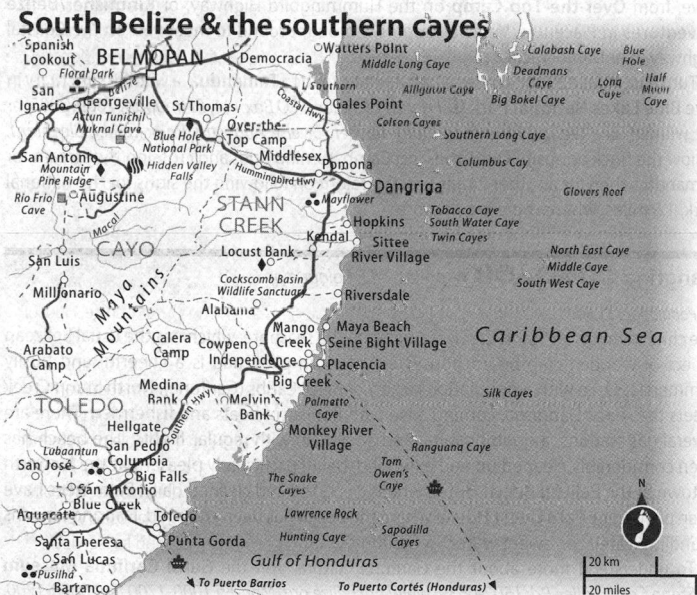

South Belize & the southern cayes

vast flood plains filled with citrus trees, which provide a spectacular backdrop for the 52-mile journey southeast to Dangriga.

The Hummingbird Highway climbs through rich tropical hardwood forest until reaching Mile 13, where a visitor centre marks a track leading off to **St Herman's Cave**. Two paths, with good birdwatching, lead through shady ferns before descending in steps to the cave entrance with its unique microclimate. You can walk for more than a mile underground but it can be slippery if wet; torch and spare batteries essential. There is a 3-mile trail to a campsite from the visitor centre.

Two miles further on is the **Blue Hole National Park** ① *daily 0800-1600, US$4, visitor centre at entrance,* an azure blue swimming hole fringed with vines and ferns, fed by a stream that comes from St Herman's Cave. This is typical karst limestone country with sinkholes, caves and underground streams. After its long journey underground, the water here is deliciously cool until it disappears again into the top of a large underwater cavern. Eventually this joins the Sibun River which enters the sea just south of Belize City. There is a rough 2½-mile trail (good hiking boots are required), through low secondary forest, between St Herman's Cave and the **Blue Hole** itself. A sign on the roadway warns visitors against thieves; lock your car and leave someone on guard if possible when swimming. An armed guard and more wardens have been hired to prevent further theft and assaults.

The peaks of the mountains dominate the south side of the highway until about Mile 30, when the valley of Stann Creek begins to widen out into Belize's most productive agricultural area, where large citrus groves stretch along the highway.

Canoeing or tubing trips can be organized down Indian Creek, visiting the imaginatively named Caves Five, Four and Three and then Daylight Cave and Darknight Cave, from **Over-the-Top Camp** on the Hummingbird Highway, or **Kingfisher/Belize Adventures** in Placencia. Vehicle support is brought round to meet you on the Coastal Highway near Democracia.

Turn east at Mile 32 for 4 miles along a gravel road to **Tamandua**, a wildlife sanctuary in **Five Blue Lakes National Park** ① *Friends of 5 Blues, PO Box 111, Belmopan, T809-2005, or the warden, Lee Wengrzyn, a local dairy farmer, or else Augustus Palacio (see Sleeping).* Follow the track opposite **Over-the-Top Camp**, turning right and crossing the stream for Tamandua, then for another 2 miles or so straight on following the signs for the national park, 1.5 miles, where there is camping.

Dangriga ●🛏●●❀▲●● ▸▸ *pp831-842. Colour map 6, A1.*

→ *Population: 11,600.*

The chief town of the Stann Creek District is on the seashore, which has the usual Belizean aspect of wooden clap-board houses elevated on piles, and is a cheerful and busily commercial place with a population largely of Black Caribs (Garífuna). North Stann Creek meets the sea at Dangriga, coming alive with flotillas of boats and fishermen. There are several gas stations, a good hospital and an airfield with regular flights. The beach has been considerably cleaned up and extended, being particularly pleasant at the far north of town at the **Pelican Beach Hotel**, where it is raked and cleaned daily. Palm trees have been planted by **Pal's Guest House** where the beach has been enlarged. Dangriga means 'standing waters' or 'sweet water' in Garífuna.

To understand more about the Garífuna culture, visit the **Gulisi Garífuna Museum** ① *Stann Creek Valley Rd, T502-0639, www.ngcbelize.org, Mon-Fri 1000-1700, Sat 0800-1200,*

US$5. The museum includes information about the origins of the Garífuna people, history and customs, with music and a working garden of traditional plants and herbs.

Cayes near Dangriga
Tobacco Caye ① *US$15, 35 mins by speedboat from Dangriga*, is a tiny and quite heavily populated island, but has lots of local flavour and charm and, though becoming a little commercialized, still has an authentic feel. It sits right on the reef and you can snorkel from the sandfly-free beach although there are no large schools of fish; snorkelling gear for rent. Boats go daily, ask at **Riverside Café** ① *US$12-15 per person*.

South Water Caye, the focus of a marine reserve, is a lovely palm-fringed tropical island with beautiful beaches, particularly at the south end.

South of Dangriga → *Colour map 6, A1.*
The Southern Highway (now completely paved except for a stretch of a mile or so) connects Dangriga with Punta Gorda in the far south. Six miles inland from Dangriga the road branches off the Hummingbird Highway and heads south through mixed tropical forests, palmettos and pines along the fringes of the Maya Mountains. West of the road, about 5 miles from the junction with the Hummingbird Highway, a track leads to **Mayflower**, a Maya ruin. Some minimal work has begun on opening it up and some say it will eventually be the biggest archaeological site in southern Belize.

Fifteen miles from Dangriga, a minor road forks off 4 miles east to the Garífuna fishing village of Hopkins. Watch out for sandflies when the weather is calm. The villagers throw household slops into the sea and garbage on to the beach.

Turning east towards the Caribbean just before Kendal a road leads down the Sittee River to **Sittee River Village** and **Possum Point Biological Station**.

Glover's Reef
Glover's Reef, part of North East Cay and about 45 miles offshore, is an atoll with beautiful diving and has been a Marine Reserve since 1993, US$10. The reef here is pristine and the cayes are generally unspoilt, but yellow blight has hit the area killing most of the existing palm trees – especially on **Long Caye**. The combination of Hurricane Mitch and high water temperatures has damaged the coral, and the snorkelling is not as good as it once was.

Placencia ⊜⚫✪▲⚫⚫ ►► *pp831-842. Colour map 6, A1.*
Placencia, a former Creole fishing village 30 miles south of Dangriga, is a small seaside community on a thin sandy peninsula promoting the delights of the offshore cayes and marinelife and is a good base for inland tours too. Continuing down the Southern Highway a couple of hotel signs indicate a turning (nothing official, look carefully) to a road that heads east to Riversdale (after 9 miles) turning south to follow the peninsula to **Maya Beach**, **Seine Bight** and, eventually, **Placencia**. The peninsula road is very rough from Riversdale to Seine Bight, with sand mixed with mud; a 4WD is advisable.

Placencia is becoming more popular among people looking for an 'end of the road' adventure. It's a relaxing combination of chilling out on the beach, fishing, snorkelling and diving. If you time the trip right or get lucky, your visit may coincide with the migrations of the whale shark – the largest fish in the world at up to 55 ft – that passes through local waters from March to May. And, between January and March, hundreds of scarlet macaws gather at nearby Red Bank. Also worth hitting if you can time it right is the **Lobster Fest**, on the last full weekend in June, with two days of music, dancing and lobster and the **Sidewalk Arts Festival** held the weekend before or after Valentine's Day. Placencia is a natural base for one- and two-day trips to **Cockscomb Basin Wildlife Sanctuary** – see page 827. **Big Creek**, on the mainland opposite Placencia, is 3 miles from Mango Creek.

There are no streets, just a network of concrete footpaths connecting the wooden houses that are set among the palms. The main sidewalk through the centre of the village is reported to be in the *Guiness Book of Records* as the world's narrowest street. The atmosphere has been described as laid back, with lots of Jamaican music, particularly after Easter and Christmas celebrations.

The local **Placencia Tourism Center** ⓘ *T523-4045, www.placencia.com, Mon-Fri 0900-1700, closed public holidays, and 1130-1300 during low season*, is in Placencia Village Square, with lots of useful information. It also produces the local monthly news-sheet, *Placencia Breeze* (www.placenciabreeze.com).

Placencia

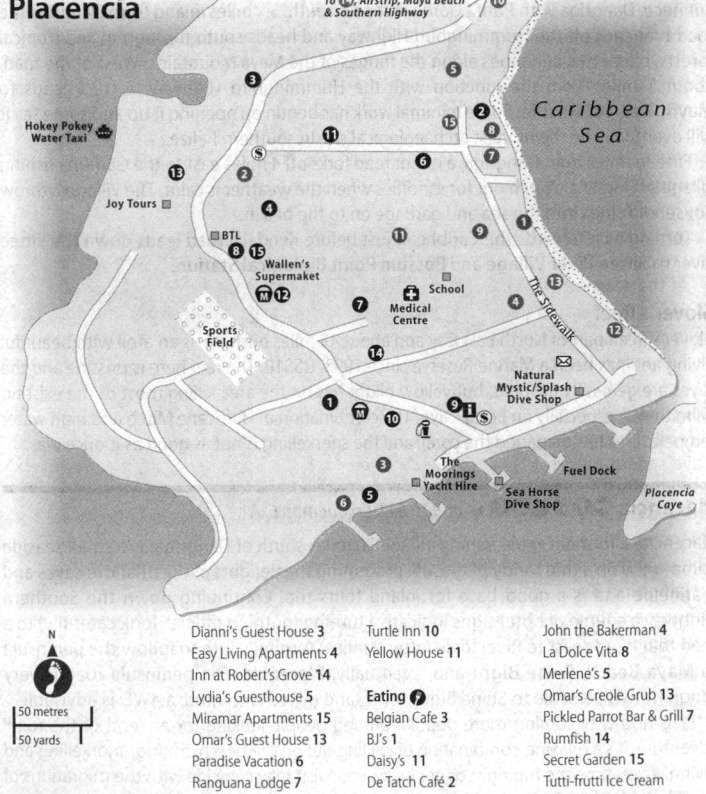

	Dianni's Guest House **3**	Turtle Inn **10**	John the Bakerman **4**
	Easy Living Apartments **4**	Yellow House **11**	La Dolce Vita **8**
	Inn at Robert's Grove **14**		Merlene's **5**
	Lydia's Guesthouse **5**	**Eating** 🍴	Omar's Creole Grub **13**
50 metres	Miramar Apartments **15**	Belgian Cafe **3**	Pickled Parrot Bar & Grill **7**
50 yards	Omar's Guest House **13**	BJ's **1**	Rumfish **14**
	Paradise Vacation **6**	Daisy's **11**	Secret Garden **15**
	Ranguana Lodge **7**	De Tatch Café **2**	Tutti-frutti Ice Cream
Sleeping 🛏	Seaspray **8**	French Connection **6**	Parlour **9**
Cozy Corner **1**	Serenade Guest House **9**	Garden Brew Coffee	Wendy's Creole **10**
Deb & Dave's Last Resort **2**	Trade Winds **12**	House **12**	

Around Placencia

Trips can be made to local cayes and the **Barrier Reef**, approximately 18 miles offshore. Day trips include snorkelling, with a beach BBQ lunch of lobster and conch. Offshore cayes include **Laughing Bird Caye**. **Gladden Spit** and **Silk Cayes Marine Reserve** (reserve fee US$10), also protected by **Friends of Nature**. Whale sharks visit the spit in March, April, May and June for 10 days after the full moon to feed on the spawn of aggregating reef fish.

Several hotels and guide services have kayaks that can be rented to explore some of the nearer islands or the quieter waters of the **Placencia Lagoon**. Those who want to keep their feet dry can go mountain biking on the peninsula or use it as a base for trips to **Cockscomb Basin Wildlife Sanctuary** and Maya ruins.

Day tours by boat south along the coast from Placencia to **Monkey River** and **Monkey River Village** are available. Monkey River tours, US$20 per person, feature howler monkeys, toucans, manatees and iguanas. Monkey River Village can be reached by a rough road, which is not recommended in wet weather. The road ends on the north side of the river and the town is on the south side, so call over for transport. Trips upriver can also be arranged here with locals but kayaking is best organized in Placencia. Trips can be arranged to Red Bank for the scarlet macaws, which gather in their hundreds between January and March. For information on travelling to or from Puerto Cortés in Honduras, see pages 974 and 991. North of Placencia is the Garífuna community of **Seine Bight**.

Cayes near Placencia

Ranguana Caye is a private caye reached from Placencia (US$5). Getting there is free if it fits in with one of the regular trips, otherwise it costs US$150 each way for up to four people. Divers must bring their own scuba equipment. Day trips for diving, snorkelling or just relaxing cost US$45-50, and include lunch. For longer stays, see Sleeping, page 836.

At the southernmost end of the Mesoamerican Barrier Reef are the **Sapodilla Cayes**, US$10. Tours are arranged from Guatemala (for example see under Río Dulce and Lívingston) or can be made from Placencia. There are settlements on a few of the Cayes including **Hunting Caye**.

The **Silk Cayes**, also known as the **Queen Cayes**, is a small group of tiny, picture-perfect islands, which sits on the outer barrier reef and, together with Gladdens Spit, has recently become the core zone of the country's newest marine reserve. The Silk Cayes have superb diving, especially on the North Wall. Coral in the deeper areas is in good condition with many tube and barrel sponges and sharks, turtles and rays often seen cruising the reef wall. The Silk Cayes are a popular destination for Placencia-based dive operators, however, it's not possible to dive in this area during periods of rough weather. The rainy season lasts from June to January.

Laughing Bird Caye (reserve fee US$4, www.friendsofnaturebelize.org), used to be the home of the Laughing Gull (*Larus articilla*), now it's home to other sea birds and has an exciting array of underwater life around its shores.

Cockscomb Basin Wildlife Sanctuary and around ☺▲☺ ►► pp831-842.
Colour map 6, A1.

ⓘ *US$5.*

Some 20 miles south of Dangriga, the Southern Highway crosses the Sittee River at the small village of **Kendal** (ruins nearby). One mile beyond is the village of **Maya Centre** from where a poor seven-mile track winds west through Cabbage Haul Gap to the

Cockscomb Basin Wildlife Sanctuary (21,000 acres), the world's first jaguar sanctuary and definitely worth an extended visit if you have two or three days. The sanctuary was created out of the Cockscomb Basin Forest Reserve in 1986 to protect the country's highest recorded density of jaguars (*Panthera onca*), and their smaller cousins the puma (red tiger), the endangered ocelot, the diurnal jaguarundi and that feline cutey, the margay. Many other mammals share the heavily forested reserve, including coatis, collared peccaries, agoutis, anteaters, Baird's tapirs and tayras (a small weasel-like animal). There are red-eyed tree frogs, boas, iguanas and fer-de-lances, as well as over 290 species of bird, including king vultures and great curassows. The sanctuary is a good place for relaxing, showering under waterfalls, tubing down the river, or listening to birds – hundreds of bird species have been spotted and there are several types of toucan, hummingbirds and scarlet macaws to be seen by early risers. The reserve is sponsored by the Belizean government, the **Audubon Society**, the **Worldwide Fund For Nature** and various private firms. Donations are very welcome.

Park HQ is at the former settlement of Quam Bank (whose milpa-farming inhabitants founded the **Maya Centre** outside the reserve). Here there is an informative visitor centre. An 18-mile network of jungle trails spreads out from the centre, ranging in distance from a few hundred yards to 2.5 miles. Walkers are unlikely to see any of the big cats as they are nocturnal, but if you fancy a walk in the dark you may be lucky. Note that the guards leave for the day at 1600. You will see birds, frogs, lizards, snakes and spiders. Longer hikes can be planned with the staff. Nearby is one of Belize's highest summits, **Victoria Peak** (3675 ft), which is an arduous four- or five-day return climb and should not be undertaken lightly. There is virtually no path, a guide is essential; February to May are the best months for the climb. ▸▸ *For guides, see Activities and tours, page 840.*

Punta Gorda ⊕⊘▲⊕⊙ ▸▸ *pp831-842. Colour map 6, B1.*

→ *Population: 5255.*
The turn-off from the Southern Highway for Mango Creek, Independence and Big Creek comes 15 miles after the Riversdale turn-off, and the road runs 4 miles east through the **Savannah Forest Reserve** to the mangrove coast opposite Placencia. About 35 miles beyond the junction, 10.5 miles north of the T-junction for Punta Gorda, half a mile west of the road, is the **Nim Li Punit** archaeological site which has a visitor centre and clean spacious housing for the stelae. Nim Li Punit ('The Big Hat') was only discovered in 1974. A score of stelae, 15-20 ft tall, were unearthed, dated AD 700-800, as well as a ball court and several groups of buildings. The site is worth visiting – look for the sign on the highway. Day trips also offered from Placencia. A short distance beyond, the highway passes **Big Falls Village**, almost completely destroyed by Hurricane Iris. Take a short hike back to the hot springs for a swim, camp or sling a hammock, but first seek permission from the landowner, Mr Peter Aleman. Four miles from Big Falls, the Highway reaches a T-junction, know locally as the 'Dump', marked by a Shell station; the road to San Antonio branches right (west), the main road turns sharp left and runs down through a forest reserve for 13 miles to Punta Gorda. The road is paved from Big Falls to Punta Gorda.

Punta Gorda is the southernmost town of any size in Belize, a marketing centre and fishing port with a varied ethnic makeup of Creoles, Q'eqchi', Mopan, Chinese, East Indians and descendants of the many races brought here over the years as labourers in ill-fated settlement attempts. Three miles north of **Toledo** are the remains of the sugar cane

Border essentials: Belize–Guatemala

Punta Gorda–Puerto Barrios

Crossing to Guatemala A boat service goes to Puerto Barrios in Guatemala from Punta Gorda. Requena Water Taxi, 12 Front St, T722-2070, has fast skiffs daily 0900 leaving from main dock in front of immigration, returning at 0200, one hour, US$20. Pichilingo, T722-2870 leaves daily at 1400, returning from Puerto Barrios at 1000. Mar Y Sol leaves Punta Gorda for Puerto Barios at 1600, returning the next day at 1300. Rigo also provides a service to Lívingston on Tue and Fri, leaving 1000 and returning from Lívingston at 0700. These companies also provide services to Puerto Barrios and Lívingston by request. Requena also offers charters and trips to the cayes. Bike and motorbike transportation has been reported as difficult. Officials in Lívingston do not have the authority to issue vehicle permits to anything other than water craft.

Exchange There are money changers at both ends of the crossing but it is better to buy quetzales in Guatemala. Neither side changes TCs. Try to get rid of any Belizean dollars in Belize.

Transport Can sometimes be arranged from Pueblo Viejo along a road to Jalacté (also reached by trail from Blue Creek and Aguacate), from where it is a 30-minute hike to Santa Cruz del Petén (often muddy). From here trucks can be caught to San Luis on the highway near Poptún.

Belizean immigration Exit stamps for people and vehicles can be obtained at the Customs House next to the pier on Front St. Be there at least one hour before departure, or two hours if loading a motorcycle. PACT exit tax payable, see page 775.

Guatemalan consulate If you need a visa it must be obtained in Belize City. Tourist cards are available in Puerto Barrios.

Shopping Although locals cross to shop in Guatemala, it's illegal to cross the land border between Guatemala and Belize. There is no Guatemalan government presence and entry stamps cannot be obtained. The area has been the focal point for border disputes locally and visitors to the area should take local advice before travelling.

settlement founded by Confederate refugees after the American Civil War. The coast, about 10 ft above sea level, is fringed with coconut palms. The seafront is clean and enjoyable – once you get away from Front Street, where the lively and colourful market on Wednesday, Friday and Saturday comes with the associated smells of fish and rotting vegetables. The *Voice of America* has an antenna complex to the south of town.

Toledo Visitors' Information Center, also called **Dem Dats Doin ①** *in booth by pier, PO Box 73, T722-2470, demdatsdoin@btl.net, free, irregular opening hours*, Alfredo and Yvonne Villoria, provide information on travel, tours, guiding, accommodation with indigenous families (Homestay Programme), message service and book exchange, for the whole of Toledo district. **Tourist Information Centre ①** *Front St, T/F722-2531, Mon-Sat 0800-1200 and 1300-1700*, provides a wealth of information about the area, including bus schedules to local Maya villages, and can organize reservations for flights and for hotels, tours and boat trips to Honduras. The **Toledo Ecotourism Association** has an office in the same building. Information on the **Village Guesthouse** and **Ecotrail** programme, as well as booking and transport to the villages.

The Crystal Skull of Lubaantun

In 1927, a young woman by the name of Anna Mitchell-Hedges woke for her 17th birthday. For her it proved more eventful than most as she explored the recently excavated Maya site of Lubaantun to discover a finely crafted crystal skull made of pure quartz – setting off a tale of intrigue that remains to this day.

The size of a small watermelon, the translucent skull of reflected light weighs just over 5 kg. The skull is one of only two ever found in Central America. Its date of manufacture is unknown – but some put it at over 3600 years old – and its purpose is equally curious. Local Maya people gave the skull to Anna's father, the British explorer FA Mitchell-Hedges as a gift, saying it was used for healing and, more sinisterly, for willing death.

Dating the skull precisely is difficult because of the purity of the crystal, but the details of the finding are equally mysterious, with speculation that the skull was 'placed' to make that birthday so special.

Around Punta Gorda

Rainfall in this region is particularly heavy, with more than 170 inches annually, and the vegetation is consequently luxuriant. There are many tours that can be enjoyed on the numerous rivers in the Toledo District. Countless species of birds make their homes along the rivers, as do troops of howler monkeys and other wildlife. Kayaking is a good way to view wildlife on the rivers. There are many white-sand beaches on the cayes off Punta Gorda for the beachcomber, or camper. Fly fishing is becoming a popular sport and sport fishing, snorkelling and scuba-diving are available. **Toledo** is off the beaten path and has some of the most spectacular views, waterfalls, rainforest, cayes and friendly people.

South of Punta Gorda 🌐 ▶ *pp831-842. Colour map 6, B1.*

San Pedro Columbia

Inland from Punta Gorda there are several interesting villages in the foothills of the Maya Mountains. Take the main road as far as the 'Dump', the road junction with the Southern Highway. Take the road west to San Antonio. After nearly 2 miles, there is a branch to San Pedro Columbia, a Q'eqchi' village where the Maya inhabitants speak the Q'eqchi' language and the women wear colourful costumes, including Guatemalan-style *huípiles*. There are many religious celebrations, at their most intense on **San Luis Rey Day** (5 August).

Lubaantun

ⓘ *0800-1600 daily, beyond San Pedro, continuing left around the church, then right and downhill to the concrete bridge, then left for a mile, a caretaker will point out things of interest. Take refreshments.*

Lubaantun ('Fallen Stones') was the major ceremonial site of southern Belize. The site has a visitor centre and has undergone extensive work to restore a large part of the ruins. It was found to date from AD 800-900, late in the Maya culture and therefore unique. A series of terraced plazas surrounded by temples and palaces ascend along a ridge from south to north. The buildings were constructed with unusual precision and some of the original lime-mortar facings can still be discerned. Excavation revealed whistle figurines, iron pyrite mirrors, obsidian knives, conch shells from Wild Cane Caye, etc. One of the great controversies of the site was the discovery in 1927 of the Crystal Skull by the daughter of the explorer FA Mitchell-Hedges (see box, page 830). This whole region is a network of hilltop sites, mostly unexcavated and unrecognizable to the untrained eye.

Blue Creek

Blue Creek is another attractive indigenous village which has a marked trail to **Blue Creek Caves** ① *US$12.50 per person, the caretaker is the guide*, and their Maya drawings. The trail leads through forest and along rock-strewn creeks. Swimming nearby is good swimming but choose a spot away from the strong current. Turn off 3 miles before San Antonio at **Roy's Cool Spot** (good restaurant; daily truck and all buses pass here).

Pusilhá

Pusilhá is one of the most interesting Maya cities, only accessible by boat. Many stelae have been found here dating from AD 573-731, and carvings are similar to those at Quiriguá, Guatemala. Rare features are a walled-in ball court and the abutments remaining from a bridge that once spanned the Moho River. Swimming in the rivers is safe. There are plenty of logging trails and hunters' tracks penetrating the southern faces of the Maya Mountains but if hiking in the forest, do not go alone.

San Antonio ●❶❷❸ ➤➤ *pp831-842. Colour map 6, B1.*

San Antonio (21 miles from Punta Gorda) was founded by refugees from San Luis in Guatemala in the late 19th century. Nearby there are Maya ruins of mainly scientific interest. There's a community phone for checking buses and other information, T702-2144. **Dem Dats Doin** in Punta Gorda (see page 829) will also be able to give information. There's a medical centre in the village.

There are no roads to the southern border with Guatemala along the Sarstún River. The **Sarstoon-Temash National Park** is a wilderness of red mangroves and unspoilt rainforest. There are no visitor facilities at present. At **Barranco**, the only coastal hamlet south of Punta Gorda, there is a village guesthouse (part of TEA, see box, page 833). A dirt road goes to Barranco through the village of Santa Ana, or you can go by boat.

◉ Southern Belize and the southern cayes listings

For Sleeping and Eating price codes and other relevant information, see Essentials pages 45-48.

● Sleeping

South to Dangriga *p823*
LL Manatee Lodge, Gales Point, T220-8040, www.manatee lodge.com. Resort on the shores of the Southern Lagoon, trips to local areas. Prices include transfers, meals and tours.
LL-E Caves Branch Jungle Lodge, ½ mile past St Herman's Cave, T/F822-2800, www.cavesbranch.com. Reached along

½-mile track, signed on the left, any bus between Belmopan and Dangriga will stop. A secluded spot on the banks of Caves Branch River, comfortable *cabañas* with private baths or **E** per person in the bunkhouse, camping US$5 per person, good, clean, shared bathrooms, great 'jungle showers', delicious meals served buffet style. More than just accommodation, this is very much an activity centre. Great trips through caves, 7-mile underground floats, guided jungle trips, overnight trips as well, tubing, kayaking, mountain biking and rappelling, including

the adrenalin-busting **Black Hole Drop**.
Excellent guides, pricey for some budgets
starting at around US$60 but highly
recommended. See also page 773.
A-D Palacios Mountain Retreat, Mile 31,
Augustus Palacio, St Martha, Hummingbird
Hwy, T822-3683, www.palacios retreat.com.
Good for relaxing, *cabañas*, bunk rooms
and camping. Friendly, helpful, family
atmosphere, safe, good local food, swimming
in river, tours to waterfall in forest, caves
and lagoon, Five Blue Lakes National Park.
Beware sandflies.
**E Gales Point Bed and Breakfast
Association**, contact Hortence Welch on
arrival or call T220-9031 in advance. Basic
accommodation, no indoor plumbing,
meals available.

Dangriga *p824*
LL Bonefish, Mahogany St, on seafront
near post office, T522-2243, www.bluemarlin
lodge.com. A/c, US cable TV, hot water,
takes Visa. Packages are all inclusive.
L-AL Pelican Beach, outside town,
on the beach north of town, T522-2044,
www.pelicanbeachbelize.com. Private bath,
hot water, a/c, veranda, pier, hammocks,
20 rooms, restaurant, bar, games lounge, gift
shop, tours arranged, helpful (taxi from town,
or 15-min walk from North Stann Creek).
B-D Pal's Guest House, 868 A Magoon
St, Dangriga, T522-2095, www.pals belize.com.
19 units on beach, all with balconies, sea views,
bath, fan, cable TV, cheaper rooms in main
building, shared bath downstairs, private
upstairs. Dangriga Dive Centre runs from
next door (see Activities and tours).
C-D Bluefield Lodge, 6 Bluefield Rd,
T522-2742, bluefield@btl.net. Bright hotel,
owner Louise Belisle very nice, spotless,
comfortable beds, very helpful, secure.
Highly recommended.
C-D Chaleanor, 35 Magoon St, T522-2587,
chaleanor@btl.net. Fairly large rooms, some
with TV and fan and a/c some with sea views,
rooftop restaurant.

E Catalina, 37 Cedar St, T522-2390.
Very small, not that clean, but family-run
and friendly, store luggage.

Cayes near Dangriga *p825*
Tobacco Caye
There is no electricity on the island, but it's
a good family atmosphere and great fun.
AL-B Lana's on the reef, T522-2571, USA
T909-9434556. Has its own fishing pier,
snorkelling equipment hire, good
Caribbean-style food, mosquito net, shared
and private shower. Recommended.
AL-B Reef's End Lodge, T522-2419,
www.reefsendlodge.com. Basic, small rooms,
boat transfer on request from Dangriga.
C Island Camps, PO Box 174 (51 Regent St,
Belize City, T227-2109). Owner Mark Bradley
will pick up guests in Dangriga, A-frame
huts, campground, meals available, reef
excursions, friendly, good value.
Recommended.

South Water Caye
LL Blue Marlin Lodge, T522-2243,
www.bluemarlinlodge.com. Excellent
dive lodge offering various packages,
small sandy island with snorkelling
off the beach, good accommodation
and food, runs tours.
LL Pelican's Pouch, rooms in a 2-storey
colonial building, and 3 secluded cottages.
Pelican University is ideal for groups
housing up to 23 people at US$60
per person per day including 3 meals.

South of Dangriga *p825*
LL Hamanasi, Sittee Point, T520-7073,
www.hamanasi.com. 17-acre resort,
18 rooms and suites with a/c. Swimming
pool, full dive operation.
LL-L Jaguar Reef Lodge, south of Hopkins,
just north of Sittee River, T520-7040,
www.jaguarreef.com. 18 a/c rooms with
fridges. Central lodge on sandy beach, pool,
diving, snorkelling, kayaking, mountain bikes,
birdwatching and wildlife excursions.

Guesthouse programme

An interesting alternative to Punta Gorda is to stay in indigenous villages as part of the Guesthouse Programme, run by villagers and the non-competitive cooperative the Toledo Ecotourism Association (TEA).

A number of villages have joined together and developed a visitor scheme. Each has built a well-appointed guesthouse, simple, but clean, with sheets, towels, mosquito nets, and oil lamps, ablutions block, and a total of eight bunks in two four-bunk rooms. Visitors stay here, but eat in the villagers' houses on rotation, so each household gains equal income and only has to put up with intrusive foreigners for short periods. Villages taking part include San Miguel, San José (Hawaii), Laguna and Blue Creek. Santa Elena is an isolated village beyond the Dump towards San Ignacio. Medina Bank is more accessible as its location is just off the southern highway. Barranco is a Garífuna village south of Punta Gorda, accessible by boat or poor road.

Local attractions include: San Antonio waterfall; caves at San José (Hawaii); Uxbenka ruins and caves 2½ hour walk from San Antonio (turn right just before Santa Cruz), with commanding view from ruins; and Río Blanco waterfalls, 10 minutes beyond the village. For Uxbenka and Santa Cruz, take Chun's bus on Wednesday and Saturday at 1300 from San Antonio and arrange return time. Do not take Cho's bus, it does not return. Many village men and children speak English. The local indigenous people have been relearning old dances from elderly villagers and are trying to rescue the art of making and playing the harp, violin, marimba and guitar for evening entertainments. Home-made excursions are arranged; these vary from a four-hour trek looking at medicinal plants and explaining

agriculture, to seeing very out-of-the-way sights like caves and creeks (take boots, even in dry season). The village tour could be skipped, although by doing this on your own you deprive the 'guide' of income.

One night for two people, with a forest tour and two meals, costs US$42.50 for a basic package or US$55 for a full package (including music and dancing) but all profits go direct to the villages, with no outsiders as middlemen. Dorms are US$11 per person. Profits are ploughed back into the villages' infrastructure, schools and other community projects. A US$5 registration fee is payable at the TEA Office at the Tourist Information Center (BTB Building) in Punta Gorda, T722-2531, before visiting the village. The staff provide information about participating villages, key attractions, tours and courses, and take bookings and arrange transport. You may have to arrange your own transport, or a vehicle can be hired. Staff at TEA will be able to advise. Hitching is not recommended as some villages are remote. 'Market' buses leave Punta Gorda every Monday, Wednesday, Friday and Saturday at 1130 or 1200 depending on the village. They come from the villages on the morning of the same days departing early at 0400, 0500 or 0600, depending on the village.

The Homestay Programme is a scheme that involves staying with the family in their house. Several villages in the area participate. As you live with the family there is less privacy and the experience is more intense. Details can be discussed with Dem Dats Doin in Punta Gorda, who will also help you arrange transport. Both programmes are a unique way to explore the Maya villages; you are unlikely to find such an experience elsewhere.

L-AL Beaches and Dreams, Sittee Point, T523-7078, www.beachesanddreams.com. 4 extremely well-furnished beachfront rooms. Price includes full breakfast, Dangriga transfer, use of bikes and kayaks.

AL Lillpat Resort, T/F520-7019. Just 4 a/c rooms on the Sittee River, pool, restaurant, bar, very convenient for Cockscomb, birdwatching and fishing. Fishing specialist.

AL-A Hopkins Inn, on beach south of centre, T523-7013, www.hopkinsinn.com. White cabins with private bathroom, very clean and friendly, German spoken. Price includes breakfast, knowledgeable owners.

AL-E Toucan Sittee, T523-7039, www.toucansittee.info. 400 yds down river from **Glover's**. Run by Neville Collins, lovely setting, rooms with screens and fans, bunkhouse, hot water, or fully equipped riverside apartments, grow most of their own fruit and veg, also over 50 medicinal plants.

C-D Sandy Beach Lodge, 20-min walk south of village, T522-2023, T523-7006. A women's cooperative, run by 14 women who work in shifts, arrive before 1900, 6 thatched beachside *cabañas*, quiet, safe, friendly, clean.

C-D Tipple Tree Beya Inn, just before Sandy Beach Lodge, T520-7006, www.tippletree.com. English/American run, 4 rooms in a wooden house and small cabin apartment, camping possible.

E Swinging Armadillos Bunk House, on the pier, T522-2016. 5 rooms, outdoor shower, seafood restaurant, bar, usually the best in the village.

E-F Glover's Guest House, on river bank, T802-2505. 5 rooms, restaurant, camping, jungle river trips, family-run and starting point for the boat to **North East Caye** (see below). Price per person.

Glover's Reef *p825*
Glover's Reef Atoll
LL-AL Manta Reef Resort, Glover's Reef Atoll, 3 Eyre St, Belize City, T223-1895, F223-2764.Just 9 individual cabins with full facilities, in perfect island setting, 1-week packages available only, reservations essential, excellent diving and fishing, good food. Highly recommended.

North East Caye
B-E Glover's Atoll Resort, T614-7177, www.glovers.com.bz. No reservations needed, 8 cabins with wood-burning stoves, US$99-269 per person per week (from camping to cabins; nightly prices also) plus 9% tax. Weekly rates include round-trip transportation from Sittee River. Occasional rice and seafood meals, bring food, some groceries and drinking water (US$1.50 a gallon) available. Best to bring everything you will need. Facilities are simple and basic. Guests are sometimes invited to help out.

Placencia *p825, map p826*
Rooms may be hard to find in the afternoon (after arrival of the bus from Dangriga). Usually several houses to rent, US$200-550 per week, see the ads at the tourist information centre.

LL The Inn at Robert's Grove, north of the air strip and Rum Point Inn, T523-3565, www.robertsgrove.com. Luxury resort with 2 pools, massage service, boats and jacuzzis set on a white-sand beach shaded by the odd palm. Rooms are spacious, comfortable and quiet and the restaurant serves good, filling food. Entertainment and tours, including PADI diving from its own marina, are organized. Friendly bar staff.

LL Turtle Inn, on beach close to airstrip, T523-3244, www.turtleinn.com. Completely destroyed by Hurricane Iris, owner Francis Ford Coppola rebuilt this impressive resort in local and Balinese style set around a circular pool with restaurant and spa.

LL-L Miramar Apartments, T503-3095. Immaculate, fully equipped apartments close to the beach that range from 1-bed studios to 3-bed apartments.

L-AL Easy Living Apartments, T523-3524, www.easyliving.bz. Well-appointed roomy apartments with space for up to 4, at which

point they represent good value – TV, fully equipped kitchen, good location at the centre of town, on the sidewalk.
AL Ranguana Lodge, T523-3112, www.ranguanabelize.com. Wooden cabins on the ocean, very clean.
AL-A Cozy Corner, on the beach, close to Serenade and Yellow House, T523-3450, cozycorner@btl.net. 10 rooms with fridge, TV, some cheaper rooms without a/c and good restaurant (Tue-Sun) in front.
AL-A Serenade Guest House, T523-3380, www.serenadeguesthouse.com. Spacious, airy rooms, all with a/c and private bath. Upstairs rooms more expensive. Welcoming owners. Restaurant next door. Parking available.
AL-B Trade Winds Hotel, South Point, T523-3122, trdewndpla@btl.net. 9 very colourful cabins in a spacious private plot on the south beach.
AL-C Seaspray, T523-3148, www.seaspray hotel.com. Very nice, comfortable and friendly. Good-value rooms across a range of prices from beachside *cabañas* to small doubles in original building. Popular De Tatch restaurant on the beach, see Eating.
A Dianni's Guest House, T523-3159, www.diannisplacencia.com. 6 spacious rooms and 3 *cabañas* with a/c, most with 1 double and single bed. Fridge, coffee and tea provided, nice balcony with hammocks, internet available.
B-D Paradise Vacation Hotel, down by the piers, T523-3179, www.paradisevacation belize.com. 12 rooms with private baths and 4 rooms with shared.
C Deb and Dave's Last Resort, on the road, T523-3207, www.toadaladventure.com. 4 very good budget rooms with shared bathroom, hot water, kayak and bike rental. Walk-ins only, no advance reservations. Also runs tours in local area.
C The Yellow House, T523-3481, www.ctbelize.com. A bright yellow building, directly behind Serenade, with 4 very comfortable rooms with communicating

doors, so excellent for a family or group of friends. Front rooms have microwave, coffee machines and fridges. Excellent value. Also runs **B-C** Garden Cabañas, www.garden cabanas.com, and **A-C** Mahogany Beach.
C-D Lydia's Guesthouse, T523-3117, lydias@btl.net. 8 double rooms with shared toilet and shower, situated across the sidewalk on a quiet part of the beach. Kitchen facilities. Simple, but very chilled and with free Wi-Fi or a PC for hire. Recommended.
D Omar's Guest House, on the sidewalk, T667-0651.
E Lucille's Rooms. Run by Lucille and family, private bath, fans, meals by arrangement.

Camping
Camping is possible on the beach or under the palms.

Around Placencia *p827*
Maya Beach
L Green Parrot Beach Houses, T523-2488, www.greenparrot-belize.com. Beach houses on stilts, all with sea view, sleep up to 5, kitchenettes, open-air restaurant and bar.
L Singing Sands Inn, T520-8022, www.singingsands.com. 6 thatched cabins with bathrooms, hot water, fans, ocean view, snorkelling in front of the resort at False Caye, restaurant and bar on the beach.
L-AL Maya Breeze Inn, T523-8012, www.mayabreezeinn.com. 4 cottages on the beach, 2 with a/c, restaurant across the road.
AL-A Barnacle Bill's, T523-8010, www.gotobelize.com/barnacle. 2 *cabañas* with queen-sized bed, sleeper/sofa in the living/dining area, full kitchen, private bath and fans.

Mango Creek/Independence
A-B Hello Hotel, Independence, T503-2028, hotelhello@yahoo.com. Run by Antonio Zabaneh at the shop where the bus stops, clean, comfortable, helpful.
C-D Ursella's Guest House, T503-2062. 9 simple rooms with shared or private bath, TV.

F Hotel above People's Restaurant.
Very basic, ask to borrow a fan and lamp,
shower is a bucket of water in a cabin,
basic restaurant.

Cayes near Placencia *p827*
L Frank's Caye, reservations through
Serenade Guesthouse, T523-3380,
www.belizecayes.com. 3 *cabañas* with
private baths, restaurant and bar.
L-AL Ranguana Caye, reservations
through Robert's Grove, T523-3565,
www.robertsgrove.com. 3 *cabañas*,
each with a double and single bed, gas
stove, private hot showers and toilet in
separate building. BBQ pits so bring food,
but meals also available.

Camping
Lime Caye (tent camping is crowded). Very
good fishing at certain times of the year
(contact local guides for information).

**Cockscomb Basin Wildlife Sanctuary
and around** *p827*
There is usually space on arrival, but to
guarantee accommodation, contact the
Belize Audubon Society, see page 774.
L Mama Noots Backabush Resort,
T422-3666, www.mamanoots.com. Electricity
from solar, wind and hydro system, most
fruits and vegetables grown organically on
the grounds of the resort. 6 double rooms
and 1 duplex thatched *cabaña* that sleeps
up to 6. Private baths.
A-E Mejen Tz'il's Lodge, T520-3032;
isaqui@btl.net. Owned by Liberato and
Araceli Saqui, screened rooms with double
beds or bunk beds, veranda, private hot
water showers and toilets in a separate
building, restaurant on premises.
B-E Park HQ. Purpose-built cabins and
dorms (**D-E** per person) with a picnic
area. Drinking water is available, also earth
toilets, but you must bring all your own food,
drinks, matches, torch, sleeping bag, eating
utensils and insect repellent. Nearest shop
is at Maya Centre.

D Nu'uk Che'il Cottages, Maya Centre,
T520-3033, nuukcheil@btl.net. Simple
thatched rooms in a garden next to the
forest, take the botanical trail and learn
about Maya medicine from Aurora Saqui;
Ernesto, her husband, can arrange transport
to the Park HQ.

Punta Gorda *p828*
AL Sea Front Inn, 4 Front St, T722-2300,
www.seafrontinn.com. 14 rooms with
private bath hot water, a/c, TV, restaurant
with great views. Maya Island Air and
Tropic Air agents.
AL-B Punta Caliente, 108 José María
Nuñez St, T722-2119. Private bath,
hot water, fan and cable TV, good
value, restaurant.
AL-C Tate's Guest House, 34 José María
Nuñez St, T722-0147, tatesguesthouse@
yahoo.com. A/c, cheaper without, clean,
hot water, bathroom, TV, parking, friendly,
breakfast before 0730, laundry.
B-D Pallavi, 19 Main St, T702-2414,
gracemcp@hotmail.com. Tidy, balcony,
clean, friendly.
C Mahung's Inn, corner North and Main St,
T722-2044, mahungsinn@hotmail.com.
Reasonable, private bath, cable TV, also
rents mountain bikes, US$5 per day.
C St Charles Inn, 23 King St, T722-2149,
stcharlespg@btl.net. All with bath, spacious
rooms, fan or a/c, cable TV, good.
C-D Nature's Way Guest House, 65 Front
St, T702-2119. Clean, friendly, good breakfast,
camping gear for rent. Recommended.
D-E Wahima, on waterfront, T722-2542.
Clean and safe, with private bath, owner
Max is friendly and informative. Also
rents kitchenettes.
F Airport Hotel. Price per person,
quiet, OK, communal bathrooms,
clean, spartan. You can flag down
the 0500 bus to Belize in front of Wahima
or Pallavi, buy a ticket the night before
to get a reserved seat.

San Pedro Columbia *p830*
L Fallen Stones Butterfly Ranch, 3 miles beyond the village, up very steep, rocky hills, leave messages at **Texaco** in Punta Gorda, T722-2167. Excellent site, ideal for visiting the ruins of Lubaantun. Owned by an Englishman, working butterfly farm exporting pupae. Price includes tax, service and breakfast, jungle tours, laundry, airport transfers.
C-D Dem Dats Doin, T722-2470, demdatsdoin@btl.net (see page 829).
E Guesthouse. Dormitory beds. You can get drinks and breakfast at the large yellow stone house.

Blue Creek *p831*
There is basic accommodation at the house at the beginning of the trail to the caves. Blue Creek is one of the villages participating in the **TEA Guesthouse Programme**, see page 833.
E Roots and Herbs, halfway to Blue Creek; turn left at **Jim's Pool Room** in Manfredi Village, then continue about 5 miles. Simple cabins with mosquito nets, Pablo is an excellent guide, good food. Price per person.

San Antonio *p831*
D Bol's Hilltop Hotel. Showers, toilets, meals extra, clean.

🅞 Eating

Dangriga *p824*
¥ Ritchie's Dinette, on main street north of police station. Creole and Spanish food, simple, large portions, popular for breakfast.
¥ Riverside Café, south bank of river, just east of main road. Nicer inside than it looks, good breakfast, good service and food, best place to get information on boats to Tobacco Caye.
¥ Ruby's Rainforest Café, past the Riverside Café, on the beach. Open sporadically but good food. Be prepared for Ruby – she's quite a character, very

friendly, and you'll get the full family history. No good if you're in a hurry!

South of Dangriga *p825*
¥¥ Ronnie's Kitchen, turquoise house on stilts north of the police station in Hopkins (follow the road left from the bus stop). 0630-2100. Excellent food, friendly, includes burritos and chicken, Ronnie also gives good local advice.

Placencia *p825, map p826*
¥¥¥ French Connection, set to move location (Apr 2009), T523-3656. Considered one of the top restaurants in Belize, this serves sumptuous, fairly priced international cuisine in a friendly but classy environment. Recommended.
¥¥¥ La Dolce Vita, near Wallen's grocery, T523-3115. Italian restaurant who claim to have the best wine selection in town.
¥¥¥ Merlene's, in the Bakeder area south of the Placencia Village dock. One of the best, opens early for good breakfast.
¥¥¥ The Secret Garden, near Wallen's grocery, T523, 3617. International cuisine served in a relaxed, chilled out atmosphere
¥¥¥-¥¥ Rumfish, T523-3293, rumfish@ btl.net. Good quality restaurant, very popular with locals.
¥¥ Belgian Cafe, above Michelo, 21 Harbour Place. Open 0700-1430, Mon-Fri. Friendly European-owned café, with Wi-Fi, great for breakfasts.
¥¥ Cozy Corner, on the beach T523-3280. Very nice beachside bar and restaurant. Good, mid-priced barbecue and grilled seafood.
¥¥ De Tatch Café, just before the north end of the sidewalk. Closed Wed. Said to be the the best coffee in town, certainly is hugely popular with excellent seafood specials at night and snappy service; a winner.
¥¥ The Garden Brew Coffee House, in a little garden next to Wallen's Hardware. Nice coffee and home-made muffins.
¥¥ Pickled Parrot Bar and Grill, close to Wallen's Hardware. Closed Sun. Good pizza, chicken and seafood.

¶¶-¶ BJ's Restaurant, see map, T523-3131.
Good fried chicken and traditional Creole
food. Recently, owners Percy and Betty have
begun to experiment and now they offer
good Asian stir-fries and pizza – inexpensive
and popular with locals.
¶ Daisy's, sidewalk, close to De Tatch.
Cheap meals and good ice cream.
¶ John the Bakerman, follow the signs.
Freshly baked bread and cinnamon buns
each afternoon at 1800 (takeaway only).
¶ Omar's Creole Grub, Creole diner.
¶ Tutti-frutti Ice Cream Parlour, Placencia
Village Square. Great Italian ice cream, made
by real Italians!
¶ Wendy's Creole Restaurant and Bar,
close to the gas station. Good food but
service can be very slow so leave plenty
of time if you're meeting transport.

Around Placencia *p827*
¶¶ Goyo's Inn/Restaurant Independence,
Mango Creek. Family-owned, good food.
¶ Lola's Café and Art Gallery, sign at south
end of Seine Bight. For an entertaining
evening with dinner, run by local artist
Lola Delgado.
¶ White house with green shutters, Mango
Creek, behind People's. Better than at
People's. Book 2 hrs in advance if possible.

Punta Gorda *p828*
Several cafés around the market area with
good views over the bay.
¶¶ Bobby's Main St. Serves excellent fish
dishes, Bobby is a local fishing guide and
arranges trips.
¶¶ Earth Runnings Café and Bukut Bar,
Main Middle St, T702-2007, bukutbar@
hotmail.com. Closed Tue. Great, idiosyncratic
bar and café with regular live music that also
provides tourist information, internet and
occasional yoga and therapeutic massage.
¶¶ Emery Restaurant, Main St, T702-2990.
Local dishes and seafood, popular with locals,
reasonable prices, friendly.
¶¶ Gomier's, behind the Sea Front Inn.
For vegan meals and soya products.

¶¶ Marian's Bayview Restaurant, 76 Front St,
T722-0129. Serves traditional Belizean and
East Indian dishes.
¶ El Cafe, opposite Mahung's Inn.
Inexpensive café fare.
¶ Marenco's Ice cream Parlour, Main St.
Serves good ice cream and food as well.

San Antonio *p831*
¶ Theodora or **Clara**, next to hotel.
Both do meals with advance notice.
Local specialities are *jippy jappa/kula*,
from a local plant, and chicken *caldo*.

⊕ Entertainment

Dangriga *p824*
Listen for local music 'Punta Rock', a
Garífuna/African-based Carib sound, now
popular throughout Belize. **Local Motion
Disco**, next to Cameleon, open weekends,
punta rock, reggae, live music. **Riviera Club**,
between bridge and Bank of Nova Scotia,
popular nightclub at weekends. Home-
made instruments are a Garífuna speciality,
particularly drums. Studios can be visited.

Placencia *p825, map p826*
Tipsy Tuna Sports Bar, popular sports
and karaoke beachside bar, from 1900.
Barefoot Beach Bar at Tipsy Tuna
is a very popular joint on the beach
with live music and a happy hour
1700-1800. Closed Mon.

⊕ Festivals and events

Dangriga *p824*
18-19 Nov Garífuna, or Settlement
Day, re-enacting the landing of the
Black Caribs in 1823, having fled a
failed rebellion in Honduras. Dancing
all night and next day; very popular.
Booking advisable for accommodation.
Private homes rent rooms, though.
Boats from Puerto Barrios to Punta Gorda

(see Transport) tend to be full, but launches take passengers for US$10 per person.

▲ Activities and tours

South to Dangriga p823
There is a wide variety of day and overnight excursions, from US$30 per boat holding 6-8 people. Contact Kevin Andrewin of **Manatee Tour Guides Association** on arrival. Community phone, T02-12031, minimum 48 hrs' notice is advisable, ask for Alice or Josephine.

Dangriga p824
Dangriga Dive Centre, T522-3262. Derek Jones arranges fabulous trips to the cayes.
Pelican Beach Hotel runs tours to Cockscomb Basin, Gales Point and citrus factories.
Rosado's Tours, 35 Lemon St, T522-2119. Government Services.
Treasured Travels, 64 Commerce St, T522-2578, is very helpful, run by Diane.

South of Dangriga p825
Second Nature Divers, T523-7038, divers@btl.net, or enquire at **Hamanasi**. English-owned, good guides and equipment, recommended spot to visit is Sharks' Cave.

Glover's Reef p825
Off The Wall Dive Center, Dangriga, T614-6348, www.offthewallbelize.com, offers dive courses. Friendly owners Jim and Kendra Schofield offer packages that include transport, accommodation, meals and diving.

Placencia p825, map p826
Scuba-diving and snorkelling
Full PADI scuba-diving courses are available at most local dive shops, around US$350. Some dive operators listed below base themselves out of high-end resorts.
Of the in-town operators **Seahorse**, **Joy Tours** and **Splash** enjoy solid reputations. However, environmental standards and genuine concern for the reef is somewhat lacking – this could be improved with a little encouragement. Prices are from about US$70, plus 9% sales tax, for 2-tank dives, US$105 to outer reef (gear extra).
Seahorse Dive Shop, T523-3166, www.belizescuba.com, ask for Brian Young. Good selection of gear. **Splash**, T523-3058, www.splashbelize.com. Owners helpful – specialize in dive training and courses. **Joy Tours**, T651-0464, www.njoybelize.com, is new but locally recommended. **Naudi Dive Shop**, T523-3595, www.nauticalinn belize.com, and **Robert's Grove Dive Shop**, T523-3565, www.robertsgrove.com.
Ocean Motion Guide Service, T523-3363, www.oceanmotion placencia.com, is a reputable snorkelling tour operator. Snorkel trips generally cost US$60-70 for a full day and US$30-45 for a half day, including gear. There is a whale shark and snorkelling fee of US$15 in operation from 1 Mar-3 Jul charged by **Friends of Nature**.

Fishing
Fishing, especially saltwater fly-fishing, is excellent, with recognized world-class permit fishing. Reputable licensed guides and tour operators include **Kurt Godfrey**, T523-3277, and **Earl Godfrey**, T523-3433, lgodfrey@ btl.net. **Destinations Belize**, offers combination cayes camping and fishing/ snorkelling trips, plus whale shark interaction tours, T523-4018, www.destinations belize.com. **Bruce Leslie**, from **Tutti-frutti**, T523-3370. Rates for a full day of light tackle and fly fishing, including lunch, average US$325, maximum 2 anglers per boat for fly-fishing.

Kayaking
Toadal Adventures, T523-3207, www.toadaladventure.com, is a reputable tour operator for multi-day kayaking trips to the cayes and Monkey River.

Cockscomb Basin Wildlife Sanctuary and around *p827*

The Belize Audobon Society, see page 774, runs the reserve. The most knowledgeable guides to the reserve live in Maya Centre; contact Julio Saqui, of **Julio's Cultural Tours**, T608-4992, www.cockscombmayatours.com, who runs the village shop and can look after any extra luggage. At **Greg's Bar**, on the main road in the middle of the village, you can contact **Greg Sho**, an experienced river and mountain guide who can arrange kayak trips.

Full-day Mopan Mayan cultural tours of Maya Centre Village are available including visits to workshops on traditional Mayan cooking, crafts, language and natural tropical medicines. Contact **Liberato** or **Araceli Saqui** at Maya Centre Village. Tour operators in Placencia run day trips for US$65.

Punta Gorda *p828*
Green Iguana Eco Adventures, T722-2475, provides a wide range of tours and services. **Tide Tours**, Main St, T722-2129, www.tidetours.org, organizes eco-tours. Also try **Sun Creek Tours**, suncreek@hughes.net.

◉ Transport

South to Dangriga *p823*
Boat
Gales Point can be reached by inland waterways from **Belize City**, but buses have largely superseded boat services.

Bus
At least 2 daily Southern Transport buses run between **Belize City** and Dangriga on the coastal road.

Dangriga *p824*
Air
Maya Island Air and Tropic Air, T522-2129, from **Belize City** several daily, also from **Punta Gorda** via Placencia. Tickets from the airstrip, or **Pelican Beach Hotel**.

Boat
A fast skiff leaves 0900 (be there at 0800) on Sat for **Puerto Cortés, Honduras**. Irregular service, departing from north bank of river by bridge, T522-3227, ask for Carlos. Check procedures for exit formalities in advance. Enquire locally about hiring a boat for around US$25 per person in a group to **Belize City**.

Bus
From **Belize City**, Southern Transport, Magazine St, several daily from 0800, returning daily from 0530, US$5, 3½-4 hrs (bus passes entrance to the Blue Hole National Park); also via Coastal Hwy, 2 hrs. Bus to **Placencia** daily at 1200 and 1700, 3 hrs, US$5, via Hopkins and Sittee River, US$4. To **Belmopan**, 2½ hrs, US$4.50. The Southern Transport bus terminal is at the junction at the south end of town.

South of Dangriga *p825*
Bus
From Dangriga or Placencia, **Southern Transport** around 0700, 1500, 1530 and 1800, which travel on to Placencia or Dangriga depending where you are going. James Bus from Dangriga to Placencia around 1130 and 1700, Placencia to Dangriga around 0600 and 1400.

To **North East Caye**, 4 daily Southern Transport buses (T522-2160) from **Dangriga** to Sittee River and Glover's Guest House at Sittee River Village (see Sleeping). Also 3 daily buses from **Placencia**. Or, take any bus going south to the Sittee junction and take a ride to the guesthouse. If you get lost, phone ahead for help. At 0800 on Sun a sailing boat leaves for the reef, 5 hrs, US$20 per person 1 way (price included in accommodation package), returns Sat. At other times, charter a boat (skiff or sailing boat, US$200 1 way, up to 8 people, diesel sloop US$350, up to 30 people).

Placencia *p825, map p826*
Air
Placencia has its own airstrip. Maya Island Air and Tropic Air (T523-3410) fly several times a day to **Belize City** (international and municipal), also to **Dangriga** and **Punta Gorda**.

Boat
The Hokie Pokie Water Taxi, T523-2376, leaves from the gas station behind the M'n M store, across the lagoon to **Independence/Mango Creek** at 0630, 0730, 0800, 1430 and 1630, 15 mins, US$5. Returning 0645, 1000, 1600, 1700. From here, buses depart for Punta Gorda and Belize City.

The Gulf Cruza, T523-4045, provides a regular weekly service linking Placencia and Puerto Cortés in Honduras. The journey can be quite choppy. From Placencia the boat leaves the dock near the petrol station at 0930 every Fri, passing Big Creek at 1000 to complete immigration formalities. It arrives in Puerto Cortés from1200, US$50. Buy tickets in the Placencia Tourism Center, US$55. Return service leaves Puerto Cortés on Mon at 1100 arriving 1330.

Bus
Placencia Peninsula Shuttle, T607-2711, runs from the Placencia dock to the Zeboz Hotel 5 times daily each way, US$2.50-5. See the tourist office for schedule.Buses to **Dangriga** direct at 0600, 0630, 1400, 3 hrs, US$5. Express, US$6. Direct busess to **Punta Gorda**, from Placencia with **Southern Transport** or **James Buses**. Alternatively take the Hokie Pokie Water Taxi, see above, to catch the James Bus Line buses from Independence Village, at 0930, 1045, 1500, 1630, 1645, 1½-2½ hrs. For buses to **Dangriga**, 1 hr, **Belmopan**, 2½ hrs and **Belize City**, 3½ hrs, also catch the boat to Independence. Buses leave at 0715, 0815, 1015, 1415 and 1645. Check times and fares at the Placencia tourist centre at the dock next to the Shell gas station.

Cockscomb Basin Wildlife Sanctuary and around *p827*
Bus
Can be booked at time of reservation, or locals will drive you from Maya Centre, otherwise it is a 6-mile, uphill walk from Maya Centre to the reserve – allow 2 hrs for the walk to Maya Centre. If you leave early in the morning going either way you are likely to see quite a lot of wildlife. All buses going south from **Dangriga** go through Maya Centre, 40 mins, US$4; and north from Placencia, return buses from 0700 onwards to Dangriga. If walking, leave all unwanted gear in Dangriga in view of the uphill stretch from Maya Centre, or you can leave luggage at Julio's little store in Maya Centre for a daily fee.

Taxi
A taxi from **Dangriga** will cost about US$50, it is not difficult to hitch back.

Punta Gorda *p828*
Air
Airstrip 5 mins' walk east of town. Daily flights with **Maya Island Air** and **Tropic Air**, T722-2008, from Dangriga, Placencia, Belize City (both airports). Tickets at **Alistair King's** (at Texaco station), **Bob Pennell's** hardware store on Main St, the **Sea Front Inn** on Front St or the offices alongside the airstrip. Advance reservations recommended.

Requena's Charter Services, T722-2070, leaves Punta Gorda for **Puerto Barrios, Guatemala**, at 0900 every day, US$20, 1 hr, return journey leaves at 1400. Guatemalan operator **Pichilingo** provides a similar service, leaving Puerto Barrios for **Punta Gorda** at 1000, returning at 1400.

Bus
James bus line to Belize City (6½ hrs, longer in heavy rain), daily at 0400, 0500, 0600, 0800, 1000 and 1200. James bus returns from Belize City daily, leaving hourly between 0515 and 1015, then 1215, 1315, 1515 and 1545. To **San Antonio** from square, see below; buses

to **San Pedro Columbia** and San José, Wed and Sat 1200, return Wed and Sat morning. Buses can be delayed in the wet season. For the latest information on schedules, contact the Tourist Information Centre or **Dem Dats Doin** at the pier by the Customs House.

San Antonio p831
Bus and car
From **Punta Gorda**, 1-1½ hrs, US$1.50, Mon, Wed, Fri, Sat 1230, from west side of Central Park, also 1200 on Wed and Sat, continuing to **Santa Cruz**, **Santa Elena** and **Pueblo Viejo** (1 hr from San Antonio). Or, hire a pickup van in **Dangriga**; or get a ride in a truck from the market or rice cooperative's mill in Punta Gorda (1 leaves early afternoon); or go to the road junction at Dump, where the northern branch goes to Independence/ Mango Creek, the other to San Antonio; 6 miles, either hitch or walk. Bus from San Antonio to Punta Gorda, Mon, Wed, Fri and Sat 0530, also 0500 Wed and Sat (having left Pueblo Viejo at 0400). If going to **Dangriga**, take the 0500, get out at Dump to catch 0530 **Southern Transport** bus going north. This area is full of places to explore and it is worth hiring a vehicle.

● Directory

Dangriga p824
Banks Bank of Nova Scotia, MasterCard and Visa, and ATM. Belize Bank (Visa cash advances). **Immigration office** South end of Commerce St. **Internet** Val's laundry and Pelican Beach Hotel. **Laundry** Val's, Mahogany Rd near Bonefish, also has internet access. **Medical services** New Southern Regional Hospital, T522-3832. **Post office** Mahogany Rd. **Telephone** BTL office is on the main street.

Placencia p825
Banks Atlantic Bank south end of the village witn ATM. Also ATM opposite Wendy's. **Internet** On the main road is Purple Space Monkey Village, and Placencia Office Supplies, on the main road near the centre. Good machines, fast access. also at De Tatch. **Medical services** Basic medical care available at Placencia Medical Center, T223-3292, behind St John's Memorial School on the sidewalk. **Post office** Mon-Fri 0800-1200, 1330-1600. **Telephone** BTL office in the centre where you can make international calls. Payphones here, at the gas station and the ballfield.

Around Placencia p827
Banks Belize Bank, Mango Creek/ Independence, is open Fri only 0900-1200.

Punta Gorda p828
Banks Belize Bank, at one end of the park, will change excess Bz$ for US$ on production of passport and ticket out of the country. They do not change quetzales and charge US$5 for advancing cash against Visa and MasterCard, changes TCs. Mon-Thu 0800-1300, Fri 0800-1630. You can change Bz$ for quetzales at Customs in Punta Gorda (ask for Emilio from **Grace** restaurant) and Puerto Barrios. **Western Union**, is run by Mahung's, corner North and Main St, Mon-Sat 0800-1200, 1330-1700. **Internet** Several places in town. Internet, next door to Sea Front Inn. Carisha's, by clock tower. **Laundry** Sony's Laundry Service near airstrip. **Telephone** The BTL office on Main St and King St.

Contents

Footprint features

Border crossings

At a glance

◉ Getting around Buses are efficient and economical.

◉ Time required 2-3 weeks would be best if you have the time.

☼ Weather High 20°Cs throughout the year, with most rainfall from May-Oct.

✖ When not to go The wettest weather and highest temperatures are in May, when it's hot and humid.

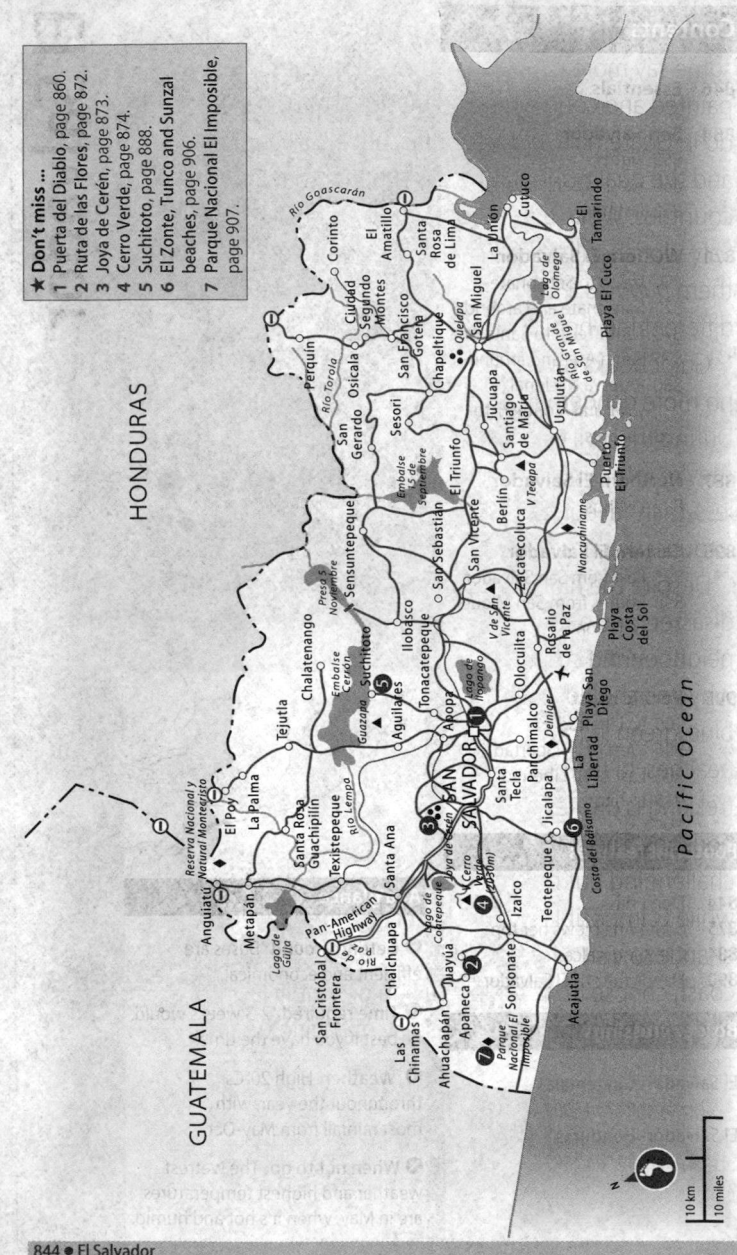

★ **Don't miss …**
1 Puerta del Diablo, page 860.
2 Ruta de las Flores, page 872.
3 Joya de Cerén, page 873.
4 Cerro Verde, page 874.
5 Suchitoto, page 888.
6 El Zonte, Tunco and Sunzal beaches, page 906.
7 Parque Nacional El Imposible, page 907.

HONDURAS

GUATEMALA

Pacific Ocean

10 km
10 miles

El Salvador is a lively country and the people are just as friendly – some say more so – than in the rest of Central America. Ornately painted and colourful buses bump from place to place, just as they do in Guatemala and Honduras, but El Salvador has better roads and the quality of the buses is superior to that of neighbouring countries. While the rest of Central America relies on tortillas, Salvadorians fill them with beans, cheese or meat and call them *pupusas*. Pinning it down is difficult but there's a slightly different feel here from neighbouring countries.

Guidebooks tend to urge caution, but in reality El Salvador is no more dangerous than other Central American countries. During the civil war, Salvadorians sought refuge abroad; now they're returning, bringing with them a gang culture and other less-than-favourable imports from the United States, although as a tourist you are rarely subjected to any of these social problems.

Despite the high rate of gang-related crime, frequent natural disasters and a tourist infrastructure less developed than its neighbouring countries, there are some compelling reasons why you should visit El Salvador: dramatic volcanic landscapes, blue-green lagoons, horizon-filling panoramas and golden beaches. In the northern hills around El Poy and Perquín the trekking is divine, with far-reaching views across staggered horizons. The stark cinder cone of Volcán Izalco offers a challenging but rewarding trek from the slopes of Cerro Verde, while El Imposible National Park provides adventurers with the chance to visit a forest newly accessible to visitors. Along the coast, choose from surfing, diving or simply lazing around and watching the endless display of Pacific sunsets.

Essentials

The smallest of the Central American republics, El Salvador's tiny territory of Pacific beaches, volcanic peaks and mountains holds a population just shy of six million – slightly more than Nicaragua with a land mass just one-sixth that of her eastern neighbour. El Salvador's main attractions have not been promoted compared with those in neighbouring countries, and the lack of a developed tourist infrastructure stops some travellers from passing through. But visitors that do take the time, always leave with memories of a friendly people, warm and helpful, and the increasingly rare experience of occasionally being the only traveller in town. The devastating earthquakes of early 2001 literally brought the country to its knees. For the visitor, the most visible sign of damage is the destruction and damage caused to hundreds of the nation's colonial churches. Today most areas are rebuilt and people and businesses are back on track once again.

Life in El Salvador focuses strongly on San Salvador. All roads lead towards the capital with just a few exceptions. Planning your trip will involve either a visit to San Salvador or at least travelling through it. Fortunately the country is so small that the capital can make a convenient base, thus avoiding the hassle of dragging your bags across the country.

Where to go

San Salvador is a cosmopolitan city with a variety of architectural styles that have been created by the multitude of rebuilding projects in a history dogged by earthquakes. The city centre is always busy and widely thought of as unsafe at night, so newcomers are best advised to head for the western areas around Boulevard de los Héroes, with its shopping malls and restaurants, and the residential districts of Escalón and the Zona Rosa with its newly opened major shopping malls – Multiplaza, Hipermall and La Gran Vía – with fancy stores, branded boutiques and a variety of restaurants and night clubs.

Throughout El Salvador volcanoes dominate the landscape, and the scenery is one of its main attractions. Close to the capital, **Parque Balboa** affords fine views through the dramatic Puerta del Diablo (Devil's Door) and from the Mirador in the centre of the mountain village of **Los Planes de Renderos**. Below Los Planes de Renderos is **Panchimalco**, an old village with a growing handicraft industry where the cultural traditions are being kept alive and hosts the yearly Procesión de Las Palmas, a spectacular floral procession in the beginning of May. **Parque Nacional Cerro Verde**, just west of San Salvador, is a popular excursion for its prospect over Izalco and Santa Ana volcanoes and the deep-blue waters of the beautiful **Lago de Coatepeque**. Closed for two years after earthquakes, Cerro Verde recuperated its very unique flora and fauna and was declared a protected natural area and is now open to foreign visitors. Also a short distance west of the capital are the country's main archaeological sites of **San Andrés** and the unique **Joya de Cerén**, where a Maya settlement has been preserved under volcanic ash. There are no grand temples and sculptures, but the dwellings and everyday objects found here are the only ones of their type preserved from the Maya era in Central America. Just north of San Salvador is **Cihuatán**, El Salvador's largest archaeological park and the largest city in Mesoamerica at the time of the Toltec. The main city of the west is **Santa Ana**, which is also a good base for visiting the sites of **Tazumal** and **Casa Blanca** to the west.

A little further south, **Sonsonate** is an interesting town leading to the **Ruta de las Flores** a handful of villages climbing the volcanic chains with good scenery and waterfalls, pleasant hiking and a smattering of crafts.

There are very few pockets of undisturbed land, mainly because El Salvador is farmed intensively. On the border with Guatemala and Honduras is **Montecristo**, a remnant of cloud forest administered jointly by the three countries, while another such survivor is **Parque Nacional El Imposible**, one of the largest national parks in Central America. Just south of El Imposible is the **Barra de Santiago** protected natural area, home to a wide variety of species in the best preserved mangrove in the country.

North of San Salvador, near the Honduran border, are the towns of **La Palma** and **San Ignacio**, where handicrafts of brightly painted wood and other styles are made. Also north, but heading more to the east, is **Suchitoto**, one of the best-preserved colonial towns currently enjoying a revival that takes advantage of the beautiful scenery around Cerrón Grande resevoir. In eastern El Salvador are the cities of **San Vicente** and **San Miguel**, the port of La Unión/Cutuco and many small traditional towns. Those interested in the recent civil war can visit **Perquín**.

The Pacific coast at **La Libertad** is only a short trip from the capital and is a good place to start exploring the Balsam coast to the west, the surfing beaches and to get a feel for the country as a whole. The beaches of the **Costa del Sol** are definitely worth a stop for their long stretches of sand and estuaries. The **Gulf of Fonseca** has islands with secluded beaches which you can explore. In some parts of the country the infrastructure for tourism is quite rudimentary, but in others (such as the capital and nearby places of interest and some of the beach resorts) it is well developed.

Suggested itinerary With so many crossings and borders, the options for travel in and around El Salvador are very flexible. Points of interest are spread throughout the country so there is no natural route to travel. If you want to visit **Parque Nacional El Imposible**, go for the La Hachadura crossing, drift through **Apaneca** and on to **San Salvador** before heading north to **Suchitoto**. If you're going to Honduras, head to **El Poy** if you want to drop into Santa Rosa de Copán or Gracias, or **Perquín** if you want Gracias or Tegucigalpa. For Nicaragua head to El Amatillo. El Salvador is subtly different to the other Central American nations. While you could shoot through the main highlights in 10 days, hang out for two to three weeks and soak up the nuances. If you've got the time, you'll enjoy the difference.

When to go
The most pleasant months are from November to January. El Salvador is fortunate in that temperatures are rarely excessively high. The average for San Salvador is 28°C with a variation of only about 3°C. March to May are the hottest months; December to February the coolest. There is one rainy season, from May to October, with April and November being transitional periods; there are only light rains for the rest of the year: the average annual rainfall is about 1830 mm. Highest temperatures and humidity will be found on the coast and in the lowlands, with the heat at its greatest from March to May.

Sport and activities

El Salvador has been a popular **surfing** destination for several decades, from La Libertad heading west. Beyond this there is some diving in the coastal area and volcano lagoons.

National parks provide opportunities for trekking and nature walks in particular at Parque Nacional Cerro Verde close to San Salvador and in the more remote parks of Montecristo and Parque Nacional El Imposible.

Getting there

Air

From Europe To Miami with any transatlantic carrier, then to San Salvador with **American Airlines** or **Taca**. **Iberia** flies from Barcelona and Madrid via Miami.

The international airport is at Comalapa, 62 km southeast of San Salvador off the Coastal Highway, reached by a four-lane toll highway. There is a tourist information desk at the airport, which is open sporadically. If closed, you can still pick up some useful leaflets. Taxis and buses provide regular links to the capital.▸▸ *See Transport, page 867.*

There is a 13% tax on international air tickets bought in El Salvador and an airport departure tax of US$32 for anyone staying more than six hours. The airport departure tax is now included in the ticket. The phone number for the airport authorities (**CEPA**) is T2339-9455. The airport has offices for all the main car rental companies and there are two banks, a tourist office and **Grupo Taca** and **American Airline** offices. Border formalities tend to be relatively brief although searches may be carried out.

From USA and Canada The main connection is with Miami. Other cities with flights to San Salvador are Atlanta, Dallas/Fort Worth, Houston, Los Angeles, Montreal, New Orleans, New York, Orlando, Phoenix, San Diego, San Francisco, Washington and Toronto.

From Central America and Mexico There are flights from all capitals and many larger cities in Mexico.

From South America Good connections to Colombia with a few flights to Barranquilla and Bogotá. Also connections with Buenos Aires, Cali, Caracas, Cartagena, Cucutá, Guayaquil, Quito, Lima, Medellín, Santa Marta and Santiago. Some flights via San José or Panama City.

Road

Several border crossings with neighbouring countries. To the west the Pan-American Highway arrives from Guatemala at San Cristóbal through Santa Ana (see page 879), Las Chinamas (to the south, see page 879) and La Hachadura (see page 909), which is handy for Parque Nacional El Imposible. To the northwest the crossing is at Anguiatú (see page 879). Also to the northwest the crossing at El Poy (see page 891) leads to southern Honduras, as does the crossing to the northeast at Perquín (see page 899) and to the east at El Amatillo (see page 899).

Getting around

Road

Bus Bus services are good and cover most areas, although the buses are usually crowded. The best time to travel by bus is 0900-1500; avoid Friday and Sunday afternoons. All bus routes have a number, some also have a letter. Strange as it may seem, the system works and the route numbers don't change. In early April 2009 there was a bus price war. That, combined with the wide variations in oil prices, means that bus prices are changing erratically. Buses are brightly painted, particularly around San Miguel.

Transport is not difficult for the budget traveller as nearly all buses have luggage racks. For bigger bags there is space at the back where a couple of seats have been removed, so sit near there if you want to stay close to your bag. However, when problems on buses do occur they are usually at the back of the bus. The cheaper alternatives to the **Pullman buses**, which cross to Guatemala and Tegucigalpa from Puerto Bus Terminal in San Salvador, have luggage compartments beneath them and the luggage is tagged.

Car At the border, after producing a driving licence and proof of ownership, you are given a *comprobante de ingreso* (which has to be stamped by immigration, customs and quarantine), this is free of charge and you get the vehicle permit for 60 days. You need to have a passport from the same country you have your drivers licence or an international drivers licence and that you have not been in the country for more than 60 days. (If you are a foreigner residing in El Salvador you need to get a Salvadorian drivers licence.) You receive a receipt, vehicle permit and vehicle check document. Under no circumstances may the 60 days be extended, even though the driver may have been granted 90 days in the country. A few kilometres from the border the *comprobante* will be checked. When you leave the country a *comprobante de ingreso* must be stamped again and, if you don't intend to return, your permit must be surrendered. Do not overstay your permitted time unless you wish to be fined. Leaving the country for a few days in order to return for a new permit is not recommended as customs officials are wise to this and may demand bribes. To bring a vehicle in permanently involves a complex procedure costing thousands of dollars.

Petrol costs per US gallon US$2.80 (super), US$2.40 (regular), US$2 (diesel). All are unleaded. **Roads** are very good throughout the country, but look out for crops being dried at the roadside or in central reservations. Take care of buses, which travel very fast. Third-party, **insurance** is compulsory in El Salvador and can be arranged at the border (enquire first at consulates). Under the 1996 law, **seat belts** must be worn; the fine for not doing so is US$57. The fine for **drink-driving** is US$57. If your alcohol level is very high you go straight to jail and have to await the sentence. Do not attempt to bribe officials. For more information, call **Ministerio de Transporte** ① *T2281-0678 0679.*

Sleeping

As the most industrialized of the Central American states El Salvador has an impressive selection of international-standard business hotels in San Salvador. The country also has a good selection of more expensive hotels for those taking weekend breaks from the capital. At the lower end there is no shortage of cheap accommodation, but there is a shortage of good, cheap accommodation. If you have the time, shop around, don't check into the first hotel you come to. If travelling at holiday times book accommodation in advance. **Ximena's Guest House** off Boulevard de Los Héroes is recognized as a hotel where backpackers meet up.

Eating

Pupusas, stuffed tortillas made of corn or ricemeal, are the quintessential Salvadorian dish. They come in several varieties including *chicharrón* (pork crackling), *queso* (cheese) and *revueltas* (mixed), and are typical, tasty and cheap. They are sold at street stalls, and are better there than at restaurants, but beware stomach infection from the accompanying *curtido* (pickled cabbage). On Saturday and Sunday nights people congregate in *pupuserías*. *Pavo* (turkey sandwiches) is common and good, as are *frijoles* (red beans). A *boca* is an appetizer, a small dish of yucca, avocado or chorizo, served with a drink before a meal. Apart from in San Salvador, restaurants tend to close early, around 2000.

Coffee makes an excellent souvenir and is good value and delicious. **Beer Suprema** is stronger than Pilsener, while **Golden Light** is a reduced-alcohol beer. *Chaparro* is El Salvador's *chicha* or *agua ardiente*. Although it is illegal to sell it, everyone has their source. *Chaparro curado* contains fruit or honey. It is a favourite at election times when alcohol sales are banned. Water bottles are emptied and filled with the clear *chaparro* for illegal swigging on the streets. Chicha is a traditional alcoholic drink made from corn, sometimes with a trace of pineapple. When made well it can taste similar to white wine. It is a trademark of the Maya and is particularly well made in the western village of Izalco. Ask at the tourist office there for a Chicha contact to purchase a sample.

Festivals and events

1 Jan New Year's Day.
Mar/Apr Holy Week (3 days, government 10 days).
1 May Labour Day.
10 May Mothers' Day.
First week of Aug Corpus Christi (half day).
15 Sep (half day).

2 and **5 Nov** (half day).
24 Dec (half day) and **Christmas Day**. Government offices are also closed on religious holidays. Look in newspapers for details of regional fiestas and other fairs. There are many craft fairs, for example at San Sebastián and San Vicente.

Shopping

The best place to buy arts and crafts is in the village where the items are originally made; **Ilobasco** for ceramics, **San Sebastián** for hammocks and **La Palma** for painted wooden boxes, **Nahuizalco** for baskets and furniture of wicker and jute. If you cannot go there in person, the markets in **San Salvador** (Mercado Ex-Cuartel and Mercado de Artesanía) sell many of these items at a slightly higher prices. Branches of Nahanché have outlets in the major shopping malls with good quality handicrafts from all over the country.

Essentials A-Z

Accident and emergency
Police: 911; Fire service: T2527-7300; Red Cross: T2222-5155; Hospitals: T2225-4481; Public hospital: Rosales T2231-9200; Public maternity: Hospital de Maternidad T2529-8200; Private Hospital Pro Familia: T2244-8000; Private Maternity: T2271-2555; Hospital Gynecologico: T2247-1122.

Customs and duty free
All personal luggage is allowed in free. Also permitted: 50 cigars or 200 cigarettes, and 2 litres of liquor, 2 used cameras or a

video recorder, 1 personal stereo, 1 portable computer and new goods up to US$1000 in value (best to have receipts). No restrictions on the import of foreign currency; up to the amount imported and declared may also be exported. Check with www.aduana.gob.sv for full information.

Phone numbers for Salvadorian border crossings: Hachadura: T2420-3767, Chinamas: T2401-3601; San Cristóbal: T2441-8109; El Poy: T2335-9401; Angiatú: T2401-0231; Amatillo: T2649-9388.

Electricity

110 volts, 60 cycles, AC (US-style flat-pin plugs). Supply is far from stable; important electrical equipment should have surge protectors.

Embassies and consulates

For more countries, visit www.rree.gob.sv.
Belgium, Av de Tervuren 171, 2nd floor, 1150 Brussels, T733-0485.
Canada, 209 Kent St K2P 1Z8, Ottawa, Ontario, T613-238-2939, also in Montreal and Vancouver.
Germany, Joachin-Karnatz-Allee 47, 10557, Berlín (Tiergarten), T30-206-4660, www.botschaft-elsalvador.de.
Israel, 4 Avigail, Apto 4, Abu-Tor, Jerusalem, Israel. 93551, T267-28411.
Italy, Via Gualtiero Castellini 13, Scala B int, 3, 00197 Roma, T06-807-6605.
Japan, Kowa 38, Building 803, Nishi Azabu 4 Ch, Tokyo, Japan 106, T33499-4461.
Spain, Calle Serrano 114, 2 Edif Izquierda, 28006 Madrid, T91-562-8002.
Mexico, Calle Temístocles 88 Col Polanco, México DF, T5281-5725.
UK, 2nd floor, 8 Dorset Sq, London, NW1 6PU, T020-7224-9800.
US: 1400 Sixteenth N.W Washington, DC 20036, T202-387-6511; with consulates in several other large cities.

Health

Gastroenteritic diseases are most common. Visitors should take care over what they eat during the first few weeks, and should drink *agua cristal* (purified bottled water). The bags of water sold in the street are not always safe and taste somewhat of rubber. Cases of denque are rare in adults. For diarrhoea, mild dysentery, amoebas and parasitic infections get *Nodik* tablets from any chemist or large supermarket, approx US$14 for a 3-day cure. El Salvador has one of the best health systems in Central America, so the capital is a good place to sort out problems. You can get a stool sample taken at the **Pro-Familia Hospital**, 25 Av Norte, near Metro Centro, which gives you the result in about 6-12 hrs. See also page 51.

Internet

Internet cafés are widespread in the capital and are now commonplace in smaller places outside San Salvador. Most hotels will offer both internet service and wireless connection.

Language

Spanish is the official language and English is widely understood in business and travel industry-related circles.

Media

Newspapers in San Salvador include *Diario de Hoy* (right wing), www.elsalvador.com, and *La Prensa Gráfica* (centre) every morning including Sun, www.laprensagrafica.com; both have the most listings of cultural events in San Salvador. *Co Latino* is a left-wing newspaper. *El Mundo* in the afternoons except Sun. US newspapers and magazines available at leading hotels.

Of the 80 **radio stations**, 1 is government owned and several are owned by churches.

There are 4 commercial **television stations**, all with national coverage, and 1 government-run station with 2 channels. There are several cable channels, all with CNN news, etc. Most hotels and many guesthouses in San Salvador have cable.

Money → *US$1=8.75 colones (fixed).*
El Salvador adopted the dollar on 1 Jan 2001 and the national currency – the colón – is now totally replaced. All US coinage and notes are widely used, although you may have problems with US$20 bills and above. There are some small shops and street merchants that still price their products in colones, but they are in the minority.

ATMs and exchange

Do not find yourself in the countryside without cash or credit cards; traveller's cheques (TCs) are of limited use outside the capital and major cities. You can use credit cards in pretty much any store (except small *tiendas*). See under San Salvador, Banks, page 868 regarding exchange of TCs. Be aware that some banks will want to see your original purchase receipt. Credit cards are widely accepted and are charged at the official rate. There are international Visa and MasterCard ATMs in El Salvador and larger cities throughout the country. For cash advances on Visa or MasterCard, go to **Aval-Visa** or **Banco de America Central de El Salvador**.

All ATMs and banks give US dollars in cash (so no need for exchange). Pretty much all gas stations have ATMs.

Cost of living and travelling

El Salvador is reasonably priced and 2 people should be able to travel for US$40 per person per day. However, the range of services open to the foreign tourist is still limited (although growing) so the quality of hotels is not as good as in neighbouring countries for the same price.

Opening hours

Banks Mon-Fri 0900-1700, Sat 0900-1200, closed between 29-30 Jun and 30-31 Dec.
Businesses Mon-Fri 0800-1200, 1400-1730; Sat 0800-1200.
Government offices Mon-Fri 0730-1530.

Post

Airmail to and from Europe can take up to a month, but is normally about 15 days; from the USA, 1 week. Certified packets to Europe cost US$9.25 per kilo and regular service is US$8.50 per kilo, good service; swifter, but more expensive, is **EMS** (US$34 per kg to Europe). Courier services are much quicker, but cost more. The correct address for any letter to the capital is 'San Salvador, El Salvador, Central America'.

Safety

Traditionally El Salvador has a reputation for violence and crime. In part this is a legacy of many years of civil war although this has been improved through a more active role of the police in later years. The reality is that most people visiting El Salvador return with reports of friendly, open people. Locals will talk incessantly about the country's problems and dangers but few actual examples materialize. Be cautious until you find your own level of comfort and always ask local advice. Statistically El Salvador has the unenviable distinction of having the worst levels of violent crime in the continent. This derives from Salvadorian gang culture (*maras*) and most visitors will see nothing of this activity. Since Mar 1996, the army and the civil police (PNC) have been patrolling the highways in an effort to reduce crime. Do not stop for lone gunmen dressed in military-looking uniforms. If renting a car, buy a steering lock. Visitors to San Salvador should seek advice on where is not safe both inside and outside the city.

Telephone → Country code T+503.

The **international direct dialling** code (to call out of El Salvador) is T00; 144+00 for Telefonica. There are no local area codes within El Salvador. There is a network of public phones for telecommunications companies – all use prepaid phone cards that only work in the company's particular machines. Available at most street corners, supermarkets, gas stations to small stores they can be used for local and international calls, but make sure the card is from the same company as the public phone. The cards come in several denominations (US$1-3, US$5, US$10, US$25, etc). Mobile phones are very cheap. You can get a SIM card for US$3 and if you need a mobile phone you can get one from as little as US$12.

Some hotels will provide direct dialling – by far the easiest option. Dial T114 for **Information** (English spoken) and details of new phone numbers in capital.

Time
- 6 hrs GMT.

Tipping

In upmarket restaurants: 10%, in others, give small change. Check your bill as most now add the 10% at the end (if they have, an additional tip is not needed). Nothing for taxi drivers except when hired for the day; airport porters, *boinas rojas* (red berets), US$2 per bag.

Tourist information
Corporación Salvadoreña de Turismo (Corsatur), at the Ministry of Tourism, Edificio Carbonel No1, Col Roma Alameda Dr Manuel Enrique Araujo Pasaje Carbonel San Salvador, T2243-7835; T2241-3200, www.elsalvador.travel. Provides information locally and on the web.
Revue, www.revuemag.com. English-language magazine published in Guatemala, with a section on El Salvador. Contains articles on places to visit and details of activities.

Useful websites
www.alfatravelguide.com Has a comprehensive listings of hotels throughout the country.
www.elsalvador.com Site of *El Diario de Hoy*– look in 'Otros Sitios' for tourist info.
www.diariocolatino.com Site of the leftist *Co Latino* newspaper.
www.laprensa.com.sv Site of *La Prensa Gráfica* newspaper.
www.mipatria.net and **www.theother elsalvador.com** Access to useful information.
www.turismo.com.sv Lists of hotels, restaurants and interesting places to visit.

www.utec.edu.sv Site of Centre for Investigation of El Salvadorian Public Opinion (CIOPS) with information in Spanish on El Salvadorian political and social issues.

Visas and immigration
Every visitor must have a valid passport. No visas are required for European, US, Canadian, Australian or New Zealand nationals. The government website www.rree.gob.sv has a full list of country requirements.

Overstaying the limit on a tourist card can result in fines. Immigration officials can authorize up to 90 days stay in the country; extensions may be permitted on application to Migración, Centro de Gobierno (see under San Salvador). As of 2006, when El Salvador signed a Central America-4 (CA-4) Border Control Agreement with Guatemala, Honduras, and Nicaragua, you have to visit a country outside of these 4 to re-enter and gain 90 days. Always check at a Salvadorian consulate for any changes to the rules.

Weights and measures
The metric system is used alongside certain local units such as the *vara* (836 mm), *manzana* (7000 sq m) and the *quintal* (45 kg). Some US weights and measures are also used; US gallons are used for gasoline and quarts for oil.

San Salvador

→ *Colour map 6, C1. Altitude: 680-1000 m. Population: 2,297,282 including suburbs).*

Surrounded by a ring of mountains in a valley known as 'Valle de las Hamacas', San Salvador has suffered from both natural and man-made disasters. El Salvador's capital is a bustling cosmopolitan city with a rich blend of architectural styles; modern, yet retaining the charm of the Spanish era with the privilege of being one of the first European cities in the New World. Today, crumbling buildings await renovation and restoration, or the arrival of the next earthquake to deliver the final death knell. As always, some areas speed to recovery, and the shopping malls and wealthy suburbs to the west stand out in the pollution-filled valley. The further northwest you get from the city centre the higher you climb and the cleaner the air becomes.

San Salvador itself does not have many natural attractions, but there are several day trips to nearby volcanoes, crater lakes and beauty spots such as Los Planes de Renderos, the Puerto del Diablo and San Salvador's own volcano, Boquerón, which has a newly inaugurated paved road all the way to the top. There are, surprisingly, many green areas and trees planted alongside the streets giving the city a refreshing atmosphere. If you spend a few days in the city and surrounding area you could be pleasantly surprised by how easy it is to get around and how much there is to do. ➤➤ *For listings, see pages 862-870.*

Ins and outs

Getting there The **international airport** (SAL) is at Comalapa, 62 km southeast of San Salvador towards Costa del Sol beach, reached by a four-lane, toll highway. Some domestic flights use the old airport at Ilopango, 13 km east of the capital. Most **international buses** arrive at the Puerto Bus terminal, although luxury services and **Ticabus** have their own terminals. Domestic bus lines use terminals at the east, south and west ends of the city. ➤➤ *See Transport, page 867.*

Getting around The main focal points of the city are the historical centre, the commercial district some 3 km to the west around Boulevard de los Héroes, and the residential and commercial districts of Escalón and Zona Rosa another 2 km further west. City buses and taxis are needed to get between the three (see page 867).

Four broad streets meet at the centre: Avenida Cuscatlán and its continuation Avenida España run south to north; Calle Delgado and its continuation Calle Arce, with a slight blip, from east to west. This principle is retained throughout: the *avenidas* run north to south and the *calles* east to west. The even-numbered *avenidas* are east of the central *avenidas*, odd numbers west; north of the central *calles*, they are dubbed Norte, south of the central *calles* Sur. The even-numbered *calles* are south of the two central *calles*, the odd numbers north. East of the central *avenidas* they are dubbed Oriente (Ote), west of the central *avenidas* Poniente (Pte). Sounding more complicated than it is, the system is straightforward and quickly grasped.

Tourist information Corporación Salvadoreña de Turismo (Corsatur) ① *Edificio Carbonel No 1, Col Roma Alameda Dr Manuel Enrique Araujo Pasaje Carbonel San Salvador, T2243-7835, www.elsalvador.travel, Mon-Fri 0800-1230, 1330-1730.* Good information on buses, archaeological sites, beaches and national parks. Texaco and Esso sell good maps at some of their service stations. The best maps of the city and country (US$3 and

US$2 respectively) are available from the **Instituto Geográfico Nacional** ① *1 Calle Pte y 43 Av Norte 02310, Col Flor Blanca, T2260-8000*. The **Instituto Salvadoreño de Turismo ISTU** ① *Calle Rubén Darío 619, San Salvador Centre, T2222-8000*, has useful information about the 13 government-run **Turicentros** recreation and water parks in the country and on Cerro Verde and Walter T Deininger national parks.

Best time to visit The climate is semi-tropical and healthy, and the water-supply relatively pure. Days are often hot, especially in the dry season, but the temperature drops in the late afternoon and nights are usually pleasantly mild. Since it is in a hollow, the city has a very bad smog problem, caused mainly by traffic pollution. Efforts are being made to reduce vehicle emissions.

Safety The city centre is considered by many to be dangerous after dark, but the area north of Bulevar de los Héroes up to around San Antonio Abad is quite safe. As a general rule, stay out of poorly lit areas and keep to main roads where there are more people around. At night, taxis are a sensible alternative if you don't know where you're going exactly.

Armed security personnel are commonplace. There is a heightened atmosphere of tension in some areas. In downtown markets, don't carry cameras, don't wear watches or jewellery and don't flash money around.

Background

San Salvador was first established by Gonzalo, brother of the conquistador Pedro de Alvarado, in 1525. The settlement was named in honour of Christ the Saviour who, Pedro believed, had saved him from death in his first attempt to conquer the peoples of **Cuscatlán**, as the region was then known. In 1528 the town was moved to a site near present-day Suchitoto, only to be relocated 20 years later to its present location. Over the next three centuries it developed into the capital of the province of San Salvador. The city has been destroyed by earthquakes 14 times since 1575, the last being in 1986. Nowadays the buildings are designed to withstand seismic shocks, and most stood up well to the earthquake of 2001.

Sights

A number of important buildings are near the intersection of the main roads in the historic centre. On the east side of Avenida Cuscatlán is the **Plaza Barrios**, the heart of the city. A fine equestrian statue looks west towards the renaissance-style **Palacio Nacional** (1904-1911). To the north is the **new cathedral**, which was left unfinished for several years after Archbishop Romero suspended its construction to use the money to reduce poverty. Work was resumed in 1990 and completed in 1999, the last consecration of a cathedral of the millennium. It now stands as a beacon of tranquillity amid the dirt and noise of the downtown capital. It commands a striking presence, gleaming white and modern, its façade flanked by two giant murals vividly splashed with the colourful work of the country's most famous artist, **Fernando Llort**. Inside it is quite bare, but for the fabulous circular stained-glass window of a dove surrounded by a hundred shards of brilliant yellow glass, which in turn is framed by yellow stars set in deep lapis lazuli-blue glass. Beneath the cathedral, a new chapel has been created to house the tomb of assassinated **Archbishop Oscar Romero**.

East of Plaza Barrios, on Calle Delgado, is the **Teatro Nacional**, whose interior has been magnificently restored. If you walk along 2 Calle Oriente you pass, on the right, **Parque Libertad** with the rebuilt church of **El Rosario** on the eastern side where José Matías Delgado, father of the Independence movement, lies buried. The interior, decked out in modern sculpture, is fascinating, although knocked slightly by the earthquake. The **Palacio Arquiepiscopal** is next door. Not far away to the southeast, on 10 Avenida Sur, is another rebuilt church, **La Merced**, whose belltower rang out Father Delgado's tocsin call to Independence in 1811.

One block north, across Calle Delgado, is the **Teatro Nacional** on Plaza Morazán, with a monument to General Morazán. Heading east along Delgado is the **Mercado Ex-Cuartel**,

⓵ San Salvador

Sleeping	Happy House 4	Ximena's Guest House 6
Alameda 1	Real Intercontinental	
Florida 3	San Salvador 2	Eating
Grecia Real 7	San Carlos 5	Pueblo Viejo 2

and the expected confusion of sounds and smells that besiege the senses. Nearby are some of the cheapest hotels in the city. Running west from the Teatro Nacional, Calle Arce leads to **Hospital Rosales** and its own gardens. On the way to the hospital is the great church of **El Sagrado Corazón de Jesús**, which is well worth a visit; don't miss the stained-glass windows. Turn left (south) here and after one block you come to the **Parque Bolívar**, with the national printing office to the south and the Department of Health to the north.

Four streets north of Calle Arce is the Alameda Juan Pablo II, an important road for bus transport, on which stands **Parque Infantil**, where you will find the Palacio de los Deportes. One block west is the **Centro de Gobierno**, with many official buildings.

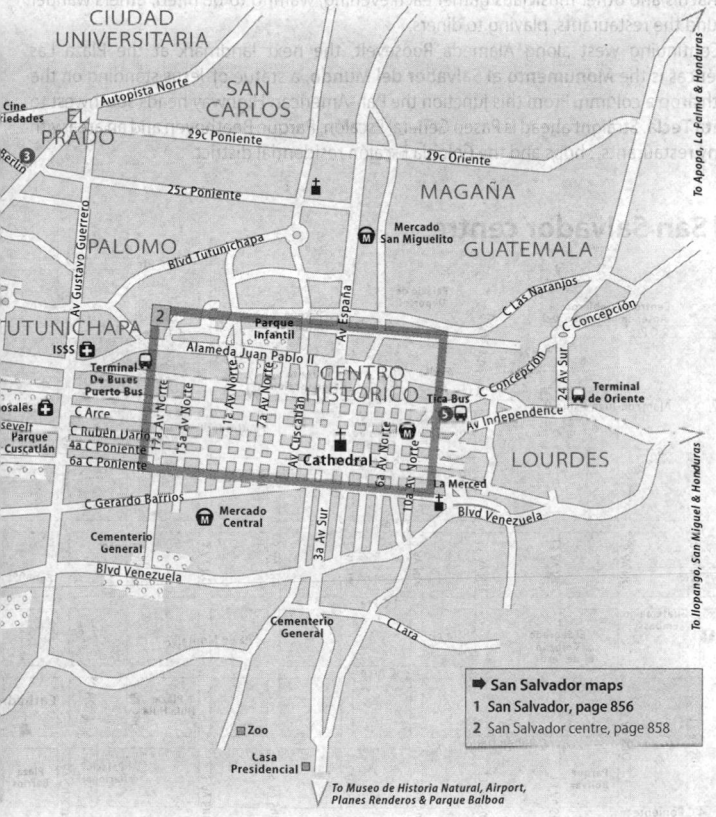

San Salvador maps
1 San Salvador, page 856
2 San Salvador centre, page 858

To Museo de Historia Natural, Airport,
Planes Renderos & Parque Balboa

Bars & clubs
Café La T 5
El Arpa 6
La Luna 3

The north side of Parque Bolívar is Calle Rubén Darío (2 Calle Poniente), which becomes Alameda Roosevelt, then Paseo General Escalón as it runs through the commercial and residential districts west of the centre. Heading west this boulevard first passes **Parque Cuscatlán**. A major junction is with 49 Avenida: to the south this avenue soon passes the national stadium, **Estadio Olímpico Flor Blanca**, before becoming the main highway to the international airport. To the north, 49 Avenida crosses Alameda Juan Pablo II beyond which it changes name to **Bulevar de los Héroes**, home to the fashionable shopping centres, **Metrocentro** and the newer **Metrosur**, the **Hotel Real Intercontinental**, some of the city's better restaurants and a glut of fast-food places, which is a busy area at all times, especially at night. At the Shell station by Metrocentro, mariachis and other musicians gather each evening, waiting to be hired; others wander around the restaurants, playing to diners.

Continuing west along Alameda Roosevelt, the next landmark at the Plaza Las Américas is the **Monumento al Salvador del Mundo**, a statue of Jesus standing on the Earth atop a column. From this junction the Pan-American Highway heads southwest to **Santa Tecla**. Straight ahead is Paseo General Escalón, Parque Beethoven and an area with many restaurants, shops and the Colonia Escalón residential district.

② San Salvador centre

Sleeping 🛏
American Guest House **1**   El Palacio **3**
Centro Histórico **2**

Another important residential and entertainment region is the **Zona Rosa** and **Colonia San Benito**, reached either from the Pan-American Highway or from Escalón. In this leafy suburb, some of the most elegant restaurants and the **Hotel Sheraton Presidente** and **Hotel Hilton Princess** (where former US president Clinton stayed while on his Central America tour) are found. **MUNA (Museo Nacional de Antropología David J Guzman)** ① *Feria Internacional, Av de la Revolución y Carretera a Santa Tecla, T2243-3750, Tue-Sun 0900-1700, US$1.50*, is a brand new museum worth visiting showcasing exhibits on the country's archaeological and historical past as well as numerous cultural events. Just north of the museum at the end of Avenida Revolución is **MARTE (Museo de Arte de El Salvador)** ① *T2243-6099, Tue-Sun 1000-1800, US$1.50, café and shop in lobby*. This new, privately run modern arts museum has permanent exhibits depicting the history of Salvadoran painters with temporary exhibits of artists from Latin America and other parts of the world.

A little further north is **El Arbol de Dios** ① *La Mascota y Av Masferrer, T2224-6200, Mon-Sat 1000-2200*, an arts and crafts store, restaurant, museum and garden, operated by the famed Salvadorian artist Fernando Llort, who designed the façade of the Metropolitan Cathedral and is known for his naïf-style wood paintings. The display here also includes the work of other artists.

In Colonia San Benito is **Museo de Ciencias Físicas Stephen Hawking** ① *Av Reforma 179, T2223-3027, Mon-Sat 1000-1400, US$1.25*, with sections on astronomy, ecology, electronics and biochemistry. Interactive exhibits about the sciences with monthly lectures on scientific topics. This area also has many art galleries such as **Galería Espacio** ① *Av La Capilla*, **Galería 1-2-3** ① *Calle La Reforma*, **La Pinacoteca** ① *Blv Hipódromo*, to name a few. See local press for details.

Worth visiting is the **María Auxiliadora church**, locally known as 'don Rua', situated in Barrio San Miguelito. This multi-coloured marble temple – a copy of the cathedral in Turin (Italy) – is one of the city's landmarks, displaying a Venetian clock tower and with a spectacular view from the belltower.

Museo Militar de las Fuerzas Armadas ① *behind the presidential palace of San Jacinto at the former Cuartel El Zapote*, has a collection of exhibits of weapons, uniforms and decorations of the armed forces, and weapons captured from FMLN guerrillas. **Mercado de San Miguelito** is an indoor market located close to don Rua. Safer than many of the other city markets and famous for its *comedores* which offer typical Salvadoran dishes (difficult to find outside a traditional Salvadorian home) at

➡ **San Salvador maps**
1 San Salvador, page 856
2 San Salvador centre, page 858

economic prices. There are several food stalls throughout the place – look for the area dedicated just to *comedores* at the far end of the market. It's a great place to watch people go about their shopping and to enjoy the display of stalls.

A good sightseeing tour of the surrounding area heads south to a couple of local places of interest. Lasting most of the day by bus (No 12) or two to three hours by car it starts a few blocks southwest of the main square on the eastern side of the Mercado Central. It includes the **San Salvador Zoo** ① *T2270-0828, Wed-Sun 0900-1600, US$0.60*, which was recently renovated and although small, is quiet and attractive. Just three blocks away is the newly restored **Museo de Historia Natural** ① *Parque Saburo Hirao*, with interesting displays on prehistoric findings and a herbal medicine garden. To get there, take bus No 2 ' Zoo', and No 12 from the centre. You then pass the **Casa Presidencial** and go on up to the new residential district in the mountain range of **Planes de Renderos**. This place is crowned by the beautiful **Parque Balboa** ① *daily 0800-1800*, and there's a good view of the city from El Mirador at the foot of the park. Parque Balboa is a **Turicentro**, with cycle paths, playground and gardens. From the park a scenic road runs to the summit of **Cerro Chulo**, from which the view, seen through the Puerta del Diablo (Devil's Door), is even better. There are local buses to Puerta del Diablo and Parque Balboa (No 12 from eastern side of Mercado Central and No 12-MC marked 'Mil Cumbres') almost hourly. Bus No 17 goes from the same location to Panchimalco through Los Planes de Renderos so you can get off at the junction there and take the No 12 to Parque Balboa and Puerta del Diablo.

The **Puerta del Diablo** consists of two enormous, nearly vertical rocks which frame a magnificent view of the Volcán San Vicente. The rocks are very steep but the sides can be climbed on reasonable paths for an even better view. A little beyond the car park and drinks stands at the Puerta del Diablo is a path climbing up a further summit, from which there are 360° views: to the coast, Lago Ilopango, the capital and volcanoes, including San Salvador, Izalco and Cerro Verde and San Vicente.

At the foot of Cerro Chulo is **Panchimalco** (see below). The route to Panchimalco (No 17 from Mercado Central) and the coast branches off the road to Parque Balboa at the village of **Los Planes**, a few kilometres before the park.

Around San Salvador

Many places can be visited in a day from San Salvador either on the frequent bus services or by car. Closest to the city is south to the indigenous village of **Panchimalco**, heading east are the beautiful setting and views around **Lago de Ilopango**; and to the southwest the crater of **Volcán San Salvador** (see Santa Tecla, page 873).

Heading west towards Santa Ana, but still manageable in a day, are the archaeological sites of **Joyo de Cerén**, El Salvador's Pompeii, and **San Andrés** and the peaks of **Volcán Izalco** and **Cerro Verde** (see page 874) with the deep blue waters of **Lago de Coatepeque** in the crater below. The limits of a comfortable weekend trip will take you to the garden park of **Ichanmichen**, which is restful (see page 909), and the pyramid of **Tazumal** (west of Santa Ana) is also worth a visit (see page 876). At weekends the coast around La Libertad (see page 905) is very popular. Bus 495 from the Terminal del Occidente goes to the seaside resort of **Costa del Sol** (see page 908).

Panchimalco

This small town and the surrounding area is home to the Pancho, descendants of the Pipil tribes, one of the region's dominant indigenous groups prior to conquest. This is one of the few places in El Salvador where you can still see indigenous people in traditional dress. Streets of large cobbles, with low adobe houses, thread their way between huge boulders at the foot of Cerro Chulo. A very fine baroque colonial church, Santa Cruz, has a white façade with statues of eight saints. Inside are splendid woodcarvings and wooden columns, altars, ceilings and benches. There is a bell inscribed with the cipher and titles of the Holy Roman Emperor Charles V, and a colourful cemetery. The Casa de La Cultura in the main street has frequent cultural events and crafts stores. The **Fiesta de Santa Cruz de Roma** is held on 12-14 September, with music and traditional dances; on 3 May (or the second Sunday of the month) there is the procession of **Las Palmas**. Bus 17 from Mercado Central at 12 Calle Poniente, San Salvador, every 45 minutes (45 minutes), or minibus from near Mercado Central, very crowded but quicker (30 minutes), and cheaper (US$0.80).

Lago de Ilopango
Beyond the four-lane highway to Ilopango airport (14.5 km east) lie the deep waters of Lago de Ilopango. Surrounded by mountains, the views around El Salvador's largest and deepest crater lake are impressive. Before the conquest local people used to appease the harvest gods by drowning four virgins here every year. Private chalets make access to the lake difficult, except at clubs and the **Turicentro Apulo**, but it is well worth a visit. The eastern shore is less polluted and is reached from Cojutepeque. There are a number of lakeside cafés and bathing clubs, some of which hire dug-outs by the hour. The cafés are busy in the dry season (try **Teresa's** for fish dishes), but often closed in the middle of the year. **Hotel Vista del Lago ①** *3 km from Apulo turn-off on the highway*, is on a hill top. Bus 15, marked Apulo, runs from the bus stop on Parque Hula Hula to the lake (via the airport), 1¼ hours, US$1. Entrance to the Turicentro **camping site** costs US$0.60.

Volcán San Salvador
This large massif at 1839 m has an impressive crater, more than 1.5 km wide and 543 m deep, known as **El Boquerón**. About 2 km to the east is the equally dramatic peak of **El Picacho** (1960 m), which dominates the capital. Buses leave a block from Plaza Merliot. By car you turn right just after the Plaza Merliot Mall and continue to the end of the road where a newly paved road take you up the volcano. A walk clockwise round the crater takes about two hours; the first half is easy, the second half rough. The views are magnificent, if somewhat spoilt by TV and radio towers. The area by Boqueron is now a park administrated by the Ministry of Tourism. The area is closed off, with guards during opening hours (0800-1500 daily). **La Laguna** botanical garden is near the summit. The inner slopes of the crater are covered with trees, and at the bottom is a smaller cone from the eruption of 1917.

You can follow the road north and then turn right through extensive coffee plantations and forest to reach the summit of **El Picacho**. This also makes an excellent climb from the Escalón suburb of San Salvador, in the early morning preferably, which takes about three to four hours return trip (take a guide). The easy access, great views and fresh climate has made the Volcano of San Salvador a popular destination for people in the capital, and as a result new restaurants have opened their doors in recent years. See Eating, page 863. Another access to the volcano from the city side is by **Ecoparque El Espino ①** *run by El Espino Cooperative T2289-0749/69 www.ecoparqueelespino.com, US$1.50*. The entrance is by the Polideportivo in Ciudad Merliot, take bus No 42 C especial and walk 100 m. They have several trails, bike rental and small cafeterias. The trails end at a mirador with a panoramic view of the city.

Hotel and guesthouse prices

LL over US$150	L US$100-150	AL US$66-99
A US$46-65	B US$31-45	C US$21-30
D US$12-20	E US$7-11	F under US$7

Restaurant prices

🍴🍴🍴 over US$15	🍴🍴 US$8-15	🍴 under US$8

See pages 45-48 for further information.

● Sleeping

San Salvador *p854, maps p856 and p858*
In the downtown area, some hotels lock their doors very early. Many cheap *hospedajes* near Terminal de Oriente are of dubious safety and not recommended for single women. Foreigners are advised not to be out in the city centre after dark.

13% VAT (IVA) is added to bills at major hotels. Most of the cheaper hotels are around the Centro Histórico. Be careful in this area, particularly at night.

LL Hotel Real Intercontinental San Salvador, Blv de los Héroes and Av Sisimiles, in front of the Metrocentro, T2211-3333, www.gruporeal.com. A useful landmark, smart, formal atmosphere (popular with business visitors), Avis car hire, Taca desk, shop selling souvenirs, postcards, US papers and magazines.

AL Radisson Plaza, 89 Av Norte and 11 Calle Pte, Col Escalón, T2257-0700, www.radisson.com. Elegant rooms with a/c and cable TV. Good value, with parking.

B Alameda, 43 Av Sur and Alameda Roosevelt 2305, T2267-0800. Good service, tour information and parking.

B Alicante Guest House, Calle las Rosas y Av Los Laureles 1, Col La Sultana, T2243-0889, www.alicante.com.sv. Telephone, cable TV, restaurant, internet access for guests, breakfast included. Discounts for extended stays.

B Internacional Puerto Bus, Alameda Juan Pablo II y 19 Av Norte, at Puerto Bus terminal, T/F2221-1000. A/c, TV, wake-up service.

B Mariscal, Paseo Escalón 3658, T2283-0220, www.hotelmariscal.com. Good apartments, a good deal for long-term stay.

B-C Good Luck, Av Los Sisimiles 2943, Col Miramonte (turn left at Real Intercontinental and go uphill 200 m), T2260-1666 hotelgoodluck@yahoo.com. TV, shower, cheaper without a/c, hot water, bright but simple, restaurant, secure parking.

B-C Grecia Real, Av Sisimiles 2922, Col Miramontes, 50 m west of Hotel Real Intercontinental, T2261-0555, www.greciareal.com. With good Greek restaurant. Recommended.

C American Guest House, 17 Av Norte 119 between Calle Arce y 1 Calle Pte, 3 blocks from Puerto Bus, T2222-8789. With bath (cheaper without), hot water, fan, helpful, will store luggage, accepts credit cards, discounts for groups. Oldest guest house downtown, run by the young at heart Irma Estradain her 70s, weekly rates, Cafetería La Amistad, parking nearby, good.

C Centro Histórico, 1 Calle Pte 124 y 1 Av Norte, 2 blocks from cathedral, T2221-5086, www.hotelescentrohistorico.com.sv. A/c, TV, parking, good choice.

C El Palacio, 4 Calle Pte125, next to National Palace, T2222-2243, www.hotelescentro historico.com.sv. A/c, cable TV, parking, good central location.

C Happy House, Av Sisimiles 2951, Col Miramonte, T/F2260-1568, www.hotelhappy house-elsalvador.com. Good, friendly, parking, good breakfast.

C Hotel Florida, Pasaje Los Almendros 15, Urbanizacón Florida and Blv de los Héroes, T2260-2540. All rooms with bath, fan, laundry service, some with a/c, thin walls but good value, secure. Recommended.

C-E International Guest House, 35 Av Norte 9 bis, Reparto Santa Fe, T2226-7343. Private baths, breakfast included.

C-E Ximena's Guest House, Calle San Salvador 202, Col Centroamérica, T2260-2481, www.ximenasguesthouse.com. With cable

TV, a variety of rooms with private bath and hot shower, cheaper in 6-bed dormitory, discounts for long stay, clean, pleasant. Breakfast, lunch and dinner, fruit shakes with purified water and organic coffee. Wi-Fi. Friendly and knowledgeable staff (ask for Lena, speaks several languages). Variety of economic tours as well as transport to their beach house **Capricho** and **Lisa Guest House** at organic farm. Conveniently located, but not easy to find (behind the Esso station on Blv de los Héroes). Recommended.

D Casa Clementina, Av Morazán y Av Washington 34, Col Libertad, T2225-5962. Very friendly, clean, pleasant, garden.

D Centro, 9 Av Sur 410, T2271-5045, hotel_centro55@hotmail.com. A bit box-like, check out 1200, cable TV, internet, TV, phone, friendly, washing facilities, clean, safe. Recommended.

D Nuevo Panamericano, 8 Av Sur 113, T2222-2959. Cold shower, safe, open 24 hours, parking. Recommended.

D San Carlos, Calle Concepción 121, T2221-1664. With bath, early morning call, doors locked 2400, cold drinks available, good. Resident cockroaches but otherwise clean. Ticabus leaves from outside (ticket reservations in lobby office hours).

F Hospedaje España, 12 Av Norte 123, T2222-5248. Fan, clean, bright, good value.

🍴 Eating

San Salvador *p854, maps p856 and p858*
In the older downtown area few places are open to eat after 1830. Restaurants are open later in the western sections of the city. Along Blv Hipódromo, San Benito, restaurants are generally very good, but expensive. On Blv de los Héroes there are many restaurants, including US-style fast-food places. The strip along Calle San Antonio Abad has several local eateries.

₩₩₩ Acajutla Restaurant and Coctelería, Residencial Cumbres de Escalón, Av Maferrer Norte 8, T2263-1722. This is the main branch of several locations (Col Miramonte T2260-1688, Zona Rosa T2237-9404) Great seafood.

₩₩₩ A Lo Nuestro, Calle La Reforma 225A, Col San Benito, T2223-5116, T2279-1900 www. alonuestro.com.sv. International gourmet food based on Salvadorian ingredients.

₩₩₩ Al Pomodoro, Paseo Escalón 3952, Col Escalón, T2257-2544, www.alpomodoro.com. Popular, good Italian, also does delivery.

₩₩₩ China Palace, Alameda Roosevelt 2731, T2298-4313. Excellent value, the oldest Chinese restaurant in San Salvador.

₩₩₩ Daruma, Blv El Hipódromo 428, Col San Benito, T2243-9416. Japanese gourmet food with home delivery.

₩₩₩ Dynasty, Blv Hipódromo 738-B, T2263-9955. Known for serving the best Chinese food in the city.

₩₩₩ El Bodegón, Paseo Escalón 3956 and 77 Av Norte, T2263-5283. The proprietor is Spanish and the food likewise. Excellent.

₩₩₩ H'ola Beto's Escalón, Pasaje Dordelly 4352 between 85 and 87 Av Norte (above Paseo Escalón). Best seafood in the city, also serves Italian. Great service, parking. Recommended.

₩₩₩ Hunan, Paseo Escalón 4999, Plaza Villavicencio, T2263-9911. Chinese restaurant with specialities from Hunan, Szechuan, Pekin and Shanghai.

₩₩₩ Kamakura, 93 Av Norte 617, Col Escalón T2263-2401. Japanese food.

₩₩₩ La Hacienda Real, just opposite of La Gran Via Mall T, Km 8, Carretera Panamericana, next to RAF offices T2243-8567. Without a doubt the best steaks in El Salvador, excellent service and fingerlicking food.

₩₩₩ La Pampa Argentina, Blv Constitución 550, T2263-6550. Highly recommended for steaks, popular.

₩₩₩ La Panetière, Plaza Villavicencio, local 5, Paseo Escalón. Delicious French pastry, crêpes, cappuccinos, popular with foreigners, a bit pricey but worth it.

₩₩₩ Paradise, corner of Reforma, Col San Benito, in front of Pizza Hut, T2224-4201. ●

Good for steak and lobster, excellent food and service. Expensive but worth it.

Pasquale Pasta e Pizza, Paseo Escalón 3931, Col Escalón T2263-5445. Excellent wines and beautiful location.

Señor Tenedor, Calle La Mascota, T2241-0700, www.senortenedor.com, and branch in **La Gran Vía**. Gourmet deli and restaurant.

Sushi Itto, Blv Hipódromo, Col San Benito, T2243-1166, and in shopping mall **La Gran Vía**. Sushi, expensive but good.

Tony Romas, Blv de los Héroes (Metrocentro) and Zona Rosa, T2298-5500. Specializes in imported ribs.

Asia Grill, at Multiplaza Mall, T2243-2309. Contemporary Asian food

Automariscos, located next to roundabout by the Don Rua church, 5a Av Norte, Blv Tutunichapa, T2226-5363, also outlet in San Benito, Av Revolución No 179 T2243-3653 (between Pizza Hut and Anthropological museum). Out of the ordinary seafood and huge portions. Recommended.

Basilea, Centro Comercial Basilea, T2223-6818, www.restaurantebasilea.com. Nice garden atmosphere and small shopping centre, restaurant and excellent cakes (from Shaw's Bakery next door; see Cafés, below).

Café Café, Calle El Tanque, 99 Av Norte y 7 y 9 Calle Pte bis 130, T2263-4034, www.cafe cafe.com.sv. Locally popular Peruvian restaurant. Recommended.

Coconut Grove, 79 Av Sur y Calle La Mascota, 7 y 8, Col Escalón, T2264-2979. Serves seafood.

El Zócalo II, 71 Av Norte, just in front of Galerías mall. Excellent Mexican food.

Felipe's, 27 Calle Pte 743, Col Layco, off Blv de los Héroes. Popular Mexican restaurant, good value. Also has a branch by the US Embassy.

Kalpataru, Calle La Mascota 928 and Calle Maquilishuat, just below **Arbol de Dios**. Open until 2230, full restaurant service and lunch buffet, nice atmosphere. Best vegetarian place in town.

KREEF, new location at Plaza Kreef, 87 Av Sur and Av los Almendros Block G, Zona 11, Urb Maquilishuat T2264-7094, www. kreef.com. Restaurant and deli, specialities meat and juicy chicken filets, imported cheese, beer and wine. Live music weekends.

Pueblo Viejo, in Metrosur, T2260-3545. Open 1100-2000. Popular for lunch, local and steak dishes, including *parrillada*, and seafood.

Restaurante Sol y Luna, Blv Universitario, in front of **Cines Reforma**, T2225-6637. Open Mon-Fri 0830-1730, Sat until 1600. Delicious vegetarian food.

Rosal, 93 Av Norte y Calle El Mirador, Col Escalón, near **Hotel Radisson**, T2263-2391. Italian, good. Try the gourmet lasagne and the garlic breads.

Sopón Típico, 71 Av Norte and 1 Calle Pte 3702, Col Escalón, T2298-3008 and Blv de Los Héroes, Pasaje Las Palmeras 130, Urbanización Florida T2260-2671, www.elsopontipico.com. Typical Salvadorian soups and other dishes.

Mercadito Merliot, Antiguo Cuscatlán. Famous food market with fresh seafood dishes (among others).

The Brother, Calle San Antonio Abad. Meats grilled on outdoor BBQ, large dishes and low prices.

Cafés, delis and juice stalls
There are numerous cafeterías serving cheap traditional meals such as *tamales*, *pupusas*, *frijoles*, rice with vegetables, etc. Often these places can be found around the major hotels.
Café de Don Pedro, Roosevelt y Alameda, next to Esso filling station. Good range of food, mariachi groups, open all night, another branch in Chiltiuapan, near Plaza Merliot Mall, also 24 hrs.
La Panetiere, outlets in most malls including Metrocentro, Plaza Villaviciencio, El Paseo, Multiplaza among others, www.lapanetiere. com.sv. Pioneer in coffee shops and also specializes in gourmet sandwiches, crepes, quiches and French pastry.

La Ventana, 83 Calle Pte 510 and 9a Av Norte in front of Plaza Palestina, Escalón, just below the Hotel Radisson, T2263-3188. Great meals and also one of the best bar selections in town.

Oh-la-la, 1 Calle Ote and 69 Av Norte 168, just around the corner of Galerías mall, T2223-0161. Fine pastries.

Shakes, 3 Calle Pte 5254, Lomas Verdes, Col Escalón, T2263-4533. Juice bar and delicious fresh cakes. Recommended.

Shaw's, Paseo Escalón, 1 block west of Plaza Beethoven, Zona Rosa (see above) and at Metrocentro. Good coffee and chocolates, also sell US magazines and greetings cards.

⊕ Entertainment

San Salvador *p854, maps p856 and p858*
Bars and clubs

Check for gigs in *La Prensa Gráfica* and *El Diario de Hoy*. All leading hotels have their own nightclub. All discos have ladies' night on Wed and Thu when women enter free and get a discount on drinks; go in a group. **Zona Rosa, Col San Benito**, has many bars/discos/open-air cafés in a 5-block area, well-lit, crowded Fri-Sat night (disco cover charge is US$10), take bus No 30 B from near Esso/Texaco/Mundo Feliz on Blv de los Héroes before 2000, taxi thereafter. Just beyond Zona Rosa the new shopping malls of Multiplaza and La Gran Vía are the new favourite places for going out with both having strips of night clubs, coffee shops and bars where youngsters gather at the weekends. Among the most popular discos in Multiplaza are Envy and Stanza and the bar La Cueva.

Café La T, run by German Anne, opposite Centro Comercial San Luis also has a fairtrade gift shop.

El Arpa Av A 137 Col San José, run by Gerry from Ireland.

La Luna, Calle Berlín 228, off Blv de los Héroes, Urbanización Buenos Aires 3, T2260-2921, www.lalunacasayarte.com,

open Wed-Sun. Great food and atmosphere, live music some nights, decor and furniture designed by local artists. Popular and fashionable place to hang out. Reasonably priced drinks and snacks; take taxi late at night.

Photo Café, Col El Roble, Pje 2 21, T2100-2469, near National University, is an artsy place run by photojournalists.

Cinema

A few older-style cinemas in the centre are being overshadowed by the multiplexes along the Blv de los Héroes. Look in local press for listings. Arthouse films are shown at La Luna and Café La T for free. See schedules for events. **Alliance Française** arranges film seasons, T2223-8084.

Music, dance and theatre

Ballet and theatre at the **Teatro Nacional de Bellas Artes**, and music or plays at the **Teatro Cámera**.

Spectator sports

Check *La Prensa Gráfica* and *El Diario de Hoy*. **Baseball** On the field opposite Mercado Nacional de Artesanías, Tue-Fri 1700, Cuban and US coaches, local teams, entrance US$1.25.

Boat racing Club Náutico, at the Estero de Jaltepeque, is famous for its boat races across the mud flats at low tide.

Football Sun and Thu at the Cuscatlán and/or Flor Blanca stadiums.

Motor racing At the new El Jabalí auto-drome on lava fields near Quetzaltepeque.

⊕ Festivals and events

San Salvador *p854, maps p856 and p858*
Mar/Apr Holy Week
Jul/Aug Celebrations of El Salvador del Mundo are held the fortnight preceding **6 Aug**. As a climax, colourful floats wend their way up the Campo de Marte (the park encompasssing Parque Infantil and Palacio

de Deportes; 9 Calle Pte and Av España). On **5 Aug**, an ancient image of the Saviour is borne before the large procession, before church services the next day, celebrating the **Feast of the Transfiguration**.

12 Dec Día del Indígena; there are colourful processions honouring the **Virgen de Guadalupe** (take bus No 101 to the Basílica de Guadalupe, on the Carretera a Santa Tecla).

O Shopping

San Salvador *p854, maps p856 and p858*
Visa and MasterCard are accepted in most establishments.

Bookshops

Magazines and newspapers in English can be bought at leading hotels and many shops sell US magazines. **Cervantes**, 9 Av Sur 114 in the Centre and Edif El Paseo 3, Paseo Escalón; **Clásicos Roxsil**, 6 Av Sur 1-6, Santa Tecla, T2228-1212; **Editorial Piedra Santa**, Av Olímpica 3428, Av 65-67 Sur, T2223-5502; **Etc Ediciones** in Centro Comercial Basilea, San Benito. Some English books at Librería Cultural Salvadoreña in Metrosur.
Olivos, also café and restaurant, just below Hotel Princess, Zona Rosa, T2245-4221, www.olivoscafe.com. Has a wide selection of books, specializing in alternative medicine and health.

Crafts

You can buy fairtrade arts and crafts at **Café La T**, Calle San Antonio Abad, and **Nahanché**. Metrocentro, Centro Comercial Basilea and Multiplaza has a great selection of handicrafts from all over the country.
El Arbol de Dios, La Mascota y Av Masferrer, T2224-6200, see page 859.
Mercado Ex-Cuartel, 8 Av Norte, 1 Calle Ote. Crafts market, a few blocks east of the Teatro Nacional, rebuilt after a fire in 1995.
Mercado Nacional de Artesanías, opposite the Estado Mayor on the road to Santa Tecla

(buses 101A, B or C, 42B, 79, 34, 30B), at prices similar to the Mercado Ex-Cuartel, open daily 0800-1800. A 1-stop craft shop with a good cross-section of items even if not that well presented. Some of the cheapest prices.

Markets and malls

Metrocentro, large shopping mall on the Blv de los Héroes, northwest of the city centre. Together with **Metrosur** this is the largest shopping mall in Central America. Another shopping centre, **Villas Españolas**, is on the Paseo Escalón, 1 block south of the Redondel Masferrer; it is more exclusive, with expensive boutiques. **Galerías Escalón**, Col Escalón, has department stores and cybercafés. **El Paseo**, is the new mall in Escalon, located just at the corner of 79 Av The area west of Zona Rosa has 3 newer malls named **Multiplaza**, **Hiper Mall Cascadas** and **La Gran Vía**.

▲ Activities and tours

San Salvador *p854, maps p856 and p858*
Tour operators
Inter Tours, Balam Quitze mall in Paseo Escalon, T2263-6188, www.viajero.com.sv. One of the most recognized travel agencies in the capital. They have excellent service and can track down that special rate you need.
OTEC Turismo Joven, Centro Comercial El Partenope , local 2, Paseo Escalón, T2264-0200, www.otec.com.sv. Official ISIC office in El Salvador and STA Travel representative, offering travel assistance, reissue of lost tickets, date changes and rerouting. Special prices for student, teacher and youth with ISIC card.
Pullmantur, Av La Revolución, T2243-1300. Luxury bus service to Guatemala and excellent package tours to Antigua.
Salva Natura, 33 Av Sur 640, Col Flor Blanca, T2279-1515, www.salvanatura.org. For information about Parque Nacional El Imposible on the coast near Guatemala.

Watersports

El Salvador Divers, Paseo Escalón 3 Calle Pte 5020, Col Escalón, T2264-0961, www.elsalvadordivers.com. Offer weekly excursions and classes. Located behind the Villavicencio Mall.

Ríos Aventuras, is part of Tropic Tours, Av Olimpica 3597, T2279-3235, www.riosaventuras. com.sv. Bilingual guides organize rafting trips to Río Paz on the Guatemalan border. Recommended.

⊖ Transport

San Salvador *p854, maps p856 and p858*

Air

The international airport (SAL), T2339-9455, at Comalapa is 62 km southeast from San Salvador towards Costa del Sol beach. **Acacya** minibus to airport, from 3 Calle Pte y 19 Av Norte, T2271-4937, airport T2339-9182, at 0600, 0700, 1000, 1400 (be there 15 mins before), US$3 one-way (leaves from airport when full, on right as you go out). **Acacya**, T2271-4937, also has a taxi service, US$25, the same as other radio taxi companies; ordinary taxis charge US$20. Taxi to La Libertad beach US$30. To **Costa del Sol** US$50. There is a post office, a tourist office, 2 exchange desks, (including Citi Bank) and duty-free shopping for both departures and arrivals.

The old airport is at Ilopango, 13 km east of the city and is primarily used by the air force and for some domestic flights.

Airline offices American Airlines, Alameda Roosevelt, Edificio Centroamericana, 3107, T2298-0777. **Copa Airlines**, T2209-2600, www.copaair.com. **Delta**, 81 Av Norte y Calle El Mirador, Edif WTC, local 107, piso 4, Col Escalón T2275-9292, www.delta.com. **Grupo TACA**, Oficinas Centrales Santa Elena (behind American Embassy), T2267-8222, www.taca.com. **Mexicana**, Edificio Mejicana de Aviación, 2 nivel, Km 4.5, Carretera Sta Tecla, T2252-9999, www.mexicana.com. **United Airlines**, T2279-3900, www.united.com.

Bus

Local Most buses stop running at 2100. City buses charge US$0.20 and microbuses charges US$0.25 within the city – have the right change or a small bill to hand. Most run 0500-2000, after which use taxis.

Some useful routes: 29 from Terminal de Oriente to Metrocentro via downtown; 30 Mercado Central to Metrocentro; 30B from Mundo Feliz (100 m up from Esso station on Blv de los Héroes) to Escalón, 79 Av Norte, Zona Rosa (San Benito), Alameda Roosevelt and back to Metrocentro along 49 Av; 34 San Benito–Mercado de Artesanías–Terminal de Occidente–Mercado Central–Terminal Oriente; 52 'Paseo' Parque Infantil–Metrocentro–Plaza Las Américas–Paseo Escalón–Plaza Masferrer; 52 'Hotel' Parque Infantil–Metrocentro–Hotel Copa Airlines–Plaza Masferrer. Route 101 buses to/from Santa Tecla are blue and white for either class of service.

Domestic services go from **Terminal de Occidente**, off Blv Venezuela, T2223-3784 (take city buses 4, 7C, 27, 44 or 34); **Terminal de Oriente**, end of Av Peralta in Centro Urbano Lourdes (take city buses No 29 from Metrocentro, 42 from Alameda, or No 4, from 7 Calle), T2281-3086, very crowded with buses and passengers, keep your eyes open for the bus you want; and **Terminal Sur**, San Marcos, Zona Franca, about 9 km from the city (take city bus No 26 from Universidad Nacional area or Av España downtown, take taxi to city after 1830). Terminal de Sonsonate, located just outside city center, by main road to Acajutla T2450-4625, Terminal de Santa Ana T2440-0938. Routes and fares are given under destinations.

Long distance and international
Heading south Recognized international bus company Ticabus departs from Hotel San Carlos, Calle Concepción 121, T2222-4808, www.ticabus.com. Also with an office in Blv del Hipódromo, Zona Rosa, T2243-9764. To **Tapachula** 0600 and 1200 noon, 11 hrs,

US$30. To **Guatemala**, 0600 and 1300, 5 hrs, US$15. To **Tegucigalpa**, 1200, 7 hrs, US$15. To **Managua**, 0500, 12 hrs, US$30. To **San José**, 33 hrs including overnight in Managua, US$50. To **Panama City**, depart 0500, arriving 1700 next day, US$75. They now have an executive coach service to **Nicaragua** for US$44, and **Costa Rica** US$58, (both depart 0300) and to **Panama** at 0500, US$93. **King Quality**, Puerto Bus Terminal, Alameda Juan Pablo II y 19 Av Norte, T2241-8704; in Zona Rosa T2271-1361, www.king-qualityca.com. You can walk there from city centre, but it's not advisable with luggage; take bus 101D from Metrocentro, or bus 29, 52 to 21 Av Norte, 2 blocks south of terminal (city buses don't permit heavy luggage). The terminal has a *casa de cambio* (good rates) and a restaurant. They have departures to Central America and Mexico. Departure times from Puerto Bus station (check office for times from Zona Rosa).

Service to Guatemala with domestic carriers include Pezzarossi, Taca, Transesmer, Melva, and Vencedora. All operate services to Guatemala City more or less hourly (5½ hrs, US$13). Departures between 0500 and 1600. Confortlines (sister company of King Quality) has departures to Guatemala at 0800 and 1400 for US$30 – higher-class bus than the regular service but no meals. Pullmantur, T2243-1300, runs a 0700 service Mon-Sat, 0830 Sun, and a daily luxury 1500 service from Hotel Marriott Presidente in Zona Rosa for US$35, with a/c, film, drinks and meals. Service to **Mexico** also from Terminal de Occidente, El Cóndor goes to Talismán, Mexico via Sonsonate, La Hachadura and Escuintla, US$12, 0330, 9½ hrs, also 0700-0800 to Guatemala City. **Transgalgos** has direct departures to Mexico from Puerto Bus.

Car

Car hire Local insurance (about US$10-15 per day plus a deductible US$1000 deposit) is mandatory and 13% IVA applies. **Avis**, 43 Av Sur 137, Col. Flor Blanca www.avis.com.sv, T2500-2847; **Budget**, Hotel Sheraton

Presidente, Col San Benito T2283-2908 and Calle Mirador and 85 Av Norte 648, Col Escalón, T2264-3888, www.budget.com; Hertz, corner of 91 Av Nte and 9 Calle Pte, T2264-2818, www.hertz.com; Sandoval & Co, T2235-4405, sub-compact late-model cars from US$10 per day, English spoken; Euro Rent-Cars, 29 Calle Pte and 7 Av Norte 1622, T2235-5232, chamba_r@hotmail.com, cheap daily rates from US$10.

Car repairs Modern service centres of **Record** and **Impressa**, are found throughout the capital. Good source of spare parts found at **Super Repuestos**, T2221-4440.

Insurance **Asesuiza** is widely used for car insurance T2209-5025 as is **La Centroamericana**, T2298-6666.

Car papers Ministerio de Hacienda, T2226-1900, 'Tres Torres', turn left on Blv de los Héroes, 300 m past Texaco station.

Taxi
Plenty (all yellow), don't have meters, ask fare before getting in. Trips within San Salvador will have a minimum cost of US$4 and most trips will be between US$4 and US$7. Airport is approximately US$25. Few drivers speak English. They will charge more in the rain. More expensive radio taxis may be hired through **Acacya**, T2271-4937.

❶ Directory

San Salvador *p854, maps p856 and p858*
Banks
Most banks open Mon-Fri 0900-1600, Sat 0900-1200. The banks have branches in all the shopping malls and in large hotels such as **Princess Hilton** and **Radisson**. ATMs only give US dollars. **Banco Agrícola Comercial de El Salvador**, Paseo Escalón 3635, T2279-1033, English spoken. **HSBC** give good rates for TCs and Visa card advances.

Most banks give cash advance on your credit card if you bring your passport. In emergency, for Visa International or MasterCard, T2224-5100; Visa TCs can only be changed by Visa cardholders. Visa ATMs can be found at **Aval** card 24-hr machines, the majority at Esso and Shell service stations (eg Esso, Blv de los Héroes), but also at Metrocentro, 8th floor food court, and Centro de Servicio, Av Olímpica. See also Yellow Pages. **Western Union** for money transfers, c/o HSCB branches, T2225-2503 (48 other branches throughout the country, look out for the black and yellow sign), head office Alameda Roosevelt 2419 between 45 y 47 Av Sur, T2298-1888, Mon-Fri 0800-1700, Sat 0800-1200, take passport and photographic ID (30 mins if from USA/Canada, 2-3 hrs from Europe). **Banco de América Central** (Ex-Credomatic), next to Siman in Metrocentro and CC San Luis gives cash advances on credit cards.

Cultural centres

Alianza Francesa, 5 Av Norte 152, Col Escalón, T2260-5807 and new location in Col San Benito: Calle La Mascota 547 , Pasaje 2, www.afelsalvador.com. **Union Church**, Calle 4 Final, Col La Mascota, T2263-8246, English-speaking interdominational international church, weekly church services and bible studies, volunteering opportunities. **Centro de Intercambio y Solidaridad (CIS)**, Blv Universitario 4, next to Cine Reforma, T2226-2623, www.cis-elsalvador.org, for language classes, FMLN (Frente Farabundo Martí para la Liberación Nacional) programmes and schools. **Instituto para el Rescate Ancestral Indígena Salvadoreño (RAIS)**, Av Santiago 20, Col San Mateo, has programmes for local aid to indigenous communities and the Nahual language and customs.

Embassies and consulates

Belize, Calle el Bosque Ote y Calle Lomas de Candelaria I, Block "P1", Col Jardines de la 1a Cima Etapa, T2248-1423. **Costa Rica**, Calle Cuscatlán 4415, between 81 and 83 Av Sur, Col Escalón, T2264-3863. **Canada**, Centro Financiero Gigante and Alameda Roosevelt y 63 Av Sur Lobby 2, local 6, T2279 4659. **France**, 1 Calle Pte 7380, Col Escalón, T2298-4260. **Germany**, 77 Av Norte y 7 Calle Pte 3972, T2263-2088. **Guatemala**, 15 Av Norte 135 between 1 Calle Pte and Calle Arce, T2271-2225. **Holland**, I Calle Pte 3796, T2298-2185. **Honduras**, 89 Av Norte 561, between 7 and 9 Calle Pte, Col Escalón, T2263-2808. **Israel**, Centro Financiero Gigante, Torre B, 11 piso, Alameda Roosevelt y 63 Av Sur, T2211-3434. **Italy**, La Reforma 158, Col San Benito, T2223-4806. **Mexico**, Pasaje 12 y Calle Circunvalación, San Benito, behind Hotel Presidente, T2248 9906. **Nicaragua**, Calle Mirador and 93 Av Norte 4814, Col Escalón, T2263-8849. **Norway**, Calle Cuscatlán 133 between 83 and 81 Av Sur, Col Escalón, T2263-8257. **Panama**, Av Buganvilia No21, Col San Francisco T2298-0773. **Spain**, Calles la Reforma 164, Col San Benito, T2257-5700. **Sweden**, Alameda Manuel E Araujo y 67 Av Sur 3515, T2281-7901. **Switzerland**, Pastelería Lucerna, 85 Av Sur y Paseo Escalón 4363, T2263-7485. **USA**, Blv Santa Elena, Antiguo Cuscatlán, T2278-4444, outside the city, reached by bus 101A.

Emergency

Fire service, T2555-7300. **Red Cross**, Av Henry Dunat y 17 Av Norte, T2224-5155, 24 hr. **Police**, T911, no coin needed from new coin phones. In San Salvador, metropolitan police respond to the tourist complaints.

Immigration

Departamento de Inmigración, Centro de Gobierno, T2221-2111, Mon-Fri 0800-1600. Will consider extending tourist visas, but be prepared with photos and plenty of patience. **Migración y Extranjería**, Plaza Merliot and I lipermall Cascadas saves the trip to Centro de Gobierno and has quicker service.

Internet

Cafés (roughly US$1 per hr) are found throughout the city, especially at shopping malls.

Language schools

Centro de Intercambio y Solidaridad, Blv Universitario 4, T2226-2623, www.cis-elsalvador.org. Spanish school in the mornings 0800-1200, English school in the afternoons 1700-1900 (volunteer English teachers needed for 10-week sessions). **Cihuatan Spanish Language Institute** (Ximena's Guest House), Calle San Salvador 202, Col Centro América (near Hotel Real Intercontinental), T2260-2481, ximenas@navegante.com.sv; US$8 per hr.

Libraries

The **UCA** library (Universidad Centro-americana), José S Cañas, Autopista Sur, is said to be the most complete collection. US information library at **American Chamber of Commerce,** 87 Av Norte 720, Apto A, Col Escalón, Apdo Postal (05) 9, Sr Carlos Chacón, speaks English, helpful. **Centro Cultural Salvadoreño,** Av Los Sisimiles, Metrocentro Norte, T2226-9103, 0800-1100, 1400-1700, English library, excellent. **Intercambios Culturales de El Salvador,** 67 Av Sur 228, Col Roma, T2245-1488, extensive Spanish and English reference library, local artistic exhibitions, computer school.

Medical services

Hospitals and clinics Hospital de la Mujer, between 81 and 83 Av Sur y Calle Juan José Cañas, Col Escalón (south of Paseo, bus 52 Paseo), T2223-8955. **Hospital Pro-Familia,** 25 Av Norte 483, 11 blocks east of Metrocentro, T2244-8000, clinics and 24-hr emergency, reasonable prices. **Hospital Rosales,** 25 Av Norte y 3 Calle Pte, T2231-9200, long waits. **Clínicas Médicas,** 25 Av Norte 640 (bus 3, 9, 44 centro from Universidad Nacional), T2225-5233. If you contract a serious stomach problem, the doctor will send you for tests, which will cost US$5-6. **Doctors** Dr Cesar Armando Solano, at Av Bernal 568, Col Yurimuri T2261-1657, excellent dentist and low prices. English spoken. **Medicentro La Esperanza,** 27 Av Norte is a good place to find doctors in most specialist fields, afternoons mostly after 1500. **Dr Jorge Panameno,** T2225-9928, English-speaking, specialist in tropical diseases, makes house calls at night for about US$50.

Post office

Central Post Office at the Centro de Gobierno with EMS, T2527-7600. Good service to Europe. Mon-Fri 0730-1700, Sat 0730-1200. **Lista de Correos,** Mon-Fri 0800-1200, 1430-1700, good service for mail collection. Branches throughout the city.

Telephone

Phone boxes throughout the city, card only, available at fast-food stores such as **Pollo Campero;** direct dialling to anywhere in the world, also collect calls. Telephone cards for sale in pharmacies and stores, denominations from US$1 upwards.

Work

UCA University Simeon Cañas, Blv Los Próceres San Salvador, T2210-6600, www.uca.edu.sv. An English-language programme always needing certified English teachers.

Western El Salvador

Compact and with good transport links, Western El Salvador combines the dramatic volcanic landscapes of Cerro Verde, Volcán Izalco and Lago de Coatepeque – essential for any visitor to the country – with the serene beauty and majesty of countless waterfalls and the colourful Ruta de las Flores around Sonsonate. Little indigenous villages and pre-Columbian ruins contrast with the vibrancy of Santa Ana, El Salvador's second largest city. Three routes lead to Guatemala, the northernmost passing close to the impressive cloud forests of Parque Nacional Montecristo on the border with Honduras. ▶▶ *For listings, see pages 880-886.*

Izalco to Sonsonate ●● ▶▶ *pp 880-886.*

From the junction with the Pan-American Highway, just west of Colón, route CA 8 heads west, past Armenia, to the town of Izalco (population: 70,959) at the foot of Izalco volcano (8 km from Sonsonate, bus 53C). The town has evolved from the gradual merging of the *ladino* village of Dolores Izalco and the indigenous village of Asunción Izalco. In colonial times this was an important trading centre and experienced a communist rebellion in 1932. Today the town is experiencing a tourist revival with good colonial architecture, a prominent and active indigenous population, and rich heritage of religious imagery which blends indigenous and Roman Catholic beliefs, and produces regular processions and festivals. A week-long festival celebrating El Salvador del Mundo runs 8-15 August and there is also a local celebration from 24 November to 10 December. The Feast of John the Baptist runs from 17-24 June.

Note The town of Izalco and Izalco volcano are not directly connected by road. A paved road branches off the Pan-American highway 14 km before the turning for Izalco town (about 22 km from Sonsonate) and goes up towards Cerro Verde, Volcán Izalco and Lago de Coatepeque (see page 874).

Sonsonate and around ●●●● ▶▶ *pp880-886. Colour map 5, C3.*

→ *Altitude: 225 m. Population: 71,541.*

Sonsonate, 64 km from the capital, is the country's chief cattle-raising region. It also produces sugar, tobacco, rice, tropical fruits, hides and balsam. The city was founded in 1552 and is hot, dirty and crowded, but worth checking to see the colonial architecture in the city centre. The beautiful **El Pilar** church (1723) is strongly reminiscent of the church of El Pilar in San Vicente. The **Cathedral** has many cupolas (the largest covered with white porcelain) and was badly damaged in the 2001 earthquake but is now fully restored. The old church of **San Antonio del Monte** (completed 1861), 1 km from the city, draws pilgrims from afar (fiesta 22-26 August). There is a small **railway museum**, look for the locomotive at the entrance to the city on the highway from San Salvador (Km 65). An important market is held each Sunday. The market outside the church is quite well organized. In the northern outskirts of the city there is a waterfall on the Río Sensunapán. Legend has it that an indigenous princess drowned there, and on the anniversary of her death a gold casket appears below the falls. The main annual event is **Feria de la Candelaria** in February. Easter Week processions are celebrated with particular fervour and are probably the most impressive in the whole country. On Easter Thursday and Holy Friday the streets are filled with thousands of members of the cofradías (brotherhoods).

Around Sonsonate

Route CA 8, northwest to Ahuachapán (see page 877), has spectacular scenery along the **Ruta de las Flores**, with frequent buses from Sonsonate (bus 249 and 285, two hours) covering the 40-km paved route. The road goes just outside the indigenous village of Nahuizalco (population: 49,081). Some of the older women here still wear the *refajo* (a doubled length of cloth made of tie-dyed threads worn over a wrap-round skirt), and various crafts are still made, including wood and rattan furniture. Although use of the indigenous language is dying out you do still encounter people who speak Nahuat. The night market, unique in El Salvador, opens at dusk and has traditional local food on sale. There's a religious festival 19-25 June, with music, **Danza de los Historiantes** and art exhibitions; also 24-25 December, with music and **Danza de los Pastores**. Take bus 53 D from Sonsonate.

Salcoatitán and Juayúa

A little further up the mountainside at Km 82 is Salcoatitán (population: 5484) at 1045 m above sea level, a colonial village with a beautiful park in front of the colonial church. This cozy village used to be only a drive-through on the way to Juayua or Apaneca but has experienced a tourist revival lately with several new restaurants, art galleries and artisans shops. **Los Patios restaurant** (same owners Las Cabañas de Apaneca) just opened a restaurant and art gallery here.

Further along, the road branches off to Juayúa 2 km further north and the same bus from Sonsonate takes a detour into the village and back. Juayua is the largest city in Ruta de Las Flores – the name means 'River of Purple Orchids' in the local Nahuatl dialect – and sits nestling in a valley dominated by volcanoes. It's a peaceful spot where you can watch people at work and kids playing in the semi-cobbled street. The surrounding region is blanketed in coffee groves; the bean was introduced to the area in 1838 and today the town produces about 10% of the coffee exported from El Salvador. Its church houses an image of the **Cristo Negro** (Black Christ) carved by Quirio Cataño at the end of the 16th century. **Tourist information** is available from Jaime Salgado, at **Juayutur** ① *T2469-2310, juayutur@navegante.com.sv*. He can provide good information about the activities available in the region including rappelling waterfalls, the hike of the seven waterfalls and the mountain lagoon with wild horses. Guides are trained local youngsters. Also check out the Casa de la Cultura, on the corner next to the park for information on Juayúa. Gaby and Julio Vega, the owners of **Akwaterra Tours** ① *www.akwaterra.com*, run a mountain cabin at Finca Portezuelo named **La Escondida**. Now they have coffee decks, a camping site. They're fluent in English and offer a wide range of activites at Portezuelo Adventure Park such as hiking, mountain biking, horseback riding, ATVs and paragliding.

There are a number of excursions you can do in the area to see wildlife including river otters, toucans, butterflies and many other animals. In the dry season **Laguna de las Ranas** (Laguna Seca) dries up, attracting numerous reptiles as it shrinks. There are also trips to the 30-m high waterfall at **Salto el Talquezal**, the 50-m high **Salto de la Lagunilla Azul** and several other waterfalls in the region seven in one day if you take a tour, with swimming and picnics on the way (see below). Every weekend Juayúa celebrates the Feria Gastronómica, an opportunity to try a variety of traditional dishes, often accompanied by local events, music and shows.

The **Feria Gastronómica Internacional** is in January and celebrates with dishes from all over the world; other festivals include **Día de los Canchules** (31 October), when people ask for candies and **Día de las Mercedes** (17 September), when the houses are decorated with branches and candles leading up to the procession of the Virgen de la Merced. Another local attraction is the newly opened **Museo del Café**, of the coffee cooperative **La Majada** ① T2467-9008 ext 1451, www.cafemajadaoro.com.sv, located in San José La Majada, just outside Juayua on the road to Los Naranjos. Tours include information on coffee processing and a trip to the processing plant. A coffee shop offers local brews and iced coffee.

Los Naranjos and around

Moving northeast of Juayúa, swirling up a scenic mountain road connecting Juayúa with Santa Ana you arrive at Los Naranjos, a small traditional coffee village located at the mountain pass between Santa Ana and the Pilón volcanoes. The lines of wind-breaking trees preventing damage to coffee trees are particularly beautiful, while the high altitude makes the climate cool with the scent of cypress forests. A series of restaurants and small cabins for lodging has popped up in recent years and is an excellent option for cool climate and countryside relaxation.

At Km 82 on the Carretera Salcoatitán to Juayúa is **Parque y Restaurante La Colina** ① T2452-2916, www.lacolinajuayua.com, with hammocks, arts and crafts, and horse riding available. **Apaneca** is a short distance uphill from Sonsonate, see page 871.

Several **waterfalls** and other sites of natural beauty can be found in the Sonsonate district. To the west, near the village of **Santo Domingo de Guzmán** (bus 246 from Sonsonate), are the falls of **El Escuco** (2 km north), **Tepechapa** (1.5 km further) and **La Quebrada** (further still up the Río Tepechapa), all within walking distance of both Santo Domingo and each other. Walk through the town, then follow the river, there are several spots to swim. Santo Domingo de Guzman is also known for its *alfarería* (pottery) of *comales*, clay plates used to create torillas and *pupusas* over open fire, and its many Nahuat speaking habitants. There's a festival in Santo Domingo, 24-25 December. A short distance north is **San Pedro Puxtla** (bus 246), with a modern church built on the remains of an 18th-century edifice. From here you can visit the **Tequendama Falls** on the Río Sihuapán. Bus 219 goes east to **Cuisnahuat** (18th-century baroque church), where the Fiesta de San Judas takes place 23 29 November. From there it is 2 km south to the Río Apancoyo, or 4 km north to **Peñón El Escalón** (covered in balsam trees) and **El Istucal Cave**, at the foot of the Escalón hill, where indigenous rites are celebrated in November.

Santa Tecla to Santa Ana ●● ⫸ pp880-886.

The new Pan-American Highway parallels the old one, continuing northwest to the border with Guatemala at San Cristóbal. Santa Ana, acting as a transport hub, has routes out to Ahuachapán to the west and the border at Las Chinamas, as well as north to Metapán and beyond to the border crossing of Anguiatú.

Fifteen kilometres from Santa Tecla, 7 km beyond the junction with the Sonsonate road, there is a junction to the right. This road forks immediately, right to **Quezaltepeque**, left (at **Joya de Cerén** café) to **San Juan Opico**. After a few kilometres on the San Juan road, you cross the railway by the Kimberley-Clark factory.

Joya de Cerén

① US$3, parking US$1, T2401-5782, www.fundar.org.sv/joyadeceren.
After the girder bridge crossing the Río Sucio there is a grain store beside which is Joya de Cerén (32 km from the capital). This is a major archaeological site and on the World

Heritage List of UNESCO (the only one in El Salvador), not for spectacular temples, but because this is the only known site where ordinary Maya houses have been preserved having been buried by the ash from the nearby Laguna Caldera volcano in about AD 600. Buildings and construction methods can be clearly seen; a painted book and household objects have been found. All the structures are covered with protective roofing. The site has a small but good museum, café, toilets and car park. Official tours are in Spanish but English language tours available upon request. ▸▸ *See Transport, page 885.*

San Andrés

① *Tue-Sun 0900-1600, US$3, popular for weekend picnics, otherwise it's quiet. Has a café. Take bus No 201 from Terminal de Occidente, US$1.50 (same bus from Santa Ana) T2319-3220, www.fundar.org.sv/sanandres.*

Back on the main road, heading west is the excavated archaeological site of San Andrés, halfway between Santa Tecla and Coatepeque on the estate of the same name (its full name is **La Campana de San Andrés**). It is located at Km 32.5 on the Pan-American Highway, just after the Hilasal towel factory. A new museum at the site displays some of the ceramics found and others can be seen at the **Museo Antrpológico David J Guzmán (MUNA)** in San Salvador. The museum also features a special indigo section with information about this natural dye. El Salvador was the number one producer of indigo in the world during the colonial era. A large indigo *obraje* (processing basin) – probably the largest found in Latin America – was found at San Andrés during an archaeological excavation and has been preserved. There are good views of the nearby hills.

Lago de Coatepeque

At El Congo, 13 km before Santa Ana, a branch road leads south to the northern shore of the beautiful Lago de Coatepeque, a favourite weekend resort, with good sailing, watersports and fishing, near the foot of Santa Ana Volcano. Many weekend homes line the north and east shores, making access to the water difficult, but there are public *balnearios*. The lakeside hotels are a good option for having a meal and use their infrastructure for the day. You can also get boat rides on the lake through the hotels or by independent fishermen. There are *aguas termales* (hot springs) on the opposite side of the lake. A ride is between US$15 and US$45.There are two islands in the lake – **Anteojos** which is close to the hotels, and **Teopán** on the far side. The local Fiesta del Santo Niño de Atocha runs from 25-29 June.

Cerro Verde, Volcán Izalco and Santa Ana Volcano

① *Park entrance US$1, passport or photocopy required, car park US$0.70. Guided tour to the summit of Izalco or Santa Ana is included, leaving from the entrance daily 1100. The guided tour through the nature trail around the Cerro Verde Summit is US$0.25 per person and is led by local trained guides. The Turicentro Cerro Verde (the summit of Cerro Verde with its trails, the parking lot and departure point for the hikes to the volcano) is run by the Ministry of Tourism, for information T2222-8000, www.elsalvador.travel. The whole area covering the volcanoes Santa Ana, Cerro Verde and Izalco and surrounding area are part of the Parque Nacional de los Volcanes, which is administrated by Salvanatura, T2279-1515, www.salvanatura.org.*

In October 2005, Santa Ana volcano erupted for the first time in more than 100 years. The area was closed for a period, but it has now reopened.

Santa Ana blows her top

In October 2005 Volcán Santa Ana awoke from a sleep of more than 100 years. The eruption killed two and forced thousands to flee the area. A fumarole rose 10 km into the air and rocks were thrown a distance of 1.5 km. Shortly after, satellite photographs showed the ash cloud covering most of western El Salvador and parts of Guatemala. Check locally for access to the area.

From El Congo another road runs south, around the east shore of Lago Coatepeque. This road is locally known as Carretera Panorámica, due to the fantastic view of Coatepeque on one side and the mountains and valleys beyond the ridge. After reaching the summit, the paved road branches right, climbing above the south end of the lake to **Parque Nacional Cerro Verde** (2030 m) with its fine and surprising views of the Izalco volcano (1910 m), and Santa Ana volcano (2381 m), the highest volcano in the country. The road up to Cerro Verde is lined with beautiful flowers and half way up there is a mirador with a great view of Lago Coatepeque. Cerro Verde is probably one of the most beautiful places in El Salvador due to the special flora and fauna, breathtaking views and fine volcano trekking.

A 30-minute walk along a nature trail leads you around the crater ridge, to a series of miradors with views of Lago Coatepeque and Santa Ana volcano. For the best view of Izalco, go in the morning, although the afternoon clouds around the cone can be enchanting. ⇥ *For information on climbing Volcán Izalco and Santa Ana, see box, page 884.*

The old hotel and its volcano-view terrace was destroyed in the 2001 earthquake but you can still go there for an amazing view over Izalco volcanic crater. There are now a couple of cabins available for US$35 55. For information call the turicentro on 17949-2751. To access Cerro Verde, take bus No 208 from Santa Ana at 0800, passing El Congo at 0815 am to catch the 1100 departure. If you come from Sonsonate side, take the No 209 bus from Sonsonate to Cerro Verde.

Santa Ana and around ◉⦿▲◉◗ ⇥ *pp880-886. Colour map 5, C3.*

→ *Altitude: 776 m. Population: 245,421.*

Santa Ana, 55 km from San Salvador and capital of its department, is the second largest city in the country. The basin of the Santa Ana volcano is exceptionally fertile, producing large amounts of coffee, with sugar cane coming a close second. The city, named Santa Ana La Grande by Fray Bernardino Villapando in 1567, is the business centre of western El Salvador. There are some fine buildings: the neo-Gothic **cathedral**, and several other churches, especially **El Calvario**, in neoclassical style. Of special interest is the classical **Teatro de Santa Ana** ① *on the north side of the plaza, a guide (small charge) will show you round on weekdays, refer to the local press for performances,* originally completed in 1910, now in the latter stages of interior restoration and one of the finest theatres in Central America. The Fiestas Julias take place from 1-26 July.

Chalchuapa → *Altitude: 640 m. Population: 96,727.*

About 16 km west of Santa Ana, on the road to Ahuachapán, lies Chalchuapa. President Barrios of Guatemala was killed in battle here in 1885, while trying to reunite Central

America by force. There are some good colonial-style domestic buildings. The church of Santiago Apóstol is particularly striking; almost the only one in El Salvador which shows strong indigenous influences (restored 1997-1998). Fiestas are on 18-21 July, Santiago Apóstol, and 12-16 August, San Roque. **Tazumal** ruins next to the cemetery in Chalchuapa, are the tallest and probably the most impressive in El Salvador. Built about AD 980 by the Pipil, with its 14-step pyramid. In 2004 the ruins suffered a partial collapse of the main pyramid due to the filtration of water which led to extensive excavations and application of new preservation techniques (descarting the old concrete) and many new discoveries were made. The excavations concluded in 2006. The site has been occupied since 5000 BC and in the **Museo Stanley H Boggs** ① *Tue-Sun 0900-1600, T2408-4295*, you find artefacts found in Tazumal since the first excavations in the 1950s.

Casa Blanca Archaeological Site ① *Km 78 Pan-American Hwy, T2408-4641, Tue-Sun 0900-1600, US$1*, is a newly opened archaeological site just outside Chalchuapa along the Pan-American Highway. There are several pyramids, ongoing excavations, and a museum that provides an insight into the archaeological history of the area and information on indigo (*añil*) production. If you want to participate in the indigo workshop the cost is US$3. It's very interesting, educational and you get to keep the products produced, recommended.

Santa Ana

Sleeping
El Faro 1
La Libertad 3
La Posada del Rey 2

Sahara 4

Eating
Expresión 1

Los Horcones 3

Atiquizaya

The road continues 12 km west to Atiquizaya, a small, quiet town with one *hospedaje*, several good *pupuserías* (1600-2100) and **Restaurante Atiquizaya**, which can be found at the intersection with the main highway to Ahuachapán. At **Cataratas del Río Malacachupán** there is a beautiful 50-m-high waterfall cascading into a lagoon; it's a 1-km hike to get there. Nearby is **Volcán Chingo** on the Guatemalan border. Another attraction is **Aguas Calientes**, a hot spring that runs into the river and is excellent for a relaxing bath and for enjoying nature. It's a short ride from Atiquizaya, but bring a local guide.

Ahuachapán → *Colour map 5, C3. Altitude: 785 m. Population: 110,511.*

A quiet town with low and simple houses, 35 km from Santa Ana. Coffee is the main product. The main local attraction is the geothermal field of **Los Ausoles**, 3 km road from Ahuachapan and marked on the road out of town to Apaneca as 'Planta Geotérmica'. You can't go into the plant, but when you arrive take the road to the right where, just a little way up the hill on the left, you come to a little house, geysers of boiling mud with plumes of steam and strong whiffs of sulphur. The *ausoles* are used for generating 30% of the country's electricity. For a small tip the house owner will take you into his back garden to see the fumaroles and boiling pools. If you want a more professional tour, with an explanation on the thermal activity including a trip through the geothermal plant, contact **Tours Universales** in the city, see page 884.

Taking the northern road from Ahuachapán, 9 km west of town near the village of **Los Toles** are the **Tehuasilla Falls**, where the Río El Molino falls 60 m (bus No 293 from Ahuachapán to Los Toles, then walk 1 km). The road continues northwest through the treeless **Llano del Espino**, with its small lake, and across the Río Paz into Guatemala.

Tacuba → *Population: 29,585.*

Tacuba is an indigenous town, around 850 m above sea level, and 15 km west of Ahuachapán. Tacuba means 'the village of the football game', probably relating to the *juego de pelota* of the Maya, and the existence of many pre-Columbian mounds in the surrounding area suggest the region was heavily populated in the past. At the entrance to the town are the largest colonial church ruins in El Salvador, torn down by the earthquake of Santa Marta, the same tremors that ruined large parts of Antigua, Guatemala, in 1773. You can also visit the Casa de la Cultura office, **Concultura** ① *3 km on main st north, daily 0900-1230, 1330-1600*, to see an interesting display of photos. The town is near the northern entrance of Parque Nacional El Imposible, which is accessed by hiking or 4WD in the dry season.

The surrounding area offers a wide range of opportunities including waterfalls, pristine rivers, mountain hikes and panoramic views. **Ceiba de los Pericos**, 15 minutes out of Tacuba by car, a 600-year-old ceiba tree where thousands of parrots flock together at dusk to sleep in its branches, ending the day with a deafening noise before resting for the night. In Tacuba centre the **Ceiba de las Garzas** is the rendezvous of hundreds of *garzas* (herons).

Local tour company **El Imposible Tours**, led by Tacuba native Manolo Gonzalez, provide tours of the Tacuba area and to Parque Nacional El Imposible. The dirt road leading from Tacuba to the cordillera, is steep and spectacular and provides impressive views; it is recommended although a 4WD is required.

Apaneca → *Altitude: 1450 m. Population: 8383.*

Between Ahuachapán and Sonsonate is Apaneca (91 km from San Salvador, 29 km from Las Chinamas on the border) an extremely peaceful town (and the highest town in the country), with small cobbled streets, marking the summit of the **Ruta de las Flores**. Founded by Pedro de Alvarado in 1543, Apaneca is known for its cool climate and winds – *apaneca* means 'rivers of wind' in Nahuatl. The town has a colonial centre, a traditional *parque* and a municipal market selling fruit, flowers and handicrafts. One of the oldest parochial churches in the country used to corner the central park but was demolished after damage caused by the 2001 earthquake. It has been partially reconstructed, with a modern twist. A new artisans market has opened – a great place to observe the local arts and crafts. Other local industries include coffee, flowers for export and furniture. Have a look at the topiary creations outside the police station. Check out the **Casa de la Cultura** in the centre of town. There are two small lakes nearby to the north, **Laguna Verde** and **Laguna Las Ninfas**, whose crater-like walls are clothed in tropical forest and cypress trees. It is possible to swim in the former, but the latter is too shallow and reedy. According to local legend, a swim is meant to be very beneficial to your health and the lakes are very popular with tourists. This is the Cordillera de Apaneca, part of the narrow highland belt running southeast of Ahuachapán.

South of Apaneca is the **Cascada del Río Cauta**. To get there, take bus No 216 from Ahuachapán towards Jujutla, alight 3 km after the turn-off to Apaneca, then walk 300 m along the trail to the waterfall.

Santa Leticia ① *archaeological site US$2; 2-hr coffee tour US$20; both combined US$35, www.coffee.com.sv. Bus No 249 from Juayúa (10 mins).* The Santa Leticia archaeological site is believed to be 2600 years old and was rediscovered in 1968 by the farm owner. Three huge monuments are buried among the coffee groves and you feel like a first-time discoverer as you travel the winding route to get there. There are three stone spheres with human characteristics weighing between 6000 and 11,000 kg.

Ataco

Concepción de Ataco, to give the town its full name, is located just below Apaneca. In the last five years the energetic Mayor of the village has lead Ataco to be a new favourite in Ruta de Las Flores. The village has undergone a complete renovation, and now boasts cobbled streets, old fashioned benches and street lights, and a popular weekend festival with food, flowers, and arts and crafts. New restaurants and coffee shops continue to open up, mainly for weekends only, making Ataco one of the most visited villages in the area.

Look for the *marimba* and the traditional dances in the main square and drop by **Diconte**, a new and artsy café that offers anything from delicious home-made pies to original arts and crafts that are giving La Palma art a run for their money. The **House of Coffee** has an espresso machine and produce excellent cups of world class coffee grown in Ataco at their own *finca* for five generations. Several restaurants, coffee shops and small hotels have made Ataco a great destination for a weekend trip.

North of Santa Ana

Texistepeque, 17 km north of Santa Ana on the road to Metapán, has an 18th-century baroque church, with fiestas on 23-27 December and 15 January. The town was one of the main areas for indigo production, and colonial processing plants known as *obrajes* exist all around the area. Visit the indigo workshop and museum of **Licenciado Marroquín** just out of town.

Border essentials: El Salvador–Guatemala

San Cristóbal
The border with Guatemala is 30 km northwest from Santa Ana along the paved Pan-American Highway at San Cristóbal. This is the Carretera Pan-americana crossing to Guatemala taken by the international buses and much heavy traffic.
Sleeping El Paso; basic, friendly.
Salvadorian immigration The border is open 0600-2000.
Transport To Santa Ana, bus No 201, US$0.80, 1½ hours, 0400-1800.

Anguiatú
This is normally a quiet border crossing except when there are special events at Esquipulas in Guatemala.
Salvadorian immigration The usual requirements apply; relaxed crossing.
Transport To Santa Ana, bus No 235A, US$0.80, 1¾ hours. To Metapán 40 minutes, US$0.25. This is the best route from San Salvador to northwest Guatemala, Tikal and Belize, but there is an alternative through Honduras (see under El Poy, page 891). There is a road of sorts from Metapán to El Poy and two buses a day, four hours, US$1.80, but the poor state of the road is more than compensated for by spectacular scenery.

Las Chinamas
This is a busy crossing as it is the fastest road link from San Salvador to Guatemala City. The road to the border is being widened and repaved for its entire length, except where it passes through Chalchuapa at Km 78 and Ahuachapán at Km 100.
Salvadorian immigration A straightforward crossing; quick service if your papers are ready.
Crossing by private vehicle If driving with non-Central American licence plates, expect about 45 minutes for formalities; you can hire a *trámite* (young boy) to hustle your papers through, US$2-3. Your vehicle will probably be searched by anti-narcotics officers (DOAN); do not refuse as your papers will be checked again 300 m into El Salvador. PNC (police) are courteous and efficient.
Transport 300 m above immigration, frequent buses to Ahuachapán, No 265, US$0.45, 25 minutes. Change there to a No 202 to San Salvador. Between 0800 and 1400 you may try for a space on one of the international Pullmans, negotiate with driver's aide, about US$3.50 to the capital.
Exchange Coming from Guatemala, cash your quetzals at the border, check what you are given. Change money with the women in front of the ex-ISTU office next to Customs. Good quetzal-dollar rate, cash only.

Metapán is about 10 km northeast of Lago de Güija and 32 km north of Santa Ana. Its colonial baroque **Catedral de San Pedro**, completed by 1743, is one of the very few to have survived in El Salvador. The altarpieces have some very good silver work, and the façade is splendid. The Fiesta de San Pedro Apóstol runs from 25-29 June. There are lots of easy walks with good views towards **Lago de Metapán** and, further on, **Lago de Güija**. If planning to walk in the hills near Metapán, seek local advice and do not walk alone.

Reserva Nacional y Natural Montecristo ➤➤ *Colour map 5, C3.*

ⓘ *20 km from Metapán to the park. Park employees (guardabosques) escort visitors and a permit is obtained (via fax or email) through MARN (Ministry of Environment) in San Salvador, T2267-6259 (with Patrimonio Natural and ask for Solicitud de Ingreso a Parque Nacional Montecristo). You need to fill out a form and pay US$6 per person. A 4WD is necessary in the wet season (mid-May to mid-Oct). To hire a 4WD and driver, contact Sr Francisco Xavier Monterosa, Calle 15 de Septiembre Casa 40, T2402-2805/T7350-1111 (mobile). It takes 1½-2 hrs to ascend, less to return. The trails to the summit take 1½ hrs. Camping is permitted.*

A mountain track from Metapán gives access to El Salvador's last remaining cloud forest, where there is an abundance of protected wildlife. It now forms part of El Trifinio, or the International Biosphere 'La Fraternidad', administered jointly by Guatemala, Honduras and El Salvador. Near the top of **Cerro Montecristo** (2418 m), which is the point where the three borders meet, there is an **orchid garden** with over 100 species (the best time to see them in flower is early spring), an orchard and a camping ground in the forest. The views are stunning, as is the change seen in flora and fauna with the altitude. This highest elevated part is closed for visitors during the mating and reproduction season of the animals (31 May to 31 October).

◉ Western El Salvador listings

For Sleeping and Eating price codes and other relevant information, see Essentials pages 45-48.

● Sleeping

Izalco *p871*
B La Casona de Los Vega, 2a Av Norte 24, in the center of Izalco. T2453-5951, www.lacasonadelosvega.com.sv. Colonial home converted into comfortable hotel and restaurant. Comfortable, with good views.
C El Chele, Final Av Roberto Carillas, Calle La Violeta, Caserío Texcalito, T2453-6740. Ricardo Salazar, T7798-8079, www.izalcoel chelerestaurant.com, some 800 m north of Izalco at a *finca* surrounded by forest. Great view of Volcán Izalco. Escorted hikes and horse rides available to Cerro Verde and its surrounding slopes and Izalco with visits to 2 pre-Columbian ruins nearby. Free transport available, call to arrange. English spoken.

Sonsonate *p871*
B Plaza, Calle 9 Oriente, Barrio del Angel, T/F2451-6626, www.hotelplazasonsonate. com. A/c rooms, good restaurant and a pool. Recommended.

B-C Agape, Km 63 on outskirts of town, take old road through Sonsonate, the hotel is on the exit street to San Salvador, just before the main roundabout on the right side, T2451-2667, www.hotelagape.com.sv. Converted convent, suites and rooms, a/c or fan, safe parking, fine restaurant, gardens, cable TV, pool and laundry service. Recommended.

Salcoatitán and Juayúa *p872*
B La Escondida, 6 km north of Juayúa at Finca El Portezuelo, T7888-4552, www.akwa terra.com. B&B in an exceptionally beautiful location, cradled between Laguna Verde and forest-clad mountains, with a view over to Ahuachapán to the north. You can use this as a base for hikes, mountain biking, horse riding and coffee tours. Fireplace, DVD, equipped kitchen. Contact Julio and Gaby (English spoken). They also offer coffee decks – a tent protected by an outer wooden structure – and camping.
B Posada El Encanto, Col La Esmeralda 7677, a couple of block outside Juayúa city centre, T2452-2187. Rooms have private bathroom, a/c and TV. Parking.

C Hotel Juayúa, Urb Esmeralda, Final 6a Av Norte, Juayúa, T2469-2109, www.hoteljuayua.com. Newest hotel in town, with great views.

C-D Doña Mercedes, 29 Av Sur, 6 Calle Oriente 3-6, Juayúa, 1 block south of Farmacia Don Bosco, T2452-2287. Discounts for longer stays. Recommended.

D-E Anahuac, 1 Calle Pte and 5 Av Norte, Juayúa, T2469-2401, www.hotelanahuac.com. Dormitories for backpackers and tours.

D-E El Mirador, a block from the park, Juayúa, T2452-2432, www.elmiradorjuayua.com. A 3-storey building with restaurant on top. Best option for low rates and central location.

Los Naranjos and around *p873*

A Hotel and Restaurant Los Trozos, located on the road down to Sonsonate. T2415-9879, www.lostrozos.com.

Lago de Coatepeque *p874*

B-C Torremolinos, on pier out above the lagoon, T2441-6037, www.torremolinos lagocoatepeque.com. Pool, good rooms (all with hot showers), restaurant and bar, boating trips, popular at weekends with music, lively. Discounts for longer stays.

D-F Amacuilco, 300 m from Telecom, T2441-6239. Very helpful manager called Sandra. 6 rooms (avoid those that overlook the kitchen). Discounts for longer stays, *marimba* classes, Spanish and Nahuatl lessons, and an art gallery. All meals available, pool, great view with jetty over the lake, secure, boat excursions on lake, tours arranged from US$30-40 per day, kayaks and bikes for rent. Recommended.

Santa Ana *p875, map p876*

Many hotels close their doors from 2000, so arrive early if you can.

B-C Sahara, 3 Calle Pte y 10 Av Sur, T2447-8865, www.hotelsahara.com.sv. Good service, but a little overpriced.

C-D La Libertad, near cathedral, 4 Calle Ote 2, T2441-2358. With bath, good-value budget choice, friendly, clean, helpful. Safe car park across the street, US$2 for 24 hrs.

D-E Casa Frolaz, 29 Calle Pte 42-B between 8 and 10 Av Sur T2440-5302. www.casafrolaz. com. Beautiful and clean hostel with art, paintings, history books and a friendly reception, hot showers, tropical garden with hammocks and barbecue.

D-E El Faro 1, 14 Av Sur 9 entre 9 y 11 Calle Pte, T2447-7787, www.hoteleselfaro.com. Clean rooms, good price.

D-E El Faro 2, 20 Av Sur and 2a Calle Pte (behind IRCA), T2447-1583, www.hotel eselfaro.com. A new branch of the same hotel at another location in Santa Ana.

E La Posada del Rey, 10 Av Sur 71, between 13 and 15 Calle Pte, east side of Mercado Colón and 50 m from bus terminal, T2440-0787, hotellaposadadelrey@hotmail.com. Low prices and nice rooms, friendly and helpful owners. A good backpacker choice and recommended.

Ahuachapán *p877*

B Casa Blanca, 2 Av Norte y Calle Gerardo Barrios, T2443-1505. 2 good, clean rooms with a/c. Recommended. Owner's husband is a doctor.

B-C El Parador, Km 102.5 Carretera a Guatemala, 1.5 km west of town, T/F2443-0331. Hotel and restaurant, a/c, good service, motel-style, relaxing. Helpful owner, Sr Nasser. Buses to border stop outside. Recommended.

E San José, 6 Calle Pte, opposite the park, T2413-0033. Clean, friendly, with bath. Parking available.

Tacuba *p877*

C-D La Cabaña de Tacuba, 50 m west of Alcaldía, T2417-4332. Nice hotel with large park grounds, access to river and swimming pools, a/c, cable TV. Great food at restaurant.

D-F Hostal de Mama y Papa, Barrio El Calvario, 1 Calle 1, T2417-4268, www.imposibletours.com. Home of the González family, dorm and private rooms with private bath available. Excellent, cheap food. The son, Manolo, runs El Imposible Tours.

Apaneca *p878*

AL Santa Leticia, Carretera Sonsonate Km 86.5, south of Apaneca, T2433-0357, www.coffee.com.sv. Comfortable double rooms, decorated in locally carved wood. Solar heated pool, gardens, live music on Sun, restaurant. Close to Santa Leticia archaeological site.

B Las Cabañas de Apaneca, T2433-0500, www.cabanasapaneca.com. 12 cabins in pleasant gardens, many with good views. More expensive with full board.

B Villas Suizas, at entrance to Apaneca, T2433-0193. Several log cabins with kitchen and living room. Lovely gardens.

C-E Las Orquídeas, Av Central Sur 4, T2433-0061. Clean rooms, accessible prices, centrally located. Also offer accommodation in a family home.

Laguna Verde

C Hotel Laguna Verde Guest House, T7859-2865, www.apanecasguesthouse. netfirms.com. A nice small domo house and a wood cabin located at the rim of a deep secondary crater with a spectacular view. Located 250 m from Laguna Verde and 3 km from Apaneca, a perfect departure point for hiking in the area. Micobuses serve the area several times a day; check current schedules.

Ataco *p878*

A-B Alicante Montaña, Km 93.5 Carr, Apaneca/Ataco, T2413-8656, www.alicante apaneca.com. 26 rooms with hot water, cable TV. Restaurant, pool, spa and jacuzzi.

B El Jardín de Celeste, Km 94, Carr Apaneca y Ataco, T2433-0277, www.eljardinde celeste.com. 10 rustic cabins with local flair located in a coffee grove and surrounded by colourful plants. The restaurant has capacity for larger parties and conventions. Beautifully decorated throughout the place with antiques, orchids, plants and arts and crafts.

B La Posada de Don Oli, Ataco, a few km west of Apaneca, T2450-5155, oogomezduarte@yahoo.com.mx. Hotel and restaurant in a colonial setting, owned by

the local mayor, Oscar Gómez. Guides available for visits to the local sights.

B-C Las Flores de Eloisa, Km 92.5 Carr Apaneca/Ataco, T2433-0415. Seven small cabins located inside a plant nursery.

North of Santa Ana *p878*

B-C San José, Carretera Internacional Km 113, Metapán, near bus station, T2442-0556, www.hotleselsalvador.com. A/c, quiet, cable TV, safe parking, restaurant on ground floor.

F Hospedaje Central, 2 Av Norte y Calle 15 de Septiembre. Clean, friendly and popular, with bath.

⑦ Eating

Izalco *p871*

⑪ Casa de Campo, across from Turicentro Atecozol, T2453-6530. The old *casco* of the *finca* **Cuyancúa** has been restored with beautiful gardens, making it a good spot for a meal (only open at weekends). The fish raised in the artificial lake is served in the restaurant. Horses available for hire.

⑨ Mariona, in the centre, T2453-6580. One of several *comedores*. They serve a 55-year-old recipe for *sopa de gallina* (Creole chicken soup) which is famous all over Izalco.

⑨ Restaurante El Cheles, located in the centre of Izalco with another branch out of town at Final Av Roberto Carillas, Calle La Violeta, Caserío Texcalito, T2453-5392, www.izalcoelchelerestaurant.com. Owner Ricardo Salazar speaks English and can arrange escorted hikes and horse riding to Cerro Verde.

Sonsonate *p871*

⑪ Doña Laura, located inside Hotel Agape (see Sleeping, above). Open 0730-2100. Highly recommended.

⑨ Burger House Plaza, Pasaje Francisco Chacón. Open 0900-2000. Hamburgers, fried chicken with potato salad.

Salcoatitán and Juayúa *p872*
Each weekend the whole central plaza of Juayua is invaded by the Gastronomical Food Fair, grab a chair and a table if you can, the event attracts folks from far and near. During the week there are several other options. Check www.juayua. com. for a complete list of hotels and restaurants in this area.

⫪ Baking Pizza, 2a Calle Ote y 4a Av Sur, Juayua, T2469-2356 – home-made pizza.

⫪ Comedor Laura's, 1 block from the park on 1 Av Sur, Juayúa, T2452-2098. Open daily 0700-2000. 'The best in town' according to one reader, serving *comida a la vista*.

⫪ La Terraza, on corner of the park, Juayúa. A café and convenience store with a tourist kiosk nearby.

⫪ Parque Restaurante La Colina, Km 82 on the turn-off between Juayúa and Salcoatitán, T2452-2916, old timer in the region, popular with families, also has hammocks for relaxation after the meal as well as cabins and horse rides for the kids.

⫪ Taquería La Guadalupana, Av Daniel Cordón Sur and 2a Calle Ote, Juayúa T2452-2195. Good Mexican food.

Cafés
Pastelería y Cafetería Festival, 4 Calle Pte and 1 Av Sur, T2452-2269. Bakery and coffee shop – try the *pastelitos de ciruela* (plum pie) or the traditional *semita*. Good view overlooking the park.

Santa Ana *p875, map p876*
Restaurants close quite early, between 2000 and 2100. *Comedores* are usually cheap and good value or try the food stalls beside the plaza or in front of the cathedral. Look for excellent pineapples in season.

⫪⫪ Los Horcones, on main plaza next to the cathedral. Like a jungle lodge inside, with pleasant balcony dining, good cheap meals.

⫪⫪ Lover's Steak House, 4 Av Sur y 17 Calle Pte, T2440-5717. Great value, recommended.

⫪⫪ Talitunal, 5 Av Sur 6. Mon-Sat 0900-1900. Vegetarian, attractive, good lunch, owner is a doctor and expert on medicinal plants.

⫪ Expresión, 11 Calle Pte 20, between Av 6 and 8, T/F2440-1410, www.expresion cultural.org. A great little coffee bar, restaurant, bookshop and internet café, with occasional art exhibitions. The owner, Angel, speaks English. An obligatory stop, recommended.

Chalchuapa *p875*
Several cheap and informal eateries with good-quality meals can be found around the newly renovated and charming central park.

⫪⫪ Los Antojitos, Calle Ramón Flores 6. Good meals.

Ahuachapán *p877*
There are now a handful of restaurants with lake views by Laguna del Espino just outside Ahuachapan.

⫪⫪ Restaurant El Paseo, **Restaurant Tanya** and **El Parador**, on the Las Chinamas road. All serve good meals.

Apaneca *p878*
Stalls in the municipal market offer cheap meals and typical dishes. Try the *Budín* at the middle stall on the right side of market entrance (might be the best in El Salvador). A definite must for those on a budget or for experiencing local food.

⫪⫪-⫪ La Cocina de Mi Abuela, in town, T2433-0100, open weekends; and **Cabañas de Apaneca**. The 2 largest restaurants, and the most popular spots. Attract people from far and wide.

⫪⫪ El Rosario, by the turnoff at Km 95 between Apaneca and Ataco, T2433-0205, www.negociosyturismoelrosario.com. Offers different grilled dishes, from regular *churrascos* to *pelibuey* (a mix between goat and sheep), *jaripeo*, (Salvadorian version of rodeo), horse shows and musical entertainments weekends.

⫪⫪ Entre Nubes, just up the road at km 93.5, T2433-0345, exceptionally beautiful nursery plants surround this fine coffee shop (open weekends) great desserts and varieties of coffee.

Climbing Izalco

Izalco, as can be seen from the lack of vegetation, is a geologically young volcano. Historical records show that activity began in the 17th century as a sulphurous smoke vent but, in February 1770, violent eruptions formed a cone that was more or less in constant activity until 1957. There was a small eruption in 1966 through a blowhole on the southeast slope testified by two 1000-m lava flows. Since that time, it has been quiescent.

A path leads off the road (signposted) just below the car park on Cerro Verde. In 20-30 minutes, descend to the saddle between Cerro Verde and Izalco, then it's 1-1½ hours up (steep but manageable). The contrast between the green forest of Cerro Verde and the coal-black lava around Izalco is impressive.The climb is three hours from base. Beware of falling rocks when climbing. There's a spectacular view from the top so try to ensure that low cloud is not expected before planning to go. For a quick descent, find a rivulet of soft volcanic sand and half-slide, half-walk down in 15 minutes, then it's about one hour back up the saddle. This 'cinder running' requires care, strong shoes and consideration for those below.

If you wish to climb the volcano you need to take the first bus to Cerro Verde, as the park rangers wait for the passengers from this bus before they start the guided climb to the volcano at 1100.

ψ Parque Ecoturístico Las Cascadas de Don Juan, T2273-1380, lascascadasdedonjuan@yahoo.com. Serving typical dishes and also offer hikes to the waterfalls, freshwater springs as well as a camping area.

ψ Artesanías y Comedor Rosita. Range of local dishes as well as arts and crafts.

ψ Laguna Verde Restaurant . Km 3.5 Carretera El Caserío by La Laguna Verde, T2261-0167. A newly opened, cosy and rustic spot serving typical dishes of the region. Only open weekends.

Ataco *p878*
A number of small restaurants and coffee shops have opened recently, most are only open at weekends.

ψ-ψ The House of Coffee, T2450-5353, thoc@hotmail.com. Open all week except Mon. A must visit, the recently opened café has the only professional espresso machine in town and thus a variety of coffee drinks available. Homemade cakes and steaming hot "Cup of Excellence" award-winning coffee is available here.

North of Santa Ana *p878*
Just before entering Metapán, 50 m off the highway, at the rim of the Lagunita Metapán, there are a couple of places with an international menu offering good fish from the lake. Both have a/c.

▲ Activities and tours

Ahuachapán *p877*
Tour operators
Tours Universales, at Agencia de Viajes Morales, 2 Av Norte 2-4, T2413-2002. Speak to Beatriz Contreras.

Tacuba *p877*
Tour operators
El Imposible Tours, see Hostal de Mama y Papa, page 881. Local guide Manolo, T2417-4268, T7283-1126, www.imposibletours.com.

⊖ Transport

Sonsonate *p871*
Bus
No 248 to **Santa Ana**, US$1.50 along CA 12 north, 39 km, a beautiful journey through high, cool coffee country, with volcanoes in view. To **Ahuachapán**, bus No 249, 2 hrs, slow, best to go early in the day. To **Barra de Santiago**, bus No 285. To **Los Cobanos** bus No 259. Take care at the bus terminal and on rural routes (eg in Nahuizalco area). From **San Salvador** to Sonsonate by bus No 530, US$0.80, 1½ hrs, very frequent.

Joya de Cerén *p873*
Bus
No 108 from **San Salvador** Terminal de Occidente to San Juan; US$0.45, 1 hr. Bus No 201 from **Santa Ana**, US$0.60, 1 hr, ask the bus driver to drop you at Desvío Opico from where you can catch another bus to Joya de Cerén.

Lago de Coatepeque *p874*
Bus
From **Santa Ana**, bus No 220 'El Lago' to the lake every 30 mins, US$0.35. From **San Salvador**, bus No 201 to El Congo (bridge at Km 50) on Pan American Hwy, US$1, then pick up the No 220 bus to the lake, US$0.45. Other buses to **Guatemala** may also stop at El Congo, so it's worth checking.

Taxi
From Santa Ana, US$10.

Cerro Verde and Volcán Izalco *p874*
Bus
From **Santa Ana**, bus No 248 goes to Santa Ana and Cerro Verde via El Congo. If you come from San Salvador wait for the bus at the other side of the main road, near the turnoff to Lake Coatepeque. The departures from Santa Ana are 0800, 1000 1100 and 1300. The bus arrives approximately 30 mins later at El Congo. Going back, the bus leaves from Cerro Verde at 1100, 1200, 1300, 1500,

1600 and 1730. The latest bus stops at El Congo and does not go all the way to Santa Ana. The journey between Cerro Verde at El Congo takes approximately 1 hr.

If you travel from **San Salvador** take the bus towards Santa Ana (No 205). Get off at the Shell gas station at El Congo, cross the bridge that goes over the highway and catch the No 248 at the junction from Santa Ana. If you come from the west take the bus from Esso gas station beween Izalco and Ateos that leads to Santa Ana and get off at junction 14 km below Cerro Verde summit and wait for No 248 that comes from El Congo.

Santa Ana *p875, map p876*
Bus
No 201 from Terminal del Occidente, **San Salvador**, US$1-US$1.25, 1 hr, every 10-15 mins, 0400-1830. To **La Libertad**, take 'autopista' route bus to San Salvador and change buses in Nueva San Salvador. Buses (**Melva**, **Pezzarossi** and others) leave frequently from 25 Calle Pte y 8 Av Sur, T2440-3606, for **Guatemala City**, full fare as from San Salvador, 4-4½ hrs including border stops. Alternatively, there are local buses to the border for US$0.45; they leave from the market. Frequent buses to **Metapán** and border at **Anguiatú**. No 238 follows a beautiful route to **Juayúa**.

Atiquizaya *p877*
Bus
There are frequent buses to the river from the central park in Atiquizaya; buses No 202 and 456 from Terminal Occidente in **San Salvador**, 2 hrs, US$0.90. From **Santa Ana**, 45 mins, US$0.40. All Ahuachapán buses stop in the Parque Central.

Ahuachapán *p877*
Bus
Ahuachapán is 100 km from **San Salvador** by bus 202, US$0.90, every 20 mins, 0430-1830 to the capital, 2 hrs via **Santa Ana**. Microbuses to border from northwest corner

of parque, US$0.45, 25 mins, slower buses same price. Frequent buses and minivans to the border at Km 117.

Tacuba *p877*
Bus
Buses leave the terminal in **Ahuachapán** every 30 mins, 0500-1530, return 1630-1700, via **Ataco**; US$0.60, 45 mins, rough road.

Apaneca *p878*
Bus
Local buses stop by the plaza, others pass on the main road, a few blocks north, leaving you with a fairly long walk. **Laguna Verde** can be reached by walking from Apaneca to Cantón Palo Verde and Hoyo de Cuajuste, then a further 1 km from where the road ends.

North of Santa Ana *p878*
Bus
From Santa Ana bus No 235, US$0.80, 1 hr. If driving San Salvador-Metapán, a bypass skirts Santa Ana. Bus No 211 to border at **Anguiatú**.

❶ Directory

Salcoatitán and Juayúa *p872*
Banks Between Sonsonate and Ahuachapan, Juayúa is the only village with a bank, including ATM. Open 0800-1600 Mon-Fri, 0800-1200 Sat. There are branches of several banks in both Sonsonate and Ahuachapán. **Internet** Mini Librería, 4 Calle Ote, half a block from main square, Juayúa.

Santa Ana *p875, map p876*
Banks Banks will change TCs. HSBC and several other banks, Av Independencia Sur, between Calle 3 and 7. **Internet** Expresión, has a couple of computers on the go in a very comfortable setting. **Laundry** Lavandería Solución, 7 Calle Pte 29, wash and dry US$2.50 per load, ironing service, recommended. **Police** Emergency T911. **Post office** 7 Calle Pte, between 2 Av and Av Independencia Sur.

Northern El Salvador

The route from San Salvador to western Honduras heads north, skirting the vast arm of the Cerrón Grande reservoir with volcanoes in the distance. Small villages are interspersed with brand new settlements tucked amongst the fields and hills as the road winds through mountainous landscape – a snapshot of the old way of life, and the emergence of the new. Currently enjoying a cultural revival, the charming colonial town of Suchitoto on the southern shore of the reservoir is definitely worth a visit. ▸▸ *For listings, see pages 892-894.*

North from San Salvador

The old highway, Troncal del Norte (CA 4) used to be the only acess to the north from the capital, but has been replaced with a modern highway. This can be accessed from Boulevard de la Constitución, in the northeastern part of San Salvador, and swirls west around the Volcán de San Salvador towards the Pan-American Highway and branches out to Nejapa, Quezaltepeque and Apopa to the north. Another advance in the northern road system is the newly improved road that connects Aguilares with Suchitoto. It is 2½ hours by car from San Salvador to La Palma, then 11 km to the border at El Poy.

Apopa and Tonacatepeque

ⓘ *Bus 38 B from San Salvador to Apopa, US$0.35.*

Apopa is a friendly town with a good market and a new shopping centre. It is the junction with a road to Quezaltepeque (12 km). A paved road runs east from Apopa to Tonacatepeque, an attractive small town on a high plateau. It has a small textile industry and is in an agricultural setting – check out the charming park and the colonial church. There has been some archaeological exploration of the town's original site, 5 km away. A paved road from Tonacatepeque runs 13 km south to the Pan-American Highway, some 5 km from the capital. In the other direction, a dry-weather road runs north to Suchitoto. Three kilometres beyond Apopa, on CA 4 Km 17, is **Finca Orgánica Las Termópilas** where **Lisa's Guest House** is located (see page 892). There is also a Spanish-language school and they arrange volunteers for the 'Working Farm' project at Termópilas organic farm. Tours are available to the archaeological site Cihuatán (see below) as well as on horseback to Suchitoto and to Volcán Guazapa, which played a prominent part in the civil war. The panoramic views are amazing and you can visit the old guerrilla hide outs. Contact Lena and René Carmona at **Ximena's** (see page 862), T2260-2481. All buses from Terminal de Oriente to Aguilares pass the entrance (US$0.25).

Aguilares

From Apopa, it's 21 km to Aguilares, 4 km beyond which are the ruins of **Cihuatán** ⓘ *Tue-Sun 0900-1600, map of the site with the Sendero Interpretativo is available from Lisa's Guest House or Ximena's Guest House; alternatively, contact chief archaeologist Paul Amaroli at FUNDAR in San Salvador, T2235-9453, www.fundar.org.sv.* The name means 'place of women' and was presided over by female royalty. This was the largest city in Mesoamerica during the Toltec period, when the city was surrounded by extended fortification measuring more than 10 sq km. The biggest archaeological site in the country has several tall pyramids, ball courts and *temazcales* (ritual saunas).

An improved road goes from Aguilares heading west to Suchitoto. If heading north, see page 890.

Suchitoto → *Population: 24,786.*

ⓘ *Good sites on Suchitoto are www.gaesuchitoto.com and www.suchitoto-el-salvador.com. For information in English, try to contact US citizen Roberto Broz who runs a Cyber Café Store and Restaurant El Gringo, just off the main plaza, see Eating, page 893.*

Suchitoto, meaning 'the place of birds and flowers' in Nahuatl, was founded by the Pipil more than 1000 years ago. In 1528 the capital was moved to Suchitoto for 15 years as the villa of San Salvador suffered attacks from local tribes. In 1853 an earthquake destroyed much of San Salvador and many affluent families moved to Suchitoto leaving a lasting impression on the town. Today it is a small, very attractive colonial town with cobbled streets, balconied houses and an interesting church. It is one of the favourite tourist spots in the country, with cultural traditions kept alive by the many artists living and working in the town. Several hotels and restaurants offer fantastic views towards Suchitlán and Volcán Guazapa. More than 200 species of bird have been identified in the area, and white-tailed deer inhabit the local woods.

The town was almost completely deserted in the early 1990s after 12 years of civil war which severely affected the region – 90% of the population left, leaving Suchitoto a virtual ghost town. However, a cultural revival has stimulated a range of activities and events, and the town is now considered the cultural capital of the country. Life centres on the main plaza which every evening becomes a bustle of people wandering the streets. Suchitoto's telegraph poles have been decorated by artist Paulo Rusconi, and Parque San Martín, to the west of town, is dotted with modern sculptures, some made using materials left over from the war. Arts and cultural festivals with internationally renowned artists take place every February. Another local festivity is the *Palo Encebado*, a competition involving attempts to clamber to the top of long greasy poles, and the *cerdo encebado* where a pig smeared with lard is chased through town and is kept by the first person who manages to grab it.

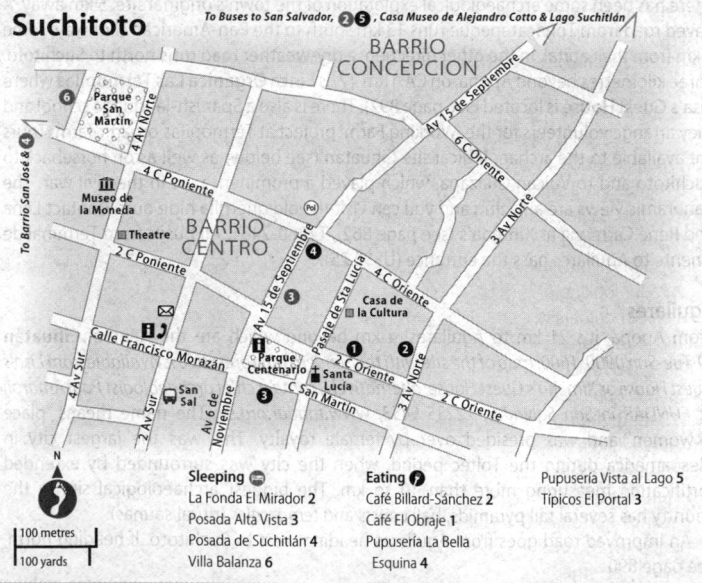

Suchitoto

To Buses to San Salvador, ② ⑤ , Casa Museo de Alejandro Cotto & Lago Suchitlán

BARRIO CONCEPCION

BARRIO CENTRO

Sleeping 🛏	Eating 🍴	Pupusería Vista al Lago 5
La Fonda El Mirador 2	Café Billard-Sánchez 2	Típicos El Portal 3
Posada Alta Vista 3	Café El Obraje 1	
Posada de Suchitlán 4	Pupusería La Bella	
Villa Balanza 6	Esquina 4	

The **Teatro de Las Ruinas** is almost fully restored and hosts concerts and events. Contact Sra Chavez, T2335 1086 for more information. **Iglesia de Santa Lucía** ① *Mon-Sat 0800-1200, 1400-1600, all day Sun*, built in 1858 with wooden and hollow columns, has also been restored with a lot of stencil work inside. There is a splendid view from the church tower. **Casa Museo de Alejandro Cotto** ① *daily 0900-1200 and 1400-1600, US$4, guided tour in Spanish (T2335-1140)*, home of movie director Alejandro Cotto, is an interesting museum with more than 132 paintings of El Salvador's most renowned artists, collections of books and music instruments.

The **tourist office** ① *Calle Francisco Morazán 7, next to the telephone office, T2335-1782, daily 0800-1700, www.suchitoto-el-salvador.com*, offers daily tours of the city centre, to Los Tercios waterfall and to Lake Suchitlán. There is also a Ministry of Tourism **tourist office** ① *Mon-Fri 0800-1700, Sat-Sun 0800-1600, T2335-1835*, in Suchito.

Around Suchitoto

A 30-minute walk north of town leads to the **Embalse Cerrón Grande** (also known as **Lago de Suchitlán**). **Proyecto Turístico Pesquero Puerto San Juan** is the newly opened harbour with boat shuttle services and, soon to open, restaurants and cafés on the lake shore. There is an area for events, parking, and arts, crafts and souvenir sales. This is the departure point for boat excursions across to remote areas in neighbouring Chalatenango, ask around and negotiate prices. Trips are available to five islands including **Isla de Los Pájaros**, which makes an interesting trip (1-1½ hours).

Ferries cross the Embalse Cerrón Grande for San Luis del Carmen (25 minutes to San Luis, frequent departures all day), where there is Comedor Carmen, and buses to Chalatenango. The ferry also makes a stop at the small village of **San Francisco Lempa**.

Los Tercios, a waterfall with striking, gigantic, black, hexagonal-shaped basaltic columns, can be reached by car, foot and by *lancha*. It is at its most impressive in the wet season when the full force of nature is on show. Walk 10-15 minutes from town down the very steep road towards the lake known as Calle al Lago de Suchitlán. Lifts can be had for about US$2-3 if you can't face the steep climb back to town afterwards, ask around. At the lake shore, where there are *comedores*, ask for a *lanchero*. A *lancha* to the base of the trail to Los Tercios is US$5-6 (negotiable) and takes 10 minutes (ask the *lanchero* to point out the trail). There are thousands of flies on the lake shore, but they don't bite. Walk upwards for 10-15 minutes in a straight line until you reach the road. You will see *flor de fuego* trees, vultures, fish eagles, blue morpho butterflies and lizards. Turn right and walk for two minutes to the third basic house on the right; take a right just before the house, through their property (if the family is there, say '*con permiso*', payment is not required). A path leads to a mirador looking out over the lake. Veering to the right on the path descends steeply down black boulders when arching to the right, you will see these impressive hexagonal structures. You can also walk from the bus terminal south along Av 6 de Noviembre. Take the first gravel road on your left until you see the town rubbish dump (*el basurero municipal*) on your left. You need to pass through the next property on your left.

La Ciudad Vieja, one-time site of the capital, is 10 km from Suchitoto. An original Pipil town, it was taken over by the Spanish who made it their central base for 17 years before electrical storms, lack of water, and cholera forced them to flee. It is a private site but can be visited. There are plans for a museum and a café.

Boat trips go to lakeside villages associated with the FMLN in the civil war. Twelve kilometres away, on the road to Aguilares, a **Bosque de la Reconciliación** is being developed at the foot of Cerro de Guazapa. Contact **CESTA** ① *T2213-1400*,

Handicrafts of El Salvador

The artists' village of **La Palma**, in a pine-covered valley under Miramundo mountain, is 84 km north of the capital 10 km south of the Honduran frontier. Here, in 1971, the artist **Fernando Llort** 'planted a seed' known as the *copinol* (a species of the locust tree) from which sprang the first artists' cooperative, now called **La Semilla de Dios** (Seed of God). The copinol seed is firm and round; on it the artisans base a spiritual motif that emanates from their land and soul.

The town and its craftspeople are now famous for their work in wood, including exotically carved *cofres* (adorned wooden chests), and traditional Christmas *muñecas de barro* (clay dolls) and ornamental angels. Wood carvings, other crafts and the designs of the original paintings by Llort, are all produced and exported from La Palma to the rest of El Salvador and thence worldwide.

In 1971 the area was almost exclusively agricultural. Today 75% of the population of La Palma and neighbouring San Ignacio are engaged directly or indirectly in producing handicrafts. The painter **Alfredo Linares** (born 1957 in Santa Ana, arrived in La Palma 1981 after studying in Guatemala and Florence) has a gallery in La Palma, employing and assisting local artists. His paintings and miniatures are marketed abroad, yet you will often find him working in the family pharmacy next to the gallery. Many of La Palma's images are displayed on the famous Hilasal towels. If you cannot get to La Palma, visit the shop/gallery/workshop of Fernando Llort in San Salvador, **Arbol de Dios**.

Twenty kilometres from the capital is the indigenous town of **Panchimalco**, where weaving on the loom and other traditional crafts are being revived. Many Nahuatl traditions, customs, dances and the language survived here as the original indigenous people hid from the Spanish conquistadors in the valley beneath the Puerta del Diablo (now in Parque Balboa). In 1996 the painter Eddie Alberto Orantes and his family opened the **Centro de Arte y Cultura Tunatiuh**, named after a Nahuatl deity who is depicted as a human face rising as a sun over a pyramid. The project employs local youths (from broken homes, or former addicts) in the production of weavings, paintings and ceramics.

In the mountains of western El Salvador, villages in the coffee zone, such as **Nahuizalco**, specialize in weaving henequen, bamboo and reed into table mats and wicker furniture. There are also local artists like Maya sculptor **Ahtzic Selis**, who works with clay and jade. East of the capital, at **Ilobasco** (60 km), many ceramic workshops produce items including the famous *sorpresas*, miniature figures enclosed in an egg shell. In the capital there are craft markets, and throughout the country, outlets range from the elegant to the rustic. Everywhere, artists and artisans welcome visitors into their workshops.

www.cesta-foe.org, in San Salvador, or contact the park directly on T2213-1403 and speak to Jesús Arriola. Also, 3 km along this road is **Aguacayo** and a large church, badly damaged during the war.

Chalatenango → *Colour map 5, C3. Altitude: 450 m. Population: 30,808.*

Highway 4 continues north from **Aguilares**, passing the western extremity of the **Cerrón Grande** reservoir. A branch to the east skirts the northern side of the reservoir to

Border essentials: El Salvador–Honduras

El Poy

The crossing between northern El Salvador and southwest Honduras at El Poy is straightforward. However, it is best to arrive early if looking to travel far beyond the border area. The border posts are 100 m either side of the border.

Transport To San Salvador, Terminal de Oriente, bus No 119, US$1.35, three to four hours, often crowded, hourly; last bus from the capital 1600. The same bus to La Palma US$0.15, 30 minutes.

Exchange Bargain with money changers at the border for the best rate for Honduran lempiras.

Chalatenango, capital of the department of the same name. Rural Chalatenango is mainly agricultural and has many remote villages, there are a number of non-governmental organizations working in the area. Chalatenango is a delightful little town with annual fairs and fiestas on 24 June and 1-2 November. It is the centre of an important region of traditional livestock farms. It has a good market and several craft shops, for example **Artesanías Chalateca**, for bags and hammocks. The weekly horse fairs, where horses, saddles and other equipment are for sale, are very popular.

La Palma and around → *Colour map 5, C3. Altitude: 1100 m. Population: 12,235.*

The main road continues north through Tejutla to La Palma, a charming village set in pine-clad mountains, and well worth a visit. It is famous for its local crafts, particularly brightly painted wood carvings and hand-embroidered tapestries. Also produced are handicrafts made from clay, metal, cane and seeds. There are a number of workshops in La Palma where the craftsmen can be seen at work and purchases made (see box, page 890). The **Fiesta del Dulce Nombre de María** takes place mid- or late February.

The picturesque village of **San Ignacio**, 6 km north of La Palma, has two or three small *talleres* producing handicrafts (20 minutes by bus, US$0.10 each way).

San Ignacio is the departure point for buses ascending a new, safe but steep road leading up to the highest mountain of El Salvador, El Pital (2730 m). As you reach the pass below the mountain top, the road branches to **Las Pilas** to the left and **Miramundo** to the right. Both Miramundo and Las Pilas have small agricultural communities, specializing in organic crops. The extensive cabbage fields combined with the pine-clad mountains make for beautiful vistas.

If you take the road from the summit to the right, you end up in Miramundo which gives a view of pretty much all El Salvador. On clear days you can see almost all the volcanoes in the country, including Volcán Pacaya and Volcán Agua In Guatemala. No doubt the best view in the country.

Border with Western Honduras

The road continues north to the border at **El Poy**, for Western Honduras. From Citalá, there is a small town with a colonial church and a potent war history (you still see bullet holes in the walls of the houses on street corners). 1 km west off the highway just before El Poy, an adventurous road leads to Metapán. Two buses daily take three hours to travel the 40 km, a rough but beautiful journey.

For Sleeping and Eating price codes and other relevant information, see Essentials pages 45-48.

⦿ Sleeping

Apopa and Tonacatepeque *p887*
D-F Lisa's Guest House, Finca Orgánica Las Termópilas, 3 km beyond Apopa, on CA 4 Km 17.5, Troncal del Norte, www.ximenasguesthouse.com. Same owners as Ximena's Guest House, T2260-2481, in San Salvador, see page 862. Budget lodging in dorms with shared bath, and spacious family rooms with TV and private bath.

Suchitoto *p888, map p888*
A-B El Tejado, 3 Av Norte 58, Barrio Concepción, T2335-1769, eltejadorestaurante@yahoo.com. Beautifully restored colonial house with just 3 rooms, pools and beautiful view of Lake Suchitlán.
A-B Los Almendros de San Lorenzo, 4 Calle Pte, next to police station, T2335-1200, www.hotelsalvador.com. In a restored colonial house with exclusive rooms and delightful gardens. Delicious meals in the restaurant – people come from the capital to lunch here at weekends. Art Gallery Pascal, across the street, has great exhibits (same owner).
B Hacienda La Bermuda 1525, Km 34.8 Carretera a Suchitoto, www.labermuda.com, T2226-1839. Hotel and restaurant with frequent cultural activities, located just outside Suchitoto.
B-C Posada de Suchitlán, Final 4 Calle Pte, at the western end of town, T2335-1064, www.laposada.com.sv. Colonial-style, beautifully tiled and decorated, excellent hotel and restaurant, stunning view.
B-D Posada Alta Vista, on Av 15 de Septiembre near the square, T2335-1645. Good rooms, although the cheaper ones can be hot. Helpful, friendly staff. Rooftop terrace with great view of the town.

D La Fonda El Mirador, Calle 15 de Septiembre, Barrio Concepción, on the road that leads to the lake, T2335-1126, quintanilladavid@yahoo.com. Next to restaurant of same name, with superb views of lake and good food too.
E Villa Balanza, in front of Parque San Martín, T2335-1408, www.villabalanzarestaurante.com.sv. 2 rooms in the restaurant of the same name. Beautiful and artistically decorated.

Chalatenango *p890*
D La Ceiba, 1a calle Pte, near 5a Av Norte, behind the military fort, Barrio Las Flores, T2301-1080. With shower and bath. A nice, new 2-storey house.

La Palma and around *p891*
AL Entre Pinos, San Ignacio, T2335-9312, www.entrepinosresortandspa.com. 1st-class resort complex, a/c, pool, cable TV, sauna and small shop.
C Hotel La Palma, Troncal del Norte, 84 km Carretera, La Palma, T2335-9012, http://lapalma.gang.net/en/tourism/lapalma.shtml. 32 large rooms, clean, with bath. Friendly, with good restaurant, beautiful gardens, nice pool, ceramics workshop, parking and gas station. Recommended.
C La Posada de Reyes, San Ignacio, just behind the park, T2352-9223. Nice private rooms with bath, also has a restaurant.
C-D Paseo El Pital, La Palma, T2305-9344. Restaurant and hotel, bit over priced but pleasant.
D Hotel Maya, Km 77.5 Troncal del Norte. Motel at the entrance of La Palma. Amazing panoramic view.
D-E Las Praderas de San Ignacio, San Ignacio, a couple of kilometres before the border, T2350-9330, www.hotelpraderasdesanignacio.com. Cabins, beautiful gardens and an economic restaurant.
D-F Hostal Miramundo, Miramundo, T2219-6251, www.hotelmiramundo.com.

Nice rooms with hot water. A restaurant, great food and great views. Recommended.
E-F Hotel Cayahuanca, San Ignacio, across the street at Km 93.5, T2335-9464. Friendly, with good but expensive restaurant.
F Casa de Huéspedes Las Orquídeas, Las Pilas. Run by a local farming family – ask for a guided trip to the mountain top nearby, for an unrivalled panoramic view and free peaches.

❶ Eating

Apopa and Tonacatepeque *p887*
♥♥ **La Posada de John Paul**, Finca Orgánica Las Termópilas. Serves food made with own-grown produce, as well as meat dishes and natural fruit juices. Excellent organic honey and coffee available, and fruit and vegetables when in season.

Suchitoto *p888, map p888*
Local specialities include *salporitas* (made of corn meal) and *chachamachas*. Try the *pupusas* in the market. Several eating options around the main plaza.
♥♥♥ **Los Almendros de San Lorenzo**, 4 a Calle Pte, Esquina PNC, Barrio El Centro, T2335-1200, plebailly@hotelelsalvador.com. Best restaurant in Suchitoto. Has a French chef, serves succulent meals and visitors come from San Salvador on weekends to dine here.
♥♥ **El Dorado**, by Lake Suchitlán, T2225-5103, www.gaesuchitoto.com. Bar and restaurant that hosts frequent concerts.
♥♥ **Estancia La Bermuda**, just out of Suchitoto, Km 34.8 Carretera a San Salvador, T2389-9078, www.labermuda.com. B&B, colonial-style restaurant with pool and cultural events.
♥♥ **Típicos El Portal**, Parque Centenario, T2335-1679. The current hot spot, open until midnight. Serves gourmet *pupusas* with home-grown herbs, Salvadorian specialities and natural teas.

♥♥ **Vista Conga Restaurant**, T2335-1679, Final pasaje Cielito Lindo No 8 Bo Concepción, vistacongasuchi@yahoo.com. Live music, only open at weekends.
♥ **Café Billard-Sánchez**, 4 Calle Pte, by El Cerrito, Barrio Santa Lucía, T2335-1464. Bar and disco.
♥ **Café El Obraje**, next to Santa Lucía church, T2335-1173. Clean and reasonably priced, with good breakfast variety, closed Tue.
♥ **Cyber Café Store and Restaurant El Gringo**, T2335-1770, 8a Av Norte No 9, Bo San José, open daily Fri-Wed. Serves *pupusas* (normal and gourmet), Tex/Mex and typical Salvadorian foods. Famous for veggie burritos.
♥ **Pupusería La Bella Esquina**, on 15 de Septiembre and 4 Calle Ote. Very good, cheap food.
♥ **Pupusería Vista al Lago**, Av 15 de Septiembre 89, T2335-1134. Good food.

Chalatenango *p890*
Several restaurants to choose from including:
♥♥♥-♥ **Rinconcitos**, next to the military fort. A la carte menu as well as *pupusas*, good

La Palma and around *p891*
In Ignacio, there are many local *comedores*, including **Comedor Elisabeth**, which offer delicious *comida a la vista* including fresh milk, cheese and cream.
♥ **El Poyeton**, Barrio San Antonio, 1 block from church, La Palma. Reliable, serves simple dishes.
♥ **La Estancia**, on Calle Principal, La Palma, T/F2335-9049. Open 0800-2000. Good menu, useful bulletin board.

❶ Shopping

La Palma and around *p891*
Handicrafts
There are more than 80 arts and crafts workshops in La Palma, www.lapalma elsalvador.com, provides a complete list of all the workshops and how to contact them.

Many workshops have come together and formed a **Placita Artesanal** – an artisans market, which is located by the Catholic church on the central plaza.

Cooperativa La Semilla de Dios, Plaza San Antonio. The original cooperative founded by Fernando Llort in 1971, it has a huge selection of crafts and paintings, helpful.

Gallery Alfredo Linares, Sr Linares' house (if gallery is unattended, ask in the pharmacy), T2335-9049. Well-known artist whose paintings sell for US$18-75. Open daily 0900-1800, friendly, recommended.

Palma City, Calle Principal behind church. Sra Alicia Mata is very helpful and will help find objects, whether she stocks them or not (wood, ceramics, *telas*, etc).

⊖ Transport

Suchitoto *p888, map p888*
Bus
To **Aguilares**, No 163 every 30 mins, 0500-1800, 30 mins on newly paved road. Regular buses (No 129) from Terminal Oriente, **San Salvador**, beginning at 0330. The bus stops at the market and leaves town for the capital from 3 Av Norte. To **Ilobasco** by dirt road, 0800 and 1000, returning 1230 and 1430.

Ferry
Cross the Embalse Cerrón Grande (Lago de Suchitlán) for **San Luis del Carmen** (25 mins to San Luis, frequent departures throughout the day) where there is **Comedor Carmen**, and buses linking to **Chalatenango**.

Chalatenango *p890*
Bus
No 125 from Oriente terminal, San Salvador, US$2, 2½ hrs.

La Palma and around *p891*
Bus
From **San Salvador**, Terminal de Oriente, No 119, US$2.25, 3 hrs, last bus at 1630.

⊕ Directory

Suchitoto *p888, map p888*
Banks Western Union available. Mon-Fri 0800-1600, Sat 0830-1200. Will cash TCs. No credit card facilities. **Internet** Cyber Café El Gringo, open daily 0800-2100, US$1per hr, free Wi-Fi for laptops; Barrio San José; 2 places on the main square either side of **Típicos El Portal**.

Eastern El Salvador

A primarily agricultural zone, the central region is lined with dramatic volcanoes, impressive scenery and the small towns of the Lempa Valley. Along the coast, quiet beaches and islands can be found on the way to the stunning Gulf of Fonseca to the east. In the north towards the mountain range bordering Honduras was an area of fierce disputes between the army and guerrillas during the civil war (1980-1992). Small communities are now rebuilt and opening up to visitors providing several small quaint villages offer ecotourism and original crafts. There are two border crossings to Honduras: to the north at Perquín, and the east at El Amatillo. ➤ *For listings, see pages 901-904.*

East from San Salvador ⊜❶❼⊜❶ ➤ *pp901-904.*

There are two roads to the port of La Unión (formerly known as Cutuco) on the Gulf of Fonseca: the Pan-American Highway, 185 km through Cojutepeque and San Miguel (see page 898); and the coastal highway, also paved, running through Santo Tomás, Olocuilta, Zacatecoluca and Usulután (see page 905).

The Pan-American Highway is dual carriageway out of the city, but becomes single carriageway for several kilometres either side of Cojutepeque – sections that are twisty, rough and seem to induce some very bad driving.

At San Martín, 18 km from the capital, a paved road heads north to Suchitoto, 25 km on the southern shore of the Embalse Cerrón Grande, also known as Lago de Suchitlán. At Km 34.8 is **Hacienda La Bermuda**, see page 892.

Cojutepeque → *Colour map 6, C1. Population: 50,315.*
The capital of the Department of Cuscatlán, 34 km from San Salvador, is the first town on the Pan American Highway encountered when heading east. There is a good weekly market. The town is famous for cigars, smoked sausages, *quesadillas* and tongue, and its annual *feria* on 29 August has fruits and sweets, saddlery, leather goods, pottery and headwear on sale from neighbouring villages, and sisal hammocks, ropes, bags and hats from the small factories of Cacaopera (Department of Morazán). There is also a sugar cane festival on 12-20 January. Lago de Ilopango is a short trip to the southwest.

Cerro de las Pavas, a conical hill near Cojutepeque, dominates Lago de Ilopango and offers splendid views of wide valleys and tall mountains. Its shrine of **Our Lady of Fátima** draws many pilgrims every year (religious ceremonies take place here on 13 May).

Ilobasco → *Population 61,510.*
From **San Rafael Cedros**, 6 km east of Cojutepeque, a 16 km paved road north to Ilobasco has a branch road east to Sensuntepeque at about Km 13. The surrounding area, devoted to cattle, coffee, sugar and indigo, is exceptionally beautiful. Many of Ilobasco's population are workers in clay; although some of its decorated pottery is now mass-produced and has lost much of its charm this is definitely the best place to buy pottery in El Salvador. Check out miniature *sorpresas*, delicately shaped microscopic sceneries the size of an egg (don't miss the naughty ones). Try **Hermanos López** ① *entrance to town, or José y Víctor Antino Herrera i Av Carlos Bonilla 61, T2332-2324, look for the 'Kiko' sign*, where there are fine miniatures for sale. The annual fiesta is on 29 September.

San Sebastián → *Population 14,411.*

Four kilometres from the turning to Ilobasco, further south along the Pan-American Highway at **Santo Domingo** (Km 44 from San Salvador), a paved road leads for 5 km to San Sebastián, where colourfully patterned cloth hammocks and bedspreads are made. You can watch them being woven on complex looms of wood and string. Behind **Funeraria Durán** there is a weaving workshop. Sr Durán will take you past the caskets to see the weavers. The **Casa de Cultura**, about 50 m from the plaza, will direct you to weaving centres and give information on handicrafts. Before buying, check prices and beware of overcharging. Market day is on Monday.

San Vicente → *Colour map 6, C1. Population: 53,213.*

Founded in 1635, San Vicente is 61 km from the capital and lies a little southeast of the Highway on the Río Alcahuapa, at the foot of the double-peaked **Volcán San Vicente** (or **Chinchontepec**), with very fine views of the Jiboa valley to the west. The town enjoys a lovely setting and is a peaceful place to spend a night or two. Its pride and joy is **El Pilar** (1762-69), the most original church in the country. It was here that the local chief, **Anastasio Aquino**, took the crown from the statue of San José and crowned himself King of the Nonualcos during the rebellion of 1832.

El Pilar stands on a small square 1½ blocks south of the Parque Central. On the latter is the cathedral, whose nave is draped with golden curtains. In the middle of the main plaza is a tall, open-work clock tower, quite a landmark when descending the hill into the city. Three blocks east of the main plaza is the *tempisque* tree under which the city's

San Vicente

Sleeping 🛏
Casa de Huéspedes
El Turista 1
Central Park 2

Eating 🍴
Acapulco 1
Comedor Rivolí 2

200 metres
200 yards

foundation charter was drawn up. The tree was decreed a national monument on 26 April 1984. An extensive market area can be found a few blocks west of the centre and hammock sellers are on nearby streets. An army barracks takes up an entire block in the centre. There's a small **war museum**; ask the FMLN office here or in San Salvador. Carnival day is 1 November.

Around San Vicente

Three kilometres southeast of the town is the **Balneario Amapulapa** ① *T2393-0412, US$0.80 entry and US$0.90 parking charges, a Turicentro*. There are three pools at different levels in a wooded setting. The Tourist Police patrols here and lately it's been considered a safe place for tourists, although women should not walk to the area alone. Reached by bus No 177 from Zacatecoluca bus station, and by pickup from the San Vicente Bus station. **Laguna de Apastepeque** ① *T2389-7172, near San Vicente off the Pan-American Hwy*, is small but picturesque. Take bus No 156 from San Vicente, or 499 from San Salvador. Ask in San Vicente for guides for climbing the San Vicente volcano.

San Miguel

Sleeping 🛏	El Mandarín 6	Motel Millián 5
China House 2	King Palace 3	Trópico Inn 8
Comfort Inn Real 4	Madrid 9	Victoria 10

San Miguel → *Colour map 6, C2. Population: 218,410.*

Set at the foot of the **Volcán San Miguel** (**Chaparrastique**), which last erupted in 1976 but has shown activity ever since, San Miguel is the third largest city in El Salvador, 136 km from San Salvador. The capital of its Department, the town was founded in 1530 as a military fortress by Don Luis de Moscoso. It now has one of the fastest growing economies in Central America, some pleasant plazas and a bare 18th-century cathedral. The city's theatre dates from 1909, but since the 1960s it has been used for various purposes other than the arts. After several years of restoration it reopened in 2003 in all its original glory. There is a Metrocentro shopping centre southeast of the centre and the **Turicentro of Altos de la Cueva** ① *T2669-0699, take bus No 94 (leaves in front of the Cathedral in San Miguel) US$0.80, bungalows US$34*, is 1 km north. It offers swimming pools, gardens, restaurants, sports facilities and bungalows for rent, and is busy at weekends.

The arid climate all year round makes the region ideal for growing maize, beans, cotton and sisal, and some silver and gold are mined here. However, the biggest industry is the *remesas* (money received from family members who have emigrated to the US), as this part of the country experienced heavy migration both during and after the civil war.

The fiesta de la Virgen de la Paz is on the third Saturday in November, and one of the biggest carnivals in Central America, known as *El Carnaval de San Miguel*, also takes place here.

Routes from San Miguel ⊖❶❷❸ → *pp901-904.*

Several routes radiate outwards from San Miguel. A paved road runs south to the Pacific Highway. Go south along it for 12 km, where a dirt road leads to Playa El Cuco (bus 320 from San Miguel, US$1.50). A mainly paved, reasonable road goes to west to San Jorge and Usulután: leave the Pan-American Highway 5 km west of San Miguel, where the road passes hills and coffee plantations with good views of the San Miguel volcano.

Another route heads northeast to the small town of Jocorro, where the road splits with options to Honduras. Heading north, San Francisco Gotera leads to the Perquín crossing; east of Jocorro the road leads to the border crossing at El Amatillo; and directly east from San Miguel lies La Unión, with connections north to El Amatillo.

San Francisco Gotera and around

The capital of Morazán Department can be reached directly from the Oriente terminal in San Salvador, or from San Miguel (bus No 328). There are places to stay (see Sleeping, page 902).

Beyond San Francisco, the road runs to **Jocaitique** (there is a bus) from where an unpaved road climbs into the mountains through pine forests to **Sabanetas**, near the Honduran border. Accommodation is available at Jocaitique and Sabanetas.

Northeast of San Francisco is **Corinto** ① *20 mins north of the village on foot, just east of the path to the Cantón Coretito, open daily*, which has two rock overhangs showing faint evidence of pre-Columbian wall paintings. Take an early bus, No 327, from San Miguel, US$1.

Ciudad Segundo Montes and around

Eight kilometres north of San Francisco Gotera is Ciudad Segundo Montes, a group of villages housing 8500 repatriated Salvadorian refugees (the community is named after one of the six Jesuit priests murdered at the Central American University in November

Border essentials: El Salvador–Honduras

Perquín

The Honduran border has been moved, by treaty, to less than 3 km north of Perquín; this area has been the subject of disputes and definition problems for many decades. It was one of the basic causes of the 'Football War' of 1969 (see page 1404) and there were military confrontations between El Salvador and Honduras before the boundary disagreement was finally and completely resolved in April 2006. There is a border crossing 5 km past the frontier here and the route to Marcala and La Esperanza (Honduras) is open. There is a bus service from Marcala to San Miguel, five hours, US$3.50, using this route, but be aware that the road may be impassable after heavy rains.

El Amatillo

Río Goascarán is the border, with El Amatillo on both sides of the bridge.
Salvadorian immigration The border closes at 1700 and may close for two hours at lunchtime. This is a very busy crossing, but is easy for those going on foot.
Crossing by private vehicle You will be hounded by *tramitadores* offering to help, but there's no need to use their services as it's a fairly relaxed crossing. Car searches are thorough at this crossing.
Sleeping Near the border are two *hospedajes*, both basic: **Anita** (with *comedor*) and **Dos Hermanos** (without).
Transport To San Miguel, bus No 330, one hour 40 minutes, US$1.50. See also Santa Rosa de Lima.

1989). Schafic Vive is a small museum with information on the community. If you wish to visit contact **PRODETUR** ① *T2680-4086*, for information. No formal accommodation is available.

Fourteen kilometres north of San Francisco is **Delicias de la Concepción**, where fine decorated hammocks and ceramics are made. The prices are good and the people are helpful; worth a visit. Buses every 20 minutes from San Francisco.

Perquín and around → *Colour map 6, C2. Altitude: 1200 m. Population: 3158.*
Perquín – meaning 'Road of the Hot Coals'– is 205 km from San Salvador and was the guerrillas' 'capital', and the scene of much military activity. War damage used to be visible around the town, but all is now peaceful and the scenery is very beautiful, surrounded by pine-topped mountains. There is a small central square with a Casa de la Cultura, post office and a PRODETUR **tourist information office** ① *T2680-4086*. Opposite is the plain Iglesia Católica Universal Progresista.

The **Museo de la Revolución** ① *T7942-3721, daily 0800-1700, US$1.20, no photos or filming allowed, guided tours in Spanish, camping permitted, US$1*, clearly signposted from the plaza, has temporary exhibits as well as one on Archbishop Romero and all the gory details of his murder – nothing is spared. The museum, run by ex-guerrillas, is badly lit, but fascinating with photographs, propaganda posters, explanations, objects, pictures of the missing, and military paraphernalia. In the garden is the wreckage of an American-made helicopter, shot down by guerrillas in 1984. Sprawled like a piece of modern art, it would look at home in a contemporary art gallery. There is also a room where a recreated cabin shows the place from where the clandestine radio *Venceremos* broadcast their programmes during the war.

Behind the town is the **Cerro de Perquín** ① *US$0.25 to climb, it is advisable to bring a guide*. The views are fantastic with the town below nestling in the tropical scenery, green parrots flying through the pine trees, and the mountains stretching towards the border with Honduras. The **Festival de Invierno**, 1-6 August, is a mixture of music, exhibitions and film. Book accommodation in advance if planning to come for the festival. The **Festival de San Sebastián** is on 21-22 January, and the celebration of the **Virgen del Tránsito**, the patron saint of the church, takes place 14-15 August.

Nearby villages such as Arambala and El Mozote can be visited, or you can take a walking tour. At **El Mozote** is a recently built memorial to a massacre that took place in 1981, during which more than 300 people, among them children, were killed. Five kilometres west of Perquín is **Arambala**, which is slowly being rebuilt. Locals will give you a tour of the town and church, which was destroyed by fire in the 1980s. Near Perquín, turn-off 2 km south, are the park and trails of **Cerro Pelón**. Nearby is **El Llano del Muerto**, a tourist area of naturally heated pools and wells. North of Perquín, straddling the new border with Honduras, is one of the few unpolluted rivers in the country. The people of Morazán are more reserved with strangers than in the rest of El Salvador. If travelling on your own, 4WD is advised.

Ruta de la Paz run by **PRODETUR** ① *T2680-4086, perkintours@yahoo.es, daily 0800-1700, 0800-2100 during the winter festival*, provides walks, culture and adventure tourism, and can organize accommodation. Tours are between 25 minutes and two days, and for one to 10 people. Ask for Serafín Gomez, who is in charge of the tours.

Santa Rosa de Lima → *Population: 27,693.*

The shortest route from San Miguel to the Honduran border takes the Ruta Militar northeast through Santa Rosa de Lima to the Goascarán bridge at El Amatillo, a total of 58 km on paved road.

Santa Rosa is a charming little place with a wonderful colonial church set in the hillside. There are gold and silver mines, a market on Wednesday, and a curiously large number of pharmacies and shoe shops. The FMLN office has details about the **Codelum Project**, a refugee camp in Monte Barrios. The fiesta is on 22-31 August.

La Unión ⚫🟠🟡🟢🔵 » *pp901-904. Colour map 6, C2.*

→ *Population: 34,045.*

It is another 42 km from San Miguel to the port of La Unión, on the Gulf of Fonseca. The spectacular setting on the west shore of the gulf does little to offset the heat and the faded glory of this port town which handles half the country's trade. Shortly before entering the town, the Pan-American Highway turns north for 33 km to the Goascarán bridge at **El Amatillo** on the border with Honduras (see box, page 899). A project to inaugurate the modern port of La Unión is scheduled to happen in the near future. This huge project includes foreign investments, such as a large Spanish tuna fish processing plant, with supporting infrastructure including new roads, hotels and a school running training in logistics and tourism.

Around la Unión

Conchagua is worth visiting to see one of the few old colonial churches in the country, and there is a good bus service from La Unión (No 382, US$0.10). The church was begun in 1693, after the original Conchagua had been moved to its present site following repeated attacks on the island settlements by the English. There are fiestas on 18-21 January and 24 July. There is also **Volcán Conchagua** (1243 m) which can be climbed but is a hard walk, particularly near the top where protective clothing is useful against the vegetation. It's about four hours up and two hours down, but you will be rewarded by superb views over Volcán San Miguel to the west and the Gulf of Fonseca, which is bordered by El Salvador, Honduras and Nicaragua (where the Cosigüina volcano is prominent) to the east.

In the Gulf of Fonseca are the Salvadoran islands of **Isla Zacatillo**, **Isla Conchagüita** and the largest, **Isla Meanguera** (about 4 km by 7 km). English and Spanish pirates occupied the island in the late 1600s, and international claims remained until the International Court of Justice in The Hague awarded the island to El Salvador in 1992, in preference to claims from Honduras and Nicaragua.

A *lancha* leaves La Union for the town of **Meanguera del Golfo**, on Meanguera. The journey across the gulf is beautiful – tranquil waters, fishing boats and views to the surrounding mountains. The island has secluded beaches with good bathing, for example Marahual (45-minute walk), fringed with palm trees. About 2400 people live on this carefree island, where painted boats float in the cove surrounded by small *tiendas* and *comedores* that serve fish, shark and prawns. The highest point on the island is **Cerro de Evaristo** at 512 m. Launches leave La Unión daily at 1000 but times change so ask locally; the journey takes two hours. It's possible to arrange transport with a local boatman to Coyolito (Honduras) and Isla Amapala, but make sure the price is agreed beforehand. You can travel to Honduras or Nicaragua if you have visited immigration in La Unión first to get the necessary paperwork.

◉ Eastern El Salvador listings

For Sleeping and Eating price codes and other relevant information, see Essentials pages 45-48.

● Sleeping

San Vicente *p896, map p896*
D-E Central Park, on Parque Central, T2393-0383. Good, clean rooms, with bath, a/c and phone. Cheaper with fan, cheaper still without TV. Café and restaurant downstairs.
E Estancia Familiar, El Calvario (corner in front of Pollo Campero), budget option in town.

San Miguel *p898, map p897*
Most hotels are on the entrance roads, although there are plenty of cheap places near the bus station.

LL-A Hotel Comfort Inn Real San Miguel, T2600-0202, www.choicehotels.com, Av Roosevelt, in front of Metrocentro.
A Trópico Inn, Av Roosevelt Sur 303, T2661-1800, tropicoinn@yahoo.com. Clean and comfortable, with reasonable restaurant, swimming pool, garden and safe parking for motorbikes. Recommended.
B El Mandarín, Av Roosevelt Norte, T2669-6969. A/c, pool, good Chinese restaurant.
C Madrid T2669-2738, Blv Ruta Militar, Av Trejo Pacheco 4, on the road to Santa Rosa de Lima. Private bath with a/c and cable TV.
C Motel Millián, Panamericana Km 136, in front of the Military Hospital, T2683-8100. Pool and a good restaurant. Recommended, value for money.
C Victoria, 8a Av Sur 101, El Calvario T2660-7208, hotelvictoriasanmiguel2008@

hotmail.com. Private bath with a/c and cable TV.

D China House, 15 Av Norte, Panamericana Km 137.5, T/F2669-5029. Clean, friendly.

E King Palace, opposite the bus station. Good breakfast.

San Francisco Gotera *p898*

C-E Hospedaje San Francisco, Av Morazán 29, T2654-0066. Nice garden and hammocks.

Perquín and around *p899*

B Hotel Perkin Lenca, Km 205.5 Carretera a Perquín, T/F2680-4080, www.perkinlenca. com. Swiss cabins. Nice cosy restaurant La Cocina de Ma'Anita, open daily 0700-1900.

B Las Margaritas, T2613-1930, at the entrance to Perquín village.

C Arizona T2634-8990, at entrance to town on main street towards El Llano del Muerto.

D La Posada de Don Manuel, 5 mins from Perquín at the bottom of the hill, CTE Perquín T2680-4037. Previously called El Gigante, countless partitioned rooms that would probably be noisy if full, but rarely are. Clean, with cold showers and meals. Have restaurant and organize tours with guides. Friendly.

F Cocina Mama Toya y Mama Juana, at the entrance of Perquin village, T2680-4045. Small rooms with 3 beds, shared bath, parking.

Camping

It's possible to camp in the grounds of the Museo de la Revolución, near a crater formed by a 227-kg bomb dropped in Aug 1981. Ask in the nearby *tiendas*.

Near the Río Zapo, PRODETUR has a great campground with facilities, and there are guides who can give you a tour of the area. Great for both trekking and hiking. There is also a simple cabin for rent here.

Santa Rosa de Lima *p900*

F Florida, Ruta Militar, T2641-2020. Helpful, fairly clean, basic, with 3 parking spaces (arrive early).

F Hospedaje Mundial, near the market. Basic rooms with fan. Friendly, lots of parking.

F Recreo, 2 blocks from town centre in front of police station and Telecom, 4 Av Norte, Barrio el Recreo, T2641-2126. Basic fan rooms, noisy but friendly. Recommended.

La Unión *p900*

E San Francisco, Calle General Menéndez 6-3, Barrio Concepción, T2604-4159. Clean and friendly, some rooms with hammocks and fan. Noisy and has some water supply problems, but OK. Safe parking.

Around La Unión *p901*

D Hotel Paraíso, Meanguera del Golfo. Has rooms with TV, private bath and hot water. Recommended.

❷ Eating

Ilobasco *p895*

There are 2 pizzerias, several local *comedores*, a Pollo Campero and a Taco Hut.

❚❚ Restaurante Ricky, at 3 Av Sur. The town's only real restaurant with à la carte dining.

San Vicente *p896, map p896*

The San Vicente Gastronomical festival is held on the last Sat of the month at the central park. Close to Hotel Central Park are Pops and La Nevería, for good ice cream.

❚ Acapulco, by the central market. Good.

❚ Casablanca, next to the park, T2393-0549. Good shrimps, steaks, and you can swim in their pool for US$1.15.

❚ Comedor Rivoli, Av María de los Angeles Miranda. Clean, offering good breakfast and lunches.

❚ Evergreen, Bar and restaurant. Open Wed-to Sun.

San Miguel *p898, map p897*

Try *bocadillos de totopostes*, maize balls with either chilli or cheese; and *tustacos*, which are like small tortillas with sugar or honey. Both are delicious and traditional.

El Gran Tejano, 4 Calle Pte, near the cathedral. Great steaks.

Restaurant Perkin Lenca, Km 205.5 Carretera a Perquín, T/F2680-4080, www.perkinlenca.com, open daily 0700-2000. Part of the hotel of the same name, this restaurant serves traditional food.

Perquín and around *p899*
Antojitos Marisol, T2680-4063, near the church on the south side of the plaza. Simple food and open late.
Comedor Blanquita, T2680-4223 near the church in the centre, *comida a la vista* and snacks.
La Cocina de Mi Abuela, at the entrance to town. T2680-4002, popular with locals with good, local dishes.

Santa Rosa de Lima *p900*
Martina, near the bridge. Good food including *sopa de apretadores* for US$7.
Chayito, Ruta Militar. Buffet, *comedor*.

La Unión *p900*
Bottled water is hard to find, but *agua helada* from clean sources is sold (US$0.25 a bag). There are several cheap *comedores* to choose from, try **Comedores Gallego** (**†**) and **Rosita** (**†**), recommended. **Comedor Tere** (**†**), Av General Menéndez 2.2, is also fairly good.
Amanecer Marino, on the waterfront. Beautiful view of the bay and good for watching the world go by. Serves seafood.
Las Lunas, 3 blocks from the central park. Nice atmosphere. Very popular among locals.
Restaurante Puerto Viejo, located in front of El Dragon. Big portions, cheap. Best seafood in town – try *tazón de sopa de pescado*.

● Transport

Cojutepeque *p895*
Bus No113 from Oriente terminal in **San Salvador** (US$0.80); buses leave from Cojutepeque on the corner of the plaza, 2 blocks from the main plaza.

San Sebastián *p896*
Bus
Bus No 110 from the Oriente terminal runs from San Salvador to San Sebastián (1½ hrs, US$1). There are also buses from Cojutepeque.

San Vicente *p896, map p896*
Bus
No116 from Oriente terminal, **San Salvador**, every 10 mins or so (1½ hrs, US$0.90). Returning to the capital, catch bus from the bus station, Av Victoriano Rodríguez y Juan Crisóstomo Segovia; outside the cathedral; or on the road out of town. To **Zacatecoluca**, bus 177 (US$0.50) from bus station. Buses to some local destinations leave from the street that runs west to east through the market. You have to take 2 buses to get to **San Miguel** (see below), the first to the Pan-American Hwy, where there is a bus and food stop, then another on to San Miguel (US$1.50 total).

San Miguel *p898, map p897*
Bus
Buses 301, 306 and 346 from Oriente terminal, **San Salvador** US$2.50, every 30 mins from 0500 to 1630, 2½ hrs. There are also 3 comfortable express buses daily, 2 hrs, US$5.

There are frequent buses to the Honduran border at **El Amatillo**, US$1. 4 buses, No 332A, daily to **Perquín**, from 0600-1240, 2¾ hrs, US$1.60.

Perquín and around *p899*
Bus
From **San Miguel**, bus No 332A (2¾ hrs, US$1.50). The bus from Terminal Oriente in **San Salvador** (4½ hrs) is very crowded, luggage a hindrance. Bus or truck from **Cd Segundo Montes**. Transport back to Cd Segundo Montes or San Miguel may be difficult in the afternoons.

Car

If you're driving fill your tank before getting to Perquín because the last petrol station is 20 mins from the city and closes at 1700.

Santa Rosa de Lima *p900*
Bus

To the Honduran border every 15 mins, US$0.50. Direct buses also to **San Salvador**, No 306, from 0400 until 1400, US$3.25, 3½ hrs.

La Unión *p900*
Bus

The terminal is at 3 Calle Pte (block 3). To **San Salvador**, bus 304, US$2, 4 hrs, many daily, direct or via San Miguel, 1 passes the harbour at 0300. Bus 320 to **San Miguel**, US$0.45. Bus to Honduran border at **El Amatillo**, No 353, US$1.80.

O Directory

San Vicente *p896, map p896*
Banks Banco Hipotecario on main plaza, exchange counter at side. Also branches of HSBC, Citi Bank and Banco Agrícola Casa de Cambio León, Calle Dr Antonio J Cañas, off northeast corner of main plaza. **Post office** In Gobernación, 2 Av Norte y Calle 1 de Julio 1823. **Telephone** Telecom, 2 Av Norte/Av Canónigo Raimundo Lazo, southeast of plaza.

San Miguel *p898, map p897*
Banks Open daily 0900-1600. Citi Bank will change TCs, but you must produce receipt of purchase. Banco Agrícola is next to Tropico Inn. Casa de Cambio Lego, 2 Calle Pte, overlooking market. **Police** Emergency T911.

La Unión *p900*
Customs 3 Av Norte 3.9. **Immigration** Av General Cabañas and 1 Av Norte. **Internet** Infocentro, 1 Calle Pte, 2-4 Av Norte, Mon-Fri. **Police station** Opposite Immigration office.

Pacific coast

Running the length of the country to the south, the Pacific coastline is a blend of stunning views, quiet beaches and private resorts. If basking in the sun isn't enough, the coast is a big hit with the surf crowd as some of the best surfing spots are located in the departments of La Libertad and Las Flores in San Miguel. For a little more activity, you can go west and visit the impressive Parque Nacional El Imposible. Heading east towards Nicaragua, the islands of the Gulf of Fonseca are equally cut off. ►► *For listings, see pages 910-914.*

La Libertad ⊜❷▲⊜❶ ►► *pp910-914. Colour map 6, C1.*

→ *Population: 35,997.*

Just before Santa Tecla, a branch road turns south for 24 km to the small fishing port of La Libertad, 34 km from San Salvador and just 25 minutes from the Comalapa International Airport. This is a popular, laid-back seaside resort in the dry season but is not very clean. However, the whole area has been recently remodelled and now boasts an amphitheatre, soccer and basketball courts and a brand new **Complejo Turístico** where the old naval building once stood, with a *malecon* and several restaurants. The pier is worth seeing for the fish market awnings and, when the fleet is in, for the boats hauled up out of the water along its length. The cemetery by the beach has tombstones painted in the national colours, blue and white. On the seafront are several hotels and restaurants. At a small plaza, by the **Punta Roca** restaurant, the road curves left to the point, offering fine views of La Libertad bay and along the coast. The market street is two blocks inland across from the central church. The coast to the east and west has good fishing, surfing and bathing. The beaches are black volcanic sand (which can get very hot).

La Libertad gets very crowded at weekends and holidays and for overnight stays the beaches to the west of La Libertad are better. Service can be off-hand. Dedicated surfers may wish to stay for a while, as the breaks at Punta Roca in Puerto La Libertad are rated among the best 10 in the world. The season runs from November to April and the surf is excellent. Watch your belongings on the beach and don't stay out alone late at night.

The town holds an annual **Gastronomic Festival** in early December and has resurrected the tradition of *lunadas* – full-moon parties in the dry season. Bonfires are lit on the beach, restaurants stay open late offering *comida típica*, and some places provide live music and themed nights. Find local information in Spanish at www.puertolalibertad.com.

Around La Libertad

The **Costa del Bálsamo** (Balsam coast), running west from La Libertad and Acajutla, gives its name to the pain-relieving balsam, once a major export of the region. On the steep slopes of the departments of Sonsonate and La Libertad, scattered balsam trees are still tapped for their aromatic juices. Buses travel along the coast to Sonsonate (at 0600 and 1300) and the journey offers stunning views of the rugged volcanic coast. The municipalities of San Julián, Cuisnahuat, Ixhuatan, Tepecoyo, Talnique, Jayaque, Chiltuipan, Comasagua and Teotepeque are all situated along the balsam coast. On the road from San Salvador to La Libertad is **Plaza Turística Zaragoza** ① *Tue-Sun 1000-1900*, where you will find handicrafts, restaurants and amenities for children.

At the very entrance of Puerto La Libertad you now have the newly inaugurated shopping center called **El Faro** where you will find the **Selectos** supermarket, shoe shop, **Nevería** ice cream shop and fried chicken **Pollo Campero**.

The eastern end of La Libertad is **Playa La Paz or Punta Roca**, 2 km beyond which is **Playa Obispo**. About 1 km east of La Curva, on the right towards San Diego is the **Fisherman's Club** ① T2262-4444, entry US$6, with pool, tennis courts and a good restaurant. The beach is good too, but beware of the rip tide; it's only advisable for surfers.

West of La Libertad ⊜❶⊜ ▸▸ pp910-914.

Continuing west from **Playa Conchalío** at Km 38 you reach **Playa El Majahual**, which does not have a safe reputation, nor is it very clean, but offers good waves for surfing. A little further on is **Playa El Cocal** and **Playa San Blas**. On both beaches several new hotels catering primarily for surfers have popped up. One of the most popular beaches for foreigner is **Playa El Tunco**. To get here take bus No 80 from La Libertad and get off at the turn-off where all the surfer hotels signs are posted (**Roca Sunzal** is the most visible one). It is then a short walk (a couple of blocks) to the seafront. This is one of the best surfing beaches in this area with the two breaks, Sunzal and La Bocana, both easily accessible. **Club Salvadoreño** ① www.clubsalvadoreno.com, and **Club Tecleño** both have their beach premises here and El Tunco itself has several hotels and restaurants. ▸▸ See listings, page 910.

Further up the road at Km 43.5 is **El Sunzal**. Although the breaks are amazing at Sunzal, the small hotels are not as safe as at El Tunco and there have been reports of theft at the beach at dusk, so choose to stay at El Tunco. The exception in El Sunzal is the brand new luxury hotel **Casa de Mar**, which is located just in front of the breaks, and is an option if you want a splurge or to dine in their gourmet seafood restaurant, Café Sunzal, which has great food and panoramic views of the beach.

At Km 49.5 is **Playa Palmarcito**. This tiny and inviting beach is great for escaping the crowds and is good for novice surfers, as the breaks are not as violent as on other beaches. Located just in front of the beach is **Restaurante Las Palmas**, offering great meals and low prices. A new option for a few night's stay is **Hotel El Palmarcito**, which also has a restaurant, surf board rental and classes. Perched atop a cliff next to Palmarcito is the **Atami Beach Club** ① T2223-9000, access for US and other non-Central American passport-holders is US$10, including a cabaña for changing, a beautiful place with a large pool, private beach, expensive restaurant, two bars and gardens. At the turn-off to the beach along the highway (next to police station) is the **Hotel Bosques del Río** (same owner as **Restaurante Las Palmeras**), where you can ask for discounts for longer stays.

Just a couple of kilometres out of La Libertad on the Carretera Litoral is **Parque Nacional Walter Deininger** ① run by the Ministry of Tourism, T2243-7835, www.el salvador.travel, for more information contact ISTU on T2222-8000, www.istu.gob.sv, simply present your passport at the gate. There are rivers and caves, and the park is great for hiking. There is even a seed bank for endangered tree species, an array of medicinal plants and a nursery. The views are fantastic and it's a good way to learn more about the flora and fauna, guides are available upon request.

At Km 53.5 is **Playa El Zonte**, is another favourite among foreign tourists. It's a bit safer and quieter than El Tunco, being further away from La Libertad. The top-notch surf breaks has made El Zonte a place people stay longer than anticipated, and there are several well-established hotels with restaurant service. There are also several informal, cheap cafés and room rentals down at the beach.

The Carretera Litoral continues for a further 40 km or so to Acajutla past rocky bays, remote black-sand beaches and through tunnels. Take great care if you bathe along this coast, as it can be dangerous.

Acajutla and around → *Colour map 5, C3. Population: 52,359.*

At the junction of San Julian, a short journey south from Sonsonate, the coastal road heads south to the lowlands city of Acajutla, El Salvador's main port serving the western and central areas, 85 km from San Salvador (the port is 8 km south of the Coastal Highway). It is a popular seaside resort during the summer for Salvadorans, but lodging in the village is not considered safe for foreigners. There are some good seafood restaurants with panoramic views.

The rocky beach of **Los Cóbanos** (14 km south of Acajutla via San Julian, bus from Sonsonate) is very popular with weekending Salvadorans and has one of only two coral reefs along the entire Central American Pacific coast, making it a popular dive spot. Fishermen arrange boat trips; negotiate a price. José Roberto Suárez at **Los Cobanos Village Lodge** ① *T2420-5248, sas_tun@hotmail.com*, speaks English and can be of assistance when renting boats and diving equipment.

The newly paved coastal road heads west running along the coast for 43 km before reaching the Guatemalan frontier at **La Hachadura**.

The black-sand beaches northwest of Acajutla at **Metalío** and Costa Azul (mostly full of private beach houses) and **Barra de Santiago** are recommended, although there are few public facilities. Barra de Santiago is a peninsula, 30 km west of Acajutla, the beach is reached along a 7 km compact dirt road or across a beautiful lagoon. The entire area is a protected natural area is in the process of being declared an ecological reserve to protect endangered species, including turtles, crocodiles and sea falcons. The Garza Axul (blue heron) is one of the amazing rare birds only found here. The mangrove is the third largest in El Salvador. This beach has an island named **El Cajete,** which has an archaeological site dating back to around AD 900. There are several pyramids but the area has not been excavated. **El Capricho Beach House** ① *T2260-2481, same owners as Ximena's in San Salvador, see page 862* has a beautiful beach front hotel here (see Sleeping, page 911).

Parque Nacional El Imposible

① *Park entrance is US$6, payable at the gate. For more information contact Salvanatura office, 33 Av Sur 640, Col Flor Blanca, San Salvador, T2279-1515, www.salvanatura.org. Voluntary donation of US$4-5 a day. To get to the park, take the San Salvador–Sonsonate bus, and then bus No 259 to Cara Sucia. Pickups leave for the park at 1100 and 1400. From Guatemala and the border, regular buses heading for San Salvador pass through Cara Sucia from where you catch the 1100 and 1400 pickups.*

So-called because of the difficulty of reaching it, this 'impossibility' has helped preserve some of the last vestiges of El Salvador's flora and fauna on the rocky slopes and forests of the coastal **Cordillera de Apaneca**. Traders used to travel through the region, navigating the steep passes from which the park takes its name.

Among the mammals are puma, ocelot, agouti and ant bear; the birds include black-crested eagle, white hawk and other birds of prey, black and white owls, and woodpeckers. There is also a wide variety of reptiles, amphibians and insects, the greatest diversity in the country. There are eight different strata of forest, and over 300 species of tree have been identified. There is a small visitor centre, and rivers and natural pools to swim in. Trained naturalist guides from the nearby community of San Miguelito accompany visitors into the park, helping to identify season specific trails and routes, and pointing out interesting plants, animals and other attractions along the way.

East of La Libertad ●❶❷● ↠ pp910-914.

The second route to La Unión runs east through the southern cotton lands. It begins on a four-lane motorway to the airport at Comalapa. The first place of any importance is at Km 13, **Santo Tomás** where there are pre-Hispanic ruins at **Cushululitán**, a short distance north. A new road to the east, rising to 1000 m, runs south of Lago de Ilopango to join the Pan-American Highway beyond Cojutepeque. Ten kilometres on from Santo Tomás is **Olocuilta**, an old town famed for its church and known throughout the world for its rice dough, *pupusas*. It hosts a colourful market on Sundays under a great tree. Both Santo Tomás and Olocuilta can be reached by bus 133 from San Salvador. The highway to the airport crosses the Carretera Litoral (CA 2) near the towns of San Luis Talpa and Comalapa. The coastal road goes east, through Rosario de la Paz, across Río Jiboa and on to Zacatecoluca.

Costa del Sol

Just after Rosario, a branch road to the south leads to **La Herradura** (bus 153 from Terminal del Sur to La Herradura, US$1.25, 1½ hours) and the Playa Costa del Sol on the Pacific, which is being developed as a tourist resort. The beach is on a narrow peninsula, the length of which are private houses which prevent access to the sand until you reach the **Turicentro** ① *0800-1800*. Here, *cabañas* can be rented for the day or for 24 hours, but they are not suitable for sleeping. Playa Costa del Sol is crowded at weekends and holidays, as there are extensive sandy beaches. However, the sea has a mild undertow; so go carefully until you are sure. Several new and expensive hotels are continuously popping up but prices are a bit over the top, budget travellers might choose some of the smaller hotels by Playa Los Blancos. On the road to Costa del Sol, there is also a great water park, **Atlantis Water Park** ① *Km 51, carretera Costa del Sol, T2211-4103, www.atlantis.com.sv, US$8, bus routes 495 and 143 (every 15 mins)*. Options from San Salvador, including hotel pick-up, small lunch and entrance from US$15-20.

Isla Tasajera

At the southeast end of the Costa del Sol road, near the **Pacific Paradise** hotel, a ferry (US$1.75) leaves for Isla Tasajera in the Estero de Jaltepeque (tidal lagoon). For boat excursions, take the Costa del Sol bus to the last stop at La Puntilla and negotiate with the local boatmen. Boat hire for the day costs US$75, including pilot. It's a great trip into the lagoon, with mangroves, dolphin watching and trips up to the river mouth of the Río Lempa (the longest river in the country).

Zacatecoluca → *Colour map 6, C1. Altitude: 201 m. Population: 65,826.*

The capital of La Paz Department is 56 km from San Salvador by road and 19 km south of San Vicente. This is a good place to buy hammocks (for example nylon 'doubles', US$13). José Simeón Cañas, who abolished slavery in Central America, was born here. There is a cathedral in the Moorish style and an excellent art gallery. A brand new mall just opened, with a supermarket and several stores.

Border essentials: El Salvador–Guatemala

La Hachadura
The border is at the bridge over the Río Paz, with a filling station and a few shops nearby.

Salvadorian immigration The immigration facilities are on either side of the bridge; a relaxed crossing.

Crossing by private vehicle The border crossing is quite straightforward but a private vehicle requires a lot of paperwork (about two hours).

Sleeping El Viajero, La Hachadura, is safe, clean, good value, with fans.

Transport To San Salvador, Terminal de Occidente, bus No 498, three hours; to Ahuachapán, by market, bus No 503, US$0.75, 50 minutes.

Ichanmichen
ⓘ *Admission and car parking US$0.75 per person, bungalow rental US$4.*

Near the town is the park and Turicentro of Ichanmichen ('the place of the little fish'). It is crossed by canals and decorated with natural spring pools where you can swim. It is very hot but there is plenty of shade.

Usulután, Playa El Espino and Laguna El Jocotal → *Colour map 6, C2.*
About 110 km from the capital is Usulután, capital of its department. It's a large, dirty and unsafe place, and only useful as a transit point (bus 302 from San Salvador, US$1.40). The coastal highway goes direct from Usulután to La Unión.

Playa El Espino can be reached from Usulután, by car (4WD), pickup or slow bus; it is very remote but lovely. Some small hotels and restaurants operate, but most only at weekends. To visit the reserve, enquire at the entrance; hire a boat to see more.

Beyond Usulután, the impressive silhouette of **Volcán Chaparrasque** rises out of the flat coastal plain. Two roads go northeast to San Miguel, the first from 10 km along at El Tránsito, the second a further 5 km east, which keeps to the low ground south and east of Volcán San Miguel. Two kilometres beyond this turning on the Carretera Litoral is a short road to the right leading to Laguna El Jocotal, a national nature reserve supported by the World Wildlife Fund, which has an abundance of birds and snakes.

Playa El Cuco
ⓘ *Bus No 320 to San Miguel, US$0.45, 1 hr, last bus 1600.*

About 12 km from the junction for San Miguel there is a turning to the right leading in 7 km to Playa El Cuco, a popular beach with several cheap places to stay near the bus station. The main beach is liable to get crowded and dirty at weekends and holidays, but is deserted mid-week. Single women should take care here; locals warn against walking along the beach after sunset. Cases of malaria have been reported. Another popular beach, **El Tamarindo**, is reached by following the coastal road a little further before taking a right turn.

Pacific coast listings

For Sleeping and Eating price codes and other relevant information, see Essentials pages 45-48.

Sleeping

La Libertad p905

B Pacific Sunrise, at the entrance of La Libertad, T2346-2000, www.hoteles elsalvador.com. A brand new hotel with pool, restaurant and rooms overlooking the Obispo beach which can be accessed via an ingenious pedestrian overpass. Best hotel in La Libertad and good rates if more people share the rooms.

C La Posada de Don Lito, Playa El Obispo at the entrance to the village, T2335-3166.

C Rick, behind **Punta Roca**. Clean rooms with bath. Friendly and good value. Has a restaurant.

D Hotel Surf Club, 2 Calle Pte 22-9. Big rooms, a/c, kitchen area. Supermarket downstairs.

F Comedor Margoth. Run-down but clean.

West of La Libertad p906
Playa El Conchalío

C El Malecón de Don Lito, T2355-3201. Good for children, plenty of space.

C Los Arcos del Mediterráneo, T2335-3490, www.hotelmedplaz.com.sv, 300 m from beach. A/c, TV, safe and quiet, with pool, garden and restaurant.

Playa El Majahual

B Hotel El Pacífico, T2310-6504. Pool, restaurant.

D Hotel y Restaurante Santa Fe, at the entrance to the Majahual beach, T2310-6508. Safe and nice, with pool. Recommended, relaxing and safe.

Playa El Cocal

B-C Punta Roca Surf Resort, T2346-1753, www.puntaroca.com.sv. Owned by National Champion Jimmy Rotherham, Punta Roca is an option for surfers (the beach has rocks!).

Playa San Blas

C-D Sol Bohemio, T2305-5193, www.sol bohemio.com. Offers reasonable rates, as do a couple of the smaller hostels, such as **Barriles**.

Playa El Tunco

B Tekuani Kal, www.tekuanikal.com, T2389-6388, *temascal* (indigenous sauna), massages and beautiful seaside pool.

B Tunco Lodge, T2389-6318, www.tunco lodge.com. New hotel with same owners as Papayas Lodge. A/c, wireless, TV and pools.

B-C Roca Sunzal, Km 42, T2389-6126, www.rocasunzal.com. Best hotel in El Tunco, beautifully located in front of the beach. Great views, pool, good food in restaurant. Value for money. They now have new suites with artsy and original decor. Good service. Recommended.

C Hotel Mopelia, T2389-6265, www.hotel mopelia-salvador.com. Owned by Frenchman Gilles, is a popular spot, also for its bar (open all week) and new pizzeria **Tunco Veloz**.

C-D La Guitarra, www.surfingeltunco.com, T2389-6390. 18 rooms with and without a/c, discounts for longer stays ,Wi-Fi.

C-D Tortuga Surf Lodge. Cozy little cabin house, surfing lessons available.

D El Tubo last building on right-hand side. Cheap rooms and board rental.

D La Sombra, info@lasombradelarte.com. Rooms with a/c and fan.

D-E El Mangle, just in front of Roca Sunzal, this is the dorm branch of that hotel, with guests welcome to use the Roca Sunzal pool.

D-E Papayas Lodge, T2389-6231, www.papayalodge.com. Family-run surf hostel. Clean rooms with fans, use of kitchen and safe. Owned by Salvadorian surf legend, Papaya. Board sales and repair and surf classes. Recommended.

D-E Roots, camping ground, beach side.

E Casa Tamanique, a couple of blocks up the road from El Tubo, fernandosgallegos@yahoo.com. Newcomer with a tiny hostel.

Playa El Sunzal

B Las Olas, T2411-7753. www.akwaterra.com. 8 nicely decorated rooms with amazing views. Food à la carte. No beach as the hotel is located on the top of a cliff. Salt-water pool.
E El Hostal at the entrance of Playa El Sunzal run by a couple of guys from the States.

Playa Palmarcito

B Atami Beach ClubT2223-9000, www.atami.com.sv. Good rooms. Swimming pool and water slide. Seafood restaurant. In the grounds of the club is a private *rancho*.
D El Palmarcito, T7942-4879, www.elpalmarcito.com, surf lessons, board rental, restaurant, beachfront.

Playa El Zonte

E Casa de Frida Hotel, T2302-6068, www.lacasadefrida.com. Lodging in cabins behind restaurant with beachfront garden. Cosy place with hammocks, now under new management
E Esencia Nativa, T7737-8879, esencia nativa@yahoo.com. Run by surfer Alex Novoa, with cheap rooms and pool. Popular restaurant serves range of options, including veggie food and is busy at weekends. Surfing lessons and board rentals available. Popular with surfers.
E Horizonte Surf Camp, El Zonte, T2323-0099, saburosurfcamp@hotmail.com. Simple bungalows, some with a/c, nice garden, pool, restaurant, board rental, clean, good service. Good choice for surfers. Beach front restaurant offers good food. New room for up to 6 people on a 3rd floor. Great view.

Acajutla and around *p907*

B Los Cóbanos Village Lodge, Carretera Acajutla, turn right at Restaurant Marsolie, T2420-5248, www.loscobanos.com.sv. Beachfront cabins with pool and restaurant. Scuba-diving, surfing, fishing on offer. TV and internet available.
B-E Capricho BeachHouse, Barra de Santiago (same owners as **Ximena's**, see page 862), contact T2260-2481, www.ximenasguesthouse.com (under: Capricho). Private rooms with bath and a/c, cabin with dorms and ceiling fan, clean and safe. Beautiful beach and located in a wildlife reserve, close to mangroves and the tip of the peninsula. Tours of the mangroves, fishing, surf lessons and board rental all available. Transport from the capital and tours to **Parque Nacional El Imposible** available. Recommended. Take direct bus No 285 to La Barra de Santiago, which departs twice daily from Sonsonate, or bus towards border and pickup from turn-off.

Parque Nacional El Imposible *p907*

B Hostal El Imposible, T2411-5484. With restaurant/bar area, swimming pool and small trail. 5 cabins sleeping 2-6 people have private bath, hot water and small terrace, also restaurant service. Information from **Salvanatura** in San Salvador, T2279-1515. www.salvanatura.org.

Costa del Sol *p908*

Cheaper accommodation can be found 1 km east at Playa Los Blancos and in La Herradura.
A Izalco Cabaña Club. 30 rooms and a pool. Good value, seafood is a speciality.
B Izalco Cabaña Club, T2338-2006 also has another hotel at Playa Torola.
D Miny Hotel y Restaurant Mila, Km 66, opposite police station. Very friendly, owner Marcos speaks English. Clean, simple, fan, pool, good food, beach access. Take bus No 495 from Terminal Sur, San Salvador;

buses are very crowded at weekends, but the resort is quiet during the week.

Playa El Cuco p909
B Trópico Club, 2.5 km along the coast from Playa El Cuco, T2682-1073, tropicoinn@yahoo.com. Several cabins, pool and open-air dining. Leads directly to the beach. Run by the **Trópico Inn** in San Miguel, (T2661-1800) see page 901.
D Cucolindo, 1 km along the coast, T2619-9012, hotelcucolindo@hotmail.com. Basic cabin for 4, with cold water. Mosquitos.
D Los Leones Marinos, El Cuco, T2619-9015. Clean and tidy with bath.

Playa Las Flores
A-B Las Flores Surf Resort, located close to Playa El Cuco, T2619-9118, www.lasfloresresort.com. Run by surf expert Rodrigo Barraza, boutique hotel, cater mostly for foreign tourists making an excellent choice for an upscale budget.

Playa Torola
B Torola Cabaña Club, Km 175, Playa Torola, El Tamarindo, T2681-5528. Pool looking out to sea, great open-air bar/restaurant, friendly. Welcoming owner, recommended.

Playa El Tamarindo
B Tropi Tamarindo, T2682-1073, www.tropicoinn.com.sv. Run by the **Trópico Inn** in San Miguel (T2661-1800), see page 901)

❶ Eating

La Libertad p905
There are cheap restaurants near the pier, in the market, and around Playa La Paz, Playa El Obispo and El Sunzal. An area with new buildings located where the old Marina used to be close to the pier now hosts a series of great seafood eateries.
❄ El Nuevo Altamar, 4 Calle Pte, Playa La Paz, T2335-3235. Good for seafood, steaks and bird.
❄ Mariscos Freddy and **La Marea**, on the beach at Playa Obispo. Good-value seafood restaurants.
❄-❄ Punta Roca, 5 Av Sur, T2335-3261. Mon-Fri 0800-2000, Sat and Sun 0800-2300. Try the shrimp soup. Owned by American ex-pat Robert Rotherham, father of the national surf champion Jimmy Rotherham.

Around La Libertad p905
East of the El Faro mall at the entrance there is a strip with very good restaurants. 2 of the best are:
❄ La Dolce Vita, Playa Las Flores, 200 m east of the Shell gas station, T2335-3592. Excellent seafood and pasta restaurant.
❄ La Curva de Don Gere, T2335-34360. Legendary place run by Geremias Alvarado with several outlets in El Salvador (and the US). One of the trademarks is their seafood cream chowder in huge sizes including king crab legs and other goodies.

West of La Libertad p906
El Sunzal
Around the Sunzal area several new very good restaurants have recently opened, such Hola Beto's,Las Pamas Mirador and La Curva de Don Gere. All have beautiful vistas over the coastline.
❄ Café Sunzal, Km 43.5 Carretera El Litoral, Playa Sunzal, T2389-6019, www.cafesunzal.com. Great seafood and steak house, exquisite international cuisine. Excellent views over the Sunzal beach.

El Tunco
Tunco is on the rise an new places keep popping up.

♟ Hotel and Restaurante Roca Sunzal, has delicious seafood and a very good bar. All with an excellent beachfront location. Recommended.

♟ Hotel Mopelia (see Sleeping) just opened a **Pizzería** and their well-stocked bar is open all week.

♟♟-♟ La Bocana, in front of the Tunco (pig). Owned and operated by Luis who's very friendly. Beachfront, offering great view from 2nd storey. Good seafood, great value.

♟ Dale Dale Café, is a new coffee shop just behind **Roca Sunzal**. They have delicious brownies, muffins and coffee to go with it.

♟ Erika, T2389-6054. Run by owner Amelia Hernández. Very popular with the locals. 2nd story palm hatch with great atmosphere.

El Zonte

♟ Escencia Nativa (see Sleeping), run by charismatic Alex Novoa, has an innovating menu and pizzas. Folks come down from the capital just to get a bite.

♟ Horizonte Surf Resort, run by Japanese Saburo, has a nice restaurant at the beachfront. The view from 2nd floor is especially lovely. Good value.

♟ La Casa de Frida, El Zonte, T2253-2949, www.lacasadefrida.com. Under new management and looking good. A great restaurant located in a large beachfront garden dotted with tables and hammocks.

Costa del Sol *p908*

♟ Restaurante Kenny Mar, Km 60, Carretera Costa del Sol, Playa San Marcelino, T2338-2578. Delicious seafood with beachfront view.

▲ Activities and tours

La Libertad *p905*
Watersports

Look for board rentals and surf lessons at hostels on the coast west of Puerto

La Libertad. Also look at www.sunzal.com, which offers great surfing tours combined with photography by local photographer, El Vaquero.

Punta Roca, restaurant in La Libertad, T2335-3261 www.puntarocarockets.com. Owner Robert Rotherham (father of Surf Champion Jimmy Rotherham) runs surfboard rental, including boards for both pros and beginners, see website for full details. He also arranges excursions including deep-sea fishing for up to 3 people, see www.punta roca.com.sv (which features webcam of area, surf and weather report) for more information. English spoken. Recommended.

⊖ Transport

La Libertad *p905*
Bus

The station for the buses going down to Puerto La Libertad is now located at the 17th Av Sur at the intersection of Blv Venezuela by the general cemetery in San Salvador. The buses going to San Salvador from Puerto La Libertad leave from the terminal at the entrance of the city centre by the ball courts. Departures from Puerto La Libertad along the coast to Sonsonate depart at 0600.

For beaches around Acajutla and west, take the direct bus from Terminal de Occidente to Sonsonate and then on: No 285 to **Barra de Santiago**, No 28 to **Cara Sucia** and the border and No 252 to **Acajutla**.

For **Costa del Sol**, **Zacatecoluca** and connections toward eastern beaches go from Terminal del Sur by San Marcos in San Salvador.

Acajutla and around *p907*
Bus

No 207 from Terminal Occidente, **San Salvador** (US$2.80), or No 252 from Sonsonate (US$0.30). 58 km from Santa Ana.

Zacatecoluca *p908*
Bus
No133 from Terminal Sur, San Salvador. Direct bus to La Libertad 1540 (US$0.85), or take San Salvador bus, change at Comalapa, 2 hrs.

Playa El Cuco *p909*
Boat
Boat from El Tamarindo across the bay leads to a short cut to La Unión.

Bus
From La Unión, 20 mins.

❻ Directory

La Libertad *p905*
Banks There are no credit card facilities or international ATMs in La Libertad. Banco de Fomento Agropecuario, Mon-Fri 0800-1600, Sat 0800-1200. Also has Western Union. HSBC, takes TCs. **Internet** Infocentros, in main street close to Puerto Bello, cheap. **Language school** 5 Av Norte, close to Punta Roca restaurant, T2449-0331, salvaspanischool@ mailcity.com. **Police** Calle Gerardo Barrios and 1 Av Sur. **Tourism police**, based here and patrol the town and beach areas at weekends. A tourist kiosk is planned for the entrance to town. **Post office** Up the side of the Telecom office, 0800-1200, 1400-1700. **Telephone** Telepunto, next to Hotel Puerto Bello, 2 Calle Pte (0630-0830). Cheap rates. **Telecom** on same road.

Contents

Honduras

At a glance

⊙ **Getting around** Buses, flights to cut out long journeys. Boats to the Bay Islands from La Ceiba, and to Belize from Puerto Cortés.

● **Time required** You could easily spend 3 weeks exploring.

☀ **Weather** Wettest Aug-Dec. From Jan-Mar it's chilly in the central highlands at night, hot on the coast.

✖ **When not to go** Rainy season if you don't like getting wet.

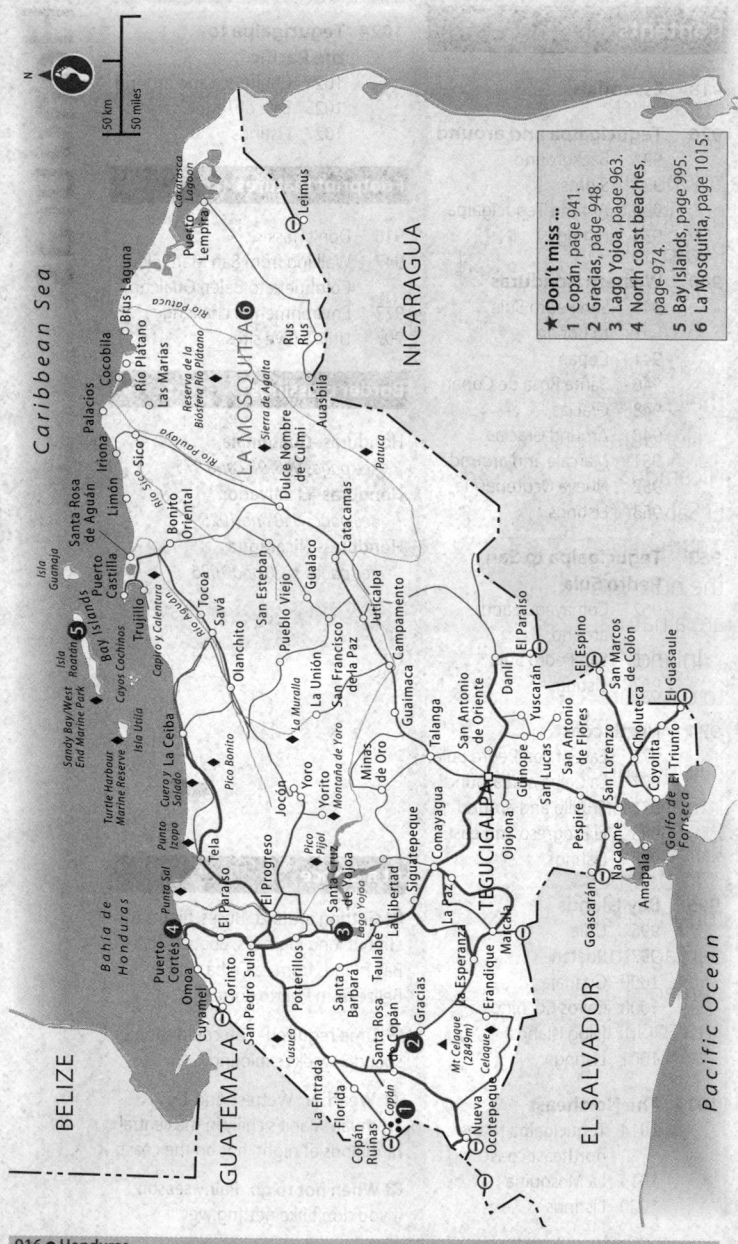

★ **Don't miss ...**
1 Copán, page 941.
2 Gracias, page 948.
3 Lago Yojoa, page 963.
4 North coast beaches, page 974.
5 Bay Islands, page 995.
6 La Mosquitia, page 1015.

Sliced, spliced and spread across a mountainous interior, Honduras is a pleasantly challenging surprise that has developed in curiously disconnected zones. In the heart of the mountains Tegucigalpa epitomizes the Latin city – a chaotic celebration of colonial architecture divided by steeply sloping cobbled streets. By contrast, the republic's second and more modern city, San Pedro Sula, on the coastal lowland plain, has a neat matrix of *calles* and *avenidas* that seem rather dull by comparison.

A world away, the Bay Islands bask in sunny skies. Utila thrives on a throw-it-together-and-see-if-it-works existence. It's easily the cheapest place to learn to dive in the western hemisphere.

Honduras is the second largest Central American republic after Nicaragua, but its population is smaller than that of neighbouring El Salvador, the smallest country. Bordered by Nicaragua, Guatemala, El Salvador and a narrow coastal Pacific strip, it is the northern Caribbean coast and beautiful Bay Islands that are a natural focus and a prime destination for visitors.

Inland, the mountainous terrain creates natural obstacles to easy, direct travel around the country. It also means that, for trekking and hiking, there are great swathes of beautiful hillside, much of which is dotted with small communities, largely disinterested in the comings and goings of the few travellers who venture so far off the beaten track.

In October 1998 Hurricane Mitch deluged Honduras with torrential rain leaving an estimated 10,000 people dead and damage to almost all parts of the country. While the physical damage has been cleaned up, eleven years on the economic and social impact continues to ripple through the country.

Essentials

Where to go

With the popularity of the Bay Islands as a diving destination, mainland Honduras is often missed in the frenzied rush towards the sea. And, while the beauty of the islands cannot be overstated, picking a route that takes in some of the smaller towns of Honduras gives a far better understanding of the country as a whole.

The capital, **Tegucigalpa**, has an old, colonial sector and a new section with modern hotels, shopping malls and businesses. Across the Río Choluteca is Tegucigalpa's twin city, **Comayagüela**, the working heart of the city with the markets and bus terminals. Around the capital, there are colonial villages, old mining towns, handicraft centres and good hiking areas, including **Parque Nacional La Tigra**, which will make ideal trips for a day or two.

West of Tegucigalpa, near the border with Guatemala, is Honduras' premier Maya archaeological site **Copán**, where new discoveries continued to be made, and some fine Maya art can be seen. A short distance from the site, the well-restored town of **Copán Ruinas** is a colonial gem and, nearby, the site of **El Puente** is beginning to reveal treasures hidden for centuries. Closer to the capital, quiet colonial towns such as **Gracias** and graceful **Santa Bárbara** are the site of opal mines, Lenca indigenous communities and the **national park** of **Mount Celaque**. There is lots of good hiking in the vicinity of the popular colonial city of **Santa Rosa de Copán**. A good way to explore this more traditional part of the country is to pick a route, travel in short distances and soak up the calm and tranquillity.

From Tegucigalpa a paved highway runs north to **San Pedro Sula**, the second city of the republic and the country's main business centre. The road passes the old colonial capital of Comayagua and beautiful Lago Yojoa. Northwest of San Pedro Sula, the **north coast** has a number of centres of interest to the visitor. The main port is **Puerto Cortés**, to the west of which is **Omoa**, an increasingly popular beach and fishing village with an old fort, from which an overland route enters Guatemala. East of San Pedro Sula are **Tela**, a more established resort, and **La Ceiba**, a good base for visiting the nearby national parks of Pico Bonito and Cuero y Salado, whitewater rafting trips on the Río Cangrejal and departure point for the Bay Islands and La Mosquitia. Further east, **Trujillo**, sitting at the southern end of a palm-fringed bay, was once the country capital.

Curving in an arc off the cost near La Ceiba, the **Bay Islands** of **Utila**, **Roatán** and **Guanaja**, plus the smaller **Hog Islands**, are some of Honduras' main tourist destinations. Travellers visiting just one part of Honduras often pick the islands. The diving is excellent and Utila is currently the cheapest dive centre in the Caribbean. The islands also have good beaches.

Northeast of Tegucigalpa is the province of Olancho, an agricultural and cattle-raising area that leads eventually to the Caribbean coast at Trujillo. Juticalpa and Catacamas are the main towns, and the mountains of the district have cloud forest, hiking trails and beautiful conservation areas. Beyond Olancho is **La Mosquitia**, most easily reached from La Ceiba, which is forested, swampy and almost uninhabited. Efforts are being made to promote sustainable development among the Miskito and the Pech. Ecotourism initiatives have been set up in some coastal communities and inland, making for adventurous and rewarding travel where the main ways of getting around are by boat, small plane or on foot.

Honduras' short **Pacific coast** on the Gulf of Fonseca is little visited, other than en route to Nicaragua and El Salvador. The main towns in the region are Choluteca and, in the gulf, Amapala, on the extinct volcanic Isla del Tigre. Another route to Nicaragua is that

east of the capital through the town of Danlí, which passes the Panamerican Agricultural School at Zamorano and the old mining town of Yuscarán.

Suggested itineraries The Honduran trail is pretty straightforward. Most people arrive from Guatemala and visit **Copán** with its nearby ruins and growing range of activities. From Copán it's a bus to San Pedro Sula and a quick change to continue to **Tela** or **La Ceiba**, both close to national parks. From La Ceiba the ferry leaves for **Roatán** and **Utila**, the budget travellers' choice for diving, snorkelling and island life. That trip will take about 10 days – add the flight or long bus journey round to Tegucigalpa. From there, it's onwards to Nicaragua. If you have more time, a circular route goes to **Santa Rosa de Copán**, through **Gracias** to **Tegucigalpa**, and then from the capital to **Comayagua**, **Lago Yojoa** and **San Pedro Sula**. That will make your stay in Honduras close to three weeks – add one more if you want to visit **La Mosquitia**.

When to go

Altitude is the main impact on climate. In Tegucigalpa, at 1000 m, temperatures range from 4°C (January-March) up to 33°C (April-May). In the lowlands to the north, temperatures in San Pedro Sula range from 20-37°C with the coolest months being November to February. On the Caribbean the dry season stretches from February to June, while the heaviest rains fall August to December. Inland, rain falls throughout the year, with the drier months being November to April. Some of the central highland areas enjoy a delightful climate, with a freshness that makes a pleasant contrast to the humidity and heat of the lowland zones.

Sport and activities

Adventure tourism
Mountain biking is increasingly popular as is horse riding around Copán. Hardcore adventure can be found in the swamp wetlands of Mosquitia, usually by taking an organized tour.

Nature tourism
Nature trips take advantage of the wide variety of national parks. Birders have known about the treasures of the country for years, but hikers and trekkers are beginning to venture out through the valleys and across the hills that are often shrouded in cloud forest.

Scuba-diving
Diving off the Bay Islands has long been the number one attraction, with some of the best and most varied diving in Central America. PADI courses are among the cheapest in the world. Snorkelling is also excellent.

Whitewater rafting
Rafting is growing steadily in Honduras with the hotspot being the River Cangrejal, close to La Ceiba, where Grade II, III and IV rapids test both the novice and experienced paddler. The sport is relatively new to Honduras and more sites are sure to be found in the coming years.

National parks ›› *See colour map 6 in the centre of the book.*

The extensive system of national parks and protected areas provides the chance to enjoy some of the best scenery Honduras has to offer, much of it unspoilt and rarely visited. The

National Parks' Office, **Conama**, is next to the Instituto Nacional Agrario in Tegucigalpa; chaotic but friendly and a good source of information. **Cohdefor** ① *10 Av 4 Calle NO, San Pedro Sula, T253-4959, www.cohdefor.hn*, the national forestry agency, is also much involved with the parks. Parks have different levels of services – see individual parks for details. Natural reserves continue to be established and all support and interest is most welcome. Parks currently in existence are **La Tigra**, outside Tegucigalpa (page 931), and the **Río Plátano** (page 1018). Under development since 1987 are **Monte Celaque** (page 948), **Cusuco** (page 966), **Punta Sal** (page 976), **Capiro y Calentura** (page 982), **Montaña Cerro Azul-Meámbar** (page 963), **Montaña de Yoro** (page 983) and **Pico Bonito** (page 979). These parks have visitor centres, hiking trails and primitive camping. The following have been designated national parks by the government: **Montecristo–Trifinio** (page 952), **Santa Bárbara** (page 964), **Pico Pijol** (page 983), **Agalta** (Olancho, page 1015) and **Montaña de Comayagua** (page 963). Wildlife refuges covered in the text are **Cuero y Salado** (page 980), **Las Trancas** (page 951) and **La Muralla-Los Higuerales** (page 1014). For information on protected areas in the **Bay Islands**, see page 995.

Getting there

Air

Tegucigalpa, La Ceiba, San Pedro Sula and Roatán all have international airports. There are no direct flights to Tegucigalpa from Europe, but connecting flights can be made via Miami, then with **American Airlines** or **Taca**. There are flights to Tegucigalpa, San Pedro Sula and Roatán from Houston with **Continental** and services to Tegucigalpa from New York. **Taca** flies daily from Guatemala City and San Salvador, with connections throughout the region via El Salvador.

   American Airlines fly daily from Miami, as do **Taca** and **Iberia**. There are also frequent services from San Pedro Sula. Services also available with **Spirit Air**, **Delta** and **Mexicana**.

Road

There are numerous border crossings. With **Guatemala** to the west you can cross near Copán Ruinas at El Florido, on the Caribbean coast at Corinto or to the south at Agua Caliente. For **El Salvador** there are crossings at El Poy, leading to Suchitoto in the west, and Perquín leading to San Miguel and the east. For **Nicaragua,** the border post town of Guasale in the south leads 116 km on a very bad road to the Nicaraguan town of León, while the inland routes at Las Manos and El Espino guide you to Estelí and Matagalpa, in the northern hills. Crossing to Nicaragua through the Mosquitia coast is not possible – officially at least.

   Taxes are charged on entry and exit at land borders, but the amount varies, despite notices asking you to denounce corruption. Entry is 60 lempiras and exit is 30 lempiras. Double is charged on Sunday. If officials make an excess charge for entry or exit, ask for a receipt. Do not attempt to enter Honduras at an unstaffed border. When it is discovered that you have no entry stamp you will either be fined US$60 or escorted to the border, and you will have to pay the guard's food and lodging; or you can spend a night in jail.

Sea

A regular weekly service departing Mondays at 1100 links Puerto Cortés with Mango Creek and Placencia, in Belize – see page 991 for details.

Getting around

Air

There are airstrips in all large towns and many of the cut-off smaller ones. Internal airlines include Isleña, www.flyislena.com, **Sosa** and **Atlantic Air**. **Atlantic Air** serves La Ceiba, San Pedro Sula, Teguc, Roatán and Utila. **Sosa**, the largest domestic carrier, serves Roatán, Utila, Guanaja, San Pedro Sula, Tegucigalpa and other destinations in Honduras. La Ceiba is the main hub for domestic flights, especially for **Sosa** and **Atlantic**, and most flights to and from the islands stop there. Airport **departure tax** is US$34 (not charged if in transit less than nine hours). There is a 10% tax on all tickets sold for domestic and international journeys.

Road

The road system throughout the country has improved rapidly in recent years and Honduras probably has the best roads in Central America. However, many roads were built and maintained with US money when Honduras was supporting the contras in Nicaragua and are now showing signs of lack of maintenance. Traffic tends to travel fast on these apparently good roads and road accidents are second only to Costa Rica in Latin America. If driving, take care and avoid driving at night. Total road length is now 15,100 km, of which 3020 km are paved, 10,000 km are all-weather roads and the remainder are passable in the dry season.

Bus There are essentially three types of service: local (*servicio a escala*), direct (*servicio directo*) and luxury (*servicio de lujo*). Using school buses, a *servicio a escala* is very slow, with frequent stops and detours and is uncomfortable for long periods. *Servicio directo* is faster, slightly more expensive and more comfortable. *Servicio de lujo* has air-conditioned European and Brazilian buses with videos.

Buses set out early in the day, with a few night buses running between major urban centres. Try to avoid bus journeys after dark as there are many more accidents and even occasional robberies.

If you suffer from motion sickness, the twisty roads can become unbearable. Avoid sitting at the back of the bus, take some water and sit by a window that will open. Minibuses are faster than buses, so the journey can be quite hair-raising. Pickups that serve out-of-the-way communities will leave you covered in dust (or soaked) – sit near the cab if possible.

Car Regular **gasoline/petrol** costs around US$2.60 per US gallon and US$2.25 for diesel. On entering with a car (from El Salvador at least), customs and the transit police give a 30-day permit for the vehicle. This must be renewed in Tegucigalpa (anywhere else authorization is valid for only one Department). Charges for motorists appear to be: on entry, US$30 in total for a vehicle with two passengers, including provisional permission from the police to drive in Honduras, US$1 (official minimum) for car papers, fumigation and baggage inspection; on exit, US$2.30 in total. Motorcyclists face similar charges. These charges are changing all the time and differ significantly from one post to another (up to US$40 sometimes). They are also substantially higher on weekends and holidays. You will have to pass through Migración, Registro, Tránsito, Cuarentena, Administración, Secretaría and then a police vehicle check. At each stage you will be asked for money, for which you will not always get a receipt. On arriving or leaving with a vehicle there are so many checks that it pays to hire a *tramitador* to steer you to the correct officials in the correct order (US$1-2 for the guide). No fresh food is allowed to cross the border. The easiest border crossing is at Las Manos. The **Pan-American Highway** in Honduras is in bad condition in parts. One reader warns to "beware of potholes that can take a car. They suddenly appear after 20 km of good road without warning." If hiring a car, make sure it has all the correct papers and emergency triangles, which are required by law.

Cycling Bicycles are regarded as vehicles but are not officially subject to entrance taxes. Bicycle repair shops are difficult to find, and parts for anything other than mountain bikes may be very hard to come by. Some buses and most local flights will take bicycles. Most main roads have hard shoulders and most drivers respect cyclists. It is common for cars to blow their horn to signal their approach.

Hitchhiking Relatively easy. Travel is still by foot and mule in many rural areas.

Taxi Widely available. Tuk-tuks have become very popular in Honduras, and are a quick and cheap way to move around in towns and cities.

Maps

The **Instituto Geográfico Nacional** produces two 1:1,000,000 maps (1995) of the country; one a tourist map which includes city maps of Tegucigalpa, San Pedro Sula and La Ceiba, and the other a good road map although it does not show all the roads. Both maps are widely available in bookshops in major cities and some hotels. **International Travel Maps (ITM)** has a 1:750,000 map of Honduras.

Sleeping

Accommodation in Honduras varies greatly. In Tegucigalpa and San Pedro Sula you will find the mix ranges from business-style hotels of international standards down to simple, but generally clean rooms. In popular tourist spots the focus is more on comfort and costs rise accordingly. Get off the beaten track and you'll find some of the most basic and cheapest accommodation in Central America – complete with accompanying insect life, it can be unbearable or a mind-broadening experience depending on your mood. There is a 4% extra tax on rooms in the better hotels.

Eating and drinking

The cheapest meals are the *comida corriente*, or the sometimes better prepared and more expensive *comida típica*, which usually contain some of the following: beans, rice, meat, avocado, egg, cabbage salad, cheese, bananas, potatoes or yucca, and always tortillas. *Carne asada* is charcoal-roasted meat and served with grated cabbage between tortillas; it is good, although rarely prepared hygienically. Make sure that pork is properly cooked. *Tajadas* are crisp, fried *plátano* chips topped with grated cabbage and sometimes meat; *nacatamales* are ground, dry maize mixed with meat and seasoning, boiled in banana leaves. *Baleadas* are soft flour tortillas filled with beans and various combinations of butter, egg, cheese and cabbage. *Pupusas* are thick corn tortillas filled with *chicharrón* (pork scratchings), or cheese, served as snacks with beer. *Tapado* is a stew with meat or fish, plantain, yucca and coconut milk. *Pinchos* are meat, poultry, or shrimp kebabs. *Sopa de mondongo* (tripe soup) is very common.

Fish is sold on the beaches at Trujillo and Cedeño. While on the north coast, look out for *pan de coco* (coconut bread) made by Garífuna (Black Carib) women, and *sopa de camarones* (prawn soup) prepared with coconut milk and lemon juice. Honduras is now a major producer of tilapia with exports to the US and fresh tilapia available in many restaurants.

Drink

Soft drinks are called *refrescos*, or *frescos* (the name also given to fresh fruit blended with water, make sure you check that bottled water is used as tap water is unsafe); *licuados* are fruit blended with milk. Bottled drinking water is available in most places. *Horchata* is morro seeds, rice water and cinnamon. Coffee is thick and sweet. The main brands of **beer** are Port Royal Export, Imperial, Nacional, Barena and Salva Vida (more malty than the others). Local **rum** is cheap, try Flor de Caña white, or seven-year-old amber. Twelve-year-old Flor de Caña Centenario is regarded as the best.

Festivals and events

Most Roman Catholic feast days are celebrated.
1 Jan New Year's Day.
14 Apr Day of the Americas.
Mar/Apr Semana Santa (Thu, Fri and Sat before Easter Sun).

1 May Labour Day.
15 Sep Independence Day.
3 Oct Francisco Morazán.
12 Oct Columbus' arrival in America.
21 Oct Army Day.

Shopping

The best articles are those made of wood. Straw items are also highly recommended. Leather is cheaper than in El Salvador and Nicaragua. As a single stopping point, the region around Santa Bárbara is one of the best places, with outlets selling handicrafts from nearby villages. Alternatively you can explore the villages yourself and see the goods being made. Coffee is OK, but not great. Sales tax is 12%; 15% on alcohol and tobacco.

Essentials A-Z

Customs and duty free

There are no customs duties on personal effects. You are allowed to bring in 200 cigarettes or 100 cigars, or 500 g of tobacco, and 2 quarts of spirit.

Electricity

Generally 110 volts but, increasingly, 220 volts is being installed. US-style plugs.

Embassies and consulates

For a full list visit www.sre.hn
Belize, 22 Gabourel Lane, Belize City, T02-245-889.

Canada, 151 Slater St, Suite 805-A, Ottawa, Ontario K1P 5H3, T613-233-8900.
El Salvador, 89 Av Norte between 7 and 9 Calle Pte 561, Col Escalón, San Salvador, T2263-2808.
France, 8 rue Crevaux, 75116 Paris, T4755-8645.
Germany, Cuxhavener Str 14, D-10555 Berlín, T30397497-10.
Guatemala, 19 Av "A", 20-19, Zona 10, T2363-5622.
Israel, Calle Zohar Tal No 1, Herzlya Pituach, CP46741, T9957-7686.
Japan, 38 Kowa Bldg, 8F No 802, 12-24 Nishi Azabu 4, Chome Minato Ku, Tokyo 106, T03-3409-1150.

Mexico, Alfonso Reyes 220, Col Condesa, México DF, T55-211-5747.
Netherlands, Nassauplein 17, 2585 EB, La Haya, T70-364-1684.
Nicaragua, Reparto Las Colinas Prado Ecuestre 298, Managua, T/F278-3043.
Spain, Calle Rafael Calvo 15, 6B, Madrid, T91-702-5157.
UK, 115 Gloucester Place, London W1H 3PJ, T020-7486-4880.
USA, 3007 Tilden St NW, Pod 4M, Washington, DC 20008, T202-966-7702.

Health
Inoculate against typhoid and tetanus. There is cholera, so eating on the street or at market stalls is not recommended. There are hospitals and private clinics in Tegucigalpa, San Pedro Sula and larger towns. See page 51 for further information.

Identification
It is advisable to carry some form of identification at all times, because spot checks have increased, especially when entering or leaving major towns.

Internet
Internet cafés are widely available in the capital and in popular locations. Prices and connections vary greatly; in cities good speeds are at about US$1 per hr. On the islands, speeds are erratic and prices expensive.

Language
Spanish is the main language, but English is often spoken in the north, in the Bay Islands, by West Indian settlers on the Caribbean coast, and in business communities.

Media
The principal newspapers in Tegucigalpa are *El Heraldo* and *La Tribuna*. In San Pedro Sula they are *El Tiempo* and *La Prensa*. Links on the net at www.honduras.com. The English weekly paper *Honduras This Week*, is now mainly online at www.hondurasthis week.com. They're frequently looking for student interns.

There are 6 television channels and 167 broadcasting stations. Cable TV is available in large towns and cities.

Money → *US$1=18.88 lempiras (June 2009)*. The unit of currency is the **lempira** (written Lps and referred to as lemps) named after a famous indigenous chief who lost his life while fighting the invasion of the Spaniards. It is reasonably stable against the US dollar. Divided into 100 centavos, there are nickel coins of 5, 10, 20 and 50 centavos. Bank notes are for 1, 2, 5, 10, 20, 50, 100 and 500 lempiras. No one has change for larger notes, especially the 500. Any amount of any currency can be taken in or out of the country.

Credit cards and traveller's cheques
Acceptance of credit cards in Honduras is patchy and commissions can be as high as 6%. Most businesses will try to tack on a service charge to credit card purchases, which is illegal. Ask the manager to call **BAC** and check if the charge is permitted. It is advisable to have traveller's cheques (TCs) available and US$ cash.

MasterCard and Visa are accepted in major hotels and most restaurants in cities and larger towns. Amex is accepted in more expensive establishments. Cash advances are available from **BAC**, **Banco Atlántida**, **Aval Card** and **Honducard** throughout the country. BAC represents Amex and issues and services Amex credit cards.

TCs can be quite a hassle as many banks and business don't accept them.

Cost of living and travelling
Honduras is not expensive: 2 people can travel together in reasonable comfort for US$25 per person per day (less if on a tight budget), but prices for tourists fluctuate greatly. Transport, including domestic flights, is still the cheapest in Central America. Diving will set you back a bit, but at US$270 or so for a PADI course, it is still the cheapest in Central America.

Opening hours

Banks In Tegucigalpa Mon-Fri 0900-1500; on the north coast Sat 0800-1100. **Post offices** Mon-Fri 0700-2000; Sat 0800-1200. **Shops** Mon-Fri 0900-1200, 1400-1800; Sat 0800-1200.

Post

Airmail takes 4-7 days to Europe and the same for the USA. Expensive for parcels. Probably worth using a courier. 20 g letter to USA US$0.80, Europe US$1.30, rest of the world US$1.75. Parcel up to 1 kg to the USA US$18, Europe US$29, rest of the world US$35.

Safety

There are serious domestic social problems in San Pedro Sula, including muggings and theft, but there is a Tourist Police in place – in Copán Ruinas, Roatán, La Ceiba, Tela and San Pedro Sula – that has reduced the problem. Take local advice and be cautious when travelling alone or off the beaten track. The vast majority of Hondurans are honest, friendly, warm and welcoming, and the general perception is that crime is now reducing.

Telephone → *Country code T+504.*
Local operator T192; General information T193, International operator T197. **Hondutel** provides international telephone services from stations throughout the country. The system has improved dramatically in recent years due to competition, with over 50% of Hondurans owning a cell phone. You can buy a cell phone for about US$10 from Tigo, Claro and Digicel, with phone cards from US$2 upwards.

Time

-6 hrs GMT.

Tipping

Normally 10% of the bill but more expensive places add a service charge.

Tourist information

Ministerio Hondureño de Turismo, main office is at Edificio Europa, Av Ramón E Cruz and Calle República de México, Col San Carlos, Tegucigalpa, T222-2124. Also an office at Toncontín Airport and several regional offices.

Useful websites

www.hondurastips.honduras.com A reliable favourite with lots of information about Honduras and links to national newspapers. The biannual publication, *HONDURAS Tips*, edited by John Dupuis in La Ceiba, Edificio Gómez, Local No 2, 4 Calle, T/F440-3383, is full of interesting and useful tourist information, in English and Spanish, free (available in Tegucigalpa from Ministerio Hondureño de Turismo).
Honduras this Week English–language information at www.hondurasthisweek.com.
www.letsgohonduras.com The official guide on the internet.
www.netsys.hn Good for business links. Several regional guides are being developed – these are mentioned within the text.

Visas and immigration

Neither a visa nor tourist card is required for nationals of Western European countries, USA, Canada, Australia, New Zealand, Japan, Argentina, Chile, Guatemala, Costa Rica, Nicaragua, El Salvador, Panama and Uruguay. Citizens of other countries need either a tourist card, which can be bought from Honduran consulates for US$2-3, or a visa, and they should enquire at a Honduran consulate in advance to see which they need. The price of a visa seems to vary depending on nationality and where it is bought. Extensions of 30 days are easy to obtain (up to a maximum of 6 months' stay, cost US$5). There are immigration offices for extensions at Tela, La Ceiba, San Pedro Sula, Santa Rosa de Copán, Siguatepeque, La Paz and Comayagua, and all are more helpful than the Tegucigalpa office.

You will have to visit a country outside of Guatemala, Honduras and Nicaragua to re-enter and gain 90 days.

Weights and measures

The metric system is official.

Tegucigalpa and around

→ *Colour map 6, C2. Altitude: 1000 m. Population: 1.1 million.*
Genuinely chaotic, Tegucigalpa – or Tegus as it is called by locals – is cramped and crowded, but still somehow retains a degree of charm in what remains of the colonial centre. If you can bear to stay away from the Caribbean for a few days, it has much more history and charisma than its rival San Pedro Sula, to the north. Surrounded by sharp, high peaks on three sides, the city is built on the lower slopes of El Picacho. The commercial centre is around Boulevard Morazán, an area known as 'zona viva', full of cafés, restaurants and shops. For contrast to the modern functional city, you can visit some of the centuries-old mining settlements set in forested valleys among the nearby mountains that are ideal for hiking. **▶▶** *For listings, see pages 933-939.*

Getting there

Toncontín international airport is 6.5 km south of the centre, US$4-5 in a taxi to the centre. The airport is in a narrow valley creating difficult landing conditions: morning fog or bad weather can cause it to close. The Carretera del Sur (Southern Highway), which brings in travellers from the south and from Toncontín Airport, runs through Comayagüela into Tegucigalpa. There is no central bus station and bus companies have offices throughout Comayagüela. On arrival it is very much easier and recommended, to take a taxi to your hotel until you get to know the city.

Getting around

The winding of streets in the city means that moving around in the first few days is as much about instinct as following any map. There are cheap buses and taxis for city transport. The Tegucigalpa section of the city uses both names and numbers for streets, but names are used more commonly. In Comayagüela, streets designated by number are the norm. Addresses tend not to be very precise, especially in the colonias around Boulevard Morazán east and south of the centre of Tegucigalpa.

Tourist information

Ministerio Hondureño de Turismo ① *Edif Europa, Av Ramón E Cruz and Calle República de México, 3rd floor, Col San Carlos, T238-3974, also at Toncontín Airport, open 0830-1530,* provides lists of hotels and sells posters and postcards. Information on cultural events around the country from **Teatro Nacional Manuel Bonilla** is better than at regional tourist offices. **El Mundo Maya** ① *behind the cathedral next to the Parque Central, T222-2946,* is a private tourist information centre.

Best time to visit

The city's altitude gives it a reliable climate: temperate during the rainy season from May to November; warm, with cool nights in March and April; and cool and dry with very cool nights from December to February. The annual mean temperature is about 23°C (74°F).

Safety

Generally speaking, Tegucigalpa is cleaner and safer (especially at night) than Comayagüela. If you have anything stolen, report it to **Dirección de Investigación Criminal (DGIC)** ① *5 Av, 7-8 Calle (next to Edificio Palermo), T237-4799.*

Background

Founded as a silver and gold mining camp in 1578, Tegucigalpa means silver hill in the original indigenous tongue; miners first discovered gold at the north end of the current Soberanía bridge. The present city is comprised of the two former towns of Comayagüela and Tegucigalpa which, although divided by the steeply banked Río Choluteca, became the capital in 1880 and are now united administratively as the Distrito Central.

Being off the main earthquake fault line, Tegucigalpa has not been subjected to disasters by fire or earthquake, unlike many of its Central American neighbours, so it has retained many traditional features. The stuccoed houses, with a single, heavily barred entrance leading to a central patio, are often attractively coloured. However, the old low skyline of the city has been punctuated by several modern tall buildings, and much of the old landscape changed with the arrival of Hurricane Mitch.

The rains of **Hurricane Mitch** in October 1998 had a devastating effect on the Distrito Central. But the damage caused by the Choluteca bursting its banks is hard to see these days, with the exception of the first avenue of Comayagüela, where abandoned homes and buildings remain empty. Bridges washed away by the floodwaters have now been replaced, power supplies are back and, in some respects, traffic is actually better now, since many routes were diverted from the heart of downtown. Today, Hurricane Mitch lives on as painful memory.

Sights

Crossing the river from Comayagüela by the colonial Mallol bridge, on the left is the old Casa Presidencial (1919), home to the National Archive. When this was a museum, visitors could see the President's office and the Salón Azul state room. Try asking – you may be lucky. (The new Palacio Presidencial is a modern building on Boulevard Juan Pablo II in Colonia Lomas del Mayab.)

Calle Bolívar leads to the Congress building and the former site of the University, founded in 1847. The site adjoining the church in Plaza La Merced is now the **Galería Nacional de Arte** ① *Tue-Sat 0900-1600, Sun 0900-1400, US$1.50*, a beautifully restored 17th-century building, housing a very fine collection of Honduran modern and colonial art, prehistoric rock carvings and some remarkable pre-Colombian ceramic pieces. There are useful descriptions of exhibits, and explanations of the mythology embodied in the prehistoric and pre-Colombian art.

Calle Bolívar leads to the main square, Plaza Morazán (commonly known as Parque Central). On the eastern side of the square are the **Palacio del Distrito Central**, and the domed and double-towered **cathedral**, built in the late 18th century but are currently undergoing a complete facelift. See the gilt colonial altarpiece, the fine examples of Spanish colonial art, the cloisters and, in Holy Week, the ceremony of the Descent from the Cross.

Avenida Miguel Paz Barahona, running through the north side of the square, is a key venue. To the east is the church of **San Francisco**, with its clangorous bells, and (on 3 Calle, called Avenida Cervantes) the old **Spanish Mint** (1770), now the national printing works.

From Plaza Morazán, heading west towards the river to Avenida Miguel Paz Barahona, opposite the Post Office is the **Museo Para La Identidad Nacional** ① *Tue-Sat 0900-1700, Sun 1000-1600, US$3.30*, a new museum that is unashamedly about Honduras for Honduras for Hondurans. Good big-screen trip, and a well-thought-out trip through Honduran history from plate tectonics to the present day. Just enough detail without getting heavy. Every capital city in Central America should have a museum like this.

Head east a block, then left (north) along 5 Calle (Calle Los Dolores), is the 18th-century church of **Iglesia de Nuestra Señora de los Dolores**. Two blocks north and three blocks west of the church is the beautiful Parque Concordia with good copies of Maya sculpture and temples. On a hilltop one block above Parque Concordia, on Calle Morelos 3A, is **Museo de la Historia Republicana Villa Roy** ① *Mon-Sat 0800-16, US$1.10, www.ihah.hn*, the former site of the Museo Nacional and, in 1936, home of the former president, Julio Lozano. The building was restored, reconstructed and reopened in 1997. There are seven

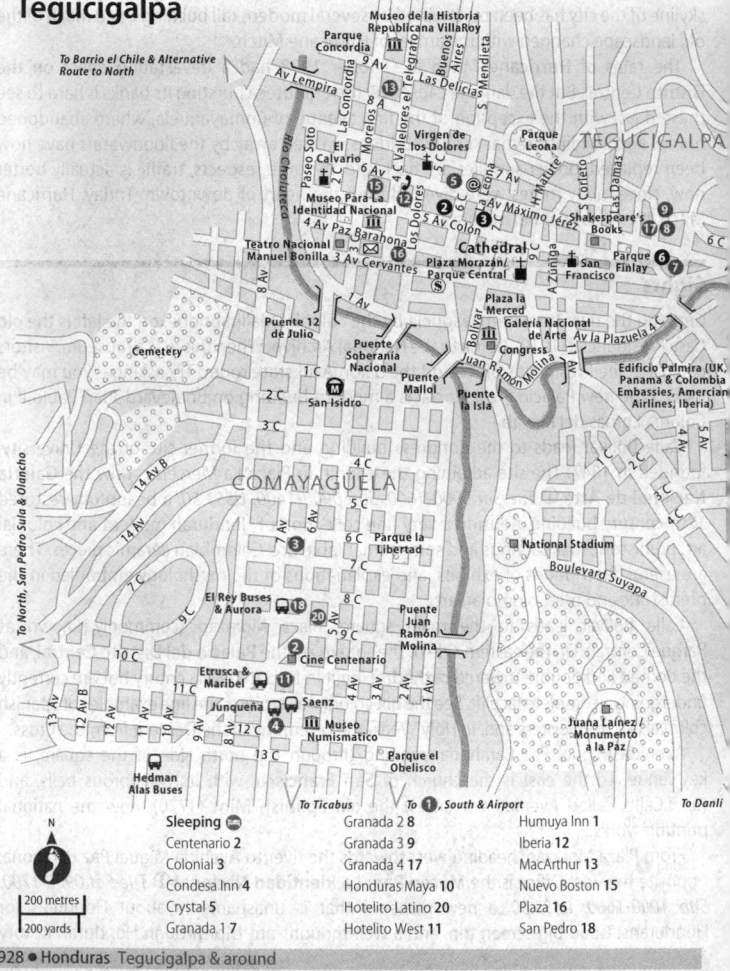

Tegucigalpa

To Barrio el Chile & Alternative Route to North

Sleeping 🛏
Centenario **2**
Colonial **3**
Condesa Inn **4**
Crystal **5**
Granada 1 **7**

Granada 2 **8**
Granada 3 **9**
Granada 4 **17**
Honduras Maya **10**
Hotelito Latino **20**
Hotelito West **11**

Humuya Inn **1**
Iberia **12**
MacArthur **13**
Nuevo Boston **15**
Plaza **16**
San Pedro **18**

main rooms presenting Honduras' history from Independence in 1821 up to 1963, as well as cultural and temporary exhibits and a collection of graceful old cars.

Back on Avenida Miguel Paz Barahona, and further west, are the **Teatro Nacional Manuel Bonilla**, with a rather grand interior (1915) inspired by the Athenée Theatre in Paris and, across the square, the beautiful old church of **El Calvario**. Built in elegant colonial style, El Calvario's roof is supported by 14 pillars.

In Colonia Palmira, to the southeast of the city, is Boulevard Morazán, with shopping and business complexes, embassies, banks, restaurants, *cafeterías* and bars. You can get a fine view of the city from the **Monumento a La Paz** ① *open till 1700*, on Juana Laínez hill, near the Estadio Nacional (National Stadium), but don't walk up alone.

The backdrop to Tegucigalpa is the summit of **El Picacho**, with the Cristo del Picacho statue looming up to the north (see Valle de Angeles, below), although this can be hard to see at times. From Plaza Morazán go up 7 Calle and the Calle de la Leona to **Parque La Leona**, a small handsome park with a railed walk overlooking the city and safer than Monumento a La Paz. Higher still is the reservoir in El Picacho, also known as the **United Nations Park**, which can be reached by a special bus from the No 9 bus stop, behind Los Dolores church (in front of Farmacia Santa Bárbara, Sunday only, US$0.15); alternatively, take a bus to El Piligüin or Corralitos (daily at 0600) from the north side of Parque Herrera in front of the Teatro Nacional Manuel Bonilla.

Comayagüela
Crossing the bridge of 12 de Julio (quite near the Teatro Nacional Manuel Bonilla, see above) you can visit Comayagüela's market of San Isidro. In the Edificio del Banco Central, is the **Pinacoteca Arturo H Medrano** ① *12 Calle entre 5 y 6 Av*, which houses approximately 500 works by five Honduran artists and the **Museo Numismático** ① *Mon-Fri 0900-1200, 1300-1600*, which has a collection of coins and banknotes from Honduras and around the world. Funds have been set aside to restore the older parts of Comayagüela, which should make the place more enjoyable to explore.

Ticamaya **20**   Taiwan **6**

Eating ⑦
Alondra **1**
Bar Mediterráneo **2**
Duncan Maya **3**

Around Tegucigalpa 😑🎭❀🟑 ⇢ pp933-939.

Heading north out of Tegucigalpa on the Olancho road, you come to **Talanga**, with a post office and Hondutel near the market on the main road. From Talanga it is a short trip to the historic and beautiful settlements of Cedros and Minas de Oro. From the Parque Central an unpaved road leads south to the Tegucigalpa-Danlí road making a triangular route possible back to the capital.

Cedros is one of Honduras' earliest settlements, dating from Pedro de Alvarado's mining operations of 1536. It is an outstanding colonial mining town with cobbled streets, perched high on an eminence amid forests. The festival of El Señor del Buen Fin takes place in the first two weeks of January. Buses to Talanga, Cedros and nearby San Ignacio leave from Reynita de San Ignacio in Mercado Zonal Belén, Comayagüela, T224-0066.

Santa Lucía → Altitude: 1400-1600 m.

Northeast of Tegucigalpa, on the way to Valle de Angeles, a right turn goes to the quaint old mining village of Santa Lucía which is perched precariously on a steep mountainside overlooking the valley with Tegucigalpa below. The town has a colonial church with a Christ statue given by King Felipe II of Spain in 1592. There is a charming legend of the

Around Tegucigalpa

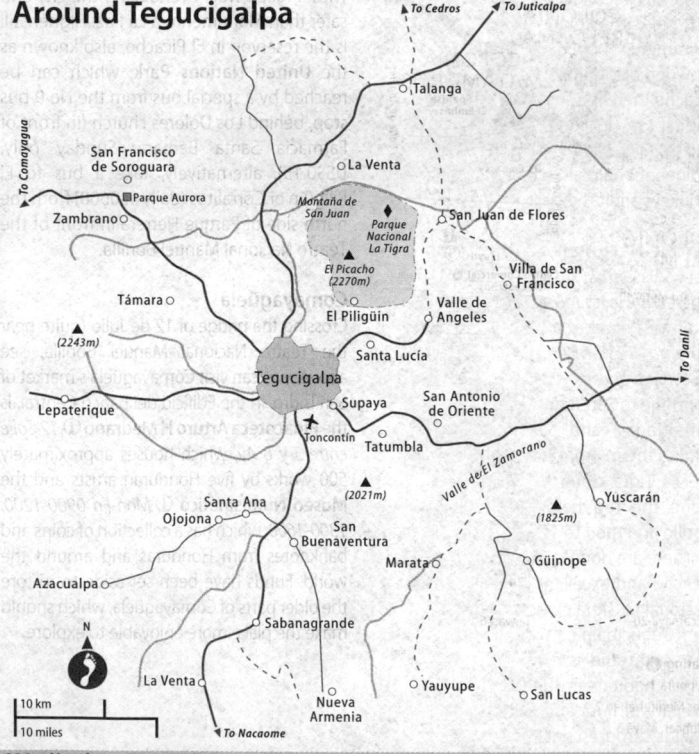

Black Christ, which the authorities ordered to be taken down to Tegucigalpa when Santa Lucía lost its former importance as a mining centre. Every step it was carried away from Santa Lucía it became heavier. When it was impossible to carry it any further they turned round, and by the time they were back in Santa Lucía, it was as light as a feather.

The town is lively with parties on Saturday night, and there is a festival in the second and third weeks of January. There are souvenir shops in the town, including **Cerámicas Ucles** just past the lagoon, second street on left, and another ceramics shop at the entrance on your right. There are good walks up the mountain on various trails, with fine views of Tegucigalpa.

A good circuit is to descend east from the mountain towards San Juan del Rancho through lovely landscapes on a good dirt road, then connect with the paved road to El Zamorano. From there continue either to El Zamorano, or return to Tegucigalpa (see below for opposite direction).

Valle de Angeles → *Altitude: 1310 m.*

About 30 minutes' drive from Tegucigalpa, Valle de Angeles is on a plain below **Monte San Juan**, with **Cerro El Picacho** (2270m) and **Cerro La Tigra** nearby. It is a popular spot for trips from the city, with a cool climate year round and is surrounded by pine forests. There are tracks going through the forests, old mines to explore, a picnic area and a swimming pool; consequently it is crowded on Sundays. At the top of Cerro El Picacho there is a stunning view of the city, and if so inclined you can visit the **zoo ①** *daily, 0800-1500, US$0.20*, of mostly indigenous animals including jaguar, spider monkeys and other animals and birds.

Parque Nacional La Tigra

① *US$10 entry. Go first to the Amitigra office, Edificio Italia, 6th floor, about 3 blocks southwest of Amex office in Av República de Panamá, T232-6771; helpful. Book a visit here in advance.*

Continue to San Juan de Flores (also called Cantarranas) and San Juancito, an old mining town. From here you can climb in the La Tigra cloud forest and even walk along the top before descending to El Hatillo and then to Tegucigalpa.

There are good climbs to the heights of Picacho and excellent hikes in the Parque Nacional La Tigra cloud forest. Only 11 km from Tegucigalpa, this cloud forest covers 238 sq km and is considered one of the richest habitats in the world with a great diversity of flora and fauna – bromeliads, orchids, arborescent ferns and over 200

North of Tegucigalpa

species of bird. Single hikers must have a guide. There are two approach routes: go to **El Piligüin** (see below) for the Jutiapa entrance, from where you can start hiking, or to Gloriales Inn in El Hatillo. You can also walk 24 km from Tegucigalpa to the Jutiapa entrance. Then hike to the visitor centre of La Tigra at El Rosario (10 km, three hours, easy hiking, superb). Alternatively, go to **San Juancito**, above which is the national park (well worth a visit, a stiff, one-hour uphill walk to El Rosario visitor centre, park offices and six trails ranging from 30 minutes to eight hours, bring insect repellent).

A recommended hike is the **Sendero La Esperanza**, which leads to the road; turn right then take the **Sendero Bosque Nublado** on your left. The whole circuit takes about one hour 20 minutes. A few quetzal birds survive here, but you will need a good eye. In the rainy season (June, July, October and November) there is a spectacular 100-m waterfall (Cascada de la Gloria), which falls on a vast igneous rock. Do not leave paths when walking as there are steep drops. Also get advice about personal safety, as robberies have occurred.

From Parque Herrera in Tegucigalpa, buses throughout the day go to the village of **El Piligüin**, north of Santa Lucía. A delightful 40-minute walk down the pine-clad mountainside leads to **El Chimbo** (meals at *pulpería* or shop, ask anyone the way), then take bus either to Valle de Angeles or Tegucigalpa.

At Km 24 on the road to Danlí, there are climbs to the highest peak through the Uyuca rainforest. Information is available from the Escuela Agrícola Panamericana in the breathtaking **Valle del Zamorano**, or from the **Amitigra** office in Tegucigalpa (see above). The school has rooms for visitors. Visits to the school are organized by some tour operators. On the northwest flank of Uyuca is the picturesque village of **Tatumbla**.

Suyapa

Southeast of Tegucigalpa, the village of Suyapa attracts pilgrims to its big church, home to a tiny wooden image of the Virgin, about 8 cm high, set into the altar. A fiesta is held 1-4 February, see page 935. Take a bus to the University or to Suyapa from 'La Isla', one block northwest of the city stadium.

Sabanagrande

Further south (40 km) is Sabanagrande, just off the main highway. This typical colonial town, complete with cobbled streets, is a good day trip from Tegucigalpa. There is an interesting colonial church (1809), Nuestra Señora del Rosario 'Apa Kun Ka' (the place of water for washing), with the **fiesta** of La Virgen de Candelaria from 1-11 February. At 1000 m, it has a mild climate, beautiful scenery with pleasant walks, including views to the Pacific and the Gulf of Fonseca. The town is famous for its *rosquillas* (a type of biscuit).

Ojojona → Altitude: 1400 m.

Ojojona is another quaint, completely unspoiled, old village about 30 minutes (24 km) south of Tegucigalpa; turn right off the Southern Highway. The village pottery is interesting but make your selection carefully as some of it is reported to be of poor quality. La Casona del Pueblo offers the best handicrafts in town, including fine rustic ceramics. Fiesta 18-20 January. There are two well-preserved colonial churches in Ojojona, with fine paintings, plus two more in nearby Santa Ana, which is passed on the way from Tegucigalpa.

Hotel and guesthouse prices		
LL over US$150	**L** US$100-150	**AL** US$66-99
A US$46-65	**B** US$31-45	**C** US$21-30
D US$12-20	**E** US$7-11	**F** under US$7

Restaurant prices		
♥♥♥ over US$15	**♥♥** US$8-15	**♥** under US$8

See pages 45-48 for further information.

● Sleeping

Tegucigalpa p926, map p928
There is a 4% tax on hotel bills, plus 12% sales tax: check if it is included in the price.
LL Honduras Maya, Av República de Chile, Col Palmira, T280-5000, www.honduras maya.hn. Rooms and apartments, casino, swimming pool, **Bar Mirador** with nightly happy hour 1700-1900, cafeterías (Black Jack's Snack Bar, Cafetería 2000), restaurant (Rosalila), conference hall and convention facilities for 1300, view over the city from upper rooms. Excellent travel agency in the basement.
AL Humuya Inn, Col Humuya 1150, 5 mins from airport, T239 2206, www.humuyainn.com. Rooms and service apartments, US owner. Recommended.
A Plaza, on Av Paz Barahona, in front of post office, T237-2111, hotelplaza_centro@ yahoo.com. good location, friendly staff, hot water, cable TV, free internet in the lobby and breakfast included.
B-C Granada 4, Av Gutemberg, T237-4004, neat, tidy rooms with a/c and Wi-Fi, parking available. 1 of 4 Granada hotels all very close to each other.
C Crystal, 2nd floor, Máximo Jerez y S Mendieta, T237-8980. TV, a/c, OK rooms.
C Granada 1, Av Gutemberg 1401, Barrio Guanacaste, T237-2381. Hot water on 2nd floor only, good, clean, safe, TV lounge. Internet café next door.
C Granada 2, T238-8066 and **C Granada 3**, T237-0843, on the street leading uphill (to Barrio Casamate) from northeast corner of Parque Finlay. Good beds, hot water, safe

parking, can be noisy from passing traffic so try to get a room at the back. Recommended.
C MacArthur, Av Lempira 454 and Telégrafo, T237-9839, www.hotelmacarthur.com. A/c, TV, private bath, cheaper without a/c, small pool. Recommended.
D Nuevo Boston, Av Máximo Jerez 321, T237-9411. Good beds, spotless, hot water, central. Good value, no credit cards, rooms on street side noisy, free coffee, mineral water and cookies in lounge, stores luggage, well-run. Simple and recommended.
E-F Iberia, Peatonal Los Dolores, T237-9267. Hot showers, clean, friendly and helpful owner happy to help guests get to know Tegus, refurbished, stores luggage, cheaper without fan.

Comayagüela p929
Convenient for buses to the north and west and there are many cheap pensiones and rooms. It is noisier and dirtier than Tegucigalpa, many places are unsuitable for travellers. If you are carrying luggage, take a taxi.
C-D Centenario, 6 Av, 9-10 Calle, T222-1050. Safe parking. Recommended.
D-E Real de Oro, Av Cabañas, 11 and 12 Calle. Clean, friendly.
E Condesa Inn, 7 Av, 12 Calle. Clean, hot shower, a/c, TV, cafetería, very friendly, a bargain. Recommended.
E-F San Pedro, 9 Calle, 6 Av. With bath (cheaper without), or with private cold shower. Popular, restaurant.
F California, 6 Av, 22-23 Calle. Private bath, friendly, close to Mi Esperanza bus station for Nicaragua.
F Colonial, 6 y 7 Av, 6 Calle 617, T237-5785. With bath, hot water, clean, secure (but unsafe area), front desk unhelpful, otherwise good service and value, restaurant next door.
F Hotelito Latino, 6 Av, 8 Calle. Very basic, friendly, safe, cafetería.
F Hotelito West, 10 Calle, 6-7 Av. Towels and soap, hot water all day, very friendly, changes TCs. Recommended.

F Ticamaya, 6 Av, 8 Calle. Soap, towels and clean sheets daily, quiet, friendly, restaurant.

Valle de Angeles *p931*

B-D Villas del Valle, 500 m north of town, T766-2534, www.villasdelvalle.com. Selection of rooms, cabins and suites. Honduran and European food in the restaurant.

C Hotel y Restaurante Posada del Angel, northeast of centre, T766-2233, hotelposada delangel@yahoo.com. Swimming pool, indifferent service, moderate prices.

Parque Nacional La Tigre *p931*

E Eco Albergue La Tigra, in the old hospital of the mining company. Price per person. Rooms named after local birds, capacity for 50.

F Hotelito San Juan, San Juancito. 6 rooms with shared bathroom.

● Eating

Tegucigalpa *p926, map p928*

Take a walk down the pedestrianised stretch of Av Paz Barahona. In the evening, take a taxi to Blv Morazón. Most places close on Sun. There are good Chinese restaurants on Calle del Telégrafo in centre; huge servings at reasonable prices.

ⵉⵉⵉ Alondra, Av República de Chile on east side of Honduras Maya. One of the best.

ⵉⵉⵉ El Arriero, Av República de Chile, near Honduras Maya. Excellent steaks and seafood.

ⵉⵉⵉ El Trapiche, Blv Suyapa, opposite National University. Colonial ranch atmosphere, good steaks and national dishes. Recommended.

ⵉⵉⵉ Roma, Av Santa Sede, Calle Las Acacias 1601, 1 block off Av República de Chile. The oldest Italian restaurant in the city, good pizzas.

ⵉⵉ Casa María, Av Ramón E Cruz, Col Los Castaños, 1 block off Blv Morazán. Colonial building, good food.

ⵉⵉ China Food, 2 blocks before the easternmost bridges on Blv Morazán, ½ block to the right. Good-value Chinese.

ⵉⵉ Daymio, Plaza Benito Juárez, Col Palmira. 1 of several Japanese restaurants in this area.

ⵉⵉ Duncan Maya, Av Colón 618, opposite central Pizza Hut. Lively place, popular with locals, occasionally has live music. Good and reasonably priced.

ⵉⵉ El Gachupín, off Blv Morazán, Col El Castaño Sur. Superb, Mediterranean-style food, garden.

ⵉⵉ El Ganadero, Calle La Isla, behind Congress building. Steaks, chicken, seafood, good.

ⵉⵉ El Padrino, 1 block off Blv Morazán, Col Montecarlo behind Popeye's. Very good pizzas and other dishes.

ⵉⵉ El Pórtico, near Blv Morazán, T236-7099. Good food but don't be in a hurry.

ⵉⵉ José y Pepe's, Av República de Panamá, near the Honduras Maya. Excellent steaks, good service and value. Warmly recommended.

ⵉⵉ Mei-Mei, Pasaje Midence Soto, central. Chinese. Recommended.

ⵉⵉ Rojo, Verde y Ajo, 1 Av B, Col Palmira. Good food, reasonable price, closed Sun.

ⵉⵉ Sushi Bar in the Bakery Center, 1 Av B, Col Palmira. Sushi and tempura.

ⵉⵉ Taco Loco, Paseo Argentina behind Blv Morazán. Mexican fast food.

ⵉⵉ Tito, ½ block off Blv Morazán on Av Juan Lindo. Good pizzas.

ⵉⵉ Tony's Mar, Blv Juan Pablo II y Av Uruguay, Col Tepeyac, T239-9379. Seafood, good, simple, New Orleans style.

ⵉ El Patio 2, easternmost end of Blv Morazán. Traditional food, good service and atmosphere, good value for the hungry. Recommended.

ⵉ Taiwan, round corner from Hotels Granada 2 and 3, on Av Máximo Jerez. Chinese food, huge portions, good value.

Bakeries

Antojitos, next door to Hotel Granada 3. Convenient for breakfast, closes at 1100, easiest place to eat in the area.

Basilio's Repostería y Panadería, Calle Peatonal between Los Dolores and S Mendieta. Good cakes, bread and pastries.

Salman's. Several outlets. Good bread/pastries.

Cafeterías

Al Natural, Calle Hipólito Matute y Av Miguel Cervantes. Some vegetarian, some meat

dishes, huge fresh fruit juices, antiques, caged birds, nice garden atmosphere.
Bar Mediterráneo, Calle S Mendieta, between Máximo Jerez and Colón. Delicious goat meat, and cheap set meals.
Café y Librería Paradiso, Av Paz Barahona 1351. Excellent coffee and snacks, good library, paintings and photos to enjoy, newspapers and magazines on sale, good meeting place.
Cafetería Típica Cubana, Parque Finlay. Open 0700-1800 (1200 Sun). Good breakfast, good service.
Chomy's Café, Centro Comercial Asfura, Av Cervantes and 2 branches in Col San Carlos (Calle Ramón Rosa and Calle San Carlos). Good quiches, desserts, coffee, tea.
Don Pepe's Terraza, Av Colón 530, upstairs, T222-1084. Central, cheap, live music, but typical Honduran atmosphere. Recommended.
Stacolosal, Paseo de Panamá y Paseo Argentina off Av República de Chile, Col Palmira. Open 0700-1900. Good cheap eating place, classical music and friendly owner.

Comayagüela p929
Cafeterías
Bienvenidos a Golosinas, 6 Av, round corner from Hotel Colonial. Friendly, basic meals, beer.
Cafetería Nueva Macao, 4 Av No 437. Large portions, Chinese.
Comedor Tulin, 4 Av between 4 and 5 Calle. Good breakfasts.

Santa Lucía p930
♥♥ **Miluska**. A Czech restaurant serving Czech and Honduran food. Recommended.
♥ **Comedor**, next to the plaza/terrace of the municipality. On Sun food is available on the streets.

Valle de Angeles p931
♥♥ **La Casa de las Abuelas**, 1 block north of Parque Central, T766-2626. Pleasant courtyard with wine bar, café, library, satellite TV, email, phone, information and art gallery.
♥♥ **Las Tejas**, opposite the Centro Turístico La Florida. A Dutch-owned restaurant.

♥ **Restaurante Turístico de Valle de Angeles**, on top of hill overlooking town. Good.

Parque Nacional La Tigra p931
♥ **Grocery store**, next door to Hotelito San Juan, San Juancito. Sells fuel, drinks and can prepare *comida corriente*; same owners as hotel, T766-2237.
♥ **Señora Amalia Elvir**, before El Rosario. Meals are available at Señora Amalia's house.

⊙ Entertainment

Tegucigalpa p926, map p928
Bars and clubs
In front of the Universidad Nacional on Blv Suyapa is **La Peña**, where every Fri at 2100 there is live music, singing and dancing, entrance US$1.40. Blv Morazán has plenty of choice in nightlife including **Taco Taco**, a good bar, sometimes with live mariachi music; next door **Tequila**, a popular drinking place only open at weekends. **Tobacco Road Tavern**, a popular gringo hang-out, in the downtown area on Calle Matute. **Iguana Rana Bar** is very popular with locals and visitors, similarly **La Puerta del Alcalá**, 3½ blocks down from Taca office on Blv Morazán, Col Castaño Sur. Pleasant open setting.

Cinemas
Plazas 1 to 5, in Centro Comercial Plaza Miraflores on Blv Miraflores. **Regis, Real, Opera,** and **Sagitario** at Centro Comercial Centroamérica, Blv Miraflores (for good US films). **Multiplaza**, Col Lomas del Mayab, 6-screens. In the city centre, **Lido Palace, Variedades** and **Aries**, 200 m up Av Gutemberg leading from Parque Finlay to Col Reforma.

⊛ Festivals and events

Suyapa p932
1-4 Feb Fiesta, with a televised *alborada* with singers, music and fireworks, from 2000-2400 on the 2nd evening.

Sabanagrande *p932*
1-11 Feb Fiesta of La Virgen de Candelaria.

Ojojona *p932*
18-20 Jan Fiesta.

○ Shopping

Tegucigalpa *p926, map p928*
Bookshops
Metromedia, Edif Casa Real, Av San Carlos, behind Centro Comercial Los Castaños, Blv Morazán, English books, new and second-hand, for sale or exchange. Librería Paradiso (see under Cafeterias above). Books in Spanish. Editorial Guaymuras, Av Miguel Cervantes 1055. Second-hand bookstalls in Mercado San Isidro (6 Av y 2 Calle, Comayagüela), cheap.

Markets
Mercado San Isidro, 6 Av at 1 Calle, Comaya-güela. Many fascinating things, but filthy; do not buy food here. Sat is busiest day. Mercado de Artesanías, 3 Av, 15 Calle, next to Parque El Soldado. Good value.

Good supermarkets: La Colonia, in Blv Morazón; Más y Menos, in Av de la Paz. Also on Calle Salvador, 1 block south of Peatonal.

Photography
Kodak on Parque Central and Blv Morazán; Fuji by the cathedral and on Blv Morazán.

▲ Activities and tours

Tegucigalpa *p926 map p928*
Columbia, Calle Principal between 11 y 12 Av, Blv Morazán, T232-3532, columbiatours@ sigmanet.hn. Excellent for national parks, including Cusuco, Pico Bonito and Cuero y Salado, as well as Punta Sal and Bay Islands. Explore Honduras Tour Service, Col Zerón 21-23 Av, 10 Calle NO, San Pedro Sula, T552-6242, www.explorehonduras.com. Copán and Bay Islands tours.

Gloria Tours across from north side of Parque Central in Casa Colonial, T/F238-2232. Information centre and tour operator.
Trek Honduras, Av Julio Lozano 1311, T239-9827. Tours of the city, Bay Islands, Copán, San Pedro Sula, Valle de Angeles and Santa Lucía.

● Transport

Tegucigalpa *p926, map p928*
Air
Toncontín Airport opens at 0530. Check in at least 2 hrs before departure; snacks, souvenir shops, several duty-free stores and internet. Buses to airport from Comayagüela, on 4 Av between 6 and 7 Calle, or from Av Máximo Jerez in downtown Tegucigalpa; into town US$0.19, every 20 mins from left-hand side outside the airport; yellow cabs, US$7-8, smaller *colectivo* taxis, US$5 or more.

Airline offices Atlantic Airline, T220-5231; Air France, Centro Comercial Galería, Av de la Paz, T237-0229; Alitalia, Col Alameda, 5 Av, 9 Calle No 821, T239-4246; American, Ed Palmira, opposite Honduras Maya, 1st floor, T232-1414; British Airways, Edif Sempe, Blv Comunidad Económica Europea, T225-5101; Continental, Av República de Chile, Col Palmira, T220-0999; Grupo Taca, Blv Morazán y Av Ramón E Cruz, T239-0148 or airport T233-5756; Iberia, Ed Palmira, opposite Honduras Maya, T232-7760; Isleña Airlines, T236-8778, also at Toncontín Airport, T233-2192, www.flyislena.com; Japan Airlines, Edif Galería La Paz, 3rd floor, Local 312, 116 Av La Paz, T237-0229; KLM, Ed Ciicsa, Av República de Chile y Av República de Panamá, Col Palmira, T232-6410; Lufthansa, Edif Plaza del Sol, No 2326, Av de la Paz, T236-7560. Sol Air in Tegucigalpa on T235-3737; Sosa Airline, at the airport, T233-7351.

Bus
Local Fares are US$0.08-0.12; stops are official but unmarked.

Long distance To **San Pedro Sula** on Northern Hwy, 3¼-4 hrs depending on service. Several companies, including: Sáenz, Centro Comercial Perisur, Blv Unión Europea, T233-4229 and **Hedman Alas**, 11 Av, 13-14 Calle, Comayagüela, T237-7143, www.hedmanalas.com, both recommended; **El Rey**, 6 Av, 9 Calle, Comayagüela, T237-6609; **Viajes Nacionales** (Viana), terminal on Blv de Las Fuerzas Armadas, T235-8185. To **Tela** and **La Ceiba**, Viana Clase Oro, and Etrusca, 8 Av, 12 y 13 Calle, T222-6881. To **Choluteca**, Mi Esperanza, 6 Av, 23-24 Calle, Comayagüela, T225-1502. To **Trujillo**, Cotraibal, 7 Av, 10-11 Calle, Comayagüela, T237-1666. To **La Esperanza**, Empresa Joelito, 4 Calle, No 834, Comayagüela. To **Comayagua**, most going to San Pedro Sula and **Transportes Catrachos**, Col Torocagua, Blv del Norte, Comayagüela. To **Valle de Angeles** and **Santa Lucía**, from stop on Av La Paz (near filling station opposite hospital). To **Juticalpa** and **Catacamas**, Empresa Aurora, 8 Calle, 6-7 Av, Comayagüela, T237-3647. For **Danlí** and **El Paraíso**, for the Nicaraguan border at Las Manos, see page 1026.

For travellers leaving Tegucigalpa, take the Tiloarque bus on Av Máximo Jerez, by Calle Palace, and get off in Comayagüela at Cine Centenario (Av 6) for nearby **Empresa Aurora** buses (for **Olancho**) and **El Rey** buses (for **San Pedro Sula**). 3 blocks northwest is Cine Lux, near which are **Empresas Unidas** and **Maribel** (8 Av, 11-12 Calle, T237-3032) for **Siguatepeque**. Tiloarque bus continues to Mi Esperanza bus terminal (for **Choluteca** and **Nicaraguan border**). Take a 'Carrizal' or 'Santa Fe' bus ascending Belén (9 Calle) for Hedman Alas buses to **San Pedro Sula** and for Comayagua buses. The **Norteño** bus line to San Pedro Sula is alongside Mamachepa market, from where there are also buses for **Nacaome** and **El Amatillo** border with El Salvador.
International Ticabus, 16 Calle, 5-6 Av, Comayagüela, T222-0590, www.ticabus.com, to **Managua** (US$20, 9 hrs), **San José** (US$40),

San Salvador (US$15), **Guatemala City** (US$30) and **Panama** (US$65) daily. Make sure you reserve several days ahead. Hedman Alas have a service to **Guatemala City** and **Antigua** that leaves Tegucigalpa for San Pedro Sula, 0600, 12 hrs, US$52. Alternatively to **Nicaragua**, take Mi Esperanza bus to San Marcos de Colón, then taxi or local bus to El Espino on border. To **San Marcos**, 4 daily from 0730, direct to border at 0400, US$2.50, 5 hrs (0730 is the latest one that will get you into Nicaragua the same day). Or Mi Esperanza bus to Río Guasaule border, several daily, 4 hrs, US$2. To **San Salvador**, Cruceros del Golfo, Barrio Guacerique, Blv Comunidad Económica Europea, Comayagüela, T233-7415, US$18, at 0600 and 1300, 6 hrs travelling, 1 hr or more at border. Connections to **Guatemala** and **Mexico**; direct bus to border at El Amatillo, US$2.50, 3 hrs, several daily; alternatively from San Pedro Sula via Nueva Ocotepeque and El Poy. To **San Salvador** and **Guatemala**, with King Quality from Tegucigalpa (T225-5415) from Cruceros del Golfo terminal, 0600 and 1300 and San Pedro Sula (T553-4547) at 0630. Alternatively, to Guatemala go to San Pedro Sula and take **Escobar**, **Impala** or **Congolón** to Nueva Ocotepeque and the border at **Agua Caliente**, or via **Copán** (see page 724).

Car
Car hire Avis, Edif Palmira and airport, T232-0088. Budget, Blv Suyapa and airport, T/F235-9531. Hertz, Centro Comercial Villa Real, Col Palmira, T239-0772. Maya, Av República de Chile 202, Col Palmira, T232-0992. Molinari, 1 Av, 2 Calle, Comayagüela and airport, T237-5335. Thrifty, Col Prados Universitarios, T235-6077. Toyota, T235-6694.
Car repairs Metal Mecánica, 1 block south of Av de los Próceres, Col Lara. Volkswagen dealer near Parque Concordia, good.

Taxi
About US$2-4 per person, but you can often bargain down to around US$1.50 a trip in the city. More after 2200, cheaper on designated routes, eg Miraflores to centre.

Santa Lucía p930

Bus To Santa Lucía from Mercado San Pablo, **Tegucigalpa**, hourly service, US$0.30, past the statue of Simón Bolívar by the Esso station, Av de los Próceres.

Valle de Angeles p931

Bus To Valle de Angeles every 45 mins, US$0.40, 1 hr, leaves from San Felipe, near the hospital. To **San Juan de Flores** 1000, 1230, 1530.

Parque Nacional La Tigra p931

Bus Buses leave from Mercado San Pablo, **Tegucigalpa**, for **San Juancito** from 1000, 1½ hrs, on Sat and Sun bus at 0800 packed with people visiting their families, US$0.75; passes turn-off to Santa Lucía and goes through Valle de Angeles. Return bus from San Juancito at 1500 from across the river and up the hill, opposite the park. On Sat, buses return at 0600 and 1200 from church, board early. For return journey double check local information. Alternatively, from behind Los Dolores church in Tegucigalpa you can take a bus to **El Piligüin/Jutiapa** at 0600; it passes through beautiful scenery by El Hatillo and other communities. From El Piligüin, it is a long, hot walk up to the park entrance.

Ojojona p932

Bus Buses leave **Comayagüela** every 15-30 mins from Calle 4, Av 6, near San Isidro market, US$0.40, 1 hr. From same location, buses go west to **Lepaterique** ('place of the jaguar'), another colonial village, over 1-hr drive through rugged, forested terrain. Distant view of Pacific on fine days from heights above village.

● Directory

Tegucigalpa p926 map p928
Banks

There are many ATMs in the city centre. All banks have several branches throughout the city; we list the main offices. Branch offices are unlikely to change TCs, only US$ cash. **HSBC**, 5 Calle (Av Colón) in the centre and at 5 Calle in front of Plaza Morazán. **Banco Atlántida**, 5 Calle in front of Plaza Morazán (may agree to change money on Sat up to 1200). **Banco de Honduras** (Citibank), Blv Suyapa. **Banco del País**, Calle Peotonal in the centre, changes TCs. **Banco de Occidente**, 3 Calle (Cervantes) y 6 Av (S Mendieta) in the centre.

Visa, MasterCard and Amex cash advances (no commission) and TCs at **BAC**, Blv Morazán, and at **Honducard**, Av de la Paz y Ramón E Cruz, and at **Aval Card**, Blv Morazán. Banks are allowed to trade at the current market rate, but there is a street market along the Calle Peatonal off the Parque Central, opposite the post office and elsewhere. Exchange can be difficult on Sat, try **Coin**, a *casa de cambio* on Av de la Paz, inside **Supermercado Más y Menos**, same rates as banks, no commission, Mon-Fri 0830-1730, Sat 0900-1200, changes TCs but will photocopy cheques and passport; another branch of **Coin** on Calle Peatonal, good rates. Recommended.

Cultural centres

Alianza Francesa, Col Lomas del Guijarro, T239-6163, cultural events Fri afternoon, French films Tue 1930. **Centro Cultural Alemán**, 8 Av, Calle La Fuente, T237-1555, German newspapers, cultural events. **Instituto Hondureño de Cultura Interamericana (IHCI)**, Calle Real de Comayagüela, T237-7539, has an English library and cultural events.

Embassies and consulates

Belize, T220-5000, Ext 7770. **Canada**, Ed Financiero Banexpo, Local 3, Col Payaqui, Blv Juan Bosco II, T232-4551. **Costa Rica**, Col El Triángulo, 1a Calle, opposite No 3451, T232-1768, bus to Lomas del Guijarro to last stop, then walk up on your left for 300 m. **Ecuador**, Av Juan Lindo 122, Col Palmira, T236-5980. **El Salvador**, 2 Av Calzada República de Uruguay, Casa 219, Col San Carlos T236-8045. **France**, Col Palmira, 3 Calle, Av Juan Lindo, T236-6432. **Germany**,

Ed Paysen, 3rd floor, Blv Morazán, T232-3161. **Guatemala**, Col Las Minitas 4 Calle, Casa 2421, T232-9704, Mon-Fri 0900-1300, take photo, visa given on the spot, US$10. **Italy**, Av Principal 2602, Col Reforma, T236-6391. **Japan**, Col San Carlos, between 4 and 5 Calle, 2 blocks off Blv Morazán and Av de la Paz, T236-6828, behind Los Castaños Shopping Mall. **Mexico**, Av República de México, Paseo República de Brasil 2402, Col Palmira, T232-6471, opens 0900, visa takes 24 hrs. **Netherlands** (Consulate), Edif Barahona, Col Alameda, next to INA, T231-5007. **Nicaragua**, Av Choluteca 1130, bloque M-1, Col Lomas del Tepeyac, T232-9025 daily, 0800-1200, US$25, visa can take up to 2 days. **Norway**, consular services in front of Residencial el Limonar, 1557-0856. **Panama**, Ed Palmira No 200, opposite Honduras Maya, 2nd floor, T239-5508. **Spain**, Col Matamoros 801, T236-6589, near Av de la Paz and US Embassy. **Sweden**(Consulate), Av Altiplano, Retorno Borneo 2758, Col Miramontes, T/F232-4935. **UK**, Edif Banexpo, 3rd floor, Col Payaqu, T232-0612. **USA**, Av La Paz, Mon-Fri 0800-1700, take any bus from north side of Parque Central in direction 'San Felipe', T236-9320.

Immigration

Dirección General de Migración, Av Máximo Jerez, next to Hotel Ronda, Tegucigalpa.

Internet

Café Don Harry, Av República de Chile 525, Edif Galerías ICB, T220-6174. **@ccess Cyber Coffee**, Centro Commercial La Ronda, Av Máximo Jerez next to Super Donuts, Mon-Sat 0800-1900, US$1.50 for 30 mins. **Café Cyberplace**, Barrio La Plazuela, Av Cervantes 1215, opposite Souvenirs Maya, T220-5200, open 0900-1830, US$2 for 30 mins. **Cyberplace Center**, Av Máximo Jérez and Las Damas, Mon-Sat 0900-1900, US$1 per hr. **Cyberiada Internet Café**, Plaza Brezani, Av Máximo Jerez, Calle H Matute, open 24 hrs, US$1.80 per hr with free coffee. **Multinet**, on Barahona, also in Blv Morazán and Centro Comerical. Lots of machines with full services,

0830-1900, Sun 0900-1700. US$1.50 per hr. **PC Cyber**, Edif Paz Barahona, Calle Peatonal, Mon-Fri 0830-1700, Sat 0830-1400.

Laundry

La Cisne, 1602 Calle La Fuente/Av Las Delicias, US$2.50 up to 5 kg, same-day service. **Lavandería Italiana**, Barrio Guadalupe, 4 blocks west of Av República de Chile 300 block. **Lavandería Super Jet**, Av Gutemberg, 300 m east of Hotel Granada, US$0.20 per kg. **Mi Lavandería**, opposite Repostería Calle Real, 3 Calle, 2 Av, Comayagüela, T237-6573, Mon-Sat 0700-1800, Sun and holidays 0800-1700.

Medical services

Dentist Dra Rosa María Cardillo de Boquín, Ed Los Jarros, Sala 206, Blv Morazán, T231-0583. Recommended. **Dr Roberto Ayala**, DDS, C Alfonso XIII 3644, Col Lomas de Guijarro, T232-2407. **Hospitals** Hospital y Clínica Viera, 11 y 12 Av, 5 Calle, Tegucigalpa, T237-7136. **Hospital la Policlínica** SA 3 Av, 7 y 8 Calle, Comayagüela, T237-3503. **Centro Médico Hondureño**, 3 Av, 3 Calle, Barrio La Granja, Comayagüela, T233-6028. **Pharmacies** Farmacia Rosna, pedestrian mall off Parque Central, T237-0605, English spoken. Recommended. **Regis Palmira**, Ed Ciicsa, Av República de Panamá, Col Palmira.

Post office

Av Paz Barahona/C del Telégrafo, Lista de Correos (Poste Restante) mail held for 1 month, 20g letter to US (US$0.80), Europe (US$1.30), rest of the world (US$1.75).

Telephone

Hondutel, Calle del Telégrafo y Av Colón, has several direct AT&T lines to USA, no waiting. Phone, fax and telegrams; open 24 hrs for phone services only. Also at 6 Av, 7-8 Calle, Comayagüela, with post office.

Work

Peace Corps, opposite Edif Ciicsa, on Av República de Chile, uphill past Hotel Honduras Maya.

Western Honduras

Close to the Guatemalan border, the serene ruins of Copán are Honduras' major Maya attraction. Treasured for its exceptional artistry when compared to other Maya sites, the ruins enjoy a calm and pleasant setting. The quiet town of Copán Ruinas nestles among hills nearby. In fact, the whole area is sprinkled with interesting towns and villages, mostly in delightful hilly surroundings; some with a colourful colonial history, others with their foundations in the Lenca communities, and many producing handicrafts. The ruins of Copán aside, one of the enjoyable aspects of western Honduras is that there are no 'must-sees' – just pick a route, take your time and enjoy the scenery and whatever else you may find. ▸▸ *For listings, see pages 953-961.*

Western Honduras

San Pedro Sula to Copán ⊜ ⋫ pp953-961.

The Western Highway runs parallel to the border from San Pedro Sula southwest along the Río Chamelecón to Canoa (58 km), from where there is a paved road south to Santa Bárbara (a further 53 km). Continuing along the Western Highway, the road from Canoa towards Guatemala runs southwest to La Entrada (115 km from San Pedro), where it forks again left for Santa Rosa (see below) and right for an attractive 60-km road through deep green scenery to Copán Ruinas.

The regular bus is recommended rather than the dangerous minibus service, which can be a bit hair-raising. The road is paved throughout and in good condition.

La Entrada is a hot, dusty town and the place to change buses. Going south takes you to Santa Rosa and towards El Salvador, west to Copán and Guatemala.

El Puente ① daily 0800-1600, US$5, is a national archaeological park reached by taking a turn-off, 4.5 km west from La Entrada on the Copán road, then turning right on a well-signposted, paved road 6 km to the visitor centre. It is near the confluence of the Chamelecón and Chinamito rivers and is thought to have been a regional centre between AD 600 and 900.

Copán Ruinas ⊜❼❷⊜⊙▲⊜❶ ⋫ pp953-961. Colour map 6, B1.

→ www.copanhonduras.org.

A charming town set in the hills just to the east of the border with Guatemala, Copán Ruinas – to give the town its full name – thrives and survives on visitors passing through to visit the nearby ruins. Nevertheless, it is arguably the best-preserved and one of the most pleasant towns in Honduras. Close to the border with Guatemala, it's a good place to stop for a few days before heading straight to San Pedro Sula (172 km) and the Bay Islands or Tegucigalpa (395 km), with the impressive ruins of Copán, good attractions, coffee plantation tours, hiking, caving, hot springs, horseback riding, language schools and volunteer opportunities.

The **Museo Copán** ① Mon-Sat 0800-1600, US$2, on the town square has good explanations in Spanish of the Maya empire and stelae. There is a good selection of artefacts, a burial site and a tomb that was unearthed during a road-building project. It is a good idea to visit the museum before the ruins. **Casa K'inich** ① up the hill from Hotel Marina Copán, US$1.10. The completely restored Old Cuartel now houses the Casa K'inich Interactive Children's Museum, an interesting museum for everyone, not just for kids, and in a nice spot with great views of the town. **Enchanted Wings Butterfly House** ① 2 blocks west of the cemetery on the road to Guatemala, T651-4133, daily 0800-1700, US$5.50, is run by Bob 'The Butterfly Guy' Gallardo, specialist in Honduran butterflies. The garden, complete with restaurant, is beautiful and has exhibits of rare butterflies, an orchid garden and birdwatching tours can be arranged. Recommended.

As in much of Honduras, tuk-tuks have arrived, providing cheap, easy transport. Short trips around town are US$0.50, Macaw Mountain Bird Park US$1.10, ruins US$0.80, Hedman Alas terminal US$1.10.

Copán archaeological site

① Daily, 0800-1600, US$15 entry to ruins and Las Sepulturas, admission valid for 1 day; US$7 to enter the museum with entrance to the tunnels an additional pricey US$15. Bilingual *guided tours available (US$25, 2 hrs), recommended. The Copán Guide Association has a kiosk in the parking area where qualified bilingual guides can be hired at a fixed rate.*

Photographs of the excavation work and a maquette of the site are located in a small exhibition room at the visitor centre. There is a cafetería by the entrance to the ruins, and also a handicrafts shop, in the Parque Arqueológico, next to the bookshop, with local and country maps, and a Spanish/English guide book for the ruins, which is rather generalized. Useful recent books are: *Scribes, Warriors and Kings: City of Copán*, by William and Barbara Fash, and *History Carved in Stone*, a guide to Copán, by William Fash and Ricardo Arguciá (3rd edition, 1998, US$3), published locally and available at the site. Luggage can be left for free.

The magnificent ruins of Copán are one of Central America's major Maya sites, certainly the most significant in Honduras, and they mark the southeastern limit of Maya dominance. Just 1 km from the village, there is a path beside the road from Copán to the ruins which passes two stelae en route. Get to the ruins as early as possible, or stay late in the day so you have a chance to be there without hordes of people.

Museo de Escultura Maya

① *US$10, ticket from main ticket office not at the museum.*

The impressive and huge two-storey Museo of Maya Sculpture and sculpture park houses the newly excavated carvings. In the middle of the museum is an open-air courtyard with a full-size reproduction of the Rosalila temple, found intact buried under Temple 16 with

1 Copán Ruinas

Buses to La Entrada

To Guatemala

To Copán Archaeological Park

Ixbalanque

Palacio Municipal

Parque Central

Cathedral

Clinic

Casa de Todo

Base Camp Tours

Yaragua Tours

Copán Net

To 4 & Hedman Alas Buses

➡ Copán maps
1 Copán Ruinas, page 942
2 Copán archeological site, page 943

N

100 metres
100 yards

Sleeping		Eating
Brisas de Copán 1	Los Jaguares 8	Café Vamos a Ver 7
Café ViaVía Copán 2	Madrugada 9	Carnitas Nía Lola 1
Camino Maya 3	Marina Copán 10	Llama del Bosque 4
Don Udo's 15	Posada 12	
En La Manzana Verde 14	Yaragua 13	Picame 8
Hacienda San Lucas 4		Pizza Copán 9
Hospedaje Los Gemelos 5		Twisted Tanya's 5
Hostel Iguana Azul 7		
La Casa de Café 7		

2 Copán archaeological site

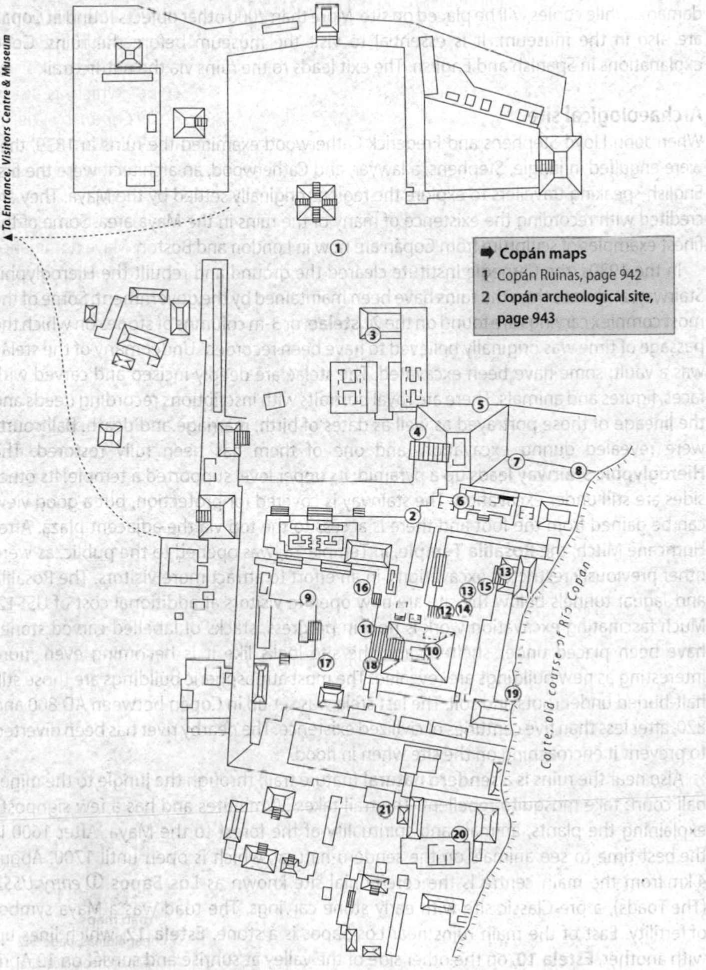

To Entrance, Visitors Centre & Museum
Corte old course of Río Copan
1
2
3
4
5
6
7
8
9
10
11
12
13
14
15
16
17
18
19
20
21
N
50 metres
50 yards

➡ **Copán maps**
1 Copán Ruinas, page 942
2 Copán archeological site, page 943

Main Plaza with Stelae **1**
Acropolis **2**
Ball Court **3**
Hieroglyphic Stairway **4**
Structure 26 **5**
Council House, Temple 22A **6**
Temple of Meditation/ Temple 22 **7**
House of Knives **8**
Structure 13 **9**
Structure 16 **10**
Altar Q **11**
Rosalila Building (within Structure 16) **12**
Entrance to Rosalila & Jaguar tunnels **13**
Hunal Building (beneath Rosalila) & Tomb of Founder **14**
East Court/Plaza de los Jaguares **15**
Plaza Occidental **16**
Altar I **17**
Altar H **18**
Temple 18 **19**
Structure 32 **20**
Zona Residencial **21**

its original paint and carvings (see below). A reproduction of the doorway to Temple 16 is on the upper floor. The new museum houses the original stelae to prevent weather damage, while copies will be placed on site. More than 2000 other objects found at Copán are also in the museum. It is essential to visit the museum before the ruins. Good explanations in Spanish and English. The exit leads to the ruins via the nature trail.

Archaeological site

When John Lloyd Stephens and Frederick Catherwood examined the ruins in 1839, they were engulfed in jungle. Stephens, a lawyer, and Catherwood, an architect, were the first English-speaking travellers to explore the regions originally settled by the Maya. They are credited with recording the existence of many of the ruins in the Maya area. Some of the finest examples of sculpture from Copán are now in London and Boston.

In the 1930s, the Carnegie Institute cleared the ground and rebuilt the Hieroglyphic Stairway, and since then the ruins have been maintained by the government. Some of the most complex carvings are found on the 21 **stelae**, or 3-m columns of stones on which the passage of time was originally believed to have been recorded. Under many of the stelae was a vault; some have been excavated. The stelae are deeply incised and carved with faces, figures and animals. There are royal portraits with inscriptions recording deeds and the lineage of those portrayed as well as dates of birth, marriage and death. Ball courts were revealed during excavation, and one of them has been fully restored. The **Hieroglyphic Stairway** leads up a pyramid; its upper level supported a temple. Its other sides are still under excavation. The stairway is covered for protection, but a good view can be gained from the foot and there is access to the top via the adjacent plaza. After Hurricane Mitch, the **Rosalila Temple**, in Temple 16, was opened to the public, as were other previously restricted excavations, in an effort to attract more visitors. The Rosalila and Jaguar tunnels below the site are now open to visitors at additional cost of US$12. Much fascinating excavation work is now in progress, stacks of labelled carved stones have been placed under shelters, and the site looks like it is becoming even more interesting as new buildings are revealed. The most atmospheric buildings are those still half-buried under roots and soil. The last stela was set up in Copán between AD 800 and 820, after less than five centuries of civilized existence. The nearby river has been diverted to prevent it encroaching on the site when in flood.

Also near the ruins is a **sendero natural** (nature trail) through the jungle to the minor ball court; take mosquito repellent. The trail takes 30 minutes and has a few signposts explaining the plants, animals and spirituality of the forest to the Maya. After 1600 is the best time to see animals on the sendero natural, which is open until 1700. About 4 km from the main centre is the ceremonial site known as **Los Sapos** ① *entry US$2* (The Toads), a pre-Classic site with early stone carvings. The toad was a Maya symbol of fertility. East of the main ruins near Los Sapos is a stone, **Estela 12**, which lines up with another, **Estela 10**, on the other side of the valley at sunrise and sunset on 12 April every year. Horse rides to Los Sapos can be arranged through **Yaragua Tours** (US$15, three hours, see Activities and tours, page 958).

One kilometre beyond the main ruins, along the road to San Pedro Sula, or connected by a new stone path from the main site, is an area called **Las Sepulturas** ① *entrance is almost 2 km from the main site, entry to this site is included in the main Copán ticket,* a residential area where ceramics dating back to 1000 BC have been found. Exhibits from the site are on display in the Copán Museum. It is a delightful site, beautifully excavated and well maintained, peaceful and in lovely surroundings.

Border essentials: Honduras–Guatemala

El Florido

Honduran immigration The office is on the border at El Florido and you get stamps there. They charge entry and exit fees (see Visas and immigration, page 925); ask for a receipt for any 'extra' charges.

Leaving Honduras If leaving with a private vehicle, you need three stamps on your strip from Migración, Tránsito (where they take your *Proviso Provisional*) and Aduana (where they take your *Pase Fronterizo* document) and cancel the stamp in your passport.

Guatemalan consulate Visas can be obtained in San Pedro Sula or Tegucigalpa. Guatemalan tourist cards are available at the border.

Transport Minibuses run all day every day until 1700 between Copán Ruinas and the border at El Florido, 30 minutes, connecting with buses to Guatemalan destinations (see below). Catch the buses behind the municipal market. The cost should be about US$2.50. If heading for Antigua, there are regular minibus services between Copán and Guatemala City/Antigua, US$12 per person. Just to visit Copán, those needing visas can get a 72-hour exit pass at the border but you must re-cross at the same border post before expiry. To enter (or return to) Guatemala an alternative route is via Santa Rosa de Copán and Nueva Ocotepeque (see below and El Florido, Guatemala, page 724 and Chiquimula, Guatemala, page 722).

Around Copán Ruinas

There are many caves around Copán to visit – some of which have unearthed Maya artefacts. Ask locally or check with Yaragua Tours (see page 958). Also here, and in the neighbouring part of Guatemala, are a few remaining Chorti indigenous villages, interesting to visit, particularly on 1 November, Día de Los Muertos, when there are family and communal ceremonies for the dead.

After all the trekking has exhausted you, a trip to the thermal springs **Agua Caliente**, ① *20 km north from Copán, 0800-2000, US$1.50*, will be just what you need. Reached by a road through villages and beautiful scenery, it's a 45-minute journey by vehicle, pickups sometimes go for about US$25, shared between passengers. Cheapest option is local transport from beside the soccer field. Best to use **Base Camp Adventures** or **Yaragua Tours** for trips, US$15. Cross the river and follow the trail up to the springs, but only swim in the river where the very hot water has mixed with the cold. There are changing facilities and toilets in the park. Take all food and water. Also on the road to Guatemala is the **Enchanted Wings Butterfly House** ① *0800-1700, US$3*.

Nine kilometres east of Copán is **Santa Rita**, a small colonial town on the Copán River with cobblestones and red roofs (**Hospedaje Santa Rita** and unnamed outdoor restaurant recommended, off main road next to Esso; speciality *tajadas*, huge portions, cheap).

Also try the **Macaw Mountain** ① *US$10, T651-4245, www.macawmountain.com*, a unique ecotourism project incorporating Honduras' largest bird park with parrots, toucans and macaws. Tour of the coffee *finca*, riverside restaurant serving good, hearty food, visitor centre, river swimming, highly recommended. Ten minutes from the town centre.

Santa Rosa de Copán ⬣🅿️🅕✳️🅞🔺🅖🅒 ➠ *pp953-961. Colour map 6, B1.*

➔ *Altitude: 1160 m.*

Santa Rosa is an important regional town with a colonial atmosphere of cobbled streets and some of the best colonial architecture in Honduras. Originally known as Los Llanos, it was made a municipality in 1812 and became capital of the Department of Copán when it was split from Gracias (now Lempira). The town is set in some of the best scenery in Honduras and the fine weather makes it ideal for hiking, horses and mountain biking.

Santa Rosa owes its wealth to the fact that it's an agricultural and cattle-raising area. Maize and tobacco are grown here, and visitors can see traditional hand-rolling at the **Flor de Copán cigar factory** ① *3 blocks east of the bus terminal, Mon-Fri until 1700, closed 1130-1300, tours in Spanish at 1000 and 1400, US$2 per person – ask the guard at the gate.* The central plaza and church are perched on a hilltop. There is a quieter plaza, the **Parque Infantil** ① *Calle Real Centenario y 6 Av SO*, a fenced playground and a nice place to relax. The main **market** ① *1 Calle and 3 Av NE*, has good leather items. **Farmers' markets** are held daily in Barrio Santa Teresa (take 4 Calle SE past 5 Avenida SE), and at 4 Calle SE and 5 Avenida SE on Sunday 0500 to 1000. ➠ *For further information, visit www.visitesantarosadecopan.org.*

Santa Rosa de Copán

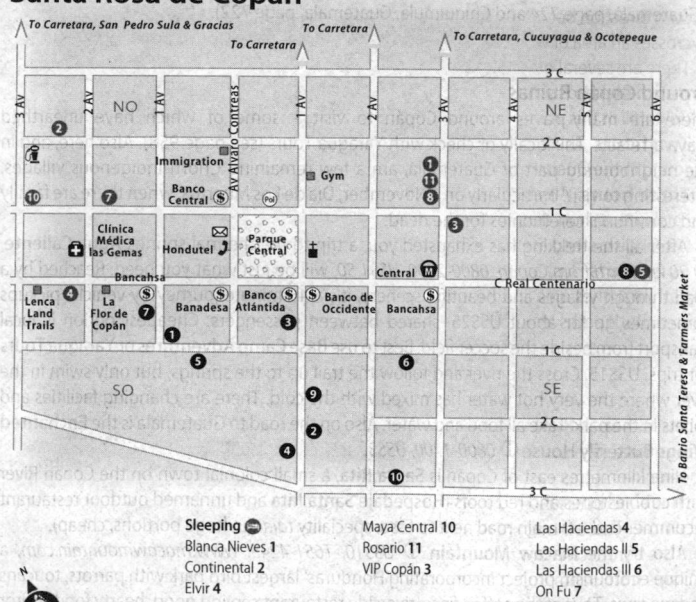

Sleeping 🛏️		Maya Central **10**	Las Haciendas **4**
Blanca Nieves **1**		Rosario **11**	Las Haciendas II **5**
Continental **2**		VIP Copán **3**	Las Haciendas III **6**
Elvir **4**			On Fu **7**
Hospedaje Calle Real **5**		**Eating** 🍴	Pizza Pizza **8**
Hospedaje Santa		Chikys **1**	Rincón Colonial **9**
Eduviges **7**		El Rodeo **2**	Well **10**
Hospedaje Santa Rosa **8**		Flamingos **3**	

Walking from San Manuel Colohuete to Belén Gualcho

There is a well-defined, well-used and easy to follow mule trail linking these two villages, which makes a good one- or two-day hike. Maps are not essential as there are communities at many points along the way where advice can be sought. If required, a map of the area is available from the Lenca Cultural Centre in Gracias.

The path leading away from the village leaves from opposite the *pulpería* and *comedor* where the bus drops you, heading west and downhill into a valley. The path is used by 4WD vehicles and continues to San Sebastián. Just after the community of San José, after passing the last house, the path to Belén branches off. A smaller path leaves the 4WD track and climbs steeply up to your right and more northwest.

One hour Just after Peña Blanca, the path direction becomes unclear after it crosses an area of white chalky rocks. There are several other paths here. The main path heads north and steeply downhill at this point.

Two hours There is water all the year round in the Quebrada de Rogán.

Three hours All year round water in Río Gualmite, a short descent. After this there is a longish, steep ascent.

Four hours Just after this point the path branches on a large flat grassy area. Both paths lead to Belén Gualcho.

The one to the left drops and crosses the river and then you are faced with a long, arduous and very steep ascent. We would recommend taking the path to the right, which exits to the far right of a grassy area by three small houses.

Five hours The path climbs as it skirts around the Cerro Capitán. Just after passing the steepest part, a small landslide forces the path into a descent almost to the river. From here, only 2 m above the river, you can walk steeply down off the path to the river bank where there is the most perfect camp site. Flat sandy soil in some shade on the edge of a coffee plantation and 2 m from the river.

Six hours From the camping site there is a long, continuous climb before dropping down sharply to cross the river. It is possible, but difficult, to cross the river at the point the path meets it. Take a small path off to the right just before the river, which leads to a suspension bridge. From the river it is a long continuous climb, not especially steep, to Belén Gualcho. It is between two small peaks that can be seen clearly after crossing the river. There are more houses after crossing the river and the odd *pulpería* where you can buy *refrescos* or food.

Around Santa Rosa de Copán

Taking time to explore some of the forested hills around Santa Rosa will lead you through spectacular scenery and give an insight into the life of agricultural Honduras.

There are buses from Santa Rosa west to the small town of **Dulce Nombre de Copán** (US$0.55). There are rooms available next to the Hondutel office. Hikers heading for Copán and the border can continue west through the mountains to stay at **San Agustín** (buses and pickups from Santa Rosa), take a hammock or sleeping bag, continuing next day through Mirasol to reach the Ruinas road at El Jaral, 11 km east of Copán ruins (see above).

South of Santa Rosa, buses pass through **Cucuyagua**, with a scenic river, good swimming and camping on its banks, and **San Pedro de Copán**, an attractive village and an entry point into the **Parque Nacional Celaque**, see below.

A mule trail (see box, page 947) connects **Belén Gualcho**, a Lenca village in the mountains and a good base for exploring the surrounding area, with **San Manuel de Colohuete** (1500 m), which has a magnificent colonial church whose façade is sculpted with figures of saints. Buses to San Manuel from Gracias at 1300, four hours, and usually a pickup returning in the evening. There are no hotels so you must ask villagers about places to stay. There is an equally fine colonial church 30 minutes by 4WD vehicle to the southwest at **San Sebastián Colosuca** (1550 m). The village has a mild climate (two *hospedajes*; or try Don Rubilio; food at Doña Clementina García or Doña Alicia Molina). The Feria de San Sebastián is on 20 January. An hour's walk away is the Cueva del Diablo and 6 km away is Cerro El Alta with a lagoon at the top. From San Sebastián, a mule trail goes via the heights of **Agua Fría** to reach the route near the border at **Tomalá**.

Gracias ⊜⊘▲⊜⊙ ›› *pp953-961. Colour map 6, B1.*

→ *Altitude: 765 m.*

One of the oldest and most historic settlements in Honduras, dominated by Montañas de Celaque, Puca and Opulaca – the country's highest peaks – Gracias is a charming, friendly town. Just 50 km from Santa Rosa, both the town and the surrounding countryside are worth a visit. Gracias was the centre from which Francisco de Montejo, thrice Governor of Honduras, put down the great indigenous revolt of 1537-1538. Alonso de Cáceres, his lieutenant, besieged Lempira the indigenous leader in his impregnable mountain-top fortress at Cerquín, finally luring him out under a flag of truce, ambushed him and treacherously killed him. When the Audiencia de los Confines was formed in 1544, Gracias became for a time the administrative centre of Central America.

The helpful **tourist office** in the middle of the Parque Central can store luggage and arrange transport to Parque Nacional Celaque.

There are three colonial churches, **San Sebastián**, **Las Mercedes** and **San Marcos** (a fourth, Santa Lucía, is southwest of Gracias), and a restored fort, with two fine Spanish cannon, on a hill five minutes' walk west of the centre. The fort, **El Castillo San Cristóbal**, has been well restored, and at the foot of the northern ramparts is the tomb of Juan Lindo, President of Honduras 1847-1852, who introduced free education through a system of state schools.

Around Gracias ⊜⊘⊛⊜⊙ ›› *pp953-961.*

Balneario Aguas Termales
ⓘ *Daily 0600-2000, US$2.50, rental of towels, hammock, inner tube, restaurant/bar.*
Some 6 km from Gracias along the road to Esperanza (side road signposted), are hot, communal thermal pools in the forest for swimming (one hour by a path, 1½ hours by road). To find the path, walk 2 km beyond the bridge over Río Arcagual to a second bridge before which turn right by a white house. Climb the hill and take the first path on the left (no sign), cross the river and continue for about 15 minutes to the pools. Good place to barbecue.

Parque Nacional Celaque
It takes at least a day to climb from Gracias to the summit of **Monte Celaque** (2849 m, the highest point in Honduras). Most people allow two days to enjoy the trip. The trail begins from behind the visitor centre of the Parque Nacional Celaque (1400 m), which is 8 km from Gracias, two hours' walk. There are several intersections, best to ask at each. You can also enjoy a day walk to **Mirador La Cascada** ⓘ *entry fee US$3 plus US$3 per night camping*

in the mountain, about three hours from the visitor centre, 1½ hours downhill going back. Transport can be arranged with the tourist office in the Plaza Central (US$10 per vehicle for up to four people). **Comedor Doña Alejandrina** just before the visitor centre, provides excellent breakfasts. Not much of the 8-km road from Gracias to the park is passable when wet, without a high-clearance or 4WD vehicle. Transport can be arranged through the Lenca Centre. Armando Mondragon (Texaco station, T898-4002) does trips, including lunch. At the centre there are seven beds, shower and cooking facilities, drinks available, well maintained. There is another cabin nearby with 10 beds. Take a torch and sleeping bag. Behind the centre is a trail going down to the river where a crystal-clear pool and waterfall make for wonderful bathing. Ask the guide the exact way or pay US$6 for the guide. There is a warden, Miguel, living nearby who can supply food and beer but it is safer to take supplies from Gracias. Contact Cohdefor or CIPANAC in Gracias before leaving for full information. There is a trail all the way to the summit (trees are marked with ribbons) which takes at least six hours: the first three are easy to a campsite at 2000 m (Campamento Don Tomás) where there is small hut, the rest of the way is steep. A better campsite if you can make it is Campamento Naranjo, with water, at about 2500 m – but you'll need a tent. Between these two sites, the climb is particularly steep and in cloud forest. Look out for spider monkeys. Above 2600 m quetzals have been seen. Many hikers don't bother with the summit as it is forested and enclosed; it's four hours down to the visitor centre. Don't forget good hiking boots, warm clothing, insect repellent and, given the dense forest and possibility of heavy cloud, a compass is also recommended for safety. Also, beware of snakes. There is a trail westward from the summit to Belén Gualcho which is steep towards Belén. It takes a couple of days, a guide might be a good idea.

Visiting the other peaks around Gracias is more complicated but interesting. Information, maps that you can photocopy, camping gear and guided tours can be found at the Lenca Cultural Centre.

Gracias

To Santa Rosa de Copán

Río Arcagual

Cohdefor

C Principal

Las Mercedes

Palacio Municipal

Parque Central

San Marcos

To Castillo San Cristóbal

To Santa Lucía & Celaque

San Sebastián

To La Esperanza & Aguas Termales

To La Campa

200 metres
200 yards

Guancascos 3
Iris 4
Posada de Don Juan 5
Rosario 6
San Antonio 7

Sleeping 🛏
Colonial 1
Erick 2

Eating 🍴
El Señorial 1
La Fonda 2

Border essentials: Honduras–El Salvador

Perquín

South of Marcala the road crosses into El Salvador, 3 km before Perquín. There have been several confrontations with the Honduran military in the area but the border dispute has been settled by treaty. Recent reports suggest there is no Salvadorian immigration post; entering the country is possible, but illegal. In addition to the US$10 tourist card, you will be fined US$8 for US citizens, US$12 for Europeans. Ask locally for security conditions and the latest regulations. There are buses along the very rough road from Marcala to San Miguel, El Salvador, and from Perquín to the border in the early morning. The immigration office is about 5 km inside Honduras.

El Poy

Take a bus from Nueva Ocotopeque to El Poy on the border, 15-20 minutes, US$0.30. Exit tax is US$5.50. Buses leave El Poy for San Salvador regularly, taking three to four hours.

Gracias to Erandique

After Gracias, the road runs 52 km to **San Juan del Caite** (a few *hospedajes*, Lempira, Sánchez, and the comfortable Hacienda, two restaurants nearby, helpful people and Peace Corps workers). From here a dirt road runs 26 km south to the small town of Erandique. Founded in 1560 and set high in pine-clad mountains not far from the border with El Salvador, it is a friendly town, and very beautiful. Lempira was born nearby, and was killed a few kilometres away. The third weekend in January is the local **Fiesta de San Sebastián**. Best time to visit is at the weekend. Market days are Friday and Sunday. Each of the three *barrios* has a nice colonial church. Ask around as there are lakes, rivers, waterfalls, springs and bathing ponds in the vicinity. Nearby is **San Antonio** where fine opals (not cut gems, but stones encased in rock) are mined and may be purchased. The many hamlets in the surrounding mountains are reached by roads that have been either resurfaced or rebuilt and the landscapes are magnificent.

There are several roads radiating from Erandique, including one to **Mapulaca** and the border with El Salvador (no immigration or customs or bridge here, at the Río Lempa), a road to San Andrés and another to Piraera (all passable in a car).

La Esperanza → *Colour map 6, C2. Altitude: 1485 m.*

Beyond San Juan del Caite the main, but still rough and stony, road winds through beautiful mountain pine forests to La Esperanza. It is 43 km from San Juan del Caite and another 98 km on a good road to Siguatepeque. Capital of Intibucá Department, La Esperanza is an old colonial town in a pleasant valley. It has an attractive church in front of the park. There is a grotto carved out of the mountainside west of the town centre, a site of religious festivals. There is a market on Thursdays and Sundays when the Lenca from nearby villages sell wares and food but no handicrafts. Nearby is the indigenous village of **Yaramanguila**. It's an excellent area for walking in forested hills, with lakes and waterfalls, although very cold December/January. You can hike to **Cerro de Ojos**, a hill to the north-west and visible from La Esperanza. It is forested with a clearing on top littered with many cylindrical holes; no one knows how they were formed, and they are a strange phenomenon. The turning to this hill is on the La Esperanza to San Juan road. Ask for directions.

→ *Altitude: 1300 m.*

From La Esperanza, an unpaved road runs southeast to Marcala in the Department of La Paz (a paved road goes to La Paz). During the hotter months from March to May, a cooler climate can be found in the highlands of La Paz, with pleasant temperatures during the day and cold (depending on altitude) at night. Ideal for hiking and with beautiful scenery and dramatic waterfalls in the surrounding area, Marcala is a good base from which to visit Yarula, Santa Elena, Opatoro, San José and Guajiquiro. The Marcala region is one of the finest coffee-producing areas of Honduras and a visit to **Comarca**, at the entrance to town, gives an idea of how coffee is processed. Semana Santa is celebrated with a large procession through the main street and there is a **fiesta** in honour of San Miguel Arcángel in the last week of September.

Around Marcala

Near Marcala is Balneario **El Manzanal**, 3 km on the road to La Esperanza; it has a restaurant, two swimming pools and a boating lake, open weekends only. For panoramic views high above Marcala, follow this hike (one hour): head north past **Hotel Medina**, turn right (east) after the hotel and follow the road up into hills. After 2 km the road branches. Take the left branch and immediately on the left is a football field. A small path leaves from this field on the west side taking you through a small area of pine trees then out onto a ridge for excellent views. The track continues down from the ridge back to town, passing an unusual cemetery on a hill.

There are caves nearby on **Musula** mountain, the Cueva de las Animas in Guamizales and Cueva de El Gigante and El León near La Estanzuela with a high waterfall close by. Other waterfalls are El Chiflador, 67 m high, Las Golondrinas, La Chorrera and Santa Rosita. Transport goes to La Florida where there is good walking to the village of **Opatoro** and climbing **Cerro Guajiquiro**. Between Opatoro and Guajiquiro is the **Reserva las Trancas**, a heavily forested mountain where quetzales have been seen.

Yarula and **Santa Elena** are two tiny municipalities, the latter about 40 km from Marcala, with beautiful views (bus Marcala–Santa Elena 1230 returns 0500 next day, 2¾ hours, enquire at Gámez bus office opposite market; truck daily 0830 returns from Santa Elena at 1300). Sometimes meals are available at *comedores* in Yarula and Santa Elena. The dirt road from Marcala gradually deteriorates, the last 20 km being terrible, high clearance essential, 4WD recommended. In **La Cueva Pintada**, south of Santa Elena, there are pre-Columbian cave paintings (*pinturas rupestres*) of snakes, men and dogs; ask for a guide in Santa Elena. Ask also in this village about the **Danza de los Negritos**, performed at the annual **fiesta** of Santiago, 24-25 March, in front of the church. A special performance may be organized, the dancers wearing their old wooden masks, if suitable payment is offered.

The village of **San José** (altitude: 1700 m) is a Lenca community where the climate can be cool and windy even in the hottest months. The scenery is superb. Good hill walking (see box, page 947 for two examples; there are many others), also rivers for swimming. Frequent pickups from Marcala, and two daily minibuses at about 0815 and 0900; from San José to Marcala minibuses depart at 0615 and 0645, one hour, US$1.

Border essentials: Honduras–Guatemala

Agua Caliente

You can cross into Guatemala at Agua Caliente, 16 km from Nueva Ocotepeque. There are three banks, a tourist office on the Honduran side, a *comedor* for food, and one *hospedaje*. This can be a busy crossing but is quicker, cheaper and more efficient than the one at El Florido (see page 945).

Honduran immigration All formalities completed at the border, daily 0700-1800. There are money changers outside the Honduran immigration building, keep lempiras for exit stamp and minibus ride Agua Caliente–Esqiupulas.

Guatemalan consulate The nearest is in San Pedro Sula.

Transport There are several buses a day from San Pedro Sula to Agua Caliente, the first at 0300, US$4.45, 6-7 hours. Buses from Nueva Ocotepeque to Agua Caliente every 30 mins from 0630, US$0.60. Money changers get on the bus between Nueva Ocotepeque and the border, good rates for US$ cash. Minibuses go to Esquipulas, US$0.25, with connections to destinations in Guatemala, see page 722.

Nueva Ocotepeque ●❼❷❸❶ ➤➤ *pp953-961. Colour map 6, B1.*

Heading south from Santa Rosa, Nueva Ocotepeque gives access to good hiking and leads to the borders with Guatemala and El Salvador. The old colonial church of La Vieja (or La Antigua) between Nueva Ocotepeque and the border, is in the village of Antigua Ocotepeque, founded in the 1540s, but destroyed by a flood from Cerro El Pital in 1934.

The **Guisayote Biological Reserve** protects 35 sq km of cloud forest, about 50% virgin and is reached from the Western Highway, where there are trails and good hiking. Access is from El Portillo, the name of the pass on the main road north. El Portillo to El Sillón, the park's southern entrance, three to five hours. Twice daily bus from El Sillón to Ocotepeque. **El Pital**, 3 km east of Nueva Ocotepeque, at 2730 m is the third highest point in Honduras with several square kilometres of cloud forest. The park has not been developed for tourism.

The **Parque Nacional Montecristo** forms part of the Trifinio/La Fraternidad project, administered jointly by Honduras, Guatemala and El Salvador. The park is quite remote from the Honduran side, two to three days to the summit, but there are easy-to-follow trails. Access is best from Metapán in El Salvador. From the lookout point at the peak you can see about 90% of El Salvador and 20% of Honduras on a clear day. The natural resources office, for information, is opposite Texaco, two blocks from **Hotel y Comedor Congolón** at the south end of town. Raymond J Sabella of the US Peace Corps has written a very thorough description of the natural and historical attractions of the Department, including hikes, waterfalls and caves.

For Sleeping and Eating price codes and other relevant information, see Essentials pages 45-48.

● Sleeping

San Pedro Sula to Copán *p941*

C-E San Carlos, La Entrada, at junction to Copán Ruinas, T898-5228. A/c, modern, cable TV, bar, swimming pool, restaurant (T/F661-2187), excellent value.

E-F Central, by Shell, La Entrada. With 2 beds (cheaper with 1), bath, cold water, fans.

F Hospedaje Golosino Yessi, La Entrada. Parking, small rooms, OK.

F Hospedaje María, La Entrada. Good, limited food.

Copán Ruinas *p941, map p942*

L Hacienda San Lucas, south out of town, T651-4495, www.haciendasanlucas.com. Great spot for calm and tranquillity. 8 rooms with hot water bath, restaurant, renovated hacienda home, lovely views of Copán river valley and hiking trails.

AL Posada Real de Copán, on hill overlooking Copán, 1651-4480, www.posadareal decopan.com. Full-service hotel, restaurant and very nice pool, US$5 for non-guests.

AL-A Don Udo's, www.donudos.com. Private bath, hot water, fan, a/c, TV, restaurant, bar, jacuzzi, sun deck.

AL-B Marina Copán, on the plaza occupying almost an entire block, T651-4070, www.hotel marinacopan.com. Swimming pool, sauna, restaurant, bar, live marimba music at weekends, also caters for tour groups, large rooms with TV, suites, very tasteful and spacious, friendly atmosphere. Recommended.

A Camino Maya, corner of main plaza, T651-4646, www.caminomayahotel.com. With bath, good restaurant, rooms bright and airy, cable TV, fans, rooms on courtyard quieter than street, English spoken, balconies on some upstairs rooms.

A La Casa de Café, 4½ blocks west of plaza, T651-4620, www.casadecafecopan.com.

Renovated colonial home, with breakfast, coffee all day, library, good information, beautifully designed garden, lovely views, friendly and interesting hosts, English spoken. Popular so best to reserve in advance, protected parking. Bamboo Patio massage pavilion offers 1-hr relaxation massage. Wi-Fi. Recommended.

A-B Yaragua, ½ block east of the plaza, T651-4147, www.yaragua.com. With bath, hot water, safe, clean, friendly.

B Brisas de Copán, T651-4118. Terrace, modern rooms with bath, hot water, quiet, limited parking. Recommended.

B Los Jaguares on plaza opposite Marina, T651-4451. Has 10 rooms, with bath, TV, a/c, hot water, friendly staff, locked parking, no restaurant.

B Madrugada, T651-4092, take street from southeast corner of Parque, go down steps and turn right, by the river. Unprepossessing exterior but nice colonial-style interior, 15 rooms (upstairs best).

C Hotel Posada, central location, T651-4059, www.laposadacopan.com. Private bath, ceiling fan and hot water.

C Patty, T651-4021. Fan, bath, no meals, good value, lots of parking. Recommended.

D-E Café VíaVía Copán, T651-4652, www.viaviacafe.com. Great rooms, newly decorated, part of a worldwide Belgian network of cafés, breakfast US$2.75, special price for students with card and discounts for more than 1 night, hot water, good beds, bar and great vegetarian food.

D-E Hostel Iguana Azul, next to La Casa de Café and under same ownership, T651-4620, www.iguanaazulcopan.com. Dormitory-style bunk beds in 2 rooms, shared bath, also 3 more private double rooms, hot water, free purified water, lockers, laundry facilities, garden patio, colonial decor, clean, comfortable, common area, books, magazines, travel guides (including Footprint), maps,

garden, fans, safe box, English spoken. Good for backpackers.

E Hospedaje Los Gemelos, 1 block down from **Banco de Occidente**, T651-4315. With shared bath, clean, fans, good value, friendly, pleasant patio, good for single women. Recommended.

F En la Manzana Verde, T651-4652, www.enlamanzanaverde.com. Great shared bunk rooms, shared bath, kitchen, same owners as **VíaVía**. Good budget choice.

Apartments

Casa Jaguar Rental Home, just 5 blocks from Parque Central, T651-4620, www.casa jaguarcopan.com. Comfortable village residence with 2 double bedrooms with a/c, newly decorated and fully equipped for self-catering. Available for the night, week or month. Contact **La Casa de Café**, see above.
La Casa de Don Santiago, www.casadedon santiagocopan.com. Same owners as Casa Jaguar, with 2 bedrooms, hot water bath, balconies with valley views, garden, fully equipped for self catering and available per night, week and month. Sparkling clean, comfortable and centrally located. Wi-Fi.

Santa Rosa de Copán *p946, map p946*
A Continental, 2 Calle NO y 2-3 Av, T662-0801, on 2nd floor. Good value with bath, hot water, fan, cable TV, friendly management.
A Elvir, Calle Real Centenario SO, 3 Av SO, T/F662-0805, hotelelvir@globalnet.hn. Safe, clean, quiet, all rooms have own bath, TV, hot water, drinking water, good but pricey meals in *cafetería* or restaurant.
B-C VIP Copán, 1 Calle, 3 Av, T662-0265. With bath, TV, cheaper without, cell-like rooms but clean, safe, hot water in morning.
C-D Rosario, 3 Av NE No 139, T662-0211. Cold water, with bath, cheaper without, friendly.
D Hospedaje Santa Eduviges, 2 Av NO y 1 Calle NO, T662-0308. Good beds, clean, pleasant, good value but some rooms damp.
D Maya Central (not to be confused with Hospedaje Maya), 1 Calle NO y 3 Av NO, T662-0073. With bath, cold shower, pleasant.

E Blanca Nieves, 3 Av NE, Barrio Mercedes, T662-1312. Safe, shared bath with cold water, laundry facilities. Going down hill but worth a look.
F Hospedaje Calle Real, Real Centenario y 6 Av NE. Clean, quiet, friendly, best of the cheaper places but sometimes water failures.
F Hospedaje Santa Rosa, 3 Av NE No 42, Barrio Mercedes, T662-1421. Basic, clean, safe, cold water, laundry facilities, welcoming.

Around Santa Rosa de Copán *p947*
In Belén Gualcho hotels fill up quickly on Sat as traders arrive for the Sun market.
F Pensión, Corquín. Good *pensión* with a charming garden. Recommended.
G Hospedaje, east of Santa Rosa de Copán Lepaera, opposite market. Very basic.
G Hospedaje Doña Carolina, Belén Gualcho. Electricity goes off at 2130 so take a torch and candle. Films are shown every evening at 1930, ask anyone, US$0.10.
G Hotelito El Carmen, Belén Gualcho, 2 blocks east down from the church in the plaza. Friendly, clean, good views. Recommended.

Gracias *p948, map p949*
AL-A Posada de Don Juan, Calle Principal opposite **Banco de Occidente**, T/F656-1020, www.posadadedonjuanhotel.com. Good beds, great hot showers, nice big towels, laundry, some rooms have TV, a pool and parking. Recommended.
B Guancascos, at the west end of Hondutel road, T656-1219, www.guancascos.com. Bath, hot water, TV, also rents 2-room cabin at **Villa Verde** adjacent to Monte Celaque visitor centre.
C Hotel Rosario, T656-0694. Hot water, private bath, pool, clean and friendly.
D Colonial, 1 block south of **Erick**, T656-1258. With bath, fan, bar, restaurant, very good.
D-E San Antonio, main street, 2 blocks from Texaco station, T656-1071. Clean, pleasant, friendly, good.
E Erick, same street as bus office, T656-1066. With bath, cheaper without (cold shower), TV,

comfortable beds, fresh, bright, clean, good value with helpful, friendly owners. Laundry facilities, stores luggage, shop selling basic supplies and can arrange transport to Mt Celaque. Very convenient and recommended.
E Finca Bavaria, quiet place at the edge of town, T656-1372. Good breakfasts. German/Honduran owned. Parking.
F Hospedaje Corazón de Jesús, on main street by market. Clean, OK.
F Iris, 3 blocks south of Plaza, 1 block west, opposite San Sebastián church, T656-1086. Closes at 2200. Clean, cold water. Disco Sat.

La Esperanza *p950*
Simple but pleasant *pensiones*.
B Hotel Mina, 1 block south of east side of market, T783-1071. Good beds, clean, very friendly, food available.
C La Esperanza, T783-0068. With bath, cheaper without, warm water, clean, TV, friendly, good meals.
D Mejía Batres, ½ block from Parque Central, T783-0051. With bath, clean, friendly, excellent value.
E El Rey, in Barrio La Morera, T783-2083. Clean, friendly.
E Rosario, on road to Siguatepeque. Basic.

Marcala and around *p951*
D-E Medina, on main road through town, T898-1866. The most comfortable, clean, modern with bath, *cafetería*, free purified water. Highly recommended.
E Hospedaje Edgar, main street, beginning of town. Clean, basic, no sheets.
E Hospedaje Jairo, 2 blocks east of main square. With bath.

Around Marcala *p951*
E Unnamed hotel, San José. Run by Brit Nigel Potter ('Nayo'). Basic but comfortable and clean, with meals. He also takes groups to stay in Lenca villages, US$5 per person plus US$10 per person for accommodation in a village; ask for the house of Doña Gloria, Profe Vinda, Nayo or Ruth. At least one of these will be present to meet visitors.

Nueva Ocotepeque *p952*
C Maya Chortis, Barrio San José, 4 Calle, 3 Av NE, T653-3377. Nice rooms with bath, double beds, hot water, fan, TV, mini-bar, phone, room service, quieter rooms at back, including breakfast, good restaurant, good value.
C Sandoval, opposite Hondutel, T653-3098. Rooms and suites, breakfast included, private bath, hot water, cable TV, mini-bar, phone, room service, restaurant attached, good value.
E-F San Antonio, 1 Calle, 3 Av, T653-3072. Small rooms but OK.
F Gran, about 250 m from town at the junction of the roads for El Salvador and Guatemala, just north of town, at Sinuapa. With bath, cold water, pleasant, clean, single beds only.
F Ocotepeque, by Transportes Toritos. Clean but noisy.

🍴 Eating

Copán Ruinas *p941, map p942*
ŦŦŦ Café Welchez next to Hotel Marina Copán. Good cakes but expensive and coffee 'unpredictable'.
ŦŦŦ Hacienda San Lucas, south out of town, T651-4106. Set menu by reservation, with 5-course meal, local ingredients, candlelight – great place for a special meal.
ŦŦŦ Twisted Tanya's, lovely open-air setting, 2nd floor, T651-4182, www.twisted tanya.com. Open 1500 to 2200 Mon-Sat. Closed Sun. Happy hour 1600-1800. Fine dining with lots of dishes you can't find anywhere else in Copán. Recommended.
ŦŦ Café Vamos a Ver, 1 block from plaza. Open daily 0700-2200. Lots of vegetables, good sandwiches and snacks, complete dinner US$5, pleasant, good value.
ŦŦ Café ViaVia Copán (see Sleeping, above). Food, fresh bread, bar, lodging.
ŦŦ Elisa's at Camino Maya. Excellent food at reasonable prices, pleasant, good service.
ŦŦ La Casa de Todo, 1 block from Central Park in a pleasant garden setting, www.casade

todo.com. Open 0700-2100. Restaurant, internet, craft shop, internet, book exchange. What more could you want?

¶¶ Llama del Bosque, 2 blocks west of plaza. Open for breakfast, lunch and dinner, pleasant, large portions of reasonable food, try their *carnitas típicas*. Recommended.

¶¶ Pizza Copán, locally known as Jim's, US expat Jim cooks up good old US of A fare: chicken grilled over wood fire, BBQ steaks, burgers and good pizza.

¶¶ Yaragua, next to the hotel. Good home-cooked Honduran country food, huge, portions, a/c, attentive service, recommended.

¶ Carnitas Nía Lola, 2 blocks south of Parque Central, at end of road. Open daily 0700-2200. *Comida típica*, busy bar, relaxed atmosphere and book exchange.

¶ Espresso Americano, Central Park location for a café serving great coffee, ideal for people-watching.

¶ Picame (see map). Good hearty food, good value, huge portions, popular with travellers. Recommended.

¶ Pupusería y Comedor Mari, ½ block from market. The best cheap, typical food in town. Clean, decent service, very popular with locals at lunchtime. Daily specials like seafood soup. Food is fresh, cheap and plentiful, popular with locals.

Santa Rosa de Copán *p946, map p946*

¶¶¶ Flamingos, 1 Av SE, off main plaza, T662-0654. Relatively expensive but good pasta and chop suey, popular with locals.

¶¶¶ Lily's, Calle Real Centanario, ½ block from Parque Central. Expensive but very good food, nice garden, good wine list and cigars for sale.

¶¶ Chikys, 1 Calle SO y 1 Av SO. Mexican, good food, atmosphere, music and beer. Recommended.

¶¶ El Rodeo, 1 Av SE. Good menu, specializes in steaks, nice atmosphere, plenty of dead animals on the walls, pricey.

¶¶ La Gran Villa, on the *carretera*. Some of the tastiest meats and meals in Santa Rosa, run by Garífuna family. Recommended.

¶¶ Las Haciendas, 1 Av Calle SE. Steak and seafood, varied menu, filling *comida corriente*, and an attractive patio bar. Recommended. **Las Haciendas II**, 1 Calle SO, smaller, more intimate, same menu. The 3rd and for some the best is **Las Haciendas III**, at 1 Calle 2-3 Av SE, same ownership, menu, and prices, in a pleasantly restored home.

¶¶ On Fu, 1 Av SO, near Chikys, 2nd floor. Chinese and local dishes, large servings, good vegetables, attentive service.

¶¶ Well, 3 Calle 2 Av SE, Chinese, a/c, huge portions, good value and service.

¶ Merenderoa El Campesino, at the bus terminal. Good *comedor*.

¶ Pizza Pizza, Real Centenario 5 Av NE, 4½ blocks from main plaza. One of the best in town, good pizza and pasta, pleasant surroundings in old colonial house, great coffee, best meeting place, US owned, good source of information, book exchange. Recommended.

¶ Rincón Colonial, 1 Av SE. Typical local cuisine. It's good and less expensive than its neighbours.

Around Santa Rosa de Copán *p947*
In Belén Gualcho there are 2 *comedores* on south side of plaza and east side on corner with store.

¶ Comedor Mery, Belén Gualcho. 1 block northwest of plaza. Good food in a welcoming family atmosphere.

¶ Las Haciendas, Belén Gualcho. Good.

Gracias *p948, map p949*
For breakfast, try the *comedores* near the market or, better, the restaurant at **Hotel Iris** (good *comida corriente* too) or **Guancascos**.

¶¶ Comedor Graciano and **Pollo Gracianito**, main street. Good value.

¶¶ La Fonda (see map). Good food, good value, attractively decorated, but no written menu – good practice for your Spanish. Recommended.

¶ El Señorial, main street. Simple meals and snacks, once house of former president Dr Juan Lindo.

Rancho de Lily, 3 blocks west of Hondutel. Value for money, rustic cabin, bar service, good snacks.

La Esperanza p950
Pizza Venezia, on edge of town towards Marcala. Good Italian dishes.
Café El Ecológico, corner of Parque Central. Home-made cakes and pastries, fruit drinks, delicious home-made jams.
Restaurant Magus, 1 block east of plaza, Good food in a video bar atmosphere.
Unnamed restaurant in front of church. Very good *comida corriente*.

Marcala and around p951
Riviera Linda, opposite Hotel Medina. Pleasant atmosphere, spacious, a little pricey but good food.
Café Express, beside Esso. Good breakfast and *comida corrida*. Recommended.
Darwin, main street in centre. Cheap breakfasts from 0700. Recommended.
El Mirador, on entering town by petrol station. Nice views from veranda, good food. Recommended.
Jarito, opposite market entrance. Good.

Around Marcala p951
Comedor, 500 m before plaza on main road. Good, clean and cheap.

Nueva Ocotepeque p952
Sandoval and **Don Chepe**, at Maya Chortis. The best options. Excellent food, small wine lists, good value. Recommended. Comedor Nora (▼), Parque Central, and Merendera Ruth (▼), 2 Calle NE, just off Parque Central, both offer economical *comida corriente*, preferable to *comedores* around bus terminal.

⊕ Entertainment

Copán Ruinas p941, map p942
Barcito, close to Sapo Rojo, small, cozy, laid-back bar.

Papa Changos, located a few blocks from downtown. After hours spot, popular with young locals and traveller crowd. Gets going at midnight on Fri and Sat. The place to let loose and party till dawn.
Red Fros (Sapo Rojo), 2nd floor open-air location. Laid-back place, cheap, popular with backpackers.
ViaVia, see Sleeping, every night till 2400. European chill-out lounge vibe, comfortable and popular, food until 2100.
Xibalba Bar, next to Hotel Camino Maya. Popular spot, opan all day including breakfast. Small and comfortable pub atmosphere.

Santa Rosa de Copán p946, map p946
Bars and clubs
Extasis, shows videos Mon-Thu night.
Luna Jaguar, at 3 Av, between 1 Calle SE and Calle Real Centenario, is the hottest disco in town, but proper dress required.
Manzanitas, is on the corner of 3 Av SE and Calle Real Centenario, if you fancy singing your heart out to a little karaoke.

Cinema
Plaza Saavedra, opposite Blanca Nieves, nightly at 1900.

⊛ Festivals and events

Santa Rosa de Copán p946, map p946
21-31 Aug Festival de Santa Rosa de Lima; the 'Tobacco Queen' is crowned at the end of the week.

La Esperanza p950
3rd week in Jul Festival de la Papa.
8 Dec Fiesta de la Virgen de la Concepción.

O Shopping

Copán Ruinas p941, map p942
Selling all sorts of local crafts are **La Casa de Todo**, just down the street from **Banco de Occidente**, is Copán's best crafts shop,

with a popular café for light meals and snacks. **Arte Acción** is across the street from Casa de Todo, and has childrens art exhibits, runs art projects for kids. Stop in for information.

Santa Rosa de Copán and around
p946, map p946
Supermercadeo Manzanitaz, C Centenario.

▲▲ Activities and tours

Copán Ruinas *p941, map p942*
Animal and birdwatching
Birding guide and naturalist **Bob Gallardo** (T651-4133, rgallardo32@hotmail.com) is the owner of the Butterfly Garden and an expert on Honduran flora and fauna. He leads birding trips, **natural history tours**, orchid and serpent tours around Copán and other parts of Honduras, including La Mosquitia.

Coffee tours
Copán Coffee Tour at **Finca Santa Isabel**, US$25-30 – see www.cafehonduras.com.

Horse riding
You will probably be approached with offers of horse hire, which is a good way of getting to nearby attractions. Riding trips are available to Los Sapos and Las Sepulturas, US$15 for 3 hrs. Watch out for taxi and on the street recommendations as the quality and price can be poor.
Finca El Cisne, T651-4695, www.fincael cisne.com, full-day tours to the coffee plantation high in the mountains including horse riding, lunch and transport. Also trips to hot springs on this working hacienda. Accommodation (**AL**). Good trip.
Yaragua Tours, next to hotel of same name, T651-4050, www.yaragua.com. Horse riding, coffee *fincas*, hot springs plunge and tubing tours, daily 0700-2100. Recommended.

Tour operators
Base Camp Adventures, T651-4695. Nature hikes US$8, treks, motocross tours US$40, horse riding US$15, expedition hikes US$20 and transport including shuttles to Guatemala City, Antigua US$12.
MC Tours, across the street from Hotel Marina, T651-4453, www.mctours-honduras.com, local and countrywide tours.
Copán Connections, T651-4182, www.copanconnections.com. Tours, hotels, transport, specializing in Copán and Bay Islands. Run by Tanya of Twisted Tanya fame.

Santa Rosa de Copán *p946, map p946*
Tour operators
Lenca Land Trails, at Hotel Elvir, T/F662-1375, www.lenca-honduras.com. Run by Max Elvir, organizes cultural tours of the Lenca mountain villages in western Honduras, hiking, mountain biking, the lot. Excellent source of information about the region.
Guide Ask at **Flor de Copán** cigar factory for **José Pineda** who runs tours to tobacco plantations at weekends, informative, only 30 mins from town, lovely countryside.

Gracias *p948, map p949*
Tour operators
Celaque Aventuras Tours, run by Christophe Condor, is based in Guancascos, T656-1219. Has walking tours, visits to La Campa, the national park, thermal baths, horse hire, US$8, includes horse riding, visit to thermal pools day or night, visiting natural caves. Hot springs only, US$4.
Guancascos Tourist Centre at the Guancascos Hotel arranges tours and expeditions to Monte Celaque Parque Nacional, local villages and other attractions.

Around Marcala *p951*
For trips to visit Lenca villages see Sleeping, page 955.

⊖ Transport

Copán Ruinas p941, map p942
Air
You can fly to Tablones in Guatemala, then cross the border to Copán.

Bus
Heading inland you normally have to go to San Pedro Sula before heading for the coast or south to the capital.

There is a 1st-class direct service to **San Pedro Sula** with connections to **Tegucigalpa** and **La Ceiba** with Hedman Alas (T651-4106, www.hedmanalas.com), 5 a day, 3 hrs to San Pedro. Also daily connection to **Tela** and **San Pedro Sula Airport**. To **Guatemala City** and **Antigua** at 1900. To **San Pedro Sula** at 0600, 0800, 1300, US$5, 1 way, with connections in San Pedro for Tegucigalpa and La Ceiba. Casasola Express for San Pedro Sula (T651-4078) at 0700 and 1400. Both services are comfortable, efficient, good value and with reclining seats.

If heading for **Santa Rosa de Copán** or **Gracias** get a bus to the junction at La Entrada and change there. Buses for **La Entrada** leave Copán Ruinas every 30 mins, 1 hr, US$1.80.

Express minibus service to **San Pedro Sula**, **Tela**, **La Ceiba**, and airport from **Hotel Patty** and **Yaragua Tours** – US$120 regardless of number of people. Numerous boys greet you on arrival to carry bags or offer directions for a small fee, while most are good kids, some will tell you hotels are closed.

For Guatemala direct – **Antigua** service with Hedman Alas to **Guatemala City** and **Antigua** daily at 1900.

Santa Rosa de Copán and around p946, map p946
Bus
Buses depart from the city bus station on Carretera Internacional.
Local 'El Urbano' bus to centre from bus station (on Carretera Internacional, 2 km below town, opposite Hotel Mayaland), US$0.15, 15 mins; taxi US$1.40.
Long distance If coming from the Guatemalan border at Nueva Ocotepeque, the bus will stop at the end of town near Av Centenario, 2 km below town, opposite **Hotel Mayaland**. To **Tegucigalpa**, Toritos leaves at 0400 from terminal Mon-Sat 0400 and 1000 Sun, US$6, 10 hrs. Alternatively, take an express bus to San Pedro Sula and an express bus on to Tegucigalpa (US$5, 6 hrs). To **Gracias**, Transportes Lempira, several 0630-1800, 1½ hrs, US$1.30. To **San Pedro Sula**, US$2.50, 4 hrs, every 45 mins 0400-1730, express service daily 2½ hrs, US$3.50 (Empresa Torito). Bus to **La Entrada**, 1 hr, US$1. To **Copán Ruinas**, 4 hrs on good road, US$2.90, several direct daily 1100, 1230 and 1400. Alternatively, take any bus to La Entrada, 1 hr, US$1, and transfer to a Copán Ruinas bus. South on paved road to **Nueva Ocotepeque**, 6 daily, US$1.80, 2 hrs. There you change buses for El Salvador and Guatemala (1 hr to border, US$1, bus leaves hourly until 1700).

Around Santa Rosa de Copán p947
Bus Numerous buses head south daily from Santa Rosa to **Corquín** (US$0.75, 2 hrs). **Belén Gualcho** to **Santa Rosa** daily at 0430 (Sun at 0930). To **Gracias** from main plaza at 0400, 0500 and 1330.

Gracias p948, map p949
Bus A bus goes to **La Esperanza** at 0530 and 0730, or take bus to Erandique, (they leave when full from La Planta)get off at San Juan from where frequent buses goes to La Esperanza (1 hr, US$2)There is a bus service to **Santa Rosa de Copán**, US$1.30, from 0530 to 1630, 5 times a day, 1½ hrs; beautiful journey through majestic scenery. Also to **San Pedro Sula** at 0500, 0800 and 0900, US$3, 4 hrs. Daily bus service to **Lepaera** 1400, 1½ hrs, US$1.50; daily bus to **San Manuel de Colohuete** at 1300. Cotral bus ticket office is 1 block north of Parque Central. Torito bus, a few metres from the main terminal, has buses

to the Guatemalan border at **Agua Caliente**, one at 1000, change buses at Nueva Ocotepeque.

Gracias to Erandique *p950*
Bus There are minibuses to Erandique from the bridge on the road to La Esperanza, 1100 daily, although most people go by truck from Gracias (there is sometimes a van service as far as San Juan) or La Esperanza (change trucks at San Juan intersection, very dusty). Return minibus to Gracias at 0500 daily, which connects with the bus to La Esperanza in San Juan. Trucks leave Erandique 0700 daily, but sometimes earlier, and occasionally a 2nd one leaves around 0800 for Gracias, otherwise be prepared for a long wait for a pickup.

La Esperanza *p950*
Bus To **Tegucigalpa** several daily, 3½ hrs, US$5 (**Cobramil**, also to **San Pedro Sula**, and **Joelito**, 4 hrs, US$2.60). To **Siguatepeque** 0700, 0900, last at 1000, US$1.50, 1 hrs; also to **Siguatepeque**, **Comayagua** at 0600; and to the **Salvadorian border**; bus stops by market. Hourly minibuses to **Yaramanguila**, 30 mins. Daily bus to **Marcala**, 2 hrs at 1230 (but check), US$0.80 (truck, US$1.20, 2¼ hrs). Minibus service at 1130, US$1.50. Daily minibus service to **San Juan**, departs between 1030-1200 from a parking space midway between the 2 bus stops, 2½ hrs, pickups also do this journey, very crowded; for **Erandique**, alight at Erandique turn-off, 1 km before San Juan and wait for truck to pass (*comedor* plus basic *hospedaje* at intersection). If going to Gracias, stay on the La Esperanza–San Juan bus until the end of the line where a pickup collects passengers 15 mins or so later, 1 hr San Juan-Gracias. Buses to **Lake Yojoa** (see page 963), 2 hrs, US$2.50.

Marcala and around *p951*
Bus To **Tegucigalpa** 0500, 0915 and 1000 daily via La Paz, 4 hrs, US$2.40 (bus from Tegucigalpa at 0800 and 1400, **Empresa Lila**, 4-5 Av, 7 Calle, No 418 Comayagüela,

opposite Hispano cinema); bus to **La Paz** only, 0700, 2 hrs, US$1; several minibuses a day, 1½ hrs, US$1.50. Bus also from Comayagua. Pickup truck to **San José** at around 1000 from market, ask for drivers, Don Santos, Torencio, or Gustavo. Bus to **La Esperanza** at about 0830, unreliable, check with driver, Don Pincho, at the supermarket next to where the bus is parked (same street as Hotel Medina), 1½-2 hrs, otherwise hitching possible, going rate US$1.20. Bus to **San Miguel**, El Salvador, Transportes Wendy Patricia, 0500, 1200, 7 hrs, US$3.50.

Nueva Ocotepeque *p952*
Bus Transportes Escobar daily service **Tegucigalpa** to Nueva Ocotepeque/Agua Caliente, via La Entrada and Santa Rosa de Copán (12 Av entre 8 y 9 Calle, Barrio Concepción, Comayagüela, T237-4897; **Hotel** Sandoval, T653-3098, Nueva Ocotepeque). Buses to **San Pedro Sula** stop at La Entrada (US$1.70), 1st at 0030, for connections to Copán. There are splendid mountain views. From **San Pedro Sula** there are regular buses via Santa Rosa south (6 hrs, US$4.50); road is well paved.

❶ Directory

Copán Ruinas *p941, map p942*
Banks Banco Atlántida with an ATM and Banco de Occidente are both on the plaza and change TCs and take Visa. **BAC**, has similar services and an ATM for MasterCard and Amex. It is possible to change Guatemalan currency in Copán but not at the banks; try where buses leave for the border or with money changers behind Hotel Marina.
Internet Copán Net, 1 block southwest of Parque Central, daily 0800-2100 (but Sat morning is for local children), La 2 per min. Maya Connections, next to Los Gemelos, US$1.50 per hr, daily 0730-1800. Casa de Todo, internet and much more. Open daily 0700-2100. **Language schools** Academia de Español Guacamaya, T/F651-4360,

www.guacamaya.com, classes US$140 a week, with homestay US$225, recommended. Ixbalanque, T/F651-4432, www.ixbalanque.com, 1-1 teaching plus board and lodging with local family, US$210 for classes and 7 days homestay. **Post office** Next to the market, Mon-Fri 0800-1200, 1300-1700, Sat 0800-1200, beautiful stamps available. Max 4 kgs by airmail. **Telephone** Phone calls can be made from the office of Hondutel 0800-2100.

Santa Rosa de Copán *p946, map p946*
Banks Atlántida (has Visa ATM, maximum withdrawal US$30) and Banco de Occidente (has ATM), both are on main plaza. **Cultural centre** ½ block south of Parque Central with live music and singing, sculpture and picture galley. **Immigration** Av Alvaro Contreras y 2 Calle NO, helpful, extensions available. **Internet** Pizza Pizza, has email at US$4 per hr, good machines. Prodigy, C Centenario, US$1 per hr, also across the road from the Hotel Copán, US$2 per hr.
Laundry Lavandaría Florencia, Calle Centenario. **Medical services** Dentist: Dr Wilfredo Urquía, at Calle Real Centenario 3-4 Av NE, speaks English. Recommended. Doctors: Clínica Médica Las Gemas, 2 Av NO, near Hotel Elvir, T666-1428, run by Dr Soheil Rajabian (speaks English among other languages), 1st-class attention. Hospital: Médico Quirúrgico, Barrio Miraflores,

Carretera Internacional, T/F662-1283, fast and efficient, but not cheap. **Post office and telephone** The post office and Hondutel are on the park, opposite side to the cathedral. **Voluntary work** Hogar San Antonio, run by nuns across the street from the Parque Infantil (city playground), welcomes volunteers, as does the Cultural Centre.

Gracias *p948, map p949*
Banks Bancafé, Bancrecer and Banco de Occidente, but none take Visa yet. **Cultural centres** Music lessons including marimba, available from Ramón Alvarenga, 2 blocks west of Parque Central on the same side as Iglesia San Marcos. **Internet** plenty to choose from. **Post office and telephone** Hondutel and post office 1 block south of Parque Central, closes 1100 on Sat.

La Esperanza *p950*
Banks Banco de Occidente, Banco Atlántida and Banadesa. **Internet** Couple of places, one near the cathedral, US$4 per hr.

Marcala and around *p951*
Banks Banco de Occidente and Bancafé.

Nueva Ocotepeque *p952*
Banks Banco de Occidente will change TCs. Banco Atlántida has Visa facilities.

Tegucigalpa to San Pedro Sula

The main road connecting Tegucigalpa and the country's second largest city, San Pedro Sula, heads north through beautiful scenery along the shore of Lago Yojoa, skirting villages of the Lenca communities. Alhough the tendency is to head north for the warmth and beauty of the beaches, a slow journey along the road is very rewarding. **➤➤** *For listings, see pages 967-973.*

Támara and Zambrano → *See Around Tegucigalpa map, page 930.*

The Northern Highway between Tegucigalpa and San Pedro Sula leaves the capital and enters the vast valley of Támara, with the village of the same name. A turning leads to the **San Matías waterfall**, in a delightful area for walking in cool forested mountains.

The road climbs to the forested heights of **Parque Aventuras** ① *open at weekends*, at Km 33, good food, swimming pools, horses, bikes, then to **Zambrano** (altitude: 1450 m) at Km 34 and, at Km 36, midway between Tegucigalpa and Comayagua, **Parque Aurora** ① *camping US$0.50 per person, admission US$0.70, food supplies nearby*. It has a small zoo, good swimming pools and a picnic area among pine-covered hills, a lake with rowing boats (hire US$1 per hour), a snack bar and lovely scenery. The birdwatching is good too.

Before descending to the Comayagua Valley, the Northern Highway reaches another forested mountainous escarpment. A track leads off to the right (ask for directions), with about 30 minutes' climb on foot to a tableland and the natural fortress of **Tenampua**, where the indigenous put up their last resistance to the conquistadores, even after the death of Lempira. It has an interesting wall and entrance portal.

Comayagua and around ●🏠🏤⛰🏧🏛🍴 ➤➤ *pp967-973. Colour map 6, B2.*

→ *Altitude: 550 m.*

Founded on 7 December 1537 as Villa Santa María de Comayagua on the site of an indigenous village by Alonzo de Cáceres, Comayagua is a colonial town in the rich Comayagua plain, 1½ hours' drive (93 km) north from the capital. On 3 September 1543, it was designated the Seat of the Audiencia de los Confines by King Felipe II of Spain. President Marco Aurelio Soto transferred the capital to Tegucigalpa in 1880.

There are many old colonial buildings in Comayagua, reflecting the importance of Honduras' first capital after Independence in 1821. The city is looking a little jaded these days, but is still worth a visit for the impressive architecture. Comayagua was declared a city in 1557, 20 years after its founding. Within a couple of centuries a rash of civic and religious buildings were constructed. The former university, the first in Central America, was founded in 1632 and closed in 1842 (it was located in the Casa Cural, Bishop's Palace, where the bishops have lived since 1558). Others include the churches of **La Merced** (1550-1558) and **La Caridad** (1730), **San Francisco** (1574) and **San Sebastián** (1575). **San Juan de Dios** (1590 but destroyed by earthquake in 1750), the church where the Inquisition sat, is now the site of the Hospital Santa Teresa. **El Carmen** was built in 1785. The wealth of colonial heritage has attracted funds for renovation, which have produced a slow transformation in the town. The most interesting building is the **cathedral** in the Parque Central, inaugurated in 1711, with its plain square tower and façade decorated with sculpted figures of the saints, which contains some of the finest examples of colonial art in Honduras (closed 1300-1500). Of the 16 original hand-carved and gilded altars, just four survive today. The clock in the tower was originally made over 800 years ago in Spain and is the oldest working clock in the Americas. It was given to Comayagua by Felipe II in 1582. At first it was in La Merced when that was the cathedral, but it was moved to the new cathedral in 1715. Half a block north of the cathedral is the **Ecclesiastical Museum** ① *daily 0930-1200, 1400-1700, US$0.60*. One block south of the cathedral, at the corner of 6 Calle and 1 Avenida NO, is the **Museo de Arqueología** ① *Wed-Fri 0800-1600, Sat and Sun 0900-1200, 1300-1600, US$1.70* (housed in the former Palacio de Gobernación), small scale but fascinating, with six rooms each devoted to a different period. Much of the collection came from digs in the El Cajón region, 47 km north of Comayagua, before the area was flooded for the hydroelectricity project.

There are two colonial plazas shaded by trees and shrubs. A stone portal and a portion of the façade of **Casa Real** (the viceroy's residence) still survives. Built in 1739-41, it was damaged by an earthquake in 1750 and destroyed by tremors in 1856. The army still uses a quaint old fortress built when Comayagua was the capital. There is a lively market area.

Parque Nacional Montaña de Comayagua is only 13 km from Comayagua, reached from the villages of San José de la Mora (4WD necessary) or San Jerónimo and Río Negro (usually passable). Contact **Fundación Ecosimco** ① *0 Calle y 1 Av NO in Comayagua, T772-4681*, for further information about the trails which lead through the cloud forest to waterfalls. The mountain (2407 m) has 6000 ha of cloud forest and is a major watershed for the area.

Siguatepeque → *Colour map 6, B2. Altitude: 1150 m.*

The Northern Highway crosses the Comayagua plain, part of the gap in the mountains which stretches from the Gulf of Fonseca to the Ulúa lowlands. Set in forested highlands 32 km northwest of Comayagua is the town of Siguatepeque, which has a cool climate. It is the site of the Escuela Nacional de Ciencias Forestales (which is worth a visit) and, being exactly halfway between Tegucigalpa and San Pedro Sula (128 km), is a collection point for the produce of the Intibucá, Comayagua and Lempira departments. The Cerro and Bosque de Calanterique, behind the Evangelical Hospital, is a 45-minute walk from the town centre. The Parque Central is pleasant, shaded by tall trees with the church of San Pablo on the north side and the cinema, **Hotel Versalles** and Boarding House Central on the east; **Hondutel** and the post office are on the south side.

Southwest from Siguatepeque, the route to La Esperanza is a beautiful paved road through lovely forested mountainous country, via **Jesús de Otoro**, where there are two basic *hospedajes* and **Balneario San Juan de Quelala** ① *US$0.30*, which has a *cafetería* and picnic sites. North from Siguatepeque, the highway goes over the forested escarpment of the continental divide, before descending towards Lago Yojoa. Just south of Taulabé on the highway are the illuminated **Caves of Taulabé** ① *daily, US$0.40, guides available*, with both stalactites and bats. North of Taulabé, and 16 km south of the lake is the turn-off northwest of a paved road to Santa Bárbara.

Lago Yojoa → *Colour map 6, B2. Altitude: 635 m.*

① *For local information contact Enrique Campos or his son at Motel Agua Azul (see below). For more information, contact Proyecto Humuya, behind Iglesia Betel, 21 de Agosto, Siguatepeque (T773-2426), or Proyecto de Desarrollo Río Yure, San Isidro, Cortés, Apdo 1149, Tegucigalpa.*

Sitting pretty among the mountains is the impressive Lake Yojoa, 22½ km long and 10 km wide. To the west rise the Montañas de Santa Bárbara which include the country's second highest peak and the **Parque Nacional de Santa Bárbara** (see page 965). To the east is the **Parque Nacional Montaña Cerro Azul-Meámbar**. Pumas, jaguars and other animals live in the forests, pine-clad slopes and the cloud forest forming part of the reservoir of the Lago Yojoa basin. The national parks also have many waterfalls. The 50-sq-km Azul-Meámbar park is 30 km north of Siguatepeque and its highest point is 2047 m. To get to any of the entry points (Meámbar, the main one, Jardines, Bacadia, Monte Verde or San Isidro) a 4WD is necessary. A local ecological group, **Ecolago** ⓘ *Edificio Midence Soto, Parque Central (Tegucigalpa), T237 9659*, has marked out the area and is to offer guided tours. **Ecolago** has guides who are expert in spotting regional birds; at least 373 species have been identified around the lake. At one time the lake was full of bass, but overfishing and pollution have decimated the stocks. Tilapia farming is now very important.

The Northern Highway follows the eastern margin to the lake's southern tip at **Pito Solo**, where sailing and motor boats can be hired. On the northern shore of Lago Yojoa is a complex of pre-Columbian settlements called **Los Naranjos** ⓘ *US$5*, which are believed to have had a population of several thousand. It is considered to be the country's third most important archaeological site spanning the period from 1000 BC to AD 1000, and includes two ball courts. The site is slowly being developed for tourism by the Institute of Anthropology and History and has a visitor centre, small museum and coffee shop and a number of forest walking trails. Excavation work is currently in progress. The local office of the institute (T557-8197) is at the **Hotel Brisas de Lago**. From the lake it is 37 km down to the hot Ulúa lowlands.

A paved road skirts the lake's northern shore for 12 km via Peña Blanca. A road heads southwest to **El Mochito**, Honduras' most important mining centre. A bus from 2 Avenida in San Pedro Sula goes to Las Vegas-El Mochito mine for walks along the west side of Lago Yojoa. Buses will generally stop anywhere along the east side of the lake. Another road heads north from the northern shore, through Río Lindo, to **Caracol** on the Northern Highway. This road gives access to the Pulhapanzak waterfall, with some unexcavated ceremonial mounds adjacent, and to Ojo de Agua, a pretty bathing spot near Caracol. **Peña Blanca** is, according to one reader, a "very ugly town" on the north side of the lake. Almost makes you want to stay.

Pulhapanzak waterfall
ⓘ *US$1. The caretaker allows camping for US$0.85.*
The impressive 42-m waterfall at Pulhapanzak is on the Río Lindo. The waterfall is beautiful during, or just after the rainy season, and in sunshine there is a rainbow at the falls. There is a picnic area, a small *cafetería* and a good *comedor* 15 minutes' walk away down in the village, but the site does get crowded at weekends and holidays.

Santa Bárbara and around → *Colour map 6, B2. Altitude: 290 m.*
Santa Bárbara, surrounded by high mountains, forested hills and rivers, lies in a hot lowland valley 32 km west of Lago Yojoa. One of the nicest main towns in Honduras, it has little of architectural or historical interest compared with Gracias, Ojojona or Yuscarán, but it is here that you will find Panama hats and other goods made from junco palm. The majority of the population is fair-skinned (some redheads) and the people are vivacious. In addition to being a pleasant place to stay, Santa Bárbara is also a good base for visiting villages throughout the Santa Bárbara Department. Nearby, the ruined colonial city of **Tencoa** has been rediscovered. A short local trek behind the town climbs the hills to the ruined site of **Castillo Bogran**, with fine views across the valley and the town. Heading south out of Santa Bárbara, the paved road joins the Northern Highway south of Lago Yojoa.

The Department of Santa Bárbara is called the Cuna de los Artesanos (cradle of artisans), with over 10,000 craftspeople involved in the manufacture of handicrafts. The main products come from the small junco palm, for example fine hats and baskets. The main towns for junco items are **La Arada**, 25 minutes from Santa Bárbara on the road to San Nicolás, and then branching off south, and **Ceguaca**, on a side road off the road to Tegucigalpa. Flowers and dolls from corn husks are made in Nueva Celilac. Mezcal is used to make carpets, rugs and hammocks, which are easy to find in towns such as **Ilama**, on the road to San Pedro Sula, which has one of the best small colonial churches in Honduras (no accommodation). People here also make *petates* (rugs) and purses.

Between Santa Bárbara and Lago Yojoa is the **Parque Nacional de Santa Bárbara** which contains the country's second highest peak, Montaña de Santa Bárbara at 2744 m. The rock is principally limestone with many subterranean caves. There is little tourist development as yet, with just one trail, and you can track down a guide in Los Andes, a village above Peña Blanca and Las Vegas. The best time to visit is the dry season, January-June. For information contact **Asociación Ecológica Corazón Verde** ① *Palacio Municipal, Santa Bárbara*. There is a **Cohdefor** office just below the market (look for the sign) but they are not helpful.

San Pedro Sula and around ⊜𝟎𝟎⊛𝟎⊙▲⊜𝟎 ⤷ *pp967-973. Colour map 6, B2.*

→ *Altitude: 60-150 m. Population: 900,000.*

San Pedro Sula is the second largest and most industrialized city in the country and a centre for the banana, coffee, sugar and timber trades. It is a distribution hub for northern and western Honduras with good road links. Its business community is mainly of Arab origin, and it is considered the fastest-growing city between Mexico and Panama. By Central American standards, San Pedro Sula is a well-planned, modern city, but it's not a city you'll be inclined to stay in for long.

Ins and outs

Getting there San Pedro Sula is a more important international gateway than Tegucigalpa. Its airport, Ramón Villeda Morales (SAP) is 15 km from the city centre along a good four-lane highway. The Gran Central Metropolitana central bus terminal opened in March 2008. It's a short US$3 taxi from the centre of San Pedro Sula. ⤷ *See Transport, page 972.*

Getting around The city is divided into four quadrants: Noreste (Northeast, NE), Noroeste (Northwest, NO), Sudeste (Southeast, SE) and Sudoeste (Southwest, SO), where most of the hotels are located, although newer hotels, shopping malls and restaurant chains are in the Noroeste. There are buses, minibuses and taxis for getting around town.

Best time to visit Although pleasant in the cooler season from November to February, temperatures are very high for the rest of the year. It is, nevertheless, a green city, clean and the traffic is not too bad. The higher and cooler suburb of Bella Vista, with its fine views over the city, affords relief from the intense heat of the town centre.

Background

The city was founded in 1536 by Pedro de Alvarado in the lush and fertile valley of the Ulúa (Sula) River, beneath the forested slopes of the Merendón mountains. There are many banana plantations.

Sights

The large neocolonial-style **cathedral** was completed in the 1950s. **Museo de Antropología e Historia** ⓘ *3 Av, 4 Calle NO, Mon, Wed-Sat 0900-1600, Sun 0900-1500, US$0.75, first Sun of the month is free*, has displays of the cultures that once inhabited the Ulúa Valley up to Spanish colonization and, on the first floor, local history since colonization. There is a museum café in the adjacent garden with fine stelae and a good set lunch. **Museo Jorge Milla Oviedo** ⓘ *3 Av 9 Calle NE, Barrio Las Acacias, T552-5060*, is run by the foundation that cares for the Cuero y Salado wildlife reserve.

Parque Nacional Cusuco

ⓘ *Entrance is US$15, which includes a guided trip; you cannot go on your own. Contact the HRPF at 5 Av, 1 Calle NO, San Pedro Sula, T552-1014. Also contact Cohdefor, 10 Av, 5 Calle NO, Barrio Guamilito, San Pedro Sula, T553-4959, or Cambio CA, who run tours. Permission from*

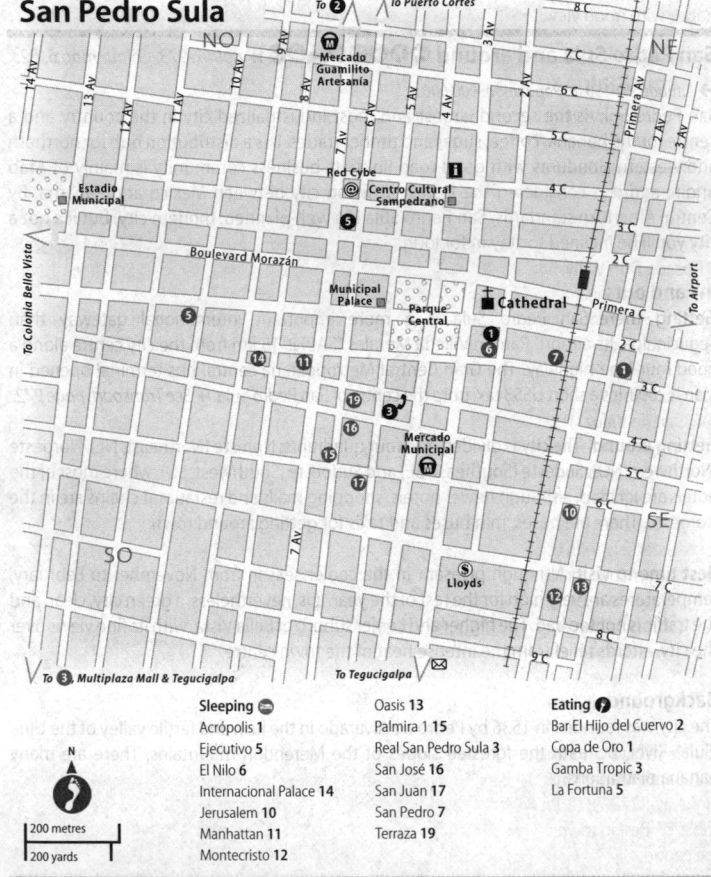

San Pedro Sula

Sleeping ⬢		Oasis **13**	Eating ⬤
Acrópolis **1**		Palmira 1 **15**	Bar El Hijo del Cuervo **2**
Ejecutivo **5**		Real San Pedro Sula **3**	Copa de Oro **1**
El Nilo **6**		San José **16**	Gamba Tropic **3**
Internacional Palace **14**		San Juan **17**	La Fortuna **5**
Jerusalem **10**		San Pedro **7**	
Manhattan **11**		Terraza **19**	
Montecristo **12**			

200 metres
200 yards

HRPF is required to walk through the park to Tegucigalpita on the coast. There is a visitor centre but bring your own food. You cannot stay or camp in the park, but camping is possible outside. Access by dirt road from Cofradía (Cafetería Negro, one block northwest of plaza, good food), on the road to Santa Rosa de Copán, then to Buenos Aires: 2 hrs by car from San Pedro Sula, 4WD recommended. ▸▸ See Transport, page 973.

Parque Nacional Cusuco, 20 km west of San Pedro Sula, offers some excellent hikes, trails and birdwatching in cloud forest. Now managed by the Fundación Ecológica Héctor Rodrigo Pastor Fasquelle (HRPF), the park was exploited for lumber until the 1950s. It was declared a protected area in 1959 when the Venezuelan ecologist, Geraldo Budowski, reported the pine trees there were the highest in Central America. Cutting was stopped and the lumber company abandoned the site. It is a splendid location and well worth the effort. The area includes tropical rainforest and cloud forest with all the associated flora and fauna. It includes both **Cerro Jilinco**, 2242 m, and **Cerro San Ildefonso**, 2228 m. There are four trails, ranging from 30 minutes to two days. They use old logging roads traversing forested ridges with good views. HRPF produces a bird checklist that includes the quetzal.

⦿ Tegucigalpa to San Pedro Sula listings

For Sleeping and Eating price codes and other relevant information, see Essentials pages 45-48.

⦿ Sleeping

Támara *p962*
F Posada Don Willy, 500 m southwest of the toll station near Balneario San Francisco. With bath (electric shower), clean, quiet, fan, excellent value.

Zambrano *p962*
L-E Caserío Valuz, 1½ km from the highway, 20 mins' walk on the road to Catarata Escondida, T898-6755 (Zambrano), T996-4294 (mob). 15 rooms with bath, most with balconies, 1- to 3-night packages including meals, also rooms for backpackers, with use of kitchen, volunteer work in exchange for room and board possible, a great place to relax, hike, read, paint.
A-C Casitas Primavera, Barrio La Primavera, 1.5 km west of main road, T898-6625/ T239-2328. Cosy houses, lovely setting, sleeps 6 (arrangements can be made for 1-2 people, **E**).

Comayagua and around *p962*
A-B Santa María, Km 82 on the Tegucigalpa highway, T772-7872. Private bath, a/c, cable TV. Best in town, although not in the centre.

B Quan, 8 Calle NO, 3 y 4 Av, T772-0070, hquan@hondutel.hn. Excellent, with private bath, popular.
C América Inc, 2 Av y 1 Calle NO, T772-0360. A/c, private bath, hot water, cheaper with fan.
D Emperador, Calle Central y 4 Av SO, Barrio Torondón, T772-0332. Good, a/c, cable TV, cheaper with fan.
D Honduras, 2 Av NO, 1 Calle, T772-1893. Clean, friendly, some rooms with bath.
D Imperial, 3 Av SO, Barrio Torondón, opposite Norymax, T772-0215. With bath, fan, TV, clean, friendly, good value, parking.
D Norymax, Calle Central y 3 Av SO, Barrio Torondón, T772-1210. Bath, a/c and TV, hot water, cheaper rooms available and car park.
E Libertad, south side of Parque Central. Nice courtyard, much choice of room size, clean apart from the toilets, cold water shower outside, helpful, good restaurant 2 doors away.
F Galaxia, Miramar, Primavera, Terminal and **Tío Luis**, are *pensiones*, all within a couple of blocks of the bus stop on the *Panamericana*.

Siguatepeque *p963*
D Zari, T773-2015. Hot water, cable TV, own generator, parking.
E-F Internacional Gómez, 21 de Junio, T773-2868. With bath (cheaper without), hot water, clean, parking.

F Boarding House Central, Parque Central, T773-2108. Very basic but good value; beware of the dog, which bites.
F Mi Hotel, 1 km from highway on road into town. With bath, parking, restaurant.
F Versalles, on Parque Central. Excellent, with restaurant, use of kitchen on request.

Lago Yojoa *p963*
L Gualiqueme, cottage at edge of lake, for information contact Richard Joint at Honduyate, T882-3129. Has 4 bedrooms in main house, 2 in annexe. Daily, weekly, monthly rental, weekend packages include ferry and fishing boat.
B Brisas del Lago, close to Peña Blanca at the northern end of the lake, T557-1433. Large hotel, good restaurant but overpriced, launches for hire.
B Finca Las Glorias, close to Peña Blanca, T566-0461, www.hotellasglorias.com. Bath, a/c, hot water, TV, bar, good restaurant, pool, great views – currently being restored.
B-C Hotel Agua Azul, at north end of lake, about 3 km west from junction at Km 166, T/F991-7244. Basic clean cabins for 2 or more persons, meals for non-residents, but food and service in restaurant is poor, beautiful gardens, manager speaks English, swimming pool, fishing, horse riding and boating, launches for hire, mosquito coils. Good reduction in low season. Recommended (except when loud karaoke is in full swing).
C Oasi Italiana, on San Pedro Sula Hwy in Yoya Cortés, some 20 km from the lake, T9991-1195. Motel rooms with fans or a/c, swimming pool and great Italian food.
C-E Boarding House Moderno, Barrio Arriba, T643-2203. Rooms with fan better value than with a/c, with hot shower, quiet, parking. Recommended.
C-E Gran Hotel Colonial, 1½ blocks from Parque Central, T643-2665. Fans in all rooms, some with a/c, cold water, sparsely furnished, friendly. Good view from roof. Recommended.
C-E Los Remos, Pito Solo, at the south end of the lake, T557-8054. Has cabins and camping facilities (**G**). Clean, beautiful setting, good

food, nice for breakfasts, no beach but swimming pool, boat trips, parking US$3.
E D&D Brewery and Guesthouse, T994-9719, dndbrew@yahoo.com. Good rooms, with a garden with a small pool, book exchange and home brewed beer.
F Hotel Maranata, Peña Blanca. Clean, near bus stop, friendly.

Santa Bárbara and around *p964*
F Ruth, Calle La Libertad, T643-2632. Rooms without windows, fan.
G Pensión, near the church, Colinas. Basic.

San Pedro Sula and around *p965,*
map p966
LL Real San Pedro Sula, Blv del Sur at Centro Comercial Multiplaza, T545-2500, www.ichotelsgroup.com. Full service and the best in town.
AL Ejecutivo, 2 Calle 10 Av SO, T552-4289, www.hotel-ejecutivo.com. A/c, cable TV, café/bar, phone, own generator.
B Acrópolis, 3 Calle 2 y 3 Av SE, T/F557-2121. A/c, cable TV, parking, café, comfortable, friendly, good value.
B Internacional Palace, 3 Calle 8 Av SO, Barrio El Benque, T550-3838. A/c, helpful, internet service, parking, pool, bar, restaurant OK.
B-C Hotel San Pedro, 3 Calle 2 Av SO, T550-1513, www.hotelsanpedrosa.com. Private bath, a/c, cheaper with fan, popular, clean, good value, rooms overlooking street are noisy, stores luggage, secure parking.
D Manhattan, 7 Av 3-4 Calle SO, T550-2316. A/c, a bit run-down.
D Palmira 1, 6 Calle 6 y 7 Av SO, T557-6522. Clean, very convenient for buses, parking.
D-E Terraza, 6 Av 4-5 Calle SO, T550-3108. Dining room dark, friendly, cheaper without a/c.
E El Nilo, 3 Calle 2 Av SO, T553-4689. Nice rooms, friendly.
E Oasis, 7 Calle 2 Av SE, T552-2650. Private bath, a/c or fan, doubles/twins, clean but noisy.
F Jerusalem, 6 Calle 1 Av SE, T946-8352. Safe, good value.
F Montecristo, 2 Av 7 Calle SE, T557-1370. Noisy, not very clean, fan, safe.

F San José, 6 Av 5 y 6 Calle SO, just round corner from Norteños bus station, T557-1208. Friendly, clean, safe, cheap and cheerful.
F-G San Juan, 6 Calle 6 Av SO, T553-1488. Modern, very noisy, clean, helpful, good value.

● Eating

Comayagua and around *p962*
Parque Central is surrounded by restaurants and fast-food establishments.
♥♥♥ Villa Real, behind the cathedral, T772-0101. Mixes colonial atmosphere with good international and Honduran cuisine.
♥♥ Hein Wong, Parque Central. Chinese and international food, good, a/c, reasonably priced.
♥♥ Las Palmeras, south side of Parque Central, T772-0352. Good breakfasts, open for dinner and lunch, good portions, reasonable prices.
♥ Fruty Tacos, 4 Calle NO, just off southwest corner of Parque Central. Snacks and *licuados*.
♥ Juanis Burger Shop, 1 Av NO 5 Calle, near southwest corner of Parque Central. Friendly, good food, OK.
♥ Venecia, in front of Supermercado Carol, T772-1734. Popular café-style restaurant.

Siguatepeque *p963*
♥♥ Granja d'Elia, one of several restaurants on the Northern Hwy. Open all day, lots of vegetables, also meat, all-you-can-eat buffet, French chef, veg from own market garden and bread on sale outside.
♥♥ Juanci's, main street. Open until 2300. US-style hamburgers, good steaks and snacks.
♥ Bicos, southwest corner of Parque Central. Nice snack bar/patisserie.
♥ Cafetería Colonial, 4 Av SE (behind church). Good pastries and coffee, outside seating.
♥ Pollos Kike, next door. Pleasant setting, fried chicken.
♥ Supermercado Food, south side of plaza. Has a good snack bar inside.

Lago Yojoa *p963*
Roadside stalls near Peña Blanca sell fruit.
♥♥ Brisas del Canal, Peña Blanca, local food. Recommended, but small portions.
♥♥-♥ Comedores, on the roadside. Serve bass fish caught in the lake, with Atenciones Evita being a popular choice.
♥ Comedor Vista Hermosa, Peña Blanca. Has good, cheap food.

Cafés and bakeries
Panadería Yoja, 1 block from Hotel Maranata, Peña Blanca, good juices and pastries.

Santa Bárbara and around *p964*
♥♥ Doña Ana, 1 block above Parque Central. No sign but restaurant in Ana's dining room, crammed with bric-a-brac, only meat, rice, beans and bananas, plentiful and good food if a little boring.
♥♥ El Brasero, ½ block below Parque Central. Extensive menu of meat, chicken, fish, Chinese, good food, well prepared. Recommended.
♥♥ Pizzería Don Juan, Av Independencia. Very good pizzas.
♥ Comedor Everest, by bus stop on Parque Central. Friendly, good *comida corriente*.
♥ Las Tejas, near Rodríguez. Friendly, good pizzeria.
♥ McPollo, main street. Clean, smart, good.
♥ Repostería Charle's, Parque Central. Excellent cakes, pastries, about the only place open for breakfast.

San Pedro Sula and around *p965,* map *p966*
International restaurants in all the top hotels.
♥♥♥ Bar El Hijo del Cuervo, 13 Calle 7-8 Av NO, Barrio Los Andes. Mexican cuisine, informal setting of *champas* in tropical garden with fountain, à la carte menu, tacos, *quesadillas*.
♥♥♥ La Huerta de España, 21 Av 2 Calle SO, Barrio Río de Piedras, 4 blocks west of Av Circunvalación. Daily until 2300. Supposedly best Spanish cuisine in town.
♥♥♥ Las Tejas, 9 Calle 16 y 17 Av, Av Circunvalación. Good steaks and fine seafood,

as also at nearby sister restaurant **La Tejana**, 16 Av 19 Calle SO, Barrio Suyapa, T557-5276.

Ψ Pamplona, on plaza, opposite Gran Hotel Sula. Pleasant decor, good food, strong coffee, excellent service.

Ψ Applebees, Circunvalación. Good food, service and prices. Highly recommended.

Ψ Chef Mariano, 16 Av 9-10 Calle SO, Barrio Suyapa, T552-5492. Garífuna management and specialities, especially seafood, Honduran and international cuisine, attentive service, a/c, not cheap but good value, open daily for lunch and dinner.

Ψ Gamba Tropic, 5 Av 4-5 Calle SO. Delicious seafood, good wine, medium prices, a/c.

Ψ La Espuela, Av Circunvalación, 16 Av 7 Calle. Good grilled meats. Recommended.

Ψ La Fortuna, 2 Calle 7 Av NO. Chinese and international, very good, not expensive, smart, good service, a/c.

Ψ Sim Kon, 17 Av 6 Calle NO, Av Circunvalación. Arguably the best Chinese in town. Enormous portions. Try *arroz con camarones* (prawns with rice).

Ψ Copa de Oro, 2 Av 2 y 3 Calle SO. Extensive Chinese and Western menu, a/c, pleasant. Recommended.

Cafés

Café Nani, 6 Av 1-2 Calle SO. Good *pastelería*.

Café Skandia, ground floor, **poolside** at the Gran Hotel Sula. Open 24 hrs, best place for late night dinners and early breakfasts, good club sandwiches, good service.

Café Venecia, 6 Av 4-5 Calle. Good juices,

Espresso Americano, 2 branches, in Calle Peatonal, 4 Av, off southwest corner of Parque Central, and in Megaplaza shopping mall. Closed Sun, great coffee, cookies.

⊕ Entertainment

San Pedro Sula and around *p965*, *map p966*

Bars and clubs

A thriving nightlife exists beyond the casinos. **Mango's**, 16 Av 8-9 Calle SO, Barrio Suyapa.

Open 1900 onwards. Open terrace, pool tables, dance floor, rock music, snacks. An exclusive option is **El Quijote**, 11 Calle 3-4 Av SO, Barrio Lempira, cover charge.

Cinemas

There are 8 cinemas, all showing Hollywood movies, look in local press for details.

Theatre

The Círculo Teatral Sampedrano stages productions (see Cultural centres, page 973). **Proyecto Teatral Futuro**, is a semi-professional company presenting contemporary theatre of Latin American countries and translations of European playwrights, as well as ballet, children's theatre, and workshops. Offices and studio-theatre at 4 Calle 3-4 Av NO, Edif INMOSA, 3rd floor, T552-3074.

⊕ Festivals and events

San Pedro Sula and around *p965*, *map p966*

End Jun **Feria Juniana**, the city's main festival.

⊙ Shopping

Siguatepeque *p963*

Leather goods A good leatherworker is Celestino Alberto Díaz, Barrio San Antonio, Casa 53, 2 Calle NE, 6 Av NE. 1 block north of Celestino's is a good shoemaker, leather shoes made for US$25.

San Pedro Sula and around *p965*, *map p966*

Bookshops La Casa del Libro, 1 Calle 5-6 Av SO. Comprehensive selection of Spanish and English-language books, good for children's books and game, just off Parque Central. **Librería Atenea**, Edif Trejo Merlo, 1 Calle 7 Av SO. Wide choice of Latin American, US and British fiction, philosophy, economics and so on. **Librería Cultura**,

1 Calle 6-7 Av SO. Cheap paperbacks, Latin American classics. **Librería Editorial Guaymuras**, 10 Av 7 Calle NO. Wide range of Hispanic authors.

Food Supermercado Los Andes, good supermarket, strategically located at the intersection of Calle Oeste and Av Circunvalación.

Handicrafts Large artisan market, **Mercado Guamilito Artesanía**, 6 Calle 7-8 Av NO. Daily 0800-1700. Typical Honduran handicrafts at good prices (bargain), with a few imported goods from Guatemala and Ecuador; also good for fruit and vegetables. **Danilo's Pura Piel**, factory and shop 18 Av B/9 Calle SO. **Honduras Souvenirs**, Calle Peatonal No 7, mahogany woodcraft. The **IMAPRO Handicraft School** in El Progreso has a retail outlet at 1 Calle 4-5 Av SE, well worth visiting, fixed prices, good value, good mahogany carvings. The **Museum Gift Shop**, at the Museo de Antropología e Historia has lots of cheap *artesanía* gifts open during museum visiting hours.

▲ Activities and tours

Comayagua and around *p962*
Cramer Tours in Pasaje Arias.
Inversiones Karice's, 4 Av NO, very friendly and helpful.
Rolando Barahona, Av Central.

San Pedro Sula and around *p965, map p966*
Maya Temple, www.mayatempletours.com, also offers travel services.

⊖ Transport

Zambrano *p962*
Bus From the capital take any bus going north to Comayagua, Siguatepeque or La Paz and tell the driver where you want to get off.

Comayagua and around *p962*
Bus To **Tegucigalpa**, US$1.10, every 45 mins, 2 hrs (Hmnos Cruz, Comayagua, T772-0850). To **Siguatepeque**, US$0.55 with Transpinares. To **San Pedro Sula**, US$1.50, 3 hrs, either catch a bus on the highway (very crowded) or go to Siguatepeque and change buses there. Incoming buses to Comayagua drop you on the main road outside town. From here you can walk or taxi into town. Buses depart from Torocagua: *colectivo* from Calle Salvador y Cervantes in town.

Siguatepeque *p963*
Bus To **San Pedro Sula**, from the west end of town every 35 mins, US$1.35. **Tegucigalpa** with **Empresas Unidas** or **Maribel**, from west plaza, south of market, US$1.50, 3 hrs. Alternatively take a taxi, US$0.50, 2 km to the highway intersection and catch a Tegucigalpa– San Pedro Sula bus which passes every 30 mins. To **Comayagua**, Transpinares, US$0.50, 45 mins. To **La Esperanza** buses leave from near Boarding House Central, 1st departure 0530, several daily, taxi from town centre US$0.50.

Lago Yojoa *p963*
Bus To lake from **San Pedro Sula**, US$1, 1½ hrs; bus from lake to **Tegucigalpa** with Hedman-Alas, US$3, 3-5 hrs, 185 km.

Pulhapanzak waterfall *p964*
Bus By car it's a 1½-hr drive from San Pedro, longer by bus. There is a bus from **Peña Blanca** every 2 hrs to the falls, or take a Mochito or Cañaveral bus from **San Pedro Sula** from the bus station near the railway (hourly 0500-1700) and get off at the sign to the falls, at the village of Santa Buena Ventura, US$0.95. Alternatively stay on the bus to Cañaveral (take identification because there is a power plant here), and walk back along the Río Lindo, 2 hrs past interesting rock formations and small falls. Last bus returns at 1630 during the week.

Santa Bárbara and around p964

Bus To **Tegucigalpa**, 0700 and 1400 daily, weekends 0900, US$3, 4½ hrs with Transportes Junqueños (passing remote villages in beautiful mountain scenery). To **San Pedro Sula**, 2 hrs, US$1.90, 7 a day between 0500 and 1630. Bus to **San Rafael** at 1200, 4 hrs. Onward bus to **Gracias** leaves next day.

San Pedro Sula and around p965, map p966

Air

A taxi to the airport costs US$12 per taxi, but bargain hard. Yellow airport taxis cost US$18. Free airport shuttle from big hotels. Buses and *colectivos* do not go to the airport terminal itself; you have to walk the final 1 km from the La Lima road. Duty free, Global One phones, banks, restaurant on 2nd floor. Flights to **Tegucigalpa** (35 mins), **La Ceiba**, **Utila** and to **Roatán**. See page 920 for international flights.

Airline offices American, Ed Firenze, Barrio Los Andes, 16 Av 2-3 Calle, T558-0524, airport T668-3241. **Atlantic**, airport, T668-7309. **Continental**, Plaza Versalles, Av Circunvalación, T557-4141, airport T668-3208. **Grupo Taca** 13 Av NO corner of Norte de la Circunvalación, Barrio Los Andes, T557-0525, airport T668-3333. **Isleña**, Edif Trejo Merlo, 1 Calle 7 Av SO, T552-8322, airport T668-3333. **Sosa**, 8 Av 1-2 Calle SO, Edif Román, T550-6548, airport 668-3128.

Bus

Local Local buses cost US$0.10, smaller minibuses cost US$0.20.

Long distance New central bus terminal opened in 2008. The Gran Central Metropolitana is clean, safe and a short US$3 taxi from the centre of San Pedro Sula. **Heading south**, buses pass **Lago Yojoa** for **Tegucigalpa**, very regular service provided by several companies, 4½ hrs, 250 km by paved road. Main bus services with comfortable coaches in the town centre are **Hedman Alas**, T553-1361, 0830, 1330 and 1730, US$7; Transportes **Sáenz**, T553-4969, US$7; **El Rey**, T553-4264, or **Express**, T557-8355; Transportes

Norteños, T552-2145, last bus at 1900; Viana, T556-9261.

Heading west from San Pedro the road leads to **Puerto Cortés**, a pleasant 45-min journey down the lush river valley. With Empresa Impala, T553-3111, from 0430 until 2200, US$1, or **Citul**, and also on to **Omoa** from 0600.

Heading east buses go to **La Lima**, **El Progreso**, **Tela** and **La Ceiba** (Tupsa and Catisa, very regular to El Progreso, hourly to La Ceiba from 0600 and 1800, 3 hrs, US$3), some with a change in El Progreso, others direct. Also 1st class to La Ceiba with **Viana** at 1030 and 1730, and with **Hedman Alas** at 1000, 1400 and 1800. To **Trujillo**, 3 per day, 6 hrs, US$5, comfortable.

Heading southwest buses go to **Santa Rosa de Copán** through the Department of Ocotepeque, with superb mountain scenery, to the **Guatemalan border**. Congolón, and Empresa Toritos y Copanecos, serve **Nueva Ocotepeque** (US$8) and **Agua Caliente** on the Guatemalan border with 7 buses a day; Congolón, T553-1174.

To **Santa Rosa de Copán**, with connections at La Entrada for **Copán Ruinas**, with Empresa Toritos y Copanecos, T563-4930, leaving every 20 mins, 0345-1715, 3 hrs, US$3.70. Take a bus to the junction of La Entrada and change for connection to Copán Ruinas if you're not going direct. 1st-class bus to **Copán Ruinas** with Hedman Alas, T553-1361, daily at 0950 and 1430, 3 hrs, US$14 with a/c, movie and bathrooms. Also direct service with Casasola-Cheny Express at 0800, 1300 and 1400.

International Services available from Tica bus covering the whole of Central America from Mexico to Panama.

Car

Car rentals Avis, 1 Calle, 6 Av NE, T553-0888; **Blitz**, Hotel Sula and airport (T552-2405 or 668-3171); **Budget**, 1 Calle 7Av NO, T552-2295, airport T668-3179; **Maya Eco Tours**, 3 Av NO, 7-8 Calle, and airport (T552-2670 or 668-3168); **Molinari**, Hotel Sula and airport

(T553-2639 or 668-6178); **Toyota**, 3 Av 5 y 6 Calle NO, T557-2666 or airport T668-3174. **Car repairs** Invandl, 13 Calle, 5 y 6 Av NE, T552-7083. Excellent service from Víctor Mora.

Parque Nacional Cusuco *p966*
Bus San Pedro Sula–Cofradía, 1 hr, US$0.15, from 5 Av, 11 Calle SO (buses drop you at turn-off 1 km from town); pickup Cofradía–Buenos Aires 1½ hrs, US$1.75, best on Mon at 1400 (wait at small shop on outskirts of town on Buenos Aires road); the park is 12 km from Buenos Aires.

● Directory

Comayagua and around *p962*
Banks Only HSBC near Parque Central changes TCs, but others for cash include Banco Atlántida, Banco de Occidente, Bancafé, Ficensa, Banadesa, Bamer and Banffaa. **Immigration** Migración is at 6 Calle NO, 1 Av, good place to get visas renewed, friendly. **Medical services** Dentist: Dr José de Jesús Berlioz, next to Colegio León Alvarado, T772-0054.

Siguatepeque *p963*
Banks HSBC, Banco Atlántida and Banco de Occidente.

Santa Bárbara and around *p964*
Banks Banadesa, Bancafé, Banco Atlántida, and Banco de Occidente.

San Pedro Sula and around *p965, map p966*
Banks HSBC, has a beautiful mural in its head office, 5 Av, 4 Calle SO and a branch at 5 Av, 6-7 Calle SO, changes TCs. Banco Atlántida, on Parque Central, changes TCs at good rates. Banco de Honduras (Citibank). Banco Continental, 3 Av, 3-5 Calle SO No 7. Banco de Occidente, 6 Av, 2-3 Calle SO. Bancafé, 1 Calle, 1 Av SE and all other local banks. BAC for Visa, MasterCard and Amex is at, 5 Av y 2 Calle NO. These are also at **Aval Card**, 14 Av NO y Circunvalación, and **Honducard**, 5 Av y 2 Calle NO. **Cultural centres** Alianza Francesa, on 23 Av 3-4 Calle SO, T/F553-1178, www.aftegucig alpa.com, offers French and Spanish classes, has a library, films and cultural events. Centro **Cultural Sampedrano**, 3 Calle, 4 Av NO No 20, T553-3911, USIS-funded library, cultural events, concerts, art exhibitions and theatrical productions. **Embassies and consulates** Belize, Km 5 Blv del Norte, Col los Castaños, T551-0124, 551-0707. El Salvador, Edif Rivera y Cía, 7th floor, local 704, 5 y 6 Av 3 Calle, T/F553-4604. France, Col Zerón, 9 Av 10 Calle 927, T557-4187. Germany, 6 Av NO, Av Circunvalación, T553-1244. Guatemala, 8 Calle 5-6 Av NO, No 38, T/F553-3560. Italy, Edif La Constancia, 3rd floor, 5 Av 1-2 Calle NO, T552-3672. Mexico, 2 Calle 20 Av SO 201, Barrio Río de Piedras, T553-2604. Netherlands, 15 Av 7-8 Calle NE, Plaza Venecia, Local 10, T557-1815. Nicaragua, Col Trejo, 23 Av A entre 11 Calle B y 11 Calle C No 145, T/F550-3394. Spain, 2 Av 3-4 Calle NO 318, Edif Agencias Panamericanas, T558-0708. UK, 13 Av 10-12 Calle SO, Suyapa No 62, T557-2046. **Immigration** Calle Peatonal, just off Parque Central, or at the airport. **Internet** Internet cafés are found throughout town. Internet Café, Multiplaza centre, T550-6077, US$1 per hr. Red Cybe Café, Calle 3, 1 block east of the Hedman Alas bus terminal, US$1per hr. **Laundry** Excelsior, 14-15 Av Blv Morazán. Lava Fácil, 7 Av, 5 Calle NO, US$1.50 per load. Lavandería Almich, 9-10 Av, 5 Calle SO No 29, Barrio El Benque. Rodgers, 4a Calle, 15-16 Av SO, No 114. **Medical services** Dentist: Clínicas Dentales Especializadas, Ed María Antonia, 3a Calle between 8 and 9 Av NO, apartamento L-1, Barrio Guamilito, T558-0464. **Post office** 3 Av SO between 9-10 Calle. **Telephone** Hondutel, 4 Calle 4 Av SO. Calls can be made from Gran Hotel Sula.

North coast

Honduras' Caribbean coast has a mixture of banana-exporting ports, historic towns and Garífuna villages. Working from west to east the main towns of interest are Omoa, Puerto Cortés, Tela, La Ceiba and Trujillo. In between the towns you will find isolated beaches and resorts, and national parks like Pico Bonito, which are perfect for hiking and whitewater rafting. The route west takes in the 'Jungle Trail' to Guatemala – which you can now do by bus.

Running parallel to the coast, a route from El Progreso runs south of the coastal mountain chain Cordillera Nombre de Dios leading to rarely visited national parks, pristine cloud forest and an alternative route to La Ceiba. **>> For listings, see pages 984-994.**

Puerto Cortés → *Colour map 6, B2.*

Stuck out on the northwestern coast of the country and backed by the large bay of Laguna de Alvarado, Puerto Cortés is hot, tempered by sea breezes and close to many beautiful palm-fringed beaches nearby. The success of the place is its location and most Honduran trade passes through the port which is just 58 km from San Pedro Sula by road and rail, and 333 km from Tegucigalpa. It has a small oil refinery, a free zone and, being two days' voyage from New Orleans, is arguably now the most important port in Central America.

The Parque Central contains many fine trees but focuses on a huge Indian poplar, planted as a sapling in 1941, in the centre that provides an extensive canopy.

Getting there If entering Puerto Cortés by boat, go to immigration immediately. Coming from Belize there is an immigration 'hut' on the dockside. Passports are often collected on the boat, handed in and returned as they are processed. There is a US$3

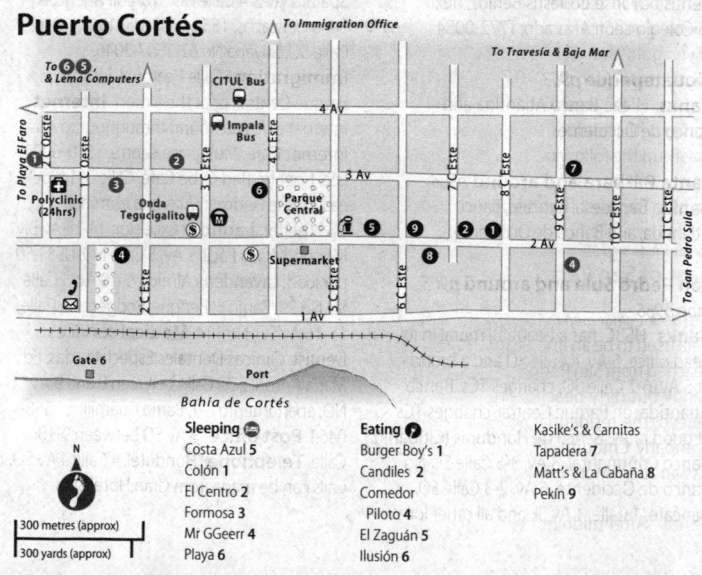

Puerto Cortés

Sleeping
Costa Azul 5
Colón 1
El Centro 2
Formosa 3
Mr GGeerr 4
Playa 6

Eating
Burger Boy's 1
Candiles 2
Comedor
  Piloto 4
El Zaguán 5
Ilusión 6

Kasike's & Carnitas
Tapadera 7
Matt's & La Cabaña 8
Pekín 9

300 metres (approx)
300 yards (approx)

Border essentials: Honduras–Guatemala

Corinto
A road now connects Puerto Cortés (Honduras) and Puerto Barrios (Guatemala), with a new bridge over the Motagua river.

Honduran immigration at Corinto if crossing from Puerto Barrios in Guatemala for Omoa and Puerto Cortés in Honduras. Immigration services are either side of the border.

Entering Honduras Buses stop at the immigration office in Guatemala, before continuing for a few minutes and dropping you at the border. After crossing the border into Honduras, complete immigration formalities and it's a few minutes' walk to where the buses head along the coast. If you enter Honduras by boat you must go to immigration in Puerto Cortés as soon as possible. Entry tax of US$3.

Entering Guatemala Buses leave Puerto Cortés for **Omoa** and **Corinto** on the border every hour or so.

entry fee, make sure that you have the stamp. This is the only official payment; if asked for more, demand a receipt.

Omoa → *Colour map 6, B2.*
Omoa, 18 km from Puerto Cortés, is set in the beautiful Bahía de Omoa where the mountains, lusciously carpeted in jungle, tumble towards the sea. You can watch fine purple sunsets from the quiet laid-back bars on the beach, and if you're lucky see dolphins in the bay. It has an 18th-century castle, Fortaleza de San Fernando, now renovated and worth a visit. It was built by the Spaniards in 1759 to protect the coast and shipments of silver, gold and cacao from British pirates. There is a **visitor centre** and a small, interesting **museum** ① *Mon-Sun 0900-1600, US$1.40, tickets on sale at gate, guides available.*

During the week Omoa is a quiet, friendly fishing village, but at weekends it gets a little busier with Hondurans from San Pedro and the place becomes littered, followed by a grand clean-up the following Monday morning. Near Omoa are two waterfalls (**Los Chorros**), with lovely walks to each, and good hiking in attractive scenery both along the coast and inland.

It's a fair walk from the main road. Get a tuk-tuk for US$0.50 to the beach.

East of San Pedro Sula ◉⊘❀▲◎◉ ›› *pp984-994.*

Tela → *Colour map 6, B2.*
Tela used to be an important banana port before the pier was partly destroyed by fire. Easily reached from San Pedro Sula with a bus service via El Progreso, it is pleasantly laid out with a sandy but dirty beach. Tela Viejo to the east is the original city joined by a bridge to Tela Nuevo, the residential area built for the executives of the American banana and farming company **Chiquita**. There is a pleasant walk along the beach east to Ensenada, or west to San Juan. More information is available at www.tela-honduras.com.

Safety After midnight take a cab, Lps 30 per person at night.

Around Tela

Local buses and trucks from the corner just east of the market go east to the Garífuna village of **Triunfo de la Cruz**, which is set in a beautiful bay. Site of the first Spanish settlement on the mainland, a sea battle between Cristóbal de Olid and Francisco de Las Casas (two of Cortés' lieutenants) was fought here in 1524.

Beyond Triunfo de la Cruz is an interesting coastal area that includes the cape, **Parque Nacional Punta Izopo** (1½-hour walk along the beach, take water – 12 km from Tela) and the mouth of the Río León. This, and its immediate hinterland, are a good place to see parrots, toucans, turtles, alligators and monkeys as well as the first landing point of the Spanish conqueror Cristóbal de Olid. For information contact **Prolansate** (see box, opposite). To get right into the forest and enjoy the wildlife, it is best to take an organized tour (see Tour operators, page 991). A trip to Punta Izopo involves kayaking through mangrove swamps up the Río Plátano, Indiana Jones style.

Further northwest, along palm-fringed beaches is **Parque Nacional Punta Sal 'Jeannette Kawas'** ① *US$2*, contact **Prolansate** for information, a lovely place now protected within the park's 80,000-ha boundaries. It is one of the most important parks in Honduras and has two parts, the peninsula and the lagoon. During the dry season some 350 species of bird live within the lagoon, surrounded by forest, mangroves and wetlands. Once inhabited only by Garífuna, the area has suffered from the immigration of cattle farmers who have cleared the forest, causing erosion, and from a palm oil extraction plant on the Río San Alejo, which has dumped waste in the river and contaminated the lagoons. Conservation and environmental protection programmes are now underway. To get there you will need a motor boat, or take a bus (three a day) to Tornabé and hitch a ride 12 km, or take the crab truck at 1300 for US$0.40 (back at 1700), on to Miami, a small, all-thatched fishing village (two hours' walk along beach from Tornabé), beer on ice available, and walk the remaining 10 km along the beach. There are also pickups from Punta Sal to Miami, contact Prolansate for information.

Jardín Botánico at Lancetilla ① *T448-1740, not well signposted – a guide is recommended, ask at the Cohdefor office; guide services daily 0800-1530, US$6; good maps*

Northwestern coast

available in English or Spanish US$0.30, is 5 km inland, and was founded (in 1926) as a plant research station. Now, it is the second largest botanical garden in the world. It has more than 1000 varieties of plant and over 200 bird species have been identified. It has fruit trees from every continent, the most extensive collection of Asiatic fruit trees in the western hemisphere, an orchid garden, and plantations of mahogany and teak alongside a 1200-ha virgin tropical rainforest. But be warned, there are many mosquitoes.

To get to Lancetilla and the Jardín Botánico, take a taxi from Tela, US$4, but there are few in the park for the return journey in the afternoon, so organize collection in advance.

La Ceiba and around 😊🖊🕐🛇🗗🛆🕐🕐 ➡ pp984-994. Colour map 6, B3.

La Ceiba, the capital of Atlántida Department and the third largest city in Honduras, stands on the narrow coastal plain between the Caribbean and the rugged Nombre de Dios mountain range crowned by the spectacular Pico Bonito (2435 m) (see page 979). The climate is hot, but tempered by sea winds. Once the country's busiest port, trade has now passed to Puerto Cortés and Puerto Castilla, but there is still some activity. The close proximity to Pico Bonito National park, Cuero y Salado Wildlife Refuge and the Cayos Cochinos Marine Reserve gives the city the ambitious target of becoming an important ecotourism centre. While the opportunities aren't immediately obvious, there is definitely a buzz about town – watch out for developments. The main plaza is worth walking around to see statues of various famous Hondurans including Lempira and a couple of ponds.

A **butterfly and insect museum** ⓘ *Col El Sauce, 2a Etapa Casa G-12, T442-2874, http:// butterflywebsite.com, Mon-Sat 0800-1200, 1300-1600, closed Wed afternoon, US$1, student reductions*, has a collection of over 10,000 butterflies, roughly 2000 other insects and snakes. Good for all ages, you get a 25-minute video in both Spanish and English and Robert and Myriam Lehman guide visitors expertly through the life of the butterfly. There is also a **Butterfly Farm** ⓘ *daily 0800-1630, entry US$6*, on the grounds of **The Lodge** at Pico Bonito.

Around La Ceiba → *See map, La Ceiba and the coast, page 979.*

Fig Tree Medical Centre ⓘ *T440-0041 (in La Ceiba), 25 km east of La Ceiba*, on the highway to Jutiapa, is a famous centre for alternative medicine. Operated by Dr Sebi, this facility is treating cancer and diabetes utilizing vegetarian diet, medications and the local hot springs. For more information or to visit call in advance. **Jutiapa** is a small dusty town with a pretty little colonial church. Contact Standard Fruit Company, Dole office in La Ceiba (off main plaza) to visit a local pineapple plantation. **Corozal** is an interesting Garífuna village near La Ceiba, at Km 209.5, with a beach, Playas de Sambrano and a hotel (see Sleeping, page 984). **Sambo Creek**, another Garífuna village, has nice beaches and a couple of hotels. Near the towns of **Esparta** and **El Porvenir**, thousands of crabs come out of the sea in July and August and travel long distances inland. The **Catarata El Bejuco** is a waterfall 7 km along the old dirt road to **Olanchito** (11 km from La Ceiba). Follow a path signposted to Balneario Los Lobos to the waterfall about 1 km upriver through the jungle.

La Ceiba

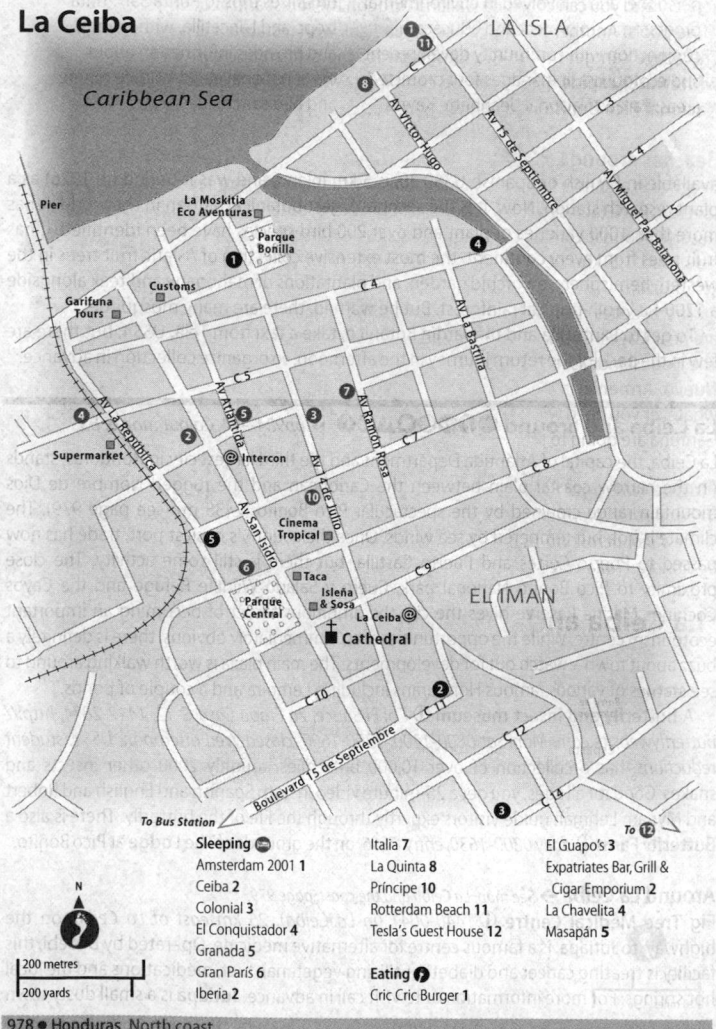

Sleeping			
Amsterdam 2001 1	Italia 7	El Guapo's 3	
Ceiba 2	La Quinta 8	Expatriates Bar, Grill &	
Colonial 3	Príncipe 10	Cigar Emporium 2	
El Conquistador 4	Rotterdam Beach 11	La Chavelita 4	
Granada 5	Tesla's Guest House 12	Masapán 5	
Gran París 6			
Iberia 2	**Eating**		
	Cric Cric Burger 1		

There is good swimming from a pebbly beach where the river broadens. Along this road is **El Naranjo** near **Omega Tours Jungle Lodge and Adventure Company**.

Yaruca, 20 km down the old road to Olanchito, is easily reached by bus and offers good views of Pico Bonito. **Eco-Zona Río María**, 5 km along the Trujillo highway (signposted path up to the foothills of the Cordillera Nombre de Dios), is a beautiful walk through the lush countryside of a protected area. Just beyond Río María is **Balneario Los Chorros** (signposted), a series of small waterfalls through giant boulders into a deep rock pool that is great for swimming (refreshments nearby). Upstream there is some beautiful scenery and you can continue walking through the forest and in the river, where there are more pools. Another bathing place, Agua Azul, with restaurant is a short distance away. The active can get on the **Río Cangrejal** for the exhilarating rush of Grade II, III and IV **whitewater rapids**, which can be combined with treks in to the wilderness of **Parque Nacional Pico Bonito** (see below).

Beaches around La Ceiba

Beaches in and near La Ceiba include **Playa Miramar** (dirty, not recommended), **La Barra** (better), **Perú** (across the Río Cangrejal at Km 205.5, better still, quiet except at weekends, deserted tourist complex, restaurant, access by road to Tocoa, 10 km, then signposted side road 1.5 km, or along the beach 6 km from La Ceiba) and **La Encenada** (close to Corozal).

The beaches near the fishing villages of Río Esteban and Balfate are very special and are near Cayos Cochinos (Hog Islands) where the snorkelling and diving is spectacular. The Hog Islands (see page 1000) can be reached by *cayuco* from Roatán, La Ceiba and **Nuevo Armenia**, a nondescript Garífuna village connected by road to Jutiapa. Take whatever you need with you as there is almost nothing on the smaller cayes. However, the Garífuna are going to and fro all the time.

Parque Nacional Pico Bonito

ⓘ *For further information on the park contact Leslie Arcantara at FUPNAPIB, at Calle 19, Av 14 de Julio, across from Suyapita Catholic church, Barrio Alvarado, T442-0618, www.pico bonito.org. Take care if you enter the forest: tracks are not yet developed, a compass is*

La Ceiba and the coast

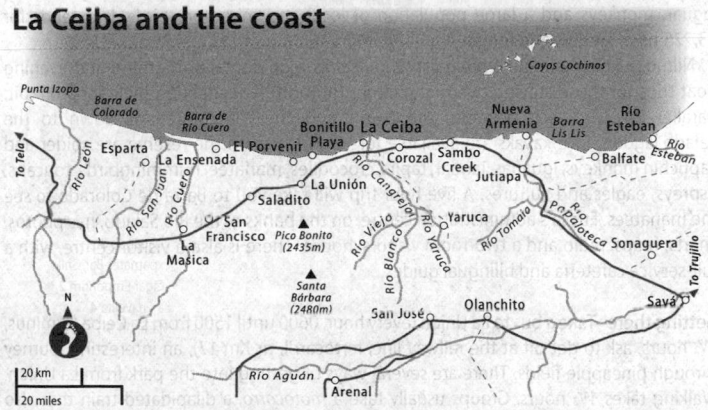

advisable. Tour companies in *La Ceiba* arrange trips to the park. A day trip, horse riding through the park, can be arranged through Omega Tours, see page 991. Trip includes food and guide, US$25. Recommended. Access to Public Trails in Pico Bonito is US$6. Go early in the morning for the best views, and to see birdlife and howler monkeys.

Parque Nacional Pico Bonito (674 sq km) is the largest national park in Honduras and is home to Pico Bonito (2435 m). The Río Cangrejal, a mecca for whitewater rafting, marks the eastern border of the park. It has deep tropical hardwood forests that shelter, among other animals, jaguars and three species of monkey, deep canyons and tumbling streams and waterfalls (including Las Gemelas, which fall vertically for some 200 m).

Parque Nacional Pico Bonito has two areas open for tourism. The first is the Río Zacate area, located past the community of El Pino, 10 km west of La Ceiba; the second is on the Río Cangrejal, near the community of El Naranjo, about 7.5 km from the paved highway.

A hanging bridge over the Río Cangrejal provides access to the visitor centre and the El Mapache Trail up to the top of El Bejuco waterfall. Further up the road in Las Mangas, Guaruma (T442-2693) there is a very nice trail with beautiful swimming holes in a pristine creek. The trail is well maintained and local guides are available.

For the Río Zacate area, access is just past the dry stream (*quebrada seca*) bridge on the main La Ceiba to Tela highway from where the road leads to the entrance through pineapple plantations to a steep trail leading up to the Río Zacate waterfall, about one hour 20 minutes' hiking. A good price range of accommodation is available in both areas.

Development of the park by **Curla** (Centro Universitario Regional del Litoral Atlántico) continues under the supervision of **Cohdefor**, the forestry office, and the **Fundación Parque Nacional Pico Bonito (FUPNAPIB)** ① *Calle 19, Av 14 de Julio, La Ceiba, T442-0618.*

Cuero y Salado Wildlife Reserve

① *US$10 to enter the reserve, which you can pay at Fucsa, keep the receipt, plus US$5 per person for accommodation. The reserve is managed by the Fundación Cuero y Salado (Fucsa) Refugio de Vida Silvestre, 1 block north and 3 blocks west of Parque Central (see map) to the left of the Standard Fruit Company, La Ceiba, T/F443-0329, Apartado Postal 674. The foundation is open to volunteers, preferably those who speak English and Spanish.*

Near the coast, between the Cuero and Salado rivers, 37 km west of La Ceiba, is the Cuero y Salado Wildlife Reserve, which has a great variety of flora and fauna, including manatee, jaguar, monkeys and a large population of local and migratory birds. It extends for 13,225 ha of swamp and forest.

Nilmo, a knowledgeable biologist who acts as a guide, takes morning and evening boat trips for those staying overnight, either through the canal dug by Standard Fruit, parallel to the beach between the palms and the mangroves, or down to the Salado lagoon. Five kayaks are available for visitors' use. In the reserve are spider and capuchin monkeys, iguanas, jaguar, tapirs, crocodiles, manatee, hummingbirds, toucans, ospreys, eagles and vultures. A five-hour trip will take you to Barra de Colorado to see the manatees. Fucsa's administration centre, on the banks of the Río Salado, has photos, charts, maps, radio and a two-room visitors' house. There is also a visitor centre, with a full-service cafeteria and bilingual guides.

Getting there Take a bus to La Unión (every hour, 0600 until 1500 from La Ceiba terminus, 1½ hours, ask to get off at the railway line, ferrocarril, or Km 17), an interesting journey through pineapple fields. There are several ways of getting into the park from La Unión. Walking takes 1½ hours. Groups usually take a *motocarro*, a dilapidated train that also transports the coconut crop. From near Doña Tina's house (meals available), take a *burra*, a flat-bed railcar propelled by two men with poles (a great way to see the countryside) to the community on the banks of the Río Salado. To return to La Unión, it is another *burra* ride or a two-hour walk along the railway, then, either wait for a La Ceiba bus (last one at 1500), or ask for the short cut through grapefruit groves, 20 minutes, which leads to the main La Ceiba–Tela road, where there are many more buses back to town.

Trujillo and around ⊙⊘⊙⊙▲⊙⊙ ▸▸ *pp984-994. Colour map 6, B3.*

→ *www.trujillohonduras.com.*

Once a major port and the former capital, Trujillo sits on the southern shore of the palm-fringed Bay of Trujillo. It is a quiet, pleasant town with clean beaches nearby and calm water that is ideal for swimming. Christopher Columbus landed close to the area on his fourth voyage to the Americas and the town was later founded in 1525 by Juan de Medina, making it the oldest town in Honduras. Hernán Cortés arrived here after his famous march overland from Yucatán in pursuit of his usurping lieutenant, Olid. Filibuster William Walker (see under Nicaragua) was shot near here in 1860; a commemorative stone marks the spot in the rear garden of the hospital, one block east of the Parque Central, and the old cemetery (near Hotel Trujillo) is his final resting place.

Fortaleza Santa Bárbara ① *US$1*, a ruined Spanish fortress overlooking the bay, is worth a visit. Most of the relics found there have been moved to the museum of Rufino Galán, but there are still a few rusty muskets and cannon balls. Twenty minutes' walk from Trujillo plaza is the **Museo y Piscina Rufino Galán Cáceres** ① *US$1, US$0.50 to swim*, which has a swimming pool filled from the Río Cristales with changing rooms and picnic

Trujillo & the coast

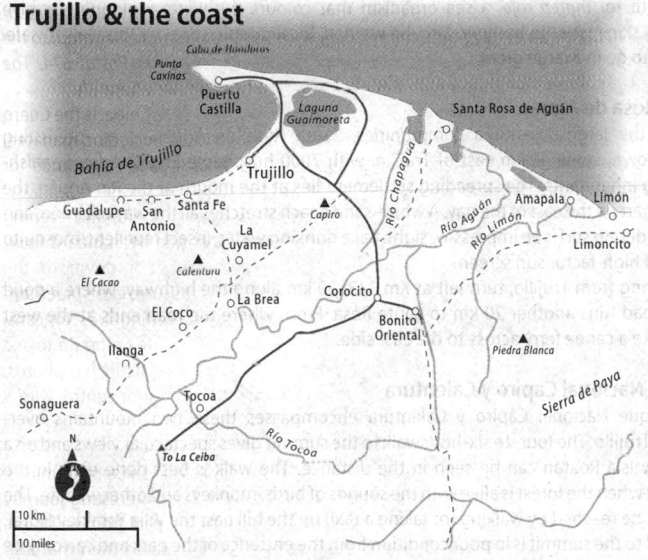

10 km
10 miles

facilities. Close by, the wreckage of a US C-80 aircraft that crashed in 1985 forms part of Sr Galán's museum. The rest of the collection is a mass of curios, some very interesting. The cemetery is rather overgrown, with collapsed and open tombs, but it does give a feel of the origins of early residents. The **Fiesta de San Juan Bautista** is in June, with participation from surrounding Garífuna settlements.

West of Trujillo, just past the football field on the Santa Fe road, is the **Río Grande**, which has lovely pools and waterfalls for river bathing, best during the rainy season. Take the path on the far side of river, after about 10 minutes cut down to the rocks and follow the river upstream along the boulders.

Beaches
Good beaches are found both on the peninsula and around Trujillo Bay. Before setting out ask which beaches are safe. Take a bus from near the Parque Central towards Puerto Castilla and ask the driver to let you off at the path about 1 km beyond the bridge over the lagoon. Other beaches around Puerto Castilla are separated by mangroves, are littered and have sandflies. The beaches in town tend to be less clean. If you're tempted to walk to find a cleaner stretch of sand don't walk alone; tourists here have been assaulted and robbed.

West of Trujillo
There are interesting Garífuna villages west of Trujillo. The road is rough, often impassable in wet weather, and jeeps are needed even in the dry season. **Santa Fe**, 10 km west of Trujillo, is a friendly place with several good Garífuna restaurants, for example **Comedor Caballero** and **Las Brisas de Santa Fe**, on the endless white sandy beach. The bus service continues to **San Antonio** (good restaurant behind the beach) and **Guadalupe**. Walk in the morning along the beach to Santa Fe and then get a bus back to Trujillo, taking plenty of water and sun block. This stretch of beach is outstanding, but watch out for *marea roja*, a sea organism that colours the water pink and can give irritating skin rashes to bathers. Also, be warned, local people consider this walk unsafe. It's best to go in a large group.

Santa Rosa de Aguán
One of the largest Garífuna communities, Santa Rosa de Aguán is an interesting coastal town, some 40 km east of Trujillo, with 7000 hospitable English- and Spanish-speaking inhabitants. The spreading settlement lies at the mouth of the Río Aguán, the greater part on the east of the bay. A white-sand beach stretches all the way to Limón, and the thundering surf is an impressive sight. Take drinking water, insect repellent, mosquito coils and high-factor sun screen.

If driving from Trujillo, turn left at Km 343, 20 km along the highway, where a good gravel road runs another 20 km to Santa Rosa. From where the road ends at the west bank, take a canoe ferry across to the east side.

Parque Nacional Capiro y Calentura
The Parque Nacional Capiro y Calentura encompasses these two mountains overlooking Trujillo. The four- to six-hour walk to the summit gives spectacular views and on a clear day Isla Roatán can be seen in the distance. The walk is best done early in the morning when the forest is alive with the sounds of birds, monkeys and other wildlife. The path can be reached by walking (or taking a taxi) up the hill past the **Villa Brinkley Hotel**. The road to the summit is in poor condition from the entrance of the park and can only be

driven in a 4WD. Insect repellent is needed if you pause. As with all walks in this area, it's safest to go in a group. The park is run by the **Fundación Capiro Calentura Guaimoreto (FUCAGUA)** ① *Parque Central, Trujillo, Mon-Fri*. They have information on all the reserves in the area and also on hiking and tours. Until a new office is built in the park, entry tickets must be bought here before going to Capiro y Calentura. They are opening up trails, improving old ones and organizing guided tours through parts of the forest. The hike along the Sendero de la Culebrina uses the remnants of a colonial stone road used to transport gold from the mines in the Valle de Aguán. Halfway up the **Cerro de las Cuevas**, 7 km beyond Cuyamel, are impressive caves showing traces of occupation by pre-Columbian Pech indigenous people.

Refugio de Vida Silvestre Laguna de Guaimoreto (RVSLG)

FUCAGUA, see above, also administers the Refugio de Vida Silvestre, Laguna de Guaimoreto (RVSLG), northeast of Trujillo, where there is a bird island (Isla de los Pájaros), monkeys and good fishing. To visit, either arrange a trip with Fucagua, a tour agency such as Turtle Tours, or take a bus from Trujillo towards Puerto Castilla, get off just after the bridge which crosses the lagoon, then walk away from the lagoon for about 200 m to a dirt track on the left. Follow this and cross a low bridge and on the left is the house of a man who rents dug-out canoes. The Isla de los Pájaros is about 3 km up the lagoon, a bit too far for a dug-out. Another alternative is to go down to the wharf and hire out a motorized canoe or launch(price depends on the number of passengers and length of trip). There are no roads, paths or facilities in the area.

El Progreso and east ●●● ➤ *pp984-994.*

El Progreso, an important but unattractive agricultural and commercial centre on the Río Ulúa, is 30 minutes' drive on the paved highway southeast of San Pedro Sula, en route to Tela. While most people make straight for the coast at Tela, heading east from El Progreso leads through mountain scenery up to the small town of Yoro, beyond to Olanchito and a link to La Ceiba. With everyone else rushing to the Bay Islands, you could well have the place to yourself.

Parque Nacional Pico Pijol → *Colour map 6, B2.*

This park protects the 2282-m summit of primary cloud forest that is home to many quetzales. It is 32 km from the town of **Morazán** in the Yoro Department, which is 41 km from Progreso (bus from Progreso or Santa Rita). In Morazán are **Hospedaje El Corazón Sagrado**, several restaurants and a disco. The lower slopes of Pico Pijol have been heavily farmed. Access by vehicle is possible as far as Subirana. A guide is needed from there to a large cave nearby and access is difficult. Another trail to the summit (2282 m) starts at **Nueva Esperanza** village (bus from Morazán, Parque Central); ask for the correct trail. The first day is tough, all uphill with no shade; the second is tougher and requires a lot of clearing. Take a compass and a topographical map. Also in the park is the waterfall at **Las Piratas**; take a bus from Morazán to Los Murillos and then walk to El Ocotillo (ask for Las Piratas).

Yoro and around → *Colour map 6, B2.*

The paved highway to the prosperous little town of Yoro passes through pleasant countryside surrounded by mountains and dotted with ranches and farms. The **Parque Nacional Montaña** de **Yoro** is 8 km to the southeast (access from Marale), comprising 257 sq km of cloud forest, home to the Tolupanes indigenous people, also known as Xicaques. The **Asociación Ecológica Amigos de la Montaña de Yoro** has an office in the Parque Central in Yoro. From Yoro a dirt road continues to **Olanchito** via **Jocón**, through attractive country as the road snakes along the pine-forested slopes of Montaña Piedra Blanca and Montaña de la Bellota, with fine views of the surrounding valleys and distant mountain ranges.

◉ North coast listings

For Sleeping and Eating price codes and other relevant information, see Essentials pages 45-48.

● Sleeping

Puerto Cortés *p974, map p974*
Avoid 4 Calle between 1 and 2 Av and the area on 1 Av opposite the dockyards; it is unpleasant by day and dangerous at night.
AL Playa, 4 km west at Cienaguita, T665-1105. Hotel complex, directly on beach, cable TV, good fish dishes in restaurant. Mountain bikes for rent, available to non-guests.
A Costa Azul, Playa El Faro, T665-2260. Restaurant, disco-bar, billiards, table tennis, pool, horse riding, volley ball, good value.
C Costa Mar, Playas de la Coca Cola, T665-1367. Pleasant, with private bath, swimming pool and restaurant.
C Mr GGeerr, 9 Calle, 2 Av E, T665-0444. No hot water, very clean, a/c, bar, video, satellite TV. Recommended.
C-E El Centro, 3 Av 2-3 Calle, T665-1160. With bath, a/c, hot water, cable TV, parking, garden, café, pleasant, well furnished.
D Frontera del Caribe, Playas de Camaguey, road to Travesía, T665-5001. Very friendly, quiet, safe, on beach, restaurant on 1st floor, open, airy, good food, 7 rooms on 2nd floor, private bath, cold water, linen changed daily, fan. Recommended.
F Colón, 3 Av 2 Calle O. Diagonally opposite Hotel Puerto Limón in clapboard building, clean, safe, basic.
F Formosa, 3 Av 2 Calle E. With bath (some without), no towel, but soap and toilet paper provided, clean, fan, good value, friendly Chinese owner.

Omoa *p975*
B Sueño del Mar, T658-9047, www.suenos demar.com. Newest hotel on the beach with a handful of rooms of differing sizes run by Canadian couple Karen and Mark. Great spot and the quiet end of the beach. Canadian breakfasts, laundry, Wi-Fi internet and a few steps from the beach. Recommended.
B Tatiana, on beach. With bath, clean and quiet.
B-C Fisherman's Hotel, great small hotel by the beach, clean, handy location, restaurant out front. A/c, cheaper with fan.
C Gemini B, on main access road to beach, T658-9137. Bath, fan, *cafetería*, parking, lawn, comfortable.
D Hospedaje Champa Julita, on beach, T658-9174. Friendly, fan, basic, run-down.
E Roli's Place, T/F658-9082, http://yaxpactours.com. 80 m from beach, clean rooms with private bath and hot water, good information here of the region, bikes and kayaks for guests' use, games, shady garden and campground. Roli will change TCs, quetzals, euro and dollars. Quiet after 2200. Great, but not a party place.
F The tienda, where the bus stops. Has cheap, basic rooms, shared bathroom, OK.

Tela *p975*
During Easter week, the town is packed: room rates double and advance booking is essential.
L Telamar, T448-2196, www.hotel telamar.com. A complex of wooden bungalows, set on a palm-fringed beach. Rooms and villas available, also restaurant, bar, golf club, swimming pool and a conference centre.

A César Mariscos, on beach, T448-2083, www.hotelcesarmariscos.com. A/c, large rooms, restaurant.

A Gran Central, just south of the centre of town, T/F448-1099, www.hotelgran central.com. French-owned, beautifully restored historic banana-port-era hotel. 1 suite, kitchen, hot water, cable TV, a/c, security, safe box in each room. Local excursions available. Highly recommended.

A Sherwood, T448-1065, www.hotelsher wood.com. On waterfront, some cheaper rooms, a/c, TV, hot water, upper rooms have balconies and are airy, pool, English-speaking owner, TCs or credit cards accepted. The staff are friendly, honest, and there's a restaurant.

A-B Maya Vista, top of hill, steep flight of steps starting opposite **Preluna**, T/F448-1497, www.mayavista.com. Canadian-owned, French and English spoken, bath, a/c, hot water, bar, restaurant, delicious French-Canadian cuisine, fantastic views. Very highly recommended.

C Ejecutivos, 8 Calle 3 Av NE, T448-1076. A/c, hot water, TV, 8 rooms with kitchenette.

C Mango B&B, 8 Calle, 5 Av, T448-0338, www.mangocafe.net. A/c, hot water, TV, comfortable, well-furnished rooms, friendly, efficient.

C Tela, 9 Calle, 3-4 Av NE, T448-2150. Clean, airy, fans, hot water, will do laundry, with restaurant, but meagre breakfast, otherwise very good.

C-D Bertha's, 8 Calle, 9 Av NE, T448-1009. Near bus terminal, with bath, a/c, cheaper with fan, clean. Recommended.

E Mar Azul, 11 Calle, 5 Av NE, T448-2313. With fan and bath, charming helpful owner. Best backpacker place in town.

E-F La Posada del Sol, 8 Calle 3 Av NE, opposite **Ejecutivos**, T448-2111. With bath (cheaper without), clean, laundry facilities, nice garden.

F Sara, 11 Calle, 6 Av, behind the restaurant Tiburón Playa, T448-1477. Basic in a rickety old building, with bath, or without, poor sanitation. Cheapest in town, popular with backpackers, friendly, noisy especially at weekends from all-night discos.

Around Tela *p976*

There are cheap houses and *cabañas* for rent in Triunfo de la Cruz. There is a small hotel in Río Tinto, near Parque Nacional Punta Sal; accommodation is also available in private houses.

A-B Caribbean Coral Inn, Triunfo de la Cruz, T669-0224, www.globalnet.hn/caribcoralinn. With bath, fan.

A-B The Last Resort, Tornabé, T/F984-3964. Has 8 bungalows for rent, some a/c, some fan, hot water, with breakfast, several cabins for different size groups.

D-F El Tucán, Triunfo de la Cruz. Backpacker place with *cabañas*.

La Ceiba and around *p977, map p978*

AL La Quinta, at the Zona Viva, right on the beach, T440-3311, quintarealhotel.com. By far the best hotel in La Ceiba. Swimming pool, a/c, cable TV, beach, restaurant and bars.

A-B Gran Hotel París, Parque Central, T/F443-2391, hotelparis@psinet.hn. A/c, own generator, swimming pool, parking, good value.

B Ceiba, Av San Isidro 5 Calle, T443-2737. With fan or a/c and bath, restaurant and bar, uncomfortable, but good breakfast.

B Iberia, Av San Isidoro, next door to **Ceiba**, T443-0401. A/c, windows without screen. Recommended.

B Paraíso, Calle 4 E, Barrio La Isla, T443-3535. Bath, a/c, hot water, TV, restaurant, 4 blocks from beach, bar, restaurant.

B Tesla's Guest House, Calle Montecristo 212, Col El Naranjal, opposite Hospital La Fe, T/F443-3893. 5 rooms, private bathrooms, hot water, a/c, pool, phone, minibar, BBQ, laundry, friendly family owners speak English, German, French and Spanish, airport collection.

C Italia, Av Ramón Rosas, T443-0150. Clean, a/c, good restaurant with reasonable prices, swimming pool, parking in interior courtyard.

C-E Posada Don Giuseppe, Av San Isidro at 13 Calle, T/F442-2812. Bath, a/c (fan cheaper), hot water, TV, bar, restaurant. Comfortable.

D Colonial, Av 14 de Julio, between 6a and 7a Calle, T443-1953. A/c, sauna, jacuzzi, cable TV, rooftop bar, restaurant with varied menu, nice atmosphere, tourist office, tours available. A bit run-down.

D El Conquistador, Av La República, T443-3670. Cheaper with fan, shared bath, safe, clean, TV.

D Príncipe, 7 Calle between Av 14 de Julio and Av San Isidro, T443-0516. Cheaper with fan and shared bath, bar/restaurant, TV.

E Amsterdam 2001, 1 Calle, Barrio La Isla, T443-2311. Run by Dutch man Jan (Don Juan), good for backpackers, dormitory beds or rooms, with laundry, bit run-down, **Dutch Corner Café** for great breakfasts.

E Granada, Av Atlántida, 5-6 Calle, T443-2451, hotelparis@psinet.hn. Bath, a/c, clean, safe, cheaper with fan.

E Rotterdam Beach, next door to Amsterdam 2001 at 1 Calle, Barrio La Isla, T440-0321. On the beach, with bath, fan, clean, friendly, pleasant garden, good value. Recommended.

E Tropical, Av Atlántida between 4 y 5 Calle, T442-2565. With bathroom, fan, basic, small rooms, noisy, sell cold drinks and water.

F Las 5 Rosas, Calle 8 near Av La Bastilla, opposite Esso. Clean, simple rooms, bath, fan, laundry, good value.

F Pelican's Beat Beach Camp and Trailer Park on Bonitillo Playa some 6 km west of La Ceiba on the road to Tela, T995-4122. Camp or sling a hammock, both available for rent. Food available, trips to nearby cayes, sea kayaking and horse riding. Regular buses from La Ceiba to Bonitillo from outside Gran Hotel París.

Around La Ceiba p977
B Hotel Canadien, Sambo Creek, T440-2099, www.hotelcanadien.com. With double suite. Can arrange trips to Hog Islands for US$80 per boat.

B Villa Rhina, near the turn-off from the main road, Corozal, T443-1222, www.honduras.com/villarhina. With pool and restaurant.

C Villa Helen's, Sambo Creek about 35 minutes east of La Ceiba, T408-1137, www.villahelens.com. Good selection of rooms from simple to luxury. Pool and on the beach, with a good selection of activities in the quiet seclusion.

E Cabañas del Caribe, in Dantillo, 5 mins out of town on the road to Tela, T441-1421, T997-8746 (mob). 6 big cabins, some with jacuzzi, and 7 rooms on the beach, restaurant serving breakfast. Video screen in restaurant. Great place to relax. Call 1 day ahead to collect from town. Buses from La Ceiba for Dantillo every 30 mins.

E Hermanos Avila, Sambo Creek, simple hotel-restaurant, clean, food OK.

E Finca El Edén, in Santa Ana, 32 km west of La Ceiba, bertiharlos@yahoo.de. Rooms, dorms, hammocks and mattresses. Good views to the sea and good food.

Beaches around La Ceiba p979
E Chichi, Nuevo Armenia. 3 small rooms, fan, mosquito net, clean, good food available.

Parque Nacional Pico Bonito p979
Río Cangrejo area
B-E Omega Tours Jungle Lodge and Adventure Company, El Naranjo, T440-0334, www.omegatours.info. With wide range of options from simple rooms to comfortable *cabañas* and good food. Rafting and kayaking are available on the Río Cangrejal and trips to La Moskitia (see page 1015).

D Jungle River Lodge, on Río Cangrejal overlooking Pico Bonito, T440-1268, www.jungleriverlodge.com. Private rooms and dorms, natural swimming pools, restaurant and breathtaking views. Rafting, canopy tours, zip wires, hiking and mountain biking tours available. Activities include a free night's accommodation. Take Yaruka bus from main bus terminal, get off at Km 7; blue kayak marks entrance on river side of the road, call for arranged transport or join a tour.

D-E Cabañas del Bosque, up the road from Jungle River at Las Mangas: Nice rustic cabins with spectacular views in rooms and dorms.

Río Zacate area
LL-L The Lodge, Pico Bonito, T440-0388, T1-888-428-0221 (in the USA), www.picobonito.com. Honduras' 1st world-class ecolodge at the base of Parque Nacional Pico Bonito. 2 rooms, full-service nature lodge, swimming pool, gourmet restaurant, tours, guides, butterfly farm.

D Natural View Ecoturism Center, in El Pino, T386-9678. Very rustic cabins with access to trails in the vicinity. Cabins are built of adobe walls and thatched room, with a private bath, mosquito screens, but no power. Set in the middle of a plant nursery with a nice restaurant on premises. Efraín can help arrange several good trips nearby including a boat trip down the lower Río Zacate through mangroves to a farm located next to the beach, adjacent to Cuero y Salado.

D Posada del Buen Pastor, T950-3404. Has 4 rustic rooms on the upper storey of a private home with private bath, cable TV and fan.

Cuero y Salado Wildlife Reserve *p980*
D-E Refuge, T/I 443-0329, Fucsa's administration centre, on the banks of the Río Salado. Has photos, charts, maps, radio and a 2-room visitors' house, sleeping 4 in basic bunks, electricity 1800-2100. No mosquito nets, so avoid Sep and Oct if you can. Don't wear open footwear as snakes and yellow scorpions can be found here. Book in advance. Food available. There's also tent space for camping at the refuge.

Trujillo and around *p981, map p981*
AL-B Christopher Columbus Beach Resort, outside town along the beach, drive across airstrip, T434-4966. Has 72 rooms and suites, a/c, cable TV, swimming pool, restaurant, watersports, tennis, painted bright turquoise.
B Resort y Spa Agua Caliente Silin, Silin, on main road southeast of Trujillo, T434-4247.

Cabañas with cable TV, pool, thermal waters, restaurant, massage given by Pech Lastenia Hernández, very relaxing.
B Villa Brinkley (known locally as Miss Peggy's), on the mountain overlooking the bay, T434-4444. Good view, large rooms, wooden furniture, big bathrooms, sunken baths, fan, cheaper rooms in annex, Bit run-down.
C Campamento, Río Grande, Trujillo, 2 km along the road, T434-4244. Has a bar, good food, and 10 rooms, lovely setting, mountain backdrop, showers, palm trees, shade, basic but clean, ask about camping.
C O'Glynn, 3 blocks south of the plaza, T434 4592. Smart, clean, good rooms and bathrooms, a/c, TV, fridge in some rooms. Highly recommended.
C Trujillo, up the hill from the market, T434-4202. Fan, clean sheets daily, rooms with shower and toilet, TV, good value. Ask for a corner room, cockroaches in ground-floor rooms, nice breeze.
D Colonial, on plaza, T434-4011. With bath, hacienda style, restaurant (**El Bucanero**, see Sleeping), a/c, safe and clean.
E Mar de Plata, up street west, T434-4174. Upstairs rooms best, with bath, fan, friendly and helpful, beautiful view from room.
E-F Casa Kiwi, in Puerto Castilla, out of town, T/F434-3050, www.casakiwi.com. A 5-km, 15-min bus journey from town in an isolated location. Private rooms and dormitories, with kitchen and restaurant facilities. On a secluded beach with the benefits of internet, book swap, boat rides, horse riding, local trips and perfect for true relaxation. Buses to Puerto Castilla from the bus station every couple of hours, US$0.40. Watch when riding bikes in the area, especially at night.
E-F Catracho, 3 blocks south of church, then a block east, T434-4439. Basic, clean, noisy, no water at night, wooden cabins facing a garden, camping space US$1.50, parking.
F Buenos Aires, opposite **Catracho**, T434-4431. Monthly rates available, pleasant,

clean, peaceful, but cabins damp and many mosquitos, organizes tours to national park.
F Coco Pando, Barrio Cristales, behind beach, T434-4748. Garífuna-owned, clean, bright airy rooms, restaurant serving typical Garífuna dishes, runs popular weekend disco nearby.

Yoro and around p983
D Hotel Olanchito, Barrio Arriba, Calle La Palma, Olanchito, T446-6385. A/c.
E Nelson, Yoro. Comfortable rooms with bath, fan, modern, good restaurant/bar and nice outdoor swimming pool on 3rd floor, bar/disco on roof with marvellous views. Warmly recommended.
E Valle Aguán y Chabelito, 1 block north of Parque Central, Olanchito, T446-6718. Under same management as **Hotel Olanchito**. Single rooms, with a/c, double rooms with fan, all rooms with cable TV, best in town, with best restaurant.
E-F Palacio, on main street, Yoro. All rooms with bath and fan and a good resaurant.
F Aníbal, corner of Parque Central, Yoro. Excellent value, private or shared bath, clean, pleasant, wide balcony, restaurant.
F Colonial, Calle del Presidio, Olanchito. Good value, bath, fan, cheaper with shared bath, restaurant, parking.
F Hospedaje, Jocón. Clean and basic.

⊕ Eating

Puerto Cortés p974, map p974
†† Candiles, 2 Av, 7-8 Calle. Good grills, reasonable prices, open-air seating.
†† Pekín, 2 Av, 6-7 Calle. Chinese, a/c, excellent, good service, a bit pricey but recommended. Supermercado Pekín next door.
† Burger Boy's, 2 Av 8 Calle. Lively, popular with local teenagers.
† Comedor Piloto, 2 Av 1-2 Calle. Mon-Sat 0700-1800. Clean, satellite TV, fans, good value and service, popular.
† El Zaguán, 2 Av 5-6 Calle, closed Sun. Popular with locals, good for refreshments.

† Ilusión, 4 Calle E opposite Parque. Pastries, bread, coffee, nice for breakfast.
† Kasike's Restaurant-Bar-Peña, 3 Av y 9 Calle and **Carnitas Tapadera**, on same block. Recommended.
† Matt's, on same block as La Cabaña, a/c, nice bar, good food, not expensive.
† Wendy's, on the Parque. With inside play centre for children.

Cafés and ice cream parlours
† Repostería y Pastelería Plata, 3 Av and 2 Calle E, near Parque Central. Good bread and pastries, excellent cheap *almuerzo*, buffet-style, kids' playroom. Recommended.

Omoa p975
† Cayuquitos, on beachfront. Good-value meals all day, but service is very slow.
† Fisherman's Hut, 200 m to right of pier. Clean, good food, seafood, recommended. Don't expect early Sun breakfasts after the partying the night before.
† Sunset Playa, on beachfront at the southern end of the beach. Good food, open all day.

Cafés and juice bars
† Stanley, on the beach next door to Cayuquitos. Good value, with good shakes and juices.

Tela p975
The best eating is in the hotel restaurants.
††† Casa Azul, Barrio El Centro. Open till 2300. Run by Mark from Texas, subs, dinner specials, book exchange. Helpful.
††† Arecifes. Open Thu-Sun. Best bar and grill in town.
††† César Mariscos (see Sleeping, above). Open from 0700. Nice location on the beach, serves good seafood, very good breakfast menu.
††† Iguana Sports Bar, on road between 2 town bridges leading out of town. Open-air, music.
††† Luces del Norte, of Doña Mercedes, 11 Calle, 2 Av NE, towards beach from

Parque Central, next to **Hotel Puerto Rico**. Delicious seafood and good typical breakfasts, very popular, also good information and book exchange.

† Maya Vista, in hotel (see Sleeping, above). Run by Québécois Pierre, fine cuisine, 1 of the best in Tela. Highly recommended.

† Merendero Tía Carmen, at the the Mango Hotel. Good food, Honduran specialities including baleadas, good *almuerzo*.

† Bahía Azul, good fresh food, excellent sea food.

† Bella Italia, Italian-owned serving pizza, on walkway by the beach.

† El Pescador, San Juan. On the beach, great seafood in a fine setting.

† Sherwood, see Sleeping, above. Good food, popular, enjoy the view from the terrace, also opens 0700 and serves excellent breakfast.

† Tuty's Café, 9 Calle NE near Parque Central. Excellent fruit drinks and good cheap lunch specials, but slow service.

Cafés and ice cream parlours
Espresso Americano, in front of Central Park. Best place in town for coffee, latte, cappuccino, with internet and international calls. Very popular.

La Ceiba and around *p977, map p978*
† Cafetería Cobel, 7 Calle between Av Atlántida and 14 de Julio, 2 blocks from Parque Central. Could be the best *cafetería* in the entire country, very popular with locals, always crowded, good fresh food, daily specials, highly recommended. Unmissable.

† El Guapo's, corner of 14 de Julio and 14 Calle. Open daily for dinner. US-Honduran owned, good combination of international and typical Honduran cuisine

† La Chavelita, end of 4 Calle E, overlooking Río Cangrejal. Open daily for lunch and dinner. Seafood, popular.

† La Plancha, Calle 9, east of the cathedral. Open daily for lunch and dinner. Best steak house in La Ceiba, with good seafood dishes.

† Toto's, Av San Isidro, 17 Calle. Good *pizzería*.

† Cric Cric Burger, Av 14 de Julio, 3 Calle, facing attractive Parque Bonilla. Good fast food, several branches. Recommended.

† Expatriates Bar, Grill and Cigar Emporium, at Final de Calle 12, above Refricón, 3 blocks south, 3 blocks east of Parque Central. Thu-Tue 1600-2400. Honduran-American owners, very affordable, with good steak and shrimps. Free internet service for clients. Also have a branch open at the Cangrejal River, Km 9.

† Gallo Pinto, Calle 9, east of the cathedral. Affordable typical Honduran cuisine in a pleasant informal setting.

† Mango Tango, on 1 Calle. The best Ceibeño cuisine in the Zona Viva. Open daily for dinner from 1730. Menu includes fish, pork, chicken and beef dishes, and the best salad bar in town! They also have a nice sports bar.

† Masapán, 7 Calle, Av San Isidro-Av República. Daily 0630-2200. Self-service, varied, well-prepared choice of dishes, fruit juices, good coffee. Recommended.

† Palace, 9 Calle, Av 14 de Julio. Large Chinese menu, surf 'n' turf. Recommended.

† The Palm Restaurant, centrally located, ½ a block from Parque Central in the Banco de Occidente building. American-style food open daily for breakfast, lunch and dinner. TVs with international news and sports. Free internet service for clients.

† Paty's, Av 14 de Julio between 6 and 7 Calle. Milkshakes, wheatgerm, cereals, donuts, etc, purified water, clean. Opposite is an excellent pastry shop. There are 2 more **Paty's**, at 8 Calle E and the bus terminal.

Around La Ceiba *p977*
† Kabasa, Sambo Creek. Seafood Garífuna-style, bar, delightful location.

Trujillo and around *p981, map p981*
Don't miss the coconut bread, a speciality of the Garífuna.

† Galaxia, 1 block west of plaza. Good seafood, popular with locals.

† Oasis, opposite HSBC. Outdoor seating, Canadian owned, good meeting place, information board, good food, bar, English books for sale, book exchange, local tours.

¶ **Bahía Bar**, T434-4770, on the beach by the landing strip next to **Christopher Columbus**. Popular with expats, also Hondurans at weekends, vegetarian food, showers, toilets.

¶ **Don Perignon**, uphill from Pantry. Some Spanish dishes, good local food, cheap.

¶ **El Bucanero**, on main plaza. A/c, video, good breakfast, *desayuno típico*.

¶ **Pantry**, 1½ blocks from the park. Garífuna cooking and standard menu, cheap pizzas, a/c.

⊙ Entertainment

La Ceiba and around *p977, map p978*
Iguana Sports Bar Discoteque is the place to go.
La Casona, 4a Calle. Thu-Sat, 2000-0400. Most popular nightspot in town. Karaoke bar, good music.
Monaster, 1 Calle. Thu-Sat 2000-0400. Nice setting, good a/c. Several others along 1 Calle.

Trujillo and around *p981, map p981*
Head to **Rincón de los Amigos** or **Rogue's** if you're looking for drink at the end of the day. Also try the **Gringo Bar** and **Bahía Bar**. In **Barrio Cristales** at weekends there's *punta* music and a lively atmosphere. Recommended.
The cinema shows current US releases.

✤ Festivals and events

Puerto Cortés *p974, map p974*
Aug Noche Veneciana on 3rd Sat.

Tela *p975*
Jun Fiesta de San Antonio.

La Ceiba and around *p977, map p978*
15-28 May San Isidro La Ceiba's patron saint's celebrations continue for 2 weeks,

the highlight being the international carnival on the 3rd Sat in May, when La Ceiba parties long and hard to the Afro-Caribbean beat of *punta* rock.

⊙ Shopping

Puerto Cortés *p974, map p974*
There is a souvenir shop, **Marthita's**, in the customs administration building (opposite Hondutel). The market in the town centre is quite interesting, 3 Calle between 2 and 3 Av. **Supertienda Paico** is on the Parque.

La Ceiba and around *p977, map p978*
Carrion Department Store, Av San Isidro with 7A Calle. **Deli Mart** late-night corner store on 14 de Julio, round corner from internet café, shuts at 2300. **El Regalito**, good-quality souvenirs at reasonable prices in small passage by large Carrión store. **T Boot**, store for hiking boots, Calle 1, east of Av San Isidro, T443-2499. **Supermarket Super Ceibena**, 2 on Av 14 de Julio and 6A Calle.

Trujillo and around *p981, map p981*
Garí-Arte Souvenir, T434-4207, in the centre of Barrio Cristales, is recommended for authentic Garífuna souvenirs. Owned by Ricardo Lacayo and open daily.
Tienda Souvenir Artesanía next to Hotel Emperador, handicrafts, hand-painted toys. 3 supermarkets in the town centre.

▲ Activities and tours

Puerto Cortés *p974, map p974*
Bahía Travel/Maya Rent-a-Car, 3 Av 3 Calle, T665-2102.
Irema, 2 Av 3-4 Calle, T665-1506.
Ocean Travel, Plaza Eng, 3 Av 2 Calle, T665-0913.

Tela *p975*
Garífuna Tours, southwest corner of Parque Central, T448-2904, www.garifunatours.com,

knowledgeable and helpful with mountain bike hire, US$5 per day. Day trips to Punta Sal (US$31), Los Micos lagoon (US$31) and Punta Izopo (US$24). La Ceiba–Cayos Cochinos (US$51), La Ceiba–Cuero Salado (US$68), Pico Bonito (US$33). Also trips further afield to La Ceiba, Mosquita (4 days, US$499) and a shuttle service between San Pedro Sula and La Ceiba, US$18 per person. Also La Ceiba to Copán, US$45. Good value. Highly recommended.
Honduras Caribbean Tours, T448-2623, www.honduras-caribbean.com. Wide range of tours and treks throughout Honduras specializing in North coast.

Around Tela p976
Garífuna Tours (address above) in Tela, run recommended tours for US$31 to Parque Nacional Punta Sal, food extra.

La Ceiba and around p977, map p978
Ask around to find a tour that suits your needs and to verify credentials.
Caribbean Travel Agency, run by Ann Crichton, Av San Isidro, Edif Hermanos Kawas, Apdo Postal 66, T/F443-1360, helpful, shares office with **Ríos Honduras**, see below.
Garífuna Tours, Av San Isidro 1 Calle, T440-3252, www.garifunatours.com. Day trips into Pico Bonito National Park (US$34 per person), Cuero y Salado (US$59), rafting on the Cangrejal (US$34), trips out to Cayos Cochinos (US$49) and a shuttle service to Tela (US$1).
Junglas River Rafting, T440-1268, www.jungleriverlodge.com.
La Ceiba Ecotours, Av San Isidro, 1st block, 50 m from beach, T/F443-4207, hiking and riding in Parque Nacional Pico Bonito, visits to other nearby reserves, whitewater rafting, trips to La Mosquitia.
La Moskitia Eco Aventuras, Av 14 de Julio at Parque Manuel Bonilla, T/F442-0104, www.honduras.com/moskitia, Jorge Satavero, very knowledgeable, enthusiastic and flexible. Specializes in trips to Mosquitia. Recommended.

Omega Tours, T440-0334, www.omega tours.info, runs rafting and kayaking trips on the Río Cangrejal, jungle hikes, and own hotel 30 mins upstream. Also tours to La Mosquitia ranging from easy adventure tours of 4 days up to 13-day expeditions. Prices drop dramatically with more than 2 people.
Ríos Honduras, T443-0780, office@ rioshonduras.com, offering whitewater rafting, trips on the Río Cangrejal, spectacular, reservations 1 day in advance.

Cuero y Salado Wildlife Reserve p980
Although it is possible to go to the Salado and hire a villager and his boat, a qualified guide will show you much more. It is essential to bring a hat and sun lotion with you. Travel agencies in La Ceiba run tours there, but **Fucsa** arranges visits and owns the only accommodation in the reserve. Before going, check with **Fucsa** in La Ceiba. Although the office only has basic information, the people are helpful and there are displays and books about the flora and fauna to be found in the park. A guide and kayak for a 1-hr trip costs about US$10. Boatmen charge about US$20 for a 2-hr trip or US$40 for 5 hrs (6-7 persons maximum), US$6-7 for the guide.

Trujillo and around p981, map p981
Hacienda Tumbador Crocodile Reserve is privately owned, accessible only by 4WD and with guide, US$5 entry.

Transport

Puerto Cortés p974, map p974
Boat
To Guatemala Information from Ocean Travel at 3 Av, 2 blocks west of plaza.

To Belize Boats connecting to Belize leave from beside the bridge over the lagoon (Barra La Laguna), buy tickets at the blue wooden shack next to *joyería* near **Los Coquitos** bar just before bridge. Daily 0800-1700. The **Gulf Cruza** launch leaves Puerto Cortés on Mon at

1100, for **Mango Creek** and on to **Placencia**, 4 hrs arriving around 1340, US$50.

Remember to get your exit stamp. To be sure of getting an exit stamp go to Immigration in town. If arriving from Belize and heading on straight away you don't need to go into town to catch a bus. Get on to the bridge, cross over the other side and keep walking 200 m to the main road. Buses going past are going to San Pedro Sula and beyond.

Bus
Virtually all buses now arrive and leave from 4 Av 2-4 Calle. Bus service at least hourly to **San Pedro Sula**, US$2.30, 45 mins, Citul (4 Av between 3 and 4 Calle) and **Impala** (4 Av y 3 Calle, T255-0606). Expresos del Caribe, Expresos de Citul and Expresos del Atlantic all have minibuses to **San Pedro Sula**. Bus to **Omoa** and **Tegucigalpita** from 4 Av, old school bus, loud music, very full, guard your belongings. Citral Costeños go to the Guatemalan border, 4-5 Av, 3C E. Regular buses leave for **Omoa** (US$0.70) at 0730 to get to **Corinto** at the Guatemalan border.

Omoa *p975*
Boat Boats leave for **Lívingston**, Guatemala, on Tue and Fri around 1000. Ask around to confirm. Ask at **Fisherman's Hut** for Sr Juan Ramón Menjivar.

Bus Frequent buses to the border at 1000, 1400 and 1700. See page 975 for border-crossing information.

Tela *p975*
Bike Hire from Garífuna Tours, 9 Calle y Parque Central (see page 990).

Bus Catisa or Tupsa lines from San Pedro Sula to **El Progreso** (US$0.50) where you must change to go on to **Tela** (3 hrs in total) and **La Ceiba** (last bus at 1900). On Catisa bus ask to be let off at the petrol station on the main road, then take a taxi to the beach,

US$0.50. Also 1st-class service with **Hedman Alas** at 1010, 1415 and 1810.

Bus from Tela to **El Progreso** every 30 mins, US$1.50. To **La Ceiba**, every 30 mins, from 0410 until 1800, 2 hrs, US$2. Direct to **Tegucigalpa**, Traliasa, 1 a day from Hotel Los Arcos, US$4.50, same bus to **La Ceiba** (this service avoids San Pedro Sula). To **Copán**, leave by 0700 via El Progreso and San Pedro Sula to arrive same day. To **Trujillo** through **Savá**, **Tocoa** and **Corocito**.

Shuttle Garífuna Tours, see page 990, offers a shuttle service direct to **San Pedro**, US$18 and **Copán Ruinas**, US$45.

Around Tela *p976*
Bus To Triunfo de la Cruz, US$0.40 (about 5 km, if no return bus, walk to main road where buses pass).

La Ceiba and around *p977, map p978*
Air
For La Mosquitia see page 1015.

Golosón (LCE), 10 km out of town. See Getting there, page 920, for international services. For details of flights to Bay Islands, see page 995. Isleña (T443-0179 airport), flies to **San Pedro Sula**, **Trujillo**, **Puerto Lempira**, **Roatán** and **Guanaja**; Taca fly to **Tegucigalpa** and **San Pedro Sula**. Sosa, the most reliable domestic airline flies to **Utila**, **Roatán**, **San Pedro Sula**, **Tegus** and others. Office on Parque Central, T443-1399. Atlantic Air, T/F440-2347. Sosa, Atlantic and Isleña all have flights. At weekends there are some charter flights that may be better than scheduled flights. Taxi to town US$8 per person or walk 200 m to the main road and share for US$2 with other passengers, also buses from bus station near Cric Cric Burger at end 3 Av, US$0.15. Intercity buses pass by the entrance.

Boat
Ferry schedules from the Muelle de Cabotaje, T445-1795 or T445-5056, with daily services as follows: La Ceiba–Utila 0815, 0930 and 1630, Utila–La Ceiba, 0630, 0945 and 1430, US$15.

La Ceiba–Roatán, 1000 and 1600, Roatán–La Ceiba, 0700 and 1300, US$18. Boats leave from Muelle de Cabotaje. Too far to walk, about 15-min taxi ride from town, US$2-3 per person if sharing with 4 people, buses available from centre of town.

Trips to the Hog Islands can be arranged, call T441-5987 or through **Garifuna Tours** restaurant. US$65 for a boat load.

Bus
Taxis from centre to bus terminal, which is a little way west of town (follow Blv 15 de Septiembre), cost US$1 per person, or there are buses from Parque Central. Most buses leave from here. **Traliasa**, **Etrusca** and **Cristina** bus service to **Tegucigalpa** via Tela several daily, US$6, avoiding San Pedro Sula (US$1 to Tela, 2 hrs); also hourly service to **San Pedro Sula**, US$2 (3-4 hrs). **Empresa Tupsa** direct to **San Pedro Sula** almost hourly from 0530 until 1800. Also 1st class with **Hedman Alas** – take taxi to separate terminal. To **Trujillo**, 3 hrs direct, 4½ hrs local (very slow), every 1½ hrs or so, US$3; daily bus La Ceiba–Trujillo–Santa Rosa de Aguán. To **Olanchito**, US$1, 3 hrs; also regular buses to **Sonaguera**, **Tocoa**, **Balfate**, **Isletas**, **San Esteban** and other regional locations.

Car
Car rental Maya Rent-a-Car, Hotel La Quinta, T443-3071. **Dino's Rent-a-Car**, Hotel Partenon Beach, T443-0404. **Molinari** in Hotel París on Parque Central, T/F443-0055.

Beaches around La Ceiba p979
Bus To Nuevo Armenia from La Ceiba at 1100 US$0.75, 2½ hrs. At the bus stop is the office where boat trips are arranged to **Cayos Cochinos**, US$10, trips start at 0700.

Trujillo and around p981, map p981
Boat Cargo boats leave for **Mosquitia** (ask all captains at the dock, wait up to 3 days, see page 1015), the **Bay Islands** (very difficult) and Honduran ports to the west. Ask at the jetty. The trip to **Puerta Lempira** costs about US$15.

Bus Trujillo can be reached by bus from **San Pedro Sula**, **Tela** and **La Ceiba** by a paved road through Savá, Tocoa and Corocito. From **La Ceiba** it is 3 hrs by direct bus, 4 hrs by local. 3 direct Cotraibal buses in early morning from Trujillo. Bus from **Tegucigalpa** (Comayagüela) with Cotraibal, 7 Av between 10 and 11 Calle, US$6, 9 hrs; some buses to the capital go via La Unión, which is not as safe a route as via San Pedro Sula. To **San Pedro Sula**, 5 daily 0200-0800, US$5. Public transport also to **San Esteban** and **Juticalpa** (leave from in front of church at 0400, but check locally, arriving 1130, US$5.20). Bus to **Santa Fe** at 0930, US$0.40, leaves from outside Glenny's Super Tienda. To **Santa Rosa de Aguán** and **Limón** daily.

Yoro and around p983
Bus Hourly bus service to **El Progreso**, several daily to **Sulaco**.

❶ Directory

Puerto Cortés p974, map p974
Banks All banks open Mon-Fri 0800-1700, Sat 0830-1130. HSBC, 2 Av, 2 Calle. Banco de Comercio cashes TCs. Banco de Occidente, 3 Av 4 Calle E, cashes Amex TCs, accepts Visa/MasterCard. Banco Ficensa has ATM for MC and Amex only, 2 Av, 2C. Banks along 2 Av E, include Atlántida (2 Av, 3-4 Calle, has Visa ATM), Bamer, and HSBC. **Immigration** Migración 5 Av y 3-4 Calle next to Port Captain's office, 0800-1800. **Internet** Lema Computers, 5-6 Av, 2C, open Mon-Sat. **Medical services** Policlínica, 3 Av just past 1 Calle, open 24 hrs. **Post office** next door to Hondutel. **Telephone** Hondutel, dock entrance, Gate 6, fax and AT&T. Direct to USA.

Omoa p975
Banks Banco de Occidente does not take credit cards, but will cash TCs. Some shops will change dollars. Ask around. **Immigration** Migración has an office on the main road opposite Texaco. If you come

from Guatemala by car you have to get a police escort from Corinto to Puerto Cortés. **Internet** Near the beach.

Tela *p975*
Banks Banco Atlántida (with ATM), HSBC, 9 C 3 Av, Visa and MasterCard cash advances and changes TCs. Also try **Bamer** and **Atlantida**. Casa de Cambio La Teleña, 4 Av, 9 Calle NE for US$, TCs and cash. Exchange dealers on street outside post office.
Immigration Migración is at the corner of 3 Av and 8 Calle. **Internet** Service at the Mango Café. **Language classes** Mango Café Spanish School, US$115 for 4 hrs a day, Mon-Fri with a local tour on Sat, T448-2856, www.mangocafe.net. **Laundry** El Centro, 4 Av 9 Calle, US$2 wash and dry. Lavandería Banegas, Pasaje Centenario, 3 Calle 1 Av. Lavandería San José, 1 block northeast of market. **Medical services** Centro Médico CEMEC, 8 Av 7 Calle NE, T/F448-2456. Open 24 hrs, X-rays, operating theatre, smart, well equipped. **Post office and telephone** Both on 4 Av NE. Fax service and collect calls to Europe available and easy at Hondutel.

La Ceiba and around *p977, map p978*
Banks HSBC, 9 Calle, Av San Isidro, and Banco Atlántida, Av San Isidro and 6-7 Calle, have ATM that accepts Visa and they will cash TCs at good rates. Cash advances on Visa and MasterCard from BAC on Av San Isidro opposite Hotel Iberia between 5 and 6 Calle; also Amex. Honducard, Av San Isidro for Visa, next to Farmacia Aurora. Better rates for US$ cash from cambistas in the bigger hotels (and at travel agency next door to Hotel Príncipe). Money exchange, at back of Supermercado Los Almendros, 7 Calle, Av San Isidro with Av 14 de Julio, daily 0800-1200, 1400-1800, T443-2720, good rates for US$ cash and TCs. **Internet** Hondusoft, in Centro Panayotti, 7A Calle between San Isidro and Av 14 de Julio, Mon-Fri 0800-2000, Sat 0800-1800, discount 1800-2000 when US$3 instead of

US$6 per hr. La Ceiba Internet Café, Barrio El Iman, 9 Calle, T440-1505, Mon-Sat 0900-2000, US$3 per hr. Iberia, next to Hotel Iberia, US$0.80 per hr. Intercon Internet Café, Av San Isidro, opposite Atlántida ATM. **Language schools** Best to do some research and look at the options. Worth considering are: Centro Internacional de Idiomas, T/F440-1557, www.honduras spanish.com, provides a range of classes 5 days for US$150, with hotel option US$290, with branches in Utila and Roatán. Central America Spanish School, Av San Isidro No 110, Calle 12 y 13, next to Foto Indio, T/F440-1707, www.ca-spanish.com, US$150 for the week, homestay also an option adding US$70, also have branches on Utila and Roatan. **Medical services** Doctors: Dr Gerardo Meradiaga, Edif Rodríguez García, Ap No 4, Blv 15 de Septiembre, general practitioner, speaks English. Dr Siegfried Seibt, Centro Médico, 1 Calle and Av San Isidro, speaks German. Hospital: Vincente D'Antoni, Av Morazán, T443-2264, private, well equipped. **Post office** Av Morazán, 13 Calle O. **Telephone** Hondutel for international telephone calls is at 2 Av, 5 y 6 Calle E.

Trujillo and around *p981, map p981*
Banks Banco Atlántida on Parque Central and HSBC, both cash US$, TCs and handle Visa. Banco de Occidente also handles MasterCard and Western Union. **Immigration** Opposite Mar de Plata. **Internet** Available in town. **Laundry** Next to Disco Orfaz, wash and dry US$2.50. **Libraries** Library in middle of square. **Medical services** Hospital on main road east off square towards La Ceiba. **Post office and telephone** Post office and Hondutel, F434-4200, 1 block up from church.

Yoro and around *p983*
Banks Banco Atlántida on Parque Central. **Post office and telephone** Post office and Hondutel 1 block from Parque Central.

Bay Islands

A string of islands off the northern coast of Honduras, the Bay Islands are the country's most popular tourist attraction. Warm, clear Caribbean waters provide excellent reef diving – some of the cheapest in the Caribbean. Equally enjoyable are the white-sand beaches, tropical sunsets and the relaxed atmosphere which positively encourages you to take to your hammock, lie back and relax. The culture is far less Latino than on the mainland. English is spoken by many and there are still Black Carib descendants of those deported from St Vincent in 1797. ⇥ *For listings, see pages 1001-1013.*

Ins and outs

Getting there Transport to the Bay Islands is easy and there are regular flights with Isleña, Sosa and **Atlantic Airlines** from La Ceiba (T440-2343) and San Pedro Sula (T433-6016) to Utila and Roatán. **Taca** has an international service from Miami to Roatán. There is also a daily boat service from La Ceiba to Roatán and Utila. **Spirit Airlines** is going to provide direct flights from Fort Lauderdale (Miami) to La Ceiba from May 2009.

The islands → *www.caribbeancoast.com/bayislands/index.cfm.*
The beautiful Bay Islands (**Islas de la Bahía**), of white sandy beaches, coconut palms and gentle sea breezes, form an arc in the Caribbean, some 32 km north of La Ceiba. The three main islands are **Utila**, **Guanaja** and, the largest and most developed, **Roatán**. At the eastern end of Roatán are three smaller islands: **Morat**, **Santa Elena**, and **Barbareta**, with many islets and cayes to explore. Closest to the mainland are the small, palm-fringed **Hog Islands**, more attractively known as **Cayos Cochinos**.

The underwater environment is one of the main attractions and is rich and extensive; **reefs** surround the islands, often within swimming distance of the shore. **Caves** and caverns are a common feature, with a wide variety of **sponges** and the best collection of **pillar coral** in the Caribbean. There are many protected areas including the **Marine Parks** of Turtle Harbour on Utila, and Sandy Bay/West End on Roatán, which has permanent mooring buoys at the popular dive sites to avoid damage from anchors. Several other areas have been proposed as marine reserves by the Asociación Hondureña de Ecología: the Santuario Marino de Utila, Parque Nacional Marino Barbareta and Parque Nacional Marino Guanaja. The Bay Islands have their own conservation association (see under Roatán, below).

The traditional industry is fishing, mostly shellfish, with fleets based at French Harbour; but the supporting boat-building is a dying industry. Tourism is now a major source of income, particularly because of the scuba-diving attractions. English-speaking blacks constitute the majority of the population, particularly on Roatán. Utila has a population which is about half black and half white, the latter of British descent mainly from the settlers from Grand Cayman who arrived in 1830. Columbus anchored here in 1502, during his fourth voyage. In the 18th century the islands were the base for English, French and Dutch buccaneers. They were in British hands for over a century, but were finally ceded to Honduras in 1859. Latin Hondurans have been moving to the islands from the mainland in recent years.

The islands are very beautiful, but beware of the strong sun (the locals bathe in T-shirts), sandflies and other insects. Basic etiquette for snorkelling and diving applies. Snorkellers and divers should not stand on or even touch the coral reefs; any contact, even the turbulence from a fin, will kill the delicate organisms.

→ *Area: 41 sq km.*

Utila is the cheapest and least developed of the islands and has a very laid-back ambience. Only 32 km from La Ceiba, it is low lying, with just two hills, Pumpkin and the smaller Stewarts, either side of the town known as **East Harbour**. The first inhabitants were the Paya and there is scant archaeological evidence of their culture. Later the island was used by pirates; Henry Morgan is reputed to have hidden booty in the caves. The population now is descended from Black Caribs and white Cayman Islanders with a recent influx from mainland Honduras. Independence Day (15 September) festivities, including boxing and climbing greased poles, are worth staying for. More information available at www.aboututila.com.

Around Utila

There are no big resorts on the island, although a couple of small, lodge-style, upmarket places have opened, otherwise the accommodation is rather basic. Sunbathing and swimming is not particularly good – people come for the diving. **Jack Neal Beach** has white sand with good snorkelling and swimming. **Chepee's White Hole** at the end of Blue Bayou peninsula has a beach for swimming. Snorkelling is also good offshore by the Blue Bayou restaurant, a 20-minute walk from town, but you will be charged US$1 for use of the facilities. There are hammocks and a jetty, which is great for fishing at sunset, and the only place to get away from the terrible sandflies. **Bandu Beach** is another option on the northern end of the island. Sunchairs, drinks and clean toilets are provided. Buy a drink or pay a US$2 charge. There is also sandfly relief at **Big Bight**, **Redcliff** and **Rocky Point**.

You can hike to **Pumpkin Hill** (about 4 km down the lane by **HSBC**, bikes recommended) where there are some freshwater caves with a beach nearby (watch out for sharp coral). It is also possible to walk on a trail from the airfield to Big Bight and the iron shore on the east coast, about 2 km, exploring tidal pools; nice views and beach but it is rocky so wear sandals.

You can visit the **Iguana Station** ⓘ *Mon, Wed and Fri 1400-1700, T2425-3946, www.utila-iguana.de, US$2.20*, a short walk up hill from the fire station – follow the signs.

Utila

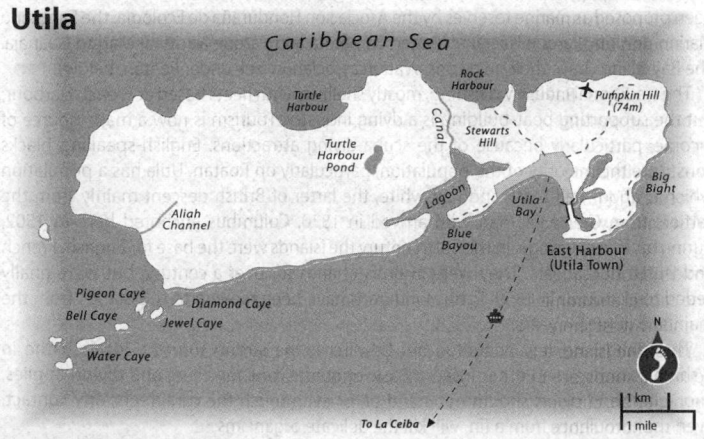

Utila's dive sites

There are currently around 50 dive sites around Utila, where permanent moorings have been established to minimize damage to the coral reef. Although the reef is colourful and varied, there are not a lot of fish, and lobster have almost disappeared. The dive sites are close to shore at about 20 m depth but they are all boat dives. Diving off the north coast is more spectacular, with drop-offs, canyons and caves. Fish are more numerous, helped by the establishment of the **Turtle Harbour Marine Reserve and Wildlife Refuge**.

Paying volunteer options possible. They also offer great trips through the mangroves to explore the more hidden parts of the island for around US$10.

Utila's cayes

A 20-minute motorboat ride from East Harbour are the cayes, a chain of small islands populated by fisherfolk off the southwest coast of Utila, which are known as the Cayitos de Utila. **Jewel Caye** and **Pigeon Caye** are connected by a bridge and are inhabited by a fishing community, which reportedly settled there to get away from the sandflies on Utila. Basic accommodation and food is available. **Diamond Caye** is privately owned, the snorkelling offshore here is excellent. **Water Caye** is a coconut island with 'white hole' sandy areas and with wonderful bathing in the afternoons. It is the only place where you can camp, sling a hammock or, in an emergency, sleep in or under the house of the caretaker; take food and fresh water, or rent the caretaker's canoe and get supplies from Jewel Caye.

Roatán ⊕⊕⊕⊖▲⊖⊕ ▶▶ pp1001-1013. Colour map 6, B3.

→ *Area:127 sq km.*

Roatán is the largest of the islands and has been developed quite extensively. But its idyllic charm is still apparent and quiet beaches are often just a short walk away. There is a paved road running from West End through to French Harbour, almost to Oak Ridge, continuing unpaved to Punta Gorda and Wilkes Point, as well as other unmade roads.

Tourist offices Bay Islands Conservation Association **(BICA)** ① *Edif Cooper, Calle Principal, Coxen Hole, T/F445-1424 (Farley Smith, an American volunteer, is extremely helpful)*, manages the Sandy Bay/West End Marine Reserve and has lots of information about the reef and its conservation. Map of the island at about 1:50,000 supplied by **Antonio E Rosales**, T445-1559. Local information maps are also available from **Librería Casi Todo**, West End, www.roatan.com provides local information about the island.

Coxen Hole

The capital and administrative centre of the department, Coxen Hole, or Roatán City, is on the southwest shore. Planes land and boats dock here and you can get transport to other parts of the island. It is a scruffy little town with not much of tourist interest but some souvenir shops are opening. Besides being the seat of the local government, it has immigration, customs and the law courts. There is a post office, supermarket, handicraft shops, photo shops, banks, travel agents, a bookshop and various other stores. Buses leave from outside the supermarket. All public transport starts or ends here. If taxis are shared, they are *colectivos* and charge the same as buses.

Sandy Bay

A short journey from Coxen Hole, en route to West End, is Sandy Bay, one of the quieter towns on the island. The **Carambola Botanical Gardens** ① *daily 0700-1700, US$3, guided tours or nature trails*, created in 1985, contain many flowering plants, ferns and varieties of trees which can be explored on a network of trails – it is well worth a visit. The **Roatán Museum** ① *US$4*, has displays covering the history of the island, with plenty of information about the pirates who called Roatán home, and a collection of artefacts.

West End

Five minutes by road beyond Sandy Bay, the popular community of West End, at the western tip of the island, is the most popular place to stay. It's a narrow beach on a palm-fringed bay with a distinctly laid-back atmosphere. The **Sandy Bay/West End Marine Park** protects marine life in the area and large numbers of fish have flourished along the coast creating spectacular snorkelling. See www.roatanmarinepark.com for more details. There are numerous good foreign and local restaurants with lots of pizza/pasta places, as well as hotels, *cabañas* and rooms to rent for all budgets. It is a stiff walk from Coxen Hole over the hills (three hours) to West End, or take the bus on the paved road (US$1; 20 minutes).

West Bay

A beautiful clean beach with excellent snorkelling on the reef, particularly at the west end, where the reef is only 10-20 m offshore and the water is shallow right up to where the wall drops off 50-75 m out and scuba-diving begins. Paradise comes at a price and the sandflies here are a nightmare, but there are a couple of jetties where you can escape them. Take your own food and drinks, and insect repellent. Developers have discovered the delights of West Bay and the atmosphere is changing fast. Apartments, hotels, bars and restaurants are springing up.

East of Coxen Hole

French Harbour, on the south coast, with its shrimping and lobster fleet, is the main fishing port of Roatán. There is no beach and there are two seafood-packing plants. The

① Roatán

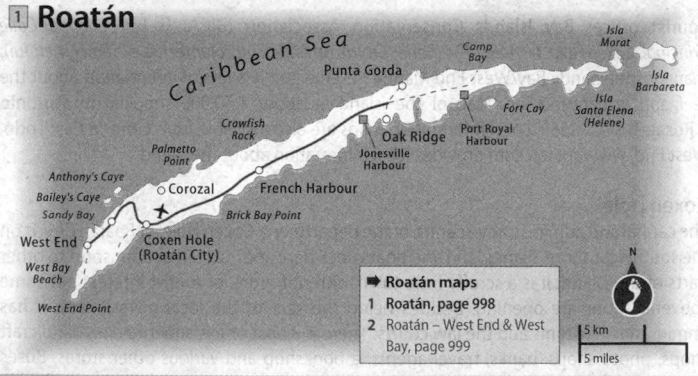

→ Roatán maps
1 Roatán, page 998
2 Roatán – West End & West Bay, page 999

5 km
5 miles

road passes Coleman's (Midway) Bakery, where you can buy freshly baked products. The bay is protected by the reef and small cayes, which provide safe anchorage. Roatan Dive and Yacht Club and Romeos Marina (at Brick Bay) offer services for visiting yachts. Several charter yachts are based here. There are a few cheap, clean places to stay, as well

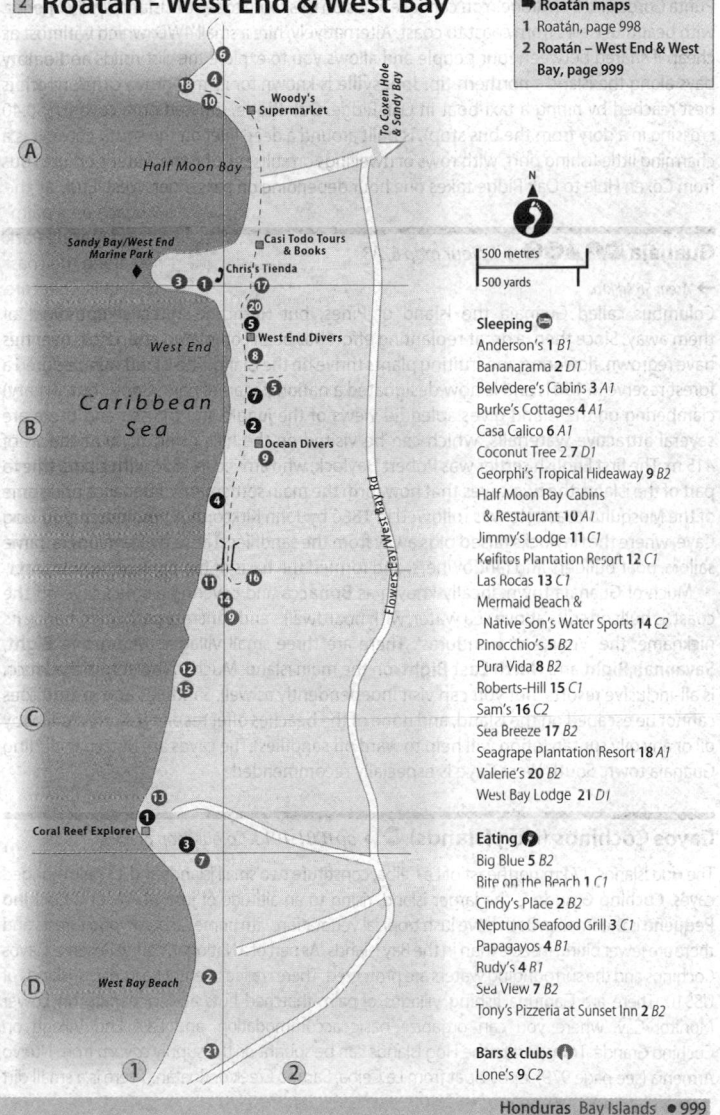

2 Roatán - West End & West Bay

Roatán maps
1 Roatán, page 998
2 Roatán – West End & West Bay, page 999

Woody's Supermarket

To Coxen Hole & Sandy Bay

Half Moon Bay

Sandy Bay/West End Marine Park

Casi Todo Tours & Books

Chris's Tienda

West End

West End Divers

Caribbean Sea

Ocean Divers

Flowers Bay/West Bay Rd

Coral Reef Explorer

West Bay Beach

500 metres
500 yards

Sleeping

Anderson's **1** *B1*
Bananarama **2** *D1*
Belvedere's Cabins **3** *A1*
Burke's Cottages **4** *A1*
Casa Calico **6** *A1*
Coconut Tree 2 **7** *D1*
Georphi's Tropical Hideaway **9** *B2*
Half Moon Bay Cabins & Restaurant **10** *A1*
Jimmy's Lodge **11** *C1*
Keifitos Plantation Resort **12** *C1*
Las Rocas **13** *C1*
Mermaid Beach & Native Son's Water Sports **14** *C2*
Pinocchio's **5** *B2*
Pura Vida **8** *B2*
Roberts-Hill **15** *C1*
Sam's **16** *C2*
Sea Breeze **17** *B2*
Seagrape Plantation Resort **18** *A1*
Valerie's **20** *B2*
West Bay Lodge **21** *D1*

Eating

Big Blue **5** *B2*
Bite on the Beach **1** *C1*
Cindy's Place **2** *B2*
Neptuno Seafood Grill **3** *C1*
Papagayos **4** *B1*
Rudy's **4** *B1*
Sea View **7** *B2*
Tony's Pizzeria at Sunset Inn **2** *B2*

Bars & clubs

Lone's **9** *C2*

as expensive hotels and dive resorts. Eldon's Supermarket is open daily and has a range of imported US food. **Gios Restaurant** and **Casa Romeos** serve top-quality seafood.

Across the island

The main road goes across the mountain ridge along the island with side roads to Jonesville, Punta Gorda and Oak Ridge. You can take a bus on this route to see the island's hilly interior, with beautiful views from coast to coast. Alternatively, hire a small 4WD, which is almost as cheap if shared between four people and allows you to explore the dirt roads and empty bays along the island's northern tip. **Jonesville** is known for its mangrove canal, which is best reached by hiring a taxi boat in Oak Ridge. **Oak Ridge**, situated on a caye (US$0.40 crossing in a dory from the bus stop), is built around a deep inlet on the south coast. It is a charming little fishing port, with rows of dwellings on stilts built on the water's edge (a bus from Coxen Hole to Oak Ridge takes one hour depending on passengers, US$1.10).

Guanaja ⊕🖉🔺⊖🌢 ➤ Colour map 6, A3.

➔ *Area: 56 sq km.*

Columbus called Guanaja the Island of Pines, but Hurricane Mitch swept most of them away. Since then, a great replanting effort has been completed and, until the pines have regrown, flowering and fruiting plants thrive on the island. The island was declared a forest reserve in 1961, and is now designated a national marine park. Good (but sweaty) clambering on the island gives splendid views of the jungle and the sea and there are several attractive waterfalls, which can be visited on the hills rising to the summit of 415 m. The first English settler was Robert Haylock, who arrived in 1856 with a land title to part of the island, the two cayes that now form the main settlement of Bonacca and some of the Mosquito coast. He was followed in 1866 by John Kirkconnell who purchased Hog Caye, where the Haylocks raised pigs away from the sandflies. These two families became sailors, boat builders and landowners, and formed the basis of the present population.

Much of Guanaja town, locally known as **Bonacca** and covering a small caye off the coast, is built on stilts above sea water, with boardwalks and concrete pathways, hence its nickname: the 'Venice of Honduras'. There are three small villages, **Mangrove Bight**, **Savannah Bight** and **North East Bight**, on the main island. Much of the accommodation is all-inclusive resorts, but you can visit independently as well. Sandflies and mosquitoes cannot be escaped on the island, and none of the beaches offer respite (coconut oil, baby oil or any oily suntan lotion will help to ward off sandflies).The cayes are better, including Guanaja town. South West Caye is especially recommended.

Cayos Cochinos (Hog Islands) ⊖ ➤ *pp1001-1013. Colour map 6, B3.*

The Hog Islands, 17 km northeast of La Ceiba, constitute two small islands and 13 palm-fringed cayes. **Cochino Grande** is the larger island, rising to an altitude of just 143 m, and **Cochino Pequeño** is the smaller. Both have lush tropical vegetation with primeval hardwood forests and there are fewer biting insects than in the Bay Islands. As part of a National Marine Reserve, Cayos Cochinos and the surrounding waters are protected. There is a fee to enter parts of the islands of US$10. There are Garífuna fishing villages of palm-thatched huts at Chachauate on Lower Monitor Cay, where you can organize basic accommodation, and East End Village on Cochino Grande. Transport to the Hog Islands can be sought on the supply *cayuco* from Nuevo Armenia (see page 979), or by boat from La Ceiba, Sambo Creek or Roatán. There is a small dirt airstrip. Dug-out canoes are the local form of transport. The islands are privately owned and access to most of the cayes is limited, being occupied only by caretakers.

◉ Bay Islands listings

For Sleeping and Eating price codes and other relevant information, see Essentials pages 45-48.

● Sleeping

Utila *p996, map p996*
L-AL Laguna Beach Resort, on point opposite Blue Bayou, T/F668-68452, www.utila.com. Comfortable lodge, with bungalows each with own jetty, 8-day package includes meals and diving US$970, non diver US$840. Fishing offered, can accommodate maximum of 40.
L-AL Utila Lodge Resort, T425-3143, www.utilalodge.com. An all-wooden building with decks and balconies, harbour view, a/c, 8 rooms, clean and modern, meals only when they have guests, dive shop (Bay Islands College of Diving) on site.
A-B Trudy's, 5 mins from airport, T/F425-3103. Rooms with a/c and hot water. Also Trudy's Suites, with colour TV, fridge and microwave. Recommended. Underwater Vision dive shop on site.
A-C Mango Inn, La Punta, T425-3326, www.mango-inn.com. With bath, cheaper without, fan, spotless, helpful, roof terrace, reduction for students with Utila Dive Centre. Pool, Mango Café and La Dolce

Vita Pizzeria for brick-oven pizzas on premises. Recommended.
B Colibri Hill Resort, T425-3329, www.colibri-resort.com, restaurant, bar, swimming pool, a/c.
B Jade Seahorse, T425-3270, www.jadeseahorse.com. 5 great cabins, artistic, unique and very funky, restaurant, bar, fantastic artistic gardens. Recommended,
C Bay View, 100 m from **Utila Lodge** T425-3114, bayviewinternet@yahoo.com. Two apartments with kitchen, living and dining room. Located on the water. With or without bath, pier, family-run.
C-D Freddy's, off the boat and turn right, it's a long walk to just over the bridge, T425-3142. Good rooms, kitchens, quiet end of town.
D Ruby's Inn, T425-3240, hot water, private bath and a/c.
D-F Margaritaville, in a pleasant location just outside town near the beach, T425-3366. Very clean, big rooms with 2 double beds, private bathroom, friendly.
E Celena, main street, T425-3228. With bath, clean with fan. Recommended.
E Countryside, 10 mins' walk out of town, T425-3216. Shared bath, rooms and apartments, quiet, clean, friendly, fan, porch, ask in town for Woody and Annie.
E Harbour View, right on water, T425-3159. Parrot's Dive on site, cheaper rooms with shared bathrooms upstairs, rooms with private bath downstairs, hot water, own generator, cleaning done only on arrival, TV, fans, run by Roger and Maimee.
E Laguna del Mar, opposite and owned by **Trudy's**, T425-3103. Clean, with terrace, fans, mosquito nets. Diving offered.
E Seaside, opposite Gunter's Dive School, T425-3150. Private and shared rooms, kitchen for use. Wi-Fi, nice place, clean, laundry service, hammocks, balcony. Popular with budget travellers. Recommended.

Cayos Cochinos/ Hog Islands

Cochino Grande
North East Cay
Cochino Pequeño
North West Cay
Timón
Lower Monitor
Pelon
Coral Reefs
Sandy Cays

N

2 km
2 miles

E Bavaria, up towards Mango Inn, offers clean, simple rooms.

E-F Cross Creek (see also Diving, page 1009), T425-3334, www.crosscreekutila.com. Good, clean rooms, with shower and shared toilets, discount for divers on courses.

F Loma Vista, up road opposite the dock, T425-3243. Clean, fan, shared bath, very friendly, washes clothes cheaply.

Utila's cayes *p997*

F Hotel Kayla. Affiliated with Captain Morgan's Dive Center on Jewell Cay. Free accommodation at Jewell Cay with PADI courses. Jewell Cay and Pigeon Cay are linked by a bridge. All hotels are small family run affairs **D-E**, 3 restaurants for food; **♥**. You can rent out Little Cay and Sandy Cay completely, details available from cayosutila@hotmail.com.

Roatán *p997, maps p998 and p999*
Coxen Hole

C Caye View, Calle Principal, T445-1222. A/c, bath, TV, phone, laundry, restaurant, bar, overlooks water, overpriced.

C-E Mom, on main road into Coxen Hole, above pharmacy, next to hospital. Private or shared bath, modern, clean, a/c, TV.

E El Paso, next door to Caye View, T445-1367. Shared bath, restaurant.

F Naomi Allen, near the bus depot. Fan, clean, good.

Sandy Bay

LL Anthony's Key Resort, T445-1003, www.anthonyskey.com. Glorious location, accommodation in small cabins, launch and diving facilities (only open to resident guests), the owner, Julio Galindo, is very serious about helping the environment and local community. Dolphin pool at the resort looked after by the Institute of Marine Sciences.

West End

AL Half Moon Bay Cabins, Half Moon Bay, T445-1075. Bungalows and cabins with bath, restaurant with excellent seafood.

AL-B Coconut Tree, West End, T445-4081, www.westbaycoconuttree.com. Private cabins (3 double beds) owned by Vincent Bush, a/c, kitchen, balcony, hot water, fan, fridge, clean, friendly, discounts in low season.

A Pura Vida, T/F445-4141, www.puravida resort.com. A/c, cheaper with fan, hot water, restaurant/bar/pizzeria open all day.

A-B Mermaid Beach, West End, T445-4335, www.roatanmermaidbeachcabins.com. Clean, quiet, with bath, fan or a/c, dive shop next door.

A-D Seagrape Plantation Resort, Half Moon Bay, T445-4428, www.seagraperoatan.com. Cabins, rooms with private bath and budget options with shared bathroom, hot water, family atmosphere, friendly, Visa accepted, nice location on rocky promontory, no beach, but snorkelling possible, full-service restaurant and bar, inclusive packages available. Fun drives for US$30 with equipment.

B Casa Calico, north of Half Moon Bay, T445-4231, www.casacalico.com. Comfortable, cable TV, videos, rooms and apartments, fan, 2 rooms with a/c, garden, huge balconies, apartments sleep 4 or more with kitchen, hot water, noisy in morning, friendly, helpful.

B Georphi's Tropical Hideaway, West End, T445-4205, www.roatangeorphis.com. 9 cabins, kitchens, coffee shop under trees with excellent cookies and pancakes, open all day.

B Pinocchio's, West End, behind Sea View Restaurant, T445-4466, www.roatan pinocchios.com. Comfortable rooms with good views of the ocean.

B Posada Arco Iris, Half Moon Bay, T445-4264, www.roatanposada.com. Apartments with kitchen, hot water, fan, large balcony, friendly owners. Restaurant specializing in grilled meats. Highly recommended.

B-C Keifitos Plantation Resort, on hillside above beach, T978-4472, www.keifitos plantation.com. Bungalows in a beautiful setting, short walk from village, mosquitoes, bar, good breakfasts to 1300, champagne breakfasts Sun, horses for rent with guide, friendly owners, very quiet, very clean. Recommended.

B-D Roberts-Hill, West End, T445-1176. Basic rooms with bath and fan, 2-storey *cabaña* and cabins on the beach next to Keifitos.

C Belvedere's Cabins, West End beach behind Chris's Tienda, T445-1171. Private bath, restaurant serving steaks, seafood, pasta and salad.

C Dolphin Resort, centre of Half Moon Bay, T445-1280. Private bathroom, a/c and fan. Recommended.

C Sea Breeze, north of West End, T445-4026, www.seabreezeroatan.com. Nice rooms, hot water, baths, a/c optional, suites and studios available with kitchens, windsurfers and kayaks for rent.

C-D Anderson's, behind Chris's Tienda, West End, T455-5365. Basic rooms, shared bath, clean, fan, lower rates for longer stays.

C-D Burke's cottages, east end of village past Half Moon Bay, T445-1252. Private bath and kitchen, laundry, cold water.

C-D Chillies, Half Moon Bay, T445-4003, www.nativesonsroatan.com/chillies.htm. Double rooms and dormitory, clean, fully equipped kitchen, lounge, big balcony, camping and hammocks available. Excellent value for money.

D-E Sam's, end of Miller Av. Double rooms and dorm, some fans, island-style dinners.

E Dora Miller (no sign), West End, 2 houses behind Jimmy's Lodge. Washing facilities, no fan, no mosquito nets, basic, noisy, friendly.

E Jimmy's Lodge, West End. Hammocks or communal rooms, popular with backpackers, extremely basic, smelly, ground-floor room has crabs at night, very friendly, cheap meals, snorkelling gear and horse riding available, it is very cheap to string a hammock here, but very exposed and tin roof, you'll be bitten by sandflies, hosepipe as a shower.

E-F Valerie's, north of West End. Dormitory accommodation, communal central area with cooker and fridge (private rooms **D**),

hospitable, but watch your belongings, reports of theft, basic but friendly.

West Bay

AL Island Pearl, on the beach, T445-5005, www.roatanpearl.com. Double storey apartments, a/c, hot water, tiled kitchen, handmade furniture, nicely decorated.

AL-A Coconut Tree 2, on the beach, T445-1648. Luxury cabins with hot water, a/c, balcony. Has merged with **Bananarama** so look for combined packages.

AL-B Las Rocas, next to Bite on the Beach, T/F445-1841, www.lasrocasresort.com. Duplex *cabañas*, very close together, hot water, balcony, smaller cabins sleep 3, larger ones sleep 6, free boat transport to West End and back, dive shop and restaurant.

A-B Bananarama, centre of West Bay beach, T992-9679. With bath, hot water, fan, PADI dive courses available, breakfast included for guests, good value. Recommended.

B West Bay Lodge, south of West Bay beach, T991-0694, www.westbaylodge.com. Cabins with hot water and fan, good breakfast.

East of Coxen Hole

L Coco View Resort, French Harbour, T911-7371, www.cocoviewresort.com. Good shore diving, on lagoon.

L Reef House Resort, Oak Ridge, T435-2297, www.reefhouseresort.com Meals and various packages, including diving. Wooden cabins with sea-view balconies, seaside bar, private natural pool, dock facilities, good snorkelling from the shore.

A-B Executivo Inn, Mount Pleasant on the road to French Harbour opposite electricity plant, T455-6708, www.executiveinn.org. Nice rooms, a/c, hot water, TV, pool, no beach.

A-B The Faro Inn, above Gios seafood restaurant, T455-5214. TV, phone, a/c, large rooms, including continental breakfast.

C Palm Tree Resort, Brick Bay, T445-1986. Cabins with bath, home cooking island style, quiet, diveshop, wall diving with boat.

E Britos, French Harbour. With fan, very good value.

E Dixon's Plaza, French Harbour, past the Buccaneer. Good.

E San José Hotel, Oak Ridge. With bath (2 rooms), cheaper without (3 rooms), clean, pleasant, good value, water shortages, good food, English-speaking owner, Louise Solórzano.

Elsewhere

B Ben's Restaurant, on coast road south out of Punta Gorda, T445-1916. Nice cabins to rent, dive shop (US$35 per dive), limited equipment, disorganized, wooden deck over sea, local food, bar, friendly, safe parking.

Guanaja p1000

C-D Harry Carter, T455-4303, ask for fan. Rooms are clean.

E Miss Melba, just before Hotel Alexander sign on left, house with flowers. 3 rooms in boarding house, run by friendly old lady with lots of island information, shared bathroom, cold water, great porch and gardens.

Cayos Cochinos (Hog Islands) p1000, map p1001

AL Plantation Beach Resort, Cochino Grande, T/F442-0974. VHF 12. Rustic cabins on hillside, hot water, fans, diving offshore, yacht moorings, good steep walk up to lighthouse for view over cayes to mainland, music festival end Jul, local bands and dancers, they charge US$30 for the trip from La Ceiba.

E Cayo Timón (also known as **North Sand Cay**) can be visited from Utila, 1¼ hrs by boat; you can rent the caye (price per person), minimum 6, 8 is comfortable, A-frame, Polynesian style, do overnight diving trips, very basic, quiet, peaceful. Phone Roy and Brenda at **Thompson's Bakery**, Utila, T425-3112, for information.

❶ Eating

Utila p996, map p996

Menus are often ruled by the supply boat: on Tue and Fri restaurants have everything, by the weekend some drinks run out.

♤♤♤ Jade Seahorse. 1100-2200, closed Thu. A variety of seafood homemade style and *licuados*, coolest decor in town, includes the very popular **Treetanic** bar, high up in the trees 1700-2400.

♤♤♤-♤♤ Mariposa Restaurant, new place, lovely spot over the water, good views overlooking bay, nice atmosphere, bright, clean, airy. One of the nicest places in town. Now under new management offers fresh seafood. More expensive but good quality.

♤♤ Bundu Café. Closed Thu. Regular typical menu. Mon is all-you-can-eat pizza and pasta. Broad selection of beach novels, romance and western novels. Great spot to watch people on the street. Recommended.

♤♤ Capt Jack's, next to Gunter's Dive Shop. Daily 0630-2100. Good,

♤♤ Driftwood Café Texan BBQ-style place with good burgers. Airy setting above the water.

♤♤ El Picante, up towards Mango Inn. Upscale Mexican restaurant in a good location.

♤♤ Indian Wok, in front of Tranquila Bar. Open Mon, Wed and Fri. Variety of Asian dishes and homemade, good potato salad.

♤♤ La Cueva, good bar, decent pizzas.

♤♤ La Piccola, pastas, garlic bread, fish, pizza, great service. Upscale yet relaxed atmosphere offering lunch and dinner. One of the best places in town.

♤♤ La Pirata. Open 1800 until 0100. Mainly steak menu with fine views form the top of the new ferry building.

♤♤ Pizza Nut, inside Coco Loco bar. Good pizza.

♤♤-♤ Seven Seas (Martha's), across the street from Cross Creek Dive Shop. Closed Mon. Good *balleadas* and comfort food.

♤♤-♤ Sir Veza Beergarden, a bit out of town on the airport road in a pleasant garden setting. Closed Tue. Great daily specials, try the falafel or chicken kebabs.

ẏ Big Mamas, recently renovated, lovely place, prettiest restaurant on Utila.

ẏ Che Pancho, inside cinema area. Hot dogs, Spanish tortillas and Argentine snacks. Great lunch option.

ẏ Dave Island Café. Closed Mon and Sun. In front of Coco Loco, very popular with locals and tourists. San Franciscan chef offers pork and chicken with a choice of sauces. Great curries and good vegetarian dishes. Great homemade chocolate cake. Big portions. Menu changes daily. Come early to get a seat.

ẏ G.B.'s, inside Bushes Supermarket. Good lunch options. Homemade Bread bvailable.

ẏ Howells's Restaurant , near the UPCO building. Popular with locals, and often overlooked. Great lunch options with local dishes.

ẏ Mermaid Restaurant. Very nice building, airy, open, wood ceiling, buffet style, some of the quickest food on the island, economical prices, popular with divers and locals. Mermaids Internet on premises – also international calls, a/c or open-air dining.

ẏ Munchie's, in a lovely restored historic building near the dock with a porch for people-watching. Nice snacks, good service. Daily specials. Also organize trips to the cayes.

ẏ RJ's BBQ and Grill House. Open Wed, Fri, Sun, 1730 to 2200. Great BBQ. Popular.

ẏ Skidrow Bar and Restaurant, in front of Ecomarine Dive shop. Great burritos, popular with expats. Mon night is pub quiz night.

ẏ Thompsons Bakery. Open 0600-1200. Very informal, friendly, good cakes, coconut bread, breakfasts, biscuits, cinnamon rolls, *baleadas*, cheap and with lots of information. Good lunch option.

ẏ Zanzibar Café, funky ramshackle place typical of Utila. Breakfasts, shakes, burgers, sandwiches, pastas.

Utila's cayes *p997*

There are a few restaurants, a Sat night disco and little else.

Roatán *p997 maps p998 and p999*

Evening meals cost US$4-10. There is a good seafood restaurant on Osgood Caye a few mins by free water taxi from wharf.

Coxen Hole

ẏẏ El Paso, next to the Caye View. Good seafood soup.

ẏẏ Qué Tal Café, on road to West End. Good coffee, herbal teas, sandwiches and pastries, shares space with bookstore.

ẏ HB Warren. Large well-stocked supermarket (best place on island for fresh fruit) with *cafetería*, mainly lunch and snacks, open 0700-1800.

ẏ Hibiscus Sweet Shop. Home-made fruit pies, cakes and biscuits.

ẏ Pizza Rey, opposite Warren's. Pizza slices.

West End

ẏẏẏ Deja Blue. Asian and Middle East specialities, good location, salad buffet, expensive but worth it.

ẏẏẏ Half Moon Bay Restaurant, Half Moon Bay. Nice location to sit on terrace overlooking sea, more expensive than most, excellent food, service can be very slow.

ẏẏẏ Punta del Ovest music village, 200 m along path behind Bamboo. Hut, exotic, clay-oven pizzas, one of the best in town. Shows a film every night.

ẏẏ Belvedere's, on water, West End. Fri-Sun1900-2100.Nice setting, tasty Italian food. Recommended.

ẏẏ Big Blue, above West End Divers, serves good Thai food.

ẏẏ Brick Oven, about 15 mins out of West End (follow the signs). Good food and movies every night.

ẏẏ Cannibal Café, in the Sea Breeze. Open 1030 until 2200, closed Sun. Excellent Mexican food, large helpings, good value.

ẏẏ Cindy's Place, next to Sunset Inn. Local family breakfast, lunches and dinner in garden, fish caught same morning, also lobster and king crab. Recommended.

The Cool Lizard, Mermaid Beach. Seafood, vegetarian and chicken, home-made bread, salads, nice atmosphere, good.

Keifito's Hangout, West End. Good breakfast, champagne on Sun, well priced.

Lighthouse, on the point after **Belvedere's**, local dishes, good coffee and breakfasts, fried chicken and seafood. A bit run-down.

Papagayos, Half Moon Bay, on a jetty, T445-1008. Good atmosphere for pre-prandial tipple, reggae music, basic meals, no sandflies, great sundeck, Thu is band/dance/party night, also rooms to rent (**B**).

Pinocchio's, West End, along same path as the **Lighthouse**, www.roatan pinocchios.com. Excellent pasta, great stir fry and delicious salads, run by Patricia and Howard.

Pura Vida, next to **West End Divers**, Italian, restaurant and pizzeria, good atmosphere.

Rick's American Café, Sandy Bay. Open from 1700, except Wed. Tree-top bar, shows all sports events, best steaks on Roatán.

Rudy's. Open all day. Good pancakes and cookies for breakfast, sandwich combos, good atmosphere but pricey.

Salt and Pepper Club, entrance to West End. Supermarket, BBQ and live music.

Sea View Restaurant, West End. Italian chef/manager, extensive menu, pasta, fish, chicken, pizza, good salads.

Tony's Pizzeria, in the Sunset Inn. Fresh fish, good food, big portions.

Twisted Toucan, West End. The place for drinking and dancing, happy hour 1600-1900.

Tyll's Kitchen, in Tyll's Dive Shop, now open for breakfast, happy hour for rum and beer goes on all day.

Velva's Place, at the far end of Half Moon Bay. Island-style seafood and chicken dishes, try the conch soup, good prices.

Sunset Playa on the beach.

Tartines and Chocolate, Half Moon Bay. French bakery, good bread and pastries.

West Bay

The Bite on the Beach, on the point over West Bay. Wed-Sun brunch, huge deck in gorgeous position excellent, fresh food and great fruit punch. Recommended and very much what Roatán is about.

Neptuno Seafood Grill, between **Fosters** and **Coconut Tree 2**. Seafood, paella, barbecued crab, extensive bar, open daily for lunch and dinner.

West Bay Lodge, see Sleeping. Good breakfasts on a nice balcony with sea view.

East of Coxen Hole

There is a *taquería* close to HSBC on the main road in French Harbour serving good tacos, burritos and hamburgers.

Gios, French Harbour. Seafood, king crab speciality.

Roatan Dive and Yacht Club, French Harbour. Daily specials, pizza, salads, sandwiches, usually very good.

BJ's Backyard Restaurant, Oak Ridge, at the harbour. Island cooking, fishburgers, smoked foods, reasonable prices. There is a pizzeria and, next door, a supermarket.

Iguana Grill, French Harbour. International cuisine and suckling pig.

Pirate's Hideaway, at Calabash Bay, east of Oak Ridge. Seafood, friendly owner.

Romeo's, French Harbour. Romeo, who is Honduran-Italian, serves good seafood, and continental cuisine.

Tres Flores, French Harbour, on the hill. Good views, Mexican specialities, they pick up groups from West End, T245-0007.

Guanaja *p1000*

Harbour Light, through **Mountain View** nightclub. Good food, reasonably priced for the island.

● Entertainment

Utila *p996, map p996*
Bars and clubs

Bar in the Bush is the place to go, 100 m beyond the **Mango Inn**, very popular, lots of dancing and always packed, Wed 1800-2330, Fri (Ladies Night) and Sun 1800-0300.

Coco Loco, on jetty at harbour front near Tranquila Bar, very popular with young divers, together with Coco Loco these 2 places are the anchors and reigning kings of late night Utila night life.

La Pirata Bar, at the dock, high up, great views, breezy.

Treetanic Bar, new hot spot on the island. Inside Jade Seahorse.

Cinema

Reef Cinema, opposite Bay Islands Originals shop, shows films at 1930 every night, at US$3 per person. Popcorn, hotdogs, a/c, comfortable seats, big screen. Also inside the cinema is **Funkytown Books and Music**, an excellent bookshop to trade, sell and rent. Stock up here before you travel anywhere else. Also trades MP3s.

Utila Centre for Marine Ecology, opposite Trudy's, www.utilaecology.org. Offers free presentations on Tropical Marine Ecology, the 1st and 3rd Mon of each month, 1830-1930.

Roatán *p997, maps p998 and p999*
Most clubs come alive about midnight, play reggae, salsa, *punta* and some rock.

Coxen Hole

Foster's, the late night hotspot, dance music Thu night as well as band nights.

Harbour View, Thu-Sun nights, late, US$0.50 entrance, very local, usually no problem with visitors, but avoid local disputes. Hot and atmospheric.

Sundowners Bar, popular happy hour from 1700-1900, Sun quiz followed by BBQ.

West End

Bahía Azul, Fri is party night, DJ, dancing.
C-bar, fantastic location on beachfront near Seagrape Plantation.
Lone's Bar, Mermaid Beach, nightly BBQ, reggae music.

East of Coxen Hole

Al's, Barrio Las Fuertes, before French Harbour. Closed Sat night, salsa and plenty of *punta*.

✪ Festivals and events

Utila *p996, map 996*
Aug **Sun Jam** on Water Caye at a weekend at the beginning of Aug, www.sunjamutila.com. Look out for details locally. They charge a US$2.50 entrance fee to the island; bring your own tent/hammock, food and water.

◯ Shopping

Utila *p996, map p996*
Arts and crafts
Bay Islands Original Shop sells T-shirts, sarongs, coffee, hats, etc. Mon-Fri 0900-1200 and 1300-1800, Sat and Sun 0900-1200. Also try **Utila Lodge Gift Shop**.

Gunter Kordovsky is a painter and sculptor with a gallery at his house, good map of Utila, paintings, cards and wood carving.

Roatán *p997, maps p998 and p999*
Supermarkets
Best to buy supplies in Coxen Hole.
Coconut Tree at West End expensive.
Woods is cheaper. **Eldon** in French Harbour is also expensive. **Ezekiel**, West End, opposite church, fruit and vegetables.

▲ Activities and tours

Utila *p996, map p996*
The **Utila Snorkel Center**, for all those who do not want to dive, organizes trips. Inside Mango Tree Business building. See also Bundu Café, page 1004.

Diving
Dive with care for yourself and the reef at all times; www.roatanet.com has plenty of information about Utila and its dive sites.

Utila is a very popular dive training centre. Learning to dive is cheaper here than anywhere else in the Caribbean, especially if you include the low living expenses. It is best to do a course of some sort; students come first in line for places on boats and recreational divers have to fit in. In recent years, Utila has developed a reputation for poor safety and there have been some accidents requiring emergency treatment in the recompression chamber on Roatán. Serious attempts have been made to change this by the diving community of Utila. 3 or 4 accidents that happen annually are a result of cowboy divers and drug or alcohol abuse.

Instructors Choose an instructor who you get on with, and one who has small classes and cares about safety; follow the rules on alcohol/drug abuse and pay attention to the dive tables. There is a rapid turnover of instructors; many stay only a season to earn money to continue their travels, and some have a lax attitude towards diving regulations and diving tables. Check that equipment looks in good condition and well maintained. Boats vary, you may find it difficult to climb into a dory if there are waves. While a dive shop has a responsibility to set standards of safety, you also have a responsibility to know about diving times. If you don't, or are a beginner, ask.

Price There is broad price agreement across dive shops in Utila. Out of the revenues the Utila Dive Supporters' Association can budget for spending, facilities and eventually conservation. Whatever you may think of the idea, one benefit, is greater safety and better organized protection of the reef. Whether this works remains to be seen, but the price of saving a few dollars could end up costing lives. Dive insurance at US$3 per day for fun divers, US$9 for students (Advanced, or Open Water), US$30 for divemasters is compulsory and is available from the BICA office. It covers air ambulance to Roatán and the recompression chamber. Treat any cuts from the coral seriously, they do not heal easily.

PADI courses A PADI Open Water course costs US$249 (including certificate) with 4 dives, an Advanced course costs US$257 with 5 dives, US$233 if you do the Open Water course with the dive shop first. You can work your way up through the courses with rescue diver (US$333) and dive master (US$750). The Open Water usually comes with 2 free fun dives. Credit cards, if accepted, are 6% extra. Not permitted by credit cards but as all companies on the island do it you can't go elsewhere. Competition is fierce with over 15 dive shops looking for business, so you can pick and choose. Once qualified, fun dives are US$50 for 2 tanks. Dive shops offer free basic accommodation with packages. Most schools offer instruction in English or German; French and Spanish are usually available somewhere, while tuition handbooks are provided in numerous languages including Japanese. A variety of courses is available up to instructor level. If planning to do a diving course, it is helpful but not essential to take passport-sized photographs with you for the PADI card.

Dive operators
Altons Dive Center, T425-3704, www.altons diveshop.com. Offers NAUI and PADI certification, weekly fish talk, recommended, popular, owned by the mayor of Utila.
Bay Islands College of Diving, on main street close to **Hondutel** tower, T425-3291, www.dive-utila.com. 5-star PADI facility, experienced and well qualified staff, good boats ranging from 50 ft, for large parties to skiff for smaller ones, environmentally sound. Only dive shop on the island with in-house pool and hot tub. The trauma centre and recompression chamber. shared by all dive shops is located here. 5-star facility.
Captain Morgan's, T425-3349, www.diving utila.com, has been recommended for small classes, good equipment, friendly staff. The only dive shop that offers accomodation on nearby Pigeon Key. Popular with travelling couples.

Cross Creek, T425-3397, www.crosscreek utila.com, 2 boats, maximum 8 people per instructor, 2-3 instructors, free use of kayaks, accommodation on site for students, 18 rooms, can also arrange transfers from the mainland.

Deep Blue Divers, T/F425-3211, www.deep blueutila.com. One of the newest operators on the island, which means new gear and the friendly owners are getting good feedback through word of mouth.

Gunter's Ecomarine Dive Shop, T/F425-3350, http://ecomarinegunters. blogspot.com. Dive school with 4 divers per group maximum, 7 languages spoken. Most laid-back dive shop and the only dive school that does not hassle divers arriving at the ferry dock.

Paradise Divers, on the seafront, T425-3148. Relaxed and friendly.

Parrot Aqua Adventures, T425-3772, tatianaluna22@yahoo.com, run by a dynamic local couple. Good reviews by divers with new boat and small classes.

Underwater Vision Dive Center at Trudy's, T425 3103, www.underwatervision.net. Brand new accommodations. Very nice location at the Bay.

Utila Dive Centre, Mango Inn, PADI CDC, T/F425 3103, www.utiladivecentre.com. Well-maintained equipment, daily trips to north coast in fast dory, recommended, all boats covered and custom-built, surface interval on cayes.

Utila Watersports, T/F425-3264, run by Troy Bodden. 4 students per class. Troy also hires out snorkelling gear, photographic and video equipment and takes boat trips. Good reports.

Whale Shark & Oceanic Research Centre (WSORC), T425-3760, www.wsorc.com, is a professional scientific organization committed to education and preserving Utila's oceans, offers speciality courses including Whale shark research, naturalist courses, research diver, fish ID, Coral ID. Free presentation 1930 Sun nights about whale sharks.

Roatán *p997, maps p998 and p999*
Diving
If you don't want to dive, the snorkelling is normally excellent. The creation of the Sandy Bay/West End Marine Park along 4 km of coast from Lawson Rock around the southwest tip to Key Hole has encouraged the return of large numbers of fish in that area and there are several interesting dive sites. Lobsters are still rare, but large grouper are now common and curious about divers.
If the sea is rough off **West End** try diving around **French Harbour** (or vice versa) where the cayes provide some protection. There are more mangroves on this side, which attract the fish. **Flowers Bay** on the south side has some spectacular wall dives, but not many fish, and it is calm during the 'Northers' which blow in Dec-Feb. Few people dive the east end except the liveaboards (Bay Islands Aggressor, The Aggressor Fleet, Romeo Tower, French Harbour, T445-1518) and people on camping trips to Pigeon Cay, so it is relatively unspoilt. Because fishing is allowed to the east, tropical fish are scarce and the reef is damaged in places. In addition to a few stormy days from Dec to Feb, you can also expect stinging hydroids in the top few feet of water around Mar and Apr which bother people who are sensitive to stings. Vinegar is the local remedy.
Courses As on Utila, the dive operators concentrate on instruction but prices vary (since Dec 1994 the municipal government has set minimum prices). You can normally find a course starting within 1 or 2 days. There is more on offer than in Utila; not everyone teaches only PADI courses. Prices for courses and diving vary with the season. In low season good deals abound. Open Water US$225, advanced US$160, fun dives US$25. Despite the huge number of dive students, Roatán has a good safety record but it still pays to shop around and find an instructor you feel confident with at a dive shop which is well organized with well-maintained equipment. As in other 'adventure' sports, the cheapest is not always the best. Dive insurance is US$2

per day, and is sometimes included in the course price. If you do not have dive insurance and need their services, the hyperbaric chamber charges a minimum of US$800.

Dive operators
Anthony's Key Resort, Sandy Bay. Mostly hotel package diving, also swim and dive with dolphins, see above.
Aquarius Divers, West End. PADI courses, fun dives, excursions to the south walls in conjunction with Scuba Romance dive shop, Brick Bay.
Bananarama, West Bay, in centre of beach, next to Cabaña Roatana, small, friendly, run by young German family, boat and shore diving.
The Last Resort, Gibson Bight, T445-1838 (in USA T305-893-2436). Mostly packages from the USA.
Native Son's Water Sports, next to Mermaid cabins, West End. Run by Alvin, local instructor, PADI and PDSI courses and fun dives.
Ocean Connections at Sunset Inn, West End, T/F3327-0935, www.ocean-connections.com, run by Carol and Phil Stevens with emphasis on safety and fun, good equipment, multilingual instructors, PADI courses, BSAC, the only shop with nitrox instruction, fast boats, also rooms and restaurant, dive/accommodation packages available. Recommended.
Scuba Romance, Dixon Cove. New shop and equipment, large diesel boat and compressor, diving the south wall and the reef at Mary's Place, overnight trips to Barbareta, 6 dives, US$80, sleeping on the boat, work with Palm Cove Resort, cabin-style accommodation, home cooking.
Sueño del Mar Divers, good, inexpensive, American-style operation, tends to dive the sites closest to home, T445-1717.
Tyll's Dive, West End, T403-8852, www.tylls dive.com, multilingual instructors, PADI, SSI courses, accommodation also available.

West End Divers, West End, T445-4289, www.westendivers.com, Italian owned, competent bilingual instructors, PADI Dive Centre.

Tour operators
At **Belvedere's Lodge** on the headland at Half Moon Bay, Dennis runs snorkelling trips to secluded bays beyond Antony's Key in a glass-bottomed yacht. He also takes charters and sunset cruises all along the coast. Horse riding available from **Keifitos** or **Jimmy's** in West End. Alex does day trips to Punta Gorda and 2/3-day trips in his sailboat *Adventure Girl*. His boat is moored at **Ocean Divers** dock, contact here or at Tyll's. **Far Tortugas** charters, trimaran *Genesis*, does sailing trips with snorkelling and reef drag (snorkellers towed behind slow-moving boat), US$45 per day, US$25 per ½ day, contact **Casi Todo**, West End, T445-1347. **Coconut Tree** have a rainforest tour to Pico Bonito, US$112 (guide, transport, lunch and snorkelling).
Submarine trips Karl Stanley offers a probably unique opportunity with deep-sea submarine trips down to 2000 ft. At US$600 per person, a little on the pricey side, but then it's not an everyday option. **Stanley Submarines**, www.stanleysubmarines.com.
Boat trips Kayak rentals and tours from **Seablades**, contact Alex at Casi Todo, 3- to 7-day kayak tours, US$150-250. Full and ½-day rental US$20 and US$12 (with instruction), kayaks available at **Tyll's**. From Rick's American Café, **Casablanca** charters on yacht *Defiance III*, sunset cruises, party trips, full-day snorkelling, also can be arranged through **Casi Todo**. At West Bay beach is a glass-bottomed boat, **Caribbean Reef Explorer**, US$20 per 1½ hrs, unfortunately includes fish feeding, which upsets the reef's ecological balance. Glass-bottomed boat and 3-person submarine tours from the dock at Half Moon Bay, US$25 per person.
Fishing Trips can be arranged through Eddie, contact at **Cindy's** next to Ocean Divers, West End, small dory, local expert, good results, US$30 per hr, but prices can

vary. Alternatively, go fishing in style from French Harbour, **Hot Rods** sports fisher, US$500 per day charter, T445-1862. See **Casi Todo**, above, for fishing tours, ½- and full day. Fishing trips also available on **Flame**, contact Darson or Bernadette, T445-1616, US$20 per hr.

Travel agents

Airport travel agency has information on hotels, will make bookings, no commission. **Bay Islands Tour and Travel Center**, in Coxen Hole (Suite 208, Cooper Building, T445-1585) and French Harbour. **Casi Todo 1** in West End or **Casi Todo 2** in Coxen Hole can arrange tours, locally and on the mainland, including fishing, kayaking, island tours, trips to Barbareta and Copán. Local and international air tickets also sold here as well as new and second-hand books, Mon-Sat, 0900-1630. **Columbia Tours**, Barrio El Centro, T445-1160, good prices for international travel, very helpful. **Tropical Travel**, in Hotel Caye View, T445-1146. **Carlos Hinds**, T445-1446, has a van for trips, reasonable and dependable.

Guanaja p1000
Diving and sailing

The most famous dive site off Guanaja is the wreck of the *Jado Trader*, sunk in 1987 in about 30 m on a flat bottom surrounded by some large coral pinnacles which rise to about 15 m. Big black groupers and moray eels live here, as does a large shy jewfish and many other fish and crustaceans.
End of The World, next to **Bayman Bay Club**, T/F402-3016, www.guanaja.com. Diving instruction, beachfront bar, restaurant, cabins, kayaks, canoes, hobie cats, white-sand beach, fishing. Highly recommended resort. **Jado Divers**, beside Melba's, T453-4326. US$26 for 2 dives, run by Matthew from US. Preston Borden will take snorkellers out for US$25 per boat load (4-6 people), larger parties accommodated with larger boat, or for customized excursions, very flexible.

● Transport

Utila *p996, map p996*
Air

Sosa, T452-3161, www.aerolineasosa.com, flies on Mon, Wed and Fri to **La Ceiba**, US$50. Also to **Roatán** (US$40), **San Pedro** (US$51) and **Tegucigalpa** (US$64). **Atlantic Air**, have 3 flights a week to La Ceiba. There is local transport between airport and hotels.

Boat

Ferry services on the Princess Utila, La Ceiba-Utila at 0930 and 1600, and Utila-La Ceiba at 0620 and 1400. Automatic ticketing US$21. Dock fee required when leaving Utila (US$1)

Cycling
Bike hire about US$5 per day. Try **Delco Bike**.

Roatán *p997, maps p998 and p999*
Air

The airport is 20 mins' walk from Coxen Hole, or you can catch a taxi from outside the airport for US$1.50. There is a hotel reservation desk in the airport, 1445-1930. Change in Coxen Hole for taxis to West End. US$1 per person for *colectivos* to West End, US$2 to Oak Ridge. If you take a taxi from the airport they charge US$10 per taxi; if you pick one up on the main road you may be able to bargain down to US$5. **Isleña**, **Sosa** and **Atlantic Air** fly from **La Ceiba**, US$20 1 way (fewer Sun); flights also to and from **Tegucigalpa**, US$60, via **San Pedro Sula** (Isleña), US$50, frequency varies according to season. No other direct flights to other islands, you have to go via **La Ceiba** (to **Utila** US$38.50, to **Guanaja** US$51). Always buy your ticket in advance (none on sale at airport), as reservations are not always honoured.

From the USA, **Taca** flies on Sat from **Houston**, on Sun from **Miami**. From Central America, daily flights from **Belize City** (Isleña), Sat from **San Salvador** (Taca).

Airlines Taca, at airport T445-1387; Isleña, airport T445-1088; Sosa, airport T445-1154. **Casi Todo**, T445-1347, sells all flights within Honduras at same price as airlines.

Boat

Galaxy II sails from **La Ceiba** to Coxen Hole. Roatán–La Ceiba 0700, La Ceiba–Roatán 0930, T445-1795. No sailings in bad weather. At times the crossing can be rough, seasickness pills available at ticket counter. Irregular boats from **Puerto Cortés** and **Utila**. Cruise ships visit from time to time, mostly visiting **Tabayana Resort** on West Bay.

Bus

From Coxen Hole to Sandy Bay is a 2-hr walk, or a US$1 bus ride, hourly 0600-1700; taxi drivers will try to charge much more.

Car

Car rental Captain Van, West End, vans, also mopeds and bicycles, good information about the islands; **Roatan Rentals**, West End, range of vehicles, pickups and vans for rent; **Sandy Bay Rent-A-Car**, US$42 per day all inclusive, jeep rental, T445-1710, agency also in West End outside Sunset Inn; **Toyota**, opposite airport, have pickups, US$46, 4WD, US$65, Starlets US$35 per day, also 12-seater bus, US$56 per day, T445-1166.

Cycling and mopeds

Captain Van's Rentals, West End; also from Ole Rentavan, T445-1819.

Taxi

If you take a private taxi, *privado*, negotiate the price in advance. The official rate from the airport to Sandy Bay/West End is US$8 per taxi regardless of the number of passengers.

Guanaja *p1000*
Air

The airport is on Guanaja but you have to get a water taxi from there to wherever you are

staying; there are no roads or cars; Sosa and Isleña (T453-4208) fly daily from **La Ceiba**, 30 mins. Other non-scheduled flights available.

Boat

The *Suyapa* sails between Guanaja, **La Ceiba** and **Puerto Cortés**. The *Miss Sheila* also does this run and on to **George Town (Grand Cayman)**. *Cable Doly Zapata*, Guanaja, for monthly sailing dates to Grand Cayman (US$75 1 way). Irregular sailings from Guanaja to **Trujillo**, 5 hrs.

❶ Directory

Utila *p996, map p996*
Banks Dollars are accepted on the island and you can pay for diving courses with dollars, TCs and credit cards, although the latter carry an 8-10% charge. Banco Atlántida Mon-Fri 0830-1530, Sat 0830-1130. HSBC Mon-Fri 0830-1530, Sat 0830-1130, changes dollars and gives cash against a Visa, but not MasterCard. There are now 2 ATM machines on the island. Thompson's Bakery and Henderson's Shack (next to La Cueva) will change dollars and TCs. Michel Bessette, owner of Paradise Divers, does Amex, Visa and MasterCard advances plus 8%. **Internet** Annie's Internet, near the dock, 0800-1730, closed Sat, extortionate at US$0.15 per min. Seaside Internet, next to Seaside Inn, Mon-Fri 0900-1400 and 1600-1800. Also Internet Café on road to Mango Inn, Mon-Sat 0900-1700. Mermaids offers good internet service for reasonable prices. **Language schools** Central American Spanish School, T425-3788, www.ca-spanish.com. 20 hrs per week instruction, 4 hrs per day, US$125 for 1st week, US$100 each subsequent week, Accommodation and food US$100 per week, just accommodation US$50 per week. Also have schools on Roatan and La Ceiba. **Medical services** Utila Community Clinic (Mon-Fri 0800-1200), has a resident doctor. **Post office** At the

pier opposite Captain Morgan's Dive Centre, Mon-Fri 0800-1200, 1400-1600, Sat 0800-1100. **Telephone** Hondutel office, Mon-Fri 0700-1100 and 1400-1700, Sat 0700-1100, is near Utila Lodge. The main service is reported as unreliable. **Hondutel** sends (and receives) faxes. The REMAX office in the Mango Tree business building offers phone calls and most internet places offer Skype services.

Roatán p997, maps p998 and p999
Banks Banco Atlántida and HSBC in Coxen Hole. There is also a **BAC** office where you can get a cash advance on your Visa/MasterCard, upstairs, before Caye View Hotel on the main street. 5 banks in French Harbour; HSBC in Oak Ridge, T245-2210, MasterCard for cash advances. No banks in West End. No exchange facilities at the airport. Dollars and lempiras can be used interchangeably for most services. **Internet** Available at the Sunset Inn. The **Lucky Lemp**, opposite Qué Tal coffee shop, main street Coxen Hole, phone, fax and email services. **Monoloco** reported to have very cheap packages. **Paradise Computer**, Coxen Hole, 10 mins'

walk down road to West End. **Medical services** Dentist: upstairs in the Cooper building for emergency treatment, but better to go to La Ceiba or San Pedro Sula. Doctor: Dr Jackie Bush has a clinic in Coxen Hole, no appointment necessary, for blood or stool tests, etc. **Ambulance and Hyperbaric Chamber,** Anthony's Key with full medical service. **Local hospital,** Ticket Mouth Rd, Coxen Hole, T445-1499. **Post office** In Coxen Hole, stamps not always available, bring them with you or try **Librería Casi Todo** in West End. **Telephone** Very expensive, you will be charged as soon as a call connects with the satellite, whether or not the call goes through. **Hondutel** in Coxen Hole, fax is often broken. **Supertienda Chris**, West End, T/F445-1171, 1 min to Europe US$10, USA, Canada US$5. Both **Librería Casi Todo** and **Rudy's Cabins** in West End have a fax, US$10 per page to Europe, US$5 to USA. Rudy's charges US$2 a min to receive phone calls.

Guanaja p1000
Banks HSBC and Banco Atlántida

The Northeast

Through the agricultural and cattle lands of Olancho State, a road runs near to the Parque Nacional Sierra de Agalta and beyond to Trujillo on the Caribbean coast. To the west, accessible only by air or sea, is the Mosquitia coast – a vast expanse of rivers and swamps, coastal lagoons and tropical forests filled with wildlife but with few people. From February to May you can taste the vino de coyol, which is extracted from a palm (a hole is made at the top of the trunk and the sap that flows out is drunk neat). With sugar added it ferments and becomes alcoholic (chicha); it is so strong it is called patada de burro (mule kick). ▶▶ *For listings, see pages 1020-1023.*

Tegucigalpa to the northeast coast ●●●●●●● ▶▶ *pp1020-1023.*

The Carretera de Olancho runs from the capital northeast to the Caribbean coast. It passes through **Guaimaca** and **San Diego**, **Campamento**, 127 km, a small, friendly village surrounded by pine forests, and on to the Río Guayape, 143 km.

By the river crossing at **Los Limones** is an unpaved road north to **La Unión** (56 km), deep in the northern moutains passing through beautiful forests and lush green countryside. To the north is the **Refugio de Vida Silvestre La Muralla-Los Higuerales** ① *US$1*, where quetzales and emerald toucanettes can be seen between March and May in the cloud forest. For those that have made the effort to get to this spot, if you're camping you may experience the frissonic pleasure of jaguars 'screaming' during the night. The park comprises the three peaks of La Muralla, 1981 m, Las Parras, 2064 m, and Los Higuerales, 1985 m. Cohdefor has an office on the main plaza for information, closed weekends. You are now required to take a guide with you on the trail. Cost is US$4, arrange in La Unión. Four trails range from 1-10 km and are recommended. There are two campsites in the forest (contact Cohdefor on T/F222-1027 for prior arrangements), or there is accommodation for one or two at the visitor centre.

Juticalpa → *Colour map 6, B3. Altitude: 420 m.*
The main road continues another 50 km from Los Limones to Juticalpa, the capital of Olancho department, in a rich agricultural area for herding cattle and growing cereals and sugar cane. There is a paved road northeast through the cattle land of Catacamas, continuing to just beyond Dulce Nombre de Culmí.

Catacamas and around → *Colour map 6, B4. Altitude: 400 m.*
Catacamas lies at the foot of Agalta mountain in the Río Guayape valley in the Department of Olancho, 210 km from Tegucigalpa. The Río Guayape (named after an indigenous dress, *guayapis*) is famous for its gold nuggets.

The town was established by the Spaniards and the colonial church dates from the early 18th century. It is an agricultural and cattle-raising district. The National School of Agriculture (ENA) is based here, ask if you wish to visit their agricultural demonstration plots in the Guayape valley, 5 km south of the town.

Hiking in the mountains behind Catacamas is beautiful. From Murmullo there are trails to coffee farms. **Río Talgua**, 4 km east of Catacamas, is interesting with caves in which significant pre-Columbian remains have been found. The area and caves are worth a visit. Hiking to **El Boquerón**, stop off at the main road near Punuare, 17 km west of Catacamas, and walk up **Río Olancho**, which has nice limestone cliffs and a pretty river canyon. Through much of the canyon the stream flows underground.

Beyond Catacamas, a rough road continues northeast up the Río Tinto Valley to **Dulce Nombre de Culmí**. Further on is **Paya** where the road becomes a mule track but, in three to four days in the dry season, a route can be made over the divide (Cerro de Will) and down the Río Paulaya to Mosquitia (see below). Local police say that there is a path in the dry season from Dulce Nombre to San Esteban (about 30 km).

Juticalpa to Trujillo

There is a fine scenic road from Juticalpa to Trujillo. From Juticalpa head northeast and turn left where the paved road ends, to **San Francisco de la Paz**. Beyond San Francisco is **Gualaco**, which has an interesting colonial church (there are several places to stay, see Sleeping, page 1020).

The town of **San Esteban** is 23 km from Gualaco. On the way you pass Agalta mountain, and some of the highest points in Honduras, and several waterfalls on the Río Babilonia.

After San Esteban the road continues to **Bonito Oriental** (via El Carbón, a mahogany collection point with the Paya communities in the vicinity). There are four hotels here. The final 38 km from Bonito Oriental to Trujillo are paved, through Corocito. There are many dirt roads between San Francisco and Trujillo. If driving, ask directions if in any doubt. Fuel is available in the larger villages but there is none between San Esteban and Bonito Oriental.

Parque Nacional Sierra de Agalta

Between the roads Juticalpa–Gualaco–San Esteban and Juticalpa–Catacamas–Dulce Nombre de Culmí lies the cloud forest of the Parque Nacional Sierra de Agalta, extending over 1200 ha and reaching a height of 2590 m at **Monte de Babilonia**, a massif with a number of interesting mountains. Several different ecosystems have been found with a wide variety of fauna and flora: 200 species of bird have been identified so far. There are several points of entry. Contact **Cohdefor** in Juticalpa, Culmí, Gualaco, San Esteban or Catacamas for information on access, maps, guides, mules and lodging. There is no infrastructure in the park, but a base camp is being built. A good trail leads to **La Picucha** mountain (2354 m). Access is from El Pacayal, 750 m, a short distance towards San Esteban from Gualaco (bus at 0700 which goes on to Tocoa). There are two campsites on the trail, the first at 1060m is just short of **La Chorrera** waterfall, which has a colony of white-collared swifts that nest in the cave behind the falls. Four to six hours above is the second campsite at 1900 m. The final section is mainly dwarf forest with low undergrowth on the summit. There is much wildlife to be seen and a good viewpoint 1 km beyond at the site of two abandoned radio towers. Hiking time is two days.

La Mosquitia ⬤❶❷❸▲❹❺ ⇥ pp1020-1023. Colour map 6, B4-5.

Forested, swampy and almost uninhabited, Mosquitia is well worth visiting if you have the time and energy. In the the Central American Little Amazon, you can hope to see rainforest wildlife including monkeys and incredible birdlife as you drift through the varied habitat that includes lowland tropical rainforest, coastal lagoons, undisturbed beaches, mangroves, grasslands and patches of pine savannah. Home to members of the Miskito and Pech tribes as well as the Garífuna ethnic group who live in small communities on the coast and along the major rivers. The Río Plátano Biosphere Reserve, a UN World Heritage Site, covers an area over 5200 sq km – one of the largest protected areas in Central America.

Ins and outs

While certainly a challenging environment, many backpackers visit the reserve either alone or with professional guides. For those travelling alone, as long as you have basic Spanish and are a reasonably confident traveller this is the cheapest option. With access by air, sea and road, you can visit any time of the year but it is usually best to avoid the heavy rains from November to January. The driest months are March to May and August to October.

What to take It's a tough environment and you should go prepared. Take a mosquito net and repellent, clothing for rain and also for cooler temperatures at night, good walking shoes and a first-aid kit. Also enough cash in small denominations for your stay (there are no banks in the area) and plastic bags to keep things dry.

Eastern Honduras

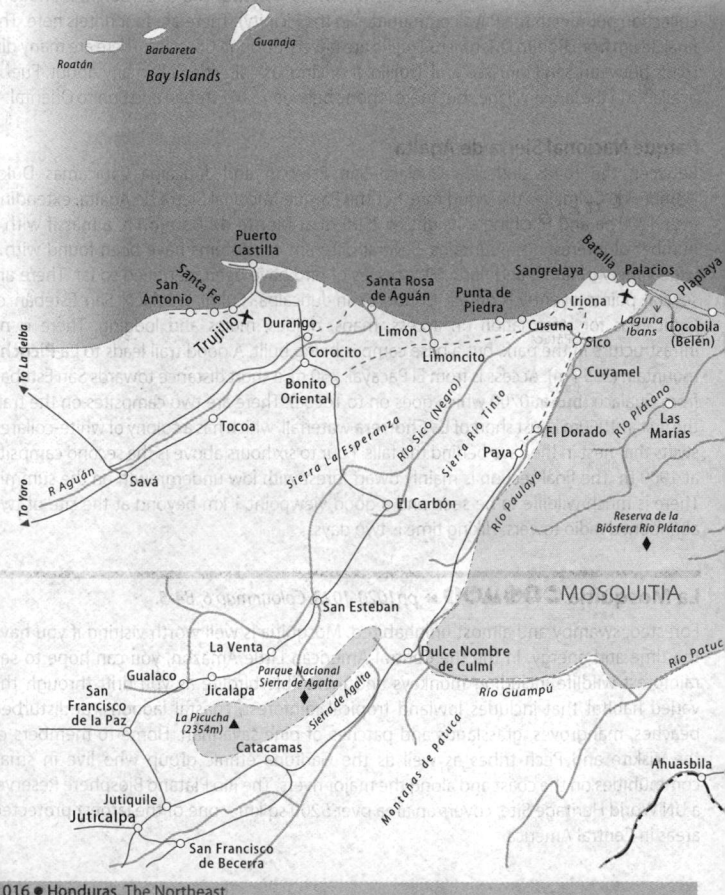

For study of the region **MOPAWI (Mosquitia Pawisa)** is the best source of information and provides the main means of access for travellers to communities in Mosquitia. It is a non-profit-making, non-sectarian organization dedicated to the development of the region and the conservation of the biodiversity of its flora and fauna. There is a **head office** ① *in Puerto Lempira, T898-7460*, another **office** ① *in Tegucigalpa, Residencias Tres Caminos 4b, lote 67, Apartado 2175, T235-8659*, plus offices in several other villages.

MOPAWI is concerned with the protection of natural and human resources throughout Mosquitia and the Department of Gracias a Dios. Among its programmes is the conservation of marine turtles and the green iguana. The Reserva Biósfera Río Plátano (525,100 ha) with the Reserva Antropólogica Tawakha, the Reserva Nacional Patuca and together with Mosquitia Nicaragüense, constitute one of the largest forest reserves north of the Amazon.

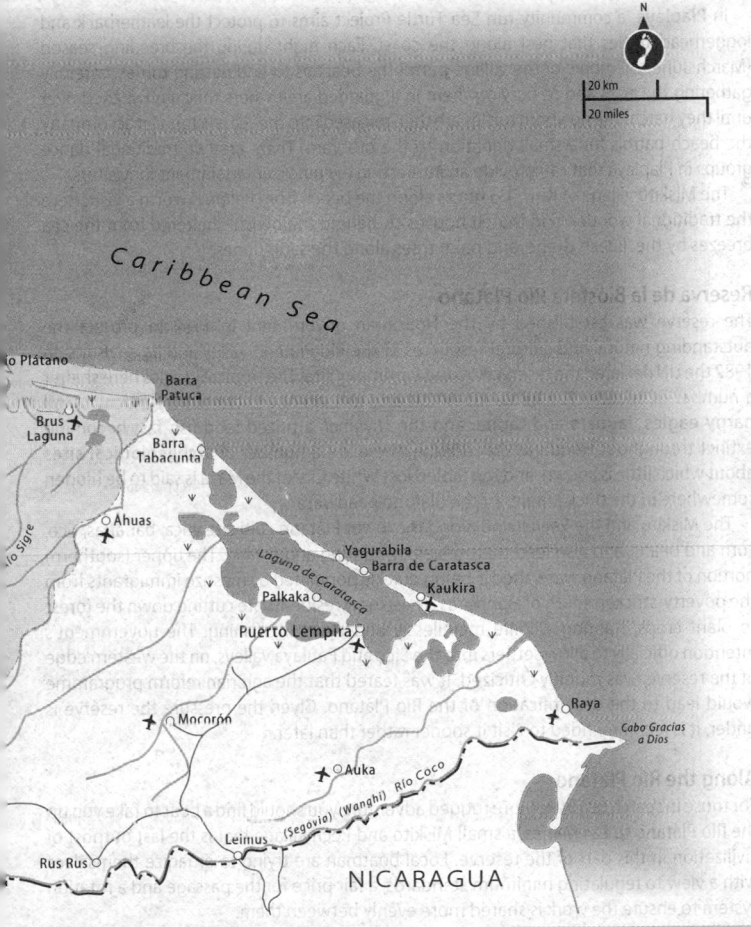

Coastal villages

A narrow strand of land divides the inland waterway and Ibans lagoon from the Caribbean. Along this pleasant setting lie a number of small native villages starting with the Garífuna village of Plaplaya and continuing through the Miskito villages of Ibans, Cocobila, Raistá, Belén, Nueva Jerusalem and Kuri. Trails connect all of these villages making exploration easy with vast expanses of unspoiled, white-sand beaches providing an easy route for getting from place to place, with the sea providing a wonderful way to cool off during the heat of the day.

Apart from generally relaxing in the slow-paced life along the coast there are several interesting things to do in the area. In **Raistá**, the butterfly farm was a pilot project, focusing on raising the colourful butterfly species of the area to sell to live butterfly exhibition houses throughout the world.

In **Plaplaya**, a community-run Sea Turtle Project aims to protect the leatherback and loggerhead turtles that nest along the coast. Each night during the breeding season (March-June) members of the village patrol the beaches to find nesting turtles, carefully gathering the eggs and re-burying them in a guarded area where they are watched over until they hatch. The newborn turtles are then released into the sea. Visitors can accompany the beach patrols for a small donation to the program. There are two traditional dance groups in Plaplaya that can provide an interesting evening's entertainment for visitors.

The Miskito village of **Kuri**, 1½ hours along the beach from Belén, is worth a visit. Here the traditional wooden and thatch houses sit behind the beach, sheltered from the sea breezes by the 'Beach Grape' and palm trees along the sand dunes.

Reserva de la Biósfera Río Plátano

The reserve was established by the Honduran government in 1980 to protect the outstanding natural and cultural resources of the Río Plátano valley and its environs. In 1982 the UN declared the reserve a World Patrimony site. The tropical jungles here shelter a number of endangered birds, mammals and fish, among them **scarlet macaws** and **harpy eagles**, **jaguars** and **tapirs**, and the *cuyamel*, a prized food fish fast becoming extinct throughout Honduras. In addition, there are a number of **archaeological sites** about which little is known, and the fabled lost White City of the Maya is said to be hidden somewhere in the thick jungles of the Plátano headwaters.

The Miskito and the Pech living along the lower Plátano cultivate yuca, bananas, rice, corn and beans, and also feed themselves by hunting and fishing. The upper (southern) portion of the Plátano watershed is being quickly populated by mestizo immigrants from the poverty-stricken south of Honduras. These new residents are cutting down the forest to plant crops, hunting wildlife mercilessly and dynamite-fishing. The government's intention officially to allow settlers into the Sico and Paulaya valleys, on the western edge of the reserve, was roundly criticized. It was feared that the agrarian reform programme would lead to the desertification of the Río Plátano. Given the pressure the reserve is under, it is recommended to visit it sooner rather than later.

Along the Río Plátano

For those in search of a little more rugged adventure you should find a boat to take you up the Río Plátano to Las Marías, a small Miskito and Pech village that is the last outpost of civilization in this part of the reserve. Local boatman are trying to organize themselves with a view to regulating minimum standards, a fair price for the passage and a rotation system to ensure the work is shared more evenly between them.

Most people stay the night in Raistá before and after visiting Las Marías. Gasoline is very expensive in La Mosquitia and this is reflected in the high cost of transportation. The ride to Las Marías costs about US$130 so put together a group of four or five people to share the cost. That price should get you a boat and boatman for three days to take you on the round trip (four to six hours each way) from the coast with a day in Las Marías to look around. If you stay longer you should negotiate a fair price with the boatman to cover his extra time. Bring food and water for the trip as well as other jungle gear. The journey upstream to Las Marías, although beautiful, can become very tedious and uncomfortable. Birdwatching can provide a diversion; there are three species of toucan as well as tanagers, herons, kingfishers, vultures, hawk eagles and oropendolas. If you are lucky you might see crocodiles or iguanas. On arrival in Las Marías, arrange return at once.

An alternative route to Las Marías is by boat across Ibans Lagoon, 45 minutes by tuk-tuk, then 6½ hours' walk through jungle (rough path, hot, mosquitoes, take lots of water and insect repellent, and wear good hiking boots). This is only recommended for fit walkers in drier weather. Expect to pay around US$30 for the guide, and if returning from Las Mariás by boat you'll probably still have to pay the return fare even if you're only travelling one way.

Las Marías

This Miskito-Pech village is the furthest limit of upstream settlement. Once in Las Marías you're normally met by a member of the *saca guia*, a representative of the Las Marías Ecotourism Committee who will let you know what trips are available in the area and help make arrangements on a rotation system that shares the work among the community. This group was set up with the help of MOPAWI and Peace Corps with the aim of developing and coordinating a system of eco tourism that benefits the local people, protects the reserve and also offers extraordinary experiences to tourists. A number of guides have been trained in Las Marías to deal with international visitors. They are coordinated by the Committee, have a set price structure with prices and rules posted on the walls of all the *hospedajes*.

Typical guided trips include day hiking on trails around the village, a three-day hike to scenic **Pico Dama** (very strenuous), a day trip by *pipante* upriver to see the **petroglyphs** at **Walpulbansirpi** left by the ancestors of the Pech or multi-day trips upriver to visit other petroglyph sites and view wildlife in the heart of the reserve. Note that it's harder to advance upriver during the rainy season from June to December. ▸▸ *See Activities and tours, page 1022.*

Brus Laguna → *Colour map 6, B5.*

It is a 15-minute scenic flight from Puerto Lempira (see below) above Caratasca Lagoon and grassy, pine-covered savannas to **Ahuas**, one-hour walk from the Patuca River (fabled for gold). There is a hospital here, four missions, some basic accommodation and a generally improving atmosphere. Irregular *cayucos* sail down to Brus Laguna for US$2.50, at the mouth of the Río Patuca, or US$12.50 (15 minutes) scenic flight in the mission plane. The airstrip is 4 km from village, take a lift for US$1. There is a disco at the riverside to the left of the bridge. Plagued by mosquitoes throughout summer and autumn.

Puerto Lempira → *Colour map 6, B5.*

Puerto Lempira is on the large Caratasca Lagoon. The main office of MOPAWI (see above) is here. The airstrip is only five minutes' walk from town. Regular tuk-tuks (motorized

Border essentials: Honduras–Nicaragua

Leimus

Honduran immigration If you wish to cross here, obtain your exit stamp in Puerto Lempira; the immigration office is open Monday to Friday until 2300. This office is helpful and a good source of information.

canoes) cross the lagoon to **Kaukira**, US$1.20 (a nice place, but nothing there), **Yagurabila** and **Palkaka**. The tuk-tuks leave Kaukira daily except Sunday at 0500, returning during the morning. In the afternoon the lagoon is usually too rough to cross.

Inland by road from Puerto Lempira are **Mocorón** and **Rus Rus**, which may be visited with difficulty (there is no public transport but any vehicle will give a lift) and is a beautiful, quiet village (accommodation at Friends of America hospital's house; meals from Capi's next door, ask Friends about transport out). A branch off this road leads southeast to **Leimus** on the Río Coco and the border with Nicaragua. Ask for Evaristo López (at whose house you can get breakfast) who can arrange transport to Leimus, most days, three to four hours for about US$3.50. He is also knowledgeable about area safety.

The road continues south to the small town of **Ahuashbila** on the upper river of the Río Coco, which marks the border with Nicaragua.

◉ The Northeast listings

For Sleeping and Eating price codes and other relevant information, see Essentials pages 45-48.

◉ Sleeping

Tegucigalpa to the northeast coast *p1014*
F Hospedaje San Carlos, La Unión. Serves good vegetarian food.
F Hospedaje Santos, Campamento. Basic.
F Hotel, on plaza, Guaimaca, above restaurant Las Cascadas. Good value, clean and friendly.
F Hotelito Granada, Campamento. Basic.

Juticalpa *p1014*
D El Paso, 1 Av NE y 6 Calle NO, 6 blocks south of Parque (on way to highway), T885-2311. Quiet, clean, bath, fan, laundry facilities. Highly recommended.
D Las Vegas, 1 Av NE, T885-2700, central, ½ block north of Parque. Clean, friendly, with *cafetería*.

D-F Antúnez, 1 Calle NO y 1 Av NO, a block west of Parque Central, T885-2250. With bath (cheaper without), friendly, clean, also annex in same street.
F Familiar, 1 Calle NO between Parque and Antúnez. Bath, clean, basic. Recommended.
F Fuente, 5 mins from bus station on left side of main road to town centre. Basic but large and clean rooms.
F Regis, 1 Calle NO. Balcony, good value.

Catacamas and around *p1014*
E Central, in Barrio El Centro, T899-4276. With bath, cheaper without, big mango tree in front.
E Juan Carlos, Barrio José Trinidad Reyes, T899-4212. Good restaurant. Recommended.
E La Colina, T899-4488. With bath, hot water, fan, TV, parking.
F Hospedaje Tania, on the main street, Dulce Nombre de Culmí. Very basic.

Juticalpa to Trujillo *p1015*
F Calle Real, Gualaco, near Parque Central. Basic, friendly, will store luggage.

F Centro, San Esteban. Very clean, nice family, best.
F Hotel Hernández, San Esteban. Cheapest.
F Hotel San Esteban, San Esteban. Very friendly, clean.
F Hotelito Central, Gualaco. Similar to Calle Real.

Coastal villages p1018
Plaplaya
F Doña Yohana, close to the village centre.
F Doña Sede, east of village centre with good meals
F Basilia, traditional and the cheapest, 15 mins west of centre.

Raistá and Belén
Choose between Eddie and Elma Bodden (**F**) on the lagoon and Doña Cecilia Bodden (**F**), just up from the lagoon towards the sea. Try the food at Elma's Kitchen (**F**) in Raistá, thought by some to be the best on the coast. Near the lagoon between Raistá and Belén is Doña Exe (**F**), and in Belén there is Doña Mendilia (**F**), near the grass airstrip.

Las Marías p1019
Balancing the benefits of tourism are difficult in such a sensitive area. Sharing the benefits is one way of offsetting the negative impact of tourism and, whenever possible, the Ecotourism Committee tries to share tourists between the 4 basic but clean *hospedajes* (all **F**) of Ovidio, Justa, Tinglas or Diana, with meals available for US$3.

Brus Laguna p1019
D-E Estancia, T433-8043 and **Paradise**, T433-8039. Rooms with a fan and optional private bath.

Puerto Lempira p1019
D Gran Hotel Flores. Some rooms with bath. Recommended.
E Villas Caratascas. Huts with bath, restaurant, disco.
F Charly's restaurant, Mocorón. Rooms available. Price per person.

F Pensión Moderno. Good, friendly, with electricity from 1800-2230.

🍴 Eating

Juticalpa p1014
¶ Casa Blanca, 1 Calle SE. Quite smart with a good cheap menu, good paella.
¶ Comedor Any, 1 Av NO. Good value and friendly.
¶ El Rancho, 2 Av NE. Specializes in meat dishes, wide menu, pleasant.
¶ El Tablado, 1 Av NE entre 3 y 4 Calle NO. Good fish, bar.

Cafés
Helados Frosty, near Parque Central. Ice creams.
La Galera, 2 Av NE. Specializes in *pinchos*.
Tropical Juices, Blv de los Poetas. Good fruit juices.

Catacamas and around p1014
In Dulce Nombre de Culmí, there are several *comedores* on the main plaza.
¶ As de Oro, Catacamas. Good beef dishes, Wild West decor.
¶ Asia, Catacamas. Chinese.
¶ Comedor Ejecutivo, Catacamas. Buffet-style meals US$2, local craft decorations.
¶ Continental, Catacamas. Chicken dishes, pizza, US beer.

Juticalpa to Trujillo p1015
There are 3 nice *comedores* in San Esteban near the Hotel San Esteban.
¶ Comedor Sharon, Gualaco. One of several places to eat.

Puerto Lempira p1019
¶ Delmy, 3 blocks north of main street. Chicken and other dishes, noisy.
¶ Doña Aida, north side of main road to landing bridge. Fresh orange juice.
¶ La Mosquitia, Centro Comercial Segovia in main street. Breakfasts and cheap fish.

🌐 Entertainment

Catacamas and around *p1014*
Fernandos and **Extasis Montefresco** are bars outside town towards Tegucigalpa, pool (US$1.20), live music 2 evenings a week
Cine Maya, Barrio El Centro, cinema.

Puerto Lempira *p1019*
Hampu, is a bar by the landing bridge.

🛍 Shopping

Juticalpa *p1014*
From 0600 on Sat, the market in Parque Central has a good selection of food, fruit, vegetables and souvenirs, said to be the best outdoor market in Olancho.

⛰ Activities and tours

La Mosquitia *p1015*
Several commercial guides organize trips into the Río Plátano Biosphere Reserve and may be a good option for those with limited Spanish. All-inclusive packages range from 3-14 days and cost about US$100 per day. In order to support ecotourism in the reserve you are encouraged to check the tour operator you are considering works with local people. For other options, see under San Pedro Sula, La Ceiba and Trujillo.
La Moskitia Eco Aventuras, with Jorge Satavero, office in La Ceiba, T442-0104, www.honduras.com/moskitia. Specializes in trips to La Mosquitia.
Mesoamerica Travel and **Fundación Patuca** (Hauke Hoops), also specialize in travel in this region. **Mesoamerica** is the only company to run tours to the Zona Arriba of the Río Patuca (5 or 10 days).
Bob 'The Butterfly, Bird and Bug Guy'
Gallardo, based in Copán Ruinas, rgallardo32 @hotmail.com, highly regarded birding and other specialized nature trips to La Mosquitia.

Las Marías *p1019*
The services of the *saca guía* are US$3.50. Guides are required even for day hikes due to the possibility of getting lost or injured on the faint jungle trails. The cost for a guide is US$6 per day for groups up to 5. Overnight hikes require 2 guides. River trips in a *pipante*, a shallow dug-out canoe manoeuvered with poles (*palancas*) and paddles (*canaletes*), require 3 guides plus US$4.20 for the canoe. 2 visitors and their gear will fit in each boat with the guides.

🚍 Transport

Tegucigalpa to the northeast coast *p1014*
Bus From **Comayagüela** to La Unión, daily, take 4 hrs. To get to the park, hire a truck from La Unión for about US$18. There's little traffic so it's difficult to hitchhike. If driving from **San Pedro Sula**, take the road east through Yoro and Mangulile; from **La Ceiba**, take the Savá–Olanchito road and turn south 13 km before Olanchito.

Juticalpa *p1014*
Bus Bus station is on 1 Av NE, 1 km southeast of Parque Central, taxis US$0.50. Hourly to **Tegucigalpa** from 0330 to 1800; to **San Esteban** from opposite Aurora bus terminal at 0800, 6 hrs, US$2.25. To **Trujillo** 0400, 9 hrs, US$5.20. To **Tocoa** at 0500.

Catcamas and around *p1014*
Bus From **Tegucigalpa** to Juticalpa/. Catacamas, **Empresa Aurora**, 8 Calle 6-7 Av, Comayagüela, T237-3647, hourly 0400-1700, 3¼ hrs, US$2 to Juticalpa, 4 hrs US$2.75 to Catacamas. **Juticalpa**–Catacamas, 40 mins, US$0.60. To **Dulce Nombre de Culmí** (see below), 3 hrs, US$1.35, several daily.

Juticalpa to Trujillo *p1015*
Bus To Juticalpa and to the north coast (Tocoa and Trujillo) are fairly frequent.

La Mosquitia p1015
Air
Alas de Socorro fly to **Ahuas**, T233-7025. This company charters planes for US$565, but per person it is US$60 1 way to Ahuas (see Medical services, below). SAMi flies to various villages from Puerto Lempira, eg **Ahuas**, **Brus Laguna**, **Belén**. There are expensive express flights to places like **Auka**, **Raya**, **Kaukira**.

Airline offices Sosa, T898-7467.

Boat
Coastal supply vessels run between La Ceiba and the coastal villages of La Mosquitia. The *Corazón* and *Mr Jim* make the trip weekly and their captains can be found at the harbour east of La Ceiba. Prices vary (US$10-20); be prepared for basic conditions. There are no passenger facilities such as beds or toilets on board and the journey takes a good 24 hrs.

Rivers, lagoons and inland waterways are the highways in the reserve and dug-out canoes provide the public transportation. Once in Palacios, you can catch *colectivo* boat transport at the landing near the Río Tinto Hotel to travel along the inland passage to coastal villages in the reserve such as Plaplaya, Raista and Belén (about US$3.50 for a 1 or 2-hr trip). There is usually a boat to meet the planes that arrive in the morning and information on prices to different locations is posted in the airline offices. If you miss the *colectivo* you will usually have to pay extra for a special trip (about US$20).

Road
An upgraded road is the cheapest and most favoured route by locals. Take a bus from La Ceiba to Tocoa (US$2). From the market in Tocoa take a series of pickups (US$16 per person) along the beach to Batalla, crossing

the various creeks that block the way in launches that wait to meet the cars. The journey to **Batalla** takes about 5½ hrs. From Batalla cross the lagoon in a boat to **Palacios** (US$0.70) and continue from there. The trip is not possible in the wetter months of the year (Jul, Oct and Nov). Some may suggest the possibility of catching a truck from Limón to Sangrilaya then walking along the beach and wading across rivers for 1-2 days to get to Batalla. While this is possible it is not recommended because of the heat, bugs and general safety issues.

ⓘ Directory

Juticalpa p1014
Banks HSNC (the only one that will change TCs), Banco Atlántida, Banco de Occidente. **Post office** 2 blocks north from Parque Central, opposite Shell station. **Telephone** Hondutel on main street, 1 block from Parque Central.

Catacamas and around p1014
Banks Banco Atlántida, Banco de Occidente, in Barrio El Centro. **Medical services** Dentist: Elvia Ayala Lobo, T899-4129.

La Mosquitia p1015
Medical services Hospitals: Alas de Socorro operates from Ahuas to collect sick people from villages to take them to Ahuas hospital. Contact the Moravian church (in Puerto Lempira Reverend Stanley Goff, otherwise local pastors will help).

Puerto Lempira p1019
Banks Banco Atlántida.

Tegucigalpa to the Pacific

From the capital to the Golfo de Fonseca the route twists through mountain valleys down to the volcanic islands and Honduras' Pacific ports of San Lorenzo and Amapala. Near the coast the Pan-American Highway leads west to El Salvador and east though the hot plains of Choluteca to the quiet but popular beaches of Cedeña and Ratón and ultimately to Nicaragua. An alternative route to Nicaragua heads east, through the agricultural town of Danlí, to the border at Las Manos. Short detours from the highway lead to picturesque colonial villages and old mining centres in the hills. ►► *For listings, see pages 1027-1030.*

Tegucigalpa to Goascarán

From the capital a paved road runs south through fine scenery. Beyond Sabanagrande (see page 932) is **Pespire**, a picturesque colonial village with the beautiful church of San Francisco, which has triple domes. Pespire produces small, delicious mangoes. At **Jícaro Galán** (92 km) the road joins the Pan-American Highway, which heads west through **Nacaome**, where there is a colonial church, to the border with El Salvador at **Goascarán**. At Jícaro Galán, Ticabus and other international buses from San Salvador, Tegucigalpa and Managua meet and exchange passengers.

San Lorenzo → *Colour map 6, C2.*

The Pan-American Highway continues south from Jícaro Galán, to the Pacific coast (46 km) at San Lorenzo, a dirty town on the shores of the Gulf of Fonseca. The climate on the Pacific litoral is very hot.

Amapala → *Colour map 6, C2.*

A 31-km road leaves the Pan-American Highway 2 km west of San Lorenzo, signed to Coyolito. It passes through scrub and mangrove swamps before crossing a causeway to a hilly island, around which it winds to the jetty at **Coyolito** (no *hospedajes* but a *comedor* and *refrescarías*).

The Pacific port of Amapala, on Isla del Tigre, has been replaced by Puerto de Henecán in San Lorenzo, and is reached by a road which leaves the Pan-American Highway at the eastern edge of San Lorenzo. The **Isla del Tigre** is yet another place reputed to be the site of hidden pirate treasure. In the 16th century it was visited by a number of pirates, including Sir Francis Drake. Amapala was capital of Honduras for a brief period in 1876 when Marco Aurelio Soto was president. Today, in addition to a naval base, Amapala is a charming, decaying backwater. The 783-m extinct Amapala volcano has a road to the summit where there is a US army unit and a DEA contingent. You can walk round the island in half a day. There is a ferry service from Coyolito, but fishermen will take you to San Lorenzo for a small fee, not by motor launch, and the trip takes half a day. The deep-sea fishing in the gulf is good. It is possible to charter boats to La Unión in El Salvador.

Choluteca and around ●❼✸❸❶ ►► *pp1027-1030. Colour map 6, C3.*

Choluteca is expanding rapidly on the back of the local industries of coffee, cotton and cattle which flourish despite the hot climate. The town was one of the earliest settlements in Honduras (1535) and still has a colonial centre. The church of **La Merced** (1643) is

Border essentials: Honduras–El Salvador

Goascarán

The Santa Clara bridge over the Río Goascarán is the border with El Salvador. A temporary pass can be purchased on the Honduran side for US$1.50 for a visit to the Salvadorian town of **El Amatillo**; many Hondurans cross to purchase household goods and clothes.

Honduran immigration The border closes at 1700. Try to avoid lunchtime when there may be a two-hour break. This border is very relaxed.

Crossing by private vehicle Expect to be besieged by young *tramitadores* touting for your business. They wear a black and white uniform of sorts with name badges, carry an identity card issued by the border station, and will take the strain out of the three-to four-hour border crossing. Expect to pay about US$25 to the various officials on both sides.

Salvadorian consulate To south of town, fast and friendly, daily 0800-1500.

Sleeping Two cheap *hospedajes*, San Andrés and Los Arcos on the Honduran side.

Transport Bus Tegucigalpa–El Amatillo, hourly, US$1.50, four hours. El Amatillo–Choluteca, US$1, three hours, every 30 minutes, microbuses.

Exchange Moderate rates of exchange from money changers.

being renovated and is due to be reconsecrated. The **Casa de la Cultura** and **Biblioteca Municipal** are in the colonial house of José Cecilio del Valle on the corner of the Parque Central. A fine steel suspension bridge crosses the broad river at the entrance into Choluteca from the north (it was built in 1937). The social centre of **San José Obrero** ① *3 Calle SO*, where handicrafts, in particular carved wood and chairs, can be bought. The **Mercado Municipal** ① *7 Av SO, 3 Calle SO*, is on outskirts of town.

Cedeño beach, on the eastern side of the Gulf of Fonseca 40 km from Choluteca, is a lovely though primitive spot, with clean sand stretching for miles and often thundering surf. Avoid public holidays, weekend crowds and take a good insect repellent. Spectacular views and sunsets over the Gulf of Fonseca south to Nicaragua and west to El Salvador, and of the volcanic islands in the bay. Hourly bus from Choluteca (US$0.60, 1½ hours). A turn-off leads from the Choluteca–Cedeño road to Ratón beach, more pleasant than Cedeño. Bus from Choluteca at 1130; returns next morning.

East of Tegucigalpa ●●❀●● ➻ *pp1027-1030. Colour map 6, C3.*

A good paved road runs east from Tegucigalpa through the hills to Danlí, 92 km away in the Department of El Paraíso. There are no signs when leaving Tegucigalpa so ask the way. Some 40 km along, in the Zambrano Valley (see page 962), is the Escuela Agrícola Panamericana, which is run for all students of the Americas with US help: it has a fine collection of tropical flowers (book visits in advance at the office in Tegucigalpa).

Yuscarán → *Colour map 6,C3. Altitude: 1070 m.*

At Km 47.5, a paved road branches south to Yuscarán, in rolling pineland country preserved by the **Reserva Biológica de Yuscarán**, which protects much of the land around Montserrat mountain. The climate here is semi-tropical. Yuscarán was an

Border essentials: Honduras–Nicaragua

Las Manos
This is recommended as the best of the three routes from Tegucigalpa to Nicaragua.
Honduran immigration Border crossing open daily 0800-1600.
Crossing by private vehicle Whether entering or leaving Honduras, you will find *tramitadores* will help you through the paperwork, and are recommended. Total costs are about US$25 and the receipts may not quite tally with what you have paid.
Transport Direct bus Las Manos to Tegucigalpa, 0930, US$2.
Exchange Buy and sell your córdobas in Nicaragua.

El Espino
Border formalities can be particularly tedious at El Espino.
Honduran immigration Immigration is 100 m from the border, daily 0800-1600 (till 1630 on Nicaraguan side). Beware of taxis offering to take you to the border after 1600.
Nicaraguan consulate In Tegucigalpa.
Transport Taxis/minibuses run from Choluteca and San Marcos (10 km) to the border. From San Marcos they only leave when full, US$1, US$0.50 for locals. To Tegucigalpa, there is a direct bus through Choluteca with **Empresa Esperanza**, 4 hours.
Exchange This is easy at this crossing for dollars and córdobas, but the rate for córdobas is better on the Nicaraguan side.

Río Guasaule
The other route from Choluteca to Nicaragua goes through El Triunfo to the border at the bridge over the Río Guasaule. This route is preferred by the international buses as the road is better. It may be worth choosing one of the many 'helpers' to steer you to the correct officials. Fix price beforehand.
Honduran immigration Open daily 0800-1600. On Ticabus, passengers' passports are collected by an official as the bus enters Honduras. Entry tax is paid to the official, who returns passports after sniffer dogs have checked the bus for drugs. No other customs checks.
Transport Bus Choluteca–Guasaule, US$1, 45 minutes.
Exchange There is a bank, but lots of money changers offer rates slightly worse than in the capital. Watch out for children who try to distract you while changing money.

important mining centre in colonial days and is a picturesque village, with cobbled streets and houses on a steep hillside. Ask to see the museum near the town plaza; you have to ask around to find the person who has the key, antiques and photographs are displayed in a restored mansion which belonged to a mining family. There is a Casa de Cultura in the former Casa Fortín, open Monday-Saturday. The Yuscarán distilleries, one in the centre, the other on the outskirts, are considered by many to produce the best *aguardiente* in Honduras (tours possible). The Montserrat mountain that looms over Yuscarán is riddled with mines. The old Guavias mine is close to Yuscarán, some 4 km along the road to Agua Fría. About 10 km further along, a narrow, winding road climbs steeply through pine woods to the summit of **Pico Montserrat** (1891 m).

Danlí → *Colour map 6, C3. Altitude: 760 m.*

Danlí, 102 km from Tegucigalpa, is noted for sugar and coffee production, a large meat-packing company (Orinsa), and is a centre of the tobacco industry. There are four cigar factories. The **Honduras-América SA factory** ① *right-hand side of Cine Aladino, Mon-Fri 0800-1200, 1300-1700, Sat 0800-1200*, produces export quality cigars at good prices. Also **Placencia Tabacos**, on the road to Tegucigalpa, where you can watch cigar-making. Better prices than at Santa Rosa. From Danlí to the north is **Cerro San Cristóbal** and the beautiful **Lago San Julián**.

El Paraíso → *Colour map 6, C3.*

A paved road goes south 18 km to El Paraíso, and beyond to the Nicaraguan border at Las Manos/Ocotal. El Paraíso is a pretty town in an area producing coffee, bananas and rice.

② Tegucigalpa to the Pacific listings

For Sleeping and Eating price codes and other relevant information, see Essentials pages 45-48.

● Sleeping

Tegucigalpa to Goascarán *p1024*
There are very basic hotels with restaurants at the border in Goascarán.
C Oasis Colonial, Jícaro Galán, T881-2220. nice rooms, good restaurant and pool and an unnamed basic guesthouse.
D Perpetuo Socorro, Barrio el Centro, Jícaro Galán, T895-4453. A/c, TV.
F Intercontinental, in centre, Jícaro Galán. Basic, tap and bucket shower, friendly.
F Suyapa, Jícaro Galán. Basic, cheap.

San Lorenzo *p1024*
C Miramar, Barrio Plaza Marina, T781-2039. Has 26 rooms, 4 with a/c, good restaurant, overpriced, in rough dockside area, best not to walk there.
E-F Perla del Pacífico, on main street, T781-3025. Fan, bath, comfortable, clean, friendly, central, charming. Recommended.

Amapala *p1024*
Ask for **Doña Marianita**, who rents the 1st floor of her house.
B Hotel Villas Playa Negra, Aldea Playa Negra, T898-8534. 7 rooms with a/c, 7 with fan, pool, beach, restaurant, isolated, lovely setting.

F Al Mar, above Playa Grande. Fan, scorpions, lovely view of mountains and sunset.
F Pensión Internacional on the harbour. Very basic, otherwise only local accommodation of low standard.

Choluteca and around *p1024*
B La Fuente, Carretera Panamericana, past bridge, T782-0253. With bath, swimming pool, a/c, meals.
D Camino Real, road to Guasaule, T882-0610. Swimming pool, good steaks in restaurant. Recommended.
D Centroamérica, near La Fuente, T882-3525. A/c, good restaurant, bar, pool, good value.
D Escuela de Español Mina Clavo Rico, El Corpus, Choluteca 51103 (east of Choluteca), T/F887-3501. Price per person, US$90 per week, full board, living with local families, language classes (US$4 per hr), riding, craft lessons, work on farms, number of excursions.
D-E Pierre, Av Valle y Calle Williams, T882-0676. With bath (ants in the taps), a/c or fan, TV, free protected parking, *cafetería* has good breakfasts, very central, credit cards accepted. Recommended.
E Brabazola, Barrio Cabañas, T782-2534. A/c, comfy beds, TV, good.
E Pacífico, near Mi Esperanza terminal, outside the city. Clean, cool rooms, fan,

cable TV, hammocks, quiet, safe parking, fresh drinking water, breakfast US$1.50.

F Hibueras, Av Bojórquez, Barrio El Centro, T882-0512. With bath and fan, clean, purified water, *comedor* attached, good value.

F San Carlos, Paz Barahona 757, Barrio El Centro. With shower, fan, very clean, pleasant.

F Santa Rosa, 3 Calle NO, in the centre, just west of market, T882-0355. Some with bath, pleasant patio, laundry facilities, clean, friendly. Recommended.

East of Tegucigalpa *p1025*
B Escuela Agrícola Panamericana. Rooms are available, but there is nowhere to eat after 1700.

Yuscarán *p1025*
D-E Hotel, T892-7213. Owned by Dutch man Freek de Haan and his Honduran wife and daughter, private or dormitory rooms, beautiful views of Nicaraguan mountains in the distance.

F Hotel Carol. 6 modern rooms with bath and hot water, annex to owner's fine colonial house, safe, family atmosphere, good value.

Danlí *p1027*
C-D Gran Hotel Granada, T883-2499. Bar, cable TV, accepts Visa. Restaurant and swimming pool, locals pay ½ price.

D-E La Esperanza, Gabriela Mistral, next to Esso station, T883-2106. Bath, hot water, fan (more expensive with a/c), TV, drinking water, friendly, parking.

F Apolo, El Canal, next to Shell station, T883-2177. With bath, clean, basic.

F Danlí, El Canal, opposite Apolo. Without bath, good.

F Eben Ezer, 3½ blocks north of Shell station, T883-2655. Basic, hot showers.

F Las Vegas, next to bus terminal. Noisy, restaurant, washing facilities, parking.

F Regis, 3 blocks north of Plaza Central. With bath, basic.

El Paraíso *p1027*
E-F 5a Av Hotel y Restaurant, 5 Av y 10 Calle, T893-4298. Bath, hot water, restaurant specializes in Mexican-American food. Parking.

F Lendy's, Barrio Nuevo Carmelo, by bus station, T893-4461. Clean, prepares food.

🍴 Eating

San Lorenzo *p1024*
🍴 **Restaurant-Bar Henecán**, on Parque Central. A/c, good food and service, not cheap but worth it.

Amapala *p1024*
🍴 **Mercado Municipal**. Several clean *comedores*.
🍴 **Restaurant-Bar Miramar** by the harbour. Overlooking the sea, pleasant, very friendly, good meals, hamburgers and *boquitas*, and you can hang your hammock.

Choluteca and around *p1024*
🍴 **Alondra**, Parque Central. Old colonial house, open Fri-Sun only.
🍴 **Comedor Central**, Parque Central. *Comida corriente* daily specials, *licuados*, sandwiches, good for breakfast. Local specialities are the drinks *posole* and *horchata de morro*.
🍴 **El Burrito**, Blv Choluteca between 4 and 5 Av N. With good-value meals and fast service.
🍴 **El Conquistador**, on Pan-American, opposite **La Fuente**. Steaks, etc, outdoor seating but you have to eat inside, good but slow service. Will change money for customers. Recommended.
🍴 **Frosty**, on main street. Owned by Hotel Pierre, good food and juices.
🍴 **Tico Rico**, Calle Vincente Williams. Has been highly recommended.

Yuscarán *p1025*
🍴 **Cafetería Colonial**, opposite Banco de Occidente. Serves excellent *desayuno típico* and *comida corriente*.

Danlí p1027

¶ Comedor Claudio. Good *comida corriente*, good information from locals.

¶ El Gaucho and **España**, town centre. Good.

¶ El Paraíso de las Hamburguesas. Cheap, good, owner very friendly.

¶ Pizzería Picolino, 2 blocks southwest of Parque Central. Good pizzas.

¶ Rancho Típico, El Canal, near Hotel Danlí. Excellent.

El Paraíso p1027

¶ Comedor Edith, on a small square on main road, after Parque Central towards border. US$0.85 for a meal.

⊛ Festivals and events

Choluteca and around p1024

8 Dec The feast day of the **Virgen de la Concepción**, a week of festivities, followed by the **Festival del Sur**, 'Ferisur'.

Danlí p1027

3rd week Aug Fiesta del Maíz lasts all week, with cultural and sporting events, all-night street party on the Sat; it gets very crowded with people from Tegucigalpa.

⊖ Transport

San Lorenzo p1024

Bus Frequent *busitos* from **Tegucigalpa** to San Lorenzo (US$1) and **Choluteca** (US$1.50).

Amapala p1024

Boat Motorized *lanchas* run between **Coyolito** and Amapala, US$0.35 per person when launch is full (about 10 passengers), about US$4 to hire a launch (but you will probably have to pay for the return trip as well). 1st boat leaves Amapala at 0700 to connect with 1st Coyolito–San Lorenzo bus at 0800; next bus from Coyolito at 0900.

Choluteca and around p1024

Bus To **El Espino** (Nicaraguan border) from Choluteca, US$1.15, 1 hr, 1st at 0700, last at 1400. Also frequent minibuses to **El Amatillo** (El Salvador border) via San Lorenzo, US$1, from bus stop at bridge. Buses to Choluteca from Tegucigalpa with **Mi Esperanza**, **Bonanza** and **El Dandy**; Bonanza continues to San Marcos and departs Tegucigalpa hourly from 0530, 4 hrs to Choluteca, US$1.90. The municipal bus terminal is about 10 blocks from the new municipal market, about 8 blocks from cathedral/Parque Central; Mi Esperanza has its own terminal 1 block from municipal terminal.

Yuscarán p1025

Bus Frequent buses to **Zamorano** and **Tegucigalpa**; from the capital buses leave from Mercado Jacaleapa. For information, ask anyone in the Parque Central in Yuscarán.

Danlí p1027

Bus From **Tegucigalpa**, US$2, from Blv Miraflores near Mercado Jacaleapa (from left-hand side of market as you face it), Col Kennedy, Tegucigalpa, hourly, 2 hrs, arrive 1½ hrs before you want to leave, long queues for tickets (take 'Kennedy' bus from C La Isla near the football stadium in central Tegucigalpa, or taxi, US$1.20, to Mercado Jacaleapa). Express bus from Col Kennedy, 0830, 1230 and 1700, US$2. One road goes east from Danlí to **Santa María** (several buses daily), crossing a mountain range with great views.

El Paraíso p1027

Bus Minibuses from **Danlí** terminal to El Paraíso, frequent (0600 to 1740), US$0.40, 30 mins, don't believe taxi drivers who say there are no minibuses. **Emtra Oriente**, Av 6, Calle 6-7, runs 4 times a day from **Tegucigalpa** to El Paraíso, 2½ hrs, US$1.50. Buses from El Paraíso to **Las Manos**, about every 1½ hrs, US$0.35, 30 mins, or taxi US$4, 15 mins.

❶ Directory

San Lorenzo p1024
Banks Bancahorro (changes US$ cash and TCs), Banco Atlántida, and Banco de Occidente (no exchange); Chinese grocery gives good rates for US$ cash.

Amapala p1024
Banks Banco El Ahorro Hondureño.

Choluteca and around p1024
Banks Of the many banks in town, Banco Atlántida has a Visa ATM, and only Banco de Comercio changes TCs. Can be difficult to exchange money in Choluteca. **Embassies and consulates**

El Salvador, to south of town, fast and friendly, daily 0800-1500. **Post office** Mon-Fri 0800-1700, Sat 0800-1200, US$0.15 per letter for Poste Restante. **Telephone** Collect calls to Spain, Italy, USA only.

Danlí p1027
Banks Banco Atlántida changes TCs without problems. Cash on Visa card, maximum US$50. Other banks as well. **Medical services** Dentist: Dr Juan Castillo, Barrio El Centro, T883-2083.

El Paraíso p1027
Banks Several branches in town including HSBC.

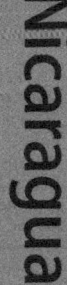

Nicaragua

Contents

Footprint features

Border crossings

Nicaragua–Costa Rica, see pages 1103 and 1118
Nicaragua–Honduras, see pages 1062 and 1078

At a glance

◎ **Getting around** Buses between large towns. Minibuses around the Managua, Masaya, Granada triangle. Boats out to the Corn Islands.

◉ **Time required** 2-3 weeks getting to know the country.

☼ **Weather** Dry season Dec-May. Wet from Jun-Oct. Always warm.

✕ **When not to go** Temperatures can be unbearably hot in May.

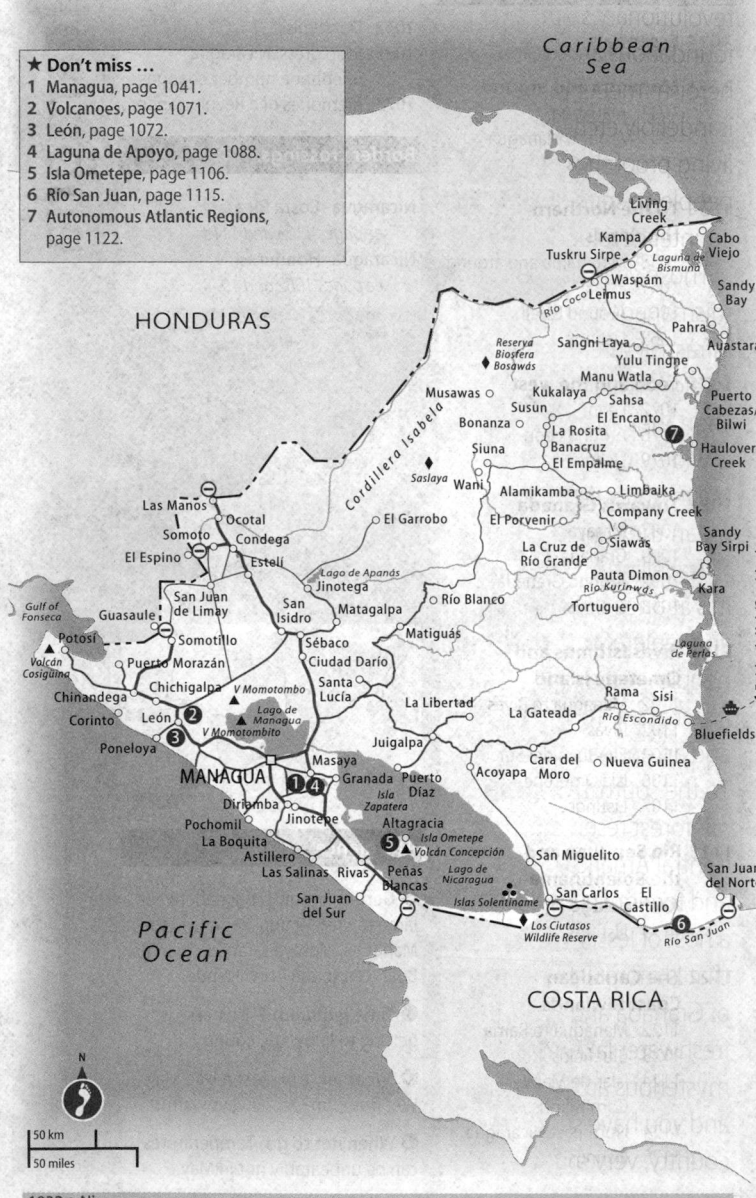

Caribbean Sea

HONDURAS

Living Creek
Kampa
Cabo Viejo
Tuskru Sirpe
Laguna de Bismuna
Waspám
Sandy Bay
Leimus
Río Coco
Pahra
Auastara
Reserva Biosfera Bosawás
Sangni Laya
Yulu Tingne
Manu Watla
Musawas
Kukalaya
Sahsa
Puerto Cabezas/Bilwi
Bonanza
Susun
El Encanto
La Rosita
Banacruz
Haulover Creek
Saslaya
Wani
Siuna
El Empalme
Alamikamba
Limbaika
El Porvenir
Company Creek
Las Manos
Ocotal
Condega
El Garrobo
La Cruz de Río Grande
Siawás
Sandy Bay Sirpi
Somoto
Estelí
Pauta Dimon
Río Kurinwás
Kara
El Espino
Lago de Apanás
Jinotega
Río Blanco
Tortuguero
Laguna de Perlas
San Juan de Limay
San Isidro
Río Blanco
Guasaule
Somotillo
Matagalpa
Matiguás
Rama
Sisi
Gulf of Fonseca
Potosí
Volcán Cosigüina
Puerto Morazán
Ciudad Darío
Santa Lucía
La Libertad
La Gateada
Río Escondido
Bluefields
Chinandega
Chichigalpa
V Momotombo
Lago de Managua
La Gateada
Corinto
León
V Momotombito
Juigalpa
Cara del Moro
Nueva Guinea
Poneloya
MANAGUA
Masaya
Granada
Puerto Díaz
Acoyapa
Diriamba
Jinotepe
Isla Zapatera
Pochomil
La Boquita
Altagracia
Isla Ometepe
Volcán Concepción
San Miguelito
Astillero
Las Salinas
Rivas
Peñas Blancas
Lago de Nicaragua
San Carlos
El Castillo
San Juan del Norte
San Juan del Sur
Islas Solentiname
Los Ciutasos Wildlife Reserve
Río San Juan

To Islas de Maíz/Corn Islands

Cordillera Isabela

Pacific Ocean

COSTA RICA

N
50 km
50 miles

Nicaragua is a nation born out of poetry, fire and indomitable, revolutionary spirit. It is a land of tempestuous geological foundations and equally tempestuous history. A land where great heroism meets wild poetic struggle. The 1979 Sandinista revolution is indelibly etched on the national psyche, and Nicaraguans are living proof that political destiny can be commandeered by the people, in spite of the US government, who sponsored years of counter-revolutionary violence during the notorious Contra War.

Those years of brutal unrest, natural disasters and economic mismanagement have effectively crippled the country's infrastructure. Today, in spite of lasting peace and burgeoning foreign investment, Nicaragua suffers blackouts and water shortages. Many towns lack paved roads, the horse and cart is widely used, and wood remains the principal source of fuel. Meanwhile, the ever rising costs of petrol and staple foods mean the sting of poverty is bound to remain for some time.

Travelling in Nicaragua is a challenging, intensive adventure. It is at once beautiful, inspirational, amusing, saddening, grotesque, and replete with endless anarchic charms. Through it all, the people – eternally decent and good humoured – are the country's finest asset. To the north, you'll find dark, entrancing mountains and an endearing Campo culture irrevocably tied to the land. To the south, the vigorous Río San Juan courses through verdant rainforest reserves, offering some of the best wildlife viewing in Central America. To the west, the Pacific coast is enticing tourists and foreign investors with its gorgeous, sandy beaches. To the east, a host of lesser visited shores possess an English-speaking culture that is more Caribbean than Nicaraguan. Add the fine colonial towns of Granada and León, the magical island of Ometepe, the largest freshwater lake in Central America, remote indigenous villages, mysterious archaeological relics, and endless smoking volcanoes, and you have some compelling reasons to visit this captivating country, very much on its way up.

Essentials

Where to go

The largest of the Central American republics, Nicaragua is located at the junction of three continental plates. Earthquakes and volcanic eruptions frequently shake the country – at times, to its foundations. The people and most of the economic activity are concentrated in the western highlands, around the two great lakes of Managua and Nicaragua, and to the west of the volcanic chain that runs parallel to the Pacific shore. Stretching inland from the Caribbean coast, the largely unpopulated lowlands are challenging country for travelling and a nature paradise for those with the energy and time to spare.

Dramatic evidence of tectonic power can be seen in the capital, **Managua**, where the centre was destroyed by an earthquake in 1972. The old cathedral stands open to the skies, a crumbling testament to what the city could have been. Other sites in the old colonial centre, close to the shores of **Lago de Managua**, reflect Nicaragua's recent civil war. Within easy reach of the capital are the Pacific beaches of **Pochomil** and **Masachapa**.

Southeast of Managua is the colonial city of **Masaya**, a major centre for handicrafts in the region and a base for visits to the smoking crater of the **Santiago** volcano. The road continues to **Granada**, one of Nicaragua's major colonial cities, passing close to the crystal-clear waters of the beautiful Apoyo crater lake. Founded on the shores of **Lago de Nicaragua** in 1524, Granada is the oldest continually inhabited city on the mainland of the Americas. It promises a stunning setting, gorgeously restored Spanish buildings, hordes of camera-toting tourists and some of the best restaurants in the country. The lake also has an archipelago of 354 islands that are great for boat trips and nature watching. **Isla Zapatera**, an extinct volcano and pre-Columbian site, is accessible from Granada. **Ometepe**, easily reached from Granada and the lakeside town of **San Jorge**, near **Rivas**, is the largest island and a peaceful, popular destination with welcoming residents, indigenous petroglyphs and two forest-covered volcanoes ideal for climbing.

San Carlos marks the southeast corner of Lake Nicaragua at the outlet of the **Río San Juan**, which flows along the Costa Rican border to **San Juan del Norte**, and passes through some of Central America's most unspoilt forest; the potential for nature tourism is enormous. A short trip from San Carlos is the **Solentiname archipelago**, a group of forested islands and home to a community of artists. On the south Pacific coast, heading towards Costa Rica, the burgeoning resort town-cum-surfers' hang-out of **San Juan del Sur** provides beach life and fabulous sunsets. Close by is the country's most important turtle nesting ground at **La Flor**.

Two routes head round Lago de Managua from the capital, heading north to **Honduras**. The main route runs south of the lake shore arriving at the former capital of **León**, a feisty city of colonial houses, beautiful churches, students and captivating festivals. As the birthplace of Rubén Darío, one of Latin America's greatest poets, the city is rightly proud of its cultural heritage. Nearby are the Pacific beaches of **Las Peñitas** and **Poneloya**. Heading north is sweltering **Chinandega** and the national park of **Cosigüina** volcano, overlooking the Gulf of Fonseca. A second route goes east of Lake Managua through the refreshing highland towns of **Matagalpa**, **Jinotega** and **Estelí**, ideal country for walking and hiking.

On the Caribbean coast, **Bluefields** and **Bilwi** are port towns with an entirely different cultural flavour. Bluefields is a bumpy bus and boat journey from Managua, Bilwi makes for a long journey on a couple of buses. Out to sea, the **Corn Islands**, fringed with coral, are popular for bathing, snorkelling and diving. All can be reached by plane from Managua.

Nicaragua telephone number changes

As of May 2009, Nicaraguan telephone numbers changed from seven to eight digits. Users will need to add '2' before dialling a land line, or '8' before dialling a mobile phone line.

Suggested itinerary If you're travelling through Central America, arriving from Honduras through Las Manos, you can stay a few days in **Estelí** and **León** to get the feel of the north. Drop in to **Managua** for a day or two to appreciate the capital's chaos if nothing else before spending a few days in **Granada**. From here you've got several options. Backtrack a bit for a few days in the isolated **Corn Islands**, or head round the southwest side of **Lake Nicaragua** and **Isla Ometepe**. **San Juan del Sur** on the Pacific coast is worth a stop before heading to Costa Rica. There are two options: straight down through **Peñas Blancas** to visit the Nicoya Peninsula, or through **San Carlos**, which is a good base for visiting the Caños Negro Wildlife Reserve, Fortuna and Volcán Arenal.

When to go

The dry season runs from December to May, with temperatures becoming unbearably hot towards the end of the season. The wettest months are June to October. The most popular time to visit is just after the rainy season in November. The higher altitudes in the north are cooler year-round and chilly at night.

Sport and activities

The national game is baseball, with a season running from November to February. There are five major league teams and Managua's Estadio Nacional stadium attracts crowds of up to 20,000. Football comes a poor second, breaking the trend of most Latin countries.

Opportunities for **nature tourism** are growing rapidly, with the lowlands of the Caribbean coast, the Río San Juan and the highlands around Matagalpa attracting keen nature watchers. **Community tourism** is also developing, allowing intrepid travellers to experience daily life in Nicaraguan communities and cooperatives. The islands of Lake Nicaragua and the Maribios volcanoes of León and Chinandega are popular destinations for **trekking**. Granada is experiencing a steady rise in interest and activities such as **mountain biking**, hiking and kayaking are growing rapidly in popularity. The Pacific coast has some good swimming beaches and there are excellent **surfing** opportunities to the south. Out on the Corn Islands, **snorkelling** and **diving** are possible on nearby coral reefs.

Getting there

Air

From **Europe** take any trans-Atlantic flight to Miami or Houston and connect to **American**, **Continental** or **Grupo Taca**. From **North America** there are regular daily flights to Managua from Miami, Atlanta and Houston with either **American**, **Continental**, **Delta**, **Iberia** or **Taca**. There are also connections from several US cities through El Salvador. From **Latin America** there are good connections from Barranquilla, Bogotá, Buenos Aires, Cali, Cancún, Caracas,

Cartagena, Guatemala City, Guayaquil, Havana, La Paz, Lima, Medellín, Mexico City, Panama City, Quito, San José, San Salvador, Santiago, Santo Domingo and São Paulo.

River
In San Carlos there is an immigration post linking with the boat journey on the Río Frío connecting to Los Chiles in Costa Rica. There is no official border crossing between San Juan del Norte and Costa Rica.

Road
The main road links to the north are at El Guasaule (page 1078) and further inland on the Pan-American Highway at Las Manos (page 1062) with a third option at the border north of Somoto at El Espino in Honduras (page 1062). Crossing the border to Costa Rica in the south, the most commonly used crossing is at Peñas Blancas (page 1103), although it is also possible to leave from San Carlos for Los Chiles (page 1118), connecting with Fortuna and Lake Arenal.

Getting around

Air
La Costeña ① T2263-1228, operates air services to Bluefields, Corn Island, Minas (Bonanza/Siuna/Rosita), Puerto Cabeza, San Carlos and Waspám. **Atlantic Airlines** ① T2270-5355, www.atlanticairlines.com, provides similar coverage and connects to Tegucigalpa and other Honduran cities. Domestic flights should be reconfirmed as soon as possible. Luggage limits are: 9 kg hand luggage; stowed luggage 13.5 kg free, maximum 45 kg. Domestic departure tax is 30 córdobas in Managua and about 5 córdobas in outlying airports.

Airport information Passengers arriving by air pay an entry tax of US$5; departing passengers pay an airport tax of US$32, payable in US dollars, often included in the price of your ticket. There is a sales tax of US$5 on tickets issued in and paid for in Nicaragua; a transport tax of 1% is levied on all tickets issued in Nicaragua. For information on Managua airport, see page 1053.

Road
The Pan-American Highway from Honduras to Costa Rica is paved the whole way (384 km) as is the shorter international road to the Honduran frontier via Chinandega. The road between Managua and Rama (for Bluefields) is also paved. Road directions are given according to landmarks, even where there are street names or numbers.

If arriving overland, there is an US$8 charge. Exit tax for foreigners is US$2 (US$5 at weekends). Always insist on a receipt and if in doubt, go to the Immigration Department in Managua to verify the charge. Officials in Las Manos may try to overcharge – be firm.

Bus Local buses are the cheapest in Central America and often the most crowded. Baggage loaded on to the roof or in the luggage compartment may be charged for, usually at half the passenger rate or a flat fee of US$0.50. International **Ticabus** buses link Nicaragua with Central America from Panama to southern Mexico.

Car and motorcycle Motorists and motorcyclists pay US$20 in cash on arrival at the border (cyclists US$2, up to US$9 at weekends) in addition to the entry tax for other overland arrivals (see above). Do not lose the receipts, or you will have to pay again when you leave. Get the correct entry stamps or you will encounter all sorts of problems once inside the country. Vehicles not cleared by 1630 are held at customs overnight. Formalities can take up to four hours. On leaving, motorists pay five córdobas, plus the exit tax. Petrol is sold by the gallon. Regular petrol is US$0.73 per gallon, US$0.79 for super, diesel US$0.68 super – all unleaded. There are 24-hour service stations in the major cities, elsewhere they close at 1800. Be careful when driving at night, few roads are lit and there are people, animals and holes in the road. Crash helmets for motocyclists are compulsory.

Car hire costs around US$30 a day for a basic car, rising to US$85 for a jeep. Weekly discount rates are significant and if you want to cover a lot of sites quickly it can work out to be worthwhile. A minimum deposit of US$500 is required along with an international driving licence or a licence from your country of origin. Insurance costs US$10-23. Before signing up check insurance and what it covers and also ask about mileage allowance. Most agents have an office at the international airport and offices in other parts of Managua.

Cycling Several cyclists have said that you should take a 'proof of purchase' of your cycle or suggest typing out a phoney 'cycle ownership' document to help at border crossings.

Hitchhiking Hitching is widely accepted, but not easy because so many people do it and there is little traffic – offer to pay a small contribution.

Sea
The main Pacific ports are Corinto, San Juan del Sur and Puerto Sandino. The two main Atlantic ports are Puerto Cabezas and Bluefields.

Sleeping
Most hotels are run by independent operators with a few upmarket international chains beginning to arrive. Standards vary greatly but there is plenty of competition in the mid- to low-budget range in most towns. In smaller towns, cheaper hotels tend to be better value.

Eating and drinking
Try *nacatamales* (cornflower dumplings stuffed with pork or chicken and vegetables, and boiled in banana leaves), an excellent value meal. *Gallo pinto* (rice and beans) is another tasty dish. Fizzy drinks are known as *gaseosas* in Nicaragua, as in neighbouring countries. Fresh fruit-based drinks and juices are *frescos*. Coffee can be terrible as most good Nicaraguan beans go for export and locals drink instant – ask for *café percolado* (filter coffee).

Festivals and events
Businesses, shops and restaurants all close for most of Holy Week; many companies also close down during the Christmas to New Year period. Holidays that fall on a Sun are taken the following Mon.

1 Jan New Year's Day.
Mar/Apr Holy Week 1200 Wed to Easter Sun.

1 May Labour Day.
19 Jul Revolution of 1979.
14 Sep Battle of San Jacinto.
15 Sep Independence Day.
2 Nov All Souls' Day (Día de los Muertos).
7-8 Dec Immaculate Conception (La Purísima).
25 Dec Christmas Day.

Shopping

Masaya is the centre for *artesanía*, selling excellent crafts, high-quality cotton hammocks, leather goods and colourful woven rugs often used as wall hangings and wicker furniture. Ceramics are produced in many parts of the country.

Essentials A-Z

Customs and duty free

Duty-free import of 500 g of tobacco products, 3 litres of alcoholic drinks and 1 large bottle (or 3 small bottles) of perfume is permitted.

Electricity

110 volts AC, 60 cycles, US-style plugs.

Embassies and consulates

Canada, contact embassy in USA
Costa Rica, Av Central 2540, Barrio La California, San José, T221-2924.
El Salvador, Calle El Mirador y 93 Av Norte, No 4814, Col Escalón, San Salvador, T263-2292.
France, 34 Av Bugeaud, 75116 Paris, T4405-9042.
Germany, Joachim-Karnatz-Allee 45 (Ecke Paulstr) 10557 Berlin, T206-4380.
Honduras, Col Tepeyac, Bloque M-1, No 1130, DC T239-5225.
Italy, Via Brescia 16, 00198 Roma, T841-4693.
Mexico, Prado Norte 470, Col Lomas de Chapultepec, esq Explanada, T5540-5625.
Spain, Paseo de la Castellana 127, 1-B, 28046 Madrid, T555-5510.
UK, Vicarage House, 58-60 Kensington Church St, London W8 4DB, T020-7938-2373.
USA, 1627 New Hampshire Av NW Washington, DC 20009, T202-939-6570.

Health

Tap water is not recommended for drinking outside Managua, León and Granada and avoid uncooked vegetables and peeled fruit. Intestinal parasites abound; if requiring treatment, take a stool sample to a lab before going to a doctor. Malaria is prevalent; high risk areas are east of the great lakes, take regular prophylaxis. Dengue fever is increasingly present; take precautions to avoid being bitten by mosquitoes. See also page 51.

Internet

Widely available in main cities and in some smaller towns.

Language

A basic knowledge of Spanish is essential for independent travel in Nicaragua. On the Caribbean coast English is widely spoken, but in the rest of the country it's Spanish only. Nicaraguan Spanish is quite distinctive and initially tricky to grasp. Drop your 's's, roll your 'r's and turn your 't's to 'd's.

Media

All newspapers are published in Managua, but many are available throughout the country: **Dailies**: *La Prensa*, centre, the country's best, especially for coverage of events outside Managua; *El Nuevo Diario*, centre-left and sensationalist; *La Noticia*, right, government paper. **Weeklies**: *El Seminario*, left-leaning, well-written with in-depth analysis; *7 Días*, pro-Government; *Tiempo del Mundo*, owned by Rev Moon, good coverage of South America, not much on Nicaragua. **Monthlies**: *El País*, pro-government, good features. *Between the Waves*, tourist magazine in English.

Money → *US$1=19.11 córdobas (June 2009)*.

The unit of currency is the **córdoba (C)**, divided into 100 centavos. Any bank in Nicaragua will change US dollars to córdobas and vice-versa. US dollars are accepted as payment almost everywhere but change is given in córdobas. It is best to carry US$ notes and sufficient local currency away from the bigger towns. Take all the cash you need when visiting the Caribbean coast or Río San Juan. Carry small bills for travelling outside cities or using public buses.

ATMs and exchange

Bank queues can be very long so allow plenty of time, especially on Mon mornings and the 15th and 31st of every month. When changing money take some ID or a copy. You cannot change currencies other than US dollars and euro (**BanCentro** only). Money changers on the street (*coyotes*) during business hours are legitimate and their rates differ little from banks.

Visa and MasterCard are accepted in many restaurants, shops and hotels in Managua, Granada and León. This applies to a lesser extent to Amex, Credomatic and Diners Club. But don't rely exclusively on credit cards. For cash advances the most useful bank is **Banco de América Central (BAC)**. BAC offers credit-card advances, uses the Cirrus debit system and changes all traveller's cheques (TCs). TCs often carry a commission of 5% so use your credit/debit card or cash if you can. TCs can only be changed in Managua at *Multicambios* in Plaza España and around the country at branches of **BAC** and **Banco de Finanzas** (Amex cheques only). Purchase receipts may be required when changing TCs in banks.

In Managua, ATM machines in the airport, at the Metrocentro and Plaza Inter shopping malls and in many gas station convenience stores. Outside the capital ATMs are hard to find, but becoming increasingly common in the main towns and at 24-hr gas stations.

Cost of living and travelling

Nicaragua is not an expensive country as far as accommodation is concerned, and public transport is also fairly cheap. For food, a *comida corriente* costs about US$1.75 (restaurant meals US$4-13, breakfast US$2.50-3.50). However, on the islands or in out-of-the-way places where supplies have to be brought in by boat or air, you should expect to pay more. A tight daily budget would be around US$20-25 a day.

Opening hours

Banks Mon-Fri 0830-1200, 1400-1600, Sat 0830-1200/1300.
Businesses Mon-Fri 0800-1200, 1430-1730.

Post

Airmail to Europe takes 7-10 days, US$0.80; to USA, 18 days, US$0.55; to Australia, US$1.

Safety

Visitors must carry their passports with them at all times. A photocopy is acceptable, but make sure you also have a copy of your visa or entrance stamp. Pickpocketing and bag slashing occur in Managua, and on buses throughout the country. Apart from Managua at night, most places are generally safe. Reports of robberies and assaults in northern Nicaragua indicate that care should be taken in this area; ask about conditions before going, especially if proposing to leave the beaten track.

Telephone → *Country code T+505.*
Phone lines are owned by the **Entel**. As of May 2009, Nicaraguan telephone numbers changed from 7 to 8 digits. Users will need to add '2' before dialling a land line, or '8' before dialling a mobile phone line. If you are phoning from inside the prefix zone you need to dial the 8 digits, but if you are dialling a different zone you put '0' in front. For example, to call Managua from Masaya it would be T02266-8689. Phone cards are available from gas stations, supermarkets and shops.

International or national calls can be made at any **Entel** office, 0700-2200. All calls paid for in córdobas. To the USA, US$3 for the 1st minute, US$1 for each following minute. Collect calls (*por cobrar*) to the USA and Europe are possible. For **SPRINT**, dial 171; **AT&T** 174 and **MCI** 166. To connect to phone services in Germany dial 169, Belgium 172, Canada 168, Spain 162, Netherlands 177, UK 175.

Time

6 hrs GMT.

Tipping

US$0.50 per bag for porters; no tip for taxi drivers. Restaurant bills include a 15% tax and 10% service is added or expected as a tip.

Tourist information

Tourist offices in Nicaragua are more concerned with internal development than public service. Tour operators and foreign-owned hotels are often better sources of information. However, the **Institute of Tourism** in Managua (see page 1041) has a range of general brochures and information packs, www.visitanicar agua.com. In the USA, contact PO Box 140357, Miami, FL 33114-0357, T1-800-737-7253.

Useful websites

www.centramerica.com Has a search engine with news links and information.
www.nicanet.org For activist issues.
www.nicaragua.com Has an e-community.
www.toursnicaragua.com Has a good selection of photographs and images.
www.vianica.com Good on hotels, transport and itineraries.

Visas and immigration

Visa rules change frequently, so check before you travel, www.cancilleria.gob.ni. Visitors need a passport with a minimum validity of 6 months and may have to show an onward ticket and proof of funds in cash or cheques for a stay of more than a week. No visa is required by nationals of EU countries, the USA, Canada, Australia or New Zealand.

If you need a visa it can be bought before arriving at the border, it costs US$25, is valid for arrival within 30 days and for a stay of up to 30 days; 2 passport photographs are required. A full 30-day visa can be bought at the border, but it is best to get it in advance. Visas take under 2 hrs to process in the embassies in Guatemala City and Tegucigalpa, but may take 48 hrs elsewhere. Extensions can be obtained at the **Dirección de Migración y Extranjería**, Semáforo Tenderí, 2 1½ c al norte, Managua, T2244-3989 ext 3 (Spanish only), www.migracion.gob.ni. Arrive at the office before 0830. From the small office on the right-hand side you must obtain the *formulario* (3 córdobas). Then queue at the *caja* in the large hall to pay US$18 for your 30-day extension or US$37 for 90 days. This can take

hours. In the meantime you can complete the forms. With the receipt of payment you queue at the window on the right. With luck you will receive the extension stamp by midday. There is a small *Migración* office in Metrocentro shopping mall where you can obtain a visa extension. Another possibility is to leave the country for 72 hrs and re-enter on a new visa.

Weights and measures

The metric system is official, but in practice a mixture is used of metric, imperial and old Spanish measurements, including the *vara* (about 1 m) and the *manzana* (0.7 ha). Petrol is measured in US gallons, liquids in quarts and pints, speed in kph, fabric in yards, with centimetres and metres for height, pounds for weight and Celsius for temperature.

Working and volunteering

Volunteer work in Nicaragua is not as common as it was during the Sandinista years. Foreigners now work in environmental brigades supporting the **FSLN**, construction projects, agricultural cooperatives and environmental organizations. Certain skills are in demand, as elsewhere in the developing world.

To find out about the current situation, try contacting non-governmental organizations in your home country, such as the **Nicaraguan Network**, 1247 East St, SE, Washington, DC 20003, T202-544-9355, www.nicanet.org; twin-town/sister-city organizations and Nicaraguan Solidarity Campaigns, such as **NSC/ENN Brigades**, 86 Durham Rd, London, N7 7DT, T020-561-4836, www.nicaraguasc.org.uk, or **Dutch Nicaragua Komitee**, Aptdo Postal 1922, Managua.

Casa Danesa, T2267-8126 (Managua), may be able to help find volunteer work, usually for 3 months. An excellent short-term non-profit volunteer experience can be had with **El Porvenir**, 1420 Ogden St, No 204, Denver, CO, 80218, T303-861-1499, www.elporvenir.org, an outgrowth of **Habitats for Humanity**. Work on drinking water, latrine and re-forestation projects.

Managua and around

→ *Colour map 7, A1. Population: 1,328,695. Altitude: 40-200 m.*

Managua, the nation's capital and commercial centre since 1852, was destroyed by an earthquake in March 1931 and then partially razed by fire five years later. Rebuilt as a modern, commercial city, the centre was again decimated by an earthquake in December 1972 when just a few modern buildings were left standing. Severe damage from the Revolution of 1978-1979 and flooding of the lakeside areas as a result of Hurricane Mitch in 1998 added to the problems. It's a tribute to the city's resilience that it still has the energy to carry on. ▶▶ For listings, see pages 1046-1057.

Ins and outs

Getting there The airport is 12 km east of the city, near the lake. Buses and taxis (US$15 to Barrio Martha Quezada, half the price if hailed from the main road) run from the airport to the city. International bus services arrive at several terminals throughout the city. **Ticabus** and **King Quality** are in Barrio Martha Quezada, close to most of the cheap hotels. **Transnica** is in Metrocentro. Provincial bus services have three main arrival/departure points. City buses and taxis serve the provincial terminals. ▶▶ *See Transport, page 1053.*

Getting around Managua is on the southern shores of Lake Managua, 60 km from the Pacific. Instead of cardinal points, the following are used: *al lago* (north), *arriba* (east), *al sur* (south), *abajo* (west). The old centre is a garden monument consisting of open spaces, ageing buildings, lakeside restaurants. Despite lying over 14 seismic faults and the warnings of seismologists, important new buildings have been built here including a presidential palace between the ruins of the cathedral and the lakefront, the epicentre of the 1972 earthquake.

Two areas now lay claim to being the heart of Managua. The older of the two is based around the **Hotel Crown Plaza** (formerly the Hotel Intercontinental and still referred to as the *'viejo Intercontinental'*), with a shopping and cinema complex, complete with US-style 'food court' and, to the west, **Barrio Martha Quezada** with many mid-range and budget hotels, and international bus services. Nearby, to the south, **Plaza España** has the country's best supermarket and numerous shops, banks, travel agents, tour companies and nearly every airline office in the country. The other heart of the city is based on the **Carretera a Masaya**, running from the new cathedral to Camino de Oriente. This stretch of four-lane highway includes the **Rotonda Rubén Darío**, the **Metrocentro** shopping complex, numerous restaurants, the Pellas family business centre with the **BAC** and **Credomatic** headquarters, and the cinema, disco and offices of **Camino de Oriente**. You'll need to take a bus or taxi to get there or to the provincial bus terminals.

Buses are cheap, crowded and infamous for pickpockets. Their routes can be hard to fathom. **Taxis** must have red number plates. Taxi-sharing in Managua is standard for non-radio taxis, so don't be surprised if the driver stops to pick someone up on roughly the same route. ▶▶ *See Transport, page 1053.*

Tourist information **Instituto Nicaragüense de Turismo (INTUR)** ① *Hotel Crown Plaza, 1 c al sur, 1 c abajo, enter by the side door, T2254-5191, www.visitanicaragua.com, Mon-Sat 0800-1700*, provides limited information about Managua and other parts of the country.

Information on national parks and conservation should be obtained from **Sistema Nacional de Areas Protegidas (Sinap)** ① *Ministerio de Medio Ambiente y Recursos Naturales (Marena), Km 12.5 Carretera Norte, T2263-2617.*

Safety Nicaraguans are incredibly friendly and Managua is one of the safest cities in Latin America, but you should still take sensible precautions. Never walk at night unless you are in a good area or shopping centre zone. Arriving in Managua after dark is not a problem, but it's best to book your hotel in advance and take a taxi. Long-distance buses are fine, but be careful in the market when you arrive to take the bus. If you prefer to avoid the bus terminals all together, get off the bus before you reach the market. When you arrive at the **Ticabus** station, make sure you know where you want to go before setting out. The **Mercado Oriental** (not to be confused with the Camino de Oriente which is safe and fun), said to be the largest informal market in Latin America, and its barrio, Ciudad Jardín, should be avoided at all costs.

Sights

In the old centre of Managua near the lake shore, the attractive neoclassical **Palacio Nacional de la Cultura**, previously the Palacio de los Héroes de la Revolución, has been beautifully restored and houses the **Museo Nacional de Nicaragua** ① *Mon-Fri 0800-1700, Sat and Sun 0900-1600, US$2.25, includes a 20-min introductory guided tour in English and French*, as well as the Archivo Nacional and the Biblioteca Nacional.

Damaged by earthquake, the **Catedral Vieja** (old cathedral) now has a roof of narrow steel girders and side-window support bars to keep it standing, the atmosphere is of a

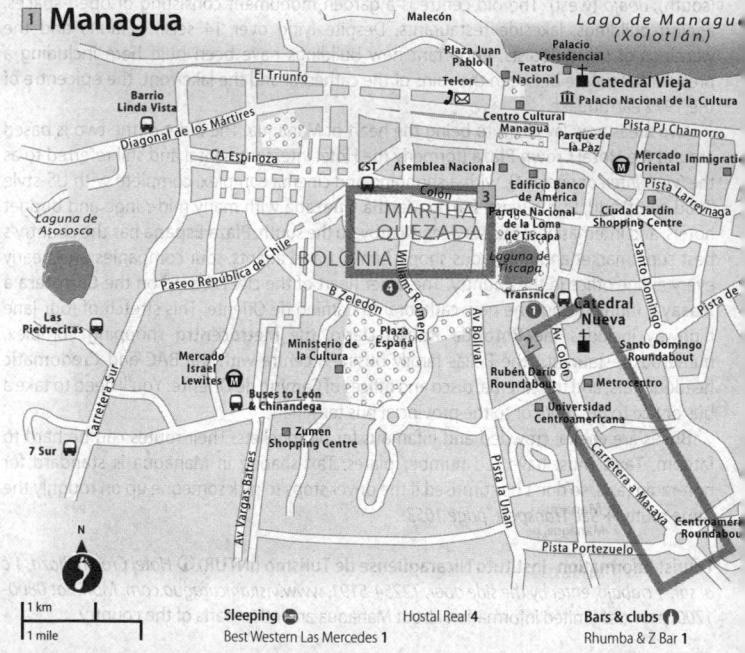

1 **Managua**

sad, old building past its prime, left in ruins, but still worth a look. The **Centro Cultural Managua**, next to the Palacio Nacional de Cultura, has a good selection of before and after photos of quake-struck Managua in 1972. The centre is also home to the national art school and the national music school. There are some art exhibits in galleries downstairs.

The garishly painted **Palacio Presidencial** is in front of the Palacio de la Cultura on the opposite corner to the old cathedral. These buildings are situated on the **Parque Central** and provide a striking contrast with the modern **Teatro Rubén Darío** ① *on the lake shore, www.tnrubendario.gob.ni, US$1.50-20 depending on show*, which hosts good plays, folkloric dances and musical events. There are usually temporary exhibitions in the theatre so, during the day, ask at the window to view the exhibit and you can probably look at the auditorium as well. The **Parque de la Paz**, just southeast of the Parque Central, is part of the rebuilding programme for the old centre. The park is a graveyard for weapons and a few dozen truckloads of AK-47s are buried there, some seen sticking out of the cement; take care here, the neighbourhood on the other side is of bad repute. Three blocks south of the Parque Central are the offices of the **Asamblea Nacional** (Nicaraguan parliament), which include the city's only high-rise building, once the Bank of America, now the offices of the *diputados* (parliamentary members).

A significant landmark is the **Hotel Crown Plaza**, which has a distinctive design similar to a Maya pyramid. Just in front is the Plaza Inter shopping centre with cinemas, restaurants and shops. The Bolívar-Buitrago junction, at the northwest corner of Plaza Inter, is on a number of important bus routes.

From the hilltop behind the Hotel Crown Plaza the **Parque Nacional de la Loma de Tiscapa** provides the best views of the capital and of the **Laguna de Tiscapa** on the south side of the hill. From the top, a giant black silhouette of **Sandino** stands looking out over the city. The spot has historical significance as it is the site of the former presidential palace; it was here that Sandino signed a peace treaty with Somoza and was abducted (and later killed) at the entrance to the access road. Underneath the park facing the *laguna* (now blocked by a fence) are the former **prison cells of the Somoza regime** ① *daily 0800-1630*, where inmates were said to have been tortured before being tossed into the lake. To get there, take the road behind the Crown Plaza to the top of the hill using an access road for the Nicaraguan military headquarters. Guards at the park are nervous about photography; ask permission and photograph only downtown and towards the stadium – do not take photos on the access road up to the park.

Nuevo Diario

eter Maps

Carretera Norte

Bello Horizonte Shopping Centre

Ciudad Xolotlán

unicipal

Pista Portezuelo

Mercado Iván Montenegro

Pista Sábana Grande

oberto Huembes/ Mercado Central

Buses to Masaya, Granada & Rivas

Centro Comercial Managua

To Airport & ⑦

Tc Mercado El Mayoreo Bus Station

Blvd Buenos Aires

➡ **Managua City maps**
1 Managua, page 1042
2 Metrocentro, page 1044
3 Martha Quezada, page 1047

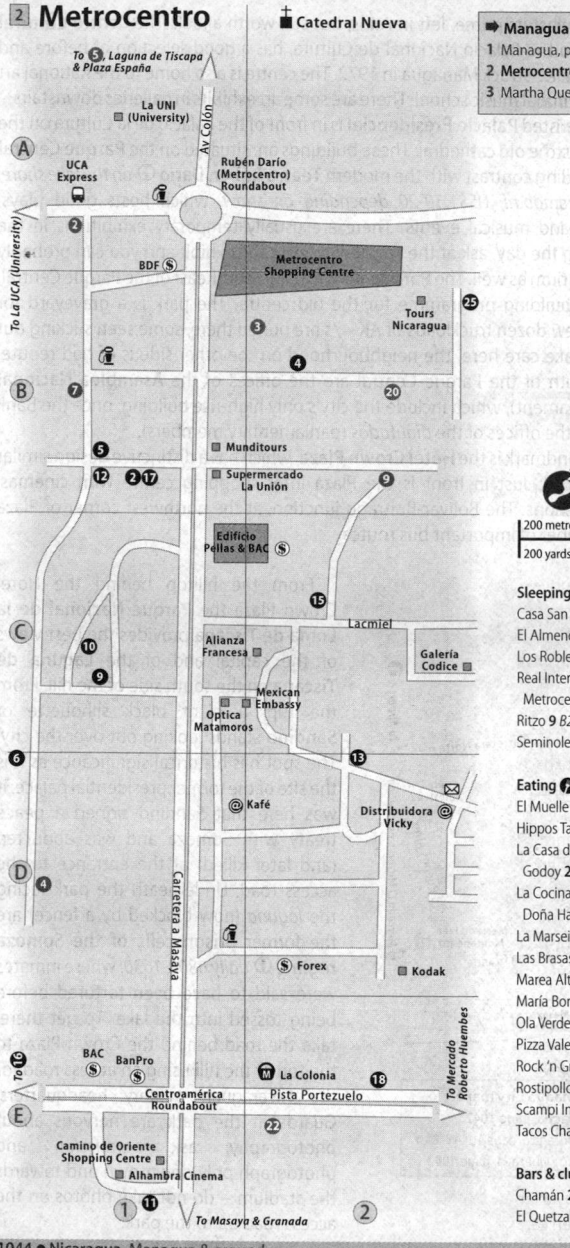

2 Metrocentro

✝ Catedral Nueva

■ Catedral Nueva

➡ **Managua City maps**
1 Managua, page 1042
2 Metrocentro, page 1044
3 Martha Quezada, page 1047

Sleeping 🛏
Casa San Juan **5** *A1*
El Almendro **2** *A1*
Los Robles **4** *D1*
Real Intercontinental
  Metrocentro **3** *B2*
Ritzo **9** *B2*
Seminole Plaza **7** *B1*

Eating 🍴
El Muelle **4** *B2*
Hippos Tavern & Grill **5** *B1*
La Casa de Los Mejía
  Godoy **25** *B2*
La Cocina de
  Doña Haydée **9** *C1*
La Marseillaise **6** *D1*
Las Brasas **11** *E1*
Marea Alta **12** *B1*
María Bonita **13** *D2*
Ola Verde **10** *C1*
Pizza Valenti **15** *C2*
Rock 'n Grill **17** *B1*
Rostipollo **16** *E1*
Scampi International **2** *B1*
Tacos Charros **18** *E2*

Bars & clubs 🍸
Chamán **20** *B2*
El Quetzal **22** *E2*

Map labels

To **5**, Laguna de Tiscapa & Plaza España
La UNI (University)
Av. Colón
UCA Express
Rubén Darío (Metrocentro) Roundabout
To La UCA (University)
BDF **$**
Metrocentro Shopping Centre
Tours Nicaragua
Munditours
Supermercado La Unión
Edificio Pellas & BAC **$**
Lacmiel
Alianza Francesa
Galería Codice
Mexican Embassy
Optica Matamoros
Kafé
Distribuidora Vicky
Carretera a Masaya
Forex
Kodak
To Mercado Roberto Huembes
BAC **$**
BanPro **$**
Centroamérica Roundabout
La Colonia
Pista Portezuelo
To **6**
Camino de Oriente Shopping Centre
Alhambra Cinema
To Masaya & Granada

200 metres
200 yards

From Tiscapa hill, the **Catedral Nueva** (new cathedral), inaugurated in 1993, can be seen 500 m to the south of the lake. Designed by the Mexican architect Ricardo Legoreto, comments on the exterior range from 'strikingly beautiful' to 'sacreligious'. The interior, which is mostly unadorned concrete, has been described as 'post-nuclear, with an altar resembling a futuristic UN Security Council meeting room'. Many visitors are fascinated by the Sangre de Cristo room, where a life-size bleeding Christ is encased in a glass and steel dome, illuminated by a domed roof with hundreds of holes for the sun to filter through. At night, the dome sparkles with the glow of lightbulbs in the holes. Pedestrian access is possible from the Metrocentro junction; vehicles need to approach from the east.

Barrio Martha Quezada, a mixture of well-to-do housing alongside poorer dwellings, is to the west of the Crown Plaza. South again, through the Bolonia district, is **Plaza España** by the Rotondo El Güengüense roundabout. Plaza España is reached either by continuing over the hill behind the Crown Plaza and branching right at the major junction, or by going south on Williams Romero, the avenue at the western edge of Barrio Martha Quezada (bus No 118).

Around Managua

Laguna de Xiloá
ⓘ *Sat and Sun only (US$0.35), US$1.60 for cars, US$0.30 for pedestrians; or take bus No 113 to Las Piedrecitas for Xiloá.*
There are several volcanic crater lakes close to Managua, some of which have become centres of residential development, with swimming, boating, fishing and picnicking facilities for the public. Among the more attractive of these lakes is Laguna de Xiloá, 16 km from Managua just off the new road to León. On Saturday and Sunday, the only days when buses run, Xiloá gets very crowded. It is quiet during the week and you can camp there, but without public transport you will have to walk or take a taxi. Other lakes within a 45-minute drive of Managua are the **Laguna de Masaya** and **Laguna de Apoyo** (see page 1088).

Museo Las Huellas de Acahualinca
ⓘ *Along the lake, 2 km due west of the Museo Nacional, T2266-5774, Mon-Fri 0800-1700, Sat and Sun 0900-1600, US$2.50; additional US$2 to take photographs, US$3 for video cameras; all explanations in Spanish; taxi recommended as it is hard to find and in an unsafe neighbourhood.*
These ancient prehistoric animal and human footprints, preserved in the sedimentary tufa and discovered when stone was being quarried, represent some of the oldest evidence of human occupation in Nicaragua. A museum has been created around the original site and the 6000-year-old footprints have been left as they were found in excavation. The museum also has a small display of ceramic artefacts found at the site and an illustration of the estimated height of the people who made the footprints.

Bus Nos 102, 12 or 6 pass the site; look for a concrete tower and a huge stone slab by a small red footbridge. Off the main road there are no signs. If you are driving, take the street that leads west (*abajo*) from the old centre. Turn right immediately before López Richardson; the pavement becomes a dirt road and the museum is on the right.

Mateare and Momotombito
Thirty kilometres northwest of Managua, **Mateare** is a pleasant fishing and agricultural town with some of the finest lake fish in Lake Managua (eat at your own risk). Distanced from the capital by a large peninsula, the lake is much cleaner here than on the Managua side. The fishermen can take you to the small volcanic island of **Momotombito** (US$60 for

a day trip). The best time of year to visit is during the rainy season, when the island is green and the swell on the lake small. Beware of snakes when hiking around the island. There are other small islands in the shadow of the smoking Momotombo volcano, which appears to loom over the lake from the mainland shore. Momotombito is a nature reserve, and has much bird and reptile life and a legendary family of albino crocodiles. There is a small military outpost on the calm side of the island. Stop there to check in if you wish to hike on the islands. Bring drinks or food as gifts for the (non-uniformed) guards, who are very friendly and usually quite bored. They might take you hiking for a small fee.

Pacific beaches near Managua

There are several beaches on the Pacific coast, about an hour's drive from Managua. Because of their proximity to the capital, they get very crowded during the high season (January to April). The nearest are Pochomil and Masachapa (54 km from Managua, bus service from terminal in Israel Lewites market every hour, US$1). **Pochomil** beach is deserted in the week out of season; it gets cleaner the further south you go, but there are rocks and strong waves here so swim with care. It is a tourist centre with a few hotels and many small family-owned restaurants. Don't sleep on the beach or the mosquitoes will eat you alive.

At the entrance to **Masachapa** is the access road to the **Montelimar Resort**. Just before the resort gates is the dirt road to the area's nicest public beach, **Montelimar Gratis** or **El Muelle de Somoza**, a long deserted stretch of clean sand from the Somoza pier to the rocky point that separates the resort from the rest of Masachapa. Take a bus to Masachapa and walk from main highway on the entrance road or drive to the pier, then walk north.

La Boquita is the nearest beach to the villages south of Managua and is visited by turtles from August to November. Just south of **Casares** (69 km from Managua) are further beaches. Access is a long hike or journey by 4WD and lodging is available.

Heading north from Managua, a visit to the broad sandy **El Velero beach** ① US$3.50, is recommended, despite the entry fee and poor road. Facilities are controlled by the **INSSBI (Instituto Nicaraguense de Seguridad Social y Bienestar)** for state employees and weekends are fully booked weeks in advance. The beach is beautiful and the sea is ideal for surfing and swimming. To get there, turn off at Km 60 on the old road to León and follow signs. **El Tránsito** is another lovely, undeveloped Pacific beach. Buses from Managua leave at 1200, 1315 and 1500 (from Terminal Lewites) and return at 0600 or 0700, US$0.70.

◉ Managua and around listings

Hotel and guesthouse prices		
LL over US$150	**L** US$100-150	**AL** US$66-99
A US$46-65	**B** US$31-45	**C** US$21-30
D US$12-20	**E** US$7-11	**F** under US$7
Restaurant prices		
▯▯▯ over US$15	▯▯ US$8-15	▯ under US$8

See pages 45-48 for further information.

◉ Sleeping

Managua *p1041, maps p1042, p1044 and p1047*
Accommodation is generally expensive in Managua. Martha Quezada has the best

budget options, but it's unsafe to walk around at night, particularly near the bus station where down-and-outs hang around. Bolonia has good mid-range hotels, while Metrocentro is the place for business and high-end travellers. A 15% tax is supposed to be added to hotel bills – ask for a receipt if you need one.

Martha Quezada and around
L-LL Hotel Crowne Plaza, 'el viejo Hotel Inter', in front of the Plaza Inter shopping centre, T2228-3530, www.crowneplaza.com. This is

one of the most historic buildings in Managua, home to the foreign press for more than a decade, as well as Howard Hughes. The Sandinista government also ran Nicaragua from here in the early 1980s. Some rooms have a lake view, but are small for the price. Use of swimming pool for non-residents on Sun is US$18.

AL Mansión Teodolinda, INTUR, 1 c al sur, ½ c abajo, T2228-1060, www.teodolinda.com.ni. Popular with business people, this hotel has good-quality room, with private bath, hot water, kitchenette, cable TV, phone. There's also a pool, bar, restaurant and laundry service.

A El Conquistador, Plaza Inter, 1 c al sur, 1 c abajo, T2222-4789, www.hotelelconquistador.com. 11 airy rooms with a/c, hot water, cable TV, telephone and Wi-Fi. Pleasant courtyard patio, and a range of services including tours, business centre and laundry.

B Los Cisneros, Ticabus, 1c al Norte, 1½ c abajo, T2222-3535, www.hotelloscisneros.com. Apartments and rooms with hot water, cable TV and Wi-Fi overlook a lush garden with hammock space. They can organize transit to the airport, serve breakfast, and speak English. Cheaper with fan (**C**). Recommended.

B María La Gorda, Iglesia El Carmen, 1 c al sur, ½ c arriba, ½ c al sur, just west of Martha QuezadaT2268-2455. Good value. 8 simple, secure rooms with a/c, private bath, hot water and cable TV. There's internet, laundry services, airport transfer, breakfast included and free local calls.

C Hospedaje Carlos, Ticabus, ½ c al lago, T2222-2554. Secure, family-run place with 8 clean good-value rooms, some have private bath. Rooms on left at the back better than on right

C Jardín de Italia, Ticabus, 1 c arriba, ½ c lago, T2222-7967. Well-known, friendly

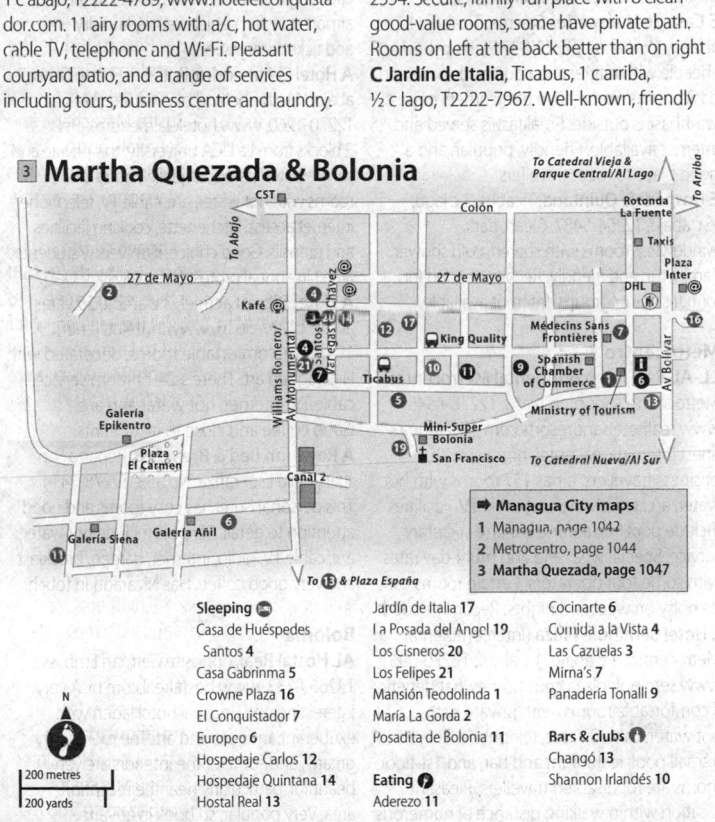

3 Martha Quezada & Bolonia

➡ **Managua City maps**
1 Managua, page 1042
2 Metrocentro, page 1044
3 Martha Quezada, page 1047

Sleeping
Casa de Huéspedes Santos **4**
Casa Gabrinma **5**
Crowne Plaza **16**
El Conquistador **7**
Europeo **6**
Hospedaje Carlos **12**
Hospedaje Quintana **14**
Hostal Real **13**
Jardín de Italia **17**
La Posada del Ángel **19**
Los Cisneros **20**
Los Felipes **21**
Mansión Teodolinda **1**
María La Gorda **2**
Posadita de Bolonia **11**

Eating
Aderezo **11**
Cocinarte **6**
Comida a la Vista **4**
Las Cazuelas **3**
Mirna's **7**
Panadería Tonalli **9**

Bars & clubs
Changó **13**
Shannon Irlandés **10**

hotel with 8 rooms. Each has private bath, a/c and cable TV. There's a garden, and services include tours, airport transfer and parking. Mixed reports. Take care of your belongings.
C Los Felipes, Ticabus, 1½ c abajo, T2222-6501, www.hotellosfelipe.com.ni. This pleasant hotel has a lovely garden filled with a plethora of coloured parrots. The 28 rooms have private bath, cable TV, Wi-Fi and telephone. There's a pool and staff are friendly. Cheaper with fan (**D**).
D Casa Gabrinma, Ticabus 1 c al sur, ½ c arriba, opposite radio *La Primerísima*, T2222-6650. This family hotel has 4 basic rooms with fan and cable TV. Cheap food, group discounts, friendly and quiet.
E Casa de Huéspedes Santos, Ticabus, 1 c al lago, 1½ c abajo, T2222-3713. Ramshackle cheapie with interesting courtyard space and basic rooms. Some have bath, others have washbasins outside. Breakfast is served and internet available. Friendly, popular, and a good place to meet travellers.
E Hospedaje Quintana, Ticabus, 1 c lago, ½ c abajo, T2254-5487. Clean, dark, windowless rooms with shared, cold shower. Family-run and friendly. Recommended for longer stays or groups. Internet available.

Metrocentro

LL-AL Real Intercontinental Metrocentro, Metrocentro shopping plaza, T2278-4545, www.realhotelsandresorts.com. Nicaragua's finest international hotel, popular with business travellers. It has 157 rooms with hot water, a/c, telephone and cable TV. Facilities include pool, restaurant, bar and secretary service. Special weekend and multi-day rates with some tour operators. Certain rooms can be noisy on weekend nights. Recommended.
L Hotel Seminole Plaza (Intercontinental Metrocentro, 1 c abajo, 1 c al sur, T2270-0061, www.seminoleplaza.com. Somewhat generic, if comfortable rooms, with private bath, hot water, cable TV, a/c, telephone. There's a small pool, restaurant and bar, and 1st-floor rooms are for disabled travellers. Pleasant location within walking distance of numerous

bars and restaurants, rooms on the pool side are quieter. Good value, recommended.
AL Hotel Los Robles, Restaurante La Marseillaise, 30 varas al sur, T2267-3008, www.hotellosrobles.com. Managua's best B&B offers comfortable rooms with classy furnishings, cable TV, a/c, hot water, Wi-Fi and luxurious bath tubs. The beautiful colonial interior is complimented by a lush, cool garden, complete with bubbling fountain. Book in advance. Recommended.
A Casa San Juan, Reparto San Juan, Calle Esperanza 560, T2278-3220. Rooms in this friendly, family-run hotel are clean, fresh and comfortable. They have a/c, bath and cable TV. Other services include internet, airport transfer, vehicle rental, laundry and ticket reservation.
A Hotel El Almendro, Rotonda Rubén Darío, 2 c abajo, ½ c sur (behind big wall, ring bell), T2270-1260, www.hotelelalmendro.com. 2 blocks from La UCA university, this private and secure hotel has good quality, good-value rooms with hot water, a/c, cable TV, telephone, internet access, kitchenette, cooking facilities and utensils. Good choice, if university students aren't in annual protest (normally Nov-Dec).
A Hotel Ritzo, Lacmiel, 3 c arriba, 25 varas al sur, T2277-5616, www.hotelritzo.net. 10 sparse, comfortable rooms, decorated with Nicaraguan art. There's 24-hr room service, cable TV, internet, hot water and a/c. Good coffee and close to restaurants.
A Royal Inn Bed & Breakfast, Reparto San Juan, Calle Esperanza, No 553, T2278-1414. This personal hotel has cosy rooms and good attention to detail. Services include hot water, a/c, cable TV, radio, internet, garden, breakfast and very good coffee. Has Nicaraguan touch.

Bolonia

AL Hostal Real, opposite German Embassy, T2266-8133, www.hostalreal.com.ni. A very interesting and unusual hotel laden with exuberant antiques and art. The rooms vary greatly, and some of the interiors are very beautiful, particularly near the reception area. Very popular, so book in advance.

A Hotel Europeo, Canal 2, 75 varas abajo, T2268-2130, www.hoteleuropeo.com.ni. Each room is different, and some have interesting furnishings. Rooms at the back are best. All rooms have a/c, private bath with hot water, cable TV. There's a restaurant, bar, fax, secure parking, laundry service, free internet in lobby and pool. Price includes continental breakfast. Staff are friendly and helpful. A quiet location.

A La Posada del Angel, opposite Iglesia San Francisco, T2268-7228, pdangel@ibw.com.ni. This hotel, filled with interesting art work and antique furniture, has lots of personality. Good, clean rooms, private bath, hot water, cable TV, a/c, minibar, Wi-Fi and telephone. Pool, laundry service. Book ahead.

A Posadita de Bolonia, Canal 2, 3 c abajo, 75 m al sur, casa 12, T2268-6692. This intimate hotel has 8 rooms with private bath, cable TV, internet. It's in a quiet area, close to several galleries. Friendly owner speaks English and is helpful. Full breakfast included.

Managua airport

AL Best Western Las Mercedes, Km 11 Carretera Norte, across from international terminal, T2263-1011, www.lasmercedes.com.ni. Convenient for flights, with large tree-filled grounds, tennis court, pool and barber shop. Rooms are comfortable, but check before accepting one. There can be noise and fumes from the airport during peak hours. Local phone calls can be made here when airport office is shut; the outdoor café is the best place to kill time near the airport.

Pacific beaches near Managua *p1046*

LL Montelimar Resort, near Pochomil and Masachapa, T2269-6769, www.barcelomontelimarbeach.com. This expensive resort is becoming popular with package tours and is often booked solid Nov-Apr. It has a broad, unspoilt sandy beach ideal for bathing and surfing. The nearest public transport is 3 km away at Masachapa, taxi from Managua US$30 (70 km), or hire a car.

A Ticomo Mar, on the nicest part of Pochomil beach, T2265-0210. Best hotel in

the region apart from Montelimar, but still poor value. Bungalows have private porches, kitchenettes, hot water, a/c, private bath.

B Hotel Palmas del Mar, La Boquita, centre of beach, T2552-8715. Beach front, private bath, a/c or fan, a bit noisy.

B Villas del Mar, just north of Pochimal centre, T2266-6661. Crowded, overpriced food, party atmosphere, use of swimming pool US$5 per person.

C-E Centro Vacacional de Trabajadores, El Tránsito. Has good-value beach flats for 4-6 people at north end, normally available mid-week. Good meals available from Señora Pérez on the beach; possible accommodation too.

D Suleyka, Centro Turístico La Boquita, T2552-8717. Shared baths and fan, 6 rooms, good restaurant with fresh fish dishes.

❶ Eating

Managua *p1041, maps p1042, p1044 and p1047*
The Metrocentro shopping centre has several good ¶-¶ restaurants in its food court. Along with US, Guatemalan and Nicaraguan (**Rostipollo, Tip-Top, Quick Burger** and others) fast-food chains, it has cheaper versions of good Nicaraguan restaurants like **Doña Haydée**, and **María Bonita**.

Most restaurants will make a big salad or a rice, banana and bean dish for vegetarians.

Martha Quezada

¶ **Anada**, Estatua de Montoya 10 varas arriba, T2228-4140. Daily 0700-2100. Nicaragua's original non-meat eatery and still one of the best. They serve wholesome vegetarian food, juices, smoothies, breakfasts and soups.

¶ **Cocinarte**, INTUR, 1 c sur, closed Sun. International and vegetarian cuisine in a rancho-style setting.

¶-¶ **Rancho Tiscapa**, gate at Military Hospital, 300 varas sur, T2268-4290. Laid-back ranch-style eatery and bar serving traditional dishes like *indio viejo, gallo pinto* and *cuajada con* tortilla. Good food and a great, breezey view of new Managua and Las Sierras. Recommended.

¶ Aderezo, Ticabus 2 c arriba, ½ c sur. Clean, pleasant little place serving home-cooked *comida típica*.

¶ Comida a la Vista Buffet, Ticabus, 2 c abajo. Often packed out at lunchtime. Economical buffet food.

¶ Las Cazuelas, CST, 2 c sur, 1 c arriba, opposite Casa de Huéspedes Santos, T2228-6090. Always music on here. Great-value breakfasts (US$1.50) with big portions, lunch and dinner too.

¶ Mirna's, near Pensión Norma, 0700-1500. Good-value breakfasts and *comidas*, lunch buffet 1200-1500, popular with travellers and Nicaraguans, friendly service.

¶ Panadería Tonalli, Ticabus, 3 c arriba, ½ c al sur. Pleasant little bakery serving nutritious wholemeal breads, cakes, cookies and coffee. Proceeds go to social projects.

Metrocentro

¶¶¶ La Marseillaise, Calle Principal Los Robles, T2277-0224. Closed Sun. Classy and expensive French restaurant with a good wine list and a sophisticated array of gastronomic offerings including salmon and lobster. Mixed reviews.

¶¶¶ Lo Stradivari, Lacmiel, ½ c abajo, T2277-2277. Low-key no-frills ambience at this Italian restaurant. Excellent home-made pastas, good salads, outdoor seating and good wine sauces. Recommended.

¶¶¶ Marea Alta, Colonial los Robles 75, T2278-2459. Daily 1200-2200. Has good fresh fish, including sushi. Skip the shellfish but try grilled dorado fish or tuna. There's outdoor seating and a relaxed ambience.

¶¶¶ María Bonita, Altamira, la Vicky, 1½ c abajo, T2270-4326. Mexican and Nicaraguan food, including a lunchtime buffet during the week. However, it's perhaps most popular on weekend nights, with live music and a noisy, happy crowd. Pleasant ambience and friendly staff.

¶¶¶ Rock 'n Grill, next to Marea Alta, 278-6906. Filled with rock memorabilia,

this fun restaurant serves steaks, ribs, burgers and shrimps. Music on Thu night. Popular with Nicaraguans and foreigners.

¶¶¶ Scampi International, ALKE 1 ½ c abajo, T2270-6013. Big, club-like space that attracts a mostly young clientele. They serve sushi and lobster, and keep live fish in a giant tank near the entrance. Seafood as fresh as it gets.

¶¶¶ Tre Fratelli, Colonial los Robles, Hotel Princess, 20 varas abajo, T2278-3334. Service is excellent at this classic Italian restaurant, but mixed reviews regarding the food; avoid the white cream sauces. There's a happy hour on the deck outside.

¶¶ El Muelle, Intercontinental Metrocentro, 1½ c arriba, T2278-0056. Managua's best seafood. There's excellent *pargo al vapor* (steamed red snapper), *dorado a la parilla*, *cocktail de pulpo* (octopus), and great *ceviche*. It's a crowded, informal setting with outdoor seating. Highly recommended.

¶¶ Hippos Tavern and Grill, Colonial los Robles, ½ c al sur, T2267-1346. Tavern-style place serving grilled food and good salads. Nice ambience and music. A popular spot for people-watching and after-work cocktails.

¶¶ La Cocina de Doña Haydée, opposite Pastelería Aurami, Planes de Altamira, T2270-6100, www.lacocina.com.ni. Daily 0730-2230. Once a popular family kitchen eatery that has gone upscale. Traditional Nicaraguan food– try the *surtido* dish for 2, the *nacatamales* and the traditional *Pio V* dessert, a sumptuous rum cake. Popular with foreign residents.

¶¶ La Hora del Taco, Monte de los Olivos, 1 c al lago, on Calle Los Robles. Good Mexican dishes including *fajitas* and *burritos*. A warm, relaxed atmosphere.

¶¶ Las Brasas, in front of Cine Alhambra, Camino Oriente. The best value in town, serving decent, traditional Nicaraguan fare in an outdoor setting. It's a good place to come with friends and order a half bottle of rum; it comes with a bowl of ice, limes, coke and 2 plates of food. Great atmosphere.

¶¶ Ola Verde, Doña Haydée, 1 c abajo, ½ c lago, T2270-3048. All organic menu of mostly veggie food, but some organic meat dishes too. Servings can be small and service mediocre, but there's a good store with organic coffee to keep you busy while you wait.

¶ Rostipollo, just west of Centroamérica roundabout, T2277-1968. Headquarters for the Nicaraguan chain that is franchised right across Central America and Mexico. Delicious chicken cooked over a wood fire, Caesar salad, lunch specials and combo dishes. You'll find it next to McDonald's inside the Metrocentro food court.

¶ Casa de Café, Lacmiel, 1 c arriba, 1½ c sur, T2278-0605. Daily 0700-2200. The mother of all cafés in Managua, with airy upstairs seating area that makes the average coffee taste much better. Good turkey sandwiches, desserts, pies and *empanadas*. There's another branch on the 2nd level of the Metrocentro shopping plaza, but it lacks the charm and fresh air. Popular and recommended.

¶ El Guapinol, Metrocentro, from 1100 daily. The best of the Food court eateries with very good grilled meat dishes, chicken, fish and a hearty veggie dish (US$4.50). Try *Copinol* dish with grilled beef, avocado, fried cheese, salad, tortilla and *gallo pinto* US$4.

¶ La Casa de los Mejía Godoy, Plaza el Sol, 2 c sur, T2270-4928. This famous terraced restaurant regularly hosts live music acts (see Bars and clubs). It serves Nicaraguan cuisine, and good, economical lunch buffets. Very popular and recommended.

¶ Pizza Valenti, Colonial Los Robles, T2278-7474. Best cheap pizza in town, packed on Sun nights – national 'eating out with the family' night. They do home delivery.

¶ Tacos Charros, Plaza el Café, 1 c abajo. The place for cold beer and tasty *tacos*. Check out the great photos of Pancho Villa, Mexico's most enigmatic revolutionary hero.

Bolonia

¶¶¶ El Churrasco, Rotonda El Güegüence. This is where the Nicaraguan president and parliamentary members decide the country's future over a big steak. Try the restaurant's namesake which is an Argentine-style cut with garlic and parsley sauce. Recommended.

¶¶ Santa Fe, across from Plaza Bolonia, T2268-9344. Tex-Mex style with walls covered in stuffed animal heads. It does a pretty good beef grill and *taco* salad, but bad *burritos*. Noisy and festive at lunchtime.

¶ Rincón Cuscalteco, behind Plaza Bolonia, T2266-4209. Daily 1200-2200. Good cheap *pupusas salvadoreñas*, also *vigorón* and *quesillos*. Cheap beer and very relaxed.

⊙ Entertainment

Managua *p1041, maps p1042, p1044 and p1047*

Bars and clubs

There are several god places on Lacmiel (and it's safe to walk at night as well).

Bar Chaman, Colonial Los Robles. Frequented by a young, wild crowd. Lots of dancing and sweating to salsa, rock and disco on tape.

Bar Changó, Plaza Inter, 2 c sur, 15 varas abajo. Where the terminally hip enjoy salsa, reggae, Brazilian hip-hop, rock, pop, jazz and world music. Pleasant setting under a large tree.

El Quelite, Enitel Villa Fontana 5 c abajo, T2267-0126. Open-air, typical Nicaraguan dance bar with good food; try the *corvina a la plancha* (sea bass) US$5. Lots of dancing and live acts Thu-Sun.

El Quetzal, Rotonda Centro América, 1 c arriba, opposite Galería Simón, T2278-1733. Fun crowd who fill big dance floor and dance non-stop. Free entry, live music, ranchera, salsa, merengue.

La Casa de los Mejía Godoy, Plaza El Sol, 2 c sur, T2278-4913, www.losmejiagodoy.org, Thu-Sat, opens 2100. This is a chance to see 2 of Nicaragua's most famous folk singers. A very intimate setting, check with programme to make sure either Carlos or Luis Enrique is playing. Fri is a good bet, entrance US$15.

Rhumba & Z Bar, Carretera a Masaya Km 3.5, opposite Galería Simón, T2278-1733. Lots of dancing, popular, weekends only.

Shannon Bar Irlandés, 1 block east and 1 block south of Ticabus, T2222-6683, open 1700-0200. Excellent food, whisky and Guinness (which often runs dry due to popularity). Recommended. Some rooms with shared bath (**F**) with breakfast available for those early-morning **Ticabus** departures.

Cinema
Alhambra 1, 2 & 3, Camino de Oriente, T2270-3835. US films, Spanish subtitles, US$3, bring sweater for polar a/c.
Alianza Francesa, Altamira, 1 block north of Mexican Embassy. Shows French films and has art exhibits during the day.
Cinemas Inter, Plaza Inter, T2222-5122. American films with Spanish subtitles. Book in advance on weekend evenings.
Metrocentro Cinemark, Metrocentro. Small, crowded theatre with 6 screens and steep seating.

Dance and theatre
Ballet Tepenahuatl, folkloric dances at the Teatro Rubén Darío.
Doña Haydée, opposite **Pastelería Aurami**, Planes de Altamira, T2270-6100. Folkloric dance on Tue.
Intermezzo del Bosque, Colegio Centroamericano 5 km al sur, T8088-30071. On Wed, food, dances, US$40, check with **Delicias del Bosque**, or **Grayline Tours**, www.graylinenicaragua.com.
Teatro Nacional Rubén Darío, Frente al Malecón de Managua, T2222-7426.

⊛ Festivals and events

Managua *p1041, maps p1042, p1044 and p1047*
1-10 Aug The Festival de Santo Domingo (Managua's patron saint) is held at El Malecón church: ceremonies, horse racing, bullfights, cockfights, a lively carnival; proceeds go to the General Hospital.
1 Aug (½ day) and **10 Aug** are local holidays.
7 Dec La Purísima, is held nationwide and is particularly celebrated in Managua. Altars are erected to the Virgin Mary, with singing, processions, fireworks and offerings of food.

○ Shopping

Managua *p1041, maps p1042, p1044 and p1047*
Bookshops
Hispamer, UCA, 1 c arriba, 1 c al sur. Best Spanish-language bookstore in the country, with maps, postcards and tourist items.

Handicrafts
Mercado Oriental is not recommended, see Safety, page 1042.
Mercado Ricardo Huembes (also called **Mercado Central**), Pista Portezuelo, take bus No 110 or 119. The best place to buy handicrafts, and just about anything else. Artesanía from all parts of the country at the northeast end of the parking lot.
Metrocentro, in Plaza Inter and in Centro Comercial Managua. Some handicrafts (goldwork, embroidery) and good general shopping.
Mi Pueblo at Km 9.5 on Carretera Sur, T8882-5650. Handicrafts and plants and there's also a good restaurant.
Takesa, del Intercontinental 2 c al sur, ½ abajo, Edif Bolívar 203, T2268-3301. A smart shop selling Nicaraguan arts and crafts, high quality and high prices.

Imported goods
Galería Simón, opposite Z-Bar on Carretera a Masaya. Imported goods, take your passport, accepts US$ and TCs (to the value of purchase).

▲ Activities and tours

Managua *p1041, maps p1042, p1044 and p1047*
Canopy tour
Tiscapa Canopy Tour, T8893-5017, Tue-Sun 0900-1630, US$13. A breathtaking zip-line ride that is operated using 3 long metal cables and 4 platforms to traverse Tiscapa lake, at times more than 70 m in the air.

Spectator sports

The national sport and passion is **baseball**, with games on Sun mornings at the Estadio Denis Martínez. The season runs Nov-Feb and tickets cost US$1-5. Other popular sports include **basketball** and **football** although none have a regular venue and season. Nicaragua has had 4 lightweight world champion **boxers** but the big fights are staged outside the country. There is also **cockfighting** and **bullfighting** (but no kill).

Tour operators

Careli Tours, Edificio Invercasa, Planes de Altamira, Frente al Colegio Pedagógico La Salle, www.carelitours.com. Guided tours through western Nicaragua and down the Río San Juan.
Grayline Nicaragua, Rotunda El Güegüense, 250 m al sur, contiguo a **Viajes América**, PO Box 91, Edificio Central Correos de Nicaragua, T2268-2412, www.grayline nicaragua.com. Day trips, tours packages, hotels, car rentals.
Schuvar Tours, Plaza España Edif Bamer No 4, T2266-3588, www.schuvartours.com. Various cultural and adventure tours, transportation, car rental and flights.
Tours Nicaragua, Shell Plaza el Sol 110, 1 c al sur, 120 varas abajo, 110, T2252-4035, www.toursnicaragua.com. One of the best, offeringa wide variety of tours to all parts of the country in vans, 4WD, boats and small plane. English-, German- and French-speaking guides. Contact Mike Newton, helpful.

⊖ Transport

Managua *p1041, maps p1042, p1044 and p1047*
Air
For **Managua International Airport (MGA)**, take any bus marked 'Tipitapa' from Mercado Huembes, Mercado San Miguel or Mercado Oriental (near Victoria brewery), US$0.25. Alternatively, take a taxi (US$7-15). Be early for international flights – formalities are slow and thorough. Artisan stalls and cheap food in between arrivals and departures. Duty free shops, café, toilets through immigration. You are not allowed to stay overnight in the airport. There are ATMs and money-changing facilities.
Domestic flights Tickets can be bought at the domestic terminal, which is located just west of the exit for arriving international passengers, or from city travel agents or tour operators. Keep luggage to a minimum, as there isn't much capacity on these little planes. Also be aware that fuel and ticket prices are rising, and schedules are subject to change at any time. To **Bilwi**, La Costeña, 0630, 1030, 1430, US$148 return, 1½ hrs. To **Bluefields**, La Costeña, 0600, 0630, 1000, 1400, US$128 return, 1 hr; **Atlantic Airlines**, 0645, 1410. To **Corn Islands**, La Costeña, 0630, 1400, US$165 return, 1½ hrs; **Atlantic Airlines**, 0645, 1410. To **Minas**, La Costeña, 0900, US$139 return, 1 hr. To **San Carlos**, La Costeña, 0925, 1425, US$120 return. To **Waspam**, La Costeña, 1000, US$155 return, 1½ hrs. For return times see individual destinations.

Airline offices AeroMéxico, Optica Visión, 75 varas arriba, 25 varas al lago, T2266-6997, www.aeromexico.com. **American Airlines**, Rotonda El Güegüense 300 varas al sur, T2255-9090, www.aa.com. **Atlantic Airlines**, T2270-5355. **Continental Airlines**, Edificio Ofiplaza, piso 2 edificio 5, T2278-7033, www.continental.com. **Copa Airlines**, Carretera a Masaya Km 4.5, edificio CAR No 6, T2233-1624, www.copaair.com. **Delta Airlines**, Rotonda El Güegüense 100 m arriba, T2254-8130, www.delta.com. **La Costeña**, T2263-2142. **Spirit Airlines**, airport, T2233-2884, www.spiritair.com. **Taca Airlines**, Edificio Barcelona, Plaza España, T2266-3136, www.taca.com.

Bus
Local Beware of pickpockets on the crowded urban buses, particularly on tourist routes. City buses run every 10 mins 0530-1800, every 15 mins 1800-2200, when last services begin their routes; buses are frequent but routes are difficult to fathom. Tickets cost about US$0.20.

The main bus routes are:

No 101 from Las Brisas, passing CST, Hotel Intercontinental, Mercado Oriental, then on to **Mercado San Miguel** and **El Mayoreo**;

No 103 from 7 Sur to Mercado Lewites, Plaza 19 de Julio, Metrocentro, **Mercado San Miguel** and **Villa Libertad**;

No 109 from Teatro Darío to the Bolívar/Buitrago junction just before Intercontinental turns east, then southeast to **Mercado Huembes/bus station**;

No 110 runs from 7 Sur to **Villa San Jacinto** passing en route Mercado Lewites, Plaza 19 de Julio, Metrocentro, Mercado Huembes/bus station and Mercado San Miguel;

No 113 from Ciudad Sandino, Las Piedrecitas, CST, Intercontinental, to **Mercado Oriental**;

No 116 runs east-west below Intercontinental, on Buitrago, also passing CST;

No 118 takes a similar route but turns south on Williams Romero to Plaza España, thence to **Israel Lewites bus station**;

No 119 runs from Plaza España to **Mercado Huembes/bus station** via Plaza 19 de Julio;

No 123 runs from Mercado Lewites via 7 Sur and Linda Vista to near Palacio Nacional de Cultura, and **Nuevo Diario**.

Long distance *Bus Expresos'* are much faster than regular routes. Check with terminal to confirm when the next express will leave. Payment is required in advance and seat reservations are becoming more common. There are also microbuses serving some of the major destinations. These are comparatively speedy and as comfortable as it gets.

La UCA, serves just a few destinations close to Managua. The *expresos* and microbuses are cheap, fast and particularly recommended if travelling to Granada, León or Masaya. To **Granada**, every 15 mins or when full, 0530-2100, US$1.10, 1 hr. To **Jinotepe**, 0600-2100, every 20 mins or when full, US$1.10, 1 hr. To **León**, every ½ hr, 0730-2100, US$1.75, 1½ hrs, To **Masaya**, every 15 mins or when full, 0-2100, US$0.65, 40 mins.

Mercado Roberto Huembes, also called Mercado Central, is used for destinations southwest. To **Granada**, every 15 mins, 0520-2200, Sun 0610-2100, US$1, 1½ hrs. To **Masaya**, every 20 mins, 0625-1930, Sun until 1600, US$0.50, 50 mins. To **Peñas Blancas**, express bus, 0400, US$3, 3½ hrs; or go to Rivas for connections. To **Rivas**, every 30 mins, 0400-1800, US$1.75, 2½ hrs; express buses, US$2.50, 2 hrs; microbuses, US$3, 1½ hrs. To **San Juan del Sur**, express bus, 0900, 1600, US$3.25, 2½ hrs; or go to Rivas for connections.

Mercado Mayoreo, for destinations east and then north or south. To **Boaco**, every 30 mins, 0500-1800, US$1.75, 2 hrs. To **Camoapa**, 8 daily, 0630-1700, US$2.25, 3 hrs. To **El Rama**, 8 daily, 0500-2200, US$8, 9 hrs. To **Estelí**, every 30 mins, 0400-1800, US$3, 3½ hrs; express buses, 12 daily, US$3.50, 2½ hrs. To **Jinotega**, express buses, 11 daily, 0400-1730, US$3.50, 3½ hrs. To **Juigalpa**, every 20 mins, 0500-1730, US$3, 2½ hrs. To **Matagalpa** every 30 mins, 0330-1800, US$2.50, 2½ hrs; express buses, 12 daily, US$3, 2 hrs. To **Ocotal**, express buses, 12 daily, 0545-1745, US$5.50, 3½ hrs. To **San Rafael del Norte**, express bus, 1500, US$6, 4 hrs. To **San Carlos**, 0500, 0600, 0700, US$9, 9½ hrs. To **Somoto**, express buses, Mon-Sat 0715, 0945, 1245, 1345, 1545, 1645, Sun no express after 1345, US$4.50, 3½ hrs.

Mercado Israel Lewites, also called Mercado Boer, for destinations west and northwest. Microbuses leave from here, particularly recommended for journeys to León. To **Chinandega**, express buses, every 30 mins, 0600-1915, US$2.50, 2½ hrs. To **Corinto**, every hour, 0500-1715, US$3.50, 3 hrs. To **Diriamba**, every 20 mins, 0530-1930, US$1.25, 1 hr 15 mins. To **El Sauce**, express buses, 0745, 1445, US$3.25, 3½ hrs. To **Guasaule**, 0430, 0530, 1530, US$3.25, 4 hrs. To **Jinotepe**, every 20 mins, 0530-1930, US$1.25, 1 hr 30 mins. To **León**, every 30 mins, 0545-1645, US$1.25, 2½ hrs; express buses, every 30 mins, 0500-1645, US$1.50,

2 hrs; microbuses, every 30 mins or when full, 0600-1700, US$1.75, 1½ hrs. To **Pochomil**, hourly, 0600-1920, US$1, 2 hrs.

International buses The cheap and efficient international buses are often booked up many days in advance and tickets will not be sold until all passport/visa documentation is complete. The best known is **Ticabus**, which parks in Barrio Martha Quezada, from Cine Dorado, 2 c arriba, T2222-6094, www.ticabus.com, with services throughout Central America. Other operators include **King Quality**, end of Calle 27 de Mayo, opposite Plaza Inter, T2228-1454, www.kingqualityca.com and **Transnica**, la Rotonda de Metrocentro 300 m al lago, 50 m arriba, T2277-3133, www.transnica.com.

To **Costa Rica** Ticabus, 0600, 0700, 1200, US$15, 8 hrs; King Quality, 1330, US$21, 8½ hrs; Transnica, 0530, 0700, 1000, 1200 (executive), US$13, executive service US$22, 8½ hrs.

To **El Salvador** Ticabus, 0500, US$30, 11 hrs; King Quality, 0330 (quality), 0530 (cruceros), 1100 (King), 'Cruceros class', US$25, 'Quality Class' US$35, 'King Class' US$51, 11 hrs; Transnica, 0500, US$18, 11 hrs.

To **Guatemala** Ticabus, 0500, US$46, 30 hrs including an overnight stay in El Salvador; King Quality, 0230 (cruceros), 1530 (quality/king), 'Cruceros class' US$52, 'Quality Class' US$62, 'King Class' US$86, 15 hrs.

To **Honduras (Tegucigalpa)** Ticabus, 0500, US$23, 8 hrs, then continues to San Pedro Sula, US$37, 10 hrs; King Quality, 0330 (king), 1130 (quality), 'Quality Class' US$30, 'King Class' US$42, 8½ hrs; Transnica, 0500, 8 hrs, US$20.

To **Mexico (Tapachula)** Ticabus, 0500, US$63, 36 hrs, including overnight stay in El Salvador; King Quality, 'Quality Class' US$74, 'King Class' US$96.

To **Panama** Ticabus, 0600, 0700, 1200, US$44, 28-32 hrs, including a 2 to 6 hr stopover in Costa Rica.

Car

All car hire agencies have rental desks at the International airport arrivals terminal. It is not a good idea to rent a car for getting around Managua, as it is a confusing city and fender benders are common and an injury accident means you could go to jail, even if not at fault. Outside the capital main roads are better marked and a rental car means you can get around more freely. (Taxis can also be hired by the hour or by the day, see below.)

For good service and 24-hr roadside assistance, the best rental agency is **Budget**, with rental cars at the airport, T2263-1222, and Holiday Inn, T2270-9669. Their main office is just off Carretera Sur at Montoya, 1 c abajo, 1 c sur, T2255-9000. Average cost of a small Toyota is US$50 per day while a 4WD (a good idea if exploring) is around US$100 per day with insurance and 200 km a day included; 4WD weekly rental rates range from US$600-750. Check website for details: www.budget.com.ni. Also at the airport is **Avis**, T2233-3011, www.avis.com.ni. **Hertz** is at the airport, T2266-8399, at Hotel Seminole Plaza, T2270-5896, and at Hotel Crowne Plaza, T2262-2531, www.hertz.com. Another reliable agency is **Toyota Rent a Car**, www.toyotarentacar.com, which has cars to match its name and is at the airport, T2266-3620, the Hotel Princess, T2270-4937, and the Camino Real, T2263-2358.

Taxi

Taxis (the best method of transport for foreigners) can be flagged down on the street. Fares range from US$1.50-US$2 for a short trip, US$2-US$3.50 across town, US$10 to airport. Fares are always per person, not per car. Taxi drivers may decide not to take you if your destination is in a different direction to other passengers. If they agree, ask how much (¿por cuánto me lleva?) before getting in. If the front seat is empty take it as the back seat will be filled en route. Street names and numbers are not universal in the city and the taxi driver may not know your destination; have the telephone number of your hotel with you. If heading for Barrio Martha Quezada, ask for the **Ticabus** if you do not know your exact destination. Taxis from the airport are 50% cheaper from the main road beyond the car park.

Radio taxis are recommended for early flights or late night transport. Companies include: **Co-op 25 de Febrero**, T2222-5218, or **Co-op 2 de Agosto**, T2263-1512, get price quote on the phone (normally 80-100% more expensive).

❶ Directory

Managua *p1041, maps p1042, p1044 and p1047*
Banks
Any bank in Nicaragua will change US$ to córdobas and vice-versa. TC purchase receipts may be required in banks when changing TCs. The best 2 banks for foreigners are **Banco de América Central (BAC)** and **Banco de Finanzas (BDF)**. BAC offers credit card advances, uses the Cirrus debit system and changes all TCs with a 5% commission. BDF changes Amex TCs only, also with a 5% commission. In Managua ATM machines are found in the airport, at the Metrocentro and Plaza Inter shopping malls and in many gas station convenience stores ('Red Total'). There are several money changers at the road junction in Altamira by the restaurant **Casa del Pomodoro** and outside **La Colonia** shopping centre in Plaza España. After 1800 and on Sun they are usually tricksters. On Sun you can change money at the **Intercontinental**, major hotels or banks inside **Metrocentro**. See page 1038 for more details.

Embassies and consulates
Austria, Rotonda El Guenguense, 1 c al norte, T2266-3316. Canada, Bolonia Los Pipitos, 2 c abajo, T2264-2723, Mon-Thu 0900-1200. Costa Rica, Los Robles, Tip Top, 25 varas abajo, T2270-3799, 0900-1500. Denmark, Bolonia Salud Integral, 2 c al lago, 50 varas abajo, T2254-5059. Finland, Hospital Militar, 1 c north, 1½ c abajo, T2264-1137, 0800-1200, 1300-1500. France, Iglesia El Carmen, 1½ c abajo, T2222-6210, 0800-1600. Germany, Plaza España, 200 m lago, T2266-3917, Mon-Fri 0900-1200. Guatemala, just after Km 11 on Carretera a Masaya, T2279-9834, fast service, 0900-1200 only. Honduras, Las Colinas No 298, T2276-2406. Italy, Rotonda El Güegüence, 1 c lago, T2266-6486, 0900-1200. Mexico, Km 4.5, Carretera a Masaya, 1 c arriba, T2277-5886. Panamá, Col Mantica, el Cuartel General de Bomberos, 1 c abajo, No 93, T/F2266-8633, 0830-1300, visa on the spot, valid 3 months for a 30-day stay, US$10, maps and information on the Canal. Spain, Las Colinas Av, Central No 13, T2276-0968. Sweden, Plaza España, 1 c abajo, 2 c lago, ½ c abajo, Apdo Postal 2307, T2266-0085, 0800-1200. Switzerland, Banpro Las Palmas, 1 c abajo, T2266-3010. UK, Reparto Los Robles, Primera Etapa, main entrance from Carretera a Masaya, 4th house on right, T2278-0014, Apdo Aéreo 169, 0900-1200. USA, Km 4.5, Carretera del Sur, T2266-6010, 0730-0900. Venezuela, Km 10.5, Carretera a Masaya, T2276-0267.

Emergencies
Police: T118 in an emergency; the local police station number will depend on what *distrito* you are in. Start with the Metrocentro area number, T2265-0651. Fire: T115 in an emergency; the central number is T2265-0162. Red Cross: T128 in an emergency.

Immigration and customs
Immigration: near Ciudad Jardín, Antiguo Edif del Seguro Social (bus No 101, 108) Mon-Fri 0800-1600, T2244-3989. Customs: Km 5 Carretera del Norte (bus No 108).

Internet
Lots of places, especially in and around Plaza Inter, María Quezada and Metrocentro. Most internet cafés are open daily, charge around US$0.60 per hr and also offer internet calls.

Language schools

Casa Nicaragüense de Español, Km 11.5 Carretera Sur, Spanish classes and a thorough introduction to Nicaragua, accommodation with families. **Huellas**, Col Centroamérica, Callejón El Ceibo G-414, T2277-2079, intensive classes, private classes and regular classes (0880-1200). **Nicaragua Spanish School**, Rotonda Bello Horizonte, 2 c al sur, 2 c arriba, T2244-4512, regular and private classes. **Universidad Americana**, Centro de Idiomas Extranjeros, T2278-3800 ext 301, open course with flexible hrs and regular 5-month course. **Universidad Centroamericana (UCA)**, Centro de Idiomas Extranjeros, T2278-3923, ext 242-351, 5-week regular classes of all levels and open classes with flexible hours.

Libraries

Casa Ben Linder Library, Estatua Monseñor Lezcano 3 c al sur, 1½ c arriba, also good book exchange, T2266-4373.

Medical services

Dentists Dr Claudia Bendaña, T2277-1842 and Dr Mario Sánchez Ramos, T2278-1409, T2278-5588 (home). **Doctors** Internal medicine, Dr Enrique Sánchez Delgado, T2278-1031; Dr Mauricio Barrios, T2255-6900. **Gynaecologists** Dr Edwin Mendieta, T2266-5855. **Ophthalmologist**: Dr Milton Eugarrios, T2278-6306. **Paediatricians**: Dr Alejandro

Ayón, T2276-2142; Dr César Gutiérrez Quant, T2278-3902, T2278-5465 (home). **Hospitals** Generally crowded, with very long queues. The best are **Hospital Bautista**, near Mercado Oriental, T2249-7070; **Hospital Militar**, south from Intercontinental and take 2nd turning on left, T2222-2763; and **Hospital Alemán-Nicaragüense**, Km 6 Carretera Norte Siemens, 3 c al sur, T2249-0701, operated with German aid. Phone for appointment first if possible. **Private clinics** These are an alternative. **Policlínica Nicaragüense**, consultation US$30. **Med-Lab**, Plaza España 300 m al sur, recommended for tests on stool samples, the director speaks English.

Post office

21 locations around Managua, the main office for the country is 1 block west of Parque Central. Wide selection of beautiful stamps. Poste Restante (*Lista de Correos*) keeps mail for 45 days, US$0.20 per letter. There is another post office in the Centro Comercial Managua and at the airport.

Telephone

Enitel, same building as post office, open 0700-2230. There is a small office in the international airport. Telephone offices are spreading around Managua.

To the Northern Highlands

A couple of routes to the Honduran border use the Pan-American Highway heading north of Lake Managua. The road rises and winds through hilly country, with fields set aside for agriculture and coffee growing, giving way to mining and pine forests. Damage from the Revolution is evident throughout the region, and particularly in the small town of Estelí. A short detour south of Estelí takes a paved road to good walking and wildlife country in Matagalpa and Jinotega. North of Estelí the road splits, leading to Somoto and Ocotal, and completing the 214-km paved road from the capital to Honduras. ▶▶ *For listings, see pages 1063-1070.*

Tipitapa and further north → *Colour map 7, A1.*
Heading east out of Managua along the southern shore of the lake is Tipitapa (21 km). The resort has reopened and you can swim in clean water in the baths. The air-conditioned restaurant attached to the thermal baths is good. There is a colourful market, and the **Fiesta del Señor de Esquipulas** takes place on 13-16 January.

The Pan-American Highway goes north through Tipitapa to **Sébaco**, passing through **Ciudad Darío**, where the poet Rubén Darío was born. You can see the house, which is maintained as a **museum** ① *Mon-Fri 0800-1200, 1400-1700.* There is an arts festival for the week of his birthday, 18 January. Sébaco and the surrounding area was badly affected by Hurricane Mitch. East of the highway is **Esquipula**, 2½ hours by bus, a good place for hiking, fishing and riding.

Matagalpa and around ⊖⊕⊕⊖⊙▲⊖⊙ ▶▶ *pp1063-1070. Colour map 6, C4.*

→ *Altitude: 672 m.*
From Sébaco a road leads to Matagalpa, and some of the best walking country in Nicaragua. Matagalpa has an old church, and while it is about the only colonial-style building left, the town retains a simple agrarian charm. It was badly damaged in the Revolution but all war damage has now been repaired. A coffee boom in the late 1990s benefitted the region greatly, but the crash in coffee prices in 2001 has subsequently decimated the fragile local economy. The local festival and holiday on 26 September celebrates the **Virgen de las Mercedes**.

Matagalpa is a small town, the main focus of the surrounding agricultural land and the birthplace of Carlos Fonseca, one of the founder members of the FSLN. The house he was born in, now the **Museo Carlos Fonseca** ① *1 block east of Parque San José*, looks certain to remain closed for the foreseeable future, but the local FSLN office has the keys. It's a busy town with just the **cathedral** and the **Galería de los Héroes y Mártires**, in the main square to the north, to consider as sights. The **Centro Popular de la Cultura** is 2½ blocks north, four blocks east from the northeast corner of the cathedral plaza. **Matagalpa Tours** ① *Banpro, ½ c arriba, T2772-0108*, is an excellent source of information, with a thorough knowledge of the city and the surrounding mountains; staff speak Dutch and English. **INTUR** ① *Alcaldía, 1 c arriba, ½ c al sur, T2772-7060*, has limited, patchy details on local attractions. You could also try **CIPTURMAT**, next door to Matagalpa tours; and **CANTUR**, in the coffee museum; but none of them speak English.

Coffee, the region's main source of employment, is harvested from November to February and can be seen drying in the sun at the southern edge of town. There is a **coffee museum** ① *Alcaldía, 1½ c norte, daily 0800-1230, 1400-1900, free*, devoted to its history and cultivation.

A 32-km road runs from Matagalpa east to the Tuma Valley. Matagalpa, with its beautiful mountains and diverse scenery, is one of the best hiking areas of Nicaragua. A nice way to discover the area on your own is with *Treasures of Matagalpa*, a brochure describing five one-day hikes ranging from four to eight hours, including a detailed map, instructions and a description of the history of the area. You can buy the brochure (US$1.75) at **Centro Girasol** ① *2 blocks south, 1 block west of Terminal Sur, T2612-6030.* All profit goes to supporting families with disabled children. You should also visit the centre if you're interested in volunteering.

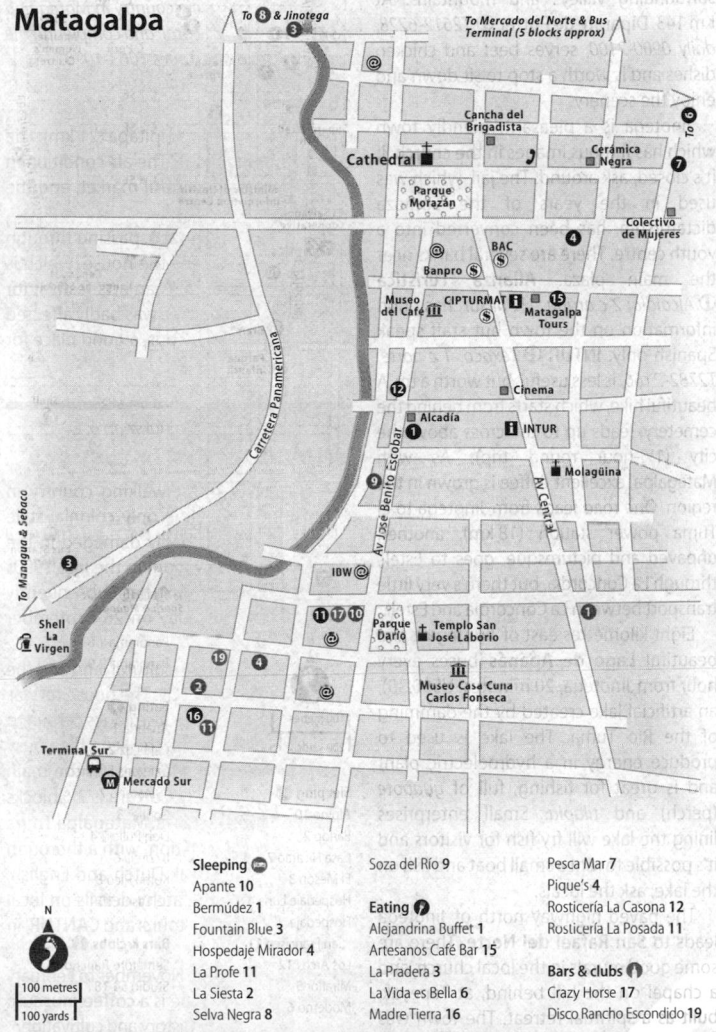

Matagalpa

Sleeping 🛏	Soza del Río 9
Apante 10	
Bermúdez 1	**Eating** 🍴
Fountain Blue 3	Alejandrina Buffet 1
Hospedaje Mirador 4	Artesanos Café Bar 15
La Profe 11	La Pradera 3
La Siesta 2	La Vida es Bella 6
Selva Negra 8	Madre Tierra 16

Pesca Mar 7
Pique's 4
Rostícería La Casona 12
Rostícería La Posada 11

Bars & clubs 🍸
Crazy Horse 17
Disco Rancho Escondido 19

N
100 metres
100 yards

Jinotega and around → *Colour map 6, C4.*
Population: 33,000. Altitude: 641 m.

A rough road spirals north from Matagalpa to Jinotega rising out of the valley and into one of the most scenic paved highways in the north, lined by highland farms, virgin cloud forest and breathtaking views of the surrounding valleys and mountains. At Km 143, **Diparate de Potter** ① *T2612-6228, daily 0900-2100,* serves beef and chicken dishes and is worth a stop to sit down and enjoy the scenery.

Jinotega is a pleasant, friendly town which has famous images in the church; if it's closed, ask around. The jail, which was used in the years of the Somoza dictatorship, has been converted into a youth centre. There are several banks near the main plaza. **Alianza Turística** ① *Alcaldía, 2 c arriba, 1½ al sur,* has good information on the town but staff speak Spanish only. **INTUR** ① *Texaco, 1 c norte, T2782-2166,* is less useful, but worth a try. A beautiful hike, which starts from behind the cemetery, leads up to the cross above the city (1½-hour round trip). As with Matagalpa, excellent coffee is grown in the region. One road leads from Jinotega to El Tuma power station (18 km); another, unpaved and picturesque, goes to Estelí, through La Concordia, but there's very little transport between La Concordia and Estelí.

Eight kilometres east of Jinotega is the beautiful **Lago de Apanás** (buses every hour from Jinotega, 20 minutes, US$0.35), an artificial lake created by the damming of the Río Tuma. The lake is used to produce energy in a hydroelectric plant and is great for fishing, full of *guapote* (perch) and *tilapia*. Small enterprises lining the lake will fry fish for visitors and it's possible to rent a small boat and fish on the lake; ask the locals.

The paved highway north of Jinotega leads to **San Rafael del Norte**. There are ~~me~~ good murals in the local church, and ~~a chapel~~ on the hill behind, at Tepeyak, ~~its~~ spiritual retreat. The town was

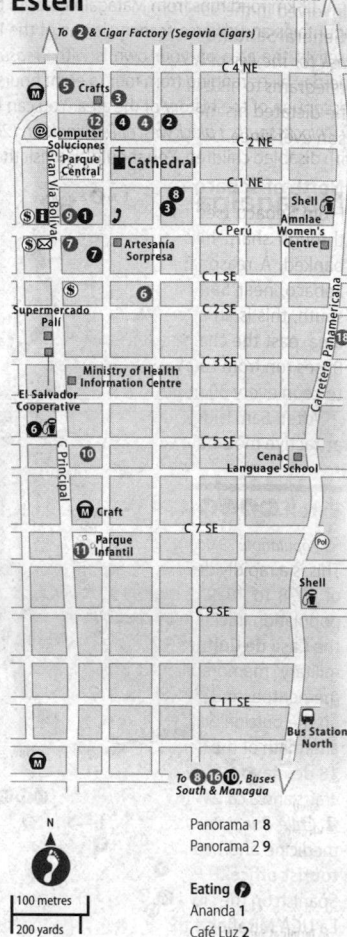

Estelí

To Somoto & Honduras
To ② & Cigar Factory (Segovia Cigars)

N

100 metres
200 yards

Sleeping 🛏
Alpino 10
Barlop 2
Casa Nicarao 7
El Mesón 3
Hospedaje Luna 4
Hospedaje
  San Francisco 11
Los Arcos 12
Miraflor 5
Moderno 6
Panorama 1 8
Panorama 2 9

Eating 🍴
Ananda 1
Café Luz 2
Cafetería El Rincón
  Pinareño 7
Cohifer 3
Don Pollo 2 4
Ixcotelli 6
Koma Rico 8
La Casita 10

Bars & clubs 🍸
Semáforo Rancho 16
Studio 54 18

involved in the Sandinista struggle and its recent history is very interesting. The **Museo General Sandino** ① *in the Casa Museo Ejército Defensor de La Soberanía Nacional; if locked, ask for the key at the mayor's house across the street*, is where Sandino used to send off telegrams to his troops in different parts of the northern hills. The young woman to whom he dictated his messages became his wife and the town has claimed him as their native son ever since.

North of Sébaco

From Sébaco (see page 1058) a 134-km journey to the border at El Espino takes you through sharp hills with steep climbs and descents, but it's smooth and quite well banked. A reasonable road leads off the Pan-American Highway 10 km northwest of Sébaco, near **San Isidro**, to join the Pacific Highway near León (110 km). If travelling south, this is an attractive route to Managua through the Chinandega cotton-growing area, past the chain of volcanoes running west from Lake Managua, and through León. Buses run from Estelí to San Isidro every 30 minutes (two hours, US$0.50), and San Isidro to León every 30 minutes (three to four hours, US$1.50.)

After San Isidro, the Pan-American Highway continues through **La Trinidad**, an attractive mountain village set in a canyon, before reaching Estelí.

Estelí ⬤🅟🅐🅞▲🅔🅖 ▸▸ pp1063-1070. Colour map 6, C3.

→ *Population: 73,000. Altitude: 844 m.*

This is a rapidly developing departmental capital, heavily damaged during the Revolution of 1978 to 1979. It's not especially attractive, but it is energetic, with a large student population injecting life into an otherwise humdrum agricultural centre. Worth visiting is the **Casa de Cultura**, which has a small exhibition of petroglyphs found in the area and of military memorabilia, and the **Galería de los Héroes y Mártires**, next door, with mementoes and photographs of those killed defending the Revolution and moving paintings on the outside walls. Many cooperatives and support organizations were developed in the aftermath of the Revolution. One of them, the **Asociación de ex-combatientes históricos 18 de mayo** ① *Calle Principal, ½ c south of the Plaza de la Cathedral*, is good and has some crafts and a café with posters all over the walls. The **Ministry of Health Information Centre** ① *Calle Principal, 4 blocks from the Plaza*, is involved with projects to revive traditional medicine and healing and offers advice on a wide range of herbal remedies. The **INTUR tourist office** ① *Parque Central, ½ c sur, on Calle Principal, T2713-6799*, has information in Spanish on the city and its surroundings. If you are interested in visiting rural communities, **La UCA Miraflor** is the best organization to approach (see Miraflor, below).

Around Estelí ⬤🅟🅔🅖 ▸▸ pp1063-1070. Colour map 6, C3.

Miraflor → *Altitude: 800-1500 m.*

Miraflor is a 5675-ha nature reserve 28 km northeast of Estelí in the Department of Jinotega. It contains the **Laguna de Miraflor** and has a wide range of flora and fauna (including the quetzal). The **Unión de Cooperativas Agropecuarias (UCA) Miraflor** ① *costado noreste de la catedral 2 c arriba, ½ c sur, T2713 2971, www.miraflor.org*, operates in the reserve, has a tourism project and is in charge of environmental protection. The cooperative can provide wooden huts, basic facilities and accommodation (**E-G**), meals, horse hire (US$7 per day) and guided walks (US$10 per person). It is recommended for a visit to see rural life and is a

Border essentials: Nicaragua–Honduras

Somoto–El Espino

There's nowhere to stay in El Espino. There's a duty-free shop and a food bar on the Nicaraguan side and several cafés on the Honduran side.

Nicaraguan immigration 20 km beyond Somoto is El Espino, 5 km from the Honduran border at La Playa. The Nicaraguan side is open 24 hours.

Crossing by private vehicle Motorists leaving Nicaragua should enquire in Somoto if an exit permit has to be obtained there or at El Espino. This also applies to cyclists.

Transport Minibuses run between Somoto and the border every hour 0615-1710. Buses to Estelí are hourly, 2½ hours, express buses are Managua-bound, 1½ hours, and will drop you off at the Shell station, just east of central Estelí. There are six daily buses to Managua, 3½ hours. On the Nicaraguan side taxis wait to take you to Somoto, they may try to overcharge; pay no more than US$8. On the Honduran side, taxis go between the border and the Mi Esperanza bus stops, when full, US$1 for foreigners, less for locals.

Directory No money changers on the Nicaraguan side but locals will oblige.

Las Manos–Ocotal

This is recommended as the best route from Tegucigalpa to Managua.

Nicaraguan immigration Open 24 hours. Arrivals must fill in an immigration card, present their luggage to the customs authorities and obtain a receipt, and then present these to the immigration authorities with passport and entry fees. Leaving the country, fill out a card, pay the tax and get your passport stamped.

Crossing by private vehicle After completing immigration procedures, go to 'Tránsito' to pay for the vehicle permit, obtain clearance from 'Revisión', and get your vehicle permit from 'Aduana' (customs). If it is busy, you could go first to customs and get your number in the queue. On leaving the country, complete the immigration requirements, then go to 'Tránsito' to have the vehicle checked, and to customs to have the vehicle stamp in the passport cancelled. Surrender the vehicle permit at customs and take another form back to 'Tránsito'; this will be stamped, signed and finally handed over at the exit gate.

Transport Las Manos–Ocotal bus, every 30 minutes or when full, 0500-1645, 45 minutes. Taxis also available, US$7-8, set fare before boarding.

Directory Money changers operate on both sides. Rates for cash and TCs are usually better in Estelí.

beautiful area for riding. Travelling to the region at night is not recommended due to crime, although police have been installed at the entrance to the Miraflor reserve.

El Sauce and around

A very poor gravel road just north of Estelí runs to El Sauce where there is a large 16th-century church (burnt down in 1997 and refurbished in 2002). It's a place of pilgrimage and people come from all over Central America to visit the black **Christ of Esquipulas**, celebrated in a giant festival that culminates 15-18 January. After 20 km, an equally rough road branches north to **Achuapa**, beyond which an unmade road continues through the *artesanía* town of **San Juan de Limay** (one *hospedaje*), famous thoughout Nicaragua for its great **soapstone carvings**. The artists are happy to invite you into their house to watch them carve (average sculpture costs US$8 or less). Further on, **Pueblo Nuevo** (two basic *hospedajes*) is near an archaeological site. From here the road goes on to join the Pan-American Highway just east of Somoto.

Condega → *Population: 8000. Altitude: 561 m.*
From Estelí, the Pan-American goes north to Condega, a quiet town. Its name means 'pottery makers' and the indigenous village was once known for its ceramics. Some of the country's most beautiful pottery is still made here and visitors are welcome at the **Ducuale Grande Ceramic Co-operative** ① *opposite Colegio Ana Velia de Guillén, T2752-2374*, a women's co-op that makes attractive red-clay earthenware; there's a small shop attached. Condega has a small and well-kept **archaeological museum** ① *Casa de Cultura de Condega, Plaza Central, Julio C Salgado, opposite the Policía Nacional, T2752-2221, Tue-Sun 0800-1200, 1400-1800*, with permanent expositions of discoveries from the region.

Somoto → *Population: 14,000. Altitude: 700 m.*
Continuing along the highway you reach Somoto, a pleasant town in a lovely setting. Recent excavations have uncovered unusual pre-Columbian remains which are on display at the **Museo Arqueológico de Somoto** ① *on the parque central, Mon-Fri 0800-1200*. The town is famous for the best *rosquillas* (a traditional toasted food, dry but tasty, made of egg, cheese, cornmeal and butter) in Nicaragua. Try the *viejita*, which also has pure cane sugar in the centre. Some 15 km north of Somoto is one of Nicaragua's most impressive canyons, a national monument well worth visiting. It's a moderate and slippery 3-km hike from a highway exit, best reached by taxi (US$4). A guide is recommended, but not essential.

Ocotal → *Colour map 6, C3. Population: 27,000. Altitude: 606 m.*
From Somoto a road turns off right to Ocotal (18 km), a clean, cool, whitewashed town on a sandy plain and well worth a visit. It is near the Honduran border, to which a road runs north (bus marked Las Manos), and the scenery is wonderful. From Ciudad Sandino – formerly Jícaro – 50 km east from Ocotal, you can get to **San Albino**, where there are many gold mines and the nearby Río Coco is used to wash the gold.

◉ To the Northern Highlands listings

For Sleeping and Eating price codes and other relevant information, see Essentials pages 45-48.

● Sleeping

Tipitapa and further north *p1058*
E El Valle, Sébaco, on the highway 1.5 km south of town, T2775-2209. Small, simple rooms with fans and TV at this quiet, motel-style place on the highway. Some have a/c.
F Casa Agricultor, Ciudad Darío, bus station, 1½ c al norte, T2776-2379. Simple, dark

rooms; 3 with bath, 5 without, all have a fan and there's secure parking. The owner, Emma López, is hospitable and friendly.
F Hotel Oscar Morales, Esquipula. Clean, with shower.

Matagalpa and around *p1058, map p1059*
Many places shut their doors by 2200-2300. The town has an erratic water supply and possible shortages Mar-Apr.
A Lomas de San Thomas, Escuela Guanuca 400 m arriba, T2772-4189, The most luxurious

in the region. 26 spacious rooms with private bath, hot water, cable TV, telephone, mini-bar. Away from the centre.

D Hotel Apante, west side of Parque Darío, T2772-6890. Clean rooms with private bath, hot water and cable TV. The management si friendly and there's free coffee 24 hrs a day.

D Hotel Fountain Blue, catedral, 3 c al norte, 2 c abajo, T2772-2733. Comfortable rooms with private bath, cable TV, hot water and fan. A simple breakfast of coffee and bread is included, and laundry service is available.

D Hotel La Siesta, Texaco, 1½ abajo, T2772-2476. Clean, tidy, good-value hotel with friendly management. Rooms have hot water, cable TV and fan. There's internet facilities, international call centre and a café, too.

D Hotel Soza del Río, Av Río Grande, T2772-3030, opposite the river. 17 economical rooms with bath, fan and cable TV. The hotel is also accessible from Restaurante Casa Casea, next to Supermercado Matagalpa. Breakfasts, buffet lunches and dinner served.

E Hotel La Profe, Shell el Progreso, 20 varas al norte, T2772-2506. A pleasant, family-run place. Tidy rooms have cable TV, fan, private bath and hot water.

F Bermúdez, Parque Darío, 2 c abajo, T2612-9876. Most rooms at this friendly and ramshackle hotel are run-down, but some aren't too bad. Cheap singles.

F Hospedaje Mirador, Parque Darío, 1½ c abajo, T2772-4084. Simple, bare-bones rooms around a courtyard. Friendly management and a vociferous parrot.

Around Matagalpa

LL-E Selva Negra, 10 km on road to Jinotega at Km 139.5, at 1200 m, T2772-3883, www.selva negra.com. Set in a gorgeous private rainforest reserve, Selva Negra has a range of mostly extravagant accommodation including Germanic cottages (**LL-A**), double rooms (**B**) and dorm beds (**E**). There's a good, if expensive restaurant serving organic food farmed on the premises. Entrance is US$3 if just want to hike the surrounding trails – ask for a map at the hotel.

C Hacienda San Rafael, on the road to La Dalia, T2612-2229. This lovely organic coffee farm is the producer of the fine **Café de los Reyes**. Lodging is in an attractive wooden lodge that affords some spectacular views of surrounding mountains above well-manicured gardens. The 270-ha farm has short nature paths, 1 leading to a small waterfall. Rooms have 1 shared bath, meals are available, reservations only.

C-F Esperanza Verde lodge, www.fincaesperanzaverde.org. This famous eco-lodge, built for the observation of butterflies, has handsome wood and brick cabins (**B**) with covered patios, solar power, private bath and bunk beds. There's also dorm rooms (**E**) and camping at US$6 per person.

Jinotega and around *p1060*

Most hotels and restaurants lock their doors at 2200, Fri-Sun 2300. Only hardy youths are out in the streets after this time.

A Hotel Café and Restaurant Borbon, Texaco, 1 c abajo, ½ c norte, T2782-2710. Well-appointed and very nice. 25 comfortable rooms with private bath, hot water, a/c, cable TV. Quiet, friendly, best in province, good restaurant ¶¶ with traditional dishes.

C Hotel Solentuna Hem, Esso, 1 c arriba, 2½ c norte, T2782-2334. Clean, safe, family hotel with 17 rooms. The owner lived in Sweden for many years, and offers a range of beauty treatments including massage and pedicure. Breakfast and dinner is served, and coffee tours are available. Pleasant and professional.

D Hotel Central, catedral, ½ c norte, T2782-2063. Offers 20 rooms of varying quality. Rooms upstairs have private bath, cable TV and a great mountain view. Cheaper rooms (**F**) are without bath or view. There's also a communal TV and purified water dispenser downstairs, and a restaurant with very cheap food. Great location, very friendly.

D Hotel La Fuente, Esso, 4 c arriba, T2782-2966. 12 rooms with private bath, hot water and cable TV. There's also parking and restaurant. Good value, but located away from the centre in a less attractive area. Friendly.

E Primavera, Esso station, 4 c norte, T2782-2400. This economical hotel has 28 clean, plain rooms, cheaper without cable TV and bath (**F**). Breakfast is served, but not included in the price. Good local atmosphere.

San Rafael del Norte
F Hospedaje Rocío, just south of the petrol station, T2652-2313. Small, homely and very clean, good value, with bath and set meals.

Estelí *p1061, map p1060*
A Hotel Los Arcos, Catedral, 1 c norte, www.familiasunidas.org/hotelosarcos.htm. This brightly painted, professionally managed and comfortable hotel has 18 rooms with private bath, a/c or fan, and cable TV. The attached restaurant, **Vuela Vuela**, is also reputable, and profits go to social projects.
A Hotel Panorama 1, Km 147, Carretera Panamericana, T2713-3147. Inconveniently located away from the centre, but good if you need to catch an early morning bus. The newer section has brightly painted, comfortable rooms with private bath, hot water, a/c and cable TV. The older section is cheaper (**B**) and less attractive, but still quite comfortable.
A-D Alpino, Almacén Sony, ½ c arriba, T2713-2828, halpino@hotmail.com. A wide range of lodgings with differing features and prices, from apartments with cable TV and a/c (**A**), to basic, economical rooms with fan (**C-D**)
C Casa Hotel Nicarao, central plaza, 1½ c sur, T2713-2490. Clean, comfortable rooms set around a relaxing courtyard filled with plants, paintings and sitting space. Very friendly management and a nice atmosphere, but the walls are thin and let lots of noise through. There are cheaper rooms without bath (**E**).
C El Mesón, Av Bolívar, central plaza, 1 c norte, T2713-2655, barlan@ibw.com.ni. Clean, comfortable rooms at this friendly, helpful hotel, all with hot water and cable TV. There's a travel agency attached, and an *artesanía* shop over the road. Recommended.

D Hotel Miraflor, Parque Central, ½ c norte, T2713-2003. Popular with Nicas. 7 rooms with hot water, cable TV and private bath. The attached restaurant serves *comida típica*.
D Hotel Panorama 2, catedral, 1 c sur, ½ c arriba, T2713-5023. Same features as **Hotel Panorama 1** (above), but much quieter at night, with good access to centre restaurants, secure parking, rooms upstairs nicer. If leaving on early bus pay in advance, ask for receipt.
D Moderno, catedral, 2½ c sur, T2713-2378. Clean and comfortable rooms with a/c, hot water and cable TV. There's a restaurant for guests, where breakfast and dinner are served.
E Barlop, Parque Central, 6 c norte, T2713-2486. This hotel has 12 rooms, 6 of which are good, 6 basic. The former have showers and cable TV. Parking available.
E Hospedaje Luna, catedral, 1 c al norte, 1 c arriba, T2441-8466, www.cafeluzyluna.com. Hostel with 2 dorms and 2 private rooms (**E**). There's hammock space, an activities board, tourist information, DVDs, tours and drinking water. Volunteer work in Miraflor can be arranged here – 3 months commitment and Spanish speakers are preferred. Discounts for longer stays and groups.
E Hospedaje San Francisco, next to Parque Infantil. Just one of a handful of cheapies in this area. Rooms are basic and clean with outside bathroom. The hotel is friendly and pleasant enough. Shabby, but the price is right.

Condega *p1063*
D Hotel Restaurante Gualca, T2715-2431. Offers 6 rooms with shared baths, clean, noisy at weekends.
E Hospedaje Framar, on main plaza next to Casa de Cultura, T2715-2393. With 14 very clean and pleasant rooms, cold showers, nice garden, safe, friendly, owner speaks English, excellent value. Safe parking for motorbikes.
E Pensión Baldovinos, opposite the park, T2715-2222. There are 20 rooms, cheaper with shared bath. Fan, group discounts, good food.

Somoto *p1063*

D Hotel Colonial, iglesia, ½ c al sur, T2722-2040. An attractive, professionally managed hotel with decent rooms; all have private bath, cable TV and fan. Popular with businessmen and NGOs.

D Hotel Panamericano, on north side of Parque Central, T2722-2355. Good-value rooms at this interesting hotel, where you'll find an orchid collection, a craft shop and a menagerie. The annexed section, a few roads away has a lovely garden and recreation area. The owners run trips to the canyon and surrounding countryside. Highly recommended.

F El Bambú, Policía Nacional, 2 c norte, T2722-2330. Close to the highway and bus station. 20 simple, economical rooms with cable TV. Some have bath, some don't.

F Hospedaje La Provedencia, Intel, 2½ c norte, T2722-2089. Offers 6 simple rooms with 2 shared baths inside a house. Friendly, family-run and basic.

Ocotal *p1063*

A Hotel Frontera, behind the Shell station on the highway to Las Manos, T2732-2668. This is the best hotel in town, even if it looks like a prison compound from outside. It has an inviting swimming pool, bar, restaurant and events room. The rooms are clean and comfortable, if uninspiring, and cheaper without a/c (**C**). They also offer internet, laundry service and international call facility.

C Hotel Benmoral, at south entrance to city, opposite FINOSA, T2732-2824. 20 dark, clean rooms with a/c or fan (**D**), cable TV and hot water. Food is available, and there's parking space. Friendly and helpful.

D Hotel Belrive, Shell station on the highway, 1 c abajo. This motel-style place has rooms with bath, hot water and cable TV. There's parking and a restaurant. Pleasant and friendly. Cheaper without a/c (**E**).

D Hotel Restaurant Mirador, opposite bus station, T2732-2496. The 22 rooms have cable TV, private bath and hot water. Some are nicer than others. As the name suggests, there's a small restaurant attached.

E Hotel El Viajero, Esso station, 3½ c abajo, T2732-2040. Clean, pleasant, economical place with 15 rooms. All have fan, most with bath. Breakfast and lunch are served, there's internet service and cable TV. Cheaper without bath (**G**).

❶ Eating

Tipitapa and further north *p1058*

†† El Sesteo, Sébaco, Del BDF, 1½ c abajo. Clean, with a/c (wonderful) and well-staffed. Their menu boasts a healthy selection of steaks, chicken, soup and shrimp dishes.

†† Los Gemelos, Sébaco, Monumento de la Virgen, 1½ c abajo. Regular buffets and a variety of meat and chicken dishes served. There's a disco on Sat and Sun evenings, playing hip-hop, salsa and dance.

† El Buen Gusto, Ciudad Darío, bus station, 3½ c al norte. This clean *comedor* serves home-cooked Nicaraguan fare and some good-looking fairy cakes.

Matagalpa and around *p1058, map p1059*

†† Restaurant La Pradera, Shell la Virgen, 2 c al norte, T2772-2543. One of the best in town, ideal for 'meat lovers', also serves good seafood.

†† Restaurante Pesca Mar, Cancha del Brigadista, 3 c arriba, T2772-3548. Open daily until 2200. Seafood specialities, shrimp in garlic butter, red snapper in onions.

††-† La Vida es Bella, T2772-5476, Col Lainez. An Italian-run restaurant, has received strong praise from a couple of readers, well worth it, reasonably priced.

††-† Restaurante Pique's, T2772-2723, Casa Pellas, 1c arriba. Atmospheric Mexican restaurant serving *tacos*, *tequila*, *tostados* and *chiliquilas*. Popular and friendly.

††-† Rosticería La Posada, T2772-2330, Parque Darío, ½ c abajo. Very fine eatery serving roasted chicken and fish *a la tipitapa*.

† Alejandrina Buffet, Alcadía, ½ c al sur. Economical buffet serving freshly cooked Nicaraguan fare. Clean, tasty and friendly.

¶ Rosticería La Casona, Museo del Café, 1½ al sur, T2772-3901. Local haunt serving a range of chicken and beef dishes, cold beer and refreshments. Not bad, and economical.

Cafés

Artesanos Café Bar, Banpro, ½ c arriba. This pleasant café-bar has a wooden, rancho-style interior. They do breakfasts, light lunches, and hot and cold drinks including *licuados*, iced coffee and really excellent cappucinos. Popular with both locals and tourists, and a good night spot too.

Madre Tierra, Texaco, 1½ abajo. Adorned with political photography, peace flags, outsider art, and iconic, revolutionary portraits, this café-bar has an alternative, intellectual feel. They serve tasty home-made burgers, light meals and cold beer. The action hots up at night, with regular live music and documentary films.

Jinotega and around *p1060*

¶¶ Roca Rancho, Esso, 1 c sur, 2½ c arriba. Tue-Sun 1200-0000. This fun, friendly restaurant looks like a bit like a beach bar. Serves up *comida típica*, shrimps, burgers, *bocas*, beer and liquors. Live music on Thu.

¶ Jinocuba No 1, Alcaldía, 5 c norte, T2782-2607. Daily 1200-1200. Widely recommended Cuban restaurant serving *Mojito cubano* and *pollo habanero* among other things.

¶ Las Marías, Esso, 2½ c sur. Good locals' lunch buffet with pork, chicken and beef-based Nica dishes. Family-run and friendly.

Estelí *p1061, map p1060*

¶¶¶-¶¶ Cohifer, Cohifer, Catedral, 1 c arriba, ½ c al sur. A very decent establishment that promises a fulfilling gastronomic experience. They serve a range of excellent steaks, chicken and fish dishes. Well established and recommended.

¶¶ Ixcotelli, Almacén Sony, ½ c arriba, T2714-2212. Fine Nicaraguan cuisine in a pleasant, ranch-style setting.

¶¶ Las Brasas, just off northeast corner of central park, T2713-4985. Tue-Sun 1130-2400.

Popular, lively place, with stacks of booze and bottles lining the walls. They serve Nicaraguan food and a range of beef dishes, including steak fillets, *brochetas* and *mixtas*. Try the *cerdo asado*. Recommended.

¶ Cafetería El Rincón Pinareño, Enitel, ½ c sur. Cuban and Nicaraguan dishes and home-made pastries, try *vaca frita* (shredded fried beef with onions and bell peppers), *sandwich cubano*, very good service and food, crowded for lunch, recommended.

¶ Don Pollo 2, catedral, 1 c norte, ½ c arriba. This popular roast chicken place is great for a cheap, tasty fill and a bottle or 2 of cold beer. Mariachis on some evenings.

¶ Koma Rico, Enitel, 1 c norte, 1½ c arriba. Some of the best street food in the city. They serve tasty grilled meats and chicken. Very popular with locals.

Cafés, juice bars and bakeries

Ananda, Enitel, 10 varas abajo. Chilled-out yoga centre adorned with a plethora of happy-looking plants. They serve delicious and healthy fresh fruit *licuados* – the perfect boost if you're feeling run-down. Highly recommended.

Café Luz, catedral, 1 c al norte, 1 c arriba. This English-owned café supports communities in Miraflor. They serve a range of breakfasts, including fruit salads with yogurt and granola, pancakes with honey, and for homesick Brits – egg and bacon buttie. They also sell *artesanías*, light lunches, and have a liquor licence for evening entertainment.

La Casita, opposite la Barranca, at south entrance to Estelí on Panamericana, T2713-4917. Nicaragua's best home-made yogurt in tropical fruit flavours. Very cute place with pleasant outdoor seating underneath trees on back patio, recommended.

Condega *p1063*

¶ La Cocina de Virfrank, Km 191, Carretera Panamericana, T2715-2391. Daily 0630-2000. Very cute roadside eatery set in a little garden with excellent food and economical prices.

Somoto p1063

¶¶-¶ Restaurante Almendro, Iglesia, ½ c al sur. Famous for its steaks, good *comida corriente*. Big tree in the centre gives the restaurant its name and is a famous Mejía Godoy song.

¶¶-¶ Restaurante Somoteño, Parque Central, 2 c abajo, 75 varas al norte, on Carreterra Panamericana, T2722-2518. Cheery outdoor seating with bamboo walls, great beef grill with friendly service and monumental portions: *corriente* (normal), semi *à la carte* (too big) and *à la carte* (way too big), Recommended.

¶ Cafetería Bambi, Enitel, 2½ c sur, T2722-2231, Tue-Sun 0900-2200. Surprisingly no deer on the menu, just sandwiches, hamburgers, hot dogs, tacos and fruit juices.

Ocotal p1063

¶¶-¶ Llamarada del Bosque, south side of Parque Central, T2732-2643. Popular locals' joint that serves tasty and economical buffet food and *comida típica*.

¶¶-¶ Restaurante La Cabaña, next to Hotel Benmoral, T2732-2415. Daily 1000-2300. Good steak dishes like *filete a la cabaña* or *jalapeño*. Lovely garden setting with banana trees and separate gazebos for the tables.

¶ Comedor la Esquinita, Esso, 1 c al sur. Clean, pleasant *comedor* with tables set around a leafy courtyard. They serve economical Nica fare.

✪ Entertainment

Matagalpa and around *p1058, map p1059*
Bars and clubs
Crazy Horse, Parque Darío, 10 varas abajo. Wild West-style drinking hole with log cabin exterior and an inside filled with cart wheels, Stetson hats and other cowboy memorabilia. They serve cold beer and Flor de Caña.
Disco Rancho Escondido, Parque Darío, 2 c abajo. Popular place for a dance and a drink.
La Posada Restaurant and Disco, Parque Darío, ½ c abajo. Another good place for dancing, popular with families.

Estelí p1061, map p1060
Bars and clubs
Rincón Legal, Textiles Kanan, 1 c abajo. This classic, must-see Sandinista bar is filled with revolutionary memorabilia and managed by an FSLN comrade. They often stage live music and play rousing Sandinista tunes.
Semáforo Rancho Bar, Hospital San Juan de Dios, 400 m al sur. Don your dancing shoes for Estelí's quintessential night spot. It hosts some of the best live music in the country, with nationally and internationally renowned acts performing regularly.
Studio 54, next to Casa Pellas. A great place for a dance, with bright, young, boisterous crowds descending en-masse.

✪ Shopping

Matagalpa and around *p1058, map p1059*
Cerámica Negra, Parque Darío. This kiosk, open irregularly, sells black pottery in the northern tradition – a style found only in parts of Chile, Nicaragua and Mexico. For more information contact Estela Rodríguez, T2772-4812.

Estelí *p1061, map p1060*
On Calle Principal there is an economical supermarket, **Palí**; on the same street closer to the centre is **Kodak** for photography supplies.
Mocha Nana Café, La Casa de la Mujer, 1½ c abajo, has a small selection of English-language books, including Footprint guides. *Artesanías* can be found opposite Hotel Mesón.

▲ Activities and tours

Matagalpa and around *p1058, map p1059*
Tour operators
Matagalpa Tours, Banpro, ½ c arriba, T2772-0108, www.matagalpatours.com. Trekking, hiking, birdwatching and rural

community tours are among their well-established repertoire. Dutch- and English-speaking, helpful and friendly. The best agency in town, for all your adventuring needs.

Estelí p1061, map p1060
Cigars
The country's finest cigars are manufactured in Estelí. Contact **INTUR** for a comprehensive factory list. All visits must be arranged in advance.

Tour operators
Tisey, Apdo Postal No 63, T2713-2655, next to **Hotel El Mesón** and run by same management as the hotel.

⊙ Transport

Tipitapa and further north p1058
Sébaco is a major transportation hub with northbound traffic to **Matagalpa** and **Jinotega** and northwest to **Estelí**, **Ocotal** and **Somoto**. Buses pass every 15 mins to/from **Estelí** US$1.20, **Matagalpa** US$1.10 and **Managua** US$1.50. Buses between Matagalpa and Sébaco pass the highway just outside **Chagüitillo** every 15 mins.

Matagalpa and around p1058, map p1059
Terminal Sur (Cotransur), is located near Mercado del Sur and used for all destinations outside the department of Matagalpa.

To **Jinotega**, every ½ hr, 0500-1900, US$1.40, 1½ hrs. To **Managua**, every ½ hr, 0335-1805, US$2.20, 3-4 hrs; express buses, every hour, 0520-1720, US$2.75, 2½ hrs. To **Estelí**, every ½ hr, 0515-1745, US$1.40, 2-3 hrs; express buses, 1000, 1630, US$1.50, 1½ hrs. Express bus to **León**, 0600, US$2.75, 3 hrs. Express bus to **Masaya**, 0700, 1400, 1530, US$2.75, 4 hrs.

Terminal Norte, by Mercado del Norte (Guanuca), is for all destinations within the province of Matagalpa including **San**

Ramón and **El Tuma**. Taxi between terminals US$0.50.

Jinotega and around p1060
Most destinations will require a change of bus in Matagalpa. To **Matagalpa**, every ½ hr, 0500-1800, US$1.50, 1½ hrs. To **Managua**, express buses, 10 daily, 0400-1600, US$4, 3½ hrs. To **San Rafael del Norte**, 10 daily, 0600-1730 US$1, 1 hr. Taxis in Jinotega are available for local transport, average fare US$0.50.

Estelí p1061, map p1060
Estelí has 2 terminals, both located on the Pan-American Hwy. The north terminal deals with northern destinations like Somoto and Ocotal. The south terminal, a short distance away, deals with southern destinations like Managua. A handful of Managua express buses also stop at the Shell station, east of the centre on the Pan-American Hwy.

North station For northern destinations. To **Somoto**, every hour, 0530-1810, US$1.10, 2½ hrs; use this service to connect to El Espino border bus. To **Ocotal**, every hour, 0600-1730, US$1.40, 2 hrs; use this for bus to Las Manos crossing. To **Jinotega**, every hour, 0445, 0730, 0830, 1330, 1600, US$2.25, 2 hrs. To **El Sauce**, 0900, US$1.25, 3 hrs. To **San Juan de Limay**, 0530, 0700, 1000, 1215, 1400, 1500, US$2.25, 3 hrs. To **Miraflor**, take a bus heading towards **San Sebastián de Yalí** (not one that goes to Condega first), 3 daily 0600, 1200, 1600, US$2, 1½ hrs. Return bus passes at 0700, 1100 and 1620. You can also come in 4WD; there are 2 rental agencies in Estelí.

South station Express bus to **León**, 0645, 3 hrs, US$2.75 To **Managua**, every ½ hour, 0330-1800, US$2, 3 hrs; express buses, roughly every hour, 0545-1515, US$2.75, 2 hrs. To **Matagalpa**, every ½ hour, 0520-1650, US$1.40, 2 hrs; express buses, 0805, 1435, US$1.50, 1½ hrs.

Ocotal *p1063*

The bus station for Ocotal is on the highway, 1 km south of the town centre, 15-20 mins' walk from Parque Central. Buses to **Las Manos/Honduras border** every 30 mins, 0500-1645, US$0.80, 45 mins. To **Somoto**, every 45 mins, 0545-1830, US$0.75, 2½ hrs. Express bus to **Managua**, 10 daily, 0400-1530, US$4.50, 4 hrs. To **Ciudad Antigua**, 0500, 1200, US$1.25, 1½ hrs. To **Estelí**, leaves the city market every hour, 0445-1800, US$1.30, 2½ hrs; express buses are Managua-bound, 2 hrs, US$1.65, they will drop you off at the Shell station, just east of central Estelí.

❸ Directory

Matagalpa and around *p1058, map p1059*
Banks Banco de América Central (BAC and Credomatic), Parque Morazán, 1 c al sur, on Av Central, changes all TCs and cash on Visa and MC and has ATM for most credit and debit cards with Cirrus logo. **Banpro**, opposite **BAC**, offers similar services.
Internet Many internet places around town, particularly along Av José Benito Escobar, most charge US$0.50 per hr.

Estelí *p1061, map p1060*
Banks Almost every bank in the city is located in 1 city block. If you go 1 block

south and 1 block east from the central park you will find the 2 banks that change TCs, **Banco de América Central** (BAC), T2713-7101, which changes all brands of TCs. **Internet** Cafés all over town, try **Computer Soluciones**, Parque Central, US$0.50 per hr. **Language schools** Centro Nicaragüense de Aprendizaje y Cultura (CENAC), Apdo 40, Estelí, T2713-5437, 2 offices: Texaco, 5 c arriba, ½ c sur, and De los Bancos 1 c sur, T2713-2025, ½ c arriba. 20 hrs of Spanish classes, living with a family, full board, travelling to countryside, meetings and seminars, opportunities to work on community projects, US$140 per week. Also teaches English to Nicaraguans and others and welcomes volunteer tutors. **Los Pipitos-Sacuanjoche Escuela de Español**, Costado Noreste Catedral, 1 c norte, ½ c abajo, T2713-3830, www.lospipitosesteli.org.ni. Social projects are a part of the course and all profits go to disabled children and their families. Excursions to local cooperatives and homestay available. US$50-175, flexible options.

Ocotal *p1063*
Bank Bancentro, Parque Central, 1 c norte, 1 c abajo, has a Visa ATM and money-changing facility; as does **Banco Procredit**, Parque Central, 1 c abajo.

León and the west

A third route to Honduras leaves the capital heading through the Pacific lowlands to the Gulf of Fonseca in the shadow of Los Maribios, a chain of volcanoes from Momotombo on Lake Managua to Cosigüina overlooking the gulf. This route takes in León, a city influential in shaping Nicaraguan history since colonial times. On the Pacific coast are the beaches at Poneloya and the major port of Corinto. From León, 88 km from Managua, the Pacific Highway continues north to the industrial town of Chinandega. From here, routes lead west to the port of Corinto, north to the Gulf of Fonseca and east to Guasaule and the Honduran border. For the adventurous traveller, León is a good base to climb one of the volcanoes of Los Maribios: Momotombo is known for its perfect shape and incredible views from the top; Cerro Negro is the youngest volcano in Central America, erupting every four to five years; Volcán Telica has bubbling mudholes at the base and glowing lava in the crater; San Cristóbal is the tallest volcano in Nicaragua and highly active; while Cosigüina is surrounded by beautiful nature and famous for its huge crater lake and spectacular views. ►► *For listings, see pages 1079-1085.*

Towards León

The old paved road to León crosses the Sierra de Managua, offering fine views of the lake. It is longer than the new Pacific Highway and not in good condition. About 60 km down the new road to León lies the village of **La Paz Centro**, with several truck-stop restaurants and accommodation. There is a good range of cheap, handmade pottery here, and you can ask to see the potters' ovens and production of bricks. Try the local speciality *quesillo* (mozzarella cheese, onions and cream wrapped in tortilla), available all along the highway. From here you can reach **Volcán Momotombo**, which dominates the Managua skyline from the west. It is possible to camp on the lakeside with great views of the volcano.

You need a permit to climb Momotombo from the south as a geothermal power station has been built on the volcano's slopes. At the time of writing, no permit was required to climb the volcano from the north but one reader has reported it as being a gruelling 11-hour climb. Take local advice and use a professional guide – ask at **Va Pues** or **Quetzaltrekkers** in León. ►► *See Tour operators, page 1084.*

León Viejo

① *US$2 entrance fee includes Spanish-speaking guide.*

At the foot of the volcano lies León Viejo, destroyed by earthquake and volcanic eruption on 31 December 1609 and now being excavated. It was here that the brutal first Spanish governor of Nicaragua Pedrarias and his wife were buried in La Merced church next to Francisco Hernández de Córdoba, the country's founder who had been beheaded under order of Pedrarias. Archaeological excavations have revealed the **cathedral**, the **Convento de la Merced**, the **Casa del Gobernador**, as well as the bodies of Hernández de Córdoba and Pedrarias, which have been placed in a special tomb in the Plaza Mayor. The ruins themselves are little more than low walls and probably only of serious interest to archaeologists, but you can see the ground plan of the old Spanish town and from the ruins of the old fortress there are breathtaking views of Volcán Mombotombo, Lake Managua and Momotombito Island and the Maribios Volcanoes range. To get to León Viejo, take a Managua bus and get out in La Paz Centro, US$1, 45 minutes. Catch a second bus (or taxi) to Puerto Momotombo, US$0.50, 30 minutes, and walk 10 minutes to the site from there.

➔ *Population: 184,792. Altitude: 50 m.*

León has a colonial charm unmatched elsewhere in Nicaragua, except perhaps by Granada. It is typified by narrow streets, red-tile roofs, low adobe houses and time-worn buildings. Founded by Hernández de Córdoba in 1524 at León Viejo, 32 km from its present site, it was moved here after the devastating earthquake of 1609. The existing city was founded in 1610. In recent years, economic factors have taken precedence over the cleaning up of old buildings, but the work continues slowly.

As the capital, León was the dominant force in Nicaragua until Managua took control in 1852. Today, it is still thought of as the 'intellectual' capital, with a university (Universidad Nacional Autónoma de Nicaragua, UNAN) founded in 1804, religious colleges, the largest cathedral in Central America, and several colonial churches. It is said that Managua became the capital, although at the time it was no more than an indigenous settlement, because it was halfway between violently Liberal León and equally violently Conservative Granada.

Ins and outs

Getting there Regular buses to León run from Managua and Chinandega, with frequent routes from Estelí and Matagalpa. International buses will drop you off, if asked, at the entrance to town. The bus terminal is at the northeastern end of town, a 20-minute walk, or short taxi ride from the centre.

Getting around Most attractions are within a few blocks of the centre so choosing a fairly central hotel will make it an easy city to explore on foot. Local buses will take you to the terminal and a network of *colectivos* work as cheap taxis (US$0.15). Taxis cost US$0.60 during the day, US$0.70 at night.

Tourist information INTUR ① *Parque Rubén Darío 2½ c al norte, T2311-1325, www.leononline.net*, has maps for sale, reference books and friendly staff.

Sights

Legend has it that the plans for the **Basílica de la Asunción** (the **cathedral**) ① *to see inside, visit between 0700-0900 or 1600-1800*, were switched with those of Lima (Peru) by mistake. However, the enormous size of the building, designed by Guatemalan architects, may be explained by the need to withstand the area's heavy seismic activity. Construction was begun in 1746 and was not completed for 113 years. Its famous shrine – 145 cm high, covered by white topazes from India given by Felipe II of Spain – is, sadly, kept in a safe in the vestry, to which the bishop holds the key. The cathedral also houses a very fine ivory Christ, the consecrated Altar of Sacrifices and the Choir of Córdoba, the great Christ of Esquipulas (in bronze with a cross of very fine silver) and statues of the 12 Apostles. At the foot of one of these statues is the tomb of Rubén Darío, the 19th-century Nicaraguan poet, and one of the greatest in Latin America, guarded by a sorrowful lion. All the entrances to the cathedral are guarded by lions said to come alive after midnight to patrol the old church. The old Plaza de Armas, in front of the cathedral, is now **Parque Jerez**, but is usually referred to as **Parque Central**; it contains a statue of General Jerez, a mid-19th-century Liberal leader.

León has the finest **colonial churches** in Nicaragua, more than 12 in all, and they are the city's most significant attraction. **La Recolección**, with a beautiful baroque Mexican

Memories of a Revolutionary

During the 1978-1979 Revolution, León was the centre of heavy fighting. There are many monuments from that time in the city. In the city centre a plaque marks the spot where the first president, Somoza, was assassinated in 1956 by poet Rigoberto López Pérez. Visitors can also see El Fortín (from the cathedral, go west about 10 blocks, then south), the ruined last stronghold of Somoza's national guard. It's best to go early in the morning for the great views of town and several volcanoes. A commemorative march goes there each 7 July. El Veinte Uno, the national guard's 21st garrison, was also ruined, and the scene of an important battle in April 1979; the jail around the corner (three blocks south of cathedral) has been converted into a garden with a statue to *El Combatiente Desconocido* (the unknown warrior). In the Barrio San Felipe, seven or eight blocks north of the market behind the cathedral, a statue of Luisa Amanda Espinoza remembers the first woman member of the FSLN to die, in 1970.

Across the street from the north side of the cathedral is an interesting mural depicting the history from pre-Columbian times to the Sandinista Revolution, dating to 1990. Sadly many of the murals are being painted over as images of the Revolution are gradually removed and replaced. It surrounds a commemorative park, the Mausoleo Héroes y Mártires. There is also the Galería Héroes y Mártires (Calle 1 NO, between Avenidas 1 and 2), which sells handicrafts and houses the twinning office with New Haven (US).

Descriptions of León's fight against the Somoza régime can be found in the book *Fire from the Mountain: The Making of a Sandinista*, by Omar Cabezas.

façade, built in 1786, has a neoclassical interior with mahogany woodwork. **La Merced**, which was built in 1615 and burned by pirates in 1685, is notable for its seven different altars. It is one of the oldest churches in León and has fine woodwork inside and a restored exterior. **San Felipe** was built at the end of the 16th century for the religious services of the black and mulatto population of the city. It was rebuilt in the 18th century in a manner true to its original form, a mixture of baroque and neoclassical. **El Calvario**, constructed during the same period, is notable for its neoclassical façade attributed to the growing French influence in Spain at the time. The **Iglesia y Convento de San Francisco** ① *US$1.50*, founded in 1639, is the oldest convent with a church in León. It still has two plateresque altars from Spain and its original pillars. In 1830, after the expulsion of the Franciscans from Nicaragua, it was used by various civic organizations and is now a gallery. The **Iglesia de San Nicolás de Laborío**, was founded in 1618 for the local indigenous population, and is the most modest of the León churches, constructed of wood and tiles over adobe walls with an unostentatious façade and a simple altar, 10 m tall. The celebration for San Nicolás is 10 September. The **Iglesia de Nuestra Señora Pilar de Zaragoza** was built from 1884-1934 and has two unusual octagonal turrets and an arched doorway with tower above. There is a pleasant walk south across the bridge, past the church of **Guadalupe**, to the cemetery.

The house of poet Rubén Darío, the famous 'Four Corners' in Calle Rubén Darío, is now the **Museo-Archivo Rubén Darío** ① *Tue-Sat 0900-1200, 1400-1700, Sun 0900 1200, entry and guided tour free but donations accepted*. It has an interesting collection of personal possessions, photographs, portraits and a library with a wide range of books of poetry in Spanish, English and French. Darío died in 1916 in another house in the northwest sector

León

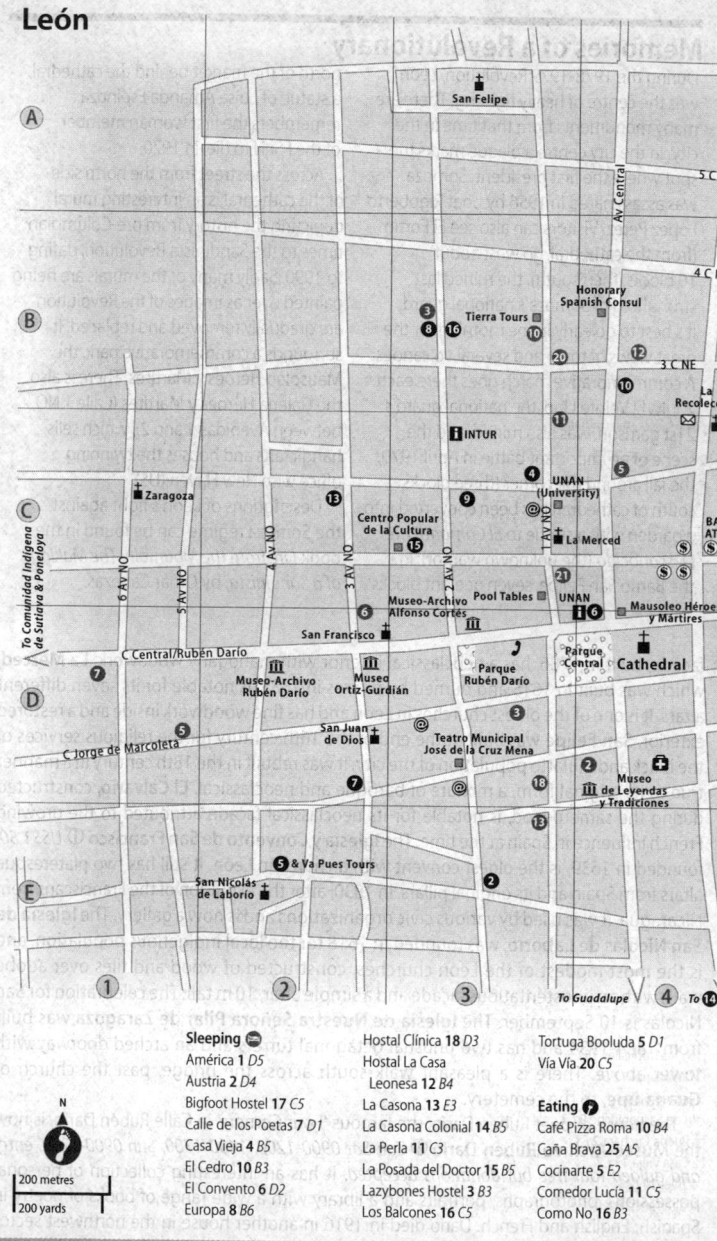

Sleeping

América **1** D5
Austria **2** D4
Bigfoot Hostel **17** C5
Calle de los Poetas **7** D1
Casa Vieja **4** B5
El Cedro **10** B3
El Convento **6** D2
Europa **8** B6

Hostal Clínica **18** D3
Hostal La Casa
  Leonesa **12** B4
La Casona **13** E3
La Casona Colonial **14** B5
La Perla **11** C3
La Posada del Doctor **15** B5
Lazybones Hostel **3** B3
Los Balcones **16** C5

Tortuga Bolouda **5** D1
Vía Vía **20** C5

Eating

Café Pizza Roma **10** B4
Caña Brava **25** A5
Cocinarte **5** E2
Comedor Lucía **11** C5
Como No **16** B3

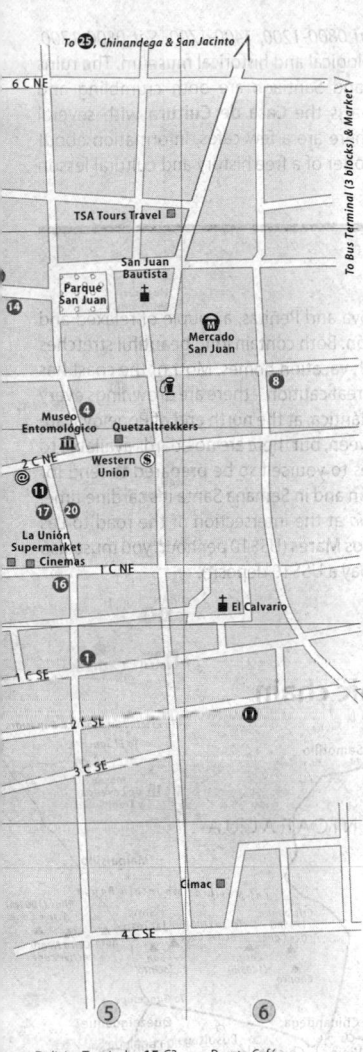

Delicias Tropicales **15** C3
El Mississippi **12** D6
El Sesteo **6** D4
Flor de Sacuanjoche **9** C3
La Buena Cuchara **2** E3
La Casa Vieja **13** C2
Lacmiel **14** E4
Mediterráneo **8** B3

Puerto Café
 Benjamín Linder **4** C3
Venivé **7** D2

Bars & clubs 🍸
Café Taquezal **3** D3
Divino Castigo **20** B3
Don Señor **21** C3
La Pasarela **5** C4

(marked with a plaque). Alfonso Cortés –
another of Nicaragua's finest poets who
wrote a famous poem while chained to
the bars in front of Rubén's old bed – went
insane while living in Darío's house in
1927 and spent the rest of his years in a
Managuan asylum until his death in 1969,
leaving behind the *museo-archivo*.

Two blocks west of La Merced church is
the **Centro Popular de la Cultura** which
has frequent exhibitions and events, and is
the only place in León to see live folk
concerts (schedule on the front door).
The **Museo de Leyendas y Tradiciones**
① *parque central, 3 c sur, Tue-Sat 0800-1200,
1400-1700, US$0.50*, has handcrafted life-
size models depicting the rich legends of
León. The **Museo Ortiz Guardián** ① *Mon-
Fri 1100-1900, US$1*, is a colonial home and
art museum. **Museo Archivo Alfonso
Cortés** ① *Mon-Sat 0800-1200, 1400-1700*,
has dusty displays of the great poet's
manuscripts. **CIMAC** ① *Costado sur del
Puente Martínez, ½ c arriba, 1 c al norte,
T2311-0752, cimac@ibw.com.ni, Mon-Fri
0800-1100, 1400-1700, Sat 0800-1100,
US$1*, which used to be a garbage plant,
has been transformed into a centre for
urban environmental initiatives, with a
self-guided trail and further information
available at site.

Sutiava

The western end of the city is the oldest,
and here is the oldest of all the churches,
the parish church of **San Juan Bautista** in
Sutiava (1530). Las Casas, the Apostle of the
Indies, preached here several times. It has a
fine façade, the best colonial altar in the
country and an interesting representation
of *El Sol* (the sun), carved in wood on the
ceiling. The church has been beautifully
reconstructed. Just south of the church on
the dirt plaza is a **museum** ① *daily 0800-
1100, 1400-1700, Sat 0800-1000, US$0.50*,
housing many colonial relics.

On the main street north of the church is
a small **Museo de la Comunidad Indígena**

Sutiava or **Museo Adiac** ① *T311-5371, Mon-Fri 0800-1200, 1400-1700, Sat 0800-1200, donations greatly appreciated*, with an anthropological and historical museum. The ruins of the nearby parish churches of Vera Cruz and Santiago are both crumbling and unapproachable. Also in the suburb of Sutiava is the **Casa de Cultura** with several interesting murals adorning the walls. Inside there are a few cafés, information about prominent Nicaraguan cultural figures and the offer of a free history and cultural lesson on Thursdays (1500) in basic Spanish.

Around León ⊕🅟🅕🅔🅢 ▶▶ pp1079-1085.

Poneloya and Las Peñitas beaches

A bumpy road from León heads west to Poneloya and Peñitas, a couple of relaxed and very friendly beach communities 19 km from León. Both contain long beautiful stretches of sand and a mixture of humble houses and rich vacation homes. Most of the coast has big waves and strong currents (swim here with great caution – there are drownings every year). The south end of Las Peñitas and Puerto Mántica, at the north end of Poneloya, are the best for swimming, with good surfing in between, but there are no boards available to rent. During the week you will have the beaches to yourself so be prepared to fend for yourself, but at weekends people come from León and in Semana Santa it's sardine time. It is possible to rent quadbikes from the *pulpería* at the intersection of the road to Las Peñitas and Poneloya, called **Licorería Estela de los Mares** (US$10 per hour, you must also show a driving licence, sign a release form and pay a US$10 deposit).

León & Los Maribios volcanic chain

San Jacinto

On the road to Estelí, 12 km north of the intersection with the Chinandega–León road, is San Jacinto. About 200 m to the west of the road is a field of steaming, bubbling **mud holes**, which is worth visiting. You should approach carefully, the ground may give and scald your legs; follow other footmarks for safety, avoiding walking on the crystallized white sulphur, and listen for hissing. It is recommended to hire a guide (ask tour operators in León) or trust one of the local children (US$0.25 tip) to show you where it is safe to walk. A visit can be combined with a hike to the edge of the spectacular crater of Telica with glowing lava inside. The climb is fairly easy but trails can be hard to find. It's best to use a professional guide and make an excursion from León – ask at **Va Pues** or **Quetzaltrekkers**. ➤ *See Tour operators, page 1084.*

Chinandega → *Colour map 6, C3. Population: 137,940. Altitude: 70 m.*

About 40 km beyond León, Chinandega is one of the hottest, driest towns in Nicaragua. Agriculturally, this is one of the richest areas in Central America producing bananas, peanuts, sugar cane and shrimps. There's a good market by the bus terminal and you can hire horse-drawn cabs. The local fiesta is on 26 July. The **tourist office** ① *Reparto Los Angeles, T2341-2040*, has a helpful representative who speaks English and Italian.

Chichigalpa

Not far away, near Chichigalpa, is the **Ingenio San Antonio**, the largest sugar mill in Nicaragua, with a railway between the town and the mill (five trains a day each way May-November, passengers taken, US$0.10; also bus US$0.30). While there are no official tours of the installations, you can apply at Gate (*Portón*) 14 to be shown around. On the edge of Chichigalpa itself is the **Flor de Caña distillery**, maker of what many believe to be the finest rum in the world, aged up to 21 years and made in over 15 flavours. On leaving you will recognize the picture on the bottle labels, a palm-shaded railway leading towards Chichigalpa with volcanoes in the background.

Corinto → *Colour map 6, C3. Population: 17,414. Altitude: 3 m.*

Twenty-one kilometres from Chinandega, Corinto is the main port in Nicaragua and the only one at which vessels of any considerable size can berth. About 60% of the country's commerce passes through here. The town itself is on a sandy island, **Punto Icaco**, connected to the mainland by long railway and road bridges. There are beautiful old wooden buildings with verandas, especially by the port. Entry to the port is barred to those without a permit.

[Map showing: To Sébaco, Matagalpa & Estelí, San Francisco Libre, San Benito, Panamerican Highway, Lago de Managua (Xolotlán), omotombo (1300m) ctive Cone, Isla Momotombito, uerto Momotombo, Apoyeque Lagoon, Chiltepe Peninsula, Jiloá Lagoon, León Viejo, La Paz Centro, Nagarote, Materare, Carretera Nueva a León, Carretera Vieja a León, MANAGUA, Las Nubes, El Crucero, To Masaya & Granada, El Velero, Carretera Masachapa, San Rafael del Sur, El Tránsito, Montelimar, Masachapa, Pochomil]

Border essentials: Nicaragua–Honduras

El Guasaule

Nicaraguan immigration The distance between the border posts is 500 m. The border is open 24 hours. To enter Nicaragua costs US$7 plus a US$1 Alcaldía charge; to exit it is US$2 plus the US$1 immigration charge.

Transport Buses run every 30 minutes from the border to Chinandega, US$1.40. Express bus to Managua, 1130, 1230 and 1700, four hours, US$3.50 via Somotillo and León. From Managua to Río Guasaule at 1810.

Directory Money changers offer the same rates for córdobas to lempiras as on the Honduran side. Banco de Crédito Centroamericano, beside immigration, is recommended, good rates, no commission, and will accept photocopy of passport if yours is being checked by immigration.

Potosí

Nicaraguan immigration and customs The border is open 0800-1700, but closed for lunch. Exit is US$2 and Nicaraguan immigration entrance is US$7.

Transport Buses from Potosí–Chinandega, 0230, 0345, 0500, 0620, 0710, 1000, 1500, US$2, three hours. If trying to leave Nicaragua, there may be a ferry. Alternatively, try a private boat to El Salvador.

On the Corinto–Chinandega road is **Paseo Cavallo beach** (Restaurante Buen Vecino). The sea is treacherous here and people drown every year. There are no facilities in Corinto's barrier islands, but they are beautiful with crashing surf on one side, calm and warm swimming water on the other. The journey can be negotiated with any fisherman. A *panga* can be rented for the whole day for US$40 so you can explore the numerous islands and mangroves. You'll see lots of birdlife but also lots of sandflies, so be sure to bring repellent.

North of Chinandega

The road north to Puerto Morazán passes through the village of **El Viejo**, US$0.20 by bus from Chinandega, 5 km, where there is an old church, **La Basílica del Viejo**, famous throughout the country for its celebration on 6 December called **La Lavada de la Plata**, which consists of devotees washing all silver parts of the altar. The Basílica has la Virgen del Hato, which leaves the altar every December in a major pilgrimage to visit Corinto, Chinandega, León and Managua.

From Chinandega there are six buses a day to **Potosí** (at least three hours, US$1.20). In the centre of the village there are warm thermal springs in which people congregate to relax each afternoon. There are also pleasant black-sand beaches; the sea, although the colour of coffee, is clean. The passenger ferry from Potosí to La Unión (El Salvador) has been suspended. Ask around for an ad hoc service or ask in Chinandega before setting out to the peninsula. Rumours suggest that there may be a service from Corinto to La Unión.

It is a four-hour hike to the cone of **Volcán Cosigüina**. The path is overgrown and very difficult to follow, so you may need a guide (see Tour operators, page 1084). There is plenty of wildlife in the area, including poisonous snakes. On 23 January 1835, one of the biggest eruptions in history blew off most of the cone, reducing it from 3000 m to its present height of 800 m, throwing ash as far as Colombia, and leaving an enormous crater lake. From the cone there are beautiful views of the Golfo de Fonseca shared by Nicaragua, Honduras and El Salvador. The volcano and the surrounding dry tropical forest are a Reserva Natural, administered by the Ministry of the Environment and Natural Resources in Managua.

Jiquilillo beach, 42 km from Chinandega, is reached by a mostly paved road branching off the El Viejo–Potosí road. Lying on a long peninsula, there are a few lodgings and small restaurants. From Chinandega a rough paved road goes to the Honduran border on the **Río Guasaule** near **Somotillo** (where the road improves) heading to Choluteca, Honduras. The bus from Chinandega takes 1¾ hours (US$1.25).

⓪ León and the west listings

For Sleeping and Eating price codes and other relevant information, see Essentials pages 45-48.

⓪ Sleeping

León *p1072, map p1074*
L La Perla, Iglesia La Merced, 1 c norte, T2311-3125, www.laperlaleon.com. This handsome old colonial building has been recently remodelled and now houses elegant rooms, suites, bar, restaurant and pool. Some rooms have bath tubs.
AL Hotel El Convento, connected to Iglesia San Francisco, T2311-7053, www.hotelel convento.com.ni. This beautiful, intriguing hotel is decorated with elegant antique art, including an impressive altar adorned with gold leaf.
A Hotel Austria, catedral, 1 c sur, T2311-1206, www.hotelaustria.com.ni. Very clean and comfortable rooms surrounding a lush central courtyard. They have hot water, a/c, telephone and cable TV. Internet and laundry service available. Continental breakfast is included in the price. Friendly and oftenfully booked.
A Hostal La Casa Leonesa, catedral, 3 c norte, 15 varas arriba, T2311-0551, www.la casaleonesa.com. This typical León house has a lovely elegant interior, a swimming pool and 10 rooms of varying size, all with private bath, hot water, cable TV, telephone. Breakfast included. Rooms upstairs are cheaper (**B**).
A La Posada del Doctor, Parque San Juan, 25 varas abajo, T2311-4343,

www.laposadadeldoctor.com. Very clean and nicely furnished rooms with private bath, hot water, cable TV, a/c. Services include laundry, parking and Wi-Fi. Pleasant little patio and relaxed atmosphere. Breakfast included.
A Los Balcones, esq de los bancos, 1 c arriba, T2311-0250, www.hotel balcones.com. A handsome colonial building with an attractive courtyard, bar and restaurant. The 20 rooms have private bath, hot water, a/c and cable TV; some have a good view. Breakfast included. Tasteful, professional and comfortable.
B Europa, 3 C NE, 4 Av, T2311-6040, www.hoteleuropaleon.com. Pleasant patios and quiet, clean comfortable rooms with Wi-Fi, safe, telephone, a/c, hot water. Services include restaurant, bar and parking. Cheaper with fan (**C**).
B La Casona Colonial, Parque San Juan, ½ c abajo, T2311-3178. This pleasant colonial house has 5 good-value homely rooms with private bath and a/c. Management is friendly and hospitable, and there's a lovely green garden, too. Cheaper with fan (**C**)
C América, catedral, 2 c arriba, T2311-5533. Plain, comfortable rooms in a friendly old house. There's a pleasant patio and garden, internet, parking and meals on request.
C-F Lazybones Hostels, Parque de los Poetas, 2½ c norte, T2311-3472, www.lazybones.com. Managed by a friendly English-Colombian couple, this quality hostel has a great pool and lots of extras including

free coffee and tea, pool table, internet, DVD rental and a daily 10 min long-distance phone call. Dorms (**F**) are clean, some private rooms have private bath (**C**), cheaper without (**D**). Check out the mural by one of Managua's finest graffiti artists. Recommended.

D Calle de los Poetas, Calle Rubén Darío, Museo Darío, 1½ c abajo, T2311-3306, rsampson@ibw.com.ni. This comfortable good-value guesthouse has a relaxed homely ambience, spacious rooms with private and shared bath, a beautiful garden and friendly hosts. It's also the base for **Sampson Expeditions** (see page 1084). Often full, so arrive early. Discounts for longer stays. Recommended.

D Hostal Clínica, 1 Av NO, Parque Central, 1½ c sur, T2311-2031, marymergalo2000@yahoo.com. Family-run and very Nicaraguan. Single and double rooms with private or shared bathroom, breakfast and drinks available. Very friendly, good reports.

D-F Vía Vía, Banco ProCredit, ½ c sur, T2311-6142, www.viaviacafe.com. Part of a worldwide network of Belgian cafés, this excellent and professionally managed hostel offers clean dorm beds (**F**) and a range of private rooms (**D-E**), some with TV. There's a tranquil garden, a well-stocked and socially aware information centre, popular restaurant-bar, community tours and classes. 'A meeting place for cultures'. Recommended.

E Casa Vieja, Parque San Juan, 1½ c sur, T2311-4235. Sociable Nica hotel with some long-term residents and a family feel. It has 9 large rooms with fan, communal bath and kitchen, cooking on request, laundry service and telephone. Friendly.

E El Cedro, T2311-4643, northwest corner of parque central, 2½ c norte. 9 clean, comfortable, good-value rooms with private bath and cable TV. There's a café and bar attached, and the friendly management speak English. Recommended.

E La Casona, Teatro González, 2 c sur, T2311-5282, lacasonahostal@hotmail.com.

This spacious house has lots of places to relax, a garden with hammocks, pool (sometimes empty), use of kitchen and washing facilities. The rooms have private and shared bath, poor mattresses and fan. Economical and popular with volunteers. Lovely hosts.

F Bigfoot Hostel, Banco ProCredit, ½ c sur, www.bigfootnicaragua.com. Sociable, buzzing and popular with the whippersnappers. This Australian-run backpackers' joint has lots of dorm space, a handful of private rooms (**E**), pool, sandboarding tours, TV, pool table, and a popular restaurant serving everything from cappuccinos to wholesome Nica fare.

F Tortuga Booluda, Iglesia San Juan de Dios, 1½ c abajo, T2311-4653, www.tortugabooluda.com. Pleasant Nica-run hostel with links to social projects, dorms, chill-out spaces, hammocks, kitchen and notice board.

Poneloya and Las Peñitas beaches
p1076

Most of the best restaurants are found at the hotels and hostels.

B Suyapa Beach Hotel, in Las Peñitas, T8885-8345 www.suyapabeach.com. A well-kept and professional hotel with a pool and 20 clean rooms, all with poor beds and private bath, some with a/c. Rooms on 2nd and 3rd floor have ocean views and a breeze. Often full with groups. Cheaper with fan (**D**).

C Oasis, Terminal de Buses, 200 varas norte, Las Peñitas, T8839-5344. 7 large rooms with poor mattresses; some rooms have phenomenal views. Lots of chill-out spaces with hammocks. Services include rental of surf boards, horse riding and laundry service. The restaurant has great views but the toilets are nasty.

C Posada de Poneloya, Playa Poneloya, from the intersection of Las Peñitas and Poneloya, 150 m to the right, T2317-1378. 19 rooms with private bath, hot water, a/c, with room service and nanny service, parking, not a great part of the beach, but lively on weekends.

D Samaki, overlooking the bay, Las Peñitas, T2640-2058, www.lasamaki.net. 4 tasteful rooms with good mattresses, safes, mosquito nets and private bath. Canadian owned, very relaxed, friendly and hospitable, and home to Nicaragua's only kite-surfing operation. Fresh food made to order, including delicious, real Asian curries. Recommended.

D-F Barca de Oro, Las Peñitas, at the end of the beach facing Isla Juan Venado Wildlife Refuge, www.barcadeoro.com.ni. Friendly, funky hotel with dorm beds (**F**) and private rooms (**D**), all with fan and bath. Services include kayaking, horse riding, body boarding, book exchange, hammocks, tours of the area and beauty treatments.

Chinandega *p1077*

AL Los Volcanes, Km 129.5, Carretera a Chinandega, at southern entrance to city, T2341-1000, www.losvolcaneshotel.com. Very pleasant, comfortable rooms with private bath, hot water, a/c, cable TV. There's a smart restaurant and bar, service is professional.

B Hotel Chinandegano, Esso El Calvario 1½ c arriba, T2341-4800. One of the best, with decent rooms, popular bar and restaurant.

B Hotel Pacífico, Iglesia San Antonio, 1½ c sur, T2341-1418, hotelpac@ibw.com.ni. Comfortable, friendly hotel with decent, modern rooms, all have a/c, cable TV, private bath and hot water. Recommended.

C Hotel San José, esq de los Bancos, 2½ c norte, T2341-2723. Clean, comfortable and friendly. 10 small, plain rooms have private bath, a/c, cable TV. Breakfast included. Laundry service and internet available.

D Casa Grande, frente de Gallo mas Gallo, T2341-0325. Management is friendly but the beds are poor. Be sure to get a room with a/c, those without (**F**) can be uncomfortably warm.

D Don Mario's, Enitel, 170 varas norte, T2341-4054, Great value rooms and friendly hosts at this homely lodging. Rooms have a/c, private bath and cable TV. The owners speak excellent English. Recommended.

Eating

León *p1072, map p1074*

††† - †† **Caña Brava**, on bypass road, T2311-5666. Daily 1100-2200. For many locals the best food in town, with excellent beef dishes, large portions and attentive service. It has very little charm though, and is far from the centre.

†† **Café Pizza Roma**, catedral, 2½ c norte, T2311-3568. 1200-2300, closed Tue. Average pizzas and good meat dishes. Popular with Nicas.

†† **Cocinarte**, Costardo norte Iglesia el Laborío, T2325-4099. Quality vegetarian restaurant with an intriguing international menu of Eastern, Middle Eastern and Nicaraguan cuisine. Lots of fresh and organic produce used, and it holds a monthly organic market. Fri evenings are romantic music nights and Sun afternoon sees chess matches with free coffee. Recommended.

†† **El Sesteo**, next to cathedral, on Parque Central, T2311-5327. The place for watching the world go by, particularly in the late afternoon. Good pork dishes, *nacatamales*, fruit drinks and *cacao con leche*. Portraits of Nicaraguan cultural greats on the wall. Begging can be frequent if you sit outside.

†† **Flor de Sacuanjoche**, northeast corner of University UNAN-León, 75 m abajo, T2311-1121. Daily 0900-2400. Popular with Nicas. Serves meat and veggie dishes, lunch and breakfast.

†† **Lacmiel**, catedral, 5 c sur. Good meat dishes and onion soup. Occasional live music. Recommended.

†† **Mediterráneo**, Parque Rubén Darío, 2½ c norte, T8895-9392. Tue-Sun 1200-2300. French and Mediterranean cuisine, including pasta and Italian wines. It has a wide range of meat and chicken dishes, and takeaway pizza too. Popular with foreigners, recommended.

†† **Venivé**, Iglesia de San Juan de Dios, 1 c sur. León's finest Spanish tapas restaurant. Smart, stylish and sadly neglected by the locals.

†† - † **La Casa Vieja**, Iglesia San Francisco, 1½ c norte. Mon-Sat 1600-2300. Lovely, intimate little restaurant-bar with a vaguely rustic feel. Serves quality meat and chicken dishes, beer and delicious home-made lemonade. Recommended.

₩-₩ Vía Vía, Banco Procredit ½ c sur. A very popular place for breakfast, lunch or dinner. The gringo-friendly menu has food glossaries and descriptions of some classic Nicaraguan dishes. It also serves favourites from other Central American countries and has live music. See under Bars and clubs.

₩ Casa Popular de Cultura, Plaza Central, 1 c norte, 2½ c abajo. Friendly little locals' spot, sometimes with passing musicians. Serves sandwiches and burgers. Good atmosphere.

₩ Comedor Lucía, Banco Procredit, ½ c sur. Reputable *comedor* serving good but slightly pricey *comida típica* and buffet food, popular with locals. Lunch only.

₩ El Cedro, northwest corner of parque central, 2½ c norte, T2311-4643. Good, filling, economical breakfasts – try the English breakfast for giant portions that will keep you fuelled till dinner time.

₩ El Mississippi, southeast corner of the cathedral, 1 c sur, 2½ c arriba. Also known as, perhaps unfortunately, '*la cucaracha*' (the cockroach), everyone raves about the bean soup here. Simple, unpretentious dining at this locals' haunt.

₩ La Buena Cuchara, Parque Rubén Darío, 3½ c sur. Friendly, homely little *comedor* with tasty and economical buffet food. Lunch only. Recommended.

Cafés, bakeries and juice bars
Como No, Parque Rubén Darío, ½ c norte. Delicious-smelling wholemeal bread, juices, shakes, economical breakfasts and sandwiches.

Delicias Tropicales, next to the Casa de Cultura. Tasty fresh fruit juices and smoothies, very refreshing after the heat of León's streets.

Puerto Café Benjamín Linder, next to UNAN (northern corner), T2311-0548. Daily 0800-2400. Coffee roasted fresh on premises at this café named after social worker who was killed by Contras in 1980s. Profits go to

the prosthetic outreach clinic in León. High-speed internet access and massage.

Sutiava *p1075*
₩ Los Pescaditos, Iglesia de San Juan, 1 c sur, 1 c abajo. Daily 1200-2230. Excellent seafood at reasonable prices, go with the waiter to choose your fish from the ice box, recommended.

₩ El Capote, Billares Lacayo, 3 c sur, ½ c arriba, T2315-3918. Mon-Sat 1100-2300, Sun 1000-1700. No frills bar and eatery with very good food, seafood, cow's tail soup, a massive *surtido* (sampler) dish for US$7.

Chinandega *p1077*
₩ Frank's Bar and Grill, southeast corner of Iglesia El Calvario, 1 c sur. One of the best in town, with good beef cuts and fine wine. Smart, clean interior.

₩ Gerry's Seafood, Shell central, 1½ c norte. Reportedly very good fish and seafood.

₩ Corona de Oro, Iglesia San Antonio, 1½ c arriba, T2341-2539. Chinese food with flavour. The chicken curry and shrimp skewers are especially tasty.

₩ El Mondongazo, south side of Colégio San Luis, T2341-4255. Traditional Nicaraguan foods like *sopa mondongo* (tripe soup), beef, chicken and meatball soup.

₩ El Refugio, Esso, El Calvario, ½ c sur, T2341-0834. Great beef specialities, try the breaded tongue.

₩ Kingdom's Plaza, enitel, 1 c arriba, ½ c sur, T2341-8911. Burgers, roast chicken and fairly decent, economical pizza. Delivers.

₩ Las Tejitas, Parque Central, 7 c arriba. Cheap and cheerful. They serve buffet food, grilled meats and *comida típica*. Very popular and always packed out. A Chinandega institution.

☺ Entertainment

León *p1072, map p1074*
Bars and clubs
León has a vibrant nightlife, owed to its large student population. The action moves between different places depending on

the night of the week.

Café Taquezal, southwest corner of Parque Central, ½ c abajo, T2311-7282. Mon-Sat 1800-0200. Pleasant atmosphere with good live folk music on Thu nights. Classic León decor. Food served.

Discoteca Dilectus, at the southern entrance to the city. Wed-Sun. Inconveniently located, but probably the best disco in town. Upmarket crowd.

Divino Castigo, UNAN, 1 c norte. Daily 1700-0100. Good atmosphere, 'bohemian nights' on Tue and Sat. Look at the *mesa maldita* (cursed table) where old newspaper articles tell you the cruel history of this house. Or ask for Sergio Ramírez's book from which the bar derives its name.

Don Señor, opposite Parque La Merced. Tue-Sun. Popular with students and young Nicas on Fri nights, with liberal doses of karaoke, dancing and beer. A good place to see the locals cut loose.

El Cedro, T2311-4643, northwest corner of parque central, 2½ c norte. Thu night is rock night in El Cedro, the only place in town to catch some decent guitar riffs. The friendly management is worldly and English-speaking. Lots of beer and popular with Nicas.

La Pasarela, UNAN, 1 c arriba. A great outdoor student venue, best attended in the dry season.

Olla Quemada, Museo Rubén Darío, ½ c abajo. Popular on Wed nights with live music acts and lots of beer. Great, friendly atmosphere.

Salón Estrella, esq de los bancos, ½ c norte. Dark, hot and steamy, with lots of raunchy reggaeton and dance. Definitely a locals' haunt, but gringos are welcome too. On its way down, reportedly.

Vía Vía, Banco ProCredit, ½ c sur. Good on most nights, but best on Fri when live music performs. There's salsa on Sat, free pool on Tue and quiz night on Mon. Good, warm atmosphere. Popular with foreigners and often recommended.

Cinema

Next to **La Unión** supermarket, 1 block north and 1 block east of El Sesteo in Plaza Siglo Nuevo, T2311-7080/83. Films shown in English with Spanish subtitles.

Chinandega *p1077*
Bars and clubs

Monserrat, main entrance Reparto Monserrat 2 c arriba, T2341-3465, Thu-Sun after 2000. Has a big dance floor, appetizers, rum and cold beer, dance music.

❀ Festivals and events

León *p1072, map p1074*
Mar/Apr Holy Week ceremonies are outstanding with sawdust street-carpet, similar to those in Guatemala, especially in Sutiava on Good Fri after 1500.
20 Jun Liberation by Sandinistas.
1 Nov All Saints' Day.
Dec Santa Lucía is celebrated in Sutiava; there are processions, religious and cultural events, sports and Pepe Cabezón (a giant head on legs) accompanies l a Gigantona (an impossibly tall princess) through the city.
7 Dec Día de la Concepción, festivities including singing, dancing and fireworks.

O Shopping

León *p1072, map p1074*
The old **market** (dirty) is near the centre, behind the cathedral, and the **new market** is at the bus terminal, 5-6 blocks east of the old railway station, which itself is now **Mercado San Juan**, not touristy, good local atmosphere.
La Unión, Calle 1 Norte, 1 block north of central market, good supermarket.
Libro Centro Don Quijote, next to **Hotelito Calle Real**, sells second-hand books, some in English.

▲ Activities and tours

León *p1072, map p1074*

Cultural and community tourism

Casa de Cultura, Iglesia La Merced, 1½ c abajo. Offers a range of courses including traditional and contemporary dance, music and painting. Ask inside for a schedule.

Via Via, Banco ProCredit, ½ c sur, T2311-6142, www.viaviacafe.com. Interesting cultural tours include 'cowboy for a day' where you milk a cow and prepare an ox cart; and 'workshop cooking', which includes trips to markets and *tortilla*-making.

Sandboarding

Bigfoot adventures, Banco ProCredit, ½ c sur, www.bigfootadventure.com. Fancy descending the slopes of an active volcano at high speed? The most professional outfit in town will kit you out with a sandboard and safety gear, and transport you to the top of Cerro Negro. The fastest boards have been clocked at 70 kph.

Tour operators

Tierra Tour, La Merced, 1½ c norte, T2311-0599, www.tierratour.com. Dutch-owned outfit with good information and affordable tours of León, the Maribios volcanoes and Isla Juan Venado reserve. Runs shuttles direct to Granada and other places.

Va Pues, North side of El Laborio church, inside Cocinarte restaurant, T2315-4099, wwwvapues.com. Popular tours include Cerro Negro, León Viejo, night turtle tours, kayaking and city tours. English, French and Spanish spoken. Also has an office in Granada and organizes trips all over the country.

Trekking

Flavio Parajón, Texaco Guadalupe, 1 c abajo, ½ c sur, T8880-8673, fparajon2003@ yahoo.es. Good, friendly, honest and experienced mountain guide for Maribios Volcanoes. He has his own 4WD, speaks Spanish and basic English.

Quetzaltrekkers, Iglesia Recolección, 1½ c arriba, T8843-7647, www.quetzaltrekkers.com. Non-profit organization, proceeds go to street kids. Multi-day hikes to Los Maribios US$20-US$70 including transport, food, water, camping equipment. Guides are foreign volunteers, check your guide's experience before trip, be sure to climb with at least one local guide who knows the volcanoes well.

Sampson Expeditions, Calle Rubén Darío, 1½ c abajo, inside **Hostal Calle de Los Poetas**, T2311-3306, rsampson@ibw.com.ni. Kayaking in Juan Venado and Laguna El Tigre, volcano expeditions, poetry tours. Rigo Sampson comes from a family of devout hikers and climbers and is Nicaragua's foremost expert on climbing the Los Maribios Volcanoes. He also works closely with social organizations to help local kids into schools. Professional and highly recommended.

⊖ Transport

Towards León *p1071*

Bus

Frequent bus service to **La Paz Centro** from Managua, Terminal Lewites, every 30 mins.

León *p1072, map p1074*

Bus

The bus terminal is in the far eastern part of town, a long walk or short taxi ride from the centre. Small trucks also ferry people between the bus terminal and town for US$0.25. Besides the regular and express buses, *compartidos* (small vans) go to most places below, often faster than the bus.

To **Managua**, express bus, every 30 mins, 0500-1600, US$1.50, 1 hr 45 mins. To **Chinandega**, every 15 mins, 0500-1800, US$1, 1 hr 45 mins. To **Corinto**, every 30 mins, 0500-1800, US$1, 2 hrs. To **Chichigalpa**, every 15 mins, US$0400-1800, US$0.75, 1 hr. To **Estelí**, express bus, 0520, 1245, 1315, 1515, US$2.50, 3 hrs; or go to

San Isidro for connections. To **Matagalpa**, express bus, 0400, 0700, 1400, US$2.75, 3 hrs, or go to San Isidro for connections. To **San Isidro**, every 30 mins, 0420-1730, US$1.50, 2½ hrs. To **El Sauce**, every hour, 0800-1600, US$1.50, 2½ hrs. To **El Guasaule**, 0500, US$2, 2½ hrs. To **Salinas Grandes**, 0600,1200, US$0.40, 1½ hrs.

Taxi
Taxis around town charge US$0.40 in the day and US$0.80 at night.

Around León *p1076*
Bus
Take No 101 from **León**'s Terminal Interurbana, or the central market west to the bus stop near Sutiava church on Calle Rubén Darío, **Poneloya**, then walk 3 mins to Terminal Poneloya outside the market, from where a small bus leaves every hour or so for **Las Peñitas** (0600-1700, 45 mins, US$0.60) at the south end of Poneloya beach.

Taxi
From León costs around US$10.

Chinandega *p1077*
Bus
Most buses leave from the new market at the southeast edge of town. To **Corinto**, every 20 mins, 0600-2100, 30 mins, US$0.40. To **Guasaule**, every 2 hrs, 0600-1600, 2 hrs, US$2.25. To **León**, every 15 mins, 0600-1700, 1¼ hr, US$1. To **Managua**, every 30 mins, 0600-1600, 3 hrs, US$2.50. To **Somotillo**, every 3 hrs, 0900-1500, 2 hrs, US$2. Buses for **Potosí**, **El Viejo** and **Puerto Morazán** leave from the Mercadito at northwest of town. A local bus connects Terminal, Mercado and Mercadito.

① Directory

León *p1072, map p1074*
Banks There are many banks on the 2 roads that lead from the front and back of the cathedral to the north. Next to the La Unión Supermarket is BAC (Banco de América Central) T2311-7247, for TCs of any kind and cash from credit cards. Cash can be changed with the *coyotes* 1 block north of the back of the cathedral or at any bank. **Internet** At nearly every hotel and almost every street in León, best high-speed hook-up at Puerto Café Benjamín Linder, next to UNAN (northern corner), T2311-0548, daily 0800-0000. **Language schools** León Spanish School, Casa de Cultura, Iglesia La Merced, 1½ c abajo, www.apc-spanishschools.com, T2311-2116. Flexible weekly or hourly 1-on-1 tuition with activities, volunteering and home-stay options. Pleasant location inside the casa de cultura. **Metropolis Academy**, www.metropolisspanish.com, La Merced, 2 c norte, 875-9325. A range of programmes from simple hourly tuition to full-time courses with daily activities and family homestay. 20 hrs of tuition costs US$115, **Vía Vía**, Banco ProCredit, ½ c sur, T2311-6142, www.viaviacafe.com. This growing cultural centre has good ties to local communities and a popular hostel-restaurant-bar on site. A convenient, sociable option. **Medical services** Hospital at catedral, 1 c sur, T2311-6990. Red Cross T2311-2627. **Police** T2311-3137. **Post office** Correos de Nicaragua, Banco Mercantil 1 c norte, T2311-2102. **Telephone** Enitel is on Parque Central at the west side, T2311-7377. Also at bus terminal.

Towards Granada

The journey from Lago de Managua to Lago de Nicaragua passes several volcanoes including Volcán Santiago whose crater spews out tonnes of sulphurous gases over Parque Nacional Volcán Masaya. Nearby, the town of Masaya is a centre for handicrafts in a coffee-growing zone. The blasted remains of Mombacho are near the historical city of Granada. The perfect cone of Concepción, on Isla de Ometepe, rises out of the waters of Lago de Nicaragua, which has a number of other islands that can be visited by boat. ►► *For listings, see pages 1093-1101.*

Parque Nacional Volcán Masaya → *Colour map 7, A1.*

ⓘ *Daily 0900-1700, US$4. The visitor centre is 1.5 km from the entrance at Km 23 on the road from Managua. There are picnic facilities, toilets and barbecues nearby. It's possible to camp, but there are no facilities after the centre closes. Soft drinks, bottled water and sometimes fresh coconut water are available at the summit of Santiago crater. Ask the bus driver to drop you off at Km 23 on the Managua–Masaya route. It's easy to hitchhike from either city, especially on Sun. At the entrance, park rangers might be available to drive you up to the summit for US$0.70.*

Created in 1979, Parque Nacional Volcán Masaya is the country's oldest national park. It covers an area of 54 sq km, and contains 20 km of trails leading to and around two volcanoes rising to around 400 m. **Volcán Nindirí** last erupted in 1670. The more active **Volcán Masaya** burst forth in 1772 and again in 1852, forming the Santiago crater between the two peaks; this in turn erupted in 1932, 1946, 1959 and 1965 before collapsing in 1985, and the resulting pall of sulphurous smoke made the soil uncultivable in a broad belt to the Pacific. Take drink, a hat and hiking boots if you're planning on doing much walking. If walking to the summit, leave early as there is little shade along the road.

Santiago's most recent eruption was on 23 April 2001. Debris pelted the parking area of the park with flaming rocks at 1427 in the afternoon, shooting tubes of lava onto the hillside just east of the parking area and setting it ablaze. Today the cone remains highly irregular with large funnels of sulphuric acid being followed by periods of little or no smoke. On 4 October 2003 Santiago emitted an eruption cloud 4.6 km in length, but no actual eruption was forthcoming. A real eruption is expected soon.

Although research into the activity of Volcán Masaya is limited, gaseous emissions range from 500 to 3000 tonnes a day, making the volcano one of the largest natural polluters in the world.

Volcán Masaya was called *Popogatepe* or 'mountain that burns' by the Chorotega people who believed that eruptions were a sign of anger from the goddess of fire, Chacitutepe. To appease her they made sacrifices to the lava pit, which often included children and young women. In the 16th century Father Francisco de Bobadilla planted a cross on the summit of Masaya to exorcize the *Boca del Infierno* (Mouth of Hell); the cross visible today commemorates the event.

The biggest natural heroes of the park are the unique **parakeets** (*chocoyos*) who nest in the active Santiago crater. These orange- or crimson-fronted parakeets are best spotted just before the park closes between March and October. They lay two to four eggs per nest in the interior cliffs of the crater in July and after incubation and rearing lasting roughly three months, leave their highly toxic home for the first time.

From the visitor centre, a short path leads up to Cerro El Comalito, with good views of Mombacho, the lakes and the extraordinary volcanic landscapes of the park; longer trails continue to Lake Masaya and the San Fernando crater.

→ *Population: 140,000. Altitude: 234 m.*

Masaya lies 29 km southeast of Managua, and is the folkloric and crafts centre of Nicaragua, home to more artisans than any other place in the country. The town is in almost constant celebration with religious festivals, including Central America's longest party, the **San Jerónimo** festival. Running for three months from 30 September, the festival includes traditional dancing, music and countless processions. Every Thursday the **Jueves de Verbena** is a smaller festival with dancing, eating and drinking late into the night. The **tourist office** in the craft market near the music stage is helpful (mostly Spanish spoken).

Ciudad de Masaya

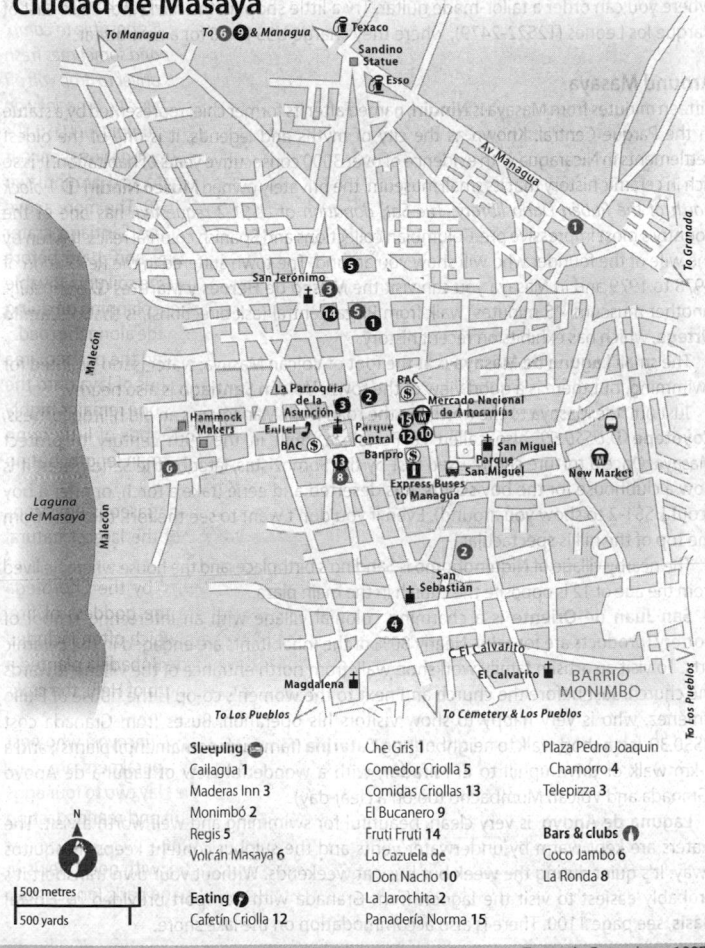

Sleeping ⚫	Che Gris 1	Plaza Pedro Joaquin
Cailagua 1	Comedor Criolla 5	Chamorro 4
Maderas Inn 3	Comidas Criollas 13	Telepizza 3
Monimbó 2	El Bucanero 9	
Regis 5	Fruti Fruti 14	**Bars & clubs** ❶
Volcán Masaya 6	La Cazuela de	Coco Jambo 6
	Don Nacho 10	La Ronda 8
Eating ❼	La Jarochita 2	
Cafetín Criolla 12	Panadería Norma 15	

500 metres
500 yards

Local handicrafts are sold in the market near the bus station and in the new **Centro de Artesanías** (closed Sundays) in the old market (also called the Centro Cultural Antiguo Mercado de Masaya). The newly restored 19th-century market was ruined during the Revolution. The 'new' market is very popular with Nicaraguans and sells excellent hammocks, leather work, colourful woven rugs and furniture. The artisan market has concerts every Thursday night with food, free admission and a range of musical and dance acts. This is the best place to see one of Masaya's more than 30 professional folkloric dance troops. The 'old' market, close to the bus park, is marginally cheaper but crowded, dirty and not recommended. Masaya is also the centre for Nicaraguan rocking chairs, which can be bought packed for transporting by air. The best place for local craftwork is the barrio of **Monimbo**. On Avenida los Leones you find several **guitar shops**, where you can order a tailor-made guitar. Try a little shop (in the backyard) 75 m east of Parque los Leones (T2522-2479), where they charge US$40-50 for a new guitar.

Around Masaya

Fifteen minutes from Masaya is **Nindirí**, named after its former chief represented by a statue in the Parque Central. Known as the city of myths and legends, it is one of the oldest settlements in Nicaragua with evidence of over 3000 consecutive years of habitation. It is so rich in ceramic history that its small museum, the privately owned **Museo Nindirí** ① *1 block north of the Rubén Darío library, Tue-Sat, donation of US$1-2 requested*, has one of the country's most impressive pre-Columbian collections and Spanish colonial relics. It is run by the wife of the founder who will show you around. The town suffered in the Revolution of 1978 to 1979 and in Masaya you can visit the **Museo de Héroes y Mártires** ① *open daily*. Another museum, 45 minutes' walk from Plaza Central (ask directions), is that of **Camilo Ortega**, which has exhibits on recent history.

The small **Laguna de Masaya** is at the foot of Volcán Masaya; water is too polluted for swimming, but there is a good view of the town. **Volcán Santiago** is also nearby.

Just outside Masaya to the north, on the road from Managua, is an old hilltop fortress, **Coyotepe** ① *US$0.50*, also called La Fortaleza, built in the 19th century to protect Masaya. Once a torture centre used first by the Somozistas, later by the Sandinistas, it is now a clubhouse for the boy scouts. It is deserted and eerie (take a torch, or offer a boy scout US$1-2 to show you around). Even if you don't want to see the fort, the view from the top of the hill is spectacular.

The nearby village of **Niquinohomo** is Sandino's birthplace, and the house where he lived from the age of 12 is opposite the church in the main plaza.

San Juan de Oriente is a charming colonial village with an interesting school of pottery (products are for sale). Nearly 80% of the inhabitants are engaged in the ceramic arts. To visit an artisan family workshop walk from north entrance of the village towards the church. Just before the church and next to the women's co-op is the house of Dulio Jiménez, who is very happy to show visitors his operation. Buses from Granada cost US$0.30. It is a short walk to neighbouring **Catarina** (famous for ornamental plants), and a 1-km walk or drive uphill to **El Mirador**, with a wonderful view of Laguna de Apoyo (Granada and Volcán Mombacho too on a clear day).

Laguna de Apoyo is very clean, beautiful for swimming and well worth a visit. The waters are kept warm by underwater vents and the sulphur content keeps mosquitos away. It's quiet during the week but busy at weekends. Without your own transport it's probably easiest to visit the lagoon from Granada with transport provided by **Hostal Oasis**, see page 1100. There is also accommodation on the lake shore.

→ *Population: 111,506. Altitude: 60 m.*

Situated on the northwest shore of vast Lake Nicaragua, and at the foot of Volcán Mombacho, Granada is increasingly popular and currently the place to hang out in Nicaragua. Founded in 1524 by Hernández de Córdoba on the site of the indigenous village of Xalteva, it is the oldest city to be continually inhabited and in its original location in continental Latin America. The prosperous city was attacked on at least three occasions by British and French pirates coming up the San Juan and Escalante rivers, and much of old Granada was burnt by filibuster William Walker in 1856. Despite it's turbulent history, Granada – the third largest city of the republic – still retains many beautiful buildings and has preserved its Castilian traditions.

Ins and outs

Getting there There are very regular and quick bus and minibus services between Managua and Granada, making it a good base even if your main interest is the capital. International buses pass the western side of town.

Getting around Small and manageable on foot, the focal point of the town is the Parque Central. Heading east takes you to Lake Nicaragua and the Complejo Turístico (tourist

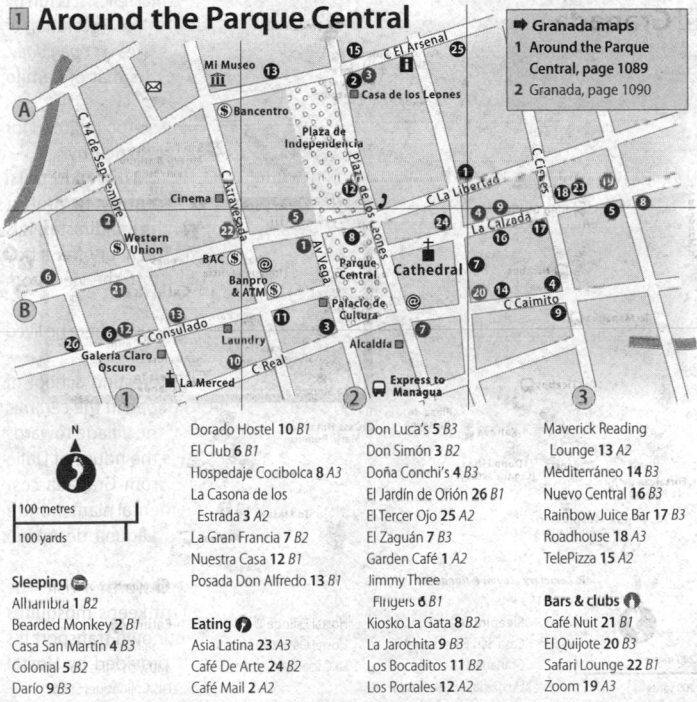

1 Around the Parque Central

➡ Granada maps
1 Around the Parque Central, page 1089
2 Granada, page 1090

N
100 metres
100 yards

Sleeping
Alhambra 1 *B2*
Bearded Monkey 2 *B1*
Casa San Martín 4 *B3*
Colonial 5 *B2*
Darío 9 *B3*
Dorado Hostel 10 *B1*
El Club 6 *B1*
Hospedaje Cocibolca 8 *A3*
La Casona de los Estrada 3 *A2*
La Gran Francia 7 *B2*
Nuestra Casa 12 *B1*
Posada Don Alfredo 13 *B1*

Eating
Asia Latina 23 *A3*
Café De Arte 24 *B2*
Café Mail 2 *A2*
Don Luca's 5 *B3*
Don Simón 3 *B2*
Doña Conchi's 4 *B3*
El Jardín de Orión 26 *B1*
El Tercer Ojo 25 *A2*
El Zaguán 7 *B3*
Garden Café 1 *A2*
Jimmy Three Fingers 6 *B1*
Kiosko La Gata 8 *B2*
La Jarochita 9 *B3*
Los Bocaditos 11 *B2*
Los Portales 12 *A2*
Maverick Reading Lounge 13 *A2*
Mediterráneo 14 *B3*
Nuevo Central 16 *B3*
Rainbow Juice Bar 17 *B3*
Roadhouse 18 *A3*
TelePizza 15 *A2*

Bars & clubs
Café Nuit 21 *B1*
El Quijote 20 *B3*
Safari Lounge 22 *B1*
Zoom 19 *A3*

centre). South of the Parque is the working heart of the city with the market and many bus departure points. East, west and north of the park, the streets are a bit quieter. Horse-drawn carriages available for hire if you want to rest your feet.

Tourist information INTUR ① *Iglesia San Fransisco, ½ c al sur, on calle Arsenal, T2552-6858.* The best INTUR office in the country, with good maps, lots of information on local and national sites, and English-speaking staff.

Sights

The centre of the city, about 10 blocks from the lake, is the **Parque Central**, with many trees and food stalls selling Granada's famous *vigorón*, a popular dish of fried pork skins, yucca, and cabbage salad served on a big banana leaf. Bordering the park are many civic buildings, the landmark **Hotel Alhambra**, the cathedral and the local tourist office (southeast corner). In between the red house of the bishop and the cathedral is the century cross with a time capsule of belongings from 1899 buried underneath in the hope of a peaceful 20th century. This practice was repeated in 1999 with another cross and time capsule in front of the La Merced church in the hope of a peaceful 21st century. The **cathedral**, rebuilt in neoclassical style, is simpler in design and ornamentation than the church of **La Merced** to the west, which was built in 1781 to 1783, half destroyed in the civil wars of 1854, restored in 1862 and is currently undergoing another restoration. Its

2 **Granada**

Sleeping 🛏
Casa San Francisco **4**
Granada **1**
Hospedaje El Maltese **7**

Hostal Esfinge **2**
Hostal Oasis Granada **3**
La Calzada **6**

Eating 🍴
Casa Maconda **1**
Kathy's Waffle House **5**
Las Colinas del Sur **6**

interior is painted in pastel shades, predominantly green and blue. It has some unusual features and interesting lighting. Away from the centre, beyond La Merced, is the church of **La Jalteva** (or *Xalteva* – the Indigenous name of Granada), which faces a park with formal ponds. Note that to view the interiors of Granada's churches you must time your visit from 0600-0800 or 1500-1700. Not far from La Jalteva is **La Pólvora** ① *donations to the caretaker*, an old fortress that has been partially restored and opened to the public. It has a pleasant rooftop with views of the church and volcano east from the turrets. The chapel of **María Auxiliadora** ① *open to public at 1600*, where Las Casas, Apostle of the Indies, often preached, is hung with local lace and needlework. Heading southwest from Jalteva, the cemetery is worth a visit as the resting place of key figures from Nicaraguan history. Heading towards the Managua bus terminal from Jalteva, you pass the beautiful, now-dilapidated **hospital**, which was built in 1886.

Directly north of Parque Central is the restored **Casa de Los Leones** ① *T2552-4176, www.c3mundos.org, free during the day, check bulletin board for events*, restored and run by the international foundation **Casa de los Tres Mundos**. It is a beautiful colonial house, with art exhibits and concerts. Heading west is the fortress-church of **San Francisco**, Nicaragua's oldest, though burned many times and now only the front steps are from 1524. There are some wonderful sculptures inside. Next door is the **Museo del Convento de San Francisco** ① *0800-1800, US$2, US$2.50 extra for photography*. Originally a convent (1524), it was then a Spanish garrison, William Walker's garrison, a university and more recently an institute. The cloister surrounds about three dozen tall palms. Restoration is now complete and it is the country's most interesting pre-Columbian museum, housing 28 sculptures from Isla Zapatera in the lake, dating from AD 800-1200. Note especially the double sculptures of standing or seated figures bearing huge animal masks, or doubles, on their heads and shoulders (including lizard, tortoise, jaguar). The museum also contains several galleries with changing exhibits of Nicaraguan art and there's a snack bar.

A road runs from the Parque Central to Plaza España by the dock on Lake Nicaragua; the church of **Guadalupe** is on this road. From Plaza España it is a 30-minute walk along the lakeshore to the **Complejo Turístico** ① *US$0.12*, an area with restaurants, bars, paths and benches. The lake beach is popular, having been cleaned up and built into a pleasant park; marimba bands stroll the beach and play a song for you for a small fee. At night everyone decants to the club and bars of the *complejo*.

Lago de Nicaragua

To San Carlos

Dock

Plaza España

C San Juan del Sur

Complejo Turístico

To Las Isletas

To Puerto Asese

➡ **Granada maps**
1 Around the Parque Central, page 1089
2 Granada, page 1090

La Terrazza La Playa **9**
Mona Lisa **7**
Querube's **8**

Bars & clubs 🎵
César **1**

Horse-drawn carriages are available for hire and are used here as taxis by the locals. The drivers are happy to take visitors around the city (US$4.50 for 30 minutes, US$9 per hour). You can see most of the city's sites in a half-hour rental. A recommended walk, or carriage ride, starts from La Pólvora and continues down Calle Real, past La Capilla María Auxiliadora, La Jalteva, La Merced to Parque Central. From the cathedral you can then continue to La Virgen de Guadalupe and to the lake front along La Calzada.

Around Granada

Reserva Natural Volcán Mombacho

① *Thu-Sun 0800-1700, US$8 including transport to the summit. To get there, take a bus towards Nandaime or Rivas from Granada or Masaya and get off at the Emapalme Guanacaste, from where it's 1 km to the entrance. You can continue hiking to the summit, passing attractive coffee fincas, but it's long, brutal and strenuous towards the end. Trucks to the summit depart 0830, 1000, 1300, 1500.*

Volcán Mombacho is the dark, eternally brooding backdrop to Granada's pretty, colonial streets. Its green slopes are home to *fincas* (farms) at the lower reaches and a small but attractive cloud forest reserve higher up. Hardcore hikers may be disappointed by the three trails, sometimes inundated with tourists. Guides are obligatory on the hardest trail (US$10). An interesting possibility is a night hike to view the salamanders unique to the region. Two canopy tours also offer high-speed experiences of the volcano; **Mombotour** and **Mombacho Canopy Tour** are both located well below the cloud forest zone. ▶▶ *See Activities and tours, page 1098.*

Archipiélago Las Isletas

Scattered like a broken necklace over the waters of Lake Nicaragua, Las Isletas are a chain of 354 tiny, jewel-like islands. Formed by a violent volcanic eruption, the islands are fertile havens for arboreal and avian species, and some are inhabited by fishermen and small communities. Some have also been snapped up by local real estate agents and are now 'for sale' to rich foreigners. You can visit the Isletas as part of a tour, with boats departing from the lake shore at Puerto Assese, 3 km from the entrance to the Complejo Turístico, or from Marina Cocibolca (see Sailing, page 1099). Perhaps the best way to experience the rich aquatic wildlife of the islands is at dawn, in a kayak. ▶▶ *See Activities and tours, page 1099.*

Parque Nacional Archipiélago Zapatera

Home to the country's most important pre-Columbian sites, the 11 islands of this archipelago contain mysterious petroglyphs, a crater lake and wonderfully active ecosystems, including tropical dry and wet forests. Zapatera is the largest and most important site. A number of massive basalt statues have been recovered there and are now on exhibition in Granada's San Fransisco convent. It's best to visit the islands as part of a tour as **MARENA** are reportedly turning away unsolicited visitors. Use an agency in Granada or Managua, or contact **La UCA Tierra y Agua** (see Cultural and community tours, page 1098), which can organize accommodation in rural communities.

For Sleeping and Eating price codes and other relevant information, see Essentials pages 45-48.

● Sleeping

Parque Nacional Volcán Masaya
p1086
B Hotel Volcán Masaya, Km 23, Carretera a Masaya, T2522-7114. Great location in front of the volcano park, with spectacular views from the shared patio. Rooms have private bath, a/c, fridge and cable TV. Lobby area is good for relaxing.

Masaya *p1087, map p1087*
B Hotel Monimbó, Iglesia San Sebastián, 1 c arriba, 1½ c norte, T2522-6867, hotelmonimbo 04@hotmail.com. 7 good-quality rooms with private bath, hot water, a/c and cable TV. There's a pleasant patio space and services include internet and transport.
B Maderas Inn, Bomberos, 2 c sur, T2522-5825. Small rooms with private bath, a/c, cable TV and continental breakfast included in the price. Cheaper without breakfast and a/c (**C**). Internet, tours, laundry service and airport transportation available.
C Cailagua, Km 30, T2522-4435. Comfortable hotel with 22 rooms with private bath, a/c and cable TV, swimming pool, restaurant. In a noisy location, quite a way from centre. Good for the exhausted driver; secure parking.
E Hotel Regis, La Parroquia, 3½ c norte, T2522-2300. Very friendly and helpful owner. Rooms are clean, with shared bath and fan. The best budget option.

Around Masaya *p1088*
B San Simian, Laguna Apoyo, beyond Norome Resort, T88813-6866, www.san simian.com. A lovely, peaceful spot with 5 great *cabañas* and amazing outdoor bathtubs, perfect for soaking under the starry sky. Facilities include bar, restaurant, hammocks, kayaks and a catamaran (US$15 per hr). Day use US$5. Recommended.

D-F Crater's Edge, Laguna Apoyo, access road, 500 m west, T8860-8689, www.craters-edge.com. A very friendly and hospitable hostel with dorm beds (**F**), private rooms (**D**) and a plenty of facilities including kayaks, restaurant-bar, Wi-Fi, book exchange and a floating platform. Day use US$7. Daily transport to and from Oasis hostel in Granada. Recommended.

Granada *p1089, maps p1089 and p1090*
L Hotel Darío, Calle La Calzada, de la Catedral, 150 varas al lago, T2552-3400, www.hoteldario.com. Right in the heart of town and housed by the smart, green and white neoclassical building you can't fail to notice. The interior is handsome, with comfortable rooms and beautiful grounds. There's a gym, and a kidney-shaped swimming pool for cooling off.
L La Gran Francia, southeast corner of Parque Central, T2552-6000, www.lagran francia.com. This traditional colonial building has handsome rooms with private bath, hot water, cable TV, a/c, minibar and internet access. Standard rooms are dark and face a wall, suites have big wooden doors that lead on to small balcony with a lovely view and lots of light; worth the extra money. Rates include a (stingy) breakfast, there's a swimming pool and staff are friendly.
L-A Hotel Alhambra, Parque Central, T2552-4486, www.alhambra.com.ni. Granada's landmark hotel has a stunning location on the plaza. Rooms vary dramatically in quality and price. They include 'classic rooms' (**A**) with a/c, cable TV and hot water; 'superior rooms' (**AL**) with king or queen size beds and minibar; and luxury 'suites' (**L**). The ones overlooking the park are best. There's a pool and terrace for drinks, and a restaurant – not owned by the hotel – that receives a lot of criticism for poor service. Often full with groups.
AL Hotel Colonial, Calle La Libertad, Parque Central, 25 varas al norte, T2552-7581,

www.hotel colonialgranada.com. This centrally located, colonial-style hotel has a range of pleasant, comfortable lodgings, including heavily decorated rooms with 4-poster beds and 10 luxury suites with jacuzzi (**A**); all have hot water, a/c, cable TV and Wi-Fi. 2 pools, the restaurant serves breakfast only.

AL La Casona de los Estrada, Iglesia San Francisco, ½ c abajo, T2552-7393, www.casona losestrada.com.ni. Decorated with fine furnishings, this small, homely hotel has 6 pleasant, well-lit rooms with private bath, hot water, a/c and cable TV. There's a pleasant plant-filled courtyard, English and French are spoken, prices include breakfast.

A Casa San Francisco, Corrales 207, T2552-8235, www.casasanfrancisco.com. This attractive, tranquil hotel comprises 2 colonial houses with 13 lodgings that vary greatly. One house has 2 suites and 2 comfortable rooms with private bath, cable TV, a/c, pool and a modern kitchen. The other has 8 rooms and 1 suite, a pool and restaurant. The friendly and helpful staff speak English.

A Casa San Martín, Calle La Calzada, catedral, 1 c lago, T2552-6185, javier_sanchez_a@ yahoo.com. 7 rooms in a beautiful colonial home, with cable TV, private bath, a/c or fan. Pleasant decor and garden terrace, very authentic Granada. Staff speak English.

A El Club, Parque Central, 3½ c abajo, T2552-4245, www.elclub-nicaragua.com. Dutch-owned hotel with 10 small, modern rooms with private bath, a/c, cable TV and Wi-Fi. There's a restaurant and bar downstairs, which can be noisy at times. The staff are friendly and helpful.

B Hospedaje El Maltese, Plaza España, 50 m sur, opposite *malecón* in Complejo Turístico, T2552-7641, www.nicatour.net. 8 very clean rooms with private bath, nice furnishings, Italian spoken, restaurant Mon-Fri 1600-2200. Don't walk here at night alone.

B Hotel Granada, opposite Iglesia Guadalupe, T2552-2974, www.hotelgranada nicaragua.com. This recently renovated hotel has smart, clean, comfortable rooms with

cable TV, Wi-Fi, a/c and hot water. A pool is being constructed, and there's a lovely view from the balcony and restaurant.

B Italiano, next to Iglesia Guadalupe, T2552-7047, italianriky@latinmail.com. Rooms have bath and a/c, nice patio, drinks available, good value, Italian spoken.

C Posada Don Alfredo, La Merced, 1 c norte, T2552-4455, alfredpaulbaganz@hotmail.com. This interesting old hotel is housed in an historic building with many original features like high, wooden ceilings and slatted windows. The rooms are dark and simple, some with a/c and hot water (**B**). The German management is hospitable and friendly.

C-F Dorado Hostel, southwest corner of Parque Central, 1½ c abajo, T2552-6932, www.hostaldorado.com. Housed in a lovely colonial building, this new hostel has a relaxing patio, free Wi-Fi and DVD movies. Lodgings include single (**D**) and double rooms (**C**), and dormitories (**E**) of various sizes, cheaper with shared bath (**F**).

D Hospedaje Cocibolca, Calle La Cazada, T2552-7223, www.hospedajecocibolca.com. A friendly, family house with 24 clean, simple rooms. There's a kitchen and internet access.

D Hostal Esfinge, opposite market, T2552-4826, esfingegra@hotmail.com.ni. Lots of character at this friendly old hotel near the market. Rooms in the newer building are smaller, but some have bath and cable TV. Friendly and clean, with motorcycle parking in the lobby.

D Nuestra Casa, La Merced, 1 c al norte, ½ abajo, T2552-8115, www.hotelnuestra casa.com. Simple rooms with and without bath, cable TV and a/c (**B** with bath, TV and a/c). There's a pleasant honeymoon suite and the owner, an ordained minister in the Universal Life Church, will marry you on request. There's a popular bar and restaurant attached.

D-F Bearded Monkey, Calle 14 de Septiembre, near the fire station, T2552-4028, www.thebeardedmonkey.com. A sociable, popular hostel with dormitories (**F**), private rooms (**D**), and hammocks for those terribly impoverished backpackers. There's a plethora of services to keep you entertained including restaurant, bar, cable TV, internet access, cheap calls, evening films, bike rentals, and free tea and coffee. Use lockers, as everybody is free to walk in and out. Runs trips to Laguna de Apoyo, see page 1088.

D-F Hostal Oasis Granada, Calle Estrada 109, south of the centre, T2552-8006. Mix of dorm, shared and private rooms (**C-D** with all mod-cons), food available, laundry service and washing facilities. Full range of entertainment from book exchange and swimming pool, through to free internet (and internet calls to Canada and USA) and DVDs. Popular; gets good reports. Daily transit to Laguna Apoyo.

E La Calzada, near Iglesia Guadalupe, T2475-9229, guesthouselacalzada@ yahoo.com. This family-run guesthouse has 8 big, simple rooms with fan and private bath; cheaper with shared bath.

⊕ Eating

Masaya *p1087, map p1087*

🍴🍴 **El Bucanero**, Km 26.5, Carretera a Masaya. A Cuban-owned favourite with sweeping views of Laguna Masaya and a loud, party atmosphere. There's a constantly changing menu of international and Nicaraguan dishes, including good beef dishes. Worth it for the views.

🍴🍴 **La Cazuela de Don Nacho**, inside artisan market, northeast side of stage, T2522-7731, Fri-Wed 1000-1800, Thu 1000-0000. There's a jaunty atmosphere at this pleasant market-place eaterie, usually buzzing with diners. They serve *comida típica* and á la carte food like shrimps, *filete mignon*, *filete de pollo* and *churrasco* steak.

🍴🍴 **La Jarochita**, La Parroquia, 75 varas norte, T2522-4831. Daily 1100-2200. The best Mexican in Nicaragua; some drive from Managua just to eat here. Try *sopa de tortilla*, and chicken *enchilada* in *mole* sauce, *chimichangas* and Mexican beer. Recommended.

🍴🍴 **Restaurante Che Gris**, Hotel Regis, ½ c sur. Very good food in huge portions, including excellent *comida típica*, *comida corriente* and à la carte food like steak, chicken and pork. Also has a branch at the southeast corner of the market.

🍴-🍴 **Telepizza**, Parque Central, ½ c norte, T2522-0170. Good wholesome pizza, thick or thin based. Delivery service.

🍴 **Cafetín Criolla**, southwest corner of the artisan market. Cheap, filling, greasy food, popular with the locals and often bustling.

🍴 **Comedor Criolla**, northeast corner of Parque Central, 5 c al norte. Popular locals' haunt serving economical Nica fare, buffet food, breakfasts and lunch.

🍴 **Comedor Criollas**, Parque Central, south side. Another local eaterie with the 'criolla' namesake. This large, clean, buffet restaurant serves up healthy portions of Nica fare.

🍴 **Plaza Pedro Joaquin Chamorro**, also known as **Tiangue de Monimbó**, in front of Iglesia San Sebastián in Monimbó. Good *fritangas* with grilled meats, *gallo pinto* and other traditional Masaya food, very cheap.

Cafés, juice bars and bakeries
Fruti Fruti, northeast corner of Parque Central, 3½ c norte. Tasty, sweet, fresh fruit smoothies, including delicious, alcohol-free piña coladas.

Panadería Norma, northwest corner of the artisan market, ½ c norte. Good, fresh-brewed coffee, bread, cakes and pastries.

Granada *p1089, maps p1089 and p1090*

🍴🍴🍴 **Casa Maconda**, Calle La Calzada, 3½ c al lago, T2680-6420, closed Mon. This Spanish restaurant serves *paella*, tapas and the strongest Sangría in Granada. There's a happy hour from 1700-2000, a musical ambience, dance classes and exhibitions.

🍴🍴🍴 **El Jardín de Orión**, northwest corner of Parque Central, 4 c abajo, ½ c al sur, T2552 1220. This buzzing French restaurant has a fabulous garden terrace and a changing menu of sophisticated European cuisine. Great atmosphere and friendly service.

La Gran Francia, corner of Parque Central. Daily 1100-2300. This beautiful restaurant is the epitome of colonial grandeur, with high ceiling dining rooms and a plethora of elegant, antique furniture. It serves expensive French-Nicaraguan cuisine, and has pleasant views from the upper floor balcony.

Mediterráneo, Calle Caimito, T2552-6764. Daily 0800-2300. Mediterranean cuisine served in a Spanish-owned colonial house with an attractive and tranquil garden setting. Mixed reviews; good seafood, bad paella. Popular with foreigners.

Doña Conchi's, Calle Caimito, T2552-7376. Wed-Mon 1100-2300. A very beautiful restaurant, completely illuminated by candles and adorned with rustic decorations like wood piles and bunches of dried flowers. They serve quality dishes like grilled salmon, seabass and lobster. There's also an interesting *artesanía* shop attached. Recommended.

El Zaguán, on road behind cathedral, T2552-2522. Mon-Fri 1200-1500 and 1800-2200, Sat and Sun1200-2200. Incredible, succulent grilled meats and steaks, cooked on a wood fire and served impeccably. Undoubtedly the best beef cuts in Granada, if not Nicaragua. Highly recommended.

Asia Latina, Calle La Calzada, 2½ c al lago. Thai and Asian fusion, with a touch of Latin. Great curries and vegetarian dishes, served in a friendly, atmospheric setting. Recommended.

Café Chavalos, corner of Calle Arsenal and Matirio, T8852-0210. An interesting training programme for 'would-be gang members', who, under supervision of chef Sergio, now learn to prepare international cuisine. Best to book in advance. Recommended.

Charly's Bar, Petronic, 5c abajo, 25 varas al sur, T2552-2942, www.charlysbar.com. Mon and Wed-Fri 1100-1500, 1800-2300, Sat-Sun 1100-2300. Great BBQ food under a relaxed, beach-bar-style *palapa*. Dishes include juicy kebabs and German sausages. Good, but a bit out of town.

Don Luca's, Calle La Calzada, catedral, 2 c al lago, T2552-7822. Excellent wood-oven pizza, *calzone*, and pasta. Pleasant setting.

El Tercer Ojo, Calle El Arsenal, south corner of the Convento San Francisco, T2552-6451. Tue-Sun 1000-2400. This lounge restaurant has interesting, exotic decor, reminiscent of some far eastern locale. It serves fairly decent, if unimaginative, international cuisine. Relaxed and pleasant, with weekly specials like Sushi night (Tue).

Jimmy Three Fingers, La Merced, 1 c al norte, ½ al abajo, T2552-8115, www.jimmythreefingers.com. Famous rib-shack serving lovingly prepared, slow-cooked baby back ribs, seafood, Italian cuisine, gourmet soups and comfort food for Granada's homesick expats. Celebrated and reassuringly creative.

La Jarochita, Alcaldía, 2 c al lago, T2552-8304. Quite possibly Nicaragua's finest Mexican restaurant, serving tacos, *burritos* and *quesadillas con mole*, among other national staples. Colourful and friendly. Also has a branch in Masaya.

La Terrazza La Playa, Complejo Turístico. Great *cerdo asado* and *filete de guapote*.

Las Colinas del Sur, Shell Palmira, 1 c sur, T2552-3492. Daily 1200-2200, Tue lunch only 1200-1500. Seafood specialities, excellent lake fish, try the *guapote* fried whole, boneless fillets, avocado salad. Far from centre, but worth it, take a taxi. Recommended.

Los Chocoyos, Calle Corrales, north corner of the Convent, inside Casa San Fransisco, T2552-8235. Daily 1200-2300. A range of tasty international cuisine including Mexican, Italian and French, served in a colonial setting.

Mona Lisa, Calle La Calzada, 3½ c al lago, T2552-8187. Undoubtedly the best pizzas in Granada; stone-baked, tasty and authentic. Recommended.

Roadhouse, Calle La Calzada, 2 c al lago. Popular with Nicaraguans, this rocking American-style restaurant serves a range of wholesome burgers. The fries, flavoured with cajun spices, are the real stand-out dish though.

♥-♥ Los Bocaditos, Calle El Comercio. Mon-Sat 0800-2200, Sun 0800-1600. A bustling but clean locals' joint with buffet from 1100-1500, breakfast and dinner menu.

♥-♥ Los Portales, opposite Cafemail on Plaza de los Leones, T2552-4115. Daily 0700-2200. Simple Mexican food, sometimes overpriced, but a great place for people-watching.

♥-♥ Nuevo Central, Calle La Calzada, 1½ c al lago. An unassuming little place, and just one of many terraced restaurants along this stretch. They do unpretentious, cheapish chicken and meat dishes with enormous portions. Popular with locals.

♥ Kiosko La Gata, Parque Central. Daily 1000-1900. Offers traditional Nica drinks like *chicha* and *cacao con leche*.

♥ Restaurant Querube's, Calle el Comercio, opposite Tiangue 1. Clean and popular locals' joint near the market. Offers Nicaraugan and Chinese fare from a buffet, as well as set lunches and breakfasts.

♥ TelePizza, Bancentro, 1½ c al lago. T2552-4219. Daily 1000-2200. Good, tasty pizzas; but not outstanding. Popular with Nicaraguans or those that have had enough of the gringo places. Delivery service.

Cafés
Café De Arte, Calle Calzada, near the cathedral, T2552-6461. Tue-Sun 1100-2200. This charming café hosts exhibitions of local artists. The desserts are 'to die for'. Recommended.

Café Isabella, 108 Calle Corrales, Bancentro, 1 c norte, ½ c abajo. Breakfast is served on a large covered balcony on the street or in the interior garden, also has vegetarian dishes.

Café Mail, next to Casa de Tres Mundos, T2552-6847. Daily 0700-2200. Check your email whilst sipping a cappucino; offers breakfasts and light meals too. Good for people-watching on the patio outside.

Don Simón, Parque Central, T8884-1393. Daily 0700-2100. Great views over the plaza. Simple breakfasts, good pastries, coffee, espresso, cappuccino, sandwiches.

Garden Café, Enitel, 1 c al lago. A very relaxed, breezey café with a lovely leafy garden and patio space. Good breakfasts, sandwiches, coffees, muffins and cookies. Friendly and pleasant. Recommended.

Kathy's Waffle House, opposite Iglesia San Francisco. 0730-1400. Kathy does the best breakfasts in Granada, and it's always busy here in the morning. You'll find everything from waffles to pancakes to *huevos rancheros*, all with free coffee refills. Highly recommended.

Maverick Reading Lounge, Telepizza, 1 c abajo. Fair-trade gourmet coffee, hot tea, good selection of magazines in English and Spanish, second-hand books, cigars.

Rainbow Juice Bar, Calle La Calzade, 2 c al lago. Sweet, tasty juices and *licuados* – great for a nutrient boost.

● Entertainment

Masaya *p1087, map p1087*
Bars and clubs
Casino Pharaoh's, 3 blocks north of the park, T2522-5222.

Chapo's, Bomberos 2½ c al sur. Mon-Fri 1200-0200, Sat and Sun 1400-0300. A trendy bar/club, good for a beer and hamburger with cable TV.

Coco Jambo, 4-5 blocks west of the Parque Central on the Malecón Masaya. Busy at weekends.

El Delfín Azul, 1½ Calle south of the fire department. Fri-Sun.

La Ronda, south side of the Parque Central. Locals also gather here.

Dance
Every Thu folkloric dances are performed behind the Mercado Artesanía in Masaya.

Granada *p1089, maps p1089 and p1090*
Bars and clubs
Café Nuit, northwest corner of parque central, 2½ c abajo, Wed-Mon 1900-0200. Great live music venue, with acts on Fri and Sat performing inside a pleasant colonial courtyard. Very cool and popular.

César, on waterfront (Complejo Turístico), Fri and Sat only. Recommended for dancing and drinking, very popular, inexpensive bar with merengue and salsa music.
El Club, northwest corner of parque central, 3 c abajo. Mon-Thu until 2400, Fri-Sun until 0200. Clean, modern bar with Euro-ambience, dance music and a mixture of locals and foreigners. Stylish and a cut above the rest.
El Quijote, southeast corner of parque central, 1 c al lago. Loud, boozy pub with a fun, foreign and mostly beer swilling crowd.
Jimmy Three Fingers, La Merced, 1 c norte. Fri-Sun 1800-0200. A renowned expat bar, also popular with Nicas and the local Harley Davidson chapter. The boss is an interesting and entertaining character. Live music and good, cold beer.
Safari Lounge, northwest corner of parque central, 1 c abajo. Complete with mock-Zebra skin upholstery, this modern bar is popular with foreigners and a great spot for people-watching over a rum or 2. The bar upstairs is more of a local affair.
Zoom Bar, Calle La Calzada, Parque Central, 3 c lago, across from Hospedaje Cocibolca. A very North American, sports themed bar with a big screen TV and football memorabilia. Very popular with beer-soaked gringos and expats. The burgers, contrary to the sign outside, are only just average.

Cinema
1 block behind **Hotel Alhambra**, good, modern, 2 screens.

⊕ Festivals and events

Granada *p1089, maps p1089 and p1090*
Mar Folklore, Artesanía and Food Festival for 3 days (check locally for dates).
Mar/Apr Holy Week.
14-30 Aug Assumption of the Virgin.
Aug La Hípica takes place 2nd weekend of Aug. The Sun preceding La Hípica is **La Fiesta de Toros** with bulls running in the streets of Granada.

25 Dec **Christmas** celebrated with masked and costumed performers.

○ Shopping

Granada *p1089, maps p1089 and p1090*
The **market** (large green building south of Parque Central) is dark, dirty and packed, but there are lots of stalls on the streets outside, as well as a horse cab rank and taxis. The main shopping street runs north-south, west of plaza.
Supermercado Pali, next to the outdoor market, is also dark and dirty, but marginally less chaotic for shopping.

▲ Activities and tours

Granada *p1089, maps p1089 and p1090*
Canopy tours
Mombacho Canopy Tour, on the road up to the Mombacho cloud forest reserve, T8888-2566, Tue-Sun 0830-1730. Not as spectacular or professional as the **Mombotour** canopy, but fun, cheaper at US$30, US$10 student discount and combines better with a visit to the cloud forest reserve which is on this side of the volcano.
Mombotour, Centro Comercial Granada No2, next to BAC, T2552-4548, www.mombotour.com. This is a world-class canopy tour designed by the inventor canopy tours, with 17 platforms 3-20 m above the ground on the lake side of Volcán Mombacho. The tour concludes with a vertical descent on a rappel line. 2 trips daily, US$38, including 4WD transfers.

Cultural and community tourism
La UCA Tierra y Agua, Shell Palmira, 75 varas abajo,T2552-0238, www.ucatierrayagua.org, Mon, Wed, Fri 0830-1400. This organization will help you organize a visit to rural communities around Granada including Isla Sonzapaota, La Granadilla, Albergue Nicaragua Libre and Aguas Agrias. Very interesting and highly recommended for

a perspective on local life and the land. Roll up your sleeves and muck in, if you wish.

Horse riding
Blue Mountain, southwest corner of Parque Central, 1½ c abajo, T2552-5323, www.bluemountainnicaragua.com. Offers daily cowboy-style tours of the region, with birdwatching, swimming and fishing options. You can bottle-feed some calves too, before they're made into burgers.

Kayaking
Inuit Kayaks, entrance to the touristic Center, 400 m sur on the lake, T2608-3646, www.inuitkayak.com. Kayak rental, sales and tours of the Isletas. Also, sailing, catamarans and windsurfing.

Mombotour, Central Comercial Granada No 2, next to BAC, T2552-4548, www.mombotour.com. Having overtaken the reputable 'Island Kayaks' agency, Mombotour offers kayak lessons and guided tours of the Isletas, which can be combined with longer birding expeditions.

Massage
Seeing Hands, inside EuroCafe, off the northwest corner of Parque Central. This excellent organization offers blind people an opportunity to earn a living as masseurs. A range of effective, professional massages are available, from a 15-min back, neck and shoulder massage, US$2.50, to a 1-hr table massage, US$12.50.

Sailing
Marina Cocibolca, www.marinacocibolca.net. Larger than Asese. Check the marina's administrative offices for information on costs and schedules for visits to the Isletas, Zapatera, and nearby private reserves.

Puerto Asese, www.aseselasisletas.com. 3 km from Granada, this low-key dock is the place to find transport to Las Isletas or Zapatera.

Zapatera Tours, Calle Palmira contiguo a la Cancha, T8842-2587, www.zapateratours.com. This company specializes in lake tours with

trips to las Isletas, Zapatera, Ometepe and the Solentiname archipelago. It also offers biking, hiking and windsurfing.

Tour operators
JB Fun Tours, on Parque Central inside artisan shop at cultural centre, T2552-6732, www.jbfuntours.com. Lots of options including fishing, manager Christian Quintanilla speaks English and is a good guide.

Oro Travel, Convento San Francisco, ½ c norte, T2552-4568, www.orotravel.com. Granada's best tour operator offers quality, specialized tours and trips, many including transfers and hotels. Owner Pascal speaks French, English and German. Friendly and helpful.

Tierra Tour, Calle la Calzada, catedral, 2 c lago, T2552-8723, www.tierratour.com. This well-established Dutch-Nicaraguan agency offers a wide range of services including economical trips to Las Isletas, cloud forest tours, birding expeditions and shuttles. Helpful and friendly.

Va Pues, Parque central, blue house next to the cathedral, T2552-8291, www.vapues.com. This award-winning agency offers canopy tours, turtle expeditions, car rental, domestic flights and a 'romantic getaway' tour to a private island.

⊝ Transport

Masaya *p1087, map p1087*
Bus Buses leave from the new market or you can also catch a non-express bus from the Carretera a Masaya towards **Granada** or **Managua**. Express buses leave from Parque San Miguel to La UCA in **Managua** when full or after 20 mins, 0600-2000, US$0.60.

Granada, every 30 mins, 0600-1800, 45 mins, US$0.60. **Jinotepe**, every 30 mins, 0500-1800, 1½ hrs, US$0.50. **Managua**, every 30 mins, 0400-1800, 1 hr, US$0.50. Express to **Managua**, every 30 mins, 0400-2100, 40 mins, US$0.80. **Matagalpa**, 0600 and 0700, 4 hrs, US$2.25. Or take a bus to **Tipitapa**, 0300-1800, 45 mins, US$2, change for Matagalpa.

Buses run to Valle de Apoyo for **Lago de Apoyo** from Masaya 2 times a day (1000, 1600, 45 mins, US$0.50) then walk down the road that drops into the crater. The bus returns to Masaya at 1130 and 1650. You will have to get off at Km 37.5 and walk down the 5-km access road (it's very dusty in the dry season, so bring a bandana). Hitching is possible though traffic is sparse on weekdays.

Taxi Fares around **Masaya** are US$0.30-0.80. **Granada**, US$15; **Managua** US$20; **airport** US$25. Horse-drawn carriages (*coches*) US$0.30.

From **Granada** to Laguna de Apoyo, US$15-20, or from **Managua**, US$35-40.

Granada *p1089, maps p1089 and p1090*

Bus

Intercity bus For the border with Costa Rica use **Rivas** bus to connect to **Peñas Blancas** service or use international buses.

Express minibuses to La UCA in **Managua** from a small lot just south of Parque Central on Calle Vega, every 20 mins, 0500-2000, 45 mins, US$1.20. Ask to be dropped on the highway exit to **Masaya**, US$0.60, from where it's a 20-min walk or 5-min taxi ride to the centre. Buses to Mercado Roberto Huembes, Managua, also leave from a station near the old hospital in Granada, west of centre, but they're slower and only marginally cheaper.

Leaving from the Shell station, Mercado, 1 c al lago. To **Rivas**, 7 daily, 0540-1510, 1½ hrs, US$1.50. To **Nandaime**, every 20 mins, 0500-1800, 20 mins, US0.70. To **Niquinohomo**, every 20 mins, 0550-1800, 45 mins, US$1, use this bus for visits to **Diriá**, **Diriomo**, **San Juan de Oriente**, **Catarina**. To **Jinotepe**, 0550, 0610, 0830, 1110, 1210 and 1710, 1½ hrs, US$1, for visits to **Los Pueblos**, including **Masatepe** and **San Marcos**. There's a 2nd terminal nearby, Shell station, 1 c abajo, 1 c norte, serving **Masaya**, every 30 mins, 0500-1800, 40 mins, US$0.50.

Shuttle To **Laguna de Apoyo**, 2 daily shuttles leave from **Hostal Oasis**, Calle Estrada 109, south of the centre, T2552-8006, www.nicaraguahostel.com, to Crater's Edge hostel at the lake, 1000, 1600, 30 mins, US$2. They return at 1100 and 1700. **Paxeos**, Parque Central, blue house next to cathedral, T2552-8291, www.paxeos.com. Daily shuttles to **Managua airport**, **León**, **San Juan del Sur** and **San Jorge**.

International bus

International buses to **San José**, **Costa Rica**, pass through Granada each day. See individual offices for schedules: King Quality, Shell Guapinol, 1½ c al Sur, opposite Ticabus, www.kingqualityca.com. Ticabus, Shell Guapinol, 1½ c al Sur, T2552-2899, www.ticabus.com. Transnica, Calle Xalteva, Frente de Iglesia Auxiliadora, T2552-6619, www.transnica.com.

Ferry

Schedules are subject to change. The ferry to **San Carlos** leaves the main dock on Mon and Thu at 1400, and stops at **Altagracia**, **Ometepe** after 4 hrs (US$4 1st class, US$2 2nd class), **Morrito** (8 hrs, US$5 1st class, US$3, 2nd class) and **San Miguelito** (10 hrs, US$5.50 1st class, US$3 2nd class). It stops in **San Carlos** after 14 hrs (US$8 1st class, US$4 2nd class). This journey is tedious, take your own food and water, and a hammock, if you have one. The ferry returns from San Carlos on Tue and Fri following the same route. For **Altagracia** you can also take a cargo boat with passenger seats on Wed and Sat (1200, 4½ hrs, US$2). It is faster (and less scary) to go overland to **San Jorge** and catch a 1-hr ferry to **Ometepe**, see page 1113.

Taxi

Granada taxi drivers are useful for finding places away from the centre, US$0.50 during the day, US$1 at night. To **Managua** US$25, but check taxi looks strong enough to make the journey.

● Directory

Masaya *p1087, map p1087*

Banks All banks will change dollars. The BAC, opposite the northwest corner of the artisan market, has an ATM; as does **Banpro**, opposite the southwest corner. There's a **Bancentro** on the west side of the plaza with a Visa ATM. You'll also find street changers around the plaza. **Internet** Intecomp, is south of the main plaza. Also try Mi PC a colores, on Sergio Delgadillo. **Medical services** Dr Gerardo Sánchez, next to town hall, speaks some English. Dr Freddy Cárdenas Ortega, near bus terminal, is a recommended gynaecologist. **Post office** Sergio Delgadillo. **Telephone** Enitel office on Parque Central.

Around Masaya *p1088*

Language schools Apoyo Intensive Spanish School, Laguna de Apoyo, T8882-3992, www.gaianicaragua.org, groups of 4, 5 hrs' tuition per day. 5-day programme, US$220 for a week including accommodation and food or US$/10 per month, family stays available. It is also possible to stay in the lodge without enrolling in the school, from US$16 plus meals, contact the school for more information.

Granada *p1089, maps p1089 and p1090*

Banks Banco de Centro América (BAC) Parque Central, 1 c abajo, on Calle La Libertad, has an ATM and will change TCs and US dollars. ATM at Esso Station (15-min walk from town centre) accepts Cirrus, Maestro, MasterCard as well. Banpro, BAC, 1 c al sur, has a less reliable ATM and money-changing facilities. Bancentro, BAC, 1 c al norte, has a Visa ATM. **Western Union**, from fire station ½ block south, Mon-Sat 0800-1300, 1400-1700. **Internet** Internet cafés can be found all over town, while most *hostales* and

hotels also offer internet access, including international calls. **Language schools** APC Spanish School, west side of Parque Central, T2552-4203, www.spanish granada.com. Flexible immersion classes in this centrally located language school. There are volunteer opportunities with local NGOs. **Casa Xalteva**, Iglesia Xalteva, ½ c al norte, T2552-2436, www.casaxalteva.com. Small Spanish classes for beginners and advanced students, 1 week to several months. Home stays arranged, and voluntary work with children, recommended. **Nicaragua Mía Spanish School**, inside Maverick's reading lounge, Calle Arsenal, behind hotel Colonial, T2552-2755, www.nicaragua-mia-spanish school.com. An established and professional language school with various learning options, from hourly to weekly tuition. The school takes an ethical approach and contributes to local causes. **One on One**, Calle La Calzada 450, T2552-6771, www.1on1 tutoring.net. One on One uses a unique teaching system where each student has 4 different tutors, thus encouraging greater aural comprehension. Instruction is flexible, by the hour or week, with homestay and activities available. There's an evening restaurant too, where you can practise your Spanish with locals. Recommended. Also see **Apoyo Intensive Spanish School**, on Laguna de Apoyo, page 1088. **Laundry** Laundry service Parque Central, 1½ c abajo, around US$3 for a medium-sized load, daily 0700-1900. **Medical services** Dr Francisco Martínez Blanco, Clínica de Especialidades Piedra Bocona, ½ block west of Cine Karawale, T2552-5989, f_mblanco@ yahoo.com, general practitioner, speaks good English, consultation US$10. **Telephone** (Enitel) on corner northeast of Parque Central. **Post office** From fire station ½ block east, ½ block north.

Rivas Isthmus and Ometepe Island

The slender isthmus of Rivas, bordered by Costa Rica to the south, is a well-travelled, mostly agricultural department served by the Pan-American highway. The department capital is a pleasant, if uninteresting transportation hub with connections to some of the country's finest attractions. To the west lie burgeoning Pacific resorts, fantastic waves and famous turtle-nesting sites. To the east lies the port of San Jorge, Lake Nicaragua and the tranquil island of Ometepe, rising mysteriously with twin volcanoes. To the south, the Pan-American highway continues its journey into Costa Rica and beyond, making Rivas an exciting department of diverse scenery, transition and international frontiers. ▸▸ *For listings, see pages 1107-1114.*

Managua to Rivas ●●● ▸▸ *pp1107-1114.*

Approximately 26 km from Managua, the Pan-American highway climbs to 900 m at Casa Colorada. Further on, at El Crucero, a paved branch road goes through the Sierra south to the Pacific beaches of Pochomil and Masachapa. The highway continues through the beautiful scenery of the sierras to **Diriamba**, in a coffee-growing district 42 km from Managua. In the centre of the town is the **Museo Ecológico de Trópico Seco** ① *Tue-Sat 0800-1200, 1400-1700, Sun 0800-1200, US$1,* with displays of local flora and fauna, including coffee and turtles, and a section on volcanoes. The local fiesta is on 20 January. There is a 32-km dirt road direct to the beach at **Masachapa** (no buses).

Five kilometres north of Diriamba a paved road branches off the main highway and runs east through **San Marcos**, Masatepe (famous for wooden and rattan furniture) and Niquinohomo to Catarina and Masaya. A road also leads to **La Concepción**, a small industrious village in the highlands, very typical of this part of Nicaragua, where few travellers go. The area is rich in pineapple, pitaya, coffee, mandarins and oranges and the people are welcoming. Access is by bus from Jinotepe, every 20 minutes, US$0.50, or from Managua's Roberto Huembes terminal, every half an hour, US$0.75.

Five kilometres beyond Diriamba is **Jinotepe**, capital of the coffee-growing district of Carazo. It has a fine neoclassical church with modern stained-glass windows from Irún, in Spain. 'Liberation Day' is celebrated on 5 July here, while the fiesta in honour of St James the Greater runs from 24-26 July.

From **Nandaime**, 21 km south of Jinotepe, a paved road runs north to Granada (bus US$0.50). Nandaime has two interesting churches, El Calvario and La Parroquia (1859-1872). The annual fiesta, 24-27 July, features masked dancers.

At Km 85 is the signed turn off that leads down a long dirt road to the private reserve and lodge of **Domitila** (see Sleeping, page 1108). About 45 km beyond Nandaime (US$0.40 by bus) is Rivas.

Rivas ●●●● ▸▸ *pp1107-1114. Colour map 7, A2.*

➔ *Population: 41,764. Altitude: 139 m.*

The Costa Rican national hero, drummer Juan Santamaría, sacrificed his life here in 1856 when setting fire to a building captured by the infamous William Walker. On the town's Parque Central is a lovely old basilica (in need of repair). In the dome you can see the fresco of the sea battle against the ships of Protestantism and Communism. The Parque has some old, arcaded buildings on one side, but also some new buildings.

Border essentials: Nicaragua–Costa Rica

Peñas Blancas

This is the only road crossing between Nicaragua and Costa Rica.

Nicaraguan immigration Daily 0600-2200. When entering Nicaragua, complete Costa Rican exit formalities and then walk the 500 m to the new border controls. International bus passengers have to disembark and queue for immigration to stamp their passports. Then unload your baggage and wait in a line for the customs official to arrive. You will be asked to open your bags, the official will give them a cursory glance and you reload. Passports and tickets will be checked again back on the bus. If you are not on a bus, there are plenty of helpers on hand. Allow 45 minutes to complete the formalities. You will have to pay US$5-8 to enter Nicaragua plus a US$1 *Alcaldía* charge. If you arrive Mon-Fri before 0800 or after 1700, or at any time at the weekend, you will have to pay US$12 plus the *Alcaldía* charge.

When leaving Nicaragua, pay US$1 *Alcaldía* charge to enter the customs area and then complete formalities in the new customs building where you pay US$2 to have your passport checked Monday-Friday 0800-1700, US$4, 0600-0800 and after 1700, or any time on Sat and Sun. Then walk the 500 m to the Costa Rican border and simply have your passport stamped. Buses and taxis are available from the border; hitching is difficult.

Crossing by private vehicle There is no fuel going into Nicaragua until Rivas (37 km). After you have been through *Migración*, find an inspector who will fill out the preliminary form to be taken to *Aduana*. At the *Vehículo Entrando* window, the vehicle permit is typed up and the vehicle stamp is put in your passport. Next, go to *Tránsito* to pay for the car permit. Finally, ask the inspector to give a final check.

On leaving Nicaragua, first pay your exit tax in the office at the end of the control station (receipt given). Then return for your exit stamp and complete the *Tarjeta de Control Migratorio*. Motorists must then go to *Aduana* to cancel vehicle papers; exit details are typed on to the vehicle permit and the stamp in your passport is cancelled. Find the inspector in *Aduana* who has to check the details and stamp your permit. If you fail to do this you will not be allowed to leave the country; you will be sent back to *Sapoá* by the officials at the final Nicaraguan checkpoint.

Transport Buses to Rivas, every 30 minutes, 0600-1800, US$0.75, one hour. From here buses connect to Managua, every 30 minutes, 0330-1800, US$2.50, two hours 45 minutes or to Granada, every 45 minutes, 0530-1625, US$2, one hour 45 minutes, try to board an express bus from Rivas to your destination. Express buses from Peñas Blancas to Managua, every 30 minutes, 0700-1800, US$3.50, 3½ hrs. There can be long waits when international buses are passing through. If you are travelling independently, a good time to cross is around 0900, before the buses arrive.

Rivas is a good stopping place if in transit by land through Nicaragua. The bus station, adjacent to the market, is on the northwest edge of town about eight blocks from the main highway. The road from the lake port of San Jorge joins this road at Rivas; 11 km beyond Rivas, at La Virgen on the shore of Lake Nicaragua, it branches south to San Juan del Sur. The **tourist office (INTUR)** ① *75 m west of the Texaco station (in front of Hospedaje Lidia), T2453-4914 (ask for Sr Francisco Cárdenas)*, has good maps of Nicaragua and general information.

Refugio de Vida Silvestre Río Escalante Chacocente
① *US$0.70, www.chacocente.info.*

Between Nandaime and Rivas are various turnings south that lead eventually to the Pacific coast (all are rough; high clearance is more important than 4WD). One of these turnings (89 km from Managua if going via Diriamba and Jinotepe; 61 km from Peñas Blancas), just south of the Río Ochomogo bridge, is signposted to the **Refugio de Vida Silvestre Río Escalante Chacocente**. This 4800-ha reserve of forest and beach is the second most important turtle nesting site in the country and one of the biggest tracts of tropical dry forest in the Pacific basin. The forest is full of mammal, reptile and birdlife and the beach is long and empty. Bring your own hammock and shade. The rough dirt road to the coast (45 km) goes to Las Salinas. Turn right here to **Astillero**, which has a fishing cooperative, and continue to the reserve. You will probably have to ask directions several times and cross a number of rivers, the last of which is impassable after rain without a very strong 4WD). Camping is safe and you can buy fish from the co-op. At **Chacocente**, there is a **Marena** office, a government-sponsored **turtle sanctuary** (signs say 'authorized personnel only'; don't be put off, they welcome visitors). The **Marena** wardens protect newly hatched turtles and help them make it to the sea (a magnificent sight from November to December). Unfortunately, turtle eggs are considered to have aphrodisiac properties and are used as a dietary supplement by the locals. **Marena** is virtually powerless to prevent egg theft, although for two months a year the reserve is protected by armed military personnel.

San Juan del Sur ⊜❼❼⊛▲❶❻ ⤻ *pp1107-1114. Colour map 7, A2.*

San Juan del Sur on the Pacific coast has a beautiful bay which is rapidly developing. A few years ago this was a humble fishing village, now tourists, expats and estate agents are transforming it into a Costa Rican-style development, driving land prices to exorbitant levels. Still, the sunsets have to be seen to be believed, and the village has retained its small-town feel, for now at least. You'll find it 28 km from Rivas, south along the Pan-American Highway and then right to the coast along a road which is in good condition. There is also a direct dirt road from Rivas going through beautiful countryside, but it is only good when dry.

The town beach is cleaned daily, but at weekends and on holidays, especially Semana Santa, San Juan is busy; otherwise the beaches are quiet during the week. The **INTUR tourist office** ① *between the beach and the market in front of Joxi, www.sanjuandel sur.org.ni, Mon-Fri 0900-1200, 1300-1700, Sat 0900-1200,* is helpful, sells maps and a guide of San Juan del Sur. Alternatively, try www.sanjuandelsurguide.com.

South of San Juan del Sur
You can take a boat to more pristine beaches such as **Playa del Coco** on the poor road to Ostional. Or ask around for a bus leaving to Ostional (1300 at the market, two hours). The surfing on nearby beaches is good, **Playa Maderas** is the current hotspot, often crowded with beginners. Shuttles leave from agencies, hostels and surf shops. ⤻ *See Transport, page 1113.*

Refugio de Vida Silvestre La Flor ① *US$10, US$2.50 student discount, access by 4WD or on foot,* covers 800 ha of tropical dry forest, mangroves, estuary and beach. A beautiful, sweeping cove with sand and many trees, it is the most important and most visited beach by nesting sea turtles from August to November. During the high season, armed guards protect the arrival of the turtle (sometimes in their thousands and usually lasting a period of three days). The rangers are very happy to explain the creatures' reproductive habits. Many birds live in the protected mangroves at the south end of the beach. Camping is provided during the turtle arrivals, US$25 per night, first come, first served. Bring a hammock and mosquito netting as insects are vicious at dusk. The ranger station sells soft drinks. To get there, the exit for the dirt path south is 200 m before the entrance to San Juan del Sur, 21 km from the highway. Several rivers, most of which have firm beds, must be crossed.

San Jorge
On the southwestern shore of Lake Nicaragua close to Rivas, San Jorge, is the main departure point for Ometepe Island, but on Sundays in summer the town itself is very lively with music, baseball, swimming and lots of excursion buses.

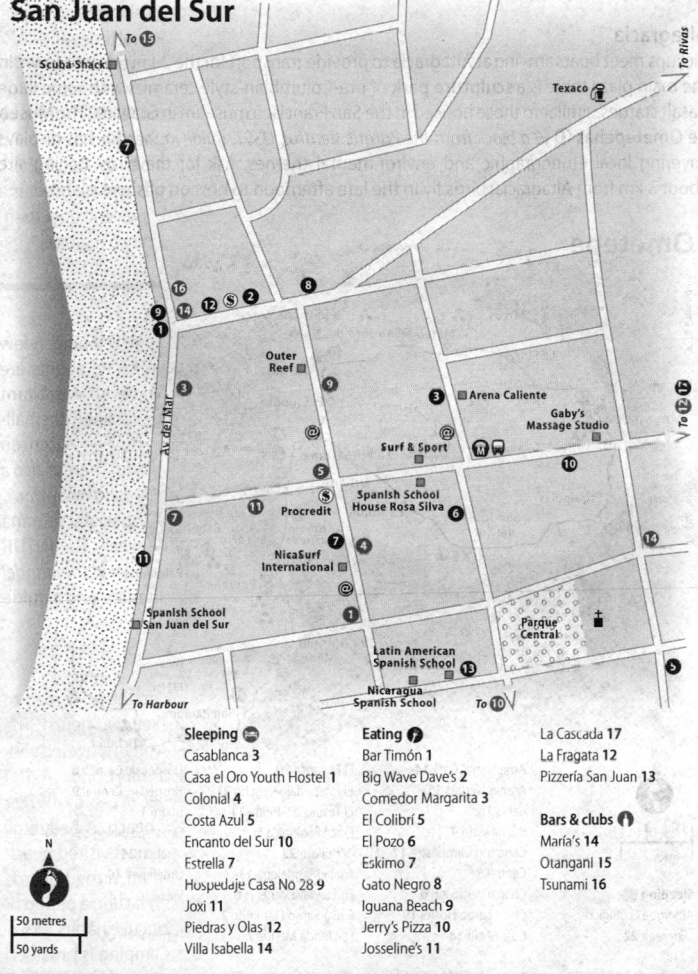

San Juan del Sur

Sleeping 🛏
Casablanca **3**
Casa el Oro Youth Hostel **1**
Colonial **4**
Costa Azul **5**
Encanto del Sur **10**
Estrella **7**
Hospedaje Casa No 28 **9**
Joxi **11**
Piedras y Olas **12**
Villa Isabella **14**

Eating 🍴
Bar Timón **1**
Big Wave Dave's **2**
Comedor Margarita **3**
El Colibrí **5**
El Pozo **6**
Eskimo **7**
Gato Negro **8**
Iguana Beach **9**
Jerry's Pizza **10**
Josseline's **11**

La Cascada **17**
La Fragata **12**
Pizzería San Juan **13**

Bars & clubs 🍸
María's **14**
Otangani **15**
Tsunami **16**

The largest freshwater island in the world, Ometepe is a highlight of any trip to Nicaragua. It has two volcanoes, one of them, **Concepción**, a perfect cone rising to 1610 m; the other, **Volcán Maderas**, rising to 1394 m. There are two main villages, on either side of Volcán Concepción: Moyogalpa and Altagracia, which are connected by bus. **Moyogalpa** is a tourist port and there is not much to keep you here unless you're catching an early boat. **Altagracia** is smaller and more charming. The people of Ometepe are said to be the kindest in Nicaragua, partly because the Revolution and Civil War were never waged here. There are many indigenous **petroglyphs** on the island, the best being near **Finca Magdalena**.

Altagracia

Pickups meet boats arriving at Altagracia to provide transport for the 2-km ride into town. In the main plaza there is a **sculpture park** of pre-Columbian-style ceramics with some large basalt statues, similar to those housed in the San Francisco museum in Granada. The **Museo de Ometepehas** ① ½ *a block from the Parque Central, US$1, guide in Spanish*, has displays covering local ethnographic and environmental themes. Ask for the birdwatching site about 3 km from Altagracia; birds fly in the late afternoon to nest on offshore islands.

Ometepe

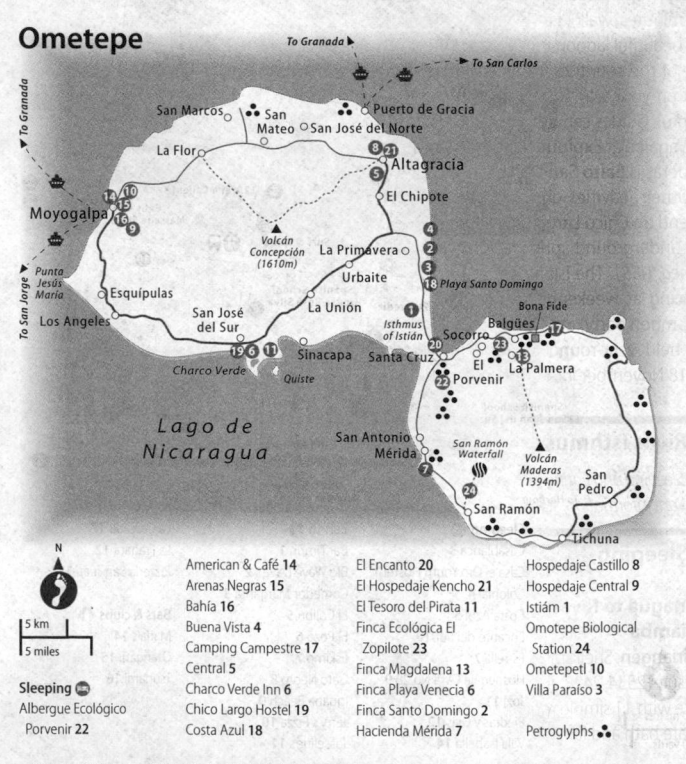

American & Café **14**	El Encanto **20**	Hospedaje Castillo **8**
Arenas Negras **15**	El Hospedaje Kencho **21**	Hospedaje Central **9**
Bahía **16**	El Tesoro del Pirata **11**	Istiám **1**
Buena Vista **4**	Finca Ecológica El	Ometepe Biological
Camping Campestre **17**	Zopilote **23**	Station **24**
Sleeping ⊖	Central **5**	Finca Magdalena **13**	Ometepetl **10**
Albergue Ecológico	Charco Verde Inn **6**	Finca Playa Venecia **6**	Villa Paraíso **3**
Porvenir **22**	Chico Largo Hostel **19**	Finca Santo Domingo **2**	
	Costa Azul **18**	Hacienda Mérida **7**	Petroglyphs ⁂

N
5 km
5 miles

You can stroll to the base of **Volcán Concepción** (which had its last major eruption in 1957), for good views of the lake In the company of many birds and howler monkeys. To climb the volcano, leave from **Cuatro Cuadros**, 2 km from Altagracia, and make for a cinder gully between forested slopes and a lava flow. There are several *fincas* on the lower part of the volcano. The ascent takes about five hours (take water), with alpine vegetation, heat from the crater and howler monkeys as attractions. It gets very steep near the summit. It's recommended that you get a guide as visibility is often restricted by clouds and it is easy to get lost, especially in the final stages (US$15 per person, minimum of three). Ask for guides near the pier; otherwise contact Eduardo Ortiz and his son José, of **Cuatro Cuadros**, or Eduardo Manzanares or Berman Gómez from **Exploring Ometepe**. There is an alternative route up Volcán Concepción from behind the church in Moyogalpa. Again, a guide is recommended as it's easy to get lost in the jungle or the cloud. The walk takes eight hours; a machete is useful. Camping is possible near the top. South of Volcán Concepción is Laguna Charco Verde (see below).

Around Isla Ometepe

For **Volcán Maderas** ① *US$1.50 to climb, US$3.50 with a guide*, take an early bus (0430 or 0530) from Altagracia to Balgües (or stay overnight) and ask for **Finca Magdalena** (20 minutes' walk). From here it's a 2½-hour walk through banana plantations and forest to the beautiful lagoon in the crater (the path can be very muddy, boots recommended). This is one of the country's finest Pacific basin cloud forests with howler monkeys accompanying you on your way to the volcano summit. The climb is not technical, but a guide may be helpful. Guides can be found at the coffee cooperative in Balgües, **Finca Magdalena** and in Moyogalpa at **Exploring Ometepe** or at **Hotel Ometepetl**. On the southwest flank of Volcán Maderas is **Salto San Ramón**, a 110-m waterfall. Take water on all hikes and climbs.

Other activities on the island include the **Laguna Charco Verde** (ask around for the legend on Chico Largo who is still said to watch the lagoon), the waterfall at San Ramon or the underground spring and water eye of **La Presa** ① *close to Santo Domingo, privately owned, US$1*. The island does not offer a lot in terms of entertainment besides some local dancing at weekends (ask around). Every month there is the **Fiesta de la Luna Llena** (full-moon party) at Charco Verde (ask around for directions and times). **Fiestas patronales** are held year-round in different villages, the festivities 22-26 July in Moyogalpa and 12-18 November in Altagracia include both religious processions and bull riding.

⦿ Rivas Isthmus and Ometepe Island listings

For Sleeping and Eating price codes and other relevant information, see Essentials pages 45-48.

⦿ Sleeping

Managua to Rivas *p1102*
Diriamba
E Diriangén, Shell station, 1 c arriba, ½ c sur, T2534-2428. A friendly, family-run place with 11 simple rooms, each with private bath and fan. Parking available.

San Marcos
B Hotel Casa Blanca, across from the Baptist church, T2535-2717, www.hotelcasa blanca.com.ni. A very friendly, pleasant hotel with 16 clean rooms, some have a/c. There's Wi-Fi, hammocks, a garden for relaxing. Breakfast included in the price.

B Hotel and Restaurante Lagos y Volcanes, La Concepción, San Marcos, 4 km sur, Instituto Guillermo Ampie, 1½ km arriba, lagosyvolcanes@hotmail.com. Surrounded by citrus trees and offering great views of

Laguna Masaya, this hotel has 15 attractive rooms with decent beds, cable TV, bath and hot water. Facilities include a good restaurant and pool.

Jinotepe

B Domitila, Km 85, T8881-1786, www.domitila.org. This tropical dry forest reserve near the shores of Lake Nicaragua and Isla Zapatera has some very fine simple, rustic lodging, with private bath, sawdust toilets. Prices are high but meals are included. Hiking trails are charged at additional high rates; visits to Isla Zapatera can be arranged and are better value.
B Hotel Casa Mateo, BDF, 1½ c abajo, T2532-3284, www.hotelcasamateo.com. This comfortable 3-storey hotel has 40 good rooms, some with a/c (**A**). There's a decent restaurant attached serving breakfasts and *comida típica*. Excellent central location and the best place in town.

Rivas *p1102*

A Nicarao Inn Hotel, Parque Central, 2 c abajo, T2563-3836, www.hotelnicaraoinn.com.ni. The finest hotel in Rivas has 18 tastefully decorated, comfortable rooms, all with a/c, cable TV, hot water and Wi-Fi. Conference centre, restaurant and bar. Breakfast included.
C Español, behind Iglesia San Pedro, T2563-0006. Offers 5 basic rooms with bath and fan. Restaurant attached.
D Hospedaje Lidia, Texaco, ½ c abajo, near bus stop, T2563-3477. 12 rooms, clean, family atmosphere, some with private bath, noisy, helpful, recommended.

San Juan del Sur *p1104, map p1105*

Hotel prices in San Juan del Sur double for Semana Santa, Christmas and New Year.
LL-L Piedras y Olas, Parroquia, 1½ c arriba, T2568-2110, www.piedrasyolas.com. Beautiful luxurious homes (**L**) and hotel suites with great furnishings, style and views of the bay. Sailing trips on the *Pelican Eyes* boat can be arranged.
AL Casablanca, opposite Bar Timón on the beach road, T2568-2135, www.sanjuandelsur.org.ni. Clean, comfortable rooms with a/c,

cable TV, private bath, refrigerator and hot water. There's a small pool, parking, free internet and continental breakfast included in the price. Friendly and relaxed.
AL Villa Isabella, behind church to the left, T2568-2568, www.sanjuandelsur.org.ni. Lovely, well-decorated wooden house with 17 clean rooms, private bath, a/c, disabled access, large windows. There's a pool, garage parking, internet, video library and breakfast included in the price. English spoken, very helpful.
A Colonial, del Mercado 1 c al mar, ½ c sur, T2568-2539, www.hotel-nicaragua.com. This well-managed hotel has a pleasant, relaxing garden, and 12 comfortable rooms with a/c, cable TV, hot water. Continental breakfast included, bikes and tours can be arranged.
C Hotel Encanto del Sur, Iglesia, 100 m sur, T2568-2222. 18 clean, tidy, comfortable rooms with private bath and a/c, cheaper with fan (**D**). Quiet, away from the action and good value.
C-E Costa Azul, mercado, 1c al mar, T2568-2294. Comfortable, economical rooms with good mattresses and a/c, cheaper with fan (**D**) or shared bath (**E**). There's internet, hammocks, parking and kitchen.
D Joxi, mercado, 1½ c al mar, T2568-2348, casajoxi@ibw.com.ni. Friendly, Norwegian-run, bunk beds, a/c, cable TV, restaurant and bar.
D-F Casa el Oro Youth Hostel, hotel colonial, 20 varas sur, T2568-2415, www.casaeloro.com. Young, popular hostel with dorm beds (**E-F**), private rooms (**D**) and a plethora of services, shuttles, tours and lessons. Good kitchen and garden. Plenty of hammocks.
E Estrella, mercado, 2c sur, T2568-2210. Weathered and fading old cheapie with simple rooms, partitioned walls, good breezes and sea views. Shared bath.
E Hospedaje Casa No 28, mercado, 1c al mar, 1c norte, T2568-2441. Good clean budget option with basic rooms and shared bath. Some rooms have private bath, a/c and hot water (**C**).

North of San Juan del Sur

LL Morgan´s Rock, Playa Ocotal, T2296-9442, www.morgansrock.com. Luxury hacienda on a secluded beach with options for activities and wildlife trips in the surrounding area.

A Marsella Beach Resort, Playa Marsella, T8887-1337, www.marsellabeachresort.com. Independent cabins with private bath, a/c and great views, restaurant, also house for rent (**LL**).

C-E Camping Matilda, Playa Maderas, T2456-3461. The best lodgings on the beach. They have 8 rooms with private bath (**C**), 2 small dorms (**D**), and some little 'camping houses' that look like dog kennels (**E**). Very friendly, relaxed and pleasant. Often full.

South of San Juan del Sur *p1104*
LL-AL Parque Marítimo El Coco, 18 km south of San Juan del Sur, T8892-0124, www.playaelcoco.com.ni. Very nice apartments, bungalows and houses for 4-10 people, some on beach, others with ocean view. Closest lodging to La Flor Wildlife Refuge.

San Jorge *p1105*
There are a few ultra-cheap *hospedajes* scattered around the port, otherwise most lodgings in San Jorge start at around US$20.
B Hotel Dalinky, the port, 200 varas abajo, T2563-4990. Large, clean double rooms with a/c, cable TV and bath. Breakfast included and parking available. There's a handful of cheaper rooms too (**D**).
B Hotel Hamacas, the port, 100 varas abajo, 25 varas sur, T2563-1709. As the name suggests, lots of hammocks, mostly slung across porches. The rooms are large and clean with a/c and cable TV. Breakfast included. **D** with fan.

Altagracia *p1106, map p1106*
D-E Hospedaje Castillo, parque central, 1 c sur, ½ c oeste, T2552-8744. Pleasant, friendly hotel with 19 rooms, most have bath outside (**E**). There's a good restaurant, bar and internet facilities attached, credit cards are accepted and travellers cheques changed. Tours to the volcanoes. Recommended.
D-E Hotel Central, Iglesia, 2 c sur, T2552-8770. 19 rooms (**E**) and 6 *cabañas* (**D**) surround an attractive courtyard, all with private bath

and fan. There's a restaurant and bar, bicycle rental, tours and hammocks to rest your weary bones. Friendly and recommended.
E El Hospedaje Kencho, T8820-2246. Basic and scruffy rooms, with or without bath.

Around Isla Ometepe *p1107, map p1106*
Moyogalpa
B American Café and Hotel, the dock, 100 varas up the hill, T2645-7193. Excellent value, comfortable and immaculately clean rooms, some with a/c, cheaper without (**C**). All have good, new mattresses and properly heated water. Italian, German, Spanish and English spoken. Recommended.
C Ometepetl, on main street from dock, T2569-4276, ometepetlng@hotmail.com (reservations for Istián, Santo Domingo also). This long-standing Moyogalpa favourite has rooms with a/c (**D** without) and bath. There's a pool and a popular restaurant attached, vehicle rental and tours on request.
D-F Hospedaje Central, from dock, 1 block right, 3 blocks up the hill, T2569-4262. This brightly coloured Moyogalpa cheapie has dorms (**F**) and private rooms (**D**), but has seen better days. Keep an eye on your stuff.
E Arenas Negras, opposite Hotel Ometepetl, T8883-6167. 10 simple rooms, small but clean, 9 with private bath and fan. Friendly and basic.
E Hotel Bahía, on main street from dock, T2470-3473. Very basic rooms with fan. Nice and breezy upstairs.

San José del Sur
A-B Hotel Charco Verde Inn, almost next to the lagoon, San José del Sur, T8887-9302, www.charcoverde.com.ni. Pleasant *cabañas* with private bath, a/c, terrace (**A**), and doubles with private bath and fan (**B**). Good reports. Watch out for the mythical Chico Largo.
B-D Finca Playa Venecia, San José del Sur, 250 m from the main road, T8872-7668, www.fincavenecia.com. Very chilled out, comfortable lodgings and a lovely lakeside garden. *Cabañas* overlooking the water are best (**B**), but regular *cabanas* (**C**) and rooms (**D**) are good too. Recommended.

C El Tesoro del Pirata, Playa Valle Verde, near Charco Verde, Km 15, Carretera a Altagracia, turn towards the lake, T8832-2429. Next to a good beach, cabins with private bath and a/c, dorms and rooms with fan and shared bath. Rustic restaurant attached.

D-F Chico Largo Hostel, next to **Finca Playa Venecia**, T8886-4069. Hostel with dorms (**F**) or private rooms (**D**), friendly ambience, poor beds.

Playa Santo Domingo

A-D Villa Paraíso, beachfront, T2563-4675, www.villaparaiso.com.ni. Ometepe's most expensive and luxurious lodging has a beautiful, peaceful setting with 13 cute, stone *cabañas* (**A**) and 5 rooms (**D**). Most have a/c, private bath, hot water, cable TV, minibar and internet. Some of the rooms have a patio and lake view.

B Hotel Costa Azul, Hotel Paraíso, 50 varas sur, T2644-0327. A hotel with 7 big, clean rooms. They have a/c, private bath and TV with DVD. There's a restaurant serving *comida típica* and breakfasts. Bike and motorbike rental, tours and guides available.

B-D Finca Santo Domingo, Playa Santo Domingo, north side of Villa Paraíso, T2485-6177, www.hotelfincasantodomingo.com. Friendly lakeside hotel with a range of rooms (**C-D**) and bungalows (**B**), all with private bath. There's an *artesanía* store, bicycle rental and various tours. The restaurant serves *comida típica* and has good views.

D Hotel Buena Vista, Playa Santo Domingo, Villa Paraíso, 150 m norte. Great views, you really feel the lake from here. 10 rooms have private bath and fan, there's a restaurant, a pleasant terrace and hammocks.

D Hotel Istiám, Villa Paraíso, 2 km sur, T8887-9891 across the road from the beach, reservations through **Ometepetl** in Moyogalpa. Basic and often seemingly abandoned, friendly, family-run place. Rooms are simple but clean, with fan and bath, cheaper shared (**E**). Good swimming. Restaurant, tours and bike rental.

Balgües

B-F Finca Magdalena, Balgües, www.fincamagdalena.com, T8880-2041.

Famous cooperative farm run by 26 families, with accommodation in a small cottages, *cabañas* (**B**) doubles (**E**), singles, dorms (**F**) and hammocks. Camping possible. Stunning views across lake and to Concepción, good meals around US$2, friendly, basic, wildly popular on the budget highway.

E-F Finca Ecológica El Zopilote, about 1 km uphill from, Balgües. Funky hostel with dormitory, hammocks, camping and *cabañas*. Full moon parties, use of kitchen and free track up to the volcano.

F Camping Campestre, 500 m east of Balgües, T2695-2071. English-owned organic farm with camping space near the banana plantation. Opportunities to volunteer, outdoor kitchen and camping equipment provided.

Santa Cruz

D Albergue Ecológico Porvenir, T8855-1426. Stunning views at this tranquil, secluded lodge at the foot of Maderas. Rooms are clean, tidy and comfortable, with private bath and fan. Nearby trails run to the crater lake and miradors.

D El Encanto, www.goelencanto.com, T8867-7128. An experimental *finca* comprising 4 ha of land. The rooms are good, clean and comfortable, and a there's very pleasant, chilled out garden. Various tours are available.

Mérida

B-F Hacienda Mérida, at the old Somoza dock in lower Mérida, T8868-8973, www.hmerida.com. Popular hostel with a beautiful setting by the lake. Lodgings have wheelchair access and include a mixture of dorms (**F**) and rooms (**C**), some with views (**B**). There's a children's school on-site where you can volunteer, kayak rental, good quality mountain bikes, internet and a range of tours available, including sailing. The restaurant serves fresh, hygienically prepared food, good for vegetarians. Recommended.

San Ramón

E Ometepe Biological Station, San Ramón, T8883-1107, for groups of students only. The station claims to 'manage' 325 ha of conservation land, partly consumed by cash crops. Rooms are simple with shared bath outside. Services include mountain bikes, kayaks, meals.

⍾ Eating

Managua to Rivas p1102
Diriamba
Ψ Mi Bohio, Museo, 1 c arriba, T2534-2437. Founded in 1972, a good, clean restaurant serving chicken in wine sauce, soups and *ceviche* among other dishes.

San Marcos
Ψ La Casona Coffee Shop, ENITEL, 1 c norte 'Where cool people hang out.' A very good eatery, popular with students and serving proper, tasty coffee, cakes, pastas and salads. Recommended.

Jinotepe
ΨΨ-Ψ Pizzería Colisseo, Parque Central, 1 c norte, T2532-2150. Tue-Sun 1200-2200. The most famous pizzas in Nicaragua. Some customers drive from Managua to eat here. Also serves pasta

Rivas p1102
Ψ El Mesón, Iglesia San Francisco, ½ c abajo, T2563-4535, Mon-Sat 1100-1500. Very good, try *pollo a la plancha* or *bistec encebollado*.
Ψ Rancho Cocteleró Mariscazo, 800 m south of Rivas stadium on best side of Pan-American Hwy. One of the best seafood restaurants in Nicaragua. Simple decor, friendly service, very good value. Highly recommended.
Ψ Chop Suey, southwest corner of the plaza, T2563-3235. Daily 1000-2100. Chinese food at Nicaraguan prices, for those intent on a change.
Ψ Pizza Hot, north side of the plaza, T2563-4662. Fast food including burgers, fried chicken and fairly good pizza.

San Juan del Sur p1104, map p1105
There are many popular, but overpriced restaurants lining the beach, where your tourist dollars buy excellent sea views and mediocre food. Only the better ones are listed below.
ΨΨ-Ψ Bar Timón, across from **Hotel Casablanca**, T2568-82243. Daily 0800-2200. Probably the best of the beachfront eateries, serving lobster, prawns and a host of other seafood dishes. No plastic furniture. Popular and Nicaraguan.
ΨΨ-Ψ Big Wave Dave's, Texaco, 200 m al mar, T2568-2203, www.bigwavedaves.net. Tue-Sun 0830-2400. Popular with foreigners out to party and hook up with others. Wholesome pub food and a buzzing, boozy atmosphere.
ΨΨ-Ψ El Colibrí, mercado, 1 c este, 2½ sur. The best restaurant in town, with an excellent and eclectic Mediterranean menu, great decor, ambience, fine wines and really good food, much of it organic. Pleasant, hospitable and highly recommended.
ΨΨ-Ψ El Pozo, mercado, ½ c sur. Smart and stylish, with a robust international menu and an attractive, young clientele. This interesting little restaurant almost belongs in London or New York.
ΨΨ-Ψ La Cascada, Piedras y Olas, parque, 1½ c arriba. Palm-thatched restaurant, excellent location overlooking the harbour, good sandwiches.
ΨΨ-Ψ Pizzería San Juan, Tue-Sun 1700-2130. Good pizza and pasta, but a rather plain interior and not much of a dining experience.
Ψ Iguana Beach, next door to Timón. Sandwiches, burgers, beer and cheese-drenched nachos, as well as seafood. Popular with tourists, often buzzing and a good place to drink.
Ψ Josseline's, on the beach. One of the better beachside eateries, offering the usual seafood fare like shrimps, fillets and lobster. Some limited meat and chicken dishes too.
Ψ Comedor Margarita, mercado, ½ c norte.
Ψ Jerry's Pizza, mercado, ½ c este. American-owned pizza joint serving reasonable fast-food and breakfasts. A nice, airy, open-front space, good for people-watching.
Ψ La Fragata, Texaco, 250 m al mar. The place for cheap and cheerful fast-food, roast chicken.

Cafés and ice cream parlours

Eskimo, seafront, 2½ c north of **Hotel Estrella**. Sweet, cold cones, sundaes and banana splits. Another branch just south of Banco Procredit.
Gato Negro, mercado, 1c al mar, 1 c norte. Popular gringo café with good coffee, reading space and snacks. This is also one of the best bookshops in the country, with what they claim is the largest collection of English-language books on Nicaragua, in Nicaragua.

☻ Entertainment

San Juan del Sur p1104, map p1105
Bars and clubs

The action revolves around **Iguana Beach**, **Maria's** and **Big Dave's Waves**, all located close to each other. You could also try:
Otangani, north on the seafront, next to **Gallo de Oro**, T8878-8384. Thu-Sun 1800-0100. Good fun dancing to techno and salsa. Female travellers should not walk here at night. Catch a cab, especially to return.
Tsunami, seafront, next to **Maria's**. Loud reggae shakes bamboo walls draped with fairy lights and rasta flags. There's a big screen TV and movies on Mon and Wed night.

▲ Activities and tours

San Juan del Sur p1104, map p1105
Canopy tour

Da' Flying Frog, just off the road to Marsella, T2568-2351, tiguacal@ibw.com.ni, US$25. Close to San Juan del Sur with 17 platforms, great views from the canopy.

Diving

The waters around San Juan del Sur are home to a wrecked Russian trawler and sea creatures including rays, turtles and eels.
Scuba Shack, seafront, 3 c north of **Hotel Estrella**, T2568-2502. This friendly, professional PADI centre offers 1 tank dives (US$46), 2 tank dives (US$86), and Open Water certification (US$345), including equipment. Training to

assistant instructor level, technical training. Also rents out equipment, runs snorkelling tours (US$92 for 4), and surfing lessons (US$30 per hr).

Massage

Gaby's Massage Studio, mercado, ½ este, T2568-2654, estrelladeluna@hotmail.com. Professionally trained in Managua, Gaby has 7 years' experience and combines techniques from Shiatsu, reflexology and aromatherapy. US$25 for 1 hr.

Sailing
Pelican Eyes Sailing Adventures,

Parroquia 1½ c arriba, T2568-2110, sailing@ piedrasyolas.com. Sails to the beach at Brasilito, US$70 per person, min 10 people, leaves San Juan at 0900, return 1700.

Surfing

The coast north and south of San Juan del Sur is among the best in Central America for surfing. Access to the best areas are by boat or long treks in 4WD. Board rental costs US$10 per day; lessons US$30 per hr.
Arena Caliente, mercado, ½ c norte, T8815-3247, www.arenacaliente.com. Friendly surf shop with board rental, surfing lessons (with transport and rash vest) and fishing trips. Also runs transport to the beaches.
NicaSurf International, mercado, 1c al mar, ½ c sur, T2568-2626, www.nicasurfint.com. Board rental, classes, trips and tons of merchandise.
Outer Reed, mercado, 1 c al mar, ½ c norte. Specializes in supplying the right board for the right person. Tours include a 4-day odyssey to surf hard-to-reach waves in the north.
Surf and Sport, Mercado, ½ c al mar, T2402-2973. Board rental, fishing equipment, tours, lessons and transportation to the beaches.

Isla Ometepe p1106
Canopy tour

Canopy Sendero Los Monos, Playa Santo Domingo. A baby canopy tour, very much for beginners, with 4 cables and 6 platforms, US$10. Suitable for children 4 and up.

Organic farming
Bona Fide, Balgües, www.projectbonafide.com. Also known as Michael's farm, Bona Fide offers innovative courses in permaculture as well as volunteer opportunities for those wishing to learn more about the science and work of organic farming. An interesting project.

Tour operators
Ometepe Expeditions, 75 m from the port in Moyogalpa (in front of **Hotel Ometepetl**), ometepexpeditions@hotmail.com, T2664-6910. A highly reputable agency that worked with the BBC to guide a group of disabled people to the summit of Concepción. Offers a range of tours including half- and full-day hikes to the volcanoes and cloud forests. Experienced, knowledgeable and helpful. English-speaking guides include **Bermán Gómez**, T8836-8360 and **Eduardo Manzanares**, T8873-7714. Recommended.

⊖ Transport

Managua to Rivas p1102
Jinotepe
Bus For **Managua** buses leave from the terminal in the northeast corner of town, every 20 mins, US$0.55. **Nandaime** every 30 mins, US$0.35. **Diriamba–Masaya** every 20 mins.

Rivas p1102
Bus Express bus to **Managua**, every 30 mins, 0630-1700, US$2.50, 2 hrs. **Granada**, every 45 mins, 0530-1625, US$2, 1 hr 45 mins. **Jinotepe**, every 30 mins, 0540-1710, US$1, 1 hr 45 mins. **San Juan del Sur**, every 30 mins, 0600-1830, US$1, 45 mins. **Peñas Blancas**, every 30 mins, 0500-1600, US$0.75, 1 hr.

Taxi From centre of Rivas to the dock at **San Jorge**, US$1.50. Beware overcharging.

San Juan del Sur p1104, map p1105
Boat Rana Tours, kiosk opposite **Hotel Estrella** on the seafront, runs transport to the northern beaches like **Michal**, **Marsella** and

Madera, US$10 per person. They depart at 1100 and return at 1630.

Bus To **Managua**, every hr 0500-1530, 3½ hrs, US$2.50. Or take a bus/taxi to Rivas and change here. To **Rivas**, every ½ hour, 0500-1700, 40 mins, US$1. For **La Flor** or **Playa El Coco** use bus to **El Ostional**, 1600, 1700, US$ 0.70, 1½ hrs. Return from El Coco at 0600, 0730 and 1630.

For the **border**, take any bus to Rivas, get off when it hits the Pan-American Hwy (this crossing is also know as 'La Virgen'); all buses heading south from here will go to **Peñas Blancas** (every 30 mins). Taxi to the border is US$10-15.

Shuttle Several companies run shuttles to the beaches around **San Juan del Sur**, including Casa Oro Youth Hostel, Arena Caliente surf shop and Indian Face Tours. Each has at least 3 daily departures to **Las Playones**, the beach next to Maderas, US$5.

San Jorge p1105
Boat To **Ometepe**, ferry and boats, 12 daily, 0730-1830, 1 hr, US$2-3. Return journeys 0530-1600. Services are greatly reduced on Sunday, with just 3 daily ferries.

Taxi From San Jorge a road runs from the shore through Rivas to the port of San Juan del Sur.

Taxi to **Rivas**, US$1.50 (per person), beware overcharging, *colectivos* US$0.50. Direct from San Jorge to **San Juan del Sur** costs US$15. It is a lot cheaper to take a taxi to Rivas and another one from Rivas to San Juan.

Isla Ometepe p1106
Boat The lake can have very big swells. The best access route to the island is from San Jorge on the lake's southwest shore to Moyogalpa. The ferry and boat offer regular services. Cars are transported with the ferry.

From Moyogalpa to **San Jorge**, 12 daily boats and ferries, hourly 0530-1600, US$2. Reduced services on Sun, 3 ferries only.

The port of Altagracia is called San Antonio and is 2 km north of the town; pickups meet the boat that passes between Granada and San Carlos. To **San Carlos**, Mon and Thu 1800-1900, US$8, 11 hrs. To **Granada**, Tue and Fri, around 0000, US$4, 3½ hrs.

Bus Buses wait for the boats in Moyogalpa and run to **Altagracia** hourly, 0530-1830, US$1, 1 hr. To **San Ramón** 0815, US$1.25, 3 hrs. To **Mérida**, 0830, 1430, 1630US$2, 2½ hrs. To **Balgües**, 1030, 1530, US$2, 2 hrs. For **Charco Verde**, take any bus to Altagracia that uses the southern route.

Car and bike hire Toyota Rent a Car, Hotel Ometepetl, T2459-4276. A strong 4WD is a must, US$35-50 for 12 hrs, US$60 for 24 hrs. A driver can also be provided, with advance notice.

Bicycle and motorbikes are widely available from hotels. **Hacienda Mérida** has some particularly good mountain bikes. Be careful on the northern road; it's rocky and dangerous.

ⓘ Directory

Rivas p1102
Banks The plaza has 2 banks: a **Banpro** on the west side, and a **Banco Procredit** with a Visa ATM on the northwest corner. There's also a BAC ATM, plaza, 2 c oeste. **Western Union**, 1 block from the Market, Mon-Fri 0830-1600, Sat 0830-1200. **Internet** Gaby Cyber, from bus terminal 5 blocks south, ½ block east, US$1 per hr, Mon-Sat 0800-2000, Sun 0900-1900. **Telephone** Enitel is 3 blocks south of Parque Central, or 7 blocks south and 3 blocks east from bus terminal.

San Juan del Sur p1104, map p1105
Banks Banco Procredit, mercado, 1 c al mar, will change dollars. There is a single ATM in town, Visa only, Mercado, 1 c al mar, 1 c norte, ½ c al mar. Some hotels might change dollars too. **Internet** Several places in town, most charge US$1 per hr. **Language schools** Karla Cruz, Parque Central, 1½ c sur (3rd house to the right after the road turns right), T2657-1658, karlacruzsjds@yahoo.com. Private instructor who also gives classes, US$5 per hr, discount for longer periods, additional US$50 for homestay in her house, recommended. **Latin American Spanish School**, southwest corner of parque central, ½ c al mar, www.nicaspanish.org, T8820-2252. Professionally led, intensive classes, activities and homestay. **Spanish School House Rosa Silva**, mercado, 50 m al mar, T2682-2938, www.spanishsilva.com. 20 hrs of 'dynamic' classes cost US$120, student accommodation or home-stay are extra. Activities include swimming, hiking and cooking. All teachers are English-speaking. Teaching by the hr, US$7. **Spanish School San Juan del Sur**, T2568-2432, www.sjdsspanish.com. Regular morning classes, tutoring with flexible hours. **Laundry** Lavandería Gaby, mercado, ½ c arriba, around US$3 for a medium sized load. **Post office** 150 m left (south) along the seafront from the main junction.

Isla Ometepe p1106
Banks Banco Procredit, pier, 500 varas uphill, with Visa ATM and dollar changing facility. There's a Western Union attached. You can also change money (no TCs) in the 2 biggest grocery stores (1 opposite Hotel Bahía) or in hotels. Best to bring all the cash you need from Rivas. **Internet** Crushingly slow at most places; expect time-outs. Hotel Central in Altagracia, US$2 per hr. Comercial Arcia in Moyogalpa, US$2 per hr.

Río San Juan and the Solentiname Archipelago

The Río San Juan, running through deep jungles, drains Lake Nicaragua from its eastern end into the Caribbean at San Juan del Norte. Over 190 km long and with more than 17 tributaries, it runs the length of the southern border of the Indio Maíz Biological Reserve and connects Lake Nicaragua to the Atlantic Ocean. It is the best area in Nicaragua to spot wildlife. This great river has played an integral part in Nicaragua's colonial and post-colonial history and is one of the most accessible of the country's many pristine nature-viewing areas.

The department's capital, San Carlos, is perched on the shores of Lake Nicaragua, providing access to the wonderful Solentiname archipelago. These idyllic islands are home to various artistic communities, where families practise a type of primitivist art that has reached galleries in New York and Paris. The archipelago has a fascinating history, and was the subject of a famous social experiment in Utopianism. ➽ *For listings, see pages 1119-1121.*

Background

First sailed by the Spanish in 1525, the complete length of the river was navigated on 24 June 1539, the day of San Juan Bautista, hence its name. In colonial times it was a vital link between the Spanish Caribbean and the port of Granada. After three attacks by Caribbean pirates on Granada, the Spanish built a fortress at El Castillo in 1675. The English tried to take the fort twice in the 18th century, failing the first time thanks to the teenage Nicaraguan national heroine Rafaela Herrera, and then succeeding with Lord (then Captain) Nelson, who later had to withdraw owing to tropical diseases. Later it became the site of many aborted canal projects. It is still a most rewarding boat journey.

San Carlos → *See map page 1116. Colour map 1, A2. Altitude: 39 m.*

Like a ragged vulture, San Carlos is perched between several transportation arteries. It is the jumping-off point for excursions to the Islas Solentiname, along the Río Frío to Los Chiles in Costa Rica and the Río San Juan itself, with irregular launches to the river from the lakeside. It's a reasonably ugly town, but not overly offensive. Nearby are the two great nature reserves of Los Guatusos and Indio Maíz. In the wet season it is very muddy. At San Carlos there are the ruins of a fortress built for defence against pirates.

Solentiname Archipelago

On **Isla San Fernando**, many locals carve and paint balsa wood figures. The diet on the island is somewhat limited but there is lots of fresh fruit. Ask for Julio Pineda or his sister Rosa, one of the local artists. The island has a new **museum** ① *US$1*, with a variety of natural and cultural history exhibits as well as a spectacular view of the archipelago, especially at sunset; if closed ask in the village if it can be opened. Apart from at the hotel, there is no electricity on the island, so take a torch.

Isla La Venada, named for its plentiful population of *venado* (deer), is also home to artists, in particular the house of Rodolpho Arellano who lives on the south side of the island. He is one of the region's best painters and his wife, daughters and grandson all paint tropical scenes and welcome visitors to see and purchase their works. On the north side of the island is a series of semi-submerged caves with some of the best examples of petroglyphs from the pre-Columbian Guatuso tribe.

Isla El Padre is privately owned and the only island inhabited by howler monkeys. If you circle the island in a boat they can usually be spotted in the trees.

Isla Mancarrón is the largest in the chain, with the highest hill at 250 m. This is where the famous revolutionary/poet/sculptor/Catholic priest/Minister of Culture, Ernesto Cardenal, made his name by founding a school of painting, poetry and sculpture, and even decorating the local parish church in naïve art. He preached a kind of Marxist liberation theology, where the trials of Christ were likened to the trials of poor Nicaraguans. There is a monument to the Sandinista flag outside the church. Hiking is possible on the island where many parrots and *Moctezuma oropendolas* make their home. The island's hotel of the same name is part of the local folklore as its founder Alejandro Guevara was a hero of the Sandinista Revolution; his widow Nubia and her brother Peter now look after the place.

Los Guatusos Wildlife Reserve

Known as the cradle of wildlife for Lake Nicaragua, Los Guatusos is home to many exotic and varied species of bird and reptile. It is also heavily populated by monkeys, especially howlers. The reserve is crossed by three rivers, Guacalito, Zapote and Papaturro, which are popular for boat touring. It is essential to be at the park for sunrise to see the best of the wildlife. After 1030 the river often becomes busier with the immigration traffic of labourers heading to Costa Rica. A new **research centre** ① *explanations in Spanish only, US$4, ask for Armando who is an enthusiastic expert on orchids*, built by Friends of the Earth

San Carlos

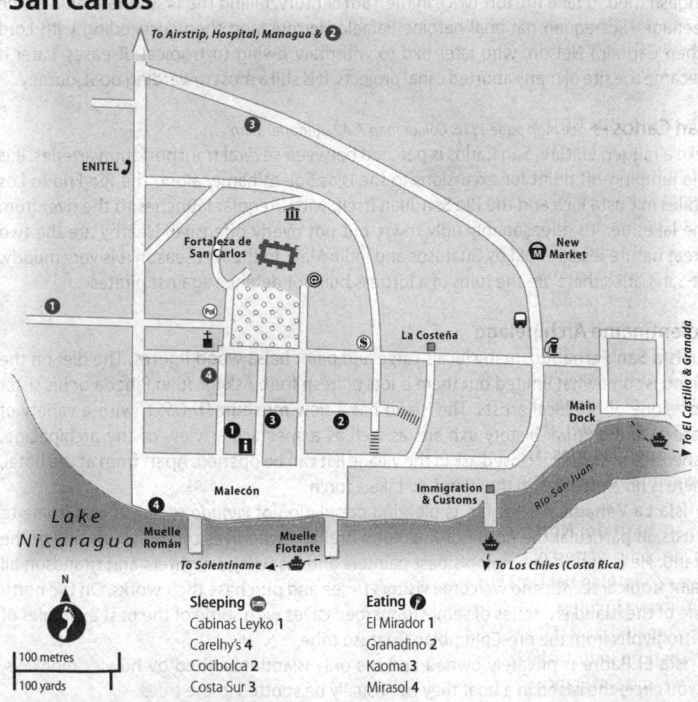

To Airstrip, Hospital, Managua & ②

ENITEL ♪

Fortaleza de
San Carlos

New Market

La Costeña

To El Castillo & Granada

Main Dock

Río San Juan

Malecón

Immigration & Customs

Lake Nicaragua

Muelle Román

Muelle Flotante

To Solentiname

To Los Chiles (Costa Rica)

N

100 metres
100 yards

Sleeping 🛏
Cabinas Leyko 1
Carelhy's 4
Cocibolca 2
Costa Sur 3

Eating 🍴
El Mirador 1
Granadino 2
Kaoma 3
Mirasol 4

and the Spanish Government, has a collection of over 90 orchids native to the region and a butterfly farm. Visitors are welcome. Lodging is also possible in the research centre. There is a public boat from San Carlos to Papaturro (Monday to Saturday 1100 and 1400, US$1, 1½ hours; check the return schedule locally).

El Castillo to the Caribbean
Some 60 km downriver is **El Castillo**, built around the restored ruins of the 18th-century Spanish fort called **La Fortaleza de la Inmaculada Concepción**. The old fort has a good history **museum** ① *closes at 1200 for lunch, US$1.50*. The **tourist office** on the quay has a leaflet about the fort and town. It was here that Nelson did battle with the Spanish forces. There are great views of the river from the fortress. The town is on a wide bend in the river where some shallow but tricky rapids run the whole width. Horse riding is possible (about US$6 per hour). El Castillo is a good place to pick up food on the river.

Reserva Biológica Indio Maíz
A few kilometres downstream is the Río Bartola and the beginning of the Reserva Biológica Indio Maíz, 3000 sq km of mostly primary rainforest and home to more than 600 species of bird, 300 species of reptile and 200 species of mammal including many big cats and howler, white-faced and spider monkeys. Sleeping is possible in **Refugio Bartola**, a research station and training ground for biologists; it has a labyrinth of well-mapped trails behind the lodge. The hotel guides are very knowledgeable. They will also take you down the Río Bartola in canoe for great wildlife viewing and birding. Neglect in recent years has made turning up without booking a bit of a gamble, so make sure you book in advance. Camping is possible; ask the park ranger (his house is across the Río Bartola from the **Refugio Bartola** lodge).

Bartola and further east
The river past **Bartola** becomes more beautiful and the Costa Rican border reaches to the south bank of the river. The Costa Rican side is partially deforested; the Nicaraguan side with the Indio Maíz Reserve is almost entirely intact. Watch out for turtles, birds and crocodiles. Two hours downriver is the **Río Sarapiquí** and immigration check-points for both Costa Rica and Nicaragua (no stamps available though).

If coming from the Río San Juan to Río Sarapiquí you will need to check in with the Costa Rican guard station if you want to spend the night, or even if you want to pick up something at the store. If continuing down the river without stopping you only need to check in at the Nicaraguan station on the Río San Juan.

Past the Sarapiquí, the San Juan branches north, and both sides of the river (heavily forested) become part of Nicaragua again as the Río Colorado heads into Costa Rica. Two hours or so later, the San Juan reaches the Caribbean via a series of magnificent forest-wrapped lagoons. The Río Indio must be taken to reach the isolated but surprisingly wealthy village of San Juan del Norte.

San Juan del Norte → *Colour map 7, A3.*
One of the wettest places on the American continent with more than 5000 mm of rain each year, San Juan del Norte (also called Santa Isabel) is also one of the most beautiful, with primary rainforest, lagoons, rivers and the Caribbean Sea. It is settled by a small population (estimated at 275), though it was once a boom town in the 19th century, when the American industrialist Cornelius Vanderbilt was running his steamship line between New York and San Francisco. Then called Greytown, San Juan del Norte was the pickup point for

Border essentials: Nicaragua–Costa Rica

San Carlos–Los Chiles

This is a frequently used crossing point between Nicaragua and Costa Rica, providing good access to and from Fortuna; it's normally quick and hassle free. There is a track of sorts from the south side of the Río San Juan, but most travellers go by boat up the Río Frío.

Nicaraguan immigration The border is now open daily 0800-1600. If travelling into Costa Rica an exit stamp must be obtained in San Carlos (US$2, Monday-Friday only). Entrance stamps into Costa Rica (US$8) are only available on arrival in Los Chiles. Check with the police for the latest information.

Transport Presently there are two launches a day from San Carlos to Los Chiles, 1000, 1600, two hours, US$9. Schedules are often subject to change, so enquire locally before setting out. You may be able to find a private boat to take you for around US$120 (eight people).

Note The Nicaragua–Costa Rica border runs along the southern bank of the Río San Juan but has been the subject of government tension and debate with regards to Costa Rica's rights to navigate the river. The Costa Rican border reaches the south banks of the Río San Juan 2 km downriver from El Castillo but the river in its length is Nicaraguan territory. It is best to travel in Nicaraguan boats on the river, as Costa Rican boats could be detained or turned back.

San Juan del Norte

This area of the Caribbean coast is a narcotics zone, with drugs being landed from San Andrés (Colombia). Before attempting to cross the border, seek information on safety.

Nicaraguan immigration There is no official immigration in San Juan del Norte. Travellers have reported being able to get stamps from the authorities here but this is not recommended. It's better to go to Bluefields or to one of the posts up the Río San Juan. Take advice on what to do on arrival in Costa Rica; the official entrance is Limón.

Transport Boats go from San Juan del Norte to Barra del Colorado in Costa Rica, but it is very expensive – ask about fishing boats and canoes.

the steamship journey to the Pacific via the Río San Juan, Lake Nicaragua to La Virgen and then by mule overland to San Juan del Sur. This service was quite popular during the 'gold rush' of San Francisco and a young Mark Twain made the crossing, later recounting his journey in the book *Travels with Mr Brown*. The town remained in its location on the Bahía San Juan del Norte, actually a coastal lagoon, until the 1980s, when fighting caused its population to flee. Re-established in its current location on the the east bank of the Río Indio, the village is separated from the Caribbean Sea by 400 m of rainforest. The population is a mix of Miskito, Creole, Rama and Hispanic. There is no land route from here to Bluefields and the boat takes about three hours, US$600. Due to its proximity to Limón, in Costa Rica, colones are the standard currency here as all the food and supplies are bought easier there than in San Carlos. In Sarapiquí and San Juan del Norte córdobas, colones and dollars are all accepted.

If in your own boat (chartered), a trip further down the **Río Indio** is recommended, with lots of wildlife, virgin forest and Rama (please respect their culture and privacy). A visit to the ruins of old **Greytown** is also interesting, with a well-marked trail that leads through various cemeteries buried in the forest and to the town centre where only foundations and the church bell remain. It has been described as 'incredibly atmospheric' with amazing wildlife and is great for birding in the morning. Note the names on some of the tombstones, which include sailors from around the world. Most of the year the entrance is underwater so rubber boots are of great use here as for the rest of the region. Swimming is best in the **Blue Lagoon**; as there are many sharks in the Caribbean. If coming on the public boat from San Carlos, Melvin can arrange tours with one of his *pangas* (expect to pay around US$15-20 for a boat).

◉ Río San Juan and the Solentiname Archipelago listings

For Sleeping and Eating price codes and other relevant information, see Essentials pages 45-48.

● Sleeping

San Carlos *p1115, map p1116*
D Cabinas Leyko, Policía Nacional, 2 c abajo, T2583-0354. The best place in town has clean, comfortable rooms with good mattresses, private bath and a/c. Cheaper with fan (**E**).
D Carelhy's Hotel, Iglesia católica, ½ c sur, T2583-0389. 10 rooms with private bath, fan and cable TV. Can help arrange tours and transport, breakfasts for large groups.
E Cocibolca, in San Miguelito north of San Carlos, at the end of the jetty, T2552-8803. Colonial style hotel with hard beds; ask for a room with a balcony. Horse riding arranged by the owner, Franklin, as well as day trips to El Boquete and El Morro Islands. The Granada–San Carlos boat stops here.
E Costa Sur, Consejo Supremo Electoral 50 m sur, T2583-0224. With 10 rooms, shared or private bath and fan, meals. Some have a/c (**C**).

Solentiname Archipelago *p1115*
It's possible to stay in basic but generally very clean private homes.
L Refugio Mancarrón, Mancarrón, up the hill from the dock and church, T2265-2716 (Managua). Includes 3 meals per day. Good spot, ideal for wildlife, hiking, with good rooms and food.
B-C Hotel Celentiname or Doña María, San Fernando, T8893-1977. This hotel has pretty grounds and owners Daniel and

María are friendly and helpful. Tiny rooms have shared bath, weak beds and no windows. The cabins have private bath and spectacular lake views. No advance booking.
D Albergue de la Comunidad de Solentiname/Doña Esperanza, Mancarrón, T2283-0083. Low-ceiling cabins in need of care, big grassy grounds, food available, library. Turn right before church and call out at the gate (¡*Buenas*!), rustic cabins with full board included, some with private bath, some with shared, owned by the famed priest Ernesto Cardenal (can be booked through his **Galería de Los Tres Mundos**, in Managua, T2278-5781).

Río Sábalo
D Hotel Sábalos, on confluence of San Juan and Sábalo rivers, T8894-9377, www.hotel sabalos.com.ni. This simple, wooden hotel has a great location, with views up and down the river, great for watching locals pass in canoes. Friendly and recommended.

Los Guatusos Wildlife Reserve *p1116*
E (per person) **Research centre**, offering bunkbeds with mosquito netting and shared bath.

El Castillo *p1117*
AL Posada del Río, 100 m north from the dock, T2616-3528. The best place in town, with very comfortable, pleasant rooms, hot water, a/c, private bath and balconies. Breakfast included.
B Hotel Victoria, north from the dock and at the end of the end road, T2583-0188, hotelvictoria01@yahoo.es. 9 rooms with fan,

private bath and hot water, 3 with a/c and 2 with shared bath (**E**), There's lots of turtles and caimans nearby, but they seem to feeding on waste from the hotel. Breakfast included.
C Albergue El Castillo, next to fortress above city dock, T2583-0195. Comfortable, if simple wooden rooms and great views from a shared balcony overlooking the river. Only 1 room has a private bath, best rooms are 1 and 10 for extra side ventilation, but noisy bats for company in 10. Good food; try the *camarones del río* (river shrimp) in garlic butter. Noisy in the early morning as the public boats warm up (0500) motors. Breakfast included.
E Universal, main dock, 50 m downriver. Friendly owners, pleasant views and small, clean, wooden rooms. A good budget choice.

Bartola and further east *p1117*
Río Sarapiquí
D Cabinas La Trinidad or **Doña Adilia's**, at confluence of Río San Juan and Río Sarapiquí on Costa Rican bank, mobile T(506) 391-7120, hurbinacom@yahoo.com. Little rooms with private bath, fan, not terribly clean, bring mosquito net. You need to check in with the Costa Rican guard station across from the lodge on the Río Sarapiquí.

Bahía de San Juan
LL Rio Indio Lodge, between Indio river and Río San Juan, near San Juan del Norte, T(506) 296-0095, www.rioindiolodge.com. Multi-million dollar lodge, designed for upscale fishing packages but excellent for wildlife safaris, birdwatching and rainforest walks. Nicaragua's finest rainforest jungle lodge, recently named one of the top 10 jungle lodges in the world.

San Juan del Norte *p1117*
E Hotel Lost Paradise or **Melvin's Place**, on the river at the south end of town. Ceiling fan, private bath, screened windows but bring coils or mosquito netting. Bar, restaurant (order well in advance), night-time generated power, gazebo on the river, bottled water is sometimes for sale, becoming neglected.

❷ Eating

San Carlos *p1115, map p1116*
†⊣ Granadino, opposite Alejandro Granja playing field, T2583-0386. Daily 0900-0200. Considered the best in town, with a relaxed ambience, good murals, pleasant river views, *Camarones en salsa*, steak and hamburgers.
†⊣ Kaoma, across from Western Union, T2583-0293. Daily from 0900 until the last customer collapses in a pool of rum. Funky place, decorated with dozens of oropendula nests, attracts a hard-drinking, friendly clientele.
† El Mirador, Iglesia católica, 1½ c sur, T2583-0377. Daily 0700-2000. Superb view from patio of Lake Nicaragua, Solentiname, Río Frío and Río San Juan and the jumbled roofs of the city. Decent chicken, fish and beef dishes starting at US$3 with friendly service.
† Mirasol, next to the Roman lake dock where the river meets the lake. Good grilled meats and decent salads, fried chicken, good place to sit in the daytime to watch life on the river and lake with nice views, ruthless mosquitoes in the evening.

El Castillo *p1117*
† Bar Cofalito, on the jetty. Good view and even better *camarones de río* considered by many the best in town, occasional fresh fish. Owner has river kayaks and can organize expeditions on the Río San Juan, rents motorboat (US$10 per hr) for tarpon and snook fishing.
† Vanessa's, north of the dock. Great spot by the rapids, with excellent fish and *camarones del río* .

San Juan del Norte *p1117*
Simple food, fresh lobster if in season, if not the fried snook is recommended. There is a pleasant bar upriver from **Doña Ester's Place** with a big palm ranch and cold beer, card-playing locals and friendly Rama. It can be hard to find someone in San Juan to cook a meal, so bring snacks and arrange meals at **Doña Ester's** or **Melvin's Place** in advance.

🎭 Entertainment

San Juan del Norte p1117
Bars and clubs
There is a disco which is full of festive locals at weekends dancing to reggae, salsa, rap and merengue. If staying at Melvin's Place he will take you to the disco to make sure you have a good time and get home safely. It's a short walk but a ride in his *super-panga*, if offered, is not to be missed. There are no police in San Juan and while the locals are very honest, be aware that this is border country and care should be taken, particularly at night.

🚌 Transport

San Carlos p1115, map p1116
Air To Managua, La Costeña, 0925, 1425, US$120 return (see Managua for outgoing schedules). Sit on the left for the best views. There is a maximum weight for flights – you will be asked your body weight. Flights land and take off within 5 mins, so early arrival is advised. Taxi from airstrip to dock US$1.

Boat *Pangas* are small motor boats; *botes*, long, narrow ones; *planos*, big broad ones. All schedules are subject to change, check locally before planning a journey. To **Granada**, Tue and Fri, 1400, 15 hrs, US$7. Bring a hammock and expect an exhausting journey. To **Solentiname Archipelago**, stopping at islands La Venada, San Fernando and Mancarrón, Tue and Fri 1200, 2½ hrs, US$4. To **Los Guatuzos Wildlife Refuge**, stopping at village of Papaturro, Tue, Wed, Thu, 0700, 5½ hrs, US$5. To **El Castillo** (and Sábalos), 0800, 1100 (express), 1300 (slow boat), 1430, 1530, 1630, 1½ (express) – 2½ hrs, US$4, US$5 (express), US$2 (slow boat), reduced services on Sun when only first 2 boats run. Avoid the slow boat if you can, it's a gruelling 6-hr ride. To **Los Chiles (Costa Rica)**, 1000, 1600, 2 hrs, US$8. To **San Juan del Norte**, Tue, Fri, 0600, 8 hrs, US$15.

Private boats are expensive but are faster. Ask at docks, restaurants, taxi drivers or at tourism office. Average round-trip rates: **El Castillo** US$190-250, **Solentiname** US$100-150. Group tours are available from tour operators in Managua.

Bus Managua to San Carlos is a brutal ride, but locals prefer it to the ferry trip. There are some lovely views during the early part and pure pain in the kidneys at the end. To **Managua**, daily 0200, 0600, 0800 and 1100, 9½ hrs, US$7. Returning from Mercado El Mayoreo at 0500, 0600, 0700 and 1300.

Solentiname Archipelago p1115
Boat Private transfers from San Carlos to **Solentiname** 1-1½ hr, US$55-85 per boat. Public boat to **San Carlos**, Tue and Fri, 0430, 2-3 hrs, US$4.

El Castillo p1117
To **San Carlos**: 0500 (slow boat), 0520 (express), 0600, 0700, 1100 (express), 1400, 1½-2½ hrs, US$2.75, US$3.75 (express), US$2 (slow boat), reduced services on Sun when only first 2 boats run. Avoid the slow boat if you can, reduced services on Sun. To **San Juan del Norte**, Tue, Fri, 0930, 5 hrs, US$10.

San Juan del Norte p1117
To **San Carlos**, stopping at El Castillo, Thu and Sun, 0430, US$15. There's little chance of connecting with Bluefields, north on the Caribbean coast, unless you have lots of patience, cash and a strong, sea-faring stomach. You might hitch a ride on a fishing boat if you're lucky, otherwise expect a challenging trip.

📖 Directory

San Carlos p1115, map p1116
Banks BDF, next to dock for Solentiname. No exchange for TCs and you can only change cash with street changers. Bring all the cash you need, as there's no ATM for miles.

The Caribbean Coast lowlands

Colour map 7, A3.

Nicaragua's eastern tropical lowlands make for a striking change from the rest of the country. Gone are the volcanoes, hills and valleys, and in their place is lush, tropical rainforest drenched between May and December with heavy rainfall. Most of the population are the African-influenced Miskito people who live in the northern lowlands, mainly around Puerto Cabezas. Their economy is based on timber, fishing and mining. To reach the Caribbean port of Bluefields and the idyllic and peaceful Corn Islands, you can fly or take the famous 'Bluefields Express' downriver. English is widely but not universally spoken. » *For listings, see pages 1125-1130.*

Background

This area, together with roughly half the coastal area of Honduras, was never colonized by Spain. From 1687 to 1894 it was a British Protectorate known as the Miskito Kingdom. It was populated then, as now, by the Miskito, whose numbers are estimated at 75,000. There are two other indigenous groups, the Sumu (5000) and the Rama, of whom only a few hundred remain, near Bluefields. Also near Bluefields are a number of Garífuna communities. Today's strong African influence has its roots in the black labourers brought in by the British to work the plantations and in Jamaican immigration. The Afro-Nicaraguan people call themselves *criollos* (Creoles). The largest number of inhabitants of this region are Spanish-speaking *mestizos*. The Sandinista Revolution, like most other political developments from the Spanish-speaking part of Nicaragua, was met with mistrust. Although the first Sandinista junta recognized the indigenous peoples' rights to organize themselves and choose their own leaders, many of the programmes failed to encompass their social, agricultural and cultural traditions. Relations deteriorated and many engaged in fighting for self-determination. A low point was reached when the Sandinista Government ordered forced resettlement of many Miskito villages, burning to the ground what was left behind. About half the Miskito population fled as refugees to Honduras, but most returned after 1985 when a greater understanding grew between the Sandinista Government and the people of the east coast. The Autonomous Atlantic Region was given the self-governing status in 1987; it is divided into Región Autonomista Atlántico Norte (RAAN) and Región Autonomista Atlántico Sur (RAAS). In Nicaragua, the Caribbean coast is almost always referred to as the Atlantic coast.

Managua to Rama ⊖❷❷❸ » *pp1125-1130.*

At **San Benito**, 35 km from Managua on the Pan-American Highway going north, the Atlantic Highway branches east, paved all the way to Rama on the Río Escondido. Shortly after Teustepe, a paved road goes northeast to Boaco. A turn-off, unpaved, goes to **Santa Lucía**, a village inside a crater, with a women's handicraft shop. There is also a cooperative here with an organic farming programme (information from **Unag** in Matagalpa). **Boaco** (84 km from Managua) is called the city of two floors because of its split-level nature. The upper floor has a nice square with good views of the countryside.

Juigalpa → *Colour map 7, A2. Population: 41,000.*

The Atlantic Highway continues through Juigalpa, a pleasant town with one of the best museums in Nicaragua, **Museo Gregorio Aguilar Barea** ① *Mon-Fri, US$0.25, T8812-0784,* housing a collection of idols resembling those at San Agustín, Colombia. The bus terminal is in the town centre near the market, up the hill. Banks accept dollars in cash only.

Rama

The main road continues east to **Santo Tomás** and smaller villages (including La Gateada, connected by air from Managua via San Carlos on Friday with **La Costeña**, T2285-0160), then to **Cara de Mono**, on the Río Mico, and finally to **Rama**, 290 km from Managua. From Rama, you can take a boat to Bluefields or the daily bus to Pearl Lagoon. This is on a new road, and is an alternative way to travel to the coast. From Pearl Lagoon, *pangas* sail to Bluefields.

Bluefields ●❶❷❸❶ ➤ *pp1125-1130. Colour map 7, A3.*

➔ *Population: 42,665.*

Dirty, chaotic yet curiously inviting, Bluefields, the most important of Nicaragua's three Caribbean ports, gets its name from the Dutch pirate Abraham Blaauwveld. It stands on a lagoon behind the bluff at the mouth of the Bluefields River (Río Escondido), which is navigable as far as Rama (96 km). In May there is a week-long local festival, **Mayo-Ya!** with elements of the British maypole tradition, local music, poetry and dancing. The local **Fiesta de San Jerónimo** is on 30 September. Tourist information is available from **INTUR** ① *opposite Salón Siu, T2572-0221*. There are bars, a couple of reggae clubs, *comedores*, restaurants and an **Almacén Internacional**. Prices are about the same as in Managua. Be prepared for frequent power and water cuts.

Laguna de Perlas

The lagoon itself is some 50 km long with mostly Creole villages round its shores, such as Pearl Lagoon, Haulover, Brown Bank, Marshall Point and San Vicente. **La Fe** and **Orinoco** are Garífuna (of African descent) villages, while **Raitipura** and **Kakabila** are indigenous villages. In Raitipura there is a Danish housing project, run by Mogens Vibe who takes on volunteers for a minimum of one week (recommended). Within walking distance is the swimming beach of **Awas** (basic accommodation). Larger vessels may be available for transport to Puerto Cabezas, but there is no transport south of Bluefields.

Outlying areas of the Región Autonomista Atlántico Sur

The **Río Kurinwás** area north of Bluefields is a fascinating, largely uninhabited jungle area, where it is possible to see monkeys. It might occasionally be possible to get a boat to **Tortuguero** (also called Nuevo Amanecer) a *mestizo* town that will really give you a taste of the frontier. Tortuguero is about a six-hour speedboat ride from Bluefields up the Kurinwás River; several days by regular boat. The **Río Grande** is the next river north of the Kurinwás, connected to the Pearl Lagoon by the Top-Lock Canal. At its mouth are five interesting villages: the four Miskito communities of **Kara**, **Karawala**, **Sandy Bay Sirpi** and **Walpa**, and the Creole village of **La Barra**. Sandy Bay Sirpi is situated on both the river and the Caribbean and has a pleasant beach.

Travelling upriver, the Río Grande is noticeably more settled than the Río Kurinwás. After some distance (about a six hour speedboat ride from Bluefields, several days by regular boat), you reach the *mestizo* town of **La Cruz de Río Grande**. It was founded in about 1922 by Chinese traders to serve workers from a banana plantation (now disused) further upriver. La Cruz has a very pretty church. The adventurous can walk between La Cruz and Tortuguero; it takes about 10 hours each way in the dry season, 12 hours in the rainy season.

The Corn Islands are two small islands fringed with white coral and slender coconut trees, perfect for relaxation. **Little Corn**, the smaller of the two and far more idyllic, escaped serious damage in the 1988 hurricane and can be visited by boat from the larger island, **Big Corn**, a one-hour ride by *panga*. On Little Corn Island there is no electricity and no phones, just pristine white-sand beaches and some of the Caribbean's finest undisturbed coral reefs. Big Corn is a popular Nicaraguan holiday resort (the best months are March and April). The nicest beaches on Big Corn are on **Long Bay** (walk across the island from Playa Coco)and **Brig Bay**, by the dock.

If you climb the mountain, wear long trousers as there are many ticks. On Little Corn you can climb the lighthouse for fantastic views of the whole island (not recommended if you are uncomfortable with heights). The language of the islands is English. The islanders are very friendly but petty thievery has been reported. Be wary of touts who greet you at the airport, posing as impartial guides; they may charge you for their services. Make sure you take enough money with you to the island as credit cards are not accepted and everything is more expensive than on the mainland; dollars are widely used.

Northeast Nicaragua ⊜❷▲⊜❻ ➤ pp1125-1130.

Puerto Cabezas → *Colour map 6, B6. Population: 50,941.*
Puerto Cabezas, capital of the Región Autonomista Atlántico Norte, has a distinctly different atmosphere from Bluefields. It is principally a large Miskito village and offers an excellent introduction to the Miskito area. You can arrange to stay in small Miskito villages, for example near Haulover, a few hours by boat south of Puerto Cabezas. There are significant minorities of *mestizos* (referred to on the coast as *españoles* or the Spanish) and Creoles, many of whom came to 'Port' by way of Las Minas. Spanish is a second language for the majority of residents; many speak at least some English, and for some, English is their native language. The local name for Puerto Cabezas is **Bilwi**, although the name is of Sumo origin. The Miskitos conquered the Sumos to obtain the town some time in the last century. There are two main roads, the only paved streets, which run parallel to each other and to the sea. At the southern end of the town is the port area; a walk along the pier at sunset is highly recommended. The airport is at the northern end. The main market occupies the central part of town.

Waspám and the Río Coco → *Population: 38,701.*
The Coco River (called *Waspán* in Spanish and *Wanghi* in Miskito) is the heart of Miskito country. There is a road from Puerto to Waspám; during the dry season the 130-km trip should take about three hours by 4WD vehicle, several hours longer by public bus (leaves Puerto at 0700, Monday to Saturday and, with luck, returns from Waspám at 1200). The bus can be boarded at several points in Puerto along the road out of town, US$5 to Waspám. The trip takes you through the pine forests, red earth, and north of Puerto towards the Coco River (the border with Honduras), and you will pass through two Miskito villages, **Sisin** and **Santa Marta**. Hitching is possible; if you cannot get all the way to Waspám, make sure you are left at Sisin, Santa Marta or La Tranquera. You can take lifts from the military; never travel at night.

Parque Nacional Saslaya → *Colour map 6, B4.*

Saslaya was the first national park in Nicaragua, located within the Reserva Biósfera Bosawás, and contains the largest tropical cloud forest in Central America. The Proyecto Ecoturístico Rosa Grande, supported by Nature Conservancy and the Peace Corps involves the community of **Rosa Grande**, 25 km from Siuna, near an area of virgin forest with a trail, waterfall on the River Labú and lots of wildlife including monkeys and large cats. One path leads to a lookout with a view over the **Cerro Saslaya**; another circular path to the northwest goes to **Rancho Alegre Falls**. Guides can be hired for US$7 a day plus food. Excursions cost US$13 per person for guide, food and camping equipment. You may have to pay for a camp guard while hiking. Tourism is in its infancy here and you may find little things 'added on' to your bill. Be certain you have enough supplies for your stay. Contact Don Trinidad at the *comedor* in Santa Rosa. In Siuna, contact **Proyecto Bosawás** ① *200 m east of airstrip; Mon-Fri 0800-1700*. Groups of five or more must reserve in advance; contact the **Amigos de Saslaya** ① *c/o Proyecto Bosawás, Siuna, RAAN*, by post or telegram.

● The Caribbean Coast lowlands listings

For Sleeping and Eating price codes and other relevant information, see Essentials pages 45-48.

● Sleeping

Managua to Rama *p1122*

E Boaco, Boaco, on the 1st level, opposite Cooperativa San Carlos, T8842-2434. Small beds, private and shared baths, friendly owners who include one of the country's finest archaeologists, Edgar Espinoza, the current director of the Museo Nacional de Nicaragua. It may be possible at the weekend to convince Edgar to guide you to hidden petroglyph sites in the hills; call ahead.

F Casa de Soya, Santa Lucía. Good food, friendly owners, single room for rent, basic. Good views from nearby mountains.

F Sobalvarro, Boaco, on the square. Simple and clean.

Juigalpa *p1122*

D La Quinta, on main road at the east end of town. Rooms with a/c or fan, bath, clean, friendly, restaurant has good food and a fine view of surrounding mountains.

E-F Rubio, on main north road. Clean, friendly, with bath (cheaper without), TV, laundry.

Bluefields *p1123*

Most hotels in Bluefields are quite basic and run-down.

AL Hotel Oasis, 150 m from Bluefields Bay, T2572-2812, www.oasiscasinohotel.com. The best hotel in town, with spacious modern rooms, comfortable furnishings and professional service. There's a casino downstairs with a handful of gaming tables, should you fancy a low-key punt. Breakfast included.

B Bluefields Bay Hotel, Barrio Pointeen, T2572-2838. Owned by the region's university, this hotel has clean, simple rooms with private bath and hot water. The rooms upstairs are better and less damp. Excursions are offered to surrounding areas.

C Caribbean Dreams, Barrio Punta Fría, opposite market, T2572-1943. With 27 rooms, private bath, a/c or fan and cable TV. Services include a restaurant with home-cooking and à la carte menu, Wi-Fi and laundry. Clean and often booked, call ahead. Helpful owners.

C Mini Hotel Central, Barrio Punta Fría, T2572-2362. Has 9 simple rooms with private bath, a/c, TV. Cheaper with fan (**D**).

C South Atlantic II, Barrio Central, next to petrol station Levy, T2572-2265. Clean rooms with fair mattresses, private bath, cable TV and a/c. The double rooms (**A**) are much

, more comfortable and more ...nsive. There's a sports bar and restaurant upstairs serving Caribbean dishes like 'rundown soup'. Friendly.

D El Aeropuerto, airport, ½ c norte, T2572-2862. Clean, 13 rooms with private bath, a/c, some with fan, also has restaurant and disco. Grouchy owner.

D Los Pipitos, Punta Fría, 50 m from Caribbean Dreams (above). 4 rooms with private bath and a/c, cheaper with fan (**E**), simple but good; bakery on premises.

D Marda Maus, Barrio Central, T2572-2429. Rooms are simple, smallish and clean. Not bad for a budget choice, but view the room before accepting it.

E El Dorado, Barrio Punta Fría, T2572-2365. Small, grotty rooms, but most have cable TV and private bath. Sketchy atmosphere, but the price is right.

E Hotel Costa Sur, Barrio Central, across from Lotería, T2572-2452. Lots of rooms, all with shared bath and fans. Bar and restaurant attached.

E Hotel Kaora View, Entrada a Las Carmelitas, ½ c norte, Barrio Teodoro Martínez, T2572-0488. 10 rooms with 1 shared bath, very clean, friendly, good service.

F Hospedaje Pearl Lagoon, Barrio Central, across from UNAG, T2572-2411. Basic, 9 rooms, not terribly pleasant, most with shared bath. Not very helpful.

Laguna de Perlas *p1123*

D Casa Blanca, in May 4 sector, T2572-0508, casa_blanca_lp@yahoo.com. The best hotel in town, with clean, light, comfortable rooms; all but 1 have shared bath. The owners are very hospitable and friendly, and offer fishing expeditions, trips to the keys and community tours. They're happy to answer questions by email, and prefer reservations in advance. Good restaurant attached. Recommended.

E Green Lodge, next to Enitel, from dock, 1 c sur, T2572-0507. This basic, homely and friendly hotel has 8 tiny, narrow rooms with shared bath, The owner, Wesley, is very knowledgeable about the area, has good

contacts and can help arrange tours. They cook cheap grub too.

Islas de Maíz/Corn Islands *p1124*
Big Corn

AL Casa Canada, South End, T2644-0925, www.casa-canada.com. Sophisticated, luxurious rooms with ocean views. Each is splendidly equipped with a DVD player, minibar, coffee-maker, leather chairs and mahogany furniture. A beautiful infinity pool overlooks the waves. Friendly and hospitable management. Recommended, if you can afford it.

A Hotel Paraíso, Brig Bay, T2575-5111, www.paraisoclub.com. A professional, friendly hotel, managed by 2 Dutch gentlemen who contribute to local social projects. They offer a range of clean, comfortable *cabañas*, all with hammocks and mosquito nets. It's right on the beach, and there's good snorkelling at the wreck off-shore.

A Princesa de la Isla, Waula Point, T8854-2403, www.laprincesadelaisla.com. The Princess has seen better days, but her setting on a windswept point is eternally romantic. The bungalow – normally reserved for honeymooners – is much better than the rooms, with lots of character and unique furnishings.

B Anastasia's, North End, T2425-9589. Located by the best snorkelling reef on the island, this hotel offers a marine park with 'snorkel trails'. There's a restaurant on stilts, and all rooms have private bath, cable TV and a/c.

B Picnic Centre, Picnic Centre Beach, T2575-5204. Great location, 8 average rooms with private bath, some with a/c. There's a very popular mid-priced ranch on the beach for eating and drinking, and worth a visit if sleeping elsewhere. Good ambience.

C Panorama, Iglesia católica, ½ c al este, T2575-5065. Motel-style place by the beach offering simple, economical rooms with mosquito nets. Cheaper without a/c (**D**).

D Silver Sand, Sally Peaches, south of rocky point, T2575-5005. Managed by the enigmatic Ira Gómez, who alone is worth a visit. Rustic fishermen's cabins in a gorgeous, secluded setting. Ira can organize fishing trips, and cook up the catch in his bar-restaurant on the beach. Look out for the happy neighbours playing reggae through their enormous speakers.

Little Corn

AL-B Casa Iguana, on southeastern bluff, www.casaiguana.net. This is a famous, popular lodging, beautifully located with stunning views of the beaches. It has 4 *cabañas* with shared bath (**B**), 9 *casitas* with private bath (**A**), and 1 'luxury' *casita* (**AL**). Food is grown in the lush, attractive gardens, great breakfasts, sociable dining and an expensive internet café (US$10 per hr). An impressive outfit, even if it is a bit of a gringo summer camp. Book in advance, especially in high season.

B Ensueños, Otto Beach, www.ensuenos-littlecornisland.com. Trippy, rustic cabins with sculpted *Lord of the Rings*-style interiors; some have electricity, some don't (**C**). The grounds are wonderfully lush and filled with exuberant fruit trees, and naturalist owner Ramón Gil is an interesting and friendly host. There's comfortable houses too (**A**), and meals are available. Recommended.

B Los Delfines, in the village just south of the boat landing, T8820-2242, www.hotellos delfines.com.ni. Little Corn's most upmarket hotel, popular with Colombian businessmen. The rooms are average for the price, comfortable, clean with a/c. Hot water is sporadic. The restaurant has nice views, but service is annoyingly slack. Ask about deals if studying at the adjoining dive shop.

C Derek's, at northernmost point of east coast, T2419-0600, www.dereksplace littlecorn.com. Southeast Asian-style cabins on stilts, all equipped with renewable energy, mosquito nets, orthopaedic mattresses and hammocks. It's a tranquil, social spot, and the cabins are very clean in spite of the backpacker clientele. Meals, snorkelling gear and bicycle rental available to guests.

C-E Sunrise Paradise, on the east coast just north of **Grace's**. Also known as Carlito's, and managed by the head of informal security, who is a real gentleman. It offers a range of simple cabins all with fan and electricity. There's also food, beer and hammocks, and the grounds are pleasant.

Puerto Cabezas *p1124*

B Liwa-Mairin, enitel, 2c este, 20 varas norte, T2792-2315. The best in town. This hotel has great big, airy double rooms with lots of light, balconies, sea views, a/c, cable TV and tasteful, comfortable furnishings. Good value and recommended.

C Miss Judy's, next to Centro de Computación Ansell, T2792-2225. Also known as Casa Museo, this lovely house has lots of interesting art and artefacts in the attached museum and gallery. Rooms have private bath, cheaper with fan (**D**). Friendly and interesting, with lots of family history. Recommended.

D Hospedaje Bilwi, in front of pier. Tucked away from the paved road, this large, basic hotel has 19 rooms, some with fan, some with a/c. Good view of the dock from the back balcony. There's a seafood restaurant downstairs.

Parque Nacional Saslaya *p1125*

E Chino, Siuna. The best and most expensive place in town.

F Bosawás Field Station, on the river Labú. Has hammocks but not many, clean but simple, locally produced and cooked food about US$1.25.

F Costeño, Siuna,100 m east of airstrip. Basic.

⊘ Eating

Managua to Rama *p1122*

Boaco is cattle country and there are many good places to enjoy a local steak.
⑪ La Casona, Boaco, next to Texaco, T8842-2421. Daily 0800-2300. Try their *lomo de costilla* or *plato típico*.

Cueva, Boaco, south side of the ?quia Santiago church, T8842-2438. ?ery good steaks.

Bluefields *p1123*
⊪ **Bay View Restaurant**, next to Tía Irene. Beautiful spot on the water to watch the world go by with a drink, popular.

⊪ **Restaurant Flotante**, built over the water at the end of the main street. Average prices, slow service, great view.

Islas de Maíz/Corn Islands *p1124*
Steer clear of baby lobsters as the harvesting threatens the local population.

Big Corn
Ask around for where meals are available; the restaurants serve mainly chicken and chop suey, but in private houses you can find much better fare. Try fresh coconut bread (from family stores), banana porridge and sorrel drink (red, and ginger-flavoured). The main market area is near **Will Bowers Wharf** and is a cheap place to eat.

⊪-⊪ **Fisherman's Cave**, next to the dock. This great little seafood restaurant overlooks the water and fishing boats. A relaxing spot. Check out the pools filled with live fish.

⊪-⊪ **Nautilus Dive Centre**, North Point, T2575-5077. Fabulously eclectic menu with Caribbean curry and classic dishes like rundown soup, containing vegetables, coconut milk and seafood.

⊪-⊪ **Seva's Place**, 500 m east of Anastasia's in Sally Peaches, T2575-5058. Quite possibly the island's best restaurant. They serve great seafood, meat and chicken from a fine location with rooftop seats and ocean views. Try the lobster *a la plancha*.

Little Corn
See hotels for most of the eating options.

⊪ **Habana Libre**, just north of boat landing, T8848-5412. Really tasty, flavourful dishes including succulent veal, fish and lobster served with interesting sauces. There's terraced seating, good music and amiable

staff. Cuban specialities are available on request and in advance. Be sure to try a mojito – they're outstanding.

⊪ **Miss Bridgette's**, in the village, north of the dock. A lovely little comedor serving wholesome, home-cooked fare. Service is very Caribbean, so bring a book for the wait.

Puerto Cabezas *p1124*
⊪-⊪ **Crisfa**, enitel, 2½ c sur, 1 c oeste. Tasty *comida típica*, meat, seafood and chicken dishes. Not bad, one of the better ones.

⊪-⊪ **Kabu Payaska**, hospital, 200 varas al mar. Often recommended by the locals, this restaurant overlooking the water serves some of the best seafood and *comida típica* in town.

Parque Nacional Saslaya *p1125*
⊪ **Comedor Jassy**, La Rosita, near the entrance of town on the Siuna side. Recommended.

⊪ **Comedor Melania**, Rosa Grande. A meal costs about US$1.

⊪ **Comedor Siuna**, opposite **Hotel Costeño**, Siuna, has good *comida corriente*.

⊪ **Desnuque**, Siuna. There are 2 *comedores* Desnuque, 1 in the market and the other on a hill near the baseball stadium and airstrip; the latter has good pizza as well as typical Nicaraguan food. Recommended.

▲▲ Activities and tours

Islas de Maíz/Corn Islands *p1124*
Big Corn
Diving **Nautilus Resort & Dive Nautilus**, North Point, T2575-5077, www.divebigcorn.com. Diving and snorkelling trips with Guatemalan NASE certified training instructor include trips to see the cannon of the old Spanish Galleon, blowing rock, PADI certification from US$275, night dives 2 tank dives from US$60-90 per person, snorkelling trips and glass-bottom boat tours at US$15 per person.

Fishing **Ira Gómez**, Silver Sands hostel, Sally Peaches, south of rocky point,

T2575-5005. One of those irresistible local characters, Ira is an enthusiastic fisherman. He can organize fishing trips to suit you.

Little Corn
Diving **Dive Little Corn**, boat landing in village, T8823-1154, www.divelittlecorn.com. There's a strong **PADI** ethos at this 5-star, gold palm centre, with training right up to assistant instructor level. Open Water training costs US$320 including equipment, and packages can combine with **Casa Iguana** stays.
Dolphin Dive, in the village, south of the dock, T2690-0225, www.dolphindivelittlecorn.com. Operated by islander Sandy Herman, a passionate and friendly instructor with many years diving experience. She offers **PADI** instruction to dive master level. Packages are available, including discounts at **Delphines**. Groups are kept small. Recommended.

Puerto Cabezas p1124
Cultural and community tourism
AMICA, supermarket Monter, 2½ c sur, T2792-2219. This women's organization can arrange tours and transportation to communities around Bilwi. The all-inclusive packages are expensive for individuals, so it's best to organize a group. They can also provide contacts and lodgings if you want to arrange your own transport.

⊖ Transport

Managua to Rama p1122
Bus 2 trucks a day to **Santa Lucía** from Boaco, US$1, 1 bus a day to/from **Managua**.
From Boaco, unpaved roads go north to **Muy Muy** and **Matagalpa**, and south to **Comoapa**. **Managua**–Boaco goes every 40 mins from Plaza Mayoreo (2 hrs 10 mins, US$1.50).

Juigalpa p1122
Bus Every 15 mins from **Managua**, US$2.50, 3 hrs.

Rama p1123
Bus From Managua, buses leave for Rama from the Mercado Mayoreo every hour, 0400-1130, 8 hrs, US$7. To **Managua**, hourly 0400-1130. To/from **Juigalpa**, hourly 0800-1500, 6 hrs, US$3.75. To **Pearl Lagoon**, 1600, 3 hrs, US$7.50; from Pearl Lagoon to Rama, 0600.

Boat To **Bluefields**, pangas depart when full, several daily, 0530-1600, US$10, 2 hrs. The ferry is slightly cheaper and much slower. It departs Mon, Wed and Fri in the early morning (around 0800 when the bus has arrived), US$8, 5-8 hrs.

Bluefields p1123
Air The airport is 3 km south of the city centre, either walk (30 mins) or take a taxi US$2. La Costeña office, T2572-2500; also on Managua and the Corn Islands route with similar times and costs is **Atlantic Airlines** T2572-1299.
La Costeña to **Managua**, daily 0710, 0840, 1120, 1610, US$128 return, 1 hr. To **Corn Islands**, daily 0740, 1510, US$98 return, 20 mins. To **Bilwi**, daily except Sun 1210, US$148 return, 1 hr.

Boat *Pangas* depart when full. The early ones are more reliable, and services on Sun are restricted. To **Pearl Lagoon**, from 0830, several daily, US$6, 1½ hrs, continues to **Tasbapauni**, US$12, 2½ hrs. To **El Rama**, 0530-1600, several daily, US$10, 2 hrs. To **Corn Islands**, ferry, 0900, every Wed, US$12, 5-6 hrs; cargo ferry, Sun, 0600.

Islas de Maíz/Corn Islands p1124
Air La Costeña flies from Big Corn to **Managua** with a stop in **Bluefields**, daily at 0810 and 15400, US$165 round trip, 90 mins with stop. Re-confirm seats before travelling. La Costeña airline office is on Big Corn, T2575-5131.

Boat

Inter-island boats Big Corn to Little Corn, daily 1000, 1630, US$6.50, 40 mins. Little Corn to Big Corn, daily 0700, 1400, US$6.50, 40 mins. Boats leave from main dock, first come, first served. US$0.20 charge to get into the dock area. Buy big blue trash bags to keep luggage dry at shop across from dock entrance, best to sit near the back.

Mainland boats Subject to change, check locally; Corn Islands to **Bluefields** leaves Tue, 0900, US$12, 5-6 hrs; and Fri and Sun 1200. To **Bilwi**, daytime departure, once per month, US$30, 3 days.

Bus Buses and *colectivos* travel clockwise and anti-clockwise round Big Corn. US$0.70 per person regardless of distance all day.

Puerto Cabezas *p1124*

Air The airstrip is 3 km from the town. Taxis will charge US$1 to any point in Puerto (it is also possible to walk).

La Costeña (T2792-2282) flies daily to **Managua**, 0820, 1220, 1610, 1½ hrs, US$148 return, in small 12-seater planes. To **Bluefields**, 1110, 1 hr, US$148 return. There are also daily flights via **Bonanza**, **Siuna** and **Rosita**. Frequent cancellations so it's best to make reservation and pay just before plane leaves. Bring your passport: there are 'immigration' checks by the police in Puerto, and sometimes in the waiting lounge in Managua; also, there is a customs check when returning from the coast by air to Managua.

Bus Public bus service is available between Puerto and **Waspám** and from **Matagalpa** (14 hrs). Furthermore, Puerto is connected by road to **Managua**; however, this 559-km trip should only be attempted in the dry season (early Jan to mid-May) in a 4WD

vehicle. With luck, it will take only 2-3 days (the road, almost all of it unpaved, is not bad from Managua to Siuna, but becomes very difficult after that); do not drive at night. If you drive back from Puerto to Managua, take the road out of town and turn left at the sign, SW Wawa.

Car It is not possible to rent a vehicle or bicycle in Puerto, but arrangements for a car and driver can be made (ask a taxi or at your *hospedaje*).

Parque Nacional Saslaya *p1125*

Air La Costeña flies daily to **Siuna**, reservations in Siuna, T2263-2142.

Bus Daily from Siuna market to the park at 0500 and 0730, sometimes at 1100, US$2.25.

Car There are 2 road links from **Managua**: 1 through Matagalpa and Waslala; the other through Boaco, Muy Muy, Matiguás and Río Blanco, a very scenic 330-km drive, about 7 hrs by 4WD in the dry season; check on the security situation before starting out.

La Rosita is 70 km east of Siuna, and it is also possible to drive on through to **Puerto Cabezas**, although the road is in poor shape.

❶ Directory

Bluefields *p1123*

Banks There are banks for money-changing, no ATMs, bring all the cash you need when visitng the Carribbean coast. Possibility of a Visa advance if stuck.

Puerto Cabezas *p1124*

Banks There is **Banpro** for changing dollars, no ATMs. Bring all the cash you need.
Hospital On the outskirts of town.

Contents

Border crossings

Costa Rica–Nicaragua,
see pages 1185, 1204 and 1267
Costa Rica–Panama,
see pages 1247 and 1266

At a glance

◉ **Getting around** Mostly by bus; boats to Tortuguero and Bahía Drake.

◉ **Time required** Ideally 4-5 weeks.

☽ **Weather** Dec-Apr is best.

✕ **When not to go** Wet season.

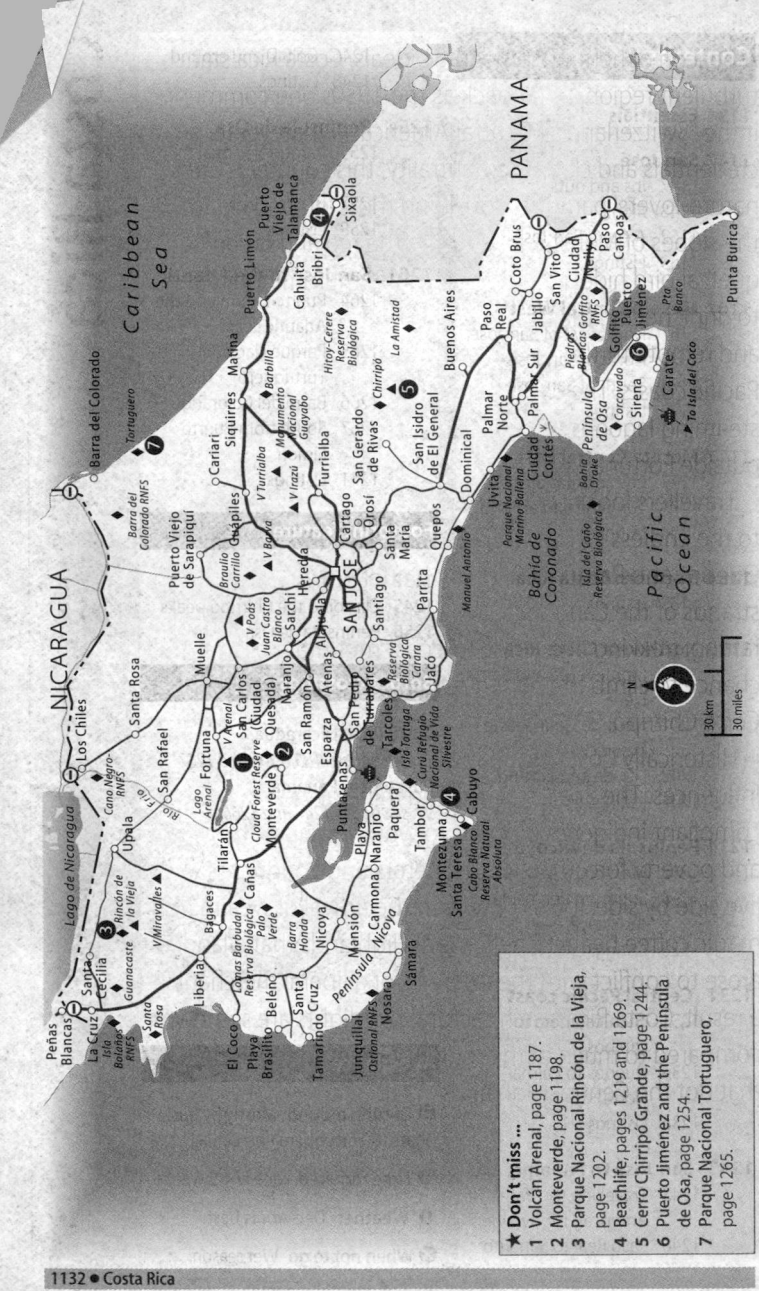

★ **Don't miss ...**

1 Volcán Arenal, page 1187.
2 Monteverde, page 1198.
3 Parque Nacional Rincón de la Vieja, page 1202.
4 Beaches, pages 1219 and 1269.
5 Cerro Chirripó Grande, page 1244.
6 Puerto Jiménez and the Península de Osa, page 1254.
7 Parque Nacional Tortuguero, page 1265.

A beacon of neutral democratic ideals, Costa Rica stands out in a turbulent region; as far back as the 1930s one commentator called it the "Switzerland of Central America". Whatever its political credentials and claims to neutrality, this country is undeniably a nature-lovers' paradise: you'll find moss-draped cloud forest on the slopes of Monteverde, where the red and green, sacred quetzal bird hides in the treetops and hummingbirds congregate to drink nectar; there's rainforest wilderness on the Osa Peninsula and remote turtle-nesting beaches on the north Atlantic and Pacific coasts. The country's volcanic peaks range from the gentle steaming lagoons of Irazú and Poás to the explosive Arenal, just outside Fortuna, where red-hot lava lights up the night sky.

Travellers looking to combine nature and comfort should head to the endless sand and surf beaches of the Nicoya Peninsula, Quepos and Parque Nacional Manuel Antonio, or to the off-beat strands of the Caribbean. For adrenalin junkies there's whitewater rafting, trekking and coast-to-coast mountain biking, and the chance to climb the barren *páramo* savannahs to the peak of Cerro Chirripó.

Historically Costa Rica has avoided the extremes of external influences. The Spanish found no mineral wealth here or compliant indigenous labour to work the land. Hard conditions and poverty forced both conquerors and conquered to work and live side by side. It was only with the arrival of wealth from the magic coffee bean in the Central Highlands that a landed gentry arose to conflict with the interests of a liberal merchant class. As a result, Costa Rica's architectural highlights are somewhat limited compared to much of the region, concentrated in the churches that dot the Central Highlands.

Essentials

Geographically Costa Rica is the smallest but two of the Central American republics (after El Salvador and Belize) and only Panama and Belize have fewer inhabitants. Despite these diminutive tendencies, the 'Rich Coast' has carved out a niche market as the nature destination in Central America with a well-developed network of national parks and biological reserves protecting large tracts of unspoilt tropical wilderness. Adventure activities are an option to sap untapped adrenaline and there are plenty of glorious beaches for lazing around and soaking up the perfect climate. Known throughout Latin America as the continent's purest democracy, Costa Rica celebrated a centenary of democracy in 1989. For Ticos, as the citizens are known, the country has the highest standard of living in Central America, the highest literacy rate (95%), the second lowest birth rate (after Panama) and the greatest degree of economic and social advancement.

Where to go

Costa Rica's main attractions are its countryside, nature and wildlife. Although the country has a colourful history, most of the colonial heritage has been lost in earthquakes over the centuries. **San José**, the capital, is a lively city, and worth enjoying for a couple of days, visiting museums and cultural attractions while organizing visits to other parts of the country.

Surrounding San José is the **Meseta Central** draped in the quirky charms and graceful air of **Zarcero**, **Sarchí**, **Heredia** and **Alajuela** in the heart of this agricultural and coffee-producing region. Just 57 km from the capital, the impressive crater and easily reached summit of **Volcán Poás** steams and puffs in a national park with a sprinkling of wildlife and a few trails. To the east, the former capital Cártago is overshadowed by **Volcán Irazú**, with spectacular views from the summit. Nearby the **Orosí Valley** leads to the hidden beauty of Costa Rica's newest reserve **Parque Nacional Tapantí**. Further east on the Caribbean slope, **Turrialba** is a prime site for world-class **whitewater rafting** on the scenic Reventazón and Pacuare rivers, staying in secluded lodges offering comfortable nature tourism and guided tours.

North to San Carlos the route leads to **Fortuna** and **Lake Arenal**, the backdrop to the most spectacular of Costa Rica's volcanoes – the active **Arenal**. A perfect cone, it is best watched at night when the red hot lava can, with luck, be seen spewing out of the top before rolling and crashing down the mountainside. In addition to being the starting point for volcano trips, **Fortuna**, at the foot of Arenal, is a good base for boat trips to the wetlands of **Caño Negro Wildlife Refuge**, a birdwatcher's paradise near **Los Chiles**, and a route between Costa Rica and Nicaragua.

South of Lake Arenal is **Monteverde Forest Reserve**, a private reserve and a guiding light in the world of conservation. Difficult to reach, the epiphyte-laden cloud forest spans the continental divide, protecting the habitat of the resplendent quetzal and many other tropical birds. Nearby **Santa Elena** and several other private reserves offer nature visits and dramatic canopy tours for visitors.

Continuing north the Pan-American Highway leads towards the Nicaraguan border. **Guanacaste**, in the northwest, is drier with open plains once used for cattle ranching inspiring a distinctive regional music, dance and culture. From the town of **Liberia**, trips to **Parque Nacional Rincón de la Vieja** reveal an array of geothermal curiosities including mud pots and hot springs. Close to the Nicaraguan border, **Parque Nacional Santa Rosa** protects rare dry tropical forest and Pacific beaches used by nesting turtles. These two

Packing for Costa Rica

Climate is generally very comfortable in Costa Rica limiting the need for specialist clothing. If you choose to go to the higher altitudes, Chirripó for example, be sure to take warm clothing and rain gear. For jungle treks take long-sleeved shirts and trousers that will protect you from insect bites.

parks, along with the adjacent Parque Nacional Guanacaste, encompass the Guanacaste Conservation Area, declared a World Heritage Site by the United Nations in 1999. Beach lovers should head for the **Nicoya Peninsula**, with miles of white-sand beaches. Resorts are springing up if you want parties, dancing and services, but smaller towns exist for solitude, sun loving and surf.

On the southern Pacific, beautiful beaches fringe the coast from the transport hub of **Puntarenas** through the surf hangout of **Jacó**, to the justifiably popular **Quepos** with treasured **Parque Nacional Manuel Antonio** nearby, and the quieter spots around **Dominical** and **Playa Hermosa**. In the far south, the **Osa Peninsula** draws naturalists to the beauty of **Parque Nacional Corcovado**'s protected primary rainforest. It's tough, hot, sweaty and not for the faint hearted, but you won't regret the effort.

The Pan-American Highway takes the high road down the southern spine of the country from San José to Panama through the spectacular mountain scenery of the Cordillera Talamanca. The country's highest mountain, **Cerro Chirripó** (3820 m), is climbed from **San Gerardo** near **San Isidro de El General**. Throughout the area, lodges catering for all budgets offer birdwatching and guided tours in the mountains, where the **Parque Nacional Chirripó** and neighbouring **Parque Internacional La Amistad** protect the country's largest area of virgin forest with the greatest biological diversity.

Puerto Limón is the main town on the Caribbean with a vibrancy and rhythm that shines through at carnival each October. While much of the region is used for banana cultivation, on the coast towards the Nicaraguan border is **Parque Nacional Tortuguero**, reached through a network of inland canals and waterways full to bursting with tropical birdlife, basking crocodiles, noisy monkeys and beaches used by nesting turtles.

South of Puerto Limón the road leads to Panama through the towns of **Cahuita, Puerto Viejo** and **Manzanillo**. Strong local cultures, a proud expatriate community and protected tropical rainforest attract backpackers and the discerning traveller to this forgotten corner of Costa Rica. It's also the best route to Bocas del Toro in Panama.

Suggested itinerary All traffic goes through San José so your visit will inevitably involve a few days in the capital. If travelling from Nicaragua, you have two options. Cross by land at Peñas Blancas to travel down the **Nicoya Peninsula** for a few days on the beach, or to **Liberia** to spend time clambering around the volcanic **Rincón de la Vieja**. The second option is to cross to Los Chiles for a trip to **Caño Negro Wildlife Reserve** before moving on to **Fortuna** and the explosive **Arenal**. The next stop might be a few days in Santa Elena to visit **Monteverde Cloud Forest**. From here, you could spend 10 days travelling down the Pacific coast, stopping at **Manuel Antonio National Park** and the **Osa Peninsula** in the south before heading to Panama. Alternatively, head to **San José** and after a few days, continue east to **Tortuguero** before heading south to **Cahuita, Puerto Viejo de Talamanca** and the border with Panama. At a push you would need two or three weeks in Costa Rica; four to five weeks would be much more relaxing.

When to go

In general, the best time to visit December to February. This is during the dry season (December to April), but before the temperatures really rise (March and April). Two main factors contribute to the local climatic conditions: altitude and location. The climate varies from the heat and humidity of the Caribbean and Atlantic lowlands, usually around the mid-20°Cs, falling to the warm temperate Meseta Central with chilly temperatures at greater heights – in the Cordillera Talamanca, the average temperature is below 16°C. On the Pacific side there is a well-defined wet season (May-November). The wetter Atlantic side has no specific dry season but there is less rainfall between March and September. Festivals are spread throughout the year, but the two biggest are Independence Day (September) and Día de la Raza (October).

Sport and activities

Nature tourism

Tourists particularly enjoy the many well-kept and well-guarded national parks and nature reserves that protect some samples of the extraordinarily varied Costa Rican ecosystems. The variety is daunting and includes some of the last patches of dry tropical forest in the **Parque Nacional Santa Rosa**, the cloud forest of **Monteverde** and the **Talamanca Mountains** and nine active volcanoes including **Rincón de la Vieja**, **Poás**, **Irazú** and of course **Arenal**. There is a standard entrance fee of US$7 for all national parks. Manuel Antonio is closed on Mondays; Cabo Blanco is closed on Mondays and Tuedays.

Birdwatchers and butterfly lovers have long flocked to Costa Rica to see some of the 850 or so species of bird (the whole of the US counts about 800) and untold varieties of butterfly. All of these can best be seen in the parks, together with monkeys, deer, coyotes, armadillos, anteaters, turtles, coatis, raccoons, snakes, and, more rarely, wild pigs, wild cats and tapirs.

Although the national parks and other privately owned reserves are a main tourist attraction, many are in remote areas and not easy to get to on public transport; buses or coaches that do go tend to stay for a short time. There is a tendency for tour companies to dominate the National Park 'market' to the exclusion of other public transport. For tight budgets, try making up a party with others and sharing taxis or hiring a car.

The **Sistema Nacional de Areas de Conservación (SINAC)** ① *T2283-8004, PO Box 10104-1000, San José, www.costarica-nationalparks.com*, administers the National Park System (write in advance or call). For information and permits to visit and/or camp or conduct research in the parks apply to **Fundación de Parques Nacionales (FPN)** ① *Av 15, San José, T2257-2239, Mon-Fri 0800-1200, 1300-1700, 300 m north and 150 m east of Santa Teresita Church, Barrio Escalante, between Calles 23-25*. Check in advance if your trip depends on gaining entrance. If you want to work as a volunteer in the parks, at US$12 per day for lodging and food, contact the **Asociación de Voluntarios (ASVO)** ① *Calle 36, Av 3, San José, T2258-4430, www.asvocr.org*. Bilingual tourist information and/or telephone numbers for individual national park offices is available by dialling T192.

Watersports

The rivers of Costa Rica have proved to be highly popular for whitewater rafting, kayaking and canoeing, both for the thrill of the rapids and the wildlife interest of the quieter sections. The fibe most commonly run rivers are the Reventazón (and the Pascua section of it), Pacuare, Corobicí, Sarapiquí and El General. You can do a day trip but to reach the Grade IV and V rapids you usually have to take two to three days. The Reventazón is perhaps the most accessible but the Pacuare has been recommended as a more beautiful experience. The Corobicí is slow and popular with birdwatchers. Ríos Tropicales (see page 1160) has been recommended. For reasons of safety heavy rain may cause cancellations, so make sure your plans are flexible.

There is swimming on both Atlantic and Pacific coasts. Offshore, sea kayaking is increasingly popular. Snorkelling and scuba-diving are offered by several hotels and most beach tour offices, but you have to pick your spot carefully. Anywhere near a river will suffer from poor visibility and the coral reef has died in many places because of agricultural pollutants washed downstream, particularly on the Caribbean coast. Generally, on the Caribbean side, you can see wrecks and coral reefs, particularly in the southeast towards the Panamanian border, while on the Pacific side you see large pelagics and sportfish. Liveaboard dive boats head for the islands of Caño and Isla del Coco. Divers are not permitted in national parks or reserves, nor within 500 m of the protected sea turtle zone north of Parque Nacional Tortuguero. Windsurfing is good along the Pacific coast, particularly in the bay close to La Cruz and world class on Lake Arenal, particularly the west end. Lots of hotels have equipment for hire and operators in San José will know where the best conditions prevail at any time. Be careful of obstacles in the water along rocky coastlines and near river mouths. Surfing is popular on the Pacific and southern Caribbean beaches, attracting professionals who follow storm surges along the coast. Beginners can take classes in some resorts like Tamarindo, Jacó and Dominical, and proficient surfers can get advice on waves from surf shops in these areas.

For sport fishing, sailfish and marlin are targeted off the Pacific; snook and tarpon are caught in the Caribbean, the largest snook being found in September and October, mostly north of Limón (where there are fishing lodges), but also towards Panama. Exciting it may be, cheap it is not. Anglers can save money in groups, since it is usually the same cost to rent a boat for one or four.

Other sports

Football (soccer) is the national sport (played every Sunday at 1100, September to May, at the Saprissa Stadium). Mountain biking is popular throughout most parts of the country with options to simply rent the bike and push out on your own, or join a guided trip. There are several golf courses close to the capital, and a growing number on the Nicoya Peninsula and at Los Sueños Marriott, near Jacó. The Meseta Central is good country for horse riding; horses can be hired by arrangement directly with owners. Most fiestas end with bullfighting in the squares, with no horses used. Bullfights are held in San José during the Christmas period. There is no kill and spectators are permitted to enter the ring to chase, and be chased by, the bull. If you're looking for a last big-spending celebration, hot-air-balloon rides take you over the trees near Arenal Volcano and also the Turrialba region. Contact **Serendipity Adventures** ① *T2558-1000, www.serendipity adventures.com*. And the final suggestion is to jump off a bridge. Bungee jumping, that is, off the Colorado bridge, close to Grecia in the Meseta Central (see page 1160).

Getting there

Air

The main international airport is at San José (see page 1147). Departure tax is a flat rate of US$26 per person, regardless of nationality or immigration status, when leaving by air. Exit taxes, by air or land, and legislation regarding visa extensions, are subject to frequent change and travellers should check these details as near to the time of travelling as possible.

From Europe From most European cities flights connect in the US at Miami, Houston, Dallas and many others with **American Airlines**, **Continental** and **Grupo Taca**. **Iberia** have daily flights between Madrid and San José. There are direct charter flights in season from several European cities including Frankfurt (**Condor**).

From North America Flights from North America are many and varied (more than 20 each week), again some stop in Miami so check if a direct flight is important. Departure points include: Atlanta, Boston, Chicago, Dallas, Houston, Los Angeles, Miami, New York, Orlando, San Francisco, Toronto, Washington DC. **Daniel Oduber International Airport**, near Liberia, is increasingly popular, conveniently located just 30 minutes from some of Guanacaste's finest beaches. Charter specials available from time to time.

From South America Flights from South American cities include Bogotá (**Copa**, **Grupo Taca**), Cali (**SAM**, **Grupo Taca**), Caracas (**Grupo Taca**), Cartagena (**SAM**), Guayaquil (**Grupo Taca**), Lima (**Grupo Taca**), Quito (**Grupo Taca**) and Santiago (**Grupo Taca**).

From Central America The **Grupo Taca** alliance provides connections with all capitals and several of the more popular tourist destinations including Cancún, Guatemala City (also **United** and **Copa**), Managua (**Copa**), Mexico City (also **Mexicana, United**), Panama City (**Copa**), San Pedro Sula, San Salvador (**Copa**) and Tegucigalpa.

From the Caribbean There are a couple of flights a week to Havana (**Cubana, Grupo Taca**) and regular charters to San Andrés, Colombia (**SAM**). Also flights to Santo Domingo (**Copa**).

Road
Road links to the north are on the Pan-American Highway at Peñas Blancas with immigration services and buses connecting to and from Nicaragua. It is possible to cross the northern border close to Los Chiles, making the journey by land or boat to San Carlos. Crossing the border on the North Pacific is possible but immigration services are non-existent and transportation is irregular.

The main crossing to Panama at Paso Canoas is straightforward and problem-free. On the Caribbean coast, Sixaola links with the Panamian town of Guabito over the old banana bridge. Immigration services on both sides but only during normal office hours.

Sea
The main ports for international cargo vessels are **Puerto Limón**, with regular sailings to and from Europe, and **Caldera**, on the central Pacific coast. Contact shipping agents, of which there are many, in Puerto Limón and San José for details. Cruise vessels arrive at Caldera, Puntarenas and Puerto Limón, normally stopping for little more than 24 hours.

Getting around

Air
There are domestic airports, with scheduled services provided by **Sansa** or **NatureAir** at Barra Colorado, Carate, Carrillo-Sámara, Coto 47, Drake Bay, Golfito, Liberia, La Fortuna,

Limón, Nosara Beach, Palmar Sur, Puerto Jiménez, Punta Islita, Quepos, Tamarindo, Tambor and Tortuguero. Several charter companies also operate out of San José. ▸▸ *See Transport, page 1161.*

Road
Costa Rica has a total of 35,700 km of roads of which 7500 km are paved. The Pan-American Highway runs the length of the country, from the Nicaraguan to the Panamanian borders. A highway has been built from Orotina to Caldera, a port on the Gulf of Nicoya, which has replaced Puntarenas as the principal Pacific port. There is also a highway from Orotina to Ciudad Colón. Another road goes from Orotina as far as Quepos greatly improving access to the Pacific beaches. Beyond Quepos, it's a dirt road down to Dominical, but continuing further south from Dominical to Ciudad Cortés, the road is generally good. All four-lane roads into San José are toll roads. It is illegal to ride in a car or taxi without wearing seatbelts.

Bus The good road network supports a regular bus service that covers most parts of the country. Frequency declines with popularity but you can get to most places with road access eventually. San José is the main hub for buses, although you can skip down the Pacific coast by making connections at Puntarenas. Coming from Nicaragua, direct to Arenal, requires cutting in and travelling through Tilaran.

Two shuttle bus companies offer transport from the capital to dozens of beach and tourism destinations in comfortable a/c minibuses. ▸▸ *See Transport, page 1162.*

Car Driving in Costa Rica allows for greater flexibility when travelling. Many of the nature parks are in remote areas; 4WD and high-clearance is recommended and sometimes essential; in the wet season some roads will be impassable. Always ask locals or bus drivers what the state of the road is before embarking on a journey. Do not assume that if the buses are running, a car can get through too.

Tourists who enter by car or motorcycle pay US$10 road tax, including mandatory insurance, and can keep their cars for an initial period of 90 days. This can be extended for a total period of six months, for about US$10 per extra month, at the **Instituto Costarricense de Turismo**, or at the **Customs office** ① *Av 3, Calle 14,* if you take your passport, car entry permit, and a piece of stamped paper (*papel sellado*) obtainable at any bookshop. Cars are fumigated on entry: exterior US$8. If you have an accident while in the country do not move the vehicle and immediately contact **Policía de Tránsito** ① *San José, T2222-9330 or T2222-9245.*

Car hire Renting a car can be a surprisingly economical way to travel if you can form a group and split the costs. As with all rentals, check your vehicle carefully as the company will try to claim for the smallest of 'damages'. Most leases do not allow the use of a normal car off paved roads. Always make sure the spare tyre is in good order, as potholes are frequent. You can have tyres fixed at any garage for about US$2 in 30 minutes. Guideline prices: smallest economy car US$21-32 per day includes unlimited mileage or US$125-200 per week; 4WD vehicle costs US$33-91 per day, US$200-550 per week, including unlimited mileage. Driver's licence from home and credit card generally required. Loss damage waiver (LDW) insurance is mandatory and costs an extra US$10-17 per day; excess is between US$750 and US$1500. Cash deposits or credit card charges range from US$800 to US$1800, so check you have sufficient credit. Discounts for car hire are available during the 'Green Season' (May to November). If you plan to drop off a hired car somewhere other than where you picked it up, check with several firms for their charges: **Elegante**, **Ada** and **National** appear to have the lowest drop-off fees. Insurance will not cover broken windscreens, driving on unsurfaced roads or damaged tyres.

Safety Never leave anything in a hired car and never leave your car on the street, even in daylight. Secure parking lots are available in most cities. Regular reports of break-ins at national parks and other popular tourism areas. Driving at night is not recommended.

Fuel Main fuel stations have regular (unleaded) US$0.84 and diesel US$0.69 per litre; super gasoline (unleaded) is available throughout the country, US$0.89 per litre. Prices are regulated by the government.

Road tolls Costa Rica has a road toll system is in place, with charges of between US$0.20 to US$0.40 for some of the busiest routes in the Central Highlands.

Cycling Cycling is easier in Costa Rica than elsewhere in Central America; there is less heavy traffic and it is generally more 'cyclist friendly'. However, paving is thin and soon deteriorates; look out for cracks and potholes, which bring traffic to a crawl. The prevailing wind is from the northeast so, if making an extensive tour, travelling in the direction of Panama is slightly more favourable.

Recommended reading for all users: Baker's *The Essential Road Guide to Costa Rica*, with detailed strip maps, kilometre by kilometre road logs, motoring information plus San José map and bus guide (Bill Baker, Apdo 1185-1011, San José). Cycle shops have sprung up around the country offering parts and repair services.

Hitchhiking Generally easy and safe by day, but take the usual precautions.

Sea

Ferries serve the southern section of the Nicoya Peninsula from Puntarenas. The Osa Peninsula has a regular ferry service linking Golfito and Puerto Jiménez, and Bahía Drake is reached on boats from Sierpe. Boats travel to Tortuguero from Moín, close to Puerto Limón, and from Cariari, north of Guápiles.

Train

All commercial lines are closed. For the truly devoted there is talk of reintroducing a tourist 'banana' train from Siquirres to Matina on the Caribbean side. Ask locally for details. A tourist train (weekends) from San José to the Pacific, departing from Estación del Pacífico, 600 m south of Parque Central, at 0600, travelling to Caldera with a stop in Orotina; returns at 1500. Tickets (US$25 return) must be purchased Monday-Wednesday for following weekend. The tours are in refurbished 1940s German wagons. Contact **America Travel** ① *T2233-3300, www.ticotraintour.com.*

Maps

The **Instituto Geográfico Nacional** ① *Calle 9, Av 20-22, open 0730-1600*, at the Ministry of Public Works and Transport in San José, supplies good topographical maps for walkers. **ITM** has a 1:500,000 travel map of Costa Rica, available at bookstores throughout the country. Maps are also available in San José at **7th Street Books** ① *Calle 7, Av 1 and Central*,

T2256-8251; **Universal** ① *Av Central, Calle 1 and Central, T2222-2222;* and **Lehmann** ① *Av Central, Calle 1-3, T2223-1212.*

Sleeping

Accommodation in Costa Rica favours couples and groups – the price of a single room is often the same as a double, and the price of a room for four is often less than double the price for two. So if you can get in a group, the cost per person falls considerably. Accommodation prices during the 'green' season (May to November), are generally much lower. A 13% sales tax plus 3.39% tourism tax (total 16.39%) are added to the basic price of hotel rooms. A deposit is advised at the more expensive hotels in San José, especially in the high season (December to April), to guarantee reservations. If you arrive late at night in the high season, even a guaranteed reservation may not be kept.

The **Costa Rica Bed & Breakfast Group**, which has 300 bed and breakfast inns and small hotels around the country in its membership, helps with reservations. The **Costa Rican Chamber of Hotels** ① *T2248-0990, www.costaricanhotels.com,* provides information about its members (mostly larger hotels) and an online reservation system. The **Costa Rican Tourist Board** ① *T2291-5740, www.turismo-sostenible.co.cr,* has an eco-rating system for hotels, an encouraging indicator of progress.

Camping opportunities in Costa Rica are limited with few offical campsites. It is possible to camp in some national parks. Contact the Fundación de Parques Nacionales in San José for details (see Nature tourism, page 1136).

Eating and drinking

Local cuisine

Sodas (small restaurants) serve local food, which is worth trying. Very common is *casado*, a cheap lunch which includes rice, beans, stewed beef or fish, fried plantain and cabbage. *Olla de carne* is a soup of beef, plantain, corn, yucca, *ñampi* and *chayote* (local vegetables). *Sopa negra* is made with black beans, and comes with a poached egg in it; *picadillo* is another meat and vegetable stew. Snacks are popular: *gallos* (filled tortillas), *tortas* (containing meat and vegetables), *arreglados* (bread filled with the same) and *empanadas*. *Pan de yuca* is a speciality, available from stalls in San José centre. For breakfast, try *gallo pinto* (rice and beans) with *natilla* (a slightly sour cream). The best ice cream can be found in *Pops* shops.

In general, eating out in Costa Rica is more expensive than elsewhere in Central America. A sales tax of 13% plus 10% service charge are added to restaurant bills.

Drink

There are many types of cold drink made either from fresh fruit or milk drinks with fruit (*batidos*) or cereal flour whisked with ice cubes. Drinks are often sugared well beyond North American or European tastes (ask for *poco azúcar*). The fruits range from the familiar to the exotic; others include *cebada* (barley flour), *pinolillo* (roasted corn), *horchata* (rice flour with cinnamon), *chan*, which according to Michael Brisco is 'perhaps the most unusual, looking like mouldy frogspawn and tasting of penicillin'. All these drinks cost the same as, or less than, bottled fizzy products. Excellent coffee. Local beers are Bavaria, Pilsen, Imperial, Rock Ice and Kaiser (which is non-alcoholic).

Festivals and events

1 Jan New Year's Day.
19 Mar St Joseph.
Mar/Apr Easter. Nearly everyone is on holiday; everywhere is shut on Thu, Fri and Sun, and many shops close on Sat and most of the previous week as well.
11 Apr Battle of Rivas.
1 May Labour Day.
Jun Corpus Christi.
29 Jun St Peter and St Paul.
25 Jul Guanacaste Day.
2 Aug Virgin of Los Angeles.
15 Aug Mothers' Day.

15 Sep Independence Day.
12 Oct Día de la Raza (Columbus Day). The main festival is **Carnival in Puerto Limón**, the week before and after Columbus Day, when the focus of the country for once dwells on the country's largest Caribbean town. There's music, dance, street processions and general festivities. Hotels book up, but it's definitely worth making the effort to go.
8 Dec Immaculate Conception.
25 Dec Christmas Day.
28-31 Dec San José only.

Shopping

The best buys are wooden items, ceramics and leather handicrafts. Many wooden handicrafts are made of rainforest hardwoods and deforestation is a critical problem. Coffee should have 'puro' on the packet or it may contain sugar or other additives.

Essentials A-Z

Accident and emergency
Police: T117/127. Fire: T118. Medical (Red Cross): T128.

For Police, Fire, Red Cross emergencies/bilingual operators: T911.

Customs and duty free
Duty-free allowances are 500 g of manufactured tobacco, 2 kg of chocolate and 5 litres of liquor. Any amount of currency may be taken in or out, but amounts over US$10,000 must be declared. Cameras, binoculars, camping equipment, laptop computers and other portable items of personal/professional/leisure use are free of duty.

Electricity
110 volts AC, 60 cycles, US-style plugs.

Embassies and consulates
Australia, De la Sala House, 11th floor, 30 Clarence St, Sydney NSW: 2000, T9-261-1177.

Belize, Room 3, 2nd floor, Capital Garden Plaza, Belmopan, T822-1582.
Canada, 325 Dalhouise St, Suite 407, Ottawa, ON, K1N 7G2, T613-562-2855.
El Salvador, 85 Av Sur y Calle Cuscatlán, 4415 Col Escalón, SS, T2264-3865.
France, 78 Av Emile Zola, 75015 Paris, T4-578-9696.
Germany, Dessauerstrasse 28-29 D-10963 Berlin, T30-2639-8990.
Guatemala, 15 Calle 7-59, Zona 10, Guatemala City, T2366-9918.
Honduras, Residencial El Triángulo Lomas del Guijamo, Calle 3451, Tegucigalpa, T232-1768.
Israel, Abba Hillel Silver St, 14 Mail Box, 38 Beit Oz, 15th floor, Ramat Gan, 52506, T3-613-5061.
Italy, Viale Liegi 2, Int 8, Roma, T4425-1046.
Japan, Kowa Building, No 38, 9th floor, 901 4-12-24 Nishi Azabu Minato, Ku Tokio, 106-0031, T3-486-1812.

Mexico, Calle Río Poo 113, Col Cuauhtémoc between Río Pánuco and Lerma, México DF, T5525 7765.
Netherlands, Laan Copes van Cattenburch 46, 2585 GB, Den Haag, T70-354-0780.
Nicaragua, de la Estatua de Montoya, 2 c al lago y ½ c arriba (Callejón Zelaya), Managua, T266-2404.
Norway (covers **Sweden** and **Denmark**), Skippergat 33, 8th floor, 0154 Oslo, Noruega, T2233-0408.
Panama, Calle Samuel Lewis Edificio Plaza Omega, 3rd floor, Contiguo Santuario Nacional Panamá, T264-2980.
Spain, Paseo de la Castellana 164, 17-A, 28046 Madrid, T91-345-9622.
Switzerland, Schwarztorstrasse 11, 3007 Berna, T031-372-7887.
UK (covers **Portugal**), Flat 1, 14 Lancaster Gate, London W2 3LH, T020-7706-8844.
USA, 2114-S St, North West Washington DC 20008, T202-234-2945.

More embassy addresses are listed at www.rree.go.cr.

Health

Drinking water is safe in all major towns; elsewhere it should be boiled, but bottled water is widely available.

Intestinal disorders are prevalent in the lowlands. Malaria is on the increase: malaria prophylaxis is advised for visitors to the lowlands, especially near the Nicaraguan and Panama border. Dengue fever has been recorded throughout the country, mostly in coastal cities. Having said all that, the standards of health and hygiene are among the best in Latin America. For further information, see page 51.

Internet

Internet cafés are popular and connections in the towns tend to be good. Prices vary but a rough guide is US$1 for 1 hr in the Central Valley; twice that in beach towns and tourism areas. Rates are lower around colleges and universities.

Language

Spanish is the first language, but you will find someone who can speak some English in most places. In the Caribbean the Afro-Caribbean population speak a regional creole dialect with elements of English.

Media

The best San José morning papers are *La Nación* (www.nacion.co.cr) and business-orientated *La República* (www.larepublica.net); there is also *Al Día*, *El Heraldo*, *Diario Extra* (the largest circulating daily) and *La Prensa Libre* (www.prensalibre.co.cr). *La Gaceta* is the official government daily paper. The *Tico Times* (www.ticotimes.net) is out on Fri, and there is the *San José*, which is great for news in English with classifieds.

There are 6 local TV stations, many MW/FM radio stations throughout the country. Local **Voz de América** (VOA) station. **Radio Dos** (95.5 FM) and **Rock Radio** (107.5 FM) have English-language DJs and music. Many hotels and private homes receive 1 of the 4 TV stations offering direct, live, 24-hour satellite TV from the USA. All US cable TV can be received in San José.

Money → *US$1=577 colones (June 2009).* The unit is the **colón**, which in most years devalues slowly against the dollar. There are 5, 10, 25, 50, 100 and 500-colon coins. Notes in use are for 1000, 2000, 5000 and 10,000 colones. US dollars are widely accepted but don't depend on being able to use them.

ATMs and exchange

US dollars can be exchanged in most banks. Most tourist and 1st-class hotels will change dollars and traveller's cheques (TCs) for guests only; the same applies in restaurants and shops if you buy something. Hardly anyone will change damaged US dollar notes. All state-run banks and some private banks will change euro, but it is almost impossible to exchange any other major currency in Costa Rica. For bank drafts and transfers commission may be charged.

Banks are starting to stay open later and several open on Sat. Most banks will process cash advances on Visa/MasterCard. ATMs that accept international Visa and/or MasterCard are widely available at most banks, and in shopping malls and at San José airport. Credomatic handles all credit card billings; they will not accept a credit card charge that does not have the imprint of the borrower's card plus an original signature. This is the result of fraud, but it makes it difficult to book tours or accommodation over the phone. If your card is lost or stolen, ring T0800-011-0184 (MasterCard/Visa) or T0800-012-3211 (AMEX).

Cost of living and travelling
Costa Rica is more expensive than countries to the north. While transport is reasonably cheap, you get less for your money in the hotels. You will be able to survive on US$30 a day, but that does not allow for much in the way of activities.

Opening hours
Banks Mon-Fri 0900-1500.
Businesses Mon-Fri 0900-1200, 1400-1730 (1600 government offices), Sat 0800-1200.
Shops Mon-Sat 0800-1200, 1300-1800 (most stay open during lunch hour).

Post
Airmail letters to Europe cost 180 c, postcards 165 c; to North/South America, letters 155 c, 135 c for postcards; to Australia, Africa and Asia, letters 240 c, postcards 195 c. Expreso letters, 140 c extra, several days quicker to USA and North Europe. Registered mail, 400 c. Airmail takes 5 to 10 days. All parcels sent out of the country by foreigners must be taken open to the post office for clearance. **Lista de Correos**, charges 75 c per letter and will keep them for 4 weeks. For information call Correos de Costa Rica, T800-900-2000.

Safety
Generally speaking, Costa Rica is very safe but, as ever, there are some problem areas. Look after your belongings in hotels – use the safe. If hiring a car do not leave valuables in the vehicle and leave nothing unattended on beaches or buses. Theft (pickpocketing, grab-and-run thieves and mugging) is on the increase in San José, especially in the centre, in the market, at the Coca Cola bus station, in the barrios of Cuba, Cristo Rey, México, 15 de Setiembre and León XIII. Keep away from these areas at night and on Sun, when few people are around, as we have received reports of violent robberies. Street gangs, known as *chapulines*, are mostly kids. The police do seem to be trying to tackle the problem but help yourself by avoiding potentially dangerous situations.

You must carry your passport (or a photocopy) with you at all times.

Tax
Departure tax US$26 per person.
Road tax US$10, when entering Costa Rica by car or motorcycle.
Sales tax 13%.

The sales tax plus 3.39% tourism tax is added to hotel room prices.

Telephone → *Country code T+506.*
There are no area codes in Costa Rica, the **international direct dialling** code (to call out of Costa Rica) is T00. Dial T116 for the operator. In Mar 2008, Costa Rica changed telephone numbers from 7 to 8 digits. All landlines now have a 2 in front of the old 7-digit number and all mobile phones now have an 8 in front of the old 8-digit number. Nationwide phone changes are taken up by organizations and people at different rates.

Many websites are still quoting the old 7-digit numbers. Be prepared when using phones and taking down numbers.

Long-distance telephone services are handled by the state-run **Instituto Costarricense de Electricidad (ICE)** and its subsidiary **Radiográfica Costarricense SA (RACSA)**, Telecommunications Centre, A 5, Calle 1, San José, Mon-Fri 0800-1900, Sat 0800-1200, closed Sun.

Standard rates to US, Canada, Mexico and South America are US$0.45 per min; Panama is US$0.40 and Europe and the rest of the world (except Central America and Belize) US$0.60 a min if you dial direct; operator-assisted calls cost up to US$3.12 per min. Only variable rates are to Central America: standard rates between 0700 and 1900 (US$0.40 a min), reduced between 1900 and 2200 (US$0.35) and reduced again between 2200 and 0700 and during the weekend (US$0.28). Add 13% sales tax.

Public phones are maddening to use, various kinds are available: some use 10 and 20 colón silver coins, others use 50 colón gold coins, and still others employ at least 2 types of calling cards, but not interchangeably. The 199 cards are recommended, but it's often easiest to call collect inside (T110) and outside (T116) the country. Assistance for hearing impaired (Spanish only) is T137.

Phone cards with 'Personal Identification Numbers' are available for between US$0.80 and US$10. These can be used for national and international direct dialling from a private phone. Calls abroad can be made from phone booths; collect calls abroad may be made from special booths in the RACSA office, or from any booth nationwide if you dial T116 for connection with the international operator (T175 for collect calls to the USA). Phone cards can be used. Dial T124 for international information. Country Direct Dialling Codes to the USA are:

MCI/World Phone 0800-012-2222, AT&T 0800-0114-114, Sprint/GlobalOne 0800-013-0123, Worldcom 0800-014-4444.

Time
-6 hrs GMT.

Tipping
A 10% service charge is automatically added to restaurant and hotel bills, as well as the 13% sales tax.

Tourist information
Instituto Costarricense de Turismo (ICT), underneath the Plaza de la Cultura, Calle 5, A Central-2, T2223-1733, www.visitcosta rica.com. Daily 0900-1700. All tourist information is given here along with a good free map of San José and the country. See page 1147 for more details. Student cards give reductions in most museums.

Useful websites
www.centralamerica.com Costa Rica's Travelnet, contains general information on tourist-related subjects.
www.infocostarica.com A Yahoo-style search engine with information, links and maps for all things Costa Rican.

Visas and immigration
Nationals of most EU nations, the US, Canada, Israel and Japan do not need visas for visits of up to 90 days. Nationals of the Republic of Ireland, Australia and New Zealand do not need a visa, but visits are limited to 30 days. For more information, check www.migracion.go.cr.

If you overstay the 30- or 90-day permitted period, you must report to immigration before leaving the country. For longer stays ask for a Prórroga de Turismo at Migración (Immigration) in San José. For this you need 4 passport photos, an airline or bus ticket out of the country and proof of funds (for example TCs); you can apply for an extension of 1 or 2 months, at 300 colones per month. The paperwork takes 3 days. If you leave the country, you must wait 72 hrs before returning, but it may be cheaper and easier to do this to get a new 30-day entry. Travel agents can arrange all extension and exit formalities for a small fee.

Monetary fines for overstaying your visa or entry permit have been eliminated; if you plan to stay longer, be aware that immigration officials have said that tourists who overstay their welcome more than once will be denied entry into the country on subsequent occasions – part of government efforts to crack down on 'perpetual tourists'.

An onward ticket (a bus ticket, which can be bought at the border immigration office or sometimes from the driver on Tica international buses, or a transatlantic ticket) is asked for, but can be refunded in San José with a loss of about US$3 on a US$20 ticket. Cashing in an air ticket is difficult because you may be asked to produce another ticket out of the country. Also, tourists may have to show at least US$300 in cash or TCs before being granted entry (especially if you have no onward ticket).

Weights and measures
Metric.

San José

→ Colour map 7, B3. Altitude: 1150 m.
Nestled in a broad, fertile valley producing coffee and sugar-cane, San José was founded in 1737 and became capital in 1823 after struggles for regional ascendency between competing towns of the Central Valley. Frequent earthquakes have destroyed most of the colonial buildings and the modern replacements do little to inspire. But, like any city, the mix of museums and general attractions make it worth a couple of days' stay. ▶▶ *For listings, see pages 1153-1166.*

Ins and outs

Getting there
Aeropuerto Internacional Juan Santamaría is 16 km from the centre along a good *autopista*. A taxi from the pre-payment booth costs US$15 and efficient buses running every 10 minutes leave from outside the terminal building for San José city centre. Long-distance buses have their terminals scattered round town (see map, page 1148) but the majority are close to the Coca Cola Terminal, in the central west of the city. Bus connections in Costa Rica and with other Central American countries are very good.

Getting around
For the most part the city conforms to a grid systems – avenidas run east-west; calles north-south. Avenidas to the north of Avenida Central are given odd numbers; those to the south even numbers. Calles to the west of Calle Central are even-numbered; those to the east are odd-numbered. The three main streets, Avenida Central, Avenida 2 and the intersecting Calle Central, encompass the business centre. The main shops are along Avenida Central, a pleasant downtown stroll in the section closed to traffic.

Some people find the narrow streets too heavily polluted with exhaust fumes preferring to stay in the suburbs of Escazú, Alajuela or Heredia and using regular bus services to make the journey to town. It's probably a good choice if you've already visited San José, but if it's your first time in the capital you should give it a try for a couple of days at least. A circular bus route travels along Avenida 3 out to La Sabana and back making a useful circuit and an impromptu city tour. Taxis can be ordered by phone or hailed in the street; they are red and are legally required to have meters and to use them. Traffic is congested especially between 0700 and 2000, so driving in the city centre is best avoided. If you do drive, watch out for no-parking zones. Seven blocks of the Avenida Central, from Banco Central running east to Plaza de la Cultura, are closed to traffic and most of the streets downtown are one-way streets.

Tourist information
Instituto Costarricense de Turismo ① *under Plaza de la Cultura, Calle 5, Av Central-2, T2223-1733, Mon-Fri 0900-1700.* Can also be found at Juan Santamaría airport (very helpful, will check hotels for you), the main post office and at borders. Free road maps of Costa Rica, San José and the metropolitan area and public transport timetables available. **OTEC** ① *Calle 3, Av 1-3, Edif Ferenz, San José, T2256-0633, www.otecviajes.com,* the youth and student travel office, is extremely helpful, and offers good special discounts for ISTC and FIYTO members.

Best time to visit

The climate is comfortable, with temperatures between 15° and 26°C, though the evenings can be chilly. The rainy season lasts roughly from May to November; the rest of the year it's mainly dry.

Sights

Many of the most interesting public buildings are near the intersection of Avenida Central and Calle Central. The **Teatro Nacional** ① *just off Av 2, on Calle 3, T2221-1329 (tours), T2221-5341 (event and ticket information), Mon-Sat 0900-1600, www.teatronacional.go.cr, from US$5*, built in 1897, has marble staircases, statues, frescoes and foyer decorated in gold with Venetian plate mirrors. It has a coffee bar run by **Café Britt** and guided tours. Nearby is **Plaza de la Cultura** ① *Av Central, Calle 3-5*, which, in addition to being a great place for people-watching, hosts public concerts. The **Museo de Oro Procolombino** ① *entrance is off Calle 5, T2243-4202, www.museosdelbancocentral.org, daily 0930-1700, US$9*, has a booty of golden treasure buried beneath the Plaza de la Cultura. Fine golden figures of frogs, spiders, raptors and other creatures glisten in this spectacular pre-Columbian gold museum sponsored by the **Banco Central**. Also here is the **Museo Numismático** with an exhibition on the history of Costa Rican money.

① San José

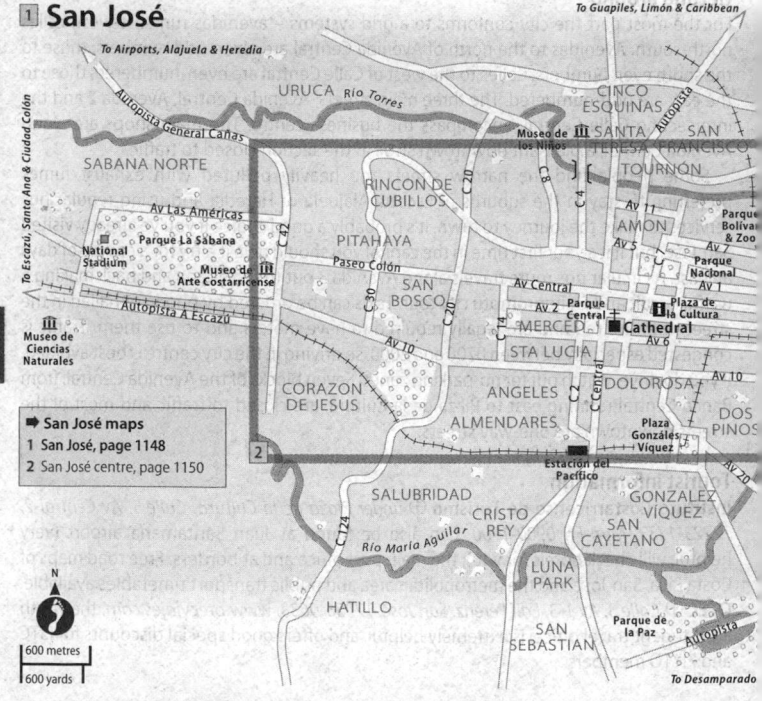

➡ **San José maps**
1 San José, page 1148
2 San José centre, page 1150

The **Museo Nacional** ① *Calle 17, Av Central-2, T2257-1433, Tue-Sat 0830-1600, Sun 0900-1600, US$4, children and students with ID free*, east from the Plaza de la Cultura, has interesting displays on archaeology, anthropology, national history, some gold and ex-President Arias' Nobel Peace Prize. Information is in Spanish and English. Facing it is the **Plaza de la Democracia**, a concrete cascade built to mark the November 1989 centenary of Costa Rican democracy. The **Palacio Nacional** ① *Av Central, Calle 15*, is home of the Legislative Assembly; any visitor can attend debates, sessions start at 1600.

Two blocks north of the Museo Nacional is the **Parque Nacional**, with a grandiloquent bronze monument representing the five Central American republics ousting the filibuster William Walker (see the Nicaragua History section) and the abolition of slavery in Central America. There is also a statue donated by the Sandinista Government of Nicaragua to the people of Costa Rica. To the north of the park is the **Biblioteca Nacional**. East of the library is the **Museo de Formas, Espacio y Sonidos** ① *Calle 17, Av 3-7, T2222-9462, Tue-Fri 0930-1600, US$1, students and children free, wheelchair accessible, signs in Braille*, housed in the old Atlantic Railway Station. In the old liquor factory west of the Biblioteca Nacional, now the Centro Nacional de la Cultura, is the **Museo de Arte y Diseño Contemporáneo** ① *Av 3, Calle 15-17, T2257-7202, Tue-Sat 1000-1700, US$3, students with ID US$0.50.*

One of the best museums in the city is the **Museo del Jade Fidel Tristan** ① *INS building 11th floor, Av 7, Calle 9-13, T2287-6034, Mon-Fri 0830-1530, Sat 0900-1300, US$3*, with the largest collection of jade carvings in Central America, pottery and sculpture.

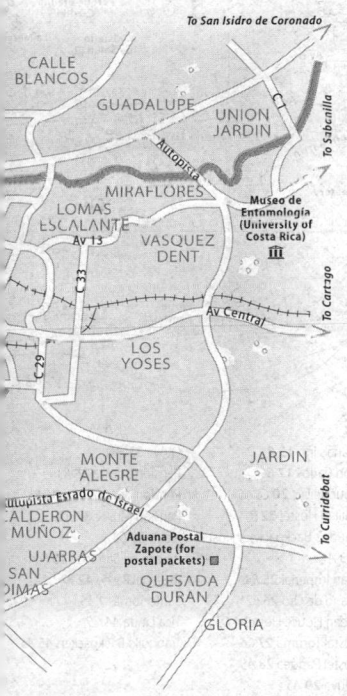

With explanations in Spanish and English, and topped off with a beautiful view over the city, it's a fascinating museum and shouldn't be missed.

Along Calle Central, west of the Teatro Nacional, is **Parque Central**, with a band-stand in the middle among trees, again with occasional performances. East of the park is the monumental architecture of the **Catedral Metropolitana**; to the north is the **Teatro Melico Salazar** ① *see press for details or call T2221-4952*, which has a good mix of performances throughout the year.

Further west, in **Parque Braulio Carrillo**, opposite the eclectic neo-Gothic design of **La Merced** church, is a huge carved granite ball brought from the Diquis archaeological site near Palmar Norte. There are other such designs at the entrance to the Museo de Ciencias Naturales.

At the end of Paseo Colón, at Calle 42, **Parque La Sabana** was converted from the former city airport in the 1950s; the old airport building on the east side is now the **Museo de Arte Costarricense** ① *T2222-7155, Tue-Sat 1000-1600, US$5, US$1 for students, Sun 1000-1400, free*, with a small but interesting display of paintings and sculptures. At the west end of the park is the **Estadio Nacional**, with seating for 20,000 spectators at (mainly) football matches, basketball, volleyball and tennis courts, a running track, lake and swimming pool.

② San José centre

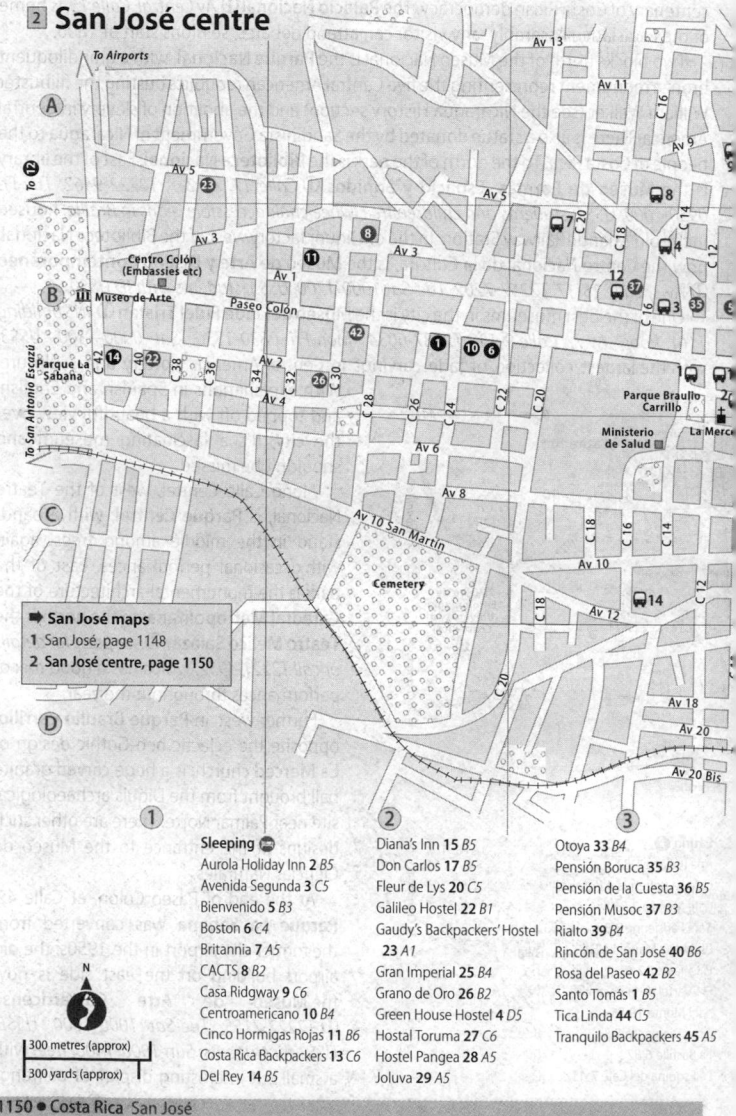

➡ San José maps
1 San José, page 1148
2 San José centre, page 1150

300 metres (approx)
300 yards (approx)

Sleeping
Aurola Holiday Inn **2** B5
Avenida Segunda **3** C5
Bienvenido **5** B3
Boston **6** C4
Britannia **7** A5
CACTS **8** B2
Casa Ridgway **9** C6
Centroamericano **10** B4
Cinco Hormigas Rojas **11** B6
Costa Rica Backpackers **13** C6
Del Rey **14** B5

Diana's Inn **15** B5
Don Carlos **17** B5
Fleur de Lys **20** C5
Galileo Hostel **22** B1
Gaudy's Backpackers' Hostel **23** A1
Gran Imperial **25** B4
Grano de Oro **26** B2
Green House Hostel **4** D5
Hostal Toruma **27** C6
Hostel Pangea **28** A5
Joluva **29** A5

Otoya **33** B4
Pensión Boruca **35** B3
Pensión de la Cuesta **36** B5
Pensión Musoc **37** B3
Rialto **39** B4
Rincón de San José **40** B6
Rosa del Paseo **42** B2
Santo Tomás **1** B5
Tica Linda **44** C5
Tranquilo Backpackers **45** A5

Opposite the southwest corner of Parque Sabana are the impressive natural displays of the **Museo de Ciencias Naturales** ① *Colegio La Salle, T2232-1306, Mon-Sat 0730-1600, Sun 0900-1700, US$1.50, children US$1*, next to the Ministry of Agriculture; take 'Sabana Estadio' bus from Avenida 2, Calle 1 to the gate.

Eating ❼			
Ana Italiana **1** *B2*	La Puriscaleña **8** *B4*	Nashville South **20** *B5*	Terminal Alfaro **8** *A3*
Café La Bohemia **4** *B4*	La Vasconia **9** *B5*	Risas **21** *B4*	Terminal Atlántico
Café Mundo **2** *B6*	Lubnan **10** *B2*		Norte **9** *A3*
Café Parisienne **3** *B5*	Machu Picchu **11** *B2*	**Buses** 🚌	Terminal Caribe
Churrería Manolo **4** *B4*	Pollo a la Leña **13** *B5*	Alajuela & Airport	(Sixaola) **10** *A4*
El Chicote **12** *A1*	Soda Tapia **14** *B1*	Buses **1** *B3*	Terminal Cartago **11** *D5*
El Cuartel de la Boca	Tin Jo **15** *C5*	Heredia Buses **2** *B3/B4*	Terminal Coca Cola **12** *B3*
del Monte **19** *B6*	Vishnu **16** *B5*	Liberia Buses **3** *B3*	Terminal Los Santos **13** *D6*
Gran Diamante **5** *B4*		Panaline Bus **4** *B3*	Terminal Puntarenas **14** *C3*
La Bastille **6** *B2*	**Bars & clubs** ❼	San Isidro Buses **5** *D4*	Terminal Turrialba **15** *C5*
La Esquina del Café **7** *A5*	Chelle's **17** *B5*	Ticabus **6** *C5*	
	Disco Salsa 54 **18** *B5*	Transnica Bus **7** *B3*	

North of Avenida Central, on Calle 2, is the **Unión Club**, the principal social centre of the country. Opposite is the **Correo Central**, general post and telegraph office which also houses an internet café, pastry shop and the **Museo Postal, Telgráfico y Filatélico** ① *upstairs, Mon-Fri 0800-1700, free.*

A couple of blocks to the west is the hustle and bustle of the **Mercado Central**, dating back to 1881, rich with the shouts, cries, smells and chaos of a fresh produce market. Good cheap meals for sale as well as some interesting nick-nacks for the passing tourist. Often crowded; watch for thieves.

The Disneyesque building on the horizon to the north of the city is the **Centro Costarricense de Ciencias y Cultura** (Scientific and Cultural Centre) in the old city penitentiary with the **Galería Nacional**, **Biblioteca Carlos Luis Sáenz**, the **Auditorio Nacional** and **Museo de Los Niños** ① *Calle 4, Av 9, T2258-4929, Tue-Fri 0800-1530, Sat-Sun 0930-1630, US$1.60, children US$1.* Interesting as much for the well-restored building as for the exhibits using former prison cells and spaces to good effect.

Along Avenida 3, north of the Plaza de la Cultura, are the four gardens of the remodelled **Parque Morazán**, with another bandstand at the centre. A little to the northeast, **Parque España**, cool, quiet, and intimate, has for neighbours the **Casa Amarilla** (Yellow House), seat of the Ministry of Foreign Affairs, and the **Edificio Metálico**, imported from Europe to become one of the country's first schools.

To the north of Parque Morazán is **Parque Simón Bolívar**, now a recreation area, with **Simón Bolívar National Zoo and Botanical Gardens** ① *Av 11, just east of Calle 7 (go down Calle 7 about 3 blocks from Av 7), T2233-6701, Mon-Sun 0900-1630, US$3.* It's been remodelled and much improved, with all native plants numbered and listed in a brochure; although the animal cages are small. There's also a restaurant and souvenir shop.

To the north of town, a reasonable walk or a short taxi ride, is **Spirogyra** ① *100 m east, 150 m south of Centro Comercial El Pueblo (near Hotel Villa Tournón), T2222-2937, daily 0800-1700, guided tours for more than 10 people (reservations required), US$6, US$5 students, US$3 children*, a fascinating butterfly farm close to the city but filled with life. To get there, take 'Calle Blancos' bus from Calle 3 and Avenida 5 to El Pueblo.

Around San José ●🟡🟢❋ ▶▶pp1153-1166.

San José is a good base for excursions into the beautiful Meseta Central. Excursions to the spectacular **Orosí Valley** and **Irazú Volcano** are given under Cártago (see page 1177). **Volcán Poás** gently simmers and steams from its elevated position at the northern limit of the Central Highlands and can be visited from San José (**TUASA** bus departs from Avenida 2, Calle 12-14 at 0830, returns 1430, US$4.75 round trip, T442-6900), Heredia or Alajuela (see page 1167). To reach **Volcán Barva** in Parque Nacional Braulio Carrillo, take a bus to San José de la Montaña (see page 1171). Enquire first about the likely weather when planning a visit to Poás, Irazú or Barva as cloud will limit the views; early morning visits recommended.

San Antonio de Escazú, a western suburb of San José popular with the expatriate community, hosts the **Día del Boyero** (National Oxcart Drivers' Day) on the second weekend in March. Festivities culminate on the Sunday in a colourful oxcart parade from the school to the centre, accompanied by typical *payasos* (clowns). Open-air dancing in the evening to music played on a marimba. ▶▶ *See Festivals and events, page 1159.*

In La **Guácima**, 35 minutes west of San José, 20 minutes south of Alajuela, is a **Butterfly Farm** ① *daily 0830-1700, US$15 adults, US$10 students, US$7.50 children under 12, includes guided tour every 2 hrs, last one at 1500*, dedicated to rearing and exporting over 120 species of butterfly. The first such farm in Latin America, now with over 100 associated farmers throughout Costa Rica, it is believed to be one of the second largest exporters of farm-bred butterflies in the world (the largest is in Taiwan). Created by Joris Brinckerhoff, a former Peace Corp volunteer and his wife in 1984, the farm opened to the public in 1990. All visitors receive a two-hour guided tour. Visit in the morning as butterflies require heat from the sun for the energy to fly so when it is cool or cloudy, there may be less activity.

Getting there The Butterfly Farm offers round trip minibus transportation from San José hotels (US$15, US$10 students, US$8 children, reservations required, T2438-0400). The public bus for La Guácima, leaves from Calle 10, Avenida 2-4, behind La Merced Church in San José (0800, 1100 and 1400, returns at 1230, 1530 and 1730, one hour, US$0.55); at the last stop walk 300 m from the school south to the butterfly sign. From Alajuela take a bus marked 'La Guácima abajo', which departs 100 m south, 100 m west of **Tikal Supermarket** (40 minutes, at 0620, 0900, 1100 and 1300; returning at 0945, 1145, 1345, 1545 and 1745).

From San José you can take a tour of **Café Britt's coffee farm** ① *near Barva de Heredia, T2277-1500, www.coffeetour.com, 1100, 1½ hrs, US$40*, where you can see the processing factory, tasting room and a multi-media presentation using professional actors of the story of coffee. You can arrange to be picked up at various points and hotels in San José. **Teatro Dionisio Chaverría** at **Café Britt** hosts weekend theatre and a children's show on Sunday afternoons.

③ San José listings

Hotel and guesthouse prices
LL over US$150	**L** US$100-150	**AL** US$66-99
A US$46-65	**B** US$31-45	**C** US$21-30
D US$12-20	**E** US$7-11	**F** under US$7

Restaurant prices
↑↑↑ over US$15   **↑↑** US$8-15   **↑** under US$8
See pages 45-48 for further information.

⊜ Sleeping

San José *p1147, maps p1148 and p1150*
There are cheap hotels between the Mercado Central, Mercado Borbón and the Coca Cola terminal. Cheaper hotels usually have only wooden partitions for walls, making them noisy. Hotels in the red-light district, Calle 6, Av 1-5, near Mercado Central, charge on average US$10 with toilet and shower for a night.

LL-AL Grano de Oro, Calle 30, Av 2, T2255-3322, www.hotelgranodeoro.com. Exquisite converted 19th-century mansion, 35 rooms and suites, beautiful terrace gardens, renowned restaurant. Friendly, good value.
L Aurola Holiday Inn, Av 5 between Calle 5-7, T2222-2424, www.aurola-holiday inn.com. Mainly business clientele, casino, good view of city from casino.
L-AL Britannia, Calle 3, Av 11, T2223-6667, www.hotelbritanniacostarica.com. 1910 Spanish-style beautifully restored mansion, high standard, antique furniture, very good service, excellent restaurant, worth the money.
L-AL Del Rey, Av 1, Calle 9, T2257-7800, www.hoteldelrey.com. Nice single, double, triple rooms, standard or deluxe, suites. Landmark hotel, centre of casino and upmarket red-light district, not recommended for families, walls a bit thin. Has a restaurant.
L-AL Fleur de Lys, Calle 13, Av 2-6, T2223-1206, www.hotelfleurdelys.com. Restored Victorian mansion house, good restaurant, bar. Stylishly elegant. Recommended.
AL Don Carlos, Calle 9, Av 7-9, T2221-6707, www.doncarloshotel.com. 36 rooms, interesting traditional building, much artwork and statuary, sun deck, free coffee, Annemarie's giftshop with good selection, credit cards accepted, airport shuttle.

AL Rosa del Paseo, Paseo Colón, Calle 28-30, T2257-3225, www.rosadelpaseo.com. Beautifully restored mansion, breakfast included. Good location for access to the city centre but not in the heart of town.

AL Santo Tomás, Av 7, Calle 3-5, T2255-3950, www.hotelsantotomas.com. French Victorian mansion, 20 rooms, pool, garden, internet access, secure parking, **Restaurant El Oasis** next door, tours arranged.

A Cinco Hormigas Rojas, Calle 15, Av 9-11, T2255-3412, www.cincohormigasrojas.com. Nice decor, small house. Prices includes taxes.

A Rincón de San José, formerly **Edelweiss**, Av 9, Calle 13-15, 100 m east of **Condovac** offices, T2221-9702, www.hotelrinconde sanjose.com. English, Dutch and Spanish spoken, clean, comfortable, native hardwood furniture and carved doors. Pleasant courtyard bar, helpful, friendly.

A-B CACTS, Av 3 bis, Calle 28-30, 3 blocks north of **Pizza Hut**, Paseo Colón, T2221-2928, www.hotelcacts.com. Safe, good service, breakfast and taxes included, TV, friendly, pets allowed. Recommended.

A-C Joluva, Calle 3b, Av 9-11, T2223-7961. With breakfast, old house, friendly, safe, good laundry service, good value. A relaxing and gay-friendly hotel.

B Diana's Inn, Calle 5, Av 3, Parque Morazán, near **Holiday Inn**, T2223-6542, dianas@rac sa.co.cr. An old building formerly used by the president, now restored, includes breakfast and taxes, discounts available, a/c, TV, hot water, noisy, free luggage storage, safe box.

C Centroamericano, Av 2, Calle 6-8, T2221-3362. Includes taxes, private bath, clean small rooms, very helpful, will arrange accommodation in other towns, free shuttle (Mon-Fri) to airport, laundry facilities.

C Pensión de la Cuesta, Av 1, Calle 11-15, T2256-7946, www.pensiondelacuesta.com. A little off the wall in style, with artwork all over this old colonial home. Shared bath, use of the kitchen and internet, includes breakfast.

C-D Casa Ridgway, Calle 15, Av 6-8, T2233-6168, www.amigosparalapaz.org. 1-4 beds in room, shared bath, use of

kitchen, very helpful, friendly, laundry possible, group rates and facilities.

C-D Green House Hotel, Plaza Gonzalez Viques, Calle 11, Av 16 y 18, T2258-0102, www.greenhousehostel.altervista.org. Very clean, both private and shared rooms come with hot water bath, free breakfast, communal kitchen, Wi-Fi, cable TV, not close to the centre, but great spot otherwise.

C-D Hostel Pangea, Av 11, Calle 3 bis, T2221-1992, www.hostelpangea.com. Friendly, clean, use of kitchen. Good local information, with free coffee, internet, breakfast and reportedly the only hostel in Central America with heated pool, jacuzzi, licensed bar and wet bar. Good spot.

C-E Tranquilo Backpackers, Calle 7, Av 9-11, T2223-3189, www.tranquiloback packers.com. Dormitory and private rooms with great, relaxed atmosphere, but not very helpful.

D Avenida Segunda, Av 2 No 913, Calle 9-11, T2222-0260, acebrisa@racsa.co.cr. Includes taxes, shared or private bath, friendly, stores luggage.

D Bienvenido, Calle 10, Av 1-3, T2233-2161. Clean, hot shower, near centre and airport bus, best hotel near Coca Cola bus terminal.

D Boston, Av 8, Calle Central-2, T2221-0563. With or without bath, good, very friendly, but noisy, will store luggage.

D JC Friends Hostel, Calle 34 y Av 3, Casa Esquinera, Paseo Colon. Owned by an extremely well-travelled Tico who has bucketfuls of local information to impart. Communal kitchen, lockers, a/c and internet access. Tuasa bus stops opposite. Also have a *hostal* in Tamarindo.

D Otoya, Calle 1, Av 3-5, T2221-3925, erickpensionotoya@24horas.com. Close to the centre, cleanish, friendly and quite popular, you're allowed to use the telephone (free local calls). Hot water throughout and some rooms with private bath, includes taxes. Luggage store, laundry service, English spoken.

D Pensión Musoc, Calle 16, Av 1-3, T2222-9437. With or without private bath, very clean, hot water, luggage stored, will do laundry. Friendly, near bus stations so somewhat noisy, but recommended.

D-E Casa Yoses, Av 8, Calle 41, 25 mins west from Spoon in Los Yoses, T2234-5486, www.casayoses.com. Popular hostel in restored mansion, located near the trendy San Pedro Mall, breakfast and internet are gratis, relaxing gardens, quiet area.

D-E Costa Rica Backpackers, Av 6, Calle 21-23, T2221-6191, www.costaricaback packers.com. Top billing at these prices with a pool, good dormitory and private rooms, kitchen and laundry services, free coffee and internet. Parking possible.

D-E Gaudy's Backpackers' Hostel, Av 5, Calle 36-38, T2258-2937, www.back packer.co.cr. Good backpacker choice, with dormitory accommodation, kitchen, communal areas and internet access. Good location and quieter than the other cheap options.

D-E Gran Imperial, on the western side of the Central Market, Calle 8, Av 1-Central, T2222-8463, www.hostelgranimperial.com. Mixed reports, small rooms, thin walls, clean, sometimes noisy, with or without private bath, limited hot showers, includes taxes, restaurant with good prices, best to reserve. Good for meeting other travellers, with balcony overlooking Central Market. A great spot for relaxing, locked luggage store, TV.

D-E Hostal Toruma, Av Central, Calle 29-31, T2234-9186. 93 beds, clean, hot water, crowded but safe, lockable storage in each room, includes breakfast. Free use of internet and kitchen for guests. A good place for meeting other travellers to arrange group travel.

E Galileo Hostel, 100 m east of SodaTapia, T2248-2094, www.hostelgalileo.com. Friendly place, charming property with dorm beds and free internet.

E Pensión Boruca, Calle 14, Av 1-3, near Coca Cola terminal, T2223-0016. Shared bath,

hot water, laundry service, rooms a bit dark but friendly owner.

E Rialto, Av 5, Calle 2, 1 block north of Correos, T2221-7456. Shared or private bath, hot water, safe, friendly but can be very noisy.

F Tica Linda, Av 10, Calle 7-9. Dormitory accommodation, use of kitchen, hot water and laundry, TV in communal area. Will store luggage, popular with travellers. No sign, just a notice on the front. Moves often which makes finding the place a problem, but popular. Ask locally.

Near the airport
See Alajuela, page 1172.

Around San José p1152
A Pico Blanco Inn, San Antonio de Escazú, T2228-1908. All rooms with balconies and views of Central Valley, several cottages. English owner, restaurant with English pub, airport pickup can be requested. It's recommended.

A-B Costa Verde Inn, 300 m south of the 2nd San Antonio de Escazú cemetery, T2228-4080, www.costaverdeinn.com. A secluded and charming country home with 14 imaginatively decorated rooms – a popular choice away from the centre of town.

Camping
Belén, San Antonio de Belén, 2 km west of intersection at Cariari and San Antonio, 5 km from airport, turn off Hwy 1 on to Route 111, turn right at soccer field then 1st left for 1 km, T2239-0421. US$10 per day, American-owned trailer park, shade, hot showers, laundry, friendly, recommended, good bus service to San José.

🍴 Eating

San José p1147, maps p1148 and p1150
Traditional dishes, feasting on a steady supply of rice and beans, tend to be a

little on the heavy side but are definitely worth trying.

At lunchtime cheaper restaurants offer a set meal called a *casado*, US$1.50-2.50, which is good value. There are several cheap Chinese places along Av 5. For reliable and seriously cheap places, try the **Mercado Central**, around the Coca Cola bus terminal and the area to the southwest of **Parque Central**. *Autoservicios* do not charge tax and service and represent the best value. There are plenty of fast-food outlets dotted throughout the city.

††† Ana Italiana, T2222-6153, Paseo Colón, Calle 24 y 26. Closed Mon. Good Italian food and friendly.

††† Café Mundo, Av 9, Calle 13-15, opposite Hotel Rincón de San José, T2222-6190. Old mansion tastefully restored, good salads, great pasta, wonderful bread, a stylish joint.

††† El Chicote, on north side of Parque Sabana, T2232-0936. Reliable favourite, country style, good grills.

††† El Cuartel de la Boca del Monte, Av 1, Calle 21-23, T2221-0327. Live music at night but a good and popular restaurant by day.

††† Jurgen's, Calle 41 and Paseo Rubén Darío, Barrio Dent in Los Yoses, T2224-2455. Closed Sun. 1st-class service, excellent international menu, sophisticated atmosphere.

††† La Bastille, Paseo Colón, Calle 22, T2255-4994. Closed Sun. Stylish French food in elegant surrounds.

††† La Cocina de Leña, north of the centre in El Pueblo, Barrio Tournón, T2255-1360. Excellent menu of the very best in Tico cuisine, upmarket, pricey, but warm, friendly ambience.

††† La Esquina del Café, Av 9, Calle 3b. Daily 0900-2200. Speciality coffee roasters with good restaurant, souvenir shop, live music twice a month.

††† La Masia de Triquell, Edif Casa España, Sabana Norte, T2296-3528. Closed Sun. Catalan, warmly recommended.

††† Le Chandelier, 50 m west and 100 m south of the main entrance of the ICE building in Los Yoses, T2225-3980. Closed Sun. One of the best French restaurants in town, reservations required.

††† Los Ranchos Steak House, Sabana Norte near **Hotel TRYP Meliá**. Reliable, good food.

††† Lubnan, Paseo Colón, Calle 22-24, T2257-6071. Authentic Lebanese menu, vegetarian selections, great service.

††† Marbella, out beyond San Pedro mall, T2224-9452. Fish, paella specialities, packed on Sun, very good.

††† Tin Jo, Calle 11, Av 6-8, T2221-7605. Probably the best Asian cuisine in town.

†† Café La Bohemia, Calle Central, Av 2, next to Teatro Melico Salazar. Pastas and meats as well as light lunches such as quiches and crêpes.

†† Gran Diamante, Av 5, Calle 4-6. With a 'lively kitchen' where you can watch the food being prepared.

†† La Vasconia, corner of Av 1, Calle 5, great little restaurant combining a passion for football and food. Basic in style, good traditional dishes.

†† Los Antojitos, on Paseo Colón, on Pavas Hwy west of Sabana, in Tibás, San Antonio de Escazú and in Centro Comercial Cocorí (road to suburb of San Pedro), T2232-2411. Serves excellent Mexican food at fair prices.

†† Machu Picchu, Calle 32, Av 1-3, T2222-7384. Open from 1700. Cosed Sun. Great Peruvian food, good service in homely atmosphere.

†† México Bar, north of the Coca Cola district in Paso de la Vaca, T2221-8461. Dead by day, comes alive at night with a flurry of music and good Mexican food.

†† Vishnu, Av 1, Calle 1-3, also on Calle 14, Av 2. Daily 02800-2000. Best known vegetarian place in town, good quality, cheap and good *plato del día*. Try their soya cheese sandwiches and ice cream, sells good wholemeal bread.

† Chicharronera Nacional, Av 1, Calle 10-12. *Autoservicio* and very popular.

† China Bonita at Av 5, Calle 2-4. One of the cheapest Chinese options in town.

† Corona de Oro, Av 3, Calle 2-4 (next to Nini). An excellent *autoservicio*.

¶ Don Sol, Av 7b No 1347. Excellent 3-course vegetarian lunch, run by integral yoga society (only open for lunch).

¶ El Merendero, Av 6, Calle Central-2. *Autoservicio* serving cheap local food, popular with Ticos.

¶ La Puriscaleña, on the corner of Calle Central and Av 5, is a good, local *comedor*. The *menú del día* is a tasty bargain.

¶ Pollo a la Leña, Calle 1, Av 3-5, which has seriously cheap chicken, popular with locals.

¶ Popular, Av 3, Calle 6-8. Good *casado*.

¶ Whapin, Calle 35, Av 13, Excellent Caribbean restaurant with extensive menu, authentic rice and beans and fried plantains, live music occasionally.

Cafés, sodas and ice cream parlours

Bagelman, Paseo Rubén Darío (Av Central), Calle 33, just east of **Hostal Toruma** in Barrio Escalante, T2224-2432. Smart and tasty fast-food bagel heaven, delivers to area hotels. Also in San Antonio de Escazú, T2288-4460.

Café del Teatro, Av 2, Calle 3, in foyer of National Theatre. Open Mon-Sat. Pricey but worth it for the sheer style and sophistication of the belle époque interior.

Café Parisienne on the Plaza de la Cultura, the street café of the **Gran Hotel Costa Rica**. Food a little overpriced, but have a coffee and watch the world go by.

Churrería Manolo, Av Central, Calle Central-2 (restaurant upstairs). Open 24 hrs. Simple, quick food with takeaway options on the street, good sandwiches and hot chocolate.

Helados Boni, Calle Central, Av 6-8. Home-made ice cream.

Helados Rena, Calle 8, Av Central. Excellent.

La Esquina del Café, Av 9, Calle 3b, Barrio Amón, T2257-9868. Daily 0900-2200. Speciality coffee roasters with beans from 6 different regions to taste, also a good restaurant with a souvenir shop. Live music twice a month.

La Nutrisoda, Edif Las Arcadas. Daily 1100-1800. Home-made natural ice cream.

Macrobiótica, Calle 11, Av 6-8. Health shop selling good bread.

Musmanni, has several outlets throughout the country, varying quality, best in the large cities and in the morning.

Pops, with several branches throughout town and the country, has excellent ice cream too.

Ruiseñor, Paseo Rubén Darío and Calle 41-43, Los Yoses, T2225-2562. The smart place to take coffee and snacks in east San José.

Soda El Parque, Calle 2, Av 4-6. Open 24 hrs. A popular spot for business people by day and relaxing entertainers by night.

Soda La Luz, Av Central, Calle 33, east towards Los Yoses. Good filling and cheap meals.

Soda Nini at Av 3, Calle 2-4. Cheap and cheerful.

Soda Tapia, Calle 42, Av 2-4, east side of Parque Sabana. Classic stopping place for Josefinos, with good food, served quickly.

Soda Vegetariana, next to **Librería Italiana**. Vegetarian with good juices and food.

Spoon has a central bakery at Av Central, Calle 5-7. Good coffee and pastries to take-out or eat in, also light lunches.

Around San José *p1152*

¶ Taj Mahal, San Antonio de Escazú, from Centro Comercial Paco, 1 km west on the old highway, T2228-0980. Indian food for a change.

⊕ Entertainment

San José *p1147, maps p1148 and p1150*

Bars and clubs

The *Tico Times* has a good listings section.

Beatles, Calle 9, Av Central. Good music, popular with ex-pats.

Calle de la Armagua, San Pedro. Happening street for young Ticos from 2230 onwards.

Centro Comercial El Pueblo, north of town in Barrio Tournón, with a cluster of fine restaurants, bars and discos. This is where Ticos party the night away until dawn.

Cocoloco is the liveliest of the discos, Infinito gets a slightly older crowd and La Plaza outside the centre, is often not as busy.

Chelle's, Av Central, Calle 9, T2221-1369. Excellent 24-hr bar and restaurant which changes its mood and clientele through the day. Great snacks and people watching.

Disco Salsa 54, Calle 3, Av 1-3. The place to go for salsa.

El Cuartel de la Boca del Monte, Av 1, Calle 21-23, T2221-0327. Live music at weekends, popular with students, hip young things but without the flashy dress. Recommended.

Key Largo, Parque Morazán. Live music, very popular with the Hotel del Rey crowd and all the stuff they get up to!

La Avispa, Calle 1, Av 8-10, and Déjà vu, Calle 2, Av 14-16. Both are gay-friendly discos, but not exclusively so.

Nashville South, Calle 5, Av 1-3. A popular Country-and-Western-style gringo bar.

Risas, Calle 1, Av Central, T2223-2803. Bars on 3 floors, good, popular with locals.

Terrau, out in San Pedro on Calle de la Armagua. The most popular of many clubs along this street. The area gets going around 2300 and keeps going till dawn. You'll need photo ID to get into the clubs.

Cinemas

Excellent modern cinemas showing latest releases are located throughout the metropolitan area, see *La Nación* for listings.

Cine Universitario at the UCR's Abelardo Bonilla law school auditorium in San Pedro, T2207-4717, shows good films at 1700 and 1900 daily, US$3-4.

El Semáforo in San Pedro shows films made in Latin America and Spain.

Sala Garbo, Av 2, Calle 28, T2222-1034, shows independent art house movies.

Variedades, Calle 5, Av Central-1, T2222-6108 is in the centre. Others can be found in Los Yoses, T2223-0085, San Pedro, T2283-5716, Rohrmoser, T2232-3271 and Heredia, T2293-3300.

Theatre

More than 20 theatres offer live productions in the San José area; check the *Tiempo Libre* entertainment supplement every Thu in *La Nación* for show times, mostly weekends.

Teatro del Angel, Av Central, Calle 13-15, T2222-8258. Has 3 modern dance companies.

Teatro Nacional, Av 2, Calle 3-5 T2221-5341 (recommended for the productions, the architecture and the bar/café), US$5 for guided tour, T2221-1329, behind it is La Plaza de la Cultura, a large complex.

Teatro Melico Salazar, Parque Central, T2233-5424, www.teatromelico.go.cr, for popular, folkloric shows.

⊛ Festivals and events

San José *p1147, maps p1148 and p1150*
Dec-Jan Christmas/New Year. Festivities last from mid-Dec to the first week of Jan, with dances, horse shows and much confetti throwing in the crowded streets. The annual El Tope horse parade starts at noon on 26 Dec and travels along the principal avenues of San José. A carnival starts next day at about 1700 in the same area. Fairs, firework displays, food and music at El Zapote, frequent buses from the centre.
Mar The International Festival of Culture assembles musicians from throughout Central America in a week of performances in the Plaza de Cultura around the 2nd week of Mar, although concern over the future of the event exists due to lack of funding.
2nd Sun in Mar Día del Boyero (Day of the Oxcart Driver) is celebrated in San Antonio de Escazú. Parades of ox-drawn carts, with music, dancing and blessings from the priesthood.
Mar/Apr Street parades during Easter week.
Sep 15 Independence Day. Bands and dance troupes move through the streets, although activities start to kick-off the night before with the traditional nationwide singing of the National Anthem at 1800.

Around San José *p1152*
San Antonio de Escazú
2nd weekend of Mar Día del Boyero
(National Oxcart Drivers' Day). Festivities
culminate on the Sun in a colourful oxcart
parade from the school to the centre.
Dancing in the evening to marimba music.

O Shopping

San José *p1147, maps p1148 and p1150*
Bookshops
Casa de la Revista, Calle 5, Av 1-3, T2256-
5092. Mon-Fri 0900-1800, Sat 0800-1700.
Good selection of maps, newspapers,
magazines and some books (mostly
paperbacks) in English. For other locations
and information, call main office of Agencia
de Publicaciones de Costa Rica, T2283-9383.
Librería Lehmann, Av Central, Calle 1-3,
T2223-1212, has a large and varied selection
of Spanish and English books and magazines.
They also stock maps including the 1:50,000
topographical maps produced by the Instituto
Geográfico Nacional de Costa Rica (IGN).
Mora Books, Av 1, Calle 3-5, T2255-4136, in
Omni building above Pizza Hut, Mon-Sat
1100-1900. Large selection of used books,
reasonable prices.
7th Street Books, Calle 7, Av Central, T2256-
8251, marroca@racsa.co.cr. A wide range of
new and used books covering all topics of
interest to visitors to Costa Rica, including
Footprint. Mon-Sat 0900-1800, Sun 1000-1700.

Crafts and markets
Market on Av Central, Calle 6-8, 0630-1800
(Sun 0630-1200), good leather suitcases and
wood. **Mercado Borbón**, Av 3-5, 8-10, fruit and
vegetables. *Artesanía* shops include: **Canapi**,
Calle 11, Av 1 (a cooperative, cheaper than
most), **Mercado Nacional de Artesanía**, Calle
11, Av 4, T2221-5012, Mon-Fri 0900-1800, Sat
0900-1700, is a good one-stop shop with a
wide variety of goods on sale. **La Casona**, Calle
Central, Av Central-1, daily 0900-1900, a
market of small *artesanía* shops, is full of

interesting little stalls. **Galería Namu**, opposite
the Alianza Francesa building on Av 7 and
Calle 5-7, Mon-Sat 0900-1630, T2256-3412,
www.galerianamu.com, is the best one-stop
shop for home-grown and indigenous art,
with the distinctly bright coloured ceramics
of Cecilia Figueres. Items can be shipped if
required and online shopping is possible. At
the **Plaza de la Democracia** in front of the
National Museum, tented stalls run the length
of a city block, great place to buy hammocks,
arts and crafts at competitive prices. Don't
be afraid to negotiate. **Centro Comercial El
Pueblo**, near the Villa Tournón Hotel, also has
a number of stalls but is mainly upmarket,
built in a traditional 'pueblo' style.
    In **Moravia** (8 km northeast of San José
with stops often included on city tours) the
block-long **Calle de la Artesanía** includes
souvenir stores, including well-known **La
Rueda**, T2297-2736, good for leatherworks.

Photography
Taller de Equipos Fotográficos, 120 m east
of kiosk Parque Morazán, Av 3, Calle 3-5,
T2223-1146. Authorized Canon workshop.
Tecfot, Av 7, Calle Central, T2221-1438.
Repairs all cameras, authorized Minolta
dealer, good service and reasonable rates.

Shopping malls
Shopping malls are popping up in different
parts of town including San Pedro, on the
eastern ring rd, complete with cinema. The
expanded **Multiplaza Mall**, near Camino Real,
Escazú, has great shops and lots of cinemas.
Across the highway toward San José is **Plaza
Itskatzú**, a colonial-style shopping centre with
restaurants and shops. Another is the **Terra
Mall** in Curridabat.

▲ Activities and tours

San José *p1147, maps p1148 and p1150*
If you're planning on staying in or around San
José for a while, look in the Calendar pages of
the *The Tico Times* for clubs and associations.

Bungee jumping

After Rafael Iglesias Bridge (Río Colorado), continue on Pan-American Hwy 1.5 km, turn right at Salón Los Alfaro, down the track to Puente Colorado. **Tropical Bungee** operates 0900-1600 daily in high season, US$65 1st jump, US$30 for the 2nd (same day only) includes transportation from San José, reservations required, T2248-2212, www.bungee.co.cr.

Cycling

Coast to Coast Adventures, T2280-8054, www.ctocadventures.com, run trips in the local area.

Night tours

Costa Rican Nights Tour, La Uruca, T2290-3035, www.puebloantiguo.co.cr. This 3-hr dinner show incorporates fireworks, marimba music, a show and a guided tour through San José in Pueblo Antiguo. Takes place Wed, Fri, Sat 1900-2200.

Swimming

The best public pool is at **Ojo de Agua**, 5 mins from the airport in Alajuela, 15 mins from San José. Daily 0800-1600, US$1.55, T2441-2808. Direct bus from Calle 10, Av 2-4 (behind La Merced Church) in San José or take bus to Alajuela and then another to San Antonio de Belén. There is also an open-air pool at **Plaza González Víquez**, in the southeast section of San José, crowded. Weekends only, US$1, T2256-6517.

Nature tours

ACTUAR, T2248-9470, www.actuarcostarica. com. An association of 26 community-based rural tourism groups.
Aguas Bravas, T2292-2072, www. aguas-bravas.co.cr. Whitewater rafting on rivers around the Central Valley, also horse riding, biking, hiking and camping.
Costa Rica Expeditions, Av 3, Calle Central 3, T2257-0766, www.costaricaexpeditions.com. Upmarket wildlife adventures include whitewater rafting (US$95 for 1-day trip on Río Pacuare, includes lunch and transport; other rivers from US$69-95) and further options. They own **Tortuga Lodge, Corcovado Lodge Tent Camp** and **Monteverde Lodge**. Daily trips, highly recommended.
Ecole Travel, lobby of Gran Hotel, T2253-8884, www.ecoletravel.com. Chilean-Dutch, highly recommended for budget tours to Tortuguero, Corcovado and tailor-made excursions off the beaten track.
Green Tropical Tours, Calle 1, Av 5-7, T2229-4192, www.greentropical.com, with options outside the norm including tours to Guayabo National Monument, Los Juncos and cloud forest.
Horizontes, Calle 28, Av 1-3, T2222-2022, www.horizontes.com. A big operator in Costa Rica, high standards, educational and special interest, advice given and arrangements made for groups and individuals.
Mitur, T2296-7378, www.mitour.com. A range of tours, including Ilan Ilan in Tortuguero US$199, 3-days, 2 nights.
Ríos Tropicales, Calle 38, between Paseo Colón and Av 2, 50 m south of Subway, T2233-6455, www.riostropicales. com. Specialists in whitewater rafting and kayaking, good selection and careful to assess your abilities, good food, excellent guides, US$250 for 2-day trip on Río Pacuare, waterfalls, rapids, including camping and food. Many other options throughout the country.
Typical Tours, Las Arcadas, next to the Gran Hotel Costa Rica, T2233-8486. City tours, volcano tours, nature reserves, rafting, cruising.

Several companies focus on trips to Tortuga Island off the southern tip of Nicoya Peninsula. Try **Bay Island Cruises**, T2258-3536, bayislan@racsa.co.cr. Daily tours to Tortuga Island, US$79 includes lunch and transport from San José area.

Tour operators

Aventuras Naturales, Av Central, Calle 33-35, T2225-3939, www.adventure costarica.com. Specialists in whitewater rafting with their own lodge on the Pacuare, which has a canopy adventure tour. Also several other trips.

COOPRENA (Simbiosis Tours), San José, T2290-8646, www.turismoruralcr.com. A group supporting small farmers, broadly working to the principle of sustainable tourism. Offers tours and accommodation around the country.

Costa Rican Trails, 325 Curridabat de la Pops, 300-m al Sur y 250 al Este, T1 888-803-3344 (USA), T1866-865-7013 (Canada), www.costaricantrails.com. Travel agency and tour operator, offering 1-day and multi-day tours and packages, selected and resorts, reliable local ground and air transport.

LA Tours, PO Box 492-1007, Centro Colón, T2221-4501. Kathia Vargas is extremely helpful in rearranging flights and reservations.

Super Viajes, American Express representative, Oficientro Ejecutivo La Sabana, Edif 1 Sabana, PO Box 3985, T2220-0400.

Swiss Travel Service, is one of the biggest tour operators with branches in many of the smarter hotels, T2282-4898, www.swiss travelcr.com. Can provide any standard tour, plus several specialist tours for birdwatchers. Good guides and warmly recommended.

● Transport

San José p1147, maps p1148 and p1150

Air
The much-improved Aeropuerto Internacional Juan Santamaría (SJO) is at El Coco, 16 km from San José along the Autopista General Cañas (5 km from Alajuela). Airport information, T2443 2622 (24 hrs). The Sansa terminal for domestic flights is next to the main terminal. Sansa runs a free bus service to the airport for its passengers. There is another terminal, about 1 km west of the main terminal, used by charter flights and private planes. Buses to city centre from main street outside ground-floor terminal. Buses to airport, continuing on to Alajuela from Av Central-2, Calle 10, every 10 mins from 0500-2100; 45 mins, US$0.50 (good service, plenty of luggage space). Taxi to and from airport, US$12. Taxis run all night from the main square. For early flights you can reserve a taxi from any San José hotel the night before. All taxi companies run a 24-hr service. Bank at the airport 0800-1600, with ATM available as well. **ICT**, open in the day time, has a helpful tourist office in the main terminal for maps, information and hotel reservations.

Internal flights Sansa and Nature Air (from Tobias Bolaños, 8 km west of San José, in Pavas) operate internal flights throughout the country. **Sansa** check-in is at office on Av Las Americas and Calle 42, free bus to and from airport. Check schedules on **Nature Air**, T2299-6000, www.natureair.com. If you made reservations before arriving in Costa Rica, confirm and collect tickets as soon as possible after arrival. Book ahead, especially for the beaches. In Feb and Mar, planes can be fully booked 3 weeks ahead. On all internal scheduled and charter flights there is a baggage allowance of 12 kg. Oversized items such as surfboards or bicycles are charged at US$15 if there is room in the cargo hold.

From San José you can fly to **Barra del Colorado**, **Coto 47**, **Drake Bay**, **Golfito**, **Liberia**, **Limón**, **Nosara**, **Palmar Sur**, **Puerto Jiménez** (with a connecting flight to **Carate**, on the border of Corcovado National Park), **Punta Islita**, **Quepos**, **Carrillo-Sámara**, **Tamarindo**, **Tambor**, **Tortuguero** and **Granada** in Nicaragua and **Bocas del Toro** in Panama.

Airline offices
International carriers Air France, Condominio Vista Real, 1st floor, 100 m east of POPs, Curridabat, T2280-0069; **Alitalia**, Calle 24, Paseo Colón, T2295-6820; **American**, Sabana Este, opposite Hotel TRYP Meliá, T2257-1266; **Avianca**, Edif Centro, p 2, Colón, Paseo Colón, Calle 38-40, T2233-3066; **British Airways**, Calle 13, Av 13, T2257-8087; **Condor Airlines**, Calle 5, Av 7-9, T2256-6161; **Continental**, Oficentro La Virgen No 2, 200 m south, 300 m east and 50 m north of American Embassy, Pavas, T2296-4911; **Copa**, Av 5, Calle 1, T2223-2672; **Delta**, 100 m east of Toyota and 50 m south,

T2257-2992; **Grupo Taca**, see **Sansa** above; **Iberia**, Paseo Colón, Calle 40, T2257-8266; **KLM**, Sabana Sur, behind Controlaría General Building, T2220-4111; **Lloyd Aéreo Boliviano**, Av 2, Calle 2-4, upstairs, T2255-1530; **LTU International Airways** (German charter airline), Condominio da Vinci, Oficina No 6, Barrio Dent, T2234-9292; **Lufthansa**, Calle 5, Av 7-9, T2243-1818; **Martinair**, Dutch charter airline – subsidiary of KLM, see above; **Mexicana**, Paseo Colón Torres Mercedes, T2295-6969, Mexican Tourist Card available here; **SAM**, Paseo Colón, Calle 38-40, Edif Centro Colón, 2nd floor, T2233-3066; **Singapore Airlines**, Edificio Isabella San Pedro, T2234-2223; **Servivensa**, Edif Centro Colón, 2nd floor, Paseo Colón, Calle 38-40, T2257-1441; **Swissair**, Calle Central, Av 1-3, T2221-6613; **United Airlines**, Sabana Sur, behind Controlaría General Building, T2220-2027; **Varig**, Sabana West 150 m south of Canal 7, T2290-5222.

National and charter airlines
Aerobell, T2290-0000, www.aerobell.com, at Pavas; **Alfa Romeo Aéreo Taxi**, in Puerto Jiménez, T2735-5112; **Helicópteros del Norte**, helicopter charters and sightseeing tours out of San José, US$350 per hr, T2232-7534; **Nature Air** (see above); **Paradise Air**, T2296-3600, www.flywith paradise.com, based in Pavas; **Sansa**, T2223-4179, www.flysansa.com.

Bus
Local Urban routes in San José cost US$0.50 or less. Hand baggage in reasonable quantities is not charged. A cheap tour of San José can be made on the bus marked *periférico* from Paseo Colón in front of the Cine Colón, or at La Sabana bus stop, a 45-min circuit of the city. A smaller circuit is made by the 'Sabana/ Cementerio' bus, pick it up at Av 2, Calle 8-10.

Regional In the majority of cases, buses start or finish their journey at San José so there are services to most towns; see under relevant destination for details of times

and prices. Check where the bus stops at your destination, some routes do not go to the centre of towns, leaving passengers some distance away.

Bus stations are scattered around town: **Alajuela** (including airport) from Av 2, Calle 12-14; **Cahuita**, **Limón**, **Manzanillo**, **Puerto Viejo de Talamanca**, **Sixaola** all served from Gran Terminal del Caribe (Guapileños, Caribeños, Sixaola); **Jacó**, **Carará**, **Quepos**, **Manuel Antonio**, **Uvita** all depart from from Terminal Coca Cola; **Santa Cruz** (½ block west), **Peñas Blancas** (100 m north) from outside Terminal Coca Cola; **Cártago** from Terminal Cártago during the day, after 2030 from Gran Hotel Costa Rica, Av 2, Calle 3-5; **Cd Quesada (San Carlos)**, **Fortuna**, **Guápiles (Braulio Carrillo)**, **Los Chiles**, **Caño Negro**, **Monteverde** (outside terminal), **Puerto Jiménez** (outside terminal), **Puerto Viejo Sarapiquí**, **Tilarán** (½ block north) from Terminal Atlántico Norte at Av 9, Calle 12; **Playa del Coco**, **Liberia** from Calle 14, Av 1-3; **Golfito**, **Nicoya**, **Nosara**, **Palmar Norte**, **Paso Canoas**, **Sámara**, **San Vito**, **Tamarindo** from Terminal Alfaro; **San Isidro de El General** (2 companies, Musoc and Tuasur), terminal down on Av 22-24, Calle Central, **Heredia** from Terminal Heredia or a minibus from Av 2, Calle 10-12; **Volcán Irazú** from Av 2, Calle 1-3, opposite Gran Hotel Costa Rica; **Volcán Poás** from Av 2, Calle 12-14; **Puntarenas** from Terminal Puntarenas, Calle 16, Av 10-12; **Santa María de Dota** from Terminal Los Santos; **Turrialba** from Terminal Turrialba.

Shuttle bus 2 companies, Interbus, T2283-5573, www.interbusonline.com, and Fantasy Tours/GrayLine, T2220-2126, www.graylinecostarica.com, offer transport from the capital to dozens of beach and tourism destinations in comfortable a/c minibuses, bilingual drivers, hotel pickup, tickets US$17-38 1 way.

International If the timing of your journey is important, book tickets: in Dec-Jan, buses are often booked 2 weeks ahead, while at other times of the year outside holiday seasons there are plenty of spaces. Ticabus terminal at Calle 9-11, Av 4, T2221-8954, www.ticabus.com, office open Mon-Sun 0600-2200. **Ticabus to Guatemala City**, 3 daily, 60 hrs, US$74, with overnight stay in Managua and San Salvador. To **Tegucigalpa**, 3 daily, 48 hrs, US$42, overnight stay in Managua. To **Managua** 3 daily, US$21, 10 hrs including 1 hr at Costa Rican side of border and another 2 hrs on Nicaraguan side while they search bags. To **Panama City** 1200 daily, US$26 1 way, 18 hrs (book in advance). To get a Panamanian tourist card you must buy a return ticket – you can get a refund in Panama but with a discount of 15%. **Transnica**, Calle 22, Av 3-5, T2223-4242, runs buses with TV, video, a/c, snacks, toilet, to **Managua** 4 daily, US$20 return. Before departure have your ticket confirmed on arrival at the terminal; when buying and confirming your ticket, you must show your passport. When boarding the bus you are given an immigration form.

Panaline goes to **Panama City** daily at 1300 from Calle 16, Av 3, T2256-8721, www.panalinecr.com, US$22 1 way, US$41 return, reduction for students, arrives 0500; a/c, payment by Visa/MasterCard accepted. To **David**, from Terminal Alfaro, 2 daily, 9 hrs, US$18; book in advance. They are modern, comfortable buses, although there is not much room for long legs, but they have the advantage of covering a scenic journey in daylight. A bus to **Changuinola** via the Sixaola–Guabito border post leaves San José at 1000 daily, 8 hrs, US$8, from opposite Terminal Alfaro, T2556-1432 for info, best to arrive 1 hr before departure; the bus goes via Siquirres and is the quick route to **Limón**.

Car

Car hire Most local agencies are on or close to Paseo Colón, with a branch or drop-off site at or close to the airport and other locations around the country.

International companies with services include **Adobe, Alamo, Avis, Budget, Dollar, Economy, Hertz, Hola, National, Payless, Thrifty, Toyota** and **Tricolor**.

Solid, T2442-6000, www.rentacarcosta rica.com, are a local company with several offices around town including **Hostal Toruma**, most competively priced in town; **Wild Rider Motorcycles**, also rents cheap 4WD vehicles (see below).

Motorcycle and bike

Rental Wild Rider Motorcycles, Paseo Colón, Calle 32 diagonal Kentucky, next to Aventuras Backpackers, T2258-4604, www.wild-rider.com, Honda XR250s, Yamaha XT600s and Suzuki DR650SE available for rent from US$60-75 a day, US$700-1300 deposit required. 4WD vehicles also available, US$240-440 per week, monthly discounts.

Cycle repairs Cyclo Quiros, Apartado 1366, Pavas, 300 m west of US Embassy. The brothers Quiros have been repairing bikes for 20 years, good place for general information and repairs, highly recommended.

Taxis

Minimum fare US$0.57 for 1st km, US$0.31 additional km. Taxis used to charge more after 2200, but that rule has been rescinded. Taxis are red and have electronic meters called *marías*, if not, get out and take another cab. For journeys over 12 km, price should be negotiated between driver and passenger. Radio cabs can be booked in advance. To order a taxi, call **Coopeguaria**, T2226-1366, **Coopeirazu**, T2254-3211, **Coopemoravia**, T2229-8882, **Coopetaxi**, T2235-9966, **Taxi San Jorge**, T2221-3434, **Taxis Guaria**, T2226-1366, **Taxis Unidos SA**, which are the official taxis of the Juan Santamaría International Airport and are orange instead of red, T2222-6865, or look in the classified adverts of *The Tico Times* for car and driver hire.

● Directory

San José p1147, maps p1148 and p1150
Banks

Queues in state-run banks tend to be long; using privately run banks is recommended. The 15th and end of the month (pay day for government employees) are especially bad. Visa and MasterCard ATMs are widespread and the best option in the capital. Queues tend to be shorter outside San José. Money can be sent through **Banco de San José** or **Banco de Costa Rica** at 4%. Credit card holders can obtain cash advances from **Banco de San José** (Visa, MasterCard) and **Credomatic Los Yoses** in colones (Master Card ATM) and **Banco Popular** (Visa ATM) minimum cash advance: US$50 equivalent. ATMs which will accept international Visa/MasterCard are available at most banks, shopping malls and San José airport. **Banco Crédito Agrícola de Cártago**, state-run, 9 branches, also makes advances on Visa, no commission, no limits. **Banco de Costa Rica**, Av 2, Calle 4, state-run, changes TCs, open 0830-1500, long queues, 1% commission. **Banco de San José**, Calle Central, Av 3-5, private, commission 2.5%. **Banco Nacional**, head office, Av 1-3, Calle 2-4, state-run, will change TCs into dollars but you pay a commission, accepts Visa credit cards as do most of the bigger banks in San José and other major towns. Many private banks are open late and Sat, including **Banco Cuscatlán**, with 12 branches around the country, Mon-Fri 0800-1800, Sat 0800-1200, T2299-0299.

An alternative to the banks for getting money are the money-transfer services: **Western Union**, T2283-6336, www.westernunion.com, which operates out of many pharmacies and other locations and **Moneygram**, T2295-9055, www.moneygram.com. Quicker than banks but you pay a price premium. **Interbank**, transfers are cheaper and you don't need an account, but take several days or more. Ask at a bank's information desk for details.

Cultural centres

Alianza Francesa, Av 7, Calle 5, French newspapers, French films every Wed evening, friendly; **Centro Cultural Costarricense Norteamericano**, Calle 37, Av 1-5, Los Yoses, T2207-7500, www.cccncr.com, open daily until 1930, free, shows good films, plays, art exhibitions and English-language library.

Embassies and consulates

Belgium, Barrio Dent, T2280-4435, 0800-1330; **Canada**, Building 5 (3rd floor) of Oficentro Ejecutivo La Sabana, Sabana Sur, T2242-4400, Mon-Thu 0800-1630, Fri 0800-1330; **El Salvador**, Paseo Colón, from Toyota 500 m north and 25 m west, T2257-7855; **France**, Curridabat, 200 m south, 25 m west of Indoor Club, T2234-4167, 0830-1200; **Germany**, Rohrmoser, 200 m north and 75 m east of Oscar Arias' house, T2232-5533, 0900-1200; **Guatemala**, 500 m south, 30 m east of POPs, Curridabat, T2283-2557, 0900-1300; **Honduras**, Rohrmoser, T2291-5143, 0900-1230; **Israel**, Edificio Colón, 11th floor, Paseo Colón, Calle 38-40, T2221-6444, 0900-1200; **Italy**, Los Yoses, Av 10, Calle 33-35, T2234-2326, 0900-1200; **Japan**, Oficentro building No 7, La Sabana, T2296-1650; **Mexico**, Consulate, Av 7, Calle 13-15, T2225-7284, 0830-1230; **Netherlands**, Oficentro Ejecutivo La Sabana, Sabana Sur, T2296-1490, Mon-Fri 0900-1200; **Nicaragua**, Av Central, Calle 25-27, opposite Pizza Hut, T2222-2373, 0830-1130 and 1330-1500, 24-hr wait for visa, US$25, dollars only, passport photo; **Norway**, Centro Colón, 10th floor, T2283-8222. Mon-Thu 1400-1700; **Panama**, San Pedro, T2281-2442, strict about onward ticket, 0900-1400, you need a photograph and photocopy of your passport, visa costs US$10 cash and takes up to 24 hrs; **Spain**, Paseo Colón, Calle 32, T2222-1933; **Sweden**, honorary consul at Almacén Font, 100 m east of La Pozuelo, La Uruca, T2232-8549; **Switzerland**, Centro Colón, p 10, Paseo Colón, Calle 38, T2221-4829, 0900-1200; **UK**, Centro Colón, p 11, end of Paseo Colón with Calle 38, T2258-2025,

0900-1200; **USA**, in the western suburb of Pavas, opposite Centro Comercial, catch a ruta 14 bus to Pavas, Zona 1 from Av 1 and Calle 16-18, T2220-3939, 0800-1630; **Venezuela**, Los Yoses, de la 5a entrada, 100 m south, 50 m west, T2225-8810, 0830-1230, visa issued same day, US$30, helpful.

Immigration

The immigration office is on the airport highway, opposite Hospital México. You need to go here for visas extensions, etc. Queues can take all day. To get there, take bus No 10 or 10A Uruca, marked 'México', then cross over highway at the bridge and walk 200 m along highway – just look for the queue or ask the driver. Better to find a travel agent who can obtain what you need for a fee, say US$5. Make sure you get a receipt if you give up your passport.

Internet

Cybercafé, in the basement of Edificio Las Arcadas, next to the Gran Hotel Costa Rica, daily 0700-2300, has a few machines. **Internet Café**, 4th floor, Av C, Calle 4, 0900-2200. A better way to spend less money as it is just 400 colones for full or part hr, but not a café. Several branches around town including at the western end of Paseo Colón in Edificio Colón, Calle 38-40, and if you want to type all night there is a 24-hr café in San Pedro, close to Banco Popular.

Language schools

The number of schools has increased rapidly. Listed below are just a selection recommended by readers. Generally, schools offer tuition in groups of 2-5 for 2-4 weeks. Lectures, films, outings and social occasions are usually included and accommodation with families is encouraged. Many schools are linked to the university and can offer credits towards a US course. Rates, including lodging, are around US$1100 a month. **Academica Tica de Español**, in San Rafael de Coronado, 10 km north of San José, T2229-0013, www.academiatica.com;

AmeriSpan, 1334 Walnut St, 6th floor, Philadelphia, PA 19107, T215-751-1100www.amerispan.com, has affiliated schools in Alajuela, Heredia, San José and 6 others locations; **Costa Rican Language Academy**, Barrio California, T2280-5834, www.spanishand more.com, run by Aída Chávez, offers language study and accommodation with local families, and instruction in Latin American music and dancing as well; **Costa Rica Spanish Institute**, Zapote in San Pedro district, T2234-1001, www.cosi.co.cr, US$350 per week, US$495 with homestay in San José, also branch in Manuel Antonio; **Instituto Británico** in Los Yoses, 1000 San José, T2225-0256, www.instituto britanico.co.cr, teaches English and Spanish; **Instituto de Español Costa Rica**, A 1, Calle Central – Calle 1, Apartado 1405-2100, Guadalupe, TT2280-6622, www.costaricaspanishschool.com. Close to the centre of San José, and complete with its own B&B. English, French and German spoken; **Universal de Idiomas**, in Moravia, T2223-9662, www.universal-edu.com, stresses conversational Spanish; **Intercultura**, Heredia, T2260-8480, www.intercultura costarica.com. Intensive courses with excursions to beaches, volcanoes, rainforest and a volunteer programme.

Laundry

Washing and dry cleaning at **Centro Comercial San José**, 2000, daily 0730-2000, US$3.75 for large load; **Lavandería Costa Rica**, Av 3, Calle 19-21, US$5 for a large load; **Lavandería Lavamex**, below Hotel Gran Imperial at Calle 7, Av 1-Central, US$4 to wash, US$4 to dry, quick service and very friendly. Book swap, very popular with travellers, much more than a laundry thanks to the helpful owners Karl and Patricia.

Libraries

Biblioteca Nacional, opposite Parque Nacional, Mon-Fri 0830-1630, also has art and photography exhibitions; **Centro Cultural**

Costarricense Norteamericano, C 37, Av 1-5, www.cccncr.com, T2207-7500, has a good English-language library.

Medical services

Dentists Clínica Dental Dr Francisco Cordero Guilarte, Rohrmoser 300 m east of Plaza Mayor, T2223-8890; **Dra Fresia Hidalgo**, Uned Building, San Pedro, 1400-1800, English spoken, reasonable prices, recommended, T2234-2840; **Fernando Baldioceda** and **Silvia Oreamuno**, 225 m north of Paseo Colón on the street that intersects at the Toyota dealership: both speak English; **Alfonso Villalobos Aguilar**, Edif Herdocía, p 2, Av 3, Calle 2-4, T2222-5709.

Doctors Dr Jorge Quesada Vargas, Clínica Internacional, Av 14, Calle 3-5, speaks German.

Hospitals and clinics Social Security hospitals have a good reputation (free to social security members, few members of staff speak English), free ambulance service run by volunteers: **Dr Calderón Guardia**, T2257-7922, **San Juan de Dios**, T2257-6282, **México**, T2232-6122; **Clínica Bíblica** Calle 1, Av 14, 24-hr pharmacy, T2257-5252, frequently recommended and the one most used by the local expatriate community and offers 24-hr emergency service at reasonable charges with staff who speak English, better than the large hospitals, where queues are long; **Clínica Católica**, northeast of San José, another private hospital with 24-hr pharmacy, T2246-3000; **Hospital CIMA**, T2208-1000, on the highway toward Escazú, country's newest and most modern private

hospital, bilingual staff, expensive rates, 24-hr pharmacy, T2208-1080.

Police

Thefts should be reported in San José to **Recepción de Denuncias**, Organismo de Investigación Judicial (OIJ), Calle 19, Av 6-8, T2295-3643. Call for nearest OIJ office in outlying areas.

Post office

Calle 2, Av 1-3, open for sale of stamps Mon-Fri, 0700-1700, Sat-Sun 0700-1800. Stamp vending machine in main post office. Lista de Correos, Mon-Fri 0800-1700, quick service. **Couriers** DHL, Pavas, Calle 34, T2209-6000, www.dhl.com; **Fed Ex**, Paseo Colón, 100 m east of León Cortés' statue, T2293-3157, www.fedex.com; UPS, 50 m east of Pizza Hut central office, Pavas, San José, T2239-0576, www.ups.com.

Telephone

Faxes and internal telegrams from main post office. Fax abroad, internet access and email from **RACSA**, Av 5, Calle 1, 0730-2200 (see also Essentials, page 1145). **ICE (Instituto Costarricense de Electricidad)**, Av 2, Calle 1, for phone calls (phone card only), and fax service, 0700-2200, 3-min call to UK US$10, friendly service (cheaper than **Radiográfica**, but check). Collect/reverse charge telephone calls can be made from any public telephone. English-speaking operators are available. See also page 1144.

Meseta Central West

Hilly and fertile with a temperate climate, the Central Highlands is a major coffee-growing area. Fairly heavily populated, picturesque and prosperous towns sit in the shadows of active volcanoes. Exploring the towns and villages of the region – each with its own character and style – gives good insight into the very heart of Costa Rica.

From San José, the Pan-American Highway heads east through the Meseta Central for 332 km along good roads to the Nicaraguan border. While CA1 will take you north, by sticking to it you'll miss visiting the remnants of colonial architecture found in Alajuela, Heredia and the countless smaller towns that enjoy the spring-like temperatures of the highlands. Although it's easier to explore the region in a private vehicle, frequent public buses and short journeys make hopping between towns fairly straightforward – if stepping out from San José it's probably worth dumping most of your luggage in the city and travelling light.
▶▶ For listings, see pages 1172-1176.

Northwest of San José ☺❶❀☻❶❻ ▶▶ *pp1172-1176.*

Alajuela → *Colour map 7, B3. Altitude: 952 m.*
The provincial capital of Alajuela has a slightly milder climate than San José, making it a popular weekend excursion for Josefinos. Famous for its flowers and market days (Saturday market is good value for food), regular buses from San José make it an easy day trip. Alternatively, stay in Alajuela, and use the regular buses to visit the capital. It is 5 km from the international airport, and is handy for early flights and late arrivals.

The town centres on the Parque Central with the 19th-century domed church on the eastern side. The unusual church of La Agonía, five blocks further east, is an interesting mix of styles. One block to the south, Juan Santamaría, the national hero who torched the building in Rivas (Nicaragua) in which William Walker's filibusters were entrenched in 1856, is commemorated by a monument. One block north of the Parque Central, the **Museo Histórico Juan Santamaría** ① *Av 3, Calle 2, Tue-Sun 1000-1800*, tells, somewhat confusingly, the story of this war.

Parque Nacional Volcán Poás → *Colour map 7, B3.*
① *Daily 0800-1530, 1 hr later Fri-Sun, Dec-Apr, US$10, good café next door, and toilets further along the road to the crater. If you wish to get in earlier you can leave your car/taxi at the gates, walk the 3 km up the hill and pay on your way out. The volcano is very crowded on Sun so go in the week if possible. Arrive early as clouds often hang low over the crater after 1000, obstructing the view. Wear good shoes, a hat and suncream.*
Volcán Poás (2708 m) sits in the centre of the Parque Nacional Volcán Poás (6506 ha), where the still-smoking volcano and bubbling turquoise sulphur pool are set within a beautiful forest. The crater is almost 1.5 km across – the second largest in the world. The park is rich with abundant birdlife given the altitude and barren nature of the terrain and home to the only true dwarf cloud forest in Costa Rica.

From Alajuela two paved roads head north for 37 km to the volcano. The first through San Pedro de Poás and Fraijanes, the second follows the road to San Miguel, branching left just before the town of Vara Blanca. In the park, trails are well marked to help guide you from the visitor centre to the geysers, lake and other places of interest. The main crater is 1 km along a road from the car park. There is a visitor centre by the car park with explanations of the recent changes in the volcano. There is also a good café run by **Café Britt**; alternatively, bring your own food and water.

From **Vara Blanca** the road runs north past the popular La Paz waterfall, round the east side of the volcano through Cinchona and Cariblanco. This area was hit by a 6.2 magnitude earthquake in January 2009, causing damage to roads in the area. **La Paz Waterfall Gardens** ① *5 km north of Vara Blanca, T2482-2720, www.waterfallgardens.com, US$32*, has forest trails past five huge falls and one of the world's largest butterfly and hummingbird gardens, a restaurant, US$12 buffet lunch and the **Peace Lodge Hotel** (**LL**), closed due to the earthquake, but expected to reopen in May 2009. The road is twisty, winding through lush forest, with several waterfalls down to the lowlands at **San Miguel**. Here the road leads either northeast heading to La Virgen and eventually Puerto Viejo de Sarapiquí (see page 1263), or northwest to Venecia (see below).

La Virgen

Ten kilometres northeast of San Miguel is La Virgen, near the Río Sarapiquí, a good spot for Grade I, II and III rafting, which is organized by the hotel **Rancho Leona**. From San José, take the Río Frío bus which passes through San Miguel, or a bus from San Carlos, and ask to get off at **Rancho Leona**. Juan Carlos in La Virgen has been recommended as a guide for rafting, T2761-1148, from US$25 per person.

Meseta Central - West

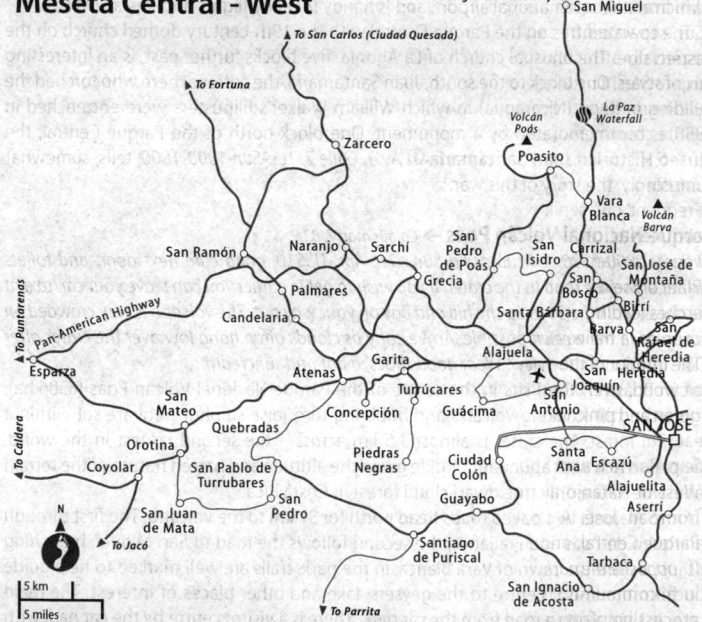

Venecia and around

Heading west from San Miguel, Venecia (two buses daily from San José, 4½ hours, US$3) has an interesting church. Near Venecia are the pre-Columbian tumuli of **Ciudad Cutris**. A good road goes to within 2 km of Cutris, from where you can walk or take a 4WD vehicle; get a permit to visit from the local *finca* owner.

West of Venecia is Aguas Zarcas, where the road splits. Heading directly north, the roads descends into the jungle lowlands, following the Río San Carlos towards the Nicaraguan border, passing through several small towns. After about 40 km, in Boca Tapada, is **La Laguna del Lagarto Lodge** (see page 1173).

Grecia

The road from Alajuela to San Carlos (see page 1184) passes through Grecia and several towns of the Meseta Central, with good paved roads leading to others. The hills are covered with green coffee bushes, interspersed with other plants for shade. Grecia is also a major pineapple producer, and has an interesting church made entirely of metal. A short distance along the road to Alajuela is **El Mundo de los Serpientes** ① *T2494-3700, snakes@ racsa.co.cr, 0800-1600, US$11, children US$6, reductions for biology students*, a snake farm with more than 50 species. On the old road about 10 km towards Tacares is **Los Chorros Recreational Park** ① *US$4*, with two massive waterfalls and picnic spots.

Sarchí and Naranjo → *Colour map 7, B3.*

Heading west is the town of Sarchí, the country's artisan centre, where you can visit the *fábricas* that produce the intricately geometric and floral designs painted on ox-carts, which are almost a national emblem. The town is divided in two, Sarchí Norte and Sarchí Sur, separated by some 4 km. The green church (until they paint it again) in Sarchí is especially attractive at sunset. Travel agents in San José charge around US$55 for a day trip to Sarchí usually combined with a trip to Volcán Poás.

The road continues north to Naranjo, a quiet agricultural town with an exquisite bright white church, and a shocking post-modern pyramidal structure in the main square.

Zarcero

Frequent bus services from San José/Alajuela pass through Zarcero, on the lip of the continental divide, en route to San Carlos (Ciudad Quesada). The town is famous for vegetable farming, dairy products and notable for the topiary creations of Evangelista Blanco Breves that fill the main plaza. Bushes are clipped, trimmed and shaped into arches leading up to the white church with twin towers, with shapes of animals, dancing couples, a helicopter, many designs of Henry Moore-like sculptures and a small grotto. The interior of the quaint church, overshadowed somewhat by the plaza, is made entirely of wood, even the pillars, painted cream and pale grey with patterns in blue, brown, green and pink; cartouches, emblems and paintings.

San Ramón and Los Angeles Cloud Forest Reserve

West of Naranjo along the Pan-American Highway is the town of San Ramón, 76 km from San José. A clean town, known locally as the City of Poets, with an attractive Parque Central, and a street market on Saturday mornings. The **Museo de San Ramón** ① *opposite the park, Tue-Fri 1300-1700, T2437-9851*, records the history and culture of the local community. There's good walking in the surrounding area. You can visit the coffee processing plant (in season) at the **Cooperativa de Café** ① *US$15-39*, in San Ramón.

Heading north the road forks, left to Zarcero. The right fork heads north to La Tigra and Fortuna, passing the Los Angeles Cloud Forest Reserve (20 km from San Ramón). The private 800-ha Reserve (see **Hotel Villablanca**, page 1173) offers hiking, guided tours, horse riding and canopy ascents. The local **fiesta** is around the day of San Ramón, 30 August, when local saints are carried on litters to the town's church.

Palmares and Atenas → *Colour map 7, B3.*

Palmares, 7 km southeast of San Ramón, has a pretty central park with lovely tall trees, where sloths are occasionally spotted. The quiet town comes alive in January for the annual **Fiestas de Palmares**, with food, carnival rides, concerts and parades.

After Palmares you can pick up the Pan-American Highway and head to the coast or return to San José, or continue south to Atenas. The church and main plaza in Atenas lie on an earthquake fault. The local speciality, *toronja rellena*, is a sweet-filled grapefruit. Atenas is reputed to have the best climate in the world, with stable temperatures of between 17 and 32°C year-round.

North of San José ●❼❸❶ » *pp1172-1176.*

Heredia → *Colour map 7, B3. Altitude: 1200 m.*

Ten kilometres north of San José, Heredia is capital of the province of the same name and an important coffee centre. It is a convenient and pleasant place to stay, away from the pollution of San José but close to the capital and the airport, and with good public transport. The town is mostly new with only the main square maintaining a colonial atmosphere in its architecture. The short squat **Basílica de la Inmaculada Concepción**, built in 1797, has survived countless earthquakes. To the north of the central plaza, with a statue to the poet Aquileo Echeverría (1866-1909), is the solitary defensive structure of **El Fortín**. Across the street the **Casa de la Cultura** is a fine colonial home that now hosts concerts and exhibitions. The School of Marine Biology at the Universidad Nacional campus has a **Museo Zoológico Marino**.

Around Heredia

One of the largest coffee *beneficios* is **La Meseta**. The bus from Heredia to Santa Bárbara will drop you at the gate and you can ask for a guided tour. A more popular tour is of **Café Britt's coffee farm** ① *US$40, tours 1100, 1½ hrs, includes lunch and show, T2277-1500, www.coffee tour.com*, near Barva de Heredia where you can see the processing factory, tasting room and multimedia presentation of the story of coffee. You can be picked up from Heredia or at various points in San José. The **Teatro Dionisio Chaverría** at Café Britt hosts weekend theatre, and a children's show on Sunday afternoons.

North of Heredia is the historic town of **Barva**, on the slopes of Volcán Barva; there frequent buses to/from Heredia. At Barva, the **Huetar Gallery** is recommended for arts, crafts and delicious food. There is also a **Museo de Cultura Popular** ① *Mon-Fri 0900-1600, US$1.50*, 500 m east of the Salón Comunal de Santa Lucía de Barva. North of Heredia through San Rafael, above Los Angeles, is **Galería Octágono** ① *T2267-6325 www.galeria octagono.com*, an arts gallery with handmade textiles by a women's community cooperative, and also a B&B, see page 1174. Beyond Barva, to the west, is **Santa Bárbara**, good seafood at the **Banco de los Mariscos**, T2269-9090, 500 m west from the central plaza. Five kilometres west of Heredia is **San Joaquín de Flores**, a small rural town with views of Barva and Poás volcanoes.

A short distance south of Heredia on the road to **Santo Domingo** is **INBio Parque** ① *T2507-8107, www.inbio.ac.cr, Tue-Sun 0800-1800, US$44*, an educational and recreational centre that explains and gives insight into Costa Rica's biological diversity. In a small area you can visit the ecosystems of central highland forest, dry forest and humid forest, with trails set out for bromelias and *guarumo*.

Volcán Barva

Parque Nacional Braulio Carrillo ① *park entry US$8, no permit needed* (see page 1261), to the north of Heredia, includes Volcán Barva, at 2906 m. This section of the park is ideal for hiking with a good trail leading up to the summit with three lagoons nearby, and excellent views and wildlife encounters for the few that make the effort. The really enthusiastic can hike all the way down to the lowlands arriving close to La Selva Biological Station near Puerto Viejo de Sarapaqui, but careful planning is required. There is a ranger station and camp site near the entrance, 4 km north of Sacramento, from where it's a 3-km easy climb to the top – still a treasure and, amazingly, a well-kept secret from the hordes.

San José de la Montaña to Sacramento

From San José de la Montaña it is four hours' walk to Sacramento but some buses continue towards Sacramento halving the walk time (otherwise walk, hitchhike, or arrange a ride with the park director). A taxi between Heredia and Sacramento costs US$10.

South of San José

Aserrí to San Pablo de Turrubares

Ten kilometres south of San José is Aserrí, a village with a beautiful white church. On Friday and Saturday evenings, street bands begin the fiesta with music from 2000, followed by marimbas. Extremely popular among locals, the dancing is fabulous, with *chicharrones*, tortillas and plenty of other things to eat and drink. Further along the same road is **Mirador Ram Luna**, a restaurant with a fine panoramic view. At the end of the road is **San Ignacio de Acosta**, again with a good church containing life-size Nativity figures. Buses from San José (Calle 8, Av 12-14 in front of the Baptist church) via Aserrí hourly from 0500 to 2230, return 0430 to 2100, one hour. The unpaved road continues to **Santiago de Puriscal**, which was the epicentre for many earthquakes in 1990. Although the church is now closed as a result, there are excellent views from the town and the road. From here it is possible to take a dirt road to the Pacific coast, joining the coastal road near Parrita (see page 1233). Alternatively, take the road to **San Pablo de Turrubares**, from where you can either head west for Orotina, via an unpaved road through San Pedro and San Juan de Mata, or for Atenas via Quebradas, then east to Escobal, next stop on railway, then 4WD necessary to Atenas.

For Sleeping and Eating price codes and other relevant information, see Essentials pages 45-48.

ⓢ Sleeping

Alajuela *p1167*
The 2 **Hampton Inns** and the **Garden Court** are the closest place to stay near the airport, 2 km east of Juan Santamaría on the main highway.

LL Xandari, T2443-2020, www.xandari.com. Once an old coffee *finca* overlooking the Central Valley, this architectural treasure has 21 private villas, health restaurant, organic gardens, trails and waterfalls, spa treatments and many facilities. One of the best hotels in Costa Rica.

L Garden Court Hotel, T2443-0043, www.gardencourtairporthotel.com. Good comforts, including pool, but you're here for the proximity to the airport.

L Hampton Inn Airport, T2436-0000, www.hamptoninn.com. 100 rooms, double glazing, a/c, free form outdoor pool, bar, fast food places nearby, children free and discounts for 3 or 4 adults sharing.

L Hampton Inn and Suites, T2442-3320, www.grupomarta.com. Luxury suites and facilities for business travellers.

AL-B Hotel 1915, Calle 2, Av 5-7, 300 m north of park central, T2440-7163, www.1915hotel.com. Old family home smartly refurbished with stylish garden patio café. Very good service. Rooms have cable TV, mini fridge, telephone, some with a/c, price includes breakfast. Best in town for the price.

A-B Islands B&B, Av 1, Calle 7-9, 50 m west of La Agonía church, T2442-0573, islandsbb@hotmail.com. A small family-run Tico-owned B&B with 8 comfortable rooms. Some rooms have cable TV, free local calls. Airport pickup available, very secure and 24-hr parking.

A Viña Romántica, up in the hills near Alajuela on road to Poás volcano, 15 mins from airport, T2430-7621 www.vina romantica.com. Great spot, gourmet meals.

B Hotel Mi Tierra, Av 2, Calle3-5 T2441-1974, www.hotelmitierra.net. Offers pool, adventure tours and parking. Popular with travellers.

B-C Charly's Place, a couple of blocks north of the central park on Av 5, Calle Central-1, T2440-6853, lilyhotel@latinmail.com. Popular place, with 14 rooms most with private bathrooms, cheaper without, some with TV. Also cheap backpackers' area. Credit cards accepted.

B-C Hotel Alajuela, on corner across from central park at Av Central and Calle 2, T2441-1241, alajuela@racsa.co.cr. 28 generally good rooms and apartments all with private bathrooms. Helpful staff, garden patio for relaxing.

C Mango Verde Hostel, Av 3, Calle 2-4, T2441-6330, mirafloresbb@hotmail.com. 6 clean rooms with private bath and hot water, close to the centre of town. Courtyard, kitchen and communal area, relaxing atmosphere. Parking.

C Pensión Alajuela, Av 9, Calle Central-2, opposite the court house, T2443-1717, www.pensionalajuela.com. Mixed bag of 12 simple rooms, some with private bath, some without. Small bar downstairs, laundry and fax service. 24-hr parking next door.

D-E Cortez Azul, Av 3, Calle 2-4, 100 m west of Museo Juan Santamaría, T2443-6145, hotelcortezazul@gmail.com. Popular spot with a handful of good, clean rooms.

D-F Central Alajuela, Av Central, Calle 8, close to the bus terminal, T2443-8437. Basic rooms, shared bathrooms have cold water but it is reasonably clean. Popular with Ticos arriving from out of town.

Parque Nacional Volcán Poás *p1167*
Camping in the park is not permitted but there are several places advertising cabins on the road up to Poás and nearby.

L-A Poás Volcano Lodge, west of Poasito, 500 m from Vara Blanca junction on road to Poasito, at El Cortijo farm, sign on gate, 1 km to house, T2482-2194, www.poas

volcanolodge.com. English-owned, includes breakfast, dinner, wholesome food, rooms in converted buildings with bath, or in farmhouse with shared bath, jungle trail, good walking, horseback riding 25 mins to volcano by car, 1½ hrs from San José.
C Alberque Ecológica La Providencia, near Poás NP (2 km from green entrance gate to volcano), T2232-2498. Private reserve, beautiful horse riding tour US$25-30 including lunch.

La Virgen *p1168*
AL-A La Quinta de Sarapiquí Lodge, Bajos de Chilamate on the Río Sardinal, T2761-1052, www.laquintasarapiqui.com. Costa Rican-owned, family-run lodge, 23 rooms with bath and fan, bar and restaurant overlooking the rainforest, tubing down rivers, popular with birdwatchers (bird list available). Also a frog and butterfly garden.
B Albergue Ecológico Islas del Río, T2292-2072 in San José, T2766-6524, in Chilamate, www.aguas-bravas.co.cr. Price per person. The operational centre of Aguas Bravas close to Puerto Viejo de Sarapiquí, includes meals, rooms with private and shared bathroom, ideal for groups, canopy tour, hiking. Río Sarapiquí trips arranged.
C-E Finca Pedro y el Lobo, 12761-1406, www.fincapedro.com. Beautiful rustic accommodation, also options for camping, kayaking, rafting and exploring waterfalls.
D Rancho Leona, T2761-1019, www. rancholeona.com. Private rooms, kayaking, meals available also jungle tours.

Venecia and around *p1169*
A La Laguna del Lagarto Lodge, Boca Tapada, T2289-8163, www.lagarto-lodge-costa-rica.com. 12 rooms with bath, 6 with shared bath, friendly, 500 ha of forest, good for watching animals, boat trips down Río San Carlos to Río San Juan.
C Recreo Verde, Marsella, near Venecia, T2472-1020. A good choice in a recreational and ecological conservation park. There are hot springs, primary forest, a few trails going to nearby caves and helpful and helpful staff.

Grecia *p1169*
L-A Posada Mimosa, Costa Rica, T2494-5868, www.mimosa.co.cr. B&B, rooms, suites and cabins set in beautiful tropical gardens, pool. Uses solar energy.

Sarchí and Naranjo *p1169*
A Rancho Mirador, on the *Panamericana*, 1 km west of the turn-off for Naranjo, T2451-1302. Good-value *cabañas*, restaurant with local food, a spectacular view of coffee *fincas* and San José in the distance. Owner Rick Vargas was formerly a stunt pilot in the US.
B Cabinas Daniel Zamora, Sarchí, T2454-4596. With bath, fan, hot water, very clean and extra blankets if cold at night.
B Hotel Villa Sarchí Lodge, 800 m north of Sarchí, T2454-5000. Has 11 rooms with private bath, hot water, cable TV and pool.
F La Bamba, Naranjo, down the hill by the football pitch. May muster up enough energy to let you stay in 1 of their simple rooms.

Zarcero *p1169*
B-C Don Beto, by the church, T2463-3137. With bath, very friendly, clean.

San Ramón and Los Angeles Cloud Forest Reserve *p1169*
LL Hotel Villablanca, north of town set in the 800-ha Los Angeles Cloud Forest Reserve, T2461-0300, www.villablanca-costarica.com. Naturalist hikes, some up to 8 hrs, canopy tour, horse riding, night walks, birdwatching, coffee plantation tour and the famous La Mariana Chapel with handpainted ceiling tiles – you don't have to stay to visit.
A-B La Posada, T2445-7359, www.posada hotel.net. 400 m north of the cathedral. 35 good rooms, with private bath, hot water, use of kitchen, laundry. Parking and small patio.
C San Ramón, 100 m east, 25m south of Banco de Costa Rica, T2447-2042. 35 spotless rooms (but pretty garish decor), with private bathroom, hot water and cable TV. Parking.
D Hotel Nuevo Jardín, 5 blocks north of the central park, T2445-5620. Simple, clean and friendly.

D Gran Hotel, 150 m west of post office, T2445-6363. Big rooms, private bathrooms, hot water, friendly, communal TV area.

Palmares and Atenas *p1170*

AL El Cafetal Inn, out of Atenas, in St Eulalia, 4.7 km towards Grecia, T2446-5785, www.cafetal.com. Nice setting on a coffee plantation, private house, large pool, 10 rooms, airport transport, recommended.

Heredia *p1170*

AL Valladolid, Calle 7, Av 7, T2260-2905, valladol@racsa.co.cr. 11 spacious rooms and suites, all with a/c, private bath, telephone and cable TV. 5th floor has sauna, jacuzzi and **Bonavista Bar** with fine views overlooking the Central Valley.

AL-B Apartotel Vargas, 800 m north of Colegio Santa Cecilia and San Francisco Church, T2237-8526, apartotelvargas@ yahoo.com. 8 large, well-furnished apartments with cooking facilities, hot water, laundry facilities, TV, internet, enclosed patio with garage and nightwatchman, English-speaking staff. Sr Vargas will collect you from airport. Excellent choice if taking language classes and in a group. Best option in town.

B-C Hotel Heredia, Calle 6, Av 3-5, T2238-0880. Has 12 rooms, some quite dark, but all have private bath and hot water, parking.

C Las Flores, Av 12, Calle 12-14, T2261-8147. With bath, clean, quiet, parking and recommended.

F Colonial, Calle 4-6, Av 4, T2237-5258. Clean, friendly and family-run, will park motorcycles in restaurant.

F El Verane, Calle 4, Av 6-8, next to central market, T2237-1616. Rooms on street side are slightly better, close to bus terminal.

Around Heredia *p1170*

LL Finca Rosa Blanca, 1.6 km from Santa Bárbara de Heredia, T2269-9392, www.fincarosablanca.com. Deluxe suites in an architectural explosion of style and eloquence, romance and exclusivity at the

extremes of imagination. Spa facilities for comfort. Quality restaurant and bar

LL-AL Bougainvillea de Santo Domingo, just west of Santo Domingo, T2244-1414, www.hb.co.cr. Excellent service, pool, sauna, spectacular mountain setting, free shuttle bus to San José. Highly recommended.

D Galería Octágono, T2267-6325 www.galeriaoctagono.com, is an arts gallery and B&B, including breakfast, other meals and transport available at additional cost, wonderful cypress cabin, hikes, and friendly and informative owners.

🍴 Eating

Alajuela *p1167*

Finding something to eat in Alajuela is not difficult, most restaurants, cafés and sodas are within 1 or 2 blocks of the Parque Central and down Calle Central.

🍴 **La Mansarda**, central plaza. Good, wholesome Tico dishes.

🍴 **Café Almibar**, Av Central, Calle 1-3. Another snacking stop popular with locals.

🍴 **Jalapeño's**, Central T2430-4027. Great Mexican food, friendly, 50 m south of the post office.

🍴 **La Cocina de Abuelita**, Av Central, Calle 1-3. Simple lunchtime, buffet menu.

🍴 **Trigo Miel**, Av 2, Calle Central-2. One of a couple of patisserie cafés in Alajuela serving divine snacks and good coffee.

Venecia and around *p1169*

🍴 **El Parque**, near church, Venecia. Good local food.

Zarcero *p1169*

The town is known for cheese and fruit preserves.

🍴 **Soda/Restaurant El Jardín**, 1st floor, overlooking the plaza. Local lunches and breakfasts. Good view of topiary.

San Ramón and Los Angeles Cloud Forest Reserve *p1169*
¶ **Tropical**, near northwest corner of the Parque. Excellent ice cream parlour.

Heredia *p1170*
¶¶-¶ **La Rambla**, Calle 7, Av 7. Services a good mix of *comida típica* and international dishes.
¶¶ **Cowboy Restaurant**, T2237-8719 Calle 9, Av 5. Grill option where the Mid-West meets Costa Rica. Lively bar in the evenings. Credit cards accepted.
¶¶ **El Gran Papa**, Calle 9, Av 3. Open for dinner, good range of *bocas*, pastas and cocktails.
¶¶ **La Luna de Valencia**, a few kilometres north of Barva, T2269-6665. Authentic paella restaurant, vegetarian options, friendly service, recommended.
¶¶ **Le Petit Paris**, Calle 5 and Av Central-2, T2262-2564, closed Sun. A little piece of France simply oozing style. The ambience shifts between the bar, restaurant and patio café. Divine food, live music on Thu.
¶¶-¶ **Baalbek Bar & Grill**, San Rafael de Heredia on the road to Monte de la Cruz, T2267-6482. Good Mediterranean food, live music Fri /Sat.
¶¶-¶ **Bulevar Bar**, Av Central, Calle 5-7. One of the happening places with a lively balcony bar upstairs and fast food and *bocas* available.
¶¶-¶ **Fresas**, Calle 7, Av 1, T2262-5555. Diner-style restaurant serving snacks, sandwiches, breakfast, full meals, fresh fruit juices and strawberries; bar upstairs.
¶¶-¶ **Las Espigas**, corner of Parque Central. Good coffee, pastries and lunch specials.
¶ **Entrepanes**, fine coffee and pastries, upstairs from Pop's diagonal to the central park.
¶ **Vishnu Mango Verde**, Calle 7, Av Central-1, T2237-2526. Good wholesome vegetarian served fast-food-style.

❀ Festivals and events

Alajuela *p1167*
11 Apr Juan Santamaría Day, a week of bands, concerts and dancing in celebration of the life of the town's most famous son.

Mid-Jul The fruitful heritage comes to the fore with a Mango Festival of parades, concerts and an arts and crafts fair.

◯ Shopping

Alajuela *p1167*
Goodlight Books, Calle 1-3, T2430-4083, quality used books, mostly English, espresso and pastries. Internet available.

Sarchí and Naranjo *p1169*
One of the largest *artesanías* is **Fábrica de Chaverri** in Sarchi Sur. **Taller Lalo Alfaro**, the oldest workshop, is in Sarchí Norte and worth a visit to see more traditional production methods. Both sell handmade furniture, cowhide rocking chairs and wooden products as well as ox-carts, which come in all sizes.

⊝ Transport

Alajuela *p1167*
Bus Service to **San José**. Depart Alajuela from main bus terminal Calle 8, Av Central-1, or Av 4, Calle 2-4 every 10 mins, 30 mins, US$0.75, with both services arriving on Av 2 in the capital. To **Heredia** from 0400 until 2200, 30 mins, US$0.50. Buses to the Butterfly Farm at **La Guácima** marked 'La Guácima abajo' leave from Av 2 between Calle 8-10, US$0.30. 1 block south of the terminal buses depart for several small villages in the area including **Laguna de Fraijanes** and **Volcán Poás**.

Parque Nacional Volcán Poás *p1167*
The volcano can be reached by car from **San José**. A taxi for 6 hrs with a side trip will cost about US$50-60. There is a daily excursion bus from the main square of Alajuela right up to the crater, leaving at 0915 (or before if full), connecting with 0830 bus from San José (from Av 2, Calle 12-14); be there early for a seat; although extra buses run if necessary, the area gets very crowded, US$5.75 return. The bus waits at the top with time to see everything

(clouds permitting), returning 1430. Daily bus **Alajuela-Poasito** 1200, US$1, will take you part way to the summit. From **Poasito** hitch a lift as it is a 10-km walk. Other options include taking the 0600 or 1600 bus from Alajuela to **San Pedro de Poás**, hitch/ taxi to Poasito and stay overnight, hiking or hitching up the mountain next morning. The 0500 bus from Alajuela to Poasito arrives 2 hrs before the park gates open.

Sarchí and Naranjo *p1169*
Express bus from **San José** to Sarchí, Calle 16, Av 1-3, 1215, 1730 and 1755, Mon-Fri, returning 0530, 0615, 1345, Sat 1200, 1½ hrs, US$1.45. Tuan T2441-3781 buses every 30 mins, 0500-2200 from Alajuela bus station, 1½ hrs, US$0.50.

Transportes Naranjo, T2451-3655, run buses to/from **San José**'s Coca Cola terminal every 40 mins, US$1.25. Buses connect other towns and villages in the area.

San Ramón and Los Angeles Cloud Forest Reserve *p1169*
San Ramón is a transport hub. A regular service from **San José Empresarios Unidos**, T2222-0064, at Calle 16, Av 10-12, go to **Puntarenas**, 10 a day, every 45 mins or so, US$1.70. There is also a regular service to **Fortuna** and **Alajuela**. Buses run to surrounding villages and towns.

Palmares and Atenas *p1170*
The library on the plaza in Atenas also serves as the bus office, **Cooptransatenas**, T2446-5767. Many daily buses to **San José**, either direct or via **Alajuela**, US$1.90.

Heredia *p1170*
Buses from **San José**, from Av 2, Calle 12-14, every 10 mins daily, 0500-0015, then every 30 mins to 0400, 25-min journey, US$0.50. Return buses from Av 6, Calle 2-1.

Local buses leave from Av 8, Calle 2-4, by the market.

Volcán Barva *p1171*
Accessible from **Heredia**, there is no route from the San José–Limón Hwy. Buses leave from the market at 0630, 1230 and 1600, returning at 0730, 1300, 1700. Arriving at **Porrosati** (a town en route to Volcán Barva). Some continue as far as Sacramento, otherwise walk 6 km to park entrance, then 4 km to lagoon. Be careful if leaving a car; there are regular reports of theft from rental cars.

ⓘ Directory

Alajuela *p1167*
Banks No shortage of banks, all within 3 blocks of each other and most with ATM, including **Banco Nacional**, Calle 2, Av Central-1, facing central park, **Scotiabank**, next door, **Banco Crédito Agrícola de Cártago**, Calle 2, Av Central-2, and **Banco de Santa Cruz**, Calle 2, Av 3, which is also the office of **Credomatic**. **Emergency** T911. **Internet** Southside of main plaza, Mon-Sun 0900-2200, US$0.60 per hr. Also with pool tables. **Interplanet**, across from La Agonía church on Av Central and Calle 9, daily 0830-2200. **Medical services** Hospital San Rafael, 200m southeast of the airport autopista intersection, T2436-1000, can help in a crisis. **Post office** Corner of Av 5 and Calle 1, Mon-Fri 0730-1700, Sat mornings.

Sarchí and Naranjo *p1169*
Banks Banco Nacional has branches in Sarchí Sur and Sarchí Norte, and on the north side of the plaza in Naranjo, with Visa and MasterCard ATM. **Post office** Services are found in both villages.

Heredia *p1170*
Language schools Centro Panamericano de Idiomas, San Joaquín de Flores, T2265-6306, www.cpi-edu.com. Accommodation with local families. **Intercultura Language and Cultural Center**, Heredia, T2260-8480, www.interculturacostarica.com. Small classes, also with a campus at Playa Samara.

Meseta Central East

The eastern Central Highlands offer relative quiet, despite being close to San José. The former capital and pilgrimage site of Cártago sits meekly at the bottom of the fuming Irazú volcano before it falls away to the beautiful Orosí Valley. The thundering Río Reventazón leads the next step down the Atlantic slope, beginning its journey to the Caribbean, passing Turrialba, a good base for whitewater adventure. Meanwhile, the slopes of nearby Turrialba volcano hide the country's main archaeological site of Guayabo and good hiking opportunities to its summit.
» *For listings, see pages 1180-1183.*

Cártago and around ●●▲●● » *pp1180-1183. Colour map 7, B3.*

→ *Altitude: 1439 m.*

Cártago, at the foot of the Irazú Volcano and 22.5 km from San José on a toll road (US$0.75), is encircled by mountains. Founded in 1563, it was the capital of Costa Rica for almost 300 years until San José assumed the role in 1823. Since then the town has failed to grow significantly and remains small, though densely populated. Earthquakes in 1841 and 1910 destroyed many of the buildings and ash from Irazú engulfed the town in 1963. While colonial-style remnants exist in one or two buildings, the town feels as if it is still reeling from the impact of so much natural devastation and is keeping quiet, waiting for the next event.

The most important attraction in town, and the focal point for pilgrims from all over Central America, is the **Basílica de Nuestra Señora de Los Angeles**, the patroness of Costa Rica, on the eastern side of town. Rebuilt in 1926 in Byzantine style, it houses the diminutive **La Negrita**, an indigenous image of the Virgin under 15 cm high, worshipped for her miraculous healing powers. The basílica houses a collection of finely made silver and gold images, no larger than 3 cm high, of various parts of the human anatomy, presumably offered in the hope of being healed. The most important date in the pilgrims' calendar is 2 August, when the image of La Negrita is carried in procession to churches in Cártago with celebrations throughout Costa Rica.

Also worth seeing is **La Parroquia** (the old parish church), roughly 1 km west of the basílica, ruined by the 1910 earthquake and now converted into a delightful garden retreat with flowers, fish and hummingbirds.

Around Cártago

Aguas Calientes, 4 km southeast of Cártago and 90 m lower, has a warm-water *balneario* ideal for picnics. On the road to Paraíso, 8 km from Cártago, is an orchid garden, the **Jardín Lankester** ① *10 mins' walk from the main road, T2552-3247, daily 0830-1630, US$5,* run by the University of Costa Rica. The best displays are between February and April. While off the beaten track, the gardens are worth a visit. The Cártago–Paraíso bus departs every 30 minutes from the south side of central park in Cártago (15 minutes); ask the driver to let you out at Campo Ayala. Taxi from Cártago, US$5.

Volcán Irazú **→** *Colour map 7, B3. Altitude: 3432 m.*
① *US$10, 0800-1530 most of the year.*

Irazú's crater is an impressive half-mile cube dug out of the earth, surrounded by desolate grey sand, which looks like the surface of the moon. President Kennedy's visit in 1963 coincided with a major eruption and, in 1994 the north wall of the volcano was destroyed by another eruption that sent detritus down as far as the Río Sucio, within sight of the the San José–Limón Highway. The views are stupendous on a clear day and the main reason for the trip. But the clouds normally move in enveloping the lower peaks and slopes by 1300 (sometimes even by 0900 or 1000 between July and November), so get there as early as you can to have a greater chance of a clear view of the mountains and the sun shining on the clouds in the valley below. There's little wildlife other than the ubiquitous Volcano Junco bird and the few plants which survive in this desert, but ongoing colonization is attracting more birds.

It's definitely worth the trip and an early start. As one traveller wrote: "In the afternoon the mountain top is buried in fog and mist or drizzle, but the ride up in the mist can be magical, for the mountainside is half displaced in time. There are new jeeps and tractors, but the herds of cattle are small, the fields are quilt-work, handcarts and ox-carts are to be seen under the fretworked porches of well-kept frame houses. The land is fertile, the pace is slow, the air is clean. It is a very attractive mixture of old and new. Irazú is a strange mountain, well worth the ride up."

Orosí Valley

Further east from Cártago a trip round the Orosí Valley makes a beautiful circular trip, or a fine place to hang out for a while in a valley that is often overlooked as the crowds rush to the more popular spots on the coast. The centrepiece of the valley is the artificial Lake Cachí used for hydro-electric generation. Heading round the lake counter-clockwise, the road passes through Orosí, clips the edge of Parque Nacional Tapantí, continuing to the Cachí Dam and completes the circuit passing through Ujarrás. Along the way there are several miradors which offer excellent views of the Reventazón Valley. For transport see each destination. Day trips can be easily arranged from San José.

In **Orosí** there is an 18th-century **mission** ① *closed Mon*, with colonial treasures, and just outside two **balnearios** ① *US$2.50*, with restaurants serving good meals at fair prices. It's a good place to hang out, take some low-key language classes, mixed with mountain biking and trips to the national park and other sites of interest.

Parque Nacional Tapantí-Macizo de la Muerte
① *Daily 0700-1700, US$7.*
Twelve kilometres beyond Orosí is the Parque Nacional Tapantí-Macizo de la Muerte, one of the wettest parts of the country (some parts reportedly receiving as much as 8 m of rain a year). From June to November/December it rains every afternoon. Approached from Orosí, and just 30 km from Cártago, the national park is suprisingly easy to reach and packs in the interest.

Covering 58,000 ha, Tapantí-Macizo includes the former Tapantí National Park and much of the Río Macho Forest Reserve. The park protects the Río Orosí basin which feeds the Cachí Dam hydro power plant. Strategically, the southern boundary of the park joins with Chirripó National Park, extending the continuous protected area that makes up La Amistad Biosphere Reserve. The park incorporates a wide range of life zones with altitudes rising from 1220 m to over 3000 m at the border with Chirripó. The diverse altitudes and relative seclusion of the park has created an impressive variety of species – 260 bird species, 45 mammals, lizards, snakes – a list which is currently incomplete due to the relatively recent creation of the park. There are picnic areas, a nature centre with slide shows (ask to see them) and good swimming in the dry season (November-June), and trout fishing season (1 April-31 October).

Cachí

Continue around the lake to Cachí and the nearby **Casa del Soñador** (Dreamer's House) which sells wood carvings from the sculpture school of the late Macedonio Quesada. The road crosses the dam wall and follows the north shore to Ujarrás, then back to Cártago. The **Charrarra tourist complex** ① *30-mins' walk from Ujarrás*, has a good campsite, restaurant, pool, boat rides on the lake and walks. It can be reached by direct bus on Sunday. Buses leave from Cártago one block north of the Cártago ruins.

Ujarrás

Ujarrás (ruins of a colonial church and village) is 6.5 km east of Paraíso, on the shores of the artificial Lago Cachí. There is a bus every 1½ hours from Paraíso that continues to Cachí. Legend has it that in 1666 English pirates, including the youthful Henry Morgan, were seen off by the citizens of Ujarrás aided by the Virgin. The event is now celebrated annually in mid-March when the saint is carried in procession from Paraíso to the ruined church.

Turrialba and around ☺❼▲☺ » *pp1180-1183. Colour map 7, B3.*

→ *Altitude: 646 m.*

Turrialba (62 km from San José) bridges the Central Valley highlands and the Caribbean lowlands, and was once a stopping point on the old Atlantic railway between Cártago and Puerto Limón. The railway ran down to Limón on a narrow ledge poised between mountains on the left, and the river to the right, but no longer operates. The **Centro Agronómico Tropical de Investigación y Enseñanza (CATIE)** ① *T2558-2000 ext 2275, www.catie.ac.cr, botanical garden open daily 0700-1600, T556-2700, US$5*, about 4 km southeast of Turrialba, covers more than 800 ha of this ecologically diverse zone (with many fine coffee farms), has one of the largest tropical fruit collections in the world and houses an important library on tropical agriculture; visitors and students are welcome for research or birdwatching. Past CATIE on the south side of the river, a large sugar mill makes for a conspicuous landmark in Atirro, the centre for macadamia nuts. Nearby, the 256-ha **Lake Angostura** has now flooded some of the whitewaters of the Río Reventazón. What has been lost as world-class whitewater is believed, by some, to be a Lake Arenal in the making. A glimpse of the vegetation-covered lake will convince you otherwise.

Around Turrialba

Many whitewater rafting companies operate out of Turrialba, with trips to the **Río Reventazón** and **Río Pacuare**. The rafting is excellent; the Pascua section of the Reventazón can be Grade V at rainy times. The Pacuare is absolutely perfect with divine scenery. By contacting the guides in Turrialba you can save about 30% on a trip booked in San José, provided they are not already contracted.

Volcán Turrialba (3329 m) may be visited from Cártago by a bus from Calle 4 y Avenida 6 to the village of San Gerardo. From Turrialba take a bus to Santa Cruz. From both, an unpaved road meets at **Finca La Central**, on the saddle between Irazú and Turrialba.

Monumento Nacional Guayabo

① *T2559-1220, Tue-Sun 0800-1530, US$6, local guides available, water, toilets, no food.*
About 19 km north of Turrialba, near Guayabo, is a 3000-year-old ceremonial centre excavated with paved streets and stone-lined water channels. The archaeological site, 232 ha and 4 km from the town of Guayabo, is now a national monument, and dates from the period

1000 BC-AD 1400. There are excellent walks in the park, where plenty of birds and wildlife can be seen. Worth a trip to see Costa Rica's most developed ancient archaeological site but small in comparison to the great sites of the Maya. There is also a camping area.

⏺ Meseta Central East listings

For Sleeping and Eating price codes and other relevant information, see Essentials pages 45-48.

⏺ Sleeping

Cártago *p1177*
A-B Los Angeles Lodge B&B, near the Basílica at Av 4, Calle 14-16, T2591-4169. Clean, nice rooms, restaurant.
D Dinastia, Calle 3, Av 6-8, close to the old railway station, at the Las Ruinas end of town, T2551-7057. Slightly more expensive with private bath. The rooms are small although better with a window. Safe hotel but in lively area north of the central market. Credit cards accepted.

Volcán Irazú *p1177*
D Hotel Gestoria Irazú, on the slopes of Irazú on the way up, in San Juan de Chicúa, T2253-0827. Simple rooms with private bath, hot water and extra blankets to get you through the cold winter nights.

Orosí Valley *p1178*
A Orosí Lodge, T2533-3578, www.orosilodge.com. 6 rooms and a house with balcony overlooking the valley towards Volcán Irazú each with private bath, hot water and kitchenette. Just about everything you could want; divine home-baked cookies, mountain bikes, kayaks and horses for rent, and an internet service. Credit cards accepted. Excellent value.
B Hotel Reventazón, T2533-3838. Rather stark and characterless rooms, with telephone, TV, fridge, internet. Clean and friendly service, good local knowledge. Credit cards accepted.

C-F Montaña Linda, T2533-3640 (local), www.montanalinda.com. A classic and well-run backpackers' place, with a range of options. Dormitory rooms, camping, and B&B service if you just can't get out of bed! There is also a language school, with package deals for lodgers. Toine and Sara are friendly and know their patch very well, organizing trips to local sights.
D Río Palomo, in Palomo, just south of Orosí, T2533-3128. Cabins, pool, laundry facilities, good restaurant.

Parque Nacional Tapantí-Macizo de la Muerte *p1178*
A-B Monte Sky Mountain Retreat, near Tapantí, T2228-0010. Cabins with shared bath, cold water, includes meals, hiking trails through forest. Camping platforms also available. In addition to the price there is a US$8 per person entrance fee to the 300 ha private reserve.
B Kiri Lodge, 1.5 km from the park entrance, T2533-2272, www.kirilodge.net. Excellent lodging and food, breakfast included. Peaceful, trout fishing, very friendly, good trails on 50-ha property.

Camping
No camping is allowed at the park. See Monte Sky Mountain Retreat, above.

Turrialba *p1179*
AL Wagelia, Av 4, entrance to Turrialba, T2556-1566, www.hotelwageliaturrialba.com. 18 rooms, bath, some a/c, restaurant.
B-D Interamericano, facing the old railway station on Av 1, T2556-0142 www.hotel

interamericano.com. Price per person. Very friendly place, family-run, popular with kayakers. Clean, private or shared bath. Safe for motorbikes. Internet service, bar and communal area with TV and books.
C Alcázar, Calle 3, Av 2-4, 25 m north of Banco Norte. Small terrace upstairs, each room has cable TV, telephone, fan and a private bath with hot water. Small, cheap bar/restaurant downstairs with frightening colour schemes.
C-D Central, next to Interamericano, T2556-0170. Price per person, with bath, restaurant, basic.
D Hotel Turrialba, Av 2, Calle 2-4, T2556-6654. Clean simple rooms with private bath, hot water and TV. There are also a couple of pool tables and drinks for sale.
E Laroche, north of Parque Central on Calle 1. Simple and basic rooms but friendly with comfortable beds. Small bar downstairs.
F Whittingham, Calle 4, Av 0-2, T2550-8927. Has 7 fairly dark but OK rooms, some with private bath – an option if other places are full.

Around Turrialba p1179
LL-L Casa Turire, 14 km southeast of Turrialba, follow the signposts, T2531-1111, www.hotelcasaturire.com. Overlooking Lake Angostura, 12 luxury rooms with bath, 4 suites, cable TV, phone, restaurant, pool, library, games room, in the middle of a 1620-ha sugar, coffee and macadamia nut plantation. Virgin rainforest nearby, trails, horses, bike rental, excursions.
A Albergue Mirador Pochotel, Pavones, T2538-1010. 10 basic cabins, restaurant, a popular spot.
A Turrialtico, on road to Siquirres, T2538-1111, www.turrialtico.com. On top of hill with extensive views. Rooms are clean with private bath, comfortable, friendly. Going northeast from Turrialba, the main

road follows the Río Reventazón down to Siquirres (see page 1263).
E San Agustín, Vereh, some 25 km southeast of Turrialba (take bus via Jicotea). Truly isolated for a real rural Costa Rica experience. Candlelight camping, river bathing, hiking and horse riding in surrounding area – basic, and a very pure rainforest experience.

Monumento Nacional Guayabo p1179
D Albergue y Restaurant La Calzada, T2559-0023. Call in advance to make a reservation and check they're open.

🍴 Eating

Cártago p1177
🍴 **Auto 88**, east of public market. Cafetería-style, with beer-drinking room adjoining dining room.
🍴 **Soda Apollo**, on northwest corner of parque, opposite La Parroquia. 24-hr snack option.

Volcán Irazú p1177
🍴🍴-🍴 **Restaurante Linda Vista**. Spectacular views, as you'd expect from Costa Rica's highest restaurant, serving good food and drinks. But most people stop to post, stick, pin or glue a business card, or some other personal item, to the wall.

Turrialba p1179
🍴🍴-🍴 **Pizzería Julián**, on the square. Popular.
🍴 **La Garza**, on main square. Cheap, local good food.
🍴 **Nuevo Hong Kong**, just east of the main square. Good, reasonable prices.
🍴 **Soda Burbuja**, a block south of square on Calle Central. Local dishes, excellent portions, very good value.

▲ Activities and tours

Cártago *p1177*
Mercatur, next to Fuji at Av 2, Calle 4-6, provides local tourist information.

Around Turrialba *p1179*
See also the companies in San José (eg Ríos Tropicales, page 1160).
Serendipity Adventures, T2558-1000, www.serendipityadventures.com. Canyoning rappelling and hot-air ballooning. Recommended.
Tico's River Adventures, T2556-1231, www.ticoriver.com. With recommended local guides.

⊖ Transport

Cártago *p1177*
Bus
A good bus service supplies the surrounding area. To **San José** every 10 mins from Av 4, Calle 2-4. Arrives and departs San José from Calle 5, Av 18-20 for the 45-min journey. After 2030 buses leave from Gran Hotel Costa Rica, Av 2, Calle 3-5. **Orosí/Río Macho**, for **Parque Nacional Tapantí** every 30 mins from Calle 6, Av 1-3, 35-55 mins. **Turrialba**, every hr from Av 3, Calle 8-10, 1 hr direct, 1 hr 20 mins *colectivo*. **Cachí**, via **Ujarrá** and **Paraíso** from Calle 6, Av 1-3, every 1½ hrs, 1 hr 20 mins. **Paraíso**, every 5 mins from Av 5, Calle 4-6. **Aguacalientes**, every 15 mins from Calle 1, Av 3-5. **Tierra Blancas** for **Irazú**, every 30 mins from Calle 4, Av 6-8.

Closest bus for **Irazú** rides to San Juan de Chichua, still some 12 km from the summit. The bus leaves Cártago from north of the central market, Av 6, Calle 1-3, at 1730, returning at 0500 the next day, so you have to spend at least 2 nights on the volcano or in a hotel if you can't

get a ride. To visit **Volcán Turrialba** take a bus from Calle 4 y Av 6 to the village of San Gerardo.

Volcán Irazú *p1177*
Bus
It is possible to get a bus from Cártago to Tierra Blanca (US$0.33) or San Juan de Chicúa (which has 1 hotel) and hitch a ride in a pickup truck. Alternatively you can take a bus from Cártago to Sanatorio. Ask the driver to drop you at the crossroads just outside Tierra Blanca. From there you walk 16 km to the summit. If you're looking for a day trip from San José, a yellow 'school' express bus run by **Buses Metropoli SA**, T2530-1064, runs from **San José**, daily 0800 from Gran Hotel Costa Rica, stops at Cártago ruins 0830 to pick up more passengers, returns 1230 with lunch stop at **Restaurant Linda Vista**, US$6.50.

Taxi
From **Cártago** is US$32 return. A taxi tour from **Orosí** costs US$10 per person, minimum 3 people, and stops at various places on the return journey, eg Cachí dam and Ujarrás ruins. Since it can be difficult to find a decent hotel in Cártago, it may be easier to take a guided tour leaving from **San José**, about US$35, 5½ hrs includes lunch, transport from San José. If driving from San José, take the turn-off at the Ferretería San Nicolás in Taras, which goes directly to Irazú, avoiding Cártago.

Orosí Valley *p1178*
Bus
From **Cártago** to Orosí/Río Macho from Calle 6, Av 1-3, every 30 mins, journey time of 35-55 mins, US$0.50.

Parque Nacional Tapantí-Macizo de la Muerte p1178

Bus

The 0600 bus from Cártago to Orosí gets to Puricil by 0700, then walk (5 km), or take any other Cártago–Orosí bus to Río Macho and walk 9 km to the refuge. Alternatively take a taxi from **Orosí** (US$7 round trip, up to 6 passengers), or **San José**, US$50.

Turrialba p1179

Bus

From **San José** every hr 0530-2200 from Terminal Turrialba, Calle 13, Av 6-8, 1½ hrs, US$2 from **Cártago**, 1 hr, US$1.25, runs until about 2200. Service to **Siquirres**, for connections to Caribbean lowlands, hourly, 40 mins, US$1.50.

Monumento Nacional Guayabo p1179

Bus

From **Turrialba**, there are buses at 1100 (returning 1250) and 1710 (returning 1750), and on Sun at 0900, return 1700 (check times, if you miss it is quite difficult to hitch as there is little traffic), US$0.45 to Guayabo. If you can't get a bus all the way to Guayabo,

several buses each day pass the turn-off to Guayabo, the town is a 2-hr walk uphill (taxi US$10, easy to hitch back). Tour operators in **San José** offer day trips to Guayabo for about US$65 per person (minimum 4 people), cheaper from Turrialba.

Directory

Cártago p1177

Banks No shortage of banks, most with ATMs. Banco de Costa Rica, Av 4, Calle 5-7. Banco Scotiabank, Park Central at Av 2, Calle 2. Banco Nacional, Av 2, Calle 1-3. **Emergencies** Call T911. **Internet** Café Línea, Av 4, Calle 6-8, the only internet place in town, looks decidedly temporary. **Medical services** Dr Max Peralta, entrance on Calle 3, Av 7. The pharmacy is along Av 4 between Calle 1-6.

Orosí Valley p1178

Language schools Montaña Linda Language School, T2533-3640, see Sleeping above. Uses local teachers to get you *hablando español* with a homestay option if you want total submersion. Recommended.

Northern Costa Rica

The Cordillera de Tilarán and the Cordillera de Guanacaste stretch to the Nicaragua border. Tucked in the eastern foothills is the vast artificial Lago Arenal, resting calmly beneath the highly active Volcán Arenal. A number of quieter spots can be found in the area with fine opportunities for fishing and seeing the wildlife, while the more active can go rafting, windsurfing, horse riding and trekking. ➤➤ *For listings, see pages 1189-1194.*

San Carlos and around → *Colour map 7, B3.*

Also known as **Ciudad Quesada**, San Carlos is the main town of the northern lowland cattle and farming region and is a hub of communications. True to form, the town has a frontier feel with an air of bravado and a pinch of indifference. Situated on the downside of the northern slopes of the central highlands mountain region, the temperature rises and the speed of life slows down. In a town without major sights, the huge church overlooking the main plaza stands out. The cavernous interior is matched for style by modern stained-glass windows and an equally massive sculpture of Christ above the altar. As a regional centre San Carlos is served by frequent buses from San José, and has good connections to La Fortuna and Los Chiles. The bus terminal, about 1 km north of town, is close to a shopping centre and cinema. From San Carlos a paved road runs northwest to **Florencia** (service station). At Platanar de San Carlos, there are a couple of sleeping options, see page 1189.

Los Chiles and Refugio Natural de Vida Silvestre Caño Negro → *Colour map 7, B3.*

Heading through the northern lowlands, a good road carves through rich red laterite soils in an almost straight line for 74 km through flat land where the shiny leaves of orange and citrus fruit plantations have replaced forest. Just short of the Nicaraguan border is Los Chiles, where boat trips head through dense, tropical vegetation into the 10,171-ha Caño Negro Natural Wildlife Refuge and Caño Negro Lake, spanning about 800-ha in the rainy season. Birdwatchers flock to the northern wetlands to see the amazing variety of birdlife which feasts at the seasonal lake created by the flood waters of the Río Frío. The lake slowly shrinks in the dry season (January to April). The variety of habitats in the refuge makes a rewarding trip for anyone interested in seeing alligators, turtles and monkeys. Fishing trips for snook and tarpon are easily arranged.

Los Chiles is a small town on the banks of the Río Frío, a few hundred metres west of Highway 35. The central plaza is also a football pitch, and most places of interest are within a block or two. The days pass slowly as children chuck themselves off the dockside in the heat of the afternoon sun. Ask about guides at **Restaurant Los Petates**, **Restaurant El Parque** or **Rancho Eco-Directa**. A three-hour tour with Esteban, Oscar Rojas (T2471-1090) and Enrique, who have all been recommended, costs about US$60. Alternatively, **Aventuras Arenal in Fortuna** run trips to Caño Negro (see below) approximately US$55. It is cheaper to get a boat from **Los Chiles** to the park (US$60 for a boat, up to four people) rather than taking a tour from elsewhere (eg Fortuna) and convenient if you are going on to Nicaragua, but there are not always boats available nor sufficient numbers to fill one economically. Call the **Caño Negro park administration** ① *T2471-1309*, for information and reservations for food and lodging. US$10 entrance to the park.

Fishing trips are likely to be beyond the budgets of many, but then what price do you put on catching a 2-m-long tarpon. A full day's fishing on the Río Frío, Río San Juan or

Los Chiles

Most people using this crossing take the boat between Los Chiles and San Carlos in Nicaragua, which is somewhat remote from the rest of the country. There is a road link to the land border along a dirt track.

Costa Rican immigration All formalities are in Los Chiles which is a few kilometres short of the border. The office is close to the river and leaving procedures are normally straightforward. Daily 0800-1600, usually closed for lunch. If entering Costa Rica, officials can be more difficult, mainly because they are sensitive about the many Nicaraguan immigrants wishing to enter the country. Crossing purely overland is possible. It is some 4 km to the border post, and a total of 14 km to San Carlos with no regular transport. See page 1103 for details.

Transport There are a couple of launches from Los Chiles to San Carlos at 0800 and 1400, 45 minutes, US$9. Launches can be hired costing US$120 for up to eight people.

Lago de Nicaragua (boat, rods and drinks included) can range from US$95 to US$500 with **No Frills Fishing Adventures** (see page 1189), depending on the boat and destination.

Fortuna → *Colour map 7, B3. Altitude: 254 m.*

The small town of Fortuna is an ideal base for exploring the Arenal region with the ominous silhouette of the active Volcán Arenal looming above the town. Reached on a paved road running west from San Carlos/Ciudad Quesada or along the northern shore of Lake Arenal from Tilaran, it's worth a few days of your travels. Once a quiet town that shuddered in the shadow of the volcano's power, it has grown rapidly to accommodate the steady increase in visitors keen to see the active volcano.

Getting there Transport between Fortuna and Santa Elena is time consuming by bus as it requires traveling to Tilarán for a connecting bus on the bumpy road up to Santa Elena. Alteratives are to get a jeep, boat, and jeep leaving Fortuna at 0830 and 1230, US$12, or horseriding to Monteverde (US$35). It is also becoming possible to get transfers to Tortuguero – ask locally for details.

Around Fortuna

About 6 km south of Fortuna are the impressive **Río Fortuna Waterfalls** ① *US$7, drinks available at the entrance*, plunging 70 m into the cloud of swirling mist and spray. It's a pleasant walk down the road for a couple of kilometres before turning off to head uphill through yucca and papaya plantations. From the entrance, a steep and slippery path leads to the falls, so take shoes with a good tread. Bathing is possible, so take swimming clothes, but it's safer 50 m downstream. If you don't want to walk, there are several options. You can drive, but 4WD is necessary. Bicycle hire (US$3 per hour, US$15 per day) is one option and hard work, or you can hire a horse for the day at around US$35. Two to three hours' climb above the falls is the crater lake of Cerro Chato. The top (1100 m) is reached through mixed tropical/cloud forest, with a good view (if you're lucky) but beware of snakes on the path. A guide, if you need one, will charge US$9.

Safari river floats down the Río Peñas Blancas (US$43) and **whitewater rafting**, best in the wet season (from US$69 for a one-day trip including all food and transport), are available through several tour operators. **Horse riding** through the forest to Monteverde costs around US$75 per person for the day trip. Luggage is taken on pack animals or by vehicles. Some operators seem to change the route once underway due to some 'unforeseen problem', so agree the route and try to arrange compensation if there are major changes. Due to competition for business, many horses are overworked on this route. Although difficult when on a budget, try not to bargain down the price, and do ask to see the horses before beginning the journey. The journey is also possible via jeep-boat-jeep (US$30-35).

A small **snake farm** ① *a few kilometres west of Fortuna, US$2*, with 40 specimens is a good opportunity to get up close and personal with these rather cool creatures.

Almost 5 km north of Fortuna is the **Baldi Thermae complex** ① *T2479-9651, daily 1000-2200, US$28*, with four thermal pools ranging from 37° up to 63°C – the limits of endurance without being poached. It's a great experience and there are poolside drinks available. A taxi from town costs US$4, a bus is bus US$1.

Ten kilometres northwest of Fortuna is **Balneario Tabacón** ① *T2460-2020, daily 1000-2200, day guests welcome, entry US$60*, a kitsch complex of thermal pools, waterfalls and (for residents) beauty treatments, with three bars and a restaurant. The water is hot and stimulating; there are a pools at descending heights and temperatures as well as water-slides and a waterfall to sit under. The food is good and the fruit drinks thirst quenching. The resort (**L**) is popular with evening coach tours from San José. Taxi from Fortuna to Tabacón US$4.50. Cheaper are the hot waters about 4 km further along the road at **Quebrada Cedeña**, which are clean and safe. There is no sign but look for local parked cars.

Also near Fortuna are the limestone **Cavernas del Venado**. Tours from Fortuna with all equipment can be arranged through **Eagle Tours** ① *T2479-9091, US$40*. Buses run from San Carlos en route to Tilarán daily; return transport to Fortuna at 2200.

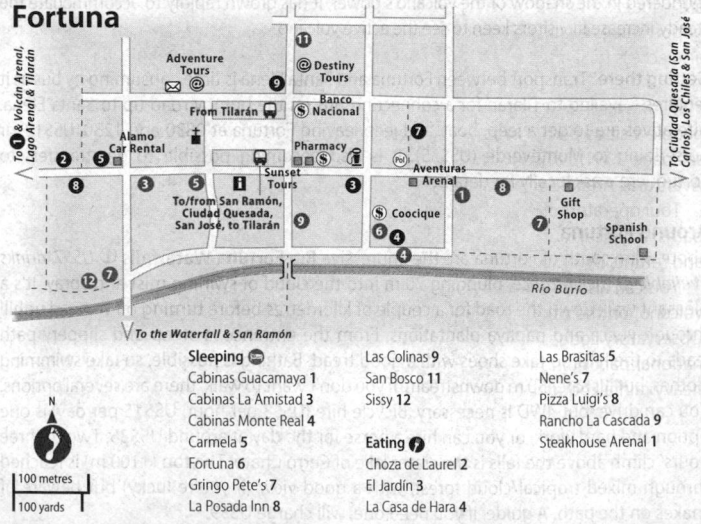

Fortuna

Sleeping
- Cabinas Guacamaya **1**
- Cabinas La Amistad **3**
- Cabinas Monte Real **4**
- Carmela **5**
- Fortuna **6**
- Gringo Pete's **7**
- La Posada Inn **8**
- Las Colinas **9**
- San Bosco **11**
- Sissy **12**

Eating
- Choza de Laurel **2**
- El Jardín **3**
- La Casa de Hara **4**
- Las Brasitas **5**
- Nene's **7**
- Pizza Luigi's **8**
- Rancho La Cascada **9**
- Steakhouse Arenal **1**

Volcán Arenal → *Colour map 7, B3.*

Skirting the slopes of the 1633-m Volcán Arenal, the road travels north around the base to the artificial **Lago Arenal** and hydroelectric dam. The highly active volcano is beautiful, a classic Stromboli-type cone shape characterized by explosions sending out hot grey clouds of sulphurous gases, which can descend the slopes at alarming speeds. The lava streams have moved from the west side to the northeast following activity in recent years. Although the side facing Fortuna is green, the side facing the lake is grey and barren, and the lava flows are clearly visible. There are three active craters and several fumaroles, with activity particularly impressive at night, as the red hot lava crashes, smashes and tumbles down the hillside accompanied by rumbles and intermittent roars (rather like someone moving furniture upstairs). Some people say there is greater volcanic activity around the full moon. The activity is fuelled by a magma chamber that vulcanologists believe is just 5 km below the surface.

Arenal has been continuously active since July 1968, when an eruption killed 78 people and more or less destroyed three villages including Tabacón, which is situated above the *balneario*. The most recent continuous major activity was in May 1998, but in 2000 a small group travelled beyond the permitted area, and were engulfed by a pyroclastic avalanche – the guide later died of third-degree burns. On no account should you walk up the volcano beyond the level of the vegetation, as it's dangerous. There is good hiking on the lower slopes from Fortuna. You can see the latest images of Arenal at www.arenal.net.

If you are visiting between May and December you may not see much as the volcano is usually obscured by clouds and rain and there can be bad weather for weeks on end. Clouds and rain are common in the afternoons all year round, but the clouds do break and you may be lucky. If you can hire a taxi for a trip at about 0400-0500, and you can get up, the sky is often clearer.

To the east, the vast Lago Arenal reflects the moods of the volcano perfectly: smooth and calm from a distance, but whipped up to a waved frenzy by strong easterlies which are squeezed by the hills on either side. The surrounding area offers a multitude of opportunities for hiking, mountain biking, windsurfing and many other activities. There is also access to Santa Elena and Monteverde on foot or horseback.

Park information Much of the area surrounding the volcano is a national park which most people visit as part of a tour. The most common entrance is through **Hotel Los Lagos**, see page 1191), which offers night tours at 1700 for hotel guests, if the sky is clear. **Aventuras Arenal** can provide dependable advice.

Tour operators offer trips to view the volcano at night followed by a visit to the thermal baths; a typical four-hour tour, costing US$35 per person, leaves Fortuna at about 1530 and returns by 1930. Make sure the entry fee to the baths is included.

You can also visit the park on your own. The entrance is on the western flank of the volcano, on the other side to Fortuna, 2 km down a bumpy road signposted to Arenal Observatory Lodge. Four interesting trails, taking up to 1½ hours each, lead through the national park going through a mixture of terrains, that flourish in the microclimate of heavy rainfall bought on by the volcano.

North to Upala

A quiet route north leads from Fortuna to **San Rafael de Guatuso**. There is a 'voluntary' toll of US$1 between Jicarito and San Rafael for reconstruction work on this road. You can come back to the lake either by turning off before San Rafael through **Venado** (where there are caves), or from San Rafael itself, where there are a couple of basic hotels. If you continue along the road from San Rafael northwest towards the Nicaraguan border you come to **Upala** and a poor road east to **Caño Negro**. There is a direct bus from San José to Upala, T2221-3318 (from Avenida 3-5, Calle 10 at 1000 and 1700, four hours).

Around Lago Arenal

A mostly paved road twists and winds round the northern shore of Lake Arenal, leading to Tilarán via Nuevo Arenal. Whether travelling by bus or car, you can get from Fortuna to Monteverde via Tilarán in a day, but set out early to make your connection with the 1230 bus in Tilarán or to avoid driving after dark. The lakeside road has improved greatly in recent years, but some sections are still unpaved. The main hazard is the winding road and some seriously pot-holed sections.

There is plenty of good accommodation around the lake shore, much of it in the higher price brackets. With only a couple of buses a day, and limited traffic, getting off the bus for a look will almost certainly delay you for a day.

If you do stop, an excellent café for a meal and drink with great views over the lake is **Toad Hall** ① *T2692-8020*, towards the northeastern end, which has an excellent souvenir shop with a good mix of Costa Rican crafts, some modern, some traditional, most desirable.

With a head count of just over 2500 (**Nuevo**) **Arenal** is a small town with not much to see. The town is new, because it moved from its original location which now lies deep below the surface of the lake.

Continuing west towards Tilarán, the western side of the lake is popular with **windsurfers** throughout the year, and between December and April the conditions are world class. A batch of hotels cater for windsurfers of all levels; there are many other options in the area so take your pick if you want to stop.

Tilarán → *Colour map 7, B2.*

Tilarán would not appear on the list of destinations for travellers were it not for its role as a small regional transport hub for people journeying between Fortuna, Santa Elena/Monteverde and Cañas on the Pan-American Highway. In town there is pretty much nothing to do, and with luck, the connecting buses will be timed perfectly to avoid you having to wait too long. But if you do, there are several places to catch a bite to eat, and several good places to stay if you need a bed for the night.

For Sleeping and Eating price codes and other relevant information, see Essentials pages 45-48.

⊖ Sleeping

San Carlos and around p1184

AL Hotel La Garza, Platanar de San Carlos, 8 km from Florencia, T2475-5222, www.hotel lagarza.com. 12 charming bungalows with bath and fan, overlooking river. Idyllic spot with good views of Arenal. Guided tours, boat trips, fishing, 230 ha of forest and cattle ranch.

AL Tilajari Resort Hotel, Muelle San Carlos, 13 km north of Platanar de San Carlos, T2462-1212, www.tilajari.com. Luxury rooms, and suites, a/c, private bath, tennis courts, 2 pools, sauna, bar, restaurant, horses and excursions available. Justifiably popular with luxury groups.

C Don Goyo, San Carlos, T2460-1780. 20 clean, well-lit rooms, with private bathrooms, fans, cable TV – best value in town.

C La Central, on west side of park, San Carlos, T2460-0301, www.hotellacentral.net. Private bath, hot water, fan, TV and phone in room.

D del Valle, Av 3, Calle 0-2, San Carlos, T2460-0718. Nothing special but friendly and secure, a good deal at this price.

D-E El Retiro, on the north side of the park, San Carlos, T2460-0463. Bath, hot water, clean and comfortable, popular with local business people.

D-E Fernando, Av 1 Calle 2-4, around corner from Banco Popular, T2460 3314. Probably the best of several basic *pensiones* if you can get one of the new rooms.

E Cabinas Kimbara, on the main road 800 m north of Muelle gas station, T2469-9100. Basic rooms, private bath, fan, includes taxes, pool.

Los Chiles p1184

A Rancho Tulipan, 1 block west of the parque central opposite the immigration offices, T2471-1414, cocas34@hotmail.com. Good restaurant, 10 clean well-appointed rooms with a/c, TV, bath and hot water, breakfast and taxes included. Can arrange a wide variety of tours in the area including river safaris and fishing trips. The manager Carlos Sequera is useful for information on travelling to Nicaragua.

C Hotel Carolina, close to main highway, T2471-1151. Clean and well maintained – the best of the budgets. Accommodation ranges from small, fairly dark rooms with shared bath to a/c cabins with TV.

D No Frills Fishing Lodge, on the main highway just before town, T2471-1410. Set on a 40-ha property, clean modern rooms, restaurant and bar, 8 boats for fishing expeditions (see page 1185).

D-E Cabinas Jabirú, 100 m from the bus stop, a few blocks from the central park, T2471-1496. Cheaper price for Youth Hostel members. Good, but simple rooms, with private bathrooms, fan, some with TV and parking. Postal service, fax and laundry and a range of interesting tours. Cheapest to Caño Negro (US$20 per person, minimum 3) and to El Castillo de la Concepción in Nicaragua.

F Onassis, southwest corner of main plaza, T2471-1447. Your best bet of the strip facing the football pitch. Basic rooms, clean, shared bath, meals upon request.

Fortuna p1185, map p1186

As one of the most popular destinations for all visitors to Costa Rica, accommodation tends to be quite pricey in high season. Conversely, generous discounts in the green/low season are common.

L-AL Arenal Country Inn, south of town, T2479-9670, www.arenalcountryinn.com. A former working hacienda with 20 large, fully equipped *cabinas* set in pleasant tropical gardens. After eating in the dining room – once a holding pen – you can rest by the pool before heading out to explore.

L-AL Las Cabañitas, 1.5 km east of town, beyond Villa Fortuna, T2479-9400. 43 cabins with private baths, a couple of pools, observatory for viewing Arenal volcano, restaurant. Recommended.

AL Fortuna, 1 block southeast of the central park, T2479-9197. One of the newest places in town, with 44 rooms (12 wheelchair accessible), all fully accessible. Price includes breakfast.

AL San Bosco, town centre, T2479-9050, www.arenal-volcano.com. All rooms with private bath, quiet, signs on main road, clean, friendly, nice gardens with terrace, pool and view of the volcano, excellent service and attention to detail, slightly less without a/c.

AL-A Cabinas Monte Real, 1 block from the main plaza, T2479-9357, www.montereal hotel.com. Close to the centre, quiet and friendly, big rooms with private bath and hot water, pool, internet, next to the river and also close to centre. Parking.

A Albergue Ecoturístico La Catarata, 2 km from town, rough road, T2479-9522, www.cataratalodge.com. Price per person. Reservations essential for these 8 cabins in cooperative with organic garden, home-made soaps and shampoos, good fresh food, butterfly farm, taxi US$2, hot water, laundry, all meals. Run by community association and supported by WWF Canada and CIDA Canada.

A Hotel Arenal Rossi, T2479-9023, www.hotelarenalrossi.com. 1 km west, towards the volcano, with breakfast, friendly owner, hot water, fan, watch the volcano from the garden, horses for rent, good value.

A Hotel Carmela, on the south side of the church, www.hotelarenalcarmela.com. 26 rooms with private bath, floor and ceiling fans, some with fridge. Very central, hot showers, can arrange tours. Apartment sleeping 5 available (**E** per person).

A-B Las Colinas, southeast of the central park, T2479-9305, www.ascolinasarenal.com 20 tidy rooms, with private bathroom, some with incredible views. Friendly management, good discounts in the low season. Internet access with Wi-Fi. Recommended.

A-E Arenal Backpacker's Resort, T2479-7000, www.arenalbackpackersresort.com. Good hostel a short distance north out of

town. Dorm and private rooms. Great spot with a pool in the garden with view of Arenal for relaxing when you want to relax.

B Cabinas Guacamaya, town centre, T2479-9393, www.cabinasguacamaya.com. 8 good-sized rooms sleeping 3 or 4, all with private bath and hot water, fridge and a/c. Clean and tidy, with plenty of parking.

B Cabinas Las Flores, west of town, 2 km on road towards the volcano, T2479-9307. Clean, basic, but a little overpriced, restaurant.

B Hotel Villa Fortuna, 500 m south of the bridge, 1 km east from the central plaza, T2479-9139. Has 12 bright and tidy cabins, with neat bathrooms, fans or a/c, nice pool and simple gardens.

C Cabinas La Amistad, central, www.hotel laamistadarenal.com, T2479-9364. Clean, friendly, hot water, firm beds.

D La Posada Inn, a couple of blocks east of the parque central, T2479-9793, laposadainn@yahoo.com. Price per person. 8 simple, but spotless rooms, bath with hot water, fans but mosquitoes reported. Small communal area out front, communal kitchen and the friendly owner Thadeo is very helpful.

D Sissy, office is 100 m south and 100 m west of church, T2479-9256. Quiet spot beside the river, basic rooms with private bathroom; others have shared bath, and there's access to a kitchen and camping spaces (US$3 per person); simple but friendly. Recommended.

F Gringo Pete's, east end of town, T2479-8521, gringopetes2003@yahoo.com. Great place, dormitory and private rooms, clean and tidy. Kitchen facilities and communal area for relaxing. Good notice board and tours arranged. Recommended. Another, bigger and better **Gringo Pete**'s opening across town soon, expected to be **C-D**.

Volcán Arenal *p1187*

Fortuna is the easiest place to stay if you don't have your own transport, but the whole area from Fortuna all along the shores of the lake is littered with hotels and eating options, each taking advantage of superb views and relative seclusion. Hotels on the southern side of the lake are slightly cut off but have fantastic views. Arenal Bungee T2479-7440 in the center of La Fortuna offers bungee, rocket launcher and big-swing adventures US$39.

LL-L Arenal Observatory Lodge, on the northwestern side of the volcano, 4 km after El Tabacón, a turn towards the lake down a (signposted) gravel road, T2290-7011, www.arenalobservatorylodge.com. 4WD recommended along this 9-km stretch (taxi-jeep from Fortuna, US$25). Set up in 1973, the observatory was purely a research station but it now has 42 rooms varying from cabins with bunk beds and bath, to newer rooms with queen-size beds. There are stunning views of the volcano (frighteningly close), Lake Arenal, and across the valley of Río Agua Caliente. The lava flows on the other side of the volcano, but the trails are beautiful and the service excellent.

LL-L Montaña de Fuego, T2479-1220, www.montanadefuego.com. 66 bungalows and rooms, with the stylish (and pricey) Acuarelas restaurant, canopy tour.

L Los Lagos, T2479-1000, www.hotellos lagos.com. 94 comfortable cabin rooms sleeping up to 4, day visits US$20, excellent food and spectacular views of the volcano over the lake, good facilities and small café. There are 3 marked footpaths towards the lava fields and lakes through the forest.

L Arenal Paraíso Resort & Spa, 7.5 km from Fortuna, T2479-1100, www.arenalparaiso. com. 124 rooms, good views of the volcano.

L Volcano Lodge, 6 km from Fortuna, T2460-6080, info@volcanolodge.com. With open-air restaurant good for viewing the volcano.

L-AL Linda Vista del Norte Lodge on the gravel road, taking the right fork (not to the Arenal Observatory Lodge), near Arenal Vista Lodge, T2479-1551, www.hotellinda vista.com. Nice views, several good, unspoilt trails in the area, horse riding tours, hot water. Recommended.

AL Arenal Vista Lodge, T2692-2079. Has 25 rooms with bath, arranges boat trips, riding and hiking, close to hanging bridges and canopy tour, also butterfly garden.

Camping

There is a small campsite just before the park entrance with hook-ups for vehicles, US$2.50 per person. Great views of the volcano and a good spot for walking.

Camping is also possible on the edge of the lake, no services, but good view of volcano at night.

North to Upala *p1188*

L Magil Forest Lodge, 3 km from Col Río Celeste, near San Rafael de Guatuso, T2221-2825. Set in 240 ha on the foothills of the 1916-m **Volcán Tenorio** (now a national park of 12,871 ha with thermal waters, boiling mud and unspoilt forest). 7 rooms with private bath, price includes meals.

F Pensión Buena Vista, Upala. Basic, food available.

Around Lago Arenal *p1188*

LL La Mansión Marina and Club, T2692-8018, www.lamansionarenal.com. On the lake, beautiful pool, very relaxing.

LL-AL Arenal Lodge, travelling round the lake from Fortuna, just north of the dam wall up 2.5-km steep road, T2460-1881, www.arenallodge.com. Stunning views to the north and south. Rooms, suites, meal extra in excellent restaurant.

L-AL Hotel Tilawa, 8 km north of Tilarán, T2695-5050, www.hotel-tilawa.com. With great rooms, restaurant, tennis and excellent opportunities for wind surfing, kayaking and birdwatching. Equipment for rent for US$55 a day. Guaranteed beginner lesson – if it's not fun it's free; try not to laugh and you've got a good deal. Good discounts off season.

L-A Hotel Los Héroes (Pequeña Helvecia), 10 km from Arenal towards Tilarán, T2692-8012, www.hotellosheroes.com. Delightful Swiss owners with inspiring energy. A superb hotel, complete with Swiss train service.

AL La Ceiba, 6 km from Arenal, T2692-8050, www.ceibatree-lodge.com. Overlooking Lake Arenal, Tico owned and run, good, helpful, great panoramic views, good breakfast.

A Chalet Nicholas, west end of lake, T2694-4041, www.chaletnicholas.com. Bed and breakfast (a speciality), run by friendly retired North Americans. Non-smokers only, children under 10 discouraged. Recommended.

A Rock River Lodge, on the road skirting the lake, T2692-1180. Rooms and bungalows, with bathroom, good restaurant. Excellent activity spot with day options for surfing (US$35) and fishing (US$55) and good mountain biking. Bikes available for hire.

B Aurora Inn B&B (Nuevo) Arenal, T2694-4590. Private bath, pool and jacuzzi, art gallery, wedding receptions overlooking Lake Arenal.

B La Alondra, west of La Mansión Marina and Clubs, T2692-8036. With simple, basic rooms sleeping up to 4 and great Tico restaurant from US$5.

Tilarán *p1188*

C Cabiñas El Sueño, 1 block north of bus terminal/central park, T2695-5347. Clean rooms around central patio, hot water, fan, TV, friendly and free coffee. Good deal.

C Naralit, on the south side of the church, T2695-5393. Clean, with a restaurant.

D Hotel Restaurant Mary, south side of church, T2695-5479. Bath, small pleasant rooms, the upstairs is recommended.

D-E Central, round the back of the church, 1 block south, T2695-5363. With shared bath (more with own bath), noisy.

❶ Eating

San Carlos and around *p1184*
Variety of sodas in the central market offer *casados*, check out the great sword collection displayed at La Ponderosa.

♨♨♨ Coca Loca Steak House, next to Hotel La Central, T2460-3208. Complete with Wild West swing door.

♨♨ Los Geranios, Av 4 and Calle. Popular bar and restaurant serving up good *bocas* and other dishes.

♨♨ Restaurant Crystal, on the western side of the plaza. Sells fast food, snacks, ice cream and good fruit dishes.

Los Chiles *p1184*

♨ El Parque on the main plaza. With good home cooking.

♨ Los Petates, on road running south of the central park. Has good food, cheap with large portions but check the bill.

Fortuna *p1185, map p1186*

♨♨♨ La Vaca Muca, out of the town on the way to Tabacón, T2479-9186. Typical Latino food, steak house.

♨♨♨ Las Brasitas, at west end of town (see map), T2479-9819. Open-air restaurant serving abundant authentic Mexican fare with a laid-back European-café style.

♨♨ Choza de Laurel, west of the church, T2479-7063. Typical food in a rustic setting, serving breakfast, lunch and dinner, US$2-US$4.50, occasionally greeted by passing hummingbirds.

♨♨ Coco Loco, south of town, T2468-0990. Coffee, smoothies and fruit drinks, gallery and souvenirs.

♨♨ El Jardín, on the main street opposite the gas station, T2479-9360. Good menu with a mix of local and fast food, pizza, good place to watch the world go by.

♨♨ Nene's, 1½ blocks east of the main square, T2479-9192. Good food, pleasant service, not expensive. Recommended.

♨♨ Pizza Luigi's, west end of town (see map), T2479-9898. Formal, open-air restaurant with distinctly Italian pretensions toward pizza and pasta. Good wine list for Fortuna.

♨♨ Rancho La Cascada, corner of Parque with high conical thatched roof, T2479-9145. Good *bocas*, films sometimes shown in evenings.

♨♨ Steakhouse Arenal next to Hotel Las Flores. Mid-priced steak house with Texan tendencies.

♨♨ Vagabondo, west end of town, T2479-8087, www.vagabondocr.com. Reasonably priced pizza and pasta, also has rooms (**A**) with breakfast.

La Casa de Hara, round the side of Hotel Fortuna. Very good local food, fast service and normal prices – where the locals eat.

Around Lago Arenal *p1188*
¶¶-¶ Caballo Negro, a couple of kilometres west of (Nuevo) Arenal, T2694-4515. The best restaurant for miles, serving vegetarian, Swiss and seasonal fish dishes with organic salads. Warm family atmosphere.
¶ Maverick's Bar & Restaurant (Nuevo) Arenal, T2694-4282. Grilled meat, pizza, excellent food, salad bar and very friendly.
¶ Restaurante Lajas (Nuevo) Arenal, T2694-4385. Tico and vegetarian fare.
¶ Típico Arenal (Nuevo) Arenal, T2694-4159. Good local dishes with seafood and vegetarian options. Large room upstairs (**C**) with private bath and hot water, the best cheap place in town.
¶ Toad Hall, northeast of the lake, T2692-8020. Café, restaurant and gift shop.

Tilarán *p1188*
¶ Restaurant La Carreta, at the back of the church, T2695-6593. The place to go and relax if you have time to kill. Excellent breakfast and lunch only, North American food, pancakes, coffee and good local information.
¶ Stefanie's, out of the bus station to the left on the corner of the main plaza. Good and quick if you need a meal between buses.

▲ Activities and tours

Fortuna *p1185, map p1186*
Tour operators
Aventuras Arenal, on the main street, T2479-9133, www.arenaladventures.com. Provides all tours in the area, and has been around for many years. Can help with enquiries about other parts of Costa Rica.
Canopy Tour, east down the main street, T2479-9769, www.crarenalcanopy.com. Offer a short horse riding journey from Fortuna, US$50, as well as quad tours, mountain bike rental and general tours.

Desafío, just off main square by thatched restaurant, T2479-9464, www.desafio costarica.com. Full range of tours, and with office in Monteverde.
Eagle Tours, T2479-9091, www.eagle tours.net. Helpful, with usual tours.
Sunset Tours, T2479-9800, www.sunset tourcr.com. Reliable, long-standing company with a selection of tours. Recommended.

⊖ Transport

San Carlos and around *p1184*
Bus Direct bus from Terminal Atlántico Norte, **San José**, hourly from 0645-1815, 2¼ hrs, US$2.20, return 0500-1930. From San Carlos buses go northwest to **Tilarán** via **Fortuna** and **Arenal** (0630 and 1400), other buses go to **Fortuna** through El Tanque, 6 daily, 1½ hrs, **San Rafael de Guatuso** and **Upala**, north to **Los Chiles**, hourly, 3 hrs, northeast to towns on the Río San Carlos and Río Sarapiquí, including **Puerto Viejo de Sarapiquí** (5 a day, 3 hrs), and east to the Río Frío district.

Los Chiles *p1184*
Bus Going into Costa Rica, there are direct buses to **San José** daily 0500, 1500, 5 hrs, from San José Atlántico Norte Terminal, Calle 12, Av 7-9, to Los Chiles at 0530, 1530, US$4 with **Auto Transportes San Carlos**, T2255-4318. Alternatively take one of the hourly buses from the same terminal in San José to **San Carlos**, US$3.25 (**Cd Quesada**) from where there are hourly services, 2 hrs, US$2.20. From **Fortuna**, take the bus to San Carlos, get off at Muelle and wait for a connection.

Fortuna *p1185, map 1186*
Bus From **San José** there are daily returning buses hourly from 0500-1930 from Terminal Atlántico Norte, with **Auto Transportes San José–San Carlos**, T2255-4318, 4½ hrs, via San Carlos, US$3.25. From **San Carlos**, 6 buses daily, 1 hr, US$1. To **Tilarán** there are 2 buses

daily at 0800 (connecting to 1230 bus Tilarán–Santa Elena/Monteverde and 1300 bus Tilarán–Puntarenas) and 1730, US$2.90, 4 hrs. Shuttle bus services to **Monteverde** and **Tamarindo** (US$26 per person, min 6). Taxis in the area overcharge. Agree on price before travelling.

Leaving Fortuna, there are frequent buses to **San Ramon** with buses to San José every 30 mins, and good connections to Puntarenas. Also regular service to **Ciudad Quesada**.

Car hire Alamo, T2479-9090, has an office in town; Poas T2479-8027.

Tilarán p1188
Bus If heading for Santa Elena and Monteverde see page 1197. Direct bus from **San José**, 4 daily, 4 hrs, from Terminal Atlántico Norte. 2 daily buses to **San Carlos** via Fortuna at 0700 and 1230. To **Fortuna**, 3 hrs, US$2.00. Daily bus to **Santa Elena** (for Monteverde), 1230, 2½ hrs, US$1.65, return 0700 daily. Tilarán–Puntarenas 0600, 1300, 3 hrs, US$3. 5 daily buses to/from **Cañas** (at 0500, 0730, 1000, 1230 and 1530, 40 mins, US$1.25), where buses head north and south along the Pan-American. If you get the 1230 Tilarán–Liberia bus you can get from there to the Nicaraguan border before it closes.

❸ Directory

San Carlos and around p1184
Banks Banco Nacional, Av Central, west of the church, T2461-9200. **Banco de Costa Rica**, east side of park and another near the

market, T2461-9006, both have ATMs. Others nearby, include **Banco Popular**, T2460-0534. **Internet** Ask around or try Café **Internet**, Av 5, Calle 2-4, 400c per hr, Mon-Fri 0800-2100, Sat 0800-1800. **Post office** Av 5, Calle 2-4.

Los Chiles p1184
Banks Banco Nacional, with ATM, on central park. **Post office** Services provided by Cabiñas Jabirú, 25 m north of market.

Fortuna p1185, map p1186
Banks Banco Nacional de Costa Rica, T2479-9022, will change TCs, US$1 commission, ATM. Banco Popular, T2479-9422, Visa ATM. Coocique, open Sat mornings 0800-1200, Visa ATM. **Internet** Prices in Fortuna are quite expensive. Try Eagle Tours, T2479-9091, or Destiny Tours. **Laundry** Lavandería La Fortuna, Mon-Sat 0800-2100, US$5 wash and dry 4 kg. **Pharmacy** Farmacia Dr Max, east down the main street, Mon-Sat 0730-2030, Sun 0800-1200. **Post office** Down main street, shares building with the police.

Around Lago Arenal p1188
Banks Banco Nacional (Nuevo) Arenal, beside the football pitch.

Tilarán p1188
Banks Banco Cootilaran, a couple of blocks north of the Parque Central, has a Visa and MasterCard ATM, and there is also a **Banco de Costa Rica** in town. **Internet** Café across from bus station.

Northwest Costa Rica

The route of the Pan-American Highway heads north passing near the world-renowned Monteverde Cloud Forest in the Cordillera de Tilarán, the marshes of the Parque Nacional Palo Verde, the active Volcán Rincón and the dry tropical forest of the Parque Nacional Santa Rosa on the Pacific coast, as it crosses the great cattle haciendas of Guanacaste before reaching the Nicaraguan border. ▸▸ *For listings, see pages 1205-1213.*

San José to Esparza and Barranca

The Pan-American Highway from San José descends from the Meseta Central to Esparza, an attractive town with a turbulent early history, as it was repeatedly sacked by pirates in the 17th century, belying its peaceful nature today.

The stretch of the highway between San Ramón and Esparza (31 km) includes the sharp fall of 800 m from the Meseta Central, often shrouded in mist and fog making conditions treacherous for road users. Beyond Esparza is the **Bar/Restaurant Mirador Enis**, a popular stopping place for tour buses breaking the journey at a service station with fruit stalls nearby, before a left turn at Barranca for Puntarenas, 15 km.

Puntarenas and around → *Colour map 7, B3.*

Puntarenas fills a 5-km spit, thrusting out into the Gulf of Nicoya, east to west, but no wider than six avenues. Although popular with locals, most visitors pass through, using it as a transport hub with links to the southern Nicoya Peninsula or to get a bus north or south to other parts of the country without returning to San José. If heading for Nicoya, see page 1214. If heading to Santa Elena/Monteverde see below, and page 1211. It is also the Pacific destination for the bright white, cruise palaces that float through the Central American ports, and dock at Muelle de Cruceros on the Calle Central.

Once the country's main Pacific port with rail links to the Central Highlands, it has since been superseded by Caldera a short distance to the south. The northern side of the peninsula, around Calle Central with the market, banks, a few hotels and the fishing docks, is run-down and neglected, typical of small tropical ports. The southern side is made up of the **Paseo de los Turistas**, drawing crowds to the hot, sometimes dirty beach, especially at weekends. There are several hotels along the strip, as well as restaurants, bars and a general seafront beach atmosphere. There is a public swimming pool at the western end of the point (US$1 entrance), close to the ferries, and good surfing off the headland. There is a **Museo de la Historia Marina** ① *T2661-5036, Tue-Sun 0945-1200, 1300-1715, US$1.80*, in the Cultural Centre by the main church and tourist office. Across the gulf are the hills of the Nicoya Peninsula. **Puntarenas Marine Park** ① *T2661-5272, daily 0900-1700, US$4 children US$2*, offers 28 large aquariums showing Costa Rica's marine life. In the gulf are several islands including the **Islas Negritas**, a biological reserve reached by passenger launches.

Monteverde and Santa Elena ⊜❼❽▲❶❸❹ ▸▸ *pp1205-1213.*

Monteverde Cloud Forest Reserve is one of the most precious natural jewels in Costa Rica's crown, and an opportunity to see plants, insects, birds and mammals in grand profusion – in theory, at least. Protected by law, this private preserve is also protected by appalling access roads on all sides (the nearest decent road is at least two hours from the town). Santa Elena and Monteverde, although separate, are often referred to as the same place; most sites of interest are between the town of Santa Elena at the bottom of the hillside and Monteverde Cloud Forest Reserve at the top.

Monteverde & Santa Elena

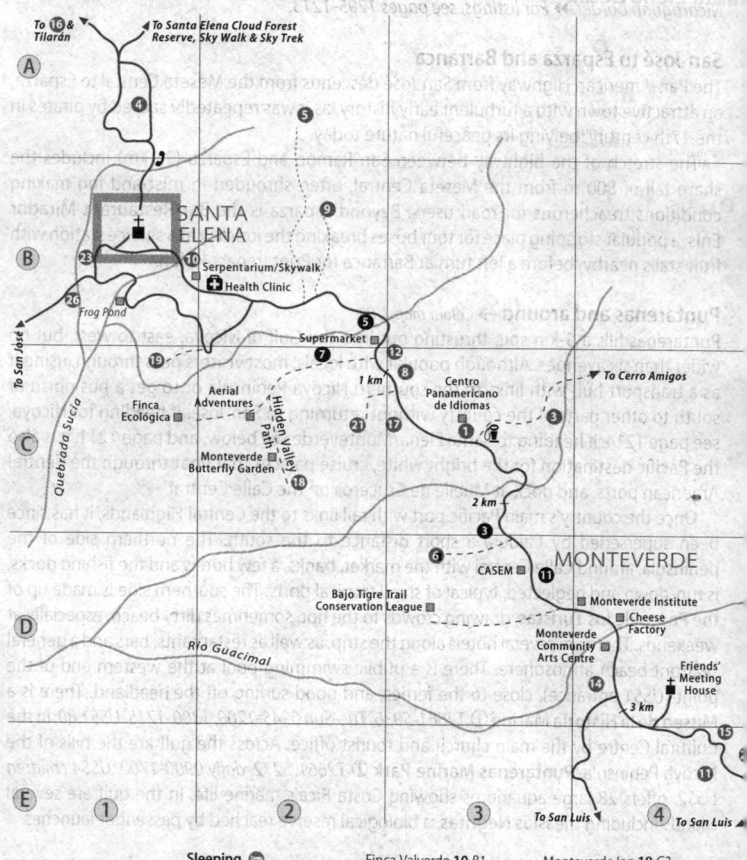

To 16 & Tilarán

To Santa Elena Cloud Forest Reserve, Sky Walk & Sky Trek

SANTA ELENA

Serpentarium/Skywalk
Health Clinic
Frog Pond

To San José
Quebrada Sucia

Supermarket

Aerial Adventures
Finca Ecológica
Hidden Valley Path

Centro Panamericano de Idiomas
To Cerro Amigos

1 km

Monteverde Butterfly Garden

2 km

Monteverde Conservation League
Bajo Tigre Trail

CASEM

MONTEVERDE

Monteverde Institute
Cheese Factory

Río Guacimal

Monteverde Community Arts Centre

Friends' Meeting House

3 km

To San Luis
To San Luis

N
400 metres

Ins and outs

From the Pan-American Highway northwest to Km 149, turn right just before the Río Lagarto. Continue for about 40 km on mostly gravel road (allow 2½ hours) to Santa Elena. Parts of the road are quite good, but in wet weather 4WD is recommended for the rough parts. If driving, check that your car rental agreement allows you to visit Monteverde. A 33-km shorter route is to take the Pipasa/Sardinal turn-off from the Pan-American Highway shortly after the Río Aranjuez. At the park in Sardinal, turn left, then go via Guacimal to the Monteverde road.

Buses come from Puntarenas via the Km 149 route. There are also buses from Tilarán to the north, linked with Fortuna by Volcán Arenal, and Cañas on the Pan-American Highway. There are two daily buses from San José.

Alternatively you can make the journey from Tilarán by bus or private transport. It's an equally poor road – a journey that takes a couple of hours, but, if driving, you can visit the quiet and dramatic **Cataratas de Viento Fresco**, some 11 km from Tilarán, 800 m down a very steep road, followed by a 400-m walk. It's a bit hairy if it's raining but worth the effort.

Santa Elena detail

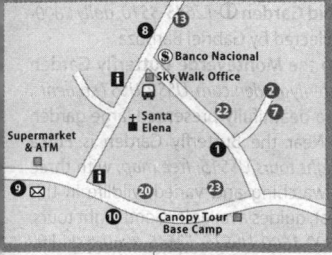

Santa Elena and around

Santa Elena is a rugged and busy place, often packed with visitors exploring the options or just passing time. It is cheaper to stay in town rather than along the single, unpaved road that twists and turns for 5 km through the village of Monteverde, with hotels and places of interest situated along the road almost to the reserve itself. **Santa Elena Reserve**, **Sky Trek** and **Sky Walk** are to the north of Santa Elena, all other places of interest are east, heading up the hill.

Five kilometres north of Santa Elena, off the road to Tilarán, **Sky Trek** ① *T2645-5238, www.skytrek.com, daily 0700-1500, US$66, student US$52, child US$42,* is a popular and a breathtaking experience, as you fly through the air on a system of cables strung out from giant forest trees. On clear days the view from the highest tower is unbelievable. Night-time zip wires have recently been

Monteverde Cloud Forest Reserve ♦

5 km

Hummingbird Gallery

Reserve Entrance & Field Station

4 km

Sleepers Sleep Cheaper
Hostel **26** *B1*
Tina's Casitas **23** *B1*
Trapp Family Lodge **24** *F5*
Villa Verde **25** *E4*

Eating ❼
Chunches **1** *Santa Elena detail*
El Bosque **3** *C3*

Johnny's Pizza **5** *B2*
Lucia's **7** *C2*
Marisquería El Márquez **8**
  Santa Elena detail
Morphos **9** *Santa Elena detail*
Pollo Asado El Campesino **10**
  Santa Elena detail
Stella's Bakery **11** *D3*

introduced. Included in the package is **Sky Tram**, which involves travelling through the canopy in six- seater cable cars.

Very close to Santa Elena, at the start of the climb to Monteverde, is the **Serpentarium** ① *T2645-6002, daily 0900-2000, US$8, US$6 students*, with specimens of snakes and amphibians found in the nearby cloud forest. Other natural history places of interest include the **Frog Pond** ① *TT2645-6320, daily 0900-2030, US$9*, with 25 species of frog, and **The Bat Jungle** ① *daily 0900-2000, T2645-5052, US$8*, where you can learn about the nocturnal habits of over 40 bats.

Just 100 m beyond **Hotel Sapo Dorado** is the **Orchid Garden** ① *T2645-5510, daily 0800-1700, US$5, US$3 students*, with about 400 species collected by Gabriel Barboza.

A dirt road opposite the **Hotel Heliconia** leads to the **Monteverde Butterfly Garden** ① *T2645-5512, daily 0930-1600, www.monteverdebutterflygarden.com, US$9, US$7 students, including guided tour, best time for a visit 1100-1300*, a beautifully presented large garden planted for breeding and researching butterflies. Near the Butterfly Garden is **Finca Ecológica**, ① *T2645-5869, 0700-1730 daily, US$10, night tours US$15, free map*, with three trails totalling around 5 km with bird lists for birdwatching and varied wildlife in this transitional zone between cloud and tropical dry forest, guides available. Good night tours. Down the same path is **Aerial Adventures** ① *daily 0800-1600, US$15, T2645-5960*, a ski-lift-style ride travelling slowly through the treetops. Ideal for birdwatching.

Santa Elena Cloud Forest Reserve
① *0700-1600, entrance US$12, students US$6, T2645-5390, www.reservasantaelena.org, for information. It is a long, steep hike from the village; alternatively hire a taxi, US$6.50.*
One kilometre along the road north from Santa Elena to Tilarán, a 5-km track is signposted to the reserve, managed by the **Centro Ecológico Bosque Nuboso de Monteverde**. It is 83% primary cloud forest and the rest is secondary forest at 1700 m, bordered by the Monteverde Cloud Forest Reserve and the Arenal Forest Reserve. There is a 12-km path network and several lookouts where, on a clear day, you can see and hear Volcán Arenal. The 'canopy tour' is recommended: you climb inside a hollow strangler fig tree then cross between two platforms along aerial runways 30 m up, good views of orchids and bromeliads, then down a 30-m hanging rope at the end. There are generally fewer visitors here than at Monteverde. The **Centro Ecológico Bosque Nuboso** is administered by the local community and profits go to five local schools. It was set up by the Costa Rican government in 1989 with collaboration from Canada. The rangers are very friendly and enthusiastic. There is a small information centre where rubber boots can be hired and a small café open at weekends. Hand-painted T-shirts are for sale.

Monteverde and around → *Colour map 7, B3.*
Strung out along the road to the cloud forest, the settlement at Monteverde – between Santa Elena and the reserve – was founded by American Quakers in the 1950s. Without a centre as such, it started life as a group of dairy farms providing milk for a cooperative cheese factory. The **cheese factory** ① *shop closes 1600*, now privately owned, still operates selling excellent cheeses of various types, fresh milk, ice cream, milkshakes to die for and *cajeta* (a butterscotch spread).

Today, Monteverde maintains an air of pastoral charm, but tourism provides more revenue for the town than dairy produce ever could. It was the vision of the dairy farmers that led to the creation of the reserve to protect the community watershed. When George Powell and his wife spent time in the region studying birds they realized the importance of protecting the area. Working with local residents they created the reserve in 1972 – foresight that has spawned the creation of many other natural attractions locally and throughout the country.

The best way of getting the full low-down on the place is at the **Museum of Monteverde History** ① *daily 0930-1930, US$5*. A spacious museum that records the history of Monteverde, beginning with the creation of the Central American isthmus three million years ago to its settlement by indigenous people – then the arrival of the Ticos, followed by the Quaker settlers, and then biologists, conservationists and ecotourism.

Reserva Sendero Tranquilo ① *daily, T2645-5010, entry restricted to 12 people at any one time,* is a private 200-ha reserve near the Monteverde cheese factory. Reservations and guides should be arranged through **El Sapo Dorado** hotel, which also offers night tours for US$25 per person.

Just before the entrance to Monteverde Cloud Forest is the **Hummingbird Gallery** ① *T2645-5030, daily 0700-1700*, where masses of different hummingbirds can be seen darting around a glade, visiting feeding dispensers filled with sugared water. Outside the entrance is a small shop/photo gallery that sells pictures and gifts, as well as **Bromeliads Nature Bookstore and Café**. There is also a slide show at **Hotel Belmar, The Hidden Rainforest** ① *1930 daily except Fri*, by Bobby Maxson.

Adjoining the Monteverde Cloud Forest is **El Bosque Eterno de los Niños (Children's Eternal Rainforest)** ① *T2645-5003, www.acmcr.org*, established in 1988 after an initiative by Swedish schoolchildren to save forests. Currently at 22,000 ha, the land has been bought and is maintained by the **Monteverde Conservation League** with children's donations from around the world. The **Bajo Tigre** trail takes 1½ hours, parking available with notice, a guide can be arranged, but no horses are allowed on the trail. Groups can arrange trips to the **San Gerardo** and **Poco Sol Field stations** ① *0800-1600, entrance US$6, students US$2, contact the Monteverde Conservation League for reservations at San Gerardo or Poco Sol, T2645-5003, www.acmcr.org*, one of Costa Rica's best-kept secrets.

Monteverde Cloud Forest Reserve

① *www.cct.or.cr. The reserve entrance is at the field station at the top of the road. Bus from Santa Elena heads up the hill leaving at 0600 and 1100 returning at 1400 and 1700. The total number of visitors to the reserve at any one time is 150, so be there before 0700 to make sure of getting in during high season (hotels will book you a place for the following day). Tour buses come in from San José daily. Entrance fee US$17 (students with ID US$9) valid for multiple entry during the day, cannot be purchased in advance. Office open daily 0700-1630; the park opens at 0700 and closes at 1700. A small shop at the office sells various checklists, postcards and APS film, gifts and excellent T-shirts, the proceeds of which help towards the conservation project.*

Straddling the continental divide, the 10,500-ha Monteverde Cloud Forest Reserve is privately owned and administered by the Tropical Science Centre – a non-profit research and educational association. The reserve is mainly primary cloud forest and spends much of the year shrouded in mist, creating stunted trees and abundant epiphytic growth. The best months to visit are January-May, especially February, March and April. It contains more than 400 species of bird, including the resplendent quetzal, best seen in the dry months between January and May, especially near the start of the Nuboso trail; the three-wattled bellbird with its distinctive 'bonk' call; and the bare-necked umbrella bird. There are more than 100 species of mammal, including monkeys; Baird's tapir; six endangered cats (jaguar, jaguarundi, margay, ocelot, tigrillo and puma); reptiles; and amphibians. But be warned, travellers have told us there is little chance of seeing much wildlife. The reserve also includes an estimated 2500 species of plant and more than 6000 species of insect. The entrance is at 1500 m, but the maximum altitude in the reserve is over 1800 m. Mean temperature is between 16° and 18°C and average annual rainfall is 3000 mm. The weather changes quickly and wind and humidity often make the air feel cooler.

The commonly used trails are in good condition and there are easy, short and interesting walks for those who do not want to hike all day. Trail walks take from two hours but you could easily spend all day just wandering around. Trails may be restricted from time to time if they need protection. There is a trail northwards to the Arenal volcano that is increasingly used, but it is not easy. There are three refuges for people wishing to spend the night within the reserve boundaries, see Sleeping. Free maps of the reserve are available at the entrance. Follow the rules, stay on the paths, leave nothing behind, take no fauna or flora out; no radios/CD players/iPods, etc are allowed.

Guides Natural history walks with biologist guides, every morning and afternoon, three to four hours, US$16 (children half price); advance reservations at the office or through your hotel are strongly recommended. If you use a private (non-reserve) guide you must pay his entrance fee too. An experienced and recommended guide is **Gary Diller** ① *T2645-9916*, he also does night tours. There are 25 others operating, of varying specialization and experience. Excellent night tours in the reserve are available normally with **Ricardo Guindon** or call **Monteverde Reserve** ① *T2645-5112, US$15*, at 1900 sharp. Day or night, a guide is recommended if you want to see wildlife, since the untrained eye misses a lot.

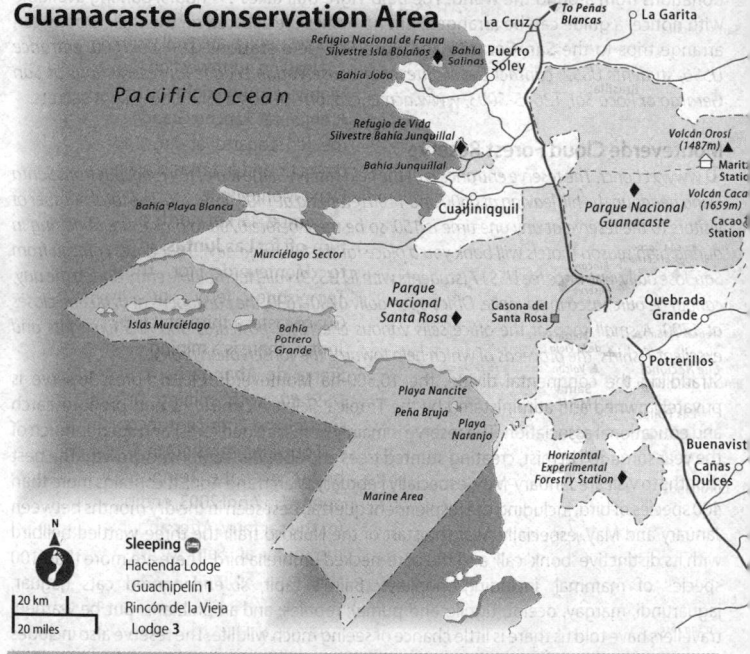

Guanacaste Conservation Area

Pacific Ocean

To Peñas Blancas
La Cruz • La Garita

Refugio Nacional de Fauna
Silvestre Isla Bolaños ◆ Bahía Salinas Puerto Soley

Bahía Jobo

Refugio de Vida
Silvestre Bahía Junquillal ◆

Bahía Junquillal

Volcán Orosí (1487m) ▲

Marit. Static

Bahía Playa Blanca

Cuajiniqguil

Volcán Caca (1659m) ▲

Parque Nacional Guanacaste Cacao Station

Murciélago Sector

Islas Murciélago

Parque Nacional Santa Rosa ◆

Casona del Santa Rosa 🏛

Quebrada Grande

Bahía Potrero Grande

Potrerillos

Playa Nancite

Peña Bruja

Playa Naranjo

Horizontal Experimental Forestry Station ◆

Buenavist

Cañas Dulces

Marine Area

N

Sleeping 🛏
Hacienda Lodge
Guachipelín **1**
Rincón de la Vieja
Lodge **3**

20 km
20 miles

Donations and volunteer work Donations are welcomed for purchasing additional land and maintaining and improving existing reserve areas. If you are interested in volunteer work, from non-skilled trail maintenance to skilled scientific assistance work, surveying, teaching or studying on a tropical biology programme, contact the reserve (US$14 per person, board and lodging, two weeks minimum). The Conservation League works with schools in the area on education regarding conservation. Donations can be made at the **Monteverde Cloud Forest Reserve** office or **Tropical Science Centre** ① *San José, T2253-3267, www.cct.or.cr*, or the **Monteverde Conservation League** ① *Apdo Postal 124-5655, San José, Costa Rica, T2645-5003, www.acmcr.org*.

North to Guanacaste Province ⊕⊘▲⊕ » *pp1205-1213*.

North of Barranca, the Pan-American Highway heads towards the province of Guanacaste – the cultural heartland of Costa Rica, home to the *sabanero* cowboy and the rolling plains of the northern ranches. The province also includes the Peninsula of Nicoya and the lowlands at the head of the gulf. Rainfall is moderate; 1000-2000 mm per year. The long dry season makes irrigation important, but the lowlands are deep in mud during the rainy season.

Guanacaste, with its capital Liberia, has a distinctive people, way of life, flora and fauna. The smallholdings of the highlands give way here to large haciendas and great cattle estates. The rivers teem with fish; there are all kinds of wildlife in the uplands.

The people are open, hospitable and fun-loving, and are famed for their music and dancing, and in fact, the Punto Guanacasteco has been officially declared the national dance. There are many fiestas in January and February in the local towns and villages, which are well worth seeing.

Heading northwest on the Pan-American Highway, turn right just after the Río Aranjuez at Rancho Grande (or just south of the Río Lagarto at Km 149) to access a dramatic and at times scenic route to Santa Elena-Monteverde.

Some 43 km north of Barranca is the turn-off for **Las Juntas**, an alternative route to Monteverde for those using the Tempisque ferry or arriving from Guanacaste; a third of it is paved. After Las Juntas, there is a mining ecomuseum at **La Sierra de Abangares** ① *daily 0600-1800, US$1.80*, with mining artefacts from a turn-of-the-20th-century gold mine.

Four kilometres north, the long-awaited bridge over the Tempisque River finally opened in April 2003, ending the long waits for the car ferry. After about 6 km, a road to the right at San Joaquín leads to the **Hacienda Solimar Lodge** (see Sleeping, page 1207), a 1300-ha cattle farm with dry tropical virgin forest bordering Parque

Nacional Palo Verde (see below) near Porozal in the lower Tempisque River basin. The freshwater Madrigal estuary on the property is one of the most important areas for waterbirds in Costa Rica (only guests staying at the Hacienda can visit). Also surrounded by gallery forest, it is recommended for serious birdwatchers. Reservations essential, contact **Birdwatch** ① *T2228-4768, www.birdwatch costarica.com.*

Sixty-seven kilometres north of Barranca, **Cañas** has little to keep the visitor for long. There are a number of interesting sights nearby and, for the traveller arriving from the north, this is the cut-through to Tilarán and connecting buses to Arenal or Fortuna. **Las Pumas** ① *behind Safaris Corobicí, Cañas, free but donations welcome and encouraged*, is a small, private, Swiss-run animal rescue centre which specializes in looking after big cats, including jaguar. It's an unmissable if rather sad experience.

Parque Nacional Palo Verde

At the south of the neck of the Nicoya Peninsula is Parque Nacional Palo Verde, currently over 18,650 ha of marshes with many water birds. Indeed, in the *laguna* more than 50,000 birds are considered resident. The views from the limestone cliffs are fantastic. **Palo Verde Biological Station** ① *T2661-4717, Reservations on T2524-0607, www.ots.ac.cr*, is a research station run by the Organization for Tropical Studies. It organizes natural history walks and basic accommodation; US$89 with three meals and a guided walk (from US$32), cheaper for researchers, make advance reservations. Turn off the Pan-American Highway at **Bagaces**, halfway between Cañas and Liberia. There is no public transport. The **Palo Verde Administration offices** ① *T2661-4717*, are in Bagaces, next to the service station. Park entrance US$10. There are two ranger stations, Palo Verde and Catalina. Check roads in wet season.

Liberia and around 🌐🚗🏨🅿️🍴🛏️🏧 ➤➤ pp1205-1213. Colour map 7, B2.

➔ *Population: 40,000.*

Known as the 'White City', Liberia is a neat, clean, cattle town with a triangular, rather unattractive modern church, and single-storey colonial houses meticulously laid out in the streets surrounding the central plaza. The town is at the junction of the Pan-American Highway and a well-paved branch road leads southwest to the Nicoya Peninsula.

There is a **tourist office** ① *3 blocks south of the plaza on Calle 1, Av 6, T2666-1606*, which is helpful, English is spoken; leave a donation as the centre is not formally funded (the information is not always accurate). In the same building is the **Museo del Sabanero (Cowboy Museum)** ① *museum and tourist office Mon-Sat 0800-1200, 1300-1600, US$0.45*, a poorly presented display of artefacts. You can also get some tourist information across the plaza from the church.

Africa Mia animal park ① *T2661-8165, www.africamia.net, US$15 entry, US$10 child*, features animals from Africa, including ostriches and giraffes, and has picnic areas, a restaurant and offers tours. Further north is the turn-off northeast to **Quebrada Grande**.

Parque Nacional Rincón de la Vieja

① *Park entry US$6. There are 2 ways into the park: the southern route, which has less traffic, goes from Puente La Victoria on the western side of Liberia and leads, in about 25 km, to the Santa María sector, closest to the hot springs. In this part, you can hike 8 km to the boiling mud pots (Las Pailas) and come back in the same day; the sulphur springs are on a different trail and only one hour away. The northern route turns right off the Pan-American Highway 5 km* *northwest of Liberia, through Curubandé (no public transport on this route). Beyond Curubandé, you cross the private property of Hacienda Lodge Guachipelin (US$2 to cross), beyond which is Rincón de la Vieja Lodge, see Sleeping. Day trips are possible to all areas, US$15 for Rincón de la Vieja, US$40 for Santa Rosa and US$50 for Palo Verde. Minimum of 4 required, prices per person. Park is closed Mon for maintenance.*

Most easily visited from Liberia, Parque Nacional Rincón de la Vieja (14,161 ha) was created to preserve the area around the Volcán Rincón de la Vieja, to the northeast of the town. It includes dry tropical forest, mud pots, hot sulphur springs and several other geothermal curiosities. The volcanic massif reaches to 1916 m and can be seen from a wide area around Liberia when not shrouded in clouds. The area is cool at night and subject to strong, gusty winds and violent rains; in the day it can be very hot, although always windy. These fluctuations mark all of the continental divide, of which the ridge is a part. From time to time the volcano erupts, the last eruption being in November 1995, when it tossed rocks and lava down its slopes.

The park is home to over 350 recorded species of bird, including toucans, parrots, three-wattled bellbirds and great curassows, along with howler monkeys, armadillos and coatis, ticks and other biting insects. It also has the largest density of Costa Rica's national flower the *guaria morada* or purple orchid. Horses can be rented in the park from some of the lodges. If you want to climb the volcano you will need to camp near the top, or at the warden's station, in order to ascend early in the morning before the

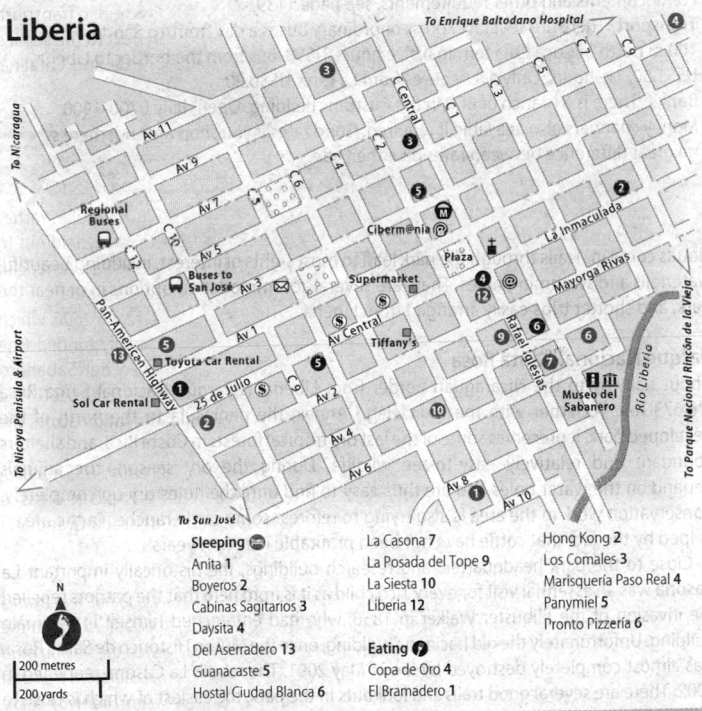

Liberia

Sleeping
Anita **1**
Boyeros **2**
Cabinas Sagitarios **3**
Daysita **4**
Del Aserradero **13**
Guanacaste **5**
Hostal Ciudad Blanca **6**

La Casona **7**
La Posada del Tope **9**
La Siesta **10**
Liberia **12**

Eating
Copa de Oro **4**
El Bramadero **1**

Hong Kong **2**
Los Comales **3**
Marisquería Paso Real **4**
Panymiel **5**
Pronto Pizzería **6**

200 metres
200 yards

Border essentials: Costa Rica–Nicaragua

Peñas Blancas

Immigration Office hours Monday-Saturday 0600-2200, Sunday 0600-2000. On leaving Costa Rica you have to go to Migración to surrender your passport to be stamped and to give in your immigration form. 'Helpers' may try and sell you the form before you arrive at the office – you do not have to buy it from them. Across the border, passports are inspected on the Nicaraguan side. Crossing to Nicaragua may be a slow process; if you arrive when a Tica, Sirca or other international bus is passing through this is especially true. When leaving Nicaragua you pay US$1 for the 'right to leave', another US$2 at customs and there are reports of a US$1 'bus station tax' on the Nicaraguan side. Visa stamps are given at the border. If you have no outward ticket for Costa Rica, and are challenged, you can buy a cheap bus ticket back to Nicaragua at the border (valid for one year).

Crossing by private vehicle Entering Costa Rica by car, first pay your entrance stamp, then go to Aduana Permiso de Vehículo for your vehicle permit (state how long you want); get insurance at the *Seguro Obligatorio* window. Your vehicle is then briefly inspected before you can depart. Fumigation cost US$3 for cars, US$4 for pickups. Leaving by car, hand over the printed vehicle permit you got on arrival.

For documents and other requirements, see page 1139.

Transport There are several express or ordinary buses a day from/to San José, 100 m north of Coca Cola terminal, five hours, US$8. Bus from the border to Liberia, US$1.50, 1½ hours. Only a few buses from La Cruz, US$0.80.

Banks There is a branch of BCR in the Customs building. Open daily 0700-1900. Money changers also available if required. Good rates if you shop around; there's no great difference between rates on either side.

---

clouds come in. Trails through the park lead to most sights of interest, including beautiful waterfalls and swimming holes. There are several accommodation options in or near the park, and shorter trips easily arranged from Liberia.

Parque Nacional Santa Rosa

About halfway to the Nicaraguan border from Liberia, is Parque Nacional Santa Rosa (38,673 ha). Together with the Murciélago Annex, the peninsula to the north of the developed park, it preserves some of the last dry tropical forests in Costa Rica, and shelters abundant and relatively easy-to-see wildlife. During the dry season, the animals depend on the water holes and are thus easy to find until the holes dry up completely. Conservation work in the area is also trying to reforest some cattle ranches in the area – helped by the fact that cattle have not been profitable in recent years.

Close to the park headquarters and research buildings, the historically important **La Casona** was an essential visit for every Tico child as it is from here that the patriots repelled the invasion of the filibuster Walker in 1856, who had entrenched himself in the main building. Unfortunately the old hacienda building, once the Museo Histórico de Santa Rosa, was almost completely destroyed by fire in May 2001. The rebuilt La Casona reopened in 2002. There are several good trails and lookouts in the park, the easiest of which is close to

La Casona. Lasting a couple of hours, it leads through dry tropical forest with many Indio Desnudo (naked Indian) trees, which periodically shed their red flaky bark.

Deeper in the park, **Playa Naranjo** (12 km, three hours' walk or more, or use 4WD, park authorities permitting) and **Playa Nancite** (about the same distance from the entrance) are major nesting sites of **leatherback** and **Olive Ridley sea turtles**. The main nesting season is between August and October (although stragglers are regularly seen up to January) when flotillas of up to 10,000 Ridley turtles arrive at night on the 7-km long Playa Nancite. Females clumsily lurch up the beach, scoop out a deep hole, deposit and bury an average of 100 ping-pong-ball sized eggs before returning exhausted to the sea. Playa Nancite is a restricted-access beach; you need a written permit to stay plus US$2 per day to camp, or US$15 in dormitories. Permits from **SPN** in San José, and the **Park Administration building** ① *Santa Rosa, T2666-5051, make sure you have permission before going*. Research has been done in the Playa Nancite area on howler monkeys, coatis and the complex interrelation between the fauna and the forest. Playa Naranjo is one of the most attractive beaches in the country. It is unspoilt, quiet and very good for surfing. There is good camping, drinking water (although occasionally salty) and BBQ facilities.

La Cruz and Isla Bolaños → *Colour map 7, B2.*

The last town before the border, La Cruz has a bank (for cash, traveller's cheques or credit card transactions), a handful of hotels and absolutely incredible sunsets from the hilltop overlooking the Bahía de Salinas. Down in the bay the Islas Bolaños Wildlife Refuge and some of the best conditions for windsurfing in Costa Rica.

Isla Bolaños is a 25-ha National Wildlife Refuge protecting the nesting sites of the brown pelican, frigate bird and American oystercatcher. The island is covered with dry forest and you can only walk round the island at low tide. The incoming tidal surge is very dangerous, be off the island before the tide comes in. No camping is allowed.

① Northwest Costa Rica listings

For Sleeping and Eating price codes and other relevant information, see Essentials pages 45-48.

● Sleeping

San José to Esparza and Barranca
p1195

L-AL Hotel Vista Golfo, 14 km off the Inter-American Hwy at Miramar, T2639-8303, www.vistagolfo.com. Wildlife, canopy tour, horse riding, waterfalls and spring-fed pool on 27 ha in what is now an adventure park.
C Hotel Castanuelas, close to the highway, T2635-5105. A/c, quiet, cooler alternative to Puntarenas.
C Hotel Río Mar, Barranca, T2663-0158. With bath and restaurant. Good.

Puntarenas and around *p1195*
Accommodation is difficult to find from Dec-Apr, especially at weekends.
L-A Tioga, on the beach front with Calle 17, T2661-0271, www.hoteltioga.com. 54 rooms; those with balconies are much better, with views. Private bath, a/c, TV and telephone. Restaurant, swimming pool, very good.
A-B La Punta, Av 1, Calle 35, T2661-0696. Good spot 1 block from car ferry, with bath, hot water, secure parking, good pool. American-owned, big rooms, friendly, clean.
A-B Las Hamacas on beach front between Calle 5-7, T2661-0398. Rooms are OK, but noisy when the bar is in full flow. Small pool. Could do with a lick of paint; for now it is overpriced.

B-C Cayuga, Calle 4, Av Central-1, T2661-0344. Has 31 rooms with private bathroom, a/c, pretty dark rooms, restaurant. There is a small garden patio but it's hardly paradise.

B-C Gran Hotel Chorotega, on the corner of Calle 1, Av 3 near the banks and market, T2661-0998. Clean rooms with private bath, cheaper with shared. Efficient and friendly service. Popular with visiting business people. A good deal.

C Gran Imperial, on the beach front, in front of the Muelle de Cruceros, T2661-0579. Pleasant rooms, although a little dark, but clean with private bath and fan. Small garden patio, and a very chilled atmosphere, restaurant. Good spot and handy for buses.

D Cabezas, Av 1, Calle 2-4, T2661-1045. Has 23 rooms, some with private bath, cheaper without. Simple rooms with no frills but bright and clean. Good deal.

D-E Río, Av 3, Calle Central-2 near market, T2661-0331. Private bath, fans, good rooms. Friendly Chinese owners keen to help, lively, sometimes noisy, but popular place.

F Monte Mar, Av 3, Calle 1-3. Very basic, some rooms with fan, but bearable on a budget.

Around Puntarenas

A Casa San Francisco, at Roble, 10 km east of Puntarenas, on the coast, T2663-0148. Near regional hospital, run by 2 Canadian women, pool, clean, laundry facilities, friendly and helpful, mainly weekly or long-term rental. Recommended.

Santa Elena *p1197, map p1196*
AL Arco Iris, southeast of Banco Nacional, T2645-5067, www.arcoirislodge.com. Rooms with bath, restaurant with good healthy breakfast, horses for rent, plenty of parking.

AL-A Finca Valverde, 300 m east of Banco Nacional up hill on road to the reserve, T2645-5157, www.monteverde.co.cr. Rooms with bath, nice gardens for birdwatching, bar and restaurant.

AL-A Miramontes, leading into Santa Elena from the north, T2645-5152, www.swisshotel miramontes.com. 8 comfortable rooms in a quiet spot, Swiss-run, wonderful restaurant.

B Pensión El Sueño, T2645-5021. Very friendly, hot shower, small but nice rooms, clean, pricey meals, car park. Run by Rafa Trejos who does horse-riding trips into the mountains to see quetzals, etc (US$35).

B-F Pensión Santa Elena, T2645-5051, www.pensionsantaelena.com. Good range of rooms of varying standards and quality – all good value for the money. Very popular, clean, good food, kitchen available.

C El Colibrí, T2645-5682, clean, friendly, timber built, with balconies.

C Hospedaje El Banco, see map. Price per person. Family-run, friendly, hot shower, clean, good information, English spoken.

D-E Tina's Casistas, T2645-5641, www.tinascasitas.de. 4 cabins with 9 rooms with private or shared bath. In a quiet part of Santa Elena and worth a look if you want a little more comfort.

F Pensión Cabinas Marín, 500 m north of the centre past the Agricultural College. Spacious rooms (room 8 has a nice view), good breakfasts, friendly.

F Sleepers Sleep Cheaper Hostel, T2645-6204, http://sleepershostel.blogspot.com. Cheap budget accommodation with dorm rooms. Kitchen and internet access too.

Monteverde *p1198, map p1196*
LL El Establo, next to Heliconia, T2645-5110, www.elestablo.com. 155 carpeted rooms with private bathroom, restaurant, 50-ha farm with 50% cloud forest, own nature guide, good birdwatching, riding stables, 35 horses, family-run, very accommodating. Recommended.

LL Monteverde Lodge, T2645-5057, www.costaricaexpeditions.com. With restaurant, jacuzzi, daily slide shows US$5 at 1800. Recommended.

L El Sapo Dorado, T2645-5010, www.sapo dorado.com. 30 suites, 10 with fireplaces, good but expensive restaurant (0700-2100).

L Fonda Vela, T2645-5125, www.fonda vela.com. Private bathroom, hot water, 40 beautiful rooms and suites spread around 5 buildings. A 25-min walk, 5-min drive to the reserve, on a 14-ha farm with forest and trail system, good birding, 2 excellent restaurants (open to public), bar, TV room, art gallery and conference room.

L Heliconia, T2645-5109, www.hotel heliconia.com. Private bathrooms, restaurant, very comfortable, excellent food, private reserve and nature rails. Highly recommended.

L-AL Belmar, 300 m behind service station, T2645-5201, www.hotelbelmar.net. Swiss chalet-style, beautiful views of Nicoya, restaurant, good.

L-AL Hotel de Moñtana Monteverde, T2645-5046, www.monteverdemountain hotel.com Comfortable, set meals, good, wholesome food, sauna, jacuzzi, good views of Nicoya, excellent birdwatching on 15-ha reserve, transport from San José available. Recommended.

AL Cloud Forest Lodge, 300 m north of Sapo Dorado, T2645-5058, www.cloudforest lodge.com. 20 rooms with bath. Restaurant, beautiful views and tours available here with Canopy Tours, see Activities and tours.

AL Trapp Family Lodge, closest to the reserve, T2645-5858, www.trappfam.com. Tidy rooms, upstairs with balconies, downstairs with terraces. Restaurant and friendly, helpful hosts.

A El Bosque, next to restaurant of same name, T2645-5158. Has 26 comfortable rooms with hot showers. Clean, fine views, beautiful gardens and short trail, safe parking.

A La Colina Lodge, between Monteverde and reserve, T2645-5009. Private bath, balconies with some rooms, cheaper in dormitory, helpful, luggage stored, small area for camping, one of the original houses of Monteverde with some nice touches. Marvin Rockwell, the former owner and one of the original Quaker settlers, pops in to give talks when requested.

A Villa Verde, 1 km from reserve, T2640-4697, www.villaverdehotel.com. Rooms with

hot showers, others with shared bath, some with kitchenette, includes breakfast. Clean, nice, with restaurant and excellent views. Good package rates for students.

B Mariposa, T2645-5013. Has 3 rooms in a single block sleeping up to 3 people, with private bath. A family atmosphere with breakfast included in the price.

B Pensión Manakin, just beyond El Establo, along a short road on the right, T2645-5080. Offers 10 simple rooms, a few with private bath, cheaper with shared bath, also fully equipped cabins. Filling breakfast and evening meals are available, in a family atmosphere great for sharing stories with other guests. A small balcony at the back makes a calm place to sit and relax. The Villegas are very knowledgeable about the area, and will help arrange tours and transport up to the reserve if required.

C-D Albergue Bellbird, just before the gas station, T2645-5518. ½ a dozen rooms in mainly dorm-style accommodation, shared bathrooms, restaurant with typical food.

D Monteverde Inn, down track opposite Heliconia, T2645-5156. Private bathroom, quiet, breakfast included. Run-down, price per person.

Monteverde Cloud Forest Reserve p1199

Shelter facilities throughout the reserve cost US$3.50-US$5 a night, reserve entry fee for each night spent in the park, plus key deposit of US$5. Bring sleeping bag and torch. You can make your own meals. Dormitory-style accommodation for up to 30 people at entrance, **Albergue Reserva Biológica de Monteverde**, T2645-5122, US$40 full board only, includes park entrance fee. Reservations only for all reserve accommodation (usually booked up by groups).

North to Guanacaste Province p1201

A Capazuri B&B, 2.5 km north of Cañas, T2669-6280. Also camping US$7 per person.

A Hacienda Solimar Lodge. 8 rooms with private or shared bathroom, includes meals,

minimum 2 nights, transport on request, local guide, horse riding. Recommended for serious birdwatchers, contact **Birdwatch**, T2228-4768, www.birdwatchcostarica.com, see page 1201. Reservations essential.
B El Corral, Pan-American, Cañas, T2669-1467. With bath.
C Cañas, Calle 2, Av 3, Cañas, T2669-0039. With bath, clean, pleasant.
E Cabinas Corobicí, Cañas, T2669-0241. Has 11 good rooms with bath and parking available. Price per person.

Liberia and around p1202, map p1203
A Las Espuelas, 2 km south of Liberia, T2666-0144, www.bestwestern.com. Good, a/c, satellite TV, swimming pool, round trip bus service from San José.
B Boyeros, on Pan-American Hwy with Av Central, T2666-0722. Pool, bath, restaurant.
B Hostal Ciudad Blanca, Av 4, Calle 1-3, from Gobernación 200 m south, 150 m east, T2666-3962. Has 12 nice but dirty rooms, a/c, hot water, TV, restaurant/bar, parking, rooster wake up call.
B Hotel del Aserradero, Pan-American Hwy and Av 3, T2666-1939. Has 16 big rooms with bath, parking and fans.
B Santa Clara Lodge, 4 km from Quebrada Grande, T2666-4054. Has 4 rooms with shared bath, 1 room with bath, cattle farm, riding, dry forest.
C Guanacaste, Calle 12, Av 3, just round corner from bus stations, T2666-0085. Clean, bath, friendly, restaurant, safe parking, money exchange, **Ticabus** agency offers transfers and tours here. Camping area, English spoken, group discount, 15% student discount, affiliated youth hostel. Recommended.
C La Siesta, Calle 4, Av 4-6, T2666-0678. Clean, with bath, restaurant, swimming pool, helpful owner who speaks English.
C-E Hotel Daysita, Av 5, Calle 11-13, T2666-0197. Restaurant, pool, quiet, not central. Cheaper to share 6-bedded room with bath.
C-E La Posada del Tope, Rafael Iglesias, 1½ blocks south from church, T2666-3876.

Clean, friendly, helpful, with shower, laundry facilities, parking, bike rentals, baggage storage. The owner Dennis has a telescope for star gazing. Price per person.
D-E La Casona, Av 6, Calle Central, T2666-2971. Rooms for up to 4 people, shared bath, washing facilities, rooms facing street get very hot; more expensive in annex with private bath.
D-E Liberia, ½ block south of main square, T2666-0161. Cheaper with shared bath, fans, clean, friendly, good information board and breakfast, laundry facilities. Recommended.
E Cabinas Sagitarios, Av 11, Calle 2, T2666-0950. With bath, run by Dutchman and Costa Rican, breakfast and dinner available on request, friendly.
F Anita, Calle 4 y Av 8, T2666-1285. Bath, clean, family-run, friendly, café, shop, parking, best of the range.

Parque Nacional Rincón de la Vieja
p1202, map p1200
AL Hacienda Lodge Guachipelín, accessed through the northern route, T2666-8075, www.guachipelin.com. Meals available, 50 rooms, internet, canopy tour, naturalist guides, riding, hot springs, sulphur springs, mud pools, waterfalls (transport from Liberia arranged, US$50 per person round trip).
AL Rincón de la Vieja Lodge, accessed through the northern route, T2200-0238, www.rincondelaviejalodge.net. Canopy tour, sulphur hot springs, tennis, horseback riding, internet. Also packages including transport from San José. The lodge is on the edge of the park and there are horses guides and tours. 3¼ hrs to the volcano, 30 mins to Las Pailas, 45 mins to the thermal springs, Azufrales, and 2¼ hrs to the Hidden Waterfalls.
A-B Buena Vista Mountain Lodge, accessed through the Santa María sector, T2661-8158. Rooms, waterslide, canopy tour, spa, internet, restaurant/bar.
F Miravieja Lodge, accessed through the Santa María sector, T2662-2004. Rustic lodge in citrus groves, meals, transport and tours.

Parque Nacional Santa Rosa *p1204*
Camping
There is a pleasant campground at Park Administration, T2679-9692, about 7 km from the entrance with giant strangler figs that shade your tent from the stupendously hot sun, and very adequate sanitary facilities, picnic tables, and so forth for US$2.15 per person per night. There is a small *comedor* for meals (breakfast 0600-0630, lunch 1100-1200, evening 1700-1800, good) and drinks near the campground but it is advised that you bring some of your own supplies; a tent is useful and essential in the wet season. You may be able to sleep on the veranda of one of the scientists' houses. Bring a mosquito net and insect repellent. If the water is not running, ask Park Administration.

La Cruz and Isla Bolaños *p1205*
L-AL Ecoplaya Beach Resort, Bahía Salinas, T2228-7146, www.ecoplaya.com. All-inclusive resort, well maintained with nice restaurant.
A-C Hotel La Mirada, on road out to the Pan-American Hwy, T/F2679-9084. Clean, tidy rooms, ample parking.
B Amalia's Inn, 100 m south of Parque Central. Stunning views, small pool, very friendly and excellent local knowledge. Extra person US$5, and 1 room sleeps 6. Excellent value for groups and recommended
C-D Cabinas Santa Rita, 150 m south of Parque Central, T2679-9062. Nice, clean, secure with good parking. Cheaper with fan. Would be great in any other town not competing with Amalia's.
D Hotel Bella Vista, ½ block northwest of the plaza, T2679-8060. Rooms, restaurant/bar, great view.

Camping
Playa Morro Trailer Park y Cabinas, west of La Cruz, on Bahía Salinas looking over to Isla Bolaños. Drinking water, showers, toilets, tennis, barbecue, fishing boats and horses to rent, 1-km beach.

● Eating

Puntarenas and around *p1195*
There are many bars and a couple of discos along the Paseo de los Turistas. A number of Chinese restaurants on Av Central and Calle 1 and there is good, cheap food from market stalls, eg *sopa de carne* (meat soup).
♥♥ Aloha, on the seafront on Calle 17. Worth checking out.
♥♥ Casa de Mariscos, Calle 7-9, T2661-1666, closed Wed. On the beach front, good seafood, reasonable prices.
♥♥ Jardín Cervecero Bierstube, on the seafront at Calle 23-25, T2661-5293. Good for sandwiches, hamburgers and a beer.
♥♥ Kayte Negro, north side of the peninsula on Av Badillo, Calle 17. Good local food.
♥♥ La Yunta, on the beachfront at Calle 19, T2661-3216. A popular steak house, open all night.
♥♥ Mariscos Kahite Blanco, near launch. Excellent and locally renowned seafood.
♥♥ Soda Brisas del Mar, on Calle Central, Av 2-4. Good for a snack.
♥ Soda Macarena, opposite the Muelle de Cruceros (dock). Handy while waiting for buses.

Around Puntarenas
♥♥ María Vargas, Roble, 10 km east of Puntarenas. Bar and restaurant, friendly, good food, reasonable prices.

Santa Elena *p1197, map p1196*
♥♥♥ Chunches, opposite Pensión Santa Elena, T2645-5147, closed Sun. A very useful place with good espresso bar and snacks, used books, magazines, laundromat, fax service.
♥♥ Marisquería El Márquez (see map), T2645-5918, closed Sun. Seafood and *casados*.
♥♥ Morphos (see map), T2645-5607. Typical and international fare, recommended, with a good atmosphere, but not cheap.
♥ Pollo Asado El Campesino (see map). Tico soda, early breakfast special.

Monteverde p1198, map p1196

♛♛-♛ Johnny's Pizza, on main road between Santa Elena and Monteverde, T2645-5066. Good wood oven-cooked pizzas in a relaxed atmosphere, café, souvenir shop. Tables outside give extra chance to see wildlife.

♛♛-♛ Restaurant Lucia's, down road opposite **Heliconia**, T2645-5337. Tasty lasagne, international and vegetarian fare.

♛♛ Restaurant El Bosque, on road to reserve, next to **Casem**, open from 0630. Shop, good food, clean.

♛ Stella's Bakery, opposite **Casem**, T2645-5560. Excellent wholemeal bread, cakes and good granola – there's a café if you want to eat in.

North to Guanacaste Province p1201

♛♛♛ Rincón Corobicí, next to **La Pacífica**, Cañas, T2669-6191. Clean and pleasant, with a small zoo and offers rafting down Río Corobicí.

♛♛ Central, main square. Good Chinese restaurant.

♛♛ Restaurant Panchitos, main square, Cañas. Good and inexpensive.

Liberia and around p1202, map p1203

♛♛♛ Marisquería Paso Real, south side of main square. Great ceviche and seafood.

♛♛ Chop Suey, Calle Central. Chinese, big helpings.

♛♛ Copa de Oro, next to **Hotel Liberia**. Chinese, huge servings, good value.

♛♛ El Bramadero, part of the **Hotel Bramadero** on the Pan-American Hwy. Popular, breakfast from 0630, lively bar in the evenings.

♛♛ Jardín de Azúcar, just off plaza, T2666-3563. Self service, good variety and tasty.

♛♛ Pronto Pizzería, Calle 1, Av 4. Good food (not just pizzas) in a charming colonial house.

♛♛-♛ Hong Kong, 1½ blocks east of church. Chinese, cheap and cheerful.

♛ Los Comales, Calle Central, Av 5-7. Daily 0630-2100. Traditional Guanacaste dishes prepared with maize, run by women's cooperative.

♛ Panymiel, Av Central, Calle 8-9, and Av 3, Calle 2. Bakery, snacks and drinks, good value.

La Cruz and Isla Bolaños p1205

♛ La Orchidea, La Cruz, T2679-9316. Seafood, cheap. Daily 0630-2200.

♛ Restaurant Telma, La Cruz, T2679-9150. Tico food, cheap.

♛ Soda Estadio, La Cruz. Good, cheap.

♛ Soda Marta, La Cruz, T2679-9347. Cheap Tico fare.

✪ Festivals and events

Puntarenas and around p1195

Jul Fiesta de la Virgen del Mar, on the Sat closest to the 16 Jul, with a week of festivities leading to a carnival and regatta of decorated fishing boats and yachts.

Monteverde p1198, map p1196

Dec-Mar Monteverde Music Festival, T2645-5053. Classical and jazz concerts at sunset, local, national and international musicians. Programme from local hotels, US$10.

Liberia and around p1202, map p1203

25 Jul, Guanacaste Day sees dancing, parades and cattle related festivities.

○ Shopping

Monteverde p1198, map p1196

Casem, a cooperative gift shop, is located just outside Monteverde on the road to the reserve next to **El Bosque** restaurant, T2645-5190. It sells embroidered shirts, T-shirts, wooden and woven articles and baskets. Next door, there's a shop selling Costa Rican coffee.

Liberia and around p1202, map p1203

Mini Galería Fulvia, on the main plaza, sells Tico Times, English papers and books. English spoken and helpful.

Tiffany's, Av C-2, Calle 2, general gifts, cigars.

▲ Activities and tours

Puntarenas and around *p1195*
Tour operators
See under San José Tour operators, page 1159, for Gulf of Nicoya cruises.

Monteverde *p1198, map p1196*
Canopy Tours, at Cloud Forest Lodge, T2645-5243. Offer tours of 5 platforms, connected by steel cables, to explore the forest canopy, US$45 per person, US$35 for students at Cloud Forest Lodge.

North to Guanacaste Province *p1201*
Tour operators
CATA Tours, Cañas, T2296-2133, full-day tours to Parque Nacional Palo Verde.
Safaris Corobicí is 4 km past Cañas on the Pan-American Hwy, 25 m before the entrance to Centro Ecológico La Pacífica, T2669-6191. Float tours down the Río Tenorio, US$37 per person for 2 hrs' rafting, US$60, ½-day, under 14 yrs ½-price.

Liberia and around *p1202, map p1203*
Tour operators
Hotel Liberia can organize tours, rent out bikes and assist with enquiries. A recommended guide for the nearby national parks is **Alejandro Vargas Rodríguez**, who lives in front of the Red Cross, T2666-1889.

⊖ Transport

San José to Esparza and Barranca
p1195
Bus If going from **San José** to Monteverde it is possible to change buses in Barranca, rather than going all the way to Puntarenas, if you leave the capital before 1230.

Puntarenas and around *p1195*
Bus Terminal for San José is at Calle 2, Av 2-4. Buses every 40 mins, 0415-1900 to **San José**, 2 hrs, US$3. Buses from San José leave from Terminal Puntarenas Calle CB16,

Av 10-12, T2222-0064, 0600-1900. Daily bus to **Santa Elena** for Monteverde, T2222-3854 0630 and 1430, US$4.25, 5 hrs. Buses south to **Quepos** from main bus station, 6 daily via **Jacó**, US$$5.00, 4 hrs, return 0430, 1030, 1630. To **Liberia** with **Empresa Pulmitan**, first at 0600, last 1500, 4 hrs, US$4.75. To **Tilarán** via **Cañas** at 1130 and 1630. Good café at bus terminal where you can wait for your bus.

Ferry Check which dock your ferry leaves from. For the **Nicoya Peninsula** see page 1214. To southern Nicoya Peninsula from the dock at Calle 35. To **Playa Naranjo** at 1000, 1420,and 1900, returning at 1250, 1700 and 2100, 1½ hrs. T2661-1069 for exact times. Pedestrians US$1.60, motorbikes US$3, cars US$12. The ferry dock is about 1 km from Puntarenas bus station, local buses run between the two, otherwise walk or get a taxi. Buses meet the ferry for **Nicoya** (through Carmona, 40 km unpaved, 30 km paved road, crowded, noisy, frequently break down, US$1.25, 2¼ hrs), **Sámara** (US$1.30), **Coyote**, **Bejuco** and **Jicaral**.

From the same dock a car ferry goes to **Paquera** at 0830, 1330, 1830 and 2230, returning at 0500, 1100, 1700 and 2030, 1½ hrs, T2641-0118 to check the times. On arrival, get on the bus (which waits for the ferry) as quickly as possible (to **Cóbano**, 2-3 hrs, US$1.25, bad road, to **Montezuma** US$2.60, 1½ hrs at least), pay on the bus, or get a taxi. **Hotel Playa Tambor** also runs a car ferry to **Paquera** 7 times daily leaving Paquera 0500, 0700, 1000,1145,1500, 1630 and 2000. A bus to **Tambor** will be waiting at Paquera on your arrival. T2661-2084 for information.

Launch **Paquera**-Puntarenas leaves from behind the central market, directly north of the bus stop at 0600, 1100 and 1515, returning at 0730, 1230 and 1700. Pedestrians US$1.50, motorbikes US$1.80, Tickets are sold when the incoming boat has docked.

Santa Elena *p1197, map p1196*

Bus From **Puntarenas**, **Terminal Empresarios Unidos**, daily at 1415, occasionally at 1315 as well, 2½-4 hrs, returns 0600, US$2.20. This bus arrives in time to catch a bus to **Quepos** for Manuel Antonio. See Monteverde Transport, below, for buses from **San José**.

To **Tilarán** the 0700 (US$1.80, 3 hrs) connects with the 1230 bus to **Fortuna** and others to **Cañas** for the Pan-American Hwy, Liberia and Nicoya Peninsula.

Car There is a service station, Mon-Sat 0700-1800, Sun 0700-1200.

Horse Several places rent horses; look for signs between Santa Elena and Monteverde or ask at your hotel. Try not to hire horses that look overworked.

Taxi Santa Elena to Monteverde, US$6, and Monteverde to the reserve, US$5.75 (hunt around for good prices). Not so easy to find a taxi for return trip, best to arrange beforehand.

Monteverde *p1198, map p1196*

Bus From **San José** a direct bus runs from Av 9, Calle 12, just outside Terminal Atlántico Norte daily at 0630 and 1430, 4½ hrs, US$4. Leaves Monteverde from **Hotel Villa Verde** also at 0630 and 1430, picking up through town, stopping at Santa Elena bus stop (be early). Check times in advance, Sat bus does not always run in low season (T2645-5159 in Santa Elena, T2222-3854, in San José). This service is not 'express', it stops to pick up passengers all along the route, and is not a comfortable ride. Keep your bag with you at all times; several cases of theft reported. Alternatively, get a bus to **Puntarenas** and change there for Santa Elena, see above.

North to Guanacaste Province *p1201*

Bus The Cañas bus station is 500 m north of the centre, where all buses depart from

except for those to San José, which leave from the terminal 300 m west of Parque Central on the Pan-American Hwy.
To **San José**, Transportes La Cañera, T2669-0145, 8 daily from 0400, 3½ hrs, arriving and departing from Calle 16, Av 1-3. To **Liberia**, 10 daily from 0530. To **Puntarenas**, 8 daily from 0600. To **Upala**, for Bijagua and Volcán Tenorio, 7 daily from 0500, 1¾ hrs, US$1.50. To **Tilarán**, 7 daily from 0600. Buses to Tilarán for **Nuevo Arenal**, past the volcano and on to **Fortuna**, or for connections to **Santa Elena** and **Monteverde**. If going by road, the turn-off for Tilarán is at the filling station, no signs.

Liberia and around *p1202, map p1203*

Air The Aeropuerto Internacional Tomás Guardia, about 13 km from Liberia (LIR) on the road to the Nicoya Peninsula was reopened in 1992, revamped in 1995 and renamed **Aeropuerto Daniel Oduber Quirós**, after the former president who came from Guanacaste. The runway can handle large jets and charter flights, and direct daily flights to **Miami**. Lacsa, T2666-0306; Sansa, T2221-9414; Nature Air, T2220-3054. There is a direct weekly flight to **New York** arriving Sat, through Air-Tech, www.airtech.com, Wed, Sat and Sun. Delta flights from **Atlanta**. American flights from **Miami**, Continental from **Houston**.

Bus To **San José** leave from Av 5, Calle 10-12, with 14 a day, US$4.25, 4 hrs. Other buses leave from the local terminal at Calle 12, Av 7-9. Liberia to **Playa del Coco**, hourly, 0500-1800, **Playa Hermosa** and **Panama**, 5 daily 0730-1730, 1½ hrs, **Puntarenas**, 7 a day, 0500-1530, **Bagaces/ Cañas**, 4 a day, 0545-1710, **Cañas Dulces**, 3 a day, 0600-1730, **La Cruz/ Peñas Blanca**, 8 a day 0530-1800. **Filedefia-Santa Cruz-Nicoya**, 0500-2020, 20 a day.

Car Car rental Sol and Toyota car rental agencies (see map) offer same prices and allow you to leave the vehicle at San José airport for US$50.

Parque Nacional Rincón de la Vieja p1202

A taxi costs US$30 1-way from Liberia. Most hotels will arrange transport for US$15 per person, min 6 passengers. Departure at 0700, 1 hr to entrance, return at 1700; take food and drink. You can also hitch; most tourist vehicles will pick you up. If you take your own transport a 4WD is best, although during the dry season a vehicle with high clearance is adequate.

Parque Nacional Santa Rosa p1204

Parque Nacional Santa Rosa is easy to reach as it lies west of the Pan-American Hwy, about 1 hr north of Liberia. Any bus going from Liberia to Peñas Blancas on the Nicaraguan border will drop you right at the entrance (US$0.70, 40 mins), from where it's a 7-km walk, but you may be able to hitch a ride. Last bus returns to Liberia about 1800. Coming from the border, any bus heading south will drop you off at the entrance.

La Cruz and Isla Bolaños p1205

Bus Regular buses to **San José** from 0545 until 1630, 5½ hrs. To **Liberia**, 5 daily 0700-1730, 1½ hrs. To **Peñas Blancas**, 5 daily 0700-1730, 1 hr. To **Playa Jobo** in Bahía Solanos, at 0530, 1030 and 1500, from main plaza.

⊙ Directory

Puntarenas and around p1195
Banks Banco Nacional and Banco de Costa Rica, on Av 3, Calle 1-3 near the Central Market, changes TCs, and with ATM. **Internet** Millennium Cyber Café, on the beach front with Calle 15, only one in town so popular, 1000-2200, 600c per hr. Free

coffee if you're lucky. **Post office** Av 3, Calle Central-1, close to Central Market. **Telephone** ICE and Radiográfica, Av C, Calle 2-4.

Santa Elena p1197, map p1196
Banks Banco Nacional, daily 0900-1500, to change TCs with commission and advance cash against Visa. ATM machine for Visa in the supermarket opposite the post office. **Internet** Several places are opening up, but with poor communication links are charging exorbitant prices. Try Treehouse Cafe, T2645-5751 US$3 per hr 0700-2200 and Pura Vida.

Monteverde p1198, map p1196
Cultural centres Galería Extasis, 250 m south of La Cascada, T2645-5548, exhibits sculptures by the Costa Rican artist, Marco Tulio Brenes. **Language schools** A branch of the **Centro Panamericano de Idiomas**, in Heredia, has opened a school on the road up to the reserve, T2645-6306. Accommodation is with local families.

Liberia and around p1202, map p1203
Banks Banco Popular and Bancrecei both have Visa ATMs. Banco de Costa Rica is on the main plaza. Credomatic, Av Central, MasterCard ATM. For money exchange, try *casa de cambio* on Calle 2 or ask around, eg Restaurant Chun San, behind the cathedral. **Internet** Planet, ½ block south of the church, cheap, with good machines, Mon-Sat 0800-2200, Sun 0900-2100. Ciberm@nia, north side of main plaza, T2666-7240, US$1.25 per hr. **Medical services** Enrique Baltodano Hospital, T2666-0011. Pharmacies close to the main plaza.

Península de Nicoya

Fringed by idyllic white-sand beaches along most of the coastline, the Nicoya Peninsula is hilly and hot. There are few towns of any size and most of the roads not connecting the main communities are in poor condition. While several large hotel resorts are increasingly taking over what were once isolated coves, they are generally grouped together and there are still many remote beaches to explore. A few small areas of the peninsula are protected to preserve wildlife, marine ecosystems and the geological formations of Barra Honda.
▶▶ *For listings, see pages 1220-1230.*

Ins and outs

Getting there There are several ways of getting to the Nicoya Peninsula. The **Taiwan Friendship Bridge** over the Tempisque saves time and gas money getting to the peninsula, eliminating the ferry. Just across the river is **Hotel Rancho Humo** ① *T2255-2463* with boat trips on the Tempisque and Bebedero rivers, visits to Palo Verde and Barra Honda national parks.

A second route takes the **Salinero car ferry** from Puntarenas across the Gulf of Nicoya to Playa Naranjo. Buses meet the ferry for Nicoya (US$1.25, 2¼ hours), Sámara (US$1.30), Coyote, Bejuco and Jicaral. A fourth route also departs from Puntarenas to Paquera from the dock at Calle 35. On arrival, get on the bus (which waits for the ferry) as quickly as possible (to Cóbano, two to three hours, US$1.25, bad road, to Montezuma US$2.60, 1½ hours at least), pay on the bus, or get a taxi. **Hotel Playa Tambor** also runs a ferry service, **Naviera–Tambor SA**, between Puntarenas and Paquera, with a bus running between Paquera and the hotel in Tambor.

Getting around All the beaches on the Nicoya Peninsula are accessible by road in the dry season. Most places can be reached by bus from Nicoya. However, the stretch from Paquera to Montezuma and the Cabo Blanco Reserve is connected to Playa Naranjo and the north only by very poor roads. There is no bus connection between Playa Naranjo and Paquera and the road is appalling even in the dry season.

Beaches Even in high season, you will be able to find a beautiful beach that is uncrowded. There are so many of them, just walk until you find what you want. You will see plenty of wildlife along the way, monkeys, iguanas and squirrels as well as many birds. There can be dangerous undertows on exposed beaches; the safest bathing is from those beaches where there is a protective headland, such as at Playa Panamá in the north.

Santa Cruz and around

Heading from Liberia by road, the first town you reach is Santa Cruz, known as Costa Rica's National Folklore City for its colourful fiestas, dancing and regional food. January is the month for the fiesta dedicated to Santo Cristo de Esquipulas, when it can be difficult to find accommodation. There is also a rodeo fiesta in January. But for the rest of the year, it's a quiet little town, with a charming modern church, providing supplies for the beach tourism industry. If you need to buy food, Santa Cruz is a good place to stock up.

In **Guaitil**, 9 km east of Santa Cruz and 19 km north of Nicoya, local artisans specialize in reproductions of indigenous Chorotegan pottery. They work with the same methods used by the indigenous long ago, with minimal or no use of a wheel and no artificial paints.

Ceramics are displayed at the local *pulpería*, or outside houses. At **San Vicente**, 2 km southeast of Guaitíl, local craftsmen work and sell their pottery.

West coast beaches ⊖⊕⊗⊙⊿⊛⊜ ➤ *pp1220-1230*.

A number of beaches are reached by unpaved roads from the Santa Cruz–Liberia road. Many can be accessed by bus from the Liberia bus station, others may require you to change buses at Santa Cruz. Each of the beaches has its appeal – Tamarindo and Playa del Coco for partying, Flamingo to the north and Junquillal for their greater seclusion, and Grande for nesting turtles and surfing.

Playa del Coco and around

After the town of **Comunidad**, a road leads east to Playa del Coco and Playa Hermosa, and the ever-pending resort development of Playa Panamá, see below.

Playa del Coco is a popular resort some 8 km from the highway, set in an attractive islet-scattered bay hemmed in by rocky headlands. It's a good place to chill out, with a mix of good services without being too developed. The best beaches are to the south. All activities concentrate on the beach and fishing. Coco is the starting point for surf trips to Santa Rosa spots by boat, such as **Witch's Rock**. Snorkelling and diving are nothing special, but for a diving expedition to the **Islas Murciélago**, see page 1228. Sightings of manta rays and bull sharks are common around Islas Catalinas and Islas Murciélago.

There are bars, restaurants and a few motels along the sandy beach. It is too small to get lost. To reach it, leave the road at Comunidad (road paved). Be wary of excursions to secluded Playa Verde, accessible by boat only, as some boatmen collaborate with thieves and reap the rewards later. A 2.5-km road heads southwest from Playa del Coco to **Playa Ocotal**.

Playa Hermosa and Playa Panamá

A spur road breaks from the main road to Playa del Coco heading north to Playa Hermosa. This is one of the nicest resorts and served by a paved road. Accommodation is mixed, but it's a good quiet alternative to other beaches in the region. Walking either to the left or the right you can find isolated beaches with crystal-clear water. The big **Papagayo** tourist complex near Playa Panamá, which once planned to provide as many as 60,000 hotel rooms, started years ago. Objections have delayed construction, but the project continues.

Playa Tamarindo and around

South of Filadelfia, close to Belén, a mostly paved but poor road heads east to the beach and popular surf spot of Playa Tamarindo, www.tamarindobeach.net, and other beaches. The sunsets are incredible and while most make their way to the beach for that magic moment, the strong beach culture makes this a popular place to hang out.

Either side of the sunset, Tamarindo is a flurry of activity, easily the liveliest beach resort on the Nicoya Peninsula and development is quickly changing the place. The beach is attractive with strong tides in places so take care if swimming. Three good breaks provide a variety of options for the surf crowd. Beyond surf and sun, the most popular excursion is an evening trip to Playa Grande and the leatherback turtle nesting sights from October to March. There's a good blend of hotels and bars to make it a good beach stop – not too busy, but not dead.

Close to Tamarindo, **Playa Avellanas** is a quiet beach with good surfing for those who want to get away from the service culture of Tamarindo. Shuttle buses run from Tamarindo, and there are a handful of accommodation options.

Playa Grande

North of Playa Tamarindo is Playa Grande and the **Parque Nacional Marino Las Baulas de Guanacaste** (485 ha terrestrial, 22,000 ha marine), well known as a nesting site for **leatherback turtles** (October-February). Organized trips to the beaches are possible from Tamarindo. Also in town is **El Mundo de La Tortuga** ① *T2653-0471*, an unusual turtle museum. The road from the main highway at Belén leads directly to Playa Grande, a sleepy town with almost no transport and no way of getting around.

Playa Flamingo and beaches to the north

North of Tamarindo and Playa Grande are the beaches of **Conchal**, **Brasilito**, **Flamingo** and **Potrero**. It's a collection of beaches with subtle changes of atmostphere. Conchal is a beautiful 3-km beach full of shells, but with only luxury accommodation; most budget travellers stay at Brasilito and walk along the beach. Further north, the bay around Playa Flamingo has white sand, although the actual beach has some fairly intrusive developments with a grab-all approach to beachfront properties; in fact, the beach is now polluted and not as beautiful as it was. Several smaller beaches retain a relaxed

Península de Nicoya

atmosphere where life is governed by little more than the sunrise and beautiful sunsets. Further north is the isolated beach of Potrero with pockets of visitors.

Playa Junquillal → Colour map 7, B2.
South of Tamarindo, Playa Junquillal is one of the cleanest beaches in Costa Rica and is still very empty. Completely off the beaten track with almost no tourist facilities, it does have a selection of stylish hotels, most of which are quite pricey, but there is also camping if you have a tent.

Nicoya → Colour map 7, B2.
Nicoya, at the heart of the peninsula, is a pleasant little town distinguished by possessing the country's second oldest church, the 17th-century church of San Blas. Damaged by an earthquake in 1822 it was restored in 1831, and is currently undergoing renovations. The Parque Central, on Calle and Avenida Central, is leafy and used for occasional concerts. Buses arrive at Avenida 1, Calle 3-5. Most hotels and banks are within a couple of blocks of the central park. The area **Conservation Offices (ACT)** are on the northern side of central park.

There is no general information for visitors, but they can assist with specific enquiries.

Parque Nacional Barra Honda →
Colour map 7, B2.
① Entry US$6, no permit required.
A small park in the north of the Nicoya Peninsula (2295 ha), Barra Honda National Park was created to protect a mesa with a few caves and the last remains of dry tropical forest in the region. The park office is near Barra Honda at Santa Ana, at the foot of the mesa, and there are two different trails to the top; two hours' hiking.

Sámara and Playa Carrillo →
Colour map 7, B2.
Sámara (www.samarabeach.com) is a smallish Tico village that has maintained some of its regular way of life alongside tourist development. The beautiful beach, 37 km from Nicoya on a paved road, is probably the safest and one of the best bathing beaches in Costa Rica. Playa Carrillo is 5 km away at the south end of the beach. The litter problem is being tackled with rubbish bins, warning signs, refuse collections and bottle banks. Both places have airstrips served by scheduled services from San José.

Nosara → *Colour map 7, B2.*

Nosara (www.nosara.com) is a small village about 26 km north of Sámara without much to see or do in it – which makes it ideal if you like lying around on beaches. Indeed most come for the three unspoiled beaches which are not particularly close to the village.

Playa Nosara is north of the village across the Río Nosara where you may see turtles (see below); Peladas is the prettiest and smallest, south of the river, and Guiones is safe for swimming and good for surfing. Expatriates have formed the Nosara Civic Association to protect the area's wildlife and forests and prevent exploitation.

Playa Ostional

North of Nosara is Playa Ostional where **Olive Ridley turtles** lay eggs in July-November along the coastal strip of the Refugio Nacional de Vida Silvestre Ostional. The turtles arrive for nesting at high tide. The villagers are allowed to harvest the eggs in a designated area of the beach, the rest are protected and monitored. Outside the egg-laying period it is very quiet. Contact the MINAE (Ministry of Environment and Energy) ranger station for details.

Southern Península de Nicoya ⊖⊕⊕⊕⊗▲⊕⊕ » *pp1220-1230.*

The southern Nicoya Peninsula is almost completely cut off from the north. Roads are appalling and those that exist are frequently flooded in part. For this reason most access the region by ferry from Puntarenas. Arriving at **Playa Naranjo** there are several expensive eating places by the dock and a gas station. Beaches and stopping points are dotted along the southern shore of the peninsula passing through low key coastal centres of Tambor, Montezuma, Cabuya, Mal País and Playa Santa Teresa.

Paquera

Paquera is a small village 22 km along the coast from Playa Naranjo. There are a few shops and some simple lodgings, for example **Cabinas Rosita** on the inland side of the village. It is separated from the quay by 1 km or so; apart from a good soda, a restaurant, a public telephone and a branch of **Banco de Costa Rica**, there are no facilities.

Tambor, Curú National Wildlife Refuge and Cóbano

The small village of **Tambor**, 19 km from Paquera, has a dark sand beach, some shops and restaurants. The beach is beautiful, 6 km long with rolling surf; 1½ hours on a bone-shaking road from the ferry. However cruise ships from Puntarenas come here, and part of the beach has been absorbed by the large and controversial **Hotel Playa Tambor**. Built around a cattle farm by the Barceló group of Spain, the resort is alleged to have encroached on the public beach and drained a swamp that was a wildfowl habitat. A second stage is planned at Punta Piedra Amarilla, with a 500-boat yacht marina, villas and a total of 1100 rooms. Buses travelling from Paquera to Montezuma, pass through Tambor, connecting with the car ferry arriving from Puntarenas, US$2.60, two hours.

North of Playa Tambor is the **Curú National Wildlife Refuge** ① *T2661-2392, in advance and ask for Doña Julieta.* Only 84 ha, but with five different habitats and 110 species of bird. Access is through private land.

Cóbano, near Montezuma, can be reached by bus from Paquera ferry terminal, and buses for Tambor, Cóbano and Montezuma meet the launches from Puntarenas (there is an airstrip with flights from San José). Roads north, west and south out of Cóbano, require 4WD. Cóbano has a petrol/gas station.

Montezuma → *Colour map 7, B2.*

No longer a quiet sleepy hamlet, Montezuma is a very popular small village on the sea. It is a well-liked backpacking destination and at busy periods hotels fill up every day, so check in early. Although it gets crowded, there are some wonderful beaches; many are rocky, with strong waves making it difficult to swim, but it's very scenic. There are beautiful walks along the beach, sometimes sandy, sometimes rocky, always lined with trees that visit impressive waterfalls. The village can be reached in four hours from Puntarenas if you get the early launch. There is a tourist office at **Aventuras Montezuma**, which is very helpful and often knows which hotel has space; ask here first before looking around. The once-popular **Cabinas Karen** are now closed. Prior to her death in 1994, Doña Karen donated her land to the National Parks in memory of her late husband creating what was to become Reserva Natural Absoluta Cabo Blanco (see below). **Cabinas Karen** now houses park guards.

Around Montezuma

Close to the village, 20 minutes up the Río Montezuma, is a beautiful, huge **waterfall** with a big, natural swimming hole, beyond which is a smaller waterfall. Intrepid walkers can carry on up to further waterfalls but it can be dangerous and accidents have been reported. There's another waterfall, 6 km north of Montezuma, with a pool right by the beach – follow the road out to the beach at the north end of town and keep going past three coves for about half an hour until you reach the trail off to the left (you can't miss it). **» See Tour operators, page 1228.**

You can use Montezuma as a base for exploring the **Reserva Natural Absoluta Cabo Blanco** ① *Wed-Sun 0800-1600, US$6, jeep/taxi from Montezuma US$7, first at 0700, returns 1600.* The 1172-ha reserve is 11 km from Montezuma. The marine birds include frigate birds, pelicans and brown boobies; there are also monkeys, anteaters, kinkajou and collared peccary. You can bathe in the sea or under a waterfall. At the beautiful **Playa Balsitas**, 6 km from the entrance, there are pelicans and howler monkeys.

At **Cabuya**, 2 km from Cabo Blanco Reserve, the sea can be cloudy after rough weather. Cabuya Island can be visited on foot at low tide. On the road west out of Cabuya, **Cafetería El Coyote** specializes in local and Caribbean dishes. On the west coast of the peninsula is the little village of **Mal País**. The coast here is virtually unspoilt with long white beaches, creeks and natural pools, and the facilities stretch north up the beach to blend with **Santa Teresa**. The surfing appeal of the area is growing with Mal Pais best suited for beginners, and the more experience crowd going up to Santa Teresa.

You can also arrange tours to **Isla Tortuga**. Many businesses rent horses; check that the horses are fit and properly cared for. Recommended for horses are **Cocozuma Traveller** and **Aventuras Montezuma**.

For Sleeping and Eating price codes and other relevant information, see Essentials pages 45-48.

● Sleeping

Santa Cruz *p1214*
B Diria, on the main road, T2680-0080. Bath, restaurant, pools.
B-C La Pampa, 25 m west of Plaza de los Mangos, T2680-0586. A/c, cheaper without, near parque, good, clean.
D-E Anatolia, 200 m south, 100 m west of plaza, T2680-0333. Plywood partitions, dirty bathrooms.
F Pensión Isabel, behind the church, T2680-0173. Price per person, simple box rooms.

Playa del Coco and around *p1215*
Good discounts (up to 40%) in green season. At Playa Ocotal, only top-end accommodation, but good diving services.
LL-AL El Ocotal Resort Hotel, Playa Ocotal, T2670-0321, www.ocotalresort.com. Rooms, suites and bungalows, PADI dive shop on beach, sport fishing, surfing, tennis, 3 pools, car hire, excursions.
AL Villa Casa Blanca, Playa Ocotal, T2670-0518. 15 idyllic rooms, with breakfast, friendly and informative, family atmosphere, small pool. Pricey but very good.
AL-A La Puerta del Sol, north of Playa del Coco, T2670-0195. Great little family-run hotel. Good food in Italian restaurant, small pool and gym, friendly atmosphere and free scuba lesson in hotel pool.
A Villa del Sol, at northern end of Playa del Coco, T2670-0085, www.villadelsol.com. Canadian-owned (from Quebec), with pool, clean, friendly, safe, big garden with parrots. Recommended.
B Coco Palms, Playa del Coco, beside football pitch, T2670-0367. German-run, large pool, gringo bar and parking.
B Pato Loco Inn, Playa del Coco, T2670-0145. Airy rooms, Italian restaurant, internet for guests.

B-D Cabinas Chale, north of Playa del Coco, T2670-0036. Double rooms and villas, with private bath. Pretty quiet, small resort-style spot, small pool, 50 m from beach. Good deal, especially villas which sleep up to 6.
C Cabinas El Coco, just north of the pier right on the beach, T2670-0110. With bath and good reasonable restaurant.
C Witch's Rock Surf Camp, Playa del Coco, T2670-1138. Simple rooms.
C-D Luna Tica, Playa del Coco, south of the plaza, T2670-0127. Also with an annex over the road (friendly, clean). Both usually full at weekends.

Playa Hermosa and Playa Panamá *p1215*
The Playa Panamá area has several all-inclusive resort-style hotels (**L**).
AL El Velero, Playa Hermosa, T2672-1017, www.costaricahotel.net. With an airy villa feel, nice rooms with a/c and bathrooms, pool, clean, good restaurant.
AL Villa del Sueño, southern end of Playa Hermosa, T2672-0026, www.villadelsueno.com. Canadian-owned, with big rooms, good restaurant, pool and live music. Apartments for longer stays.
B Hotel Playa Hermosa, southern end of Playa Hermosa, T2672-0046. Italian-run, 22 clean rooms, better prices for groups, very good Italian restaurant overlooking gardens. Recommended.
B Iguana Inn, 100 m from the beach, T2672-0065. Has 9 rooms, some with kitchen. Relaxed, laid-back spot, with use of kitchen, and laundry.

Playa Tamarindo and around *p1215*
Plenty of accommodation – best in each budget range listed. Book in advance at Christmas and New Year.
LL Capitán Suizo, a long way south of the centre towards Playa Langosta, T2653-0075, www.hotelcapitansuizo.com. 8 bungalows, 22 rooms with patio or balcony, a/c, pool,

restaurant, kayaking, scuba-diving, surfing, sport fishing available, riding on hotel's own horses, Swiss management. One of Costa Rica's distinctive hotels.

L VOEC, on the beach, T2653-0852, www.voecretreats.com. A women's retreat, which offers a 6-night package that includes accommodation, meals, daily surf and yoga lessons, 1 private surf lesson, 2 spa treatments at Coco Spa, a surf excursion to remote waves and the use of surfing equipment. Price per person.

L-AL Tamarindo Diria, near centre of town, T2653-0032, www.eldiria.com. Full range of services, good restaurants, beautiful pool, expensive tours offered with good guide, now with a golf course nearby.

A-B Cabinas Hotel Zullymar, at the southern end of town, T2653-0140, www.zullymar.com. Rooms with a/c and cheaper cabins, good beach bar. Recommended.

B Cabinas Marielos, near the bus stop, T2653-0141, www.cabinasmarieloscr.com. Clean basic rooms, with bath, use of kitchen, popular, book ahead.

B Pozo Azul, at the northern entrance to town, T2653-0280. Cabins, a/c, cheaper in low season, cooking facilities, clean, good, swimming pool.

C Frutas Tropicales, just south of Tamarindo Vista Best Western, T2653-0041. Has 3 simple, spotless and quiet rooms.

C Villas Macondo, 1 block back from the beach, T2653-0812, www.villasmacondo.com. Rooms with shared kitchen, and apartments. Swimming pool, washing machine, safety boxes, fridge and friendly people too.

D Botella de Leche, at the southern end of town, T2653-0189, www.labotelladeleche.com. Hostel rooms, very clean, use of kitchen, big communal lounge. Good choice.

E Rodamar, 50 m from Tamarindo Vista, T2653-0109. No a/c or fan, no mosquito nets, but clean, helpful, kitchen, shared bath. Family atmosphere and cheapest good deal.

F Tsunami, at the northern end of town. Basic, tidy rooms, private bath and use of the kitchen. Turn up and see if there's space, it's probably full of surfers more interested in water than comfort. Great value.

Playa Avellanes *p1215*
D Casa Surf, T2652-9075, www.casa-surf.com. Friendly, good place, with helpful owners who produce marvellous food from their own bakery.

Playa Grande *p1216*
AL-A Hotel Las Tortugas, right on the beach in the centre of town, T2653-0423, www.lastortugashotel.com. 11 rooms with bathroom, pool, restaurant, meals included, tours arranged.

A-B Playa Grande Inn, T2653-0719, www.playagrandeinn.com. Formerly **Rancho Diablo**. 10 rooms with fan, good set up for surfers.

E Cabinas/Restaurante Playa Grande, 500 m before beach at the entrance to town, T8354-7661 (mob). 8 cabins with bath and kitchen, also has camping. Price per person.

Playa Flamingo and beaches to the north *p1216*
AL Mariner Inn, Playa Flamingo, T2654-4081. Has 12 rooms with bath, a/c, free camping on the beach.

A Bahía Potrero Beach Resort, Playa Potrero, T2654-4183. Bar, pool, 10 rooms with bath.

A-B Cabinas Bahía Esmeralda, Playa Potrero, T2654-4480. Garden, pool, hot water, roof ventilator, Italian restaurant.

A-B Cabinas Isolina, Playa Potrero, T2654-4333, www.isolinabeach.com. 250 m from beach, nice garden, roof ventilator.

B-C Hotel Brasilito, Playa Brasilito, close to beach on plaza, T2654-4237, www.brasilito.com. Good rooms. Horses, kayaks and bikes to rent. **Los Arcades Restaurant**, run by Charlie and Claire, mixing Thai and local dishes, closed Mon.

C Cabinas Mayra, Playa Potrero, T2654-4213. On beach, friendly, with pretty, basically equipped cabins. Camping on the beach.

C Ojos Azules, Playa Brasilito, T2654-4343. Run by Swiss couple, 18 cabins, good breakfasts with home-baked bread, nightmare decor.

F Brasilito Lodge, Playa Brasilito, right on the beach, T2654-4452, www.brasilito-conchal.com. Big rooms, good beds, bit of a bargain really. Internet service, several tours available. Also camping. Price per person.

Playa Junquillal *p1217*

A-AL Iguanazul, T2658-8124, www.iguana zul.com. 24 different sizes of tiled-roof cabins on a cliff, great spot, hot water, fan or a/c, pool, restaurant, bar, sport fishing on 27-ft *Marlin Genie*, close to good surfing.

A El Lugarcito, T2658-8436, ellugarcito@ racsa.co.cr. B&B, ocean views, restaurant/bar, tours, diving, boutique.

A Tatanka, T2658-8426, tatanka@racsa.co.cr. 10 cabins with a pool. Good restaurant serving Italian, French and Tico dishes.

A-C Guacamaya Lodge, T2658-8431, www.guacamayalodge.com. Immaculate bungalows and 1 fully equipped house with pool, ocean views, Swiss cuisine.

B El Castillo Divertido, T2658-8428, www.costarica-adventureholidays.com. Castle rooms, restaurant, gardens, rooftop star-gazing deck, music.

B Playa Junquillal, on the beach, T2653-0432. Sleeping 2-4. Ideal for surfers and beach lovers.

B-C Hibiscus, close to the beach, T2658-8437. Big rooms with big windows, seafood restaurant with German specialities, garden, 50 m to beach, German-run.

Camping

Camping Los Malinches, after Iguanazul at the northern entrance to town off main road down a dirt track. Spectacular location, clean bathroom provided. Worth the effort, but bring all your own food.

Nicoya *p1217*

A-AL Hotel Turístico Curime, 500 m south of the centre on road to Sámara, T2685-

5238. Fully equipped bungalows, 3-m-deep pool.

D Jenny, or **Yenny** as the sign says, on the corner of Calle 1, Av 4, T2685-5050. Spotless, with bath, a/c, towels, soap and TV. Cavernous rooms – book in with a friend and play hide and seek. Recommended.

D Las Tinajas, opposite Liberia bus stop on Av 1, T2685-5081. With bath, modern, clean, good value.

D-E Pensión Venecia, opposite old church on square, T2685-5325. Squidgy beds but good value for the price. Recommended.

E-F Chorotega, Calle Central, Av 4-6, T2685-5245. With bath (cheaper without), very good value, clean, quiet. Rooms at back have windows. Clothes-washing facilities (good Chinese soda opposite).

Sámara *p1217*

AL Hotel Fénix, on beach about 2 km east of the village, T2656-0158, www.fenix hotel.com. 6 slightly cramped double units with fans, kitchenettes, hot water, small pool, friendly. Internet for guests.

AL Mirador de Sámara Aparthotel, rising up the hill above the village, T2656-0044, www.miradordesamara.com. Very friendly, German-owned. 6 large, cool and comfortable suites with bath and kitchen. Recommended.

A-B Belvedere, sloping up the hill, T2656-0213. Very friendly German owners. A cosy hotel with 10 small rooms, very clean. Recommended.

B Marbella, inland, road going south, T2656-0362. German-run, beautiful grounds, pool, good service, close to beach. Recommended.

B-C Casa Valeria, on the beach near the supermarket, T2656-0511. Friendly and good value, especially for 3 sharing, breakfast included, various different rooms, some with sea view, all nicely decorated, most with bath, hot water. Kitchen and laundry available, small bar, tours, tickets and car rental arranged. Recommended.

D Arenas, at the western end of town, T2656-0320. Comfortable, cheaper for longer stays, good restaurant opposite, pleasant bar next door.

Camping
Camping Coco, near the beach, T2656-0496. With toilets, electricity until 2200. The same family own **Camping San Martín**, T2656-0336, same deal, also offers **La Tigre Tours** kayak, snorkel, diving, trips to see dolphins. **Camping Los Mangos**, slightly further from the beach.

Nosara *p1218*
A Villaggio, Punta Guiones de Garza, close to Nosara, 17 km north of Sámara, T2654-4664, www.flordepacifico.com. An upmarket yet simply furnished beach hotel with vacation ownership plan, 30 bungalows, international restaurant, club house, bars, pool, disco, good packages arranged in San José, T2233-2476.
B Blew Dog's Surf Camp, near Playa Guiones, T2682-0080, www.blewdogs.com. Comfortable cabins, also flop house for US$10 per person, pool table, videos, full service reggae bar/restaurant.
B Rancho Suizo Lodge, Playa Pelada, T2682-0057, www.nosara.ch. Swiss owned bungalows, restaurant, credit cards accepted, whirlpool, hiking, riding, bird and turtle watching.
C Casa Río Nosara, on the road to the airstrip, T2682-0117. Rancho-style house with cabins and nice garden, clean, friendly, camping, canoe tours and horse riding arranged, German owners.
D Cabinas Agnell, in the village, T2682-0142. With bath, good value.
E Cabinas Chorotega, in the village near the supermarket, T2682-0129. Has 8 simple, clean rooms, shared or own bath. Bar and restaurant downstairs, so can be noisy.

Playa Ostional *p1218*
You can camp on the beach.
F Cabinas Guacamaya, T2682-0430. With bath, clean, good food on request. Price per person.

F Cabinas Ostional, next to the village shop. Very basic accommodation in cabins with bath, clean, friendly.

Southern Península de Nicoya *p1218*
A-B Oasis del Pacífico, on beach, Playa Naranjo, T2661-0209. A/c, old building, clean, quiet, with pool, good restaurant and free transport from ferry. Recommended.
C El Paso, north of ferry, Playa Naranjo, T2641-8133. With bath, cheaper without, cold water, clean, restaurant and pool.
E Cabinas Maquinay, 1.3 km towards Jicaral, Playa Naranjo, T2661-1763. Simple rooms with a pool and the attached **Disco Maquinay**.

Tambor, Curú National Wildlife Refuge and Cóbano *p1218*
LL Tango Mar, 3 km from Tambor, T2683-0001, www.tangomar.com. All services including golf course and its own waterfall.
C Dos Lagartos, Tambor, T2683-0236. Cheap, clean, good value.
C-D Cabinas Cristina, on the beach, Tambor. With bath, T2683-0028, cheaper without, good food.

Montezuma *p1219*
Montezuma is a very small place; hotels furthest from the centre are a 10-min walk.
L-A El Jardín, T642 0074, www.hotelel jardin.com. 15 rooms and 2 fully equipped villas located on the hill overlooking the town and ocean beyond. Shower, hot water, a/c, private terraces and hammocks. In the grounds is a pool with a little waterfall, very restful and great views, superb spot.
AL El Tajalín, T2642-0061, www.tajalin.com. Very smart hotel, spotlessly clean, rooms come with private hot water shower and a/c, located in a quiet out of the way spot and yet moments from the high street. Hammock terrace for relaxing.
AL-B Los Mangos, a short walk south of the village, T2642-0076, www.hotellosmangos. com. Large site comprising 9 bungalows, each accommodating 3 people, with bath,

hot water and fan. Also 10 rooms, some with shared bath, some for 4 people. Yoga classes run from an open-sided pagoda on the grounds. Different and fun and lots of free mangos (when in season).

AL-C Amor de Mar, T2642-0262, www.amordemar.com. This well-loved hotel has the feeling of a special place. Rooms are pristine with private bath and hot water. Breakfast and brunch is served on a very pretty terrace that joins well-manicured gardens, where visitors can recline in hammocks and stare out to sea.

A Horizontes, on road to Cóbano, T2642-0534, www.horizontes-montezuma.com. Language school, restaurant, pool, hot water. Highly recommended.

B Cabinas Mar y Cielo, on the beach, T2642-0261. Has 6 rooms, sleeping 2-5 people, all with bath, fan and sea view. Recommended.

B Montezuma Paradise, 10 mins' walk out of town, on the road to Cabuya, past the waterfall entrance, T2642-0271. Very friendly owners have rooms with shared bath and 1 with private, overlooking the ocean and minutes from a secluded beach cove.

B Pargo Feliz, T2642-0065, elpargofeliz@costarricense.cr. Cabins with bath. Serves good food in a peaceful atmosphere – something the owners are keen on.

B-C La Cascada, 5 mins' walk out of town, on the road to Cabo Blanco, close to the entrance to the waterfalls, T2642-0057. Lovely hotel with pretty, well-kept rooms and a wide hammock terrace overlooking the ocean for relaxing. Restaurant serves local food for breakfast, lunch and dinner.

B-C Montezuma Pacific, 50 m west of the church, next to El Tajalin, T2642-0204. With private bath, hot water and a/c.

D Lucy, follow road south past **Los Mangos**, T2642-0273. One of the oldest hotels in town and one of the most popular budget options, due to its location on the sea. 10 rooms with fans, some with sea view. Shared bath, pleasant balcony. Ultra-friendly Tica owner. Restaurant next door opens during high season. Recommended.

D-F El Tucán, at the top of the road down to the beach, T2642-0284. Wooden hotel on stilts, clean, small wood-panelled rooms, shared shower and toilet, fan, mosquito net on window. Recommended.

E Hotel El Capitán, on the main street, T2642-0069. Old wooden house with an endless variety of rooms, most with shared cold water bath, but some with private. Very friendly owners and good location, can get a little noisy, good for backpackers.

E Pensión Arenas, on the beach, T2642-0308. Run by Doña Meca, rustic small rooms, with fan, shared bath, no frills but pleasant balcony and sea view. Free camping. Laundry service.

E Pensión Jenny, at the end of the track by the football field, T2642-0306. Basic lodging with shared bath, cheap and clean, nice out of the way location. Laundry service.

Around Montezuma *p1219*
L Milarepa, Playa Santa Teresa, on beach, T2640-0023, www.milarepahotel.com. Nice bamboo bungalows, open-air bathroom.

AL Celaje, Cabuya, on beach, T2640-0374. Very good Italian restaurant. Pool, rooms with bath, hot water, good.

AL-A Los Caballos, 3 km north on road to Cóbano from Montezuma, T2642-0124. Has 8 rooms with bath, pool, outdoor restaurant, ocean views, gardens. 5 mins from beach, horses are a speciality.

AL-C Mal País Surf Camp, Mal País, T2640-0031, www.malpaissurfcamp.com. Restaurant, pool, also has camping.

AL-D Funky Monkey Lodge, Santa Teresa, T2640-0317, www.funky-monkey-lodge.com. The same very friendly and hospitable owners have extended their relaxed and very attractive resort. They now have one bungalow sleeping 8 people, 3 private bungalows and 2 apartments, sleeping 2-4 and a suite with a large balcony overlooking the ocean. They also have a rather upmarket dormitory with individual beds. The apartments have a/c, ocean view, access to the kitchen and face the swimming pool. They have a restaurant, bar, TV, DVD, ping-pong table, surfboard rental and organize surf lessons, local tours, car or ATV rental. Recommended.

A-C Cabinas Las Rocas, 20 mins south of Montezuma, T2642-0393, www.caboblanco park.com. Good but quite expensive meals, small, seashore setting, isolated.

A-E Frank's Place, Mal País, the road junction, T2640-0096. Set in tropical gardens. Wide variety of rooms with private or shared bath, and self-catering options available. Good range of services and local advice.

B-C Cabañas Bosque Mar, Mal País, T2640-0074. Clean, large rooms, hot water shower, attractive grounds, good restaurant on beach nearby, 3 km to Cabo Blanco Reserve.

B-C Cabañas Playa Santa Teresa, Playa Santa Teresa, 150 m from beach, T2640-0137. Surfboard rental, horses, German-run.

C Cabinas Mar Azul, Mal País, T2642-0298, Run by Jeannette Stewart, camping possible, delicious fried fish, shrimp, lobster.

C Linda Vista, on the hill over Montezuma, T2642-0274. Units sleep 6, with bath (cold water) and fan, ocean views.

C Mochila Inn, 300 m outside Montezuma, T2642-0030. *Cabinas* from US$30, also houses and apartments for around US$350 per month.

C-E Cabinas y Restaurante El Ancla de Oro, Cabuya, T2642-0369. Some cabins with bath, others shared bathroom, seafood restaurant, lobster dinners US$10, filling breakfasts, owned by Alex Villalobos, horses US$20 per day with local guide, mountain bike rental, transport from Paquera launch available. El Delfín restaurant at crossroads, friendly, good-value local food.

D Casa Zen, Santa Teresa. Smart, budget accommodation with shared bath and one fully furnished apartment. Camping area also available. Close to the beach, restaurant on site.

E-F Cabañas Playa El Carmen, Playa Santa Teresa, T2683-0281. Basic cabins and camping, shared bath and kitchen. Jungle Juice, vegetarian restaurant, serves smoothies and meals from US$4.

Camping
Rincón de los Monos, 500 m along the beach from the centre of Montezuma, T2643-0048. Clean, well organized, lockers for rent. Lots of monkeys around.

● Eating

Santa Cruz *p1214*
Ψ Coopetortilla, 3 blocks east of the church. A local institution— a women's cooperative cooking local dishes. Cheap and enjoyable.

Playa del Coco and around *p1215*
ΨΨΨ Mariscos la Guajira, on southern beach. Popular and beautiful beach-front location.
ΨΨΨ Papagayo, near the beach, T2670-0298. Good seafood, recommended.
ΨΨ Bananas, on the road out of town. The place to go drinking and dancing until the early hours.
ΨΨ Cocos, on the plaza, T2670-0235. Bit flashy and pricey for the area, good seafood.
ΨΨ El Roble, beside the main plaza. A popular bar/disco.
ΨΨ Playa del Coco, on the beach. Popular, open from 0600
Ψ Jungle Bar, on the road into town. Another lively, slightly rougher option.

Playa Tamarindo and around *p1215*
ΨΨΨ Flesta del Mar, on the loop at the end of town. Large thatched open barn, good food, good value.
ΨΨΨ Ginger, at the northern end of town, T2672-0041. Tue-Sun. Good Thai restaurant.
ΨΨΨ Iguana Surf restaurant on road to Playa Langosta. Good atmosphere and food.
ΨΨ Coconut Café, on beach near Tamarindo Vista. Pizzas, pastries and good fish. Check for good breakfasts and cheap evening meals.
ΨΨ El Arrecife, on roundabout. Popular spot to hang out, with Tico fare, good chicken and pizzas.
ΨΨ The Lazy Wave, on road leading away from the beach, T2653-0737. Menu changes daily, interesting mix of cuisine, seafood.

Portofino, at end of road by roundabout. Italian specialities and good ice cream.

Stellas, on road leading away from the beach. Very good seafood, try dorado with mango cream. Recommended.

Arco Iris, on road heading inland. Cheap vegetarian, great atmosphere.

Frutas Tropicales, near Tamarindo Vista. Snacks and breakfast.

Playa Flamingo and beaches to the north p1216

La Casita del Pescado, Playa Brasilito. Some reasonably priced fish dishes which you have to eat quickly because the stools are made of concrete.

Marie's Restaurant, Playa Flamingo, T2654-4136. Breakfast, seafood, *casados* and international dishes.

Pizzeria Il Forno, Playa Brasilito. Serves a mean pizza.

Restaurant La Boca de la Iguana, Playa Brasilito. Good value.

Las Brisas, at the northern end of Playa Potrero. A great spot for a beer and a snack, and surprisingly popular for its cut-off location.

Costa Azul, Playa Potrero, by the football pitch. One of several restaurants in the area, popular with locals.

Cyber Shack, Playa Brasilito. Internet, coffee, breakfast and UPS service.

Playa Junquillal p1217

La Puesta del Sol, T2658-8442. The only restaurant along the strip, but then nothing could compete with the dishes from this ittle piece of Italy. Spectacular setting. Very popular so reservations required.

Nicoya p1217

Café de Blita, 2 km outside Nicoya towards Sámara. Good.

Soda El Triángulo, opposite Chorotega. Good juices and snacks, friendly owners.

Teyet, near Hotel Jenny. Good, with quick service.

Daniela, 1 block east of plaza. Breakfast, lunches, coffee, *refrescos*, good.

Sámara p1217

There are several cheap sodas around the football pitch in the centre of town.

Restaurant Delfín, on the beach. Very good value and French owned. They also have *cabinas*.

El Ancla Restaurant, on the beach, T2656-0716. Seafood.

Las Brasas, by the football pitch, T2656-0546. Spanish restaurant and bar.

Restaurant Acuario, on the beach. Serves Tico and other food.

Soda Sol y Mar, on the road to Nosara. Costa Rican and International food.

Nosara p1218

Gilded Iguana, Playas Guiones. Gringo food and good company.

La Dolce Vita, south along the road out of town. Good but pricey Italian food.

Casa Romántica, Playas Guiones. The European restaurant.

Corky Carroll's Surf School, T2682-0385. Surf lessons and a good Mexican/Thai restaurant (closed Sun).

Giardino Tropicale, in the middle section. Pizza.

Hotel Almost Paradise, Playas Guiones, T2682-0173. Good food with a great view.

La Luna, slightly up the hill. Good food and ambience.

Olga's, Playa Peladas. Seafood on the beach.

Soda Vanessa, Playas Guiones. One of several sodas in the village. Good, very cheap.

Playa Ostional p1218

Mirador de los Tortugueros, 1 km south of Cabinas Guacamaya. Good restaurant with coffee and pancakes. Great atmosphere. Recommended.

Montezuma p1219

Playa de Los Artistas/Cocina Mediterránea, about 5 mins south of town on the road to Cabuya. Best restaurant in town.

Bakery Café, north end of town. Great for breakfast, with bread, cakes and excellent vegetarian food.

Brisas del Mar, just south of the soccer ground in Santa Teresa. Offers great local seafood – tuna or *mahi mahi* straight from the boats at Mal País. Great service and atmosphere. Highly recommended.

Chico's Playa Bar, on the beach. Popular hangout, great sushi. They stop serving food in the low season.

Cocolores, on the beach behind El Pargo Feliz, T2642-0096. Closed Mon. Good for seafood and nice veggie options.

El Pulpo Pizzeria, Santa Teresa, good-value pizzeria that also delivers.

El Sano Banano, on the road to the beach. Health-food restaurant, good vegetarian food, large helpings, daily change of menu, milkshakes, fresh fruit and yoghurt, owned by Dutch/Americans, free movies with dinner.

Pizza Romana, opposite El Capitán. Good Italian food cooked by Italians, pizzas, pesto, fresh pastas, etc.

Tayrona, behind Taganga. Great pizza, Italian owned, attractive restaurant off the main street.

Soda El Caracol, located by the football field. One of several sodas around town serving good Tico food, very cheap.

Soda Monte Sol, on the road to Cabo Blanco. Recommended for good Mexican burritos, good value, big helpings.

Taganga, located at the top of the high street, opposite El Tucan hostel. Argentine grills, chicken and meat.

⊕ Entertainment

Playa Tamarindo and around *p1215*
With a long beachside strip, it's a question of exploring town until you find something that works. Call it bar surfing if you like.

Sámara *p1217*
Bar La Góndola is popular and has a dart board. Opposite is **Bar Colocho**. **Dos Lagartos** disco is on the beach near **Al Manglar** and the disco at **Isla Chora** is the place to be during the season if you like resort discos.

Nosara *p1218*
Some of the nightlife is in the village as well – **Rambú**, **Disco Tropicana** and various others line the football pitch.

Montezuma *p1219*
Bar Moctezuma, usually open the latest, but not as loud as the others.
Chico's Bar and **Chico's Playa Bar**, a relaxing cocktail by the beach, or late night salsa dancing ad very loud reggaeton parties.
Congo Azul Bar, reggae nights Thu and Sat.

Around Montezuma *p1219*
New bars are opening up every year along the beach front at Mal País. For a treat, try a *mojito* on the terrace at the exclusive resort of **Flor Blanca** at the northern edge of Santa Teresa.
Bar Tabu, Santa Teresa. Probably the most popular bar in the area, great location on the beach; good music, always lively, open late.
La Llora Amarilla, Santa Teresa. Now very popular, large venue that hosts regular disco and party nights.
Mal País Surf Camp, Mal País. Bar open every night, live jam night on Wed.

O Shopping

Playa Tamarindo and around *p1215*
The town is increasingly a retail outlet selling everything you need for the beach, as well as general living with a couple of general stores in the centre of town.

Sámara *p1217*
The **supermarket**, near **Casa del Mar**, is well stocked and you can get fresh bread and croissants from **Chez Joel**. **Free Radical** super/soda on main road, 1 km east of town centre, offers fresh *ceviche*, delightful pastries, beer, wine, natural juices, local honey and unusual hand-blown glass products.

Montezuma *p1219*

There are now a number of rather pricey, boutique-style souvenir and clothes shops in Montezuma, most sell a very similar range. **Librería Topsy**, T2642-0576. Mon-Fri 0800-1400, Sat 0800-1200. Sells books and maps and will take postcards and small letters to the post office for you.

▲▲ Activities and tours

Playa del Coco and around *p1215*

Agua Rica Charters, T2670-0473, www.agua ricacharters.com, or contact them through the internet café. Can arrange transport to Witch's Rock for surfers, approx US$400 for up to 10.

Deep Blue Diving, beside Hotel Coco Verde, T2670-1004, www.deepblue-diving.com, has diving trips to Islas Catalinas and Islas Murciélago, where sightings of manta rays and bull sharks are common. 2-tank dive from US$55. Will also rent gear.

Rich Coast Diving, TT2670-0176, www.richcoastdiving.com.

Playa Hermosa and Playa Panamá *p1215*

Diving Safari, based at the Sol Playa Hermosa Resort on Playa Hermosa, T2453-5044, www.billbeardcostarica.com. One of the longest-running diving operations in the country, offering a wide range of options in the region.

Playa Tamarindo and around *p1215*
Diving

Try the Pacific Coast Dive Center, T2653-0267, or Agua Rica Dive Center, T2653-0094.

Surfing and yoga

VOEC, on the beach, T2653-0852, www. voecretreats.com. A woman's retreat that offers 6-night packages, which include surf and yoga lessons. See Sleeping, page 1221.

Tour operators

There are many tours on offer to see the turtles nesting at night in Playa Grande. **Hightide Adventures and Surfcamp**, T2653-0108, www.tamarindoadventures.net, offers a full range of tours.

Iguana Surf Tours, T2653-0148, rent surfboards, they have one outlet near the beach, opposite the supermarket, the other in the restaurant of the same name.

Sámara *p1217*

Most hotels will arrange tours for you. You can rent bikes from near the *ferretería* on the road to Cangrejal. Recommended, though, is **Tip Top Tours**, T2656-0650, run by a very nice French couple, offering dolphin tours (from US$45 per person), mangrove tours (US$43 per person) and waterfall tours (US$20 per person). Naturalist guided tours to Barra Honda and Isla Chora (US$70 per person), as well as slightly more unusual trips like *Journée Cowboy* where you spend a day on the ranch roping cattle and eat with a Tico family. **Wing Nuts Canopy Tour**, T2656-0153 US$40, kids US$25, family-run, friendly service, spectacular ocean views from the treetops, with 12 platforms, lots of wildlife close up, great photo opportunity, 1st-class equipment.

Nosara *p1218*

Casa Río Nosara for horse or river tours, and Gilded Iguana for kayaking and fishing. For turtle tours, try **Rancho Suizo**, T2682-0057, or **Lagarta Lodge**, T2682-0035, who are both sensitive to the turtles and don't exploit or bother them.

Montezuma *p1219*

Aventuras en Montezuma, T2642-0050. Offers a similar range, snorkelling to Tortuga Island, canopy, sunset and wildlife tours for similar prices, also taxi boat to Jacó, US$35, minimum 5 people. Ivan and his staff are also very helpful as a tourist office and can advise on hotels and other matters locally and nationally. They also book and confirm flights.

Cocozuma Traveller, T2642-0911, www.cocozumacr.com. Tico-owned company, now one of the best in Montezuma. Runs all the usual tours including horse rides and Isla Tortuga. Their boat taxi now runs to Jacó (US$35), Sámara (US$50) and Puntarenas (US$40). They will also arrange hotels, transfers, car rental and have quadbikes for hire. Very helpful staff are happy to give information about the area.

Eco Tours Montezuma, T2642-0058, on the corner opposite **Soda Monte Sol**. Offer a wide range of tours, including shuttle to Cabo Blanco (US$3), kayaking/snorkelling at Isla Cabuya (US$25 per person), day trip to Isla Tortuga (US$25 per person), horse rental (US$25) and bike rental (US$5 per day). Also boat/road transfers to Jacó/Tamarindo for around US$150 for up to 6 people.

Montezuma Expeditions, top of the high street, T2642-0919, www.montezumaexpeditions.com. Very efficient set up – organize private and group transport around the country, trips between US$35 and US$48 per person, these include, San José, Fortuna (Arenal), Monteverde and Jacó.

Zuma Tours, Cóbano, T8849-8569, www.zumatours.net. Lots of information available on their website.

☉ Transport

Santa Cruz p1214
Bus Buses leave and arrive from terminals on Plaza de los Mangos. From **San José**, 9 daily, 0700-1800, 4½ hrs, US$5, Calle 18-20, Av 3, ½ block west of Terminal Coca Cola, return 0300-1700. To **Tamarindo**, 2030, return 0645, US$1, also to **Playa Flamingo** and nearby beaches, 0630, 1500, return 0900, 1700, 64 km. To **Liberia** every hr, US$1, 0530-1930. To **Nicoya** hourly 0630-2130, US$0.35.

Taxi To Nicoya, US$10.50 for 2 people.

Playa del Coco and around p1215
Bus From **San José** from Calle 14, Av 1-3, 0800, 1400, 5 hrs, return 0800, 1400 US$1.50. 6 buses daily from **Liberia**, 0530-1815, return 0530-1800.

Playa Hermosa and Playa Panamá p1215
Bus From **Liberia**, Empresa Esquivel, 0730, 1130, 1530, 1730, 1900, return 0500, 0600, 1000, 1600, 1700, US$0.80.

Playa Tamarindo and around p1215
Air Several daily flights from **San José** with Sansa (US$78 1 way) and NatureAir (US$90) from **San José**. Daily flight from **Fortuna** with Sansa.

Bus From **Santa Cruz**, 0410, 1330, 1500 daily. To Santa Cruz first bus at 0600, US$1. Express bus from **San José** daily from Terminal Alfaro, 1530, return 0600 Mon-Sat, 0600, Sun 1230, 5½ hrs. Bus back to San José, can be booked through Hotel Tamarindo Diria, US$5.

Playa Flamingo and beaches to the north p1216
Bus From **San José** to Flamingo, Brasilito and Potrero, daily from Av 3, Calle 18-20, 0800, 1000, 6 hrs, return 0900, 1400. From **Santa Cruz** daily 0630, 1500, return 0900, 1700, 64 km to Potrero.

Playa Junquillal p1217
Bus Daily from **Santa Cruz** departs 1030, returns to Santa Cruz at 1530.

Nicoya p1217
Bus From **San José**, 8 daily from Terminal Alfaro, 6 hrs; from **Liberia** every 30 mins from 0430-2200; from **Santa Cruz** hourly 0630-2130. To **Playa Naranjo** at 0500 and 1300, US$1.45, 2¼ hrs. 12 buses per day to **Sámara**, 37 km by paved road, 1 to **Nosara**.

Sámara p1217
Air Daily flights from **San José**, Sansa US$78, Nature Air, US$90.

Bus From **Nicoya**, 45 km, US$1.15, 1½ hrs, 0800, 1500, 1600, return 0530, 0630, 1130, 1330, 1630. Express bus from Terminal Alfaro, **San José** daily at 1230, return Mon-Sat 0430, Sun 1300, 5-6 hrs. School bus to **Nosara** around 1600; ask locally for details. It is not possible to go from Sámara along the coast to Montezuma, except in 4WD vehicle; not enough traffic for hitching.

Taxis Official and others stop outside bus station (US$20 to **Nosara**, US$10 to **Nicoya**).

Nosara *p1218*
Air Sansa has daily flights to **San José**, US$78, **Nature Air**, US$90.

Bus Daily from **Nicoya** to Nosara, Garza, Guiones daily from main station, 1300, return 0600, US$2, 2 hrs; from **San José** daily from Terminal Alfaro at 0600, 6 hrs, return 1245.

Playa Ostional *p1218*
Bus 1 daily at 0500 to **Santa Cruz** and **Liberia**, returns 1230 from Santa Cruz, 3 hrs, US$1.75.

Montezuma *p1219*
Bus To **Paquera** daily at 0530, 0815, 1000, 1215, 1400 and 1600, connecting with the car and passenger ferry to **Puntarenas** central docks. Tickets available in advance from tourist information centre; be at bus stop outside **Hotel Moctezuma**, in good time as the bus fills up quickly, US$2.60, 1 hr (the road has been paved). To **Cabuya** US$1, buses run 4 times a day. Change at Cóbano for **Mal País** – 2 buses run daily from Cóbano, 1100 and 1400 (check as times can change).

Taxi To **Cóbano** US$5. To **Paquera** US$20.

⊙ Directory

Santa Cruz *p1214*
Banks Banco Nacional, with ATM, on main road. **Post office** 400 m west of Plaza de los Mangos.

Playa del Coco and around *p1215*
Banks Banco Nacional, closed Sat.
Internet Café Internet 2000, on road out of town, also try E-Juice Bar, T2670-05563 and Leslie Café.

Playa Tamarindo and around *p1215*
Banks Banco Nacional, opposite Hotel Diria. **Internet** Tamarindo Internet, T2653-0404.

Nicoya *p1217*
Banks With ATMs on main square and Calle 3, with very welcome a/c. **Post office** On corner of main square.

Sámara *p1217*
Banks There is no bank in Sámara, although hotels may change money. **Internet** Tropical Latitudes Internet Café in centre of town, and hotels may offer access.
Post office Almost on the beach.

Nosara *p1218*
Internet and telephone Nosara Office Centre, offering email, fax, photocopies and international calls. **Language schools** Rey de Nosara language school is in the village, T2682 0215, www.reydenosara. itgo.com. Classes from US$18 per hr. They can often advise about other things to see and do in the area and arrange tours and homestays.

Montezuma *p1219*
Banks Change money at Hotel Moctezuma, Aventuras en Montezuma and Cocozuma Traveller (otherwise go to the Banco Nacional in Cóbano, T2642-0210). **Internet** There is an internet café in Pizz@net next to the Hotel Moctezuma, US$2 per hr. Sano Banano has an all-Mac internet, a little pricey at US$3 per hr and can be slow. Another is located behind El Parque Hotel. **Laundry** Laundrette in Pensión Jenny and Hotel Arenas (on the beach). **Medical services** If you need a pharmacy, you will have to go to Cóbano.

Central Pacific coast

West of the Central Highlands lies a slim lowland strip of African palm with just the occasional cattle ranch. But, for the visitor, it is the miles of beaches stretching from Jacó almost continuously south to Uvita that are the real attraction. Parque Nacional Manuel Antonio is a major destination with developed services. Further south, the beaches are quieter and the Parque Nacional Marino Ballena, which is harder to get to, is barely developed; but it's of interest to divers and whalewatchers. ▶▶ *For listings, see pages 1236-1242.*

Esparza to the Pacific coast

From Esparza on the Pan-American Highway a road runs 21 km southeast to **San Mateo** (from where a road runs northeast to Atenas and the Central Highlands – see Meseta Central section). Just before San Mateo, at Higuito de San Mateo, is **Las Candelillas** ① *T2428-9157*, a 26-ha farm and reforestation project with fruit trees and sugar cane. There is a day use recreational area with showers, pool and riding, trails and bar/restaurant.

From San Mateo a road runs south to **Orotina**, which used to be an important road/rail junction on the San José-Puntarenas route. Today the area is home to **Original Canopy Tour** at **Mahogany Park** ① *T2257-5149*, which charges US$45 to fly through the trees; transportation is available.

West of Orotina the road forks northwest to the port of **Caldera,** via Cascajal, and southwest to the Pacific coast at Tárcoles.

The Costanera to Quepos ●●●▲●● ▶▶ *pp1236-1242.*

The Costanera or coastal road passes through Jacó, Manuel Antonio and Quepos and on to Dominical before heading inland to San Isidro de El General or continuing south to Palmar Norte. If you want a popular beach, pick somewhere before Manuel Antonio. Beyond Manuel Antonio, although not deserted, you'll find things a lot quieter. If driving yourself, check the state of the roads and bridges before setting out to San Isidro. Just because buses are getting through, it doesn't mean cars can. Leave nothing of value in your vehicle; thefts, robberies and scams are regularly reported in the area. The road is paved as far as Quepos and with few potholes. Thereafter it is a good, but dusty, gravel road, paved in villages until Paquita, just before Quepos. After Quepos, the road is unpaved to Dominical. From Dominical the road inland through Barú to San Isidro is paved but landslides can make this section hazardous. High clearance is needed if a bridge is down. South from Dominical, the Costanera drifts through small expat communities that are only just being explored by visitors. They cover a range of budgets, but all are for people seeking solitude while it lasts.

Reserva Biológica Carara

① *Daily 0700-1600, US$7.*
Between Orotina and Jacó the Carara Biological Reserve (5242 ha) is rich in wildlife. Three trails lead through the park: one lasting a couple of hours leaves from close to Tarcoles bridge; the others lasting a little over one hour from the ranger station to the south. The reserve protects a transitional zone from the dry north coast of the country to the very humid region of the southeast. Spider monkeys, scarlet macaws and coatis can all be seen in the reserve.

One of the most popular free experiences in Costa Rica is to peer over the side of the Río Tárcoles bridge to see the opaque sediment-filled waters broken by the bony backs of the somnolent crocodiles below. It's easy to find the spot to stop, as cars cram the roadside, especially at dawn and dusk when scarlet macaws can be seen returning to their roosts from Carara Biological Reserve on the southern banks of the river.

You can get a closer look by taking a boat tour with **Jungle Crocodile Safari** ① *T2292-2316*, or **Crocodile ECO Tour** ① *T2637-0426*, US$25 per person from the dock in Tárcoles, US$35 round trip from Jacó.

Next to Carara is **La Catarata** ① *T2236-4140, 0800-1500, 15 Dec-15 Apr, US$7.50*, a private reserve with an impressive waterfall with natural pools for bathing. Take the gravel road up the hill beside **Hotel Villa Lapas**: it's 5 km to the entrance, and a 2½-km hike to falls and pools, but it's worth the effort. There are signs on the main road. **Bijagual Waterfall Tours** ① *T2661-8263*, offer horse riding or 4WD to the falls.

Jacó

A short distance from Carara is Jacó, a large stretch of sandy beach, with a lively and youthful energy. It is popular with surfers and weekenders from San José, and comes with a rough'n'ready, earthy commercial appeal. If you want to learn to surf, this is as good a

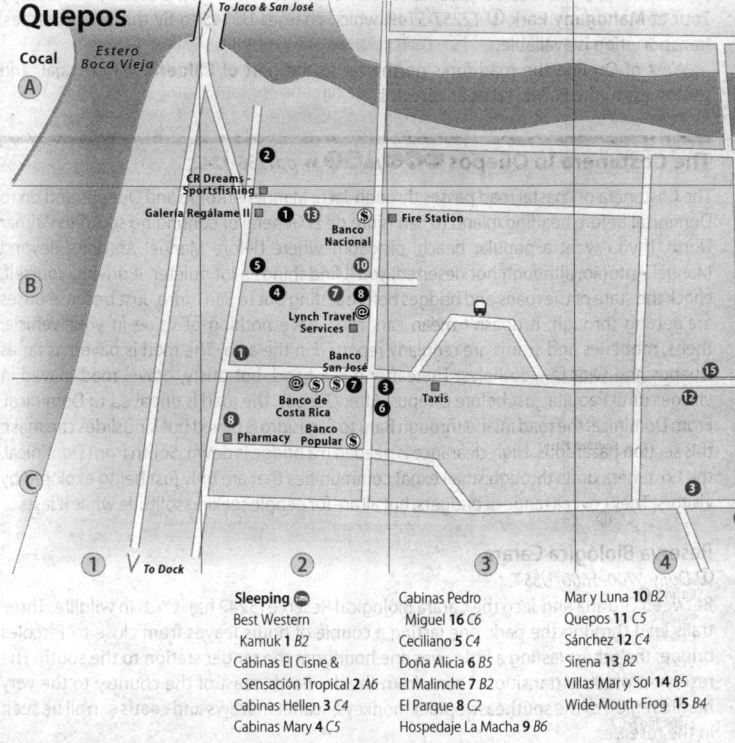

Sleeping ⬤	Cabinas Pedro	Mar y Luna **10** *B2*
Best Western	Miguel **16** *C6*	Quepos **11** *C5*
Kamuk **1** *B2*	Ceciliano **5** *C4*	Sánchez **12** *C4*
Cabinas El Cisne &	Doña Alicia **6** *B5*	Sirena **13** *B2*
Sensación Tropical **2** *A6*	El Malinche **7** *B2*	Villas Mar y Sol **14** *B5*
Cabinas Hellen **3** *C4*	El Parque **8** *C2*	Wide Mouth Frog **15** *B4*
Cabinas Mary **4** *C5*	Hospedaje La Macha **9** *B6*	

place as any, with several surf shops offering courses and boards for rent. If you want to party with crowds on their annual holiday, it's a great spot. If you're looking for peace and quiet, go elsewhere.

Jacó to Quepos

From Jacó the potholed road runs down the coastline with lovely views of the ocean. The beaches are far quieter and, if you have a car, you can take your pick. A few kilometres south is **Playa Hermosa**, which is right on the main road and has a popular surfing beach. If travelling by car, 20 km further and a few kilometres off the road is **Playa Bejuco**, **Esterillos Centro** and **Playa Palma**, near Parrita; definitely worth exploring. Beyond **Parrita** (Banco Nacional, Banco de Costa Rica, a gas station and a few stores) the road travels through a flat landscape of endless African palm plantations. Many of the plantation villages are of passing interest for their two-storey, balconied houses laid out around a central football pitch, a church of some denomination and the obligatory branch of AA. The carriageway narrows to single track on bridges along this road so take care if you're driving, especially at night.

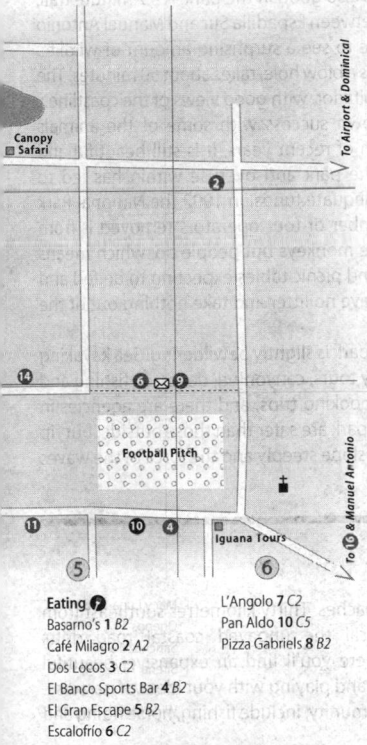

Quepos → *Colour map 7, B3.*

Developed as a banana exporting port by United Brands, Quepos was forced to recreate itself following the devastation of banana plantations in the region overwhelmed by Panama disease, in the early 1950s. Endless rows of oil-producing African Palm have replaced the bananas and Quepos has long since shrugged off the portside image, to the extent that few even bother to explore the dock at the southern end of town.

South of Quepos, a winding road, lined with hotels, bars, restaurants and stores rises and falls for 7 km before reaching the beautiful coastline of Parque Nacional Manuel Antonio (see below) and nearby beautiful beaches. The impact on what was once an attractive stretch of jungle-clad coastline is indisputable. For some it is an environmental catastrophe, for others it is a demonstration of the importance of planning to protect. Quepos plays an important role as a service town for local and foreign tourists. It is cheaper than the Manuel Antonio road, there is no shortage of restaurants, bars and shops, and regular buses make the journey to the national park. Tell the bus driver where you are going and he will drop you at your chosen hotel.

Eating 🍴
Basarno's **1** *B2*
Café Milagro **2** *A2*
Dos Locos **3** *C2*
El Banco Sports Bar **4** *B2*
El Gran Escape **5** *B2*
Escalofrío **6** *C2*

L'Angolo **7** *C2*
Pan Aldo **10** *C5*
Pizza Gabriels **8** *B2*

Parque Nacional Manuel Antonio

① *Tue-Sun 0700-1600, closed Mon, US$7. Guides available, but not essential, at entrance. Early and late are the best times to see the wildlife. Breakfast and other meals available from stalls just before the river, where cars can be parked and minded for US$1 by the stallholders. Basic toilets, picnic tables and drinks available by the beaches, cold water showers at Manuel Antonio and Espadilla Sur beaches.*

From the southeastern corner of Quepos, a road winds up, over and round the peninsula of Punta Quepos, passing the flourishing hotels, restaurants, bars and stores along the length of this rocky outcrop. Travelling the road for the first time, you can't fail to be impressed by the beauty of the views. And at night, you can't help being blinded by the neon lights that speckle the hillside – evidence of the vibrant tourist trade. At times it is difficult to believe a national park flourishes on the other side of the watershed.

With 683 ha of mangrove swamps and beaches, home to a rich variety of fauna and flora, Manuel Antonio National Park can rightly claim to be one of Costa Rica's most popular protected areas – second only to Volcán Poás. Just 7 km south of Quepos on a paved road, three beautiful, forest-fringed beaches stretch along the coastline and around the headland of Punta Catedral: **Espadilla Sur**, **Manuel Antonio** and **Puerto Escondido**. Iguanas and white-faced monkeys often come down to the sand.

In addition to enjoying the beaches, hiking is also good in the park. A 45-minute trail, steep in places, runs round the Punta Catedral between Espadilla Sur and Manuel Antonio beaches. If you're early, and quiet, it is possible to see a surprising amount of wildlife. A second walk to Puerto Escondido, where there is a blow hole, takes about 50 minutes. The map sold at the entrance shows a walk up to a mirador, with good views of the coastline.

Manuel Antonio has been a victim of its own success with some of the animals becoming almost tame. But for all the criticism of recent years, it is still beautiful and highly enjoyable. Overdevelopment outside the park and overuse within has led to problems of how to manage the park with inadequate funds. In 1992 the National Park Service (SPN) threatened to close it and a number of tour operators removed it from their itineraries. You are not allowed to feed the monkeys but people do, which means that they can be a nuisance, congregating around picnic tables expecting to be fed and rummaging through bags given the chance. Leave no litter and take nothing out of the park, not even seashells.

The range of activities in the area outside the park is slightly bewildering. Sea kayaking is possible, as is mountain biking, hiking, canopy tours, canyoning, deep-sea fishing and even quad biking. Most hotels can assist with booking trips, and there are agencies in Quepos that can also advise. The beaches in the park are safer than those outside, but rip tides are dangerous all along the coast. Beaches slope steeply and the force of the waves can be too strong for children.

Quepos to Palmar Norte

Playa Matapalo

Beaches, beaches, endless stretches of sandy beaches. Thirty kilometres southeast from the congestion of Quepos towards Dominical the unpaved coastal road drifts almost unnoticed through Playa Matapalo, where you'll find an expansive, beautiful sandy beach recommended for surfing, relaxing and playing with your ideas of paradise. Other activities, in an overwhelmingly Swiss community, include fishing, horse riding and hiking to mountain waterfalls.

Dominical → *Colour map 7, B2.*

Twelve kilometres further on, at the mouth of the Río Barú, is Dominical (www.dominical.biz), a small town with a population of a few hundred. No more than 500 m from one end to the other it's popular with surfers and often busy. It's a great spot for surfing. Hotel prices soar in high season and most hotels are close to noisy bars. Treks and horse riding trips to waterfalls are possible if the beach is too much to bear. Just north of the town **Hacienda Barú** has a **national wildlife preserve**, with activities like abseiling, canopy tours and nature walks (see below). If you want to touch up your Spanish try the **Adventure Education Center** ① *T2787-0023, www.adventurespanishschool.com*, with an immersion Spanish school. They have schools in Arenal and Turrialba as well. Most people come here for the surfing; if you want to learn visit the **Green Iguana Surf Camp** ① *T8825-1381, www.greeniguanasurfcamp.com*, who provide board hire, group lessons, individual lessons and package deals.

Punta Dominical is 4 km south of town (no transport). A poor dirt road follows a steep path inland up the Escaleras (stairs) to some secluded accommodation blending beach and rainforest.

Uvita

If you get the impression the southern Pacific coast is about beaches, you'd be right. The village of Uvita, 18 km south of Dominical, has beautiful beaches all along the coastline. You can walk in the nearby forests, swim in nearby waterfalls or at the beach, take a boat trip and watch birds. Ballena National Marine Park (see below) protects over 5000 ha of Pacific coral reef, and humpback whales can be sighted at nearby Isla Ballena between December and April.

The road south from Uvita is being repaved as far as Ciudad Cortés, and access to the beaches of Playa Ballena and Playa Bahía is getting easier with consequent development of the area.

Parque Nacional Marino Ballena

The vast majority of Ballena (Whale) Marine National Park is coastal waters – 5161 ha against 116 ha of protected land – which may go some way to explaining why there isn't a lot to see at this least-developed national park. The underwater world is home to coral reefs and abundant marine life that includes common and bottle-nosed dolphins as well as occasional visits from humpback whales at times seen with their calves.

Although there is a rarely staffed **rangers station** ① *T2786-7161*, in Bahía, and signposts line the Costanera, the infrastructure in the park is non-existent. There is a nominal entrance fee of US$6 which is rarely collected. Along the beach at Bahía is a turtle-nesting project administered by the local community. As with the park itself, the organization is very ad hoc – visitors and volunteers are welcome. Beachcombing is good, as is snorkelling when the tides are favourable. Boat trips to the island can be arranged from Bahía, and diving is starting up with the most recommended local being Máximo Vásquez, or Chumi as he is known. The coastal road continues south beside **Playa Tortuga**, passing small communities of foreigners hiding and enjoying one of the quietest spots near a beach in Costa Rica, to join the Pan-American Highway at Palmar Norte (see page 1245).

For Sleeping and Eating price codes and other relevant information, see Essentials pages 45-48.

◉ Sleeping

Esparza to the Pacific coast *p1231*
AL El Rancho Oropéndola, San Mateo, T2428-8600. Cabins with private bath or rooms with shared bath, rustic and peaceful, pool, nature trails.
C Cabinas Kalim, Orotina, near plaza, T2428-8082.

Reserva Biológica Carara *p1231*
LL Villa Caletas, Punta Leona, to the south of the reserve, T2637-0505, www.hotelvillacaletas.com. One of the distinctive hotels of Costa Rica. French-owned, divine rooms and 14 villas atop a mountain with amazing views, spectacular sunsets, lush gardens, pool, restaurant, boat and nature tours.

Jacó *p1232*
Accommodation in Jacó is overpriced; look for discounts May-Nov.
L-AL Cocal, on beach near the centre of town, T2643-3067, www.hotelcocalandcasino.com. 2 pools, hammocks, German-owned, restaurant. Highly recommended.
AL-B Cabinas Las Palmas, northern end of town, T2643-3005. Neat rooms, some with kitchenette, all with bath and fan, clean. Pretty gardens.
A-B Alice, south of centre, T2643-3061. Tidy rooms with private bath, small terrace and pool.
A-B Los Ranchos, central and close to the beach, T2643-3070. 4 bungalows and 8 rooms sleeping 4-8 people, lively spot.
A-B Pochote Grande, northern end of town, T2643-3236, www.hotelpochotegrande.net. Beautiful, German-owned hotel with bar and restaurant. Good rooms, free-form pool and a superb 500-year-old *pochote* tree shading the grounds. Good value.

B Cabinas La Cometa, central, T2643-3615. With fan and hot water, very clean.
B El Jardín, at northern end of town, close to the beach, T2643-3050. Has 10 rooms in quiet spot, friendly with small pool.
B Hotel Paraíso Escondido, 150 m east of the Catholic church on calle Los Cholos, T2643-2883, www.hoteljaco.com. All rooms with a private bath, patio and a/c, rooms cheaper with fan. Swimming pool and laundry service. The owner often meets arriving buses. Good spot and worth the price.
B-E Hotel Kangaroo, at the southern end of town, T2643-3351, www.hotel-kangaroo.com. Mix of dorms and private rooms, but it's the atmosphere that keeps people happy and recommending this place.
C Bohío, central and near beach, T2643-3017. Private bath, cold water, fan, camping.
D Cabinas Gipsy Italiano, near beach at northern end, T2643-3448. With bath and hot water.
D Cabinas Wahoo, behind the restaurant of the same name not far from buses, T2643-3513. Simple rooms, with private bath and fan. Good value.
E Hotel de Haan, at the beach end of Calle Bohio, T2643-1795, www.hoteldehaan.com. Popular backpacker spot, with pool, laundry, kitchen facilities. Good choice.

Camping
Camping El Hicaco, slightly south of the centre, T2643-3226, and **Restaurant Los Hicacos** are both down same access route to the beach.
Camping Madrigal, at the southern end of the beach, T2643-3329. A quiet spot.

Jacó to Quepos *p1233*
AL Hotel El Delfín, Esterillos Centro and Playa Bejuco, T/F2778-8054. Completely renovated with swimming pool, all rooms with breezy balcony, secluded, clean, good restaurant, considered by many to be one of the best beach hotels in Costa Rica. Recommended.

AL La Isla, Playa Palo Seco, T2779-9016. Bar, pool, horse and canoe trips, hot water, a/c.

A Beso del Viento, Playa Palo Seco, 5 km, T2779-9674, www.besodelviento.com. Swimming pool, French owners, stylish rooms.

A La Felicidad Country Inn, Esterillos Centro and Playa Bejuco, T2778-6824, www.lafelicidad.com. Oceanfront, pool and restaurant.

A Vista Hermosa, Playa Hermosa, T2643-3422. Pool, simple rooms with a/c, restaurant, secure parking.

A-B Auberge du Pelican, Esterillos Este, T2778-8105, www.aubergepelican.com. Café, French-Canadian owners, restaurant. Great spot, private airstrip out back, beach out front.

A-B Hotel Sandpiper Inn, T2643-7042, www.sandpipercostarica.com. Spacious cabins, pool, restaurant, sportfishing.

B-C Cabinas Maldonado, Playa Palma, T2227-5400. Rooms sleeping 4, with bath, cold water, kitchen.

D Finca Don Herbert, Playa Palma. With bath, clean, parking.

D Rooms/Restaurant Alex, Playa Palma, T2779 6667. 2.6 km south, with bath, fan. Recommended.

D-F Jungle Surf Café, Playa Hermosa. Basic cabins with a Tex-Mex burger bar.

E Rancho Grande, Playa Hermosa, T2643-3529. Large wooden house with communal kitchen, popular with surfers, great atmosphere. Small store for supplies.

F Las Brisas, Playa Palma. Simple rooms near beach.

Quepos p1233, map p1232
It's difficult to find accommodation on Sat Dec-Apr, and when schools are on holiday.

A Best Western Kamuk, central, near the bus terminal, T2777-0811, www.kamuk.co.cr. Shower, TV, a/c, some ocean views, bar and restaurant with large-screen videos.

A Cabinas Pedro Miguel, towards Manuel Antonio, T2777-0035, www.cabinaspedromiguel.com. Simple rooms, small pool and very friendly Tico owners. Next door is Centro de Idiomas del Pacífico.

A Hotel Sirena, near bus station, T2777-0528. Has 14 quite good rooms with private bathroom, a/c. Restaurant and pool.

B Cabinas El Cisne and Sensación Tropical, 75 m north of Catholic church and football pitch, T2777-0719. Safe, family-run, secure parking, bigger rooms on left. Recommended.

B-C El Malinche, close to bus station, T2777-0093. Has 27 clean and good rooms, simply decorated, some with a/c much cheaper without.

B-E Wide Mouth Frog, short distance from the bus terminal, T2777-2798, www.widemouthfrog.org. Private rooms and dorms.

C Villas Mar y Sol, towards the eastern side of town, T2777-0307. Has 8 rooms with private bath and hot shower. Relaxed spot, parking.

C-D Ceciliano, towards the eastern side of town, on the road leading to Manuel Antonio, T2777-0192. Family-run, quiet, small rooms, with bath, hot.

C-D Hotel Quepos, eastern side of town, T2777-0274. With bath, cheaper without, simple, recommended.

D Cabinas Hellen, eastern side of town, T2777-0504. Quite small rooms with private bath and fan, but clean and plenty of parking.

D Cabinas Mary, by football pitch close to **Iguana Tours**, T2777-0128. Clean, friendly, OK.

D-F Hospedaje La Macha, next to post office on walkway by the football pitch, T2777-0216. Includes the cheapest beds in town. Very basic but clean.

E Doña Alicia, on walkway by football pitch, T2777-0419. Big cabin with bath, friendly, quiet, parking, can wash clothes.

E El Parque, on waterfront road, T2777-0063, Price per person, friendly, clean, a bit run-down but good value, private bath, fan.

E Mar y Luna, central, T2777-0394. With or without bath, quiet, clean, friendly, popular.

E Sánchez, a couple of blocks east of the bus terminal, T2777-0491. Without bath, OK.

Parque Nacional Manuel Antonio *p1234*

There are hotels all along the road from Quepos to Manuel Antonio, many of them expensive. Many shut in the low season; in high season, it's best to book ahead. The area is full to bursting at weekends with locals camping on the beach. The parked Second World War plane – decked out as a bar – marks the start of the downhill to the beach.

LL Makanda by the Sea, down a dirt road leading to Punta Quepos from opposite **Café Milagro**, T2777-0442, www.makanda.com. 11 villas and studios with superb open design. An idyllic and romantic paradise spot.

LL Sí Como No, T2777-0777, www.sicomo no.com. A superb hotel with beautiful touches of design using stunning stained glass, all the comforts you would expect, and service par excellence plus a cinema.

L-AL Costa Verde, at the train carriage restaurant and reception, T2777-0584, www.costaverde.com. Apartments for 2-4 people, with kitchenette and bath, 2-bedroom villas available, well-appointed, pool and a couple of restaurants. Several nature trails out the back. Recommended.

L-AL Karahé, along the main road towards the beach, on private road, T2777-0170, www.karahe.com. Includes breakfast, cabins on a steep hillside with lovely view, sleep 3-4, recommended, fridge, bath, a/c or fan, good restaurant, swimming pool across the road, access to beach, walk to park along the beach.

L-A La Arboleda, T2777-1056, www.hotel-arboleda.com. Cabins on hillside leading down to beach sleep 2-3, bath, fan, Uruguayan restaurant, 8-ha wood. Beware snakes, crabs and monkeys in the yard at night. Recommended.

AL Villa de la Selva, overlooking the bay, T2777-0434. Has 5 simple rooms, some with kitchenettes. Up above most of the activity, this is a charming spot away from the mêlée. Recommended.

A Hotel del Mar, on the main road towards Quepos, T2777-0543, www.gohoteldelmar. com. Rents surfboards, sells drinks and light meals and has a collection of English novels to read in the bar.

A Hotel Manuel Antonio, T2777-1237. Good breakfast, camping possible nearby, ask in the restaurant. Handy, just minutes from the national park and the beach.

A Vela Bar, T2777-0413, www.velabar.com. Large rooms with bath, fans, safes, very good restaurant, fishing and other trips, also has a fully equipped house to rent.

A-B B&B Casa Buena Vista, T2777-1002. Offers a breathtaking view and wonderful breakfast terrace, friendly owner.

B Mono Azul, T2777-1954, monoazul@ racsa.co.cr. 20 rooms, conference rooms, library, internet, 2 nightly movies, international headquarters of **Kids Saving the Rainforest** and souvenir store with profits going to save the rainforest. Friendly place with a couple of pools, and a good restaurant.

C Cabinas Ramírez, towards the end of the road, T2777-5044. With bath, food and bar, free hammocks and camping, guests can help with cooking in exchange.

C-E Vista Serena Hostel, at the start of the road, T2777-5132, www.vistaserena.com. Good quality budget option on the Manuel Antonio strip. Good rooms, private or dorms, and balconies with hammocks looking out to the coast.

E Costa Linda, up the side road just before the park, T2777-0304. Double rooms or 4-bedded room, fan, water shortage, watch out for racoons raiding the outdoor kitchen in the night, good breakfasts; dinner rather pricey.

Dominical *p1235*

Booking hotels is slightly easier in the Dominical and Uvita area using regional specialists and booking service **Selva Mar**, T2771-4582, www.exploringcostarica.com.

AL Diuwak, back from the beach, T2787-0087, www.diuwak.com. Rooms and suites, sleeping up to 4 people, with private bath. Mini supermarket and internet service, pool.

AL Hotel/Restaurant Roca Verde, on the beachfront about 1 km south of Dominical, T2787-0036, www.rocaverde.net. Tropical rooms with a/c. Small balcony or terraces, with a pool. Big bar and restaurant. Recommended.

AL Villas Río Mar Jungle and Beach Resort, out of town, 500 m from beach, T2787-0052, www.villasriomar.com. 40 bungalows with bath, fridge and fan, pool, jacuzzi, tennis court, trails, riding, all inclusive.

AL-B Hotel Pacífico Edge, Punta Dominical, T2771-4582, www.exploringcostarica.com. Selva Mar service. 4 large cabins with great views of ocean and rainforest.

A Hacienda Barú, about 2 km north of Dominical, T2787-0003, www.hacienda baru.com. A 332-ha reserve that began life as a private reserve in 1972. Cabins sleeping 3 or more with private bath, hiking, riding. So much to see and do in such a small area. There is a canopy observation platform, tree climbing, night walks in the jungle and several self-guided trails and a butterfly garden.

B Bella Vista Lodge, Punta Dominical, T2388-0155 or T2771-4582 (through the Selva Mar reservation service). Great view, good large meals, owned by local American 'Woody Dyer', organizes trips in the area. There are also houses to rent.

B Posada del Sol, 100 m from beach, T2787-0085. Owned by local historian Mariela Badilla, 20-odd rooms, bath, fan, patio with hammocks, also 2-bedroom apartment with kitchen for US$150 per week. Rooms vary.

B-C Río Lindo, at the entrance to town, T2787-0028. Clean, tidy rooms with a balcony or terrace. Private bath with fan or a/c. Pool and bar area.

B-C Tortilla Flats, formerly Cabinas Nayarit right on the sea front, T2787-0033. Rooms sleeping up to 3 people, with private bath and hot water. A bit overpriced if just for 2.

B-E Cabinas San Clemente, on beach, T2787-0026. Clean, with or without a/c, friendly, US-owned, restaurant, also cheaper, basic dorm rooms, shared bath, fan; **San Clemente Bar and Grill**, under same ownership, good, big portions.

C-E Cabinas El Coco, at end of main street, T2787-0235. With or without bath, negotiate price, unfriendly, noisy, a last option. Camping possible.

Uvita *p1235*
The central booking service **Selva Mar**, T2771-4582, www.exploringcostarica.com, makes booking a hotel in this area easier.

AL Canto de Ballenas, 6 km south of Uvita, close to Parque Nacional Marino Ballena, T2248-2538, www.turismoruralcr.com. Rustic, but fine, wooden cabins in a simple landscaped garden. Great spot in a quiet location.

AL Villa María Luisa Lodge, Bahía Uvita, T2743-8094. Simple cabins sleeping up to 6.

B Cabinas El Chamán, 2 km south on the beach, T2771-2555. Nice location, 8 simple *cabinas* with private bathroom, camping US$4 per person.

C-D Coco Tico Ecolodge, Uvita village, T2743-8032. 6 clean *cabinas*, sleep 3, with private bathroom and trails outback.

D Cabinas Las Gemelas, Playa Bahía Uvita, T2743-8009. Simple rooms, with showers and bathrooms. Quiet spot with gardens for camping.

D Cabinas Los Laureles, Uvita village, 200 m turn on the left from the main road, T2771-8008. Nice location, 3 *cabinas* with private bathroom, simple and quite good.

D Roca Paraíso, near Cabinas El Chamán, T2220-4263 for information. Basic.

E Cabinas Punta Uvita, opposite Restaurant Los Almendros close to the beach. Simple, basic *cabinas* with private bathroom.

E-F Cascada Verde, Uvita village, up the hill, www.cascadaverde.org. *Hostal*, educational retreat and organic farm, German-run, vegetarian food, yoga and meditation workshops available. Pay for a bed, hammock or camp, or work for your lodgings. Long-term lodgings preferred, great spot if you take to the place.

F The Tucan Hotel, Uvita village, just off the main road, T2743-8140, www.tucan hotel.com. Low-key and pleasant spot in Uvita. Dormitory and private rooms, kitchen available, advice on local travel options and Wi-Fi.

Parque Nacional Marino Ballena
p1235
AL Hotel Villas Gaia, Playa Tortuga, 200 m to the beach, T2244-0316, www.villasgaia.com. 12 spacious cabins with private bathrooms (hot water), fan and terrace. Swimming pool and restaurant serving Swiss, international and vegetarian dishes. Ocean view, diving school, horses. Several other quiet secluded options opening up.
A Posada Playa Tortuga, Playa Tortuga, T2384-5489. Run by Gringo Mike, a great spot and place to stay, and Mike knows everything there is to know about the area.

Eating

Jacó *p1232*
There are lots of *sodas* in Jacó.
Sunrise Grill Breakfast Place, centre of town. Breakfast from 0700, closed Wed.
Wishbone, on the main street. Big plates of Mexican food, from US$6.
Chatty Cathy's, on the main drag. A popular dining spot.
La Ostra, centre of town. Good fish in this pleasant open-air restaurant open all day.
Wahoo, just within the centre to the north. Good Tico food, mainly fish.

Jacó to Quepos *p1233*
Doña María's Soda, small central market, Parrita, T8842-3047. Tasty *casados*.

Quepos *p1233, map p1232*
There are many good restaurants along the road towards Manuel Antonio.
Basarno's, near the entrance to town. Bar, restaurant, club. Daily 1000-0100. Good mix of snacks and a lively spot later in the night.
El Gran Escape, central, T2777-0395. Lively collection of restaurants and bars offering Tex Mex, pizza and sushi. Good food and service, recommended.

Dos Locos, central, T2777-1526. Popular with Mexican and Tico fare, open to the street, occasional live music.
El Banco Restaurant and Sports Bar, near El Gran Escape, T2777-0478. Remodelled long bar with bright neon, good Tex Mex food and will cook your catch.
Escalofrío, next to Dos Locos. Pizza, pasta and ice cream to die for from US$4.
Gardin Gourmet, opposite Escalofrío. Great deli with lots of imported treats.
Pizza Gabriels, central, T2777-1085. Popular little spot with a lively undercurrent. Fine pizza and pasta from US$6.

Cafés, snacks and bakeries
The municipal market (for fruit and bread) is at the bus station.
Café Milagro, on the waterfront, T2777-0794, www.cafemilagro.com. Best expresso, cakes, pies, Cuban cigars, souvenirs, freshly roasted coffee for sale; another branch on the road to Manuel Antonio.
L'Angolo, opposite Dos Locos. Serves a mix of breads, olives, hams and everything you'd need for self-catering or picnicking in style.
La Buena Nota, on road near the beach in Manuel Antonio, T2777-1002. Sells English-language newspapers. A good place to seek local information, run by Anita Myketuk, who has initiated publicity on rip tides.
Pan Aldo, right in front of the soccer pitch, T2777-2697. Italian specialities, wholewheat sourdough, pastries, great bread and pastries.

Dominical *p1235*
Jazzy's River House, down the main street. More an open-house cum cultural centre, occassionally have meals followed by an open mike set up on Wed.
Restaurant El Coco, in town. Serves good food and rents budget rooms.
San Clemente, in town. A good mix of Tex Mex with big servings.
Thrusters, in town. A hip spot for the surf crowd, with sushi in the front restaurant.
Soda Nanyoa, Dominical, offers Costa Rican specialities.

⦿ Entertainment

Jacó *p1232*
Discos in town include **Central**, close to the beach, T2643-3076, **Los Tucanes**, **El Zarpe Sports Bar**, T2643-3473, **Club Olé**, T2643-1576, restaurant, bar, disco and games.

▲ Activities and tours

Quepos *p1233, map p1232*
Amigos del Río, opposite the football pitch, T2777-0082, www.amigosdelrio.net. River rafting, kayaking, canopy and horse riding tours, good guides.
Iguana Tours, close to the church on the football pitch, T2777-2052, www.iguana tours.com. Excellent local knowledge with many tours available. Friendly and helpful.
Lynch Travel Services, right in the centre of town, T2777-0161, www.lynch travel.com.

⦿ Transport

Jacó *p1232*
Bus
From **San José** Coca Cola bus station, 3 daily, 3½ or 4½ hrs, US$3.80 or US$4.60, arrive at Plaza Jacó-Complex terminal at north end of town, next to Pizza Hut. Also several buses to **Quepos**.

Quepos *p1233, map p1232*
Air
There are several daily flights from **San José**, with **Sansa** and **Nature Air** (US$50 1 way). The Sansa office is under Hotel Quepos, T2777-0683.

Bus
There are 3 express buses a day leaving **San José** Coca Cola bus station, T2223-5567, at 0600, 1200 and 1800, returning at 0600, 0930, 1200 and 1700, 3½ hrs, US$4.50, book a day in advance, 6 regular buses, 4½ hrs, US$4. There are buses northwest along the coast to **Puntarenas**, 3½ hrs, 0430, 1030, and 1500, return 0500, 1100, 1430, US$2.10. 2 daily buses via **Dominical** to **San Isidro de El General**, T2771-4744, 0500, and 1330, 3½ hrs, US$2.00, connections can be made there to get to the Panamanian border, return 0700, 1330.

Taxi
Taxis congregate opposite the bus terminal, just up from **Dos Locos** restaurant. Minibuses meet flights.

Parque Nacional Manuel Antonio *p1234*
Bus
There are 3 express buses a day, direct from **San José**, 4 hrs, US$4.50. At weekends buy ticket the day before; buses fill to standing room only very quickly. Roads back to San José on Sun evening are packed. A regular bus service runs roughly ½-hourly from beside **Quepos** market, starting at 0545, to Manuel Antonio, last bus back at 1700, US$0.35.

Car
If driving, there is ample guarded parking in the area, US$6.

Taxi
From **Quepos**, approximately US$10. Minibuses meet flights from San José to the airport at Quepos (see above), US$2.25.

Dominical *p1235*
Bus
To **Quepos** 0545, 0815, 1350 (Sat and Sun) and 1450. To **San Isidro**, 0645, 0705, 1450, 1530, 1 hr. To **Uvita** at 0950, 1010, 1130 (weekends) 1710 and 2000. To **Cd Cortés** and **Cd Neily** 0420 and 1000. To **San José**, 0545, 1340 (Sat and Sun), 7 hrs.

Uvita *p1235*
Bus
From **San José** Terminal Coca Cola, Mon-Fri 1500, Sat and Sun 0500, 1500, return Mon-Fri 0530, Sat and Sun 0530, 1300, 7 hrs. From **San Isidro** daily 0800, 1600, return 0600, 1400. From **Dominical**, last bus 1700 or 1800.

● Directory

Jacó *p1232*
Banks Banco Nacional in centre of town. **Internet** Iguana Mar, Centro de Computación and Mexican Joe's Internet Café. **Language schools** City Playa Language Institute, T2643-4023, service@ costaricareisen.com, offers Spanish classes with or without homestay, and the novel option of free surfing lessons. **Post office** Near Municipalidad offices.

Quepos *p1233, map p1232*
Banks Several branches in town including Banco Nacional, which has a Visa ATM as does Banco Popular and Banco San José. The best place to exchange TCs or US$ cash is at **Distribuidora Puerto Quepos**, opposite Banco de Costa Rica, 0900-1700, no paperwork, no commission, all done in 2 mins, same rate as banks. **Immigration** On the same street as the Banco de Costa Rica. **Internet** Access available from Internet Quepos, fast machines, good service, US$1.50 per hr. Several others in town, including **Arte Net, Quepos Diner & Internet Café, Internet Tropical, CyberLoco** and **Internet Cantina**. **Language schools** Escuela D'Amore, in a great setting overlooking the ocean, halfway between Quepos and the national park, T2777-1143, www.escueladamore.com. Believes in the immersion technique, living with local families. **Costa Rica Spanish Institute**, T2234-1001, www.cosi.co.cr. **Laundry** Lavanderías de Costa Rica, near the football pitch, good. **Medical services** The hospital is out of town, T2777-0922. Red Cross, T2777-0118. **Police** T2777-0196. **Post office** On the walkway by the football pitch, 0800-1700.

San José to Panama

Heading through the Talamanca mountains, the Pan-American Highway reaches its highest point at Cerro de la Muerte (Peak of Death) and passes El Chirripó, Costa Rica's highest peak at 3820 m, as the scenic road drops down through the valley of the Río de El General to the tropical lowlands of the Pacific coast and the border with Panama. Private reserves along the route are ideal for birdwatching – here the resplendent quetzal enjoys a quieter life than his Monteverde relations – and mountain streams are stocked with trout providing both sport and food. Lodges and hotels are usually isolated, dotted along the highway. Towards Costa Rica's most southerly point, the Península de Osa is a nature haven of beautiful pathways, palm-fringed beaches and protected rainforest – well worth the effort if you have the time.
» *For listings, see pages 1248-1253.*

Travelling the Pan-American Highway ⊖🚗⛰😊🚌 » *pp1248-1253.*

From San José the Pan-American Highway runs for 352 km to the Panama border. It's a spectacular journey but challenging if you're driving, with potholes, frequent rockslides during the rainy season, roadworks and generally difficult conditions.

From Cártago, the route heads south over the mountains, beginning with the ascent of **Cerro Buena Vista** (3490 m), a climb of almost 2050 m to the continental divide. A little lower than the peak, the highest point of the road is 3335 m at Km 89, which travels through barren *páramo* scenery. Those unaccustomed to high altitude should beware of mountain sickness brought on by a too rapid ascent. For 16 km the road follows the crest of the Talamanca ridge, with views of the Pacific 50 km away, and on clear days of the Atlantic, 80 km to the east.

Some 4.5 km east of Km 58 (Cañón church) is **Genesis II**, a privately owned 40-ha cloud forest National Wildlife Refuge, at 2360 m, bordering the **Tapantí–Macizo de la Muerte National Park**. Accommodation is available here and at several other places along the way. At Km 78 is **Casa Refugio de Ojo de Agua**, a historic pioneer home overlooked but for a couple of picnic tables in front of the house. At Km 80 a steep, dramatic road leads down the spectacular valley of the Río Savegre to **San Gerardo de Dota**, a birdwatchers' paradise. The highest point is at Km 89.5, where temperatures are below zero at night.

San Isidro de El General → *Colour map 7, B3. Altitude: 702 m.*

The drop in altitude from the highlands to the growing town of San Isidro passes through fertile valleys growing coffee and raising cattle. The huge **cathedral** on the main plaza is a bold architectural statement, with refreshing approaches to religious iconography inside. The **Museo Regional del Sur** ① *Calle 2, Av 1-0, T2771-5273, Mon-Fri 0800-1200, 1330-1630, free,* is in the old marketplace, now the Complejo Cultural. The 750-ha **Centro Biológico Las Quebradas** ① *7 km north of San Isidro, T2771-4131, Tue-Fri 0800-1400, Sat and Sun 0800-1500, closed Oct,* has trails and dormitory lodging for researchers. San Isidro de El General is also the place to stock up for a trip into Parque Nacional Chirripó and to climb Cerro Chirripó Grande (3820 m), see page 1245.

Parque Nacional Chirripó

① *US$7, crowded in season, make reservations in Oficina de los Parques Nacionales (OPN), Calle 4, Av Central-2, San Isidro de El General, T2771-3155, open 0600-1700. If you want to* *walk or climb in the park, get food in San Isidro and book accommodation at the OPN. Take the 0500 Pueblo Nuevo bus from northwest corner of Parque Central, or the 1400 from the bus station to San Gerardo de Rivas (US$1.05, 1½ hrs, return at 0700 and 1600), which passes the entrance to the park. Interesting trip up the Río Chirripó valley.*

San Isidro de El General is west of Costa Rica's highest mountain **Cerro Chirripó Grande** (3820 m) in the middle of Parque Nacional Chirripó (50,150 ha). Treks starts from San Gerardo de Rivas (see below). The views from the hilltops are splendid and the high plateau near the summit is an interesting alpine environment with lakes of glacial origin and diverse flora and fauna. The park includes a considerable portion of cloud forest and the walk is rewarding.

Parque Nacional Chirripó neighbours **Parque Internacional La Amistad** (193,929 ha), established in 1982, and together they extend along the Cordillera de Talamanca to the Panamanian border, comprising the largest area of virgin forest in the country with the greatest biological diversity.

San Gerardo de Rivas
In a cool, pleasant spot, San Gerardo de Rivas is at the confluence of the Río Blanco and the Río Pacífico Chirripó. Close to Parque Nacional Chirripó entrance, it is the starting point for the climb up **Cerro Chirripó Grande** (3820 m). If you haven't booked accommodation at the refugio in San Isidro you can book it at the **MINAE office** (see box, opposite).

As interest in this quiet area grows, new tours are appearing including horse riding up to Llano Bonito (US$50), trips to local waterfalls (US$40) and nature tours.

Handy for weary legs after the climb, there are **hot springs** ① *daily 0700-1800, entrance US$1*, in the area. Before crossing the concrete bridge turn left to 'Herradura' for 10 minutes then look for the sign after Parque Las Rosas; go down to the suspension bridge, cross the river and continue for 10 minutes to the house where you pay. Information about the town can be found on www.sangerardocostarica.com.

Buenos Aires to Paso Real
Continuing southeast, a good road sinks slowly through the Río General valley where the Talamanca Mountains dominate the skyline. At Km 197 (from San José), the change from coffee to fruit is complete; at the junction for **Buenos Aires** is the huge **Del Monte** cannery. The town, a few kilometres off the Pan-American Highway, has some simple accommodation.

Heading 17 km east towards the mountains is the **Reserva Biológica Durika**, a privately owned reserve of roughly 800 ha, aiming to create a self-sustained community in the Talamanca mountains. Accommodation is available in some rustic cabins.

South along the highway, the small towns of Térraba and Boruca are the most prominent remains of the nation's indigenous population. The community of **Boruca**, with a small *hostal* (F), has a small, poorly maintained museum, but every year the **Fiesta de los Diablitos** on the last day of December and first two days of January, and the last day of January and the first two days of February in **Rey Curre,** see the culture come alive in a festival of music, dance and costume. There is a daily bus to Boruca from Buenos Aires at 1130 (1½ hours).

At **Paso Real** the highway heads west to Palmar Norte, with a turn heading towards San Vito (see below) and the Panamanian border.

Climbing the Chirripó peaks

The early morning climb to the summit of Cerro Chirripó, Costa Rica's highest mountain, is a refreshing slog after the relative comforts often encountered in Costa Rica. The hike takes you through magnificent cloud forest draped in mosses and ephiphytes before entering a scorched area of *paramo* grasslands with incredible views to the Pacific and Atlantic coastlines on clear days. The widlife – birdlife in particularly – is incredible and, even if you don't see it, you will certainly hear it. The trek itself is not difficult but it is tiring being almost consistently uphill on the way and a knee-crunching, blister-bursting journey down.

From the *refugio* inside the park, you can also explore the nearby Crestones, a volcanic outcrop that has been etched on to the minds of every Costa Rican, and the creatively named Sabana de los Leones and Valle de los Conejos.

If you wish to climb the 3820 m Cerro Chirripó, Costa Rica's highest mountain, you must make advance reservations by calling the park service office in San Gerardo, T2771-5116, located to the east of San Isidro de El General. After phoning for reservations you are given a couple of days to pay by bank deposit to guarantee your space. Visitors are not allowed into the park without reservations at the *refugio*. During the dry season it's often full, so it's a good idea to make arrangements as soon as possible. Start in the early morning for the 8- to 10-hour hike to the *refugio*. The cost is US$7 entry for each day spent in the park, plus US$6 shelter fee per night. The *refugio* has simple but adequate accommodation, with space for about 80 people and a large kitchen area.

The cold – often frosty in the morning – is a bit of a shock in contrast to the rest of Costa Rica, but you can rent blankets and sleeping bags from the *refugio* (US$1 each). Gas cookers are also available for hire (US$2). There are sufficient water supplies en route so you will need only to carry your food supplies. Electrical power at the *refugio* is only for a couple of hours each night, so be sure to bring a flashlight. The top of Chirripó is located another 5.1 km from the Crestones base camp.

In addition to the high camp there is a shelter about halfway up, **Refugio Llano Bonito** (2500 m), which is simple and occasionally clean, with wooden floor, two levels to sleep on, no door but wind protection, drinking water and toilet. It's about four hours' walk from San Gerardo and three hours' walk on to **Refugios Base Crestones**. Plan for at least two nights on the mountain – although you can do it with only one night if you're tight for time, rising very early to summit on the second day in time to go all the day down in one hit. While nights can be cold, daytime temperatures tend to be warm to hot, so go prepared with sunscreen and hat. In the rainy season, trails up the plateau are slippery and muddy, and fog obscures the views. Time your descent to catch the afternoon bus back to San Isidro.

For a general update on San Gerardo and climbing Chirripó, visit www.sangerardocostarica.com.

Palmar Norte and Palmar Sur

Taking a sharp turn at Paso Real (straight on for San Vito – see below), the Pan-American Highway heads west to Palmar Norte (Km 257 – with gas station) from where a paved road leads to Ciudad Cortés. A road heads northwest to Dominical (see page 1235).

Crossing the Río Grande de Terraba leads to Palmar Sur, which is 90 km from the Panamanian border. There are several stone spheres in the area. A banana plantation close to town has stone spheres – 1.5 m in diameter and accurate within 5 mm – of pre-Columbian manufacture, though their use is a matter of conjecture. Recent theories are that they were made to represent the planets of the solar system, or that they were border markers.

From Palmar Sur the Pan-American Highway heads southeast to Chacarita (33 km) where a road turns off to the Osa Peninsula, to Río Claro (another 26 km) where a road leads to Golfito, another 15 km leads to Ciudad Neily which is 16 km from the border at Paso Canoas.

Sierpe
Through a matrix of cooperative banana and African plantations, a road leads to Sierpe, on the Río Sierpe, where there are several small hotels and the departure point for boats to Bahía Drake, see page 1255.

Paso Real to San Vito 😊🟠🟡🟢🔵 ▶▶ pp1248-1253. Colour map 7, B4.
The road from Paso Real to San Vito is now paved and has lovely views. **La Amistad International Park** has few facilities for visitors at present, but one lodge is found way up in the hills beyond Potrero Grande, just south of the Paso Real junction on the way to San Vito. Near the border is **San Vito**. Originally built by Italian immigrants among denuded hills, it is a prosperous but undistinguished town.

On the road from San Vito to Ciudad Neily at Las Cruces are the world-renowned **Wilson Botanical Gardens** ① T2773-4004, www.ots.ac.cr, owned by the **Organization for Tropical Studies**, 6 km from San Vito. In 360 ha of forest reserve are over 5000 species of tropical plants, orchids, other epiphytes and trees with 331 resident bird species. It is possible to spend the night here if you arrange it first with the **OTS** ① T2240-6696, in San José: **L** per person all inclusive, US$32 per person for day visits with lunch. On the same road is **Finca Cántaros** ① T2773-3760, specializing in local arts and crafts, owned by Gail Hewson Gómez. It's one of the best craft shops in Costa Rica – worth a look even if you don't buy anything.

Border with Panama–Sabalito
The road south from San Vito to Ciudad Neily is paved, in good condition and offers some of the best coastal views in the country as the road rapidly falls through the hills. Heading east from San Vito, a good gravel road, paved in places, runs via Sabalito (Banco Nacional) to the Panama border at Río Sereno. There are buses from Sabalito to San José. See Panama chapter, page 1370, for details of this border crossing.

Golfito and around 😊🟠🔺🟡🟢🔵 ▶▶ pp1248-1253. Colour map 7, B4.
Thirty-one kilometres north of the border a road branches south at Río Claro (several pensiones and a fuel station) to the former banana port of Golfito, a 6-km long linear settlement bordering the Golfo Dulce and steep forested hills. While elements of hard sweat and dock labour remain, Golfito's prominence today comes from being Costa Rica's only free port, set up in 1990, selling goods tax free at about 60% of normal prices. Popular with shoppers from throughout the country, it can be difficult to get a hotel room at weekends. Check out www.golfito-costarica.com for information on lodging and activities in the area.

Border essentials: Costa Rica–Panama

Paso Canoas
Shops sell 'luxury' items brought from Panama at prices considerably lower than those of Costa Rica (for example sunglasses, stereo equipment, kitchen utensils, etc).

Immigration Border open 0600-2200 (Costa Rica time). Costa Rica is one hour behind Panama. For information on entering Panama, see page 1145.

Crossing by private vehicle Those motoring north can get insurance cover at the border for US$17, this will cover public liability and property damage.

Golfito also provides boat and ferry access to Puerto Jiménez and the Osa Peninsula, and popular fishing and surfing beaches to the south of the town.

Entering the town from the south heading north there are a few hotels where the road meets the coast. In 2 km is the small town centre of painted buildings with saloon bars, open-fronted restaurants and cheap accommodation – probably the best stop for budget travellers. Nearby is the dilapidated *muellecito* used by the ferries to Puerto Jiménez and water taxis. A further kilometre north are the container port facilities and the **Standard Fruit Company**'s local HQ, though many of the banana plantations have been turned over to oil palm and other crops. Beyond the dock is the free port, airstrip and another set of hotels.

The **Refugio Nacional de Fauna Silvestre Golfito**, in the steep forested hills over-looking Golfito, was created to protect Golfito's watershed. Rich in rare and medicinal plants with abundant fauna, there are some excellent hikes in the refuge. Supervised by the University of Costa Rica, they have a field office in Golfito.

Thirty minutes by water taxi from Golfito, you can visit **Casa Orquídeas** ① 12775-1614, *tours last about 2½ hrs, US$5 per person, US$20 minimum, closed Fri,* a family-owned botanical garden with a large collection of herbs, orchids and local flowers and trees, that you can see, smell, touch and taste.

To the north of Golfito is the **Parque Nacional Piedras Blancas** tropical wet forest. The area was being exploited for wood products, but has been steadily purchased since 1991 with help from the Austrian government and private interests, notably the classical Austrian violinist Michael Schnitzler. All logging has now ceased and efforts are devoted to a research centre and ecotourism, concentrated in an area designated **Parque Nacional Esquinas**. Near the village of **La Gamba** a tourist lodge has been built (see Sleeping, below). La Gamba is 6 km along a dirt road from Golfito, or 4 km from Briceño on the Pan-American Highway between Piedras Blancas and Río Claro.

Beaches around Golfito
Playa de Cacao is about 6 km (1½-hour walk) north of Golfito round the bay, or a short trip by water taxi. Further north is the secluded beach of **Playa San Josecito** with a couple of adventure-based lodges.

About 15 km by sea south of Golfito, and reached by water taxi or a long bus journey (US$2 by *colectivo* ferry from the small dock; 0600 and 1200, return 0500, 1300), **Playa Zancudo** is a long stretch of clean golden sound, dotted with a few rustic hotels ideal for relaxing and lazing away the days. Still further south is **Pavones**, where a world record left-hand wave has elevated the rocky beach to the realm of surfing legend. South of Pavones, towards the end of the peninsula and at the mouth of the Golfo Dulce is **Punta Banco**.

Ciudad Neily, Paso Canoas and the Panama border

Ciudad Neily is an uninspiring town providing useful transport links between San Vito in the highlands and the coastal plain, and is roughly 16 km from Paso Canoas on the border with Panama. Paso Canoas is a little piece of chaos with traders buying and selling to take advantage of the difference in prices between Costa Rica and Panama. With little to hold you, there is little reason to visit unless heading to Panama. If misfortune should find you having to stay the night, there are some reasonable options.

⦿ San José to Panama listings

For Sleeping and Eating price codes and other relevant information, see Essentials pages 45-48.

⦿ Sleeping

Travelling the Pan-American Highway *p1243*
L Hotel de Montaña Savegre, San Gerardo de Dota, T2740-1028, www.savegre.co.cr. Waterfalls, trout fishing, prices include meals.
A-B Trogón Lodge, San Gerardo de Dota, T2740-1051, www.grupomawamba.com. 23 fine wooden cabins with private bathroom, set amongst beautiful gardens connected by paths used by dive-bombing hummingbirds.
B Finca Eddie Serano Mirador de Quetzales, Km 70, T2381-8456. A 43-ha forest property at 2650 m. Eddie Serrano has passed away, but one of his sons will show visitors quetzals (almost guaranteed, but don't tell anyone at Monteverde Cloud Forest) and other endemic species of the highlands. 10 cabins, sleeping 2-5, with wonderful views, private bath, price per person includes breakfast, dinner and guided hike.
D Hotel and Restaurant Georgina, Km 95, T2770-8043. At almost 3300 m, Costa Rica's highest hotel, basic, clean, friendly, good food (used by southbound **Tracopa** buses), good birdwatching; ask owners for directions for a nice walk to see quetzals.

Camping

Los Ranchos, San Gerardo de Dota, at the bottom of the hill, T2771-2376. Camping in perfect surroundings. No transport down here, but pickups from the highway can be arranged.

San Isidro de El General *p1243*
A Rancho La Botija, out of town on the road to San Gerardo, T2770-2147, www.ranchola botija.com. Restaurant, pool, hiking to nearby petroglyphs, open 0900 at weekends, great restaurant littered with fragments of *botijas*. Recommended.
B Talari Mountain Lodge, 10 mins from San Isidro on the road to San Gerardo, T2771-0341, www.talari.co.cr. 8-ha farm, with bath, riverside cabins, known for birdwatching, rustic.
C Hotel Los Crestones, in town, T2770-1200, www.hotelloscrestones.com. Big rooms, complete with TV, poo. Wheelchair accessible.
C-D Astoria, on north side of square, T2771-0914. Tiny but clean rooms.
D El Valle, Calle 2, Av Central-2, T2771-0246. Cleanish, one of the better cheapies.
D Hotel/Restaurant Amaneli, in town, T2771-0352. 41 quite good rooms with private bathroom, fan, some noisy.
D Hotel Iguazu, Calle Central, Av 1, T2771-2571. Hot water, cable TV, clean, safe with parking.
D-E Hotel Chirripó, south side of Parque Central, T2771-0529. Private or shared bath, clean, very good restaurant, free covered parking, recommended.
E Lala, Calle Central, Av 1, T2771-0291. Basic and simple.

San Gerardo de Rivas *p1244*

All accommodation is on the road up to the park

D El Urán, at the very top, closest to the park entrance, T2742-5003, www.hoteluran.com. Simple, clean rooms, lots of blankets and a restaurant that will feed you early before setting out.

D Marín, next to MINAE office, T2742-5099. Basic but friendly and good value.

D Pelícano, T2742-5050, www.hotel pelicano.net. 11 rooms sleeping between 2 and 5 people, with great views, a bar and restaurant. Beautiful setting with countless birds. Also has a pool.

D-E Roca Dura, opposite the football pitch, T2742-5071, rocadurasangerardo@ hotmail.com. Built on a huge boulder, 7 rooms with hot showers, good *comedor*, nice view, shop next door, friendly owners.

E Cabinas El Descanso, T2742-5061, eldescanso@hotmail.com. 7 bunks, bathroom, hearty meals available, gas stove for hire, horses for rent and guide services offered, recommended. Price per person.

E Cabinas/Restaurant Elimar, 500 m out of village. Swimming pool, simple restaurant, 4 quite good *cabinas* with private bathroom, hot water.

E El Bosque, T2742-5021, elbosque@ gmail.com. With a small bar and restaurant. Looks a bit scruffy from the outside, but spotless rooms and great views over the valley from some rooms.

Camping

You can camp at Roca Dura and El Bosque, or near the park office, in San Gerardo near the bus stop. Check in first and pay US$0.30.

Buenos Aires to Paso Real *p1244*

B-C Cabañas, Durika Biological Reserve, T2730-0657, www.durika.org. Rustic cabins. Includes 3 vegetarian meals a day, with a wide range of activities including walks, hikes to the summit of Cerro Durika and cultural tours. Around US$10 per person on top of the daily rate.

E Cabinas Violeta, Buenos Aires, next to the fire station, 200 m west of the plaza, T2730 0104. Clean, simple, central and OK if you're stuck for the night.

F Cabinas Mary, Buenos Aires, 800 m south of the centre close to the **Aridikes** office, T2730-0187. Quiet spot which tries to be clean.

Palmar Norte and Palmar Sur *p1245*

C-E Hotel y Cabinas Casa Amarilla, 300 m east of bus station on the plaza, T2786-6251. With fan, cabins are more expensive than the hotel rooms, rooms at back quieter, rooms over restaurant noisy but cheaper.

D Cabinas Tico-Alemán, on the highway near the gas station, T2786-6232. 25 *cabinas* with private bathroom. Best in town.

F Hotel Xinia, 150 m east from bus station, T2786-6129. 26 rooms, very basic but OK, shared bathroom.

Sierpe *p1246*

A Río Sierpe Lodge, T2384-5595. All-inclusive plan with an emphasis on fishing.

B Oleaje Sereno, T2786-7580. Good rooms, with restaurant on river bank.

E-F Margarita, T2786-7574. Has 13 good rooms. Friendly owners and good value.

Paso Real to San Vito *p1246*

B El Ceibo, just down from main plaza, T2773-3025. With bath, hot water and TV, good restaurant.

C-D Cabinas Rino, right in the centre of town, T2773-3071. Clean and well maintained. Good deal.

D Cabinas Las Huacas, near Cabinas Firenze, T2773-3115. 13 OK cabinas with private bathroom, hot water, TV, which were looking very run-down when last visited.

E Las Mirlas, 500 m out of town on road to Sabalito, T2773-3714. In same location as **Hotel Pitier**, but more attractive.

F Cabinas Firenze, close to the gas station, on the road from San Isidro, T2773-3741. Has 6 basic *cabinas*, sleep 5, with private bathroom.

F Colono, plaza area, T2773-4543. Cheap and central.

F Hotel Pitier, 500 m out of town on road to Sabalito, T2773-3027. Clean, with bath.

Golfito p1246
L Esquinas Rainforest Lodge, near La Gamba, 6 km from Golfito, T2741-8001, www.esquinaslodge.com. Full board, private baths, verandas overlooking the forest, tours, all profits to the local community.

B Las Gaviotas, next to El Gran Ceibo, T2775-0062, lasgaviotas@hotmail.com. 21 cabins and rooms, with bath, a/c and with excellent restaurant looking out over the waterfront.

B Sierra, at the northernmost part of town, near the airport and free zone, T2775-0666. 72 double rooms, a/c, a couple of pools, restaurant. Rooms are better than the place looks from the outside.

C Golfo Azul, T2775-0871. Has 20 comfortable large rooms, with bath and a/c, good restaurant.

C La Purruja Lodge, 4 km south of Golfito, T2775-5054, www.purruja.com. 5 duplex cabins with bath, plus camping US$2 per tent.

D Delfina, town centre, T2775-0043. Shared bath, fan, friendly, basic. Some rooms with private bath much better. Rooms on street are noisy, parking available.

D Mar y Luna, T2775-0192. Has 8 rooms sleeping 2-4, with bath, fan, restaurant on stilts above the sea, quiet spot, good deal.

D Melissa, behind Delfina, T2775-0443. Has 4 simple rooms, with private bath, clean and quiet, great spot overlooking bay. Parking available. Recommended.

D-E Del Cerro, close to the docks, T2775-0006. Offering 20 simple rooms sleeping 1-6, private bathroom, laundry services, fishing boat rentals.

D-E Golfito, central, T2775-0047. Quiet, with a couple of rooms overlooking the bay and an apartment at US$30. A little run-down but OK.

E Costa Rica Surf, T2775-0034. Has 25 dark rooms, most with private bath. Big bar downstairs. Not the best in town, but OK.

F El Uno, above Chinese restaurant of same name, T2775-0061. Very basic and mildly amusing if you fancy pretending to be a banana in a packing case, but friendly.

Beaches around Golfito p1247
L Tiskita Jungle Lodge, Punta Banco, T2296-8125, www.tiskita-lodge.co.cr. A 162-ha property including a fruit farm, with excellent birdwatching, 14 cabins overlooking ocean. Overlooks beach, cool breezes, waterfall, jungle pools, trails through virgin forest – great spot.

L-A Cabinas La Ponderosa, Pavones, T8824-4145 (T954-771-9166 in USA), www.cabinaslaponderosa.com. Owned by 2 surfers, large cabins, fan or a/c, with bath (hot water), walking, horse riding, fishing, diving and surfing; also house for rent (sleeps 6), restaurant.

A-B Oasis on the Beach, Playa Zancudo, T2776-0087, www.oasisonthebeach. com. Cabins and apartments with kitchenettes, internet and tours. Great spot and atmosphere.

A Latitude 8, Playa Zancudo, T2776-0168, www.latitude8lodge.com. A couple of secluded, tranquil cabins with full kitchen and hot water.

A Los Cocos, Playa Zancudo, Golfito, T2776-0012, www.loscocos.com. Beach front cabins at the ocean with private bathroom, hot water, mosquito net, fan, kitchenette, refrigerator, veranda. Also provide boat tours and taxi service. Discounts for longer stays. Heavenly.

B Pavones Surf Lodge, Pavones, T2222-2224 (San José). Includes meals, 2 cabins with bath, 6 rooms with shared bath.

B-C Coloso Del Mar, Playa Zancudo, T2776-0050, www.coloso-del-mar.com. Great little spot with 4 simple cabins overlooking the beach and a Tico/Caribbean restaurant.

B-C Mira Olas, Pavones, T2393-7742. Cabins with kitchen and fan, low monthly rates, jungle trail.

B-C Sol y Mar, Playa Zancudo, T2776-0014, www.zancudo.com. 4 screened cabins, hot water, fan, 3-storey rental house (US$700 per month), 50 m from ocean, bar/restaurant, meals 0700-2000, home-baked bread, great fruit shakes, volleyball with lights for evening play, badminton, paddleball, boogie boards, library. Highly recommended.

D-E The Yoga Farm, Punta Banco, www.yogafarmcostarica.org. A laid-back retreat, set on a mountainside surrounded by primary rainforest and near the beach. A great place to get back to nature, it offers a range of activities (see Activities and tours, page 1252). Price includes accommodation, food and yoga. Price per person.

E Pensión Fin del Mundo, Playa Zancudo, over Restaurant Tranquilo. 6 simple rooms with fan, mosquito net, clean, shared bathroom. English book exchange at Tienda Buen Precio.

E Rancho Burica, Pavones. With thatched cabins, horse riding, fishing, tours to Guaymí indigenous reserve.

Ciudad Neily, Paso Canoas and the Panama border *p1248*
Ciudad Neily
C Cabinas Andrea, T2783-3784. 18 clean *cabinas* with private bathroom, a/c or fan, TV. Popular with Ticos coming through town, handy for main bus terminal.
D-E El Rancho, just off the highway, T2783-3060. Has 50 resort-style cabins with bath, TV (cheaper without). Restaurant open 1600.
E Cabinas Heileen, north of plaza, T2783-3080. Simple *cabinas* with private bathroom, fan.
E Hotel Musuco, just off the Pan-American Hwy, T2783-3048. With bath, cheaper without, fan, clean and quiet. Good deal.
F Hotel Villa, north of Hotel Musoc, T2783-5120. Cheapest and last option in town.

Paso Canoas
D Cabinas Interamericano, T2732-2041. With bath and fan, some with a/c, good value upstairs, restaurant.

E Cabinas Jiménez, T2732-2258. Quite good *cabinas* with private bathroom, fan. Very clean, good deal.
E Hilda, south of town, T2732-2873. Good rooms, very clean, restaurant over the road. Recommended.
F Cabinas El Paso, T2732-2740. OK rooms with shower.

Eating

San Isidro de El General *p1243*
¶ **La Cascada**, Av 2 and Calle 2, T2771-6479. Balcony bar where the bright young things hang out.
¶ **Restaurant Crestones**, south of the main plaza, T2771-1218. Serves a good mix of snacks, drinks and lively company.
¶ **Restaurant El Tenedor**, Calle Central, Av Central-1, T2771-0881. Good food, friendly, big pizzas, recommended.
¶ **Soda Chirripó**, south side of the main plaza. Gets the vote from the current gringo crowd in town.
† **La Marisquería**, corner of Av 0 and Calle 4. Simple setting but great *ceviche*.
† **Soda J&P**, indoor market south of the main plaza. The best of many.

Paso Real to San Vito *p1246*
¶ **Lilianas**, San Vito. Still showing homage to the town's Italian heritage with good pasta dishes and pizza.
† **Restaurant Nelly**, San Vito, near Cabinas Las Huacas. Good wholesome truck-drivers' fare.

Golfito *p1246*
Many seafood places along the seafront.
¶ **Cubana**, near post office. Good, try *batidos*.
¶ **El Uno**, near Cubana. Good, reasonably priced seafood.
¶ **La Dama del Delfín Restaurant**, downtown. Breakfast from 0700, snacks, home-baked goods, closed for dinner and Sun.
† **Le Eurekita**, centre. Serves a mean breakfast of *huevos rancheros*.

Beaches around Golfito *p1247*
🍴 **Bar y Restaurant Tranquilo**, Playa
Zancudo. A lively spot between **Zancudo
Beach Club** and **Coloso del Mar**.
🍴 **Macondo**, Playa Zancudo. Italian
restaurant which also has a couple
of rooms.
🍴 **Soda Katherine**, Playa Zancudo, T2776-
0124. From US$4, great Tico fare; also
simple cabins.

▲ Activities and tours

San Isidro de El General *p1243*
Ciprotur, Calle 4, Av 1-3, T2771-
6096, www.ecotourism.co.cr. Good
information on services throughout
the southern region.
Selvamar, Calle 1, Av 2-4, T2771-4582,
www.exploringcostarica.com. General
tours and the main contact for out of the
way destinations in the southern region.

Golfito *p1246*
Land Sea Tours, T2775-1614, landsea@
racsa.co.cr. Know everything there is to
know about the area. They can organize
almost anything including national and
international flights, and can advise on
crewing on yachts heading up and down
the coast.

Beaches around Golfito *p1247*
The Yoga Farm, Punta Banco, www.yoga
farmcostarica.org. Yoga, horseback riding and
hikes through the rainforest. Also organize
homestay with an indigenous family.

❂ Transport

San Isidro de El General *p1243*
Bus Terminal at Av 6, Calle Central-2 at
the back of the market and adjacent streets
but most arrive and depart from bus depots
along the Pan-American Hwy. From **San
José** (just outside Terminal Coca Cola), hourly

service 0530-1730, US$3.30, 3 hrs (buses to
the capital leave from the highway, Calle 2-4).
To **Quepos** via **Dominical** at 0500 and 1330,
3 hrs. However, **Tracopa** buses coming from
San José, going south go from Calle 3/Pan-
American Hwy, behind church, to **Palmar
Norte**, US$2.25; **Paso Canoas**, 0830-1545,
1930 (direct), 2100; **David** (Panama) direct,
1000 and 1500; **Golfito** direct at 1800; **Puerto
Jiménez**, 0630, 0900 and 1500. Waiting room
but no reservations or tickets sold. **Musoc**
buses leave from the intersection of Calle
2-4 with the Pan-American Hwy.
　Most local buses leave from bus terminal
to the south of the main plaza. Buses to **San
Gerardo de Rivas** and **Cerro Chirripó** leave
0500 and 1400, return 0700 and 1600.

Taxi　A 4WD taxi to San Gerardo costs
about US$20 for up to 4 people.

Palmar Norte and Palmar Sur *p1245*
Air　Daily flights with Sansa (US$72)and
Nature Air, **San José**–Palmar Sur (US$73
1 way).

Bus　Express bus to **Palmar Norte** from
Terminal Alfaro, with **Tracopa** from **San José**,
7 daily 0600-1800, 5 hrs, via **San Isidro de
El General**, 5 buses return to the capital
0445-1300. 5 buses daily to **Sierpe** for the
boat to **Bahía Drake** (page 1255) 45 mins.
Also buses north to **Dominical**, and south
to the **Golfito** and the Panamanian border.

Sierpe *p1246*
Bus and boat　5 buses daily to **Palmar
Norte**, 0530-1530, 45 mins. Boats down Río
Sierpe to **Bahía Drake**, 1½ hrs, US$70 per
boat. Many hotels in Drake have boats,
may be able to get a lift, US$15 per person.

Paso Real to San Vito *p1246*
Bus　Direct buses **San José** to San Vito,
4 daily, 0545, 0815, 1130 and 1445, from
Terminal Alfaro, Calle 14, Av 5; direct bus
San Vito-San José 0500, 0730, 1000, 1500,
6 hrs, corriente buses take 8 hrs. Alternative

route, not all paved, via Cd Neily (see below); from San Vito to **Las Cruces** at 0530 and 0700; sit on the left coming up, right going down, to admire the wonderful scenery; return buses pass Las Cruces at 1510.

Golfito p1246
Air Several daily flights to **San José**, with Sansa (US$75 1 way). Runway is all weather, tight landing between trees; 2 km from town, taxi US$0.50.

Bus From **San José** 0700 (8½ hrs) and 1500 (6 hrs express) daily from Terminal Alfaro, return 0500 (express), 1300, US$6; from **San Isidro de El General**, take 0730 bus to Río Claro and wait for bus coming from Cd Neily. To **Paso Canoas**, US$1.25, hourly from outside Soda Pavo, 1½ hrs. To **Pavones** at 1000 and 1500, and return at 0430 and 1230, 3 hrs, US$2.50. A spit of land continues south to Punta Burica with no roads and only a couple of villages.

Sea There is a boat service between Golfito and **Puerto Jiménez**, leaving the dock in Golfito at 1130, US$2.50, 1½ hrs, returning at 0600, or chartering a water taxi for US$60, up to 8 passengers, is possible.

Water taxis in and around Golfito, Froylan Lopez, T8824-6571, to **Cacao Beach**, **Punta Zancudo**, **Punta Encanto** or to order, US$20 per hr up to 5 persons.

Docks Land Sea Tours (see above) and Banana Bay Marina (T2775-0838, www.ban anabaymarina.com) accommodate boats up to 150 ft – either of these places might be an option if heading south on a boat, but you'll need to ask nicely and be a bit lucky.

Ciudad Neily, Paso Canoas and the Panama border p1248
Bus The terminal in Cd Neily is at the northern end of town, beside the Mercado Central. Daily bus to **San José**, with Tracopa, from main square (6 daily, US$6, 7 hrs, on Sun buses from the border are full by the time they reach Cd Neily). Buses arrive at

Av 5 and Calle 14 in San José. Services to **San Vito** inland, and to **Palmar**, **Cortés** and **Dominical** (0600 and 1430, 3 hrs). Also to **Puerto Jiménez** at 0700 and 1400, 4 hrs. Bus for **Golfito** leaves from the centre of town every 30 mins. The Pan-American Hwy goes south (plenty of buses, 20 mins, US$0.35) to Paso Canoas on the Panamanian border. *Colectivo* US$1.10, very quick.

San José–Paso Canoas, US$9, 8 hrs from Terminal Alfaro at 0500, 1100 (direct), 1300, 1800, return 0400, 0730, 0900, 1500 (T2223-7685). Not all buses go to the border. International buses that reach the border after closing time wait there till the following day. Hourly buses to Cd Neily, ½ hourly to Golfito.

⊙ Directory

San Isidro de El General p1243
Banks Banco Nacional, on north side of plaza, Mon-Fri, 0830-1545. **Internet** Bruncanet, on north side of plaza, and MS Internet Café. **Post office** 3 blocks south of the church. **Telephone** ICE office on Calle 4, Av 3-PAH.

Paso Real to San Vito p1246
Banks There are branches of Banco Nacional and Banco Popular in San Vito. **Post office and internet** Post office at northern end of town.

Golfito p1246
Banks Banco Nacional near dock, Mon-Fri 0830-1535, T2775-1622. **Internet** Internet café, on ground floor below Hotel Golfito.

Ciudad Neily, Paso Canoas and the Panama border p1248
Banks In Cd Neily, there are branches of Banco Nacional and Banco de Costa Rica. At Paso Canoas, banks on either side of border close at 1600 local time. Slightly better dollar rate for colones on the Costa Rican side. **Internet** Planet Internet at the northern end of Cd Neily.

Península de Osa

Across the Golfo Dulce is the hook-shaped appendage of the Osa Peninsula. Some distance from most other places of interest in the country, the journey is worthwhile as the peninsula is world famous for the diversity of flora and fauna in Parque Nacional Corcovado, with some of the best rainforest trekking and trails in the country. ▶ *For listings, see pages 1258-1260.*

Ins and outs

Getting to the peninsula is becoming easier. There is a daily ferry service from Golfito arriving at the small dock in Puerto Jiménez; bus services run from San José, passing through San Isidro de El General, Palmar North, and from the south at Ciudad Neily; and boats ply the coastal route from Sierpe to Bahía Drake. You can also fly from San José.

Puerto Jiménez → *Colour map 7, B4.*

Getting there To reach Puerto Jiménez from the Pan-American Highway (70 km), turn right about 30 km south of Palmar Sur; the road is paved to Rincón, thereafter it is

Puerto Jiménez

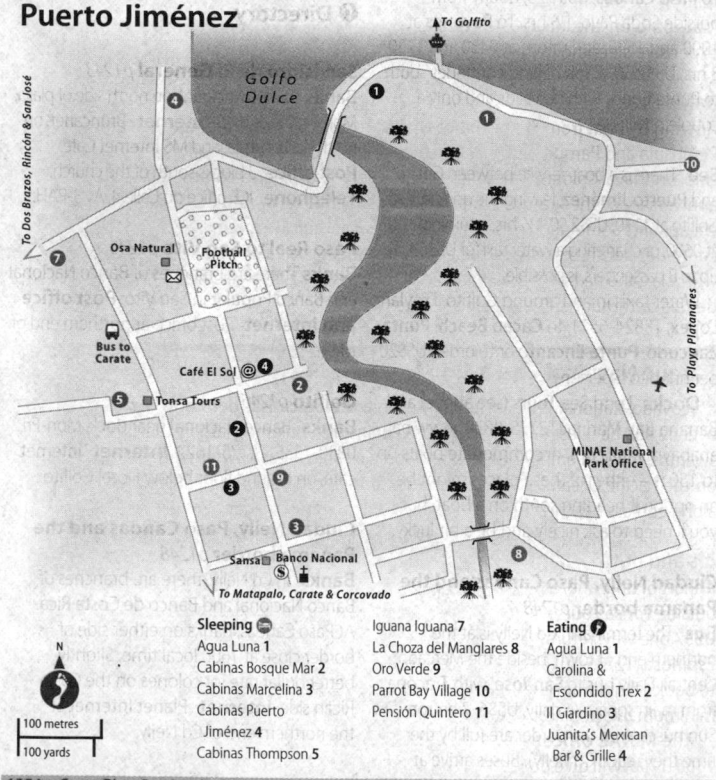

Sleeping
Agua Luna **1**
Cabinas Bosque Mar **2**
Cabinas Marcelina **3**
Cabinas Puerto
Jiménez **4**
Cabinas Thompson **5**

Iguana Iguana **7**
La Choza del Manglares **8**
Oro Verde **9**
Parrot Bay Village **10**
Pensión Quintero **11**

Eating
Agua Luna **1**
Carolina &
Escondido Trex **2**
Il Giardino **3**
Juanita's Mexican
Bar & Grille **4**

driveable with many bridge crossings. There is a police check point 47 km from the Pan-American Highway.

Once a gold-mining centre, Puerto Jiménez still has the feel of a frontier town although most miners were cleared from the Parque Nacional Corcovado area over 20 years ago.

Today, Puerto Jiménez is a popular destination with its laid-back, occasionally lively atmosphere, reasonable beaches nearby and, of course, the beautiful national park on the Pacific side of the peninsula. Look out for *El Sol de Osa*, www.soldeosa.com, an up-to-date community-information service. A particular charm of Puerto Jiménez, barely five blocks square, is its relative freedom from road traffic – Scarlet macaws can be seen roosting in the trees around the football pitch. There are good local walks to the jungle, where you will see monkeys and many birds, and to beaches and mangroves. There is a seasonal migration of humpbacks between October and March.

Geological treasures can be seen at the gold mine at **Dos Brazos** about 15 km west of town; ask for the road that goes uphill beyond the town, to see the local gold mines. Several *colectivo* taxis a day to Dos Brazos, last bus back at 1530 (often late); taxi US$7.25. You can also take a long walk to **Carate** (see below), which has a gold mine. Branch to the right and in 4 km there are good views of the peninsula. A topographical map is a big help, obtainable from Instituto Geográfico in San José. At **Cabo Matapalo** on the tip of the peninsula, 18 km south of Puerto Jiménez, are several expensive sleeping options.

Bahía Drake

Arriving by boat from Sierpe, Bahía Drake provides a northern entrance point to the Osa Peninsula and Parque Nacional Corcovado. In March 1579, Sir Francis Drake careened his ship on Playa Colorada in Bahía Drake. There is a plaque commemorating the 400th anniversary of the famous pirate's nautical aberration in Agujitas. Life in the bay is not cheap, and combined with transport, costs can quickly mount up. Bahía Drake, which continues south merging seamlessly with Agujitas, is a popular destination for **divers** with Isla Caño nearby. Open Water PADI courses (US$325) are available at **Cabinas Jinetes de Osa** or through **Caño Divers** at Pirate Cove.

Parque Nacional Corcovado ● ›› pp1258-1260. Colour map 7, C4.

Corcovado National Park, including **Reserva Biológica Isla del Caño** (84 ha), comprises over 42,469 ha – just under half the Osa Peninsula. Consisting largely of tropical rainforest, swamps, miles of empty beaches, and some cleared areas now growing back, it is located on the Pacific Ocean at the western end of the peninsula. An ideal spot for just walking along endless beaches, the park is also filled with birds, mammals and six species of cat.

Ins and outs

If short of time and/or money, the simplest way to the park is to take the pickup truck from outside **Tonsa Tours** in Puerto Jiménez to Playa Carate (most days at 0600 and 1400, 2½ hrs, US$7 one way, returning at 0800 and 1600, ask in advance about departure). Or call **Cirilo Espinosa** (T2735-5075), or **Ricardo González** (T2735-5068), for a 4WD jeep taxi. It is possible to book a flight from Puerto Jiménez to Carate or La Sirena in the park for US$99 per person, minimum five people. Ask at the airstrip or call T2735-5178.

The **MINAE office** ① *Puerto Jiménez, near the airport, T2735-5036, daily 0830-1200, 1300-1700,* will give permits for entering the park (US$7) and will book accommodation at **La Sirena**, see page 1260. Hiking boots and sandals are useful if you are walking in the park.

Around the park

At **Carate** there is a dirt airstrip and a store, run by Gilberto Morales and his wife Roxana (they rent rooms, but they are often full of gold miners; they also have a tent for hire, but take a sleeping bag). There are several luxury options here and a couple more lodges 30 minutes' walk west along the beach.

Five minutes' walk further down the beach is **La Leona** park wardens' station and entrance to the park. To go beyond here costs US$7 per day, whether you are walking along the beach to La Sirena (18 km, six hours, take sun protection), or just visiting for the day. Beyond here to the end of **Playa Madrigal** is another 2½-hours' walk, partly sandy, partly rocky, with some rock pools and rusty shipwrecks looking like modern art sculptures. The shore rises steeply into the jungle, which grows thickly with mangroves, almonds and coconut palms. Check with wardens about high tide so you don't get stuck. There are a couple of rivers along the beach, the first, Río Madrigal, is only about 15 minutes beyond La Leona (lovely and clear, deep enough for swimming about 200 m upstream, a good place for spotting wildlife). The best place for seeing

Southern Costa Rica & the Osa Peninsula

wildlife, though, is La Sirena, where there are paths inland and the terrain is flatter and more isolated.

You can head inland from Sirena on a trail past three conveniently spaced shelters to **Los Patos**, after passing several rivers full of reptiles (20 km, six to nine hours depending on conditions). The wooden house is the ranger station with electricity and TV, and four beds available at US$1.75 per night; meals possible if you do not bring your own food. Its balcony is a great observation point for birds, especially the redheaded woodpecker. From Los Patos you can carry on to the park border then, crisscrossing the Río Rincón to La Palma (small *hostal*), a settlement on the opposite side of the peninsula (13 km, six more hours), from which there are several 'taxis' making the one-hour trip to Puerto Jiménez (see above). An offshoot of this trail will lead you to a raffia swamp that rings the **Corcovado Lagoon**. The lagoon is only accessible by boat, but there are no regular trips. Caymans and alligators survive here, sheltered from the hunters.

From Sirena you can walk north along the coast to the shelter at Llorona (plenty of waterfalls), from which there is a trail to the interior with a shelter at the end. From Llorona you can proceed north through a forest trail and along the beach to the station at **San Pedrillo** on the edge of the park. You can stay here, camping or under roof, and eat with the rangers, who love company. From San Pedrillo you can take the park boat (not cheap) to Isla del Caño; a lovely (staffed) park outpost.

Isla del Coco

This has to be one of the world's most distant island destinations: the steep-sided and thickly wooded island and national park of 24 sq km lies 320 km off the Osa Peninsula, on the Cocos Ridge, which extends some 1400 km southwest to the Galápagos Islands. There is virtually nothing on the island, apart from a few endemic species, but you can visit for some of the world's best diving. The BBC/Discovery Channel shot some dramatic silhouetted images of tiger sharks here for their *Blue Planet* series. Historically, though, it was a refuge for pirates who are supposed to have buried great treasure here, though none has been found by the 500 or so expeditions looking for the 'x' that marked the spot. Travel by chartered boat can be made in Puntarenas, after a government permit has been obtained, or you can take a scuba-diving cruise on the **Okeanos Agressor** ① *T2232-0572 ext 60 (in US: PO Drawer K, Morgan City, LA 70381, T504-385-2416)*. The twice-monthly 10-day trips are understandably expensive (about US$3095 for 10 days).

Península de Osa – rain, snakes and mosquitoes

Avoid the rainy season. Bring umbrellas (not raincoats, which are too hot), because it will rain, unless you are hiking, in which case you may prefer to get wet. There are a few shelters, so only mosquito netting is indispensable. Bring all your food if you haven't arranged otherwise; food can only be obtained at Puerto Jiménez and Agujitas in the whole peninsula, and lodging likewise. The cleared areas (mostly outside the park, or along the beach) can be devastatingly hot. Chiggers (*coloradillas*) and horseflies infest the horse pastures and can be a nuisance, similarly sandflies on the beaches; bring spray-on insect repellent. Another suggestion is vitamin B1 pills (called thiamine, or *tiamina*). Mosquitoes are supposed to detest the smell and leave you alone. Get the Instituto Geográfico maps, scale 1:50,000. Remember finally that, as in any tropical forest, you may find some unfriendly wildlife like snakes (fer-de-lance and bushmaster snakes may attack without provocation), and herds of peccaries. You should find the most suitable method for keeping your feet dry and protecting your ankles; for some, rubber boots are the thing, for others light footwear that dries quickly.

Península de Osa listings

For Sleeping and Eating price codes and other relevant information, see Essentials pages45-48.

Sleeping

Puerto Jiménez *p1254, map p1254*

There is a website covering Jiménez hotels: www.jimenezhotels.com.

L Parrot Bay Village, left from the pier, T2735-5180, www.parrotbayvillage.com. Fully equipped wooden cabins sleeping 1-5, restaurant, beautiful spot, almost private beach. Cheaper in groups.

A Iguana Lodge, 5 km southeast of Puerto Jiménez behind the airstrip, T8829-5865, www.iguanalodge.com. 4 cabins, good swimming and surfing.

A La Choza del Manglares, right beside the mangrove on the river, T2735-5002, www.manglares.com. Clean, well-maintained cabins with private bath. In the day regular visits from monkeys, scarlet macaws and the occasional crocodile in the grounds by the river. Completely renovated.

A-B Agua Luna, facing pier, T2735-3593. Rooms sleeping 2-4 with bath, good, although pricey; restaurant next door.

A-B Cabinas Puerto Jiménez, on the gulf shore with good views, T2735-5090, www.cabinasjimenez.com. Remodelled big rooms, many with private decks looking out to the gulf, spotless. Wi-Fi internet access.

B-C Cabinas Marcelina, down main street, T2735-5007. With bath, big clean, friendly, nice front yard, totally renovated, small discount for youth hostelling members.

D Cabinas Bosque Mar, T2735-5681. Clean, large rooms and restaurant.

D Hotel Oro Verde, down main street, T2735-5241. Run by Silvia Duirós Rodríguez, 10 clean, comfortable rooms, with bath and fan, some overlooking the street.

D Iguana Iguana, on road leading out of town, T2735-5158. Simple rooms with private bath, restaurant, small bar, pool.

E Pizzería Cabinas Mariel, T2735-5071. Simple cabins.

F Cabinas Thompson, 50 m from the centre, T2735-5910. With bath, fan, clean but dark.

F Pensión Quintero, just off main street, T2735-5087. Very simple wooden building, but clean and good value; will store luggage. Ask for Fernando Quintero, who rents horses and has a boat for up to 6 passengers, good value; he is also a guide, recommended. Price per person.

Cabo Matapalo

LL Lapa Ríos Wilderness Resort, T2735-5130, www.laparios.com. The cream of the crop. Includes meals. 14 luxury palm-thatched bungalows on private 2400-ha reserve (80% virgin forest, US owners Karen and John Lewis), camping trips, boats can be arranged from Golfito. Idyllic, fantastic views, recommended.

AL-A El Remanso Rainforest Beach Lodge, Cabo Matapalo, T2735-5569, www.elremanso.com. Houses and cabins for rent, all fully equipped and with ocean views, an oasis of peace.

Bahía Drake p1255

LL Aguila de Osa Inn, the normal landing point, T2296-2190, www.aguiladeosa.com. Includes meals; fishing, hiking, canoeing and horse riding available, comfortable cabins made with exotic hardwoods. Recommended.

LL La Paloma Jungle Lodge, T2239-0954, www.lapalomalodge.com. Price per person includes meals. 9 cabins with bath, guided tours with resident biologist. Packages.

L Drake Bay Wilderness Camp, opposite Aguila de Osa Inn, T2770-8012, www.drakebay.com. Price per person, with meals, cabins, tents available, pleasant family atmosphere, pool, 2 restaurants. Great views. Wide range of tours available.

AL Cabinas Jinete de Osa, T2236-5637, www.costaricadiving.com. Good hotel, run by 2 brothers from Colorado. Diving a speciality, PADI courses offered. Spacious and airy rooms, all with bath, hot water, fan. Recommended.

AL-A Pirate Cove, northern end of the beach, T2786-7845, www.piratecove.com. Very nice tent-like cabins emulate an outdoor experience minus the mud. US$55

per person shared bath, US$70 with bath, 3 meals included.

B Rancho Corcovado Lodge, in the middle of the beach, T2786-7059. Price per person. Simple, rustic rooms, many with view, all with bath. Friendly Tico owners, nice open-air restaurant on beach serves *comida típica*. Camping permitted.

D Bella Vista Lodge, on the beach at the southern end of town, T2770-8051. The only budget option in town and disappointing. Basic rooms, 2 with bath, 3 shared (even more basic), meals (US$3-5) not included.

Camping

Camping is allowed outside **Rancho Corcovado** (use of electricity and bathrooms included) or outside **Pirate Cove** (north end of beach), no fixed price, small charge for baths.

Parque Nacional Corcovado p1255

MINAE office, facing the airstrip, Puerto Jiménez, T2735-5036. For booking dormitory accommodation and camping facilities in Corcovado National Park.

LL Casa Corcovado Jungle Lodge, along the coast from San Pedrillo, T2256-3181, www.casacorcovado.com. Outside the park in the forest, but with 500 m of beach more or less opposite Isla del Cano, 14 bungalows, many facilities, packages from 2 nights full board with boat transport (2 hrs) from Sierpe.

L-AL Corcovado Lodge, 30 mins' walk west of Carate along the beach, T2257-0766, www.costaricaexpeditions.com. 20 walk-in tents with 2 camp-beds in each, in a beautiful coconut grove with hammocks overlooking the beach; to be sure of space book through **Costa Rica Expeditions** in San José, see page 1160. Clean showers and toilets; good food, take a torch. Behind the camp is a trail into the jungle with a great view of the bay; many birds to be seen, plus monkeys and frogs.

A La Leona Eco-Lodge, 30 mins' walk west of Carate along the beach, T2735-5705, www.laleonaecolodge.com. Rustic tent cabins, crocodile spotting, rappelling, yoga and night hikes. Price per person.

F La Leona park wardens' station, at entrance to the park. Maximum 12 people in basic rooms or camping, meals available. Book in high season through SINAC.

F La Sirena, book through **MINAE**, Puerto Jiménez, near the airport, T2735-5036. In dorms, maximum 20 people (reservation essential), take sheets/sleeping bag. Also camping, no reservation needed, 3 meals available. Bring mosquito netting.

🍴 Eating

Puerto Jiménez *p1254, map p1254*
Ⅲ Agua Luna, on the seashore near the dock, T2735-5033. Stylish setting, beautifully presented but pricey.
Ⅲ Il Giardino, just off the main street. Quiet little Italian, intimate setting, and good food.
Ⅲ-Ⅱ Carolina, down the main street, T2735-5185. Highly recommended for fish (everything actually), good prices. **Escondido Trex** office at back of restaurant.
Ⅱ Juanita's Mexican Bar and Grille, central, T2735-5056. Happy hour, crab races, good Mexican fare, seafood from US$4.
Ⅰ Pollo Frito Opi Opi, north end of town, T2735-5192. Fried chicken, hamburgers, fries.
Ⅰ Soda Bosquemar, on main street, T2735-5681. Good food at good prices.

🥾 Activities and tours

Puerto Jiménez *p1254, map p1254*
Aventuras Tropicales, opposite the football pitch, T2735-5195, www.aventuras tropicales.com. Can book accommodation and has a couple of computers with internet.
Escondido Trex, in the back of **Carolina**, T2735-5210, www.escondidotrex.com. Excellent local information, treks, kayaking and jungle trips.

MINAE office, facing the airstrip, T2735-5036, for booking dormitory lodging and camping facilities in Corcovado National Park.
Tonsa Tours, see map. Run by the quiet Jaime, provides many of the normal tours, and also jungle treks across to Carate. Not for the faint-hearted, but certain to be fascinating.

🚌 Transport

Puerto Jiménez *p1254, map p1254*
Air There are daily flights to Puerto Jiménez and **Golfito** with Sansa (US$78) and Nature Air (US$65 1 way) from **San José**.

Bus 1 block west of the main street. A café by the bus terminal is open Sat 0430 for a cheap and reasonable breakfast. From **San José**, just outside Terminal Atlántico Norte (C 12, Av 9-11), there are 2 buses daily to Puerto Jiménez at 0600 and 1200 via San Isidro, US$7, 8 hrs, return 0500, T2735-5189. There are also buses from **San Isidro**, leaving from the Pan-American Hwy at 0930 and 1500, US$4.50, returns at 0400 and 1300, 5 hrs. To **Cd Neily** at 0500 and 1400, 3 hrs, US$3. A few *colectivos* to **Carate** depart from outside **Restaurant Carolina** daily 0530 and 0600, cost US$7. Service may be restricted in the wet season.

Sea There is a boat service between **Golfito** and Puerto Jiménez, leaving the dock in Golfito at 1130, US$2.50, 1½ hrs, returning at 0600, or chartering a water taxi for US$60, up to 8 passengers, is possible.

ℹ Directory

Puerto Jiménez *p1254, map p1254*
Banks Branch of Banco Nacional, T2735-5155. **Internet** Café El Sol, on main street, 0700-1900, US$8 per hr.
Post office Opposite the football pitch.

San José to the Atlantic

Heading east from San José, the Central Highlands quickly fall away to the sparsely populated flat Caribbean lowlands. The tropical rainforest national parks of Tortuguero and Barra del Colorado, leading through coastal canals and waterways, are a nature lover's paradise with easily arranged trips, normally from San José, into the rainforest. South of the distinctly Caribbean city of Puerto Limón, coastal communities have developed to provide comfortable hangouts and laid-back beach life for all budgets. ➡ *For listings, see pages 1271-1285.*

There are two routes from San José to Puerto Limón on the Atlantic coast. The newer main route goes over the Cordillera Central, through the Parque Nacional Braulio Carrillo down to Guápiles and Siquirres. This highland section is prone to fog and if driving yourself, requires extra care. The second, more scenic but considerably longer, route follows the old Atlantic railway to Cártago, south of Irazú volcano to Turrialba, joining the main highway at Siquirres.

Parque Nacional Braulio Carrillo → *Colour map 7, B3.*

The third largest of Costa Rica's national parks Parque Nacional Braulio Carrillo was created to protect the high rainforest north of San José from the impact of the San José–Guápiles–Puerto Limón highway. It extends for 47,583 ha, and encompasses five different types of forest with abundant wildlife including hundreds of species of bird, jaguar, ocelot and Baird's tapir. Various travel agencies offer naturalist tours, approximately US$65 from San José. San José to Guápiles and Puerto Limón buses go through the park.

The entrance to the **Quebrada González centre** ① *daily 0800-1530 US$7*, is on the highway, 23 km beyond the Zurquí tunnel, just over the Río Sucio at the Guápiles end and has an administration building. To get there, take any bus to the Atlantic and ask to be dropped off. There are three trails: **Las Palmas**, 1.6 km (you need rubber boots); across the road are **El Ceibo**, 1 km, circular; and **Botarrama**, entry 2 km from Quebrada González. The trail has good birdwatching and the views down the Río Patria canyon are impressive. The Zurquí centre near the tunnel has been closed but may open again soon so ask at headquarters. It has services and the 250-m Los Jilqueros trail to the river.

South Caribbean coast

Beyond Quebrada González (1.5 km) is **Los Heliconios** ① *entry US$7*, butterfly garden with an insect museum and amphibians. Adjoining it, **Reserva Turística El Tapir** ① *entry US$7*, has a 20-minute trail and others of one to two hours.

An ingenious **Rainforest Aerial Tram** ① *Tue-Sun 0630-1600, Mon 0900-1530, 90 mins' ride costs US$49.50, students with ID and children ½-price, children under 5 are not allowed*, lifts visitors high into the rainforest, providing a fascinating up-close and personal view of the canopy life. The price includes a guided nature walk. It's best to go as early as possible for birds. Tourist buses arrive 0800. There's a guarded car park for private vehicles and restaurant for meals in the park. It can be difficult to get reservations during the high season. There's a **Rainforest Aerial Tram office in San José** ① *Av 7, Calle 7, behind Aurola Holiday Inn, T2257-5961; there's an all-inclusive package from San José leaving around 0800 daily, US$78.50, students and under 11s US$53.75, with pickups at most major hotels.*

Parque Nacional Braulio Carrillo & Puerto Viejo loop

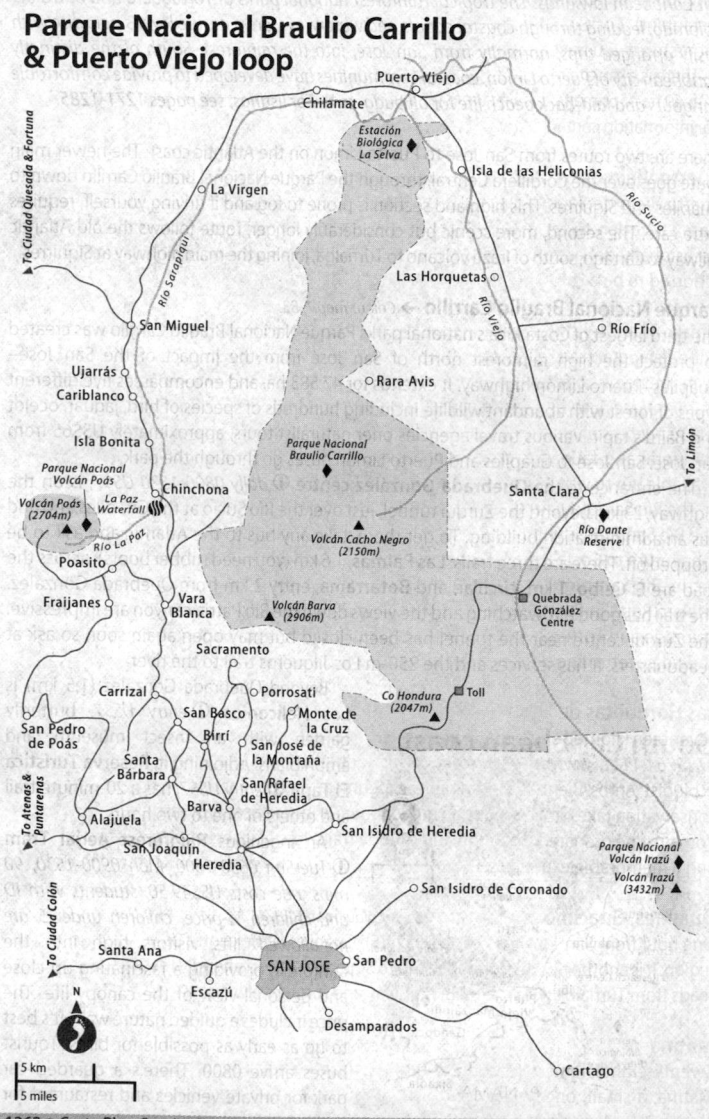

Further on, at the Soda Gallo Pinto is the **Bosque Lluvioso** ① *T2224-0819, daily 0700-1700, entry US$15*, a 170-ha private reserve. It is at Km 56 on the Guápiles highway (Rancho Redondo), with a restaurant and trails in primary and secondary forest.

The turn-off at Santa Clara to Puerto Viejo de Sarapiquí is 13 km before Guápiles. At the junction is **Rancho Robertos**, T2711-0050, a good, popular and reasonable roadside restaurant). For Guápiles see below. Nearby is a **Tropical Frog Garden**, an interesting short stop if you have the time.

There is a private reserve bordering the Parque Nacional Braulio Carrillo called **Río Danta**, with 60 ha of primary rainforest and short limited treks (US$4) arranged with meals (US$6-9). For information contact **Mawamba Group** ① *T2223-2421, must be pre-arranged, no drop-ins*.

Puerto Viejo de Sarapiquí → *Colour map 7, B3*.

Puerto Viejo de Sarapiquí is 40 km north of the San José–Limón highway and 20 km from La Virgen to the southwest. Once an important port on the Río Sarapiquí, only occasionally launches ply the Río Colorado to the Canales de Tortuguero. There is reported to be a cargo boat once a week to Barra del Colorado (no facilities, bring your own food, hammock, sleeping bag), and on to Moín, about 10 km by road from Puerto Limón. There is little traffic, so you will need luck and a fair amount of cash. There is good fishing on the Río Sarapiquí.

In the neighbourhood is **La Selva Biological Station** ① *T2766-6565, www.ots.ac.cr, 3½-hr guided natural history walk with bilingual naturalists daily at 0800 and 1330-1600, US$36 per person*, on the Río Puerto Viejo, run by the Organization for Tropical Studies. The floral and faunal diversity is unbelievable. Several guided and self-led walks are available but to visit it is essential to book in advance. Accommodation is also available.

The Río Sarapiquí flows into the San Juan, forming the northern border of Costa Rica. The Río San Juan is wholly in Nicaragua, so you technically have to cross the border and then return to Costa Rica. This will cost US$5 and you will need a passport and visa. Trips on the **Río Sarapiquí** and on the **Río Sucio** are beautiful (US$15 for two hours); contact William Rojas in Puerto Viejo (T2766-6108) for trips on the Río Sarapiquí or to Barra del Colorado and Tortuguero. There is a regular boat service to Tortuguero on Monday and Thursday, returning on Tuesday and Friday, costing US$55 per person.

Las Horquetas de Sarapiquí

Seventeen kilometres south of Puerto Viejo, near Las Horquetas de Sarapiquí, is **Rara Avis** ① *T2764-1111, www.rara-avis.com*, rustic lodges in a 600-ha forest reserve owned by ecologist Amos Bien. This admirable experiment in educating visitors about rainforest conservation takes small groups on guided tours (rubber boots provided), led by biologists. You must be prepared for rough and muddy trails, lots of insects but great birdwatching and a memorable experience.

Guápiles, Guácimo and Siquirres → *Colour map 7, B3/4*.

One hour from San José (bus costs US$1.45), Guápiles is the centre of the Río Frío banana region. It is another 25 km from Guácimo to Siquirres, a clean, friendly town and junction for roads from Turrialba with the main highway and former railways.

Matina

Twenty-eight kilometres beyond Siquirres, heading north at the 'techo rojo' junction is Matina, a small, once-busy town on the railway but off the highway. Today, it is an access point to Tortuguero and the less well-known private **Reserva Natural Pacuare**, 30 km north of Puerto Limón, which is accessible by canal from Matina. Run by Englishman John Denham, it has a 6-km stretch of **leatherback turtle nesting beach**, protected and guarded by the reserve. Volunteers patrol the beach in May and June, measuring and tagging these magnificent marine turtles (US$50 per person per week, includes good meals and accommodation). For volunteer work, contact Carlos Fernández, **Corporación de Abogados** ① *Av 8-10, Calle 19, No 837, San José, T2233-0508, fdezlaw@racsa.co.cr, organization information at www.turtleprotection.org.*

Puerto Limón and the Atlantic coast ⊖❼❶❻ ›› pp1271-1285.

On a rocky outcrop on an almost featureless coastline, Puerto Limón is the country's most important port. Between Puerto Limón and the Río San Juan on the Nicaraguan border, the long stretch of Atlantic coastline and its handful of small settlements is linked by a canal system that follows the coastline. The region encompasses Parque Nacional Tortuguero, famed for its wildlife and turtle nesting beaches, and Refugio Nacional de Fauna Silvestre Barra del Colorado. The Río San Juan forms the border between Costa Rica and Nicaragua, however the border is not mid-river, but on the Costa Rican bank. English is widely spoken along the coast.

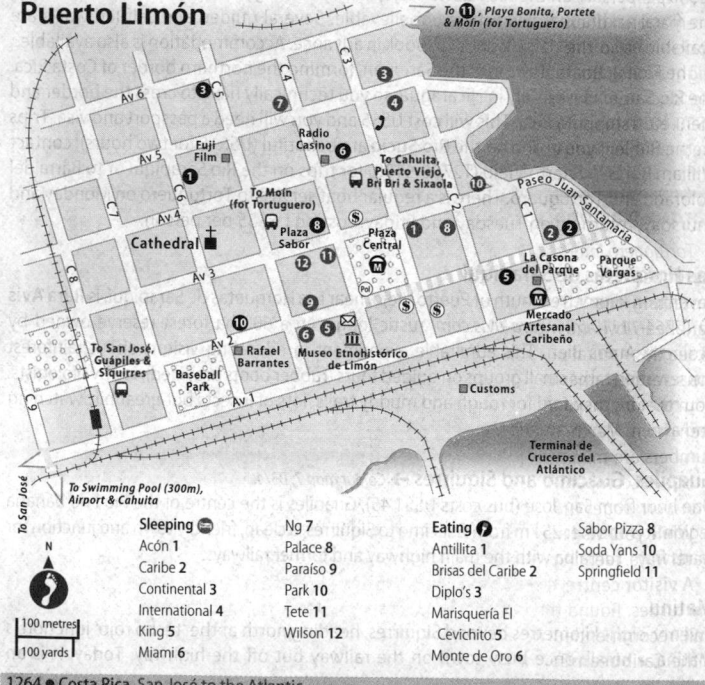

Puerto Limón

To ⑪ , Playa Bonita, Portete & Moín (for Tortuguero)

To Cahuita, Puerto Viejo, Bri Bri & Sixaola

Paseo Juan Santamaría

To Moín (for Tortuguero)

Fuji Film

Radio Casino

Plaza Sabor

Plaza Central

Cathedral

La Casona del Parque

Parque Vargas

Mercado Artesanal Caribeño

To San José, Guápiles & Siquirres

Rafael Barrantes

Baseball Park

Museo Etnohistórico de Limón

Customs

Terminal de Cruceros del Atlántico

To San José

To Swimming Pool (300m), Airport & Cahuita

100 metres
100 yards

Sleeping		**Eating**	
Acón 1	Ng 7	Antillita 1	Sabor Pizza 8
Caribe 2	Palace 8	Brisas del Caribe 2	Soda Yans 10
Continental 3	Paraíso 9	Diplo's 3	Springfield 11
International 4	Park 10	Marisquería El	
King 5	Tete 11	Cevichito 5	
Miami 6	Wilson 12	Monte de Oro 6	

Puerto Limón → *Colour map 7, B4.*

Built on the site of the ancient indigenous village of Cariari, Columbus dropped anchor at Punta Uvita, the island off the coastline, on his fourth and final voyage. The climate is very humid and it rains almost every day. With a mainly black population and a large Chinese contingent, the town has a distinctly Caribbean feel, expressed particularly during carnival but in most bars every weekend.

Parque Vargas and the seafront promenade at the rocky headland are popular places for social gatherings and killing time, making for ideal people-watching territory, especially in the evening. Parque Vargas, sadly rather run-down, is an impressive botanical display with a colourful mural depicting the history of Limón and a bandstand.

On the upside, the nightlife is good, particularly for Caribbean music and dancing, culminating in carnival every October, Costa Rica's largest festival. There is a small **Museo Etnohistórico de Limón** ① *Calle 2, Av 2, Mon-Fri 0900-1200, 1300-1600*, featuring material relating to Columbus' arrival in Limón. The cargo docks are still active with international crews making regular journeys, as well as being the landing point for pristine floating palaces cruising the Caribbean. The **carnival**, which takes place just before 12 October, is Costa Rica's biggest; it's crowded and prices rise, but it's definitely worth seeing.

Around Puerto Limón

Playa Bonita and **Portete** have pleasant beaches about 5 km along the coastal road from Puerto Limón. **Moín**, a further 1.5 km east along the road, is the sight of the international docks, which exports some 2.8 million bunches of bananas annually. The docks are also the departure point for barges to Tortuguero and Barra del Colorado (eight hours). Boats also run from Moín to Tortuguero (see below) and may be hired at the dockside. Buses run to Moín every 40 minutes from 0600-1740, 30 minutes, US$0.10. If shipping a vehicle, check which dock. Some simple accommodation options are available if you end up waiting here.

Parque Nacional Tortuguero 🌐🚹🚰🚻 » *pp1271-1285. Colour map 7, B4.*

① *Tortuguero Information Centre, T8833-0827, safari@racsa.co.cr.*

Tortuguero is a 29,068-ha national park, with a marine extension of over 50,000 ha, protecting the Atlantic nesting sites of the green and leatherback turtle and the Caribbean lowland rainforest inland. As with much of Costa Rica, getting the timing right to see this natural phenomenon is essential. The green turtles lay their eggs at night on the scrappy, rather untidy beach from June to October, with the hatchlings emerging from the depths of their sandy nests until November at the latest. Leatherbacks can be seen from March to June. Hawksbill and loggerheads also nest at Tortuguero but numbers are minimal. Trips to look for nesting turtles are carefully monitored and you must be accompanied by a licensed guide at all times. » *For details, see Tour operators and Transport, pages 1281 and 1283.*

While your visit may not coincide with those of the turtles, the canals of jungle fringed waterways, teeming with bird and insect life, behind the beach are always a pleasure.

A **visitor centre**, close to the village of Tortuguero, has information on the park and the turtles. Round the back of the headquarters there is a well-marked 1.4-km nature trail, recommended. In the centre is a small gift shop. To the northern end of the village is the **Caribbean Conservation Corporation**, which has played a fundamental role in

Sixaola

Costa Rican immigration Straightforward crossing, with formalities either side of the bridge. The border is open 0700-1700. They shut for lunch for 45 minutes on Saturday and Sunday. The immigration office is just before the railway bridge, over the river Sixaola, which marks the border with Panama. Panama is one hour ahead of Costa Rica.

Sleeping At the entrance to town is Imperio (**E**), eight basic cabins with ventilator, shared bath; and Cabinas Sánchez (**E**), T2754-2105, clean and tidy, best option.

Transport Moving on in Panama, the simplest and most enjoyable option is to get a taxi to Changuinola Marine Terminal for the fast boat along the Snyder Canal to Bocas del Toro. A railway runs to Almirante (Panama) from Guabito, on the Panamanian side. If crossing to Panama take the earliest bus possible to Sixaola (see Panama, North-western Caribbean coast, page 1376). Direct San José–Sixaola from Terminal del Caribe, Autotransportes Mepe (T2221-0524), 0600, 1000, 1400 and 1600, return 0600, 0800, 1000 and 1500, 5½ hours. Also six daily from Puerto Limón (Radio Casino), four hours.

Banks There are no banks in Sixaola, but you can change money in the supermarket. Rates, especially to the US dollar, are very poor. Shops near the border in Panama will accept colones but shops in Changuinola and beyond do not. Dollars are used as national currency in Panama.

---

the creation and continued research of the turtle nesting grounds. There's an interesting and very informative **natural history museum** ① *T2224-9215 (San José), www.cccturtle.org, daily 1000-1200, 1400-1730, donation US$1*. Information about all this and more can be found on the village website, www.tortugerovillage.com.

A guide is required for trips along the beach at night and recommended for trips through the waterways. Do not swim at Tortuguero as there area sharks. If travelling with a lodge, tours will be arranged for you. If organizing independently, contact the information kiosk in the village for instructions and to link up with a registered guide. To visit the turtles at night you must pay US$7 park entrance fee, and US$5 each for a guide. A guide and tour in no way guarantees you will see a turtle or hatchlings.

Tours through the water channels are the best way to see the rainforest, ideally in a boat without a motor. The canal, bordered with primary rainforest, gives way to smaller channels, and, drifting slowly through forest darkened streams, the rainforest slowly comes alive with wildlife including birds – over half of those found in Costa Rica – monkeys, sloths and, for the lucky, alligators, tapirs, jaguars, ocelots, peccaries, anteaters and even manatees. You can hire a canoe and guide for about US$6 per hour per person in a boat without motor, or US$12 with a motor, minimum of four people. Night tours cost US$15 per person per hour. Fishing tours, with all equipment included, cost US$35 per person, with a minimum of two people. Take insect repellent. ▶▶ *See Tour operators, page 1281.*

Barra del Colorado ●● ▶▶ *pp1271-1285.*

The canals are part artificial, part natural; originally they were narrow lagoons running parallel to the sea separated by a small strip of land. Now the lagoons are linked, and it is

Border essentials: Costa Rica–Nicaragua

Barra del Colorado
Costa Rican immigration This is not a regular border crossing and there are no formal facilities on the Costa Rican side. Do not leave for Nicaragua by boat or on foot without checking with the Guardia Civil in Barra del Colorado or Tortuguero, who are very helpful. Similarly, check with them if arriving from Nicaragua.
Transport Transport is available on a twice weekly boat services between Puerto Viejo de Sarapiqui and Tortuguero on Tuesdays and Fridays, US$55. Privately hired boats will be expensive, unless you can hitch a ride with a local boat service.

possible to sail as far as Barra del Colorado, in the extreme northeast of Costa Rica, 25 km beyond Tortuguero. They pass many settlements. The town is divided by the river, the main part being on the northern bank. Secluded and difficult to get to, the **Refugio Nacional de Fauna Silvestre Barra del Colorado** (81,213 ha) is a national wildlife refuge. The reserve and the Parque Nacional Tortuguero share some boundaries, making for a far more effective protected zone. The fame of the region's fauna extends to the waters, which are world-renowned for fishing.

Once across the Río Colorado (which in fact is the south arm of the Río San Juan delta), you can walk to Nicaragua (see under Nicaragua, San Juan del Norte, page 1117) along the coast, but it is a long 30-km beach walk, take food and lots of water. Most hikers overnight en route. Seek advice before setting out.

South from Puerto Limón ⊙❶❷❸▲❺❻ ⇒ pp1271-1285.

Penshurst
South of Limón, a paved road shadows the coastline normally separated by little more than a thin line of palms. Beyond Penshurst is the **Hitoy Cerere Biological Reserve**. If you have time, camping is easy in the hills and there are plenty of rivers for swimming. Further south the road leads to Cahuita, Puerto Viejo and on towards Manzanillo – all sleepy beach towns, with lively centres, comfortable hideaways, and coastal and nature opportunities to explore. If heading for the border, heading inland just north of Puerto Viejo takes you through Bri Bri and on to Sixaola.

From Penshurst it is 11.5 km to **Cahuita**; this stretch of the road is paved to the edge of Cahuita.

Cahuita and Parque Nacional Cahuita → Colour map 7, B4.
ⓘ *Entry to the park US$7. The official entrance to the park is at Puerto Vargas, about 5 km south of Cahuita, where the park headquarters, a nature trail, camping facilities and toilets are situated. Take the bus to Km 5, then turn left at the sign. You can enter the park for free from the southern side of Cahuita, which is ideal for relaxing on the beach, but leave a donation. If you have the option, visit during the week when it is quieter. There is a tourist complex in the area, and the restaurant Marisquería, at Puerto Vargas park entrance, is an Italian, with a jovial host who also has rooms.*
The small town of Cahuita hides 1 km back from the main road, and enjoys a sleepy feel. A laid-back community, it's a good place to hide away in one of the secluded spots or to

party in the centre of town. North of the town there is a beautiful black-sand beach ideal for swimming or just lazing about in a hammock, while to the south is the national park. Most people stay in Cahuita to explore the park.

Cahuita National Park (1068 ha) is a narrow strip of beach protecting a coral reef off shore and a marine area of 22,400 ha. The length of the beach can be walked in about three hours, and passes endless coconut palms and interesting tropical forest, through which there is also a path. It is hot and humid, so take drinking water, but a wide range of fauna can be seen, as well as howler monkeys, white face monkeys, coatis, snakes, butterflies and hermit crabs. Over 500 species of fish inhabit the surrounding waters and reef tours are available. An old Spanish shipwreck can be seen and reached without a boat. Snorkellers should take care to stay away from the coral, which is already badly damaged by agricultural chemicals and other pollutants. The park extends from the southern limit of Cahuita town southeast to Puerto Vargas.

Note Cahuita and Puerto Viejo have suffered from what locals believe is a lack of support and investment from central government. An undercurrent of problems, partially

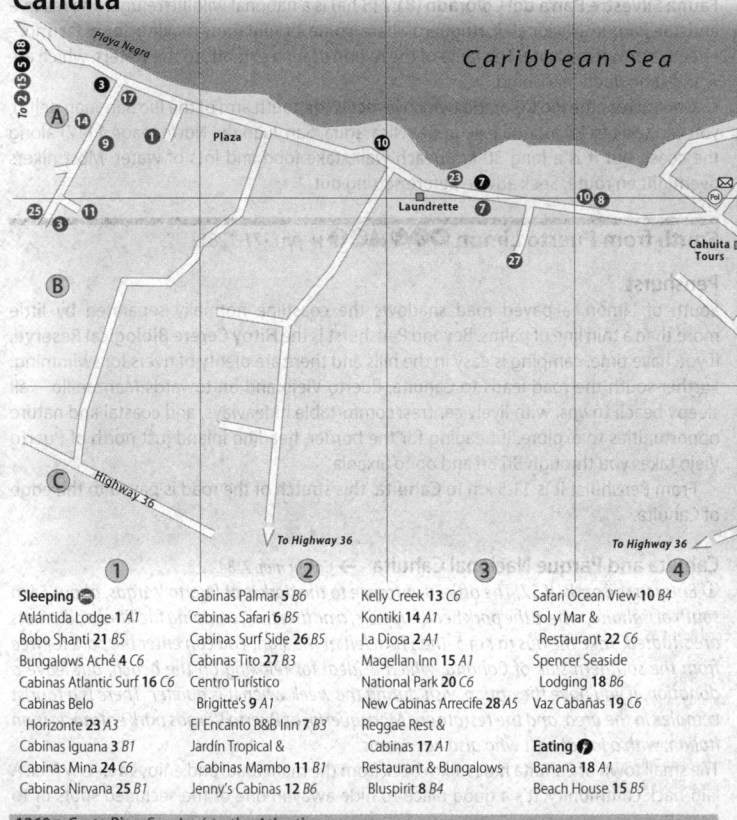

Cahuita

Sleeping	Cabinas Palmar **5** *B6*	Kelly Creek **13** *C6*	Safari Ocean View **10** *B4*
Atlántida Lodge **1** *A1*	Cabinas Safari **6** *B5*	Kontiki **14** *A1*	Sol y Mar &
Bobo Shanti **21** *B5*	Cabinas Surf Side **26** *B5*	La Diosa **2** *A1*	Restaurant **22** *C6*
Bungalows Aché **4** *C6*	Cabinas Tito **27** *B3*	Magellan Inn **15** *A1*	Spencer Seaside
Cabinas Atlantic Surf **16** *C6*	Centro Turístico	National Park **20** *C6*	Lodging **18** *B6*
Cabinas Belo	Brigitte's **9** *A1*	New Cabinas Arrecife **28** *A5*	Vaz Cabañas **19** *C6*
Horizonte **23** *A3*	El Encanto B&B Inn **7** *B3*	Reggae Rest &	
Cabinas Iguana **3** *B1*	Jardín Tropical &	Cabinas **17** *A1*	Eating
Cabinas Mina **24** *C6*	Cabinas Mambo **11** *B1*	Restaurant & Bungalows	Banana **18** *A1*
Cabinas Nirvana **25** *B1*	Jenny's Cabinas **12** *B6*	Bluspirit **8** *B4*	Beach House **15** *B5*

based on the perception that everyone on the Caribbean coast takes drugs, does mean that you may be offered drugs. If you are not interested, just say no.

Puerto Viejo de Talamanca → *Colour map 7, B4.*

Puerto Viejo is a good base and a quietly happening party town, with a number of good beaches stretching out to the south. Activities in the area are numerous and you could spend many days exploring the options. There is reef diving nearby, or you can head south to Mandoca for lagoon diving from canoes. Surfers seek out the glorious **Salsa Brava** wave, which peaks from December to February. Away from the beach, nature trips range from tough treks in Gandoca–Manzanillo Wildlife Refuge (see below) through to gentle strolls around the self-guided botanical gardens to the north of town. There are also several cultural trips to KeKöLdi and BriBri indigenous reserves and options to take dug-outs to the inland town of Yorkin. The **Asociación Talamanqueña de Ecoturism y Conservación** ① *ATEC, T2750-0191, www.ateccr.org,* provides tourist information, sells locally made crafts and T-shirts, and also offers guide services, rainforest hikes, snorkelling and fishing trips. The **South Caribbean Music Festival** takes place in the lead up to Easter.

Around Puerto Viejo

There are a number of popular beaches southeast along the road from Puerto Viejo. Traffic is limited, buses occasional, but it is walkable. About 4 km away is **Playa Cocles**, which has some of the best surfing on this coast, and 2 km further on is **Playa Chiquita**, with many places to stay. Next is **Punta Uva**, beyond which, after another 5 km, you arrive in **Manzanillo**, followed by white-sand beaches and rocky headlands to **Punta Mona** and the **Gandoca–Manzanillo Wildlife Refuge** ① *ANAI, T2224-6090,* a celebration of Costa Rican diversity largely left alone by prospectors and tourists alike. Among other projects, marine scientists are studying protecting the giant leatherback turtle. Volunteer work is possible.

Bribri

At **Hotel Creek**, north of Puerto Viejo, the paved road heads through the hills to the village of Bribri, at the foot of the Talamanca Range Indigenous Reserve. Halfway between is **Violeta's Pulpería**. From Limón, **Aerovías Talamaqueñas**

N

100 metres
100 yards

School

Laundrette

& Willies Tours

Roberto's Tours

To Coastal Path

Parque Nacional Cahuita

Cha Cha Cha 2 *B5*
Chao's Paradise 3 *A1*
Coral Reef 1 *B5*
La Casa Creole 5 *A1*
Le Fe 8 *B5*
Mango Tango Pizzeria 17 *B5*
Miss Edith's 6 *A4*
Palenque Luisa 4 *B5*
Pastry Shop 7 *B3*
Relax & Rikki's Bar 13 *B5*

Sobre las Olas 10 *A2*
Soda Priscilla 16 *C6*

Bars & clubs
Cocos 14 *B5* ●

Indígenas fly cheaply to **Amubri** in the reserve (there is a *casa de huéspedes* run by nuns in Amubri). Villages such as Bribri, Chase, Bratsi, Shiroles and San José Cabécar can be reached by bus from Cahuita. Several buses daily to Bribri from Limón. Continuing south is Sixaola, on the border with Panama (see page 1266).

Puerto Viejo de Talamanca

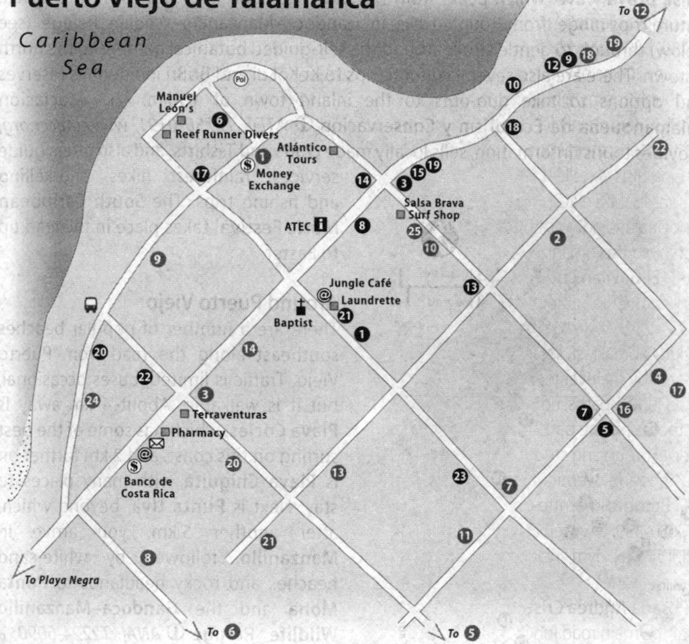

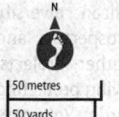

Caribbean Sea
Pol
Manuel León's
Reef Runner Divers
Atlántico Tours
Money Exchange
ATEC
Salsa Brava Surf Shop
Jungle Café
Laundrette
Baptist
Terraventuras
Pharmacy
Banco de Costa Rica
To Playa Negra
To 6
To 5
To 12

N
50 metres
50 yards

Sleeping
Bull Inn 20
Cabinas Casa Verde 2
Cabinas Grant 3
Cabinas Lika 21
Cabinas Los Almendros 1
Cabinas Popular 17
Cabinas Soda Mitchell 16
Cabinas Tropical 4
Cabinas Yucca 19
Cashew Hill 5
Coco Loco Lodge 6
Fortaleza 14
Guaraná 13
Jacaranda 7
Las Olas Camping & Cabinas 18
Los Sueños 8
Maritza 9
Puerto Viejo 10
Pura Vida 11
Rocking J's 12
Tamandua Lodge 22

Eating
Amimodo 9
Bread & Chocolate 1
El Parquecito 3
Hot Rocks 14
Jammin Juices & Jerk Chicken 17
La Terraza 15
Lidia's Place 5
Monchies 23
Pan Pay 6
Peace & Love Coffee 22
Pizza Boruca 21
Pizzeria Rusticone 13
Pollo Frito 18
Red Stripe Café 20
Salsa Brava 12
Soda Miss Sam 7
Soda Palmer 19
Stanford's 10
Tamara 8

Bars & clubs
Baba Yaga 25
Sunset 24

For Sleeping and Eating price codes and other relevant information, see Essentials pages 45-48.

Sleeping

Puerto Viejo de Sarapiquí *p1263*

AL Selva Verde Lodge, out of town, heading west a few kilometres towards La Virgen, T2766-6800, www.holbrooktravel.com. On over 200 ha of virgin rainforest reserve, 40 double rooms, 5 bungalows for 4, includes meals, caters mainly for tour groups. Sensitively set in among the rainforest, evening lectures by biologists, excellent for birdwatchers and naturalists with extensive trail system, rafting, canoeing and riding through property; tours with biologists organized.

AL-B El Gavilán Lodge, on the southern bank of the Río Sarapiquí, reached by taxi, T2234-9507, www.gavilanlodge.com. Includes breakfast, set in 100-ha private reserve by the river pier, good restaurant, good jungle paths, riding and river tours, 12 rooms private bath, garden jacuzzi, special group and student/researcher rates, day trips and overnight trips from San José.

A El Bambú, in centre north of park, T2766-6359, www.elbambu.com. Bath, fan, TV, pool, gym, including breakfast, very pleasant.

B Posada Andrea Cristina, just out of town near the main road junction, T2766-6265, www.andreacristina.com. Comfortable small cabins, set amongst tropical gardens. Good local knowledge.

C Mi Lindo Sarapiquí, overlooking park, T2766-6074. Has 6 spotless rooms with bath, fan, hot water and restaurant downstairs. Recommended.

E Cabinas Monteverde, next to El Bambú, T2766-6236. Bath, restaurant, but pretty dirty.

E Hospedaje Gonar, on road to the dock above hardware store (*ferretería*) without signpost, T8844-4677. Basic rooms, ones with windows slightly better. Shared bath, pretty dirty.

Las Horquetas de Sarapiquí *p1263*

AL River-Edge Cabin and **Waterfall Lodge**, T2764-3131, www.rara-avis.com. Accommodation at Rara Avis, the Lodge is beautiful 8-room jungle lodge in an idyllic setting, the Cabin is deeper in the rainforest for even more seclusion. There is also treetop accommodation and rates for backpackers at Las Casitas.

Guápiles, Guácimo and Siquirres *p1263*

A Casa Río Blanco, Guápiles, about 6 km west of Guápiles look out for the big yellow road sign on, take first right before the Río Blanco bridge and follow signpost for 1 km, T2710-4124, www.casarioblanco.com. Accommodates 12 guests in comfortable cabins, with breakfast, run by Herbie and Annette from Amsterdam. Beautiful gardens and a great spot for people interested in the environment. Recommended.

B Río Palmas, Guácimo, 1 km past EARTH School, T2760-0330. Has 30 rooms, private bathroom, pool, restaurant. The 200-ha property includes ornamental plant farm and rainforest.

C Cabinas Car, Guápiles, 50 m west of church, T2710-0035. Has 10 clean, tidy rooms, with private bath, hot water, fan and TV.

C Centro Turístico Pacuare, Siquirres, T2768-6482. Renovated, with large pool.

C Centro Turístico Río Blanco, Guápiles, on main road at entrance to town, T2710-7857. With bath, fan. Recommended.

D Alcema, Siquirres, 50 m east of market, T2768-6004. Some dark rooms, with fan, clean, shared bath.

D Cabinas de Oro, Guápiles, northeast of bus terminal, T2710-6663. Clean rooms, private bath with hot water, cheaper without. Restaurant nearby.

D Don Quito, 3.5 km towards Siquirres, T2768-8533. Pleasant, good restaurant.

E Hotel Alfaro (El Tunel), Guápiles, 50 m west of bus terminal, T2710-6293. Simple rooms, no frills, but clean. Open 24 hrs, with a rather funky aluminium stairway. Good value.

Puerto Limón *p1265, map p1264*
Beware of theft at night, and remember it is a port; there are a lot of drunks roaming the streets.
A-B Park, Av 3, Calle 1-2, T2798-0555. Neat little hotel with 34 rooms, sea-facing rooms, quiet and cool, restaurant good.
B-C Acón, on corner of main square, Calle 3, Av 3, T2758-1010. Big rooms with private bath, a/c, clean, safe, good restaurant, a bit run-down, popular daily disco **Aquarius** except Mon.
B-C Caribe, facing Parque Vargas, Av 2, Calle 1-2, T2758-0138. Big, immaculate rooms with private bath, hot water and big fan. Good deal.
C-D Miami, next to King on Av 2, Calle 4-5, T2758-0490. Has 35 rooms, all with private bath, some with a/c, others with fans. Secure and efficient. Credit cards accepted.
C-D Tete, 1 block west of main square, Av 3, Calle 4-5, T2758-1122. Clean rooms, bright and good beds. Some rooms sleeping up to 6 and some with balconies overlooking the square.
D Palace, 1 block north of bus stops, Calle 2-3, Av 2. Family-run hotel, with 33 mostly big rooms. Pretty clean, balcony overlooking street, popular with travellers and good place to make up groups for Tortuguero.
D-E International, opposite the Continental, Av 5, Calle 2-3, T2758-0434. Private bath, some with a/c other with fan, good deal.
E Continental, a little north of the centre, Av 5, Calle 2-3, T2798-0532. Has 25 big, good and clean rooms with ceiling fans.
E King, next to post office near main square on Av 2, T2758-1033. Simple rooms, pretty dark, but clean and secure.
F Hotel Wilson, on street west of main square, Av 3, Calle 4-5, T2758-5028. Clean, tidy and central, OK.

F Ng, Calle 4, Av 5-6, T2758-2134. Has 15 basic rooms some with bath, cheaper without. Basic and a bit untidy, but friendly. Price per person. Good for the price.
F Paraíso, Av 2, Calle 4-5. Plyboard partitions divide a once-beautiful house into tiny, dark, box rooms. Hard core roughing it and a little sad.

Parque Nacional Tortuguero *p1265*
Top-end hotels normally target package deals; walk-in rates given where available. There are many cheap *cabañas* in town; the boatmen or villagers will help you find them. Staying in town is better for the local economy.

In town
B Casa Marbella, in front of the Catholic church, T2709-8011, http://casamarbella. tripod.com. B&B with 4 small rooms, with private bath. Run by local guide Daryl Loth. Good source of information and in the centre of the village.
B Miss Junie's, T2709-8102. Has 12 good cabins at the north end of town.
D Cabinas Tortuguero, T2709-8114, tinamon@racsa.co.cr. 5 little cabins, each sleeping 3 with private bath, pleasant little garden with hammocks. Nice spot.
D Yoruki Lodge, T2709-8068. Clean, simple rooms looking over the river.
D-E Cabinas Sabina's, T2709-8069. Winding down, the end of an era, with just 16 rooms remaining. Good views looking out over to the Caribbean.
D-E Mary Scar, T2711-0671. Basic stuff: foam mattresses, but friendly enough if things elsewhere are full.

Out of town
Places out of town, best visited as part of a package, include:
LL Jungle Lodge Hotel, north end of the lagoon, T2233-0133, www.grupopapagayo. com. 50 big, wooden panelled rooms, complete with pool, wet bar, games room and disco.

L Tortuga Lodge, T2257-0766 (San José), www.costaricaexpeditions.com. Price per person Includes meals. Very comfortable accommodation, in big rooms each with veranda or balcony.

AL Mawamba Lodge, T2293-8181, www.grupomawamba.com. Comfortable cabins with fans, pool, walking distance to town. Turtle beaches are behind property.

AL Pachira Lodge, across the canal from the town, T2223-1682, www.pachiralodge.com. 3-day/2-night package includes transport, food, tours with bilingual guide, US$269.

AL Turtle Beach Lodge, T2248-0707, www.turtlebeachlodge.com. 2- to 7-day packages from US$210 in 48 ha of beautifully landscaped tropical grounds.

A Laguna Lodge, T2225-3740, www.laguna tortuguero.com. 50-odd cabins, with bath and fan, restaurant, bar, beautiful gardens, pool and conference room.

B Caribbean Paradise, 1 channel back from Tortuguero, T2223-0238 (difficult to reach, try going direct when you arrive). Run by Tico Carlos and his wife Ana, includes 3 meals. 16 simple rooms, no set itinerary, personal service, activities as you want them. A refreshing change from the general offering and very enjoyable.

B El Manati, T2534-7256. Tico family-run, simple rooms with a terrace. Relaxing spot, work with Ecole Travel in San José. Price includes breakfast, good value.

B-E Tortuguero Caribe Lodge, near Ilan Ilan, T2385-4676. Offers 10 simple cabins, friendly Tico-run and owned. Book direct or as package through **Ecole Travel** in San José. More expensive price includes breakfast and dinner.

D Ilan Ilan, through the **Agencia Mitur** in San José, T2296-7378, www.ilan-ilan lodge.com. All-inclusive packages, simple rooms in a line, with small terrace. Pool, jacuzzi and riverside bar. 2-day pacakage US$160. Recommended.

F Caño Palma Biological Station, 6 km north of Tortuguero, administered by the **Canadian Organization for Tropical Education and Rainforest Conservation** (in Canada T905-683-2116). Basic rooms for volunteer staff. Price per person, Includes meals. A good place for serious naturalists or just for unwinding, accommodation for up to 16 in wooden cabin, freshwater well for drinking and washing. Minimum stay 2 weeks.

Camping
You can sometimes camp at the national park office for US$2.50.

Barra del Colorado *p1266*
L Silver King Lodge, T2711-0708, www.silver kinglodge.com. Price per person. Deluxe sport-fishing hotel, 5-night packages includes flights, meals, rooms with bath, a/c, pool.

D Tarponland Lodge, T2710-2141. Cabins, run by Guillermo Cunningham, very helpful and knowledgeable. If you have a tent you may be able to camp at **Soda La Fiesta**, lots of mosquitoes.

Penshurst *p1267*
AL Los Aviarios del Caribe, 30 km south of Limón just north of Penshurst, T2750-0775, www.slothrescue.org. A sloth rescue sanctuary with a small nature reserve. The friendly owners offer canoe trips in the Estrella river delta and there's a volunteer programme if you have time to spare. They also have a number of comfortable rooms. Recommended.

AL Selva Bananita Lodge, 20 km from Puerto Limón at Cerro Mochila heading inland at Bananito, T2253-8118, www.selva bananito.com. 7 cabins on secluded farm, solar heating, primary rainforest tours, tree climbing, horses and bikes to rent.

Cahuita and Parque Nacional Cahuita *p1267, map p1268*
Beware of theft on the beach and drug pushers who may be undercover police.

L-A La Diosa, Playa Grande, past Playa Negra, T2755-0055, www.hotelladiosa.net. Colourful bungalows with luxury jacuzzi, a/c, private hot water bath, hammocks, pool, gym, massage, games room, internet, surf/kayak equipment – all this and on the beach. Cheaper out of season.

AL La Casa de las Flores, Cahuita, T2755-0326, www.lacasadelasflores hotel.com. Centrally located, this Italian-run hotel is modern and very clean. The black and white minimalism is quite harsh in the bedrooms.

AL Magellan Inn, 2 km north of Cahuita, T2755-0035, www.magellaninn.com. Includes breakfast, 6 beautifully decorated rooms with bath and fan, and 10,000-year-old pool (honestly) set in peaceful gardens and with renowned French Creole restaurant.

AL-A El Encanto Bed and Breakfast Inn, Playa Negra, T2755-0113, www.elencantobed andbreakfast.com. Attractive place built by very stylish French owners, among shady gardens with pool. 3 bungalows with private bath, hot water, fan, mosquito net, terrace and hammocks and 1 3-bedroom apartment. Yoga and massage are available.

AL-C Kayas Place, Playa Negra, T2750-0690, www.kayasplace.com. Beautifully hand built with reclaimed wood, each room is a little different and accommodation ranges from simple to more luxurious *cabinas*. Opposite the beach, a nice chilled spot.

A Resort style Atlántida Lodge, Playa Negra, north of Cahuita, on the main road, T755-0115. With private bath and ceiling fan. Pleasant gardens, pool, jacuzzi, massage, safe parking for cars and motorcycles. Bar and restaurant onsite.

A-B Bungalows Aché, by the entrance to the national park, T2755-0119, www.bunga lowsache.com. A little off the beaten track in a very tranquil and attractive location. Well-kept bungalows with private hot water bath, mosquito nets, coffee maker, fridge and hammocks, friendly owners.

A-C Jardín Tropical and Cabinas Mambo, Playa Negra, north of Cahuita, T2755-0033, http://jardintropical.ch. 2 decent bungalows sleeping 2-4, or a house with kitchen for 5. Poison dart frogs in the gardens.

B Kelly Creek, within a couple of blocks of the centre of town, by entrance to national

park, T2755-0007, kellycr@racsa.co.cr. Large rooms with veranda, ceiling fan to assist fresh sea breezes, good service and great spot.

B-C Cabinas Iguana, 800 m north of Cahuita, T2755-0005. Swiss-owned, very friendly, cabins or houses to rent, kitchen, fan, mosquito netting, balcony, clean, waterfall-fed pool, nice location. Big 2-for-1 book swap. Very good value. Recommended.

C Cabinas Palmar, down a little road from the bus stop which goes straight to the seafront, T2755-0243. Tico-run, clean, good, friendly and very helpful. Internet café.

C Cabinas Tito, Playa Negra, north of Cahuita, T2755-0286. Clean, quiet cabins sleeping 2-3, good for families, good value.

C Jenny's Cabinas, heading to the beach, T2755-0256. Balconies with view, Canadian owned, bath, fan, breakfast available, running water, close to the sea but surrounding area a bit scruffy.

C Spencer Seaside Lodging, on beach close to Jenny's Cabinas, T2755-0027. Beachfront basic rooms, internet, community kitchen. Price per person.

C-D Cabinas Atlantic Surf, south end of town near the beach, T2755-0116. Wooden hotel with communal balconies and hammocks and relaxed vibe. Rooms come with private hot water bath, fan and mosquito nets.

C-D Centro Turístico Brigitte's, Playa Negra, north of Cahuita, down a small track, T2755-0053, www.brigittecahuita.com. Friendly, quiet, Swiss-run, good restaurant, wildlife, 2 small cabins sleeping 2 – one with kitchen, excellent local information, internet, laundry service, bike rentals, horse riding and many different tours. Recommended.

C-D Hotel National Park, opposite **Kelly Creek**, by entrance to national park, T2755-0244. Bright rooms, fan, just about friendly, the beach-front restaurant makes it a good spot.

C-D Reggae Rest and Cabinas, near Chao's Paradise in Play Negra, T2755-0515. Basic *cabinas* all with private bath in nice location by the beach.

C-D Restaurant and Bungalows Bluspirit, just out of town on the road to Playa Negra. Gorgeous split-level bungalows with private bath, hot water and hammocks, by the beach. Run by a very friendly couple who also serve fresh fish and Italian home-cooked meals in their bar and restaurant.

C-D Safari Ocean View, towards Play Negra, T2755-0393. 5 decent *cabinas* with private bath and hot water, also terrace and hammocks, great location a short amble to the shore and good value for the price.

D Cabinas Belo Horizonte, Playa Negra, north of Cahuita, T2755-0206. A couple of good rooms, quite simple but on the beach, rent for US$200 per month or US$20 per day.

D Cabinas Mina, main street. Very friendly owners offer very basic rooms with private bath and cold water.

D Cabinas Nirvana, towards Playa Negra, T2755-0110, nirvana99@racsa.co.cr. Wooden rooms in a very tranquil spot, hot water private bath, swimming pool in gardens.

D Cabinas Safari, opposite Cabinas Palmar, T2755-0405. Simple rooms with fan and shared bath and hot water, friendly owner Wayne Palmer, clean, price per person, good value.

D Cabinas Surf Side, facing the school, T2755-0246. Clean, good value. Parking.

D New Cabinas Arrecife, right on the coast close to Miss Edith's, T2755-0081. OK rooms, but great spot and view from restaurant.

D Sol y Mar, on the road to parque nacional, T2755-0237. Friendly owners have rooms that sleep 2-6 people, with private hot-water bath. Rooms are a little tatty, but fine and some very spacious. Their local restaurant is good for breakfast.

D Vaz Cabañas, towards the park entrance, T2755-0218. Friendly, cold shower, some fans, quite clean, good restaurant, safe parking. Recommended. Same owners have now opened more *cabañas* (**C**), under the same name, in front of the bus station. Clean and bright with private hot water showers.

D Villa Delmar, close to national park entrance, T2755-0392. Rooms with private shower, cold and hot water. Bicycle rental, laundry service and parking.

D-E Bobo Shanti, around the corner from Cabinas Safari. Colourfully painted in red, green and gold. Rooms have private bath, hot and cold water. Chilled vibes.

D-E Cabinas Margarita, Playa Negra, north of Cahuita, down a 200-m path, T2755-0205. Simple rooms, quiet spot, nice atmosphere, clean.

Camping

It's possible to camp in Cahuita National Park.
Kontiki, near Playa Negra, T2755-0261. With laundry, showers and toilets, also a few cabins.
Colibrís Paradise, out of village close to Playa Negra.

Puerto Viejo de Talamanca *p1269, map p1270*

Discounts are often available May-Nov.
L-AL Samasati Lodge & Retreat Center, near Hone Creek on junction between Cahuita and Puerto Viejo, T2750-0315, www.samasati.com. Beautiful mountain location with 100-ha reserve, vegetarian restaurant, meditation courses, reservation recommended.

AL-A Cabinas Los Almendros (see map), T2750-0235, flchwg@racsa.co.cr. 3 fully equipped apartments and a complex of conventional rooms with private hot water bath, a/c and cable TV in the more expensive ones. None of the Caribbean charm but good facilities, especially for families. Cash exchange, credit card advances, tour advice, good, friendly service.

A Escape Caribeño, 500 m along road to Punta Uva, T2750-0103. German-run, well-furnished cottages, fully equipped, some a/c.

A Lizard King, out of town, heading north, T2750-0614/0630. Smart *cabinas* located upstairs at their Mexican restaurant, not always open. Swimming pool.

A-B Bungalows Calalú, on the road to Cocles, T2750-0042, www.bungalows calalu.com. Bungalows with and without kitchen, also swimming pool and beautiful butterfly garden in the grounds.

A-B Cabinas Casa Verde, central, T2750-0015, www.cabinascasaverde.com. Comfortable rooms with hammocks, private bath, cracked tile showers in beautiful gardens. A pool and open-air jacuzzi add to the relaxation. The owner collects Central American poison dart frogs and keeps them in tanks dotted around the grounds; ask to take a look, even if you are not a guest. Very nice owners and staff, recommended.

A-C Cashew Hill, south of town, T2750-0256, www.cashewhilllodge.co.cr. Re-developed in the last few years, although retaining rustic charm. 6 family-orientated rooms, with both private and shared bath, fans and mosquito nets. Set in 1 ha of beautiful gardens on the rolling hills above the town, mirador looks out over the jungle tops to the sea. Yoga massage retreats and classes available. Quiet, very chilled atmosphere.

A-C Coco Loco Lodge, south of town, T2750-0281, www.cocolocolodge.com. Quiet spot in expansive garden south of town, nice thatched wooden and stone cabins, some fully equipped with kitchen and cable TV. Popular. English, German and Spanish spoken.

B Guaraná, opposite Lulu Berlu Gallery, T2750-0244, www.hotelguarana.com. Very attractive hotel if a little pricey, well kept. All rooms with private, hot water bath, fans, mosquito nets, private balconies and hammocks. They also have a communal kitchen and parking space.

B Maritza, central, T2750-0003. In cabins, with bath, clean, clean, friendly. Affiliated to International Youth Hostel Association, English spoken. A map in the bar shows all the hotels and cabinas in the area. Highly recommended.

B-C Cabinas David, just out of town past Lizard King, T2750-0542, cabinas_david@yahoo.com. Cabinas with private, hot water shower, individual terrace with hammocks.

B-C Jacaranda, a few blocks back (see map), T2750-0069, www.cabinasjacaranda.net. A very relaxed spot away from the beach

set in beautiful gardens, with coloured mosaic pathways and private areas to read and relax. Rooms are fixed with colourful throws and side lights, showers are spacious. Very attractive place, hot water throughout, fans, mosquito nets. Communal kitchen. Massages can be booked to take place in a pagoda in their flower garden.

C Cabinas Grant, on the road out of town (see map), T2752-0292. Local ownership, large clean rooms, with private bath and fan. Each with a small terrace. Restaurant upstairs is now a seafood eatery.

C Cabinas Tropical, close to the coast, T2750-0283, www.cabinastropical.com. 8 spotless rooms, some with fridges, with good mattresses, private bath and hot water. Pleasant gardens with shaded garden house for relaxing, small bar/café. The German owner, Rolf Blancke, is a tropical biologist and runs tours. Recommended.

C Cabinas Yucca, north of town, T2750-0285. Has 5 cabinas with private hot water showers, good value and great spot, nice beach garden, parking, friendly, German-run.

C Hotel Fortaleza, on main street in the middle of town, T2750-0028. Rooms with private hot water bath, not a particularly special building, but fine, clean and a very relaxed friendly atmosphere with communal terrace for watching street life.

C-D Cabinas Soda Mitchell, close to Soda Lidia. 3 sparkling rooms sleeping 2-3 people, with private shower and (usually) hot water. Very pleasant owner and quiet out-of-the-way location.

C-D Café Rico, north end of town. Coffee shop with a couple of rooms with private shower and hot water. Very friendly English owner and probably the best coffee in town.

C-D Pura Vida, a few blocks back from the main street (see map),T2750-0002, German-Chilean run, friendly, very clean, hammocks. Sadly lacking in character but recommended.

C-E Puerto Viejo, just off the main street (see map), T2750-0620. Great management make the place the most chilled in town.

78 beds in basic rooms sleep 1 to 5, 3 have private hot-water bath, the rest are shared hot and cold water showers. There is a communal kitchen and large areas to eat, chat and be social. 1 fully equipped apartment for monthly rental (approx US$500). Owners are all surfers and they offer board rental, buy and sell, also wave info. Scooter rental available. Popular with surfers.

C-F Las Olas Camping and Cabinas, next to **Salsa Brava Restaurant**. Basic for the price – camping from US$6, rooms from US$25 – rooms with private bath and hot water, but great spot on the beach and friendly local owners. Showers and toilet facilities for campers.

D Bull Inn, first left after **Harbor Supermarket**. Locally owned, very clean and bright rooms with private bath, hot water, and a communal balcony.

D Los Sueños, main steret (on map), T2750-0369, www.costaricaguide.info/lossuenos.htm. Laid-back and very relaxing, just 4 colourful and bright rooms.

D-E Cabinas Popular, opposite the back entrance of **Casa Verde**. Nicely located at the back of the town – very peaceful with rural backdrop – rather basic rooms and a little dark, but extremely good value, private shower, but cold water.

D-F Rocking J's, on the beach out of town, towards Cocles, T2750-0657, www.rocking js.com. A sprawling multi-coloured campers' paradise. Huge covered hammock hotel and area for tents – bring your own or rent one of theirs. They also have a 'tree house' room, with double bed under a retractable ceiling so you can watch the stars, also a music system and fridge (you need never come down) and the 'King Suite', an open-sided, colourful room, with private bath. Coloured mosaic murals, communal kitchen, toilets and restaurant, all done by guests. They also offer kayak, surfboard and hike rentals, and the occasional full moon party.

E Cabinas Lika, southern end of town (see map). Friendly backpackers set-up with private rooms, dorms and hammocks, shared kitchen and laid-back vibe.

E Cabañas Yoli, 250 m from bus stop. Clean, basic, fan, OK – one of the last Tico-owned places.

E Sol y Sombre, at entrance to town, with the style of the French. 5 clean rooms, with fan and mosquito nets. Small restaurant downstairs.

F Cabinas Salsa Brava, popular with surfers.

F Tamandua Lodge, behind **Cabinas Dolce Vida**. Very basic budget accommodation, with shared rooms, shared bathroom and shared kitchen.

Around Puerto Viejo p1269

LL-A Aguas Claras, 4.5 km from Puerto Viejo on road to Manzanillo, T2750-0131, www.aguasclaras-cr.com. 5 beautiful cottages each painted a different colour with pretty white wooden gables and balconies. All fully equipped and very close to the beach. **Restaurant Miss Holly** serves gourmet breakfast and lunch. Recommended.

L Tree House Lodge, Punta Uva, T2750-0706, www.costaricatreehouse.com. Dutch owner Edsart has 3 apartments – 2 of which are the most unusual in Costa Rica: the treehouse and the beach suite (there is also a beach house). All are fully equipped with kitchen facilities and hot water, and all are equally luxurious.

L-AL Shawandha, Playa Chiquita, T2750-0018, www.shawandhalodge.com. Beautiful bungalows in the jungle with a calm and private feel and fantastic mosaic showers. Massages now available. Very stylish restaurant serving French Caribbean fusion, pricey.

AL Hotel Kasha, Playa Chiquita, T2750-0205, www.costarica-hotelkasha.com. 14 bungalows in lush gardens on the beach, beautiful pool, jacuzzi and restaurant.

AL Hotel Las Palmas, Playa Uva, T2759-0303, www.laspalmashotel.com. Cabins, 26 rooms, pool, snorkelling, rainforest, tours, transport from San José on Wed, Fri, Sun, US$30 return, US$20 1 way.

AL-A Banana Azul Guest House, Playa Negra, T2750-2035, toll free T1-800-821-5352, www.bananaazul.com. Neat and comfortable rooms with private bath as well as beach houses. Breakfast included.

AL-A Cariblue Bungalows, Playa Cocles, T2750-0035, www.cariblue.com. Nice natural complex with palm roofs, set in beautiful garden. Restaurant and bar on site along with a games room and library.

A Almonds and Corals Tent Camp, Playa Uva, T2272-2024, www.almondsandcorals.com. Luxury camping with bath and hot water in tents on platforms in the forest, pool, restaurant, trips arranged to Punta Mona, snorkelling, bike hire, breakfast and dinner included. Sleeping in the wild, with some comfort thrown in.

A Playa Chiquita Lodge, Playa Chiquita, T2750-0408, www.playachiquitalodge.com. The lodge labels itself a beach jungle hotel and that's exactly what it feels like. They have 11 rooms and 3 houses (monthly rentals accepted) all with hot water, hammocks and plenty of space, easy beach access and breakfast included.

A Totem Cabinas, Playa Cocles, T2750-0758, www.totemsite.com. Surf-orientated hotel heavy on the bamboo furniture. Luxury rooms with lounge areas, private shower, hot water, cable TV and private balconies overlooking Playa Cocles. Italian bar and restaurant, internet room and swimming pool. Surf board rental and surf and kite school.

A-B La Costa de Papito, Playa Cocles, T2750-0080, www.lacostadepapito.com. 11 beautifully designed bungalows with all the style you'd expect from Eddie Ryan (**Carlton Arms Hotel**, New York). Rooms with fan and bath. Great owners who love to make their guests happy, recommended. **Costa de Papito** now host **Pure Jungle Spa**, T2750-0536, www.purejunglespa.com, Tue-Sat, or by appointment. Treatments are organic and handmade and sound good enough to eat … They range from chocolate facials to banana body wraps.

A-B Miraflores Lodge and Restaurant, Playa Chiquita, T2750-0038, www.miraflores lodge.com. 10 rooms (2 with kitchen), a/c, breakfast included, with bath, fan, gardens, lots of wildlife. English and French spoken. Cheaper rates in low season.

B Azania, Playa Cocles, T2750-0540, www.azania-costarica.com. Beautiful thatched-roof bungalows with great facilities in garden setting, restaurant, pool and jacuzzi, parking.

B Cabinas Pangea, Manzanillo, behind **Aquamor**, T2759-9012, www.greencoast. com/aquamor.htm. 2 nice rooms with bath, also house on beach with kitchen.

C-D Cabinas Something Different, T2759-9014, Manzanillo. 10 very clean rooms, 6 with a/c, all with private bath and hot water, big parking area and kitchen use available, friendly local people.

E Cabinas Las Veraneras, Manzanillo. Rooms with shared bath.

E Cabinas/Restaurant Maxi, Manzanillo, T2754-2266. Basic rooms, highly respected seafood restaurant.

E Selvin Cabins and restaurant, Playa Uva. With room and dormitory accommodation.

🍴 Eating

Puerto Limón *p1265, map p1264*
Cheap food is available in and around the Central Market. *Casados* in market in the day, outside it at night, good, cheap food. Try *pan bon*, spicy bread from Creole recipe, sold near bus stop for San José.

🍴 **Springfield**, north of town opposite the hospital. Stylish with a mix of Tico and international dishes. Best restaurant in town.

🍴 **Antillita**, Calle 6, Av 4-5. Caribbean rice and beans, meat, open evenings only.

🍴 **Brisas del Caribe**, facing Parque Vargas, Av 2, Calle 1, T2758-0138. Cheap noodles, meat, seafood, and good service.

🍴 **Marisquería El Cevichito**, Av 2, Calle 1-2, T2758-1380. Good fish, steaks and *ceviche* and good spot for people-watching.

Monte de Oro, Av 4, Calle 3-4. Serves good local dishes, in a rough and ready atmosphere.
Park Hotel, Av 3, Calle 1-2. Does good meals overlooking the sea.
Sabor Pizza, corner of Av 3 and Calle 4. Good pizza.
Soda Yans, Av 2, Calle 5-6. Popular spot.
Diplo's, Av 6, Calle 5-6. The best, and cheapest, Caribbean food in town.
Milk Bar La Negra Mendoza, at the central market. Good milk shakes and snacks.
Samkirson, Calle 3, Av 3-4. One of several Chinese restaurants. Good value.
Soda Mares, overlooking market square. Daily 0700-1400. Good food.

Parque Nacional Tortuguero *p1265*
Café Caoba, Tortuguero village. Cheap and has excellent pizza, sandwiches and shrimp.
Miss Junie's, north end of Tortuguero village. Very popular, has good local dishes, reservation necessary.
The Vine, Tortuguero village. Pizzas and sandwiches.
El Dolar, Tortuguero village. Simple restaurant, small menu, good *casado*.
Restaurant El Muellecito, Tortuguero village, T2710-6716. Also 3 simple cabins.

Cahuita and Parque Nacional Cahuita *p1267, map p1268*
If the catch is good restaurants have lobster.
La Casa Creole, Playa Negra, by the Magellan Inn, 2 km north of Cahuita, T2755-0104 (for reservations). Mon-Sat 0600-0900. A culinary feast of French and Creole creations, from US$8. Recommended.
Cha Cha Cha, Cahuita, T2755-0191. Opens at 1700, closed Mon International menu, great food and service, refreshing chic decor, very good pasta from US$4.
Chao's Paradise, T2755-0421, Playa Negra. Typical Caribbean food and seafood specials, good little reggae bar, with oropendula nests overlooking the beach.
Coral Reef, next to Coco's Bar, Cahuita. Very accommodating local management

can cook to your tastes, great local food with seafood specialities.
Mango Tango Pizzeria, Cahuita. Great home-made pasta with a wide variety if Italian sauces, quite a rarity in these parts, good pizza, good restaurant.
Miss Edith's, Cahuita, T2755-0248. Open daily until 2130. Almost legendary. Delicious Caribbean and vegetarian food, nice people, good value, no alcohol licence, take your own, many recommendations for breakfast and dinner, but don't expect quick service.
Pizz n' Love, Cahuita, Excellent restaurant run by a Dutch hippy, pizzas named after celebrities with loads of good toppings such as ricotta, parmesan and ginger prawns, served on tables painted with slogans such as 'give pizza a chance'. Recommended.
Restaurant Banana, top of Playa Negra. A good restaurant and bar away from the crowds. Recommended.
Restaurant Palenque Luisa, Cahuita. Has the distinctly tropical feel with split-bamboo walls, sand floors and a good *menú típico*.
Restaurant Relax, Cahuita, over Rikki's Bar. Fantastic pizzas, pastas, some Mexican and fish, good Italian wines.
Sobre las Olas, Playa Negra, T2755-0109. Closed Tue. On the beach serving Tico and Italian, popular bar in the evening.
Sol y Mar, Cahuita. Open 0730-1200, 1630-2000, need to arrive early and wait at least 45 mins for food. Red snapper and volcano potato especially wicked, US$5; also good breakfasts, try cheese, egg and tomato sandwich, US$2. Good value.
100% Natural Coffee Shop, Cahuita. Snacks, tapas and cocktails, and of course, natural coffees. Internet.
The Beach House, Cahuita. Bar and restaurant, cocktails served, laid-back establishment on the high street. Surf lessons and information available.
Rest Le Fe, opposite Coco's Bar, Cahuita. Large variety of dishes all centred round rice and beans, good typical food.
Ice Cream Shop, high street, Cahuita. Ice cream and juice kiosk.

The Pastry Shop, Playa Negra, T2755-0275. Delicious breads, brownies and pies.

Soda Priscilla, opposite **Sol y Mar**, Cahuita. Good budget breakfast *pinto*, eggs and fresh juices.

Puerto Viejo de Talamanca *p1269, map p1270*

Amimodo, north end of town, overlooking the beach, beyond **Standord's**. Fine Italian restaurant with prices to match. Reputedly fantastic. Weekend Latin nights. Doesn't always come with a smile.

Stanford's, Upstairs restaurant has a rather pricey, but good menu in arty surroundings.

Chili Rojo, is east of town, past Stanfords. Thai, Eastern and vegetarian food including humous and falafel platters and coconut curries and delicious home-made ice cream.

El Parquecito, facing sea in the centre. Nice breezy atmosphere, specializes in pizza and Italian dishes.

Grant Seafood, main street. Seafood restaurant located over **Cabinas Grant**.

Jammin Juices and Jerk Chicken, by the coast. Roast chicken with a variety of home-made sauces and salsas, also great vegetarian selection, open for breakfast, lunch and early dinners. Recommended.

La Terraza, main street, above **Frutería Ivone**. Lovely Italian owner and chef, will cook to your requirements – ravioli, lasagne, pastas and seafood and tiramisu for afters.

Pizzeria Rusticone, 1 block back from main street (see map). Best pizzas in town cooked in original ovens, excellent pastas including home-made ones, all at good prices, recommended.

Salsa Brava, north end of town (see map). Spanish food, closed Sun. Recommended.

Tamara, on main street, T2750-0148. Open 0600-2100. Local good fish dishes, popular throughout the day and packed at weekends.

Bread and Chocolate, centre of town (see map). A breakfast café well-renowned for home baking and the morning menu is filled with good, home-made choices,

ranging from eggs, bacon and fresh bread to oatmeal with apple and cinnamon. Breads and cakes, mint and nut brownies and divine chocolate truffles are home-made and the café is well recommended.

Hot Rocks, main street. American joint that serves steak, nachos and pizzas, cocktails and beers served in front of cinema-size movie screen – they show 3 films a night, free with dinner or drinks.

Carlos Pool Bar, 1 block from the main street, behind **Pollo Frito**. Locally owned bar that serves cheap and large *casados*, soda included in the price. Pool tables and sometimes a movie showing.

Lidia's Place, south of centre. Good typical food and to-die-for chocolate cake that does not hang round.

Peace and Love Coffee, south end of town. Ex-Bambú owners. Italians making fantastic home-made breads and pizzas, lasagnes and other mouthwatering delicatessen items at surprisingly reasonable prices.

Pizza Boruca, opposite the church (see map). Best pizza slices in all Costa Rica, cheap and delicious – this man is always busy.

Pollo Frito, north end of town, opposite **Stanford's** (see map). Affectionately named the 'fried chicken place' – no one ever remembers its real name. A late-opening café, perfect for late-night snacking, serves mainly (as you would guess) fried chicken and yucca, but also rice and beans, *casados* and sandwiches.

Red Stripe Café, south end of town (see map). Snacks and smoothies.

Soda Miss Sam, south of the centre, good local food piled high, good value.

Soda Palmer, north end of town (see map). Cheap Chinese food, big plates, nice people.

Cafés and bakeries

Monchies, 2 blocks off the main street (see map). Delicious baked goods.

Pan Pay, beachfront. Good bakery. Also serve great breakfasts: eggs with avocado, fresh bread and tomato salsa, omelettes, pastries, etc. A good place to read the paper and nod at the locals – a very popular spot in the morning.

Around Puerto Viejo *p1269*

🍴 **El Living**, Playa Cocles. Pizza, drinks and music, very laid back, and good prices.

🍴 **La Isla Inn**, Playa Cocles. Serves Japanese Caribbean fusion, including sushi, soups, salads, and stir-fry.

🍴 **Magic Ginger**, Hotel Kasha, Playa Chiquita. Restaurant and bar serving gourmet French cooking, seafood specials and exotic salads.

🍴 **Rest Maxi**, Manzanillo. Reggae-style restaurant serving typical Caribbean food and seafood specials.

🍴 **Aguas Dulce**, Playa Cocles. Ice creams, pastries and sandwiches.

☺ Entertainment

Cahuita and Parque Nacional Cahuita *p1267, map p1268*

Rikki's Bar and **Cocos Bar** in the centre of Cahuita; the latter is the livelier of the 2 and hosts reggae nights on Fri and live music. **Coffee Bar**, on the shore near **Cabinas Jenny**, is a good reggae spot.

Puerto Viejo de Talamanca *p1269, map p1270*

Puerto probably has the most lively nightlife on Costa Rica's entire Caribbean coast and has always run on an unspoken rota – each bar having a particular night, and this is still (loosely) the case. Various bars have bid for **Bambu's** Mon and Fri reggae nights, which now run between **Sunset Bar** (by the bus stop) and **Baba Yaga** (next to **Hotel Puerto Viejo**). (Bambu was a bar that burnt down several years ago.) Sunset has live events and pool tables, they have also taken over **Jam Night** on Wed (that used to be held at **Tesoro** in Cocles). **Baba Yaga** is smaller and more intimate; and they run the occasional dance music event.

Jhonny's Bar (or **Mike's Playground**, depending on how local you are – Jhonny's is the original) is perhaps the best night now in town on Thu, Sat and Sun. Right on the beach, with Puerto's reggae/dancehall best.

Stanford's Disco, tends to be the quietest, despite being one of the originals. **Dubliner Irish Bar** is past Salsa Brava, Don't get too excited, they're apparently often out of Guinness and there's nothing in the way of traditional ale, but there's a flag on the wall and lots of Irish music, so if you fancy something not very tropical. **Bar In and In**, over **Rest Tamara** in the high street is a much more laid back reggae bar for pre-party drinks and cocktails. There is a small bar at **Café Puerto Viejo**, with olives and expensive cocktails – ambient and chilled music makes a change from the reggae everywhere else.

▲ Activities and tours

Parque Nacional Tortuguero *p1265*
Tour operators

Most people visit Tortuguero as part of a tour from San José flying into the airport, or catching an agency bus and boat from Matina. It is possible to travel to Tortuguero independently (see Transport, below). Tours from San José include transport, meals, 2 nights' lodging, guide and boat trips for US$215-330 per person (double occupancy). **Caño Blanco Marina**, 2 Av, 1-3 C, San José, T2256-9444 (San José), T2710-0523 (Tortuguero). Runs a daily bus-boat service San José-Tortuguero at 0700, US$50 return, Book in advance – if you miss the boat, there is nothing else in Caño Blanco Marina. **Mawamba**, T2223 2421, www.grupoma wamba.com. Minimum 2 people, 3 days/ 2 nights, daily, private launch so you can stop en route, with launch tour of national park included. Accommodation at the very comfortable **Mawamba Lodge**, 3-day/ 2-night package, Tue, Fri, Sun US$330. Other accommodations have very similar packages, with the difference being the level of comfort in the hotel. Ilan Ilan Lodge, T2255-3031, www.ilan-ilan lodge.com is one of the more affordable at US$199 for 2 nights.

OTEC (see page 1147) runs 3-day/2-night tours for US$180, with small student discount; a trip to see the turtles in Jul-Sep costs extra. Tours from Puerto Viejo de Sarapiquí, including boat trip to Tortuguero, meals, 2 nights' lodging, guide and transport to San José cost US$275-400 per person (double occupancy). *Riverboat Francesca*, T2226-0986, www.tortuguero canals.com, costs US$195 per person 2 day-1 night trips exploring the canals for exquisite wildlife, sportfishing. Longer packages are also available.

Organizing a package trip from **Puerto Limón** is more difficult. Viajes Tropicales Laura, T2795-2410, www.viajestropicales laura.net, have been highly recommended, daily service, open return US$60 if phoned direct, more through travel agencies, pickup from hotel, will store luggage, lunch provided, excellent for pointing out wildlife on the way. An inclusive 2-day, 1-night package a from Puerto Limón with basic accommodation, turtle-watching trip and transport (no food) costs from US$99 per person.

Guides Several local guides have been recommended, including Johnny Velázquez; Alberto, who lives next to Hotel Mary Scar; Rubén Bananero, who lives in the last house before you get to the National Park office, sign on pathway, recommended for 4-hr tour at dusk and in the dark; Chico, who lives behind Sabina's Cabinas, US$2 per hr, and will take you anywhere in his motor boat; Ernesto, who was born in Tortuguero, and has 15 years' experience as a guide, contact him at Tropical Lodge or through his mother, who owns Sabina's Cabinas; Rafael, a biologist who speaks Spanish and English (his wife speaks French), and lives 500 m behind Park Rangers' office (ask rangers for

directions); he also rents canoes. Ross Ballard, a Canadian biologist who can be contacted through Casa Marbella.

Daryl Loth lives locally and runs **Tortuguero Safaris**, T8833-0827, safari@racsa.co.cr. Barbara Hartung of **Tinamon Tours**, T2709-8004, www.tinamon tours.de, a biologist who speaks English, German, French and Spanish, is recommended for boat, hiking and turtle tours in Tortuguero (US$5 per person per hr; all-inclusive trips from Limón 3-days, 2-nights, US$140 per person). Both Daryl and Barbara are strong supporters of using **paddle power**, or at most electric motors. Provide the latest details of how to get to Tortuguero yourself.

There are several **boats for rent** from Tortuguero, ask at the *pulpería*. The use of polluting 2-stroke motors is outlawed in Tortuguero, and the use of 4-stroke engines is limited to 3 of the 4 main water channels.

Cahuita and Parque Nacional
Cahuita *p1267, map p1268*
Snorkelling equipment and surfboards available for rent. Horses can be hired, but try to ensure they are in good shape. Bicycles can be hired for about US$7 per day and you can cycle to Puerto Viejo and the Panamanian border through some beautiful scenery.

Tour operators
Wide range of activities available including water sports and nature tours.
Cahuita Tours, T2755-0232, exotica@ racsa.co.cr, excursions by jeep and glass-bottomed boat tours over the reefs, bike, diving and snorkelling equipment rental, international telephone service (ICE) and Western Union money transfer. GrayLine bus travel can be arranged here.
Roberto's Tours, office located at his restaurant (Roberto's) on the main street. Very nice people run all the usual tours of the area including snorkelling and diving.

Willies Tours, T2755-0267, www.willies-costarica-tours.com. Willie is most helpful and knows everything about Cahuita and surrounding areas. He runs tours to Tortuguero, Panama, Bri Bri indigenous reserve and whitewater rafting in the Pacuare river. The office is located opposite Restaurant Palenque on the main street, where he also runs an internet café.

Puerto Viejo de Talamanca *p1269, map p1270*

Tours in Puerto Viejo include canopy, snorkelling, boat trips and diving in Cahuita and Manzanillo, trips to an indigenous reserve, rafting in Pacuare, kayaking, bird watching, etc. ATEC is the easiest source of information (www.ateccr.org) and the original provider of information and tours combining ecotourism and conservation but you can also try **Canopy Tour** and **Terraventuras**, T2750-0750, www.terraventuras.com, **Exploradores Outdoors**, T2750-6262, www.exploradores outdoors.com, **Atlántico Tours**, T2750-0004, offer several trips. **Reef Runner Divers**, T2750-0480, www.reefrunnerdivers.com, **Yuppi and Tino**, T2750-0621, **Dragon Scooter Rental**, T2750-0728, www.dragonscooter rentals.com in Puerto Viejo, and **Aguamar Adventures**, in Manzanillo, who have been operating since 1993, offer diving courses and local trips. Prices from US$35.

● Transport

Puerto Viejo de Sarapiquí *p1263*

Bus Buses stop on north side of park. From **San José** 7 daily from Gran Terminal del Caribe, 1½ hrs through PN Braulio Carrillo, or through Heredia, 4 daily, 3½ hrs. From **Cd Quesada**, 5 daily, 2½ hrs.

Car To get there by car from **San José**, after passing through the PN Braulio Carrillo take Route 4, a paved road which turns off near Santa Clara to Puerto Viejo; it bypasses Río Frío and goes via Las Horquetas. A more scenic but longer route leaves from Heredia via San Miguel and La Virgen, and on to Puerto Viejo.

Guápiles, Guácimo and Siquirres *p1263*

Bus In Guápiles, buses leave from a central terminal a block to the north of the church. Regular buses to **San José** and **Puerto Limón**. Buses to **Puerto Viejo de Sarapiquí** ever 2½ hrs, and to **Río Frío** every 1½ hrs.

For Siquirres, at least 1 bus per hr leaves Gran Terminal del Caribe in **San José**, 2½-hr journey.

Puerto Limón *p1265, map p1264*

Bus Town bus service is irregular and crowded. Service from **San José** with CoopeLimón, T2233-3646 and Caribeño, T2222-0610, at least every hour, 0500-2000, daily. Arrive and depart from Calle 2, Av 1-2, US$3, 2½ hrs. Also services to **Guápiles** and **Siquirres**. From same stop buses to Siquirres/ Guápiles, 13 daily, 8 direct. Near Radio Casino on Av 4, Calle 3-4, buses leave for **Sixaola**, first 0500, last 1800, US$2.50, stopping at Cahuita, Puerto Viejo and Bri Bri en route. To **Manzanillo**, at 0600, 1430, returning 1130, 1900, 1½ hrs, US$1.50. To **Moín** from Calle 5, Av 3-4, every 30 mins between 0600-2200.

Parque Nacional Tortuguero *p1265*

Air Daily flights from **San José** with Nature Air (US$$70).

Bus and boat It is quite possible to travel to Tortuguero independently, but more challenging than the all-inclusive packages. There are a couple of options. From **Limón**, regular vessels leaves from the Tortuguero dock in **Moín**, north of Limón, US$50 return. It is a loosely run cooperative, with boats leaving at 1000. There is also a 1500 service that runs less frequently. If possible, book in advance through the Tortuguero Information Centre (check the times; they change frequently). If you are in a group you may be able to charter a boat for approximately US$200.

An alternative route is between Puerto Veijo de Sarapiqui and Tortuguero. Boats leave Puerto Viejo on Mon and Thu, returning on Tue and Fri. US$55 per person.

From **San José**, the bus/boat combination is the cheapest option and a mini-adventure in itself. Take the 0900 bus to Cariari from the Terminal Gran Caribe, arriving around 1045. Walk 500 m north to the ticket booth behind the police station where you can buy you bus/boat ticket to Tortuguero. Take the 1200 bus to **La Pavona**, arriving around 1330. Take 1 of the boats to Tortuguero, which will arrive about 1500. The journey is about US$10 1-way. Don't be talked into a package if you're not interested – there are plenty of services to choose from in Tortuguero. The return service leaves at 0830 and 1330 giving you 1 or 2 nights in Tortuguero. (There appears to be an attempt to monopolize this service but for the time being at least, there are a couple of boats in operation.)

Alternative routes include the 1030 bus from San José to Cariari, changing to get the 1400 bus to La Geest and the 1530 boat to Tortuguero. Or 1300 bus San José-Cariari, 1500 bus Cariari to La Pavona, 1630 boat La Pavone to Tortuguero.

It is also possible to take a bus from Siquirres to **Freeman** (unpaved road), a Del Monte banana plantation, from where unscheduled boats go to Tortuguero; ask around at the bank of the Río Pacuare, or call the public phone office in Tortuguero (T2710-6716, open 0730-2000) and ask for **Johnny Velázquez** to come and pick you up, US$57, maximum 4 passengers, 4 hrs. Sometimes heavy rains block the canals, preventing passage there or back. Contact **Willis Rankin** (T2798-1556) an excellent captain who will negotiate rampaging rivers. All riverboats for the major lodges (see below) leave from Hamburgo or Freeman. If the

excursion boats have a spare seat you may be allowed on.

Barra del Colorado *p1266*
Air Flights to **San José** daily with Sansa (US$63).

Boat To **Tortuguero** takes 1½ hr and costs US$50. A motorized canoe can take 8 people and costs up to US$80, 2 hrs. Try and arrive in a group as boats are infrequent.

Penshurst *p1267*
Bus Small buses leave **Limón** (Calle 4, Av 6) for Valle de Estrella/Pandora, 7 a day from 0500, at 2-hourly intervals, last at 1800, 1½ hrs (returning from Pandora at similar times).

Cahuita and Parque Nacional Cahuita *p1267, map p1268*
Bus Service direct from **San José**'s Terminal del Caribe, to **Cahuita** at 0600, 1000, 1200, 1400 and 1600, return 0700, 0800, 0930, 1130 and 1630, 3½ hrs, US$6.50, T2257-8129, Trans Mepá, 4 hrs, US$4.50, and from **Puerto Limón**, in front of Radio Casino, 0500-1800, return 0630-2000, 1 hr, US$0.80, T2758-1572, both continuing to Bribri, and Sixaola (dirt road) on the Panamanian border (US$1, 2 hrs). The bus drops you at the crossing of the 2 main roads in Cahuita.

Puerto Viejo de Talamanca *p1269, map p1270*
Bus Daily services from **San José** from Gran Terminal del Caribe at 0600, 1000, 1200, 1400 and 1600, return at 0730, 0900, 1100 and 1600, 4 hrs, US$7.50; from **Limón** daily from Radio Casino, 0500-1800, return 0600-2000, 1½ hrs; 30 mins from **Cahuita**, US$0.45. To **Manzanillo** at 0700, 1530, 1900, returning 0500, 0830, 1700, ½ hr, US$0.80. To **Sixaola** 5 daily, 0545 until 1845, 2 hrs, US$1.80.

Around Puerto Viejo *p1269*
Express bus to **Manzanillo** from Terminal Sixaola, **San José**, daily, 1600, return 0630. From **Limón** daily 0600, 1430, return 1130, 1900, 1½ hrs.

● Directory

Puerto Limón *p1265, map p1264*
Banks Usual hours and services, all with ATMs at **Banco de Costa Rica**, Av 2, Calle 1, Mon-Fri 0900-1400; **Banco Nacional**, Av 2, Calle 3, with ATM; **Banco Popular**, Calle 3, Av 1-2, with ATM. **Banco de San José**, Av 3, Calle 3-4, with ATM. **Internet** Edutec Internet, on 2nd level above Plaza Caribe, US$2.30 per hr. Also 24-hr access at **Internet**, 1 block from Mas X Menos, US$1 per hr. **Laundry** Av 2, Calle 5-6, price per item, not that cheap, but 2-hr turnaround. **Medical services** Red Cross, Calle 3, Av 1-2, T2758-0125. **Hospital**, on road to Moín, T2758-2222. **Post office** Opposite central for international calls at Av 2, Calle 5-6 and at Calle 3, Av 4-5, Mon-Thu 0800-1700, Fri 02800-1600.

Cahuita and Parque Nacional Cahuita *p1267, map p1268*
Banks None. Money exchange is difficult except occasionally for cash dollars

(Cahuita Tours changes dollars and TCs). Take plenty of colones from Limón. Nearest banks are is in **Puerto Viejo** and **Bribri** (20 km) but several places accept credit cards.
Internet Cyberbet, part of Cabinas Safari, US$1.60 per hr. **Willies Tours** has internet, opposite the bus station. **Post office** Next to police station at northern end of town.

Puerto Viejo de Talamanca *p1269, map p1270*
Banks Banco Nacional is 3 blocks south of ATEC, with ATM machine, but only take Visa or Plus (not MasterCard or Cirrus). The bank in Bribri does accept MasterCard credit card. You can change TCs and cash at **Manuel León's general store** on the beach. **Cabinas Los Almendros** changes TCs, euro and US dollars, and give credit card advance. **Internet** From ATEC, US$2.50 per hr. Also **Jungle Café**, fastest internet in town, but pricey and pre-pay cards only. **Books, Librería & Bazar Internet**, also fast, US$2.50 per hr. Internet next to Hot Rocks, slow, but open late. **Medical services** Chemist at the shopping area by the bank. **Police** On sea front. **Post office** At the shopping area by the bank. US$2 to send, US$1 to receive, atecmail@racsa.co.cr. **Telephone** There is a public telephone outside the ATEC office.

Contents

Border crossings

Panama–Costa Rica, *see pages 1358 and 1370*

Panama

At a glance

⊖ **Getting around** Buses up to a point; flights at times; taxis best in Panama City and cheap for groups.

⊘ **Time required** 2-3 weeks.

☼ **Weather** From Dec-Apr, the dry season, temperatures are in the high 20°Cs .

✖ **When not to go** The wettest months are Oct and Nov.

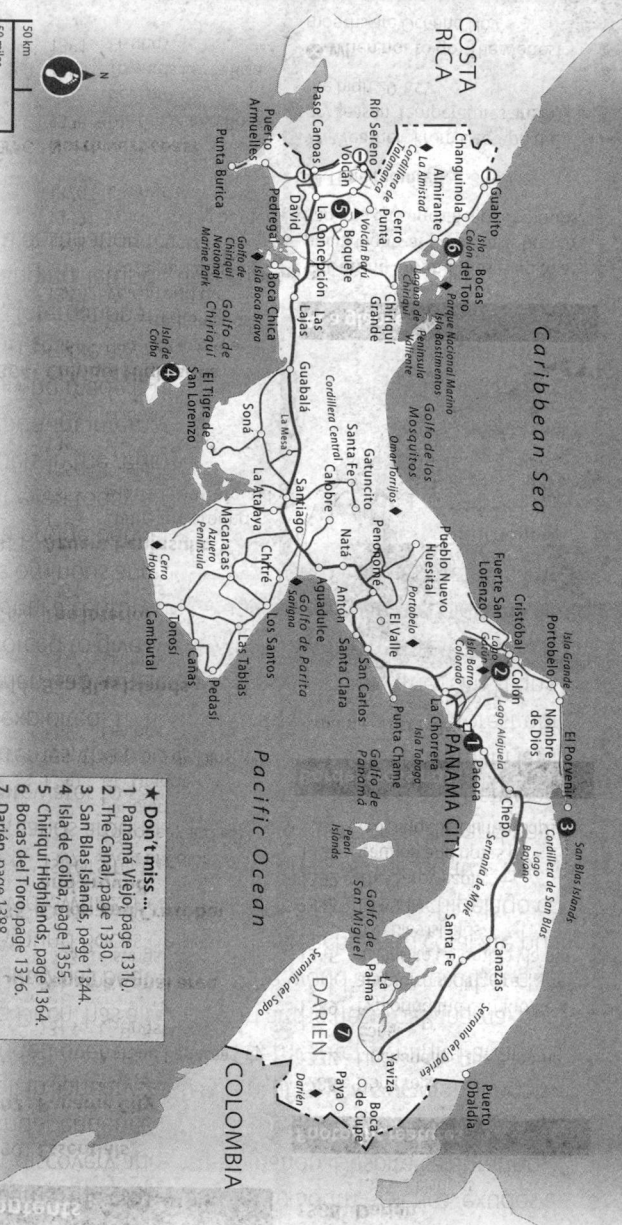

Panama, the crossing point to South America, exudes a sense of self-discovery and determination. Despite celebrating 100 years of independence in 2003, the country only really took control of itself in January 2000 when, after years of wrangling, the US finally handed over the running of the inter-oceanic Panama Canal. The 'Big Ditch' has always been at the heart of Panama, but now the country has begun to tell the world about its other claims to fame.

Around Bocas del Toro the beaches and coral are pulling in the crowds, while the islands of the San Blas archipelago continue to draw visitors to this distant corner of the country. The cool highlands around Boquete are ideal for hiking and have enough whitewater to satisfy river rafters. Beyond and between these extremes, the opportunities for exploration remain largely unexploited. To the west is the expansive rainforest of the Darién Gap, where even the great Pan-American Highway is forced to give way to the power of nature.

Until a century ago, Panama was part of Colombia, linked by the ominous and daunting Darién Gap. Its strategic importance as a bridge between two oceans has given Panama a global role but even today it is not thought of as part of Central America by others in the region. Secretive banking practices made it an important international finance centre, while impressive standards of living made it the destination of choice for a handful of high-profile asylum seekers and a useful dumping ground for the international community. However, Panama is now changing, letting go of its past and exploring new ground as a destination for adventurous travellers.

Essentials

Where to go

The S-shaped isthmus of Panama, just 80 km at its narrowest and 193 km at its widest, is one of the world's great crossroads – its destiny has been entirely shaped by this junction. To the north there are connections and links with the great civilizations of Central America and Mexico, while to the south, the wilderness of the Darién leads to Colombia and the great wealth of South America.

For thousands of years, people and animals have used the Panamanian corridor as a channel of communication. At the time of conquest, the Spaniards used it as a crossing point between the Atlantic and Pacific Oceans and forays north and south along the coast. In part Panama owes its creation to this positioning (the outcome of a squabble between Colombia and the United States in 1903), and the make-up of its population and their distribution has been affected by this corridor ever since. Today, over 40% of Panamanians live in two cities – Panama City and Colón – which control access to the canal. International control continued until 31 December 1999, when the Canal Area, formerly the US Canal Zone, was returned to Panamanian jurisdiction.

Panama City is a modern city, spread round the Bahía de Panamá. From the hilltop lookout of the unique Parque Natural Metropolitano, visitors enjoy spectacular views of the banks and high-rise buildings of the capital with the Canal in the distance. The rubble and ruins of Panamá Viejo lie to the east, the city's original location sacked by the pirate Henry Morgan. The younger replacement of Casco Viejo dates from 1673 and is slowly being restored to its former glory.

The city lies at the Pacific end of the **Panama Canal**, a feat of engineering that lifts ocean-going liners 26 m to Lago Gatún on the 67.5-km voyage between the Caribbean Sea and the Pacific Ocean. The financial cost of the canal was staggering; the price in human terms was over 22,000 lives. The Canal is surprisingly beautiful, consisting of the river-fed **Lago Gatún**, which is reached by a series of locks on the Pacific and Caribbean sides. Within the lake is **Reserva Biológica de la Isla Barro Colorado**, to which animals fled when the basin flooded. **Parque Nacional Soberanía**, which forms part of the watershed of Lake Gatún, is an easier trip, just 30 minutes from the capital.

At the Caribbean end of the Canal is **Colón**, the country's major port for container traffic, shipping and, for the dedicated shopper, the second largest tax-free zone in the world. To the east is **Portobelo**, the site of flamboyant 16th- and 17th-century markets, where warehouses filled with Peruvian gold and silver were guarded against pirate raids. Off the coast lies the marine burial site of the British buccaneering seaman Sir Francis Drake. Quiet, beautiful beaches await the visitor today. Further east, the 365-island **Archipiélago de San Blas** of crystalline waters and palms continues its autonomous existence under the guidance of the Kuna nation. The islands can be visited and hotels, lodges and simple cabinas are opening to cater for the growing tourist interest.

The Pan-American Highway runs almost parallel to the Pacific coastline from Panama City to Costa Rica, running through agricultural zones, Pacific beaches, colonial towns and mountain landscapes. The **Península de Azuero** is dotted with old colonial towns, beaches perfect for surfing, and nature reserves of wetland birds, nesting turtles and quiet solitude. Open pastures and savannahs give way to sugar plantations on approach to **David**, the hot and humid third city of the Republic. It is an attractive city, both colonial and modern with good communications and an ideal base for the mountain resorts of

Boquete and **Volcán**. Up in the cooler **Chiriquí Highlands** dominated by **Volcán Barú**, there is good hiking, horseriding, river rafting and other adventure sports.

North of the **Talamanca Mountains**, banana plantations stretch across the northern Caribbean lowlands that surround **Laguna de Chiriquí**. The offshore islands of **Bocas del Toro** and the **Parque Nacional Marino Isla Bastimentos** are home to nesting turtles, birds and other wildlife. Once cut off and difficult to reach, the islands are growing in popularity. If lying around relaxing on idyllic beaches isn't appealing enough, the snorkelling and diving on the unspoilt reefs is excellent.

Darién in the east is the most inhospitable part of Panama where all roads, including the Pan-American Highway, eventually just peter out. With no land links between Panama and Colombia, the fit and adventurous are tempted to cross one of the world's last great wildernesses by foot or boat to the border and Colombia beyond. While not impossible, several high-profile kidnappings have occurred. It is extremely dangerous.

Suggested itinerary Most people arrive in Panama overland from Costa Rica and head straight for **Bocas del Toro** – it's chilled, relaxed and there's a lot going on. From there it's a long haul to **Panama City**. You can break the journey, with a rather circuitous detour stopping off at David for a trip into the mountains at Boquete for great trekking, white-water rafting and exploring. When you get to Panama City, it's a short trip to see or to travel the **Panama Canal** is essential. From **Colón** on the Caribbean it's a short trip out to the **San Blas Islands**. A couple of weeks should cover the main areas. If you're heading to South America, you can improvise a journey working along the coast to **Puerto Obaldía** or catch a boat to Cartagena from Colón. The overland journey through the **Darién Gap** is not to be undertaken lightly. If in any doubt, fly.

When to go

The most popular time to visit is in the dry season from mid-December to mid-April. Temperatures vary little throughout the country ranging year round temperatures from 30-32°C (85-90°F) in the day dropping to 21-22°C (70-72°F) at night. Above 500 m, temperatures fall, making the highland towns attractive spots to cool off.

Rainfall, however, varies greatly. The Caribbean side of the central Cordillera is soaked with around 4000 mm annually. On the Pacific slope, it is much lighter with an average of 1700 mm. Both areas have pronounced seasonal variations. Rainfall begins to taper off sometime in December for the dry season. At this time rainfall on the Pacific side is scarce, or absent altogether, though on the Atlantic side you can expect a downpour 365 days a year. Even in the rainy season, however, the downpours, though heavy, usually last only an hour or two, and almost always come in mid-afternoon.

Sport and activities

Panama's tourism potential for special interest travel is only now being truly appreciated. It is a paradise for fishermen and birdwatchers alike; there are fine beaches and beautiful islands along both Atlantic and Pacific coasts; several indigenous as well as colonist communities provide considerable cultural interest; ecotourists can find a variety of challenging activities; and there are few routes as appealing to the long-distance traveller as crossing the Darién Gap (get local advice on levels of safety). Visitor facilities in Panama are well developed for those engaged in international commerce, off-shore banking and for bargain-hunting shoppers, and many other aspects of tourism are developing quickly.

Birdwatching

Birdlife is abundant and varied in Panama and the country is an important destination for many birdwatchers. The Darién jungle, both coastlines, the forest fringe along the Canal, and the Chiriquí highlands (where quetzales, among many other species, may be seen) all provide their own special attractions for the birder. Those interested are referred to *A Guide to the Birds of Panama*, by R S Ridgely and J A Gwynne Jr (Princeton University Press, 1992.)

Diving

Diving is the best locally developed sport. The Caribbean coral reefs are similar to those of Belize and Honduras, extending southeast for 100 km along from the Costa Rica border and then from Colón 300 km to the border with Colombia. For information on these areas, see under Bocas del Toro, Portobelo and the San Blas Islands. The Pacific has quite different ecosystems owing to the much greater tidal ranges, differing water temperature and density. Places to go include Taboga, the Pearl Islands, Iguana Island and Parque Nacional Coiba. A third, and perhaps unique experience, is diving in the lakes of the Panama Canal, mainly to visit wrecks, submerged villages and the odd train left behind by the filling of the canal. **Scuba Panama** have a good website, www.scubapanama.com.

Hiking

Volcán Barú, Panama's highest peak at 3475 m, and nearby Cerro Punta are the two best climbs in the country but there are several excellent long walks. The hike from Cañita on the Darién road over the continental divide to Cartí is an alternative to flying to San Blas. The Caminos de Cruces and Real are jungle walks that follow in the steps of the Conquistadors crossing the continental divide and, if combined into an ocean-to-ocean hike, take eight days. A good range for hiking is the Serranía de Majé east of Panama City, visiting Embera villages and its howler monkey population. Closer is the Parque Nacional Chagres and a three-day walk from Cerro Azul to the coast.

Nature tourism

Some 43% of Panama remains forested and a quarter of the land has protected status, which includes 14 national parks, wildlife refuges and forest reserves that are home to over 900 recorded bird species – including the endangered great green macaw and the harpy eagle, the national bird. Most national parks can be visited without hindrance if you can get there – there is supposed to be a US$3 entry fee but it is rarely charged. Transport can be very difficult and facilities non-existent; the largest, Darién National Park, is a good example. Slowly the value of the National Park system to tourism is being realized and some parks now have accommodation in huts for US$5 a bed. Contact **Asociación Nacional de Conservación de la Naturaleza (ANCON)** ① *Amelia Denis de Icaza, Edif No 153, Cerro Ancón, Quarry Heights, Apdo 153, T314-0052, www.ancon.org*, or **ANAM** ① *Edif 804, Albrook, Balboa, Ancón, near the domestic terminal at Albrook, T500-0855, www.anam.gob.pa*.

Surfing

Surfing is best at Isla Grande, Playa Venado on the Azuero Peninsula, Santa Catalina on the Pacific coast of Veraguas and Bocas del Toro. In the capital, Kenny Myers, T6671-7777, www.panamasurftours.com, offers tours to the more out of the way beaches. Also check out Playa Rio Mar near San Carlos, just 1.5 km from Panama City, and Rio Mar Surf Camp, T6516-5031, www.riomar surf.com. Options range from turn-up-and-surf to rooms, boards, classes and transport.

Whitewater rafting and river running

Whitewater rafting is best in the Chiriquí river system near David – Grades III to IV on the Río Chiriquí (all year round) – and the Chiriquí Viejo Palon section (December to April) when the river is not in full speight. Also in the Parque Nacional Chagres area, north of Panama City, with Grades II and III, which some consider better for **tubing** – floating down river on an inflated inner tube (generally best August to December). There are a selection of operators in Boquete, see page 1374.

Getting there

Air

Tocumen International Airport is 27 km east of the city centre. Taxis (US$25) and buses run to Panama City. For a lower price, take a shared cab (*compartivo*), and while you may wait a little longer, the price becomes US$10-15 for two or three people respectively. We received a report that there is a US$5 arrival tax in addition to the airport departure tax of US$20 that has to be paid by all passengers (cash only). There is a US$4 tax on air tickets over US$100 purchased in Panama.

From Europe No direct services. Connecting flights go to Miami, then by **American Airlines** or **Copa** to Panama City. **Iberia** goes from Madrid via Miami. From Frankfurt, Paris, Madrid and London, there is a connection via Bogotá with **Avianca** and **SAM**.

From the USA Direct flights from Atlanta, Baltimore, Houston, Los Angeles, Miami, New York (some change planes in San José), Orlando and Portland. For other US cities, connections are made in Miami or Houston.

From Central America Direct flights from Cancún and Mexico City, Guatemala City, Managua, San José and San Salvador. No direct flights to Tegucigalpa, but connections with **Lacsa** through San José or **Taca** in San Salvador.

From South America Lots of flights from Colombia with **Copa** (Barranquilla, Bogotá, Cartagena, Cali, Medellín) and **SAM** (Bogotá). One-way tickets are not available from Colombia to Panama on **SAM** or **Copa**, but a refund on an unused return portion is possible, less 17% taxes, on **SAM**. **LAB** fly from Santa Cruz (Bolivia). From Guayaquil and Quito, **Continental, Ecuatoriana** and **Copa**. **Copa** from Santiago de Chile and Lima. From Caracas, **Mexicana, Copa** and **Aeropostal**.

From the Caribbean Copa has flights from Havana, Kingston, Port-au-Prince, San Juan and Santo Domingo.

Road

Overland passage to Panama from Costa Rica on the Pacific side is at Paso Canoas, where crossing is straightforward, simple and fast. International buses make the journey from Costa Rica to David and on to Panama City stopping briefly for paperwork at the border (see page 1358). A less popular but more entertaining crossing point is Sixaola/Guabito on the Caribbean coast, on the road between Almirante and Chiriquí Grande that links the region to the rest of the country. Passengers and vehicles (car or motorcycle) are given 30 days at the border.

Overland routes to Colombia are possible through the Darién Gap, where the purist has a difficult, but not impossible, challenge. Alternatively it is possible to hop, skip and jump your way along the Caribbean coast taking canoes, but the cost can be considerable. For details see the Darién section, page 1388.

Sea

The Panama Canal is on the itineraries of many shipping services from Europe and the USA that take passengers, but charges are high.

There are several boats that make the journey from Isla Grande on the Caribbean across to Cartagena, charging US$150-200 for the journey. It is also possible to travel by sea to/from Colombia. See page 1344 for San Blas connections. A couple of boats travel weekly from Colón to San Andrés Island, Colombia, from where there are connections to Cartagena; the **Johnny Walker** takes 30 hours, but the service is very irregular and travellers have sometimes had to wait over a week in vain. There are (contraband) boats from Coco Solo, Colón, to the Guajira Peninsula, Colombia. The uncomfortable three-day journey is undertaken entirely at your own risk and you may have to wait days for a sailing. You have to bargain for your fare on these boats and accommodation is a little primitive.

Staying closer to the coastline it is possible to cross the border to Colombia on the Caribbean side close to Puerto Obaldía, and on the Pacific coast via Jaqué and possibly La Palma. These routes are not cheap and can take several days (see page 1393).

Getting around

Air

There are local flights to most parts of Panama by several airlines. The most reliable is **Aeroperlas** ① T315-7500, www.aeroperlas.com, the **Grupo Taca** subsidiary, with destinations throughout the country. Other services include: **Mapiex** ① T315-0344, www.mapiex.com, offering charter flights between Bocas del Toro, David and Panama City. **Air Panama** ① T316-9000, www.flyairpanama.com, offers a wide range of domestic services. **Ansa** ① T226-7891, which flies to San Blas; **Parsa** ① T226-3883, provides a charter service; **Transpasa** ① T236-0842, has charter flights to San Blas; **Chitreana** ① T226-4116, flies to Chitré, Los Santos, Las Tablas and Guararé, and **Aerotaxi** ① T226-7891, operates a service to San Blas and charter flights.

On internal flights passengers must present their identity documents and have their luggage weighed. As excess baggage charges are frequent, ask if it is cheaper to ship excess as air freight (*carga*) on the same flight.

Road

There are now about 9700 km of roads, of which 3100 km are paved. The highway running from Colón to Panama City is the only fully paved road crossing the isthmus. A well-maintained scenic road traverses the isthmus from Gualaca in Chiriquí to the town of Chiriquí Grande in Bocas del Toro, crossing the Swedish-built Fortuna hydroelectric dam. The road continues to Almirante and the regional centre of Changuinola, opening up a beautiful route along the Caribbean. The Pan-American Highway, usually called the *Interamericana* in Panama, runs east from Panama City to Chepo and into the province of Darién, and west to the Costa Rican border. It is paved throughout (as far east as the Panama/Darién provincial border) and is being improved. There is a modern toll road between Panama City and La Chorrera, and the section between David and La Concepción is a modern, four-lane highway. There are expressways in and around Panama City.

Bus The bus network covers the entire country, generally with efficient, timely services. Some of the long-distance buses are small 'mini' buses, normally modern and comfortable, but large, modern air-conditioned buses are being introduced. They are more expensive than elsewhere in Central America. Slower 'regular' buses run in country areas. 'Express' buses with air conditioning operate between Panama City and Colón and to David and the border with Costa Rica.

Car Average **car hire** rates range from US$24 per day for a small saloon to US$65 for 4WD jeep, free mileage, insurance US$8 per day, 5% tax, US$500 deposit (can be paid by credit card), minimum age 23, home driver's licence acceptable. If you require a 4WD it is better to book a few days in advance. If planning to rent from an international company, consult them before leaving home. Sometimes deals are available that cannot be made in Panama. Rental cars are not allowed out of the country; these are marked by special licence plates.

Super grade gasoline (called *super*) costs about US$3.40 per US gallon (3.78 litres); unleaded is available in larger towns. Low octane (*regular* or *normal*) costs about US$3.20; diesel is about US$3. For motorcyclists, note that a crash helmet must be worn.

Taking a car with Panamanian plates to Costa Rica requires a permit from the Traffic Police (*Tránsito*) obtainable on presentation of the ownership certificate and a document from the Judicial Police (*PTJ*) indicating that the vehicle has not been reported stolen. A travel agency, for example **Chadwick's** in Balboa, will arrange this for you for US$30.

Sea
Boats and comfortable yachts provide tours all or part way through the canal. Contact tour operators in Panama City or Colón for details. It is also possible to travel through offering linehandling services, if you have sailing experience and turn up at the right time.

A regular ferry makes the journey to the island of Bocas del Toro from Almirante and Chiriquí Grande on the western Caribbean coast. To the east, canoes serves the archipelago of San Blas.

Access to and from Colombia is possible by sea, along the Caribbean or Pacific coasts, although the journey takes several days and can be costly, see page 1393.

Shipping a vehicle Taking a vehicle out of Panama to Colombia, Venezuela or Ecuador is not easy or cheap. The best advice is to shop around the agencies in Panama City or Colón to see what is available when you want to go. Both local and international lines take vehicles, and sometimes passengers, but schedules and prices are very variable.

To Panama, the recommended agency is **Panalpina** ① *Los Andes 2, Ojo de Aqua, Vía Transmística, Panama City, T273-7066, www.panalpina.com*. Jürgen Lahntaler speaks German, English and Spanish. Panalpina can also arrange shipment of vehicles to Ecuador, Venezuela and Chile.

To Colombia, agents include: **CSAV** ① *PO Box: 0832-2775, Edificio Frontenac, Local 2-B, Calle 50 y esq 54 Este, Panama City, T269-1613, www.csav.com*, who also sail to other countries in South America on both the Atlantic and Pacific side.

To Barranquilla, Vicente Simones' Colón ① *T195-1262, beeper 270-0000, code 700283*, will arrange all paperwork for US$25: car passage US$800, motorcycle US$50, plus US$50 per passenger, no accommodation on ship other than hammock space, take food and drink for a week (even though voyage should be three days).

To Cartagena, **Captain Newball** ① *Edificio Los Cristales, Piso 3, Calle 38 y Av Cuba, Panama City*. On the same route, **Central American Lines** ① *agent in Panama, Colón T441-2880, Panama City T236-1036*, sail once a week. Also **Géminis Shipping Co SA** ① *Apdo Postal No 3016, Zona Libre de Colón, República de Panamá, T441-6269, F441-6571*. Mr Ricardo Gil is helpful and reliable. Another agent, **Barwil** ① *Galerías Balboa Suite 35, Av Balboa, Panama City, T263-7755, www.barwil-panama.com*, arranges shipments to Colombia (Cartagena) and elsewhere in Latin America from Balboa or Cristóbal.

Customs formalities at the Colombian end will take up to three days to clear (customs officials do not work at weekends). Cartagena is the best port because it is privately run, more secure and more efficient. Go first to customs: **DIAN** ① *Manga CL27 A 24-83, Diagonal DIAN, Jefe División de Servicio al Comercio Exterior*. Here you will receive, for free, the necessary documents to enter the port (this takes about 24 hours).

To Ecuador, weekly (sometimes more often) sailings with combined services of **Maersk Line** ① *Blv Costa del Este, Complejo Business Park, Edificio Norte, piso 5, Panama City, T206-2200, www.maerskline.com*, visit the website to find your nearest office. **Hapaglloyd** agents are **AGENCO** ① *Edif Eurocentro, PB, Av Abel Bravo, Urbanización Obarrio, Panama City, T300-1400, www.hapag-lloyd.com*, about US$900 for a 6-m container. Shipping to Guayaquil from Panama's container port of Manzanillo, next to Colón, is the best choice, preferable to Colombia or Venezuela. **TNE (Transportes Navieros Ecuatorianos)** ① *T269-2022*, ship vehicles to Guayaquil; agent in Cristóbal, Agencia Continental SA, T445-1818. Another agent recommended in Cristóbal is **Associated Steamships** ① *Balboa, T211-9400, www.shipsagent.com*. Customs agents cost US$60 in Colón, US$120 in Guayaquil; 12 days from starting arrangements in Panama to leaving Guayaquil docks. Seek advice on paperwork from the Ecuadorean consul in Panama. **Barwil** (see above for Colombia) will ship vehicles to Arica, Chile.

To Venezuela, in addition to those mentioned above, agents include: **Cia Transatlántica España** ① *T269-6300*, to La Guaira. **Vencaribe** (a Venezuelan line), agent in Cristóbal: **Associated Steamship (Wilford and McKay**, see above), T252-1258 (Panama), T445-0461 (Cristóbal). There are several agencies in Colón/Cristóbal. Formalities before leaving can be completed through a travel agency – recommended is **Continental Travel Agency** ① *at the Hotel Continental, T263-6162*. In Venezuela there are customs complications (without carnet) and this route is not really recommended.

Maps

Topographic maps and aerial photos are sold by the **Instituto Geográfico Nacional Tommy Guardia (IGNTG)** ① *Vía Simón Bolívar, opposite the National University (footbridge nearby, fortunately), T236-2444, www.ignpanama.gob.pa, take Transístmica or Tumba Muerto bus, Mon-Fri 0800-1530*. Maps from 1:500,000 to 1:50,000 available. **ITM** (www.itmb.com) have a 1:800,000 travel map of Panama.

Sleeping

The very best in five-star luxury is available in Panama City and several comfortable lodges are found in the larger towns and mountain and jungle hideaways. If travelling further afield, accommodation in the **C** category and below is available in most towns of interest. Camping is generally tolerated.

Eating

In Panama City the range of food available is very broad with a profusion of restaurants and well-stocked supermarkets. In the interior tastes are simpler and available ingredients less varied. Most food is boiled or fried in vegetable oil (usually soybean oil). Virtually every restaurant will have a *comida corriente* (meal of the day), which will include a serving of meat, chicken or fish, white rice and a salad, a dish of boiled beans garnished with a *tajada* (slice) of fried ripe plantain. It will cost about US$2 in towns, perhaps more in the city, less in villages. A bowl of *sopa de carne* (beef broth with vegetables) or *de pescado* (fish chowder) is usually available as a first course for US$0.50. Breakfast normally consists of eggs, a small beefsteak or a slice of liver fried with onions and tomatoes, bread and butter and some combination of *frituras*.

The staple of Panamanian food is white rice, grown not in paddies but on dry land, and usually served at every meal, often with the addition of chicken, shrimp, vegetables, etc. Meat is usually fried (*frita*) or braised (*guisada*), rarely grilled except in the better restaurants. Beef is common; pork, chicken and the excellent fish are usually a better choice.

The national dish is *sancocho de gallina*, a stew of chicken, yuca, *ñame* (dasheen), plantain, cut-up pieces of corn on the cob, potatoes and onions and strongly flavoured with *culantro*, an aromatic leaf similar in flavour to coriander (*cilantro*). *Ropa vieja* ('old clothes') is beef boiled or steamed until it can be shredded, then sautéed with onions, garlic, tomatoes and green or red peppers, often served with yellow rice (coloured with *achiote*). Piquant *ceviche*, eaten as a first course or a snack with cold beer, is usually raw corvina or shellfish seasoned with tiny red and yellow peppers, thin slices of onion and marinated in lime juice; it is served very cold with crackers (beware of the bite). A speciality of the Caribbean coast is *sao*, pigs' feet pickled with lime and hot peppers. Also try *arroz con coco*, coconut rice, or the same with *tití*, tiny shrimp; also *fufú*, a fish chowder with coconut milk. *Mondongo* is the stewed tripe dish called *menudo* in Mexico; the Panamanian version is less spicy, but very well seasoned.

Most *panaderías* sell good pastries: in Panama City most of the European standards are available; in the country, try *orejas*, *costillas* or *ma'mellena* ('fills me up more', a sweet bread-pudding with raisins); *dulces* (of coconut, pineapple, etc), are cakes or pastries, not sweets/candies as elsewhere (the latter are *confites*). Among the items sold at the roadside you may see bottles stopped with a corncob, filled with *nance*, a strong-flavoured, yellow-green fruit packed with water and allowed to ripen and ferment slightly; *pifá/pixbae*, a bright orange fruit which, when boiled, tastes much like sweet potato (two or three will see you though to your next meal); *níspero*, the tasty, acidic yellow fruit of the chicle tree.

There are dozens of sweetened fruit drinks found everywhere in the country, making excellent use of the many delicious tropical and temperate fruits grown here: *naranja* (orange), *maracuyá* (passion fruit), *guayaba, zarzamora* (blackberry), *guanábana*, etc. The generic term is *chicha dulce*, which also includes drinks made with rice or corn. Most common carbonated canned drinks are available. Panamanian beer tends to be low in alcohol, *Panamá* and *Soberana* are the most popular locally. *Chicha fuerte* is the alcoholic form of corn or rice drink fermented with sugar, brewed mostly in the countryside. Sample with care. The local rum, for example *Carta Vieja*, is not bad. *Seco*, a harsh brand of 'white lightning' made from the juice of sugar cane, brand name *Herrerano*, deserves respect.

Festivals and events

1 Jan New Year's Day.	**3 Nov** Independence Day.
9 Jan Martyrs' Day.	**4 Nov** Flag Day.
Feb/Mar Shrove Tuesday Carnival.	**5 Nov** Independence Day
Mar/Apr Good Friday.	(Colón only).
1 May Labour Day (Republic).	**10 Nov** First Call of Independence.
15 Aug Panama City only.	**28 Nov** Independence from Spain.
1 Nov National Anthem Day.	**8 Dec** Mothers' Day.
2 Nov All Souls' Day.	**25 Dec** Christmas Day.

The school holidays are December to March, and during these times the popular tourists spots are busy so make reservations in advance.

The fiestas in the towns are well worth seeing. Panama City at **Carnival** time, held on the four days before Shrove Tuesday, is the best. During carnival, women who can afford it wear the voluminous *pollera* dress, a shawl folded across the shoulders, velvet slippers, tinkling pearl and polished fish-scale hair ornaments (called *tembleques* from their quivering motion) in spirited shapes and colours. The men wear a *montuno* outfit: round straw hats, embroidered blouses and trousers sometimes to below the knee only, and carry the *chácara*, or small purse.

At the **Holy Week** ceremonies at Villa de Los Santos the farces and acrobatics of the big devils – with their debates and trials in which the main devil accuses and an angel defends the soul – the dance of the 'dirty little devils' and the dancing drama of the Montezumas are all notable. The ceremonies at **Pesé** (near Chitré) are famous all over Panama. At **Portobelo**, near Colón, there is a procession of little boats in the canals of the city. **Bullfights**, where the bull survives, are an important part of rural fairs, as are rodeo events.

The indigenous Ngöbe-Bugle (Guaymí) of Chiriquí province meet around 12 February to transact tribal business, hold feasts and compete for brides by tossing balsa logs at one another; those unhurt in this contest, known as *Las Balserías*, are viewed as heroes.

Shopping

More traditional Panamanian crafts include the colourful *molas* embroidered by the Kuna people of the San Blas islands. Masks, costumes, ceramics and woven hats can be found in several small villages dotted around the Azuero Peninsula. These are on sale in many places. Straw, leather and ceramic items are also available, as are carvings of wildlife made from wood, nuts and other natural materials. And of course, don't forget the quintessential **Panama hat**. Good ones are expensive. Duty-free imported goods including stereos, photographic equipment, perfume and clothes are cheap in the Colón Free Zone on the Caribbean coast. Most items are cheaper than at point of origin.

Essentials A-Z

Customs and duty free

Panamanian Customs are strict; drugs without a doctor's prescription may be confiscated. Cameras, binoculars, etc, 500 cigarettes or 500 g of tobacco and 3 bottles of alcoholic drinks for personal use can be taken in free of duty. However, passengers leaving Panama by land are not entitled to any duty-free goods.

Electricity

110 volts AC, 60 cycles, US-style plugs. 220 volts is occasionally available in homes and hotels.

Embassies and consulates

Embassies/consulates in these and other countries can be checked at www.mire.gob.pa.
Australia, 39 Wardell Rd, Earlwood, Sydney NSW 2206, T9558-2500.
Austria, Elisabethstr 4/5/4/10, A-1010 Vienna, T587-2347.
Belgium, Av Louise 390-392, 1050 Brussels, T649-0729.
Canada, 130 Albert St, Suite 300 Ottawa, ON, Kip 564, T236-7177.
Costa Rica, Calle 38, Av 7 y 9, San José, 1257-3241.
France, 145 Av de Suffren, 75015 Paris, T4566-4244.
Germany, Joachim-Karnatz-Allee 45, 3 OG, 10557 Berlín, T30-226-05811.
Israel, Rehov Hei Be'iyar 10/3, Tel Aviv 62998, T696-0849.
Italy, Viale Regina Margherta No 239, Cuarto Piso, Interno 11, 00198 Roma, T1156-60707.
New Zealand, Shortland St, Auckland, T379-8550.
Nicaragua, del Cuartel de Bomberos 1 cuadra abajo, Managua, T266-2224.
South Africa, 832 Duncan St, Brooklyn, Pretoria, 0181, T/F1236-22629.
Spain, Claudio Coello 86, 1° 28006, Madrid T576-7668.
Sweden, Ostermalmsgatan 59, 114 50, 102 04 Stockholm, T662-6535.
UK, 40 Hertford St, London W1Y 7TG, T020-7493-4646.
USA, 2862 McGill Terrace NW, Washington DC 20008, T202-483-1407, www.embassyofpanama.org.

Health

Water in Panama City and Colón is safe to drink. Drink bottled water outside the cities, especially in Bocas del Toro where the expanding water system is not as clean as desired. In smaller towns, it is best to drink bottled or boiled water to avoid minor problems. Yellow fever vaccination is recommended before visiting Darién. Travellers to Darién Province and San Blas Province in Panama (including the San Blas Islands) should treat these as malarial areas in which there is resistance to chloroquine. Treatment is expensive; insurance underwritten by a US company would be helpful. See page 51 for further information.

Internet

Internet access is available throughout the country. Charges average out at about US$1-2 per hr.

Language

Spanish is the national language, but English is widely understood. The older generation of West Indian immigrants speak Wari-Wari, a dialect of English incomprehensible to most other English speakers. In rural areas, indigenous people use their own languages and many are bilingual.

Media

La Prensa, www.prensa.com, is the major local daily newspaper. Others are *La Estrella de Panamá*, *El Universal de Panamá*, *El Panamá América*, www.epasa.com, and 2 tabloids, *Crítica Libre*, www.critica.com.pa, and *El Siglo*. *Colón News* is a weekly publication in Spanish and English. In English is the bi-weekly *Panama News*, www.thepanamanews.com.

The international edition of the *Miami Herald* is printed in Panama and many other US newspapers are widely available in the capital.

Money → *US$1=1 balboa (June 2009).*
The unit of currency in Panama is the balboa, but Panama is one of the few countries in the world which issues no paper money; US banknotes are used exclusively, and US notes and coins are legal tender. There are 'silver' coins of 50c (called a *peso*), 25c (called *cinco reales* or *cuara*, from US 'quarter'), 10c,

nickel of 5c (called a *real*) and copper of 1c. All coins are used interchangeably with US equivalents, which are the same in size and composition. There is great reluctance in Panama to accept US$50 and US$100 dollar notes because of counterfeiting. Do not be offended if asked to produce ID and sign a register when spending them. You can take in or out any amount of currency. If travelling north, remember that US dollar notes, especially smaller denominations, are useful in all Central American countries and may be difficult to obtain in other republics. Stocking up on a supply of US$5 and US$1 notes greatly facilitates border crossings and traffic problems in Central America where 'fees' and 'instant fines' can become exorbitant if you only have a US$20 note.

ATMs and credit cards
Visa ATMs are available at branches of **Telered**, call T001-800-111-0016, if card is lost or stolen. MasterCard/Cirrus ATMs are available at **Caja de Ahorros** offices and others in the Pronto system. MasterCard emergency number is T001-800-307-7309; Western Union is T269-1055. See Panama City Directory, page 1327, for other credit card phone numbers.

Cost of living and travelling
Prices are somewhat higher than in the rest of Central America, although food costs much the same as in Costa Rica. The annual average increase in consumer prices fluctuates in line with US trends.

Opening hours
Banks Open at different times, but are usually open all morning, and often on Sat. **Government departments** Mon-Fri 0800-1200, 1230-1630. **Shops** Mon-Sat 0700/0800-1200, 1400-1800/1900.

Post
When sending mail, great care should be taken to address all mail as 'Panama' or 'RP' (Republic of Panama). Airmail takes up to 10 days, sea mail 3-5 weeks from Europe. Example rates for airmail (up to 15 g) are as follows: Central, North and South America and Caribbean, 35c; Europe, 45c up to 10 g, 5c for every extra 5 g; Africa, Asia, Oceania, 60c. Parcels to Europe can only be sent from the post office in the El Dorado shopping centre in Panama City (bus from Calle 12 to Tumba Muerto). Post offices, marked with blue and yellow signs, are the only places permitted to sell stamps.

Tax
US$5 arrival tax in addition to the airport departure tax of US$20, payable by all passengers (cash only). US$4 tax on air tickets over US$100 purchased in Panama. There is a 10% tax on all hotel prices

Telephone → *Country code T+507.*
The **international direct dialling** code (to call out of Panama) is T00; **Telecarrier** T088+00; **Clarocom** T055+00. Dial T102 for the local operator and T106 for an international operator. Collect calls are permitted, 3 mins minimum, rates are higher than direct, especially to USA. **Cable & Wireless** now run the telephone system and have offices in most towns. Cost of direct dialled calls, per minute, are between US$1-3.20. Calls are roughly 20-30% cheaper for most, but not all destinations from 1700-2200. Lowest rates apply Sun all day. Many cheap international call centres in Panama City, check the the internet cafés on Vía Veneto, off Vía España for best offers.

Public payphones take 5, 10 and sometimes 25 cent coins. Phone cards are available in denominations of US$3, 5, 10, 20 and 50, for local, national and international calls. There are prepaid *Aló Panamá* cards – dial 165 for connection in US$10, US$20, US$30 and US$50 denominations, but they are 50% more expensive than payphone cards. For *AT&T* dial T109. For *SPRINT* (collect calls only) T115 and for **MCI** T108. **BT Chargecard** calls to the UK can be made through the local operator.

Time
-5 hrs GMT.

Tipping
In restaurants, tip 10% of the bill, often added to the bill in Panama City. Porters expect US$1 for assistance at the airport. Taxi drivers don't expect tips.

Tourist information
Instituto Panameño de Turismo (IPAT) toll-free T011-800-SIPANAMA from the US or Canada, www.visitpanama.com, or contact your nearest embassy. Once in country, IPAT have an office in Panama City (see page 1302).

Useful websites
www.businesspanama.com Economic, political and business information.
www.panama-guide.com Expatriate community forum, news, chat and information.
www.panamainfo.com An excellent site in English with good general information on Panama and links to several other national sites including newspapers, government organizations and tourist services.
www.panamatours.com A pure tourism site with a good overview of the country.
www.stri.org The Smithsonian Tropical Research Institute, whose headquarters are in Panama.

Visas and Immigration
Visitors must have a passport, and in most cases a tourist card (issued for 90 days and renewable for another 90 at the Immigration Office in Panama City, David or other provincial offices, eg Changuinola) or a visa (issued for 90 days, extendable for a further 90 days). Tourist cards are available at borders, from Panamanian consulates, *Ticabus* or airlines. To enter Panama officially you must have an onward flight ticket, travel agent confirmation of the same, or be able to demonstrate that you have sufficient funds (in cash, credit card or valid traveller's cheques) to cover your stay and departure. Recent travellers report these are asked for on the land frontier with Costa Rica and at Puerto Obaldía (Darién); generally officers are not very strict unless they fear you may be destitute.

Citizens of most European (including the United Kingdom) and Central American countries do not need a tourist card or a visa. Citizens of the United States, Canada, most Caribbean, South American and some Asian countries need a tourist card (US$5) available at airlines and travel agencies. Citizens of Egypt, Peru, Dominican Republic, many African, Eastern European and Asian countries require a visa – check before travelling with your nearest Consulate office.

Nationals not requiring visas can renew their 90-day tourist cards once for a total of 180 days, after which you must leave the country for 3 days. The necessary documents must all be obtained in advance: a photo-ID card (*carnet*), to be surrendered when you return for an exit visa, will be issued; allow 1-2 hrs for this. Requirements are 2 passport photos, a ticket out of the country or proof of sufficient funds, a brief letter explaining why you wish to extend your stay, a letter from a permanent resident accepting legal and financial responsibility for you during your extra days in Panama, and 2 photocopies of the name page and the entry stamp page of your passport. All papers must be presented at *Prórrogas* in the immigration office and a fee of US$11 paid for each 90-day extension before the photo ID card is issued. Requirements for renewing a visa are similar, but include 2 photocopies of the original visa.

Weights and measures
Metric and imperial systems are both used.

Panama City

→ *Colour map 8, B1.*

Panama City is a curious blend of old Spain, US-style mall developments and the bazaar atmosphere of the east. Hardly surprising then that it has a polyglot population unrivalled in any other Latin American city. Beyond the new developments and skyscrapers that mushroomed along the southern end of the Canal, the palm-shaded beaches, islands in the bay and encircling hills still constitute a large part of Panama City's charm. And its cabarets and nightlife are an added attraction for any self-respecting hedonist. ►► *For listings, see pages 1314-1329.*

Ins and outs

Getting there Tocumen International Airport is 27 km from the city centre. For flights, see page 1293. Set-price taxis (US$25), cheaper if shared (*compartido*) and buses are available for getting into Panama City. The bus journey should take one hour but can take up to three in rush hour. Car rental companies also have offices at the airport. The city is well served by international buses from countries throughout Central America, with offices in the centre of town. ►► *See Transport, page 1324.*

Getting around The old part of the city, Casco Viejo, can easily be toured on foot. There are old, usually crowded and very cheap buses for getting to other districts. The reasonably priced taxis charge on a zone system and can be shared if you wish to economize. Taxis can be hired by the hour for a city tour. At night, radio taxis are preferable. Many *avenidas* have both names and numbers, although locals are most likely to use the names, so asking for directions can be a bit complicated. Also, because there is no postal delivery to homes or businesses, few buildings display their numbers, so try to find out the nearest cross street.

The wider metropolitan area has a population of approximately 720,000. Adjacent to the city, but constituting a separate administrative district, is the town of San Miguelito, a residential area for over 330,000 people. Once a squatter community, every available square inch of hillside has been built on and it is increasingly considered to be a part of greater Panama City.

Tourist offices Information office of the **Instituto Panameño de Turismo** (IPAT) ① *Av Samuel Lewis y Calle Gerardo Ortega, Edif Central, T526-7000, www.ipat.gob.pa,* have good lists of lodgings and other services. There are other **IPAT kiosks** ① *Tocumen Airport in Panamá Viejo, Tue-Sun 0800-2200; on the pedestrian mall on Av Central, Mon-Fri 0900-1700; and opposite Hotel Continental on España,* and in all regions of the country.

Safety Tourist police on mountain bikes are present in the downtown areas of the city, recognizable by their broad armbands. Panamanians are generally very friendly and helpful. Accustomed to foreigners, they are casual about tourists. However, as in any large city with many poor people, certain areas can be dangerous after dark and reasonable precautions should be taken at all times. Attacks have been reported in Casco Viejo (although this area is now well patrolled by police during the daytime) and Panamá Viejo. Marañón (around the market), San Miguelito (on the way in from Tocumen Airport) and Calidonia can all be dangerous; never walk there at night and take care in daylight, too. Poor districts like Chorillo, Curundú and Hollywood are best avoided altogether. Probably the safest area for budget travellers to stay is Bella Vista, although it is deserted after dark and street crime can take place here at any hour. Taxis are the safest way to travel around the city and drivers will give you good advice on where not to go. If concerned, lock the doors of the taxi.

Background

Modern Panama City was founded on its present site in 1673. The capital was moved from Old Panama (Panamá Viejo), 6.5 km to the east, after Henry Morgan looted the South American treasure chest depot of Golden Panama in 1671. Today, it is a thoroughly modern city complete with congested streets and noisy traffic. Uncollected trash mouldering in the tropical heat and the liberal use of razor-wire are other eyesores but, despite its blemishes, the city does possess considerable charm. The old quarter, called Casco Viejo or San Felipe, massively fortified by Spain as the era of widespread piracy was coming to an end, lies at the tip of the peninsula at the eastern end of the Bay of Panama.

Sights

The principal districts of interest to vistors include El Cangrejo, Campo Alegre, Paitilla, and Coco del Mar, where the international banks, luxury hotels and restaurants are located. Calidonia, Bella Vista and Perejil are bustling with commerce, traffic, and mid-price hotels.

Casco Viejo

Casco Viejo (the 'Old Compound' or San Felipe), which occupies the narrow peninsula east of Calle 11, is an unusual combination of beautifully restored public buildings, churches, plazas, monuments and museums alongside inner-city decay which, after decades of neglect, is now gradually being gentrified. Several budget hotels are found here, some very badly run-down but not without their faded glory. Created in 1673 after the sacking of old Panama, Casco Viejo is a treasure trove of architectural delights, some restored, others in a desperate state of repair, but most demanding a gentle meander through the shady streets. In 1992 local authorities began reviving some of the area's past glory by painting the post-colonial houses in soft pastels and their decorations and beautiful wrought-iron railings in relief. New shops and restaurants are moving into restored buildings in an attempt to make Casco Viejo a tourist attraction.

At the walled tip of the peninsula is the picturesque **Plaza de Francia**, with its bright red poinciana trees and obelisk topped by a cockerel (symbol of the Gallic nation), which has a document with 5000 signatures buried beneath it. Twelve large narrative plaques and many statues recall the French Canal's construction history and personalities; the work of Cuban doctor Carlos Finlay in establishing the cause of yellow fever is commemorated on one tablet. Facing the plaza is the French Embassy, housed in a pleasant early 20th-century building; it stubbornly refused to relocate during the years when the neighbourhood declined and is now one of the main focus points in the area's renaissance. Built flush under the old seawalls around the plaza are **Las Bóvedas** (The Vaults), the thick-walled colonial dungeons where prisoners in tiny barred cells were immersed up to their necks during high tides. Nine 'vaults' were restored by the Instituto Panameño de Turismo (IPAT) in 1982 and converted into an art gallery – **Galería Las Bóvedas** ① *Tue-Sun 1100-1900; students offer walking tours of the Casco Viejo from here during these hrs, copies of 'Focus on Panama' are available here*, – and handicraft centre. The French restaurant **Las Bóvedas** occupies another two 'vaults' next to the former Palacio de Justicia, partly burned during 'Operation

Just Cause' and now housing the **Instituto Nacional de Cultura** (INC), with an interesting mural by Esteban Palomino on the ground floor.

Steps lead up from the Plaza de Francia to the **Paseo de las Bóvedas** promenade along the top of the defensive walls surrounding the peninsula on three sides. This is a popular place for an evening stroll; it is ablaze with bougainvillea and affords good views of the Bahía de Panamá, the Serranía de Majé on the Panama/Darién provincial border (on a clear day), Calzada Amador (known during the Canal Zone era as the Causeway) and the islands beyond.

1 Panama City

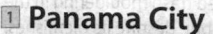

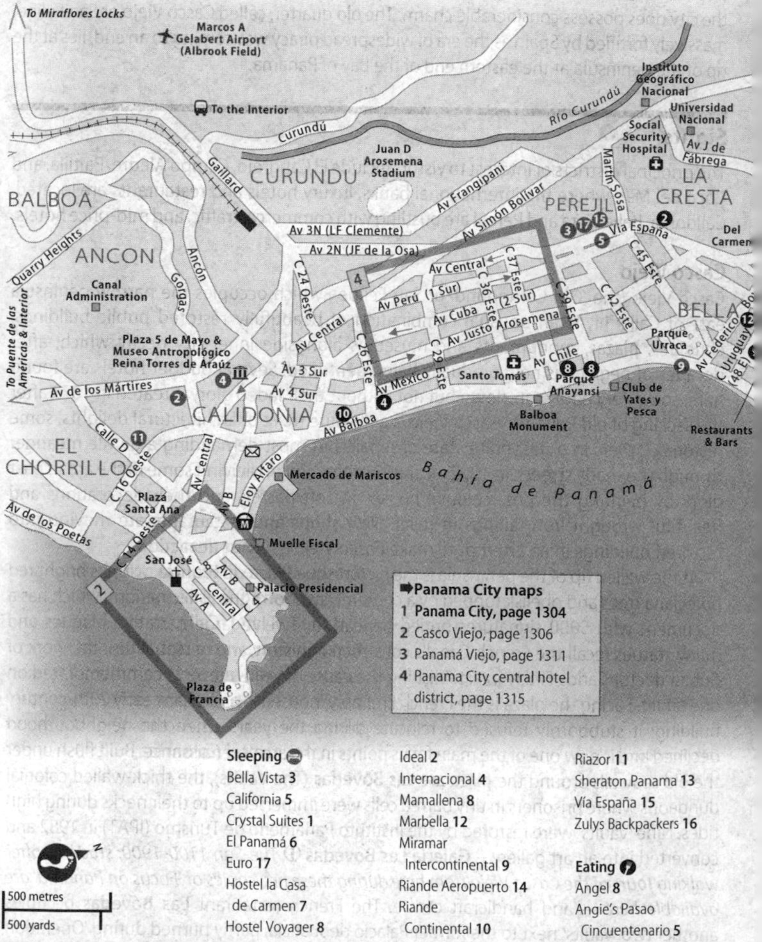

To Miraflores Locks
Marcos A Gelabert Airport (Albrook Field)
To the Interior
Curundú
Río Curundú
Instituto Geográfico Nacional
Universidad Nacional
Social Security Hospital
Av J de Fábrega
Juan D Arosemena Stadium
CURUNDU
Gaillard
BALBOA
Av Frangipani
Av Simón Bolívar
PEREJIL
Martín Sosa
LA CRESTA
Vía España
Del Carmen
Quarry Heights
ANCON
Av 3N (LF Clemente)
Av 2N (JF de la Osa)
C 24 Oeste
Ancón
Gorgas
Canal Administration
Av Central
Av Perú (1 Sur)
Av Cuba
(2 Sur)
Av Justo Arosemena
C 36 Este
C 37 Este
C 39 Este
C 42 Este
C 45 Este
BELLA
Parque Urraca
Av Federico Boyd
C Uruguay (48 E)
To Puente de las Américas & Interior
Plaza 5 de Mayo & Museo Antropológico Reina Torres de Araúz
Av 3 Sur
Av 4 Sur
C 26 Este
C 29 Este
Av México
Santo Tomás
Av Chile
Parque Anayansi
Club de Yates y Pesca
Av de los Mártires
CALIDONIA
Av Balboa
Balboa Monument
Restaurants & Bars
Calle D
EL CHORRILLO
C 16 Oeste
Av Central
Eloy Alfaro
Mercado de Mariscos
Bahía de Panamá
Plaza Santa Ana
Av de los Poetas
Av B
Muelle Fiscal
C 14 Oeste
San José
C 8
Av B
Central
Av A
C 4
Palacio Presidencial
Plaza de Francia
Panama City maps
1 Panama City, page 1304
2 Casco Viejo, page 1306
3 Panamá Viejo, page 1311
4 Panama City central hotel district, page 1315
Sleeping
Bella Vista 3
California 5
Crystal Suites 1
El Panamá 6
Euro 17
Hostel la Casa de Carmen 7
Hostel Voyager 8
Ideal 2
Internacional 4
Mamallena 8
Marbella 12
Miramar Intercontinental 9
Riande Aeropuerto 14
Riande Continental 10
Riazor 11
Sheraton Panama 13
Vía España 15
Zulys Backpackers 16
Eating
Angel 8
Angie's Pasao Cincuentenario 5
N
500 metres
500 yards

Two blocks northwest of the Plaza (Avenida A and Calle 3) are the restored ruins of the impressive **Church and Convent of Santo Domingo** (1673, later destroyed by fires in 1737 and 1756), both with paired columns and brick inlaying on their façades. The famous 15-m long flat arch, **Arco Chato**, which formed the base of the choir, was built entirely of bricks and mortar with no internal support. When the great debate as to where the Canal should be built was going on in the United States Congress, a Nicaraguan postage stamp showing a volcano, with all its implications of earthquakes, and the stability of this arch – a supposed proof of no earthquakes – are said to have played a large part in determining the choice in Panama's favour. A chapel on the site has been converted into the interesting **Museo de Arte Colonial Religioso** ① *Tue-Sat 0830-1630, admission US$0.75, students and seniors US$0.25, T228-2897,* whose treasures include a precious Golden Altar, a delicate snail staircase, silver relics and wooden sculptures from Lima and Mexico, 19th-century engravings of the city, and the skeleton of a woman found during excavation of the church.

Not far from Santo Domingo, across Avenida Central, the neoclassical **Teatro Nacional** ① *T262-3525, Mon-Fri 0800-1600, US$0.50*, with 850-seat capacity, opened in 1908 with Verdi's *Aida* being performed in what was then considered the state of the art in acoustics. French-influenced sculptures and friezes enliven the façade, while Roberto Lewis' paintings depicting the birth of the nation adorn the theatre's dome. The ballerina Dame Margot Fonteyn, who married a member of the prominent Arias family and was a long-time resident of Panama until her death in 1991, danced at the theatre's re-inauguration in 1974.

Diagonally opposite the Teatro Nacional (Avenida B and Calle 3) is the peaceful **Plaza Bolívar**, with a statue of the liberator Simón Bolívar, draped in robes, standing below a large condor surrounded by plaques of his deeds. Around the square are the former **Hotel Colombia**, the **Church of San Felipe Neri**, and many 19th-century houses still displaying roofs of red-clay tiles bearing the stamp 'Marseilles 1880'. On the east side stand **San Francisco Church** ① *Mon-Sat 1430-1800, Sun all day*, colonial but 'modified' in 1917 and modernized in 1983, and the **San Francisco Convent**

Caffé Pomodoro 1
Calypso 2
El Trapiche 3
Gauchos Steak House 9
Gran China 4
Jimmy's 5
La Cascada 10
Las Costillitas 11
Las Tinajas 12

Manolo 6
Matsul 13
Niko's Café 7
Parrillada Martín Fierro 14
Pavo Real 17
Pizzeria Sorrento 15
Sushi Itto 16

(1678), the largest of all the religious buildings, which was restored by Peruvian architect Leonardo Villanueva. The Bolivarian Congress of June 1826, at which Bolívar proposed a United States of South America, was also held in the Chapter Room of the Convent, now known as the **Salón Bolívar**, and the 1904 Constitution was also drafted here. This northern wing was dedicated as the **Instituto Bolívar** in 1956; its wood panelling, embossed leather benches and paintings (restored in part by the government of Ecuador) may be viewed with an authorized guide from the Bolivarian Society (T262-2947). The adjacent Colegio Bolívar, built on a pier over the water, is due to become the new Cancillería (Ministry of Foreign Affairs).

Another long block west of Plaza Bolívar, and one block north on the seafront (Avenida Eloy Alfaro) between Calles 5 y 6, is the **Palacio Presidencial**, the most impressive building in the city, built as an opulent residence in 1673 for successive colonial auditors and governors, enlarged and restored under President Belisario Porras in 1922.

A few blocks west, Avenida Alfaro curves north around the waterfront to the colourful **Central Market**, Mercado San Felipe (see Shopping, page 1321) and the **Muelle Fiscal**

2 Casco Viejo

wharf where coastal vessels anchor and small cargo boats leave for Darién and sometimes Colombia. Two blocks further north, where Avenida Alfaro meets Avenida Balboa by the pier, is the modern **Mercado de Mariscos** (fish and seafood market), where fishermen land their catch.

Returning to Casco Viejo, two blocks south of the Palacio Presidencial is the heart of the old town, the **Plaza Catedral** or **Independencia**, with busts of the Republic's founders, and surrounding public buildings. On the west is the **cathedral** (1688-1794, refurbished in 1999), with its twin towers, domes, classical façade encrusted with mother-of-pearl and three of the tower bells brought from the Old Panama Cathedral. To the right of the main altar is a subterranean passage that leads to other *conventos* and the sea. On the southwest corner with Calle 7 is the neoclassical **Palacio Municipal** (City Hall), on the first floor of which is the **Museo de Historia de Panamá** ① *Mon-Fri 0800-1600, US$0.50*, which covers the nation's history since European landfall, and includes highlights of the treaty between Panama and the USA which led to the construction of the Canal. The former post office next door, originally built in 1875 as the **Grand Hotel** ("the largest edifice of that kind between San Francisco and Cape Horn" according to a contemporary newspaper), is the city's best example of French architecture. It became de Lesseps' headquarters during Canal excavations in the 1880s and was sold back to Panama in 1912. It has been entirely gutted and converted into the **Museo del Canal Interoceánico** ① *Plaza Catedral, T/F211-1650, Tue-Sun 0900-1700, US$2, concessions US$0.75, www.museodelcanal. com, photography not allowed, English- and French-speaking guides are available, other languages available if booked in advance, hand-held English audio commentaries cost US$5.* It has an interesting and comprehensive history of Panama – mainly the central provinces – as shaped by its pass route. Recommended.

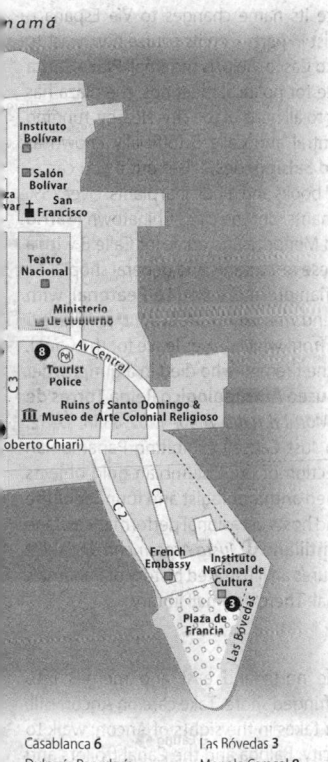

The east side of the Plaza is dominated by the former **Archbishop's Palace**. Later occupied by a university, this was a shelter for runaway kids and then spent a period as the **Central Hotel** (1884), once the most luxurious in Central America. The interior featured a palm garden, restaurants, barber shop, 100 rooms with private baths and a wooden staircase imported from New York, and it was the centre of Panama's social life for decades. Today it is decrepit and may, in time, benefit from the creeping regeneration of the old city.

There are a number of other interesting religious structures within two or three

Map labels:
namá

- Instituto Bolívar
- Salón Bolívar
- San Francisco
- Teatro Nacional
- Ministerio de Gobierno
- Av Central
- Tourist Police
- Ruins of Santo Domingo & Museo de Arte Colonial Religioso
- oberto Chiari)
- French Embassy
- Instituto Nacional de Cultura
- Plaza de Francia
- Las Bóvedas

Casablanca **6**
Dulcería Panadería
La Gran Vida **2**
Las Róvedas **3**
Monolo Caracol **8**
Mostaza **7**

blocks of the cathedral, but the most-visited is the **Church of San José** ① *Av A and Calle 8, 1 block west and 2 south of the Plaza Catedral, T228-0190*, with its famous Altar de Oro, a massive baroque altar carved from mahogany and, according to common belief, veneered with gold. This was one of the few treasures saved from Henry Morgan's attack on Old Panama in 1671 and legend records different versions of how it was concealed from the buccaneers: whitewashed by the priest, or even covered in mud by nuns.

A block to the south on Calle 9 is the run-down **Plaza Herrera**. French influence is evident in the windows and flower-filled cast-iron balconies of the green and pale pink houses and *pensiones*. Behind Plaza Herrera are the ruins of the **Tiger's Hand Bulwark**, where the defensive wall ended and the landward-side moat began. The strongpoint held a 50-man military post and 13 cannon; it was demolished in 1856 as the town expanded but restored in 1983. Portions of the moat can still be detected.

Avenida Central and Calidonia
From Calle 10 heading north, Avenida Central, Panama City's main commercial street, enters the 'mainland', curves northwest then sweeps northeast running almost parallel with the shore through the whole town. En route its name changes to Vía España – although signs reading 'Avenida Central España' exist in parts – on its course northeast to Tocumen Airport. At its crossing with Calle B, close to Casco Viejo, is the small **Plaza Santa Ana** with a colonial church (1764), a favourite place for political meetings; the plaza has many restaurants and is a good place to catch buses to all parts of the city. Nearby, running towards the Central Market between Avenida Central and Calle B (officially known as Carrera de Chiriquí), is an exotic, narrow alley called **Salsipuedes** – 'Get out if you can' – where crowded stalls sell everything from fruit to old books and medicinal plants. Over 75% of the street's residents in 1892 were Chinese merchants, but the city's Chinatown (**Barrio Chino**) is now largely confined to nearby Calle Juan Mendoza and adjacent Calle B with a typical Chinese archway at the entrance; good Chinese restaurants and general shops.

The next section of Avenida Central is a pedestrian precinct called **La Peatonal**, with trees and decorations, modern department stores and wandering street vendors. **Plaza 5 de Mayo**, at Calle 22 Este, is another busy bus stop from which buses leave for the Canal. In the centre of the Plaza is an obelisk honouring the firemen who died in a gunpowder magazine explosion on the site in May 1914. The **Museo Antropológico Reina Torres de Araúz** ① *Av Ascanio Villalaz, Metropolitan Park, Mon-Fri 0900-1600, T262-8338, US$2*. It has five salons (partly looted during 'Operation Just Cause') exhibiting Panamanian history, anthropology and archaeology, rare collection of pre-Columbian gold objects and ceramics (Profesora Torres de Araúz, a renowned anthropologist and founder of the museum, died in 1982). It was renovated in 1999 and hosts occasional performances. One block east of Plaza 5 de Mayo is the **Museo Afro-Antillano** ① *Justo Arosemena and Calle 24, T262-5348, Tue-Sat 0830-1530, US$1*, which features an illustrated history of Panama's West Indian community and their work on the Canal. There's a small library.

Ancón
Ancón curves round the hill of the same name north and east and merges into Panama City. It has picturesque views of the palm-fringed shore. Take care on Ancón Hill, as robberies sometimes occur. The following **walk** takes in the sights of Ancón: walk to the top of the hill in the morning for views of the city, Balboa and the Canal (toilets and water fountain at the top – you may have to climb part of the radio tower to see anything); the entrance is on Avenida de los Mártires (formerly Avenida de Julio and briefly Avenida

Presidente Kennedy). From Avenida de los Mártires take a clockwise route around the hill, bearing right on to Balboa Road (Avenida Estado de Jamaica), you will soon come upon the **Kuna Artesans** market on your left where the Kuna sell their multicolored *molas*, Further on down and to the left is the **Mercado Artesanal** where a wider variety of handicrafts, woven baskets from the Wounaan-Embera people, and Ecuadorian sweaters can be found. You will come upon **Chase Manhattan** and **Citibank** shortly after passing the Mercado Artesanal. The post office and a café follow. Then walk down the Prado lined with royal palms to the **Goethals Memorial** ① *free, identity must be shown to the guards*, in honour of the engineer George Washington Goethals, behind the building of the Canal. The steps lead to the administration building to see the restored murals of the Construction of the Canal. Follow Heights Road until it becomes Gorgas Road where you will pass the headquarters of the **Smithsonian Tropical Research Institute** ① *opposite Plaza 5 de Mayo, Mon-Fri 0900-1700, Sat 0900-1200, café Mon-Fri 1000-0430, T212-8000, www.stri.org*, an English-language scientific research library where applications to visit Barro Colorado Island are made. The café/bookshop sells environmental books and nature guides, including national park maps.

A little further, among trees and flowers, is the former **Gorgas Army Community Hospital.** Named after William Crawford Gorgas, the physician who is credited with clearing the Canal Zone of the more malignant tropical diseases before construction began in the beginning of the 20th century. Gorgas Road leads back to Avenida de los Mártires, but look out for the sign to the **Museo de Arte Contemporáneo** ① *Av de los Mártires, entrance on Av San Blas, T262-8012, Tue-Sun 0900-1700, US$1.* Housed in a former Masonic Lodge (1936), the permanent collection of national and international modern paintings and sculptures has special exhibitions from time to time, with marquetry, silkscreen and engraving workshops, and a library of contemporary visual art open to students. At the foot of Ancón Hill the **Instituto Nacional** stands on the four-lane Avenida de los Mártires. At **Mi Pueblito** ① *north of Av de los Mártires, east of the Quarry Heights entrance, open till 2200, small admission charge*, you'll find nostalgic replicas of three different villages: one colonial from the Central Provinces, one Afro-Antillian and one indigenous. It's on a busy road so best to take a taxi. To continue further west into Balboa, see Transport, page 1326.

La Exposición
East of Plaza 5 de Mayo, along the oceanside Avenida Balboa (a popular stretch for jogging), on a semi-circular promontory jutting out into the water by Calle 34, is a great monument to **Vasco Núñez de Balboa**, who stands sword aloft as he did when he strode into the Pacific on 15 September 1513. The 1924 statue stands on a white marble globe poised on the shoulders of a supporting group representing the so-called 'four races of Man'. To the east is **Parque Anayansi**, a pleasant shady park, popular with local couples and flocks of parrots in the late afternoon.

Two more pleasant plazas, Porras and Arias, can be found west of Hospital Santo Tomás across Avenida 3 Sur (Justo Arosemena). This central part of the city is known as La Exposición because of the international exhibition held here in 1916 to celebrate the building of the Canal. There are two museums nearby: **Museo de Ciencias Naturales** ① *Av Cuba y Calle 30, T225-0645, Tue-Sat 0900-1530, Sun 1300-1630, US$1, students and seniors US$0.25*, which has good sections on geology, palaeontology, entomology and marine biology, and **Museo Casa del Banco Nacional** ① *Calle 34 between Av Cuba and Av Justo Arosemena, Mon-Fri 0800-1230, 1330-1630, free*, which, although not widely known, is worth a visit. It contains a large numismatic and stamp collection and a history of banking from the 19th century, old postal and telephone items and historic photos.

Further east, as Avenida Balboa begins to curve around the other end of the Bay of Panama to Punta Paitilla, is **Bella Vista**, once a very pleasant residential district and site of many hotels in our B and C ranges. It includes the neighbourhood of **Perejil** ('parsley'), originally called Perry Hill. Bordering this on the north, where Vía España passes the Iglesia del Carmen, is **El Cangrejo** ('the crab') apartment and restaurant district, with many upmarket stores and boutiques. The University City is on the Transisthmian Highway. Opposite the campus is the Social Security Hospital. All these areas are evidence of Panama City's sensational growth since the post-war economic boom and the spread of the centre eastwards; the attractive residential suburb of Punta Paitilla was an empty hill where hunting was practised as recently as the 1960s.

The 265-ha **Parque Natural Metropolitano** ① *between Av Juan Pablo II and the Camino de la Amistad, west of El Cangrejo along the Río Curundú, T232-5552, www.parque metropolitano.org, Tue-Sun 0800-1600, park open 0730-1800,* has a mirador (150 m) with a great view over the city and a glimpse of the Canal, as well as two interpretive walking trails from which *tití* monkeys, agoutis, coatis, white-tailed deer, sloths, turtles and up to 200 species of bird may be glimpsed (go early morning for best viewing); green iguanas sun themselves on every available branch. To get there, take the bus marked 'Tumba Muerto', from Avenida Central, and ask to be dropped at the Depósito. The park is signposted from here, otherwise make for the crane and the tree-covered hill. The **Smithsonian Institute** has installed a unique construction crane for studying the little-known fauna in the canopy of this remnant of tropical semi-deciduous lowland forest, which can be visited while walking the paths of the Metropolitan Park. Researchers and students wishing to use the crane need to apply through the Smithsonian Institute. The **visitor centre** ① *Av Juan Pablo II, T232-5516,* runs guided one-hour tours and holds regular slide shows. No ANAM permit is required; it's a recommended, easy excursion.

Parque Municipal and Botanical Summit Gardens ① *Carretera Gaillard towards Gamboa, 20 mins from Panama City, Mon-Fri 0800-1600, Sat/Sun 0800-1800, T232-4854/ 4007, nominal entrance fee,* has a small zoo in the gardens with most of the animals found in Panama. The cages are reported to be a bit small. There is a harpy eagle at the zoo providing an opportunity to see and appreciate the size of these incredible birds. There is also information on their conservation in the small visitor centre.

Around Panama City ⊝❼🔺⊜❶ ►► pp 1314-1329.

Panamá Viejo

① *Tue-Sun 0900-1700, US$3, T226-8915, www.panamaviejo.org, US$4 for the cathedral lookout, US$6 for museum and lookout. Getting there: taxi from the city centre, US$10; buses from Vía España or Avenida Balboa, US$0.80. Panamá Viejo also makes a good excursion for passengers with a little time to kill at nearby Tocumen Airport; taxis can be as much as US$5 but still reasonable, especially if this is the only chance you'll have to see Panamá. Alternatively, take any bus marked Vía España, get off at Vía Cincuentenario, then take a bus to Panamá Viejo.* A recommended short trip is to the ruins of Panamá Viejo, 6.5 km northeast along the coast. A wander among the ruins still gives an idea of the site's former glory, although many of the structures have been worn by time, fungus and the sea. The narrow **King's Bridge** (1620) at the north end of the town's limits is a good starting point; it marked the beginning of the three trails across the isthmus and took seven years to build. Walking south brings you to the **Convento de San José**, where the Golden Altar originally stood (see page 1305); it was spared by the great fire that swept the town during Morgan's attack (which side started the fire is still debated). Several blocks further south is the main plaza, where the square stone tower of the **cathedral** (1535-1580) is a prominent feature (US$4 extra). In the immediate vicinity are the Cabildo, with imposing arches and columns, the remnants of **Convento de Santo Domingo**, the **Bishop's Residence**, and the **Slave Market** (or House of the Genovese), whose gaol-like structure was the hub of the American slave trade. There were about 4000 African slaves in 1610, valued at about 300 pesos apiece. Beyond the plazas to the south, on a rocky eminence overlooking the bay, stand the **Royal Houses**, the administrative stronghold including the **Quartermaster's House**, the **Court** and **Chancellery**, the **Real Audiencia** and the **Governor's Residence**.

Further west along the Pacific strand are the dungeons, kitchens and meat market (now almost obliterated by the sea); a store and refreshment stands cluster here on the south side of the plaza, and handicrafts from the Darién are sold along the beach. Across Calle de la Carrera stands another great complex of religious convents: **La Concepción** (1598) and the **Compañía de Jesús** (1621). These too were outside the area destroyed by the 1671 fire but are today little more than rubble. Only a wall remains of the Franciscan **Hospital de San Juan de Dios**, once a huge structure encompassing wards, courtyards and a church. Another block west can be seen part of the **Convento de San Francisco** and its gardens, facing the rocky beach. About 100 m west is the beautiful **Convento de La Merced**, where Pizarro, Almagro and their men attended Mass on the morning they sailed

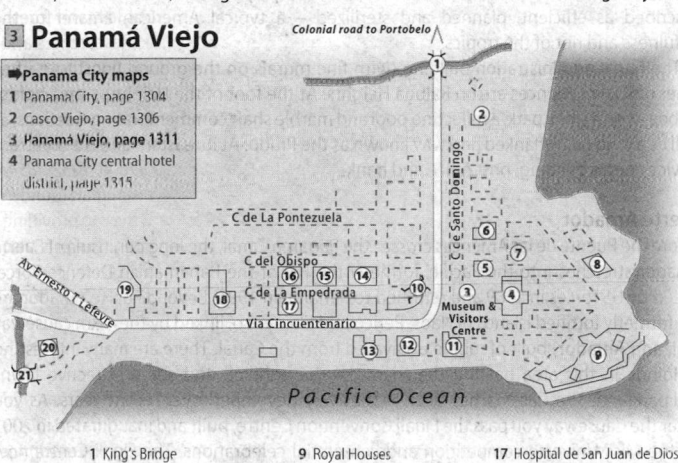

③ Panamá Viejo

➡**Panama City maps**
1 Panama City, page 1304
2 Casco Viejo, page 1306
3 Panamá Viejo, page 1311
4 Panama City central hotel district, page 1315

1 King's Bridge	9 Royal Houses	17 Hospital de San Juan de Dios
2 Convento de San José	10 Emperor's Bridge	18 Convento de San Francisco
3 Main Plaza	11 Dungeons	19 Convento de la Merced
4 Cathedral	12 Kitchens	20 La Navidad Fort
5 Cabildo	13 Meat Market	21 Matadero/
6 Convento de Santo Domingo	14 Convento de Compañía	Slaughterhouse Bridge
7 Bishop's Residence	de Jesús	
8 Slave's House/	15 Convento La Concepción	
House of the Genovese	16 Church of La Concepción	

Not to scale

on their final and momentous expedition to Peru. Decades later Morgan stored his plunder here until it could be counted, divided up and sent back to the Atlantic side. At the western limit of Panamá Viejo stands **La Navidad Fort** (1658). Its purpose was merely to defend the **Matadero (Slaughterhouse) Bridge** across the Río Agarroba but its 50-man garrison and half-dozen cannon were no match for the determined force of privateers; it is also known as Morgan's Bridge because it was here that the attack began.

There is a **visitor centre**, with exhibitions in Spanish, as well as maps, pictures and models of how Panama's first city would have looked. There are also opportunities for students to volunteer in future excavations (check www.panamaviejo.org). By the ruins is **Museo de Panamá Viejo** ① *Vía Cincuentenario, T226-89156, Mon-Sun 0900-1700, US$2.*

The whole area (unfenced) is attractively landscaped, with plenty of benches to rest on, and floodlit at night. Late afternoon when the sun is low is an especially nice time to visit, although at least two hours should be allowed to appreciate the site fully. The main ruins are patrolled by police and reasonably safe. **Dame Margot Fonteyn**, the ballerina, is buried alongside her husband Roberto Arias Guardia in the Jardín de la Paz cemetery behind Panamá Viejo. IPAT organizes free folklore events and local dance displays on Saturdays in the dry season (*verano*), which are worth seeing. The tourist office in Panama City (T226-7000) has a list of programmes and can supply professional guides if required.

Balboa → *Colour map 8, B1.*

The town and docks of Balboa are just over 3 km west of Panama City (10 minutes by taxi, US$5) and stand attractively between the Canal quays and Ancón Hill. It has been described as efficient, planned and sterilized – a typical American answer to the wilfulness and riot of the tropics.

The Canal administration building (with fine murals on the ground floor) and a few other official residences are on Balboa Heights. At the foot of the Heights is the town of Balboa, with a small park, a reflecting pool and marble shaft commemorating Goethals, as well as a long palm-flanked parkway known as the Prado. At its eastern end is a theatre, a service centre building, post office and bank.

Fuerte Amador

Before the Puente de las Américas crosses the Panama Canal, the long peninsula of Fuerte Amador stretches into the Pacific, formerly the HQ of the Panamanian Defence Force, seized by US forces in 1989 and returned to Panama in 1994. Beyond Fuerte Amador are the formerly fortified islands of Naos, Perico and Flamenco, linked by the 4-km causeway (**Calzada Amador**) built of rubble excavated from the Canal. There are many interesting buildings in this area bearing the marks of the conflict, and some attractive lawns and parkland. The Calzada has been extensively developed over recent years. As you enter the Causeway you pass the Figali Convention Centre, built and inaugurated in 2003 for the Miss Universe competition and centennial celebrations. The Figali Centre now hosts major music and sports events. It has fine views of the Puente de las Américas and the ships lined up to enter the Canal. There are small charges for entry and for swimming at Solidaridad beach on **Naos** (crowded at weekends and the water is polluted – not recommended). There is a small marine park with local marine life on show. At Punta Culebra on Naos is the **Marine Exhibition Center** ① *T212-8793, Tue-Fri 1300-1800, Sat-Sun 1000-1800, US$2* (of the Smithsonian Tropical Research Institute), with interesting aquaria and exhibitions on marine fauna. As the road reaches **Isla Perico**, there is a block of restaurants, bars and some shops underneath what is set to be an apartment-style hotel. A 'mega resort' is in process at Naos Harbour – a 300 room hotel, 114 room apartment-hotel, casino, shops, condos and new beach, and there is a proposal for a cable car to the Causeway descending from the top of Ancón Hill. **Flamenco**, the last of the islands, is the headquarters for the National Maritime Service and home to the Flamenco Yacht Club, a large duty-free store and a pristine mall of boutiques, expensive souvenir shops and lively range of restaurants, bars and clubs. Most popular between Wednesday and Saturday nights.

The **Bridge of Life Biodiversity Museum** ① *T314-1395, www.biomuseopanama.org*, currently being developed on the Causeway, is designed by architect Frank Gehry with botanical gardens designed by New York specialist Edwina von Gal. Labelled a learning centre and 'hub of an interchange of nature, culture, the economy and life' the museum is an impressive and modern testament to Panama's location as a major ecological crossroads.

Taboga Island
There are launch services to Taboga Island (**Calypso Queen**, T226-1991/1551, **Canal & Bay Tours**, T314-1349), about 20 km offshore. The island is a favourite year-round resort, produces delicious pineapples and mangoes and has one of the oldest churches in the Western hemisphere. Admission to the beach at **Hotel Taboga** is US$10, redeemable in tokens to buy food and drink (covered picnic huts cost extra). There are other good places to swim around the island, but its south side is rocky and sharks visit regularly.

The trip out to Taboga is very interesting, passing the naval installations at the Pacific end of the Canal, the great bridge linking the Americas, tuna boats and shrimp fishers in for supplies, visiting yachts from all over the world at what remains of the Balboa Yacht Club, and the Calzada Amador. Part of the route follows the channel of the Canal, with its busy traffic. Taboga itself, with a promontory rising to 488 m, is carpeted with flowers at certain times of year. There are few cars in the meandering, helter-skelter streets, and just one footpath as a road. All items are expensive on the island, so make sure you bring plenty of cash as there is no bank.

Pearl Islands → *Colour map 8, B2.*
A longer trip, 75 km southwest by launch, takes you to the Pearl Islands, visited mostly by sea anglers for the Pacific mackerel, red snapper, corvina, sailfish, marlin and the other species that abound in these waters. High mountains rise from the sea, and there is a little fishing village on a shelf of land at the water's edge. There was much pearl fishing in colonial days. **Contadora**, one of the smallest Pearl Islands (three-hour boat trip), has become quite famous since its name became associated with a Central American peace initiative. It was also where the last Shah of Iran, Mohammed Rezá Pahlaví, was exiled, in a house called Puntalara, after the Iranian Revolution. Contadora is popular with Canadian, Spanish and Italian holidaymakers and is becoming crowded, built-up and consequently is not as peaceful as it once was. Lack of drinking water is now harming the tourist development. There are beautiful beaches with crystal-clear water, good skin-diving and sailing, and lots of sharks.

Hotel and guesthouse prices
LL over US$150 **L** US$100-150 **AL** US$66-99
A US$46-65 **B** US$31-45 **C** US$21-30
D US$12-20 **E** US$7-11 **F** under US$7
Restaurant prices
♥♥♥ over US$15 **♥♥** US$8-15 **♥** under US$8
See pages 45-48 for further information.

● Sleeping

Panama City p1302, maps p1304, p1306, p1311 and p1315
There is a 10% tax on all hotel prices. Most hotels are a/c, all others have fans. Cheaper accommodation can be found in *pensiones* and there are cheap places on Av México.
LL Miramar Intercontinental, Av Balboa, T206-8888, www.miramarpanama.com. On the seafront with excellent views. 3 restaurants, huge pool, gym and exclusive marina. Broadband internet available. President Bush stayed here.
LL-L Sheraton Panama, Vía Israel y Calle 77, T305-5100, www.starwoodhotels.com. 4 restaurants, 1 with excellent view over the bay, another offering Southeast Asian cuisine, casino and sports bar, outdoor swimming pool.
L El Panamá, Vía España 111, T215-9000, www.elpanama.com. Tropical art deco style, vast rooms, good pool and vast 'Vegas'-style casino, a bit inefficient but generally good.
L Euro Hotel, Vía España 33, opposite the **Bella Vista**, T263-0802. A/c, private bath, cable TV, pool, restaurant and bar on a busy street.
AL Riande Aeropuerto, near Tocumen Airport (5 mins), T290-3333, www.hoteles riande.com. A/c, clean, free transport to airport, good breakfasts, pool (loud music all day), tennis, casino.
AL Riande Continental, Vía España and Ricardo Arias, T263-9999. Sister hotel to the Riande Aeropuerto and a landmark in the modern city centre. Good value with prices including buffet breakfast. Casino on site.
A Roma Plaza, Av Justo Arosemena y Calle 33, T227-3844, www.hotelromaplaza.com.

Rooms are clean and airy but expensive given competition in the area, rooftop pool. Couple of restaurants, **Italian Garden** offers a good buffet breakfast for US$5.25.
A-B Costa Inn, Av Perú y Calle 39, T227-1522, www.hotelcostainn.com. Very good value, sparklingly clean, rooftop pool with great views of the city. Double rooms feature 2 bathrooms. Breakfast included.
B Caribe Av Perú y Calle 28, T225-0404, caribehotel@hotmail.com. 153 very large rooms, one of the city's older hotels, rooftop pool and bar, casino, restaurant.
B Hostal La Casa de Carmen, Calle 1, Urbanización El Carmen Casa 32, Vía Brasil, 1 block back from Vía España, T/F263-4366, www.lacasadecarmen.net. Good, cheap place close to the business centre of town.
B Hotel Internacional, Plaza 5 de Mayo, T262-4933, hinterpan@cwpanama.net. Spacious rooms with a/c and cable TV, although a little tatty for the price, the views of the city and ocean are almost worth it.
B-C Hotel Vía España, Calle Martín Sosa (on the corner of Vía España), T264-0800. Clean rooms and comfy beds, a/c, private bath, telephone, TV with cable. A few suites have a jacuzzi for a very good price. Restaurant on site and internet (US$1 for 30 mins) available. Friendly, recommended.
C Acapulco, Calle 30 Este y Av Perú, T225-3832. A/c, clean, TV, private bath, some rooms a little musty but ones with balcony are better, excellent restaurant, safe parking. Conveniently located and recommended.
C Andino, Calle 35 y Av Perú, beside Parque Parades, T225-1162, andino@cableonda.net. Large rooms and all mod cons including TV, fridge and telephone. Some rooms a little smoky. Family-run, friendly, free internet access, laundry, quiet street. Highly recommended.
C Bella Vista, Vía España N 31 y Calle 42, T264-4029. A/c, cable TV, private bath, safe deposit. Recommended.

C California, Vía España y Calle 43, Bella Vista, T263-7736, www.hotelcalifornia panama.com. With bath, a/c, modern, good value and with discounts for long-stay clientele, TV, nice restaurant, friendly, safe.

C Covadonga, Calle 29, Av Perú, T225-5275. Small rooms but good rooftop terrace pool with views over the bay.

C Hotel Latino, Av Cuba y Calle 36 Este, T227-2994, hlatino@hotmail.com. Slightly dingy rooms, a/c, private bath, cable TV.

C Hotel Marbella, Calle D (between Calle 55 and Calle Eusebio A Morales), El Cangrejo, T263-2220, www.hmarbella.com. Plush rooms with a/c, cable TV and private bath in safe, central area of town.

C Lisboa, Av Cuba y Calle 31, T227-5916. Modern, a/c, TV, restaurant, good value. Decoration is very 'red', so if you like your accommodation fiery, you'll love this place.

C Veracruz, Av Perú y Calle 30, T227-3022, www.hotelveracruz.com.pa. Very good

restaurant, helpful staff and elegant reception area, but rooms in need of decoration and noisy next to the street. Recommended.

C-D Centro Americano, Av Justo Arosemena y Av Ecuador, T227-4555, www.hotelcentroamericano.com. Very clean, hot water, good reading lights, TV, restaurant and ice machine on every floor, good value. Recommended.

C-D Residencial La Alameda, Calle 30 Este, Av Cuba, T225-1758. Clean, modern, a/c, hot water, cable TV, parking.

C-D Venecia, Av Perú, between Calle 36 and 37, T227-7881, hotelvenecia@hotmail.com. Small, box-like rooms, some smelly, others are much better. Range of prices for rooms.

C-E Mamallena, Calle Manuel María Ycaza, opposite Restaurante Jimmy, T6676-6163, www.mamallena.com. Newish hostel with private rooms and dorms, kitchen and plenty of places to hang out. Often full with backpackers. They've done their research,

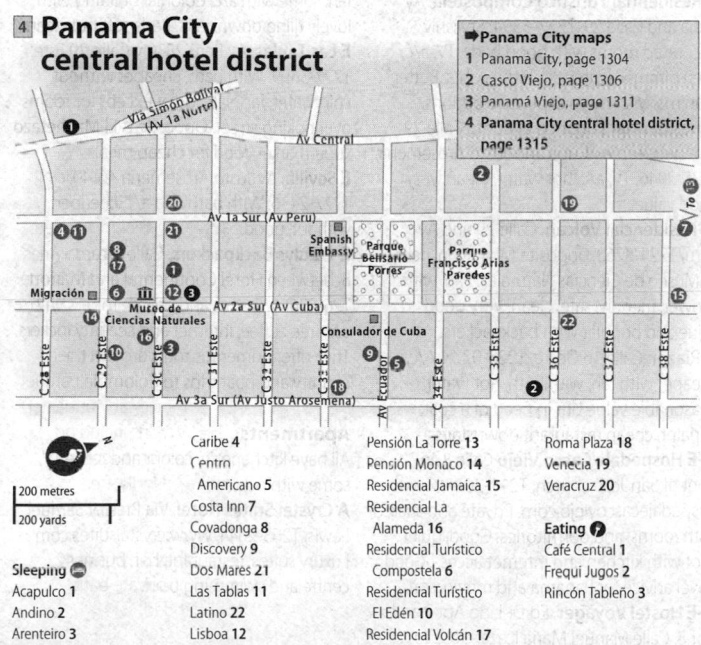

4 Panama City central hotel district

➡ **Panama City maps**
1 Panama City, page 1304
2 Casco Viejo, page 1306
3 Panamá Viejo, page 1311
4 Panama City central hotel district, page 1315

Caribe **4**	Pensión La Torre **13**	Roma Plaza **18**
Centro	Pensión Mónaco **14**	Venecia **19**
Americano **5**	Residencial Jamaica **15**	Veracruz **20**
Costa Inn **7**	Residencial La	
Covadonga **8**	Alameda **16**	**Eating**
Discovery **9**	Residencial Turístico	Café Central **1**
Dos Mares **21**	Compostela **6**	Frequi Jugos **2**
Las Tablas **11**	Residencial Turístico	Rincón Tableño **3**
Latino **22**	El Edén **10**	
Lisboa **12**	Residencial Volcán **17**	

200 metres
200 yards

Sleeping
Acapulco **1**
Andino **2**
Arenteiro **3**

and have details about sail boats to Colombia on the website.

D Arenteiro, Calle 30 Este y Av Cuba, T227-5883. Hot water, TV, modern, very clean, excellent value. New bar and restaurant.

D Discovery, Av Ecuador, T225-1140. Clean, fairly quiet, safe parking and free airport pickup, very good value. Bar.

D Dos Mares, Calle 30 between Perú and Cuba, T/F227-6150. A/c, bath but rooms in need of renovation, hot water, pool on roof, good restaurant, TV, phone.

D Ideal, Calle 17 Oeste just off Av Central, between Plaza Santa Ana y Plaza 5 de Mayo, T262-2400. A/c (cold), shared hot shower, pool, cable TV, internet at US$1 per hr, safe.

D Pensión Monaco, Av Cuba y Calle 29, T225-2573. Unfriendly staff but very well appointed rooms with TV and a/c.

D Residential Jamaica, Av Cuba and Calle 38, T225-9870. Smart-looking building with very clean rooms, colour TV, a/c. Good.

D Residential Turístico Compostela, Av Cuba and Calle 29, T227-6394. Stylishly decorated rooms with good beds, TV, a/c, even dimmer switches on the lights. Better than many far more expensive options.

D Residential Turístico El Edén, Calle 29 Este between Av Cuba and Justo Arosemena, T225-2946. TV, a/c, hot water. Clean, very good value.

D Residencial Volcán, Calle 29 and Av Perú, T225-5263, opposite Migración, next to Museo de Ciencias Naturales. Fan, with shower, friendly, safe, clean. Very good value and popular with backpackers.

D Riazor, Calle 16 Oeste, T228-0777. A/c, cheaper with fan, with bath, hot water. Reasonable value but in need of a coat of paint, cheap restaurant downstairs.

D-E Hospedaje Casco Viejo Calle 8, in front of San José church, T211-2027, www.hospedajecascoviejo.com. Private and shared bath rooms, and dormitories. Good, quiet spot with kitchen and internet access. Good travel advice for Panama and moving on.

D-E Hostel Voyager, Ed Di-Lido Apt 3 and Apt 8, Calle Manuel Maria Icaza, close to Jimmys Restaurant, T223-3687, www.voyagerhostelpanama.net. Dormitory rooms (US$8 per person), price includes continental breakfast, laundry service, TV, use of kitchen and free internet service for guests – great place to meet other travellers, but mixed reports on the rooms. Recommended.

D-E Pensión La Torre Av Perú (south side), Calle 39, T225-0172. A/c (cheaper without), TV, cleanish, cheap, but this is a real by-the-hour place, rooms dark.

E Caracas, Calle 12 on Plaza Santa Ana, T228-7232. Large, clean rooms, friendly, a/c (cheaper with a fan), hot showers, be wary of rooms with outside windows.

E Casa Grande, Av Central, Calle 8-9, T211-3316, 1 block behind the cathedral. Good location but basic rooms with shared bath.

E Hotel Colón, just off Calle 12, 1 block from the Plaza Santa Ana, T228-8510, elhotelcolon@pa.inter.net. Most rooms with fan, some with a/c. Colonial building with lovely tiling downstairs. Beds soft but clean.

E Las Tablas, Av Perú 2830 y Calle 29 Este, T227-3699. With bath, cheaper without, cold water, fan, safe, quiet except for rooms overlooking street. Opposite is **El Machetazo** supermarket, food for cheap meals.

E Sevilla, Av Justo Arosemena 46-40, T227-2436. With bath and a/c, cheaper without, good.

E-F Zulys Backpackers, Calle Ricardo Arias 8, between **Hotel Continental** and **Mariott**, T269-2665. Dorms and private rooms with a/c, free coffee, internet and security lockers. They offer numerous tours around the country and boat trips to Colombia.

Apartments

All have kitchenette, colour and cable TV, some with pool.

A Crystal Suites Hotel, Vía Brasil y Samuel Lewis, T263-2644, www.crystalsuites.com. Luxury suites, restaurant, bar, business centre and swimming pool.

Camping

There are no official sites but it is possible to camp on some beaches or, if in great need, in the **Balboa Yacht Club** car park. It is also possible to camp in the **Hipódromo** grounds (11 km east of the city, on Vía España) but there are no facilities; this is allowed if you are waiting to ship your vehicle out of the country. Also possible, by previous arrangement, at La **Patria** swimming pool nearby, and at the **Chorrera** (La Herradura) and La Siesta beaches on the Pan-American Highway.

Taboga Island *p1313*

You may be able to find locals to stay with; ask around.

AL-A Cerrito Tropical, north end of town, T390-8999, www.cerritotropicalpanama.com. Small B&B overlooking the bay leading to the Canal. 6 comfortable rooms, all with a/c, including breakfast.

A Taboga, T250-2122, htaboga@sinfo.net. Apdo 550357, Paitilla, Panamá, 300 m east of wharf. A/c, TV, restaurant, café, pool, beach.

C Chu, on main street, 200 m left of wharf, T250-2036. Wooden colonial style, thin walls, shared bath, beautiful views, own beach, terrace restaurant serving traditional fish and chicken dishes.

Pearl Islands *p1313*

L Contadora Resort, T214-3719, www.hotel contadora.com. Same ownership as El Panamá in Panama City, chalet complex, nice location on beach, but reportedly run-down.

A Contadora Island Inn, T6699-6414, www.contadoraislandinn.com. A selection of rooms, all with private bath, with B&B service. Good range of relaxation and adventure activities – take your pick.

● Eating

Panama City *p1302, maps p1304, p1306, p1311 and p1315*

There is a wide range of international restaurants in all styles and price ranges.

There are also good restaurants in most of the more expensive hotels.

¶¶¶ Casablanca, Plaza Bolívar In Casco Viejo. Long-established reputable restaurant with tables al fresco in the picturesque plaza in Casco Viejo.

¶¶¶ Gauchos Steak House, Calle Uruguay y Calle 48. Choose your own steak, a must for meat lovers. Good.

¶¶¶ La Cocotte, Uruguay 138, T213-8250. In former private house, excellent French cuisine, expensive, Hilary Clinton slipped out of the embassy to eat here – but not on a Sun as it's closed.

¶¶¶ Las Bóvedas, in converted dungeons at seaward end of Casco Viejo (take a taxi), T228-8068. Good French food, art galleries adjoining, live jazz Thu-Sat, closed Sun.

¶¶¶ Limoncillo, Calle 47 y Uruguay, Marbella, T263-5350, www.limoncillo.com. Contemporary award-winning international cuisine, with good reviews over the years.

¶¶¶ Matsui, Av Eusebio A Morales A-12. Open 1200-2000 Japanese, excellent all-you-can-eat.

¶¶¶ Miraflores Restaurant, Miraflores Visitor Centre. Mon-Sat 1200-2300. A little out of town, but thoroughly different. Classy dining with an up-close view of passing ships. Great salads, North American style meats and pastas, and buffet. Used as a location in the movie *The Tailor of Panama*.

¶¶¶ Rendezvous, at the **Riande Continental**. Open 24 hrs, superb Sun brunch.

¶¶¶ Sushi Itto, between Av Samuel Lewis y Calle 55, at the back of Plaza Obarrio building, T265 1222. Mexican owned, mixing sushi and Japanese dishes with Latin food.

¶¶¶-¶¶ Monolo Caracol, Av Central, Casco Viejo, across from Palacio Nacional de Gobierno y Justicia. Excellent food, tapas and seafood, can get noisy.

¶¶¶-¶¶ Mostaza, Calle A opposite Arco Chato. One of the best restaurants in Casco Viejo, with large portions and live music at weekends.

¶¶ Athen's, corner of Av Uruguay and Av 4 Sur, Obarrio, behind the Delta petrol station.

Excellent pizza, also Greek and Middle Eastern food including stuffed pitta breads and good salads, lively atmosphere, young crowd, very good.

†† Café de Nire, Av Central y Calle 3. Offers a covered outside dining area, popular place, food average.

†† Caffé Pomodoro, Av Eusebio A Morales, north of Calle 55, in patio of **Apartotel Las Vegas**. Garden setting, also has a/c. Serves Northern Italian pasta and sauces. Informal, moderately priced.

†† Calypso, Vía España y Calle 46, La Cresta, T223-0749. French restaurant and bar.

†† El Trapiche, Vía Argentina 10, T221-5241. Many dishes including *empanadas* (meat filled fritters) and *mondongo* (seasoned tripe), also in Panamá Viejo, Vía Cincuentenario. Panamanian food with traditional music and dance programmes, call for information.

†† Gran China, Av Balboa, between Calle 26 y 27. Good-value Chinese.

†† Jimmy's, Paseo Cincuentenario just beyond Atlapa Centre, T226-1096. Panamanian, good grills, seafood, fast food and fish, served under a thatched roof, very popular, also on Av Samuel Lewis opposite **Riande Continental**. A/c, self service, good for breakfast and lunch.

†† La Cascada, Av Balboa y Calle 25. Closed Sun. Beef, pork, seafood, enormous helpings, open-air, kitsch decor but good service. Menus in charming English. 'Doggy bags' available. Highly recommended. Credit cards not accepted.

†† La Tablita, Transisthmian Hwy, Los Angeles district, T260-1458. Good steaks, reasonable prices.

†† Las Costillitas on Vía Argentina. Closed Sun. Same management as **La Cascada**, same huge menu (which takes 30 mins to read), and same reasonable prices .

†† Las Tinajas, on Calle 51, near **Ejecutivo Hotel**, T263-7890. Panamanian, traditional entertainment Tue and Thu-Sat from 2100, craft shop, closed Sun. Recommended.

†† Le Sandwich de Paris, Calle 51, just before **EcoMargo Tours** on the opposite side of the road. French. Good crunchy baguettes and crêpes at reasonable prices; good for lunch.

†† Manolo, Vía Argentina, sidewalk terrace. A favourite for politicians and young people in evenings and Sun morning, draught beer served with Spanish *tapas*, *churros* a speciality, also on Vía Venetto y Calle Eusebio A Morales, tables or counter, same menu, prices and service.

†† Marbella, Av Balboa y Calle 39. Spanish seafood, *cazuela de mariscos, paella,* good.

†† Ozone Café, Calle Uruguay. Food from all over the world, upmarket, good and popular, many other restaurants in same area.

†† Parrillada Martín Fierro, Calle Eusebio A Morales, T264-1927. Surf 'n'turf.

†† Pavo Real, Vía Argentina and Calle José Martí. Mon-Tue 1200-2400, Wed-Sat 1200-0330, live music from 2200, closed Sun. Upmarket English pub with restaurant, darts, good food, expat hangout.

†† Pencas, Amador Causeway, in front of Plaza Iberoamericana, T211-3671, www.pencas.com. Panamanian food and live 'Panamanian Expressions' – folkloric nights with music and dancing on Wed nights. Call ahead and make a reservation as it gets busy.

††-† Restaurant y Pizzeria Sorrento, Vía Ricardo Arias 11, T269-0055. One of the best meal deals in town. Excellent pizza, pasta and more traditional Panamanian dishes at good prices.

† Angel, Vía Argentina 68, T263-6411. Closed Sun. Spanish, seafood, imported mussels, and eel, *bacalao* (cod).

† Angie's Pasao Cincuentenario, opposite **Jimmy's**. Buffet style with huge portions and low prices. Very popular around lunchtime.

† Benihana, Calle 60, Obarrio. Closed Sat. Favoured by Japanese locals.

† Casa Vegetarian Kuan Yin, Ricardo Arias, just before the **Continental Hotel**. Chinese-orientated vegetarian buffet; very cheap.

† Centolla's Place, Vía España, Río Abajo, T221-7056. Caribbean seafood, catering to

Antillean community, friendly, worth
a taxi ride. Recommended.

¶ Frequi Jugos, Av Justo Arosemena,
Edificio Hatillo, between Calle 35 and 36.
Not entirely vegetarian, but a good place
for a fresh fruit juice/fruit salad. Has a good
lunch buffet. Convenient for the hotel district.

¶ Govinda's, Calle 47, No 24, Marbella.
Many vegetarian specialities.

¶ La Victoria, Av Central, next to **Minimercado
Teresa**. 1100-2300. Very cheap (US$1 a meal)
with juke box and a/c. Recommended. Also
recommended is the unnamed restaurant
opposite, very popular with locals.

¶ Mango's Pub & Grill, Calle Uruguay 1-24,
T269-4856. US-style bar and food, many
imported beers, best hamburger south
of Houston, live music Tue and Sat,
recommended for lunch and evening.

¶ Mireya, Calle Ricardo Arango y Ricardo Arias,
near **Continental Hotel**, T269-1876. Health
food bakery, good value, recommended,
also Calle 39 y Av Balboa, Bella Vista.

¶ Mi Salud, Calle 31 y Av México 3-30. Mon-
Sat 0700-1900. Owned by dietary specialist
Carlos Raúl Moreno, vegetarian options.

¶ Niko's Café with 4 locations at Vía España
near **El Rey** supermarket, T264-0136;
El Dorado Shopping Centre, T260-0022;
Paitilla, past old airport T270-2555; and
behind the former Balboa High School
in the Canal Zone T228-8888. Very good,
cheap, self-service.

¶ Palacio Imperial, Calle 17 near **Ticabus**
office. Good and cheap Chinese.

¶ Riazor, Calle 16, 15-105, T228-2541.
Just as it was 40-50 years ago, cheap
local food with style. Recommended.
Take a taxi at night.

¶ Rincón Tableño, Av Cuba No 5 y Calle 31.
Panamanian. Several locations, good *comida
criolla*, lunchtimes only. Recommended.

¶ Tang, Calle A y Cenbule, off Plaza Santa Ana.
Cheap, friendly, Chinese. Recommended.

Cafés and snacks

Café Central, Av Central, between Calle 28
and 29, Calidonia. Basic and cheap food, OK.

Café Coca Cola, Av Central and Plaza Santa
Ana, not the safest area. Pleasant, friendly,
reasonably priced – US$3 for set lunch.

Café Jaime, corner of Calle 12 and
Av Central. Good *chichas* (natural drinks).

Dulcería Panadería La Gran Vida,
Av Central 11-64 (between Calle 11 y 12).
Good *chicha* juice, good cheap ice cream,
empanadas and cakes. Recommended.

Groovy Café, Vía Venetto, Edificio Torres
de Alba. A bit hit and miss, and not quite
as groovy as its name suggests, generally
decent filled potatoes, salads and
sandwiches. Not much in the way of coffee.

Markany, Av Cuba y Av Ecuador. Serves
good snacks.

Panadería y Dulcería Río de Oro, opposite
Rey Supermarket on Vía España, lower level
of the shopping center. Good place for a
cheap snack with cakes and pastries.

Fuerte Amador *p1312*

¶¶¶ Café Barko, Calzado de Amador.
One of the most established restaurants in
Flamenco Mall, specializing in seafood and
Panamanian dishes, beautifully prepared.

¶¶ Crêpes and Waffles, located upstairs at
the Flamenco Mall. Pleasant, light dishes.

¶¶-¶ Mi Ranchito, by Naos Isla, T228-4909.
This charming, simple, outdoor restaurant
is highly recommended in the evening for
seeing the skyline, as well as for good,
cheap traditional food and drink.

Pearl Islands *p1313*

¶¶ Gallo Nero, by runway. Good seafood
especially lobster, pizza and pasta, at
reasonable prices. Run by German
couple Gerald and Sabine.

¶ Fonda Sagitario, near **Gallo Nero**.
A café, offering cheap eats; also a
supermarket and a duty-free shop.

¶ Michael's, opposite **Gallo Nero**.
Good pizzas, ice cream.

● Entertainment

Panama City *p1302, maps p1304, p1306, p1311 and p1315*

Bars and clubs

La Chiva Parrandera is an open-sided bus that tours the hot-spots from 2000-2400. Call T263-3144, for information, US$25 per person.

Many late night haunts are concentrated in the Marbella district such as **La Cantina, Galerías Marbella**, Calle 5 East, T264-4958, Wed-Sat, ladies nights and live music; **Mangos; Café Dalí**; and **Fonda Antioqueña**.

Café Bolívar, Plaza Bolívar, Casco Viejo. Small, snug bar with outside tables.

Casablanca, Plaza Bolívar, Casco Viejo. Fancy, hip bar and restaurant offering Provençale/Thai cuisine, mixed reports on the food, a/c.

Deep Room, Calle Uruguay area of Bella Vista. An excellent club. Tribal house and electronica. Late start, sometimes 0400.

La Parrillita, Av 11 de Octubre, Hato Pintado. Restaurant/disco in a railway carriage.

Las Bóvedas, Plaza de Francia, Casco Viejo, T228-8068. Jazz on the weekends from 2100-0100.

Las Molas, entrance to **Chase Manhattan Bank**, Vía España, Los Angeles district. Small bands, rural decor, drinks US$1.50.

Liquid, Calle 50 and Calle José de la Cruz. If there's any big pop music names in town, they're likely to be playing here, hosts electronic events and late night dance parties.

Next, Av Balboa, T265-8746. Wed-Sat, commercial disco, pricey cover charge.

Oz Bar and Lounge, Calle 53 Este, Marbella. Well established chill-out lounge bar with house nights and good DJ's. Ladies drink free on Fri.

Panamá Viejo, T221-1268. Colombian restaurant, bar and disco, open 24 hrs.

Unplugged, Calle 48, Bella Vista. Mon-Sat, rock 'n' roll club.

Voodoo Lounge, Plaza Pacífica, Punta Pacífica, T215-1581. Fri house music, live DJs Sat electronic music.

Wasabi Sushi Lounge, Marbella, T264-1863, Electronic music and sushi, ladies nights, sangria and live DJs.

Cabarets, casinos and gambling

There are more than 20 state-managed casinos, some in the main hotels with profits intended for charitable public institutions. Most offer blackjack, baccarat, poker, roulette and slot machines (*traganikles*). Winnings are tax-free and paid without deductions. The **National Lottery** is solemnly drawn (and televized) Wed and Sun at 1300 in Plaza de la Lotería between Av Perú y Cuba; 4-digit tickets, called *billetes* or *pedazos*, cost US$1, a win pays up to US$2000; 'chance' tickets, with only 2 digits cost US$0.25, and pay up to US$14.

Josephine's, Calle 50 y Av Uruguay, El Cangrejo. Cover charge US$20, continuous show Mon-Sat 2100-0400.

Le Palace, Calle 52, opposite **Hotel El Ejecutivo**, T269-1844. No cover, shows from 2030.

Cinema and theatre

La Prensa and other newspapers publish daily programming (*cartelera*) of cultural events. Good range of cinemas including **Cine Balboa** near Steven's Circle, **MultiPlaza Mall** at Punta Pacífica, modern multi-screen **Albrook Mall**, www.albrookmall.com, and **Multi Centro** in Paitilla.

Anayansi Theatre, in the Atlapa Convention Centre, Vía Israel, San Francisco. With a 3000-seat capacity, good acoustics, regular recitals and concerts.

Balboa Theatre, near Steven's Circle and post office in Balboa. Folkloric groups and jazz concerts sponsored by National Institute of Culture.

Cine Universitario, in the National University, T264-2737. US$1.50 for general public, shows international and classic movies, daily (not holidays) at 1700, 1900 and 2100.

Guild Theatre, in the Canal Area at Ancón. Mounts amateur productions mainly in English.

Teatro Nacional, see page 1305, occasionally has shows and performances. There are regular folklore sessions every other Sun and monthly National Ballet performances when not on tour. Check the press for details.

Live music
Bar Platea, opposite the old Club Union building, Casco Viejo. Good jazz lounge and bar, open late – live music here starts around 10pm.
Café El Aleph, Vía Argentina north of Vía España, T264-2844. Coffee house atmosphere, snacks and full meals, internet facilities, occasional art shows, live jazz at weekends, phone for programme.
Café Gardel, Vía Argentina, T269-3710. Small restaurant, tiny bar, perfect atmosphere for jazz.
Giorgio's, 1 block south of Vía Porras.
Hotels Granada and **Soloy** (Bar Maitai, T227-1133) are recommended for live Latin music at weekends.
Las Bóvedas, on Plaza de Francia, T228-8068. Jazz on weekends 2100-0100.
Nottingham, Fernández de Córdoba, Vista Hermosa, T261-0314. Live salsa at weekends, no cover charge, restaurant.
Vino's Bar, Calle 51 y Colombia, Bella Vista, T264-0520. Live salsa at weekends, cover charge, restaurant.

⊛ Festivals and events

Panama City *p1302, maps p1304, p1306, p1311 and p1315*
Feb/Mar Carnival activities include a parade on Shrove Tue and have become more elaborate in recent years.
3 Nov Independence Day, practically the whole city – or so it seems – marches in a colourful and noisy parade through the old part of the city lasting over 3 hrs. Another parade takes place the following day.
Dec Christmas parade, with US influence much in evidence, rather than the Latin American emphasis on the *Nacimiento* and the Three Kings.

O Shopping

Panama City *p1302, maps p1304, p1306, p1311 and p1315*
Duty-free imported luxuries of all kinds are an attraction at the Zona Libre in Colón, but Panama City is a booming shopping centre where bargains are not hard to find; anything from crystal to cashmere may be cheaper than at their point of origin.

The smartest shops are along **Calle 50** (Av 4 Sur) in Campo Alegre, and **Vía España** in Bella Vista and El Cangrejo, but **Av Central** is cheaper, the best and the most popular.

Of the various commercial centres, with banking, entertainment and parking facilities, the largest is **Los Pueblos**, on Vía Tocumen, with buses leaving from 5 de Mayo, or take a taxi for US$5. It's a huge complex of mega stores drawing in large numbers. **Multi Plaza** is a new mall located at Punta Pacífica, close to Atlapa, with department stores, shops, restaurants, banks and an 8 screen cinema. **Multi Centro** is at Punta Paitilla and easily accessible from the centre of town. **Albrook**, by the national bus terminal, have a mall that includes a large cinema.

Arts and crafts
Traditional Panamanian *artesanía* includes *molas* (see page 1346), eg Emma Vence, T261-8009; straw, leather and ceramic items; *chunga nawala* (palm fibre) canasters; the *pollera* circular dress, the *montuno* shirts (embroidered), the *chácara* (a popular bag or purse), the *chaquira* necklace made by Ngöbe-Buglé (Guaymí) people, and jewellery. Indigenous Darién (Embera) carvings of jungle birds and animals from cocobolo wood or *tagua* nut (small, extremely intricate, also *tagua* necklaces) make interesting souvenirs (from US$10 up to US$250 for the best, museum-quality pieces). The tourist

office has a full list of *artesanía* shops, including those in the main hotels.

Artesanías Nacionales Several indigenous co-ops selling a good selection direct from open-air outlets, eg in Panamá Viejo, Canal Area at Balboa and along road to Miraflores Locks at Corozal (daily if not raining).

Colecciones, Vía Italia opposite **Hotel Plaza Paitilla Inn**, has a wide selection. Plenty of straw articles available, including baskets, bags, traditional masks and Panama hats (US$150 for the best quality).

Flory Salzman on Vía Venetto at the back of El Panamá Hotel, T223-6963. The best place outside San Blas Islands for *molas*, huge selection, sorted by theme, ask for discounts.

Inovación, or **Indutípica**, Av A y Calle 8 Ote (opposite San José Church) for reproductions of pre-Columbian ceramics and jewellery, necklaces, Kuna *molas* (prices starting from US$2.50) from the Darién, and Ngöbe-Buglé dresses from Bocas del Toro.

Mercardo Artesanal de Cinco de Mayo, behind the old Museo Antropológico Dra Reina. Stalls selling Kuna, Ngöbe-Buglé and Embera crafts as well as local Panamanian work. They also have a selection of hammocks and artefacts from neighbouring countries.

Reprosa, Av Samuel Lewis y Calle 54, T269-0457. A unique collection of pre-Columbian gold artefacts reproduced in sterling silver vermeil; David and Norma Dickson make and sell excellent reproductions (**Panamá Guacas**, T266-6176).

Books and music
Gran Morrison, Vía Espana, T269-2211, and 4 other locations around the city. Books, travel guides and magazines in English.

La Garza, Av José de Fábrega y Calle 47, near the University. Bookshop with good supply of Latin American literature (Spanish only).

Legends, Calle 50, San Francisco, diagonal to the Iglesia de Guadalupe de Panamá, T270-0097. A cultural oasis – CDs, books, T-shirts and posters.

Librería Argosy, Vía Argentina north of Vía España, El Cangrejo, T223-5344. Very good selection in English, Spanish and French, also sells tickets for musical and cultural events. Recommended.

National University Bookshop, on campus between Av Manuel Espinosa Batista and Vía Simón Bolívar, T223-3155. For excellent range of specialized books on Panama, national authors, social sciences and history, Mon-Fri 0800-1600. Highly recommended.

The campus **Simón Bolívar Library** has extensive Panamanian material, only for registered students but visitors engaged in special research can obtain a temporary permit from the director, Mon-Fri 0800-2000, Sat 0900-1300.

Librería Cultural Panameña, SA, Vía España y Calle 1, Perejil, T223-5628, www.libreria cultural.com. Mon-Fri 0900-1800, Sat 0900-1700. Excellent, mostly Spanish bookshop with obscure Panamanian prints as well as regular titles and very helpful staff.

The Smithsonian Tropical Research Institute (see page 1309), Edif Tupper, Av de los Mártires (opposite National Assembly), has a bookshop and the best English-language scientific library in Panama, Mon-Fri 0800-1600.

Camping equipment
Army Force, east end pedestrianized section of Av Central, west of Plaza 5 de Mayo.

Army-Navy store, Av Central near Plaza 5 de Mayo, for various pieces of camping and hiking equipment.

Markets and supermarkets
Bargain hard as prices are extremely competitive. The central **Mercado San Felipe**, close to the docks and Palacio Presidencial, is the place for fresh produce (pigs, ducks, poultry and geese) and pets. The most interesting part is the chaotic shopping area along Calle 13 and the waterfront (Terraplen). It's the best place

to buy second-hand jungle and military supplies (eg powerful insect repellents, machetes and cooking equipment) for a trek into the forested interior.

Supermercado El Rey has a branch on Vía España just east of **Hotel Continental**, at El Dorado, and at several other locations. Super 99, Farmacias Arrocha, Casa de la Carne (expensive) and Machetazo, also a department store (on Av Central, Calidonia) are said to be the city's best.

Newspapers and magazines
The international edition of the *Miami Herald* is widely available at newsstands and hotels, as are leading US papers and magazines. Spanish and English magazines at branches of **Farmacias Arrocha, Super 99** and **Gago** supermarkets/drugstores.

Photography
There are many places for equipment such as **Foto Decor** and **Foto Enodi**, Vía Porras. **Relojería**, Calle Medusín, off Av Central in Calidonia. Watch shop for camera repairs.

▲ Activities and tours

Panama City *p1302, maps p1304, p1306, p1311 and p1315*
Beaches
Many are within 1½ hrs' drive of the city. **Fort Kobbe** beach (US$7.50, with vouchers given for drinks and hot dogs, bus from Canal Area bus station US$0.75, 30 mins) and **Naos** beach (US$1, Amador bus from same station, US$0.30, then 2-km walk along causeway) have been recommended. Veracruz beach is not recommended as it is both dirty and dangerous. All are dangerous at night.

Golf
Coronado Beach Golf Club, part of the **Hotel Coronado Club Suites Resort** (open to tourists who get guest cards

at Coronado office on Calle 50), www.coronadoresort.com. **Summit Golf and Resort**, 20 mins out of the city along Carretera Gaillard, T232-4653, www.summitgolfpanama.com. Tourists welcome, green fees and rented clubs.

Horse races
President Ramón racetrack, Juan Díaz. Thu, Sat, Sun and holidays. Entry from US$0.50-2.50. Take a bus to Juan Díaz.

Swimming
Piscina Adán Gordón, between Av Cuba and Av Justo Arosemena, near Calle 31, 0900-1200, 1300-1700 (except weekends to 1700 only). Admission US$0.50 (take ID) Women must wear bathing caps; take a padlock for locker.
Piscina Patria (the Olympic pool), San Pedro or Juan Díaz bus, US$0.25.

Tour operators
Adventuras in Panama, Edi Celma, Ofic 3, El Paical, T260-0044, www.adventuresin panama.com. Specialist in hiking, rock climbing, canyoning, very knowledgeable about Darién and the old colonial roads, very active on looking for new opportunities. Many trips focus on the nearby Chagres National Park including the 'Jungle Challenge', which involves rappelling off a series of waterfalls – great fun! Good store of equipment with the unusual option of naturist hiking if the mood takes you and weather suits
Airemar, Calle 52 y Ricardo Arias 21, T269-2533. Highly recommended for flights to South America.
Ancon Expeditions, Calle Elvira Méndez, next to **Marriott Hotel**, T269-9415, www.anconexpeditions.com. This is the tour operator for the environmental agency ANCON. Excellent guides and service, with especially recommended programmes in the Darién region (Cana Valley and Punta Patiño), but can arrange programmes to most of Panama's wilderness areas. Trans-

Darién treks and specialist birding programmes available.

Arco Iris, Apdo. 6-2544 El Dorado, T225-7414, www.arcoirispanama.com. Full range of local tours.

Cinco Continentes, Av Principal La Alameda, Edif Plaza San Marcos, T260-8447. Helpful with shipping a car. Recommended.

Eco Circuitos, T314-0068, www.ecocircuitos. com. Expertly run with conservation an utmost priority. Good range of creative tours include hiking, diving, cultural exchange and educational programs.

EcoMargo Tours, Calle 50 San Francisco, local 1, next to Farmacias Arrocha, T302-0390, www.margotours.com. Specializes in ecotourism for small groups with emphasis on using local guides, can book various lodges and excursions.

Panama Jones, T/F726-2621, www.panama canal.com. English spoken, specialists in adventure tourism. Their 11-night Panama Explorer tour gives a good look at the diverse aspects of the country.

Panama Pete Adventures, Av Miguel Brostella, Plaza Camino de Cruces No 35, bear Country Inn & Suites El Dorado, T/F6673-6436, www.panamapete adventures.com. All the adventure options available in Panama.

Panama Star Tours, Calle Ricardo Arias, Edif Comi PB, T265-7970, www.panamastar. com. Arranges itineraries and books accommodation throughout the country.

Panama Trails, Edif Plaza Morica, piso 11, Oficina 1104, Calle 50 y 71, T393-8334, www.panamatrails.com. Offers a wide selection of multi-day packages.

Panama Travellers, Vía Argentina, in front of El Parque Andrés Bello, Edif Yolanda, T214-7345, www.panamatravellers.com. The usual tours, Canal, eco-exploring, birdwatching, jungles, kayaks, etc.

Scubapanama, Urbanización El Carmen, Av 6 Norte y Calle 62a No 29-B, T261-3841, www.scubapanama.com. Respected local dive operator. Offers dives in the Caribbean (near Portobelo), Pacific and the Canal.

One option includes all 3 areas in 1 day. Longer trips can be arranged on request, including options in Pearl Islands and Isla Coiba. Given sufficient numbers all-inclusive multi-day trips to Isla Coiba start at around US$450-500. Certification courses available.

Tanager Tourism, in the town of Palmilla, 8 km south of Mariato, T6715-7471, www.tanagertourism.com. New Dutch-owned tour operator, based on the Azuero Peninsula, developing ecotourism options in this undiscovered and remote part of Panama.

Pearl Islands p1313

Argonaut Steamship Agency, Calle 55 No 7-82, Panama City, T264-3459. Launch cruises.

⊖ Transport

Panama City *p1302, maps p1304, p1306, p1311 and p1315*

Air

Airport information T238-4160, T238-4322 or T226-1622.

Tocumen International Airport (PTY), 27 km. Official taxi fare is US$25 to or from Panama City, maximum 2 passengers in same party, US$14 each sharing with 1 other, or US$10 per person if you share making it a *colectivo*. US$2 extra if you go by the toll road – much quicker. Bargaining is possible with regular cabs but not with tourist taxis at the airport.

From the airport to the city, walk out of the terminal and across the main road to the bus shelter. Another option is to walk 300 m to the traffic circle where there is a bus shelter (safe but hot during the day). For about US$3 (should only be US$1.20) driver takes you by Panamá Viejo, just off the main airport road.

Buses to the airport are marked 'España-Tocumen', 1 hr, US$0.35, but if going at a busy time, eg in the morning rush hour, allow 1½-3 hrs.

There is a 24-hr **left-luggage** office near the **Budget** car rental desk for US$1 per article per day (worth it, since theft in the departure lounge is common). The official IPAT tourist office at the airport remains open to meet late flight arrivals. There are duty-free shops at the airport with a wide selection and good prices. Most facilities are found in upper level departure area **Banco Nacional de Panamá**, **Cable & Wireless** office for international phone, fax and internet access); car rental is downstairs at Arrivals.

Domestic flights operate from Marcos A Gelabert airport at Albrook in the Canal Area. There is no convenient bus service, taxis charge US$1-2. Good self-service café especially for fried breakfast before early flight to San Blas. **Aeroperlas** operates daily flights to 17 destinations throughout the country (eg from Panama City to **Colón** US$26, **David** US$65, **Bocas del Toro** US$66, **Yaviza/El Real** US$55, all fares 1 way). **Air Panama** have flights to 22 destinations, including **San José** in Costa Rica. **Mapiex Aéreo** and **Aviatur** also fly to several destinations throughout the country, and there are charter flights to many **Darién** outposts. Sample hourly rates for private hire: Twin Otter 20 passenger, US$630. Rodolfo Causadias of **Transpasa**, T226-0842 is an experienced pilot for photographic work.

Airline offices For international airline websites see page 37. **Aerolíneas Argentinas**, Vía Brasil y Av Ramón Arias, T269-3815; **AeroMéxico**, Av 1B Norte, El Cangrejo, T263-3033; **Aeroperlas**, reservations T315-7500, www.aeroperlas. com; **Air France**, Calle Abel Bravo y 59 Obarrio T269-7381; **Alitalia**, Calle Alberto Navarro, T269-2161; **American Airlines**, Calle 50 Plaza New York, T269-6022; **Avianca**, 223-5225; **Aviatur**, T315-0311; **Cathy Pacific**, Av 1-B Norte, El Cangrejo, T263-3033; **Continental**, Av Balboa y Av 4, Ed Galerías Balboa, Planta Baja, T263-9177; **Copa**, Av Justo Arosemena y Calle 39, T217-2672; **Cubana**, Av Justo Arosamena, T227-2291;

Delta, Edif World Trade Centre, Calle 53E, Marbella, T214-8118; **Grupo Taca**, Centro Comercial Camino de Cruces, Local 2, Vía Ricardo J Alfaro, T360-2093; **Iberia**, Av Balboa y Calle 34, T227-3966; **KLM**, Av Balboa y Calle Uruguay, Edif Plaza Miramar, T264-6395; **LAB**, Calle 50 No 78, Ed Bolivia, T263-6771; **LanChile**, Calle 72, San Francisco, T226-7119; **Lufthansa**, Calle Abel Bravo y 59 Obarrio, Ed Eurocentro, T269-1549; **Mapiex Aéreo**, T315-0344; **Mexicana**, Vía Argentina, Ed Torre el Cangrejo oficina 64, T264-9855; **United Airlines**, Bella Vista, L-1, T225-6519;

Bus

Local The traditional small buses known as *chivas*, consisting of locally made wooden bodies grafted onto truck chassis, have all but disappeared. Most buses in urban areas are old US school buses brightly painted in fanciful designs, but poor condition. They are known as *diablos rojos* (red devils) and are notorious for roaring engines and aggressive drivers. Most outbound (east) buses travel along Av Perú, through Bella Vista, before fanning out to their various destinations. Inbound (west) buses travel along Vía España and Av Central through the Calidonia shopping district. Basic fare US$0.25, usually paid to the driver upon descending; if there is a fare box, deposit upon entering. To stop at the next authorized stop, call out '*parada*' to the driver.

Long distance All buses apart from the Orange buses leave from the bus terminal in Albrook, near the domestic airport. Taxi US$2 to centre. Facilities at the vast terminal include ATMs, internet access, clothes shops, luggage shops, bakeries and basic restaurants.

Most long-distance buses are fairly modern and in good condition. Except for the longest routes, most are 24-seater 'Coaster'-type minibuses. Check if a/c on next bus out is functioning. Offices are arranged in long line from right to left in the terminal.

Orange buses to all **Canal Area** destinations (Balboa, Miraflores, Paraíso, Kobbe, etc) leave from SACA terminal near Plaza 5 de Mayo; from the Plaza, walk past the National Assembly tower and turn left.

From the Gran Terminal de Transporte, Albrook (T232-5803): **Bocas del Toro**, 0800 and 2000, 12 hrs; **Chitre**, 14 daily, 3½ hrs, US$7.50; **Colón**, every 30 mins, 30 daily, 2 hrs, US$2-US$2.50; **David**, 30 daily, 5½ to 7 hrs, US$12.50-US$15; **Las Tablas**, 13 per day, 0600-1900, 5 hrs, US$6.50; **Paso Canoas** (border with Costa Rica), 10 daily, 8 hrs, US$14; **Penonome**, every 15 mins, 2¼ hrs, US$4.50; **Santiago**, every 30 mins, 3½ hrs, US$7.50.

International buses Buses going north through Central America get booked up so reserve a seat in advance and never later than the night before departure. Ticabus, in the Gran Terminal de Transporte, Albrook, T314-6385, www.ticabus.com, run a/c buses to **San José**, daily at 1100, arriving at 0200 the next day, US$25 1 way (but check times, which change at regular intervals); continuing to **Managua**, US$45; **Tegucigalpa**, US$65, and on as far as **Tapachula** on the Mexico–Guatemala Pacific coast border, US$110, via **Guatemala City**, US$95 (3½ days, overnight in Managua and El Salvador). Tickets are refundable; they pay on the same day, minus 15%. **Panaline** to **San José** from the Albrook Gran Terminal de Transporte, T314-6383, www.panalinecr. com and the main terminal leaves daily at 2200 arriving at 1530 the following day. You can also travel with **Padafront**, T314-6263, www.padafront.com, Panama City–Paso Canoas then change to **Tracopa** or other Costa Rican buses for San José and other destinations en route to the Costa Rican capital.

Car

Several major downtown arteries become 1-way during weekday rush hours, eg Av 4 Sur/Calle 50, 1-way heading west 0600-0900, east 1600-1900. The Puente de las Américas can be used only to go into or out of town depending on time and day, mostly weekends; these directions are not always clearly signed.

Car rental At the airport: Avis, T238-4056; Budget, T238-4068; Dollar, T238-4032; Hertz, T238-4081 and National, T238-4144.

In El Cangrejo: Avis, Vía Venetto, T264-0722; Barriga, Edif Wonaga 1 B, Calle D, T269-0221; Budget, T263-9190; Dollar, T269-7542. Gold, Calle 55, T264-1711; Hertz, Hotel Sheraton, T226-4077 ext 6202, Calle 50, T264-1111, El Cangrejo T263-6663; International, Vía Venetto, T264-4540.

Cycling

Almacén The Bike, Calle 50 opposite Telemetro. Good selection of cycle parts.

Taxi

Service is generally good, but can be scarce during peak hours and many drivers have little clue where many streets are – it's good to have a rough idea of the address location. Voluntary sharing is common but not recommended after dark. Most newer taxis have a/c. If a taxi already has a passenger, the driver will ask your destination to see if it coincides with the other passenger's. If you do not wish to share, waggle your index finger or say 'No, gracias'. Similarly, if you are in a taxi and the driver stops for additional passengers, you may refuse politely. Zone system: US$1 for 1 passenger within 1 zone, US$0.25 for each additional zone (US$2 is a common overcharge in zone 1). Additional passengers US$0.25 each regardless of zones; sharing passengers each pay full fare. Panamanians rarely tip, but foreigners may add US$0.25 or US$0.50 to the fare. Hourly hire, advised for touring dubious areas, US$7 per hr, US$8 with a/c. Radio taxis summoned by telephone are highly recommended. They are listed in yellow pages under 'Taxis'. Add US$0.40 to fare for pickup. 'Tourist taxis' at major hotels (aged, large American cars with 'SET' number plates) have a separate rate structure: they are more expensive than those you flag down.

Train
A luxury train now runs daily from Corozal Passenger Station in Panama City to **Colón** US$22 1 way, US$44 return, 0715, returns 1715, 1¼ hrs. Turn up on the day or book in advance through tour operators. More details available at www.panarail.com. A cab to the station from Panama City costs about US2.50.

Taboga Island *p1313*
Boat Taboga is reached in 1-1½ hrs from Pier 17-18 in **Balboa** (check the times in advance, 1314-1730); taxi from Panama City about US$4 per person. Daily at 0830,with additional 1500 service on Mon, Wed and Fri. Sat-Sun 0800, 1030 and 1600. Return at 1630 daily, with 0930 service on Mon, Wed and Fri. Sat-Sun 0900, 1500 and 1700. Return fare US$10.

Pearl Islands *p1313*
Air Return air ticket to **Contadora** from Paitilla, US$61 by **Aeroperlas**, T250-4026 in Contadora.
Mountain bike hire By entrance to Caesar Park, US$5 per hr.

● Directory

Panama City *p1302, maps p1304, p1306, p1311 and p1315*
Banks
Try to avoid 15th and last working day of the month, as they are pay days. Panamanian banks' hours vary, but most open Mon-Fri 0800-1500, Sat 0800-1200. **Visa** T264-0988; **MasterCard** T263-5221; **Diners** T263-8195. **American Express**, Agencia de Viajes Fidanque, Av Balboa, Torre Banco BBVA, Piso 9, T225-5858, Mon-Fri 0800-1715, does not exchange TCs. International Service Center, T001-800-111-0006. ATM for withdrawals at

Banco Continental near hotel of same name. Banistmo, Calle 50, Mon-Fri 0800-1530, Sat 0900-1200, changes TCs, no commission on AMEX, US$5 per transaction for other TCs. **Banco General** takes Amex, Bank of America and Thomas Cook TCs, 1% commission, minimum US$2 per transaction. Branch at Av Central y 4 Sur (Balboa) can be used for cash advances from ATMs on Visa. **Bank of America**, Vía José de la Cruz Herrera, Calle 53 Este, no commission on own TCs, US$0.10 tax. You can buy AMEX TCs at **Banco Mercantil del Istmo** on Vía España (they also give cash advances on MasterCard). **Banco Nacional de Panamá**, Vía España opposite the Hotel Continental, T205-2000, changes AMEX TCs with 1% commision. **Chase Manhattan Bank**, US$0.65 commission on each TC, Visa advances. **Citibank** has plenty of ATMs for cash withdrawals for its own debit or credit card holders, also Visa cash advances. **Lloyds Bank**, Calle Aquilino de la Guardia y Calle 48, Bella Vista, T263-6277, T263-8693 for foreign exchange, offers good rates for sterling (the only bank which will change sterling cash, and only if its sterling limit has not been exhausted). It is possible to change South American currencies (poor rates) at **Panacambios**, ground floor, Plaza Regency, behind Adam's Store, Vía España, near the Banco Nacional de Panamá and opposite Hotel Riande Continental (it also has postage stamps for collectors).

Conservation
Asociación Nacional de Conservación de la Naturaleza (ANCON), Calle Amela Dennis de Icaza, Ancón Hill, past Panama's Supreme Court, in former Quarry Heights, Casa 153, T314-0052, www.ancon.org, for comprehensive information on the country's natural attractions and environmental matters. They also run a chain of lodges throughout the country eg in Darién and Bocas.

Embassies and consulates
Canada, World Trade Center, Galería Comecial, piso 1, Calle 53e, Marbella, T264-

9731; **Chile**, Vía España, Edif Banco de Boston, T223-9748, 0900-1200, 1400-1600; **Colombia**, MM Icaza 12, Edif Grobman, 6th floor, T264-9266, 0800-1300; **Costa Rica**, Calle Samuel Lewis, T264-2980, 0900-1600; **El Salvador**, Av Manuel Espinoza Batista, Edif Metropolis 4A, T223-3020, 0900-1300; **France**, Plaza de Francia, Zona 1, T211-6200; **Germany**, Edif Bank of America, Calle 50 y 53, T263-7733, 0900-1700; **Guatemala**, Edif Altamira, 9th floor, 9-25, Vía Argentina, T269-3406, 0800-1300; **Honduras**, Av Justo Arosemena y Calle 31, Edif Tapia, 2nd floor, T225-8200, 0900-1400; **Israel**, Edif Grobman, Calle MM Icaza, 5th floor, PO Box 6357, T264-8022; **Italy**, Av Bal boa Edif Banco Exterior, T225-8948, 0900-1200; **Mexico**, Edif Credicorp, Calle 50, T210-1523, 0800-1200; **Netherlands**, Altos de Algemene Bank, Calle MM Icaza, 4, T264-7257, 0830-1300, 1400-1630; **Nicaragua**, Edif de Lessep's, 4th floor, Calle Manuel María Icaza, T264-3080; **Norway**, Edif Comasa, 5th floor, Av Samuel Lewis, T263-1955, 0900-1230, 1430-1630; **Spain**, Plaza Porras, entre Av Cuba y Av Perú, Calle 33A, T227-5122, 0900-1300; **Sweden**, consulate at Av Balboa y Calle Uruguay, T264-3748, 0900-1200, 1400-1600; **Switzerland**, Av Samuel Lewis y Calle Gerardo Ortega, Edif Banco Central Cancellería, 4th floor, T264-9731, PO Box 499 (Zona 9A), 0845-1145; **UK**, Torre Swiss Bank, Calle 53, Zona 1, T269-0866; **USA**, PAS Building 783, Demetrio Basilio Lakas Avenue Clayton, T207-7000, http://panama.us embassy.gov ; **Venezuela**, Edif Hong Kong Bank, 5th floor, Av Samuel Lewis, T264-2524, 0830-1100.

Immigration

Migración y Naturalización, Av Cuba (2 Sur) y Calle 29, T225-8925; visa extensions and exit permits issued Mon-Fri 0800-1530. **Ministerio de Hacienda y Tesoro**, Av Perú/Calle 36, T227-4879, for tax compliance certificate (*paz y salvo*) required for exit visa (*permiso de salida*) if you stay more than 30 days. **Customs** For renewal of permits and obtaining exit papers for vehicles at Paitilla airport.

Internet

Internet cafés are everywhere in Panama City, and are especially concentrated in the commercial centre around Vía España. Rates can be as low as US$0.50 per hr. New places are constantly opening, with many offering perks to clients, such as free coffee.

Language schools

ILERI, 42G Vía La Amistad, El Dorado T/F260-4424, www.ileripanama.com. Small school offering homestays, US$450 per wk 1-to-1 tuition.

Laundry

Lavamático Lavarápido, Calle 7 Central No 7-45, ½ block from Plaza Catedral, Mon-Sat 0800-2000, Sun 0900-1400. Many around Plaza Catedral; wash and dry US$2. **Lavandería y Lavamático America**, Av Justo Arosemana and Calle 27. Self service was and dry only US$1.50. Very convenient for the hotel district.

Medical services

Hospitals and clinics Private clinics charge high prices; normally visitors are treated at either the **Clínica San Fernando**, T229-2004, or the **Clínica Paitilla**, T269-6060, which both have hospital annexes. For inoculations, buy vaccine at a chemist and ask them to recommend a clinic; plenty in La Exposición around Parque Belisario Porras. **Dentist** Balboa Dental Clinic, El Prado, Balboa, T228-0338, good, fair price. Dr Daniel Wong, Clínica Dental Marbella, Edif Alfil (ground floor), near Centro Comercial Marbella, T263-8998. Dr D Lindo, T223-8383, very good but fix price before treatment.

Post office

There is no home postal delivery service in Panama. Recipients either have a post office box (*apartado*), or receive mail via General Delivery/Poste Restante (*Entrega General*). The main post office is close to Casco Viejo at the west end of Av Balboa at Av B, opposite the Mercado de Mariscos, Mon-Fri 0700-1745,

Sat 0700-1645; 'Poste Restante' items are held for a month. Official name and zone must be included in the address. **Main Post office.** 'Zona 1, Central, Av Balboa opposite Mercado de Mariscos'; **Calle 30 East/Av Balboa**: 'Zona 5, La Exposición'; **El Dorado Shopping Centre**, Tumba Muerto: 'Zona 6A, El Dorado'; **Vía España, Bella Vista** (in front of Piex store): 'Zona 7, Bella Vista'. Parcels sent 'poste restante' are delivered either to **Encomiendas Postales Transístmicas** at the El Dorado Centro Comercial or the main post office if there is no duty to pay on the goods. The post office operates a courier system called **EMS** to most Central and South American countries, Europe, US and some Asian countries. Packages up to 20 kg: 2-3 days to USA (500 g documents to Miami US$13); 3-4 days Europe US$20; Asia US$25. Also private courier services, eg UPS, Edif Fina, Calle 49, El Cangrejo, ½ kg to London or Paris, 3-4 days, US$30; **Jet Express (Federal Express)**, Edif Helga, Vía España y Av 4 Sur/Calle 50, ½ kg to Miami, 2 days, US$19.

Telephone
Cable & Wireless has its main office in Vía España, on the ground floor of Banco Nacional building. It offers excellent but expensive international telephone, telex, fax and modem (use Bell 212A type) facilities. Collect calls to 21 countries, dial T106. For the cost of phone cards and international calls, see page 1300. Local calls in Panama City, US$0.10 for 3 mins, US$0.05 for each additional min; anywhere else in the country, US$0.15 per min.

Balboa *p1312*
Banks Chase Manhattan Bank and Citibank. **Post office** Av Balboa and El Prado. **Telephone** Cable & Wireless.

Panama Canal area

→ *Colour map 8, B1.*

Whether travelling through the Canal, or just standing at its side, watching the vast ocean-going vessels rise and fall as they pass through the huge canal locks is a spectacular sight. In the middle of Lago Gatún is Parque Nacional Isla Barro Colorado, a popular destination for nature lovers and birdwatchers. On the eastern side of the canal, 2 km after Miraflores Lock, is the entrance to the Parque Nacional Camino de Cruces, which has several designated hiking trails including the Camino de Cruces colonial gold route which continues through Parque Nacional Soberanía as far as the Chagres River. ➤➤ *For listings, see pages 1333-1334.*

Background

The Panama Canal was created from the artificial, river-fed Lago Gatún, 26 m above sea level, which supplies the water for the lock system to function. Ships sail across the lake after having been raised from sea level by a series of locks on either the Atlantic or the Pacific approach. They are then lowered by the locks on the opposite side. As the crow flies, the distance across the isthmus is 55 km. From shore to shore the Canal is 67.5 km, or 82 km (44.08 nautical miles) from deep water to deep water. It has been widened to 150 m in most places. The trip normally takes eight or nine hours for the 30 to 40 ships passing through each day. On the Atlantic side there is a normal variation of 30 cm between high and low tides, and on the Pacific of about 380 cm, rising sometimes to 640 cm.

From the Pacific, the Canal channel goes beneath the Puente de las Américas and passes the port of Balboa. The waterway has to rise 16.5 m to Lago Miraflores. The first stage of the process is the Miraflores Locks, 1.5 km before the lake. A taxi to the locks from the city costs US$10. At the far end of the lake, ships are raised another 9.5 m by the single-step Pedro Miguel Locks, after which the 13 km Gaillard, or Culebra Cut is entered, a narrow rock defile leading to Lago Gatún. Opposite Miraflores Locks, there is a swing bridge. Gaillard Cut can be seen from Contractor's Hill, on the west side, reached by car (no buses) by turning right 3 km past Puente de las Américas, passing Cocolí, then turning as signed. The road beyond Cocolí goes on to Posa, where there are good views of the locks, the cut and former Canal Zone buildings.

Barro Colorado

For 37 km the Canal passes through Lago Gatún. Enough water must be accumulated in the reservoir during the rainy season to operate the locks throughout the three to four month dry season, since a single ship's transit can use up to 50 million gallons. (A high level reservoir, Lago Alajuela, formerly Madden Lake, feeds the lake and maintains its level; see below.) In the lake is **Barro Colorado Island**, to which animals fled as the basin slowly filled. It is a formally protected area called the **Barro Colorado Nature Monument** and has been a site of scientific research for over 70 years. The excursion is highly recommended for seeing wildlife, especially monkeys, and includes a walk around a guided trail with over 50 points of interest.

> ● *Everything that crosses the Canal pays by weight, although there are plans to introduce a flat fee. The record for the smallest sum is held by Richard Halliburton, who swam from ocean to ocean between 14 and 23 August 1928, paying US$0.36 for his 150 lbs.*

Gatún Locks

Continuing north, 10 km southwest of Colón are the Gatún Locks (*Esclusas de Gatún*) with their neat, attendant town. Here is the **observation point** ① *daily 1000-1630*, perhaps the best spot in the Canal area for photographing the passage of ships. The most magnificent of the Canal's locks, Gatún integrates all three lock 'steps' on the Atlantic side, raising or lowering ships to or from 26 m in one operation. The flights are in duplicate to allow ships to pass in opposite directions simultaneously. Passage through the locks takes about one hour.

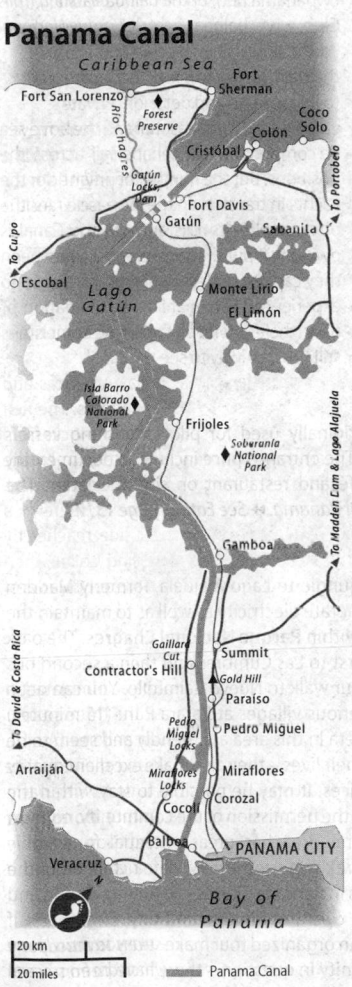

Panama Canal

After crossing the lock, the road forks with the left-hand branch bridging the Chagres River just downstream from the graceful Gatún Dam – the largest earth dam in the world when it was built in 1906. Opposite the power plant is the **Tarpon Club** ① *T443-5316*, a fishing club which has a very nice restaurant, disco and bar. A short distance further south is an attractive lakeside picnic area and small boat-launching area. The road goes on down the lake to Escobal and Cuipo through lovely scenery, good for birding. There are no hotels in Cuipo but there are plenty of buses to/from Colón (US$1.60, two hours, US$0.25 to the locks). A bus from Colón to Gatún Locks costs US$0.75.

Canal tours

Most people are surprised by the stunning beauty of the scenery around the Canal, and it is also interesting to see the mechanics of the passage. Full and partial transits can be organized through Panama Canal Tours, see Activities and tours, page 1334.

Another way of seeing the Canal is on the **luxury daily train** ① *US$22 1 way, US$44 return, 0715, returns 1715, 1¼ hrs, contact T317-6070, www.panarail.com*, which runs to Colón.

It's also possible to visit the **Miraflores Locks** and the **Miraflores Visitor Centre** ① *Mon–Sun 0900-1630, www.pancanal. com, US$8 entrance to the museum and Canal viewing platform, US$5 for platform only*, which was constructed as part of Centenial celebrations at a cost of US$6 million. The museum is spread over four

Linehandling the Panama Canal

The best way to see the Panama Canal is by boat. If you don't have your own, it is possible to sail through as a linehandler on a yacht. Each yacht is required to have four onboard linehandlers plus the helmsman for what is normally a two-day journey. While many Panamanians work full-time as linehandlers, people with experience, or at least a modicum of common sense, may be able to get a position as a linehandler and work their way through. One experienced captain in Costa Rica said the task is not difficult, but you do have to work when it is time to work – so don't expect to sunbathe all the way through.

An additional benefit is that as well as getting to see the canal from the inside, the yacht's owners are required to feed linehandlers three meals a day and, if the journey takes more than one day (for most yachts transit requires two days), accommodation.

If you are interested go to the Panama Canal Yacht Club in Colón on the Caribbean side (email pcyachtclub@cwpanama.net), or the Balboa Yacht Club, www.balboa yachtclub.com, on the Pacific side. Ask in the club or office for the best person to speak to. Don't expect to just turn up and get a job. Private yacht transits are seasonal and there may be competition for linehandling positions. But the number of private yachts in transit is on the increase. Transit obviously has its risks, and no yacht owner will put their vessel at risk when they can use professional and experienced Panamanians. But nevertheless, with all these caveats, it is still the best way to see the canal.

floors and includes a training simulator originally used for pilots transiting vessels through the Canal, it is a good half-day trip. The entrance price includes a documentary film in English and Spanish. There is a café and restaurant on site, the latter, **The Miraflores** was used in the movie *The Tailor of Panama*. ▸▸ *See Eating, page 1317.*

Lago Alajuela

It is a two-hour drive through picturesque jungle to Lago Alajuela, formerly Madden Lake, east of the Canal. The lake, used to generate electricity as well as to maintain the level of Lago Gatún, covers 50 sq km and is within **Parque Nacional Chagres**. The park can be reached by bus from Panama City, first to Las Cumbres and then a second bus to Caimitillo. After that it is a 3½- to four-hour walk to Nuevo Caimitillo. You can get a dugout canoe to take you to Emberá indigenous villages at Parara Puru (15 minutes) and Embera Drua (30-40 minutes). The Emberá in this area are friendly and seem to be coping well with the impacts of tourism on their lives – they also make excellent quality crafts, which are sold at very reasonable prices. It may be possible to stay within the village of Parara Puro for a small fee and with the permission of the community, giving a greater insight into village life. The Chagres area has great potential for wildlife watching and jungle adventure. Multi-day trekking trips into wildlife rich parts of the forest can be arranged with some companies in Panama City, as can tubing, rafting and abseiling within the watershed – see Tour operators in Panama City, page 1323. If visiting the villages on the Chagres River on an organized tour make sure your company pays the correct visitation fee to the community in question – there have been several incidents of payment being withheld. On a similar note all trips made in the area should involve the employment of Emberá guides/assistants to ensure that these villages benefit from tourism on their lands. The Camino Real passes through the park. There is another refuge at Cerro Azul, marking the start of a challenging three-day hike to the north coast, guide essential. Take a bus for Chepo from Panama City and get off at Vista Hermosa, then walk the 6 km to the ranger hut.

The canal drive runs from Balboa along the Gaillard Highway. Beyond Fort Clayton there is a fine view of the Miraflores and Pedro Miguel locks. Beyond Pedro Miguel town, a road branches off to the left to **Summit** (Las Cumbres), where there are experimental gardens containing tropical plants from all over the world (closed Monday) and a good, small zoo containing native wildlife. **La Hacienda** restaurant serves native dishes. The alternative road to Lago Alajuela (37 km) crosses the Las Cruces trail (an old cannon marks the spot), and beyond is deep jungle. If walking the trail, take machete and compass. Halfway along the Las Cruces trail (1¼ hours) a gravel track, the Plantation Road, turns left, emerging after 1¼ hours on the Gamboa highway 1.5 km north of Summit.

A large area of rainforest between Lago Gatún and Lago Alajuela has been set aside as **Parque Nacional Soberanía** with many walking trails. The park is very popular with birdwatchers with just under 400 species recorded to date, and is reputedly one of the finest observation areas for birds in the world. It once held the world record for the most birds counted in a 24-hour period. The park has two fabulous trails for wildlife observation and also has an aviary for harpy eagles. Plantation Trail begins right at the entrance of the road that leads to the Canopy Tower and Pipeline Road is about 17 km long in total, accessed from the Gaillard highway running along the canal, just north of Gamboa, the old American dredging port. The now-abandoned coast-to-coast pipeline was built during the Second World War by the United States and hidden in the jungle as a guarantee of oil supply should the canal be sabotaged. The park has an information centre at the Summit Garden.

◉ Panama Canal area listings

For Sleeping and Eating price codes and other relevant information, see Essentials pages 45-48.

◉ Sleeping

Lago Alajuela *p1332*
LL-L Canopy Tower Ecolodge and Nature Observancy, signposted from just beyond Summit Gardens on the Transisthmus Hwy, T264-5720, www.canopytower.com. A hotel and ecolodge that rises to the rainforest canopy in a converted old communications tower. 7 quirky little rooms, with private bath, price includes meals and guided walks. Some cheaper rooms available off season. Excellent for wildlife. Day trips and guided tours welcome.

LL-L Gamboa Rainforest Resort, on the hill above Gamboa overlooking the Chagres River, T314-5000, www.gamboaresort.com. This looming green and white resort built on old American golf course has a restaurant (a bit soulless) and swimming pool. There is an ancient tree dividing the complex. Cheapest rooms are in apartments formerly occupied by US dredging engineers. An aerial tramway runs silently through the canopy to a mirador with good views of the canal (at US$35 not cheap but an easy way to see monkeys, sloths and crocodiles). Tour available to non-residents.
C Cabañas Flotantes in the Chagres River. Interesting place to stay with thatched 'floating cabins' moored between Lago Alajuela and the Canal. For further information, contact **Panama Paradise**, T269-9860.

Barro Colorado *p1330*

Visitors without permits will be turned away on arrival.

Smithsonian Institute, at the Tupper Building in Ancón, US$40, T212-8000, www.stri.org. Arrange daily trips which last 4-6 hrs, including boat, audio-visual display and lunch, but take water. Take a Gamboa Summit bus from next to Plaza 5 de Mayo (0600 and 0615) to the Dredging Division dock at Gamboa (US$0.65), from where the boat leaves. Make arrangements with the Institute in Ancón. Tours don't go Mon or Thu, max 12 people Tue and Wed, 15 on Fri, 25-30 Sat and Sun – book in advance, especially at weekends. ID required when booking.

Gatún Locks *p1331*

Agencia Giscomes, T/F264-0111. Offers trips through the canal every 2nd and 4th Sat or Sun of the month, leaving at 0730. Partial boat trips are also offered on the canal, through Miraflores Locks as far as Pedro Miguel locks.

Aerotours, T262-8710, fly Piper J3 Cub trips, 30 mins US$60 per person, full coast to coast, 2 hrs, US$200.

Canal tours *p1331*

Panama Canal Tours, Vía Porras y Calle Belén No 106, T226-8917, www.pmatours. net. Full and partial transits organized. Partial transit US$115, full transit US$165. Trips are every Sun, with additional services subject to demand.

◎ Transport

Gatún Locks *p1331*

Orange bus from Panama City to **Miraflores Locks** leaves from the bus station next to Plaza 5 de Mayo (direction Paraíso), 20 mins, US$0.35. Ask driver to let you off at the stop for 'Esclusas de Miraflores', from where it's a 10-min walk to the locks. Taxi to the locks, US$10 per hr. Another good way to see the Panama Canal area is to rent a car.

Lago Alajuela *p1332*

The trip to **Summit** may be made by train on Sun or buses marked Gamboa, every 1-1½ hrs, from bus station next to Plaza 5 de Mayo, US$0.45, 1½-hr ; the Paraíso bus will also take you to the **Miraflores** and **Pedro Miguel** locks.

Colón and Cristóbal and around

→ Colour map 8, B1.
Landfall on the Caribbean side for the passage of the Canal is made at the twin cities of Cristóbal and Colón, the one merging into the other almost imperceptibly and both built on Manzanillo Island at the entrance of the Canal in Bahía Limón. The island has now been connected with the mainland. Colón was founded in 1852 as the terminus of the railway across the isthmus; Cristóbal came into being as the port of entry for the supplies used in building the Canal.

Avenida del Frente is the main commercial street and is quite active but has lost its past splendour: the famous Bazar Francés closed in 1990, the curio shops are not noteworthy and the railway station stands virtually deserted except for the movement of a few freight trains. Nevertheless, there is talk of declaring the whole of Colón a free zone (the Zona Libre being the city's main attraction), the authorities are moving to give the city new housing and employment (residential estates like 'Rainbow City' and 'Puerto Escondido' are being extended on the landward side to relocate entire neighbourhoods of slums), and the demands on Cristóbal's busy port facilities (200 million tons of cargo a year) continue to increase. It is hoped that, if these plans are realized, Colón may become a pleasant place again. ▶ *For listings, see pages 1341-1343.*

Ins and outs
At Cristóbal ships usually dock at Pier No 9, five minutes from the shops of Colón. Vehicles wait at the docks for those wanting to visit Colón and other places.

Safety Mugging, even in daylight, is a real threat in both Colón and Cristóbal. The situation has improved now that the two main streets and some of the connecting ones are guarded by police officers; you are still strongly recommended not to stray too far from their range of sight. Keep a few dollars handy for muggers in case the worst happens.

Tourist office IPAT tourist office ① *Calle 13 between Central y Domingo Díaz (just before Ley supermarket, opposite Silenciadores Colón), T441-4460, Mon-Fri 0830-1630,* are helpful. Also try **Cámara de Comercio** ① *Plaza 5 de Mayo,* if your tourism involves business.

Colón
Colón was originally called Aspinwall, after one of the founders of the Transisthmian Railway. The French-influenced **cathedral** ① *C 5 y Av Herrera, 1400-1745 daily,* has an attractive altar and good stained-glass windows. **The Washington Hotel** ① *on the seafront at the north end of the town,* is the town's most historic structure and is worth a look. The original wooden hotel was built in 1850 for employees of the Railroad Company. President Taft ordered a new fireproof hotel to be built in 1912 and the old one was later razed. Although remodelled a number of times, today's building, with its broad verandas, waving palms, splendid chandelier, plush carpets and casino, still conjures up a past age, while the café provides an excellent view of ships waiting to enter the Canal.

Next door is the **Casa de Lesseps**, home of the Suez Canal's chief engineer during the 1880s (not open to the public). Across from the **Washington** is the **Old Stone Episcopal Church**, built in 1865 for the railway workers; it was then the only Protestant church in Colombia (of which Panama was a province).

Running north through the centre of Colón is the palm-lined **Avenida Central**, with many statues (including one of *Columbus and the Indian Girl*, a gift from the Empress of France). The public market is at the corner of Calle 11. Avenida del Frente, facing the Bahía de Limón, has many old wooden buildings with wide verandas.

Colón

N

200 metres
200 yards

Sleeping 🛏
Andros 1
Astor 2
Carlton 3
García 4
Internacional 5

Meryland 6
Nuevo Washington 7
Pensión Acrópolis 8
Pensión Anita 9
Pensión Plaza 10
Sotelo 11

Eating 🍴
Antonio 1
Fenix 3
La Cabaña Avila 4
Recession 6
Veteranos 7

The main reason to come to Colón is to shop at the **Zona Libre** ① *Mon-Fri 0800-1700 (a few places retail on Sat morning), if you have a car, pay a minder US$1 to watch it while in the zone.* It's the second-largest free zone in the world, an extensive compound of international stores and warehouses established in 1949 and surrounded by a huge wall – pick up a free map from hotels or tourist office showing who sells what. A passport or official ID must be shown to gain entry to the zone.

The 30-minute beach drive around Colón's perimeter is pleasant and cool in the evening; despite the slums at the south end there are some nice homes along the east shore of the peninsula. Permission from the Port Authority security officer is required to enter the port area, where agents for all the world's great shipping lines are located in colonial Caribbean-style buildings dating from 1914. Almost lost in a forest of containers is the **Panama Canal Yacht Club** ① *T441-5882*, whose open-air restaurant and historically decorated bar offer very good food (seafood and Chinese). This is the place to ask about sailing boat charters to the San Blas Islands or shorter trips aboard visiting yachts.

Around Colón and Cristóbal

A well-paved road branches off the TransIsthmus Highway at Sabanitas, 14 km east of Colón, and runs northeast along the coast for 33 km to the historic Spanish garrison port of **Portobelo** (see below). The rocky **Costa Arriba** is very attractive, with a number of lovely white-sand beaches (crowded at weekends). Playa María Chiquita (14 km) has a bathing pavilion, toilets, bar and restaurant managed by the government tourist bureau. A local speciality is *sao*, Jamaican-style pig's feet pickled with lime and chillies, sold from roadside stalls. Playa Langosta, also with swimming, bar and restaurant, is 3 km further on. There are plenty of small restaurants along this road serving fresh seafood. A group of people can rent a boat at Puerto Pilón, close to Sabanita (US$100-150 a day) for a ride to Portobelo, seas are often rough, take precautions. In **Buenavista**, just before entering Portobelo, a cannon marks the spot where Henry Morgan landed for his devastating 15-day sack of the town in 1668.

West of Colón ⊖ ➤ *pp1341-1343*.

From Colón, the Caribbean Costa Abajo, stretching west of the Canal, can also be visited. The road leaves Colón through new housing developments (on the left is the modern city of Margarita) and runs 10 km southwest to the Gatún Locks (see page 1331).

Fuerte San Lorenzo → *Colour map 8, B1*.

Perched on a cliff-top promontory overlooking the mouth of the Río Chagres with great views of the coast, Fort San Lorenzo is one of the oldest and best-preserved Spanish fortifications in the Americas. Construction began the year before Drake launched a 23-ship attack on the post (1596) and proceeded up the Chagres in an unsuccessful attempt to reach Panama City. The following century, Morgan fought a bloody 11-day battle to take the fort as a prelude to his decisive swoop on Panamá Viejo in 1671. Although new defences were then built, they were unable to prevent British Admiral Edward Vernon's successful attack in 1740 (one of Vernon's cannon with the 'GR' monogram can still be seen). Engineer Hernández then spent seven years strengthening the garrison (1760-1767), but the threat to San Lorenzo gradually receded as Spanish galleons were diverted to the Cape Horn route and the era of the freebooters approached its end.

The last Royalist soldiers left the fort in 1821 as Colombia declared its Independence from Spain. The earliest artillery sheds can be seen on the lower cliff level but most of the bulwarks, arched stone rooms and lines of cannon are 18th century. The site has undergone an extensive UNESCO renovation programme and is well worth a visit. There is a picnic area and a tiny beach is accessible by a steep path down the cliff.

Costa Abajo
There is no crossing of the Chagres at San Lorenzo. To continue down the Costa Abajo, you have to return to the Gatún Dam and take the gravel road along the west side of the river, which winds its way through pristine forest to the coastal village of Piña and its kilometre-long beach. The road runs west along a steep and rocky shore to Nuevo Chagres and Palmas Bellas, quiet fishing resorts in coconut palm groves, but with few facilities. You'll need a 4WD to continue to Río Indio and Miguel de la Borda, where the road comes to an end. The villages beyond, including historic Río Belén where one of Columbus' ships was abandoned in 1502, are still only accessible by sea.

If you want a real adventure, you can travel from Penonemé in Coclé Province across the continental divide to Coclecito, and then, with collective boat transport, down the Coclé del Norte River to the coast and the town of the same name – a true jungle adventure for those prepared to rough it and get away from it all. For more information contact Sven and Vivi on T993-3620 or T674-1162 (mobile).

Portobelo and east of Colón ●●●●● ▸▸ pp1341-1343. Colour map 8, B1.
East of Colón along the Caribbean coastline is Portobelo, founded in 1519 on the protected bay in which **Columbus** sought shelter in 1502. Researchers believe they have now located the wreck of the *Vizcaiína*, abandoned by Columbus, in shallow waters somewhere off the coast of Portobelo. Now little more than a large village, the 'Beautiful Port' was once the northern terminus of the **Camino Real**, where Peruvian treasure, carried on mule trains across the isthmus from Panama City, was stored in fortified warehouses. The gold moved on when the periodic arrival of the Spanish Armada created famed fairs where the wealth of the New World was exchanged for goods and supplies from Europe. The fair of 1637 saw so much material change hands that, according to the Englishman Thomas Gage, it took 30 days for the loading and unloading to be completed. In the **Royal Contaduría**, or Customs House, bars of gold and silver were piled up like firewood. Such riches could hardly fail to attract foreign pirates. Portobelo was one of **Francis Drake**'s favourite targets but it was also his downfall; he died here of dysentery in 1596 and was buried in a lead-lined coffin in the bay off Isla Drake. Divers are currently attempting to discover the exact spot, intending to return Drake's body to his home city of Plymouth. By the beginning of the 17th century several *castillos* (Santiago, San Gerónimo and San Fernando) had been built of coral stone quarried nearby to protect the harbour. Attacks continued, until in 1740 the treasure fleets were rerouted around the Horn and the Portobelo Fairs ended. The fortifications were rebuilt after Vernon's attack in 1744 but they were no longer seriously challenged, leaving the fortresses visible today. The largest, the aptly named 'Iron Castle', was largely dismantled during Canal construction. But there are many other interesting ruined fortresses, walls, rows of cannon and remains of the town's 120 houses and public buildings still to be seen standing along the foreshore amid the present-day village. In 1980 the remains of the colonial structure, known as the **Monumental Complex** ① *US$1, closed Sun*, was declared a World Cultural Heritage monument by UNESCO. The Contaduría

Exploring the Camino Real and surrounding area

Although little of the Camino Real remains, its two branches from Madden Lake/Lago Alajuela across the mountains to Nombre de Dios (30 km) and Portobelo can still be hiked.

The trail starts at the old manganese mining zone (Mina 1, on the dirt road that runs from the Transístmica to a little way up the Río Boquerón). Buses run occasionally from the Transístmica to Salamanca, roughly where the Río Boquerón empties into Madden Lake. The trail follows the Río Boquerón up to the continental divide and the Río Nombre de Dios down the northern watershed to the coast near the present-day town.

This historic trek is easy for anyone with reasonable fitness, as one can drive to entry and exit points. Guides are not really necessary, the rivers are beautiful (and carry little water in the dry season) and the jungle is almost untouched; the trail is straightforward and rises only to 330 m at the divide. Allow about three days for the Boquerón–Nombre de Dios trek. The trail to Portobelo branches off the Boquerón trail at the Río Diablo or Río Longue. After you leave the Boquerón you will need to navigate by compass. The Diablo takes the trekker higher into the divide (700 m) than the Longue (350 m, the route that the treasure-laden mules followed) and the terrain is more broken; both lead to the Río Cascajal (higher reaches are strewn with large boulders), which descends to the Caribbean.

The highest point in the region, Cerro Brujo (979 m), is passed en route. There are jaguars in this forested refuge, but they are unlikely to present any danger to hikers – indeed, you'd be lucky to see one. The Cascajal reaches the road about 1 km east of Portobelo. The Boquerón–Portobelo hike is more demanding than the other and takes four days maximum, a good machete is essential, and solitude guaranteed for at least two days.To the south and east of the Camino Real are the rivers of the Chagres system, which flow into Lago Alajuela. Some of these are now being exploited for rafting. Check with tourist agencies in Panama City for Camino Real treks. Also see page 1340 for description of part of the Camino Real.

(1630) has been restored, with similar plans for the Plaza, Hospital Chapel and the Fernández House. There is a small museum with a collection of arms.

In **San Felipe Church** (1776) is the 17th-century cocobolo-wood statue of the Black Christ, about whose origin there are many legends. One tells of how fishermen found it floating in the sea during an epidemic of cholera in the town. It was brought ashore and immediately the epidemic began to wane. Another says that the life-size image was on its way to Cartagena when the ship put in to Portobelo for supplies. After being thwarted five times by rough weather to leave port, the crew decided the statue wished to remain in Panama. It was thrown overboard, floated ashore and was rescued by the locals.

The Tourist office (IPAT) ① *just west of the square behind the Alcadía, T448-2073, Mon-Fri 0830-1630*, can provide guides, schedules of Congos and other performances, as well as comprehensive information about the many local points of interest, including the surrounding 34,846-ha **Portobelo National Park**, which has 70 km of coast line with beautiful beaches, superb scuba-diving sites and boat rental to visit secluded beaches nearby, such as La Huerta. Services in town are limited with no bank or post office and just one minimart.

Isla Grande 😊🚹📱📵 » pp1341-1343. Colour map 8, B1.

A paved road continues northeast from Portobelo to Isla Grande, and another heads east to Nombre de Dios (25 km) and Palenque. Scuba-diving is offered at several places along the way. The road passes through **Garrote** and **La Guaira**, from where *pangas* can be hired (US$1, although they might try and charge US$2 if you take the boat on your own) at the car park to cross to **Isla Grande**. The island is a favourite because of its relaxed lifestyle, fishing, scuba-diving and snorkelling, windsurfing and dazzling white palm-fringed beaches. The best beaches are enclosed in front of the two expensive hotels, but you should be able to use them. A good, more public beach, is on a spit before **Hotel Isla Grande**. The island's 300 black inhabitants make a living from fishing and coconut cultivation, and a powerful French-built lighthouse crowns the small island's northern point, where there is a mirador, reached by steep path. There are a number of colourful African-tinged festivals held here throughout the year, particularly on 24 June, 16 July and the pre-Lenten Carnival with *Congos*. The part of the village to the right of the landing stage is more lively with competing salsa sounds.

Nombre de Dios 😊 » pp1341-1343. Colour map 8, B1.

The beautiful, deserted mainland beaches continue as the 'road' heads east to Nombre de Dios. The historic town (1520) near the present village was once the thriving trading port that first hosted the famed fairs, located at the end of the stone-paved Camino Real from the capital. By the 1550s, more than half the trade between Spain and its colonies was passing through its lightly defended harbour, but in 1594 the decision was made to move operations to the more sheltered site of Portobelo. The Camino Real was diverted and Nombre de Dios was already dying when Drake captured and burnt it two years later, so that William Dampier could describe the site some years later as "only a name ... everything is covered by the jungle with no sign that it was ever populated." Excavations have taken place revealing the Spanish town, parts of the Camino Real, a broken cannon and other objects, most of which are now in the National Museum.

The modern village is built on either side of a freshwater channel; a footbridge links the two. The church is built on a plaza on the west side, the main square is on the east. It has few facilities, one hotel and a restaurant on the square, but there's a beautiful beach for the few who get this far. A *cayuco* (US$3 per person, 12 minutes) can be taken to Playa Damas, an unusual beach where alternating patches of red and white sand resemble a chess board. The beach is owned by an amateur ecologist who has built some rustic huts and a campsite, **Costa El Oro** (T263-5955), on a small island here, he also offers expert guidance on local fishing and diving spots. Buses come into the centre en route to Portobelo or Cuango; while most go as far as the main square before coming back the same way, some turn round before this at the little plaza beside the police station.

The track staggers on for another 25 km linking the peaceful fishing villages of the Costa Arriba. Locals eagerly await the paved road's eventual extension through the succession of seaside villages to the Golfo de San Blas opposite El Porvenir, the capital of the Kunas' self-governed area of **Kuna Yala** (Kuna Earth).

Not far beyond Nombe de Dios, near Viento Frío, is **Diver's Haven**, which is recommended for diving tours (see Sleeping, page 1342). The next village is **Palenque**, unspoilt, with a good beach and very rudimentary huts being built for visitors. **Miramar** is the cleanest of all the *pueblitos* along this coastline. The occasional smuggling boat puts in here and a few Panama City tourists come to stay in the three houses on the tiny Isla

Bellavista (ask Niano at **Bohio Miramar** bar/restaurant) – US$70 for house with three double beds, no beach but you can swim off the jetty). Boats can take you on to **Santa Isabel** (beyond the reach of the dirt road), US$35 for the boat, or to **San Blas** US$25 each, minimum eight people. The village at the end of the road is **Cuango**, a bit run-down and dusty between rains, with a littered beach.

◉ Colón and Cristóbal listings

For Sleeping and Eating price codes and other relevant information, see Essentials pages 45-48.

● Sleeping

Colón and Cristóbal *p1335, map p1336*
AL Meryland, Calle 7 y Santa Isabel, T441-7128. New with restaurant.
AL Nuevo Washington, Av del Frente Final, T441-7133, nwh@sinfo.net. Art deco style, guarded enclave, clean, restaurant, good view of ships entering the canal, also the small **Pharaoh** casino and the 24-hrs **Los Piratas** bar.
B Carlton, Calle 10 y Av Meléndez, T447-0112. A good choice and one of the better hotels.
C Andros, Av Herrera, between Calle 9 y 10, T441-0477. Modern, clean, fan or a/c, bath, TV, good restaurant, *cafetería*.
C Internacional, Av Bolívar, y Calle 11, T441-8870. Well-furnished, bar, restaurant.
C Sotelo, Guerrero y Calle 11, T441-7702. Small but clean rooms.
D-E Astor, Frente, between Calle 7 y Calle 8, T441-0233. Big airy rooms, some with option for a/c – best at front, with plant-filled balcony. Recommended.
D-E García, Calle 4, 75 m east of Av Central, T441-0860. Basic, but airier than some others in this category, pay a little more and get a/c.
D-E Pensión Plaza, Av Central y Calle 7, T441-3216. Clean and cheap, more expensive rooms have a/c and TV
E Pensión Acrópolis, Av Amador Guerrero y Calle 11, opposite Sotelo, T441-1456. Shared bath.
E Pensión Anita, Amador Guerrero y Calle 10, T441-2080. Dark rooms, basic.

Fuerte San Lorenzo *p1337*
D Las Bahías, on the edge of the roadless Golfo de los Mosquitos, 4 km west of Coclé del Norte and 60 km from Colón. A small rustic lodge. 4 *cabañas* on the beach with 1 double and 2 single beds in each. Las Bahías is only accessible by boat, either by collective *cayuco* from Gobea or Río Indio (US$8) or from Muelle de Calle 5 in Colón.

Portobelo and east of Colón *p1338*
B Cabañas el Mar, in Buenaventura, 5 km west on road to Colón, T448-2102. With a/c, cheaper with fan, quiet location by the sea.
B Scuba Portobelo, also in Buenaventura, T448-2147 or T261-3841. Scuba gear for hire.
D Aquatic Park, on road towards Colón. Dormitory accommodation, expensive.
E Hospedaje La Aduana, in town on main square. Somewhat noisy bar.

Isla Grande *p1340*
During holidays and dry season weekends, make reservations in advance; prices often double during high season. All hotels have bars and simple restaurants.
LL Bananas Village Resort, north side of the island, usually accessed by boat but also by path over the steep hill, T263-9510, www.bananasresort.com. Relatively discreet luxury hotel, on the best beach on the island, with a good but expensive bar.
B Damaris, 300 m to right of the dock, T687-8202. **Turquesa** bar/restaurant, popular with Panamanians.
B Isla Grande, T225-6722. US$45 for 4 beds, with a/c. Bungalows scattered along an excellent sandy beach. Popular with Panamanians, restaurant, pool table, ping pong, a little run-down but good value.

B Villa Ensueño, right at the landing stage, T/F448-2964. Large lawns (big enough to play football) with gardens and a hammock on each balcony.

D Cabañas Jackson, immediately behind main landing stage, T441-5656. Many huts/bungalows available.

Nombre de Dios *p1340*
C Diver's Haven, not far beyond Nombre de Dios, near Viento Frío, T448-2248. Recommended for diving tours.

E Bohío, to left of road, on beach 50 m before the quay. 2 small but light rooms with TV and fan; the restaurant at the back of the jetty rents out 2 dark rooms. Boats can take you on to **Santa Isabel** (beyond the reach of the dirt road), US$35 for the boat, or to **San Blas** US$25 per person, minimum 8 people.
E Casa de Huéspedes, on main square. With restaurant. A beautiful beach can be enjoyed by those few who get this far. A *cayuco* (US$3 per person, 12 mins) can be taken to Playa Damas, an unusual beach where alternating patches of red and white sand resemble a chess board. The beach is owned by an amateur ecologist who has built some rustic huts and a campsite (**Costa El Oro**, T263-5955) on a small island here, also offers expert guidance on fishing and diving spots.
F Nameless hospedaje, Cuango. Ask for María Meneses at 1st house on the left on east side of square. There is also one restaurant and store here.

❶ Eating

Colón and Cristóbal *p1335, map p1336*
See Sleeping for **Panama Canal Yacht Club**. Hotels **Carlton** and **Washington** also have good restaurants (♔♔). There are several fast food outlets.
♔♔ **Hotel Andros**, Av Herrera y Calle 9, T441-0477. Modern, self-service, open till 2000, except Sun. Check out the mirrors.

♔♔ **Veteranos**, Calle 9 y Av del Frente, T441-3563. Popular with visiting business men, port officials and lately with younger clientele.
♔ **Antonio**, Av Herrera y Calle 11. Unremarkable but decent.
♔ **Fenix**, Central y Calle 8. Basic local fare.
♔ **La Cabaña Avila**, Av Central y Calle 8, Caribbean food.
♔ **Nacional**, esquina Guerrero y Calle 11. Popular with locals, good for breakfast.
♔ **Recession**, Calle 13 y Central. Good soups, Chinese and other dishes, cheap.

Portobelo and east of Colón *p1338*
A number of small *fondas* serving coconut rice with fresh shrimps, spicy Caribbean food with octopus or fish, or *fufú* (fish soup cooked with coconut milk and vegetables).
♔♔ **Los Cañones**, in Buenaventura, 5 km west on the road to Colón, good food in a lovely setting by the water, not cheap.
♔ **El Hostal del Rey**, corner of Parque Central, Portobelo. Good meals and value.
♔ **La Torre**, T448-2039, in La Escucha, 3 km before the town. Good food.

Isla Grande *p1340*
♔♔ **Kiosco Milly Mar**, just west of landing pier. Excellent fish dishes, moderate prices.
♔ **Candy Rose**. Serves drinks with a special octopus cooked in coconut milk.

❀ Festivals and events

Portobelo and east of Colón *p1338*
21 Oct The miraculous reputation of the **Black Christ** is celebrated annually; purple-clad pilgrims come from all over the country and the statue is paraded through the town at 1800 on a flower- and candle-covered litter carried by 80 men (who take 3 steps forward and 2 steps back to musical accompaniment); feasting and dancing till dawn.
Jan-Mar/Apr Other fiestas in the Portobelo region – for example **Carnival**, **Patron Saint's Day** (20 Mar) – are opportunities to experience the *congos*. Unlike the dance of

the same name found elsewhere on the Caribbean coast, the *congo* here is the name given both to the main, male participants and a slowly unfolding ritual that lasts from the Día de los Reyes (6 Jan) to Easter. Among the various explanations of its symbolism are elements of the people's original African religions, their capture into slavery, their conversion to Catholicism and mockery of the colonial Spaniards. Members of the audience are often 'imprisoned' in a makeshift palisade and have to pay a 'ransom' to be freed.

● Transport

Colón and Cristóbal *p1335, map p1336*
Air
Former US France Field AFB has replaced Colón's old airstrip as the busy local airport, on the mainland east of the city, taxi under US$1, but barter. **Aeroperlas** has daily flights Mon-Thu to **Panama City**; T430-1038, US$26 1 way. Flights are hectic with Free Zone executives; no reservations so allow plenty of time or plan to stay the night in Colón.

Bus
Bus station on Av del Frente and Calle 12. Express (a/c) US$2.25, and regular buses, US$1.75, daily to **Panama City** every 20 mins, less frequent at weekends, about 2 hrs. Hourly to **Portobelo** daily, US$2, 1 hr.

Boat
For shipping a vehicle, see page 1295. For **San Blas** try asking at Coco Solo pier, T430-7327.

Taxi
Tariffs vary, US$0.75 in Colón, US$1.25 to outskirts, US$5-7 per hr. Car rental and taxis on Av del Frente facing Calle 11; most drivers speak some English and can advise on 'no-go' areas.

Train
US$20, 1 way, US$35 return, to **Panama City**, leaves 1730, station on west side of town just off the centre.

Portobelo and east of Colón *p1338*
Bus Buses from **Colón**, every hr from 0700 from the bus station on Av del Frente y Calle 13, 1 hr, US$1; **María**, **Chiquita**, 40 mins, US$0.80. Portobelo can be visited from Panama City in a day without going into Colón by taking an early bus to the Sabanitas turn-off (US$1) and waiting for a Colón–Portobelo service (US$1).

To villages further east, take buses marked 'Costa Arriba' from stop at back of square: **Nombre de Dios**, 45 mins US$1; **Palenque**, 70 mins, US$1.50; **Miramar**, 80 mins US$3, **Cuango**, 1½ hrs, US$3.50. Road paved until just beyond Nombre de Dios.
Boat Launch to **Santa Isabel** (beyond reach of Costa Arriba road), 2 hrs, to **San Blas** 3 hrs.

Isla Grande *p1340*
On Sun the last bus from La Guaira back to **Portobelo** leaves at 1500 and is always packed. Hitching with Panamanian weekenders is possible, all the way to **Panama City** if you're lucky!

● Directory

Colón and Cristóbal *p1335, map p1336*
Banks Banco Nacional de Panamá. Caja de Ahorros. Chase Manhattan Bank. Citibank. Lloyds Bank agency in Colón Free Zone, at Av Santa Isabel y Calle 14, T445-2177. Mon-Fri 0800-1300. **Internet** Explonet, Frente, between Calle 9 y Calle 10, Mon-Sat 0800-2300, Sun 1300-2000, US$2.50 per hr. **Dollar Rent-a-Computer**, Calle 11 Y Av Guerrero, above Café Nacional, T441-7632, US$2.50 per hr, net phones US$0.61per min to England. **Post office** in Cristóbal Administration Building, on corner of Av Bolívar and Calle 9. **Telephone** Cable & Wireless in Cristóbal.

Isla Grande *p1340*
Telephone There are 2 pay phones; 150 m to the left of the landing jetty, on a small plaza, to the right beside the basketball court.

San Blas Islands

→ *Colour map 8, B2.*

The Archipiélago de San Blas (or Las Mulatas) is a broad string of 365 islands ranging in size from deserted islets with just a few coconut palms to inhabited islands, about 50 in total and home to hundreds of Kuna people. Lying off the Caribbean coast east of Colón, the archipelago stretches along the coast for over 200 km from the Gulf of San Blas to the Colombian border. The islands' distance from the mainland ranges from 100 m to several kilometres. ➡ *For listings, see pages 1347-1348.*

Ins and outs

There are about 20 basic airstrips in the San Blas Islands and province. They include: El Porvenir, Cartí, Río Sidra, Río Azúcar, Narganá, Corazón, Río Tigre, Playón Chico, Tupile, Tikankiki, Ailigandi, Achutupu (also known as Uaguitupu), Mamitupu, Ogóbsucum, Ustupu, Mansucum, Mulatupu, Tubuala, Calidonia and Puerto Obaldía. You can be dropped off at any island or village and picked up later, subject to negotiations with the pilot, but though this may sound appealing, it is probably not wise since there is no drinking water or food. One of the best islands to visit from the Porvenir area is **Dog Island** with a superb beach and great snorkelling on a wreck just 20 m off shore. Hotel prices usually include a trip here. There is a 'local' tax of US$1 per island. Any travel agent in Panama can book a San Blas tour.

An alternative route to San Blas is to walk over the continental divide from Cañita to Sarti. Take a bus from Panama City towards Darién and get off at Cañita, then walk two to three hours to the **EcoLodge** at Burbayar (there is also a lodge at Nusagrande). The following day, camp on the coastal side of the Serranía de San Blas and on the third day make sure that you reach **Cartí** before 1600 when the last boat leaves for the islands – US$20-30 to El Porvenir, or US$10 (20 minutes) to Isla Naranjos. At Cartí there is a museum of Kuna culture.

The most common point of entry into the San Blas, **El Porvenir** is taken up with an airstrip, customs and immigration. On a sailing journey this is the place to obtain your final exit stamp from Panama, or to check in if coming from Colombia. El Porvenir has a rustic hotel and is not unattractive, with a palm-fringed beach at the north end. Reef systems around the island invite snorkelling but intensive fishing means large marine life is scarce.

Background

The Kuna (Cuna or Tule) are the most sophisticated and politically organized of the country's seven indigenous groups (Kuna, Embera, Waounan, Ngobe, Bugle, Nassau and Terribe). They run the San Blas Territory virtually on their own terms after a rebellion in 1925, with internal autonomy and, uniquely among Panama's indigenous groups, they send their representative to the National Assembly. Each community is presided over by a *sáhila* (chief). Land is communally owned but coconut trees may belong to individuals. The Kuna have their own language, although Spanish is widely spoken. The women wear gold noserings and earrings, costumes with unique designs and *molas*, see box, page 1346, based on local themes, geometric patterns, stylized fauna and flora and pictorial representations of current events or political propaganda. They are outside the Panamanian tax zone and have negotiated a treaty perpetuating their long-standing trade with small craft from Colombia. Photographers need to have plenty of cash when they visit, as the set price for a Kuna to pose is US$1 per photo.

Sailing to Colombia via the San Blas Islands

With the price of a plane ticket to Cartagena costing around US$170, an alternative, more adventurous route to Colombia could be spending several days travelling by boat. It's adventurous, a true travel experience and a chance to see part of the world normally reserved for those with very big budgets.

Two types of boat can take you to Colombia. The first are local trading vessels, which occasionally head to Colombia stopping at many of the more inhabited Kuna islands and settlements along the coast. These are usually around US$200 per person, all the way to Cartagena, Barranquilla or Santa Marta. You may be able to track one down at the Colón port.

A second option is recreational yachts, often foreign-owned and travelling between Panama and Cartagena, Colombia. Some boats are on round-the-world trips, but a small number make it their business to ferry adventurous travellers to and from Colombia. Price is between US$300-400, including basic food. These boats usually leave from Portobelo or Isla Grande. In Panama and in Hostel Voyager in Panama City or visit Hostel Mamallena (www.mamallena.com) or Hostel Wunderbar (www.hostelwunderbar.com) or , contact Sr Burgos at Hotel San Blas. If coming from Cartagena in Colombia visit Casa Viena, www.casaviena.com.

Sailing vessels usually head along the coast using the most northerly islands of the San Blas, such as Cayos Holandés as overnight stops before the two- to three-day sail across the open sea to Colombia. Prevailing winds and currents make it a rougher ride from Panama to Colombia.

Choosing a boat and captain is important. Sailing is not a risk-free business as demonstrated by the multitude of wrecks in the San Blas area. Talk to your captain about previous experience and look at the boat. If in doubt, listen to your instincts. Bear in mind there is no set schedule for departures – you may have to wait to get enough people together. And as ever, when leaving a country, paperwork is important. Make sure you've completed exit formalities as directed by your captain.

Wichub-Huala and Nalunega

Just south of Porvenir, Wichub-Huala and Nalunega are heavily inhabited labyrinths of huts and alleys and are culturally fascinating. Both have communal halls where the political decisions of the villages are made, and both have simple accommodation and general stores. The shop on the south side of Wichub-Huala (the island closer to Porvenir) seems to be better stocked; it's a good place for last minute supplies.

Cayos Chichime

Not more than a couple of hours sail to the east lie the idyllic islands of the Cayos Chichime, also known as Wichudup or Wichitupo in the Kuna language. The deep-water channel entering the harbour is only 30 m wide with reefs on both sides, and requires care even from experienced captains. Both islands are beautiful and inhabited by only a handful of Kuna who survive through a combination of fishing, harvesting coconuts and selling *molas* to passing boats. The Kuna are friendly, easy-going people and interesting to talk to. Many of the Kuna who live on the islands only do so for four to five months per year before returning to the more inhabited islands or moving on to another island. One of the Panama San Blas Islands' more

La mola

You might not know what it is until you see one, but the *mola* – literal translation a 'blouse' – is the most colourful artistic expression of Kuna Yala – the San Blas archipelago. A mola is a reverse appliqué, or 'cut-out', decorative textile made by Kuna women. First created in the mid-19th century it is still worn daily on the front and back of a blouse.

Usually measuring 40 by 33 cm, *molas* are made out of up to seven (but on average three to four) superimposed, differently coloured materials. Each layer is cut to make up a design element constituted by the unveiled layer beneath it. The ragged hem is folded over and sewn down with concealed stitching. This careful craftwork and step-by-step process slowly reveals a design of a bird, aquatic creature, monster, a generic scene such as fishing or even perhaps a protecting spirit or a wild dance of colours, but always something personal to the creator's imagination.

The traditional *mola*, the 'serkan' design, with its small range of totemic objects, has been added to by the Kuna encounter with modern Panama and you are as likely to see a mola depicting an aeroplane, map, flag, political leanings, or an American invasion, which can be just as interesting. Another development is machine-made *molas* with simplistic motifs and gaudy colours.

As gifts and souvenirs, *molas* make great miniature wall-hangings and have the advantage of being light and small, so they don't take up too much precious space in the backpack. It's worth seeking out a good quality one. Don't worry about exact symmetry, but do look for fine and even outlines, the narrower, the better. The larger pattern should come out of the top layer, often black or maroon, and the detail mainly from lower layers. Some *molas* have appliqué – sewn on, as opposed to cut away, motifs – and they can create additional depth and enliven the surface, but try to avoid those with fill-in – dots and triangles and small circles roughly applied to fill up space. Stitching should be even and usually hidden, never substituted with tape, and where there is decorative surface stitching it shouldn't compete with the more graphic cut-away. Check the quality of the material in the lower layers and run your hand across the surface of the *mola* to make sure the layers are not scrunching up.

permanent residents seems to be Umburto who, if he has space, will let you stay in a hut for US$5 per night – he might even throw in some food. And for a small fee the family will also cook locally caught seafood (through don't accept lobster or crab due to over-fishing, and certainly not the meat or eggs of sea turtles, which are sometimes caught). Umburto has a boat with a motor and will take you to Porvenir for a negotiated price.

The Kuna will try and sell you *molas*, one of their few methods of obtaining cash income – if you're not interested, it will be sufficient to decline politely.

Cayos Holandés

To the east of Chichime lies a long chain of sparsely inhabited islands known as Cayos Holandés or Dutch Keys. Some of the islands have no permanent residents, but most have at least one family of Kuna harvesting coconuts. These *cayos* are the furthest from the mainland in Kuna Yala and have a rugged, remote feel. Washed by strong Caribbean swells, the Cayos Holandés harbor abundant marine life along the barrier reef and in the deepwater channels at either end of the group – in these areas Caribbean reef sharks, tarpon and rays are often seen. Even on the sheltered southern side there exist some pristine patch reefs only metres from islands themselves. Toward the eastern end of the chain is an excellent protected anchorage known to local yacht types as 'the swimming pool', due to its clear, calm water and location surrounded on all sides by islands. As with Chichime, caution and good navigational charts are required when entering this area.

San Blas Islands listings

For Sleeping and Eating price codes and other relevant information, see Essentials pages 45-48.

Sleeping

San Blas Islands *p1344*
Camping is generally discouraged on the islands but if you want to, make sure that you speak to the *sáhila* first.

It may be possible to book direct with a hotel; bear in mind that when coming to these islands, you will always need to book somewhere for the first night.
LL Dolphin Lodge, Narganá, about halfway along the coast between El Porvenir and the Colombian border, T225-8435. Owned by a Kuna family on Uaguitupu, US$139 including air fare, meals and overnight stay.
LL Iskardup Ecoresort, on Isla Tigre, a short canoe trip east from Narganá, T269-6047. With cabins, bar, restaurant, solar power, package tours include trips to the mainland.
L Kwadule, near Corazón de Jesús and Narganá. Very nice restaurant/bar over the reef, some cabins over the water, with bath.
L Sapibenega, T215-1406, www.sapibenega. com. Beautiful, stilted cabins, with private bath. Good restaurant. Accessed through Playa Chicón.
A Kuanidup, Achutupo Island, T227-6026. Has 7 huts, good food, lovely beaches, no electricity, bathrooms in centre of island.
B Hotel El Porvenir, El Porvenir, T221-1397, simple option close to airstrip. Good for boat trips.
D Narganá Lodge Hotel, Narganá. The best option, with a basic hotel (**F**) and restaurant, El Caprichito, serving good crab dishes.

D Sugtupu Hotel, Cartí-Sugtupu, south of El Porvenir, reached by boat from El Porvenir or the coastal town of Soledad. Simple option.

Wichub-Huala and Nalunega, *p1345*
A Hotel Anai, Wichub-Huala, T239-3025. Price includes food. Ask for Israel Fernández on arrival at El Porvenir.
B Hotel San Blas, Nalunega Island, 10 mins by boat from the El Porvenir airstrip. T262-5410. Traditional cane and thatch, shared showers, price includes breakfast, lunch, lobster dinner and 2 excursions. Owner Sr Burgos meets incoming flights every morning and boats to Cartagena pick up passengers from here.
C Cabañas Ukuptupu, Wichub-Huala, T220-4781 or T299-9011. Run by the family Juan García, canoes for hire. Recommended.

Festivals and events

San Blas Islands *p1344*
All the following fiestas involve dances, games, meals and speeches, and are traditional. Those on Narganá have a stronger Western element (but also typical dancing and food).
Feb Anniversary of the Tule Revolution, at Playón Chico, Tupile, Ailigandi and Ustupu.
19 Mar Fiesta patronal on Narganá.
8 Jul Anniversary of Inakiña on Mulatupo.
29-31 Jul Fiesta patronal on Fulipe.
20 Aug Charles Robinson anniversary on Narganá.
3 Sep Anniversary of Nele-Kantule on Ustupo.
11 Sep Anniversary of Yabilikiña on Tuwala.

O Shopping

San Blas Islands p1344

Molas (see box, page 1346) cost upwards of US$10 each. You can also try the San Blas perfume *Kantule*. Both are also obtainable in many Panama City and Colón shops.

▲ Activities and tours

San Blas Islands p1344

It's quite easy to arrange a trip by talking to the Kuna selling souvenirs on the tip of the Casco Viejo Peninsula in Panama City.

⊖ Transport

San Blas Islands p1344

Air

Several companies fly from **Panama City** (Albrook) including **Aeroperlas** (T315-7500), **Ansa** (T315-0300), **Transpasa** (T236-0842) and **Aerotaxi** (T264-8644).

The most popular destination is **El Porvenir**, on the north side of the Golfo de San Blas, where tourists are picked up by boat to go to a neighbouring island, about 20 mins. One-way fares to the islands are US$32 to **El Porvenir** and US$52 to **Puerto Obaldía**. All other air fares are scaled in between. All flights leave between 0600 and 0630, Mon-Sat, returning 0800-0830. Evening and Sun flights must be booked privately. Baggage over 15 kg is charged at US$0.50 per kg, so wear your heavy stuff.

Sea

There are occasional boats to the San Blas Islands from **Colón**, but there is no scheduled service and the trip can be rough. One ship that goes from time to time is the *Almirante*; try to find the captain, Figueres Cooper, who charges US$30 for the trip. The port captain's office at Coco Solo may have information on boat departures, T441-5231 or 445-1055, although most boats are not keen to take gringos. Alternatively, go to Portobelo and try for a boat from there, 9 hrs to **El Porvenir**, every other day, US$17.

The Interior

→ Colour map 8, B1

Cross the Puente de las Américas from Panama City and you enter the most densely populated rural quarter of the country, a Panama that is in great contrast to the cosmopolitan capital and the Canal: colonial towns, varied agriculture, traditional crafts and music, Pacific beaches and beautiful mountain landscapes with good walking options. The Pan-American Highway crosses the region known as 'El Interior' (though the term can refer to any area outside the capital), en route to Costa Rica. ►► For listings, see pages 1351-1352.

Panama City to Costa Rica

The Pan-American Highway, also known as the *Interamericana*, heads westwards along a well graded and completely paved road from Panama City through Concepción to the Costa Rican border for 489 km. Leaving Panama City, the Pan-American Highway crosses the **Puente de las Américas** over the Canal at the Pacific entrance (if on a bus, sit on the right-hand side – north – for the best views). The bridge was built between 1958 and 1962 by the USA to replace the ferry crossing. It is 1653 m long and, with a road surface to seaway distance of 117 m, there is ample room for all ships to pass below. The bridge, which has three lanes, is the only vehicular crossing on the Pacific side of the canal. There is also a pedestrian walkway for the length of the bridge, but muggings have occurred on the bridge even in broad daylight so take care. Buses run to a *mirador* on the far side of the bridge from the city.

La Chorrera → Colour map 8, B1.

The first place you reach, 13 km from Panama City, is the small town of **Arraiján**. Another 21 km by four-lane highway (toll US$0.50) takes you to La Chorrera with an interesting store, **Artes de las Américas**, filled with wooden carvings. A branch road (right) leads 1.5 km to **El Chorro**, the waterfall from which the town takes its name. At Km 20, among hills, is the old town of **Capira** (good food is on offer next to the Shell station, Chinese-run). Just west of Capira is a sign indicating the turn-off to **Lídice**, 4 km north of the highway, at the foot of Cerro Trinidad (which local tradition calls 'the end of the Andes'). The town was the home of Czech immigrants who in 1945 succeeded in having the name changed from Potero to commemorate Lídice in their homeland, which suffered heavily in the Second World War.

The highway passes through the orange groves of Campana, where a 4-km road climbs to **Parque Nacional Altos de Campana**. Created in 1966, the 4816 ha park – the first in Panama – protects humid tropical forest growing on mountainous volcanic rock that forms picturesque cliffs ideal for walking and hiking.

San Carlos and beaches → Colour map 8, B1.

At Bejuco, 5 km east of Chame, the road stretches down a 28-km peninsula to **Punta Chame**, with a white-sand beach, a few houses, and just one hotel/restaurant. At low tide, the sand is alive with legions of small pink crabs. There is a splendid view northeast to Taboga Island and the entrance to the Canal in the distance. Food is prepared by the beach, there are several bars and a pickup running between the highway and the beach costing US$1 is your link to the outside world.

Beyond Chame are two beaches: **Nueva Gorgona**, 3 to 4 km long, waves increasing in size from west to east, and a well-stocked grocery store. A little further along the Pan-American is **Playa Coronado**, the most popular beach in Panama, but rarely crowded. Homeowners from Playa Coronado have installed a checkpoint at the turning, unaffiliated with the police station opposite. Be polite, but do not be deterred from using the public beach.

Opposite the turning to Playa Coronado is a road inland to Las Lajas and beyond to the hills and **Lagunas del Valle**, about one hour from the highway. Ten kilometres beyond Playa Coronado is the town of **San Carlos**, where there's good river and sea bathing (beware of jelly fish and do not bathe in the estuarine lake). There are not many restaurants in San Carlos, but there are plenty of food shops.

El Valle

Five kilometres on, a road to the right leads, after a few kilometres, to a climb through fine scenery to the summit of **Los Llanitos** (792 m) (direct bus from Panama City US$3.50, or US$1 from San Carlos), and then down 200 m to a mountain-rimmed plateau (7 by 5.5 km) on which is the comparatively cool, summer resort of El Valle. Four kilometres before El Valle is a parking spot with fine views of the village and a waterfall nearby. Soapstone carvings of animals, straw birds, painted gourds (*totumas*), carved wood tableware, pottery and *molas* are sold in the famous Sunday market, which is very popular with Panamanians and tourists. There is also a colourful flower market. The orchid nursery has a small zoo and Panama's best-known **petroglyphs** can be seen near the town. This is one of many good walks in the vicinity (ask directions); another is to the cross in the hills to the west of town.

Beyond El Valle is the **Canopy Adventure** ① *T983-6547 (in El Valle, Spanish only), T264-5720 (in Panama City) http://adventure.panamabirding.com, daily 0600-1700, US$50*, with a series of cables and wires whizzing you through the forest; the last stage swoops across the face of a waterfall. It's good for all ages and the whole experience takes about 1½ hours and includes a short hike through the forest. To get there from El Valle take a bus to El Chorro Macho or taxi to La Mesa.

Santa Clara and Antón

Santa Clara, with its famous beach, 115 km from Panama City, is the usual target for motorists. The beach is about 20 minutes from the Pan-American Highway, with fishing, launches for hire and riding. About 13 km beyond is Antón, which has a special local *manjar blanco* (a gooey fudge) and a crucifix reputed to be miraculous.

Penonomé → *Colour map 8, B1.*

A further 20 km is the capital of Coclé province, Penonomé, an old town even when the Spaniards arrived. An advanced culture which once thrived here was overwhelmed by volcanic eruption. Objects revealed by archaeologists are now in Panama City, in the American Museum of Natural History in New York, and in the local **Museo Conte de Penonomé** ① *Tue-Sat 0900-1230, 1330-1600, Sun 0830-1300*. The local university and the **Mercado de Artesanato** on the highway are worth a visit. There is a delightful central plaza with the air of a tiny provincial capital of times past. The town is often a lunch stop for motorists making the trip from Panama City to the western border.

Balneario Las Mendozas and Churuquita Grande
Just under 1 km northwest of Penonomé is Balneario Las Mendozas, on a street of the same name, an excellent, deep river pool for bathing in. Further down the Río Zaratí, also known as the Santa María, is **La Angostura** where the river dives down a canyon. The dirt access road is usually suitable for ordinary cars. There are copper- and gold-mining activities in this area and further north, beyond La Pintada, where a 35-km road has been built to **Coclecito** on the Caribbean side of the Continental Divide. The mining company is also involved in conservation work including reforestation near La Angostura. Northeast of Penonomé is **Churuquita Grande** (camping is possible near the river with a waterfall and swimming hole). There's a **Feria de la Naranja** (orange festival) held on the last weekend of January, see page 1352. From Penonomé you can visit **La Pintada** (buses every 30 minutes), a mountain village that makes a quiet stopping-off point for hiking and horse riding.

El Caño, El Copé and Natá
El Caño is 24 km west of Penonomé, and 3.5 km from the main road is the **Parque Arqueológico del Caño** ① *Tue-Fri 0900-1600, Sat-Sun 1030-1300, US$1*, which has a small museum, some excavations (several human skeletons have been found in the burial site) and standing stones.

From El Caño (the ruins) you can take a *chiva* up into the mountains, changing to another at Río Grande, to the village of **El Copé** (direct buses from Panama City), which gives access to the **Parque Nacional Omar Torrijos** a protected forest of rubber trees with some good trails.

A further 7 km along the Pan-American Highway is **Natá**, one of the oldest towns in Panama and the Americas (1520). The early colonists fought constant attacks led by Urracá. The Iglesia de Santiago Apóstol (1522) is impressive, with interesting wood carvings. It is sadly run-down now; donations gratefully received for restoration work.

Aguadulce → *Colour map 8, B1. Population: 14,800.*
Some 10 km beyond is Aguadulce, a prosperous supply centre (bus from Panama, US$6), with local pottery for sale and *salinas* (saltworks) nearby.

Another 17 km further on, just after the large Santa Rosa sugar plantation, a road leads off right to the mountain spa of **Calobre** (31 km). The hot springs are, however, a good hour's drive away, on a very rough road, through great mountain scenery.

⦿ The Interior listings

For Sleeping and Eating price codes and other relevant information, see Essentials pages 45-48.

⦿ Sleeping

La Chorrera *p1349*
D Hospedaje Lamas, on side street just right of Tropical. A/c or fan, clean, big rooms, TV. Recommended.
D Tropical, pink and green building on Pan-American Hwy. With fan and private bath. Recommended.

San Carlos and beaches *p1349*
A Río Mar, beyond San Carlos on the Río Mar beach, T223-0192. Has a good seafood restaurant.
B Cabañas de Playa Gorgona, San Carlos, T269-2433. Cheaper, with kitchenettes, BBQ, pool, shade, hammocks, on the ocean.
B Gorgona Hayes, San Carlos, T223-7775. With pleasant pool, fountain, tennis court, restaurant. Good.

Camping

Camping is possible on Palmar Beach.

El Valle *p1350*

The town has no real centre; everyone cycles. Accommodation is hard to find at weekends. Private houses near **Pensión Niña Dali** rent cheaper rooms.

B Cabañas Las Mozas, T983-6071. The restaurant serves Arabic food.

B Hotel Campestre, at the foot of Cara Coral Hill, T983-6146, www.hotelcampestre.com. 40 tidy rooms and restaurant serving Swiss-style lunch dishes from US$6.

D El Greco Motel, Calle Central, T983-6149. With a restaurant.

E-F Pensión Niña Dalia. No towels or soap. Will look after bags.

Santa Clara and Antón *p1350*

L-AL Cabañas Las Sirenas, Santa Clara, T223-0132, www.lasirenas.com. *Cabañas* to rent for 5 or 8 people in an attractive landscaped environment.

D Hotel Rivera, Antón, Km 131, T987-2245. With bath and a/c or fan, cheaper without bath, clean.

E Pensión Panamá, Antón, across the Pan-American Hwy. Friendly, clean, safe, a/c.

Penonomé *p1350*

C-D Dos Continentes, Av Juan D Arosemena, T997-9325. With shower, a/c, pool, restaurant.

D-E Pensión Los Pinos, on left of highway to Panama City. With bath and a/c (cheaper with fan).

E Pensión Dos Reales, Calle Juan Vásquez. Basic, mosquitoes, noisy.

E Residencial El País, Calle Juan Arosemena near church and Parque, no sign but look for black lanterns on wall. With bath, good value.

Balneario Las Mendozas and Churuquita Grande *p1351*

AL Posada del Cerro La Vieja, Chiguirí Arriba, Coclé (Apdo 543 Estafeta 9A Carrasquilla, Panama City), T223-4553, posada97@hotmail.com. An excellent purpose-built lodge for walkers and ecotourists. It offers guided treks on foot or mule, including through the mountains to El Valle, or across the isthmus to the Atlantic coast with the final stage by dugout canoe.

E No Name, La Pintada, in front of the church. Juan Cedeno has a house with a couple of large, clean rooms, a/c, hot water.

Aguadulce *p1351*

C El Interamericano, on Pan-American Hwy, T997-4148. Clean rooms with bath, a/c, TV and balcony. Also has a swimming pool.

D Pensión Sarita, T997-4437, and others. It may be possible to sleep by the fire station.

✪ Festivals and events

Balneario Las Mendozas and Churuquita Grande *p1351*

Jan Feria de la Naranja (orange festival), last weekend in Jan. The inauguration and dancing is on Sat; the big day, Sun, includes a colourful parade and huge displays of fruit.

⊖ Transport

San Carlos and beaches *p1349*

Bus Panama City-San Carlos, frequent from 0615, US$3.50. To **David**, US$10.

Azuero Peninsula

→ *Colour map 8, C1.*

The small town of Divisa, 61 km beyond Penonomé, is the crossroads for a major paved road that branches south into the Azuero Peninsula, one of the earliest parts of Panama to be settled. Despite road paving in the south and east, many of the peninsula's small towns are still remote and preserve much of their 400-year-old colonial traditions, costumes and a number of white churches. In addition to its tranquillity, the region's cleanliness and prosperity are a welcome change from Panama City. Most towns of any size on the peninsula have annual carnivals (the four days before Ash Wednesday) but the one in Las Tablas is especially picturesque and popular with visitors. Accommodation is in short supply at this time throughout the region. » *For listings, see pages 1358-1363.*

Chitré and around ⬤🅰⬤⬤⬤ » *pp1358-1363. Colour map 8, C1.*

Passing through **Parita**, with a church dating from 1556, the road reaches the cattle centre of Chitré (37 km), capital of Herrera Province and the best base for exploration. The **cathedral** (1578) is imposing and beautifully preserved. The small **Museo de Herrera** ① *C Manuel Correa, Tue-Sat 0900-1230, 1330-1500, Sun 0900-1200, US$1,* has historical exhibits, a few archaeological artefacts, and some local ethnographic displays. The town is known primarily for its red clay pottery, especially its roofing and floor tiles, which are exported, and for its woven mats and carpets.

There are some nice beaches close to Chitré served by local buses, for example **Playa Monagre** and **El Rompio** ① *take the Santa Ana bus from Chitré terminal, frequent services during the day, 30 mins, US$1 to Monagre,* which are busy at weekends and holidays. It is a 30-minute walk south along the beach from Monagre to El Rompio, where you can catch a bus back to Chitré or head further south at low tide for mangroves and solitude. There are a few restaurants at Monagre, but no accommodation.

At **Puerto Agallito**, 15 minutes by bus from Chitré, many migratory birds congregate and are studied at the **Humboldt Ecological Station**. Along the swampy coast just to the north is the 8000-ha **Parque Nacional Sarigua**, established in 1984 to preserve the distinctive tropical desert and mangrove margins of the Bahía de Parita. Ancient artefacts have been unearthed within the park's boundaries. The pre-Columbian site of **Monegrillo** is considered very significant but there is little for the non-specialist to appreciate.

La Arena, the centre for Panamanian pottery, is 2 km west of Chitré. The Christmas festivities here, 22-25 December, are worth seeing, see page 1361. To get there, take a bus from Chitré (US$0.30; taxi US$1.50). Alternatively, tour operators in Panama City can arrange shopping tours here.

Los Santos, only 4 km across the Río La Villa from Chitré in Los Santos province, is a charming old town with a fine 18th-century church (San Anastasio) containing many images. The first call for Independence came from here, recognized in the interesting **Museo de la Nacionalidad** ① *Plaza Bolívar, Tue-Sat 0900-1600, Sun 0900-1200, US$1,* set in a lovely house where the Declaration was signed on 10 November 1821. **Azuero regional IPAT office** ① *T966-8072, Mon-Fri 0830-1630,* is next door.

The main road continues 22 km southeast through agricultural country to the tiny town of **Guararé**, notable only for its folkloric museum, the **Museo Manuel Zárate** ① *2 blocks behind the church, T996-2535,* where examples of Azuero's many traditional costumes, masks and crafts are exhibited in a turn-of-the-20th-century house. There is also a wealth of traditional dance, music and singing contests during the annual National Festival of **La Mejorana** (24 September).

Las Tablas and around → *Colour map 8, C1.*

Las Tablas (6 km further) is capital of Los Santos province and the peninsula's second largest city, 67 km from the Divisa turn-off. The central **Iglesia de Santa Librada** with its gold-leaf altar and majestic carvings is one of the finest churches in this part of Panama and is now a National Historic Monument. **El Pausilipo**, former home of thrice-President Porras – known to Panamanians as 'the great man' – is in the process of being turned into a museum. Las Tablas is widely known for its **Fiesta de Santa Librada**, 19-23 July, see page 1361).

The lovely and unspoilt beach of **El Uverito** is located about 10 km to the east of town but has no public transport (taxi US$4.50). A paved road runs to **Mensabé**.

Smaller paved roads fan out from Las Tablas to the beaches along the south coast and the small villages in the hills of the peninsula. A circular tour around the eastern mountain range can be done by continuing south to **Pocrí** and **Pedasí** (42 km), then west to **Tonosí**, all with their ancient churches and lack of spectacular sights, but typical of the Azuero Peninsula. Another 57 km of paved road runs directly over the hills from Tonosí to Las Tablas.

Pedasí → *Colour map 8, C1.*

Pedasí is a peaceful little town and the municipal library near the church has many old volumes. The local festival, on 29 June is **Patronales de San Pablo**. President Mireya Moscoso was born in Pedasí and the family figures prominently in the town's history. Beautiful empty beaches (**Playa del Toro**, **Playa La Garita** and **Playa Arena**) and crystal-clear seas are 3 km away, but beware of dangerous cross-currents when swimming. There is no public transport to the beaches but it is a pleasant walk early in the morning. You can also walk along the seashore from one beach to another, best at low tide. The local fishing craft are based at **Playa Arena** (also the safest for swimming) and boats can be hired for sport fishing, whale watching and visits to **Isla Iguana**, a wildlife sanctuary 8 km offshore, protecting the island's birdlife, reptiles (including turtles) and forest. Locally hired boats cost about US$40 for half a day. The **IPAT** office in Los Santos arranges tours with knowledgeable naturalist René Chan who lives locally.

Playa Venado and Tonosí

About 31 km from Pedasí, and 12 km before Cañas, a small sign points to the black-sand beach of **Playa Venado**, a surfers' paradise. There are five *cabañas* for rent here. The road onwards goes to **Cañas** (no hotel), running near the Pacific coast for a short distance, with a string of lovely coves and sandy beaches accessible by rough tracks.

From Tonosí a branch road goes a few kilometres further south to **Cambutal**, west of which begins **Parque Nacional Cerro Hoya**, where sea turtles come ashore to lay their eggs from July to November. There is also a 20-km long beach at Guánico Abajo, 20 minutes' drive from Tonosí, but no public transport.

An alternative to the main road returning to Las Tablas takes the inland road north following the Río Tonosí. Crossing a saddle between the two mountain ranges that occupy the centre of the Peninsula (picturesque views of forested Cerro Quema, 950 m), the road arrives at **Macaracas**, another attractive but unremarkable colonial town, from where two paved roads return to Los Santos and Chitré (35 km).

Ocú

About 45 km west of Chitré is Ocú, an old colonial town, whose inhabitants celebrate a few notable fiestas during the year with traditional dress, music, masks and dancing. Ocú is also known for its woven hats, which are cheaper than elsewhere in Panama.

The central mountains effectively cut off the western side of the peninsula from the more developed eastern half. There is only one road down from the highway, a gruelling gravel/dirt ribbon that staggers from near Santiago down the western coastline of the Peninsula as far south as the village of Arenas (80 km) before giving up in the face of the surrounding scrubby mountain slopes. Eastward from here the Peninsula reaches its highest point at Cerro Hoya (1559 m). No roads penetrate either to the coast or into the mountains, ensuring solitude for the **Parque Nacional Cerro Hoya**, which protects most of the southwest tip. The 32,557-ha park protects four life zones in a region that has been devastated by agriculture, over-grazing, season burning and human population pressure. More than 30 species of endemic plant have been recorded in the park and it is one of the last known sites to see the red macaw. One research trip in 1987 even found an endemic species of howler monkey. Turtles also use the coastal beaches for nesting from July to November. There are no refuges.

Santiago and around 😊😊 ➤➤ pp1358-1363. Colour map 7, C6.

Back on the Pan-American Highway, from the junction at Divisa the roads enters the Province of Veraguas – the only one with seaboards on both oceans – and arrives after 37 km in Santiago. Capital of the province, Santiago is one of the oldest towns in the country, in a grain-growing region that is very dry in summer. Very good and cheap *chácaras* – macramé bags used by male *campesinos* as a convenient holdall for lunch and other necessities in the fields – are sold in the market here. Heading north for 18 km is **San Francisco**; which has a wonderful old church with wooden images, altar pieces and pulpit. The swimming pool is adjacent to the church.

East of Santiago is the turn-off to **La Atalaya**, site of a major pilgrimage and festival in honour of a miraculous statue of Christ, and home of the **Instituto Jesús Nazareno** ① *open to visitors on Sun*, an important agricultural school for rural boys. West of Santiago is **La Mesa** (turn-off at Km 27), with a beautiful, white colonial church. The old rough road heads south through **Soná** and rejoins the Pan-American at **Guabalá**. The paved highway from Santiago to Guabalá saves a couple of hours.

Las Lajas ① *20 km west of Guabalá*, has good beaches. Facilities are limited: there is a small restaurant, La Estrella del Pacífico, about 1 km to the east, but apart from that remember to bring your own food and drink from town. Watch out for strong waves and sharks. To get there, take the turn-off at San Félix or take a bus from David to Las Lajas at 1145 and 1245, US$4. From there it's a short taxi trip to the beach (taxis US$3), or you can walk the 3 km from San Félix. A turning left, 38 km west of Las Lajas, leads to Horconcitos and 13 km beyond on a dirt road, is the tiny fishing village of Boca Chica. From there you can cross in a few minutes to the island of **Boca Brava** ① *US$1 per person* in the **Parque Nacional Marítimo Golfo de Chiriquí**.

Isla de Coiba

Some 80 km to the southeast is Isla de Coiba, which, at 503 sq km, is the largest island within Panamanian territory. A former penal colony, the limited interaction has ensured the protection of the plant, animal and marine life in the area which has been protected since

1992 as **Parque Nacional Coiba**. The park itself covers over 2700 sq km and includes areas of rich open ocean, Coiba and outlying islands and the second largest coral reef in the Eastern Pacific. On land the mostly untouched rainforest supports Panama's largest surviving colony of scarlet macaws, along with 146 other avian species. The marine environment, which in terms of pelagic life can only be rivalled by islands such as Cocos and the Galapagos, boasts 23 recorded species of whale and dolphin, including humpback, sperm and killer whales, some of which can spotted on dive trips to the island. Marine life of the fishy kind includes whitetip, bull, hammerhead and whale sharks in addition to manta and eagle rays. **Santa Catalina**, accessible from Santiago and then the small town of Sona, a route served by a few local buses per day, is a relaxed but fast-developing coastal village. Santa Catalina's main claim to fame has been as the location of some of Central America's best surfing breaks. **ScubaCoiba** ① *on the main street, T202-2171, www.scubacoiba.com*, provides access to Coiba's unique submarine world. Numerous hotels in Santa Catalina cater to a wide range of budgets. There's also a surf school. It may be possible to arrange an independent trip to Coiba for US$50-60 by chartering a local boat.

David ⊜❶❷❊▲❸❶ ▸▸ *pp1358-1363. Colour map 7, C5.*

David, capital of Chiriquí Province and a hot and humid city, rich in timber, coffee, cacao, sugar, rice, bananas and cattle, is the second city of the republic. Founded in colonial times as San José de David, it has managed to keep its traditions intact while modernizing itself. The attractive city is safe and friendly and a gateway to the Chiriquí Highlands and the Caribbean province of Bocas del Toro. With a wide selection of hotels and restaurants, it is a good place to break the trip from Costa Rica to become acquainted with Panama and its people.

Ins and outs

Getting around David presents a significant navigational challenge to the visitor. It is perfectly flat with no prominent landmarks, the central plaza is not central, there are no street signs, some streets have two names and the locals use neither, preferring nostalgic points of reference (eg across the street from where the old oak used to be) to genuinely useful guidance. City bus routes are circuitous and generate additional confusion. When you get hopelessly lost take a taxi – for US$0.65 it's not such a bad idea. The **IPAT tourist office** ① *Av 3 Este y Calle A Norte on Parque Cervantes, T775-4120, Mon-Fri, 0830-1630*, is friendly and helpful.

Sights

The city of David focuses on the fine central plaza, **Parque Cervantes**, which teems with birds in the early morning, providing good birdwatching from the balconies of the Hotel Occidental or Iris. The colonial-style **Iglesia de San José** is on the west side of the park. The bell tower in Barrio Bolívar was built separately as a defence against tribal attacks. The Palacio Municipal is opposite Hotel Nacional on Avenida and Calle Central. The **Museo José de Obaldía** ① *Av 8 Este 5067 y Calle A, Norte, 4 blocks from Plaza, Mon-Sat 0830-1630, US$0.25*, is a museum of history and art in the house of the founder of Chiriquí Province.

A few kilometres north of David on the Boquete road is **Balneario Majagua**, where you can swim in a river under a waterfall (cold drinks for sale). There is another bathing place on the right 10 km further on. Take a Dolega or Boquete bus and ask the driver to drop you off.

About 2 km along the main road to the border is the **Carta Vieja rum factory** ① *Mon-Fri 0800-1600*, offering free tours and something to take away with you.

About 10 km east of David is the small town of **Chiriquí**. A paved road through Gualaca leads north to the mountains and over the divide to Chiriquí Grande (page 1376).

West of David ⚫🔵🟢🟢 ►► *pp1358-1363*.

Heading towards the Costa Rican border, a dirt road turns off to the left to **Las Palmas**, a pleasant orange-growing village which welcomes tourists. Just before the village is a **waterfall** where a single column of water falls into a pool, delightful for swimming and camping. Ask in David for directions.

The Pan-American Highway, now a modern divided highway, goes through cattle land for 26 km west to **La Concepción**, which also goes by the name of Bugaba, the local name for the district. It is an important agricultural shipping point, also widely known for its handmade saddles. There are several decent hotels, but better can be found in Volcán,

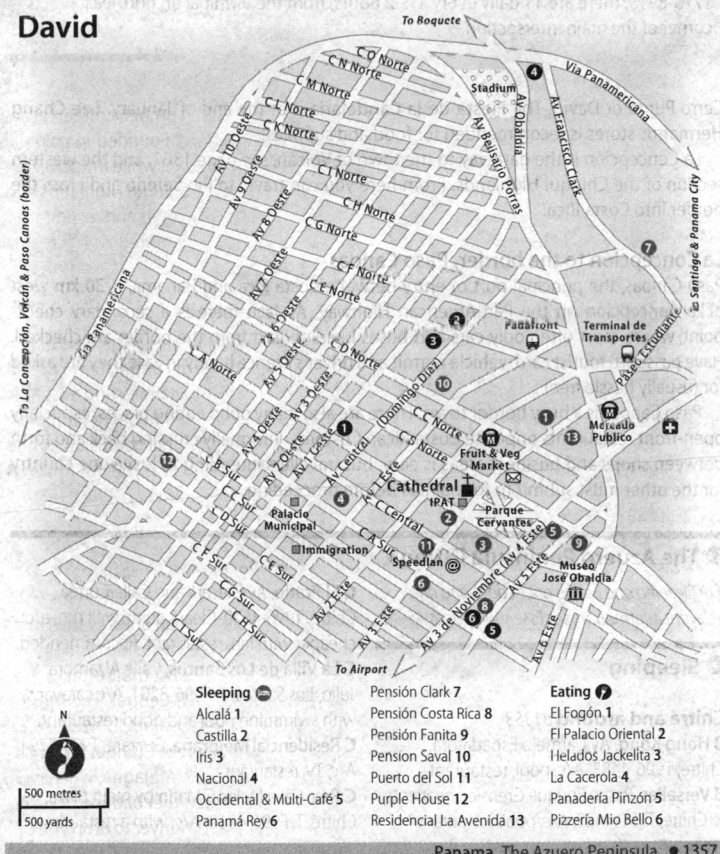

David

To Boquete

To La Concepción, Volcán & Paso Canoas (border)

To Santiago & Panama City

To Airport

Sleeping 🛏	**Pensión Clark 7**	**Eating** 🍴
Alcalá **1**	Pensión Costa Rica **8**	El Fogón **1**
Castilla **2**	Pensión Fanita **9**	El Palacio Oriental **2**
Iris **3**	Pension Saval **10**	Helados Jackelita **3**
Nacional **4**	Puerto del Sol **11**	La Cacerola **4**
Occidental & Multi-Café **5**	Purple House **12**	Panadería Pinzón **5**
Panamá Rey **6**	Residencial La Avenida **13**	Pizzería Mío Bello **6**

N

500 metres
500 yards

Border essentials: Panama–Costa Rica

Pasa Canoas

Currency exchange Money changers will change colones into dollars at a good rate; the Banco Nacional de Panama cashes TCs and also has Visa ATM.

Panamanian immigration Panamanian customs are open 24 hours; the Costa Rican side is open 0500-2100 Panama time. After checking in at Entrada, buy a tourist card from the IPAT tourist office around the corner of the building to the left. Return to Entrada for an entry stamp. All relatively quick and painless, unless an international bus has arrived just before you. Free maps of Panama available at IPAT.

Sleeping Palace, basic but clean bathroom. There is a reasonable restaurant at the border. Greater choice, although not necessarily better, on the Costa Rican side.

Time Panama is one hour ahead of Costa Rica.

Transport Buses to Panama City via La Concepción and David with Padafront, T775-8913, there are 11 daily every 1½-2 hours, from the terminal on northeast corner of the main intersection.

Cerro Punta or David. The **Fiesta de la Candelaria** is at the end of January. **Lee Chang Hermanos** stores is recommended for food and supplies.

La Concepción is the gateway to the town of Volcán, see page 1367, and the western section of the Chiriqui Highlands. From here you can travel to Río Sereno and cross the border into Costa Rica.

La Concepción to the border, Paso Canoas

Paso Canoas, the principal port of entry between Costa Rica and Panama, is 30 km west of La Concepción on the Pan-American Highway. At Jacú there is a secondary checkpoint, where most often only cars and buses heading east from the border are checked. Have passport, tourist card, vehicle permit and driver's licence handy in case they are asked for (usually hassle free).

Paso Canoas is a busy border town. There are also many good eating places, especially open-front restaurants opposite Costa Rican Customs. Informally crossing back and forth between shops and business areas is easy, but travellers intending to leave one country for the other must submit to formalities before proceeding.

⊙ The Azuero Peninsula listings

For Sleeping and Eating price codes and other relevant information, see Essentials pages 45-48.

● Sleeping

Chitré and around *p1353*
B Hong Kong, Av Carmelo Espadafora, Chitré, T996-4483. A/c, pool, restaurant.
B Versalles, Paseo Enrique Grensier, near entry to Chitré, T996-4422. A/c, pool, restaurant.

C El Prado, Av Herrera and Calle Correa, Chitré, T996-4620. Clean, quiet, well run, a/c, cheaper with fan, restaurant. Recommended.
C La Villa de Los Santos, Calle Alzamora Julio, Los Santos, T/F996-8201. A/c caravans, with swimming pool and good restaurant.
C Residencial Mejorana, Guararé, T994-5794. A/c, TV, restaurant.
C Rex, Calle Maliton Matín by main plaza, Chitré, T/F996-4310. A/c, with a restaurant.

D Cabañas Bayano Mar, near El Rompío. Pleasant cabins with private bath and fan, nice setting, restaurant and bar.
D Pensión Central, Av Herrera next to El Prado, Chitré, T996-0059. With bath, a/c, cheaper with fan, noisy in front rooms.
D Pensión Colombia, Calle Manuel Correa near museum (3 blocks from plaza), Chitré, T996-1856. Fan, private bath, basic.
D Santa Rita, Calle Manuel Correa y Av Herrera, Chitré, T996-4610. Friendly, clean, restaurant, good value. Recommended.
E Pensión Deportiva, Los Santos. No single rooms, private showers.
E Pensión Herrerana, Av Herrera 4072, Chitré, I996-4356. Small rooms with fan, private bath, very hot, clean, parking, basic.

Las Tablas and around *p1354*
D Zafiro, Av Belisario Porras, across from main plaza, T/F994-8200. Modern, a/c, TV.
E Pensión Mariela, Av Belisario Porras, opposite Zafiro. Basic and run-down.

Pedasí *p1354*
C Hotel Residencial Pedasí, at the entrance to town, T995-2322. A/c, spacious grounds.
D Dim's, Av Principal, T995-2303. A/c, lovely garden with hammocks.
D-E Residencial Moscoso, T995-2203. With shower, TV, a/c, cheaper with fan, clean, good, friendly, meals arranged by owner at nearby bar.

Playa Venado and Tonosí *p1354*
D Pensión Boamy, Playa Tonosí, T995-8142. With a/c, cheaper with fan, friendly.
D Playa Venado. There are 5 *cabañas* for rent here (no electricity, very basic, overpriced), and plenty of idyllic **camping** spots (camping free, showers cost US$0.25), as well as a combined open-air restaurant.
D-E Pensión Roslyn, Playa Tonosí. A/c, cheaper with fan, basic.
E Playa Tonosí. There are *cabañas* for rent (price per person), plenty of idyllic camping spots and a small restaurant.

Ocú *p1355*
E Posada San Sebastián, on the plaza. Fan, clean bathrooms, patio, charming.

Santiago and around *p1355*
C Roselas Apartotel, Vía San Francisco, T998-7269. Apartments with kitchen, a/c, hot water, clean, friendly, safe parking for motorcycles.
C-E Gran David, on Pan-American Hwy, T998-4510. A/c, TV, cheaper with fan, private bath, clean. Has pool, good restaurant and is recommended.
D Piramidal, on Pan-Am Hwy nearing stopping point for David–Panama buses, T998-3123. A/c, TV, shower, clean, quiet, good pool. Recommended.
D Santiago, Calle 2 near the cathedral, T998-4824. Clean, with a/c, TV and shower, cheaper with shared bath. Noisy and run-down.
D-F Restaurante Boca Brava, Boca Brava, T774-3117. With cabins, cane huts and camping. Lots of wildlife and interesting flora, snorkelling on nearby rocks. German owners.
E Cabañas La Lajas, Las Lajas. Sleeps 2-4 people with views out to sea, cold showers, kitchen and friendly people.
E Central, next to Jigoneva, T998-6116. Basic, all rooms with shower, Chinese owner.
E Jigoneva, Av Central 2038. Basic, friendly.

Camping
Campamento Evagelico 'La Buena Esperanza', some 28 km west of Santiago, off the road to Canazas, T999-6237, www.elcampamento.net. A beautiful setting on a lake with a few cabins.

David *p1356, map p1357*
Most cheap hotels are on Av 5 Este.
A Nacional, Av and Calle Central, T775-2221, www.hotelnacionalpanama.com. Clean rooms, with good restaurant and games room.
B Castilla, Calle A Norte between Av 2 and 3 Este, T774-5260, www.hotelcastilla panama.com. Modern and comfortable, centrally located.

B Puerto del Sol, Av 3 Este y Calle Central, T774-8422. New, clean, well furnished, TV, a/c, internet US$1 per hr.

C Alcalá, Av 3 Este between Calle D and E Norte, T774-9018, hotelalcala@cw panama.net. Comfortable and pleasant. Has parking.

C Panamá Rey, Av 3 Este y Calle A Sur, T775-0253. Modern high-rise building, with restaurant.

C-D Iris, Calle A Norte, on Parque Cervantes T775-2251. With bath and a/c, cheaper with fan. Friendly and clean.

D Occidental, Av 4 Este on Parque Cervantes, T775-4695. With bath and a/c, cheaper with fan, nice balcony overlooking park, good value. Recommended.

D Pensión Costa Rica, Av 5 Este, Calle A Sur, T775-1241. Variety of rooms, with shower and/or a/c, basic, clean, safe, friendly and good value, but a bit run-down and noisy.

D Residencial La Avenida, Av 3 Este between Calle D and E Norte, T774-0451. With bath and a/c, cheaper with fan, parking, good value.

D-E Pensión Saval, Calle D Norte between Cincuentenario and Av 1 Este, across Plaza Oteima, T775-3543. With bath and a/c, cheaper with fan, basic, run-down but friendly.

D-E The Purple House, Calle C Sur and Av 6 Oeste, Barrio San Mateo, T774-4059, www.purplehousehostel.com. Hostel close to the centre of town with private and dormitory rooms. Also use of kitchen, free internet access and good information on travel throughout the country and Central America. Good reports but cold showers. Taxi from bus terminal is US$2.50.

E Pensión Clark, Av Francisco Clark, north of bus terminal, T774-3452. With bath.

E-F Pensión Fanita, Calle 5 between 5 Este and 6 Este, T775-3718. Family-run in an old wooden house.

West of David *p1357*
C Koco's Place, Puerto Armuelles, T770-7049. A/c, TV and small restaurant.

● Eating

Chitré and around *p1353*
Many restaurants serving economical *comida corriente*, plus a few Chinese.
¶¶ El Mesón in the Hotel Rex. Upmarket, national and international dishes.
¶ El Chitreano, Calle Antonio Burgos. Good food and large portions.

Pedasí *p1354*
¶¶¶ Turístico JR's, T995-2176. Owner was formerly head chef at El Panamá (see page 1314). Swiss/French dishes, good quality and variety, expensive. Recommended.
¶ Angela, Pedasí. Local fare, good.

David *p1356, map p1357*
¶ El Fogón, Av 1 Este y Calle B Norte. Good, reasonable prices.
¶ El Palacio Oriental, Av Domingo Díaz (Central) y Calle E Norte. Chinese.
¶ Ely's, Av 3 E y Calle A Norte, also at Plaza OTEIMA. Good bread and pastries.
¶ Helados Jackelita, Calle E Norte y Av Domingo Díaz. Very good fresh fruit ice cream.
¶ La Cacerola, Av Obaldía behind Super Barú, just off Pan-American Hwy. Self-service, clean, fresh Panamanian dishes all day, a/c, good value. Highly recommended.
¶ Multi-Café, in Hotel Occidental, Av 4 Este on Parque Cervantes. Popular with locals, good quality, variety and value.
¶ Nueva China, Av Obaldía. Chinese.
¶ Panadería Pinzón, Av 5 Este, Calle A Sur, opposite Pensión Costa Rica. Excellent shop/café with sandwiches, cakes.
¶ Pizzería Mio Bello, Calle A Sur y Av 5 Este. Good Italian.

West of David *p1357*
Puerto Armuelles has plenty of cheap eating places.
¶ Club Social, Puerto Armuelles, on water (ask any taxi). Chicken and rice dishes.

🎉 Festivals and events

Chitré and around *p1353*
May/Jun Feast of Corpus Christi (40 days after Easter) is a 4-day feast celebrated in Los Santos with one of the country's most famous and popular festivals, a glorious distillation of the Peninsula's strong Spanish roots and well worth attending.
End Apr The Feria de Azuero. 'Little devil' (*diablito*) and other masks featuring in the fiestas are the local handicraft speciality and may be purchased from stalls or workshops around town and in Parita.
24 Jun Fiesta de San Juan Bautista, and the preceding week.
19 Oct The district's founding (1848) is celebrated with colourful parades and historical events.
22-25 Dec Christmas festivities at La Arena, with music, dancing, bull running in the Plaza de Toros and cock fights.

Las Tablas *p1354*
19-23 Jul Fiesta de Santa Librada and incorporated Fiesta de la Pollera. Las Tablas is widely known for this festival. The *pollera* is a ruffled, intricately embroidered in a single colour, off-the-shoulder dress based on colonial fashions and is now the national costume of Panama; *polleras* are made in villages near Las Tablas, the most beautiful coming from Santo Domingo (5 km east).

Ocú *p1355*
19-24 Jan San Sebastián, the district's patron saint, is celebrated with costumed folklore groups.
Aug El Matrimonio Campesino, El Penitente de la Otra Vida and El Duelo del Tamarindo, are straight from medieval Spain and well worth witnessing.
15 Aug The Festival del Manito at the Assumption.

David *p1356, map p1357*
Mid-Mar Major week-long international fair and fiesta.

🅰 Activities and tours

David *p1356, map p1357*
Servicios Turísticos, Calle Central, T775-4644. Regional tours.
Travesías, Calle B Norte between Av 5 and 6 Este, T/F774-5352, www.travesias panama.com. Regional tours.

🚍 Transport

Chitré and around *p1353*
Bus
Chitré is the transport hub of the peninsula, there is a bus terminal just outside town, take city bus **Las Arenas**.
To **Panama City** (250 km), regular buses, 4 hrs, US$6. To **Santiago**, frequent service, 1 hr, US$2. There is no direct service to **David**, change at Santiago. To **Divisa**, 30 mins, US$1.30; same fare and time to **Las Tablas** (buses leave when full). To **Tonosí** 3 hrs, US$4.15. To **Santiago**, 1½ hrs, US$2.50.

Las Tablas and around *p1354*
Bus
To **Panama City**, several daily, 4½ hrs, US$7. To **Santo Domingo**, 10 mins, US$0.40. To **Tonosí**, 2½ hrs, US$4.25. Last bus from Los Santos to **Las Tablas** at 1800.
From Las Tablas buses to **Pedasí** leave when full, 1 hr, US$2, bumpy trip.

Playa Venado and Tonosí *p1354*
Bus
1 a day to Playa Venado from **Las Tablas** at 1300, about 2 hrs, US$3.20, return at 0700. No direct bus between Pedasí and Tonosí.

Pedasí to Cañas around 0700 and 1500, US$2; **Cañas** to Tonosí 1 a day. Tonosí to **Las Tablas**, 4 a day between 0700 and 1300, US$3, 1 hrs, leave when full.

A milk truck leaves Tonosí at 0700 for **Chitré**, via Cañas, Playa Venado, Pedasí and Las Tablas, takes passengers, returns 1230.

Tonosí to **Chitré** via Macaracas, 4 a day before 1100, 3 hrs, US$4, mostly paved road.

Hitching
Difficult as there is little traffic.

Ocú p1355
Bus
Several buses a day from Chitré, 1 hr, US$1.75, and buses on to **Panama City**, US$7.

Those with limited time can get a glimpse of the Peninsula and villages by taking a bus from **Chitré** to **Pesé**, **Los Pozos** or **Las Minas**, all in the foothills of the western range, and then another to Ocú; staying the night and taking another bus on to Santiago to return to the Panama City–David Hwy.

Santiago and around p1355
Bus
From **Penonomé**, US$4; from **Aguadulce**, US$2.50. Panama City–David buses stop outside **Hotel Piramidal**. To **David**, US$7. To **Panama City** US$7.

David p1356, map p1357
Air
Aeroperlas, Calle A Norte y Av 3 Este next to Hotel Castilla, T721-1195. Several flights a day from **Panama City**, US$59 1 way. Also to **Bocas del Toro** and **Changuinola**, both US$32 1 way (occasional seasonal offers, eg US$20). Daily service to **San José**, Costa Rica, US$83, 1 way.

Bus
Local US$0.20; taxis US$0.65 in city.

Long distance The main bus terminal is at Av 2 Este, 1 block north of Av Obaldía. Taxi to centre US$1. All companies use this except Padafront, whose terminal is nearby at Av 2 Este y Av Obaldía, T775-8913.

To **Panama City** regular buses US$10.60, express US$15, 3 hrs, 10 daily with **Padafront**.

To **Paso Canoas** (border with Costa Rica), US$1.50, 1½ hrs, every 15 mins 0500-1830. Direct to **San José** with **Tracopa**, 0830 daily, US$12, 8 hrs, with stop in San Isidro.

Regular buses to **Boquete** every 25 mins, 0600-2145, 1 hr, US$1.20; **Volcán**, every 15 mins, 0700-1800, 1½ hrs, US$2.30; **Chiriquí Grande**, every 90 mins, 0630-1600, 3 hrs, US$7; buses to **Almirante** every 40 mins, 0500-1900, 4 hrs, US$8; **Cerro Punto**, 2¼ hrs, US$3.

Car
Budget, T775-5597; Hertz, T775-6828; Mike's, T775-4963. Rent a 4WD vehicle in David if going to Volcán Barú.

Ocú can be reached directly from the Pan-American Hwy (19 km) by a paved turn-off south just past the Río Conaca bridge (11 km west of Divisa); *colectivos* run from here for US$0.80. Alternatively, a mostly gravel road runs west from Parita along the Río Parita valley, giving good views of the fertile landscapes of the northern Peninsula.

West of David p1357
Bus
From David via **Concepción** and **Paso Canoas** buses run every 15 mins, 0500-2000, 2½ hr, US$3.

Train
Chiriquí Railway: passenger service Puerto Armuelles-**Progreso** (halfway to Paso Canoas), 2 a day each way, 2 hrs, US$1. There is also a 'Finca Train', 4 decrepit, converted banana trucks, leaving at 1500 for the banana *fincas*, returning, by a different route, at 1800. No charge for passengers. Minibuses also leave all day for the *fincas*.

O Directory

Chitré and around *p1353*

Internet At Éconoútiles stationary store, Av Herrera 1 block from cathedral, US$3 per hr. Also at **Abacus**, Belarmino Urriola, US$2.50 per hr.

David *p1356, map p1357*

Banks Banistmo, Av 2 Este y Calle A Norte, also on Av Obaldía, for Visa cash advances, changes AMEX TCs without commission. Banco Nacional de Panamá, 0800-1330 (generally very convenient, but guards have been known to turn away travellers wearing shorts), changes Amex TCs, 1% commission plus US$0.10 tax per cheque. Banco General, Av 3 Este y Calle C Norte, changes TCs, 1% commission, Visa ATM. Caja de Ahorro (Caja Pronto), Av 2 Este y Calle Central, for MasterCard and Amex TCs.

Embassies and consulates Costa Rica, Urbanización El Bosque, 2 blocks west of clinic, best take a taxi, T774-1923.

Immigration Immigration office Calle C Sur between Av Central and 1 Este, T775-4515, Mon-Fri 0800-1500. **Ministerio de Hacienda y Tesoro** Calle C Norte, 1 block from Parque Cervantes, near the post office.

Internet Sinfonet, Calle E Norte y Av Domingo Díaz, daily 0800-0000, US$1 per hr; **Speedlan**, Av 3 este y Calle A Sur, beside Panamá Rey hotel, T777-2438, US$1 per hr. **Instituto OTEIMA**, C D N between Av 1 and 2 Este, daily 0800-1200, 1330-2000, US$1 per hr; **Electrónica Nacional**, Av Obaldía, opposite Domino's Pizza, US$1.50 per hr. **Laundry** Lavandería One, Av Centenario Central y 1A Sur; Lavafast, 1 Av Obaldia. **Post office** Calle C Norte y Av 3 Este.

Chiriquí Highlands

The Tierras Altas de Chiriquí include the highland areas around Boquete, Volcán Barú and Cerro Punta. The mingling of Atlantic and Pacific winds creates a year-round spring-like climate. The so-called 'bajareque' (literally 'falling down') shrouds the area in a fine mist, creating cloud forests at higher altitudes. Closer to the ground, the black volcanic soil creates highly fertile conditions. Coffee fincas and intensive farming that produces most of the country's vegetables are interspersed with tourist resorts, popular with Panameños seeking to escape the tropical heat during vacations (December to March). It's an ideal place to spend some time hiking, horse riding, fishing, rafting and birdwatching.

Daytime temperatures are cool; evenings and nights chilly. Some days can be rather windy in the dry season. Mornings are especially clear and beautiful all year round. Travellers entering Panama from the north should consider a visit before pushing on to Panama City.
▶ For listings, see pages 1370-1375.

Boquete and the Eastern Highlands ⬤🅿️🅕❀▲🅐🅒 ▶ pp1370-1375.
Colour map 7, B5.

Heading north towards Boquete in the heart of the cool Eastern Highlands, a well-paved road climbs gently from David, passing (after 10 km) a waterfall with a swimming hole, open-air restaurant/bar and space for wild camping. It passes through **Dolega** (swimming pool, one *pensión*, notable for its carnival four days before Ash Wednesday), before reaching (after 40 km) the popular mountain resort of Boquete, at 1060 m in the valley of the Río Caldera, with the slopes of Volcán Barú to the west. It is a beautiful panorama of coffee plantations and orange groves, strawberry fields and gardens.

Good lodging and facilities make Boquete an excellent base for fishing, riding, river rafting and hiking in the area. It is a slow-paced, predominantly wood-built town with several attractive landscaped parks, including the main plaza and the nearby Parque de las Madres. The fairground east of the river is the site for the annual **Feria de las Flores y del Café**, usually held mid-January. In April, a **Feria de las Orquídeas** is held with many varieties of local and exotic orchids, as well as other flowers. The **cemetery** ① *Mon-Sat 0930-1300, 1400-1800*, is worth a visit, there is a small museum of *huacas* (funerary sculptures) in the centre and a fine panoramic view from the 'Bienvenidos a Boquete' arch at the entrance to the town. ▶ *See Activities and tours, page 1374.*

Boquete has gained international recognition as a producer of fine coffees and freelance tour guides Terry van Niekerk and Hans van der Vooren provide tours (daily 0900, US$25 per person) of fine local coffee operations, see page 1374. Very comprehensive, informative 2½- to three-hour tours that cover everything from plant to production, harvesting to roasting to a tasting of the final product. Tours in English, Spanish and Dutch, minimum two people. The tours visit **Café Kotowa** ① *T720-1430*. There is a **Tourist Office (CEFATI)** ① *T720-4060, daily 0900-1800*, at the entrance to town. Helpful staff provide information about the area and there is a café, shop and small museum upstairs.

Volcán Barú

The highest point in the country, Volcán Barú rises to an altitude of 3475 m and is reached easily from Boquete, 21 km to the east, and not so easily from Volcán to the west. The summit lies within the boundaries of **Parque Nacional Volcán Barú**, which covers some 14,000 ha and borders the vast La Amistad International Park, to the north, which itself spans the Panamanian-Costa Rican border covering much of the Cordillera Talamanca. Rainfall in the park ranges between 3000 and 4000 mm a year, and temperatures range from a subtropical 17°C to a distinctly chilly 7°C. Rich cloud forest makes ideal conditions for reptiles, amphibians and birds, with around 40 species endemic to the park.

From Boquete it is 21 km to the summit. The first 7 km is paved, sometimes lined with aromatic pines and goes through coffee groves, most numerous in the area during the year-end harvest season, mainly tended by Ngöbe-Buglé (Guaymí) people. The paved road ends at a small, usually unstaffed, ANAM office, from where the track winds up from the office through tall, impressive cloud forest, thick with hanging creepers, lichen and bromeliads. The steep cuttings are carpeted with a glorious array of ferns and colourful flowers; many birds can be seen, including bee hummingbirds, as well as wild turkeys and squirrels. The perfume from the flowers, especially in the wet season when there are many more blooms, is magnificent.

As the road rises, increasingly steeply, there are wonderful views of the Boquete valley, the Río Caldera running through a steep gorge, and the misty plain beyond stretching to the Pacific. Some 9 km from the park entrance is a sign on the right, 'La Nevera' (the ice-box). A small side-trail here leads to a cool mossy gully where there is a stream for water, but no flat ground to camp. This is the only reliable water source during the dry season, so take plenty with you.

At the summit the cloud forest is replaced by a forest of TV and radio aerials in fenced-off enclosures. A short path leads to a small cross and a trigonometric point, from where the best views of dusty craters and the valleys of Volcán, Bambito and Cerro Punta stretch out below. The high-altitude brush contrasts spectacularly with the dark green forest, wisps of mist and cloud clinging to the treetops. Occasionally horizontal rainbows can be seen in the haze, formed in the *bajareque* drizzle. There

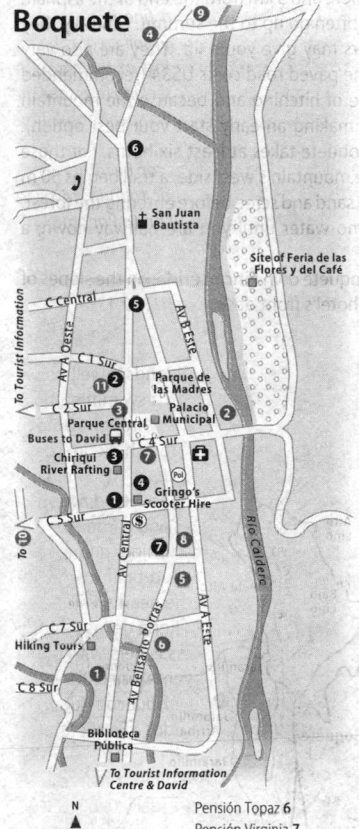

Boquete

San Juan Bautista

Site of Feria de las Flores y del Café

C Central

To Tourist Information

AV Oeste

C 1 Sur

Parque de las Madres

C 2 Sur

Palacio Municipal

Parque Central

Buses to David

C 4 Sur

Chiriquí River Rafting

Gringo's Scooter Hire

C 5 Sur

AV Central

Río Caldera

C 7 Sur

Hiking Tours

AV Este

AV Belisario Porras

C 8 Sur

Biblioteca Pública

To Tourist Information Centre & David

N

100 metres

100 yards

Sleeping
Cabañas Isla Verde 10
Fundadores 1
Hostal Boquete 2
Hostal Palacios 3
Hostel Nomba 11
Panamonte 4
Pensión Marilós 5

Pensión Topaz 6
Pensión Virginia 7
Rebequet 8
Villa Lorena Cabañas 9

Eating
Bistro Boquete 2
Casona Mexicana 1
Delicias del Perú 6
Lourdes 3
Macchu Picchu 7
Pizzería La Volcánica 4
Sabrosón 5

are many craters around the main summit, with dwarf vegetation, lichens and orchids. Even in the dry season, you will be lucky to have a clear view of both oceans.

In a suitable vehicle it takes about two hours to the top (depending on the weather); or it's a 4½- to six-hour hike up, three hours down, from the park office. Zona Urbana minibuses (US$1) go to El Salto, 4 km from Boquete and 3 km from the end of the asphalt. Vehicles that service the antenna installations often go up to the summit. Officially they are not allowed to take passengers, but drivers may give you a lift. They are also very friendly and like to chat. A taxi to the end of the paved road costs US$4 (recommended during the wet season as there is little chance of hitching and because the mountain summit usually clouds over in the afternoon, making an early start your best option). Hiking from the summit all the way back to Boquete takes at least six hours. For those wishing to continue over Barú to Volcán on the mountain's west side, a trail begins 50 m before the cross, descending steeply over loose sand and scree before entering the forest. It's eight to 12 hours to Volcán, and there's no water until you are halfway down; a challenging and rewarding hike (see opposite).

The managers of the **Hotel Panamonte** in Boquete own **Finca Lérida**, on the slopes of Volcán Barú, tours can be arranged. Ask at the hotel's front desk.

Around Boquete

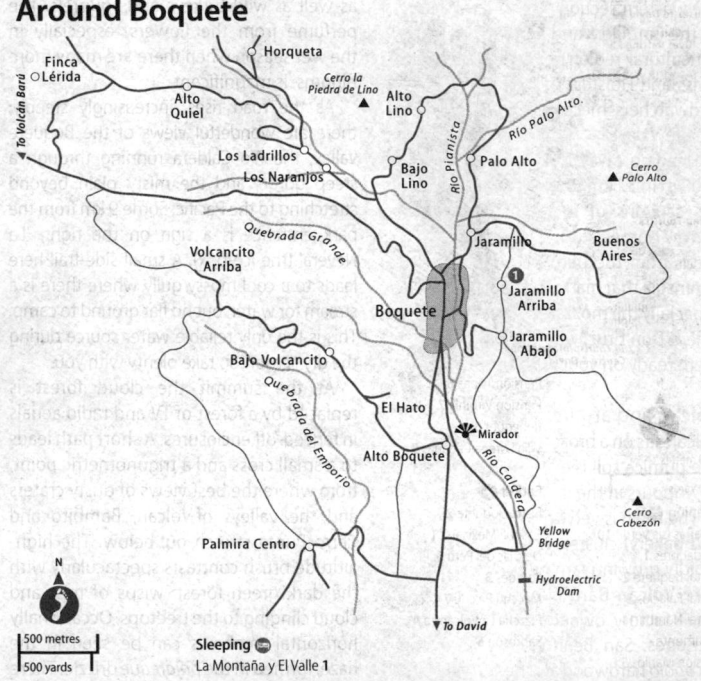

500 metres
500 yards

Sleeping
La Montaña y El Valle 1

Other hikes and excursions

Twenty-seven kilometres north of the Pan-American Highway (13 km south of Boquete) is a turn-off east to Caldera (14 km), from where a 25- to 30-minute walk leads to **Los Pozos de Caldera** ① *no facilities, options for camping, entry US$1*, a well-known series of hot springs said to be good for rheumatism sufferers. River-rafting trips on the Chiriquí start from Caldera (see Activities and tours, page 1374). There are six buses a day from David to Caldera, four a day from Boquete to Caldera, and pickups from the main road to the village.

Across the suspension bridge, **Conservas de Antaño** ① *T720-1539*, is a very friendly family-owned business that makes old-fashioned fruit preserves. **Café Ruiz** ① *2 km north of Boquete, T720-1392*, is a small factory known for its premium-grade roasted coffees. They welcome visitors for a guided tour (Don José Ruiz speaks English, starting 0900, three hours, US$14), explaining the whole process from harvesting to hand selecting only the best beans and vacuum packing the product. Next door is **Villa Marta**, a private mansion with a huge landscaped garden open to the public, and a sign: '*Mi jardín es su jardín*'. **Los Ladrillos**, a few kilometres further up the Caldera Valley, is a small area of basalt cliffs with octagonal fingers of rock in clusters. Beyond is **Horqueta**, a picturesque hillside area of coffee groves, with a roadside waterfall and banks of pink impatiens; beautiful views to the south.

Volcán and the Western Highlands ●●●●●● ➤➤ *pp1370-1375*.

The western section of the Tierras Altas (highlands) de Chiriquí is bounded on the north by the Cordillera and on the west by the Costa Rican border, a prosperous and dynamic agricultural region renowned for vegetables, flowers, superb coffees, and the brown Swiss and Holstein dairy herds that thrive in the cool highland pastures. The area is a birdwatchers' mecca and is also popular with residents of Panama City wishing to cool off for a few days.

Heading away from La Concepción there is a very good paved road north, rising 1200 m in 32 km to Volcán. From Cuesta de Piedra, a turning to the right will take you to the canyons of the **Macho de Monte**, a rather small river that has worn deep, narrow gorges. Further on, to the left, is the **Mirador Alan Her** ① *US$0.10*, with good views from the purpose-built tower to the sea, and on a clear day, the Punto Burica peninsula that marks the Panama–Costa Rica border. Local cheeses on sale are very good, especially the mozzarella. Near Volcán, you can get excellent wood carvings at **Artes Cruz** where Don Cruz, who speaks English, will make charming souvenirs to order and have them ready on your return trip.

Volcán and around ➤ *Colour map 7, B5*.

Volcán sits on a broad 1450-m high plateau formed by an ancient eruption of Volcán Barú. The pumice soil is extremely porous and dries within minutes of the frequent torrential downpours in the rainy season; in summer the area is tinder dry.

The town is very spread out. The centre (with police station, gas station, supermarket and bakery) clusters around the crossroads to Cerro Punta and Río Sereno. Volcán is a rapidly growing farming town, with nurseries cultivating ferns for export, the **Beneficio Café Volcán Barú** (interesting tours during October-February harvest season), and a small factory owned by the Swiss Bérard family producing excellent European-style sausages. San Benito school is noted for hardwood furniture, woodcarvings using *cocobolo* hardwood and hand-painted ceramics sold for the benefit of the school. Brother

Alfred will let you browse through his warehouse full of English books from the now-closed Canal Zone libraries and you can take away what you will. **Cerámica Beija-Flor** is run by local women who market their own wares.

Southwest of town is the **Las Lagunas de Volcán** nature reserve, with two beautiful lakes, abundant aquatic and other birdlife. High vehicles or 4WDs are required in the wet season. **Sitio Barriles**, 6 km from town on the road to Caizán (several buses daily, US$0.50), has interesting petroglyphs; also past Fina Palo Santo, 5 km from town on the road to Río Sereno. **La Fuente Park** ⓘ *US$0.25* (signed from the main road) has playing fields and a spring-fed swimming hole (source of Río Gariché) that's excellent for children.

Volcán is a good jumping-off place for the ascent of **Volcán Barú**. It is possible to climb the west side in one or two days, camping about halfway by a small spring (the only reliable water in the dry season) or in a crater near the top (no water), descending the following day to Boquete on the vehicle road (see page 1364). The trail is beautiful, climbing gently at first through lush cloud forest (many birds, butterflies, and orchids), then scrambling steeply over loose volcanic sand and scree – a challenging but rewarding hike. Guides can be arranged in Volcán; climbers sometimes get lost. For **tourist information**, Angel Rodríguez at Hotel Don Tavo speaks fluent English and is very knowledgeable about the area.

The road divides at the police station in Volcán. The right branch continues north to tiny **Bambito** and **Cerro Punta** (22 km), following the Chiriquí Viejo river valley up the northwest foothills of Volcán Barú. Cross the dry plain known as **Paso Ancho**, with coffee farms in the hill to the west.

Cerro Punta ⊜ ↠ *pp1370-1375. Colour map 7, B5.*

→ *Altitude: 2130 m.*

Heading north from Volcán, at the end of the road is Cerro Punta (buses from David via La Concepción and Volcán, two hours, US$2.65). Set in a beautiful valley, it is at the heart of a vegetable- and flower-growing zone, and a region of dairy farms and racehorse stables. It is sometimes called 'Little Switzerland' because of its Alpine-style houses and the influence of Swiss and former-Yugoslav settlers (there is a settlement called **Nueva Suiza** just south of town). The countryside, full of orchids, is beautiful, though economic pressures push the potato fields ever higher up the hillsides, to the cost of the wooded areas, and sadly encourage the extensive use of agro-chemicals. There are many fine walks in the crisp mountain air. Continue through Cerro Punta to follow the main street as it curves to the left. **Haras Cerro Punta** (topiary initials clipped in the hedge) and **Haras Carinthia** (name visible on stable roof) are well-known thoroughbred farms who will usually receive visitors and show them round. Further on is the small bridge at Bajo Grande. The right fork leads to **Respingo**, where there is a small forest ranger station.

Hikes and nature trails
Camino Los Quetzales Continuing along the main road in Cerro Punta through town is the starting point of the easy six-hour hike, mostly downhill after an initial climb, to Boquete. The track is clear in places and there are a few signs showing the direction and time to Boquete, with the last section following the Río Caldera canyon. It is easier in the dry season (December-April), but can be enjoyed throughout the year. Take food, insect repellent and rain gear. This hike is also recommended for birdwatching; quetzales and many other species may be seen. Take a taxi (4WD) from Cerro Punta to the Respingo ranger station, US$10. You can stay overnight here in the rangers' quarters (**F** per person), clean, shared bath and kitchen.

The Camino Los Quetzales leads to **Bajo Mono**, from which there are irregular local buses to Boquete (20 minutes, US$1). The walk can also be done in the opposite direction (uphill). It is possible to set out from and return to Boquete in one (very long) day.

Parque la Amistad ① *7 km from the centre of Cerro Punta (signposted at road junction, entrance fee US$1, payable at Las Nubes)*, has been open since 1991, with two trails, good for birdwatching, including quetzales. Nature buffs should also visit Los Quetzales reserve inside Parque La Amistad. See Sleeping, page 1372.

Volcán to the border ●●❷ ➤➤ *pp1370-1375. Colour map 7, B5.*

From the fork at the police station in Volcán, the left branch loops 48 very scenic kilometres west, climbing over the Cerro Pando, and passing through beautiful cattle country and coffee plantations on a well-paved, little-travelled, winding road to the Costa Rican border. **Los Pozos**, an area of small thermal pools beside a rushing river, is a good campsite, but only accessible by 4WD vehicles and hard to find as the turn-off from Volcán-Río Sereno road is unmarked. Enquire at **Panadería Mollek** (good espresso and pastries), opposite the police station in Volcán. Sr Juan Mollek has a farm at Los Pozos and can provide information. At **Río Colorado**, 15 km from Volcán, **Beneficio Café Durán**, a coffee processing plant whose delicious aroma of fermenting pulp and drying beans will announce its proximity from kilometres away, is hospitable to visitors. At **Santa Clara**, 25 km from Volcán, is the **Finca Hartmann**, 1300-1800 m, where the US **Smithsonian Tropical Research Institute** maintains a biological research station devoted to ecological studies. Enter the unmarked drive 50 m west of petrol station, next to a green house with 'Ab Santa Clara No 2' sign and proceed 1 km on a dirt road. Latest birdwatching checklist compiled by researchers lists 277 species observable on the densely wooded coffee and cattle farm which borders La Amistad International Park to the north. Biologists and the Hartmann family welcome visitors and have information in Spanish and English.

Border with Costa Rica – Río Sereno
The village of Río Sereno has the air of a cowboy town. The Panamanian businesses are centred around the plaza (including **Banco Nacional** – changes traveller's cheques), and the Costa Rican businesses along a street right on the border. Approaching the village from Volcán, abandoned installations from the era of military government are visible on the right. The bus station is just to the right of the *alto* (stop) sign. Follow the main street left along the plaza to where it ends at a steep road crossing diagonally. This is the border with Costa Rica, otherwise unmarked. Numerous vendors' stalls, especially Sunday during coffee harvest (October to December or January). It is safe to park (and lock) your vehicle in the open area of **Almacén Universal**. Costa Rican shops selling leather goods, a few crafts, clothing, gladly accept US dollars at current rates. Do not miss the upper floor of **Super Universal** and **Supermercado Xenia**. If crossing into Panama, sell your colones here; it will be much more difficult in Volcán or David and rates are worse in Panama City.

Río Sereno to Paso Canoas
A paved winding road runs 50 km south along the Panama side of the border to Paso Canoas, about two to two and a half hours by bus. At Km 41 an impressive cascade over 100 m high pours over a cliff on the left of the Río Chiriquí Viejo below. For information on whitewater rafting on the Río Chiriquí Viejo from Breñón during the dry season, see

ZOLL DOUANE

Border Essentials: Panama–Costa Rica

Río Sereno

Crossing to Costa Rica This is a minor international crossing post, recommended because the area is prettier and cooler than Paso Canoas (see page 1358), but only for those using public transport. Private vehicles cannot complete formalities here, and Panamanian tourist cards are not available.

Panamanian immigration Immigration and customs are in the wooden police station visible on the hill north of the main Panamanian street. Departing travellers who have been in Panama for over 30 days should see Essentials for details on exit permits. Those entering Panama with a visa, or from countries that require neither visa nor tourist card, will be admitted; those requiring a tourist card or a visa will be directed to Paso Canoas.

Costa Rican immigration The office is in a new white building at Río Sereno, open 0800-1600 Costa Rican time, Sunday till 1400. Departing travellers who have overstayed their 90-day permit will be directed to Paso Canoas for the required tax payments and fines.

Transport There is a frequent bus service dawn to dusk from David to Río Sereno, three hours, via La Concepción, Volcán, Santa Clara; several minibuses daily Río Sereno-Paso Canoas, 2½ hours. On the Costa Rican side bus from San Vito via Sabalito (see page 1247) to the border.

Boquete, Activities and tours. There is a good view of the river valley at Km 47, with Volcán Barú visible to the northeast.

◉ Chirquí Highlands listings

For Sleeping and Eating price codes and other relevant information, see Essentials pages 45-48.

◒ Sleeping

Boquete and the Eastern Highlands
p1364, map p1365
Accommodation is difficult to find during the *feria*.

AL La Montaña y el Valle – The Coffee Estate Inn, Jaramillo Arriba, T/F720-2211, www.coffeeestateinn.com. 2.5 km from San Juan Bautista church in Boquete (pass church, turn right at fork, cross river, turn left at intersection, then follow signs), Canadian-run, 3 deluxe cottages in 2.5 ha (with kitchen, hot water, spacious), fine views, breakfast and dinner available. DirecTV and freshly roasted coffee from

their farm is available to guests. Also camping (dry season only) US$10 for 2.

AL Panamonte, Av Central, north of town, T720-1324, www.panamonte.com. With bath, some with kitchen, dinner is highly recommended, popular, garden has over 200 varieties of orchid, very attractive surroundings, built in 1919 and well maintained, charming, run by the Collins family (Swedish/American), day spa introduced (massages, facials and aromatherapy). Tours available.

A Tinamou Cottage, 10 mins from town, T720-3852, habbusdekwie@cwpanama.net. 1 cottage for up to 3 people (1 double, 1 single) set on a private coffee farm. Cost includes breakfast. Perfect for nature lovers. Can arrange pick up in town.

A-C Cabañas Isla Verde, convenient location off main street, follow signs posted just before the Casona Mexi restaurant. T/F720-2533, www.islaverdepanama.com. 6, 2-storey *cabañas*, 2 'suites' overlooking a small stream and a cheaper room with outside bathroom. Good value with lots of space and in a very relaxing environment. German owner Eva Kipp is friendly and knowledgeable. Discounts available in the low season.

B Villa Lorena Cabañas, by bridge near **Panamonte**, T/F720-1848. Comfortable cottages for 4-6 persons, overlooking the Río Caldera.

C Fundadores, Av Central at south end of town, T720-1298, hotfundland@cwp.net.pa. Restaurant, beautiful grounds with stream.

C Hostal Mozart, on the Volcancito road, 5 mins' drive from central Boquete, T720-3764. Charming, brightly decorated house with outside patio offering nice views. Friendly owner Lorenza speaks German, English and Spanish. Breakfast and dinners are delicious. Camping also available.

C Rebequet, Av A Este y Calle 6 Sur, T/F720-1365. Excellent spacious rooms and cabins around a garden, with bath, TV and fridge, kitchen and eating area for guests' use, popular, friendly and helpful. Recommended.

C-E Hostel Nomba, 100 m from Parque Central, behind Bistro Boquete, T6497-5672, New hostel already becoming very popular with backpackers, offers simple but comfortable dorms and private rooms, communal kitchen, library, in-room security lockers and bike rental.

D Hostal Boquete, just off Calle 4 Sur to left of bridge, T720-2573. clean, TV, terrace and garden overlooking river. Recommended.

D-E Hostal Palacios, Av Central on main plaza, T720-1653. With bath and hot water (cheaper without), basic, use of kitchen. Friendly with good information on hiking. Recommended.

D-E Pensión Topaz, behind Texaco station at south end of town, T/F720-1005. With bath, cheaper without, garden with view of Volcán Barú, small pool, good breakfasts, run

by Schöb family (artist/anthropologist), tours arranged, beer garden at the family *finca* during the dry season.

E Pensión Marilós, Av A Este y Calle 6 Sur, opposite **Rebequet**, T720-1380, with bath, hot water, English spoken, very clean and well run, motorcycle parking. Often full but permits sharing, tours organized, stores bags. Recommended.

E Pensión Virginia, main plaza, T720-1260. The food and lodging isn't remarkable, but the owners are extremely helpful and speak several languages, internet and laundry service available.

Volcán and around *p1367*

Hotels are often fully booked during holidays. Price categories shown for cottages are for 1 or 2 people, but most for larger groups for the same price or slightly more.

L-AL Bambito Camping Resort, Bambito, T771-4265, www.hotelbambito.com. 47 rooms with all expected comforts in a fine country setting,

AL Hostal Cielito Sur B&B, 9 km from Volcán, past Hotel Bambito but before town of Cerro Punta, T/F771-2038, www.cielitosur.com. A lovely place to stay, personal attention, each room is decorated with artwork from Panama's indigenous groups, delicious country-style breakfast is included. Good information about the area from owners Janet and Glenn Lee.

A Cabañas Dr Esquivel, on the road behind **Supermercado Bérard**, Volcán, T771-4770. Several large houses in a compound, friendly.

A Las Huacas, main street at west end of Volcán, T771-4363. Nice cottages, hot water, clubhouse, elaborate gardens, interesting aviaries, English spoken.

C Cabañas Las Reinas, Volcán, signed from main road, T771-4338. Self-contained units with a kitchen in lawn setting.

C Don Tavo, main street, Volcán, T/F771-5144. Comfortable, garden, private baths, hot water, restaurant, clean, friendly. Recommended.

C Dos Ríos, Volcán, T771-4271. Older wooden building (upper-floor rooms quieter), restaurant, bar, garden with stream, private baths, hot water unreliable.

D Cabañas Señorial, main street at entrance to town, Volcán, T771-4239. Basic, for short-stay couples.

D El Oasis, behind restaurant Calle La Fuente, El Valle, Volcán, T771-4644. Bar can be noisy, owner also rents rooms in her home by La Fuente pool.

D La Nona, Calle La Fuente, El Valle, T771-4284. Cabins for up to 5, friendly, good value.

D Motel California, on main street, Volcán, T771-4272. Friendly Croatian owner (Sr Zizic Jr) speaks English, clean private baths, hot water, parking, larger units for up to 7, restaurant, bar, quiet, good but check beds, some are very old and soft.

Cerro Punta *p1368*

LL-A Los Quetzales Lodge & Spa, T771-2182, www.losquetzales.com, at Guadalupe. A true forest hideaway, with 5 self-contained cabins, 3 dormitories or 5 separate chalets. All with baths, hot water and the chalets have no electricity. Los Quetzales is on a cloud forest reserve at 2020 m, inside Volcán Barú National Park, nearly 100 bird species, including quetzales, visible from porches, streams, trout hatchery, primeval forest, 4WD vehicles only, a hike from parking area, but worth it. Owner Carlos Alfaro, fluent in English, can arrange transport or cook.

B Hotel Cerro Punta, T720-2020. With 9 simple rooms and a quite good restaurant, just before the turning to La Amistad.

D Pensión Eterna Primavera, in Cerro Punta town. Basic.

Volcán to the border *p1369*

AL The Hartmanns, 1 km beyond the end of the dirt road, Santa Clara, T/F775-5223, www.fincahartmann.com, have comfortable wooden cabins available in the woods, no electricity but with bath and hot water on a working coffee *finca*. They're also excellent auto mechanics.

Border with Costa Rica *p1369*

D Hotel Los Andes, Río Sereno. Good.

⊘ Eating

Boquete and the Eastern Highlands
p1364, map p1365

†††-†† Hibiscus, Calle A Este. Intimate French restaurant serving escargot and chicken cordon bleu, popular among Boquette's burgeoning ex-pat community.

†† Bistro Boquete, Av Central, American owner Loretta once cooked for a US president in her previous establishment in Colorado. Her bistro here is renowned for excellent filet mignon at very reasonable prices.

†† Deli Baru, main street. Tempting array of cheeses, meats and wine as well as sandwiches, salad and soup

†† Delicias del Peru, Av Central, Good place to take in Boquete's gorgeous verdant, forest and garden views. Popular spot for *pisco* sour and ceviche, everything nicely presented.

†† El Explorador, a 45-min walk from Boquete (past **Hotel Panamonte**) across from La Montaña and El Valle. Beautiful location, picnic area, children's playground, hammocks, etc. Entrance to area, US$1, but free to restaurant (excellent local food, breakfast and dinner), open weekends and holidays only.

†† Machu Picchu, Av Belisario Porras. Fantastic Peruvian food cooked by a very friendly Peruvian, long established in Panama. Impressive menu, mostly meat, fish and seafood.

†† Palo Alto, past the Hotel Panamonte, cross bridge, take left and 400 m after that on the left. Beautiful country-style decor set beside the gurgling Río Caldera. Lunch and dinner. International fare and good coffee.

†† Snoopy's, over bridge on Calle 4, opposite flower fair grounds. Run by Englishman Roy Knight, Snoopy's has become a very popular spot for laid-back eating with good views, burgers, snacks and some main meals.

♈-♈ Restaurante Hotel Panamonte, Av Central, north end of town. Open for breakfast, lunch and dinner. Fantastic meals, pricey but well worth the treat. Quaint and charming, succulent trout, fresh juices and delicious desserts.

♈ Sabrosón, on Av Central near church. Good quality and value.

♈ Salvatore, Av Central at south end of town. Good Italian and pizza.

♈ Bistrot Boquete, on main street past the Mandarin supermarket. Open Thu-Mon 1100-2200. A Boquete hang-out, great atmosphere, menu includes chicken curry salad and filet mignon. Excellent brownies.

♈ Casona Mexicana, Av Central, near Lourdes. Good Mexican food.

♈ Java Juice, Av Central, cheap smoothies, burgers, sandwiches and snacks.

♈ La Huaca, near Hotel Panamonte. Serves pizza, US-owned.

♈ Los Arcos, Calle 1 Sur ½ block from Av Central. Open 1600-2400. Good seafood, popular disco at night.

♈ Los Puentes, just past Da' Sandwich Shop, main street diagonal to the Texaco gas station. Great value and excellent typical Panamanian food. Breakfast is good and cheap, the best corn tortillas in town!

♈ Lourdes, Av Central. Good spot with an outside terrace, but mixed reports on the food.

♈ Pizzería La Volcánica, Av Central, ½ block from main plaza. Good pizzas and pasta at reasonable prices, popular.

♈ Punto de Encuentro, Av A Este, near Pensión Marilo's. Breakfast only, pancakes, fruit salad and juices.

♈ Santa Fe, east of river, near the *feria* ground. A nice place to watch sporting events on cable. US-owned serving US-style food, nachos, burgers, sandwiches and bar in a nice spot.

Bakeries

Da' Sandwich Shop, main street diagonal to the Texaco gas station. US-style deli sandwiches, large portions, fresh juices and fruit salads. Cheap.

King's, Av B Este near Parque a las Madres. A particularly good bakery.

Pastelería Alemana, south of the arch at the entrance to town. Delicious coffee and pastries.

Volcán and around *p1367*

♈ La Hacienda Restaurant, Bambito, T771-4152. Fresh trout, barbecued chicken. Recommended.

♈ Hotel Don Tavo, Volcán. Restaurant in hotel, serving pizza and local dishes.

♈ La Luna, 4 km on the road to Cerro Punta in Paso Ancho. Good Chinese food.

♈ Lizzy's, near post office, Volcán. Fast food, English spoken.

♈ Lorena, on road to Río Sereno. Tables on porch. Good fish brought from coast daily.

♈ Marisquería El Pacífico, main road east of main intersection, Volcán. Recommended.

Border with Costa Rica *p1369*

♈♈ Bar Universal, Río Sereno. Recommended for fried chicken with plantain chips (family atmosphere during the day, more raucous Sat evenings and on pay day during the coffee harvest).

♈♈ Sr Lli, top end of the Costa Rican street. Unnamed restaurant, serving good food, friendly and helpful.

😃 Entertainment

Boquete and the Eastern Highlands
p1364, map p1365

Not renowned for nightlife Boquete is usually a ghost-town after 2200, however, the recent influx of tourists and ex-pats are obviously having some impact. African themed **Zanzibar**, Av Central, is open till midnight and serves cocktails (closed Mon) and **Snoopy's Sports bar**, over the bridge on Calle 4, opposite the flower fair grounds, has a large hall and hosts various (mostly weekend) events.

Volcán and around *p1367*
Weekend discos at **Eruption** and **Kalahari**, rustic, good places to meet young locals.

⊛ Festivals and events

Boquete and the Eastern Highlands
p1364, map p1365
Jan Feria de las Flores y del Café is a 2-week-long festival (starts 2nd week of Jan) highlighting Boquete's abundance of exotic and colorful flowers. This time of year coffee harvesting season is in full swing and the fair exhibits coffee and coffee-based products. Vendors come from all over Central America to sell their wares. Lodgings fill up, so make reservations in advance.
28 Nov Independence from Spain. Boquete erupts in a day-long parade hosting marching bands of schools from all over Panama.

Volcán and around *p1367*
Dec Feria de las Tierras Altas is held during the 2nd week of Dec in La Fuente Park. Rodeo, dancing, crafts fair and many other attractions.

▲ Activities and tours

Boquete and the Eastern Highlands
p1364, map p1365
River rafting
Chiriquí River Rafting, Av Central, next to Lourdes, T720-1505, www.panama-rafting.com. Open 0830-1730. Bilingual father-and-son team Héctor and Ian Sánchez, offer 2- to 4-hr Grade II, III and IV trips with modern equipment on Río Chiriquí and surrounding area, US$60-105 per person. They can arrange lodging and transport to starting-point or vehicle delivery to landing point. Offer trip during dry season, Dec-Apr, as well on Río Chiriquí Viejo (Grade III/IV Technical, US$90-100) and Río Esti (Grade II and III). Recommended.

Panama Rafters, just below the square on Av Central, T/F720-2712, www.panamarafters.com. Good, solid rafting operation with quality gear, guides and a strong emphasis on safety. Kayak and multi-day trips are available, but most trips are run on the excellent Río Chiriquí Viejo. ½-day on the Grade III Harpia section US$75, full day on the Grade IV Jaguar section US$90.

Tour operators
Aventurist, T720-1635, www.aventurist. com. Mountain bike hire, hiking, coffee tours.
Boquete Mountain Safari Tours, T627-8829, www.boquetemountainsafari tours.com. Good selection of ½- and full-day tours, from hikes to full on adventures.
Coffee Adventures, T720-3852, www.coffeeadventures.net. Coffee tours and visits to local indigenous villages. The same company offer Boquette Tree Trek canopy tours, www.canopypanama.com.
Feliciano Tours, T624-9940, provides tours and transport of the area US$20-US$60. Good for those needing guidance on trails of the area, some English spoken.
Hiking/Birdwatching Tours, T720-3852. Run by Terry Van Niekerk, who speaks English, Spanish and Dutch, and provides hiking and birdwatching tours of the area surrounding Boquete. Highly recommended for the **Los Quetzales** hike (5 hrs) which also includes transport back from Cerro Punta to Boquete (2 hrs). Tours include fresh coffee and snacks and some include a light breakfast. Prices from US$20-US$60 per person depending on tour.
Hiking Tours, Av A Ote on road to cemetery, T/F720-2726. Friendly and helpful owner Sr Bouttet arranges guided tours in the area including Volcán Barú, Cerro Punta (around US$50 per day for a group of up to 3) and can give advice on where to stay overnight.
Hotel Panamonte, Av Central, north end of town, organizes day trips to Volcán Barú, birdwatching and coffee plantations, US$150 for a group of up to 4.

Sr Frank Glavas at Pensión Marilo's, Av A Este y Calle 6 Sur, organizes guides and trips throughout the area.

⊖ Transport

Boquete and the Eastern Highlands
p1364, map p1365
Bike and scooter
Estate Office-Gringo's Scooter Hire, Av Central near park. Infomation on hiking, bike hire (US$2.50 per hr, US$10 day 8 hrs), scooter hire (US$6.50 per hr, US$20 day), pay deposit.

Bus
Local buses depart from the main plaza, called El Parque, old fashioned and pretty, every 20 mins to **Volcán** (US$1.65), **David** (US$0.50), and **Paso Canoas** (US$0.75). 10 buses daily to **Panama City** via David with **Padafront**, US$11, 7 hr; terminal beside Delta petrol station next to El Sótano restaurant, east of Volcán intersection on Pan-American Hwy, T770-4485.

⚐ Directory

Boquete and the Eastern Highlands
p1364, map p1365
Banks Global Bank, Mon-Fri, 0800-1500, Sat 0800-1500 changes TCs with a commission of US$1 per cheque and has an ATM. Same hours at Banco Nacional and Banolar, on the main street, who will both cash TCs. **Internet** Oasis Internet, near Pastelería Alemán; Kelnix, beside Chiriquí River Rafting, T720-2803, daily 0800-2000, US$1.80 per hr. **Language schools** Habla Ya, Central Avenue, Los Establos Plaza 20-22, Boquete, T720-1294, www.hablaya panama.com. Recommended by one traveller for great Spanish tuition with homestay options. US$220 for 1 week, US$700 for 4. Can also provide excursion advice. **Laundry** Lavomático Las Burbujas, just south of church, very friendly, US$1 to wash. **Post office** In the Palacio Municipal.

Volcán and around *p1367*
Banks Banco Nacional and Banco de Istmo, Mon-Fri 0800-1500, Sat 0800-1200, both change dollar TCs. **Internet** Sinfonet, in Hotel Don Tavo, US$1 per hr, friendly and helpful. Hardware store Ferremax, main road opposite police station, T771-4461, sends and receives international faxes, 0700-1200, 1400-1800, US$1.50 per page plus telephone charge, English spoken **Laundry** Lava mático Volcán, main road opposite Jardín Alegría dancehall. Service only US$2.50, wash, dry and fold, reliable, Doña Miriam will have washing ready when promised.

Northwest coast

Panama's Caribbean banana-growing region has historical links with Columbus' fourth voyage and with the black slaves imported to work the plantations. Ports of varying age and activity lie on the Laguna de Chiriquí, providing an alternative land route to Costa Rica. This region is subject to heavy rainfall, which may take the form of daily afternoon downpours or violent tropical storms. Only from January to March is there much respite from the regular soakings. ▶▶ *For listings, see pages 1381-1387.*

Towards Laguna de Chiriquí

From Chiriquí on the Pan-American Highway, 14 km east of David, there is a road north over the mountains to Chiriquí Grande (98 km). Beyond Gualaca the road passes the Fortuna hydroelectric plant, the Cricamola Indigenous Reservation and descends through virgin rainforest to the Caribbean. On the way up the hill, just north of Valle de la Mina is **Mary's**, a simple restaurant. If travelling under your own steam you can stop to admire the views across Lago Fortuna resevoir, from where the road is a tough, steep and twisting climb to the the continental divide, 62 km from the Pan-American Highway, and marked by nothing more than an altitude marker sign.

There is a 10-m waterfall 2.5 km north of the divide. Going north from the continental divide to Chiriquí Grande is a cyclist's delight – good road, spectacular views, little traffic and downhill all the way, but nowhere to eat until Punta Pena, just outside Chiriquí Grande. The road reaches the sea at **Chiriquí Grande**, once the embarkation point for travellers catching the ferry to Almirante and beyond, but now, with the new road heading north, rarely visited.

Banana coast

Fifty kilometres north of Chiriquí Grande, one of Central America's most important banana-growing regions extends from **Almirante** northwest across the border to Costa Rica. Today Almirante is a small commercial port, usually just a transit point for tourists heading to or from the Bocas archipelago. The banana railway starts/ends here. In the 1940s and 50s, disease virtually wiped out the business and plantations were converted to *abacá* and cacao. With the development of disease resistant strains of banana, the *abacá* and cacao have been all but replaced, and banana plantations once again thrive. The main players in the industry are large multinational companies. **Cobanat**, who export through **Chiquirí Land Company** (a subsidiary of **Chiquita Brands**) and **Dole** (a subsidiary of **Standard Brands**), who export bananas to Europe and the US from Almirante. In April 1991 a devastating earthquake struck northwest Panama and southeast Costa Rica. An island in the bay which sank during the earthquake now shows as nothing more than a patch of shallow turquoise water.

Isla Colón and Bocas del Toro ⊜❼❻▲❸❶ ▶▶ *pp1381-1387. Colour map 7, B5.*

Across the bay are the rainforest, reefs and beaches of the **Bocas Islands**, the most important of which is **Isla Colón**. The protected bay offers all forms of watersport and diving, beautiful sunrises and sunsets. All the islands harbour plenteous wildlife but especially those east of Colón where tropical birds, butterflies, red, yellow and orange frogs and a great variety of other wildlife abounds. For some, this is being called the new

Galápagos, but, as in that fragile paradise, attraction and concern walk hand in hand. Formerly a major banana producer, the industry failed to revive alongside the mainland plantations and the main sources of income are now fishing and tourism. Bocas del Toro town, where most visitors stay, is on the southeast tip of the island. Most activity takes

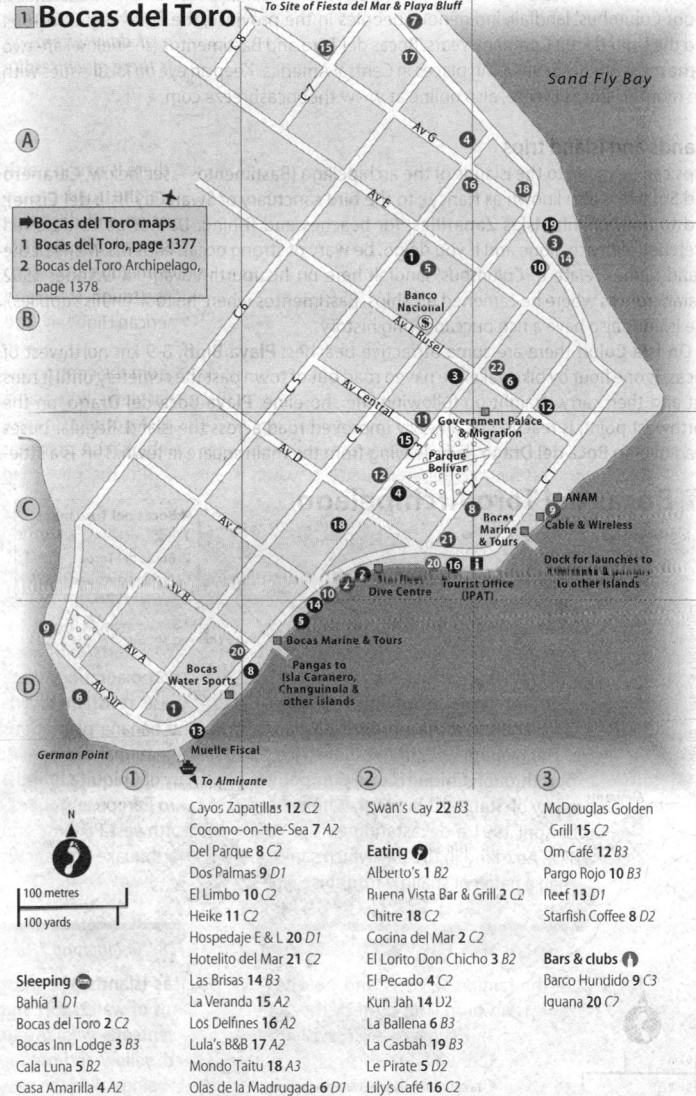

Bocas del Toro

To Site of Fiesta del Mar & Playa Bluff

Sand Fly Bay

➡ Bocas del Toro maps
1 Bocas del Toro, page 1377
2 Bocas del Toro Archipelago, page 1378

Banco Nacional

Government Palace & Migration

Parque Bolívar

ANAM

Cable & Wireless

Bocas Marine & Tours

Dock for launches to Almirante & pangas to other Islands

Star Fleet Dive Centre

Tourist Office (IPAT)

Bocas Marine & Tours

Bocas Water Sports

Pangas to Isla Caranero, Changuinola & other islands

German Point

Muelle Fiscal

To Almirante

N

100 metres
100 yards

Sleeping 🛏
Bahía 1 *D1*
Bocas del Toro 2 *C2*
Bocas Inn Lodge 3 *B3*
Cala Luna 5 *B2*
Casa Amarilla 4 *A2*

Cayos Zapatillas 12 *C2*
Cocomo-on-the-Sea 7 *A2*
Del Parque 8 *C2*
Dos Palmas 9 *D1*
El Limbo 10 *C2*
Heike 11 *C2*
Hospedaje E & L 20 *D1*
Hotelito del Mar 21 *C2*
Las Brisas 14 *B3*
La Veranda 15 *A2*
Los Delfines 16 *A2*
Lula's B&B 17 *A2*
Mondo Taitu 18 *A3*
Olas de la Madrugada 6 *D1*

Swan's Cay 22 *B3*

Eating 🍴
Alberto's 1 *B2*
Buena Vista Bar & Grill 2 *C2*
Chitre 18 *C2*
Cocina del Mar 2 *C2*
El Lorito Don Chicho 3 *B2*
El Pecado 4 *C2*
Kun Jah 14 *D2*
La Ballena 6 *B3*
La Casbah 19 *B3*
Le Pirate 5 *D2*
Lily's Café 16 *C2*

McDouglas Golden
  Grill 15 *C2*
Om Café 12 *B3*
Pargo Rojo 10 *B3*
Reef 13 *D1*
Starfish Coffee 8 *D2*

Bars & clubs 🍸
Barco Hundido 9 *C3*
Iguana 20 *C2*

place around the broad main street – Calle 3 – and the leafy square. The **Feria del Mar** is at the end of September/early October, but for most of the rest of the year it is peaceful and quiet, although more hotels are appearing each year. English is spoken by most of the black population. At the **tourist office** ⓘ *on the seafront, T757-9642, www.bocas.com, Mon-Fri 0830-1630*, there is an informative permanent exhibit, with English translations, about Columbus' landfall, indigenous peoples in the province, the fire at Bocas in 1904 and the United Fruit Company years. Bocas del Toro and Bastimentos (see below) are two of the most rapidly developing places in Central America. Keep an eye on local issues with the monthly Bocas Breeze, also online at www.thebocasbreeze.com.

Islands and island trips

Trips can be made to the islands of the archipelago (Bastimentos – see below, **Caranero** and **Solarte** – also known as Nancy); to the bird sanctuary of **Swan Cay** (**Isla del Cisne**); and to the beautiful **Islas Zapatillas**, for beaches and fishing. Do not go to deserted stretches of beach alone and if you do go, be wary of strong ocean currents. Many of the island names relate to Columbus' landfall on his fourth voyage in October 1502 (Caranero was where he careened his ships, Bastimentos where he took on his supplies). The islands also have a rich buccaneering history.

On Isla Colón there are some attractive beaches: **Playa Bluff**, 8-9 km northwest of Bocas, is one hour by bike; take the paved road out of town past the cemetery until it runs out and then carry straight on following the shoreline; **Playa Boca del Drago**, on the northwest point, is reached by a newly improved road across the island. Regular buses head over to **Boca del Drago** daily, leaving from the main square in town. This is a little-

2 Bocas del Toro Archipelago

➡ Bocas del Toro maps
1 Bocas del Toro, page 1377
2 Bocas del Toro Archipelago, page 1378

visited part of the island. Behind the beach there's a good restaurant and a cheap hostel. A local conservation project has an office here and it might be possible to hire dive and snorkel gear.

Colón also has **La Gruta del Drago**, a cave occupied by long-beaked white bats, which fly out at dusk (tour US$10 plus US$5 for lunch on beach). You can walk to the cave, a pleasant day, but ask locals for directions and advice on safety.

Opposite Bocas, 200 m across the channel, is the small island of **Caranero**, reached by *panga* either flagged down from a waterfront restaurant/bar, or boarded at the small quay just beyond Le Pirate or Taxi 25's quay next to the tourist office.

A 15-minute boat ride from Bocas town, the quiet island of **Solarte** is a very quiet retreat and good for day trips. For those into frogs, **Hospital Point** (good snorkelling) is the orange frog hangout.

The **National Marine Park** ① *tours US$15-20 per person, US$75 per boat, 0900-1600, entry to the Cayos Zapatillas section of the park is US$10 extra, see Tour operators, page 1386,* on **Isla Bastimentos** encompasses virtually the whole island, bar the small town of Bastimentos on the western tip. Both this island and Isla Colón are turtle-nesting grounds and their protection is being improved with the help of organizations like **Caribaro**, on Calle 3, who set up beach patrols. There is snorkelling and a lunch stop at Cayo Crawl. Many tour boats also visit **Laguna Bocatorito** (no snorkelling), part of Isla Cristóbal, to view dolphins before going on to the Zapatillas Cays in the park.

On **Bastimentos** it's a 30-minute walk to northern beaches with soft off-white sand and strong undertow; ask directions, take food and drink, or ask if anywhere is open selling meals. **Red Frog Beach** is the best known; it has a strong rip tide, but **Polo's Beach** (with red-and-black frog accompaniment) is also recommended – look out for sloths and monkeys. **Playa Larga**, halfway along the north shore, is best reached by boat, as is nearby Polo's Beach. The Ngobe indigenous community of Bahía Honda on the South Side of Bastimentos have opened a restaurant and small ecotourism project the 'Trail of the Sloth', which involves a dugout canoe trip and hike through the rainforest to a cave that plays host to an important bat colony. The restaurant offers traditional food in addition to the more common Panamanian dishes. For more information call T6669-6269 (mobile), or check the website bocas.com/indians/bahiahonda.htm.

Bastimentos village is a stilted, ramshackle, wooden affair clinging to a steep slope on the leeward side of the island. Tourism once skirted round it, helping the place hold on to its old-style Caribbean charm; now a few smart places are opening up, but it is still very quiet.

Cayos Zapatillas Norte is the quieter of the two Zapatillas because the tour boats do not generally stop here.

Isla Popa and **Cayo Agua**, the other main islands in the area, are sparsely settled, heavily forested and have no beaches.

Diving

Several places throughout the archipelago are popular for diving. The joy of diving in Bocas lies in the details, with some wonderful intact coral gardens (74 out of 79 Caribbean coral species exist here) that seem to play host to a multitude of little gems. Brittle stars, spotted morays, arrow crabs, toadfish and squid are just some of the inhabitants you can expect to see, along with most of the common Caribbean reef fish. Occasionally larger grouper, rays and nurse sharks also put in an appearance.

Good dive sites include: **Tiger Rock** with stronger currents, deeper dives, larger fish and sometimes nurse and whitetip reef sharks; dolphin and wash rocks with rock pinnacles, overhangs and caverns and **La Gruta Polo** with good coral, canyons and caverns. **Hospital Point** is popular for both day and night dives. Several good locations near the resort for scuba-diving and for snorkelling in the clear waters around **Mangrove Point**.

Cavern diving at **Polo's Beach**, only in calm sea, **Punta Vieja** on the northeast shore of Bastimentos and boat dives at **Cayos Zapatillas**.

The best **snorkelling** sites are **Hospital Point** on Cayo Nancy, **Punta Vieja**, **Islas Zapatillas**, but only outside the reef – tour boats will just drop you off at North Cay for snorkelling off the beach (points en route on tours are also disappointing – **Cayo Crawl** has two great sites with very colourful coral, known as Cayo Crawl Inside and Outside, referring to reefs several hundred meters offshore to the east and west – the area directly around the island is seagrass only; hire a boat and guide from one of the dive shops to see the best of the reef. Some areas, such as the islands around the entrance to **Laguna Bocatorito**, harbour habitats where large coral and sponge colonies run right up to the edges of the mangroves creating the unique and fascinating ecosystem. These areas are as a beautiful as they are fragile and require great caution to avoid damaging the reef and its inhabitants, so if not experienced and confident with your snorkelling ability it's best to leave these areas alone and stick to corals in deeper water.

Surfing
The break on the point of Bastimentos where the island curves away from Carenero to meet First Beach (or Playa Wizard) is the renowned and occasionally terrifying (reaching up to 25 ft) **Silver Back**, which attracts surfers from around the globe (peaks December to February).

Playa Bluff is a good beach break, **Playa Paunch** is mostly reef, both are excellent breaks on Colón, and the northeast point of **Caranero**, a full reef, and the most popular of the island breaks. ➤➤ *For board rental, see Activities and tours, page 1385.*

Towards Costa Rica ●●●● ➤➤ *pp1381-1387.*

Changuinola
Between Almirante and the Costa Rica border is sprawling Changuinola, the main commercial centre in the region which, although architecturally not attractive, has an airport and lively nightlife with local bars. Changuinola is good for shopping (the food markets are great), there are also several banks where you can change traveller's cheques and use ATMs. Changuinola's main interest to travellers is as a stepping off or arrival point for fast water taxis to Bocas del Toro, see page 1387. The trip is very enjoyable, weaving through the coastal Snyder Canal offering a fleeting insight into life along the waterway. Visitors should take care going out at night here; women alone will almost certainly be approached if they enter bars, and maybe also on the street. Excursions can be made to Naso/Teribe indigenous villages. The most commonly known trip is the **Wekso Ecolodge**, reached by taxi to El Silencio (US$5), then on the Río Teribe (US$30 per boat, or US$5 on local boat). Organize in advance through **National Organization for Sustainable Ecotourism Development** (**ODESEN**) ① *T6569-3869, www.bocas.com/odesen.htm.* Simple (**D**) accommodation is also available.

For Sleeping and Eating price codes and other relevant information, see Essentials pages 45-48.

● Sleeping

Towards Laguna de Chiriquí *p1376*
For nature lovers and those looking for a fantastic location, the **Cloudforest Jungle Lodge** can be found just inside the Fortuna Forest Reserve.

B Finca La Suiza, on the southern side of the Fortuna Reserve, Quadrifoglio, 16615-3774 (in David), www.panama.net.tc. To get there from Gualaca: pass the sign to Los Planes (16.4 km) and the turning to Chiriquicito; 300 m after this junction is the sign for the Fortuna Reserve, 1 km beyond the sign is the gate to the *finca* on the right Owned by a Swiss couple, Herbert Brüllmann and Monika Kohler, excellent for birdwatching on 20 km of forest trails, very good food, comfortable accommodation with bath and hot water, breakfast US$5, dinner US$14.50.

D Pensión Emperador, Chiriquí Grande, T757-9656. With balconies overlooking the wharf. Clean and friendly.

E Buena Vista, Chiriquí Grande, T756-9726. Friendly, breakfast available, shared baths.

Banana coast *p1376*
D-E San Francisco, Almirante. A/c or fan, small dark rooms, overpriced.

E Albergue Bahía, Almirante, T778-9211. Clean, friendly owner, will store belongings.

Isla Colón and Bocas del Toro *p1376*
LL-AL El Limbo, on the front street next to Bocas del Toro, T757-9062, www.ellimbo. com. Great location overlooking the channel between Isla Colón and Carenero. Good but pricey restaurant, businesslike rooms with a/c, TV, fridge. Rooms with balconies are better. Also with a place on Isla Bastamientos.

AL Bocas del Toro, Calle 2 y Av C, T/F757-9018, www.hotelbocasdeltoro.com. On the seafront, large clean rooms, some with excellent sea views.

AL Cocomo-on-the-Sea, Av Norte y Calle 6, Bocas del Toro, T/F757-9259, www.coco moonthesea.com. 4 rooms on the seafront with a/c, private bathroom, huge breakast included, simple and clean, home-cooked meals, book swap. US owner Douglas is very helpful. Sundeck and free use of 2 kayaks. Good.

AL Swan's Cay, opposite the municipal building on main street, Bocas del Toro, T757-9090, www.swanscayhotel.com. Pricey and upmarket, 2 restaurants, internet, laundry, swimming pool in 2nd building on the seafront.

AL-D Las Brisas, Bocas, on the sea at north end of the main street (formerly **Botel Thomas**), T/F757-9549, hotel_lasbrisas@ yahoo.com. Wooden building on stilts with nice veranda over the sea. Cheaper rooms upstairs have private bath and fan, good but the occasional cockroach and thin walls. Downstairs rooms are more expensive rooms have a/c, cable TV and some have fridge. They have fully equipped rooms with kitchenettes.

AL-E Hotel La Rumba, 1.5 km out of town at Big Creek, T757-9961, www.hotellarumba. com. Rooms of varying sizes and facilities in a round, thatched hotel, with restaurant and bar overlooking the sea. Games, happy hours and satellite showing sport.

A Bocas Inn Lodge, north end of Main St, Bocas, T757-9600, www.ancon expeditions.com. Run by tour operator Ancon Expeditions (see page 1323), comfortable and simple with pleasant, spacious bar and terrace and communal veranda upstairs, good platform for swimming. Water heated with solar panels, Crab and lobster off the menu due to overfishing concerns. Good reviews.

A Hotelito del Mar, Calle 1, T757-9861, www.hotelitodelmar.com. Friendly owner, sparkling clean rooms, all very conventional with private bath, hot water and a/c. Good central location. Tours arranged.

A Lula's B&B, Av Norte, across street from Cocomo on the Sea, T757-9057, www.lulabb.com. Old style and homely with huge kitchen and living area downstairs, continental breakfast included. All rooms with a/c and private bath, family-run. Recommended.

A-B Bahía, south end of main street, Bocas, T757-9626, www.hotelbahia.biz. Building formerly the HQ of the **United Fruit Company** built in 1905, remodelled rooms with balcony are more expensive, all rooms with hot water, TV and a/c. Laundry service available and restaurant in front.

A-B Cala Luna, behind **Alberto's Restaurant**, Calle 5 and Av E, Bocas, T757-9066, www.calalunabocas.com. A hidden gem in the backstreets. Rooms are spacious with a very appealing, sparse, almost Japanese style. Same owners as **Alberto's**.

A-B La Estrella de Bocas, Calle 1, T757-9011, www.bocas.com/estrella.htm. Accommodation ranges from apartments with fully equipped kitchen and rooms with a/c, cable TV and private bath. Mixed reports.

A-B Los Delfines, Av G y Calle 5, Bocas, T/F757-9963, www.bocasdelfines.com. Clean, reasonable-sized rooms with cable TV and a/c. Restaurant.

A-B Punta Manglar (formerly Mangrove Point), T/F757-9541. Cabins sleeping 2-8 set amongst the mangroves and accessible by boat – the hotel offers dive courses up to dive master and fun dives.

B-C Casa Amarilla, Calle 5 y Av G, Bocas, behind Mondo Taitu, T757-9938, dennis@cwp.net. 4 Large airy rooms with good beds, a/c, fridge, digital safe and large cable TV. Owner lives upstairs and is very helpful. Free coffee and fruit in the morning. Good value and recommended.

B-C La Veranda, Calle 7, Av G, 1 block after Supermarket Ahorros, T757-9211, laverandapanama.tripod.com. Beautiful wooden, original Bocas-style house, rooms come with private or shared bath and hot water – feels like home. Large veranda on 1st floor has a communal kitchen and a spacious area to eat or relax.

C Del Parque, seaward side of square, Bocas, T757-9008. Well-kept old town house with light rooms and good beds, hot water, free coffee and fruit. Discounts in low season.

C Dos Palmas, Av Sur y Calle 6, Bocas, T757-9906. Quaint with lots of local charm, built over water, a/c, cheaper with fan, clean, swim off platform at back, free coffee before midday.

C Hotel Olas de la Madrugada, Av Sur, T757-9930, www.hotelolas.com. New and already popular hotel built over the water. Clean and bright rooms, all with a/c, cable TV and private hot water shower, good for the price. Friendly owners are opening a bar and restaurant, they also have jet-ski and wakeboard rental.

D Hotel Cayos Zapatillas, on the High St, odd-looking building overlooking the park. Good rooms, very reasonably priced for location and with private hot-water shower and cable TV. Laundry service.

D Sagitarius, 1 block from main street on Av D, Bocas, T757-9578. With hot water, bath, a/c, cheaper with fan, TV. Clean and good.

D-E Heike, on main square, Bocas, T757-9708, www.bocas.com/heike.htm. 9 rooms, shared bathrooms, kitchen for lodgers and a communal veranda. Inexpensive, friendly and highly recommended.

D-E Hospedaje E & L, Main St, T757-9206. Friendly, budget accommodation, conveniently located, cold water, shared kitchen available.

D-E Mondo Taitu, Bocas, T757-9425, www.mondotaitu.com. Cheap surfers' hostel at far end of island near **Hotel Las Brisas**. Good place to meet other travellers, hang out and get groups for trips. Good kitchen, dorms and some private rooms, shared hot water bath, apartment with private bath for couples and a cool little bar tucked in at the back. Breakfast included. Movies and bikes for local use. International calls and surf board rental.

Islands and island trips *p1378*
LL-AL Buccaneer Resort, on the east side of Isla Carenero, T/F757-9042, www.bocas buccaneer.com. High-end suites and cabins, all with a/c, on the beach. Breakfast included.
L-AL Al Natural, Old Point, Bastimentos, T/F757-9004, www.alnaturalresort.com. Belgian-owned ecolodge bungalows using traditional techniques and native fallen trees – electricity provided by solar power. Bungalows consist of 3 walls, leaving 1 side open and exposed to a spectacular view of the ocean and Zapatillas Keys in the distance – a truly natural experience. Price includes transport from Isla Colón, 3 meals with wine, use of kayaks and snorkelling gear. Highly recommended.
L-AL Careening Cay Resort, Isla Carenero – facing Isla Colón, T757-9157, www.careeningcay.com. Cottages in a tranquil, well-manicured location, some equipped with gas stove, microwave and fridge, others without, all with a/c and sleep 1-6. Their **Sunset Grill** restaurant serves dinner Tue-Sun.
AL Coral Cay, east of Bastimentos island, T6626-1919, www.bocas.com/coralcay.htm. Rustic cabins built over the water. Beautiful surroundings and outstanding seafood. Price includes 2 meals per day, snorkelling equipment and the use of a traditional dugout canoe. Watch out for the sandflies.
AL Solarte del Caribe, Isla Solarte (Cayo Nancy), T6593-2245, www.solarteinn.com. B&B on the southern side of the island. Comfortable beds, colourful, tropical surroundings and good food. Breakfast and roundtrip transport included.
A Acuario, Isla Caranero, T757-9565, www.bocas.com/casa-acuario.htm. Nicely situated on a pontoon, rooms come with TV, a/c and balconies over the water, there is a kitchen and bar, American owned.
A El Limbo, on Isla Bastamientos, T757-9062, www.ellimbo.com. Beach-front location, good mix of activities. A little pricey for the package.
A-B Hotel Tierra Verde, Isla Carenero. T757-9903, www.hoteltierraverde.com.

Well-maintained hotel situated among the palms a stone's throw from the shore. Rooms have private showers and hot water, internet available.
B Caribbean View Hotel, Bastimentos Town, T757-9442, www.bocas.com/caribbean-view. htm. Wooden, traditional-style hotel, with lovely local owners, upmarket for rustic Bastimentos Town. Rooms available with a/c or fan, all have private shower, hot water and TV. There is a communal deck over the water.
C-D Hotel Bastimentos, Bastimentos Town. An elevated position overlooking the town, islands and surrounding waters. Attractive budget accommodation, with shared dorms and private rooms with showers. Communal kitchen and TV, friendly owners.
D-E Pensión Tío Tom, Bastimentos Town, T757-9831, www.tio-tom.com. Rustic, budget accommodation on the water, rooms with mosquito nets and private bath. Chilled vibe, friendly and helpful owners who also run the internet café a couple of doors down. Recommended.

Changuinola *p1380*
C Alhambra, on the main street (Calle 17 de Abril), T758-9819. Large rooms, hot water TV, a/c, telephone.
C Semiramis, diagonally opposite the Alhambra, T758-6006. Dark rooms with outstandingly kitsch pictures, a/c, TV, restaurant serving Chinese plus standard Panamanian food.
D Taliali, 150 m from bus station, set back from Calle 17 de Abril. A/c, TV, hot water.
D-E Carol, T758-8731, 200 m from bus station. With bath, hot water, a/c (cheaper rooms without), TV, small dark rooms, restaurant next door same ownership.

🍴 Eating

Towards Laguna de Chiriquí *p1376*
🍴 **Café**, Chiriquí Grande. Good.
🍴 **Dallys**, Chiriquí Grande, to right of wharf. Popular.

Isla Colón and Bocas del Toro *p1376*

Cocina del Mar, next to Buena Vista. Very pricey, but top-end seafood cuisine, with views of the bay.

La Ballena, next to Swan Cay Hotel, Bocas. Bit pricey but delicious Italian seafood pastas and cappuccinos, good for breakfast and tables outside.

-Bongos, main St. Slightly overpriced American-style food.

-El Pecado, on southwest corner of parque, Bocas. Panamanian and international food including Lebanese, one of the best restaurants in town, not too expensive. Great drinks and good wines worth splashing out on, also try their early evening houmous with warm Johnny Cakes (coconut bread).

Alberto's Restaurant, Calle 5, Bocas. Great pizza, pasta and lasagne, r easonable prices.

Bar y Restaurante Le Pirate, Calle 3, next to El Limbo Hotel, Bocas. Outstanding lobster for very reasonable prices. Built over the water, full bar, mixed drinks and happy hour.

Crazy Charlie's, main St. Caribbean and local food, they also rent DVDs.

Lemongrass, Calle 2, next to Buena Vista, upstairs. Owner here has experience of cooking in Asia so expect good, authentic Thai curries and lots of seafood. Good views over the bay and excellent bar for cocktails.

Pargo Rojo, new location opposite Hotel Las Brisas. Long-standing Iranian chef Bernard has moved his restaurant from Carenero to Bocas, bringing his excellent culinary delights to town. In a very attractive, renovated building overlooking the street. Recommended.

The Reef, end of main st, opposite Super Gourmet. Local food with seafood specials and a cocktail bar with terrace over the water.

Restaurant Claudios, at Hotel Laguna, opposite the park on main st. Reasonably priced, good Italian food, pizzas and pastas are home-made. Big breakfast menu.

Shelly's BBQ Mexican Food, located behind Claudios, T757-9979. First Mexican eatery in Bocas, with enchiladas, mole, guacamole and barbecued meats. They also do home delivery (plus taxi cost) and sell a range of frozen specials in Bocas's Super Gourmet store.

Starfish Coffee, coffee shop on Calle 3, just before Bocas Water Sports, Bocas. Cappuccino, pastries, croissants and brownies. Excellent breakfast deals at reasonable prices. Owner offers yoga classes in the morning and tours of their environmentally friendly coffee plantation on the mainland on request.

-Flip Flops Bar & Grill, main St. Seafood, grills and burgers. On the water.

Buena Vista Bar and Grill, Bocas. Long-standing American-style sports bar, shows games on directTV, run by very friendly Panamanian and his American girlfriend. Good menu for both bar snacks and main meals, grills, tacos, fish and veggie options. Nice spot over the water to relax and chat with a beer or cocktail.

El Lorito Don Chicho, main st, Bocas. Most popular – and oldest – local café in town, cheap, good dishes and cakes. Ask for the delicious pudding – unique to Bocas – and their malted milkshakes.

Kun Jah, close to Hotel Limbo. Very reasonable Chinese food, huge plates – fried rice, noodles, sweet 'n' sour, etc, good food, great for those on a budget. Terrace over the water.

La Casbah, main street. Offers reasonably priced Mediterranean food.

Lily's Café, next to Tropical Suites Hotel. Open for breakfast and lunch only. Caribbean food with a health food twist. Pastas, soups, salads and sandwiches.

McDouglas Golden Grill, opposite park, main st. The fast-food emporium of Bocas – burgers, chips and hotdogs, cheap. Also pizzas with loads of cheese, and breakfast eggs and pancakes – good for those on a budget, but not on a diet.

Om Café, now located over Flow Surf Shop, close to La Ballena. Closed Wed. Excellent, home-made Indian food served in very relaxing and ambient surroundings. Tables are available on the balcony or private rooms for larger parties. **Om** also serves good breakfasts with home-made granola and yoghurt, lassis, fruit salads and bagels. Recommended.

¶ Restaurant Chitre, main street. Best *fonda* in town, local food, nice owners, and good spot for watching street traffic.

Islands and island trips *p1378*
¶¶ Pickled Parrot, Carenero. Bar and restaurant. Draft beers and American BBQs, happy hour 1500-1700 every day. Lovely spot at sunset, facing Bastimentos Island.

¶¶-¶ Blue Marble, next to Roots, on the water in Bastimentos. Breakfasts, sandwiches, salads, cakes and pastries and an endless list of teas. Friendly people, great spot to chill in the afternoon with a cup of tea and slice of cake. Owners also run island eco tours, including night tours.

¶ Restaurant Doña Mara, Carenero. Excellent seafood and typical Panamanian food.

¶ Roots, Bastimentos village, just east of the centre. Bar and restaurant with a nice terrace, run by Oscar who will also guide tourists to the lake in the middle of the island.

⊙ Entertainment

Isla Colón and Bocas del Toro *p1376*
Barco Hundido, Calle 1, next to Cable & Wireless office, Bocas. Thatched-roof watering hole, affectionately known as the **Wreck Deck** (its original name) built over the water and above a wrecked, sunken boat. Lights illuminate the boat at night making it a perfect spot to watch the local marine life and the thumping local nightlife. The place to hang out; dancing, Caribbean scene, mixed drinks, 3 dance floors, good music and on occasion – at the owners whim – 'pizza and movie night.'

El Encanto, main St. The only truly local spot, they play salsa at volume and have a pool hall.

Flip Flops Bar & Grill (at Piña Colada), main street. Big deck over the water, happy hours and seafood. Also movies shown on large screen, ping pong and Wi-Fi.

Iguana Bar, Bocas. New smart establishment, surf videos and gringos, good music, another pre-**Barco** spot.

Lemongrass, Calle 2, next to **Buena Vista**, upstairs. Excellent bar for cocktails and moonlit views over the bay. Occasionally hosts live music.

Mondo Taitu, at the north end of Bocas, T757-9425. Relaxed, good for cocktails and for warming up for the **Barco Hundido** or **Blue Monday** (see below).

Islands and island trips *p1378*
Every Mon anyone who wants to party heads over to Isla Bastimentos to **Blue Mondays**, a largely local event with live Calypso music and the full Caribbean vibe. Hugely popular.

▲ Activities and tours

Isla Colón and Bocas del Toro *p1376*
Diving and snorkelling
Starfleet, near tourist office, T/F757 0630, www.starfleetscuba.com. Have years of experience in the Bocas waters, German and Dutch spoken. Discover scuba dives from US$65, PADI Open Water course US$235, scuba review US$25, snorkel trips, US$15. Safe, with good instructors and equipment.

Bocas Watersports, Main Street, T757-9541, www.bocaswatersports.com. Dive courses, waterskiing and kayak rental. Night dives run at US$50, with longer 2-tank trips to Tiger Rock and the Zapatilla Cayes running at around US$75. Snorkelling gear can be hired from several places, US$5 a day. Affiliated to the Punta Manglar resort.

Surfing
You can rent boards from a small shop next to **The Yellow House** or in **Mondo Taitu**. There are 2 surf shops in town, **Tropix**,

on main st (T757-9415) who make custom boards and **Flow**, located under **Om Café**.

Tour operators
There are now numerous tour operators; so many that you should be able to plan your own day if you have a big enough group and know where you want to go. Most operators have maps and pictures of the surrounding islands. Usual tours visit either Dolphin Bay, Hospital Point, Cayo Coral and Red Frog Beach (Bastimentos), or Boca del Drago and Swans Cay (Bird Island). For a little extra you can add Cayos Zapatilla to the first tour.
Blue Marble Tours, located on Bastimentos, T6632-6269. Very enthusiastic guide, a knowledgeable biologist, offers day- and, unusually, night-time wildlife tours in their jungle grounds on Isla Solarte. Recommended.
Cap'n Don's, T6487-8460. Private boat rental, windsurfing equipment, kayaks, hobie cats, pedal boats and snorkelling.
Catamaran Sailing Adventures, 3rd St, beside Almacen Rosa Blanca, T757-9710, www.bocassailing.com. Owner Marcel offers popular day sailing tours on his 12-m catamaran around the Bocas Islands for US$40, including lunch and snorkelling gear. Very knowledgeable when it comes to finding the best reef areas – you can also hire the whole boat for an overnight trip for US$300 and do a customized trip.
J&J Transparente Tours, main st beside Le Pirate, T757-9915, transparentetours@hotmail.com, US$17 to Laguna Bocatorito, Cayo Crawl, Zapatillas or Red Frog Beach, and sometimes snorkelling at Hospital Point.
Mouth of the Bull Adventures, T6561-0460, organized or customized adventure tours, snorkelling and jungle tours.

○ Transport

Towards Laguna de Chiriquí *p1376*
Bicycle Plenty of bike rentals, and some scooter rentals. US$1.50 per hr, US$7.50 day.

Boat Water taxi from Almirante to **Bocas** US$3. To get to the *muelle* from bus station, cross over railway line, bear left following far side of fence across scrub land to road, head left along road 2 blocks to the quay.

Bus From Almirante to **David**, every 40 mins, 4 hrs, US$7; **Changuinola**, 30 mins, US$1.

Car The road between Chiriquí Grande and Almirante is in excellent condition for the 74 km length of the new road.

Train See under Changuinola, page 1387.

Isla Colón and Bocas del Toro *p1376*
Air Bocas del Toro can be reached by **Aeroperlas** twice daily from Albrook Airport, Panama City, T757-9341, www.aeroperlas.com, US$70 1 way. **David** daily, US$32; Changuinola, US$7. **Nature Air** (Costa Rica, www.nature air.com) now operate flights between Bocas del Toro and San José; Costa Rica, US$110 1 way. Call **Bocas International Airport** for details, T757-9841.

Boat Water taxis To and from **Almirante** run daily 0530-1830, 30 mins minimum, US$3. Hire boats or water taxis in Bocas del Toro to Bastimentos and the other islands. Boat to **Bastimentos**, US$2 per person 1 way, ask around **Le Pirate Bar** or **Taxi 25** dock next to IPAT, elsewhere along waterfront. Inter-island boats also go from the water taxi *muelle*, near the tourist office. From Carenero or Bastimentos town it is easy to flag down a passing boat taxi. Don't forget to arrange a time to be picked up. If hiring a boat, try to arrange it the day before, at least US$60 per day, depending on the boatman (4 hrs minimum, can take 9 people or more, depending on boat size). If going on to Costa Rica from Bocas, get the first water taxi for connections at Sixaola. It is better to travel early if you are headed to Costa Rica; a bus leaves Changuinola direct for San José at 1000. However, if you are simply going to **Puerto Viejo** or **Cahuita**, you can leave anytime before lunch. The border closes at 1700 and Costa Rica is 1 hr behind Panama.

Palanga, the car ferry, runs between **Almirante** and Bocas every day, leaving at 0900 and returning from Bocas at 1200. US$15 per car (more for large vehicles), US$1 for foot passengers.

Costa Rica immigration at the Sixaola border crossing requires you to have proof of a return flight out of the country or back to Panama and will ask to see it. Currently you can buy bus tickets at the border that are sufficient, however Costa Rica are cracking down on their '72 hour' law (you can re-enter the country after leaving for 72 hrs) and are toughening up on those foreigners who appear to be 'living' permanently in Costa Rica without official residence.

Towards Costa Rica *p1380*
Changuinola
Air To **David**, daily Mon-Fri, US$32 with Aeroperlas, T758-7521.

Bus There is a road from Changuinola to **Almirante** (buses every 30 mins till 2000, 30 mins, US$1.25). Bus to **San José** leaves Changuinola 1000 daily (no office, pay on bus) US$8, 6-7 hrs, 1 stop for refreshments in Limón, but many police checks (this bus may not always run). Bus to **David**, 4 hrs, US$7.

Boat Going to and from Costa Rica the best route is a fast water taxi along the historic Snyder Canal, a 15-km canal built in the late 1800s to transport bananas from Changuinola to awaiting ships in the open sea. Today, it's a great way to zip through the narrow canals at speed. **Bocas Marine & Tours**, T757-9033, on Calle 3 next to Le Pirate, offer routes between **Bocas–Changuinola**, US$6 each way. You avoid going through Almirante, catching a bus from Changuinola, or a taxi (US$20) to Guabito on the border with Costa Rica. If coming from Costa Rica,

get to Changuinola for a boat to Bocas (see page 1380).

Trains The banana railways provide links between **Guabito** on the Costa Rican border, Changuinola and **Almirante**. There are no passenger trains, and banana trains are incredibly slow, although passage can be negotiated with officials. Schedules and fares should be checked with the **Chiriquí Land Company**, Almirante T758-3215. Should leave for border every day.

● Directory

Isla Colón and Bocas del Toro *p1376*
Banks Banco Nacional de Panamá, Calle 4 and Av E, T757-5948, Mon-Fri 0800-1500, Sat 0900-1200, 24-hour ATM. **Immigration** Migración office, at the back of the Palacio, is for visitors arriving by air or boat. Officials are at the airport to stamp passports of those arriving nationals covered by the '*convenio*' and to provide tourist cards for others (eg US citizens arriving from Costa Rica; see page 1301). Those requiring visas must go to the Banco Nacional to purchase the relevant documentation (US$10) and then go to the office in the Palacio. This office does not renew tourist cards or visas. **Internet** Bocas Internet Café, next to the M/S Isla Colón Supermarket on main st, US$2 per hr; Don Chicho's Internet, next to El Loríto restaurant, US$2 per hr. **Bravo Centre** is fast and has an international call centre US$2 per hr. **Laundry** Lavamático, on the right, just beyond Hostal Ancón at north end of town, US$3 per load, pick up following day.

Changuinola *p1380*
Bank Bancistmo Mon-Fri 0800-1500, Sat 0900-1200, changes AMEX TCs. Cash advances on Visa and MasterCard. **Immigration** Oficina de Migración, renewal of visas and tourist cards.

Darién

➔ Colour map 8, B3.

East of Chepo, the Darién stretches out over a third of the area of Panama and is almost undeveloped. Most villages are accessible only by air, river or on foot. The Pan-American Highway ends at Yaviza; from there, if you want to cross by land to South America, it's on foot through the jungles of Darién.

As one of the great impenetrable wildernesses of the world, crossing the Darién Gap is the dream of many, but not a trip to be undertaken lightly. By all accounts good Spanish, good guides, serious planning and lots of money are essential. If you're looking for an exciting route to Colombia, the river crossings and jungle treks of the Darién are one option; alternatively, you can use sea launches and canoes to skip along the Pacific or Caribbean coastline. The overland journey is in fact more expensive than by air – and considerably more dangerous.

At the end of 1992, Panama and Colombia revealed a plan to build a road through the Darién Gap, which includes environmental protection. Construction of a previous project had been halted in the 1970s by a lawsuit filed by US environmental groups who feared deforestation, soil erosion, endangerment of indigenous groups and the threat of foot-and-mouth disease reaching the USA. Even if the plan is completed, the Darién Gap road linking Panama with Colombia will not be open for many years. ➤➤ *For listings, see page 1395.*

Towards Colombia

The Pan-American Highway runs east 60 km from Panama City to the town of **Chepo**. There are no hotels or *pensiones* here, but if you are stuck, ask at the fire station, they will be able to find a place for you. There is a document check in Chepo and at one or two other places. From Chepo the highway has been completed as far as **Yaviza** (225 km). It is gravel from Chepo until the last 30 km which are of earth (often impassable in the rainy season).

From **El Llano**, 18 km east of Chepo, a road goes north to the Caribbean coast. After 27 km it passes the **Nusagandi Nature Lodge** in the Pemansky Nature Park. The lodge is in Kuna (Cuna) territory, in an area of mostly primary forest. The coast is reached at Cartí, 20 km from Nusagandi. From here there is access to the Archipiélago de San Blas (see page 1344).

Thirty-five kilometres east of Chepo the Pan-American crosses the Lago Bayano dam by bridge (the land to the north of the highway as far as Cañazas is the **Reserva Indígena del Bayano**). Lago Bayano dam supplies a significant amount of Panama's electricity, and has been a source of friction with the Kuna people who occupy the land around the lake and especially above in the catchment area.

The main villages (Yaviza, Púcuro, Paya and Cristales) have electricity and radios; canned food (but no gasoline) is available in Yaviza, Pinogana, Unión de Chocó, Púcuro and Paya, only the Emberá-Wunan (also spelt Wunaan) of the Chocó and Kuna women retain traditional dress. Organized **jungle tours** to Kuna and Emberá-Wunan villages and the Río Bayano costing from US$65 to over US$300 can be purchased through **Extreme Tours** in Panama City. Two of the easiest villages to visit on your own are Mogue, 45 minutes upriver from La Palma (at high tide), US$10 (possible to see harpy eagles in this area) and at Puerto Lara – an hour's walk from turning off the main road just south of Santa Fe (four-person huts, US$20 per person, including meals).

The private **Punta Patiño Nature Reserve** owned by the Panamanian NGO **ANCON** is 25 km southwest of La Palma. Covering some 260 sq km, the reserve protects diverse habitats ranging from rare Pacific Dry forest through to mangroves. Punta Patiño is a good place to get a feel for the Darién and offers rewarding wildlife viewing, including 130 species of bird including the possibility of seeing a harpy eagle, and marmosets, kinkajous, tamanduas and at times, big cats. Heading back from Punta Patiño you pass the small fishing village of **Punta Alegre**, known for frequent fiestas, with a population of Colombian immigrants and Emberá tribesmen. Access within the region is by collective boat (US$3.50 to Mogué, similar to Punto Alegre). Trips can be arranged through **Ancon Expeditions**, see Panama City page 1323, T269-9415, www.anconexpeditions.com.

The bus service from Panama City (see below) has its problems: the road is bad and may be washed out after rains. Find out before you leave how far you can get. Alternatively, there is an irregular boat to Yaviza, going about once a week, US$12 including meals, leaving from the harbour by the market in the old city, information from Muelle Fiscal, Calle 13 next to the Mercado Público. The only sleeping accommodation is the deck (take a hammock) and there is one primitive toilet for about 120 people. The advertised travel time is 16 hours, but it can take as long as two days.

Yaviza/El Real
Another possibility is to fly to La Palma and take the shorter boat trip to Yaviza, or direct to El Real (three a week, US$68 return), which is about 10 km from Yaviza. There is only one hotel at **Yaviza**; there is also a TB clinic and a hospital. Crossing the river in Yaviza costs US$0.25. From Yaviza it is an easy two-hours' walk to **Pinogana** (small and primitive), where you have to cross the Río Tuira by dugout, US$1 per person. From Pinogana you can walk on, keeping the river to your left, to Vista Alegre (three hours), recross the river and walk 30 minutes to **Unión de Chocó** (some provisions and you can hammock overnight; you can sleep in the village hall but use a net to protect against *vinchucas* – Chagas disease). It's 1 km upriver to Yape, on the tributary of the same name, then three to four hours' walk to Boca de Cupe. Alternatively, you can go by motor dugout from Pinogana to Boca de Cupe (about US$65 per boat). Or take a boat from Yaviza to **El Real** (US$10), where there is a basic place to stay (**F El Nazareno**, T228-3673). Opposite there is a lady who will prepare meals if given notice. From there, take a motor dugout to Boca de Cupe, about US$15-20 per person, five hours (if possible, take a banana dugout, otherwise bargain hard on boats). A boat to Paya costs about US$35 per person for groups of four or five. Boats from El Real are infrequent and may only go to Unión de Chocó or Pinogana. A jeep track runs from El Real to Pinogana.

There are various other combinations of going on foot or by boat, prices for boat trips vary widely, so negotiate. They tend to be lower going downstream than up. It is wise to make payment always on arrival.

Boca de Cupe → *Colour map 8, B3.*
You can stay overnight at Boca de Cupe with a family. Food and cold beer is on sale here (last chance if you are going through to Colombia), and **Restaurant Nena** (blue building near landing dock) serves meals for US$2 and is a good source of information. Lodging (**D**) in Boca de Cupe with Antonio (son of María who helped many hikers crossing Darién, but who died in 1989). Don Ramón will prepare meals for US$2 and let you sleep on his floor. You can go with Emberá-Wunan people to Unión de Chocó, stay one or two days with them and share some food (they won't charge for lodging). The Emberá-Wunan are very friendly and shy, and it's best not to take pictures. In Boca de Cupe get your exit stamp (though you may be told to get it at Púcuro) and keep an eye on your luggage. From Boca de Cupe to Púcuro by dugout, US$20-50, to Paya (if river level is high enough), US$80. Boca de Cupe–Púcuro is also possible on foot.

Púcuro

Púcuro is a Kuna village and it is customary to ask the chief's permission to stay (he will ask to see your passport). Immigration here, if arriving from Colombia, can be very officious. The women wear colourful ornamented *molas* and gold rings through their noses. There is a small shop selling basic provisions, such as tinned meats and salted biscuits. Visitors usually stay in the assembly house. People show little interest in travellers. From Púcuro you can walk through lush jungle to Paya, six hours (guide costs US$20, not really necessary, do not pay in advance), which was the capital of the Kuna Empire. From Púcuro to Paya there are four river crossings. The path is clear after the first kilometre.

Paya

In Paya you may be able to stay in the assembly house at the village, but it is usual to stay 2 km away eastwards in the barracks; US$2.50 per person, recommended. There's a passport check, baggage search and, on entry into Panama at least, all gear is treated with a chemical that eats plastic and ruins leather – wash it off as soon as possible. For

Darién

US$2-2.50 you will get meals. The Kuna people in Paya are more friendly than in Púcuro. From Paya there are two routes.

Paya to Turbo

Route one From Paya, the next step is four to six hours' walk to **Palo de las Letras**, the frontier stone, where you enter Los Katíos, one of Colombia's national parks (see below). The path is not difficult, but is frequently blocked up to the border. From there you go down until you reach the left bank of the Río Tulé (three hours, no water between these points), you follow it downstream, which involves seven crossings (at the third crossing the trail almost disappears, so walk along the river bed – if possible – to the next crossing). If any of these watercourses are dry, watch out for snakes. About 30 minutes after leaving this river you cross a small creek; 45 minutes further on is the abandoned camp of the Montadero, near where the Tulé and Pailón rivers meet to form the Río Cacarica. Cross the Cacarica and follow the trail to the MA (**Ministerio del Medio Ambiente** – Colombian National Parks) abandoned rangers' hut at **Cristales** (seven hours from Palo de las Letras).

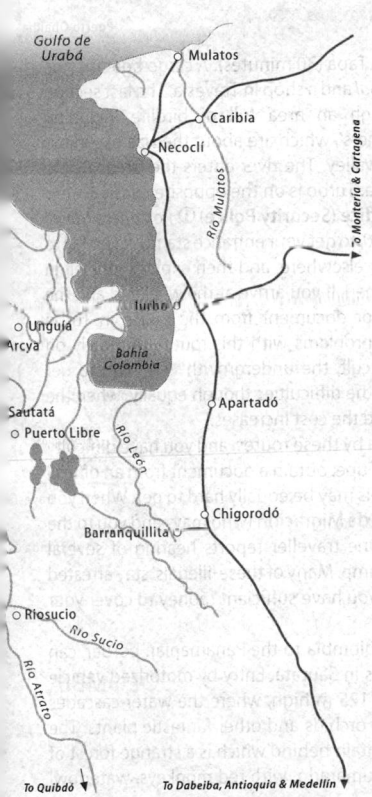

Guides from Paya to Cristales (they work in a rota and always go in pairs), charge US$55-200. They each carry a gun and a small bag of provisions and travel very fast.

If you insist on walking beyond Montadero, a machete, compass and fishing gear (or extra food) are essential. The path is so overgrown that it is easier, when the river is low, to walk and swim down it (Cristales is on the left bank, so perhaps it would be better to stick to this side). Occasional dugout will take you to **Bijao** (or Viajado), two hours, for around US$120 per boat. There is no village nearby, so arrive prepared. It is possible to walk to Bijao down the right (west) bank of the Río Cacarica (heavy going). From the bend to the east of the river the path improves and it is one hour to Bijao. At Bijao ask for the ANAM station, where you can eat and sleep (floor space, or camp). At the end of 1998 guerrillas seized Bijao, killing several people and driving out others, so it is unclear what facilities are available now.

From Bijao a motor dugout used to run to **Travesía** (also called Puerto América) for US$40 per person (two to five hours), from where motorboats go to Turbo for US$10 (in scheduled boat – if it stops; if not it'll cost you about US$250 to hire a boat). Travesía has some accommodation and provisions but has been reported as expensive and anti-gringo. Once again, there is a walking

The harpy eagle

The wildest and most remote forests of Panama still play host to one of Latin America's most magnificent predator, the harpy eagle (*harpia harpyja*). Standing 1 m tall and with 5-cm talons that rival the claws of a grizzly bear, the harpy is the world's most powerful bird of prey. In comparison to its huge body size, the eagle's wingspan (around 2.1 m) is not large, an adaptation that allows it to glide between the trees with exceptional stealth and agility, searching for its favoured prey of monkeys and sloths.

Harpy eagles need huge territories with good wildlife populations in order to survive. Massive deforestation in Panama and elsewhere in Latin America has resulted in its disappearance from vast swathes of its former habitat. Due to its rarity, and the fact that the harpy does not often soar, this bird is tough to track down. But Panama is perhaps the harpy's greatest stronghold in Central America, and several nest sites have been identified in the Darién and Canal areas. Agencies in Panama City can arrange trips to these nest sites.

route south to Limón (two hours) and east to La Tapa (30 minutes). A cargo boat may be caught from here to Turbo. There is one *residencial* and a shop in Travesía. The last section from Travesía down the Atrato goes through an area full of birdlife including hummingbirds, kingfishers, herons, and 'screamers', which are about the size of turkeys and are believed to be endemic to the Atrato valley. The river enters the Great Atrato swamp and from there to the Bahía de Colombia. Turbo is on the opposite coast.

On arrival in Turbo, you must go to the **DAS office (Security Police)** ① *Postadero Naval, north along Carrera 13 near airport, open 0800-1630*, to get your entrance stamp. If you fail to do this, you will have to wait until Cartagena, or elsewhere, and then explain yourself in great detail to DAS and quite likely you will be fined. If you arrive at the weekend and the DAS is closed, make sure you obtain a letter or document from the police in Turbo that states when you arrived in Colombia. The problems with this route are mostly on the Colombian side, where route finding is difficult, the undergrowth very hard to get through, and the terrain steep. Any rain adds to the difficulties though equally, when the water is low, boats need more pole assistance and the cost increases.

If you are coming into Panama from Colombia by these routes, and you have difficulty in obtaining entry stamps at Púcuro or Boca de Cupe, obtain a document from an official en route stating when you arrived in Panama. This may be equally hard to get. When you arrive in Panama City, go to the **Oficina Nacional de Migración** (who may send you to the port immigration) and explain the problem. One traveller reports hearing of several arrests of travellers caught without their entry stamp. Many of these 'illegals' stay arrested for weeks. It may help to be able to prove that you have sufficient money to cover your stay in Panama.

The **Parque Nacional Katios**, extending in Colombia to the Panamanian border, can be visited with mules from the MA headquarters in Sautatá. Entry by motorized vehicle is prohibited. Look out for the Tilupo waterfall, 125 m high, where the water cascades down a series of rock staircases, surrounded by orchids and other fantastic plants. The Alto de la Guillermina is also in the park, a mountain behind which is a strange forest of palms called 'mil pesos', and the Ciénagas de Tumaradó, with red monkeys, waterfowl and alligators.

Cautions and notes on crossing the Darién Gap

When planning your trip by land or along the coast to Colombia, remember there are strict rules on entry into Colombia and you must aim for either Turbo or Buenaventura to obtain your entry stamp. Failure to do this will almost certainly involve you in significant fines, accusations of illegal entry, or worse in Colombia. Do not enter Darién without full details of which areas to avoid because of the activities of drug traffickers, bandits and guerrilla groups, mostly from Colombia, but operating on both sides of the border.

The best time to go is in the dry months (January to mid-April); the trip would be considerably harder in the wet season (May to December). Even when totally covered in mosquito repellent you will get bitten and run the risk of contracting dengue fever. Travel with a reliable companion or two. Talk to knowledgeable locals for the best advice. Hire at least one indigenous guide, but do it through the village *corregidor*, whose involvement may add to the reliability of the selected guides. (Budget up to US$10 per day for the guide and his food. Negotiate with the chief, but do not begrudge the cost.) Travel light and move fast. The journeys described here takes about seven days to Turbo.

Route two The second route is a strenuous hike up the Río Paya valley through dense jungle (machete country) for about 16 hours to the last point on the Paya (fill up with water), then a further three hours to the continental divide where you cross into Colombia. Down through easier country (three to four hours) brings you to **Unguía** where motor boats are available to take you down the Río Tarena, out into the Gulf of Urabá, across to Turbo. This trip should not be taken without a guide, though you may be lucky and find some local people making the journey and willing to take you along. They will appreciate a gift when you arrive in Unguía. Hazards include blood-sucking ticks, the inevitable mosquitoes and, if those weren't enough, thirst.

There are many other possible routes from Panama crossing the land border used by locals. Most involve river systems and are affected by water levels. There are few tracks and no reliable maps. We have heard of successful crossings using the Salaqui and Balsas rivers, and a land route Jaqué–Jurado–Río Sucio. Good Spanish and guides, serious planning and money are essential. See below for sea routes.

By sea: the Caribbean route via Puerto Obaldía

Boats leave, irregularly, from the Coco Solo wharf in Colón (minibus from Calle 12, 15 minutes, US$0.80, taxi US$4) for Puerto Obaldía, via the San Blas Islands. These are small boats and give a rough ride in bad weather, cost around US$30 per person, take your own food, water and shade; with stops, the journey takes two to four days. There are flights with **Ansa** ① *T226-7891/6881*, and **Transpasa** ① *T226-0932/0843*, at 0600-0630 from Panama City to Puerto Obaldía, daily except Sunday for US$44 single (book well in advance). There are also flights with **Aerotaxi**. Puerto Obaldía is a few kilometres from the Colombian border. Arriving in Puerto Obaldía you have to pass through the military control for baggage search, immigration (proof of funds and onward ticket asked for) and malaria control. In Puerto Obaldía there are shops, **Colombian Consulate**, **Panamanian Immigration**, but nowhere to change traveller's cheques until well into Colombia (not

Turbo); changing cash is possible. There are *expresos* (speedboats) from Puerto Obaldía (after clearing Customs) to Capurganá, and then another on to **Acandí** (**F Hotel Central**, clean, safe; **F Hotel Pilar**, safe). From Acandí you can go on to Turbo, on the Gulf of Urabá, no fixed schedule (you cannot get to Turbo in the same day; take shade and drinks and be prepared for seasickness). Medellín can be reached by road from Turbo. Walk from Puerto Obaldía to Zapzurro, just beyond the border, for a dugout to Turbo, US$15, where you must get your Colombia entry stamp. It seems that most vessels leaving Puerto Obaldía for Colombian ports are contraband boats. As in other parts of Darién seek security advice.

Capurganá (Colombia)
Alternatively, you can get from Puerto Obaldía to Acandí on the Colombian side of the border, either by walking for nine hours or by hiring a dugout or a launch to Capurganá (US$8), and then another launch, which takes one hour and costs US$3. The snorkelling is good in Capurganá. There is a Panamanian consul (Roberto) who issues visas for Panama. There are **Twin Otter** flights to Medellín. To walk to Capurganá from Puerto Oaldía takes four hours, guide recommended (they charge US$10); first go to **La Miel** (two hours), then to **Zapzurro** (20 minutes), where there are shops and cabins for rent, then an hour to 90 minutes to Capurganá. Most of the time the path follows the coast, but there are some hills to cross (it's hot; take drinking water). From Acandí a daily boat is scheduled to go at 0800 to Turbo (US$15, three hours). Take pesos, if possible, to these Colombian places, the rate of exchange for dollars is poor.

The Pacific route
Although not quick, the Pacific coastline provides another relatively straightforward route across the Darién (Spanish is essential). Take a bus from Panama City (Plaza 5 de Mayo) to **Metetí** (**D-E Hospedaje Feliz**, basic 'box' rooms), 50 km from Yaviza, the junction for transport to **Puerto Quimba**, where boats can be taken to La Palma. Alternatively, take a bus to **Santa Fe**, which is 75 km short of Yaviza and off to the south, a rough but scenic six to eight hours (US$8, three a day, check times). In Santa Fe it is possible to camp near the police post. Then hitch a ride on a truck (scarce), or walk two hours to the Río Sabanas at Puerto Larda (11 km) where you must take a dugout or launch to La Palma, or hire one (US$5, two hours). **La Palma** is also reached by boat from Yaviza (US$3, eight hours). It is the capital of Darién – you can change cash and traveller's cheques – has one *pensión* (**F**, friendly, English-speaking owners, with cooking and laundry facilities), or see if you can stay with the *guardia*). **Jaqué** is on the Pacific coast, near Puerto Piña, 50 km north of the Colombian border (one hotel). **Bahía Piña** has a runway, used mainly by the expensive fishing resort. If you want to stay in the area, there are a range of options provided as part of the **Darién Paradise Trail** ① *T226-7000, www.darientrail.tripod.com*, a community-based ecotourism circuit with accommodation in Santa Fe, Boca Lara, La Palma, Sambu, Meteti-Canglón and Ipeti Embera. Hotels tend to be in the **E** category.

These isolated settlements on the Pacific coast are close to the **Parque Nacional Darién**, Panama's largest and wildest protected area. Cana and Cerro Pirre are at its heart but at present it is not advisable to visit because of the various armed bands that use the jungle as cover. From **Jaqué** you can catch a launch to **Jurado** in Colombia (US$25, four 'murderous' hours, take something to sit on). The launch continues to **Bahía Solano** or there are weekly cargo boats to Buenaventura (**M/N Fronteras** US$45 including food, 36 hours, bunks but OK), where there is a DAS office where you can sort out your paperwork.

Alternatively, at the Muelle Fiscal in Panama City (by the main waterfront market, near Calle 13), ask for a passenger boat going to Jaqué. The journey takes 18 hours, is cramped and passengers cook food themselves, but costs only US$12. Jaqué is only reached by sea or air (the airstrip is used mostly by wealthy visitors going sports fishing); there are small stores, a good *comedor*, and one *hospedaje*.

The guard post is open every day and gives exit stamps. Canoes from Jaqué go to Juradó (US$20, 4½ hours) or Bahía Solano (US$45, 160 km, with two overnight stops) in Chocó. The first night is in Jurado. There are flights from Jurado to Turbo, but you can get stuck in Jurado for several days. Bahía Solano is a deep-sea fishing resort with an airport and *residencias*. Flights from Bahía Solano go to Quibdó, connecting to Cali, or Medellín (book flights in advance; the town is popular with Colombian tourists). On this journey, you sail past the lush, mountainous Pacific coast of Darién and Chocó, with its beautiful coves and beaches, and you will see a variety of marine life.

ⓓ Darién listings

For Sleeping and Eating price codes and other relevant information, see Essentials pages 45-48.

E Guacamaya, Santa Fe, T299-6727.
F Chavela, Jaqué, clean, basic, friendly.

ⓢ Sleeping

Yavisa/El Real *p1389*
E Tres Américas, pay in Casa Indira shop next door. Take mosquito coils – there isn't anywhere to hang a net – basic, but friendly.

Paya to Turbo *p1391*
F Doña Julia, Unguia. With bath.
F Residencias Viajero, Unguia. With bath.

Puerto Obaldía *p1393*
E Residencia Cande. A good *pensión*, nice and clean, which also serves very good meals for US$1.50, order meals in advance.

Capurganá (Columbia) *p1394*
Several hotels including **B** Calypso, **D** Náutico, **E** Al Mar, and **E** Uvita. Also *pensiones*, or you can camp by the beach.

The Pacific route *p1394*
It is easy to find accommodation with local families and camping is possible on the beach.
LL Cana Field Station, Cana, T269-9415 (Panama City), www.anconexpeditions.com. Mainly used by groups and ornithologists for set trips.

ⓣ Transport

Towards Columbia *p1388*
Bus From bus terminal in Panama City, buses leave every 2 hrs 0630-1430 for **Pacora**, US$0.80, **Chepo**, US$1.60, **Cañitas**, 4 hrs, US$3.10, **Arretí**, 6 hrs, US$9, **Metetí** and **Canglón**, 8 hrs, US$11.20. Beyond, to **Yaviza**, in the dry season only (Jan-Apr), US$15, 10 hrs minimum. Plenty of pickups run on the last stretch to Yaviza, eg about 3 hrs from Metetí to Yaviza.

The Pacific route *p1394*
Air and boat There are 2 daily Aeroperlas flights from Panama City to **La Palma**, US$40, and 1 a day to **Jaqué** on the Pacific shore, US$49; also to **Yaviza** 3 days a week, but check with the airline Parsa, T226-3883. They have an office at the domestic airport in Panama City. If you cannot get a plane from **La Palma** to **Jaqué**, there are boats, US$15. En route there is an Ancon Lodge at Punta Patino. Details from **Ancon Expediciones** in Panama City, page 1323.

Contents

Background

Regional history

Arrival of the American people

While controversy continues to surround the precise date humans arrived in the Americas, the current prevailing view suggests the first wave of emigrants travelled across the Bering Strait ice bridge created in the last Ice Age between Siberia and Alaska approximately 15,000 years ago. Small groups of peoples quickly moved through the region as the migratory lifestyle of the hunter-gatherer explored the Americas. In fertile lands the development of farming and the reduced reliance on hunting and migrating encouraged groups to settle. By 1500 BC, villages were developing and growing in many parts of the Americas including Mesoamerica.

Pre-Columbian civilizations

The **Aztec** Empire that Spanish conqueror Hernán Cortés encountered in 1519 and subsequently destroyed was the third major power to have dominated what is now known as Mexico. Before it, the empires of **Teotihuacán** and **Tula** each unified what had essentially been an area of separate indigenous groups. All three, together with their neighbours such as the Maya (see page 1400) and their predecessors, belong to a more or less common culture called **Mesoamerica**. Despite the wide variety of climates and terrains that fall within Mesoamerica's boundaries, from the deserts of northern Mexico to El Salvador and Honduras, the civilizations that developed were interdependent, sharing the same agriculture (based on maize, beans and squash) and many sociological features. They also shared an enormous pantheon (in which the god of rain and the feathered serpent-hero were predominant); the offering of blood to the gods, from oneself and from sacrificial victims usually taken in war; pyramid-building; a game played with a rubber ball; trade in feathers, jade and other valuable objects, possibly from as far away as the Andean region of South America; hieroglyphic writing; astronomy; and an elaborate calendar.

The **Mesoamerican Calendar** was a combination of a 260-day almanac year and the 365-day solar year. A given day in one of the years would only coincide with that in the other every 52 years, a cycle called the **Calendar Round**. In order to give the Calendar Round a context within a larger timescale, a starting date for both years was devised; the date chosen by the Classic Maya was equivalent to 3113 BC in Christian time. Dates measured from this point are called Long Count dates. Historians divide Mesoamerican civilizations into three periods, the **pre-Classic**, which lasted until about AD 300, the **Classic**, until AD 900, and the **post-Classic**, from 900 until the Spanish conquest. An alternative delineation is: Olmec, Teotihuacán and Aztec, named after the dominant civilizations within each of those periods.

Olmecs

Who precisely the Olmecs were, where they came from and why they disappeared is a matter of debate. It is known that they flourished from about **1400-400 BC**, that they lived in the **Mexican Gulf coast** region between Veracruz and Tabasco, and that all later civilizations have their roots ultimately in Olmec culture. They carved **colossal heads**, stelae (tall, flat monuments), jade figures and altars; they gave great importance to the jaguar and the serpent in their imagery; they built large ceremonial centres such as **San Lorenzo** and **La Venta**. Possibly derived from the Olmecs and gaining importance in the first millennium BC was the centre in the Valley of Oaxaca at **Monte Albán**. This was a major city, with certain changes of influence, right through until the end of the Classic period. Also derived from the Olmecs was the **Izapa** civilization, on the Pacific border of present-day Mexico and Guatemala. The progression from the Olmec to the Maya civilization seems to have taken place here with obvious connections in artistic style, calendar use, ceremonial architecture and the transformation of the Izapa long-lipped god into the Maya long-nosed god.

Teotihuacán

Almost as much mystery surrounds the origins of Teotihuacán as those of the Olmecs. Teotihuacán, '**the place where men become gods**', was a great urban state, holding in its power most of the **Central Highlands** of Mexico. Its influence can be detected in the Maya area, Oaxaca and the civilizations on the Gulf coast that succeeded the Olmecs. The monumental pyramids in the city itself, which still stands beyond the northern outskirts of Mexico City, are enormous, the planning precise; it is estimated that by the seventh century AD some 125,000 people were living in its immediate vicinity. Early evidence did not suggest Teotihuacán's power was gained by force, but research indicates both **human sacrifice** and **sacred warfare** took place. For reasons unknown, Teotihuacán's influence over its neighbours ended around 600 AD. Its glory coincided with that of the Classic Maya, but the latter's decline occurred some 300 years later, at which time a major change affected all Mesoamerica.

Toltecs

The start of the post-Classic period, between the Teotihuacán and Aztec horizons, was marked by an upsurge in militarism. In the semi-deserts to the north of the settled societies of central Mexico and Veracruz lived groups of nomadic hunters. These people, who were given the general name of **Chichimecs**, began to invade the central region and were quick to adopt the urban characteristics of the groups they overthrew. The **Toltecs** of **Tula** were one such invading force, rapidly building up an empire stretching from the Gulf of Mexico to the Pacific in central Mexico. Infighting by factions within the Toltecs split the rulers and probably hastened the empire's demise sometime after 1150. The exiled leader **Topíltzin Quetzalcóatl** (Feathered Serpent) is possibly the founder of the Maya-Toltec rule in the Yucatán (the Maya spoke of a Mexican invader named Kukulcán – Feathered Serpent). He is certainly the mythical figure the Aztec ruler, Moctezuma II, took Cortés to be, returning by sea from the east.

Zapotecs and Mixtecs

Another important culture to develop in the first millennium AD was the Mixtec, in western Oaxaca, southern Mexico. The Mixtecs infiltrated all the territory held by the Zapotecs, who had ruled Monte Albán during the Classic period and had built many other sites in the Valley of Oaxaca, including Mitla. The Mixtecs, in alliance with the Zapotecs, successfully withstood invasion by the Aztecs.

Aztecs

The process of transition from semi-nomadic hunter-gathering to city and empire-building continued with the **Aztecs**, who bludgeoned their way into the midst of rival city states in

Central America and Mexico in figures

	Population	Area (sq km)	People (per sq km)
Mexico	105,300,000	1,958,000	54
Guatemala	13,300,000	108,900	122
Belize	300,000	23,000	13
El Salvador	6,900,000	21,000	329
Honduras	7,10,000	112,100	63
Nicaragua	5,60,000	130,000	43
Costa Rica	4,400,000	51,100	88
Panama	3,300,000	75,500	44
Comparison figures			
UK	61,000,000	243,600	250
EU	318,700,000	2,536,100	126
USA	301,600,000	9,632,000	31
Australia	21,000,000	7,741,200	3

Source: World Development Indicators 2007

the vacuum left by the destruction of Tula around 1150. They rose from practically nothing to achieve power almost as great as Teotihuacán in about 200 years. From their base at **Tenochtitlán in Lake Texcoco** in the Valley of Mexico they aggressively extended their sphere of influence from the Tarascan Kingdom in the north to the Maya lands in the south. Not only did the conquered pay heavy tribute to their Aztec overlords, but they also supplied the flow of **sacrificial victims** needed to satisfy the deities, at whose head was **Huitzilopochtli**, the warrior god of the Sun. The speed with which the Aztecs adapted to a settled existence and fashioned an effective political state is remarkable. Their ability in sculpting stone, in pottery, in writing books, and in architecture (from what we can gather from what the Spaniards did not destroy) was great. Surrounding all this activity was a strictly ritual existence, with ceremonies and feasts dictated by the two enmeshing calendars. It is impossible to say whether the Aztec Empire would have gone the way of its predecessors had the Spaniards not arrived to precipitate its collapse. Undoubtedly, the Europeans received much assistance from people who had been oppressed by the Aztecs and wished to be rid of them. Within two years Cortés, with his horses, an array of military equipment and relatively few soldiers, brought to an end an extraordinary culture.

Maya
The best known of the pre-Conquest indigenous civilizations of the present Central American area was the Maya, thought to have evolved in a formative period in the **Pacific highlands** of Guatemala and El Salvador between **1500 BC** and about **AD 100**. After 200 years of growth it entered what is known today as its Classic period when the civilization flourished in Guatemala, El Salvador, Belize, Honduras and Southern Mexico (Chiapas, Campeche and Yucatán). The Maya civilization was based on independent and antagonistic city states, including Tikal, Uaxactún, Kaminaljuyú, Iximché, Zaculeu and Quiriguá in Guatemala; Copán in Honduras; Altún Ha, Caracol and Lamanai in Belize; Tazumal and San

Population growth	Life expectancy (years)	GNI (US$ per capita)	GDP (US$billion)
1%	74	8340	893.40
2.4%	70	2440	33.40
2.1%	72	3800	1.30
1.3%	72	2850	20.20
1.7%	70	1600	12.60
1.3%	72	980	5.70
1.4%	79	5560	25.20
1.6%	75	5510	19.70
0.7%	79	42,740	2727.80
0.6%	80	36,329	12,179.30
0.7%	78	46,040	13,811.20
1.5%	81	35,960	821.70

Andrés in El Salvador; and Palenque and Bonampak (both in Chiapas), Chichén Itzá, Uxmal, Mayapán, Tulum, Cobá and the Puuc cities of Sayil, Labná and Kabah (all on the Yucatán Peninsula) in Mexico. Recent research has revealed that these cities, far from being the peaceful ceremonial centres once imagined, were warring adversaries, striving to capture victims for sacrifice. Furthermore, much of the cultural activity, controlled by a theocratic minority of priests and nobles, involved blood-letting, by even the highest members of society. Royal blood was the most precious offering that could be made to the gods. This change in perception of the Maya was the result of the discovery of defended cities and of a greater understanding of the Maya's hieroglyphic writing. Although John Lloyd Stephens' prophecy that "a key surer than that of the Rosetta stone will be discovered" has not yet been fulfilled, the painstaking decipherment of the glyphs has uncovered many secrets of Maya society (see Breaking the Maya Code by Michael D Coe, Thames and Hudson).

Alongside the preoccupation with blood was an artistic tradition rich in ceremony, folklore and dance. The Maya achieved paper codices and glyphic writing, which also appears on stone monuments and their fine ceramics; they were skilful weavers and traded over wide areas, though they did not use the wheel and had no beasts of burden. The cities were all meticulously dated. Maya art is a mathematical art: each column, figure, face, animal, frieze, stairway and temple expresses a date or a time relationship. When, for example, an ornament on the ramp of the Hieroglyphic Stairway at Copán was repeated some 15 times, it was to express that number of elapsed 'leap' years. The 75 steps stand for the number of elapsed intercalary days. The Maya calendar was a nearer approximation to sidereal time than either the Julian or the Gregorian calendars of Europe; it was only .000069 of a day out of true in a year. They used the zero centuries in advance of the Old World, plotted the movements of the sun, moon, Venus and other planets, and conceived a cycle of more than 1800 million days.

Their tools and weapons were flint and hard stone, obsidian and fire-hardened wood, and yet with these they hewed out and transported great monoliths over miles of difficult country, and carved them over with intricate glyphs and figures that would be difficult enough with modern chisels. Also with those tools they cultivated lavish crops. To support urban populations now believed to number tens of thousands, and a population density of 150 per sq km (compared with less than one per sq km today), an agricultural system was developed of raised fields, fertilized by fish and vegetable matter from surrounding canals.

The height of the Classic period lasted until AD 900-1000, after which the Maya concentrated into Yucatán after a successful invasion of their other lands by non-Maya people (this is only one theory; another is that they were forced to flee due to drought and a peasant rebellion). They then came under the influence of the Toltecs who invaded Yucatán (Chichén Itzá is seen as an example of a Maya city that displays many Toltec features). From then on their culture declined. The Toltecs gradually spread their empire as far as the southern borders of Guatemala. They in turn were conquered by the Aztecs, who did not penetrate Central America.

Conquest

It was only during his fourth voyage, in 1502, that **Columbus** reached the mainland of Central America; he landed in **Costa Rica** and **Panama**, which he called **Veragua**, and founded the town of Santa María de Belén. In 1508 Alonso de Ojeda received a grant of land on the Pearl coast east of Panama, and in 1509 he founded the town of San Sebastián, later moved to a new site called Santa María la Antigua del Darién (now in Colombia). In 1513 the governor of the colony at Darién was **Vasco Núñez de Balboa**. Taking 190 men he crossed the isthmus in 18 days and caught the first glimpse of the Pacific; he claimed it and all neighbouring lands in the name of the King of Spain. But from the following year, when Pedrarias de Avila replaced him as Governor, Núñez de Balboa fell on evil days, and he was executed by Pedrarias in 1519. That same year Pedrarias crossed the isthmus and founded the town of Panamá on the Pacific side. It was in April 1519, too, that **Cortés** began his conquest of Mexico. Central America was explored from these two nodal points of Panama and Mexico. By 1525 Cortés' lieutenant, **Pedro de Alvarado**, had conquered as far south as San Salvador. Meanwhile Pedrarias was sending forces into Panama and Costa Rica (the latter was abandoned due to the hostile natives, but was finally colonized from Mexico City when the rest of Central America had been taken). In 1522-1524, Andrés Niño and Gil González Dávila invaded **Nicaragua** and **Honduras**. Many towns were founded by these forces from Panama. Spanish forces from the north and south sometimes met and fought bitterly. At this time the gentle **Bartolomé de las Casas**, the 'apostle of the Indies', was active as a Dominican missionary in Central America in the 1530s.

Settlement

The groups of Spanish settlers were few and widely scattered, a fundamental point in explaining the **political fragmentation** of Central America today. Panama was ruled from Bogotá, but the rest of Central America was subordinate to the Viceroyalty at Mexico City, with Antigua, Guatemala, as an Audiencia for the area until 1773, and thereafter Guatemala City. Panama was of paramount importance for colonial Spanish America for its strategic position, and for the trade passing across the isthmus to and from the southern colonies. The other provinces were of comparatively little value.

The small number of **Spaniards intermarried** freely with the locals, accounting for the predominance of mestizos in present-day Central America. But the picture has regional variations. In Guatemala, where there was the highest native population density, intermarriage affected fewer of the natives, and over half the population today is still purely *indígena* (**indigenous**). On the Meseta Central of Costa Rica, the natives were all but wiped out by disease and, as a consequence of this great disaster, there is a community of over two million whites, with little *indígena* admixture, in the highlands. **Blacks** predominate along the Caribbean coast of Central America. Most were brought in as cheap labour to work as railway builders and banana planters in the 19th century and canal cutters in the 20th. The **Garífuna** people, living from southern Belize to Nicaragua, arrived in the area as free people after African slaves and indigenous Caribbean people intermingled following a shipwreck off St Vincent.

Independence and after

On 5 November 1811, **José Matías Delgado**, a priest and jurist born in San Salvador, organized a revolt with another priest, Manuel José Arce. They proclaimed the independence of El Salvador, but the Audiencia at Guatemala City suppressed the revolt and took Delgado prisoner.

It was the revolution of 1820 in Spain itself that precipitated the independence of Central America. When on 24 February 1821, the Mexican **General Agustín de Iturbide** announced his *Plan de Iguala* for an independent Mexico, the Central American *criollos* decided to follow his example, and a **declaration of independence**, drafted by José Cecilio del Valle, was announced in Guatemala City on 15 September 1821. Iturbide invited the provinces of Central America to join with him and, on 5 January 1822, Central America was declared annexed to Mexico. Delgado refused to accept this decree and Iturbide, who had now assumed the title of **Emperor Agustín I**, sent an army south under Vicente Filísola to enforce it in the regions under Delgado's influence. Filísola had completed his task when he heard of Iturbide's abdication, and at once convened a general congress of the Central American provinces. It met on 24 June 1823, and established the **Provincias Unidas del Centro de América**. The Mexican Republic acknowledged their independence on 1 August 1824, and Filísola's soldiers were withdrawn.

The congress, presided over by Delgado, appointed a provisional governing *junta* that promulgated a constitution modelled on that of the United States in November 1824. The Province of Chiapas was not included in the Federation, as it had already adhered to Mexico in 1821. Guatemala City, by force of tradition, soon became the seat of government.

The first President under the new constitution was **Manuel José Arce**, a liberal. One of his first acts was to **abolish slavery**. El Salvador, protesting that he had exceeded his powers, rose in December 1826. Honduras, Nicaragua and Costa Rica joined the revolt, and in 1828 **General Francisco Morazán**, in charge of the army of Honduras, defeated the federal forces, entered San Salvador and marched against Guatemala City. He captured the city on 13 April 1829, and established that contradiction in terms: a liberal dictatorship. Many conservative leaders were expelled and church and monastic properties confiscated. Morazán himself became President of the Federation in 1830. He was a man of considerable ability; he encouraged education, fostered trade and industry, opened the country to immigrants, and reorganized the administration. In 1835 the capital was moved to San Salvador.

These reforms antagonized the conservatives and there were several uprisings. The most serious revolt was among the *indígenas* of Guatemala, led by Rafael Carrera, an illiterate mestizo conservative and a born leader. Years of continuous warfare followed, during the course of which the Federation withered away. As a result, the federal congress passed an act that allowed each province to assume the government it chose, but the idea of a federation was not quite dead. Morazán became President of El Salvador. Carrera, who was by then in control of Guatemala, defeated Morazán in battle and forced him to leave the country. But in 1842, Morazán overthrew Braulio Carrillo, then dictator of Costa Rica, and became president himself. At once he set about rebuilding the Federation, but was defeated by the united forces of the other states and was shot on 15 September 1842. With him perished any practical hope of Central American political union.

The separate states

The history of **Guatemala**, **El Salvador**, **Honduras** and **Nicaragua** since the breakdown of federation has been tempestuous in the extreme (**Costa Rica**, with its mainly white population and limited economic value at the time, is a country apart, and **Panama** was Colombian territory until 1903). In each the ruling class was divided into pro-clerical conservatives and anti-clerical liberals, with constant changes of power. Each was weak, and tried repeatedly to buttress its weakness by alliances with others, which invariably broke up because one of the allies sought a position of mastery. The wars were mainly ideological wars between conservatives and liberals, or wars motivated by inflamed nationalism. Nicaragua was riven internally by the mutual hatreds of the Conservatives of Granada and the Liberals of León, and there were repeated conflicts between the Caribbean and interior parts of Honduras.

Of the four republics, **Guatemala** was the strongest and in some ways the most stable. While the other states were skittling their presidents like ninepins, Guatemala had a succession of strong dictators: Rafael Carrera (1844-1865), Justo Rufino Barrios (1873-1885), Manuel Cabrera (1898-1920), and Jorge Ubico (1931-1944). These were separated by intervals of constitutional government, anarchy, or attempts at dictatorship that failed. (Few presidents handed over power voluntarily, most were forcibly removed or assassinated.)

Despite the permutations and combinations of external and civil war there was a recurrent desire to re-establish some form of *La Gran Patria Centroamericana*. Throughout the 19th century, and far into the 20th, there were ambitious projects for political federation, usually involving El Salvador, Honduras and Nicaragua; none of them lasted more than a few years.

Regional integration

Poverty, the fate of the great majority, has brought about closer economic cooperation between the five republics, and in 1960 they established the **Central American Common Market** (CACM). Surprisingly, the Common Market appeared to be a great success until 1968, when integration fostered national antagonisms, and there was a growing conviction in Honduras and Nicaragua, which were doing least well out of integration, that they were being exploited by the others. In 1969 the 'Football War' broke out between El Salvador and Honduras, basically because of a dispute about illicit emigration by Salvadoreans into Honduras, and relations between the two were not normalized until 1980. Hopes for improvement were revived in 1987 when the Central American Peace Plan, drawn up by President Oscar Arias Sánchez of Costa Rica, was signed by the Presidents of Guatemala, El Salvador, Honduras, Nicaragua and Costa Rica. The plan proposed formulae to end the civil strife in individual countries, achieving this aim first in

Nicaragua (1989), then in El Salvador (1991). In Guatemala, a ceasefire after 36 years of war led to the signing of a peace accord at the end of 1996. With the signing of peace accords, emphasis has shifted to regional, economic and environmental integration.

In October 1993, the presidents of Guatemala, El Salvador, Honduras, Nicaragua and Costa Rica signed a new **Central American Integration Treaty Protocol**, to replace that of 1960 and set up new mechanisms for regional integration. The Treaty was the culmination of a series of annual presidential summits held since 1986 which, besides aiming for peace and economic integration, established a Central American Parliament and a Central American Court of Justice.

Attempts at further economic and regional integration continue. Plans to create the a **Free Trade Area of the Americas** (FTAA) by 2005 (agreed in Monterrey, in January 2004), stalled. The **Central American Free Trade Agreement** (CAFTA) was signed by El Salvador, Guatemala, Honduras and Nicaragua in 2003. After protracted debate, Costa Rica agreed to sign up to join in October 2007. The Trade Agreement went into effect on 1 March 2006 for El Salvador following completion of all necessary steps, including delivery of signed Treaty copies to the OAS, which was the final step. Honduras, Nicaragua and Guatemala all signed in 2006. Costa Rica still has to pass several acts of legislation to meet the requirements. This Central American regional integration supports the wider **Plan Puebla-Panama**, the development of an economic corridor stretching from Puebla, west of Mexico City, as far as Panama. Supporters of the plan see it as a means for economic development. Critics – of which there are many in each Central American nation, as well as Mexico and the United States – see it as a way of draining cheap labour resources with little concern for environmental concerns and long-term progress.

While the Plan Puebla may continue to simmer on the back burner, the desire for Central American nations to strengthen ties is regularly voiced. This is most apparent in the creation of the Central America 4 (CA-4), a 2006 border control agreement between Guatemala, El Salvador, Honduras and Nicaragua, that opens up travel between the four nations.

Regional meetings occur periodically to promote and encourage trust and cooperation, and while the final destination of such cooperation is far from clear, the Central America of today is far more productive and safer than it was in the 1980s and early 1990s.

Wildlife

Mexico alone has over 430 mammal species, more than 960 different birds, around 720 reptiles and almost 300 amphibians and as for insects, definitely more than you want to know about, from beautiful butterflies to biting bugs. Even the smallest country in the area, El Salvador, which has little natural habitat remaining, can boast a total of 680 species of vertebrates, the UK has just 280 or so. This diversity is due to the fact that the area is the meeting place of two of the world's major biological regions – the Nearctic to the north and the Neotropical to the south. It has a remarkable geological and climatic complexity and consequently an enormous range of habitats, from desert in the north of Mexico to rainforests, dry forests, cloud forests, mangroves and stretches of wetlands further south in the tropical areas of the region.

When to go?

In terms of wildlife, the best time to visit depends, obviously, on where you are and what you want to see. For instance, if its whale watching you want off Baja California, then go between mid December and mid-March, but if it's the sight of hundreds of thousands of migrating raptors passing over Central America then it will have to be between August and December, or the spectacular mass of Monarch butterflies in the Reserva Ecológica El Campanario, just west of Mexico City, are best visited in January or February. Likewise, the sight of nesting turtles from Mexico to Panama requires planning to get the timing right.

Spotting wildlife

Use local, **experienced guides** as these people will know what species are around and where to look for them and will often recognize bird calls and use these as an aid to spotting them. You should take **binoculars**; get a pair with a reasonable magnification and good light-gathering configurations (ie 10x40 or 8x40) for use in the dim light of the rainforests. They will also need to be reasonably waterproof. Another enormous aid to wildlife watching is a strong torch or, better still, a powerful **headlamp**. The latter not only leaves your hands free but it also helps when trying to spot eye shine of nocturnal mammals, the light reflected back from their eyes direct to yours. Some places, such as Monteverde Cloud Forest Reserve in Costa Rica and the Community Baboon Sanctuary in Belize, offer excellent night walks with guides, but with care you can equally well arrange your own. Another strategy to use is to select a likely looking spot – such as a fruiting fig or a watering hole (in dry country) – and wait for the animals to come to you.

Mammals

In Central America and Mexico mammals tend to be secretive, indeed the majority are nocturnal; hence the need for night walks if you are serious about finding them, though, even then, good views are comparatively rare. That said, you will certainly see some delightful creatures, with views of primates being more or less guaranteed. The rainforests throughout the region contain **spider monkeys**, **howler monkeys** and/or **capuchin monkeys**. The howlers are probably the most noticeable because, as their name suggests, they are inclined to make a huge row at times, especially early in the mornings and in the late afternoons. The **Community Baboon Sanctuary** in **Belize** was set up especially for the conservation of the black howler monkey and you've a good chance of seeing them in **Tikal, Guatemala**, in **Parque Nacional Pico Bonito** in **Honduras**, on the **Omotepe Islands** in **Nicaragua** and the rainforests of **Costa Rica**. The **spider monkey** is a much more agile, slender primate, swinging around high in the canopy, using its prehensile tail as a fifth limb and again found throughout the region. The smaller, white-throated **capuchins** are also commonly seen, moving around quite noisily in groups, searching for fruit and insects in the trees and even coming down to the ground to find food. Smaller again, and restricted to **Panama** and **Costa Rica**, is the red-backed squirrel monkey. The most likely places to see them are **Parques Nacionales Corcovado** and **Manuel Antonio** in **Costa Rica**. Finally, for the daytime species, you may see a **tamarin**, both Geoffroy's and the cotton-top tamarin are present, but only in **Panama** (try Darién or Natural Metropolitano NPs). The New World, unlike Africa and Asia, has only one group (10 species) of nocturnal primates and this, appropriately enough, is the **night monkey**. Panama is the only country in the region to contain night monkeys. Another mammal you are very likely to see in the southern countries of the region are sloths, good places to look are **Reserva Monteverde** and the forests of **Tortuguero** and **Manuel Antonio** in **Costa Rica**. As they tend to stay in one area for days at a time, local guides are excellent in pointing them out. The most easily seen of the carnivores is not, sadly, the longed for **jaguar**, but the ubiquitous **white-nosed coati**, a member of the racoon family. The females and their offspring go around in groups and are unmistakable with their long, ringed tails, frequently held in the air, and their long snouts sniffing around for insects and fruit in trees and on the ground. At many tourist sites, they hang around waiting to be fed by the visitors, in particular around Tikal and in the popular lowland National Parks of Costa Rica. Members of the cat family are rarely seen, those in the area include the bobcat (in Mexico only), jaguar, puma, ocelot and margay. All are more likely to be seen at night, or, possibly, at dawn and dusk. In Belize, Cockscomb Basin Wildlife Sanctuary is also known as the Jaguar Reserve, so this area is as good a place as any to try your luck. Río Bravo and Chan Chich Lodge in Belize, Corcovado and Tortuguero NPs in Costa Rica and Reserva Biológica Indio Maíz in Nicaragua are also possibilities for the jaguar and the other small cats. The largest land mammal in Central America is Baird's tapir, weighing up to 300 kg. It is a forest species and very secretive, particularly so in areas where it is hunted. Corcovado and Santa Rosa NPs in Costa Rica are all places it might be seen, at least there is a reasonable chance of seeing its hoof prints. They might be seen at waterholes or be spotted swimming in rivers. More likely to be seen are peccaries, especially the collared peccary, medium sized pig-like animals that are active both day and night. The collared peccary can be found in both dry and rain forests throughout the region, while the white-lipped peccary is more common in wetter, evergreen forests. Both live in herds, of up to 100 individuals in the case of the white-lipped species. Found throughout the area, in drier, woodland patches, the white-tailed deer can easily be spotted, especially at dawn or dusk, or their bright eyeshine can be seen at night if you are out in a car or on foot with a torch. Also found from Mexico down into South America is the smaller red brocket, this, though, is a rainforest species and is more elusive. Rodent species you might see include the agouti, which looks rather like a long-legged guinea pig, it can be seen moving around on the forest floor. Considerably larger and stockier is the nocturnal paca (gibnut in Belize), another forest species found throughout the region, often near water where they hide when chased by predators. The world's largest rodent, the capybara, is also found near water, but in this region can be seen only in Panama, in Darién, for instance. Bats will usually be a quick fly past at night, impossible to identify but for the jagged flight path which is clearly not that of a bird. Perhaps one of the strangest is the Mexican long-nosed bat, which forages in groups of 25, feeding on nectar from agaves, in particular, in the desert regions of the country. The nightly exodus of bats from caves near to El Zotz, in Petén, Guatemala is a spectacular sight. Others feed on fish, frogs, fruit and insects; probably the most notorious is the blood-sucking vampire bat, though it rarely attacks humans, instead feeding almost exclusively on domestic stock, such as cattle and goats.

Finally, marine mammals in the area include whales, dolphins and manatees. The last of these can be seen in Belize's Southern Lagoon, Lago Izabal in Guatemala or Cuero Y Salado Wildlife Reserve in Honduras. Whales and dolphins occur along both the Pacific and Atlantic coasts and can be watched at a number of sites from El Vizcaíno Biosphere Reserve in Baja California down the Pacific coast to Puero Vallarta, Escondido and other places along the coast as far south as Isla Iguana Wildlife Reserve in Panama.

Birds

It is true, the early bird gets the worm and the earlier you get up, the more species you'll see! All countries have very high numbers of birds on their lists but Panama is the haven for birdwatchers in this area; though relatively tiny, it boasts almost as many (922) bird species as Mexico. One of the best places to go in Panama is the Pipeline Road (Sendero Oleoducto) in Parque Nacional Soberanía. In this lowland rainforest area, brilliantly coloured species such as the violaceous and slaty-tailed **trogans** or the blue-crowned **motmot** can be seen, along with **parrots, tanagers, hummingbirds, antbirds** and many others during the day. It is also a good place to see the spectacular keel-billed **toucan**. At night, eight species of owl, including the crested, can be found, along with potoos and a variety of nightjars. Also, for serious birders, not to be missed in Panama is **Parque Nacional Darién** with mangroves, lowland and montane rainforest where numerous raptors can be seen, including king and black **vultures**, crested **eagles** and, if you're really lucky, the huge, monkey-eating **harpy eagle** with its 2-m wing span. **Macaws, parrots** and **parakeets** are common, along with toucans, hummingbirds, aracaris and tanagers. At higher altitudes in this park (Cerro Pirre), the golden-headed quetzal can be seen at higher altitudes in Parque Nacional Darién (around Pirre Camp) and nowhere else in Central America.

Many of these birds can be seen outside Panama. Toucans and the smaller toucanets are widespread throughout the tropical areas of the region with the ruins of **Tikal** offering good siting opportunities. Another popular sighting is the scarlet macaw easily spotted near **Puerto Juárez, Costa Rica**, and the region of El Perú and the **Río San Juan** in **Guatemala**. Hummingbirds too are a common sighting throughout the region, frequently drawn to sugar-feeders. The harpy eagle is extremely rare with sightings on the **Osa Peninsula, Costa Rica** a possibility and the in rainforest region of northern Guatemala, Belize and southern Mexico.

To find the **resplendent quetzal**, a brilliant emerald green bird, with males having a bright scarlet breast and belly and ostentatious long green streamers extending as much as 50 cm beyond the end of its tail, **Monteverde Cloud Forest Reserve** or the less atmospheric **Eddie Serrano Mirador** in Costa Rica are a couple of the best places to go. You'll also have a good chance of spotting the quetzal in the **Quetzal Biosphere Reserve** in the Sierra de las Minas, **Guatemala**, where the bird is on name of the currency and national symbol.

In addition to the quetzal, Costa Rica, containing around 850 bird species, follows close on the heels of Panama as being a good country to visit for birdwatchers and **Monteverde** is a hotspot. Species there include black **guans, emerald toucanets, violet sabrewings, long-tailed manakins, three wattled bellbirds** and the threatened **bare-necked umbrellabird**. Mixed flocks of small birds such as **warblers, tanagers, woodcreepers** and **wood-wrens** can also be seen in the area. **La Selva Biological Station**, an area of rainforest in Costa Rica, is another area rich in rainforest species such as the **chestnut-billed toucan, mealy parrot** and **squirrel cuckoo**. A very different habitat, with, consequently, different birds, is found in the large wetland area of **Parque Nacional Palo Verde** in Costa Rica. Here one can see **jabirus, black-necked stilts, spotted rails, bare-throated tiger heron, purple gallinule** and many other water birds. In the dry season, **ducks**, including the **black-bellied whistling duck, blue-billed teal, ring-necked duck** and **northern pintail**, congregate in this area in their thousands. More rarely seen here is the **white-faced whistling duck**. Many of these waterbirds can also be seen in **Crooked Tree Wildlife Sanctuary** in Belize.

Of course, all along the coasts are masses of different seabirds, including **pelicans, boobies** and the **magnificent frigate bird**. And in Mexico coastal wetlands near Celestún and in Río Lagarto on the Yucután Peninsula, provide good sightings of **pink flamingoes**.

Maybe you are looking for real rarities, then try spotting the threatened **horned guam**, a highly distinctive and striking bird, that can be found only in high cloud forests of **Mexico** and **Guatemala**, for example, in **El Triunfo Biosphere Reserve** in Mexico. Another species you might consider searching for is the maroon-fronted parrot, endemic to the pine forests of the **Sierra Madre Occidental** in Mexico. This species, strangely for a parrot, nests exclusively in holes in limestone cliffs. The **El Tary Sanctuary**, between the cities of

Monterrey and Saltillo, has been created to protect the largest known nesting cliff of this bird, where 100 pairs, a quarter of the breeding population, are found.

Reptiles

This covers **snakes, lizards, crocodilians** and **turtles**. Mexico has more of these animals than any other country in the world. Throughout the whole region, though, you are not particularly likely to see snakes in the wild; for those wishing to do so, a snake farm or zoo is the best place to go. You might, though, be lucky on one of your walks and see a **boa constrictor**, or, again, a guide might know where one is resting. In contrast, **lizards** are everywhere, from small geckos walking up walls in your hotel room, catching insects attracted to the lights, to the large **iguanas** sunbathing in the tree tops. The **American crocodile** and **spectacled caiman** are both found throughout the area, with the latter being seen quite frequently. **Morlet's crocodile**, on the other hand, is found only in Mexico, Belize and Guatemala. Several species of both freshwater and sea **turtles** are present in the region. **Parque Nacional Tortuguero** in **Costa Rica** is a good place to see freshwater and four species of marine turtles, while at **Ostional Beach** in Santa Rosa National Park you can watch masses of olive Ridley turtles coming in to lay their eggs, particularly in September and October. You'll also be able to see nesting turtles along the Pacific coastal beaches of Nicaragua, in La Mosquitia, Honduras, Monterrico, Guatemala and Mexico, in particular along the southern Pacific around Mazunte and near Bahías de Huatulco.

Amphibians

You'll certainly hear frogs and toads, even if you do not see them. However, the brightly coloured **poison-dart frogs** and some of the tree frogs are well worth searching out. Look for them in damp places, under logs and moist leaf litter, in rock crevices and by ponds and streams, many will be more active at night. **Monteverde** and **La Selva Reserves** are both rich in amphibians, and a visit to **Bocas del Toro** will also reveal colourful amphibians on appropriately named Red Frog Beach.

Invertebrates

There are uncounted different species of invertebrates in the area. Probably, most desirable for ecotourists are the **butterflies**, though some of the **beetles**, such as the jewel **scarabs**, are also pretty spectacular. If you are fascinated by spiders, you can always go hunting for nocturnal **tarantulas**; Lamanai in Belize harbours four different species. The gathering of **Monarch butterflies** near Angangueo in Central Mexico is certainly worth a special visit. There are also butterfly farms in some of the countries, including in Nicaragua (Los Guatusos Wildlife Reserve) and Costa Rica (eg el Jardín de Mariposas In Monteverde) that will give you a close up view of many different species. Watching **leaf-cutter ants** marching in long columns from a bush they are systematically destroying and taking the pieces of leaf to their nest, huge mounds on the forest floor, can be a absorbing sight, while marching columns of army ants, catching and killing all small beasts in their path, are best avoided.

Marine wildlife

Predicting the movement and location of marine animals is difficult, and often sightings of sharks and rays is chance. However, the **whale shark** makes a seasonal migration through the coastal waters of Belize and Honduras between March and May. Less natural shark encounters can be had off **Caye Caulker**, Belize, and **Isla Mujeres**, on the Yutatán, Mexico, where hand-feeding brings in **sting rays** and **nurse sharks** for close but safe encounters.

Books

Literature

Books covering the region look like a Who's Who of literature with classic contributions:

Banks, Iain *Canal Dreams.*
Greene, Graham *The Lawless Road, The Power and the Glory, The Captain and the Enemy* and *Getting to Know the General.*
Huxley, Aldous *Eyeless in Gaza* and *Beyond the Mexique Bay.*
Kerouac, Jack *On the Road.*
Lawrence, DH *The Plumed Serpent.*
Lewis, Norman *The Volcanoes Above Us.*
Lowry, Malcolm Under the Volcano.
Theroux, Paul *The Old Patagonian Express* and *The Mosquito Coast.*

And that, without touching on the home-grown talents of **Miguel Angel Asturias, Cardenal, Ernesto, Darío, Rubén, Fuentes, Carlos, Rulfo, Juan** and the rest. Any of these books would make an excellent choice to accompany the start of your travels.

Wilson, Jason, *Traveller's Literary Companion, South and Central America* (Brighton, UK: in Print, 1993), a general guide to the literature of the region with extracts from works by Latin American writers and by non-Latin Americans about the various countries; it also has very useful bibliographies.

History

Coe, Michael D *The Maya* (Thames and Hudson), an excellent overview of the Maya.
Coe, Michael D *Breaking the Maya Code*, an in-depth account of how the hieroglyphics of the Maya were eventually read.

Dunkerley, James *Power in the Isthmus: A Political History of Modern Central America* (1989), a good history of the smaller republics.

Wildlife

If wildlife spotting is the primary reason for your trip, then plan carefully. Specialist advice on where and when to visit should be researched, using advice from detailed sources such as websites or tour companies mentioned throughout this book.

Useful guide books, covering all **vertebrate** groups, include:
Beletsky, Les *Ecotravellers' Wildlife Guides* (one for Costa Rica, one for Tropical Mexico and one for Belize and Northern Guatemala).
Reid, F *Field Guide to the Mammals of Central America and Southeast Mexico,* is worth finding.
Emmon, Louise *Neotropical Rainforest Mammals: A Field Guide*, will help with identifying wildlife.

For birds:
Howell, Steve and Webb, Sophie *A Guide to the Birds of Mexico and Northern Central America.*
Howell, Steven *A Guide to the Birds of Mexico and Northern Central America.*
Peterson, R *Field Guide to Mexican Birds.*
Ridgeley, R and Gwynne, J *Field Guide to the Birds of Panama.*
Stiles, G, Skutch, A and Gardner, D *A Field Guide to the Birds of Costa Rica.*
www.lab.org.uk (Latin American Bureau) An excellent specialist online guide and bookstore, with country specific titles and international delivery.

Contents

Footnotes

Basic Spanish for travellers

Learning Spanish is a useful part of the preparation for a trip to Latin America and no volumes of dictionaries, phrase books or word lists will provide the same enjoyment as being able to communicate directly with the people of the country you are visiting. It is a good idea to make an effort to grasp the basics before you go. As you travel you will pick up more of the language and the more you know, the more you will benefit from your stay.

General pronunciation

Whether you have been taught the 'Castilian' pronunciation (z and c followed by i or e are pronounced as the *th* in think) or the 'American' pronunciation (they are pronounced as s), you will encounter little difficulty in understanding either. Regional accents and usages vary, but the basic language is essentially the same everywhere.

Vowels

a	as in English *cat*
e	as in English *best*
i	as the *ee* in English *feet*
o	as in English *shop*
u	as the *oo* in English *food*
ai	as the *i* in English *ride*
ei	as *ey* in English *they*
oi	as *oy* in English *toy*

Consonants

Most consonants can be pronounced more or less as they are in English. The exceptions are:

g	before *e* or *i* is the same as *j*
h	is always silent (except in *ch* as in *chair*)
j	as the *ch* in Scottish *loch*
ll	as the *y* in *yellow*
ñ	as the *ni* in English *onion*
rr	trilled much more than in English
x	depending on its location, pronounced *x, s, sh* or *j*

Spanish words and phrases

Greetings, courtesies

hello	*hola*
good morning	*buenos días*
good afternoon/ evening/night	*buenas tardes/noches*
goodbye	*adiós/chao*
pleased to meet you	*mucho gusto*
see you later	*hasta luego*
how are you?	*¿cómo está? ¿cómo estás?*
I'm fine, thanks	*estoy muy bien, gracias*
I'm called...	*me llamo...*
what is your name?	*¿cómo se llama? ¿cómo te llamas?*
yes/no	*sí/no*
please	*por favor*

thank you (very much)	*(muchas) gracias*
I speak Spanish	*hablo español*
I don't speak Spanish	*no hablo español*
do you speak English?	*¿habla inglés?*
I don't understand	*no entiendo/ no comprendo*
please speak slowly	*hable despacio por favor*
I am very sorry	*lo siento mucho/ disculpe*
what do you want?	*¿qué quiere? ¿qué quieres?*
I want	*quiero*
I don't want it	*no lo quiero*
leave me alone	*déjeme en paz/ no me moleste*
good/bad	*bueno/malo*

Questions and requests

Have you got a room for two people?	Is tax included?
¿Tiene una habitación para dos personas?	*¿Están incluidos los impuestos?*
How do I get to_?	When does the bus leave (arrive)?
¿Cómo llego a_?	*¿A qué hora sale (llega) el autobús?*
How much does it cost?	When? *¿cuándo?*
¿Cuánto cuesta? ¿cuánto es?	Where is_? *¿dónde está_?*
I'd like to make a long-distance phone call	Where can I buy tickets?
Quisiera hacer una llamada de larga distancia	*¿Dónde puedo comprar boletos?*
Is service included?	Where is the nearest petrol station?
¿Está incluido el servicio?	*¿Dónde está la gasolinera más cercana?*
	Why? *¿por qué?*

Basics

bank	*el banco*	market	*el mercado*
bathroom/toilet	*el baño*	note/coin	*le billete/la moneda*
bill	*la factura/la cuenta*	police (policeman)	*la policía (el policía)*
cash	*el efectivo*	post office	*el correo*
cheap	*barato/a*	public telephone	*el teléfono público*
credit card	*la tarjeta de crédito*	supermarket	*el supermercado*
exchange house	*la casa de cambio*	ticket office	*la taquilla*
exchange rate	*el tipo de cambio*	traveller's cheques	*los cheques de viajero/*
expensive	*caro/a*		*los travelers*

Getting around

aeroplane	*el avión*	insured person	*el/la asegurado/a*
airport	*el aeropuerto*	to insure yourself against	*asegurarse contra*
arrival/departure	*la llegada/salida*	luggage	*el equipaje*
avenue	*la avenida*	motorway, freeway	*el autopista/la*
block	*la cuadra*		*carretera*
border	*la frontera*	north, south, west, east	*norte, sur, oeste*
bus station	*la terminal de*		*(occidente), este*
	autobuses/camiones		*(oriente)*
bus	*el bus/el autobús/*	Oil	*el aceite*
	el camión	to park	*estacionarse*
collective/		passport	*el pasaporte*
fixed-route taxi	*el colectivo*	petrol/gasoline	*la gasolina*
corner	*la esquina*	puncture	*el pinchazo/*
customs	*la aduana*		*la ponchadura*
first/second class	*primera/segunda clase*	street	*la calle*
left/right	*izquierda/derecha*	that way	*por allí/por allá*
ticket	*el boleto*	this way	*por aquí/por acá*
empty/full	*vacío/lleno*	tourist card/visa	*la tarjeta de turista*
highway, main road	*la carretera*	tyre	*la llanta*
immigration	*la inmigración*	unleaded	*sin plomo*
insurance	*el seguro*	to walk	*caminar/andar*

Accommodation

air conditioning	*el aire acondicionado*	power cut	*el apagón/corte*
all-inclusive	*todo incluido*	restaurant	*el restaurante*
bathroom, private	*el baño privado*	room/bedroom	*el cuarto/la habitación*
bed, double/single	*la cama matrimonial/ sencilla*	sheets	*las sábanas*
		shower	*la ducha/regadera*
blankets	*las cobijas/mantas*	soap	*el jabón*
to clean	*limpiar*	toilet	*el sanitario/excusado*
dining room	*el comedor*	toilet paper	*el papel higiénico*
guesthouse	*la casa de huéspedes*	towels, clean/dirty	*las toallas limpias/ sucias*
hotel	*el hotel*		
noisy	*ruidoso*	water, hot/cold	*el agua caliente/fría*
pillows	*las almohadas*		

Health

aspirin	*la aspirina*	diarrhoea	*la diarrea*
blood	*la sangre*	doctor	*el médico*
chemist	*la farmacia*	fever/sweat	*la fiebre/el sudor*
condoms	*los preservativos, los condones*	pain	*el dolor*
		head	*la cabeza*
contact lenses	*los lentes de contacto*	period/sanitary towels	*la regla/ las toallas femeninas*
contraceptives	*los anticonceptivos*		
contraceptive pill	*la píldora anti- conceptiva*	stomach	*el estómago*
		altitude sickness	*el soroche*

Family

family	*la familia*	boyfriend/girlfriend	*el novio/la novia*
brother/sister	*el hermano/la hermana*	friend	*el amigo/la amiga*
daughter/son	*la hija/el hijo*	married	*casado/a*
father/mother	*el padre/la madre*	single/unmarried	*soltero/a*
husband/wife	*el esposo (marido)/ la esposa*		

Months, days and time

January	*enero*	Monday	*lunes*
February	*febrero*	Tuesday	*martes*
March	*marzo*	Wednesday	*miércoles*
April	*abril*	Thursday	*jueves*
May	*mayo*	Friday	*viernes*
June	*junio*	Saturday	*sábado*
July	*julio*	Sunday	*domingo*
August	*agosto*		
September	*septiembre*	at one o'clock	*a la una*
October	*octubre*	at half past two	*a las dos y media*
November	*noviembre*	at a quarter to three	*a cuarto para las tres/ a las tres menos quince*
December	*diciembre*		
		it's one o'clock	*es la una*

it's seven o'clock	*son las siete*	in ten minutes	*en diez minutos*
it's six twenty	*son las seis y veinte*	five hours	*cinco horas*
it's five to nine	*son las nueve menos cinco*	does it take long?	*¿tarda mucho?*

Numbers

one	*uno/una*	sixteen	*dieciséis*
two	*dos*	seventeen	*diecisiete*
three	*tres*	eighteen	*dieciocho*
Four	*cuatro*	nineteen	*diecinueve*
five	*cinco*	twenty	*veinte*
six	*seis*	twenty-one	*veintiuno*
seven	*siete*	thirty	*treinta*
eight	*ocho*	forty	*cuarenta*
nine	*nueve*	fifty	*cincuenta*
ten	*diez*	sixty	*sesenta*
eleven	*once*	seventy	*setenta*
twelve	*doce*	eighty	*ochenta*
thirteen	*trece*	ninety	*noventa*
fourteen	*catorce*	hundred	*cien/ciento*
fifteen	*quince*	thousand	*mil*

Food

avocado	*el aguacate*	goat	*el chivo*
baked	*al horno*	grapefruit	*la toronja/el pomelo*
bakery	*la panadería*	grill	*la parrilla*
banana	*el plátano*	grilled/griddled	*a la plancha*
beans	*los frijoles/ las habichuelas*	guava	*la guayaba*
		ham	*el jamón*
beef	*la carne de res*	hamburger	*la hamburguesa*
beef steak or pork fillet	*el bistec*	hot, spicy	*picante*
boiled rice	*el arroz blanco*	ice cream	*el helado*
bread	*el pan*	jam	*la mermelada*
breakfast	*el desayuno*	knife	*el cuchillo*
butter	*la mantequilla*	lime	*el limón*
cake	*el pastel*	lobster	*la langosta*
chewing gum	*el chicle*	lunch	*el almuerzo/la comida*
chicken	*el pollo*	meal	*la comida*
chilli or green pepper	*el ají/pimiento*	meat	*la carne*
clear soup, stock	*el caldo*	minced meat	*el picadillo*
cooked	*cocido*	onion	*la cebolla*
dining room	*el comedor*	orange	*la naranja*
egg	*el huevo*	pepper	*el pimiento*
Fish	*el pescado*	pasty, turnover	*la empanada/ el pastelito*
fork	*el tenedor*	pork	*el cerdo*
fried	*frito*	potato	*la papa*
garlic	*el ajo*		

prawns	*los camarones*	spoon	*la cuchara*
raw	*crudo*	squash	*la calabaza*
restaurant	*el restaurante*	squid	*los calamares*
salad	*la ensalada*	supper	*la cena*
salt	*la sal*	sweet	*dulce*
sandwich	*el bocadillo*	to eat	*comer*
sauce	*la salsa*	toasted	*tostado*
sausage	*la longaniza/el chorizo*	turkey	*el pavo*
scrambled eggs	*los huevos revueltos*	vegetables	*los legumbres/vegetales*
seafood	*los mariscos*	without meat	*sin carne*
soup	*la sopa*	yam	*el camote*

Drink

beer	*la cerveza*	ice/without ice	*el hielo/sin hielo*
boiled	*hervido/a*	juice	*el jugo*
bottled	*en botella*	lemonade	*la limonada*
camomile tea	*la manzanilla*	milk	*la leche*
canned	*en lata*	mint	*la menta*
coffee	*el café*	rum	*el ron*
coffee, white	*el café con leche*	soft drink	*el refresco*
cold	*frío*	sugar	*el azúcar*
cup	*la taza*	tea	*el té*
drink	*la bebida*	to drink	*beber/tomar*
drunk	*borracho/a*	water	*el agua*
firewater	*el aguardiente*	water, carbonated	*el agua mineral con gas*
fruit milkshake	*el batido/licuado*	water, still mineral	*el agua mineral sin gas*
glass	*el vaso*	wine, red	*el vino tinto*
hot	*caliente*	wine, white	*el vino blanco*

Key verbs

to go	**ir**	there is/are	*hay*
I go	*voy*	there isn't/aren't	*no hay*
you go (familiar)	*vas*		
he, she, it goes,		**to be**	**ser**	**estar**
you (formal) go	*va*	I am	*soy*	*estoy*
we go	*vamos*	you are	*eres*	*estás*
they, you (plural) go	*van*	he, she, it is,		
		you (formal) are	*es*	*está*
to have (possess)	**tener**	we are	*somos*	*estamos*
I have	*tengo*	they, you (plural) are	*son*	*están*
you (familiar) have	*tienes*		
he, she, it,		This section has been assembled on the basis of glossaries
you (formal) have	*tiene*	compiled by André de Mendonça and David Gilmour of
we have	*tenemos*	South American Experience, London, and the Latin American
they, you (plural) have	*tienen*	Travel Advisor, No 9, March 1996

Index → *Entries in bold refer to maps*

Advertisers' index

Acknowledgements

A great deal of work goes into the creation of Footprint's Central America and Mexico Handbook. It's an almost non-stop process, which in some respects is made easier by the internet but in others the digital age makes the task even more daunting. There are no short cuts to getting the latest and most up-to-date information possible. A large team of people contribute to this guide, not all of whom are mentioned below: in-country correspondents – both old and new – provide the inside track on developments in each country in a way that only residence allows; readers' letters provide personal experiences and stories, while trips by experienced researchers capture the spirit of the very latest happenings in the region.

As author of the book I have the pleasure of meeting and working with a wide range of people from varied backgrounds and being able to see, first hand, the changing face of the region. I also get the pleasure of working with a varied bunch of people, who are passionate about the region, or their particular patch.

Specific people should quite rightly be thanked for their contribution particular to the Central America and Mexico Handbook 18th Edition.

Thanks to Ria Gane at the Footprint office who quite rightly keeps the critical eye of an editor on the text for style and sense. Thanks to Sarah Sorenson for pushing improvements on the maps. And to Felicity Laughton who is blessed with the challenge of trying to extract copy from overly clingy authors.

Starting from the northernmost country, Mexico has benefited from the research on Footprint's Mexico Handbook, which has been coordinated by Richard Arghiris with his usual steady and dependable flair. Geoff Groesbeck researched a fair chunk of the northern area, and Anna Maria Espsater took on the tropics of the south. Their work is this book's gain.

Peter Hutchison revisited Guatemala after the country was under the guardianship of Claire Boobbyer (Footprint Guatemala Handbook). It was great to travel through the country again, daunting to see how much it has changed in recent years, and devastating to see the massive landslide on the road between Nebaj and Cobán that took place in early 2009.

Matthew Hamilton, resident in La Antigua, also provided updates to the country, in addition to his main task of updating Belize. Great to meet up Matt and hope to keep working with you in the future.

Honduras was entertaining as usual. Peter Hutchison took a meandering route, through lesser visited areas. Howard Rosenzweig checked out the information in Copán Ruinas which was, as ever, extremely useful. Thanks to Nicole Backhaus for updating the information about the ever-changing island of Utila. And to Steve Box at the Utila Centre for Marine Ecology for checking out the text for La Ceiba.

Thanks to the many colleagues in Nicaragua, Costa Rica and Panama who provided updates to augment the detailed overhaul these chapters received in the 17th edition.

For specialist contributions from this or previous years, we would like to thank: Caroline Harcourt for wildlife; Nigel Gallop for music and dance; John Alton for details on cargo ship cruises; Binka and Robin le Breton for motoring; Ashley Rawlings for motorcycling; Hallam Murray for cycling; Hilary Bradt for hiking and trekking; David Fishlow for language and Mark Eckstein for responsible tourism. Finally, many thanks to Beth and Shaun Tierney for supplying all the text and images for the colour diving section.

About the author

Peter Hutchison first travelled through Central and South America between 1993 and 1995 after gaining a degree in Development Studies specializing in Latin American Studies from Reading University. During his travels he used both versions of The Bible – Central and South – to guide his path, taking time to stop for almost two years to work on the *Bolivian Times* in La Paz. Leaving South America he headed north from Bolivia, straight through the Amazon. Since then regular trips to Latin America travelling popular routes and journeying roads less travelled, have kept the passion alive.

The draw of the Amazon continued and in February and March 2002 a team of five, led by Peter, made the first recorded descent of the River Parapeti (www.coursingthe parapeti.com) – the Amazon's most southern tributary – with the support of the Royal Geographic Society and funding from a Travelling Fellowship provided by the Winston Churchill Memorial Trust.

River travel by canoe continued in Belize 2003 when Peter entered the Macal River Race in Belize with Marc Gussen and Max. Paddling the Devizes Westminster Canoe Marathon down the River Thames in 2004, 2005 and 2008 has kept the long-distance race going.

Peter now lives in Hanwell, West London, using this base to work as a freelance journalist and travel writer. Having trained on the kayaking course used in the Mexican Olympics in 1968, he is very excited about watching the developments in London in the build up to 2012.

Travellers' letters

Travelling through Central America and Mexico you're bombarded with experiences – good and bad. While it's up to you to decide where you go, how you travel and what you do, we try our best to provide up-to-date information to help you on your way. Many travellers assist us in this task by writing to us with information about new hotels that have opened, established hotels that have gone downhill or been refurbished, restaurants that provide a welcome change from the norm, changes in transport prices, routes and options and so on.

All comments are extremely welcome. Many thanks to the following readers who have taken the time to write notes as they travel and to share their experiences with us by post or, increasingly, by email. It's great to receive letters, from short pithy corrections to colourful, sometimes humorous descriptions of personal journeys:

Paul Goossens, The Netherlands (Mex); Maura Leahy (Mex); Dave Maynard, Canada (Nic); Natalie and Christian Nguyen, Switzerland (Bel); Hilary Prowse, UK (Mex).

Also many thanks to the many hoteliers, restaurateurs, tour operators and others mentioned in Footprint's Central America and Mexico Handbook who have kindly taken the time to inform us when their contact details have changed. While we are unlikely to include the details of a new establishment without specific recommendations or, ideally, a visit, it is very useful to receive details about changes in telephone numbers, email and postal addresses, services provided, prices and so on. Thanks.

If you want to let us know about your experiences – good, bad or ugly – then don't delay; go to www.footprintbooks.com and send in your comments.

Credits

Footprint credits

Editor: Ria Gane
Map editor: Sarah Sorensen
Colour section: Kassia Gawronski

Managing Director: Andy Riddle
Commercial Director: Patrick Dawson
Publisher: Alan Murphy
Editorial: Sara Chare, Nicola Gibbs, Jen Haddington, Alice Jell, Felicity Laughton
Cartography: Robert Lunn, Kevin Feeney, Emma Bryers
Cover design: Robert Lunn
Design: Mytton Williams
Marketing: Liz Harper, Hannah Bonnell
Sales: Jeremy Parr
Advertising: Renu Sibal
Business development: Zoë Jackson,
Finance and administration: Elizabeth Taylor

Photograpy credits

Front cover: Kasiakorsieko/Shutterstock
Back cover: Hemis.fr/Superstock
Diving section: Shaun Tierney/Seafocus

Manufactured in India by Nutech Print Services, Delhi

Pulp from sustainable forests

Footprint feedback

We try as hard as we can to make each Footprint guide as up to date as possible but, of course, things always change. If you want to let us know about your experiences – good, bad or ugly – then don't delay, go to **www.footprintbooks.com** and send in your comments.

Publishing information

Footprint Central America and Mexico
18th edition
© Footprint Handbooks Ltd
October 2009

ISBN: 978 1 906098 69 8
CIP DATA: A catalogue record for this book is available from the British Library

® Footprint Handbooks and the Footprint mark are a registered trademark of Footprint Handbooks Ltd

Published by Footprint
6 Riverside Court
Lower Bristol Road
Bath BA2 3DZ, UK
T +44 (0)1225 469141
F +44 (0)1225 469461
www.footprintbooks.com

Distributed in the USA by Globe Pequot Press, Guilford, Connecticut

Discover the Magic & Beauty of Guatemala... our way!
Villa Colonial Antigua
Villa Santa Catarina Atitlán
Villa Caribe Livingston
Villa Maya Tikal
Hotel Maya Internacional Flores
Reservations:
PBX: (502) 2223-5000
info@villasdeguatemala.com
HOTELS
VILLAS DE GUATEMALA
We are 100% Guatemala
www.villasdeguatemala.com

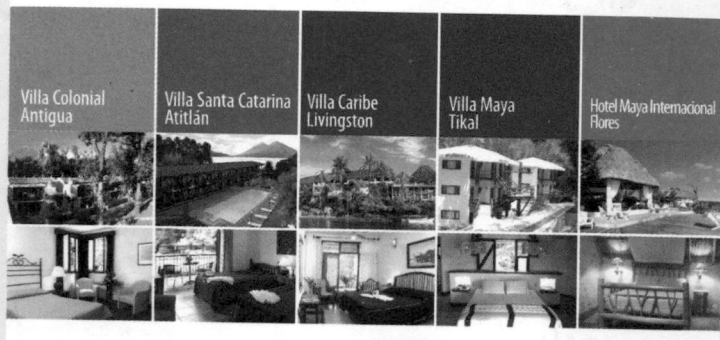

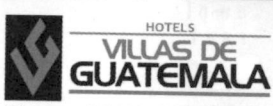

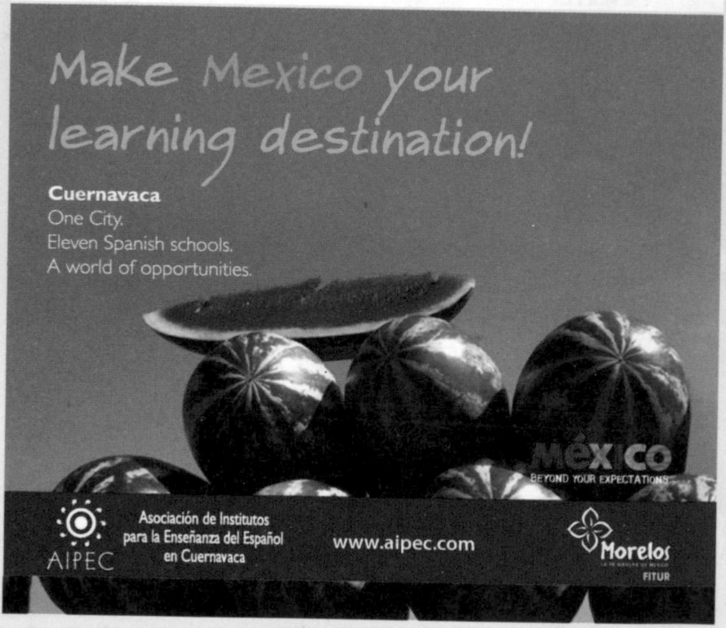
Make Mexico your learning destination!
Cuernavaca
One City.
Eleven Spanish schools.
A world of opportunities.
MÉXICO
BEYOND YOUR EXPECTATIONS
AIPEC
Asociación de Institutos para la Enseñanza del Español en Cuernavaca
www.aipec.com
Morelos
FITUR